Account Title	Classification	Financial Statement	Normal Balance
L			
Land	Plant Asset	Balance Sheet	Debit
Loss on Disposal of Plant Assets	Other Expense	Income Statement	Debit
M			
Maintenance and Repairs Expense	Operating Expense	Income Statement	Debit
Mortgage Payable	Long-Term Liability	Balance Sheet	Credit
N			
Notes Payable	Current Liability/ Long-Term Liability	Balance Sheet	Credit
P			
Patents	Intangible Asset	Balance Sheet	Debit
Paid-in Capital in Excess of Par Value—Common Stock	Stockholders' Equity	Balance Sheet	Credit
Paid-in Capital in Excess of Par Value—Preferred Stock	Stockholders' Equity	Balance Sheet	Credit
Preferred Stock	Stockholders' Equity	Balance Sheet	Credit
Premium on Bonds Payable	Long-Term Liability—Contra	Balance Sheet	Credit
Prepaid Insurance	Current Asset	Balance Sheet	Debit
Prepaid Rent	Current Asset	Balance Sheet	Debit
R			
Rent Expense	Operating Expense	Income Statement	Debit
Retained Earnings	Stockholders' Equity	Balance Sheet and Retained Earnings Statement	Credit
S			
Salaries and Wages Expense	Operating Expense	Income Statement	Debit
Salaries and Wages Payable	Current Liability	Balance Sheet	Credit
Sales Discounts	Revenue—Contra	Income Statement	Debit
Sales Returns and Allowances	Revenue—Contra	Income Statement	Debit
Sales Revenue	Revenue	Income Statement	Credit
Selling Expenses	Operating Expense	Income Statement	Debit
Service Revenue	Revenue	Income Statement	Credit
Stock Investments	Current Asset/Long-Term Investment	Balance Sheet	Debit
Supplies	Current Asset	Balance Sheet	Debit
Supplies Expense	Operating Expense	Income Statement	Debit
T			
Treasury Stock	Stockholders' Equity	Balance Sheet	Debit
U			
Unearned Service Revenue	Current Liability	Balance Sheet	Credit
Utilities Expense	Operating Expense	Income Statement	Debit

(1) The normal balance for Income Summary will be credit when there is a net income, debit when there is a net loss. The Income Summary account does not appear on any financial statement.

(2) If a periodic system is used, Inventory also appears on the income statement in the calculation of cost of goods sold.

The following is a sample chart of accounts. It does not represent a comprehensive chart of all the accounts used in this textbook but rather those accounts that are commonly used. This sample chart of accounts is for a company that generates both service revenue as well as sales revenue. It uses the perpetual approach to inventory. If a periodic system was used, the following temporary accounts would be needed to record inventory purchases: Purchases; Freight-in; Purchase Returns and Allowances; and Purchase Discounts.

CHART OF ACCOUNTS

Assets	Liabilities	Stockholders' Equity	Revenues	Expenses
Cash	Notes Payable	Common Stock	Service Revenue	Administrative Expenses
Accounts Receivable	Accounts Payable	Paid-in Capital in Excess of Par Value—Common Stock	Sales Revenue	Amortization Expense
Allowance for Doubtful Accounts	Unearned Service Revenue		Sales Discounts	
	Salaries and Wages Payable	Preferred Stock	Sales Returns and Allowances	Bad Debt Expense
Interest Receivable	Interest Payable	Paid-in Capital in Excess of Par Value—Preferred Stock	Interest Revenue	Cost of Goods Sold
Inventory	Dividends Payable		Gain on Disposal of Plant Assets	Depreciation Expense
Supplies	Income Taxes Payable	Treasury Stock		Freight-Out
Prepaid Insurance	Bonds Payable	Retained Earnings		Income Tax Expense
Prepaid Rent	Discount on Bonds Payable	Dividends		Insurance Expense
Land	Premium on Bonds Payable	Income Summary		Interest Expense
Equipment	Mortgage Payable			Loss on Disposal of Plant Assets
Accumulated Depreciation—Equipment				Maintenance and Repairs Expense
Buildings				Rent Expense
Accumulated Depreciation—Buildings				Salaries and Wages Expense
Copyrights				Selling Expenses
Goodwill				Supplies Expense
Patents				Utilities Expense

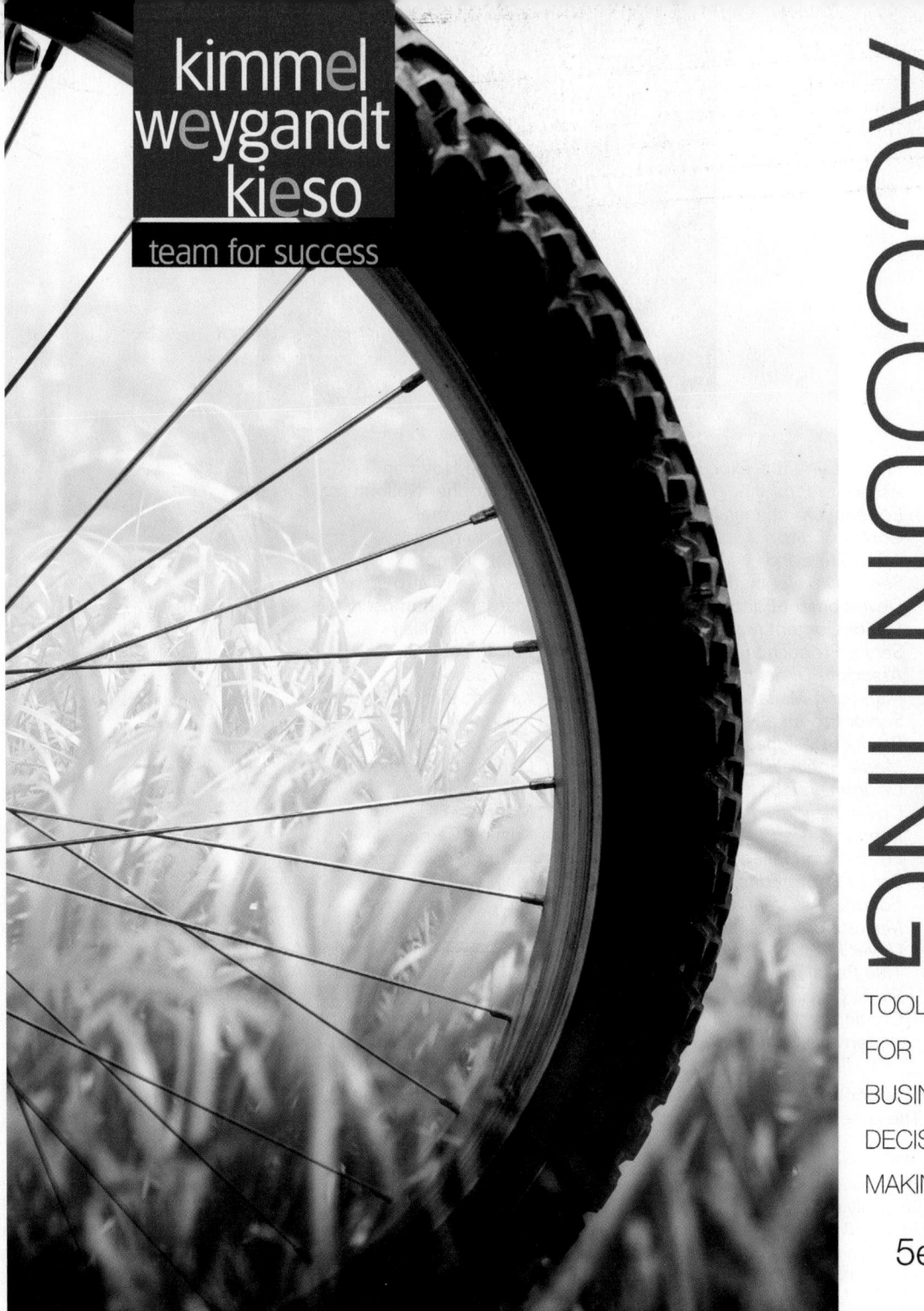

Paul D. Kimmel PhD, CPA
University of Wisconsin—Milwaukee
Milwaukee, Wisconsin

Jerry J. Weygandt PhD, CPA
University of Wisconsin—Madison
Madison, Wisconsin

Donald E. Kieso PhD, CPA
Northern Illinois University
DeKalb, Illinois

kimmel
weygandt
kieso
team for success

ACCOUNTING

TOOLS FOR BUSINESS DECISION MAKING

5e

WILEY

Vice President & Executive Publisher	George Hoffman
Associate Publisher	Christopher DeJohn
Editorial Operations Manager	Yana Mermel
Content Editor	Ed Brislin
Associate Editor	Sarah Vernon
Senior Development Editor	Terry Ann Tatro
Development Editor	Margaret Thompson
Senior Content Manager	Dorothy Sinclair
Senior Production Editor	Erin Bascom
Associate Director of Marketing	Amy Scholz
Marketing Manager	Karolina Zarychta Honsa
Senior Product Designer	Allison Morris
Product Designer	Greg Chaput
Media Specialist	Daniela DiMaggio
Design Director	Harry Nolan
Cover Design	Maureen Eide
Interior Design	Kristine Carney
Production Management Services	Furino Production
Senior Photo Editor	Mary Ann Price
Editorial Assistant	Jaclyn MacKenzie
Marketing Assistant	Justine Kay
Cover Photo	I Dream Stock Collection/Age Fotostock America, Inc.
Title Page and Brief Contents Image	I Dream Stock Collection/Age Fotostock America, Inc.
Sierra Corporation Icon	© Ben Blankenburg/iStockphoto
Continuing Cookie Chronicle Icon	© Fekete Tibor/iStockphoto
Waterways Continuing Problem Icon	© Perry Kroll/iStockphoto

This book was set in New Aster by Aptara®, Inc. and printed and bound by Courier-Kendallville. The cover was printed by Courier-Kendallville.

Founded in 1807, John Wiley & Sons, Inc. has been a valued source of knowledge and understanding for more than 200 years, helping people around the world meet their needs and fulfill their aspirations. Our company is built on a foundation of principles that include responsibility to the communities we serve and where we live and work. In 2008, we launched a Corporate Citizenship Initiative, a global effort to address the environmental, social, economic, and ethical challenges we face in our business. Among the issues we are addressing are carbon impact, paper specifications and procurement, ethical conduct within our business and among our vendors, and community and charitable support. For more information, please visit our website: www.wiley.com/go/citizenship.

ISBN-13 978-1-118-12816-9

Binder-Ready Version ISBN 978-1-118-34276-3

Printed in the United States of America

10 9 8 7 6 5 4

Brief Contents

*Available at the book's companion website, **www.wiley.com/college/kimmel**.

From the Authors

Dear Student,

Why This Course? *Remember your biology course in high school? Did you have one of those "invisible man" models (or maybe something more high-tech than that) that gave you the opportunity to look "inside" the human body? This accounting course offers something similar. To understand a business, you have to understand the financial insides of a business organization. An accounting course will help you understand the essential financial components of businesses. Whether you are looking at a large multinational company like Apple or Starbucks or a single-owner software consulting business or coffee shop, knowing the fundamentals of accounting will help you understand what is happening. As an employee, a manager, an investor, a business owner, or a director of your own personal finances—any of which roles you will have at some point in your life—you will make better decisions for having taken this course.*

> "Whether you are looking at a large multinational company like Apple or Starbucks or a single-owner software consulting business or coffee shop, knowing the fundamentals of accounting will help you understand what is happening."

Why This Book? *Hundreds of thousands of students have used this textbook. Your instructor has chosen it for you because of its trusted reputation. The authors have worked hard to keep the book fresh, timely, and accurate.*

This textbook contains features to help you learn best, whatever your learning style. We invite you to browse through pages xxvi–xxx. These pages describe the main features you will find in this textbook and explain their purpose.

How To Succeed? *We've asked many students and many instructors whether there is a secret for success in this course. The nearly unanimous answer turns out to be not much of a secret: "Do the homework." This is one course where doing is learning. The more time you spend on the homework assignments—using the various tools that this textbook provides—the more likely you are to learn the essential concepts, techniques, and methods of accounting. Besides the textbook itself, the book's companion website also offers various support resources.*

Good luck in this course. We hope you enjoy the experience and that you put to good use throughout a lifetime of success the knowledge you obtain in this course. We are sure you will not be disappointed.

Paul D. Kimmel
Jerry J. Weygandt
Donald E. Kieso

Your Team for Success in Accounting

Wiley Accounting is your partner in accounting education. We want to be the first publisher you think of when it comes to quality content, reliable technology, innovative resources, professional training, and unparalleled support for your accounting classroom.

Your Wiley Accounting Team for Success is comprised of three distinctive advantages that you won't find with any other publisher:

WileyPLUS

An Experienced Team
of Support Professionals

The *WileyPLUS* Account Managers understand the time constraints of busy instructors who want to provide the best resources available to their students with minimal headaches and planning time. They know how intimidating new software can be, so they are sure to make the transition easy and painless.

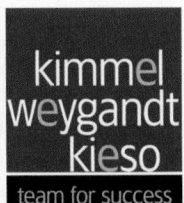

Author Commitment

A Proven Author Team
of Inspired Teachers

The Team for Success authors bring years of industry and academic experience to the development of each textbook that relates accounting concepts to real-world experiences. This cohesive team brings continuity of writing style, pedagogy, and problem material to each course from Principles to Intermediate so you and your students can seamlessly progress from introductory through advanced courses in accounting.

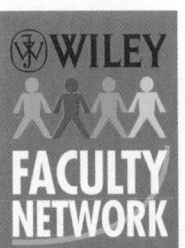

Wiley Faculty Network

A Team of Educators Dedicated
to Your Professional Development

The Wiley Faculty Network (WFN) is a global group of seasoned instructors who share best practices in teaching with their peers. Our Virtual Guest Lecture Series provides the opportunity you need for professional development in an online environment that is relevant, convenient, and collaborative. We are proud to be able to offer valuable CPE credits to attendees of these seminars and workshops.

www.wileyteamforsuccess.com

Author Commitment
Collaboration. Innovation. Experience.

After decades of success as authors of textbooks like this one, Paul Kimmel, Jerry Weygandt, and Don Kieso understand that teaching accounting goes beyond simply presenting data. The authors are truly effective because they know that teaching is about telling compelling stories in ways that make each concept come-to-life.

Teacher / Author / Professional

Through their textbooks, supplements, online learning tools, and classrooms, these authors have developed a comprehensive pedagogy that engages students in learning and faculty with teaching.

These authors collaborate throughout the entire process. The end result is a true collaboration where each author brings his individual experience and talent to the development of every paragraph, page, and chapter, thus creating a truly well-rounded, thorough view on any given accounting topic.

Many Ways in One Direction

Our **Team for Success** has developed a teaching system that addresses every learning style. Each year brings new insights, feedback, ideas, and improvements on how to deliver the material to every student with a passion for the subject in a format that gives them the best chance to succeed.

The key to the team's approach is in understanding that, just as there are many different ways to learn, there are also many different ways to teach.

In Their Own Words

Visit the Wiley **Team for Success** website to hear from the authors first-hand as they discuss their teaching styles, collaboration, and the future of accounting.

www.wileyteamforsuccess.com

Author Commitment

Jerry Weygandt

Jerry J. Weygandt, PhD, CPA, is Arthur Andersen Alumni Emeritus Professor of Accounting at the University of Wisconsin—Madison. He holds a Ph.D. in accounting from the University of Illinois. Articles by Professor Weygandt have appeared in the *Accounting Review*, *Journal of Accounting Research*, *Accounting Horizons*, *Journal of Accountancy*, and other academic and professional journals. These articles have examined such financial reporting issues as accounting for price-level adjustments, pensions, convertible securities, stock option contracts, and interim reports. Professor Weygandt is author of other accounting and financial reporting books and is a member of the American Accounting Association, the American Institute of Certified Public Accountants, and the Wisconsin Society of Certified Public Accountants. He has served on numerous committees of the American Accounting Association and as a member of the editorial board of the Accounting Review; he also has served as President and Secretary-Treasurer of the American Accounting Association. In addition, he has been actively involved with the American Institute of Certified Public Accountants and has been a member of the Accounting Standards Executive Committee (AcSEC) of that organization. He has served on the FASB task force that examined the reporting issues related to accounting for income taxes and served as a trustee of the Financial Accounting Foundation. Professor Weygandt has received the Chancellor's Award for Excellence in Teaching and the Beta Gamma Sigma Dean's Teaching Award. He is on the board of directors of M & I Bank of Southern Wisconsin. He is the recipient of the Wisconsin Institute of CPA's Outstanding Educator's Award and the Lifetime Achievement Award. In 2001 he received the American Accounting Association's Outstanding Educator Award.

Paul Kimmel

Paul D. Kimmel, PhD, CPA, received his bachelor's degree from the University of Minnesota and his doctorate in accounting from the University of Wisconsin. He is an Associate Professor at the University of Wisconsin—Milwaukee, and has public accounting experience with Deloitte & Touche (Minneapolis). He was the recipient of the UWM School of Business Advisory Council Teaching Award, the Reggie Taite Excellence in Teaching Award and a three-time winner of the Outstanding Teaching Assistant Award at the University of Wisconsin. He is also a recipient of the Elijah Watts Sells Award for Honorary Distinction for his results on the CPA exam. He is a member of the American Accounting Association and the Institute of Management Accountants and has published articles in *Accounting Review*, *Accounting Horizons*, *Advances in Management Accounting*, *Managerial Finance*, *Issues in Accounting Education*, *Journal of Accounting Education*, as well as other journals. His research interests include accounting for financial instruments and innovation in accounting education. He has published papers and given numerous talks on incorporating critical thinking into accounting education, and helped prepare a catalog of critical thinking resources for the Federated Schools of Accountancy.

Don Kieso

Donald E. Kieso, PhD, CPA, received his bachelor's degree from Aurora University and his doctorate in accounting from the University of Illinois. He has served as chairman of the Department of Accountancy and is currently the KPMG Emeritus Professor of Accountancy at Northern Illinois University. He has public accounting experience with Price Waterhouse & Co. (San Francisco and Chicago) and Arthur Andersen & Co. (Chicago) and research experience with the Research Division of the American Institute of Certified Public Accountants (New York). He has done post doctorate work as a Visiting Scholar at the University of California at Berkeley and is a recipient of NIU's Teaching Excellence Award and four Golden Apple Teaching Awards. Professor Kieso is the author of other accounting and business books and is a member of the American Accounting Association, the American Institute of Certified Public Accountants, and the Illinois CPA Society. He has served as a member of the Board of Directors of the Illinois CPA Society, then AACSB's Accounting Accreditation Committees, the State of Illinois Comptroller's Commission, as Secretary-Treasurer of the Federation of Schools of Accountancy, and as Secretary-Treasurer of the American Accounting Association. Professor Kieso is currently serving on the Board of Trustees and Executive Committee of Aurora University, as a member of the Board of Directors of Kishwaukee Community Hospital, and as Treasurer and Director of Valley West Community Hospital. From 1989 to 1993 he served as a charter member of the national Accounting Education Change Commission. He is the recipient of the Outstanding Accounting Educator Award from the Illinois CPA Society, the FSA's Joseph A. Silvoso Award of Merit, the NIU Foundation's Humanitarian Award for Service to Higher Education, a Distinguished Service Award from the Illinois CPA Society, and in 2003 an honorary doctorate from Aurora University.

The Wiley Faculty Network

The Place Where Faculty Connect ...

The Wiley Faculty Network is a global community of faculty connected by a passion for teaching and a drive to learn and share. Connect with the Wiley Faculty Network to collaborate with your colleagues, find a mentor, attend virtual and live events, and view a wealth of resources all designed to help you grow as an educator. Embrace the art of teaching—great things happen where faculty connect!

Attend

Discover innovative ideas and gain knowledge you can use.

- Training
- Virtual Guest Lectures
- Live Events

View

Explore your resources and development opportunities.

- Teaching Resources
- Archived Guest Lectures
- Recorded Presentations
- Professional Development Modules

Collaborate

Connect with colleagues—your greatest resource.

- Find a Mentor
- Interest Groups
- Blog

Find out more at
www.WHEREFACULTYCONNECT.com

Virtual Guest Lectures
Connect with recognized leaders across disciplines and collaborate with your peers on timely topics and discipline-specific issues, many of which offer CPE credit.

Live and Virtual Events
These invitation-only, discipline-specific events are organized through a close partnership between the WFN, Wiley, and the academic community near the event location.

Technology Training
Discover a wealth of topic- and technology-specific training presented by subject matter experts, authors, and faculty where and when you need it.

Teaching Resources
Propel your teaching and student learning to the next level with quality peer-reviewed case studies, testimonials, classroom tools, and checklists.

Connect with Colleagues
Achieve goals and tackle challenges more easily by enlisting the help of your peers. Connecting with colleagues through the WFN can help you improve your teaching experience.

What's New?

The Fifth Edition expands our emphasis on student learning and improves upon a teaching and learning package that instructors and students have rated the highest in customer satisfaction in the following ways:

Increased Managerial Accounting Coverage

This edition reflects our continuing commitment to provide thorough coverage of all managerial accounting topics. We now offer separate chapters on incremental analysis (Chapter 20) and capital budgeting (Chapter 24), as well as a new Appendix J on pricing.

Continued Emphasis on Helping Students Learn Accounting Concepts

Especially with this edition of the textbook, we have carefully scrutinized all chapter material to help students learn accounting concepts. We revised existing explanations and illustrations as well as added more explanations, examples, and illustrations. For example, we have added T-accounts in the margin to illustrate the effect of accounting procedures as well as discussed how tight credit policies nearly prevented Apple from fulfilling its first sale.

Corporate Social Responsibility

Today's companies are evaluating not just their profitability but also their corporate social responsibility. In this edition, we have profiled some of these companies in the new People, Planet, and Profit Insight boxes, such as PepsiCo, to highlight their sustainable business practices. We have also added a new *Broadening Your Perspective* problem, Considering People, Planet, and Profit, which offers students the opportunity to analyze current business practices.

Student-Friendly Companies

One of the goals of the financial accounting course is to orient students to the application of accounting principles and techniques in practice. Accordingly, we have expanded our practice of using numerous examples from real companies throughout the textbook to add more high-interest enterprises that we hope will increase student engagement, such as Clif Bar, Groupon, REI, and Skechers. Also, beginning in Chapter 14, we introduce Current Designs, a kayak-making company, and then follow-up with a new decision-making problem in every chapter based on this real-world company.

Managerial Accounting Video Series

Through the use of real-world, cutting-edge companies, these videos (available in *WileyPLUS*) engage students with a dynamic overview of managerial accounting topics. Students are then motivated to further review the detailed tools, examples, and discussions presented in their textbook, *WileyPLUS* course, and classroom lectures.

Enhanced Homework Material

In each chapter, we have updated Self-Test Questions, Questions, Brief Exercises, Do it! Review, Exercises, Problems, and Research Cases. Financial analysis and reporting problems have been updated in accordance with the new Tootsie Roll and Hershey financial statements. New Considering People, Planet, and Profit problems are included to offer students experience in evaluating corporate social responsibility, and new Considering Your Costs and Benefits problems require students to weigh the pros and cons of two alternatives.

Accuracy and Relevance

This edition was also subject to an overall, comprehensive revision to ensure that it is technically accurate, relevant, and up-to-date. A chapter-by-chapter summary of content changes is provided in the chart on the next two pages.

Content Changes by Chapter

Chapter 1: Introduction to Financial Statements
- New Feature Story, on Clif Bar and its ESOP and open-book management program.
- New discussion of LLCs and S corporations, to reflect more current business practices.
- New People, Planet, and Profit Insight, on evaluating companies on social practices as well as on financial results.
- New Research Case on possible expanding role of auditors.

Chapter 2: A Further Look at Financial Statements
- Updated to reflect new conceptual framework terminology.

Chapter 3: The Accounting Information System
- Heavily revised Feature Story, now on MF Global's failure to segregate company accounts from customer accounts.
- New Ethics Insight, on Credit Suisse Group's failure to properly write down value of its securities.
- New Research Case based on Green Bay Packers' annual report publication.

Chapter 4: Accrual Accounting Concepts
- New Feature Story, on Groupon and complexity of accounting for its revenues.
- New People, Planet, and Profit Insight, on costs of disposing discarded, possibly toxic, materials.

Chapter 5: Merchandising Operations and the Multiple-Step Income Statement
- New Feature Story, on REI and its unique business model.
- New use of recent REI and Dick's Sporting Goods financial statement information.
- Revised Ethics Insight box on improving company clarity of financial disclosures by citing eBay's recent sale of Skype.
- New People, Planet, and Profit Insight, about whether PepsiCo should market green.

Chapter 6: Reporting and Analyzing Inventory
- Added new Accounting Across the Organization box, on Sony's inventory management practices.
- New Research Case, on U.S. companies use of LIFO.
- New Considering People, Planet, and Profit Insight, about Caterpillar's annual Sustainability Report.

Chapter 7: Fraud, Internal Control, and Cash
- New People, Planet and Profit Insight, about the need for an effective system of internal controls for sustainability reporting.
- New Interpreting Financial Statements problem, based on recent Ernst & Young global survey on fraud.

Chapter 8: Reporting and Analyzing Receivables
- New Feature Story, about Nike, its products, and its receivables management.
- Featured companies in chapter are now Nike and Skechers, to increase student engagement.
- New example of Apple's first sale, to demonstrate importance of extending credit.

Chapter 9: Reporting and Analyzing Long-Lived Assets
- Revised Feature Story and in-chapter examples, to focus on JetBlue as well as include more recent information about the airline industry.
- New People, Planet, and Profit Insight, about Billiton's sustainability report.
- New Research Cases, about goodwill and Best Buy's profitability.

Chapter 10: Reporting and Analyzing Liabilities
- Expanded EOC material: 2 new Questions, 3 new Brief Exercises, 2 new Exercises, new Real-World Focus problem, new Interpreting Financial Statements problem, new Considering People, Planet, and Profit problem, and new All About You problem.

Chapter 11: Reporting and Analyzing Stockholders' Equity
- New Feature Story, about why Mark Zuckerberg delayed taking Facebook public.
- New People, Planet, and Profit Insight, about rising level of support for shareholder proposals requesting action related to social and environmental issues.
- New Accounting Across the Organization box, about how the recent financial crisis affected companies' dividend payouts.
- New Research Case, new Considering People, Planet, and Profit problem, and new IFRS Concepts and Application problem.

Chapter 12: Statement of Cash Flows
- Revamped Feature Story, to include more recent information about Apple's cash flow status.
- New Accounting Across the Organization box, about Kodak's need to sell plant assets to raise cash.
- New Investor Insight, about how 42% of companies going public had audit opinions warning about the companies' risk of failure.

Chapter 13: Financial Analysis: The Big Picture
- Revised Feature Story, to include more recent information about Warren Buffett as well as to improve readability.
- New Investor Insight, about how recently some companies have altered their pension-plan accounting to avoid prior-year events to distort current-year results.
- New Do it! box on ratio analysis.

Chapter 14 Managerial Accounting
- New Feature Story, on history and operations of Current Designs (kayak-making company).
- New Management Insight, about importance of U.S. factory jobs.
- New Corporate Social Responsibility section.
- Deleted chapter appendix (Accounting Cycle for a Manufacturing Company).

Chapter 15 Job Order Costing
- New Feature Story, on Lynn Tilton, founder and CEO of Patriarch Partners, the largest, woman-owned U.S. business.
- Added more explanations and details (such as T-accounts), to increase student understanding.

Chapter 16 Process Costing
- Changed example of company in Process Cost Flow section to roller blade/skateboard wheel manufacturer, to increase student appeal.
- New People, Planet, and Profit Insight, about costs/benefits of remanufactured goods.

Chapter 17 Activity-Based Costing
- New Feature Story, on why Precor switched from traditional costing to activity-based costing.
- Changed example company, in Example of ABC versus Traditional Costing section, to producing abdominal trainers to tie in with Precor.
- Rewrote definition/explanation of value-added and non–value-added activities, as well as of activity levels, to ensure student understanding.

- New Management Insight, summarizing a recent survey of ABC practices by companies worldwide.
- New Real-World Focus problem, on use of ABC in the financial services industry.

Chapter 18 Cost-Volume-Profit
- New Feature Story, on how Jeff Bezos started and expanded Amazon.com's operations.
- New People, Planet, and Profit Insight, on hydroponic farming/vertical farming.
- Added material on use of scatter plots in High-Low Method section, as well as provided supplement on regression analysis on book's companion website.
- New Real-World Focus problem, on how Barnes and Noble's current structure left it ill-prepared for an e-book environment.

Chapter 19 Cost-Volume-Profit Analysis: Additional Issues
- New Feature Story, still about Intel, but now explaining why the computer chip giant experiences huge swings in its earnings.
- Provided more step-by-step explanations and illustrations, so students will improve their understanding of why and how to compute break-even points, target net income, and margin of safety.
- New Service Company Insight, about why Warren Buffett acquired Burlington Northern Railroad.
- New Real-World Focus problem, on Smart Balance's employment and cost structure.

Chapter 20 Incremental Analysis (previously part of Chapter 23)
- New Service Company Insight, about the relevant revenues and costs of Amazon.com's Prime free shipping program.
- Expanded sunk cost discussion and illustrations, to improve student understanding.
- New material on how behavioral decision-making can affect whether or not to replace equipment.
- Expanded discussion of elimination of an unprofitable segment to include fixed cost analysis.
- New section on other considerations in decision-making, e.g., qualitative factors and relationship of incremental analysis and ABC.

Chapter 21 Budgetary Planning (previously Chapter 20)
- Added more detailed explanation to the Budgeting and Human Behavior section about participative budgeting.

- Added marginal T-accounts to Production Budget and Direct Materials Budget sections, to illustrate flow of costs.
- New Service Company Insight, on the implications of budgetary optimism as it pertains to governments.
- New Management Insight, on the potential costs and benefits of a company stockpiling raw materials.
- Added a second Comprehensive Do It! problem on budgeted income statement and balance sheet.
- New Considering Your Costs and Benefits problem about whether student loans should be considered as a source of income.

Chapter 22 Budgetary Control and Responsibility Accounting (previously Chapter 21)
- New Service Company Insight, about NBCUniversal's response to Fox wanting to reduce its TV licensing fee.
- Added graph to the solution for the Do It! on flexible budgets, to increase student understanding.
- Moved Management by Exception to within Performance Evaluation discussion, for better flow of chapter topics.

Chapter 23 Standard Costs and Balanced Scorecard (previously Chapter 22)
- New Feature Story (and accompanying video) on Starbucks' origins and vision.
- New material and illustrations added, to enhance explanation of the components of variances as well as how to compute them.

- New People, Planet, and Profit Insight, highlighting Starbucks' 10th annual Global Responsibility Report and the company's commitment to corporate social responsibility.
- New Real-World Focus problem referencing the *Wall Street Journal* article, "In Risky Move, GM to Run Plants Around Clock."
- New Considering Your Costs and Benefits problem, addressing the extent to which financial measures should influence medical care.

Chapter 24 Planning for Capital Investments (previously part of Chapter 23)
- New Feature Story, on how timing can affect capital investments by the cruise-line industry.
- New section on additional considerations for capital budgeting, such as intangible benefits, profitability index for mutually exclusive projects, risk analysis, and post-audit of investment projects.
- New Management Insights, about whether Verizon's investment in its 4G wireless service will pay off and whether there is too much plant capacity for manufacturing big-screen TVs.
- New Considering Your Costs and Benefits problem, about calculating the NPVs of solar panels.

Appendix J Pricing
- New appendix that discusses pricing goods for external sales, pricing services, transfer pricing for internal sales, transfers between divisions in different countries, and other cost approaches to pricing.

Active Teaching and Learning Supplementary Material

For Instructors

In addition to the support instructors receive from *WileyPLUS* and the Wiley Faculty Network, we offer the following useful supplements.

Textbook Companion Website.   On this website, **www.wiley.com/college/kimmel**, instructors will find the Solutions Manual, Test Bank, Instructor's Manual, Computerized Test Bank, and other resources.

Solutions Manual.   The Solutions Manual contains detailed solutions to all questions, brief exercises, exercises, and problems in the textbook, as well as suggested answers to the questions and cases. The estimated time to complete exercises, problems, and cases is provided.

Instructor's Manual.   Included in each chapter are lecture outlines with teaching tips, chapter reviews, and review quizzes.

Test Bank and Computerized Test Bank.   The test bank and computerized test bank allow instructors to tailor examinations according to learning objectives and learning outcomes, including AACSB, AICPA, and IMA professional standards. Achievement tests, comprehensive examinations, and a final exam are included.

PowerPoint™.   The PowerPoint™ presentations contain a combination of key concepts, images, and problems from the textbook. They are a useful, animated tool for classroom lectures.

For Students

Textbook Companion Website.   On this website, **www.wiley.com/college/kimmel**, students will find support materials that include *Exercises: Set B, Challenge Exercises, Problems: Set C, Continuing Cookie Chronicle* and *Waterways Continuing Problems, Appendices F–J,* and *Cases for Managerial Decision-Making.*

Study Guide.   The Study Guide includes a chapter review and provides opportunities for practice through problems and multiple-choice exercises.

Working Papers.   The working papers are partially completed accounting templates that will help students correctly format their textbook accounting solutions. Working paper templates are available for all end-of-chapter brief exercises, exercises, problems, and cases. Excel working papers are available in *WileyPLUS*.

Quantum Tutors.   Adaptive learning and assessment software that will help students master the core accounting topics and skills necessary to be successful in this course.

Mobile Applications.   Quizzing and reviewing content is available for download on iTunes.

Managerial Accounting Video Series.   Through the examples of real-world, cutting-edge companies, these videos (available in *WileyPLUS*) engage students with a dynamic overview of managerial accounting topics. Students are then motivated to further review the detailed tools, examples, and discussions presented in their textbook, *WileyPLUS* course, and classroom lectures.

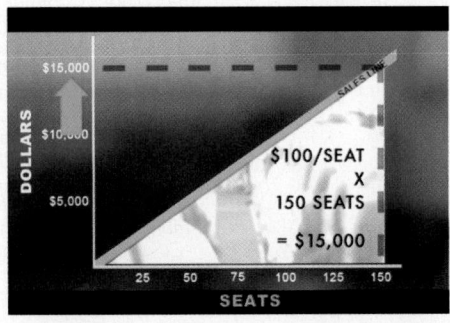

Acknowledgments

Accounting, Fifth Edition, has benefitted greatly from the input of focus group participants, manuscript reviewers, those who have sent comments by letter or e-mail, ancillary authors, and proofers. We greatly appreciate the constructive suggestions and innovative ideas of reviewers and the creativity and accuracy of the ancillary authors and checkers.

Prior Edition

Thanks to the following reviewers, focus group participants, and others who provided suggestions for the Fourth Edition:

Sylvia Allen	*Los Angeles Valley College*
Juanita Ardavany	*Los Angeles Valley College*
Eric Blazer	*Millersville University*
Evangelie Brodie	*North Carolina State University*
Thane Butt	*Champlain College*
Sandra Byrd	*Missouri State University*
Lisa Capozzoli	*College of DuPage*
Siu Chung	*Los Angeles Valley College*
Leslie Cohen	*University of Arizona*
Rita Kingery Cook	*University of Delaware*
Cheryl Copeland	*California State University—Fresno*
Cheryl Crespi	*Central Connecticut State University*
Sue Counte	*St. Louis Community College—Meramec*
Robin D'Agati	*Palm Beach Community College*
Brent W. Darwin	*Allan Hancock College*
Michael Deschamps	*Mira Costa College*
Gadis Dillon	*Oakland University*
Rafik Elias	*University of California, Los Angeles*
Alan Falcon	*Loyola Marymount University*
Annette Fisher	*Glendale Community College*
Lance Fisher	*Oklahoma State University*
Roger Gee	*San Diego Mesa College*
Lisa Gray	*Seminole State College and Valencia Community College*
Michael Haselkorn	*Bentley University*
Hassan Hefzi	*California State PolyTech University—Pomona*
M.A. "Maggie" Houston	*Wright State University*
Ryan Huldah	*Iona College*
Ann Kelly	*Providence College*
Mehmet Kocakulah	*University of Southern Indiana*
Wikil Kwak	*University of Nebraska—Omaha*
Barbara Lamberton	*University of Hartford*
Lihon Liang	*Syracuse University*
D. Jordan Lowe	*Arizona State University*
James Lukawitz	*University of Memphis*
Sue Marcum	*American University*
Sal Marino	*Westchester Community College*
Florence McGovern	*Bergen Community College*
Noel McKeon	*Florida Community College at Jacksonville*
Paul Mihalek	*Central Connecticut State University*
Jeanne Miller	*Cypress College*
William J. Nealon	*Schenectady County Community College*
Joseph M. Nicassio	*Westmoreland County Community College*
Garth Novack	*University of Washington*
Rosemary Nurre	*San Mateo Community College*
Marge O'Reilly-Allen	*Rider University*
Terry Patton	*Midwestern State University*
Sandra Pelfrey	*Oakland University*
Ronald Pierno	*Florida State University*
John Purisky	*Salem State University*
Karl Putnam	*University of Texas—El Paso*
Ray Reisig	*Pace University, Pleasantville*
Rod Ridenour	*Montana State University—Bozeman*
Larry Rittenberg	*University of Wisconsin*
Cecile M. Roberti	*Community College of Rhode Island*
Lawrence Roman	*Cuyahoga Community College*
Luther L. Ross	*Central Piedmont Community College*
Robert Russ	*Northern Kentucky University*
Nancy Sill	*Modesto Junior College*
Gerald Smith	*University of Northern Iowa*
Vic Stanton	*University of California, Berkley*
Howard Switkay	*Community College of Philadelphia*
Diane Tanner	*University of North Florida*
Michael Tydlaska	*Mountain View College*
Joan Van Hise	*Fairfield University*
Richard Van Ness	*Schenectady County Community College*
Ron Vogel	*College of Eastern Utah*
Barbara Warschawski	*Schenectady County Community College*
Wendy Wilson	*Southern Methodist University*

Fifth Edition

Thanks to the following reviewers, focus group participants, and others who provided suggestions for the Fifth Edition:

Dawn Addington	*Central New Mexico Community College*
Bruce Bradford	*Fairfield University*
Duane Brandon	*Auburn University*
Gary Braun	*University of Texas—El Paso*
Jerold K. Braun	*Daytona State College*
Robert Braun	*Southeastern Louisiana University*
Leroy Bugger	*Edison State College*
Sandra Byrd	*Missouri State University*
Lisa Capozzoli	*College of DuPage*
Renee Castrigano	*Cleveland State University*
Gayle Chaky	*Dutchess Community College*
Toni Clegg	*Delta College*
Cheryl Copeland	*California State University—Fresno*
Cheryl Corke	*Genesee Community College*
Paquita Davis-Friday	*Baruch College*
Larry DeGaetano	*Montclair State University*
Ron Dustin	*Fresno City College*
Barbara Eide	*University of Wisconsin—La Crosse*
Ann Escaro	*McHenry County College*
Janet Farler	*Pima Community College*
Annette Fisher	*Glendale Community College*
Hubert Glover	*Drexel University*
Gloria Grayless	*Sam Houston State University*
Siriyama Kanthi Herath	*Georgia Institute of Technology*
Bambi Hora	*University of Central Oklahoma*
Robert Kenny	*The College of New Jersey*
Marinilka Kimbro	*Gonzaga University*
Don Kovacic	*California State University—San Marcos*
Joseph Larkin	*Saint Joseph's University*
Richard Larkin	
David Laurel	*South Texas College*
Maria Leach	*Auburn University*
Jason Lee	*SUNY Plattsburgh*
Harold Little	*Western Kentucky University*
Nancy Lynch	*West Virginia University*
Lois Mahoney	*Eastern Michigan University*
Florence McGovern	*Bergen Community College*
Mary Michel	*Manhattan College*
Earl Mitchell	*Santa Ana College*
Kathy Munter	*Pima Community College*
Michael Newman	*University of Houston*
Judy Peterson	*Monmouth College*

Janice Pitera	*Broome Community College*
Robert Rambo	*Roger Williams University*
Ruthie G. Reynolds	*Howard University*
John Ribezzo	*Community College of Rhode Island*
Luther Ross	*Central Piedmont Community College*
Susan Sadowski	*Shippensburg University/UMUC*
Richard Sarkisian	*Camden County College*
Mary Jane Sauceda	*University of Texas—Brownsville*
Karl Schindl	*University of Wisconsin—Manitowoc*
Debbie Seifert	*Illinois State University*
Valerie Simmons	*University of Southern Mississippi*
Jaye Simpson	*Tarrant County College Northwest*
Mike Skaff	*College of the Sequoias*
Pam Smith	*Northern Illinois University*
Nancy Snow	*University of Toledo*
Naomi Soderstrom	*University of Colorado—Boulder*
Patrick Stegman	*College of Lake County*
Paul Swanson	*Illinois Central College*
Karen Tabak	*Maryville University*
Diane Tanner	*University of North Florida*
Margaret Tanner	*University of Arkansas*
Joan Van Hise	*Fairfield University*
Sheila Viel	*University of Wisconsin—Milwaukee*
Christopher Wallace	*California State University—Sacramento*
Kathryn Yarbrough	*University of North Carolina—Charlotte*
Judith Zander	*Grossmont College*

Advisory Board Members

Lisa Capozzoli	*College of DuPage*
Marina Grau	*Houston Community College*
Michael Gurevitz	*Montgomery College—Rockville*
Marcye Hampton	*University of Central Florida*
Merrily Hoffman	*San Jacinto College Central*
Jeffrey Jones	*College of Southern Nevada*
James Racic	*Lakeland Community College*
Steve Teeter	*Utah Valley University*
Geoffrey Tickell	*Indiana University of Pennsylvania*
Bob Urell	*Irvine Valley College*
Wanda Wong	*Chabot College*
Judith Zander	*Grossmont College*

Ancillary Authors, Contributors, Proofers, and Accuracy Checkers

We sincerely thank the following individuals for their hard work in preparing the content that accompanies this textbook:

LuAnn Bean	*Florida Institute of Technology*
Jack Borke	*University of Wisconsin—Platteville*
Richard Campbell	*University of Rio Grande*
Sandra Cohen	*Columbia College—Chicago*
Terry Elliott	*Morehead State University*
James M. Emig	*Villanova University*
Larry R. Falcetto	*Emporia State University*
Cecelia M. Fewox	*College of Charleston*
Coby Harmon	*University of California—Santa Barbara*
Harry Howe	*SUNY—Geneseo*
Doug Kieso	*Aurora University*
Kirk Lynch	*Sandhills Community College*
Laura McNally	*Black Hills State College*
Kevin McNelis	*New Mexico State University*
Jill Misuraca	*University of Tampa*
Barb Muller	*Arizona State University*
Yvonne Phang	*Borough of Manhattan Community College*
John Plouffe	*California State University—Los Angeles*
Laura Prosser	*Black Hills State University*
Eileen M. Shifflett	*James Madison University*
Ellen Sweatt	*Georgia Perimeter College*
Diane Tanner	*University of North Florida*
Joan Van Hise	*Fairfield University*
Sheila Viel	*University of Wisconsin—Milwaukee*
Alice Sineath	*Forsyth Technical Community College*
Teresa Speck	*Saint Mary's University of Minnesota*
Lynn Stallworth	*Appalachian State University*
Doris Warmflash	*SUNY, Westchester Community College*
Dick Wasson	*Southwestern College*
Andrea Weickgenannt	*Xavier University*
Bernie Weinrich	*Lindenwood University*
Melanie Yon	

We thank Benjamin Huegel and Teresa Speck of St. Mary's University for their extensive efforts in the preparation of the homework materials related to Current Designs. We also appreciate the considerable support provided to us by the following people at Current Designs: Mike Cichanowski, Jim Brown, Diane Buswell, and Jake Greseth. We also benefited from the assistance and suggestions provided to us by Joan Van Hise in the preparation of materials related to sustainability.

We appreciate the exemplary support and commitment given to us by associate publisher Chris DeJohn, marketing manager Karolina Zarychta Honsa, operations manager Yana Mermel, content editor Ed Brislin, development editors Terry Ann Tatro and Margaret Thompson, lead product designer Allie Morris, product designer Greg Chaput, vice president of content management Sesha Bolisetty, designers Maureen Eide and Kristine Carney, illustration editor Anna Melhorn, photo editor Mary Ann Price, project editor Jeanine Furino of Furino Production, Denise Showers at Aptara, Cyndy Taylor, project manager Matt Gauthier at Integra, and Katie Trotta at ANSR. All of these professionals provided innumerable services that helped the textbook take shape.

Finally, our thanks to Amy Scholz, Susan Elbe, George Hoffman, Tim Stookesberry, Joe Heider, and Steve Smith for their support and leadership in Wiley's College Division. We will appreciate suggestions and comments from users—instructors and students alike. You can send your thoughts and ideas about the textbook to us via email at AccountingAuthors@yahoo.com.

Paul D. Kimmel
Milwaukee, Wisconsin

Jerry J. Weygandt
Madison, Wisconsin

Donald E. Kieso
DeKalb, Illinois

Contents

read it!

Feature Stories introduce chapter topics in fun ways using real-world companies that are engaging.

Issues that affect today's business world are highlighted in the textbook.

CHAPTER 11

facebook

REPORTING AND ANALYZING STOCKHOLDERS' EQUITY

Paul Sakuma/AP/Wide World Photos

Real World

INTEL CORPORATION Balance Sheets December 31, 2011 and 2010 (in millions)		
Assets	**2011**	**2010**
Current assets	$25,872	$31,611
Noncurrent assets	45,247	31,575
Total as		

KEEPING AN EYE ON CASH

The balance sheet presents the balances of a company's s accounts at a point in time. Companies report in the "Finan tion of the statement of cash flows information regarding ca flows during the year that resulted from equity transactions. presents the cash flows from financing activities from the stat of Sara Lee Corporation in a recent year: From this informatic company's purchases of treasury stock during the period fa

Broadening Your Perspective

Financial Reporting and Analysis

FINANCIAL REPORTING PROBLEM: *Tootsie Roll Industries, Inc.*

BYP11-1 The stockholders' equity section of Tootsie Roll Industries' balance sheet is shown in the Consolidated Statement of Financial Position in Appendix A. You will also find data relative to this problem on other pages of Appendix A. (Note that Tootsie Roll has two classes of common stock. To answer the following questions, add the two classes of stock together.)

A Look at IFRS

The accounting for transactions related to stockholders' equity, such as issuance of share purchase of treasury stock, and declaration and payment of dividends, are similar und both IFRS and GAAP. Major differences relate to terminology used, introduction of iter such as revaluation surplus, and presentation of stockholders' equity information.

Insight Boxes frame real-world company issues through inter-national, ethical, and other perspectives.

Investor Insight
Morrow Snowboards Improves Its Stock Appeal

Investors are often eager to invest in a company that has a hot new product. However, when snowboard maker Morrow Snowboards, Inc., issued shares of stock to the public for the first time, some investors expressed reluctance to invest in Morrow because of a number of accounting control problems. To reduce investor concerns, Morrow implemented a perpetual inventory system to improve its control over inventory. In addition, it stated that it would perform a physical inventory count every quarter until it felt that the perpetual inventory system was reliable.

? If a perpetual system keeps track of inventory on a daily basis, why do companies ever need to do a physical count?

© Ben Blankenburg/iStockphoto

see it

CONTENT FOR ALL LEARNING STYLES

In addition to a textbook consistently reviewed as very readable, over 50% of the textbook provides visual presentations and interpretations of content.

Equation Analysis Illustrations visually walk you through the steps of journal transactions.

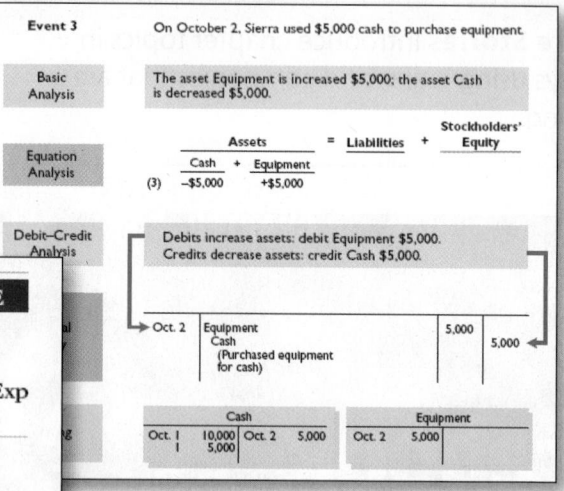

Event 3	On October 2, Sierra used $5,000 cash to purchase equipment.
Basic Analysis	The asset Equipment is increased $5,000; the asset Cash is decreased $5,000.

Cash Flow Analyses visually summarize the effects of transactions on cash flows.

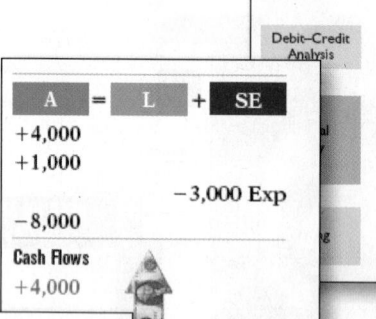

A	=	L	+	SE
+4,000				
+1,000				
				−3,000 Exp
−8,000				

Cash Flows
+4,000

Retailer receives cash more quickly from credit card issuer

Infographics reinforce important textual concepts. Infographics were revised in the Fifth Edition.

Illustrations are clearly identified and often present data in a real-world format.

CANDLESTICK, INC.
Bond Premium Amortization Schedule
Straight-Line Method—Annual Interest Payments
$100,000 of 10%, 5-Year Bonds

www.wileyteamforsuccess.com

do it!

WAGES AND PAYROLL TAXES

Do it! During the month of September, Lake Corporation's employees ea[rned] wages of $60,000. Withholdings related to these wages were $3,500 for Social Sec[urity] (FICA), $6,500 for federal income tax, and $2,000 for state income tax. Costs incurr[ed] unemployment taxes were $90 for federal and $150 for state.

Prepare the September 30 journal entries for (a) salaries and wages expense and [sala]ries and wages payable, assuming that all September wages will be paid in October [and] (b) the company's payroll tax expense.

Action Plan

- Remember that wages earned are an expense to the company, but withholdings reduce the amount due to be paid to the employee.
- Payroll taxes are taxes the company incurs related to its employees.

Solution

(a) To determine wages payable, reduce wages expense by the withholdings for [FICA,] federal income tax, and state income tax.

Sept. 30	Salaries and Wages Expense	60,000	
	FICA Taxes Payable		3,50[0]
	Federal Income Taxes Payable		6,50[0]
	State Income Taxes Payable		2,00[0]
	Salaries and Wages Payable		48,00[0]

(b) Payroll taxes would be for the company's share of FICA, as well as for federal and [state] unemployment tax.

Clear **Do it! exercises** in the textbook narrative provide step-by-step applications of a concept at the precise moment you acquire the knowledge. Each Do it! in the textbook narrative includes a solution, an Action Plan, and a path of related homework exercises.

Comprehensive Do it!'s at the end of each chapter apply the Do it! and address **multiple** topics.

Comprehensive **Do it!**

Snyder Software Inc. successfully developed a new spreadsheet program. However, to produce and market the program, the company needed additional financing. On January 1, 2013, Snyder borrowed money as follows.

1. Snyder issued $500,000, 11%, 10-year bonds. The bonds sold at face value and pay interest on January 1.

2. Snyder issued $1.0 million, 10%, 10-year bonds for $886,996. Interest is payable on [Ju]ine method of amortization.

Do it! Review

Do It! 10-1 You and several classmates are studying for the next accounting examination. They ask you to answer the following questions:

1. If cash is borrowed on a $60,000, 9-month, 10% note on August 1, how much interest expense would be incurred by December 31?
2. The cash register total including sales taxes is $42,000, and the sales tax rate is 5%. What is the sales taxes payable?
3. If $42,000 is collected in advance on November 1 for 6-month magazine subscriptions, what amount of subscription revenue should be recognized on December 31?

Do It! 10-2 During the month of February, Morrisey Corporation's employees earned wages of $74,000. Withholdings related to these wages were $5,661 for Social Security (FICA), $7,100 for federal income tax, and $1,900 for state income tax. Costs incurred for unemployment taxes were $110 for federal and $160 for state.

Prepare the February 28 journal entries for (a) salaries and wages expense and salaries and wages payable assuming that all February wages will be paid in March and (b) the company's payroll tax expense.

End-of-Chapter Do it! exercises provide further practice with alternate versions of the in-chapter Do It! exercises.

get it!

TOOLS FOR DECISION-MAKING

As an employee, manager, or even a director of your own personal finances, you will make better decisions by learning how to analyze and solve business problems using tools provided throughout each chapter.

🧰 DECISION TOOLKIT

DECISION CHECKPOINTS	INFO NEEDED FOR DECISION	TOOL TO USE FOR DECISION	HOW TO EVALUATE RESULTS
What is the company's policy toward dividends and growth?	Retained earnings statement	How much of this year's income did the company pay out in dividends to shareholders?	A company striving for rapid growth will pay a low (or no) dividend.

The Decision Toolkit and **the Decision Toolkit Summary** direct you to the tools and information you need when evaluating business issues.

🧰 USING THE DECISION TOOLKIT

The Hershey Company, located in Hershey, Pennsylvania, is the leading North American manufacturer of chocolate. Its products include Hershey's Kisses, Reese's Peanut Butter Cups, Kit Kat, and Take 5 bars. Imagine that you are considering the purchase of shares of Hershey's common stock.

Instructions

Answer these questions related to your decision whether t
(a) What financial statements should you evaluate?
(b) What should these financial statements tell you?

Using the Decision Toolkit asks you to apply toolkit lessons to a financial statement analysis exercise. Suggested solutions are provided.

18. What is the purpose of the management discussion and analysis section (MD&A)?

19. Why is it important for financial statements to receive an unqualified auditor's opinion?

20. What types of information are presented in the notes to the financial statements?

21. ✏️ The accounting equation is Assets = Liabilities + Stockholders' Equity. Appendix A, at the end of this textbook, reproduces Tootsie Roll's financial statements. Replacing words in the equation with dollar amounts, what is Tootsie Roll's accounting equation at December 31, 2011?

The tool icon indicates that an activity employs one of the decision tools presented in the chapter. The ← indicates that an activity relates to a business function beyond accounting. The pencil icon ✏️

A wrench icon next to select end-of-chapter homework exercises highlights opportunities where you will practice decision-making tools.

kieso
weygandt
kimmel
warfield

www.wileyteamforsuccess.com

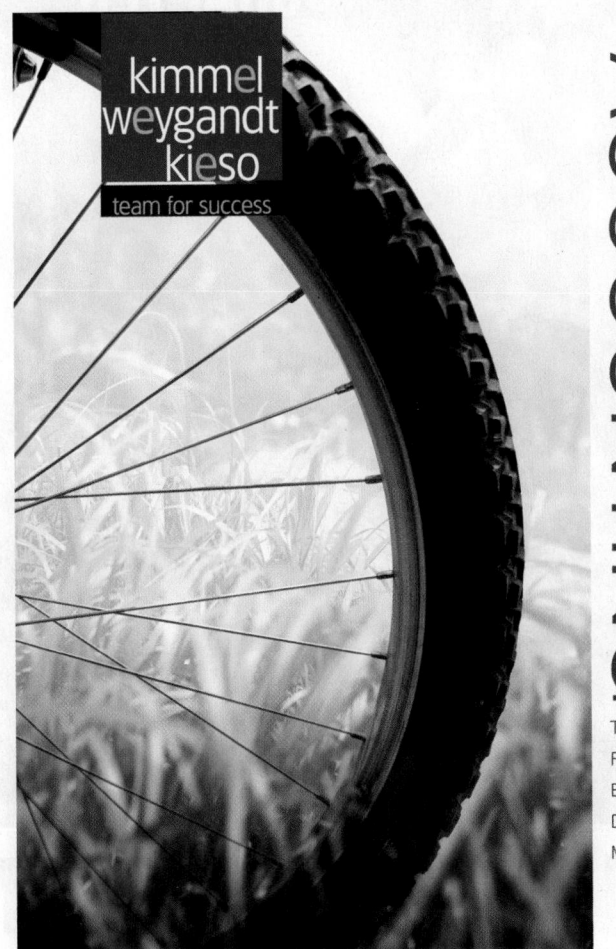

kimmel
weygandt
kieso
team for success

ACCOUNTING

TOOLS
FOR
BUSINESS
DECISION
MAKING

5e

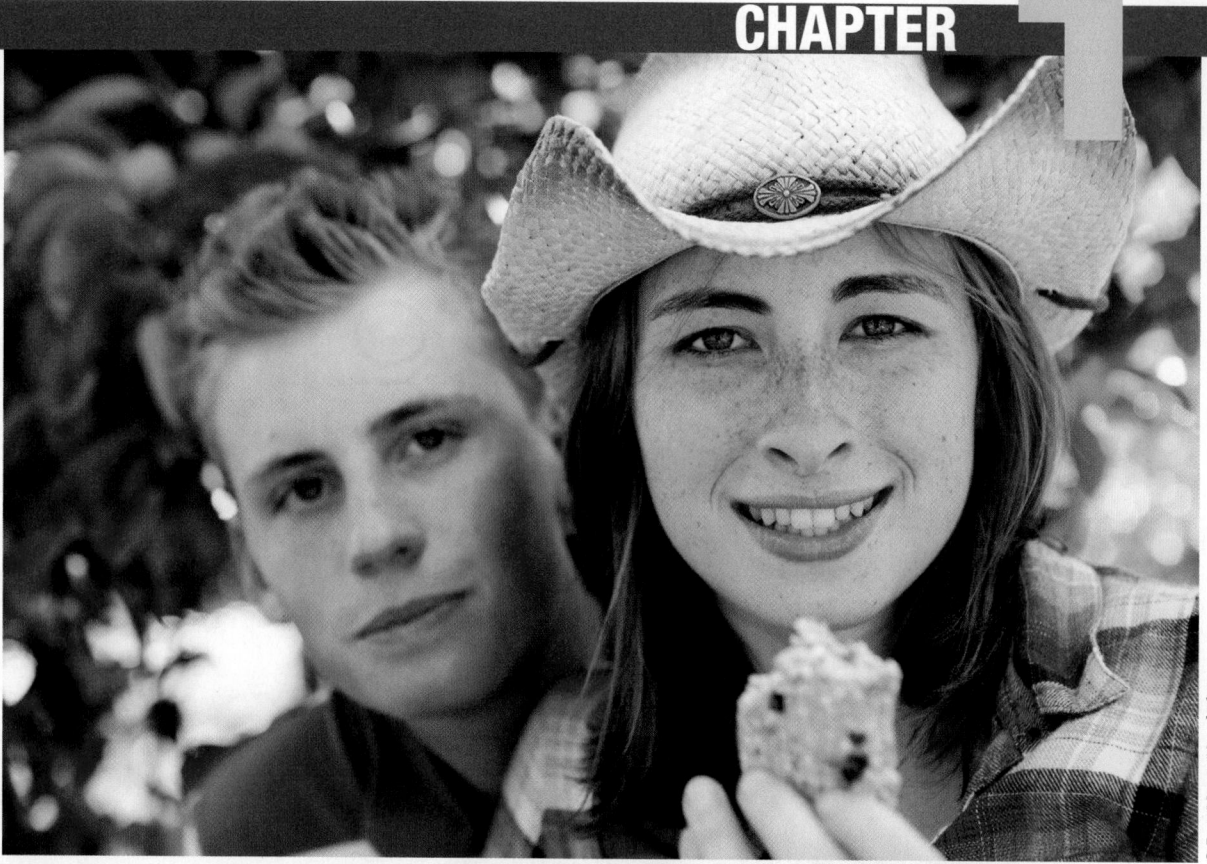

© Dan Moore/iStockphoto

CHAPTER 1

INTRODUCTION TO FINANCIAL STATEMENTS

✔The Navigator

- Scan Learning Objectives
- Read Feature Story
- Scan Preview
- Read Text and Answer **Do it!**
  ○ p. 5 ○ p. 11 ○ p. 18 ○ p. 21
- Work Using the Decision Toolkit
- Review Summary of Learning Objectives
- Work Comprehensive **Do it!** p. 24
- Answer Self-Test Questions
- Complete Assignments
- Go to WileyPLUS for practice and tutorials

🌐 Read A Look at IFRS p. 43

LEARNING OBJECTIVES

After studying this chapter, you should be able to:

1 Describe the primary forms of business organization.
2 Identify the users and uses of accounting information.
3 Explain the three principal types of business activity.
4 Describe the content and purpose of each of the financial statements.
5 Explain the meaning of assets, liabilities, and stockholders' equity, and state the basic accounting equation.
6 Describe the components that supplement the financial statements in an annual report.

The Navigator is a learning system designed to prompt you to use the learning aids in the chapter and to set priorities as you study.

Many students who take this course do not plan to be accountants. If you are in that group, you might be thinking, "If I'm not going to be an accountant, why do I need to know accounting?" Well, consider this quote from Harold Geneen, the former chairman of IT&T: "To be good at your business, you have to know the numbers—cold." In business, accounting and financial statements are the means for communicating the numbers. If you don't know how to read financial statements, you can't really know your business.

KNOWING THE NUMBERS

Many businesses agree with this view. They see the value of their employees being able to read financial statements and understand how their actions affect the company's financial results. For example, consider Clif Bar & Company. The original Clif Bar® energy bar was created in 1990 after six months of experimentation by Gary Erickson and his mother in her kitchen. Today, the company has almost 300 employees and is considered one of the leading Landor's Breakaway Brands®.

Clif Bar is guided by what it calls its Five Aspirations—Sustaining Our Business, Our Brands, Our People, Our Community, and the Planet. Its website documents its efforts and accomplishments in these five areas. Just a few examples include the company's use of organic products to protect soil, water, and biodiversity; the "smart" solar array (the largest in North America), which provides nearly all the electrical needs

for its 115,000-square-foot building; and the incentives Clif Bar provides to employees to reduce their personal environmental impact, such as $6,500 toward the purchase of an efficient car or $1,000 per year for eco-friendly improvements toward their homes.

One of the company's proudest moments was the creation of an employee stock ownership plan (ESOP) in 2010. This plan gives its employees 20% ownership of the company (Gary and his wife Kit own the other 80%). The ESOP also resulted in Clif Bar enacting an open-book management program, including the commitment to educate all employee-owners about its finances. Armed with this basic financial knowledge, employees are more aware of the financial impact of their actions, which leads to better decisions.

Even in companies that do not practice open-book management, today's employers generally assume that managers in all areas of the company are "financially literate." To help prepare you for that, in this textbook you will learn how to read and prepare financial statements, and how to use basic tools to evaluate financial results. In this first chapter, we will introduce you to the financial statements of a real company whose products you are probably familiar with—Tootsie Roll. Tootsie Roll's presentation of its financial results is complete, yet also relatively easy to understand.

✔The Navigator

INSIDE CHAPTER 1 . . .

How do you start a business? How do you determine whether your business is making or losing money? How should you finance expansion—should you borrow, should you issue stock, should you use your own funds? How do you convince banks to lend you money or investors to buy your stock? Success in business requires making countless decisions, and decisions require financial information.

The purpose of this chapter is to show you what role accounting plays in providing financial information. The content and organization of the chapter are as follows.

Introduction to Financial Statements

Forms of Business Organization	Users and Uses of Financial Information	Business Activities	Communicating with Users
• Sole proprietorship • Partnership • Corporation	• Internal users • External users • Ethics in financial reporting	• Financing • Investing • Operating	• Income statement • Retained earnings statement • Balance sheet • Statement of cash flows • Interrelationships of statements • Other elements of an annual report

 The Navigator

LEARNING OBJECTIVE 1

Describe the primary forms of business organization.

Sole Proprietorship
-Simple to establish
-Owner controlled
-Tax advantages

Partnership
-Simple to establish
-Shared control
-Broader skills and resources
-Tax advantages

Corporation
-Easier to transfer ownership
-Easier to raise funds
-No personal liability

Forms of Business Organization

Suppose you graduate with a business degree and decide you want to start your own business. But what kind of business? You enjoy working with people, especially teaching them new skills. You also spend most of your free time outdoors, kayaking, backpacking, skiing, rock climbing, and mountain biking. You think you might be successful in opening an outdoor guide service where you grew up, in the Sierra Nevada mountains.

Your next decision is to determine the organizational form of your business. You have three choices—sole proprietorship, partnership, or corporation.

You might choose the sole proprietorship form for your outdoor guide service. A business owned by one person is a **sole proprietorship**. It is **simple to set up** and **gives you control** over the business. Small owner-operated businesses such as barber shops, law offices, and auto repair shops are often sole proprietorships, as are farms and small retail stores.

Another possibility is for you to join forces with other individuals to form a partnership. A business owned by two or more persons associated as partners is a **partnership**. Partnerships often are formed because one individual does not have **enough economic resources** to initiate or expand the business. Sometimes **partners bring unique skills or resources** to the partnership. You and your partners should formalize your duties and contributions in a written partnership agreement. Retail and service-type businesses, including professional practices (lawyers, doctors, architects, and certified public accountants), often organize as partnerships.

As a third alternative, you might organize as a corporation. A business organized as a separate legal entity owned by stockholders is a **corporation**. Investors in a corporation receive shares of stock to indicate their ownership claim. Buying stock in a corporation is often more attractive than investing in a partnership because shares of stock are **easy to sell** (transfer ownership). Selling a proprietorship or partnership interest is much more involved. Also, individuals can become **stockholders** by investing relatively small amounts of money. Therefore, it is **easier for corporations to raise funds**. Successful corporations often have thousands of stockholders, and their stock is traded on organized stock exchanges like the New York Stock Exchange. Many businesses start as sole proprietorships or partnerships and eventually incorporate. For example, in 1896 Leo Hirshfield started Tootsie Roll as a sole proprietorship, and by 1919 the company had incorporated.

Other factors to consider in deciding which organizational form to choose are **taxes and legal liability**. If you choose a sole proprietorship or partnership, you generally receive more favorable tax treatment than a corporation. However, proprietors and partners are personally liable for all debts and legal obligations of the business; corporate stockholders are not. In other words, corporate stockholders generally pay higher taxes but have no personal legal liability. We will discuss these issues in more depth in a later chapter.

Finally, while sole proprietorships, partnerships, and corporations represent the main types of business organizations, hybrid forms are now allowed in all states. These hybrid business forms combine the tax advantages of partnerships with the limited liability of corporations. Probably the most common among these hybrids types are limited liability companies (LLCs) and subchapter S corporations. These forms are discussed extensively in business law classes.

The combined number of proprietorships and partnerships in the United States is more than five times the number of corporations. However, the revenue produced by corporations is eight times greater. Most of the largest businesses in the United States—for example, Coca-Cola, ExxonMobil, General Motors, Citigroup, and Microsoft—are corporations. Because the majority of U.S. business is done by corporations, the emphasis in this textbook is on the corporate form of organization.

Alternative Terminology
Stockholders are sometimes called *shareholders*.

Alternative Terminology notes present synonymous terms that you may come across in practice.

Do it!

In choosing the organizational form for your outdoor guide service, you should consider the pros and cons of each. Identify each of the following organizational characteristics with the organizational form or forms with which it is associated.

1. Easier to raise funds.
2. Simple to establish.
3. No personal legal liability.
4. Tax advantages.
5. Easier to transfer ownership.

Solution

1. Easier to raise funds: Corporation.
2. Simple to establish: Sole proprietorship and partnership.
3. No personal legal liability: Corporation.
4. Tax advantages: Sole proprietorship and partnership.
5. Easier to transfer ownership: Corporation.

Related exercise material: **BE1-1** and *Do it!* **1-1**.

BUSINESS ORGANIZATION FORMS

Do it! exercises prompt you to stop and review the key points you have just studied.

Action Plans give you tips about how to approach the problem.

Action Plan

• Know which organizational form best matches the business type, size, and preferences of the owner(s).

The Navigator

Users and Uses of Financial Information

The purpose of financial information is to provide inputs for decision-making. Accounting is the information system that identifies, records, and communicates the economic events of an organization to interested users. **Users** of accounting information can be divided broadly into two groups: internal users and external users.

INTERNAL USERS

Internal users of accounting information are managers who plan, organize, and run a business. These include **marketing managers, production supervisors, finance directors, and company officers**. In running a business, managers must answer many important questions, as shown in Illustration 1-1.

Questions Asked by Internal Users

Finance	**Marketing**	**Human Resources**	**Management**
Is cash sufficient to pay dividends to Microsoft stockholders?	What price should Apple charge for an iPod to maximize the company's net income?	Can General Motors afford to give its employees pay raises this year?	Which PepsiCo product line is the most profitable? Should any product lines be eliminated?

Illustration 1-1 Questions that internal users ask

Illustrations help you visualize and apply the ideas as you study.

To answer these and other questions, you need detailed information on a timely basis. For internal users, accounting provides internal reports, such as financial comparisons of operating alternatives, projections of income from new sales campaigns, and forecasts of cash needs for the next year. In addition, companies present summarized financial information in the form of financial statements.

© Agnieszka Pastuszak-Maksim/iStockphoto

Accounting Across the Organization stories show applications of accounting information in various business functions.

 ## Accounting Across the Organization
The Scoop on Accounting

Accounting can serve as a useful recruiting tool even for the human resources department. Rhino Foods, located in Burlington, Vermont, is a manufacturer of specialty ice cream. Its corporate website includes the following:

> "Wouldn't it be great to work where you were part of a team? Where your input and hard work made a difference? Where you weren't kept in the dark about what management was thinking? . . . Well—it's not a dream! It's the way we do business . . . Rhino Foods believes in family, honesty and open communication— we really care about and appreciate our employees—and it shows. Operating results are posted and monthly group meetings inform all employees about what's happening in the Company. Employees also share in the Company's profits, in addition to having an excellent comprehensive *benefits* package."

Source: www.rhinofoods.com/workforus/workforus.html.

 What are the benefits to the company and to the employees of making the financial statements available to all employees? (See page 42.)

EXTERNAL USERS

There are several types of **external users** of accounting information. **Investors** (owners) use accounting information to make decisions to buy, hold, or sell stock. **Creditors** such as suppliers and bankers use accounting information to evaluate the risks of selling on credit or lending money. Some questions that investors and creditors may ask about a company are shown in Illustration 1-2.

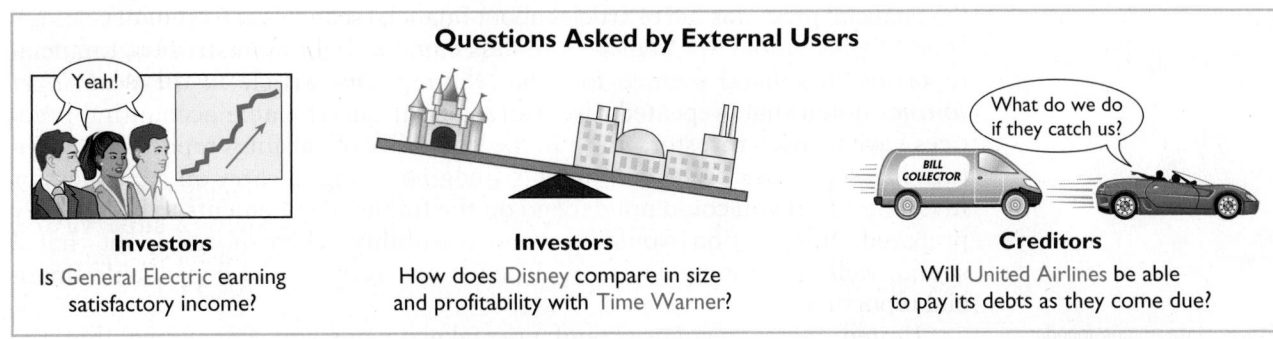

Questions Asked by External Users

Investors
Is General Electric earning satisfactory income?

Investors
How does Disney compare in size and profitability with Time Warner?

Creditors
Will United Airlines be able to pay its debts as they come due?

Illustration 1-2 Questions that external users ask

The information needs and questions of other external users vary considerably. **Taxing authorities**, such as the Internal Revenue Service, want to know whether the company complies with the tax laws. **Customers** are interested in whether a company like General Motors will continue to honor product warranties and otherwise support its product lines. **Labor unions**, such as the Major League Baseball Players Association, want to know whether the owners have the ability to pay increased wages and benefits. **Regulatory agencies**, such as the Securities and Exchange Commission or the Federal Trade Commission, want to know whether the company is operating within prescribed rules. For example, Enron, Dynegy, Duke Energy, and other big energy-trading companies reported record profits at the same time as California was paying extremely high prices for energy and suffering from blackouts. This disparity caused regulators to investigate the energy traders to make sure that the profits were earned by legitimate and fair practices.

Accounting Across the Organization

Spinning the Career Wheel

How will the study of accounting help you? A working knowledge of accounting is desirable for virtually every field of business. Some examples of how accounting is used in business careers include:

General management: Managers of Ford Motors, Massachusetts General Hospital, California State University–Fullerton, a McDonald's franchise, and a Trek bike shop all need to understand accounting data in order to make wise business decisions.

Marketing: A marketing specialist at Procter & Gamble must be sensitive to costs and benefits, which accounting helps them quantify and understand. Making a sale is meaningless unless it is a profitable sale.

Finance: Do you want to be a banker for Citicorp, an investment analyst for Goldman Sachs, or a stock broker for Merrill Lynch? These fields rely heavily on accounting knowledge to analyze financial statements. In fact, it is difficult to get a good job in a finance function without two or three courses in accounting.

Real estate: Are you interested in being a real estate broker for Prudential Real Estate? Because a third party—the bank—is almost always involved in financing a real estate transaction, brokers must understand the numbers involved: Can the buyer afford to make the payments to the bank? Does the cash flow from an industrial property justify the purchase price? What are the tax benefits of the purchase?

Josef Volavka/iStockphoto

? How might accounting help you? (See page 42.)

ETHICS IN FINANCIAL REPORTING

People won't gamble in a casino if they think it is "rigged." Similarly, people won't "play" the stock market if they think stock prices are rigged. At one time, the financial press was full of articles about financial scandals at Enron, WorldCom, HealthSouth, and AIG. As more scandals came to light, a mistrust of financial reporting in general seemed to be developing. One article in the *Wall Street Journal* noted that "repeated disclosures about questionable accounting practices have bruised investors' faith in the reliability of earnings reports, which in turn has sent stock prices tumbling."[1] Imagine trying to carry on a business or invest money if you could not depend on the financial statements to be honestly prepared. Information would have no credibility. There is no doubt that a sound, well-functioning economy depends on accurate and dependable financial reporting.

Ethics Note Circus-founder P.T. Barnum is alleged to have said, "Trust everyone, but cut the deck." What Sarbanes-Oxley does is to provide measures that (like cutting the deck of playing cards) help ensure that fraud will not occur.

United States regulators and lawmakers were very concerned that the economy would suffer if investors lost confidence in corporate accounting because of unethical financial reporting. Congress passed the **Sarbanes-Oxley Act (SOX)** to reduce unethical corporate behavior and decrease the likelihood of future corporate scandals. As a result of SOX, top management must now certify the accuracy of financial information. In addition, penalties for fraudulent financial activity are much more severe. Also, SOX increased the independence of the outside auditors who review the accuracy of corporate financial statements, and increased the oversight role of boards of directors.

Effective financial reporting depends on sound ethical behavior. To sensitize you to ethical situations and to give you practice at solving ethical dilemmas, we address ethics in a number of ways in this textbook. (1) A number of the *Feature Stories* and other parts of the text discuss the central importance of ethical behavior to financial reporting. (2) *Ethics Insight boxes* and marginal *Ethics Notes* highlight ethics situations and issues in actual business settings. (3) Many of the *People, Planet, and Profit Insight boxes* focus on ethical issues that companies face in measuring and reporting social and environmental issues. (4) At the end of the chapter, an *Ethics Case* simulates a business situation and asks you to put yourself in the position of a decision-maker in that case.

When analyzing these various ethics cases and your own ethical experiences, you should apply the three steps outlined in Illustration 1-3.

Illustration 1-3 Steps in analyzing ethics cases

Solving an Ethical Dilemma

1. Recognize an ethical situation and the ethical issues involved.	2. Identify and analyze the principal elements in the situation.	3. Identify the alternatives, and weigh the impact of each alternative on various stakeholders.
Use your personal ethics to identify ethical situations and issues. Some businesses and professional organizations provide written codes of ethics for guidance in some business situations.	Identify the **stakeholders**—persons or groups who may be harmed or benefited. Ask the question: What are the responsibilities and obligations of the parties involved?	Select the most ethical alternative, considering all the consequences. Sometimes there will be one right answer. Other situations involve more than one right solution; these situations require you to evaluate each alternative and select the best one.

#1 ALT   #2 ALT

---

[1]"U.S. Share Prices Slump," *Wall Street Journal* (February 21, 2002).

Ethics Insight

The Numbers Behind Not-for-Profit Organizations

Accounting plays an important role for a wide range of business organizations worldwide. Just as the integrity of the numbers matters for business, it matters at least as much at not-for-profit organizations. Proper control and reporting help ensure that money is used the way donors intended. Donors are less inclined to give to an organization if they think the organization is subject to waste or theft. The accounting challenges of some large international not-for-profits rival those of the world's largest businesses. For example, after the Haitian earthquake, the Haitian-born musician Wyclef Jean was criticized for the poor accounting controls in a relief fund that he founded. In response, he hired a new accountant and improved the transparency regarding funds raised and spent.

 What benefits does a sound accounting system provide to a not-for-profit organization? (See page 43.)

Gemunu Amarasinghe/AP Photo

Insights provide examples of business situations from various perspectives—ethics, investor, international, and corporate social responsibility.

Business Activities

All businesses are involved in three types of activity—financing, investing, and operating. For example, Leo Hirshfield, the founder of Tootsie Roll, obtained cash through financing to start and grow his business. Some of this **financing** came from personal savings, and some likely came from outside sources like banks. Hirshfield then **invested** the cash in equipment to run the business, such as mixing equipment and delivery vehicles. Once this equipment was in place, he could begin the **operating** activities of making and selling candy.

The **accounting information system** keeps track of the results of each of the various business activities—financing, investing, and operating. Let's look at each type of business activity in more detail.

FINANCING ACTIVITIES

It takes money to make money. The two primary sources of outside funds for corporations are borrowing money (debt financing) and issuing (selling) shares of stock in exchange for cash (equity financing).

Tootsie Roll may borrow money in a variety of ways. For example, it can take out a loan at a bank or borrow directly from investors by issuing debt securities called bonds. Persons or entities to whom Tootsie Roll owes money are its **creditors**. Amounts owed to creditors—in the form of debt and other obligations—are called liabilities. Specific names are given to different types of liabilities, depending on their source. Tootsie Roll may have a **note payable** to a bank for the money borrowed to purchase delivery trucks. Debt securities sold to investors that must be repaid at a particular date some years in the future are **bonds payable**.

Corporations also obtain funds by selling shares of stock to investors. Common stock is the term used to describe the total amount paid in by stockholders for the shares they purchase.

The claims of creditors differ from those of stockholders. If you loan money to a company, you are one of its creditors. In lending money, you specify a payment schedule (e.g., payment at the end of three months). As a creditor, you have a legal right to be paid at the agreed time. In the event of nonpayment, you may legally force the company to sell property to pay its debts. In the case of financial difficulty, creditor claims must be paid before stockholders' claims.

LEARNING OBJECTIVE 3
Explain the three principal types of business activity.

Financing

Essential terms are printed in blue. They are defined again in the **glossary** at the end of the chapter.

Stockholders, on the other hand, have no claim to corporate cash until the claims of creditors are satisfied. Suppose you buy a company's stock instead of loaning it money. You have no legal right to expect any payments from your stock ownership until all of the company's creditors are paid. However, many corporations make payments to stockholders on a regular basis as long as there is sufficient cash to cover required payments to creditors. These cash payments to stockholders are called dividends.

INVESTING ACTIVITIES

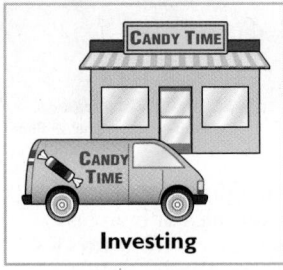
Investing

Once the company has raised cash through financing activities, it uses that cash in investing activities. Investing activities involve the purchase of the resources a company needs in order to operate. A growing company purchases many resources, such as computers, delivery trucks, furniture, and buildings. Resources owned by a business are called assets. Different types of assets are given different names. For example, Tootsie Roll's mixing equipment is a type of asset referred to as **property**, **plant**, **and equipment**.

Alternative Terminology
Property, plant, and equipment is sometimes called *fixed assets*.

Cash is one of the more important assets owned by Tootsie Roll or any other business. If a company has excess cash that it does not need for a while, it might choose to invest in securities (stocks or bonds) of other corporations. **Investments** are another example of an investing activity.

OPERATING ACTIVITIES

Operating

Once a business has the assets it needs to get started, it begins operations. Tootsie Roll is in the business of selling all things that taste, look, or smell like candy. It sells Tootsie Rolls, Tootsie Pops, Blow Pops, Caramel Apple Pops, Mason Dots, Mason Crows, Sugar Daddy, and Sugar Babies. We call amounts earned on the sale of these products **revenues**. Revenue is the increase in assets or decrease in liabilities resulting from the sale of goods or the performance of services in the normal course of business. For example, Tootsie Roll records revenue when it sells a candy product.

Revenues arise from different sources and are identified by various names depending on the nature of the business. For instance, Tootsie Roll's primary source of revenue is the sale of candy products. However, it also generates interest revenue on debt securities held as investments. Sources of revenue common to many businesses are **sales revenue**, **service revenue**, and **interest revenue**.

The company purchases its longer-lived assets through investing activities as described earlier. Other assets with shorter lives, however, result from operating activities. For example, **supplies** are assets used in day-to-day operations. Goods available for future sales to customers are assets called **inventory**. Also, if Tootsie Roll sells goods to a customer and does not receive cash immediately, then the company has a right to expect payment from that customer in the near future. This right to receive money in the future is called an **account receivable**.

Before Tootsie Roll can sell a single Tootsie Roll, Tootsie Pop, or Blow Pop, it must purchase sugar, corn syrup, and other ingredients, mix these ingredients, process the mix, and wrap and ship the finished product. It also incurs costs like salaries, rents, and utilities. All of these costs, referred to as **expenses**, are necessary to produce and sell the product. In accounting language, expenses are the cost of assets consumed or services used in the process of generating revenues.

Expenses take many forms and are identified by various names depending on the type of asset consumed or service used. For example, Tootsie Roll keeps track of these types of expenses: **cost of goods sold** (such as the cost of ingredients); **selling expenses** (such as the cost of salespersons' salaries); **marketing expenses** (such as the cost of advertising); **administrative expenses** (such as the salaries of administrative staff, and telephone and heating costs incurred at the corporate office); **interest expense** (amounts of interest paid on various debts); and **income taxes** (corporate taxes paid to the government).

Tootsie Roll may also have liabilities arising from these expenses. For example, it may purchase goods on credit from suppliers. The obligations to pay for these goods are called **accounts payable**. Additionally, Tootsie Roll may have **interest payable** on the outstanding amounts owed to the bank. It may also have **wages payable** to its employees and **sales taxes payable**, **property taxes payable**, and **income taxes payable** to the government.

Tootsie Roll compares the revenues of a period with the expenses of that period to determine whether it earned a profit. When revenues exceed expenses, net income results. When expenses exceed revenues, a net loss results.

Do it! Classify each item as an asset, liability, common stock, revenue, or expense.

BUSINESS ACTIVITIES

1. Cost of renting property.
2. Truck purchased.
3. Notes payable.
4. Issuance of ownership shares.
5. Amount earned from performing service.
6. Amounts owed to suppliers.

Action Plan

- Classify each item based on its economic characteristics. Proper classification of items is critical if accounting is to provide useful information.

Solution

1. Cost of renting property: Expense.
2. Truck purchased: Asset.
3. Notes payable: Liabilities.
4. Issuance of ownership shares: Common stock.
5. Amount earned from performing service: Revenue.
6. Amounts owed to suppliers: Liabilities.

 The Navigator

Related exercise material: **BE1-3**, **Do it!** **1-2**, and **E1-3**.

Communicating with Users

Assets, liabilities, expenses, and revenues are of interest to users of accounting information. This information is arranged in the format of four different **financial statements**, which form the backbone of financial accounting:

LEARNING OBJECTIVE **4**

Describe the content and purpose of each of the financial statements.

- To show how successfully your business performed during a period of time, you report its revenues and expenses in an **income statement**.
- To indicate how much of previous income was distributed to you and the other owners of your business in the form of dividends, and how much was retained in the business to allow for future growth, you present a **retained earnings statement**.
- To present a picture at a point in time of what your business owns (its assets) and what it owes (its liabilities), you prepare a **balance sheet**.
- To show where your business obtained cash during a period of time and how that cash was used, you present a **statement of cash flows**.

To introduce you to these statements, we have prepared the financial statements for your outdoor guide service, Sierra Corporation, after your first month of operations. To summarize, you officially started your business in Truckee,

International Note The primary types of financial statements required by International Financial Reporting Standards (IFRS) and U.S. generally accepted accounting principles (GAAP) are the same. Neither IFRS nor GAAP is very specific regarding format requirements for the primary financial statements. However, in practice, some format differences do exist in presentations commonly employed by IFRS companies as compared to GAAP companies.

California, on October 1, 2014. Sierra provides guide services in the Lake Tahoe area of the Sierra Nevada mountains. Its promotional materials describe outdoor day trips, such as rafting, snowshoeing, and hiking, as well as multi-day backcountry experiences. To minimize your initial investment, at this point the company has limited outdoor equipment for customer use. Instead, your customers either bring their own equipment or rent equipment through local outfitters. The financial statements for Sierra's first month of business are provided in the following pages.

INCOME STATEMENT

The **income statement** reports a company's revenues and expenses and resulting net income or loss for a period of time. To indicate that its income statement reports the results of operations for a **specific period of time**, Sierra dates the income statement "For the Month Ended October 31, 2014." The income statement lists the company's revenues followed by its expenses. Finally, Sierra determines the net income (or net loss) by deducting expenses from revenues. Sierra Corporation's income statement is shown in Illustration 1-4. Congratulations, you are already showing a profit!

Illustration 1-4 Sierra Corporation's income statement

Helpful Hint The financial statement heading identifies the company, the type of statement, and the time period covered. Sometimes, another line indicates the unit of measure, e.g., "in thousands" or "in millions."

SIERRA CORPORATION
Income Statement
For the Month Ended October 31, 2014

Revenues		
Service revenue		$10,600
Expenses		
Salaries and wages expense	$5,200	
Rent expense	900	
Supplies expense	1,500	
Depreciation expense	40	
Interest expense	50	
Insurance expense	50	
Total expenses		7,740
Net income		$ 2,860

Ethics Note When companies find errors in previously released income statements, they restate those numbers. Perhaps because of the increased scrutiny shortly after Sarbanes-Oxley was implemented, companies filed a record 1,195 restatements.

Why are financial statement users interested in net income? **Investors are interested in a company's past net income because it provides useful information for predicting future net income**. Investors buy and sell stock based on their beliefs about a company's future performance. If investors believe that Sierra will be successful in the future and that this will result in a higher stock price, they will buy its stock. Creditors also use the income statement to predict future earnings. When a bank loans money to a company, it believes that it will be repaid in the future. If it didn't think it would be repaid, it wouldn't loan the money. Therefore, prior to making the loan the bank loan officer uses the income statement as a source of information to predict whether the company will be profitable enough to repay its loan. Thus, reporting a strong profit will make it easier for Sierra to raise additional cash either by issuing shares of stock or borrowing.

Amounts received from issuing stock are not revenues, and amounts paid out as dividends are not expenses. As a result, they are not reported on the income statement. For example, Sierra Corporation does not treat as revenue the $10,000 of cash received from issuing new stock (see Illustration 1-7), nor does it regard as a business expense the $500 of dividends paid (see Illustration 1-5).

🧰 DECISION TOOLKIT

DECISION CHECKPOINTS	INFO NEEDED FOR DECISION	TOOL TO USE FOR DECISION	HOW TO EVALUATE RESULTS
Are the company's operations profitable?	Income statement	The income statement reports a company's revenues and expenses and resulting net income or loss for a period of time.	If the company's revenue exceeds its expenses, it will report net income; otherwise, it will report a net loss.

Decision Toolkits summarize the financial decision-making process.

RETAINED EARNINGS STATEMENT

If Sierra is profitable, at the end of each period it must decide what portion of profits to pay to shareholders in dividends. In theory, it could pay all of its current-period profits, but few companies do this. Why? Because they want to retain part of the profits to allow for further expansion. High-growth companies, such as Google and Facebook, often pay no dividends. **Retained earnings** is the net income retained in the corporation.

The **retained earnings statement** shows the amounts and causes of changes in retained earnings for a specific time period. The time period is the same as that covered by the income statement. The beginning retained earnings amount appears on the first line of the statement. Then, the company adds net income and deducts dividends to determine the retained earnings at the end of the period. If a company has a net loss, it deducts (rather than adds) that amount in the retained earnings statement. Illustration 1-5 presents Sierra Corporation's retained earnings statement.

SIERRA CORPORATION
Retained Earnings Statement
For the Month Ended October 31, 2014

Retained earnings, October 1	$ 0
Add: Net income	2,860
	2,860
Less: Dividends	500
Retained earnings, October 31	$2,360

Illustration 1-5 Sierra Corporation's retained earnings statement

Helpful Hint The heading of this statement identifies the company, the type of statement, and the time period covered by the statement.

By monitoring the retained earnings statement, financial statement users can evaluate dividend payment practices. Some investors seek companies, such as Dow Chemical, that have a history of paying high dividends. Other investors seek companies, such as Amazon.com, that reinvest earnings to increase the company's growth instead of paying dividends. Lenders monitor their corporate customers' dividend payments because any money paid in dividends reduces a company's ability to repay its debts.

🧰 DECISION TOOLKIT

DECISION CHECKPOINTS	INFO NEEDED FOR DECISION	TOOL TO USE FOR DECISION	HOW TO EVALUATE RESULTS
What is the company's policy toward dividends and growth?	Retained earnings statement	How much of this year's income did the company pay out in dividends to shareholders?	A company striving for rapid growth will pay a low (or no) dividend.

BALANCE SHEET

LEARNING OBJECTIVE 5

Explain the meaning of assets, liabilities, and stockholders' equity, and state the basic accounting equation.

The **balance sheet** reports assets and claims to assets at a specific **point** in time. Claims to assets are subdivided into two categories: claims of creditors and claims of owners. As noted earlier, claims of creditors are called **liabilities**. The owners' claim to assets is called stockholders' equity.

Illustration 1-6 shows the relationship among the categories on the balance sheet in equation form. This equation is referred to as the basic accounting equation.

Illustration 1-6 Basic accounting equation

$$\textbf{Assets = Liabilities + Stockholders' Equity}$$

This relationship is where the name "balance sheet" comes from. Assets must balance with the claims to assets.

As you can see from looking at Sierra's balance sheet in Illustration 1-7, the balance sheet presents the company's financial position as of a specific date—in this case, October 31, 2014. It lists assets first, followed by liabilities and stockholders' equity. Stockholders' equity is comprised of two parts: (1) common stock and (2) retained earnings. As noted earlier, common stock results when the company sells new shares of stock; retained earnings is the net income retained in the corporation. Sierra has common stock of $10,000 and retained earnings of $2,360, for total stockholders' equity of $12,360.

Alternative Terminology Liabilities are also referred to as *debt*.

Illustration 1-7 Sierra Corporation's balance sheet

Helpful Hint The heading of a balance sheet must identify the company, the statement, and the date.

SIERRA CORPORATION
Balance Sheet
October 31, 2014

Assets

Cash	$15,200
Accounts receivable	200
Supplies	1,000
Prepaid insurance	550
Equipment, net	4,960
Total assets	$21,910

Liabilities and Stockholders' Equity

Liabilities		
Notes payable	$ 5,000	
Accounts payable	2,500	
Unearned service revenue	800	
Salaries and wages payable	1,200	
Interest payable	50	
Total liabilities		$ 9,550
Stockholders' equity		
Common stock	10,000	
Retained earnings	2,360	
Total stockholders' equity		12,360
Total liabilities and stockholders' equity		$21,910

Creditors analyze a company's balance sheet to determine the likelihood that they will be repaid. They carefully evaluate the nature of the company's assets and liabilities. In operating the Sierra Corporation guide service, the balance sheet will be used to determine whether cash on hand is sufficient for immediate cash needs. The balance sheet will also be used to evaluate the relationship between debt and stockholders' equity to determine whether the company has a satisfactory proportion of debt and common stock financing.

DECISION TOOLKIT

DECISION CHECKPOINTS	INFO NEEDED FOR DECISION	TOOL TO USE FOR DECISION	HOW TO EVALUATE RESULTS
Does the company rely primarily on debt or stockholders' equity to finance its assets?	Balance sheet	The balance sheet reports the company's resources and claims to those resources. There are two types of claims: liabilities and stockholders' equity.	Compare the amount of debt versus the amount of stockholders' equity to determine whether the company relies more on creditors or owners for its financing.

STATEMENT OF CASH FLOWS

The primary purpose of a statement of cash flows is to provide financial information about the cash receipts and cash payments of a business for a specific period of time. To help investors, creditors, and others in their analysis of a company's cash position, the statement of cash flows reports the cash effects of a company's **operating**, **investing**, and **financing** activities. In addition, the statement shows the net increase or decrease in cash during the period, and the amount of cash at the end of the period.

Users are interested in the statement of cash flows because they want to know what is happening to a company's most important resource. The statement of cash flows provides answers to these simple but important questions:

- Where did cash come from during the period?
- How was cash used during the period?
- What was the change in the cash balance during the period?

The statement of cash flows for Sierra, in Illustration 1-8, shows that cash increased $15,200 during the month. This increase resulted because operating

SIERRA CORPORATION
Statement of Cash Flows
For the Month Ended October 31, 2014

Cash flows from operating activities		
Cash receipts from operating activities	$11,200	
Cash payments for operating activities	(5,500)	
Net cash provided by operating activities		$ 5,700
Cash flows from investing activities		
Purchased office equipment	(5,000)	
Net cash used by investing activities		(5,000)
Cash flows from financing activities		
Issuance of common stock	10,000	
Issuance of note payable	5,000	
Payment of dividend	(500)	
Net cash provided by financing activities		14,500
Net increase in cash		15,200
Cash at beginning of period		0
Cash at end of period		$15,200

Illustration 1-8 Sierra Corporation's statement of cash flows

Helpful Hint The heading of this statement identifies the company, the type of statement, and the time period covered by the statement. Negative numbers are shown in parentheses.

activities (services to clients) increased cash $5,700, and financing activities increased cash $14,500. Investing activities used $5,000 of cash for the purchase of equipment.

© Marek Uliasz/iStockphoto

People, Planet, and Profit Insight

Beyond Financial Statements

Should we expand our corporate reports beyond the income statement, retained earnings statement, balance sheet, and statement of cash flows? Some believe we should take into account ecological and social performance, in addition to financial results, in evaluating a company. The argument is that a company's responsibility lies with anyone who is influenced by its actions. In other words, a company should be interested in benefiting many different parties, instead of only maximizing stockholders' interests.

A socially responsible business does not exploit or endanger any group of individuals. It follows fair trade practices, provides safe environments for workers, and bears responsibility for environmental damage. Granted, measurement of these factors is difficult. How to report this information is also controversial. But many interesting and useful efforts are underway. Throughout this textbook, we provide additional insights into how companies are attempting to meet the challenge of measuring and reporting their contributions to society, as well as their financial results, to stockholders.

? Why might a company's stockholders be interested in its environmental and social performance? (See page 43.)

DECISION TOOLKIT

DECISION CHECKPOINTS	INFO NEEDED FOR DECISION	TOOL TO USE FOR DECISION	HOW TO EVALUATE RESULTS
Does the company generate sufficient cash from operations to fund its investing activities?	Statement of cash flows	The statement of cash flows shows the amount of cash provided or used by operating activities, investing activities, and financing activities.	Compare the amount of cash provided by operating activities with the amount of cash used by investing activities. Any deficiency in cash from operating activities must be made up with cash from financing activities.

INTERRELATIONSHIPS OF STATEMENTS

Illustration 1-9 shows simplified financial statements of Tootsie Roll Industries, Inc. (We have simplified the financial statements to assist your learning.) Tootsie Roll's **actual financial statements** are presented in **Appendix A**, at the end of the textbook. Note that the numbers in Tootsie Roll's statements are presented in thousands—that is, the last three 000s are omitted. Thus, Tootsie Roll's net income in 2011 is $43,938,000, not $43,938. Because the results on some financial statements become inputs to other statements, the statements are interrelated. These interrelationships can be seen in Tootsie Roll's financial statements, as follows.

1. The retained earnings statement uses the results of the income statement. Tootsie Roll reported net income of $43,938,000 for the period. Net income is added to the beginning amount of retained earnings to determine ending retained earnings.

Illustration 1-9 Tootsie Roll's financial statements

TOOTSIE ROLL INDUSTRIES, INC.
Income Statement
For the Year Ended December 31, 2011 (in thousands)

Revenues		$532,505
Expenses		
Cost of goods sold	$365,225	
Selling, marketing, and administrative expense and other	106,368	
Income tax expense	16,974	
Total expenses		488,567
Net income		$ 43,938

Helpful Hint Note that final sums are double-underlined.

TOOTSIE ROLL INDUSTRIES, INC.
Retained Earnings Statement
For the Year Ended December 31, 2011 (in thousands)

Retained earnings, January 1, 2011	$135,866
Add: Net income	43,938
	179,804
Less: Dividends and other (net)	65,535
Retained earnings, December 31, 2011	$114,269

Helpful Hint The arrows in this illustration show interrelationships of the four financial statements.

TOOTSIE ROLL INDUSTRIES, INC.
Balance Sheet
December 31, 2011 (in thousands)

Assets

Cash		$ 78,612
Investments		10,895
Accounts receivable		41,895
Inventories		71,760
Prepaid expenses		5,070
Property, plant and equipment, net		212,162
Other assets		437,462
Total assets		$857,856

Liabilities and Stockholders' Equity

Liabilities		
Accounts payable	$ 10,683	
Dividends payable	4,603	
Accrued liabilities	43,069	
Deferred income taxes payable	43,521	
Bonds payable	7,500	
Employee benefits payable and other	82,545	$191,921
Stockholders' equity		
Common stock	551,666	
Retained earnings	114,269	665,935
Total liabilities and stockholders' equity		$857,856

TOOTSIE ROLL INDUSTRIES, INC.
Statement of Cash Flows
For the Year Ended December 31, 2011 (in thousands)

Cash flows from operating activities		
Cash receipts from operating activities	$528,004	
Cash payments for operating activities	(477,614)	
Net cash provided by operating activities		$ 50,390
Cash flows from investing activities		
Capital expenditures and acquisitions	(16,351)	
Net purchases/sales of investment securities and other	(34,806)	
Net cash used by investing activities		(51,157)
Cash flows from financing activities		
Repurchase of common stock	(18,190)	
Dividends paid in cash	(18,407)	
Net cash used by financing activities		(36,597)
Net increase (decrease) in cash		(37,364)
Cash at beginning of year		115,976
Cash at end of year		$ 78,612

Helpful Hint Negative amounts in the statement of cash flows are presented in parentheses.

2. The balance sheet and retained earnings statement are also interrelated. Tootsie Roll reports the ending amount of $114,269,000 on the retained earnings statement as the retained earnings amount on the balance sheet.

3. Finally, the statement of cash flows relates to information on the balance sheet. The statement of cash flows shows how the Cash account changed during the period. It shows the amount of cash at the beginning of the period, the sources and uses of cash during the period, and the $78,612,000 of cash at the end of the period. The ending amount of cash shown on the statement of cash flows must agree with the amount of cash on the balance sheet.

Study these interrelationships carefully. **To prepare financial statements, you must understand the sequence in which these amounts are determined and how each statement impacts the next.**

FINANCIAL STATEMENTS

Do it!

CSU Corporation began operations on January 1, 2014. The following information is available for CSU Corporation on December 31, 2014:

Accounts receivable	1,800	Retained earnings	?	Supplies expense	200
Accounts payable	2,000	Equipment	16,000	Cash	1,400
Rent expense	9,000	Insurance expense	1,000	Dividends	600
Notes payable	5,000	Service revenue	17,000		
Common stock	10,000	Supplies	4,000		

Prepare an income statement, a retained earnings statement, and a balance sheet.

Action Plan

• Report the revenues and expenses for a period of time in an income statement.

• Show the amounts and causes (net income and dividends) of changes in retained earnings during the period in the retained earnings statement.

• Present the assets and claims to those assets (liabilities and equity) at a specific point in time in the balance sheet.

Solution

CSU CORPORATION
Income Statement
For the Year Ended December 31, 2014

Revenues		
Service revenue		$17,000
Expenses		
Rent expense	$9,000	
Insurance expense	1,000	
Supplies expense	200	
Total expenses		10,200
Net income		$ 6,800

CSU CORPORATION
Retained Earnings Statement
For the Year Ended December 31, 2014

Retained earnings, January 1	$ 0
Add: Net income	6,800
	6,800
Less: Dividends	600
Retained earnings, December 31	$6,200

CSU CORPORATION
Balance Sheet
December 31, 2014

Assets

Cash	$ 1,400
Accounts receivable	1,800
Supplies	4,000
Equipment	16,000
Total assets	$23,200

Liabilities and Stockholders' Equity

Liabilities		
Notes payable	$ 5,000	
Accounts payable	2,000	
Total liabilities		$ 7,000
Stockholders' equity		
Common stock	10,000	
Retained earnings	6,200	
Total stockholders' equity		16,200
Total liabilities and stockholders' equity		$23,200

Related exercise material: **BE1-5, BE1-6, BE1-7, BE1-8, BE1-9, BE1-10, Do it! 1-3, E1-4, E1-5, E1-6, E1-7, E1-8, E1-9, E1-10, E1-11,** and **E1-14.**

✔ The Navigator

OTHER ELEMENTS OF AN ANNUAL REPORT

Publicly traded U.S. companies must provide shareholders with an **annual report**. The annual report always includes the financial statements introduced in this chapter. The annual report also includes other important information such as a management discussion and analysis section, notes to the financial statements, and an independent auditor's report. No analysis of a company's financial situation and performance is complete without a review of these items.

LEARNING OBJECTIVE 6

Describe the components that supplement the financial statements in an annual report.

Management Discussion and Analysis

The **management discussion and analysis (MD&A)** section presents management's views on the company's **ability to pay near-term obligations, its ability to fund operations and expansion, and its results of operations**. Management must highlight favorable or unfavorable trends and identify significant events and uncertainties that affect these three factors. This discussion obviously involves a number of subjective estimates and opinions. A brief excerpt from the MD&A section of Tootsie Roll's annual report is presented in Illustration 1-10.

  TOOTSIE ROLL INDUSTRIES, INC.
Management's Discussion and Analysis of
Financial Condition and Results of Operations

The Company has a relatively straightforward financial structure and has historically maintained a conservative financial position. Except for an immaterial amount of operating leases, the Company has no special financing arrangements or "off-balance sheet" special purpose entities. Cash flows from operations plus maturities of short-term investments are expected to be adequate to meet the Company's overall financing needs, including capital expenditures, in 2012.

Illustration 1-10 Tootsie Roll's management discussion and analysis

Notes to the Financial Statements

Explanatory notes and supporting schedules accompany every set of financial statements and are an integral part of the statements. The **notes to the financial statements** clarify the financial statements, and provide additional detail. Information in the notes does not have to be quantifiable (numeric). Examples of notes are descriptions of the significant accounting policies and methods used in preparing the statements, explanations of uncertainties and contingencies, and various statistics and details too voluminous to be included in the statements. The notes are essential to understanding a company's operating performance and financial position.

Illustration 1-11 is an excerpt from the notes to Tootsie Roll's financial statements. It describes the methods that Tootsie Roll uses to account for revenues.

Illustration 1-11 Notes to Tootsie Roll's financial statements

 TOOTSIE ROLL INDUSTRIES, INC.
Notes to Financial Statements

Revenue recognition
Revenue, net of applicable provisions for discounts, returns, allowances, and certain advertising and promotional costs, is recognized when products are delivered to customers based on a customer purchase order, and collectibility is reasonably assured.

Auditor's Report

An **auditor's report** is prepared by an independent outside auditor. It states the auditor's opinion as to the fairness of the presentation of the financial position and results of operations and their conformance with generally accepted accounting principles.

An **auditor** is an accounting professional who conducts an independent examination of a company's financial statements. Only accountants who meet certain criteria and thereby attain the designation **certified public accountant (CPA)** may perform audits. If the auditor is satisfied that the financial statements provide a fair representation of the company's financial position and results of operations in accordance with generally accepted accounting principles, then the auditor expresses an **unqualified opinion**. If the auditor expresses anything other than an unqualified opinion, then readers should only use the financial statements with caution. That is, without an unqualified opinion, we cannot have complete confidence that the financial statements give an accurate picture of the company's financial health. For example, recently Blockbuster, Inc.'s auditor stated that its financial situation raised "substantial doubt about the Company's ability to continue as a going concern."

Illustration 1-12 is an excerpt from the auditor's report from Tootsie Roll's 2011 annual report. Tootsie Roll received an unqualified opinion from its auditor, PricewaterhouseCoopers.

Illustration 1-12 Excerpt from auditor's report on Tootsie Roll's financial statements

 TOOTSIE ROLL INDUSTRIES, INC.
Excerpt from Auditor's Report

To the Board of Directors and Shareholders of Tootsie Roll Industries, Inc.

In our opinion, the accompanying consolidated statements of financial position and the related consolidated statements of earnings, comprehensive earnings and retained earnings, and of cash flows present fairly, in all material respects, the financial position of Tootsie Roll Industries, Inc. and its subsidiaries at December 31, 2011 and December 31, 2010, and the results of their operations and their cash flows for each of the three years in the period ended December 31, 2011 in conformity with accounting principles generally accepted in the United States of America. Also in our opinion, the Company maintained, in all material respects, effective internal control over financial reporting as of December 31, 2011, based on criteria established in *Internal Control—Integrated Framework* issued by the Committee of Sponsoring Organizations of the Treadway Commission (COSO).

Do it! State whether each of the following items is most closely associated with the management discussion and analysis (MD&A), the notes to the financial statements, or the auditor's report.

1. Descriptions of significant accounting policies.
2. Unqualified opinion.
3. Explanations of uncertainties and contingencies.
4. Description of ability to fund operations and expansion.
5. Description of results of operations.
6. Certified public accountant (CPA).

Action Plan

- Realize that financial statements provide information about a company's performance and financial position.
- Be familiar with the other elements of the annual report in order to gain a fuller understanding of a company.

 The Navigator

Solution

1. Descriptions of significant accounting policies: Notes.
2. Unqualified opinion: Auditor's report.
3. Explanations of uncertainties and contingencies: Notes.
4. Description of ability to fund operations and expansion: MD&A.
5. Description of results of operations: MD&A.
6. Certified public accountant (CPA): Auditor's report.

Related exercise material: **BE1-11,** **Do it!** **1-4,** and **E1-17.**

USING THE DECISION TOOLKIT

The Hershey Company, located in Hershey, Pennsylvania, is the leading North American manufacturer of chocolate. Its products include Hershey's Kisses, Reese's Peanut Butter Cups, Kit Kat, and Take 5 bars. Imagine that you are considering the purchase of shares of Hershey's common stock.

Using the Decision Toolkit exercises ask you to use information from financial statements to make financial decisions.

Instructions

Answer these questions related to your decision whether to invest.
(a) What financial statements should you evaluate?
(b) What should these financial statements tell you?
(c) Do you care if the financial statements have been audited? Explain.
(d) Appendix B at the end of this textbook contains financial statements for Hershey. What comparisons can you make between Tootsie Roll and Hershey in terms of their respective results from operations and financial position?

Solution

(a) Before you invest, you should evaluate the income statement, retained earnings statement, balance sheet, and statement of cash flows.
(b) You would probably be most interested in the income statement because it tells about past performance and thus gives an indication of future performance. The retained earnings statement provides a record of the company's dividend history. The balance sheet reveals the relationship between assets and liabilities. The statement of cash flows reveals where the company is getting and spending its cash. This is especially important for a company that wants to grow.
(c) You would want audited financial statements. These statements indicate that a CPA (certified public accountant) has examined and expressed an opinion that the statements present fairly the financial position and results of operations of

the company. Investors and creditors should not make decisions without studying audited financial statements.

(d) Many interesting comparisons can be made between the two companies. Tootsie Roll is smaller, with total assets of $857,856,000 versus $4,412,199,000 for Hershey, and it has lower revenue—$532,505,000 versus $6,080,788,000 for Hershey. In addition, Tootsie Roll's cash provided by operating activities of $50,390,000 is less than Hershey's $580,867,000.

While useful, these basic measures are not enough to determine whether one company is a better investment than the other. In later chapters, you will learn of tools that will allow you to compare the relative profitability and financial health of these and other companies.

Summary of Learning Objectives

1 Describe the primary forms of business organization. A sole proprietorship is a business owned by one person. A partnership is a business owned by two or more people associated as partners. A corporation is a separate legal entity for which evidence of ownership is provided by shares of stock.

2 Identify the users and uses of accounting information. Internal users are managers who need accounting information to plan, organize, and run business operations. The primary external users are investors and creditors. Investors (stockholders) use accounting information to help them decide whether to buy, hold, or sell shares of a company's stock. Creditors (suppliers and bankers) use accounting information to assess the risk of granting credit or loaning money to a business. Other groups who have an indirect interest in a business are taxing authorities, customers, labor unions, and regulatory agencies.

3 Explain the three principal types of business activity. Financing activities involve collecting the necessary funds to support the business. Investing activities involve acquiring the resources necessary to run the business. Operating activities involve putting the resources of the business into action to generate a profit.

4 Describe the content and purpose of each of the financial statements. An income statement presents the revenues and expenses of a company for a specific period of time. A retained earnings statement summarizes

the changes in retained earnings that have occurred for a specific period of time. A balance sheet reports the assets, liabilities, and stockholders' equity of a business at a specific date. A statement of cash flows summarizes information concerning the cash inflows (receipts) and outflows (payments) for a specific period of time.

5 Explain the meaning of assets, liabilities, and stockholders' equity, and state the basic accounting equation. Assets are resources owned by a business. Liabilities are the debts and obligations of the business. Liabilities represent claims of creditors on the assets of the business. Stockholders' equity represents the claims of owners on the assets of the business. Stockholders' equity is subdivided into two parts: common stock and retained earnings. The basic accounting equation is Assets = Liabilities + Stockholders' Equity.

6 Describe the components that supplement the financial statements in an annual report. The management discussion and analysis provides management's interpretation of the company's results and financial position as well as a discussion of plans for the future. Notes to the financial statements provide additional explanation or detail to make the financial statements more informative. The auditor's report expresses an opinion as to whether the financial statements present fairly the company's results of operations and financial position.

DECISION TOOLKIT *A SUMMARY*

DECISION CHECKPOINTS	INFO NEEDED FOR DECISION	TOOL TO USE FOR DECISION	HOW TO EVALUATE RESULTS
Are the company's operations profitable?	Income statement	The income statement reports a company's revenues and expenses and resulting net income or loss for a period of time.	If the company's revenue exceeds its expenses, it will report net income; otherwise, it will report a net loss.
What is the company's policy toward dividends and growth?	Retained earnings statement	How much of this year's income did the company pay out in dividends to shareholders?	A company striving for rapid growth will pay a low (or no) dividend.
Does the company rely primarily on debt or stockholders' equity to finance its assets?	Balance sheet	The balance sheet reports the company's resources and claims to those resources. There are two types of claims: liabilities and stockholders' equity.	Compare the amount of debt versus the amount of stockholders' equity to determine whether the company relies more on creditors or owners for its financing.
Does the company generate sufficient cash from operations to fund its investing activities?	Statement of cash flows	The statement of cash flows shows the amount of cash provided or used by operating activities, investing activities, and financing activities.	Compare the amount of cash provided by operating activities with the amount of cash used by investing activities. Any deficiency in cash from operating activities must be made up with cash from financing activities.

Glossary

Accounting *(p. 6)* The information system that identifies, records, and communicates the economic events of an organization to interested users.

Annual report *(p. 19)* A report prepared by corporate management that presents financial information including financial statements, a management discussion and analysis section, notes, and an independent auditor's report.

Assets *(p. 10)* Resources owned by a business.

Auditor's report *(p. 20)* A report prepared by an independent outside auditor stating the auditor's opinion as to the fairness of the presentation of the financial position and results of operations and their conformance with generally accepted accounting principles.

Balance sheet *(p. 14)* A financial statement that reports the assets and claims to those assets at a specific point in time.

Basic accounting equation *(p. 14)* Assets = Liabilities + Stockholders' Equity.

Certified public accountant (CPA) *(p. 20)* An individual who has met certain criteria and is thus allowed to perform audits of corporations.

Common stock *(p. 9)* Term used to describe the total amount paid in by stockholders for the shares they purchase.

Corporation *(p. 4)* A business organized as a separate legal entity owned by stockholders.

Dividends *(p. 10)* Payments of cash from a corporation to its stockholders.

Expenses *(p. 10)* The cost of assets consumed or services used in the process of generating revenues.

Income statement *(p. 12)* A financial statement that reports a company's revenues and expenses and resulting net income or net loss for a specific period of time.

Liabilities *(p. 9)* Amounts owed to creditors in the form of debts and other obligations.

Management discussion and analysis (MD&A) *(p. 19)* A section of the annual report that presents management's views on the company's ability to pay near-term obligations, its ability to fund operations and expansion, and its results of operations.

Net income *(p. 11)* The amount by which revenues exceed expenses.

Net loss *(p. 11)* The amount by which expenses exceed revenues.

Notes to the financial statements *(p. 20)* Notes clarify information presented in the financial statements and provide additional detail.

Partnership *(p. 4)* A business owned by two or more persons associated as partners.

Retained earnings *(p. 13)* The amount of net income retained in the corporation.

Retained earnings statement *(p. 13)* A financial statement that summarizes the amounts and causes of changes in retained earnings for a specific time period.

Revenue *(p. 10)* The increase in assets or decrease in liabilities resulting from the sale of goods or the performance of services in the normal course of business.

Sarbanes-Oxley Act (SOX) *(p. 8)* Regulations passed by Congress to reduce unethical corporate behavior.

Sole proprietorship *(p. 4)* A business owned by one person.

Statement of cash flows *(p. 15)* A financial statement that provides financial information about the cash receipts and cash payments of a business for a specific period of time.

Stockholders' equity *(p. 14)* The owners' claim to assets.

Comprehensive Do it!

The Comprehensive Do it! is a final review before you begin homework.

Jeff Andringa, a former college hockey player, quit his job and started Ice Camp, a hockey camp for kids ages 8 to 18. Eventually, he would like to open hockey camps nationwide. Jeff has asked you to help him prepare financial statements at the end of his first year of operations. He relates the following facts about his business activities.

In order to get the business off the ground, he decided to incorporate. He sold shares of common stock to a few close friends, as well as buying some of the shares himself. He initially raised $25,000 through the sale of these shares. In addition, the company took out a $10,000 loan at a local bank.

Ice Camp purchased, for $12,000 cash, a bus for transporting kids. The company also bought hockey goals and other miscellaneous equipment with $1,500 cash. The company earned camp tuition during the year of $100,000 but had collected only $80,000 of this amount. Thus, at the end of the year, its customers still owed $20,000. The company rents time at a local rink for $50 per hour. Total rink rental costs during the year were $8,000, insurance was $10,000, salary expense was $20,000, and supplies used totaled $9,000, all of which were paid in cash. The company incurred $800 in interest expense on the bank loan, which it still owed at the end of the year.

The company paid dividends during the year of $5,000 cash. The balance in the corporate bank account at December 31, 2014, was $49,500.

Instructions

Using the format of the Sierra Corporation statements in this chapter, prepare an income statement, retained earnings statement, balance sheet, and statement of cash flows. (*Hint:* Prepare the statements in the order stated to take advantage of the flow of information from one statement to the next, as shown in Illustration 1-9 on page 17.)

Action Plan

- On the income statement: Show revenues and expenses for a period of time.

- On the retained earnings statement: Show the changes in retained earnings for a period of time.

- On the balance sheet: Report assets, liabilities, and stockholders' equity at a specific date.

- On the statement of cash flows: Report sources and uses of cash from operating, investing, and financing activities for a period of time.

Solution to Comprehensive Do it!

ICE CAMP		
Income Statement		
For the Year Ended December 31, 2014		
Revenues		
Service revenue		$100,000
Expenses		
Salaries and wages expense	$20,000	
Insurance expense	10,000	
Supplies expense	9,000	
Rent expense	8,000	
Interest expense	800	
Total expenses		47,800
Net income		$ 52,200

ICE CAMP
Retained Earnings Statement
For the Year Ended December 31, 2014

Retained earnings, January 1, 2014	$ 0
Add: Net income	52,200
	52,200
Less: Dividends	5,000
Retained earnings, December 31, 2014	$47,200

ICE CAMP
Balance Sheet
December 31, 2014

Assets

Cash	$49,500
Accounts receivable	20,000
Equipment	13,500
Total assets	$83,000

Liabilities and Stockholders' Equity

Liabilities		
Notes payable	$10,000	
Interest payable	800	
Total liabilities		$10,800
Stockholders' equity		
Common stock	25,000	
Retained earnings	47,200	
Total stockholders' equity		72,200
Total liabilities and stockholders' equity		$83,000

ICE CAMP
Statement of Cash Flows
For the Year Ended December 31, 2014

Cash flows from operating activities		
Cash receipts from operating activities	$80,000	
Cash payments for operating activities	(47,000)	
Net cash provided by operating activities		$33,000
Cash flows from investing activities		
Purchase of equipment	(13,500)	
Net cash used by investing activities		(13,500)
Cash flows from financing activities		
Issuance of common stock	25,000	
Issuance of notes payable	10,000	
Dividends paid	(5,000)	
Net cash provided by financing activities		30,000
Net increase in cash		49,500
Cash at beginning of period		0
Cash at end of period		$49,500

The Navigator

Self-Test, Brief Exercises, Exercises, Problem Set A, and many more resources are available for practice in WileyPLUS.

This would be a good time to look at the Preface to this textbook. Knowing the purpose of the different types of homework will help you understand what each contributes to your accounting skills and competencies.

Self-Test Questions

Answers are on page 43.

(LO 1) **1.** Which is **not** one of the three forms of business organization?
  (a) Sole proprietorship.   (c) Partnership.
  (b) Creditorship.   (d) Corporation.

(LO 1) **2.** Which is an advantage of corporations relative to partnerships and sole proprietorships?
  (a) Lower taxes.
  (b) Harder to transfer ownership.
  (c) Reduced legal liability for investors.
  (d) Most common form of organization.

(LO 2) **3.** Which statement about users of accounting information is **incorrect**?
  (a) Management is considered an internal user.
  (b) Taxing authorities are considered external users.
  (c) Present creditors are considered external users.
  (d) Regulatory authorities are considered internal users.

(LO 2) **4.** Which of the following did **not** result from the Sarbanes-Oxley Act?
  (a) Top management must now certify the accuracy of financial information.
  (b) Penalties for fraudulent activity increased.
  (c) Independence of auditors increased.
  (d) Tax rates on corporations increased.

(LO 3) **5.** Which is **not** one of the three primary business activities?
  (a) Financing.   (c) Advertising.
  (b) Operating.   (d) Investing.

(LO 3) **6.** Which of the following is an example of a financing activity?
  (a) Issuing shares of common stock.
  (b) Selling goods on account.
  (c) Buying delivery equipment.
  (d) Buying inventory.

(LO 4) **7.** Net income will result during a time period when:
  (a) assets exceed liabilities.
  (b) assets exceed revenues.
  (c) expenses exceed revenues.
  (d) revenues exceed expenses.

(LO 4) **8.** The financial statements for Joseph Corporation contained the following information.

Accounts receivable	$ 5,000
Sales revenue	75,000
Cash	15,000
Salaries and wages expense	20,000
Rent expense	10,000

What was Joseph Corporation's net income?
  (a) $60,000.   (c) $65,000.
  (b) $15,000.   (d) $45,000.

(LO 4, 5) **9.** What section of a statement of cash flows indicates the cash spent on new equipment during the past accounting period?
  (a) The investing activities section.
  (b) The operating activities section.
  (c) The financing activities section.
  (d) The statement of cash flows does not give this information.

(LO 4, 5) **10.** Which statement presents information as of a specific point in time?
  (a) Income statement.
  (b) Balance sheet.
  (c) Statement of cash flows.
  (d) Retained earnings statement.

(LO 5) **11.** Which financial statement reports assets, liabilities, and stockholders' equity?
  (a) Income statement.
  (b) Retained earnings statement.
  (c) Balance sheet.
  (d) Statement of cash flows.

(LO 5) **12.** Stockholders' equity represents:
  (a) claims of creditors.
  (b) claims of employees.
  (c) the difference between revenues and expenses.
  (d) claims of owners.

(LO 5) **13.** As of December 31, 2014, Stoneland Corporation has assets of $3,500 and stockholders' equity of $1,500. What are the liabilities for Stoneland Corporation as of December 31, 2014?
  (a) $1,500.   (c) $2,500.
  (b) $1,000.   (d) $2,000.

(LO 6) **14.** The element of a corporation's annual report that describes the corporation's accounting methods is/are the:
  (a) notes to the financial statements.
  (b) management discussion and analysis.
  (c) auditor's report.
  (d) income statement.

(LO 6) **15.** The element of the annual report that presents an opinion regarding the fairness of the presentation of the financial position and results of operations is/are the:
  (a) income statement.
  (b) auditor's opinion.
  (c) balance sheet.
  (d) comparative statements.

Go to the book's companion website, **www.wiley.com/college/kimmel**, to access additional Self-Test Questions.

Questions

1. ◄ What are the three basic forms of business organizations?

2. What are the advantages to a business of being formed as a corporation? What are the disadvantages?

3. What are the advantages to a business of being formed as a partnership or sole proprietorship? What are the disadvantages?

4. "Accounting is ingrained in our society and is vital to our economic system." Do you agree? Explain.

5. ◄ Who are the internal users of accounting data? How does accounting provide relevant data to the internal users?

6. Who are the external users of accounting data? Give examples.

7. What are the three main types of business activity? Give examples of each activity.

8. Listed here are some items found in the financial statements of Finzelberg. Indicate in which financial statement(s) each item would appear.
   (a) Service revenue. (d) Accounts receivable.
   (b) Equipment. (e) Common stock.
   (c) Advertising expense. (f) Interest payable.

9. ◄ ⌐══C Why would a bank want to monitor the dividend payment practices of the corporations to which it lends money?

10. "A company's net income appears directly on the income statement and the retained earnings statement, and it is included indirectly in the company's balance sheet." Do you agree? Explain.

11. ⌐══C What is the primary purpose of the statement of cash flows?

12. What are the three main categories of the statement of cash flows? Why do you think these categories were chosen?

13. What is retained earnings? What items increase the balance in retained earnings? What items decrease the balance in retained earnings?

14. What is the basic accounting equation?

15. (a) Define the terms assets, liabilities, and stockholders' equity.
    (b) What items affect stockholders' equity?

16. Which of these items are liabilities of White Glove Cleaning Service?
    (a) Cash. (f) Equipment.
    (b) Accounts payable. (g) Salaries and wages
    (c) Dividends.   payable.
    (d) Accounts receivable. (h) Service revenue.
    (e) Supplies. (i) Rent expense.

17. How are each of the following financial statements interrelated? (a) Retained earnings statement and income statement. (b) Retained earnings statement and balance sheet. (c) Balance sheet and statement of cash flows.

18. ⌐══C What is the purpose of the management discussion and analysis section (MD&A)?

19. ⌐══C Why is it important for financial statements to receive an unqualified auditor's opinion?

20. ⌐══C What types of information are presented in the notes to the financial statements?

21. ✏ The accounting equation is Assets = Liabilities + Stockholders' Equity. Appendix A, at the end of this textbook, reproduces Tootsie Roll's financial statements. Replacing words in the equation with dollar amounts, what is Tootsie Roll's accounting equation at December 31, 2011?

The tool icon ⌐══C indicates that an activity employs one of the decision tools presented in the chapter. The ◄ indicates that an activity relates to a business function beyond accounting. The pencil icon ✏ indicates that an activity requires written communication.

Brief Exercises

BE1-1 Match each of the following forms of business organization with a set of characteristics: sole proprietorship (SP), partnership (P), corporation (C).
(a) _____ Shared control, tax advantages, increased skills and resources.
(b) _____ Simple to set up and maintains control with owner.
(c) _____ Easier to transfer ownership and raise funds, no personal liability.

Describe forms of business organization.
(LO 1), K

BE1-2 Match each of the following types of evaluation with one of the listed users of accounting information.
  1. Trying to determine whether the company complied with tax laws.
  2. Trying to determine whether the company can pay its obligations.
  3. Trying to determine whether an advertising proposal will be cost-effective.
  4. Trying to determine whether the company's net income will result in a stock price increase.
  5. Trying to determine whether the company should employ debt or equity financing.
(a) _____ Investors in common stock. (d) _____ Chief Financial Officer.
(b) _____ Marketing managers. (e) _____ Internal Revenue Service.
(c) _____ Creditors.

Identify users of accounting information.
(LO 2), K
◄

Classify items by activity.
(LO 3), **K**

BE1-3 Indicate in which part of the statement of cash flows each item would appear: operating activities (O), investing activities (I), or financing activities (F).
(a) _____ Cash received from customers.
(b) _____ Cash paid to stockholders (dividends).
(c) _____ Cash received from issuing new common stock.
(d) _____ Cash paid to suppliers.
(e) _____ Cash paid to purchase a new office building.

Determine effect of transactions on stockholders' equity.
(LO 4), **C**

BE1-4 Presented below are a number of transactions. Determine whether each transaction affects common stock (C), dividends (D), revenue (R), expense (E), or does not affect stockholders' equity (NSE). Provide titles for the revenues and expenses.
(a) Costs incurred for advertising.
(b) Assets received for services performed.
(c) Costs incurred for insurance.
(d) Amounts paid to employees.
(e) Cash distributed to stockholders.
(f) Assets received in exchange for allowing the use of the company's building.
(g) Costs incurred for utilities used.
(h) Cash purchase of equipment.
(i) Cash received from investors.

Prepare a balance sheet.
(LO 4, 5), **AP**

BE1-5 In alphabetical order below are balance sheet items for Burnett Company at December 31, 2014. Prepare a balance sheet following the format of Illustration 1-7 (page 14).

Accounts payable	$65,000
Accounts receivable	71,000
Cash	22,000
Common stock	18,000
Retained earnings	10,000

Determine where items appear on financial statements.
(LO 4, 5), **K**

BE1-6 Eskimo Pie Corporation markets a broad range of frozen treats, including its famous Eskimo Pie ice cream bars. The following items were taken from a recent income statement and balance sheet. In each case, identify whether the item would appear on the balance sheet (BS) or income statement (IS).
(a) _____ Income tax expense.
(b) _____ Inventory.
(c) _____ Accounts payable.
(d) _____ Retained earnings.
(e) _____ Equipment.
(f) _____ Sales revenue.
(g) _____ Cost of goods sold.
(h) _____ Common stock.
(i) _____ Accounts receivable.
(j) _____ Interest expense.

Determine proper financial statement.
(LO 4), **K**

BE1-7 Indicate which statement you would examine to find each of the following items: income statement (IS), balance sheet (BS), retained earnings statement (RES), or statement of cash flows (SCF).
(a) Revenue during the period.
(b) Supplies on hand at the end of the year.
(c) Cash received from issuing new bonds during the period.
(d) Total debts outstanding at the end of the period.

Use basic accounting equation.
(LO 5), **AP**

BE1-8 Use the basic accounting equation to answer these questions.
(a) The liabilities of Jantz Company are $90,000 and the stockholders' equity is $230,000. What is the amount of Jantz Company's total assets?
(b) The total assets of Foley Company are $170,000 and its stockholders' equity is $80,000. What is the amount of its total liabilities?
(c) The total assets of Sundberg Co. are $800,000 and its liabilities are equal to one-fourth of its total assets. What is the amount of Sundberg Co.'s stockholders' equity?

Use basic accounting equation.
(LO 5), **AP**

BE1-9 At the beginning of the year, Goren Company had total assets of $800,000 and total liabilities of $500,000. (Treat each item independently.)
(a) If total assets increased $150,000 during the year and total liabilities decreased $80,000, what is the amount of stockholders' equity at the end of the year?
(b) During the year, total liabilities increased $100,000 and stockholders' equity decreased $70,000. What is the amount of total assets at the end of the year?
(c) If total assets decreased $80,000 and stockholders' equity increased $110,000 during the year, what is the amount of total liabilities at the end of the year?

BE1-10 Indicate whether each of these items is an asset (A), a liability (L), or part of stockholders' equity (SE).
(a) Accounts receivable.
(b) Salaries and wages payable.
(c) Equipment.
(d) Supplies.
(e) Common stock.
(f) Notes payable.

Identify assets, liabilities, and stockholders' equity.
(LO 5), **K**

BE1-11 Which is **not** a required part of an annual report of a publicly traded company?
(a) Statement of cash flows.
(b) Notes to the financial statements.
(c) Management discussion and analysis.
(d) All of these are required.

Determine required parts of annual report.
(LO 6), **K**

Do it! Review

Do it! **1-1** Identify each of the following organizational characteristics with the organizational form or forms with which it is associated.
(a) Easier to transfer ownership.
(b) Easier to raise funds.
(c) More owner control.
(d) Tax advantages.
(e) No personal legal liability.

Identify benefits of business organization forms.
(LO 1), **C**

Do it! **1-2** Classify each item as an asset, liability, common stock, revenue, or expense.
(a) Issuance of ownership shares.
(b) Land purchased.
(c) Amounts owed to suppliers.
(d) Bonds payable.
(e) Amount earned from selling a product.
(f) Cost of advertising.

Classify business activities.
(LO 3), **K**

Do it! **1-3** Marsh Corporation began operations on January 1, 2014. The following information is available for Marsh Corporation on December 31, 2014.

Accounts payable	$ 5,000	Notes payable	$ 7,000
Accounts receivable	2,000	Rent expense	10,000
Advertising expense	4,000	Retained earnings	?
Cash	3,100	Service revenue	25,000
Common stock	15,000	Supplies	1,900
Dividends	2,500	Supplies expense	1,700
Equipment	26,800		

Prepare an income statement, a retained earnings statement, and a balance sheet for Marsh Corporation.

Prepare financial statements.
(LO 4, 5), **AP**

Do it! **1-4** Indicate whether each of the following items is most closely associated with the management discussion and analysis (MD&A), the notes to the financial statements, or the auditor's report.
(a) Description of ability to pay near-term obligations.
(b) Unqualified opinion.
(c) Details concerning liabilities, too voluminous to be included in the statements.
(d) Description of favorable and unfavorable trends.
(e) Certified public accountant (CPA).
(f) Descriptions of significant accounting policies.

Identify components of annual reports.
(LO 6), **C**

Exercises

E1-1 Here is a list of words or phrases discussed in this chapter:
1. Corporation
2. Creditor
3. Accounts receivable
4. Partnership
5. Stockholder
6. Common stock
7. Accounts payable
8. Auditor's opinion

Match items with descriptions.
(LO 1, 2, 4, 6), **K**

Instructions

Match each word or phrase with the best description of it.

_____ (a) An expression about whether financial statements conform with generally accepted accounting principles.

_____ (b) A business that raises money by issuing shares of stock.

_____ (c) The portion of stockholders' equity that results from receiving cash from investors.

_____ (d) Obligations to suppliers of goods.

_____ (e) Amounts due from customers.

_____ (f) A party to whom a business owes money.

_____ (g) A party that invests in common stock.

_____ (h) A business that is owned jointly by two or more individuals but does not issue stock.

Identify business activities.
(LO 3), **C**

E1-2 All businesses are involved in three types of activities—financing, investing, and operating. Listed below are the names and descriptions of companies in several different industries.

Abitibi Consolidated Inc.—manufacturer and marketer of newsprint
Cal State–Northridge Stdt Union—university student union
Oracle Corporation—computer software developer and retailer
Sportsco Investments—owner of the Vancouver Canucks hockey club
Grant Thornton LLP—professional accounting and business advisory firm
Southwest Airlines—discount airline

Instructions

(a) For each of the above companies, provide examples of (1) a financing activity, (2) an investing activity, and (3) an operating activity that the company likely engages in.

(b) Which of the activities that you identified in (a) are common to most businesses? Which activities are not?

Classify accounts.
(LO 3, 4), **C**

E1-3 The Clear View Golf & Country Club details the following accounts in its financial statements.

	(a)	(b)
Accounts payable	___	___
Accounts receivable	___	___
Equipment	___	___
Sales revenue	___	___
Service revenue	___	___
Inventory	___	___
Mortgage payable	___	___
Supplies expense	___	___
Rent expense	___	___
Salaries and wages expense	___	___

Instructions

(a) Classify each of the above accounts as an asset (A), liability (L), stockholders' equity (SE), revenue (R), or expense (E) item.

(b) Classify each of the above accounts as a financing activity (F), investing activity (I), or operating activity (O). If you believe a particular account doesn't fit in any of these activities, explain why.

Prepare income statement and retained earnings statement.
(LO 4), **AP**

E1-4 This information relates to Molina Co. for the year 2014.

Retained earnings, January 1, 2014	$67,000
Advertising expense	1,800
Dividends	6,000
Rent expense	10,400
Service revenue	58,000
Utilities expense	2,400
Salaries and wages expense	30,000

Instructions

After analyzing the data, prepare an income statement and a retained earnings statement for the year ending December 31, 2014.

E1-5 Suppose the following information was taken from the 2014 financial statements of pharmaceutical giant Merck and Co. (All dollar amounts are in millions.)

Prepare income statement and retained earnings statement.

(LO 4), **AP**

Retained earnings, January 1, 2014	$43,698.8
Cost of goods sold	9,018.9
Selling and administrative expenses	8,543.2
Dividends	3,597.7
Sales revenue	38,576.0
Research and development expense	5,845.0
Income tax expense	2,267.6

Instructions

(a) After analyzing the data, prepare an income statement and a retained earnings statement for the year ending December 31, 2014.

(b) Suppose that Merck decided to reduce its research and development expense by 50%. What would be the short-term implications? What would be the long-term implications? How do you think the stock market would react?

E1-6 Presented here is information for DeVito Inc. for 2014.

Prepare a retained earnings statement.

(LO 4), **AP**

Retained earnings, January 1	$130,000
Service revenue	400,000
Total expenses	175,000
Dividends	65,000

Instructions

Prepare the 2014 retained earnings statement for DeVito Inc.

E1-7 Consider each of the following independent situations.

(a) The retained earnings statement of Grant Corporation shows dividends of $68,000, while net income for the year was $75,000.

(b) The statement of cash flows for Remington Corporation shows that cash provided by operating activities was $10,000, cash used in investing activities was $110,000, and cash provided by financing activities was $130,000.

Interpret financial facts.

(LO 4), **AP**

Instructions

For each company, provide a brief discussion interpreting these financial facts. For example, you might discuss the company's financial health or its apparent growth philosophy.

E1-8 The following items and amounts were taken from Motte Inc.'s 2014 income statement and balance sheet.

Identify financial statement components and prepare income statement.

(LO 4, 5), **C**

_____ Cash	$ 84,700		_____ Accounts receivable	$ 88,419
_____ Retained earnings	123,192		_____ Sales revenue	584,951
_____ Cost of goods sold	438,458		_____ Notes payable	6,499
_____ Salaries and wages expense	115,131		_____ Accounts payable	49,384
_____ Prepaid insurance	7,818		_____ Service revenue	4,806
_____ Inventory	64,618		_____ Interest expense	1,882

Instructions

(a) In each, case, identify on the blank line whether the item is an asset (A), liability (L), stockholder's equity (SE), revenue (R), or expense (E) item.

(b) Prepare an income statement for Motte Inc. for the year ended December 31, 2014.

E1-9 Here are incomplete financial statements for Riedy, Inc.

Calculate missing amounts.

(LO 4, 5), **AP**

RIEDY, INC.
Balance Sheet

Assets		Liabilities and Stockholders' Equity	
Cash	$ 7,000	Liabilities	
Inventory	10,000	Accounts payable	$ 5,000
Buildings	45,000	Stockholders' equity	
Total assets	$62,000	Common stock	(a)
		Retained earnings	(b)
		Total liabilities and	
		stockholders' equity	$62,000

Income Statement

Revenues	$85,000
Cost of goods sold	(c)
Salaries and wages expense	10,000
Net income	$ (d)

Retained Earnings Statement

Beginning retained earnings	$12,000
Add: Net income	(e)
Less: Dividends	5,000
Ending retained earnings	$27,000

Instructions

Calculate the missing amounts.

Compute net income and prepare a balance sheet.

(LO 4, 5), **AP**

E1-10 Flint Hills Park is a private camping ground near the Lathom Peak Recreation Area. It has compiled the following financial information as of December 31, 2014.

Service revenue (from camping fees)	$132,000	Dividends	$ 9,000
Sales revenue (from general store)	25,000	Notes payable	50,000
Accounts payable	11,000	Expenses during 2014	126,000
Cash	8,500	Supplies	5,500
Equipment	114,000	Common stock	40,000
		Retained earnings (1/1/2014)	5,000

Instructions

(a) Determine Flint Hills Park's net income for 2014.

(b) Prepare a retained earnings statement and a balance sheet for Flint Hills Park as of December 31, 2014.

(c) Upon seeing this income statement, Joe Winsor, the campground manager, immediately concluded, "The general store is more trouble than it is worth—let's get rid of it." The marketing director isn't so sure this is a good idea. What do you think?

Identify financial statement components and prepare an income statement.

(LO 4, 5), **AP**

E1-11 Kellogg Company is the world's leading producer of ready-to-eat cereal and a leading producer of grain-based convenience foods such as frozen waffles and cereal bars. Suppose the following items were taken from its 2014 income statement and balance sheet. (All dollars are in millions.)

____ Retained earnings	$5,481	____ Bonds payable	$ 4,835
____ Cost of goods sold	7,184	____ Inventory	910
____ Selling and		____ Sales revenue	12,575
administrative expenses	3,390	____ Accounts payable	1,077
____ Cash	334	____ Common stock	105
____ Notes payable	44	____ Income tax expense	498
____ Interest expense	295		

Instructions

Perform each of the following.

(a) In each case, identify whether the item is an asset (A), liability (L), stockholders' equity (SE), revenue (R), or expense (E).

(b) Prepare an income statement for Kellogg Company for the year ended December 31, 2014.

Prepare a statement of cash flows.

(LO 5), **AP**

E1-12 This information is for Dyckman Corporation for the year ended December 31, 2014.

Cash received from lenders	$20,000
Cash received from customers	50,000
Cash paid for new equipment	28,000
Cash dividends paid	8,000
Cash paid to suppliers	16,000
Cash balance 1/1/14	12,000

Instructions

(a) Prepare the 2014 statement of cash flows for Dyckman Corporation.

(b) Suppose you are one of Dyckman's creditors. Referring to the statement of cash flows, evaluate Dyckman's ability to repay its creditors.

E1-13 Suppose the following data are derived from the 2014 financial statements of Southwest Airlines. (All dollars are in millions.) Southwest has a December 31 year-end.

Prepare a statement of cash flows.

(LO 5), **AP**

Cash balance, January 1, 2014	$1,390
Cash paid for repayment of debt	122
Cash received from issuance of common stock	144
Cash received from issuance of long-term debt	500
Cash received from customers	9,823
Cash paid for property and equipment	1,529
Cash paid for dividends	14
Cash paid for repurchase of common stock	1,001
Cash paid for goods and services	6,978

Instructions

(a) After analyzing the data, prepare a statement of cash flows for Southwest Airlines for the year ended December 31, 2014.

(b) Discuss whether the company's net cash provided by operating activities was sufficient to finance its investing activities. If it was not, how did the company finance its investing activities?

E1-14 Edward Waltz is the bookkeeper for Edminson Company. Edward has been trying to get the balance sheet of Edminson Company to balance. It finally balanced, but now he's not sure it is correct.

Correct an incorrectly prepared balance sheet.

(LO 5), **AP**

EDMINSON COMPANY
Balance Sheet
December 31, 2014

Assets		Liabilities and Stockholders' Equity	
Cash	$18,000	Accounts payable	$16,000
Supplies	9,500	Accounts receivable	(12,000)
Equipment	40,000	Common stock	40,000
Dividends	8,000	Retained earnings	31,500
Total assets	$75,500	Total liabilities and	
		stockholders' equity	$75,500

Instructions

Prepare a correct balance sheet.

E1-15 Suppose the following items were taken from the balance sheet of Nike, Inc. (All dollars are in millions.)

Classify items as assets, liabilities, and stockholders' equity and prepare accounting equation.

(LO 5), **AP**

1.	Cash	$2,291.1	7.	Inventory	$2,357.0
2.	Accounts receivable	2,883.9	8.	Income taxes payable	86.3
3.	Common stock	2,874.2	9.	Equipment	1,957.7
4.	Notes payable	342.9	10.	Retained earnings	5,818.9
5.	Buildings	3,759.9	11.	Accounts payable	2,815.8
6.	Mortgage payable	1,311.5			

Instructions

Perform each of the following.

(a) Classify each of these items as an asset, liability, or stockholders' equity and determine the total dollar amount for each classification.

(b) Determine Nike's accounting equation by calculating the value of total assets, total liabilities, and total stockholders' equity.

(c) To what extent does Nike rely on debt versus equity financing?

E1-16 The summaries of data from the balance sheet, income statement, and retained earnings statement for two corporations, Colaw Corporation and Hunter Enterprises, are presented on the next page for 2014.

Use financial statement relationships to determine missing amounts.

(LO 5), **AP**

	Colaw Corporation	Hunter Enterprises
Beginning of year		
Total assets	$110,000	$150,000
Total liabilities	70,000	(d)
Total stockholders' equity	(a)	70,000
End of year		
Total assets	(b)	180,000
Total liabilities	120,000	55,000
Total stockholders' equity	60,000	(e)
Changes during year in retained earnings		
Dividends	(c)	5,000
Total revenues	215,000	(f)
Total expenses	165,000	80,000

Instructions

Determine the missing amounts. Assume all changes in stockholders' equity are due to changes in retained earnings.

Classify various items in an annual report.

(LO 6), K

E1-17 The annual report provides financial information in a variety of formats, including the following.

> Management discussion and analysis (MD&A)
> Financial statements
> Notes to the financial statements
> Auditor's opinion

Instructions

For each of the following, state in what area of the annual report the item would be presented. If the item would probably not be found in an annual report, state "Not disclosed."
(a) The total cumulative amount received from stockholders in exchange for common stock.
(b) An independent assessment concerning whether the financial statements present a fair depiction of the company's results and financial position.
(c) The interest rate that the company is being charged on all outstanding debts.
(d) Total revenue from operating activities.
(e) Management's assessment of the company's results.
(f) The names and positions of all employees hired in the last year.

Exercises: Set B and Challenge Exercises

Visit the book's companion website, at **www.wiley.com/college/kimmel**, and choose the Student Companion site to access Exercise Set B and Challenge Exercises.

Problems: Set A

Determine forms of business organization.

(LO 1), C

P1-1A Presented below are five independent situations.
(a) Three physics professors at MIT have formed a business to improve the speed of information transfer over the Internet for stock exchange transactions. Each has contributed an equal amount of cash and knowledge to the venture. Although their approach looks promising, they are concerned about the legal liabilities that their business might confront.
(b) Al Bolt, a college student looking for summer employment, opened a bait shop in a small shed at a local marina.
(c) Rita Benedict and Joe Freeze each owned separate shoe manufacturing businesses. They have decided to combine their businesses. They expect that within the coming year they will need significant funds to expand their operations.

(d) Andrea, Diane, and Steve recently graduated with marketing degrees. They have been friends since childhood. They have decided to start a consulting business focused on marketing sporting goods over the Internet.

(e) Jack Yaeger has developed a low-cost GPS device that can be implanted into pets so that they can be easily located when lost. He would like to build a small manufacturing facility to make the devices and then sell them to veterinarians across the country. Jack has no savings or personal assets. He wants to maintain control over the business.

Instructions ◼▦▶

In each case, explain what form of organization the business is likely to take—sole proprietorship, partnership, or corporation. Give reasons for your choice.

P1-2A   Financial decisions often place heavier emphasis on one type of financial statement over the others. Consider each of the following hypothetical situations independently.

(a) The North Face is considering extending credit to a new customer. The terms of the credit would require the customer to pay within 30 days of receipt of goods.

(b) An investor is considering purchasing common stock of Amazon.com. The investor plans to hold the investment for at least 5 years.

(c) JPMorgan Chase Bank is considering extending a loan to a small company. The company would be required to make interest payments at the end of each year for 5 years, and to repay the loan at the end of the fifth year.

(d) The president of Campbell Soup is trying to determine whether the company is generating enough cash to increase the amount of dividends paid to investors in this and future years, and still have enough cash to buy equipment as it is needed.

Identify users and uses of financial statements.

(LO 2, 4, 5), **K**

Instructions ◼▦▶

In each situation, state whether the decision-maker would be most likely to place primary emphasis on information provided by the income statement, balance sheet, or statement of cash flows. In each case provide a brief justification for your choice. Choose only one financial statement in each case.

P1-3A   On June 1, Hightower Service Co. was started with an initial investment in the company of $22,100 cash. Here are the assets, liabilities, and common stock of the company at June 30, and the revenues and expenses for the month of June, its first month of operations:

Prepare an income statement, retained earnings statement, and balance sheet; discuss results.

(LO 4, 5), **AP**

Cash	$ 4,600	Notes payable	$12,000
Accounts receivable	4,000	Accounts payable	500
Service revenue	7,500	Supplies expense	1,000
Supplies	2,400	Maintenance and repairs expense	600
Advertising expense	400	Utilities expense	300
Equipment	26,000	Salaries and wages expense	1,400
Common stock	22,100		

In June, the company issued no additional stock but paid dividends of $1,400.

Instructions

(a) Prepare an income statement and a retained earnings statement for the month of June and a balance sheet at June 30, 2014.

(b) Briefly discuss whether the company's first month of operations was a success.

(c) Discuss the company's decision to distribute a dividend.

Marginal check figures (in blue) provide a key number to let you know you are on the right track.

(a) Net income $ 3,800
    Ret. earnings $ 2,400
    Tot. assets $37,000

P1-4A   Presented below is selected financial information for Wenger Corporation for December 31, 2014.

Determine items included in a statement of cash flows, prepare the statement, and comment.

(LO 5), **AP**

Inventory	$ 25,000	Cash paid to purchase equipment	$ 12,000
Cash paid to suppliers	104,000	Equipment	40,000
Buildings	200,000	Service revenue	100,000
Common stock	50,000	Cash received from customers	132,000
Cash dividends paid	7,000	Cash received from issuing	
Cash at beginning of period	9,000	common stock	22,000

Instructions

(a) Determine which items should be included in a statement of cash flows and then prepare the statement for Wenger Corporation.

(b) Comment on the adequacy of net cash provided by operating activities to fund the company's investing activities and dividend payments.

(a) Net increase $31,000

Comment on proper accounting treatment and prepare a corrected balance sheet.

(LO 5), **AP**

P1-5A Merando Corporation was formed on January 1, 2014. At December 31, 2014, Bill Jensen, the president and sole stockholder, decided to prepare a balance sheet, which appeared as follows.

MERANDO CORPORATION
Balance Sheet
December 31, 2014

Assets		Liabilities and Stockholders' Equity	
Cash	$20,000	Accounts payable	$30,000
Accounts receivable	50,000	Notes payable	15,000
Inventory	36,000	Boat loan	22,000
Boat	24,000	Stockholders' equity	64,000

Bill willingly admits that he is not an accountant by training. He is concerned that his balance sheet might not be correct. He has provided you with the following additional information.

1. The boat actually belongs to Jensen, not to Merando Corporation. However, because he thinks he might take customers out on the boat occasionally, he decided to list it as an asset of the company. To be consistent, he also listed as a liability of the corporation his personal loan that he took out at the bank to buy the boat.
2. The inventory was originally purchased for $25,000, but due to a surge in demand Bill now thinks he could sell it for $36,000. He thought it would be best to record it at $36,000.
3. Included in the accounts receivable balance is $10,000 that Bill loaned to his brother 5 years ago. Bill included this in the receivables of Merando Corporation so he wouldn't forget that his brother owes him money.

Instructions

(a) Comment on the proper accounting treatment of the three items above.

(b) Tot. assets $85,000

(b) Provide a corrected balance sheet for Merando Corporation. (*Hint:* To get the balance sheet to balance, adjust stockholders' equity.)

Problems: Set B

Determine forms of business organization.

(LO 1), **C**

P1-1B Presented below are five independent situations.

(a) Randy Gentry, a college student looking for summer employment, opened a produce stand along a busy local highway. Each morning he buys produce from local farmers, then sells it in the afternoon as people return home from work.

(b) Dave Boyce and Davey Lopez each owned separate swing-set manufacturing businesses. They have decided to combine their businesses and try to expand their reach beyond their local market. They expect that within the coming year they will need significant funds to expand their operations.

(c) Three chemistry professors at LU have formed a business to employ enzymes to clean up toxic waste sites. Each has contributed an equal amount of cash and knowledge to the venture. The use of enzymes in this situation is experimental, and legal obligations could result.

(d) Marty Wells has run a successful, but small cooperative vitamin store for over 20 years. The increased sales of her store have made her believe that the time is right to open a national chain of vitamin stores across the country. Of course, this will require a substantial investment in stores, inventory, and employees in each store. Marty has no savings or personal assets. She wants to maintain control over the business.

(e) Charles Kuehl and Peg Lambing recently graduated with masters degrees in business. They have decided to start a consulting business focused on teaching the basics of exporting to small business owners interested in exporting.

Instructions

In each case, explain what form of organization the business is likely to take—sole proprietorship, partnership, or corporation. Give reasons for your choice.

P1-2B Financial decisions often place heavier emphasis on one type of financial statement over the others. Consider each of the following hypothetical situations independently.

Identify users and uses of financial statements.

(LO 2, 4, 5), **K**

(a) An investor is considering purchasing common stock of the 24/7 Fitness company. The investor plans to hold the investment for at least 3 years.

(b) Xerox is considering extending credit to a new customer. The terms of the credit would require the customer to pay within 60 days of receipt of goods.

(c) The president of American Airlines is trying to determine whether the company is generating enough cash to increase the amount of dividends paid to investors in this and future years, and still have enough cash to buy new flight equipment as it is needed.

(d) PNC Bank is considering extending a loan to a small company. The company would be required to make interest payments at the end of each year for 5 years, and to repay the loan at the end of the fifth year.

Instructions ▰▰▰➤

In each of the situations above, state whether the decision-maker would be most likely to place primary emphasis on information provided by the income statement, balance sheet, or statement of cash flows. In each case, provide a brief justification for your choice. Choose only one financial statement in each case.

P1-3B Shaw's Garden was started on May 1 with an investment of $45,000 cash. Following are the assets, liabilities, and common stock of the company on May 31, 2014, and the revenues and expenses for the month of May, its first month of operations.

Prepare an income statement, retained earnings statement, and balance sheet; discuss results.

(LO 4, 5), **AP**

Accounts receivable	$ 8,400	Notes payable	$26,000
Service revenue	10,400	Salaries and wages expense	1,900
Advertising expense	1,800	Equipment	58,800
Accounts payable	4,400	Maintenance and repairs expense	2,100
Cash	10,800	Insurance expense	400
Common stock	45,000		

No additional common stock was issued in May, but a dividend of $1,600 in cash was paid.

Instructions

(a) Prepare an income statement and a retained earnings statement for the month of May and a balance sheet at May 31, 2014.

(b) Briefly discuss whether the company's first month of operations was a success.

(c) Discuss the company's decision to distribute a dividend.

(a) Net income $ 4,200
Ret. earnings $ 2,600
Tot. assets $78,000

P1-4B Presented below are selected financial statement items for Preacher Corporation for December 31, 2014.

Determine items included in a statement of cash flows, prepare the statement, and comment.

(LO 5), **AP**

Inventory	$ 55,000	Cash paid to purchase equipment	$ 20,000
Cash paid to suppliers	154,000	Equipment	40,000
Buildings	400,000	Service revenue	200,000
Common stock	20,000	Cash received from customers	162,000
Cash dividends paid	2,000	Cash received from issuing	
Cash at beginning of period	11,000	bonds payable	40,000

Instructions

(a) Determine which items should be included in a statement of cash flows, and then prepare the statement for Preacher Corporation.

(b) Comment on the adequacy of net cash provided by operating activities to fund the company's investing activities and dividend payments.

(a) Net increase $26,000

P1-5B Walters Corporation was formed during 2013 by John Walters. John is the president and sole stockholder. At December 31, 2014, John prepared an income statement for Walters Corporation. John is not an accountant, but he thinks he did a reasonable job preparing the income statement by looking at the financial statements of

Comment on proper accounting treatment and prepare a corrected income statement.

(LO 4, 5), **AP**

other companies. He has asked you for advice. John's income statement appears as follows.

WALTERS CORPORATION
Income Statement
For the Year Ended December 31, 2014

Accounts receivable	$17,000
Service revenue	40,000
Rent expense	10,000
Insurance expense	7,000
Vacation expense	6,000
Net income	$34,000

John has also provided you with these facts.

1. Included in the service revenue account is $3,000 of revenue that the company provided service for and received payment for in 2013. He forgot to include it in the 2013 income statement, so he put it in this year's statement.

2. John operates his business out of the basement of his parents' home. They do not charge him anything, but he thinks that if he paid rent it would cost him about $10,000 per year. He, therefore, included $10,000 of rent expense in the income statement.

3. To reward himself for a year of hard work, John went to Turkey. He did not use company funds to pay for the trip, but he reported it as an expense on the income statement since it was his job that made him need the vacation.

Instructions ✏️➤

(a) Comment on the proper accounting treatment of the three items above.

(b) Net income $30,000

(b) Prepare a corrected income statement for Walters Corporation.

Problems: Set C

Visit the book's companion website, at **www.wiley.com/college/kimmel**, and choose the Student Companion site to access Problem Set C.

Continuing Cookie Chronicle

This serial problem starts in Chapter 1 and continues in every chapter. You can also find this problem at the book's companion website, **www.wiley.com/college/kimmel**.

CCC1 Natalie Koebel spent much of her childhood learning the art of cookie-making from her grandmother. They spent many happy hours mastering every type of cookie imaginable and later devised new recipes that were both healthy and delicious. Now at the start of her second year in college, Natalie is investigating possibilities for starting her own business as part of the entrepreneurship program in which she is enrolled.

A long-time friend insists that Natalie has to include cookies in her business plan. After a series of brainstorming sessions, Natalie settles on the idea of operating a cookie-making school. She will start on a part-time basis and offer her services in people's homes. Now that she has started thinking about it, the possibilities seem endless. During the fall, she will concentrate on holiday cookies. She will offer group sessions (which will probably be more entertainment than education) and individual lessons. Natalie also decides to include children in her target market. The first difficult decision is coming up with the perfect name for her business. She settles on "Cookie Creations," and then moves on to more important issues.

Instructions

(a) What form of business organization—proprietorship, partnership, or corporation—do you recommend that Natalie use for her business? Discuss the benefits and weaknesses of each form that Natalie might consider.

(b) Will Natalie need accounting information? If yes, what information will she need and why? How often will she need this information?

(c) Identify specific asset, liability, revenue, and expense accounts that Cookie Creations will likely use to record its business transactions.

(d) Should Natalie open a separate bank account for the business? Why or why not?

(e) Natalie expects she will have to use her car to drive to people's homes and to pick up supplies, but she also needs to use her car for personal reasons. She recalls from her first-year accounting course something about keeping business and personal assets separate. She wonders what she should do for accounting purposes. What do you recommend?

Broadening Your Perspective

Financial Reporting and Analysis

FINANCIAL REPORTING PROBLEM: *Tootsie Roll Industries, Inc.*

BYP1-1 The 2011 financial statements of Tootsie Roll Industries, Inc. are provided in Appendix A.

Instructions

Refer to Tootsie Roll's financial statements to answer the following questions.
(a) What were Tootsie Roll's total assets at December 31, 2011? At December 31, 2010?
(b) How much cash did Tootsie Roll have on December 31, 2011?
(c) What amount of accounts payable did Tootsie Roll report on December 31, 2011? On December 31, 2010?
(d) What were Tootsie Roll's total revenues in 2011? In 2010?
(e) What is the amount of the change in Tootsie Roll's net income from 2010 to 2011?

COMPARATIVE ANALYSIS PROBLEM: *Tootsie Roll vs. Hershey*

BYP1-2 Tootsie Roll's financial statements are presented in Appendix A. The financial statements of The Hershey Company are presented in Appendix B.

Instructions

(a) Based on the information in these financial statements, determine the following for each company.
(1) Total assets at December 31, 2011.
(2) Net property, plant, and equipment at December 31, 2011.
(3) Total revenue for 2011.
(4) Net income for 2011.
(b) What conclusions concerning the two companies can you draw from these data?

RESEARCH CASE

BYP1-3 The June 22, 2011, issue of the *Wall Street Journal Online* includes an article by Michael Rapoport entitled "Auditors Urged to Tell More." It provides an interesting discussion of the possible expanding role of CPAs.

Instructions

Read the article and answer the following questions.
(a) What are some of the ideas that the Public Company Accounting Oversight Board proposed for expanding the role of auditors in "passing judgment on more of what a company does and says?"
(b) How might the financial crisis influence the public's opinion regarding the need for more information from auditors?
(c) Describe the proposed "Auditor's Discussion and Analysis."
(d) Discuss whether you think that auditors will view these proposals positively or negatively.

INTERPRETING FINANCIAL STATEMENTS

BYP1-4 Xerox was not having a particularly pleasant year. The company's stock price had already fallen in the previous year from $60 per share to $30. Just when it seemed things couldn't get worse, Xerox's stock fell to $4 per share. The data below were taken from the statement of cash flows of Xerox. (All dollars are in millions.)

Cash used in operating activities		$ (663)
Cash used in investing activities		(644)
Financing activities		
Dividends paid	$ (587)	
Net cash received from issuing debt	3,498	
Cash provided by financing activities		2,911

Instructions

Analyze the information, and then answer the following questions.
(a) If you were a creditor of Xerox, what reaction might you have to the above information?
(b) If you were an investor in Xerox, what reaction might you have to the above information?
(c) If you were evaluating the company as either a creditor or a stockholder, what other information would you be interested in seeing?
(d) Xerox decided to pay a cash dividend. This dividend was approximately equal to the amount paid in the previous year. Discuss the issues that were probably considered in making this decision.

REAL-WORLD FOCUS

BYP1-5 *Purpose:* Identify summary information about companies. This information includes basic descriptions of the company's location, activities, industry, financial health, and financial performance.

Address: **http://biz.yahoo.com/i**, or go to **www.wiley.com/college/kimmel**

Steps
  1. Type in a company name, or use the index to find company name.
  2. Choose **Quote**, then choose **Profile**, then choose **Income Statement**. Perform instructions (a) and (b) below.
  3. Choose **Industry** to identify others in this industry. Perform instructions (c)–(e) below.

Instructions

Answer the following questions.
(a) What is the company's net income? Over what period was this measured?
(b) What is the company's total sales? Over what period was this measured?
(c) What is the company's industry?
(d) What are the names of four companies in this industry?
(e) Choose one of the competitors. What is this competitor's name? What is its total sales? What is its net income?

Critical Thinking

DECISION-MAKING ACROSS THE ORGANIZATION

BYP1-6 Sue Hartley recently accepted a job in the production department at Tootsie Roll. Before she starts work, she decides to review the company's annual report to better understand its operations.

Instructions

Use the annual report provided in Appendix A to answer the following questions.
(a) What CPA firm performed the audit of Tootsie Roll's financial statements?
(b) What was the amount of Tootsie Roll's earnings per share in 2011?
(c) What are the company's net sales in foreign countries in 2011?
(d) What did management suggest as the cause of the decrease in the earnings from operations in 2011?
(e) What were net sales in 2007?
(f) How many shares of Class B common stock have been authorized?
(g) How much cash was spent on capital expenditures in 2011?
(h) Over what life does the company depreciate its buildings?
(i) What was the value of raw material and supplies inventory in 2010?

COMMUNICATION ACTIVITY

BYP1-7 Lori Milner is the bookkeeper for Philco Company, Inc. Lori has been trying to get the company's balance sheet to balance. She finally got it to balance, but she still isn't sure that it is correct.

PHILCO COMPANY, INC.
Balance Sheet
For the Month Ended December 31, 2014

Assets		Liabilities and Stockholders' Equity	
Equipment	$18,000	Common stock	$12,000
Cash	9,000	Accounts receivable	(6,000)
Supplies	1,000	Dividends	(2,000)
Accounts payable	(4,000)	Notes payable	10,000
Total assets	$24,000	Retained earnings	10,000
		Total liabilities and stockholders' equity	$24,000

Instructions

Explain to Lori Milner in a memo (a) the purpose of a balance sheet, and (b) why this balance sheet is incorrect and what she should do to correct it.

ETHICS CASE

BYP1-8   Rules governing the investment practices of individual certified public accountants prohibit them from investing in the stock of a company that their firm audits. The Securities and Exchange Commission (SEC) became concerned that some accountants were violating this rule. In response to an SEC investigation, PricewaterhouseCoopers fired 10 people and spent $25 million educating employees about the investment rules and installing an investment tracking system.

Instructions

Answer the following questions.
(a) Why do you think rules exist that restrict auditors from investing in companies that are audited by their firms?
(b) Some accountants argue that they should be allowed to invest in a company's stock as long as they themselves aren't involved in working on the company's audit or consulting. What do you think of this idea?
(c) Today, a very high percentage of publicly traded companies are audited by only four very large public accounting firms. These firms also do a high percentage of the consulting work that is done for publicly traded companies. How does this fact complicate the decision regarding whether CPAs should be allowed to invest in companies audited by their firm?
(d) Suppose you were a CPA and you had invested in IBM when IBM was not one of your firm's clients. Two years later, after IBM's stock price had fallen considerably, your firm won the IBM audit contract. You will be involved in working with the IBM audit. You know that your firm's rules require that you sell your shares immediately. If you do sell immediately, you will sustain a large loss. Do you think this is fair? What would you do?
(e) Why do you think PricewaterhouseCoopers took such extreme steps in response to the SEC investigation?

ALL ABOUT YOU

BYP1-9   Some people are tempted to make their finances look worse to get financial aid. Companies sometimes also manage their financial numbers in order to accomplish certain goals. Earnings management is the planned timing of revenues, expenses, gains, and losses to smooth out bumps in net income. In managing earnings, companies' actions vary from being within the range of ethical activity, to being both unethical and illegal attempts to mislead investors and creditors.

Instructions

Provide responses for each of the following questions.
(a) Discuss whether you think each of the following actions (adapted from **www.finaid.org/fafsa/ maximize.phtml**) to increase the chances of receiving financial aid is ethical.
   (i)   Spend down the student's assets and income first, before spending parents' assets and income.
   (ii) Accelerate necessary expenses to reduce available cash. For example, if you need a new car, buy it before applying for financial aid.
   (iii) State that a truly financially dependent child is independent.
   (iv) Have a parent take an unpaid leave of absence for long enough to get below the "threshold" level of income.

(b) What are some reasons why a **company** might want to overstate its earnings?

(c) What are some reasons why a **company** might want to understate its earnings?

(d) Under what circumstances might an otherwise ethical person decide to illegally overstate or understate earnings?

FASB CODIFICATION ACTIVITY

BYP1-10 The FASB has developed the Financial Accounting Standards Board Accounting Standards Codification (or more simply "the Codification"). The FASB's primary goal in developing the Codification is to provide in one place all the authoritative literature related to a particular topic. To provide easy access to the Codification, the FASB also developed the Financial Accounting Standards Board Codification Research System (CRS). CRS is an online, real-time database that provides easy access to the Codification. The Codification and the related CRS provide a topically organized structure, subdivided into topic, subtopics, sections, and paragraphs, using a numerical index system.

You may find this system useful in your present and future studies, and so we have provided an opportunity to use this online system as part of the *Broadening Your Perspective* section.

Instructions

Academic access to the FASB Codification is available through university subscriptions, obtained from the American Accounting Association (at **http://aaahq.org/FASB/Access.cfm**), for an annual fee of $150. This subscription covers an unlimited number of students within a single institution. Once this access has been obtained by your school, you should log in (at **http://aaahq.org/ascLogin.cfm**) and familiarize yourself with the resources that are accessible at the FASB Codification site.

CONSIDERING PEOPLE, PLANET, AND PROFIT

BYP1-11 This chapter's Feature Story discusses the fact that although Clif Bar & Company is not a public company, it does share its financial information with its employees as part of its open-book management approach. Further, although it does not publicly share its financial information, it does provide a different form of an annual report to external users. In this report, the company provides information regarding its sustainability efforts.

Address: **www.clifbar.com/uploads/default/ClifBar_AA2010.pdf**

Instructions

Access the 2010 annual report of Clif Bar & Company at the site shown above and then answer the following questions.

(a) What are the Five Aspirations?

(b) How does this annual report differ from the annual report discussed in the chapter (see pages 17 and 19)? Are there any similarities?

(c) What are the four key goals of the company's sustainability efforts related to the planet? Give one example of a recent initiative, and a measurable outcome for that initiative, that the company has taken related to each goal.

Answers to Insight and Accounting Across the Organization Questions

p. 6 The Scoop on Accounting Q: What are the benefits to the company and to the employees of making the financial statements available to all employees? **A:** If employees can read and use financial reports, a company will benefit in the following ways. The **marketing department** will make better decisions about products to offer and prices to charge. The **finance department** will make better decisions about debt and equity financing and how much to distribute in dividends. The **production department** will make better decisions about when to buy new equipment and how much inventory to produce. The **human resources department** will be better able to determine whether employees can be given raises. Finally, **all employees** will be better informed about the basis on which they are evaluated, which will increase employee morale.

p. 7 Spinning the Career Wheel Q: How might accounting help you? **A:** You will need to understand financial reports in any business with which you are associated. Whether you become a manager, a doctor, a lawyer, a social worker, a teacher, an engineer, an architect, or an entrepreneur, a working knowledge of accounting is relevant.

p. 9 The Numbers Behind Not-for-Profit Organizations Q: What benefits does a sound accounting system provide to a not-for-profit organization? **A:** Accounting provides at least two benefits to not-for-profit organizations. First, it helps to ensure that money is used in the way that donors intended. Second, it assures donors that their money is not going to waste and thus increases the likelihood of future donations.

p. 16 Beyond Financial Statements Q: Why might a company's stockholders be interested in its environmental and social performance? **A:** Many companies now recognize that being a socially responsible organization is not only the right thing to do, but it also is good for business. Many investment professionals understand, for example, that environmental, social, and proper corporate governance of companies affects the performance of their investment portfolios. For example, British Petroleum's oil spill disaster is a classic example of the problems that can occur for a company and its stockholders. BP's stock price was slashed, its dividend reduced, its executives replaced, and its reputation badly damaged. It is interesting that socially responsible investment funds are now gaining momentum in the marketplace such that companies now recognize this segment as an important investment group.

Answers to Self-Test Questions

1. b **2.** c **3.** d **4.** d **5.** c **6.** a **7.** d **8.** d **9.** a **10.** b **11.** c **12.** d **13.** d **14.** a **15.** b

A Look at IFRS

Many people feel that there is a need for one set of international accounting standards. Here is why:

LEARNING OBJECTIVE 7

Describe the impact of international accounting standards on U.S. financial reporting.

Multinational corporations. Today's companies view the entire world as their market. For example, Coca-Cola, Intel, and McDonald's generate more than 50% of their sales outside the United States, and many foreign companies, such as Toyota, Nestlé, and Sony, find their largest market to be the United States.

Mergers and acquisitions. The mergers between Fiat/Chrysler and Vodafone/Mannesmann suggest that we will see even more such business combinations in the future.

Information technology. As communication barriers continue to topple through advances in technology, companies and individuals in different countries and markets are becoming more comfortable buying and selling goods and services from one another.

Financial markets. Financial markets are of international significance today. Whether it is currency, equity securities (stocks), bonds, or derivatives, there are active markets throughout the world trading these types of instruments.

KEY POINTS

- International standards are referred to as **International Financial Reporting Standards (IFRS)**, developed by the International Accounting Standards Board (IASB). Over 115 countries require or permit use of IFRS.

- Recent events in the global capital markets underscore the importance of financial disclosure and transparency not only in the United States but in markets around the world. As a result, many are examining which accounting and financial disclosure rules should be followed.

- U.S standards, referred to as generally accepted accounting principles (GAAP), are developed by the Financial Accounting Standards Board (FASB). The fact that there are differences between what is in this textbook (which is based on U.S. standards) and IFRS should not be surprising because the FASB and IASB have responded to different user needs. In some countries, the primary users of financial statements are private investors. In others, the primary users are tax authorities or central government planners. It appears that the United States and the international standard-setting environment are primarily driven by meeting the needs of investors and creditors.

- The internal control standards applicable to Sarbanes-Oxley (SOX) apply only to large public companies listed on U.S. exchanges. There is a continuing debate as to whether non-U.S. companies should have to comply with this extra layer of regulation. Debate about international companies (non-U.S.) adopting SOX-type standards centers on whether the benefits exceed the costs. The concern is that the higher costs of SOX compliance are making the U.S. securities markets less competitive.

- The textbook mentions a number of ethics violations, such as Enron, WorldCom, and AIG. These problems have also occurred internationally, for example, at Satyam Computer Services (India), Parmalat (Italy), and Royal Ahold (the Netherlands).

- IFRS tends to be simpler in its accounting and disclosure requirements; some people say it is more "principles-based." GAAP is more detailed; some people say it is more "rules-based." This difference in approach has resulted in a debate about the merits of "principles-based" versus "rules-based" standards.

- U.S. regulators have recently eliminated the need for foreign companies that trade shares in U.S. markets to reconcile their accounting with GAAP.

- The three most common forms of business organization, proprietorships, partnerships, and corporations, are also found in countries that use IFRS. Because the choice of business organization is influenced by factors such as legal environment, tax rates and regulations, and degree of entrepreneurism, the relative use of each form will vary across countries.

- The conceptual framework that underlies IFRS is very similar to that used to develop GAAP. The basic definitions provided in this textbook for the key elements of financial statements, that is, assets, liabilities, equity, revenues, and expenses, are simplified versions of the official definitions provided by the FASB. The more substantive definitions, using the IASB definitional structure, are as follows.

  Assets. A resource controlled by the entity as a result of past events and from which future economic benefits are expected to flow to the entity.

  Liabilities. A present obligation of the entity arising from past events, the settlement of which is expected to result in an outflow from the entity of resources embodying economic benefits. Liabilities may be legally enforceable via a contract or law, but need not be; i.e., they can arise due to normal business practice or customs.

  Equity. A residual interest in the assets of the entity after deducting all its liabilities.

  Income. Increases in economic benefits that result in increases in equity (other than those related to contributions from shareholders). Income includes both revenues (resulting from ordinary activities) and gains.

  Expenses. Decreases in economic benefits that result in decreases in equity (other than those related to distributions to shareholders). Expenses includes losses that are not the result of ordinary activities.

LOOKING TO THE FUTURE

Both the IASB and the FASB are hard at work developing standards that will lead to the elimination of major differences in the way certain transactions are accounted for and reported. In fact, at one time the IASB stated that no new major standards would be issued for a period of time. The reason for this policy was to provide companies the time to translate and implement IFRS into practice, as much had happened in a very short period of time. Consider, for example, that as a result of a joint project on the conceptual framework, the definitions of the most fundamental elements (assets, liabilities, equity, revenues, and expenses) may actually change. However, whether the IASB adopts internal control provisions similar to those in SOX remains to be seen.

IFRS PRACTICE

IFRS SELF-TEST QUESTIONS

1. Which of the following is **not** a reason why a single set of high-quality international accounting standards would be beneficial?
   (a) Mergers and acquisition activity.
   (b) Financial markets.
   (c) Multinational corporations.
   (d) GAAP is widely considered to be a superior reporting system.

2. The Sarbanes-Oxley Act determines:
  (a) international tax regulations.
  (b) internal control standards as enforced by the IASB.
  (c) internal control standards of U.S. publicly traded companies.
  (d) U.S. tax regulations.

3. IFRS is considered to be more:
  (a) principles-based and less rules-based than GAAP.
  (b) rules-based and less principles-based than GAAP.
  (c) detailed than GAAP.
  (d) None of the above.

4. Which of the following statements is **false**?
  (a) IFRS is based on a conceptual framework that is similar to that used to develop GAAP.
  (b) Assets are defined by the IASB as resources controlled by the entity as a result of past events and from which future economic benefits are expected to flow to the entity.
  (c) Non-U.S. companies that trade shares in U.S. markets must reconcile their accounting with GAAP.
  (d) Proprietorships, partnerships, and corporations are also found in countries that use IFRS.

5. Which of the following statements is **true**?
  (a) Under IFRS, the term *income* refers to what would be called revenues and gains under GAAP.
  (b) The term *income* is not used under IFRS.
  (c) The term *income* refers only to gains on investments.
  (d) Under IFRS, expenses include distributions to owners.

IFRS CONCEPTS AND APPLICATION

IFRS1-1 Who are the two key international players in the development of international accounting standards? Explain their role.

IFRS1-2 What might explain the fact that different accounting standard-setters have developed accounting standards that are sometimes quite different in nature?

IFRS1-3 What is the benefit of a single set of high-quality accounting standards?

IFRS1-4 Discuss the potential advantages and disadvantages that countries outside the United States should consider before adopting regulations, such as those in the Sarbanes-Oxley Act, that increase corporate internal control requirements.

INTERNATIONAL FINANCIAL REPORTING PROBLEM: *Zetar plc*

IFRS1-5 The financial statements of Zetar plc are presented in Appendix C. The company's complete annual report, including the notes to its financial statements, is available in the Investors section at **www.zetarplc.com**.

Instructions
Visit Zetar's corporate website and answer the following questions from Zetar's 2011 annual report.
  (a) What accounting firm performed the audit of Zetar's financial statements?
  (b) Over what life does the company depreciate its buildings?
  (c) What is the address of the company's corporate headquarters?
  (d) What is the company's reporting currency?
  (e) What two segments does the company operate in, and what were the sales for each segment in the year ended April 30, 2011?

Answers to IFRS Self-Test Questions

1. d **2.** c **3.** a **4.** c **5.** a

Remember to go back to The Navigator box on the chapter opening page and check off your completed work.

© mattjeacock/iStockphoto

✔ The Navigator

- Scan Learning Objectives
- Read Feature Story
- Scan Preview
- Read Text and Answer **Do it!**
  ○ p. 52 ○ p. 53 ○ p. 62 ○ p. 66
- Work Using the Decision Toolkit
- Review Summary of Learning Objectives
- Work Comprehensive **Do it!** p. 71
- Answer Self-Test Questions
- Complete Assignments
- Go to WileyPLUS for practice and tutorials

💭 Read A Look at IFRS p. 95

A FURTHER LOOK AT FINANCIAL STATEMENTS

LEARNING OBJECTIVES

After studying this chapter, you should be able to:

1 Identify the sections of a classified balance sheet.

2 Identify tools for analyzing financial statements and ratios for computing a company's profitability.

3 Explain the relationship between a retained earnings statement and a statement of stockholders' equity.

4 Identify and compute ratios for analyzing a company's liquidity and solvency using a balance sheet.

5 Use the statement of cash flows to evaluate solvency.

6 Explain the meaning of generally accepted accounting principles.

7 Discuss financial reporting concepts.

✔ The Navigator

Few people could have predicted how dramatically the Internet would change the investment world. One of the most interesting results is how it has changed the way ordinary people invest their savings. More and more people are striking out on their own, making their own investment decisions.

Two early pioneers in providing investment information to the masses were Tom and David Gardner, brothers who created an online investor website called The Motley Fool. The name comes from Shakespeare's *As You Like It*. The fool in Shakespeare's plays was the only one who could speak unpleasant truths to kings and queens without being killed. Tom and David view themselves as 21st-century "fools," revealing the "truths" of Wall Street to the small investor, who they feel has been taken advantage of by Wall Street insiders. The Motley Fool's online bulletin board enables investors to exchange information and insights about companies.

Critics of these bulletin boards contend that they are simply high-tech rumor mills that cause investors to bid up stock prices to unreasonable levels. For example, the stock of PairGain Technologies jumped 32 percent in a single day as a result of a bogus takeover rumor on an investment bulletin board. Some observers are concerned that small investors—ironically, the very people the

JUST FOOLING AROUND?

Gardner brothers are trying to help—will be hurt the most by misinformation and intentional scams.

To show how these bulletin boards work, suppose that in a recent year you had $10,000 to invest. You were considering Best Buy Company, the largest seller of electronics equipment in the United States. You scanned the Internet investment bulletin boards and found messages posted by two different investors. Here are excerpts from actual postings during the same year:

TMPVenus: "Where are the prospects for positive movement for this company? Poor margins, poor management, astronomical P/E!"

broachman: "I believe that this is a LONG TERM winner, and presently at a good price."

One says sell, and one says buy. Whom should you believe? If you had taken "broachman's" advice and purchased the stock, the $10,000 you invested would have been worth over $300,000 five years later. Best Buy was one of America's best-performing stocks during that period of time.

Rather than getting swept away by rumors, investors must sort out the good information from the bad. One thing is certain—as information services such as The Motley Fool increase in number, gathering information will become even easier. Evaluating it will be the harder task.

✔ The Navigator

INSIDE CHAPTER 2 . . .

If you are thinking of purchasing Best Buy stock, or any stock, how can you decide what the stock is worth? If you manage J. Crew's credit department, how should you determine whether to extend credit to a new customer? If you are a financial executive of IBM, how do you decide whether your company is generating adequate cash to expand operations without borrowing? Your decision in each of these situations will be influenced by a variety of considerations. One of them should be your careful analysis of a company's financial statements. The reason: Financial statements offer relevant and reliable information, which will help you in your decision-making.

In this chapter, we take a closer look at the balance sheet and introduce some useful ways for evaluating the information provided by the financial statements. We also examine the financial reporting concepts underlying the financial statements. We begin by introducing the classified balance sheet.

A Further Look at Financial Statements

The Classified Balance Sheet	Using the Financial Statements	Financial Reporting Concepts
• Current assets • Long-term investments • Property, plant, and equipment • Intangible assets • Current liabilities • Long-term liabilities • Stockholders' equity	• Ratio analysis • Using the income statement • Using the statement of stockholders' equity • Using a classified balance sheet • Using the statement of cash flows	• The standard-setting environment • Qualities of useful information • Assumptions • Principles • Cost constraint

✔ The Navigator

The Classified Balance Sheet

LEARNING OBJECTIVE 1

Identify the sections of a classified balance sheet.

In Chapter 1, you learned that a balance sheet presents a snapshot of a company's financial position at a point in time. It lists individual asset, liability, and stockholders' equity items. However, to improve users' understanding of a company's financial position, companies often use a **classified** balance sheet instead. A classified balance sheet groups together similar assets and similar liabilities, using a number of standard classifications and sections. This is useful because items within a group have similar economic characteristics. A classified balance sheet generally contains the standard classifications listed in Illustration 2-1.

Illustration 2-1 Standard balance sheet classifications

Assets	Liabilities and Stockholders' Equity
Current assets	Current liabilities
Long-term investments	Long-term liabilities
Property, plant, and equipment	Stockholders' equity
Intangible assets	

These groupings help financial statement readers determine such things as (1) whether the company has enough assets to pay its debts as they come due, and (2) the claims of short- and long-term creditors on the company's total assets. Many of these groupings can be seen in the balance sheet of Franklin Corporation shown in Illustration 2-2. In the sections that follow, we explain each of these groupings.

CURRENT ASSETS

Current assets are assets that a company expects to convert to cash or use up within one year or its operating cycle, whichever is longer. In Illustration 2-2, Franklin Corporation had current assets of $22,100. For most businesses, the cutoff for classification as current assets is one year from the balance sheet date. For example, accounts receivable are current assets because the company will

Illustration 2-2 Classified balance sheet

FRANKLIN CORPORATION
Balance Sheet
October 31, 2014

Assets

Current assets			
Cash		$ 6,600	
Debt investments		2,000	
Accounts receivable		7,000	
Notes receivable		1,000	
Inventory		3,000	
Supplies		2,100	
Prepaid insurance		400	
Total current assets			$22,100
Long-term investments			
Stock investments		5,200	
Investment in real estate		2,000	7,200
Property, plant, and equipment			
Land		10,000	
Equipment	$24,000		
Less: Accumulated depreciation—equipment	5,000	19,000	29,000
Intangible assets			
Patents			3,100
Total assets			$61,400

Liabilities and Stockholders' Equity

Current liabilities			
Notes payable		$11,000	
Accounts payable		2,100	
Unearned sales revenue		900	
Salaries and wages payable		1,600	
Interest payable		450	
Total current liabilities			$16,050
Long-term liabilities			
Mortgage payable		10,000	
Notes payable		1,300	
Total long-term liabilities			11,300
Total liabilities			27,350
Stockholders' equity			
Common stock		14,000	
Retained earnings		20,050	
Total stockholders' equity			34,050
Total liabilities and stockholders' equity			$61,400

Helpful Hint Recall that the accounting equation is Assets = Liabilities + Stockholders' Equity.

collect them and convert them to cash within one year. Supplies is a current asset because the company expects to use the supplies in operations within one year.

Some companies use a period longer than one year to classify assets and liabilities as current because they have an operating cycle longer than one year. The **operating cycle** of a company is the average time required to go from cash to cash in producing revenue—to purchase inventory, sell it on account, and then collect cash from customers. For most businesses, this cycle takes less than a year, so they use a one-year cutoff. But for some businesses, such as vineyards or airplane manufacturers, this period may be longer than a year. **Except where noted, we will assume that companies use one year to determine whether an asset or liability is current or long-term.**

Common types of current assets are (1) cash, (2) investments (such as short-term U.S. government securities), (3) receivables (accounts receivable, notes receivable, and interest receivable), (4) inventories, and (5) prepaid expenses (insurance and supplies). **Companies list current assets in the order in which they expect to convert them into cash.** *Follow this rule when doing your homework.*

Illustration 2-3 presents the current assets of Southwest Airlines Co. in a recent year.

Illustration 2-3 Current assets section

Real World	**SOUTHWEST AIRLINES CO.** Balance Sheet (partial) (in millions)	
Current assets		
Cash and cash equivalents		$1,390
Short-term investments		369
Accounts receivable		241
Inventories		181
Prepaid expenses and other current assets		420
Total current assets		$2,601

As explained later in the chapter, a company's current assets are important in assessing its short-term debt-paying ability.

LONG-TERM INVESTMENTS

Alternative Terminology
Long-term investments are often referred to simply as *investments.*

Long-term investments are generally: (1) investments in stocks and bonds of other corporations that are held for more than one year, (2) long-term assets such as land or buildings that a company is not currently using in its operating activities, and (3) long-term notes receivable. In Illustration 2-2, Franklin Corporation reported total long-term investments of $7,200 on its balance sheet.

Yahoo! Inc. reported long-term investments on its balance sheet in a recent year as shown in Illustration 2-4.

Illustration 2-4 Long-term investments section

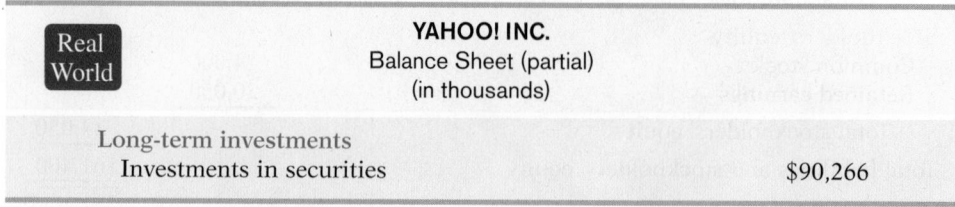

Real World	**YAHOO! INC.** Balance Sheet (partial) (in thousands)	
Long-term investments		
Investments in securities		$90,266

PROPERTY, PLANT, AND EQUIPMENT

Property, plant, and equipment are assets with relatively long useful lives that are currently used in operating the business. This category includes land, buildings, equipment, delivery vehicles, and furniture. In Illustration 2-2, Franklin Corporation reported property, plant, and equipment of $29,000.

Depreciation is the allocation of the cost of an asset to a number of years. Companies do this by systematically assigning a portion of an asset's cost as an expense each year (rather than expensing the full purchase price in the year of purchase). The assets that the company depreciates are reported on the balance sheet at cost less accumulated depreciation. The **accumulated depreciation** account shows the total amount of depreciation that the company has expensed thus far in the asset's life. In Illustration 2-2, Franklin Corporation reported accumulated depreciation of $5,000.

Illustration 2-5 presents the property, plant, and equipment of Cooper Tire & Rubber Company in a recent year.

Alternative Terminology Property, plant, and equipment is sometimes called *fixed assets* or *plant assets*.

International Note In 2007, China adopted International Financial Reporting Standards (IFRS). This was done in an effort to reduce fraud and increase investor confidence in financial reports. Under these standards, many items, such as property, plant, and equipment, may be reported at current fair values rather than historical cost.

Illustration 2-5 Property, plant, and equipment section

COOPER TIRE & RUBBER COMPANY Balance Sheet (partial) (in thousands)		
Property, plant, and equipment		
Land and land improvements	$ 41,553	
Buildings	298,706	
Machinery and equipment	1,636,091	
Molds, cores, and rings	268,158	$2,244,508
Less: Accumulated depreciation		1,252,692
		$ 991,816

INTANGIBLE ASSETS

Many companies have assets that do not have physical substance and yet often are very valuable. We call these assets **intangible assets**. One common intangible is goodwill. Others include patents, copyrights, and trademarks or trade names that give the company **exclusive right** of use for a specified period of time. Franklin Corporation reported intangible assets of $3,100.

Illustration 2-6 shows the intangible assets of media giant Time Warner, Inc. in a recent year.

Helpful Hint Sometimes intangible assets are reported under a broader heading called "*Other assets.*"

Illustration 2-6 Intangible assets section

TIME WARNER, INC. Balance Sheet (partial) (in millions)	
Intangible assets	
Goodwill	$40,953
Film library	2,690
Customer lists	2,540
Cable television franchises	38,048
Sports franchises	262
Brands, trademarks, and other intangible assets	8,313
	$92,806

ASSETS SECTION OF CLASSIFIED BALANCE SHEET

Do it! Baxter Hoffman recently received the following information related to Hoffman Corporation's December 31, 2014, balance sheet.

Prepaid insurance	$ 2,300	Inventory	$3,400
Cash	800	Accumulated depreciation—	
Equipment	10,700	equipment	2,700
		Accounts receivable	1,100

Prepare the assets section of Hoffman Corporation's classified balance sheet.

Solution

Action Plan

- Present current assets first. Current assets are cash and other resources that the company expects to convert to cash or use up within one year.
- Present current assets in the order in which the company expects to convert them into cash.
- Subtract accumulated depreciation–equipment from equipment to determine net equipment.

HOFFMAN CORPORATION
Balance Sheet (partial)
December 31, 2014

Assets

Current assets		
Cash	$ 800	
Accounts receivable	1,100	
Inventory	3,400	
Prepaid insurance	2,300	
Total current assets		$ 7,600
Property, plant, and equipment		
Equipment	10,700	
Less: Accumulated depreciation—equipment	2,700	8,000
Total assets		$15,600

✔ The Navigator

Related exercise material: **BE2-2, Do it! 2-1**, and **E2-4**.

CURRENT LIABILITIES

In the liabilities and stockholders' equity section of the balance sheet, the first grouping is current liabilities. **Current liabilities** are obligations that the company is to pay within the next year or operating cycle, whichever is longer. Common examples are accounts payable, salaries and wages payable, notes payable, interest payable, and income taxes payable. Also included as current liabilities are current maturities of long-term obligations—payments to be made within the next year on long-term obligations. In Illustration 2-2, Franklin Corporation reported five different types of current liabilities, for a total of $16,050.

Illustration 2-7 shows the current liabilities section adapted from the balance sheet of Marcus Corporation in a recent year.

Illustration 2-7 Current liabilities section

Real World

MARCUS CORPORATION
Balance Sheet (partial)
(in thousands)

Current liabilities	
Notes payable	$ 239
Accounts payable	24,242
Current maturities of long-term debt	57,250
Other current liabilities	27,477
Income taxes payable	11,215
Salary and wages payable	6,720
Total current liabilities	$127,143

LONG-TERM LIABILITIES

Long-term liabilities (long-term debt) are obligations that a company expects to pay **after** one year. Liabilities in this category include bonds payable, mortgages payable, long-term notes payable, lease liabilities, and pension liabilities. Many companies report long-term debt maturing after one year as a single amount in the balance sheet and show the details of the debt in notes that accompany the financial statements. Others list the various types of long-term liabilities. In Illustration 2-2, Franklin Corporation reported long-term liabilities of $11,300.

Illustration 2-8 shows the long-term liabilities that The Procter & Gamble Company reported in its balance sheet in a recent year.

Illustration 2-8 Long-term liabilities section

Real World	THE PROCTER & GAMBLE COMPANY Balance Sheet (partial) (in millions)	
	Long-term liabilities	
	Long-term debt	$23,375
	Deferred income taxes	12,015
	Other noncurrent liabilities	5,147
	Total long-term liabilities	$40,537

STOCKHOLDERS' EQUITY

Stockholders' equity consists of two parts: common stock and retained earnings. Companies record as **common stock** the investments of assets into the business by the stockholders. They record as **retained earnings** the income retained for use in the business. These two parts, combined, make up **stockholders' equity** on the balance sheet. In Illustration 2-2 (page 49), Franklin reported common stock of $14,000 and retained earnings of $20,050.

Alternative Terminology
Common stock is sometimes called *capital stock*.

Do it!

BALANCE SHEET CLASSIFICATIONS

The following financial statement items were taken from the financial statements of Callahan Corp.

_____ Salaries and wages payable
_____ Service revenue
_____ Interest payable
_____ Goodwill
_____ Debt investments (short-term)
_____ Mortgage payable (due in 3 years)
_____ Investment in real estate

_____ Equipment
_____ Accumulated depreciation— equipment
_____ Depreciation expense
_____ Retained earnings
_____ Unearned service revenue

Match each of the items to its proper balance sheet classification, shown below. If the item would not appear on a balance sheet, use "NA."

Current assets (CA)
Long-term investments (LTI)
Property, plant, and equipment (PPE)
Intangible assets (IA)

Current liabilities (CL)
Long-term liabilities (LTL)
Stockholders' equity (SE)

Action Plan

• Analyze whether each financial statement item is an asset, liability, or stockholders' equity item.

• Determine if asset and liability items are current or long-term.

Solution

CL	Salaries and wages payable		LTI	Investment in real estate
NA	Service revenue		PPE	Equipment
CL	Interest payable		PPE	Accumulated depreciation— equipment
IA	Goodwill		NA	Depreciation expense
CA	Debt investments (short-term)		SE	Retained earnings
LTL	Mortgage payable (due in 3 years)		CL	Unearned service revenue

✔ The Navigator

Related exercise material: **BE2-1,** *Do it!* **2-2, E2-1, E2-2, E2-3, E2-5** and **E2-6.**

Using the Financial Statements

LEARNING OBJECTIVE 2

Identify tools for analyzing financial statements and ratios for computing a company's profitability.

In Chapter 1, we introduced the four financial statements. We discussed how these statements provide information about a company's performance and financial position. In this chapter, we extend this discussion by showing you specific tools that you can use to analyze financial statements in order to make a more meaningful evaluation of a company.

RATIO ANALYSIS

Ratio analysis expresses the relationship among selected items of financial statement data. A **ratio** expresses the mathematical relationship between one quantity and another. For analysis of the primary financial statements, we classify ratios as follows.

Illustration 2-9 Financial ratio classifications

Profitability Ratios

Measure the income or operating success of a company for a given period of time

Liquidity Ratios

Measure short-term ability of the company to pay its maturing obligations and to meet unexpected needs for cash

Solvency Ratios

Measure the ability of the company to survive over a long period of time

A single ratio by itself is not very meaningful. Accordingly, in this and the following chapters, we will use various comparisons to shed light on company performance:

1. **Intracompany comparisons** covering two years for the same company.
2. **Industry-average comparisons** based on average ratios for particular industries.
3. **Intercompany comparisons** based on comparisons with a competitor in the same industry.

Next, we'll use some ratios and comparisons to analyze the financial statements of Best Buy Company.

USING THE INCOME STATEMENT

Best Buy Company generates profits for its stockholders by selling electronics. The income statement reports how successful it is at generating a profit from its sales. The income statement reports the amount earned during the period (revenues) and the costs incurred during the period (expenses). Illustration 2-10 shows a simplified income statement for Best Buy.

From this income statement, we can see that Best Buy's sales increased but net income decreased during the period. Net income decreased from $1,317 million to $1,277 million. A much smaller competitor of Best Buy is hhgregg.

Illustration 2-10 Best Buy's income statement

Real World

BEST BUY CO., INC.
Income Statements
For the Years Ended February 26, 2011,
and February 27, 2010 (in millions)

	2011	2010
Revenues		
Net sales and other revenue	$50,325	$49,749
Expenses		
Cost of goods sold	37,635	37,534
Selling, general, and administrative expenses and other	10,699	10,096
Income tax expense	714	802
Total expenses	49,048	48,432
Net income	$ 1,277	$ 1,317

hhgregg operates 173 stores in 15 states and is headquartered in Indianapolis, Indiana. It reported net income of $48.2 million for the year ended March 31, 2011.

To evaluate the profitability of Best Buy, we will use ratio analysis. **Profitability ratios**, such as earnings per share, measure the operating success of a company for a given period of time.

Earnings per Share

Earnings per share (EPS) measures the net income earned on each share of common stock. We compute EPS by dividing net income minus preferred dividends by the average number of common shares outstanding during the year. Stockholders usually think in terms of the number of shares they own or plan to buy or sell, so stating net income earned as a per share amount provides a useful perspective for determining the investment return. Advanced accounting courses present more refined techniques for calculating earnings per share.

For now, a basic approach for calculating earnings per share is to divide earnings available to common stockholders by average common shares outstanding during the year. What is "earnings available to common stockholders"? It is an earnings amount calculated as net income less dividends paid on another type of stock, called preferred stock (Net income − Preferred dividends).

By comparing earnings per share of **a single company over time**, we can evaluate its relative earnings performance from the perspective of a stockholder—that is, on a per share basis. It is very important to note that comparisons of earnings per share across companies are **not meaningful** because of the wide variations in the numbers of shares of outstanding stock among companies.

Illustration 2-11 (page 56) shows the earnings per share calculation for Best Buy in 2011 and 2010, based on the information presented below. (Note that to simplify our calculations, we assumed that any change in the number of shares for Best Buy occurred in the middle of the year.)

(in millions)	**2011**	**2010**
Net income	$1,277	$1,317
Preferred dividends	–0–	–0–
Shares outstanding at beginning of year	419	414
Shares outstanding at end of year	393	419

Illustration 2-11 Best Buy's earnings per share

	Earnings per Share	=	Net Income − Preferred Dividends
			Average Common Shares Outstanding

($ and shares in millions)	2011	2010
Earnings per share	$\dfrac{\$1{,}277 - \$0}{(393 + 419)/2} = \$3.14$	$\dfrac{\$1{,}317 - \$0}{(419 + 414)/2} = \$3.16$

🧰 DECISION TOOLKIT

DECISION CHECKPOINTS	INFO NEEDED FOR DECISION	TOOL TO USE FOR DECISION	HOW TO EVALUATE RESULTS
How does the company's earnings performance compare with that of previous years?	Net income available to common stockholders and average common shares outstanding	Earnings per share $=$ $\dfrac{\text{Net income} - \text{Preferred dividends}}{\text{Average common shares outstanding}}$	A higher measure suggests improved performance, although the number is subject to manipulation. Values should not be compared across companies.

USING THE STATEMENT OF STOCKHOLDERS' EQUITY

LEARNING OBJECTIVE 3

Explain the relationship between a retained earnings statement and a statement of stockholders' equity.

As discussed in Chapter 1, the retained earnings statement describes the changes in retained earnings during the year. This statement adds net income to beginning retained earnings and then subtracts dividends to arrive at ending retained earnings.

Stockholders' equity is comprised of two parts: retained earnings and common stock. Therefore, the stockholders' equity of most companies is affected by factors other than just changes in retained earnings. For example, the company may issue or retire shares of common stock. Most companies, therefore, use what is called a **statement of stockholders' equity** rather than a retained earnings statement. This statement presents the causes of changes to stockholders' equity during the period, including those that caused retained earnings to change. Illustration 2-12 is a simplified statement of stockholders' equity for Best Buy.

Illustration 2-12 Best Buy's statement of stockholders' equity

Real World

BEST BUY CO., INC.
Statement of Stockholders' Equity
(in millions)

	Common Stock	Retained Earnings
Balances at February 28, 2009	$ 246	$4,397
Issuance of common stock	237	
Net income		1,317
Dividends		(234)
Other adjustments		1,001
Balances at February 27, 2010	483	6,481
Issuance of common stock	303	
Repurchase of common stock	(729)	
Net income		1,277
Dividends		(238)
Other adjustments		(285)
Balances at February 26, 2011	$ 57	$7,235

We can observe from this financial statement that Best Buy's common stock increased in the first year as the result of an issuance of shares. However, Best Buy's common stock decreased during the second year. Even though it had an issuance of common stock, that increase was much smaller than the decrease caused by a stock repurchase. Another observation from this financial statement is that Best Buy paid dividends each year. This is a relatively recent practice for Best Buy. For many years, it did not pay dividends, even though it was profitable and could do so. You might wonder why Best Buy paid no dividends during years when it was profitable. In fact, in a prior year, two Best Buy stockholders discussed this question about the company's dividend policy on an investor bulletin board. Here are excerpts:

Katwoman: "Best Buy has a nice price increase. Earnings are on the way up. But why no dividends?"

AngryCandy: "I guess they feel they can make better use of the money by investing back in the business. They still view Best Buy as a rapidly growing company and would prefer to invest in expanding the infrastructure (building new stores, advertising, etc.) than in paying out dividends. . . . If Best Buy gets to the stage of 'stable, big company' with little room for expansion, then I'm sure you'll see them elect to pay out a dividend."

AngryCandy's response is an excellent explanation of the thought process that management goes through in deciding whether to pay a dividend. Management must evaluate what its cash needs are. If it has uses for cash that will increase the value of the company (for example, building a new warehouse), then it should retain cash in the company. However, if it has more cash than it has valuable opportunities, it should distribute its excess cash as a dividend.

USING A CLASSIFIED BALANCE SHEET

You can learn a lot about a company's financial health by also evaluating the relationship between its various assets and liabilities. Illustration 2-13 provides a simplified balance sheet for Best Buy.

LEARNING OBJECTIVE 4

Identify and compute ratios for analyzing a company's liquidity and solvency using a balance sheet.

Illustration 2-13 Best Buy's balance sheet

BEST BUY CO., INC.
Balance Sheets
(in millions)

Assets	February 26, 2011	February 27, 2010
Current assets		
Cash and cash equivalents	$ 1,103	$ 1,826
Short-term investments	22	90
Receivables	2,348	2,020
Merchandise inventories	5,897	5,486
Other current assets	1,103	1,144
Total current assets	10,473	10,566
Property and equipment	7,905	7,453
Less: Accumulated depreciation	4,082	3,383
Net property and equipment	3,823	4,070
Other assets	3,553	3,666
Total assets	$17,849	$18,302

(continued)

Illustration 2-13 (continued)

Liabilities and Stockholders' Equity

Current liabilities		
Accounts payable	$ 4,894	$ 5,276
Accrued liabilities	1,471	1,681
Accrued income taxes	256	316
Accrued compensation payable	570	544
Other current liabilities	1,472	1,161
Total current liabilities	8,663	8,978
Long-term liabilities		
Long-term debt	711	1,104
Other long-term liabilities	1,183	1,256
Total long-term liabilities	1,894	2,360
Total liabilities	10,557	11,338
Stockholders' equity		
Common stock	57	483
Retained earnings	7,235	6,481
Total stockholders' equity	7,292	6,964
Total liabilities and stockholders' equity	$17,849	$18,302

Liquidity

Suppose you are a banker at CitiGroup considering lending money to Best Buy, or you are a sales manager at Hewlett-Packard interested in selling computers to Best Buy on credit. You would be concerned about Best Buy's liquidity—its ability to pay obligations expected to become due within the next year or operating cycle. You would look closely at the relationship of its current assets to current liabilities.

WORKING CAPITAL. One measure of liquidity is working capital, which is the difference between the amounts of current assets and current liabilities:

Illustration 2-14 Working capital

> **Working Capital = Current Assets − Current Liabilities**

When current assets exceed current liabilities, working capital is positive. When this occurs, there is greater likelihood that the company will pay its liabilities. When working capital is negative, a company might not be able to pay short-term creditors, and the company might ultimately be forced into bankruptcy. Best Buy had working capital in 2011 of $1,810 million ($10,473 million − $8,663 million).

CURRENT RATIO. Liquidity ratios measure the short-term ability of the company to pay its maturing obligations and to meet unexpected needs for cash. One liquidity ratio is the current ratio, computed as current assets divided by current liabilities.

The current ratio is a more dependable indicator of liquidity than working capital. Two companies with the same amount of working capital may have significantly different current ratios. Illustration 2-15 shows the 2011 and 2010 current ratios for Best Buy and for hhgregg, along with the 2011 industry average.

What does the ratio actually mean? Best Buy's 2011 current ratio of 1.21:1 means that for every dollar of current liabilities, Best Buy has $1.21 of current assets. Best Buy's current ratio increased in 2011. When compared to the industry average of 1.5:1, Best Buy's liquidity seems low. It is also less than hhgregg's.

Illustration 2-15 Current ratio

Current Ratio =	Current Assets / Current Liabilities		
Best Buy ($ in millions)		hhgregg	Industry Average
2011	2010	2011	2011
$\dfrac{\$10,473}{\$8,663} = 1.21{:}1$	1.18:1	2.00:1	1.50:1

One potential weakness of the current ratio is that it does not take into account the **composition** of the current assets. For example, a satisfactory current ratio does not disclose whether a portion of the current assets is tied up in slow-moving inventory. The composition of the current assets matters because a dollar of cash is more readily available to pay the bills than is a dollar of inventory. For example, suppose a company's cash balance declined while its merchandise inventory increased substantially. If inventory increased because the company is having difficulty selling its products, then the current ratio might not fully reflect the reduction in the company's liquidity.

Ethics Note A company that has more current assets than current liabilities can increase the ratio of current assets to current liabilities by using cash to pay off some current liabilities. This gives the appearance of being more liquid. Do you think this move is ethical?

Accounting Across the Organization

Can a Company Be Too Liquid?

There actually is a point where a company can be too liquid—that is, it can have too much working capital. While it is important to be liquid enough to be able to pay short-term bills as they come due, a company does not want to tie up its cash in extra inventory or receivables that are not earning the company money.

By one estimate from the REL Consultancy Group, the thousand largest U.S. companies had cumulative excess working capital of $1.017 trillion in a recent year. This was an 18% increase, which REL said represented a "deterioration in the management of operations." Given that managers throughout a company are interested in improving profitability, it is clear that they should have an eye toward managing working capital. They need to aim for a "Goldilocks solution"—not too much, not too little, but just right.

Source: Maxwell Murphy, "The Big Number," *Wall Street Journal* (November 9, 2011).

? What can various company managers do to ensure that working capital is managed efficiently to maximize net income? (See page 95.)

Jorge Salcedo/iStockphoto

Solvency

Now suppose that instead of being a short-term creditor, you are interested in either buying Best Buy's stock or extending the company a long-term loan. Long-term creditors and stockholders are interested in a company's solvency—its ability to pay interest as it comes due and to repay the balance of a debt due at its maturity. Solvency ratios measure the ability of the company to survive over a long period of time.

DEBT TO ASSETS RATIO. The debt to assets ratio is one measure of solvency. It is calculated by dividing total liabilities (both current and long-term) by total assets. It measures the percentage of total financing provided by creditors rather than stockholders. Debt financing is more risky than equity financing because debt must be repaid at specific points in time, whether the company is performing well or not. Thus, the higher the percentage of debt financing, the riskier the company.

The higher the percentage of total liabilities (debt) to total assets, the greater the risk that the company may be unable to pay its debts as they come due. Illustration 2-16 shows the debt to assets ratios for Best Buy and hhgregg, along with the 2011 industry average.

Illustration 2-16 Debt to assets ratio

Debt to Assets Ratio = $\dfrac{\text{Total Liabilities}}{\text{Total Assets}}$			
Best Buy ($ in millions)		**hhgregg**	**Industry Average**
2011	2010	2011	2011
$\dfrac{\$10,557}{\$17,849} = 59\%$	62%	42%	57%

The 2011 ratio of 59% means that every dollar of assets was financed by 59 cents of debt. Best Buy's ratio exceeds the industry average of 57% and is significantly higher than hhgregg's ratio of 42%. The higher the ratio, the more reliant the company is on debt financing. This means the company has a lower equity "buffer" available to creditors if the company becomes insolvent. Thus, from the creditors' point of view, a high ratio of debt to assets is undesirable. Best Buy's solvency appears lower than hhgregg's and lower than the average company in the industry.

The adequacy of this ratio is often judged in the light of the company's earnings. Generally, companies with relatively stable earnings, such as public utilities, can support higher debt to assets ratios than can cyclical companies with widely fluctuating earnings, such as many high-tech companies. In later chapters, you will learn additional ways to evaluate solvency.

Investor Insight

When Debt Is Good

Debt financing differs greatly across industries and companies. Here are some debt to assets ratios for selected companies in a recent year:

	Debt to Assets Ratio
American Pharmaceutical Partners	19%
Callaway Golf Company	20%
Microsoft	21%
Sears Holdings Corporation	73%
Eastman Kodak Company	78%
General Motors Corporation	94%

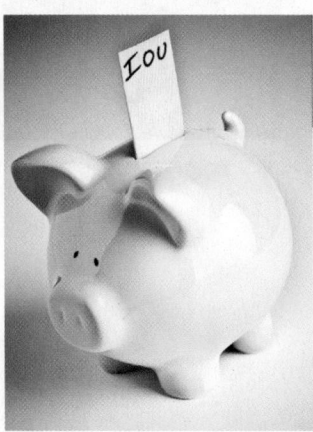
© David Crockett/iStockphoto

? Discuss the difference in the debt to assets ratio of Microsoft and General Motors. (See page 95.)

DECISION TOOLKIT

DECISION CHECKPOINTS	INFO NEEDED FOR DECISION	TOOL TO USE FOR DECISION	HOW TO EVALUATE RESULTS
Can the company meet its near-term obligations?	Current assets and current liabilities	$\text{Current ratio} = \dfrac{\text{Current assets}}{\text{Current liabilities}}$	Higher ratio suggests favorable liquidity.
Can the company meet its long-term obligations?	Total liabilities and total assets	$\dfrac{\text{Debt to assets ratio}} = \dfrac{\text{Total liabilities}}{\text{Total assets}}$	Lower value suggests favorable solvency.

KEEPING AN EYE ON CASH

LEARNING OBJECTIVE 5
Use the statement of cash flows to evaluate solvency.

In the statement of cash flows, net cash provided by operating activities is intended to indicate the cash-generating capability of the company. Analysts have noted, however, that **net cash provided by operating activities fails to take into account that a company must invest in new property, plant, and equipment** (capital expenditures) just to maintain its current level of operations. Companies also must at least **maintain dividends at current levels** to satisfy investors. A measurement to provide additional insight regarding a company's cash-generating ability is free cash flow. Free cash flow describes the net cash provided by operating activities after adjusting for capital expenditures and dividends paid.

Consider the following example. Suppose that MPC produced and sold 10,000 personal computers this year. It reported $100,000 net cash provided by operating activities. In order to maintain production at 10,000 computers, MPC invested $15,000 in equipment. It chose to pay $5,000 in dividends. Its free cash flow was $80,000 ($100,000 − $15,000 − $5,000). The company could use this $80,000 to purchase new assets to expand the business, pay off debts, or increase its dividend distribution. In practice, analysts often calculate free cash flow with the formula shown below. (Alternative definitions also exist.)

$$\text{Free Cash Flow} = \text{Net Cash Provided by Operating Activities} - \text{Capital Expenditures} - \text{Cash Dividends}$$

We can calculate Best Buy's 2011 free cash flow as follows (dollars in millions).

Net cash provided by operating activities	$1,190
Less: Expenditures on property, plant, and equipment	744
Dividends paid	237
Free cash flow	$ 209

Best Buy generated free cash flow of $209 million which is available for the acquisition of new assets, the retirement of stock or debt, or the payment of additional dividends. Long-term creditors consider a high free cash flow amount an indication of solvency. hhgregg's free cash flow for 2011 is a negative $0.9 million. Given that hhgregg is considerably smaller than Best Buy, we would expect its free cash flow to be much lower. But, negative free cash flow could be cause for concern.

DECISION TOOLKIT

DECISION CHECKPOINTS	INFO NEEDED FOR DECISION	TOOL TO USE FOR DECISION	HOW TO EVALUATE RESULTS
How much cash did the company generate to expand operations, pay off debts, or distribute dividends?	Net cash provided by operating activities, cash spent on fixed assets, and cash dividends	$\text{Free cash flow} = \text{Net cash provided by operating activities} - \text{Capital expenditures} - \text{Cash dividends}$	Significant free cash flow indicates greater potential to finance new investment and pay additional dividends.

RATIO ANALYSIS

Do it!

The following information is available for Ozone Inc.

	2014	2013
Current assets	$ 88,000	$ 60,800
Total assets	400,000	341,000
Current liabilities	40,000	38,000
Total liabilities	120,000	150,000
Net income	100,000	50,000
Net cash provided by operating activities	110,000	70,000
Preferred dividends	10,000	10,000
Common dividends	5,000	2,500
Expenditures on property, plant, and equipment	45,000	20,000
Shares outstanding at beginning of year	60,000	40,000
Shares outstanding at end of year	120,000	60,000

(a) Compute earnings per share for 2014 and 2013 for Ozone, and comment on the change. Ozone's primary competitor, Frost Corporation, had earnings per share of $2 in 2014. Comment on the difference in the ratios of the two companies.

(b) Compute the current ratio and debt to assets ratio for each year, and comment on the changes.

(c) Compute free cash flow for each year, and comment on the changes.

Action Plan

- Use the formula for earnings per share (EPS): (Net income − Preferred dividends) ÷ (Average common shares outstanding).
- Use the formula for the current ratio: Current assets ÷ Current liabilities.
- Use the formula for the debt to assets ratio: Total liabilities ÷ Total assets.
- Use the formula for free cash flow: Net cash provided by operating activities − Capital expenditures − Cash dividends.

Solution

(a) Earnings per share

2014	2013
$\dfrac{(\$100,000 - \$10,000)}{(120,000 + 60,000)/2} = \$1.00$	$\dfrac{(\$50,000 - \$10,000)}{(60,000 + 40,000)/2} = \$0.80$

Ozone's profitability, as measured by the amount of income available to each share of common stock, increased by 25% [($1.00 − $0.80) ÷ $0.80] during 2014. Earnings per share should not be compared across companies because the number of shares issued by companies varies widely. Thus, we cannot conclude that Frost Corporation is more profitable than Ozone based on its higher EPS.

(b)

	2014	2013
Current ratio	$\dfrac{\$88,000}{\$40,000} = 2.20{:}1$	$\dfrac{\$60,800}{\$38,000} = 1.60{:}1$
Debt to assets ratio	$\dfrac{\$120,000}{\$400,000} = 30\%$	$\dfrac{\$150,000}{\$341,000} = 44\%$

The company's liquidity, as measured by the current ratio, improved from 1.60:1 to 2.20:1. Its solvency also improved, as measured by the debt to assets ratio, which declined from 44% to 30%.

(c) Free cash flow

2014: $110,000 − $45,000 − ($10,000 + $5,000) = $50,000
2013: $70,000 − $20,000 − ($10,000 + $2,500) = $37,500

The amount of cash generated by the company above its needs for dividends and capital expenditures increased from $37,500 to $50,000.

✔ The Navigator

Related exercise material: **BE2-3, BE2-5, BE2-6, Do it! 2-3, E2-7, E2-9, E2-10,** and **E2-11.**

Financial Reporting Concepts

You have now learned about the four financial statements and some basic ways to interpret those statements. In this last section, we will discuss concepts that underlie these financial statements. It would be unwise to make business decisions based on financial statements without understanding the implications of these concepts.

THE STANDARD-SETTING ENVIRONMENT

How does Best Buy decide on the type of financial information to disclose? What format should it use? How should it measure assets, liabilities, revenues, and expenses? Accounting professionals at Best Buy and all other U.S. companies get guidance from a set of accounting standards that have authoritative support, referred to as **generally accepted accounting principles (GAAP)**. Standard-setting bodies, in consultation with the accounting profession and the business community, determine these accounting standards.

The **Securities and Exchange Commission (SEC)** is the agency of the U.S. government that oversees U.S. financial markets and accounting standard-setting bodies. The **Financial Accounting Standards Board (FASB)** is the primary accounting standard-setting body in the United States. The **International Accounting Standards Board (IASB)** issues standards called **International Financial Reporting Standards (IFRS)**, which have been adopted by many countries outside of the United States. Today, the FASB and IASB are working closely together to minimize the differences in their standards. Recently, the SEC announced that foreign companies that wish to have their shares traded on U.S stock exchanges no longer have to prepare reports that conform with GAAP, as long as their reports conform with IFRS. The SEC is currently evaluating whether the United States should eventually adopt IFRS as the required set of standards for U.S. publicly traded companies. Another relatively recent change to the financial reporting environment was that, as a result of the Sarbanes-Oxley Act, the **Public Company Accounting Oversight Board (PCAOB)** was created. Its job is to determine auditing standards and review the performance of auditing firms. If the United States adopts IFRS for its accounting standards, it will also have to coordinate its auditing regulations with those of other countries.

International Note Over 115 countries use international standards (called IFRS). For example, all companies in the European Union follow IFRS. In this textbook, we highlight any significant differences using International Notes like this one, as well as a more in-depth discussion in the *A Look at IFRS* section at the end of each chapter.

International Insight

The Korean Discount

If you think that accounting standards don't matter, consider recent events in South Korea. For many years, international investors complained that the financial reports of South Korean companies were inadequate and inaccurate. Accounting practices there often resulted in huge differences between stated revenues and actual revenues. Because investors did not have faith in the accuracy of the numbers, they were unwilling to pay as much for the shares of these companies relative to shares of comparable companies in different countries. This difference in share price was often referred to as the "Korean discount."

In response, Korean regulators decided that, beginning in 2011, companies would have to comply with international accounting standards. This change was motivated by a desire to "make the country's businesses more transparent" in order to build investor confidence and spur economic growth. Many other Asian countries, including China, India, Japan, and Hong Kong, have also decided either to adopt international standards or to create standards that are based on the international standards.

SeongJoon Cho/Bloomberg/Getty Images, Inc.

Source: Evan Ramstad, "End to 'Korea Discount'?" *Wall Street Journal* (March 16, 2007).

? What is meant by the phrase "make the country's businesses more transparent"? Why would increasing transparency spur economic growth? (See page 95.)

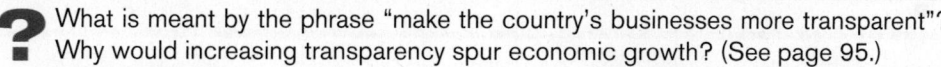

QUALITIES OF USEFUL INFORMATION

LEARNING OBJECTIVE 7
Discuss financial reporting concepts.

Recently, the FASB and IASB completed the first phase of a joint project in which they developed a conceptual framework to serve as the basis for future accounting standards. The framework begins by stating that the primary objective of financial reporting is to provide financial information that is **useful** to investors and creditors for making decisions about providing capital. According to the FASB, useful information should possess two fundamental qualities, relevance and faithful representation, as shown in Illustration 2-17.

Illustration 2-17 Fundamental qualities of useful information

Relevance   Accounting information has relevance if it would make a difference in a business decision. Information is considered relevant if it provides information that has **predictive value**, that is, helps provide accurate expectations about the future, and has **confirmatory value**, that is, confirms or corrects prior expectations. Materiality is a company-specific aspect of relevance. An item is material when its **size** makes it likely to influence the decision of an investor or creditor.

Faithful Representation   Faithful representation means that information accurately depicts what really happened. To provide a faithful representation, information must be **complete** (nothing important has been omitted), **neutral** (is not biased toward one position or another), and **free from error**.

Enhancing Qualities

In addition to the two fundamental qualities, the FASB and IASB also describe a number of enhancing qualities of useful information. These include **comparability, consistency, verifiability, timeliness,** and **understandability.** In

Accounting Across the Organization

What Do These Companies Have in Common?

Another issue related to comparability is the accounting time period. An accounting period that is one-year long is called a **fiscal year**. But a fiscal year need not match the calendar year. For example, a company could end its fiscal year on April 30, rather than December 31.

Why do companies choose the particular year-ends that they do? For example, why doesn't every company use December 31 as the accounting year-end? Many companies choose to end their accounting year when inventory or operations are at a low point. This is advantageous because compiling accounting information requires much time and effort by managers, so they would rather do it when they aren't as busy operating the business. Also, inventory is easier and less costly to count when its volume is low.

Some companies whose year-ends differ from December 31 are Delta Air Lines, June 30; Walt Disney Productions, September 30; and Dunkin' Donuts, Inc., October 31. In the notes to its financial statements, Best Buy states that its accounting year-end is the Saturday nearest the end of February.

 What problems might Best Buy's year-end create for analysts? (See page 95.)

accounting, comparability results when different companies use the same accounting principles. Another characteristic that enhances comparability is consistency. Consistency means that a company uses the same accounting principles and methods from year to year. Information is verifiable if independent observers, using the same methods, obtain similar results. As noted in Chapter 1, certified public accountants (CPAs) perform audits of financial statements to verify their accuracy. For accounting information to have relevance, it must be timely. That is, it must be available to decision-makers before it loses its capacity to influence decisions. The SEC requires that public companies provide their annual reports to investors within 60 days of their year-end. Information has the quality of understandability if it is presented in a clear and concise fashion, so that reasonably informed users of that information can interpret it and comprehend its meaning.

ASSUMPTIONS IN FINANCIAL REPORTING

To develop accounting standards, the FASB relies on some key assumptions, as shown in Illustration 2-18. These include assumptions about the monetary unit, economic entity, periodicity, and going concern.

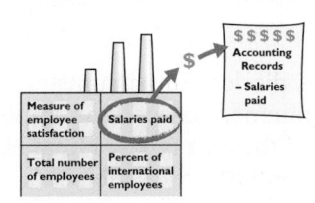

Monetary Unit Assumption The monetary unit assumption requires that only those things that can be expressed in money are included in the accounting records. This means that certain important information needed by investors, creditors, and managers, such as customer satisfaction, is not reported in the financial statements.

Economic Entity Assumption The economic entity assumption states that every economic entity can be separately identified and accounted for. In order to assess a company's performance and financial position accurately, it is important to not blur company transactions with personal transactions (especially those of its managers) or transactions of other companies.

Periodicity Assumption Notice that the income statement, retained earnings statement, and statement of cash flows all cover periods of one year, and the balance sheet is prepared at the end of each year. The periodicity assumption states that the life of a business can be divided into artificial time periods and that useful reports covering those periods can be prepared for the business.

Going Concern Assumption The going concern assumption states that the business will remain in operation for the foreseeable future. Of course, many businesses do fail, but in general, it is reasonable to assume that the business will continue operating.

Illustration 2-18 Key assumptions in financial reporting

Ethics Note The importance of the economic entity assumption is illustrated by scandals involving Adelphia. In this case, senior company employees entered into transactions that blurred the line between the employees' financial interests and those of the company. For example, Adelphia guaranteed over $2 billion of loans to the founding family.

PRINCIPLES IN FINANCIAL REPORTING
Measurement Principles

GAAP generally uses one of two measurement principles, the historical cost principle or the fair value principle. Selection of which principle to follow generally relates to trade-offs between relevance and faithful representation.

HISTORICAL COST PRINCIPLE. The historical cost principle (or cost principle) dictates that companies record assets at their cost. This is true not only at the time the asset is purchased but also over the time the asset is held. For example, if land that was purchased for $30,000 increases in value to $40,000, it continues to be reported at $30,000.

FAIR VALUE PRINCIPLE. The fair value principle indicates that assets and liabilities should be reported at fair value (the price received to sell an asset or settle a liability). Fair value information may be more useful than historical cost for certain types of assets and liabilities. For example, certain investment securities are reported at fair value because market price information is often readily available for these types of assets. In choosing between cost and fair value, the FASB uses two qualities that make accounting information useful for decision-making—relevance and faithful representation. In determining which measurement principle to use, the FASB weighs the factual nature of cost figures versus the relevance of fair value. In general, the FASB indicates that most assets must follow the historical cost principle because market values may not be representationally faithful. Only in situations where assets are actively traded, such as investment securities, is the fair value principle applied.

Full Disclosure Principle

The full disclosure principle requires that companies disclose all circumstances and events that would make a difference to financial statement users. If an important item cannot reasonably be reported directly in one of the four types of financial statements, then it should be discussed in notes that accompany the statements.

COST CONSTRAINT

Providing information is costly. In deciding whether companies should be required to provide a certain type of information, accounting standard-setters consider the cost constraint. It weighs the cost that companies will incur to provide the information against the benefit that financial statement users will gain from having the information available.

FINANCIAL ACCOUNTING CONCEPTS AND PRINCIPLES

Do it!

The following items guide the FASB when it creates accounting standards.

Relevance	Periodicity assumption
Faithful representation	Going concern assumption
Comparability	Historical cost principle
Consistency	Full disclosure principle
Monetary unit assumption	Materiality
Economic entity assumption	

Match each item above with a description below.

1. _____ Ability to easily evaluate one company's results relative to another's.

2. _____ Belief that a company will continue to operate for the foreseeable future.

3. _____ The judgment concerning whether an item is large enough to matter to decision-makers.

4. _____ The reporting of all information that would make a difference to financial statement users.

5. _____ The practice of preparing financial statements at regular intervals.

6. _____ The quality of information that indicates the information makes a difference in a decision.

7. _____ A belief that items should be reported on the balance sheet at the price that was paid to acquire the item.

8. _____ A company's use of the same accounting principles and methods from year to year.

9. _____ Tracing accounting events to particular companies.

10. _____ The desire to minimize errors and bias in financial statements.

11. _____ Reporting only those things that can be measured in dollars.

Action Plan

- Understand the need for conceptual guidelines in accounting.
- List the characteristics of useful financial information.
- Review the assumptions, principles, and constraint that comprise the guidelines in accounting.

Solution

1. Comparability	7. Historical cost principle
2. Going concern assumption	8. Consistency
3. Materiality	9. Economic entity assumption
4. Full disclosure principle	10. Faithful representation
5. Periodicity assumption	11. Monetary unit assumption
6. Relevance	

 The Navigator

Related exercise material: **BE2-8, BE2-9, BE2-10, BE2-11, Do it! 2-4, E2-12,** and **E2-13.**

 # USING THE DECISION TOOLKIT

In this chapter, we evaluated a home electronics giant, Best Buy. Tweeter Home Entertainment sold consumer electronics products from 154 stores on the East Coast under various names. It specialized in products with high-end features. Tweeter filed for bankruptcy in June 2007 and was acquired by another company in July 2007. Financial data for Tweeter, prior to its bankruptcy, are provided below.

	September 30	
(amounts in millions)	2006	2005
Current assets	$146.4	$158.2
Total assets	258.6	284.0
Current liabilities	107.1	119.0
Total liabilities	190.4	201.1
Total common stockholders' equity	68.2	82.9
Net income (loss)	(16.5)	(74.4)
Net cash provided (used) by operating activities	15.6	(26.7)
Capital expenditures (net)	17.4	22.2
Dividends paid	0	0
Average shares of common stock (millions)	25.2	24.6

Instructions

Using the data provided, answer the following questions and discuss how these results might have provided an indication of Tweeter's financial troubles.

1. Calculate the current ratio for Tweeter for 2006 and 2005 and discuss its liquidity position.
2. Calculate the debt to assets ratio and free cash flow for Tweeter for 2006 and 2005 and discuss its solvency.

3. Calculate the earnings per share for Tweeter for 2006 and 2005, and discuss its change in profitability.
4. Best Buy's accounting year-end was February 28, 2007; Tweeter's was September 30, 2006. How does this difference affect your ability to compare their profitability?

Solution

1. Current ratio:

   2006: $\$146.4 \div \$107.1 = 1.37{:}1$ *2005:* $\$158.2 \div \$119.0 = 1.33{:}1$

   Tweeter's liquidity improved slightly from 2005 to 2006, but in both years it would most likely have been considered inadequate. In 2006, Tweeter had only $1.37 in current assets for every dollar of current liabilities. Sometimes larger companies, such as Best Buy, can function with lower current ratios because they have alternative sources of working capital. But a company of Tweeter's size would normally want a higher ratio.

2. Debt to assets:

   2006: $\$190.4 \div \$258.6 = 73.6\%$ *2005:* $\$201.1 \div \$284.0 = 70.8\%$

   Tweeter's solvency, as measured by its debt to assets ratio, declined from 2005 to 2006. Its ratio of 73.6% meant that every dollar of assets was financed by 73.6 cents of debt. For a retailer, this is extremely high reliance on debt. This low solvency suggests Tweeter's ability to meet its debt payments was questionable.

   Free cash flow:

   2006: $\$15.6 - \$17.4 - \$0 = -\$1.8$ million
   2005: $-\$26.7 - \$22.2 - \$0 = -\$48.9$ million

   Tweeter's free cash flow was negative in both years. The company did not generate enough net cash provided by operating activities even to cover its capital expenditures, and it was not paying a dividend. While this is not unusual for new companies in their early years, it is also not sustainable for very long. Part of the reason that its debt to assets ratio, discussed above, was so high was that it had to borrow money to make up for its deficient free cash flow.

3. Loss per share:

   2006: $-\$16.5 \div 25.2 = -\$0.65$ per share
   2005: $-\$74.4 \div 24.6 = -\$3.02$ per share

   Tweeter's loss per share declined substantially. However, this was little consolation for its shareholders, who experienced losses in previous years as well. The company's lack of profitability, combined with its poor liquidity and solvency, increased the likelihood that it would eventually file for bankruptcy.

4. Tweeter's income statement covers 7 months not covered by Best Buy's. Suppose that the economy changed dramatically during this 7-month period, either improving or declining. This change in the economy would be reflected in Tweeter's income statement but would not be reflected in Best Buy's income statement until the following March, thus reducing the usefulness of a comparison of the income statements of the two companies.

The Navigator

Summary of Learning Objectives

1 Identify the sections of a classified balance sheet. In a classified balance sheet, companies classify assets as current assets; long-term investments; property, plant, and equipment; and intangibles. They classify liabilities as either current or long-term. A stockholders' equity section shows common stock and retained earnings.

2 Identify tools for analyzing financial statements and ratios for computing a company's profitability. Ratio analysis expresses the relationship among selected items of financial statement data. Profitability ratios, such as earnings per share (EPS), measure aspects of the operating success of a company for a given period of time.

3 **Explain the relationship between a retained earnings statement and a statement of stockholders' equity.** The retained earnings statement presents the factors that changed the retained earnings balance during the period. A statement of stockholders' equity presents the factors that changed stockholders' equity during the period, including those that changed retained earnings. Thus, a statement of stockholders' equity is more inclusive.

4 **Identify and compute ratios for analyzing a company's liquidity and solvency using a balance sheet.** Liquidity ratios, such as the current ratio, measure the short-term ability of a company to pay its maturing obligations and to meet unexpected needs for cash. Solvency ratios, such as the debt to assets ratio, measure the ability of a company to survive over a long period.

5 **Use the statement of cash flows to evaluate solvency.** Free cash flow indicates a company's ability to generate net cash provided by operating activities that is sufficient to pay debts, acquire assets, and distribute dividends.

6 **Explain the meaning of generally accepted accounting principles.** Generally accepted accounting principles are a set of rules and practices recognized as a general guide for financial reporting purposes. The basic objective of financial reporting is to provide information that is useful for decision-making.

7 **Discuss financial reporting concepts.** To be judged useful, information should have the primary characteristics of relevance and faithful representation. In addition, useful information is comparable, consistent, verifiable, timely, and understandable.

The **monetary unit assumption** requires that companies include in the accounting records only transaction data that can be expressed in terms of money. The **economic entity assumption** states that economic events can be identified with a particular unit of accountability. The **periodicity assumption** states that the economic life of a business can be divided into artificial time periods and that meaningful accounting reports can be prepared for each period. The **going concern assumption** states that the company will continue in operation long enough to carry out its existing objectives and commitments.

The **historical cost principle** states that companies should record assets at their cost. The **fair value principle** indicates that assets and liabilities should be reported at fair value. The **full disclosure principle** requires that companies disclose circumstances and events that matter to financial statement users.

The **cost constraint** weighs the cost that companies incur to provide a type of information against its benefit to financial statement users.

DECISION TOOLKIT *A SUMMARY*

DECISION CHECKPOINTS	INFO NEEDED FOR DECISION	TOOL TO USE FOR DECISION		HOW TO EVALUATE RESULTS
How does the company's earnings performance compare with that of previous years?	Net income available to common stockholders and average common shares outstanding	Earnings per share	$= \dfrac{\text{Net income} - \text{Preferred dividends}}{\text{Average common shares outstanding}}$	A higher measure suggests improved performance, although the number is subject to manipulation. Values should not be compared across companies.
Can the company meet its near-term obligations?	Current assets and current liabilities	Current ratio	$= \dfrac{\text{Current assets}}{\text{Current liabilities}}$	Higher ratio suggests favorable liquidity.
Can the company meet its long-term obligations?	Total liabilities and total assets	Debt to assets ratio	$= \dfrac{\text{Total liabilities}}{\text{Total assets}}$	Lower value suggests favorable solvency.
How much cash did the company generate to expand operations, pay off debts, or distribute dividends?	Net cash provided by operating activities, cash spent on fixed assets, and cash dividends	Free cash flow	$= \begin{array}{c}\text{Net cash} \\ \text{provided by} \\ \text{operating} \\ \text{activities}\end{array} - \begin{array}{c}\text{Capital} \\ \text{expenditures}\end{array} - \begin{array}{c}\text{Cash} \\ \text{dividends}\end{array}$	Significant free cash flow indicates greater potential to finance new investment and pay additional dividends.

Glossary

Classified balance sheet *(p. 48)* A balance sheet that groups together similar assets and similar liabilities, using a number of standard classifications and sections.

Comparability *(p. 65)* Ability to compare the accounting information of different companies because they use the same accounting principles.

Consistency *(p. 65)* Use of the same accounting principles and methods from year to year within a company.

Cost constraint *(p. 66)* Constraint that weighs the cost that companies will incur to provide the information against the benefit that financial statement users will gain from having the information available.

Current assets *(p. 49)* Assets that companies expect to convert to cash or use up within one year or the operating cycle, whichever is longer.

Current liabilities *(p. 52)* Obligations that a company expects to pay within the next year or operating cycle, whichever is longer.

Current ratio *(p. 58)* A measure of liquidity computed as current assets divided by current liabilities.

Debt to assets ratio *(p. 59)* A measure of solvency calculated as total liabilities divided by total assets. It measures the percentage of total financing provided by creditors.

Earnings per share (EPS) *(p. 55)* A measure of the net income earned on each share of common stock; computed as net income minus preferred dividends divided by the average number of common shares outstanding during the year.

Economic entity assumption *(p. 65)* An assumption that every economic entity can be separately identified and accounted for.

Fair value principle *(p. 66)* Assets and liabilities should be reported at fair value (the price received to sell an asset or settle a liability).

Faithful representation *(p. 64)* Information that is complete, neutral, and free from error.

Financial Accounting Standards Board (FASB) *(p. 63)* The primary accounting standard-setting body in the United States.

Free cash flow *(p. 61)* Net cash provided by operating activities after adjusting for capital expenditures and cash dividends paid.

Full disclosure principle *(p. 66)* Accounting principle that dictates that companies disclose circumstances and events that make a difference to financial statement users.

Generally accepted accounting principles (GAAP) *(p. 63)* A set of accounting standards that have substantial authoritative support, that guide accounting professionals.

Going concern assumption *(p. 65)* The assumption that the company will continue in operation for the foreseeable future.

Historical cost principle *(p. 66)* An accounting principle that states that companies should record assets at their cost.

Intangible assets *(p. 51)* Assets that do not have physical substance.

International Accounting Standards Board (IASB) *(p. 63)* An accounting standard-setting body that issues standards adopted by many countries outside of the United States.

International Financial Reporting Standards (IFRS) *(p. 63)* Accounting standards, issued by the IASB, that have been adopted by many countries outside of the United States.

Liquidity *(p. 58)* The ability of a company to pay obligations that are expected to become due within the next year or operating cycle.

Liquidity ratios *(p. 58)* Measures of the short-term ability of the company to pay its maturing obligations and to meet unexpected needs for cash.

Long-term investments *(p. 50)* Generally, (1) investments in stocks and bonds of other corporations that companies hold for more than one year; (2) long-term assets, such as land and buildings, not currently being used in the company's operations; and (3) long-term notes receivable.

Long-term liabilities (long-term debt) *(p. 53)* Obligations that a company expects to pay after one year.

Materiality *(p. 64)* Whether an item is large enough to likely influence the decision of an investor or creditor.

Monetary unit assumption *(p. 65)* An assumption that requires that only those things that can be expressed in money are included in the accounting records.

Operating cycle *(p. 50)* The average time required to purchase inventory, sell it on account, and then collect cash from customers—that is, go from cash to cash.

Periodicity assumption *(p. 65)* An assumption that the life of a business can be divided into artificial time periods and that useful reports covering those periods can be prepared for the business.

Profitability ratios *(p. 55)* Measures of the operating success of a company for a given period of time.

Property, plant, and equipment *(p. 51)* Assets with relatively long useful lives that are currently used in operating the business.

Public Company Accounting Oversight Board (PCAOB) *(p. 63)* The group charged with determining auditing standards and reviewing the performance of auditing firms.

Ratio *(p. 54)* An expression of the mathematical relationship between one quantity and another.

Ratio analysis *(p. 54)* A technique that expresses the relationship among selected items of financial statement data.

Relevance *(p. 64)* The quality of information that indicates the information makes a difference in a decision.

Securities and Exchange Commission (SEC) *(p. 63)* The agency of the U.S. government that oversees

U.S. financial markets and accounting standard-setting bodies.

Solvency *(p. 59)* The ability of a company to pay interest as it comes due and to repay the balance of debt due at its maturity.

Solvency ratios *(p. 59)* Measures of the ability of the company to survive over a long period of time.

Statement of stockholders' equity *(p. 56)* A financial statement that presents the causes of changes to stockholders' equity during the period, including those that caused retained earnings to change.

Timely *(p. 65)* Information that is available to decision-makers before it loses its capacity to influence decisions.

Understandability *(p. 65)* Information presented in a clear and concise fashion so that users can interpret it and comprehend its meaning.

Verifiable *(p. 65)* The quality of information that occurs when independent observers, using the same methods, obtain similar results.

Working capital *(p. 58)* The difference between the amounts of current assets and current liabilities.

Comprehensive **Do it!**

Listed here are items taken from the income statement and balance sheet of Bargain Electronics, Inc. for the year ended December 31, 2014. Certain items have been combined for simplification. (Amounts are given in thousands.)

Notes payable (due in 3 years)	$ 50.5
Cash	141.1
Salaries and wages expense	2,933.6
Common stock	454.9
Accounts payable	922.2
Accounts receivable	723.3
Equipment, net	921.0
Cost of goods sold	9,501.4
Income taxes payable	7.2
Interest expense	1.5
Mortgage payable	451.5
Retained earnings	1,336.3
Inventory	1,636.5
Sales revenue	12,456.9
Debt investments (short-term)	382.6
Income tax expense	30.5
Goodwill	202.7
Notes payable (due in 6 months)	784.6

Instructions

Prepare an income statement and a classified balance sheet using the items listed. Do not use any item more than once.

Solution to Comprehensive **Do it!**

Action Plan

• In preparing the income statement, list revenues, then expenses.

• In preparing a classified balance sheet, list current assets in order of liquidity.

BARGAIN ELECTRONICS, INC.
Income Statement
For the Year Ended December 31, 2014
(in thousands)

Revenues		
Sales revenue		$12,456.9
Expenses		
Cost of goods sold	$9,501.4	
Salaries and wages expense	2,933.6	
Interest expense	1.5	
Income tax expense	30.5	
Total expenses		12,467.0
Net loss		$ (10.1)

BARGAIN ELECTRONICS, INC.
Balance Sheet
December 31, 2014
(in thousands)

Assets

Current assets		
Cash	$ 141.1	
Debt investments	382.6	
Accounts receivable	723.3	
Inventory	1,636.5	
Total current assets		$2,883.5
Equipment, net		921.0
Goodwill		202.7
Total assets		$4,007.2

Liabilities and Stockholders' Equity

Current liabilities		
Notes payable	$ 784.6	
Accounts payable	922.2	
Income taxes payable	7.2	
Total current liabilities		$1,714.0
Long-term liabilities		
Mortgage payable	451.5	
Notes payable	50.5	502.0
Total liabilities		2,216.0
Stockholders' equity		
Common stock	454.9	
Retained earnings	1,336.3	
Total stockholders' equity		1,791.2
Total liabilities and stockholders' equity		$4,007.2

 The
Navigator

 PLUS   **Self-Test, Brief Exercises, Exercises, Problem Set A, and many more resources are available for practice in WileyPLUS.**

Self-Test Questions

Answers are on page 95.

(LO 1) **1.** In a classified balance sheet, assets are usually classified as:
(a) current assets; long-term assets; property, plant, and equipment; and intangible assets.
(b) current assets; long-term investments; property, plant, and equipment; and common stock.
(c) current assets; long-term investments; tangible assets; and intangible assets.
(d) current assets; long-term investments; property, plant, and equipment; and intangible assets.

(LO 1) **2.** Current assets are listed:
(a) by order of expected conversion to cash.
(b) by importance.
(c) by longevity.
(d) alphabetically.

3. The correct order of presentation in a classified bal- (LO 1) ance sheet for the following current assets is:
(a) accounts receivable, cash, prepaid insurance, inventory.
(b) cash, inventory, accounts receivable, prepaid insurance.
(c) cash, accounts receivable, inventory, prepaid insurance.
(d) inventory, cash, accounts receivable, prepaid insurance.

(LO 1) **4.** A company has purchased a tract of land. It expects to build a production plant on the land in approximately 5 years. During the 5 years before construction, the land will be idle. The land should be reported as:
(a) property, plant, and equipment.
(b) land expense.
(c) a long-term investment.
(d) an intangible asset.

(LO 2) **5.** Which is an indicator of profitability?
(a) Current ratio.
(b) Earnings per share.
(c) Debt to assets ratio.
(d) Free cash flow.

(LO 2) **6.** For 2014, Ganos Corporation reported net income $26,000; net sales $400,000; and average shares outstanding 4,000. There were preferred dividends of $2,000. What was the 2014 earnings per share?
(a) $6.00.   (c) $99.50.
(b) $6.50.   (d) $100.00.

(LO 3) **7.** The balance in retained earnings is **not** affected by:
(a) net income.
(b) net loss.
(c) issuance of common stock.
(d) dividends.

(LO 4) **8.** Which of these measures is an evaluation of a company's ability to pay current liabilities?
(a) Earnings per share.
(b) Current ratio.
(c) Both (a) and (b).
(d) None of the above.

(LO 2, 4) **9.** The following ratios are available for Bachus Inc. and Newton Inc.

	Current Ratio	Debt to Assets Ratio	Earnings per Share
Bachus Inc.	2:1	75%	$3.50
Newton Inc.	1.5:1	40%	$2.75

Compared to Newton Inc., Bachus Inc. has:
(a) higher liquidity, higher solvency, and higher profitability.
(b) lower liquidity, higher solvency, and higher profitability.

(c) higher liquidity, lower solvency, and higher profitability.
(d) higher liquidity and lower solvency, but profitability cannot be compared based on information provided.

10. Companies can use free cash flow to: (LO 5)
(a) pay additional dividends.
(b) acquire property, plant, and equipment.
(c) pay off debts.
(d) All of the above.

11. Generally accepted accounting principles are: (LO 6)
(a) a set of standards and rules that are recognized as a general guide for financial reporting.
(b) usually established by the Internal Revenue Service.
(c) the guidelines used to resolve ethical dilemmas.
(d) fundamental truths that can be derived from the laws of nature.

12. What organization issues U.S. accounting standards? (LO 6)
(a) Financial Accounting Standards Board.
(b) International Accounting Standards Committee.
(c) International Auditing Standards Committee.
(d) None of the above.

13. What is the primary criterion by which accounting (LO 7) information can be judged?
(a) Consistency.
(b) Predictive value.
(c) Usefulness for decision-making.
(d) Comparability.

14. Neutrality is an ingredient of: (LO 7)

	Faithful representation	Relevance
(a)	Yes	Yes
(b)	No	No
(c)	Yes	No
(d)	No	Yes

15. The characteristic of information that evaluates (LO 7) whether it is large enough to impact a decision.
(a) Comparability.   (c) Cost.
(b) Materiality.   (d) Consistency.

Go to the book's companion website, **www.wiley.com/college/kimmel**, to access additional Self-Test Questions.

Questions

1. What is meant by the term operating cycle?

2. Define current assets. What basis is used for ordering individual items within the current assets section?

3. Distinguish between long-term investments and property, plant, and equipment.

4. How do current liabilities differ from long-term liabilities?

5. Identify the two parts of stockholders' equity in a corporation and indicate the purpose of each.

6.
(a) Lorie Power believes that the analysis of financial statements is directed at two characteristics of a company: liquidity and profitability. Is Lorie correct? Explain.
(b) Are short-term creditors, long-term creditors, and stockholders primarily interested in the same characteristics of a company? Explain.

7. Name ratios useful in assessing (a) liquidity, (b) solvency, and (c) profitability.

8. Tim Sands, the founder of Waterboots Inc., needs to raise $500,000 to expand his company's operations. He has been told that raising the money through debt will increase the riskiness of his company much more than issuing stock. He doesn't understand why this is true. Explain it to him.

9. What do these classes of ratios measure?
   (a) Liquidity ratios.
   (b) Profitability ratios.
   (c) Solvency ratios.

10. Holding all other factors constant, indicate whether each of the following signals generally good or bad news about a company.
    (a) Increase in earnings per share.
    (b) Increase in the current ratio.
    (c) Increase in the debt to assets ratio.
    (d) Decrease in free cash flow.

11. Which ratio or ratios from this chapter do you think should be of greatest interest to:
    (a) a pension fund considering investing in a corporation's 20-year bonds?
    (b) a bank contemplating a short-term loan?
    (c) an investor in common stock?

12. (a) What are generally accepted accounting principles (GAAP)?
    (b) What body provides authoritative support for GAAP?

13. (a) What is the primary objective of financial reporting?
    (b) Identify the characteristics of useful accounting information.

14. Joe Merando, the president of Lane Company, is pleased. Lane substantially increased its net income in 2014 while keeping its unit inventory relatively the same. Donald Jantz, chief accountant, cautions Joe, however. Jantz says that since Lane changed its method of inventory valuation, there is a consistency problem and it is difficult to determine whether Lane is better off. Is Jantz correct? Why or why not?

15. What is the distinction between comparability and consistency?

16. Describe the constraint inherent in the presentation of accounting information.

17. Your roommate believes that accounting standards are uniform throughout the world. Is your roommate correct? Explain.

18. Glenda Wine is president of Better Books. She has no accounting background. Wine cannot understand why fair value is not used as the basis for all accounting measurement and reporting. Discuss.

19. What is the economic entity assumption? Give an example of its violation.

20. What was Tootsie Roll's largest current asset, largest current liability, and largest item under "Other assets" at December 31, 2011?

Brief Exercises

Classify accounts on balance sheet.
(LO 1), K

BE2-1 The following are the major balance sheet classifications:

Current assets (CA)   Current liabilities (CL)
Long-term investments (LTI) Long-term liabilities (LTL)
Property, plant, and equipment (PPE) Common stock (CS)
Intangible assets (IA)   Retained earnings (RE)

Match each of the following accounts to its proper balance sheet classification.

_____ Accounts payable   _____ Income taxes payable
_____ Accounts receivable   _____ Investment in long-term bonds
_____ Accumulated depreciation _____ Land
_____ Buildings   _____ Inventory
_____ Cash   _____ Patent
_____ Goodwill   _____ Supplies

Prepare the current assets section of a balance sheet.
(LO 1), AP

BE2-2 A list of financial statement items for Morales Company includes the following: accounts receivable $14,000; prepaid insurance $2,600; cash $10,400; supplies $3,800; and debt investments (short-term) $8,200. Prepare the current assets section of the balance sheet listing the items in the proper sequence.

Compute earnings per share.
(LO 2), AP

BE2-3 The following information (in millions of dollars) is available for Limited Brands for a recent year: sales revenue $9,043; net income $220; preferred dividend $0; and average shares outstanding 333 million. Compute the earnings per share for Limited Brands.

Identify items affecting stockholders' equity.
(LO 3), K

BE2-4 For each of the following events affecting the stockholders' equity of Noland, indicate whether the event would: increase retained earnings (IRE), decrease retained earnings (DRE), increase common stock (ICS), or decrease common stock (DCS).

_____ (a) Issued new shares of common stock.
_____ (b) Paid a cash dividend.
_____ (c) Reported net income of $75,000.
_____ (d) Reported a net loss of $20,000.

BE2-5 These selected condensed data are taken from a recent balance sheet of Bob Evans Farms (in millions of dollars).

Calculate liquidity ratios.
(LO 4), **AP**

Cash	$ 29.3
Accounts receivable	20.5
Inventory	28.7
Other current assets	24.0
Total current assets	$102.5
Total current liabilities	$201.2

Compute working capital and the current ratio.

BE2-6 Gray's Books & Music Inc. reported the following selected information at March 31.

Calculate liquidity and solvency ratios.
(LO 4, 5), **AP**

	2014
Total current assets	$262,787
Total assets	439,832
Total current liabilities	293,625
Total liabilities	376,002
Net cash provided by operating activities	62,300

Calculate (a) the current ratio, (b) the debt to assets ratio, and (c) free cash flow for March 31, 2014. The company paid dividends of $12,000 and spent $24,787 on capital expenditures.

BE2-7 Indicate whether each statement is true or false.
(a) GAAP is a set of rules and practices established by accounting standard-setting bodies to serve as a general guide for financial reporting purposes.
(b) Substantial authoritative support for GAAP usually comes from two standards-setting bodies: the FASB and the IRS.

Recognize generally accepted accounting principles.
(LO 6), **K**

BE2-8 The accompanying chart shows the qualitative characteristics of useful accounting information. Fill in the blanks.

Identify characteristics of useful information.
(LO 7), **K**

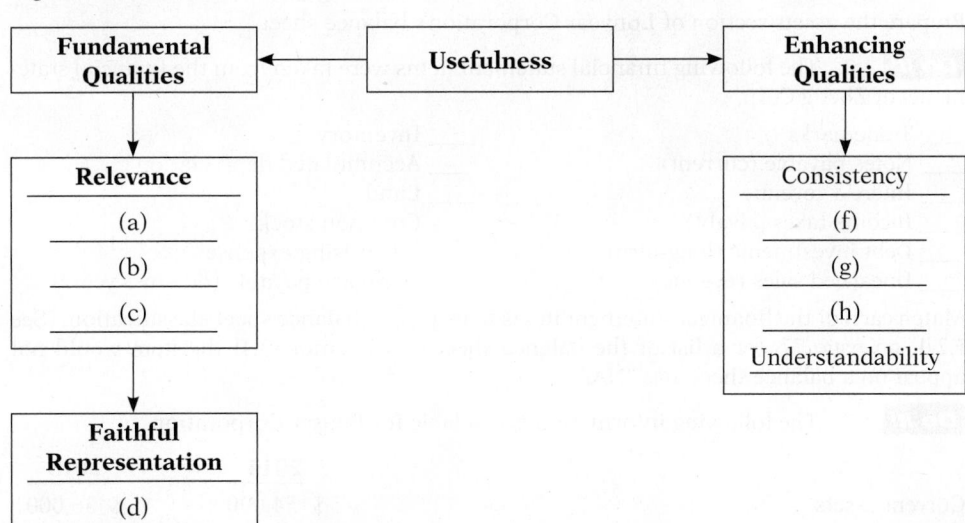

BE2-9 Given the characteristics of useful accounting information, complete each of the following statements.
(a) For information to be _____, it should have predictive and confirmatory value.
(b) _____ means that information accurately depicts what really happened.
(c) _____ means using the same accounting principles and methods from year to year within a company.

Identify characteristics of useful information.
(LO 7), **K**

Identify characteristics of useful information.

(LO 7), K

BE2-10 Here are some qualitative characteristics of useful accounting information:

1. Predictive value
2. Neutral
3. Verifiable
4. Timely

Match each qualitative characteristic to one of the following statements.

_____ (a) Accounting information should help provide accurate expectations about future events.

_____ (b) Accounting information cannot be selected, prepared, or presented to favor one set of interested users over another.

_____ (c) The quality of information that occurs when independent observers, using the same methods, obtain similar results.

_____ (d) Accounting information must be available to decision-makers before it loses its capacity to influence their decisions.

Define full disclosure principle.

(LO 7), K

BE2-11 The full disclosure principle dictates that:

(a) financial statements should disclose all assets at their cost.

(b) financial statements should disclose only those events that can be measured in dollars.

(c) financial statements should disclose all events and circumstances that would matter to users of financial statements.

(d) financial statements should not be relied on unless an auditor has expressed an unqualified opinion on them.

Do it! Review

Prepare assets section of balance sheet.

(LO 1), AP

Do it! 2-1 Lonyear Corporation has collected the following information related to its December 31, 2014, balance sheet.

Accounts receivable	$22,000	Equipment	$180,000
Accumulated depreciation—equipment	50,000	Inventory	58,000
Cash	13,000	Supplies	7,000

Prepare the assets section of Lonyear Corporation's balance sheet.

Classify financial statement items by balance sheet classification.

(LO 1), AP

Do it! 2-2 The following financial statement items were taken from the financial statements of Zheng Corp.

_____ Trademarks
_____ Notes payable (current)
_____ Interest revenue
_____ Income taxes payable
_____ Debt investments (long-term)
_____ Unearned sales revenue

_____ Inventory
_____ Accumulated depreciation
_____ Land
_____ Common stock
_____ Advertising expense
_____ Mortgage payable (due in 3 years)

Match each of the financial statement items to its proper balance sheet classification. (See E2-1, on page 77, for a list of the balance sheet classifications.) If the item would not appear on a balance sheet, use "NA."

Compute ratios and analyze.

(LO 4, 5), AP

Do it! 2-3 The following information is available for Benser Corporation.

	2014	2013
Current assets	$ 54,000	$ 36,000
Total assets	240,000	205,000
Current liabilities	22,000	30,000
Total liabilities	72,000	100,000
Net income	80,000	40,000
Net cash provided by operating activities	90,000	56,000
Preferred dividends	6,000	6,000
Common dividends	3,000	1,500
Expenditures on property, plant, and equipment	27,000	12,000
Shares outstanding at beginning of year	40,000	30,000
Shares outstanding at end of year	75,000	40,000

(a) Compute earnings per share for 2014 and 2013 for Benser, and comment on the change. Benser's primary competitor, Matile Corporation, had earnings per share of $1 per share in 2014. Comment on the difference in the ratios of the two companies.

(b) Compute the current ratio and debt to assets ratio for each year, and comment on the changes.

(c) Compute free cash flow for each year, and comment on the changes.

Do it! 2-4   The following characteristics, assumptions, principles, and constraint guide the FASB when it creates accounting standards.

Identify financial accounting concepts and principles.
(LO 7), **K**

Relevance	Periodicity assumption
Faithful representation	Going concern assumption
Comparability	Historical cost principle
Consistency	Full disclosure principle
Monetary unit assumption	Materiality
Economic entity assumption	Cost constraint

Match each item above with a description below.

1. _____ Items not easily quantified in dollar terms are not reported in the financial statements.
2. _____ Accounting information must be complete, neutral, and free from error.
3. _____ Personal transactions are not mixed with the company's transactions.
4. _____ The cost to provide information should be weighed against the benefit that users will gain from having the information available.
5. _____ A company's use of the same accounting principles from year to year.
6. _____ Assets are recorded and reported at original purchase price.
7. _____ Accounting information should help users predict future events, and should confirm or correct prior expectations.
8. _____ The life of a business can be divided into artificial segments of time.
9. _____ The reporting of all information that would make a difference to financial statement users.
10. _____ The judgment concerning whether an item's size makes it likely to influence a decision-maker.
11. _____ Assumes a business will remain in operation for the foreseeable future.
12. _____ Different companies use the same accounting principles.

Exercises

E2-1   The following are the major balance sheet classifications.

Classify accounts on balance sheet.
(LO 1), **AP**

Current assets (CA)	Current liabilities (CL)
Long-term investments (LTI)	Long-term liabilities (LTL)
Property, plant, and equipment (PPE)	Stockholders' equity (SE)
Intangible assets (IA)	

Instructions
Classify each of the following financial statement items taken from Mordica Corporation's balance sheet.

____ Accounts payable	____ Income taxes payable
____ Accounts receivable	____ Inventory
____ Accumulated depreciation— equipment	____ Stock investments (to be sold in 7 months)
____ Buildings	____ Land (in use)
____ Cash	____ Mortgage payable
____ Interest payable	____ Supplies
____ Goodwill	____ Equipment
	____ Prepaid rent

Classify financial statement items by balance sheet classification.

(LO 1), AP

E2-2 The major balance sheet classifications are listed in E2-1.

Instructions

Classify each of the following financial statement items based upon the major balance sheet classifications listed in E2-1.

____ Prepaid advertising ____ Patents
____ Equipment ____ Bonds payable
____ Trademarks ____ Common stock
____ Salaries and wages payable ____ Accumulated depreciation—
____ Income taxes payable   equipment
____ Retained earnings ____ Unearned sales revenue
____ Accounts receivable ____ Inventory
____ Land (held for future use)

Classify items as current or noncurrent, and prepare assets section of balance sheet.

(LO 1), AP

E2-3 Suppose the following items were taken from the December 31, 2014, assets section of the Boeing Company balance sheet. (All dollars are in millions.)

Inventory	$16,933	Patents	$12,528
Notes receivable—due after		Buildings	21,579
December 31, 2015	5,466	Cash	9,215
Notes receivable—due before		Accounts receivable	5,785
December 31, 2015	368	Debt investments (short-term)	2,008
Accumulated depreciation—buildings	12,795		

Instructions

Prepare the assets section of a classified balance sheet, listing the current assets in order of their liquidity.

Prepare assets section of a classified balance sheet.

(LO 1), AP

E2-4 Suppose the following information (in thousands of dollars) is available for H.J. Heinz Company—famous for ketchup and other fine food products—for the year ended April 30, 2014.

Prepaid insurance	$ 125,765	Buildings	$4,033,369
Land	76,193	Cash	373,145
Goodwill	3,982,954	Accounts receivable	1,171,797
Trademarks	757,907	Accumulated depreciation—	
Inventory	1,237,613	buildings	2,131,260

Instructions

Prepare the assets section of a classified balance sheet, listing the items in proper sequence and including a statement heading.

Prepare a classified balance sheet.

(LO 1), AP

E2-5 These items are taken from the financial statements of Donavan Co. at December 31, 2014.

Buildings	$105,800
Accounts receivable	12,600
Prepaid insurance	3,200
Cash	11,840
Equipment	82,400
Land	61,200
Insurance expense	780
Depreciation expense	5,300
Interest expense	2,600
Common stock	60,000
Retained earnings (January 1, 2014)	40,000
Accumulated depreciation—buildings	45,600
Accounts payable	9,500
Notes payable	93,600
Accumulated depreciation—equipment	18,720
Interest payable	3,600
Service revenue	14,700

Instructions

Prepare a classified balance sheet. Assume that $13,600 of the note payable will be paid in 2015.

E2-6 Suppose the following items were taken from the 2014 financial statements of Texas Instruments, Inc. (All dollars are in millions.)

Prepare a classified balance sheet.

(LO 1), **AP**

Common stock	$2,826	Accumulated depreciation—	
Prepaid rent	164	equipment	$3,547
Equipment	6,705	Accounts payable	1,459
Stock investments (long-term)	637	Patents	2,210
Debt investments (short-term)	1,743	Notes payable (long-term)	810
Income taxes payable	128	Retained earnings	6,896
Cash	1,182	Accounts receivable	1,823
		Inventory	1,202

Instructions

Prepare a classified balance sheet in good form as of December 31, 2014.

E2-7 Suppose the following information is available for Callaway Golf Company for the years 2014 and 2013. (Dollars are in thousands, except share information.)

Compute and interpret profitability ratio.

(LO 2), **AP**

	2014	2013
Net sales	$1,117,204	$1,124,591
Net income (loss)	66,176	54,587
Total assets	855,338	838,078
Share information		
Shares outstanding at year-end	64,507,000	66,282,000
Preferred dividends	–0–	–0–

There were 73,139,000 shares outstanding at the end of 2012.

Instructions

(a) What was the company's earnings per share for each year?

(b) Based on your findings above, how did the company's profitability change from 2013 to 2014?

(c) Suppose the company had paid dividends on preferred stock and on common stock during the year. How would this affect your calculation in part (a)?

E2-8 These financial statement items are for Barfield Corporation at year-end, July 31, 2014.

Prepare financial statements.

(LO 1, 3, 4), **AP**

Salaries and wages payable	$ 2,080
Salaries and wages expense	57,500
Supplies expense	15,600
Equipment	18,500
Accounts payable	4,100
Service revenue	66,100
Rent revenue	8,500
Notes payable (due in 2017)	1,800
Common stock	16,000
Cash	29,200
Accounts receivable	9,780
Accumulated depreciation—equipment	6,000
Dividends	4,000
Depreciation expense	4,000
Retained earnings (beginning of the year)	34,000

Instructions

(a) Prepare an income statement and a retained earnings statement for the year. Barfield Corporation did not issue any new stock during the year.

(b) Prepare a classified balance sheet at July 31.

(c) Compute the current ratio and debt to assets ratio.

(d) Suppose that you are the president of Crescent Equipment. Your sales manager has approached you with a proposal to sell $20,000 of equipment to Barfield. He would like to provide a loan to Barfield in the form of a 10%, 5-year note payable. Evaluate how this loan would change Barfield's current ratio and debt to assets ratio, and discuss whether you would make the sale.

Compute liquidity ratios and compare results.

(LO 4), **AP**

E2-9 Nordstrom, Inc. operates department stores in numerous states. Selected financial statement data (in millions of dollars) for a recent year follow.

	End of Year	Beginning of Year
Cash and cash equivalents	$ 72	$ 358
Receivables (net)	1,942	1,788
Merchandise inventory	900	956
Other current assets	303	259
Total current assets	$3,217	$3,361
Total current liabilities	$1,601	$1,635

Instructions

(a) Compute working capital and the current ratio at the beginning of the year and at the end of the year.

(b) Did Nordstrom's liquidity improve or worsen during the year?

(c) Using the data in the chapter, compare Nordstrom's liquidity with Best Buy's (see page 57).

Compute liquidity measures and discuss findings.

(LO 4), **AP**

E2-10 The chief financial officer (CFO) of Grienke Corporation requested that the accounting department prepare a preliminary balance sheet on December 30, 2014, so that the CFO could get an idea of how the company stood. He knows that certain debt agreements with its creditors require the company to maintain a current ratio of at least 2:1. The preliminary balance sheet is as follows.

GRIENKE CORP.

Balance Sheet

December 30, 2014

Current assets			Current liabilities		
Cash	$25,000		Accounts payable	$ 20,000	
Accounts receivable	30,000		Salaries and wages payable	10,000	$ 30,000
Prepaid insurance	5,000	$ 60,000	Long-term liabilities		
Equipment (net)		200,000	Notes payable		80,000
Total assets		$260,000	Total liabilities		110,000
			Stockholders' equity		
			Common stock	100,000	
			Retained earnings	50,000	150,000
			Total liabilities and stockholders' equity		$260,000

Instructions

(a) Calculate the current ratio and working capital based on the preliminary balance sheet.

(b) Based on the results in (a), the CFO requested that $20,000 of cash be used to pay off the balance of the accounts payable account on December 31, 2014. Calculate the new current ratio and working capital after the company takes these actions.

(c) Discuss the pros and cons of the current ratio and working capital as measures of liquidity.

(d) Was it unethical for the CFO to take these steps?

E2-11 Suppose the following data were taken from the 2014 and 2013 financial statements of American Eagle Outfitters. (All dollars are in thousands.)

Compute and interpret solvency ratios.
(LO 4, 5), **AP**

	2014	2013
Current assets	$ 925,359	$1,020,834
Total assets	1,963,676	1,867,680
Current liabilities	401,763	376,178
Total liabilities	554,645	527,216
Net income	179,061	400,019
Net cash provided by operating activities	302,193	464,270
Capital expenditures	265,335	250,407
Dividends paid on common stock	82,394	80,796
Weighted-average shares outstanding	205,169	216,119

Instructions
Perform each of the following.
(a) Calculate the current ratio for each year.
(b) Calculate earnings per share for each year.
(c) Calculate the debt to assets ratio for each year.
(d) Calculate the free cash flow for each year.
(e) Discuss American Eagle's solvency in 2014 versus 2013.
(f) Discuss American Eagle's ability to finance its investment activities with net cash provided by operating activities, and how any deficiency would be met.

E2-12 Presented below are the assumptions and principles discussed in this chapter.

Identify accounting assumptions and principles.
(LO 7), **K**

1. Full disclosure principle.
2. Going concern assumption.
3. Monetary unit assumption.
4. Periodicity assumption.
5. Historical cost principle.
6. Economic entity assumption.

Instructions
Identify by number the accounting assumption or principle that is described below. Do not use a number more than once.

_____ (a) Is the rationale for why plant assets are not reported at liquidation value. (*Note:* Do not use the historical cost principle.)
_____ (b) Indicates that personal and business record-keeping should be separately maintained.
_____ (c) Assumes that the dollar is the "measuring stick" used to report on financial performance.
_____ (d) Separates financial information into time periods for reporting purposes.
_____ (e) Measurement basis used when a reliable estimate of fair value is not available.
_____ (f) Dictates that companies should disclose all circumstances and events that make a difference to financial statement users.

E2-13 Garcia Co. had three major business transactions during 2014.

Identify the assumption or principle that has been violated.
(LO 7), **C**

(a) Reported at its fair value of $260,000 merchandise inventory with a cost of $208,000.
(b) The president of Garcia Co., Sal Garcia, purchased a truck for personal use and charged it to his expense account.
(c) Garcia Co. wanted to make its 2014 income look better, so it added 2 more weeks to the year (a 54-week year). Previous years were 52 weeks.

Instructions
In each situation, identify the assumption or principle that has been violated, if any, and discuss what the company should have done.

Exercises: Set B and Challenge Exercises

Visit the book's companion website, at **www.wiley.com/college/kimmel**, and choose the Student Companion site to access Exercise Set B and Challenge Exercises.

Problems: Set A

Prepare a classified balance sheet.
(LO 1), **AP**

P2-1A Suppose the following items are taken from the 2014 balance sheet of Yahoo! Inc. (All dollars are in millions.)

Goodwill	$3,927
Common stock	6,283
Equipment	1,737
Accounts payable	152
Patents	234
Stock investments (long-term)	3,247
Accounts receivable	1,061
Prepaid rent	233
Debt investments (short-term)	1,160
Retained earnings	6,108
Cash	2,292
Notes payable (long-term)	734
Unearned sales revenue	413
Accumulated depreciation—equipment	201

Tot. current assets $4,746
Tot. assets $13,690

Instructions

Prepare a classified balance sheet for Yahoo! Inc. as of December 31, 2014.

Prepare financial statements.
(LO 1, 3), **AP**

P2-2A These items are taken from the financial statements of Tresh Corporation for 2014.

Retained earnings (beginning of year)	$31,000
Utilities expense	2,000
Equipment	66,000
Accounts payable	18,300
Cash	10,100
Salaries and wages payable	3,000
Common stock	12,000
Dividends	12,000
Service revenue	68,000
Prepaid insurance	3,500
Maintenance and repairs expense	1,800
Depreciation expense	3,600
Accounts receivable	11,700
Insurance expense	2,200
Salaries and wages expense	37,000
Accumulated depreciation—equipment	17,600

Net income $21,400
Tot. assets $73,700

Instructions

Prepare an income statement, a retained earnings statement, and a classified balance sheet as of December 31, 2014.

Prepare financial statements.
(LO 1, 3), **AP**

P2-3A You are provided with the following information for Ramirez Enterprises, effective as of its April 30, 2014, year-end.

Accounts payable	$ 834
Accounts receivable	810
Accumulated depreciation—equipment	670
Cash	1,270
Common stock	900
Cost of goods sold	1,060
Depreciation expense	335
Dividends	325
Equipment	2,420
Income tax expense	165
Income taxes payable	135
Insurance expense	210
Interest expense	400
Inventory	967
Land	3,100
Mortgage payable	3,500
Notes payable	61

Prepaid insurance	$ 60
Retained earnings (beginning)	1,600
Salaries and wages expense	700
Salaries and wages payable	222
Sales revenue	5,100
Stock investments (short-term)	1,200

Instructions

(a) Prepare an income statement and a retained earnings statement for Ramirez Enterprises for the year ended April 30, 2014.

(b) Prepare a classified balance sheet for Ramirez Enterprises as of April 30, 2014.

(a) Net income	$2,230
(b) Tot. current assets	$4,307
Tot. assets	$9,157

P2-4A Comparative financial statement data for Bosch Corporation and Fielder Corporation, two competitors, appear below. All balance sheet data are as of December 31, 2014.

Compute ratios; comment on relative profitability, liquidity, and solvency.

(LO 2, 4, 5), **AN**

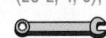

	Bosch Corporation 2014	Fielder Corporation 2014
Net sales	$1,800,000	$620,000
Cost of goods sold	1,175,000	340,000
Operating expenses	283,000	98,000
Interest expense	9,000	3,800
Income tax expense	85,000	36,000
Current assets	407,200	190,336
Plant assets (net)	532,000	139,728
Current liabilities	66,325	33,716
Long-term liabilities	108,500	40,684
Net cash provided by operating activities	138,000	36,000
Capital expenditures	90,000	20,000
Dividends paid on common stock	36,000	15,000
Average number of shares outstanding	80,000	50,000

Instructions

(a) Comment on the relative profitability of the companies by computing the net income and earnings per share for each company for 2014.

(b) Comment on the relative liquidity of the companies by computing working capital and the current ratio for each company for 2014.

(c) Comment on the relative solvency of the companies by computing the debt to assets ratio and the free cash flow for each company for 2014.

P2-5A Here and on page 84 are financial statements of Ogleby Company.

Compute and interpret liquidity, solvency, and profitability ratios.

(LO 2, 4, 5), **AP**

OGLEBY COMPANY
Income Statement
For the Year Ended December 31, 2014

Net sales	$2,218,500
Cost of goods sold	1,012,400
Selling and administrative expenses	906,000
Interest expense	78,000
Income tax expense	69,000
Net income	$ 153,100

OGLEBY COMPANY
Balance Sheet
December 31, 2014

Assets

Current assets	
Cash	$ 60,100
Debt investments	84,000
Accounts receivable (net)	169,800
Inventory	145,000
Total current assets	458,900
Plant assets (net)	575,300
Total assets	$1,034,200

Liabilities and Stockholders' Equity

Current liabilities		
Accounts payable	$ 160,000	
Income taxes payable	35,500	
Total current liabilities		195,500
Bonds payable		200,000
Total liabilities		395,500
Stockholders' equity		
Common stock	350,000	
Retained earnings	288,700	
Total stockholders' equity		638,700
Total liabilities and stockholders' equity		$1,034,200

Additional information: The net cash provided by operating activities for 2014 was $190,800. The cash used for capital expenditures was $92,000. The cash used for dividends was $31,000. The average number of shares outstanding during the year was 50,000.

Instructions

(a) Compute the following values and ratios for 2014. (We provide the results from 2013 for comparative purposes.)
  (i) Working capital. (2013: $160,500)
  (ii) Current ratio. (2013: 1.65:1)
  (iii) Free cash flow. (2013: $48,700)
  (iv) Debt to assets ratio. (2013: 31%)
  (v) Earnings per share. (2013: $3.15)
(b) Using your calculations from part (a), discuss changes from 2013 in liquidity, solvency, and profitability.

Compute and interpret liquidity, solvency, and profitability ratios.

(LO 2, 4, 5), **AP**

P2-6A Condensed balance sheet and income statement data for Sadecki Corporation are presented here and on the next page.

SADECKI CORPORATION
Balance Sheets
December 31

Assets	2014	2013
Cash	$ 28,000	$ 20,000
Receivables (net)	70,000	62,000
Other current assets	90,000	73,000
Long-term investments	62,000	60,000
Property, plant, and equipment (net)	510,000	470,000
Total assets	$760,000	$685,000

Liabilities and Stockholders' Equity	2014	2013
Current liabilities	$ 75,000	$ 70,000
Long-term liabilities	80,000	90,000
Common stock	330,000	300,000
Retained earnings	275,000	225,000
Total liabilities and stockholders' equity	$760,000	$685,000

SADECKI CORPORATION
Income Statements
For the Years Ended December 31

	2014	2013
Sales revenue	$750,000	$680,000
Cost of goods sold	440,000	400,000
Operating expenses (including income taxes)	240,000	220,000
Net income	$ 70,000	$ 60,000

Additional information:

Net cash provided by operating activities	$82,000	$56,000
Cash used for capital expenditures	$45,000	$38,000
Dividends paid	$20,000	$15,000
Average number of shares outstanding	33,000	30,000

Instructions

Compute these values and ratios for 2013 and 2014.
(a) Earnings per share.
(b) Working capital.
(c) Current ratio.
(d) Debt to assets ratio.
(e) Free cash flow.
(f) ◀▬▬▶Based on the ratios calculated, discuss briefly the improvement or lack thereof in financial position and operating results from 2013 to 2014 of Sadecki Corporation.

P2-7A Selected financial data of two competitors, Target and Wal-Mart, are presented here. (All dollars are in millions.) Suppose the data were taken from the 2014 financial statements of each company.

Compute ratios and compare liquidity, solvency, and profitability for two companies.

(LO 2, 4, 5), **AP**

	Target (1/31/14)	Wal-Mart (1/31/14)
	Income Statement Data for Year	
Net sales	$64,948	$401,244
Cost of goods sold	44,157	306,158
Selling and administrative expenses	16,389	76,651
Interest expense	894	2,103
Other income	28	4,213
Income taxes	1,322	7,145
Net income	$ 2,214	$ 13,400

	Target	Wal-Mart
	Balance Sheet Data (End of Year)	
Current assets	$17,488	$ 48,949
Noncurrent assets	26,618	114,480
Total assets	$44,106	$163,429
Current liabilities	$10,512	$ 55,390
Long-term liabilities	19,882	42,754
Total stockholders' equity	13,712	65,285
Total liabilities and stockholders' equity	$44,106	$163,429
Net cash provided by operating activities	$4,430	$23,147
Cash paid for capital expenditures	$3,547	$11,499
Dividends declared and paid on common stock	$465	$3,746
Average shares outstanding (millions)	774	3,951

Instructions

For each company, compute these values and ratios.
(a) Working capital.
(b) Current ratio.
(c) Debt to assets ratio.
(d) Free cash flow.
(e) Earnings per share.
(f) Compare the liquidity and solvency of the two companies.

P2-8A A friend of yours, Sue Yaeger, recently completed an undergraduate degree in science and has just started working with a biotechnology company. Sue tells you that the owners of the business are trying to secure new sources of financing which are needed in order for the company to proceed with development of a new health care product. Sue said that her boss told her that the company must put together a report to present to potential investors.

Comment on the objectives and qualitative characteristics of financial reporting.

(LO 6, 7), **E**

Sue thought that the company should include in this package the detailed scientific findings related to the Phase I clinical trials for this product. She said, "I know that the biotech industry sometimes has only a 10% success rate with new products, but if we report all the scientific findings, everyone will see what a sure success this is going to be! The president was talking about the importance of following some set of accounting principles. Why do we need to look at some accounting rules? What they need to realize is that we have scientific results that are quite encouraging, some of the most talented employees around, and the start of some really great customer relationships. We haven't made any sales yet, but we will. We just need the funds to get through all the clinical testing and get government approval for our product. Then these investors will be quite happy that they bought in to our company early!"

Instructions

(a) What is accounting information? Explain to Sue what is meant by generally accepted accounting principles.

(b) Comment on how Sue's suggestions for what should be reported to prospective investors conforms to the qualitative characteristics of accounting information. Do you think that the things that Sue wants to include in the information for investors will conform to financial reporting guidelines?

Problems: Set B

Prepare a classified balance sheet.
(LO 1), **AP**

P2-1B Suppose the following items are taken from the 2014 balance sheet of Starbucks Corporation. (All dollars are in millions.)

Goodwill	$ 477
Common stock	40
Equipment	3,036
Accounts payable	391
Stock investments (long-term)	280
Accounts receivable	288
Prepaid rent	278
Debt investments (current)	157
Retained earnings	2,244
Cash	281
Notes payable (noncurrent)	550
Notes payable (current)	1,468
Unearned sales revenue (current)	297
Bonds payable	354
Inventory	692
Accumulated depreciation—equipment	145

Tot. current assets $1,696
Tot. assets $5,344

Instructions

Prepare a classified balance sheet for Starbucks Corporation as of September 30, 2014.

Prepare financial statements.
(LO 1, 3), **AP**

P2-2B These items are taken from the financial statements of Mueller, Inc.

Prepaid insurance	$ 2,400
Equipment	30,000
Salaries and wages expense	34,000
Utilities expense	2,100
Accumulated depreciation—equipment	7,600
Accounts payable	7,200
Cash	6,100
Accounts receivable	2,900
Salaries and wages payable	3,000
Common stock	6,000
Depreciation expense	4,300
Retained earnings (beginning)	14,000

Dividends	2,600
Service revenue	51,000
Maintenance and repairs expense	2,600
Insurance expense	1,800

Instructions

Prepare an income statement, a retained earnings statement, and a classified balance sheet as of December 31, 2014.

P2-3B You are provided with the following information for Vern Corporation, effective as of its April 30, 2014, year-end.

Prepare financial statements.
(LO 1, 3), **AP**

Accounts payable	$ 3,100
Accounts receivable	10,150
Accumulated depreciation—equipment	6,600
Depreciation expense	3,200
Cash	20,955
Common stock	20,000
Dividends	2,800
Equipment	24,250
Sales revenue	20,450
Income tax expense	700
Income taxes payable	300
Interest expense	350
Interest payable	175
Notes payable (due in 2018)	4,700
Prepaid rent	380
Rent expense	660
Retained earnings, beginning	13,960
Salaries and wages expense	5,840

Instructions

(a) Prepare an income statement and a retained earnings statement for Vern Corporation for the year ended April 30, 2014.

(b) Prepare a classified balance sheet for Vern as of April 30, 2014.

(a) Net income	$9,700
(b) Tot. current assets	$31,485
Tot. assets	$49,135

P2-4B Comparative statement data for Omaz Company and Wise Company, two competitors, are presented below. All balance sheet data are as of December 31, 2014.

Compute ratios; comment on relative profitability, liquidity, and solvency.
(LO 2, 4, 5), **AN**

	Omaz Company 2014	Wise Company 2014
Net sales	$450,000	$900,000
Cost of goods sold	225,000	450,000
Operating expenses	130,000	150,000
Interest expense	6,000	10,000
Income tax expense	15,000	75,000
Current assets	180,000	700,000
Plant assets (net)	600,000	800,000
Current liabilities	75,000	230,000
Long-term liabilities	190,000	200,000
Net cash provided by operating activities	46,000	180,000
Capital expenditures	20,000	50,000
Dividends paid	-0-	5,000
Average number of shares outstanding	200,000	500,000

Instructions

(a) Compute the net income and earnings per share for each company for 2014.

(b) Comment on the relative liquidity of the companies by computing working capital and the current ratio for each company for 2014.

(c) Comment on the relative solvency of the companies by computing the debt to assets ratio and the free cash flow for each company for 2014.

Compute and interpret liquidity, solvency, and profitability ratios.

(LO 2, 4, 5), **AP**

P2-5B The financial statements of Divine Company are presented here.

DIVINE COMPANY
Income Statement
For the Year Ended December 31, 2014

Net sales	$700,000
Cost of goods sold	400,000
Selling and administrative expenses	150,000
Interest expense	7,800
Income tax expense	43,000
Net income	$ 99,200

DIVINE COMPANY
Balance Sheet
December 31, 2014

Assets

Current assets	
Cash	$ 22,100
Debt investments	34,800
Accounts receivable (net)	90,700
Inventory	155,000
Total current assets	302,600
Plant assets (net)	461,300
Total assets	$763,900

Liabilities and Stockholders' Equity

Current liabilities	
Accounts payable	$119,700
Income taxes payable	29,000
Total current liabilities	148,700
Bonds payable	110,000
Total liabilities	258,700
Stockholders' equity	
Common stock	170,000
Retained earnings	335,200
Total stockholders' equity	505,200
Total liabilities and stockholders' equity	$763,900
Net cash provided by operating activities	$61,300
Capital expenditures	$42,000
Dividends paid	$10,000
Average number of shares outstanding	65,000

Instructions

(a) Compute the following values and ratios for 2014. (We provide the results from 2013 for comparative purposes.)
   (i) Current ratio. (2013: 2.4:1)
   (ii) Working capital. (2013: $178,000)
   (iii) Debt to assets ratio. (2013: 31%)
   (iv) Free cash flow. (2013: $13,000)
   (v) Earnings per share. (2013: $1.35)

(b) Using your calculations from part (a), discuss changes from 2013 in liquidity, solvency, and profitability.

P2-6B   Condensed balance sheet and income statement data for Fellini Corporation are presented below.

Compute and interpret liquidity, solvency, and profitability ratios.
(LO 2, 4, 5), AP

FELLINI CORPORATION
Balance Sheets
December 31

Assets	2014	2013
Cash	$ 50,000	$ 30,000
Receivables (net)	80,000	55,000
Other current assets	74,000	73,000
Long-term investments	78,000	54,000
Property, plant, and equipment (net)	520,000	407,000
Total assets	$802,000	$619,000

Liabilities and Stockholders' Equity	2014	2013
Current liabilities	$ 88,000	$ 65,000
Long-term liabilities	90,000	70,000
Common stock	370,000	320,000
Retained earnings	254,000	164,000
Total liabilities and stockholders' equity	$802,000	$619,000

FELLINI CORPORATION
Income Statements
For the Years Ended December 31

	2014	2013
Sales revenue	$770,000	$800,000
Cost of goods sold	420,000	400,000
Operating expenses (including income taxes)	250,000	287,000
Net income	$100,000	$113,000
Net cash provided by operating activities	$165,000	$178,000
Cash used for capital expenditures	$85,000	$45,000
Dividends paid	$20,000	$13,000
Average number of shares outstanding	370,000	320,000

Instructions

Compute the following values and ratios for 2013 and 2014.
(a) Earnings per share.
(b) Working capital.
(c) Current ratio.
(d) Debt to assets ratio.
(e) Free cash flow.
(f) Based on the ratios calculated, discuss briefly the improvement or lack thereof in the financial position and operating results of Fellini from 2013 to 2014.

P2-7B   Selected financial data of two competitors, Home Depot and Lowe's, are presented here. (All dollars are in millions.) Suppose the data were taken from the 2014 financial statements of each company.

Compute ratios and compare liquidity, solvency, and profitability for two companies.
(LO 2, 4, 5), AP

	Home Depot	Lowe's
	Income Statement Data for Year	
Net sales	$77,349	$48,283
Cost of goods sold	51,352	31,556
Selling and administrative expenses	18,570	12,022
Interest expense	696	239
Other income	74	45
Income taxes	2,410	1,702
Net income	$ 4,395	$ 2,809

	Home Depot	Lowe's
	Balance Sheet Data (End of Year)	
Current assets	$14,674	$ 8,686
Noncurrent assets	29,650	22,183
Total assets	$44,324	$30,869
Current liabilities	$12,706	$ 7,751
Long-term liabilities	13,904	7,020
Total stockholders' equity	17,714	16,098
Total liabilities and stockholders' equity	$44,324	$30,869
Net cash provided by operating activities	$5,727	$4,347
Cash paid for capital expenditures	$3,558	$4,010
Dividends paid	$1,709	$428
Average shares outstanding	1,849	1,481

Instructions

For each company, compute these values and ratios.
(a) Working capital.
(b) Current ratio. (Round to two decimal places.)
(c) Debt to assets ratio.
(d) Free cash flow.
(e) Earnings per share.
(f) ▬▬▬➤Compare the liquidity, profitability, and solvency of the two companies.

Comment on the objectives and qualitative characteristics of accounting information.
(LO 6, 7), E

P2-8B Yocum Software International Inc., headquartered in Toronto, specializes in Internet safety and computer security products for both the home and commercial markets. In a recent balance sheet, it reported a deficit (negative retained earnings) of US$5,678,288. It has reported only net losses since its inception. In spite of these losses, Yocum's common shares have traded anywhere from a high of $3.70 to a low of $0.32 on the Canadian Venture Exchange.

Yocum's financial statements have historically been prepared in Canadian dollars. Recently, the company adopted the U.S. dollar as its reporting currency.

Instructions ▬▬▬➤
(a) What is the objective of financial reporting? How does this objective meet or not meet Yocum's investors' needs?
(b) Why would investors want to buy Yocum's shares if the company has consistently reported losses over the last few years? Include in your answer an assessment of the relevance of the information reported on Yocum's financial statements.
(c) Comment on how the change in reporting information from Canadian dollars to U.S. dollars likely affected the readers of Yocum's financial statements. Include in your answer an assessment of the comparability of the information.

Problems: Set C

Visit the book's companion website, at **www.wiley.com/college/kimmel**, and choose the Student Companion site to access Problem Set C.

Continuing Cookie Chronicle

(*Note:* This is a continuation of the Cookie Chronicle from Chapter 1.)

CCC2 After investigating the different forms of business organization, Natalie Koebel decides to operate her business as a corporation, Cookie Creations Inc., and she begins the process of getting her business running.

While at a trade show, Natalie is introduced to Gerry Richards, operations manager of "Biscuits," a national food retailer. After much discussion, Gerry asks Natalie to consider being Biscuits' major supplier of oatmeal chocolate chip cookies. He provides Natalie with the most recent copy of the financial statements of Biscuits. He expects that Natalie will need to supply Biscuits' Watertown warehouse with approximately 1,500 dozen cookies a week. Natalie is to send Biscuits a monthly invoice, and she will be paid approximately 30 days from the date the invoice is received in Biscuits' Chicago office.

Natalie is thrilled with the offer. However, she has recently read in the newspaper that Biscuits has a reputation for selling cookies and donuts with high amounts of sugar and fat, and as a result, consumer demand for the company's products has decreased.

Instructions

Natalie has several questions. Answer the following questions for Natalie.
(a) What type of information does each financial statement provide?
(b) What financial statements would Natalie need in order to evaluate whether Biscuits will have enough cash to meet its current liabilities? Explain what to look for.
(c) What financial statements would Natalie need in order to evaluate whether Biscuits will be able to survive over a long period of time? Explain what to look for.
(d) What financial statement would Natalie need in order to evaluate Biscuits' profitability? Explain what to look for.
(e) Where can Natalie find out whether Biscuits has outstanding debt? How can Natalie determine whether Biscuits would be able to meet its interest and debt payments on any debts it has?
(f) How could Natalie determine whether Biscuits pays a dividend?
(g) In deciding whether to go ahead with this opportunity, are there other areas of concern that Natalie should be aware of?

Broadening Your Perspective

Financial Reporting and Analysis

FINANCIAL REPORTING PROBLEM: *Tootsie Roll Industries, Inc.*

BYP2-1 The financial statements of Tootsie Roll Industries, Inc., appear in Appendix A at the end of this textbook.

Instructions

Answer the following questions using the financial statements and the notes to the financial statements.
(a) What were Tootsie Roll's total current assets at December 31, 2011, and December 31, 2010?
(b) Are the assets included in current assets listed in the proper order? Explain.
(c) How are Tootsie Roll's assets classified?
(d) What were Tootsie Roll's current liabilities at December 31, 2011, and December 31, 2010?

COMPARATIVE ANALYSIS PROBLEM: *Tootsie Roll vs. Hershey*

BYP2-2 The financial statements of The Hershey Company appear in Appendix B, following the financial statements for Tootsie Roll in Appendix A. Assume Hershey's average number of shares outstanding was 227,514,000, and Tootsie Roll's was 56,997,000.

Instructions

(a) For each company calculate the following values for 2011.
    (1) Working capital.   (4) Free cash flow.
    (2) Current ratio.   (5) Earnings per share.
    (3) Debt to assets ratio.
    (*Hint:* When calculating free cash flow, **do not** consider business acquisitions to be part of capital expenditures.)
(b) Based on your findings above, discuss the relative liquidity and solvency of the two companies.

RESEARCH CASE

BYP2-3 The July 6, 2011, edition of the *Wall Street Journal Online* includes an article by Michael Rapoport entitled "U.S. Firms Clash Over Accounting Rules." The article discusses why some U.S. companies favored adoption of International Financial Reporting Standards (IFRS) while other companies opposed it.

Instructions

Read the article and answer the following questions.
(a) The articles says that the switch to IFRS tends to be favored by "larger companies, big accounting firms, and rule makers." What reasons are given for favoring the switch?
(b) What two reasons are given by many smaller companies that oppose the switch?
(c) What criticism of IFRS is raised with regard to regulated companies?
(d) Explain what is meant by "condorsement."

INTERPRETING FINANCIAL STATEMENTS

BYP2-4 The following information was reported by Gap, Inc. in its 2010 annual report.

	2010	2009	2008	2007	2006
Total assets (millions)	$7,065	$7,985	$7,564	$7,838	$8,544
Working capital	$1,831	$2,533	$1,847	$1,653	$2,757
Current ratio	1.87:1	2.19:1	1.86:1	1.68:1	2.21:1
Debt to assets ratio	.42:1	.39:1	.42:1	.45:1	.39:1
Earnings per share	$1.89	$1.59	$1.35	$1.05	$0.94

(a) Determine the overall percentage decrease in Gap's total assets from 2006 to 2010. What was the average decrease per year?
(b) Comment on the change in Gap's liquidity. Does working capital or the current ratio appear to provide a better indication of Gap's liquidity? What might explain the change in Gap's liquidity during this period?
(c) Comment on the change in Gap's solvency during this period.
(d) Comment on the change in Gap's profitability during this period. How might this affect your prediction about Gap's future profitability?

REAL-WORLD FOCUS

BYP2-5 *Purpose:* Identify summary liquidity, solvency, and profitability information about companies, and compare this information across companies in the same industry.

Address: **http://biz.yahoo.com/i**, or go to **www.wiley.com/college/kimmel**

Steps
1. Type in a company name, or use the index to find a company name. Choose **Profile**. Choose **Key Statistics**. Perform instruction (a) below.
2. Go back to **Profile**. Click on the company's particular industry behind the heading "Industry." Perform instructions (b), (c), and (d).

Instructions

Answer the following questions.
(a) What is the company's name? What was the company's current ratio and debt to equity ratio (a variation of the debt to assets ratio)?
(b) What is the company's industry?
(c) What is the name of a competitor? What is the competitor's current ratio and its debt to equity ratio?
(d) Based on these measures, which company is more liquid? Which company is more solvent?

BYP2-6 The Feature Story described the dramatic effect that investment bulletin boards are having on the investment world. This exercise will allow you to evaluate a bulletin board discussing a company of your choice.

Address: **http://biz.yahoo.com/i**, or go to **www.wiley.com/college/kimmel**

Steps

1. Type in a company name, or use the index to find a company name.
2. Choose **Msgs** or **Message Board**. (for messages).
3. Read the 10 most recent messages.

Instructions

Answer the following questions.

(a) State the nature of each of these messages (e.g., offering advice, criticizing company, predicting future results, ridiculing other people who have posted messages).

(b) For those messages that expressed an opinion about the company, was evidence provided to support the opinion?

(c) What effect do you think it would have on bulletin board discussions if the participants provided their actual names? Do you think this would be a good policy?

Critical Thinking

DECISION-MAKING ACROSS THE ORGANIZATION

BYP2-7   As a financial analyst in the planning department for Shonrock Industries, Inc., you have been requested to develop some key ratios from the comparative financial statements. This information is to be used to convince creditors that Shonrock Industries, Inc. is liquid, solvent, and profitable, and that it deserves their continued support. Lenders are particularly concerned about the company's ability to continue as a going concern.

Here are the data requested and the computations developed from the financial statements:

	2014	2013
Current ratio	3.1	2.1
Working capital	Up 22%	Down 7%
Free cash flow	Up 25%	Up 18%
Debt to assets ratio	0.60	0.70
Net income	Up 32%	Down 8%
Earnings per share	$2.40	$1.15

Instructions

Shonrock Industries, Inc. asks you to prepare brief comments stating how each of these items supports the argument that its financial health is improving. The company wishes to use these comments to support presentation of data to its creditors. With the class divided into groups, prepare the comments as requested, giving the implications and the limitations of each item regarding Shonrock's financial well-being.

COMMUNICATION ACTIVITY

BYP2-8   F. P. Fernetti is the chief executive officer of Tomorrow's Products. Fernetti is an expert engineer but a novice in accounting.

Instructions

Write a letter to F. P. Fernetti that explains (a) the three main types of ratios; (b) examples of each, how they are calculated, and what they measure; and (c) the bases for comparison in analyzing Tomorrow's Products' financial statements.

ETHICS CASE

BYP2-9   At one time, Boeing closed a giant deal to acquire another manufacturer, McDonnell Douglas. Boeing paid for the acquisition by issuing shares of its own stock to the stockholders of McDonnell Douglas. In order for the deal not to be revoked, the value of Boeing's stock could not decline below a certain level for a number of months after the deal.

During the first half of the year, Boeing suffered significant cost overruns because of inefficiencies in its production methods. Had these problems been disclosed in the quarterly financial statements during the first and second quarters of the year, the company's stock most likely would have plummeted, and the deal would have been revoked. Company managers spent considerable time debating when the bad news should be disclosed. One public relations manager suggested that the company's problems be revealed on the date of either Princess Diana's or Mother Teresa's funeral, in the hope that it would be lost among those big stories that day. Instead, the company waited until October 22 of that year to announce a $2.6 billion write-off due to cost overruns. Within one week, the company's stock price had fallen 20%, but by this time the McDonnell Douglas deal could not be reversed.

Instructions

Answer the following questions.
(a) Who are the stakeholders in this situation?
(b) What are the ethical issues?
(c) What assumptions or principles of accounting are relevant to this case?
(d) Do you think it is ethical to try to "time" the release of a story so as to diminish its effect?
(e) What would you have done if you were the chief executive officer of Boeing?
(f) Boeing's top management maintains that it did not have an obligation to reveal its problems during the first half of the year. What implications does this have for investors and analysts who follow Boeing's stock?

ALL ABOUT YOU

BYP2-10 Every company needs to plan in order to move forward. Its top management must consider where it wants the company to be in three to five years. Like a company, you need to think about where you want to be three to five years from now, and you need to start taking steps now in order to get there.

Instructions

Provide responses to each of the following items.
(a) Where would you like to be working in three to five years? Describe your plan for getting there by identifying between five and 10 specific steps that you need to take in order to get there.
(b) In order to get the job you want, you will need a résumé. Your résumé is the equivalent of a company's annual report. It needs to provide relevant and reliable information about your past accomplishments so that employers can decide whether to "invest" in you. Do a search on the Internet to find a good résumé format. What are the basic elements of a résumé?
(c) A company's annual report provides information about a company's accomplishments. In order for investors to use the annual report, the information must be reliable; that is, users must have faith that the information is accurate and believable. How can you provide assurance that the information on your résumé is reliable?
(d) Prepare a résumé assuming that you have accomplished the five to 10 specific steps you identified in part (a). Also, provide evidence that would give assurance that the information is reliable.

FASB CODIFICATION ACTIVITY

BYP2-11 If your school has a subscription to the FASB Codification, go to **http://aaahq.org/ ascLogin.cfm** to log in and prepare responses to the following.

Instructions

(a) Access the glossary ("Master Glossary") at the FASB Codification website to answer the following.
   (1) What is the definition of current assets?
   (2) What is the definition of current liabilities?
(b) A company wants to offset its accounts payable against its cash account and show a cash amount net of accounts payable on its balance sheet. Identify the criteria (found in the FASB Codification) under which a company has the right of set off. Does the company have the right to offset accounts payable against the cash account?

CONSIDERING PEOPLE, PLANET, AND PROFIT

BYP2-12 Auditors provide a type of certification of corporate financial statements. Certification is used in many other aspects of business as well. For example, it plays a critical role in the sustainability movement. The February 7, 2012, issue of the *New York Times* contained an article by S. Amanda Caudill entitled "Better Lives in Better Coffee," which discusses the role of certification in the coffee business.

Address: **http://scientistatwork.blogs.nytimes.com/2012/02/07/better-lives-in-better-coffee/**

Instructions

Read the article and answer the following questions.

(a) The article mentions three different certification types that coffee growers can obtain from three different certification bodies. Using financial reporting as an example, what potential problems might the existence of multiple certification types present to coffee purchasers?

(b) According to the author, which certification is most common among coffee growers? What are the possible reasons for this?

(c) What social and environmental benefits are coffee certifications trying to achieve? Are there also potential financial benefits to the parties involved?

Answers to Insight and Accounting Across the Organization Questions

p. 59 Can a Company Be Too Liquid? Q: What can various company managers do to ensure that working capital is managed efficiently to maximize net income? **A:** Marketing and sales managers must understand that by extending generous repayment terms, they are expanding the company's receivables balance and slowing the company's cash flow. Production managers must strive to minimize the amount of excess inventory on hand. Managers must coordinate efforts to speed up the collection of receivables, while also ensuring that the company pays its payables on time but never too early.

p. 60 When Debt Is Good Q: Discuss the difference in the debt to assets ratio of Microsoft and General Motors. **A:** Microsoft has a very low debt to assets ratio. The company is in a rapidly changing industry and thus should try to minimize the risk associated with increased debt. Also, because Microsoft generates significant amounts of cash and has minimal needs for large investments in plant assets, it does not need to borrow a lot of cash. General Motors needs to make huge investments in plant assets, and it has a very large credit operation. Thus, it has large borrowing needs.

p. 63 The Korean Discount Q: What is meant by the phrase "make the country's businesses more transparent"? Why would increasing transparency spur economic growth? **A:** Transparency refers to the extent to which outsiders have knowledge regarding a company's financial performance and financial position. If a company lacks transparency, its financial reports do not adequately inform investors of critical information that is needed to make investment decisions. If corporate transparency is increased, investors will be more willing to supply the financial capital that businesses need in order to grow, which would spur the country's economic growth.

p. 64 What Do These Companies Have in Common? Q: What problems might Best Buy's year-end create for analysts? **A:** First, if Best Buy's competitors use a different year-end, then when you compare their financial results, you are not comparing performance over the same period of time or financial position at the same point in time. Also, by not picking a particular date, the number of weeks in Best Buy's fiscal year will change. For example, fiscal years 2008 and 2009 had 52 weeks, but fiscal year 2007 had 53 weeks.

Answers to Self-Test Questions

1. d **2.** a **3.** c **4.** c **5.** b **6.** a ($26,000 − $4,000) **7.** c **8.** b **9.** d **10.** d **11.** a **12.** a
13. c **14.** c **15.** b

A Look at IFRS

The classified balance sheet, although generally required internationally, contains certain variations in format when reporting under IFRS.

LEARNING OBJECTIVE 8

Compare the classified balance sheet format under GAAP and IFRS.

KEY POINTS

• IFRS recommends but does not require the use of the title "statement of financial position" rather than balance sheet.

- The format of statement of financial position information is often presented differently under IFRS. Although no specific format is required, most companies that follow IFRS present statement of financial position information in this order:
  - Noncurrent assets
  - Current assets
  - Equity
  - Noncurrent liabilities
  - Current liabilities
- IFRS requires a classified statement of financial position except in very limited situations. IFRS follows the same guidelines as this textbook for distinguishing between current and noncurrent assets and liabilities.
- Under IFRS, current assets are usually listed in the reverse order of liquidity. For example, under GAAP cash is listed first, but under IFRS it is listed last.
- Some companies report the subtotal **net assets**, which equals total assets minus total liabilities. See, for example, the statement of financial position of Zetar in Appendix C.
- IFRS has many differences in terminology that you will notice in this textbook. For example, in the sample statement of financial position illustrated below, notice in the investment category that stock is called shares, and in the equity section common stock is called share capital—ordinary.

FRANKLIN CORPORATION
Statement of Financial Position
October 31, 2014

Assets

Intangible assets			
Patents			$ 3,100
Property, plant, and equipment			
Land		$10,000	
Equipment	$24,000		
Less: Accumulated depreciation—equipment	5,000	19,000	29,000
Long-term investments			
Share investments		5,200	
Investment in real estate		2,000	7,200
Current assets			
Prepaid insurance		400	
Supplies		2,100	
Inventory		3,000	
Notes receivable		1,000	
Accounts receivable		7,000	
Debt investments		2,000	
Cash		6,600	22,100
Total assets			$61,400

Equity and Liabilities

Equity			
Share capital—ordinary		$20,000	
Retained earnings		14,050	$34,050
Non-current liabilities			
Mortgage payable		10,000	
Notes payable		1,300	11,300
Current liabilities			
Notes payable		11,000	
Accounts payable		2,100	
Salaries and wages payable		1,600	
Unearned sales revenue		900	
Interest payable		450	16,050
Total equity and liabilities			$61,400

- Both IFRS and GAAP require disclosures about (1) accounting policies followed, (2) judgments that management has made in the process of applying the entity's accounting policies, and (3) the key assumptions and estimation uncertainty that could result in a material adjustment to the carrying amounts of assets and liabilities within the next financial year.
- Comparative prior period information must be presented and financial statements must be prepared annually.
- Both GAAP and IFRS are increasing the use of fair value to report assets. However, at this point IFRS has adopted it more broadly. As examples, under IFRS companies can apply fair value to property, plant, and equipment; natural resources; and in some cases intangible assets.
- Recently, the IASB and FASB completed the first phase of a jointly created conceptual framework. In this first phase, they agreed on the objective of financial reporting and a common set of desired qualitative characteristics. These were presented in the Chapter 2 discussion.
- The monetary unit assumption is part of each framework. However, the unit of measure will vary depending on the currency used in the country in which the company is incorporated (e.g., Chinese yuan, Japanese yen, and British pound).
- The economic entity assumption is also part of each framework, although some cultural differences result in differences in its application. For example, in Japan many companies have formed alliances that are so strong that they act similar to related corporate divisions, although they are not actually part of the same company.

LOOKING TO THE FUTURE

The IASB and the FASB are working on a project to converge their standards related to financial statement presentation. A key feature of the proposed framework is that each of the statements will be organized in the same format, to separate an entity's financing activities from its operating and investing activities and, further, to separate financing activities into transactions with owners and creditors. Thus, the same classifications used in the statement of financial position would also be used in the income statement and the statement of cash flows. The project has three phases. You can follow the joint financial presentation project at the following link: **http://www.fasb.org/project/financial_statement_presentation.shtml**.

The IASB and the FASB face a difficult task in attempting to update, modify, and complete a converged conceptual framework. For example, how do companies choose between information that is highly relevant but difficult to verify versus information that is less relevant but easy to verify? How do companies define control when developing a definition of an asset? Is a liability the future sacrifice itself or the obligation to make the sacrifice? Should a single measurement method, such as historical cost or fair value, be used, or does it depend on whether it is an asset or liability that is being measured? It appears that the new document will be a significant improvement over its predecessors and will lead to principle-based standards, which will help financial statement users make better decisions.

IFRS PRACTICE

IFRS SELF-TEST QUESTIONS

1. Which of the following statements is **false**?
   (a) The monetary unit assumption is used under IFRS.
   (b) Under IFRS, companies sometimes net liabilities against assets to report "net assets."
   (c) The FASB and IASB are working on a joint conceptual framework project.
   (d) Under IFRS, the statement of financial position is usually referred to as the statement of assets and equity.
2. A company has purchased a tract of land and expects to build a production plant on the land in approximately 5 years. During the 5 years before construction, the land will be idle. Under IFRS, the land should be reported as:
   (a) land expense.
   (b) property, plant, and equipment.
   (c) an intangible asset.
   (d) a long-term investment.

3. Current assets under IFRS are listed generally:
   (a) by importance.
   (b) in the reverse order of their expected conversion to cash.
   (c) by longevity.
   (d) alphabetically.
4. Companies that use IFRS:
   (a) may report all their assets on the statement of financial position at fair value.
   (b) may offset assets against liabilities and show net assets and net liabilities on their statement of financial positions, rather than the underlying detailed line items.
   (c) may report noncurrent assets before current assets on the statement of financial position.
   (d) do not have any guidelines as to what should be reported on the statement of financial position.
5. Companies that follow IFRS to prepare a statement of financial position generally use the following order of classification:
   (a) current assets, current liabilities, noncurrent assets, noncurrent liabilities, equity.
   (b) noncurrent assets, noncurrent liabilities, current assets, current liabilities, equity.
   (c) noncurrent assets, current assets, equity, noncurrent liabilities, current liabilities.
   (d) equity, noncurrent assets, current assets, noncurrent liabilities, current liabilities.

IFRS CONCEPTS AND APPLICATION

IFRS2-1 In what ways does the format of a statement of financial of position under IFRS often differ from a balance sheet presented under GAAP?

IFRS2-2 Do the IFRS and GAAP conceptual frameworks differ in terms of the objective of financial reporting? Explain.

IFRS2-3 What terms commonly used under IFRS are synonymous with common stock and balance sheet?

IFRS2-4 The statement of financial position for Ruiz Company includes the following accounts (in British pounds): Accounts Receivable £12,500; Prepaid Insurance £3,600; Cash £15,400; Supplies £5,200; and Debt Investments (short-term) £6,700. Prepare the current assets section of the statement of financial position, listing the accounts in proper sequence.

IFRS2-5 Widmer Company recently received the following information related to the company's December 31, 2014, statement of financial position (in Swiss francs).

Inventory	CHF 2,900	Debt investments (short-term)	CHF 120
Cash	13,400	Accumulated depreciation—	
Equipment	21,700	equipment	5,700
Share investments		Accounts receivable	4,300
(long-term)	6,500		

Prepare the assets section of the company's classified statement of financial position.

IFRS2-6 The following information is available for Cole Bowling Alley at December 31, 2014.

Buildings	$128,800	Share Capital—Ordinary	$100,000
Accounts Receivable	14,520	Retained Earnings	15,000
Prepaid Insurance	4,680	Accumulated Depreciation—Buildings	42,600
Cash	18,040	Accounts Payable	12,300
Equipment	62,400	Notes Payable	97,780
Land	64,000	Accumulated Depreciation—Equipment	18,720
Insurance Expense	780	Interest Payable	2,600
Depreciation Expense	7,360	Service Revenue	14,180
Interest Expense	2,600		

Prepare a classified statement of financial position; assume that $13,900 of the notes payable will be paid in 2015.

IFRS2-7 Steve Trevino is interested in comparing the liquidity and solvency of a U.S. software company with a Chinese competitor. Is this possible if the two companies report using different currencies?

INTERNATIONAL COMPARATIVE ANALYSIS PROBLEM: *Tootsie Roll vs. Zetar plc*

IFRS2-8 The financial statements of Zetar plc are presented in Appendix C. The company's complete annual report, including the notes to its financial statements, is available in the Investors section at **www.zetarplc.com**.

Instructions

Identify five differences in the format of the statement of financial position used by Zetar compared to a company, such as Tootsie Roll, that follows GAAP. (Tootsie Roll's financial statements are available in Appendix A.)

Answers to IFRS Self-Test Questions

1. d **2.** d **3.** b **4.** c **5.** c

✔ The Navigator

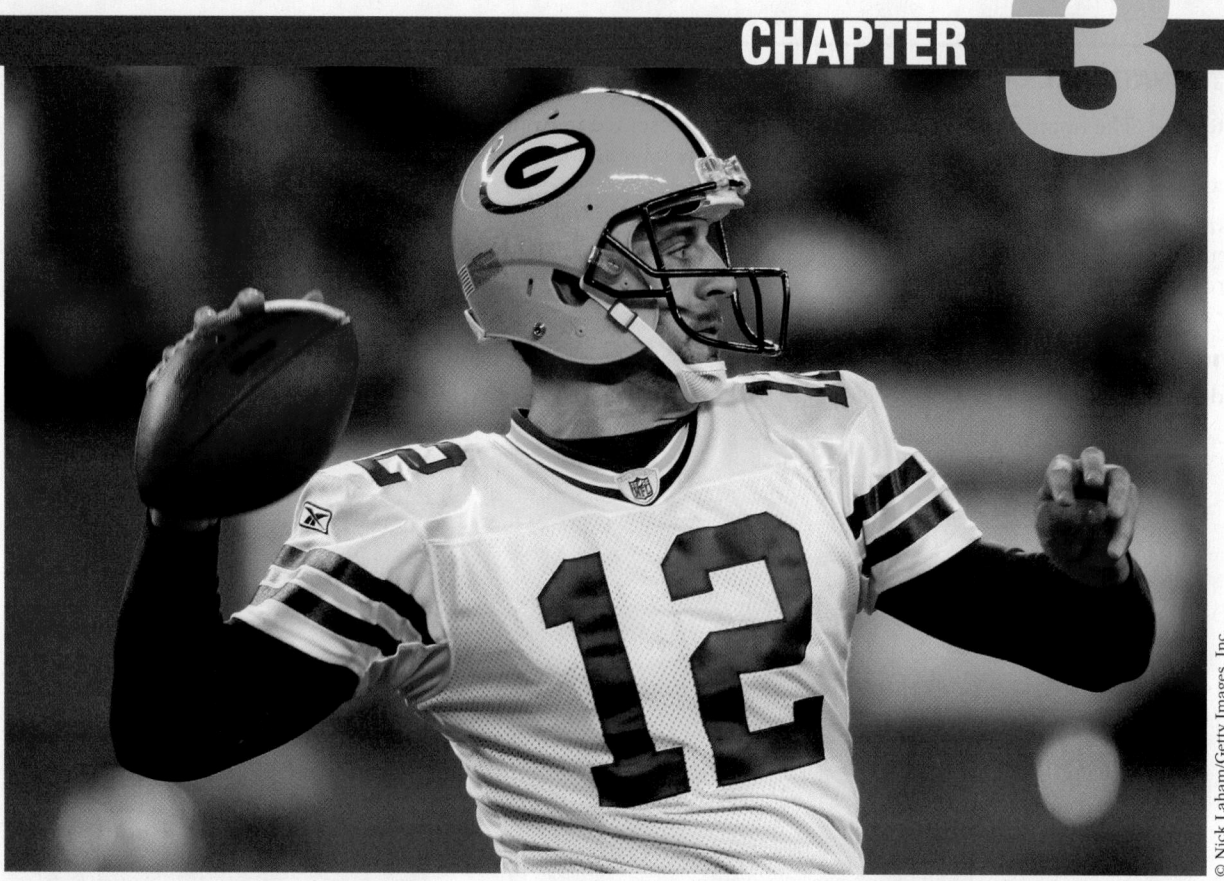

CHAPTER 3

© Nick Laham/Getty Images, Inc.

The Navigator

- Scan Learning Objectives
- Read Feature Story
- Scan Preview
- Read Text and Answer **Do it!**
  ○ p. 110 ○ p. 116 ○ p. 119 ○ p. 128
- Work Using the Decision Toolkit
- Review Summary of Learning Objectives
- Work Comprehensive **Do it!** p. 133
- Answer Self-Test Questions
- Complete Assignments
- Go to WileyPLUS for practice and tutorials

Read A Look at IFRS p. 159

THE ACCOUNTING INFORMATION SYSTEM

LEARNING OBJECTIVES

After studying this chapter, you should be able to:

1 Analyze the effect of business transactions on the basic accounting equation.

2 Explain what an account is and how it helps in the recording process.

3 Define debits and credits and explain how they are used to record business transactions.

4 Identify the basic steps in the recording process.

5 Explain what a journal is and how it helps in the recording process.

6 Explain what a ledger is and how it helps in the recording process.

7 Explain what posting is and how it helps in the recording process.

8 Explain the purposes of a trial balance.

9 Classify cash activities as operating, investing, or financing.

✓ The Navigator

How organized are you financially? Take a short quiz. Answer yes or no to each question:

- Does your wallet contain so many cash machine receipts that you've been declared a walking fire hazard?

- Is your wallet such a mess that it is often faster to fish for money in the crack of your car seat than to dig around in your wallet?

- Was Aaron Rodgers (the quarterback for the Green Bay Packers) playing high school football the last time you verified the accuracy of your bank account?

ACCIDENTS HAPPEN

If you think it is hard to keep track of the many transactions that make up *your* life, imagine how difficult it is for a big corporation to do so. Not only that, but now consider how important it is for a big company to have good accounting records, especially if it has control of *your* life savings. MF Global Holdings Ltd is such a company. As a large investment broker, it held billions of dollars of investments for clients. If you had your life savings invested at MF Global, you might be slightly displeased if you heard this from one of its representatives: "You know, I kind of remember an account for someone with a name like yours—now what did we do with that?"

Unfortunately, that is almost exactly what happened to MF Global's clients shortly before it recently filed for bankruptcy. During the days immediately following the bankruptcy filing, regulators and auditors struggled to piece things together. In the words of one regulator, "Their books are a disaster . . . we're trying to figure out what numbers are real numbers." One company that considered buying an interest in MF Global walked away from the deal because it "couldn't get a sense of what was on the balance sheet." That company said the information that should have been instantly available instead took days to produce.

It now appears that MF Global did not properly segregate customer accounts from company accounts. And, because of its sloppy record-keeping, customers were not protected when the company had financial troubles. Total customer losses were approximately $1 billion. As you can see, accounting matters!

Source: S. Patterson and A. Lucchetti, "Inside the Hunt for MF Global Cash," *Wall Street Journal Online* (November 11, 2011).

✔The Navigator

INSIDE CHAPTER 3 . . .

As indicated in the Feature Story, a reliable information system is a necessity for any company. The purpose of this chapter is to explain and illustrate the features of an accounting information system. The organization and content of the chapter are as follows.

The Accounting Information System			
Accounting Information System	**The Account**	**Steps in the Recording Process**	**The Trial Balance**
• Accounting transactions • Analyzing transactions • Summary of transactions	• Debits and credits • Debit and credit procedures • Stockholders' equity relationships • Summary of debit/credit rules	• The journal • The ledger • Chart of accounts • Posting • The recording process illustrated	• Limitations of a trial balance

✔ The Navigator

The Accounting Information System

LEARNING OBJECTIVE 1

Analyze the effect of business transactions on the basic accounting equation.

The system of collecting and processing transaction data and communicating financial information to decision-makers is known as the **accounting information system**. Factors that shape an accounting information system include the nature of the company's business, the types of transactions, the size of the company, the volume of data, and the information demands of management and others.

Most businesses use computerized accounting systems—sometimes referred to as electronic data processing (EDP) systems. These systems handle all the steps involved in the recording process, from initial data entry to preparation of the financial statements. In order to remain competitive, companies continually improve their accounting systems to provide accurate and timely data for decision-making. For example, in a recent annual report, Tootsie Roll states, "We also invested in additional processing and data storage hardware during the year. We view information technology as a key strategic tool, and are committed to deploying leading edge technology in this area." In addition, many companies have upgraded their accounting information systems in response to the requirements of Sarbanes-Oxley.

In this chapter, in order to emphasize the underlying concepts and principles, we focus on a manual accounting system. The accounting concepts and principles do not change whether a system is computerized or manual.

ACCOUNTING TRANSACTIONS

To use an accounting information system, you need to know which economic events to recognize (record). Not all events are recorded and reported in the financial statements. For example, suppose General Motors hired a new employee and purchased a new computer. Are these events entered in its accounting records? The first event would not be recorded, but the second event would. We call economic events that require recording in the financial statements accounting transactions.

An accounting transaction occurs when assets, liabilities, or stockholders' equity items change as a result of some economic event. The purchase of a computer by General Motors, the payment of rent by Microsoft, and the sale of a multi-day guided trip by Sierra Corporation are examples of events that change a company's assets, liabilities, or stockholders' equity. Illustration 3-1 summarizes the decision process companies use to decide whether or not to record economic events.

Illustration 3-1 Transaction identification process

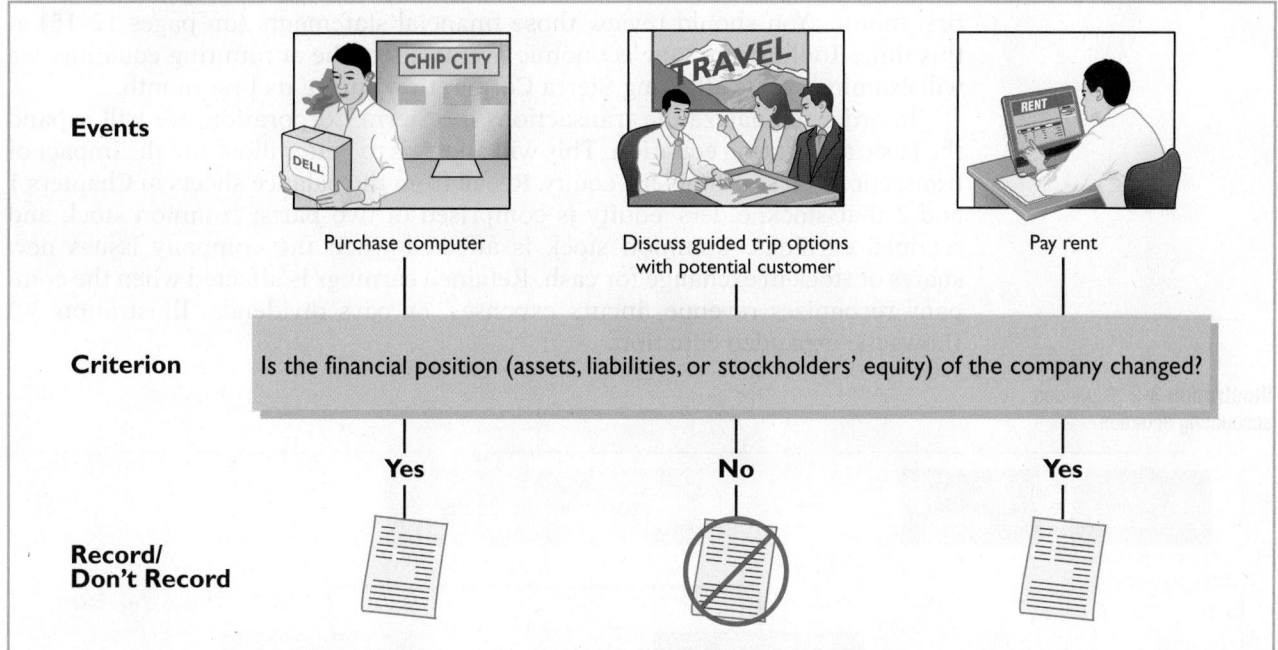

Events — Purchase computer | Discuss guided trip options with potential customer | Pay rent

Criterion — Is the financial position (assets, liabilities, or stockholders' equity) of the company changed?

Yes | No | Yes

Record/ Don't Record

ANALYZING TRANSACTIONS

In Chapter 1, you learned the basic accounting equation:

$$\textbf{Assets = Liabilities + Stockholders' Equity}$$

In this chapter, you will learn how to analyze transactions in terms of their effect on assets, liabilities, and stockholders' equity. **Transaction analysis** is the process of identifying the specific effects of economic events on the accounting equation.

The accounting equation must always balance. Each transaction has a dual (double-sided) effect on the equation. For example, if an individual asset is increased, there must be a corresponding:

Decrease in another asset, *or*

Increase in a specific liability, *or*

Increase in stockholders' equity.

Two or more items could be affected when an asset is increased. For example, if a company purchases a computer for $10,000 by paying $6,000 in cash and signing a note for $4,000, one asset (equipment) increases $10,000, another asset (cash) decreases $6,000, and a liability (notes payable) increases $4,000. The result is that the accounting equation remains in balance—assets increased by a net $4,000 and liabilities increased by $4,000, as shown below.

Assets	=	Liabilities	+	Stockholders' Equity
+$10,000		+$4,000		
− 6,000				
$ 4,000	=	$4,000		

Chapter 1 presented the financial statements for Sierra Corporation for its first month. You should review those financial statements (on pages 12–15) at this time. To illustrate how economic events affect the accounting equation, we will examine events affecting Sierra Corporation during its first month.

In order to analyze the transactions for Sierra Corporation, we will expand the basic accounting equation. This will allow us to better illustrate the impact of transactions on stockholders' equity. Recall from the balance sheets in Chapters 1 and 2 that stockholders' equity is comprised of two parts: common stock and retained earnings. Common stock is affected when the company issues new shares of stock in exchange for cash. Retained earnings is affected when the company recognizes revenue, incurs expenses, or pays dividends. Illustration 3-2 shows the expanded equation.

Illustration 3-2 Expanded accounting equation

If you are tempted to skip ahead after you've read a few of the following transaction analyses, don't do it. Each has something unique to teach, something you'll need later. (We assure you that we've kept them to the minimum needed!)

EVENT (1). INVESTMENT OF CASH BY STOCKHOLDERS. On October 1, cash of $10,000 is invested in the business by investors (primarily your friends and family) in exchange for $10,000 of common stock. This event is an accounting transaction because it results in an increase in both assets and stockholders' equity.

Basic Analysis	The asset Cash is increased $10,000; stockholders' equity (specifically Common Stock) is increased $10,000.

		Assets	=	Liabilities	+	Stockholders' Equity	
Equation Analysis		Cash	=			Common Stock	
	(1)	+$10,000				+$10,000	Issued stock

The equation is in balance after the issuance of common stock. Keeping track of the source of each change in stockholders' equity is essential for later accounting activities. In particular, items recorded in the revenue and expense columns are used for the calculation of net income.

EVENT (2). NOTE ISSUED IN EXCHANGE FOR CASH. On October 1, Sierra borrowed $5,000 from Castle Bank by signing a 3-month, 12%, $5,000 note payable. This transaction results in an equal increase in assets and liabilities. The specific effect of this transaction and the cumulative effect of the first two transactions are:

Basic Analysis	The asset Cash is increased $5,000; the liability Notes Payable is increased $5,000.

		Assets	=	Liabilities	+	Stockholders' Equity
		Cash	=	Notes Payable	+	Common Stock
Equation Analysis		$10,000				$10,000
	(2)	+5,000		+$5,000		
		$15,000	=	$5,000	+	$10,000
				$15,000		

Total assets are now $15,000, and liabilities plus stockholders' equity also total $15,000.

EVENT (3). PURCHASE OF OFFICE EQUIPMENT FOR CASH. On October 2, Sierra purchased equipment by paying $5,000 cash to Superior Equipment Sales Co. This event is a transaction because an equal increase and decrease in Sierra's assets occur.

Basic Analysis	The asset Equipment is increased $5,000; the asset Cash is decreased $5,000.

		Assets			=	Liabilities	+	Stockholders' Equity
		Cash	+	Equipment	=	Notes Payable	+	Common Stock
Equation Analysis		$15,000				$5,000		$10,000
	(3)	−5,000		+$5,000				
		$10,000	+	$5,000	=	$5,000	+	$10,000
			$15,000				$15,000	

The total assets are now $15,000, and liabilities plus stockholders' equity also total $15,000.

EVENT (4). RECEIPT OF CASH IN ADVANCE FROM CUSTOMER. On October 2, Sierra received a $1,200 cash advance from R. Knox, a client. This event is a transaction because Sierra received cash (an asset) for guide services for multi-day trips that are expected to be completed by Sierra in the future. Although Sierra received cash, **it does not record revenue until it has performed the work**. In some industries, such as the magazine and airline industries, customers are expected to prepay. These companies have a liability to the customer until they deliver the magazines or provide the flight. When the company eventually provides the product or service, it records the revenue.

Since Sierra received cash prior to performance of the service, Sierra has a liability for the work due.

Basic Analysis	The asset Cash is increased $1,200; the liability Unearned Service Revenue is increased $1,200 because the service has not been performed yet. That is, when an advance payment is received, an unearned revenue (a liability) should be recorded in order to recognize the obligation that exists.

Equation Analysis

	Assets			=	Liabilities			+	Stockholders' Equity
	Cash	+	Equip-ment	=	Notes Payable	+	Unearned Service Revenue	+	Common Stock
	$10,000		$5,000		$5,000				$10,000
(4)	+1,200						+$1,200		
	$11,200	+	$5,000	=	$5,000	+	$1,200	+	$10,000

$16,200 $16,200

EVENT (5). SERVICES PERFORMED FOR CASH. On October 3, Sierra received $10,000 in cash from Copa Company for guide services performed for a corporate event. This event is a transaction because Sierra received an asset (cash) in exchange for services.

Guide service is the principal revenue-producing activity of Sierra. **Revenue increases stockholders' equity.** This transaction, then, increases both assets and stockholders' equity.

Basic Analysis	The asset Cash is increased $10,000; the revenue Service Revenue is increased $10,000.

Equation Analysis

	Assets			=	Liabilities			+	Stockholders' Equity					
	Cash	+	Equip-ment	=	Notes Pay.	+	Unearned Serv. Rev.	+	Common Stock	+	Rev.	− Exp.	− Div.	
	$11,200		$5,000		$5,000		$1,200		$10,000					
(5)	+10,000										+$10,000			Service Revenue
	$21,200	+	$5,000	=	$5,000	+	$1,200	+	$10,000	+	$10,000			

$26,200 $26,200

Often companies perform services "on account." That is, they perform services for which they are paid at a later date. Revenue, however, is recorded when services are performed. Therefore, revenues would increase when services are performed, even though cash has not been received. Instead of receiving cash, the company receives a different type of asset, an **account receivable**. Accounts receivable represent the right to receive payment at a later date. Suppose that Sierra had provided these services on account rather than for cash. This event would be reported using the accounting equation as:

Assets	=	Liabilities	+	Stockholders' Equity
Accounts Receivable	=			Revenues
+$10,000				+$10,000 Service Revenue

Later, when Sierra collects the $10,000 from the customer, Accounts Receivable decreases by $10,000, and Cash increases by $10,000.

	Assets	=	Liabilities	+	Stockholders' Equity
Cash	Accounts Receivable				
+$10,000	−$10,000				

Note that in this case, revenues are not affected by the collection of cash. Instead we record an exchange of one asset (Accounts Receivable) for a different asset (Cash).

EVENT (6). PAYMENT OF RENT. On October 3, Sierra Corporation paid its office rent for the month of October in cash, $900. This rent payment is a transaction because it results in a decrease in an asset, cash.

Rent is a cost incurred by Sierra Corporation in its effort to generate revenues. It is treated as an expense because it pertains only to the current month. **Expenses decrease stockholders' equity.** Sierra records the rent payment by decreasing cash and increasing expenses to maintain the balance of the accounting equation.

Basic Analysis	The expense account Rent Expense is increased $900 because the payment pertains only to the current month; the asset Cash is decreased $900.

Equation Analysis

		Assets			=	Liabilities			+		Stockholders' Equity				
				Equip-		Notes		Unearned		Common			Retained Earnings		
	Cash	+	ment	=	Pay.	+	Serv. Rev.	+	Stock	+	Rev.	−	Exp.	−	Div.
	$21,200		$5,000		$5,000		$1,200		$10,000		$10,000				
(6)	−900												−$900		Rent Expense
	$20,300	+	$5,000	=	$5,000	+	$1,200	+	$10,000	+	$10,000	−	$900		
		$25,300								$25,300					

EVENT (7). PURCHASE OF INSURANCE POLICY FOR CASH. On October 4, Sierra paid $600 for a one-year insurance policy that will expire next year on September 30. Payments of expenses that will benefit more than one accounting period are identified as assets called prepaid expenses or prepayments.

Basic Analysis	The asset Cash is decreased $600; the asset Prepaid Insurance is increased $600.

Equation Analysis

			Assets				=	Liabilities			+		Stockholders' Equity				
			Prepaid		Equip-		Notes		Unearned		Common			Retained Earnings		
	Cash	+	Insurance	+	ment	=	Pay.	+	Serv. Rev.	+	Stock	+	Rev.	−	Exp.	−	Div.
	$20,300				$5,000		$5,000		$1,200		$10,000		$10,000		$900	
(7)	−600		+$600													
	$19,700	+	$600	+	$5,000	=	$5,000	+	$1,200	+	$10,000	+	$10,000	−	$900	
			$25,300									$25,300				

The balance in total assets did not change; one asset account decreased by the same amount that another increased.

EVENT (8). PURCHASE OF SUPPLIES ON ACCOUNT. On October 5, Sierra purchased an estimated three months of supplies on account from Aero Supply for $2,500. In this case, "on account" means that the company receives goods or services that it will pay for at a later date.

Basic Analysis	The asset Supplies is increased $2,500; the liability Accounts Payable is increased $2,500.

Equation Analysis

	Assets				=	Liabilities			+	Stockholders' Equity			
	Cash +	Supplies +	Prepd. Insur. +	Equip- ment	=	Notes Pay. +	Accounts Payable +	Unearned Serv. Rev. +		Common Stock +	Rev.	− Exp.	− Div.
	$19,700		$600	$5,000		$5,000		$1,200		$10,000	$10,000	$900	
(8)		+$2,500					+$2,500						
	$19,700 +	$2,500 +	$600 +	$5,000	=	$5,000 +	$2,500 +	$1,200	+	$10,000 +	$10,000	− $900	
		$27,800						$27,800					

EVENT (9). HIRING OF NEW EMPLOYEES. On October 9, Sierra hired four new employees to begin work on October 15. Each employee will receive a weekly salary of $500 for a five-day work week, payable every two weeks. Employees will receive their first paychecks on October 26. On the date Sierra hires the employees, there is no effect on the accounting equation because the assets, liabilities, and stockholders' equity of the company have not changed.

Basic Analysis	An accounting transaction has not occurred. There is only an agreement that the employees will begin work on October 15. (See Event (11) for the first payment.)

EVENT (10). PAYMENT OF DIVIDEND. On October 20, Sierra paid a $500 dividend. **Dividends** are a reduction of stockholders' equity but not an expense. Dividends are not included in the calculation of net income. Instead, a dividend is a distribution of the company's assets to its stockholders.

Basic Analysis	The dividends account is increased $500; the asset Cash is decreased $500.

Equation Analysis

	Assets				=	Liabilities			+	Stockholders' Equity			
	Cash +	Sup- plies +	Prepd. Insur. +	Equip- ment	=	Notes Pay. +	Accts. Pay. +	Unearned Serv. Rev. +		Common Stock +	Rev.	− Exp.	− Div.
	$19,700	$2,500	$600	$5,000		$5,000	$2,500	$1,200		$10,000	$10,000	$900	
(10)	−500												− $500
	$19,200 +	$2,500 +	$600 +	$5,000	=	$5,000 +	$2,500 +	$1,200	+	$10,000 +	$10,000	− $900	− $500
		$27,300						$27,300					

EVENT (11). PAYMENT OF CASH FOR EMPLOYEE SALARIES. Employees have worked two weeks, earning $4,000 in salaries, which were paid on October 26.

Salaries and Wages Expense is an expense that reduces stockholders' equity. This event is a transaction because assets and stockholders' equity are affected.

Basic Analysis	The asset Cash is decreased $4,000; the expense account Salaries and Wages Expense is increased $4,000.

Equation Analysis

	Assets				=	Liabilities			+	Stockholders' Equity				
		Sup-	Prepd.	Equip-		Notes	Accts.	Unearned		Common		Retained Earnings		
	Cash +	plies +	Insur. +	ment	=	Pay. +	Pay. +	Serv. Rev. +		Stock +	Rev. −	Exp. −	Div.	
	$19,200	$2,500	$600	$5,000		$5,000	$2,500	$1,200		$10,000	$10,000	$ 900	$500	
(11)	−4,000											− 4,000		Sal./Wages
	$15,200 +	$2,500 +	$600 +	$5,000	=	$5,000 +	$2,500 +	$1,200	+	$10,000 +	$10,000 −	$4,900 −	$500	Expense

$23,300 $23,300

Investor Insight
Why Accuracy Matters

    While most companies record transactions very carefully, the reality is that mistakes still happen. For example, bank regulators fined Bank One Corporation (now JPMorgan Chase) $1.8 million because they felt that the unreliability of the bank's accounting system caused it to violate regulatory requirements.

    Also, in recent years Fannie Mae, the government-chartered mortgage association, announced a series of large accounting errors. These announcements caused alarm among investors, regulators, and politicians because they fear that the errors may suggest larger, undetected problems. This is important because the home-mortgage market depends on Fannie Mae to buy hundreds of billions of dollars of mortgages each year from banks, thus enabling the banks to issue new mortgages.

    Finally, before a major overhaul of its accounting system, the financial records of Waste Management Company were in such disarray that of the company's 57,000 employees, 10,000 were receiving pay slips that were in error.

    The Sarbanes-Oxley Act was created to minimize the occurrence of errors like these by increasing every employee's responsibility for accurate financial reporting.

© Enviromatic/iStockphoto

? In order for these companies to prepare and issue financial statements, their accounting equations (debits and credits) must have been in balance at year-end. How could these errors or misstatements have occurred? (See page 159.)

SUMMARY OF TRANSACTIONS

Illustration 3-3 (page 110) summarizes the transactions of Sierra Corporation to show their cumulative effect on the basic accounting equation. It includes the transaction number in the first column on the left. The right-most column shows the specific effect of any transaction that affects stockholders' equity. Remember that Event (9) did not result in a transaction, so no entry is included for that event. The illustration demonstrates three important points:

1. Each transaction is analyzed in terms of its effect on assets, liabilities, and stockholders' equity.

2. The two sides of the equation must always be equal.

3. The cause of each change in stockholders' equity must be indicated.

Illustration 3-3 Summary of transactions

	Assets				=	Liabilities			+	Stockholders' Equity				
		Sup-	Prepd.	Equip-		Notes	Accts.	Unearned		Common		Retained Earnings		
	Cash +	plies +	Insur. +	ment =		Pay. +	Pay. +	Serv. Rev. +		Stock +	Rev. −	Exp. −	Div.	
(1)	+$10,000				=					+$10,000				Issued stock
(2)	+5,000					+$5,000								
(3)	−5,000			+$5,000										
(4)	+1,200							+$1,200						
(5)	+10,000										+$10,000			Service Revenue
(6)	−900											−$ 900		Rent Expense
(7)	−600		+$600											
(8)	+$2,500						+ $2,500							
(10)	−500												−$500	Dividends
(11)	−4,000											−4,000		Sal./Wages Expense
	$15,200 +	$2,500 +	$600 +	$5,000 =		$5,000 +	$2,500 +	$1,200 +		$10,000 +	$10,000 −	$4,900 −	$500	

$23,300 $23,300

DECISION TOOLKIT

DECISION CHECKPOINTS	INFO NEEDED FOR DECISION	TOOL TO USE FOR DECISION	HOW TO EVALUATE RESULTS
Has an accounting transaction occurred?	Details of the event	Accounting equation	If the event affected assets, liabilities, or stockholders' equity, then record as a transaction.

TRANSACTION ANALYSIS

Do it! A tabular analysis of the transactions made by Roberta Mendez & Co., a certified public accounting firm, for the month of August is shown below. Each increase and decrease in stockholders' equity is explained.

	Assets		=	Liabilities	+	Stockholders' Equity			
				Accounts		Common		Retained Earnings	
	Cash +	Equipment =		Payable +		Stock +	Revenue −	Expenses	
1.	+$25,000					+$25,000			Issued stock
2.		+$7,000 =		+$7,000					
3.	+8,000						+$8,000		Service Revenue
4.	−850							−$850	Rent Expense
	$32,150 +	$7,000 =		$7,000 +		$25,000 +	$8,000 −	$850	

$39,150 $39,150

Action Plan

- Analyze the tabular analysis to determine the nature and effect of each transaction.
- Keep the accounting equation in balance.
- Remember that a change in an asset will require a change in another asset, a liability, or in stockholders' equity.

Describe each transaction that occurred for the month.

Solution

1. The company issued shares of stock to stockholders for $25,000 cash.
2. The company purchased $7,000 of equipment on account.
3. The company received $8,000 of cash in exchange for services performed.
4. The company paid $850 for this month's rent.

Related exercise material: **BE3-1, BE3-2, BE3-3, Do it! 3-1, E3-1, E3-2, E3-3,** and **E3-4.**

The Navigator

The Account

Rather than using a tabular summary like the one in Illustration 3-3 for Sierra Corporation, an accounting information system uses accounts. An **account** is an individual accounting record of increases and decreases in a specific asset, liability, stockholders' equity, revenue, or expense item. For example, Sierra Corporation has separate accounts for Cash, Accounts Receivable, Accounts Payable, Service Revenue, Salaries and Wages Expense, and so on. (Note that whenever we are referring to a specific account, we capitalize the name.)

In its simplest form, an account consists of three parts: (1) the title of the account, (2) a left or debit side, and (3) a right or credit side. Because the alignment of these parts of an account resembles the letter T, it is referred to as a **T-account**. The basic form of an account is shown in Illustration 3-4.

LEARNING OBJECTIVE 2

Explain what an account is and how it helps in the recording process.

Title of Account

| Left or debit side | Right or credit side |

Illustration 3-4 Basic form of account

We use this form of account often throughout this book to explain basic accounting relationships.

DEBITS AND CREDITS

The term **debit** indicates the left side of an account, and **credit** indicates the right side. They are commonly abbreviated as **Dr.** for debit and **Cr.** for credit. They **do not** mean increase or decrease, as is commonly thought. We use the terms debit and credit repeatedly in the recording process to describe **where** entries are made in accounts. For example, the act of entering an amount on the left side of an account is called **debiting** the account. Making an entry on the right side is **crediting** the account.

When comparing the totals of the two sides, an account shows a **debit balance** if the total of the debit amounts exceeds the credits. An account shows a **credit balance** if the credit amounts exceed the debits. Note the position of the debit side and credit side in Illustration 3-4.

The procedure of recording debits and credits in an account is shown in Illustration 3-5 for the transactions affecting the Cash account of Sierra Corporation. The data are taken from the Cash column of the tabular summary in Illustration 3-3.

LEARNING OBJECTIVE 3

Define debits and credits and explain how they are used to record business transactions.

Illustration 3-5 Tabular summary and account form for Sierra Corporation's Cash account

Tabular Summary	Account Form

Cash
$10,000
5,000
−5,000
1,200
10,000
−900
−600
−500
−4,000
$15,200

Cash			
(Debits)	10,000	**(Credits)**	5,000
	5,000		900
	1,200		600
	10,000		500
			4,000
Balance	15,200		
(Debit)			

Every positive item in the tabular summary represents a receipt of cash; every negative amount represents a payment of cash. **Notice that in the account form we record the increases in cash as debits, and the decreases in cash as credits.** For example, the $10,000 receipt of cash (in red) is debited to Cash, and the −$5,000 payment of cash (in blue) is credited to Cash.

Having increases on one side and decreases on the other reduces recording errors and helps in determining the totals of each side of the account as well as the account balance. The balance is determined by netting the two sides (subtracting one amount from the other). The account balance, a debit of $15,200, indicates that Sierra had $15,200 more increases than decreases in cash. That is, since it started with a balance of zero, it has $15,200 in its Cash account.

DEBIT AND CREDIT PROCEDURES

International Note Rules for accounting for specific events sometimes differ across countries. For example, European companies rely less on historical cost and more on fair value than U.S. companies. Despite the differences, the double-entry accounting system is the basis of accounting systems worldwide.

Each transaction must affect two or more accounts to keep the basic accounting equation in balance. In other words, **for each transaction, debits must equal credits**. The equality of debits and credits provides the basis for the double-entry accounting system.

Under the double-entry system, the two-sided effect of each transaction is recorded in appropriate accounts. This system provides a logical method for recording transactions. The double-entry system also helps to ensure the accuracy of the recorded amounts and helps to detect errors such as those at MF Global as discussed in the Feature Story. If every transaction is recorded with equal debits and credits, then the sum of all the debits to the accounts must equal the sum of all the credits. The double-entry system for determining the equality of the accounting equation is much more efficient than the plus/minus procedure used earlier.

Dr./Cr. Procedures for Assets and Liabilities

In Illustration 3-5 for Sierra Corporation, increases in Cash—an asset—were entered on the left side, and decreases in Cash were entered on the right side. We know that both sides of the basic equation (Assets = Liabilities + Stockholders' Equity) must be equal. It therefore follows that increases and decreases in liabilities will have to be recorded **opposite from** increases and decreases in assets. Thus, increases in liabilities must be entered on the right or credit side, and decreases in liabilities must be entered on the left or debit side. The effects that debits and credits have on assets and liabilities are summarized in Illustration 3-6.

Illustration 3-6 Debit and credit effects–assets and liabilities

Debits	Credits
Increase assets	Decrease assets
Decrease liabilities	Increase liabilities

Asset accounts normally show debit balances. That is, debits to a specific asset account should exceed credits to that account. Likewise, **liability accounts normally show credit balances.** That is, credits to a liability account should exceed debits to that account. The **normal balances** may be diagrammed as in Illustration 3-7.

Illustration 3-7 Normal balances–assets and liabilities

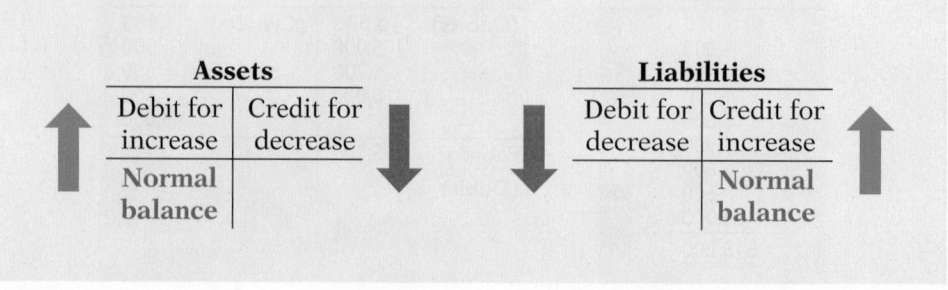

Knowing which is the normal balance in an account may help when you are trying to identify errors. For example, a credit balance in an asset account, such as Land, or a debit balance in a liability account, such as Salaries and Wages Payable, usually indicates errors in recording. Occasionally, however, an abnormal balance may be correct. The Cash account, for example, will have a credit balance when a company has overdrawn its bank balance (written a check that "bounced"). In automated accounting systems, the computer is programmed to flag violations of the normal balance and to print out error or exception reports. In manual systems, careful visual inspection of the accounts is required to detect normal balance problems.

Helpful Hint The normal balance is the side where increases in the account are recorded.

Dr./Cr. Procedures for Stockholders' Equity

In Chapter 1, we indicated that stockholders' equity is comprised of two parts: common stock and retained earnings. In the transaction events earlier in this chapter, you saw that revenues, expenses, and the payment of dividends affect retained earnings. Therefore, the subdivisions of stockholders' equity are common stock, retained earnings, dividends, revenues, and expenses.

COMMON STOCK. Common stock is issued to investors in exchange for the stockholders' investment. The Common Stock account is increased by credits and decreased by debits. For example, when cash is invested in the business, Cash is debited and Common Stock is credited. The effects of debits and credits on the Common Stock account are shown in Illustration 3-8.

Debits	Credits
Decrease Common Stock	Increase Common Stock

Illustration 3-8 Debit and credit effects–Common Stock

The normal balance in the Common Stock account may be diagrammed as in Illustration 3-9.

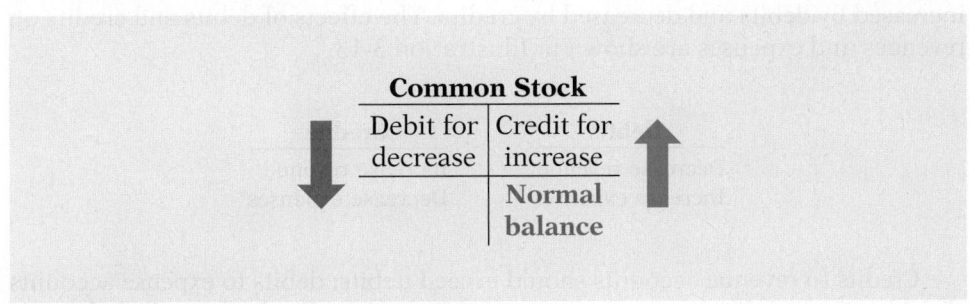

Illustration 3-9 Normal balance–Common Stock

RETAINED EARNINGS. Retained earnings is net income that is retained in the business. It represents the portion of stockholders' equity that has been accumulated through the profitable operation of the company. Retained Earnings is increased by credits (for example, by net income) and decreased by debits (for example, by a net loss), as shown in Illustration 3-10.

Debits	Credits
Decrease Retained Earnings	Increase Retained Earnings

Illustration 3-10 Debit and credit effects–Retained Earnings

The normal balance for Retained Earnings may be diagrammed as in Illustration 3-11.

Illustration 3-11 Normal balance–Retained Earnings

DIVIDENDS. A dividend is a distribution by a corporation to its stockholders. The most common form of distribution is a cash dividend. Dividends result in a reduction of the stockholders' claims on retained earnings. Because dividends reduce stockholders' equity, increases in the Dividends account are recorded with debits. As shown in Illustration 3-12, the Dividends account normally has a debit balance.

Illustration 3-12 Normal balance–Dividends

REVENUES AND EXPENSES. When a company recognizes revenues, stockholders' equity is increased. Revenue accounts are increased by credits and decreased by debits.

Expenses decrease stockholders' equity. Thus, expense accounts are increased by debits and decreased by credits. The effects of debits and credits on revenues and expenses are shown in Illustration 3-13.

Illustration 3-13 Debit and credit effects–revenues and expenses

Debits	Credits
Decrease revenue	Increase revenue
Increase expenses	Decrease expenses

Credits to revenue accounts should exceed debits; debits to expense accounts should exceed credits. Thus, **revenue accounts normally show credit balances, and expense accounts normally show debit balances**. The normal balances may be diagrammed as in Illustration 3-14.

Illustration 3-14 Normal balances–revenues and expenses

Investor Insight

Keeping Score

The Chicago Cubs baseball team has these major revenue and expense accounts:

Revenues	Expenses
Admissions (ticket sales)	Players' salaries
Concessions	Administrative salaries
Television and radio	Travel
Advertising	Ballpark maintenance

? Do you think that the Chicago Bears football team would be likely to have the same major revenue and expense accounts as the Cubs? (See page 159.)

© Jonathan Daniel/Getty Images, Inc.

STOCKHOLDERS' EQUITY RELATIONSHIPS

Companies report the subdivisions of stockholders' equity in various places in the financial statements:

- Common stock and retained earnings: in the stockholders' equity section of the balance sheet.
- Dividends: on the retained earnings statement.
- Revenues and expenses: on the income statement.

Dividends, revenues, and expenses are eventually transferred to retained earnings at the end of the period. As a result, a change in any one of these three items affects stockholders' equity. Illustration 3-15 shows the relationships of the accounts affecting stockholders' equity.

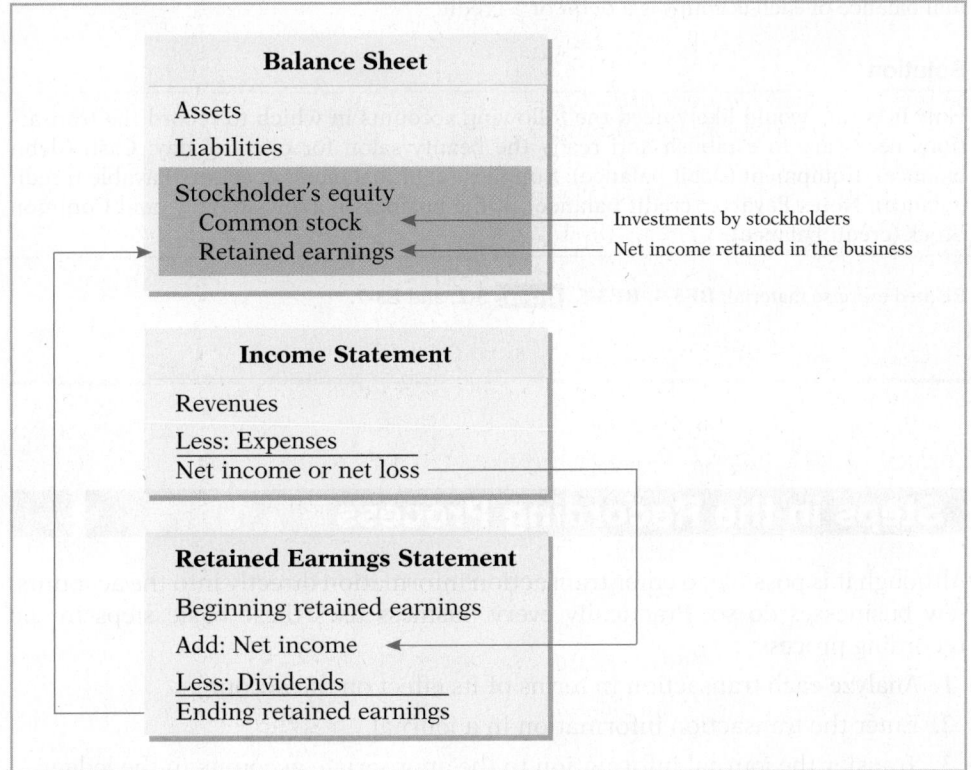

Illustration 3-15
Stockholders' equity relationships

SUMMARY OF DEBIT/CREDIT RULES

Illustration 3-16 summarizes the debit/credit rules and effects on each type of account. **Study this diagram carefully.** It will help you understand the fundamentals of the double-entry system. No matter what the transaction, total debits must equal total credits in order to keep the accounting equation in balance.

Illustration 3-16 Summary of debit/credit rules

DEBITS AND CREDITS FOR BALANCE SHEET ACCOUNTS

Action Plan

- First identify asset accounts for each different type of asset invested in the business.

- Then identify liability accounts for debts incurred by the business.

- Hair It Is Inc. needs only one stockholders' equity account, Common Stock, when it begins the business. The other stockholders' equity account, Retained Earnings, will be needed after the business is operating.

Do it! Kate Browne, president of Hair It Is Inc., has just rented space in a shopping mall for the purpose of opening and operating a beauty salon. Long before opening day and before purchasing equipment, hiring assistants, and remodeling the space, Kate was strongly advised to set up a double-entry set of accounting records in which to record all of her business transactions.

Identify the balance sheet accounts that Hair It Is Inc. will likely need to record the transactions necessary to establish and open for business. Also, indicate whether the normal balance of each account is a debit or a credit.

Solution

Hair It Is Inc. would likely need the following accounts in which to record the transactions necessary to establish and ready the beauty salon for opening day: Cash (debit balance); Equipment (debit balance); Supplies (debit balance); Accounts Payable (credit balance); Notes Payable (credit balance), if the business borrows money; and Common Stock (credit balance).

Related exercise material: **BE3-4, BE3-5, Do it! 3-2,** and **E3-7.**

Steps in the Recording Process

Although it is possible to enter transaction information directly into the accounts, few businesses do so. Practically every business uses these basic steps in the recording process:

1. Analyze each transaction in terms of its effect on the accounts.

2. Enter the transaction information in a journal.

3. Transfer the journal information to the appropriate accounts in the ledger.

The actual sequence of events begins with the transaction. Evidence of the transaction comes in the form of a **source document**, such as a sales slip, a check, a bill, or a cash register document. This evidence is analyzed to determine the effect of the transaction on specific accounts. The transaction is then entered in the **journal**. Finally, the journal entry is transferred to the designated accounts in the **ledger**. The sequence of events in the recording process is shown in Illustration 3-17.

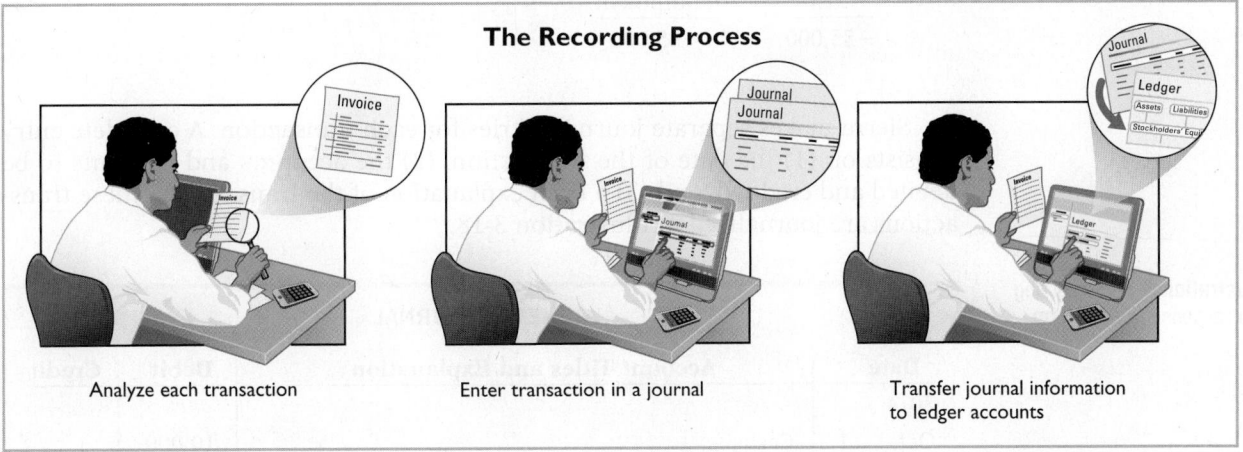

The Recording Process

Analyze each transaction — Enter transaction in a journal — Transfer journal information to ledger accounts

Illustration 3-17 The recording process

THE JOURNAL

Transactions are initially recorded in chronological order in journals before they are transferred to the accounts. For each transaction, the journal shows the debit and credit effects on specific accounts. (In a computerized system, journals are kept as files, and accounts are recorded in computer databases.)

Companies may use various kinds of journals, but every company has at least the most basic form of journal, a general journal. **The journal makes three significant contributions to the recording process:**

LEARNING OBJECTIVE 5

Explain what a journal is and how it helps in the recording process.

1. It discloses in one place the **complete effect of a transaction**.
2. It provides a **chronological record** of transactions.
3. It **helps to prevent or locate errors** because the debit and credit amounts for each entry can be readily compared.

Entering transaction data in the journal is known as journalizing. To illustrate the technique of journalizing, let's look at the first three transactions of Sierra Corporation in equation form.

On October 1, Sierra issued common stock in exchange for $10,000 cash:

Assets	=	Liabilities	+	Stockholders' Equity
				Common
Cash	=			Stock
+$10,000				+$10,000 Issued stock

On October 1, Sierra borrowed $5,000 by signing a note:

$$\text{Assets} = \text{Liabilities} + \text{Stockholders' Equity}$$

		Notes	
Cash	=	Payable	
+$5,000		+$5,000	

On October 2, Sierra purchased equipment for $5,000:

$$\text{Assets} = \text{Liabilities} + \text{Stockholders' Equity}$$

| Cash | Equipment | | |
| −$5,000 | +$5,000 | | |

Sierra makes separate journal entries for each transaction. A complete entry consists of: (1) the date of the transaction, (2) the accounts and amounts to be debited and credited, and (3) a brief explanation of the transaction. These transactions are journalized in Illustration 3-18.

Illustration 3-18 Recording transactions in journal form

GENERAL JOURNAL

Date		Account Titles and Explanation	Debit	Credit
2014				
Oct.	1	Cash	10,000	
		Common Stock		10,000
		(Issued stock for cash)		
	1	Cash	5,000	
		Notes Payable		5,000
		(Issued 3-month, 12% note payable for cash)		
	2	Equipment	5,000	
		Cash		5,000
		(Purchased equipment for cash)		

Note the following features of the journal entries.

1. The date of the transaction is entered in the Date column.
2. The account to be debited is entered first at the left. The account to be credited is then entered on the next line, indented under the line above. The indentation differentiates debits from credits and decreases the possibility of switching the debit and credit amounts.
3. The amounts for the debits are recorded in the Debit (left) column, and the amounts for the credits are recorded in the Credit (right) column.
4. A brief explanation of the transaction is given.

It is important to use correct and specific account titles in journalizing. Erroneous account titles lead to incorrect financial statements. Some flexibility exists initially in selecting account titles. The main criterion is that each title must appropriately describe the content of the account. For example, a company could use any of these account titles for recording the cost of delivery trucks: Equipment, Delivery Equipment, Delivery Trucks, or Trucks. Once the company chooses the specific title to use, however, it should record under that account title all subsequent transactions involving the account.

Accounting Across the Organization
Boosting Microsoft's Profits

At one time, Microsoft's Home and Entertainment Division lost over $4 billion, mostly due to losses on the original Xbox videogame console. With the Xbox 360 videogame console, the division's head of finance, Bryan Lee, hoped the division would become profitable. He set strict goals for sales, revenue, and profit. "A manager seeking to spend more on a feature such as a disk drive has to find allies in the group to cut spending elsewhere, or identify new revenue to offset the increase," he explained.

For example, Microsoft originally designed the Xbox 360 to have 256 megabytes of memory. But the design department said that amount of memory wouldn't support the best special effects. The purchasing department said that adding more memory would cost $30–which was 10% of the estimated selling price of $300. The marketing department, however, "determined that adding the memory would let Microsoft reduce marketing costs and attract more game developers, boosting royalty revenue. It would also extend the life of the console, generating more sales." As a result, Microsoft doubled the memory to 512 megabytes. Today, the division enjoys great success.

© flyfloor/iStockphoto

Source: Robert A. Guth, "New Xbox Aim for Microsoft: Profitability," *Wall Street Journal* (May 24, 2005), p. C1.

? In what ways is this Microsoft division using accounting to assist in its effort to become more profitable? (See page 159.)

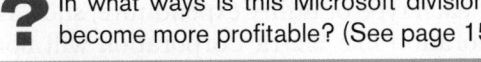

Do it!

JOURNAL ENTRIES

The following events occurred during the first month of business of Hair It Is Inc., Kate Browne's beauty salon:

1. Issued common stock to shareholders in exchange for $20,000 cash.
2. Purchased $4,800 of equipment on account (to be paid in 30 days).
3. Interviewed three people for the position of stylist.

In what form (type of record) should the company record these three activities? Prepare the entries to record the transactions.

Solution

Each transaction that is recorded is entered in the general journal. The three activities are recorded as follows.

1. Cash	20,000	
Common Stock		20,000
(Issued stock for cash)		
2. Equipment	4,800	
Accounts Payable		4,800
(Purchased equipment on account)		

3. No entry because no transaction occurred.

Related exercise material: **BE3-6, BE3-9, Do it! 3-3, E3-6, E3-8,** and **E3-9.**

Action Plan

- Record the transactions in a journal, which is a chronological record of the transactions.
- Make sure to provide a complete and accurate representation of the transactions' effects on the assets, liabilities, and stockholders' equity of the business.

 The Navigator

THE LEDGER

LEARNING OBJECTIVE 6
Explain what a ledger is and how it helps in the recording process.

The entire group of accounts maintained by a company is referred to collectively as the **ledger**. The ledger provides the balance in each of the accounts as well as keeps track of changes in these balances.

Companies may use various kinds of ledgers, but every company has a general ledger. A **general ledger** contains all the assets, liabilities, stockholders' equity, revenue, and expense accounts, as shown in Illustration 3-19 (page 120). Whenever we use the term **ledger** in this textbook without additional specification, it will mean the general ledger.

Illustration 3-19 The general ledger

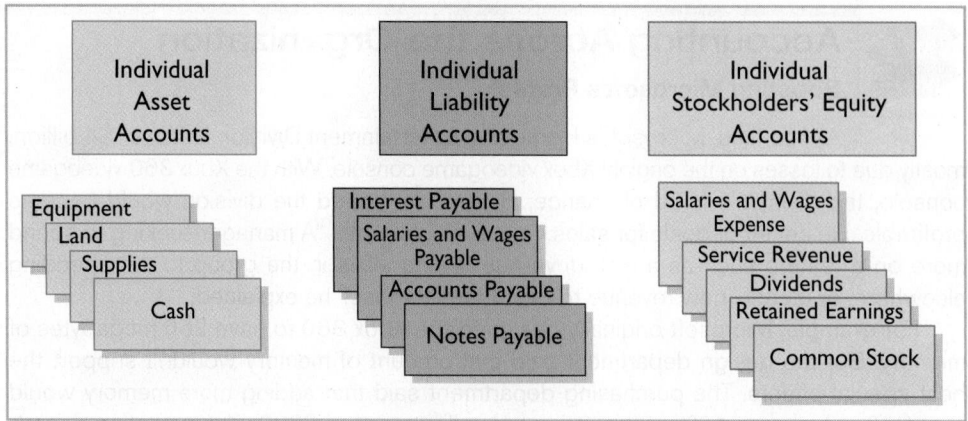

CHART OF ACCOUNTS

The number and type of accounts used differ for each company, depending on the size, complexity, and type of business. For example, the number of accounts depends on the amount of detail desired by management. The management of one company may want one single account for all types of utility expense. Another may keep separate expense accounts for each type of utility expenditure, such as gas, electricity, and water. A small corporation like Sierra Corporation will not have many accounts compared with a corporate giant like Ford Motor Company. Sierra may be able to manage and report its activities in 20 to 30 accounts, whereas Ford requires thousands of accounts to keep track of its worldwide activities.

Most companies list the accounts in a **chart of accounts**. They may create new accounts as needed during the life of the business. Illustration 3-20 shows the chart of accounts for Sierra Corporation in the order that they are typically listed (assets, liabilities, stockholders' equity, revenues, and expenses). **Accounts shown in red are used in this chapter**; accounts shown in black are explained in later chapters.

Illustration 3-20 Chart of accounts for Sierra Corporation

SIERRA CORPORATION—CHART OF ACCOUNTS

Assets	Liabilities	Stockholders' Equity	Revenues	Expenses
Cash	Notes Payable	Common Stock	Service Revenue	Salaries and Wages
Accounts Receivable	Accounts Payable	Retained Earnings		Expense
Supplies	Interest Payable	Dividends		Supplies Expense
Prepaid Insurance	Unearned	Income Summary		Rent Expense
Equipment	Service Revenue			Insurance Expense
Accumulated Depreciation—	Salaries and Wages			Interest Expense
Equipment	Payable			Depreciation Expense

POSTING

LEARNING OBJECTIVE 7

Explain what posting is and how it helps in the recording process.

The procedure of transferring journal entry amounts to ledger accounts is called posting. **This phase of the recording process accumulates the effects of journalized transactions in the individual accounts.** Posting involves these steps:

1. In the ledger, enter in the appropriate columns of the debited account(s) the date and debit amount shown in the journal.
2. In the ledger, enter in the appropriate columns of the credited account(s) the date and credit amount shown in the journal.

Ethics Insight

A Convenient Overstatement

Sometimes a company's investment securities suffer a permanent decline in value below their original cost. When this occurs, the company is supposed to reduce the recorded value of the securities on its balance sheet ("write-them down" in common financial lingo) and record a loss. It appears, however, that during the financial crisis, employees at some financial institutions chose to look the other way as the value of their investments skidded. A number of Wall Street traders that worked for the investment bank Credit Suisse Group were charged with intentionally overstating the value of securities that had suffered declines of approximately $2.85 billion. One reason that they may have been reluctant to record the losses is out of fear that the company's shareholders and clients would panic if they saw the magnitude of the losses. However, personal self-interest might have been equally to blame—the bonuses of the traders were tied to the value of the investment securities.

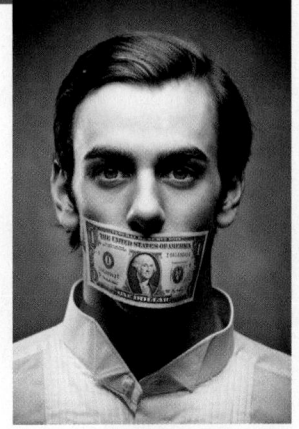

© Nuno Silva/iStockphoto

Source: S. Pulliam, J. Eaglesham, and M. Siconolfi, "U.S. Plans Changes on Bond Fraud," *Wall Street Journal Online* (February 1, 2012).

? What incentives might employees have had to overstate the value of these investment securities on the company's financial statements? (See page 159.)

THE RECORDING PROCESS ILLUSTRATED

Illustrations 3-21 through 3-31 on the following pages show the basic steps in the recording process using the October transactions of Sierra Corporation. Sierra's accounting period is a month. A basic analysis and a debit–credit analysis precede the journalizing and posting of each transaction. Study these transaction analyses carefully. **The purpose of transaction analysis is first to identify the type of account involved and then to determine whether a debit or a credit to the account is required.** You should always perform this type of analysis before preparing a journal entry. Doing so will help you understand the journal entries discussed in this chapter as well as more complex journal entries to be described in later chapters.

Illustration 3-21 Investment of cash by stockholders

Cash flow analyses show the impact of each transaction on cash.

Cash Flows
+10,000

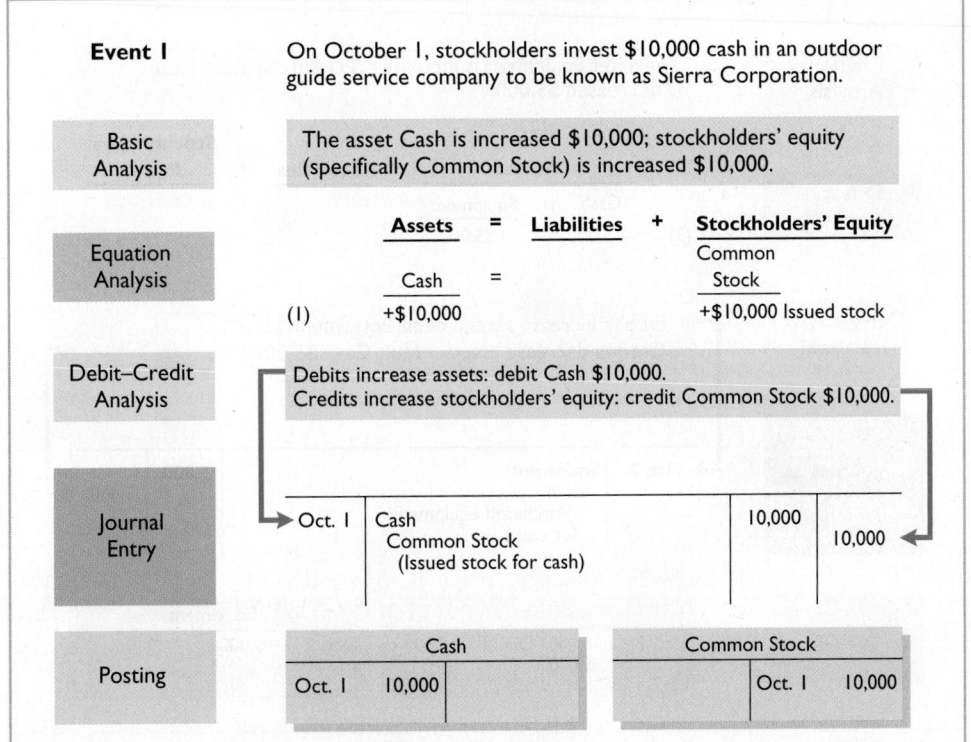

	Event 1	On October 1, stockholders invest $10,000 cash in an outdoor guide service company to be known as Sierra Corporation.

Basic Analysis — The asset Cash is increased $10,000; stockholders' equity (specifically Common Stock) is increased $10,000.

Equation Analysis

	Assets	=	Liabilities	+	Stockholders' Equity
	Cash	=			Common Stock
(1)	+$10,000				+$10,000 Issued stock

Debit–Credit Analysis — Debits increase assets: debit Cash $10,000.
Credits increase stockholders' equity: credit Common Stock $10,000.

Journal Entry

Oct. 1	Cash	10,000	
	Common Stock		10,000
	(Issued stock for cash)		

Posting

Cash			Common Stock		
Oct. 1	10,000			Oct. 1	10,000

Illustration 3-22 Issue of note payable

Cash Flows
+5,000

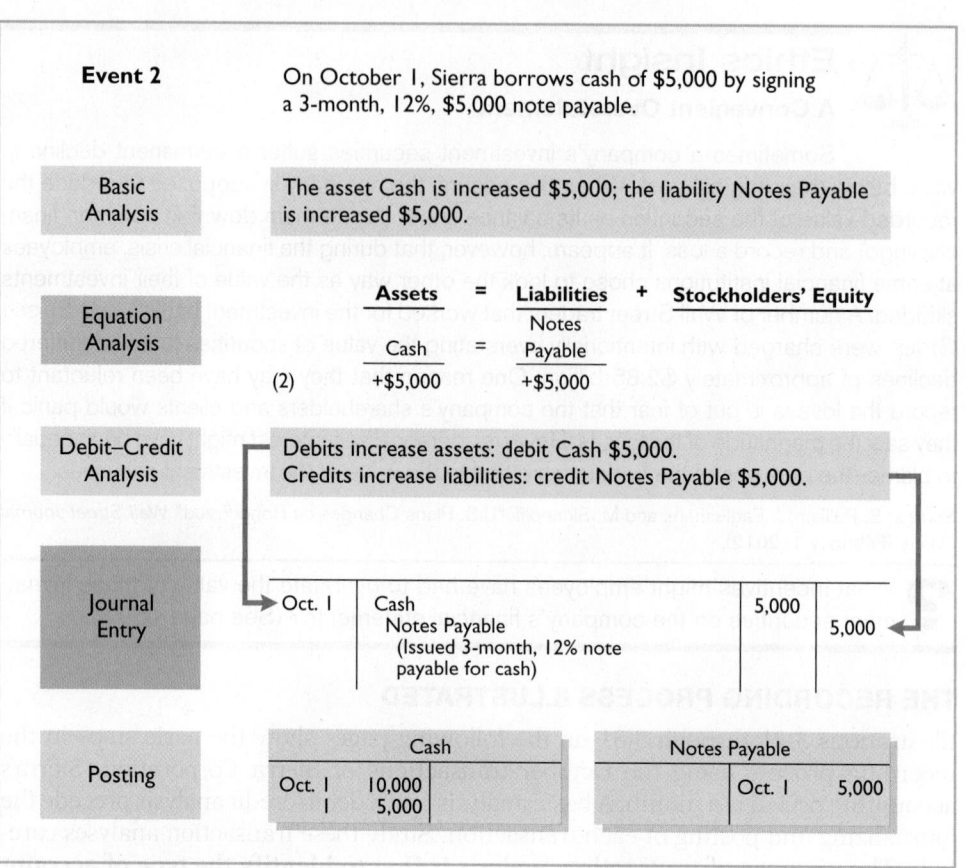

	Event 2	On October 1, Sierra borrows cash of $5,000 by signing a 3-month, 12%, $5,000 note payable.
	Basic Analysis	The asset Cash is increased $5,000; the liability Notes Payable is increased $5,000.

Equation Analysis

	Assets	=	Liabilities	+	Stockholders' Equity
	Cash	=	Notes Payable		
(2)	+$5,000		+$5,000		

Debit–Credit Analysis

Debits increase assets: debit Cash $5,000.
Credits increase liabilities: credit Notes Payable $5,000.

Journal Entry

Oct. 1	Cash	5,000	
	Notes Payable		5,000
	(Issued 3-month, 12% note payable for cash)		

Posting

Cash			Notes Payable		
Oct. 1	10,000			Oct. 1	5,000
1	5,000				

Illustration 3-23 Purchase of equipment

Cash Flows
−5,000

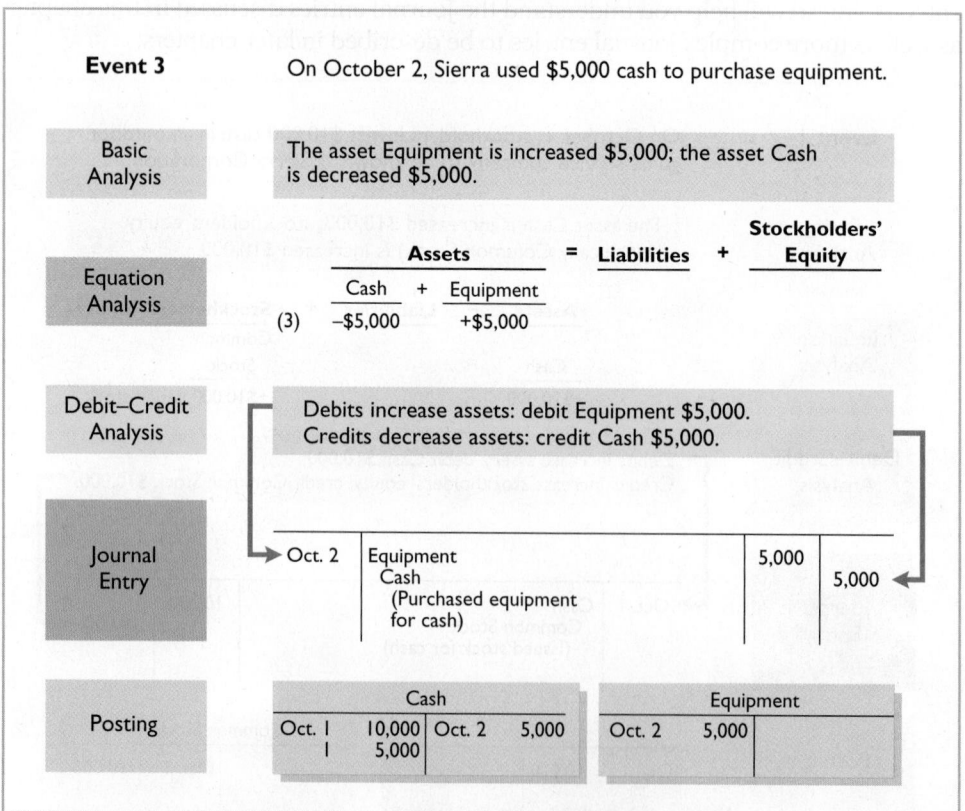

	Event 3	On October 2, Sierra used $5,000 cash to purchase equipment.
	Basic Analysis	The asset Equipment is increased $5,000; the asset Cash is decreased $5,000.

Equation Analysis

	Assets			=	Liabilities	+	Stockholders' Equity
	Cash	+	Equipment				
(3)	−$5,000		+$5,000				

Debit–Credit Analysis

Debits increase assets: debit Equipment $5,000.
Credits decrease assets: credit Cash $5,000.

Journal Entry

Oct. 2	Equipment	5,000	
	Cash		5,000
	(Purchased equipment for cash)		

Posting

Cash				Equipment	
Oct. 1	10,000	Oct. 2	5,000	Oct. 2	5,000
1	5,000				

Illustration 3-24 Receipt of cash in advance from customer

Event 4 On October 2, Sierra received a $1,200 cash advance from R. Knox, a client, for guide services for multi-day trips that are expected to be completed in the future.

Basic Analysis The asset Cash is increased $1,200; the liability Unearned Service Revenue is increased $1,200 because the service has not been performed yet. That is, when an advance payment is received, an unearned revenue (a liability) should be recorded in order to recognize the obligation that exists.

Helpful Hint Many liabilities have the word "payable" in their title. But, note that Unearned Service Revenue is considered a liability even though the word *payable* is not used.

Equation Analysis

	Assets	=	Liabilities	+	Stockholders' Equity
	Cash	=	Unearned Serv. Rev.		
(4)	+$1,200		+$1,200		

Cash Flows
+1,200

Debit–Credit Analysis Debits increase assets: debit Cash $1,200. Credits increase liabilities: credit Unearned Service Revenue $1,200.

Journal Entry

Oct. 2	Cash	1,200	
	Unearned Service Revenue (Received advance from R. Knox for future service)		1,200

Posting

Cash				Unearned Service Revenue	
Oct. 1	10,000	Oct. 2	5,000	Oct. 2	1,200
1	5,000				
2	1,200				

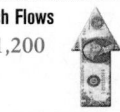

Illustration 3-25 Services performed for cash

Event 5 On October 3, Sierra received $10,000 in cash from Copa Company for guide services performed in October.

Basic Analysis The asset Cash is increased $10,000; the revenue Service Revenue is increased $10,000.

Equation Analysis

	Assets	=	Liabilities	+	Stockholders' Equity
	Cash	=			Revenues
(5)	+$10,000				+$10,000 Service Revenue

Cash Flows
+10,000

Debit–Credit Analysis Debits increase assets: debit Cash $10,000. Credits increase revenues: credit Service Revenue $10,000.

Journal Entry

Oct. 3	Cash	10,000	
	Service Revenue (Received cash for services performed)		10,000

Posting

Cash				Service Revenue	
Oct. 1	10,000	Oct. 2	5,000	Oct. 3	10,000
1	5,000				
2	1,200				
3	10,000				

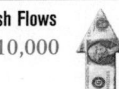

Illustration 3-26 Payment of rent with cash

Cash Flows
−900

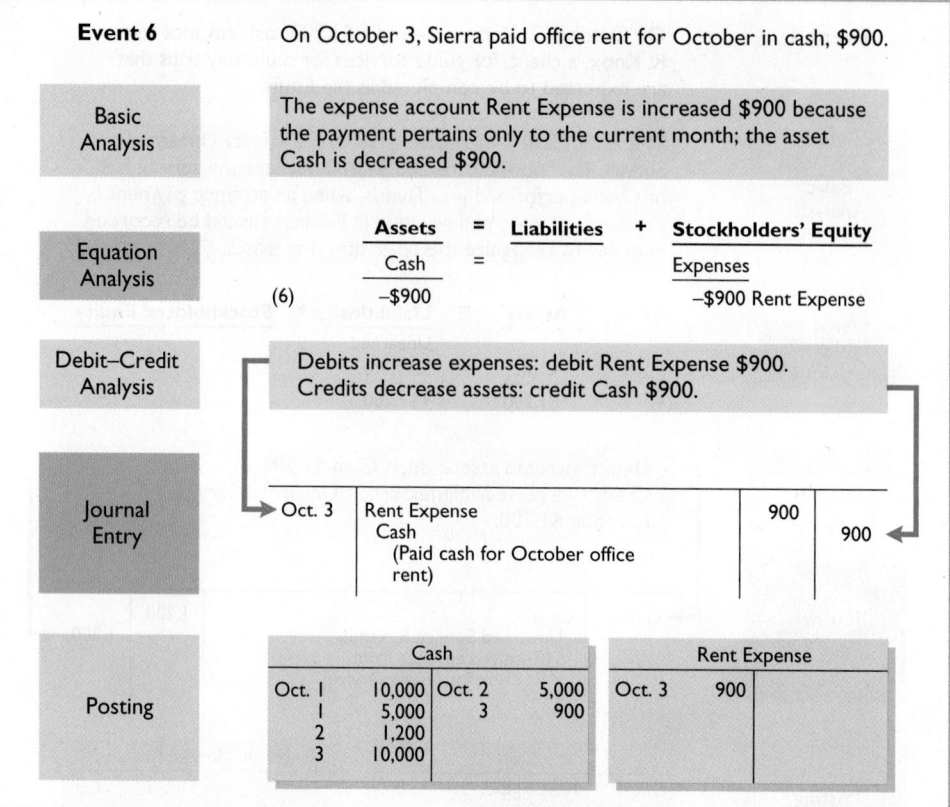

Event 6 — On October 3, Sierra paid office rent for October in cash, $900.

Basic Analysis — The expense account Rent Expense is increased $900 because the payment pertains only to the current month; the asset Cash is decreased $900.

Equation Analysis

	Assets	=	Liabilities	+	Stockholders' Equity
	Cash	=			Expenses
(6)	−$900				−$900 Rent Expense

Debit–Credit Analysis — Debits increase expenses: debit Rent Expense $900. Credits decrease assets: credit Cash $900.

Journal Entry

Oct. 3	Rent Expense	900	
	Cash		900
	(Paid cash for October office rent)		

Posting

Cash					Rent Expense		
Oct. 1	10,000	Oct. 2	5,000		Oct. 3	900	
1	5,000	3	900				
2	1,200						
3	10,000						

Illustration 3-27 Purchase of insurance policy with cash

Cash Flows
−600

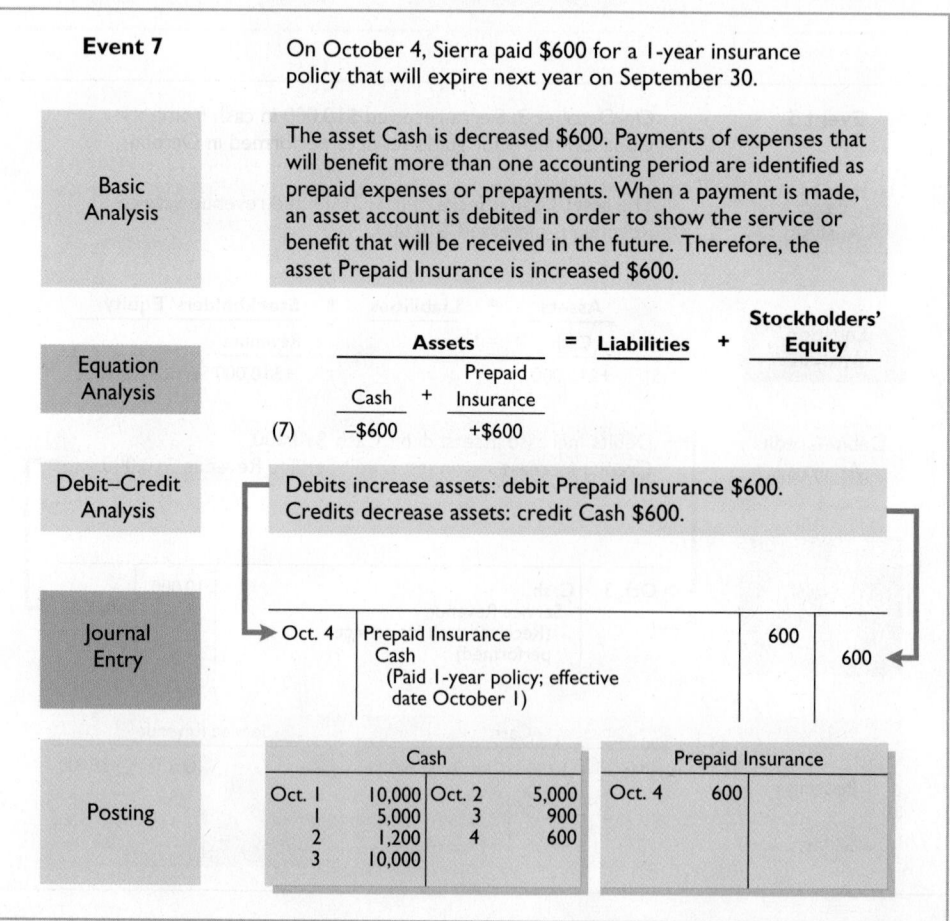

Event 7 — On October 4, Sierra paid $600 for a 1-year insurance policy that will expire next year on September 30.

Basic Analysis — The asset Cash is decreased $600. Payments of expenses that will benefit more than one accounting period are identified as prepaid expenses or prepayments. When a payment is made, an asset account is debited in order to show the service or benefit that will be received in the future. Therefore, the asset Prepaid Insurance is increased $600.

Equation Analysis

	Assets			=	Liabilities	+	Stockholders' Equity
	Cash	+	Prepaid Insurance				
(7)	−$600		+$600				

Debit–Credit Analysis — Debits increase assets: debit Prepaid Insurance $600. Credits decrease assets: credit Cash $600.

Journal Entry

Oct. 4	Prepaid Insurance	600	
	Cash		600
	(Paid 1-year policy; effective date October 1)		

Posting

Cash					Prepaid Insurance		
Oct. 1	10,000	Oct. 2	5,000		Oct. 4	600	
1	5,000	3	900				
2	1,200	4	600				
3	10,000						

Illustration 3-28 Purchase of supplies on account

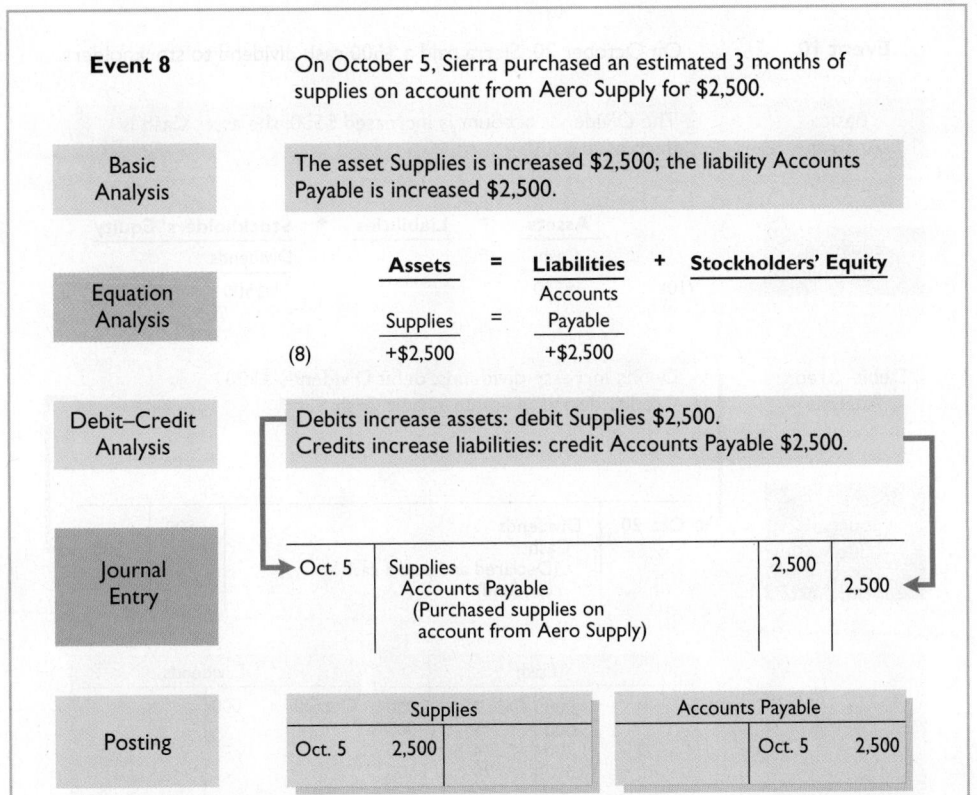

Event 8	On October 5, Sierra purchased an estimated 3 months of supplies on account from Aero Supply for $2,500.
Basic Analysis	The asset Supplies is increased $2,500; the liability Accounts Payable is increased $2,500.

		Assets	**=**	**Liabilities**	**+**	**Stockholders' Equity**
Equation Analysis				Accounts		
		Supplies	=	Payable		
	(8)	+$2,500		+$2,500		

Cash Flows
no effect

Debit–Credit Analysis	Debits increase assets: debit Supplies $2,500. Credits increase liabilities: credit Accounts Payable $2,500.

Journal Entry		Oct. 5	Supplies		2,500	
			Accounts Payable			2,500
			(Purchased supplies on account from Aero Supply)			

Posting	**Supplies**	**Accounts Payable**
	Oct. 5 2,500	Oct. 5 2,500

Illustration 3-29 Hiring of new employees

Event 9	On October 9, Sierra hired four employees to begin work on October 15. Each employee will receive a weekly salary of $500 for a 5-day work week, payable every 2 weeks—first payment made on October 26.
Basic Analysis	An accounting transaction has not occurred. There is only an agreement that the employees will begin work on October 15. Thus, a debit–credit analysis is not needed because there is no accounting entry. (See transaction of October 26 (Event 11) for first payment.)

Illustration 3-30 Payment of dividend

Cash Flows
−500

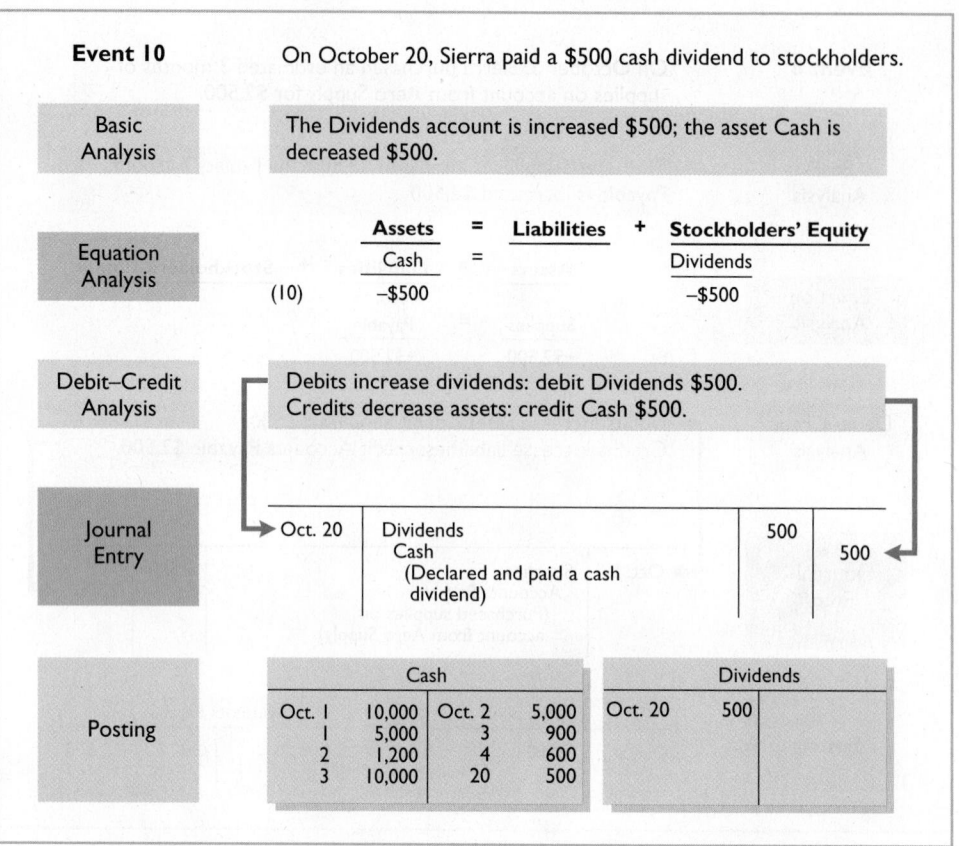

Event 10	On October 20, Sierra paid a $500 cash dividend to stockholders.
Basic Analysis	The Dividends account is increased $500; the asset Cash is decreased $500.

Equation Analysis

	Assets	=	Liabilities	+	Stockholders' Equity
	Cash	=			Dividends
(10)	−$500				−$500

Debit–Credit Analysis

Debits increase dividends: debit Dividends $500.
Credits decrease assets: credit Cash $500.

Journal Entry

Oct. 20	Dividends		500	
	Cash			500
	(Declared and paid a cash dividend)			

Posting

Cash						Dividends		
Oct. 1	10,000	Oct. 2	5,000		Oct. 20	500	
1	5,000	3	900				
2	1,200	4	600				
3	10,000	20	500				

Illustration 3-31 Payment of cash for employee salaries

Cash Flows
−4,000

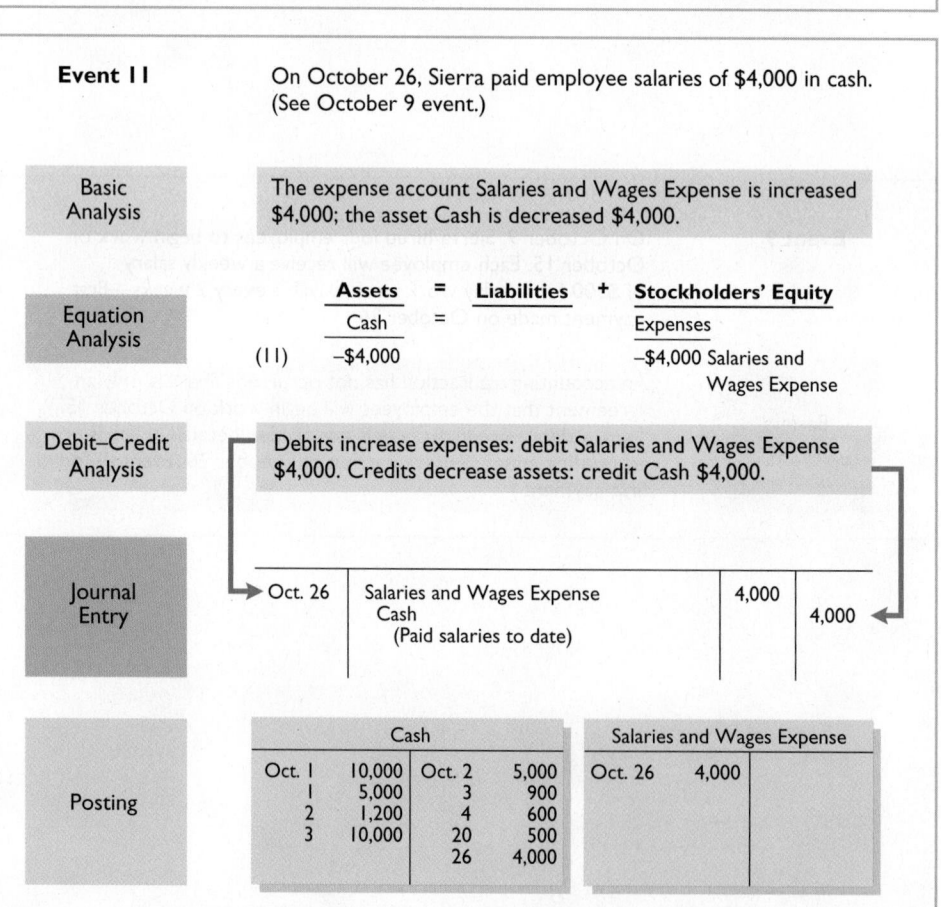

Event 11	On October 26, Sierra paid employee salaries of $4,000 in cash. (See October 9 event.)
Basic Analysis	The expense account Salaries and Wages Expense is increased $4,000; the asset Cash is decreased $4,000.

Equation Analysis

	Assets	=	Liabilities	+	Stockholders' Equity
	Cash	=			Expenses
(11)	−$4,000				−$4,000 Salaries and Wages Expense

Debit–Credit Analysis

Debits increase expenses: debit Salaries and Wages Expense $4,000. Credits decrease assets: credit Cash $4,000.

Journal Entry

Oct. 26	Salaries and Wages Expense		4,000	
	Cash			4,000
	(Paid salaries to date)			

Posting

Cash						Salaries and Wages Expense		
Oct. 1	10,000	Oct. 2	5,000		Oct. 26	4,000	
1	5,000	3	900				
2	1,200	4	600				
3	10,000	20	500				
		26	4,000				

SUMMARY ILLUSTRATION OF JOURNALIZING AND POSTING

The journal for Sierra Corporation for the month of October is summarized in Illustration 3-32. The ledger is shown in Illustration 3-33 (on page 128) with all balances highlighted in red.

Illustration 3-32 General journal for Sierra Corporation

GENERAL JOURNAL

Date		Account Titles and Explanation	Debit	Credit
2014				
Oct.	1	Cash	10,000	
		Common Stock		10,000
		(Issued stock for cash)		
	1	Cash	5,000	
		Notes Payable		5,000
		(Issued 3-month, 12% note payable for cash)		
	2	Equipment	5,000	
		Cash		5,000
		(Purchased equipment for cash)		
	2	Cash	1,200	
		Unearned Service Revenue		1,200
		(Received advance from R. Knox for future service)		
	3	Cash	10,000	
		Service Revenue		10,000
		(Received cash for services performed)		
	3	Rent Expense	900	
		Cash		900
		(Paid cash for October office rent)		
	4	Prepaid Insurance	600	
		Cash		600
		(Paid 1-year policy; effective date October 1)		
	5	Supplies	2,500	
		Accounts Payable		2,500
		(Purchased supplies on account from Aero Supply)		
	20	Dividends	500	
		Cash		500
		(Declared and paid a cash dividend)		
	26	Salaries and Wages Expense	4,000	
		Cash		4,000
		(Paid salaries to date)		

Illustration 3-33 General ledger for Sierra Corporation

GENERAL LEDGER

	Cash								Unearned Service Revenue		
Oct.	1	10,000	Oct.	2	5,000					Oct.	2	1,200
	1	5,000		3	900							
	2	1,200		4	600					Bal.		1,200
	3	10,000		20	500							
				26	4,000							
Bal.		15,200										

	Supplies				Common Stock		
Oct.	5	2,500				Oct.	1	10,000
Bal.		2,500				Bal.		10,000

	Prepaid Insurance				Dividends	
Oct.	4	600		Oct.	20	500
Bal.		600		Bal.		500

	Equipment				Service Revenue		
Oct.	2	5,000				Oct.	3	10,000
Bal.		5,000				Bal.		10,000

	Notes Payable				Salaries and Wages Expense	
			Oct.	1	5,000	Oct. 26	4,000
			Bal.		5,000	Bal.	4,000

	Accounts Payable				Rent Expense	
			Oct.	5	2,500	Oct. 3	900
			Bal.		2,500	Bal.	900

POSTING

Do it!

Selected transactions from the journal of Faital Inc. during its first month of operations are presented below. Post these transactions to T-accounts.

Date		Account Titles	Debit	Credit
July	1	Cash	30,000	
		Common Stock		30,000
	9	Accounts Receivable	6,000	
		Service Revenue		6,000
	24	Cash	4,000	
		Accounts Receivable		4,000

Action Plan

- Journalize transactions to keep track of financial activities (receipts, payments, receivables, payables, etc.).
- To make entries useful, classify and summarize them by posting the entries to specific ledger accounts.

✔ The Navigator

Solution

	Cash				Accounts Receivable		
July	1	30,000		July	9	6,000	July 24	4,000
	24	4,000					

	Common Stock				Service Revenue	
		July	1	30,000		July	9	6,000

Related exercise material: **BE3-10**, *Do it!* **3-4**, and **E3-11**.

The Trial Balance

A **trial balance** lists accounts and their balances at a given time. A company usually prepares a trial balance at the end of an accounting period. The accounts are listed in the order in which they appear in the ledger. Debit balances are listed in the left column and credit balances in the right column. The totals of the two columns must be equal.

The trial balance proves the mathematical equality of debits and credits after posting. Under the double-entry system, this equality occurs when the sum of the debit account balances equals the sum of the credit account balances. **A trial balance may also uncover errors in journalizing and posting.** For example, a trial balance may well have detected the error at MF Global discussed in the Feature Story. **In addition, a trial balance is useful in the preparation of financial statements.**

These are the procedures for preparing a trial balance:

1. List the account titles and their balances.

2. Total the debit column and total the credit column.

3. Verify the equality of the two columns.

Illustration 3-34 presents the trial balance prepared from the ledger of Sierra Corporation. Note that the total debits, $28,700, equal the total credits, $28,700.

Illustration 3-34 Sierra Corporation trial balance

SIERRA CORPORATION
Trial Balance
October 31, 2014

	Debit	Credit
Cash	$ 15,200	
Supplies	2,500	
Prepaid Insurance	600	
Equipment	5,000	
Notes Payable		$ 5,000
Accounts Payable		2,500
Unearned Service Revenue		1,200
Common Stock		10,000
Dividends	500	
Service Revenue		10,000
Salaries and Wages Expense	4,000	
Rent Expense	900	
	$28,700	$28,700

Helpful Hint Note that the order of presentation in the trial balance is:

Assets
Liabilities
Stockholders' equity
Revenues
Expenses

LIMITATIONS OF A TRIAL BALANCE

A trial balance does not prove that all transactions have been recorded or that the ledger is correct. Numerous errors may exist even though the trial balance column totals agree. For example, the trial balance may balance even when any of the following occurs: (1) a transaction is not journalized, (2) a correct journal entry is not posted, (3) a journal entry is posted twice, (4) incorrect accounts are used in journalizing or posting, or (5) offsetting errors are made in recording the amount of a transaction. In other words, as long as equal debits and credits are posted, even to the wrong account or in the wrong amount, the total debits will equal the total credits. Nevertheless, despite these limitations, the trial balance is a useful screen for finding errors and is frequently used in practice.

Ethics Note An **error** is the result of an unintentional mistake. It is neither ethical nor unethical. An **irregularity** is an intentional misstatement, which is viewed as unethical.

DECISION TOOLKIT

DECISION CHECKPOINTS	INFO NEEDED FOR DECISION	TOOL TO USE FOR DECISION	HOW TO EVALUATE RESULTS
How do you determine that debits equal credits?	All account balances	Trial balance	List the account titles and their balances; total the debit and credit columns; verify equality.

KEEPING AN EYE ON CASH

LEARNING OBJECTIVE 9

Classify cash activities as operating, investing, or financing.

The Cash account shown below reflects all of the inflows and outflows of cash that occurred during October for Sierra Corporation (see Illustrations 3-21 to 3-31). We have also provided a description of each transaction that affected the Cash account.

1. Oct. 1 Issued stock for $10,000 cash.
2. Oct. 1 Issued note payable for $5,000 cash.
3. Oct. 2 Purchased equipment for $5,000 cash.
4. Oct. 2 Received $1,200 cash in advance from customer.
5. Oct. 3 Received $10,000 cash for services performed.
6. Oct. 3 Paid $900 cash for October rent.
7. Oct. 4 Paid $600 cash for one-year insurance policy.
8. Oct. 20 Paid $500 cash dividend to stockholders.
9. Oct. 26 Paid $4,000 cash salaries.

The Cash account and the related cash transactions indicate why cash changed during October. However, to make this information useful for analysis, it is summarized in a statement of cash flows. The statement of cash flows classifies each transaction as an operating activity, an investing activity, or a financing activity. A user of this statement can then determine the amount of net cash provided by operating activities, the amount of cash used for investing purposes, and the amount of cash provided by financing activities.

Operating activities are the types of activities the company performs to generate profits. Sierra Corporation is an outdoor guide business, so its operating activities involve providing guide services. Activities 4, 5, 6, 7, and 9 relate to cash received or spent to directly support its guide services.

Investing activities include the purchase or sale of long-lived assets used in operating the business, or the purchase or sale of investment securities (stocks and bonds of companies other than Sierra). Activity 3, the purchase of equipment, is an investment activity.

The primary types of **financing activities** are borrowing money, issuing shares of stock, and paying dividends. The financing activities of Sierra Corporation are Activities 1, 2, and 8.

Cash

Oct.	1	10,000	Oct.	2	5,000
	1	5,000		3	900
	2	1,200		4	600
	3	10,000		20	500
				26	4,000
Bal.		15,200			

 USING THE DECISION TOOLKIT

The Kansas Farmers' Vertically Integrated Cooperative, Inc. (K-VIC) was formed by over 200 northeast Kansas farmers in the late 1980s. Its purpose is to use raw materials, primarily grain and meat products grown by K-VIC's members, to process this material into end-user food products, and to distribute the products nationally. Profits not needed for expansion or investment are returned to the members annually, on a pro rata basis, according to the fair value of the grain and meat products received from each farmer.

Assume that the following trial balance was prepared for K-VIC.

KANSAS FARMERS' VERTICALLY INTEGRATED COOPERATIVE, INC.
Trial Balance
December 31, 2014
(in thousands)

	Debit	Credit
Accounts Receivable	$ 712,000	
Accounts Payable		$ 673,000
Buildings	365,000	
Cash	32,000	
Cost of Goods Sold	2,384,000	
Notes Payable (due in 2015)		12,000
Inventory	1,291,000	
Land	110,000	
Mortgage Payable		873,000
Equipment	63,000	
Retained Earnings		822,000
Sales Revenue		3,741,000
Salaries and Wages Payable		62,000
Salaries and Wages Expense	651,000	
Maintenance and Repairs Expense	500,000	
	$6,108,000	$6,183,000

Because the trial balance is not in balance, you have checked with various people responsible for entering accounting data and have discovered the following.

1. The purchase of 35 new trucks, costing $7 million and paid for with cash, was not recorded.

2. A data entry clerk accidentally deleted the account name for an account with a credit balance of $472 million, so the amount was added to the Mortgage Payable account in the trial balance.

3. December cash sales revenue of $75 million was credited to the Sales Revenue account, but the other half of the entry was not made.

4. $50 million of salaries expense were mistakenly charged to Maintenance and Repairs Expense.

Instructions

Answer these questions.

(a) Which mistake(s) have caused the trial balance to be out of balance?

(b) Should all of the items be corrected? Explain.

(c) What is the name of the account the data entry clerk deleted?

(d) Make the necessary corrections and prepare a correct trial balance with accounts listed in proper order.

(e) On your trial balance, write BAL beside the accounts that go on the balance sheet and INC beside those that go on the income statement.

Solution

(a) Only mistake #3 has caused the trial balance to be out of balance.

(b) All of the items should be corrected. The misclassification error (mistake #4) on the salaries expense would not affect bottom-line net income, but it does affect the amounts reported in the two expense accounts.

(c) There is no Common Stock account, so that must be the account that was deleted by the data entry clerk.

(d) and (e):

KANSAS FARMERS' VERTICALLY INTEGRATED COOPERATIVE, INC.
Trial Balance
December 31, 2014
(in thousands)

	Debit	Credit	
Cash ($32,000 − $7,000 + $75,000)	$ 100,000		BAL
Accounts Receivable	712,000		BAL
Inventory	1,291,000		BAL
Land	110,000		BAL
Buildings	365,000		BAL
Equipment ($63,000 + $7,000)	70,000		BAL
Accounts Payable		$ 673,000	BAL
Salaries and Wages Payable		62,000	BAL
Notes Payable (due in 2015)		12,000	BAL
Mortgage Payable ($873,000 − $472,000)		401,000	BAL
Common Stock		472,000	BAL
Retained Earnings		822,000	BAL
Sales Revenue		3,741,000	INC
Cost of Goods Sold	2,384,000		INC
Salaries and Wages Expense ($651,000 + $50,000)	701,000		INC
Maintenance and Repairs Expense ($500,000 − $50,000)	450,000		INC
	$6,183,000	$6,183,000	

The Navigator

Summary of Learning Objectives

1 Analyze the effect of business transactions on the basic accounting equation. Each business transaction must have a dual effect on the accounting equation. For example, if an individual asset is increased, there must be a corresponding (a) decrease in another asset, or (b) increase in a specific liability, or (c) increase in stockholders' equity.

2 Explain what an account is and how it helps in the recording process. An account is an individual accounting record of increases and decreases in specific asset, liability, and stockholders' equity items.

3 Define debits and credits and explain how they are used to record business transactions. The terms debit and credit are synonymous with left and right. Assets, dividends, and expenses are increased by debits and decreased by credits. Liabilities, common stock, retained earnings, and revenues are increased by credits and decreased by debits.

4 Identify the basic steps in the recording process. The basic steps in the recording process are (a) analyze each transaction in terms of its effect on the accounts, (b) enter the transaction information in a journal, and (c) transfer the journal information to the appropriate accounts in the ledger.

5 Explain what a journal is and how it helps in the recording process. The initial accounting record of a transaction is entered in a journal before the data are entered in the accounts. A journal (a) discloses in one place the complete effect of a transaction, (b) provides a chronological record of transactions, and (c) prevents or locates errors because the debit and credit amounts for each entry can be readily compared.

6 Explain what a ledger is and how it helps in the recording process. The entire group of accounts maintained by a company is referred to collectively as a ledger. The ledger provides the balance in each of the accounts as well as keeps track of changes in these balances.

7 Explain what posting is and how it helps in the recording process. Posting is the procedure of transferring journal entries to the ledger accounts. This phase of the recording process accumulates the effects of journalized transactions in the individual accounts.

8 Explain the purposes of a trial balance. A trial balance is a list of accounts and their balances at a given time. The primary purpose of the trial balance is to prove the mathematical equality of debits and credits after posting. A trial balance also uncovers errors in journalizing and posting and is useful in preparing financial statements.

9 Classify cash activities as operating, investing, or financing. Operating activities are the types of activities the company performs to generate profits. Investing activities relate to the purchase or sale of long-lived assets used in operating the business, or to the purchase or sale of investment securities (stock and bonds of other companies). Financing activities are borrowing money, issuing shares of stock, and paying dividends.

 The Navigator

🧰 DECISION TOOLKIT *A SUMMARY*

DECISION CHECKPOINTS	INFO NEEDED FOR DECISION	TOOL TO USE FOR DECISION	HOW TO EVALUATE RESULTS
Has an accounting transaction occurred?	Details of the event	Accounting equation	If the event affected assets, liabilities, or stockholders' equity, then record as a transaction.
How do you determine that debits equal credits?	All account balances	Trial balance	List the account titles and their balances; total the debit and credit columns; verify equality.

Glossary

Account *(p. 111)* An individual accounting record of increases and decreases in specific asset, liability, stockholders' equity, revenue or expense items.

Accounting information system *(p. 102)* The system of collecting and processing transaction data and communicating financial information to decision-makers.

Accounting transactions *(p. 102)* Events that require recording in the financial statements because they affect assets, liabilities, or stockholders' equity.

Chart of accounts *(p. 120)* A list of a company's accounts.

Credit *(p. 111)* The right side of an account.

Debit *(p. 111)* The left side of an account.

Double-entry system *(p. 112)* A system that records the two-sided effect of each transaction in appropriate accounts.

General journal *(p. 117)* The most basic form of journal.

General ledger *(p. 119)* A ledger that contains all asset, liability, stockholders' equity, revenue, and expense accounts.

Journal *(p. 117)* An accounting record in which transactions are initially recorded in chronological order.

Journalizing *(p. 117)* The procedure of entering transaction data in the journal.

Ledger *(p. 119)* The group of accounts maintained by a company.

Posting *(p. 120)* The procedure of transferring journal entry amounts to the ledger accounts.

T-account *(p. 111)* The basic form of an account.

Trial balance *(p. 129)* A list of accounts and their balances at a given time.

Comprehensive *Do it!*

Bob Sample and other student investors opened Campus Carpet Cleaning, Inc. on September 1, 2014. During the first month of operations, the following transactions occurred.

Sept. 1 Stockholders invested $20,000 cash in the business.
  2 Paid $1,000 cash for store rent for the month of September.
  3 Purchased industrial carpet-cleaning equipment for $25,000, paying $10,000 in cash and signing a $15,000 6-month, 12% note payable.
  4 Paid $1,200 for 1-year accident insurance policy.
  10 Received bill from the *Daily News* for advertising the opening of the cleaning service, $200.
  15 Performed services on account for $6,200.
  20 Paid a $700 cash dividend to stockholders.
  30 Received $5,000 from customers billed on September 15.

The chart of accounts for the company is the same as for Sierra Corporation except for the following additional account: Advertising Expense.

Instructions

(a) Journalize the September transactions.

(b) Open ledger accounts and post the September transactions.

(c) Prepare a trial balance at September 30, 2014.

Action Plan

- Proceed through the accounting cycle in the following sequence:
  1. Make separate journal entries for each transaction.
  2. Note that all debits precede all credit entries.
  3. In journalizing, make sure debits equal credits.
  4. In journalizing, use specific account titles taken from the chart of accounts.
  5. Provide an appropriate explanation of each journal entry.
  6. Arrange ledger in statement order, beginning with the balance sheet accounts.
  7. Post in chronological order.
  8. Prepare a trial balance, which lists accounts in the order in which they appear in the ledger.
  9. List debit balances in the left column and credit balances in the right column.

Solution to Comprehensive Do it!

(a)

GENERAL JOURNAL

Date	Account Titles and Explanation	Debit	Credit
2014			
Sept. 1	Cash	20,000	
	Common Stock		20,000
	(Issued stock for cash)		
2	Rent Expense	1,000	
	Cash		1,000
	(Paid September rent)		
3	Equipment	25,000	
	Cash		10,000
	Notes Payable		15,000
	(Purchased cleaning equipment for cash and 6-month, 12% note payable)		
4	Prepaid Insurance	1,200	
	Cash		1,200
	(Paid 1-year insurance policy)		
10	Advertising Expense	200	
	Accounts Payable		200
	(Received bill from *Daily News* for advertising)		
15	Accounts Receivable	6,200	
	Service Revenue		6,200
	(Services performed on account)		
20	Dividends	700	
	Cash		700
	(Declared and paid a cash dividend)		
30	Cash	5,000	
	Accounts Receivable		5,000
	(Collection of accounts receivable)		

(b)

GENERAL LEDGER

Cash

Sept.	1	20,000	Sept.	2	1,000
	30	5,000		3	10,000
				4	1,200
				20	700
Bal.		12,100			

Common Stock

			Sept.	1	20,000
			Bal.		20,000

Accounts Receivable

Sept.	15	6,200	Sept.	30	5,000
Bal.		1,200			

Dividends

Sept.	20	700			
Bal.		700			

Prepaid Insurance				Service Revenue		
Sept. 4	1,200				Sept. 15	6,200
Bal.	1,200				Bal.	6,200

Equipment				Advertising Expense		
Sept. 3	25,000			Sept. 10	200	
Bal.	25,000			Bal.	200	

Notes Payable				Rent Expense		
		Sept. 3	15,000	Sept. 2	1,000	
		Bal.	15,000	Bal.	1,000	

Accounts Payable			
		Sept. 10	200
		Bal.	200

(c)

CAMPUS CARPET CLEANING, INC.
Trial Balance
September 30, 2014

	Debit	Credit
Cash	$12,100	
Accounts Receivable	1,200	
Prepaid Insurance	1,200	
Equipment	25,000	
Notes Payable		$15,000
Accounts Payable		200
Common Stock		20,000
Dividends	700	
Service Revenue		6,200
Advertising Expense	200	
Rent Expense	1,000	
	$41,400	$41,400

The Navigator

Self-Test, Brief Exercises, Exercises, Problem Set A, and many more resources are available for practice in WileyPLUS.

Self-Test Questions

Answers are on page 159.

(LO 1)   1. The effects on the basic accounting equation of performing services for cash are to:
   (a) increase assets and decrease stockholders' equity.
   (b) increase assets and increase stockholders' equity.
   (c) increase assets and increase liabilities.
   (d) increase liabilities and increase stockholders' equity.

2. Genesis Company buys a $900 machine on credit. (LO 1)
   This transaction will affect the:
   (a) income statement only.
   (b) balance sheet only.
   (c) income statement and retained earnings statement only.
   (d) income statement, retained earnings statement, and balance sheet.

(LO 1) **3.** Which of the following events is **not** recorded in the accounting records?
(a) Equipment is purchased on account.
(b) An employee is terminated.
(c) A cash investment is made into the business.
(d) Company pays dividend to stockholders.

(LO 1) **4.** During 2014, Gibson Company assets decreased $50,000 and its liabilities decreased $90,000. Its stockholders' equity therefore:
(a) increased $40,000.
(b) decreased $140,000.
(c) decreased $40,000.
(d) increased $140,000.

(LO 2) **5.** Which statement about an account is **true**?
(a) In its simplest form, an account consists of two parts.
(b) An account is an individual accounting record of increases and decreases in specific asset, liability, and stockholders' equity items.
(c) There are separate accounts for specific assets and liabilities but only one account for stock-holders' equity items.
(d) The left side of an account is the credit or decrease side.

(LO 3) **6.** Debits:
(a) increase both assets and liabilities.
(b) decrease both assets and liabilities.
(c) increase assets and decrease liabilities.
(d) decrease assets and increase liabilities.

(LO 3) **7.** A revenue account:
(a) is increased by debits.
(b) is decreased by credits.
(c) has a normal balance of a debit.
(d) is increased by credits.

(LO 3) **8.** Which accounts normally have debit balances?
(a) Assets, expenses, and revenues.
(b) Assets, expenses, and retained earnings.
(c) Assets, liabilities, and dividends.
(d) Assets, dividends, and expenses.

(LO 3) **9.** Paying an account payable with cash affects the components of the accounting equation in the following way:
(a) Decreases stockholders' equity and decreases liabilities.
(b) Increases assets and decreases liabilities.
(c) Decreases assets and increases stockholders' equity.
(d) Decreases assets and decreases liabilities.

10. Which is **not** part of the recording process? (LO 4)
(a) Analyzing transactions.
(b) Preparing a trial balance.
(c) Entering transactions in a journal.
(d) Posting transactions.

11. Which of these statements about a journal is **false**? (LO 5)
(a) It contains only revenue and expense accounts.
(b) It provides a chronological record of transactions.
(c) It helps to locate errors because the debit and credit amounts for each entry can be readily compared.
(d) It discloses in one place the complete effect of a transaction.

12. A ledger: (LO 6)
(a) contains only asset and liability accounts.
(b) should show accounts in alphabetical order.
(c) is a collection of the entire group of accounts maintained by a company.
(d) provides a chronological record of transactions.

13. Posting: (LO 7)
(a) normally occurs before journalizing.
(b) transfers ledger transaction data to the journal.
(c) is an optional step in the recording process.
(d) transfers journal entries to ledger accounts.

14. A trial balance: (LO 8)
(a) is a list of accounts with their balances at a given time.
(b) proves that proper account titles were used.
(c) will not balance if a correct journal entry is posted twice.
(d) proves that all transactions have been recorded.

15. A trial balance will **not** balance if: (LO 8)
(a) a correct journal entry is posted twice.
(b) the purchase of supplies on account is debited to Supplies and credited to Cash.
(c) a $100 cash dividend is debited to Dividends for $1,000 and credited to Cash for $100.
(d) a $450 payment on account is debited to Accounts Payable for $45 and credited to Cash for $45.

Go to the book's companion website, **www.wiley.com/college/kimmel**, to access additional Self-Test Questions.

✔ **The Navigator**

Questions

1. Describe the accounting information system.

2. Can a business enter into a transaction that affects only the left side of the basic accounting equation? If so, give an example.

3. Are the following events recorded in the accounting records? Explain your answer in each case.
(a) A major stockholder of the company dies.
(b) Supplies are purchased on account.
(c) An employee is fired.
(d) The company pays a cash dividend to its stockholders.

4. Indicate how each business transaction affects the basic accounting equation.
(a) Paid cash for janitorial services.
(b) Purchased equipment for cash.

(c) Issued common stock to investors in exchange for cash.

(d) Paid an account payable in full.

5. Why is an account referred to as a T-account?

6. The terms debit and credit mean "increase" and "decrease," respectively. Do you agree? Explain.

7. Terry Rabas, a fellow student, contends that the double-entry system means each transaction must be recorded twice. Is Terry correct? Explain.

8. Misty Reno, a beginning accounting student, believes debit balances are favorable and credit balances are unfavorable. Is Misty correct? Discuss.

9. State the rules of debit and credit as applied to (a) asset accounts, (b) liability accounts, and (c) the Common Stock account.

10. What is the normal balance for each of these accounts?
   (a) Accounts Receivable.
   (b) Cash.
   (c) Dividends.
   (d) Accounts Payable.
   (e) Service Revenue.
   (f) Salaries and Wages Expense.
   (g) Common Stock.

11. Indicate whether each account is an asset, a liability, or a stockholders' equity account, and whether it would have a normal debit or credit balance.
   (a) Accounts Receivable.   (d) Dividends.
   (b) Accounts Payable.   (e) Supplies.
   (c) Equipment.

12. For the following transactions, indicate the account debited and the account credited.
   (a) Supplies are purchased on account.
   (b) Cash is received on signing a note payable.
   (c) Employees are paid salaries in cash.

13. For each account listed here, indicate whether it generally will have debit entries only, credit entries only, or both debit and credit entries.
   (a) Cash.
   (b) Accounts Receivable.
   (c) Dividends.
   (d) Accounts Payable.

   (e) Salaries and Wages Expense.
   (f) Service Revenue.

14. What are the normal balances for the following accounts of Tootsie Roll Industries? (a) Accounts Receivable, (b) Income Taxes Payable, (c) Sales, and (d) Selling, Marketing, and Administrative Expenses.

15. What are the basic steps in the recording process?

16. (a) When entering a transaction in the journal, should the debit or credit be written first?
   (b) Which should be indented, the debit or the credit?

17. (a) Should accounting transaction debits and credits be recorded directly in the ledger accounts?
   (b) What are the advantages of first recording transactions in the journal and then posting to the ledger?

18. Journalize these accounting transactions.
   (a) Stockholders invested $12,000 in the business in exchange for common stock.
   (b) Insurance of $800 is paid for the year.
   (c) Supplies of $1,800 are purchased on account.
   (d) Cash of $7,500 is received for services rendered.

19. (a) What is a ledger?
   (b) Why is a chart of accounts important?

20. What is a trial balance and what are its purposes?

21. Tyler Bazil is confused about how accounting information flows through the accounting system. He believes information flows in this order:
   (a) Debits and credits are posted to the ledger.
   (b) Accounting transaction occurs.
   (c) Information is entered in the journal.
   (d) Financial statements are prepared.
   (e) Trial balance is prepared.

   Indicate to Tyler the proper flow of the information.

22. Two students are discussing the use of a trial balance. They wonder whether the following errors, each considered separately, would prevent the trial balance from balancing. What would you tell them?
   (a) The bookkeeper debited Cash for $600 and credited Salaries and Wages Expense for $600 for payment of wages.
   (b) Cash collected on account was debited to Cash for $800, and Service Revenue was credited for $80.

Brief Exercises

BE3-1 Presented below are three economic events. On a sheet of paper, list the letters (a), (b), and (c) with columns for assets, liabilities, and stockholders' equity. In each column, indicate whether the event increased (+), decreased (−), or had no effect (NE) on assets, liabilities, and stockholders' equity.
(a) Purchased supplies on account.
(b) Received cash for providing a service.
(c) Expenses paid in cash.

Determine effect of transactions on basic accounting equation.
(LO 1), **C**

BE3-2 During 2014, Damon Corp. entered into the following transactions.
1. Borrowed $60,000 by issuing bonds.
2. Paid $9,000 cash dividend to stockholders.
3. Received $13,000 cash from a previously billed customer for services performed.
4. Purchased supplies on account for $3,100.

Determine effect of transactions on basic accounting equation.
(LO 1), **AP**

Using the following tabular analysis, show the effect of each transaction on the accounting equation. Put explanations for changes to Stockholders' Equity in the right-hand margin. For Retained Earnings, use separate columns for Revenues, Expenses, and Dividends if necessary. Use Illustration 3-3 (page 110) as a model.

Assets			=	Liabilities		+	Stockholders' Equity	
	Accounts			Accounts	Bonds		Common	Retained
Cash +	Receivable +	Supplies =		Payable +	Payable +		Stock +	Earnings

Determine effect of transactions on basic accounting equation.

(LO 1), AP

BE3-3 During 2014, Comstock Company entered into the following transactions.
1. Purchased equipment for $286,176 cash.
2. Issued common stock to investors for $137,590 cash.
3. Purchased inventory of $68,480 on account.

Using the following tabular analysis, show the effect of each transaction on the accounting equation. Put explanations for changes to Stockholders' Equity in the right-hand margin. For Retained Earnings, use separate columns for Revenues, Expenses, and Dividends if necessary. Use Illustration 3-3 (page 110) as a model.

Assets			=	Liabilities	+	Stockholders' Equity	
				Accounts		Common	Retained
Cash +	Inventory +	Equipment =		Payable	+	Stock +	Earnings

Indicate debit and credit effects.

(LO 3), K

BE3-4 For each of the following accounts, indicate the effect of a debit or a credit on the account and the normal balance.
(a) Accounts Payable. (d) Accounts Receivable.
(b) Advertising Expense. (e) Retained Earnings.
(c) Service Revenue. (f) Dividends.

Identify accounts to be debited and credited.

(LO 3), C

BE3-5 Transactions for Grover Company for the month of June are presented below. Identify the accounts to be debited and credited for each transaction.

June 1 Issues common stock to investors in exchange for $5,000 cash.
    2 Buys equipment on account for $1,100.
    3 Pays $740 to landlord for June rent.
    12 Bills Matt Wilfer $700 for welding work done.

Journalize transactions.

(LO 5), AP

BE3-6 Use the data in BE3-5 and journalize the transactions. (You may omit explanations.)

Identify steps in the recording process.

(LO 4), C

BE3-7 Rachelle Mohling, a fellow student, is unclear about the basic steps in the recording process. Identify and briefly explain the steps in the order in which they occur.

Indicate basic debit-credit analysis.

(LO 4), C

BE3-8 Upton Corporation has the following transactions during August of the current year. Indicate (a) the basic analysis and (b) the debit-credit analysis illustrated on pages 121–126.

Aug. 1 Issues shares of common stock to investors in exchange for $10,000.
    4 Pays insurance in advance for 3 months, $1,500.
    16 Receives $900 from clients for services rendered.
    27 Pays the secretary $620 salary.

Journalize transactions.

(LO 5), AP

BE3-9 Use the data in BE3-8 and journalize the transactions. (You may omit explanations.)

Post journal entries to T-accounts.

(LO 7), AP

BE3-10 Selected transactions for Perez Company are presented below in journal form (without explanations). Post the transactions to T-accounts.

Date		Account Title	Debit	Credit
May	5	Accounts Receivable	3,800	
		Service Revenue		3,800
	12	Cash	1,600	
		Accounts Receivable		1,600
	15	Cash	2,000	
		Service Revenue		2,000

BE3-11 From the ledger balances below, prepare a trial balance for Yeager Company at June 30, 2014. All account balances are normal.

Prepare a trial balance.
(LO 8), **AP**

Accounts Payable	$ 1,000	Service Revenue	$8,600
Cash	5,400	Accounts Receivable	3,000
Common Stock	18,000	Salaries and Wages Expense	4,000
Dividends	1,200	Rent Expense	1,000
Equipment	13,000		

BE3-12 An inexperienced bookkeeper prepared the following trial balance that does not balance. Prepare a correct trial balance, assuming all account balances are normal.

Prepare a corrected trial balance.
(LO 8), **AP**

CINELLI COMPANY
Trial Balance
December 31, 2014

	Debit	Credit
Cash	$20,800	
Prepaid Insurance		$ 3,500
Accounts Payable		2,500
Unearned Service Revenue	1,800	
Common Stock		10,000
Retained Earnings		6,600
Dividends		5,000
Service Revenue		25,600
Salaries and Wages Expense	14,600	
Rent Expense		2,600
	$37,200	$55,800

Do it! Review

Do it! 3-1 Transactions made by Huddleston Co. for the month of March are shown below. Prepare a tabular analysis that shows the effects of these transactions on the expanded accounting equation, similar to that shown in Illustration 3-3 (page 110).

Prepare tabular analysis.
(LO 1), **C**

1. The company performed $20,000 of services for customers on account.
2. The company received $20,000 in cash from customers who had been billed for services [in transaction (1)].
3. The company received a bill for $1,800 of advertising but will not pay it until a later date.
4. Huddleston Co. paid a cash dividend of $3,000.

Do it! 3-2 Joel Blocker has just rented space in a strip mall. In this space, he will open a photography studio, to be called Picture This! A friend has advised Joel to set up a double-entry set of accounting records in which to record all of his business transactions.

Identify normal balances.
(LO 2, 3), **C**

Identify the balance sheet accounts that Joel will likely need to record the transactions needed to open his business (a corporation). Indicate whether the normal balance of each account is a debit or credit.

Do it! 3-3 Joel Blocker engaged in the following activities in establishing his photography studio, Picture This!:

Record business activities.
(LO 4, 5), **AP**

1. Opened a bank account in the name of Picture This! and deposited $8,000 of his own money into this account in exchange for common stock.
2. Purchased photography supplies at a total cost of $950. The business paid $400 in cash, and the balance is on account.
3. Obtained estimates on the cost of photography equipment from three different manufacturers.

In what form (type of record) should Joel record these three activities? Prepare the entries to record the transactions.

Post transactions.
(LO 6, 7), **AP**

Do it! 3-4   Joel Blocker recorded the following transactions during the month of April.

Apr.	3	Cash	3,400	
		Service Revenue		3,400
	16	Rent Expense	500	
		Cash		500
	20	Salaries and Wages Expense	300	
		Cash		300

Post these entries to the Cash account of the general ledger to determine the ending balance in cash. The beginning balance in cash on April 1 was $1,900.

Exercises

Analyze the effect of transactions.
(LO 1), **C**

E3-1   Selected transactions for Warner Advertising Company, Inc., are listed here.

1. Issued common stock to investors in exchange for cash received from investors.
2. Paid monthly rent.
3. Received cash from customers when service was performed.
4. Billed customers for services performed.
5. Paid dividend to stockholders.
6. Incurred advertising expense on account.
7. Received cash from customers billed in (4).
8. Purchased additional equipment for cash.
9. Purchased equipment on account.

Instructions

Describe the effect of each transaction on assets, liabilities, and stockholders' equity. For example, the first answer is (1) Increase in assets and increase in stockholders' equity.

Analyze the effect of transactions on assets, liabilities, and stockholders' equity.
(LO 1), **AP**

E3-2   Manning Company entered into these transactions during May 2014, its first month of operations.

1. Stockholders invested $40,000 in the business in exchange for common stock of the company.
2. Purchased computers for office use for $30,000 from Dell on account.
3. Paid $4,000 cash for May rent on storage space.
4. Performed computer services worth $19,000 on account.
5. Performed computer services to Lawton Construction Company for $5,000 cash.
6. Paid Southern States Power Co. $8,000 cash for energy usage in May.
7. Paid Dell for the computers purchased in (2).
8. Incurred advertising expense for May of $1,300 on account.
9. Received $12,000 cash from customers for contracts billed in (4).

Instructions

Using the following tabular analysis, show the effect of each transaction on the accounting equation. Put explanations for changes to Stockholders' Equity in the right-hand margin. Use Illustration 3-3 (page 110) as a model.

Assets			=	Liabilities	+		Stockholders' Equity			
	Accounts			Accounts		Common		Retained Earnings		
Cash	+ Receivable	+ Equipment	=	Payable	+	Stock	+ Revenues	− Expenses	−	Dividends

Determine effect of transactions on basic accounting equation.
(LO 1), **AP**

E3-3   During 2014, its first year of operations as a delivery service, Persinger Corp. entered into the following transactions.

1. Issued shares of common stock to investors in exchange for $100,000 in cash.
2. Borrowed $45,000 by issuing bonds.
3. Purchased delivery trucks for $60,000 cash.
4. Received $16,000 from customers for services performed.
5. Purchased supplies for $4,700 on account.
6. Paid rent of $5,200.

7. Performed services on account for $10,000.
8. Paid salaries of $28,000.
9. Paid a dividend of $11,000 to shareholders.

Instructions

Using the following tabular analysis, show the effect of each transaction on the accounting equation. Put explanations for changes to Stockholders' Equity in the right-hand margin. Use Illustration 3-3 (page 110) as a model.

Assets					=	Liabilities		+	Stockholders' Equity				
											Retained Earnings		
		Accounts		Equip-		Accounts	Bonds		Common				
Cash	+	Receivable	+ Supplies +	ment	=	Payable	+ Payable	+	Stock	+ Revenues	− Expenses	− Dividends

E3-4 A tabular analysis of the transactions made during August 2014 by Colaw Company during its first month of operations is shown below. Each increase and decrease in stockholders' equity is explained.

Analyze transactions and compute net income.
(LO 1), **AP**

	Assets							=	Liabilities	+	Stockholders' Equity					
									Accounts		Common			Retained Earnings		
	Cash	+	A/R	+	Supp.	+	Equip.	=	Payable	+	Stock	+	Rev.	− Exp.	− Div.	
1.	+$20,000										+$20,000					Com. Stock
2.	−1,000						+$5,000		+$4,000							
3.	−750				+$750											
4.	+4,100		+$5,400										+$9,500			Serv. Rev.
5.	−1,500								−1,500							
6.	−2,000														−$2,000 Div.	
7.	−800													−$ 800		Rent Exp.
8.	+450		−450													
9.	−3,000													−3,000		Salar. Exp.
10.									+300					−300		Util. Exp.

Instructions

(a) Describe each transaction.
(b) Determine how much stockholders' equity increased for the month.
(c) Compute the net income for the month.

E3-5 The tabular analysis of transactions for Colaw Company is presented in E3-4.

Prepare an income statement, retained earnings statement, and balance sheet.
(LO 1), **AP**

Instructions

Prepare an income statement and a retained earnings statement for August and a classified balance sheet at August 31, 2014.

E3-6 Selected transactions for Home Place, an interior decorator corporation, in its first month of business, are as follows.

Identify debits, credits, and normal balances and journalize transactions.
(LO 3, 5), **AP**

1. Issued stock to investors for $15,000 in cash.
2. Purchased used car for $10,000 cash for use in business.
3. Purchased supplies on account for $300.
4. Billed customers $3,700 for services performed.
5. Paid $200 cash for advertising start of the business.
6. Received $1,100 cash from customers billed in transaction (4).
7. Paid creditor $300 cash on account.
8. Paid dividends of $400 cash to stockholders.

Instructions

(a) For each transaction indicate (a) the basic type of account debited and credited (asset, liability, stockholders' equity); (b) the specific account debited and credited (Cash, Rent Expense, Service Revenue, etc.); (c) whether the specific account is increased or decreased; and (d) the normal balance of the specific account. Use the format shown on page 142, in which transaction 1 is given as an example.

	Account Debited				Account Credited			
	(a)	**(b)**	**(c)**	**(d)**	**(a)**	**(b)**	**(c)**	**(d)**
Trans-action	**Basic Type**	**Specific Account**	**Effect**	**Normal Balance**	**Basic Type**	**Specific Account**	**Effect**	**Normal Balance**
1	Asset	Cash	Increase	Debit	Stock-holders' equity	Common Stock	Increase	Credit

(b) Journalize the transactions. Do not provide explanations.

Analyze transactions and determine their effect on accounts.

(LO 3), C

E3-7 This information relates to Crofoot Real Estate Agency.

Oct. 1 Stockholders invest $30,000 in exchange for common stock of the corporation.
   2 Hires an administrative assistant at an annual salary of $36,000.
   3 Buys office furniture for $3,800, on account.
   6 Sells a house and lot for M.E. Graves; commissions due from Graves, $10,800 (not paid by Graves at this time).
   10 Receives cash of $140 as commission for acting as rental agent renting an apartment.
   27 Pays $700 on account for the office furniture purchased on October 3.
   30 Pays the administrative assistant $3,000 in salary for October.

Instructions

Prepare the debit–credit analysis for each transaction, as illustrated on pages 121–126.

Journalize transactions.

(LO 5), AP

E3-8 Transaction data for Crofoot Real Estate Agency are presented in E3-7.

Instructions

Journalize the transactions. Do not provide explanations.

Journalize a series of transactions.

(LO 4, 5), AP

E3-9 The May transactions of Hanschu Corporation were as follows.

May 4 Paid $700 due for supplies previously purchased on account.
   7 Performed advisory services on account for $6,800.
   8 Purchased supplies for $850 on account.
   9 Purchased equipment for $1,000 in cash.
   17 Paid employees $530 in cash.
   22 Received bill for equipment repairs of $900.
   29 Paid $1,200 for 12 months of insurance policy. Coverage begins June 1.

Instructions

Journalize the transactions. Do not provide explanations.

Post journal entries and prepare a trial balance.

(LO 7, 8), AP

E3-10 Transaction data and journal entries for Crofoot Real Estate Agency are presented in E3-7 and E3-8.

Instructions

(a) Post the transactions to T-accounts.
(b) Prepare a trial balance at October 31, 2014.

Analyze transactions, prepare journal entries, and post transactions to T-accounts.

(LO 1, 5, 7), AP

E3-11 Selected transactions for Protheroe Corporation during its first month in business are presented below.

Sept. 1 Issued common stock in exchange for $20,000 cash received from investors.
   5 Purchased equipment for $9,000, paying $3,000 in cash and the balance on account.
   8 Performed services on account for $18,000.
   14 Paid salaries of $1,200.
   25 Paid $4,000 cash on balance owed for equipment.
   30 Paid $500 cash dividend.

Protheroe's chart of accounts shows Cash, Accounts Receivable, Equipment, Accounts Payable, Common Stock, Dividends, Service Revenue, and Salaries and Wages Expense.

Instructions

(a) Prepare a tabular analysis of the September transactions. The column headings should be Cash + Accounts Receivable + Equipment = Accounts Payable + Stockholders' Equity. For transactions affecting stockholders' equity, provide explanations in the right margin, as shown on page 110.
(b) Journalize the transactions. Do not provide explanations.
(c) Post the transactions to T-accounts.

E3-12 The T-accounts below summarize the ledger of Wheeling Gardening Company, Inc. at the end of the first month of operations.

Journalize transactions from T-accounts and prepare a trial balance.
(LO 5, 8), **AP**

	Cash			
Apr.	1	15,000	Apr. 15	800
	12	700	25	3,500
	29	800		
	30	900		

	Unearned Service Revenue		
		Apr. 30	900

	Accounts Receivable			
Apr.	7	3,400	Apr. 29	800

	Common Stock		
		Apr. 1	15,000

	Supplies	
Apr.	4	5,200

	Service Revenue		
		Apr. 7	3,400
		12	700

	Accounts Payable			
Apr.	25	3,500	Apr. 4	5,200

	Salaries and Wages Expense	
Apr.	15	800

Instructions

(a) Prepare the journal entries (including explanations) that resulted in the amounts posted to the accounts. Present them in the order they occurred.

(b) Prepare a trial balance at April 30, 2014. (*Hint:* Compute ending balances of T-accounts first.)

E3-13 Selected transactions from the journal of Eberle Inc. during its first month of operations are presented here.

Post journal entries and prepare a trial balance.
(LO 7, 8), **AP**

Date		Account Titles	Debit	Credit
Aug.	1	Cash	8,000	
		Common Stock		8,000
	10	Cash	1,700	
		Service Revenue		1,700
	12	Equipment	6,200	
		Cash		1,200
		Notes Payable		5,000
	25	Accounts Receivable	3,400	
		Service Revenue		3,400
	31	Cash	600	
		Accounts Receivable		600

Instructions

(a) Post the transactions to T-accounts.

(b) Prepare a trial balance at August 31, 2014.

E3-14 Here is the ledger for Keisler Co.

Journalize transactions from T-accounts and prepare a trial balance.
(LO 5, 8), **AP**

	Cash			
Oct.	1	7,000	Oct. 4	400
	10	980	12	1,500
	10	8,000	15	250
	20	700	30	300
	25	2,000	31	500

	Common Stock		
		Oct. 1	7,000
		25	2,000

	Accounts Receivable			
Oct.	6	800	Oct. 20	700
	20	920		

	Dividends		
Oct.	30	300	

	Supplies			
Oct.	4	400	Oct. 31	180

	Service Revenue		
		Oct. 6	800
		10	980
		20	920

Equipment				Salaries and Wages Expense		
Oct. 3	3,000			Oct. 31	500	

Notes Payable				Supplies Expense		
		Oct. 10	8,000	Oct. 31	180	

Accounts Payable				Rent Expense		
Oct. 12	1,500	Oct. 3	3,000	Oct. 15	250	

Instructions

(a) Reproduce the journal entries for only the transactions that **occurred on October 1, 10, and 20,** and provide explanations for each.

(b) Prepare a trial balance at October 31, 2014. (*Hint:* Compute ending balances of T-accounts first.)

Analyze errors and their effects on trial balance.

(LO 8), **AN**

E3-15 The bookkeeper for Willingham Corporation made these errors in journalizing and posting.

1. A credit posting of $400 to Accounts Receivable was omitted.
2. A debit posting of $750 for Prepaid Insurance was debited to Insurance Expense.
3. A collection on account of $100 was journalized and posted as a debit to Cash $100 and a credit to Accounts Payable $100.
4. A credit posting of $300 to Income Taxes Payable was made twice.
5. A cash purchase of supplies for $250 was journalized and posted as a debit to Supplies $25 and a credit to Cash $25.
6. A debit of $395 to Advertising Expense was posted as $359.

Instructions

For each error, indicate (a) whether the trial balance will balance; if the trial balance will not balance, indicate (b) the amount of the difference and (c) the trial balance column that will have the larger total. Consider each error separately. Use the following form, in which error 1 is given as an example.

	(a)	(b)	(c)
Error	**In Balance**	**Difference**	**Larger Column**
1	No	$400	Debit

Prepare a trial balance and financial statements.

(LO 8), **AP**

E3-16 The accounts in the ledger of Bastin Delivery Service contain the following balances on July 31, 2014.

Accounts Receivable	$13,400	Prepaid Insurance	$ 2,200
Accounts Payable	8,400	Service Revenue	15,500
Cash	?	Dividends	700
Equipment	59,360	Common Stock	40,000
Maintenance and		Salaries and Wages Expense	7,428
Repairs Expense	1,958	Salaries and Wages Payable	820
Insurance Expense	900	Retained Earnings	5,200
Notes Payable (due 2017)	28,450	(July 1, 2014)	

Instructions

(a) Prepare a trial balance with the accounts arranged as illustrated in the chapter, and fill in the missing amount for Cash.

(b) Prepare an income statement, a retained earnings statement, and a classified balance sheet for the month of July 2014.

Identify normal account balance and corresponding financial statement.

(LO 3), **K**

E3-17 The following accounts, in alphabetical order, were selected from recent financial statements of Krispy Kreme Doughnuts, Inc.

Accounts payable	Interest income
Accounts receivable	Inventories
Common stock	Prepaid expenses
Depreciation expense	Property and equipment
Interest expense	Revenues

Instructions

For each account, indicate (a) whether the normal balance is a debit or a credit, and (b) the financial statement—balance sheet or income statement—where the account should be presented.

E3-18   Review the transactions listed in E3-1 for Warner Advertising Company and classify each transaction as either an operating activity, investing activity, or financing activity, or if no cash is exchanged, as a noncash event.

Classify transactions as cash-flow activities.
(LO 9), **AP**

E3-19   Review the transactions listed in E3-3 for Persinger Corp. and classify each transaction as either an operating activity, investing activity, or financing activity, or if no cash is exchanged, as a noncash event.

Classify transactions as cash-flow activities.
(LO 9), **AP**

Exercises: Set B and Challenge Exercises

Visit the book's companion website, at **www.wiley.com/college/kimmel**, and choose the Student Companion site to access Exercise Set B and Challenge Exercises.

Problems: Set A

P3-1A   On April 1, DeDonder Travel Agency Inc. was established. These transactions were completed during the month.
1. Stockholders invested $30,000 cash in the company in exchange for common stock.
2. Paid $900 cash for April office rent.
3. Purchased office equipment for $3,400 cash.
4. Purchased $200 of advertising in the *Chicago Tribune*, on account.
5. Paid $500 cash for office supplies.
6. Performed services worth $12,000. Cash of $3,000 is received from customers, and the balance of $9,000 is billed to customers on account.
7. Paid $400 cash dividends.
8. Paid *Chicago Tribune* amount due in transaction (4).
9. Paid employees' salaries $1,800.
10. Received $9,000 in cash from customers billed previously in transaction (6).

Analyze transactions and compute net income.
(LO 1), **AP**

Instructions
(a) Prepare a tabular analysis of the transactions using these column headings: Cash, Accounts Receivable, Supplies, Equipment, Accounts Payable, Common Stock, and Retained Earnings (with separate columns for Revenues, Expenses, and Dividends). Include margin explanations for any changes in Retained Earnings.
(b) From an analysis of the Retained Earnings columns, compute the net income or net loss for April.

(a) Cash $34,800
    Total assets $38,700

P3-2A   Nina Finzelberg started her own consulting firm, Finzelberg Consulting Inc., on May 1, 2014. The following transactions occurred during the month of May.

Analyze transactions and prepare financial statements.
(LO 1), **AP**

May	1	Stockholders invested $15,000 cash in the business in exchange for common stock.
	2	Paid $600 for office rent for the month.
	3	Purchased $500 of supplies on account.
	5	Paid $150 to advertise in the *County News*.
	9	Received $1,400 cash for services performed.
	12	Paid $200 cash dividend.
	15	Performed $4,200 of services on account.
	17	Paid $2,500 for employee salaries.
	20	Paid for the supplies purchased on account on May 3.
	23	Received a cash payment of $1,200 for services performed on account on May 15.
	26	Borrowed $5,000 from the bank on a note payable.
	29	Purchased office equipment for $2,000 paying $200 in cash and the balance on account.
	30	Paid $180 for utilities.

Instructions
(a) Show the effects of the previous transactions on the accounting equation using the following format. Assume the note payable is to be repaid within the year.

(a) Cash $18,270
    Total assets $23,770

	Assets				=	Liabilities		+	Stockholders' Equity		
		Accounts				Notes	Accounts	Common	Retained Earnings		
Date	Cash	+ Receivable	+ Supplies	+ Equipment	= Payable	+ Payable	+ Stock	+ Revenues	− Expenses	− Dividends

Include margin explanations for any changes in Retained Earnings.

(b) Net income $2,170

(b) Prepare an income statement for the month of May 2014.

(c) Prepare a classified balance sheet at May 31, 2014.

Analyze transactions and prepare an income statement, retained earnings statement, and balance sheet.

(LO 1), **AP**

P3-3A Cindy Braun created a corporation providing legal services, Cindy Braun Inc., on July 1, 2014. On July 31 the balance sheet showed Cash $4,000; Accounts Receivable $2,500; Supplies $500; Equipment $5,000; Accounts Payable $4,200; Common Stock $6,200; and Retained Earnings $1,600. During August, the following transactions occurred.

Aug. 1 Collected $1,100 of accounts receivable due from customers.
4 Paid $2,700 cash for accounts payable due.
9 Performed services worth $5,400, of which $3,600 is collected in cash and the balance is due in September.
15 Purchased additional office equipment for $4,000, paying $700 in cash and the balance on account.
19 Paid salaries $1,400, rent for August $700, and advertising expenses $350.
23 Paid a cash dividend of $700.
26 Borrowed $5,000 from Standard Federal Bank; the money was borrowed on a 4-month note payable.
31 Incurred utility expenses for the month on account $380.

Instructions

(a) Cash $7,150

(a) Prepare a tabular analysis of the August transactions beginning with July 31 balances. The column heading should be Cash + Accounts Receivable + Supplies + Equipment = Notes Payable + Accounts Payable + Common Stock + Retained Earnings + Revenues − Expenses − Dividends. Include margin explanations for any changes in Retained Earnings.

(b) Net income $2,570
Ret. earnings $3,470

(b) Prepare an income statement for August, a retained earnings statement for August, and a classified balance sheet at August 31.

Journalize a series of transactions.

(LO 4, 5), **AP**

P3-4A Friendley's Miniature Golf and Driving Range Inc. was opened on March 1 by Dean Barley. These selected events and transactions occurred during March.

Mar. 1 Stockholders invested $50,000 cash in the business in exchange for common stock of the corporation.
3 Purchased Arnie's Golf Land for $38,000 cash. The price consists of land $23,000, building $9,000, and equipment $6,000. (Record this in a single entry.)
5 Advertised the opening of the driving range and miniature golf course, paying advertising expenses of $1,200 cash.
6 Paid cash $2,400 for a 1-year insurance policy.
10 Purchased golf clubs and other equipment for $5,500 from Golden Bear Company, payable in 30 days.
18 Received golf fees of $1,600 in cash from customers for golf services performed.
19 Sold 100 coupon books for $25 each in cash. Each book contains ten coupons that enable the holder to play one round of miniature golf or to hit one bucket of golf balls. (*Hint:* The revenue should not be recognized until the customers use the coupons.)
25 Paid a $500 cash dividend.
30 Paid salaries of $800.
30 Paid Golden Bear Company in full for equipment purchased on March 10.
31 Received $900 in cash from customers for golf services performed.

The company uses these accounts: Cash, Prepaid Insurance, Land, Buildings, Equipment, Accounts Payable, Unearned Service Revenue, Common Stock, Retained Earnings, Dividends, Service Revenue, Advertising Expense, and Salaries and Wages Expense.

Instructions

Journalize the March transactions, including explanations. Friendley's records golf fees as service revenue.

P3-5A Foyle Architects incorporated as licensed architects on April 1, 2014. During the first month of the operation of the business, these events and transactions occurred:

Journalize transactions, post, and prepare a trial balance.
(LO 5, 6, 7, 8), **AP**

Apr. 1   Stockholders invested $18,000 cash in exchange for common stock of the corporation.
  1   Hired a secretary-receptionist at a salary of $375 per week, payable monthly.
  2   Paid office rent for the month $900.
  3   Purchased architectural supplies on account from Burlington Company $1,300.
  10   Completed blueprints on a carport and billed client $1,900 for services.
  11   Received $700 cash advance from J. Madison to design a new home.
  20   Received $2,800 cash for services completed and delivered to M. Svetlana.
  30   Paid secretary-receptionist for the month $1,500.
  30   Paid $300 to Burlington Company for accounts payable due.

The company uses these accounts: Cash, Accounts Receivable, Supplies, Accounts Payable, Unearned Service Revenue, Common Stock, Service Revenue, Salaries and Wages Expense, and Rent Expense.

Instructions

(a) Journalize the transactions, including explanations.
(b) Post to the ledger T-accounts.
(c) Prepare a trial balance on April 30, 2014.

(c) Cash $18,800
   Tot. trial balance $24,400

P3-6A This is the trial balance of Solis Company on September 30.

Journalize transactions, post, and prepare a trial balance.
(LO 5, 6, 7, 8), **AP**

SOLIS COMPANY
Trial Balance
September 30, 2014

	Debit	Credit
Cash	$19,200	
Accounts Receivable	2,600	
Supplies	2,100	
Equipment	8,000	
Accounts Payable		$ 4,800
Unearned Service Revenue		1,100
Common Stock		15,000
Retained Earnings		11,000
	$31,900	$31,900

The October transactions were as follows.

Oct. 5   Received $1,300 in cash from customers for accounts receivable due.
  10   Billed customers for services performed $5,100.
  15   Paid employee salaries $1,200.
  17   Performed $600 of services in exchange for cash.
  20   Paid $1,900 to creditors for accounts payable due.
  29   Paid a $300 cash dividend.
  31   Paid utilities $400.

Instructions

(a) Prepare a general ledger using T-accounts. Enter the opening balances in the ledger accounts as of October 1. Provision should be made for these additional accounts: Dividends, Service Revenue, Salaries and Wages Expense, and Utilities Expense.
(b) Journalize the transactions, including explanations.
(c) Post to the ledger accounts.
(d) Prepare a trial balance on October 31, 2014.

(d) Cash $17,300
   Tot. trial balance $35,700

Prepare a correct trial balance.

(LO 8), **AN**

P3-7A This trial balance of Swisher Co. does not balance.

SWISHER CO.
Trial Balance
June 30, 2014

	Debit	Credit
Cash		$ 3,090
Accounts Receivable	$ 3,190	
Supplies	800	
Equipment	3,000	
Accounts Payable		3,686
Unearned Service Revenue	1,200	
Common Stock		9,000
Dividends	800	
Service Revenue		3,480
Salaries and Wages Expense	3,600	
Utilities Expense	910	
	$13,500	$19,256

Each of the listed accounts has a normal balance per the general ledger. An examination of the ledger and journal reveals the following errors:

1. Cash received from a customer on account was debited for $780, and Accounts Receivable was credited for the same amount. The actual collection was for $870.
2. The purchase of a printer on account for $340 was recorded as a debit to Supplies for $340 and a credit to Accounts Payable for $340.
3. Services were performed on account for a client for $900. Accounts Receivable was debited for $90 and Service Revenue was credited for $900.
4. A debit posting to Salaries and Wages Expense of $700 was omitted.
5. A payment on account for $206 was credited to Cash for $206 and credited to Accounts Payable for $260.
6. Payment of a $600 cash dividend to Swisher's stockholders was debited to Salaries and Wages Expense for $600 and credited to Cash for $600.

Instructions

Tot. trial balance $16,900

Prepare the correct trial balance. (*Hint:* All accounts have normal balances.)

Journalize transactions, post, and prepare a trial balance.

(LO 5, 6, 7, 8), **AP**

P3-8A The Sequel Theater Inc. was recently formed. It began operations in March 2014. The Sequel is unique in that it will show only triple features of sequential theme movies. On March 1, the ledger of The Sequel showed Cash $16,000; Land $38,000; Buildings (concession stand, projection room, ticket booth, and screen) $22,000; Equipment $16,000; Accounts Payable $12,000; and Common Stock $80,000. During the month of March, the following events and transactions occurred.

Mar. 2 Rented the three *Star Wars* movies (*Star Wars®*, *The Empire Strikes Back*, and *The Return of the Jedi*) to be shown for the first three weeks of March. The film rental was $10,000; $2,000 was paid in cash and $8,000 will be paid on March 10.

3 Ordered the first three *Star Trek* movies to be shown the last 10 days of March. It will cost $500 per night.

9 Received $9,900 cash from admissions.

10 Paid balance due on *Star Wars* movies' rental and $2,900 on March 1 accounts payable.

11 The Sequel Theater contracted with J. Russo to operate the concession stand. Russo agrees to pay The Sequel 15% of gross receipts, payable monthly, for the rental of the concession stand.

12 Paid advertising expenses $500.

20 Received $8,300 cash from customers for admissions.

20 Received the *Star Trek* movies and paid rental fee of $5,000.

31 Paid salaries of $3,800.

31   Received statement from J. Russo showing gross receipts from concessions of $10,000 and the balance due to The Sequel of $1,500 ($10,000 × .15) for March. Russo paid half the balance due and will remit the remainder on April 5.

31   Received $20,000 cash from customers for admissions.

In addition to the accounts identified above, the chart of accounts includes Accounts Receivable, Service Revenue, Rent Revenue, Advertising Expense, Rent Expense, and Salaries and Wages Expense.

Instructions
(a)   Using T-accounts, enter the beginning balances to the ledger.
(b)   Journalize the March transactions, including explanations. The Sequel records admission revenue as service revenue, concession revenue as sales revenue, and film rental expense as rent expense.
(c)   Post the March journal entries to the ledger.
(d)   Prepare a trial balance on March 31, 2014.

(d) Cash $ 32,750
Tot. trial balance $128,800

P3-9A   The bookkeeper for Ginger's dance studio made the following errors in journalizing and posting.

1.   A credit to Supplies of $600 was omitted.
2.   A debit posting of $300 to Accounts Payable was inadvertently debited to Accounts Receivable.
3.   A purchase of supplies on account of $450 was debited to Supplies for $540 and credited to Accounts Payable for $540.
4.   A credit posting of $680 to Interest Payable was posted twice.
5.   A debit posting to Income Taxes Payable for $250 and a credit posting to Cash for $250 were made twice.
6.   A debit posting for $1,200 of Dividends was inadvertently posted to Salaries and Wages Expense instead.
7.   A credit to Service Revenue for $450 was inadvertently posted as a debit to Service Revenue.
8.   A credit to Accounts Receivable of $250 was credited to Accounts Payable.

Analyze errors and their effects on the trial balance.
(LO 8), **AN**

Instructions
For each error, indicate (a) whether the trial balance will balance; (b) the amount of the difference if the trial balance will not balance; and (c) the trial balance column that will have the larger total. Consider each error separately. Use the following form, in which error 1 is given as an example.

Error	(a) In Balance	(b) Difference	(c) Larger Column
1.	No	$600	Debit

Problems: Set B

P3-1B   Hyman Inc. was started on May 1. Here is a summary of the May transactions.

1.   Stockholders invested $30,000 cash in the company in exchange for common stock.
2.   Purchased equipment for $10,000 cash.
3.   Paid $700 cash for May office rent.
4.   Paid $300 cash for supplies.
5.   Purchased $750 of advertising in the *Evening Times* on account.
6.   Received $8,000 in cash from customers for service.
7.   Paid a $500 cash dividend.
8.   Paid part-time employee salaries $1,000.
9.   Paid utility bills $140.
10.   Performed service on account to customers $2,000.
11.   Collected cash of $1,000 for services billed in transaction (10).

Analyze transactions and compute net income.
(LO 1), **AP**

Instructions

(a) Prepare a tabular analysis of the transactions using these column headings: Cash, Accounts Receivable, Supplies, Equipment, Accounts Payable, Common Stock, and Retained Earnings (with separate columns for Revenues, Expenses, and Dividends). Revenue is called Service Revenue. Include margin explanations for any changes in Retained Earnings.

(b) From an analysis of the Retained Earnings columns, compute the net income or net loss for May.

Analyze transactions and prepare financial statements.
(LO 1), **AP**

P3-2B Ned Walz started his own delivery service, Walz Service Inc., on June 1, 2014. The following transactions occurred during the month of June.

June 1   Stockholders invested $20,000 cash in the business in exchange for common stock.

      2   Purchased a used van for deliveries for $10,000. Walz paid $2,000 cash and signed a note payable for the remaining balance.

      3   Paid $600 for office rent for the month.

      5   Performed $3,000 of services on account.

      9   Paid $300 in cash dividends.

    12   Purchased supplies for $240 on account.

    15   Received a cash payment of $1,000 for services performed on June 5.

    17   Received a bill for $200 to cover advertisements in *Tri-State News*.

    20   Received a cash payment of $1,500 for services performed.

    23   Made a cash payment of $1,000 on the note payable.

    26   Paid $180 for utilities.

    29   Paid for the supplies purchased on account on June 12.

    30   Paid $750 for employee salaries.

Instructions

(a) Show the effects of the previous transactions on the accounting equation using the following format. Assume the note payable is to be repaid within the year.

	Assets			=	Liabilities	+	Stockholders' Equity			
Date	Cash + Receivable Accounts	+ Supplies	+ Equipment	=	Notes Payable	+ Accounts Payable	+ Common Stock	+ Retained Earnings Revenues − Expenses − Dividends		

Include margin explanations for any changes in Retained Earnings.

(b) Prepare an income statement for the month of June.

(c) Prepare a classified balance sheet at June 30, 2014.

Analyze transactions and prepare an income statement, retained earnings statement, and balance sheet.
(LO 1), **AP**

P3-3B Joe Thyme opened Thyme Company, a veterinary business in Neosho, Missouri, on August 1, 2014. On August 31, the balance sheet showed Cash $9,000; Accounts Receivable $1,700; Supplies $600; Equipment $5,000; Accounts Payable $3,600; Common Stock $10,000; and Retained Earnings $2,700. During September, the following transactions occurred.

Sept. 2   Paid $3,400 cash for accounts payable due.

      5   Received $1,200 from customers in payment of accounts receivable.

      8   Purchased additional office equipment for $5,100, paying $1,000 in cash and the balance on account.

    13   Performed services worth $10,600, of which $2,300 is paid in cash and the balance is due in October.

    17   Paid a $600 cash dividend.

    22   Paid salaries $900, rent for September $1,100, and advertising expense $250.

    26   Incurred utility expenses for the month on account $220.

    30   Received $5,000 from Hilldale Bank on a 6-month note payable.

Instructions

(a) Prepare a tabular analysis of the September transactions beginning with August 31 balances. The column headings should be Cash + Accounts Receivable + Supplies + Equipment = Notes Payable + Accounts Payable + Common Stock + Retained Earnings + Revenues − Expenses − Dividends. Include margin explanations for any changes in Retained Earnings.

(b) Prepare an income statement for September, a retained earnings statement for September, and a classified balance sheet at September 30, 2014.

P3-4B Beefeaters RV Park was started on April 1 by Sarah Rhodes. These selected events and transactions occurred during April.

Journalize a series of transactions.
(LO 4, 5), **AP**

Apr. 1 Stockholders invested $100,000 cash in the business in exchange for common stock.
4 Purchased land costing $250,000 for cash.
8 Purchased advertising in local newspaper for $1,200 on account.
11 Paid salaries to employees $3,000.
12 Hired park manager at a salary of $3,600 per month, effective May 1.
13 Paid $7,200 for a 1-year insurance policy.
17 Paid $600 cash dividends.
20 Received $6,000 in cash from customers for admission fees.
25 Sold 100 coupon books for $90 each. Each book contains ten coupons that entitle the holder to one admission to the park. (*Hint:* The revenue should not be recognized until the coupons are used.)
30 Received $7,900 in cash from customers for admission fees.
30 Paid $400 of the balance owed for the advertising purchased on account on April 8.

The company uses the following accounts: Cash, Prepaid Insurance, Land, Accounts Payable, Unearned Service Revenue, Common Stock, Dividends, Service Revenue, Advertising Expense, and Salaries and Wages Expense.

Instructions

Journalize the April transactions, including explanations. (*Note*: Beefeaters RV Park records admission revenue as service revenue.)

P3-5B Bob Royce incorporated Royce Consulting, an accounting practice, on May 1, 2014. During the first month of operations, these events and transactions occurred.

Journalize transactions, post, and prepare a trial balance.
(LO 5, 6, 7, 8), **AP**

May 1 Stockholders invested $100,000 cash in exchange for common stock of the corporation.
2 Hired a secretary-receptionist at a salary of $2,500 per month.
3 Purchased $800 of supplies on account from Pickering Supply Company.
7 Paid office rent of $1,400 for the month.
11 Completed a tax assignment and billed client $2,500 for services performed.
12 Received $4,200 advance on a management consulting engagement.
17 Received cash of $3,300 for services completed for Woodman Co.
31 Paid secretary-receptionist $2,500 salary for the month.
31 Paid 50% of balance due Pickering Supply Company.

The company uses the following chart of accounts: Cash, Accounts Receivable, Supplies, Accounts Payable, Unearned Service Revenue, Common Stock, Service Revenue, Salaries and Wages Expense, and Rent Expense.

Instructions
(a) Journalize the transactions, including explanations.
(b) Post to the ledger T-accounts.
(c) Prepare a trial balance on May 31, 2014.

(c) Cash $103,200
Tot. trial balance $110,400

P3-6B The trial balance of American Dry Cleaners on June 30 is given here.

Journalize transactions, post, and prepare a trial balance.
(LO 5, 6, 7, 8), **AP**

AMERICAN DRY CLEANERS
Trial Balance
June 30, 2014

	Debit	Credit
Cash	$15,532	
Accounts Receivable	10,536	
Supplies	3,592	
Equipment	25,950	
Accounts Payable		$15,800
Unearned Service Revenue		1,810
Common Stock		25,000
Retained Earnings		13,000
	$55,610	$55,610

The July transactions were as follows.

July	8	Received $10,189 in cash on June 30 accounts receivable.
	9	Paid employee salaries $2,100.
	11	Received $7,320 in cash for services performed.
	14	Paid creditors $4,810 of accounts payable.
	17	Purchased supplies on account $720.
	22	Billed customers for services performed $4,700.
	30	Paid employee salaries $3,114, utilities $1,767, and repairs $386.
	31	Paid $400 cash dividend.

Instructions
(a) Prepare a general ledger using T-accounts. Enter the opening balances in the ledger accounts as of July 1. Provision should be made for the following additional accounts: Dividends, Service Revenue, Maintenance and Repairs Expense, Salaries and Wages Expense, and Utilities Expense.

(b) Journalize the transactions, including explanations.

(d) Cash $20,464
Tot. trial balance $63,540

(c) Post to the ledger accounts.

(d) Prepare a trial balance on July 31, 2014.

Prepare a correct trial balance.
(LO 8), AN

P3-7B This trial balance of Lindbergh Company does not balance.

LINDBERGH COMPANY
Trial Balance
May 31, 2014

	Debit	Credit
Cash	$ 5,340	
Accounts Receivable		$ 2,750
Prepaid Insurance	700	
Equipment	9,000	
Accounts Payable		4,100
Income Taxes Payable	850	
Common Stock		5,700
Retained Earnings		6,000
Service Revenue	7,690	
Salaries and Wages Expense	4,200	
Advertising Expense		1,100
Income Tax Expense	900	
	$28,680	$19,650

Your review of the ledger reveals that each account has a normal balance. You also discover the following errors.

1. The totals of the debit sides of Prepaid Insurance, Accounts Payable, and Income Tax Expense were each understated $100.
2. Transposition errors were made in Accounts Receivable and Service Revenue. Based on postings made, the correct balances were $2,570 and $7,960, respectively.
3. A debit posting to Salaries and Wages Expense of $500 was omitted.
4. A $600 cash dividend was debited to Common Stock for $600 and credited to Cash for $600.
5. A $350 purchase of supplies on account was debited to Equipment for $350 and credited to Cash for $350.
6. A cash payment of $490 for advertising was debited to Advertising Expense for $49 and credited to Cash for $49.
7. A collection from a customer for $240 was debited to Cash for $240 and credited to Accounts Payable for $240.

Instructions
Prepare the correct trial balance, assuming all accounts have normal balances. (*Note:* The chart of accounts also includes the following: Dividends and Supplies.)

P3-8B Roxy Theater Inc. was recently formed. All facilities were completed on March 31. On April 1, the ledger showed: Cash $6,300; Land $10,000; Buildings (concession stand, projection room, ticket booth, and screen) $58,000; Equipment $6,000; Accounts Payable $2,300; Mortgage Payable $38,000; and Common Stock $40,000. During April, the following events and transactions occurred.

Apr.	2	Paid film rental fee of $1,800 on first movie.
	3	Ordered two additional films at $750 each.
	9	Received $5,700 cash from admissions.
	10	Paid $2,000 of mortgage payable and $1,200 of accounts payable.
	11	Roxy Theater contracted with M. Gavin to operate the concession stand. Gavin agrees to pay Roxy Theater 17% of gross receipts, payable monthly.
	12	Paid advertising expenses $410.
	20	Received one of the films ordered on April 3 and was billed $750. The film will be shown in April.
	25	Received $3,000 cash from customers for admissions.
	29	Paid salaries $1,900.
	30	Received statement from M. Gavin showing gross receipts of $2,000 and the balance due to Roxy Theater of $340 ($2,000 × .17) for April. Gavin paid half of the balance due and will remit the remainder on May 5.
	30	Prepaid $1,200 rental fee on special film to be run in May.

In addition to the accounts identified above, the chart of accounts shows Accounts Receivable, Prepaid Rent, Service Revenue, Rent Revenue, Advertising Expense, Rent Expense, Salaries and Wages Expense.

Instructions
(a) Enter the beginning balances in the ledger T-accounts as of April 1.
(b) Journalize the April transactions, including explanations. (*Note:* Roxy records admission revenue as service revenue, concession revenue as sales revenue, and film rental expense as rent expense.)
(c) Post the April journal entries to the ledger T-accounts.
(d) Prepare a trial balance on April 30, 2014.

P3-9B A first year co-op student working for Solutia Inc. recorded the transactions for the month. He wasn't exactly sure how to journalize and post, but he did the best he could. He had a few questions, however, about the following transactions.

1. Cash received from a customer on account was recorded as a debit to Cash of $360 and a credit to Accounts Receivable of $630, instead of $360.
2. A service performed for cash was posted as a debit to Cash of $2,000 and a credit to Service Revenue of $2,000.
3. A debit of $880 for services performed on account was neither recorded nor posted. The credit was recorded correctly.
4. The debit to record $1,000 of cash dividends was posted to the Salaries and Wages Expense account.
5. The purchase, on account, of a computer that cost $2,500 was recorded as a debit to Supplies and a credit to Accounts Payable.
6. A cash payment of $495 for salaries was recorded as a debit to Dividends and a credit to Cash.
7. Payment of month's rent was debited to Rent Expense and credited to Cash, $850.
8. Issue of $5,000 of common shares was credited to the Common Stock account, but no debit was recorded.

Instructions
(a) Indicate which of the above transactions are correct, and which are incorrect.
(b) For each error identified in (a), indicate (1) whether the trial balance will balance; (2) the amount of the difference if the trial balance will not balance; and (3) the trial

(margin notes)

Cash	$ 5,249
Tot. trial balance	$25,220

Journalize transactions, post, and prepare a trial balance.
(LO 5, 6, 7, 8), **AP**

(d) Cash	$ 6,660
Tot. trial balance	$86,890

Analyze errors and their effects on the trial balance.
(LO 8), **AN**

balance column that will have the larger total. Consider each error separately. Use the following form, in which transaction 1 is given as an example.

	(1)	(2)	(3)
Error	**In Balance**	**Difference**	**Larger Column**
1.	No	$270	Credit

Problems: Set C

Visit the book's companion website, at **www.wiley.com/college/kimmel**, and choose the Student Companion site to access Problem Set C.

Continuing Cookie Chronicle

(*Note*: This is a continuation of the Cookie Chronicle from Chapters 1 and 2.)

CCC3 In November 2014, after having incorporated Cookie Creations Inc., Natalie begins operations. She has decided not to pursue the offer to supply cookies to Biscuits. Instead, she will focus on offering cooking classes. The following events occur.

Nov. 8   Natalie cashes in her U.S. Savings Bonds and receives $520, which she deposits in her personal bank account.

   8   Natalie opens a bank account for Cookie Creations Inc.

   8   Natalie purchases $500 of Cookie Creations' common stock.

   11   Cookie Creations purchases paper and other office supplies for $95. (Use Supplies.)

   14   Cookie Creations pays $125 to purchase baking supplies, such as flour, sugar, butter, and chocolate chips. (Use Supplies.)

   15   Natalie starts to gather some baking equipment to take with her when teaching the cookie classes. She has an excellent top-of-the-line food processor and mixer that originally cost her $550. Natalie decides to start using it only in her new business. She estimates that the equipment is currently worth $300, and she transfers the equipment into the business in exchange for additional common stock.

   16   The company needs more cash to sustain its operations. Natalie's grandmother lends the company $2,000 cash, in exchange for a two-year, 9% note payable. Interest and the principal are repayable at maturity.

   17   Cookie Creations pays $900 for additional baking equipment.

   18   Natalie schedules her first class for November 29. She will receive $100 on the date of the class.

   25   Natalie books a second class for December 5 for $150. She receives a $60 cash down payment, in advance.

   29   Natalie teaches her first class, booked on November 18, and collects the $100 cash.

   30   Natalie's brother develops a website for Cookie Creations Inc. that the company will use for advertising. He charges the company $600 for his work, payable at the end of December. (Because the website is expected to have a useful life of two years before upgrades are needed, it should be treated as an asset called Website.)

   30   Cookie Creations pays $1,200 for a one-year insurance policy.

   30   Natalie teaches a group of elementary school students how to make Santa Claus cookies. At the end of the class, Natalie leaves an invoice for $300 with the school principal. The principal says that he will pass it along to the business office and it will be paid some time in December.

   30   Natalie receives a $50 invoice for use of her cell phone. She uses the cell phone exclusively for Cookie Creations Inc. business. The invoice is for services performed in November, and payment is due on December 15.

Instructions

(a) Prepare journal entries to record the November transactions.
(b) Post the journal entries to the general ledger accounts.
(c) Prepare a trial balance at November 30, 2014.

(c) Trial balance total $3,910

Broadening Your Perspective

Financial Reporting and Analysis

FINANCIAL REPORTING PROBLEM: *Tootsie Roll Industries Inc.*

BYP3-1 The financial statements of Tootsie Roll in Appendix A at the back of this textbook contain the following selected accounts, all in thousands of dollars.

Common Stock	$ 25,040
Accounts Payable	9,791
Accounts Receivable	37,394
Selling, Marketing, and Administrative Expenses	106,316
Prepaid Expenses	6,499
Net Property, Plant, and Equipment	215,492
Net Product Sales	517,149

Instructions

(a) What is the increase and decrease side for each account? What is the normal balance for each account?
(b) Identify the probable other account in the transaction and the effect on that account when:
  (1) Accounts Receivable is decreased.
  (2) Accounts Payable is decreased.
  (3) Prepaid Expenses is increased.
(c) Identify the other account(s) that ordinarily would be involved when:
  (1) Interest Expense is increased.
  (2) Property, Plant, and Equipment is increased.

COMPARATIVE ANALYSIS PROBLEM: *Tootsie Roll vs. Hershey*

BYP3-2 The financial statements of The Hershey Company appear in Appendix B, following the financial statements for Tootsie Roll in Appendix A.

Instructions

(a) Based on the information contained in these financial statements, determine the normal balance for:

Tootsie Roll Industries	**The Hershey Company**
(1) Accounts Receivable	(1) Inventories
(2) Net Property, Plant, and Equipment	(2) Provision for Income Taxes
(3) Accounts Payable	(3) Accrued Liabilities
(4) Retained Earnings	(4) Common Stock
(5) Net Product Sales	(5) Interest Expense

(b) Identify the other account ordinarily involved when:
  (1) Accounts Receivable is increased.
  (2) Notes Payable is decreased.
  (3) Machinery is increased.
  (4) Interest Revenue is increased.

RESEARCH CASE

BYP3-3 The January 27, 2011, edition of the *New York Times* contains an article by Richard Sandomir entitled "N.F.L. Finances, as Seen Through Packers' Records." The article discusses the fact that the Green Bay Packers are the only NFL team that publicly publishes its annual report.

Instructions

Read the article and answer the following questions.

(a) Why are the Green Bay Packers the only professional football team to publish and distribute an annual report?

(b) Why is the football players' labor union particularly interested in the Packers' annual report?

(c) In addition to the players' labor union, what other outside party might be interested in the annual report?

(d) Even though the Packer's revenue increased in recent years, the company's operating profit fell significantly. How does the article explain this decline?

INTERPRETING FINANCIAL STATEMENTS

BYP3-4 Chieftain International, Inc., is an oil and natural gas exploration and production company. A recent balance sheet reported $208 million in assets with only $4.6 million in liabilities, all of which were short-term accounts payable.

During the year, Chieftain expanded its holdings of oil and gas rights, drilled 37 new wells, and invested in expensive 3-D seismic technology. The company generated $19 million cash from operating activities and paid no dividends. It had a cash balance of $102 million at the end of the year.

Instructions

(a) Name at least two advantages to Chieftain from having no long-term debt. Can you think of disadvantages?

(b) What are some of the advantages to Chieftain from having this large a cash balance? What is a disadvantage?

(c) Why do you suppose Chieftain has the $4.6 million balance in accounts payable, since it appears that it could have made all its purchases for cash?

REAL-WORLD FOCUS

BYP3-5 *Purpose:* This activity provides information about career opportunities for CPAs.

Address: **www.startheregoplaces.com/why-accounting**, or go to **www.wiley.com/college/kimmel**

Steps

1. Go to the address shown above and click on **Students/Educators**.
2. Click on **High School**, then **CPA101** for parts (a), (b), and (c).
3. Click **College** to answer part (d).

Instructions

Answer the following questions.

(a) Where do CPAs work?

(b) What skills does a CPA need?

(c) What is the salary range for a CPA at a large firm during the first three years? What is the salary range for chief financial officers and treasurers at large corporations?

Critical Thinking

DECISION-MAKING ACROSS THE ORGANIZATION

BYP3-6 Sally Saia operates Double S Riding Academy, Inc. The academy's primary sources of revenue are riding fees and lesson fees, which are provided on a cash basis. Sally also boards horses for owners, who are billed monthly for boarding fees. In a few cases, boarders pay in advance of expected use. For its revenue transactions, the academy maintains these accounts: Cash, Accounts Receivable, Unearned Service Revenue, and Service Revenue.

The academy owns 10 horses, a stable, a riding corral, riding equipment, and office equipment. These assets are accounted for in the following accounts: Horses, Buildings, and Equipment.

The academy employs stable helpers and an office employee, who receive weekly salaries. At the end of each month, the mail usually brings bills for advertising, utilities, and veterinary service. Other expenses include feed for the horses and insurance. For its expenses, the academy maintains the following accounts: Supplies, Prepaid Insurance, Accounts Payable, Salaries and Wages Expense, Advertising Expense, Utilities Expense, Maintenance and Repairs Expense, Supplies Expense, and Insurance Expense.

Sally Saia's sole source of personal income is dividends from the academy. Thus, the corporation declares and pays periodic dividends. To account for stockholders' equity in the business and dividends, two accounts are maintained: Common Stock and Dividends.

During the first month of operations an inexperienced bookkeeper was employed. Sally Saia asks you to review the following eight entries of the 50 entries made during the month. In each case, the explanation for the entry is correct.

May 1	Cash	15,000	
	Unearned Service Revenue		15,000
	(Issued common stock in exchange for		
	$15,000 cash)		
5	Cash	250	
	Service Revenue		250
	(Received $250 cash for lesson fees)		
7	Cash	500	
	Service Revenue		500
	(Received $500 for boarding of horses		
	beginning June 1)		
9	Supplies Expense	1,500	
	Cash		1,500
	(Purchased estimated 5 months' supply		
	of feed and hay for $1,500 on account)		
14	Equipment	80	
	Cash		800
	(Purchased desk and other office		
	equipment for $800 cash)		
15	Salaries and Wages Expense	400	
	Cash		400
	(Issued check to Sally Saia for		
	personal use)		
20	Cash	145	
	Service Revenue		154
	(Received $154 cash for riding fees)		
31	Maintenance and Repairs Expense	75	
	Accounts Receivable		75
	(Received bill of $75 from carpenter		
	for repair services performed)		

Instructions

With the class divided into groups, answer the following.
(a) For each journal entry that is correct, so state. For each journal entry that is incorrect, prepare the entry that should have been made by the bookkeeper.
(b) Which of the incorrect entries would prevent the trial balance from balancing?
(c) What was the correct net income for May, assuming the bookkeeper originally reported net income of $4,500 after posting all 50 entries?
(d) What was the correct cash balance at May 31, assuming the bookkeeper reported a balance of $12,475 after posting all 50 entries?

COMMUNICATION ACTIVITY

BYP3-7 Clean Sweep Company offers home cleaning service. Two recurring transactions for the company are billing customers for services performed and paying employee salaries. For example, on March 15 bills totaling $6,000 were sent to customers, and $2,000 was paid in salaries to employees.

Instructions

Write a memorandum to your instructor that explains and illustrates the steps in the recording process for each of the March 15 transactions. Use the format illustrated in the textbook under the heading "The Recording Process Illustrated" (pp. 121–126).

ETHICS CASES

BYP3-8 Jennifer VanPelt is the assistant chief accountant at BIT Company, a manufacturer of computer chips and cellular phones. The company presently has total sales of $20 million. It is the end of the first quarter and Jennifer is hurriedly trying to prepare a trial balance so that quarterly financial statements can be prepared and released to management and the regulatory agencies. The total credits on the trial balance exceed the debits by $1,000.

In order to meet the 4 P.M. deadline, Jennifer decides to force the debits and credits into balance by adding the amount of the difference to the Equipment account. She chose Equipment because it is one of the larger account balances; percentage-wise it will be the least misstated. Jennifer plugs the difference! She believes that the difference is quite small and will not affect anyone's decisions. She wishes that she had another few days to find the error but realizes that the financial statements are already late.

Instructions

(a) Who are the stakeholders in this situation?
(b) What ethical issues are involved?
(c) What are Jennifer's alternatives?

BYP3-9 The July 28, 2007, issue of the *Wall Street Journal* includes an article by Kathryn Kranhold entitled "GE's Accounting Draws Fresh Focus on News of Improper Sales Bookings."

Instructions

Read the article and answer the following questions.
(a) What improper activity did the employees at GE engage in?
(b) Why might the employees have engaged in this activity?
(c) What were the implications for the employees who engaged in this activity?
(d) What does it mean to "restate" financial results? Why didn't GE restate its results to correct for the improperly reported locomotive sales?

ALL ABOUT YOU

BYP3-10 In their annual reports to stockholders, companies must report or disclose information about all liabilities, including potential liabilities related to environmental clean-up. There are many situations in which you will be asked to provide personal financial information about your assets, liabilities, revenue, and expenses. Sometimes you will face difficult decisions regarding what to disclose and how to disclose it.

Instructions

Suppose that you are putting together a loan application to purchase a home. Based on your income and assets, you qualify for the mortgage loan, but just barely. How would you address each of the following situations in reporting your financial position for the loan application? Provide responses for each of the following questions.

(a) You signed a guarantee for a bank loan that a friend took out for $20,000. If your friend doesn't pay, you will have to pay. Your friend has made all of the payments so far, and it appears he will be able to pay in the future.
(b) You were involved in an auto accident in which you were at fault. There is the possibility that you may have to pay as much as $50,000 as part of a settlement. The issue will not be resolved before the bank processes your mortgage request.
(c) The company at which you work isn't doing very well, and it has recently laid off employees. You are still employed, but it is quite possible that you will lose your job in the next few months.

Answers to Insight and Accounting Across the Organization Questions

p. 109 Why Accuracy Matters Q: In order for these companies to prepare and issue financial statements, their accounting equations (debit and credits) must have been in balance at year-end. How could these errors or misstatements have occurred? **A:** A company's accounting equation (its books) can be in balance yet its financial statements have errors or misstatements because of the following: entire transactions were not recorded; transactions were recorded at wrong amounts; transactions were recorded in the wrong accounts; transactions were recorded in the wrong accounting period. Audits of financial statements uncover some, but obviously not all, errors or misstatements.

p. 115 Keeping Score Q: Do you think that the Chicago Bears football team would be likely to have the same major revenue and expense accounts as the Cubs? **A:** Because their businesses are similar—professional sports—many of the revenue and expense accounts for the baseball and football teams might be similar.

p. 119 Boosting Microsoft's Profits Q: In what ways is this Microsoft division using accounting to assist in its effort to become more profitable? **A:** The division has used accounting to set very strict sales, revenue, and profit goals. In addition, the managers in this division use accounting to keep a tight rein on product costs. Also, accounting serves as the basis of communication so that the marketing managers and product designers can work with production managers, engineers, and accountants to create an exciting product within specified cost constraints.

p. 121 A Convenient Overstatement Q: What incentives might employees have had to overstate the value of these investment securities on the company's financial statements? **A:** One reason that they may have been reluctant to record the losses is out of fear that the company's shareholders and clients would panic if they saw the magnitude of the losses. However, personal self-interest might have been equally to blame—the bonuses of the traders were tied to the value of the investment securities.

Answers to Self-Test Questions

1. b **2.** b **3.** b **4.** a ($-\$50,000 = -\$90,000 + \$40,000$) **5.** b **6.** c **7.** d **8.** d **9.** d **10.** b
11. a **12.** c **13.** d **14.** a **15.** c

A Look at IFRS

International companies use the same set of procedures and records to keep track of transaction data. Thus, the material in Chapter 3 dealing with the account, general rules of debit and credit, and steps in the recording process—the journal, ledger, and chart of accounts—is the same under both GAAP and IFRS.

LEARNING OBJECTIVE 10
Compare the procedures for the recording process under GAAP and IFRS.

KEY POINTS

- Transaction analysis is the same under IFRS and GAAP but, as you will see in later chapters, different standards sometimes impact how transactions are recorded.
- Rules for accounting for specific events sometimes differ across countries. For example, European companies rely less on historical cost and more on fair value than U.S. companies. Despite the differences, the double-entry accounting system is the basis of accounting systems worldwide.
- Both the IASB and FASB go beyond the basic definitions provided in this textbook for the key elements of financial statements, that is, assets, liabilities, equity, revenues, and expenses. The more substantive definitions, using the IASB definitional structure, are provided in the Chapter 1 *A Look at IFRS* discussion.
- A trial balance under IFRS follows the same format as shown in the textbook.

- As shown in the textbook, dollar signs are typically used only in the trial balance and the financial statements. The same practice is followed under IFRS, using the currency of the country in which the reporting company is headquartered.
- The SEC has expressed a desire to continue working toward a single set of high-quality standards. In deciding whether the United States should adopt IFRS, some of the issues the SEC stated should be considered are:
  - Whether IFRS is sufficiently developed and consistent in application.
  - Whether the IASB is sufficiently independent.
  - Whether IFRS is established for the benefit of investors.
  - The issues involved in educating investors about IFRS.
  - The impact of a switch to IFRS on U.S. laws and regulations.
  - The impact on companies including changes to their accounting systems, contractual arrangements, corporate governance, and litigation.
  - The issues involved in educating accountants, so they can prepare statements under IFRS.

LOOKING TO THE FUTURE

The basic recording process shown in this textbook is followed by companies across the globe. It is unlikely to change in the future. The definitional structure of assets, liabilities, equity, revenues, and expenses may change over time as the IASB and FASB evaluate their overall conceptual framework for establishing accounting standards.

IFRS PRACTICE

IFRS SELF-TEST QUESTIONS

1. Which statement is **correct** regarding IFRS?
   (a) IFRS reverses the rules of debits and credits; that is, debits are on the right and credits are on the left.
   (b) IFRS uses the same process for recording transactions as GAAP.
   (c) The chart of accounts under IFRS is different because revenues follow assets.
   (d) None of the above statements are correct.
2. The expanded accounting equation under IFRS is as follows:
   (a) Assets = Liabilities + Share Capital + Dividends + Revenues − Expenses.
   (b) Assets + Liabilities = Share Capital + Dividends + Revenues − Expenses.
   (c) Assets = Liabilities + Share Capital − Dividends + Revenues − Expenses.
   (d) Assets = Liabilities + Share Capital + Dividends − Revenues − Expenses.
3. A trial balance:
   (a) is the same under IFRS and GAAP.
   (b) proves that transactions are recorded correctly.
   (c) proves that all transactions have been recorded.
   (d) will not balance if a correct journal entry is posted twice.
4. One difference between IFRS and GAAP is that:
   (a) GAAP uses accrual-accounting concepts and IFRS uses primarily the cash basis of accounting.
   (b) IFRS uses a different posting process than GAAP.
   (c) IFRS uses more fair value measurements than GAAP.
   (d) the limitations of a trial balance are different between IFRS and GAAP.
5. The general policy for using proper currency signs (dollar, yen, pound, etc.) is the same for both IFRS and this textbook. This policy is as follows:
   (a) Currency signs only appear in ledgers and journal entries.
   (b) Currency signs are only shown in the trial balance.
   (c) Currency signs are shown for all compound journal entries.
   (d) Currency signs are shown in trial balances and financial statements.

IFRS CONCEPTS AND APPLICATION

IFRS3-1 Describe some of the issues the SEC must consider in deciding whether the United States should adopt IFRS.

INTERNATIONAL FINANCIAL REPORTING PROBLEM: *Zetar plc*

IFRS3-2 The financial statements of Zetar plc are presented in Appendix C. The company's complete annual report, including the notes to its financial statements, is available in the Investors section at **www.zetarplc.com**.

Instructions
Describe in which statement each of the following items is reported, and the position in the statement (e.g., current asset).

    (a) Share capital.
    (b) Goodwill.
    (c) Borrowings and overdrafts.
    (d) Amortization of intangible assets.
    (e) Derivative financial asset.

Answers to IFRS Self-Test Questions

1. b   **2.** c   **3.** a   **4.** c   **5.** d

Rudy Archuleta/Redux Pictures

CHAPTER 4

ACCRUAL ACCOUNTING CONCEPTS

✔ The Navigator

- Scan Learning Objectives
- Read Feature Story
- Scan Preview
- Read Text and Answer **Do it!**
  ○ p. 175 ○ p. 180 ○ p. 187 ○ p. 190
- Work Using the Decision Toolkit
- Review Summary of Learning Objectives
- Work Comprehensive **Do it!** p. 198
- Answer Self-Test Questions
- Complete Assignments
- Go to WileyPLUS for practice and tutorials

 Read A Look at IFRS p. 225

LEARNING OBJECTIVES

After studying this chapter, you should be able to:

1 Explain the revenue recognition principle and the expense recognition principle.

2 Differentiate between the cash basis and the accrual basis of accounting.

3 Explain why adjusting entries are needed, and identify the major types of adjusting entries.

4 Prepare adjusting entries for deferrals.

5 Prepare adjusting entries for accruals.

6 Describe the nature and purpose of the adjusted trial balance.

7 Explain the purpose of closing entries.

8 Describe the required steps in the accounting cycle.

9 Understand the causes of differences between net income and net cash provided by operating activities.

 ✔ The Navigator

Who doesn't like buying things at a discount? That's why it's not surprising that three years after it started as a company, Groupon was estimated to be worth $16 billion. This translates into an average increase in value of almost $15 million per day.

Now consider that Groupon had previously been estimated to be worth even more than that. What happened? Well, accounting regulators and investors began to question the way that Groupon had accounted for some of its transactions. But if Groupon sells only coupons ("Groupons"), you're probably wondering how hard can it be to accurately account for that? It turns out that accounting for coupons is not as easy as you might think.

First, consider what happens when Groupon makes a sale. Suppose it sells a Groupon for $30 for Highrise Hamburgers. When it receives the $30 from the customer, it must turn over half of that amount ($15) to Highrise Hamburgers. So should Groupon record revenue for the full $30 or just $15? Until recently, Groupon recorded the full $30. But, in response to an SEC ruling on the issue, Groupon now records revenue of $15 instead. Groupon also had to restate its previous financial statements. This restatement reduced annual revenue by $312.9 million.

A second issue is a matter of timing. When should Groupon record this $15 revenue? Should it record the revenue when it sells the Groupon, or must it wait until the customer uses

KEEPING TRACK OF GROUPONS

the Groupon at Highrise Hamburgers? You can find the answer to this question in the notes to Groupon's financial statements. It recognizes the revenue once "the number of customers who purchase the daily deal exceeds the predetermined threshold, the Groupon has been electronically delivered to the purchaser and a listing of Groupons sold has been made available to the merchant."

The accounting becomes even more complicated when you consider the company's loyalty programs. Groupon offers free or discounted Groupons to its subscribers for doing things such as referring new customers or participating in promotions. These Groupons are to be used for future purchases, yet the company must record the expense at the time the customer receives the Groupon. The cost of these programs is huge for Groupon, so the timing of this expense can definitely affect its reported income.

The final kicker is that Groupon, like all other companies, must rely on many estimates in its financial reporting. For example, Groupon reports that "estimates are utilized for, but not limited to, stock-based compensation, income taxes, valuation of acquired goodwill and intangible assets, customer refunds, contingent liabilities and the depreciable lives of fixed assets." It concludes by saying that "actual results could differ materially from those estimates." So, next time you use a coupon, think about what that means for the company's accountants!

✔ The Navigator

As indicated in the Feature Story, making adjustments is necessary to avoid misstatement of revenues and expenses such as those at Groupon. In this chapter, we introduce you to the accrual accounting concepts that make such adjustments possible.

The organization and content of the chapter are as follows.

Accrual Accounting Concepts

Timing Issues	The Basics of Adjusting Entries	The Adjusted Trial Balance and Financial Statements	Closing the Books
• Revenue recognition principle • Expense recognition principle • Accrual versus cash basis of accounting	• Types of adjusting entries • Adjusting entries for deferrals • Adjusting entries for accruals • Summary of basic relationships	• Preparing the adjusted trial balance • Preparing financial statements • Quality of earnings	• Preparing closing entries • Preparing a post-closing trial balance • Summary of the accounting cycle

✔ The Navigator

Timing Issues

Most businesses need immediate feedback about how well they are doing. For example, management usually wants monthly reports on financial results, most large corporations are required to present quarterly and annual financial statements to stockholders, and the Internal Revenue Service requires all businesses to file annual tax returns. **Accounting divides the economic life of a business into artificial time periods.** As indicated in Chapter 2, this is the periodicity assumption. **Accounting time periods are generally a month, a quarter, or a year.**

Helpful Hint An accounting time period that is one year long is called a fiscal year.

Many business transactions affect more than one of these arbitrary time periods. For example, a new building purchased by Citigroup or a new airplane purchased by Delta Air Lines will be used for many years. It doesn't make sense to expense the full cost of the building or the airplane at the time of purchase because each will be used for many subsequent periods. Instead, we determine the impact of each transaction on specific accounting periods.

Determining the amount of revenues and expenses to report in a given accounting period can be difficult. Proper reporting requires an understanding of the nature of the company's business. Two principles are used as guidelines: the revenue recognition principle and the expense recognition principle.

Revenue Recognition

Service performed

Customer requests service — Cash received

Revenue should be recognized in the accounting period in which the service is performed.

THE REVENUE RECOGNITION PRINCIPLE

When a company agrees to perform a service or sell a product to a customer, it has a performance obligation. The revenue recognition principle requires that companies recognize revenue in the accounting period **in which the performance obligation is satisfied.** To illustrate, assume Conrad Dry Cleaners cleans clothing on June 30, but customers do not claim and pay for their clothes until the first week of July. Under the revenue recognition principle, Conrad records revenue in June when it performs the service, not in July when it receives the cash. At June 30, Conrad would report a receivable on its balance sheet and revenue in its income statement for the service performed. The journal entries for June and July would be as follows.

June	Accounts Receivable	xxx	
	Service Revenue		xxx
July	Cash	xxx	
	Accounts Receivable		xxx

DECISION TOOLKIT

DECISION CHECKPOINTS	INFO NEEDED FOR DECISION	TOOL TO USE FOR DECISION	HOW TO EVALUATE RESULTS
At what point should the company record revenue?	Need to understand the nature of the company's business	Record revenue in the period in which the performance obligation is satisfied.	Recognizing revenue too early overstates current period revenue; recognizing it too late understates current period revenue.

THE EXPENSE RECOGNITION PRINCIPLE

In recognizing expenses, a simple rule is followed: "Let the expenses follow the revenues." Thus, expense recognition is tied to revenue recognition. Applied to the preceding example, this means that the salary expense Conrad incurred in performing the cleaning service on June 30 should be reported in the same period in which it recognizes the service revenue. The critical issue in expense recognition is determining when the expense makes its contribution to revenue. This may or may not be the same period in which the expense is paid. If Conrad does not pay the salary incurred on June 30 until July, it would report salaries and wages payable on its June 30 balance sheet.

The practice of expense recognition is referred to as the **expense recognition principle** (often referred to as the **matching principle**). It dictates that efforts (expenses) be matched with results (revenues). Illustration 4-1 shows these relationships.

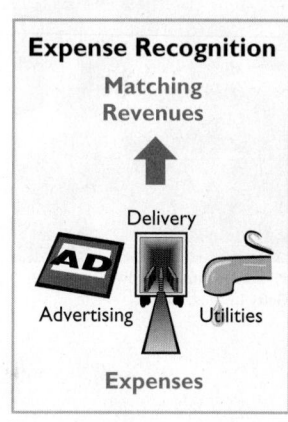

Illustration 4-1 GAAP relationships in revenue and expense recognition

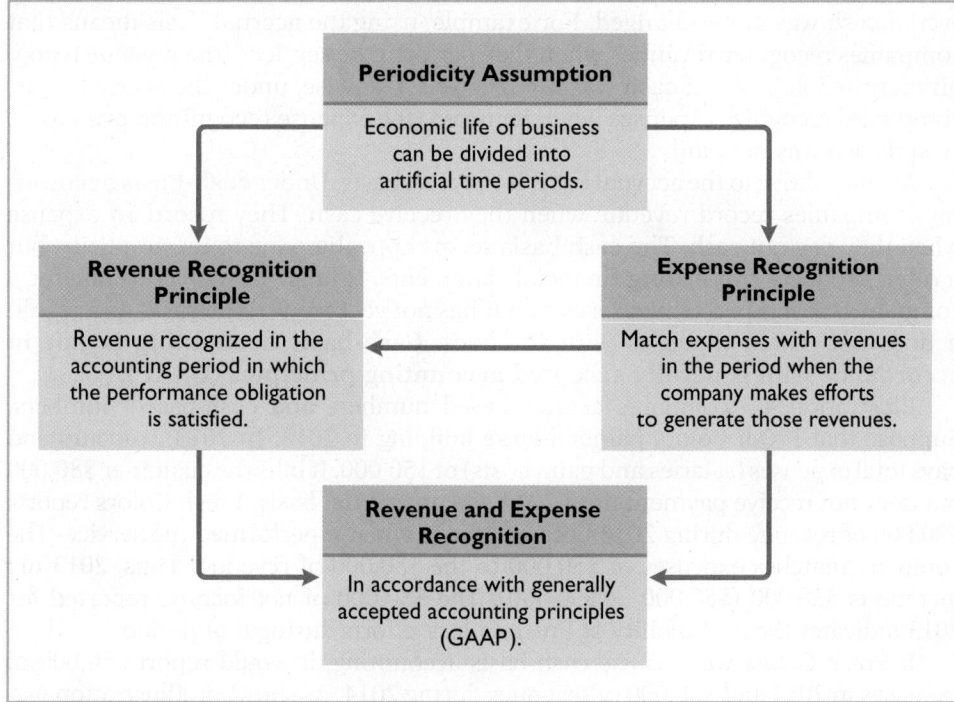

DECISION TOOLKIT

DECISION CHECKPOINTS	INFO NEEDED FOR DECISION	TOOL TO USE FOR DECISION	HOW TO EVALUATE RESULTS
At what point should the company record expenses?	Need to understand the nature of the company's business	Expenses should "follow" revenues—that is, match the effort (expense) with the result (revenue).	Recognizing expenses too early overstates current period expense; recognizing them too late understates current period expense.

PhotoAlto/James Hardy/ Getty Images, Inc.

Investor Insight

Reporting Revenue Accurately

Until recently, electronics manufacturer Apple was required to spread the revenues from iPhone sales over the two-year period following the sale of the phone. Accounting standards required this because it was argued that Apple was obligated to provide software updates after the phone was sold. Therefore, since Apple had service obligations after the initial date of sale, it was forced to spread the revenue over a two-year period. However, since the company received full payment upfront, the cash flows from iPhones significantly exceeded the revenue reported from iPhone sales in each accounting period. It also meant that the rapid growth of iPhone sales was not fully reflected in the revenue amounts reported in Apple's income statement. A new accounting standard now enables Apple to report nearly all of its iPhone revenue at the point of sale. It was estimated that under the new rule revenues would have been about 17% higher and earnings per share almost 50% higher.

? In the past, why was it argued that Apple should spread the recognition of iPhone revenue over a two-year period, rather than recording it upfront? (See page 224.)

ACCRUAL VERSUS CASH BASIS OF ACCOUNTING

Accrual-basis accounting means that transactions that change a company's financial statements are recorded **in the periods in which the events occur**, even if cash was not exchanged. For example, using the accrual basis means that companies recognize revenues when they perform the services (the revenue recognition principle), even if cash was not received. Likewise, under the accrual basis, companies recognize expenses when incurred (the expense recognition principle), even if cash was not paid.

An alternative to the accrual basis is the cash basis. Under **cash-basis accounting**, companies record revenue when they receive cash. They record an expense when they pay out cash. The cash basis seems appealing due to its simplicity, but it often produces misleading financial statements. It fails to record revenue for a company that has performed services but has not yet received the cash. As a result, it does not match expenses with revenues. **Cash-basis accounting is not in accordance with generally accepted accounting principles (GAAP).**

Illustration 4-2 compares accrual-based numbers and cash-based numbers. Suppose that Fresh Colors paints a large building in 2013. In 2013, it incurs and pays total expenses (salaries and paint costs) of $50,000. It bills the customer $80,000 but does not receive payment until 2014. On an accrual basis, Fresh Colors reports $80,000 of revenue during 2013 because that is when it performed the service. The company matches expenses of $50,000 to the $80,000 of revenue. Thus, 2013 net income is $30,000 ($80,000 − $50,000). The $30,000 of net income reported for 2013 indicates the profitability of Fresh Colors' efforts during that period.

If Fresh Colors were to use cash-basis accounting, it would report $50,000 of expenses in 2013 and $80,000 of revenues during 2014. As shown in Illustration 4-2,

	2013	2014
Activity	Purchased paint, painted building, paid employees	Received payment for work done in 2013
Accrual basis	Revenue $80,000 Expense 50,000 Net income $30,000	Revenue $ 0 Expense 0 Net income $ 0
Cash basis	Revenue $ 0 Expense 50,000 Net loss $(50,000)	Revenue $80,000 Expense 0 Net income $80,000

Illustration 4-2 Accrual-versus cash-basis accounting

it would report a loss of $50,000 in 2013 and would report net income of $80,000 in 2014. Clearly, the cash-basis measures are misleading because the financial performance of the company would be misstated for both 2013 and 2014.

 ## International Insight

Cashing In on Accrual Accounting

The Chinese government, like most governments, uses cash accounting. It is therefore interesting that for about $38 billion of expenditures in a recent budget projection, the Chinese government used accrual accounting instead of cash accounting. It decided to expense the amount in the year in which it was originally allocated rather than when the payments would be made. Why did it do this? It enabled the government to keep its projected budget deficit below a 3% threshold. While it was able to keep its projected shortfall below 3%, China did suffer some criticism for its inconsistent accounting. Critics charge that this inconsistent treatment reduces the transparency of China's accounting information. That is, it is not easy for outsiders to accurately evaluate what is really going on.

Günay Mutlu/iStockphoto

Source: Andrew Batson, "China Altered Budget Accounting to Reduce Deficit Figure," *Wall Street Journal Online* (March 15, 2010).

? Accrual accounting is often considered superior to cash accounting. Why, then, were some people critical of China's use of accrual accounting in this instance? (See page 224.)

The Basics of Adjusting Entries

In order for revenues to be recorded in the period in which the performance obligations are satisfied, and for expenses to be recognized in the period in which they are incurred, companies make adjusting entries. **Adjusting entries** **ensure that the revenue recognition and expense recognition principles are followed.**

LEARNING OBJECTIVE 3

Explain why adjusting entries are needed, and identify the major types of adjusting entries.

Adjusting entries are necessary because the **trial balance**—the first pulling together of the transaction data—may not contain up-to-date and complete data. This is true for several reasons:

1. Some events are not recorded daily because it is not efficient to do so. Examples are the use of supplies and the earning of wages by employees.
2. Some costs are not recorded during the accounting period because these costs expire with the passage of time rather than as a result of recurring daily transactions. Examples are charges related to the use of buildings and equipment, rent, and insurance.
3. Some items may be unrecorded. An example is a utility service bill that will not be received until the next accounting period.

Adjusting entries are required every time a company prepares financial statements. The company analyzes each account in the trial balance to determine whether it is complete and up-to-date for financial statement purposes. **Every adjusting entry will include one income statement account and one balance sheet account.**

TYPES OF ADJUSTING ENTRIES

Adjusting entries are classified as either deferrals or accruals. As Illustration 4-3 shows, each of these classes has two subcategories.

Illustration 4-3 Categories of adjusting entries

Deferrals:

1. Prepaid expenses: Expenses paid in cash before they are used or consumed.
2. Unearned revenues: Cash received before services are performed.

Accruals:

1. Accrued revenues: Revenues for services performed but not yet received in cash or recorded.
2. Accrued expenses: Expenses incurred but not yet paid in cash or recorded.

Subsequent sections give examples of each type of adjustment. Each example is based on the October 31 trial balance of Sierra Corporation from Chapter 3. It is reproduced in Illustration 4-4. Note that Retained Earnings has been added to this trial balance with a zero balance. We will explain its use later.

Illustration 4-4 Trial balance

SIERRA CORPORATION
Trial Balance
October 31, 2014

	Debit	Credit
Cash	$15,200	
Supplies	2,500	
Prepaid Insurance	600	
Equipment	5,000	
Notes Payable		$ 5,000
Accounts Payable		2,500
Unearned Service Revenue		1,200
Common Stock		10,000
Retained Earnings		0
Dividends	500	
Service Revenue		10,000
Salaries and Wages Expense	4,000	
Rent Expense	900	
	$28,700	$28,700

We assume that Sierra Corporation uses an accounting period of one month. Thus, monthly adjusting entries are made. The entries are dated October 31.

ADJUSTING ENTRIES FOR DEFERRALS

To defer means to postpone or delay. Deferrals are costs or revenues that are recognized at a date later than the point when cash was originally exchanged. Companies make adjusting entries for deferred expenses to record the portion that was incurred during the period. Companies also make adjusting entries for deferred revenues to record services performed during the period. The two types of deferrals are prepaid expenses and unearned revenues.

Prepaid Expenses

Companies record payments of expenses that will benefit more than one accounting period as assets. These **prepaid expenses** or **prepayments** are expenses paid in cash before they are used or consumed. When expenses are prepaid, an asset account is increased (debited) to show the service or benefit that the company will receive in the future. Examples of common prepayments are insurance, supplies, advertising, and rent. In addition, companies make prepayments when they purchase buildings and equipment.

Prepaid expenses are costs that expire either with the passage of time (e.g., rent and insurance) **or through use** (e.g., supplies). The expiration of these costs does not require daily entries, which would be impractical and unnecessary. Accordingly, companies postpone the recognition of such cost expirations until they prepare financial statements. At each statement date, they make adjusting entries to record the expenses applicable to the current accounting period and to show the remaining amounts in the asset accounts.

Prior to adjustment, assets are overstated and expenses are understated. Therefore, as shown in Illustration 4-5, **an adjusting entry for prepaid expenses results in an increase (a debit) to an expense account and a decrease (a credit) to an asset account**.

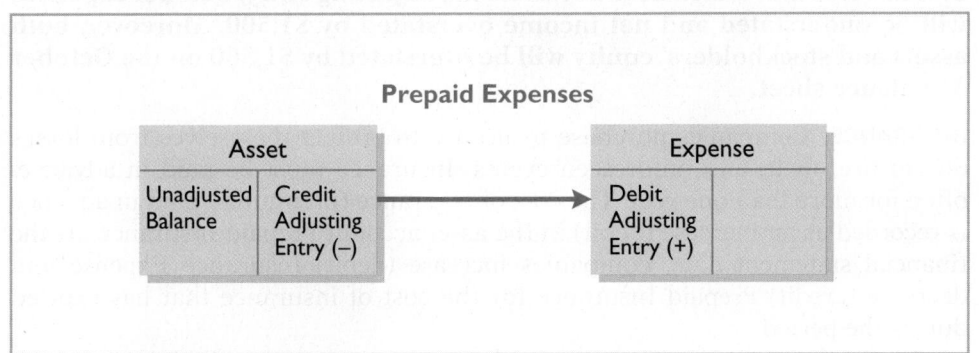

Illustration 4-5 Adjusting entries for prepaid expenses

Let's look in more detail at some specific types of prepaid expenses, beginning with supplies.

SUPPLIES. The purchase of supplies, such as paper and envelopes, results in an increase (a debit) to an asset account. During the accounting period, the company uses supplies. Rather than record supplies expense as the supplies are used, companies recognize supplies expense at the **end** of the accounting period. At the end of the accounting period, the company counts the remaining supplies. The difference between the unadjusted balance in the Supplies (asset) account and the actual cost of supplies on hand represents the supplies used (an expense) for that period.

Recall from Chapter 3 that Sierra Corporation purchased supplies costing $2,500 on October 5. Sierra recorded the purchase by increasing (debiting) the asset Supplies. This account shows a balance of $2,500 in the October 31 trial

Supplies

Oct. 5

Supplies purchased; record asset

Oct. 31
Supplies used; record supplies expense

balance. A physical count of the inventory at the close of business on October 31 reveals that $1,000 of supplies are still on hand. Thus, the cost of supplies used is $1,500 ($2,500 − $1,000). This use of supplies decreases an asset, Supplies. It also decreases stockholders' equity by increasing an expense account, Supplies Expense. This is shown in Illustration 4-6.

Illustration 4-6
Adjustment for supplies

Helpful Hint Due to their nature, adjusting entries have **no effect** on cash flows. As a result, we do not show the cash flow effects as we did in Chapter 3.

After adjustment, the asset account Supplies shows a balance of $1,000, which is equal to the cost of supplies on hand at the statement date. In addition, Supplies Expense shows a balance of $1,500, which equals the cost of supplies used in October. **If Sierra does not make the adjusting entry, October expenses will be understated and net income overstated by $1,500. Moreover, both assets and stockholders' equity will be overstated by $1,500 on the October 31 balance sheet.**

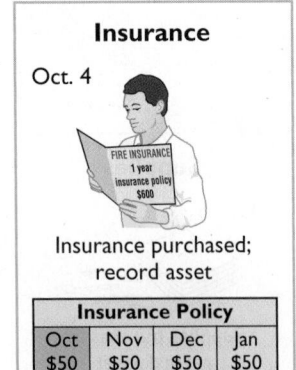

Insurance

Oct. 4

Insurance purchased; record asset

Insurance Policy			
Oct $50	Nov $50	Dec $50	Jan $50
Feb $50	March $50	April $50	May $50
June $50	July $50	Aug $50	Sept $50
I YEAR $600			

Oct. 31
  Insurance expired; record insurance expense

INSURANCE. Companies purchase insurance to protect themselves from losses due to fire, theft, and unforeseen events. Insurance must be paid in advance, often for more than one year. The cost of insurance (premiums) paid in advance is recorded as an increase (debit) in the asset account Prepaid Insurance. At the financial statement date, companies increase (debit) Insurance Expense and decrease (credit) Prepaid Insurance for the cost of insurance that has expired during the period.

On October 4, Sierra Corporation paid $600 for a one-year fire insurance policy. Coverage began on October 1. Sierra recorded the payment by increasing (debiting) Prepaid Insurance. This account shows a balance of $600 in the October 31 trial balance. Insurance of $50 ($600 ÷ 12) expires each month. The expiration of prepaid insurance decreases an asset, Prepaid Insurance. It also decreases stockholders' equity by increasing an expense account, Insurance Expense.

As shown in Illustration 4-7, the asset Prepaid Insurance shows a balance of $550, which represents the unexpired cost for the remaining 11 months of coverage. At the same time, the balance in Insurance Expense equals the insurance cost that expired in October. If Sierra does not make this adjustment, October expenses are understated by $50 and net income is overstated by $50. Moreover, as the accounting equation shows, both assets and stockholders' equity will be overstated by $50 on the October 31 balance sheet.

Illustration 4-7
Adjustment for insurance

DEPRECIATION. A company typically owns a variety of assets that have long lives, such as buildings, equipment, and motor vehicles. The period of service is referred to as the useful life of the asset. Because a building is expected to provide service for many years, it is recorded as an asset, rather than an expense, on the date it is acquired. As explained in Chapter 2, companies record such assets **at cost**, as required by the historical cost principle. To follow the expense recognition principle, companies allocate a portion of this cost as an expense during each period of the asset's useful life. Depreciation is the process of allocating the cost of an asset to expense over its useful life.

Need for adjustment. The acquisition of long-lived assets is essentially a long-term prepayment for the use of an asset. An adjusting entry for depreciation is needed to recognize the cost that has been used (an expense) during the period and to report the unused cost (an asset) at the end of the period. One very important point to understand: **Depreciation is an allocation concept, not a valuation concept.** That is, depreciation **allocates an asset's cost to the periods in which it is used. Depreciation does not attempt to report the actual change in the value of the asset.**

For Sierra Corporation, assume that depreciation on the equipment is $480 a year, or $40 per month. As shown in Illustration 4-8 (page 172), rather than decrease (credit) the asset account directly, Sierra instead credits Accumulated Depreciation—Equipment. Accumulated Depreciation is called a contra asset account. Such an account is offset against an asset account on the balance sheet. Thus, the Accumulated Depreciation—Equipment account offsets the asset Equipment. This account keeps track of the total amount of depreciation expense taken over the life of the asset. To keep the accounting equation in balance, Sierra decreases stockholders' equity by increasing an expense account, Depreciation Expense.

The balance in the Accumulated Depreciation—Equipment account will increase $40 each month, and the balance in Equipment remains $5,000.

Statement presentation. As noted above, Accumulated Depreciation—Equipment is a contra asset account. It is offset against Equipment on the balance sheet. The normal balance of a contra asset account is a credit. A theoretical alternative to using a contra asset account would be to decrease (credit) the asset account by the amount of depreciation each period. But using the contra account

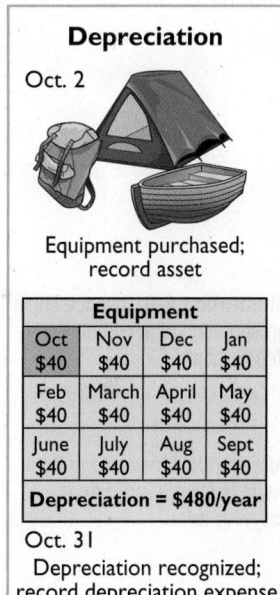

Depreciation

Oct. 2

Equipment purchased; record asset

Equipment			
Oct $40	Nov $40	Dec $40	Jan $40
Feb $40	March $40	April $40	May $40
June $40	July $40	Aug $40	Sept $40
Depreciation = $480/year			

Oct. 31
Depreciation recognized; record depreciation expense

Helpful Hint All contra accounts have increases, decreases, and normal balances opposite to the account to which they relate.

Illustration 4-8
Adjustment for
depreciation

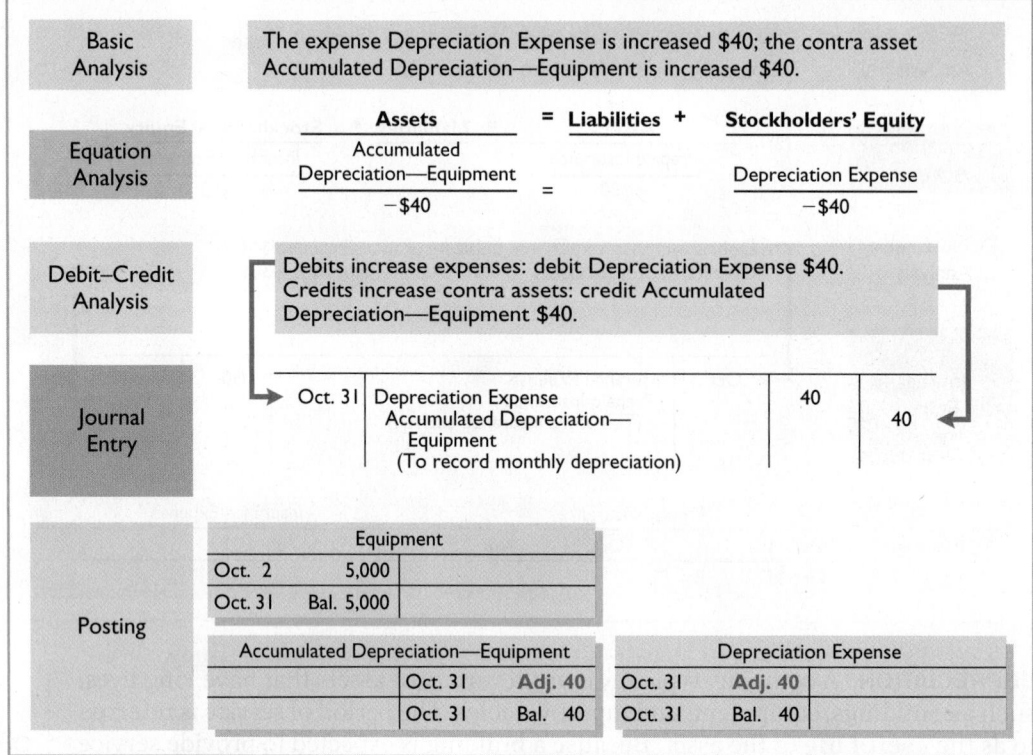

is preferable for a simple reason: It discloses both the original cost of the equipment and the total cost that has expired to date. Thus, in the balance sheet, Sierra deducts Accumulated Depreciation—Equipment from the related asset account, as shown in Illustration 4-9.

Illustration 4-9 Balance sheet
presentation of accumulated
depreciation

Equipment	$ 5,000
Less: Accumulated depreciation—equipment	40
	$4,960

Alternative Terminology Book
value is also referred to as
carrying value.

Book value is the difference between the cost of any depreciable asset and its related accumulated depreciation. In Illustration 4-9, the book value of the equipment at the balance sheet date is $4,960. The book value and the fair value of the asset are generally two different values. As noted earlier, **the purpose of depreciation is not valuation but a means of cost allocation**.

Depreciation expense identifies the portion of an asset's cost that expired during the period (in this case, in October). The accounting equation shows that without this adjusting entry, total assets, total stockholders' equity, and net income are overstated by $40 and depreciation expense is understated by $40.

Illustration 4-10 summarizes the accounting for prepaid expenses.

Illustration 4-10 Accounting
for prepaid expenses

ACCOUNTING FOR PREPAID EXPENSES

Examples	Reason for Adjustment	Accounts Before Adjustment	Adjusting Entry
Insurance, supplies, advertising, rent, depreciation	Prepaid expenses recorded in asset accounts have been used.	Assets overstated. Expenses understated.	Dr. Expenses Cr. Assets or Contra Assets

Unearned Revenues

Companies record cash received before services are performed by increasing (crediting) a liability account called **unearned revenues**. In other words, the company has a performance obligation to transfer a service to one of its customers. Items like rent, magazine subscriptions, and customer deposits for future service may result in unearned revenues. Airlines such as United, American, and Delta, for instance, treat receipts from the sale of tickets as unearned revenue until the flight service is provided.

Unearned revenues are the opposite of prepaid expenses. Indeed, unearned revenue on the books of one company is likely to be a prepaid expense on the books of the company that has made the advance payment. For example, if identical accounting periods are assumed, a landlord will have unearned rent revenue when a tenant has prepaid rent.

When a company receives payment for services to be performed in a future accounting period, it increases (credits) an unearned revenue account. Unearned revenue is a liability account used to recognize the obligation that exists. The company subsequently recognizes revenues when it performs the service. During the accounting period, it is not practical to make daily entries as the company performs services. Instead, the company delays recognition of revenue until the adjustment process. The company then makes an adjusting entry to record the revenue for services performed during the period and to show the liability that remains at the end of the accounting period. Prior to adjustment, liabilities are typically overstated and revenues are understated. Therefore, as shown in Illustration 4-11, **the adjusting entry for unearned revenues results in a decrease (a debit) to a liability account and an increase (a credit) to a revenue account**.

Unearned Revenues

Oct. 2

Thank you in advance for your work

I will finish by Dec. 31

$1,200

Cash is received in advance; liability is recorded

Oct. 31
Some service has been performed; some revenue is recorded

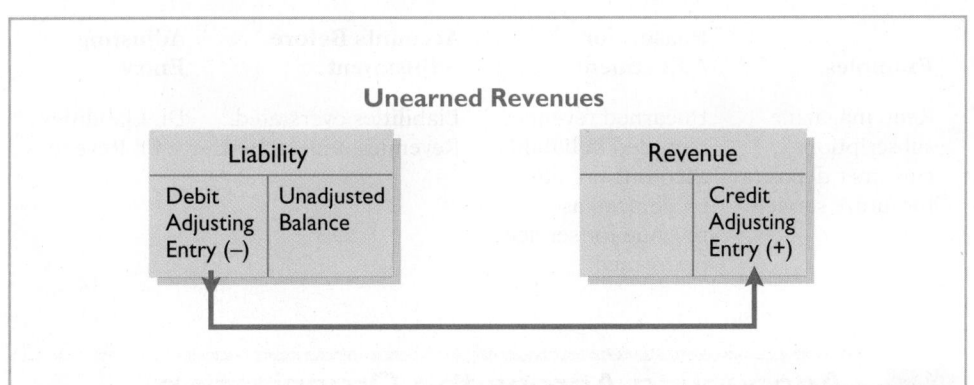

Illustration 4-11 Adjusting entries for unearned revenues

Sierra Corporation received $1,200 on October 2 from R. Knox for guide services for multi-day trips expected to be completed by December 31. Sierra credited the payment to Unearned Service Revenue. This liability account shows a balance of $1,200 in the October 31 trial balance. From an evaluation of the service Sierra performed for Knox during October, the company determines that it should recognize $400 of revenue in October. The liability (Unearned Service Revenue) is therefore decreased and stockholders' equity (Service Revenue) is increased.

As shown in Illustration 4-12 (page 174), the liability Unearned Service Revenue now shows a balance of $800. That amount represents the remaining guide services expected to be performed in the future. Service Revenue shows total revenue for October of $10,400. **Without this adjustment, revenues and net income are understated by $400 in the income statement. Moreover, liabilities are overstated and stockholders' equity is understated by $400 on the October 31 balance sheet.**

Illustration 4-12
Service revenue
accounts after
adjustment

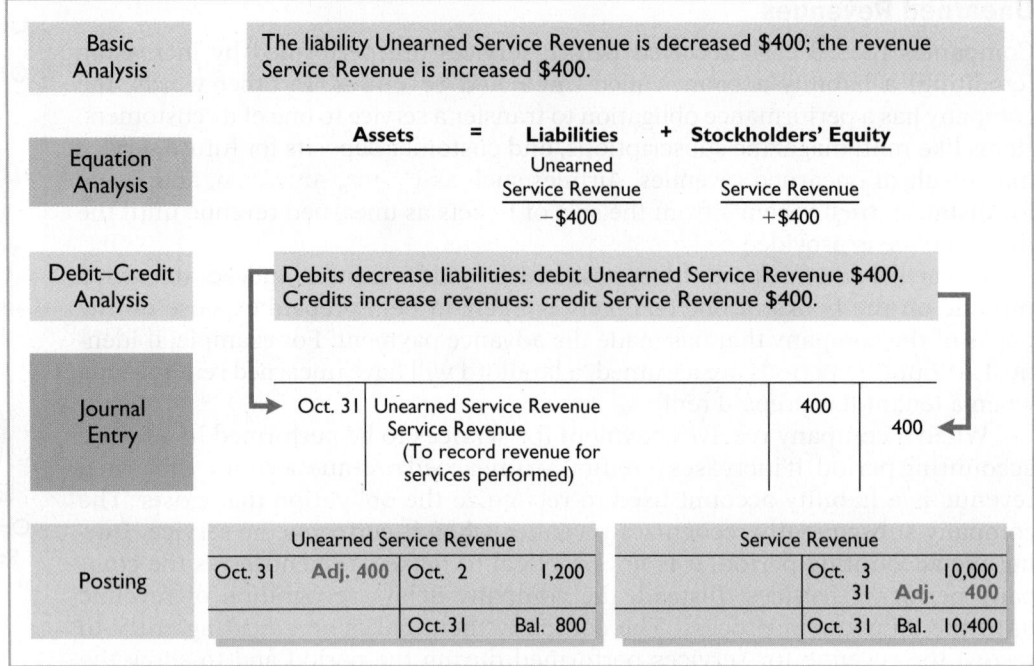

| Basic Analysis | The liability Unearned Service Revenue is decreased $400; the revenue Service Revenue is increased $400. |

Equation Analysis

Assets	=	Liabilities	+	Stockholders' Equity
		Unearned Service Revenue		Service Revenue
		−$400		+$400

Debit–Credit Analysis

Debits decrease liabilities: debit Unearned Service Revenue $400.
Credits increase revenues: credit Service Revenue $400.

Journal Entry

Oct. 31	Unearned Service Revenue	400	
	Service Revenue		400
	(To record revenue for services performed)		

Posting

Unearned Service Revenue					Service Revenue		
Oct. 31	Adj. 400	Oct. 2	1,200			Oct. 3	10,000
						31 Adj.	400
		Oct. 31	Bal. 800			Oct. 31 Bal.	10,400

Illustration 4-13 summarizes the accounting for unearned revenues.

Illustration 4-13 Accounting
for unearned revenues

ACCOUNTING FOR UNEARNED REVENUES

Examples	Reason for Adjustment	Accounts Before Adjustment	Adjusting Entry
Rent, magazine subscriptions, customer deposits for future service	Unearned revenues recorded in liability accounts are now recognized as revenue for services performed.	Liabilities overstated. Revenues understated.	Dr. Liabilities Cr. Revenues

Accounting Across the Organization

Turning Gift Cards into Revenue

Those of you who are marketing majors (and even most of you who are not) know that gift cards are among the hottest marketing tools in merchandising today. Customers purchase gift cards and give them to someone for later use. In a recent year, gift-card sales topped $95 billion.

Although these programs are popular with marketing executives, they create accounting questions. Should revenue be recorded at the time the gift card is sold, or when it is exercised? How should expired gift cards be accounted for? In a recent balance sheet, Best Buy reported unearned revenue related to gift cards of $479 million.

Source: Robert Berner, "Gift Cards: No Gift to Investors," *BusinessWeek* (March 14, 2005), p. 86.

? Suppose that Robert Jones purchases a $100 gift card at Best Buy on December 24, 2013, and gives it to his wife, Mary Jones, on December 25, 2013. On January 3, 2014, Mary uses the card to purchase $100 worth of CDs. When do you think Best Buy should recognize revenue and why? (See page 224.)

© Skip ODonnell/iStockphoto

Do it!

The ledger of Hammond, Inc., on March 31, 2014, includes these selected accounts before adjusting entries are prepared.

	Debit	Credit
Prepaid Insurance	$ 3,600	
Supplies	2,800	
Equipment	25,000	
Accumulated Depreciation—Equipment		$5,000
Unearned Service Revenue		9,200

An analysis of the accounts shows the following.

1. Insurance expires at the rate of $100 per month.
2. Supplies on hand total $800.
3. The equipment depreciates $200 a month.
4. During March, services were performed for one-half of the unearned service revenue.

Prepare the adjusting entries for the month of March.

Solution

1. Insurance Expense	100	
Prepaid Insurance		100
(To record insurance expired)		
2. Supplies Expense	2,000	
Supplies		2,000
(To record supplies used)		
3. Depreciation Expense	200	
Accumulated Depreciation—Equipment		200
(To record monthly depreciation)		
4. Unearned Service Revenue	4,600	
Service Revenue		4,600
(To record revenue for services performed)		

Action Plan

- Make adjusting entries at the end of the period for revenues recognized and expenses incurred in the period.
- Don't forget to make adjusting entries for deferrals. Failure to adjust for deferrals leads to overstatement of the asset or liability and understatement of the related expense or revenue.

 The Navigator

Related exercise material: **BE4-4, BE4-5, BE4-6, BE4-7,** and **Do it! 4-1.**

ADJUSTING ENTRIES FOR ACCRUALS

The second category of adjusting entries is **accruals**. Prior to an accrual adjustment, the revenue account (and the related asset account) or the expense account (and the related liability account) are understated. Thus, the adjusting entry for accruals will **increase both a balance sheet and an income statement account**.

Accrued Revenues

Revenues for services performed but not yet recorded at the statement date are accrued revenues. Accrued revenues may accumulate (accrue) with the passing of time, as in the case of interest revenue. These are unrecorded because the earning of interest does not involve daily transactions. Companies do not record interest revenue on a daily basis because it is often impractical to do so. Accrued revenues also may result from services that have been performed but not yet billed nor collected, as in the case of commissions and fees. These may be unrecorded because only a portion of the total service has been performed and the clients won't be billed until the service has been completed.

    An adjusting entry records the receivable that exists at the balance sheet date and the revenue for the services performed during the period. Prior to adjustment, both assets and revenues are understated. As shown in Illustration 4-14 (page 176),

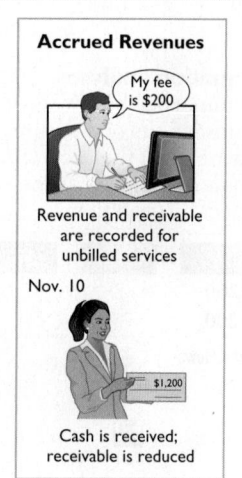

Accrued Revenues

My fee is $200

Revenue and receivable are recorded for unbilled services

Nov. 10

$1,200

Cash is received; receivable is reduced

an adjusting entry for accrued revenues results in an increase (a debit) to an asset account and an increase (a credit) to a revenue account.

Illustration 4-14 Adjusting entries for accrued revenues

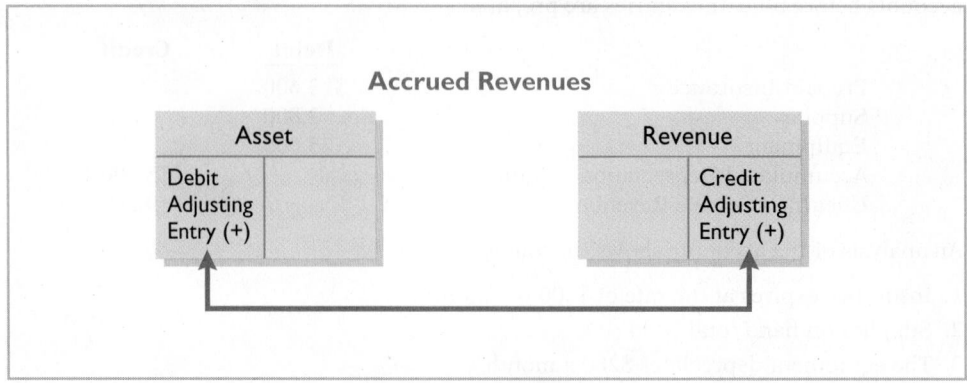

Helpful Hint For accruals, there may have been no prior entry, and the accounts requiring adjustment may both have zero balances prior to adjustment.

In October, Sierra Corporation performed guide services worth $200 that were not billed to clients on or before October 31. Because these services are not billed, they are not recorded. The accrual of unrecorded service revenue increases an asset account, Accounts Receivable. It also increases stockholders' equity by increasing a revenue account, Service Revenue, as shown in Illustration 4-15.

Illustration 4-15
Adjustment for accrued revenue

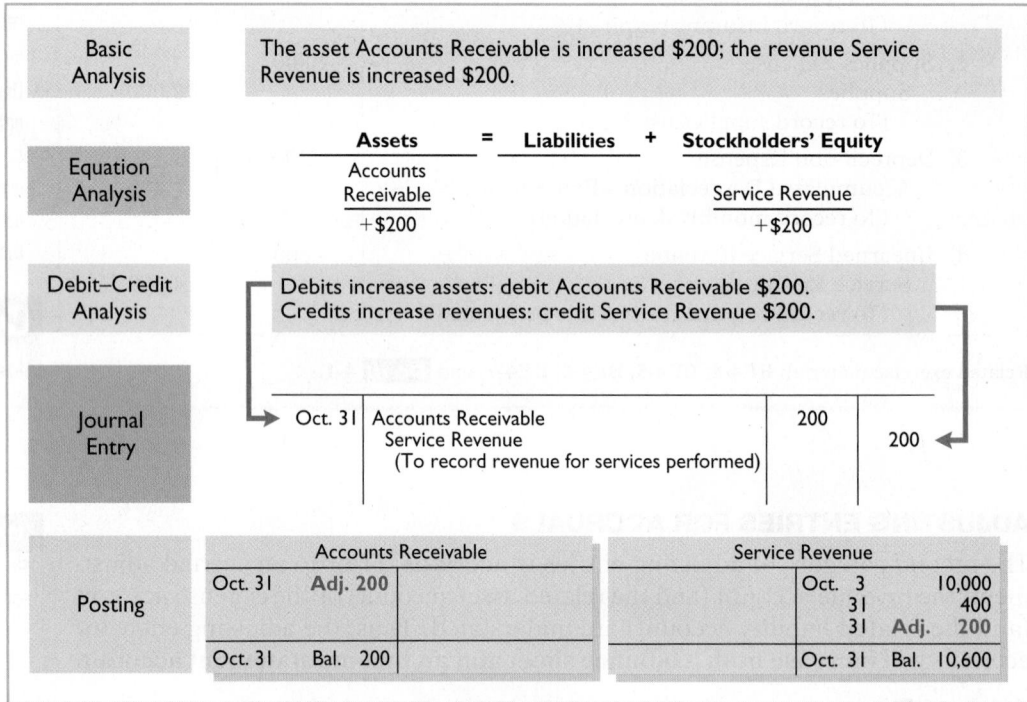

Equation analyses summarize the effects of transactions on the three elements of the accounting equation, as well as the effect on cash flows.

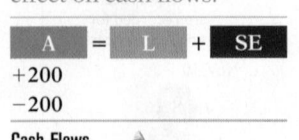

+200
−200

Cash Flows
+200

The asset Accounts Receivable shows that clients owe Sierra $200 at the balance sheet date. The balance of $10,600 in Service Revenue represents the total revenue for services Sierra performed during the month ($10,000 + $400 + $200). **Without the adjusting entry, assets and stockholders' equity on the balance sheet and revenues and net income on the income statement are understated.**

On November 10, Sierra receives cash of $200 for the services performed in October and makes the following entry.

Nov. 10	Cash	200	
	Accounts Receivable		200
	(To record cash collected on account)		

The company records the collection of the receivables by a debit (increase) to Cash and a credit (decrease) to Accounts Receivable.

Illustration 4-16 summarizes the accounting for accrued revenues.

Illustration 4-16
Accounting for accrued revenues

ACCOUNTING FOR ACCRUED REVENUES

Examples	Reason for Adjustment	Accounts Before Adjustment	Adjusting Entry
Interest, rent, services	Services performed but not yet received in cash or recorded.	Assets understated. Revenues understated.	Dr. Assets Cr. Revenues

Accrued Expenses

Expenses incurred but not yet paid or recorded at the statement date are called accrued expenses. Interest, taxes, utilities, and salaries are common examples of accrued expenses.

Companies make adjustments for accrued expenses to record the obligations that exist at the balance sheet date and to recognize the expenses that apply to the current accounting period. Prior to adjustment, both liabilities and expenses are understated. Therefore, **an adjusting entry for accrued expenses results in an increase (a debit) to an expense account and an increase (a credit) to a liability account**.

Ethics Note A report released by Fannie Mae's board of directors stated that improper adjusting entries at the mortgage-finance company resulted in delayed recognition of expenses caused by interest-rate changes. The motivation for this improper accounting apparently was the desire to meet earnings targets.

Illustration 4-17
Adjusting entries for accrued expenses

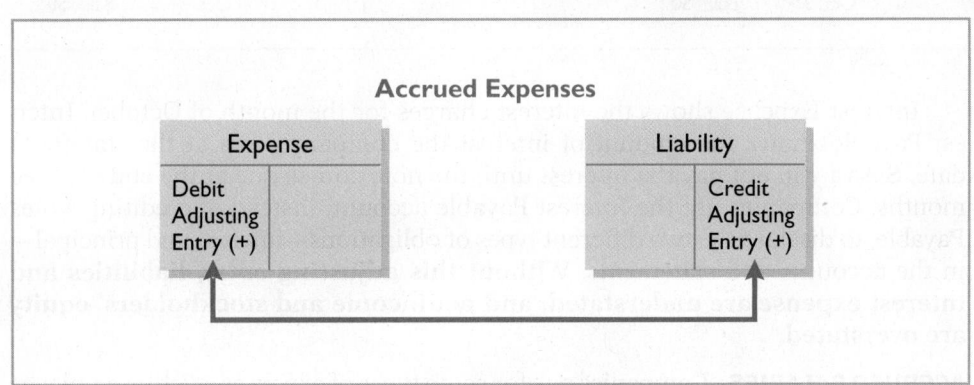

Let's look in more detail at some specific types of accrued expenses, beginning with accrued interest.

ACCRUED INTEREST. Sierra Corporation signed a three-month note payable in the amount of $5,000 on October 1. The note requires Sierra to pay interest at an annual rate of 12%.

The amount of the interest recorded is determined by three factors: (1) the face value of the note; (2) the interest rate, which is always expressed as an annual rate; and (3) the length of time the note is outstanding. For Sierra, the total interest due on the $5,000 note at its maturity date three months in the future is $150 ($5,000 × 12% × $\frac{3}{12}$), or $50 for one month. Illustration 4-18 shows the formula for computing interest and its application to Sierra Corporation for the month of October.

Illustration 4-18 Formula for computing interest

Helpful Hint In computing interest, we express the time period as a fraction of a year.

Face Value of Note		Annual Interest Rate		Time in Terms of One Year		Interest
$5,000	×	12%	×	$\frac{1}{12}$	=	$50

As Illustration 4-19 shows, the accrual of interest at October 31 increases a liability account, Interest Payable. It also decreases stockholders' equity by increasing an expense account, Interest Expense.

Illustration 4-19
Adjustment for
accrued interest

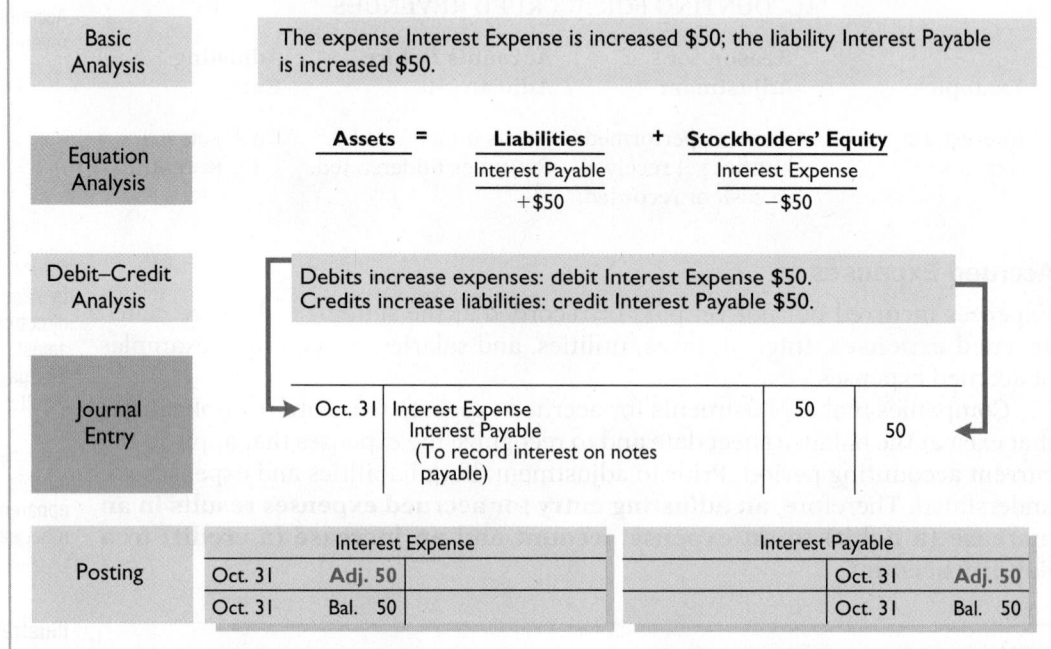

Interest Expense shows the interest charges for the month of October. Interest Payable shows the amount of interest the company owes at the statement date. Sierra will not pay the interest until the note comes due at the end of three months. Companies use the Interest Payable account, instead of crediting Notes Payable, to disclose the two different types of obligations—interest and principal—in the accounts and statements. **Without this adjusting entry, liabilities and interest expense are understated, and net income and stockholders' equity are overstated.**

ACCRUED SALARIES. Companies pay for some types of expenses, such as employee salaries and wages, after the services have been performed. Sierra paid salaries on October 26 for its employees' first two weeks of work; the next payment of salaries will not occur until November 9. As Illustration 4-20 shows, three working days remain in October (October 29–31).

Illustration 4-20 Calendar
showing Sierra Corporation's
pay periods

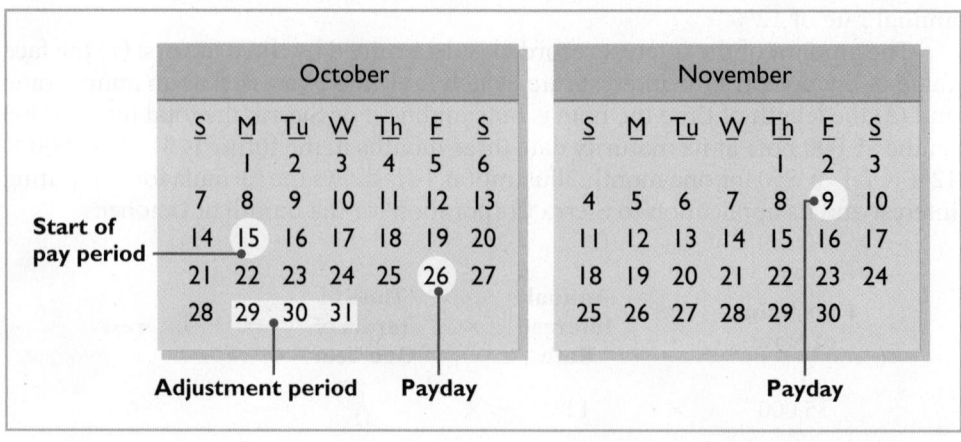

At October 31, the salaries for these three days represent an accrued expense and a related liability to Sierra. The employees receive total salaries of $2,000 for a five-day work week, or $400 per day. Thus, accrued salaries at October 31 are $1,200 ($400 × 3). This accrual increases a liability, Salaries and Wages Payable. It also decreases stockholders' equity by increasing an expense account, Salaries and Wages Expense, as shown in Illustration 4-21.

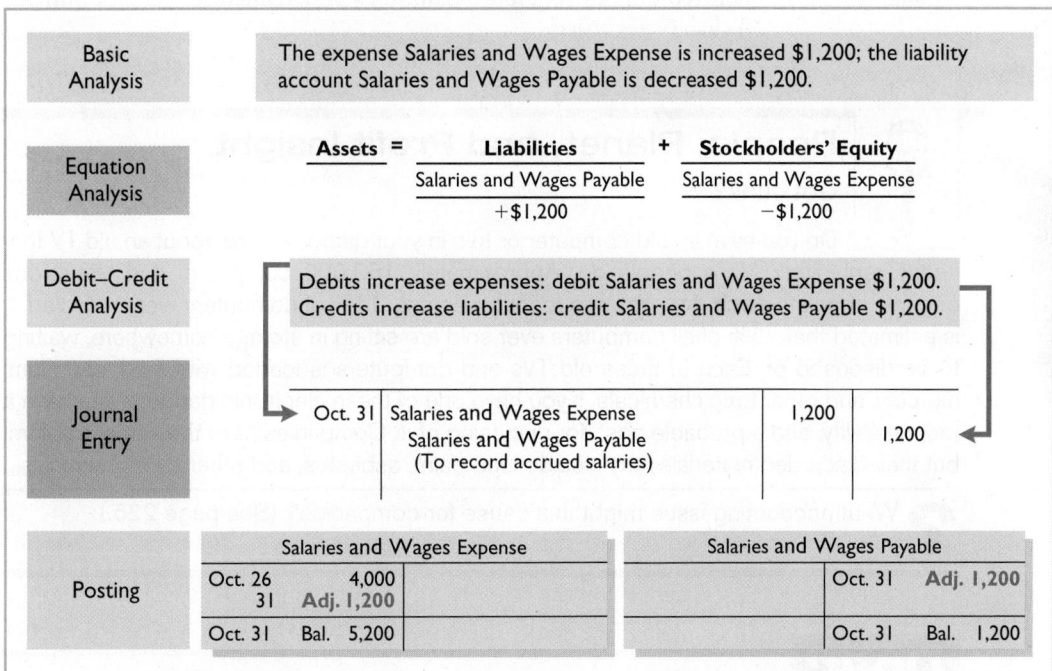

Illustration 4-21
Adjustment for accrued salaries

After this adjustment, the balance in Salaries and Wages Expense of $5,200 (13 days × $400) is the actual salary expense for October. (The employees worked 13 days in October after being hired on October 15.) The balance in Salaries and Wages Payable of $1,200 is the amount of the liability for salaries Sierra owes as of October 31. **Without the $1,200 adjustment for salaries, Sierra's expenses are understated $1,200 and its liabilities are understated $1,200.**

Sierra Corporation pays salaries every two weeks. Consequently, the next payday is November 9, when the company will again pay total salaries of $4,000. The payment consists of $1,200 of salaries and wages payable at October 31 plus $2,800 of salaries and wages expense for November (7 working days, as shown in the November calendar × $400). Therefore, Sierra makes the following entry on November 9.

Nov. 9	Salaries and Wages Payable	1,200	
	Salaries and Wages Expense	2,800	
	Cash		4,000
	(To record November 9 payroll)		

This entry eliminates the liability for Salaries and Wages Payable that Sierra recorded in the October 31 adjusting entry, and it records the proper amount of Salaries and Wages Expense for the period between November 1 and November 9.

Illustration 4-22 summarizes the accounting for accrued expenses.

Illustration 4-22
Accounting for accrued expenses

ACCOUNTING FOR ACCRUED EXPENSES

Examples	Reason for Adjustment	Accounts Before Adjustment	Adjusting Entry
Interest, rent, salaries	Expenses have been incurred but not yet paid in cash or recorded.	Expenses understated. Liabilities understated.	Dr. Expenses Cr. Liabilities

© Nathan Gleave/iStockphoto

People, Planet, and Profit Insight

Got Junk?

Do you have an old computer or two in your garage? How about an old TV that needs replacing? Many people do. Approximately 163,000 computers and televisions become obsolete **each day**. Yet, in a recent year, only 11% of computers were recycled. It is estimated that 75% of all computers ever sold are sitting in storage somewhere, waiting to be disposed of. Each of these old TVs and computers is loaded with lead, cadmium, mercury, and other toxic chemicals. If you have one of these electronic gadgets, you have a responsibility, and a probable cost, for disposing of it. Companies have the same problem, but their discarded materials may include lead paint, asbestos, and other toxic chemicals.

 What accounting issue might this cause for companies? (See page 225.)

ADJUSTING ENTRIES FOR ACCRUALS

Do it! Micro Computer Services Inc. began operations on August 1, 2014. At the end of August 2014, management attempted to prepare monthly financial statements. The following information relates to August.

1. At August 31, the company owed its employees $800 in salaries that will be paid on September 1.

2. On August 1, the company borrowed $30,000 from a local bank on a 15-year mortgage. The annual interest rate is 10%.

3. Revenue for services performed but unrecorded for August totaled $1,100.

Prepare the adjusting entries needed at August 31, 2014.

Action Plan

- Make adjusting entries at the end of the period to recognize revenue for services performed and for expenses incurred.

- Don't forget to make adjusting entries for accruals. Adjusting entries for accruals will increase both a balance sheet and an income statement account.

 The Navigator

Solution

1. Salaries and Wages Expense	800	
Salaries and Wages Payable		800
(To record accrued salaries)		
2. Interest Expense	250	
Interest Payable		250
(To record accrued interest:		
$30,000 \times 10\% \times \frac{1}{12} = \$250$)		
3. Accounts Receivable	1,100	
Service Revenue		1,100
(To record revenue for services performed)		

Related exercise material: **BE4-8, Do it! 4-2, E4-8, E4-9, E4-10,** and **E4-11.**

SUMMARY OF BASIC RELATIONSHIPS

Illustration 4-23 summarizes the four basic types of adjusting entries. Take some time to study and analyze the adjusting entries. Be sure to note that **each adjusting entry affects one balance sheet account and one income statement account**.

Type of Adjustment	Accounts Before Adjustment	Adjusting Entry
Prepaid expenses	Assets overstated. Expenses understated.	Dr. Expenses Cr. Assets or Contra Assets
Unearned revenues	Liabilities overstated. Revenues understated.	Dr. Liabilities Cr. Revenues
Accrued revenues	Assets understated. Revenues understated.	Dr. Assets Cr. Revenues
Accrued expenses	Expenses understated. Liabilities understated.	Dr. Expenses Cr. Liabilities

Illustration 4-23
Summary of adjusting entries

Illustrations 4-24 and 4-25 show the journalizing and posting of adjusting entries for Sierra Corporation on October 31. When reviewing the general ledger in Illustration 4-25, note that for learning purposes we have highlighted the adjustments in color.

GENERAL JOURNAL

Date	Account Titles and Explanation	Debit	Credit
2014	*Adjusting Entries*		
Oct. 31	Supplies Expense	1,500	
	Supplies		1,500
	(To record supplies used)		
31	Insurance Expense	50	
	Prepaid Insurance		50
	(To record insurance expired)		
31	Depreciation Expense	40	
	Accumulated Depreciation—Equipment		40
	(To record monthly depreciation)		
31	Unearned Service Revenue	400	
	Service Revenue		400
	(To record revenue for services performed)		
31	Accounts Receivable	200	
	Service Revenue		200
	(To record revenue for services performed)		
31	Interest Expense	50	
	Interest Payable		50
	(To record interest on notes payable)		
31	Salaries and Wages Expense	1,200	
	Salaries and Wages Payable		1,200
	(To record accrued salaries)		

Illustration 4-24 General journal showing adjusting entries

Illustration 4-25 General
ledger after adjustments

GENERAL LEDGER

Cash

Oct.	1	10,000	Oct.	2	5,000
	1	5,000		3	900
	2	1,200		4	600
	3	10,000		20	500
				26	4,000
Oct. 31	Bal. 15,200				

Accounts Receivable

Oct. 31	200		
Oct. 31	Bal. 200		

Supplies

Oct.	5	2,500	Oct. 31	1,500
Oct. 31	Bal. 1,000			

Prepaid Insurance

Oct.	4	600	Oct. 31	50
Oct. 31	Bal. 550			

Equipment

Oct.	2	5,000	
Oct. 31	Bal. 5,000		

Accumulated Depreciation— Equipment

	Oct. 31	40
	Oct. 31	Bal. 40

Notes Payable

	Oct. 1	5,000
	Oct. 31	Bal. 5,000

Accounts Payable

	Oct. 5	2,500
	Oct. 31	Bal. 2,500

Interest Payable

	Oct. 31	50
	Oct. 31	Bal. 50

Unearned Service Revenue

Oct. 31	400	Oct. 2	1,200
		Oct. 31	Bal. 800

Salaries and Wages Payable

	Oct. 31	1,200
	Oct. 31	Bal. 1,200

Common Stock

	Oct. 1	10,000
	Oct. 31	Bal. 10,000

Retained Earnings

	Oct. 31	Bal. 0

Dividends

Oct. 20	500	
Oct. 31	Bal. 500	

Service Revenue

		Oct. 3	10,000
		31	400
		31	200
		Oct. 31	Bal. 10,600

Salaries and Wages Expense

Oct. 26	4,000		
31	1,200		
Oct. 31	Bal. 5,200		

Supplies Expense

Oct. 31	1,500	
Oct. 31	Bal. 1,500	

Rent Expense

Oct. 3	900	
Oct. 31	Bal. 900	

Insurance Expense

Oct. 31	50	
Oct. 31	Bal. 50	

Interest Expense

Oct. 31	50	
Oct. 31	Bal. 50	

Depreciation Expense

Oct. 31	40	
Oct. 31	Bal. 40	

The Adjusted Trial Balance and Financial Statements

After a company has journalized and posted all adjusting entries, it prepares another trial balance from the ledger accounts. This trial balance is called an **adjusted trial balance**. It shows the balances of all accounts, including those adjusted, at the end of the accounting period. The purpose of an adjusted trial balance is to **prove the equality** of the total debit balances and the total credit balances in the ledger after all adjustments. Because the accounts contain all data needed for financial statements, the adjusted trial balance is the **primary basis for the preparation of financial statements**.

| LEARNING OBJECTIVE | 6 |

Describe the nature and purpose of the adjusted trial balance.

PREPARING THE ADJUSTED TRIAL BALANCE

Illustration 4-26 presents the adjusted trial balance for Sierra Corporation prepared from the ledger accounts in Illustration 4-25. The amounts affected by the adjusting entries are highlighted in color.

SIERRA CORPORATION
Adjusted Trial Balance
October 31, 2014

	Dr.	Cr.
Cash	$ 15,200	
Accounts Receivable	200	
Supplies	1,000	
Prepaid Insurance	550	
Equipment	5,000	
Accumulated Depreciation—Equipment		$ 40
Notes Payable		5,000
Accounts Payable		2,500
Interest Payable		50
Unearned Service Revenue		800
Salaries and Wages Payable		1,200
Common Stock		10,000
Retained Earnings		0
Dividends	500	
Service Revenue		10,600
Salaries and Wages Expense	5,200	
Supplies Expense	1,500	
Rent Expense	900	
Insurance Expense	50	
Interest Expense	50	
Depreciation Expense	40	
	$30,190	$30,190

Illustration 4-26
Adjusted trial balance

PREPARING FINANCIAL STATEMENTS

Companies can prepare financial statements directly from an adjusted trial balance. Illustrations 4-27 and 4-28 (page 185) present the relationships between the data in the adjusted trial balance of Sierra Corporation and the corresponding financial statements. As Illustration 4-27 shows, companies prepare the income statement from the revenue and expense accounts. Similarly, they derive the retained earnings statement from the Retained Earnings account, Dividends account, and the net income (or net loss) shown in the income statement. As Illustration 4-28 shows, companies then prepare the balance sheet from the asset, liability, and stockholders' equity accounts. They obtain the amount reported for retained earnings on the balance sheet from the ending balance in the retained earnings statement.

Illustration 4-27
Preparation of the income statement and retained earnings statement from the adjusted trial balance

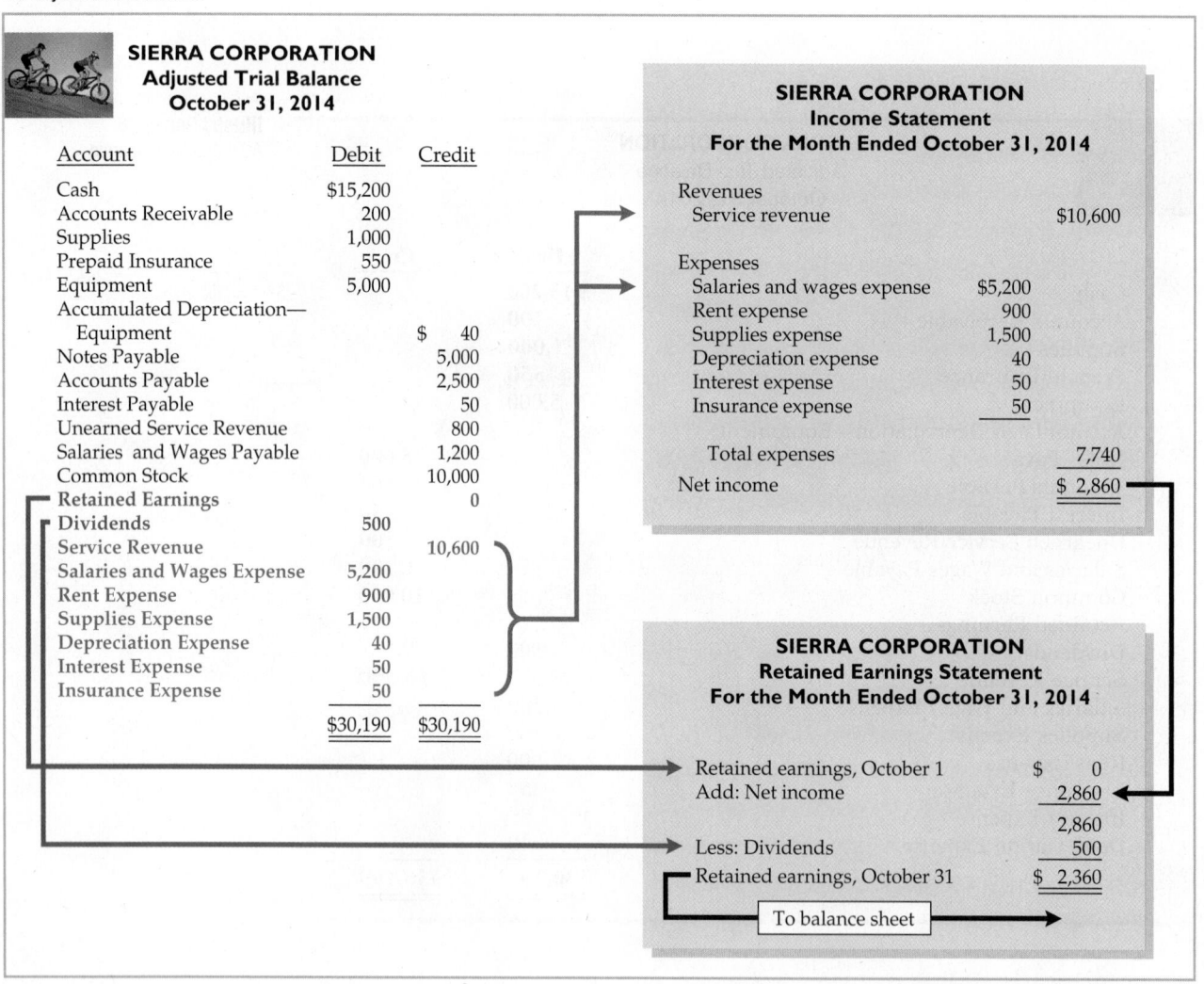

Illustration 4-28
Preparation of the balance sheet from the adjusted trial balance

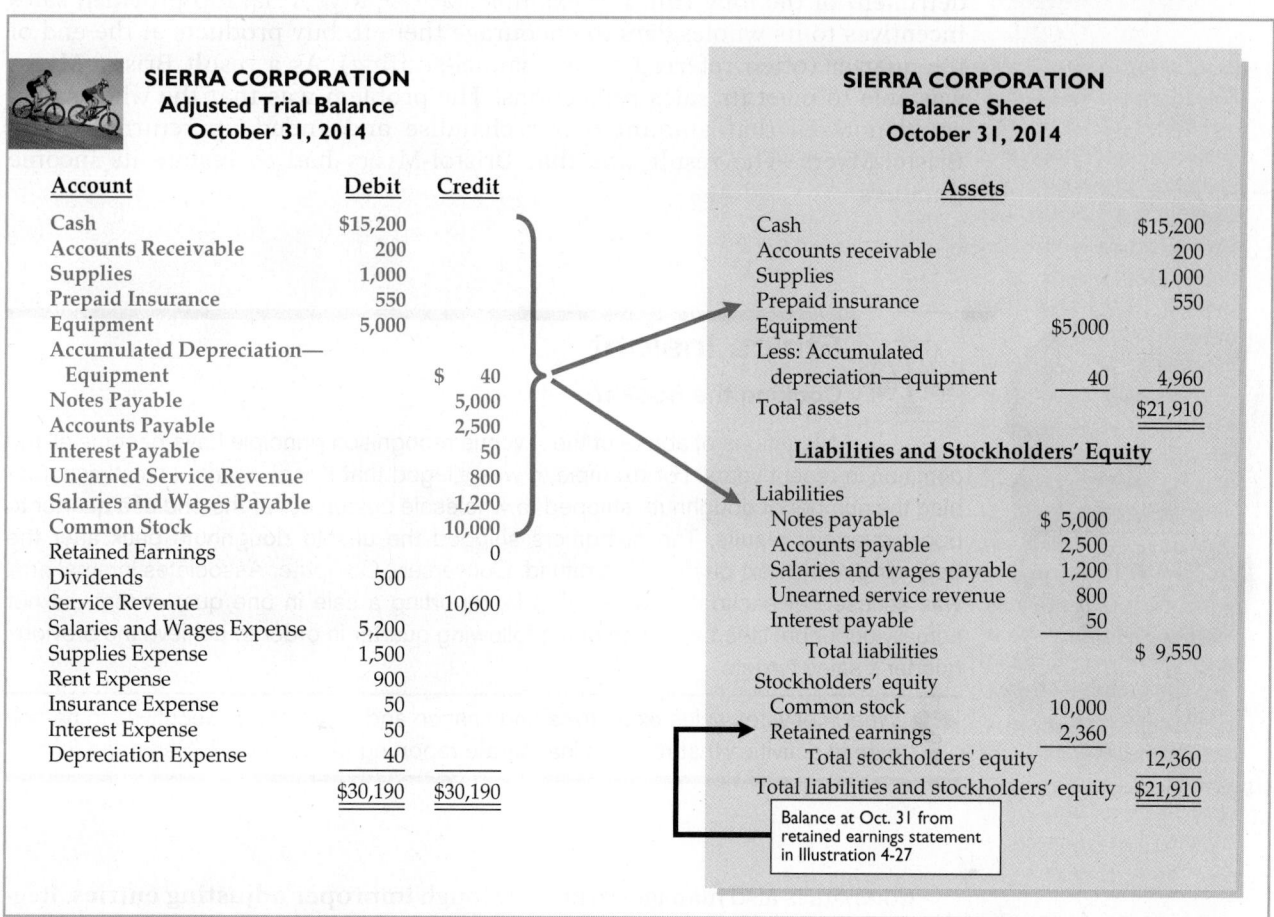

QUALITY OF EARNINGS

"Did you make your numbers today?" is a question asked often in both large and small businesses. Companies and employees are continually under pressure to "make the numbers"—that is, to have earnings that are in line with expectations. Therefore, it is not surprising that many companies practice earnings management. **Earnings management** is the planned timing of revenues, expenses, gains, and losses to smooth out bumps in net income. The quality of earnings is greatly affected when a company manages earnings up or down to meet some targeted earnings number. A company that has a high **quality of earnings** provides full and transparent information that will not confuse or mislead users of the financial statements. A company with questionable quality of earnings may mislead investors and creditors, who believe they are relying on relevant and reliable information. As a result, investors and creditors lose confidence in financial reporting, and it becomes difficult for our capital markets to work efficiently.

Companies manage earnings in a variety of ways. One way is through the use of **one-time items** to prop up earnings numbers. For example, ConAgra Foods recorded a nonrecurring gain from the sale of Pilgrim's Pride stock for $186 million to help meet an earnings projection for the quarter.

Another way is to **inflate revenue** numbers in the short-run to the detriment of the long-run. For example, Bristol-Myers Squibb provided sales incentives to its wholesalers to encourage them to buy products at the end of the quarter (often referred to as channel-stuffing). As a result Bristol-Myers was able to meet its sales projections. The problem was that the wholesalers could not sell that amount of merchandise and ended up returning it to Bristol-Myers. The result was that Bristol-Myers had to restate its income numbers.

© Dean Turner/iStockphoto

Ethics Insight
Cooking the Books?

Allegations of abuse of the revenue recognition principle have become all too common in recent years. For example, it was alleged that Krispy Kreme sometimes doubled the number of doughnuts shipped to wholesale customers at the end of a quarter to boost quarterly results. The customers shipped the unsold doughnuts back after the beginning of the next quarter for a refund. Conversely, Computer Associates International was accused of backdating sales—that is, reporting a sale in one quarter that did not actually occur until the beginning of the following quarter in order to achieve the previous quarter's sales targets.

? What motivates sales executives and finance and accounting executives to participate in activities that result in inaccurate reporting of revenues? (See page 225.)

International Note Internal controls are a system of checks and balances designed to detect and prevent fraud and errors. The Sarbanes-Oxley Act requires U.S. companies to enhance their systems of internal control. However, many foreign companies do not have to meet strict internal control requirements. Some U.S. companies believe that this gives foreign firms an unfair advantage because developing and maintaining internal controls can be very expensive.

Companies also manage earnings through **improper adjusting entries**. Regulators investigated Xerox for accusations that it was booking too much revenue upfront on multi-year contract sales. Financial executives at Office Max resigned amid accusations that the company was recognizing rebates from its vendors too early and therefore overstating revenue. Finally, WorldCom's abuse of adjusting entries to meet its net income targets is unsurpassed. It used adjusting entries to increase net income by reclassifying liabilities as revenue and reclassifying expenses as assets. Investigations of the company's books after it went bankrupt revealed adjusting entries of more than a billion dollars that had no supporting documentation.

The good news is that, as a result of investor pressure as well as the **Sarbanes-Oxley Act**, many companies are trying to improve the quality of their financial reporting. For example, hotel operator Marriott is now providing detailed information on the write-offs it has on loan guarantees it gives hotels. General Electric has decided to provide more detail on its revenues and operating profits for individual businesses it owns. IBM is attempting to provide a better breakdown of its earnings. At the same time, regulators are taking a tough stand on the issue of quality of earnings. For example, one regulator noted that companies may be required to restate their financials every single time that they account for any transaction that had no legitimate purpose but was done solely for an accounting purpose, such as to smooth net income.

Do it!

Skolnick Co. was organized on April 1, 2014. The company prepares quarterly financial statements. The adjusted trial balance amounts at June 30 are shown below.

	Debit		Credit
Cash	$ 6,700	Accumulated Depreciation—Equipment	$ 850
Accounts Receivable	600	Notes Payable	5,000
Prepaid Rent	900	Accounts Payable	1,510
Supplies	1,000	Salaries and Wages Payable	400
Equipment	15,000	Interest Payable	50
Dividends	600	Unearned Rent Revenue	500
Salaries and Wages Expense	9,400	Common Stock	14,000
Rent Expense	1,500	Retained Earning	0
Depreciation Expense	850	Service Revenue	14,200
Supplies Expense	200	Rent Revenue	800
Utilities Expense	510		
Interest Expense	50		
	$37,310		$37,310

(a) Determine the net income for the quarter April 1 to June 30.

(b) Determine the total assets and total liabilities at June 30, 2014, for Skolnick Co.

(c) Determine the balance in Retained Earnings at June 30, 2014.

Solution

(a) The net income is determined by adding revenues and subtracting expenses. The net income is computed as follows.

Revenues		
Service revenue	$14,200	
Rent revenue	800	
Total revenues		$15,000
Expenses		
Salaries and wages expense	9,400	
Rent expense	1,500	
Depreciation expense	850	
Utilities expense	510	
Supplies expense	200	
Interest expense	50	
Total expenses		12,510
Net income		$ 2,490

(b) Total assets and liabilities are computed as follows.

Assets			Liabilities	
Cash		$ 6,700	Notes payable	$5,000
Accounts receivable		600	Accounts payable	1,510
Supplies		1,000	Unearned rent revenue	500
Prepaid rent		900	Salaries and wages	
Equipment	$15,000		payable	400
Less: Accumulated			Interest payable	50
depreciation—				
equipment	850	14,150		
Total assets		$23,350	Total liabilities	$7,460

(c)

Retained earnings, April 1	$ 0
Add: Net income	2,490
Less: Dividends	600
Retained earnings, June 30	$1,890

Action Plan

- In an adjusted trial balance, all asset, liability, revenue, and expense accounts are properly stated.

- To determine the ending balance in Retained Earnings, add net income and subtract dividends.

The Navigator

Related exercise material: **BE4-9, BE4-10, BE4-11, BE4-12, Do it! 4-3, E4-12, E4-13, E4-15, and E4-16.**

Closing the Books

In previous chapters, you learned that revenue and expense accounts and the Dividends account are subdivisions of retained earnings, which is reported in the stockholders' equity section of the balance sheet. Because revenues, expenses, and dividends relate only to a given accounting period, they are considered **temporary accounts**. In contrast, all balance sheet accounts are considered **permanent accounts** because their balances are carried forward into future accounting periods. Illustration 4-29 identifies the accounts in each category.

Illustration 4-29
Temporary versus permanent accounts

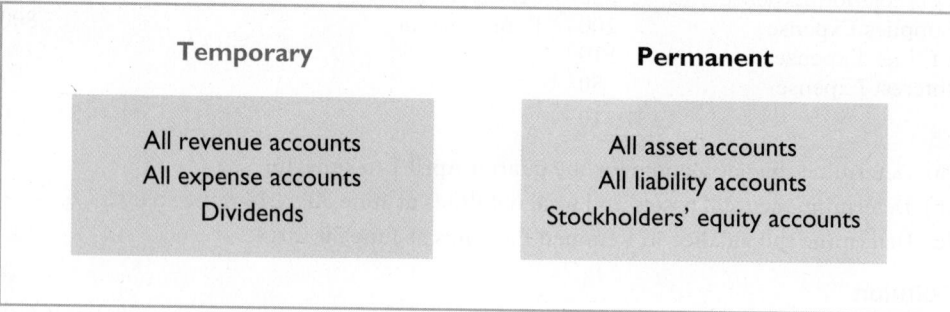

PREPARING CLOSING ENTRIES

Alternative Terminology
Temporary accounts are sometimes called *nominal accounts*, and permanent accounts are sometimes called *real accounts*.

At the end of the accounting period, companies transfer the temporary account balances to the permanent stockholders' equity account—Retained Earnings—through the preparation of closing entries. **Closing entries** transfer net income (or net loss) and dividends to Retained Earnings, so the balance in Retained Earnings agrees with the retained earnings statement. For example, in the adjusted trial balance in Illustration 4-24 (page 181), Retained Earnings has a balance of zero. Prior to the closing entries, the balance in Retained Earnings is its beginning-of-the-period balance. (For Sierra, this is zero because it is Sierra's first month of operations.)

In addition to updating Retained Earnings to its correct ending balance, closing entries produce a **zero balance in each temporary account**. As a result, these accounts are ready to accumulate data about revenues, expenses, and dividends that occur in the next accounting period. **Permanent accounts are not closed.**

When companies prepare closing entries, they could close each income statement account directly to Retained Earnings. However, to do so would result in excessive detail in the Retained Earnings account. Instead, companies close the revenue and expense accounts to another temporary account, **Income Summary**. The balance in Income Summary is the net income or loss for the year. Income Summary is then closed, which transfers the net income or net loss from this account to Retained Earnings. Illustration 4-30 depicts the closing process. While it still takes the average large company seven days to close, some companies such as Cisco employ technology that allows them to do a so-called "virtual close" almost instantaneously any time during the year. Besides dramatically reducing the cost of closing, the virtual close provides companies with accurate data for decision-making whenever they desire it.

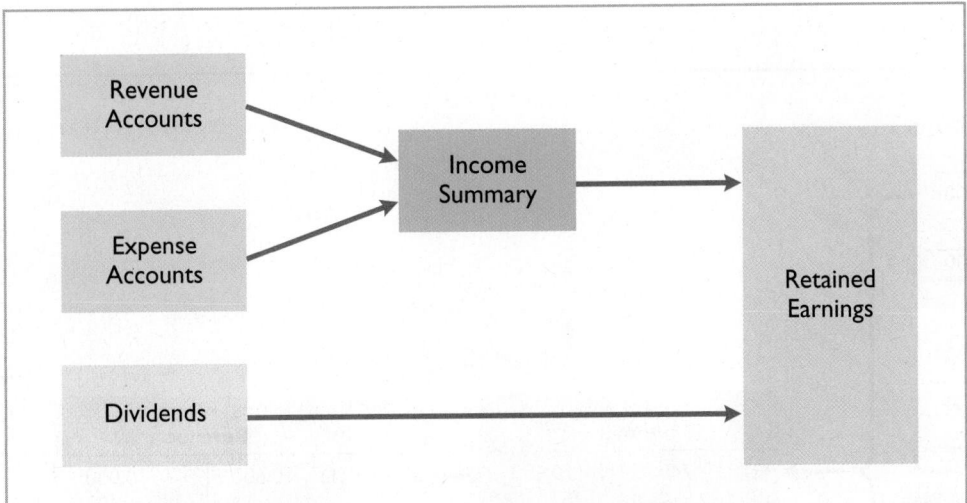

Illustration 4-30 The closing process

Illustration 4-31 shows the closing entries for Sierra Corporation. Illustration 4-32 (page 190) diagrams the posting process for Sierra Corporation's closing entries.

Illustration 4-31 Closing entries journalized

	GENERAL JOURNAL		
Date	**Account Titles and Explanation**	**Debit**	**Credit**
	Closing Entries		
	(1)		
2014			
Oct. 31	Service Revenue	10,600	
	Income Summary		10,600
	(To close revenue account)		
	(2)		
31	Income Summary	7,740	
	Salaries and Wages Expense		5,200
	Supplies Expense		1,500
	Rent Expense		900
	Insurance Expense		50
	Interest Expense		50
	Depreciation Expense		40
	(To close expense accounts)		
	(3)		
31	Income Summary	2,860	
	Retained Earnings		2,860
	(To close net income to retained earnings)		
	(4)		
31	Retained Earnings	500	
	Dividends		500
	(To close dividends to retained earnings)		

Helpful Hint Income Summary is a very descriptive title: Companies close total revenues to Income Summary and total expenses to Income Summary. The balance in Income Summary in this case is net income of $2,860.

PREPARING A POST-CLOSING TRIAL BALANCE

After a company journalizes and posts all closing entries, it prepares another trial balance, called a post-closing trial balance, from the ledger. A post-closing trial balance is a list of all permanent accounts and their balances after closing entries are journalized and posted. **The purpose of this trial balance is to prove the equality of the total debit balances and total credit balances of the permanent account balances that the company carries forward into the next accounting period.** Since all temporary accounts will have zero balances, **the post-closing trial balance will contain only permanent—balance sheet—accounts**.

Illustration 4-32 Posting of closing entries

Salaries and Wages Expense		
4,000	(2)	5,200
1,200		
5,200		5,200

Supplies Expense		
1,500	(2)	1,500

Rent Expense		
900	(2)	900

Insurance Expense		
50	(2)	50

Interest Expense		
50	(2)	50

Depreciation Expense		
40	(2)	40

2

Income Summary			
(2)	7,740	(1)	10,600
(3)	2,860		
	10,600		10,600

1

Service Revenue		
(1)	10,600	10,000
		400
		200
	10,600	10,600

3

Retained Earnings			
(4)	500		—0—
		(3)	2,860
		Bal.	2,360

4

Dividends		
500	(4)	500

CLOSING ENTRIES

Do it!

After making entries to close its revenue and expense accounts to Income Summary, Hancock Company has the following balances.

Dividends	$15,000
Retained Earnings	42,000
Income Summary	18,000 (credit balance)

Prepare the remaining closing entries at December 31.

Action Plan

- Close Income Summary to Retained Earnings.
- Close Dividends to Retained Earnings.

 The Navigator

Solution

Dec. 31	Income Summary	18,000	
	Retained Earnings		18,000
	(To close net income to retained earnings)		
31	Retained Earnings	15,000	
	Dividends		15,000
	(To close dividends to retained earnings)		

Related exercise material: **BE4-13, BE4-14, Do it! 4-4, E4-14,** and **E4-18.**

SUMMARY OF THE ACCOUNTING CYCLE

Illustration 4-33 shows the required steps in the accounting cycle. You can see that the cycle begins with the analysis of business transactions and ends with the preparation of a post-closing trial balance. Companies perform the steps in the cycle in sequence and repeat them in each accounting period.

LEARNING OBJECTIVE 8
Describe the required steps in the accounting cycle.

Illustration 4-33
Required steps in the accounting cycle

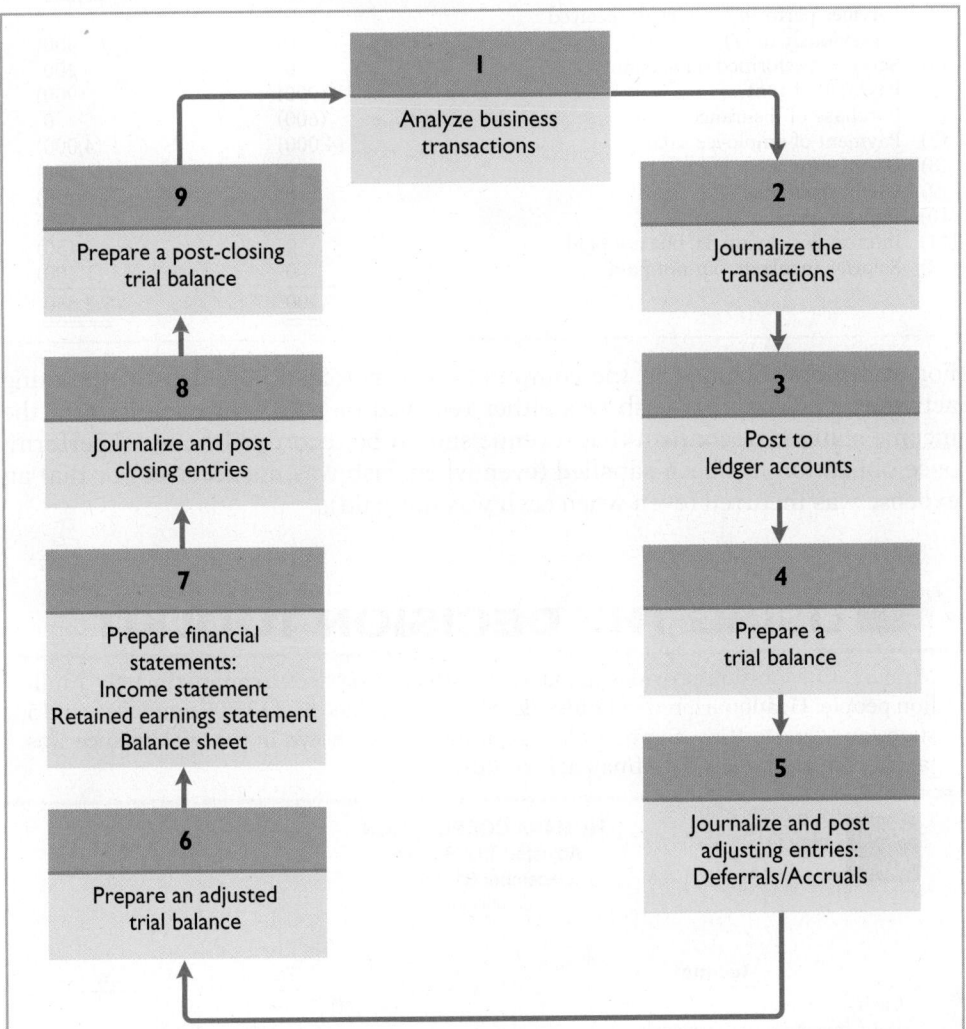

Steps 1–3 may occur daily during the accounting period, as explained in Chapter 3. Companies perform Steps 4–7 on a periodic basis, such as monthly, quarterly, or annually. Steps 8 and 9, closing entries and a post-closing trial balance, usually take place only at the end of a company's **annual** accounting period.

Helpful Hint Some companies reverse certain adjusting entries at the beginning of a new accounting period. The company makes a reversing entry at the beginning of the next accounting period. This entry is the exact opposite of the adjusting entry made in the previous period.

KEEPING AN EYE ON CASH

In this chapter, you learned that adjusting entries are used to adjust numbers that would otherwise be stated on a cash basis. Sierra Corporation's income statement (Illustration 4-27, page 184) shows net income of $2,860. The statement of cash flows reports a form of cash-basis income referred to as "Net cash provided by operating activities." For example, Illustration 1-8 (page 15), which shows a statement of cash flows, reports net cash provided by operating activities of $5,700 for Sierra. Net income and net cash provided by operating activities often differ. The difference for Sierra is $2,840 ($5,700 − $2,860). The following summary shows the causes of this difference of $2,840.

LEARNING OBJECTIVE 9
Understand the causes of differences between net income and net cash provided by operating activities.

		Computation of Net Cash Provided by Operating Activities	Computation of Net Income
(1)	Cash received in advance from customer	$ 1,200	$ 0
(2)	Cash received from customers for services performed	10,000	10,000
(3)	Services performed for cash received previously in (1)	0	400
(4)	Services performed on account	0	200
(5)	Payment of rent	(900)	(900)
(6)	Purchase of insurance	(600)	0
(7)	Payment of employee salaries	(4,000)	(4,000)
(8)	Use of supplies	0	(1,500)
(9)	Use of insurance	0	(50)
(10)	Depreciation	0	(40)
(11)	Interest cost incurred, but not paid	0	(50)
(12)	Salaries incurred, but not paid	0	(1,200)
		$ 5,700	$ 2,860

For each item included in the computation of net cash provided by operating activities, confirm that cash was either received or paid. For each item in the income statement, confirm that revenue should be recorded because a performance obligation has been satisfied (even when cash was not received) or that an expense was incurred (even when cash was not paid).

 # USING THE DECISION TOOLKIT

Humana Corporation provides managed health care services to approximately 7 million people. Headquartered in Louisville, Kentucky, it has over 13,700 employees in 15 states and Puerto Rico. Suppose that the information shown in the trial balance was taken from Humana's 2014 financial records.

Real World

HUMANA CORPORATION
Adjusted Trial Balance
December 31, 2014
(in millions)

Account	Dr.	Cr.
Cash	$ 1,613	
Debt Investments (current)	6,190	
Accounts Receivable	824	
Other Current Assets	626	
Equipment	2,402	
Accumulated Depreciation—Equipment		$ 1,723
Stock Investments (noncurrent)	1,307	
Goodwill	1,993	
Other Long-Term Assets	921	
Benefits Payable		3,222
Accounts Payable		1,308
Other Current Liabilities		730
Notes Payable (noncurrent)		3,117
Common Stock		1,690
Dividends	0	
Retained Earnings		3,046
Revenues		30,960
Medical Cost Expense	24,775	
Selling and Administrative Expenses	4,227	
Depreciation Expense	250	
Interest Expense	106	
Income Tax Expense	562	
	$45,796	$45,796

Instructions

From the trial balance, prepare an income statement, retained earnings statement, and classified balance sheet. **Be sure to prepare them in that order since each statement depends on information determined in the preceding statement.**

Solution

Real World

HUMANA CORPORATION
Income Statement
For the Year Ended December 31, 2014
(in millions)

Revenues		$30,960
Medical cost expense	$24,775	
Selling and administrative expenses	4,227	
Depreciation expense	250	
Interest expense	106	
Income tax expense	562	29,920
Net income		$ 1,040

Real World

HUMANA CORPORATION
Retained Earnings Statement
For the Year Ended December 31, 2014
(in millions)

Beginning retained earnings	$3,046
Add: Net income	1,040
Less: Dividends	0
Ending retained earnings	$4,086

Real World

HUMANA CORPORATION
Balance Sheet
December 31, 2014
(in millions)

Assets

Current assets		
Cash	$1,613	
Debt investments	6,190	
Accounts receivable	824	
Other current assets	626	
Total current assets		$ 9,253
Long-term investments		
Stock investments		1,307
Property, plant, and equipment		
Equipment	2,402	
Accumulated depreciation—equipment	1,723	679
Intangible assets		
Goodwill		1,993
Other long-term assets		921
Total assets		$14,153

Liabilities and Stockholders' Equity

Liabilities		
Current liabilities		
Accounts payable	$1,308	
Benefits payable	3,222	
Other current liabilities	730	
Total current liabilities		$ 5,260
Long-term liabilities		
Notes payable		3,117
Total liabilities		8,377
Stockholders' equity		
Common stock	1,690	
Retained earnings	4,086	
Total stockholders' equity		5,776
Total liabilities and stockholders' equity		$14,153

The
Navigator

Summary of Learning Objectives

1 **Explain the revenue recognition principle and the expense recognition principle.** The revenue recognition principle dictates that companies recognize revenue when a performance obligation has been satisfied. The expense recognition principle dictates that companies recognize expenses in the period when the company makes efforts to generate those revenues.

2 **Differentiate between the cash basis and the accrual basis of accounting.** Under the cash basis, companies record events only in the periods in which the company receives or pays cash. Accrual-based accounting means that companies record, in the periods in which the events occur, events that change a company's financial statements even if cash has not been exchanged.

3 **Explain why adjusting entries are needed, and identify the major types of adjusting entries.** Companies make adjusting entries at the end of an accounting period. These entries ensure that companies record revenues in the period in which the performance obligation is satisfied and that companies recognize expenses in the period in which they are incurred. The major types of adjusting entries are prepaid expenses, unearned revenues, accrued revenues, and accrued expenses.

4 **Prepare adjusting entries for deferrals.** Deferrals are either prepaid expenses or unearned revenues. Companies make adjusting entries for deferrals at the statement date to record the portion of the deferred item that represents the expense incurred or the revenue for services performed in the current accounting period.

5 **Prepare adjusting entries for accruals.** Accruals are either accrued revenues or accrued expenses. Adjusting entries for accruals record revenues for services performed and expenses incurred in the current accounting period that have not been recognized through daily entries.

6 **Describe the nature and purpose of the adjusted trial balance.** An adjusted trial balance is a trial balance that shows the balances of all accounts, including those that have been adjusted, at the end of an accounting period. The purpose of an adjusted trial balance is to show the effects of all financial events that have occurred during the accounting period.

7 **Explain the purpose of closing entries.** One purpose of closing entries is to transfer net income or net loss for the period to Retained Earnings. A second purpose is to "zero-out" all temporary accounts (revenue accounts, expense accounts, and Dividends) so that they start each new period with a zero balance. To accomplish this, companies "close" all temporary accounts at the end of an accounting period. They make separate entries to close revenues and expenses to Income Summary, Income Summary to Retained Earnings, and Dividends to Retained Earnings. Only temporary accounts are closed.

8 **Describe the required steps in the accounting cycle.** The required steps in the accounting cycle are (a) analyze business transactions, (b) journalize the transactions, (c) post to ledger accounts, (d) prepare a trial balance, (e) journalize and post adjusting entries, (f) prepare an adjusted trial balance, (g) prepare financial statements, (h) journalize and post closing entries, and (i) prepare a post-closing trial balance.

9 **Understand the causes of differences between net income and net cash provided by operating activities.** Net income is based on accrual accounting, which relies on the adjustment process. Net cash provided by operating activities is determined by adding cash received from operating the business and subtracting cash expended during operations.

✔ The Navigator

 # DECISION TOOLKIT *A SUMMARY*

DECISION CHECKPOINTS	INFO NEEDED FOR DECISION	TOOL TO USE FOR DECISION	HOW TO EVALUATE RESULTS
At what point should the company record revenue?	Need to understand the nature of the company's business	Record revenue in the period in which the performance obligation is satisfied.	Recognizing revenue too early overstates current period revenue; recognizing it too late understates current period revenue.
At what point should the company record expenses?	Need to understand the nature of the company's business	Expenses should "follow" revenues—that is, match the effort (expense) with the result (revenue).	Recognizing expenses too early overstates current period expense; recognizing them too late understates current period expense.

Adjusting Entries in an Automated World—Using a Worksheet

In the previous discussion, we used T-accounts and trial balances to arrive at the amounts used to prepare financial statements. Accountants frequently use a device known as a worksheet to determine these amounts. A worksheet is a multiple-column form that may be used in the adjustment process and in preparing financial statements. Accountants can prepare worksheets manually, but today most use computer spreadsheets.

> **LEARNING OBJECTIVE** 10
>
> Describe the purpose and the basic form of a worksheet.

As its name suggests, the worksheet is a working tool for the accountant. **A worksheet is not a permanent accounting record**; it is neither a journal nor a part of the general ledger. The worksheet is merely a supplemental device used to make it easier to prepare adjusting entries and the financial statements. Small companies with relatively few accounts and adjustments may not need a worksheet. In large companies with numerous accounts and many adjustments, a worksheet is almost indispensable.

Illustration 4A-1 (page 196) shows the basic form and procedures for preparing a worksheet. Note the headings: The worksheet starts with two columns for the Trial Balance. The next two columns record all Adjustments. Next is the Adjusted Trial Balance. The last two sets of columns correspond to the Income Statement and the Balance Sheet. All items listed in the Adjusted Trial Balance columns are included in either the Income Statement or the Balance Sheet columns.

Summary of Learning Objective for Appendix 4A

10 **Describe the purpose and the basic form of a worksheet.** The worksheet is a device to make it easier to prepare adjusting entries and the financial statements. Companies often prepare a worksheet using a computer spreadsheet. The sets of columns of the worksheet are, from left to right, the unadjusted trial balance, adjustments, adjusted trial balance, income statement, and balance sheet.

Illustration 4A-1
Form and procedure
for a worksheet

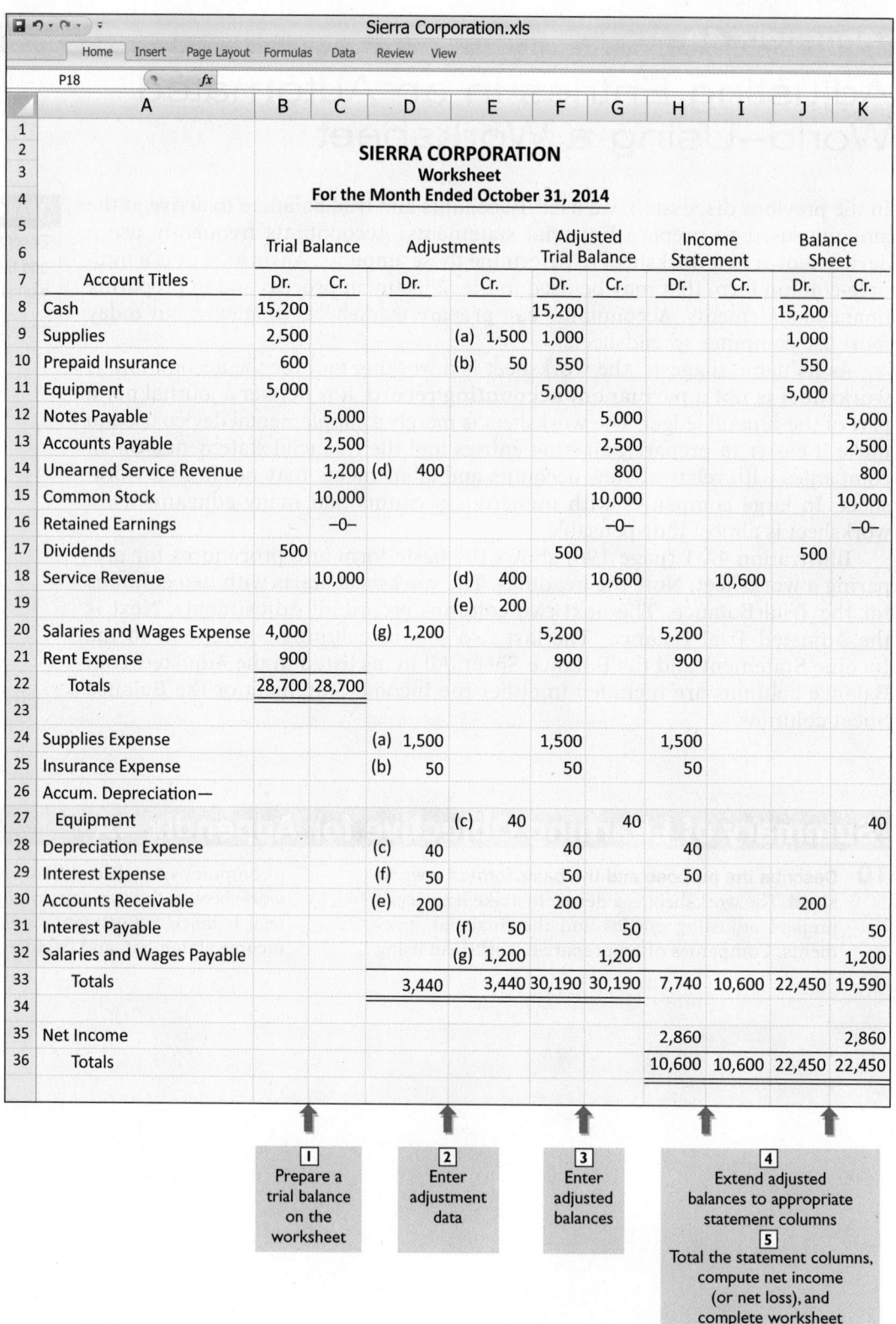

	A	B	C	D	E	F	G	H	I	J	K
					SIERRA CORPORATION						
					Worksheet						
					For the Month Ended October 31, 2014						
		Trial Balance		Adjustments		Adjusted Trial Balance		Income Statement		Balance Sheet	
7	Account Titles	Dr.	Cr.	Dr.	Cr.	Dr.	Cr.	Dr.	Cr.	Dr.	Cr.
8	Cash	15,200				15,200				15,200	
9	Supplies	2,500			(a) 1,500	1,000				1,000	
10	Prepaid Insurance	600			(b) 50	550				550	
11	Equipment	5,000				5,000				5,000	
12	Notes Payable		5,000				5,000				5,000
13	Accounts Payable		2,500				2,500				2,500
14	Unearned Service Revenue		1,200	(d) 400			800				800
15	Common Stock		10,000				10,000				10,000
16	Retained Earnings		–0–				–0–				–0–
17	Dividends	500				500				500	
18	Service Revenue		10,000		(d) 400		10,600		10,600		
19					(e) 200						
20	Salaries and Wages Expense	4,000		(g) 1,200		5,200		5,200			
21	Rent Expense	900				900		900			
22	Totals	28,700	28,700								
23											
24	Supplies Expense			(a) 1,500		1,500		1,500			
25	Insurance Expense			(b) 50		50		50			
26	Accum. Depreciation—										
27	Equipment				(c) 40		40				40
28	Depreciation Expense			(c) 40		40		40			
29	Interest Expense			(f) 50		50		50			
30	Accounts Receivable			(e) 200		200				200	
31	Interest Payable				(f) 50		50				50
32	Salaries and Wages Payable				(g) 1,200		1,200				1,200
33	Totals			3,440	3,440	30,190	30,190	7,740	10,600	22,450	19,590
34											
35	Net Income							2,860			2,860
36	Totals							10,600	10,600	22,450	22,450

1 Prepare a trial balance on the worksheet

2 Enter adjustment data

3 Enter adjusted balances

4 Extend adjusted balances to appropriate statement columns

5 Total the statement columns, compute net income (or net loss), and complete worksheet

Glossary

Accrual-basis accounting *(p. 166)* Accounting basis in which companies record, in the periods in which the events occur, transactions that change a company's financial statements, even if cash was not exchanged.

Accrued expenses *(p. 177)* Expenses incurred but not yet paid in cash or recorded.

Accrued revenues *(p. 175)* Revenues for services performed but not yet received in cash or recorded.

Adjusted trial balance *(p. 183)* A list of accounts and their balances after all adjustments have been made.

Adjusting entries *(p. 167)* Entries made at the end of an accounting period to ensure that the revenue recognition and expense recognition principles are followed.

Book value *(p. 172)* The difference between the cost of a depreciable asset and its related accumulated depreciation.

Cash-basis accounting *(p. 166)* Accounting basis in which a company records revenue only when it receives cash and an expense only when it pays cash.

Closing entries *(p. 188)* Entries at the end of an accounting period to transfer the balances of temporary accounts to a permanent stockholders' equity account, Retained Earnings.

Contra asset account *(p. 171)* An account that is offset against an asset account on the balance sheet.

Depreciation *(p. 171)* The process of allocating the cost of an asset to expense over its useful life.

Earnings management *(p. 185)* The planned timing of revenues, expenses, gains, and losses to smooth out bumps in net income.

Expense recognition principle (matching principle) *(p. 165)* The principle that matches expenses with revenues in the period when the company makes efforts to generate those revenues.

Fiscal year *(p. 164, in margin)* An accounting period that is one year long.

Income Summary *(p. 188)* A temporary account used in closing revenue and expense accounts.

Periodicity assumption *(p. 164)* An assumption that the economic life of a business can be divided into artificial time periods.

Permanent accounts *(p. 188)* Balance sheet accounts whose balances are carried forward to the next accounting period.

Post-closing trial balance *(p. 189)* A list of permanent accounts and their balances after a company has journalized and posted closing entries.

Prepaid expenses (prepayments) *(p. 169)* Expenses paid in cash before they are used or consumed.

Quality of earnings *(p. 185)* Indicates the level of full and transparent information that a company provides to users of its financial statements.

Revenue recognition principle *(p. 164)* The principle that companies recognize revenue in the accounting period in which the performance obligation is satisfied.

Reversing entry *(p. 191, in margin)* An entry made at the beginning of the next accounting period; the exact opposite of the adjusting entry made in the previous period.

Temporary accounts *(p. 188)* Revenue, expense, and dividend accounts whose balances a company transfers to Retained Earnings at the end of an accounting period.

Unearned revenues *(p. 173)* Cash received and a liability recorded before services are performed.

Useful life *(p. 171)* The length of service of a productive asset.

Worksheet *(p. 195)* A multiple-column form that companies may use in the adjustment process and in preparing financial statements.

Comprehensive Do it!

Terry Thomas and a group of investors incorporate the Green Thumb Lawn Care Corporation on April 1. At April 30, the trial balance shows the following balances for selected accounts.

Prepaid Insurance	$ 3,600
Equipment	28,000
Notes Payable	20,000
Unearned Service Revenue	4,200
Service Revenue	1,800

Analysis reveals the following additional data pertaining to these accounts.

1. Prepaid insurance is the cost of a 2-year insurance policy, effective April 1.
2. Depreciation on the equipment is $500 per month.
3. The note payable is dated April 1. It is a 6-month, 6% note.
4. Seven customers paid for the company's 6-month lawn service package of $600 beginning in April. These customers received the first month of services in April.
5. Lawn services performed for other customers but not billed at April 30 totaled $1,500.

Instructions

Prepare the adjusting entries for the month of April. Show computations.

Action Plan

- Note that adjustments are being made for one month.
- Make computations carefully.
- Select account titles carefully.
- Make sure debits are made first and credits are indented.
- Check that debits equal credits for each entry.

Solution to Comprehensive Do it!

	GENERAL JOURNAL		
Date	**Account Titles and Explanation**	**Debit**	**Credit**
	Adjusting Entries		
Apr. 30	Insurance Expense	150	
	Prepaid Insurance		150
	(To record insurance expired:		
	$3,600 ÷ 24 = $150 per month)		
30	Depreciation Expense	500	
	Accumulated Depreciation—Equipment		500
	(To record monthly depreciation)		
30	Interest Expense	100	
	Interest Payable		100
	(To accrue interest on notes payable:		
	$20,000 × 6% × $\frac{1}{12}$ = $100)		
30	Unearned Service Revenue	700	
	Service Revenue		700
	(To record revenue for services performed:		
	$600 ÷ 6 = $100; $100 per month × 7 = $700)		
30	Accounts Receivable	1,500	
	Service Revenue		1,500
	(To accrue revenue for services performed)		

 The Navigator

Self-Test, Brief Exercises, Exercises, Problem Set A, and many more resources are available for practice in WileyPLUS.

Note: All Questions, Exercises, and Problems marked with an asterisk relate to material in the appendix to the chapter.

Self-Test Questions

Answers are on page 225.

(LO 1) **1.** What is the periodicity assumption?
   (a) Companies should recognize revenue in the accounting period in which services are performed.
   (b) Companies should match expenses with revenues.
   (c) The economic life of a business can be divided into artificial time periods.
   (d) The fiscal year should correspond with the calendar year.

(LO 1) **2.** Which principle dictates that efforts (expenses) be recorded with accomplishments (revenues)?
   (a) Expense recognition principle.
   (b) Historical cost principle.
   (c) Periodicity principle.
   (d) Revenue recognition principle.

(LO 2) **3.** Which one of these statements about the accrual basis of accounting is **false**?
   (a) Companies record events that change their financial statements in the period in which events occur, even if cash was not exchanged.
   (b) Companies recognize revenue in the period in which the performance obligation is satisfied.
   (c) This basis is in accord with generally accepted accounting principles.
   (d) Companies record revenue only when they receive cash, and record expense only when they pay out cash.

(LO 3) **4.** Adjusting entries are made to ensure that:
   (a) expenses are recognized in the period in which they are incurred.
   (b) revenues are recorded in the period in which the performance obligation is satisfied.
   (c) balance sheet and income statement accounts have correct balances at the end of an accounting period.
   (d) All of the above.

(LO 4, 5) **5.** Each of the following is a major type (or category) of adjusting entry **except**:
   (a) prepaid expenses.   (c) accrued expenses.
   (b) accrued revenues.   (d) unearned expenses.

(LO 4) **6.** The trial balance shows Supplies $1,350 and Supplies Expense $0. If $600 of supplies are on hand at the end of the period, the adjusting entry is:
   (a) Supplies | 600 |
          Supplies Expense | | 600
   (b) Supplies | 750 |
          Supplies Expense | | 750
   (c) Supplies Expense | 750 |
          Supplies | | 750
   (d) Supplies Expense | 600 |
          Supplies | | 600

7. Adjustments for unearned revenues: (LO 4)
   (a) decrease liabilities and increase revenues.
   (b) increase liabilities and increase revenues.
   (c) increase assets and increase revenues.
   (d) decrease revenues and decrease assets.

8. Adjustments for prepaid expenses: (LO 4)
   (a) decrease assets and increase revenues.
   (b) decrease expenses and increase assets.
   (c) decrease assets and increase expenses.
   (d) decrease revenues and increase assets.

9. Queenan Company computes depreciation on delivery (LO 4) equipment at $1,000 for the month of June. The adjusting entry to record this depreciation is as follows:
   (a) Depreciation Expense | 1,000 |
          Accumulated Depreciation—
             Queenan Company | | 1,000
   (b) Depreciation Expense | 1,000 |
          Equipment | | 1,000
   (c) Depreciation Expense | 1,000 |
          Accumulated Depreciation—
             Equipment | | 1,000
   (d) Equipment Expense | 1,000 |
          Accumulated Depreciation—
             Equipment | | 1,000

10. Adjustments for accrued revenues: (LO 5)
   (a) increase assets and increase liabilities.
   (b) increase assets and increase revenues.
   (c) decrease assets and decrease revenues.
   (d) decrease liabilities and increase revenues.

11. Colleen Mooney earned a salary of $400 for the last (LO 5) week of September. She will be paid on October 1. The adjusting entry for Colleen's employer at September 30 is:
   (a) No entry is required.
   (b) Salaries and Wages Expense | 400 |
          Salaries and Wages Payable | | 400
   (c) Salaries and Wages Expense | 400 |
          Cash | | 400
   (d) Salaries and Wages Payable | 400 |
          Cash | | 400

12. Which statement is **incorrect** concerning the adjusted (LO 6) trial balance?
   (a) An adjusted trial balance proves the equality of the total debit balances and the total credit balances in the ledger after all adjustments are made.
   (b) The adjusted trial balance provides the primary basis for the preparation of financial statements.
   (c) The adjusted trial balance does not list temporary accounts.

(d) The company prepares the adjusted trial balance after it has journalized and posted the adjusting entries.

(LO 7) **13.** Which account will have a zero balance after a company has journalized and posted closing entries?
(a) Service Revenue.
(b) Supplies.
(c) Prepaid Insurance.
(d) Accumulated Depreciation.

(LO 7) **14.** Which types of accounts will appear in the post-closing trial balance?
(a) Permanent accounts.
(b) Temporary accounts.

(c) Expense accounts.
(d) None of the above.

15. All of the following are required steps in the account- (LO 8) ing cycle **except**:
(a) journalizing and posting closing entries.
(b) preparing an adjusted trial balance.
(c) preparing a post-closing trial balance.
(d) reversing entries.

Go to the book's companion website, **www.wiley.com/college/kimmel**, to access additional Self-Test Questions.

 The Navigator

Questions

1. (a) How does the periodicity assumption affect an accountant's analysis of accounting transactions?
(b) Explain the term fiscal year.

2. Identify and state two generally accepted accounting principles that relate to adjusting the accounts.

3. Sam Milner, a lawyer, accepts a legal engagement in March, performs the work in April, and is paid in May. If Milner's law firm prepares monthly financial statements, when should it recognize revenue from this engagement? Why?

4. In completing the engagement in Question 3, Milner pays no costs in March, $2,500 in April, and $2,200 in May (incurred in April). How much expense should the firm deduct from revenues in the month when it recognizes the revenue? Why?

5. "The historical cost principle of accounting requires adjusting entries." Do you agree? Explain.

6. Why may the financial information in an unadjusted trial balance not be up-to-date and complete?

7. Distinguish between the two categories of adjusting entries, and identify the types of adjustments applicable to each category.

8. What types of accounts does a company debit and credit in a prepaid expense adjusting entry?

9. "Depreciation is a process of valuation that results in the reporting of the fair value of the asset." Do you agree? Explain.

10. Explain the differences between depreciation expense and accumulated depreciation.

11. Remington Company purchased equipment for $15,000. By the current balance sheet date, the company had depreciated $7,000. Indicate the balance sheet presentation of the data.

12. What types of accounts are debited and credited in an unearned revenue adjusting entry?

13. Ace Technologies provides maintenance service for computers and office equipment for companies throughout the Northeast. The sales manager is elated because she closed a $300,000, three-year maintenance contract on December 29, 2013, two days before the company's year-end. "Now we will hit this year's net income target for sure," she crowed. The customer is required to pay $100,000 on December 29 (the day the deal was closed). Two more payments of $100,000 each are also required on December 29, 2014 and 2015. Discuss the effect that this event will have on the company's financial statements.

14. ValuMart, a large national retail chain, is nearing its fiscal year-end. It appears that the company is not going to hit its revenue and net income targets. The company's marketing manager, Steve Edmiston, suggests running a promotion selling $50 gift cards for $45. He believes that this would be very popular and would enable the company to meet its targets for revenue and net income. What do you think of this idea?

15. A company fails to recognize revenue for services performed but not yet received. Which of the following types of accounts are involved in the adjusting entry: (a) asset, (b) liability, (c) revenue, or (d) expense? For the accounts selected, indicate whether they would be debited or credited in the entry.

16. A company fails to recognize an expense incurred but not paid. Indicate which of the following types of accounts is debited and which is credited in the adjusting entry: (a) asset, (b) liability, (c) revenue, or (d) expense.

17. A company makes an accrued revenue adjusting entry for $780 and an accrued expense adjusting entry for $510. How much was net income understated or overstated prior to these entries? Explain.

18. On January 9, a company pays $6,200 for salaries, of which $1,100 was reported as Salaries and Wages Payable on December 31. Give the entry to record the payment.

19. For each of the following items before adjustment, indicate the type of adjusting entry—prepaid expense, unearned revenue, accrued revenue, and accrued expense—that is needed to correct the misstatement. If an item could result in more than one type of adjusting entry, indicate each of the types.
(a) Assets are understated.

(b) Liabilities are overstated.
(c) Liabilities are understated.
(d) Expenses are understated.
(e) Assets are overstated.
(f) Revenue is understated.

20. One-half of the adjusting entry is given below. Indicate the account title for the other half of the entry.
    (a) Salaries and Wages Expense is debited.
    (b) Depreciation Expense is debited.
    (c) Interest Payable is credited.
    (d) Supplies is credited.
    (e) Accounts Receivable is debited.
    (f) Unearned Service Revenue is debited.

21. "An adjusting entry may affect more than one balance sheet or income statement account." Do you agree? Why or why not?

22. [image] Which balance sheet account provides evidence that Tootsie Roll records sales on an accrual basis rather than a cash basis? Explain.

23. Why is it possible to prepare financial statements directly from an adjusted trial balance?

24. [image]
    (a) What information do accrual-basis financial statements provide that cash-basis statements do not?
    (b) What information do cash-basis financial statements provide that accrual-basis statements do not?

25. What is the relationship, if any, between the amount shown in the adjusted trial balance column for an account and that account's ledger balance?

26. Identify the account(s) debited and credited in each of the four closing entries, assuming the company has net income for the year.

27. [image] Some companies employ technologies that allow them to do a so-called "virtual close." This enables them to close their books nearly instantaneously any time during the year. What advantages does a "virtual close" provide?

28. Describe the nature of the Income Summary account, and identify the types of summary data that may be posted to this account.

29. What items are disclosed on a post-closing trial balance, and what is its purpose?

30. Which of these accounts would not appear in the post-closing trial balance? Interest Payable, Equipment, Depreciation Expense, Dividends, Unearned Service Revenue, Accumulated Depreciation— Equipment, and Service Revenue.

31. Indicate, in the sequence in which they are made, the three required steps in the accounting cycle that involve journalizing.

32. Identify, in the sequence in which they are prepared, the three trial balances that are required in the accounting cycle.

33. [image] Explain the terms earnings management and quality of earnings.

34. [image] Give examples of how companies manage earnings.

*35. What is the purpose of a worksheet?

*36. What is the basic form of a worksheet?

Brief Exercises

BE4-1 Transactions that affect earnings do not necessarily affect cash. Identify the effect, if any, that each of the following transactions would have upon cash and net income. The first transaction has been completed as an example.

Identify impact of transactions on cash and net income.
(LO 2, 9), C

	Cash	Net Income
(a) Purchased $100 of supplies for cash.	−$100	$ 0

(b) Recorded an adjusting entry to record use of $20 of the above supplies.
(c) Made sales of $1,300, all on account.
(d) Received $800 from customers in payment of their accounts.
(e) Purchased equipment for cash, $2,500.
(f) Recorded depreciation of building for period used, $600.

BE4-2 The ledger of Berkman Company includes the following accounts. Explain why each account may require adjustment.
(a) Prepaid Insurance.
(b) Depreciation Expense.
(c) Unearned Service Revenue.
(d) Interest Payable.

Indicate why adjusting entries are needed.
(LO 3), C

BE4-3 Molina Company accumulates the following adjustment data at December 31. Indicate (1) the type of adjustment (prepaid expense, accrued revenue, and so on) and (2) the status of the accounts before adjustment (overstated or understated).
(a) Supplies of $400 are on hand. Supplies account shows $1,600 balance.

Identify the major types of adjusting entries.
(LO 3), AN

(b) Services performed but unbilled total $700.

(c) Interest of $300 has accumulated on a note payable.

(d) Rent collected in advance totaling $1,100 has been earned.

Prepare adjusting entry for supplies.

(LO 4), **AP**

BE4-4 Foley Advertising Company's trial balance at December 31 shows Supplies $8,800 and Supplies Expense $0. On December 31, there are $1,100 of supplies on hand. Prepare the adjusting entry at December 31 and, using T-accounts, enter the balances in the accounts, post the adjusting entry, and indicate the adjusted balance in each account.

Prepare adjusting entry for depreciation.

(LO 4), **AP**

BE4-5 At the end of its first year, the trial balance of Boyer Company shows Equipment $22,000 and zero balances in Accumulated Depreciation—Equipment and Depreciation Expense. Depreciation for the year is estimated to be $2,750. Prepare the adjusting entry for depreciation at December 31, post the adjustments to T-accounts, and indicate the balance sheet presentation of the equipment at December 31.

Prepare adjusting entry for prepaid expense.

(LO 4), **AP**

BE4-6 On July 1, 2014, Seng Co. pays $12,400 to Nance Insurance Co. for a 2-year insurance contract. Both companies have fiscal years ending December 31. For Seng Co., journalize and post the entry on July 1 and the adjusting entry on December 31.

Prepare adjusting entry for unearned revenue.

(LO 4), **AP**

BE4-7 Using the data in BE4-6, journalize and post the entry on July 1 and the adjusting entry on December 31 for Nance Insurance Co. Nance uses the accounts Unearned Service Revenue and Service Revenue.

Prepare adjusting entries for accruals.

(LO 5), **AP**

BE4-8 The bookkeeper for Beltran Company asks you to prepare the following accrual adjusting entries at December 31. Use these account titles: Service Revenue, Accounts Receivable, Interest Expense, Interest Payable, Salaries and Wages Expense, and Salaries and Wages Payable.

(a) Interest on notes payable of $300 is accrued.

(b) Services performed but unbilled totals $1,700.

(c) Salaries of $780 earned by employees have not been recorded.

Analyze accounts in an adjusted trial balance.

(LO 6), **AN**

BE4-9 The trial balance of Goodwin Company includes the following balance sheet accounts. Identify the accounts that might require adjustment. For each account that requires adjustment, indicate (1) the type of adjusting entry (prepaid expenses, unearned revenues, accrued revenues, and accrued expenses) and (2) the related account in the adjusting entry.

(a) Accounts Receivable.

(b) Prepaid Insurance.

(c) Equipment.

(d) Accumulated Depreciation—Equipment.

(e) Notes Payable.

(f) Interest Payable.

(g) Unearned Service Revenue.

Prepare an income statement from an adjusted trial balance.

(LO 6), **AP**

BE4-10 The adjusted trial balance of Ravine Corporation at December 31, 2014, includes the following accounts: Retained Earnings $17,200; Dividends $6,000; Service Revenue $32,000; Salaries and Wages Expense $14,000; Insurance Expense $1,800; Rent Expense $3,900; Supplies Expense $1,500; and Depreciation Expense $1,000. Prepare an income statement for the year.

Prepare a retained earnings statement from an adjusted trial balance.

(LO 6), **AP**

BE4-11 Partial adjusted trial balance data for Ravine Corporation are presented in BE4-10. The balance in Retained Earnings is the balance as of January 1. Prepare a retained earnings statement for the year assuming net income is $10,400.

Identify financial statement for selected accounts.

(LO 6), **K**

BE4-12 The following selected accounts appear in the adjusted trial balance for Baden Company. Indicate the financial statement on which each account would be reported.

(a) Accumulated Depreciation.

(b) Depreciation Expense.

(c) Retained Earnings (beginning).

(d) Dividends.

(e) Service Revenue.

(f) Supplies.

(g) Accounts Payable.

Identify post-closing trial balance accounts.

(LO 7), **K**

BE4-13 Using the data in BE4-12, identify the accounts that would be included in a post-closing trial balance.

Prepare and post closing entries.

(LO 7), **AP**

BE4-14 The income statement for the Four Oaks Golf Club Inc. for the month ended July 31 shows Service Revenue $16,000; Salaries and Wages Expense $8,400; Maintenance and Repairs Expense $2,500; and Income Tax Expense $1,000. The statement of retained earnings shows an opening balance for Retained Earnings of $20,000 and Dividends $1,300.

(a) Prepare closing journal entries.

(b) What is the ending balance in Retained Earnings?

BE4-15 The required steps in the accounting cycle are listed in random order below. List the steps in proper sequence.

List required steps in the accounting cycle sequence.
(LO 8), **K**

(a) Prepare a post-closing trial balance.
(b) Prepare an adjusted trial balance.
(c) Analyze business transactions.
(d) Prepare a trial balance.
(e) Journalize the transactions.
(f) Journalize and post closing entries.
(g) Prepare financial statements.
(h) Journalize and post adjusting entries.
(i) Post to ledger accounts.

Do it! Review

Do it! 4-1 The ledger of Columbia, Inc. on March 31, 2014, includes the following selected accounts before adjusting entries.

Prepare adjusting entries for deferrals.
(LO 4), **AP**

	Debit	Credit
Supplies	2,500	
Prepaid Insurance	2,400	
Equipment	30,000	
Unearned Service Revenue		10,000

An analysis of the accounts shows the following.

1. Insurance expires at the rate of $300 per month.
2. Supplies on hand total $900.
3. The equipment depreciates $200 per month.
4. During March, services were performed for two-fifths of the unearned service revenue.

Prepare the adjusting entries for the month of March.

Do it! 4-2 Kathy Gannon is the new owner of Kathy's Computer Services. At the end of July 2014, her first month of ownership, Kathy is trying to prepare monthly financial statements. She has the following information for the month.

Prepare adjusting entries for accruals.
(LO 5), **AP**

1. At July 31, Kathy owed employees $1,100 in salaries that the company will pay in August.
2. On July 1, Kathy borrowed $20,000 from a local bank on a 10-year note. The annual interest rate is 9%.
3. Service revenue unrecorded in July totaled $1,600.

Prepare the adjusting entries needed at July 31, 2014.

Do it! 4-3 Indicate in which financial statement each of the following adjusted trial balance accounts would be presented.

Prepare financial statements from adjusted trial balance.
(LO 6), **C**

Service Revenue   Accounts Receivable
Notes Payable   Accumulated Depreciation
Common Stock   Utilities Expense

Do it! 4-4 After closing revenues and expense, Alomar Company shows the following account balances.

Prepare closing entries.
(LO 7), **AP**

Dividends	$22,000
Retained Earnings	70,000
Income Summary	36,000 (credit balance)

Prepare the remaining closing entries at December 31.

Exercises

E4-1 The following independent situations require professional judgment for determining when to recognize revenue from the transactions.

(a) Southwest Airlines sells you an advance-purchase airline ticket in September for your flight home at Christmas.

(b) Ultimate Electronics sells you a home theater on a "no money down and full payment in three months" promotional deal.

(c) The Toronto Blue Jays sell season tickets online to games in the Skydome. Fans can purchase the tickets at any time, although the season doesn't officially begin until April. The major league baseball season runs from April through October.

(d) You borrow money in August from RBC Financial Group. The loan and the interest are repayable in full in November.

(e) In August, you order a sweater from Sears using its online catalog. The sweater arrives in September, which you charged to your Sears credit card. You receive and pay the Sears bill in October.

Instructions

Identify when revenue should be recognized in each of the above situations.

E4-2 These accounting concepts were discussed in this and previous chapters.

1. Economic entity assumption.
2. Expense recognition principle.
3. Monetary unit assumption.
4. Periodicity assumption.
5. Historical cost principle.

6. Materiality.
7. Full disclosure principle.
8. Going concern assumption.
9. Revenue recognition principle.
10. Cost constraint.

Instructions

Identify by number the accounting concept that describes each situation below. Do not use a number more than once.

_____ (a) Is the rationale for why plant assets are not reported at liquidation value. (Do not use the historical cost principle.)

_____ (b) Indicates that personal and business record-keeping should be separately maintained.

_____ (c) Ensures that all relevant financial information is reported.

_____ (d) Assumes that the dollar is the "measuring stick" used to report on financial performance.

_____ (e) Requires that accounting standards be followed for all items of **significant** size.

_____ (f) Separates financial information into time periods for reporting purposes.

_____ (g) Requires recognition of expenses in the same period as related revenues.

_____ (h) Indicates that fair value changes subsequent to purchase are not recorded in the accounts.

E4-3 Here are some accounting reporting situations.

(a) Bonilla Company recognizes revenue at the end of the production cycle but before sale. The price of the product, as well as the amount that can be sold, is not certain.

(b) Barto Company is in its fifth year of operation and has yet to issue financial statements. (Do not use the full disclosure principle.)

(c) Lopez, Inc. is carrying inventory at its original cost of $100,000. Inventory has a fair value of $110,000.

(d) Ryno Hospital Supply Corporation reports only current assets and current liabilities on its balance sheet. Equipment and bonds payable are reported as current assets and current liabilities, respectively. Liquidation of the company is unlikely.

(e) Liu Company has inventory on hand that cost $400,000. Liu reports inventory on its balance sheet at its current fair value of $425,000.

(f) Sara Toney, president of Classic Music Company, bought a computer for her personal use. She paid for the computer by using company funds and debited the "Computers" account.

Instructions

For each situation, list the assumption, principle, or constraint that has been violated, if any. (Some were presented in earlier chapters.) List only one answer for each situation.

E4-4 Your examination of the records of a company that follows the cash basis of accounting tells you that the company's reported cash-basis earnings in 2014 are $33,640. If this firm had followed accrual-basis accounting practices, it would have reported the following year-end balances.

Convert earnings from cash to accrual basis.
(LO 2, 4, 5, 9), **AP**

	2014	2013
Accounts receivable	$3,400	$2,800
Supplies on hand	1,300	1,460
Unpaid wages owed	2,000	2,400
Other unpaid expenses	1,400	1,100

Instructions

Determine the company's net earnings on an accrual basis for 2014. Show all your calculations in an orderly fashion.

E4-5 In its first year of operations, Ramirez Company recognized $28,000 in service revenue, $6,000 of which was on account and still outstanding at year-end. The remaining $22,000 was received in cash from customers.

Determine cash-basis and accrual-basis earnings.
(LO 2, 9), **AP**

The company incurred operating expenses of $15,800. Of these expenses, $12,000 were paid in cash; $3,800 was still owed on account at year-end. In addition, Ramirez prepaid $2,400 for insurance coverage that would not be used until the second year of operations.

Instructions

(a) Calculate the first year's net earnings under the cash basis of accounting, and calculate the first year's net earnings under the accrual basis of accounting.
(b) Which basis of accounting (cash or accrual) provides more useful information for decision-makers?

E4-6 Kaffen Company, a ski tuning and repair shop, opened on November 1, 2013. The company carefully kept track of all its cash receipts and cash payments. The following information is available at the end of the ski season, April 30, 2014.

Convert earnings from cash to accrual basis; prepare accrual-based financial statements.
(LO 2, 4, 5, 9), **AP**

	Cash Receipts	Cash Payments
Issuance of common shares	$20,000	
Payment to purchase repair shop equipment		$ 9,200
Rent payments		1,225
Newspaper advertising payment		375
Utility bill payments		970
Part-time helper's wage payments		2,600
Income tax payment		10,000
Cash receipts from ski and snowboard repair services	32,150	
Subtotals	52,150	24,370
Cash balance		27,780
Totals	$52,150	$52,150

The repair shop equipment was purchased on November 1 and has an estimated useful life of 4 years. The company rents space at a cost of $175 per month on a one-year lease. The lease contract requires payment of the first and last months' rent in advance, which was done. The part-time helper is owed $420 at April 30, 2014, for unpaid wages. At April 30, 2014, customers owe Kaffen Company $540 for services they have received but have not yet paid for.

Instructions

(a) Prepare an accrual-basis income statement for the 6 months ended April 30, 2014.
(b) Prepare the April 30, 2014, classified balance sheet.

E4-7 VidGam, a consulting firm, has just completed its first year of operations. The company's sales growth was explosive. To encourage clients to hire its services, VidGam

Identify differences between cash and accrual accounting.
(LO 2, 3, 9), **C**

offered 180-day financing—meaning its largest customers do not pay for nearly 6 months. Because VidGam is a new company, its equipment suppliers insist on being paid cash on delivery. Also, it had to pay up front for 2 years of insurance. At the end of the year, VidGam owed employees for one full month of salaries, but due to a cash shortfall, it promised to pay them the first week of next year.

Instructions ━━▶

(a) Explain how cash and accrual accounting would differ for each of the events listed above and describe the proper accrual accounting.

(b) Assume that at the end of the year, VidGam reported a favorable net income, yet the company's management is concerned because the company is very short of cash. Explain how VidGam could have positive net income and yet run out of cash.

Identify types of adjustments and accounts before adjustment.

(LO 3, 4, 5), **AN**

E4-8 Kwun Company accumulates the following adjustment data at December 31.

(a) Services performed but unbilled totals $600.
(b) Store supplies of $160 are on hand. The supplies account shows a $1,900 balance.
(c) Utility expenses of $275 are unpaid.
(d) Services performed of $490 collected in advance.
(e) Salaries of $620 are unpaid.
(f) Prepaid insurance totaling $400 has expired.

Instructions

For each item, indicate (1) the type of adjustment (prepaid expense, unearned revenue, accrued revenue, or accrued expense) and (2) the status of the accounts before adjustment (overstated or understated).

Prepare adjusting entries from selected account data.

(LO 4, 5), **AP**

E4-9 The ledger of Beckett Rental Agency on March 31 of the current year includes the selected accounts below before adjusting entries have been prepared.

	Debit	Credit
Supplies	$ 3,000	
Prepaid Insurance	3,600	
Equipment	25,000	
Accumulated Depreciation—Equipment		$ 8,400
Notes Payable		20,000
Unearned Rent Revenue		12,400
Rent Revenue		60,000
Interest Expense	0	
Salaries and Wages Expense	14,000	

An analysis of the accounts shows the following.

1. The equipment depreciates $280 per month.
2. Half of the unearned rent revenue was earned during the quarter.
3. Interest of $400 is accrued on the notes payable.
4. Supplies on hand total $850.
5. Insurance expires at the rate of $400 per month.

Instructions

Prepare the adjusting entries at March 31, assuming that adjusting entries are made quarterly. Additional accounts are Depreciation Expense, Insurance Expense, Interest Payable, and Supplies Expense.

Prepare adjusting entries.

(LO 4, 5), **AP**

E4-10 Jim Haught, D.D.S., opened an incorporated dental practice on January 1, 2014. During the first month of operations, the following transactions occurred.

1. Performed services for patients who had dental plan insurance. At January 31, $760 of such services was completed but not yet billed to the insurance companies.
2. Utility expenses incurred but not paid prior to January 31 totaled $450.
3. Purchased dental equipment on January 1 for $80,000, paying $20,000 in cash and signing a $60,000, 3-year note payable (interest is paid each December 31). The equipment depreciates $400 per month. Interest is $500 per month.
4. Purchased a 1-year malpractice insurance policy on January 1 for $24,000.
5. Purchased $1,750 of dental supplies (recorded as increase to Supplies). On January 31, determined that $550 of supplies were on hand.

Instructions

Prepare the adjusting entries on January 31. Account titles are Accumulated Depreciation— Equipment, Depreciation Expense, Service Revenue, Accounts Receivable, Insurance Expense, Interest Expense, Interest Payable, Prepaid Insurance, Supplies, Supplies Expense, Utilities Expense, and Accounts Payable.

E4-11 The unadjusted trial balance for Sierra Corp. is shown in Illustration 4-4 (page 168). Instead of the adjusting entries shown in the text at October 31, assume the following adjustment data.

Prepare adjusting entries.
(LO 4, 5), **AP**

1. Supplies on hand at October 31 total $500.
2. Expired insurance for the month is $100.
3. Depreciation for the month is $75.
4. As of October 31, services worth $800 related to the previously recorded unearned revenue had been performed.
5. Services performed but unbilled (and no receivable has been recorded) at October 31 are $280.
6. Interest expense accrued at October 31 is $70.
7. Accrued salaries at October 31 are $1,400.

Instructions

Prepare the adjusting entries for the items above.

E4-12 The income statement of Garska Co. for the month of July shows net income of $2,000 based on Service Revenue $5,500; Salaries and Wages Expense $2,100; Supplies Expense $900; and Utilities Expense $500. In reviewing the statement, you discover the following:

Prepare a correct income statement.
(LO 1, 4, 5, 6), **AP**

1. Insurance expired during July of $350 was omitted.
2. Supplies expense includes $200 of supplies that are still on hand at July 31.
3. Depreciation on equipment of $150 was omitted.
4. Accrued but unpaid wages at July 31 of $360 were not included.
5. Services performed but unrecorded totaled $700.

Instructions

Prepare a correct income statement for July 2014.

E4-13 This is a partial adjusted trial balance of Barone Company.

Analyze adjusted data.
(LO 1, 4, 5, 6), **AN**

BARONE COMPANY
Adjusted Trial Balance
January 31, 2014

	Debit	Credit
Supplies	$ 700	
Prepaid Insurance	1,560	
Salaries and Wages Payable		$1,060
Unearned Service Revenue		750
Supplies Expense	950	
Insurance Expense	520	
Salaries and Wages Expense	1,800	
Service Revenue		4,000

Instructions

Answer these questions, assuming the year begins January 1.
(a) If the amount in Supplies Expense is the January 31 adjusting entry, and $300 of supplies was purchased in January, what was the balance in Supplies on January 1?
(b) If the amount in Insurance Expense is the January 31 adjusting entry, and the original insurance premium was for 1 year, what was the total premium and when was the policy purchased?
(c) If $2,500 of salaries was paid in January, what was the balance in Salaries and Wages Payable at December 31, 2013?
(d) If $1,800 was received in January for services performed in January, what was the balance in Unearned Service Revenue at December 31, 2013?

Prepare closing entries.
(LO 7), **AP**

E4-14 A partial adjusted trial balance for Barone Company is given in E4-13.

Instructions

Prepare the closing entries at January 31, 2014.

Journalize basic transactions and adjusting entries.

(LO 4, 5, 6), **AN**

E4-15 Selected accounts of Castle Company are shown here.

Supplies Expense				Salaries and Wages Payable		
July 31	750				July 31	1,000

Salaries and Wages Expense				Accounts Receivable		
July 15	1,000			July 31	500	
31	1,000					

Service Revenue				Unearned Service Revenue		
	July 14	3,800		July 31	900	July 1 Bal. 1,500
	31	900				20 600
	31	500				

Supplies			
July 1 Bal. 1,100		July 31	750
10 200			

Instructions

After analyzing the accounts, journalize (a) the July transactions and (b) the adjusting entries that were made on July 31. (*Hint:* July transactions were for cash.)

Prepare adjusting entries from analysis of trial balance.

(LO 4, 5, 6), **AP**

E4-16 The trial balances shown below are before and after adjustment for Bere Company at the end of its fiscal year.

BERE COMPANY
Trial Balance
August 31, 2014

	Before Adjustment		After Adjustment	
	Dr.	Cr.	Dr.	Cr.
Cash	$10,900		$10,900	
Accounts Receivable	8,800		9,400	
Supplies	2,500		500	
Prepaid Insurance	4,000		2,500	
Equipment	16,000		16,000	
Accumulated Depreciation—Equipment		$ 3,600		$ 4,800
Accounts Payable		5,800		5,800
Salaries and Wages Payable		0		1,100
Unearned Rent Revenue		1,800		800
Common Stock		10,000		10,000
Retained Earnings		5,500		5,500
Dividends	2,800		2,800	
Service Revenue		34,000		34,600
Rent Revenue		12,100		13,100
Salaries and Wages Expense	17,000		18,100	
Supplies Expense	0		2,000	
Rent Expense	10,800		10,800	
Insurance Expense	0		1,500	
Depreciation Expense	0		1,200	
	$72,800	$72,800	$75,700	$75,700

Instructions

Prepare the adjusting entries that were made.

E4-17   The adjusted trial balance for Bere Company is given in E4-16.

Prepare financial statements from adjusted trial balance.
(LO 6), **AP**

Instructions

Prepare the income and retained earnings statements for the year and the classified balance sheet at August 31.

E4-18   The adjusted trial balance for Bere Company is given in E4-16.

Prepare closing entries.
(LO 7), **AP**

Instructions

Prepare the closing entries for the temporary accounts at August 31.

Exercises: Set B and Challenge Exercises

Visit the book's companion website, at **www.wiley.com/college/kimmel**, and choose the Student Companion site to access Exercise Set B and Challenge Exercises.

Problems: Set A

P4-1A   The following selected data are taken from the comparative financial statements of American Curling Club. The club prepares its financial statements using the accrual basis of accounting.

Record transactions on accrual basis; convert revenue to cash receipts.
(LO 2, 4, 9), **AP**

September 30	2014	2013
Accounts receivable for member dues	$ 15,000	$ 19,000
Unearned sales revenue	20,000	23,000
Service revenue (from member dues)	151,000	135,000

Dues are billed to members based upon their use of the club's facilities. Unearned sales revenues arise from the sale of tickets to events, such as the Skins Game.

Instructions

(*Hint:* You will find it helpful to use T-accounts to analyze the following data. You must analyze these data sequentially, as missing information must first be deduced before moving on. Post your journal entries as you progress, rather than waiting until the end.)

(a) Prepare journal entries for each of the following events that took place during 2014.
   1. Dues receivable from members from 2013 were all collected during 2014.
   2. During 2014, goods were provided for all of the unearned sales revenue at the end of 2013.
   3. Additional tickets were sold for $44,000 cash during 2014; a portion of these were used by the purchasers during the year. The entire balance remaining in Unearned Sales Revenue relates to the upcoming Skins Game in 2014.
   4. Dues for the 2013–2014 fiscal year were billed to members.
   5. Dues receivable for 2014 (i.e., those billed in item (4) above) were partially collected.

(b) Determine the amount of cash received by American from the above transactions during the year ended September 30, 2014.

(b) Cash received $199,000

Prepare adjusting entries, post to ledger accounts, and prepare adjusted trial balance.
(LO 4, 5, 6), **AP**

P4-2A   Ken Lumas started his own consulting firm, Lumas Consulting, on June 1, 2014. The trial balance at June 30 is as follows.

LUMAS CONSULTING
Trial Balance
June 30, 2014

	Debit	Credit
Cash	$ 6,850	
Accounts Receivable	7,000	
Supplies	2,000	
Prepaid Insurance	2,880	
Equipment	15,000	
Accounts Payable		$ 4,230
Unearned Service Revenue		5,200
Common Stock		22,000
Service Revenue		8,300
Salaries and Wages Expense	4,000	
Rent Expense	2,000	
	$39,730	$39,730

In addition to those accounts listed on the trial balance, the chart of accounts for Lumas also contains the following accounts: Accumulated Depreciation—Equipment, Salaries and Wages Payable, Depreciation Expense, Insurance Expense, Utilities Expense, and Supplies Expense.

Other data:
1. Supplies on hand at June 30 total $720.
2. A utility bill for $180 has not been recorded and will not be paid until next month.
3. The insurance policy is for a year.
4. Services were performed for $4,100 of unearned service revenue by the end of the month.
5. Salaries of $1,250 are accrued at June 30.
6. The equipment has a 5-year life with no salvage value and is being depreciated at $250 per month for 60 months.
7. Invoices representing $3,900 of services performed during the month have not been recorded as of June 30.

Instructions
(a) Prepare the adjusting entries for the month of June.
(b) Service rev. $16,300   (b) Post the adjusting entries to the ledger accounts. Enter the totals from the trial balance as beginning account balances. (Use T-accounts.)
(c) Tot. trial balance $45,310   (c) Prepare an adjusted trial balance at June 30, 2014.

Prepare adjusting entries, adjusted trial balance, and financial statements.

(LO 4, 5, 6, 7), **AP**

P4-3A The Solo Hotel opened for business on May 1, 2014. Here is its trial balance before adjustment on May 31.

SOLO HOTEL
Trial Balance
May 31, 2014

	Debit	Credit
Cash	$ 2,500	
Supplies	2,600	
Prepaid Insurance	1,800	
Land	15,000	
Buildings	70,000	
Equipment	16,800	
Accounts Payable		$ 4,700
Unearned Rent Revenue		3,300
Mortgage Payable		36,000
Common Stock		60,000
Rent Revenue		9,000
Salaries and Wages Expense	3,000	
Utilities Expense	800	
Advertising Expense	500	
	$113,000	$113,000

Other data:
1. Insurance expires at the rate of $450 per month.
2. A count of supplies shows $1,050 of unused supplies on May 31.
3. Annual depreciation is $3,600 on the building and $3,000 on equipment.
4. The mortgage interest rate is 6%. (The mortgage was taken out on May 1.)
5. Unearned rent of $2,500 has been earned.
6. Salaries of $900 are accrued and unpaid at May 31.

Instructions
(a) Journalize the adjusting entries on May 31.
(b) Prepare a ledger using T-accounts. Enter the trial balance amounts and post the adjusting entries.
(c) Prepare an adjusted trial balance on May 31.
(d) Prepare an income statement and a retained earnings statement for the month of May and a classified balance sheet at May 31.
(e) Identify which accounts should be closed on May 31.

(c) Rent revenue $11,500
    Tot. adj. trial
        balance $114,630
(d) Net income $3,570

P4-4A Wolf Creek Golf Inc. was organized on July 1, 2014. Quarterly financial statements are prepared. The trial balance and adjusted trial balance on September 30 are shown here.

Prepare adjusting entries and financial statements; identify accounts to be closed.

(LO 4, 5, 6, 7), **AP**

WOLF CREEK GOLF INC.
Trial Balance
September 30, 2014

| | Unadjusted | | Adjusted | |
	Dr.	Cr.	Dr.	Cr.
Cash	$ 6,700		$ 6,700	
Accounts Receivable	400		1,000	
Supplies	1,200		180	
Prepaid Rent	1,800		900	
Equipment	15,000		15,000	
Accumulated Depreciation—Equipment				$ 350
Notes Payable		$ 5,000		5,000
Accounts Payable		1,070		1,070
Salaries and Wages Payable				600
Interest Payable				50
Unearned Rent Revenue		1,000		800
Common Stock		14,000		14,000
Retained Earnings		0		0
Dividends	600		600	
Service Revenue		14,100		14,700
Rent Revenue		700		900
Salaries and Wages Expense	8,800		9,400	
Rent Expense	900		1,800	
Depreciation Expense			350	
Supplies Expense			1,020	
Utilities Expense	470		470	
Interest Expense			50	
	$35,870	$35,870	$37,470	$37,470

Instructions
(a) Journalize the adjusting entries that were made.
(b) Prepare an income statement and a retained earnings statement for the 3 months ending September 30 and a classified balance sheet at September 30.
(c) Identify which accounts should be closed on September 30.
(d) If the note bears interest at 12%, how many months has it been outstanding?

(b) Net income $2,510
    Tot. assets $23,430

P4-5A A review of the ledger of Dempsey Company at December 31, 2014, produces these data pertaining to the preparation of annual adjusting entries.

Prepare adjusting entries.
(LO 4, 5), **AP**

1. Prepaid Insurance $15,200. The company has separate insurance policies on its buildings and its motor vehicles. Policy B4564 on the building was purchased on

July 1, 2013, for $9,600. The policy has a term of 3 years. Policy A2958 on the vehicles was purchased on January 1, 2014, for $7,200. This policy has a term of 18 months.

2. Rent revenue $84,000

2. Unearned Rent Revenue $429,000. The company began subleasing office space in its new building on November 1. At December 31, the company had the following rental contracts that are paid in full for the entire term of the lease.

Date	Term (in months)	Monthly Rent	Number of Leases
Nov. 1	9	$5,000	5
Dec. 1	6	$8,500	4

3. Notes Payable $40,000. This balance consists of a note for 6 months at an annual interest rate of 7%, dated October 1.
4. Salaries and Wages Payable $0. There are eight salaried employees. Salaries are paid every Friday for the current week. Five employees receive a salary of $600 each per week, and three employees earn $700 each per week. Assume December 31 is a Wednesday. Employees do not work weekends. All employees worked the last 3 days of December.

Instructions

Prepare the adjusting entries at December 31, 2014.

Prepare adjusting entries and a corrected income statement.
(LO 4, 5), **AN**

P4-6A Astromech Travel Court was organized on July 1, 2013, by Jessica Browning. Jessica is a good manager but a poor accountant. From the trial balance prepared by a part-time bookkeeper, Jessica prepared the following income statement for her fourth quarter, which ended June 30, 2014.

ASTROMECH TRAVEL COURT
Income Statement
For the Quarter Ended June 30, 2014

Revenues		
Rent revenue		$212,000
Operating expenses		
Advertising expense	$ 3,800	
Salaries and wages expense	80,500	
Utilities expense	900	
Depreciation expense	2,700	
Maintenance and repairs expense	4,300	
Total operating expenses		92,200
Net income		$119,800

Jessica suspected that something was wrong with the statement because net income had never exceeded $30,000 in any one quarter. Knowing that you are an experienced accountant, she asks you to review the income statement and other data.

You first look at the trial balance. In addition to the account balances reported above in the income statement, the trial balance contains the following additional selected balances at June 30, 2014.

Supplies	$ 8,200
Prepaid Insurance	14,400
Notes Payable	14,000

You then make inquiries and discover the following.
1. Travel court rental revenues include advanced rental payments received for summer occupancy, in the amount of $57,000.
2. There were $1,800 of supplies on hand at June 30.
3. Prepaid insurance resulted from the payment of a one-year policy on April 1, 2014.
4. The mail in July 2014 brought the following bills: advertising for the week of June 24, $110; repairs made June 18, $4,450; and utilities for the month of June, $215.
5. There are three employees who receive wages that total $300 per day. At June 30, four days' wages have been incurred but not paid.

6. The note payable is a 6% note dated May 1, 2014, and due on July 31, 2014.
7. Income tax of $13,400 for the quarter is due in July but has not yet been recorded.

Instructions
(a) Prepare any adjusting journal entries required at June 30, 2014.
(b) Prepare a correct income statement for the quarter ended June 30, 2014.
(c) Explain to Jessica the generally accepted accounting principles that she did not recognize in preparing her income statement and their effect on her results.

(b) Net income $33,285

P4-7A On November 1, 2014, the following were the account balances of Rijo Equipment Repair.

Journalize transactions and follow through accounting cycle to preparation of financial statements.
(LO 4, 5, 6), **AP**

	Debit		**Credit**
Cash	$ 2,790	Accumulated Depreciation—Equipment	$ 500
Accounts Receivable	2,910	Accounts Payable	2,300
Supplies	1,120	Unearned Service Revenue	400
Equipment	10,000	Salaries and Wages Payable	620
		Common Stock	10,000
		Retained Earnings	3,000
	$16,820		$16,820

During November, the following summary transactions were completed.

Nov. 8 Paid $1,220 for salaries due employees, of which $600 is for November and $620 is for October salaries payable.
10 Received $1,800 cash from customers in payment of account.
12 Received $3,700 cash for services performed in November.
15 Purchased store equipment on account $3,600.
17 Purchased supplies on account $1,300.
20 Paid creditors $2,500 of accounts payable due.
22 Paid November rent $480.
25 Paid salaries $1,000.
27 Performed services on account worth $900 and billed customers.
29 Received $750 from customers for services to be provided in the future.

Adjustment data:

1. Supplies on hand are valued at $1,100.
2. Accrued salaries payable are $480.
3. Depreciation for the month is $250.
4. Services were performed to satisfy $500 of unearned service revenue.

Instructions
(a) Enter the November 1 balances in the ledger accounts. (Use T-accounts.)
(b) Journalize the November transactions.
(c) Post to the ledger accounts. Use Service Revenue, Depreciation Expense, Supplies Expense, Salaries and Wages Expense, and Rent Expense.
(d) Prepare a trial balance at November 30.
(e) Journalize and post adjusting entries.
(f) Prepare an adjusted trial balance.
(g) Prepare an income statement and a retained earnings statement for November and a classified balance sheet at November 30.

(f) Cash $3,840
   Tot. adj. trial
      balance $24,680
(g) Net income $970

P4-8A Mike Greenberg opened Clean Window Washing Inc. on July 1, 2014. During July, the following transactions were completed.

Complete all steps in accounting cycle.
(LO 4, 5, 6, 7, 8), **AP**

July 1 Issued 12,000 shares of common stock for $12,000 cash.
1 Purchased used truck for $8,000, paying $2,000 cash and the balance on account.
3 Purchased cleaning supplies for $900 on account.
5 Paid $1,800 cash on a 1-year insurance policy effective July 1.
12 Billed customers $3,700 for cleaning services.
18 Paid $1,000 cash on amount owed on truck and $500 on amount owed on cleaning supplies.
20 Paid $2,000 cash for employee salaries.

21   Collected $1,600 cash from customers billed on July 12.
25   Billed customers $2,500 for cleaning services.
31   Paid $290 for maintenance of the truck during month.
31   Declared and paid $600 cash dividend.

The chart of accounts for Clean Window Washing contains the following accounts: Cash, Accounts Receivable, Supplies, Prepaid Insurance, Equipment, Accumulated Depreciation—Equipment, Accounts Payable, Salaries and Wages Payable, Common Stock, Retained Earnings, Dividends, Income Summary, Service Revenue, Maintenance and Repairs Expense, Supplies Expense, Depreciation Expense, Insurance Expense, Salaries and Wages Expense.

Instructions

(a) Journalize the July transactions.
(b) Post to the ledger accounts. (Use T-accounts.)
(c) Prepare a trial balance at July 31.
(d) Journalize the following adjustments.
     (1) Services performed but unbilled and uncollected at July 31 were $1,700.
     (2) Depreciation on equipment for the month was $180.
     (3) One-twelfth of the insurance expired.
     (4) An inventory count shows $320 of cleaning supplies on hand at July 31.
     (5) Accrued but unpaid employee salaries were $400.
(e) Post adjusting entries to the T-accounts.

(f) Cash $5,410
(g) Tot. assets $21,500

(f) Prepare an adjusted trial balance.
(g) Prepare the income statement and a retained earnings statement for July and a classified balance sheet at July 31.
(h) Journalize and post closing entries and complete the closing process.
(i) Prepare a post-closing trial balance at July 31.

Problems: Set B

Record transactions on accrual basis; convert revenue to cash receipts.
(LO 2, 4, 9), **AP**

P4-1B   The following data are taken from the comparative balance sheets of Golfview Inn, which prepares its financial statements using the accrual basis of accounting.

December 31	2014	2013
Accounts receivable for member fees	$18,000	$20,000
Unearned service revenue	17,000	10,000

Fees are billed to members based upon their use of the club's facilities. Unearned service revenues arise from the sale of gift certificates, which members can apply to their future use of club facilities. The 2014 income statement for the club showed that service revenue of $190,000 was recognized during the year.

Instructions

(*Hint:* You will find it helpful to use T-accounts to analyze these data.)

(a) Prepare journal entries for each of the following events that took place during 2014.
     1. Fees receivable from 2013 were all collected during 2014.
     2. Gift certificates outstanding at the end of 2013 were all redeemed during 2014.
     3. An additional $40,000 worth of gift certificates were sold during 2014; a portion of these were used by the recipients during the year; the remainder were still outstanding at the end of 2014.

(b) Cash received $199,000

Prepare adjusting entries, post to ledger accounts, and prepare an adjusted trial balance.
(LO 4, 5, 6), **AP**

     4. Fees for 2014 were billed to members.
     5. Fees receivable for 2014 (i.e., those billed in item (4) above) were partially collected.
(b) Determine the amount of cash received by the club with respect to fees during 2014.

P4-2B   Pat Okendo started her own consulting firm, Okendo Consulting, on May 1, 2014. The trial balance at May 31 is as shown on the next page.

OKENDO CONSULTING
Trial Balance
May 31, 2014

	Debit	Credit
Cash	$ 7,500	
Accounts Receivable	3,000	
Supplies	2,500	
Prepaid Insurance	3,600	
Equipment	12,000	
Accounts Payable		$ 3,500
Unearned Service Revenue		4,000
Common Stock		19,100
Service Revenue		7,500
Salaries and Wages Expense	4,000	
Rent Expense	1,500	
	$34,100	$34,100

In addition to those accounts listed on the trial balance, the chart of accounts for Okendo Consulting also contains the following accounts: Accumulated Depreciation—Equipment, Salaries and Wages Payable, Depreciation Expense, Insurance Expense, Utilities Expense, and Supplies Expense.

Other data:

1. $1,000 of supplies have been used during the month.
2. Utility costs incurred but not paid are $300.
3. The insurance policy is for 3 years.
4. $1,500 of the balance in the Unearned Service Revenue account remains unearned at the end of the month.
5. Assume May 31 is a Tuesday and employees are paid on Fridays. Okendo Consulting has two employees that are paid $600 each for a 5-day work week.
6. The equipment has a 5-year life with no salvage value and is being depreciated at $200 per month for 60 months.
7. Invoices representing $1,500 of services performed during the month have not been recorded as of May 31.

Instructions
(a) Prepare the adjusting entries for the month of May.
(b) Post the adjusting entries to the ledger accounts. Enter the totals from the trial balance as beginning account balances. (Use T-accounts.)
(c) Prepare an adjusted trial balance at May 31, 2014.

(c) Tot. trial balance $36,580

P4-3B   Death Valley Resort opened for business on June 1 with eight air-conditioned units. Its trial balance before adjustment on August 31 is presented here.

Prepare adjusting entries, adjusted trial balance, and financial statements.

(LO 4, 5, 6, 7), **AP**

DEATH VALLEY RESORT
Trial Balance
August 31, 2014

	Debit	Credit
Cash	$ 24,600	
Supplies	4,300	
Prepaid Insurance	5,400	
Land	40,000	
Buildings	132,000	
Equipment	36,000	
Accounts Payable		$ 6,500
Unearned Rent Revenue		6,800
Mortgage Payable		120,000
Common Stock		100,000

	Debit	Credit
Dividends	5,000	
Rent Revenue		80,000
Salaries and Wages Expense	53,000	
Utilities Expense	9,400	
Maintenance and Repairs Expense	3,600	
	$313,300	$313,300

Other data:

1. Insurance expires at the rate of $500 per month.
2. A count of supplies on August 31 shows $900 of supplies on hand.
3. Annual depreciation is $6,600 on buildings and $4,000 on equipment.
4. Unearned rent of $4,000 was earned prior to August 31.
5. Salaries of $600 were unpaid at August 31.
6. Rentals of $1,600 were due from tenants at August 31. (Use Accounts Receivable.)
7. The mortgage interest rate is 6% per year. (The mortgage was taken out August 1.)

Instructions
(a) Journalize the adjusting entries on August 31 for the 3-month period June 1–August 31.
(b) Prepare a ledger using T-accounts. Enter the trial balance amounts and post the adjusting entries.
(c) Prepare an adjusted trial balance on August 31.
(d) Prepare an income statement and a retained earnings statement for the 3 months ended August 31 and a classified balance sheet as of August 31.
(e) Identify which accounts should be closed on August 31.

(c) Tot. adj. trial
  balance $318,750
(d) Net income $ 10,850

Prepare adjusting entries and financial statements; identify accounts to be closed.

(LO 4, 5, 6, 7), **AP**

 GLS

P4-4B AbDulla Advertising Agency was founded by Miriam AbDulla in January 2009. Presented here are both the adjusted and unadjusted trial balances as of December 31, 2014.

ABDULLA ADVERTISING AGENCY
Trial Balance
December 31, 2014

	Unadjusted Dr.	Unadjusted Cr.	Adjusted Dr.	Adjusted Cr.
Cash	$ 11,000		$ 11,000	
Accounts Receivable	16,000		19,000	
Supplies	9,400		7,000	
Prepaid Insurance	3,350		1,790	
Equipment	60,000		60,000	
Accumulated Depreciation— Equipment		$ 25,000		$ 30,000
Notes Payable		8,000		8,000
Accounts Payable		2,000		2,000
Interest Payable		0		560
Unearned Service Revenue		5,000		3,100
Salaries and Wages Payable		0		820
Common Stock		20,000		20,000
Retained Earnings		5,500		5,500
Dividends	10,000		10,000	
Service Revenue		57,600		62,500
Salaries and Wages Expense	9,000		9,820	
Insurance Expense			1,560	
Interest Expense			560	
Depreciation Expense			5,000	
Supplies Expense			2,400	
Rent Expense	4,350		4,350	
	$123,100	$123,100	$132,480	$132,480

Instructions

(a) Journalize the annual adjusting entries that were made.

(b) Prepare an income statement and a retained earnings statement for the year ended December 31, and a classified balance sheet at December 31.

(c) Identify which accounts should be closed on December 31.

(d) If the note has been outstanding 10 months, what is the annual interest rate on that note?

(e) If the company paid $10,000 in salaries in 2014, what was the balance in Salaries and Wages Payable on December 31, 2013?

(b) Net income $38,810
     Tot. assets $68,790

P4-5B A review of the ledger of Garner Company at December 31, 2014, produces these data pertaining to the preparation of annual adjusting entries.

Prepare adjusting entries.
(LO 4, 5), **AP**

1. Prepaid Insurance $16,400. The company has separate insurance policies on its buildings and its motor vehicles. Policy B4564 on the building was purchased on January 1, 2013, for $11,400. The policy has a term of 3 years. Policy A2958 on the vehicles was purchased on July 1, 2014, for $8,800. This policy has a term of 2 years.

2. Unearned Rent Revenue $450,000. The company began subleasing office space in its new building on November 1. At December 31, the company had the following rental contracts that are paid in full for the entire term of the lease.

2. Rent revenue $90,000

Date	Term (in months)	Monthly Rent	Number of Leases
Nov. 1	9	$6,000	5
Dec. 1	6	$7,500	4

3. Notes Payable $20,000. This balance consists of a note for 8 months at an annual interest rate of 9%, dated August 1.

4. Salaries and Wages Payable $0. There are six salaried employees. Salaries are paid every Friday for the current week. Four employees receive a salary of $480 each per week, and two employees earn $600 each per week. December 31 is a Thursday. Employees do not work weekends. All employees worked the last 4 days of December.

Instructions

Prepare the adjusting entries at December 31, 2014.

P4-6B Tutors-Plus Test Prep was organized on May 1, 2013, by Jan Cooper. Jan is a good manager but a poor accountant. From the trial balance prepared by a part-time bookkeeper, Jan prepared the following income statement for her fourth quarter, which ended April 30, 2014.

Prepare adjusting entries and a corrected income statement.
(LO 4, 5), **AN**

TUTORS-PLUS TEST PREP
Income Statement
For the Quarter Ended April 30, 2014

Revenues		
Service revenue		$240,000
Operating expenses		
Advertising expense	$ 6,400	
Salaries and wages expense	92,000	
Utilities expense	1,300	
Depreciation expense	2,400	
Maintenance and repairs expense	1,700	
Total operating expenses		103,800
Net income		$136,200

Jan suspected that something was wrong with the statement because net income had never exceeded $40,000 in any one quarter. Knowing that you are an experienced accountant, she asks you to review the income statement and other data.

You first look at the trial balance. In addition to the account balances reported above in the income statement, the ledger contains the following additional selected balances at April 30, 2014.

Supplies	$ 9,800
Prepaid Insurance	12,000
Notes Payable	15,000

You then make inquiries and discover the following.

1. Service revenue includes advance payments received for summer classes, in the amount of $75,000.
2. There were $2,600 of supplies on hand at April 30.
3. Prepaid insurance resulted from the payment of a one-year policy on February 1, 2014.
4. The mail in May 2014 brought the following bills: advertising for the week of April 24, $80; repairs made April 18, $2,560; and utilities for the month of April, $530.
5. There are six employees who receive wages that total $1,380 per day. At April 30, three days' wages have been incurred but not paid.
6. The note payable is a 8% note dated February 1, 2014, and due on May 31, 2014.
7. Income tax of $15,200 for the quarter is due in May but has not yet been recorded.

Instructions
(a) Prepare any adjusting journal entries required as at April 30, 2014.
(b) Prepare a correct income statement for the quarter ended April 30, 2014.
(c) Explain to Jan the generally accepted accounting principles that she did not recognize in preparing her income statement and their effect on her results.

(b) Net income $28,190

Journalize transactions and follow through accounting cycle to preparation of financial statements.

(LO 4, 5, 6), **AP**

P4-7B On August 1, 2014, the following were the account balances of D&D Repair Services.

	Debit		Credit
Cash	$ 6,040	Accumulated Depreciation—Equipment	$ 600
Accounts Receivable	2,910	Accounts Payable	2,300
Supplies	1,030	Unearned Service Revenue	1,260
Equipment	10,000	Salaries and Wages Payable	1,420
		Common Stock	10,000
		Retained Earnings	4,400
	$19,980		$19,980

During August, the following summary transactions were completed.

Aug. 5	Received $1,200 cash from customers in payment of account.
10	Paid $3,120 for salaries due employees, of which $1,700 is for August and $1,420 is for July salaries payable.
12	Received $2,800 cash for services performed in August.
15	Purchased store equipment on account $2,000.
17	Purchased supplies on account $860.
20	Paid creditors $2,000 of accounts payable due.
22	Paid August rent $380.
25	Paid salaries $2,900.
27	Performed services worth $3,130 on account and billed customers.
29	Received $780 from customers for services to be provided in the future.

Adjustment data:

1. Supplies on hand are valued at $960.
2. Accrued salaries payable are $1,540.
3. Depreciation for the month is $320.
4. Services were performed to satisfy $800 of unearned service revenue.

Instructions
(a) Enter the August 1 balances in the ledger accounts. (Use T-accounts.)
(b) Journalize the August transactions.

(c) Post to the ledger accounts. Use Service Revenue, Depreciation Expense, Supplies Expense, Salaries and Wages Expense, and Rent Expense.
(d) Prepare a trial balance at August 31.
(e) Journalize and post adjusting entries.
(f) Prepare an adjusted trial balance.
(g) Prepare an income statement and a retained earnings statement for August and a classified balance sheet at August 31.

(f) Cash	$2,420
Tot. adj. trial balance	$27,990
(g) Net loss	$1,040

P4-8B Geog Lav opened Geog Cleaners on March 1, 2014. During March, the following transactions were completed.

Complete all steps in accounting cycle.
(LO 4, 5, 6, 7, 8), **AP**

GLS

Mar. 1   Issued 10,000 shares of common stock for $15,000 cash.
      1   Purchased used truck for $8,000, paying $3,000 cash and the balance on account.
      3   Purchased cleaning supplies for $2,000 on account.
      5   Paid $2,400 cash on a 6-month insurance policy effective March 1.
     14   Billed customers $3,700 for cleaning services.
     18   Paid $1,500 cash on amount owed on truck and $500 on amount owed on cleaning supplies.
     20   Paid $1,750 cash for employee salaries.
     21   Collected $1,600 cash from customers billed on March 14.
     28   Billed customers $4,200 for cleaning services.
     31   Paid $350 for gas and oil used in truck during month (use Maintenance and Repairs Expense).
     31   Declared and paid a $900 cash dividend.

The chart of accounts for Geog Cleaners contains the following accounts: Cash, Accounts Receivable, Supplies, Prepaid Insurance, Equipment, Accumulated Depreciation—Equipment, Accounts Payable, Salaries and Wages Payable, Common Stock, Retained Earnings, Dividends, Income Summary, Service Revenue, Maintenance and Repairs Expense, Supplies Expense, Depreciation Expense, Insurance Expense, Salaries and Wages Expense.

Instructions
(a) Journalize the March transactions.
(b) Post to the ledger accounts. (Use T-accounts.)
(c) Prepare a trial balance at March 31.
(d) Journalize the following adjustments.
    1. Services performed but unbilled at March 31 was $200.
    2. Depreciation on equipment for the month was $250.
    3. One-sixth of the insurance expired.
    4. An inventory count shows $280 of cleaning supplies on hand at March 31.
    5. Accrued but unpaid employee salaries were $1,080.
(e) Post adjusting entries to the T-accounts.
(f) Prepare an adjusted trial balance.
(g) Prepare the income statement and a retained earnings statement for March and a classified balance sheet at March 31.
(h) Journalize and post closing entries and complete the closing process.
(i) Prepare a post-closing trial balance at March 31.

(f) Tot. adj. trial balance	$29,430
(g) Tot. assets	$22,730

Problems: Set C

Visit the book's companion website, at **www.wiley.com/college/kimmel**, and choose the Student Companion site to access Problem Set C.

Continuing Cookie Chronicle

(*Note:* This is a continuation of the Cookie Chronicle from Chapters 1 through 3.)

CCC4 Cookie Creations is gearing up for the winter holiday season. During the month of December 2014, the following transactions occur.

Dec. 1   Natalie hires an assistant at an hourly wage of $8 to help with cookie making and some administrative duties.

5   Natalie teaches the class that was booked on November 25. The balance outstanding is received.

8   Cookie Creations receives a check for the amount due from the neighborhood school for the class given on November 30.

9   Cookie Creations receives $750 in advance from the local school board for five classes that the company will give during December and January.

15   Pays the cell phone invoice outstanding at November 30.

16   Issues a check to Natalie's brother for the amount owed for the design of the website.

19   Receives a deposit of $60 on a cookie class scheduled for early January.

23   Additional revenue during the month for cookie-making classes amounts to $4,000. (Natalie has not had time to account for each class individually.) $3,000 in cash has been collected and $1,000 is still outstanding. (This is in addition to the December 5 and December 9 transactions.)

23   Additional baking supplies purchased during the month for sugar, flour, and chocolate chips amount to $1,250 cash.

23   Issues a check to Natalie's assistant for $800. Her assistant worked approximately 100 hours from the time in which she was hired until December 23.

28   Pays a dividend of $500 to the common shareholder (Natalie).

As of December 31, Cookie Creations' year-end, the following adjusting entry data are provided.

1. A count reveals that $45 of brochures and posters were used.
2. Depreciation is recorded on the baking equipment purchased in November. The baking equipment has a useful life of 5 years. Assume that 2 months' worth of depreciation is required.
3. Amortization (which is similar to depreciation) is recorded on the website. (Credit the Website account directly for the amount of the amortization.) The website is amortized over a useful life of 2 years and was available for use on December 1.
4. Interest on the note payable is accrued. (Assume that 1.5 months of interest accrued during November and December.) Round to the nearest dollar.
5. One month's worth of insurance has expired.
6. Natalie is unexpectedly telephoned on December 28 to give a cookie class at the neighborhood community center on December 31. In early January, Cookie Creations sends an invoice for $450 to the community center.
7. A count reveals that $1,025 of baking supplies were used.
8. A cell phone invoice is received for $75. The invoice is for services provided during the month of December and is due on January 15.
9. Because the unexpected cookie-making class on December 31 was for such a large group of children, Natalie's assistant helps out. Her assistant worked 7 hours at a rate of $8 per hour.
10. An analysis of the Unearned Service Revenue account reveals that two of the five classes paid for by the local school board on December 9 still have not been taught by the end of December. The $60 deposit received on December 19 for another class also remains unearned.

Instructions

Using the information that you have gathered and the general ledger accounts that you have prepared through Chapter 3, plus the new information above, do the following.

(a) Journalize the above transactions.

(b) Post the December transactions. (Use the general ledger accounts prepared in Chapter 3.)

(c) Totals $8,160

(c) Prepare a trial balance at December 31, 2014.

(d) Prepare and post adjusting journal entries for the month of December.

(e) Totals $8,804

(e) Prepare an adjusted trial balance as of December 31, 2014.

(f) Net income $3,211

(f) Prepare an income statement and a retained earnings statement for the 2-month period ending December 31, 2014, and a classified balance sheet as of December 31, 2014.

(g) Prepare and post closing entries as of December 31, 2014.

(h) Totals $6,065

(h) Prepare a post-closing trial balance.

Broadening Your Perspective

Financial Reporting and Analysis

FINANCIAL REPORTING PROBLEM: *Tootsie Roll Industries, Inc.*

BYP4-1 The financial statements of Tootsie Roll are presented in Appendix A at the end of this textbook.

Instructions
(a) Using the consolidated income statement and balance sheet, identify items that may result in adjusting entries for deferrals.
(b) Using the consolidated income statement, identify two items that may result in adjusting entries for accruals.
(c) What was the amount of depreciation expense for 2011 and 2010? (You will need to examine the notes to the financial statements or the statement of cash flows.) Where was accumulated depreciation reported?
(d) What was the cash paid for income taxes during 2011, reported at the bottom of the consolidated statement of cash flows? What was income tax expense (provision for income taxes) for 2011?

COMPARATIVE ANALYSIS PROBLEM: *Tootsie Roll vs. Hershey*

BYP4-2 The financial statements of The Hershey Company are presented in Appendix B, following the financial statements for Tootsie Roll in Appendix A.

Instructions
(a) Identify two accounts on Hershey's balance sheet that provide evidence that Hershey uses accrual accounting. In each case, identify the income statement account that would be affected by the adjustment process.
(b) Identify two accounts on Tootsie Roll's balance sheet that provide evidence that Tootsie Roll uses accrual accounting (different from the two you listed for Hershey). In each case, identify the income statement account that would be affected by the adjustment process.

RESEARCH CASE

BYP4-3 The February 13, 2010, issue of the *Wall Street Journal* includes an article by Scott Thurm entitled "For Some Firms, a Case of 'Quadrophobia'."

Instructions
Read the article and answer the following.
(a) What method did the study's authors use to determine that companies were "managing" their earnings per share calculation?
(b) For the average company in the study, how much would the company have to boost earnings in order to increase earnings per share by 1/10 of a cent?
(c) What examples did the authors cite of accounting adjustments that companies can make to boost net income enough that they can round up to the next highest cent? Why aren't these methods of adjustment considered illegal?
(d) What is an earnings restatement? What relationship did the authors identify about companies that restate earnings?
(e) What incentive do companies have to round up their earnings per share to the next highest cent?

INTERPRETING FINANCIAL STATEMENTS

BYP4-4 Laser Recording Systems, founded in 1981, produces disks for use in the home market. The following is an excerpt from Laser Recording Systems' financial statements (all dollars in thousands).

LASER RECORDING SYSTEMS
Management Discussion

Accrued liabilities increased to $1,642 at January 31, from $138 at the end of the previous fiscal year. Compensation and related accruals increased $195 due primarily to increases in accruals for severance, vacation, commissions, and relocation expenses. Accrued professional services increased by $137 primarily as a result of legal expenses related to several outstanding contractual disputes. Other expenses increased $35, of which $18 was for interest payable.

Instructions

(a) Can you tell from the discussion whether Laser Recording Systems has prepaid its legal expenses and is now making an adjustment to the asset account Prepaid Legal Expenses, or whether the company is handling the legal expense via an accrued expense adjustment?

(b) Identify each of the adjustments Laser Recording Systems is discussing as one of the four types of possible adjustments discussed in the chapter. How is net income ultimately affected by each of the adjustments?

(c) What journal entry did Laser Recording make to record the accrued interest?

REAL-WORLD FOCUS

BYP4-5 *Purpose:* To learn about the functions of the Securities and Exchange Commission (SEC).

Address: **www.sec.gov/about/whatwedo.shtml**, or go to **www.wiley.com/college/kimmel**

Instructions

Use the information in this site to answer the following questions.

(a) What event spurred the creation of the SEC? Why was the SEC created?

(b) What are the five divisions of the SEC? Briefly describe the purpose of each.

(c) What are the responsibilities of the chief accountant?

Critical Thinking

DECISION-MAKING ACROSS THE ORGANIZATION

BYP4-6 Lincoln Park was organized on April 1, 2013, by Judy Tercek. Judy is a good manager but a poor accountant. From the trial balance prepared by a part-time bookkeeper, Judy prepared the following income statement for the quarter that ended March 31, 2014.

LINCOLN PARK
Income Statement
For the Quarter Ended March 31, 2014

Revenues		
Rent revenue		$83,000
Operating expenses		
Advertising expense	$ 4,200	
Salaries and wages expense	27,600	
Utilities expense	1,500	
Depreciation expense	800	
Maintenance and repairs expense	2,800	
Total operating expenses		36,900
Net income		$46,100

Judy knew that something was wrong with the statement because net income had never exceeded $20,000 in any one quarter. Knowing that you are an experienced accountant, she asks you to review the income statement and other data.

You first look at the trial balance. In addition to the account balances reported in the income statement, the ledger contains these selected balances at March 31, 2014.

Supplies	$ 4,500
Prepaid Insurance	7,200
Notes Payable	20,000

You then make inquiries and discover the following.

1. Rent revenue includes advanced rentals for summer-month occupancy, $21,000.
2. There were $600 of supplies on hand at March 31.
3. Prepaid insurance resulted from the payment of a 1-year policy on January 1, 2014.
4. The mail on April 1, 2014, brought the following bills: advertising for week of March 24, $110; repairs made March 10, $1,040; and utilities $240.
5. There are four employees who receive wages totaling $290 per day. At March 31, 3 days' wages have been incurred but not paid.
6. The note payable is a 3-month, 7% note dated January 1, 2014.

Instructions

With the class divided into groups, answer the following.
(a) Prepare a correct income statement for the quarter ended March 31, 2014.
(b) Explain to Judy the generally accepted accounting principles that she did not follow in preparing her income statement and their effect on her results.

COMMUNICATION ACTIVITY

BYP4-7 On numerous occasions, proposals have surfaced to put the federal government on the accrual basis of accounting. This is no small issue because if this basis were used, it would mean that billions in unrecorded liabilities would have to be booked and the federal deficit would increase substantially.

Instructions

(a) What is the difference between accrual-basis accounting and cash-basis accounting?
(b) Comment on why politicians prefer a cash-basis accounting system over an accrual-basis system.
(c) Write a letter to your senators explaining why you think the federal government should adopt the accrual basis of accounting.

ETHICS CASE

BYP4-8 Eaton Company is a pesticide manufacturer. Its sales declined greatly this year due to the passage of legislation outlawing the sale of several of Eaton's chemical pesticides. During the coming year, Eaton will have environmentally safe and competitive replacement chemicals to replace these discontinued products. Sales in the next year are expected to greatly exceed those of any prior year. Therefore, the decline in this year's sales and profits appears to be a one-year aberration.

Even so, the company president believes that a large dip in the current year's profits could cause a significant drop in the market price of Eaton's stock and make it a takeover target. To avoid this possibility, he urges Mark Trane, controller, to accrue every possible revenue and to defer as many expenses as possible in making this period's year-end adjusting entries. The president says to Mark, "We need the revenues this year, and next year we can easily absorb expenses deferred from this year. We can't let our stock price be hammered down!" Mark didn't get around to recording the adjusting entries until January 17, but he dated the entries December 31 as if they were recorded then. Mark also made every effort to comply with the president's request.

Instructions

(a) Who are the stakeholders in this situation?
(b) What are the ethical considerations of the president's request and Mark's dating the adjusting entries December 31?
(c) Can Mark accrue revenues and defer expenses and still be ethical?

ALL ABOUT YOU

BYP4-9   Companies prepare balance sheets in order to know their financial position at a specific point in time. This enables them to make a comparison to their position at previous points in time and gives them a basis for planning for the future. In order to evaluate *your* financial position, you can prepare a personal balance sheet. Assume that you have compiled the following information regarding your finances. (*Hint:* Some of the items might not be used in your personal balance sheet.)

Amount owed on student loan balance (long-term)	$5,000
Balance in checking account	1,200
Certificate of deposit (6-month)	3,000
Annual earnings from part-time job	11,300
Automobile	7,000
Balance on automobile loan (current portion)	1,500
Balance on automobile loan (long-term portion)	4,000
Home computer	800
Amount owed to you by younger brother	300
Balance in money market account	1,800
Annual tuition	6,400
Video and stereo equipment	1,250
Balance owed on credit card (current portion)	150
Balance owed on credit card (long-term portion)	1,650

Instructions

Prepare a personal balance sheet using the format you have learned for a classified balance sheet for a company. For the equity account, use M. Y. Own, Capital.

FASB CODIFICATION ACTIVITY

BYP4-10   If your school has a subscription to the FASB Codification, go to **http://aaahq.org/ ascLogin.cfm** to log in and prepare responses to the following.

Instructions

Access the glossary ("Master Glossary") to answer the following.
(a)   What is the definition of revenue?
(b)   What is the definition of compensation?

Answers to Insight and Accounting Across the Organization Questions

p. 166 Reporting Revenue Accurately Q: In the past, why was it argued that Apple should spread the recognition of iPhone revenue over a two-year period, rather than recording it upfront? **A:** Apple promises to provide software updates over the life of the phone's use. Because this represents an unfulfilled performance obligation, it was argued that Apple should spread its revenue recognition over a two-year estimated life of the phone.

p. 167 Cashing In on Accrual Accounting Q: Accrual accounting is often considered superior to cash accounting. Why, then, were some people critical of China's use of accrual accounting in this instance? **A:** In this case, some people were critical because, in general, China uses cash accounting. By switching to accrual accounting for this transaction, China was not being consistent in its accounting practices. Lack of consistency reduces the transparency and usefulness of accounting information.

p. 174 Turning Gift Cards into Revenue Q: Suppose that Robert Jones purchases a $100 gift card at Best Buy on December 24, 2013, and gives it to his wife, Mary Jones, on December 25, 2013. On January 3, 2014, Mary uses the card to purchase $100 worth of CDs. When do you think Best Buy should recognize revenue and why? **A:** According to the revenue recognition principle, companies should recognize revenue when the performance obligation is satisfied. In this case, revenue results when Best Buy provides the goods. Thus, when Best Buy receives cash in exchange for the gift card on December 24, 2013, it should recognize a liability, Unearned Sales Revenue, for $100. On January 3, 2014, when Mary Jones exchanges the card for merchandise, Best Buy should recognize revenue and eliminate $100 from the balance in the Unearned Sales Revenue account.

p. 180 Got Junk? Q: What accounting issue might this cause for companies? **A:** The balance sheet should provide a fair representation of what a company owns and what it owes. If significant obligations of the company are not reported on the balance sheet, the company's net worth (its equity) will be overstated. While it is true that it is not possible to estimate the **exact** amount of future environmental cleanup costs, it is becoming clear that companies will be held accountable. Therefore, it doesn't seem reasonable to not accrue for environmental costs. Recognition of these liabilities provides a more accurate picture of the company's financial position. It also has the potential to improve the environment. As companies are forced to report these amounts on their financial statements, they will start to look for more effective and efficient means to reduce toxic waste and therefore reduce their costs.

p. 186 Cooking the Books? Q: What motivates sales executives and finance and accounting executives to participate in activities that result in inaccurate reporting of revenues? **A:** Sales executives typically receive bonuses based on their ability to meet quarterly sales targets. In addition, they often face the possibility of losing their jobs if they miss those targets. Executives in accounting and finance are very aware of the earnings targets of Wall Street analysts and investors. If they fail to meet these targets, the company's stock price will fall. As a result of these pressures, executives sometimes knowingly engage in unethical efforts to misstate revenues. As a result of the Sarbanes-Oxley Act, the penalties for such behavior are now much more severe.

Answers to Self-Test Questions

1. c **2.** a **3.** d **4.** d **5.** d **6.** c ($1,350 − $600 = $750) **7.** a **8.** c **9.** c **10.** b **11.** b **12.** c **13.** a **14.** a **15.** d

A Look at IFRS

It is often difficult for companies to determine in what time period they should report particular revenues and expenses. Both the IASB and FASB are working on a joint project to develop a common conceptual framework, as well as a revenue recognition project, that will enable companies to better use the same principles to record transactions consistently over time.

LEARNING OBJECTIVE 11

Compare the procedures for revenue recognition under GAAP and IFRS.

KEY POINTS

- In this chapter, you learned accrual-basis accounting applied under GAAP. Companies applying IFRS also use accrual-basis accounting to ensure that they record transactions that change a company's financial statements in the period in which events occur.

- Similar to GAAP, cash-basis accounting is not in accordance with IFRS.

- IFRS also divides the economic life of companies into artificial time periods. Under both GAAP and IFRS, this is referred to as the **periodicity assumption**.

- IFRS requires that companies present a complete set of financial statements, including comparative information annually.

- GAAP has more than 100 rules dealing with revenue recognition. Many of these rules are industry-specific. In contrast, revenue recognition under IFRS is determined primarily by a single standard. Despite this large disparity in the amount of detailed guidance devoted to revenue recognition, the **general** revenue recognition principles required by GAAP that are used in this textbook are similar to those under IFRS.

- Revenue recognition fraud is a major issue in U.S. financial reporting. The same situation occurs in other countries, as evidenced by revenue recognition breakdowns at Dutch software company Baan NV, Japanese electronics giant NEC, and Dutch grocer AHold NV.

- A specific standard exists for revenue recognition under IFRS *(IAS 18)*. In general, the standard is based on the **probability that the economic benefits associated with the transaction will flow to the company** selling the goods, providing the service, or receiving investment income. In addition, the revenues and costs **must be capable of being measured reliably**.
- Under IFRS, revaluation of items such as land and buildings is permitted. IFRS allows depreciation based on revaluation of assets, which is not permitted under GAAP.
- The terminology used for revenues and gains, and expenses and losses, differs somewhat between IFRS and GAAP. For example, income under IFRS is defined as:

> Increases in economic benefits during the accounting period in the form of inflows or enhancements of assets or decreases of liabilities that result in increases in equity, other than those relating to contributions from shareholders.

Income includes **both** revenues, which arise during the normal course of operating activities, and gains, which arise from activities outside of the normal sales of goods and services. The term **income** is not used this way under GAAP. Instead, under GAAP income refers to the net difference between revenues and expenses. Expenses under IFRS are defined as:

> Decreases in economic benefits during the accounting period in the form of outflows or depletions of assets or incurrences of liabilities that result in decreases in equity other than those relating to distributions to shareholders.

Note that under IFRS expenses include both those costs incurred in the normal course of operations, as well as losses that are not part of normal operations. This is in contrast to GAAP, which defines each separately.

- The procedures of the closing process are applicable to all companies whether they are using IFRS or GAAP.

LOOKING TO THE FUTURE

The IASB and FASB are now involved in a joint project on revenue recognition. The purpose of this project is to develop comprehensive guidance on when to recognize revenue. Presently, the Boards are considering an approach that focuses on changes in assets and liabilities (rather than on earned and realized) as the basis for revenue recognition. It is hoped that this approach will lead to more consistent accounting in this area. For more on this topic, see **www.fasb.org/project/revenue_recognition.shtml**.

IFRS PRACTICE

IFRS SELF-TEST QUESTIONS

1. GAAP:
   (a) provides very detailed, industry-specific guidance on revenue recognition, compared to the general guidance provided by IFRS.
   (b) provides only general guidance on revenue recognition, compared to the detailed guidance provided by IFRS.
   (c) allows revenue to be recognized when a customer makes an order.
   (d) requires that revenue not be recognized until cash is received.
2. Which of the following statements is **false**?
   (a) IFRS employs the periodicity assumption.
   (b) IFRS employs accrual accounting.
   (c) IFRS requires that revenues and costs must be capable of being measured reliably.
   (d) IFRS uses the cash basis of accounting.
3. As a result of the revenue recognition project being undertaken by the FASB and IASB:
   (a) revenue recognition will place more emphasis on when revenue is earned.
   (b) revenue recognition will place more emphasis on when revenue is realized.
   (c) revenue recognition will place more emphasis on when changes occur in assets and liabilities.
   (d) revenue will no longer be recorded unless cash has been received.
4. Which of the following is **false**?
   (a) Under IFRS, the term **income** describes both revenues and gains.
   (b) Under IFRS, the term **expenses** includes losses.

(c) Under IFRS, firms do not engage in the closing process.

(d) IFRS has fewer standards than GAAP that address revenue recognition.

5. Accrual-basis accounting:

(a) is optional under IFRS.

(b) results in companies recording transactions that change a company's financial statements in the period in which events occur.

(c) will likely be eliminated as a result of the IASB/FASB joint project on revenue recognition.

(d) is not consistent with the IASB conceptual framework.

IFRS CONCEPTS AND APPLICATION

IFRS4-1 Compare and contrast the rules regarding revenue recognition under IFRS versus GAAP.

IFRS4-2 Under IFRS, do the definitions of revenues and expenses include gains and losses? Explain.

INTERNATIONAL FINANCIAL REPORTING PROBLEM: *Zetar plc*

IFRS4-3 The financial statements of Zetar plc are presented in Appendix C. The company's complete annual report, including the notes to its financial statements, is available in the Investors section at **www.zetarplc.com**.

Instructions

Visit Zetar's corporate website and answer the following questions from Zetar's 2011 annual report.

(a) From the notes to the financial statements, how does the company determine the amount of revenue to record at the time of a sale?

(b) From the notes to the financial statements, how does the company determine whether a sale has occurred?

(c) Using the consolidated income statement and consolidated statement of financial position, identify items that may result in adjusting entries for deferrals.

(d) Using the consolidated income statement, identify two items that may result in adjusting entries for accruals.

Answers to IFRS Self-Test Questions

1. a **2.** d **3.** c **4.** c **5.** b

© omgimages/iStockphoto

✔ The Navigator

- Scan Learning Objectives
- Read Feature Story
- Scan Preview
- Read Text and Answer **Do it!**
  - ○ p. 237 ○ p. 241 ○ p. 245 ○ p. 247
- Work Using the Decision Toolkit
- Review Summary of Learning Objectives
- Work Comprehensive **Do it!** p. 256
- Answer Self-Test Questions
- Complete Assignments
- Go to WileyPLUS for practice and tutorials

🌐 Read A Look at IFRS p. 279

MERCHANDISING OPERATIONS AND THE MULTIPLE-STEP INCOME STATEMENT

LEARNING OBJECTIVES

After studying this chapter, you should be able to:

1 Identify the differences between a service company and a merchandising company.

2 Explain the recording of purchases under a perpetual inventory system.

3 Explain the recording of sales revenues under a perpetual inventory system.

4 Distinguish between a single-step and a multiple-step income statement.

5 Determine cost of goods sold under a periodic system.

6 Explain the factors affecting profitability.

7 Identify a quality of earnings indicator.

✔ The Navigator

Have you ever shopped for outdoor gear at an REI (Recreational Equipment Incorporated) store? If so, you might have been surprised if a sales-clerk asked if you were a member. A member? What do you mean a member? You soon realize that REI might not be your typical store. In fact, there's a lot about REI that makes it different.

REI is a consumer cooperative, or "co-op" for short. To figure out what that means, consider this quote from the company's annual report:

BUY NOW, VOTE LATER

> As a cooperative, the Company is owned by its members. Each member is entitled to one vote in the election of the Company's Board of Directors. Since January 1, 2008, the nonrefundable, nontransferable, one-time membership fee has been $20 dollars. As of December 31, 2010, there were approximately 10.8 million members.

Voting rights? Now that's something you don't get from shopping at Wal-Mart. REI members get other benefits as well, including sharing in the company's profits through a dividend at the end of the year, which can be used for purchases at REI stores during the next two years. The more you spend, the bigger your dividend.

Since REI is a co-op, you might wonder whether management's incentives might be a little different. For example, is management still concerned about making a profit? The answer is yes, as it ensures the long-term viability of the company. At the same time, REI's members want the company to be run efficiently, so that prices remain low. In order for its members to evaluate just how well management is doing, REI publishes an audited annual report, just like publicly traded companies do. So, while profit maximization might not be the ultimate goal for REI, the accounting and reporting issues are similar to those of a typical corporation.

How well is this business model working for REI? Well, it has consistently been rated as one of the best places to work in the United States. It was ranked 8th on *Fortune*'s 2012 list. Also, REI had sustainable business practices long before social responsibility became popular at other companies. The CEO's Stewardship Report states "we reduced the absolute amount of energy we use despite opening four new stores and growing our business; we grew the amount of FSC-certified paper we use to 58.4 percent of our total paper footprint—including our cash register receipt paper; we facilitated 2.2 million volunteer hours and we provided $3.7 million to more than 330 conservation and recreation nonprofits."

So, while REI, like other retailers, closely monitors its financial results, it also strives to succeed in other areas. And, with over 10 million votes at stake, REI's management knows that it has to deliver.

 The Navigator

Merchandising is one of the largest and most influential industries in the United States. It is likely that a number of you will work for a merchandiser. Therefore, understanding the financial statements of merchandising companies is important. In this chapter, you will learn the basics about reporting merchandising transactions. In addition, you will learn how to prepare and analyze a commonly used form of the income statement—the multiple-step income statement. The content and organization of the chapter are as follows.

Merchandising Operations

LEARNING OBJECTIVE 1

Identify the differences between a service company and a merchandising company.

REI, Wal-Mart, and Amazon.com are called merchandising companies because they buy and sell merchandise rather than perform services as their primary source of revenue. Merchandising companies that purchase and sell directly to consumers are called **retailers**. Merchandising companies that sell to retailers are known as **wholesalers**. For example, retailer Walgreens might buy goods from wholesaler McKesson; retailer Office Depot might buy office supplies from wholesaler United Stationers. The primary source of revenues for merchandising companies is the sale of merchandise, often referred to simply as sales revenue or **sales**. A merchandising company has two categories of expenses: the cost of goods sold and operating expenses.

The cost of goods sold is the total cost of merchandise sold during the period. This expense is directly related to the revenue recognized from the sale of goods. Illustration 5-1 shows the income measurement process for a merchandising

Illustration 5-1 Income measurement process for a merchandising company

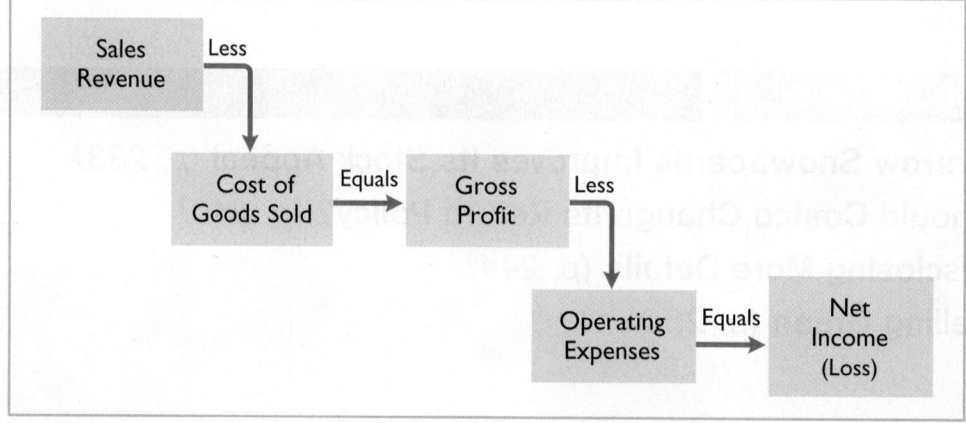

company. The items in the two blue boxes are unique to a merchandising company; they are not used by a service company.

OPERATING CYCLES

The operating cycle of a merchandising company ordinarily is longer than that of a service company. The purchase of inventory and its eventual sale lengthen the cycle. Illustration 5-2 contrasts the operating cycles of service and merchandising companies. Note that the added asset account for a merchandising company is the Inventory account.

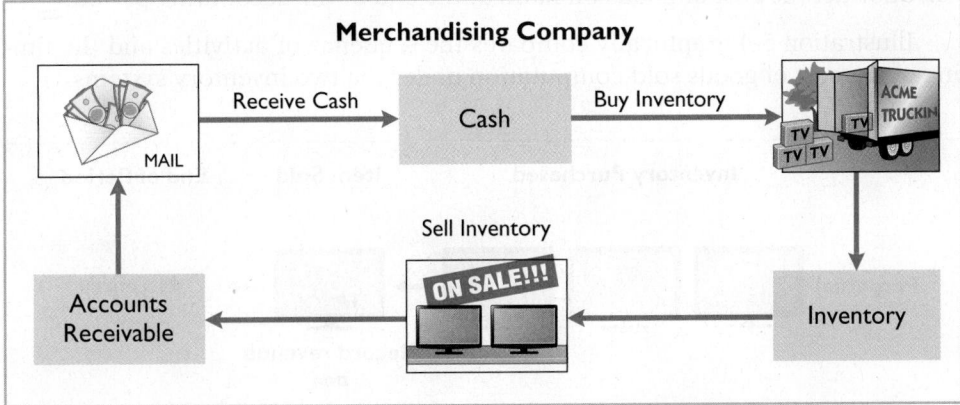

Illustration 5-2 Operating cycles for a service company and a merchandising company

FLOW OF COSTS

The flow of costs for a merchandising company is as follows. Beginning inventory plus the cost of goods purchased is the cost of goods available for sale. As goods are sold, they are assigned to cost of goods sold. Those goods that are not sold by the end of the accounting period represent ending inventory. Illustration 5-3 describes these relationships. Companies use one of two systems to account for inventory: a **perpetual inventory system** or a **periodic inventory system**.

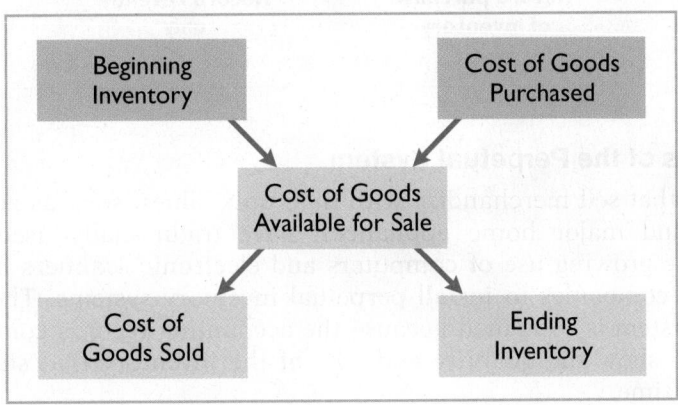

Illustration 5-3 Flow of costs

Perpetual System

Helpful Hint Even under perpetual inventory systems, companies perform physical inventories. This is done as a control procedure to verify inventory levels, in order to detect theft or "shrinkage."

In a **perpetual inventory system**, companies maintain detailed records of the cost of each inventory purchase and sale. These records continuously— perpetually—show the inventory that should be on hand for every item. For example, a Ford dealership has separate inventory records for each automobile, truck, and van on its lot and showroom floor. Similarly, a grocery store uses bar codes and optical scanners to keep a daily running record of every box of cereal and every jar of jelly that it buys and sells. Under a perpetual inventory system, a company determines the cost of goods sold **each time a sale occurs**.

Periodic System

In a **periodic inventory system**, companies do not keep detailed inventory records of the goods on hand throughout the period. They determine the cost of goods sold **only at the end of the accounting period**—that is, periodically. At that point, the company takes a physical inventory count to determine the cost of goods on hand.

To determine the cost of goods sold under a periodic inventory system, the following steps are necessary:

1. Determine the cost of goods on hand at the beginning of the accounting period.
2. Add to it the cost of goods purchased.
3. Subtract the cost of goods on hand at the end of the accounting period.

Illustration 5-4 graphically compares the sequence of activities and the timing of the cost of goods sold computation under the two inventory systems.

Illustration 5-4 Comparing perpetual and periodic inventory systems

Advantages of the Perpetual System

Companies that sell merchandise with high unit values, such as automobiles, furniture, and major home appliances, have traditionally used perpetual systems. The growing use of computers and electronic scanners has enabled many more companies to install perpetual inventory systems. The perpetual inventory system is so named because the accounting records continuously— perpetually—show the quantity and cost of the inventory that should be on hand at any time.

A perpetual inventory system provides better control over inventories than a periodic system. Since the inventory records show the quantities that should be on hand, the company can count the goods at any time to see whether the amount of goods actually on hand agrees with the inventory records. If shortages are uncovered, the company can investigate immediately. Although a perpetual inventory system requires additional clerical work and additional cost to maintain inventory records, a computerized system can minimize this cost. Much of Amazon.com's success is attributed to its sophisticated inventory system.

Some businesses find it either unnecessary or uneconomical to invest in a sophisticated, computerized perpetual inventory system such as Amazon's. However, many small merchandising businesses find that basic computerized accounting packages provide some of the essential benefits of a perpetual inventory system. Yet, managers of some small businesses still find that they can control their merchandise and manage day-to-day operations using a periodic inventory system.

Because of the widespread use of the perpetual inventory system, we illustrate it in this chapter. An appendix to this chapter describes the journal entries for the periodic system.

Investor Insight

Morrow Snowboards Improves Its Stock Appeal

Investors are often eager to invest in a company that has a hot new product. However, when snowboard maker Morrow Snowboards, Inc., issued shares of stock to the public for the first time, some investors expressed reluctance to invest in Morrow because of a number of accounting control problems. To reduce investor concerns, Morrow implemented a perpetual inventory system to improve its control over inventory. In addition, it stated that it would perform a physical inventory count every quarter until it felt that the perpetual inventory system was reliable.

 If a perpetual system keeps track of inventory on a daily basis, why do companies ever need to do a physical count? (See page 278.)

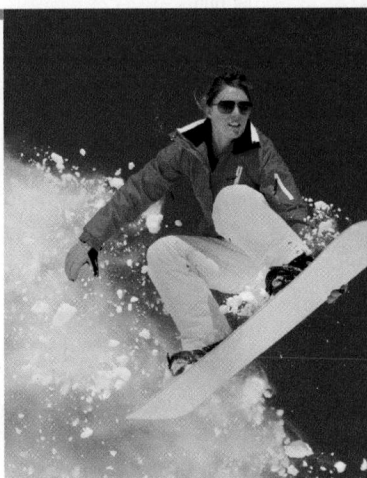

© Ben Blankenburg/iStockphoto

Recording Purchases of Merchandise

Companies may purchase inventory for cash or on account (credit). They normally record purchases when they receive the goods from the seller. Every purchase should be supported by business documents that provide written evidence of the transaction. Each cash purchase should be supported by a canceled check or a cash register receipt indicating the items purchased and amounts paid. Companies record cash purchases by an increase (debit) in Inventory and a decrease (credit) in Cash.

Each purchase should be supported by a **purchase invoice**, which indicates the total purchase price and other relevant information. However, the purchaser does not prepare a separate purchase invoice. Instead, the purchaser uses as a purchase invoice the copy of the sales invoice sent by the seller. In Illustration 5-5 (page 234), for example, Sauk Stereo (the buyer) uses as a purchase invoice the sales invoice prepared by PW Audio Supply, Inc. (the seller).

The associated entry for Sauk Stereo for the invoice from PW Audio Supply increases (debits) Inventory and increases (credits) Accounts Payable.

LEARNING OBJECTIVE | **2**

Explain the recording of purchases under a perpetual inventory system.

May 4	Inventory	3,800	
	Accounts Payable		3,800
	(To record goods purchased on account from PW Audio Supply)		

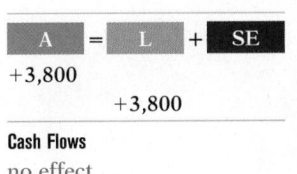

A	=	L	+	SE
+3,800				
				+3,800

Cash Flows
no effect

Illustration 5-5 Sales invoice used as purchase invoice by Sauk Stereo

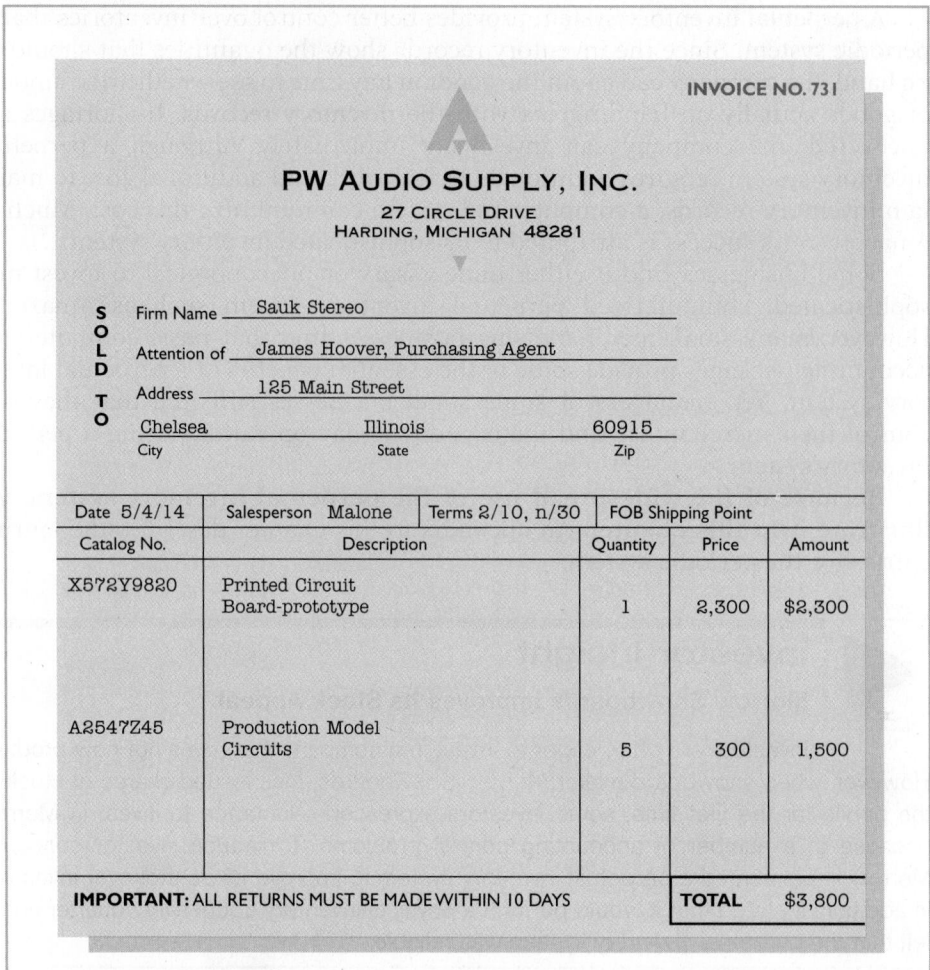

Helpful Hint To better understand the contents of this invoice, identify these items:
1. Seller
2. Invoice date
3. Purchaser
4. Salesperson
5. Credit terms
6. Freight terms
7. Goods sold: catalog number, description, quantity, price per unit
8. Total invoice amount

Under the perpetual inventory system, companies record purchases of merchandise for sale in the Inventory account. Thus, REI would increase (debit) Inventory for clothing, sporting goods, and anything else purchased for resale to customers. Not all purchases are debited to Inventory, however. Companies record purchases of assets acquired for use and not for resale, such as supplies, equipment, and similar items, as increases to specific asset accounts rather than to Inventory. For example, to record the purchase of materials used to make shelf signs or for cash register receipt paper, REI would increase (debit) Supplies.

FREIGHT COSTS

The sales agreement should indicate who—the seller or the buyer—is to pay for transporting the goods to the buyer's place of business. When a common carrier such as a railroad, trucking company, or airline transports the goods, the carrier prepares a freight bill in accord with the sales agreement.

Freight terms are expressed as either FOB shipping point or FOB destination. The letters FOB mean **free on board**. Thus, **FOB shipping point** means that the seller places the goods free on board the carrier, and the buyer pays the freight costs. Conversely, **FOB destination** means that the seller places the goods free on board to the buyer's place of business, and the seller pays the freight. For example, the sales invoice in Illustration 5-5 indicates FOB shipping point.

Thus, the buyer (Sauk Stereo) pays the freight charges. Illustration 5-6 illustrates these shipping terms.

Illustration 5-6 Shipping terms

Freight Costs Incurred by Buyer

When the buyer pays the transportation costs, these costs are considered part of the cost of purchasing inventory. As a result, the account **Inventory is increased (debited)**. For example, if Sauk Stereo (the buyer) pays Public Freight Company $150 for freight charges on May 6, the entry on Sauk Stereo's books is:

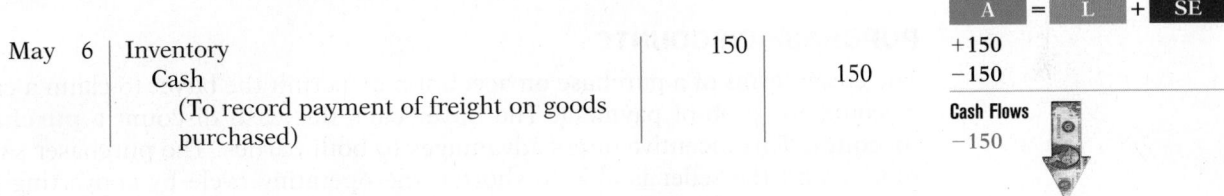

May 6	Inventory		150	
	Cash			150
	(To record payment of freight on goods purchased)			

A = L + SE
+150
−150

Cash Flows
−150

Thus, any freight costs incurred by the buyer are part of the cost of merchandise purchased. The reason: Inventory cost should include all costs to acquire the inventory, including freight necessary to deliver the goods to the buyer. Companies recognize these costs as cost of goods sold when inventory is sold.

Freight Costs Incurred by Seller

In contrast, **freight costs incurred by the seller on outgoing merchandise are an operating expense to the seller**. These costs increase an expense account titled Freight-Out (sometimes called Delivery Expense). For example, if the freight terms on the invoice in Illustration 5-5 had required that PW Audio Supply (the seller) pay the $150 freight charges, the entry by PW Audio Supply would be:

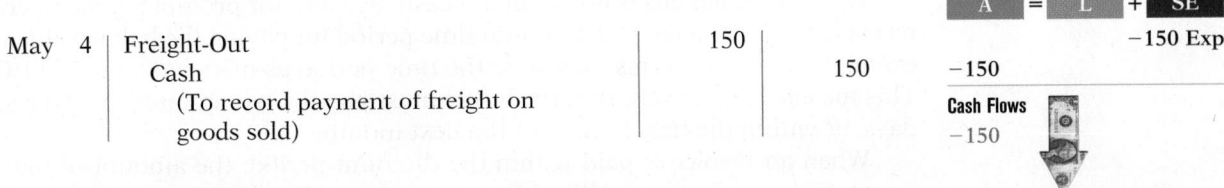

May 4	Freight-Out		150	
	Cash			150
	(To record payment of freight on goods sold)			

A = L + SE
−150 Exp
−150

Cash Flows
−150

When the seller pays the freight charges, the seller will usually establish a higher invoice price for the goods, to cover the expense of shipping.

PURCHASE RETURNS AND ALLOWANCES

A purchaser may be dissatisfied with the merchandise received because the goods are damaged or defective, of inferior quality, or do not meet the purchaser's specifications. In such cases, the purchaser may return the goods to the seller for credit if the sale was made on credit, or for a cash refund if the purchase was for cash. This transaction is known as a **purchase return**. Alternatively, the purchaser may choose to keep the merchandise if the seller is willing to grant a reduction of the purchase price. This transaction is known as a **purchase allowance**.

Assume that Sauk Stereo returned goods costing $300 to PW Audio Supply on May 8. The following entry by Sauk Stereo for the returned merchandise decreases (debits) Accounts Payable and decreases (credits) Inventory.

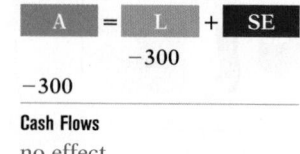

−300
−300

Cash Flows
no effect

May	8	Accounts Payable	300	
		Inventory		300
		(To record return of goods purchased from PW Audio Supply)		

Because Sauk Stereo increased Inventory when the goods were received, Inventory is decreased (credited) when Sauk Stereo returns the goods.

Suppose instead that Sauk Stereo chose to keep the goods after being granted a $50 allowance (reduction in price). It would reduce (debit) Accounts Payable and reduce (credit) Inventory for $50.

PURCHASE DISCOUNTS

The credit terms of a purchase on account may permit the buyer to claim a cash discount for prompt payment. The buyer calls this cash discount a **purchase discount**. This incentive offers advantages to both parties. The purchaser saves money, and the seller is able to shorten the operating cycle by converting the accounts receivable into cash earlier.

The **credit terms** specify the amount of the cash discount and time period during which it is offered. They also indicate the length of time in which the purchaser is expected to pay the full invoice price. In the sales invoice in Illustration 5-5 (page 234), credit terms are 2/10, n/30, which is read "two-ten, net thirty." This means that a 2% cash discount may be taken on the invoice price, less ("net of") any returns or allowances, if payment is made within 10 days of the invoice date (the **discount period**). Otherwise, the invoice price, less any returns or allowances, is due 30 days from the invoice date. Alternatively, the discount period may extend to a specified number of days following the month in which the sale occurs. For example, 1/10 EOM (end of month) means that a 1% discount is available if the invoice is paid within the first 10 days of the next month.

When the seller elects not to offer a cash discount for prompt payment, credit terms will specify only the maximum time period for paying the balance due. For example, the credit terms may state the time period as n/30, n/60, or n/10 EOM. This means, respectively, that the buyer must pay the net amount in 30 days, 60 days, or within the first 10 days of the next month.

When an invoice is paid within the discount period, the amount of the discount decreases Inventory. Why? Because the merchandiser records inventory at its cost and, by paying within the discount period, it has reduced that cost. To illustrate, assume Sauk Stereo pays the balance due of $3,500 (gross invoice price of $3,800 less purchase returns and allowances of $300) on May 14, the last day of the discount period. The cash discount is $70 ($3,500 × 2%), and the amount of cash Sauk Stereo paid is $3,430 ($3,500 − $70). The entry Sauk Stereo makes to record its May 14 payment decreases (debits) Accounts Payable by the amount of the gross invoice price, reduces (credits) Inventory by the $70 discount, and reduces (credits) Cash by the net amount owed.

Helpful Hint The term *net* in "net 30" means the remaining amount due after subtracting any returns and allowances and partial payments.

May 14	Accounts Payable	3,500	
	Cash		3,430
	Inventory		70
	(To record payment within discount period)		

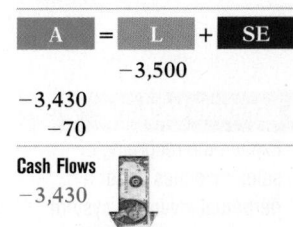

A = L + SE
−3,500
−3,430
−70

Cash Flows
−3,430

If Sauk Stereo failed to take the discount and instead made full payment of $3,500 on June 3, Sauk Stereo would reduce (debit) Accounts Payable and reduce (credit) Cash for $3,500 each.

June 3	Accounts Payable	3,500	
	Cash		3,500
	(To record payment with no discount taken)		

A = L + SE
−3,500
−3,500

Cash Flows
−3,500

A merchandising company usually should take all available discounts. Passing up the discount may be viewed as **paying interest** for use of the money. For example, passing up the discount offered by PW Audio Supply would be like Sauk Stereo paying an interest rate of 2% for the use of $3,500 for 20 days. This is the equivalent of an annual interest rate of approximately 36.5% (2% × 365/20). Obviously, it would be better for Sauk Stereo to borrow at prevailing bank interest rates of 6% to 10% than to lose the discount.

SUMMARY OF PURCHASING TRANSACTIONS

The following T-account (with transaction descriptions in blue) provides a summary of the effect of the previous transactions on Inventory. Sauk Stereo originally purchased $3,800 worth of inventory for resale. It then returned $300 of goods. It paid $150 in freight charges, and finally, it received a $70 discount off the balance owed because it paid within the discount period. This results in a balance in Inventory of $3,580.

		Inventory			
Purchase	May 4	3,800	May 8	300	Purchase return
Freight-in	6	150	14	70	Purchase discount
Balance		3,580			

Do it!

On September 5, De La Hoya Company buys merchandise on account from Junot Diaz Company. The selling price of the goods is $1,500. On September 8, De La Hoya returns defective goods with a selling price of $200. Record the transactions on the books of De La Hoya Company.

**PURCHASE
TRANSACTIONS**

Solution

Sept. 5	Inventory	1,500	
	Accounts Payable		1,500
	(To record goods purchased on account)		
8	Accounts Payable	200	
	Inventory		200
	(To record return of defective goods)		

Action Plan

• Purchaser records goods at cost.
• When goods are returned, purchaser reduces Inventory.

✔ The Navigator

Related exercise material: **BE5-4**, **Do it!** **5-1**, and **E5-1**.

Recording Sales of Merchandise

In accordance with the revenue recognition principle, companies record sales revenue, like service revenue, when the performance obligation is satisfied. Typically, that performance obligation is satisfied when the goods are transferred from the seller to the buyer. At this point, the sales transaction is completed and the sales price is established.

Sales may be made on credit or for cash. Every sales transaction should be supported by a **business document** that provides written evidence of the sale. **Cash register documents** provide evidence of cash sales. A sales invoice, like the one that was shown in Illustration 5-5 (page 234), provides support for each sale. The original copy of the invoice goes to the customer, and the seller keeps a copy for use in recording the sale. The invoice shows the date of sale, customer name, total sales price, and other relevant information.

The seller makes two entries for each sale. (1) It increases (debits) Accounts Receivable or Cash, as well as increases (credits) Sales Revenue. (2) It increases (debits) Cost of Goods Sold and decreases (credits) Inventory. As a result, the Inventory account will show at all times the amount of inventory that should be on hand.

To illustrate a credit sales transaction, PW Audio Supply records the sale of $3,800 on May 4 to Sauk Stereo (see Illustration 5-5) as follows (assume the merchandise cost PW Audio Supply $2,400).

A	=	L	+	SE
+3,800				
				+3,800 Rev

Cash Flows
no effect

A	=	L	+	SE
				−2,400 Exp
−2,400				

Cash Flows
no effect

May	4	Accounts Receivable		3,800	
		Sales Revenue			3,800
		(To record credit sale to Sauk Stereo			
		per invoice #731)			
	4	Cost of Goods Sold		2,400	
		Inventory			2,400
		(To record cost of merchandise sold on			
		invoice #731 to Sauk Stereo)			

Helpful Hint The merchandiser credits the Sales Revenue account only for sales of goods held for resale. Sales of assets not held for resale, such as equipment or land, are credited directly to the asset account.

For internal decision-making purposes, merchandising companies may use more than one sales account. For example, PW Audio Supply may decide to keep separate sales accounts for its sales of TVs, DVD players, and microwave ovens. REI might use separate accounts for camping gear, children's clothing, and ski equipment—or it might have even more narrowly defined accounts. By using separate sales accounts for major product lines, rather than a single combined sales account, company management can monitor sales trends more closely and respond more strategically to changes in sales patterns. For example, if TV sales are increasing while microwave oven sales are decreasing, the company might reevaluate both its advertising and pricing policies on each of these items to ensure they are optimal.

Ethics Note Many companies are trying to improve the quality of their financial reporting. For example, General Electric now provides more detail on its revenues and operating profits.

On its income statement presented to outside investors, a merchandising company would normally provide only a single sales figure—the sum of all of its individual sales accounts. This is done for two reasons. First, providing detail on all of its individual sales accounts would add considerable length to its income statement. Second, companies do not want their competitors to know the details of their operating results. However, at one time Microsoft expanded its disclosure of revenue from three to five types. The reason: The additional categories enabled financial statement users to better evaluate the growth of the company's consumer and Internet businesses.

ANATOMY OF A FRAUD[1]

Holly Harmon was a cashier at a national superstore for only a short while when she began stealing merchandise using three methods. Under the first method, her husband or friends took UPC labels from cheaper items and put them on more expensive items. Holly then scanned the goods at the register. Using the second method, Holly scanned an item at the register but then voided the sale and left the merchandise in the shopping cart. A third approach was to put goods into large plastic containers. She scanned the plastic containers but not the goods within them. One day, Holly did not call in sick or show up for work. In such instances, the company reviews past surveillance tapes to look for suspicious activity by employees. This enabled the store to observe the thefts and to identify the participants.

Total take: $12,000

THE MISSING CONTROLS

Human resource controls. A background check would have revealed Holly's previous criminal record. She would not have been hired as a cashier.

Physical controls. Software can flag high numbers of voided transactions or a high number of sales of low-priced goods. Random comparisons of video records with cash register records can ensure that the goods reported as sold on the register are the same goods that are shown being purchased on the video recording. Finally, employees should be aware that they are being monitored.

Source: Adapted from Wells, *Fraud Casebook* (2007), pp. 251–259.

At the end of "Anatomy of a Fraud" stories, which describe real-world frauds, we discuss the missing control activity that would likely have presented or uncovered the fraud.

SALES RETURNS AND ALLOWANCES

We now look at the "flip side" of purchase returns and allowances, which the seller records as **sales returns and allowances**. These are transactions where the seller either accepts goods back from a purchaser (a return) or grants a reduction in the purchase price (an allowance) so that the buyer will keep the goods. PW Audio Supply's entries to record credit for returned goods involve (1) an increase (debit) in Sales Returns and Allowances (a contra account to Sales Revenue) and a decrease (credit) in Accounts Receivable at the $300 selling price, and (2) an increase (debit) in Inventory (assume a $140 cost) and a decrease (credit) in Cost of Goods Sold, as shown below. (We assumed that the goods were not defective. If they were defective, PW Audio Supply would make an entry to the Inventory account to reflect their decline in value.)

May	8	Sales Returns and Allowances	300	
		Accounts Receivable		300
		(To record credit granted to Sauk Stereo		
		for returned goods)		
	8	Inventory	140	
		Cost of Goods Sold		140
		(To record cost of goods returned)		

A = L + SE
−300   −300 Rev

Cash Flows
no effect

A = L + SE
+140   +140 Exp

Cash Flows
no effect

Suppose instead that the goods were not returned but the seller granted the buyer an allowance by reducing the purchase price. In this case, the seller would debit Sales Returns and Allowances and credit Accounts Receivable for the amount of the allowance. An allowance has no impact on Inventory or Cost of Goods sold.

---

[1]The "Anatomy of a Fraud" stories in this textbook are adapted from *Fraud Casebook: Lessons from the Bad Side of Business,* edited by Joseph T. Wells (Hoboken, NJ: John Wiley & Sons, Inc., 2007). Used by permission. The names of some of the people and organizations in the stories are fictitious, but the facts in the stories are true.

Sales Returns and Allowances is a *contra revenue account* to Sales Revenue, which means it is offset against a revenue account on the income statement. The normal balance of Sales Returns and Allowances is a debit. Companies use a contra account, instead of debiting Sales Revenue, to disclose in the accounts and in the income statement the amount of sales returns and allowances. Disclosure of this information is important to management. Excessive returns and allowances suggest problems—inferior merchandise, inefficiencies in filling orders, errors in billing customers, or mistakes in delivery or shipment of goods. Moreover, a decrease (debit) recorded directly to Sales Revenue would obscure the relative importance of sales returns and allowances as a percentage of sales. It also could distort comparisons between total sales in different accounting periods.

Accounting Across the Organization

Should Costco Change Its Return Policy?

In most industries, sales returns are relatively minor. But returns of consumer electronics can really take a bite out of profits. Recently, the marketing executives at Costco Wholesale Corp. faced a difficult decision. Costco has always prided itself on its generous return policy. Most goods have had an unlimited grace period for returns. A new policy will require that certain electronics must be returned within 90 days of their purchase. The reason? The cost of returned products such as high-definition TVs, computers, and iPods cut an estimated 8¢ per share off Costco's earnings per share, which was $2.30.

Source: Kris Hudson, "Costco Tightens Policy on Returning Electronics," *Wall Street Journal* (February 27, 2007), p. B4.

© Jacob Wackerhausen/iStockphoto

? If a company expects significant returns, what are the implications for revenue recognition? (See page 278.)

SALES DISCOUNTS

As mentioned in our discussion of purchase transactions, the seller may offer the customer a cash discount—called by the seller a *sales discount*—for the prompt payment of the balance due. Like a purchase discount, a sales discount is based on the invoice price less returns and allowances, if any. The seller increases (debits) the Sales Discounts account for discounts that are taken. The entry by PW Audio Supply to record the cash receipt on May 14 from Sauk Stereo within the discount period is:

A	=	L	+	SE
+3,430				
				−70 Rev
−3,500				

Cash Flows
+3,430

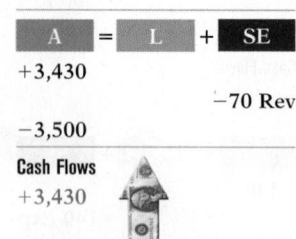

May 14	Cash	3,430	
	Sales Discounts	70	
	Accounts Receivable		3,500
	(To record collection within 2/10, n/30		
	discount period from Sauk Stereo)		

Like Sales Returns and Allowances, Sales Discounts is a **contra revenue account** to Sales Revenue. Its normal balance is a debit. Sellers use this account, instead of debiting Sales Revenue, to disclose the amount of cash discounts taken by customers. If the customer does not take the discount, PW Audio Supply increases (debits) Cash for $3,500 and decreases (credits) Accounts Receivable for the same amount at the date of collection.

The following T-accounts summarize the three sales-related transactions and show their combined effect on net sales.

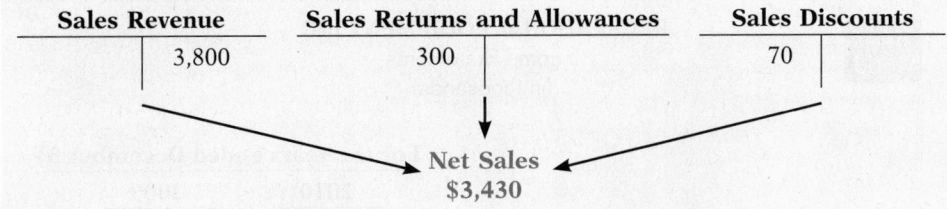

Sales Revenue	Sales Returns and Allowances	Sales Discounts
3,800	300	70

Net Sales
$3,430

Do it!

On September 5, De La Hoya Company buys merchandise on account from Junot Diaz Company. The selling price of the goods is $1,500, and the cost to Diaz Company was $800. On September 8, De La Hoya returns goods with a selling price of $200 and a cost of $105. Record the transactions on the books of Junot Diaz Company.

SALES TRANSACTIONS

Solution

Sept.	5	Accounts Receivable	1,500	
		Sales Revenue		1,500
		(To record credit sale)		
	5	Cost of Goods Sold	800	
		Inventory		800
		(To record cost of goods sold)		
Sept.	8	Sales Returns and Allowances	200	
		Accounts Receivable		200
		(To record credit granted for receipt of		
		returned goods)		
	8	Inventory	105	
		Cost of Goods Sold		105
		(To record cost of goods returned)		

Action Plan

- Seller records both the sale and the cost of goods sold at the time of the sale.
- When goods are returned, the seller records the return in a contra account, Sales Returns and Allowances, and reduces Accounts Receivable.
- Any goods returned increase Inventory and reduce Cost of Goods Sold. The inventory should be recorded at the lower of its cost or its fair value (scrap value).

The Navigator

Related exercise material: **BE5-2, BE5-3, Do it! 5-2, E5-2, E5-3,** and **E5-4.**

Income Statement Presentation

Companies widely use two forms of the income statement. One is the **single-step income statement**. The statement is so named because only one step, subtracting total expenses from total revenues, is required in determining net income (or net loss).

In a single-step statement, all data are classified into two categories: (1) **revenues**, which include both operating revenues and nonoperating revenues and gains (for example, interest revenue and gain on sale of equipment); and (2) **expenses**, which include cost of goods sold, operating expenses, and nonoperating expenses and losses (for example, interest expense, loss on sale of equipment, or income tax expense). The single-step income statement is the form we have used thus far in the text. Illustration 5-7 (page 242) shows a single-step statement for REI.

There are two primary reasons for using the single-step form. (1) A company does not realize any type of profit or income until total revenues exceed total expenses, so it makes sense to divide the statement into these two categories. (2) The form is simple and easy to read.

LEARNING OBJECTIVE 4

Distinguish between a single-step and a multiple-step income statement.

Illustration 5-7 Single-step income statements

RECREATIONAL EQUIPMENT, INC.
Income Statements
(in thousands)

	For the years ended December 31	
	2010	**2009**
Revenues		
Net sales	$1,658,751	$1,455,351
Other revenues	14,190	14,010
	1,672,941	1,469,361
Expenses		
Cost of goods sold	929,787	804,834
Payroll-related expenses	331,159	281,502
Occupancy, general and administrative	282,368	268,455
Patronage refunds	79,848	67,222
Income taxes	19,549	17,541
	1,642,711	1,439,554
Net income	$ 30,230	$ 29,807

International Note The IASB and FASB are involved in a joint project to evaluate the format of financial statements. The first phase of that project involves a focus on how to best present revenues and expenses. One longer-term result of the project may well be an income statement format that better reflects how businesses are run.

A second form of the income statement is the **multiple-step income statement**. The multiple-step income statement is often considered more useful because it highlights the components of net income. The REI income statement in Illustration 5-8 is an example.

The multiple-step income statement has three important line items: gross profit, income from operations, and net income. They are determined as follows.

1. Subtract cost of goods sold from net sales to determine **gross profit**.

2. Deduct operating expenses from gross profit to determine **income from operations**.

3. Add or subtract the results of activities not related to operations to determine **net income**.

Illustration 5-8 Multiple-step income statements

RECREATIONAL EQUIPMENT, INC.
Income Statements
(in thousands)

	For the years ended December 31	
	2010	**2009**
Net sales	$1,658,751	$1,455,351
Cost of goods sold	929,787	804,834
Gross profit	728,964	650,517
Operating expenses		
Payroll-related expenses	331,159	281,502
Occupancy, general and administrative	282,368	268,455
Total operating expenses	613,527	549,957
Income from operations	115,437	100,560
Other revenues and gains		
Other revenues	14,190	14,010
Other expenses and losses		
Patronage refunds	79,848	67,222
Income before income taxes	49,779	47,348
Income tax expense	19,549	17,541
Net income	$ 30,230	$ 29,807

Note that companies report income tax expense in a separate section of the income statement before net income. The net incomes in Illustrations 5-7 and 5-8 are the same. The two income statements differ in the amount of detail displayed and the order presented. The following discussion provides additional information about the components of a multiple-step income statement.

SALES REVENUES

The income statement for a merchandising company typically presents gross sales revenues for the period. The company deducts sales returns and allowances and sales discounts (both contra accounts) from sales revenue in the income statement to arrive at **net sales**. Illustration 5-9 shows the sales section of the income statement for PW Audio Supply.

Illustration 5-9 Statement presentation of sales section

PW AUDIO SUPPLY, INC. Income Statement (partial)		
Sales		
Sales revenue		$ 480,000
Less: Sales returns and allowances	$12,000	
Sales discounts	8,000	20,000
Net sales		**$460,000**

GROSS PROFIT

The excess of net sales over cost of goods sold is gross profit. It is determined by deducting **cost of goods sold** from sales revenue. As shown in Illustration 5-8, REI had a gross profit of $729 million in 2010. This computation uses **net sales**, which takes into account sales returns and allowances and sales discounts.

Alternative Terminology Gross profit is sometimes referred to as *gross margin*.

On the basis of the PW Audio Supply sales data presented in Illustration 5-9 (net sales of $460,000) and the cost of goods sold (assume a balance of $316,000), PW Audio Supply's gross profit is $144,000, computed as follows.

Net sales	$ 460,000
Cost of goods sold	316,000
Gross profit	**$144,000**

It is important to understand what gross profit is—and what it is not. Gross profit represents the **merchandising profit** of a company. Because operating expenses have not been deducted, it is **not a measure of the overall profit** of a company. Nevertheless, management and other interested parties closely watch the amount and trend of gross profit. Comparisons of current gross profit with past amounts and rates and with those in the industry indicate the effectiveness of a company's purchasing and pricing policies.

OPERATING EXPENSES

Operating expenses are the next component in measuring net income for a merchandising company. At REI, for example, operating expenses were $613.5 million in 2010.

At PW Audio Supply, operating expenses were $114,000. The firm determines its income from operations by subtracting operating expenses from gross profit. Thus, income from operations is $30,000, as shown below.

Gross profit	$144,000
Operating expenses	114,000
Income from operations	$ 30,000

NONOPERATING ACTIVITIES

Nonoperating activities consist of various revenues and expenses and gains and losses that are unrelated to the company's main line of operations. When nonoperating items are included, the label "**Income from operations**" (or "Operating income") precedes them. This label clearly identifies the results of the company's normal operations, an amount determined by subtracting cost of goods sold and operating expenses from net sales. The results of nonoperating activities are shown in the categories "**Other revenues and gains**" and "**Other expenses and losses**." Illustration 5-10 lists examples of each.

Illustration 5-10 Examples of nonoperating activities

Other Revenues and Gains
Interest revenue from notes receivable and marketable securities.
Dividend revenue from investments in capital stock.
Rent revenue from subleasing a portion of the store.
Gain from the sale of property, plant, and equipment.

Other Expenses and Losses
Interest expense on notes and loans payable.
Casualty losses from recurring causes, such as vandalism and accidents.
Loss from the sale or abandonment of property, plant, and equipment.
Loss from strikes by employees and suppliers.

Nonoperating income is sometimes very significant. For example, in a recent quarter, Sears Holdings earned more than half of its net income from investments in derivative securities.

The distinction between operating and nonoperating activities is crucial to external users of financial data. These users view operating income as sustainable and many nonoperating activities as nonrecurring. When forecasting next year's income, analysts put the most weight on this year's operating income and less weight on this year's nonoperating activities.

Ethics Note Companies manage earnings in various ways. ConAgra Foods recorded a nonrecurring gain for $186 million from the sale of Pilgrim's Pride stock to help meet an earnings projection for the quarter.

ImageRite/Getty Images, Inc.

Ethics Insight
Disclosing More Details

After Enron, increased investor criticism and regulator scrutiny forced many companies to improve the clarity of their financial disclosures. For example, IBM began providing more detail regarding its "Other gains and losses." It had previously included these items in its selling, general, and administrative expenses, with little disclosure.

Disclosing other gains and losses in a separate line item on the income statement will not have any effect on bottom-line income. However, analysts complained that burying these details in the selling, general, and administrative expense line reduced their ability to fully understand how well IBM was performing. For example, previously if IBM sold off one of its buildings at a gain, it would include this gain in the selling, general, and administrative expense line item, thus reducing that expense. This made it appear that the company had done a better job of controlling operating expenses than it actually had.

As another example, when eBay recently sold the remainder of its investment in Skype to Microsoft, it reported a gain in "Other revenues and gains" of $1.7 billion. Since eBay's total income from operations was $2.4 billion, it was very important that the gain from the Skype sale not be buried in operating income.

? Why have investors and analysts demanded more accuracy in isolating "Other gains and losses" from operating items? (See page 278.)

Nonoperating activities are reported in the income statement immediately after operating activities. Included among "Other revenues and gains" in Illustration 5-8 (page 242) are Interest Revenue and Gain on Disposal of Plant Assets. Included in "Other expenses and losses" are Interest Expense and Casualty Loss from Vandalism.

In Illustration 5-11, we have provided the multiple-step income statement of PW Audio Supply. This statement provides more detail than that of REI and thus is useful as a guide for homework. *For homework problems, use the multiple-step form of the income statement unless the requirements state otherwise.*

Illustration 5-11 Multiple-step income statement

PW AUDIO SUPPLY, INC.
Income Statement
For the Year Ended December 31, 2014

Sales		
Sales revenue		$480,000
Less: Sales returns and allowances	$12,000	
Sales discounts	8,000	20,000
Net sales		460,000
Cost of goods sold		316,000
Gross profit		144,000
Operating expenses		
Salaries and wages expense	64,000	
Utilities expense	17,000	
Advertising expense	16,000	
Depreciation expense	8,000	
Freight-out	7,000	
Insurance expense	2,000	
Total operating expenses		114,000
Income from operations		30,000
Other revenues and gains		
Interest revenue	3,000	
Gain on disposal of plant assets	600	3,600
Other expenses and losses		
Interest expense	1,800	
Casualty loss from vandalism	200	2,000
Income before income taxes		31,600
Income tax expense		10,100
Net income		$ 21,500

Calculation of gross profit

Calculation of income from operations

Results of activities not related to operations

Do it!

The following information is available for Art Center Corp. for the year ended December 31, 2014.

Other revenues and gains	$ 8,000	Sales revenue	$462,000
Other expenses and losses	3,000	Operating expenses	187,000
Cost of goods sold	147,000	Sales discounts	20,000

Prepare a multiple-step income statement for Art Center Corp. The company has a tax rate of 25%.

MULTIPLE-STEP INCOME STATEMENT

Action Plan

- Subtract cost of goods sold from net sales to determine gross profit.
- Subtract operating expenses from gross profit to determine income from operations.
- Add/subtract nonoperating items to determine income before tax.
- Multiply the tax rate by income before tax to determine tax expense.

The Navigator

Solution

ART CENTER CORP.
Income Statement
For the Year Ended December 31, 2014

Sales		
Sales revenue		$462,000
Sales discounts		20,000
Net sales		442,000
Cost of goods sold		147,000
Gross profit		295,000
Operating expenses		187,000
Income from operations		108,000
Other revenues and gains	$8,000	
Other expenses and losses	3,000	5,000
Income before income taxes		113,000
Income tax expense		28,250
Net income		$ 84,750

Related exercise material: **BE5-5, BE5-6, Do it! 5-3,** and **E5-5.**

DETERMINING COST OF GOODS SOLD UNDER A PERIODIC SYSTEM

LEARNING OBJECTIVE 5
Determine cost of goods sold under a periodic system.

Determining cost of goods sold is different when a periodic inventory system is used rather than a perpetual system. As you have seen, a company using a **perpetual system** makes an entry to record cost of goods sold and to reduce inventory **each time a sale is made.** A company using a **periodic system** does not determine cost of goods sold **until the end of the period.** At the end of the period, the company performs a count to determine the ending balance of inventory. It then **calculates cost of goods sold by subtracting ending inventory from the goods available for sale.** Goods available for sale is the sum of beginning inventory plus purchases, as shown in Illustration 5-12.

Illustration 5-12 Basic formula for cost of goods sold using the periodic system

	Beginning Inventory
+	Cost of Goods Purchased
	Cost of Goods Available for Sale
−	Ending Inventory
	Cost of Goods Sold

Another difference between the two approaches is that the perpetual system directly adjusts the Inventory account for any transaction that affects inventory (such as freight costs, purchase returns, and purchase discounts). The periodic system does not do this. Instead, it creates different accounts for purchases, freight costs, purchase returns, and purchase discounts. These various accounts are shown in Illustration 5-13 (page 247), which presents the calculation of cost of goods sold for PW Audio Supply using the periodic approach. Note that the basic elements from Illustration 5-12 are highlighted in Illustration 5-13. You will learn more in Chapter 6 about how to determine cost of goods sold using the periodic system.

The use of the periodic inventory system does not affect the form of presentation in the balance sheet. As under the perpetual system, a company reports inventory in the current assets section.

Appendix 5A provides further detail on the use of the periodic system.

Illustration 5-13 Cost of goods sold for a merchandiser using a periodic inventory system

PW AUDIO SUPPLY, INC.
Cost of Goods Sold
For the Year Ended December 31, 2014

Cost of goods sold			
Inventory, January 1			$ 36,000
Purchases		$325,000	
Less: Purchase returns and			
allowances	$10,400		
Purchase discounts	6,800	17,200	
Net purchases		307,800	
Add: Freight-in		12,200	
Cost of goods purchased			320,000
Cost of goods available for sale			356,000
Inventory, December 31			40,000
Cost of goods sold			$316,000

Helpful Hint The far right column identifies the primary items that make up cost of goods sold of $316,000. The middle column explains cost of goods purchased of $320,000. The left column reports contra purchase items of $17,200.

Do it!

Aerosmith Company's accounting records show the following at the year-end December 31, 2014.

Purchase Discounts	$ 3,400
Freight-In	6,100
Purchases	162,500
Beginning Inventory	18,000
Ending Inventory	20,000
Purchase Returns and Allowances	5,200

Assuming that Aerosmith Company uses the periodic system, compute (a) cost of goods purchased and (b) cost of goods sold.

COST OF GOODS SOLD–PERIODIC SYSTEM

Solution

(a) Cost of goods purchased = $160,000:

Purchases − Purchase returns and allowances − Purchase discounts + Freight-in

$162,500 − $5,200 − $3,400 + $6,100 = $160,000

(b) Cost of goods sold = $158,000:

Beginning inventory + Cost of goods purchased − Ending inventory

$18,000 + $160,000 − $20,000 = $158,000

Action Plan

• To determine cost of goods purchased, adjust purchases for returns, discounts, and freight-in.
• To determine cost of goods sold, add cost of goods purchased to beginning inventory, and subtract ending inventory.

✔ The Navigator

Related exercise material: **BE5-7, BE5-8, BE5-9, Do it! 5-4, E5-10,** and **E5-11.**

Evaluating Profitability

GROSS PROFIT RATE

A company's gross profit may be expressed as a **percentage** by dividing the amount of gross profit by net sales. This is referred to as the gross profit rate. For PW Audio Supply, the gross profit rate is 31.3% ($144,000 ÷ $460,000).

Analysts generally consider the gross profit **rate** to be more informative than the gross profit **amount** because it expresses a more meaningful (qualitative) relationship between gross profit and net sales. For example, a gross profit amount of $1,000,000 may sound impressive. But if it was the result of sales of $100,000,000, the company's gross profit rate was only 1%. A 1% gross profit rate is acceptable in very few industries. Illustration 5-14 (page 248) demonstrates that gross profit rates differ greatly across industries.

LEARNING OBJECTIVE 6
Explain the factors affecting profitability.

Illustration 5-14 Gross profit rate by industry

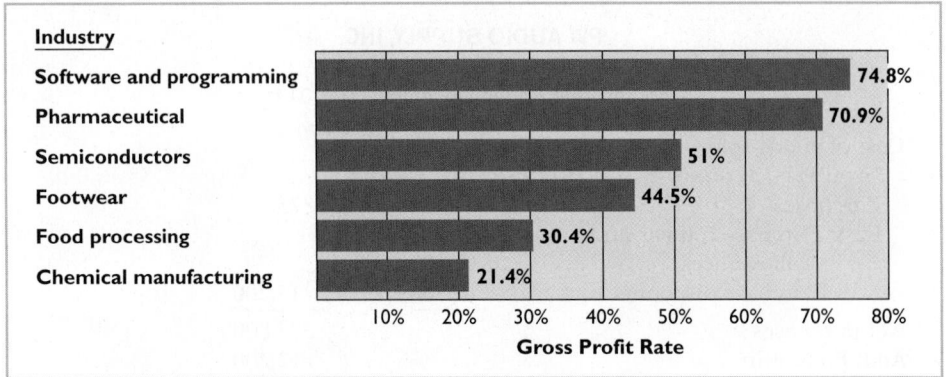

A decline in a company's gross profit rate might have several causes. The company may have begun to sell products with a lower "markup"—for example, budget blue jeans versus designer blue jeans. Increased competition may have resulted in a lower selling price. Or, the company may be forced to pay higher prices to its suppliers without being able to pass these costs on to its customers. The gross profit rates for REI and Dick's Sporting Goods, and the industry average, are presented in Illustration 5-15.

Illustration 5-15 Gross profit rate

Gross Profit Rate = $\dfrac{\text{Gross Profit}}{\text{Net Sales}}$			
REI ($ in thousands)		**Dick's Sporting Goods**	**Industry Average**
2010	2009	2010	2010
$\dfrac{\$728{,}964}{\$1{,}658{,}751} = 43.9\%$	44.7%	29.7%	34.0%

REI's gross profit rate decreased from 44.7% in 2009 to 43.9% in 2010. What might cause changes in REI's gross profit rate? When the economy slows, retailers must reduce selling prices in order to sell merchandise. This cuts into the gross profit rate. Changes in national weather patterns can also affect the amount of time people spend outdoors—and therefore impact their purchases of REI merchandise. For example, if winter provides below-average snow or extreme cold, or if summer is cooler and wetter than normal, then REI will have to discount its goods to sell them.

Why does REI's gross profit rate differ so much from that of Dick's Sporting Goods and the industry average? The gross profit rate often differs across retailers because of differences in the nature of their goods. First, REI focuses on outdoor equipment, while Dick's also sells sporting goods and hunting gear. The markup may differ significantly in these different product sectors. Also, although REI and Dick's both sell outdoor equipment, the quality of the equipment they sell differs. REI tends to sell more "high-end" goods, while Dick's tends to sell goods in a more "affordable" range. Higher-quality goods demand a higher markup. However, the retailer also sells fewer of them. In general, retailers adopt either a high-volume–low-margin approach (e.g., Wal-Mart) or a low-volume–high-margin approach (e.g., Saks Fifth Avenue). The strategic choice is often revealed in differences in the companies' gross profit rate.

 DECISION TOOLKIT

DECISION CHECKPOINTS	INFO NEEDED FOR DECISION	TOOL TO USE FOR DECISION	HOW TO EVALUATE RESULTS
Is the price of goods keeping pace with changes in the cost of inventory?	Gross profit and net sales	$\text{Gross profit rate} = \dfrac{\text{Gross profit}}{\text{Net sales}}$	Higher ratio suggests the average margin between selling price and inventory cost is increasing. Too high a margin may result in lost sales.

PROFIT MARGIN

The **profit margin** measures the percentage of each dollar of sales that results in net income. We compute this ratio by dividing net income by net sales (revenue) for the period.

How do the gross profit rate and profit margin differ? The gross profit rate measures the margin by which selling price exceeds cost of goods sold. **The profit margin measures the extent by which selling price covers all expenses** (including cost of goods sold). A company can improve its profit margin by either increasing its gross profit rate and/or by controlling its operating expenses and other costs. For example, at one time Radio Shack reported increased profit margins which it accomplished by closing stores and slashing costs. While its total sales have been declining, its profitability as measured by its profit margin has increased.

Profit margins vary across industries. Businesses with high turnover, such as grocery stores (Safeway and Kroger) and discount stores (Target and Wal-Mart), generally experience low profit margins. Low-turnover businesses, such as high-end jewelry stores (Tiffany and Co.) or major drug manufacturers (Merck), have high profit margins. Illustration 5-16 shows profit margins from a variety of industries.

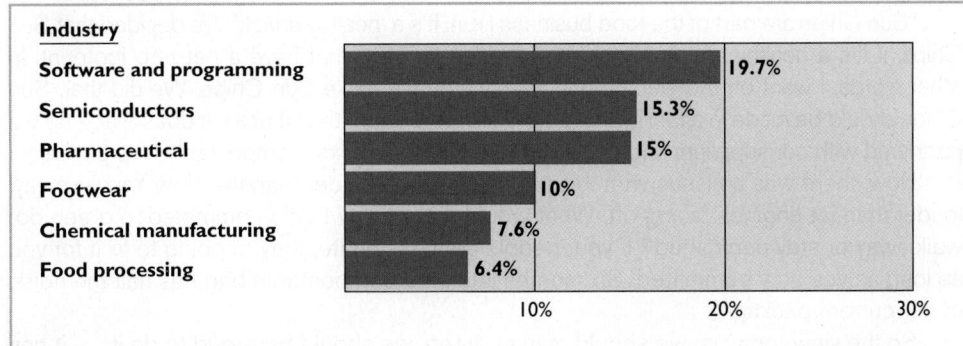

Illustration 5-16 Profit margins by industry

Profit margins for REI and Dick's Sporting Goods and the industry average are presented in Illustration 5-17 (page 250).

REI's profit margin declined from 2.0% to 1.8% between 2009 and 2010. This means that the company generated 1.8¢ of profit on each dollar of sales. This decline occurred partly because the gross profit rate decreased.

Illustration 5-17 Profit margin

Profit Margin = Net Income / Net Sales			
REI ($ in thousands)		**Dick's Sporting Goods**	**Industry Average**
2010	2009	2010	2010
$\frac{\$30,230}{\$1,658,751} = 1.8\%$	2.0%	3.7%	5.1%

A change in the profit margin can be caused by a change in the gross profit rate, a change in the amount of operating expenses relative to sales, or a change in the amount of other items (other revenues and gains, or other expenses and losses) relative to sales. In Illustration 5-8, we can see that neither operating expenses nor other items increased significantly in proportion to sales. (That is, the percentage of these items relative to sales did not change significantly. For example, sales increased by almost 14% in 2010, but operating expenses also increased by a similar amount, so that operating expenses as a percentage of sales in 2010 was about the same as in 2009.) Therefore, in 2010, most of the decline in REI's profit margin occurred because of the decline in the gross profit rate. When the gross profit rate declines, the company has less profit available to cover its operating costs.

How does REI compare to its competitors? Its profit margin was lower than Dick's in 2010 and was less than the industry average. Thus, its profit margin does not suggest exceptional profitability.

Helen Sessions/Alamy

People, Planet, and Profit Insight

Selling Green

Here is a question an executive of PepsiCo was asked: Should PepsiCo market green? The executive indicated that the company should, as he believes it's the No. 1 thing consumers all over the world care about. Here are some of his thoughts on this issue:

"Sun Chips are part of the food business I run. It's a 'healthy snack.' We decided that Sun Chips, if it's a healthy snack, should be made in facilities that have a net-zero footprint. In other words, I want off the electric grid everywhere we make Sun Chips. We did that. Sun Chips should be made in a facility that puts back more water than it uses. It does that. And we partnered with our suppliers and came out with the world's first compostable chip package.

Now, there was an issue with this package: It was louder than the New York subway, louder than jet engines taking off. What would a company that's committed to green do: walk away or stay committed? If your people are passionate, they're going to fix it for you as long as you stay committed. Six months later, the compostable bag has half the noise of our current package.

So the view today is: we should market green, we should be proud to do it . . . it has to be a 360 process, both internal and external. And if you do that, you can monetize environmental sustainability for the shareholders."

Source: "Four Problems–and Solutions," *Wall Street Journal* (March 7, 2011), p. R2.

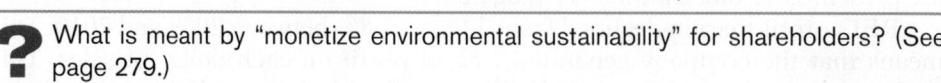

? What is meant by "monetize environmental sustainability" for shareholders? (See page 279.)

DECISION TOOLKIT

DECISION CHECKPOINTS	INFO NEEDED FOR DECISION	TOOL TO USE FOR DECISION	HOW TO EVALUATE RESULTS
Is the company maintaining an adequate margin between sales and expenses?	Net income and net sales	$\text{Profit margin} = \dfrac{\text{Net income}}{\text{Net sales}}$	Higher value suggests favorable return on each dollar of sales.

KEEPING AN EYE ON CASH

In Chapter 4, you learned that **earnings have high quality if they provide a full and transparent depiction of how a company performed**. In order to quickly assess earnings quality, analysts sometimes employ the quality of earnings ratio. It is calculated as net cash provided by operating activities divided by net income.

LEARNING OBJECTIVE 7

Identify a quality of earnings indicator.

$$\text{Quality of Earnings Ratio} = \frac{\text{Net Cash Provided by Operating Activities}}{\text{Net Income}}$$

In general, a measure significantly less than 1 suggests that a company may be using more aggressive accounting techniques in order to accelerate income recognition (record income in earlier periods). A measure significantly greater than 1 suggests that a company is using conservative accounting techniques, which cause it to delay the recognition of income.

Measures that are significantly less than 1 do not provide definitive evidence of low-quality earnings. Low measures do, however, indicate that analysts should investigate the company's earnings quality by evaluating the causes of the difference between net income and net cash provided by operating activities. Examples of factors that would cause differences are presented in Chapter 4 (pages 191–192).

Here are recent quality of earnings ratios for a number of well-known companies, all of which have measures in excess of 1.

Company Name ($ in millions)	Net Cash Provided by Operating Activities	÷ Net Income	= Quality of Earnings Ratio
DuPont	$4,741	$1,769	2.7
Intel	$11,170	$4,369	2.6
Nike	$1,736	$1,487	1.2
Microsoft	$19,037	$14,569	1.3
Wal-Mart	$26,249	$14,335	1.8

 USING THE DECISION TOOLKIT

Like REI, Mountain Equipment Cooperative (MEC) is a retailer of outdoor equipment organized as a cooperative (though MEC *only* sells to its members, who pay a one-time fee of $5). Also like REI, MEC has a significant commitment to sustainability. Many of its stores employ state-of-the-art building techniques to minimize energy use, and it pledges 1% of annual sales revenue to environmental causes. Since MEC is a Canadian company, it follows International Financial Reporting Standards (IFRS) rather than U.S. GAAP. The *A Look at IFRS* section at the end of each chapter of this textbook discusses some of the main accounting differences that you would need to be aware of to make a thorough comparison of REI and MEC. Here is recent data for MEC.

| | Year ended | |
($ in thousands)	12/26/10	12/27/09
Net income	$ 815	$ 300
Sales revenue	261,374	262,056
Cost of goods sold	174,871	175,606

Instructions

Using the basic facts in the table, evaluate the following components of MEC's profitability for the years ended December 26, 2010, and December 27, 2009.

> Profit margin
> Gross profit rate

How do MEC's profit margin and gross profit rate compare to those of REI and Dick's Sporting Goods for 2010?

Solution

| | Year ended | |
($ in thousands)	12/26/10	12/27/09
Profit margin	$\dfrac{\$815}{\$261,374} = 0.3\%$	$\dfrac{\$300}{\$262,056} = 0.1\%$
Gross profit rate	$\dfrac{\$86,503^*}{\$261,374} = 33.1\%$	$\dfrac{\$86,450^{**}}{\$262,056} = 33.0\%$

*$261,374 − $174,871   **$262,056 − $175,606

MEC's profit margin (income per dollar of sales) increased from 0.1% to 0.3%. This is well below both REI's (1.8%) and Dick's (3.7%). Thus, MEC is not as effective at turning its sales into net income as these two competitors.

MEC's gross profit rate improved from 33.0% to 33.1%. This suggests that its ability to maintain its markup above its cost of goods sold improved slightly during this period. MEC's gross profit rate of 33.1% is lower than REI's (43.9%) but higher than Dick's (29.7%). Dick's gross profit is depressed by the fact that it sells many low-margin products. REI is superior to MEC both in its ability to maintain its markup above its costs of goods sold (its gross profit rate) and in its ability to control operating costs (its profit margin).

The Navigator

Summary of Learning Objectives

1 Identify the differences between a service company and a merchandising company. Because of the presence of inventory, a merchandising company has sales revenue, cost of goods sold, and gross profit. To account for inventory, a merchandising company must choose between a perpetual inventory system and a periodic inventory system.

2 Explain the recording of purchases under a perpetual inventory system. The Inventory account is debited for all purchases of merchandise and for freight costs, and it is credited for purchase discounts and purchase returns and allowances.

3 Explain the recording of sales revenues under a perpetual inventory system. When inventory is sold, Accounts Receivable (or Cash) is debited and Sales

Revenue is credited for the selling price of the merchandise. At the same time, Cost of Goods Sold is debited and Inventory is credited for the cost of inventory items sold. Separate contra revenue accounts are maintained for Sales Returns and Allowances and Sales Discounts. These accounts are debited as needed to record returns, allowances, or discounts related to the sale.

4 Distinguish between a single-step and a multiple-step income statement. In a single-step income statement, companies classify all data under two categories, revenues or expenses, and net income is determined in one step. A multiple-step income statement shows numerous steps in determining net income, including results of nonoperating activities.

5 **Determine cost of goods sold under a periodic system.** The periodic system uses multiple accounts to keep track of transactions that affect inventory. To determine cost of goods sold, first calculate cost of goods purchased by adjusting purchases for returns, allowances, discounts, and freight-in. Then calculate cost of goods sold by adding cost of goods purchased to beginning inventory and subtracting ending inventory.

6 **Explain the factors affecting profitability.** Profitability is affected by gross profit, as measured by the gross profit rate, and by management's ability to control costs, as measured by the profit margin.

7 **Identify a quality of earnings indicator.** Earnings have high quality if they provide a full and transparent depiction of how a company performed. An indicator of the quality of earnings is the quality of earnings ratio, which is net cash provided by operating activities divided by net income. Measures above 1 suggest the company is employing conservative accounting practices. Measures significantly below 1 might suggest the company is using aggressive accounting to accelerate the recognition of income.

✔ The Navigator

 DECISION TOOLKIT *A SUMMARY*

DECISION CHECKPOINTS	INFO NEEDED FOR DECISION	TOOL TO USE FOR DECISION	HOW TO EVALUATE RESULTS
Is the price of goods keeping pace with changes in the cost of inventory?	Gross profit and net sales	$\text{Gross profit rate} = \dfrac{\text{Gross profit}}{\text{Net sales}}$	Higher ratio suggests the average margin between selling price and inventory cost is increasing. Too high a margin may result in lost sales.
Is the company maintaining an adequate margin between sales and expenses?	Net income and net sales	$\text{Profit margin} = \dfrac{\text{Net income}}{\text{Net sales}}$	Higher value suggests favorable return on each dollar of sales.

Appendix 5A

Periodic Inventory System

As described in this chapter, companies may use one of two basic systems of accounting for inventories: (1) the perpetual inventory system or (2) the periodic inventory system. In the chapter, we focused on the characteristics of the perpetual inventory system. In this appendix, we discuss and illustrate the **periodic inventory system**. One key difference between the two systems is the point at which the company computes cost of goods sold. For a visual reminder of this difference, you may want to refer back to Illustration 5-4 on page 232.

> **LEARNING OBJECTIVE** **8**
> Explain the recording of purchases and sales of inventory under a periodic inventory system.

RECORDING MERCHANDISE TRANSACTIONS

In a **periodic inventory system**, companies record revenues from the sale of merchandise when sales are made, just as in a perpetual system. Unlike the perpetual system, however, companies **do not attempt on the date of sale to record the cost of the merchandise sold**. Instead, they take a physical inventory count at the **end of the period** to determine (1) the cost of the merchandise then on hand and (2) the cost of the goods sold during the period. And, **under a periodic system**, **companies record purchases of merchandise in the Purchases account rather than the Inventory account**. Also, in a periodic system, purchase returns and allowances, purchase discounts, and freight costs on purchases are recorded in separate accounts.

To illustrate the recording of merchandise transactions under a periodic inventory system, we will use purchase/sale transactions between PW Audio Supply, Inc. and Sauk Stereo, as illustrated for the perpetual inventory system in this chapter.

RECORDING PURCHASES OF MERCHANDISE

On the basis of the sales invoice (Illustration 5-5, shown on page 234) and receipt of the merchandise ordered from PW Audio Supply, Sauk Stereo records the $3,800 purchase as follows.

May	4	Purchases	3,800	
		Accounts Payable		3,800
		(To record goods purchased on account		
		from PW Audio Supply)		

Purchases is a temporary account whose normal balance is a debit.

FREIGHT COSTS

When the purchaser directly incurs the freight costs, it debits the account Freight-In (or Transportation-In). For example, if Sauk Stereo pays Public Freight Company $150 for freight charges on its purchase from PW Audio Supply on May 6, the entry on Sauk Stereo's books is:

May	6	Freight-In (Transportation-In)	150	
		Cash		150
		(To record payment of freight on		
		goods purchased)		

Like Purchases, Freight-In is a temporary account whose normal balance is a debit. **Freight-In is part of cost of goods purchased.** The reason is that cost of goods purchased should include any freight charges necessary to bring the goods to the purchaser. Freight costs are not subject to a purchase discount. Purchase discounts apply on the invoice cost of the merchandise.

Purchase Returns and Allowances

Because $300 of merchandise received from PW Audio Supply is inoperable, Sauk Stereo returns the goods and prepares the following entry to recognize the return.

May	8	Accounts Payable	300	
		Purchase Returns and Allowances		300
		(To record return of goods purchased		
		from PW Audio Supply)		

Purchase Returns and Allowances is a temporary account whose normal balance is a credit.

Purchase Discounts

On May 14, Sauk Stereo pays the balance due on account to PW Audio Supply, taking the 2% cash discount allowed by PW Audio Supply for payment within 10 days. Sauk Stereo records the payment and discount as follows.

May	14	Accounts Payable ($3,800 − $300)	3,500	
		Purchase Discounts ($3,500 ×.02)		70
		Cash		3,430
		(To record payment within the		
		discount period)		

Purchase Discounts is a temporary account whose normal balance is a credit.

RECORDING SALES OF MERCHANDISE

The seller, PW Audio Supply, records the sale of $3,800 of merchandise to Sauk Stereo on May 4 (sales invoice No. 731, Illustration 5-5, page 234) as follows.

May	4	Accounts Receivable	3,800	
		Sales Revenue		3,800
		(To record credit sales to Sauk Stereo per invoice #731)		

Sales Returns and Allowances

To record the returned goods received from Sauk Stereo on May 8, PW Audio Supply records the $300 sales return as follows.

May	8	Sales Returns and Allowances	300	
		Accounts Receivable		300
		(To record credit granted to Sauk Stereo for returned goods)		

Sales Discounts

On May 14, PW Audio Supply receives payment of $3,430 on account from Sauk Stereo. PW Audio Supply honors the 2% cash discount and records the payment of Sauk Stereo's account receivable in full as follows.

May	14	Cash	3,430	
		Sales Discounts ($3,500 × .02)	70	
		Accounts Receivable ($3,800 − $300)		3,500
		(To record collection within 2/10, n/30 discount period from Sauk Stereo)		

COMPARISON OF ENTRIES–PERPETUAL vs. PERIODIC

ENTRIES ON SAUK STEREO'S BOOKS

	Transaction	Perpetual Inventory System		Periodic Inventory System	

May 4	Purchase of merchandise on credit.	Inventory
		  Accounts Payable
			3,800
			3,800
				Purchases
				  Accounts Payable
					3,800
					3,800

May 6	Freight costs on purchases.	Inventory
		  Cash
			150
			150
				Freight-In
				  Cash
					150
					150

May 8	Purchase returns and allowances.	Accounts Payable
		  Inventory
			300
			300
				Accounts Payable
				  Purchase Returns
				    and Allowances
					300
					300

May 14	Payment on account with a discount.	Accounts Payable
		  Cash
		  Inventory
			3,500
			3,430
			70
				Accounts Payable
				  Cash
				  Purchase Discounts
					3,500
					3,430
					70

ENTRIES ON PW AUDIO SUPPLY'S BOOKS

	Transaction	Perpetual Inventory System		Periodic Inventory System	

May 4	Sale of merchandise on credit.	Accounts Receivable
		  Sales Revenue
			3,800
			3,800
				Accounts Receivable
				  Sales Revenue
					3,800
					3,800

		Cost of Goods Sold Inventory	2,400 2,400	No entry for cost of goods sold	

May 8	Return of merchandise sold.	Sales Returns and Allowances
		  Accounts Receivable
			300
			300
				Sales Returns and Allowances
				  Accounts Receivable
					300
					300

		Inventory Cost of Goods Sold	140 140	No entry	

May 14	Cash received on account with a discount.	Cash
		Sales Discounts
		  Accounts Receivable
			3,430
			70
			3,500
				Cash
				Sales Discounts
				  Accounts Receivable
					3,430
					70
					3,500

Summary of Learning Objective for Appendix 5A

8 **Explain the recording of purchases and sales of inventory under a periodic inventory system.** To record purchases, entries are required for (a) cash and credit purchases, (b) purchase returns and allowances, (c) purchase discounts, and (d) freight costs. To record sales, entries are required for (a) cash and credit sales, (b) sales returns and allowances, and (c) sales discounts.

Glossary

Contra revenue account *(p. 240)* An account that is offset against a revenue account on the income statement.

Cost of goods sold *(p. 230)* The total cost of merchandise sold during the period.

Gross profit *(p. 243)* The excess of net sales over the cost of goods sold.

Gross profit rate *(p. 247)* Gross profit expressed as a percentage by dividing the amount of gross profit by net sales.

Net sales *(p. 243)* Sales less sales returns and allowances and sales discounts.

Periodic inventory system *(p. 232)* An inventory system in which a company does not maintain detailed records of goods on hand throughout the period and determines the cost of goods sold only at the end of an accounting period.

Perpetual inventory system *(p. 232)* A detailed inventory system in which a company maintains the cost of each inventory item, and the records continuously show the inventory that should be on hand.

Profit margin *(p. 249)* Measures the percentage of each dollar of sales that results in net income, computed by dividing net income by net sales.

Purchase allowance *(p. 236)* A deduction made to the selling price of merchandise, granted by the seller, so that the buyer will keep the merchandise.

Purchase discount *(p. 236)* A cash discount claimed by a buyer for prompt payment of a balance due.

Purchase invoice *(p. 233)* A document that provides support for each purchase.

Purchase return *(p. 236)* A return of goods from the buyer to the seller for cash or credit.

Quality of earnings ratio *(p. 251)* A measure used to indicate the extent to which a company's earnings provide a full and transparent depiction of its performance; computed as net cash provided by operating activities divided by net income.

Sales discount *(p. 240)* A reduction given by a seller for prompt payment of a credit sale.

Sales invoice *(p. 238)* A document that provides support for each sale.

Sales returns and allowances *(p. 239)* Transactions in which the seller either accepts goods back from the purchaser (a return) or grants a reduction in the purchase price (an allowance) so that the buyer will keep the goods.

Sales revenue *(p. 230)* Primary source of revenue for a merchandising company.

Comprehensive Do it!

The adjusted trial balance for the year ended December 31, 2014, for Dykstra Company is shown below.

DYKSTRA COMPANY
Adjusted Trial Balance
For the Year Ended December 31, 2014

	Dr.	Cr.
Cash	$ 14,500	
Accounts Receivable	11,100	
Inventory	29,000	
Prepaid Insurance	2,500	
Equipment	95,000	
Accumulated Depreciation—Equipment		$ 18,000
Notes Payable		25,000
Accounts Payable		10,600
Common Stock		70,000
Retained Earnings		11,000
Dividends	12,000	

	Dr.	Cr.
Sales Revenue		$536,800
Sales Returns and Allowances	$ 6,700	
Sales Discounts	5,000	
Cost of Goods Sold	363,400	
Freight-Out	7,600	
Advertising Expense	12,000	
Salaries and Wages Expense	56,000	
Utilities Expense	18,000	
Rent Expense	24,000	
Depreciation Expense	9,000	
Insurance Expense	4,500	
Interest Expense	3,600	
Interest Revenue		2,500
	$673,900	$673,900

Instructions

Prepare a multiple-step income statement for Dykstra Company. Assume a tax rate of 30 percent.

Solution to Comprehensive Do it!

DYKSTRA COMPANY
Income Statement
For the Year Ended December 31, 2014

Sales		
Sales revenue		$536,800
Less: Sales returns and allowances	$ 6,700	
Sales discounts	5,000	11,700
Net sales		525,100
Cost of goods sold		363,400
Gross profit		161,700
Operating expenses		
Salaries and wages expense	56,000	
Rent expense	24,000	
Utilities expense	18,000	
Advertising expense	12,000	
Depreciation expense	9,000	
Freight-out	7,600	
Insurance expense	4,500	
Total operating expenses		131,100
Income from operations		30,600
Other revenues and gains		
Interest revenue		2,500
Other expenses and losses		
Interest expense		3,600
Income before income taxes		29,500
Income tax expense		8,850
Net income		$ 20,650

Action Plan

• In preparing the income statement, remember that the key components are net sales, cost of goods sold, gross profit, total operating expenses, other revenues and gains, other expenses and losses, income tax expense, and net income (loss). These components are reported in the right-hand column of the income statement.

• Present nonoperating items after income from operations.

The Navigator

Self-Test, Brief Exercises, Exercises, Problem Set A, and many more resources are available for practice in WileyPLUS.

Note: All Questions, Exercises, and Problems marked with an asterisk relate to material in the appendix to the chapter.

Self-Test Questions

Answers are on page 279.

(LO 1) **1.** Which of the following statements about a periodic inventory system is **true**?
  (a) Companies determine cost of goods sold only at the end of the accounting period.
  (b) Companies continuously maintain detailed records of the cost of each inventory purchase and sale.
  (c) The periodic system provides better control over inventories than a perpetual system.
  (d) The increased use of computerized systems has increased the use of the periodic system.

(LO 2) **2.** Which of the following items does **not** result in an adjustment in the Inventory account under a perpetual system?
  (a) A purchase of merchandise.
  (b) A return of merchandise to the supplier.
  (c) Payment of freight costs for goods shipped to a customer.
  (d) Payment of freight costs for goods received from a supplier.

(LO 3) **3.** Which sales accounts normally have a debit balance?
  (a) Sales discounts.
  (b) Sales returns and allowances.
  (c) Both (a) and (b).
  (d) Neither (a) nor (b).

(LO 3) **4.** A company makes a credit sale of $750 on June 13, terms 2/10, n/30, on which it grants a return of $50 on June 16. What amount is received as payment in full on June 23?
  (a) $700.   (c) $685.
  (b) $686.   (d) $650.

(LO 3) **5.** To record the sale of goods for cash in a perpetual inventory system:
  (a) only one journal entry is necessary to record cost of goods sold and reduction of inventory.
  (b) only one journal entry is necessary to record the receipt of cash and the sales revenue.
  (c) two journal entries are necessary: one to record the receipt of cash and sales revenue, and one to record the cost of goods sold and reduction of inventory.
  (d) two journal entries are necessary: one to record the receipt of cash and reduction of inventory, and one to record the cost of goods sold and sales revenue.

(LO 4) **6.** Gross profit will result if:
  (a) operating expenses are less than net income.
  (b) sales revenues are greater than operating expenses.
  (c) sales revenues are greater than cost of goods sold.
  (d) operating expenses are greater than cost of goods sold.

7. If sales revenues are $400,000, cost of goods sold is (LO 4) $310,000, and operating expenses are $60,000, what is the gross profit?
  (a) $30,000.   (c) $340,000.
  (b) $90,000.   (d) $400,000.

8. The multiple-step income statement for a merchan- (LO 4) dising company shows each of these features **except**:
  (a) gross profit.
  (b) cost of goods sold.
  (c) a sales section.
  (d) All of these are present.

9. If beginning inventory is $60,000, cost of goods (LO 5) purchased is $380,000, and ending inventory is $50,000, what is cost of goods sold under a periodic system?
  (a) $390,000.
  (b) $370,000.
  (c) $330,000.
  (d) $420,000.

10. Bufford Corporation had reported the follow- (LO 5) ing amounts at December 31, 2014: sales revenue $184,000; ending inventory $11,600; beginning inventory $17,200; purchases $60,400; purchase discounts $3,000; purchase returns and allowances $1,100; freight-in $600; freight-out $900. Calculate the cost of goods available for sale.
  (a) $69,400.   (c) $56,900.
  (b) $74,100.   (d) $197,700.

11. Which of the following would affect the (LO 6) gross profit rate? (Assume sales remains constant.)
  (a) An increase in advertising expense.
  (b) A decrease in depreciation expense.
  (c) An increase in cost of goods sold.
  (d) A decrease in insurance expense.

12. The gross profit rate is equal to: (LO 6)
  (a) net income divided by sales.
  (b) cost of goods sold divided by sales.
  (c) net sales minus cost of goods sold, divided by net sales.
  (d) sales minus cost of goods sold, divided by cost of goods sold.

13. During the year ended December 31, 2014, Bjornstad (LO 6) Corporation had the following results: sales revenue $267,000; cost of good sold $107,000; net income $92,400; operating expenses $55,400; net cash provided by operating activities $108,950. What was the company's profit margin?
  (a) 40%.   (c) 20.5%.
  (b) 60%.   (d) 34.6%.

(LO 7) **14.** A quality of earnings ratio:
   (a) is computed as net income divided by net cash provided by operating activities.
   (b) that is less than 1 indicates that a company might be using aggressive accounting tactics.
   (c) that is greater than 1 indicates that a company might be using aggressive accounting tactics.
   (d) is computed as net cash provided by operating activities divided by total assets.

*15. When goods are purchased for resale by a company (LO 8) using a periodic inventory system:
   (a) purchases on account are debited to Inventory.
   (b) purchases on account are debited to Purchases.
   (c) purchase returns are debited to Purchase Returns and Allowances.
   (d) freight costs are debited to Purchases.

Go to the book's companion website, **www.wiley.com/college/kimmel**, to access additional Self-Test Questions.

Questions

1. (a) "The steps in the accounting cycle for a merchandising company differ from the steps in the accounting cycle for a service company." Do you agree or disagree?
   (b) Is the measurement of net income in a merchandising company conceptually the same as in a service company? Explain.

2. How do the components of revenues and expenses differ between a merchandising company and a service company?

3. Laurie Massoth, CEO of Bargain Den Stores, is considering a recommendation made by both the company's purchasing manager and director of finance that the company should invest in a sophisticated new perpetual inventory system to replace its periodic system. Explain the primary difference between the two systems, and discuss the potential benefits of a perpetual inventory system.

4. (a) Explain the income measurement process in a merchandising company.
   (b) How does income measurement differ between a merchandising company and a service company?

5. Dillard Co. has sales revenue of $100,000, cost of goods sold of $70,000, and operating expenses of $18,000. What is its gross profit?

6. Angie Milner believes revenues from credit sales may be recorded before they are collected in cash. Do you agree? Explain.

7. (a) What is the primary source document for recording (1) cash sales and (2) credit sales?
   (b) Using XXs for amounts, give the journal entry for each of the transactions in part (a), assuming perpetual inventory.

8. A credit sale is made on July 10 for $900, terms 1/15, n/30. On July 12, the purchaser returns $100 of goods for credit. Give the journal entry on July 19 to record the receipt of the balance due within the discount period.

9. As the end of Petit Company's fiscal year approached, it became clear that the company had considerable excess inventory. Ronald Morel, the head of marketing and sales, ordered salespeople to "add 20% more units to each order that you ship. The custom-ers can always ship the extra back next period if they decide they don't want it. We've got to do it to meet this year's sales goal." Discuss the accounting implications of Ronald's action.

10. To encourage bookstores to buy a broader range of book titles and to discourage price discounting, the publishing industry allows bookstores to return unsold books to the publisher. This results in very significant returns each year. To ensure proper recognition of revenues, how should publishing companies account for these returns?

11. Goods costing $1,900 are purchased on account on July 15 with credit terms of 2/10, n/30. On July 18, the purchaser receives a $300 credit from the supplier for damaged goods. Give the journal entry on July 24 to record payment of the balance due within the discount period.

12. Scribner Company reports net sales of $800,000, gross profit of $560,000, and net income of $230,000. What are its operating expenses?

13. Luo Company has always provided its customers with payment terms of 1/10, n/30. Members of its sale force have commented that competitors are offering customers 2/10, n/45. Explain what these terms mean, and discuss the implications to Luo of switching its payment terms to those of its competitors.

14. In its year-end earnings announcement press release, Brantley Corp. announced that its earnings increased by $15 million relative to the previous year. This represented a 20% increase. Inspection of its income statement reveals that the company reported a $20 million gain under "Other revenues and gains" from the sale of one of its factories. Discuss the implications of this gain from the perspective of a potential investor.

15. Identify the distinguishing features of an income statement for a merchandising company.

16. Why is the normal operating cycle for a merchandising company likely to be longer than for a service company?

17. What title does Tootsie Roll use for gross profit? How did it present gross profit? By how much did its total gross profit change, and in what direction, in 2011?

18. What merchandising account(s) will appear in the post-closing trial balance?

19. What types of businesses are most likely to use a perpetual inventory system?

20. Identify the accounts that are added to or deducted from purchases to determine the cost of goods purchased under a periodic system. For each account, indicate (a) whether it is added or deducted, and (b) its normal balance.

21. In the following cases, use a periodic inventory system to identify the item(s) designated by the letters X and Y.
    (a) Purchases $-X - Y =$ Net purchases.
    (b) Cost of goods purchased $-$ Net purchases $= X$.
    (c) Beginning inventory $+ X =$ Cost of goods available for sale.
    (d) Cost of goods available for sale $-$ Cost of goods sold $= X$.

22. ◖▬▬◗ What two ratios measure factors that affect profitability?

23. ◖▬▬◗ What factors affect a company's gross profit rate—that is, what can cause the gross profit rate to increase and what can cause it to decrease?

24. ◀▬ Mark Elarton, director of marketing, wants to reduce the selling price of his company's products by 15% to increase market share. He says, "I know this will reduce our gross profit rate, but the increased number of units sold will make up for the lost margin." Before this action is taken, what other factors does the company need to consider?

25. George Mallein is considering investing in Wigginton Pet Food Company. Wigginton's net income increased considerably during the most recent year even though many other companies in the same industry reported disappointing earnings. George wants to know whether the company's earnings provide a reasonable depiction of its results. What initial step can George take to help determine whether he needs to investigate further?

*26. On July 15, a company purchases on account goods costing $1,900, with credit terms of 2/10, n/30. On July 18, the company receives a $400 credit memo from the supplier for damaged goods. Give the journal entry on July 24 to record payment of the balance due within the discount period assuming a periodic inventory system.

Brief Exercises

Compute missing amounts in determining net income.
(LO 1, 4), AP

BE5-1 Presented here are the components in Casilla Company's income statement. Determine the missing amounts.

Sales Revenue	Cost of Goods Sold	Gross Profit	Operating Expenses	Net Income
$ 71,200	(b)	$ 30,000	(d)	$12,100
$108,000	$70,000	(c)	(e)	$29,500
(a)	$71,900	$109,600	$46,200	(f)

Journalize perpetual inventory entries.
(LO 2, 3), AP

BE5-2 Gerish Company buys merchandise on account from Mangus Company. The selling price of the goods is $900 and the cost of the goods sold is $590. Both companies use perpetual inventory systems. Journalize the transactions on the books of both companies.

Journalize sales transactions.
(LO 3), AP

BE5-3 Prepare the journal entries to record the following transactions on Horst Company's books using a perpetual inventory system.
(a) On March 2, Horst Company sold $800,000 of merchandise to Bernadina Company, terms 2/10, n/30. The cost of the merchandise sold was $540,000.
(b) On March 6, Bernadina Company returned $140,000 of the merchandise purchased on March 2. The cost of the merchandise returned was $94,000.
(c) On March 12, Horst Company received the balance due from Bernadina Company.

Journalize purchase transactions.
(LO 2), AP

BE5-4 From the information in BE5-3, prepare the journal entries to record these transactions on Bernadina Company's books under a perpetual inventory system.

Prepare sales section of income statement.
(LO 4), AP

BE5-5 Alvarado Company provides this information for the month ended October 31, 2014: sales on credit $300,000; cash sales $150,000; sales discounts $5,000; and sales returns and allowances $19,000. Prepare the sales section of the income statement based on this information.

Identify placement of items on a multiple-step income statement.
(LO 4), AP

BE5-6 Explain where each of these items would appear on a multiple-step income statement: gain on disposal of plant assets; cost of goods sold; depreciation expense; and sales returns and allowances.

Determine cost of goods sold using basic periodic formula.
(LO 5), AP

BE5-7 Sands Company sold goods with a total selling price of $800,000 during the year. It purchased goods for $380,000 and had beginning inventory of $67,000. A count of its ending inventory determined that goods on hand was $50,000. What was its cost of goods sold?

BE5-8 Assume that Tracy Company uses a periodic inventory system and has these account balances: Purchases $404,000; Purchase Returns and Allowances $13,000; Purchase Discounts $9,000; and Freight-In $16,000. Determine net purchases and cost of goods purchased.

Compute net purchases and cost of goods purchased.
(LO 5), AP

BE5-9 Assume the same information as in BE5-8 and also that Tracy Company has beginning inventory of $60,000, ending inventory of $90,000, and net sales of $612,000. Determine the amounts to be reported for cost of goods sold and gross profit.

Compute cost of goods sold and gross profit.
(LO 5), C

BE5-10 Durbin Corporation reported net sales of $250,000, cost of goods sold of $150,000, operating expenses of $50,000, net income of $32,500, beginning total assets of $520,000, and ending total assets of $600,000. Calculate each of the following values and explain what they mean: (a) profit margin and (b) gross profit rate.

Calculate profitability ratios.
(LO 6), AP

BE5-11 Barten Corporation reported net sales $800,000; cost of goods sold $520,000; operating expenses $210,000; and net income $68,000. Calculate the following values and explain what they mean: (a) profit margin and (b) gross profit rate.

Calculate profitability ratios.
(LO 6), AP

BE5-12 Moritz Corporation reported net income of $346,000, cash of $67,800, and net cash provided by operating activities of $221,200. What does this suggest about the quality of the company's earnings? What further steps should be taken?

Evaluate quality of earnings.
(LO 7), C

*BE5-13 Prepare the journal entries to record these transactions on Kimbrel Company's books using a periodic inventory system.
(a) On March 2, Kimbrel Company purchased $800,000 of merchandise from Pineda Company, terms 2/10, n/30.
(b) On March 6, Kimbrel Company returned $95,000 of the merchandise purchased on March 2.
(c) On March 12, Kimbrel Company paid the balance due to Pineda Company.

Journalize purchase transactions.
(LO 8), AP

Do it! Review

Do it! 5-1 On October 5, Narveson Company buys merchandise on account from Rossi Company. The selling price of the goods is $5,000, and the cost to Rossi Company is $3,000. On October 8, Narveson returns defective goods with a selling price of $640 and a scrap value of $240. Record the transactions of Narveson Company, assuming a perpetual approach.

Record transactions of purchasing company.
(LO 2), AP

Do it! 5-2 Assume information similar to that in 5-1. That is: On October 5, Narveson Company buys merchandise on account from Rossi Company. The selling price of the goods is $5,000, and the cost to Rossi Company is $3,000. On October 8, Narveson returns defective goods with a selling price of $640 and a scrap value of $240. Record the transactions on the books of Rossi Company, assuming a perpetual approach.

Record transactions of selling company.
(LO 3), AP

Do it! 5-3 The following information is available for Vogt Corp. for the year ended December 31, 2014:

Other revenues and gains	$ 12,700	Sales revenue	$592,000
Other expenses and losses	13,300	Operating expenses	186,000
Cost of goods sold	156,000	Sales returns and allowances	40,000

Prepare a multiple-step income statement for Vogt Corp. The company has a tax rate of 30%.

Prepare multiple-step income statement.
(LO 4), AP

Do it! 5-4 Mountain Lake Corporation's accounting records show the following at year-end December 31, 2014:

Purchase Discounts	$ 5,900	Beginning Inventory	$31,720
Freight-In	8,400	Ending Inventory	27,950
Freight-Out	11,100	Purchase Returns and	
Purchases	162,500	Allowances	3,600

Assuming that Mountain Lake Corporation uses the periodic system, compute (a) cost of goods purchased and (b) cost of goods sold.

Determine cost of goods sold using periodic system.
(LO 5), AP

Exercises

Journalize purchase transactions.
(LO 2), **AP**

E5-1 This information relates to Crisp Co.
1. On April 5, purchased merchandise from Frost Company for $28,000, terms 2/10, n/30.
2. On April 6, paid freight costs of $700 on merchandise purchased from Frost.
3. On April 7, purchased equipment on account for $30,000.
4. On April 8, returned $3,600 of April 5 merchandise to Frost Company.
5. On April 15, paid the amount due to Frost Company in full.

Instructions
(a) Prepare the journal entries to record the transactions listed above on Crisp Co.'s books. Crisp Co. uses a perpetual inventory system.
(b) Assume that Crisp Co. paid the balance due to Frost Company on May 4 instead of April 15. Prepare the journal entry to record this payment.

Journalize perpetual inventory entries.
(LO 2, 3), **AP**

E5-2 Assume that on September 1, Office Depot had an inventory that included a variety of calculators. The company uses a perpetual inventory system. During September, these transactions occurred.

Sept.	6	Purchased calculators from Dragoo Co. at a total cost of $1,650, terms n/30.
	9	Paid freight of $50 on calculators purchased from Dragoo Co.
	10	Returned calculators to Dragoo Co. for $66 credit because they did not meet specifications.
	12	Sold calculators costing $520 for $690 to Fryer Book Store, terms n/30.
	14	Granted credit of $45 to Fryer Book Store for the return of one calculator that was not ordered. The calculator cost $34.
	20	Sold calculators costing $570 for $760 to Heasley Card Shop, terms n/30.

Instructions
Journalize the September transactions.

Journalize sales transactions.
(LO 3), **AP**

E5-3 The following transactions are for Solarte Company.
1. On December 3, Solarte Company sold $500,000 of merchandise to Rooney Co., terms 1/10, n/30. The cost of the merchandise sold was $330,000.
2. On December 8, Rooney Co. was granted an allowance of $25,000 for merchandise purchased on December 3.
3. On December 13, Solarte Company received the balance due from Rooney Co.

Instructions
(a) Prepare the journal entries to record these transactions on the books of Solarte Company. Solarte uses a perpetual inventory system.
(b) Assume that Solarte Company received the balance due from Rooney Co. on January 2 of the following year instead of December 13. Prepare the journal entry to record the receipt of payment on January 2.

Journalize perpetual inventory entries.
(LO 2, 3), **AP**

E5-4 On June 10, Purcey Company purchased $9,000 of merchandise from Guyer Company, terms 3/10, n/30. Purcey pays the freight costs of $400 on June 11. Goods totaling $600 are returned to Guyer for credit on June 12. On June 19, Purcey Company pays Guyer Company in full, less the purchase discount. Both companies use a perpetual inventory system.

Instructions
(a) Prepare separate entries for each transaction on the books of Purcey Company.
(b) Prepare separate entries for each transaction for Guyer Company. The merchandise purchased by Purcey on June 10 cost Guyer $5,000, and the goods returned cost Guyer $310.

Prepare sales section of income statement.
(LO 4), **AP**

E5-5 The adjusted trial balance of Hodges Company shows these data pertaining to sales at the end of its fiscal year, October 31, 2014: Sales Revenue $900,000; Freight-Out $14,000; Sales Returns and Allowances $22,000; and Sales Discounts $13,500.

Instructions
Prepare the sales section of the income statement.

E5-6 Presented below is information for Zhou Co. for the month of January 2014.

Cost of goods sold	$212,000	Rent expense	$ 32,000
Freight-out	7,000	Sales discounts	8,000
Insurance expense	12,000	Sales returns and allowances	20,000
Salaries and wages expense	60,000	Sales revenue	370,000

Prepare an income statement and calculate profitability ratios.
(LO 4, 6), **AP**

Instructions
(a) Prepare an income statement using the format presented on page 245. Assume a 25% tax rate.
(b) Calculate the profit margin and the gross profit rate.

E5-7 Financial information is presented here for two companies.

	Yanik Company	Nunez Company
Sales revenue	$90,000	?
Sales returns and allowances	?	$ 5,000
Net sales	84,000	100,000
Cost of goods sold	58,000	?
Gross profit	?	40,000
Operating expenses	14,380	?
Net income	?	17,000

Compute missing amounts and calculate profitability ratios.
(LO 4, 6), **AP**

Instructions
(a) Fill in the missing amounts. Show all computations.
(b) Calculate the profit margin and the gross profit rate for each company.
(c) Discuss your findings in part (b).

E5-8 In its income statement for the year ended December 31, 2014, Gavin Company reported the following condensed data.

Salaries and wages expense	$465,000	Loss on disposal of plant assets	$ 83,500
Cost of goods sold	987,000	Sales revenue	2,210,000
Interest expense	71,000	Income tax expense	25,000
Interest revenue	65,000	Sales discounts	160,000
Depreciation expense	310,000	Utilities expense	110,000

Prepare multiple-step income statement and calculate profitability ratios.
(LO 4, 6), **AP**

Instructions
(a) Prepare a multiple-step income statement.
(b) Calculate the profit margin and gross profit rate.
(c) In 2013, Gavin had a profit margin of 5%. Is the decline in 2014 a cause for concern? (Ignore income tax effects.)

E5-9 Suppose in its income statement for the year ended June 30, 2014, The Clorox Company reported the following condensed data (dollars in millions).

Salaries and wages expense	$ 460	Research and development expense	$ 114
Depreciation expense	90		
Sales revenue	5,730	Income tax expense	276
Interest expense	161	Loss on disposal of plant assets	46
Advertising expense	499	Cost of goods sold	3,104
Sales returns and allowances	280	Rent expense	105
		Utilities expense	60

Prepare multiple-step income statement and calculate profitability ratios.
(LO 4, 6), **C**

Instructions
(a) Prepare a multiple-step income statement.
(b) Calculate the gross profit rate and the profit margin and explain what each means.
(c) Assume the marketing department has presented a plan to increase advertising expenses by $340 million. It expects this plan to result in an increase in both net sales and cost of goods sold of 25%. (*Hint:* Increase both sales revenue and sales returns and allowances by 25%.) Redo parts (a) and (b) and discuss whether this plan has merit. (Assume a tax rate of 34%, and round all amounts to whole dollars.)

Prepare cost of goods sold section using periodic system.
(LO 5), **AP**

E5-10 The trial balance of Sanchez Company at the end of its fiscal year, August 31, 2014, includes these accounts: Beginning Inventory $18,700; Purchases $154,000; Sales Revenue $190,000; Freight-In $8,000; Sales Returns and Allowances $3,000; Freight-Out $1,000; and Purchase Returns and Allowances $5,000. The ending inventory is $21,000.

Instructions
Prepare a cost of goods sold section (periodic system) for the year ending August 31, 2014.

Prepare cost of goods sold section using periodic system.
(LO 5), **AP**

E5-11 Below is a series of cost of goods sold sections for companies A, L, N, and R.

	A	L	N	R
Beginning inventory	$ 250	$ 120	$ 700	$ (j)
Purchases	1,500	1,080	(g)	43,590
Purchase returns and allowances	80	(d)	290	(k)
Net purchases	(a)	1,040	7,410	42,290
Freight-in	130	(e)	(h)	2,240
Cost of goods purchased	(b)	1,230	8,050	(l)
Cost of goods available for sale	1,800	1,350	(i)	49,530
Ending inventory	310	(f)	1,150	6,230
Cost of goods sold	(c)	1,230	7,600	43,300

Instructions
Fill in the lettered blanks to complete the cost of goods sold sections.

Evaluate quality of earnings.
(LO 7), **C**

E5-12 Dorcas Corporation reported sales revenue of $257,000, net income of $45,300, cash of $9,300, and net cash provided by operating activities of $23,200. Accounts receivable have increased at three times the rate of sales during the last 3 years.

Instructions
(a) Explain what is meant by high quality of earnings.
(b) Evaluate the quality of the company's earnings. Discuss your findings.
(c) What factors might have contributed to the company's quality of earnings?

Journalize purchase transactions.
(LO 8), **AP**

*E5-13 This information relates to Woodward Co.
1. On April 5, purchased merchandise from Cozart Company for $27,000, terms 2/10, n/30.
2. On April 6, paid freight costs of $1,200 on merchandise purchased from Cozart Company.
3. On April 7, purchased equipment on account for $30,000.
4. On April 8, returned some of the April 5 merchandise to Cozart Company, which cost $3,600.
5. On April 15, paid the amount due to Cozart Company in full.

Instructions
(a) Prepare the journal entries to record these transactions on the books of Woodward Co. using a periodic inventory system.
(b) Assume that Woodward Co. paid the balance due to Cozart Company on May 4 instead of April 15. Prepare the journal entry to record this payment.

Exercises: Set B and Challenge Exercises

Visit the book's companion website, at **www.wiley.com/college/kimmel**, and choose the Student Companion site to access Exercise Set B and Challenge Exercises.

Problems: Set A

Journalize, post, prepare partial income statement, and calculate ratios.
(LO 2, 3, 4, 6), **AP**

GLS

P5-1A Waters Hardware Store completed the following merchandising transactions in the month of May. At the beginning of May, Waters' ledger showed Cash of $8,000 and Common Stock of $8,000.

May 1 Purchased merchandise on account from Hauke Wholesale Supply for $8,000, terms 1/10, n/30.

2 Sold merchandise on account for $4,400, terms 2/10, n/30. The cost of the merchandise sold was $3,300.

    5   Received credit from Hauke Wholesale Supply for merchandise returned $200.

    9   Received collections in full, less discounts, from customers billed on May 2.

   10   Paid Hauke Wholesale Supply in full, less discount.

   11   Purchased supplies for cash $900.

   12   Purchased merchandise for cash $3,100.

   15   Received $230 refund for return of poor-quality merchandise from supplier on cash purchase.

   17   Purchased merchandise from Friedrich Distributors for $2,500, terms 2/10, n/30.

   19   Paid freight on May 17 purchase $250.

   24   Sold merchandise for cash $5,500. The cost of the merchandise sold was $4,100.

   25   Purchased merchandise from Fasteners Inc. for $800, terms 3/10, n/30.

   27   Paid Friedrich Distributors in full, less discount.

   29   Made refunds to cash customers for returned merchandise $124. The returned merchandise had cost $90.

   31   Sold merchandise on account for $1,280, terms n/30. The cost of the merchandise sold was $830.

Waters Hardware's chart of accounts includes Cash, Accounts Receivable, Inventory, Supplies, Accounts Payable, Common Stock, Sales Revenue, Sales Returns and Allowances, Sales Discounts, and Cost of Goods Sold.

Instructions
(a) Journalize the transactions using a perpetual inventory system.
(b) Post the transactions to T-accounts. Be sure to enter the beginning cash and common stock balances.
(c) Prepare an income statement through gross profit for the month of May 2014.
(d) Calculate the profit margin and the gross profit rate. (Assume operating expenses were $1,400.)

(c) Gross profit $2,828

P5-2A McCoy Warehouse distributes hardback books to retail stores and extends credit terms of 2/10, n/30 to all of its customers. During the month of June, the following merchandising transactions occurred.

Journalize purchase and sale transactions under a perpetual system.

(LO 2, 3), **AP**

  June   1   Purchased books on account for $1,040 (including freight) from Carlin Publishers, terms 2/10, n/30.

        3   Sold books on account to the Goldschmidt bookstore for $1,200. The cost of the merchandise sold was $720.

        6   Received $40 credit for books returned to Carlin Publishers.

        9   Paid Carlin Publishers in full.

     15   Received payment in full from the Goldschmidt bookstore.

     17   Sold books on account to Town Crier for $1,200. The cost of the merchandise sold was $730.

     20   Purchased books on account for $720 from Good Book Publishers, terms 1/15, n/30.

     24   Received payment in full from Town Crier.

     26   Paid Good Book Publishers in full.

     28   Sold books on account to Emporia Bookstore for $1,300. The cost of the merchandise sold was $780.

     30   Granted Emporia Bookstore $130 credit for books returned costing $80.

Instructions
Journalize the transactions for the month of June for McCoy Warehouse, using a perpetual inventory system.

P5-3A At the beginning of the current season on April 1, the ledger of Flint Hills Pro Shop showed Cash $2,500; Inventory $3,500; and Common Stock $6,000. The following transactions were completed during April 2014.

Journalize, post, and prepare trial balance and partial income statement.

(LO 2, 3, 4), **AP**

  Apr.   5   Purchased golf bags, clubs, and balls on account from Akers Co. $1,500, terms 3/10, n/60.

        7   Paid freight on Akers purchase $80.

        9   Received credit from Akers Co. for merchandise returned $200.

10 Sold merchandise on account to members $1,340, terms n/30. The merchandise sold had a cost of $820.

12 Purchased golf shoes, sweaters, and other accessories on account from Palmer Sportswear $830, terms 1/10, n/30.

14 Paid Akers Co. in full.

17 Received credit from Palmer Sportswear for merchandise returned $30.

20 Made sales on account to members $810, terms n/30. The cost of the merchandise sold was $550.

21 Paid Palmer Sportswear in full.

27 Granted an allowance to members for clothing that did not fit properly $80.

30 Received payments on account from members $1,220.

The chart of accounts for the pro shop includes Cash, Accounts Receivable, Inventory, Accounts Payable, Common Stock, Sales Revenue, Sales Returns and Allowances, and Cost of Goods Sold.

Instructions

(a) Journalize the April transactions using a perpetual inventory system.

(b) Using T-accounts, enter the beginning balances in the ledger accounts and post the April transactions.

(c) Tot. trial balance $8,150   (c) Prepare a trial balance on April 30, 2014.

(d) Gross profit $ 700   (d) Prepare an income statement through gross profit for the month of April 2014.

Prepare financial statements and calculate profitability ratios.

(LO 4, 6), **AP**

P5-4A Lambert Department Store is located in midtown Metropolis. During the past several years, net income has been declining because suburban shopping centers have been attracting business away from city areas. At the end of the company's fiscal year on November 30, 2014, these accounts appeared in its adjusted trial balance.

Accounts Payable	$ 26,800
Accounts Receivable	17,200
Accumulated Depreciation—Equipment	68,000
Cash	8,000
Common Stock	35,000
Cost of Goods Sold	614,300
Freight-Out	6,200
Equipment	157,000
Depreciation Expense	13,500
Dividends	12,000
Gain on Disposal of Plant Assets	2,000
Income Tax Expense	10,000
Insurance Expense	9,000
Interest Expense	5,000
Inventory	26,200
Notes Payable	43,500
Prepaid Insurance	6,000
Advertising Expense	33,500
Rent Expense	34,000
Retained Earnings	14,200
Salaries and Wages Expense	117,000
Sales Revenue	904,000
Salaries and Wages Payable	6,000
Sales Returns and Allowances	20,000
Utilities Expense	10,600

Additional data: Notes payable are due in 2018.

Instructions

(a) Net income $ 32,900   (a) Prepare a multiple-step income statement, a retained earnings statement, and a classified balance sheet.

Tot. assets $146,400

(b) Calculate the profit margin and the gross profit rate.

(c) The vice president of marketing and the director of human resources have developed a proposal whereby the company would compensate the sales force on a strictly commission basis. Given the increased incentive, they expect net sales to increase by 15%. As a result, they estimate that gross profit will increase by $40,443 and expenses by

$58,600. Compute the expected new net income. (*Hint:* You do not need to prepare an income statement.) Then, compute the revised profit margin and gross profit rate. Comment on the effect that this plan would have on net income and on the ratios, and evaluate the merit of this proposal. (Ignore income tax effects.)

P5-5A An inexperienced accountant prepared this condensed income statement for Sundberg Company, a retail firm that has been in business for a number of years.

Prepare a correct multiple-step income statement.
(LO 4), **AP**

SUNDBERG COMPANY
Income Statement
For the Year Ended December 31, 2014

Revenues	
Net sales	$850,000
Other revenues	22,000
	872,000
Cost of goods sold	555,000
Gross profit	317,000
Operating expenses	
Selling expenses	109,000
Administrative expenses	103,000
	212,000
Net earnings	$105,000

As an experienced, knowledgeable accountant, you review the statement and determine the following facts.

1. Net sales consist of sales $911,000, less freight-out on merchandise sold $33,000, and sales returns and allowances $28,000.
2. Other revenues consist of sales discounts $18,000 and rent revenue $4,000.
3. Selling expenses consist of salespersons' salaries $80,000; depreciation on equipment $10,000; advertising $13,000; and sales commissions $6,000. The commissions represent commissions paid. At December 31, $3,000 of commissions have been earned by salespersons but have not been paid. All compensation should be recorded as Salaries and Wages Expense.
4. Administrative expenses consist of office salaries $47,000; dividends $18,000; utilities $12,000; interest expense $2,000; and rent expense $24,000, which includes prepayments totaling $6,000 for the first quarter of 2015.

Instructions
Prepare a correct detailed multiple-step income statement. Assume a 25% tax rate.

Net income $67,500

P5-6A The trial balance of Customer Choice Wholesale Company contained the accounts shown at December 31, the end of the company's fiscal year.

Journalize, post, and prepare adjusted trial balance and financial statements.
(LO 4), **AP**

CUSTOMER CHOICE WHOLESALE COMPANY
Trial Balance
December 31, 2014

	Debit	Credit
Cash	$ 31,400	
Accounts Receivable	37,600	
Inventory	70,000	
Land	92,000	
Buildings	200,000	
Accumulated Depreciation—Buildings		$ 60,000
Equipment	83,500	
Accumulated Depreciation—Equipment		40,500
Notes Payable		54,700
Accounts Payable		17,500
Common Stock		160,000
Retained Earnings		67,200
Dividends	10,000	

	Debit	Credit
Sales Revenue		$ 922,100
Sales Discounts	$ 6,000	
Cost of Goods Sold	709,900	
Salaries and Wages Expense	51,300	
Utilities Expense	11,400	
Maintenance and Repairs Expense	8,900	
Advertising Expense	5,200	
Insurance Expense	4,800	
	$1,322,000	$1,322,000

Adjustment data:

1. Depreciation is $8,000 on buildings and $7,000 on equipment. (Both are operating expenses.)
2. Interest of $4,500 is due and unpaid on notes payable at December 31.
3. Income tax due and unpaid at December 31 is $24,000.

Other data: $15,000 of the notes payable are payable next year.

Instructions
(a) Journalize the adjusting entries.
(b) Create T-accounts for all accounts used in part (a). Enter the trial balance amounts into the T-accounts and post the adjusting entries.
(c) Prepare an adjusted trial balance.
(d) Prepare a multiple-step income statement and a retained earnings statement for the year, and a classified balance sheet at December 31, 2014.

(c) Tot. trial balance $1,365,500
(d) Net income $ 81,100
    Tot. assets $ 399,000

Determine cost of goods sold and gross profit under a periodic system.

(LO 4, 5), **AP**

P5-7A At the end of Ermler Department Store's fiscal year on November 30, 2014, these accounts appeared in its adjusted trial balance.

Freight-In	$ 5,060
Inventory (beginning)	41,300
Purchases	613,000
Purchase Discounts	7,000
Purchase Returns and Allowances	6,760
Sales Revenue	902,000
Sales Returns and Allowances	20,000

Additional facts:
1. Inventory on November 30, 2014, is $36,200.
2. Note that Ermler Department Store uses a periodic system.

Instructions

Gross profit $272,600

Prepare an income statement through gross profit for the year ended November 30, 2014.

Calculate missing amounts and assess profitability.

(LO 4, 5, 6), **AN**

P5-8A Yang Inc. operates a retail operation that purchases and sells snowmobiles, among other outdoor products. The company purchases all inventory on credit and uses a periodic inventory system. The Accounts Payable account is used for recording inventory purchases only; all other current liabilities are accrued in separate accounts. You are provided with the following selected information for the fiscal years 2012 through 2015, inclusive.

	2012	2013	2014	2015
Income Statement Data				
Sales revenue		$96,890	$ (e)	$82,220
Cost of goods sold		(a)	28,060	26,490
Gross profit		67,800	59,620	(i)
Operating expenses		63,640	(f)	52,870
Net income		$ (b)	$ 3,510	$ (j)
Balance Sheet Data				
Inventory	$13,000	$ (c)	$14,700	$ (k)
Accounts payable	5,800	6,500	4,600	(l)
Additional Information				
Purchases of inventory				
on account		$25,890	$ (g)	$24,050
Cash payments to suppliers		(d)	(h)	24,650

Instructions

(a) Calculate the missing amounts.

(b) The vice presidents of sales, marketing, production, and finance are discussing the company's results with the CEO. They note that sales declined over the 3-year fiscal period, 2013–2015. Does that mean that profitability necessarily also declined? Explain, computing the gross profit rate and the profit margin for each fiscal year to help support your answer.

*P5-9A   At the beginning of the current season on April 1, the ledger of Flint Hills Pro Shop showed Cash $2,500; Inventory $3,500; and Common Stock $6,000. The following transactions occurred during April 2014.

Apr.	5	Purchased golf bags, clubs, and balls on account from Akers Co. $1,500, terms 3/10, n/60.
	7	Paid freight on Akers Co. purchases $80.
	9	Received credit from Akers Co. for merchandise returned $200.
	10	Sold merchandise on account to members $1,340, terms n/30.
	12	Purchased golf shoes, sweaters, and other accessories on account from Palmer Sportswear $830, terms 1/10, n/30.
	14	Paid Akers Co. in full.
	17	Received credit from Palmer Sportswear for merchandise returned $30.
	20	Made sales on account to members $810, terms n/30.
	21	Paid Palmer Sportswear in full.
	27	Granted credit to members for clothing that did not fit properly $80.
	30	Received payments on account from members $1,220.

The chart of accounts for the pro shop includes Cash, Accounts Receivable, Inventory, Accounts Payable, Common Stock, Sales Revenue, Sales Returns and Allowances, Purchases, Purchase Returns and Allowances, Purchase Discounts, and Freight-In.

Instructions

(a) Journalize the April transactions using a periodic inventory system.

(b) Using T-accounts, enter the beginning balances in the ledger accounts and post the April transactions.

(c) Prepare a trial balance on April 30, 2014.

(d) Prepare an income statement through gross profit, assuming inventory on hand at April 30 is $4,263.

Journalize, post, and prepare trial balance and partial income statement under a periodic system.
(LO 5, 8), **AP**

(c) Tot. trial balance $8,427
(d) Gross profit $ 700

Problems: Set B

P5-1B   Krey Distributing Company completed these merchandising transactions in the month of April. At the beginning of April, the ledger of Krey showed Cash of $10,000 and Common Stock of $10,000.

Apr.	2	Purchased merchandise on account from Am-Bev Co. $8,700, terms 2/10, n/30.
	4	Sold merchandise on account $6,000, terms 2/10, n/30. The cost of the merchandise sold was $3,700.
	5	Paid $200 freight on April 4 sale.
	6	Received credit from Am-Bev Co. for merchandise returned $400.
	11	Paid Am-Bev Co. in full, less discount.
	13	Received collections in full, less discounts, from customers billed on April 4.
	14	Purchased merchandise for cash $4,700.
	16	Received refund from supplier for returned merchandise on cash purchase of April 14, $500.
	18	Purchased merchandise from Lohr Distributors $5,500, terms 2/10, n/30.
	20	Paid freight on April 18 purchase $180.
	23	Sold merchandise for cash $8,300. The cost of the merchandise sold was $5,580.
	26	Purchased merchandise for cash $2,300.
	27	Paid Lohr Distributors in full, less discount.

Journalize, post, prepare partial income statement, and calculate ratios.
(LO 2, 3, 4, 6), **AP**

29 Made refunds to cash customers for returned merchandise $180. The returned merchandise had a cost of $120.

30 Sold merchandise on account $3,980, terms n/30. The cost of the merchandise sold was $2,500.

Krey Distributing Company's chart of accounts includes Cash, Accounts Receivable, Inventory, Accounts Payable, Common Stock, Sales Revenue, Sales Returns and Allowances, Sales Discounts, Cost of Goods Sold, and Freight-Out.

Instructions

(a) Journalize the transactions.

(b) Post the transactions to T-accounts. Be sure to enter the beginning cash and common stock balances.

(c) Gross profit $6,320

(c) Prepare the income statement through gross profit for the month of April 2014.

(d) Calculate the profit margin and the gross profit rate. (Assume operating expenses were $3,000.)

Journalize purchase and sale transactions under a perpetual inventory system.

(LO 2, 3), **AP**

P5-2B Cosmotologist Warehouse distributes commercial hair care products in one-gallon bottles to hair salons and extends credit terms of 3/10, n/30 to all of its customers. During the month of April, the following merchandising transactions occurred.

Apr. 1 Purchased 190 bottles on account for $6 each (including freight) from Luminous Hair, terms 2/10, n/30.

3 Sold 40 bottles on account to the Jane's Hair Salon for $10 each.

6 Received $90 credit for 15 bottles returned to Luminous Hair.

9 Paid Luminous Hair in full.

12 Received payment in full from the Jane's Hair Salon.

13 Sold 25 bottles on account to Luxury Salon for $12 each.

20 Purchased 200 bottles on account for $6 each from Blond Beauty, terms 1/15, n/30.

24 Received payment in full from Luxury Salon.

26 Paid Blond Beauty in full.

28 Sold 160 bottles on account to Beautiful Cuts salons for $10 each.

30 Granted Beautiful Cuts $120 credit for 12 bottles returned costing $72.

Instructions

Journalize the transactions for the month of April for Cosmotologist Warehouse, using a perpetual inventory system. Assume the cost of each bottle sold was $6.

Journalize, post, and prepare trial balance and partial income statement.

(LO 2, 3, 4), **AP**

P5-3B At the beginning of the current season, the ledger of Connors' Tennis Shop showed Cash $3,500; Inventory $1,700; and Common Stock $5,200. The following transactions were completed during April 2014.

Apr. 4 Purchased racquets and balls from Rawlings Co. $980, terms 2/10, n/30.

6 Paid freight on Rawlings Co. purchase $60.

8 Sold merchandise to members $750, terms n/30. The merchandise sold cost $480.

10 Received credit of $130 from Rawlings Co. for damaged racquets that were returned.

11 Purchased tennis shoes from Fast Feet for cash $300.

13 Paid Rawlings Co. in full.

14 Purchased tennis shirts and shorts from Armour Sportswear $1,300, terms 3/10, n/60.

15 Received cash refund of $50 from Fast Feet for damaged merchandise that was returned.

17 Paid freight on Armour Sportswear purchase $60.

18 Sold merchandise to members $660, terms n/30. The cost of the merchandise sold was $440.

20 Received $500 in cash from members in partial settlement of their accounts.

21 Paid Armour Sportswear in full.

27 Granted an allowance of $30 to members for tennis clothing that did not fit properly.

30 Received cash payments on account from members $550.

The chart of accounts for the tennis shop includes Cash, Accounts Receivable, Inventory, Accounts Payable, Common Stock, Sales Revenue, Sales Returns and Allowances, and Cost of Goods Sold.

Instructions
(a) Journalize the April transactions using a perpetual inventory system.
(b) Using T-accounts, enter the beginning balances in the ledger accounts and post the April transactions.
(c) Prepare a trial balance on April 30, 2014.
(d) Prepare an income statement through gross profit for the month of April 2014.

P5-4B Parker Department Store is located near the Mark Twain Shopping Mall. At the end of the company's fiscal year on December 31, 2014, the following accounts appeared in its adjusted trial balance.

Prepare financial statements and calculate profitability ratios.

(LO 4, 6), **AP**

Accounts Payable	$ 73,300
Accounts Receivable	43,500
Accumulated Depreciation—Buildings	52,500
Accumulated Depreciation—Equipment	42,600
Buildings	140,000
Cash	30,000
Common Stock	140,000
Cost of Goods Sold	412,000
Depreciation Expense	23,400
Dividends	15,000
Equipment	100,000
Gain on Disposal of Plant Assets	4,300
Income Tax Expense	15,000
Insurance Expense	8,400
Interest Expense	7,000
Interest Payable	2,000
Inventory	43,000
Land	50,000
Mortgage Payable	62,500
Prepaid Insurance	2,400
Maintenance and Repairs Expense	6,200
Retained Earnings	19,200
Salaries and Wages Expense	111,000
Sales Revenue	626,000
Salaries and Wages Payable	3,500
Sales Returns and Allowances	8,000
Utilities Expense	11,000

Additional data: $20,000 of the mortgage payable is due for payment next year.

Instructions
(a) Prepare a multiple-step income statement, a retained earnings statement, and a classified balance sheet.
(b) Calculate the profit margin and the gross profit rate.
(c) The vice president of marketing and the director of human resources have developed a proposal whereby the company would compensate the sales force on a strictly commission basis. Given the increased incentive, they expect net sales to increase by 25%. As a result, they estimate that gross profit will increase by $50,500 and expenses by $27,800. Compute the expected new net income. (*Hint:* You do not need to prepare an income statement.) Then, compute the revised profit margin and gross profit rate. Comment on the effect that this plan would have on net income and the ratios, and evaluate the merit of this proposal.

(a) Net income $28,300
Tot. assets $313,800

P5-5B An inexperienced accountant prepared this condensed income statement for Wright Company, a retail firm that has been in business for a number of years.

Prepare a correct multiple-step income statement.

(LO 4), **AP**

WRIGHT COMPANY
Income Statement
For the Year Ended December 31, 2014

Revenues		
Net sales	$952,000	
Other revenues	16,000	
		968,000

Cost of goods sold	548,000
Gross profit	420,000
Operating expenses	
Selling expenses	160,000
Administrative expenses	104,000
	264,000
Net earnings	$156,000

As an experienced, knowledgeable accountant, you review the statement and determine the following facts.

1. Net sales consist of sales $972,000, less freight-out on merchandise sold $20,000.
2. Other revenues consist of sales discounts $12,000 and interest revenue $4,000.
3. Selling expenses consist of salespersons' salaries $88,000; depreciation on equipment $4,000; sales returns and allowances $46,000; advertising $12,000; and sales commissions $10,000. All compensation should be recorded as Salaries and Wages Expense.
4. Administrative expenses consist of office salaries $54,000; dividends $14,000; utilities $13,000; interest expense $3,000; and rent expense $20,000, which includes prepayments totaling $2,000 for the first month of 2015. The utilities represent utilities paid. At December 31, utility expense of $3,000 has been incurred but not paid.

Instructions

Net income $145,000

Prepare a correct detailed multiple-step income statement.

Journalize, post, and prepare adjusted trial balance and financial statements.

(LO 4), **AP**

P5-6B The trial balance of Buse's Fashion Center contained the accounts below at November 30, the end of the company's fiscal year.

BUSE'S FASHION CENTER
Trial Balance
November 30, 2014

	Debit	Credit
Cash	$ 37,700	
Accounts Receivable	33,700	
Inventory	43,000	
Supplies	8,800	
Equipment	143,000	
Accumulated Depreciation—Equipment		$ 41,000
Notes Payable		62,000
Accounts Payable		17,800
Common Stock		80,000
Retained Earnings		30,000
Dividends	12,000	
Sales Revenue		757,200
Sales Returns and Allowances	6,200	
Cost of Goods Sold	505,400	
Salaries and Wages Expense	110,000	
Advertising Expense	26,400	
Utilities Expense	14,000	
Maintenance and Repairs Expense	12,100	
Freight-Out	11,700	
Rent Expense	24,000	
	$988,000	$988,000

Adjustment data:

1. Store supplies on hand total $4,000.
2. Depreciation is $14,000 on the store equipment and $6,000 on the delivery equipment.
3. Interest of $4,400 is accrued on notes payable at November 30.
4. Income tax due and unpaid at November 30 is $3,000.

Other data: $24,000 of notes payable are due for payment next year.

Instructions

(a) Journalize the adjusting entries.

(b) Prepare T-accounts for all accounts used in part (a). Enter the trial balance amounts into the T-accounts and post the adjusting entries.

(c) Prepare an adjusted trial balance.

(d) Prepare a multiple-step income statement and a retained earnings statement for the year, and a classified balance sheet at November 30, 2014.

(c) Tot. trial balance	$1,015,400
(d) Net income	$15,200
Tot. assets	$200,400

P5-7B At the end of Alma's Department Store's fiscal year on December 31, 2014, these accounts appeared in its adjusted trial balance.

Determine cost of goods sold and gross profit under a periodic system.

(LO 4, 5), **AP**

Freight-In	$ 7,200
Inventory (beginning)	40,500
Purchases	456,000
Purchase Discounts	12,000
Purchase Returns and Allowances	6,400
Sales Revenue	702,000
Sales Returns and Allowances	8,000

Additional facts:

1. Inventory on December 31, 2014, is $48,300.
2. Note that Alma's Department Store uses a periodic system.

Instructions

Prepare an income statement through gross profit for the year ended December 31, 2014.

Gross profit $257,000

P5-8B Sandy Melon operates a clothing retail operation. She purchases all inventory on credit and uses a periodic inventory system. The Accounts Payable account is used for recording inventory purchases only; all other current liabilities are accrued in separate accounts. You are provided with the following selected information for the fiscal years 2012, 2013, 2014, and 2015.

Calculate missing amounts and assess profitability.

(LO 4, 5, 6), **AN**

	2012	**2013**	**2014**	**2015**
Inventory (ending)	$16,000	$ 11,300	$ 16,400	$ 14,200
Accounts payable (ending)	17,000			
Sales revenue		229,700	227,600	220,000
Purchases of inventory on account		146,900	155,700	139,200
Cash payments to suppliers		135,900	159,000	127,000

Instructions

(a) Calculate cost of goods sold for each of the 2013, 2014, and 2015 fiscal years.

(b) Calculate the gross profit for each of the 2013, 2014, and 2015 fiscal years.

(c) Calculate the ending balance of accounts payable for each of the 2013, 2014, and 2015 fiscal years.

(d) The vice presidents of sales, marketing, production, and finance are discussing the company's results with the CEO. They note that sales declined in fiscal 2015. They wonder whether that means that profitability, as measured by the gross profit rate, necessarily also declined. Explain, calculating the gross profit rate for each fiscal year to help support your answer.

(a) 2014	$150,600
(c) 2014	$24,700

***P5-9B** At the beginning of the current season on November 1, the ledger of Winona Sports showed Cash $3,300, Inventory $4,700, and Common Stock $8,000. The following transactions occurred during November 2014.

Journalize, post, and prepare trial balance and partial income statement under a periodic system.

(LO 5, 8), **AP**

Nov. 5 Purchased hockey sticks and pucks on account from Hi-Stick Co. $1,600, terms 2/10, n/60.

7 Paid freight on Hi-Stick Co. purchases $90.

9 Received credit from Hi-Stick Co. for merchandise returned $350.

10 Sold merchandise on account for $1,000, terms n/30.

12 Purchased gloves, socks, and other accessories on account from Twin City Sportswear $945, terms 1/10, n/30.

14 Paid Hi-Stick Co. in full.

17 Received credit from Twin City Sportswear for merchandise returned $45.

20 Made sales on account for $1,330, terms n/30.

21 Paid Twin City Sportswear in full.

27 Granted credit to customers for clothing that did not fit properly $150.
30 Received payments on account for $1,900.

The chart of accounts for Winona Sports includes Cash, Accounts Receivable, Inventory, Accounts Payable, Common Stock, Sales Revenue, Sales Returns and Allowances, Purchases, Purchase Returns and Allowances, Purchase Discounts, and Freight-In.

Instructions
(a) Journalize the November transactions using a periodic inventory system.
(b) Using T-accounts, enter the beginning balances in the ledger accounts and post the November transactions.
(c) Prepare a trial balance on November 30, 2014.
(d) Prepare an income statement through Gross profit, assuming inventory on hand at November 30 is $5,196.

(c) Tot. trial balance $10,759
(d) Net income $470

Problems: Set C

Visit the book's companion website, at **www.wiley.com/college/kimmel**, and choose the Student Companion site to access Problem Set C.

Comprehensive Problem

CP5 On December 1, 2014, Boline Distributing Company had the following account balances.

	Debit		Credit
Cash	$ 7,200	Accumulated Depreciation—	
Accounts Receivable	4,600	Equipment	$ 2,200
Inventory	12,000	Accounts Payable	4,500
Supplies	1,200	Salaries and Wages Payable	1,000
Equipment	22,000	Common Stock	15,000
	$47,000	Retained Earnings	24,300
			$47,000

During December, the company completed the following summary transactions.

Dec. 6 Paid $1,600 for salaries due employees, of which $600 is for December and $1,000 is for November salaries payable.
8 Received $1,900 cash from customers in payment of account (no discount allowed).
10 Sold merchandise for cash $6,300. The cost of the merchandise sold was $4,100.
13 Purchased merchandise on account from Gong Co. $9,000, terms 2/10, n/30.
15 Purchased supplies for cash $2,000.
18 Sold merchandise on account $12,000, terms 3/10, n/30. The cost of the merchandise sold was $8,000.
20 Paid salaries $1,800.
23 Paid Gong Co. in full, less discount.
27 Received collections in full, less discounts, from customers billed on December 18.

Adjustment data:
1. Accrued salaries payable $800.
2. Depreciation $200 per month.
3. Supplies on hand $1,500.
4. Income tax due and unpaid at December 31 is $200.

Instructions
(a) Journalize the December transactions using a perpetual inventory system.
(b) Enter the December 1 balances in the ledger T-accounts and post the December transactions. Use Cost of Goods Sold, Depreciation Expense, Salaries and Wages Expense,

Sales Revenue, Sales Discounts, Supplies Expense, Income Tax Expense, and Income Taxes Payable.
(c) Journalize and post adjusting entries.
(d) Prepare an adjusted trial balance.
(e) Prepare an income statement and a retained earnings statement for December and a classified balance sheet at December 31.

(d) Totals $65,500
(e) Net income $540

Continuing Cookie Chronicle

(*Note:* This is a continuation of the Cookie Chronicle from Chapters 1 through 4.)

CCC5 Because Natalie has had such a successful first few months, she is considering other opportunities to develop her business. One opportunity is to become the exclusive distributor of a line of fine European mixers. Natalie comes to you for advice on how to account for these mixers.

Go to the book's companion website, at **www.wiley.com/college/kimmel**, to see the completion of this problem.

Broadening Your Perspective

Financial Reporting and Analysis

FINANCIAL REPORTING PROBLEM: *Tootsie Roll Industries, Inc.*

BYP5-1 The financial statements for Tootsie Roll Industries appear in Appendix A at the end of this textbook.

Instructions
Answer these questions using the Consolidated Income Statement.
(a) What was the percentage change in total revenue and in net income from 2010 to 2011?
(b) What was the profit margin in each of the 3 years? (Use "Total Revenue.") Comment on the trend.
(c) What was Tootsie Roll's gross profit rate in each of the 3 years? (Use "Net Product Sales" amounts.) Comment on the trend.

COMPARATIVE ANALYSIS PROBLEM: *Tootsie Roll vs. Hershey*

BYP5-2 The financial statements of The Hershey Company appear in Appendix B, following the financial statements for Tootsie Roll in Appendix A.

Instructions
(a) Based on the information contained in these financial statements, determine the following values for each company.
  (1) Profit margin for 2011. (For Tootsie Roll, use "Total Revenue.")
  (2) Gross profit for 2011. (For Tootsie Roll, use "Product" amounts.)
  (3) Gross profit rate for 2011. (For Tootsie Roll, use "Product" amounts.)
  (4) Operating income for 2011.
  (5) Percentage change in operating income from 2011 to 2010.
(b) What conclusions concerning the relative profitability of the two companies can be drawn from these data?

RESEARCH CASE

BYP5-3 The February 21, 2012, edition of the *New York Times* contains an article by Stephanie Clifford entitled "High-End Retailers Report Strong Profits, but Wal-Mart Still Struggles."

Instructions

Read the article and answer the following questions.

(a) Explain why Wal-Mart's gross profit margin fell even though its total sales revenue increased.

(b) Saks Fifth Avenue experienced an increase in its gross profit rate for the year. What factors contributed to this increase?

(c) Macy's experienced a decline in its gross profit rate. The article said that the decline could be attributed to two factors: a free-shipping promotion and markdowns on cold-weather gear. Discuss whether this explanation is consistent with what you learned in this chapter about the financial presentation of these items in the income statement.

(d) The article mentions that Home Depot experienced increases in "same store sales." What does "increase in same store sales" mean? What implications does an increase in same store sales have for the profit margin?

INTERPRETING FINANCIAL STATEMENTS

BYP5-4 Recently, it was announced that two giant French retailers, Carrefour SA and Promodes SA, would merge. A headline in the *Wall Street Journal* blared, "French Retailers Create New Wal-Mart Rival." While Wal-Mart's total sales would still exceed those of the combined company, Wal-Mart's international sales are far less than those of the combined company. This is a serious concern for Wal-Mart, since its primary opportunity for future growth lies outside of the United States.

Below are basic financial data for the combined corporation (in euros) and Wal-Mart (in U.S. dollars). Even though their results are presented in different currencies, by employing ratios we can make some basic comparisons.

	Carrefour (in millions)	Wal-Mart (in millions)
Sales revenue	€70,486	$256,329
Cost of goods sold	54,630	198,747
Net income	1,738	9,054
Total assets	39,063	104,912
Current assets	14,521	34,421
Current liabilities	13,660	37,418
Total liabilities	29,434	61,289

Instructions

Compare the two companies by answering the following.

(a) Calculate the gross profit rate for each of the companies, and discuss their relative abilities to control cost of goods sold.

(b) Calculate the profit margin, and discuss the companies' relative profitability.

(c) Calculate the current ratio and debt to assets ratios for the two companies, and discuss their relative liquidity and solvency.

(d) What concerns might you have in relying on this comparison?

REAL-WORLD FOCUS

BYP5-5 *Purpose:* No financial decision-maker should ever rely solely on the financial information reported in the annual report to make decisions. It is important to keep abreast of financial news. This activity demonstrates how to search for financial news on the Internet.

Address: **http://biz.yahoo.com/i**, or go to **www.wiley.com/college/kimmel**

Steps

1. Type in either Wal-Mart, Target Corp., or Kmart.
2. Choose **News**.
3. Select an article that sounds interesting to you and that would be relevant to an investor in these companies.

Instructions

(a) What was the source of the article (e.g., Reuters, Businesswire, Prnewswire)?

(b) Assume that you are a personal financial planner and that one of your clients owns stock in the company. Write a brief memo to your client summarizing the article and explaining the implications of the article for their investment.

Critical Thinking

DECISION-MAKING ACROSS THE ORGANIZATION

BYP5-6 Three years ago, Sue Kienholz and her brother-in-law Jeremy Reyes opened Megamart Department Store. For the first 2 years, business was good, but the following condensed income statement results for 2014 were disappointing.

MEGAMART DEPARTMENT STORE
Income Statement
For the Year Ended December 31, 2014

Net sales		$700,000
Cost of goods sold		560,000
Gross profit		140,000
Operating expenses		
Selling expenses	$100,000	
Administrative expenses	20,000	
		120,000
Net income		$ 20,000

Sue believes the problem lies in the relatively low gross profit rate of 20%. Jeremy believes the problem is that operating expenses are too high. Sue thinks the gross profit rate can be improved by making two changes. (1) Increase average selling prices by 15%; this increase is expected to lower sales volume so that total sales dollars will increase only 4%. (2) Buy merchandise in larger quantities and take all purchase discounts; these changes are expected to increase the gross profit rate from 20% to 25%. Sue does not anticipate that these changes will have any effect on operating expenses.

Jeremy thinks expenses can be cut by making these two changes. (1) Cut 2014 sales salaries of $60,000 in half and give sales personnel a commission of 2% of net sales. (2) Reduce store deliveries to one day per week rather than twice a week; this change will reduce 2014 delivery expenses of $40,000 by 40%. Jeremy feels that these changes will not have any effect on net sales.

Sue and Jeremy come to you for help in deciding the best way to improve net income.

Instructions

With the class divided into groups, answer the following.
(a) Prepare a condensed income statement for 2015 assuming (1) Sue's changes are implemented and (2) Jeremy's ideas are adopted.
(b) What is your recommendation to Sue and Jeremy?
(c) Prepare a condensed income statement for 2015 assuming both sets of proposed changes are made.
(d) Discuss the impact that other factors might have. For example, would increasing the quantity of inventory increase costs? Would a salary cut affect employee morale? Would decreased morale affect sales? Would decreased store deliveries decrease customer satisfaction? What other suggestions might be considered?

COMMUNICATION ACTIVITY

BYP5-7 The following situation is presented in chronological order.
1. Shafer decides to buy a surfboard.
2. He calls Surfing USA Co. to inquire about their surfboards.
3. Two days later, he requests Surfing USA Co. to make him a surfboard.
4. Three days later, Surfing USA Co. sends him a purchase order to fill out.
5. He sends back the purchase order.
6. Surfing USA Co. receives the completed purchase order.
7. Surfing USA Co. completes the surfboard.
8. Shafer picks up the surfboard.
9. Surfing USA Co. bills Shafer.
10. Surfing USA Co. receives payment from Shafer.

Instructions

In a memo to the president of Surfing USA Co., answer the following questions.
(a) When should Surfing USA Co. record the sale?
(b) Suppose that with his purchase order, Shafer is required to make a down payment. Would that change your answer to part (a)?

ETHICS CASE

BYP5-8 Andrea Tabares was just hired as the assistant treasurer of Northshore Stores, a specialty chain store company that has nine retail stores concentrated in one metropolitan area. Among other things, the payment of all invoices is centralized in one of the departments Andrea will manage. Her primary responsibility is to maintain the company's high credit rating by paying all bills when due and to take advantage of all cash discounts.

William Parks, the former assistant treasurer, who has been promoted to treasurer, is training Andrea in her new duties. He instructs Andrea that she is to continue the practice of preparing all checks "net of discount" and dating the checks the last day of the discount period. "But," William continues, "we always hold the checks at least 4 days beyond the discount period before mailing them. That way we get another 4 days of interest on our money. Most of our creditors need our business and don't complain. And, if they scream about our missing the discount period, we blame it on the mail room or the post office. We've only lost one discount out of every hundred we take that way. I think everybody does it. By the way, welcome to our team!"

Instructions

(a) What are the ethical considerations in this case?

(b) What stakeholders are harmed or benefited?

(c) Should Andrea continue the practice started by William? Does she have any choice?

ALL ABOUT YOU

BYP5-9 There are many situations in business where it is difficult to determine the proper period in which to record revenue. Suppose that after graduation with a degree in finance, you take a job as a manager at a consumer electronics store called Midwest Electronics. The company has expanded rapidly in order to compete with Best Buy.

Midwest has also begun selling gift cards. The cards are available in any dollar amount and allow the holder of the card to purchase an item for up to 2 years from the time the card is purchased. If the card is not used during those 2 years, it expires.

Instructions

Answer the following questions.

At what point should the revenue from the gift cards be recognized? Should the revenue be recognized at the time the card is sold, or should it be recorded when the card is redeemed? Explain the reasoning to support your answers.

FASB CODIFICATION ACTIVITY

BYP5-10 If your school has a subscription to the FASB Codification, go to **http://aaahg.org/ ascLogin.cfm** to log in and prepare responses to the following.

(a) Access the glossary ("Master Glossary") to answer the following.

 (1) What is the definition provided for inventory?

 (2) What is a customer?

(b) What guidance does the Codification provide concerning reporting inventories above cost?

Answers to Insight and Accounting Across the Organization Questions

p. 233 Morrow Snowboards Improves Its Stock Appeal Q: If a perpetual system keeps track of inventory on a daily basis, why do companies ever need to do a physical count? **A:** A perpetual system keeps track of all sales and purchases on a continuous basis. This provides a constant record of the number of units in the inventory. However, if employees make errors in recording sales or purchases, or if there is theft, the inventory value will not be correct. As a consequence, all companies do a physical count of inventory at least once a year.

p. 240 Should Costco Change Its Return Policy? Q: If a company expects significant returns, what are the implications for revenue recognition? **A:** If a company expects significant returns, it should make an adjusting entry at the end of the year to increase Sales Returns and Allowances by the estimated amount of sales returns. This is necessary so as not to overstate the amount of revenue recognized in the period.

p. 244 Disclosing More Details Q: Why have investors and analysts demanded more accuracy in isolating "Other gains and losses" from operating items? **A:** Greater accuracy in the classification of operating versus nonoperating ("Other gains and losses") items permits investors and analysts to judge the real operating margin, the results of continuing operations, and management's ability to control operating expenses.

p. 250 Selling Green Q: What is meant by "monetize environmental sustainability" for shareholders? **A:** By marketing green, not only does PepsiCo help the environment in the long run, but it also leads to long-term profitability as well. In other words, sound sustainability practices are good business and lead to sound financial results.

Answers to Self-Test Questions

1. a **2.** c **3.** c **4.** b (($750 − $50) ×.98) **5.** c **6.** c **7.** b ($400,000 − $310,000) **8.** d **9.** a ($60,000 + $380,000 − $50,000) **10.** b ($17,200 + ($60,400 − $3,000 − $1,100 + $600)) **11.** c **12.** c **13.** d ($92,400 ÷ $267,000) **14.** b ***15.** b

A Look at IFRS

The basic accounting entries for merchandising are the same under both GAAP and IFRS. The income statement is a required statement under both sets of standards. The basic format is similar although some differences do exist.

LEARNING OBJECTIVE 9

Compare the accounting procedures for merchandising under GAAP and IFRS.

KEY POINTS

- Under both GAAP and IFRS, a company can choose to use either a perpetual or a periodic system.

- Inventories are defined by IFRS as held-for-sale in the ordinary course of business, in the process of production for such sale, or in the form of materials or supplies to be consumed in the production process or in the providing of services.

- Under GAAP, companies generally classify income statement items by function. Classification by function leads to descriptions like administration, distribution, and manufacturing. Under IFRS, companies must classify expenses by either nature or function. Classification by nature leads to descriptions such as the following: salaries, depreciation expense, and utilities expense. If a company uses the functional-expense method on the income statement, disclosure by nature is required in the notes to the financial statements.

- Presentation of the income statement under GAAP follows either a single-step or multiple-step format. IFRS does not mention a single-step or multiple-step approach.

- Under IFRS, revaluation of land, buildings, and intangible assets is permitted. The initial gains and losses resulting from this revaluation are reported as adjustments to equity, often referred to as **other comprehensive income**. The effect of this difference is that the use of IFRS results in more transactions affecting equity (other comprehensive income) but not net income.

- *IAS 1*, "Presentation of Financial Statements," provides general guidelines for the reporting of income statement information. Subsequently, a number of international standards have been issued that provide additional guidance to issues related to income statement presentation.

- Similar to GAAP, comprehensive income under IFRS includes unrealized gains and losses (such as those on certain types of investment securities) that are not included in the calculation of net income.

- IFRS requires that two years of income statement information be presented, whereas GAAP requires three years.

LOOKING TO THE FUTURE

The IASB and FASB are working on a project that would rework the structure of financial statements. Specifically, this project will address the issue of how to classify various items in the income statement. A main goal of this new approach is to provide information that better represents how businesses are run. In addition, this approach draws attention away from just one number—net income. It will adopt major groupings similar to those currently used by the statement of cash flows (operating, investing, and financing), so that numbers can be more readily traced across statements. For example, the amount of income that is generated by operations would be traceable to the assets and liabilities used to generate the income. Finally, this approach would also provide detail, beyond that currently seen in most statements (either GAAP or IFRS), by requiring that line items be presented both by function and by nature. The new financial statement format was heavily influenced by suggestions from financial statement analysts.

IFRS PRACTICE

IFRS SELF-TEST QUESTIONS

1. Which of the following would **not** be included in the definition of inventory under IFRS?
   (a) Photocopy paper held for sale by an office-supply store.
   (b) Stereo equipment held for sale by an electronics store.
   (c) Used office equipment held for sale by the human relations department of a plastics company.
   (d) All of the above would meet the definition.
2. Which of the following would **not** be a line item of a company reporting costs by nature?
   (a) Depreciation expense.
   (b) Salaries expense.
   (c) Interest expense.
   (d) Manufacturing expense.
3. Which of the following would **not** be a line item of a company reporting costs by function?
   (a) Administration.
   (b) Manufacturing.
   (c) Utilities expense.
   (d) Distribution.
4. Which of the following statements is **false**?
   (a) IFRS specifically requires use of a multiple-step income statement.
   (b) Under IFRS, companies can use either a perpetual or periodic system.
   (c) The proposed new format for financial statements was heavily influenced by the suggestions of financial statement analysts.
   (d) The new income statement format will try to de-emphasize the focus on the "net income" line item.
5. Under the new format for financial statements being proposed under a joint IASB/FASB project:
   (a) all financial statements would adopt headings similar to the current format of the balance sheet.
   (b) financial statements would be presented consistent with the way management usually run companies.
   (c) companies would be required to report income statement line items by function only.
   (d) the amount of detail shown in the income statement would decrease compared to current presentations.

IFRS CONCEPTS AND APPLICATION

IFRS5-1 Explain the difference between the "nature-of-expense" and "function-of-expense" classifications.

IFRS5-2 For each of the following income statement line items, state whether the item is a "by nature" expense item or a "by function" expense item.

_____ Cost of goods sold
_____ Depreciation expense
_____ Salaries and wages expense
_____ Selling expenses
_____ Utilities expense
_____ Delivery expense
_____ General and administrative expenses

IFRS5-3 Reinsch Company reported the following amounts (in euros) in 2014: Net income, €150,000; Unrealized gain related to revaluation of buildings, €10,000; and Unrealized loss on nontrading securities, €(35,000). Determine Reinsch's total comprehensive income for 2014.

INTERNATIONAL FINANCIAL REPORTING PROBLEM: *Zetar plc*

IFRS5-4   The financial statements of Zetar plc are presented in Appendix C. The company's complete annual report, including the notes to its financial statements, is available in the Investors section at **www.zetarplc.com**.

Instructions

Visit Zetar's corporate website and answer the following questions from Zetar's 2011 annual report.
   (a) Does Zetar use a multiple-step or a single-step income statement format? Explain how you made your determination.
   (b) Instead of "interest expense," what label does Zetar use for interest costs that it incurs?
   (c) What is the approximate tax rate of Zetar's "Tax on profit from continuing activities"?
   (d) Using the notes to the company's financial statements, explain what each of the following are:
      (1) Adjusted results.
      (2) One-off items.

Answers to IFRS Self-Test Questions
1. c   **2.** d   **3.** c   **4.** a   **5.** b

CHAPTER 6

James Porter/Workbook Stock/Getty Images, Inc.

REPORTING AND ANALYZING INVENTORY

The Navigator

- Scan Learning Objectives
- Read Feature Story
- Scan Preview
- Read Text and Answer **Do it!**
  ○ p. 287 ○ p. 294 ○ p. 299 ○ p. 301
- Work Using the Decision Toolkit
- Review Summary of Learning Objectives
- Work Comprehensive **Do it!** p. 310
- Answer Self-Test Questions
- Complete Assignments
- Go to WileyPLUS for practice and tutorials

 Read A Look at IFRS p. 331

LEARNING OBJECTIVES

After studying this chapter, you should be able to:

1 Determine how to classify inventory and inventory quantities.

2 Explain the basis of accounting for inventories and apply the inventory cost flow methods under a periodic inventory system.

3 Explain the financial statement and tax effects of each of the inventory cost flow assumptions.

4 Explain the lower-of-cost-or-market basis of accounting for inventories.

5 Compute and interpret the inventory turnover.

6 Describe the LIFO reserve and explain its importance for comparing results of different companies.

✔ The Navigator

Let's talk inventory—big, bulldozer-size inventory. Caterpillar Inc. is the world's largest manufacturer of construction and mining equipment, diesel and natural gas engines, and industrial gas turbines. It sells its products in over 200 countries, making it one of the most successful U.S. exporters. More than 70% of its productive assets are located domestically, and nearly 50% of its sales are foreign.

In the past, Caterpillar's profitability suffered, but today it is very successful. A big part of this turnaround can be attributed to effective management of its inventory. Imagine what a bulldozer costs. Now imagine what it costs Caterpillar to have too many bulldozers sitting around in inventory—a situation the company definitely wants to avoid. Conversely, Caterpillar must make sure it has enough inventory to meet demand.

At one time during a 7-year period, Caterpillar's sales increased by 100%, while its inventory increased by only 50%. To achieve this dramatic reduction in the amount of resources tied up in inventory, while continuing to meet customers' needs, Caterpillar used a two-pronged approach. First, it completed a factory modernization program, which dramatically increased its production efficiency. The program reduced by

"WHERE IS THAT SPARE BULLDOZER BLADE?"

60% the amount of inventory the company processed at any one time. It also reduced by an incredible 75% the time it takes to manufacture a part.

Second, Caterpillar dramatically improved its parts distribution system. It ships more than 100,000 items daily from its 23 distribution centers strategically located around the world (10 million square feet of warehouse space—remember, we're talking bulldozers). The company can virtually guarantee that it can get any part to anywhere in the world within 24 hours.

After these changes, Caterpillar had record exports, profits, and revenues. It would have seemed that things couldn't have been better. But industry analysts, as well as the company's managers, thought otherwise. In order to maintain Caterpillar's position as the industry leader, management began another major overhaul of inventory production and inventory management processes. The goal: to cut the number of repairs in half, increase productivity by 20%, and increase inventory turnover by 40%. In short, Caterpillar's ability to manage its inventory has been a key reason for its past success, and inventory management will very likely play a huge part in its ability to succeed in the future.

✔ The Navigator

INSIDE CHAPTER 6 . . .

In the previous chapter, we discussed the accounting for merchandise inventory using a perpetual inventory system. In this chapter, we explain the methods used to calculate the cost of inventory on hand at the balance sheet date and the cost of goods sold. We conclude by illustrating methods for analyzing inventory.

The content and organization of this chapter are as follows.

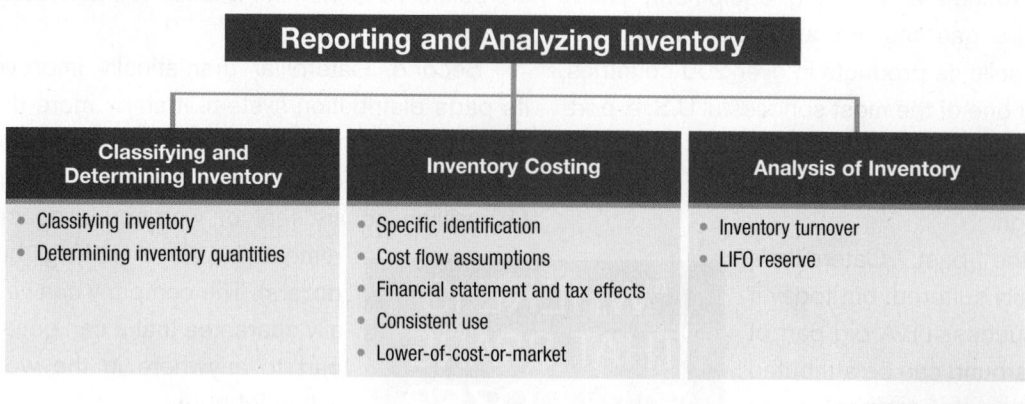

Classifying and Determining Inventory

LEARNING OBJECTIVE 1

Determine how to classify inventory and inventory quantities.

Two important steps in the reporting of inventory at the end of the accounting period are the classification of inventory based on its degree of completeness and the determination of inventory amounts.

CLASSIFYING INVENTORY

How a company classifies its inventory depends on whether the firm is a merchandiser or a manufacturer. In a **merchandising** company, such as those described in Chapter 5, inventory consists of many different items. For example, in a grocery store, canned goods, dairy products, meats, and produce are just a few of the inventory items on hand. These items have two common characteristics: (1) They are owned by the company, and (2) they are in a form ready for sale to customers in the ordinary course of business. Thus, merchandisers need only one inventory classification, **merchandise inventory**, to describe the many different items that make up the total inventory.

In a **manufacturing** company, some inventory may not yet be ready for sale. As a result, manufacturers usually classify inventory into three categories: finished goods, work in process, and raw materials. Finished goods inventory is manufactured items that are completed and ready for sale. Work in process is that portion of manufactured inventory that has begun the production process but is not yet complete. Raw materials are the basic goods that will be used in production but have not yet been placed into production.

For example, Caterpillar classifies earth-moving tractors completed and ready for sale as **finished goods**. It classifies the tractors on the assembly line in various stages of production as **work in process**. The steel, glass, tires, and other components that are on hand waiting to be used in the production of tractors are identified as **raw materials**. Illustration 6-1 shows an excerpt from Note 7 of Caterpillar's annual report, which shows the significant increases in each type of Caterpillar's inventory levels as the economy began to recover during this period.

Helpful Hint Regardless of the classification, companies report all inventories under Current Assets on the balance sheet.

Illustration 6-1 Composition of Caterpillar's inventory

(millions of dollars)	December 31		
	2011	**2010**	**2009**
Raw materials	$3,872	$2,766	$1,979
Work-in-process	2,845	1,483	656
Finished goods	7,570	5,098	3,465
Other	257	240	260
Total inventories	$14,544	$9,587	$6,360

By observing the levels and changes in the levels of these three inventory types, financial statement users can gain insight into management's production plans. For example, low levels of raw materials and high levels of finished goods suggest that management believes it has enough inventory on hand, and production will be slowing down—perhaps in anticipation of a recession. On the other hand, high levels of raw materials and low levels of finished goods probably signal that management is planning to step up production.

Many companies have significantly lowered inventory levels and costs using **just-in-time (JIT) inventory** methods. Under a just-in-time method, companies manufacture or purchase goods just in time for use. Dell is famous for having developed a system for making computers in response to individual customer requests. Even though it makes computers to meet a customer's particular specifications, Dell is able to assemble the computer and put it on a truck in less than 48 hours. The success of a JIT system depends on reliable suppliers. By integrating its information systems with those of its suppliers, Dell reduced its inventories to nearly zero. This is a huge advantage in an industry where products become obsolete nearly overnight.

The accounting concepts discussed in this chapter apply to the inventory classifications of both merchandising and manufacturing companies. Our focus throughout most of this chapter is on merchandise inventory. Additional issues specific to manufacturing companies are discussed in managerial accounting courses.

Accounting Across the Organization

A Big Hiccup

JIT can save a company a lot of money, but it isn't without risk. An unexpected disruption in the supply chain can cost a company a lot of money. Japanese automakers experienced just such a disruption when a 6.8-magnitude earthquake caused major damage to the company that produces 50% of their piston rings. The rings themselves cost only $1.50, but without them you cannot make a car. No other supplier could quickly begin producing sufficient quantities of the rings to match the desired specifications. As a result, the automakers were forced to shut down production for a few days—a loss of tens of thousands of cars.

Similarly, a major snowstorm halted production at Canadian plants of General Motors and Ford. A Ford spokesperson said, "Because the plants run with just-in-time inventory, we don't have large stockpiles of parts sitting around. When you have a somewhat significant disruption, you can pretty quickly run out of parts."

Source: Amy Chozick, "A Key Strategy of Japan's Car Makers Backfires," *Wall Street Journal* (July 20, 2007); Kate Linebaugh, "Canada Military Evacuates Motorists Stranded by Snow," *Wall Street Journal* (December 15, 2010).

? What steps might the companies take to avoid such a serious disruption in the future? (See page 331.)

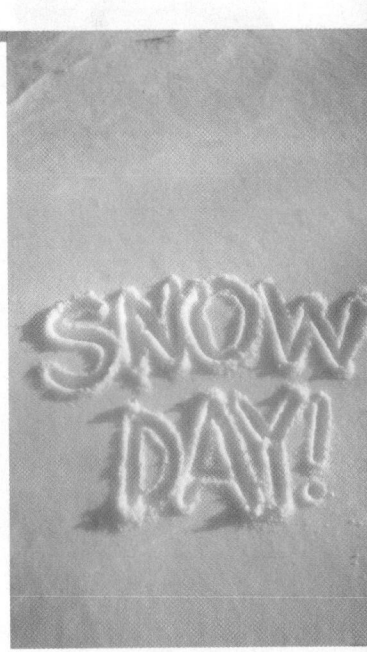

DETERMINING INVENTORY QUANTITIES

No matter whether they are using a periodic or perpetual inventory system, all companies need to determine inventory quantities at the end of the accounting period. If using a perpetual system, companies take a physical inventory for the following reasons. The first is to check the accuracy of their perpetual inventory records. The second is to determine the amount of inventory lost due to wasted raw materials, shoplifting, or employee theft.

Companies using a periodic inventory system must take a physical inventory for two different purposes: to determine the inventory on hand at the balance sheet date, and to determine the cost of goods sold for the period.

Determining inventory quantities involves two steps: (1) taking a physical inventory of goods on hand and (2) determining the ownership of goods.

Taking a Physical Inventory

Ethics Note In a famous fraud, a salad oil company filled its storage tanks mostly with water. The oil rose to the top, so auditors thought the tanks were full of oil. The company also said it had more tanks than it really did: it repainted numbers on the tanks to confuse auditors.

Companies take the physical inventory at the end of the accounting period. Taking a physical inventory involves actually counting, weighing, or measuring each kind of inventory on hand. In many companies, taking an inventory is a formidable task. Retailers such as Target, True Value Hardware, or Home Depot have thousands of different inventory items. An inventory count is generally more accurate when a limited number of goods are being sold or received during the counting. Consequently, companies often "take inventory" when the business is closed or when business is slow. Many retailers close early on a chosen day in January—after the holiday sales and returns, when inventories are at their lowest level—to count inventory. Wal-Mart, for example, has a year-end of January 31.

© Greg Brookes/iStockphoto

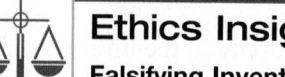 ## Ethics Insight

Falsifying Inventory to Boost Income

Managers at women's apparel maker Leslie Fay were convicted of falsifying inventory records to boost net income—and consequently to boost management bonuses. In another case, executives at Craig Consumer Electronics were accused of defrauding lenders by manipulating inventory records. The indictment said the company classified "defective goods as new or refurbished" and claimed that it owned certain shipments "from overseas suppliers" when, in fact, Craig either did not own the shipments or the shipments did not exist.

 What effect does an overstatement of inventory have on a company's financial statements? (See page 331.)

Determining Ownership of Goods

One challenge in determining inventory quantities is making sure a company owns the inventory. To determine ownership of goods, two questions must be answered: Do all of the goods included in the count belong to the company? Does the company own any goods that were not included in the count?

GOODS IN TRANSIT. A complication in determining ownership is **goods in transit** (on board a truck, train, ship, or plane) at the end of the period. The company may have purchased goods that have not yet been received, or it may have sold goods that have not yet been delivered. To arrive at an accurate count, the company must determine ownership of these goods.

Goods in transit should be included in the inventory of the company that has legal title to the goods. Legal title is determined by the terms of the sale, as shown in Illustration 6-2 and described on the next page.

Illustration 6-2 Terms of sale

1. When the terms are **FOB (free on board) shipping point**, ownership of the goods passes to the buyer when the public carrier accepts the goods from the seller.

2. When the terms are **FOB destination**, ownership of the goods remains with the seller until the goods reach the buyer.

CONSIGNED GOODS. In some lines of business, it is common to hold the goods of other parties and try to sell the goods for them for a fee, but without taking ownership of the goods. These are called **consigned goods**.

For example, you might have a used car that you would like to sell. If you take the item to a dealer, the dealer might be willing to put the car on its lot and charge you a commission if it is sold. Under this agreement, the dealer **would not take ownership** of the car, which would still belong to you. If an inventory count were taken, the car would not be included in the dealer's inventory because the dealer does not own it.

Many car, boat, and antique dealers sell goods on consignment to keep their inventory costs down and to avoid the risk of purchasing an item that they will not be able to sell. Today, even some manufacturers are making consignment agreements with their suppliers in order to keep their inventory levels low.

Do it!

RULES OF OWNERSHIP

Hasbeen Company completed its inventory count. It arrived at a total inventory value of $200,000. You have been given the information listed below. Discuss how this information affects the reported cost of inventory.

1. Hasbeen included in the inventory goods held on consignment for Falls Co., costing $15,000.

2. The company did not include in the count purchased goods of $10,000, which were in transit (terms: FOB shipping point).

3. The company did not include in the count inventory that had been sold with a cost of $12,000, which was in transit (terms: FOB shipping point).

Action Plan

• Apply the rules of ownership to goods held on consignment.

• Apply the rules of ownership to goods in transit.

Solution

The goods of $15,000 held on consignment should be deducted from the inventory count. The goods of $10,000 purchased FOB shipping point should be added to the inventory count. Item 3 was treated correctly. Sold goods of $12,000 which were in transit FOB shipping point should not be included in the ending inventory. Inventory should be $195,000 ($200,000 − $15,000 + $10,000).

Related exercise material: **BE6-1**, Do it! **6-1**, **E6-1**, **E6-2**, and **E6-3**.

ANATOMY OF A FRAUD

Ted Nickerson, CEO of clock manufacturer Dally Industries, was feared by all of his employees. Ted had expensive tastes. To support his expensive tastes, Ted took out large loans, which he collateralized with his shares of Dally Industries stock. If the price of Dally's stock fell, he was required to provide the bank with more shares of stock. To achieve target net income figures and thus maintain the stock price, Ted coerced employees in the company to alter inventory figures. Inventory quantities were manipulated by changing the amounts on inventory control tags after the year-end physical inventory count. For example, if a tag said there were 20 units of a particular item, the tag was changed to 220. Similarly, the unit costs that were used to determine the value of ending inventory were increased from, for example, $125 per unit to $1,250. Both of these fraudulent changes had the effect of increasing the amount of reported ending inventory. This reduced cost of goods sold and increased net income.

Total take: $245,000

THE MISSING CONTROL

Independent internal verification. The company should have spot-checked its inventory records periodically, verifying that the number of units in the records agreed with the amount on hand and that the unit costs agreed with vendor price sheets.

Source: Adapted from Wells, *Fraud Casebook* (2007), pp. 502–509.

Inventory Costing

LEARNING OBJECTIVE 2

Explain the basis of accounting for inventories and apply the inventory cost flow methods under a periodic inventory system.

Inventory is accounted for at cost. Cost includes all expenditures necessary to acquire goods and place them in a condition ready for sale. For example, freight costs incurred to acquire inventory are added to the cost of inventory, but the cost of shipping goods to a customer are a selling expense. After a company has determined the quantity of units of inventory, it applies unit costs to the quantities to determine the total cost of the inventory and the cost of goods sold. This process can be complicated if a company has purchased inventory items at different times and at different prices.

For example, assume that Crivitz TV Company purchases three identical 50-inch TVs on different dates at costs of $700, $750, and $800. During the year, Crivitz sold two sets at $1,200 each. These facts are summarized in Illustration 6-3.

Illustration 6-3 Data for inventory costing example

Purchases		
February 3	1 TV at	$700
March 5	1 TV at	$750
May 22	1 TV at	$800
Sales		
June 1	2 TVs for	$2,400 ($1,200 × 2)

Cost of goods sold will differ depending on which two TVs the company sold. For example, it might be $1,450 ($700 + $750), or $1,500 ($700 + $800), or $1,550 ($750 + $800). In this section, we discuss alternative costing methods available to Crivitz.

SPECIFIC IDENTIFICATION

If Crivitz can positively identify which particular units it sold and which are still in ending inventory, it can use the **specific identification method** of inventory costing. For example, if Crivitz sold the TVs it purchased on February 3 and May 22, then its cost of goods sold is $1,500 ($700 + $800), and its ending inventory is

$750 (see Illustration 6-4). Using this method, companies can accurately determine ending inventory and cost of goods sold.

Illustration 6-4 Specific identification method

Specific identification requires that companies keep records of the original cost of each individual inventory item. Historically, specific identification was possible only when a company sold a limited variety of high-unit-cost items that could be identified clearly from the time of purchase through the time of sale. Examples of such products are cars, pianos, or expensive antiques.

Today, with bar coding, electronic product codes, and radio frequency identification, it is theoretically possible to do specific identification with nearly any type of product. The reality is, however, that this practice is still relatively rare. Instead, rather than keep track of the cost of each particular item sold, most companies make assumptions, called **cost flow assumptions**, about which units were sold.

> **Ethics Note** A major disadvantage of the specific identification method is that management may be able to manipulate net income. For example, it can boost net income by selling units purchased at a low cost, or reduce net income by selling units purchased at a high cost.

COST FLOW ASSUMPTIONS

Because specific identification is often impractical, other cost flow methods are permitted. These differ from specific identification in that they **assume** flows of costs that may be unrelated to the actual physical flow of goods. There are three assumed cost flow methods:

1. First-in, first-out (FIFO)
2. Last-in, first-out (LIFO)
3. Average-cost

There is no accounting requirement that the cost flow assumption be consistent with the physical movement of the goods. Company management selects the appropriate cost flow method.

To demonstrate the three cost flow methods, we will use a **periodic** inventory system. We assume a periodic system because very few companies use **perpetual** LIFO, FIFO, or average-cost to cost their inventory and related cost of goods sold. Instead, companies that use perpetual systems, as shown in Chapter 5, often use an assumed cost (called a standard cost) to record cost of goods sold at the time of sale. Then, at the end of the period when they count their inventory, they **recalculate** cost of goods sold using **periodic** FIFO, LIFO, or average-cost as shown in this chapter and adjust cost of goods sold to this recalculated number.[1]

---

[1]Also, some companies use a perpetual system to keep track of units, but they do not make an entry for perpetual cost of goods sold. In addition, firms that employ LIFO tend to use **dollar-value LIFO**, a method discussed in upper-level courses. FIFO periodic and FIFO perpetual give the same result. Therefore, firms should not incur the additional cost to use FIFO perpetual. Few firms use perpetual average-cost because of the added cost of record-keeping. Finally, for instructional purposes, we believe it is easier to demonstrate the cost flow assumptions under the periodic system, which makes it more pedagogically appropriate.

To illustrate the three inventory cost flow methods, we will use the data for Houston Electronics' Astro condensers, shown in Illustration 6-5.

Illustration 6-5 Data for
Houston Electronics

HOUSTON ELECTRONICS
Astro Condensers

Date	Explanation	Units	Unit Cost	Total Cost
Jan. 1	Beginning inventory	100	$10	$ 1,000
Apr. 15	Purchase	200	11	2,200
Aug. 24	Purchase	300	12	3,600
Nov. 27	Purchase	400	13	5,200
	Total units available for sale	1,000		$12,000
	Units in ending inventory	450		
	Units sold	550		

From Chapter 5, the cost of goods sold formula in a periodic system is:

(Beginning Inventory + Purchases) − Ending Inventory = Cost of Goods Sold

Houston Electronics had a total of 1,000 units available to sell during the period (beginning inventory plus purchases). The total cost of these 1,000 units is $12,000, referred to as **cost of goods available for sale**. A physical inventory taken at December 31 determined that there were 450 units in ending inventory. Therefore, Houston sold 550 units (1,000 − 450) during the period. To determine the cost of the 550 units that were sold (the cost of goods sold), we assign a cost to the ending inventory and subtract that value from the cost of goods available for sale. The value assigned to the ending inventory **will depend on which cost flow method we use**. No matter which cost flow assumption we use, though, the sum of cost of goods sold plus the cost of the ending inventory must equal the cost of goods available for sale—in this case, $12,000.

First-In, First-Out (FIFO)

The first-in, first-out (FIFO) method assumes that the **earliest goods** purchased are the first to be sold. FIFO often parallels the actual physical flow of merchandise because it generally is good business practice to sell the oldest units first. Under the FIFO method, therefore, the **costs** of the earliest goods purchased are the first to be recognized in determining cost of goods sold, regardless of which units were actually sold. (Note that this does not mean that the oldest units **are** sold first, but that the costs of the oldest units are **recognized** first. In a bin of picture hangers at the hardware store, for example, no one really knows, nor would it matter, which hangers are sold first.) Illustration 6-6 shows the allocation of the cost of goods available for sale at Houston Electronics under FIFO.

Under FIFO, since it is assumed that the first goods purchased were the first goods sold, ending inventory is based on the prices of the most recent units purchased. That is, **under FIFO, companies determine the cost of the ending inventory by taking the unit cost of the most recent purchase and working backward until all units of inventory have been costed**. In this example, Houston Electronics prices the 450 units of ending inventory using the **most recent** prices. The last purchase was 400 units at $13 on November 27. The remaining 50 units are priced using the unit cost of the second most recent purchase, $12, on August 24. Next, Houston Electronics calculates cost of goods sold by subtracting the cost of the units **not sold** (ending inventory) from the cost of all goods available for sale.

Illustration 6-6 Allocation of costs-FIFO method

COST OF GOODS AVAILABLE FOR SALE

Date	Explanation	Units	Unit Cost	Total Cost
Jan. 1	Beginning inventory	100	$10	$ 1,000
Apr. 15	Purchase	200	11	2,200
Aug. 24	Purchase	300	12	3,600
Nov. 27	Purchase	400	13	5,200
	Total	1,000		$12,000

Helpful Hint Note the sequencing of the allocation: (1) compute ending inventory, and (2) determine cost of goods sold.

STEP 1: ENDING INVENTORY   STEP 2: COST OF GOODS SOLD

Date	Units	Unit Cost	Total Cost
Nov. 27	400	$13	$5,200
Aug. 24	50	12	600
Total	450		$5,800

Cost of goods available for sale $12,000
Less: Ending inventory **5,800**
Cost of goods sold $ 6,200

Helpful Hint Another way of thinking about the calculation of FIFO **ending inventory** is the *LISH assumption*—last in still here.

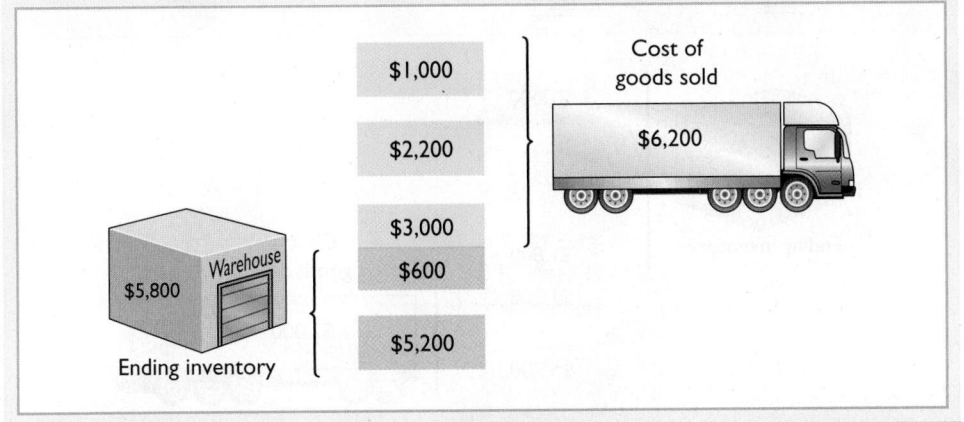

Illustration 6-7 demonstrates that companies also can calculate cost of goods sold by pricing the 550 units sold using the prices of the first 550 units acquired. Note that of the 300 units purchased on August 24, only 250 units are assumed sold. This agrees with our calculation of the cost of ending inventory, where 50 of these units were assumed unsold and thus included in ending inventory.

Illustration 6-7 Proof of cost of goods sold

Date	Units	Unit Cost	Total Cost
Jan. 1	100	$10	$1,000
Apr. 15	200	11	2,200
Aug. 24	250	12	3,000
Total	550		$6,200

Last-In, First-Out (LIFO)

The last-in, first-out (LIFO) method assumes that the **latest goods** purchased are the first to be sold. LIFO seldom coincides with the actual physical flow of inventory. (Exceptions include goods stored in piles, such as coal or hay, where goods are removed from the top of the pile as they are sold.) Under the LIFO method, the **costs** of the latest goods purchased are the first to be recognized in determining cost of goods sold. Illustration 6-8 (page 292) shows the allocation of the cost of goods available for sale at Houston Electronics under LIFO.

Illustration 6-8 Allocation of costs—LIFO method

COST OF GOODS AVAILABLE FOR SALE

Date	Explanation	Units	Unit Cost	Total Cost
Jan. 1	Beginning inventory	100	$10	$ 1,000
Apr. 15	Purchase	200	11	2,200
Aug. 24	Purchase	300	12	3,600
Nov. 27	Purchase	400	13	5,200
	Total	1,000		$12,000

Helpful Hint Another way of thinking about the calculation of LIFO **ending inventory** is the *FISH assumption*—first in still here.

STEP 1: ENDING INVENTORY

Date	Units	Unit Cost	Total Cost
Jan. 1	100	$10	$1,000
Apr. 15	200	11	2,200
Aug. 24	150	12	1,800
Total	450		$5,000

STEP 2: COST OF GOODS SOLD

Cost of goods available for sale	$12,000
Less: Ending inventory	5,000
Cost of goods sold	$ 7,000

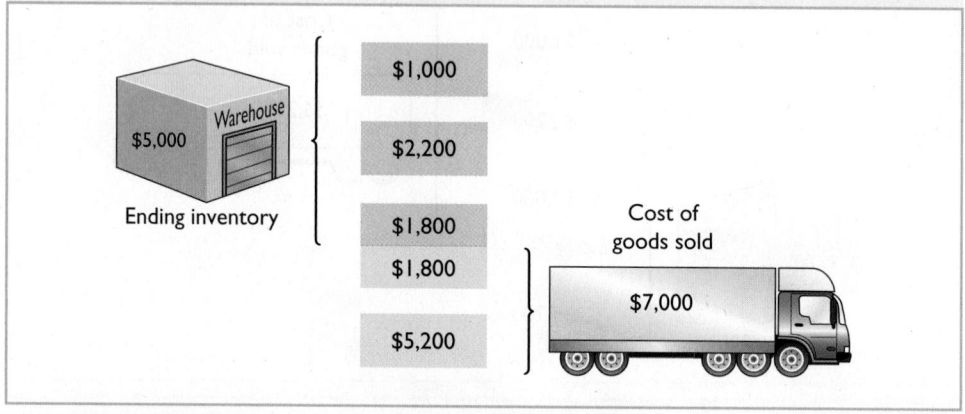

Under LIFO, since it is assumed that the first goods sold were those that were most recently purchased, ending inventory is based on the prices of the oldest units purchased. That is, **under LIFO, companies obtain the cost of the ending inventory by taking the unit cost of the earliest goods available for sale and working forward until all units of inventory have been costed**. In this example, Houston Electronics prices the 450 units of ending inventory using the **earliest** prices. The first purchase was 100 units at $10 in the January 1 beginning inventory. Then, 200 units were purchased at $11. The remaining 150 units needed are priced at $12 per unit (August 24 purchase). Next, Houston Electronics calculates cost of goods sold by subtracting the cost of the units **not sold** (ending inventory) from the cost of all goods available for sale.

Illustration 6-9 demonstrates that we can also calculate cost of goods sold by pricing the 550 units sold using the prices of the last 550 units acquired. Note that of the 300 units purchased on August 24, only 150 units are assumed sold. This agrees with our calculation of the cost of ending inventory, where 150 of these units were assumed unsold and thus included in ending inventory.

Illustration 6-9 Proof of cost of goods sold

Date	Units	Unit Cost	Total Cost
Nov. 27	400	$13	$5,200
Aug. 24	150	12	1,800
Total	550		$7,000

Under a periodic inventory system, which we are using here, **all goods purchased during the period are assumed to be available for the first sale, regardless of the date of purchase**.

Average-Cost

The **average-cost method** allocates the cost of goods available for sale on the basis of the **weighted-average unit cost** incurred. Illustration 6-10 presents the formula and a sample computation of the weighted-average unit cost.

Cost of Goods Available for Sale		Total Units Available for Sale		Weighted-Average Unit Cost
$12,000	÷	1,000	=	**$12.00**

Illustration 6-10 Formula for weighted-average unit cost

The company then applies the weighted-average unit cost to the units on hand to determine the cost of the ending inventory. Illustration 6-11 shows the allocation of the cost of goods available for sale at Houston Electronics using average-cost.

Illustration 6-11 Allocation of costs—average-cost method

COST OF GOODS AVAILABLE FOR SALE

Date	Explanation	Units	Unit Cost	Total Cost
Jan. 1	Beginning inventory	100	$10	$ 1,000
Apr. 15	Purchase	200	11	2,200
Aug. 24	Purchase	300	12	3,600
Nov. 27	Purchase	400	13	5,200
	Total	1,000		$12,000

STEP 1: ENDING INVENTORY

$12,000 ÷ 1,000 = $12.00

Units	×	Unit Cost	=	Total Cost
450		$12.00		$5,400

STEP 2: COST OF GOODS SOLD

Cost of goods available for sale	$12,000
Less: Ending inventory	5,400
Cost of goods sold	$ 6,600

$$\frac{\$12,000}{1,000 \text{ units}} = \$12 \text{ per unit}$$

Cost per unit

450 units × $12 = $5,400   Warehouse

Ending inventory

$12,000 − $5,400 = $6,600

Cost of goods sold

We can verify the cost of goods sold under this method by multiplying the units sold times the weighted-average unit cost (550 × $12 = $6,600). Note that this method does not use the simple average of the unit costs. The simple average is $11.50 ($10 + $11 + $12 + $13 = $46; $46 ÷ 4). The average-cost method instead uses the average **weighted by** the quantities purchased at each unit cost.

COST FLOW METHODS

 Do it! The accounting records of Shumway Ag Implement show the following data.

Beginning inventory	4,000 units at $3
Purchases	6,000 units at $4
Sales	7,000 units at $12

Determine (a) the cost of goods available for sale and (b) the cost of goods sold during the period under a periodic system using (i) FIFO, (ii) LIFO, and (iii) average-cost.

Action Plan

- Understand the periodic inventory system.
- Allocate costs between goods sold and goods on hand (ending inventory) for each cost flow method.
- Compute cost of goods sold for each cost flow method.

✔ **The Navigator**

Solution

(a) Cost of goods available for sale: (4,000 × $3) + (6,000 × $4) = $36,000

(b) Cost of goods sold using:
   (i) FIFO: $36,000 − (3,000* × $4) = $24,000
  (ii) LIFO: $36,000 − (3,000 × $3) = $27,000
 (iii) Average-cost: Weighted-average price = ($36,000 ÷ 10,000) = $3.60
        $36,000 − (3,000 × $3.60) = $25,200

*(4,000 + 6,000 − 7,000)

Related exercise material: **BE6-2, BE6-3, Do it! 6-2, E6-4,** and **E6-5.**

FINANCIAL STATEMENT AND TAX EFFECTS OF COST FLOW METHODS

LEARNING OBJECTIVE 3

Explain the financial statement and tax effects of each of the inventory cost flow assumptions.

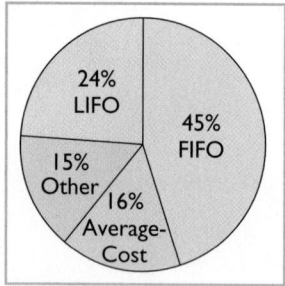

Illustration 6-12 Use of cost flow methods in major U.S. companies

Each of the three assumed cost flow methods is acceptable for use under GAAP. For example, Reebok International Ltd. and Wendy's International currently use the FIFO method of inventory costing. Campbell Soup Company, Krogers, and Walgreens use LIFO for part or all of their inventory. Bristol-Myers Squibb, Starbucks, and Motorola use the average-cost method. In fact, a company may also use more than one cost flow method at the same time. Stanley Black & Decker Manufacturing Company, for example, uses LIFO for domestic inventories and FIFO for foreign inventories. Illustration 6-12 shows the use of the three cost flow methods in 500 large U.S. companies.

The reasons companies adopt different inventory cost flow methods are varied, but they usually involve at least one of the following three factors:

1. Income statement effects
2. Balance sheet effects
3. Tax effects

Income Statement Effects

To understand why companies might choose a particular cost flow method, let's examine the effects of the different cost flow assumptions on the financial statements of Houston Electronics. The condensed income statements in Illustration 6-13 assume that Houston sold its 550 units for $18,500, had operating expenses of $9,000, and is subject to an income tax rate of 30%.

Note the cost of goods available for sale ($12,000) is the same under each of the three inventory cost flow methods. However, the ending inventories and the costs of goods sold are different. This difference is due to the unit costs that the company allocated to cost of goods sold and to ending inventory. Each dollar of difference in ending inventory results in a corresponding dollar difference in

HOUSTON ELECTRONICS
Condensed Income Statements

	FIFO	LIFO	Average-Cost
Sales revenue	$18,500	$18,500	$18,500
Beginning inventory	1,000	1,000	1,000
Purchases	11,000	11,000	11,000
Cost of goods available for sale	12,000	12,000	12,000
Less: Ending inventory	5,800	5,000	5,400
Cost of goods sold	6,200	7,000	6,600
Gross profit	12,300	11,500	11,900
Operating expenses	9,000	9,000	9,000
Income before income taxes	3,300	2,500	2,900
Income tax expense (30%)	990	750	870
Net income	$ 2,310	$ 1,750	$ 2,030

Illustration 6-13 Comparative effects of cost flow methods

income before income taxes. For Houston, an $800 difference exists between FIFO and LIFO cost of goods sold.

In periods of changing prices, the cost flow assumption can have a significant impact on income and on evaluations based on income. In most instances, prices are rising (inflation). In a period of inflation, FIFO produces a higher net income because the lower unit costs of the first units purchased are matched against revenues. In a period of rising prices (as is the case in the Houston example), FIFO reports the highest net income ($2,310) and LIFO the lowest ($1,750); average-cost falls in the middle ($2,030). If prices are falling, the results from the use of FIFO and LIFO are reversed: FIFO will report the lowest net income and LIFO the highest.

To management, higher net income is an advantage: It causes external users to view the company more favorably. In addition, management bonuses, if based on net income, will be higher. Therefore, when prices are rising (which is usually the case), companies tend to prefer FIFO because it results in higher net income.

Some argue that the use of LIFO in a period of inflation reduces the likelihood that the company will report **paper** (or **phantom**) **profit** as economic gain. To illustrate, assume that Kralik Company buys 200 units of a product at $20 per unit on January 10 and 200 more on December 31 at $24 each. During the year, Kralik sells 200 units at $30 each. Illustration 6-14 shows the results under FIFO and LIFO.

	FIFO		LIFO	
Sales revenue (200 × $30)	$6,000		$6,000	
Cost of goods sold	4,000	(200 × $20)	4,800	(200 × $24)
Gross profit	$2,000		$1,200	

Illustration 6-14 Income statement effects compared

Under LIFO, Kralik Company has recovered the current replacement cost ($4,800) of the units sold. Thus, the gross profit in economic terms is real. However, under FIFO, the company has recovered only the January 10 cost ($4,000). To replace the units sold, it must reinvest $800 (200 × $4) of the gross profit. Thus, $800 of the gross profit is said to be phantom or illusory. As a result, reported net income is also overstated in real terms.

Balance Sheet Effects

A major advantage of the FIFO method is that in a period of inflation, the costs allocated to ending inventory will approximate their current cost. For example, for Houston Electronics, 400 of the 450 units in the ending inventory are costed under FIFO at the higher November 27 unit cost of $13.

Conversely, a major shortcoming of the LIFO method is that in a period of inflation, the costs allocated to ending inventory may be significantly understated in terms of current cost. The understatement becomes greater over prolonged periods of inflation if the inventory includes goods purchased in one or more prior accounting periods. For example, Caterpillar has used LIFO for 50 years. Its balance sheet shows ending inventory of $14.5 billion. But the inventory's actual current cost if FIFO had been used is $17.0 billion.

Tax Effects

Helpful Hint A tax rule, often referred to as the *LIFO conformity rule*, requires that if companies use LIFO for tax purposes, they must also use it for financial reporting purposes. This means that if a company chooses the LIFO method to reduce its tax bills, it will also have to report lower net income in its financial statements.

We have seen that both inventory on the balance sheet and net income on the income statement are higher when companies use FIFO in a period of inflation. Yet, many companies use LIFO. Why? The reason is that LIFO results in the lowest income taxes (because of lower net income) during times of rising prices. For example, in Illustration 6-13 (page 295) income taxes are $750 under LIFO, compared to $990 under FIFO. The tax savings of $240 makes more cash available for use in the business.

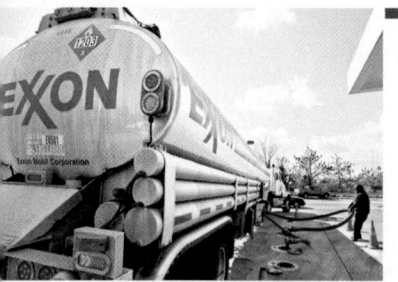

©AP/Wide World Photos

International Insight

Is LIFO Fair?

ExxonMobil Corporation, like many U.S. companies, uses LIFO to value its inventory for financial reporting and tax purposes. In one recent year, this resulted in a cost of goods sold figure that was $5.6 billion higher than under FIFO. By increasing cost of goods sold, ExxonMobil reduces net income, which reduces taxes. Critics say that LIFO provides an unfair "tax dodge." As Congress looks for more sources of tax revenue, some lawmakers favor the elimination of LIFO. Supporters of LIFO argue that the method is conceptually sound because it matches current costs with current revenues. In addition, they point out that this matching provides protection against inflation.

International accounting standards do not allow the use of LIFO. Because of this, the net income of foreign oil companies, such as BP and Royal Dutch Shell, are not directly comparable to U.S. companies, which makes analysis difficult.

Source: David Reilly, "Big Oil's Accounting Methods Fuel Criticism," *Wall Street Journal* (August 8, 2006), p. C1.

? What are the arguments for and against the use of LIFO? (See page 331.)

KEEPING AN EYE ON CASH

You have just seen that when prices are rising the use of LIFO can have a big effect on taxes. The lower taxes paid using LIFO can significantly increase cash flows. To demonstrate the effect of the cost flow assumptions on cash flow, we will calculate net cash provided by operating activities, using the data for Houston Electronics from Illustration 6-13. To simplify our example, we assume that Houston's sales and purchases are all cash transactions. We also assume that operating expenses, other than $4,600 of depreciation, are cash transactions.

	FIFO	LIFO	Average-Cost
Cash received from customers	$18,500	$18,500	$18,500
Cash purchases of goods	11,000	11,000	11,000
Cash paid for operating expenses ($9,000 − $4,600)	4,400	4,400	4,400
Cash paid for taxes	990	750	870
Net cash provided by operating activities	$ 2,110	$ 2,350	$ 2,230

LIFO has the highest net cash provided by operating activities because it results in the lowest tax payments. Since cash flow is the lifeblood of any organization, the choice of inventory method is very important.

LIFO also impacts the quality of earnings ratio. Recall that the quality of earnings ratio is net cash provided by operating activities divided by net income. Here, we calculate the quality earnings ratio under each cost flow assumption.

	FIFO	LIFO	Average-Cost
Net income (from Illustration 6-13)	$2,310	$1,750	$2,030
Quality of earnings ratio	0.91	1.34	1.1

LIFO has the highest quality of earnings ratio for two reasons: (1) It has the highest net cash provided by operating activities, which increases the ratio's numerator. (2) It reports a conservative measure of net income, which decreases the ratio's denominator. As discussed earlier, LIFO provides a conservative measure of net income because it does not include the phantom profits reported under FIFO.

🧰 DECISION TOOLKIT

DECISION CHECKPOINTS	INFO NEEDED FOR DECISION	TOOL TO USE FOR DECISION	HOW TO EVALUATE RESULTS
Which inventory costing method should be used?	Are prices increasing, or are they decreasing?	Income statement, balance sheet, and tax effects	Depends on objective. In a period of rising prices, income and inventory are higher and cash flow is lower under FIFO. LIFO provides opposite results. Average-cost can moderate the impact of changing prices.

USING INVENTORY COST FLOW METHODS CONSISTENTLY

Whatever cost flow method a company chooses, it should use that method consistently from one accounting period to another. Consistent application enhances the ability to analyze a company's financial statements over successive time periods. In contrast, using the FIFO method one year and the LIFO method the next year would make it difficult to compare the net incomes of the two years.

Although consistent application is preferred, it does not mean that a company may never change its method of inventory costing. When a company adopts a different method, it should disclose in the financial statements the change and its effects on net income. A typical disclosure is shown in Illustration 6-15 (page 298), using information from recent financial statements of Quaker Oats Company.

Helpful Hint As you learned in Chapter 2, consistency and comparability are important characteristics of accounting information.

Illustration 6-15 Disclosure of change in cost flow method

QUAKER OATS COMPANY
Notes to the Financial Statements

Note 1: Effective July 1, the Company adopted the LIFO cost flow assumption for valuing the majority of U.S. Grocery Products inventories. The Company believes that the use of the LIFO method better matches current costs with current revenues. The effect of this change on the current year was to decrease net income by $16.0 million.

LOWER-OF-COST-OR-MARKET

LEARNING OBJECTIVE 4
Explain the lower-of-cost-or-market basis of accounting for inventories.

The value of inventory for companies selling high-technology or fashion goods can drop very quickly due to changes in technology or changes in fashions. These circumstances sometimes call for inventory valuation methods other than those presented so far. For example, in a recent year, purchasing managers at Ford decided to make a large purchase of palladium, a precious metal used in vehicle emission devices. They made this large purchase because they feared a future shortage. The shortage did not materialize, and by the end of the year the price of palladium had plummeted. Ford's inventory was then worth $1 billion less than its original cost. Do you think Ford's inventory should have been stated at cost, in accordance with the historical cost principle, or at its lower replacement cost?

International Note Under U.S. GAAP, companies cannot reverse inventory write-downs if inventory increases in value in subsequent periods. IFRS permits companies to reverse write-downs in some circumstances.

As you probably reasoned, this situation requires a departure from the cost basis of accounting. This is done by valuing the inventory at the **lower-of-cost-or-market (LCM)** in the period in which the price decline occurs. LCM is a basis whereby inventory is stated at the lower of either its cost or market value as determined by current replacement cost. LCM is an example of the accounting **convention of conservatism**. Conservatism means that the approach adopted among accounting alternatives is the method that is least likely to overstate assets and net income.

Companies apply LCM to the items in inventory after they have used one of the cost flow methods (specific identification, FIFO, LIFO, or average-cost) to determine cost. Under the LCM basis, market is defined as **current replacement cost**, not selling price. For a merchandising company, current replacement cost is the cost of purchasing the same goods at the present time from the usual suppliers in the usual quantities. Current replacement cost is used because a decline in the replacement cost of an item usually leads to a decline in the selling price of the item.

To illustrate the application of LCM, assume that Ken Tuckie TV has the following lines of merchandise with costs and market values as indicated. LCM produces the results shown in Illustration 6-16. Note that the amounts shown in the final column are the lower-of-cost-or-market amounts for each item.

Illustration 6-16 Computation of inventory at lower-of-cost-or-market

	Cost	Market	Lower-of-Cost-or-Market
Flat-panel TVs	$60,000	$55,000	$ 55,000
Satellite radios	45,000	52,000	45,000
DVD recorders	48,000	45,000	45,000
DVDs	15,000	14,000	14,000
Total inventory			$159,000

Adherence to LCM is important. Acer Inc. recently took a charge of $150 million on personal computers, which declined in value before they could be sold. A Chinese manufacturer of silicon wafers for solar energy panels, LDK Solar Co., was accused of violating LCM. When the financial press reported accusations that two-thirds of its inventory of silicon was unsuitable for processing, the company's stock price fell by 40%.

Do it!

LCM BASIS

Tracy Company sells three different types of home heating stoves (gas, wood, and pellet). The cost and market value of its inventory of stoves are as follows.

	Cost	Market
Gas	$ 84,000	$ 79,000
Wood	250,000	280,000
Pellet	112,000	101,000

Determine the value of the company's inventory under the lower-of-cost-or-market approach.

Solution

The lower value for each inventory type is gas $79,000, wood $250,000, and pellet $101,000. The total inventory value is the sum of these figures, $430,000.

Related exercise material: **BE6-7**, **Do it! 6-3**, and **E6-9**.

Action Plan

- Determine whether cost or market value is lower for each inventory type.
- Sum the lower value of each inventory type to determine the total value of inventory.

✔ The Navigator

Analysis of Inventory

For companies that sell goods, managing inventory levels can be one of the most critical tasks. Having too much inventory on hand costs the company money in storage costs, interest cost (on funds tied up in inventory), and costs associated with the obsolescence of technical goods (e.g., computer chips) or shifts in fashion (e.g., clothes). But having too little inventory on hand results in lost sales. In this section, we discuss some issues related to evaluating inventory levels.

LEARNING OBJECTIVE 5
Compute and interpret the inventory turnover.

INVENTORY TURNOVER

The **inventory turnover** is calculated as cost of goods sold divided by average inventory. It indicates the liquidity of inventory by measuring the number of times the average inventory "turns over" (is sold) during the year. Inventory turnover can be divided into 365 days to compute **days in inventory**, which indicates the average number of days inventory is held.

High inventory turnover (low days in inventory) indicates the company has minimal funds tied up in inventory—that it has a minimal amount of inventory on hand at any one time. Although minimizing the funds tied up in inventory is efficient, too high an inventory turnover may indicate that the company is losing sales opportunities because of inventory shortages. For example, investment analysts at one time suggested that Office Depot had gone too far in reducing its inventory—they said they were seeing too many empty shelves. Thus, management should closely monitor this ratio to achieve the best balance between too much and too little inventory.

In Chapter 5, we discussed the increasingly competitive environment of retailers, such as Wal-Mart and Target. Wal-Mart has implemented **just-in-time inventory procedures** as well as many technological innovations to improve the efficiency of its inventory management. The following data are available for Wal-Mart.

(in millions)	2011	2010
Ending inventory	$ 36,318	$32,713
Cost of goods sold	315,287	

Illustration 6-17 presents the inventory turnovers and days in inventory for Wal-Mart and Target, using data from the financial statements of those corporations for 2011 and 2010.

Illustration 6-17 Inventory turnovers and days in inventory

$$\text{Inventory Turnover} = \frac{\text{Cost of Goods Sold}}{\text{Average Inventory}}$$

$$\text{Days in Inventory} = \frac{365}{\text{Inventory Turnover}}$$

Ratio	Wal-Mart ($ in millions)		Target	Industry Average
	2011	2010	2011	2011
Inventory turnover	$\frac{\$315,287}{(\$36,318 + \$32,713)/2} = 9.1$ times	9.1 times	6.2 times	8.4 times
Days in inventory	$\frac{365 \text{ days}}{9.1} = 40.1$ days	40.1 days	58.9 days	43.5 days

The calculations in Illustration 6-17 show that Wal-Mart turns its inventory more frequently than Target and the industry average (9.1 times for Wal-Mart versus 6.2 times for Target and 8.4 for the industry). Consequently, the average time an item spends on a Wal-Mart shelf is shorter (40.1 days for Wal-Mart versus 58.9 days for Target and 43.5 days for the industry).

This analysis suggests that Wal-Mart is more efficient than Target in its inventory management. Wal-Mart's sophisticated inventory tracking and distribution system allows it to keep minimum amounts of inventory on hand, while still keeping the shelves full of what customers are looking for.

© Dmitry Kutlayev/iStockphoto

Accounting Across the Organization
Too Many TVs or Too Few?

Financial analysts closely monitored the inventory management practices of companies during the recent recession. For example, some analysts following Sony expressed concern because the company built up its inventory of televisions in an attempt to sell 25 million liquid crystal display (LCD) TVs–a 60% increase over the prior year. A year earlier, Sony had cut its inventory levels so that its quarterly days in inventory was down to 38 days, compared to 61 days for the same quarter a year before that. But now, as a result of its inventory build-up, days in inventory rose to 59 days. While management was saying that it didn't think that Sony's inventory levels were now too high, analysts were concerned that the company would have to engage in very heavy discounting in order to sell off its inventory. Analysts noted that the losses from discounting can be "punishing."

Source: Daisuke Wakabayashi, "Sony Pledges to Corral Inventory," *Wall Street Journal Online* (November 2, 2010).

? For Sony, what are the advantages and disadvantages of having a low days in inventory measure? (See page 331.)

🧰 DECISION TOOLKIT

DECISION CHECKPOINTS	INFO NEEDED FOR DECISION	TOOL TO USE FOR DECISION	HOW TO EVALUATE RESULTS
How long is an item in inventory?	Cost of goods sold; beginning and ending inventory	$$\text{Inventory turnover} = \frac{\text{Cost of goods sold}}{\text{Average inventory}}$$ $$\text{Days in inventory} = \frac{365 \text{ days}}{\text{Inventory turnover}}$$	A higher inventory turnover or lower average days in inventory suggests that management is reducing the amount of inventory on hand, relative to cost of goods sold.

Do it!   INVENTORY TURNOVER

Early in 2014, Westmoreland Company switched to a just-in-time inventory system. Its sales, cost of goods sold, and inventory amounts for 2013 and 2014 are shown below.

	2013	2014
Sales revenue	$2,000,000	$1,800,000
Cost of goods sold	1,000,000	910,000
Beginning inventory	290,000	210,000
Ending inventory	210,000	50,000

Determine the inventory turnover and days in inventory for 2013 and 2014. Discuss the changes in the amount of inventory, the inventory turnover and days in inventory, and the amount of sales across the two years.

Solution

	2013	2014
Inventory turnover	$$\frac{\$1,000,000}{(\$290,000 + \$210,000)/2} = 4$$	$$\frac{\$910,000}{(\$210,000 + \$50,000)/2} = 7$$
Days in inventory	$365 \div 4 = 91.3$ days	$365 \div 7 = 52.1$ days

The company experienced a very significant decline in its ending inventory as a result of the just-in-time inventory. This decline improved its inventory turnover and its days in inventory. However, its sales declined by 10%. It is possible that this decline was caused by the dramatic reduction in the amount of inventory that was on hand, which increased the likelihood of "stockouts." To determine the optimal inventory level, management must weigh the benefits of reduced inventory against the potential lost sales caused by stockouts.

Action Plan

- To find the inventory turnover, divide cost of goods sold by average inventory.
- To determine days in inventory, divide 365 days by the inventory turnover.
- Just-in-time inventory reduces the amount of inventory on hand, which reduces carrying costs. Reducing inventory levels by too much has potential negative implications for sales.

✔ The Navigator

Related exercise material: **BE6-8,** *Do it!* **6-4,** and **E6-10.**

ANALYSTS' ADJUSTMENTS FOR LIFO RESERVE

Earlier, we noted that using LIFO rather than FIFO can result in significant differences in the results reported in the balance sheet and the income statement. With increasing prices, FIFO will result in higher income than LIFO. On the balance sheet, FIFO will result in higher reported inventory. The financial statement differences from using LIFO normally increase the longer a company uses LIFO.

Use of different inventory cost flow assumptions complicates analysts' attempts to compare companies' results. Fortunately, companies using LIFO are required to report the difference between inventory reported using LIFO and inventory using FIFO. This amount is referred to as the **LIFO reserve**. Reporting

LEARNING OBJECTIVE   **6**

Describe the LIFO reserve and explain its importance for comparing results of different companies.

the LIFO reserve enables analysts to make adjustments to compare companies that use different cost flow methods.

Illustration 6-18 presents an excerpt from the notes to Caterpillar's 2011 financial statements that discloses and discusses Caterpillar's LIFO reserve.

Illustration 6-18 Caterpillar's LIFO reserve

CATERPILLAR INC.
Notes to the Financial Statements

Inventories: Inventories are stated at the lower of cost or market. Cost is principally determined using the last-in, first-out (LIFO) method . . . . If the FIFO (first-in, first-out) method had been in use, inventories would have been $2,422, $2,575, and $3,022 million higher than reported at December 31, 2011, 2010, and 2009, respectively.

Caterpillar has used LIFO for over 50 years. Thus, the cumulative difference between LIFO and FIFO reflected in the Inventory account is very large. In fact, the 2011 LIFO reserve of $2,422 million is nearly 17% of the 2011 LIFO inventory of $14,544 million. Such a huge difference would clearly distort any comparisons you might try to make with one of Caterpillar's competitors that used FIFO.

To adjust Caterpillar's inventory balance, we add the LIFO reserve to reported inventory, as shown in Illustration 6-19. That is, if Caterpillar had used FIFO all along, its inventory would be $16,966 million, rather than $14,544 million.

Illustration 6-19 Conversion of inventory from LIFO to FIFO

	(in millions)
2011 inventory using LIFO	$14,544
2011 LIFO reserve	2,422
2011 inventory assuming FIFO	$16,966

The LIFO reserve can have a significant effect on ratios that analysts commonly use. Using the LIFO reserve adjustment, Illustration 6-20 calculates the value of the current ratio (current assets ÷ current liabilities) for Caterpillar under both the LIFO and FIFO cost flow assumptions.

Illustration 6-20 Impact of LIFO reserve on ratios

($ in millions)	LIFO	FIFO
Current ratio	$\dfrac{\$38,128}{\$28,561} = 1.33{:}1$	$\dfrac{\$38,128 + \$2,422}{\$28,561} = 1.42{:}1$

As Illustration 6-20 shows, if Caterpillar used FIFO, its current ratio would be 1.42:1 rather than 1.33:1 under LIFO. Thus, Caterpillar's liquidity appears stronger if a FIFO assumption were used in valuing inventories. If a similar adjustment is made for the inventory turnover, Caterpillar's inventory turnover actually would look worse under FIFO than under LIFO, dropping from 3.6 times for LIFO to 3.0 times for FIFO.[2] The reason: LIFO reports low inventory amounts, which cause inventory turnover to be higher.

CNH Global, a competitor of Caterpillar, uses FIFO to account for its inventory. Comparing Caterpillar to CNH without converting Caterpillar's inventory to FIFO would lead to distortions and potentially erroneous decisions.

---

[2]The LIFO reserve also affects cost of goods sold although typically by a much less material amount. The cost of goods sold adjustment is discussed in more advanced financial statement analysis texts.

DECISION TOOLKIT

DECISION CHECKPOINTS	INFO NEEDED FOR DECISION	TOOL TO USE FOR DECISION	HOW TO EVALUATE RESULTS
What is the impact of LIFO on the company's reported inventory?	LIFO reserve, cost of goods sold, ending inventory, current assets, current liabilities	$\text{LIFO inventory} + \text{LIFO reserve} = \text{FIFO inventory}$	If these adjustments are material, they can significantly affect such measures as the current ratio and the inventory turnover.

USING THE DECISION TOOLKIT

The Manitowoc Company is located in Manitowoc, Wisconsin. In recent years, it has made a series of strategic acquisitions to grow and enhance its market-leading positions in each of its three business segments. These include: cranes and related products (crawler cranes, tower cranes, and boom trucks); food service equipment (commercial ice-cube machines, ice-beverage dispensers, and commercial refrigeration equipment); and marine operations (shipbuilding and ship-repair services). The company reported inventory of $668.7 million for 2011 and of $558.8 million for 2010. Here is the inventory note taken from the 2011 financial statements.

Real World

THE MANITOWOC COMPANY
Notes to the Financial Statements

Inventories: The components of inventories at December 31 are summarized as follows (in millions).

	2011	2010
Inventories—gross		
Raw materials	$249.7	$223.9
Work-in-process	168.1	119.8
Finished goods	357.6	326.4
Total	775.4	670.1
Less: Excess and obsolete inventory reserve	(75.3)	(80.3)
Net inventories at FIFO cost	700.1	589.8
Less: Excess of FIFO costs over LIFO value	(31.4)	(31.0)
Inventories—net (as reported on balance sheet)	$668.7	$558.8

Manitowoc carries inventory at the lower-of-cost-or-market using the first-in, first-out (FIFO) method for approximately 89% and 87% of total inventory for 2011 and 2010, respectively. The remainder of the inventory is costed using the last-in, first-out (LIFO) method.

Additional facts:

2011 Current liabilities	$1,104.6
2011 Current assets (as reported)	1,239.8
2011 Cost of goods sold	2,813.9

Instructions

Answer the following questions.
1. Why does the company report its inventory in three components?
2. Why might the company use two methods (LIFO and FIFO) to account for its inventory?
3. Perform each of the following.
   (a) Calculate the inventory turnover and days in inventory using the LIFO inventory.
   (b) Calculate the 2011 current ratio using LIFO and the current ratio using FIFO. Discuss the difference.

Solution

1. The Manitowoc Company is a manufacturer, so it purchases raw materials and makes them into finished products. At the end of each period, it has some goods that have been started but are not yet complete (work in process).

   By reporting all three components of inventory, a company reveals important information about its inventory position. For example, if amounts of raw materials have increased significantly compared to the previous year, we might assume the company is planning to step up production. On the other hand, if levels of finished goods have increased relative to last year and raw materials have declined, we might conclude that sales are slowing down—that the company has too much inventory on hand and is cutting back production.

2. Companies are free to choose different cost flow assumptions for different types of inventory. A company might choose to use FIFO for a product that is expected to decrease in price over time. One common reason for choosing a method other than LIFO is that many foreign countries do not allow LIFO; thus, the company cannot use LIFO for its foreign operations.

3. (a) $\text{Inventory turnover} = \dfrac{\text{Cost of goods sold}}{\text{Average inventory}} = \dfrac{\$2,813.9}{(\$668.7 + \$558.8)/2} = 4.6$

   $\dfrac{\text{Days in}}{\text{inventory}} = \dfrac{365}{\text{Inventory turnover}} = \dfrac{365}{4.6} = 79.3 \text{ days}$

   (b) Current ratio

LIFO	**FIFO**
$\dfrac{\text{Current assets}}{\text{Current liabilities}} = \dfrac{\$1,239.8}{\$1,104.6} = 1.12{:}1$	$\dfrac{\$1,239.8 + \$31.4}{\$1,104.6} = 1.15{:}1$

   This represents a 2.7% increase in the current ratio $(1.15 - 1.12)/1.12$.

Summary of Learning Objectives

1 Determine how to classify inventory and inventory quantities. Merchandisers need only one inventory classification, merchandise inventory, to describe the different items that make up total inventory. Manufacturers, on the other hand, usually classify inventory into three categories: finished goods, work in process, and raw materials. To determine inventory quantities, manufacturers (1) take a physical inventory of goods on hand and (2) determine the ownership of goods in transit or on consignment.

2 Explain the basis of accounting for inventories and apply the inventory cost flow methods under a periodic inventory system. The primary basis of accounting for inventories is cost. Cost includes all expenditures necessary to acquire goods and place them in a condition ready for sale. Cost of goods available for sale includes (a) cost of beginning inventory and (b) cost of goods purchased. The inventory cost flow methods are specific identification and three assumed cost flow methods—FIFO, LIFO, and average-cost.

3 Explain the financial statement and tax effects of each of the inventory cost flow assumptions. The cost of goods available for sale may be allocated to cost of goods sold and ending inventory by specific identification or by a method based on an assumed cost flow. When prices are rising, the first-in, first-out (FIFO) method results in lower cost of goods sold and higher net income than the average-cost and the last-in, first-out (LIFO) methods.

The reverse is true when prices are falling. In the balance sheet, FIFO results in an ending inventory that is closest to current value, whereas the inventory under LIFO is the farthest from current value. LIFO results in the lowest income taxes (because of lower taxable income).

4 Explain the lower-of-cost-or-market basis of accounting for inventories. Companies use the lower-of-cost-or-market (LCM) basis when the current replacement cost (market) is less than cost. Under LCM, companies recognize the loss in the period in which the price decline occurs.

5 Compute and interpret the inventory turnover. Inventory turnover is calculated as cost of goods sold divided by average inventory. It can be converted to average days in inventory by dividing 365 days by the inventory turnover. A higher inventory turnover or lower average days in inventory suggests that management is trying to keep inventory levels low relative to its sales level.

6 Describe the LIFO reserve and explain its importance for comparing results of different companies. The LIFO reserve represents the difference between ending inventory using LIFO and ending inventory if FIFO were employed instead. For some companies this difference can be significant, and ignoring it can lead to inappropriate conclusions when using the current ratio or inventory turnover.

🧰 DECISION TOOLKIT *A SUMMARY*

DECISION CHECKPOINTS	INFO NEEDED FOR DECISION	TOOL TO USE FOR DECISION	HOW TO EVALUATE RESULTS
Which inventory costing method should be used?	Are prices increasing, or are they decreasing?	Income statement, balance sheet, and tax effects	Depends on objective. In a period of rising prices, income and inventory are higher and cash flow is lower under FIFO. LIFO provides opposite results. Average-cost can moderate the impact of changing prices.
How long is an item in inventory?	Cost of goods sold; beginning and ending inventory	$$\text{Inventory turnover} = \frac{\text{Cost of goods sold}}{\text{Average inventory}}$$ $$\text{Days in inventory} = \frac{365 \text{ days}}{\text{Inventory turnover}}$$	A higher inventory turnover or lower average days in inventory suggests that management is reducing the amount of inventory on hand, relative to cost of goods sold.
What is the impact of LIFO on the company's reported inventory?	LIFO reserve, cost of goods sold, ending inventory, current assets, current liabilities	$$\text{LIFO inventory} + \text{LIFO reserve} = \text{FIFO inventory}$$	If these adjustments are material, they can significantly affect such measures as the current ratio and the inventory turnover.

Appendix 6A

Inventory Cost Flow Methods in Perpetual Inventory Systems

Each of the inventory cost flow methods described in the chapter for a periodic inventory system may be used in a perpetual inventory system. To illustrate the application of the three assumed cost flow methods (FIFO, LIFO, and average-cost), we will use the data shown in Illustration 6A-1 and in this chapter for Houston Electronics' Astro condensers.

> **LEARNING OBJECTIVE   7**
>
> Apply the inventory cost flow methods to perpetual inventory records.

Illustration 6A-1 Inventoriable units and costs

HOUSTON ELECTRONICS
Astro Condensers

Date	Explanation	Units	Unit Cost	Total Cost	Balance in Units
1/1	Beginning inventory	100	$10	$ 1,000	100
4/15	Purchase	200	11	2,200	300
8/24	Purchase	300	12	3,600	600
9/10	Sale	550			50
11/27	Purchase	400	13	5,200	450
				$12,000	

FIRST-IN, FIRST-OUT (FIFO)

Under FIFO, the cost of the earliest goods on hand **prior to each sale** is charged to cost of goods sold. Therefore, the cost of goods sold on September 10 consists of the units on hand January 1 and the units purchased April 15 and August 24. Illustration 6A-2 shows the inventory under a FIFO method perpetual system.

Illustration 6A-2 Perpetual system—FIFO

Date	Purchases	Cost of Goods Sold	Balance
Jan. 1			(100 @ $10) $1,000
Apr. 15	(200 @ $11) $2,200		(100 @ $10) (200 @ $11) } $3,200
Aug. 24	(300 @ $12) $3,600		(100 @ $10) (200 @ $11) } $6,800 (300 @ $12)
Sept. 10		(100 @ $10) (200 @ $11) (250 @ $12) ——— $6,200	(50 @ $12) $ 600
Nov. 27	(400 @ $13) $5,200		(50 @ $12) } $5,800 (400 @ $13)

The ending inventory in this situation is $5,800, and the cost of goods sold is $6,200 [(100 @ $10) + (200 @ $11) + (250 @ $12)].

The results under FIFO in a perpetual system are the **same as in a periodic system**. (See Illustration 6-6 on page 291 where, similarly, the ending inventory is $5,800 and cost of goods sold is $6,200.) Regardless of the system, the first costs in are the costs assigned to cost of goods sold.

LAST-IN, FIRST-OUT (LIFO)

Under the LIFO method using a perpetual system, the cost of the most recent purchase prior to sale is allocated to the units sold. Therefore, the cost of the goods sold on September 10 consists of all the units from the August 24 and April 15 purchases plus 50 of the units in beginning inventory. The ending inventory under the LIFO method is computed in Illustration 6A-3.

Illustration 6A-3 Perpetual system—LIFO

Date	Purchases	Cost of Goods Sold	Balance
Jan. 1			(100 @ $10) $1,000
Apr. 15	(200 @ $11) $2,200		(100 @ $10) (200 @ $11) } $3,200
Aug. 24	(300 @ $12) $3,600		(100 @ $10) (200 @ $11) } $6,800 (300 @ $12)
Sept. 10		(300 @ $12) (200 @ $11) (50 @ $10) ——— $6,300	(50 @ $10) $ 500
Nov. 27	(400 @ $13) $5,200		(50 @ $10) } $5,700 (400 @ $13)

The use of LIFO in a perpetual system will usually produce cost allocations that differ from use of LIFO in a periodic system. In a perpetual system, the latest units purchased **prior to each sale** are allocated to cost of goods sold. In contrast, in a periodic system, the latest units purchased **during the period** are allocated to cost of goods sold. Thus, when a purchase is made after the last sale, the LIFO periodic system will apply this purchase to the previous sale. See Illustration 6-9 (on page 292) where the proof shows the 400 units at $13 purchased on November 27 applied to the sale of 550 units on September 10.

As shown above, under the LIFO perpetual system the 400 units at $13 purchased on November 27 are all applied to the ending inventory.

The ending inventory in this LIFO perpetual illustration is $5,700 and cost of goods sold is $6,300. Compare this to the LIFO periodic illustration (Illustration 6-8 on page 292) where the ending inventory is $5,000 and cost of goods sold is $7,000.

AVERAGE-COST

The average-cost method in a perpetual inventory system is called the **moving-average method**. Under this method, the company computes a new average **after each purchase**. The average cost is computed by dividing the cost of goods available for sale by the units on hand. The average cost is then applied to (1) the units sold, to determine the cost of goods sold, and (2) the remaining units on hand, to determine the ending inventory amount. Illustration 6A-4 shows the application of the average-cost method by Houston Electronics.

Date	Purchases	Cost of Goods Sold	Balance
Jan. 1			(100 @ $10) $1,000
Apr. 15	(200 @ $11) $2,200		(300 @ $10.667) $3,200
Aug. 24	(300 @ $12) $3,600		(600 @ $11.333) $6,800
Sept. 10		(550 @ $11.333) $6,233	(50 @ $11.333) $ 567
Nov. 27	(400 @ $13) $5,200		(450 @ $12.816) $5,767

Illustration 6A-4 Perpetual system—average-cost method

As indicated above, the company computes **a new average each time it makes a purchase**. On April 15, after 200 units are purchased for $2,200, a total of 300 units costing $3,200 ($1,000 + $2,200) are on hand. The average unit cost is $10.667 ($3,200 ÷ 300). On August 24, after 300 units are purchased for $3,600, a total of 600 units costing $6,800 ($1,000 + $2,200 + $3,600) are on hand at an average cost per unit of $11.333 ($6,800 ÷ 600). Houston Electronics uses this unit cost of $11.333 in costing sales until another purchase is made, when the company computes a new unit cost. Accordingly, the unit cost of the 550 units sold on September 10 is $11.333, and the total cost of goods sold is $6,233. On November 27, following the purchase of 400 units for $5,200, there are 450 units on hand costing $5,767 ($567 + $5,200) with a new average cost of $12.816 ($5,767 ÷ 450).

Compare this moving-average cost under the perpetual inventory system to Illustration 6-11 (on page 293) showing the weighted-average method under a periodic inventory system.

Summary of Learning Objective for Appendix 6A

7 **Apply the inventory cost flow methods to perpetual inventory records.** Under FIFO, the cost of the earliest goods on hand prior to each sale is charged to cost of goods sold. Under LIFO, the cost of the most recent purchase prior to sale is charged to cost of goods sold. Under the average-cost method, a new average cost is computed after each purchase.

Appendix 6B

Inventory Errors

LEARNING OBJECTIVE **8**

Indicate the effects of inventory errors on the financial statements.

Unfortunately, errors occasionally occur in accounting for inventory. In some cases, errors are caused by failure to count or price the inventory correctly. In other cases, errors occur because companies do not properly recognize the transfer of legal title to goods that are in transit. When inventory errors occur, they affect both the income statement and the balance sheet.

INCOME STATEMENT EFFECTS

Under a periodic inventory system, both the beginning and ending inventories appear in the income statement. The ending inventory of one period automatically becomes the beginning inventory of the next period. Thus, inventory errors affect the computation of cost of goods sold and net income in two periods.

The effects on cost of goods sold can be computed by entering incorrect data in the formula in Illustration 6B-1 and then substituting the correct data.

Illustration 6B-1 Formula for cost of goods sold

Beginning Inventory	+	Cost of Goods Purchased	−	Ending Inventory	=	Cost of Goods Sold

If **beginning** inventory is understated, cost of goods sold will be understated. If **ending** inventory is understated, cost of goods sold will be overstated. Illustration 6B-2 shows the effects of inventory errors on the current year's income statement.

Illustration 6B-2 Effects of inventory errors on current year's income statement

Inventory Error	Cost of Goods Sold	Net Income
Beginning inventory understated	Understated	Overstated
Beginning inventory overstated	Overstated	Understated
Ending inventory understated	Overstated	Understated
Ending inventory overstated	Understated	Overstated

Ethics Note Inventory fraud increases during recessions. Such fraud includes pricing inventory at amounts in excess of its actual value, or claiming to have inventory when no inventory exists. Inventory fraud is usually done to overstate ending inventory, thereby understating cost of goods sold and creating higher income.

An error in the ending inventory of the current period will have a **reverse effect on net income of the next accounting period**. This is shown in Illustration 6B-3. Note that the understatement of ending inventory in 2013 results in an understatement of beginning inventory in 2014 and an overstatement of net income in 2014.

Over the two years, total net income is correct because the errors offset each other. Notice that total two-year income using incorrect data is $35,000 ($22,000 + $13,000), which is the same as the total two-year income of $35,000 ($25,000 + $10,000) using correct data. Also note in this example that an error in the beginning inventory does not result in a corresponding error in the ending inventory for that period. The correctness of the ending inventory depends entirely on the accuracy of taking and costing the inventory at the balance sheet date under the periodic inventory system.

SAMPLE COMPANY
Condensed Income Statements

	2013				2014			
	Incorrect		**Correct**		**Incorrect**		**Correct**	
Sales revenue		$80,000		$80,000		$90,000		$90,000
Beginning inventory	$20,000		$20,000		$12,000		$15,000	
Cost of goods purchased	40,000		40,000		68,000		68,000	
Cost of goods available for sale	60,000		60,000		80,000		83,000	
Ending inventory	12,000		15,000		23,000		23,000	
Cost of goods sold		48,000		45,000		57,000		60,000
Gross profit		32,000		35,000		33,000		30,000
Operating expenses		10,000		10,000		20,000		20,000
Net income		$22,000		$25,000		$13,000		$10,000

$(3,000)
Net income
understated

$3,000
Net income
overstated

The errors cancel. Thus, the combined total
income for the 2-year period is correct.

Illustration 6B-3 Effects of inventory errors on two years' income statements

BALANCE SHEET EFFECTS

The effect of ending inventory errors on the balance sheet can be determined by using the basic accounting equation: Assets = Liabilities + Stockholders' Equity. Errors in the ending inventory have the effects shown in Illustration 6B-4.

Illustration 6B-4 Effects of ending inventory errors on balance sheet

Ending Inventory Error	Assets	Liabilities	Stockholders' Equity
Overstated	Overstated	No effect	Overstated
Understated	Understated	No effect	Understated

The effect of an error in ending inventory on the subsequent period was shown in Illustration 6B-3. Recall that if the error is not corrected, the combined total net income for the two periods would be correct. Thus, total stockholders' equity reported on the balance sheet at the end of 2014 will also be correct.

Summary of Learning Objective for Appendix 6B

8 **Indicate the effects of inventory errors on the financial statements.** In the income statement of the current year: (1) An error in beginning inventory will have a reverse effect on net income (e.g., overstatement of inventory results in understatement of net income, and vice versa). (2) An error in ending inventory will have a similar effect on net income (e.g., overstatement of inventory results in overstatement of net income). If ending inventory errors are not corrected in the following period, their effect on net income for that period is reversed, and total net income for the two years will be correct.

In the balance sheet: Ending inventory errors will have the same effect on total assets and total stockholders' equity and no effect on liabilities.

Glossary

Average-cost method *(p. 293)* An inventory costing method that uses the weighted-average unit cost to allocate the cost of goods available for sale to ending inventory and cost of goods sold.

Consigned goods *(p. 287)* Goods held for sale by one party although ownership of the goods is retained by another party.

Current replacement cost *(p. 298)* The cost of purchasing the same goods at the present time from the usual suppliers in the usual quantities.

Days in inventory *(p. 299)* Measure of the average number of days inventory is held; calculated as 365 divided by inventory turnover.

Finished goods inventory *(p. 284)* Manufactured items that are completed and ready for sale.

First-in, first-out (FIFO) method *(p. 290)* An inventory costing method that assumes that the earliest goods purchased are the first to be sold.

FOB destination *(p. 287)* Freight terms indicating that ownership of goods remains with the seller until the goods reach the buyer.

FOB shipping point *(p. 287)* Freight terms indicating that ownership of goods passes to the buyer when the public carrier accepts the goods from the seller.

Inventory turnover *(p. 299)* A ratio that indicates the liquidity of inventory by measuring the number of times average inventory sold during the period; computed by

dividing cost of goods sold by the average inventory during the period.

Just-in-time (JIT) inventory *(p. 285)* Inventory system in which companies manufacture or purchase goods just in time for use.

Last-in, first-out (LIFO) method *(p. 291)* An inventory costing method that assumes that the latest units purchased are the first to be sold.

LIFO reserve *(p. 301)* For a company using LIFO, the difference between inventory reported using LIFO and inventory using FIFO.

Lower-of-cost-or-market (LCM) *(p. 298)* A basis whereby inventory is stated at the lower of either its cost or its market value as determined by current replacement cost.

Raw materials *(p. 284)* Basic goods that will be used in production but have not yet been placed in production.

Specific identification method *(p. 288)* An actual physical-flow costing method in which particular items sold and items still in inventory are specifically costed to arrive at cost of goods sold and ending inventory.

Weighted-average unit cost *(p. 293)* Average cost that is weighted by the number of units purchased at each unit cost.

Work in process *(p. 284)* That portion of manufactured inventory that has begun the production process but is not yet complete.

Comprehensive Do it!

Englehart Company has the following inventory, purchases, and sales data for the month of March.

Inventory, March 1	200 units @ $4.00	$ 800
Purchases		
March 10	500 units @ $4.50	2,250
March 20	400 units @ $4.75	1,900
March 30	300 units @ $5.00	1,500
Sales		
March 15	500 units	
March 25	400 units	

The physical inventory count on March 31 shows 500 units on hand.

Instructions

Under a **periodic inventory system**, determine the cost of inventory on hand at March 31 and the cost of goods sold for March under (a) the first-in, first-out (FIFO) method; (b) the last-in, first-out (LIFO) method; and (c) the average-cost method. (For average-cost, carry cost per unit to three decimal places.)

Solution to Comprehensive `Do it!`

The cost of goods available for sale is $6,450:

Inventory, March 1	200 units @ $4.00	$ 800
Purchases		
March 10	500 units @ $4.50	2,250
March 20	400 units @ $4.75	1,900
March 30	300 units @ $5.00	1,500
Total cost of goods available for sale		$6,450

(a)   **FIFO Method**

Ending inventory:

Date	Units	Unit Cost	Total Cost	
Mar. 30	300	$5.00	$1,500	
Mar. 20	200	4.75	950	$2,450
Cost of goods sold: $6,450 − $2,450 =				$4,000

(b)   **LIFO Method**

Ending inventory:

Date	Units	Unit Cost	Total Cost	
Mar. 1	200	$4.00	$ 800	
Mar. 10	300	4.50	1,350	$2,150
Cost of goods sold: $6,450 − $2,150 =				$4,300

(c)   **Average-Cost Method**

Weighted-average unit cost: $6,450 ÷ 1,400 = $4.607
Ending inventory: 500 × $4.607 = $2,303.50
    Cost of goods sold: $6,450 − $2,303.50 = $4,146.50

Action Plan

- For FIFO, allocate the latest costs to inventory.
- For LIFO, allocate the earliest costs to inventory.
- For average-cost, use a weighted average.
- Remember, the costs allocated to cost of goods sold can be proved.
- Total purchases are the same under all three cost flow assumptions.

 The Navigator

 Self-Test, Brief Exercises, Exercises, Problem Set A, and many more resources are available for practice in WileyPLUS.

Note: All Questions, Exercises, and Problems marked with an asterisk relate to material in the appendices to the chapter.

Self-Test Questions

Answers are on page 331.

(LO 1)   **1.** When is a physical inventory usually taken?
     (a) When the company has its greatest amount of inventory.
     (b) When a limited number of goods are being sold or received.
     (c) At the end of the company's fiscal year.
     (d) Both (b) and (c).

(LO 1)   **2.** Which of the following should **not** be included in the physical inventory of a company?
     (a) Goods held on consignment from another company.
     (b) Goods shipped on consignment to another company.

     (c) Goods in transit from another company shipped FOB shipping point.
     (d) All of the above should be included.

3. As a result of a thorough physical inventory, Rail-(LO 1) way Company determined that it had inventory worth $180,000 at December 31, 2014. This count did not take into consideration the following facts. Rogers Consignment store currently has goods worth $35,000 on its sales floor that belong to Railway but are being sold on consignment by Rogers. The selling price of these goods is $50,000. Railway purchased $13,000 of goods that were shipped on December 27, FOB destination, that will be

received by Railway on January 3. Determine the correct amount of inventory that Railway should report.
(a) $230,000.   (c) $228,000.
(b) $215,000.   (d) $193,000.

(LO 2) **4.** Kam Company has the following units and costs.

	Units	Unit Cost
Inventory, Jan. 1	8,000	$11
Purchase, June 19	13,000	12
Purchase, Nov. 8	5,000	13

If 9,000 units are on hand at December 31, what is the cost of the ending inventory under FIFO?
(a) $99,000.   (c) $113,000.
(b) $108,000.   (d) $117,000.

(LO 2) **5.** From the data in Question 4, what is the cost of the ending inventory under LIFO?
(a) $113,000.   (c) $99,000.
(b) $108,000.   (d) $100,000.

(LO 2) **6.** Davidson Electronics has the following:

	Units	Unit Cost
Inventory, Jan. 1	5,000	$ 8
Purchase, April 2	15,000	10
Purchase, Aug. 28	20,000	12

If Davidson has 7,000 units on hand at December 31, the cost of ending inventory under the average-cost method is:
(a) $84,000.   (c) $56,000.
(b) $70,000.   (d) $75,250.

(LO 3) **7.** In periods of rising prices, LIFO will produce:
(a) higher net income than FIFO.
(b) the same net income as FIFO.
(c) lower net income than FIFO.
(d) higher net income than average-cost.

(LO 3) **8.** Considerations that affect the selection of an inventory costing method do **not** include:
(a) tax effects.
(b) balance sheet effects.
(c) income statement effects.
(d) perpetual versus periodic inventory system.

(LO 4) **9.** The lower-of-cost-or-market rule for inventory is an example of the application of:
(a) the conservatism convention.
(b) the historical cost principle.
(c) the materiality concept.
(d) the economic entity assumption.

(LO 5) **10.** Which of these would cause inventory turnover to increase the most?
(a) Increasing the amount of inventory on hand.
(b) Keeping the amount of inventory on hand constant but increasing sales.

(c) Keeping the amount of inventory on hand constant but decreasing sales.
(d) Decreasing the amount of inventory on hand and increasing sales.

(LO 5) **11.** Carlos Company had beginning inventory of $80,000, ending inventory of $110,000, cost of goods sold of $285,000, and sales of $475,000. Carlos's days in inventory is:
(a) 73 days.   (c) 102.5 days.
(b) 121.7 days.   (d) 84.5 days.

(LO 6) **12.** The LIFO reserve is:
(a) the difference between the value of the inventory under LIFO and the value under FIFO.
(b) an amount used to adjust inventory to the lower-of-cost-or-market.
(c) the difference between the value of the inventory under LIFO and the value under average-cost.
(d) an amount used to adjust inventory to historical cost.

(LO 7) *13. In a perpetual inventory system,
(a) LIFO cost of goods sold will be the same as in a periodic inventory system.
(b) average costs are based entirely on unit-cost simple averages.
(c) a new average is computed under the average-cost method after each sale.
(d) FIFO cost of goods sold will be the same as in a periodic inventory system.

(LO 8) *14. Fran Company's ending inventory is understated by $4,000. The effects of this error on the current year's cost of goods sold and net income, respectively, are:
(a) understated and overstated.
(b) overstated and understated.
(c) overstated and overstated.
(d) understated and understated.

(LO 4) *15. Harold Company overstated its inventory by $15,000 at December 31, 2014. It did not correct the error in 2014 or 2015. As a result, Harold's stockholders' equity was:
(a) overstated at December 31, 2014, and understated at December 31, 2015.
(b) overstated at December 31, 2014, and properly stated at December 31, 2015.
(c) understated at December 31, 2014, and understated at December 31, 2015.
(d) overstated at December 31, 2014, and overstated at December 31, 2015.

Go to the book's companion website, **www. wiley.com/college/kimmel**, to access additional Self-Test Questions.

 The Navigator

Questions

1. "The key to successful business operations is effective inventory management." Do you agree? Explain.

2. An item must possess two characteristics to be classified as inventory. What are these two characteristics?

3. ◀ What is just-in-time inventory management? What are its potential advantages?

4. Your friend Jill Wurtz has been hired to help take the physical inventory in Proehl's Hardware Store. Explain to Jill what this job will entail.

5. (a) Millar Company ships merchandise to Branyan Corporation on December 30. The merchandise reaches the buyer on January 5. Indicate the terms of sale that will result in the goods being included in (1) Millar's December 31 inventory and (2) Branyan's December 31 inventory.
   (b) Under what circumstances should Millar Company include consigned goods in its inventory?

6. Nida Hat Shop received a shipment of hats for which it paid the wholesaler $2,940. The price of the hats was $3,000, but Nida was given a $60 cash discount and required to pay freight charges of $75. What amount should Nida include in inventory? Why?

7. What is the primary basis of accounting for inventories? What is the major objective in accounting for inventories?

8. Stan Koevner believes that the allocation of cost of goods available for sale should be based on the actual physical flow of the goods. Explain to Stan why this may be both impractical and inappropriate.

9. What is the major advantage and major disadvantage of the specific identification method of inventory costing?

10. ◀ "The selection of an inventory cost flow method is a decision made by accountants." Do you agree? Explain. Once a method has been selected, what accounting requirement applies?

11. Which assumed inventory cost flow method:
   (a) usually parallels the actual physical flow of merchandise?
   (b) divides cost of goods available for sale by total units available for sale to determine a unit cost?
   (c) assumes that the latest units purchased are the first to be sold?

12. In a period of rising prices, the inventory reported in Long Company's balance sheet is close to the current cost of the inventory, whereas Windsor Company's inventory is considerably below its current cost. Identify the inventory cost flow method used by each company. Which company probably has been reporting the higher gross profit?

13. Espinosa Corporation has been using the FIFO cost flow method during a prolonged period of inflation. During the same time period, Espinosa has been paying out all of its net income as dividends. What adverse effects may result from this policy?

14. George Orear, a mid-level product manager for Theresa's Shoes, thinks his company should switch from LIFO to FIFO. He says, "My bonus is based on net income. If we switch it will increase net income and increase my bonus. The company would be better off and so would I." Is he correct? Explain.

15. Discuss the impact the use of LIFO has on taxes paid, cash flows, and the quality of earnings ratio relative to the impact of FIFO when prices are increasing.

16. ◼ What inventory cost flow method does Tootsie Roll Industries use for U.S. inventories? What method does it use for foreign inventories? (*Hint:* You will need to examine the notes for Tootsie Roll's financial statements.) Why does it use a different method for foreign inventories?

17. Alison Hinck is studying for the next accounting midterm examination. What should Alison know about (a) departing from the cost basis of accounting for inventories and (b) the meaning of "market" in the lower-of-cost-or-market method?

18. Rondeli Music Center has five TVs on hand at the balance sheet date that cost $400 each. The current replacement cost is $350 per unit. Under the lower-of-cost-or-market basis of accounting for inventories, what value should Rondeli report for the TVs on the balance sheet? Why?

19. ▭ What cost flow assumption may be used under the lower-of-cost-or-market basis of accounting for inventories?

20. Why is it inappropriate for a company to include freight-out expense in the Cost of Goods Sold account?

21. Dipoto Company's balance sheet shows Inventory $162,800. What additional disclosures should be made?

22. ◀ ▭ Under what circumstances might inventory turnover be too high—that is, what possible negative consequences might occur?

23. ▭ What is the LIFO reserve? What are the consequences of ignoring a large LIFO reserve when analyzing a company?

*24. "When perpetual inventory records are kept, the results under the FIFO and LIFO methods are the same as they would be in a periodic inventory system." Do you agree? Explain.

*25. How does the average-cost method of inventory costing differ between a perpetual inventory system and a periodic inventory system?

*26. Marshall Company discovers in 2014 that its ending inventory at December 31, 2013, was $5,000 understated. What effect will this error have on (a) 2013 net income, (b) 2014 net income, and (c) the combined net income for the 2 years?

Brief Exercises

Identify items to be included in taking a physical inventory.
(LO 1), C

BE6-1 Tiffee Company identifies the following items for possible inclusion in the physical inventory. Indicate whether each item should be included or excluded from the inventory taking.
(a) 900 units of inventory shipped on consignment by Tiffee to another company.
(b) 3,000 units of inventory in transit from a supplier shipped FOB destination.
(c) 1,200 units of inventory sold but being held for customer pickup.
(d) 500 units of inventory held on consignment from another company.

Compute ending inventory using FIFO and LIFO.
(LO 2), AP

BE6-2 In its first month of operations, Giffin Company made three purchases of merchandise in the following sequence: (1) 300 units at $6, (2) 400 units at $8, and (3) 500 units at $9. Assuming there are 200 units on hand at the end of the period, compute the cost of the ending inventory under (a) the FIFO method and (b) the LIFO method. Giffin uses a periodic inventory system.

Compute the ending inventory using average-cost.
(LO 2), AP

BE6-3 Data for Giffin Company are presented in BE6-2. Compute the cost of the ending inventory under the average-cost method. (Round the cost per unit to three decimal places.)

Explain the financial statement effect of inventory cost flow assumptions.
(LO 3), C

BE6-4 The management of Rosenquist Corp. is considering the effects of various inventory-costing methods on its financial statements and its income tax expense. Assuming that the price the company pays for inventory is increasing, which method will:
(a) provide the highest net income?
(b) provide the highest ending inventory?
(c) result in the lowest income tax expense?
(d) result in the most stable earnings over a number of years?

Explain the financial statement effect of inventory cost flow assumptions.
(LO 3), AP

BE6-5 In its first month of operation, Kuhlman Company purchased 100 units of inventory for $6, then 200 units for $7, and finally 140 units for $8. At the end of the month, 180 units remained. Compute the amount of phantom profit that would result if the company used FIFO rather than LIFO. Explain why this amount is referred to as phantom profit. The company uses the periodic method.

Identify the impact of LIFO versus FIFO.
(LO 3), C

BE6-6 For each of the following cases, state whether the statement is true for LIFO or for FIFO. Assume that prices are rising.
(a) Results in a higher quality of earnings ratio.
(b) Results in higher phantom profits.
(c) Results in higher net income.
(d) Results in lower taxes.
(e) Results in lower net cash provided by operating activities.

Determine the LCM valuation.
(LO 4), AP

BE6-7 Sadowski Video Center accumulates the following cost and market data at December 31.

Inventory Categories	Cost Data	Market Data
Cameras	$12,500	$13,400
Camcorders	9,000	9,500
DVDs	13,000	12,200

Compute the lower-of-cost-or-market valuation for Sadowski inventory.

Compute inventory turnover and days in inventory.
(LO 5), AP

BE6-8 Suppose at December 31 of a recent year, the following information (in thousands) was available for sunglasses manufacturer Oakley, Inc.: ending inventory $155,377; beginning inventory $119,035; cost of goods sold $349,114; and sales revenue $761,865. Calculate the inventory turnover and days in inventory for Oakley, Inc.

Determine ending inventory and cost of goods sold using LIFO reserve.
(LO 6), C

BE6-9 Winnebago Industries, Inc. is a leading manufacturer of motor homes. Suppose Winnebago reported ending inventory at August 29, 2014, of $46,850,000 under the LIFO inventory method. In the notes to its financial statements, assume Winnebago reported a LIFO reserve of $30,346,000 at August 29, 2014. What would Winnebago Industries' ending inventory have been if it had used FIFO?

Apply cost flow methods to perpetual inventory records.
(LO 7), AP

*BE6-10 Hogan's Department Store uses a perpetual inventory system. Data for product E2-D2 include the purchases shown on page 315.

Date	Number of Units	Unit Price
May 7	50	$10
July 28	30	15

On June 1, Hogan sold 25 units, and on August 27, 30 more units. Compute the cost of goods sold using (a) FIFO, (b) LIFO, and (c) average-cost. (Round the cost per unit to three decimal places.)

*BE6-11 Nickels Company reports net income of $92,000 in 2014. However, ending inventory was understated by $7,000. What is the correct net income for 2014? What effect, if any, will this error have on total assets as reported in the balance sheet at December 31, 2014?

Determine correct financial statement amount.
(LO 8), **AN**

Do it! Review

Do it! 6-1   Dobler Company just took its physical inventory on December 31. The count of inventory items on hand at the company's business locations resulted in a total inventory cost of $300,000. In reviewing the details of the count and related inventory transactions, you have discovered the following items that had not been considered.

Apply rules of ownership to determine inventory cost.
(LO 1), **AN**

1. Dobler has sent inventory costing $28,000 on consignment to Phillips Company. All of this inventory was at Phillips's showrooms on December 31.
2. The company did not include in the count inventory (cost, $20,000) that was sold on December 28, terms FOB shipping point. The goods were in transit on December 31.
3. The company did not include in the count inventory (cost, $13,000) that was purchased with terms of FOB shipping point. The goods were in transit on December 31.

Compute the correct December 31 inventory.

Do it! 6-2   The accounting records of Tuel Electronics show the following data.

Beginning inventory	3,000 units at $5
Purchases	8,000 units at $7
Sales	9,400 units at $10

Compute cost of goods sold under different cost flow methods.
(LO 2), **AP**

Determine cost of goods sold during the period under a periodic inventory system using (a) the FIFO method, (b) the LIFO method, and (c) the average-cost method. (Round unit cost to three decimal places.)

Do it! 6-3   Farwell Company sells three different categories of tools (small, medium and large). The cost and market value of its inventory of tools are as follows.

Compute inventory value under LCM.
(LO 4), **AP**

	Cost	Market
Small	$ 64,000	$ 61,000
Medium	290,000	260,000
Large	152,000	167,000

Determine the value of the company's inventory under the lower-of-cost-or-market approach.

Do it! 6-4   Early in 2014, Defoor Company switched to a just-in-time inventory system. Its sales and inventory amounts for 2013 and 2014 are shown below.

Compute inventory turnover and assess inventory level.
(LO 5), **AN**

	2013	2014
Sales revenue	$3,120,000	$3,713,000
Cost of goods sold	1,200,000	1,425,000
Beginning inventory	170,000	210,000
Ending inventory	210,000	90,000

Determine the inventory turnover and days in inventory for 2013 and 2014. Discuss the changes in the amount of inventory, the inventory turnover and days in inventory, and the amount of sales across the two years.

Exercises

Determine the correct inventory amount.
(LO 1), **AN**

E6-1 Columbia Bank and Trust is considering giving Gallup Company a loan. Before doing so, it decides that further discussions with Gallup's accountant may be desirable. One area of particular concern is the Inventory account, which has a year-end balance of $275,000. Discussions with the accountant reveal the following.

1. Gallup sold goods costing $55,000 to Bazil Company FOB shipping point on December 28. The goods are not expected to reach Bazil until January 12. The goods were not included in the physical inventory because they were not in the warehouse.
2. The physical count of the inventory did not include goods costing $95,000 that were shipped to Gallup FOB destination on December 27 and were still in transit at year-end.
3. Gallup received goods costing $25,000 on January 2. The goods were shipped FOB shipping point on December 26 by Lynch Co. The goods were not included in the physical count.
4. Gallup sold goods costing $51,000 to Lamey of Canada FOB destination on December 30. The goods were received in Canada on January 8. They were not included in Gallup's physical inventory.
5. Gallup received goods costing $42,000 on January 2 that were shipped FOB destination on December 29. The shipment was a rush order that was supposed to arrive December 31. This purchase was included in the ending inventory of $275,000.

Instructions

Determine the correct inventory amount on December 31.

Determine the correct inventory amount.
(LO 1), **AN**

E6-2 Kevin Farley, an auditor with Koews CPAs, is performing a review of Knight Company's Inventory account. Knight did not have a good year, and top management is under pressure to boost reported income. According to its records, the inventory balance at year-end was $740,000. However, the following information was not considered when determining that amount.

1. Included in the company's count were goods with a cost of $228,000 that the company is holding on consignment. The goods belong to Mather Corporation.
2. The physical count did not include goods purchased by Knight with a cost of $40,000 that were shipped FOB shipping point on December 28 and did not arrive at Knight's warehouse until January 3.
3. Included in the Inventory account was $17,000 of office supplies that were stored in the warehouse and were to be used by the company's supervisors and managers during the coming year.
4. The company received an order on December 29 that was boxed and was sitting on the loading dock awaiting pick-up on December 31. The shipper picked up the goods on January 1 and delivered them on January 6. The shipping terms were FOB shipping point. The goods had a selling price of $40,000 and a cost of $29,000. The goods were not included in the count because they were sitting on the dock.
5. On December 29, Knight shipped goods with a selling price of $80,000 and a cost of $50,000 to Houchins Sales Corporation FOB shipping point. The goods arrived on January 3. Houchins Sales had only ordered goods with a selling price of $10,000 and a cost of $6,000. However, a sales manager at Knight had authorized the shipment and said that if Houchins wanted to ship the goods back next week, it could.
6. Included in the count was $50,000 of goods that were parts for a machine that the company no longer made. Given the high-tech nature of Knight's products, it was unlikely that these obsolete parts had any other use. However, management would prefer to keep them on the books at cost, "since that is what we paid for them, after all."

Instructions

Prepare a schedule to determine the correct inventory amount. Provide explanations for each item above, stating why you did or did not make an adjustment for each item.

Identify items in inventory.
(LO 1), **K**

E6-3 Mateo Inc. had the following inventory situations to consider at January 31, its year-end.
(a) Goods held on consignment for Schrader Corp. since December 12.
(b) Goods shipped on consignment to Lyman Holdings Inc. on January 5.
(c) Goods shipped to a customer, FOB destination, on January 29 that are still in transit.

(d) Goods shipped to a customer, FOB shipping point, on January 29 that are still in transit.

(e) Goods purchased FOB destination from a supplier on January 25, that are still in transit.

(f) Goods purchased FOB shipping point from a supplier on January 25, that are still in transit.

(g) Office supplies on hand at January 31.

Instructions

Identify which of the preceding items should be included in inventory. If the item should not be included in inventory, state in what account, if any, it should have been recorded.

E6-4 Delmott sells a snowboard, Xpert, that is popular with snowboard enthusiasts. Below is information relating to Delmott's purchases of Xpert snowboards during September. During the same month, 102 Xpert snowboards were sold. Delmott uses a periodic inventory system.

Compute inventory and cost of goods sold using periodic FIFO and LIFO.

(LO 2), **AP**

Date	Explanation	Units	Unit Cost	Total Cost
Sept. 1	Inventory	12	$100	$ 1,200
Sept. 12	Purchases	45	103	4,635
Sept. 19	Purchases	50	104	5,200
Sept. 26	Purchases	20	105	2,100
	Totals	127		$13,135

Instructions

Compute the ending inventory at September 30 and the cost of goods sold using the FIFO, LIFO, and average-cost methods. (For average-cost, round the average unit cost to three decimal places.) Prove the amount allocated to cost of goods sold under each method.

E6-5 Horne Inc. uses a periodic inventory system. Its records show the following for the month of May, in which 74 units were sold.

Calculate inventory and cost of goods sold using FIFO, average-cost, and LIFO in a periodic inventory system.

(LO 2), **AP**

Date	Explanation	Units	Unit Cost	Total Cost
May 1	Inventory	30	$ 9	$270
15	Purchase	25	10	250
24	Purchase	38	11	418
	Total	93		$938

Instructions

Calculate the ending inventory at May 31 using the (a) FIFO, (b) LIFO, and (c) average-cost methods. (For average-cost, round the average unit cost to three decimal places.) Prove the amount allocated to cost of goods sold under each method.

E6-6 On December 1, Quality Electronics has three DVD players left in stock. All are identical, all are priced to sell at $85. One of the three DVD players left in stock, with serial #1012, was purchased on June 1 at a cost of $52. Another, with serial #1045, was purchased on November 1 for $48. The last player, serial #1056, was purchased on November 30 for $40.

Calculate cost of goods sold using specific identification and FIFO periodic.

(LO 2, 3), **AN**

Instructions

(a) Calculate the cost of goods sold using the FIFO periodic inventory method, assuming that two of the three players were sold by the end of December, Quality Electronics' year-end.

(b) If Quality Electronics used the specific identification method instead of the FIFO method, how might it alter its earnings by "selectively choosing" which particular players to sell to the two customers? What would Quality's cost of goods sold be if the company wished to minimize earnings? Maximize earnings?

(c) Which inventory method, FIFO or specific identification, do you recommend that Quality use? Explain why.

Compute inventory and cost of goods sold using periodic FIFO, LIFO, and average-cost.

(LO 2, 3), **AP**

E6-7 Eggers Company reports the following for the month of June.

Date	Explanation	Units	Unit Cost	Total Cost
June 1	Inventory	120	$5	$ 600
12	Purchase	370	6	2,220
23	Purchase	200	7	1,400
30	Inventory	230		

Instructions

(a) Compute the cost of the ending inventory and the cost of goods sold under (1) FIFO, (2) LIFO, and (3) average-cost. (Round average unit cost to three decimal places).

(b) Which costing method gives the highest ending inventory? The highest cost of goods sold? Why?

(c) How do the average-cost values for ending inventory and cost of goods sold relate to ending inventory and cost of goods sold for FIFO and LIFO?

(d) Explain why the average cost is not $6.

Evaluate impact of LIFO and FIFO on cash flows and earnings quality.

(LO 3), **AP**

E6-8 The following comparative information is available for Keysor Company for 2014.

	LIFO	FIFO
Sales revenue	$86,000	$86,000
Cost of goods sold	38,000	29,000
Operating expenses (including depreciation)	27,000	27,000
Depreciation	10,000	10,000
Cash paid for inventory purchases	32,000	32,000

Instructions

(a) Determine net income under each approach. Assume a 30% tax rate.

(b) Determine net cash provided by operating activities under each approach. Assume that all sales were on a cash basis and that income taxes and operating expenses, other than depreciation, were on a cash basis.

(c) Calculate the quality of earnings ratio under each approach and explain your findings.

Determine LCM valuation.

(LO 4), **AP**

E6-9 Birk Camera Shop Inc. uses the lower-of-cost-or-market basis for its inventory. The following data are available at December 31.

	Units	Cost/Unit	Market Value/Unit
Cameras			
Minolta	5	$170	$158
Canon	7	145	152
Light Meters			
Vivitar	12	125	114
Kodak	10	120	135

Instructions

What amount should be reported on Birk Camera Shop's financial statements, assuming the lower-of-cost-or-market rule is applied?

Compute inventory turnover, days in inventory, and gross profit rate.

(LO 5), **AP**

E6-10 Suppose this information is available for PepsiCo, Inc. for 2012, 2013, and 2014.

(in millions)	2012	2013	2014
Beginning inventory	$ 1,926	$ 2,290	$ 2,522
Ending inventory	2,290	2,522	2,618
Cost of goods sold	18,038	20,351	20,099
Sales revenue	39,474	43,251	43,232

Instructions

Calculate the inventory turnover, days in inventory, and gross profit rate for PepsiCo., Inc. for 2012, 2013, and 2014. Comment on any trends.

Compute inventory turnover and determine the effect of the LIFO reserve on current ratio.

(LO 5, 6), **AP**

E6-11 Deere & Company is a global manufacturer and distributor of agricultural, construction, and forestry equipment. Suppose it reported the following information in its 2014 annual report.

(in millions)	**2014**	**2013**
Inventories (LIFO)	$ 2,397	$3,042
Current assets	30,857	
Current liabilities	12,753	
LIFO reserve	1,367	
Cost of goods sold	16,255	

Instructions
(a) Compute Deere's inventory turnover and days in inventory for 2014.
(b) Compute Deere's current ratio using the 2014 data as presented, and then again after adjusting for the LIFO reserve.
(c) Comment on how ignoring the LIFO reserve might affect your evaluation of Deere's liquidity.

*E6-12 Inventory data for Eggers Company are presented in E6-7.

Instructions
(a) Calculate the cost of the ending inventory and the cost of goods sold for each cost flow assumption, using a perpetual inventory system. Assume a sale of 410 units occurred on June 15 for a selling price of $8 and a sale of 50 units on June 27 for $9. (*Note:* For the moving-average method, round unit cost to three decimal places.)
(b) How do the results differ from E6-7?
(c) Why is the average unit cost not $6 [($5 + $6 + $7) ÷ 3 = $6]?

Calculate inventory and cost of goods sold using three cost flow methods in a perpetual inventory system.
(LO 7), AP

*E6-13 Information about Delmott is presented in E6-4. Additional data regarding the company's sales of Xpert snowboards are provided below. Assume that Delmott uses a perpetual inventory system.

Apply cost flow methods to perpetual records.
(LO 7), AP

Date		**Units**
Sept. 5	Sale	8
Sept. 16	Sale	48
Sept. 29	Sale	46
	Totals	102

Instructions
Compute ending inventory at September 30 using FIFO, LIFO, and moving-average. (*Note:* For moving-average, round unit cost to three decimal places.)

*E6-14 Foyle Hardware reported cost of goods sold as follows.

Determine effects of inventory errors.
(LO 8), AN

	2014	**2013**
Beginning inventory	$ 30,000	$ 20,000
Cost of goods purchased	175,000	164,000
Cost of goods available for sale	205,000	184,000
Less: Ending inventory	37,000	30,000
Cost of goods sold	$168,000	$154,000

Foyle made two errors:
1. 2013 ending inventory was overstated by $2,000.
2. 2014 ending inventory was understated by $5,000.

Instructions
Compute the correct cost of goods sold for each year.

*E6-15 Holcomb Company reported these income statement data for a 2-year period.

Prepare correct income statements.
(LO 8), AN

	2014	**2013**
Sales revenue	$250,000	$210,000
Beginning inventory	40,000	32,000
Cost of goods purchased	202,000	173,000
Cost of goods available for sale	242,000	205,000
Less: Ending inventory	55,000	40,000
Cost of goods sold	187,000	165,000
Gross profit	$ 63,000	$ 45,000

Holcomb Company uses a periodic inventory system. The inventories at January 1, 2013, and December 31, 2014, are correct. However, the ending inventory at December 31, 2013, is overstated by $8,000.

Instructions

(a) Prepare correct income statement data for the 2 years.

(b) What is the cumulative effect of the inventory error on total gross profit for the 2 years?

(c) ✏️➡️ Explain in a letter to the president of Holcomb Company what has happened—that is, the nature of the error and its effect on the financial statements.

Exercises: Set B and Challenge Exercises

Visit the book's companion website, at **www.wiley.com/college/kimmel**, and choose the Student Companion site to access Exercise Set B and Challenge Exercises.

Problems: Set A

Determine items and amounts to be recorded in inventory.

(LO 1), **AN**

P6-1A Aber Limited is trying to determine the value of its ending inventory as of February 28, 2014, the company's year-end. The accountant counted everything that was in the warehouse, as of February 28, which resulted in an ending inventory valuation of $48,000. However, she didn't know how to treat the following transactions so she didn't record them.

(a) On February 26, Aber shipped to a customer goods costing $800. The goods were shipped FOB shipping point, and the receiving report indicates that the customer received the goods on March 2.

(b) On February 26, Landis Inc. shipped goods to Aber FOB destination. The invoice price was $350 plus $25 for freight. The receiving report indicates that the goods were received by Aber on March 2.

(c) Aber had $500 of inventory at a customer's warehouse "on approval." The customer was going to let Aber know whether it wanted the merchandise by the end of the week, March 4.

(d) Aber also had $400 of inventory at a Newten craft shop, on consignment from Aber.

(e) On February 26, Aber ordered goods costing $750. The goods were shipped FOB shipping point on February 27. Aber received the goods on March 1.

(f) On February 28, Aber packaged goods and had them ready for shipping to a customer FOB destination. The invoice price was $350 plus $25 for freight; the cost of the items was $280. The receiving report indicates that the goods were received by the customer on March 2.

(g) Aber had damaged goods set aside in the warehouse because they are no longer saleable. These goods originally cost $400 and, originally, Aber expected to sell these items for $600.

Instructions

For each of the above transactions, specify whether the item in question should be included in ending inventory, and if so, at what amount. For each item that is not included in ending inventory, indicate who owns it and what account, if any, it should have been recorded in.

Determine cost of goods sold and ending inventory using FIFO, LIFO, and average-cost with analysis.

(LO 2, 3), **AP**

(b) Cost of goods sold:
FIFO $105,000
LIFO $115,500
Average $109,601

P6-2A Dunbar Distribution markets CDs of numerous performing artists. At the beginning of March, Dunbar had in beginning inventory 2,500 CDs with a unit cost of $7. During March, Dunbar made the following purchases of CDs.

| March 5 | 2,000 @ $8 | March 21 | 5,000 @ $10 |
| March 13 | 3,500 @ $9 | March 26 | 2,000 @ $11 |

During March 12,000 units were sold. Dunbar uses a periodic inventory system.

Instructions

(a) Determine the cost of goods available for sale.

(b) Determine (1) the ending inventory and (2) the cost of goods sold under each of the assumed cost flow methods (FIFO, LIFO, and average-cost). Prove the accuracy of the cost of goods sold under the FIFO and LIFO methods. (*Note:* For average-cost, round cost per unit to three decimal places.)

(c) Which cost flow method results in (1) the highest inventory amount for the balance sheet and (2) the highest cost of goods sold for the income statement?

P6-3A Groves Company Inc. had a beginning inventory of 100 units of Product MLN at a cost of $8 per unit. During the year, purchases were:

| Feb. 20 | 600 units at $ 9 | Aug. 12 | 400 units at $11 |
| May 5 | 500 units at $10 | Dec. 8 | 100 units at $12 |

Groves Company uses a periodic inventory system. Sales totaled 1,500 units.

Determine cost of goods sold and ending inventory using FIFO, LIFO, and average-cost in a periodic inventory system and assess financial statement effects.

*(LO 2, 3), **AP***

Instructions
(a) Determine the cost of goods available for sale.
(b) Determine the ending inventory and the cost of goods sold under each of the assumed cost flow methods (FIFO, LIFO, and average-cost). Prove the accuracy of the cost of goods sold under the FIFO and LIFO methods. (Round average unit cost to three decimal places.)
(c) Which cost flow method results in the lowest inventory amount for the balance sheet? The lowest cost of goods sold for the income statement?

(b) Cost of goods sold:
FIFO	$14,500
LIFO	$15,100
Average	$14,824

P6-4A The management of Tinker Inc. asks your help in determining the comparative effects of the FIFO and LIFO inventory cost flow methods. For 2014, the accounting records show these data.

Inventory, January 1 (10,000 units)	$ 35,000
Cost of 120,000 units purchased	468,500
Selling price of 98,000 units sold	750,000
Operating expenses	124,000

Units purchased consisted of 35,000 units at $3.70 on May 10; 60,000 units at $3.90 on August 15; and 25,000 units at $4.20 on November 20. Income taxes are 28%.

Compute ending inventory, prepare income statements, and answer questions using FIFO and LIFO.

*(LO 2, 3), **AN***

Instructions
(a) Prepare comparative condensed income statements for 2014 under FIFO and LIFO. (Show computations of ending inventory.)
(b) ➡ Answer the following questions for management in the form of a business letter.
  (1) Which inventory cost flow method produces the inventory amount that most closely approximates the amount that would have to be paid to replace the inventory? Why?
  (2) Which inventory cost flow method produces the net income amount that is a more likely indicator of next period's net income? Why?
  (3) Which inventory cost flow method is most likely to approximate the actual physical flow of the goods? Why?
  (4) How much more cash will be available under LIFO than under FIFO? Why?
  (5) How much of the gross profit under FIFO is illusionary in comparison with the gross profit under LIFO?

(a) Gross profit:
FIFO	$378,800
LIFO	$362,900

P6-5A You have the following information for Vincent Inc. for the month ended October 31, 2014. Vincent uses a periodic method for inventory.

Calculate ending inventory, cost of goods sold, gross profit, and gross profit rate under periodic method; compare results.

*(LO 2, 3), **AP***

Date	Description	Units	Unit Cost or Selling Price
Oct. 1	Beginning inventory	60	$24
Oct. 9	Purchase	120	26
Oct. 11	Sale	100	35
Oct. 17	Purchase	100	27
Oct. 22	Sale	60	40
Oct. 25	Purchase	70	29
Oct. 29	Sale	110	40

Instructions
(a) Calculate (i) ending inventory, (ii) cost of goods sold, (iii) gross profit, and (iv) gross profit rate under each of the following methods.
  (1) LIFO.
  (2) FIFO.
  (3) Average-cost. (Round cost per unit to three decimal places.)
(b) Compare results for the three cost flow assumptions.

(a) Gross profit:
LIFO	$2,970
FIFO	$3,310
Average	$3,133

Compare specific identification, FIFO, and LIFO under periodic method; use cost flow assumption to influence earnings.

(LO 2, 3), **AP**

P6-6A You have the following information for Wooderson Gems. Wooderson uses the periodic method of accounting for its inventory transactions. Wooderson only carries one brand and size of diamonds—all are identical. Each batch of diamonds purchased is carefully coded and marked with its purchase cost.

March 1   Beginning inventory 150 diamonds at a cost of $310 per diamond.
March 3   Purchased 200 diamonds at a cost of $350 each.
March 5   Sold 180 diamonds for $600 each.
March 10 Purchased 330 diamonds at a cost of $375 each.
March 25 Sold 390 diamonds for $650 each.

Instructions

(a) Gross profit:
Maximum	$162,500
Minimum	$155,350

(a) Assume that Wooderson Gems uses the specific identification cost flow method.
  (1) Demonstrate how Wooderson could maximize its gross profit for the month by specifically selecting which diamonds to sell on March 5 and March 25.
  (2) Demonstrate how Wooderson could minimize its gross profit for the month by selecting which diamonds to sell on March 5 and March 25.
(b) Assume that Wooderson uses the FIFO cost flow assumption. Calculate cost of goods sold. How much gross profit would Wooderson report under this cost flow assumption?
(c) Assume that Wooderson uses the LIFO cost flow assumption. Calculate cost of goods sold. How much gross profit would the company report under this cost flow assumption?
(d) Which cost flow method should Wooderson Gems select? Explain.

Compute inventory turnover and days in inventory; compute current ratio based on LIFO and after adjusting for LIFO reserve.

(LO 5, 6), **AP**

P6-7A Suppose this information (in millions) is available for the Automotive and Other Operations Divisions of General Motors Corporation for a recent year. General Motors uses the LIFO inventory method.

Beginning inventory	$ 13,921
Ending inventory	14,939
LIFO reserve	1,423
Current assets	60,135
Current liabilities	70,308
Cost of goods sold	166,259
Sales revenue	178,199

Instructions

(a) Calculate the inventory turnover and days in inventory.
(b) Calculate the current ratio based on inventory as reported using LIFO.
(c) Calculate the current ratio after adjusting for the LIFO reserve.
(d) Comment on any difference between parts (b) and (c).

Calculate cost of goods sold, ending inventory, and gross profit for LIFO, FIFO, and moving-average under the perpetual system; compare results.

(LO 3, 7), **AP**

***P6-8A** Pember Inc. is a retailer operating in Edmonton, Alberta. Pember uses the perpetual inventory method. Assume that there are no credit transactions; all amounts are settled in cash. You are provided with the following information for Pember Inc. for the month of January 2014.

Date	Description	Quantity	Unit Cost or Selling Price
Dec. 31	Ending inventory	160	$20
Jan. 2	Purchase	100	22
Jan. 6	Sale	180	40
Jan. 9	Purchase	75	24
Jan. 10	Sale	50	45
Jan. 23	Purchase	100	25
Jan. 30	Sale	130	48

Instructions

(a) Gross profit:
LIFO	$7,490
FIFO	$7,865
Average	$7,763

(a) For each of the following cost flow assumptions, calculate (i) cost of goods sold, (ii) ending inventory, and (iii) gross profit.
  (1) LIFO.
  (2) FIFO.
  (3) Moving-average. (Round cost per unit to three decimal places.)
(b) Compare results for the three cost flow assumptions.

*P6-9A Lambert Center began operations on July 1. It uses a perpetual inventory system. During July, the company had the following purchases and sales.

Determine ending inventory under a perpetual inventory system.

(LO 3, 7), **AP**

	Purchases		
Date	**Units**	**Unit Cost**	**Sales Units**
July 1	7	$62	
July 6			5
July 11	3	$66	
July 14			3
July 21	4	$71	
July 27			3

Instructions

(a) Determine the ending inventory under a perpetual inventory system using (1) FIFO, (2) moving-average (round unit cost to three decimal places), and (3) LIFO.

(b) Which costing method produces the highest ending inventory valuation?

(a) FIFO $213
    Average $207
    LIFO $195

Problems: Set B

P6-1B Sun Company is trying to determine the value of its ending inventory as of March 31, 2014, the company's year-end. The following transactions occurred, and the accountant asked your help in determining whether they should be recorded or not.

Determine items and amounts to be recorded in inventory.

(LO 1), **AN**

(a) On March 30, Sun shipped to a customer goods costing $1,000. The goods were shipped FOB destination, and the receiving report indicates that the customer received the goods on April 1.

(b) On March 28, Wholesale Inc. shipped goods to Sun FOB shipping point. The invoice price was $600 plus $20 for freight. The receiving report indicates that the goods were received by Sun on April 2.

(c) Sun had $750 of consigned goods from Frederick Inc.

(d) Sun had $380 of inventory at Stephen's Variety, on consignment from Sun.

(e) On March 29, Sun ordered goods costing $640. The goods were shipped FOB destination on March 31. Sun received the goods on April 3.

(f) A customer returned goods to Sun on March 31. Upon inspection, the goods were found to be undamaged and were accepted as returned goods. These goods originally cost $400 and Sun sold them for $640.

Instructions

For each of the above transactions, specify whether the item in question should be included in ending inventory, and if so, at what amount. For each item that is not included in ending inventory, indicate who owns it and what account, if any, it should have been recorded in.

P6-2B Lifetime Distribution markets classic children's books. At the beginning of June, Lifetime had in beginning inventory 1,200 books with a unit cost of $3. During June, Lifetime made the following purchases of books.

Determine cost of goods sold and ending inventory using FIFO, LIFO, and average cost, with analysis.

(LO 2, 3), **AP**

June 3	4,000 @ $3	June 29	4,000 @ $6
June 18	7,500 @ $5		

During June, 10,500 books were sold. Lifetime uses a periodic inventory system.

Instructions

(a) Determine the cost of goods available for sale.

(b) Determine (1) the ending inventory and (2) the cost of goods sold under each of the assumed cost flow methods (FIFO, LIFO, and average-cost). Prove the accuracy of the cost of goods sold under the FIFO and LIFO methods. (*Note:* For average-cost, round cost per unit to three decimal places.)

(c) Which cost flow method results in (1) the highest inventory amount for the balance sheet and (2) the highest cost of goods sold for the income statement?

(a) Cost of goods sold:
    FIFO $42,100
    LIFO $56,500
    Average $48,475

Determine cost of goods sold and ending inventory using FIFO, LIFO, and average-cost in a periodic inventory system and assess financial statement effects.

(LO 2, 3), **AP**

(b) Cost of goods sold:

FIFO	$14,500
LIFO	$15,950
Average	$15,281

Compute ending inventory, prepare income statements, and answer questions using FIFO and LIFO.

(LO 2, 3), **AN**

(a) Gross profit:

FIFO	$456,050
LIFO	$450,550

P6-3B Smythe Company Inc. had a beginning inventory of 200 units of Product ERV at a cost of $6 per unit. During the year, purchases were:

Jan. 24	800 units at $7	Aug. 19	600 units at $ 9
Apr. 12	400 units at $8	Nov. 30	350 units at $10

Smythe Company uses a periodic inventory system. Sales totaled 1,900 units.

Instructions

(a) Determine the cost of goods available for sale.

(b) Determine the ending inventory and the cost of goods sold under each of the assumed cost flow methods (FIFO, LIFO, and average-cost). Prove the accuracy of the cost of goods sold under the FIFO and LIFO methods. (Round average unit cost to three decimal places.)

(c) Which cost flow method results in the lowest inventory amount for the balance sheet? The lowest cost of goods sold for the income statement?

P6-4B The management of Weigel Inc. asks your help in determining the comparative effects of the FIFO and LIFO inventory cost flow methods. For 2014 the accounting records show these data.

Inventory, January 1 (4,000 units)	$ 16,000
Cost of 105,000 units purchased	470,500
Selling price of 100,000 units sold	900,000
Operating expenses	185,000

Units purchased consisted of 35,000 units at $4.21 on March 20; 65,000 units at $4.60 on July 24; and 5,000 units at $4.83 on December 12. Income taxes are 30%.

Instructions

(a) Prepare comparative condensed income statements for 2014 under FIFO and LIFO. (Show computations of ending inventory.)

(b) ➤ Answer the following questions for management in the form of a business letter.

(1) Which inventory cost flow method produces the most meaningful inventory amount for the balance sheet? Why?

(2) Which inventory cost flow method produces the most meaningful net income? Why?

(3) Which inventory cost flow method is most likely to approximate the actual physical flow of the goods? Why?

(4) How much more cash will be available under LIFO than under FIFO? Why?

(5) How much of the gross profit under FIFO is illusionary in comparison with the gross profit under LIFO?

Calculate ending inventory, cost of goods sold, gross profit, and gross profit rate under periodic method; compare results.

(LO 2, 3), **AP**

(a) Gross profit:

LIFO	$2,250
FIFO	$2,570
Average	$2,420

Compare specific identification, FIFO, and LIFO under periodic method; use cost flow assumption to influence earnings.

(LO 2, 3), **AP**

P6-5B You have the following information for Crystal Inc. for the month ended May 31, 2014. Crystal uses a periodic method for inventory.

Date	Description	Units	Unit Cost or Selling Price
May 1	Beginning inventory	40	$20
May 6	Purchase	110	23
May 7	Sale	90	32
May 15	Purchase	70	25
May 18	Sale	40	37
May 24	Purchase	60	26
May 30	Sale	80	38

Instructions

(a) Calculate (i) ending inventory, (ii) cost of goods sold, (iii) gross profit, and (iv) gross profit rate under each of the following methods.

(1) LIFO.

(2) FIFO.

(3) Average-cost. (Round cost per unit to three decimal places.)

(b) Compare results for the three cost flow assumptions.

P6-6B You have the following information for Limex Watches. Limex uses the periodic method of accounting for its inventory transactions. Limex carries only one brand of hand-crafted jeweled watches—all are identical. Each batch of watches purchased is carefully coded and marked with its purchase cost.

July 1	Beginning inventory 220 watches at a cost of $420 per watch.
July 2	Purchased 200 watches at a cost of $450 each.
July 5	Sold 180 watches for $700 each.
July 14	Purchased 350 watches at a cost of $480 each.
July 28	Sold 480 watches for $720 each.

Instructions

(a) Assume that Limex uses the specific identification cost flow method.
  (1) Demonstrate how Limex could maximize its gross profit for the month by specifically selecting which watches to sell on July 5 and July 28.
  (2) Demonstrate how Limex could minimize its gross profit for the month by selecting which watches to sell on July 5 and July 28.
(b) Assume that Limex uses the FIFO cost flow assumption. Calculate cost of goods sold. How much gross profit would Limex report under this cost flow assumption?
(c) Assume that Limex uses the LIFO cost flow assumption. Calculate cost of goods sold. How much gross profit would the company report under this cost flow assumption?
(d) Which cost flow method should Limex Watches select? Explain.

(a) Gross profit:

Maximum	$174,000
Minimum	$167,400

P6-7B Suppose this information is available for the Automotive Sector of NoGo Motor Company for 2014. NoGo uses the LIFO inventory method.

Compute inventory turnover and days in inventory; compute current ratio based on LIFO and after adjusting for LIFO reserve.

(LO 5, 6), **AP**

(in millions)	
Beginning inventory	$ 10,017
Ending inventory	10,121
LIFO reserve	1,100
Current assets	54,243
Current liabilities	50,218
Cost of goods sold	130,460
Sales	154,379

Instructions

(a) Calculate the inventory turnover and days in inventory.
(b) Calculate the current ratio based on inventory as reported using LIFO.
(c) Calculate the current ratio after adjusting for the LIFO reserve.
(d) Comment on any difference between parts (b) and (c).

P6-8B Liberty Inc. is a retailer operating in Centralia. Liberty uses the perpetual inventory method. All sales returns from customers result in the goods being returned to inventory. (Assume that the inventory is not damaged.) Assume that there are no credit transactions; all amounts are settled in cash. You are provided with the following information for Liberty Inc. for the month of January 2014.

Calculate cost of goods sold, ending inventory, and gross profit for LIFO, FIFO, and moving-average under the perpetual system; compare results.

(LO 3, 7), **AP**

Date	Description	Quantity	Unit Cost or Selling Price
Dec. 31	Ending inventory	140	$14
Jan. 2	Purchase	120	15
Jan. 6	Sale	150	30
Jan. 9	Purchase	85	17
Jan. 10	Sale	70	35
Jan. 23	Purchase	100	20
Jan. 30	Sale	110	42

Instructions

(a) For each of the following cost flow assumptions, calculate (i) cost of goods sold, (ii) ending inventory, and (iii) gross profit.
  (1) LIFO.
  (2) FIFO.
  (3) Moving-average. (Round cost per unit to three decimal places.)
(b) Compare results for the three cost flow assumptions.

(a) Gross profit:

LIFO	$5,990
FIFO	$6,620
Average	$6,382

Determine ending inventory under a perpetual inventory system.

(LO 3, 7), **AP**

P6-9B Shiraz Rugs began operations on February 1. It uses a perpetual inventory system. During February, the company had the following purchases and sales.

	Purchases		
Date	**Units**	**Unit Cost**	**Sales Units**
Feb. 1	12	$150	
Feb. 6			9
Feb. 11	8	$168	
Feb. 14			5
Feb. 21	6	$182	
Feb. 27			4

Instructions

(a) FIFO $1,428
Average $1,381
LIFO $1,318

(a) Determine the ending inventory under a perpetual inventory system using (1) FIFO, (2) moving-average (round unit cost to three decimal places), and (3) LIFO.

(b) Which costing method produces the highest ending inventory valuation?

Problems: Set C

Visit the book's companion website, at **www.wiley.com/college/kimmel**, and choose the Student Companion site to access Problem Set C.

Comprehensive Problem

CP6 On December 1, 2014, Harrisen Company had the account balances shown below.

	Debit		**Credit**
Cash	$ 4,800	Accumulated Depreciation—Equipment	$ 1,500
Accounts Receivable	3,900	Accounts Payable	3,000
Inventory	1,800*	Common Stock	10,000
Equipment	21,000	Retained Earnings	17,000
	$31,500		$31,500

*(3,000 × $0.60)

The following transactions occurred during December.

Dec. 3 Purchased 4,000 units of inventory on account at a cost of $0.72 per unit.

5 Sold 4,400 units of inventory on account for $0.90 per unit. (It sold 3,000 of the $0.60 units and 1,400 of the $0.72.)

7 Granted the December 5 customer $180 credit for 200 units of inventory returned costing $150. These units were returned to inventory.

17 Purchased 2,200 units of inventory for cash at $0.80 each.

22 Sold 2,000 units of inventory on account for $0.95 per unit. (It sold 2,000 of the $0.72 units.)

Adjustment data:

1. Accrued salaries and wages payable $400.
2. Depreciation on equipment $200 per month.
3. Income tax expense was $215, to be paid next year.

Instructions

(a) Journalize the December transactions and adjusting entries, assuming Harrisen uses the perpetual inventory method.

(b) Enter the December 1 balances in the ledger T-accounts and post the December transactions. In addition to the accounts mentioned above, use the following additional accounts: Income Taxes Payable, Salaries and Wages Payable, Sales Revenue, Sales Returns and Allowances, Cost of Goods Sold, Depreciation Expense, Salaries and Wages Expense, and Income Tax Expense.

(c) Prepare an adjusted trial balance as of December 31, 2014.

(d) Prepare an income statement for December 2014 and a classified balance sheet at December 31, 2014.

(e) Compute ending inventory and cost of goods sold under FIFO, assuming Harrisen Company uses the periodic inventory system.

(f) Compute ending inventory and cost of goods sold under LIFO, assuming Harrisen Company uses the periodic inventory system.

Continuing Cookie Chronicle

(*Note:* This is a continuation of the Cookie Chronicle from Chapters 1 through 5.)

CCC6 Natalie is busy establishing both divisions of her business (cookie classes and mixer sales) and completing her business degree. Her goals for the next 11 months are to sell one mixer per month and to give two to three classes per week. Natalie has decided to use a periodic inventory system and now must choose a cost flow assumption for her mixer inventory.

> Go to the book's companion website, at **www.wiley.com/college/kimmel**, to see the completion of this problem.

Broadening Your Perspective

Financial Reporting and Analysis

FINANCIAL REPORTING PROBLEM: *Tootsie Roll Industries, Inc.*

BYP6-1 The notes that accompany a company's financial statements provide informative details that would clutter the amounts and descriptions presented in the statements. Refer to the financial statements of Tootsie Roll and the accompanying Notes to Consolidated Financial Statements in Appendix A.

Instructions

Answer the following questions. (Give the amounts in thousands of dollars, as shown in Tootsie Roll's annual report.)

(a) What did Tootsie Roll report for the amount of inventories in its Consolidated Balance Sheet at December 31, 2011? At December 31, 2010?

(b) Compute the dollar amount of change and the percentage change in inventories between 2010 and 2011. Compute inventory as a percentage of current assets for 2011.

(c) What are the (product) cost of goods sold reported by Tootsie Roll for 2011, 2010, and 2009? Compute the ratio of (product) cost of goods sold to net (product) sales in 2011.

COMPARATIVE ANALYSIS PROBLEM: *Tootsie Roll vs. Hershey*

BYP6-2 The financial statements of The Hershey Company appear in Appendix B, following the financial statements for Tootsie Roll in Appendix A.

Instructions

(a) Based on the information in the financial statements, compute these 2011 values for each company. (Do not adjust for the LIFO reserve.)
  (1) Inventory turnover. (Use product cost of goods sold and total inventory.)
  (2) Days in inventory.

(b) What conclusions concerning the management of the inventory can you draw from these data?

RESEARCH CASE

BYP6-3 The July 15, 2010, edition of *CFO.com* contains an article by Marie Leone entitled "Sucking the LIFO out of Inventory."

Instructions

Read the article, which can be found at **www.cfo.com/printable/article.cfm/14508745**, and answer the following questions.

(a) What type of company benefits most from the use of LIFO?

(b) What is the estimated boost in federal tax receipts over 10 years if the use of LIFO for taxes was not allowed?

(c) If the United States decides to adopt International Financial Reporting Standards (IFRS), what would be the implications for IFRS?

(d) What conceptual justification for LIFO do its proponents provide?

(e) What types of companies prefer to use FIFO?

INTERPRETING FINANCIAL STATEMENTS

BYP6-4 Suppose the following information is from the 2014 annual report of American Greetings Corporation (all dollars in thousands).

	Feb. 28, 2014	Feb. 28, 2013
Inventories		
Finished goods	$232,893	$244,379
Work in process	7,068	10,516
Raw materials and supplies	49,937	43,861
	289,898	298,756
Less: LIFO reserve	86,025	82,085
Total (as reported)	$203,873	$216,671
Cost of goods sold	$809,956	$780,771
Current assets (as reported)	$561,395	$669,340
Current liabilities	$343,405	$432,321

The notes to the company's financial statements also include the following information.

Finished products, work in process, and raw material inventories are carried at the lower-of-cost-or-market. The last-in, first-out (LIFO) cost method is used for approximately 75% of the domestic inventories in 2014 and approximately 70% in 2013. The foreign subsidiaries principally use the first-in, first-out (FIFO) method. Display material and factory supplies are carried at average-cost.

Instructions
(a) Define each of the following: finished goods, work in process, and raw materials.
(b) What might be a possible explanation for why the company uses FIFO for its nondomestic inventories?
(c) Calculate the company's inventory turnover and days in inventory for 2013 and 2014. (2012 inventory was $182,618.) Discuss the implications of any change in the ratios.
(d) What percentage of total inventory does the 2014 LIFO reserve represent? If the company used FIFO in 2014, what would be the value of its inventory? Do you consider this difference a "material" amount from the perspective of an analyst? Which value accurately represents the value of the company's inventory?
(e) Calculate the company's 2014 current ratio with the numbers as reported, then recalculate after adjusting for the LIFO reserve.

REAL-WORLD FOCUS

BYP6-5 *Purpose:* Use SEC filings to learn about a company's inventory accounting practices.

Address: **http://biz.yahoo.com/p/_capgds-bldmch.html**,
or go to **www.wiley.com/college/kimmel**

Steps
1. Go to this site and click on the name of an equipment manufacturer other than those discussed in the chapter.
2. Click on **SEC filings**.
3. Under "Recent filings" choose **Form 10K** (annual report) and click on **Full Filing at Edgar Online**.
4. Choose option "3," **Online HTML Version**.

If the 10K is not listed among the recent filings, then click on **View All Filings on EDGAR Online**.

Instructions
Review the 10K to answer the following questions.
(a) What is the name of the company?
(b) How has its inventory changed from the previous year?
(c) What is the amount of raw materials, work in process, and finished goods inventory?
(d) What inventory method does the company use?
(e) Calculate the inventory turnover and days in inventory for the current year.
(f) If the company uses LIFO, what was the amount of its LIFO reserve?

Critical Thinking

DECISION-MAKING ACROSS THE ORGANIZATION

BYP6-6 Heineken Electronics has enjoyed tremendous sales growth during the last 10 years. However, even though sales have steadily increased, the company's CEO, Beth Dains, is concerned about certain aspects of its performance. She has called a meeting with the corporate controller and the vice presidents of finance, operations, sales, and marketing to discuss the company's performance. Beth begins the meeting by making the following observations:

> We have been forced to take significant write-downs on inventory during each of the last three years because of obsolescence. In addition, inventory storage costs have soared. We rent four additional warehouses to store our increasingly diverse inventory. Five years ago inventory represented only 20% of the value of our total assets. It now exceeds 35%. Yet, even with all of this inventory, "stockouts" (measured by complaints by customers that the desired product is not available) have increased by 40% during the last three years. And worse yet, it seems that we constantly must discount merchandise that we have too much of.

Beth asks the group to review the following data and make suggestions as to how the company's performance might be improved.

(in millions)	**2014**	**2013**	**2012**	**2011**
Inventory				
Raw materials	$242	$198	$155	$128
Work in process	116	77	49	33
Finished goods	567	482	398	257
Total inventory	$925	$757	$602	$418
Current assets	$1,800	$1,423	$1,183	$841
Total assets	$2,643	$2,523	$2,408	$2,090
Current liabilities	$600	$590	$525	$420
Sales revenue	$9,428	$8,674	$7,536	$6,840
Cost of goods sold	$6,328	$5,474	$4,445	$3,557
Net income	$754	$987	$979	$958

Instructions

Using the information provided, answer the following questions.
(a) Compute the current ratio, gross profit rate, profit margin, inventory turnover, and days in inventory for 2012, 2013, and 2014.
(b) Discuss the trends and potential causes of the changes in the ratios in part (a).
(c) Discuss potential remedies to any problems discussed in part (b).
(d) What concerns might be raised by some members of management with regard to your suggestions in part (c)?

COMMUNICATION ACTIVITIES

BYP6-7 In a discussion of dramatic increases in coffee-bean prices, a *Wall Street Journal* article noted the following fact about Starbucks.

> Before this year's bean-price hike, Starbucks added several defenses that analysts say could help it maintain earnings and revenue. The company last year began accounting for its coffee-bean purchases by taking the average price of all beans in inventory.

Prior to this change, the company was using FIFO.

Instructions

Your client, the CEO of Supreme Coffee, Inc., read this article and sent you an e-mail message requesting that you explain why Starbucks might have taken this action. Your response should explain what impact this change in accounting method has on earnings, why the company might want to do this, and any possible disadvantages of such a change.

*BYP6-8   You are the controller of Fagan Inc. K. L. Howard, the president, recently mentioned to you that she found an error in the 2013 financial statements which she believes has corrected itself. She determined, in discussions with the purchasing department, that 2013 ending inventory was overstated by $1 million. K. L. says that the 2014 ending inventory is correct, and she assumes that 2014 income is correct. K. L. says to you, "What happened has happened—there's no point in worrying about it anymore."

Instructions

You conclude that K. L. is incorrect. Write a brief, tactful memo to her, clarifying the situation.

ETHICS CASE

BYP6-9   Reagen Wholesale Corp. uses the LIFO cost flow method. In the current year, profit at Reagen is running unusually high. The corporate tax rate is also high this year, but it is scheduled to decline significantly next year. In an effort to lower the current year's net income and to take advantage of the changing income tax rate, the president of Reagen Wholesale instructs the plant accountant to recommend to the purchasing department a large purchase of inventory for delivery 3 days before the end of the year. The price of the inventory to be purchased has doubled during the year, and the purchase will represent a major portion of the ending inventory value.

Instructions

(a) What is the effect of this transaction on this year's and next year's income statement and income tax expense? Why?

(b) If Reagen Wholesale had been using the FIFO method of inventory costing, would the president give the same directive?

(c) Should the plant accountant order the inventory purchase to lower income? What are the ethical implications of this order?

ALL ABOUT YOU

BYP6-10   Some of the largest business frauds ever perpetrated have involved the misstatement of inventory. Two classics were at Leslie Fay and McKesson Corporation.

Instructions

There is considerable information regarding inventory frauds available on the Internet. Search for information about one of the two cases mentioned above, or inventory fraud at any other company, and prepare a short explanation of the nature of the inventory fraud.

FASB CODIFICATION ACTIVITY

BYP6-11   If your school has a subscription to the FASB Codification, go to **http://aaahq.org/ascLogin.cfm** to log in and prepare responses to the following.

(a) The primary basis for accounting for inventories is cost. How is cost defined in the Codification?

(b) What does the Codification state regarding the use of consistency in the selection or employment of a basis for inventory?

(c) What does the Codification indicate is a justification for the use of the lower-of-cost-or-market for inventory valuation?

CONSIDERING PEOPLE, PLANET, AND PROFIT

BYP6-12   Caterpillar publishes an annual Sustainability Report to explain its position on sustainability, describe its goals, and report on its achievements. The report can be found at **http://www.caterpillar.com/sustainability/sustainability-report**.

Instructions

Access the report and answer the following questions.

(a) Page 24 of the report describes Caterpillar's efforts in the area of coke oven gas. Read this section and discuss how the company's efforts address both sustainability and profitability.

(b) Page 43 describes the company's goals for the year 2020. What are these goals?

(c) Page 44 describes the company's results relative to 2003 with regard to worker safety. Summarize the company's progress in this area.

(d) Page 48 describes the company's results regarding energy use. Explain how the company measures its progress, and comment on its results thus far.

Answers to Insight and Accounting Across the Organization Questions

p. 285 A Big Hiccup Q: What steps might the companies take to avoid such a serious disruption in the future? **A:** The manufacturer of the piston rings should spread its manufacturing facilities across a few locations that are far enough apart that they would not all be at risk at once. In addition, the automakers might consider becoming less dependent on a single supplier as well as having weather contingency plans.

p. 286 Falsifying Inventory to Boost Income Q: What effect does an overstatement of inventory have on a company's financial statements? **A:** The balance sheet looks stronger because inventory and retained earnings are overstated. The income statement looks better because cost of goods sold is understated and income is overstated.

p. 296 Is LIFO Fair? Q: What are the arguments for and against the use of LIFO? **A:** Proponents of LIFO argue that it is conceptually superior because it matches the most recent cost with the most recent selling price. Critics contend that it artificially understates the company's net income and consequently reduces tax payments. Also, because most foreign companies are not allowed to use LIFO, its use by U.S. companies reduces the ability of investors to compare U.S. companies with foreign companies.

p. 300 Too Many TVs or Too Few? Q: For Sony, what are the advantages and disadvantages of having a low days in inventory measure? **A:** If Sony has a low days in inventory, it reduces the amount of cash it has tied up in inventory. It also minimizes the risk that it will be stuck with excess inventory that could force it to provide big discounts, resulting in punishing losses. Sony also faces the risk that the TVs will become obsolete before they are sold. However, Sony increases the risk that it will encounter "stockouts," that is, it will not have adequate inventory to meet customer demand.

Answers to Self-Test Questions

1. d **2.** a **3.** b ($180,000 + $35,000) **4.** c ((5,000 × $13) + (4,000 × $12)) **5.** d ((8,000 × $11) + (1,000 × $12)) **6.** d ((5,000 × $8) + (15,000 × $10) + (20,000 × $12)) ÷ 40,000 = $10.75; $10.75 × 7,000 **7.** c **8.** d **9.** a **10.** d **11.** b ($285,000 ÷ (($80,000 + 110,000) ÷ 2) = 3; 365 ÷ 3) **12.** a ***13.** d ***14.** b ***15.** b

A Look at IFRS

The major IFRS requirements related to accounting and reporting for inventories are the same as GAAP. The major differences are that IFRS prohibits the use of the LIFO cost flow assumption and determines market in the lower-of-cost-or-market inventory valuation differently.

LEARNING OBJECTIVE **9**

Compare the accounting procedures for inventories under GAAP and IFRS.

KEY POINTS

- The requirements for accounting for and reporting inventories are more principles-based under IFRS. That is, GAAP provides more detailed guidelines in inventory accounting.

- The definitions for inventory are essentially similar under IFRS and GAAP. Both define inventory as assets held-for-sale in the ordinary course of business, in the process of production for sale (work in process), or to be consumed in the production of goods or services (e.g., raw materials).

- Who owns the goods—goods in transit or consigned goods—as well as the costs to include in inventory, are accounted for the same under IFRS and GAAP.

- Both GAAP and IFRS permit specific identification where appropriate. IFRS actually requires that the specific identification method be used where the inventory items are not interchangeable (i.e., can be specifically identified). If the inventory items are not specifically identifiable, a cost flow assumption is used. GAAP does not specify situations in which specific identification must be used.

- A major difference between IFRS and GAAP relates to the LIFO cost flow assumption. GAAP permits the use of LIFO for inventory valuation. IFRS prohibits its use. FIFO and average-cost are the only two acceptable cost flow assumptions permitted under IFRS.

- IFRS requires companies to use the same cost flow assumption for all goods of a similar nature. GAAP has no specific requirement in this area.

- In the lower-of-cost-or-market test for inventory valuation, IFRS defines market as net realizable value. Net realizable value is the estimated selling price in the ordinary course of business, less the estimated costs of completion and estimated selling expenses. In other words, net realizable value is the best estimate of the net amounts that inventories are expected to realize. GAAP, on the other hand, defines market as essentially replacement cost.

- Under GAAP, if inventory is written down under the lower-of-cost-or-market valuation, the new value becomes its cost basis. As a result, the inventory may not be written back up to its original cost in a subsequent period. Under IFRS, the write-down may be reversed in a subsequent period up to the amount of the previous write-down. Both the write-down and any subsequent reversal should be reported on the income statement as an expense. An item-by-item approach is generally followed under IFRS.

- An example of the use of lower-of-cost-or-net realizable value under IFRS follows.

Mendel Company has the following four items in its ending inventory as of December 31, 2014. The company uses the lower-of-cost-or-net realizable value approach for inventory valuation following IFRS.

Item No.	Cost	Net Realizable Value
1320	$3,600	$3,400
1333	4,000	4,100
1428	2,800	2,100
1510	5,000	4,700

The computation of the ending inventory value to be reported in the financial statements at December 31, 2014, is as follows.

Item No.	Cost	Net Realizable Value	Lower-of-Cost-or-NRV
1320	$ 3,600	$ 3,400	$ 3,400
1333	4,000	4,100	4,000
1428	2,800	2,100	2,100
1510	5,000	4,700	4,700
Total	$15,400	$14,300	$14,200

- Unlike property, plant, and equipment, IFRS does not permit the option of valuing inventories at fair value. As indicated above, IFRS requires inventory to be written down, but inventory cannot be written up above its original cost.

- Similar to GAAP, certain agricultural products and mineral products can be reported at net realizable value using IFRS.

- IFRS allows companies to report inventory at standard cost if it does not differ significantly from actual cost. Standard cost is addressed in managerial accounting courses.

LOOKING TO THE FUTURE

One convergence issue that will be difficult to resolve relates to the use of the LIFO cost flow assumption. As indicated, IFRS specifically prohibits its use. Conversely, the LIFO cost flow assumption is widely used in the United States because of its favorable tax advantages. In addition, many argue that LIFO from a financial reporting point of view provides a better matching of current costs against revenue and, therefore, enables companies to compute a more realistic income.

With a new conceptual framework being developed, it is highly probable that the use of the concept of conservatism will be eliminated. Similarly, the concept of "prudence" in the IASB literature will also be eliminated. This may ultimately have implications for the application of the lower-of-cost-or-net realizable value.

IFRS PRACTICE

IFRS SELF-TEST QUESTIONS

1. Which of the following should **not** be included in the inventory of a company using IFRS?
   (a) Goods held on consignment from another company.
   (b) Goods shipped on consignment to another company.
   (c) Goods in transit from another company shipped FOB shipping point.
   (d) None of the above.

2. Which method of inventory costing is prohibited under IFRS?
(a) Specific identification.   (c) FIFO.
(b) LIFO.   (d) Average-cost.

3. Yang Company purchased 2,000 phones and has 400 phones in its ending inventory at a cost of $90 each and a current replacement cost of $80 each. The net realizable value of each phone in the ending inventory is $70. The ending inventory under lower-of-cost-or-net realizable value is:
(a) $36,000.   (c) $28,000.
(b) $32,000.   (d) None of the above.

4. Specific identification:
(a) must be used under IFRS if the inventory items are not interchangeable.
(b) cannot be used under IFRS.
(c) cannot be used under GAAP.
(d) must be used under IFRS if it would result in the most conservative net income.

5. IFRS requires the following:
(a) Ending inventory is written up and down to net realizable value each reporting period.
(b) Ending inventory is written down to net realizable value but cannot be written up.
(c) Ending inventory is written down to net realizable value and may be written up in future periods to its net realizable value but not above its original cost.
(d) Ending inventory is written down to net realizable value and may be written up in future periods to its net realizable value.

IFRS CONCEPTS AND APPLICATION

IFRS6-1   Briefly describe some of the similarities and differences between GAAP and IFRS with respect to the accounting for inventories.

IFRS6-2   LaTour Inc. is based in France and prepares its financial statements in accordance with IFRS. In 2014, it reported cost of goods sold (in euros) of €578 million and average inventory of €154 million. Briefly discuss how analysis of LaTour's inventory turnover (and comparisons to a company using GAAP) might be affected by differences in inventory accounting between IFRS and GAAP.

IFRS6-3   Franklin Company has the following four items in its ending inventory as of December 31, 2014. The company uses the lower-of-cost-or-net realizable value approach for inventory valuation following IFRS.

Item No.	Cost	Net Realizable Value
AB	$1,700	$1,400
TRX	2,200	2,300
NWA	7,800	7,100
SGH	3,000	3,700

Compute the lower-of-cost-or-net realizable value.

INTERNATIONAL FINANCIAL REPORTING PROBLEM: *Zetar plc*

IFRS6-4   The financial statements of Zetar plc are presented in Appendix C. The company's complete annual report, including the notes to its financial statements, is available in the Investors section at **www.zetarplc.com**.

Instructions
Using the notes to the company's financial statements, answer the following questions.
(a) What cost flow assumption does the company use to value inventory?
(b) What was the amount of expense that the company reported for inventory write-downs during 2011?
(c) What amount of raw materials, work in process, and finished goods inventory did the company report at April 30, 2011?

Answers to IFRS Self-Test Questions

1. a   2. b   3. c   4. a   5. c

✔ Remember to go back to The Navigator box on the chapter opening page and check off your completed work.

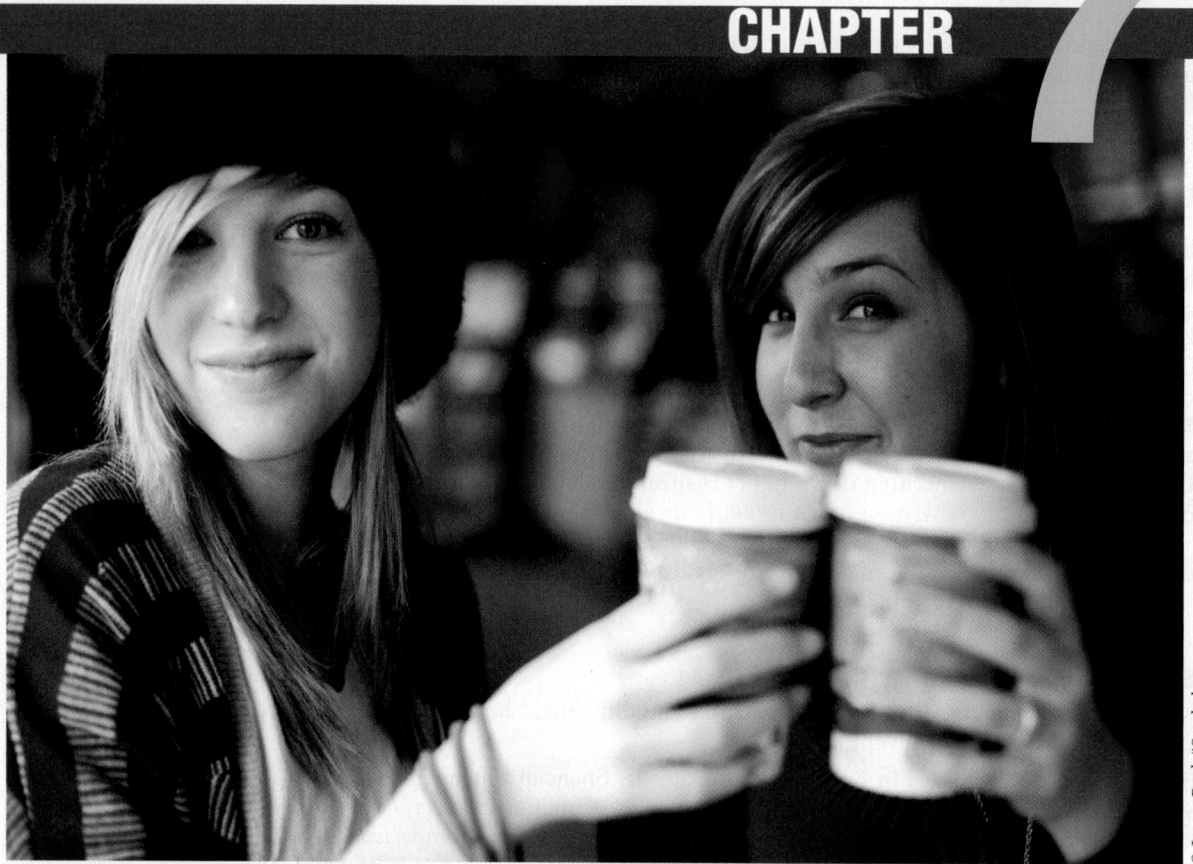

© James Pauls/iStockphoto

FRAUD, INTERNAL CONTROL, AND CASH

LEARNING OBJECTIVES

After studying this chapter, you should be able to:

1 Define fraud and internal control.

2 Identify the principles of internal control activities.

3 Explain the applications of internal control principles to cash receipts.

4 Explain the applications of internal control principles to cash disbursements.

5 Prepare a bank reconciliation.

6 Explain the reporting of cash.

7 Discuss the basic principles of cash management.

8 Identify the primary elements of a cash budget.

✔ The Navigator

If you're ever looking for a cappuccino in Moose Jaw, Saskatchewan, stop by Stephanie's Gourmet Coffee and More, located on Main Street. Staff there serve, on average, 650 cups of coffee a day, including both regular and specialty coffees, not to mention soups, Italian sandwiches, and a wide assortment of gourmet cheesecakes.

"We've got high school students who come here, and students from the community college," says owner/manager Stephanie Mintenko, who has run the place since opening it in 1995. "We have customers who are retired, and others who are working people and have only 30 minutes for lunch. We have to be pretty quick."

MINDING THE MONEY IN MOOSE JAW

That means that the cashiers have to be efficient. Like most businesses where purchases are low-cost and high-volume, cash control has to be simple.

"We have an electronic cash register, but it's not the fancy new kind where you just punch in the item," explains Ms. Mintenko. "You have to punch in the prices." The machine does keep track of sales in several categories, however. Cashiers punch a button to indicate whether each item is a beverage, a meal, or other type of item. An internal tape in the machine keeps a record of all transactions; the customer receives a receipt only upon request.

There is only one cash register. "Up to three of us might operate it on any given shift, including myself," says Ms. Mintenko.

She and her staff do two "cashouts" each day—one with the shift change at 5:00 p.m. and one when the shop closes at 10:00 p.m. At each cashout, they count the cash in the register drawer. That amount, minus the cash change carried forward (the float), should match the shift total on the register tape. If there's a discrepancy, they do another count. Then, if necessary, "we go through the whole tape to find the mistake," she explains. "It usually turns out to be someone who punched in $18 instead of $1.80, or something like that."

Ms. Mintenko sends all the cash tapes and float totals to a bookkeeper, who double-checks everything and provides regular reports. "We try to keep the accounting simple, so we can concentrate on making great coffee and food."

✔ The Navigator

INSIDE CHAPTER 7 . . .

As the story about recording cash sales at Stephanie's Gourmet Coffee and More indicates, control of cash is important to ensure that fraud does not occur. Companies also need controls to safeguard other types of assets. For example, Stephanie's undoubtedly has controls to prevent the theft of food and supplies, and controls to prevent the theft of tableware and dishes from its kitchen.

In this chapter, we explain the essential features of an internal control system and how it prevents fraud. We also describe how those controls apply to a specific asset–cash. The applications include some controls with which you may be already familiar, such as the use of a bank.

The content and organization of Chapter 7 are as follows.

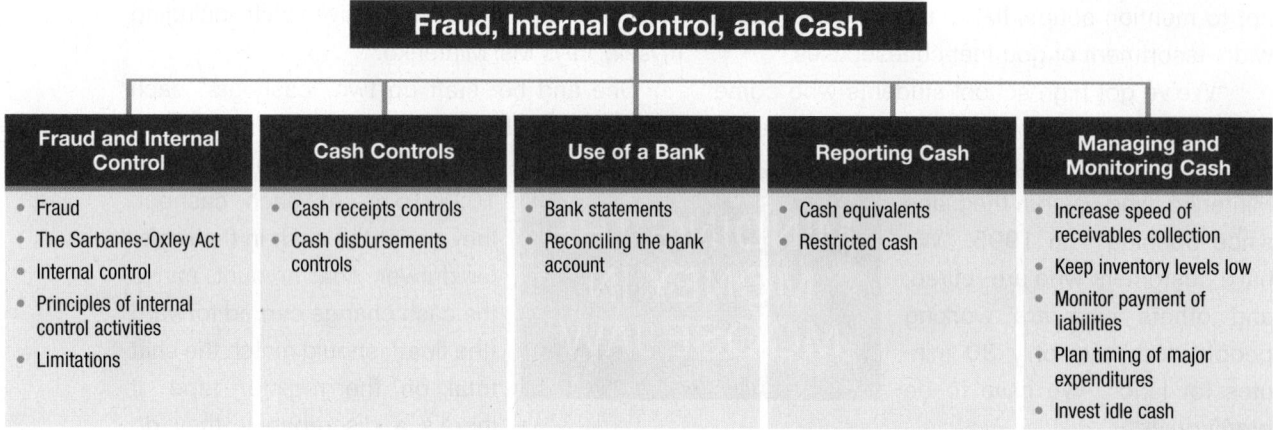

Fraud and Internal Control	Cash Controls	Use of a Bank	Reporting Cash	Managing and Monitoring Cash
• Fraud • The Sarbanes-Oxley Act • Internal control • Principles of internal control activities • Limitations	• Cash receipts controls • Cash disbursements controls	• Bank statements • Reconciling the bank account	• Cash equivalents • Restricted cash	• Increase speed of receivables collection • Keep inventory levels low • Monitor payment of liabilities • Plan timing of major expenditures • Invest idle cash

✔ The Navigator

Fraud and Internal Control

The Feature Story describes many of the internal control procedures used by Stephanie's Gourmet Coffee and More. These procedures are necessary to discourage employees from fraudulent activities.

FRAUD

A **fraud** is a dishonest act by an employee that results in personal benefit to the employee at a cost to the employer. Examples of fraud reported in the financial press include:

* A bookkeeper in a small company diverted $750,000 of bill payments to a personal bank account over a three-year period.
* A shipping clerk with 28 years of service shipped $125,000 of merchandise to himself.
* A computer operator embezzled $21 million from Wells Fargo Bank over a two-year period.
* A church treasurer "borrowed" $150,000 of church funds to finance a friend's business dealings.

Why does fraud occur? The three main factors that contribute to fraudulent activity are depicted by the **fraud triangle** in Illustration 7-1.

The most important element of the fraud triangle is **opportunity**. For an employee to commit fraud, the workplace environment must provide opportunities that an employee can exploit. Opportunities occur when the workplace lacks sufficient controls to deter and detect fraud. For example, inadequate monitoring of employee actions can create opportunities for theft and can embolden employees because they believe they will not be caught.

A second factor that contributes to fraud is **financial pressure**. Employees sometimes commit fraud because of personal financial problems caused by too much debt. Or they might commit fraud because they want to lead a lifestyle that they cannot afford on their current salary.

The third factor that contributes to fraud is **rationalization**. In order to justify their fraud, employees rationalize their dishonest actions. For example, employees sometimes justify fraud because they believe they are underpaid while the employer is making lots of money. These employees feel justified in stealing because they believe they deserve to be paid more.

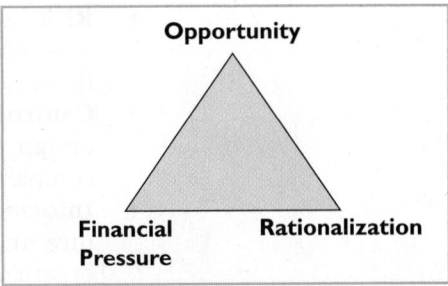

Illustration 7-1 Fraud triangle

THE SARBANES-OXLEY ACT

What can be done to prevent or to detect fraud? After numerous corporate scandals came to light in the early 2000s, Congress addressed this issue by passing the Sarbanes-Oxley Act (SOX). Under SOX, all publicly traded U.S. corporations are required to maintain an adequate system of internal control. Corporate executives and boards of directors must ensure that these controls are reliable and effective. In addition, independent outside auditors must attest to the adequacy of the internal control system. Companies that fail to comply are subject to fines, and company officers can be imprisoned. SOX also created the Public Company Accounting Oversight Board (PCAOB) to establish auditing standards and regulate auditor activity.

One poll found that 60% of investors believe that SOX helps safeguard their stock investments. Many say they would be unlikely to invest in a company that fails to follow SOX requirements. Although some corporate executives have criticized the time and expense involved in following the SOX requirements, SOX appears to be working well. For example, the chief accounting officer of Eli Lily noted that SOX triggered a comprehensive review of how the company documents controls. This review uncovered redundancies and pointed out controls that needed to be added. In short, it added up to time and money well spent. And the finance chief at General Electric noted, "We have seen value in SOX. It helps build investors' trust and gives them more confidence."[1]

INTERNAL CONTROL

Internal control consists of all the related methods and measures adopted within an organization to safeguard assets, enhance the reliability of accounting records, increase efficiency of operations, and ensure compliance with laws and regulations. Internal control systems have five primary components as listed below.[2]

- **A control environment.** It is the responsibility of top management to make it clear that the organization values integrity and that unethical activity will not be tolerated. This component is often referred to as the "tone at the top."

---

[1]"Corporate Regulation Must Be Working—There's a Backlash," *Wall Street Journal* (June 16, 2004), p. C1; and Judith Burns, "Is Sarbanes-Oxley Working?" *Wall Street Journal* (June 21, 2004), pp. R8–R9.

[2]The Committee of Sponsoring Organizations of the Treadway Commission, "Internal Control—Integrated Framework," **www.coso.org/publications/executive_summary_integrated_framework .htm** (accessed March 2008).

- **Risk assessment.** Companies must identify and analyze the various factors that create risk for the business and must determine how to manage these risks.
- **Control activities.** To reduce the occurrence of fraud, management must design policies and procedures to address the specific risks faced by the company.
- **Information and communication.** The internal control system must capture and communicate all pertinent information both down and up the organization, as well as communicate information to appropriate external parties.
- **Monitoring.** Internal control systems must be monitored periodically for their adequacy. Significant deficiencies need to be reported to top management and/or the board of directors.

© Karl Dolenc/iStockphoto

PEOPLE, PLANET, AND PROFIT INSIGHT
And the Controls Are . . .

Internal controls are important for an effective financial reporting system. The same is true for sustainability reporting. An effective system of internal controls for sustainability reporting will help in the following ways: (1) prevent the unauthorized use of data; (2) provide reasonable assurance that the information is accurate, valid, and complete; and (3) report information that is consistent with overall sustainability accounting policies. With these types of controls, users will have the confidence that they can use the sustainability information effectively.

Some regulators are calling for even more assurance through audits of this information. Companies that potentially can cause environmental damage through greenhouse gases are subject to reporting requirements as well as companies in the mining and extractive industries. And, as demand for more information in the sustainability area expands, the need for audits of this information will grow.

 Why is sustainability information important to investors? (See page 393.)

PRINCIPLES OF INTERNAL CONTROL ACTIVITIES

LEARNING OBJECTIVE 2
Identify the principles of internal control activities.

Each of the five components of an internal control system is important. Here, we will focus on one component, the control activities. The reason? These activities are the backbone of the company's efforts to address the risks it faces, such as fraud. The specific control activities used by a company will vary, depending on management's assessment of the risks faced. This assessment is heavily influenced by the size and nature of the company.

The six principles of control activities are as follows.

- Establishment of responsibility
- Segregation of duties
- Documentation procedures
- Physical controls
- Independent internal verification
- Human resource controls

We explain these principles in the following sections. You should recognize that they apply to most companies and are relevant to both manual and computerized accounting systems.

Establishment of Responsibility

An essential principle of internal control is to assign responsibility to specific employees. **Control is most effective when only one person is responsible for a given task.**

To illustrate, assume that the cash on hand at the end of the day in a Safeway supermarket is $10 short of the cash entered in the cash register. If only one person has operated the register, the shift manager can quickly determine responsibility for the shortage. What happens, though, if two or more individuals work the register? For example, in the Feature Story, the principle of establishing responsibility does not appear to be strictly applied by Stephanie's Gourmet Coffee and More since three people operate the cash register on any given shift. Many retailers solve this problem by having registers with multiple drawers. This makes it possible for more than one person to operate a register but still allows identification of a particular employee with a specific drawer. Only the signed-in cashier has access to his or her drawer.

Establishing responsibility often requires limiting access only to authorized personnel, and then identifying those personnel. For example, the automated systems used by many companies have mechanisms such as identifying passcodes that keep track of who made a journal entry, who entered a sale, or who went into an inventory storeroom at a particular time. Use of identifying passcodes enables the company to establish responsibility by identifying the particular employee who carried out the activity.

It's your shift now. I'm turning in my cash drawer and heading home.

Transfer of cash drawers

ANATOMY OF A FRAUD

Maureen Frugali was a training supervisor for claims processing at Colossal Healthcare. As a standard part of the claims-processing training program, Maureen created fictitious claims for use by trainees. These fictitious claims were then sent to the accounts payable department. After the training claims had been processed, she was to notify Accounts Payable of all fictitious claims, so that they would not be paid. However, she did not inform Accounts Payable about every fictitious claim. She created some fictitious claims for entities that she controlled (that is, she would receive the payment), and she let Accounts Payable pay her.

Total take: $11 million

THE MISSING CONTROL

Establishment of responsibility. The health-care company did not adequately restrict the responsibility for authorizing and approving claims transactions. The training supervisor should not have been authorized to create claims in the company's "live" system.

Source: Adapted from Wells, *Fraud Casebook* (2007), pp. 61–70.

Segregation of Duties

Segregation of duties is indispensable in an internal control system. There are two common applications of this principle:

1. Different individuals should be responsible for related activities.
2. The responsibility for record-keeping for an asset should be separate from the physical custody of that asset.

The rationale for segregation of duties is this: **The work of one employee should, without a duplication of effort, provide a reliable basis for evaluating the work of another employee.** For example, the personnel that design and program computerized systems should not be assigned duties related to day-to-day use of the system. Otherwise, they could design the system to benefit them personally and conceal the fraud through day-to-day use.

SEGREGATION OF RELATED ACTIVITIES. Making one individual responsible for related activities increases the potential for errors and irregularities. Instead, companies should, for example, assign related **purchasing activities** to different individuals. Related purchasing activities include ordering merchandise, order approval, receiving goods, authorizing payment, and paying for goods or services. Various frauds are possible when one person handles related purchasing activities:

- If a purchasing agent is allowed to order goods without supervisory approval, the likelihood of the agent receiving kickbacks from suppliers increases.
- If an employee who orders goods also handles receipt of the goods and invoice, as well as payment authorization, he or she might authorize payment for a fictitious invoice.

These abuses are less likely to occur when companies divide the purchasing tasks.

Similarly, companies should assign related **sales activities** to different individuals. Related selling activities include making a sale, shipping (or delivering) the goods to the customer, billing the customer, and receiving payment. Various frauds are possible when one person handles related sales activities. For example:

- If a salesperson can make a sale without obtaining supervisory approval, he or she might make sales at unauthorized prices to increase sales commissions.
- A shipping clerk who also has access to accounting records could ship goods to himself.
- A billing clerk who handles billing and cash receipts could understate the amount billed for sales made to friends and relatives.

These abuses are less likely to occur when companies divide the sales tasks: the salespeople make the sale; the shipping department ships the goods on the basis of the sales order; and the billing department prepares the sales invoice after comparing the sales order with the report of goods shipped.

ANATOMY OF A FRAUD

Lawrence Fairbanks, the assistant vice-chancellor of communications at Aesop University, was allowed to make purchases of under $2,500 for his department without external approval. Unfortunately, he also sometimes bought items for himself, such as expensive antiques and other collectibles. How did he do it? He replaced the vendor invoices he received with fake vendor invoices that he created. The fake invoices had descriptions that were more consistent with communications department purchases. He submitted these fake invoices to the accounting department as the basis for their journal entries and to the accounts payable department as the basis for payment.

Total take: $475,000

THE MISSING CONTROL

Segregation of duties. The university had not properly segregated related purchasing activities. Lawrence was ordering items, receiving the items, and receiving the invoice. By receiving the invoice, he had control over the documents that were used to account for the purchase and thus was able to substitute a fake invoice.

Source: Adapted from Wells, *Fraud Casebook* (2007), pp. 3–15.

SEGREGATION OF RECORD-KEEPING FROM PHYSICAL CUSTODY. The accountant should have neither physical custody of the asset nor access to it. Likewise, the custodian of the asset should not maintain or have access to the accounting records. **The custodian of the asset is not likely to convert the asset to personal use when one employee maintains the record of the asset, and a different employee has physical custody of the asset.** The separation of accounting responsibility from the custody of assets is especially important for cash and inventories because these assets are very vulnerable to fraud.

Accounting employee A
Maintains cash balances per books

Segregation of duties
(Accountability for assets)

Assistant cashier B
Maintains custody of cash on hand

ANATOMY OF A FRAUD

Angela Bauer was an accounts payable clerk for Aggasiz Construction Company. Angela prepared and issued checks to vendors and reconciled bank statements. She perpetrated a fraud in this way: She wrote checks for costs that the company had not actually incurred (e.g., fake taxes). A supervisor then approved and signed the checks. Before issuing the check, though, Angela would "white-out" the payee line on the check and change it to personal accounts that she controlled. She was able to conceal the theft because she also reconciled the bank account. That is, nobody else ever saw that the checks had been altered.

Total take: $570,000

THE MISSING CONTROL

Segregation of duties. Aggasiz Construction Company did not properly segregate record-keeping from physical custody. Angela had physical custody of the blank checks, which essentially was control of the cash. She also had record-keeping responsibility because she prepared the bank reconciliation.

Source: Adapted from Wells, *Fraud Casebook* (2007), pp. 100–107.

Documentation Procedures

Documents provide evidence that transactions and events have occurred. At Stephanie's Gourmet Coffee and More, the cash register tape is the restaurant's documentation for the sale and the amount of cash received. More sophisticated registers, called point-of-sale terminals, do not rely on tapes. Rather, they are networked with the company's computing and accounting records, which results in direct documentation. Similarly, a shipping document indicates that the goods have been shipped, and a sales invoice indicates that the company has billed the customer for the goods. By requiring signatures (or initials) on the documents, the company can identify the individual(s) responsible for the transaction or event. Companies should document transactions when the transaction occurs.

Companies should establish procedures for documents. First, whenever possible, companies should use **prenumbered documents, and all documents should be accounted for**. Prenumbering helps to prevent a transaction from being recorded more than once, or conversely, from not being recorded at all. Second, the control system should require that employees **promptly forward source documents for accounting entries to the accounting department**. **This control measure helps to ensure timely recording of the transaction** and contributes directly to the accuracy and reliability of the accounting records.

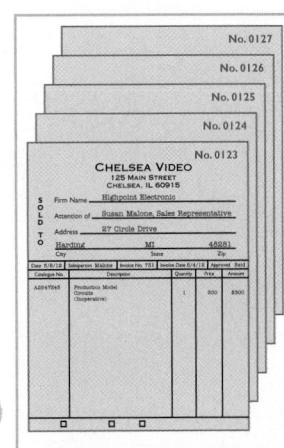

Prenumbered invoices

ANATOMY OF A FRAUD

To support their reimbursement requests for travel costs incurred, employees at Mod Fashions Corporation's design center were required to submit receipts. The receipts could include the detailed bill provided for a meal, or the credit card receipt provided when the credit card payment is made, or a copy of the employee's monthly credit card bill that listed the item. A number of the designers who frequently traveled together came up with a fraud scheme: They submitted claims for the same expenses. For example, if they had a meal together that cost $200, one person submitted the detailed meal bill, another submitted the credit card receipt, and a third submitted a monthly credit card bill showing the meal as a line item. Thus, all three received a $200 reimbursement.

Total take: $75,000

THE MISSING CONTROL

Documentation procedures. Mod Fashions should require the original, detailed receipt. It should not accept photocopies, and it should not accept credit card statements. In addition, documentation procedures could be further improved by requiring the use of a corporate credit card (rather than personal credit card) for all business expenses.

Source: Adapted from Wells, *Fraud Casebook* (2007), pp. 79–90.

Physical Controls

Use of physical controls is essential. **Physical controls** relate to the safeguarding of assets and enhance the accuracy and reliability of the accounting records. Illustration 7-2 shows examples of these controls.

ANATOMY OF A FRAUD

At Centerstone Health, a large insurance company, the mailroom each day received insurance applications from prospective customers. Mailroom employees scanned the applications into electronic documents before the applications were processed. Once the applications are scanned, they can be accessed online by authorized employees.

Insurance agents at Centerstone Health earn commissions based upon successful applications. The sales agent's name is listed on the application. However, roughly 15% of the applications are from customers who did not work with a sales agent. Two friends—Alex, an employee in record-keeping, and Parviz, a sales agent—thought up a way to perpetrate a fraud. Alex identified scanned applications that did not list a sales agent. After business hours, he entered the mailroom and found the hardcopy applications that did not show a sales agent. He wrote in Parviz's name as the sales agent and then rescanned the application for processing. Parviz received the commission, which the friends then split.

Total take: $240,000

THE MISSING CONTROL

Physical controls. Centerstone Health lacked two basic physical controls that could have prevented this fraud. First, the mailroom should have been locked during nonbusiness hours, and access during business hours should have been tightly controlled. Second, the scanned applications supposedly could be accessed only by authorized employees using their password. However, the password for each employee was the same as the employee's user ID. Since employee user ID numbers were available to all other employees, all employees knew all other employees' passwords. Thus, Alex could enter the system using another employee's password and access the scanned applications.

Source: Adapted from Wells, *Fraud Casebook* (2007), pp. 316–326.

Physical Controls

Safes, vaults, and safety deposit boxes for cash and business papers	Locked warehouses and storage cabinets for inventories and records	Computer facilities with pass key access or fingerprint or eyeball scans	Alarms to prevent break-ins	Television monitors and garment sensors to deter theft	Time clocks for recording time worked

Illustration 7-2 Physical controls

Independent Internal Verification

Most internal control systems provide for **independent internal verification**. This principle involves the review of data prepared by employees. To obtain maximum benefit from independent internal verification:

1. Companies should verify records periodically or on a surprise basis.

2. An employee who is independent of the personnel responsible for the information should make the verification.

3. Discrepancies and exceptions should be reported to a management level that can take appropriate corrective action.

Independent internal verification is especially useful in comparing recorded transactions with existing assets. The reconciliation of the cash register tape with the cash in the register at Stephanie's Gourmet Coffee and More is an example of this internal control principle. Another common example is the reconciliation of a company's cash balance per books with the cash balance per bank and the verification of the perpetual inventory records through a count of physical inventory. Illustration 7-3 shows the relationship between this principle and the segregation of duties principle.

Accounting Employee
Maintains cash balances per books

Segregation of Duties

Assistant Cashier
Maintains custody of cash on hand

Independent Internal Verification
Assistant Treasurer
Makes monthly comparisons; reports any unreconcilable differences to treasurer

Illustration 7-3 Comparison of segregation of duties principle with independent internal verification principle

Large companies often assign independent internal verification to internal auditors. Internal auditors are company employees who continuously evaluate the effectiveness of the company's internal control systems. They review the activities of departments and individuals to determine whether prescribed internal controls are being followed. They also recommend improvements when needed. In fact, most fraud is discovered by the company through internal mechanisms such as existing internal controls and internal audits. For example, WorldCom was at one time the second largest U.S. telecommunications company. The fraud that caused its bankruptcy (the largest ever when it occurred) involved billions of dollars. It was uncovered by an internal auditor.

ANATOMY OF A FRAUD

Bobbi Jean Donnelly, the office manager for Mod Fashions Corporation's design center, was responsible for preparing the design center budget and reviewing expense reports submitted by design center employees. Her desire to upgrade her wardrobe got the better of her, and she enacted a fraud that involved filing expense-reimbursement requests for her own personal clothing purchases. She was able to conceal the fraud because she was responsible for reviewing all expense reports, including her own. In addition, she sometimes was given ultimate responsibility for signing off on the expense reports when her boss was "too busy." Also, because she controlled the budget, when she submitted her expenses, she coded them to budget items that she knew were running under budget, so that they would not catch anyone's attention.

Total take: $275,000

THE MISSING CONTROL

Independent internal verification. Bobbi Jean's boss should have verified her expense reports. When asked what he thought her expenses for a year were, the boss said about $10,000. At $115,000 per year, her actual expenses were more than 10 times what would have been expected. However, because he was "too busy" to verify her expense reports or to review the budget, he never noticed.

Source: Adapted from Wells, *Fraud Casebook* (2007), pp. 79–90.

Human Resource Controls

Human resource control activities include the following.

If I take a vacation they will know that I've been stealing.

1. **Bond employees who handle cash.** Bonding involves obtaining insurance protection against theft by employees. It contributes to the safeguarding of cash in two ways. First, the insurance company carefully screens all individuals before adding them to the policy and may reject risky applicants. Second, bonded employees know that the insurance company will vigorously prosecute all offenders.

2. **Rotate employees' duties and require employees to take vacations.** These measures deter employees from attempting thefts since they will not be able to permanently conceal their improper actions. Many banks, for example, have discovered employee thefts when the employee was on vacation or assigned to a new position.

3. **Conduct thorough background checks.** Many believe that the most important and inexpensive measure any business can take to reduce employee theft and fraud is for the human resources department to conduct thorough background checks. Two tips: (1) Check to see whether job applicants actually graduated from the schools they list. (2) Never use telephone numbers for previous employers provided by the applicant; always look them up yourself.

ANATOMY OF A FRAUD

Ellen Lowry was the desk manager and Josephine Rodriquez was the head of housekeeping at the Excelsior Inn, a luxury hotel. The two best friends were so dedicated to their jobs that they never took vacations, and they frequently filled in for other employees. In fact, Ms. Rodriquez, whose job as head of housekeeping did not include cleaning rooms, often cleaned rooms herself, "just to help the staff keep up." These two "dedicated" employees, working as a team, found a way to earn a little more cash. Ellen, the desk manager, provided significant discounts to guests who paid with cash. She kept the cash and did not register the guest in the hotel's computerized system. Instead, she took the room out of circulation "due to routine maintenance." Because the room did not show up as being used, it did not receive a normal housekeeping assignment. Instead, Josephine, the head of housekeeping, cleaned the rooms during the guests' stay.

Total take: $95,000

THE MISSING CONTROL

Human resource controls. Ellen, the desk manager, had been fired by a previous employer after being accused of fraud. If the Excelsior Inn had conducted a thorough background check, it would not have hired her. The hotel fraud was detected when Ellen missed work for a few days due to illness. A system of mandatory vacations and rotating days off would have increased the chances of detecting the fraud before it became so large.

Source: Adapted from Wells, *Fraud Casebook* (2007), pp. 145–155.

LIMITATIONS OF INTERNAL CONTROL

Companies generally design their systems of internal control to provide **reasonable assurance** of proper safeguarding of assets and reliability of the accounting records. The concept of reasonable assurance rests on the premise that the costs of establishing control procedures should not exceed their expected benefit.

To illustrate, consider shoplifting losses in retail stores. Stores could eliminate such losses by having a security guard stop and search customers as they leave the store. But store managers have concluded that the negative effects of such a procedure cannot be justified. Instead, they have attempted to control shoplifting losses by less costly procedures. They post signs saying, "We reserve the right to inspect all packages" and "All shoplifters will be prosecuted." They use hidden TV cameras and store detectives to monitor customer activity, and they install sensor equipment at exits.

Helpful Hint Controls may vary with the risk level of the activity. For example, management may consider cash to be high risk and maintaining inventories in the stockroom as lower risk. Thus, management would have stricter controls for cash.

Accounting Across the Organization

SOX Boosts the Role of Human Resources

Under SOX, a company needs to keep track of employees' degrees and certifications to ensure that employees continue to meet the specified requirements of a job. Also, to ensure proper employee supervision and proper separation of duties, companies must develop and monitor an organizational chart. When one corporation went through this exercise it found that out of 17,000 employees, there were 400 people who did not report to anyone. The corporation had 35 people who reported to each other. In addition, SOX also mandates that, if an employee complains of an unfair firing and mentions financial issues at the company, HR must refer the case to the company audit committee and possibly to its legal counsel.

 Why would unsupervised employees or employees who report to each other represent potential internal control threats? (See page 393.)

Stockbyte/Getty Images, Inc.

The **human element** is an important factor in every system of internal control. A good system can become ineffective as a result of employee fatigue, carelessness, or indifference. For example, a receiving clerk may not bother to count goods received and may just "fudge" the counts. Occasionally, two or more individuals work together to get around prescribed controls. Such **collusion** can significantly reduce the effectiveness of a system, eliminating the protection offered by segregation of duties. No system of internal control is perfect.

The **size of the business** also may impose limitations on internal control. Small companies often find it difficult to segregate duties or to provide for independent internal verification. A study by the Association of Certified Fraud Examiners (*2012 Report to the Nation on Occupational Fraud and Abuse*) indicates that businesses with fewer than 100 employees are most at risk for employee theft. In fact, 31.8% of frauds occurred at companies with fewer than 100 employees. The median loss at small companies was $147,000, which was higher than the median fraud at companies with more than 10,000 employees ($140,000). A $147,000 loss can threaten the very existence of a small company.

DECISION TOOLKIT

DECISION CHECKPOINTS	INFO NEEDED FOR DECISION	TOOL TO USE FOR DECISION	HOW TO EVALUATE RESULTS
Are the company's financial statements supported by adequate internal controls?	Auditor's report, management discussion and analysis, articles in financial press	The principles of internal control activities are (1) establishment of responsibility, (2) segregation of duties, (3) documentation procedures, (4) physical controls, (5) independent internal verification, and (6) human resource controls.	If any indication is given that these or other controls are lacking, use the financial statements with caution.

CONTROL ACTIVITIES

Do it!

Identify which control activity is violated in each of the following situations, and explain how the situation creates an opportunity for a fraud.

1. The person with primary responsibility for reconciling the bank account and making all bank deposits is also the company's accountant.

2. Wellstone Company's treasurer received an award for distinguished service because he had not taken a vacation in 30 years.

3. In order to save money on order slips, and to reduce time spent keeping track of order slips, a local bar/restaurant does not buy prenumbered order slips.

Action Plan

- Familiarize yourself with each of the control activities listed on page 338.
- Understand the nature of the frauds that each control activity is intended to address.

Solution

1. Violates the control activity of segregation of duties. Record-keeping should be separate from physical custody. As a consequence, the employee could embezzle cash and make journal entries to hide the theft.

2. Violates the control activity of human resource controls. Key employees, such as a treasurer, should be required to take vacations. The treasurer, who manages the company's cash, might embezzle cash and use his position to conceal the theft.

3. Violates the control activity of documentation procedures. If prenumbered documents are not used, then it is virtually impossible to account for the documents. As a consequence, an employee could write up a dinner sale, receive the cash from the customer, and then throw away the order slip and keep the cash.

✔ The Navigator

Related exercise material: **BE7-1, BE7-2, BE7-3, Do it! 7-1, E7-1,** and **E7-2**.

Cash Controls

Cash is the one asset that is readily convertible into any other type of asset. It also is easily concealed and transported, and is highly desired. Because of these characteristics, **cash is the asset most susceptible to fraudulent activities**. In addition, because of the large volume of cash transactions, numerous errors may occur in executing and recording them. To safeguard cash and to ensure the accuracy of the accounting records for cash, effective internal control over cash is critical.

> **LEARNING OBJECTIVE** **3**
>
> Explain the applications of internal control principles to cash receipts.

CASH RECEIPTS CONTROLS

Illustration 7-4 shows how the internal control principles explained earlier apply to cash receipts transactions. As you might expect, companies vary considerably in how they apply these principles. To illustrate internal control over cash receipts, we will examine control activities for a retail store with both over-the-counter and mail receipts.

Cash Receipts Controls

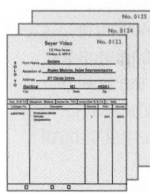

Establishment of Responsibility
Only designated personnel are authorized to handle cash receipts (cashiers)

Segregation of Duties
Different individuals receive cash, record cash receipts, and hold the cash

Documentation Procedures
Use remittance advice (mail receipts), cash register tapes or computer records, and deposit slips

Physical Controls
Store cash in safes and bank vaults; limit access to storage areas; use cash registers

Independent Internal Verification
Supervisors count cash receipts daily; assistant treasurer compares total receipts to bank deposits daily

Human Resource Controls
Bond personnel who handle cash; require employees to take vacations; conduct background checks

Illustration 7-4 Application of internal control principles to cash receipts

Over-the-Counter Receipts

In retail businesses, control of over-the-counter receipts centers on cash registers that are visible to customers. A cash sale is entered in a cash register with the amount clearly visible to the customer. This activity prevents the cashier from entering a lower amount and pocketing the difference. The customer receives an itemized cash register receipt slip and is expected to count the change received. (One weakness at Stephanie's Gourmet Coffee and More in the Feature Story is that customers were only given a receipt if they requested it.) The cash register's tape is locked in the register until a supervisor removes it. This tape accumulates the daily transactions and totals. Alternatively, cash registers called point-of-sale terminals are often networked with the company's computers for direct recording in its records.

At the end of the clerk's shift, the clerk counts the cash and sends the cash and the count to the cashier. The cashier counts the cash, prepares a deposit slip, and deposits the cash at the bank. The cashier also sends a duplicate of the deposit slip to the accounting department to indicate cash received. The supervisor removes the cash register tape and sends it to the accounting department (in a non-point-of-sale system) as the basis for a journal entry to record the cash received. The tape is compared to the deposit slip for any discrepancies. Illustration 7-5 summarizes this process.

Illustration 7-5 Control of over-the-counter receipts

Helpful Hint Flowcharts such as this one enhance the understanding of the flow of documents, the processing steps, and the internal control procedures.

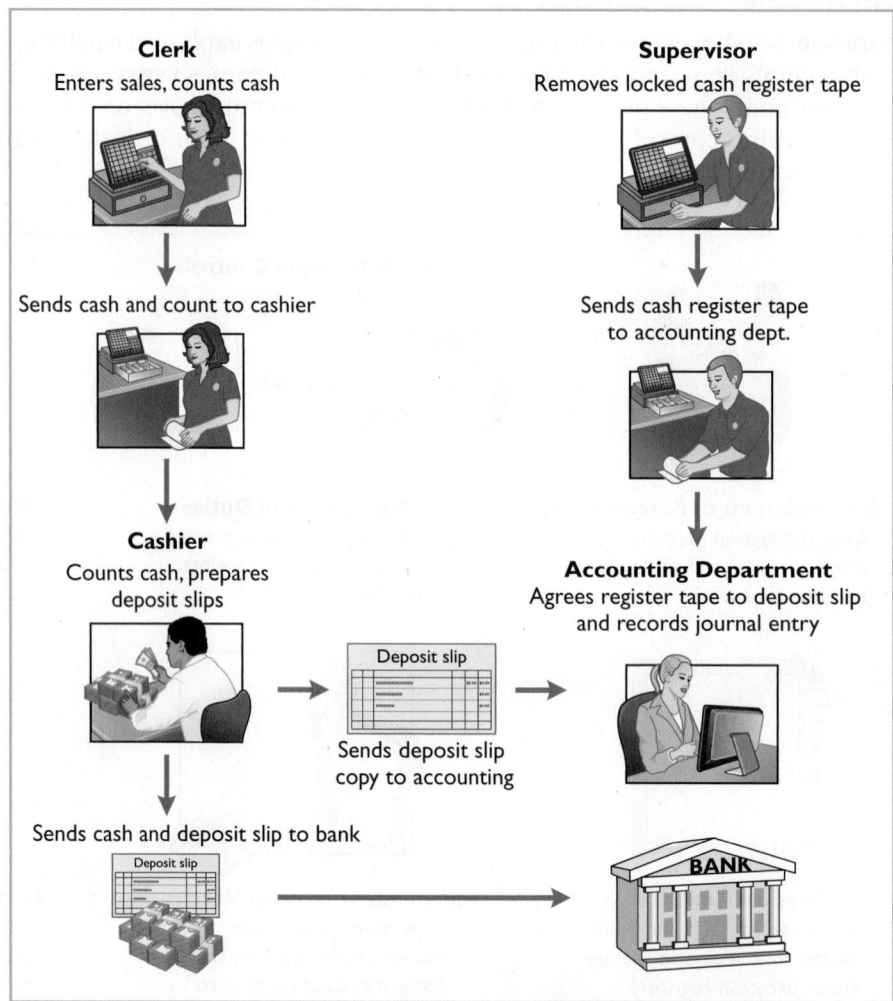

Clerk
Enters sales, counts cash

Sends cash and count to cashier

Cashier
Counts cash, prepares deposit slips

Deposit slip

Sends deposit slip copy to accounting

Sends cash and deposit slip to bank

Deposit slip

BANK

Supervisor
Removes locked cash register tape

Sends cash register tape to accounting dept.

Accounting Department
Agrees register tape to deposit slip and records journal entry

This system for handling cash receipts uses an important internal control principle—segregation of record-keeping from physical custody. The supervisor has access to the cash register tape, but **not** to the cash. The clerk and the cashier have access to the cash, but **not** to the register tape. In addition, the cash register tape provides documentation and enables independent internal verification with the deposit slip. Use of these three principles of internal control (segregation of record-keeping from physical custody, documentation, and independent internal verification) provides an effective system of internal control. Any attempt at fraudulent activity should be detected unless there is collusion among the employees.

In some instances, the amount deposited at the bank will not agree with the cash recorded in the accounting records based on the cash register tape. These differences often result because the clerk hands incorrect change back to the retail customer. In this case, the difference between the actual cash and the amount reported on the cash register tape is reported in a Cash Over and Short account. For example, suppose that the cash register tape indicated sales of $6,956.20 but the amount of cash was only $6,946.10. A cash shortfall of $10.10 exists. To account for this cash shortfall and related cash, the company makes the following entry.

Cash	6,946.10	
Cash Over and Short	10.10	
Sales Revenue		6,956.20
(To record cash shortfall)		

A	=	L	+	SE
+6,946.10				
				−10.10
				+6,956.20

Cash Flows
+6,946.10

Cash Over and Short is an income statement item. It is reported as miscellaneous expense when there is a cash shortfall, and as miscellaneous revenue when there is an overage. Clearly, the amount should be small. Any material amounts in this account should be investigated.

Mail Receipts

All mail receipts should be opened in the presence of at least two mail clerks. These receipts are generally in the form of checks. A mail clerk should endorse each check "For Deposit Only." This restrictive endorsement reduces the likelihood that someone could divert the check to personal use. Banks will not give an individual cash when presented with a check that has this type of endorsement.

The mail clerks prepare, in triplicate, a list of the checks received each day. This list shows the name of the check issuer, the purpose of the payment, and the amount of the check. Each mail clerk signs the list to establish responsibility for the data. The original copy of the list, along with the checks, is then sent to the cashier's department. A copy of the list is sent to the accounting department for recording in the accounting records. The clerks also keep a copy.

This process provides excellent internal control for the company. By employing two clerks, the chance of fraud is reduced. Each clerk knows he or she is being observed by the other clerk(s). To engage in fraud, they would have to collude. The customers who submit payments also provide control because they will contact the company with a complaint if they are not properly credited for payment. Because the cashier has access to cash but not the records, and the accounting department has access to records but not cash, neither can engage in undetected fraud.

Do it!

L. R. Cortez is concerned about the control over cash receipts in his fast-food restaurant, Big Cheese. The restaurant has two cash registers. At no time do more than two employees take customer orders and enter sales. Work shifts for employees range from 4 to 8 hours. Cortez asks your help in installing a good system of internal control over cash receipts.

Solution

Cortez should assign a separate cash register drawer to each employee at the start of each work shift, with register totals set at zero. Each employee should have access to only the assigned register drawer to enter all sales. Each customer should be given a receipt. At the end of the shift, the employee should do a cash count. A separate employee should compare the cash count with the register tape to be sure they agree. In addition, Cortez should install an automated system that would enable the company to compare orders entered in the register to orders processed by the kitchen.

Related exercise material: **BE7-4, BE7-5, Do it! 7-2,** and **E7-3.**

CONTROL OVER CASH RECEIPTS

Action Plan

- Differentiate among the internal control principles of (1) establishment of responsibility, (2) physical controls, and (3) independent internal verification.
- Design an effective system of internal control over cash receipts.

 The Navigator

CASH DISBURSEMENTS CONTROLS

Companies disburse cash for a variety of reasons, such as to pay expenses and liabilities or to purchase assets. **Generally, internal control over cash disbursements is more effective when companies pay by check or electronic funds transfer (EFT) rather than by cash.** One exception is **payments for incidental amounts that are paid out of petty cash**.[3]

Companies generally issue checks only after following specified control procedures. Illustration 7-6 shows how principles of internal control apply to cash disbursements.

Cash Disbursements Controls

  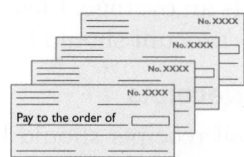

Establishment of Responsibility
Only designated personnel are authorized to sign checks (treasurer) and approve vendors

Segregation of Duties
Different individuals approve and make payments; check-signers do not record disbursements

Documentation Procedures
Use prenumbered checks and account for them in sequence; each check must have an approved invoice; require employees to use corporate credit cards for reimbursable expenses; stamp invoices "paid"

Physical Controls
Store blank checks in safes, with limited access; print check amounts by machine in indelible ink

Independent Internal Verification
Compare checks to invoices; reconcile bank statement monthly

Human Resource Controls
Bond personnel who handle cash; require employees to take vacations; conduct background checks

Illustration 7-6 Application of internal control principles to cash disbursements

Voucher System Controls

Most medium and large companies use vouchers as part of their internal control over cash disbursements. A voucher system is a network of approvals by authorized individuals, acting independently, to ensure that all disbursements by check are proper.

The system begins with the authorization to incur a cost or expense. It ends with the issuance of a check for the liability incurred. A voucher is an authorization form prepared for each expenditure in a voucher system. Companies require vouchers for all types of cash disbursements except those from petty cash.

The starting point in preparing a voucher is to fill in the appropriate information about the liability on the face of the voucher. The vendor's invoice provides most of the needed information. Then, an employee in accounts payable records

---

[3]We explain the operation of a petty cash fund in the appendix to this chapter on pages 367–369.

the voucher (in a journal called a **voucher register**) and files it according to the date on which it is to be paid. The company issues and sends a check on that date, and stamps the voucher "paid." The paid voucher is sent to the accounting department for recording (in a journal called the **check register**). A voucher system involves two journal entries, one to record the liability when the voucher is issued and a second to pay the liability that relates to the voucher.

The use of a voucher system, whether done manually or electronically, improves internal control over cash disbursements. First, the authorization process inherent in a voucher system establishes responsibility. Each individual has responsibility to review the underlying documentation to ensure that it is correct. In addition, the voucher system keeps track of the documents that back up each transaction. By keeping these documents in one place, a supervisor can independently verify the authenticity of each transaction. Consider, for example, the case of Aesop University presented on page 340. Aesop did not use a voucher system for transactions under $2,500. As a consequence, there was no independent verification of the documents, which enabled the employee to submit fake invoices to hide his unauthorized purchases.

Petty Cash Fund

As you learned earlier in the chapter, better internal control over cash disbursements is possible when companies make payments by check. However, using checks to pay such small amounts as those for postage due, employee working lunches, and taxi fares is both impractical and a nuisance. A common way of handling such payments, while maintaining satisfactory control, is to use a petty cash fund. A petty cash fund is a cash fund used to pay relatively small amounts. We explain the operation of a petty cash fund in the appendix at the end of this chapter.

Ethics Note Internal control over a petty cash fund is strengthened by: (1) having a supervisor make surprise counts of the fund to confirm whether the paid petty cash receipts and fund cash equal the fund amount, and (2) canceling or mutilating the paid petty cash receipts so they cannot be resubmitted for reimbursement.

Ethics Insight

How Employees Steal

A recent study by the Association of Certified Fraud Examiners found that two-thirds of all employee thefts involved a fraudulent disbursement by an employee. The most common form (24.9% of cases) was fraudulent billing schemes. In these, the employee causes the company to issue a payment to the employee by submitting a bill for nonexistent goods or services, purchases of personal goods by the employee, or inflated invoices. The graph below shows various types of fraudulent disbursements and the median loss from each.

Chris Fernig/iStockphoto

Source: 2012 Report to the Nation on Occupational Fraud and Abuse, Association of Certified Fraud Examiners, *www.acfe.com/uploadedfiles/ACFE_website/content/rttn/2012-report-to-nations.pdf,* p. 12.

 How can companies reduce the likelihood of fraudulent disbursements? (See page 393.)

Control Features: Use of a Bank

The use of a bank contributes significantly to good internal control over cash. A company can safeguard its cash by using a bank as a depository and clearinghouse for checks received and checks written. The use of a bank checking account minimizes the amount of currency that must be kept on hand. It also facilitates control of cash because a double record is maintained of all bank transactions—one by the business and the other by the bank. The asset account Cash maintained by the company is the "flip-side" of the bank's liability account for that company. A **bank reconciliation** is the process of comparing the bank's balance with the company's balance, and explaining the differences to make them agree.

Many companies have more than one bank account. For efficiency of operations and better control, national retailers like Wal-Mart and Target often have regional bank accounts. Similarly, a company such as ExxonMobil with more than 100,000 employees may have a payroll bank account as well as one or more general bank accounts. In addition, a company may maintain several bank accounts in order to have more than one source for short-term loans.

BANK STATEMENTS

Each month, the company receives from the bank a **bank statement** showing its bank transactions and balances.[4] For example, the statement for Laird Company in Illustration 7-7 shows the following: (1) checks paid and other debits (such as debit card transactions or direct withdrawals for bill payments) that reduce the balance in the depositor's account, (2) deposits and other credits that increase the balance in the depositor's account, and (3) the account balance after each day's transactions.

Remember that **bank statements are prepared from the *bank's* perspective**. For example, **every deposit the bank receives is an increase in the bank's liabilities (an account payable to the depositor)**. Therefore, in Illustration 7-7, National Bank and Trust **credits** to Laird Company every deposit it received from Laird. The reverse occurs when the bank "pays" a check issued by Laird Company on its checking account balance: Payment reduces the bank's liability and is therefore **debited** to Laird's account with the bank.

The bank statement lists in numerical sequence all paid checks along with the date the check was paid and its amount. Upon paying a check, the bank stamps the check "paid"; a paid check is sometimes referred to as a **canceled** check. In addition, the bank includes with the bank statement memoranda explaining other debits and credits it made to the depositor's account.

A check that is not paid by a bank because of insufficient funds in a bank account is called an **NSF check** (not sufficient funds). The bank uses a debit memorandum when a previously deposited customer's check "bounces" because of insufficient funds. In such a case, the customer's bank marks the check NSF (not sufficient funds) and returns it to the depositor's bank. The bank then debits (decreases) the depositor's account, as shown by the symbol NSF in Illustration 7-7, and sends the NSF check and debit memorandum to the depositor as notification of the charge. The NSF check creates an account receivable for the depositor and reduces cash in the bank account.

Helpful Hint Essentially, the bank statement is a copy of the bank's records sent to the customer or made available online for review.

---

[4]Our presentation assumes that a company makes all adjustments at the end of the month. In practice, a company may also make journal entries during the month as it reviews information from the bank regarding its account.

Illustration 7-7 Bank statement

National Bank & Trust
Midland, Michigan 48654   Member FDIC

ACCOUNT STATEMENT

LAIRD COMPANY
77 WEST CENTRAL AVENUE
MIDLAND, MICHIGAN 48654

Statement Date/Credit Line Closing Date

April 30, 2014

457923

ACCOUNT NUMBER

Balance Last Statement	Deposits and Credits		Checks and Debits		Balance This Statement
	No.	Total Amount	No.	Total Amount	
13,256.90	20	34,805.10	26	32,154.55	15,907.45

CHECKS AND DEBITS			DEPOSITS AND CREDITS		DAILY BALANCE	
Date	No.	Amount	Date	Amount	Date	Amount
4-2	435	644.95	4-2	4,276.85	4-2	16,888.80
4-5	436	3,260.00	4-3	2,137.50	4-3	18,249.65
4-4	437	1,185.79	4-5	1,350.47	4-4	17,063.86
4-3	438	776.65	4-7	982.46	4-5	15,154.33
4-8	439	1,781.70	4-8	1,320.28	4-7	14,648.89
4-7	440	1,487.90	4-9 CM	1,035.00	4-8	11,767.47
4-8	441	2,420.00	4-11	2,720.00	4-9	12,802.47
4-11	442	1,585.60	4-12	757.41	4-11	13,936.87
4-12	443	1,226.00	4-13	1,218.56	4-12	13,468.28
4-29	NSF	425.60	4-27	1,545.57	4-27	13,005.45
4-29	459	1,080.30	4-29	2,929.45	4-29	14,429.00
4-30	DM	30.00	4-30	2,128.60	4-30	15,907.45
4-30	461	620.15				

Symbols: **CM** Credit Memo   **EC** Error Correction   **NSF** Not Sufficient Funds   Reconcile Your Account Promptly
DM Debit Memo   **INT** Interest Earned   **SC** Service Charge

RECONCILING THE BANK ACCOUNT

Because the bank and the company maintain independent records of the company's checking account, you might assume that the respective balances will always agree. In fact, the two balances are seldom the same at any given time, and both balances differ from the "correct or true" balance. Therefore, it is necessary to make the balance per books and the balance per bank agree with the correct or true amount—a process called **reconciling the bank account**. The need for reconciliation has two causes:

1. **Time lags** that prevent one of the parties from recording the transaction in the same period.

2. **Errors** by either party in recording transactions.

Time lags occur frequently. For example, several days may elapse between the time a company pays by check and the date the bank pays the check. Similarly, when a company uses the bank's night depository to make its deposits, there will be a difference of one day between the time the company records the receipts and the time the bank does so. A time lag also occurs whenever the bank mails a debit or credit memorandum to the company.

You might think that if a company never writes checks (for example, if a small company uses only a debit card or electronic bill payment), it does not need to reconcile its account. However, **the possibility of errors or fraud still necessitates periodic reconciliation**. The incidence of errors or fraud depends on the effectiveness of the internal controls maintained by the company and the bank. Bank errors are infrequent. However, either party could accidentally record a $450 check as $45 or $540. In addition, the bank might mistakenly charge a check drawn by C. D. Berg to the account of C. D. Burg.

Reconciliation Procedure

In reconciling the bank account, it is customary to reconcile the balance per books and balance per bank to their adjusted (correct or true) cash balances. **To obtain maximum benefit from a bank reconciliation, an employee who has no other responsibilities related to cash should prepare the reconciliation.** When companies do not follow the internal control principle of independent internal verification in preparing the reconciliation, cash embezzlements may escape unnoticed. For example, in the Anatomy of a Fraud box on page 341, a bank reconciliation by someone other than Angela Bauer might have exposed her embezzlement.

Illustration 7-8 shows the reconciliation process. The starting point in preparing the reconciliation is to enter the balance per bank statement and balance

Illustration 7-8 Bank reconciliation adjustments

Helpful Hint Deposits in transit and outstanding checks are reconciling items because of time lags.

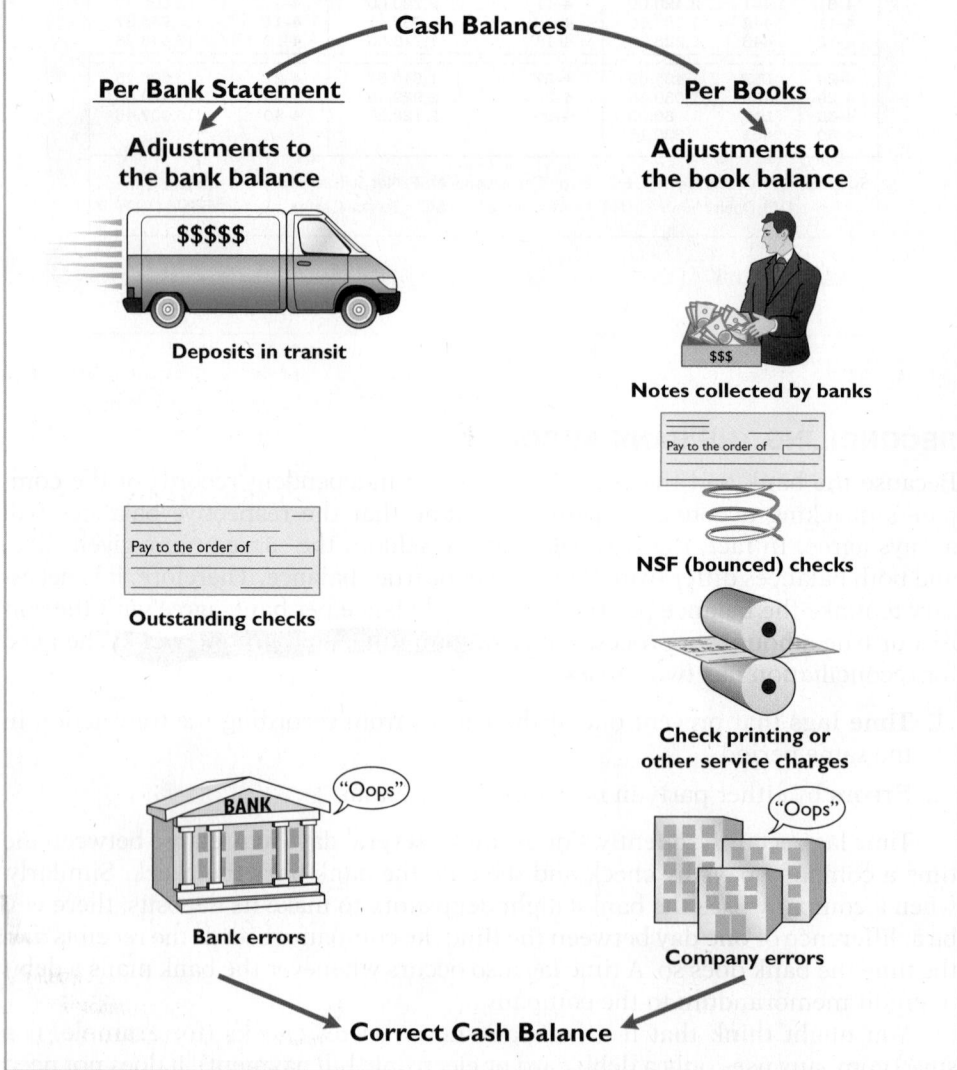

per books on a schedule. The following steps should reveal all the reconciling items that cause the difference between the two balances.

Step 1. Deposits in transit. Compare the individual deposits on the bank statement with the deposits in transit from the preceding bank reconciliation and with the deposits per company records or copies of duplicate deposit slips. Deposits recorded by the depositor that have not been recorded by the bank represent deposits in transit. Add these deposits to the balance per bank.

Step 2. Outstanding checks. Compare the paid checks shown on the bank statement or the paid checks returned with the bank statement with (a) checks outstanding from the preceding bank reconciliation, and (b) checks issued by the company as recorded in the cash payments journal. Issued checks recorded by the company that have not been paid by the bank represent outstanding checks. Deduct outstanding checks from the balance per the bank.

Step 3. Errors. Note any errors discovered in the previous steps and list them in the appropriate section of the reconciliation schedule. For example, if the company mistakenly recorded as $159 a paid check correctly written for $195, the company would deduct the error of $36 from the balance per books. All errors made by the depositor are reconciling items in determining the adjusted cash balance per books. In contrast, all errors made by the bank are reconciling items in determining the adjusted cash balance per the bank.

Step 4. Bank memoranda. Trace bank memoranda to the depositor's records. The company lists in the appropriate section of the reconciliation schedule any unrecorded memoranda. For example, the company would deduct from the balance per books a $5 debit memorandum for bank service charges. Similarly, it would add to the balance per books a $32 credit memorandum for interest earned.

Bank Reconciliation Illustrated

Illustration 7-7 presented the bank statement for Laird Company which the company accessed online. It shows a balance per bank of $15,907.45 on April 30, 2014. On this date the balance of cash per books is $11,589.45. From the foregoing steps, Laird determines the following reconciling items.

Step 1. Deposits in transit: April 30 deposit (received by bank on May 1). $2,201.40

Step 2. Outstanding checks: No. 453, $3,000.00; No. 457, $1,401.30; No. 460, $1,502.70.   5,904.00

Step 3. Errors: Check No. 443 was correctly written by Laird for $1,226.00 and was correctly paid by the bank. However, Laird recorded the check as $1,262.00.   36.00

Step 4. Bank memoranda:
   (a) Debit—NSF check from J. R. Baron for $425.60   425.60
   (b) Debit—Printing company checks charge, $30   30.00
   (c) Credit—Collection of note receivable for $1,000 plus
            interest earned $50, less bank collection fee $15   1,035.00

Helpful Hint Note in the bank statement that the bank has paid checks No. 459 and 461, but check No. 460 is not listed. Thus, this check is outstanding. If a complete bank statement were provided, checks No. 453 and 457 also would not be listed. Laird obtains the amounts for these three checks from its cash payments records.

Illustration 7-9 shows Laird's bank reconciliation.

Illustration 7-9 Bank reconciliation

LAIRD COMPANY
Bank Reconciliation
April 30, 2014

Cash balance per bank statement		$ 15,907.45
Add: Deposits in transit		2,201.40
		18,108.85
Less: Outstanding checks		
No. 453	$3,000.00	
No. 457	1,401.30	
No. 460	1,502.70	5,904.00
Adjusted cash balance per bank		**$12,204.85** ←
Cash balance per books		$ 11,589.45
Add: Collection of note receivable for $1,000 plus interest earned $50, less collection fee $15	$1,035.00	
Error in recording check No. 443	36.00	1,071.00
		12,660.45
Less: NSF check	425.60	
Bank service charge	30.00	455.60
Adjusted cash balance per books		**$12,204.85** ←

Alternative Terminology The terms *adjusted cash balance, true cash balance,* and *correct cash balance* are used interchangeably.

Helpful Hint These entries are adjusting entries. In prior chapters, we considered Cash an account that did not require adjustment because we had not yet explained a bank reconciliation.

Entries from Bank Reconciliation

The depositor (that is, the company) next must record each reconciling item used to determine the **adjusted cash balance per books**. If the company does not journalize and post these items, the Cash account will not show the correct balance. The adjusting entries for the Laird Company bank reconciliation on April 30 are as follows.

COLLECTION OF NOTE RECEIVABLE. This entry involves four accounts. Assuming that the interest of $50 has not been recorded and the collection fee is charged to Miscellaneous Expense, the entry is:

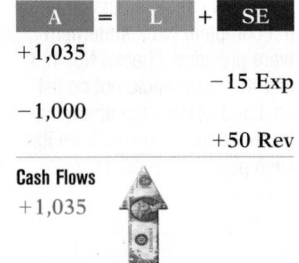

A = L + SE
+1,035
−15 Exp
−1,000
+50 Rev

Cash Flows
+1,035

Apr. 30	Cash		1,035	
	Miscellaneous Expense		15	
		Notes Receivable		1,000
		Interest Revenue		50
		(To record collection of note receivable by bank)		

BOOK ERROR. An examination of the cash disbursements journal shows that check No. 443 was a payment on account to Andrea Company, a supplier. The correcting entry is:

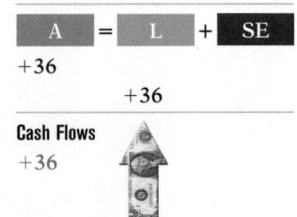

A = L + SE
+36
+36

Cash Flows
+36

Apr. 30	Cash		36	
		Accounts Payable—Andrea Company		36
		(To correct error in recording check No. 443)		

NSF CHECK. As indicated earlier, an NSF check becomes an accounts receivable to the depositor. The entry is:

Apr. 30	Accounts Receivable—J. R. Baron	425.60	
	Cash		425.60
	(To record NSF check)		

A = L + SE
+425.60
−425.60

Cash Flows
−425.60

BANK SERVICE CHARGES. Companies typically debit to Miscellaneous Expense the check printing charges (DM) and other bank service charges (SC) because they are usually small in amount. Laird's entry is:

Apr. 30	Miscellaneous Expense	30	
	Cash		30
	(To record charge for printing company checks)		

A = L + SE
−30 Exp
−30

Cash Flows
−30

The foregoing entries could also be combined into one compound entry.

After Laird posts the entries, the Cash account will appear as in Illustration 7-10. The adjusted cash balance in the ledger should agree with the adjusted cash balance per books in the bank reconciliation in Illustration 7-9 (page 356).

Cash

Apr. 30	Bal.	11,589.45	Apr. 30		425.60
	30	1,035.00	30		30.00
	30	36.00			
Apr. 30	Bal.	**12,204.85**			

Illustration 7-10
Adjusted balance in Cash account

What entries does the bank make? If the company discovers any bank errors in preparing the reconciliation, it should notify the bank so the bank can make the necessary corrections on its records. The bank does not make any entries for deposits in transit or outstanding checks. Only when these items reach the bank will the bank record these items.

Electronic Funds Transfer (EFT) System

It is not surprising that companies and banks have developed approaches to transfer funds among parties without the use of paper (deposit tickets, checks, etc.). Such procedures, called electronic funds transfers (EFTs), are disbursement systems that use wire, telephone, or computers to transfer cash from one location to another. Use of EFT is quite common. For example, many employees receive no formal payroll checks from their employers. Instead, employers send electronic payroll data to the appropriate banks. Also, individuals and companies now frequently make regular payments such as those for house, car, and utilities by EFT.

EFT transactions normally result in better internal control since no cash or checks are handled by company employees. This does not mean that opportunities for fraud are eliminated. In fact, the same basic principles related to internal control apply to EFT transactions. For example, without proper segregation of duties and authorizations, an employee might be able to redirect electronic payments into a personal bank account and conceal the theft with fraudulent accounting entries.

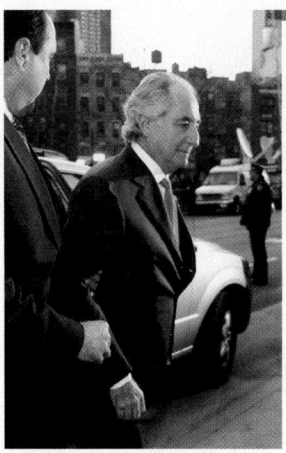

Mary Altaffer/©AP/Wide World Photos

Investor Insight

Madoff's Ponzi Scheme

No recent fraud has generated more interest and rage than the one perpetrated by Bernard Madoff. Madoff was an elite New York investment fund manager who was highly regarded by securities regulators. Investors flocked to him because he delivered steady returns of between 10% and 15%, no matter whether the market was going up or going down. However, for many years, Madoff did not actually invest the cash that people gave to him. Instead, he was running a Ponzi scheme: He paid returns to existing investors using cash received from new investors. As long as the size of his investment fund continued to grow from new investments at a rate that exceeded the amounts that he needed to pay out in returns, Madoff was able to operate his fraud smoothly. To conceal his misdeeds, he fabricated false investment statements that were provided to investors. In addition, Madoff hired an auditor that never verified the accuracy of the investment records but automatically issued unqualified opinions each year. A competing fund manager warned the SEC a number of times over a nearly 10-year period that he thought Madoff was engaged in fraud. The SEC never aggressively investigated the allegations. Investors, many of which were charitable organizations, lost more than $18 billion. Madoff was sentenced to a jail term of 150 years.

? How was Madoff able to conceal such a giant fraud? (See page 393.)

BANK RECONCILIATION

Do it!

Sally Kist owns Linen Kist Fabrics. Sally asks you to explain how she should treat the following reconciling items when reconciling the company's bank account: (1) a debit memorandum for an NSF check, (2) a credit memorandum for a note collected by the bank, (3) outstanding checks, and (4) a deposit in transit.

Action Plan

- Understand the purpose of a bank reconciliation.
- Identify time lags and explain how they cause reconciling items.

 The Navigator

Solution

Sally should treat the reconciling items as follows.

(1) NSF check: Deduct from balance per books.

(2) Collection of note: Add to balance per books.

(3) Outstanding checks: Deduct from balance per bank.

(4) Deposit in transit: Add to balance per bank.

Related exercise material: **BE7-8, BE7-9, BE7-10, BE7-11, Do it! 7-3, E7-6, E7-7, E7-8, E7-9, E7-10,** and **E7-11.**

Reporting Cash

LEARNING OBJECTIVE 6

Explain the reporting of cash.

Cash consists of coins, currency (paper money), checks, money orders, and money on hand or on deposit in a bank or similar depository. Checks that are dated later than the current date (post-dated checks) are not included in cash. Companies report cash in two different statements: the balance sheet and the statement of cash flows. The balance sheet reports the amount of cash available at a given point in time. The statement of cash flows shows the sources and uses of cash during a period of time. The statement of cash flows was introduced in Chapters 1 and 2 and will be discussed in much detail in Chapter 12. In this section, we discuss some important points regarding the presentation of cash in the balance sheet.

When presented in a balance sheet, cash on hand, cash in banks, and petty cash are often combined and reported simply as **Cash**. Because it is the most liquid asset owned by the company, cash is listed first in the current assets section of the balance sheet.

CASH EQUIVALENTS

Many companies use the designation "Cash and cash equivalents" in reporting cash. (See Illustration 7-11 for an example.) Cash equivalents are short-term, highly liquid investments that are both:

1. Readily convertible to known amounts of cash, and
2. So near their maturity that their market value is relatively insensitive to changes in interest rates.

Real World	**DELTA AIR LINES, INC.** Balance Sheet (partial) December 31, 2011 (in millions)	

Assets	
Current assets	
Cash and cash equivalents	$2,657
Short-term investments	958
Restricted cash	305
Accounts receivable and other, net	1,563
Parts inventories	367
Prepaid expenses and other	1,879
Total current assets	$ 7,729

Illustration 7-11 Balance sheet presentation of cash

Examples of cash equivalents are Treasury bills, commercial paper (short-term corporate notes), and money market funds. All typically are purchased with cash that is in excess of immediate needs.

Occasionally a company will have a net negative balance in its bank account. In this case, the company should report the negative balance among current liabilities. For example, farm equipment manufacturer Ag-Chem recently reported "Checks outstanding in excess of cash balances" of $2,145,000 among its current liabilities.

RESTRICTED CASH

A company may have restricted cash, cash that is not available for general use but rather is restricted for a special purpose. For example, landfill companies are often required to maintain a fund of restricted cash to ensure they will have adequate resources to cover closing and clean-up costs at the end of a landfill site's useful life. McKesson Corp. recently reported restricted cash of $962 million to be paid out as the result of investor lawsuits.

Cash restricted in use should be reported separately on the balance sheet as restricted cash. If the company expects to use the restricted cash within the next year, it reports the amount as a current asset. When this is not the case, it reports the restricted funds as a noncurrent asset.

Illustration 7-11 shows restricted cash reported in the financial statements of Delta Air Lines. The company is required to maintain restricted cash as collateral to support insurance obligations related to workers' compensation claims. Delta does not have access to these funds for general use, and so it must report them separately, rather than as part of cash and cash equivalents.

Ethics Note Recently, some companies were forced to restate their financial statements because they had too broadly interpreted which types of investments could be treated as cash equivalents. By reporting these items as cash equivalents, the companies made themselves look more liquid.

DECISION TOOLKIT

DECISION CHECKPOINTS	INFO NEEDED FOR DECISION	TOOL TO USE FOR DECISION	HOW TO EVALUATE RESULTS
Is all of the company's cash available for general use?	Balance sheet and notes to financial statements	Does the company report any cash as being restricted?	A restriction on the use of cash limits management's ability to use those resources for general obligations. This might be considered when assessing liquidity.

Managing and Monitoring Cash

LEARNING OBJECTIVE 7

Discuss the basic principles of cash management.

Many companies struggle, not because they fail to generate sales, but because they can't manage their cash. A real-life example of this is a clothing manufacturing company owned by Sharon McCollick. McCollick gave up a stable, high-paying marketing job with Intel Corporation to start her own company. Soon she had more orders from stores such as JC Penney and Dayton Hudson (now Target) than she could fill. Yet she found herself on the brink of financial disaster, owing three mortgage payments on her house and $2,000 to the IRS. Her company could generate sales, but it was not collecting cash fast enough to support its operations. The bottom line is that a business must have cash.[5]

A merchandising company's operating cycle is generally shorter than that of a manufacturing company. Illustration 7-12 shows the cash to cash operating cycle of a merchandising operation.

Illustration 7-12
Operating cycle of a merchandising company

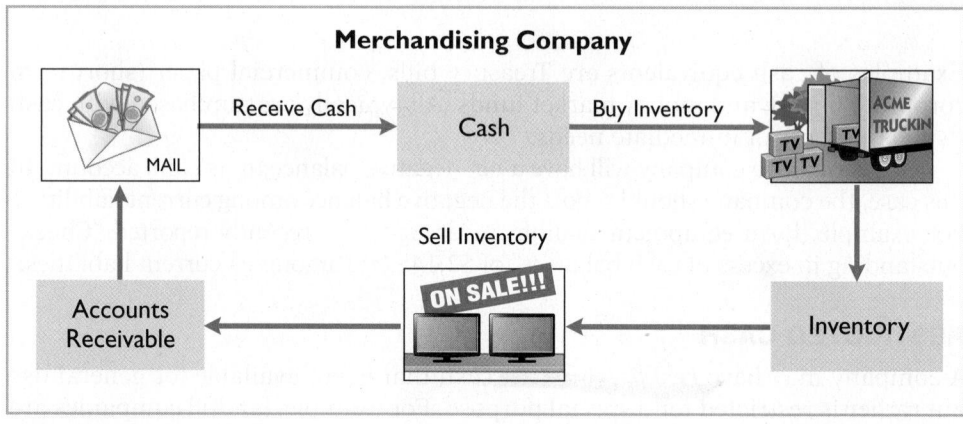

To understand cash management, consider the operating cycle of Sharon McCollick's clothing manufacturing company. First, it purchases cloth. Let's assume that it purchases the cloth on credit provided by the supplier, so the company owes its supplier money. Next, employees convert the cloth to clothing. Now the company also owes its employees money. Next, it sells the clothing to retailers, on credit. McCollick's company will have no money to repay suppliers or employees until it receives payments from customers. In a manufacturing operation there

---

[5]Adapted from T. Petzinger, Jr., "The Front Lines—Sharon McCollick Got Mad and Tore Down a Bank's Barriers," *Wall Street Journal* (May 19, 1995), p. B1.

may be a significant lag between the original purchase of raw materials and the ultimate receipt of cash from customers.

Managing the often-precarious balance created by the ebb and flow of cash during the operating cycle is one of a company's greatest challenges. The objective is to ensure that a company has sufficient cash to meet payments as they come due, yet minimize the amount of non-revenue-generating cash on hand.

BASIC PRINCIPLES OF CASH MANAGEMENT

Management of cash is the responsibility of the company treasurer. Any company can improve its chances of having adequate cash by following five basic principles of cash management.

1. **Increase the speed of receivables collection.** Money owed Sharon McCollick by her customers is money that she can't use. The more quickly customers pay her, the more quickly she can use those funds. Thus, rather than have an average collection period of 30 days, she may want an average collection period of 15 days. However, she must carefully weigh any attempt to force her customers to pay earlier against the possibility that she may anger or alienate customers. Perhaps her competitors are willing to provide a 30-day grace period. As noted in Chapter 5, one common way to encourage customers to pay more quickly is to offer cash discounts for early payment under such terms as 2/10, n/30.

2. **Keep inventory levels low.** Maintaining a large inventory of cloth and finished clothing is costly. It ties up large amounts of cash, as well as warehouse space. Increasingly, companies are using techniques to reduce the inventory on hand, thus conserving their cash. Of course, if Sharon McCollick has inadequate inventory, she will lose sales. The proper level of inventory is an important decision.

3. **Monitor payment of liabilities.** Sharon McCollick should monitor when her bills are due, so she avoids paying bills too early. Let's say her supplier allows 30 days for payment. If she pays in 10 days, she has lost the use of that cash for 20 days. Therefore, she should use the full payment period. But, she should not pay late. This could damage her credit rating (and future borrowing ability). Also, late payments to suppliers can damage important supplier relationships and may even threaten a supplier's viability. Sharon McCollick's company also should conserve cash by taking cash discounts offered by suppliers, when possible.

4. **Plan the timing of major expenditures.** To maintain operations or to grow, all companies must make major expenditures. These often require some form of outside financing. To increase the likelihood of obtaining outside financing, McCollick should carefully consider the timing of major expenditures in light of her company's operating cycle. If at all possible, she should make any major expenditure when the company normally has excess cash—usually during the off-season.

5. **Invest idle cash.** Cash on hand earns nothing. An important part of the treasurer's job is to ensure that the company invests any excess cash, even if it is only overnight. Many businesses, such as Sharon McCollick's clothing company, are seasonal. During her slow season, when she has excess cash, she should invest it.

   To avoid a cash crisis, however, it is very important that investments of idle cash be highly liquid and risk-free. A **liquid investment** is one with a market in which someone is always willing to buy or sell the investment. A **risk-free investment** means there is no concern that the party will default on its promise to pay its principal and interest. For example, using excess cash to purchase stock in a small company because you heard that it was probably going to increase in value in the near term is totally inappropriate. First, the stock of small companies is often illiquid. Second, if the stock suddenly

International Note International sales complicate cash management. For example, if Nike must repay a Japanese supplier 30 days from today in Japanese yen, Nike will be concerned about how the exchange rate of U.S. dollars for yen might change during those 30 days. Often, corporate treasurers make investments known as *hedges* to lock in an exchange rate to reduce the company's exposure to exchange-rate fluctuation.

decreases in value, you might be forced to sell the stock at a loss in order to pay your bills as they come due. The most common form of liquid investments is interest-paying U.S. government securities.

Illustration 7-13 summarizes these five principles of cash management.

Illustration 7-13 Five principles of sound cash management

1. **Increase the speed of receivables collection**

2. **Keep inventory low**

3. **Monitor payment of liabilities**

4. **Plan timing of major expenditures**

5. **Invest idle cash**

KEEPING AN EYE ON CASH

LEARNING OBJECTIVE 8

Identify the primary elements of a cash budget.

Because cash is so vital to a company, **planning the company's cash needs** is a key business activity. It enables the company to plan ahead to cover possible cash shortfalls and to make investments of idle funds. The cash budget shows anticipated cash flows, usually over a one- to two-year period. In this section, we introduce the basics of cash budgeting. More advanced discussion of cash budgets and budgets in general is provided in managerial accounting texts.

As shown below, the cash budget contains three sections—cash receipts, cash disbursements, and financing—and the beginning and ending cash balances.

ANY COMPANY Cash Budget	
Beginning cash balance	$X,XXX
Add: **Cash receipts** (itemized)	X,XXX
Total available cash	X,XXX
Less: **Cash disbursements** (itemized)	X,XXX
Excess (deficiency) of available cash over cash disbursements	X,XXX
Financing	
Add: Borrowings	X,XXX
Less: Repayments	X,XXX
Ending cash balance	$X,XXX

The **Cash receipts** section includes expected receipts from the company's principal source(s) of cash, such as cash sales and collections from customers on credit sales. This section also shows anticipated receipts of interest and dividends, and proceeds from planned sales of investments, plant assets, and the company's capital stock.

The **Cash disbursements** section shows expected payments for inventory, labor, overhead, and selling and administrative expenses. It also includes projected payments for income taxes, dividends, investments, and plant assets. Note that it does not include depreciation since depreciation expense does not use cash.

The **Financing** section shows expected borrowings and repayments of borrowed funds plus interest. Financing is needed when there is a cash deficiency or when the cash balance is less than management's minimum required balance.

Companies must prepare multi-period cash budgets in sequence because the ending cash balance of one period becomes the beginning cash balance for the next period. In practice, companies often prepare cash budgets for the next 12 months on a monthly basis.

To minimize detail, we will assume that Hayes Company prepares an annual cash budget by quarters. Preparing a cash budget requires making some assumptions. For example, Hayes makes assumptions regarding collection of accounts receivable, sales of securities, payments for materials and salaries, and purchases of property, plant, and equipment. The accuracy of the cash budget is very dependent on the accuracy of these assumptions.

Below we present the cash budget for Hayes Company. The budget indicates that the company will need $3,000 of financing in the second quarter to maintain a minimum cash balance of $15,000. Since there is an excess of available cash over disbursements of $22,500 at the end of the third quarter, Hayes will repay the borrowing, plus $100 interest, in that quarter.

A cash budget contributes to more effective cash management. For example, it can show when a company will need additional financing well before the actual need arises. Conversely, it can indicate when the company will have excess cash available for investments or other purposes.

HAYES COMPANY
Cash Budget
For the Year Ending December 31, 2014

	Quarter			
	1	**2**	**3**	**4**
Beginning cash balance	$ 38,000	$ 25,500	$ 15,000	$ 19,400
Add: **Cash receipts**				
Collections from customers	168,000	198,000	228,000	258,000
Sale of securities	2,000	0	0	0
Total receipts	170,000	198,000	228,000	258,000
Total available cash	208,000	223,500	243,000	277,400
Less: **Cash disbursements**				
Inventory	23,200	27,200	31,200	35,200
Salaries	62,000	72,000	82,000	92,000
Selling and administrative expenses (excluding depreciation)	94,300	99,300	104,300	109,300
Purchase of truck	0	10,000	0	0
Income tax expense	3,000	3,000	3,000	3,000
Total disbursements	182,500	211,500	220,500	239,500
Excess (deficiency) of available cash over disbursements	25,500	12,000	22,500	37,900
Financing				
Add: Borrowings	0	3,000	0	0
Less: Repayments—plus $100 interest	0	0	3,100	0
Ending cash balance	$ 25,500	$ 15,000	$ 19,400	$ 37,900

DECISION TOOLKIT

DECISION CHECKPOINTS	INFO NEEDED FOR DECISION	TOOL TO USE FOR DECISION	HOW TO EVALUATE RESULTS
Will the company be able to meet its projected cash needs?	Cash budget (typically available only to management)	The cash budget shows projected sources and uses of cash. If cash uses exceed internal cash sources, then the company must look for outside sources.	Two issues: (1) Are management's projections reasonable? (2) If outside sources are needed, are they available?

CASH BUDGET

Do it!

Martian Company's management wants to maintain a minimum monthly cash balance of $15,000. At the beginning of March, the cash balance is $16,500; expected cash receipts for March are $210,000; and cash disbursements are expected to be $220,000. How much cash, if any, must Martian borrow to maintain the desired minimum monthly balance?

Action Plan

- Add the beginning cash balance to receipts to determine total available cash.
- Subtract disbursements to determine excess or deficiency.
- Compare excess or deficiency with desired minimum cash to determine borrowing needs.

The Navigator

Solution

Beginning cash balance	$ 16,500
Add: Cash receipts for March	210,000
Total available cash	226,500
Less: Cash disbursements for March	220,000
Excess of available cash over cash disbursements	6,500
Financing	
Add: **Borrowings**	8,500
Ending cash balance	$ 15,000

To maintain the desired minimum cash balance of $15,000, Martian Company must borrow $8,500 of cash.

Related exercise material: **BE7-13**, **Do it!** **7-4**, and **E7-14**.

USING THE DECISION TOOLKIT

Presented below is hypothetical financial information for Mattel Corporation. Included in this information is financial statement data from the year ended December 31, 2013, which should be used to evaluate Mattel's cash position.

Selected Financial Information
Year Ended December 31, 2013
(in millions)

Net cash provided by operating activities	$325
Capital expenditures	162
Dividends paid	80
Total expenses	680
Depreciation expense	40
Cash balance	206

Also provided on the next page are projected data which are management's best estimate of its sources and uses of cash during the year ended December 31, 2014. This information should be used to prepare a cash budget for 2014.

Projected Sources and Uses of Cash
(in millions)

Beginning cash balance	$206
Cash receipts from sales of product	355
Cash receipts from sale of short-term investments	20
Cash payments for inventory	357
Cash payments for selling and administrative costs	201
Cash payments for property, plant, and equipment	45
Cash payments for taxes	17

Mattel Corporation's management believes it should maintain a balance of $200 million cash.

Instructions

(a) Using the hypothetical projected sources and uses of cash information presented above, prepare a cash budget for 2014 for Mattel Corporation.

(b) Comment on the company's cash adequacy, and discuss steps that might be taken to improve its cash position.

Solution

(a)

MATTEL CORPORATION
Cash Budget
For the Year Ending December 31, 2014
(in millions)

Beginning cash balance		$206
Add: Cash receipts		
From sales of product	$355	
From sale of short-term investments	20	375
Total available cash		581
Less: Cash disbursements		
Payments for inventory	357	
Payments for selling and administrative costs	201	
Payments for property, plant, and equipment	45	
Payments for taxes	17	
Total disbursements		620
Excess (deficiency) of available cash over disbursements		(39)
Financing		
Add: **Borrowings**		239
Ending cash balance		$200

(b) Using these hypothetical data, Mattel's cash position appears adequate. For 2014, Mattel is projecting a cash shortfall. This is not necessarily of concern, but it should be investigated. Its primary line of business is toys. Most toys are sold during December. We would expect Mattel's cash position to vary significantly during the course of the year. After the holiday season, once its customers have paid Mattel, it probably has a lot of excess cash. However, when it is making and selling its product but has not yet been paid, it may need to borrow to meet any temporary cash shortfalls.

    If Mattel's management is concerned with its cash position, it could take the following steps: (1) Offer its customers cash discounts for early payment, such as 2/10, n/30. (2) Implement inventory management techniques to reduce the need for large inventories of such things as the plastics used to make its toys. (3) Carefully time payments to suppliers by keeping track of when payments are due, so as not to pay too early. (4) If it has plans for major expenditures, time those expenditures to coincide with its seasonal period of excess cash.

The Navigator

Summary of Learning Objectives

1 Define fraud and internal control. A fraud is a dishonest act by an employee that results in personal benefit to the employee at a cost to the employer. The fraud triangle refers to the three factors that contribute to fraudulent activity by employees: opportunity, financial pressure, and rationalization. Internal control consists of all the related methods and measures adopted within an organization to safeguard assets, enhance the reliability of accounting records, increase efficiency of operations, and ensure compliance with laws and regulations.

2 Identify the principles of internal control activities. The principles of internal control are establishment of responsibility; segregation of duties; documentation procedures; physical controls; independent internal verification; and human resource controls.

3 Explain the applications of internal control principles to cash receipts. Internal controls over cash receipts include: (a) designating only personnel such as cashiers to handle cash; (b) assigning the duties of receiving cash, recording cash, and having custody of cash to different individuals; (c) obtaining remittance advices for mail receipts, cash register tapes or computer records for over-the-counter receipts, and deposit slips for bank deposits; (d) using company safes and bank vaults to store cash with access limited to authorized personnel, and using cash registers in executing over-the-counter receipts; (e) making independent daily counts of register receipts and daily comparisons of total receipts with total deposits; and (f) conducting background checks and bonding personnel who handle cash, as well as requiring them to take vacations.

4 Explain the applications of internal control principles to cash disbursements. Internal controls over cash disbursements include: (a) having only specified individuals such as the treasurer authorized to sign checks; (b) assigning the duties of approving items for payment, paying the items, and recording the payment to different individuals; (c) using prenumbered checks and accounting for all checks, with each check supported by an approved invoice; after payment, stamping each approved invoice "paid"; (d) storing blank checks in a safe or vault with access restricted to authorized personnel, and using a machine with indelible ink to imprint amounts on checks; (e) comparing each check with the approved invoice before issuing the check, and making monthly reconciliations of bank and book balances; and (f) bonding personnel who handle cash, requiring employees to take vacations, and conducting background checks.

5 Prepare a bank reconciliation. In reconciling the bank account, it is customary to reconcile the balance per books and the balance per bank to their adjusted balance. The steps reconciling the Cash account are to determine deposits in transit, outstanding checks, errors by the depositor or the bank, and unrecorded bank memoranda.

6 Explain the reporting of cash. Cash is listed first in the current assets section of the balance sheet. Companies often report cash together with cash equivalents. Cash restricted for a special purpose is reported separately as a current asset or as a noncurrent asset, depending on when the company expects to use the cash.

7 Discuss the basic principles of cash management. The basic principles of cash management include: (a) increase the speed of receivables collection, (b) keep inventory levels low, (c) monitor the timing of payment of liabilities, (d) plan timing of major expenditures, and (e) invest idle cash.

8 Identify the primary elements of a cash budget. The three main elements of a cash budget are the cash receipts section, cash disbursements section, and financing section.

✔ The Navigator

🧰 DECISION TOOLKIT *A SUMMARY*

DECISION CHECKPOINTS	INFO NEEDED FOR DECISION	TOOL TO USE FOR DECISION	HOW TO EVALUATE RESULTS
Are the company's financial statements supported by adequate internal controls?	Auditor's report, management discussion and analysis, articles in financial press	The principles of internal control activities are (1) establishment of responsibility, (2) segregation of duties, (3) documentation procedures, (4) physical controls, (5) independent internal verification, and (6) human resource controls.	If any indication is given that these or other controls are lacking, use the financial statements with caution.

(continued)

Is all of the company's cash available for general use?	Balance sheet and notes to financial statements	Does the company report any cash as being restricted?	A restriction on the use of cash limits management's ability to use those resources for general obligations. This might be considered when assessing liquidity.
Will the company be able to meet its projected cash needs?	Cash budget (typically available only to management)	The cash budget shows projected sources and uses of cash. If cash uses exceed internal cash sources, then the company must look for outside sources.	Two issues: (1) Are management's projections reasonable? (2) If outside sources are needed, are they available?

Appendix 7A

Operation of the Petty Cash Fund

The operation of a petty cash fund involves (1) establishing the fund, (2) making payments from the fund, and (3) replenishing the fund.

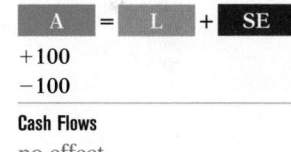

LEARNING OBJECTIVE 9
Explain the operation of a petty cash fund.

ESTABLISHING THE PETTY CASH FUND

Two essential steps in establishing a petty cash fund are: (1) appointing a petty cash custodian who will be responsible for the fund, and (2) determining the size of the fund. Ordinarily, a company expects the amount in the fund to cover anticipated disbursements for a three- to four-week period.

When the company establishes the petty cash fund, it issues a check payable to the petty cash custodian for the stipulated amount. If Laird Company decides to establish a $100 fund on March 1, the entry in general journal form is:

Mar.	1	Petty Cash	100	
		Cash		100
		(To establish a petty cash fund)		

A	=	L	+	SE
+100				
−100				

Cash Flows
no effect

The fund custodian cashes the check and places the proceeds in a locked petty cash box or drawer. Most petty cash funds are established on a fixed-amount basis. Moreover, the company will make no additional entries to the Petty Cash account unless the stipulated amount of the fund is changed. For example, if Laird Company decides on July 1 to increase the size of the fund to $250, it would debit Petty Cash $150 and credit Cash $150.

Ethics Note Petty cash funds are authorized and legitimate. In contrast, "slush" funds are unauthorized and hidden (under the table).

MAKING PAYMENTS FROM PETTY CASH

The custodian of the petty cash fund has the authority to make payments from the fund that conform to prescribed management policies. Usually, management limits the size of expenditures that come from petty cash and does not permit use of the fund for certain types of transactions (such as making short-term loans to employees).

Each payment from the fund must be documented on a prenumbered petty cash receipt (or petty cash voucher). The signatures of both the custodian and the individual receiving payment are required on the receipt. If other supporting

Helpful Hint From the standpoint of internal control, the receipt satisfies two principles: (1) establishing responsibility (signature of custodian), and (2) documentation procedures.

documents such as a freight bill or invoice are available, they should be attached to the petty cash receipt.

The custodian keeps the receipts in the petty cash box until the fund is replenished. As a result, the sum of the petty cash receipts and money in the fund should equal the established total at all times. This means that management can make surprise counts at any time by an independent person, such as an internal auditor, to determine the correctness of the fund.

The company does not make an accounting entry to record a payment at the time it is taken from petty cash. It is considered both inexpedient and unnecessary to do so. Instead, the company recognizes the accounting effects of each payment when the fund is replenished.

REPLENISHING THE PETTY CASH FUND

When the money in the petty cash fund reaches a minimum level, the company replenishes the fund. The petty cash custodian initiates a request for reimbursement. This individual prepares a schedule (or summary) of the payments that have been made and sends the schedule, supported by petty cash receipts and other documentation, to the treasurer's office. The receipts and supporting documents are examined in the treasurer's office to verify that they were proper payments from the fund. The treasurer then approves the request, and a check is prepared to restore the fund to its established amount. At the same time, all supporting documentation is stamped "paid" so that it cannot be submitted again for payment.

Helpful Hint Replenishing involves three internal control procedures: segregation of duties, documentation procedures, and independent internal verification.

To illustrate, assume that on March 15 the petty cash custodian requests a check for $87. The fund contains $13 cash and petty cash receipts for postage $44, supplies $38, and miscellaneous expenses $5. The entry, in general journal form, to record the check is:

A	=	L	+	SE
				−44 Exp
+38				
				−5 Exp
−87				

Cash Flows
−87

Mar. 15	Postage Expense	44	
	Supplies	38	
	Miscellaneous Expense	5	
	Cash		87
	(To replenish petty cash fund)		

Note that the reimbursement entry does not affect the Petty Cash account. Replenishment changes the composition of the fund by replacing the petty cash receipts with cash, but it does not change the balance in the fund.

Occasionally, in replenishing a petty cash fund the company may need to recognize a cash shortage or overage. To illustrate, assume in the preceding example that the custodian had only $12 in cash in the fund plus the receipts as listed. The request for reimbursement would therefore be for $88, and the following entry would be made.

A	=	L	+	SE
				−44 Exp
+38				
				−5 Exp
				−1 Exp
−88				

Cash Flows
−88

Mar. 15	Postage Expense	44	
	Supplies	38	
	Miscellaneous Expense	5	
	Cash Over and Short	1	
	Cash		88
	(To replenish petty cash fund)		

Conversely, if the custodian had $14 in cash, the reimbursement request would be for $86, and Cash Over and Short would be credited for $1. A debit balance in Cash Over and Short is reported in the income statement as miscellaneous expense; a credit balance is reported as miscellaneous revenue. The company closes Cash Over and Short to Income Summary at the end of the year.

Companies should replenish a petty cash fund **at the end of the accounting period**, **regardless of the cash in the fund**. Replenishment at this time is necessary in order to recognize the effects of the petty cash payments on the financial statements.

Internal control over a petty cash fund is strengthened by (1) having a supervisor make surprise counts of the fund to ascertain whether the paid petty cash receipts and fund cash equal the designated amount, and (2) canceling or mutilating the paid petty cash receipts so they cannot be resubmitted for reimbursement.

Summary of Learning Objective for Appendix 7A

9 **Explain the operation of a petty cash fund.** In operating a petty cash fund, a company establishes the fund by appointing a custodian and determining the size of the fund. The custodian makes payments from the fund for documented expenditures. The company replenishes the fund as needed, and at the end of each accounting period. Accounting entries to record payments are made each time the fund is replenished.

Glossary

Bank reconciliation (*p. 352*) The process of comparing the bank's account balance with the company's balance, and explaining the differences to make them agree.

Bank statement (*p. 352*) A statement received monthly from the bank that shows the depositor's bank transactions and balances.

Bonding (*p. 344*) Obtaining insurance protection against theft by employees.

Cash (*p. 358*) Resources that consist of coins, currency, checks, money orders, and money on hand or on deposit in a bank or similar depository.

Cash budget (*p. 362*) A projection of anticipated cash flows, usually over a one- to two-year period.

Cash equivalents (*p. 359*) Short-term, highly liquid investments that can be readily converted to a specific amount of cash and which are relatively insensitive to interest rate changes.

Deposits in transit (*p. 355*) Deposits recorded by the depositor that have not been recorded by the bank.

Electronic funds transfer (EFT) (*p. 357*) A disbursement system that uses wire, telephone, or computer to transfer cash from one location to another.

Fraud (*p. 336*) A dishonest act by an employee that results in personal benefit to the employee at a cost to the employer.

Fraud triangle (*p. 336*) The three factors that contribute to fraudulent activity by employees: opportunity, financial pressure, and rationalization.

Internal auditors (*p. 344*) Company employees who continuously evaluate the effectiveness of the company's internal control systems.

Internal control (*p. 337*) All the related methods and measures adopted within an organization to safeguard assets and enhance the reliability of accounting records, increase efficiency of operations, and ensure compliance with laws and regulations.

NSF check (*p. 352*) A check that is not paid by a bank because of insufficient funds in a bank account.

Outstanding checks (*p. 355*) Checks issued and recorded by a company that have not been paid by the bank.

Petty cash fund (*p. 351*) A cash fund used to pay relatively small amounts.

Restricted cash (*p. 359*) Cash that is not available for general use but instead is restricted for a particular purpose.

Sarbanes-Oxley Act (SOX) (*p. 337*) Law that requires publicly traded companies to maintain adequate systems of internal control.

Treasurer (*p. 361*) Employee responsible for the management of a company's cash.

Voucher (*p. 350*) An authorization form prepared for each expenditure in a voucher system.

Voucher system (*p. 350*) A network of approvals by authorized individuals, acting independently, to ensure that all disbursements by check are proper.

Comprehensive Do it!

Trillo Company's bank statement for May 2014 shows these data.

Balance May 1	$12,650	Balance May 31	$14,280
Debit memorandum:		Credit memorandum:	
NSF check	175	Collection of note receivable plus interest	505

The cash balance per books at May 31 is $13,319. Your review of the data reveals the following.

1. The NSF check was from Hup Co., a customer.
2. The note collected by the bank was a $500, 3-month, 12% note. The bank charged a $10 collection fee. No interest has been previously accrued.
3. Outstanding checks at May 31 total $2,410.
4. Deposits in transit at May 31 total $1,752.
5. A Trillo Company check for $352 dated May 10 cleared the bank on May 25. This check, which was a payment on account, was journalized for $325.

Instructions

(a) Prepare a bank reconciliation at May 31.
(b) Journalize the entries required by the reconciliation.

Action Plan

- Follow the four steps used in reconciling items (p. 355).
- Work carefully to minimize mathematical errors in the reconciliation.
- Prepare entries based on reconciling items per books.
- Make sure the cash ledger balance after posting the reconciling entries agrees with the adjusted cash balance per books.

Solution to Comprehensive Do it!

(a)

Cash balance per bank statement		$14,280
Add: Deposits in transit		1,752
		16,032
Less: Outstanding checks		2,410
Adjusted cash balance per bank		$13,622
Cash balance per books		$13,319
Add: Collection of note receivable $500,		
plus $15 interest less collection fee $10		505
		13,824
Less: NSF check	$175	
Error in recording check	27	202
Adjusted cash balance per books		$13,622

(b)

May 31	Cash		505	
	Miscellaneous Expense		10	
	Notes Receivable			500
	Interest Revenue			15
	(To record collection of note by bank)			
31	Accounts Receivable—Hup Co.		175	
	Cash			175
	(To record NSF check from Hup Co.)			
31	Accounts Payable		27	
	Cash			27
	(To correct error in recording check)			

The Navigator

Self-Test, Brief Exercises, Exercises, Problem Set A, and many more resources are available for practice in WileyPLUS.

Note: All Questions, Exercises, and Problems marked with an asterisk relate to material in the appendix to the chapter.

Self-Test Questions

Answers are on page 393.

(LO 1) **1.** Which of the following is **not** an element of the fraud triangle?
  (a) Rationalization.
  (b) Financial pressure.
  (c) Segregation of duties.
  (d) Opportunity.

(LO 1) **2.** Internal control is used in a business to enhance the accuracy and reliability of its accounting records and to:
  (a) safeguard its assets.
  (b) create fraud.
  (c) analyze financial statements.
  (d) determine employee bonuses.

(LO 2) **3.** The principles of internal control do **not** include:
  (a) establishment of responsibility.
  (b) documentation procedures.
  (c) financial performance measures.
  (d) independent internal verification.

(LO 2) **4.** Physical controls do **not** include:
  (a) safes and vaults to store cash.
  (b) independent bank reconciliations.
  (c) locked warehouses for inventories.
  (d) bank safety deposit boxes for important papers.

(LO 1) **5.** Which of the following was **not** a result of the Sarbanes-Oxley Act?
  (a) Companies must file financial statements with the Internal Revenue Service.
  (b) All publicly traded companies must maintain adequate internal controls.
  (c) The Public Company Accounting Oversight Board was created to establish auditing standards and regulate auditor activity.
  (d) Corporate executives and boards of directors must ensure that controls are reliable and effective, and they can be fined or imprisoned for failure to do so.

(LO 3) **6.** Permitting only designated personnel such as cashiers to handle cash receipts is an application of the principle of:
  (a) documentation procedures.
  (b) establishment of responsibility.
  (c) independent internal verification.
  (d) other controls.

(LO 4) **7.** The use of prenumbered checks in disbursing cash is an application of the principle of:
  (a) establishment of responsibility.
  (b) segregation of duties.
  (c) physical controls.
  (d) documentation procedures.

(LO 4) **8.** The control features of a bank account do **not** include:
  (a) having bank auditors verify the correctness of the bank balance per books.
  (b) minimizing the amount of cash that must be kept on hand.
  (c) providing a double record of all bank transactions.
  (d) safeguarding cash by using a bank as a depository.

(LO 2) **9.** Which of the following control activities is **not** relevant when a company uses a computerized (rather than manual) accounting system?
  (a) Establishment of responsibility.
  (b) Segregation of duties.
  (c) Independent internal verification.
  (d) All of these control activities are relevant to a computerized system.

(LO 5) **10.** In a bank reconciliation, deposits in transit are:
  (a) deducted from the book balance.
  (b) added to the book balance.
  (c) added to the bank balance.
  (d) deducted from the bank balance.

(LO 6) **11.** Which of the following items in a cash drawer at November 30 is **not** cash?
  (a) Money orders.
  (b) Coins and currency.
  (c) A customer check dated December 1.
  (d) A customer check dated November 28.

(LO 6) **12.** Which statement correctly describes the reporting of cash?
  (a) Cash cannot be combined with cash equivalents.
  (b) Restricted cash funds may be combined with cash.
  (c) Cash is listed first in the current assets section.
  (d) Restricted cash funds cannot be reported as a current asset.

(LO 7) **13.** Which of the following would **not** be an example of good cash management?
  (a) Provide discounts to customers to encourage early payment.
  (b) Invest temporary excess cash in stock of a small company.
  (c) Carefully monitor payments so that payments are not made early.
  (d) Employ just-in-time inventory methods to keep inventory low.

(LO 8) **14.** Which of the following is **not** one of the sections of a cash budget?
(a) Cash receipts section.
(b) Cash disbursements section.
(c) Financing section.
(d) Cash from operations section.

(LO 9)*** 15.** A check is written to replenish a $100 petty cash fund when the fund contains receipts of $94 and $2 in cash. In recording the check:

(a) Cash Over and Short should be debited for $4.
(b) Petty Cash should be debited for $94.
(c) Cash should be credited for $94.
(d) Petty Cash should be credited for $4.

Go to the book's companion website, **www.wiley.com/college/kimmel**, to access additional Self-Test Questions.

✔ The Navigator

Questions

1. A local bank reported that it lost $150,000 as the result of employee fraud. Fred Raburn is not clear on what is meant by "employee fraud." Explain the meaning of fraud to Fred and give an example of fraud that might occur at a bank.

2. Fraud experts often say that there are three primary factors that contribute to employee fraud. Identify the three factors and explain what is meant by each.

3. Identify the five components of a good internal control system.

4. "Internal control is concerned only with enhancing the accuracy of the accounting records." Do you agree? Explain.

5. Discuss how the Sarbanes-Oxley Act has increased the importance of internal control to top managers of a company.

6. What principles of internal control apply to most businesses?

7. In the corner grocery store, all sales clerks make change out of one cash register drawer. Is this a violation of internal control? Why?

8. Donald Bowen is reviewing the principle of segregation of duties. What are the two common applications of this principle?

9. How do documentation procedures contribute to good internal control?

10. What internal control objectives are met by physical controls?

11. (a) Explain the control principle of independent internal verification.
(b) What practices are important in applying this principle?

12. ➤ As the company accountant, explain the following ideas to the management of Jurgens Company.
(a) The concept of reasonable assurance in internal control.
(b) The importance of the human factor in internal control.

13. ➤ Discuss the human resources department's involvement in internal controls.

14. Hoskins Inc. owns the following assets at the balance sheet date.

Cash in bank—savings account	$ 8,000
Cash on hand	1,100
Cash refund due from the IRS	1,000
Checking account balance	12,000
Postdated checks	500

What amount should be reported as Cash in the balance sheet?

15. What principle(s) of internal control is (are) involved in making daily cash counts of over-the-counter receipts?

16. Assume that Kohl's Department Stores installed new cash registers in its stores. How do cash registers improve internal control over cash receipts?

17. At Solis Wholesale Company, two mail clerks open all mail receipts. How does this strengthen internal control?

18. "To have maximum effective internal control over cash disbursements, all payments should be made by check." Is this true? Explain.

19. Napoli Company's internal controls over cash disbursements provide for the treasurer to sign checks imprinted by a checkwriter after comparing the check with the approved invoice. Identify the internal control principles that are present in these controls.

20. How do these principles apply to cash disbursements?
(a) Physical controls.
(b) Human resource controls.

21. What is the essential feature of an electronic funds transfer (EFT) procedure?

22. "The use of a bank contributes significantly to good internal control over cash." Is this true? Why?

23. Chris Hite is confused about the lack of agreement between the cash balance per books and the balance per bank. Explain the causes for the lack of agreement to Chris and give an example of each cause.

24. Identify the basic principles of cash management.

25. Marcia Tague asks your help concerning an NSF check. Explain to Marcia (a) what an NSF check is, (b) how it is treated in a bank reconciliation, and (c) whether it will require an adjusting entry on the company's books.

26.
    (a) Describe cash equivalents and explain how they are reported.
    (b) How should restricted cash funds be reported on the balance sheet?

27. What was Tootsie Roll's balance in cash and cash equivalents at December 31, 2011? Did it report any restricted cash? How did Tootsie Roll define cash equivalents?

*28. (a) Identify the three activities that pertain to a petty cash fund, and indicate an internal control principle that is applicable to each activity.
    (b) When are journal entries required in the operation of a petty cash fund?

Brief Exercises

BE7-1 Match each situation with the fraud triangle factor (opportunity, financial pressure, or rationalization) that best describes it.
(a) An employee's monthly credit card payments are nearly 75% of their monthly earnings.
(b) An employee earns minimum wage at a firm that has reported record earnings for each of the last five years.
(c) An employee has an expensive gambling habit.
(d) An employee has check writing and signing responsibilities for a small company, and is also responsible for reconciling the bank account.

Identify fraud-triangle concepts.
(LO 1), **C**

BE7-2 Beth Pitchford is the new owner of Brigham Co. She has heard about internal control but is not clear about its importance for her business. Explain to Beth the four purposes of internal control, and give her one application of each purpose for Brigham Co.

Explain the importance of internal control.
(LO 2), **C**

BE7-3 The internal control procedures in Edmiston Company make the following provisions. Identify the principles of internal control that are being followed in each case.
(a) Employees who have physical custody of assets do not have access to the accounting records.
(b) Each month, the assets on hand are compared to the accounting records by an internal auditor.
(c) A prenumbered shipping document is prepared for each shipment of goods to customers.

Identify internal control principles.
(LO 2), **C**

BE7-4 Halleran Company has the following internal control procedures over cash receipts. Identify the internal control principle that is applicable to each procedure.
(a) All over-the-counter receipts are entered in cash registers.
(b) All cashiers are bonded.
(c) Daily cash counts are made by cashier department supervisors.
(d) The duties of receiving cash, recording cash, and having custody of cash are assigned to different individuals.
(e) Only cashiers may operate cash registers.

Identify the internal control principles applicable to cash receipts.
(LO 3), **C**

BE7-5 While examining cash receipts information, the accounting department determined the following information: opening cash balance $150, cash on hand $1,125.74, and cash sales per register tape $988.62. Prepare the required journal entry based upon the cash count sheet.

Make journal entry using cash count sheet.
(LO 3), **AP**

BE7-6 Catt Company has the following internal control procedures over cash disbursements. Identify the internal control principle that is applicable to each procedure.
(a) Company checks are prenumbered.
(b) The bank statement is reconciled monthly by an internal auditor.
(c) Blank checks are stored in a safe in the treasurer's office.
(d) Only the treasurer or assistant treasurer may sign checks.
(e) Check-signers are not allowed to record cash disbursement transactions.

Identify the internal control principles applicable to cash disbursements.
(LO 4), **C**

BE7-7 Roy Luber is uncertain about the control features of a bank account. Explain the control benefits of (a) a checking account and (b) a bank statement.

Identify the control features of a bank account.
(LO 4), **C**

BE7-8 The following reconciling items are applicable to the bank reconciliation for Nuessen Co. Indicate how each item should be shown on a bank reconciliation.
(a) Outstanding checks.
(b) Bank debit memorandum for service charge.
(c) Bank credit memorandum for collecting a note for the depositor.
(d) Deposit in transit.

Indicate location of reconciling items in a bank reconciliation.
(LO 5), **C**

Identify reconciling items that require adjusting entries.
(LO 5), **C**

BE7-9 Using the data in BE7-8, indicate (a) the items that will result in an adjustment to the depositor's records and (b) why the other items do not require adjustment.

Prepare partial bank reconciliation.
(LO 5), **AP**

BE7-10 At July 31, Farmer Company has this bank information: cash balance per bank $7,291; outstanding checks $762; deposits in transit $1,350; and a bank service charge $40. Determine the adjusted cash balance per bank at July 31.

Analyze outstanding checks.
(LO 5), **AP**

BE7-11 In the month of November, Halladay Company Inc. wrote checks in the amount of $9,750. In December, checks in the amount of $11,762 were written. In November, $8,800 of these checks were presented to the bank for payment, and $10,889 in December. What is the amount of outstanding checks at the end of November? At the end of December?

Explain the statement presentation of cash balances.
(LO 6), **C** ○━━━━━━○

BE7-12 Span Company has these cash balances: cash in bank $12,742; payroll bank account $6,000; and plant expansion fund cash $25,000. Explain how each balance should be reported on the balance sheet.

Prepare a cash budget.
(LO 8), **AP** ○━━━━━━○

BE7-13 The following information is available for Conger Company for the month of January: expected cash receipts $59,000; expected cash disbursements $67,000; and cash balance on January 1, $12,000. Management wishes to maintain a minimum cash balance of $9,000. Prepare a basic cash budget for the month of January.

Prepare entry to replenish a petty cash fund.
(LO 9), **AP**

*BE7-14** On March 20, Garber's petty cash fund of $100 is replenished when the fund contains $19 in cash and receipts for postage $40, supplies $26, and travel expense $15. Prepare the journal entry to record the replenishment of the petty cash fund.

Do it! Review

Identify violations of control activities.
(LO 2), **C**

Do it! 7-1 Identify which control activity is violated in each of the following situations, and explain how the situation creates an opportunity for fraud or inappropriate accounting practices.
1. Once a month, the sales department sends sales invoices to the accounting department to be recorded.
2. Nick Sewell orders merchandise for Silo Company; he also receives merchandise and authorizes payment for merchandise.
3. Several clerks at Guillen's Groceries use the same cash register drawer.

Design system of internal control over cash receipts.
(LO 3), **C**

Do it! 7-2 Jack Woodling is concerned with control over mail receipts at Yount Sporting Goods. All mail receipts are opened by Bill Morten. Bill sends the checks to the accounting department, where they are stamped "For Deposit Only." The accounting department records and deposits the mail receipts weekly. Jack asks your help in installing a good system of internal control over mail receipts.

Explain treatment of items in bank reconciliation.
(LO 5), **K**

Do it! 7-3 Doug Nicklas owns Doug Blankets. Doug asks you to explain how he should treat the following reconciling items when reconciling the company's bank account.
1. Outstanding checks
2. A deposit in transit
3. The bank charged to our account a check written by another company
4. A debit memorandum for a bank service charge

Prepare a cash budget.
(LO 8), **AP**

Do it! 7-4 Hull Corporation's management wants to maintain a minimum monthly cash balance of $8,000. At the beginning of September, the cash balance is $12,270; expected cash receipts for September are $97,200; cash disbursements are expected to be $115,000. How much cash, if any, must Hull borrow to maintain the desired minimum monthly balance? Determine your answer by using the basic form of the cash budget.

Exercises

E7-1   Bank employees use a system known as the "maker-checker" system. An employee will record an entry in the appropriate journal, and then a supervisor will verify and approve the entry. These days, as all of a bank's accounts are computerized, the employee first enters a batch of entries into the computer, and then the entries are posted automatically to the general ledger account after the supervisor approves them on the system.

Access to the computer system is password-protected and task-specific, which means that the computer system will not allow the employee to approve a transaction or the supervisor to record a transaction.

Identify the principles of internal control.
(LO 2), **C**

Instructions
Identify the principles of internal control inherent in the "maker-checker" procedure used by banks.

E7-2   Rosa's Pizza operates strictly on a carryout basis. Customers pick up their orders at a counter where a clerk exchanges the pizza for cash. While at the counter, the customer can see other employees making the pizzas and the large ovens in which the pizzas are baked.

Identify the principles of internal control.
(LO 2), **C**

Instructions
Identify the six principles of internal control and give an example of each principle that you might observe when picking up your pizza. (*Note:* It may not be possible to observe all the principles.)

E7-3   The following control procedures are used in Kelton Company for over-the-counter cash receipts.
1. Each store manager is responsible for interviewing applicants for cashier jobs. They are hired if they seem honest and trustworthy.
2. All over-the-counter receipts are registered by three clerks who share a cash register with a single cash drawer.
3. To minimize the risk of robbery, cash in excess of $100 is stored in an unlocked attaché case in the stock room until it is deposited in the bank.
4. At the end of each day the total receipts are counted by the cashier on duty and reconciled to the cash register total.
5. The company accountant makes the bank deposit and then records the day's receipts.

List internal control weaknesses over cash receipts and suggest improvements.
(LO 2, 3), **E**

Instructions
(a) For each procedure, explain the weakness in internal control and identify the control principle that is violated.
(b) For each weakness, suggest a change in the procedure that will result in good internal control.

E7-4   The following control procedures are used in Penny's Boutique Shoppe for cash disbursements.
1. Each week, 100 company checks are left in an unmarked envelope on a shelf behind the cash register.
2. The store manager personally approves all payments before she signs and issues checks.
3. The store purchases used goods for resale from people that bring items to the store. Since that can occur anytime that the store is open, all employees are authorized to purchase goods for resale by issuing cash from the register. The purchase is documented by having the store employee write on a piece of paper a description of the item that was purchased and the amount that was paid. The employee then signs the paper and puts it in the register.
4. After payment, bills are "filed" in a paid invoice folder.
5. The company accountant prepares the bank reconciliation and reports any discrepancies to the owner.

List internal control weaknesses for cash disbursements and suggest improvements.
(LO 2, 4), **E**

Instructions
(a) For each procedure, explain the weakness in internal control and identify the internal control principle that is violated.
(b) For each weakness, suggest a change in the procedure that will result in good internal control.

Identify internal control weaknesses for cash disbursements and suggest improvements.

(LO 2, 4), **E**

E7-5 At Nunez Company, checks are not prenumbered because both the purchasing agent and the treasurer are authorized to issue checks. Each signer has access to unissued checks kept in an unlocked file cabinet. The purchasing agent pays all bills pertaining to goods purchased for resale. Prior to payment, the purchasing agent determines that the goods have been received and verifies the mathematical accuracy of the vendor's invoice. After payment, the invoice is filed by vendor name and the purchasing agent records the payment in the cash disbursements journal. The treasurer pays all other bills following approval by authorized employees. After payment, the treasurer stamps all bills "paid," files them by payment date, and records the checks in the cash disbursements journal. Nunez Company maintains one checking account that is reconciled by the treasurer.

Instructions
(a) List the weaknesses in internal control over cash disbursements.
(b) Identify improvements for correcting these weaknesses.

Prepare bank reconciliation and adjusting entries.

(LO 5), **AP**

E7-6 Sally Rice is unable to reconcile the bank balance at January 31. Sally's reconciliation is shown here.

Cash balance per bank	$3,677.20
Add: NSF check	450.00
Less: Bank service charge	28.00
Adjusted balance per bank	$4,099.20
Cash balance per books	$3,975.20
Less: Deposits in transit	590.00
Add: Outstanding checks	770.00
Adjusted balance per books	$4,155.20

Instructions
(a) What is the proper adjusted cash balance per bank?
(b) What is the proper adjusted cash balance per books?
(c) Prepare the adjusting journal entries necessary to determine the adjusted cash balance per books.

Determine outstanding checks.

(LO 5), **AP**

E7-7 At April 30, the bank reconciliation of Longacre Company shows three outstanding checks: No. 254 $650, No. 255 $700, and No. 257 $410. The May bank statement and the May cash payments journal are given here.

Bank Statement Checks Paid			Cash Payments Journal Checks Issued		
Date	**Check No.**	**Amount**	**Date**	**Check No.**	**Amount**
5-4	254	$650	5-2	258	$159
5-2	257	410	5-5	259	275
5-17	258	159	5-10	260	925
5-12	259	275	5-15	261	500
5-20	260	925	5-22	262	750
5-29	263	480	5-24	263	480
5-30	262	750	5-29	264	360

Instructions
Using step 2 in the reconciliation procedure (see page 355), list the outstanding checks at May 31.

Prepare bank reconciliation and adjusting entries.

(LO 5), **AP**

XLS

E7-8 The following information pertains to Joyce Company.
1. Cash balance per bank, July 31, $7,328.
2. July bank service charge not recorded by the depositor $38.
3. Cash balance per books, July 31, $7,364.
4. Deposits in transit, July 31, $2,700.
5. Note for $2,000 collected for Joyce Company in July by the bank, plus interest $36 less fee $20. The collection has not been recorded by Joyce Company, and no interest has been accrued.
6. Outstanding checks, July 31, $686.

Instructions

(a) Prepare a bank reconciliation at July 31, 2014.

(b) Journalize the adjusting entries at July 31 on the books of Joyce Company.

E7-9 This information relates to the Cash account in the ledger of Treanor Company.

Prepare bank reconciliation and adjusting entries.

(LO 5), **AP**

> Balance September 1—$16,400; Cash deposited—$64,000
> Balance September 30—$17,600; Checks written—$62,800

The September bank statement shows a balance of $16,500 at September 30 and the following memoranda.

Credits		Debits	
Collection of $1,800 note plus interest $30	$1,830	NSF check: H. Kane	$560
Interest earned on checking account	45	Safety deposit box rent	60

At September 30, deposits in transit were $4,738 and outstanding checks totaled $2,383.

Instructions

(a) Prepare the bank reconciliation at September 30, 2014.

(b) Prepare the adjusting entries at September 30, assuming (1) the NSF check was from a customer on account, and (2) no interest had been accrued on the note.

E7-10 The cash records of Downs Company show the following.

Compute deposits in transit and outstanding checks for two bank reconciliations.

(LO 5), **AP**

For July:

1. The June 30 bank reconciliation indicated that deposits in transit total $580. During July, the general ledger account Cash shows deposits of $16,900, but the bank statement indicates that only $15,600 in deposits were received during the month.

2. The June 30 bank reconciliation also reported outstanding checks of $940. During the month of July, Downs Company books show that $17,500 of checks were issued, yet the bank statement showed that $16,400 of checks cleared the bank in July.

For September:

3. In September, deposits per bank statement totaled $25,900, deposits per books were $26,400, and deposits in transit at September 30 were $2,200.

4. In September, cash disbursements per books were $23,500, checks clearing the bank were $24,000, and outstanding checks at September 30 were $2,100.

There were no bank debit or credit memoranda, and no errors were made by either the bank or Downs Company.

Instructions

Answer the following questions.

(a) In situation 1, what were the deposits in transit at July 31?

(b) In situation 2, what were the outstanding checks at July 31?

(c) In situation 3, what were the deposits in transit at August 31?

(d) In situation 4, what were the outstanding checks at August 31?

E7-11 Werth Inc.'s bank statement from Hometown Bank at August 31, 2014, gives the following information.

Prepare bank reconciliation and adjusting entries.

(LO 5), **AP**

Balance, August 1	$18,400	Bank debit memorandum:		
August deposits	71,000	Safety deposit box fee	$	25
Checks cleared in August	68,678	Service charge		50
Bank credit memorandum:		Balance, August 31	20,692	
Interest earned	45			

A summary of the Cash account in the ledger for August shows the following: balance, August 1, $18,700; receipts $74,000; disbursements $73,570; and balance, August 31, $19,130. Analysis reveals that the only reconciling items on the July 31 bank reconciliation were a deposit in transit for $4,800 and outstanding checks of $4,500. In addition, you determine that there was an error involving a company check drawn in August: A check for $400 to a creditor on account that cleared the bank in August was journalized and posted for $40.

Instructions

(a) Determine deposits in transit.

(b) Determine outstanding checks. (*Hint:* You need to correct disbursements for the check error.)

(c) Prepare a bank reconciliation at August 31.

(d) Journalize the adjusting entry(ies) to be made by Werth Inc. at August 31.

Identify reporting of cash.
(LO 6), **AP**

E7-12 A new accountant at Leftwich Inc. is trying to identify which of the amounts shown below should be reported as the current asset "Cash and cash equivalents" in the year-end balance sheet, as of April 30, 2014.

1. $60 of currency and coin in a locked box used for incidental cash transactions.
2. A $10,000 U.S. Treasury bill, due May 31, 2014.
3. $260 of April-dated checks that Leftwich has received from customers but not yet deposited.
4. An $85 check received from a customer in payment of its April account, but postdated to May 1.
5. $2,500 in the company's checking account.
6. $4,800 in its savings account.
7. $75 of prepaid postage in its postage meter.
8. A $25 IOU from the company receptionist.

Instructions

(a) What balance should Leftwich report as its "Cash and cash equivalents" balance at April 30, 2014?

(b) In what account(s) and in what financial statement(s) should the items not included in "Cash and cash equivalents" be reported?

Review cash management practices.
(LO 7), **C**

E7-13 Canzer, Morel, and Wang, three law students who have joined together to open a law practice, are struggling to manage their cash flow. They haven't yet built up sufficient clientele and revenues to support their legal practice's ongoing costs. Initial costs, such as advertising, renovations to their premises, and the like, all result in outgoing cash flow at a time when little is coming in. Canzer, Morel, and Wang haven't had time to establish a billing system since most of their clients' cases haven't yet reached the courts, and the lawyers didn't think it would be right to bill them until "results were achieved."

Unfortunately, Canzer, Morel, and Wang's suppliers don't feel the same way. Their suppliers expect them to pay their accounts payable within a few days of receiving their bills. So far, there hasn't even been enough money to pay the three lawyers, and they are not sure how long they can keep practicing law without getting some money into their pockets.

Instructions

Can you provide any suggestions for Canzer, Morel, and Wang to improve their cash management practices?

Prepare a cash budget for two months.
(LO 8), **AP**

E7-14 Enright Company expects to have a cash balance of $46,000 on January 1, 2014. These are the relevant monthly budget data for the first two months of 2014.

1. Collections from customers: January $71,000, February $146,000.
2. Payments to suppliers: January $40,000, February $75,000.
3. Wages: January $30,000, February $40,000. Wages are paid in the month they are incurred.
4. Administrative expenses: January $21,000, February $24,000. These costs include depreciation of $1,000 per month. All other costs are paid as incurred.
5. Selling expenses: January $15,000, February $20,000. These costs are exclusive of depreciation. They are paid as incurred.
6. Sales of short-term investments in January are expected to realize $12,000 in cash. Enright has a line of credit at a local bank that enables it to borrow up to $25,000. The company wants to maintain a minimum monthly cash balance of $20,000.

Instructions

Prepare journal entries for a petty cash fund.
(LO 9), **AP**

Prepare a cash budget for January and February.

*E7-15 During October, Wichita Light Company experiences the following transactions in establishing a petty cash fund.

Oct. 1 A petty cash fund is established with a check for $150 issued to the petty cash custodian.

31 A check was written to reimburse the fund and increase the fund to $200. A count of the petty cash fund disclosed the following items:

Currency	$59.00
Coins	0.70
Expenditure receipts (vouchers):	
Supplies	$26.10
Telephone, Internet, and fax	16.40
Postage	39.70
Freight-out	6.80

Instructions

Journalize the entries in October that pertain to the petty cash fund.

*E7-16 Lyle Company maintains a petty cash fund for small expenditures. These transactions occurred during the month of August.

Journalize and post petty cash fund transactions.
(LO 9), AP

Aug. 1 Established the petty cash fund by writing a check on Westown Bank for $200.

15 Replenished the petty cash fund by writing a check for $175. On this date, the fund consisted of $25 in cash and these petty cash receipts: freight-out $74.40, entertainment expense $36, postage expense $33.70, and miscellaneous expense $27.50.

16 Increased the amount of the petty cash fund to $400 by writing a check for $200.

31 Replenished the petty cash fund by writing a check for $283. On this date, the fund consisted of $117 in cash and these petty cash receipts: postage expense $145, entertainment expense $90.60, and freight-out $46.40.

Instructions

(a) Journalize the petty cash transactions.
(b) Post to the Petty Cash account.
(c) What internal control features exist in a petty cash fund?

Exercises: Set B and Challenge Exercises

Visit the book's companion website, at **www.wiley.com/college/kimmel**, and choose the Student Companion site to access Exercise Set B and Challenge Exercises.

Problems: Set A

P7-1A Granada Theater is in the Greenbelt Mall. A cashier's booth is located near the entrance to the theater. Two cashiers are employed. One works from 1:00 to 5:00 P.M., the other from 5:00 to 9:00 P.M. Each cashier is bonded. The cashiers receive cash from customers and operate a machine that ejects serially numbered tickets. The rolls of tickets are inserted and locked into the machine by the theater manager at the beginning of each cashier's shift.

Identify internal control weaknesses for cash receipts.
(LO 2, 3), C

After purchasing a ticket, the customer takes the ticket to a doorperson stationed at the entrance of the theater lobby some 60 feet from the cashier's booth. The doorperson tears the ticket in half, admits the customer, and returns the ticket stub to the customer. The other half of the ticket is dropped into a locked box by the doorperson.

At the end of each cashier's shift, the theater manager removes the ticket rolls from the machine and makes a cash count. The cash count sheet is initialed by the cashier. At the end of the day, the manager deposits the receipts in total in a bank night deposit vault located in the mall. In addition, the manager sends copies of the deposit slip and the initialed cash count sheets to the theater company treasurer for verification and to the company's accounting department. Receipts from the first shift are stored in a safe located in the manager's office.

Instructions

(a) Identify the internal control principles and their application to the cash receipts transactions of Granada Theater.

(b) If the doorperson and cashier decided to collaborate to misappropriate cash, what actions might they take?

Identify internal control weaknesses in cash receipts and cash disbursements.
(LO 2, 3, 4), C

P7-2A Flint Hills Middle School wants to raise money for a new sound system for its auditorium. The primary fund-raising event is a dance at which the famous disc jockey Jay Dee will play classic and not-so-classic dance tunes. Trent Greeley, the music and theater instructor, has been given the responsibility for coordinating the fund-raising efforts. This is Trent's first experience with fund-raising. He decides to put the eighth-grade choir in charge of the event; he will be a relatively passive observer.

Trent had 500 unnumbered tickets printed for the dance. He left the tickets in a box on his desk and told the choir students to take as many tickets as they thought they could sell for $5 each. In order to ensure that no extra tickets would be floating around, he told them to dispose of any unsold tickets. When the students received payment for the tickets, they were to bring the cash back to Trent, and he would put it in a locked box in his desk drawer.

Some of the students were responsible for decorating the gymnasium for the dance. Trent gave each of them a key to the money box and told them that if they took money out to purchase materials, they should put a note in the box saying how much they took and what it was used for. After two weeks, the money box appeared to be getting full, so Trent asked Sandy Overbay to count the money, prepare a deposit slip, and deposit the money in a bank account Trent had opened.

The day of the dance, Trent wrote a check from the account to pay Jay Dee. The DJ said, however, that he accepted only cash and did not give receipts. So Trent took $200 out of the cash box and gave it to Jay. At the dance, Trent had Deb Younger working at the entrance to the gymnasium, collecting tickets from students and selling tickets to those who had not pre-purchased them. Trent estimated that 400 students attended the dance.

The following day, Trent closed out the bank account, which had $250 in it, and gave that amount plus the $180 in the cash box to Principal Ramirez. Principal Ramirez seemed surprised that, after generating roughly $2,000 in sales, the dance netted only $430 in cash. Trent did not know how to respond.

Instructions

Identify as many internal control weaknesses as you can in this scenario, and suggest how each could be addressed.

Prepare a bank reconciliation and adjusting entries.
(LO 5), AP

P7-3A On July 31, 2014, Redeker Company had a cash balance per books of $6,140. The statement from Nashota State Bank on that date showed a balance of $7,690.80. A comparison of the bank statement with the Cash account revealed the following facts.

1. The bank service charge for July was $25.
2. The bank collected a note receivable of $1,500 for Redeker Company on July 15, plus $30 of interest. The bank made a $10 charge for the collection. Redeker has not accrued any interest on the note.
3. The July 31 receipts of $1,193.30 were not included in the bank deposits for July. These receipts were deposited by the company in a night deposit vault on July 31.
4. Company check No. 2480 issued to T. Laird, a creditor, for $384 that cleared the bank in July was incorrectly entered in the cash payments journal on July 10 for $348.
5. Checks outstanding on July 31 totaled $1,860.10.
6. On July 31, the bank statement showed an NSF charge of $575 for a check received by the company from K. Wagner, a customer, on account.

Instructions

(a) Adjusted cash bal. $7,024.00

(a) Prepare the bank reconciliation as of July 31.
(b) Prepare the necessary adjusting entries at July 31.

P7-4A The bank portion of the bank reconciliation for LaRoche Company at October 31, 2014, is shown below.

Prepare a bank reconciliation and adjusting entries from detailed data.

(LO 5), **AP**

LAROCHE COMPANY
Bank Reconciliation
October 31, 2014

Cash balance per bank		$12,367.90
Add: Deposits in transit		1,530.20
		13,898.10
Less: Outstanding checks		

Check Number	Check Amount	
2451	$1,260.40	
2470	684.20	
2471	844.50	
2472	426.80	
2474	1,050.00	4,265.90

Adjusted cash balance per bank		$ 9,632.20

The adjusted cash balance per bank agreed with the cash balance per books at October 31. The November bank statement showed the following checks and deposits.

	Bank Statement				
	Checks			**Deposits**	
Date	**Number**	**Amount**	**Date**	**Amount**	
11-1	2470	$ 684.20	11-1	$ 1,530.20	
11-2	2471	844.50	11-4	1,211.60	
11-5	2474	1,050.00	11-8	990.10	
11-4	2475	1,640.70	11-13	2,575.00	
11-8	2476	2,830.00	11-18	1,472.70	
11-10	2477	600.00	11-21	2,945.00	
11-15	2479	1,750.00	11-25	2,567.30	
11-18	2480	1,330.00	11-28	1,650.00	
11-27	2481	695.40	11-30	1,186.00	
11-30	2483	575.50	Total	$16,127.90	
11-29	2486	940.00			
	Total	$12,940.30			

The cash records per books for November showed the following.

	Cash Payments Journal						**Cash Receipts Journal**	
Date	**Number**	**Amount**	**Date**	**Number**	**Amount**		**Date**	**Amount**
11-1	2475	$1,640.70	11-20	2483	$ 575.50		11-3	$ 1,211.60
11-2	2476	2,830.00	11-22	2484	829.50		11-7	990.10
11-2	2477	600.00	11-23	2485	974.80		11-12	2,575.00
11-4	2478	538.20	11-24	2486	940.00		11-17	1,472.70
11-8	2479	1,705.00	11-29	2487	398.00		11-20	2,954.00
11-10	2480	1,330.00	11-30	2488	800.00		11-24	2,567.30
11-15	2481	695.40	Total		$14,469.10		11-27	1,650.00
11-18	2482	612.00					11-29	1,186.00
							11-30	1,304.00
							Total	$15,910.70

The bank statement contained two bank memoranda:

1. A credit of $2,242 for the collection of a $2,100 note for LaRoche Company plus interest of $157 and less a collection fee of $15. LaRoche Company has not accrued any interest on the note.
2. A debit for the printing of additional company checks $85.

At November 30, the cash balance per books was $11,073.80 and the cash balance per bank statement was $17,712.50. The bank did not make any errors, but **LaRoche Company made two errors.**

Instructions

(a) Adjusted cash bal. $13,176.80

(a) Using the four steps in the reconciliation procedure described on page 355, prepare a bank reconciliation at November 30, 2014.

(b) Prepare the adjusting entries based on the reconciliation. (*Note:* The correction of any errors pertaining to recording checks should be made to Accounts Payable. The correction of any errors relating to recording cash receipts should be made to Accounts Receivable.)

Prepare a bank reconciliation and adjusting entries.
(LO 5), **AP**

P7-5A Zimmerman Company of Shawnee, Kansas, spreads herbicides and applies liquid fertilizer for local farmers. On May 31, 2014, the company's Cash account per its general ledger showed a balance of $6,738.90.

The bank statement from Shawnee State Bank on that date showed the following balance.

SHAWNEE STATE BANK

Checks and Debits	Deposits and Credits	Daily Balance
XXX	XXX	5-31 6,968.00

A comparison of the details on the bank statement with the details in the Cash account revealed the following facts.

1. The statement included a debit memo of $40 for the printing of additional company checks.
2. Cash sales of $883.15 on May 12 were deposited in the bank. The cash receipts journal entry and the deposit slip were incorrectly made for $933.15. The bank credited Zimmerman Company for the correct amount.
3. Outstanding checks at May 31 totaled $276.25, and deposits in transit were $1,880.15.
4. On May 18, the company issued check No. 1181 for $685 to M. Hartley, on account. The check, which cleared the bank in May, was incorrectly journalized and posted by Zimmerman Company for $658.
5. A $2,600 note receivable was collected by the bank for Zimmerman Company on May 31 plus $110 interest. The bank charged a collection fee of $20. No interest has been accrued on the note.
6. Included with the canceled checks was a check issued by Zinderberg Company to P. Conard for $360 that was incorrectly charged to Zimmerman Company by the bank.
7. On May 31, the bank statement showed an NSF charge of $380 for a check issued by Bev Sullivan, a customer, to Zimmerman Company on account.

Instructions

(a) Adjusted cash bal. $8,931.90

(a) Prepare the bank reconciliation at May 31, 2014.
(b) Prepare the necessary adjusting entries for Zimmerman Company at May 31, 2014.

Prepare a cash budget.
(LO 8), **AP**

P7-6A You are provided with the following information taken from Langerhan Inc.'s March 31, 2014, balance sheet.

Cash	$ 11,000
Accounts receivable	20,000
Inventory	36,000
Property, plant, and equipment, net of depreciation	120,000
Accounts payable	22,400
Common stock	150,000
Retained earnings	11,600

Additional information concerning Langerhan Inc. is as follows.

1. Gross profit is 25% of sales.
2. Actual and budgeted sales data:

March (actual)	$46,000
April (budgeted)	70,000

3. Sales are both cash and credit. Cash collections expected in April are:

March	$18,400	(40% of $46,000)
April	42,000	(60% of $70,000)
	$60,400	

4. Half of a month's purchases are paid for in the month of purchase and half in the following month. Cash disbursements expected in April are:

Purchases March	$22,400
Purchases April	28,100
	$50,500

5. Cash operating costs are anticipated to be $11,200 for the month of April.
6. Equipment costing $2,500 will be purchased for cash in April.
7. The company wishes to maintain a minimum cash balance of $9,000. An open line of credit is available at the bank. All borrowing is done at the beginning of the month, and all repayments are made at the end of the month. The interest rate is 12% per year, and interest expense is accrued at the end of the month and paid in the following month.

Instructions

Prepare a cash budget for the month of April. Determine how much cash Langerhan Inc. must borrow, or can repay, in April.

Apr. borrowings $1,800

P7-7A Castle Corporation prepares monthly cash budgets. Here are relevant data from operating budgets for 2014.

Prepare a cash budget.
(LO 8), **AP**

	January	February
Sales	$360,000	$400,000
Purchases	120,000	130,000
Salaries	84,000	81,000
Administrative expenses	72,000	75,000
Selling expenses	79,000	88,000

All sales and purchases are on account. Budgeted collections and disbursement data are given below. All other expenses are paid in the month incurred except for administrative expenses, which include $1,000 of depreciation per month.

Other data.

1. Collections from customers: January $326,000; February $378,000.
2. Payments for purchases: January $110,000; February $135,000.
3. Other receipts: January: collection of December 31, 2013, notes receivable $15,000; February: proceeds from sale of securities $4,000.
4. Other disbursements: February $10,000 cash dividend.

The company's cash balance on January 1, 2014, is expected to be $46,000. The company wants to maintain a minimum cash balance of $40,000.

Instructions

Prepare a cash budget for January and February.

Jan. 31 adjusted cash bal. $43,000

P7-8A Heisey Company is a very profitable small business. It has not, however, given much consideration to internal control. For example, in an attempt to keep clerical and office expenses to a minimum, the company has combined the jobs of cashier and bookkeeper. As a result, Terry Baden handles all cash receipts, keeps the accounting records, and prepares the monthly bank reconciliations.

Prepare a comprehensive bank reconciliation with theft and internal control deficiencies.
(LO 2, 3, 4, 5), **E**

The balance per the bank statement on October 31, 2014, was $18,380. Outstanding checks were: No. 62 for $140.75, No. 183 for $180, No. 284 for $253.25, No. 862 for $190.71, No. 863 for $226.80, and No. 864 for $165.28. Included with the statement was a credit memorandum of $185 indicating the collection of a note receivable for Heisey Company by the bank on October 25. This memorandum has not been recorded by Heisey.

The company's ledger showed one Cash account with a balance of $21,877.72. The balance included undeposited cash on hand. Because of the lack of internal controls, Terry took for personal use all of the undeposited receipts in excess of $3,795.51. He then prepared the following bank reconciliation in an effort to conceal his theft of cash.

Cash balance per books, October 31		$21,877.72
Add: Outstanding checks		
No. 862	$190.71	
No. 863	226.80	
No. 864	165.28	482.79
		22,360.51
Less: Undeposited receipts		3,795.51
Unadjusted balance per bank, October 31		18,565.00
Less: Bank credit memorandum		185.00
Cash balance per bank statement, October 31		$18,380.00

Instructions

(a) Adjusted cash bal. $21,018.72

(a) Prepare a correct bank reconciliation. (*Hint:* Deduct the amount of the theft from the adjusted balance per books.)

(b) Indicate the three ways that Terry attempted to conceal the theft and the dollar amount involved in each method.

(c) What principles of internal control were violated in this case?

Problems: Set B

Identify internal control weaknesses for cash receipts.
(LO 2, 3), C

P7-1B The Soccer Club decided to sell coupon books as a fund-raising activity. The books allow users to enjoy restaurants, entertainment, and services such as oil changes, at substantial discounts. The club bought 100 books for $16 each, and members will sell them for $20. About 20 members attended the last club meeting, and most took one or two books to sell. Since the club had already paid for the books and didn't have other immediate cash needs, members do not have to pay for the books until they sell them.

Extra books are stored on a book shelf in the club's on-campus office. The office is in a great location with plenty of student traffic. It is shared with the Marketing and Information Systems clubs. Each club has four sets of keys that are used by its officers and members.

As students sell books, they bring the cash or checks to the club's office. Students with unusual class schedules who arrive when the office is locked can put payments under the door. Payments are stored in a desk drawer until the treasurer has time to make a bank deposit. Students can pick up more books to sell as needed.

Instructions

(a) Indicate the weaknesses in internal accounting control in the club's fund-raising plan.

(b) Indicate improvements in internal control procedures for the club's fund-raising plan.

Identify internal control weaknesses in cash receipts and cash disbursements.
(LO 2, 3, 4), C

P7-2B Tom Hall has worked for Dr. Johnson for several years. Tom demonstrates a loyalty that is rare among employees. He is always willing to "cover" for other employees and hasn't taken a vacation in three years.

One of Tom's primary duties at the dental office is to open the mail, list checks received, and prepare the bank deposit form.

He also collects cash from patients at the cashier window as patients leave. At times, it is so hectic that Tom doesn't bother to give patients a receipt for the cash paid on their accounts. He assures them he will see to it that they receive the proper credit. He is so well known by most patients that no one has ever complained.

When traffic is slow in the office, Tom offers to help another employee, Sue, post the payments to patients' accounts receivable. Dr. Johnson installed a computerized accounting program that requires a user ID and password to log in, but Tom and Sue have found that it is more efficient to just leave the computer on and the receivables file open all the time, and minimize the file when it is not in use.

Instructions
Identify the principles of internal control that may be violated in this situation.

P7-3B   On March 31, 2014, Taggert Company had a cash balance per books of $5,174.20. The statement from Western Bank on that date showed a balance of $6,041.40. A comparison of the bank statement with the cash account revealed the following facts.

Prepare a bank reconciliation and adjusting entries.
(LO 5), **AP**

1. The bank service charge for March was $28.
2. The bank collected a note receivable of $2,000 for Taggert Company on March 15, plus $115 of interest. The bank made a $20 charge for the collection. Taggert has not accrued any interest on the note.
3. The March 31 receipts of $1,481.60 were not included in the bank deposits for March. These receipts were deposited by the company in a night deposit vault on March 31.
4. Company check No. 1245 issued to T. Gilroy, a creditor, for $672 that cleared the bank in March was incorrectly entered in the cash payments journal on March 8 for $627.
5. Checks outstanding on March 31 totaled $1,360.00.
6. On March 31 the bank statement showed an NSF charge of $1,033.20 for a check received by the company from R. Fross, a customer, on account.

Instructions
(a) Prepare the bank reconciliation as of March 31.
(b) Prepare the necessary adjusting entries at March 31.

(a) Adjusted cash bal.   *$6,163*

P7-4B   The bank portion of the bank reconciliation for Triad Imports, Inc. at July 31, 2014, is shown below.

Prepare a bank reconciliation and adjusting entries from detailed data.
(LO 5), **AP**

TRIAD IMPORTS, INC.
Bank Reconciliation
July 31, 2014

Cash balance per bank		$ 9,596
Add: Deposits in transit		930
		$10,526

Less: Outstanding checks

Check Number	Check Amount	
3151	$ 290	
3170	812	
3171	1,538	
3172	1,000	
3174	1,172	4,812
Adjusted cash balance per bank		$ 5,714

The adjusted cash balance per bank agreed with the cash balance per books at July 31. The August bank statement showed the following checks and deposits.

Bank Statement

Checks			Deposits	
Date	**Number**	**Amount**	**Date**	**Amount**
8-1	3170	$ 812	8-1	$ 930
8-2	3171	1,538	8-4	1,325
8-5	3174	1,172	8-8	1,152
8-4	3175	802	8-13	1,104
8-8	3176	132	8-18	1,587
8-10	3177	737	8-21	1,159
8-15	3179	1,325	8-25	1,054
8-18	3180	900	8-28	1,830
8-27	3181	596	8-30	1,067
8-30	3183	93	Total	$11,208
8-29	3187	734		
	Total	$8,841		

The cash records per books for August showed the following.

Cash Payments Journal

Date	Number	Amount	Date	Number	Amount
8-1	3175	$ 802	8-20	3183	$ 93
8-2	3176	132	8-22	3184	760
8-2	3177	737	8-23	3185	1,038
8-4	3178	1,598	8-24	3186	455
8-8	3179	1,325	8-29	3187	734
8-10	3180	900	8-30	3188	273
8-15	3181	569	Total		$10,924
8-18	3182	$1,508			

Cash Receipts Journal

Date	Amount
8-3	$ 1,325
8-7	1,152
8-12	1,014
8-17	1,587
8-20	1,159
8-24	1,054
8-27	1,830
8-29	1,067
8-30	500
Total	$10,668

The bank statement contained two bank memoranda:

1. A credit of $1,670 for the collection of a $1,600 note for Triad Imports plus interest of $80 and less a collection fee of $10. Triad Imports has not accrued any interest on the note.
2. A debit for the printing of additional company checks $70.

At August 31, the cash balance per books was $5,478, and the cash balance per bank statement was $13,563. The bank did not make any errors, but **Triad Imports, Inc. made two errors.**

Instructions

(a) Adjusted cash bal. $7,141

(a) Using the four steps in the reconciliation procedure described in the textbook, prepare a bank reconciliation at August 31, 2014.
(b) Prepare the adjusting entries based on the reconciliation. (*Note:* The correction of any errors pertaining to recording checks should be made to Accounts Payable. The correction of any errors relating to recording cash receipts should be made to Accounts Receivable.)

Prepare a bank reconciliation and adjusting entries.
(LO 5), **AP**

P7-5B Bug Busters Company performs insect extermination services. On October 31, 2014, the company's cash account per its general ledger showed a balance of $4,632.

The bank statement from Central Bank on that date showed the following balance.

CENTRAL BANK

Checks and Debits	Deposits and Credits	Daily Balance
XXX	XXX	10-31 4,070

A comparison of the details on the bank statement with the details in the cash account revealed the following facts.

1. The statement included a debit memo of $50 for the printing of additional company checks.

2. Cash sales of $342 on October 6 were deposited in the bank. The cash receipts journal entry and the deposit slip were incorrectly made for $372. The bank credited Bug Busters Company for the correct amount.

3. Outstanding checks at October 31 totaled $1,250, and deposits in transit were $2,390.

4. On October 13, the company issued check No. 4263 for $196 to T. Grey, on account. The check, which cleared the bank in May, was incorrectly journalized and posted by Bug Busters Company for $169.

5. A $1,000 note receivable was collected by the bank for Bug Busters Company on October 31 plus $50 interest. The bank charged a collection fee of $15. No interest has been accrued on the note.

6. Included with the canceled checks was a check issued by Fig Leaf Company for $120 that was incorrectly charged to Bug Busters Company by the bank.

7. On October 31, the bank statement showed an NSF charge of $230 for a check issued by Jon Simpson, a customer, to Bug Busters Company on account.

Instructions

(a) Prepare the bank reconciliation at October 31, 2014.

(b) Prepare the necessary adjusting entries for Bug Busters Company at October 31, 2014.

(a) Adjusted cash bal. $5,330

P7-6B   You are provided with the following information taken from Items Inc.'s May 31, 2014, balance sheet.

Prepare a cash budget.

(LO 8), **AP**

Cash	$ 19,000
Accounts receivable	47,600
Inventory	21,000
Property, plant, and equipment, net of depreciation	70,400
Accounts payable	18,200
Common stock	110,000
Retained earnings	21,800

Additional information concerning Items Inc. is as follows.

1. Gross profit is 40% of sales.
2. Actual and budgeted sales data:

May (actual)	$68,000
June (budgeted)	60,000

3. Sales are both cash and credit. Cash collections expected in June are:

May	$47,600	(70% of $68,000)
June	18,000	(30% of $60,000)
	$65,600	

4. Half of a month's purchases are paid for in the month of purchase and half in the following month. Cash disbursements expected in June are:

Purchases May	$18,200
Purchases June	27,500
	$45,700

5. Cash operating costs are anticipated to be $21,300 for the month of June.
6. Equipment costing $6,000 will be purchased for cash in June.
7. The company wishes to maintain a minimum cash balance of $11,000. An open line of credit is available at the bank. All borrowing is done at the beginning of the month, and all repayments are made at the end of the month. The interest rate is 9% per year, and interest expense is accrued at the end of the month and paid in the following month.

Instructions

Prepare a cash budget for the month of June. Determine how much cash Items Inc. must borrow, or can repay, in June.

Prepare a cash budget.

P7-7B   Noble Corporation prepares monthly cash budgets. Relevant data from operating budgets for 2014 are shown on page 388.

(LO 8), **AP**

	January	February
Sales	$260,000	$318,000
Purchases	112,000	120,000
Salaries	72,000	78,000
Administrative expenses	58,000	60,000
Selling expenses	30,000	36,000

All sales and purchases are on account. Budgeted collections and disbursement data are given below. All other expenses are paid in the month incurred except for administrative expenses, which include $2,000 of depreciation per month.

Other data:
1. Collections from customers: January $279,500; February $298,000.
2. Payment for purchases: January $106,000; February $116,000.
3. Other receipts—January: collection of December 31, 2013, interest receivable $7,500; February: proceeds from sale of securities $8,000
4. Other disbursements—January: pay $35,000 note payable due January 1, 2014; February: pay $5,000 cash dividend
5. The company's cash balance on January 1, 2014 is expected to be $52,000. The company wants to maintain a minimum cash balance of $40,000.

Instructions

Jan. 31 adjusted cash bal. $40,000

Prepare a cash budget for January and February.

Prepare a comprehensive bank reconciliation with theft and internal control deficiencies.

(LO 2, 3, 4, 5), E

P7-8B   Elite Service Company is a very profitable small business. It has not, however, given much consideration to internal control. For example, in an attempt to keep clerical and office expenses to a minimum, the company has combined the jobs of cashier and bookkeeper. As a result, Steve Evans handles all cash receipts, keeps the accounting records, and prepares the monthly bank reconciliations.

The balance per the bank statement on March 31, 2014, was $5,931.51. Outstanding checks were: No. 206 for $358.53, No. 441 for $292, No. 590 for $283.00, No. 781 for $286.00, No. 782 for $319.47, and No. 783 for $303.14. Included with the statement was a credit memorandum of $175 indicating the collection of a note receivable for Elite Service Company by the bank on March 21. This memorandum has not been recorded by Elite Service.

The company's ledger showed one cash account with a balance of $6,889.53. The balance included undeposited cash on hand. Because of the lack of internal controls, Steve took for personal use all of the undeposited receipts in excess of $1,591.63. He then prepared the following bank reconciliation in an effort to conceal his theft of cash.

Cash balance per books, March 31		$6,889.53
Add: Outstanding checks		
No. 781	$286.00	
No. 782	319.47	
No. 783	303.14	808.61
		7,698.14
Less: Undeposited receipts		1,591.63
Unadjusted balance per bank, March 31		6,106.51
Less: Bank credit memorandum		175.00
Cash balance per bank statement, March 31		$5,931.51

Instructions

(a) Adjusted cash bal. $5,681.00

(a) Prepare a correct bank reconciliation. (*Hint:* Deduct the amount of the theft from the adjusted balance per books.)
(b) Indicate the three ways that Steve attempted to conceal the theft and the dollar amount involved in each method.
(c) What principles of internal control were violated in this case?

Problems: Set C

Visit the book's companion website, at **www.wiley.com/college/kimmel**, and choose the Student Companion site to access Problem Set C.

Comprehensive Problem

CP7   On December 1, 2014, Havenhill Company had the following account balances.

	Debit		**Credit**
Cash	$18,200	Accumulated Depreciation—	
Notes Receivable	2,000	Equipment	$ 3,000
Accounts Receivable	7,500	Accounts Payable	6,100
Inventory	16,000	Common Stock	50,000
Prepaid Insurance	1,600	Retained Earnings	14,200
Equipment	28,000		$73,300
	$73,300		

During December, the company completed the following transactions.

Dec. 7   Received $3,600 cash from customers in payment of account (no discount allowed).

12   Purchased merchandise on account from Brown Co. $12,000, terms 1/10, n/30.

17   Sold merchandise on account $16,000, terms 2/10, n/30. The cost of the merchandise sold was $10,000.

19   Paid salaries $2,200.

22   Paid Brown Co. in full, less discount.

26   Received collections in full, less discounts, from customers billed on December 17.

31   Received $2,700 cash from customers in payment of account (no discount allowed).

Adjustment data:

1. Depreciation $200 per month.
2. Insurance expired $400.
3. Income tax expense was $425. It was unpaid at December 31.

Instructions

(a) Journalize the December transactions. (Assume a perpetual inventory system.)

(b) Enter the December 1 balances in the ledger T-accounts and post the December transactions. Use Cost of Goods Sold, Depreciation Expense, Insurance Expense, Salaries and Wages Expense, Sales Revenue, Sales Discounts, Income Taxes Payable, and Income Tax Expense.

(c) The statement from Jackson County Bank on December 31 showed a balance of $25,930. A comparison of the bank statement with the Cash account revealed the following facts.

1. The bank collected a note receivable of $2,000 for Havenhill Company on December 15.
2. The December 31 receipts were deposited in a night deposit vault on December 31. These deposits were recorded by the bank in January.
3. Checks outstanding on December 31 totaled $1,210.
4. On December 31, the bank statement showed a NSF charge of $680 for a check received by the company from L. Menke, a customer, on account.

Prepare a bank reconciliation as of December 31 based on the available information. (*Hint:* The cash balance per books is $26,100. This can be proven by finding the balance in the Cash account from parts (a) and (b).)

(d) Journalize the adjusting entries resulting from the bank reconciliation and adjustment data.

(e) Post the adjusting entries to the ledger T-accounts.

(f) Prepare an adjusted trial balance.

(g) Prepare an income statement for December and a classified balance sheet at December 31.

(f) Totals	$89,500
(g) Net income	$ 2,455
Total assets	$73,180

Continuing Cookie Chronicle

(*Note:* This is a continuation of the Cookie Chronicle from Chapters 1 through 6.)

CCC7 Part 1 Natalie is struggling to keep up with the recording of her accounting transactions. She is spending a lot of time marketing and selling mixers and giving her cookie classes. Her friend John is an accounting student who runs his own accounting service. He has asked Natalie if she would like to have him do her accounting. John and Natalie meet and discuss her business.

Part 2 Natalie decides that she cannot afford to hire John to do her accounting. One way that she can ensure that her Cash account does not have any errors and is accurate and up-to-date is to prepare a bank reconciliation at the end of each month. Natalie would like you to help her.

Go to the book's companion website, at **www.wiley.com/college/kimmel**, to see the completion of this problem.

Broadening Your Perspective

Financial Reporting and Analysis

FINANCIAL REPORTING PROBLEM: *Tootsie Roll Industries, Inc.*

BYP7-1 The financial statements of Tootsie Roll are presented in Appendix A of this book, together with an auditor's report—Report of Independent Auditors.

Instructions
Using the financial statements and reports, answer these questions about Tootsie Roll's internal controls and cash.
(a) What comments, if any, are made about cash in the "Report of Independent Registered Public Accounting Firm"?
(b) What data about cash and cash equivalents are shown in the consolidated balance sheet (statement of financial position)?
(c) What activities are identified in the consolidated statement of cash flows as being responsible for the changes in cash during 2011?
(d) How are cash equivalents defined in the Notes to Consolidated Financial Statements?
(e) Read the section of the report titled "Management's Report on Internal Control Over Financial Reporting." Summarize the statements made in that section of the report.

COMPARATIVE ANALYSIS PROBLEM: *Tootsie Roll vs. Hershey*

BYP7-2 The financial statements of The Hershey Company are presented in Appendix B, following the financial statements for Tootsie Roll in Appendix A.

Instructions
Answer the following questions for each company.
(a) What is the balance in cash and cash equivalents at December 31, 2011?
(b) What percentage of total assets does cash represent for each company over the last two years? Has it changed significantly for either company?
(c) How much cash was provided by operating activities during 2011?
(d) Comment on your findings in parts (a) through (c).

RESEARCH CASE

BYP7-3 The website **www.cpa2biz.com** has an article dated February 4, 2010, by Mary Schaeffer entitled "Emerging Issues: Demise of Paper Checks."

Instructions
Go to the website and do a search on the article title. Read the article and answer the following questions.
(a) How many different forms of payment types does the article list? What are the payment types?

(b) What problems does the shift away from paper checks to alternative payment options present for companies?

(c) What five controls does the article suggest incorporating, to decrease problems associated with multiple payment options?

INTERPRETING FINANCIAL STATEMENTS

BYP7-4 The international accounting firm Ernst & Young performed a global survey on fraud. The results of that survey are summarized in a report titled "Driving Ethical Growth—New Markets, New Challenges" (Ernst & Young, *11th Global Fraud Survey*). You can find this report by doing an Internet search on the title, or go to **http://www.ey.com/Publication/vwLUAssets/Driving_ethical_growth_-_new_markets,_new_challenges:_11th_Global_Fraud_Survey/$FILE/EY_11th_Global_Fraud_Survey.pdf**.

Instructions
Read the Executive Summary section, and then skim the remainder of the report to answer the following questions.

(a) What was the global percentage of companies that experienced fraud during the period covered by the survey, and what region of the world had the highest rate?

(b) What percentage of survey respondents performed a fraud risk assessment in the six months prior to the survey? What percentage of survey respondents have never performed a fraud risk assessment?

(c) What percentage of respondents thought members of the board of directors were either "very concerned" or "fairly concerned" about board members' personal legal liability resulting from fraud at their companies?

(d) What are the top three issues of concern to compliance officers according to the survey?

REAL-WORLD FOCUS

BYP7-5 The Financial Accounting Standards Board (FASB) is a private organization established to improve accounting standards and financial reporting. The FASB conducts extensive research before issuing a "Statement of Financial Accounting Standards," which represents an authoritative expression of generally accepted accounting principles.

Address: **www.fasb.org**, or go to **www.wiley.com/college/kimmel**

Steps
Choose **About FASB**.

Instructions
Answer the following questions.

(a) What is the mission of the FASB?

(b) How are topics added to the FASB technical agenda? (*Hint:* See Project Plans in Our Rules of Procedure.)

(c) What characteristics make the FASB's procedures an "open" decision-making process? (*Hint:* See Due Process in Our Rules of Procedure.)

BYP7-6 The Public Company Accounting Oversight Board (PCAOB) was created as a result of the Sarbanes-Oxley Act. It has oversight and enforcement responsibilities over accounting firms in the United States.

Address: **http://www.pcaobus.org/**, or go to **www.wiley.com/college/kimmel**

Instructions
Answer the following questions.

(a) What is the mission of the PCAOB?

(b) Briefly summarize its responsibilities related to inspections.

(c) Briefly summarize its responsibilities related to enforcement.

Critical Thinking

DECISION-MAKING ACROSS THE ORGANIZATION

BYP7-7 Alternative Distributor Corp., a distributor of groceries and related products, is headquartered in Medford, Massachusetts.

During a recent audit, Alternative Distributor Corp. was advised that existing internal controls necessary for the company to develop reliable financial statements were inadequate. The audit report stated that the current system of accounting for sales, receivables, and cash receipts constituted a material weakness. Among other items, the report focused on nontimely deposit of cash receipts, exposing Alternative Distributor to potential loss or misappropriation, excessive past due accounts receivable due to lack of collection efforts, disregard of advantages offered by vendors for prompt payment of invoices, absence of appropriate segregation of duties by personnel consistent with appropriate control objectives, inadequate procedures for applying accounting principles, lack of qualified management personnel, lack of supervision by an outside board of directors, and overall poor record-keeping.

Instructions
(a) Identify the principles of internal control violated by Alternative Distributor Corporation.
(b) Explain why managers of various functional areas in the company should be concerned about internal controls.

COMMUNICATION ACTIVITY

BYP7-8 As a new auditor for the CPA firm of Good and Rich, you have been assigned to review the internal controls over mail cash receipts of Lyman Company. Your review reveals that checks are promptly endorsed "For Deposit Only," but no list of the checks is prepared by the person opening the mail. The mail is opened either by the cashier or by the employee who maintains the accounts receivable records. Mail receipts are deposited in the bank weekly by the cashier.

Instructions
Write a letter to D. A. Flynn, owner of the Lyman Company, explaining the weaknesses in internal control and your recommendations for improving the system.

ETHICS CASES

BYP7-9 Banks charge fees for "bounced" checks—that is, checks that exceed the balance in the account. It has been estimated that processing bounced checks costs a bank roughly $1.50 per check. Thus, the profit margin on bounced checks is very high. Recognizing this, some banks have started to process checks from largest to smallest. By doing this, they maximize the number of checks that bounce if a customer overdraws an account. For example, NationsBank (now Bank of America) projected a $14 million increase in fee revenue as a result of processing largest checks first. In response to criticism, banks have responded that their customers prefer to have large checks processed first, because those tend to be the most important. At the other extreme, some banks will cover their customers' bounced checks, effectively extending them an interest-free loan while their account is overdrawn.

Instructions
Answer each of the following questions.
(a) Richard Coulsen had a balance of $1,500 in his checking account at First National Bank on a day when the bank received the following five checks for processing against his account.

Check Number	Amount	Check Number	Amount
3150	$ 35	3165	$ 550
3162	400	3166	1,510
		3169	180

Assuming a $30 fee assessed by the bank for each bounced check, how much fee revenue would the bank generate if it processed checks (1) from largest to smallest, (2) from smallest to largest, and (3) in order of check number?
(b) Do you think that processing checks from largest to smallest is an ethical business practice?
(c) In addition to ethical issues, what other issues must a bank consider in deciding whether to process checks from largest to smallest?
(d) If you were managing a bank, what policy would you adopt on bounced checks?

BYP7-10 The National Fraud Information Center (NFIC) was originally established in 1992 by the National Consumers League, the oldest nonprofit consumer organization in the United States, to fight the growing menace of telemarketing fraud by improving prevention and enforcement. It maintains a website that provides many useful fraud-related resources.

Address: **www.fraud.org/scamsagainstbusinesses/bizscams.htm** or go to **www.wiley.com/college/kimmel**

Instructions
Go to the site and find an item of interest to you. Write a short summary of your findings.

ALL ABOUT YOU

BYP7-11 The print and electronic media are full of stories about potential security risks that can arise from your personal computer. It is important to keep in mind, however, that there are also many ways that your identity can be stolen other than from your computer. The federal government provides many resources to help protect you from identity thieves.

Instructions
Go to **http://onguardonline.gov/idtheft.html**, and click Games, then click ID Theft Faceoff. Complete the quiz provided there.

FASB CODIFICATION ACTIVITY

BYP7-12 If your school has a subscription to the FASB Codification, go to **http://aaahq.org/ascLogin.cfm** to log in and prepare responses to the following.
(a) How is cash defined in the Codification?
(b) How are cash equivalents defined in the Codification?
(c) What are the disclosure requirements related to cash and cash equivalents?

Answers to Insight and Accounting Across the Organization Questions

p. 338 And the Controls Are . . . Q: Why is sustainability information important to investors? **A:** Investors, customers, suppliers, and employees want more information about companies' long-term impact on society. There is a growing awareness that sustainability issues can affect a company's financial performance. Proper reporting on sustainability issues develops a solid reputation for transparency and provides confidence to shareholders.

p. 345 SOX Boosts the Role of Human Resources Q: Why would unsupervised employees or employees who report to each other represent potential internal control threats? **A:** An unsupervised employee may have a fraudulent job (or may even be a fictitious person)—e.g., a person drawing a paycheck without working. Or, if two employees supervise each other, there is no real separation of duties, and they can conspire to defraud the company.

p. 351 How Employees Steal Q: How can companies reduce the likelihood of fraudulent disbursements? **A:** To reduce the occurrence of fraudulent disbursements, a company should follow the procedures discussed in this chapter. These include having only designated personnel sign checks; having different personnel approve payments and make payments; ensuring that check-signers do not record disbursements; using prenumbered checks and matching each check to an approved invoice; storing blank checks securely; reconciling the bank statement; and stamping invoices paid.

p. 358 Madoff's Ponzi Scheme Q: How was Madoff able to conceal such a giant fraud? **A:** Madoff fabricated false investment statements that were provided to investors. In addition, his auditor never verified these investment statements even though the auditor gave him an unqualified opinion each year.

Answers to Self-Test Questions

1. c **2.** a **3.** c **4.** b **5.** a **6.** b **7.** d **8.** a **9.** d **10.** c **11.** c **12.** c **13.** b **14.** d
***15.** a ($100 − ($94 + $2))

A Look at IFRS

Fraud can occur anywhere. And because the three main factors that contribute to fraud are universal in nature, the principles of internal control activities are used globally by companies. While Sarbanes-Oxley (SOX) does not apply to international companies, most large international companies have internal controls similar to those indicated in the chapter. IFRS and GAAP are very similar in accounting for cash. *IAS No. 1 (revised),* "Presentation of Financial Statements," is the only standard that discusses issues specifically related to cash.

LEARNING OBJECTIVE **10**
Compare the accounting procedures for fraud, internal control, and cash under GAAP and IFRS.

KEY POINTS

- The fraud triangle discussed in this chapter is applicable to all international companies. Some of the major frauds on an international basis are Parmalat (Italy), Royal Ahold (the Netherlands), and Satyam Computer Services (India).

- Rising economic crime poses a growing threat to companies, with nearly half of all organizations worldwide being victims of fraud in a recent two-year period (*PricewaterhouseCoopers' Global Economic Crime Survey*, 2005). Specifically, 44% of Romanian companies surveyed experienced fraud in the past two years.

- Globally, the number of companies reporting fraud increased from 37% to 45% since 2003, a 22% increase. The cost to companies was an average $1.7 million in losses from "tangible frauds," that is, those that result in an immediate and direct financial loss. These include asset misappropriation, false pretenses, and counterfeiting (*PricewaterhouseCoopers' Global Economic Crime Survey*, 2005).

- Accounting scandals both in the United States and internationally have re-ignited the debate over the relative merits of GAAP, which takes a "rules-based" approach to accounting, versus IFRS, which takes a "principles-based" approach. The FASB announced that it intends to introduce more principles-based standards.

- On a lighter note, at one time the Ig Nobel Prize in Economics went to the CEOs of those companies involved in the corporate accounting scandals of that year for "adapting the mathematical concept of imaginary numbers for use in the business world." A parody of the Nobel Prizes, the Ig Nobel Prizes (read Ignoble, as not noble) are given each year in early October for 10 achievements that "first make people laugh, and then make them think." Organized by the scientific humor magazine *Annals of Improbable Research* (*AIR*), they are presented by a group that includes genuine Nobel laureates at a ceremony at Harvard University's Sanders Theater. (See **en.wikipedia.org/wiki/Ig_Nobel_Prize**.)

- Internal controls are a system of checks and balances designed to prevent and detect fraud and errors. While most companies have these systems in place, many have never completely documented them, nor had an independent auditor attest to their effectiveness. Both of these actions are required under SOX.

- Companies find that internal control review is a costly process but badly needed. One study estimates the cost of SOX compliance for U.S. companies at over $35 billion, with audit fees doubling in the first year of compliance. At the same time, examination of internal controls indicates lingering problems in the way companies operate. One study of first compliance with the internal-control testing provisions documented material weaknesses for about 13% of companies reporting in a two-year period (*PricewaterhouseCoopers' Global Economic Crime Survey*, 2005).

- The SOX internal control standards apply only to companies listed on U.S. exchanges. There is continuing debate over whether foreign issuers should have to comply with this extra layer of regulation.

- The accounting and internal control procedures related to cash are essentially the same under both IFRS and this textbook. In addition, the definition used for cash equivalents is the same.

- Most companies report cash and cash equivalents together under IFRS, as shown in this textbook. In addition, IFRS follows the same accounting policies related to the reporting of restricted cash.

- IFRS defines cash and cash equivalents as follows.

  - **Cash** is comprised of cash on hand and demand deposits.

  - **Cash equivalents** are short-term, highly liquid investments that are readily convertible to known amounts of cash and which are subject to an insignificant risk of changes in value.

- Under IFRS, cash and cash equivalents are often shown last in the statement of financial position.

LOOKING TO THE FUTURE

Ethics has become a very important aspect of reporting. Different cultures have different perspectives on bribery and other questionable activities, and consequently penalties for engaging in such activities vary considerably across countries.

High-quality international accounting requires both high-quality accounting standards and high-quality auditing. Similar to the convergence of GAAP and IFRS, there is movement to improve international auditing standards. The International Auditing and Assurance Standards Board (IAASB) functions as an independent standard-setting body. It works to establish high-quality auditing and assurance and quality-control standards throughout the world. Whether the IAASB adopts internal control provisions similar to those in SOX remains to be seen. You can follow developments in the international audit arena at **http://www.ifac.org/iaasb/**.

Under proposed new standards for financial statements, companies would not be allowed to combine cash equivalents with cash.

IFRS PRACTICE

IFRS SELF-TEST QUESTIONS

1. Non-U.S companies that follow IFRS:
    (a) do not normally use the principles of internal control activities described in this textbook.
    (b) often offset cash with accounts payable on the statement of financial position.
    (c) are not required to follow SOX.
    (d) None of the above.
2. Which of the following is the correct reporting under IFRS for cash?
    (a) Cash cannot be combined with cash equivalents.
    (b) Restricted cash funds may be reported as a current or non-current asset depending on the circumstances.
    (c) Restricted cash funds cannot be reported as a current asset.
    (d) Cash on hand is not reported on the statement of financial position as Cash.
3. The Sarbanes-Oxley Act applies to:
    (a) all U.S. companies listed on U.S. exchanges.
    (b) all companies that list shares on any securities exchange in any country.
    (c) all European companies listed on European exchanges.
    (d) Both (a) and (c).
4. High-quality international accounting requires both high-quality accounting standards and:
    (a) a reconsideration of SOX to make it less onerous.
    (b) high-quality auditing standards.
    (c) government intervention to ensure that the public interest is protected.
    (d) the development of new principles of internal control activities.
5. Cash equivalents under IFRS:
    (a) are significantly different than the cash equivalents discussed in the textbook.
    (b) are generally disclosed separately from cash.
    (c) may be required to be reported separately from cash in the future.
    (d) None of the above.

IFRS CONCEPTS AND APPLICATION

IFRS7-1 Some people argue that the internal control requirements of the Sarbanes-Oxley Act (SOX) put U.S. companies at a competitive disadvantage to companies outside the United States. Discuss the competitive implications (both pros and cons) of SOX.

IFRS7-2 State whether each of the following is true or false. For those that are false, explain why.
    (a) A proposed new financial accounting standard would not allow cash equivalents to be reported in combination with cash.
    (b) Perspectives on bribery and penalties for engaging in bribery are the same across all countries.
    (c) Cash equivalents are comprised of cash on hand and demand deposits.
    (d) SOX was created by the International Accounting Standards Board.

INTERNATIONAL FINANCIAL REPORTING PROBLEM: *Zetar plc*

IFRS7-3 The financial statements of Zetar plc are presented in Appendix C. The company's complete annual report, including the notes to its financial statements, is available in the Investors section at **www.zetarplc.com**.

Instructions
Use the company's annual report to answer the following questions.
    (a) Which committee of the board of directors is responsible for considering management's reports on internal control?
    (b) What are the company's key control procedures?
    (c) Does the company have an internal audit department?
    (d) In what section or sections does Zetar report its bank overdrafts?

Answers to IFRS Self-Test Questions

1. c **2.** b **3.** a **4.** b **5.** c

Remember to go back to The Navigator box on the chapter opening page and check off your completed work.

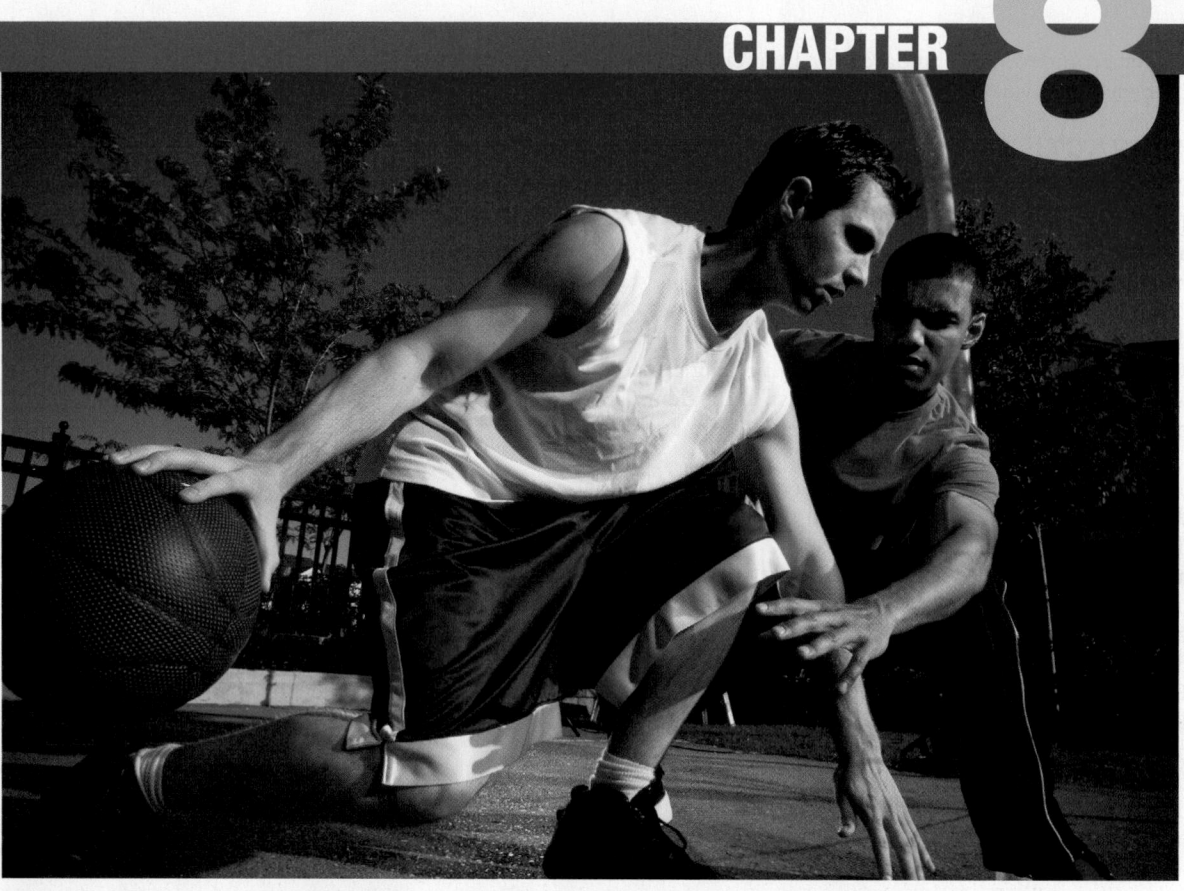

CHAPTER 8

© Arthur Kwiatkowski/iStockphoto

✔ The Navigator

- Scan Learning Objectives
- Read Feature Story
- Scan Preview
- Read Text and Answer **Do it!**
  ○ p. 407 ○ p. 411 ○ p. 417 ○ p. 420
- Work Using the Decision Toolkit
- Review Summary of Learning Objectives
- Work Comprehensive **Do it!** p. 424
- Answer Self-Test Questions
- Complete Assignments
- Go to WileyPLUS for practice and tutorials

🌐 Read A Look at IFRS p. 444

REPORTING AND ANALYZING RECEIVABLES

LEARNING OBJECTIVES

After studying this chapter, you should be able to:

1 Identify the different types of receivables.

2 Explain how accounts receivable are recognized in the accounts.

3 Describe the methods used to account for bad debts.

4 Compute the interest on notes receivable.

5 Describe the entries to record the disposition of notes receivable.

6 Explain the statement presentation of receivables.

7 Describe the principles of sound accounts receivable management.

8 Identify ratios to analyze a company's receivables.

9 Describe methods to accelerate the receipt of cash from receivables.

✔ The Navigator

What major U.S corporation got its start 38 years ago with a waffle iron? *Hint:* It doesn't sell food. *Another hint:* Swoosh. *Another hint:* "Just do it." That's right, Nike. In 1971, Nike co-founder Bill Bowerman put a piece of rubber into a kitchen waffle iron, and the trademark waffle sole was born. It seems fair to say that at Nike, "They don't make 'em like they used to."

Nike, was co-founded by Bowerman and Phil Knight, a member of Bowerman's University of Oregon track team. Each began in the shoe business independently during the early 1960s. Bowerman got his start by making hand-crafted running shoes for his University of Oregon track team. Knight, after completing graduate school, started a small business importing low-cost, high-quality shoes from Japan. In 1964, the two joined forces, each contributing $500, and formed Blue Ribbon Sports, a partnership that marketed Japanese shoes.

It wasn't until 1971 that the company began manufacturing its own line of shoes. With the new shoes came a new corporate name—Nike—the Greek goddess of victory. It is hard to imagine that the company that now boasts a stable full of world-class athletes as promoters at one time had part-time employees selling shoes out of car trunks at track meets on a cash-and-carry basis.

WHAT'S COOKING?

As the business grew, Nike sold its shoes to sporting good shops and department stores on a credit basis. This necessitated receivables management. Today, with sales of $20.8 billion and accounts receivable of $3.1 billion, managing accounts receivable is vitally important to Nike's success. If it makes a major mistake with its receivables, it will definitely affect the bottom line.

In recent years, Nike has expanded its product line to a diverse range of products, including performance equipment such as soccer balls and golf clubs. While this has increased sales revenue, it has also complicated Nike's receivables management efforts. Now, instead of selling shoes at a limited number of retail outlets, it sells its vast number of products to a diverse array of stores, large and small. For example, Nike golf clubs are sold at local country clubs and golf shops across the country, while soccer equipment can be sold directly to customers through Internet sales. This diversification of its customer list complicates matters because Nike has to approve each new store or customer for credit sales, monitor cash collections, and pursue slow-paying accounts. That's a lot of work. Maybe cash-and-carry wasn't so bad after all.

✔ The Navigator

INSIDE CHAPTER 8 . . .

In this chapter, we discuss some of the decisions related to reporting and analyzing receivables. As indicated in the Feature Story, receivables are a significant asset on the books of Nike. Receivables are important to companies in other industries as well because a larger portion of sales are made on credit in the United States. As a consequence, companies must pay close attention to their receivables balances and manage them carefully. In this chapter, we will look at the accounting and management of receivables at Nike and one of its competitors, Skechers USA.

The organization and content of the chapter are as follows.

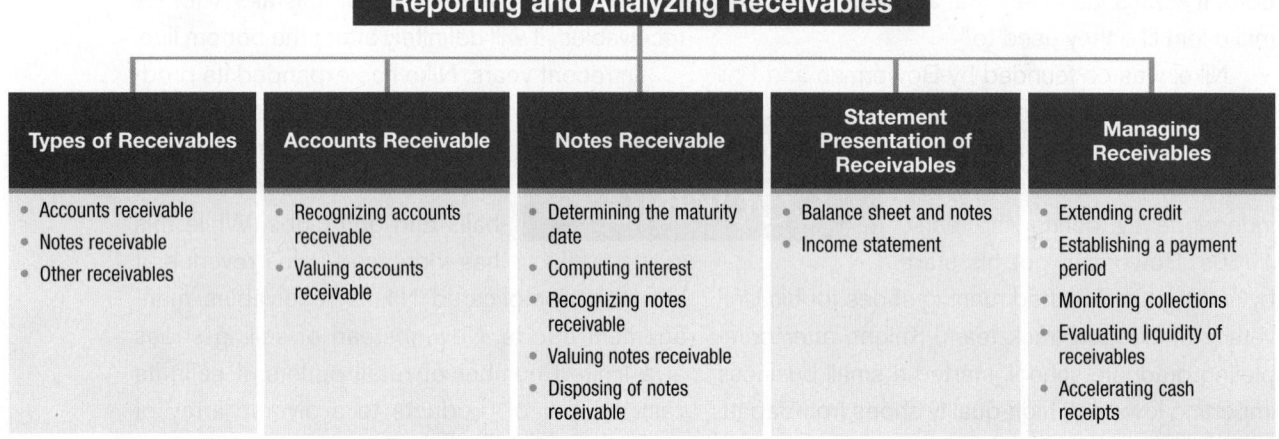

Reporting and Analyzing Receivables				
Types of Receivables	**Accounts Receivable**	**Notes Receivable**	**Statement Presentation of Receivables**	**Managing Receivables**
• Accounts receivable • Notes receivable • Other receivables	• Recognizing accounts receivable • Valuing accounts receivable	• Determining the maturity date • Computing interest • Recognizing notes receivable • Valuing notes receivable • Disposing of notes receivable	• Balance sheet and notes • Income statement	• Extending credit • Establishing a payment period • Monitoring collections • Evaluating liquidity of receivables • Accelerating cash receipts

✔ The Navigator

Types of Receivables

LEARNING OBJECTIVE 1

Identify the different types of receivables.

The term **receivables** refers to amounts due from individuals and companies. Receivables are claims that are expected to be collected in cash. The management of receivables is a very important activity for any company that sells goods or services on credit.

Receivables are important because they represent one of a company's most liquid assets. For many companies, receivables are also one of the largest assets. For example, receivables represent 20% of the assets of Nike. Illustration 8-1 lists receivables as a percentage of total assets for five other well-known companies in a recent year.

Illustration 8-1 Receivables as a percentage of assets

Company	Receivables as a Percentage of Total Assets
General Electric	52%
Ford Motor Company	42%
Minnesota Mining and Manufacturing Company (3M)	14%
DuPont Co.	17%
Intel Corporation	5%

The relative significance of a company's receivables as a percentage of its assets depends on various factors: its industry, the time of year, whether it extends long-term financing, and its credit policies. To reflect important differences among receivables, they are frequently classified as (1) accounts receivable, (2) notes receivable, and (3) other receivables.

Accounts receivable are amounts customers owe on account. They result from the sale of goods and services. Companies generally expect to collect accounts receivable within 30 to 60 days. They are usually the most significant type of claim held by a company.

Notes receivable are a written promise (as evidenced by a formal instrument) for amounts to be received. The note normally requires the collection of interest and extends for time periods of 60–90 days or longer. Notes and accounts receivable that result from sales transactions are often called trade receivables.

Other receivables include nontrade receivables such as interest receivable, loans to company officers, advances to employees, and income taxes refundable. These do not generally result from the operations of the business. Therefore, they are generally classified and reported as separate items in the balance sheet.

Ethics Note Companies report receivables from employees separately in the financial statements. The reason: Sometimes those assets are not the result of an "arm's-length" transaction.

Accounts Receivable

Two accounting issues associated with accounts receivable are:

1. **Recognizing** accounts receivable.
2. **Valuing** accounts receivable.

A third issue, accelerating cash receipts from receivables, is discussed later in the chapter.

LEARNING OBJECTIVE 2

Explain how accounts receivable are recognized in the accounts.

RECOGNIZING ACCOUNTS RECEIVABLE

Recognizing accounts receivable is relatively straightforward. A service organization records a receivable when it performs service on account. A merchandiser records accounts receivable at the point of sale of merchandise on account. When a merchandiser sells goods, it increases (debits) Accounts Receivable and increases (credits) Sales Revenue.

The seller may offer terms that encourage early payment by providing a discount. Sales returns also reduce receivables. The buyer might find some of the goods unacceptable and choose to return the unwanted goods.

To review, assume that Jordache Co. on July 1, 2014, sells merchandise on account to Polo Company for $1,000, terms 2/10, n/30. On July 5, Polo returns merchandise worth $100 to Jordache Co. On July 11, Jordache receives payment from Polo Company for the balance due. The journal entries to record these transactions on the books of Jordache Co. are as follows. **(Cost of goods sold entries are omitted.)**

July	1	Accounts Receivable—Polo Company	1,000	
		Sales Revenue		1,000
		(To record sales on account)		
July	5	Sales Returns and Allowances	100	
		Accounts Receivable—Polo Company		100
		(To record merchandise returned)		
July	11	Cash ($900 − $18)	882	
		Sales Discounts ($900 × .02)	18	
		Accounts Receivable—Polo Company		900
		(To record collection of accounts receivable)		

Helpful Hint These entries are the same as those described in Chapter 5. For simplicity, we have omitted inventory and cost of goods sold from this set of journal entries and from end-of-chapter material.

Some retailers issue their own credit cards. When you use a retailer's credit card (JCPenney, for example), the retailer charges interest on the balance due if not paid within a specified period (usually 25–30 days).

To illustrate, assume that you use your JCPenney Company credit card to purchase clothing with a sales price of $300 on June 1, 2014. JCPenney will increase (debit) Accounts Receivable for $300 and increase (credit) Sales Revenue for $300 (cost of goods sold entry omitted), as follows.

June 1	Accounts Receivable	300	
	Sales Revenue		300
	(To record sales on account)		

Assuming that you owe $300 at the end of the month and JCPenney charges 1.5% per month on the balance due, the adjusting entry that JCPenney makes to record interest revenue of $4.50 ($300 × 1.5%) on June 30 is as follows.

June 30	Accounts Receivable	4.50	
	Interest Revenue		4.50
	(To record interest on amount due)		

Interest revenue is often substantial for many retailers.

ANATOMY OF A FRAUD

Tasanee was the accounts receivable clerk for a large non-profit foundation that provided performance and exhibition space for the performing and visual arts. Her responsibilities included activities normally assigned to an accounts receivable clerk, such as recording revenues from various sources that included donations, facility rental fees, ticket revenue, and bar receipts. However, she was also responsible for handling all cash and checks from the time they were received until the time she deposited them, as well as preparing the bank reconciliation. Tasanee took advantage of her situation by falsifying bank deposits and bank reconciliations so that she could steal cash from the bar receipts. Since nobody else logged the donations or matched the donation receipts to pledges prior to Tasanee receiving them, she was able to offset the cash that was stolen against donations that she received but didn't record. Her crime was made easier by the fact that her boss, the company's controller, only did a very superficial review of the bank reconciliation and thus didn't notice that some numbers had been cut out from other documents and taped onto the bank reconciliation.

Total take: $1.5 million

THE MISSING CONTROLS

Segregation of duties. The foundation should not have allowed an accounts receivable clerk, whose job was to record receivables, to also handle cash, record cash, and make deposits, and especially prepare the bank reconciliation.

Independent internal verification. The controller was supposed to perform a thorough review of the bank reconciliation. Because he did not, he was terminated from his position.

Source: Adapted from Wells, *Fraud Casebook* (2007), pp. 183–194.

VALUING ACCOUNTS RECEIVABLE

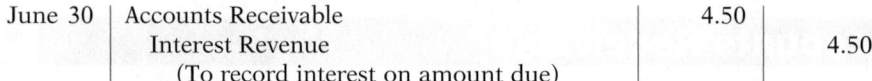

Once companies record receivables in the accounts, the next question is: How should they report receivables in the financial statements? Companies report accounts receivable on the balance sheet as an asset. Determining the **amount** to report is sometimes difficult because some receivables will become uncollectible.

Although each customer must satisfy the credit requirements of the seller before the credit sale is approved, inevitably some accounts receivable become uncollectible. For example, a corporate customer may not be able to pay because it experienced a sales decline due to an economic downturn. Similarly, individuals may be laid off from their jobs or be faced with unexpected hospital bills. The seller records these losses that result from extending credit as **Bad Debt Expense**. Such losses are a normal and necessary risk of doing business on a credit basis.

Recently, when U.S. home prices fell, home foreclosures rose, and the economy in general slowed, lenders experienced huge increases in their bad debt expense. For example, during a recent quarter Wachovia, a large U.S. bank now owned by Wells Fargo, increased bad debt expense from $108 million to $408 million. Similarly, American Express increased its bad debt expense by 70%.

Accounting uses two methods for uncollectible accounts: (1) the direct write-off method, and (2) the allowance method. We explain each of these methods in the following sections.

Alternative Terminology You will sometimes see *Bad Debt Expense* called *Uncollectible Accounts Expense.*

Direct Write-Off Method for Uncollectible Accounts

Under the **direct write-off method**, when a company determines receivables from a particular company to be uncollectible, it charges the loss to Bad Debt Expense. Assume, for example, that Warden Co. writes off M. E. Doran's $200 balance as uncollectible on December 12. Warden's entry is:

Dec. 12	Bad Debt Expense	200	
	Accounts Receivable—M. E. Doran		200
	(To record write-off of M. E. Doran account)		

A	=	L	+	SE
				−200 Exp
−200				

Cash Flows
no effect

Under this method, bad debt expense will show only **actual losses** from uncollectibles. The company reports accounts receivable at its gross amount without any adjustment for estimated losses for bad debts.

Use of the direct write-off method can reduce the usefulness of both the income statement and balance sheet. Consider the following example. In 2014 Quick Buck Computer Company decided it could increase its revenues by offering computers to college students without requiring any money down, and with no credit-approval process. It went on campuses across the country and sold one million computers at a selling price of $800 each. This promotion increased Quick Buck's revenues and receivables by $800,000,000. It was a huge success: The 2014 balance sheet and income statement looked wonderful. Unfortunately, during 2015, nearly 40% of the college student customers defaulted on their loans. The 2015 income statement and balance sheet looked terrible. Illustration 8-2 shows the effect of these events on the financial statements using the direct write-off method.

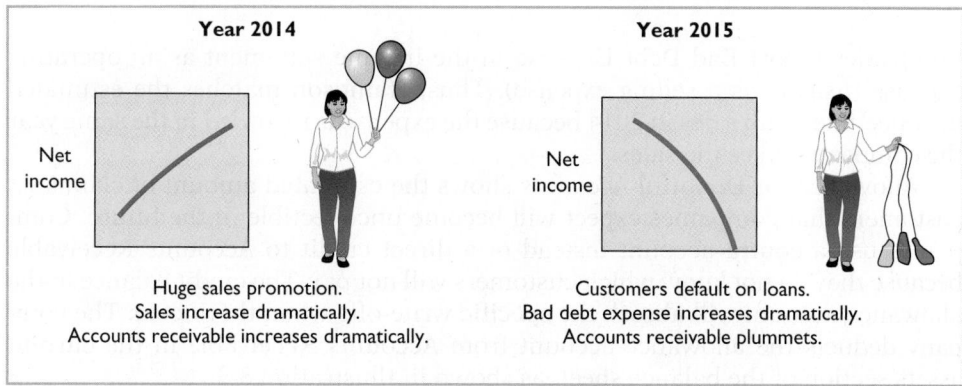

Year 2014

Net income

Huge sales promotion.
Sales increase dramatically.
Accounts receivable increases dramatically.

Year 2015

Net income

Customers default on loans.
Bad debt expense increases dramatically.
Accounts receivable plummets.

Illustration 8-2 Effects of direct write-off method

Under the direct write-off method, companies often record bad debt expense in a period different from the period in which they recorded the revenue. Thus, no attempt is made to match bad debt expense to sales revenues in the income statement. Nor does the company try to show accounts receivable in the balance sheet at the amount actually expected to be received. Consequently, unless a company expects bad debt losses to be insignificant, **the direct write-off method is not acceptable for financial reporting purposes.**

Allowance Method for Uncollectible Accounts

The allowance method of accounting for bad debts involves estimating uncollectible accounts at the end of each period. This provides better matching of expenses with revenues on the income statement. It also ensures that receivables are stated at their cash (net) realizable value on the balance sheet. Cash (net) realizable value is the net amount a company expects to receive in cash from receivables. It excludes amounts that the company estimates it will not collect. Estimated uncollectible receivables therefore reduce receivables on the balance sheet through use of the allowance method.

Helpful Hint In this context, *material* means significant or important to financial statement users.

Companies must use the allowance method for financial reporting purposes when bad debts are material in amount. It has three essential features:

1. Companies **estimate** uncollectible accounts receivable and **match them against revenues** in the same accounting period in which the revenues are recorded.

2. Companies record estimated uncollectibles as an increase (a debit) to Bad Debt Expense and an increase (a credit) to Allowance for Doubtful Accounts through an adjusting entry at the end of each period. Allowance for Doubtful Accounts is a contra account to Accounts Receivable.

3. Companies debit actual uncollectibles to Allowance for Doubtful Accounts and credit them to Accounts Receivable at the time the specific account is written off as uncollectible.

RECORDING ESTIMATED UNCOLLECTIBLES. To illustrate the allowance method, assume that Hampson Furniture has credit sales of $1,200,000 in 2014, of which $200,000 remains uncollected at December 31. The credit manager estimates that $12,000 of these sales will prove uncollectible. The adjusting entry to record the estimated uncollectibles increases (debits) Bad Debt Expense and increases (credits) Allowance for Doubtful Accounts, as follows.

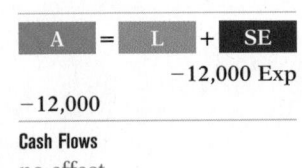

-12,000

Cash Flows
no effect

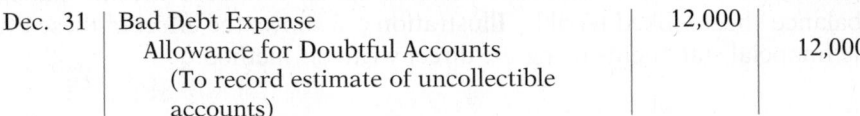

Dec. 31	Bad Debt Expense		12,000	
	Allowance for Doubtful Accounts			12,000
	(To record estimate of uncollectible accounts)			

Companies report Bad Debt Expense in the income statement as an operating expense (usually as a selling expense). Thus, Hampson matches the estimated uncollectibles with sales in 2014 because the expense is recorded in the same year the company makes the sales.

Allowance for Doubtful Accounts shows the estimated amount of claims on customers that companies expect will become uncollectible in the future. Companies use a contra account instead of a direct credit to Accounts Receivable because they do not know which customers will not pay. The credit balance in the allowance account will absorb the specific write-offs when they occur. The company deducts the allowance account from Accounts Receivable in the current assets section of the balance sheet, as shown in Illustration 8-3.

Illustration 8-3 Presentation of allowance for doubtful accounts

HAMPSON FURNITURE
Balance Sheet (partial)

Current assets		
Cash		$ 14,800
Accounts receivable	$200,000	
Less: Allowance for doubtful accounts	12,000	188,000
Inventory		310,000
Supplies		25,000
Total current assets		$537,800

The amount of $188,000 in Illustration 8-3 represents the expected **cash realizable value** of the accounts receivable at the statement date. **Companies do not close Allowance for Doubtful Accounts at the end of the fiscal year.**

RECORDING THE WRITE-OFF OF AN UNCOLLECTIBLE ACCOUNT. Various methods are used to collect past-due accounts. When a company exhausts all means of collecting a past-due account and collection appears unlikely, the company writes off the account. In the credit card industry, it is standard practice to write off accounts that are 210 days past due. To prevent premature or unauthorized write-offs, authorized management personnel should formally approve each write-off. **To maintain segregation of duties, the employee authorized to write off accounts should not have daily responsibilities related to cash or receivables.**

To illustrate a receivables write-off, assume that the vice president of finance of Hampson Furniture on March 1, 2015, authorizes a write-off of the $500 balance owed by R. A. Ware. The entry to record the write-off is:

Mar.	1	Allowance for Doubtful Accounts	500	
		Accounts Receivable—R. A. Ware		500
		(Write-off of R. A. Ware account)		

A	=	L	+	SE

+500
−500

Cash Flows
no effect

The company does not increase Bad Debt Expense when the write-off occurs. **Under the allowance method, a company debits every bad debt write-off to the allowance account and not to Bad Debt Expense.** A debit to Bad Debt Expense would be incorrect because the company has already recognized the expense when it made the adjusting entry for estimated bad debts. Instead, the entry to record the write-off of an uncollectible account reduces both Accounts Receivable and Allowance for Doubtful Accounts. After posting, the general ledger accounts appear as shown in Illustration 8-4.

Illustration 8-4 General ledger balances after write-off

Accounts Receivable			Allowance for Doubtful Accounts		
Jan. 1 Bal. 200,000	Mar. 1	500	Mar. 1	500	Jan. 1 Bal. 12,000
Mar. 1 Bal. 199,500					Mar. 1 Bal. 11,500

A write-off affects only balance sheet accounts. Cash realizable value in the balance sheet, therefore, remains the same before and after the write-off, as shown in Illustration 8-5.

Illustration 8-5 Cash realizable value comparison

	Before Write-Off	After Write-Off
Accounts receivable	$200,000	$199,500
Allowance for doubtful accounts	12,000	11,500
Cash realizable value	$188,000	$188,000

RECOVERY OF AN UNCOLLECTIBLE ACCOUNT. Occasionally, a company collects from a customer after the account has been written off as uncollectible. The company must make two entries to record the recovery of a bad debt: (1) It reverses the entry made in writing off the account. This reinstates the customer's account. (2) It journalizes the collection in the usual manner.

To illustrate, assume that on July 1, R. A. Ware pays the $500 amount that Hampson Furniture had written off on March 1. Hampson makes these entries:

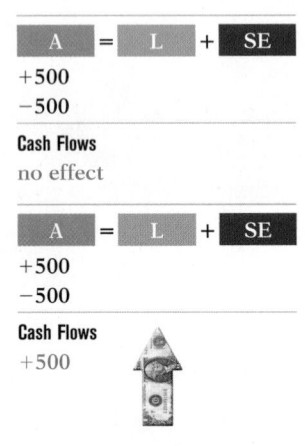

Cash Flows
no effect

Cash Flows
+500

(1)

July 1	Accounts Receivable—R. A. Ware		500	
	Allowance for Doubtful Accounts			500
	(To reverse write-off of R. A. Ware account)			

(2)

1	Cash		500	
	Accounts Receivable—R. A. Ware			500
	(To record collection from R. A. Ware)			

Note that the recovery of a bad debt, like the write-off of a bad debt, affects only balance sheet accounts. The net effect of the two entries is an increase in Cash and an increase in Allowance for Doubtful Accounts for $500. Accounts Receivable and Allowance for Doubtful Accounts both increase in entry (1) for two reasons. First, the company made an error in judgment when it wrote off the account receivable. Second, R. A. Ware did pay, and therefore the Accounts Receivable account should show this reinstatement and collection for possible future credit purposes.

Helpful Hint Like the write-off, a recovery does not involve the income statement.

ESTIMATING THE ALLOWANCE. For Hampson Furniture in Illustration 8-3, the amount of the expected uncollectibles was given. However, in "real life," companies must estimate the amount of expected uncollectible accounts if they use the allowance method. Illustration 8-6 shows an excerpt from the notes to Nike's financial statements discussing its use of the allowance method.

Illustration 8-6 Nike's allowance method disclosure

NIKE, INC.
Notes to the Financial Statements

Allowance for Uncollectible Accounts Receivable

We make ongoing estimates relating to the ability to collect our accounts receivable and maintain an allowance for estimated losses resulting from the inability of our customers to make required payments. In determining the amount of the allowance, we consider our historical level of credit losses and make judgments about the creditworthiness of significant customers based on ongoing credit evaluations. Since we cannot predict future changes in the financial stability of our customers, actual future losses from uncollectible accounts may differ from our estimates.

Helpful Hint Where appropriate, the percentage-of-receivables basis may use only a single percentage rate.

Allowance for Doubtful Accounts

	Dec. 31 Unadj.
	Bal. 1,500
	Dec. 31 Adj. 8,500
Dec. 31 Bal. 10,000	

Frequently, companies estimate the allowance as a percentage of the outstanding receivables. Under the **percentage-of-receivables basis**, management establishes a percentage relationship between the amount of receivables and expected losses from uncollectible accounts. For example, suppose Steffen Company has an ending balance in Accounts Receivable of $200,000, and an unadjusted credit balance in Allowance for Doubtful Accounts of $1,500. It estimates that 5% of its accounts receivable will eventually be uncollectible. It should report a balance in Allowance for Doubtful Accounts of $10,000 (.05 × $200,000). To increase the balance in Allowance for Doubtful Accounts from $1,500 to $10,000, the company debits (increases) Bad Debt Expense and credits (increases) Allowance for Doubtful Accounts by $8,500 ($10,000 − $1,500).

To more accurately estimate the ending balance in the allowance account, a company often prepares a schedule, called **aging the accounts receivable**. This schedule classifies customer balances by the length of time they have been unpaid.

After the company arranges the accounts by age, it determines the expected bad debt losses by applying percentages, based on past experience, to the totals of each category. The longer a receivable is past due, the less likely it is to be collected. As a result, the estimated percentage of uncollectible debts increases as the number of days past due increases. Illustration 8-7 shows an aging schedule for Dart Company. Note the increasing uncollectible percentages from 2% to 40%.

| Customer | Total | Not Yet Due | Number of Days Past Due | | | |
			1–30	31–60	61–90	Over 90
T. E. Adert	$ 600		$ 300		$ 200	$ 100
R. C. Bortz	300	$ 300				
B. A. Carl	450		200	$ 250		
O. L. Diker	700	500			200	
T. O. Ebbet	600			300		300
Others	36,950	26,200	5,200	2,450	1,600	1,500
	$39,600	$27,000	$5,700	$3,000	$2,000	$1,900
Estimated percentage uncollectible		2%	4%	10%	20%	40%
Total estimated uncollectible accounts	$ 2,228	$ 540	$ 228	$ 300	$ 400	$ 760

Illustration 8-7 Aging schedule

Total estimated uncollectible accounts for Dart Company ($2,228) represent the existing customer claims expected to become uncollectible in the future. Thus, this amount represents the **required balance** in Allowance for Doubtful Accounts at the balance sheet date. Accordingly, **the amount of bad debt expense that should be recorded in the adjusting entry is the difference between the required balance and the existing balance in the allowance account**. The existing, unadjusted balance in Allowance for Doubtful Accounts is the net result of the beginning balance (a normal credit balance) less the write-offs of specific accounts during the year (debits to the allowance account).

For example, if the unadjusted trial balance shows Allowance for Doubtful Accounts with a credit balance of $528, then an adjusting entry for $1,700 ($2,228 − $528) is necessary:

Dec. 31	Bad Debt Expense	1,700	
	Allowance for Doubtful Accounts		1,700
	(To adjust allowance account to total estimated uncollectibles)		

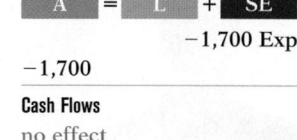

−1,700 Exp

−1,700

Cash Flows
no effect

After Dart posts the adjusting entry, its accounts appear as shown in Illustration 8-8.

Bad Debt Expense	**Allowance for Doubtful Accounts**
Dec. 31 Adj. **1,700**	Dec. 31 Unadj. Bal. 528
	Dec. 31 Adj. **1,700**
	Dec. 31 Bal. 2,228

Illustration 8-8 Bad debt accounts after posting

An important aspect of accounts receivable management is simply maintaining a close watch on the accounts. Studies have shown that accounts more than

60 days past due lose approximately 50% of their value if no payment activity occurs within the next 30 days. For each additional 30 days that pass, the collectible value halves once again.

Occasionally, the allowance account will have a **debit balance** prior to adjustment. This occurs because the debits to the allowance account from write-offs during the year **exceeded** the beginning balance in the account which was based on previous estimates for bad debts. In such a case, the company **adds the debit balance to the required balance** when it makes the adjusting entry. Thus, if there was a $500 **debit** balance in the allowance account before adjustment, the adjusting entry would be for $2,728 ($2,228 + $500) to arrive at a credit balance of $2,228 (see T-account in margin).

The percentage-of-receivables basis provides an estimate of the cash realizable value of the receivables. It also provides a reasonable matching of expense to revenue.

Allowance for Doubtful Accounts

Dec. 31 Unadj. Bal. 500	
	Dec. 31 Adj. 2,728
	Dec. 31 Bal. 2,228

DECISION TOOLKIT

DECISION CHECKPOINTS	INFO NEEDED FOR DECISION	TOOL TO USE FOR DECISION	HOW TO EVALUATE RESULTS
Is the amount of past due accounts increasing? Which accounts require management's attention?	List of outstanding receivables and their due dates	Prepare an aging schedule showing the receivables in various stages: outstanding 0–30 days, 31–60 days, 61–90 days, and over 90 days.	Accounts in the older categories require follow-up: letters, phone calls, and possible renegotiation of terms.

The following note regarding accounts receivable comes from the annual report of the shoe company Skechers USA.

Illustration 8-9 Skechers USA's note disclosure of accounts receivable

Real World

SKECHERS USA
Notes to the Financial Statements

Gross trade accounts receivable balance were $196.4 million and $285.8 million and the allowance for bad debts, returns, sales allowances and customer chargebacks was $20.4 million and $19.7 million, at December 31, 2011 and 2010, respectively. The Company's credit losses due to write-offs for the years ended December 31, 2011, 2010 and 2009 were $7.0 million, $4.8 million and $1.2 million, respectively.

Ethics Insight
When Investors Ignore Warning Signs

At one time, Nortel Networks announced that half of its previous year's earnings were "fake." Should investors have seen this coming? Well, there were issues in its annual report that should have caused investors to ask questions. The company had cut its allowance for doubtful accounts on all receivables from $1,253 million to $544 million even though its total balance of receivables remained relatively unchanged.

This reduction in bad debt expense was responsible for a very large part of the company's earnings that year. At the time, it was unclear whether Nortel might have set the reserves too high originally and needed to reduce them, or whether it slashed the allowance to artificially boost earnings. But one thing is certain—when a company makes an accounting change of this magnitude, investors need to ask questions.

Source: Jonathan Weil, "Outside Audit: At Nortel, Warning Signs Existed Months Ago," *Wall Street Journal* (May 18, 2004), p. C3.

 When would it be appropriate for a company to lower its allowance for doubtful accounts as a percentage of its receivables? (See page 443.)

Do it!

Brule Corporation has been in business for 5 years. The unadjusted trial balance at the end of the current year shows Accounts Receivable $30,000; Sales Revenue $180,000; and Allowance for Doubtful Accounts with a debit balance of $2,000. Brule estimates bad debts to be 10% of accounts receivable. Prepare the entry necessary to adjust Allowance for Doubtful Accounts.

Solution

Brule should make the following entry to bring the debit balance in Allowance for Doubtful Accounts up to a normal, credit balance of $3,000 (10% × $30,000):

Bad Debt Expense [(10% × $30,000) + $2,000]	5,000	
Allowance for Doubtful Accounts		5,000
(To record estimate of uncollectible accounts)		

Related exercise material: **BE8-3, BE8-4, BE8-5,** *Do it!* **8-1, E8-3, E8-4, E8-5,** and **E8-6.**

The Navigator

BAD DEBT EXPENSE

Action Plan

- Report receivables at their cash (net) realizable value—that is, the amount the company expects to collect in cash.
- Estimate the amount the company does not expect to collect.
- Consider the existing balance in the allowance account when using the percentage-of-receivables-basis.

Notes Receivable

Companies also may grant credit in exchange for a formal credit instrument known as a promissory note. A **promissory note** is a written promise to pay a specified amount of money on demand or at a definite time. Promissory notes may be used (1) when individuals and companies lend or borrow money, (2) when the amount of the transaction and the credit period exceed normal limits, and (3) in settlement of accounts receivable.

In a promissory note, the party making the promise to pay is called the **maker**. The party to whom payment is to be made is called the **payee**. The promissory note may specifically identify the payee by name or may designate the payee simply as the bearer of the note.

In the note shown in Illustration 8-10, Brent Company is the maker, and Wilma Company is the payee. To Wilma Company, the promissory note is a note receivable. To Brent Company, the note is a note payable.

LEARNING OBJECTIVE **4**

Compute the interest on notes receivable.

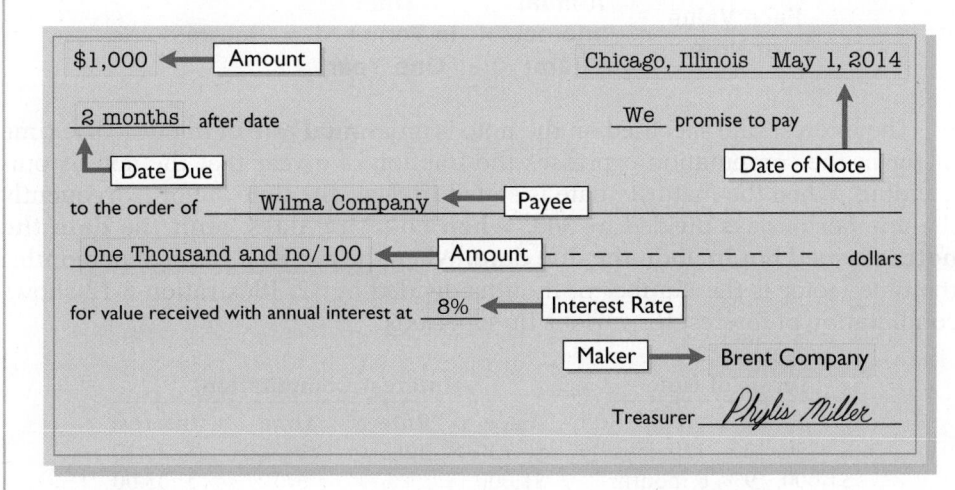

Illustration 8-10
Promissory note

Helpful Hint Who are the two key parties to a note? What entry does each party make when the note is issued?
Answer:
1. The maker, Brent Company, credits Notes Payable.
2. The payee, Wilma Company, debits Notes Receivable.

Notes receivable give the holder a stronger legal claim to assets than do accounts receivable. Like accounts receivable, notes receivable can be readily sold to another party. Promissory notes are negotiable instruments (as are checks), which means that, when sold, the seller can transfer them to another party by endorsement.

Companies frequently accept notes receivable from customers who need to extend the payment of an outstanding account receivable. Companies also often require notes from high-risk customers. In some industries (e.g., the pleasure and sport boat industry), all credit sales are supported by notes. The majority of notes, however, originate from lending transactions.

There are five issues in accounting for notes receivable:

1. **Determining** the maturity date.
2. **Computing** interest.
3. **Recognizing** notes receivable.
4. **Valuing** notes receivable.
5. **Disposing** of notes receivable.

We look at each of these issues.

DETERMINING THE MATURITY DATE

The maturity date of a promissory note may be stated in one of three ways: (1) on demand, (2) on a stated date, and (3) at the end of a stated period of time. When it is stated to be at the end of a period of time, the parties to the note will need to determine the maturity date.

When the life of a note is expressed in terms of months, you find the date when it matures by counting the months from the date of issue. For example, the maturity date of a three-month note dated May 1 is August 1. A note drawn on the last day of a month matures on the last day of a subsequent month. That is, a July 31 note due in two months matures on September 30.

When the due date is stated in terms of days, you need to count the exact number of days to determine the maturity date. In counting, **omit the date the note is issued but include the due date.**

Helpful Hint The maturity date of a 60-day note dated July 17 is determined as follows.

Term of note		60 days
July (31 − 17)	14	
August	31	45
September		15
(Maturity date)		

COMPUTING INTEREST

Illustration 8-11 gives the basic formula for computing interest on an interest-bearing note.

Illustration 8-11 Formula for computing interest

$$\text{Face Value of Note} \times \text{Annual Interest Rate} \times \text{Time in Terms of One Year} = \text{Interest}$$

The interest rate specified on the note is an **annual** rate of interest. The time factor in the computation expresses the fraction of a year that the note is outstanding. When the maturity date is stated in days, the time factor is frequently the number of days divided by 360. **When counting days, omit the date the note is issued but include the due date.** When the due date is stated in months, the time factor is the number of months divided by 12. Illustration 8-12 shows computation of interest for various time periods.

Illustration 8-12 Computation of interest

Terms of Note	Interest Computation			
	Face	× Rate ×	Time	= Interest
$ 730, 12%, 120 days	$ 730 ×	12% ×	120/360	= $ 29.20
$1,000, 9%, 6 months	$1,000 ×	9% ×	6/12	= $ 45.00
$2,000, 6%, 1 year	$2,000 ×	6% ×	1/1	= $120.00

There are different ways to calculate interest. For example, the computation in Illustration 8-12 assumes 360 days for the year. Most financial institutions use

365 days to compute interest. *For homework problems, assume 360 days to simplify computations.*

RECOGNIZING NOTES RECEIVABLE

To illustrate the basic entry for notes receivable, we will use Brent Company's $1,000, two-month, 8% promissory note dated May 1. Assuming that Brent Company wrote the note to settle an open account, Wilma Company makes the following entry for the receipt of the note.

May 1	Notes Receivable	1,000	
	Accounts Receivable—Brent Company		1,000
	(To record acceptance of Brent Company note)		

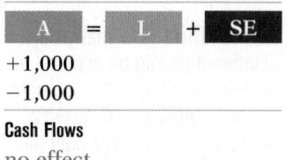

A	=	L	+	SE

+1,000
−1,000

Cash Flows
no effect

The company records the note receivable at its **face value**, the value shown on the face of the note. No interest revenue is reported when the company accepts the note because the revenue recognition principle does not recognize revenue until the performance obligation is satisfied. Interest is earned (accrued) as time passes.

If a company issues cash in exchange for a note, the entry is a debit to Notes Receivable and a credit to Cash in the amount of the loan.

VALUING NOTES RECEIVABLE

Like accounts receivable, companies report short-term notes receivable at their **cash (net) realizable value**. The notes receivable allowance account is Allowance for Doubtful Accounts. Valuing short-term notes receivable is the same as valuing accounts receivable. The computations and estimations involved in determining cash realizable value and in recording the proper amount of bad debt expense and related allowance are similar.

Long-term notes receivable, however, pose additional estimation problems. As an example, we need only look at the problems large U.S. banks sometimes have in collecting their receivables. Loans to less-developed countries are particularly worrisome. Developing countries need loans for development but often find repayment difficult. In some cases, developed nations have intervened to provide financial assistance to the financially troubled borrowers so as to minimize the political and economic turmoil to the borrower and to ensure the survival of the lender.

International Insight

Can Fair Value Be Unfair?

The FASB and the International Accounting Standards Board (IASB) are considering proposals for how to account for financial instruments. The FASB has proposed that loans and receivables be accounted for at their fair value (the amount they could currently be sold for), as are most investments. The FASB believes that this would provide a more accurate view of a company's financial position. It might be especially useful as an early warning when a bank is in trouble because of poor-quality loans. But, banks argue that fair values are difficult to estimate accurately. They are also concerned that volatile fair values could cause large swings in a bank's reported net income.

Source: David Reilly, "Banks Face a Mark-to-Market Challenge," *Wall Street Journal Online* (March 15, 2010).

? What are the arguments in favor of and against fair value accounting for loans and receivables? (See page 443.)

© Andrzej Tokarski/iStockphoto

DISPOSING OF NOTES RECEIVABLE

Notes may be held to their maturity date, at which time the face value plus accrued interest is due. In some situations, the maker of the note defaults, and the payee must make an appropriate adjustment. In other situations, similar to accounts receivable, the holder of the note speeds up the conversion to cash by selling the receivables (as described later in this chapter).

Honor of Notes Receivable

A note is **honored** when its maker pays in full at its maturity date. For each interest-bearing note, the **amount due at maturity** is the face value of the note plus interest for the length of time specified on the note.

Helpful Hint How many days of interest should be accrued at September 30 for a 90-day note issued on August 16? Answer: 45 days (15 days in August plus 30 days in September).

To illustrate, assume that Wolder Co. lends Higley Inc. $10,000 on June 1, accepting a five-month, 9% interest note. In this situation, interest is $375 ($10,000 $\times$ 9% $\times \frac{5}{12}$). The amount due, the **maturity value**, is $10,375 ($10,000 + $375). To obtain payment, Wolder (the payee) must present the note either to Higley Inc. (the maker) or to the maker's agent, such as a bank. If Wolder presents the note to Higley Inc. on November 1, the maturity date, Wolder's entry to record the collection is:

A	=	L	+	SE
+10,375				
−10,000				
				+375 Rev

Cash Flows
+10,375

Nov. 1	Cash	10,375	
	Notes Receivable		10,000
	Interest Revenue ($10,000 $\times$ 9% $\times \frac{5}{12}$)		375
	(To record collection of Higley Inc. note and interest)		

Accrual of Interest Receivable

Suppose instead that Wolder Co. prepares financial statements as of September 30. The timeline in Illustration 8-13 presents this situation.

Illustration 8-13 Timeline of interest earned

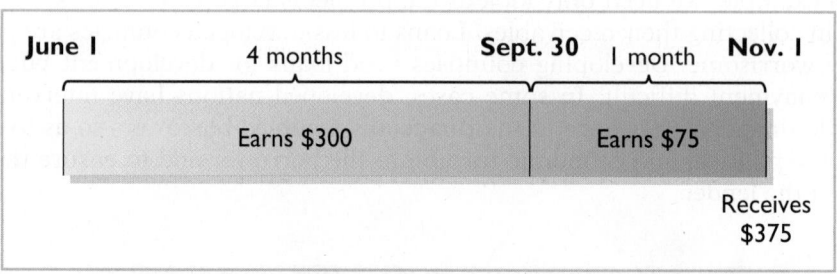

To reflect interest earned but not yet received, Wolder must accrue interest on September 30. In this case, the adjusting entry by Wolder is for four months of interest, or $300, as shown below.

A	=	L	+	SE
+300				
				+300 Rev

Cash Flows
no effect

Sept. 30	Interest Receivable ($10,000 $\times$ 9% $\times \frac{4}{12}$)	300	
	Interest Revenue		300
	(To accrue 4 months' interest on Higley note)		

At the note's maturity on November 1, Wolder receives $10,375. This amount represents repayment of the $10,000 note as well as five months of interest, or $375, as shown on the next page. The $375 is comprised of the $300 Interest

Receivable accrued on September 30 plus $75 earned during October. Wolder's entry to record the honoring of the Higley note on November 1 is:

Nov. 1	Cash [$10,000 + ($10,000 × 9% × $\frac{5}{12}$)]	10,375	
	Notes Receivable		10,000
	Interest Receivable		300
	Interest Revenue ($10,000 × 9% × $\frac{1}{12}$)		75
	(To record collection of Higley Inc. note and interest)		

A = L + SE
+10,375
−10,000
−300
+75 Rev

Cash Flows
+10,375

In this case, Wolder credits Interest Receivable because the receivable was established in the adjusting entry on September 30.

Dishonor of Notes Receivable

A **dishonored (defaulted) note** is a note that is not paid in full at maturity. A dishonored note receivable is no longer negotiable. However, the payee still has a claim against the maker of the note for both the note and the interest. If the lender expects that it eventually will be able to collect, the two parties negotiate new terms to make it easier for the borrower to repay the debt. If there is no hope of collection, the payee should write off the face value of the note.

Do it!

Gambit Stores accepts from Leonard Co. a $3,400, 90-day, 6% note dated May 10 in settlement of Leonard's overdue open account. The note matures on August 8. What entry does Gambit make at the maturity date, assuming Leonard pays the note and interest in full at that time?

Solution

The interest payable at maturity date is $51, computed as follows.

$$\text{Face} \times \text{Rate} \times \text{Time} = \text{Interest}$$
$$\$3,400 \times 6\% \times \frac{90}{360} = \$51$$

Gambit Stores records this entry at the maturity date:

Cash	3,451	
Notes Receivable		3,400
Interest Revenue		51
(To record collection of Leonard note and interest)		

Related exercise material: **BE8-6, BE8-7, Do it! 8-2, E8-7,** and **E8-8.**

NOTES RECEIVABLE

Action Plan
- Determine whether interest was accrued.
- Compute the accrued interest.
- Prepare the entry for payment of the note and the interest. The entry to record interest at maturity in this solution assumes that no interest has been previously accrued on this note.

The Navigator

Financial Statement Presentation of Receivables

Companies should identify in the balance sheet or in the notes to the financial statements each of the major types of receivables. Short-term receivables are reported in the current assets section of the balance sheet, below short-term investments. Short-term investments appear before short-term receivables because these investments are nearer to cash. Companies report both the gross amount of receivables and the allowance for doubtful accounts.

Receivables represent 53% of the total assets of heavy equipment manufacturer Deere & Company. Illustration 8-14 (page 412) shows a presentation of receivables for Deere & Company from its balance sheet and notes in a recent year.

LEARNING OBJECTIVE 6
Explain the statement presentation of receivables.

Illustration 8-14 Balance sheet presentation of receivables

Real World	DEERE & COMPANY Balance Sheet (partial) (in millions)	
Receivables		
Receivables from unconsolidated subsidiaries		$ 38
Trade accounts and notes receivable		2,694
Financing receivables		15,469
Restricted financing receivables		3,108
Other receivables		864
Total receivables		22,173
Less: Allowance for doubtful trade receivables		290
Net receivables		$21,883

In the income statement, companies report bad debt expense under "Selling expenses" in the operating expenses section. They show interest revenue under "Other revenues and gains" in the nonoperating section of the income statement.

If a company has significant risk of uncollectible accounts or other problems with its receivables, it is required to discuss this possibility in the notes to the financial statements.

Managing Receivables

LEARNING OBJECTIVE 7

Describe the principles of sound accounts receivable management.

Managing accounts receivable involves five steps:

1. Determine to whom to extend credit.
2. Establish a payment period.
3. Monitor collections.
4. Evaluate the liquidity of receivables.
5. Accelerate cash receipts from receivables when necessary.

EXTENDING CREDIT

Every entrepreneur struggles with financing issues. For example, the very first order that Apple's founders received was 50 circuit boards to a computer hobby shop. To produce the $25,000 order, Steve Jobs and Steve Wozniak needed $15,000 of parts. To purchase the parts, they borrowed $5,000 from friends but then were turned down when they applied for a bank loan for the $10,000 balance. They approached two parts suppliers in an effort to negotiate a purchase on credit, but both suppliers said no. Finally, a third supplier agreed to sell them the parts on 30-day credit after he called the computer hobby shop to confirm that it had, in fact, placed a $25,000 order to purchase goods.

A critical part of managing receivables is determining who should be extended credit and who should not. Many companies increase sales by being generous with their credit policy. However, they sometimes extend credit to risky customers who do not pay. But if your credit policy is too tight, you will lose sales. If it is too loose, you may sell to "deadbeats" who will pay either very late or not at all. One CEO noted that prior to getting his credit and collection department in order, his salespeople had 300 square feet of office space **per person**, while the people in credit and collections had six people crammed into a single 300-square-foot space. Although this focus on sales boosted sales revenue, it had very expensive consequences in bad debt expense.

Companies can take certain steps to help minimize losses due to bad debts when they decide to relax credit standards for new customers. They might require risky customers to provide letters of credit or bank guarantees. Then, if the customer does not pay, the bank that provided the guarantee will do so. Particularly risky customers might be required to pay cash on delivery. For example, at one time retailer Linens'n Things, Inc. reported that its largest suppliers were requiring cash payment before delivery. The suppliers had cut off shipments because the company had been slow in paying. Kmart's suppliers also required it to pay cash in advance when it was financially troubled.

In addition, companies should ask potential customers for references from banks and suppliers, to determine their payment history. It is important to check references of potential new customers as well as periodically to check the financial health of continuing customers. Many resources are available for investigating customers. For example, *The Dun & Bradstreet Reference Book of American Business* (**www.dnb.com**) lists millions of companies and provides credit ratings for many of them.

Accounting Across the Organization
Bad Information Can Lead to Bad Loans

Many factors contributed to the recent credit crisis. One significant factor that resulted in many bad loans was a failure by lenders to investigate loan customers sufficiently. For example, Countrywide Financial Corporation wrote many loans under its "Fast and Easy" loan program. That program allowed borrowers to provide little or no documentation for their income or their assets. Other lenders had similar programs, which earned the nickname "liars' loans." One study found that in these situations, 60% of applicants overstated their incomes by more than 50% in order to qualify for a loan. Critics of the banking industry say that because loan officers were compensated for loan volume, and because banks were selling the loans to investors rather than holding them, the lenders had little incentive to investigate the borrowers' creditworthiness.

Source: Glenn R. Simpson and James R. Hagerty, "Countrywide Loss Focuses Attention on Underwriting," *Wall Street Journal* (April 30, 2008), p. B1; and Michael Corkery, "Fraud Seen as Driver in Wave of Foreclosures," *Wall Street Journal* (December 21, 2007), p. A1.

 What steps should the banks have taken to ensure the accuracy of financial information provided on loan applications? (See page 443.)

© Andy Dean/iStockphoto

ESTABLISHING A PAYMENT PERIOD

Companies that extend credit should determine a required payment period and communicate that policy to their customers. It is important that the payment period is consistent with that of competitors. For example, if you require payment within 15 days but your competitors allow payment within 45 days, you may lose sales to your competitors. To match your competitors' generous terms yet still encourage prompt payment of accounts, you might allow up to 45 days to pay but offer a sales discount for people paying within 15 days.

MONITORING COLLECTIONS

We discussed preparation of the accounts receivable aging schedule earlier in the chapter (pages 404–406). Companies should prepare an accounts receivable aging schedule at least monthly. In addition to estimating the allowance for doubtful accounts, the aging schedule has other uses. It helps managers estimate the timing of future cash inflows, which is very important to the treasurer's efforts to prepare a cash budget. It provides information about the overall collection experience of the company and identifies problem accounts. For example, management would compute and compare the percentage of receivables that are over 90 days past due. Illustration 8-15 contains an excerpt from the notes to Skechers' financial statements discussing how it monitors receivables.

Illustration 8-15 Note on monitoring Skechers' receivables

SKECHERS USA
Notes to the Financial Statements

To minimize the likelihood of uncollectibility, customers' credit-worthiness is reviewed periodically based on external credit reporting services, financial statements issued by the customer and our experience with the account, and it is adjusted accordingly. When a customer's account becomes significantly past due, we generally place a hold on the account and discontinue further shipments to that customer, minimizing further risk of loss.

The aging schedule identifies problem accounts that the company needs to pursue with phone calls, letters, and occasionally legal action. Sometimes, special arrangements must be made with problem accounts. For example, it was reported that Intel Corporation (a major manufacturer of computer chips) required that Packard Bell (at one time one of the largest U.S. sellers of personal computers) exchange its past-due account receivable for an interest-bearing note receivable. This caused concern within the investment community. The move suggested that Packard Bell was in trouble, which worried Intel investors concerned about Intel's accounts receivable.

 DECISION TOOLKIT

DECISION CHECKPOINTS	INFO NEEDED FOR DECISION	TOOL TO USE FOR DECISION	HOW TO EVALUATE RESULTS
Is the company's credit risk increasing?	Customer account balances and due dates	Accounts receivable aging schedule	Compute and compare the percentage of receivables over 90 days old.

If a company has significant concentrations of credit risk, it must discuss this risk in the notes to its financial statements. A **concentration of credit risk** is a threat of nonpayment from a single large customer or class of customers that could adversely affect the financial health of the company. Illustration 8-16 shows an excerpt from the credit risk note from the 2011 annual report of Skechers. Skechers reports that its five largest customers account for 17.8% of its net sales, and two of its customers account for 22.5% of its receivables.

Illustration 8-16 Excerpt from Skechers' note on concentration of credit risk

SKECHERS USA
Notes to the Financial Statements

We Depend Upon a Relatively Small Group of Customers for a Large Portion of Our Sales.
During 2011, 2010 and 2009, our net sales to our five largest customers accounted for approximately 17.8%, 24.9% and 25.1% of total net sales, respectively. No customer accounted for more than 10.0% of our net sales during 2011, 2010 and 2009. One customer accounted for 12.5% and another accounted for 10.0% of net trade receivables at December 31, 2011. No customer accounted for more than 10% of net trade receivables at December 31, 2010. If we lose a major customer, experience a significant decrease in sales to a major customer or are unable to collect the accounts receivable of a major customer, our business could be harmed.

This note to Skechers' financial statements indicates it has a relatively high concentration of credit risk. A default by any of these large customers could have a significant negative impact on its financial performance.

DECISION TOOLKIT

DECISION CHECKPOINTS	INFO NEEDED FOR DECISION	TOOL TO USE FOR DECISION	HOW TO EVALUATE RESULTS
Does the company have significant concentrations of credit risk?	Note to the financial statements on concentrations of credit risk	If risky credit customers are identified, the financial health of those customers should be evaluated to gain an independent assessment of the potential for a material credit loss.	If a material loss appears likely, the potential negative impact of that loss on the company should be carefully evaluated, along with the adequacy of the allowance for doubtful accounts.

EVALUATING LIQUIDITY OF RECEIVABLES

LEARNING OBJECTIVE 8

Identify ratios to analyze a company's receivables.

Investors and managers keep a watchful eye on the relationship among sales, accounts receivable, and cash collections. If sales increase, then accounts receivable are also expected to increase. But a disproportionate increase in accounts receivable might signal trouble. Perhaps the company increased its sales by loosening its credit policy, and these receivables may be difficult or impossible to collect. Such receivables are considered less liquid. Recall that liquidity is measured by how quickly certain assets can be converted to cash.

The ratio that analysts use to assess the liquidity of receivables is the **accounts receivable turnover**, computed by dividing net credit sales (net sales less cash sales) by the average net accounts receivable during the year. This ratio measures the number of times, on average, a company collects receivables during the period. Unless seasonal factors are significant, **average** accounts receivable outstanding can be computed from the beginning and ending balances of the net receivables.[1]

A popular variant of the accounts receivable turnover is the **average collection period**, which measures the average amount of time that a receivable is outstanding. This is done by dividing the accounts receivable turnover into 365 days. Companies use the average collection period to assess the effectiveness of a company's credit and collection policies. The average collection period should not greatly exceed the credit term period (i.e., the time allowed for payment).

The following data (in millions) are available for Nike.

	For the year ended March 31,	
	2011	**2010**
Sales	$20,862	$19,014
Accounts receivable (net)	3,138	2,650

Illustration 8-17 (page 416) shows the accounts receivable turnover and average collection period for Nike and Skechers, along with comparative industry data. These calculations assume that all sales were credit sales.

---

[1]If seasonal factors are significant, determine the average accounts receivable balance by using monthly or quarterly amounts.

	Nike ($ in millions)			Skechers USA	Industry Average
Ratio	2011		2010	2011	2010
Accounts receivable turnover	$\dfrac{\$20{,}862}{(\$3{,}138 + \$2{,}650)/2} = 7.2$ times		6.9 times	7.3 times	12.2 times
Average collection period	$\dfrac{365 \text{ days}}{7.2} = 50.7$ days		52.9 days	50.0 days	29.9 days

Illustration 8-17 Accounts receivable turnover and average collection period

Nike's accounts receivable turnover was 7.2 times in 2011, with a corresponding average collection period of 50.7 days. This was slightly faster than its 2010 collection period. It was slower than the industry average collection period of 29.9 days and slightly higher than Skechers, which was 50 days. What this means is that Nike turned its receivables into cash more slowly than most other companies in its industry. Therefore, it was less likely to pay its current obligations than a company with a quicker accounts receivable turnover (all else equal) and is more likely to need outside financing to meet cash shortfalls.

🧰 DECISION TOOLKIT

DECISION CHECKPOINTS	INFO NEEDED FOR DECISION	TOOL TO USE FOR DECISION	HOW TO EVALUATE RESULTS
Are collections being made in a timely fashion?	Net credit sales and average net accounts receivable balance	$\text{Accounts receivable turnover} = \dfrac{\text{Net credit sales}}{\text{Average net accounts receivable}}$ $\text{Average collection period} = \dfrac{365 \text{ days}}{\text{Accounts receivable turnover}}$	Average collection period should be consistent with corporate credit policy. An increase may suggest a decline in financial health of customers.

In some cases, accounts receivable turnover may be misleading. Some large retail chains that issue their own credit cards encourage customers to use these cards for purchases. If customers pay slowly, the stores earn a healthy return on the outstanding receivables in the form of interest at rates of 18% to 22%. On the other hand, companies that sell (factor) their receivables on a consistent basis will have a faster turnover than those that do not. Thus, to interpret accounts receivable turnover, you must know how a company manages its receivables. In general, the faster the turnover, the greater the reliability of the current ratio for assessing liquidity.

Do it!

In 2014, Lebron James Company had net credit sales of $923,795 for the year. It had a beginning accounts receivable (net) balance of $38,275 and an ending accounts receivable (net) balance of $35,988. Compute Lebron James Company's (a) accounts receivable turnover and (b) average collection period in days.

ANALYSIS OF RECEIVABLES

Solution

(a)

Net credit sales	÷	Average net accounts receivable	=	Accounts receivable turnover
$923,795	÷	$\dfrac{\$38,275 + \$35,988}{2}$	=	24.9 times

(b)

Days in year	÷	Accounts receivable turnover	=	Average collection period in days
365	÷	24.9 times	=	14.7 days

Related exercise material: **BE8-10**, **Do it! 8-3**, **E8-11**, and **E8-12**.

Action Plan
- Review the formula to compute the accounts receivable turnover.
- Make sure that both the beginning and ending accounts receivable are considered in the computation.
- Review the formula to compute the average collection period in days.

✔ The Navigator

ACCELERATING CASH RECEIPTS

In the normal course of events, companies collect accounts receivable in cash and remove them from the books. However, as credit sales and receivables have grown in size and significance, the "normal course of events" has changed. Two common expressions apply to the collection of receivables: (1) "Time is money"— that is, waiting for the normal collection process costs money. (2) "A bird in the hand is worth two in the bush"—that is, getting the cash now is better than getting it later or not at all. Therefore, in order to accelerate the receipt of cash from receivables, companies frequently sell their receivables to another company for cash, thereby shortening the cash-to-cash operating cycle.

LEARNING OBJECTIVE 9
Describe methods to accelerate the receipt of cash from receivables.

There are three reasons for the sale of receivables. The first is their **size**. In recent years, for competitive reasons, sellers (retailers, wholesalers, and manufacturers) often have provided financing to purchasers of their goods. For example, many major companies in the automobile, truck, industrial and farm equipment, computer, and appliance industries have created companies that accept responsibility for accounts receivable financing. Caterpillar has Caterpillar Financial Services, General Electric has GE Capital, and Ford has Ford Motor Credit Corp. (FMCC). These companies are referred to as **captive finance companies** because they are owned by the company selling the product. The purpose of captive finance companies is to encourage the sale of the company's products by assuring financing to buyers. However, the parent companies involved do not necessarily want to hold large amounts of receivables, so they may sell them.

Second, **companies may sell receivables because they may be the only reasonable source of cash**. When credit is tight, companies may not be able to borrow money in the usual credit markets. Even if credit is available, the cost of borrowing may be prohibitive.

A final reason for selling receivables is that **billing and collection are often time-consuming and costly**. As a result, it is often easier for a retailer to sell the receivables to another party that has expertise in billing and collection matters. Credit card companies such as MasterCard, Visa, American Express, and Discover specialize in billing and collecting accounts receivable.

Sale of Receivables to a Factor

A common way to accelerate receivables collection is a sale to a factor. A **factor** is a finance company or bank that buys receivables from businesses for a fee and then collects the payments directly from the customers.

Factoring was traditionally associated with the textiles, apparel, footwear, furniture, and home furnishing industries. It has now spread to other types of businesses and is a multibillion dollar industry. For example, Sears, Roebuck & Co. (now Sears Holdings) once sold $14.8 billion of customer accounts receivable. McKesson has a pre-arranged agreement allowing it to sell up to $700 million of its receivables.

Factoring arrangements vary widely, but typically the factor charges a commission. It ranges from 1% to 3% of the amount of receivables purchased. To illustrate, assume that Hendredon Furniture factors $600,000 of receivables to Federal Factors, Inc. Federal Factors assesses a service charge of 2% of the amount of receivables sold. The following journal entry records Hendredon's sale of receivables on April 2, 2014.

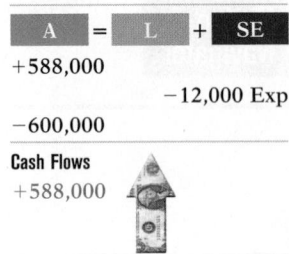

International Note GAAP has less stringent requirements regarding the sale of receivables. Thus, GAAP companies can more easily use factoring transactions as a form of financing without showing a related liability on their books. Some argue that this type of so-called "off-balance-sheet financing" would be more difficult to achieve under IFRS.

A	=	L	+	SE
+588,000				
				−12,000 Exp
−600,000				

Cash Flows
+588,000

Apr. 2	Cash	588,000	
	Service Charge Expense (2% × $600,000)	12,000	
	Accounts Receivable		600,000
	(To record the sale of accounts receivable)		

If the company usually sells its receivables, it records the service charge expense as a selling expense. If the company sells receivables infrequently, it may report this amount under "Other expenses and losses" in the income statement.

© Emrah Turudu/iStockphoto

Accounting Across the Organization

eBay for Receivables

The credit crunch has hit small businesses especially hard. Because banks have been very reluctant to loan, entrepreneurs have had to look more frequently to factoring as a source of cash. This created an opportunity for a new business called The Receivables Exchange. It offers a website where small companies can anonymously display a list of their receivables that they would like to factor in exchange for cash. Parties that are interested in providing cash in exchange for the receivables can also view the receivables and bid on those they like without revealing their identity. It has been described as "eBay for receivables." Because of his continued use of the service, one experienced participant has reduced the monthly rate that he pays to The Receivables Exchange from 4% to below 3%.

Source: Simona Covel, "Getting Your Due," *Wall Street Journal Online* (May 11, 2009).

? What issues should management consider in deciding whether to factor its receivables? (See page 444.)

National Credit Card Sales

Approximately one billion credit cards were in use recently—more than three credit cards for every man, woman, and child in this country. A common type of credit card is a national credit card such as Visa and MasterCard. Three parties are involved when national credit cards are used in making retail sales: (1) the credit card issuer, who is independent of the retailer; (2) the retailer; and (3) the customer. **A retailer's acceptance of a national credit card is another form of selling—factoring—the receivable by the retailer.**

The use of national credit cards translates to more sales and zero bad debts for the retailer. Both are powerful reasons for a retailer to accept such cards. Illustration 8-18 shows the major advantages of national credit cards to the retailer. In exchange for these advantages, the retailer pays the credit card issuer a fee of 2% to 4% of the invoice price for its services.

Ethics Note In exchange for lower interest rates, some companies have eliminated the 25-day grace period before finance charges kick in. Be sure you read the fine print in any credit agreement you sign.

Illustration 8-18 Advantages of credit cards to the retailer

The retailer considers sales resulting from the use of Visa and MasterCard as **cash sales**. Upon notification of a credit card charge from a retailer, the bank that issued the card immediately adds the amount to the seller's bank balance. Companies therefore record these credit card charges in the same manner as checks deposited from a cash sale.

To illustrate, Morgan Marie purchases $1,000 of compact discs for her restaurant from Sondgeroth Music Co., and she charges this amount on her Visa First Bank Card. The service fee that First Bank charges Sondgeroth Music is 3%. Sondgeroth Music's entry to record this transaction on March 22, 2014, is:

			A = L + SE
Mar. 22	Cash	970	+970
	Service Charge Expense	30	−30 Exp
	Sales Revenue	1,000	+1,000 Rev
	(To record Visa credit card sales)		

Cash Flows
+970

Illustration 8-19 (page 420) summarizes the basic principles of managing accounts receivable.

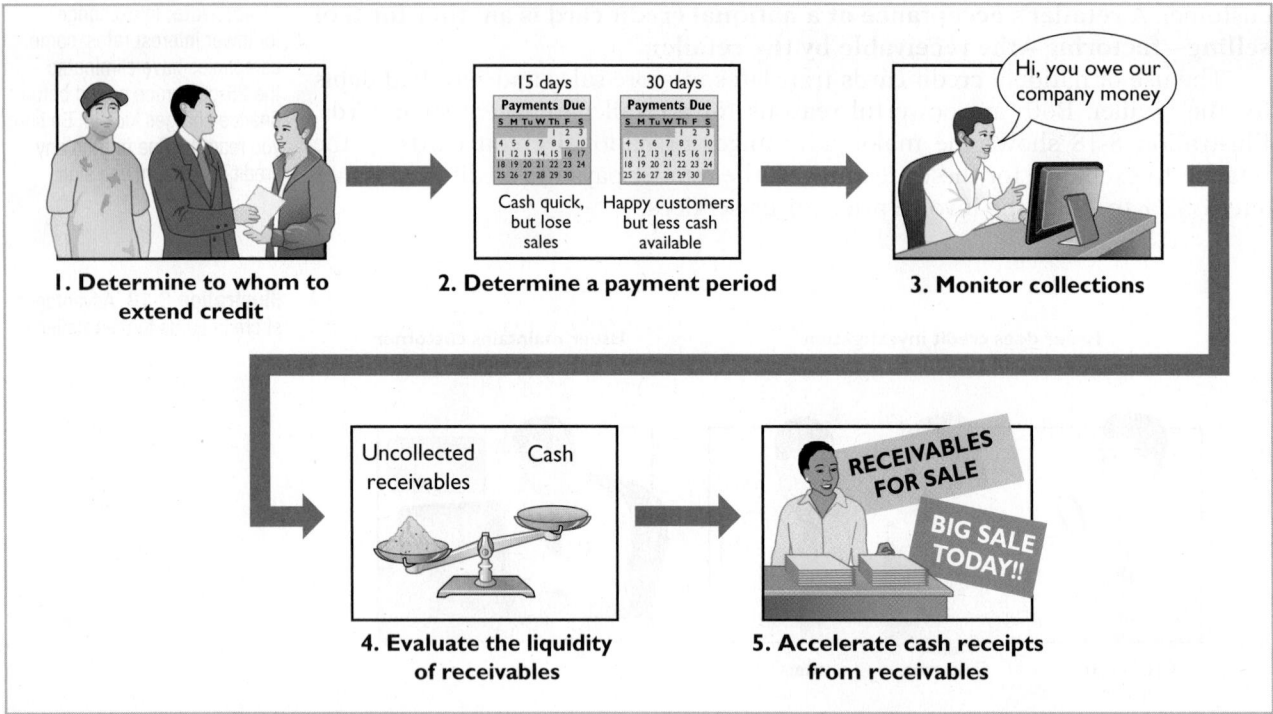

Illustration 8-19
Managing receivables

FACTORING

Do it!

Peter M. Kell Wholesalers Co. needs to raise $120,000 in cash to safely cover next Friday's employee payroll. Kell has reached its debt ceiling. Kell's present balance of outstanding receivables totals $750,000. Kell decides to factor $125,000 of its receivables on September 7, 2014, to alleviate this cash crunch. Record the entry that Kell would make when it raises the needed cash. (Assume a 1% service charge.)

Action Plan

- Consider sale of receivables to a factor.
- Weigh cost of factoring against benefit of having cash in hand.

The Navigator

Solution

Assuming that Kell Co. factors $125,000 of its accounts receivable at a 1% service charge, it would make this entry:

Sept. 7	Cash	123,750	
	Service Charge Expense (1% × $125,000)	1,250	
	Accounts Receivable		125,000
	(To record sale of receivables to factor)		

Related exercise material: **BE8-11**, **Do it!** **8-4**, **E8-13**, and **E8-14**.

KEEPING AN EYE ON CASH

A lot of companies report strong sales growth but have cash flow problems. How can this be? The reason for the difference is timing: Sales revenue is recorded when goods are delivered even if cash is not received until later. For example, Nike had sales of $20,862 million during 2011. Does that mean it received cash of $20,862 million from its customers? Most likely not. So how do we determine the amount of cash related to sales revenue that is actually received from customers? We analyze the changes that take place in Accounts Receivable.

To illustrate, suppose Bestor Corporation started the year with $10,000 in accounts receivable. During the year, it had credit sales of $100,000. At the end of the year, the balance in accounts receivable was $25,000. As a result, accounts receivable increased $15,000 during the year. How much cash did Bestor collect from customers during the year? Using the following T-account, we can determine that collections were $85,000.

Accounts Receivable			
Beginning balance	10,000	85,000	Collections
Sales	100,000		
Ending balance	25,000		

As shown, the difference between sales and cash collections is explained by the change in Accounts Receivable. Accounts Receivable increased by $15,000. Therefore, since credit sales were $100,000, cash collections were only $85,000.

To illustrate another situation, let's use Nike (see data on page 415). Recall that it had credit sales of $20,862 million. Its ending receivables balance was $3,138 million, and its beginning receivables balance was $2,650 million—an increase of $488 million. Given this change, we can determine that the cash collected from customers during the year was $20,374 million ($20,862 − $488). This is shown in the following T-account.

Accounts Receivable			
Beginning balance	2,650	20,374	Collections
Sales	20,862		
Ending balance	3,138		

 # USING THE DECISION TOOLKIT

The information below was taken from the 2011 financial statements of adidas. Similar to Nike and Skechers, adidas sells shoes as well as other products.

Instructions

Comment on adidas' accounts receivable management and liquidity relative to that of Nike, using (1) the current ratio and (2) the accounts receivable turnover and average collection period. Nike's current ratio was 2.85:1. The other ratio values for Nike were calculated earlier in the chapter (page 416).

Real World

ADIDAS AG
Selected Financial Information
(in millions)

	2011	2010
Sales	$13,344	$11,990
Current assets		
Cash and cash equivalents	$ 906	$ 1,156
Short-term investment securities	465	233
Accounts receivable (net)	1,707	1,667
Merchandise inventories	2,482	2,119
Other	875	705
Total current assets	$ 6,435	$ 5,880
Total current liabilities	$ 4,281	$ 3,908

Solution

1. Here is the 2011 current ratio (Current assets ÷ Current liabilities) for each company.

Nike	**adidas**
2.85:1	$\dfrac{\$6,435}{\$4,281} = 1.50:1$

Nike's current ratio far exceeds that of adidas. In fact, Nike's might be excessive. A company of its size would not normally want to have so much capital tied up in current assets.

2. The accounts receivable turnover and average collection period for each company are:

	Nike	**adidas**
Accounts receivable turnover	7.2 times	$\dfrac{\$13,344}{(\$1,707 + \$1,667)/2} = 7.9$ times
Average collection period	50.7 days	$\dfrac{365}{7.9} = 46.2$ days

adidas' accounts receivable turnover of 7.9 compared to Nike's 7.2, and its average collection period of 46.2 days versus Nike's 50.7 days, suggest that adidas is able to collect from its customers slightly more quickly. It is important to note, however, that adidas is a German corporation. It reports under IFRS. A thorough comparison of adidas and Nike would require consideration of differences in the treatment of accounts receivable under IFRS and GAAP.

The Navigator

Summary of Learning Objectives

1 Identify the different types of receivables. Receivables are frequently classified as accounts, notes, and other. Accounts receivable are amounts customers owe on account. Notes receivable represent claims that are evidenced by formal instruments of credit. Other receivables include nontrade receivables such as interest receivable, loans to company officers, advances to employees, and income taxes refundable.

2 Explain how accounts receivable are recognized in the accounts. Companies record accounts receivable when they perform a service on account or at the point-of-sale of merchandise on account. Sales returns and allowances, and cash discounts reduce the amount received on accounts receivable.

3 Describe the methods used to account for bad debts. The two methods of accounting for uncollectible accounts are the allowance method and the direct write-off method. Under the allowance method, companies estimate uncollectible accounts as a percentage of receivables. It emphasizes the cash realizable value of the accounts receivable. An aging schedule is frequently used with this approach.

4 Compute the interest on notes receivable. The formula for computing interest is: Face value of note × Annual interest rate × Time in terms of one year.

5 Describe the entries to record the disposition of notes receivable. Notes can be held to maturity, at which time the borrower (maker) pays the face value plus accrued interest and the payee removes the note from the accounts. In many cases, however, similar to accounts receivable, the holder of the note speeds up the conversion by selling the receivable to another party. In some situations, the maker of the note dishonors the note (defaults), and the note is written off.

6 Explain the statement presentation of receivables. Companies should identify each major type of receivable in the balance sheet or in the notes to the financial statements. Short-term receivables are considered current assets. Companies report the gross amount of receivables and allowance for doubtful accounts. They report bad debt and service charge expenses in the income statement as operating (selling) expenses, and interest revenue as other revenues and gains in the nonoperating section of the statement.

7 Describe the principles of sound accounts receivable management. To properly manage receivables, management must (a) determine to whom to extend credit, (b) establish a payment period, (c) monitor collections, (d) evaluate the liquidity of receivables, and (e) accelerate cash receipts from receivables when necessary.

8 Identify ratios to analyze a company's receivables. The accounts receivable turnover and the average collection period both are useful in analyzing management's effectiveness in managing receivables. The accounts receivable aging schedule also provides useful information.

9 Describe methods to accelerate the receipt of cash from receivables. If the company needs additional cash, management can accelerate the collection of cash from receivables by selling (factoring) its receivables or by allowing customers to pay with bank credit cards.

The Navigator

🧰 DECISION TOOLKIT *A SUMMARY*

DECISION CHECKPOINTS	INFO NEEDED FOR DECISION	TOOL TO USE FOR DECISION	HOW TO EVALUATE RESULTS
Is the amount of past due accounts increasing? Which accounts require management's attention?	List of outstanding receivables and their due dates	Prepare an aging schedule showing the receivables in various stages: outstanding 0–30 days, 31–60 days, 61–90 days, and over 90 days.	Accounts in the older categories require follow-up: letters, phone calls, and possible renegotiation of terms.
Is the company's credit risk increasing?	Customer account balances and due dates	Accounts receivable aging schedule	Compute and compare the percentage of receivables over 90 days old.
Does the company have significant concentrations of credit risk?	Note to the financial statements on concentrations of credit risk	If risky credit customers are identified, the financial health of those customers should be evaluated to gain an independent assessment of the potential for a material credit loss.	If a material loss appears likely, the potential negative impact of that loss on the company should be carefully evaluated, along with the adequacy of the allowance for doubtful accounts.
Are collections being made in a timely fashion?	Net credit sales and average net receivables balance	$$\text{Accounts receivable turnover} = \frac{\text{Net credit sales}}{\text{Average net accounts receivable}}$$ $$\text{Average collection period} = \frac{365 \text{ days}}{\text{Accounts receivable turnover}}$$	Average collection period should be consistent with corporate credit policy. An increase may suggest a decline in financial health of customers.

Glossary

Accounts receivable *(p. 399)* Amounts customers owe on account.

Accounts receivable turnover *(p. 415)* A measure of the liquidity of accounts receivable, computed by dividing net credit sales by average net accounts receivable.

Aging the accounts receivable *(p. 405)* A schedule of customer balances classified by the length of time they have been unpaid.

Allowance method *(p. 402)* A method of accounting for bad debts that involves estimating uncollectible accounts at the end of each period.

Average collection period *(p. 415)* The average amount of time that a receivable is outstanding, calculated by dividing 365 days by the accounts receivable turnover.

Bad Debt Expense *(p. 401)* An expense account to record losses from extending credit.

Cash (net) realizable value *(p. 402)* The net amount a company expects to receive in cash from receivables.

Concentration of credit risk *(p. 414)* The threat of non-payment from a single large customer or class of customers that could adversely affect the financial health of the company.

Direct write-off method *(p. 401)* A method of accounting for bad debts that involves charging receivable balances to

Bad Debt Expense at the time receivables from a particular company are determined to be uncollectible.

Dishonored (defaulted) note *(p. 411)* A note that is not paid in full at maturity.

Factor *(p. 418)* A finance company or bank that buys receivables from businesses for a fee and then collects the payments directly from the customers.

Maker *(p. 407)* The party in a promissory note who is making the promise to pay.

Notes receivable *(p. 399)* Written promise (as evidenced by a formal instrument) for amounts to be received.

Payee *(p. 407)* The party to whom payment of a promissory note is to be made.

Percentage-of-receivables basis *(p. 404)* A method of estimating the amount of bad debt expense whereby management establishes a percentage relationship between the amount of receivables and the expected losses from uncollectible accounts.

Promissory note *(p. 407)* A written promise to pay a specified amount of money on demand or at a definite time.

Receivables *(p. 398)* Amounts due from individuals and companies that are expected to be collected in cash.

Trade receivables *(p. 399)* Notes and accounts receivable that result from sales transactions.

Comprehensive **Do it!**

Presented here are selected transactions related to B. Dylan Corp.

Mar. 1 Sold $20,000 of merchandise to Potter Company, terms 2/10, n/30.
11 Received payment in full from Potter Company for balance due on existing accounts receivable.
12 Accepted Juno Company's $20,000, 6-month, 12% note for balance due on outstanding account receivable.
13 Made B. Dylan Corp. credit card sales for $13,200.
15 Made Visa credit sales totaling $6,700. A 5% service fee is charged by Visa.
Apr. 11 Sold accounts receivable of $8,000 to Harcot Factor. Harcot Factor assesses a service charge of 2% of the amount of receivables sold.
13 Received collections of $8,200 on B. Dylan Corp. credit card sales.
May 10 Wrote off as uncollectible $16,000 of accounts receivable. (B. Dylan Corp. uses the percentage-of-receivables basis to estimate bad debts.)
June 30 The balance in accounts receivable at the end of the first 6 months is $200,000. The company estimates that 10% of accounts receivable will become uncollectible. At June 30 the credit balance in the allowance account prior to adjustment is $3,500. Recorded bad debt expense.
July 16 One of the accounts receivable written off in May pays the amount due, $4,000, in full.

Instructions

Prepare the journal entries for the transactions. (Omit cost of goods sold entries.)

Action Plan

- Generally, record accounts receivable at invoice price.
- Recognize that sales returns and allowances and cash discounts reduce the amount received on accounts receivable.
- Record a service charge expense on the seller's books when accounts receivable are sold.
- Prepare an adjusting entry for bad debt expense.
- Consider the balance in the allowance account under the percentage-of-receivables basis.
- Record write-offs of accounts receivable only in balance sheet accounts.

Solution to Comprehensive **Do it!** *

Mar. 1	Accounts Receivable—Potter Company		20,000	
	Sales Revenue			20,000
	(To record sales on account)			
11	Cash		19,600	
	Sales Discounts (2% × $20,000)		400	
	Accounts Receivable—Potter Company			20,000
	(To record collection of accounts receivable)			
12	Notes Receivable		20,000	
	Accounts Receivable—Juno Company			20,000
	(To record acceptance of Juno Company note)			
13	Accounts Receivable		13,200	
	Sales Revenue			13,200
	(To record company credit card sales)			
15	Cash		6,365	
	Service Charge Expense (5% × $6,700)		335	
	Sales Revenue			6,700
	(To record credit card sales)			
Apr. 11	Cash		7,840	
	Service Charge Expense (2% × $8,000)		160	
	Accounts Receivable			8,000
	(To record sale of receivables to factor)			
13	Cash		8,200	
	Accounts Receivable			8,200
	(To record collection of accounts receivable)			

May 10	Allowance for Doubtful Accounts		16,000	
	Accounts Receivable			16,000
	(To record write-off of accounts			
	receivable)			
June 30	Bad Debt Expense		16,500	
	Allowance for Doubtful Accounts			16,500
	[($200,000 × 10%) − $3,500]			
	(To record estimate of uncollectible			
	accounts)			
July 16	Accounts Receivable		4,000	
	Allowance for Doubtful Accounts			4,000
	(To reverse write-off of accounts			
	receivable)			
	Cash		4,000	
	Accounts Receivable			4,000
	(To record collection of accounts			
	receivable)			

✔ The Navigator

*Cost of goods sold entries are omitted here as well as in homework material.

PLUS **Self-Test, Brief Exercises, Exercises, Problem Set A, and many more resources are available for practice in WileyPLUS.**

Self-Test Questions

Answers are on page 444.

(LO 1) 1. A receivable that is evidenced by a formal instrument and that normally requires the payment of interest is:
    (a) an account receivable.
    (b) a trade receivable.
    (c) a note receivable.
    (d) a classified receivable.

(LO 2) 2. Kersee Company on June 15 sells merchandise on account to Soo Eng Co. for $1,000, terms 2/10, n/30. On June 20, Eng Co. returns merchandise worth $300 to Kersee Company. On June 24, payment is received from Eng Co. for the balance due. What is the amount of cash received?
    (a) $700.   (c) $686.
    (b) $680.   (d) None of the above.

(LO 3, 6) 3. Accounts and notes receivable are reported in the current assets section of the balance sheet at:
    (a) cash (net) realizable value
    (b) net book value.
    (c) lower-of-cost-or-market value.
    (d) invoice cost.

(LO 3) 4. Net credit sales for the month are $800,000. The accounts receivable balance is $160,000. The allowance is calculated as 7.5% of the receivables balance using the percentage-of-receivables basis. If Allowance for Doubtful Accounts has a credit balance of $5,000 before adjustment, what is the balance after adjustment?
    (a) $12,000.   (c) $17,000.
    (b) $7,000.   (d) $31,000.

(LO 3) 5. In 2014, Patterson Wholesale Company had net credit sales of $750,000. On January 1, 2014, Allowance for Doubtful Accounts had a credit balance of $18,000. During 2014, $30,000 of uncollectible accounts receivable were written off. Past experience indicates that the allowance should be 10% of the balance in receivables (percentage-of-receivables basis). If the accounts receivable balance at December 31 was $200,000, what is the required adjustment to Allowance for Doubtful Accounts at December 31, 2014?
    (a) $20,000.   (c) $32,000.
    (b) $75,000.   (d) $30,000.

(LO 3) 6. An analysis and aging of the accounts receivable of Raja Company at December 31 reveal these data:

Accounts receivable	$800,000
Allowance for doubtful accounts per	
books before adjustment (credit)	50,000
Amounts expected to become	
uncollectible	65,000

What is the cash realizable value of the accounts receivable at December 31, after adjustment?
    (a) $685,000.   (c) $800,000.
    (b) $750,000.   (d) $735,000.

(LO 4) 7. Which of these statements about promissory notes is **incorrect?**
   (a) The party making the promise to pay is called the maker.
   (b) The party to whom payment is to be made is called the payee.
   (c) A promissory note is not a negotiable instrument.
   (d) A promissory note is more liquid than an account receivable.

(LO 4) 8. Michael Co. accepts a $1,000, 3-month, 12% promissory note in settlement of an account with Tani Co. The entry to record this transaction is:

(a) Notes Receivable	1,030	
Accounts Receivable		1,030
(b) Notes Receivable	1,000	
Accounts Receivable		1,000
(c) Notes Receivable	1,000	
Sales Revenue		1,000
(d) Notes Receivable	1,020	
Accounts Receivable		1,020

(LO 5) 9. Schleis Co. holds Murphy Inc.'s $10,000, 120-day, 9% note. The entry made by Schleis Co. when the note is collected, assuming no interest has previously been accrued, is:

(a) Cash	10,300	
Notes Receivable		10,300
(b) Cash	10,000	
Notes Receivable		10,000
(c) Accounts Receivable	10,300	
Notes Receivable		10,000
Interest Revenue		300
(d) Cash	10,300	
Notes Receivable		10,000
Interest Revenue		300

(LO 7) 10. If a company is concerned about extending credit to a risky customer, it could do any of the following **except:**
   (a) require the customer to pay cash in advance.
   (b) require the customer to provide a letter of credit or a bank guarantee.
   (c) contact references provided by the customer, such as banks and other suppliers.
   (d) provide the customer a lengthy payment period to increase the chance of paying.

(LO 8) 11. Eddy Corporation had net credit sales during the year of $800,000 and cost of goods sold of $500,000. The balance in receivables at the beginning of the year was $100,000 and at the end of the year was $150,000. What was the accounts receivable turnover?
   (a) 6.4   (c) 5.3
   (b) 8.0   (d) 4.0

(LO 8) 12. Prall Corporation sells its goods on terms of 2/10, n/30. It has an accounts receivable turnover of 7. What is its average collection period (days)?
   (a) 2,555   (c) 52
   (b) 30   (d) 210

(LO 9) 13. Which of these statements about Visa credit card sales is **incorrect?**
   (a) The credit card issuer conducts the credit investigation of the customer.
   (b) The retailer is not involved in the collection process.
   (c) The retailer must wait to receive payment from the issuer.
   (d) The retailer receives cash more quickly than it would from individual customers.

(LO 9) 14. Good Stuff Retailers accepted $50,000 of Citibank Visa credit card charges for merchandise sold on July 1. Citibank charges 4% for its credit card use. The entry to record this transaction by Good Stuff Retailers will include a credit to Sales Revenue of $50,000 and a debit(s) to:
   (a) Cash $48,000 and Service Charge Expense $2,000.
   (b) Accounts Receivable $48,000 and Service Charge Expense $2,000.
   (c) Cash $50,000.
   (d) Accounts Receivable $50,000.

(LO 9) 15. A company can accelerate its cash receipts by all of the following **except:**
   (a) offering discounts for early payment.
   (b) accepting national credit cards for customer purchases.
   (c) selling receivables to a factor.
   (d) writing off receivables.

Go to the book's companion website, **www.wiley.com/college/kimmel**, to access additional Self-Test Questions.

 The Navigator

Questions

1. What is the difference between an account receivable and a note receivable?

2. What are some common types of receivables other than accounts receivable or notes receivable?

3. What are the essential features of the allowance method of accounting for bad debts?

4. Mitch Lang cannot understand why the cash realizable value does not decrease when an uncollectible account is written off under the allowance method. Clarify this point for Mitch.

5. Mendosa Company has a credit balance of $2,200 in Allowance for Doubtful Accounts before adjustment. The estimated uncollectibles under the percentage-of-receivables basis is $5,100. Prepare the adjusting entry.

6. What types of receivables does Tootsie Roll report on its balance sheet? Does it use the allowance

method or the direct write-off method to account for uncollectibles?

7. How are bad debts accounted for under the direct write-off method? What are the disadvantages of this method?

8. ➤ Debbie Trevino, the vice president of sales for Tropical Pools and Spas, wants the company's credit department to be less restrictive in granting credit. "How can we sell anything when you guys won't approve anybody?" she asks. Discuss the pros and cons of "easy credit." What are the accounting implications?

9. Your roommate is uncertain about the advantages of a promissory note. Compare the advantages of a note receivable with those of an account receivable.

10. How may the maturity date of a promissory note be stated?

11. Compute the missing amounts for each of the following notes.

Principal	Annual Interest Rate	Time	Total Interest
(a)	6%	60 days	$ 270
$30,000	8%	3 years	(d)
$60,000	(b)	5 months	$2,500
$50,000	11%	(c)	$2,750

12. Carrera Company dishonors a note at maturity. What are the options available to the lender?

13. General Motors Company has accounts receivable and notes receivable. How should the receivables be reported on the balance sheet?

14. ➤ ⊙▬▬C What are the steps to good receivables management?

15. ⊙▬▬C How might a company monitor the risk related to its accounts receivable?

16. ⊙▬▬C What is meant by a concentration of credit risk?

17. ⊙▬▬C The president of Dickerson Inc. proudly announces her company's improved liquidity since its current ratio has increased substantially from one year to the next. Does an increase in the current ratio always indicate improved liquidity? What other ratio or ratios might you review to determine whether or not the increase in the current ratio is an improvement in financial health?

18. ➤ Since hiring a new sales director, Hilson Inc. has enjoyed a 50% increase in sales. The CEO has also noticed, however, that the company's average collection period has increased from 17 days to 38 days. What might be the cause of this increase? What are the implications to management of this increase?

19. ⊙▬▬C The Coca-Cola Company's accounts receivable turnover was 9.05 in 2011, and its average amount of net receivables during the period was $3,424 million. What is the amount of its net credit sales for the period? What is the average collection period in days?

20. ➤ ⊙▬▬C JCPenney Company accepts both its own credit cards and national credit cards. What are the advantages of accepting both types of cards?

21. ➤ ⊙▬▬C An article in the *Wall Street Journal* indicated that companies are selling their receivables at a record rate. Why do companies sell their receivables?

22. Calico Corners decides to sell $400,000 of its accounts receivable to Quick Central Factors Inc. Quick Central Factors assesses a service charge of 3% of the amount of receivables sold. Prepare the journal entry that Calico Corners makes to record this sale.

23. Pine Corp. has experienced tremendous sales growth this year, but it is always short of cash. What is one explanation for this occurrence?

24. How can the amount of collections from customers be determined?

Brief Exercises

BE8-1 Presented below are three receivables transactions. Indicate whether these receivables are reported as accounts receivable, notes receivable, or other receivables on a balance sheet.
(a) Advanced $10,000 to an employee.
(b) Received a promissory note of $34,000 for services performed.
(c) Sold merchandise on account for $60,000 to a customer.

Identify different types of receivables.
(LO 1), **C**

BE8-2 Record the following transactions on the books of Cohen Co. (Omit cost of goods sold entries.)
(a) On July 1, Cohen Co. sold merchandise on account to Tracy Inc. for $23,000, terms 2/10, n/30.
(b) On July 8, Tracy Inc. returned merchandise worth $2,400 to Cohen Co.
(c) On July 11, Tracy Inc. paid for the merchandise.

Record basic accounts receivable transactions.
(LO 2), **AP**

BE8-3 At the end of 2013, Morley Co. has accounts receivable of $700,000 and an allowance for doubtful accounts of $25,000. On January 24, 2014, it is learned that the company's

Prepare entry for write-off, and determine cash realizable value.
(LO 3), **AP**

receivable from Spears Inc. is not collectible and therefore management authorizes a write-off of $4,300.

(a) Prepare the journal entry to record the write-off.

(b) What is the cash realizable value of the accounts receivable (1) before the write-off and (2) after the write-off?

Prepare entries for collection of bad debt write-off.
(LO 3), **AP**

BE8-4 Assume the same information as BE8-3 and that on March 4, 2014, Morley Co. receives payment of $4,300 in full from Spears Inc. Prepare the journal entries to record this transaction.

Prepare entry using percentage-of-receivables method.
(LO 3), **AP**

BE8-5 Hirdt Co. uses the percentage-of-receivables basis to record bad debt expense and concludes that 2% of accounts receivable will become uncollectible. Accounts receivable are $400,000 at the end of the year, and the allowance for doubtful accounts has a credit balance of $2,800.

(a) Prepare the adjusting journal entry to record bad debt expense for the year.

(b) If the allowance for doubtful accounts had a debit balance of $900 instead of a credit balance of $2,800, prepare the adjusting journal entry for bad debt expense.

Compute interest and determine maturity dates on notes.
(LO 4), **AP**

BE8-6 Compute interest and find the maturity date for the following notes.

Date of Note	Principal	Interest Rate (%)	Terms
(a) June 10	$80,000	6%	60 days
(b) July 14	$50,000	7%	90 days
(c) April 27	$12,000	8%	75 days

Determine maturity dates and compute interest and rates on notes.
(LO 4), **AP**

BE8-7 Presented below are data on three promissory notes. Determine the missing amounts.

Date of Note	Terms	Maturity Date	Principal	Annual Interest Rate	Total Interest
(a) April 1	60 days	?	$600,000	9%	?
(b) July 2	30 days	?	90,000	?	$600
(c) March 7	6 months	?	120,000	10%	?

Prepare entry for note receivable exchanged for accounts receivable.
(LO 4), **AP**

BE8-8 On January 10, 2014, Tolleson Co. sold merchandise on account to Simmons for $8,000, terms n/30. On February 9, Simmons gave Tolleson Co. a 7% promissory note in settlement of this account. Prepare the journal entry to record the sale and the settlement of the accounts receivable. (Omit cost of goods sold entries.)

Prepare entry for estimated uncollectibles and classifications, and compute ratios.
(LO 3, 6, 7, 8), **AP**

BE8-9 During its first year of operations, Gehrig Company had credit sales of $3,000,000, of which $400,000 remained uncollected at year-end. The credit manager estimates that $18,000 of these receivables will become uncollectible.

(a) Prepare the journal entry to record the estimated uncollectibles. (Assume an unadjusted balance of zero in Allowance for Doubtful Accounts.)

(b) Prepare the current assets section of the balance sheet for Gehrig Company, assuming that in addition to the receivables it has cash of $90,000, merchandise inventory of $180,000, and supplies of $13,000.

(c) Calculate the accounts receivable turnover and average collection period. Assume that average net accounts receivable were $300,000. Explain what these measures tell us.

Analyze accounts receivable.
(LO 8), **AP**

BE8-10 Suppose the 2014 financial statements of 3M Company report net sales of $23.1 billion. Accounts receivable (net) are $3.2 billion at the beginning of the year and $3.25 billion at the end of the year. Compute 3M's accounts receivable turnover. Compute 3M's average collection period for accounts receivable in days.

Prepare entries for credit card sale and sale of accounts receivable.
(LO 9), **AP**

BE8-11 Consider these transactions:

(a) Draber Restaurant accepted a Visa card in payment of a $200 lunch bill. The bank charges a 3% fee. What entry should Draber make?

(b) Marin Company sold its accounts receivable of $65,000. What entry should Marin make, given a service charge of 3% on the amount of receivables sold?

Determine cash collections.
(LO 9), **AP**

BE8-12 Richman Corp. had a beginning balance in accounts receivable of $70,000 and an ending balance of $91,000. Credit sales during the period were $598,000. Determine cash collections.

Do it! Review

Do it! 8-1 Ruth Company has been in business several years. At the end of the current year, the unadjusted trial balance shows:

Prepare entry for uncollectible accounts.
(LO 3), AP

Accounts Receivable	$ 310,000 Dr.
Sales Revenue	2,200,000 Cr.
Allowance for Doubtful Accounts	5,700 Cr.

Bad debts are estimated to be 7% of receivables. Prepare the entry to adjust Allowance for Doubtful Accounts.

Do it! 8-2 Berkman Wholesalers accepts from Almonte Stores a $6,200, 4-month, 9% note dated May 31 in settlement of Almonte's overdue account. The maturity date of the note is September 30. What entry does Berkman make at the maturity date, assuming Almonte pays the note and interest in full at that time?

Prepare entries for notes receivable.
(LO 4, 5), AP

Do it! 8-3 In 2014, Grossfeld Company has net credit sales of $1,600,000 for the year. It had a beginning accounts receivable (net) balance of $108,000 and an ending accounts receivable (net) balance of $120,000. Compute Grossfeld Company's (a) accounts receivable turnover and (b) average collection period in days.

Compute ratios for receivables.
(LO 8), AP

Do it! 8-4 Lounow Distributors is a growing company whose ability to raise capital has not been growing as quickly as its expanding assets and sales. Lounow's local banker has indicated that the company cannot increase its borrowing for the foreseeable future. Lounow's suppliers are demanding payment for goods acquired within 30 days of the invoice date, but Lounow's customers are slow in paying for their purchases (60–90 days). As a result, Lounow has a cash flow problem.

Prepare entry for factored accounts.
(LO 9), AP

Lounow needs $160,000 to cover next Friday's payroll. Its balance of outstanding accounts receivable totals $800,000. To alleviate this cash crunch, the company sells $170,000 of its receivables. Record the entry that Lounow would make. (Assume a 2% service charge.)

Exercises

E8-1 On January 6, Aaron Co. sells merchandise on account to Foley Inc. for $9,200, terms 1/10, n/30. On January 16, Foley pays the amount due.

Prepare entries for recognizing accounts receivable.
(LO 2), AP

Instructions

Prepare the entries on Aaron Co.'s books to record the sale and related collection. (Omit cost of goods sold entries.)

E8-2 On January 10, Allison Milo uses her Crawford Co. credit card to purchase merchandise from Crawford Co. for $1,700. On February 10, Milo is billed for the amount due of $1,700. On February 12, Milo pays $1,100 on the balance due. On March 10, Milo is billed for the amount due, including interest at 1% per month on the unpaid balance as of February 12.

Prepare entries for recognizing accounts receivable.
(LO 2), AP

Instructions

Prepare the entries on Crawford Co.'s books related to the transactions that occurred on January 10, February 12, and March 10. (Omit cost of goods sold entries.)

E8-3 At the beginning of the current period, Griffey Corp. had balances in Accounts Receivable of $200,000 and in Allowance for Doubtful Accounts of $9,000 (credit). During the period, it had net credit sales of $800,000 and collections of $763,000. It wrote off as uncollectible accounts receivable of $7,300. However, a $3,100 account previously written off as uncollectible was recovered before the end of the current period. Uncollectible accounts are estimated to total $25,000 at the end of the period. (Omit cost of goods sold entries.)

Journalize receivables transactions.
(LO 2, 3), AP

Instructions

(a) Prepare the entries to record sales and collections during the period.
(b) Prepare the entry to record the write-off of uncollectible accounts during the period.

(c) Prepare the entries to record the recovery of the uncollectible account during the period.
(d) Prepare the entry to record bad debt expense for the period.
(e) Determine the ending balances in Accounts Receivable and Allowance for Doubtful Accounts.
(f) What is the net realizable value of the receivables at the end of the period?

Prepare entries to record allowance for doubtful accounts.

(LO 3), AP

E8-4 The ledger of Wainwright Company at the end of the current year shows Accounts Receivable $78,000; Credit Sales $810,000; and Sales Returns and Allowances $40,000.

Instructions
(a) If Wainwright uses the direct write-off method to account for uncollectible accounts, journalize the adjusting entry at December 31, assuming Wainwright determines that Hiller's $900 balance is uncollectible.
(b) If Allowance for Doubtful Accounts has a credit balance of $1,100 in the trial balance, journalize the adjusting entry at December 31, assuming bad debts are expected to be 10% of accounts receivable.
(c) If Allowance for Doubtful Accounts has a debit balance of $500 in the trial balance, journalize the adjusting entry at December 31, assuming bad debts are expected to be 8% of accounts receivable.

Determine bad debt expense, and prepare the adjusting entry.

(LO 3), AP

E8-5 Stine Company has accounts receivable of $95,400 at March 31, 2014. An analysis of the accounts shows these amounts.

| | Balance, March 31 | |
Month of Sale	2014	2013
March	$65,000	$75,000
February	12,900	8,000
December and January	10,100	2,400
November and October	7,400	1,100
	$95,400	$86,500

Credit terms are 2/10, n/30. At March 31, 2014, there is a $2,100 credit balance in Allowance for Doubtful Accounts prior to adjustment. The company uses the percentage-of-receivables basis for estimating uncollectible accounts. The company's estimates of bad debts are as shown below.

Age of Accounts	Estimated Percentage Uncollectible
Current	2%
1–30 days past due	5
31–90 days past due	30
Over 90 days past due	50

Instructions
(a) Determine the total estimated uncollectibles.
(b) Prepare the adjusting entry at March 31, 2014, to record bad debt expense.
(c) Discuss the implications of the changes in the aging schedule from 2013 to 2014.

Prepare entry for estimated uncollectibles, write-off, and recovery.

(LO 3), AP

E8-6 On December 31, 2013, when its Allowance for Doubtful Accounts had a debit balance of $1,400, Hunt Co. estimates that 9% of its accounts receivable balance of $90,000 will become uncollectible and records the necessary adjustment to Allowance for Doubtful Accounts. On May 11, 2014, Hunt Co. determined that J. Byrd's account was uncollectible and wrote off $1,200. On June 12, 2014, Byrd paid the amount previously written off.

Instructions
Prepare the journal entries on December 31, 2013, May 11, 2014, and June 12, 2014.

Prepare entries for notes receivable transactions.

(LO 4, 5), AP

E8-7 Malone Supply Co. has the following transactions related to notes receivable during the last 2 months of the year. The company does not make entries to accrue interest except at December 31.

Nov. 1   Loaned $60,000 cash to B. Carr on a 12-month, 7% note.
Dec. 11   Sold goods to R. P. Kiner, Inc., receiving a $3,600, 90-day, 8% note.
     16   Received a $12,000, 180-day, 9% note to settle an open account from M. Adcock.
     31   Accrued interest revenue on all notes receivable.

Instructions

Journalize the transactions for Malone Supply Co. (Omit cost of goods sold entries.)

E8-8   These transactions took place for Glavine Co.

Journalize notes receivable transactions.

(LO 4, 5), **AP**

2013

May   1   Received a $5,000, 12-month, 6% note in exchange for an outstanding account receivable from S. Rooney.

Dec. 31   Accrued interest revenue on the S. Rooney note.

2014

May   1   Received principal plus interest on the S. Rooney note. (No interest has been accrued since December 31, 2013.)

Instructions

Record the transactions in the general journal. The company does not make entries to accrue interest except at December 31.

E8-9   Shannon Corp. had the following balances in receivable accounts at October 31, 2014 (in thousands): Allowance for Doubtful Accounts $52; Accounts Receivable $2,910; Other Receivables $189; Notes Receivable $1,353.

Prepare a balance sheet presentation of receivables.

(LO 6), **AP**

Instructions

Prepare the balance sheet presentation of Shannon Corp.'s receivables in good form.

E8-10   The following is a list of activities that companies perform in relation to their receivables.

Identify the principles of receivables management.

(LO 7), **K**

1. Selling receivables to a factor.
2. Reviewing company ratings in *The Dun and Bradstreet Reference Book of American Business*.
3. Collecting information on competitors' payment period policies.
4. Preparing monthly accounts receivable aging schedule and investigating problem accounts.
5. Calculating the accounts receivable turnover and average collection period.

Instructions

Match each of the activities listed above with a purpose of the activity listed below.

(a) Determine to whom to extend credit.
(b) Establish a payment period.
(c) Monitor collections.
(d) Evaluate the liquidity of receivables.
(e) Accelerate cash receipts from receivable when necessary.

E8-11   Suppose the following information was taken from the 2014 financial statements of FedEx Corporation, a major global transportation/delivery company.

Compute ratios to evaluate a company's receivables balance.

(LO 7, 8), **AN**

(in millions)	2014	2013
Accounts receivable (gross)	$ 3,587	$ 4,517
Accounts receivable (net)	3,391	4,359
Allowance for doubtful accounts	196	158
Sales revenue	35,497	37,953
Total current assets	7,116	7,244

Instructions

Answer each of the following questions.

(a) Calculate the accounts receivable turnover and the average collection period for 2014 for FedEx.
(b) Is accounts receivable a material component of the company's total current assets?
(c) Evaluate the balance in FedEx's allowance for doubtful accounts.

E8-12   The following ratios are available for Lin Inc.

Evaluate liquidity.

(LO 7, 8, 9), **AN**

	2014	2013
Current ratio	1.3:1	1.5:1
Accounts receivable turnover	12 times	10 times
Inventory turnover	11 times	9 times

Instructions

(a) Is Lin's short-term liquidity improving or deteriorating in 2014? Be specific in your answer, referring to relevant ratios.

(b) Do changes in turnover ratios affect profitability? Explain.

(c) Identify any steps Lin might have taken, or might wish to take, to improve its management of its accounts receivable and inventory turnovers.

Prepare entry for sale of accounts receivable.
(LO 9), **AP**

E8-13 On March 3, Beachy Appliances sells $710,000 of its receivables to National Factors Inc. National Factors Inc. assesses a service charge of 4% of the amount of receivables sold.

Instructions

Prepare the entry on Beachy Appliances' books to record the sale of the receivables.

Identify reason for sale of receivables.
(LO 9), **C**

E8-14 In a recent annual report, Office Depot, Inc. notes that the company entered into an agreement to sell all of its credit card program receivables to financial service companies.

Instructions

Explain why Office Depot, a financially stable company with positive cash flow, would choose to sell its receivables.

Prepare entry for credit card sale.
(LO 9), **AP**

E8-15 On May 10, Renn Company sold merchandise for $4,000 and accepted the customer's First Business Bank MasterCard. At the end of the day, the First Business Bank MasterCard receipts were deposited in the company's bank account. First Business Bank charges a 3.8% service charge for credit card sales.

Instructions

Prepare the entry on Renn Company's books to record the sale of merchandise.

Prepare entry for credit card sale.
(LO 9), **AP**

E8-16 On July 4, Susie's Restaurant accepts a Visa card for a $250 dinner bill. Visa charges a 4% service fee.

Instructions

Prepare the entry on Susie's books related to the transaction.

Determine cash flows and evaluate quality of earnings.
(LO 9), **AN**

E8-17 Kimbrel Corp. significantly reduced its requirements for credit sales. As a result, sales during the current year increased dramatically. It had receivables at the beginning of the year of $38,000 and ending receivables of $191,000. Credit sales were $380,000.

Instructions

(a) Determine cash collections during the period.

(b) Discuss how your findings in part (a) would affect Kimbrel Corp.'s quality of earnings ratio. (Do not compute.)

(c) What concerns might you have regarding Kimbrel's accounting?

Exercises: Set B and Challenge Exercises

Visit the book's companion website, at **www.wiley.com/college/kimmel**, and choose the Student Companion site to access Exercise Set B and Challenge Exercises.

Problems: Set A

Journalize transactions related to bad debts.
(LO 2, 3), **AP**

P8-1A Reynolds.com uses the allowance method of accounting for bad debts. The company produced the following aging of the accounts receivable at year-end.

| | Total | Number of Days Outstanding | | | | |
		0–30	31–60	61–90	91–120	Over 120
Accounts receivable	$377,000	$222,000	$90,000	$38,000	$15,000	$12,000
% uncollectible		1%	4%	5%	8%	10%
Estimated bad debts						

Instructions

(a) Calculate the total estimated bad debts based on the above information.

(b) Prepare the year-end adjusting journal entry to record the bad debts using the aged uncollectible accounts receivable determined in (a). Assume the unadjusted balance in Allowance for Doubtful Accounts is a $4,000 debit.

(c) Of the above accounts, $5,000 is determined to be specifically uncollectible. Prepare the journal entry to write off the uncollectible account.

(d) The company collects $5,000 subsequently on a specific account that had previously been determined to be uncollectible in (c). Prepare the journal entry(ies) necessary to restore the account and record the cash collection.

(e) Comment on how your answers to (a)–(d) would change if Reynolds.com used 3% of total accounts receivable, rather than aging the accounts receivable. What are the advantages to the company of aging the accounts receivable rather than applying a percentage to total accounts receivable?

(a) Tot. est.
bad debts $10,120

P8-2A At December 31, 2013, Weiss Imports reported this information on its balance sheet.

Accounts receivable	$600,000
Less: Allowance for doubtful accounts	37,000

Prepare journal entries related to bad debt expense, and compute ratios.

(LO 2, 3, 8), AP

During 2014, the company had the following transactions related to receivables.

1. Sales on account	$2,500,000
2. Sales returns and allowances	50,000
3. Collections of accounts receivable	2,200,000
4. Write-offs of accounts receivable deemed uncollectible	41,000
5. Recovery of bad debts previously written off as uncollectible	15,000

Instructions

(a) Prepare the journal entries to record each of these five transactions. Assume that no cash discounts were taken on the collections of accounts receivable. (Omit cost of goods sold entries.)

(b) Enter the January 1, 2014, balances in Accounts Receivable and Allowance for Doubtful Accounts, post the entries to the two accounts (use T-accounts), and determine the balances.

(c) Prepare the journal entry to record bad debt expense for 2014, assuming that aging the accounts receivable indicates that estimated bad debts are $46,000.

(d) Compute the accounts receivable turnover and average collection period.

(b) A/R bal. $809,000

P8-3A Presented below is an aging schedule for Bosworth Company.

Journalize transactions related to bad debts.

(LO 2, 3), AP

Customer	Total	Not Yet Due	Number of Days Past Due			
			1–30	31–60	61–90	Over 90
Aneesh	$ 24,000		$ 9,000	$15,000		
Bird	30,000	$ 30,000				
Cope	50,000	5,000	5,000		$40,000	
DeSpears	38,000					$38,000
Others	120,000	72,000	35,000	13,000		
	$262,000	$107,000	$49,000	$28,000	$40,000	$38,000
Estimated percentage uncollectible		3%	7%	12%	24%	60%
Total estimated bad debts	$ 42,400	$ 3,210	$ 3,430	$ 3,360	$ 9,600	$22,800

At December 31, 2013, the unadjusted balance in Allowance for Doubtful Accounts is a credit of $8,000.

Instructions

(a) Journalize and post the adjusting entry for bad debts at December 31, 2013. (Use T-accounts.)

(b) Journalize and post to the allowance account these 2014 events and transactions:
1. March 1, a $600 customer balance originating in 2013 is judged uncollectible.
2. May 1, a check for $600 is received from the customer whose account was written off as uncollectible on March 1.

(c) Journalize the adjusting entry for bad debts at December 31, 2014, assuming that the unadjusted balance in Allowance for Doubtful Accounts is a debit of $1,400 and the aging schedule indicates that total estimated bad debts will be $36,700.

Compute bad debt amounts.
(LO 3), **AP**

P8-4A Here is information related to Freeman Company for 2014.

Total credit sales	$1,500,000
Accounts receivable at December 31	840,000
Bad debts written off	37,000

Instructions

(a) What amount of bad debt expense will Freeman Company report if it uses the direct write-off method of accounting for bad debts?

(b) Assume that Freeman Company decides to estimate its bad debt expense based on 4% of accounts receivable. What amount of bad debt expense will the company record if Allowance for Doubtful Accounts has a credit balance of $3,000?

(c) Assume the same facts as in part (b), except that there is a $1,000 debit balance in Allowance for Doubtful Accounts. What amount of bad debt expense will Freeman record?

(d) ▬▬▶ What is a weakness of the direct write-off method of reporting bad debt expense?

Journalize entries to record transactions related to bad debts.
(LO 2, 3), **AP**

P8-5A At December 31, 2014, the trial balance of Sloane Company contained the following amounts before adjustment.

	Debit	**Credit**
Accounts Receivable	$180,000	
Allowance for Doubtful Accounts		$ 1,500
Sales Revenue		875,000

Instructions

(a) Prepare the adjusting entry at December 31, 2014, to record bad debt expense, assuming that the aging schedule indicates that $10,200 of accounts receivable will be uncollectible.

(b) Repeat part (a), assuming that instead of a credit balance there is a $1,500 debit balance in Allowance for Doubtful Accounts.

(c) During the next month, January 2015, a $2,100 account receivable is written off as uncollectible. Prepare the journal entry to record the write-off.

(d) Repeat part (c), assuming that Sloane Company uses the direct write-off method instead of the allowance method in accounting for uncollectible accounts receivable.

(e) ▬▬▶ What are the advantages of using the allowance method in accounting for uncollectible accounts as compared to the direct write-off method?

Journalize various receivables transactions.
(LO 2, 4, 5), **AP**

P8-6A On January 1, 2014, Oswalt Company had Accounts Receivable of $54,200 and Allowance for Doubtful Accounts of $3,700. Oswalt Company prepares financial statements annually. During the year, the following selected transactions occurred.

Jan.	5	Sold $4,000 of merchandise to Ross Company, terms n/30.
Feb.	2	Accepted a $4,000, 4-month, 9% promissory note from Ross Company for balance due.
	12	Sold $12,000 of merchandise to Cano Company and accepted Cano's $12,000, 2-month, 10% note for the balance due.
	26	Sold $5,200 of merchandise to Meachum Co., terms n/10.
Apr.	5	Accepted a $5,200, 3-month, 8% note from Meachum Co. for balance due.
	12	Collected Cano Company note in full.
June	2	Collected Ross Company note in full.
	15	Sold $2,000 of merchandise to Glanvile Inc. and accepted a $2,000, 6-month, 12% note for the amount due.

Instructions

Journalize the transactions. (Omit cost of goods sold entries.)

P8-7A The president of Giraldi Enterprises asks if you could indicate the impact certain transactions have on the following ratios.

Explain the impact of transactions on ratios.
(LO 8), **C**

Transaction	Current Ratio (2:1)	Accounts Receivable Turnover (10×)	Average Collection Period (36.5 days)
1. Received $5,000 on cash sale. The cost of the goods sold was $2,600.			
2. Recorded bad debt expense of $500 using allowance method.			
3. Wrote off a $100 account receivable as uncollectible (Uses allowance method.)			
4. Recorded $2,500 sales on account. The cost of the goods sold was $1,500.			

Instructions

Complete the table, indicating whether each transaction will increase (I), decrease (D), or have no effect (NE) on the specific ratios provided for Giraldi Enterprises.

P8-8A Kolton Company closes its books on its July 31 year-end. The company does not make entries to accrue for interest except at its year-end. On June 30, the Notes Receivable account balance is $23,800. Notes Receivable include the following.

Prepare entries for various credit card and notes receivable transactions.
(LO 4, 5, 6, 9), **AP**
GLS

Date	Maker	Face Value	Term	Maturity Date	Interest Rate
April 21	Booth Inc.	$ 6,000	90 days	July 20	8%
May 25	Manning Co.	7,800	60 days	July 24	10%
June 30	ANF Corp.	10,000	6 months	December 31	6%

During July, the following transactions were completed.

July	5	Made sales of $4,500 on Kolton credit cards.
	14	Made sales of $600 on Visa credit cards. The credit card service charge is 3%.
	20	Received payment in full from Booth Inc. on the amount due.
	24	Received payment in full from Manning Co. on the amount due.

Instructions

(a) Journalize the July transactions and the July 31 adjusting entry for accrued interest receivable. (Interest is computed using 360 days; omit cost of goods sold entries.)

(b) Enter the balances at July 1 in the receivable accounts and post the entries to all of the receivable accounts. (Use T-accounts.)

(c) Show the balance sheet presentation of the receivable accounts at July 31.

(b) A/R bal. $ 4,500

(c) Tot. receivables $14,550

P8-9A Suppose the amounts presented here are basic financial information (in millions) from the 2014 annual reports of Nike and adidas.

Calculate and interpret various ratios.
(LO 7, 8), **AN**

	Nike	adidas
Sales revenue	$19,176.1	$10,381
Allowance for doubtful accounts, beginning	78.4	119
Allowance for doubtful accounts, ending	110.8	124
Accounts receivable balance (gross), beginning	2,873.7	1,743
Accounts receivable balance (gross), ending	2,994.7	1,553

Instructions

Calculate the accounts receivable turnover and average collection period for both companies. Comment on the difference in their collection experiences.

Problems: Set B

P8-1B The following represents selected information taken from a company's aging schedule to estimate uncollectible accounts receivable at year-end.

Journalize transactions related to bad debts.
(LO 2, 3), **AP**

	Total	0–30	31–60	61–90	91–120	Over 120
		Number of Days Outstanding				
Accounts receivable	$305,000	$107,000	$60,000	$50,000	$38,000	$50,000
% uncollectible		2%	5%	7.5%	10%	25%
Estimated bad debts						

Instructions

(a) Calculate the total estimated bad debts based on the above information.

(b) Prepare the year-end adjusting journal entry to record the bad debts using the allowance method and the aged uncollectible accounts receivable determined in (a). Assume the unadjusted balance in Allowance for Doubtful Accounts is a $7,000 credit.

(c) Of the above accounts, $2,600 is determined to be specifically uncollectible. Prepare the journal entry to write off the uncollectible accounts.

(d) The company subsequently collects $1,200 on a specific account that had previously been determined to be uncollectible in (c). Prepare the journal entry(ies) necessary to restore the account and record the cash collection.

(e) Explain how establishing an allowance account satisfies the expense recognition principle.

(a) Tot. est. bad debts $25,190

Prepare journal entries related to bad debt expense, and compute ratios.
(LO 2, 3, 8), AP

P8-2B At December 31, 2013, Dustin Company reported this information on its balance sheet.

Accounts receivable	$960,000
Less: Allowance for doubtful accounts	78,000

During 2014, the company had the following transactions related to receivables.

1. Sales on account	$3,600,000
2. Sales returns and allowances	150,000
3. Collections of accounts receivable	3,100,000
4. Write-offs of accounts receivable deemed uncollectible	92,000
5. Recovery of bad debts previously written off as uncollectible	28,000

Instructions

(a) Prepare the journal entries to record each of these five transactions. Assume that no cash discounts were taken on the collections of accounts receivable. (Omit cost of goods sold entries.)

(b) Enter the January 1, 2014, balances in Accounts Receivable and Allowance for Doubtful Accounts, post the entries to the two accounts (use T-accounts), and determine the balances.

(c) Prepare the journal entry to record bad debt expense for 2014, assuming that aging the accounts receivable indicates that expected bad debts are $140,000.

(d) Compute the accounts receivable turnover and average collection period.

(b) A/R bal. $1,218,000

Journalize transactions related to bad debts.
(LO 2, 3), AP

XLS

P8-3B Presented below is an aging schedule for Harper Company.

Customer	Total	Not Yet Due	1–30	31–60	61–90	Over 90
			Number of Days Past Due			
Allen	$ 18,000		$12,000	$ 6,000		
Brian	24,000				$24,000	
Charles	40,000	$ 25,000	15,000			
Dwight	52,000					$52,000
Others	196,000	97,000	60,000	39,000		
	$330,000	$122,000	$87,000	$45,000	$24,000	$52,000
Estimated percentage uncollectible		1%	3%	9%	20%	40%
Total estimated uncollectible accounts	$ 33,480	$ 1,220	$ 2,610	$ 4,050	$ 4,800	$20,800

At December 31, 2013, the unadjusted balance in Allowance for Doubtful Accounts is a credit of $9,000.

Instructions
(a) Journalize and post the adjusting entry for bad debts at December 31, 2013. (Use T-accounts.)
(b) Journalize and post to the allowance account these 2014 events and transactions:
  1. February 1, a $900 customer balance originating in 2013 is judged uncollectible.
  2. July 1, a check for $900 is received from the customer whose account was written off as uncollectible on February 1.
(c) Journalize the adjusting entry for bad debts at December 31, 2014, assuming that the unadjusted balance in Allowance for Doubtful Accounts is a debit of $2,800 and the aging schedule indicates that total estimated uncollectible accounts will be $30,600.

P8-4B Here is information related to Orson Company for 2014.

Total credit sales	$1,800,000
Accounts receivable at December 31	500,000
Bad debts written off	15,000

Compute bad debt amounts.
(LO 3), **AP**

Instructions
(a) What amount of bad debt expense will Orson Company report if it uses the direct write-off method of accounting for bad debts?
(b) Assume that Orson Company decides to estimate its bad debt expense based on 4% of accounts receivable. What amount of bad debt expense will the company record if it has an Allowance for Doubtful Accounts credit balance of $3,700?
(c) Assume the same facts as in part (b), except that there is a $2,000 debit balance in Allowance for Doubtful Accounts. What amount of bad debt expense will Orson record?
(d) ▭▭▭▷ What is the weakness of the direct write-off method of reporting bad debt expense?

P8-5B At December 31, 2014, the trial balance of Valcik Company contained the following amounts before adjustment.

Journalize entries to record transactions related to bad debts.
(LO 2, 3), **AP**

	Debit	**Credit**
Accounts Receivable	$120,000	
Allowance for Doubtful Accounts		$ 2,800
Sales Revenue		680,000

Instructions
(a) Prepare the adjusting entry at December 31, 2014, to record bad debt expense, assuming that the aging schedule indicates that $7,600 of accounts receivable will be uncollectible.
(b) Repeat part (a) assuming that instead of a credit balance there is a $2,500 debit balance in Allowance for Doubtful Accounts.
(c) During the next month, January 2015, a $750 account receivable is written off as uncollectible. Prepare the journal entry to record the write-off.
(d) Repeat part (c), assuming that Valcik Company uses the direct write-off method instead of the allowance method in accounting for uncollectible accounts receivable.
(e) ▭▭▭▷ What are the advantages of using an aging schedule and the allowance method in accounting for uncollectible accounts as compared to the direct write-off method?

P8-6B On January 1, 2014, Alter Company had Accounts Receivable $154,000; Notes Receivable of $12,000; and Allowance for Doubtful Accounts of $13,200. The note receivable is from Hartwig Company. It is a 4-month, 9% note dated December 31, 2013. Alter Company prepares financial statements annually. During the year, the following selected transactions occurred.

Journalize various receivables transactions.
(LO 2, 4, 5), **AP**

Jan.	5	Sold $10,000 of merchandise to Flynn Company, terms n/15.
	20	Accepted Flynn Company's $10,000, 3-month, 6% note for balance due.
Feb.	18	Sold $4,000 of merchandise to Mink Company and accepted Mink's $4,000, 6-month, 8% note for the amount due.
Apr.	20	Collected Flynn Company note in full.
	30	Received payment in full from Hartwig Company on the amount due.
May	25	Accepted Creech Inc.'s $9,000, 6-month, 4% note in settlement of a past-due balance on account.
Aug.	18	Received payment in full from Mink Company on note due.
Sept.	1	Sold $5,000 of merchandise to Glazer Company and accepted a $5,000, 6-month, 6% note for the amount due.

Explain the impact of transactions on ratios.
(LO 8), **C**

Instructions

Journalize the transactions. (Omit cost of goods sold entries.)

P8-7B The president of Thompson Enterprises asks if you could indicate the impact certain transactions have on the following ratios.

Transaction	Current Ratio (2:1)	Accounts Receivable Turnover (10×)	Average Collection Period (36.5 days)
1. Recorded $4,300 sales on account. The cost of the goods sold was $2,000.			
2. Recorded bad debt expense of $700 using allowance method.			
3. Wrote off a $300 account receivable as uncollectible (uses allowance method).			
4. Collected a $200 account receivable that had previously been written off.			

Instructions

Complete the table, indicating whether each transaction will increase (I), decrease (D), or have no effect (NE) on the specific ratios provided for Thompson Enterprises.

Prepare entries for various credit card and notes receivable transactions.
(LO 4, 5, 6, 9), **AP**

P8-8B Durhan Company closes its books on its October 31 year-end. The company does not make entries to accrue for interest except at its year-end. On September 30, the Notes Receivable account balance is $22,800. Notes Receivable include the following.

Date	Maker	Face Value	Term	Maturity Date	Interest Rate
Aug. 16	Stuhmer Inc.	$10,000	60 days	Oct. 15	6%
Aug. 25	Moberg Co.	3,000	2 months	Oct. 25	7%
Sept. 30	Earnest Corp.	9,800	6 months	Mar. 30	6%

Interest is computed using a 360-day year. During October, the following transactions were completed.

Oct.	7	Made sales of $4,600 on Durhan credit cards.
	12	Made sales of $600 on Visa credit cards. The credit card service charge is 3%.
	15	Received payment in full from Stuhmer Inc. on the amount due.
	25	Received payment in full from Moberg Co. on amount due.

Instructions

(a) Journalize the October transactions and the October 31 adjusting entry for accrued interest receivable. (Interest is computed using 360 days; omit cost of goods sold entries.)

(b) A/R bal. $4,600

(b) Enter the balances at October 1 in the receivable accounts and post the entries to all of the receivable accounts. (Use T-accounts.)

(c) Tot. receivables $14,449

(c) Show the balance sheet presentation of the receivable accounts at October 31, 2014.

Calculate and interpret various ratios.
(LO 7, 8), **AN**

P8-9B Suppose the following financial information (in millions) is from the 2014 annual reports of Redbird Sportswear and The Carwright Company.

	Redbird	Carwright
Sales revenue	$1,200.0	$1,350.0
Allowance for doubtful accounts, Jan. 1	6.7	12.5
Allowance for doubtful accounts, Dec. 31	7.4	14.8
Accounts receivable balance (gross), Jan. 1	293.3	216.5
Accounts receivable balance (gross), Dec. 31	307.2	202.9

Instructions

Calculate the accounts receivable turnover and average collection period for both companies. Comment on the difference in their collection experiences.

Problems: Set C

Visit the book's companion website, at **www.wiley.com/college/kimmel**, and choose the Student Companion site to access Problem Set C.

Comprehensive Problem

CP8   Madson Corporation's balance sheet at December 31, 2013, is presented below.

MADSON CORPORATION
Balance Sheet
December 31, 2013

Cash	$13,100	Accounts payable	$ 8,750
Accounts receivable	19,780	Common stock	20,000
Allowance for doubtful accounts	(800)	Retained earnings	12,730
Inventory	9,400		
	$41,480		$41,480

During January 2014, the following transactions occurred. Madson uses the perpetual inventory method.

Jan.   1   Madson accepted a 4-month, 8% note from Matheny Company in payment of Matheny's $1,200 account.

3   Madson wrote off as uncollectible the accounts of Payton Corporation ($450) and Cruz Company ($280).

8   Madson purchased $17,200 of inventory on account.

11   Madson sold for $25,000 on account inventory that cost $17,500.

15   Madson sold inventory that cost $700 to Rich Jenson for $1,000. Jenson charged this amount on his Visa First Bank card. The service fee charged Madson by First Bank is 3%.

17   Madson collected $22,900 from customers on account.

21   Madson paid $16,300 on accounts payable.

24   Madson received payment in full ($280) from Cruz Company on the account written off on January 3.

27   Madson purchased advertising supplies for $1,400 cash.

31   Madson paid other operating expenses, $3,218.

Adjustment data:

1. Interest is recorded for the month on the note from January 1.
2. Bad debts are expected to be 6% of the January 31, 2014, accounts receivable.
3. A count of advertising supplies on January 31, 2014, reveals that $560 remains unused.
4. The income tax rate is 30%. (*Hint:* Prepare the income statement up to "Income before taxes" and multiply by 30% to compute the amount; round to whole dollars.)

Instructions

(You may want to set up T-accounts to determine ending balances.)

(a) Prepare journal entries for the transactions listed above and adjusting entries. (Include entries for cost of goods sold using the perpetual inventory system.)

(b) Prepare an adjusted trial balance at January 31, 2014.

(c) Prepare an income statement and a retained earnings statement for the month ending January 31, 2014, and a classified balance sheet as of January 31, 2014.

Continuing Cookie Chronicle

(*Note:* This is a continuation of the Cookie Chronicle from Chapters 1 through 7.)

CCC8 One of Natalie's friends, Curtis Lesperance, runs a coffee shop where he sells specialty coffees and prepares and sells muffins and cookies. He is eager to buy one of Natalie's fine European mixers, which would enable him to make larger batches of muffins and cookies. However, Curtis cannot afford to pay for the mixer for at least 30 days. He asks Natalie if she would be willing to sell him the mixer on credit. Natalie comes to you for advice.

Go to the book's companion website, at **www.wiley.com/college/kimmel**, to see the completion of this problem.

Broadening Your Perspective

Financial Reporting and Analysis

FINANCIAL REPORTING PROBLEM: *Tootsie Roll Industries, Inc.*

BYP8-1 Refer to the financial statements of Tootsie Roll Industries and the accompanying notes to its financial statements in Appendix A.

Instructions
(a) Calculate the accounts receivable turnover and average collection period for 2011. (Use "Net Product Sales." Assume all sales were credit sales.)
(b) Did Tootsie Roll have any potentially significant credit risks in 2011? (*Hint:* Review Note 1 under Revenue recognition and Note 9 to the financial statements.)
(c) What conclusions can you draw from the information in parts (a) and (b)?

COMPARATIVE ANALYSIS PROBLEM: *Tootsie Roll vs. Hershey*

BYP8-2 The financial statements of The Hershey Company are presented in Appendix B, following the financial statements for Tootsie Roll in Appendix A.

Instructions
(a) Based on the information contained in these financial statements, compute the following 2011 values for each company.
   (1) Accounts receivable turnover. (For Tootsie Roll, use "Net product sales." Assume all sales were credit sales.)
   (2) Average collection period for accounts receivable.
(b) What conclusions concerning the management of accounts receivable can be drawn from these data?

RESEARCH CASE

BYP8-3 The August 31, 2009, issue of the *Wall Street Journal* includes an article by Serena Ng and Cari Tuna entitled "Big Firms Are Quick to Collect, Slow to Pay."

Instructions

Read the article and answer the following questions.
(a) How many days did InBev tell its suppliers that it was going to take to pay? How many days did it take previously?
(b) What steps did General Electric take to free up cash? How much cash did it free up?
(c) On average, how many days did companies with more than $5 billion take to pay suppliers, and how many days did they take to collect from their customers? How did this compare to companies with less than $500 million in sales?
(d) Are there any risks involved with being too tough in negotiating delayed payment terms with suppliers?

INTERPRETING FINANCIAL STATEMENTS

BYP8-4 Suppose the information below is from the 2014 financial statements and accompanying notes of The Scotts Company, a major manufacturer of lawn-care products.

(in millions)	2014	2013
Accounts receivable	$ 270.4	$ 259.7
Allowance for uncollectible accounts	10.6	11.4
Sales revenue	2,981.8	2,871.8
Total current assets	1,044.9	999.3

THE SCOTTS COMPANY
Notes to the Financial Statements

Note 19. Concentrations of Credit Risk

Financial instruments which potentially subject the Company to concentration of credit risk consist principally of trade accounts receivable. The Company sells its consumer products to a wide variety of retailers, including mass merchandisers, home centers, independent hardware stores, nurseries, garden outlets, warehouse clubs, food and drug stores and local and regional chains. Professional products are sold to commercial nurseries, greenhouses, landscape services and growers of specialty agriculture crops. Concentrations of accounts receivable at September 30, net of accounts receivable pledged under the terms of the New MARP Agreement whereby the purchaser has assumed the risk associated with the debtor's financial inability to pay ($146.6 million and $149.5 million for 2014 and 2013, respectively), were as follows.

	2014	2013
Due from customers geographically located in North America	53%	52%
Applicable to the consumer business	61%	54%
Applicable to Scotts LawnService®, the professional businesses (primarily distributors), Smith & Hawken® and Morning Song®	39%	46%
Top 3 customers within consumer business as a percent of total consumer accounts receivable	0%	0%

The remainder of the Company's accounts receivable at September 30, 2014 and 2013, were generated from customers located outside of North America, primary retailers, distributors, nurseries and growers in Europe. No concentrations of customers of individual customers within this group account for more than 10% of the Company's accounts receivable at either balance sheet date.

The Company's three largest customers are reported within the Global Consumer segment, and are the only customers that individually represent more than 10% of reported consolidated net sales for each of the last three fiscal years. These three customers accounted for the following percentages of consolidated net sales for the fiscal years ended September 30:

	Largest Customer	2nd Largest Customer	3rd Largest Customer
2014	21.0%	13.5%	13.4%
2013	20.2%	10.9%	10.2%
2012	21.5%	11.2%	10.5%

Instructions

Answer each of the following questions.
(a) Calculate the accounts receivable turnover and average collection period for 2014 for the company.
(b) Is accounts receivable a material component of the company's total 2014 current assets?
(c) Scotts sells seasonal products. How might this affect the accuracy of your answer to part (a)?
(d) Evaluate the credit risk of Scotts' 2014 concentrated receivables.
(e) Comment on the informational value of Scotts' Note 19 on concentrations of credit risk.

REAL-WORLD FOCUS

BYP8-5 *Purpose:* To learn more about factoring from websites that provide factoring services.

Address: **www.ccapital.net**, or go to **www.wiley.com/college/kimmel**

Instructions

Go to the website, click on **Invoice Factoring**, and answer the following questions.
(a) What are some of the benefits of factoring?
(b) What is the range of the percentages of the typical discount rate?
(c) If a company factors its receivables, what percentage of the value of the receivables can it expect to receive from the factor in the form of cash, and how quickly will it receive the cash?

Critical Thinking

DECISION-MAKING ACROSS THE ORGANIZATION

BYP8-6 Jan and Roy Falcon own Club Fab. From its inception, Club Fab has sold merchandise on either a cash or credit basis, but no credit cards have been accepted. During the past several months, the Falcons have begun to question their credit-sales policies. First, they have lost some sales because of their refusal to accept credit cards. Second, representatives of two metropolitan banks have convinced them to accept their national credit cards. One bank, City National Bank, has stated that (1) its credit card fee is 4% and (2) it pays the retailer 96 cents on each $1 of sales within 3 days of receiving the credit card billings.

The Falcons decide that they should determine the cost of carrying their own credit sales. From the accounting records of the past 3 years, they accumulate these data:

	2014	2013	2012
Net credit sales	$500,000	$600,000	$400,000
Collection agency fees for slow-paying customers	2,900	2,600	1,600
Salary of part-time accounts receivable clerk	4,400	4,400	4,400

Credit and collection expenses as a percentage of net credit sales are as follows: uncollectible accounts 1.6%, billing and mailing costs .5%, and credit investigation fee on new customers .2%.

Jan and Roy also determine that the average accounts receivable balance outstanding during the year is 5% of net credit sales. The Falcons estimate that they could earn an average of 10% annually on cash invested in other business opportunities.

Instructions

With the class divided into groups, answer the following.
(a) Prepare a tabulation for each year showing total credit and collection expenses in dollars and as a percentage of net credit sales.
(b) Determine the net credit and collection expenses in dollars and as a percentage of sales after considering the revenue not earned from other investment opportunities. (*Note:* The income lost on the cash held by the bank for 3 days is considered to be immaterial.)
(c) Discuss both the financial and nonfinancial factors that are relevant to the decision.

COMMUNICATION ACTIVITY

BYP8-7 Santana Corporation is a recently formed business selling the "World's Best Doormat." The corporation is selling doormats faster than Santana can make them. It has been selling the product on a credit basis, telling customers to "pay when they can." Oddly, even though sales are tremendous, the company is having trouble paying its bills.

Instructions

Write a memo to the president of Santana Corporation discussing these questions:
(a) What steps should be taken to improve the company's ability to pay its bills?
(b) What accounting steps should be taken to measure its success in improving collections and in recording its collection success?
(c) If the corporation is still unable to pay its bills, what additional steps can be taken with its receivables to ease its liquidity problems?

ETHICS CASE

BYP8-8   As its year-end approaches, it appears that Ortiz Corporation's net income will increase 10% this year. The president of Ortiz Corporation, nervous that the stockholders might expect the company to sustain this 10% growth rate in net income in future years, suggests that the controller increase the allowance for doubtful accounts to 4% of receivables in order to lower this year's net income. The president thinks that the lower net income, which reflects a 6% growth rate, will be a more sustainable rate of growth for Ortiz Corporation in future years. The controller of Ortiz Corporation believes that the company's yearly allowance for doubtful accounts should be 2% of receivables.

Instructions
(a) Who are the stakeholders in this case?
(b) Does the president's request pose an ethical dilemma for the controller?
(c) Should the controller be concerned with Ortiz Corporation's growth rate in estimating the allowance? Explain your answer.

ALL ABOUT YOU

BYP8-9   Credit card usage in the United States is substantial. Many startup companies use credit cards as a way to help meet short-term financial needs. The most common forms of debt for start-ups are use of credit cards and loans from relatives.

Suppose that you start up Spangles Sandwich Shop. You invested your savings of $20,000 and borrowed $70,000 from your relatives. Although sales in the first few months are good, you see that you may not have sufficient cash to pay expenses and maintain your inventory at acceptable levels, at least in the short term. You decide you may need to use one or more credit cards to fund the possible cash shortfall.

Instructions
(a) Go to the Internet and find two sources that provide insight into how to compare credit card terms.
(b) Develop a list, in descending order of importance, as to what features are most important to you in selecting a credit card for your business.
(c) Examine the features of your present credit card. (If you do not have a credit card, select a likely one online for this exercise.) Given your analysis above, what are the three major disadvantages of your present credit card?

FASB CODIFICATION ACTIVITY

BYP8-10   If your school has a subscription to the FASB Codification, go to **http://aaahq.org/ ascLogin.cfm** to log in and prepare responses to the following.
(a) How are receivables defined in the Codification?
(b) What are the conditions under which losses from uncollectible receivables (Bad Debt Expense) should be reported?

Answers to Insight and Accounting Across the Organization Questions

p. 406 When Investors Ignore Warning Signs Q: When would it be appropriate for a company to lower its allowance for doubtful accounts as a percentage of its receivables? **A:** It would be appropriate for a company to lower its allowance for doubtful accounts as a percentage of its receivables if the company's collection experience had improved, or was expected to improve, and therefore the company expected lower defaults as a percentage of receivables.

p. 409 Can Fair Value Be Unfair? Q: What are the arguments in favor of and against fair value accounting for loans and receivables? **A:** Arguments in favor of fair value accounting for loans and receivables are that fair value would provide a more accurate view of a company's financial position. This might provide a useful early warning of when a bank or other financial institution was in trouble because its loans were of poor quality. But, banks argue that estimating fair values is very difficult to do accurately. They are also concerned that volatile fair values could cause large swings in a bank's reported net income.

p. 413 Bad Information Can Lead to Bad Loans Q: What steps should the banks have taken to ensure the accuracy of financial information provided on loan applications? **A:** At a minimum, the bank should have requested copies of recent income tax forms and contacted the supposed employer to verify income. To verify ownership and value of assets, it should have examined bank statements, investment statements, and title documents, and should have employed appraisers.

p. 418 eBay for Receivables Q: What issues should management consider in deciding whether to factor its receivables? **A:** Management must prepare a cash budget and evaluate its projected cash needs. If it projects a cash deficiency, it should first pursue traditional bank financing since it tends to be less expensive than factoring. If traditional financing is not available, management could pursue factoring. If carefully structured, a factoring arrangement can be cost-effective since it can enable the company to outsource many billing and collection activities.

Answers to Self-Test Questions

1. c **2.** c ($1,000 − $300) × (100% − 2%) **3.** a **4.** a ($160,000 × .075) **5.** c ($200,000 ×.10) + ($30,000 − $18,000) **6.** d ($800,000 − $65,000) **7.** c **8.** b **9.** d **10.** d **11.** a $800,000 ÷ (($100,000 + $150,000) ÷ 2) **12.** c (365 days ÷ 7) **13.** c **14.** a **15.** d

A Look at IFRS

LEARNING OBJECTIVE 10

Compare the accounting procedures for receivables under GAAP and IFRS.

The basic accounting and reporting issues related to recognition and measurement of receivables, such as the use of allowance accounts, how to record discounts, use of the allowance method to account for bad debts, and factoring, are essentially the same between IFRS and GAAP.

KEY POINTS

- IFRS requires that loans and receivables be accounted for at amortized cost, adjusted for allowances for doubtful accounts. IFRS sometimes refers to these allowances as **provisions**. The entry to record the allowance would be:

Bad Debt Expense	xxxxxx	
Allowance for Doubtful Accounts		xxxxxx

- Although IFRS implies that receivables with different characteristics should be reported separately, there is no standard that mandates this segregation.

- The FASB and IASB have worked to implement fair value measurement (the amount they currently could be sold for) for financial instruments. Both Boards have faced bitter opposition from various factions. As a consequence, the Boards have adopted a piecemeal approach. The first step is disclosure of fair value information in the notes. The second step is the **fair value option**, which permits, but does not require, companies to record some types of financial instruments at fair values in the financial statements.

- IFRS requires a two-tiered approach to test whether the value of loans and receivables are impaired. First, a company should look at specific loans and receivables to determine whether they are impaired. Then, the loans and receivables as a group should be evaluated for impairment. GAAP does not prescribe a similar two-tiered approach.

- IFRS and GAAP differ in the criteria used to determine how to record a factoring transaction. IFRS is a combination of an approach focused on risks and rewards and loss of control. GAAP uses loss of control as the primary criterion. In addition, IFRS permits partial derecognition of receivables; GAAP does not.

LOOKING TO THE FUTURE

It appears likely that the question of recording fair values for financial instruments will continue to be an important issue to resolve as the Boards work toward convergence. Both the IASB and the FASB have indicated that they believe that financial statements would be more transparent and understandable if companies recorded and reported all financial instruments at fair value. That said, in *IFRS 9*, which was issued in 2009, the IASB created a split model, where some financial instruments are recorded at fair value, but other financial assets, such as loans and receivables, can be accounted for at amortized cost if certain criteria are met. Critics say that this can result in two companies with identical securities accounting for those securities in different ways. A proposal by the FASB would require that nearly all financial instruments, including loans and receivables, be accounted for at fair value. It has been suggested that *IFRS 9* will likely be changed or replaced as the FASB and IASB continue to deliberate the best treatment for financial instruments. In fact, one past member of the IASB said that companies should ignore *IFRS 9* and continue to report under the old standard because in his opinion, it was extremely likely that it would be changed before 2013, the mandatory adoption date of the standard. An ongoing FASB/IASB project on financial instruments addresses a number of issues with implications for receivables.

IFRS PRACTICE

IFRS SELF-TEST QUESTIONS

1. Under IFRS, loans and receivables are to be reported on the statement of financial position at:
   - (a) amortized cost.
   - (b) amortized cost adjusted for estimated loss provisions.
   - (c) historical cost.
   - (d) replacement cost.
2. Which of the following statements is **false**?
   - (a) Loans and receivables include equity securities purchased by the company.
   - (b) Loans and receivables include credit card receivables.
   - (c) Loans and receivables include amounts owed by employees as a result of company loans to employees.
   - (d) Loans and receivables include amounts resulting from transactions with customers.
3. In recording a factoring transaction:
   - (a) IFRS focuses on loss of control.
   - (b) GAAP focuses on loss of control and risks and rewards.
   - (c) IFRS and GAAP allow partial derecognition.
   - (d) IFRS allows partial derecognition
4. Under IFRS:
   - (a) the entry to record estimated uncollected accounts is the same as GAAP.
   - (b) loans and receivables should only be tested for impairment as a group.
   - (c) it is always acceptable to use the direct write-off method.
   - (d) all financial instruments are recorded at fair value.
5. Which of the following statements is **true**?
   - (a) The fair value option requires that some types of financial instruments be recorded at fair value.
   - (b) The fair value option permits, but does not require, that some types of financial instruments be recorded at fair value.
   - (c) The fair value option requires that all types of financial instruments be recorded at fair value.
   - (d) The FASB and IASB would like to reduce the reliance on fair value accounting for financial instruments in the future.

IFRS CONCEPTS AND APPLICATION

IFRS8-1 What are some steps taken by both the FASB and IASB to move to fair value measurement for financial instruments? In what ways have some of the approaches differed?

INTERNATIONAL FINANCIAL REPORTING PROBLEM: *Zetar plc*

IFRS8-2 The financial statements of Zetar plc are presented in Appendix C. The company's complete annual report, including the notes to its financial statements, is available in the Investors section at **www.zetarplc.com**.

Instructions
Use the company's annual report to answer the following questions.
   - (a) According to the Operational Review of Financial Performance, what was one reason why the balance in receivables increased relative to the previous year?
   - (b) According to the notes to the financial statements, how are loans and receivables defined?
   - (c) Using the notes to the financial statements, what amount of trade receivables were written off (utilised) during 2011?
   - (d) Using information in the notes to the financial statements, determine what percentage the provision for impairment of receivables was as a percentage of total trade receivables for 2011 and 2010. How did the ratio change from 2010 to 2011, and what does this suggest about the company's receivables?

Answers to IFRS Self-Test Questions
1. b **2.** a **3.** d **4.** a **5.** b

✔ The Navigator

✔ Remember to go back to The Navigator box on the chapter opening page and check off your completed work.

CHAPTER 9

REPORTING AND ANALYZING LONG-LIVED ASSETS

The Navigator

- Scan Learning Objectives
- Read Feature Story
- Scan Preview
- Read Text and Answer **Do it!**
  ○ p. 453 ○ p. 457 ○ p. 460
  ○ p. 463 ○ p. 472
- Work Using the Decision Toolkit
- Review Summary of Learning Objectives
- Work Comprehensive **Do it!** p. 480
- Answer Self-Test Questions
- Complete Assignments
- Go to WileyPLUS for practice and tutorials

 Read A Look at IFRS p. 500

LEARNING OBJECTIVES

After studying this chapter, you should be able to:

1 Describe how the historical cost principle applies to plant assets.

2 Explain the concept of depreciation.

3 Compute periodic depreciation using the straight-line method, and contrast its expense pattern with those of other methods.

4 Describe the procedure for revising periodic depreciation.

5 Explain how to account for the disposal of plant assets.

6 Describe methods for evaluating the use of plant assets.

7 Identify the basic issues related to reporting intangible assets.

8 Indicate how long-lived assets are reported in the financial statements.

The Navigator

© Linda & ColinMcKie/iStockphoto

So, you're interested in starting a new business. Have you thought about the airline industry? Is your only experience with airlines as a passenger? Don't let that stop you. Today, the most profitable airlines in the industry are not well-known majors like American Airlines and United. In fact, most giant, older airlines are either bankrupt or on the verge of bankruptcy. In a recent year, five major airlines representing 24% of total U.S. capacity were operating under bankruptcy protection.

Not all airlines are hurting. The growth and profitability in the airline industry today is found at relative newcomers like Southwest Airlines and, more recently, JetBlue Airways. These and other new airlines compete primarily on ticket prices. During a recent five-year period, the low-fare airline market share increased by 47%, reaching 22% of U.S. airline capacity.

Southwest was the first upstart to make it big. It did so by taking a different approach. It bought small, new, fuel-efficient planes. Also, instead of the "hub-and-spoke" approach used by the majors, it opted for direct, short hop, no frills flights. It was all about controlling costs—getting the most out of its efficient new planes.

JetBlue, founded by former employees of Southwest, was recently ranked as the number 1 airline in the United States by the airline rating company SkyTrax. Management initially attempted to differentiate JetBlue by offering amenities not found on other airlines, such as TVs in every seatback, while adopting Southwest's low-fare model. This approach was successful during JetBlue's early years, as it enjoyed both profitability and rapid growth. However, more recently the company has had to take aggressive steps to rein in costs in order to return to profitability.

In the past, upstarts such as Valujet chose a different approach. They bought planes that were 20 to 30 years old (known in the industry as *zombies*). By buying used planes, Valujet was able to add one or two planes a month to its fleet—an unheard of expansion. Valujet started with a $3.4 million investment and grew to be worth $630 million in its first three years.

But with fuel costs at record high levels, airlines are no longer in the market for old planes. In fact, the old Boeing 727, which until very recently was a mainstay of nearly every airline, is no longer used for passenger flights because it couldn't be operated efficiently. Today, success in the airline business comes from owning the newest and most efficient equipment, and knowing how to get the most out of it.

A TALE OF TWO AIRLINES

✔ The Navigator

INSIDE CHAPTER 9 . . .

For airlines and many other companies, making the right decisions regarding long-lived assets is critical because these assets represent huge investments. Management must make many ongoing decisions about long-lived assets—what assets to acquire and when, how to finance them, how to account for them, and when to dispose of them.

In this chapter, we address these and other issues surrounding long-lived assets. The discussion is in two parts: plant assets and intangible assets. **Plant assets** are the property, plant, and equipment (physical assets) that commonly come to mind when we think of what a company owns. Companies also have many important **intangible assets**. These assets, such as copyrights and patents, lack physical substance but can be extremely valuable and vital to a company's success.

The content and organization of this chapter are as follows.

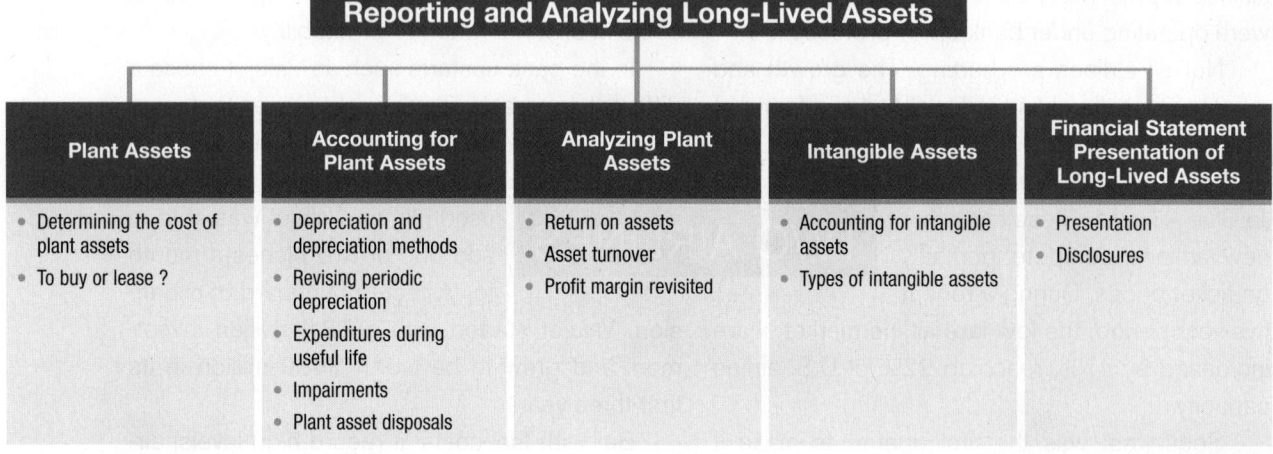

Reporting and Analyzing Long-Lived Assets				
Plant Assets	**Accounting for Plant Assets**	**Analyzing Plant Assets**	**Intangible Assets**	**Financial Statement Presentation of Long-Lived Assets**
• Determining the cost of plant assets • To buy or lease ?	• Depreciation and depreciation methods • Revising periodic depreciation • Expenditures during useful life • Impairments • Plant asset disposals	• Return on assets • Asset turnover • Profit margin revisited	• Accounting for intangible assets • Types of intangible assets	• Presentation • Disclosures

✔ The Navigator

Plant Assets

LEARNING OBJECTIVE 1

Describe how the historical cost principle applies to plant assets.

Plant assets are resources that have physical substance (a definite size and shape), are used in the operations of a business, and are not intended for sale to customers. They are called various names—property, plant, and equipment; plant and equipment; and fixed assets. By whatever name, these assets are expected to provide service to the company for a number of years. Except for land, plant assets decline in service potential (ability to produce revenue) over their useful lives.

Plant assets are critical to a company's success because they determine the company's capacity and therefore its ability to satisfy customers. With too few planes, for example, JetBlue Airways and Southwest Airlines would lose customers to their competitors. But with too many planes, they would be flying with empty seats. Management must constantly monitor its needs and acquire assets accordingly. Failure to do so results in lost business opportunities or inefficient use of existing assets and is likely to show up eventually in poor financial results.

It is important for a company to (1) keep assets in good operating condition, (2) replace worn-out or outdated assets, and (3) expand its productive assets as needed. The decline of rail travel in the United States can be traced in part to the failure of railroad companies to maintain and update their assets. Conversely, the growth of air travel in this country can be attributed in part to the general willingness of airline companies to follow these essential guidelines.

For many companies, investments in plant assets are substantial. Illustration 9-1 shows the percentages of plant assets in relation to total assets in various companies in a recent year.

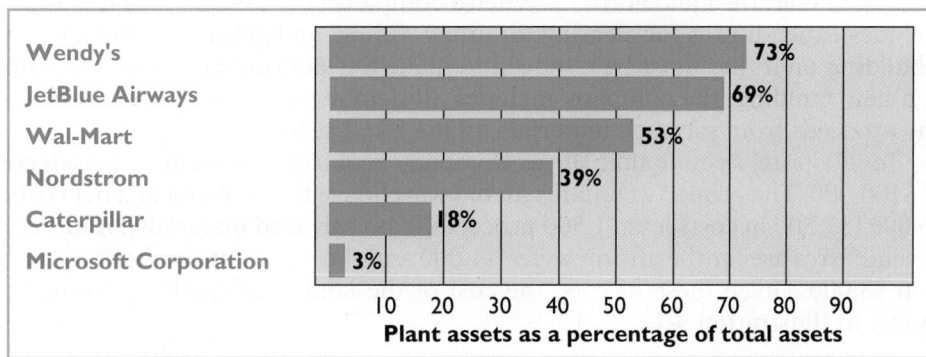

Illustration 9-1 Percentages of plant assets in relation to total assets

DETERMINING THE COST OF PLANT ASSETS

The **historical cost principle** requires that companies record plant assets at cost. Thus, JetBlue Airways and Southwest Airlines record their planes at cost. **Cost consists of all expenditures necessary to acquire an asset and make it ready for its intended use.** For example, when Boeing buys equipment, the purchase price, freight costs paid by Boeing, and installation costs are all part of the cost of the equipment.

Determining which costs to include in a plant asset account and which costs not to include is very important. If a cost is not included in a plant asset account, then it must be expensed immediately. Such costs are referred to as revenue expenditures. On the other hand, costs that are not expensed immediately but are instead included in a plant asset account are referred to as capital expenditures. JetBlue reported capital expenditures of $480 million during 2011.

This distinction is important; it has immediate, and often material, implications for the income statement. Some companies, in order to boost current income, have **improperly capitalized expenditures** that they should have expensed. For example, suppose that a company improperly capitalizes to a building account $1,000 of maintenance costs incurred at the end of the year. (That is, the costs are included in the asset account Buildings rather than being expensed immediately as Maintenance and Repairs Expense.) If the company is allocating the cost of the building as an expense (depreciating it) over a 40-year life, then the maintenance cost of $1,000 will be incorrectly spread across 40 years instead of being expensed in the current year. As a result, the company will understate current-year expenses by approximately $1,000, and will overstate current-year income by approximately $1,000. Thus, determining which costs to capitalize and which to expense is very important.

Cost is measured by the cash paid in a cash transaction or by the **cash equivalent price** paid when companies use noncash assets in payment. **The cash equivalent price is equal to the fair value of the asset given up or the fair value of the asset received, whichever is more clearly determinable.** Once cost is established, it becomes the basis of accounting for the plant asset over its useful life. Current fair value is not used to increase the recorded cost after acquisition. We explain the application of the historical cost principle to each of the major classes of plant assets in the following sections.

International Note IFRS is flexible regarding asset valuation. Companies revalue to fair value when they believe this information is more relevant.

Land

Companies often use land as a building site for a manufacturing plant or office site. The cost of land includes (1) the cash purchase price, (2) closing costs such as title and attorney's fees, (3) real estate brokers' commissions, and (4) accrued property taxes and other liens on the land assumed by the purchaser. For example, if the cash price is $50,000 and the purchaser agrees to pay accrued taxes of $5,000, the cost of the land is $55,000.

All necessary costs incurred in making land **ready for its intended use** increase (debit) the Land account. When a company acquires vacant land, its cost includes expenditures for clearing, draining, filling, and grading. If the land has a building on it that must be removed to make the site suitable for construction of a new building, the company includes all demolition and removal costs, less any proceeds from salvaged materials, in the Land account.

To illustrate, assume that Hayes Company acquires real estate at a cash cost of $100,000. The property contains an old warehouse that is razed at a net cost of $6,000 ($7,500 in costs less $1,500 proceeds from salvaged materials). Additional expenditures are for the attorney's fee $1,000 and the real estate broker's commission $8,000. Given these factors, the cost of the land is $115,000, computed as shown in Illustration 9-2.

Illustration 9-2 Computation of cost of land

Land	
Cash price of property	$ 100,000
Net removal cost of warehouse	6,000
Attorney's fee	1,000
Real estate broker's commission	8,000
Cost of land	**$115,000**

When Hayes records the acquisition, it debits Land and credits Cash for $115,000.

Land Improvements

Land improvements are structural additions made to land, such as driveways, parking lots, fences, landscaping, and underground sprinklers. The cost of land improvements includes all expenditures necessary to make the improvements ready for their intended use. For example, the cost of a new company parking lot includes the amount paid for paving, fencing, and lighting. Thus, the company would debit the total of all of these costs to Land Improvements.

Land improvements have limited useful lives, and their maintenance and replacement are the responsibility of the company. As a result, companies expense (depreciate) the cost of land improvements over their useful lives.

Buildings

Buildings are facilities used in operations, such as stores, offices, factories, warehouses, and airplane hangars. Companies charge to the Buildings account all necessary expenditures relating to the purchase or construction of a building. When a building is **purchased**, such costs include the purchase price, closing costs (attorney's fees, title insurance, etc.), and real estate broker's commission. Costs to make the building ready for its intended use consist of expenditures for remodeling rooms and offices and replacing or repairing the roof, floors, electrical wiring, and plumbing. When a new building is **constructed**, its cost consists of the contract price plus payments made by the owner for architects' fees, building permits, and excavation costs.

In addition, companies add certain interest costs to the cost of a building. Interest costs incurred to finance a construction project are included in the cost of the asset when a significant period of time is required to get the asset ready for use. In these circumstances, interest costs are considered as necessary as materials and labor. However, the inclusion of interest costs in the cost of a constructed building is **limited to interest costs incurred during the construction period**. When construction has been completed, subsequent interest payments on funds borrowed to finance the construction are recorded as increases (debits) to Interest Expense.

Equipment

Equipment includes assets used in operations, such as store check-out counters, office furniture, factory machinery, and delivery trucks. JetBlue Airways' equipment includes aircraft, in-flight entertainment systems, and trucks for ground operations. The cost of equipment consists of the cash purchase price, sales taxes, freight charges, and insurance during transit paid by the purchaser. It also includes expenditures required in assembling, installing, and testing the unit. However, companies treat as expenses the costs of motor vehicle licenses and accident insurance on company trucks and cars. Such items are **annual recurring expenditures and do not benefit future periods**. Two criteria apply in determining the cost of equipment: (1) the frequency of the cost—one time or recurring, and (2) the benefit period—the life of the asset or one year.

To illustrate, assume that Lenard Company purchases a delivery truck at a cash price of $22,000. Related expenditures are sales taxes $1,320, painting and lettering $500, motor vehicle license $80, and a three-year accident insurance policy $1,600. The cost of the delivery truck is $23,820, computed as shown in Illustration 9-3.

Delivery Truck	
Cash price	$ 22,000
Sales taxes	1,320
Painting and lettering	500
Cost of delivery truck	**$23,820**

Illustration 9-3 Computation of cost of delivery truck

Lenard treats the cost of a motor vehicle license as an expense and the cost of an insurance policy as a prepaid asset. Thus, the company records the purchase of the truck and related expenditures as follows.

Equipment	23,820	
License Expense	80	
Prepaid Insurance	1,600	
Cash		25,500
(To record purchase of delivery truck and related expenditures)		

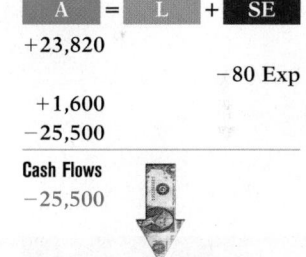

For another example, assume Merten Company purchases factory machinery at a cash price of $50,000. Related expenditures are sales taxes $3,000, insurance during shipping $500, and installation and testing $1,000. The cost of the factory machinery is $54,500, computed as in Illustration 9-4.

Factory Machinery	
Cash price	$ 50,000
Sales taxes	3,000
Insurance during shipping	500
Installation and testing	1,000
Cost of factory machinery	**$54,500**

Illustration 9-4 Computation of cost of factory machinery

Thus, Merten records the purchase and related expenditures as follows.

Equipment	54,500	
Cash		54,500
(To record purchase of factory machinery and related expenditures)		

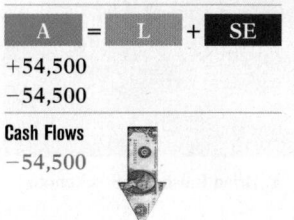

TO BUY OR LEASE?

In this chapter, we focus on purchased assets, but we want to expose you briefly to an alternative—leasing. A lease is a contractual agreement in which the owner of an asset (the **lessor**) allows another party (the **lessee**) to use the asset for a period of time at an agreed price. In many industries, leasing is quite common. For example, one-third of heavy-duty commercial trucks are leased.

Some advantages of leasing an asset versus purchasing it are:

1. **Reduced risk of obsolescence.** Frequently, lease terms allow the party using the asset (the lessee) to exchange the asset for a more modern one if it becomes outdated. This is much easier than trying to sell an obsolete asset.

2. **Little or no down payment.** To purchase an asset, most companies must borrow money, which usually requires a down payment of at least 20%. Leasing an asset requires little or no down payment.

3. **Shared tax advantages.** Startup companies typically earn little or no profit in their early years, and so they have little need for the tax deductions available from owning an asset. In a lease, the lessor gets the tax advantage because it owns the asset. It often will pass these tax savings on to the lessee in the form of lower lease payments.

4. **Assets and liabilities not reported.** Many companies prefer to keep assets and especially liabilities off their books. Reporting lower assets improves the return on assets (discussed later in this chapter). Reporting fewer liabilities makes the company look less risky. Certain types of leases, called **operating leases**, allow the lessee to account for the transaction as a rental, with neither an asset nor a liability recorded.

Airlines often choose to lease many of their airplanes in long-term lease agreements. In recent financial statements, JetBlue Airways stated that it leased 60 of its 169 planes under operating leases. Because operating leases are accounted for as rentals, these 60 planes were not presented on its balance sheet.

Under another type of lease, a **capital lease**, lessees show both the asset and the liability on the balance sheet. The lessee accounts for capital lease agreements in a way that is very similar to debt-financed purchases: The lessee shows the leased item as an asset on its balance sheet, and the obligation owed to the lessor as a liability. The lessee depreciates the leased asset in a manner similar to purchased assets. Only four of JetBlue's aircraft were held under capital leases. We discuss leasing further in Chapter 10.

Accounting Across the Organization

Many U.S. Firms Use Leases

Leasing is big business for U.S. companies. For example, in a recent year leasing accounted for about 31% of all business investment ($218 billion).

Who does the most leasing? Interestingly, major banks such as Continental Bank, J.P. Morgan Leasing, and US Bancorp Equipment Finance are the major lessors. Also, many companies have established separate leasing companies, such as Boeing Capital Corporation, Dell Financial Services, and John Deere Capital Corporation. As an example of the magnitude of leasing, leased planes account for nearly 40% of the U.S. fleet of commercial airlines. Lease Finance Corporation in Los Angeles owns more planes than any airline in the world.

In addition, leasing is becoming increasingly common in the hotel industry. Marriott, Hilton, and InterContinental are increasingly choosing to lease hotels that are owned by someone else.

? Why might airline managers choose to lease rather than purchase their planes? (See page 499.)

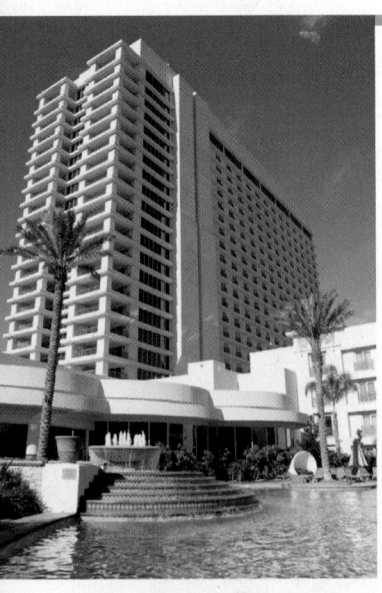

© Brian Raisbeck/iStockphoto

Do it! Assume that Drummond Corp. purchases a delivery truck for $15,000 cash plus sales taxes of $900 and delivery costs of $500. The buyer also pays $200 for painting and lettering, $600 for an annual insurance policy, and $80 for a motor vehicle license. Explain how the company should account for each of these costs.

Solution

The first four payments ($15,000 purchase price, $900 sales taxes, $500 delivery, and $200 painting and lettering) are expenditures necessary to make the truck ready for its intended use. Thus, the cost of the truck is $16,600. The payments for insurance and the license are operating expenses incurred during the useful life of the asset.

Related exercise material: **BE9-1, BE9-2,** **Do it!** **9-1, E9-1, E9-2,** and **E9-3.**

COST OF PLANT ASSETS

Action Plan

- Identify expenditures made in order to get delivery equipment ready for its intended use.
- Expense operating costs incurred during the useful life of the equipment.

✔ The Navigator

Accounting for Plant Assets

DEPRECIATION

As explained in Chapter 4, **depreciation is the process of allocating to expense the cost of a plant asset over its useful (service) life in a rational and systematic manner**. Such cost allocation is designed to properly match expenses with revenues. (See Illustration 9-5.)

LEARNING OBJECTIVE 2
Explain the concept of depreciation.

Illustration 9-5 Depreciation as a cost allocation concept

Depreciation affects the balance sheet through accumulated depreciation, which companies report as a deduction from plant assets. It affects the income statement through depreciation expense.

It is important to understand that **depreciation is a cost allocation process, not an asset valuation process**. No attempt is made to measure the change in an asset's fair value during ownership. Thus, the **book value**—cost less accumulated depreciation—of a plant asset may differ significantly from its **fair value**. In fact, if an asset is fully depreciated, it can have zero book value but still have a significant fair value.

Depreciation applies to **three classes of plant assets**: land improvements, buildings, and equipment. Each of these classes is considered to be a **depreciable asset** because the usefulness to the company and the revenue-producing ability of each class decline over the asset's useful life. Depreciation **does not apply to land** because its usefulness and revenue-producing ability generally remain intact as long as the land is owned. In fact, in many cases, the usefulness of land increases over time because of the scarcity of good sites. Thus, **land is not a depreciable asset**.

During a depreciable asset's useful life, its revenue-producing ability declines because of wear and tear. A delivery truck that has been driven 100,000 miles will be less useful to a company than one driven only 800 miles.

A decline in revenue-producing ability may also occur because of obsolescence. **Obsolescence** is the process by which an asset becomes out of date before it physically wears out. The rerouting of major airlines from Chicago's Midway

Helpful Hint Remember that depreciation is the process of *allocating cost* over the useful life of an asset. It is not a measure of value.

Helpful Hint Land does not depreciate because it does not wear out.

Ethics Note When a business is acquired, proper allocation of the purchase price to various asset classes is important since different depreciation treatment can materially affect income. For example, buildings are depreciated, but land is not.

Airport to Chicago-O'Hare International Airport because Midway's runways were too short for giant jets is an example. Similarly, many companies replace their computers long before they originally planned to do so because improvements in new computers make their old computers obsolete.

Recognizing depreciation for an asset does not result in the accumulation of cash for replacement of the asset. The balance in Accumulated Depreciation represents the total amount of the asset's cost that the company has charged to expense to date; **it is not a cash fund**.

FACTORS IN COMPUTING DEPRECIATION

Three factors affect the computation of depreciation, as shown in Illustration 9-6.

Illustration 9-6 Three factors in computing depreciation

Cost: all expenditures necessary to acquire the asset and make it ready for intended use

Useful life: estimate of the expected life based on need for repair, service life, and vulnerability to obsolescence

Salvage value: estimate of the asset's value at the end of its useful life

Helpful Hint Depreciation expense is reported on the income statement. Accumulated depreciation is reported on the balance sheet as a deduction from plant assets.

1. **Cost.** Earlier in the chapter, we explained the considerations that affect the cost of a depreciable asset. Remember that companies record plant assets at cost, in accordance with the historical cost principle.

2. **Useful life.** Useful life is an estimate of the expected productive life, also called service life, of the asset for its owner. Useful life may be expressed in terms of time, units of activity (such as machine hours), or units of output. Useful life is an estimate. In making the estimate, management considers such factors as the intended use of the asset, repair and maintenance policies, and vulnerability of the asset to obsolescence. The company's past experience with similar assets is often helpful in deciding on expected useful life.

3. **Salvage value.** Salvage value is an estimate of the asset's value at the end of its useful life for its owner. Companies may base the value on the asset's worth as scrap or on its expected trade-in value. Like useful life, salvage value is an estimate. In making the estimate, management considers how it plans to dispose of the asset and its experience with similar assets.

DEPRECIATION METHODS

LEARNING OBJECTIVE 3

Compute periodic depreciation using the straight-line method, and contrast its expense pattern with those of other methods.

Although a number of methods exist, depreciation is generally computed using one of three methods:

1. Straight-line
2. Declining-balance
3. Units-of-activity

Like the alternative inventory methods discussed in Chapter 6, each of these depreciation methods is acceptable under generally accepted accounting principles. Management selects the method it believes best measures an asset's contribution to revenue over its useful life. Once a company chooses a method, it should apply that method consistently over the useful life of the asset. Consistency enhances the ability to analyze financial statements over multiple years.

Illustration 9-7 shows the distribution of the primary depreciation methods in a sample of the largest U.S. companies. Clearly, straight-line depreciation is the most widely used approach. In fact, because some companies use more than one method, **straight-line depreciation is used for some or all of the depreciation taken by more than 95% of U.S. companies**. For this reason, we illustrate procedures for straight-line depreciation and discuss the alternative depreciation approaches only at a conceptual level. This coverage introduces you to the basic idea of depreciation as an allocation concept without entangling you in too much procedural detail. (Also, note that many hand-held calculators are preprogrammed to perform the basic depreciation methods.) Details on the alternative approaches are presented in Appendix 9A (pages 476–478).

Our illustration of depreciation methods, both here and in the appendix, is based on the following data relating to a small delivery truck purchased by Bill's Pizzas on January 1, 2014.

Cost	$13,000
Expected salvage value	$1,000
Estimated useful life (in years)	5
Estimated useful life (in miles)	100,000

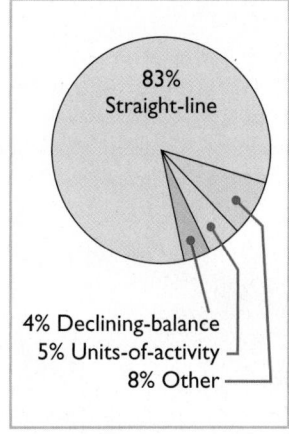

Illustration 9-7 Use of depreciation methods in major U.S. companies

Straight-Line

Under the straight-line method, companies expense an equal amount of depreciation each year of the asset's useful life. Management must choose the useful life of an asset based on its own expectations and experience.

To compute the annual depreciation expense, we divide depreciable cost by the estimated useful life. Depreciable cost represents the total amount subject to depreciation; it is calculated as the cost of the plant asset less its salvage value. Illustration 9-8 shows the computation of depreciation expense in the first year for Bill's Pizzas' delivery truck.

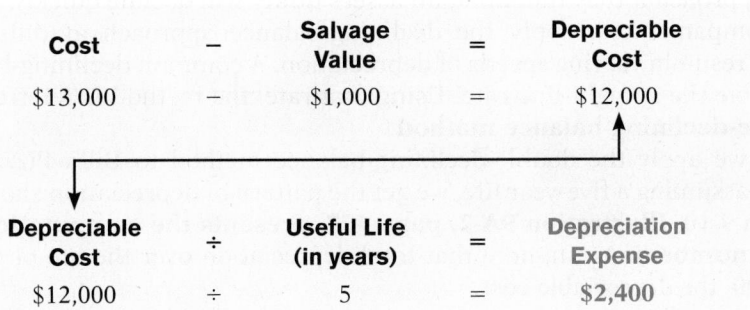

Illustration 9-8 Formula for straight-line method

Alternatively, we can compute an annual **rate** at which the company depreciates the delivery truck. In this case, the rate is 20% (100% ÷ 5 years). When an annual rate is used under the straight-line method, the company applies the percentage rate to the depreciable cost of the asset, as shown in the **depreciation schedule** in Illustration 9-9.

Illustration 9-9 Straight-line depreciation schedule

BILL'S PIZZAS

	Computation			Annual	End of Year	
Year	Depreciable Cost	×	Depreciation Rate	= Depreciation Expense	Accumulated Depreciation	Book Value
2014	$12,000		20%	$ 2,400	$ 2,400	$10,600*
2015	12,000		20	2,400	4,800	8,200
2016	12,000		20	2,400	7,200	5,800
2017	12,000		20	2,400	9,600	3,400
2018	12,000		20	2,400	12,000	1,000
			Total	$12,000		

*$13,000 − $2,400

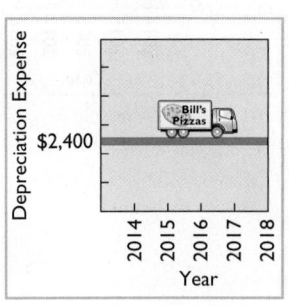

Note that the depreciation expense of $2,400 is the same each year. The book value at the end of the useful life is equal to the estimated $1,000 salvage value.

What happens when an asset is purchased **during** the year, rather than on January 1 as in our example? In that case, it is necessary to **prorate the annual depreciation** for the portion of a year used. If Bill's Pizzas had purchased the delivery truck on April 1, 2014, the company would use the truck for 9 months in 2014. The depreciation for 2014 would be $1,800 ($12,000 × 20% × $\frac{9}{12}$ of a year).

As indicated earlier, the straight-line method predominates in practice. For example, such large companies as Campbell Soup, Marriott, and General Mills use the straight-line method. It is simple to apply, and it matches expenses with revenues appropriately when the use of the asset is reasonably uniform throughout the service life. The types of assets that give equal benefits over useful life generally are those for which daily use does not affect productivity. Examples are office furniture and fixtures, buildings, warehouses, and garages for motor vehicles.

Declining-Balance

The **declining-balance method** computes depreciation expense using a constant rate applied to a declining book value. This method is called an **accelerated-depreciation method** because it results in higher depreciation in the early years of an asset's life than does the straight-line approach. However, because the total amount of depreciation (the depreciable cost) taken over an asset's life is the same **no matter what approach** is used, the declining-balance method produces a decreasing annual depreciation expense over the asset's useful life. In early years, declining-balance depreciation expense will exceed straight-line, but in later years, it will be less than straight-line. Managers might choose an accelerated approach if they think that an asset's utility will decline quickly.

Companies can apply the declining-balance approach at different rates, which result in varying speeds of depreciation. A common declining-balance rate is double the straight-line rate. Using that rate, the method is referred to as the **double-declining-balance method**.

If we apply the double-declining-balance method to Bill's Pizzas' delivery truck, assuming a five-year life, we get the pattern of depreciation shown in Illustration 9-10. **Illustration 9A-2, page 477, presents the computations behind these numbers.** Again, note that total depreciation over the life of the truck is $12,000, the depreciable cost.

Illustration 9-10 Declining-balance depreciation schedule

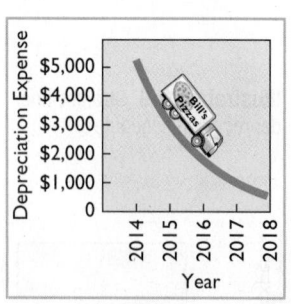

| | | BILL'S PIZZAS | |
| | Annual | End of Year | |
Year	Depreciation Expense	Accumulated Depreciation	Book Value
2014	$ 5,200	$ 5,200	$7,800
2015	3,120	8,320	4,680
2016	1,872	10,192	2,808
2017	1,123	11,315	1,685
2018	685	12,000	1,000
Total	$12,000		

Units-of-Activity

As indicated earlier, useful life can be expressed in ways other than a time period. Under the **units-of-activity method**, useful life is expressed in terms of the total units of production or the use expected from the asset. The units-of-activity method is ideally suited to factory machinery: Companies can measure production in terms of units of output or in terms of machine hours used in operating the machinery. It is also possible to use the method for such items as delivery equipment (miles driven) and airplanes (hours in use). The units-of-activity method is generally not suitable for such assets as buildings or furniture because activity levels are difficult to measure for these assets.

Applying the units-of-activity method to the delivery truck owned by Bill's Pizzas, we first must know some basic information. Bill's expects to be able to drive the truck a total of 100,000 miles. Illustration 9-11 shows depreciation over the five-year life based on an assumed mileage pattern. **Illustration 9A-4, page 478, presents the computations used to arrive at these results.**

Illustration 9-11 Units-of-activity depreciation schedule

BILL'S PIZZAS

Year	Units of Activity (miles)	Annual Depreciation Expense	End of Year Accumulated Depreciation	End of Year Book Value
2014	15,000	$ 1,800	$ 1,800	$11,200
2015	30,000	3,600	5,400	7,600
2016	20,000	2,400	7,800	5,200
2017	25,000	3,000	10,800	2,200
2018	10,000	1,200	12,000	1,000
Total	100,000	$12,000		

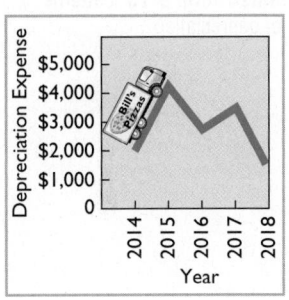

As the name implies, under units-of-activity depreciation, the amount of depreciation is proportional to the activity that took place during that period. For example, the delivery truck was driven twice as many miles in 2015 as in 2014, and depreciation was exactly twice as much in 2015 as it was in 2014.

Do it!

STRAIGHT-LINE DEPRECIATION

On January 1, 2014, Iron Mountain Ski Corporation purchased a new snow grooming machine for $50,000. The machine is estimated to have a 10-year life with a $2,000 salvage value. What journal entry would Iron Mountain Ski Corporation make at December 31, 2014, if it uses the straight-line method of depreciation?

Solution

$$\text{Depreciation expense} = \frac{\text{Cost} - \text{Salvage value}}{\text{Useful life}} = \frac{\$50,000 - \$2,000}{10} = \$4,800$$

Iron Mountain would record the first year's depreciation as follows.

Dec. 31	Depreciation Expense	4,800	
	Accumulated Depreciation—Equipment		4,800
	(To record annual depreciation on snow grooming machine)		

Related exercise material: **BE9-3, BE9-4, Do it! 9-2,** and **E9-5.**

Action Plan

- Calculate depreciable cost (Cost − Salvage value).
- Divide the depreciable cost by the asset's estimated useful life.

 The Navigator

Management's Choice: Comparison of Methods

Illustration 9-12 (page 458) compares annual and total depreciation expense for Bill's Pizzas under the three methods.

Illustration 9-12 Comparison of depreciation methods

Year	Straight-Line	Declining-Balance	Units-of-Activity
2014	$ 2,400	$ 5,200	$ 1,800
2015	2,400	3,120	3,600
2016	2,400	1,872	2,400
2017	2,400	1,123	3,000
2018	2,400	685	1,200
	$12,000	$12,000	$12,000

Annual depreciation expense varies considerably among the methods, but **total depreciation expense is the same ($12,000) for the five-year period.** Each method is acceptable in accounting because each recognizes the decline in service potential of the asset in a rational and systematic manner. Illustration 9-13 graphs the depreciation expense pattern under each method.

Illustration 9-13 Patterns of depreciation

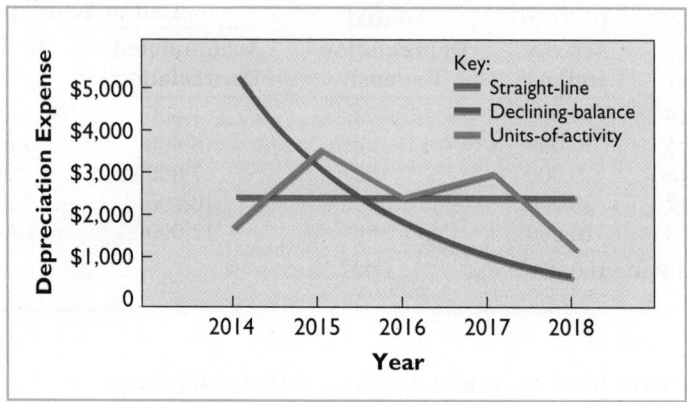

Depreciation and Income Taxes

Helpful Hint Depreciation per financial statements is usually different from depreciation per tax returns.

The Internal Revenue Service (IRS) allows corporate taxpayers to deduct depreciation expense when computing taxable income. However, the tax regulations of the IRS do not require the taxpayer to use the same depreciation method on the tax return that it uses in preparing financial statements.

Consequently, many large corporations use straight-line depreciation in their financial statements in order to maximize net income; at the same time, they use a special accelerated-depreciation method on their tax returns in order to minimize their income taxes. For tax purposes, taxpayers must use on their tax returns either the straight-line method or a special accelerated-depreciation method called the **Modified Accelerated Cost Recovery System** (MACRS).

Depreciation Disclosure in the Notes

Companies must disclose the choice of depreciation method in their financial statements or in related notes that accompany the statements. Illustration 9-14 shows excerpts from the "Property and equipment" notes from the financial statements of Southwest Airlines.

Illustration 9-14 Disclosure of depreciation policies

SOUTHWEST AIRLINES
Notes to the Financial Statements

Property and equipment Depreciation is provided by the straight-line method to estimated residual values over periods ranging from 20 to 25 years for flight equipment and 5 to 30 years for ground property and equipment once the asset is placed in service. Amortization of property under capital leases is on a straight-line basis over the lease term and is included in depreciation expense.

From this note, we learn that Southwest Airlines uses the straight-line method to depreciate its planes over periods of 20 to 25 years.

REVISING PERIODIC DEPRECIATION

LEARNING OBJECTIVE **4**
Describe the procedure for revising periodic depreciation.

Management should periodically review annual depreciation expense. If wear and tear or obsolescence indicates that annual depreciation is either inadequate or excessive, the company should change the depreciation expense amount.

When a change in an estimate is required, the company makes the change in **current and future years but not to prior periods**. Thus, when making the change, the company (1) does not correct previously recorded depreciation expense, but (2) revises depreciation expense for current and future years. The rationale for this treatment is that continual restatement of prior periods would adversely affect users' confidence in financial statements.

To determine the new annual depreciation expense, the company first computes the asset's depreciable cost at the time of the revision. It then allocates the revised depreciable cost to the remaining useful life.

Helpful Hint Use a step-by-step approach: (1) determine new depreciable cost; (2) divide by remaining useful life.

To illustrate, assume that Bill's Pizzas decides at the end of 2017 (prior to the year-end adjusting entries) to extend the estimated useful life of the truck one year (a total life of six years) and increase its salvage value to $2,200. The company has used the straight-line method to depreciate the asset to date. Depreciation per year was $2,400 (($13,000 − $1,000) ÷ 5). Accumulated depreciation after three years (2014–2016) is $7,200 ($2,400 × 3), and book value is $5,800 ($13,000 − $7,200). The new annual depreciation is $1,200, computed on December 31, 2017, as follows.

Illustration 9-15 Revised depreciation computation

Book value, 1/1/17	$ 5,800
Less: New salvage value	2,200
Depreciable cost	$ 3,600
Remaining useful life	3 years (2017–2019)
Revised annual depreciation ($3,600 ÷ 3)	**$1,200**

Bill's Pizzas does not make a special entry for the change in estimate. On December 31, 2017, during the preparation of adjusting entries, it records depreciation expense of $1,200.

Companies must disclose in the financial statements significant changes in estimates. Although a company may have a legitimate reason for changing an estimated life, financial statement users should be aware that some companies might change an estimate simply to achieve financial statement goals. For example, extending an asset's estimated life reduces depreciation expense and increases current period income.

In a recent year, AirTran Airways (now owned by Southwest Airlines) increased the estimated useful lives of some of its planes from 25 to 30 years and increased the estimated lives of related aircraft parts from 5 years to 30 years. It disclosed that the change in estimate decreased its net loss for the year by approximately $0.6 million, or about $0.01 per share. Whether these changes were appropriate depends on how reasonable it is to assume that planes will continue to be used for a long time. Our Feature Story suggests that although in the past many planes lasted a long time, it is also clear that because of high fuel costs, airlines are now scrapping many of their old, inefficient planes.

REVISED DEPRECIATION

 Chambers Corporation purchased a piece of equipment for $36,000. It estimated a 6-year life and $6,000 salvage value. Thus, straight-line depreciation was $5,000 per year (($36,000 − $6,000) ÷ 6). At the end of year three (before the depreciation adjustment), it estimated the new total life to be 10 years and the new salvage value to be $2,000. Compute the revised depreciation.

Action Plan

- Calculate remaining depreciable cost.
- Divide remaining depreciable cost by new remaining life.

Solution

Original depreciation expense = ($36,000 − $6,000 ÷ 6) = $5,000
Accumulated depreciation after 2 years = 2 × $5,000 = $10,000
Book value = $36,000 − $10,000 = $26,000

Book value after 2 years of depreciation	$26,000
Less: New salvage value	2,000
Depreciable cost	$24,000
Remaining useful life	8 years
Revised annual depreciation ($24,000 ÷ 8)	$ 3,000

✔ **The Navigator**

Related exercise material: **BE9-5**, **Do it!** **9-3**, and **E9-6**.

EXPENDITURES DURING USEFUL LIFE

During the useful life of a plant asset, a company may incur costs for ordinary repairs, additions, and improvements. Ordinary repairs are expenditures to maintain the operating efficiency and expected productive life of the unit. They usually are fairly small amounts that occur frequently throughout the service life. Examples are motor tune-ups and oil changes, the painting of buildings, and the replacing of worn-out gears on factory machinery. Ordinary repairs are debited to Maintenance and Repairs Expense as incurred.

In contrast, additions and improvements are costs incurred to **increase** the operating efficiency, productive capacity, or expected useful life of the plant asset. These expenditures are usually material in amount and occur infrequently during the period of ownership. Expenditures for additions and improvements increase the company's investment in productive facilities and are generally debited to the plant asset affected. Thus, they are **capital expenditures**. The accounting for capital expenditures varies depending on the nature of the expenditure.

Northwest Airlines at one time spent $120 million to spruce up 40 jets. The improvements were designed to extend the lives of the planes, meet stricter government noise limits, and save money. The capital expenditure was expected to extend the life of the jets by 10 to 15 years and save about $560 million compared to the cost of buying new planes. The jets were, on average, 24 years old.

ANATOMY OF A FRAUD

Bernie Ebbers was the founder and CEO of the phone company WorldCom. The company engaged in a series of increasingly large, debt-financed acquisitions of other companies. These acquisitions made the company grow quickly, which made the stock price increase dramatically. However, because the acquired companies all had different accounting systems, WorldCom's financial records were a mess. When WorldCom's performance started to flatten out, Bernie coerced WorldCom's accountants to engage in a number of fraudulent activities to make net income look better than it really was and thus prop up the stock price. One of these frauds involved treating $7 billion of line costs as capital expenditures. The line costs, which were rental fees paid to other phone companies to use their phone lines, had always been properly expensed in previous years. Capitalization delayed expense recognition to future periods and thus boosted current-period profits.

THE MISSING CONTROLS

Documentation procedures. The company's accounting system was a disorganized collection of non-integrated systems, which resulted from a series of corporate acquisitions. Top management took advantage of this disorganization to conceal its fraudulent activities.

Independent internal verification. A fraud of this size should have been detected by a routine comparison of the actual physical assets with the list of physical assets shown in the accounting records.

IMPAIRMENTS

As noted earlier, the book value of plant assets is rarely the same as the fair value. In instances where the value of a plant asset declines substantially, its fair value might fall materially below book value. This may happen because a machine has become obsolete, or the market for the product made by the machine has dried up or has become very competitive. A **permanent decline** in the fair value of an asset is referred to as an impairment. So as not to overstate the asset on the books, the company writes the asset down to its new fair value during the year in which the decline in value occurs. Recently, Disney recorded a $200 million write-down on its action movie *John Carter*. Disney spent more than $300 million producing the film.

In the past, some companies **improperly** delayed recording losses on impairments until a year when it was "convenient" to do so—when the impact on the company's reported results was minimized. For example, in a year when a company has record profits, it can afford to write down some of its bad assets without hurting its reported results too much. As discussed in Chapter 4, the practice of timing the recognition of gains and losses to achieve certain income results is known as **earnings management**. Earnings management reduces earnings quality. To minimize earnings management, accounting standards now require immediate loss recognition on impaired assets.

Write-downs can create problems for users of financial statements. Critics of write-downs note that after a company writes down assets, its depreciation expense will be lower in all subsequent periods. Some companies improperly inflate asset write-downs in bad years, when they are going to report poor results anyway. (This practice is referred to as "taking a big bath.") Then in subsequent years, when the company recovers, its results will look even better because of lower depreciation expense.

PLANT ASSET DISPOSALS

Companies dispose of plant assets that are no longer useful to them. Illustration 9-16 shows the three ways in which companies make plant asset disposals.

Whatever the disposal method, the company must determine the book value of the plant asset at the time of disposal in order to determine the gain or loss. Recall that the book value is the difference between the cost of the plant asset and the accumulated depreciation to date. If the disposal occurs at any time prior to

LEARNING OBJECTIVE **5**

Explain how to account for the disposal of plant assets.

Illustration 9-16 Methods of plant asset disposal

Sale
Equipment is sold to another party.

Retirement
Equipment is scrapped or discarded.

Exchange
Existing equipment is traded for new equipment.

the end of the year, the company must record depreciation for the fraction of the year to the date of disposal. The company then eliminates the book value by reducing (debiting) Accumulated Depreciation for the total depreciation associated with that asset to the date of disposal and reducing (crediting) the asset account for the cost of the asset.

Sale of Plant Assets

In a disposal by sale, the company compares the book value of the asset with the proceeds received from the sale. If the proceeds from the sale **exceed** the book value of the plant asset, a **gain on disposal** occurs. If the proceeds from the sale **are less than** the book value of the plant asset sold, a **loss on disposal** occurs.

Only by coincidence will the book value and the fair value of the asset be the same at the time the asset is sold. Gains and losses on sales of plant assets are therefore quite common. As an example, Delta Air Lines reported a $94 million gain on the sale of five Boeing B-727-200 aircraft and five Lockheed L-1011-1 aircraft.

GAIN ON SALE. To illustrate a gain on sale of plant assets, assume that on July 1, 2014, Wright Company sells office furniture for $16,000 cash. The office furniture originally cost $60,000 and as of January 1, 2014, had accumulated depreciation of $41,000. Depreciation for the first six months of 2014 is $8,000. Wright records depreciation expense and updates accumulated depreciation to July 1 as follows.

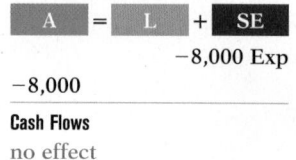

A = L + SE
−8,000 Exp
−8,000

Cash Flows
no effect

July 1	Depreciation Expense	8,000	
	Accumulated Depreciation—Equipment		8,000
	(To record depreciation expense for the first 6 months of 2014)		

After the accumulated depreciation balance is updated, the company computes the gain or loss as the difference between the proceeds from sale and the book value at the date of disposal. Wright Company has a gain on disposal of $5,000, as computed in Illustration 9-17.

Illustration 9-17 Computation of gain on disposal

Cost of office furniture	$60,000
Less: Accumulated depreciation ($41,000 + $8,000)	49,000
Book value at date of disposal	11,000
Proceeds from sale	16,000
Gain on disposal of plant asset	**$ 5,000**

Wright records the sale and the gain on sale of the plant asset as follows.

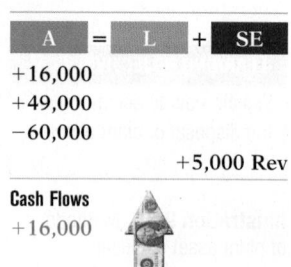

A = L + SE
+16,000
+49,000
−60,000
+5,000 Rev

Cash Flows
+16,000

July 1	Cash	16,000	
	Accumulated Depreciation—Equipment	49,000	
	Equipment		60,000
	Gain on Disposal of Plant Assets		5,000
	(To record sale of office furniture at a gain)		

Companies report a gain on disposal of plant assets in the "Other revenues and gains" section of the income statement. Recently, the shares of Sears Holdings Corporation rose 19% when the company announced its intention to sell 1,200 stores to raise cash.

LOSS ON SALE. Assume that instead of selling the office furniture for $16,000, Wright sells it for $9,000. In this case, Wright experiences a loss of $2,000, as computed in Illustration 9-18.

Cost of office furniture	$60,000
Less: Accumulated depreciation	49,000
Book value at date of disposal	11,000
Proceeds from sale	9,000
Loss on disposal of plant asset	**$ 2,000**

Illustration 9-18 Computation of loss on disposal

Wright records the sale and the loss on sale of the plant asset as follows.

July 1	Cash	9,000	
	Accumulated Depreciation—Equipment	49,000	
	Loss on Disposal of Plant Assets	2,000	
	Equipment		60,000
	(To record sale of office furniture at		
	a loss)		

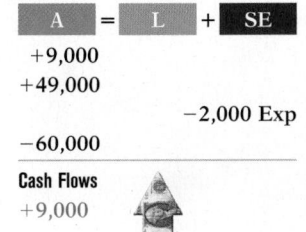

A = L + SE
+9,000
+49,000
        −2,000 Exp
−60,000

Cash Flows
+9,000

Companies report a loss on disposal of the plant asset in the "Other expenses and losses" section of the income statement.

Retirement of Plant Assets

Companies simply retire, rather than sell, some assets at the end of their useful life. For example, some productive assets used in manufacturing may have very specific uses, and they consequently have no ready market when the company no longer needs them. In such a case, the asset is simply retired.

Companies record retirement of an asset as a special case of a disposal where no cash is received. They decrease (debit) Accumulated Depreciation for the full amount of depreciation taken over the life of the asset and decrease (credit) the asset account for the original cost of the asset. The loss (a gain is not possible on a retirement) is equal to the asset's book value on the date of retirement.[1]

Do it! Overland Trucking has an old truck that cost $30,000 and has accumulated depreciation of $16,000. Assume two different situations:

1. The company sells the old truck for $17,000 cash.
2. The truck is worthless, so the company simply retires it.

What entry should Overland use to record each scenario?

PLANT ASSET DISPOSALS

Solution

1. Sale of truck for cash:		
Cash	17,000	
Accumulated Depreciation—Equipment	16,000	
Equipment		30,000
Gain on Disposal of Plant Assets		3,000
[$17,000 − ($30,000 − $16,000)]		
(To record sale of truck at a gain)		
2. Retirement of truck:		
Accumulated Depreciation—Equipment	16,000	
Loss on Disposal of Plant Assets	14,000	
Equipment		30,000
(To record retirement of truck at a loss)		

Action Plan

- Compare the asset's book value and its fair value to determine whether a gain or loss has occurred.
- Make sure that both the Equipment account and Accumulated Depreciation–Equipment are reduced upon disposal.

The Navigator

Related exercise material: **BE9-7, BE9-8, Do it! 9-4, E9-7,** and **E9-8.**

---

[1]More advanced courses discuss the accounting for exchanges, the third method of plant asset disposal.

Analyzing Plant Assets

LEARNING OBJECTIVE | **6**

Describe methods for evaluating the use of plant assets.

The presentation of financial statement information about plant assets enables decision makers to analyze the company's use of its plant assets. We will use two measures to analyze plant assets: return on assets and asset turnover. We also show how profit margin relates to both.

RETURN ON ASSETS

An overall measure of profitability is the **return on assets**. This ratio is computed by dividing net income by average assets. (Average assets are commonly calculated by adding the beginning and ending values of assets and dividing by 2.) Return on assets indicates the amount of net income generated by each dollar of assets. Thus, the higher the return on assets, the more profitable the company.

Information is provided below related to JetBlue Airways.

	JetBlue (in millions)
Net income, 2011	$ 86
Total assets, 12/31/11	7,071
Total assets, 12/31/10	6,593
Net sales, 2011	4,504

Illustration 9-19 presents the 2011 and 2010 return on assets of JetBlue Airways, Southwest Airlines, and industry averages.

Illustration 9-19 Return on assets for JetBlue and Southwest

$$\text{Return on Assets} = \frac{\text{Net Income}}{\text{Average Total Assets}}$$

JetBlue Airways ($ in millions)		**Southwest Airlines**	**Industry Average**
2011	2010	2011	2011
$\dfrac{\$86}{(\$7,071 + \$6,593)/2} = 1.3\%$	1.5%	1.1%	4.0%

JetBlue's return on assets was better than that of Southwest's but significantly lower than the airline industry. The airline industry has experienced financial difficulties in recent years as it attempted to cover high labor, fuel, and security costs while offering fares low enough to attract customers. Such difficulties are reflected in the low industry average for return on assets and the very low values for JetBlue and Southwest. Recently, Southwest announced that it would not add additional planes beyond the 700 it already had until it met its investment-return targets. Instead, the company is adding seats to existing planes and replacing some smaller planes with larger ones.

Accounting Across the Organization

Marketing ROI as Profit Indicator

Marketing executives use the basic finance concept underlying return on assets to determine "marketing return on investment (ROI)." They calculate *marketing ROI* as the profit generated by a marketing initiative divided by the investment in that initiative.

It can be tricky to determine what to include in the "investment" amount and how to attribute profit to a particular marketing initiative. However, many firms feel that measuring marketing ROI is worth the effort because it allows managers to evaluate the relative effectiveness of various programs. In addition, it helps quantify the benefits that marketing provides to the organization. In periods of tight budgets, the marketing ROI number can provide particularly valuable evidence to help a marketing manager avoid budget cuts.

Source: James O. Mitchel, "Marketing ROI," *LIMRA's MarketFacts Quarterly* (Summer 2004), p. 15.

? How does measuring marketing ROI support the overall efforts of the organization? (See page 499.)

© Walter G Arce/Cal Sport Media/NewsCom

DECISION TOOLKIT

DECISION CHECKPOINTS	INFO NEEDED FOR DECISION	TOOL TO USE FOR DECISION	HOW TO EVALUATE RESULTS
Is the company using its assets effectively?	Net income and average assets	$\text{Return on assets} = \dfrac{\text{Net income}}{\text{Average total assets}}$	Higher value suggests favorable efficiency (use of assets).

ASSET TURNOVER

Asset turnover indicates how efficiently a company uses its assets to generate sales—that is, how many dollars of sales a company generates for each dollar invested in assets. It is calculated by dividing net sales by average total assets. When we compare two companies in the same industry, the one with the higher asset turnover is operating more efficiently. It is generating more sales per dollar invested in assets. Illustration 9-20 presents the asset turnovers for JetBlue Airways and Southwest Airlines.

Illustration 9-20 Asset turnovers for JetBlue and Southwest

$\text{Asset Turnover} = \dfrac{\text{Net Sales}}{\text{Average Total Assets}}$			
JetBlue Airways ($ in millions)		**Southwest Airlines**	**Industry Average**
2011	2010	2011	2011
$\dfrac{\$4,504}{(\$7,071 + \$6,593)/2} = 0.66$ times	0.58 times	0.93 times	0.80 times

These asset turnover values tell us that for each dollar of assets, JetBlue generates sales of $0.66 and Southwest $0.93. Southwest is more successful in generating sales per dollar invested in assets. The average asset turnover for the airline industry is 0.80 times. In recent years, airlines have reduced both the number of planes used and routes flown to try to pack more customers on a plane. This would increase the asset turnover.

Asset turnovers vary considerably across industries. During a recent year, the average asset turnover for electric utility companies was 0.34. The grocery industry had an average asset turnover of 2.89. Asset turnover values, therefore, are only comparable within—not between—industries.

PROFIT MARGIN REVISITED

In Chapter 5, you learned about **profit margin**. That ratio is calculated by dividing net income by net sales. It tells how effective a company is in turning its sales into income—that is, how much income each dollar of sales provides. Illustration 9-21 shows that return on assets can be computed as the product of profit margin and asset turnover.

Illustration 9-21 Composition of return on assets

Profit Margin	×	Asset Turnover	=	Return on Assets
$\dfrac{\text{Net Income}}{\text{Net Sales}}$	×	$\dfrac{\text{Net Sales}}{\text{Average Total Assets}}$	=	$\dfrac{\text{Net Income}}{\text{Average Total Assets}}$

This relationship has very important strategic implications for management. From Illustration 9-21, we can see that if a company wants to increase its return on assets, it can do so in two ways: (1) by increasing the margin it generates from each dollar of goods that it sells (the profit margin), or (2) by increasing the volume of goods that it sells (the asset turnover). For example, most grocery stores have very low profit margins, often in the range of 1 or 2 cents for every dollar of goods sold. Grocery stores, therefore, focus on asset turnover: They rely on high turnover to increase their return on assets. Alternatively, a store selling luxury goods, such as expensive jewelry, doesn't generally have a high turnover. Consequently, a seller of luxury goods focuses on having a high profit margin. Recently, Apple decided to offer a less expensive version of its popular iPod. This new product would provide a lower margin, but higher volume, than Apple's more expensive version.

Let's evaluate the return on assets of JetBlue Airways for 2011 by evaluating its components—profit margin and asset turnover. See Illustration 9-22.

Illustration 9-22 Components of rate of return for JetBlue and Southwest

	Profit Margin	×	Asset Turnover	=	Return on Assets
JetBlue Airways	1.9%	×	0.66	=	1.3%
Southwest Airlines	1.2%	×	0.93	=	1.1%

JetBlue's return on asset of 1.3% versus Southwest's 1.1% means that JetBlue generates 1.3 cents per each dollar invested in assets, while Southwest generates 1.1 cents. Illustration 9-22 reveals that although these two airlines have similar return on asset values, they achieve this return in a slightly different fashion. First, JetBlue's profit margin of 1.9% versus Southwest's of 1.2% means that for every dollar of sales, JetBlue generates approximately 1.9 cents of net income, while Southwest generates approximately 1.2 cents. Second, JetBlue's asset turnover of 0.66 means that it generates 66 cents of sales per each dollar invested in assets, while Southwest generates 93 cents. Therefore, in 2011, Southwest was more effective at generating sales from its assets, while JetBlue was better at deriving profit from those sales.

 ## DECISION TOOLKIT

DECISION CHECKPOINTS	INFO NEEDED FOR DECISION	TOOL TO USE FOR DECISION	HOW TO EVALUATE RESULTS
How effective is the company at generating sales from its assets?	Net sales and average total assets	$\text{Asset turnover} = \dfrac{\text{Net sales}}{\text{Average total assets}}$	Indicates the sales dollars generated per dollar of assets. A high value suggests the company is effective in using its resources to generate sales.

 ## People, Planet, and Profit Insight
Sustainability Report Please

Sustainability reports identify how the company is meeting its corporate social responsibilities. Many companies, both large and small, are now issuing these reports. For example, companies such as Disney, Best Buy, Microsoft, Ford, and ConocoPhilips issue these reports. Presented below is an adapted section of BHP Billiton's (a global mining, oil, and gas company) sustainability report on its environmental policies. These policies are to (1) take action to address the challenges of climate change, (2) set and achieve targets that reduce pollution, and (3) enhance biodiversity by assessing and considering ecological values and land-use aspects. Here is how BHP Billiton measures the success or failure of some of these policies:

© Christian Uhrig/iStockphoto

Environment	Result	Trend	Commentary	Target Date
Aggregate Group target of 6% reduction in greenhouse gas emissions per unit of production	On track	Improvement	Our greenhouse gas emissions intensity index has reduced 7% on our FY2006 baseline year	30 June 2012
Aggregate Group target of 13% reduction in carbon-based energy use per unit of production	On track	Improvement	Our energy intensity index has reduced 6% on our FY2006 baseline year	30 June 2012
Aggregate Group target of a 10% improvement in the ratio of water recycled/reused to high-quality water consumed	On track	Deterioration	Our water use index has improved 7% on our FY2007 baseline year	30 June 2012

In addition to the environment, BHP Billiton has sections in its sustainability report which discuss people, safety, health, and community.

Source: BHP Billiton, *2010 Sustainability Report.*

 Why do you believe companies issue sustainability reports? (See page 500.)

Intangible Assets

Intangible assets are rights, privileges, and competitive advantages that result from ownership of long-lived assets that do not possess physical substance. Many companies' most valuable assets are intangible. Some widely known intangibles are Microsoft's patents, McDonalds's franchises, the trade name iPod, and Nike's trademark "swoosh."

LEARNING OBJECTIVE 7
Identify the basic issues related to reporting intangible assets.

Analysts estimated that in the early 1980s, the fair value of intangible assets to total assets was close to 40%. By 2000, the percentage was over 80%—quite a difference. What has happened is that research and development (e.g., hi-tech and bio-tech) has grown substantially. At the same time, many companies (e.g., Nike and Microsoft) have developed brand power which enables them to maintain their market position.

As you will learn in this section, financial statements do report numerous intangibles. Yet, many other financially significant intangibles are not reported. To give an example, according to its financial statements in a recent year, Google had total stockholders' equity of $22.7 billion. But its market value—the total market price of all its shares on that same date—was roughly $178.5 billion. Thus, its actual market value was about $155.8 billion greater than the amount reported for stockholders' equity on the balance sheet. It is not uncommon for a company's reported book value to differ from its market value because balance sheets are reported at historical cost. But such an extreme difference seriously diminishes the usefulness of the balance sheet to decision-makers. In the case of Google, the difference is due to unrecorded intangibles. For many high-tech or so-called intellectual-property companies, most of their value is from intangibles, many of which are not reported under current accounting rules.

Intangibles may be evidenced by contracts, licenses, and other documents. Intangibles may arise from the following sources:

1. Government grants, such as patents, copyrights, licenses, trademarks, and trade names.

2. Acquisition of another business in which the purchase price includes a payment for goodwill.

3. Private monopolistic arrangements arising from contractual agreements, such as franchises and leases.

ACCOUNTING FOR INTANGIBLE ASSETS

Companies record intangible assets at cost. Intangibles are categorized as having either a limited life or an indefinite life. If an intangible has a **limited life**, the company allocates its cost over the asset's useful life using a process similar to depreciation. The process of allocating to expense the cost of intangibles is referred to as amortization. The cost of intangible assets with **indefinite lives should not be amortized**.

To record amortization of an intangible asset, a company increases (debits) Amortization Expense, and decreases (credits) the specific intangible asset. (Unlike depreciation, no contra account, such as Accumulated Amortization, is usually used.)

Intangible assets are typically amortized on a straight-line basis. For example, the legal life of a patent is 20 years. Companies **amortize the cost of a patent over its 20-year life or its useful life, whichever is shorter**. To illustrate the computation of patent amortization, assume that National Labs purchases a patent at a cost of $60,000 on June 30. If National estimates the useful life of the patent to be eight years, the annual amortization expense is $7,500 ($60,000 ÷ 8) per year. National records $3,750 ($7,500 × $\frac{6}{12}$) of amortization for the six-month period ended December 31 as follows.

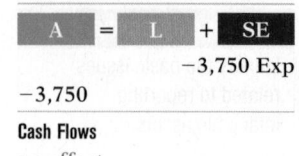

A = L + SE

−3,750 Exp
−3,750

Cash Flows
no effect

Dec. 31	Amortization Expense	3,750	
	Patent		3,750
	(To record patent amortization)		

When a company has significant intangibles, analysts should evaluate the reasonableness of the useful life estimates that the company discloses in the notes to its financial statements. In determining useful life, the company should consider obsolescence, inadequacy, and other factors. These may cause a patent or other intangible to become economically ineffective before the end of its legal life.

For example, suppose Intel obtained a patent on a new computer chip it had developed. The legal life of the patent is 20 years. From experience, however, we know that the useful life of a computer chip patent is rarely more than five years. Because new superior chips are developed so rapidly, existing chips become obsolete. Consequently, we would question the amortization expense of Intel if it amortized its patent on a computer chip for a life significantly longer than a five-year period. Amortizing an intangible over a period that is too long will understate amortization expense, overstate Intel's net income, and overstate its assets.

 DECISION TOOLKIT

DECISION CHECKPOINTS	INFO NEEDED FOR DECISION	TOOL TO USE FOR DECISION	HOW TO EVALUATE RESULTS
Is the company's amortization of intangibles reasonable?	Estimated useful life of intangibles from notes to financial statements of this company and its competitors	If the company's estimated useful life significantly exceeds that of competitors or does not seem reasonable in light of the circumstances, the reason for the difference should be investigated.	Too high an estimated useful life will result in understating amortization expense and overstating net income.

TYPES OF INTANGIBLE ASSETS

Patents

A **patent** is an exclusive right issued by the U.S. Patent Office that enables the recipient to manufacture, sell, or otherwise control an invention for a period of 20 years from the date of the grant. **The initial cost of a patent is the cash or cash equivalent price paid to acquire the patent.**

The saying "A patent is only as good as the money you're prepared to spend defending it" is very true. Most patents are subject to some type of litigation by competitors. A well-known example is the patent infringement suit brought by Amazon.com against Barnes & Noble.com regarding its online shopping software. If the owner incurs legal costs in successfully defending the patent in an infringement suit, such costs are considered necessary to establish the validity of the patent. Thus, **the owner adds those costs to the Patent account and amortizes them over the remaining life of the patent**.

Research and Development Costs

Research and development costs are expenditures that may lead to patents, copyrights, new processes, and new products. Many companies spend considerable sums of money on research and development (R&D) in an ongoing effort to develop new products or processes. For example, in a recent year IBM spent over $5.1 billion on research and development. There are uncertainties in identifying the extent and timing of the future benefits of these expenditures. As a result, companies usually record research and development costs **as an expense when incurred**, whether the R&D is successful or not.

Helpful Hint Research and development costs are not intangible costs, but because these expenditures may lead to patents and copyrights, we discuss them in this section.

International Note IFRS allows capitalization of some development costs. This may contribute to differences in R&D expenditures across nations.

To illustrate, assume that Laser Scanner Company spent $3 million on research and development that resulted in two highly successful patents. It spent $20,000 on legal fees for the patents. It can include the legal fees in the cost of the patents but cannot include the R&D costs in the cost of the patents. Instead, Laser Scanner records the R&D costs as an expense when incurred.

Many disagree with this accounting approach. They argue that to expense these costs leads to understated assets and net income. Others argue that capitalizing these costs would lead to highly speculative assets on the balance sheet. Who is right is difficult to determine.

Copyrights

The federal government grants copyrights, which give the owner the exclusive right to reproduce and sell an artistic or published work. Copyrights last for the life of the creator plus 70 years. The cost of the copyright consists of the **cost of acquiring and defending it**. The cost may be only the small fee paid to the U.S. Copyright Office, or it may amount to a great deal more if a copyright is acquired from another party. The useful life of a copyright generally is significantly shorter than its legal life.

Trademarks and Trade Names

A trademark or trade name is a word, phrase, jingle, or symbol that distinguishes or identifies a particular enterprise or product. Trade names like Wheaties, Monopoly, Sunkist, Kleenex, Coca-Cola, Big Mac, and Jeep create immediate product identification and generally enhance the sale of the product. The creator or original user may obtain the exclusive legal right to the trademark or trade name by registering it with the U.S. Patent Office. Such registration provides 20 years' protection and may be renewed indefinitely as long as the trademark or trade name is in use.

If a company purchases the trademark or trade name, the cost is the purchase price. If the company develops the trademark or trade name itself, the cost includes attorney's fees, registration fees, design costs, successful legal defense costs, and other expenditures directly related to securing it. Because trademarks and trade names have indefinite lives, they are not amortized.

Franchises

When you purchase a RAV4 from a Toyota dealer, fill up your tank at the corner Shell station, eat lunch at Subway, or make reservations at a Marriott hotel, you are dealing with franchises. A franchise is a contractual arrangement under which the franchisor grants the franchisee the right to sell certain products, to perform specific services, or to use certain trademarks or trade names, usually within a designated geographic area.

Another type of franchise is a license. Licenses granted by a governmental body permit a business to use public property in performing its services. Examples are the use of city streets for a bus line or taxi service; the use of public land for telephone, electric, and cable television lines; and the use of airwaves for radio or TV broadcasting. In a recent license agreement, Fox, CBS, and NBC agreed to pay $27.9 billion for the right to broadcast NFL football games over an eight-year period.

Franchises and licenses may be granted for a definite period of time, or the time period may be indefinite or perpetual. **When a company can identify costs with the acquisition of the franchise or license, it should recognize an intangible asset.** Companies record as **operating expenses** annual payments made under a franchise agreement in the period in which they are incurred. In the case of a limited life, a company amortizes the cost of a franchise (or license) as operating expense over the useful life. If the life is indefinite or perpetual, the cost is not amortized.

Goodwill

Usually, the largest intangible asset that appears on a company's balance sheet is goodwill. Goodwill represents the value of all favorable attributes that relate to a company that are not attributable to any other specific asset. These include exceptional management, desirable location, good customer relations, skilled employees, high-quality products, fair pricing policies, and harmonious relations with labor unions. Goodwill is unique because unlike other assets such as investments, plant assets, and even other intangibles, which can be sold **individually** in the marketplace, goodwill can be identified only with the business **as a whole**.

If goodwill can be identified only with the business as a whole, how can it be determined? Certainly, many business enterprises have many of the factors cited above (exceptional management, desirable location, and so on). However, to determine the amount of goodwill in these situations would be difficult and very subjective. In other words, to recognize goodwill without an exchange transaction that puts a value on the goodwill would lead to subjective valuations that do not contribute to the reliability of financial statements. **Therefore, companies record goodwill only when there is an exchange transaction that involves the purchase of an entire business. When an entire business is purchased, goodwill is the excess of cost over the fair value of the net assets (assets less liabilities) acquired.**

In recording the purchase of a business, a company debits the identifiable acquired assets and credits liabilities at their fair values, credits cash for the purchase price, and records the difference as the cost of goodwill. Goodwill is not amortized because it is considered to have an indefinite life. However, it must be written down if a company determines the value of goodwill has been permanently impaired.

 ## International Insight
Should Companies Write Up Goodwill?

Softbank Corp. was Japan's biggest Internet company. At one time, it boosted the profit margin of its mobile-phone unit from 3.2% to 11.2% through what appeared to some as accounting tricks. What did it do? It wrote down the value of its mobile-phone-unit assets by half. This would normally result in a huge loss. But rather than take a loss, the company wrote up goodwill by the same amount. How did this move increase earnings? The assets were being depreciated over 10 years, but the company amortizes goodwill over 20 years. (Amortization of goodwill was allowed under the accounting standards it followed at that time.) While the new treatment did not break any rules, the company was criticized by investors for not providing sufficient justification or a detailed explanation for the sudden shift in policy.

Source: Andrew Morse and Yukari Iwatani Kane, "Softbank's Accounting Shift Raises Eyebrows," *Wall Street Journal* (August 28, 2007), p. C1.

 Do you think that this treatment would be allowed under U.S. GAAP? (See page 500.)

© Pixtal/SuperStock

CLASSIFICATION CONCEPTS

Do it!

Match the statement with the term most directly associated with it.

Copyright	Amortization
Intangible assets	Franchise
Research and development costs	

1. _____ The allocation to expense of the cost of an intangible asset over the asset's useful life.

2. _____ Rights, privileges, and competitive advantages that result from the ownership of long-lived assets that do not possess physical substance.

3. _____ An exclusive right granted by the federal government to reproduce and sell an artistic or published work.

4. _____ A right to sell certain products or services or to use certain trademarks or trade names within a designated geographic area.

5. _____ Costs incurred by a company that often lead to patents or new products. These costs must be expensed as incurred.

Action Plan

- Know that the accounting for intangibles often depends on whether the item has a finite or indefinite life.
- Recognize the many similarities and differences between the accounting for plant assets and intangible assets.

✔ The Navigator

Solution

1. Amortization	4. Franchise
2. Intangible assets	5. Research and development costs
3. Copyright	

Related exercise material: **BE9-10**, *Do it!* **9-5, E9-13, E9-14,** and **E9-15.**

Financial Statement Presentation of Long-Lived Assets

LEARNING OBJECTIVE 8

Indicate how long-lived assets are reported in the financial statements.

Usually, companies show plant assets in the financial statements under "Property, plant, and equipment," and they show intangibles separately under "Intangible assets." Illustration 9-23 shows a typical balance sheet presentation of long-lived assets, adapted from a recent The Coca-Cola Company balance sheet.

Illustration 9-23
Presentation of property, plant, and equipment and intangible assets

Real World	THE COCA-COLA COMPANY Balance Sheet (partial) (in millions)	
Property, plant, and equipment		
Land		$ 699
Buildings and improvements		3,816
Machinery and equipment		10,355
Containers and other		1,597
		16,467
Less: Accumulated depreciation		6,906
		9,561
Intangible assets		
Trademarks with indefinite lives		6,183
Goodwill		4,224
Other intangible assets		2,421
		$12,828

Intangibles do not usually use a contra asset account like the contra asset account Accumulated Depreciation used for plant assets. Instead, companies record amortization of intangibles as a direct decrease (credit) to the asset account.

Either within the balance sheet or in the notes, companies should disclose the balances of the major classes of assets, such as land, buildings, and equipment, and of accumulated depreciation by major classes or in total. In addition, they should describe the depreciation and amortization methods used and disclose the amount of depreciation and amortization expense for the period.

KEEPING AN EYE ON CASH

Depreciation and amortization expense are among the biggest causes of differences between accrual-accounting net income and net cash provided by operating activities. Depreciation and amortization reduce net income, but they do not use up any cash. Therefore, to determine net cash provided by operating activities, companies add depreciation and amortization back to net income. For example, if a company reported net income of $175,000 during the year and had depreciation expense of $40,000, net cash provided by operating activities would be $215,000 (assuming no other accrual-accounting differences). The operating activities section of Coca-Cola's statement of cash flows reports the following adjustment for depreciation and amortization.

Real World

THE COCA-COLA COMPANY
Statement of Cash Flows (partial)
(in millions)

Cash flow from operating activities	
Net income	$6,906
Plus: Depreciation and amortization	1,236

The adjustment for depreciation and amortization was more than twice as big as any other adjustment required to convert net income to net cash provided by operating activities.

It is also interesting to examine the statement of cash flows to determine the amount of property, plant, and equipment a company purchased and the cash it received from property, plant, and equipment sold in a given year. For example, the investing activities section of Coca-Cola reports the following.

Real World

THE COCA-COLA COMPANY
Statement of Cash Flows (partial)
(in millions)

Cash flow from investing activities	
Acquisitions and investments	$(2,452)
Purchases of property, plant, and equipment	(1,993)
Proceeds from disposals of property, plant, and equipment	104
Other	192

As indicated, Coca-Cola made significant purchases and sales of property, plant, and equipment. The level of purchases suggests that Coca-Cola believes that it can earn a reasonable rate of return on these assets.

USING THE DECISION TOOLKIT

Delta Air Lines, Inc., headquartered in Atlanta, Georgia, is one of the largest airlines in the world. It serves 342 destinations in 61 countries.

Instructions

Review the excerpts from the company's 2011 annual report that follow and then answer the following questions.

1. What method does the company use to depreciate its aircraft? Over what period is the company depreciating these aircraft?
2. What type of intangible assets does the company have, and how are they being accounted for?
3. Compute the company's return on assets ratio, asset turnover ratio, and profit margin ratio for 2011 and 2010. Comment on your results.

(in millions)	2011	2010
Net income (loss)	$ 854	$ 593
Net sales	35,115	31,755
Beginning total assets	43,188	43,539
Ending total assets	43,499	43,188

DELTA AIR LINES, INC.
Notes to the Financial Statements (Partial)

Long-Lived Assets

The following table shows our property and equipment:

(in millions, except for estimated useful life)	Estimated Useful Life	December 31,	
		2011	2010
Flight equipment	21–30 years	$21,001	$20,312
Ground property and equipment	3–40 years	3,256	3,123
Flight and ground equipment under capital leases	Shorter of lease term or estimated useful life	1,127	988
Assets constructed for others	30 years	234	—
Advance payments for equipment		77	48
Less: accumulated depreciation and amortization		(5,472)	(4,164)
Total property and equipment, net		$20,223	$20,307

We record property and equipment at cost and depreciate or amortize these assets on a straight-line basis to their estimated residual values over their estimated useful lives.

Goodwill and Other Intangible Assets

Goodwill. As of December 31, 2011 and 2010, our goodwill balance was $9.8 billion. In evaluating goodwill for impairment, we estimate the fair value of our reporting unit by considering market capitalization and other factors if it is more likely than not that the fair value of our reporting unit is less than its carrying value. If the reporting unit's fair value exceeds its carrying value, no further testing is required. If, however, the reporting unit's carrying value exceeds its fair value, we then determine the amount of the impairment charge, if any. We recognize an impairment charge if the carrying value of the reporting unit's goodwill exceeds its estimated fair value.

Identifiable Intangible Assets. Our identifiable intangible assets had a net carrying amount of $4.8 billion at December 31, 2011. Indefinite-lived assets are not amortized and consist primarily of routes, slots, the Delta tradename, and assets related to SkyTeam. Definite-lived intangible assets consist primarily of marketing agreements and contracts and are amortized on a straight-line basis or under the undiscounted cash flows method over the estimated economic life of the respective agreements and contracts. Costs incurred to renew or extend the term of an intangible asset are expensed as incurred.

We perform the impairment test for indefinite-lived intangible assets by comparing the asset's fair value to its carrying value. . . . We recognize an impairment charge if the asset's carrying value exceeds its estimated fair value.

Solution

1. The company depreciates property and equipment using the straight-line approach. It depreciates aircraft over a 21–30-year life.
2. The company has a goodwill balance of $9.8 billion which it tests for impairment. It also has other identifiable intangible assets with a carrying value of $4.8 billion. These include indefinite-life assets such as routes, slots, the Delta tradename, and assets related to SkyTeam. Indefinite-life intangibles are tested for impairment. Definite-life intangibles, including marketing agreements and contracts, are amortized on a straight-line basis or using the undiscounted cash flows method.

3.

	2011	**2010**
Return on assets	$\dfrac{\$854}{(\$43,188 + \$43,499)/2} = 2.0\%$	$\dfrac{\$593}{(\$43,539 + \$43,188)/2} = 1.4\%$
Asset turnover	$\dfrac{\$35,115}{(\$43,188 + \$43,499)/2} = 0.81 \text{ times}$	$\dfrac{\$31,755}{(\$43,539 + \$43,188)/2} = 0.73 \text{ times}$
Profit margin	$\dfrac{\$854}{\$35,115} = 2.4\%$	$\dfrac{\$593}{\$31,755} = 1.9\%$

Delta's return on assets increased from 2011 to 2010. While its profit margin was low in both years, Delta was able to increase its asset turnover and profit margin. This suggests that its ability to generate sales from its planes and its ability to generate profits from sales both increased.

Summary of Learning Objectives

1 Describe how the historical cost principle applies to plant assets. The cost of plant assets includes all expenditures necessary to acquire the asset and make it ready for its intended use. Once cost is established, a company uses that amount as the basis of accounting for the plant asset over its useful life.

2 Explain the concept of depreciation. Depreciation is the process of allocating to expense the cost of a plant asset over its useful (service) life in a rational and systematic manner. Depreciation is not a process of valuation, and it is not a process that results in an accumulation of cash. Depreciation reflects an asset's decreasing usefulness and revenue-producing ability, resulting from wear and tear and from obsolescence.

3 Compute periodic depreciation using the straight-line method, and contrast its expense pattern with those of other methods. The formula for straight-line depreciation is:

$$\frac{\text{Cost} - \text{Salvage value}}{\text{Useful life (in years)}}$$

The expense patterns of the three depreciation methods are as follows.

Method	Annual Depreciation Pattern
Straight-line	Constant amount
Declining-balance	Decreasing amount
Units-of-activity	Varying amount

4 Describe the procedure for revising periodic depreciation. Companies make revisions of periodic depreciation in present and future periods, not retroactively.

5 Explain how to account for the disposal of plant assets. The procedure for accounting for the disposal of a plant asset through sale or retirement is: (a) Eliminate the book value of the plant asset at the date of disposal. (b) Record cash proceeds, if any. (c) Account for the difference between the book value and the cash proceeds as a gain or a loss on disposal.

6 Describe methods for evaluating the use of plant assets. Plant assets may be analyzed using return on assets and asset turnover. Return on assets consists of two components: asset turnover and profit margin.

7 Identify the basic issues related to reporting intangible assets. Companies report intangible assets at their cost less any amounts amortized. If an intangible asset has a limited life, its cost should be allocated (amortized) over its useful life. Intangible assets with indefinite lives should not be amortized.

8 Indicate how long-lived assets are reported in the financial statements. Companies usually show plant assets under "Property, plant, and equipment"; they show intangibles separately under "Intangible assets." Either within the balance sheet or in the notes, companies disclose the balances of the major classes of assets, such as land, buildings, and equipment, and accumulated depreciation by major classes or in total. They describe the depreciation and amortization methods used, and disclose the amount of depreciation and amortization expense for the period. In the statement of cash flows, depreciation and amortization expense are added back to net income to determine net cash provided by operating activities. The investing section reports cash paid or received to purchase or sell property, plant, and equipment.

DECISION TOOLKIT A SUMMARY

DECISION CHECKPOINTS	INFO NEEDED FOR DECISION	TOOL TO USE FOR DECISION	HOW TO EVALUATE RESULTS
Is the company using its assets effectively?	Net income and average assets	$\text{Return on assets} = \dfrac{\text{Net income}}{\text{Average total assets}}$	Higher value suggests favorable efficiency (use of assets).
How effective is the company at generating sales from its assets?	Net sales and average total assets	$\text{Asset turnover} = \dfrac{\text{Net income}}{\text{Average total assets}}$	Indicates the sales dollars generated per dollar of assets. A high value suggests the company is effective in using its resources to generate sales.
Is the company's amortization of intangibles reasonable?	Estimated useful life of intangibles from notes to financial statements of this company and its competitors	If the company's estimated useful life significantly exceeds that of competitors or does not seem reasonable in light of the circumstances, the reason for the difference should be investigated.	Too high an estimated useful life will result in understating amortization expense and overstating net income.

Appendix 9A

Calculation of Depreciation Using Other Methods

LEARNING OBJECTIVE 9

Compute periodic depreciation using the declining-balance method and the units-of-activity method.

In this appendix, we show the calculations of the depreciation expense amounts that we used in the chapter for the declining-balance and units-of-activity methods.

DECLINING-BALANCE

The **declining-balance method** produces a decreasing annual depreciation expense over the useful life of the asset. The method is so named because the computation of periodic depreciation is based on a **declining book value** (cost less accumulated depreciation) of the asset. Annual depreciation expense is computed by multiplying the book value at the beginning of the year by the declining-balance depreciation rate. **The depreciation rate remains constant from year to year, but the book value to which the rate is applied declines each year.**

Book value for the first year is the cost of the asset because the balance in accumulated depreciation at the beginning of the asset's useful life is zero. In subsequent years, book value is the difference between cost and accumulated depreciation at the beginning of the year. **Unlike other depreciation methods, the declining-balance method ignores salvage value in determining the amount to which the declining-balance rate is applied.** Salvage value, however, does limit the total depreciation that can be taken. Depreciation stops when the asset's book value equals its expected salvage value.

As noted in the chapter, a common declining-balance rate is double the straight-line rate—the **double-declining-balance method**. If Bill's Pizzas uses the double-declining-balance method, the depreciation rate is 40% (2 × the straight-line rate of 20%). Illustration 9A-1 presents the formula and computation of depreciation for the first year on the delivery truck.

Helpful Hint The straight-line rate is approximated as 1 ÷ Estimated life. In this case, it is 1 ÷ 5 = 20%.

Illustration 9A-1 Formula for declining-balance method

Book Value at Beginning of Year	×	Declining-Balance Rate	=	Depreciation Expense
$13,000	×	40%	=	$5,200

Illustration 9A-2 presents the depreciation schedule under this method.

Illustration 9A-2 Double-declining-balance depreciation schedule

BILL'S PIZZAS

	Computation			Annual	End of Year	
Year	Book Value Beginning of Year	× Depreciation Rate	=	Depreciation Expense	Accumulated Depreciation	Book Value
2014	$13,000	40%		$5,200	$ 5,200	$7,800*
2015	7,800	40		3,120	8,320	4,680
2016	4,680	40		1,872	10,192	2,808
2017	2,808	40		1,123	11,315	1,685
2018	1,685	40		685**	12,000	1,000

*$13,000 − $5,200
**Computation of $674 ($1,685 × 40%) is adjusted to $685 in order for book value to equal salvage value.

Helpful Hint Depreciation stops when the asset's book value equals its expected salvage value.

The delivery equipment is 69% depreciated ($8,320 ÷ $12,000) at the end of the second year. Under the straight-line method, it would be depreciated 40% ($4,800 ÷ $12,000) at that time. Because the declining-balance method produces higher depreciation expense in the early years than in the later years, it is considered an **accelerated-depreciation method**.

The declining-balance method is compatible with the expense recognition principle. It matches the higher depreciation expense in early years with the higher benefits received in these years. Conversely, it recognizes lower depreciation expense in later years when the asset's contribution to revenue is less. Also, some assets lose their usefulness rapidly because of obsolescence. In these cases, the declining-balance method provides a more appropriate depreciation amount.

When an asset is purchased during the year, it is necessary to prorate the declining-balance depreciation in the first year on a time basis. For example, if Bill's Pizzas had purchased the delivery equipment on April 1, 2014, depreciation for 2014 would be $3,900 ($13,000 × 40% × $\frac{9}{12}$). The book value for computing depreciation in 2015 then becomes $9,100 ($13,000 − $3,900), and the 2015 depreciation is $3,640 ($9,100 × 40%).

UNITS-OF-ACTIVITY

Under the **units-of-activity method**, useful life is expressed in terms of the total units of production or use expected from the asset. The units-of-activity method is ideally suited to equipment whose activity can be measured in units of output, miles driven, or hours in use. The units-of-activity method is generally not suitable for assets for which depreciation is a function more of time than of use.

Alternative Terminology Another term often used is the *units-of-production method*.

To use this method, a company estimates the total units of activity for the entire useful life and divides that amount into the depreciable cost to determine the depreciation cost per unit. It then multiplies the depreciation cost per unit by the units of activity during the year to find the annual depreciation for that year.

To illustrate, assume that Bill's Pizzas estimates it will drive its new delivery truck 15,000 miles in the first year. Illustration 9A-3 presents the formula and computation of depreciation expense in the first year.

Illustration 9A-3 Formula for units-of-activity method

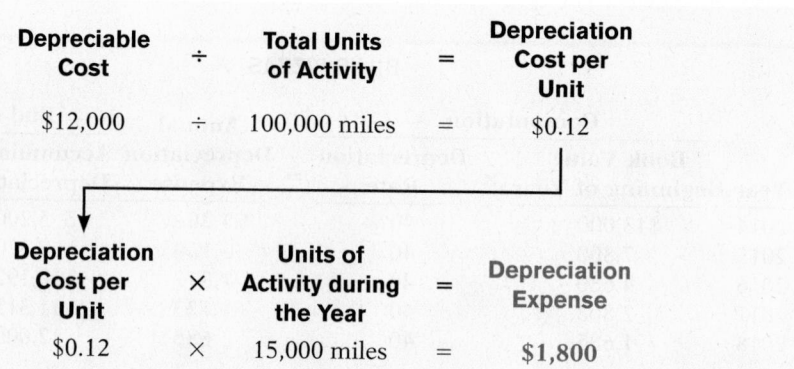

Illustration 9A-4 shows the depreciation schedule, using assumed mileage data.

Illustration 9A-4 Units-of-activity depreciation schedule

BILL'S PIZZAS

	Computation			Annual	End of Year	
Year	Units of Activity	×	Depreciation Cost/Unit	= Depreciation Expense	Accumulated Depreciation	Book Value
2014	15,000		$0.12	$1,800	$ 1,800	$11,200*
2015	30,000		0.12	3,600	5,400	7,600
2016	20,000		0.12	2,400	7,800	5,200
2017	25,000		0.12	3,000	10,800	2,200
2018	10,000		0.12	1,200	12,000	1,000

*$13,000 − $1,800

Helpful Hint Depreciation stops when the asset's book value equals its expected salvage value.

The units-of-activity method is not nearly as popular as the straight-line method, primarily because it is often difficult to make a reasonable estimate of total activity. However, this method is used by some very large companies, such as Standard Oil Company of California and Boise Cascade Corporation. When the productivity of the asset varies significantly from one period to another, the units-of-activity method results in the best matching of expenses with revenues.

This method is easy to apply when assets are purchased during the year. In such a case, companies use the productivity of the asset for the partial year in computing the depreciation.

Summary of Learning Objective for Appendix 9A

9 **Compute periodic depreciation using the declining-balance method and the units-of-activity method.** The depreciation expense calculation for each of these methods is:

Declining-balance:

$$\text{Book value at beginning of year} \times \text{Declining-balance rate} = \text{Depreciation expense}$$

Units-of-activity:

$$\text{Depreciable cost} \div \text{Total units of activity} = \text{Depreciation cost per unit}$$

$$\text{Depreciation cost per unit} \times \text{Units of activity during year} = \text{Depreciation expense}$$

Glossary

Accelerated-depreciation method *(p. 456)* A depreciation method that produces higher depreciation expense in the early years than the straight-line approach.

Additions and improvements *(p. 460)* Costs incurred to increase the operating efficiency, productive capacity, or expected useful life of a plant asset.

Amortization *(p. 468)* The process of allocating to expense the cost of an intangible asset.

Asset turnover *(p. 465)* Indicates how efficiently a company uses its assets to generate sales; calculated as net sales divided by average total assets.

Capital expenditures *(p. 449)* Expenditures that increase the company's investment in plant assets.

Capital lease *(p. 452)* A contractual agreement allowing one party (the lessee) to use another party's asset (the lessor); accounted for like a debt-financed purchase by the lessee.

Cash equivalent price *(p. 449)* An amount equal to the fair value of the asset given up or the fair value of the asset received, whichever is more clearly determinable.

Copyright *(p. 470)* An exclusive right granted by the federal government allowing the owner to reproduce and sell an artistic or published work.

Declining-balance method *(pp. 456, 476)* A depreciation method that applies a constant rate to the declining book value of the asset and produces a decreasing annual depreciation expense over the asset's useful life.

Depreciable cost *(p. 455)* The cost of a plant asset less its salvage value.

Depreciation *(p. 453)* The process of allocating to expense the cost of a plant asset over its useful life in a rational and systematic manner.

Franchise *(p. 470)* A contractual arrangement under which the franchisor grants the franchisee the right to sell certain products, to perform specific services, or to use certain trademarks or trade names, usually within a designated geographic area.

Goodwill *(p. 471)* The value of all favorable attributes that relate to a company that are not attributable to any other specific asset.

Impairment *(p. 461)* A permanent decline in the fair value of an asset.

Intangible assets *(p. 467)* Rights, privileges, and competitive advantages that result from the ownership of long-lived assets that do not possess physical substance.

Lessee *(p. 452)* A party that has made contractual arrangements to use another party's asset for a period at an agreed price.

Lessor *(p. 452)* A party that has agreed contractually to let another party use its asset for a period at an agreed price.

Operating lease *(p. 452)* A contractual agreement allowing one party (the lessee) to use the asset of another party (the lessor); accounted for as a rental by the lessee.

Ordinary repairs *(p. 460)* Expenditures to maintain the operating efficiency and expected productive life of the asset.

Patent *(p. 469)* An exclusive right issued by the U.S. Patent Office that enables the recipient to manufacture, sell, or otherwise control an invention for a period of 20 years from the date of the grant.

Plant assets *(p. 448)* Resources that have physical substance, are used in the operations of the business, and are not intended for sale to customers.

Research and development costs *(p. 469)* Expenditures that may lead to patents, copyrights, new processes, and new products; must be expensed as incurred.

Return on assets *(p. 464)* A profitability measure that indicates the amount of net income generated by each dollar of assets; computed as net income divided by average assets.

Revenue expenditures *(p. 449)* Expenditures that are immediately charged against revenues as an expense.

Straight-line method *(p. 455)* A method in which companies expense an equal amount of depreciation for each year of the asset's useful life.

Trademark (trade name) *(p. 470)* A word, phrase, jingle, or symbol that distinguishes or identifies a particular enterprise or product.

Units-of-activity method *(pp. 456, 477)* A depreciation method in which useful life is expressed in terms of the total units of production or use expected from the asset.

Comprehensive Do it! 1

DuPage Company purchased a factory machine at a cost of $18,000 on January 1, 2014. DuPage expected the machine to have a salvage value of $2,000 at the end of its 4-year useful life.

Instructions

Prepare a depreciation schedule using the straight-line method.

Action Plan

- Under the straight-line method, apply the depreciation rate to depreciable cost.

Solution to Comprehensive Do it! 1

DUPAGE COMPANY
Depreciation Schedule—Straight-Line Method

	Computation			Annual	End of Year	
Year	Depreciable Cost (a)	×	Depreciation Rate (b)	= Annual Depreciation Expense	Accumulated Depreciation	Book Value (c)
2014	$16,000		25%	$4,000	$ 4,000	$14,000
2015	16,000		25	4,000	8,000	10,000
2016	16,000		25	4,000	12,000	6,000
2017	16,000		25	4,000	16,000	2,000

(a) $18,000 − $2,000   (b) $\frac{1}{4}$ = 25%   (c) Cost less accumulated depreciation.

Comprehensive Do it! 2

On January 1, 2011, Skyline Limousine Co. purchased a limousine at an acquisition cost of $28,000. Skyline depreciated the vehicle by the straight-line method using a 4-year service life and a $4,000 salvage value. The company's fiscal year ends on December 31.

Instructions

Prepare the journal entry or entries to record the disposal of the limousine, assuming that it was:

(a) Retired and scrapped with no salvage value on January 1, 2015.
(b) Sold for $5,000 on July 1, 2014.

Action Plan

- Calculate accumulated depreciation (Depreciation expense per year × Years in use).
- At the time of disposal, determine the book value of the asset.
- Recognize any gain or loss from disposal of the asset.

Solution to Comprehensive Do it! 2

(a) Jan. 1, 2015	Accumulated Depreciation—Equipment	24,000*	
	Loss on Disposal of Plant Assets	4,000	
	Equipment		28,000
	(To record retirement of limousine)		

*(($28,000 − $4,000) ÷ 4) × 4

(b) July 1, 2014	Depreciation Expense	3,000*	
	Accumulated Depreciation—Equipment		3,000
	(To record depreciation to date of disposal)		

*(($28,000 − $4,000) ÷ 4) × $\frac{1}{2}$

	Cash	5,000	
	Accumulated Depreciation—Equipment	21,000*	
	Loss on Disposal of Plant Assets	2,000	
	Equipment		28,000
	(To record sale of limousine)		

*(($28,000 − $4,000) ÷ 4) × 3.5

Self-Test, Brief Exercises, Exercises, Problem Set A, and many more resources are available for practice in WileyPLUS.

Note: All Questions, Exercises, and Problems marked with an asterisk relate to material in the appendix to the chapter.

Self-Test Questions

Answers are on page 500.

(LO 1) **1.** Corrieten Company purchased equipment and incurred these costs:

Cash price	$24,000
Sales taxes	1,200
Insurance during transit	200
Installation and testing	400
Total costs	$25,800

What amount should be recorded as the cost of the equipment?
(a) $24,000.
(b) $25,200.
(c) $25,400.
(d) $25,800.

(LO 1) **2.** Harrington Corporation recently leased a number of trucks from Andre Corporation. In inspecting the books of Harrington Corporation, you notice that the trucks have not been recorded as assets on its balance sheet. From this, you can conclude that Harrington is accounting for this transaction as a/an:
(a) operating lease.
(b) capital lease.
(c) purchase.
(d) None of the above.

(LO 2) **3.** Depreciation is a process of:
(a) valuation.
(b) cost allocation.
(c) cash accumulation.
(d) appraisal.

(LO 3) **4.** Cuso Company purchased equipment on January 1, 2013, at a total invoice cost of $400,000. The equipment has an estimated salvage value of $10,000 and an estimated useful life of 5 years. What is the amount of accumulated depreciation at December 31, 2014, if the straight-line method of depreciation is used?
(a) $80,000.
(b) $160,000.
(c) $78,000.
(d) $156,000.

(LO 3) **5.** A company would minimize its depreciation expense in the first year of owning an asset if it used:
(a) a high estimated life, a high salvage value, and declining-balance depreciation.
(b) a low estimated life, a high salvage value, and straight-line depreciation.
(c) a high estimated life, a high salvage value, and straight-line depreciation.
(d) a low estimated life, a low salvage value, and declining-balance depreciation.

(LO 4) **6.** When there is a change in estimated depreciation:
(a) previous depreciation should be corrected.
(b) current and future years' depreciation should be revised.
(c) only future years' depreciation should be revised.
(d) None of the above.

7. Able Towing Company purchased a tow truck for (LO 4) $60,000 on January 1, 2014. It was originally depreciated on a straight-line basis over 10 years with an assumed salvage value of $12,000. On December 31, 2016, before adjusting entries had been made, the company decided to change the remaining estimated life to 4 years (including 2016) and the salvage value to $2,000. What was the depreciation expense for 2016?
(a) $6,000.
(b) $4,800.
(c) $15,000.
(d) $12,100.

8. Additions to plant assets: (LO 4)
(a) decrease liabilities.
(b) increase a repair expense account.
(c) increase a purchases account.
(d) are capital expenditures.

9. Bennie Razor Company has decided to sell one of its (LO 5) old manufacturing machines on June 30, 2014. The machine was purchased for $80,000 on January 1, 2010, and was depreciated on a straight-line basis for 10 years assuming no salvage value. If the machine was sold for $26,000, what was the amount of the gain or loss recorded at the time of the sale?
(a) $18,000 loss.
(b) $54,000 loss.
(c) $22,000 gain.
(d) $46,000 gain.

10. Which of the following measures provides an indication (LO 6) of how efficient a company is in employing its assets?
(a) Current ratio.
(b) Profit margin.
(c) Debt to assets ratio.
(d) Asset turnover.

11. Lake Coffee Company reported net sales of $180,000, (LO 6) net income of $54,000, beginning total assets of $200,000, and ending total assets of $300,000. What was the company's asset turnover?
(a) 0.90
(b) 0.20
(c) 0.72
(d) 1.39

12. Pierce Company incurred $150,000 of research and (LO 7) development costs in its laboratory to develop a new product. It spent $20,000 in legal fees for a patent granted on January 2, 2014. On July 31, 2014, Pierce paid $15,000 for legal fees in a successful defense of the patent. What is the total amount that should be debited to Patents through July 31, 2014?
(a) $150,000.
(b) $35,000.
(c) $185,000.
(d) Some other amount.

13. Indicate which one of these statements is **true**. (LO 7)
(a) Since intangible assets lack physical substance, they need to be disclosed only in the notes to the financial statements.

(b) Goodwill should be reported as a contra account in the stockholders' equity section.

(c) Totals of major classes of assets can be shown in the balance sheet, with asset details disclosed in the notes to the financial statements.

(d) Intangible assets are typically combined with plant assets and inventory and then shown in the property, plant, and equipment section.

(LO 7) **14.** If a company reports goodwill as an intangible asset on its books, what is the one thing you know with certainty?

(a) The company is a valuable company worth investing in.

(b) The company has a well-established brand name.

(c) The company purchased another company.

(d) The goodwill will generate a lot of positive business for the company for many years to come.

(LO 7) **15.** Which of the following statements is **false**?

(a) If an intangible asset has a finite life, it should be amortized.

(b) The amortization period of an intangible asset can exceed 20 years.

(c) Goodwill is recorded only when a business is purchased.

(d) Research and development costs are expensed when incurred, except when the research and development expenditures result in a successful patent.

*16. Kant Enterprises purchased a truck for $11,000 on (LO 9) January 1, 2013. The truck will have an estimated salvage value of $1,000 at the end of 5 years. If you use the units-of-activity method, the balance in accumulated depreciation at December 31, 2014, can be computed by the following formula:

(a) ($11,000 ÷ Total estimated activity) × Units of activity for 2014.

(b) ($10,000 ÷ Total estimated activity) × Units of activity for 2014.

(c) ($11,000 ÷ Total estimated activity) × Units of activity for 2013 and 2014.

(d) ($10,000 ÷ Total estimated activity) × Units of activity for 2013 and 2014.

Go to the book's companion website, **www.wiley.com/college/kimmel**, to access additional Self-Test Questions.

Questions

1. Mrs. Betancourt is uncertain about how the historical cost principle applies to plant assets. Explain the principle to Mrs. Betancourt.

2. How is the cost for a plant asset measured in a cash transaction? In a noncash transaction?

3. Carington Company acquires the land and building owned by Ankiel Company. What types of costs may be incurred to make the asset ready for its intended use if Carington Company wants to use only the land? If it wants to use both the land and the building?

4. Malor Inc. needs to upgrade its diagnostic equipment. At the time of purchase, Malor had expected the equipment to last 8 years. Unfortunately, it was obsolete after only 4 years. Ronald Nolan, CFO of Malor Inc., is considering leasing new equipment rather than buying it. What are the potential benefits of leasing?

5. In a recent newspaper release, the president of Ferguson Company asserted that something has to be done about depreciation. The president said, "Depreciation does not come close to accumulating the cash needed to replace the asset at the end of its useful life." What is your response to the president?

6. Adriana is studying for the next accounting examination. She asks your help on two questions: (a) What is salvage value? (b) How is salvage value used in determining depreciable cost under the straight-line method? Answer Adriana's questions.

7. Contrast the straight-line method and the units-of-activity method in relation to (a) useful life and (b) the pattern of periodic depreciation over useful life.

8. Contrast the effects of the three depreciation methods on annual depreciation expense.

9. In the fourth year of an asset's 5-year useful life, the company decides that the asset will have a 6-year service life. How should the revision of depreciation be recorded? Why?

10. Distinguish between ordinary repairs and capital expenditures during an asset's useful life.

11. How is a gain or a loss on the sale of a plant asset computed?

12. Lakeland Corporation owns a machine that is fully depreciated but is still being used. How should Lakeland account for this asset and report it in the financial statements?

13. What does Tootsie Roll use as the estimated useful life on its buildings? On its machinery and equipment?

14. What are the similarities and differences between depreciation and amortization?

15. During a recent management meeting, David Bryce, director of marketing, proposed that the company begin capitalizing its marketing expenditures as goodwill. In his words, "Marketing expenditures create goodwill for the company which benefits the company for multiple periods. Therefore it doesn't make good sense to have to expense it as it is incurred. Besides, if we capitalize it as goodwill, we won't have to amortize it, and this will boost reported income." Discuss the merits of David's proposal.

16. Berwik Company hires an accounting intern who says that intangible assets should always be amortized over their legal lives. Is the intern correct? Explain.

17. Goodwill has been defined as the value of all favorable attributes that relate to a business enterprise. What types of attributes could result in goodwill?

18. Megan Keen, a business major, is working on a case problem for one of her classes. In this case problem, the company needs to raise cash to market a new product it developed. Jeff Denton, an engineering major, takes one look at the company's balance sheet and says, "This company has an awful lot of goodwill. Why don't you recommend that they sell some of it to raise cash?" How should Megan respond to Jeff?

19. Under what conditions is goodwill recorded? What is the proper accounting treatment for amortizing goodwill?

20. Often research and development costs provide companies with benefits that last a number of years. (For example, these costs can lead to the development of a patent that will increase the company's income for many years.) However, generally accepted accounting principles require that such costs be recorded as an expense when incurred. Why?

21. ⚲══╾🔧 Suppose in 2014, Campbell Soup Company reported average total assets of $6,265 million, net sales of $7,586 million, and net income of $736 million. What was Campbell Soup's return on assets?

22. ⬅ Diane Carey, a marketing executive for Fresh Views Inc., has proposed expanding its product line of framed graphic art by producing a line of lower-quality products. These would require less processing by the company and would provide a lower profit margin. Joe Moreb, the company's CFO, is concerned that this new product line would reduce the company's return on assets. Discuss the potential effect on return on assets that this product might have.

23. ⬅ ⚲══╾🔧 Give an example of an industry that would be characterized by (a) a high asset turnover and a low profit margin, and (b) a low asset turnover and a high profit margin.

24. ⚲══╾🔧 Gooden Corporation and Perron Corporation operate in the same industry. Gooden uses the straight-line method to account for depreciation, whereas Perron uses an accelerated method. Explain what complications might arise in trying to compare the results of these two companies.

25. ⬅ ⚲══╾🔧 Garcia Corporation uses straight-line depreciation for financial reporting purposes but an accelerated method for tax purposes. Is it acceptable to use different methods for the two purposes? What is Garcia Corporation's motivation for doing this?

26. ⚲══╾🔧 You are comparing two companies in the same industry. You have determined that Leslie Corp. depreciates its plant assets over a 40-year life, whereas Camby Corp. depreciates its plant assets over a 20-year life. Discuss the implications this has for comparing the results of the two companies.

27. Explain how transactions related to plant assets and intangibles are reported in the statement of cash flows.

Brief Exercises

BE9-1 These expenditures were incurred by Dunston Company in purchasing land: cash price $60,000; accrued taxes $5,000; attorney's fees $2,100; real estate broker's commission $3,300; and clearing and grading $3,500. What is the cost of the land?

Determine the cost of land.
(LO 1), **AP**

BE9-2 Tolbert Company incurs these expenditures in purchasing a truck: cash price $24,000; accident insurance (during use) $2,000; sales taxes $1,080; motor vehicle license $300; and painting and lettering $1,700. What is the cost of the truck?

Determine the cost of a truck.
(LO 1), **AP**

BE9-3 Howe Chemicals Company acquires a delivery truck at a cost of $31,000 on January 1, 2014. The truck is expected to have a salvage value of $4,000 at the end of its 4-year useful life. Compute annual depreciation for the first and second years using the straight-line method.

Compute straight-line depreciation.
(LO 3), **AP**

BE9-4 Iris Company purchased land and a building on January 1, 2014. Management's best estimate of the value of the land was $100,000 and of the building $250,000. However, management told the accounting department to record the land at $230,000 and the building at $120,000. The building is being depreciated on a straight-line basis over 20 years with no salvage value. Why do you suppose management requested this accounting treatment? Is it ethical?

Compute depreciation and evaluate treatment.
(LO 3), **AN**

BE9-5 On January 1, 2014, the Ferman Company ledger shows Equipment $36,000 and Accumulated Depreciation $13,600. The depreciation resulted from using the straight-line method with a useful life of 10 years and a salvage value of $2,000. On this date, the

Compute revised depreciation.
(LO 4), **AP**

company concludes that the equipment has a remaining useful life of only 2 years with the same salvage value. Compute the revised annual depreciation.

Prepare entries for delivery truck costs.

(LO 4), AP

BE9-6 Harmon Company had the following two transactions related to its delivery truck.
1. Paid $38 for an oil change.
2. Paid $400 to install special shelving units, which increase the operating efficiency of the truck.

Prepare Harmon's journal entries to record these two transactions.

Journalize entries for disposal of plant assets.

(LO 5), AP

BE9-7 Prepare journal entries to record these transactions: (a) Rangel Company retires its delivery equipment, which cost $41,000. Accumulated depreciation is also $41,000 on this delivery equipment. No salvage value is received. (b) Assume the same information as in part (a), except that accumulated depreciation for the equipment is $37,200 instead of $41,000.

Journalize entries for sale of plant assets.

(LO 5), AP

BE9-8 Quinn Company sells office equipment on July 31, 2014, for $21,000 cash. The office equipment originally cost $72,000 and as of January 1, 2014, had accumulated depreciation of $42,000. Depreciation for the first 7 months of 2014 is $4,600. Prepare the journal entries to (a) update depreciation to July 31, 2014, and (b) record the sale of the equipment.

Compute return on assets and asset turnover.

(LO 6), AP

BE9-9 Suppose in its 2014 annual report, McDonald's Corporation reports beginning total assets of $28.46 billion; ending total assets of $30.22 billion; net sales of $22.74 billion; and net income of $4.55 billion.
(a) Compute McDonald's return on assets.
(b) Compute McDonald's asset turnover.

Account for intangibles— patents.

(LO 7), AP

BE9-10 Downs Company purchases a patent for $156,000 on January 2, 2014. Its estimated useful life is 6 years.
(a) Prepare the journal entry to record amortization expense for the first year.
(b) Show how this patent is reported on the balance sheet at the end of the first year.

Classification of long-lived assets on balance sheet.

(LO 8), AP

BE9-11 Suppose Nike, Inc. reported the following plant assets and intangible assets for the year ended May 31, 2014 (in millions): other plant assets $965.8; land $221.6; patents and trademarks (at cost) $515.1; machinery and equipment $2,094.3; buildings $974.0; goodwill (at cost) $193.5; accumulated amortization $47.7; and accumulated depreciation $2,298.0. Prepare a partial balance sheet for Nike for these items.

Determine net cash provided by operating activities.

(LO 8), AP

BE9-12 Gant Company reported net income of $157,000. It reported depreciation expense of $12,000 and accumulated depreciation of $47,000. Amortization expense was $8,000. Gant purchased new equipment during the year for $50,000. Show how this information would be used to determine net cash provided by operating activities.

Compute declining-balance depreciation.

(LO 9), AP

*BE9-13** Depreciation information for Howe Chemicals Company is given in BE9-3. Assuming the declining-balance depreciation rate is double the straight-line rate, compute annual depreciation for the first and second years under the declining-balance method.

Compute depreciation using units-of-activity method.

(LO 9), AP

*BE9-14** Speedy Taxi Service uses the units-of-activity method in computing depreciation on its taxicabs. Each cab is expected to be driven 150,000 miles. Taxi 10 cost $27,500 and is expected to have a salvage value of $500. Taxi 10 was driven 32,000 miles in 2013 and 33,000 miles in 2014. Compute the depreciation for each year.

Do it! Review

Explain accounting for cost of plant assets

(LO 1), C

Do it! 9-1 Shellhammer Company purchased a delivery truck. The total cash payment was $30,020, including the following items.

Negotiated purchase price	$24,000
Installation of special shelving	1,100
Painting and lettering	900
Motor vehicle license	180
Annual insurance policy	2,400
Sales tax	1,440
Total paid	$30,020

Explain how each of these costs would be accounted for.

Do it! 9-2 On January 1, 2014, Wolf Creek Country Club purchased a new riding mower for $15,000. The mower is expected to have a 10-year life with a $1,000 salvage value. What journal entry would Wolf Creek make on December 31, 2014, if it uses straight-line depreciation?

Calculate depreciation expense and make journal entry.
(LO 3), **AP**

Do it! 9-3 Relaford Corporation purchased a piece of equipment for $50,000. It estimated an 8-year life and $2,000 salvage value. At the end of year four (before the depreciation adjustment), it estimated the new total life to be 10 years and the new salvage value to be $4,000. Compute the revised depreciation.

Calculated revised depreciation
(LO 4), **AP**

Do it! 9-4 Thornton Company has an old factory machine that cost $50,000. The machine has accumulated depreciation of $28,000. Thornton has decided to sell the machine.
(a) What entry would Thornton make to record the sale of the machine for $25,000 cash?
(b) What entry would Thornton make to record the sale of the machine for $15,000 cash?

Make journal entries to record plant asset disposal.
(LO 5), **AP**

Do it! 9-5 Match the statement with the term most directly associated with it.

Match intangible assets with concepts.
(LO 7), **C**

Goodwill	Amortization
Intangible assets	Franchise
Research and development costs	

1. _____ Rights, privileges, and competitive advantages that result from the ownership of long-lived assets that do not possess physical substance.
2. _____ The allocation of the cost of an intangible asset to expense in a rational and systematic manner.
3. _____ A right to sell certain products or services, or use certain trademarks or trade names within a designated geographic area.
4. _____ Costs incurred by a company that often lead to patents or new products. These costs must be expensed as incurred.
5. _____ The excess of the cost of a company over the fair value of the net assets required.

Exercises

E9-1 The following expenditures relating to plant assets were made by Watkens Company during the first 2 months of 2014.
1. Paid $7,000 of accrued taxes at the time the plant site was acquired.
2. Paid $200 insurance to cover a possible accident loss on new factory machinery while the machinery was in transit.
3. Paid $850 sales taxes on a new delivery truck.
4. Paid $21,000 for parking lots and driveways on the new plant site.
5. Paid $250 to have the company name and slogan painted on the new delivery truck.
6. Paid $8,000 for installation of new factory machinery.
7. Paid $900 for a 1-year accident insurance policy on the new delivery truck.
8. Paid $75 motor vehicle license fee on the new truck.

Determine cost of plant acquisitions.
(LO 1), **C**

Instructions
(a) ☞ Explain the application of the historical cost principle in determining the acquisition cost of plant assets.
(b) List the numbers of the transactions, and opposite each indicate the account title to which each expenditure should be debited.

E9-2 Petrino Company incurred the following costs.

Determine property, plant, and equipment costs.
(LO 1), **C**

1. Sales tax on factory machinery purchased	$ 5,000
2. Painting of and lettering on truck immediately upon purchase	700
3. Installation and testing of factory machinery	2,000
4. Real estate broker's commission on land purchased	3,500
5. Insurance premium paid for first year's insurance on new truck	880
6. Cost of landscaping on property purchased	7,200
7. Cost of paving parking lot for new building constructed	17,900
8. Cost of clearing, draining, and filling land	13,300
9. Architect's fees on self-constructed building	10,000

Instructions
Indicate to which account Petrino would debit each of the costs.

Determine acquisition costs of land.

(LO 1), **AP**

E9-3 On March 1, 2014, Zobrist Company acquired real estate, on which it planned to construct a small office building, by paying $80,000 in cash. An old warehouse on the property was demolished at a cost of $8,200; the salvaged materials were sold for $1,700. Additional expenditures before construction began included $1,900 attorney's fee for work concerning the land purchase, $5,200 real estate broker's fee, $9,100 architect's fee, and $14,000 to put in driveways and a parking lot.

Instructions
(a) Determine the amount to be reported as the cost of the land.
(b) For each cost not used in part (a), indicate the account to be debited.

Understand depreciation concepts.

(LO 2), **C**

E9-4 Melissa Adduci has prepared the following list of statements about depreciation.
1. Depreciation is a process of asset valuation, not cost allocation.
2. Depreciation provides for the proper matching of expenses with revenues.
3. The book value of a plant asset should approximate its fair value.
4. Depreciation applies to three classes of plant assets: land, buildings, and equipment.
5. Depreciation does not apply to a building because its usefulness and revenue-producing ability generally remain intact over time.
6. The revenue-producing ability of a depreciable asset will decline due to wear and tear and to obsolescence.
7. Recognizing depreciation on an asset results in an accumulation of cash for replacement of the asset.
8. The balance in accumulated depreciation represents the total cost that has been charged to expense since placing the asset in service.
9. Depreciation expense and accumulated depreciation are reported on the income statement.
10. Four factors affect the computation of depreciation: cost, useful life, salvage value, and residual value.

Instructions
Identify each statement as true or false. If false, indicate how to correct the statement.

Determine straight-line depreciation for partial period.

(LO 3), **AP**

E9-5 Hinshaw Company purchased a new machine on October 1, 2014, at a cost of $90,000. The company estimated that the machine has a salvage value of $8,000. The machine is expected to be used for 70,000 working hours during its 8-year life.

Instructions
Compute the depreciation expense under the straight-line method for 2014 and 2015, assuming a December 31 year-end.

Compute revised annual depreciation.

(LO 3, 4), **AN**

E9-6 Danny Venable, the new controller of Seratelli Company, has reviewed the expected useful lives and salvage values of selected depreciable assets at the beginning of 2014. Here are his findings:

Type of Asset	Date Acquired	Cost	Accumulated Depreciation, Jan. 1, 2014	Useful Life (in years) Old	Proposed	Salvage Value Old	Proposed
Building	Jan. 1, 2006	$700,000	$130,000	40	48	$50,000	$35,000
Warehouse	Jan. 1, 2009	120,000	23,000	25	20	5,000	3,600

All assets are depreciated by the straight-line method. Seratelli Company uses a calendar year in preparing annual financial statements. After discussion, management has agreed to accept Danny's proposed changes. (The "Proposed" useful life is total life, not remaining life.)

Instructions
(a) Compute the revised annual depreciation on each asset in 2014. (Show computations.)
(b) Prepare the entry (or entries) to record depreciation on the building in 2014.

Journalize transactions related to disposals of plant assets.

(LO 5), **AP**

E9-7 Wang Co. has delivery equipment that cost $50,000 and has been depreciated $24,000.

Instructions
Record entries for the disposal under the following assumptions.
(a) It was scrapped as having no value.
(b) It was sold for $37,000.
(c) It was sold for $20,000.

E9-8   Here are selected 2014 transactions of Cleland Corporation.

Record disposal of equipment.
(LO 5), **AP**

Jan.   1   Retired a piece of machinery that was purchased on January 1, 2004. The machine cost $62,000 and had a useful life of 10 years with no salvage value.

June 30   Sold a computer that was purchased on January 1, 2012. The computer cost $36,000 and had a useful life of 3 years with no salvage value. The computer was sold for $5,000 cash.

Dec. 31   Sold a delivery truck for $9,000 cash. The truck cost $25,000 when it was purchased on January 1, 2011, and was depreciated based on a 5-year useful life with a $4,000 salvage value.

Instructions

Journalize all entries required on the above dates, including entries to update depreciation on assets disposed of, where applicable. Cleland Corporation uses straight-line depreciation.

E9-9   The following situations are independent of one another.

Apply accounting concepts.
(LO 1, 2, 6, 7), **C**

1. An accounting student recently employed by a small company doesn't understand why the company is only depreciating its buildings and equipment, but not its land. The student prepared journal entries to depreciate all the company's property, plant, and equipment for the current year-end.

2. The same student also thinks the company's amortization policy on its intangible assets is wrong. The company is currently amortizing its patents but not its goodwill. As a result, the student added goodwill to her adjusting entry for amortization at the end of the current year. She told a fellow employee that she felt she had improved the consistency of the company's accounting policies by making these changes.

3. The same company has a building still in use that has a zero book value but a substantial fair value. The student felt that this practice didn't benefit the company's users— especially the bank—and wrote the building up to its fair value. After all, she reasoned, you can write down assets if fair values are lower. Writing them up if fair value is higher is yet another example of the improved consistency that she has brought to the company's accounting practices.

Instructions

Explain whether or not the accounting treatment in each of the above situations is in accordance with generally accepted accounting principles. Explain what accounting principle or assumption, if any, has been violated and what the appropriate accounting treatment should be.

E9-10   Suppose during 2014 that Federal Express reported the following information (in millions): net sales of $35,497 and net income of $98. Its balance sheet also showed total assets at the beginning of the year of $25,633 and total assets at the end of the year of $24,244.

Calculate asset turnover and return on assets.
(LO 6), **AP**

Instructions

Calculate the (a) asset turnover and (b) return on assets.

E9-11   Shonrock International is considering a significant expansion to its product line. The sales force is excited about the opportunities that the new products will bring. The new products are a significant step up in quality above the company's current offerings, but offer a complementary fit to its existing product line. Richard Farley, senior production department manager, is very excited about the high-tech new equipment that will have to be acquired to produce the new products. Donna Beson, the company's CFO, has provided the following projections based on results with and without the new products.

Calculate and interpret ratios.
(LO 6), **AP**

	Without New Products	**With New Products**
Sales revenue	$10,000,000	$16,000,000
Net income	$500,000	$960,000
Average total assets	$5,000,000	$12,000,000

Instructions

(a) Compute the company's return on assets, profit margin, and asset turnover, both with and without the new product line.

(b) Discuss the implications that your findings in part (a) have for the company's decision.

Calculate and interpret ratios.

(LO 6), **AP**

E9-12 Bakely Company reports the following information (in millions) during a recent year: net sales, $11,408.5; net earnings, $264.8; total assets, ending, $4,312.6; and total assets, beginning, $4,254.3.

Instructions

(a) Calculate the (1) return on assets, (2) asset turnover, and (3) profit margin.

(b) Prove mathematically how the profit margin and asset turnover work together to explain return on assets, by showing the appropriate calculation.

(c) Bakely Company owns Villas (grocery), Bakely Theaters, Kurt Drugstores, and Derosa (heavy equipment), and manages commercial real estate, among other activities. Does this diversity of activities affect your ability to interpret the ratios you calculated in (a)? Explain.

Prepare adjusting entries for amortization.

(LO 7), **AN**

E9-13 These are selected 2014 transactions for Amarista Corporation:

Jan. 1   Purchased a copyright for $120,000. The copyright has a useful life of 6 years and a remaining legal life of 30 years.

Mar. 1   Purchased a patent with an estimated useful life of 4 years and a legal life of 20 years for $54,000.

Sept. 1   Purchased a small company and recorded goodwill of $150,000. Its useful life is indefinite.

Instructions

Prepare all adjusting entries at December 31 to record amortization required by the events.

Prepare entries to set up appropriate accounts for different intangibles; calculate amortization.

(LO 7), **AN**

E9-14 Haley Company, organized in 2014, has these transactions related to intangible assets in that year:

Jan. 2   Purchased a patent (5-year life) $280,000.

Apr. 1   Goodwill acquired as a result of purchased business (indefinite life) $360,000.

July 1   Acquired a 9-year franchise; expiration date July 1, 2023, $540,000.

Sept. 1   Research and development costs $185,000.

Instructions

(a) Prepare the necessary entries to record these transactions related to intangibles. All costs incurred were for cash.

(b) Make the entries as of December 31, 2014, recording any necessary amortization.

(c) Indicate what the intangible asset account balances should be on December 31, 2014.

Discuss implications of amortization period.

(LO 7), **C**

E9-15 Alliance Atlantis Communications Inc. changed its accounting policy to amortize broadcast rights over the contracted exhibition period, which is based on the estimated useful life of the program. Previously, the company amortized broadcast rights over the lesser of 2 years or the contracted exhibition period.

Instructions

 Write a short memo to your client explaining the implications this has for the analysis of Alliance Atlantis's results.

Answer questions on depreciation and intangibles.

(LO 2, 7), **C**

E9-16 The questions listed below are independent of one another.

Instructions

Provide a brief answer to each question.

(a) Why should a company depreciate its buildings?

(b) How can a company have a building that has a zero reported book value but substantial fair value?

(c) What are some examples of intangibles that you might find on your college campus?

(d) Give some examples of company or product trademarks or trade names. Are trade names and trademarks reported on a company's balance sheet?

Determine net cash provided by operating activities.

(LO 8), **AN**

E9-17 Gonzalez Corporation reported net income of $58,000. Depreciation expense for the year was $132,000. The company calculates depreciation expense using the straight-line method, with a useful life of 10 years. Top management would like to switch to a 15-year useful life because depreciation expense would be reduced to $88,000. The CEO says, "Increasing the useful life would increase net income and net cash provided by operating activities."

Instructions

Provide a comparative analysis showing net income and net cash provided by operating activities (ignoring other accrual adjustments) using a 10-year and a 15-year useful life. (Ignore income taxes.) Evaluate the CEO's suggestion.

*E9-18 Jayhawk Bus Lines uses the units-of-activity method in depreciating its buses. One bus was purchased on January 1, 2014, at a cost of $100,000. Over its 4-year useful life, the bus is expected to be driven 160,000 miles. Salvage value is expected to be $8,000.

Compute depreciation under units-of-activity method.
(LO 9), **AP**

Instructions

(a) Compute the depreciation cost per unit.
(b) Prepare a depreciation schedule assuming actual mileage was: 2014, 40,000; 2015, 52,000; 2016, 41,000; and 2017, 27,000.

*E9-19 Basic information relating to a new machine purchased by Hinshaw Company is presented in E9-5.

Compute declining-balance and units-of-activity depreciation.
(LO 9), **AP**

Instructions

Using the facts presented in E9-5, compute depreciation using the following methods in the year indicated.
(a) Declining-balance using double the straight-line rate for 2014 and 2015.
(b) Units-of-activity for 2014, assuming machine usage was 3,900 hours. (Round depreciation per unit to the nearest cent.)

Exercises: Set B and Challenge Exercises

Visit the book's companion website, at **www.wiley.com/college/kimmel**, and choose the Student Companion site to access Exercise Set B and Challenge Exercises.

Problems: Set A

P9-1A Seger Company was organized on January 1. During the first year of operations, the following plant asset expenditures and receipts were recorded in random order.

Determine acquisition costs of land and building.
(LO 1), **C**

Debit

1. Cost of real estate purchased as a plant site (land $255,000 and building $25,000)	$ 280,000
2. Installation cost of fences around property	6,800
3. Cost of demolishing building to make land suitable for construction of new building	31,000
4. Excavation costs for new building	23,000
5. Accrued real estate taxes paid at time of purchase of real estate	3,170
6. Cost of parking lots and driveways	29,000
7. Architect's fees on building plans	33,000
8. Real estate taxes paid for the current year on land	6,400
9. Full payment to building contractor	640,000
	$1,052,370

Credit

10. Proceeds from salvage of demolished building	$ 12,000

Instructions

Analyze the transactions using the following table column headings. Enter the number of each transaction in the Item column, and enter the amounts in the appropriate columns. For amounts in the Other Accounts column, also indicate the account title.

Item	Land	Buildings	Other Accounts

Land $302,170

Journalize equipment transactions related to purchase, sale, retirement, and depreciation.

(LO 3, 5, 8), **AP**

P9-2A At December 31, 2014, Navaro Corporation reported the following plant assets.

Land		$ 3,000,000
Buildings	$26,500,000	
Less: Accumulated depreciation—buildings	11,925,000	14,575,000
Equipment	40,000,000	
Less: Accumulated depreciation—equipment	5,000,000	35,000,000
Total plant assets		$52,575,000

During 2015, the following selected cash transactions occurred.

Apr. 1 Purchased land for $2,200,000.

May 1 Sold equipment that cost $600,000 when purchased on January 1, 2008. The equipment was sold for $170,000.

June 1 Sold land for $1,600,000. The land cost $1,000,000.

July 1 Purchased equipment for $1,100,000.

Dec. 31 Retired equipment that cost $700,000 when purchased on December 31, 2005. No salvage value was received.

Instructions

(a) Journalize the transactions. (*Hint:* You may wish to set up T-accounts, post beginning balances, and then post 2015 transactions.) Navaro uses straight-line depreciation for buildings and equipment. The buildings are estimated to have a 40-year useful life and no salvage value; the equipment is estimated to have a 10-year useful life and no salvage value. Update depreciation on assets disposed of at the time of sale or retirement.

(b) Record adjusting entries for depreciation for 2015.

(c) Tot. plant assets $50,037,500

(c) Prepare the plant assets section of Navaro's balance sheet at December 31, 2015.

Journalize entries for disposal of plant assets.

(LO 5), **AP**

P9-3A Presented here are selected transactions for Pine Company for 2014.

Jan. 1 Retired a piece of machinery that was purchased on January 1, 2004. The machine cost $71,000 on that date and had a useful life of 10 years with no salvage value.

June 30 Sold a computer that was purchased on January 1, 2011. The computer cost $30,000 and had a useful life of 5 years with no salvage value. The computer was sold for $12,000.

Dec. 31 Discarded a delivery truck that was purchased on January 1, 2009. The truck cost $33,400 and was depreciated based on an 8-year useful life with a $3,000 salvage value.

Instructions

Journalize all entries required on the above dates, including entries to update depreciation, where applicable, on assets disposed of. Pine Company uses straight-line depreciation. (Assume depreciation is up to date as of December 31, 2013.)

Prepare entries to record transactions related to acquisition and amortization of intangibles; prepare the intangible assets section and note.

(LO 7, 8), **AP**

P9-4A The intangible assets section of Cedeno Corporation's balance sheet at December 31, 2014, is presented here.

Patents ($60,000 cost less $6,000 amortization)	$54,000
Copyrights ($36,000 cost less $25,200 amortization)	10,800
Total	$64,800

The patent was acquired in January 2014 and has a useful life of 10 years. The copyright was acquired in January 2008 and also has a useful life of 10 years. The following cash transactions may have affected intangible assets during 2015.

Jan. 2 Paid $46,800 legal costs to successfully defend the patent against infringement by another company.

Jan.–June Developed a new product, incurring $230,000 in research and development costs. A patent was granted for the product on July 1, and its useful life is equal to its legal life. Legal and other costs for the patent were $20,000.

Sept. 1 Paid $40,000 to a quarterback to appear in commercials advertising the company's products. The commercials will air in September and October.

Oct. 1 Acquired a copyright for $200,000. The copyright has a useful life and legal life of 50 years.

Instructions
(a) Prepare journal entries to record the transactions.
(b) Prepare journal entries to record the 2015 amortization expense for intangible assets.
(c) Prepare the intangible assets section of the balance sheet at December 31, 2015.
(d) Prepare the note to the financial statements on Cedeno Corporation's intangible assets as of December 31, 2015.

(c) Tot. intangibles $315,300

P9-5A Due to rapid employee turnover in the accounting department, the following transactions involving intangible assets were improperly recorded by Eveland Corporation in 2014.

Prepare entries to correct errors in recording and amortizing intangible assets.

(LO 7), **AP**

1. Eveland developed a new manufacturing process, incurring research and development costs of $160,000. The company also purchased a patent for $40,000. In early January, Eveland capitalized $200,000 as the cost of the patents. Patent amortization expense of $10,000 was recorded based on a 20-year useful life.
2. On July 1, 2014, Eveland purchased a small company and as a result acquired goodwill of $80,000. Eveland recorded a half-year's amortization in 2014, based on a 20-year life ($2,000 amortization). The goodwill has an indefinite life.

Instructions
Prepare all journal entries necessary to correct any errors made during 2014. Assume the books have not yet been closed for 2014.

P9-6A Danner Corporation and London Corporation, two companies of roughly the same size, are both involved in the manufacture of shoe-tracing devices. Each company depreciates its plant assets using the straight-line approach. An investigation of their financial statements reveals the information shown below.

Calculate and comment on return on assets, profit margin, and asset turnover.

(LO 6), **AN**

	Danner Corp.	**London Corp.**
Net income	$ 240,000	$ 300,000
Sales revenue	1,150,000	1,200,000
Total assets (average)	3,200,000	3,000,000
Plant assets (average)	2,400,000	1,800,000
Intangible assets (goodwill)	300,000	0

Instructions
(a) For each company, calculate these values:
   (1) Return on assets.
   (2) Profit margin.
   (3) Asset turnover.
(b) Based on your calculations in part (a), comment on the relative effectiveness of the two companies in using their assets to generate sales. What factors complicate your ability to compare the two companies?

*P9-7A In recent years, Farr Company has purchased three machines. Because of frequent employee turnover in the accounting department, a different accountant was in charge of selecting the depreciation method for each machine, and various methods have been used. Information concerning the machines is summarized in the table below.

Compute depreciation under different methods.

(LO 3, 9), **AP**

Machine	Acquired	Cost	Salvage Value	Useful Life (in years)	Depreciation Method
1	Jan. 1, 2012	$96,000	$12,000	8	Straight-line
2	July 1, 2013	85,000	10,000	5	Declining-balance
3	Nov. 1, 2013	66,000	6,000	6	Units-of-activity

For the declining-balance method, Farr Company uses the double-declining rate. For the units-of-activity method, total machine hours are expected to be 30,000. Actual hours of use in the first 3 years were: 2013, 800; 2014, 4,500; and 2015, 6,000.

Instructions
(a) Compute the amount of accumulated depreciation on each machine at December 31, 2015.
(b) If machine 2 was purchased on April 1 instead of July 1, what would be the depreciation expense for this machine in 2013? In 2014?

(a) Machine 2 $60,520

Compute depreciation under *different methods.*
(LO 3, 9), **AP**

*P9-8A Boscan Corporation purchased machinery on January 1, 2014, at a cost of $250,000. The estimated useful life of the machinery is 4 years, with an estimated salvage value at the end of that period of $30,000. The company is considering different depreciation methods that could be used for financial reporting purposes.

Instructions

(a) Double-declining-balance
    expense 2016 $31,250

(a) Prepare separate depreciation schedules for the machinery using the straight-line method, and the declining-balance method using double the straight-line rate. (Round to the nearest dollar.)

(b) Which method would result in the higher reported 2014 income? In the highest total reported income over the 4-year period?

(c) Which method would result in the lower reported 2014 income? In the lowest total reported income over the 4-year period?

Problems: Set B

Determine acquisition costs of land and building.
(LO 1), **C**

P9-1B Derose Company was organized on January 1. During the first year of operations, the following plant asset expenditures and receipts were recorded in random order.

Debit

1.	Cost of real estate purchased as a plant site (land $200,000 and building $70,000)	$ 270,000
2.	Accrued real estate taxes paid at time of purchase of real estate	6,000
3.	Cost of demolishing building to make land suitable for construction of new building	31,000
4.	Cost of filling and grading the land	7,700
5.	Excavation costs for new building	21,900
6.	Architect's fees on building plans	44,000
7.	Full payment to building contractor	629,500
8.	Cost of parking lots and driveways	36,000
9.	Real estate taxes paid for the current year on land	7,300
		$1,053,400

Credit

10.	Proceeds for salvage of demolished building	$ 12,700

Instructions
Analyze the transactions using the table column headings provided here. Enter the number of each transaction in the Item column, and enter the amounts in the appropriate columns. For amounts in the Other Accounts column, also indicate the account titles.

Land $302,000

Item	**Land**	**Buildings**	**Other Accounts**

Journalize equipment transactions related to purchase, sale, retirement, and depreciation.
(LO 3, 5, 8), **AP**

P9-2B At December 31, 2013, Tong Corporation reported these plant assets.

Land		$ 4,000,000
Buildings	$28,800,000	
Less: Accumulated depreciation—buildings	11,520,000	17,280,000
Equipment	48,000,000	
Less: Accumulated depreciation—equipment	5,000,000	43,000,000
Total plant assets		$64,280,000

During 2014, the following selected cash transactions occurred.

Apr.   1   Purchased land for $2,600,000.

May   1   Sold equipment that cost $750,000 when purchased on January 1, 2009. The equipment was sold for $367,000.

June   1   Sold land purchased on June 1, 2002, for $2,000,000. The land cost $800,000.

Sept.   1   Purchased equipment for $840,000.

Dec.   31   Retired equipment that cost $470,000 when purchased on December 31, 2004. No salvage value was received.

Instructions

(a) Journalize the transactions. (*Hint:* You may wish to set up T-accounts, post beginning balances, and then post 2014 transactions.) Tong uses straight-line depreciation for buildings and equipment. The buildings are estimated to have a 40-year life and no salvage value; the equipment is estimated to have a 10-year useful life and no salvage value. Update depreciation on assets disposed of at the time of sale or retirement.

(b) Record adjusting entries for depreciation for 2014.

(c) Prepare the plant assets section of Tong's balance sheet at December 31, 2014.

(c) Tot. plant assets $81,072,000

P9-3B   Here are selected transactions for Evan's Corporation for 2014.

Journalize entries for disposal of plant assets.
(LO 5), AP

Jan.	1	Retired a piece of machinery that was purchased on January 1, 2004. The machine cost $47,000 and had a useful life of 10 years with no salvage value.
Mar.	31	Sold a computer that was purchased on January 1, 2011. The computer cost $43,400 and had a useful life of 7 years with no salvage value. The computer was sold for $25,000.
Dec.	31	Discarded a delivery truck that was purchased on January 1, 2011. The truck cost $30,000 and was depreciated based on a 6-year useful life with a $3,000 salvage value.

Instructions

Journalize all entries required on the above dates, including entries to update depreciation on assets disposed of, where applicable. Evan's Corporation uses straight-line depreciation.

P9-4B   The intangible assets section of the balance sheet for Venable Company at December 31, 2014, is presented here.

Prepare entries to record transactions related to acquisition and amortization of intangibles; prepare the intangible assets section and note.
(LO 7, 8), AP

Patents ($70,000 cost less $7,000 amortization)	$63,000
Copyrights ($48,000 cost less $18,000 amortization)	30,000
Total	$93,000

The patent was acquired in January 2014 and has a useful life of 10 years. The copyright was acquired in January 2012 and also has a useful life of 8 years. The following cash transactions may have affected intangible assets during 2015.

Jan.	2	Paid $45,000 legal costs to successfully defend the patent against infringement by another company.
Jan.–June		Developed a new product, incurring $220,000 in research and development costs. A patent was granted for the product on July 1, and its useful life is equal to its legal life. Legal and other costs for the patent were $22,000.
Sept.	1	Paid $110,000 to an extremely large defensive lineman to appear in commercials advertising the company's products. The commercials will air in September and October.
Oct.	1	Acquired a copyright for $120,000. The copyright has a useful life and legal life of 50 years.

Instructions

(a) Prepare journal entries to record the transactions.

(b) Prepare journal entries to record the 2015 amortization expense.

(c) Prepare the intangible assets section of the balance sheet at December 31, 2015.

(c) Tot. intangibles $260,850

(d) Prepare the note to the financial statements on Venable Company's intangible assets as of December 31, 2015.

P9-5B   Due to rapid employee turnover in the accounting department, the following transactions involving intangible assets were improperly recorded by Maxwell Corporation in 2014.

Prepare entries to correct errors in recording and amortizing intangible assets.
(LO 7), AP

1. Maxwell developed a new manufacturing process, incurring research and development costs of $225,000. The company also purchased a patent for $48,000. In early January, Maxwell capitalized $273,000 as the cost of the patents. Patent amortization expense of $13,650 was recorded based on a 20-year useful life.

2. On July 1, 2014, Maxwell purchased a small company and as a result acquired goodwill of $40,000. Maxwell recorded a half-year's amortization in 2014, based on a 10-year life ($2,000 amortization). The goodwill has an indefinite life.

Instructions

Prepare all journal entries necessary to correct any errors made during 2014. Assume the books have not yet been closed for 2014.

Calculate and comment on return on assets, profit margin, and asset turnover.

(LO 6), **AN**

⌐○━━━━○⌐

P9-6B Quiver Corporation and Swaze Corporation, two corporations of roughly the same size, are both involved in the manufacture of umbrellas. Each company depreciates its plant assets using the straight-line approach. An investigation of their financial statements reveals the following information.

	Quiver Corp.	Swaze Corp.
Net income	$ 800,000	$ 920,000
Sales revenue	2,400,000	2,500,000
Total assets (average)	3,000,000	2,700,000
Plant assets (average)	1,400,000	1,200,000
Intangible assets (goodwill)	480,000	0

Instructions

(a) For each company, calculate these values:
  (1) Return on assets.
  (2) Profit margin.
  (3) Asset turnover.
(b) ▅▅▶ Based on your calculations in part (a), comment on the relative effectiveness of the two companies in using their assets to generate sales. What factors complicate your ability to compare the two companies?

Compute depreciation under different methods.

(LO 3, 9), **AP**

*P9-7B In recent years Howard Company has purchased three machines. Because of frequent employee turnover in the accounting department, a different accountant was in charge of selecting the depreciation method for each machine, and various methods have been used. Information concerning the machines is summarized in the table below.

Machine	Acquired	Cost	Salvage Value	Useful Life (in years)	Depreciation Method
1	July 1, 2012	$68,000	$5,000	7	Straight-line
2	Apr. 1, 2013	64,000	6,000	4	Declining-balance
3	Sept. 1, 2013	84,000	4,000	8	Units-of-activity

For the declining-balance method, Howard Company uses the double-declining rate. For the units-of-activity method, total machine hours are expected to be 40,000. Actual hours of use in the first 3 years were: 2013, 1,200; 2014, 6,400; and 2015, 7,000.

Instructions

(a) Machine 2 $54,000

(a) Compute the amount of accumulated depreciation on each machine at December 31, 2015.
(b) If machine 2 was purchased on November 1 instead of April 1, what would be the depreciation expense for this machine in 2013? In 2014? (Round to the nearest dollar.)

Compute depreciation under different methods.

(LO 3, 9), **AP**

*P9-8B Miriam Corporation purchased machinery on January 1, 2014, at a cost of $380,000. The estimated useful life of the machinery is 5 years, with an estimated salvage value at the end of that period of $20,000. The company is considering different depreciation methods that could be used for financial reporting purposes.

Instructions

(a) Double-declining-balance exp. 2015 $91,200

(a) Prepare separate depreciation schedules for the machinery using the straight-line method, and the declining-balance method using double the straight-line rate.
(b) Which method would result in the higher reported 2014 income? In the higher total reported income over the 5-year period?
(c) Which method would result in the lower reported 2014 income? In the lower total reported income over the 5-year period?

Problems: Set C

Visit the book's companion website, at **www.wiley.com/college/kimmel**, and choose the Student Companion site to access Problem Set C.

Comprehensive Problem

CP9 Kenseth Corporation's unadjusted trial balance at December 1, 2014, is presented below.

	Debit	Credit
Cash	$ 22,000	
Accounts Receivable	36,800	
Notes Receivable	10,000	
Interest Receivable	–0–	
Inventory	36,200	
Prepaid Insurance	3,600	
Land	20,000	
Buildings	150,000	
Equipment	60,000	
Patent	9,000	
Allowance for Doubtful Accounts		$ 500
Accumulated Depreciation—Buildings		50,000
Accumulated Depreciation—Equipment		24,000
Accounts Payable		27,300
Salaries and Wages Payable		–0–
Notes Payable (due April 30, 2015)		11,000
Income Taxes Payable		–0–
Interest Payable		–0–
Notes Payable (due in 2020)		35,000
Common Stock		50,000
Retained Earnings		63,600
Dividends	12,000	
Sales Revenue		900,000
Interest Revenue		–0–
Gain on Disposal of Plant Assets		–0–
Bad Debt Expense	–0–	
Cost of Goods Sold	630,000	
Depreciation Expense	–0–	
Income Tax Expense	–0–	
Insurance Expense	–0–	
Interest Expense	–0–	
Other Operating Expenses	61,800	
Amortization Expense	–0–	
Salaries and Wages Expense	110,000	
Total	$1,161,400	$1,161,400

The following transactions occurred during December.

Dec. 2 Purchased equipment for $16,000, plus sales taxes of $800 (paid in cash).
   2 Kenseth sold for $3,500 equipment which originally cost $5,000. Accumulated depreciation on this equipment at January 1, 2014, was $1,800; 2014 depreciation prior to the sale of equipment was $825.
   15 Kenseth sold for $5,000 on account inventory that cost $3,500.
   23 Salaries and wages of $6,600 were paid.

Adjustment data:

1. Kenseth estimates that uncollectible accounts receivable at year-end are $4,000.
2. The note receivable is a one-year, 8% note dated April 1, 2014. No interest has been recorded.
3. The balance in prepaid insurance represents payment of a $3,600, 6-month premium on September 1, 2014.
4. The building is being depreciated using the straight-line method over 30 years. The salvage value is $30,000.
5. The equipment owned prior to this year is being depreciated using the straight-line method over 5 years. The salvage value is 10% of cost.
6. The equipment purchased on December 2, 2014, is being depreciated using the straight-line method over 5 years, with a salvage value of $1,800.

7. The patent was acquired on January 1, 2014, and has a useful life of 9 years from that date.
8. Unpaid salaries at December 31, 2014, total $2,200.
9. Both the short-term and long-term notes payable are dated January 1, 2014, and carry a 10% interest rate. All interest is payable in the next 12 months.
10. Income tax expense was $15,000. It was unpaid at December 31.

Instructions
(a) Prepare journal entries for the transactions listed above and adjusting entries.
(b) Prepare an adjusted trial balance at December 31, 2014.
(c) Prepare a 2014 income statement and a 2014 retained earnings statement.
(d) Prepare a December 31, 2014, balance sheet.

(b) Totals $1,205,775
(c) Net income $50,775
(d) Total assets $247,475

Continuing Cookie Chronicle

(*Note:* This is a continuation of the Cookie Chronicle from Chapters 1 through 8.)

CCC9

Part 1 Now that she is selling mixers and her customers can use credit cards to pay for them, Natalie is thinking of upgrading her website so that she can sell mixers online, to broaden her range of customers. She will need to know how to account for the costs of upgrading the site.

Part 2 Natalie is also thinking of buying a van that will be used only for business. Natalie is concerned about the impact of the van's cost on her income statement and balance sheet. She has come to you for advice on calculating the van's depreciation.

> Go to the book's companion website, at **www.wiley.com/college/kimmel**, to see the completion of this problem.

Broadening Your Perspective

Financial Reporting and Analysis

FINANCIAL REPORTING PROBLEM: *Tootsie Roll Industries, Inc.*

BYP9-1 Refer to the financial statements and the Notes to Consolidated Financial Statements of Tootsie Roll Industries in Appendix A.

Instructions
Answer the following questions.
(a) What were the total cost and book value of property, plant, and equipment at December 31, 2011?
(b) What method or methods of depreciation are used by Tootsie Roll for financial reporting purposes?
(c) What was the amount of depreciation expense for each of the 3 years 2009–2011? (*Hint:* Use the statement of cash flows.)
(d) Using the statement of cash flows, what are the amounts of property, plant, and equipment purchased (capital expenditures) in 2011 and 2010?
(e) Explain how Tootsie Roll accounted for its intangible assets in 2011.

COMPARATIVE ANALYSIS PROBLEM: *Tootsie Roll vs. Hershey*

BYP9-2 The financial statements of The Hershey Company are presented in Appendix B, following the financial statements for Tootsie Roll Industries in Appendix A.

Instructions
(a) Based on the information in these financial statements and the accompanying notes and schedules, compute the following values for each company in 2011.
  (1) Return on assets.
  (2) Profit margin (use "Total Revenue").
  (3) Asset turnover.
(b) What conclusions concerning the management of plant assets can be drawn from these data?

RESEARCH CASE

BYP9-3 The November 16, 2011, edition of the *Wall Street Journal Online* contains an article by Maxwell Murphy entitled "The Big Number: 51."

Instructions

Read the article and answer the following questions.

(a) What do the 51 companies referred to in the title have in common? What implications does this have regarding the fair value of a company's assets?

(b) What significance does the common trait referred to in part (a) have for a company's goodwill?

(c) How does a company get to record goodwill on its books—that is, what must have occurred for goodwill to show up on a company's books?

(d) If these companies write down their goodwill, will this reduce their cash?

INTERPRETING FINANCIAL STATEMENTS

BYP9-4 The March 29, 2012, edition of the *Wall Street Journal Online* contains an article by Miguel Bustillo entitled, "Best Buy Forced to Rethink Big Box." The article explains how the 1,100 giant stores, which enabled Best Buy to obtain its position as the largest retailer of electronics, are now reducing the company's profitability and even threatening its survival. The problem is that many customers go to Best Buy stores to see items but then buy them for less from online retailers. As a result, Best Buy recently announced that it would close 50 stores and switch to smaller stores. However, some analysts think that these changes are not big enough.

The following data were extracted from the 2011 and 2006 annual reports of Best Buy. (All amounts are in millions.)

	2011	2010	2006	2005
Total assets at year-end	$17,849	$18,302	$11,864	$10,294
Net sales	50,272		30,848	
Net income	1,277		1,140	

Instructions

Using the data above, answer the following questions.

(a) How might the return on assets and asset turnover of Best Buy differ from an online retailer?

(b) Compute the profit margin, asset turnover, and return on assets for 2011 and 2006.

(c) Present the ratios calculated in part (b) in the equation format shown in Illustration 9-21 (page 466).

(d) Discuss the implications of the ratios calculated in parts (b) and (c).

REAL-WORLD FOCUS

BYP9-5 **Purpose:** Use an annual report to identify a company's plant assets and the depreciation method used.

Address: **www.annualreports.com**, or go to **www.wiley.com/college/kimmel**

Steps

1. Select a particular company.
2. Search by company name.
3. Follow instructions below.

Instructions

Answer the following questions.

(a) What is the name of the company?

(b) What is the Internet address of the annual report?

(c) At fiscal year-end, what is the net amount of its plant assets?

(d) What is the accumulated depreciation?

(e) Which method of depreciation does the company use?

Critical Thinking

DECISION-MAKING ACROSS THE ORGANIZATION

BYP9-6 Payton Furniture Corp. is nationally recognized for making high-quality products. Management is concerned that it is not fully exploiting its brand power. Payton's production managers are also concerned because their plants are not operating at anywhere near full capacity. Management is currently considering a proposal to offer a new line of affordable furniture.

Those in favor of the proposal (including the vice president of production) believe that, by offering these new products, the company could attract a clientele that it is not currently servicing. Also, it could operate its plants at full capacity, thus taking better advantage of its assets.

The vice president of marketing, however, believes that the lower-priced (and lower-margin) product would have a negative impact on the sales of existing products. The vice president believes that $10,000,000 of the sales of the new product will be from customers that would have purchased the more expensive product but switched to the lower-margin product because it was available. (This is often referred to as cannibalization of existing sales.) Top management feels, however, that even with cannibalization, the company's sales will increase and the company will be better off.

The following data are available.

(in thousands)	Current Results	Proposed Results without Cannibalization	Proposed Results with Cannibalization
Sales revenue	$45,000	$60,000	$50,000
Net income	$12,000	$13,500	$12,000
Average total assets	$100,000	$100,000	$100,000

Instructions

(a) Compute Payton's return on assets, profit margin, and asset turnover, both with and without the new product line.

(b) Discuss the implications that your findings in part (a) have for Payton's decision.

(c) Are there any other options that Payton should consider? What impact would each of these have on the above ratios?

COMMUNICATION ACTIVITY

BYP9-7 The chapter presented some concerns regarding the current accounting standards for research and development expenditures.

Instructions

Assume that you are either (a) the president of a company that is very dependent on ongoing research and development, writing a memo to the FASB complaining about the current accounting standards regarding research and development, or (b) the FASB member defending the current standards regarding research and development. Your memo should address the following questions.

1. By requiring expensing of R&D, do you think companies will spend less on R&D? Why or why not? What are the possible implications for the competitiveness of U.S. companies?

2. If a company makes a commitment to spend money for R&D, it must believe it has future benefits. Shouldn't these costs therefore be capitalized just like the purchase of any long-lived asset that you believe will have future benefits?

ETHICS CASE

BYP9-8 Fresh Air Anti-Pollution Company is suffering declining sales of its principal product, nonbiodegradable plastic cartons. The president, Tyler Weber, instructs his controller, Robin Cain, to lengthen asset lives to reduce depreciation expense. A processing line of automated plastic extruding equipment, purchased for $3.5 million in January 2014, was originally estimated to have a useful life of 8 years and a salvage value of $400,000. Depreciation has been recorded for 2 years on that basis. Tyler wants the estimated life changed to 12 years total and the straight-line method continued. Robin is hesitant to make the change, believing it is unethical to increase net income in this manner. Tyler says, "Hey, the life is only an estimate, and I've heard that our competition uses a 12-year life on their production equipment."

Instructions

(a) Who are the stakeholders in this situation?

(b) Is the proposed change in asset life unethical, or is it simply a good business practice by an astute president?

(c) What is the effect of Tyler's proposed change on income before taxes in the year of change?

ALL ABOUT YOU

BYP9-9 A company's tradename is a very important asset to the company, as it creates immediate product identification. Companies invest substantial sums to ensure that their product is well-known to the consumer. Test your knowledge of who owns some famous brands and their impact on the financial statements.

Instructions

(a) Provide an answer to the five multiple-choice questions below.

    (1) Which company owns both Taco Bell and Pizza Hut?

        (a) McDonald's.   (b) CKE.   (c) Yum Brands.   (d) Wendy's.

    (2) Dairy Queen belongs to:

        (a) Breyer.   (b) Berkshire Hathaway.   (c) GE.   (d) The Coca-Cola Company.

    (3) Phillip Morris, the cigarette maker, is owned by:

        (a) Altria.   (b) GE.   (c) Boeing.   (d) ExxonMobil.

    (4) AOL, a major Internet provider, belongs to:

        (a) Microsoft.   (b) Cisco.   (c) NBC.   (d) Time Warner.

    (5) ESPN, the sports broadcasting network, is owned by:

        (a) Procter & Gamble.   (b) Altria.   (c) Walt Disney.   (d) The Coca-Cola Company.

(b) How do you think the value of these brands is reported on the appropriate company's balance sheet?

FASB CODIFICATION ACTIVITY

BYP9-10 If your school has a subscription to the FASB Codification, go to **http://aaahq.org/ascLogin.cfm** to log in and prepare responses to the following.

(a) What does it mean to capitalize an item?

(b) What is the definition provided for an intangible asset?

(c) Your great-uncle, who is a CPA, is impressed that you are taking an accounting class. Based on his experience, he believes that depreciation is something that companies do based on past practice, not on the basis of authoritative guidance. Provide the authoritative literature to support the practice of fixed-asset depreciation.

CONSIDERING PEOPLE, PLANET, AND PROFIT

BYP9-11 The March 6, 2012, edition of the *Wall Street Journal Online* contains an article by David Kesmodel entitled "Air War: 'Winglet' Versus 'Sharklet.'" This article demonstrates how a company focused on green technology has also been profitable.

Instructions

Read the article and answer the following questions.

(a) Why did Airbus file a lawsuit against Aviation Partners?

(b) What are the percentage fuel savings provided by Aviation Partners' Winglets on Boeing jetliners? How much total jet fuel did Aviation Partners say that its Winglets have provided at the time the article was written?

(c) Describe the history of the relationship between Aviation Partners and Airbus, and the development of the Airbus Sharklet.

(d) What would be the likely accounting implications if Aviation Partners were to lose the lawsuit?

Answers to Insight and Accounting Across the Organization Questions

p. 452 Many U.S. Firms Use Leases Q: Why might airline managers choose to lease rather than purchase their planes? **A:** The reasons for leasing include favorable tax treatment, better financing options, increased flexibility, reduced risk of obsolescence, and often less debt shown on the balance sheet.

p. 465 Marketing ROI as Profit Indicator Q: How does measuring marketing ROI support the overall efforts of the organization? **A:** Top management is ultimately concerned about maximizing the company's return on assets. Holding marketing managers accountable for the marketing ROI will contribute to the company's overall goal of maximizing return on assets.

p. 467 Sustainability Report Please Q: Why do you believe companies issue sustainability reports? **A:** It is important that companies clearly describe the things they value in addition to overall profitability. Most companies recognize that the health, safety, and environmental protections of their workforce and community are important components in developing strategies for continued growth and longevity. Without a strong commitment to the principles of corporate social responsibility, it is unlikely that a company will be able to maintain long-term stability and profitability. The development of a sustainability report helps companies to consider these issues and develop measures to assess whether they are meeting their goals in this area.

p. 471 Should Companies Write Up Goodwill? Q: Do you think that this treatment would be allowed under U.S. GAAP? **A:** The write-down of assets would have been allowed if it could be shown that the assets had declined in value (an impairment). However, the creation of goodwill to offset the write-down would not have been allowed. Goodwill can be recorded only when it results from the acquisition of a business. It cannot be recorded as the result of being created internally.

Answers to Self-Test Questions

1. d ($24,000 + $1,200 + $200 + $400) **2.** a **3.** b **4.** d (($400,000 − $10,000) ÷ 5) × 2 **5.** c **6.** b **7.** d (($60,000 − $12,000) ÷ 10) × 2 = $9,600; ($60,000 − $9,600 − $2,000) ÷ 4 **8.** d **9.** a (($80,000 − 0) ÷ 10) × 4.5 = $36,000; ($26,000 − ($80,000 − $36,000)) **10.** d **11.** c $180,000 ÷ (($200,000 + $300,000) ÷ 2) **12.** b ($20,000 + $15,000) **13.** c **14.** c **15.** d ***16.** d

A Look at IFRS

LEARNING OBJECTIVE 10

Compare the accounting procedures for long-lived assets under GAAP and IFRS.

IFRS related to property, plant, and equipment is found in *IAS 16* ("Property, Plant and Equipment") and *IAS 23* ("Borrowing Costs"). IFRS follows most of the same principles as GAAP in the accounting for property, plant, and equipment. There are, however, some significant differences in the implementation. IFRS allows the use of revaluation of property, plant, and equipment, and it also requires the use of component depreciation. In addition, there are some significant differences in the accounting for both intangible assets and impairments. IFRS related to intangible assets is presented in *IAS 38* ("Intangible Assets"). IFRS related to impairments is found in *IAS 36* ("Impairment of Assets").

KEY POINTS

- The definition for plant assets for both IFRS and GAAP is essentially the same.
- Both IFRS and GAAP follow the historical cost principle when accounting for property, plant, and equipment at date of acquisition. Cost consists of all expenditures necessary to acquire the asset and make it ready for its intended use.
- Under both IFRS and GAAP, interest costs incurred during construction are capitalized. Recently, IFRS converged to GAAP requirements in this area.
- IFRS, like GAAP, capitalizes all direct costs in self-constructed assets such as raw materials and labor. IFRS does not address the capitalization of fixed overhead, although in practice these costs are generally capitalized.
- IFRS also views depreciation as an allocation of cost over an asset's useful life. IFRS permits the same depreciation methods (e.g., straight-line, accelerated, and units-of-activity) as GAAP. However, a major difference is that IFRS requires component depreciation. **Component depreciation** specifies that any significant parts of a depreciable asset that have different estimated useful lives should be separately depreciated. Component depreciation is allowed under GAAP but is seldom used.

  To illustrate, assume that Lexure Construction builds an office building for $4,000,000, not including the cost of the land. If the $4,000,000 is allocated over the 40-year useful life of the building, Lexure reports $100,000 of depreciation per year, assuming straight-line depreciation and no disposal value. However, assume that $320,000 of the cost of the building relates to personal property and $600,000 relates to land improvements. The personal property has a depreciable life of 5 years, and the land improvements have a depreciable life of 10 years. In accordance with IFRS, Lexure must use component depreciation. It must reclassify $320,000 of the cost of the building to personal property and $600,000 to the cost of land improvements.

Assuming that Lexure uses straight-line depreciation, component depreciation for the first year of the office building is computed as follows.

Building cost adjusted ($4,000,000 − $320,000 − $600,000)	$3,080,000
Building cost depreciation per year ($3,080,000/40)	$ 77,000
Personal property depreciation ($320,000/5)	64,000
Land improvements depreciation ($600,000/10)	60,000
Total component depreciation in first year	$ 201,000

- IFRS uses the term **residual value**, rather than salvage value, to refer to an owner's estimate of an asset's value at the end of its useful life for that owner.
- IFRS allows companies to revalue plant assets to fair value at the reporting date. Companies that choose to use the revaluation framework must follow revaluation procedures. If revaluation is used, it must be applied to all assets within the same class. Assets that are experiencing rapid price changes must be revalued on an annual basis. Otherwise, less frequent revaluation is acceptable.

    To illustrate asset revaluation accounting, assume that Pernice Company applies revaluation to plant assets with a carrying value of $1,000,000, a useful life of 5 years, and no residual value. Pernice makes the following journal entries in year 1, assuming straight-line depreciation.

Depreciation Expense	200,000	
Accumulated Depreciation—Plant Assets		200,000
(To record depreciation expense in year 1)		

After this entry, Pernice's plant assets have a carrying amount of $800,000 ($1,000,000 − $200,000). At the end of year 1, independent appraisers determine that the assets have a fair value of $850,000. To report the plant assets at fair value, or $850,000, Pernice eliminates the Accumulated Depreciation—Plant Assets account, reduces Plant Assets to its fair value of $850,000, and records Revaluation Surplus of $50,000. The entry to record the revaluation is as follows.

Accumulated Depreciation—Plant Assets	200,000	
Plant Assets		150,000
Revaluation Surplus		50,000
(To record adjusting the plant assets to fair value)		

Thus, Pernice follows a two-step process. First, Pernice records depreciation based on the cost basis of $1,000,000. As a result, it reports depreciation expense of $200,000 on the income statement. Second, it records the revaluation. It does this by eliminating any accumulated depreciation, adjusting the recorded value of the plant assets to fair value, and debiting or crediting the Revaluation Surplus account. In this example, the revaluation surplus is $50,000, which is the difference between the fair value of $850,000 and the book value of $800,000. Revaluation surplus is an example of an item reported as other comprehensive income, as discussed in the *A Look at IFRS* section of Chapter 5. Pernice now reports the following information in its statement of financial position at the end of year 1.

Plant assets ($1,000,000 − $150,000)	$850,000
Accumulated depreciation—plant assets	0
	$850,000
Revaluation surplus (equity)	$ 50,000

As indicated, $850,000 is the new basis of the assets. Pernice reports depreciation expense of $200,000 in the income statement and $50,000 in other comprehensive income. Assuming no change in the total useful life, depreciation in year 2 will be $212,500 ($850,000 ÷ 4).

- Under both IFRS and GAAP, changes in the depreciation method used and changes in useful life are handled in current and future periods. Prior periods are not affected. GAAP recently conformed to IFRS in the accounting for changes in depreciation methods.
- The accounting for subsequent expenditures, such as ordinary repairs and additions, are essentially the same under IFRS and GAAP.
- The accounting for plant asset disposals is essentially the same under IFRS and GAAP.
- Initial costs to acquire natural resources are essentially the same under IFRS and GAAP.
- The definition of intangible assets is essentially the same under IFRS and GAAP.
- Intangibles generally arise when a company buys another company. In this case, specific criteria are needed to separate goodwill from other intangibles. Both IFRS and GAAP follow the same approach to make this separation; that is, companies recognize an intangible asset separately from goodwill if the intangible represents contractual or legal rights or is capable of being separated or divided

and sold, transferred, licensed, rented, or exchanged. In addition, under both IFRS and GAAP, companies recognize acquired in-process research and development (IPR&D) as a separate intangible asset if it meets the definition of an intangible asset and its fair value can be measured reliably.

- As in GAAP, under IFRS the costs associated with research and development are segregated into the two components. Costs in the research phase are always expensed under both IFRS and GAAP. Under IFRS, however, costs in the development phase are capitalized as Development Costs once technological feasibility is achieved.

    To illustrate, assume that Laser Scanner Company spent $1 million on research and $2 million on development of new products. Of the $2 million in development costs, $500,000 was incurred prior to technological feasibility and $1,500,000 was incurred after technological feasibility had been demonstrated. The company would record these costs as follows.

Research Expense	1,000,000	
Development Expense	500,000	
Development Costs	1,500,000	
Cash		3,000,000
(To record research and development costs)		

- IFRS permits revaluation of intangible assets (except for goodwill). GAAP prohibits revaluation of intangible assets.

- IFRS requires an impairment test at each reporting date for plant assets and intangibles and records an impairment if the asset's carrying amount exceeds its recoverable amount. The recoverable amount is the higher of the asset's fair value less costs to sell or its value-in-use. **Value-in-use** is the future cash flows to be derived from the particular asset, discounted to present value. Under GAAP, impairment loss is measured as the excess of the carrying amount over the asset's fair value.

- IFRS allows reversal of impairment losses when there has been a change in economic conditions or in the expected use of the asset. Under GAAP, impairment losses cannot be reversed for assets to be held and used; the impairment loss results in a new cost basis for the asset. IFRS and GAAP are similar in the accounting for impairments of assets held for disposal.

- The accounting for exchanges of nonmonetary assets has recently converged between IFRS and GAAP. GAAP now requires that gains on exchanges of nonmonetary assets be recognized if the exchange has commercial substance. This is the same framework used in IFRS.

LOOKING TO THE FUTURE

With respect to revaluations, as part of the conceptual framework project, the Boards will examine the measurement bases used in accounting. It is too early to say whether a converged conceptual framework will recommend fair value measurement (and revaluation accounting) for plant assets and intangibles. However, this is likely to be one of the more contentious issues, given the long-standing use of historical cost as a measurement basis in GAAP.

The IASB and FASB have identified a project that would consider expanded recognition of internally generated intangible assets. IFRS permits more recognition of intangibles compared to GAAP. Thus, it will be challenging to develop converged standards for intangible assets, given the long-standing prohibition on capitalizing internally generated intangible assets and research and development costs in GAAP.

IFRS PRACTICE

IFRS SELF-TEST QUESTIONS

1. Which of the following statements is **correct**?
    (a) Both IFRS and GAAP permit revaluation of property, plant, and equipment and intangible assets (except for goodwill).
    (b) IFRS permits revaluation of property, plant, and equipment and intangible assets (except for goodwill).
    (c) Both IFRS and GAAP permit revaluation of property, plant, and equipment but not intangible assets.
    (d) GAAP permits revaluation of property, plant, and equipment but not intangible assets.

2. International Company has land that cost $450,000 but now has a fair value of $600,000. International Company decides to use the revaluation method specified in IFRS to account for the land. Which of the following statements is **correct**?
    (a) International Company must continue to report the land at $450,000.
    (b) International Company would report a net income increase of $150,000 due to an increase in the value of the land.

(c) International Company would debit Revaluation Surplus for $150,000.

(d) International Company would credit Revaluation Surplus by $150,000.

3. Francisco Corporation is constructing a new building at a total initial cost of $10,000,000. The building is expected to have a useful life of 50 years with no residual value. The building's finished surfaces (e.g., roof cover and floor cover) are 5% of this cost and have a useful life of 20 years. Building services systems (e.g., electric, heating, and plumbing) are 20% of the cost and have a useful life of 25 years. The depreciation in the first year using component depreciation, assuming straight-line depreciation with no residual value, is:

(a) $200,000.   (b) $215,000.   (c) $255,000.   (d) None of the above.

4. Research and development costs are:

(a) expensed under GAAP.   (c) expensed under both GAAP and IFRS.

(b) expensed under IFRS.   (d) None of the above.

5. Under IFRS, value-in-use is defined as:

(a) net realizable value.   (c) future cash flows discounted to present value.

(b) fair value.   (d) total future undiscounted cash flows.

IFRS CONCEPTS AND APPLICATION

IFRS9-1 What is component depreciation, and when must it be used?

IFRS9-2 What is revaluation of plant assets? When should revaluation be applied?

IFRS9-3 Some product development expenditures are recorded as development expenses and others as development costs. Explain the difference between these accounts and how a company decides which classification is appropriate.

IFRS9-4 Holland Company constructed a warehouse for $280,000. Holland estimates that the warehouse has a useful life of 20 years and no residual value. Construction records indicate that $40,000 of the cost of the warehouse relates to its heating, ventilation, and air conditioning (HVAC) system, which has an estimated useful life of only 10 years. Compute the first year of depreciation expense using straight-line component depreciation.

IFRS9-5 At the end of its first year of operations, Mordica Company chose to use the revaluation framework allowed under IFRS. Mordica's ledger shows Plant Assets $480,000 and Accumulated Depreciation—Plant Assets $60,000. Prepare journal entries to record the following.

(a) Independent appraisers determine that the plant assets have a fair value of $460,000.

(b) Independent appraisers determine that the plant assets have a fair value of $400,000.

IFRS9-6 Parman Industries spent $300,000 on research and $600,000 on development of a new product. Of the $600,000 in development costs, $400,000 was incurred prior to technological feasibility and $200,000 after technological feasibility had been demonstrated. Prepare the journal entry to record research and development costs.

INTERNATIONAL FINANCIAL STATEMENT ANALYSIS: *Zetar plc*

IFRS9-7 The financial statements of Zetar plc are presented in Appendix C.

Instructions

Use the company's annual report, available in the Investors section at **www.zetarplc.com**, to answer the following questions.

(a) According to the notes to the financial statements, what method or methods does the company use to depreciate "plant and equipment?" What rate does it use to depreciate plant and equipment?

(b) According to the notes to the financial statements, how often is goodwill tested for impairment?

(c) Using the notes to the financial statements, as well as information from the statement of cash flows, prepare the journal entry to record the disposal of property, plant and equipment during 2011. (Round your amounts to the nearest thousand.)

Answers to IFRS Self-Test Questions

1. b **2.** d **3.** c (($10,000,000 × .05)/20) + (($10,000,000 × .20)/25) + (($10,000,000 × .75)/50) **4.** a **5.** c

The Navigator

✔ Remember to go back to The Navigator box on the chapter opening page and check off your completed work.

CHAPTER 10

© Henrik Jonsson/iStockphoto

✔ The Navigator

- Scan Learning Objectives
- Read Feature Story
- Scan Preview
- Read Text and Answer **Do it!**
  ○ p. 509 ○ p. 512 ○ p. 515
  ○ p. 520 ○ p. 521
- Work Using the Decision Toolkit
- Review Summary of Learning Objectives
- Work Comprehensive **Do it!** p. 538
- Answer Self-Test Questions
- Complete Assignments
- Go to WileyPLUS for practice and tutorials

🌐 Read A Look at IFRS p. 564

REPORTING AND ANALYZING LIABILITIES

LEARNING OBJECTIVES

After studying this chapter, you should be able to:

1 Explain a current liability and identify the major types of current liabilities.

2 Describe the accounting for notes payable.

3 Explain the accounting for other current liabilities.

4 Identify the types of bonds.

5 Prepare the entries for the issuance of bonds and interest expense.

6 Describe the entries when bonds are redeemed.

7 Identify the requirements for the financial statement presentation and analysis of liabilities.

✔ The Navigator

Debt can help a company acquire the things it needs to grow, but it is often the very thing that kills a company. A brief history of Maxwell Car Company illustrates the role of debt in the U.S. auto industry. In 1920, Maxwell Car Company was on the brink of financial ruin. Because it was unable to pay its bills, its creditors stepped in and took over. They hired a former General Motors (GM) executive named Walter Chrysler to reorganize the company. By 1925, he had taken over the company and renamed it Chrysler. By 1933, Chrysler was booming, with sales surpassing even those of Ford.

But the next few decades saw Chrysler make a series of blunders. By 1980, with its creditors pounding at the gates, Chrysler was again on the brink of financial ruin.

At that point, Chrysler brought in a former Ford executive named Lee Iacocca to save the company. Iacocca argued that the United States could not afford to let Chrysler fail because of the loss of jobs. He convinced the federal government to grant loan guarantees—promises that if Chrysler failed to pay its creditors, the government would pay them. Iacocca then streamlined

AND THEN THERE WERE TWO

operations and brought out some profitable products. Chrysler repaid all of its government-guaranteed loans by 1983, seven years ahead of the scheduled final payment.

To compete in today's global vehicle market, you must be big—really big. So in 1998, Chrysler merged with German automaker Daimler-Benz to form DaimlerChrysler. For a time, this left just two U.S.-based auto manufacturers—GM and Ford. But in 2007, DaimlerChrysler sold 81% of Chrysler to Cerberus, an investment group, to provide much-needed cash infusions to the automaker. In 2009, Daimler turned over its remaining stake to Cerberus. Three days later, Chrysler filed for bankruptcy. But by 2010, it was beginning to show signs of a turnaround.

The car companies are giants. GM and Ford typically rank among the top five U.S. firms in total assets. But GM and Ford accumulated truckloads of debt on their way to getting big. Although debt made it possible to get so big, the Chrysler story, and GM's recent bankruptcy, make it clear that debt can also threaten a company's survival.

✔The Navigator

INSIDE CHAPTER 10 . . .

The Feature Story suggests that General Motors (GM) and Ford accumulated tremendous amounts of debt in their pursuit of auto industry dominance. It is unlikely that they could have grown so large without this debt, but at times the debt threatens their very existence. Given this risk, why do companies borrow money? Why do they sometimes borrow short-term and other times long-term? Besides bank borrowings, what other kinds of debts do companies incur? In this chapter, we address these issues.

The content and organization of the chapter are as follows.

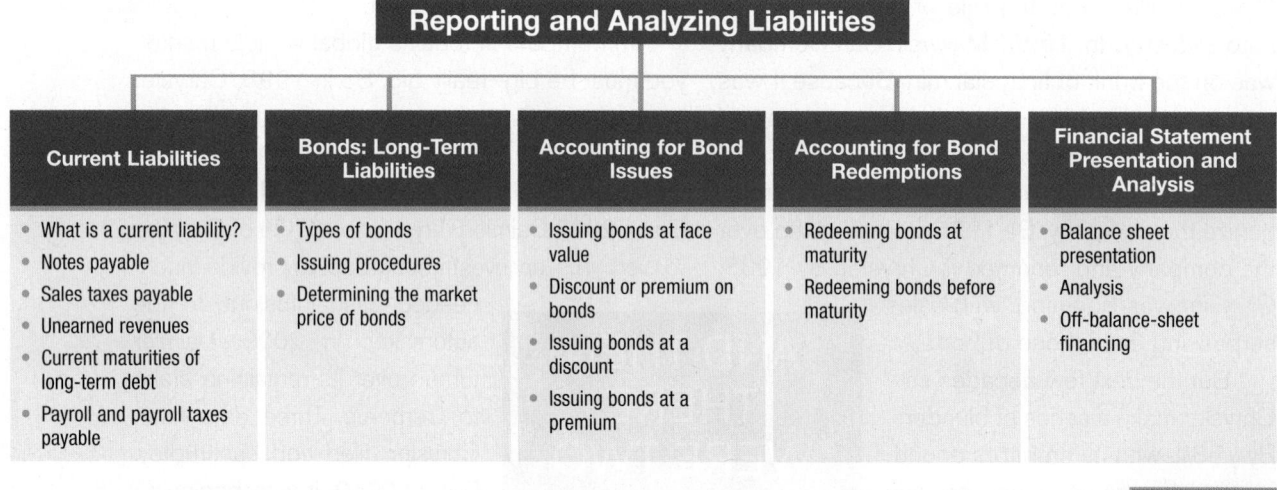

Reporting and Analyzing Liabilities

Current Liabilities	Bonds: Long-Term Liabilities	Accounting for Bond Issues	Accounting for Bond Redemptions	Financial Statement Presentation and Analysis
• What is a current liability? • Notes payable • Sales taxes payable • Unearned revenues • Current maturities of long-term debt • Payroll and payroll taxes payable	• Types of bonds • Issuing procedures • Determining the market price of bonds	• Issuing bonds at face value • Discount or premium on bonds • Issuing bonds at a discount • Issuing bonds at a premium	• Redeeming bonds at maturity • Redeeming bonds before maturity	• Balance sheet presentation • Analysis • Off-balance-sheet financing

✔ The Navigator

Current Liabilities

WHAT IS A CURRENT LIABILITY?

LEARNING OBJECTIVE 1

Explain a current liability and identify the major types of current liabilities.

You have learned that liabilities are defined as "creditors' claims on total assets" and as "existing debts and obligations." Companies must settle or pay these claims, debts, and obligations at some time in the future by transferring assets or services. The future date on which they are due or payable (the maturity date) is a significant feature of liabilities.

As explained in Chapter 2, a **current liability** is a debt that a company reasonably expects to pay (1) from existing current assets or through the creation of other current liabilities, and (2) within one year or the operating cycle, whichever is longer. Debts that do not meet both criteria are **long-term liabilities**.

Financial statement users want to know whether a company's obligations are current or long-term. A company that has more current liabilities than current assets often lacks liquidity, or short-term debt-paying ability. In addition, users want to know the types of liabilities a company has. If a company declares bankruptcy, a specific, predetermined order of payment to creditors exists. Thus, the amount and type of liabilities are of critical importance.

The different types of current liabilities include notes payable, accounts payable, unearned revenues, and accrued liabilities such as taxes, salaries and wages, and interest. In the sections that follow, we discuss a few of the common types of current liabilities.

Helpful Hint In previous chapters, we explained the entries for accounts payable and the adjusting entries for some current liabilities.

NOTES PAYABLE

Companies record obligations in the form of written notes as notes payable. They often use notes payable instead of accounts payable because notes payable provide written documentation of the obligation in case legal remedies are needed to collect the debt. Companies frequently issue notes payable to meet short-term financing needs. Notes payable usually require the borrower to pay interest.

Notes are issued for varying periods of time. **Those due for payment within one year of the balance sheet date are usually classified as current liabilities.**

To illustrate the accounting for notes payable, assume that on September 1, 2014, Cole Williams Co. signs a $100,000, 12%, four-month note maturing on January 1 with First National Bank. When a company issues an interest-bearing note, the amount of assets it receives generally equals the note's face value. Cole Williams Co. therefore will receive $100,000 cash and will make the following journal entry.

LEARNING OBJECTIVE 2
Describe the accounting for notes payable.

Sept. 1	Cash	100,000	
	Notes Payable		100,000
	(To record issuance of 12%, 4-month note to First National Bank)		

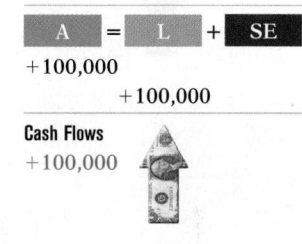

Interest accrues over the life of the note, and the issuer must periodically record that accrual. (You may find it helpful to review the discussion of interest computations that was provided in Chapter 8, page 408, with regard to notes receivable.) If Cole Williams Co. prepares financial statements annually, it makes an adjusting entry at December 31 to recognize four months of interest expense and interest payable of $4,000 ($100,000 \times 12\% \times \frac{4}{12}$):

Dec. 31	Interest Expense	4,000	
	Interest Payable		4,000
	(To accrue interest for 4 months on First National Bank note)		

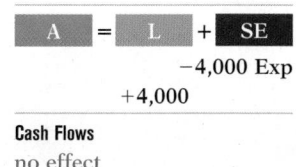

In the December 31 financial statements, the current liabilities section of the balance sheet will show notes payable $100,000 and interest payable $4,000. In addition, the company will report interest expense of $4,000 under "Other expenses and losses" in the income statement.

At maturity (January 1), Cole Williams Co. must pay the face value of the note ($100,000) plus $4,000 interest ($100,000 \times 12\% \times \frac{4}{12}$). It records payment of the note and accrued interest as follows.

Jan. 1	Notes Payable	100,000	
	Interest Payable	4,000	
	Cash		104,000
	(To record payment of First National Bank interest-bearing note and accrued interest at maturity)		

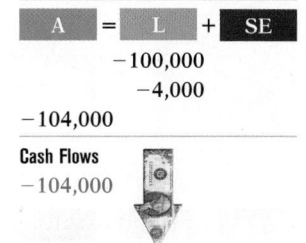

Appendix 10C at the end of this chapter discusses the accounting for long-term installment notes payable.

SALES TAXES PAYABLE

Many of the products we purchase at retail stores are subject to sales taxes. Many states are now implementing sales taxes on purchases made on the Internet as well. Sales taxes are expressed as a percentage of the sales price. The selling company collects the tax from the customer when the sale occurs and periodically (usually monthly) remits the collections to the state's department of revenue. Collecting

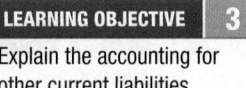

LEARNING OBJECTIVE 3
Explain the accounting for other current liabilities.

sales taxes is important. For example, the State of New York recently sued Sprint Nextel Corporation for $300 million for its alleged failure to collect sales taxes on phone calls.

Under most state laws, the selling company must enter separately on the cash register the amount of the sale and the amount of the sales tax collected. (Gasoline sales are a major exception.) The company then uses the cash register readings to credit Sales Revenue and Sales Taxes Payable. For example, if the March 25 cash register readings for Cooley Grocery show sales of $10,000 and sales taxes of $600 (sales tax rate of 6%), the journal entry is:

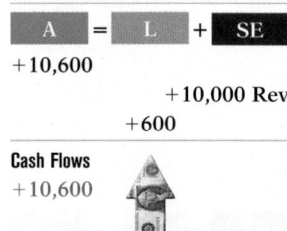

Helpful Hint Check your sales receipts from local retailers to see whether the sales tax is computed separately.

A	=	L	+	SE
+10,600				
				+10,000 Rev
		+600		

Cash Flows
+10,600

Mar. 25	Cash	10,600	
	Sales Revenue		10,000
	Sales Taxes Payable		600
	(To record daily sales and sales taxes)		

When the company remits the taxes to the taxing agency, it decreases (debits) Sales Taxes Payable and decreases (credits) Cash. The company does not report sales taxes as an expense. It simply forwards to the government the amount paid by the customer. Thus, Cooley Grocery serves only as a **collection agent** for the taxing authority.

Sometimes companies do not enter sales taxes separately on the cash register. To determine the amount of sales in such cases, divide total receipts by 100% plus the sales tax percentage. For example, assume that Cooley Grocery enters total receipts of $10,600. Because the amount received from the sale is equal to the sales price (100%) plus 6% of sales, or 1.06 times the sales total, we can compute sales as follows: $10,600 ÷ 1.06 = $10,000. Thus, we can find the sales tax amount of $600 by either (1) subtracting sales from total receipts ($10,600 − $10,000) or (2) multiplying sales by the sales tax rate ($10,000 × 6%).

UNEARNED REVENUES

A magazine publisher such as Sports Illustrated collects cash when customers place orders for magazine subscriptions. An airline company such as American Airlines often receives cash when it sells tickets for future flights. Season tickets for concerts, sporting events, and theatre programs are also paid for in advance. How do companies account for unearned revenues that are received before goods are delivered or services are performed?

1. When the company receives an advance, it increases (debits) Cash and increases (credits) a current liability account identifying the source of the unearned revenue.

2. When the company recognizes revenue, it decreases (debits) the unearned revenue account and increases (credits) a revenue account.

To illustrate, assume that Superior University sells 10,000 season football tickets at $50 each for its five-game home schedule. The university makes the following entry for the sale of season tickets.

A	=	L	+	SE
+500,000		+500,000		

Cash Flows
+500,000

Aug. 6	Cash	500,000	
	Unearned Ticket Revenue		500,000
	(To record sale of 10,000 season tickets)		

As each game is completed, Superior records the recognition of revenue with the following entry.

A	=	L	+	SE
		−100,000		
				+100,000 Rev

Cash Flows
no effect

Sept. 7	Unearned Ticket Revenue	100,000	
	Ticket Revenue		100,000
	(To record football ticket revenues)		

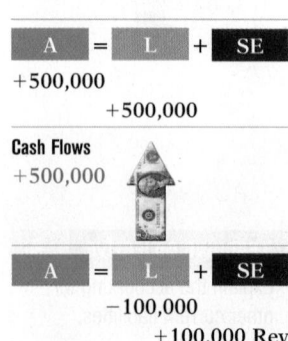

The account Unearned Ticket Revenue represents unearned revenue, and Superior reports it as a current liability. As the school recognizes revenue, it reclassifies the amount from unearned revenue to Ticket Revenue. Unearned revenue is material for some companies. In the airline industry, tickets sold for future flights represent almost 50% of total current liabilities. At United Air Lines, unearned ticket revenue is its largest current liability, recently amounting to more than $1 billion.

Illustration 10-1 shows specific unearned revenue and revenue accounts used in selected types of businesses.

Illustration 10-1 Unearned revenue and revenue accounts

Type of Business	Account Title	
	Unearned Revenue	**Revenue**
Airline	Unearned Ticket Revenue	Ticket Revenue
Magazine publisher	Unearned Subscription Revenue	Subscription Revenue
Hotel	Unearned Rental Revenue	Rental Revenue

CURRENT MATURITIES OF LONG-TERM DEBT

Companies often have a portion of long-term debt that comes due in the current year. As an example, assume that Wendy Construction issues a five-year, interest-bearing $25,000 note on January 1, 2013. This note specifies that each January 1, starting January 1, 2014, Wendy should pay $5,000 of the note. When the company prepares financial statements on December 31, 2013, it should report $5,000 as a current liability and $20,000 as a long-term liability. (The $5,000 amount is the portion of the note that is due to be paid within the next 12 months.) Companies often identify current maturities of long-term debt on the balance sheet as **long-term debt due within one year**. In a recent year, General Motors had $724 million of such debt.

It is not necessary to prepare an adjusting entry to recognize the current maturity of long-term debt. At the balance sheet date, all obligations due within one year are classified as current, and all other obligations are long-term.

Do it! You and several classmates are studying for the next accounting examination. They ask you to answer the following questions.

1. If cash is borrowed on a $50,000, 6-month, 12% note on September 1, how much interest expense would be incurred by December 31?
2. How is the sales tax amount determined when the cash register total includes sales taxes?
3. If $15,000 is collected in advance on November 1 for 3-months' rent, what amount of rent should be recognized by December 31?

Solution

1. $50,000 × 12% × 4/12 = $2,000
2. First, divide the total cash register receipts by 100% plus the sales tax percentage to find the sales amount. Second, subtract the sales amount from the total cash register receipts to determine the sales taxes.
3. $15,000 × 2/3 = $10,000

Related exercise material: **BE10-2, BE10-3, BE10-4, Do it! 10-1, E10-1, E10-2, E10-3, E10-4, E10-6,** and **E10-7.**

CURRENT LIABILITIES

Action Plan

• Use the interest formula: Face value of note × Annual interest rate × Time in terms of one year.

• Divide total receipts by 100% plus the tax rate to determine sales; then subtract sales from the total receipts.

• Determine what fraction of the total unearned rent should be recognized this year.

✔ The Navigator

PAYROLL AND PAYROLL TAXES PAYABLE

Assume that Susan Alena works 40 hours this week for Pepitone Inc., earning a wage of $10 per hour. Will Susan receive a $400 check at the end of the week? Not likely. The reason: Pepitone is required to withhold amounts from her wages to pay various governmental authorities. For example, Pepitone will withhold amounts for Social Security taxes[1] and for federal and state income taxes. If these withholdings total $100, Susan will receive a check for only $300. Illustration 10-2 summarizes the types of payroll deductions that normally occur for most companies.

Illustration 10-2 Payroll deductions

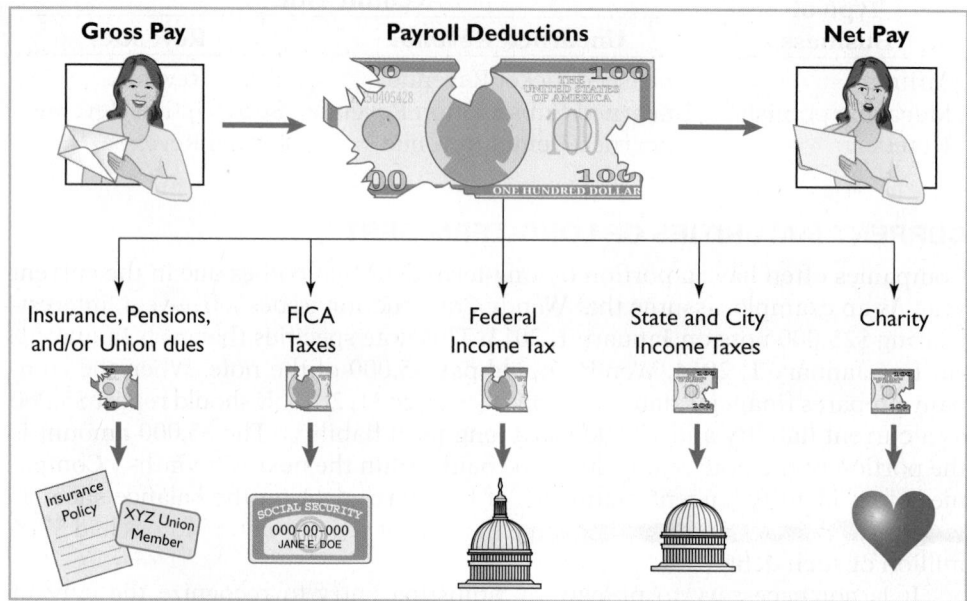

As a result of these deductions, companies withhold from employee paychecks amounts that must be paid to other parties. Pepitone therefore has incurred a liability to pay these third parties and must report this liability in its balance sheet.

As a second illustration, assume that Cargo Corporation records its payroll for the week of March 7 with the journal entry shown below.

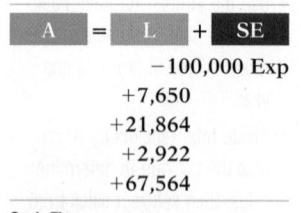

A = L + SE	
−100,000 Exp	
+7,650	
+21,864	
+2,922	
+67,564	

Cash Flows
no effect

Mar. 7	Salaries and Wages Expense		100,000	
	FICA Taxes Payable			7,650
	Federal Income Taxes Payable			21,864
	State Income Taxes Payable			2,922
	Salaries and Wages Payable			67,564
	(To record payroll and withholding taxes for the week ending March 7)			

---

[1]Social Security taxes are commonly called FICA taxes. In 1937, Congress enacted the Federal Insurance Contribution Act (FICA). As can be seen in the journal entry and the payroll tax journal entry on the next page, the employee and employer must make equal contributions to Social Security. The Social Security rate in 2012 was 7.65% for each except employees received a 2% reduction of the rate for 2012. *Our examples and homework use 7.65% for both.*

Cargo then records payment of this payroll on March 7 as follows.

Mar. 7	Salaries and Wages Payable		67,564	
	Cash			67,564
	(To record payment of the March 7 payroll)			

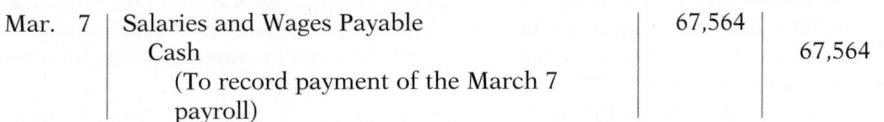

A = L + SE
−67,564
−67,564

Cash Flows
−67,564

In this case, Cargo reports $100,000 in salaries and wages expense. In addition, it reports liabilities for the salaries and wages payable as well as liabilities to governmental agencies. Rather than pay the employees $100,000, Cargo instead must withhold the taxes and make the tax payments directly. In summary, Cargo is essentially serving as a tax collector.

In addition to the liabilities incurred as a result of withholdings, employers also incur a second type of payroll-related liability. With every payroll, the employer incurs liabilities to pay various **payroll taxes** levied upon the employer. These payroll taxes include the **employer's share** of Social Security (FICA) taxes and state and federal unemployment taxes. Based on Cargo Corp.'s $100,000 payroll, the company would record the employer's expense and liability for these payroll taxes as follows.

Mar. 7	Payroll Tax Expense		13,850	
	FICA Taxes Payable			7,650
	Federal Unemployment Taxes Payable			800
	State Unemployment Taxes Payable			5,400
	(To record employer's payroll taxes on March 7 payroll)			

A = L + SE
−13,850 Exp
+7,650
+800
+5,400

Cash Flows
no effect

Companies classify the payroll and payroll tax liability accounts as current liabilities because they must be paid to employees or remitted to taxing authorities periodically and in the near term. Taxing authorities impose substantial fines and penalties on employers if the withholding and payroll taxes are not computed correctly and paid on time.

ANATOMY OF A FRAUD

Art was a custodial supervisor for a large school district. The district was supposed to employ between 35 and 40 regular custodians, as well as 3 or 4 substitute custodians to fill in when regular custodians were missing. Instead, in addition to the regular custodians, Art "hired" 77 substitutes. In fact, almost none of these people worked for the district. Instead, Art submitted time cards for these people, collected their checks at the district office, and personally distributed the checks to the "employees." If a substitute's check was for $1,200, that person would cash the check, keep $200, and pay Art $1,000.

Total take: $150,000

THE MISSING CONTROLS

Human Resource Controls. Thorough background checks should be performed. No employees should begin work until they have been approved by the Board of Education and entered into the payroll system. No employees should be entered into the payroll system until they have been approved by a supervisor. All paychecks should be distributed directly to employees at the official school locations by designated employees.

Independent internal verification. Budgets should be reviewed monthly to identify situations where actual costs significantly exceed budgeted amounts.

Source: Adapted from Wells, *Fraud Casebook* (2007), pp. 164–171.

WAGES AND PAYROLL TAXES

Do it!

During the month of September, Lake Corporation's employees earned wages of $60,000. Withholdings related to these wages were $3,500 for Social Security (FICA), $6,500 for federal income tax, and $2,000 for state income tax. Costs incurred for unemployment taxes were $90 for federal and $150 for state.

Prepare the September 30 journal entries for (a) salaries and wages expense and salaries and wages payable, assuming that all September wages will be paid in October, and (b) the company's payroll tax expense.

Action Plan

- Remember that wages earned are an expense to the company, but withholdings reduce the amount due to be paid to the employee.
- Payroll taxes are taxes the company incurs related to its employees.

Solution

(a) To determine wages payable, reduce wages expense by the withholdings for FICA, federal income tax, and state income tax.

Sept. 30	Salaries and Wages Expense	60,000	
	FICA Taxes Payable		3,500
	Federal Income Taxes Payable		6,500
	State Income Taxes Payable		2,000
	Salaries and Wages Payable		48,000

(b) Payroll taxes would be for the company's share of FICA, as well as for federal and state unemployment tax.

Sept. 30	Payroll Tax Expense	3,740	
	FICA Taxes Payable		3,500
	Federal Unemployment Taxes Payable		90
	State Unemployment Taxes Payable		150

Related exercise material: **BE10-5, BE10-6, *Do it!* 10-2,** and **E10-5.**

Bonds: Long-Term Liabilities

LEARNING OBJECTIVE **4**
Identify the types of bonds.

Long-term liabilities are obligations that a company expects to pay more than one year in the future. In this section, we explain the accounting for the principal types of obligations reported in the long-term liabilities section of the balance sheet. These obligations often are in the form of bonds or long-term notes.

Bonds are a form of interest-bearing note payable issued by corporations, universities, and governmental agencies. Bonds, like common stock, are sold in small denominations (usually $1,000 or multiples of $1,000). As a result, bonds attract many investors. When a corporation issues bonds, it is borrowing money. The person who buys the bonds (the bondholder) is investing in bonds.

Convertible Bonds

TYPES OF BONDS

Bonds may have different features. In the following sections, we describe some commonly issued types of bonds.

Secured and Unsecured Bonds

Secured bonds have specific assets of the issuer pledged as collateral for the bonds. **Unsecured bonds** are issued against the general credit of the borrower. Large corporations with good credit ratings use unsecured bonds extensively. For example, at one time DuPont reported more than $2 billion of unsecured bonds outstanding.

Callable Bonds

Convertible and Callable Bonds

Bonds that can be converted into common stock at the bondholder's option are **convertible bonds**. Bonds that the issuing company can redeem (buy back) at a stated dollar amount prior to maturity are **callable bonds**. Convertible bonds have features that are attractive both to bondholders and to the issuer. The conversion feature often gives bondholders an opportunity to benefit if the market price of the common stock increases substantially. Furthermore, until conversion, the bondholder receives interest on the bond. For the issuer, the bonds sell at a higher price and pay a lower rate of interest than comparable debt securities that do not have a conversion option. Many corporations, such as USAir, United States Steel Corp., and General Motors Corporation, have issued convertible bonds.

Accounting Across the Organization

When Convertible Bonds Don't

During the boom times of the late 1990s, many rapidly growing companies issued large quantities of convertible bonds. Investors found the convertible bonds attractive because they paid regular interest but also had the upside potential of being converted to stock if the stock price increased. At the time, stock prices were increasing rapidly, so many investors viewed convertible bonds as a cheap and safe way to buy stock.

As a consequence, companies were able to pay much lower interest rates on convertible bonds than on standard bonds. When the bonds were issued, company managers assumed that the bonds would be converted. Thus, the company would never have to repay the debt with cash. It seemed too good to be true—and it was.

When stock prices plummeted in the early 2000s, investors no longer had an incentive to convert, since the market price was below the conversion price. When many of these massive bonds came due, companies were forced either to pay them off or to issue new debt at much higher rates.

 The drop in stock prices did not change the debt to assets ratios of these companies. Discuss how the perception of a high debt to assets ratio changed before and after the fall in stock prices. (See page 563.)

Nicolas McComber/iStockphoto

ISSUING PROCEDURES

A bond certificate is issued to the investor to provide evidence of the investor's claim against the company. As Illustration 10-3 (page 514) shows, the bond certificate provides information such as the name of the company that issued the bonds, the face value of the bonds, the maturity date of the bonds, and the contractual interest rate. The face value is the amount of principal due at the maturity date. The maturity date is the date that the final payment is due to the investor from the issuing company. The contractual interest rate is the rate used to determine the amount of cash interest the borrower pays and the investor receives. Usually, the contractual rate is stated as an annual rate, and interest is generally paid semi-annually. (We use annual payments in our examples to simplify.)

Alternative Terminology The contractual rate is often referred to as the *stated rate*.

DETERMINING THE MARKET PRICE OF BONDS

If you were an investor wanting to purchase a bond, how would you determine how much to pay? To be more specific, assume that Coronet, Inc. issues a zero-interest (pays no interest) bond with a face value of $1,000,000 due in 20 years. For this bond, the only cash you receive is $1 million at the end of 20 years. Would you pay $1 million for this bond? We hope not because $1 million received 20 years from now is not the same as $1 million received today.

The term time value of money is used to indicate the relationship between time and money—that a dollar received today is worth more than a dollar promised at some time in the future. If you had $1 million today, you would invest it and earn interest so that at the end of 20 years, your investment would be worth much more than $1 million. Thus, if someone is going to pay you $1 million 20 years

Same dollars at different times are not equal.

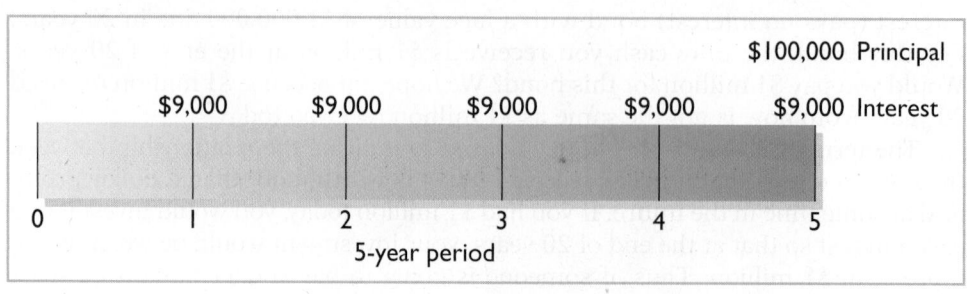

Illustration 10-3 Bond certificate

from now, you would want to find its equivalent today, or its present value. In other words, you would want to determine the value today of the amount to be received in the future after taking into account current interest rates.

The current market price (present value) of a bond is therefore a function of three factors: (1) the dollar amounts to be received, (2) the length of time until the amounts are received, and (3) the market interest rate. The market interest rate is the rate investors demand for loaning funds. The process of finding the present value is referred to as **discounting** the future amounts.

To illustrate, assume that Acropolis Company on January 1, 2014, issues $100,000 of 9% bonds, due in five years, with interest payable annually at year-end. The purchaser of the bonds would receive the following two types of cash payments: (1) **principal** of $100,000 to be paid at maturity, and (2) five $9,000 **interest payments** ($100,000 × 9%) over the term of the bonds. Illustration 10-4 shows a time diagram depicting both cash flows.

Illustration 10-4 Time diagram depicting cash flows

					$100,000 Principal
$9,000	$9,000	$9,000	$9,000	$9,000	Interest
0	1	2	3	4	5

5-year period

The current market price of a bond is equal to the present value of all the future cash payments promised by the bond. Illustration 10-5 lists and totals the present values of these amounts, assuming the market rate of interest is 9%.

Present value of $100,000 received in 5 years	$ 64,993
Present value of $9,000 received annually for 5 years	+ 35,007
Market price of bonds	**$100,000**

Illustration 10-5 Computing the market price of bonds

Tables are available to provide the present value numbers to be used, or these values can be determined mathematically or with financial calculators.[2] Appendix D, near the end of the textbook, provides further discussion of the concepts and the mechanics of the time value of money computations.

Do it!

State whether each of the following statements is true or false.

_____ 1. Secured bonds have specific assets of the issuer pledged as collateral.

_____ 2. Callable bonds can be redeemed by the issuing company at a stated dollar amount prior to maturity.

_____ 3. The contractual rate is the rate investors demand for loaning funds.

_____ 4. The face value is the amount of principal the issuing company must pay at the maturity date.

_____ 5. The market price of a bond is equal to its maturity value.

BOND TERMINOLOGY

Solution

1. True.
2. True.
3. False. The contractual interest rate is used to determine the amount of cash interest the borrower pays.
4. True.
5. False. The market price of a bond is equal to the present value of all the future cash payments promised by the bond.

Related exercise material: **Do it!** 10-3.

Action Plan

• Review the types of bonds and the basic terms associated with bonds.

 The Navigator

Accounting for Bond Issues

A corporation records bond transactions when it issues (sells) or redeems (buys back) bonds and when bondholders convert bonds into common stock. If bondholders sell their bond investments to other investors, the issuing firm receives no further money on the transaction, **nor does the issuing corporation journalize the transaction** (although it does keep records of the names of bondholders in some cases).

Bonds may be issued at face value, below face value (discount), or above face value (premium). Bond prices for both new issues and existing bonds are quoted as **a percentage of the face value of the bond. Face value is usually $1,000.**

LEARNING OBJECTIVE 5
Prepare the entries for the issuance of bonds and interest expense.

[2]For those knowledgeable in the use of present value tables, the computations in this example are $100,000 \times .64993 = $64,993 and $9,000 \times 3.88965 = $35,007 (rounded).

Thus, a $1,000 bond with a quoted price of 97 means that the selling price of the bond is 97% of face value, or $970.

ISSUING BONDS AT FACE VALUE

To illustrate the accounting for bonds issued at face value, assume that Devor Corporation issues 100, five-year, 10%, $1,000 bonds dated January 1, 2014, at 100 (100% of face value). The entry to record the sale is:

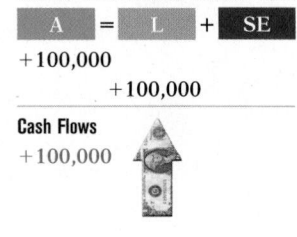

Jan. 1	Cash	100,000	
	Bonds Payable		100,000
	(To record sale of bonds at face value)		

Devor reports bonds payable in the long-term liabilities section of the balance sheet because the maturity date is January 1, 2019 (more than one year away).

Over the term (life) of the bonds, companies make entries to record bond interest. Interest on bonds payable is computed in the same manner as interest on notes payable, as explained earlier. If we assume that interest is payable annually on January 1 on the bonds described above, Devor accrues interest of $10,000 ($100,000 × 10% × $\frac{12}{12}$) on December 31. At December 31, Devor recognizes the $10,000 of interest expense incurred with the following adjusting entry.

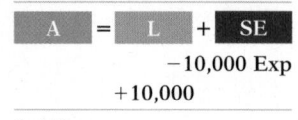

Dec. 31	Interest Expense	10,000	
	Interest Payable		10,000
	(To accrue bond interest)		

The company classifies **interest payable as a current liability** because it is scheduled for payment within the next year. When Devor pays the interest on January 1, 2015, it decreases (debits) Interest Payable and decreases (credits) Cash for $10,000. Devor records the payment on January 1 as follows.

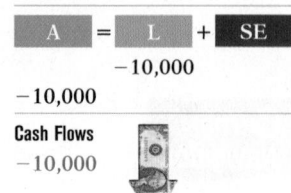

Jan. 1	Interest Payable	10,000	
	Cash		10,000
	(To record payment of bond interest)		

DISCOUNT OR PREMIUM ON BONDS

The previous illustrations assumed that the contractual (stated) interest rate and the market (effective) interest rate paid on bonds were the same. Recall that the **contractual interest rate** is the rate applied to the face (par) value to arrive at the interest paid in a year. The **market interest rate** is the rate investors demand for loaning funds to the corporation. When the contractual interest rate and the market interest rate are the same, **bonds sell at face value**.

However, market interest rates change daily. The type of bond issued, the state of the economy, current industry conditions, and the company's individual performance all affect market interest rates. As a result, the contractual and market interest rates often differ. To make bonds salable when the two rates differ, bonds sell below or above face value.

To illustrate, suppose that a company issues 10% bonds at a time when other bonds of similar risk are paying 12%. Investors will not be interested in buying the 10% bonds, so their value will fall below their face value. When a bond is sold for less than its face value, the difference between the face value of a bond and its selling price is called a discount. As a result of the decline in the bonds' selling price, the actual interest rate incurred by the company increases to the level of the current market interest rate.

Conversely, if the market rate of interest is **lower than** the contractual interest rate, investors will have to pay more than face value for the bonds. That is, if the market rate of interest is 8% but the contractual interest rate on the bonds is 10%, the price on the bonds will be bid up. When a bond is sold for more than its face value, the difference between the face value and its selling price is called a premium. Illustration 10-6 shows these relationships graphically.

Helpful Hint Bond prices *vary inversely* with changes in the market interest rate. As market interest rates decline, bond prices increase. When a bond is issued, if the market interest rate is below the contractual rate, the bond price is higher than the face value.

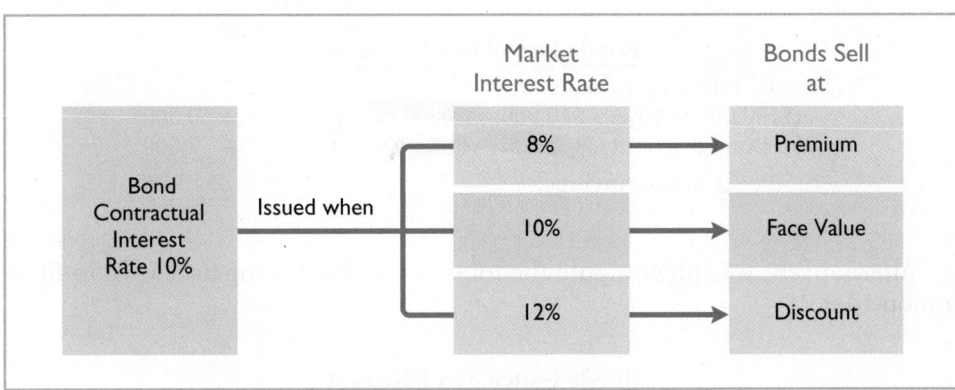

Illustration 10-6 Interest rates and bond prices

Issuance of bonds at an amount different from face value is quite common. By the time a company prints the bond certificates and markets the bonds, it will be a coincidence if the market rate and the contractual rate are the same. Thus, the issuance of bonds at a discount does not mean that the financial strength of the issuer is suspect. Conversely, the sale of bonds at a premium does not indicate that the financial strength of the issuer is exceptional.

Helpful Hint Some bonds are sold at a discount by design. "Zero-coupon" bonds, which pay no interest, sell at a deep discount to face value.

ISSUING BONDS AT A DISCOUNT

To illustrate the issuance of bonds at a discount, assume that on January 1, 2014, Candlestick Inc. sells $100,000, five-year, 10% bonds at 98 (98% of face value) with interest payable on January 1. The entry to record the issuance is:

Jan. 1	Cash	98,000	
	Discount on Bonds Payable	2,000	
	Bonds Payable		100,000
	(To record sale of bonds at a discount)		

A = L + SE
+98,000
−2,000
+100,000
Cash Flows
+98,000

Although Discount on Bonds Payable has a debit balance, **it is not an asset**. Rather it is a **contra account**, which is **deducted from bonds payable** on the balance sheet as shown in Illustration 10-7.

Illustration 10-7 Statement presentation of discount on bonds payable

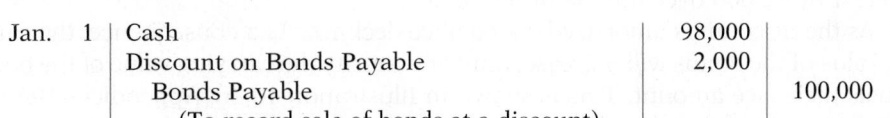

CANDLESTICK INC.
Balance Sheet (partial)

Long-term liabilities		
Bonds payable	$100,000	
Less: Discount on bonds payable	− 2,000	$98,000

Helpful Hint The carrying value (book value) of bonds issued at a discount is determined by subtracting the balance of the discount account from the balance of the Bonds Payable account.

The $98,000 represents the **carrying (or book) value** of the bonds. On the date of issue, this amount equals the market price of the bonds.

The issuance of bonds below face value causes the total cost of borrowing to differ from the bond interest paid. That is, the issuing corporation not only must pay the contractual interest rate over the term of the bonds but also must pay the face value (rather than the issuance price) at maturity. Therefore, the difference between the issuance price and the face value of the bonds—the discount—is an **additional cost of borrowing**. The company records this cost as **interest expense** over the life of the bonds. The total cost of borrowing $98,000 for Candlestick Inc. is $52,000, computed as shown in Illustration 10-8.

Illustration 10-8
Computation of total cost of borrowing—bonds issued at discount

Bonds Issued at a Discount	
Annual interest payments	
($100,000 × 10% = $10,000; $10,000 × 5)	$ 50,000
Add: Bond discount ($100,000 − $98,000)	+ 2,000
Total cost of borrowing	$52,000

Alternatively, we can compute the total cost of borrowing as shown in Illustration 10-9.

Illustration 10-9 Alternative computation of total cost of borrowing—bonds issued at discount

Bonds Issued at a Discount	
Principal at maturity	$100,000
Annual interest payments ($10,000 × 5)	+ 50,000
Cash to be paid to bondholders	150,000
Cash received from bondholders	− 98,000
Total cost of borrowing	$ 52,000

To follow the expense recognition principle, companies allocate bond discount to expense in each period in which the bonds are outstanding. This is referred to as **amortizing the discount**. Amortization of the discount **increases** the amount of interest expense reported each period. That is, after the company amortizes the discount, the amount of interest expense it reports in a period will exceed the contractual amount. As shown in Illustration 10-8, for the bonds issued by Candlestick Inc., total interest expense will exceed the contractual interest by $2,000 over the life of the bonds.

As the discount is amortized, its balance declines. As a consequence, the carrying value of the bonds will increase, until at maturity the carrying value of the bonds equals their face amount. This is shown in Illustration 10-10. Appendices 10A and 10B at the end of this chapter discuss procedures for amortizing bond discount.

Illustration 10-10
Amortization of bond discount

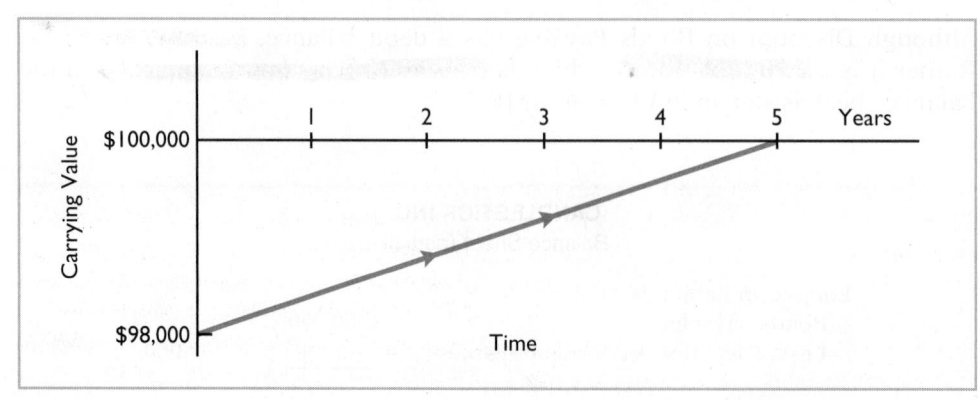

ISSUING BONDS AT A PREMIUM

We can illustrate the issuance of bonds at a premium by now assuming the Candlestick Inc. bonds described above sell at 102 (102% of face value) rather than at 98. The entry to record the sale is:

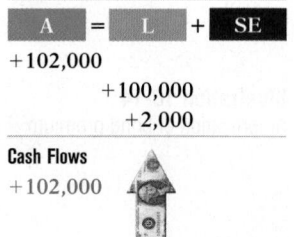

Jan. 1	Cash	102,000	
	Bonds Payable		100,000
	Premium on Bonds Payable		2,000
	(To record sale of bonds at a premium)		

A	=	L	+	SE
+102,000				
		+100,000		
		+2,000		

Cash Flows
+102,000

Candlestick adds the premium on bonds payable **to the bonds payable** amount on the balance sheet, as shown in Illustration 10-11.

CANDLESTICK INC.
Balance Sheet (partial)

Long-term liabilities		
Bonds payable	$100,000	
Add: Premium on bonds payable	**2,000**	$102,000

Illustration 10-11 Statement presentation of bond premium

Helpful Hint Both a discount and a premium account are valuation accounts. A *valuation account* is one that is needed to value properly the item to which it relates.

The sale of bonds above face value causes the total cost of borrowing to be **less than the bond interest paid** because the borrower is not required to pay the bond premium at the maturity date of the bonds. Thus, the premium is considered to be **a reduction in the cost of borrowing** that reduces bond interest expense over the life of the bonds. The total cost of borrowing $102,000 for Candlestick Inc. is $48,000, computed as in Illustration 10-12.

Bonds Issued at a Premium

Annual interest payments	
($100,000 × 10% = $10,000; $10,000 × 5)	$ 50,000
Less: Bond premium ($102,000 − $100,000)	− 2,000
Total cost of borrowing	**$48,000**

Illustration 10-12 Computation of total cost of borrowing—bonds issued at a premium

Alternatively, we can compute the cost of borrowing as shown in Illustration 10-13.

Bonds Issued at a Premium

Principal at maturity	$100,000
Annual interest payments ($10,000 × 5)	+ 50,000
Cash to be paid to bondholders	150,000
Cash received from bondholders	− 102,000
Total cost of borrowing	**$ 48,000**

Illustration 10-13 Alternative computation of total cost of borrowing—bonds issued at a premium

Similar to bond discount, companies allocate bond premium to expense in each period in which the bonds are outstanding. This is referred to as **amortizing the premium**. Amortization of the premium **decreases** the amount of interest expense reported each period. That is, after the company amortizes the premium, the amount of interest expense it reports in a period will be less than the contractual amount. As shown in Illustration 10-12, for the bonds issued by Candlestick Inc., contractual interest will exceed the interest expense by $2,000 over the life of the bonds.

As the premium is amortized, its balance declines. As a consequence, the carrying value of the bonds will decrease, until at maturity the carrying value of the bonds equals their face amount. This is shown in Illustration 10-14. Appendices 10A and 10B at the end of this chapter discuss procedures for amortizing bond premium.

Illustration 10-14
Amortization of bond premium

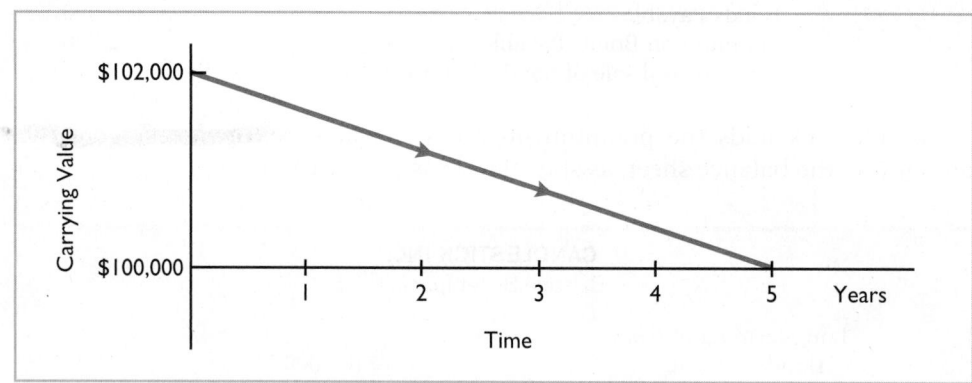

Do it!

BOND ISSUANCE

Giant Corporation issues $200,000 of bonds for $189,000. (a) Prepare the journal entry to record the issuance of the bonds, and (b) show how the bonds would be reported on the balance sheet at the date of issuance.

Action Plan

- Record cash received, bonds payable at face value, and the difference as a discount or premium.
- Report discount as a deduction from bonds payable and premium as an addition to bonds payable.

The Navigator

Solution

(a)

	Debit	Credit
Cash	189,000	
Discount on Bonds Payable	† 11,000	
Bonds Payable		200,000
(To record sale of bonds at a discount)		

(b)

Long-term liabilities		
Bonds payable	$200,000	
Less: Discount on bonds payable	~ 11,000	$189,000

Related exercise material: **BE10-8, BE10-9, BE10-10, Do it! 10-4, E10-8, E10-9,** and **E10-10.**

Accounting for Bond Redemptions

LEARNING OBJECTIVE 6

Describe the entries when bonds are redeemed.

Bonds are redeemed when the issuing corporation buys them back. The appropriate entries for these transactions are explained next.

REDEEMING BONDS AT MATURITY

Regardless of the issue price of bonds, the book value of the bonds at maturity will equal their face value. Assuming that the company pays and records separately the interest for the last interest period, Candlestick records the redemption of its bonds at maturity as:

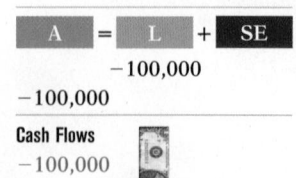

A	=	L	+	SE
		−100,000		
−100,000				

Cash Flows
−100,000

Bonds Payable	100,000	
Cash		100,000
(To record redemption of bonds at maturity)		

REDEEMING BONDS BEFORE MATURITY

Bonds may be redeemed before maturity. A company may decide to redeem bonds before maturity in order to reduce interest cost and remove debt from its balance sheet. A company should redeem debt early only if it has sufficient cash resources.

When bonds are redeemed before maturity, it is necessary to (1) eliminate the carrying value of the bonds at the redemption date, (2) record the cash paid, and (3) recognize the gain or loss on redemption. The **carrying value** of the bonds is the face value of the bonds less unamortized bond discount or plus unamortized bond premium at the redemption date.

To illustrate, assume at the end of the fourth period, Candlestick Inc., having sold its bonds at a premium, redeems the $100,000 face value bonds at 103 after paying the annual interest. Assume that the carrying value of the bonds at the redemption date is $100,400 (principal $100,000 and premium $400). Candlestick records the redemption at the end of the fourth interest period (January 1, 2018) as:

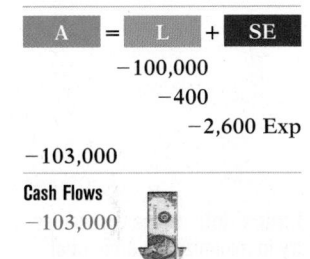

			debit	*credit*
Jan. 1	Bonds Payable		100,000	
	Premium on Bonds Payable		400	
	Loss on Bond Redemption	†	2,600	
	Cash			103,000
	(To record redemption of bonds at 103)			

A	=	L	+	SE
		−100,000		
		−400		
				−2,600 Exp
−103,000				

Cash Flows
−103,000

Note that the loss of $2,600 is the difference between the $103,000 cash paid and the $100,400 carrying value of the bonds.

Do it!

R & B Inc. issued $500,000, 10-year bonds at a discount. Prior to maturity, when the carrying value of the bonds is $496,000, the company redeems the bonds at 98. Prepare the entry to record the redemption of the bonds.

Solution

There is a loss on redemption. The cash paid, $490,000 ($500,000 × 98%), is less than the carrying value of $496,000. The entry is:

	Debit	*credit*
Bonds Payable	500,000	
Cash		490,000
Discount on Bonds Payable		4,000
Gain on Bond Redemption	†	6,000
(To record redemption of bonds at 98)		

Related exercise material: **BE10-11, Do it! 10-5, E10-13, and E10-14.**

BOND REDEMPTION

Action Plan

- Determine and eliminate the carrying value of the bonds.
- Record the cash paid.
- Compute and record the gain or loss (the difference between the first two items).

✔ The Navigator

Financial Statement Presentation and Analysis

BALANCE SHEET PRESENTATION

Current liabilities are the first category under "Liabilities" on the balance sheet. Companies list each of the principal types of current liabilities separately within the category. Within the current liabilities section, companies often list notes payable first, followed by accounts payable.

LEARNING OBJECTIVE 7

Identify the requirements for the financial statement presentation and analysis of liabilities.

Companies report long-term liabilities in a separate section of the balance sheet immediately following "Current liabilities." Illustration 10-15 shows an example.

Illustration 10-15
Balance sheet presentation of liabilities

MARAIS COMPANY
Balance Sheet (partial)

Liabilities		
Current liabilities		
Notes payable	$ 250,000	
Accounts payable	125,000	
Current maturities of long-term debt	300,000	
Accrued liabilities	75,000	
Total current liabilities		$ 750,000
Long-term liabilities		
Bonds payable	1,000,000	
Less: Discount on bonds payable	80,000	920,000
Notes payable, secured by plant assets		540,000
Lease liability		500,000
Total long-term liabilities		1,960,000
Total liabilities		$2,710,000

Ethics Note Some companies try to minimize the amount of debt reported on their balance sheet by not reporting certain types of commitments as liabilities. This subject is of intense interest in the financial community.

Disclosure of debt is very important. Failures at Enron, WorldCom, and Global Crossing have made investors very concerned about companies' debt obligations. Summary data regarding debts may be presented in the balance sheet with detailed data (such as interest rates, maturity dates, conversion privileges, and assets pledged as collateral) shown in a supporting schedule in the notes. Companies should report current maturities of long-term debt as a current liability.

KEEPING AN EYE ON CASH

The balance sheet presents the balances of a company's debts at a point in time. The statement of cash flows also presents information about a company's debts. Information regarding cash inflows and outflows during the year that resulted from the principal portion of debt transactions appears in the "Financing activities" section of the statement of cash flows. Interest expense is reported in the "Operating activities" section even though it resulted from debt transactions.

The statement of cash flows shown below presents the cash flows from financing activities for General Motors Company (Automotive Division). From this we learn that the company issued new debt of $476 million and repaid debt of $1,471 million.

GENERAL MOTORS COMPANY—Automotive Division
Real World
Statement of Cash Flows (partial)
2011
(in millions)

Cash flows from financing activities	
Proceeds from issuance of stock	$ 11
Proceeds from issuance of debt	476
Payments of debt	(1,471)
Increase in short-term borrowings	131
Dividends paid	(916)
Other	(100)
Net cash provided by (used in) financing activities	$(1,869)

ANALYSIS

Careful examination of debt obligations helps you assess a company's ability to pay its current and long-term obligations. It also helps you determine whether a company can obtain debt financing in order to grow. We will use the following information from the financial statements of the nonfinancial services division (primarily the Automotive Division) of Toyota Motor Corporation to illustrate the analysis of a company's liquidity and solvency.

Illustration 10-16
Simplified balance sheets for
Toyota Motor Corporation

TOYOTA MOTOR CORPORATION—Automotive Division
Balance Sheets
December 31, 2011 and 2010
(in millions)

Assets	2011	2010
Total current assets	$ 78,273	$ 88,643
Noncurrent assets	125,487	102,601
Total assets	$203,760	$191,244
Liabilities and Stockholders' Equity		
Total current liabilities	$ 60,319	$ 59,315
Noncurrent liabilities	24,713	25,506
Total liabilities	85,032	84,821
Total stockholders' equity	118,728	106,423
Total liabilities and stockholders' equity	$203,760	$191,244

Liquidity

Liquidity ratios measure the short-term ability of a company to pay its maturing obligations and to meet unexpected needs for cash. A commonly used measure of liquidity is the current ratio (presented in Chapter 2). The current ratio is calculated as current assets divided by current liabilities. Illustration 10-17 presents the current ratio for the Automotive Division of Toyota along with the industry average.

Illustration 10-17
Current ratio

	Toyota (Automotive Division) ($ in millions)		Industry Average
Ratio	2011	2010	2011
Current Ratio	$\dfrac{\$78,273}{\$60,319} = 1.30{:}1$	$\dfrac{\$88,643}{\$59,315} = 1.49{:}1$	1.00:1

Toyota's current ratio declined from 1.49:1 to 1.30:1 from 2010 to 2011. Although Toyota's ratio declined, it still exceeds the industry average current ratio for manufacturers of autos and trucks of 1.00:1.

Toyota's current ratio, like the industry average, is quite low. Many companies today minimize their liquid assets (such as accounts receivable and inventory) in order to improve profitability measures, such as return on assets. This is particularly true of large companies such as Ford, GM, and Toyota. Companies that keep fewer liquid assets on hand must rely on other sources of liquidity. One such source is a **bank line of credit**. A line of credit is a prearranged agreement between a company and a lender that permits the company, should it be necessary, to borrow up to an agreed-upon amount. For example, a recent disclosure regarding debt in Toyota's financial statements states that it has $23.5 billion of unused lines of credit. This represents a substantial amount of available cash.

DECISION TOOLKIT

DECISION CHECKPOINTS	INFO NEEDED FOR DECISION	TOOL TO USE FOR DECISION	HOW TO EVALUATE RESULTS
Can the company obtain short-term financing when necessary?	Available lines of credit, from notes to the financial statements.	Compare available lines of credit to current liabilities. Also, evaluate liquidity ratios.	If liquidity ratios are low, then lines of credit should be high to compensate.

Solvency

Solvency ratios measure the ability of a company to survive over a long period of time. The Feature Story in this chapter mentioned that, although there once were many U.S. automobile manufacturers, only three U.S.-based companies remain today. Many of the others went bankrupt. This highlights the fact that when making a long-term loan or purchasing a company's stock, you must give consideration to a company's solvency.

To reduce the risks associated with having a large amount of debt during an economic downturn, some U.S. automobile manufacturers took two precautionary steps while they enjoyed strong profits. First, they built up large balances of cash and cash equivalents to avoid a cash crisis. Second, they were reluctant to build new plants or hire new workers to meet their production needs. Instead, they asked workers to put in overtime, or they "outsourced" work to other companies. In this way, when the economic downturn occurred, they hoped to avoid having to make debt payments on idle production plants and to minimize layoffs. As a result, when the crisis first hit, Ford had cash of $29 billion, about double the amount of cash it would expect to use over a two-year period.

In Chapter 2, you learned that one measure of a company's solvency is the debt to assets ratio. This is calculated as total liabilities (debt) divided by total assets. This ratio indicates the extent to which a company's assets are financed with debt.

Another useful solvency measure is the times interest earned. It provides an indication of a company's ability to meet interest payments as they come due. It is computed by dividing income before interest expense and income taxes by interest expense. It uses income before interest expense and taxes because this number best represents the amount available to pay interest.

We can use the balance sheet information presented on page 523 and the additional information below to calculate solvency ratios for the Automotive Division of Toyota.

($ in millions)	2011	2010
Net income	$2,254	$904
Interest expense	350	560
Income tax expense	2,150	455

The debt to assets ratios and times interest earned for the Automotive Division of Toyota and averages for the industry are shown in Illustration 10-18.

Toyota's debt to assets ratio was 42%. The industry average for manufacturers of autos and trucks is 62%. Thus, Toyota is less reliant on debt financing than the average firm in the auto and truck industry.

Toyota's times interest earned increased from 3.4 times in 2010 to 13.6 in 2011. This means that in 2011 Toyota had earnings before interest and taxes that were more than 13 times the amount needed to pay interest. The higher the multiple, the lower the likelihood that the company will default on interest payments. Because many of the companies in this industry were still recovering from the recent recession, the industry average was only 3.2. This suggests that while Toyota's ability to meet interest payments was high, the average company in the industry had a lower ability to meet interest payments in 2011.

$$\text{Debt to Assets Ratio} = \frac{\text{Total Liabilities}}{\text{Total Assets}}$$

$$\text{Times Interest Earned} = \frac{\text{Net Income} + \text{Interest Expense} + \text{Tax Expense}}{\text{Interest Expense}}$$

Ratio	Toyota (Automotive Division) ($ in millions)		Industry Average
	2011	2010	2011
Debt to Assets Ratio	$\dfrac{\$85,032}{\$203,760} = 42\%$	44%	62%
Times Interest Earned	$\dfrac{\$2,254 + \$350 + \$2,150}{\$350} = 13.6 \text{ times}$	3.4 times	3.2 times

Illustration 10-18
Solvency ratios

Investor Insight

Debt Masking

In the wake of the financial crisis, many financial institutions are wary of reporting too much debt on their financial statements, for fear that investors will consider them too risky. The Securities and Exchange Commission (SEC) is concerned that some companies engage in "debt masking" to make it appear that they use less debt than they actually do. These companies enter into transactions at the end of the accounting period that essentially remove debt from their books. Shortly after the end of the period, they reverse the transaction and the debt goes back on their books. The *Wall Street Journal* reported that 18 large banks "had consistently lowered one type of debt at the end of each of the past five quarters, reducing it on average by 42% from quarterly peaks."

Source: Tom McGinty, Kate Kelly, and Kara Scannell, "Debt 'Masking' Under Fire," *Wall Street Journal Online* (April 21, 2010).

 What implications does debt masking have for an investor that is using the debt to assets ratio to evaluate a company's solvency? (See page 563.)

© Yenwen Lu/iStockphoto

 ## DECISION TOOLKIT

DECISION CHECKPOINTS	INFO NEEDED FOR DECISION	TOOL TO USE FOR DECISION	HOW TO EVALUATE RESULTS
Can the company meet its obligations in the long term?	Interest expense and net income before interest and taxes	$\text{Times interest earned} = \dfrac{\text{Net income} + \text{Interest expense} + \text{Tax expense}}{\text{Interest expense}}$	High ratio indicates ability to meet interest payments as scheduled.

OFF-BALANCE-SHEET FINANCING

A concern for analysts when they evaluate a company's liquidity and solvency is whether that company has properly recorded all of its obligations. The bankruptcy of Enron Corporation, one of the largest bankruptcies in U.S. history, demonstrated how much damage can result when a company does not properly record or disclose all of its debts. Many would say Enron was practicing off-balance-sheet financing. **Off-balance-sheet financing** is an intentional effort by a company to structure its financing arrangements so as to avoid showing liabilities on its balance sheet. Two common types of off-balance-sheet financing result from unreported contingencies and lease transactions.

Contingencies

One reason a company's balance sheet might not fully reflect its potential obligations is due to contingencies. Contingencies are events with uncertain outcomes that may represent potential liabilities. A common type of contingency is lawsuits. Suppose, for example, that you were analyzing the financial statements of a cigarette manufacturer and did not consider the possible negative implications of existing unsettled lawsuits. Your analysis of the company's financial position would certainly be misleading. Other common types of contingencies are product warranties and environmental cleanup obligations. For example, in a recent year, Novartis AG began offering a money-back guarantee on its blood-pressure medications. This guarantee would necessitate an accrual for the estimated claims that will result from returns.

Accounting rules require that companies disclose contingencies in the notes. In some cases, they must accrue them as liabilities. For example, suppose that Waterbury Inc. is sued by a customer for $1 million due to an injury sustained by a defective product. If at the company's year-end the lawsuit had not yet been resolved, how should Waterbury account for this event? If the company can determine **a reasonable estimate** of the expected loss and if it is **probable** it will lose the suit, then the company should accrue for the loss. It records the loss by increasing (debiting) a loss account and increasing (crediting) a liability such as Lawsuit Liability. If **both** of these conditions are not met, then the company discloses the basic facts regarding this suit in the notes to its financial statements.

Leasing

One common type of off-balance-sheet financing results from leasing. Most lessees do not like to report leases on their balance sheets because the lease increases the company's total liabilities. Recall from Chapter 9 that operating leases are treated like rentals—no asset or liabilities show on the books. Capital leases are treated like a debt-financed purchase—increasing both assets and liabilities. **As a result, many companies structure their lease agreements to avoid meeting the criteria of a capital lease.**

Recall from Chapter 9 that many U.S. airlines lease a large portion of their planes without showing any debt related to them on their balance sheets. For example, the total increase in assets and liabilities that would result if Southwest Airlines recorded on the balance sheet its off-balance-sheet **"operating" leases** would be approximately $2.3 billion. Illustration 10-19 presents Southwest Airlines' debt to assets ratio for a recent year using the numbers presented in its balance sheet. It also shows the ratio after adjusting for the off-balance-sheet leases. After those adjustments, Southwest has a ratio of 62% versus 67% before. This means that of every dollar of assets, 67 cents was funded by debt. This would be of interest to analysts evaluating Southwest's solvency.

Ethics Note Accounting standard-setters are attempting to rewrite rules on lease accounting because of concerns that abuse of the current standards is reducing the usefulness of financial statements.

Illustration 10-19 Debt to assets ratio adjusted for leases

International Note GAAP accounting for leases is more "rules-based" than IFRS. GAAP relies on precisely defined cut-offs to determine whether an item is treated as a capital or operating lease. This rules-based approach may enable companies to structure leases "around the rules." Creating a jointly prepared leasing standard is a top priority for the IASB and FASB.

	Using numbers as presented on balance sheet	Adjusted for off-balance-sheet leases
Debt to assets ratio	$\dfrac{\$8,803}{\$14,269} = 62\%$	$\dfrac{\$8,803 + \$2,371}{\$14,269 + \$2,371} = 67\%$

Critics of off-balance-sheet financing contend that many leases represent unavoidable obligations that meet the definition of a liability. Therefore, companies should report them as liabilities on the balance sheet. To reduce these concerns, companies are required to report their operating lease obligations for subsequent years in a note. This allows analysts and other financial statement users to adjust a company's financial statements by adding leased assets and lease liabilities if they feel that this treatment is more appropriate.

DECISION TOOLKIT

DECISION CHECKPOINTS	INFO NEEDED FOR DECISION	TOOL TO USE FOR DECISION	HOW TO EVALUATE RESULTS
Does the company have any contingent liabilities?	Knowledge of events with uncertain negative outcomes	Notes to financial statements and financial statements	If negative outcomes are possible, determine the probability, the amount of loss, and the potential impact on financial statements.
Does the company have significant off-balance-sheet financing, such as unrecorded lease obligations?	Information on unrecorded obligations, such as a schedule of minimum lease payments from the notes to the financial statements	Compare liquidity and solvency ratios with and without unrecorded obligations included	If ratios differ significantly after including unrecorded obligations, these obligations should not be ignored in analysis.

Investor Insight
"Covenant-Lite" Debt

In many corporate loans and bond issuances, the lending agreement specifies **debt covenants**. These covenants typically are specific financial measures, such as minimum levels of retained earnings, cash flows, times interest earned, or other measures that a company must maintain during the life of the loan. If the company violates a covenant, it is considered to have violated the loan agreement. The creditors can then demand immediate repayment, or they can renegotiate the loan's terms. Covenants protect lenders because they enable lenders to step in and try to get their money back before the borrower gets too deep into trouble.

During the 1990s, most traditional loans specified between three to six covenants or "triggers." In more recent years, however, when there was lots of cash available, lenders began reducing or completely eliminating covenants from loan agreements in order to be more competitive with other lenders. When the economy declined, these lenders lost big money when companies defaulted.

Source: Cynthia Koons, "Risky Business: Growth of 'Covenant-Lite' Debt," *Wall Street Journal* (June 18, 2007), p. C2.

 How can financial ratios such as those covered in this chapter provide protection for creditors? (See page 564.)

© Arnd Rockser/iStockphoto

USING THE DECISION TOOLKIT

Ford Motor Company has enjoyed some tremendous successes, including its popular Taurus and Explorer vehicles. Yet observers are looking for the next big hit. Development of a new vehicle costs billions. A flop is financially devastating, and the financial effect is magnified if the company has large amounts of outstanding debt.

The balance sheets on the next page provide financial information for the Automotive Division of Ford Motor Company as of December 31, 2011 and 2010. We have chosen to analyze only the Automotive Division rather than the total corporation, which includes Ford's giant financing division. In an actual analysis, you would want to analyze the major divisions individually as well as the combined corporation as a whole.

Instructions

1. Evaluate Ford's liquidity using appropriate ratios, and compare to those of Toyota and to industry averages.
2. Evaluate Ford's solvency using appropriate ratios, and compare to those of Toyota and to industry averages.
3. Comment on Ford's available lines of credit.

FORD MOTOR COMPANY—Automotive Division
Balance Sheets
December 31, 2011 and 2010
(in millions)

Assets	2011	2010
Current assets	$38,147	$34,368
Noncurrent assets	40,639	30,238
Total assets	$78,786	$64,606
Liabilities and Shareholders' Equity		
Current liabilities	$32,825	$34,516
Noncurrent liabilities	39,226	40,388
Total liabilities	72,051	74,904
Total shareholders' equity (deficit)	6,735	(10,298)
Total liabilities and shareholders' equity	$78,786	$64,606
Other Information		
Net income	$ 6,250	$ 4,146
Tax expense*	563	373
Interest expense	817	1,807
Available lines of credit (Automotive Division)	9,000	

*Estimated based on 2010 effective rate.

Solution

1. Ford's liquidity can be measured using the current ratio:

	2011	2010
Current ratio	$\dfrac{\$38,147}{\$32,825} = 1.16{:}1$	$\dfrac{\$34,368}{\$34,516} = 1.00{:}1$

Ford's current ratio improved from 2010 to 2011. Ford's 2011 current ratio exceeds the industry average of 1.00:1 but is somewhat less than Toyota's. These are increasingly common levels for large companies that have reduced the amount of inventory and receivables they hold. As noted earlier, these low current ratios are not necessarily cause for concern, but they do require more careful monitoring. Ford must also make sure to have other short-term financing options available, such as lines of credit.

2. Ford's solvency can be measured with the debt to assets ratio and the times interest earned:

	2011	2010
Debt to assets ratio	$\dfrac{\$72,051}{\$78,786} = 91\%$	$\dfrac{\$74,904}{\$64,606} = 116\%$
Times interest earned	$\dfrac{\$6,250 + \$817 + \$563}{\$817} = 9.4 \text{ times}$	$\dfrac{\$4,146 + \$1,807 + \$373}{\$1,807} = 3.5 \text{ times}$

The debt to assets ratio suggests that Ford relies very heavily on debt financing. The ratio decreased from 2010 to 2011, indicating that the company's solvency improved slightly. In 2010, it exceeded 100%. This is possible because we have calculated the ratio for the Automotive Division only, rather than for the whole company. The debt to assets ratio for the entire company in 2011 is 92%. This is extremely high.

The times interest earned is 9.4 times in 2011 and 3.5 times in 2010. This exceeds the industry average of 3.2 times. It is likely that the company's solvency was a concern to investors and creditors during the recession and was closely monitored. However, as Ford's income rose in 2010 and 2011, its solvency improved.

3. Ford has available lines of credit of $9 billion. These financing sources significantly improve its liquidity and help reduce the concerns of its short-term creditors.

Summary of Learning Objectives

1 **Explain a current liability and identify the major types of current liabilities.** A current liability is a debt that a company can reasonably expect to pay (a) from existing current assets or through the creation of other current liabilities, and (b) within one year or the operating cycle, whichever is longer. The major types of current liabilities are notes payable, accounts payable, sales taxes payable, unearned revenues, and accrued liabilities such as taxes, salaries and wages, and interest payable.

2 **Describe the accounting for notes payable.** When a note payable is interest-bearing, the amount of assets received upon the issuance of the note is generally equal to the face value of the note, and interest expense is accrued over the life of the note. At maturity, the amount paid is equal to the face value of the note plus accrued interest.

3 **Explain the accounting for other current liabilities.** Companies record sales taxes payable at the time the related sales occur. The company serves as a collection agent for the taxing authority. Sales taxes are not an expense to the company. Companies hold employee withholding taxes, and credit them to appropriate liability accounts, until they remit these taxes to the governmental taxing authorities. Unearned revenues are initially recorded in an unearned revenue account. As a company recognizes revenue, a transfer from unearned revenue to revenue occurs. Companies report the current maturities of long-term debt as a current liability in the balance sheet.

4 **Identify the types of bonds.** The following different types of bonds may be issued: secured and unsecured bonds, and convertible and callable bonds.

5 **Prepare the entries for the issuance of bonds and interest expense.** When companies issue bonds, they debit Cash for the cash proceeds and credit Bonds Payable for the face value of the bonds. In addition, they use the accounts Premium on Bonds Payable and Discount on Bonds Payable to show the bond premium and bond discount, respectively. Bond discount and bond premium are amortized over the life of the bond, which increases or decreases interest expense, respectively.

6 **Describe the entries when bonds are redeemed.** When companies redeem bonds at maturity, they credit Cash and debit Bonds Payable for the face value of the bonds. When companies redeem bonds before maturity, they (a) eliminate the carrying value of the bonds at the redemption date, (b) record the cash paid, and (c) recognize the gain or loss on redemption.

7 **Identify the requirements for the financial statement presentation and analysis of liabilities.** Current liabilities appear first on the balance sheet, followed by long-term liabilities. Companies should report the nature and amount of each liability in the balance sheet or in schedules in the notes accompanying the statements. They report inflows and outflows of cash related to the principal portion of long-term debt in the financing section of the statement of cash flows.

The liquidity of a company may be analyzed by computing the current ratio. The long-run solvency of a company may be analyzed by computing the debt to assets ratio and the times interest earned. Other factors to consider are contingent liabilities and lease obligations.

✔ The Navigator

🧰 DECISION TOOLKIT *A SUMMARY*

DECISION CHECKPOINTS	INFO NEEDED FOR DECISION	TOOL TO USE FOR DECISION	HOW TO EVALUATE RESULTS
Can the company obtain short-term financing when necessary?	Available lines of credit, from notes to the financial statements	Compare available lines of credit to current liabilities. Also, evaluate liquidity ratios.	If liquidity ratios are low, then lines of credit should be high to compensate.
Can the company meet its obligations in the long term?	Interest expense and net income before interest and taxes	$\text{Times interest earned} = \dfrac{\text{Net income} + \text{Interest expense} + \text{Tax expense}}{\text{Interest expense}}$	High ratio indicates ability to meet interest payments as scheduled.
Does the company have any contingent liabilities?	Knowledge of events with uncertain negative outcomes	Notes to financial statements and financial statements	If negative outcomes are possible, determine the probability, the amount of loss, and the potential impact on financial statements.
Does the company have significant off-balance-sheet financing, such as unrecorded lease obligations?	Information on unrecorded obligations, such as a schedule of minimum lease payments from the notes to the financial statements	Compare liquidity and solvency ratios with and without unrecorded obligations included	If ratios differ significantly after including unrecorded obligations, these obligations should not be ignored in analysis.

Appendix 10A

Straight-Line Amortization

Apply the straight-line method of amortizing bond discount and bond premium.

AMORTIZING BOND DISCOUNT

To follow the expense recognition principle, companies allocate bond discount to expense in each period in which the bonds are outstanding. The **straight-line method of amortization** allocates the same amount to interest expense in each interest period. The calculation is presented in Illustration 10A-1.

Illustration 10A-1 Formula for straight-line method of bond discount amortization

Bond Discount	÷	Number of Interest Periods	=	Bond Discount Amortization

In the Candlestick Inc. example (page 517), the company sold $100,000, five-year, 10% bonds on January 1, 2014, for $98,000. This resulted in a $2,000 bond discount ($100,000 − $98,000). The bond discount amortization is $400 ($2,000 ÷ 5) for each of the five amortization periods. Candlestick records the first accrual of bond interest and the amortization of bond discount on December 31 as follows.

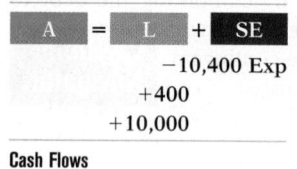

A	=	L	+	SE

−10,400 Exp
+400
+10,000

Cash Flows
no effect

Dec. 31	Interest Expense	10,400	
	Discount on Bonds Payable		400
	Interest Payable		10,000
	(To record accrued bond interest and amortization of bond discount)		

Alternative Terminology The amount in the Discount on Bonds Payable account is often referred to as *Unamortized Discount on Bonds Payable.*

Over the term of the bonds, the balance in Discount on Bonds Payable will decrease annually by the same amount until it has a zero balance at the maturity date of the bonds. Thus, the carrying value of the bonds at maturity will be equal to the face value of the bonds.

Preparing a bond discount amortization schedule, as shown in Illustration 10A-2, is useful to determine interest expense, discount amortization, and the carrying value of the bond. As indicated, the interest expense recorded each period is $10,400. Also note that the carrying value of the bond increases $400 each period until it reaches its face value of $100,000 at the end of period 5.

Illustration 10A-2 Bond discount amortization schedule

	Candlestick Inc.xls				
Home Insert Page Layout Formulas Data Review View					
P18	fx				
A	B	C	D	E	F

	(A) Interest to Be Paid (10% × $100,000)	(B) Interest Expense to Be Recorded (A) + (C)	(C) Discount Amortization ($2,000 ÷ 5)	(D) Unamortized Discount (D) – (C)	(E) Bond Carrying Value ($100,000 – D)
Interest Periods					
Issue date				$2,000	$ 98,000
1	$10,000	$10,400	$ 400	1,600	98,400
2	10,000	10,400	400	1,200	98,800
3	10,000	10,400	400	800	99,200
4	10,000	10,400	400	400	99,600
5	10,000	10,400	400	0	100,000
	$50,000	$52,000	$2,000		

CANDLESTICK, INC.
Bond Discount Amortization Schedule
Straight-Line Method—Annual Interest Payments
$100,000 of 10%, 5-Year Bonds

Column **(A)** remains constant because the face value of the bonds ($100,000) is multiplied by the annual contractual interest rate (10%) each period.

Column **(B)** is computed as the interest paid (Column A) plus the discount amortization (Column C).

Column **(C)** indicates the discount amortization each period.

Column **(D)** decreases each period by the same amount until it reaches zero at maturity.

Column **(E)** increases each period by the amount of discount amortization until it equals the face value at maturity.

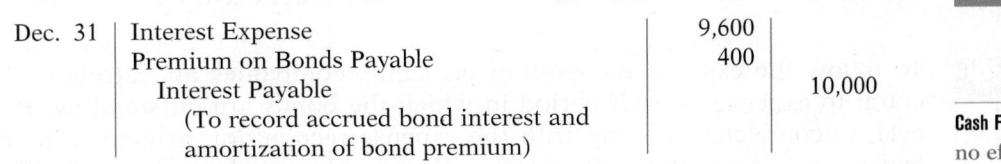

Bond Premium	÷	Number of Interest Periods	=	Bond Premium Amortization

Illustration 10A-3 Formula for straight-line method of bond premium amortization

AMORTIZING BOND PREMIUM

The amortization of bond premium parallels that of bond discount. Illustration 10A-3 presents the formula for determining bond premium amortization under the straight-line method.

Continuing our example, assume Candlestick Inc., sells the bonds described above for $102,000, rather than $98,000 (see page 519). This results in a bond premium of $2,000 ($102,000 − $100,000). The premium amortization for each interest period is $400 ($2,000 ÷ 5). Candlestick records the first accrual of interest on December 31 as follows.

Dec. 31	Interest Expense	9,600	
	Premium on Bonds Payable	400	
	Interest Payable		10,000
	(To record accrued bond interest and amortization of bond premium)		

A	=	L	+	SE
				−9,600 Exp
		−400		
		+10,000		

Cash Flows
no effect

Over the term of the bonds, the balance in Premium on Bonds Payable will decrease annually by the same amount until it has a zero balance at maturity.

A bond premium amortization schedule, as shown in Illustration 10A-4, is useful to determine interest expense, premium amortization, and the carrying value of the bond. As indicated, the interest expense Candlestick records each period is $9,600. Note that the carrying value of the bond decreases $400 each period until it reaches its face value of $100,000 at the end of period 5.

Illustration 10A-4 Bond premium amortization schedule

	Candlestick Inc.xls					
Home Insert Page Layout Formulas Data Review View						
P18	fx					
	A	B	C	D	E	F
1		CANDLESTICK, INC.				
2		Bond Premium Amortization Schedule				
3		Straight-Line Method—Annual Interest Payments				
4		$100,000 of 10%, 5-Year Bonds				
5		(A)	(B)	(C)	(D)	(E)
6		Interest to	Interest Expense	Premium	Unamortized	Bond
7	Interest	Be Paid	to Be Recorded	Amortization	Premium	Carrying Value
8	Periods	(10% × $100,000)	(A) – (C)	($2,000 ÷ 5)	(D) – (C)	($100,000 + D)
9	Issue date				$2,000	$102,000
10	1	$ 10,000	$ 9,600	$ 400	1,600	101,600
11	2	10,000	9,600	400	1,200	101,200
12	3	10,000	9,600	400	800	100,800
13	4	10,000	9,600	400	400	100,400
14	5	10,000	9,600	400	0	100,000
15		$50,000	$48,000	$2,000		
16						
17	Column (A) remains constant because the face value of the bonds ($100,000) is multiplied by the annual contractual interest rate (10%) each period.					
18	Column (B) is computed as the interest paid (Column A) less the premium amortization (Column C).					
19	Column (C) indicates the premium amortization each period.					
20	Column (D) decreases each period by the same amount until it reaches zero at maturity.					
21	Column (E) decreases each period by the amount of premium amortization until it equals the face value at maturity.					

Summary of Learning Objective for Appendix 10A

8 Apply the straight-line method of amortizing bond discount and bond premium. The straight-line method of amortization results in a constant amount of amortization and interest expense per period.

Appendix 10B

Effective-Interest Amortization

LEARNING OBJECTIVE 9

Apply the effective-interest method of amortizing bond discount and bond premium.

To follow the expense recognition principle, companies allocate bond discount to expense in each period in which the bonds are outstanding. However, to completely comply with the expense recognition principle, interest expense as a percentage of carrying value should not change over the life of the bonds.

This percentage, referred to as the effective-interest rate, is established when the bonds are issued and remains constant in each interest period. Unlike the straight-line method, the effective-interest method of amortization accomplishes this result.

Under the effective-interest method, the amortization of bond discount or bond premium results in periodic interest expense equal to a constant percentage of the carrying value of the bonds. The effective-interest method results in **varying amounts** of amortization and interest expense per period but a **constant percentage rate.** In contrast, the straight-line method results in constant amounts of amortization and interest expense per period but a varying percentage rate.

Companies follow three steps under the effective-interest method:

1. Compute the **bond interest expense** by multiplying the carrying value of the bonds at the beginning of the interest period by the effective-interest rate.
2. Compute the **bond interest paid** (or accrued) by multiplying the face value of the bonds by the contractual interest rate.
3. Compute the **amortization amount** by determining the difference between the amounts computed in steps (1) and (2).

Illustration 10B-1 depicts these steps.

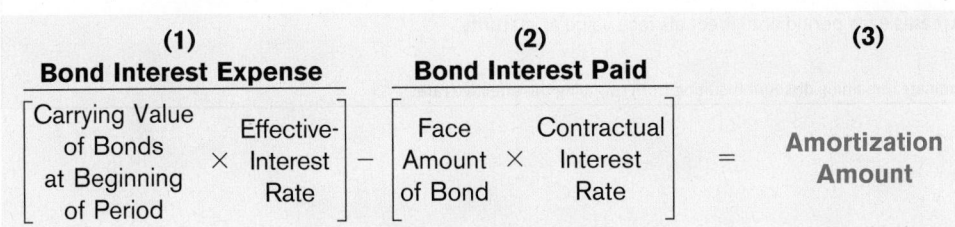

Illustration 10B-1
Computation of amortization using effective-interest method

Both the straight-line and effective-interest methods of amortization result in the same total amount of interest expense over the term of the bonds. Furthermore, interest expense each interest period is generally comparable in amount. However, **when the amounts are materially different, generally accepted accounting principles (GAAP) require use of the effective-interest method.**

AMORTIZING BOND DISCOUNT

In the Candlestick Inc. example (page 517), the company sold $100,000, five-year, 10% bonds on January 1, 2014, for $98,000. This resulted in a $2,000 bond discount ($100,000 − $98,000). This discount results in an effective-interest rate of approximately 10.53%. (The effective-interest rate can be computed using the techniques shown in Appendix D at the end of this book.)

Preparing a bond discount amortization schedule as shown in Illustration 10B-2 (page 534) facilitates the recording of interest expense and the discount amortization. Note that interest expense as a percentage of carrying value remains constant at 10.53%.

Helpful Hint Note that the amount of periodic interest expense increases over the life of the bonds when the effective-interest method is used for bonds issued at a discount. The reason is that a constant percentage is applied to an increasing bond carrying value to compute interest expense. The carrying value is increasing because of the amortization of the discount.

	A	B	C	D	E	F
						Candlestick Inc.xls
	P18		fx			
	A	**B**	**C**	**D**	**E**	**F**
1			**CANDLESTICK, INC.**			
2			**Bond Discount Amortization Schedule**			
3			**Effective-Interest Method—Annual Interest Payments**			
4			**10% Bonds Issued at 10.53%**			
5						
6		**(A)**	**(B)**	**(C)**	**(D)**	**(E)**
7	**Interest**	**Interest to Be Paid**	**Interest Expense to Be Recorded (10.53% × Preceding**	**Discount Amortization**	**Unamortized Discount**	**Bond Carrying Value**
8	**Periods**	**(10% × $100,000)**	**Bond Carrying Value)**	**(B) – (A)**	**(D) – (C)**	**($100,000 – D)**
9	Issue date				$2,000	$98,000
10	1	$10,000	$ 10,319 (10.53% × $98,000)	$ 319	1,681	98,319
11	2	10,000	10,353 (10.53% × $98,319)	353	1,328	98,672
12	3	10,000	10,390 (10.53% × $98,672)	390	938	99,062
13	4	10,000	10,431 (10.53% × $99,062)	431	507	99,493
14	5	10,000	10,507* (10.53% × $99,493)	507*	–0–	100,000
15		$50,000	$52,000	$2,000		
16						
17	Column **(A)** remains constant because the face value of the bonds ($100,000) is multiplied by the annual contractual interest rate (10%) each period.					
18	Column **(B)** is computed as the preceding bond carrying value times the annual effective-interest rate (10.53%).					
19	Column **(C)** indicates the discount amortization each period.					
20	Column **(D)** decreases each period until it reaches zero at maturity.					
21	Column **(E)** increases each period until it equals face value at maturity.					
22						
23	*Rounded to eliminate remaining discount resulting from rounding the effective rate.					

Illustration 10B-2 Bond discount amortization schedule

For the first interest period, the computations of bond interest expense and the bond discount amortization are as follows.

Illustration 10B-3
Computation of bond discount amortization

Bond interest expense ($98,000 × 10.53%)	$10,319
Bond interest paid ($100,000 × 10%)	10,000
Bond discount amortization	**$ 319**

As a result, Candlestick Inc. records the accrual of interest and amortization of bond discount on December 31 as follows.

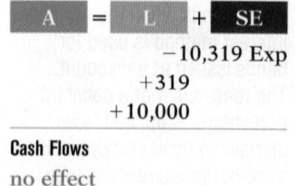

A = L + SE
−10,319 Exp
+319
+10,000

Cash Flows
no effect

Dec. 31	Interest Expense	10,319	
	Discount on Bonds Payable		319
	Interest Payable		10,000
	(To record accrued interest and amortization of bond discount)		

For the second interest period, bond interest expense will be $10,353 ($98,319 × 10.53%), and the discount amortization will be $353. At December 31, Candlestick makes the following adjusting entry.

Dec. 31	Interest Expense	10,353	
	Discount on Bonds Payable		353
	Interest Payable		10,000
	(To record accrued interest and		
	amortization of bond discount)		

A	=	L	+	SE

−10,353 Exp
+353
+10,000

Cash Flows
no effect

AMORTIZING BOND PREMIUM

Continuing our example, assume Candlestick Inc. sells the bonds described above for $102,000 rather than $98,000 (see page 519). This would result in a bond premium of $2,000 ($102,000 − $100,000). This premium results in an effective-interest rate of approximately 9.48%. (The effective-interest rate can be solved for using the techniques shown in Appendix D at the end of this book.) Illustration 10B-4 shows the bond premium amortization schedule.

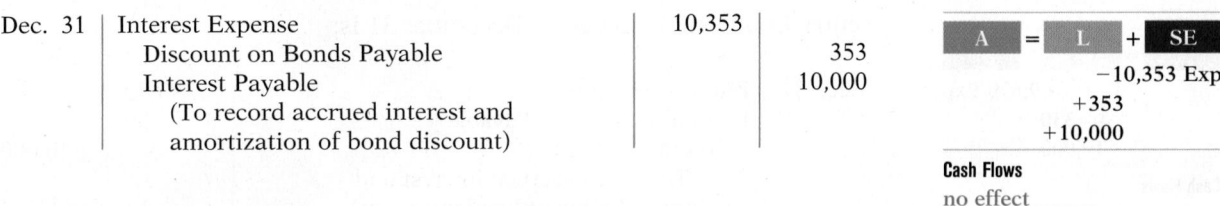

CANDLESTICK, INC.
Bond Premium Amortization Schedule
Effective-Interest Method—Annual Interest Payments
10% Bonds Issued at 9.48%

Interest Periods	(A) Interest to Be Paid (10% × $100,000)	(B) Interest Expense to Be Recorded (9.48% × Preceding Bond Carrying Value)		(C) Premium Amortization (A) − (B)	(D) Unamortized Premium (D) − (C)	(E) Bond Carrying Value ($100,000 + D)
Issue date					$2,000	$102,000
1	$10,000	$ 9,670	(9.48% × $102,000)	$ 330	1,670	101,670
2	10,000	9,638	(9.48% × $101,670)	362	1,308	101,308
3	10,000	9,604	(9.48% × $101,308)	396	912	100,912
4	10,000	9,566	(9.48% × $100,912)	434	478	100,478
5	10,000	9,522*	(9.48% × $100,478)	478*	–0–	100,000
	$50,000	$48,000		$2,000		

Column **(A)** remains constant because the face value of the bonds ($100,000) is multiplied by the contractual interest rate (10%) each period.

Column **(B)** is computed as the carrying value of the bonds times the annual effective-interest rate (9.48%).

Column **(C)** indicates the premium amortization each period.

Column **(D)** decreases each period until it reaches zero at maturity.

Column **(E)** decreases each period until it equals face value at maturity.

*Rounded to eliminate remaining discount resulting from rounding the effective rate.

Illustration 10B-4 Bond premium amortization schedule

For the first interest period, the computations of bond interest expense and the bond premium amortization are:

Bond interest paid ($100,000 × 10%)	$10,000
Bond interest expense ($102,000 × 9.48%)	9,670
Bond premium amortization	$ 330

Illustration 10B-5
Computation of bond premium amortization

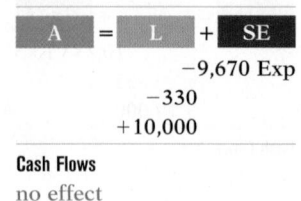

A = L + SE
−9,670 Exp
−330
+10,000

Cash Flows
no effect

The entry Candlestick makes on December 31 is:

Dec. 31	Interest Expense	9,670	
	Premium on Bonds Payable	330	
	Interest Payable		10,000
	(To record accrued interest and		
	amortization of bond premium)		

For the second interest period, interest expense will be $9,638, and the premium amortization will be $362. Note that the amount of periodic interest expense decreases over the life of the bond when companies apply the effective-interest method to bonds issued at a premium. The reason is that a constant percentage is applied to a decreasing bond carrying value to compute interest expense. The carrying value is decreasing because of the amortization of the premium.

Summary of Learning Objective for Appendix 10B

9 **Apply the effective-interest method of amortizing bond discount and bond premium.** The effective-interest method results in varying amounts of amortization and interest expense per period but a constant per- centage rate of interest. When the difference between the straight-line and effective-interest method is material, GAAP requires use of the effective-interest method.

Appendix 10C

Accounting for Long-Term Notes Payable

LEARNING OBJECTIVE 10
Describe the accounting for long-term notes payable.

Helpful Hint Computer spreadsheet programs can create a schedule of installment loan payments. This allows you to put in the data for your own mortgage loan and get an illustration that really hits home.

The use of notes payable in long-term debt financing is quite common. Long-term notes payable are similar to short-term interest-bearing notes payable except that the terms of the notes exceed one year. In periods of unstable interest rates, lenders may tie the interest rate on long-term notes to changes in the market rate for comparable loans. Examples are the 8.03% adjustable rate notes issued by General Motors (GM) and the floating-rate notes issued by American Express Company.

A long-term note may be secured by a document called a **mortgage** that pledges title to specific assets as security for a loan. Individuals widely use **mortgage notes payable** to purchase homes, as do many small and some large companies to acquire plant assets. For example, at one time approximately 18% of McDonald's long-term debt related to mortgage notes on land, buildings, and improvements.

Like other long-term notes payable, the mortgage loan terms may stipulate either a fixed or an adjustable interest rate. Typically, the terms require the borrower to make equal installment payments over the term of the loan. Each payment consists of (1) interest on the unpaid balance of the loan and (2) a reduction of loan principal. While the total amount paid remains constant, the interest decreases each period and the portion applied to the loan principal increases.

Companies initially record mortgage notes payable at face value, and subsequently make entries for each installment payment. To illustrate, assume that Porter Technology Inc. issues a $500,000, 12%, 20-year mortgage note on December 31, 2014, to obtain needed financing for the construction of a new research laboratory. The terms provide for semiannual installment payments of $33,231 (not including real estate taxes and insurance). The installment payment schedule for the first two years is as follows.

Illustration 10C-1 Mortgage installment payment schedule

Semiannual Interest Period	(A) Cash Payment	(B) Interest Expense (D) × 6%	(C) Reduction of Principal (A) − (B)	(D) Principal Balance (D) − (C)
Issue date				$500,000
1	$33,231	$30,000	$3,231	496,769
2	33,231	29,806	3,425	493,344
3	33,231	29,601	3,630	489,714
4	33,231	29,383	3,848	485,866

Porter Technology records the mortgage loan on December 31, 2014, as follows.

Dec. 31	Cash	500,000	
	Mortgage Payable		500,000
	(To record mortgage loan)		

A = L + SE
+500,000
+500,000

Cash Flows
+500,000

On June 30, 2015, Porter records the first installment payment as follows.

June 30	Interest Expense	30,000	
	Mortgage Payable	3,231	
	Cash		33,231
	(To record semiannual payment on mortgage)		

A = L + SE
−30,000 Exp
−3,231
−33,231

Cash Flows
−33,231

In the balance sheet, the company reports the reduction in principal for the next year as a current liability, and classifies the remaining unpaid principal balance as a long-term liability. At December 31, 2015 (the end of semiannual period 2), the total liability is $493,344, of which $7,478 ($3,630 + $3,848) is current and $485,866 ($493,344 − $7,478) is long-term.

Summary of Learning Objective for Appendix 10C

10 Describe the accounting for long-term notes payable. Each payment consists of (1) interest on the unpaid balance of the loan, and (2) a reduction of loan principal. The interest decreases each period, while the portion applied to the loan principal increases each period.

Glossary

Bond certificate *(p. 513)* A legal document that indicates the name of the issuer, the face value of the bonds, and other data such as the contractual interest rate and the maturity date of the bonds.

Bonds *(p. 512)* A form of interest-bearing notes payable issued by corporations, universities, and governmental entities.

Callable bonds *(p. 512)* Bonds that the issuing company can redeem (buy back) at a stated dollar amount prior to maturity.

Capital lease *(p. 526)* A contractual agreement allowing one party (the lessee) to use the assets of another party (the lessor); accounted for like a debt-financed purchase by the lessee.

Contingencies *(p. 526)* Events with uncertain outcomes that may represent potential liabilities.

Contractual (stated) interest rate *(p. 513)* Rate used to determine the amount of interest the borrower pays and the investor receives.

Convertible bonds *(p. 512)* Bonds that can be converted into common stock at the bondholder's option.

Current liability *(p. 506)* A debt that a company reasonably expects to pay (1) from existing current assets or through the creation of other current liabilities, and (2) within one year or the operating cycle, whichever is longer.

Discount (on a bond) *(p. 516)* The difference between the face value of a bond and its selling price when a bond is sold for less than its face value.

Effective-interest method of amortization *(p. 533)* A method of amortizing bond discount or bond premium that results in periodic interest expense equal to a constant percentage of the carrying value of the bonds.

Effective-interest rate *(p. 533)* Rate established when bonds are issued that maintains a constant value for interest expense as a percentage of bond carrying value in each interest period.

Face value *(p. 513)* Amount of principal due at the maturity date of the bond.

Long-term liabilities *(p. 512)* Obligations that a company expects to pay more than one year in the future.

Market interest rate *(p. 514)* The rate investors demand for loaning funds to the corporation.

Maturity date *(p. 513)* The date on which the final payment on a bond is due from the bond issuer to the investor.

Mortgage note payable *(p. 536)* A long-term note secured by a mortgage that pledges title to specific assets as security for the loan.

Notes payable *(p. 507)* An obligation in the form of a written note.

Off-balance-sheet financing *(p. 525)* The intentional effort by a company to structure its financing arrangements so as to avoid showing liabilities on its balance sheet.

Operating lease *(p. 526)* A contractual agreement allowing one party (the lessee) to use the asset of another party (the lessor); accounted for as a rental.

Premium (on a bond) *(p. 517)* The difference between the selling price and the face value of a bond when a bond is sold for more than its face value.

Present value *(p. 514)* The value today of an amount to be received at some date in the future after taking into account current interest rates.

Secured bonds *(p. 512)* Bonds that have specific assets of the issuer pledged as collateral.

Straight-line method of amortization *(p. 530)* A method of amortizing bond discount or bond premium that allocates the same amount to interest expense in each interest period.

Times interest earned *(p. 524)* A measure of a company's solvency, calculated by dividing income before interest expense and taxes by interest expense.

Time value of money *(p. 513)* The relationship between time and money. A dollar received today is worth more than a dollar promised at some time in the future.

Unsecured bonds *(p. 512)* Bonds issued against the general credit of the borrower.

Comprehensive Do it!

Snyder Software Inc. successfully developed a new spreadsheet program. However, to produce and market the program, the company needed additional financing. On January 1, 2013, Snyder borrowed money as follows.

1. Snyder issued $500,000, 11%, 10-year bonds. The bonds sold at face value and pay interest on January 1.

2. Snyder issued $1.0 million, 10%, 10-year bonds for $886,996. Interest is payable on January 1. Snyder uses the straight-line method of amortization.

Instructions

(a) For the 11% bonds, prepare journal entries for the following items.
 (1) The issuance of the bonds on January 1, 2013.
 (2) Accrue interest expense on December 31, 2013.
 (3) The payment of interest on January 1, 2014.

(b) For the 10-year, 10% bonds:
 (1) Journalize the issuance of the bonds on January 1, 2013.
 (2) Prepare the entry for the redemption of the bonds at 101 on January 1, 2016, after paying the interest due on this date. The carrying value of the bonds at the redemption date was $920,897.

Solution to Comprehensive Do it!

Action Plan

- Record the discount on bonds issued as a contra liability account.
- Compute the loss on bond redemption as the excess of the cash paid over the carrying value of the redeemed bonds.

(a)	(1) 2013			
	Jan. 1	Cash	500,000	
		Bonds Payable		500,000
		(To record issue of 11%, 10-year bonds at face value)		
	(2) 2013			
	Dec. 31	Interest Expense	55,000	
		Interest Payable		55,000
		(To record accrual of bond interest)		
	(3) 2014			
	Jan. 1	Interest Payable	55,000	
		Cash		55,000
		(To record payment of accrued interest)		
(b)	(1) 2013			
	Jan. 1	Cash	886,996	
		Discount on Bonds Payable	113,004	
		Bonds Payable		1,000,000
		(To record issuance of bonds at a discount)		
	(2) 2016			
	Jan. 1	Bonds Payable	1,000,000	
		Loss on Bond Redemption	89,103*	
		Discount on Bonds Payable		79,103
		Cash		1,010,000
		(To record redemption of bonds at 101)		
		*($1,010,000 − $920,897)		

The Navigator

Self-Test, Brief Exercises, Exercises, Problem Set A, and many more resources are available for practice in WileyPLUS.

Note: All Questions, Exercises, and Problems marked with an asterisk relate to material in the appendices to the chapter.

Self-Test Questions

Answers are on page 564.

(LO 1) **1.** The time period for classifying a liability as current is one year or the operating cycle, whichever is:
(a) longer. (c) probable.
(b) shorter. (d) possible.

(LO 1) **2.** To be classified as a current liability, a debt must be expected to be paid:
(a) out of existing current assets.
(b) by creating other current liabilities.
(c) within 2 years.
(d) Either (a) or (b).

(LO 2) **3.** Ottman Company borrows $88,500 on September 1, 2014, from Farley State Bank by signing an $88,500,

12%, one-year note. What is the accrued interest at December 31, 2014?
(a) $2,655. (c) $4,425.
(b) $3,540. (d) $10,620.

(LO 2) **4.** JD Company borrowed $70,000 on December 1 on a 6-month, 12% note. At December 31:
(a) neither the note payable nor the interest payable is a current liability.
(b) the note payable is a current liability but the interest payable is not.
(c) the interest payable is a current liability but the note payable is not.
(d) both the note payable and the interest payable are current liabilities.

(LO 3) **5.** Alexis Company has total proceeds from sales of $4,515. If the proceeds include sales taxes of 5%, what is the amount to be credited to Sales Revenue?
(a) $4,000.
(b) $4,300.
(c) $4,289.25.
(d) The correct answer is not given.

(LO 3) **6.** When recording payroll:
(a) gross earnings are recorded as salaries and wages payable.
(b) net pay is recorded as salaries and wages expense.
(c) payroll deductions are recorded as liabilities.
(d) More than one of the above.

(LO 3) **7.** No Fault Insurance Company collected a premium of $18,000 for a 1-year insurance policy on April 1. What amount should No Fault report as a current liability for Unearned Insurance Premiums at December 31?
(a) $0.
(b) $4,500.
(c) $13,500.
(d) $18,000.

(LO 4) **8.** What term is used for bonds that have specific assets pledged as collateral?
(a) Callable bonds.
(b) Convertible bonds.
(c) Secured bonds.
(d) Discount bonds.

(LO 4) **9.** The market interest rate:
(a) is the contractual interest rate used to determine the amount of cash interest paid by the borrower.
(b) is listed in the bond indenture.
(c) is the rate investors demand for loaning funds.
(d) More than one of the above is true.

(LO 5) **10.** Laurel Inc. issues 10-year bonds with a maturity value of $200,000. If the bonds are issued at a premium, this indicates that:
(a) the contractual interest rate exceeds the market interest rate.
(b) the market interest rate exceeds the contractual interest rate.
(c) the contractual interest rate and the market interest rate are the same.
(d) no relationship exists between the two rates.

(LO 5) **11.** On January 1, 2014, Kelly Corp. issues $200,000, 5-year, 7% bonds at face value. The entry to record the issuance of the bonds would include a:
(a) debit to Cash for $14,000.
(b) debit to Bonds Payable for $200,000.
(c) credit to Bonds Payable for $200,000.
(d) credit to Interest Expense of $14,000.

(LO 5) **12.** Prescher Corporation issued bonds that pay interest every July 1 and January 1. The entry to accrue bond interest at December 31 includes a:
(a) debit to Interest Payable.
(b) credit to Cash.
(c) credit to Interest Expense.
(d) credit to Interest Payable.

(LO 6) **13.** Goethe Corporation redeems its $100,000 face value bonds at 105 on January 1, following the payment of interest. The carrying value of the bonds at the redemption date is $103,745. The entry to record the redemption will include a:

(a) credit of $3,745 to Loss on Bond Redemption.
(b) debit of $3,745 to Premium on Bonds Payable.
(c) credit of $1,255 to Gain on Bond Redemption.
(d) debit of $5,000 to Premium on Bonds Payable.

14. In a recent year, Derek Corporation had net (LO 7) income of $150,000, interest expense of $30,000, and income tax expense of $20,000. What was Derek Corporation's times interest earned for the year?
(a) 5.00.
(b) 4.00.
(c) 6.67.
(d) 7.50.

15. Which of the following is **not** a measure of (LO 7) liquidity?
(a) Debt to assets ratio.
(b) Working capital.
(c) Current ratio.
(d) Current cash debt coverage.

*16. On January 1, Xiang Corporation issues $500,000, (LO 8) 5-year, 12% bonds at 96 with interest payable on January 1. The entry on December 31 to record accrued bond interest and the amortization of bond discount using the straight-line method will include a:
(a) debit to Interest Expense, $57,600.
(b) debit to Interest Expense, $60,000.
(c) credit to Discount on Bonds Payable, $4,000.
(d) credit to Discount on Bonds Payable, $2,000.

*17. For the bonds issued in Question 16, what is the car- (LO 8) rying value of the bonds at the end of the third interest period?
(a) $492,000.
(b) $488,000.
(c) $472,000.
(d) $464,000.

*18. On January 1, Holly Ester Inc. issued $1,000,000, (LO 9) 10-year, 9% bonds for $938,554. The market rate of interest for these bonds is 10%. Interest is payable annually on December 31. Holly Ester uses the effective-interest method of amortizing bond discount. At the end of the first year, Holly Ester should report unamortized bond discount of:
(a) $54,900.
(b) $57,591.
(c) $51,610.
(d) $51,000.

*19. On January 1, Nicholas Corporation issued (LO 9) $1,000,000, 14%, 5-year bonds with interest payable on December 31. The bonds sold for $1,072,096. The market rate of interest for these bonds was 12%. On the first interest date, using the effective-interest method, the debit entry to Interest Expense is for:
(a) $120,000.
(b) $125,581.
(c) $128,652.
(d) $140,000.

*20. Sampson Corp. purchased a piece of equipment by (LO 10) issuing a $20,000, 6% installment note payable. Quarterly payments on the note are $1,165. What will be the reduction in the principal portion of the note payable that results from the first payment?
(a) $1,165.
(b) $300.
(c) $865.
(d) $1,200.

Go to the book's companion website, **www.wiley.com/college/kimmel**, to access additional Self-Test Questions.

Questions

1. Peggy Jantzen believes a current liability is a debt that can be expected to be paid in one year. Is Peggy correct? Explain.

2. Trayer Company obtains $20,000 in cash by signing a 9%, 6-month, $20,000 note payable to First Bank on July 1. Trayer's fiscal year ends on September 30. What information should be reported for the note payable in the annual financial statements?

3. (a) Your roommate says, "Sales taxes are reported as an expense in the income statement." Do you agree? Explain.
   (b) Amanda's Cafe has cash proceeds from sales of $8,550. This amount includes $550 of sales taxes. Give the entry to record the proceeds.

4. Dakota University sold 9,000 season football tickets at $100 each for its five-game home schedule. What entries should be made (a) when the tickets are sold and (b) after each game?

5. Identify three taxes commonly withheld by the employer from an employee's gross pay.

6. (a) Identify three taxes commonly paid by employers on employees' salaries and wages.
   (b) Where in the financial statements does the employer report taxes withheld from employees' pay?

7. Identify the liabilities classified by Tootsie Roll as current.

8. (a) What are long-term liabilities? Give two examples.
   (b) What is a bond?

9. Contrast these types of bonds:
   (a) Secured and unsecured.
   (b) Convertible and callable.

10. Explain each of these important terms in issuing bonds:
    (a) Face value.
    (b) Contractual interest rate.
    (c) Bond certificate.

11. (a) What is a convertible bond?
    (b) Discuss the advantages of a convertible bond from the standpoint of the bondholders and of the issuing corporation.

12. Describe the two major obligations incurred by a company when bonds are issued.

13. Assume that Ziegler Inc. sold bonds with a face value of $100,000 for $104,000. Was the market interest rate equal to, less than, or greater than the bonds' contractual interest rate? Explain.

14. Jack and Lance are discussing how the market price of a bond is determined. Jack believes that the market price of a bond is solely a function of the amount of the principal payment at the end of the term of a bond. Is he right? Discuss.

15. If a 6%, 10-year, $800,000 bond is issued at face value and interest is paid annually, what is the amount of the interest payment at the end of the first period?

16. If the Bonds Payable account has a balance of $700,000 and the Discount on Bonds Payable account has a balance of $36,000, what is the carrying value of the bonds?

17. Which accounts are debited and which are credited if a bond issue originally sold at a premium is redeemed before maturity at 97 immediately following the payment of interest?

18. Natalie Pendlay, the chief financial officer of Mullins Inc., is considering the options available to her for financing the company's new plant. Short-term interest rates right now are 6%, and long-term rates are 8%. The company's current ratio is 2.2:1. If she finances the new plant with short-term debt, the current ratio will fall to 1.5:1. Briefly discuss the issues that Natalie should consider.

19. (a) In general, what are the requirements for the financial statement presentation of long-term liabilities?
    (b) What ratios may be computed to evaluate a company's liquidity and solvency?

20. Samuel Engels says that liquidity and solvency are the same thing. Is he correct? If not, how do they differ?

21. The management of Hinrichs Corporation is concerned because survey data suggest that many potential customers do not buy vehicles due to quality concerns. It is considering taking the bold step of increasing the length of its warranty from the industry standard of 3 years up to an unprecedented 10 years in an effort to increase confidence in its quality. Discuss the business as well as accounting implications of this move.

22. Matt Higgins needs a few new trucks for his business. He is considering buying the trucks but is concerned that the additional debt he will need to borrow will make his liquidity and solvency ratios look bad. What options does he have other than purchasing the trucks, and how will these options affect his financial statements?

23. Norman Corporation has a current ratio of 1.1. Tim has always been told that a corporation's current ratio should exceed 2.0. The company maintains that its ratio is low because it has a minimal amount of inventory on hand so as to reduce operating costs. Norman also has significant available lines of credit. Is Tim still correct? What do some companies do to compensate for having fewer liquid assets?

24. What are the implications for analysis if a company has significant operating leases?

25. What criteria must be met before a contingency must be recorded as a liability? How should the contingency be disclosed if the criteria are not met?

*26. ◖▬▬▬◗ Explain the straight-line method of amortizing discount and premium on bonds payable.

*27. Knobler Corporation issues $200,000 of 6%, 5-year bonds on January 1, 2014, at 103. Assuming that the straight-line method is used to amortize the premium, what is the total amount of interest expense for 2014?

*28. Glenda Hope is discussing the advantages of the effective-interest method of bond amortization with her accounting staff. What do you think Glenda is saying?

*29. Whitson Corporation issues $400,000 of 9%, 5-year bonds on January 1, 2014, at 104. If Whitson uses the effective-interest method in amortizing the premium, will the annual interest expense increase or decrease over the life of the bonds? Explain.

*30. Your friend just received a car loan. It is a 7-year installment note. He does not understand the mechanics of how the loan works. Explain the important aspects of the installment note.

*31. Roy Toth, a friend of yours, has recently purchased a home for $125,000, paying $25,000 down and the remainder financed by a 6.5%, 20-year mortgage, payable at $745.57 per month. At the end of the first month, Roy receives a statement from the bank indicating that only $203.90 of principal was paid during the month. At this rate, he calculates that it will take over 40 years to pay off the mortgage. Is he right? Discuss.

Brief Exercises

Identify whether obligations are current liabilities.
(LO 1), C

BE10-1 Linton Company has these obligations at December 31: (a) a note payable for $100,000 due in 2 years, (b) a 10-year mortgage payable of $200,000 payable in ten $20,000 annual payments, (c) interest payable of $15,000 on the mortgage, and (d) accounts payable of $60,000. For each obligation, indicate whether it should be classified as a current liability.

Prepare entries for an interest-bearing note payable.
(LO 2), AP

BE10-2 Graves Company borrows $90,000 on July 1 from the bank by signing a $90,000, 7%, 1-year note payable. Prepare the journal entries to record (a) the proceeds of the note and (b) accrued interest at December 31, assuming adjusting entries are made only at the end of the year.

Compute and record sales taxes payable.
(LO 3), AP

BE10-3 Bluestem Supply does not segregate sales and sales taxes at the time of sale. The register total for March 16 is $10,388. All sales are subject to a 6% sales tax. Compute sales taxes payable and make the entry to record sales taxes payable and sales.

Prepare entries for unearned revenues.
(LO 3), AP

BE10-4 Washburn University sells 3,500 season basketball tickets at $80 each for its 10-game home schedule. Give the entry to record (a) the sale of the season tickets and (b) the revenue recognized after playing the first home game.

Compute gross earnings and net pay.
(LO 3), AP

BE10-5 Susan Braun's regular hourly wage rate is $16, and she receives an hourly rate of $24 for work in excess of 40 hours. During a January pay period, Susan works 47 hours. Susan's federal income tax withholding is $95, and she has no voluntary deductions. Compute Susan Braun's gross earnings and net pay for the pay period. Assume that the FICA tax rate is 7.65%.

Record a payroll and the payment of wages.
(LO 3), AP

BE10-6 Data for Susan Braun are presented in BE10-5. Prepare the employer's journal entries to record (a) Susan's pay for the period and (b) the payment of Susan's wages. Use January 15 for the end of the pay period and the payment date.

Prepare entries for payroll taxes.
(LO 3), AP

BE10-7 Data for Susan Braun are presented in BE10-5. Prepare the employer's journal entry to record payroll taxes for the period. Ignore unemployment taxes.

Prepare entries for issuance of bonds.
(LO 5), AP

BE10-8 Saddle Inc. issues $300,000, 10-year, 8% bonds at 98. Prepare the journal entry to record the sale of these bonds on March 1, 2014.

Prepare entries for issuance of bonds.
(LO 5), AP

BE10-9 Range Company issues $400,000, 20-year, 7% bonds at 101. Prepare the journal entry to record the sale of these bonds on June 1, 2014.

Prepare journal entries for bonds issued at face value.
(LO 5), AP

BE10-10 Rooney Corporation issued 3,000 7%, 5-year, $1,000 bonds dated January 1, 2014, at face value. Interest is paid each January 1.
(a) Prepare the journal entry to record the sale of these bonds on January 1, 2014.
(b) Prepare the adjusting journal entry on December 31, 2014, to record interest expense.
(c) Prepare the journal entry on January 1, 2015, to record interest paid.

BE10-11 The balance sheet for Fogelberg Company reports the following information on July 1, 2014.

FOGELBERG COMPANY
Balance Sheet (partial)

Long-term liabilities		
Bonds payable	$2,000,000	
Less: Discount on bonds payable	45,000	$1,955,000

Fogelberg decides to redeem these bonds at 102 after paying annual interest. Prepare the journal entry to record the redemption on July 1, 2014.

BE10-12 Presented here are long-term liability items for Evenson Inc. at December 31, 2014. Prepare the long-term liabilities section of the balance sheet for Evenson Inc.

Bonds payable (due 2018)	$700,000
Notes payable (due 2016)	80,000
Discount on bonds payable	28,000

BE10-13 Presented here are liability items for Desmond Inc. at December 31, 2014. Prepare the liabilities section of Desmond's balance sheet.

Accounts payable	$157,000	FICA taxes payable	$ 7,800
Notes payable	20,000	Interest payable	40,000
(due May 1, 2015)		Notes payable (due 2016)	80,000
Bonds payable (due 2018)	900,000	Income taxes payable	3,500
Unearned		Sales taxes payable	1,700
rent revenue	240,000		
Discount on bonds payable	41,000		

BE10-14 Suppose the 2014 adidas financial statements contain the following selected data (in millions).

Current assets	$4,485	Interest expense	$169
Total assets	8,875	Income taxes	113
Current liabilities	2,836	Net income	245
Total liabilities	5,099		
Cash	775		

Compute the following values and provide a brief interpretation of each.
(a) Working capital.   (c) Debt to assets ratio.
(b) Current ratio.   (d) Times interest earned.

BE10-15 Suppose the Canadian National Railway Company's (CN) total assets in a recent year were $24,004 million and its total liabilities were $14,180 million. That year, CN reported operating lease commitments for its locomotives, freight cars, and equipment totaling $740 million. If these assets had been recorded as capital leases, assume that assets and liabilities would have risen by approximately $740 million.

(a) Calculate CN's debt to assets ratio, first using the figures reported, and then after increasing assets and liabilities for the unrecorded operating leases.
(b) Discuss the potential effect of these operating leases on your assessment of CN's solvency.

*BE10-16 Verlin Company issues $2 million, 10-year, 7% bonds at 99, with interest payable on December 31. The straight-line method is used to amortize bond discount.

(a) Prepare the journal entry to record the sale of these bonds on January 1, 2014.
(b) Prepare the journal entry to record interest expense and bond discount amortization on December 31, 2014, assuming no previous accrual of interest.

*BE10-17 Oxford Inc. issues $4 million, 5-year, 8% bonds at 102, with interest payable on January 1. The straight-line method is used to amortize bond premium.

(a) Prepare the journal entry to record the sale of these bonds on January 1, 2014.
(b) Prepare the journal entry to record interest expense and bond premium amortization on December 31, 2014, assuming no previous accrual of interest.

Use effective-interest method of bond amortization.

(LO 9), **AP**

*BE10-18 Presented below is the partial bond discount amortization schedule for Pape Corp., which uses the effective-interest method of amortization.

Interest Periods	Interest to Be Paid	Interest Expense to Be Recorded	Discount Amortization	Unamortized Discount	Bond Carrying Value
Issue date				$38,609	$961,391
1	$45,000	$48,070	$3,070	35,539	964,461
2	45,000	48,223	3,223	32,316	967,684

Instructions
(a) Prepare the journal entry to record the payment of interest and the discount amortization at the end of period 1.
(b) ▰▰▰▶Explain why interest expense is greater than interest paid.
(c) ▰▰▰▶Explain why interest expense will increase each period.

Prepare entries for long-term notes payable.

(LO 10), **AP**

BE10-19 Leihsing Inc. issues a $600,000, 10%, 10-year mortgage note on December 31, 2013, to obtain financing for a new building. The terms provide for semiannual installment payments of $48,145. Prepare the entry to record the mortgage loan on December 31, 2013, and the first installment payment.

Do it! Review

Answer questions about current liabilities.

(LO 2, 3), **C**

Do it! 10-1 You and several classmates are studying for the next accounting examination. They ask you to answer the following questions:
1. If cash is borrowed on a $60,000, 9-month, 10% note on August 1, how much interest expense would be incurred by December 31?
2. The cash register total including sales taxes is $42,000, and the sales tax rate is 5%. What is the sales taxes payable?
3. If $42,000 is collected in advance on November 1 for 6-month magazine subscriptions, what amount of subscription revenue should be recognized on December 31?

Prepare entries for payroll and payroll taxes.

(LO 3), **AP**

Do it! 10-2 During the month of February, Morrisey Corporation's employees earned wages of $74,000. Withholdings related to these wages were $5,661 for Social Security (FICA), $7,100 for federal income tax, and $1,900 for state income tax. Costs incurred for unemployment taxes were $110 for federal and $160 for state.

Prepare the February 28 journal entries for (a) salaries and wages expense and salaries and wages payable assuming that all February wages will be paid in March and (b) the company's payroll tax expense.

Evaluate statements about bonds.

(LO 4), **C**

Do it! 10-3 State whether each of the following statements is true or false.
_____1. Convertible bonds are also known as callable bonds.
_____2. The market rate is the rate investors demand for loaning funds.
_____3. Semiannual interest on bonds is equal to the face value times the stated rate times 6/12.
_____4. The present value of a bond is the value at which it should sell in the market.

Prepare journal entry for bond issuance and show balance sheet presentation.

(LO 5), **AP**

Do it! 10-4 Dilley Corporation issues $300,000 of bonds for $315,000. (a) Prepare the journal entry to record the issuance of the bonds, and (b) show how the bonds would be reported on the balance sheet at the date of issuance.

Prepare entry for bond redemption.

(LO 6), **AP**

Do it! 10-5 Loveland Corporation issued $400,000 of 10-year bonds at a discount. Prior to maturity, when the carrying value of the bonds was $388,000, the company redeemed the bonds at 99. Prepare the entry to record the redemption of the bonds.

Exercises

E10-1 Jenny Kane and Cindy Travis borrowed $15,000 on a 7-month, 8% note from Golden State Bank to open their business, KT's Coffee House. The money was borrowed on June 1, 2014, and the note matures January 1, 2015.

Prepare entries for interest-bearing notes.
(LO 2), **AP**

Instructions
(a) Prepare the entry to record the receipt of the funds from the loan.
(b) Prepare the entry to accrue the interest on June 30.
(c) Assuming adjusting entries are made at the end of each month, determine the balance in the interest payable account at December 31, 2014.
(d) Prepare the entry required on January 1, 2015, when the loan is paid back.

E10-2 On May 15, Criqui Outback Clothiers borrowed some money on a 4-month note to provide cash during the slow season of the year. The interest rate on the note was 8%. At the time the note was due, the amount of interest owed was $480.

Prepare entries for interest-bearing notes.
(LO 2), **AP**

Instructions
(a) Determine the amount borrowed by Criqui.
(b) Assume the amount borrowed was $18,500. What was the interest rate if the amount of interest owed was $555?
(c) Prepare the entry for the initial borrowing and the repayment for the facts in part (a).

E10-3 On June 1, Fancher Company Ltd. borrows $60,000 from First Bank on a 6-month, $60,000, 8% note. The note matures on December 1.

Prepare entries for interest-bearing notes.
(LO 2), **AP**

Instructions
(a) Prepare the entry on June 1.
(b) Prepare the adjusting entry on June 30.
(c) Prepare the entry at maturity (December 1), assuming monthly adjusting entries have been made through November 30.
(d) What was the total financing cost (interest expense)?

E10-4 In providing accounting services to small businesses, you encounter the following situations pertaining to cash sales.

Journalize sales and related taxes.
(LO 3), **AP**

1. Furcal Company enters sales and sales taxes separately on its cash register. On April 10, the register totals are sales $22,000 and sales taxes $1,100.
2. Crystal Company does not segregate sales and sales taxes. Its register total for April 15 is $13,780, which includes a 6% sales tax.

Instructions
Prepare the entries to record the sales transactions and related taxes for (a) Furcal Company and (b) Crystal Company.

E10-5 During the month of March, Olinger Company's employees earned wages of $64,000. Withholdings related to these wages were $4,896 for Social Security (FICA), $7,500 for federal income tax, $3,100 for state income tax, and $400 for union dues. The company incurred no cost related to these earnings for federal unemployment tax but incurred $700 for state unemployment tax.

Journalize payroll entries.
(LO 3), **AP**

Instructions
(a) Prepare the necessary March 31 journal entry to record salaries and wages expense and salaries and wages payable. Assume that wages earned during March will be paid during April.
(b) Prepare the entry to record the company's payroll tax expense.

E10-6 Season tickets for the Wildcats are priced at $320 and include 16 games. Revenue is recognized after each game is played. When the season began, the amount credited to Unearned Ticket Revenue was $1,728,000. By the end of October, $1,188,000 of the Unearned Ticket Revenue had been recognized as revenue.

Journalize unearned revenue transactions.
(LO 3), **AP**

Instructions
(a) How many season tickets did the Wildcats sell?
(b) How many home games had the Wildcats played by the end of October?
(c) Prepare the entry for the initial recording of the Unearned Ticket Revenue.
(d) Prepare the entry to recognize the revenue after the first home game had been played.

Journalize unearned subscription revenue.

(LO 3), **AP**

E10-7 Valenti Company Ltd. publishes a monthly sports magazine, *Fishing Preview*. Subscriptions to the magazine cost $28 per year. During November 2014, Valenti sells 6,300 subscriptions for cash, beginning with the December issue. Valenti prepares financial statements quarterly and recognizes subscription revenue at the end of the quarter. The company uses the accounts Unearned Subscription Revenue and Subscription Revenue. The company has a December 31 year-end.

Instructions
(a) Prepare the entry in November for the receipt of the subscriptions.
(b) Prepare the adjusting entry at December 31, 2014, to record subscription revenue in December 2014.
(c) Prepare the adjusting entry at March 31, 2015, to record subscription revenue in the first quarter of 2015.

Prepare journal entries for issuance of bonds and payment and accrual of interest.

(LO 5), **AP**

E10-8 On August 1, 2014, Ortega Corporation issued $600,000, 7%, 10-year bonds at face value. Interest is payable annually on August 1. Ortega's year-end is December 31.

Instructions
Prepare journal entries to record the following events.
(a) The issuance of the bonds.
(b) The accrual of interest on December 31, 2014.
(c) The payment of interest on August 1, 2015.

Prepare journal entries for issuance of bonds and payment and accrual of interest.

(LO 5), **AP**

E10-9 On January 1, Newkirk Company issued $300,000, 8%, 10-year bonds at face value. Interest is payable annually on January 1.

Instructions
Prepare journal entries to record the following events.
(a) The issuance of the bonds.
(b) The accrual of interest on December 31.
(c) The payment of interest on January 1.

Prepare entries for issuance of bonds, balance sheet presentation, and cause of deviations from face value.

(LO 5), **AP**

E10-10 Canyon Company issued $600,000, 10-year, 6% bonds at 103.

Instructions
(a) Prepare the journal entry to record the sale of these bonds on January 1, 2014.
(b) Suppose the remaining Premium on Bonds Payable was $10,800 on December 31, 2017. Show the balance sheet presentation on this date.
(c) Explain why the bonds sold at a price above the face amount.

Prepare entries for issuance of bonds, balance sheet presentation, and cause of deviations from face value.

(LO 5), **AP**

E10-11 Riot Company issued $500,000, 15-year, 7% bonds at 96.

Instructions
(a) Prepare the journal entry to record the sale of these bonds on January 1, 2014.
(b) Suppose the remaining Discount on Bonds Payable was $12,000 on December 31, 2019. Show the balance sheet presentation on this date.
(c) Explain why the bonds sold at a price below the face amount.

Prepare entries for issue of bonds.

(LO 5), **AN**

E10-12 Assume that the following are independent situations recently reported in the *Wall Street Journal*.
1. General Electric (GE) 7% bonds, maturing January 28, 2015, were issued at 111.12.
2. Boeing 7% bonds, maturing September 24, 2029, were issued at 99.08.

Instructions
(a) Were GE and Boeing bonds issued at a premium or a discount?
(b) Explain how bonds, both paying the same contractual interest rate, could be issued at different prices.
(c) Prepare the journal entry to record the issue of each of these two bonds, assuming each company issued $800,000 of bonds in total.

Prepare journal entries to record issuance of bonds, payment of interest, and redemption at maturity.

(LO 5, 6), **AP**

E10-13 Romine Company issued $350,000 of 8%, 20-year bonds on January 1, 2014, at face value. Interest is payable annually on January 1.

Instructions
Prepare the journal entries to record the following events.
(a) The issuance of the bonds.
(b) The accrual of interest on December 31, 2014.

(c) The payment of interest on January 1, 2015.

(d) The redemption of the bonds at maturity, assuming interest for the last interest period has been paid and recorded.

E10-14 The situations presented here are independent of each other.

Prepare journal entries for redemption of bonds.

(LO 6), **AP**

Instructions

For each situation, prepare the appropriate journal entry for the redemption of the bonds.

(a) Pelfer Corporation redeemed $140,000 face value, 9% bonds on April 30, 2014, at 101. The carrying value of the bonds at the redemption date was $126,500. The bonds pay annual interest, and the interest payment due on April 30, 2014, has been made and recorded.

(b) Youngman, Inc., redeemed $170,000 face value, 12.5% bonds on June 30, 2014, at 98. The carrying value of the bonds at the redemption date was $184,000. The bonds pay annual interest, and the interest payment due on June 30, 2014, has been made and recorded.

E10-15 Santana, Inc. reports the following liabilities (in thousands) on its January 31, 2014, balance sheet and notes to the financial statements.

Prepare liabilities section of balance sheet.

(LO 7), **AP**

Accounts payable	$4,263.9	Mortgage payable	$6,746.7
Accrued pension liability	1,115.2	Operating leases	1,641.7
Unearned rent revenue	1,058.1	Notes payable (due in 2017)	335.6
Bonds payable	1,961.2	Salaries and wages payable	858.1
Current portion of		Notes payable (due in 2015)	2,563.6
mortgage payable	1,992.2	Unused operating line of credit	3,337.6
Income taxes payable	265.2	Warranty liability—current	1,417.3

Instructions

(a) Identify which of the above liabilities are likely current and which are likely long-term. List any items that do not fit in either category. Explain the reasoning for your selection.

(b) Prepare the liabilities section of Santana's balance sheet as at January 31, 2014.

E10-16 Suppose McDonald's 2014 financial statements contain the following selected data (in millions).

Calculate liquidity and solvency ratios; discuss impact of unrecorded obligations on liquidity and solvency.

(LO 7), **AP**

Current assets	$ 3,416.3	Interest expense	$ 473.2
Total assets	30,224.9	Income taxes	1,936.0
Current liabilities	2,988.7	Net income	4,551.0
Total liabilities	16,191.0		

Instructions

(a) Compute the following values and provide a brief interpretation of each.

(1) Working capital.　　(3) Debt to assets ratio.

(2) Current ratio.　　　(4) Times interest earned.

(b) Suppose the notes to McDonald's financial statements show that subsequent to 2014 the company will have future minimum lease payments under operating leases of $10,717.5 million. If these assets had been purchased with debt, assets and liabilities would rise by approximately $8,800 million. Recompute the debt to assets ratio after adjusting for this. Discuss your result.

E10-17 Suppose 3M Company reported the following financial data for 2014 and 2013 (in millions).

Calculate current ratio before and after paying accounts payable.

(LO 7), **AN**

3M COMPANY
Balance Sheet (partial)

	2014	2013
Current assets		
Cash and cash equivalents	$ 3,040	$1,849
Accounts receivable, net	3,250	3,195
Inventories	2,639	3,013
Other current assets	1,866	1,541
Total current assets	$10,795	$9,598
Current liabilities	$ 4,897	$5,839

Instructions

(a) Calculate the current ratio for 3M for 2014 and 2013.

(b) Suppose that at the end of 2014, 3M management used $300 million cash to pay off $300 million of accounts payable. How would its current ratio change?

Calculate current ratio before and after paying accounts payable.

(LO 7), **AN**

E10-18 Sedgewick Boutique reported the following financial data for 2014 and 2013.

SEDGEWICK BOUTIQUE
Balance Sheet (partial)
September 30 (in thousands)

	2014	2013
Current assets		
Cash and short-term deposits	$2,574	$1,021
Accounts receivable	2,147	1,575
Inventories	1,201	1,010
Other current assets	322	192
Total current assets	$6,244	$3,798
Current liabilities	$4,503	$2,619

Instructions

(a) Calculate the current ratio for Sedgewick Boutique for 2014 and 2013.

(b) Suppose that at the end of 2014, Sedgewick Boutique used $1.5 million cash to pay off $1.5 million of accounts payable. How would its current ratio change?

(c) At September 30, Sedgewick Boutique has an undrawn operating line of credit of $12.5 million. Would this affect any assessment that you might make of Sedgewick Boutique's short-term liquidity? Explain.

Discuss contingent liabilities.

(LO 7), **C**

E10-19 A large retailer was sued nearly 5,000 times in a recent year—about once every two hours every day of the year. It has been sued for everything imaginable—ranging from falls on icy parking lots to injuries sustained in shoppers' stampedes to a murder with a rifle purchased at one of its stores. The company reported the following in the notes to its financial statements:

> The Company and its subsidiaries are involved from time to time in claims, proceedings, and litigation arising from the operation of its business. The Company does not believe that any such claim, proceeding, or litigation, either alone or in the aggregate, will have a material adverse effect on the Company's financial position or results of its operations.

Instructions

(a) Explain why the company does not have to record these contingent liabilities.

(b) Comment on any implications for analysis of the financial statements.

Prepare journal entries to record issuance of bonds, payment of interest, amortization of premium using straight-line, and redemption at maturity.

(LO 5, 6, 8), **AP**

*E10-20 Prophet Company issued $500,000, 6%, 30-year bonds on January 1, 2014, at 103. Interest is payable annually on January 1. Prophet uses straight-line amortization for bond premium or discount.

Instructions

Prepare the journal entries to record the following events.

(a) The issuance of the bonds.

(b) The accrual of interest and the premium amortization on December 31, 2014.

(c) The payment of interest on January 1, 2015.

(d) The redemption of the bonds at maturity, assuming interest for the last interest period has been paid and recorded.

Prepare journal entries to record issuance of bonds, payment of interest, amortization of discount using straight-line, and redemption at maturity.

(LO 5, 6, 8), **AP**

*E10-21 Dailey Company issued $300,000, 8%, 15-year bonds on December 31, 2013, for $288,000. Interest is payable annually on December 31. Dailey uses the straight-line method to amortize bond premium or discount.

Instructions

Prepare the journal entries to record the following events.

(a) The issuance of the bonds.

(b) The payment of interest and the discount amortization on December 31, 2014.

(c) The redemption of the bonds at maturity, assuming interest for the last interest period has been paid and recorded.

*E10-22 Cole Corporation issued $400,000, 7%, 20-year bonds on January 1, 2014, for $360,727. This price resulted in an effective-interest rate of 8% on the bonds. Interest is payable annually on January 1. Cole uses the effective-interest method to amortize bond premium or discount.

Prepare journal entries for issuance of bonds, payment of interest, and amortization of discount using effective-interest method.
(LO 5, 9), **AP**

Instructions
Prepare the journal entries to record (round to the nearest dollar):
(a) The issuance of the bonds.
(b) The accrual of interest and the discount amortization on December 31, 2014.
(c) The payment of interest on January 1, 2015.

*E10-23 Gomez Company issued $380,000, 7%, 10-year bonds on January 1, 2014, for $407,968. This price resulted in an effective-interest rate of 6% on the bonds. Interest is payable annually on January 1. Gomez uses the effective-interest method to amortize bond premium or discount.

Prepare journal entries for issuance of bonds, payment of interest, and amortization of premium using effective-interest method.
(LO 5, 9), **AP**

Instructions
Prepare the journal entries (rounded to the nearest dollar) to record:
(a) The issuance of the bonds.
(b) The accrual of interest and the premium amortization on December 31, 2014.
(c) The payment of interest on January 1, 2015.

*E10-24 Nance Co. receives $280,000 when it issues a $280,000, 6%, mortgage note payable to finance the construction of a building at December 31, 2014. The terms provide for semiannual installment payments of $14,285 on June 30 and December 31.

Prepare journal entries to record mortgage note and installment payments.
(LO 10), **AP**

Instructions
Prepare the journal entries to record the mortgage loan and the first two installment payments.

*E10-25 Goins Corporation issued a $50,000, 10%, 10-year installment note payable on January 1, 2014. Payments of $8,137 are made each January 1, beginning January 1, 2015.

Balance sheet presentation of installment note payable.
(LO 10), **AP**

Instructions
(a) What amounts should be reported under current liabilities related to the note on December 31, 2014?
(b) What should be reported under long-term liabilities?

Exercises: Set B and Challenge Exercises

Visit the book's companion website, at **www.wiley.com/college/kimmel**, and choose the Student Companion site to access Exercise Set B and Challenge Exercises.

Problems: Set A

P10-1A On January 1, 2014, the ledger of Hiatt Company contained these liability accounts.

Prepare current liability entries, adjusting entries, and current liabilities section.
(LO 1, 2, 3, 7), **AP**
GLS

Accounts Payable	$42,500
Sales Taxes Payable	6,600
Unearned Service Revenue	19,000

During January, the following selected transactions occurred.

Jan. 1 Borrowed $18,000 in cash from Premier Bank on a 4-month, 5%, $18,000 note.
5 Sold merchandise for cash totaling $6,254, which includes 6% sales taxes.
12 Performed services for customers who had made advance payments of $10,000. (Credit Service Revenue.)
14 Paid state treasurer's department for sales taxes collected in December 2013, $6,600.
20 Sold 500 units of a new product on credit at $48 per unit, plus 6% sales tax.

During January, the company's employees earned wages of $70,000. Withholdings related to these wages were $5,355 for Social Security (FICA), $5,000 for federal income tax, and $1,500 for state income tax. The company owed no money related to these earnings for federal or state unemployment tax. Assume that wages earned during January will be paid during February. No entry had been recorded for wages or payroll tax expense as of January 31.

Instructions

(a) Journalize the January transactions.

(b) Journalize the adjusting entries at January 31 for the outstanding note payable and for salaries and wages expense and payroll tax expense.

(c) Tot. current liabilities $146,724

(c) Prepare the current liabilities section of the balance sheet at January 31, 2014. Assume no change in Accounts Payable.

Journalize and post note transactions; show balance sheet presentation.

(LO 2, 7), AP

P10-2A Ermlar Corporation sells rock-climbing products and also operates an indoor climbing facility for climbing enthusiasts. During the last part of 2014, Ermlar had the following transactions related to notes payable.

Sept.	1	Issued a $12,000 note to Lippert to purchase inventory. The 3-month note payable bears interest of 6% and is due December 1. (Ermlar uses a perpetual inventory system.)
Sept.	30	Recorded accrued interest for the Lippert note.
Oct.	1	Issued a $16,500, 8%, 4-month note to Shanee Bank to finance the purchase of a new climbing wall for advanced climbers. The note is due February 1.
Oct.	31	Recorded accrued interest for the Lippert note and the Shanee Bank note.
Nov.	1	Issued a $26,000 note and paid $8,000 cash to purchase a vehicle to transport clients to nearby climbing sites as part of a new series of climbing classes. This note bears interest of 6% and matures in 12 months.
Nov.	30	Recorded accrued interest for the Lippert note, the Shanee Bank note, and the vehicle note.
Dec.	1	Paid principal and interest on the Lippert note.
Dec.	31	Recorded accrued interest for the Shanee Bank note and the vehicle note.

Instructions

(a) Prepare journal entries for the transactions noted above.

(b) Interest Payable $590

(b) Post the above entries to the Notes Payable, Interest Payable, and Interest Expense accounts. (Use T-accounts.)

(c) Show the balance sheet presentation of notes payable and interest payable at December 31.

(d) How much interest expense relating to notes payable did Ermlar incur during the year?

Prepare journal entries to record interest payments and redemption of bonds.

(LO 5, 6), AP

P10-3A The following section is taken from Mareska's balance sheet at December 31, 2013.

Current liabilities	
Interest payable	$ 40,000
Long-term liabilities	
Bonds payable (8%, due January 1, 2017)	500,000

Interest is payable annually on January 1. The bonds are callable on any annual interest date.

Instructions

(a) Journalize the payment of the bond interest on January 1, 2014.

(b) Loss $6,000

(b) Assume that on January 1, 2014, after paying interest, Mareska calls bonds having a face value of $200,000. The call price is 103. Record the redemption of the bonds.

(c) Prepare the adjusting entry on December 31, 2014, to accrue the interest on the remaining bonds.

Prepare journal entries to record issuance of bonds, interest, balance sheet presentation, and bond redemption.

(LO 5, 6, 7), AP

P10-4A On October 1, 2013, Koppa Corp. issued $700,000, 5%, 10-year bonds at face value. The bonds were dated October 1, 2013, and pay interest annually on October 1. Financial statements are prepared annually on December 31.

Instructions

(a) Prepare the journal entry to record the issuance of the bonds.

(b) Prepare the adjusting entry to record the accrual of interest on December 31, 2013.

(c) Show the balance sheet presentation of bonds payable and bond interest payable on December 31, 2013.

(d) Prepare the journal entry to record the payment of interest on October 1, 2014.
(e) Prepare the adjusting entry to record the accrual of interest on December 31, 2014.
(f) Assume that on January 1, 2015, Koppa pays the accrued bond interest and calls the bonds. The call price is 104. Record the payment of interest and redemption of the bonds.

(f) Loss $28,000

P10-5A Slocombe Company sold $6,000,000, 7%, 15-year bonds on January 1, 2014. The bonds were dated January 1, 2014, and pay interest on December 31. The bonds were sold at 98.

Prepare journal entries to record issuance of bonds, show balance sheet presentation, and record bond redemption.
(LO 5, 6, 7), **AP**

Instructions
(a) Prepare the journal entry to record the issuance of the bonds on January 1, 2014.
(b) At December 31, 2014, $8,000 of the bond discount had been amortized. Show the long-term liability balance sheet presentation of the bond liability at December 31, 2014.
(c) At January 1, 2016, when the carrying value of the bonds was $5,896,000, the company redeemed the bonds at 102. Record the redemption of the bonds assuming that interest for the year had already been paid.

(c) Loss $224,000

P10-6A Suppose you have been presented with selected information taken from the financial statements of Southwest Airlines Co., shown below.

Calculate and comment on ratios.
(LO 7), **AN**

SOUTHWEST AIRLINES CO.
Balance Sheet (partial)
December 31
(in millions)

	2014	2013
Total current assets	$ 2,893	$ 4,443
Noncurrent assets	11,415	12,329
Total assets	$14,308	$16,772
Current liabilities	$ 2,806	$ 4,836
Long-term liabilities	6,549	4,995
Total liabilities	9,355	9,831
Shareholders' equity	4,953	6,941
Total liabilities and shareholders' equity	$14,308	$16,772

Other information:

	2014	2013
Net income (loss)	$ 178	$ 645
Income tax expense	100	413
Interest expense	130	119
Cash provided by operations	(1,521)	2,845
Capital expenditures	923	1,331
Cash dividends	13	14

Note 8. Leases
The majority of the Company's terminal operations space, as well as 82 aircraft, were under operating leases at December 31, 2014. Future minimum lease payments under noncancelable operating leases are as follows: 2015, $376,000; 2016, $324,000; 2017, $249,000; 2018, $208,000; 2019, $152,000; after 2020, $728,000.

Instructions
(a) Calculate each of the following ratios for 2014 and 2013.
  (1) Current ratio.
  (2) Free cash flow.
  (3) Debt to assets ratio.
  (4) Times interest earned.
(b) Comment on the trend in ratios.

(c) Read the company's note on leases. If the operating leases had instead been accounted for like a purchase, assets and liabilities would increase by approximately $1,600 million. Recalculate the debt to assets ratio for 2014 in light of this information, and discuss the implications for analysis.

Prepare journal entries to record interest payments, straight-line discount amortization, and redemption of bonds.

(LO 5, 6, 8), **AP**

*P10-7A The following information is taken from Oler Corp.'s balance sheet at December 31, 2013.

Current liabilities		
Interest payable		$ 96,000
Long-term liabilities		
Bonds payable (4%, due January 1, 2024)	$2,400,000	
Less: Discount on bonds payable	24,000	2,376,000

Interest is payable annually on January 1. The bonds are callable on any annual interest date. Oler uses straight-line amortization for any bond premium or discount. From December 31, 2013, the bonds will be outstanding for an additional 10 years (120 months).

Instructions

(Round all computations to the nearest dollar.)

(a) Journalize the payment of bond interest on January 1, 2014.

(b) Prepare the entry to amortize bond discount and to accrue the interest on December 31, 2014.

(c) Loss $11,600

(c) Assume on January 1, 2015, after paying interest, that Oler Corp. calls bonds having a face value of $400,000. The call price is 102. Record the redemption of the bonds.

(d) Prepare the adjusting entry at December 31, 2015, to amortize bond discount and to accrue interest on the remaining bonds.

Prepare journal entries to record issuance of bonds, interest, and straight-line amortization, and balance sheet presentation.

(LO 5, 7, 8), **AP**

*P10-8A Yung Corporation sold $2,000,000, 7%, 5-year bonds on January 1, 2014. The bonds were dated January 1, 2014, and pay interest on January 1. Yung Corporation uses the straight-line method to amortize bond premium or discount.

Instructions

(a) Prepare all the necessary journal entries to record the issuance of the bonds and bond interest expense for 2014, assuming that the bonds sold at 102.

(b) Prepare journal entries as in part (a) assuming that the bonds sold at 97.

(c) Show the balance sheet presentation for the bond issue at December 31, 2014, using (1) the 102 selling price, and then (2) the 97 selling price.

Prepare journal entries to record issuance of bonds, interest, and straight-line amortization, and balance sheet presentation.

(LO 5, 7, 8), **AP**

*P10-9A Wempe Co. sold $3,000,000, 8%, 10-year bonds on January 1, 2014. The bonds were dated January 1, 2014, and pay interest on January 1. The company uses straight-line amortization on bond premiums and discounts. Financial statements are prepared annually.

Instructions

(a) Prepare the journal entries to record the issuance of the bonds assuming they sold at:
   (1) 103.
   (2) 98.

(b) Prepare amortization tables for both assumed sales for the first three interest payments.

(c) (2) 12/31/14 Interest Expense $246,000

(c) Prepare the journal entries to record interest expense for 2014 under both of the bond issuances assumed in part (a).

(d) Show the long-term liabilities balance sheet presentation for both of the bond issuances assumed in part (a) at December 31, 2014.

Prepare journal entries to record issuance of bonds, payment of interest, and amortization of bond discount using effective-interest method.

(LO 5, 9), **AP**

*P10-10A On January 1, 2014, Lock Corporation issued $1,800,000 face value, 5%, 10-year bonds at $1,667,518. This price resulted in an effective-interest rate of 6% on the bonds. Lock uses the effective-interest method to amortize bond premium or discount. The bonds pay annual interest January 1.

Instructions

(Round all computations to the nearest dollar.)

(a) Prepare the journal entry to record the issuance of the bonds on January 1, 2014.

(b) Prepare an amortization table through December 31, 2016 (three interest periods) for this bond issue.

(c) Interest Expense $100,051

(c) Prepare the journal entry to record the accrual of interest and the amortization of the discount on December 31, 2014.

(d) Prepare the journal entry to record the payment of interest on January 1, 2015.

(e) Prepare the journal entry to record the accrual of interest and the amortization of the discount on December 31, 2015.

*P10-11A   On January 1, 2014, Jade Company issued $2,000,000 face value, 7%, 10-year bonds at $2,147,202. This price resulted in a 6% effective-interest rate on the bonds. Jade uses the effective-interest method to amortize bond premium or discount. The bonds pay annual interest on each January 1.

Prepare journal entries to record issuance of bonds, payment of interest, and effective-interest amortization, and balance sheet presentation.
(LO 5, 7, 9), **AP**

Instructions

(a) Prepare the journal entries to record the following transactions.
  (1) The issuance of the bonds on January 1, 2014.
  (2) Accrual of interest and amortization of the premium on December 31, 2014.
  (3) The payment of interest on January 1, 2015.
  (4) Accrual of interest and amortization of the premium on December 31, 2015.

(a) (4) Interest
        Expense $128,162

(b) Show the proper long-term liabilities balance sheet presentation for the liability for bonds payable at December 31, 2015.

(c) Provide the answers to the following questions in narrative form.
  (1) What amount of interest expense is reported for 2015?
  (2) Would the bond interest expense reported in 2015 be the same as, greater than, or less than the amount that would be reported if the straight-line method of amortization were used?

*P10-12A   Frevert purchased a new piece of equipment to be used in its new facility. The $370,000 piece of equipment was purchased with a $50,000 down payment and with cash received through the issuance of a $320,000, 8%, 3-year mortgage note payable issued on October 1, 2014. The terms provide for quarterly installment payments of $30,259 on December 31, March 31, June 30, and September 30.

Prepare installment payments schedule, journal entries, and balance sheet presentation for a mortgage note payable.
(LO 7, 10), **AP**

Instructions

(Round all computations to the nearest dollar.)

(a) Prepare an installment payments schedule for the first five payments of the notes payable.

(b) Prepare the journal entry related to the notes payable for December 31, 2014.

(c) Show the balance sheet presentation for this obligation for December 31, 2014. (*Hint:* Be sure to distinguish between the current and long-term portions of the note.)

(c) Current portion $100,304

*P10-13A   Grace Herron has just approached a venture capitalist for financing for her new business venture, the development of a local ski hill. On July 1, 2013, Grace was loaned $150,000 at an annual interest rate of 7%. The loan is repayable over 5 years in annual installments of $36,584, principal and interest, due each June 30. The first payment is due June 30, 2014. Grace uses the effective-interest method for amortizing debt. Her ski hill company's year-end will be June 30.

Prepare journal entries to record payments for long-term note payable, and balance sheet presentation.
(LO 7, 10), **AP**

Instructions

(a) Prepare an amortization schedule for the 5 years, 2013–2018. (Round all calculations to the nearest dollar.)

(b) Prepare all journal entries for Grace Herron for the first 2 fiscal years ended June 30, 2014, and June 30, 2015. (Round all calculations to the nearest dollar.)

(c) Show the balance sheet presentation of the note payable as of June 30, 2015. (*Hint:* Be sure to distinguish between the current and long-term portions of the note.)

(b) 6/30/14 Interest
        Expense $10,500

Problems: Set B

P10-1B   On January 1, 2014, the ledger of Flaming Company contained the following liability accounts.

Prepare current liability entries, adjusting entries, and current liabilities section.
(LO 1, 2, 3, 7), **AP**

Accounts Payable	$52,000
Sales Taxes Payable	8,200
Unearned Service Revenue	11,000

During January, the following selected transactions occurred.

Jan. 1 Borrowed $18,000 from TriCounty Bank on a 3-month, 8%, $18,000 note.

5 Sold merchandise for cash totaling $18,480, which includes 6.25% sales taxes.

12 Performed services for customers who had made advance payments of $8,000. (Credit Service Revenue.)

14 Paid state revenue department for sales taxes collected in December 2013 ($8,200).

20 Sold 500 units of a new product on credit at $50 per unit, plus 6.25% sales tax.

During January, the company's employees earned wages of $54,000. Withholdings related to these wages were $4,131 for Social Security (FICA), $3,900 for federal income tax, and $1,200 for state income tax. The company owed no money related to these earnings for federal or state unemployment tax. Assume that wages earned during January will be paid during February. No entry had been recorded for wages or payroll tax expense as of January 31.

Instructions

(a) Journalize the January transactions.

(b) Journalize the adjusting entries at January 31 for the outstanding notes payable and for salaries and wages expense and payroll tax expense.

(c) Tot. current liabilities $133,901

(c) Prepare the current liabilities section of the balance sheet at January 31, 2014. Assume no change in accounts payable.

Journalize and post note transactions; show balance sheet presentation.

(LO 2, 7), AP

P10-2B Skate City Corporation sells skateboard products and also operates an indoor skating facility. During the last part of 2014, Skate City had the following transactions related to notes payable.

Aug. 1 Issued a $6,000 note to Wheeler to purchase inventory. The 3-month note payable bears interest of 9% and is due November 1.

Aug. 31 Recorded accrued interest for the Wheeler note.

Sept. 1 Issued a $15,000, 8%, 6-month note to Commerce Bank to finance the purchase of a new ramp for advanced boarders. The note is due March 1.

Sept. 30 Recorded accrued interest for the Wheeler note and the Commerce Bank note.

Oct. 1 Issued a $40,000 note and paid $10,000 cash to repair and improve its building. This note bears interest of 8% and matures in 12 months.

Oct. 31 Recorded accrued interest for the Wheeler note, the Commerce Bank note, and the improvement note.

Nov. 1 Paid principal and interest on the Wheeler note.

Nov. 30 Recorded accrued interest for the Commerce Bank note and the improvement note.

Dec. 31 Recorded accrued interest for the Commerce Bank note and the improvement note.

Instructions

(a) Prepare journal entries for the transactions noted above.

(b) Interest Payable $1,201

(b) Post the above entries to the Notes Payable, Interest Payable, and Interest Expense accounts. (Use T-accounts.)

(c) Show the balance sheet presentation of notes payable and interest payable at December 31.

(d) How much interest expense relating to notes payable did Skate City incur during the year?

Prepare journal entries to record interest payments and redemption of bonds.

(LO 5, 6), AP

P10-3B The following section is taken from Lyons Corp.'s balance sheet at December 31, 2013.

Current liabilities
    Interest payable $ 96,000
Long-term liabilities
    Bonds payable (8%, due January 1, 2018)   1,200,000

Interest is payable annually on January 1. The bonds are callable on any annual interest date.

Instructions

(a) Journalize the payment of the bond interest on January 1, 2014.

(b) Loss $24,000

(b) Assume that on January 1, 2014, after paying interest, Lyons Corp. calls bonds having a face value of $300,000. The call price is 108. Record the redemption of the bonds.

(c) Prepare the adjusting entry on December 31, 2014, to accrue the interest on the remaining bonds.

P10-4B   On April 1, 2013, CMV Corp. issued $600,000, 5%, 5-year bonds at face value. The bonds were dated April 1, 2013, and pay interest annually on April 1. Financial statements are prepared annually on December 31.

Prepare journal entries to record issuance of bonds, interest, balance sheet presentation, and bond redemption.

(LO 5, 6, 7), **AP**

Instructions

(a) Prepare the journal entry to record the issuance of the bonds.

(b) Prepare the adjusting entry to record the accrual of interest on December 31, 2013.

(c) Show the balance sheet presentation of bonds payable and bond interest payable on December 31, 2013.

(d) Prepare the journal entry to record the payment of interest on April 1, 2014.

(e) Prepare the adjusting entry to record the accrual of interest on December 31, 2014.

(f) Assume that on January 1, 2016, CMV pays the accrued bond interest and calls the bonds. The call price is 102.5. Record the payment of interest and redemption of the bonds.

(f) Loss $15,000

P10-5B   Union Electric sold $5,000,000, 5%, 10-year bonds on January 1, 2014. The bonds were dated January 1 and pay interest on January 1. The bonds were sold at 103.

Prepare journal entries to record issuance of bonds, show balance sheet presentation, and record bond redemption.

(LO 5, 6, 7), **AP**

Instructions

(a) Prepare the journal entry to record the issuance of the bonds on January 1, 2014.

(b) At December 31, 2014, $15,000 of the bond premium had been amortized. Show the long-term liability balance sheet presentation of the bond liability at December 31, 2014.

(c) At January 1, 2016, when the carrying value of the bonds was $5,120,000, the company redeemed the bonds at 104. Record the redemption of the bonds assuming that interest for the year had already been paid.

(c) Loss $80,000

P10-6B   Suppose you have been presented with the following selected information taken from the financial statements of Kellogg Company.

Calculate and comment on ratios.

(LO 7), **AN**

KELLOGG COMPANY
Balance Sheet (partial)
December 31
(in millions)

	2014	2013
Total current assets	$ 2,717	$ 2,427
Noncurrent assets	8,680	8,287
Total assets	$11,397	$10,714
Current liabilities	$ 4,044	$ 4,020
Long-term liabilities	4,827	4,625
Total liabilities	8,871	8,645
Shareholders' equity	2,526	2,069
Total liabilities and shareholders' equity	$11,397	$10,714

Other information:

	2014	2013
Net income (loss)	$ 1,103	$ 1,004
Income tax expense	444	467
Interest expense	319	307
Cash provided by operations	1,503	1,410
Capital expenditures	472	453
Cash dividends	475	450

Note 6. Leases and Other Commitments

The Company's leases are generally for equipment and warehouse space. Future minimum annual lease payments under noncancelable operating leases were as follows: 2015, $159; 2016, $137; 2017, $112; 2018, $83; 2019, $56; after 2019, $183.

Instructions

(a) Calculate each of the following ratios for 2014 and 2013.
   (1) Current ratio.
   (2) Free cash flow.
   (3) Debt to assets ratio.
   (4) Times interest earned.
(b) Comment on the trend in ratios.
(c) Read the company's note on leases. If the operating leases had instead been accounted for like a purchase, assets and liabilities would increase by approximately $584 million. Recalculate the debt to assets ratio for 2014 in light of this information, and discuss the implications for analysis.

Prepare journal entries to record interest payments, straight-line premium amortization, and redemption of bonds

(LO 5, 6, 8), AP

*P10-7B The following section is taken from Zenith Oil Company's balance sheet at December 31, 2013.

Current liabilities		
Interest payable		$ 144,000
Long-term liabilities		
Bonds payable (4%, due January 1, 2024)	$3,600,000	
Add: Premium on bonds payable	280,000	3,880,000

Interest is payable annually on January 1. The bonds are callable on any annual interest date. Zenith uses straight-line amortization for any bond premium or discount. From December 31, 2013, the bonds will be outstanding for an additional 10 years (120 months).

Instructions

(Round all computations to the nearest dollar.)
(a) Journalize the payment of bond interest on January 1, 2014.
(b) Prepare the entry to amortize bond premium and to accrue interest due on December 31, 2014.

(c) Gain $90,000

(c) Assume on January 1, 2015, after paying interest, that Zenith Company calls bonds having a face value of $1,800,000. The call price is 102. Record the redemption of the bonds.
(d) Prepare the adjusting entry at December 31, 2015, to amortize bond premium and to accrue interest on the remaining bonds.

Prepare journal entries to record issuance of bonds, interest, and straight-line amortization, and balance sheet presentation.

(LO 5, 7, 8), AP

*P10-8B Holmes Corporation sold $2,200,000, 8%, 5-year bonds on January 1, 2014. The bonds were dated January 1, 2014, and pay interest on January 1. Holmes Corporation uses the straight-line method to amortize bond premium or discount.

Instructions

(a) Prepare all the necessary journal entries to record the issuance of the bonds and bond interest expense for 2014, assuming that the bonds sold at 102.
(b) Prepare journal entries as in part (a) assuming that the bonds sold at 98.
(c) Show the balance sheet presentation for the bond issue at December 31, 2014, using (1) the 102 selling price, and then (2) the 98 selling price.

Prepare journal entries to record issuance of bonds, interest, and straight-line amortization, and balance sheet presentation.

(LO 5, 7, 8), AP

*P10-9B Wentworth Co. sold $3,000,000, 7%, 8-year bonds on January 1, 2014. The bonds were dated January 1, 2014, and pay interest on January 1. The company uses straight-line amortization on bond premiums and discounts. Financial statements are prepared annually.

Instructions

(a) Prepare the journal entries to record the issuance of the bonds assuming they sold at:
   (1) 103.
   (2) 99.
(b) Prepare amortization tables for both assumed sales for the first three interest payments.

(c) (1) Interest Expense $198,750

(c) Prepare the journal entries to record interest expense for 2014 under both assumed sales.
(d) Show the balance sheet presentation for both assumed sales at December 31, 2014.

Prepare journal entries to record issuance of bonds, payment of interest, and amortization of bond premium using effective-interest method.

(LO 5, 9), AP

*P10-10B On January 1, 2014, Imelda Corporation issued $2,000,000 face value, 6%, 10-year bonds at $2,154,434. This price resulted in an effective-interest rate of 5% on the bonds. Imelda uses the effective-interest method to amortize bond premium or discount. The bonds pay annual interest January 1.

Instructions

(Round all computations to the nearest dollar.)

(a) Prepare the journal entry to record the issuance of the bonds on January 1, 2014.

(b) Prepare an amortization table through December 31, 2016 (three interest periods) for this bond issue.

(c) Prepare the journal entry to record the accrual of interest and the amortization of the discount on December 31, 2014.

(d) Prepare the journal entry to record the payment of interest on January 1, 2015.

(e) Prepare the journal entry to record the accrual of interest and the amortization of the discount on December 31, 2015.

(c) Interest
    Expense $107,722

P10-11B On January 1, 2014, Murphy Company issued $1,600,000 face value, 7%, 10-year bonds at $1,717,761. This price resulted in a 6% effective-interest rate on the bonds. Murphy uses the effective-interest method to amortize bond premium or discount. The bonds pay annual interest on each January 1.

Prepare journal entries to record issuance of bonds, payment of interest, and effective-interest amortization, and balance sheet presentation.
(LO 5, 7, 9), **AP**

Instructions

(a) Prepare the journal entries to record the following transactions.
  (1) The issuance of the bonds on January 1, 2014.
  (2) Accrual of interest and amortization of the premium on December 31, 2014.
  (3) The payment of interest on January 1, 2015.
  (4) Accrual of interest and amortization of the premium on December 31, 2015.

(b) Show the proper balance sheet presentation for the liability for bonds payable on the December 31, 2015, balance sheet.

(c) Provide the answers to the following questions in narrative form.
  (1) What amount of interest expense is reported for 2015?
  (2) Would the bond interest expense reported in 2015 be the same as, greater than, or less than the amount that would be reported if the straight-line method of amortization were used?

(a) (4) Interest
    Expense $102,530

P10-12B Lyman purchased a new piece of equipment to be used in its new facility. The $380,000 piece of equipment was purchased with a $40,000 down payment and with cash received through the issuance of a $340,000, 8%, 5-year mortgage note payable issued on October 1, 2014. The terms provide for quarterly installment payments of $20,792 on December 31, March 31, June 30, and September 30.

Prepare installment payments schedule, journal entries, and balance sheet presentation for a mortgage note payable.
(LO 7, 10), **AP**

Instructions

(Round all computations to the nearest dollar.)

(a) Prepare an installment payments schedule for the first five payments of the notes payable.

(b) Prepare the journal entry related to the notes payable for December 31, 2014.

(c) Show the balance sheet presentation for this obligation for December 31, 2014. (*Hint:* Be sure to distinguish between the current and long-term portions of the note.)

(c) Current portion $58,822

P10-13B Ronald Allerton has just approached a venture capitalist for financing for a new business venture, the development of a local ski hill. On July 1, 2013, Ronald was loaned $140,000 at an annual interest rate of 8%. The loan is repayable over 5 years in annual installments of $35,064, principal and interest, due each June 30. The first payment is due June 30, 2014. Ronald uses the effective-interest method for amortizing debt. The ski hill company's year-end will be June 30.

Prepare journal entries to record payments for long-term note payable, and balance sheet presentation.
(LO 7, 10), **AP**

Instructions

(a) Prepare an amortization schedule for the 5 years, 2013–2018. (Round all calculations to the nearest dollar.)

(b) Prepare all journal entries for Ronald Allerton for the first 2 fiscal years ended June 30, 2014, and June 30, 2015. (Round all calculations to the nearest dollar.)

(c) Show the balance sheet presentation of the note payable as of June 30, 2015. (*Hint:* Be sure to distinguish between the current and long-term portions of the note.)

(b) 6/30/14 Interest
    Expense $11,200

Problems: Set C

Visit the book's companion website, at **www.wiley.com/college/kimmel**, and choose the Student Companion site to access Problem Set C.

Comprehensive Problem

CP10 Trevor Corporation's balance sheet at December 31, 2013, is presented below.

TREVOR CORPORATION
Balance Sheet
December 31, 2013

Cash	$ 30,000	Accounts payable	$ 13,750
Inventory	30,750	Interest payable	2,500
Prepaid insurance	5,600	Bonds payable	50,000
Equipment	38,000	Common stock	25,000
	$104,350	Retained earnings	13,100
			$104,350

During 2014, the following transactions occurred.
1. Trevor paid $2,500 interest on the bonds on January 1, 2014.
2. Trevor purchased $241,100 of inventory on account.
3. Trevor sold for $480,000 cash inventory which cost $265,000. Trevor also collected $28,800 sales taxes.
4. Trevor paid $230,000 on accounts payable.
5. Trevor paid $2,500 interest on the bonds on July 1, 2014.
6. The prepaid insurance ($5,600) expired on July 31.
7. On August 1, Trevor paid $10,200 for insurance coverage from August 1, 2014, through July 31, 2015.
8. Trevor paid $17,000 sales taxes to the state.
9. Paid other operating expenses, $91,000.
10. Redeemed the bonds on December 31, 2014, by paying $48,000 plus $2,500 interest.
11. Issued $90,000 of 8% bonds on December 31, 2014, at 103. The bonds pay interest every June 30 and December 31.

Adjustment data:
1. Recorded the insurance expired from item 7.
2. The equipment was acquired on December 31, 2013, and will be depreciated on a straight-line basis over 5 years with a $3,000 salvage value.
3. The income tax rate is 30%. (*Hint:* Prepare the income statement up to income before taxes and multiply by 30% to compute the amount.)

Instructions
(You may want to set up T-accounts to determine ending balances.)
(a) Prepare journal entries for the transactions listed above and adjusting entries.

(b) Totals $687,695
(c) N.I. $72,905

(b) Prepare an adjusted trial balance at December 31, 2014.
(c) Prepare an income statement and a retained earnings statement for the year ending December 31, 2014, and a classified balance sheet as of December 31, 2014.

Continuing Cookie Chronicle

(*Note:* This is a continuation of the Cookie Chronicle from Chapters 1 through 9.)

CCC10 Recall that Cookie Creations borrowed $2,000 from Natalie's grandmother. Natalie now is thinking of repaying all amounts outstanding on that loan. She needs to know the amounts of interest payable and interest expense to make the correct journal entries for repayment of the loan.

Go to the book's companion website, at **www.wiley.com/college/kimmel**, to see the completion of this problem.

Broadening Your Perspective

Financial Reporting and Analysis

FINANCIAL REPORTING PROBLEM: *Tootsie Roll Industries, Inc.*

BYP10-1 Refer to the financial statements of Tootsie Roll Industries and the Notes to Consolidated Financial Statements in Appendix A.

Instructions

Answer the following questions.
(a) What were Tootsie Roll's total current liabilities at December 31, 2011? What was the increase/decrease in Tootsie Roll's total current liabilities from the prior year?
(b) How much were the accounts payable at December 31, 2011?
(c) What were the components of total current liabilities on December 31, 2011 (other than accounts payable already discussed above)?

COMPARATIVE ANALYSIS PROBLEM: *Tootsie Roll vs. Hershey*

BYP10-2 The financial statements of The Hershey Company are presented in Appendix B, following the financial statements for Tootsie Roll Industries in Appendix A.

Instructions

(a) Based on the information contained in these financial statements, compute the current ratio for 2011 for each company. What conclusions concerning the companies' liquidity can be drawn from these ratios?
(b) Based on the information contained in these financial statements, compute the following 2011 ratios for each company.
  (1) Debt to assets ratio.
  (2) Times interest earned. (Hershey's total interest expense for 2011 was $94,780,000. See Tootsie Roll's Note 6 for its interest expense.)

What conclusions about the companies' long-run solvency can be drawn from the ratios?

RESEARCH CASE

BYP10-3 The September 1, 2009, edition of *CFO.com* contains an article by Marie Leone and Tim Reason entitled "Dirty Secrets." You can access this article at **www.cfo.com/article. cfm/14292477?f=singlepage**.

Instructions

Read the article and answer the following questions.
(a) Summarize the accounting for contingent items that is provided in this textbook.
(b) The authors of the article suggest that many companies are basically accounting for contingencies on a cash basis. Is this consistent with the approach you described in part (a)?
(c) The article suggests that many companies report one set of liability estimates to insurers and a different (lower) set of numbers in their financial statements. How is this possible, and what are the implications for investors?
(d) How do international accounting standards differ in terms of the amounts reported in these types of situations?

INTERPRETING FINANCIAL STATEMENTS

BYP10-4 Hechinger Co. and Home Depot are two home improvement retailers. Compared to Hechinger, founded in the early 1900s, Home Depot is a relative newcomer. But in recent years, while Home Depot was reporting large increases in net income, Hechinger was reporting increasingly large net losses. Finally, largely due to competition from Home Depot, Hechinger was forced to file for bankruptcy. Here are financial data for both companies (in millions).

	Hechinger	Home Depot
Cash	$ 21	$ 62
Receivables	0	469
Total current assets	1,153	4,933
Beginning total assets	1,668	11,229
Ending total assets	1,577	13,465
Beginning current liabilities	935	2,456
Ending current liabilities	938	2,857
Beginning total liabilities	1,392	4,015
Ending total liabilities	1,339	4,716
Interest expense	67	37
Income tax expense	3	1,040
Cash provided (used) by operations	(257)	1,917
Net income	(93)	1,614
Net sales	3,444	30,219

Instructions

Using the data provided, perform the following analysis.

(a) Calculate working capital and the current ratio for each company. Discuss their relative liquidity.

(b) Calculate the debt to assets ratio and times interest earned for each company. Discuss their relative solvency.

(c) Calculate the return on assets and profit margin for each company. Comment on their relative profitability.

(d) The notes to Home Depot's financial statements indicate that it leases many of its facilities using operating leases. If these assets had instead been purchased with debt, assets and liabilities would have increased by approximately $2,347 million. Calculate the company's debt to assets ratio employing this adjustment. Discuss the implications.

BYP10-5 For many years, Borders Group and Barnes and Noble were the dominant booksellers in the United States. They experienced rapid growth, and in the process they forced many small, independent bookstores out of business. Recently, Borders filed for bankruptcy. It was the victim of its inability to change with the times. It did not develop a viable business plan for dealing with digital books and online sales. Below is financial information (in millions) for the two companies, taken from the annual reports of each company one year before Borders filed for bankruptcy.

	Borders	Barnes and Noble
Current assets	$ 978.7	$1,719.5
Total assets	1,415.6	3,705.7
Current liabilities	918.1	1,724.4
Total liabilities	1,257.3	2,802.3
Net income/(loss)	(109.4)	36.7
Interest expense	24.1	28.2
Tax expense/(income tax benefit)	(31.3)	8.4

Instructions

(a) Compute the current ratio for each company.

(b) Compute the debt to assets ratio and times interest earned for each company. (*Hint:* A tax benefit means that rather than pay taxes, the company was due a refund because of its losses. For ratio purposes, a tax benefit is treated the opposite of tax expense.)

(c) Discuss the relative liquidity and solvency of each company. Did the bankruptcy of Borders seem likely?

REAL-WORLD FOCUS

BYP10-6 Bond or debt securities pay a stated rate of interest. This rate of interest is dependent on the risk associated with the investment. Also, bond prices change when the risks associated with those bonds change. Standard & Poor's provides ratings for companies that issue debt securities.

Address: **www.standardandpoors.com/ratings/definitions-and-faqs/en/us**, or go to **www.wiley.com/college/kimmel**

Instructions

Go to the website shown and answer the following questions.

(a) Explain the meaning of an "A" rating. Explain the meaning of a "C" rating.

(b) What types of things can cause a change in a company's credit rating?

(c) Explain the relationship between a company's credit rating and the merit of an investment in that company's bonds.

Critical Thinking

DECISION-MAKING ACROSS THE ORGANIZATION

BYP10-7   On January 1, 2012, Kenard Corporation issued $3,000,000, 5-year, 8% bonds at 97. The bonds pay interest annually on January 1. By January 1, 2014, the market rate of interest for bonds of risk similar to those of Kenard Corporation had risen. As a result, the market price of these bonds was $2,500,000 on January 1, 2014—below their carrying value of $2,946,000.

Mel Garner, president of the company, suggests repurchasing all of these bonds in the open market at the $2,500,000 price. But to do so the company will have to issue $2,500,000 (face value) of new 10-year, 12% bonds at par. The president asks you, as controller, "What is the feasibility of my proposed repurchase plan?"

Instructions

With the class divided into groups, answer the following.

(a) Prepare the journal entry to redeem the 5-year bonds on January 1, 2014. Prepare the journal entry to issue the new 10-year bonds.

(b) Prepare a short memo to the president in response to his request for advice. List the economic factors that you believe should be considered for his repurchase proposal.

COMMUNICATION ACTIVITY

BYP10-8   Harry Jackman, president of Weast, Inc., is considering the issuance of bonds to finance an expansion of his business. He has asked you to do the following: (1) discuss the advantages of bonds over common stock financing, (2) indicate the types of bonds he might issue, and (3) explain the issuing procedures used in bond transactions.

Instructions

Write a memorandum to the president, answering his request.

ETHICS CASES

BYP10-9   The July 1998 issue of *Inc.* magazine includes an article by Jeffrey L. Seglin entitled "Would You Lie to Save Your Company?" It recounts the following true situation:

"A Chief Executive Officer (CEO) of a $20-million company that repairs aircraft engines received notice from a number of its customers that engines that it had recently repaired had failed, and that the company's parts were to blame. The CEO had not yet determined whether his company's parts were, in fact, the cause of the problem. The Federal Aviation Administration (FAA) had been notified and was investigating the matter.

What complicated the situation was that the company was in the midst of its year-end audit. As part of the audit, the CEO was required to sign a letter saying that he was not aware of any significant outstanding circumstances that could negatively impact the company—in accounting terms, of any contingent liabilities. The auditor was not aware of the customer complaints or the FAA investigation.

The company relied heavily on short-term loans from eight banks. The CEO feared that if these lenders learned of the situation, they would pull their loans. The loss of these loans would force the company into bankruptcy, leaving hundreds of people without jobs. Prior to this problem, the company had a stellar performance record."

Instructions

Answer the following questions.

(a) Who are the stakeholders in this situation?

(b) What are the CEO's possible courses of action? What are the potential results of each course of action? (Take into account the two alternative outcomes: the FAA determines the company (1) was not at fault, and (2) was at fault.)

(c) What would you do, and why?

(d) Suppose the CEO decides to conceal the situation, and that during the next year the company is found to be at fault and is forced into bankruptcy. What losses are incurred by the stakeholders in this situation? Do you think the CEO should suffer legal consequences if he decides to conceal the situation?

BYP10-10   During the summer of 2002, the financial press reported that Citigroup was being investigated for allegations that it had arranged transactions for Enron so as to intentionally misrepresent the nature of the transactions and consequently achieve favorable balance sheet treatment. Essentially, the deals were structured to make it appear that money was coming into Enron from trading activities, rather than from loans.

A July 23, 2002, *New York Times* article by Richard Oppel and Kurt Eichenwald entitled "Citigroup Said to Mold Deal to Help Enron Skirt Rules" suggested that Citigroup intentionally kept certain parts of a secret oral agreement out of the written record for fear that it would change the accounting treatment. Critics contend that this had the effect of significantly understating Enron's liabilities, thus misleading investors and creditors. Citigroup maintains that, as a lender, it has no obligation to ensure that its clients account for transactions properly. The proper accounting, Citigroup insists, is the responsibility of the client and its auditor.

Instructions
Answer the following questions.

(a) Who are the stakeholders in this situation?

(b) Do you think that a lender, in general, in arranging so-called "structured financing" has a responsibility to ensure that its clients account for the financing in an appropriate fashion, or is this the responsibility of the client and its auditor?

(c) What effect did the fact that the written record did not disclose all characteristics of the transaction probably have on the auditor's ability to evaluate the accounting treatment of this transaction?

(d) The *New York Times* article noted that in one presentation made to sell this kind of deal to Enron and other energy companies, Citigroup stated that using such an arrangement "eliminates the need for capital markets disclosure, keeping structure mechanics private." Why might a company wish to conceal the terms of a financing arrangement from the capital markets (investors and creditors)? Is this appropriate? Do you think it is ethical for a lender to market deals in this way?

(e) Why was this deal more potentially harmful to shareholders than other off-balance-sheet transactions (for example, lease financing)?

ALL ABOUT YOU

BYP10-11   For most U.S. families, medical costs are substantial and rising. But will medical costs be your most substantial expense over your lifetime? Not likely. Will it be housing or food? Again, not likely. The answer: Taxes are likely to be your biggest expense. On average, Americans work 74 days to afford their federal taxes. Companies, too, have large tax burdens. They look very hard at tax issues in deciding where to build their plants and where to locate their administrative headquarters.

Instructions

(a) Determine what your state income taxes are if your taxable income is $60,000 and you file as a single taxpayer in the state in which you live.

(b) Assume that you own a home worth $200,000 in your community and the tax rate is 2.1%. Compute the property taxes you would pay.

(c) Assume that the total gasoline bill for your automobile is $1,200 a year (300 gallons at $4 per gallon). What are the amounts of state and federal taxes that you pay on the $1,200?

(d) Assume that your purchases for the year total $9,000. Of this amount, $5,000 was for food and prescription drugs. What is the amount of sales tax you would pay on these purchases?
    (*Note:* Many states do not have a sales tax for food or prescription drug purchases. Does yours?)

(e) Determine what your Social Security taxes are if your income is $60,000.

(f) Determine what your federal income taxes are if your taxable income is $60,000 and you file as a single taxpayer.

(g) Determine your total taxes paid based on the above calculations, and determine the percentage of income that you would pay in taxes based on the following formula: Total taxes paid ÷ Total income.

BYP10-12 Some employees are encouraging and setting up preventive healthcare programs. Here are the percentages for five unhealthy behaviors for individuals with some college education: current cigarette smoker (22.9%), five or more alcoholic drinks at one sitting at least once in the past year (30%), physically inactive (30%), obese (25.2%), or sleep less than 6 hours per day (30.3%).

Suppose you own a business. About a quarter of your employees smoke, and an even higher percentage are overweight. You decide to implement a mandatory health program that requires employees to quit smoking and to exercise regularly, with regular monitoring. If employees do not participate in the program, they will have to pay their own insurance premiums. Is this fair?

YES: It is the responsibility of management to try to maximize a company's profit. Employees with unhealthy habits drive up the cost of health insurance because they require more frequent and more costly medical attention.

NO: What people do on their own time is their own business. This represents an invasion of privacy, and is a form of discrimination.

Instructions
Write a response indicating your position regarding the situation. Provide support for your view.

FASB CODIFICATION ACTIVITY

BYP10-13 If your school has a subscription to the FASB Codification, go to **http://aaahq.org/asclogin.cfm** to log in and prepare responses to the following.
(a) What is the definition of current liabilities?
(b) What is the definition of long-term obligations?
(c) What guidance does the Codification provide for the disclosure of long-term obligations?

CONSIDERING PEOPLE, PLANET, AND PROFIT

BYP10-14 The December 10, 2011, edition of *The Economist* contains an article entitled "Helping the Poor to Save: Small Wonder." This article discusses how many of the world's poorest people benefit from borrowing small amounts of money.

Instructions
Read the article and answer the following questions. (The article can be accessed by doing an Internet search that includes the title of the article and magazine.)
(a) What monthly rate of interest do people pay on the loans they borrow from the microfinance organizations described in the article? What would these rates be on an annualized basis?
(b) The rates described in your answer to part (a) are very high. Explain how somebody can pay such high rates and yet still benefit from borrowing.
(c) Describe the structure of the typical village savings and loan organization.

Answers to Insight and Accounting Across the Organization Questions

p. 513 When Convertible Bonds Don't Q: The drop in stock prices did not change the debt to assets ratios of these companies. Discuss how the perception of a high debt to assets ratio changed before and after the fall in stock prices. **A:** When stock prices fell, the debt to assets of these companies was unchanged. The debt was outstanding before the fall, and it was outstanding after the fall. However, before the fall, many investors did not worry if a company had a high debt to assets ratio. They assumed that the debt would be converted to stock and so would never have to be repaid with cash. After the fall, it became clear that the debt would not be converted to stock. Suddenly, a high debt to assets ratio was a real concern.

p. 525 Debt Masking Q: What implications does debt masking have for an investor that is using the debt to assets ratio to evaluate a company's solvency? **A:** Since the debt to assets ratio is calculated using financial statement numbers from the end of the accounting period, debt masking could result in investors making incorrect assumptions about a company's solvency. By engaging in debt masking, a company is misleading investors because what it is disclosing at the end of the period does not reflect what its normal financial position was during most of the accounting period.

p. 527 "Covenant-Lite" Debt Q: How can financial ratios such as those covered in this chapter provide protection for creditors? **A:** Financial ratios such as the current ratio, debt to assets ratio, and the times interest earned provide indications of a company's liquidity and solvency. By specifying minimum levels of liquidity and solvency, as measured by these ratios, a creditor creates triggers that enable it to step in before a company's financial situation becomes too dire.

Answers to Self-Test Questions

1. a **2.** d **3.** b ($88,500 × .12 × $\frac{4}{12}$) **4.** d **5.** b ($4,515 ÷ 1.05) **6.** c **7.** b ($18,000 × $\frac{3}{12}$) **8.** c **9.** c **10.** a **11.** c **12.** d **13.** b ($103,745 − $100,000) **14.** c ($150,000 + $30,000 + $20,000) ÷ $30,000 **15.** a ***16.** c (($500,000 × .04) ÷ 5) ***17.** a ($500,000 − ($20,000 − (3 × $4,000))) ***18.** b (($938,554 × .10) − ($1,000,000 × .09)) = $3,855; ($1,000,000 − $938,554) − $3,855 ***19.** c ($1,072,096 × .12) ***20.** c ($1,165 − ($20,000 ×.015))

A Look at IFRS

LEARNING OBJECTIVE	11

Compare the accounting procedures for liabilities under GAAP and IFRS.

IFRS and GAAP have similar definitions of liabilities. IFRSs related to reporting and recognition of liabilities are found in *IAS 1 (revised)* ("Presentation of Financial Statements") and *IAS 37* ("Provisions, Contingent Liabilities, and Contingent Assets"). The general recording procedures for payroll are similar although differences occur depending on the types of benefits that are provided in different countries.

KEY POINTS

- The basic definition of a liability under GAAP and IFRS is very similar. In a more technical way, liabilities are defined by the IASB as a present obligation of the entity arising from past events, the settlement of which is expected to result in an outflow from the entity of resources embodying economic benefits. Liabilities may be legally enforceable via a contract or law but need not be. That is, they can arise due to normal business practices or customs.

- IFRS requires that companies classify liabilities as current or non-current on the face of the statement of financial position (balance sheet) except in industries where a **presentation** based on liquidity would be considered to provide more useful information (such as financial institutions). When current liabilities (also called short-term liabilities) are presented, they are generally presented in order of liquidity.

- Under IFRS, liabilities are classified as current if they are expected to be paid within 12 months.

- Similar to GAAP, items are normally reported in order of liquidity. Companies sometimes show liabilities before assets. Also, they will sometimes show non-current (long-term) liabilities before current liabilities.

- Under both GAAP and IFRS, preferred stock that is required to be redeemed at a specific point in time in the future must be reported as debt, rather than being presented as either equity or in a "mezzanine" area between debt and equity.

- Under IFRS, companies sometimes will net current liabilities against current assets to show working capital on the face of the statement of financial position. (This is evident in the Zetar financial statements in Appendix C.)

- IFRS requires use of the effective-interest method for amortization of bond discounts and premiums. GAAP allows use of the straight-line method where the difference is not material. Under IFRS, companies do not use a premium or discount account but instead show the bond at its net amount. For example, if a $100,000 bond was issued at 97, under IFRS a company would record:

Cash	97,000	
Bonds Payable		97,000

- The accounting for convertible bonds differs across IFRS and GAAP. Unlike GAAP, IFRS splits the proceeds from the convertible bond between an equity component and a debt component. The equity conversion rights are reported in equity.

To illustrate, assume that Harris Corp. issues convertible 7% bonds with a face value of $1,000,000 and receives $1,000,000. Comparable bonds without a conversion feature would have required a 9% rate of interest. To determine how much of the proceeds would be allocated to debt and how much to equity, the promised payments of the bond obligation would be discounted at the market rate of 9%. Suppose that this results in a present value of $850,000. The entry to record the issuance would be:

Cash	1,000,000	
Bonds Payable		850,000
Equity Conversion Rights (Equity)		150,000

- The IFRS leasing standard is *IAS 17*. Both Boards share the same objective of recording leases by lessees and lessors according to their economic substance—that is, according to the definitions of assets and liabilities. However, GAAP for leases is much more "rules-based," with specific bright-line criteria (such as the "90% of fair value" test) to determine if a lease arrangement transfers the risks and rewards of ownership. IFRS is more conceptual in its provisions. Rather than a 90% cut-off, it asks whether the agreement transfers substantially all of the risks and rewards associated with ownership.

- Under GAAP, some contingent liabilities are recorded in the financial statements, others are disclosed, and in some cases no disclosure is required. Unlike GAAP, IFRS reserves the use of the term **contingent liability** to refer only to possible obligations that are **not** recognized in the financial statements but may be disclosed if certain criteria are met. Contingent liabilities are defined in *IAS 37* as being:

  ◆ A possible obligation that arises from past events and whose existence will be confirmed only by the occurrence or non-occurrence of one or more uncertain future events not wholly within the control of the entity; or

  ◆ A present obligation that arises from past events but is not recognized because:

    ○ It is not probable that an outflow of resources embodying economic benefits will be required to settle the obligation; or

    ○ The amount of the obligation cannot be measured with sufficient reliability.

- For those items that GAAP would treat as recordable contingent liabilities, IFRS instead uses the term provisions. **Provisions** are defined as liabilities of uncertain timing or amount. Examples of provisions would be provisions for warranties, employee vacation pay, or anticipated losses. Under IFRS, the measurement of a provision related to an uncertain obligation is based on the best estimate of the expenditure required to settle the obligation.

LOOKING TO THE FUTURE

The FASB and IASB are currently involved in two projects, each of which has implications for the accounting for liabilities. One project is investigating approaches to differentiate between debt and equity instruments. The other project, the elements phase of the conceptual framework project, will evaluate the definitions of the fundamental building blocks of accounting. The results of these projects could change the classification of many debt and equity securities.

In addition to these projects, the FASB and IASB have also identified leasing as one of the most problematic areas of accounting. A joint project will initially focus primarily on lessee accounting. One of the first areas to be studied is, "What are the assets and liabilities to be recognized related to a lease contract?" Should the focus remain on the leased item or the right to use the leased item? This question is tied to the Boards' joint project on the conceptual framework—defining an "asset" and a "liability."

IFRS PRACTICE

IFRS SELF-TEST QUESTIONS

1. Which of the following is **false**?
   (a) Under IFRS, current liabilities must always be presented before non-current liabilities.
   (b) Under IFRS, an item is a current liability if it will be paid within the next 12 months.
   (c) Under IFRS, current liabilities are shown in order of liquidity.
   (d) Under IFRS, a liability is only recognized if it is a present obligation.

2. Under IFRS, a contingent liability is:
   (a) disclosed in the notes if certain criteria are met.
   (b) reported on the face of the financial statements if certain criteria are met.
   (c) the same as a provision.
   (d) not addressed by IFRS.

3. Stevens Corporation issued 5% convertible bonds with a total face value of $3,000,000 for $3,000,000. If the bonds had not had a conversion feature, they would have sold for $2,600,000. Under IFRS, the entry to record the transaction would require a credit to:
   (a) Bonds Payable for $3,000,000.
   (b) Bonds Payable for $400,000.
   (c) Equity Conversion Rights for $400,000.
   (d) Discount on Bonds Payable for $400,000.

4. Under IFRS, if preference shares (preferred stock) have a requirement to be redeemed at a specific point in time in the future, they are treated:
   (a) as a type of asset account.
   (b) as ordinary shares (common stock).
   (c) in the same fashion as other types of preference shares.
   (d) as a liability.

5. The joint projects of the FASB and IASB could potentially:
   (a) change the definition of liabilities.
   (b) change the definition of equity.
   (c) change the definition of assets.
   (d) All of the above.

IFRS CONCEPTS AND APPLICATION

IFRS10-1 Explain how IFRS defines a provision and give an example.

IFRS10-2 Explain how IFRS defines a contingent liability and give an example.

IFRS10-3 Briefly describe some of the similarities and differences between GAAP and IFRS with respect to the accounting for liabilities.

IFRS10-4 Ratzlaff Company issues €2 million, 10-year, 8% bonds at 97, with interest payable on July 1 and January 1.

Instructions
   (a) Prepare the journal entry to record the sale of these bonds on January 1, 2014.
   (b) Assuming instead that the above bonds sold for 104, prepare the journal entry to record the sale of these bonds on January 1, 2014.

IFRS10-5 Many multinational companies find it beneficial to have their shares listed on securities exchanges in foreign countries. In order to do this, they must comply with the securities laws of those countries. Some of these laws relate to the form of financial disclosure the company must provide, including disclosures related to contingent liabilities. This exercise investigates the Tokyo Stock Exchange, the largest securities exchange in Japan.

Address: **www.tse.or.jp/english/**, or go to **www.wiley.com/college/kimmel**

Steps
1. Choose **About TSE**.
2. Choose **History of TSE**. Answer questions (a) and (b).
3. Choose **Listed Company information**.
4. Choose **Disclosure**. Answer questions (c) and (d).
5. Answer the following questions.
   (a) When was the first securities exchange opened in Japan? How many exchanges does Japan have today?
   (b) What event caused trading to stop for a period of time in Japan?
   (c) What are four examples of decisions by corporations that must be disclosed at the time of their occurrence?
   (d) What are four examples of "occurrence of material fact" that must be disclosed at the time of their occurrence?

INTERNATIONAL FINANCIAL STATEMENT ANALYSIS: *Zetar plc*

IFRS10-6 The financial statements of Zetar plc are presented in Appendix C. The company's complete annual report, including the notes to its financial statements, is available in the Investors section at **www.zetarplc.com**.

Instructions
Use the company's annual report to answer the following questions.
   (a) According to the notes to the financial statements, what types of transactions do trade payables relate to? What was the average amount of time it took the company to pay its payables?
   (b) Note 4.2 discusses provisions that the company records for certain types of activities. What do the provisions relate to, what are the estimates based on, and what could cause those estimates to change in subsequent periods?
   (c) What was the average interest rate paid on bank loans and overdrafts?

Answers to IFRS Self-Test Questions
1. a   2. a   3. c   4. d   5. d

CHAPTER 11

Paul Sakuma/AP/Wide World Photos

✔ The Navigator

- Scan Learning Objectives
- Read Feature Story
- Scan Preview
- Read Text and Answer **Do it!**
  ○ p. 577 ○ p. 579 ○ p. 581
  ○ p. 583 ○ p. 589 ○ p. 593
- Work Using the Decision Toolkit
- Review Summary of Learning Objectives
- Work Comprehensive **Do it!** p. 600
- Answer Self-Test Questions
- Complete Assignments
- Go to WileyPLUS for practice and tutorials

 Read A Look at IFRS p. 621

REPORTING AND ANALYZING STOCKHOLDERS' EQUITY

LEARNING OBJECTIVES

After studying this chapter, you should be able to:

1. Identify and discuss the major characteristics of a corporation.
2. Record the issuance of common stock.
3. Explain the accounting for the purchase of treasury stock.
4. Differentiate preferred stock from common stock.
5. Prepare the entries for cash dividends and understand the effect of stock dividends and stock splits.
6. Identify the items that affect retained earnings.
7. Prepare a comprehensive stockholders' equity section.
8. Evaluate a corporation's dividend and earnings performance from a stockholder's perspective.

Suppose you started one of the fastest-growing companies in the history of business. Now suppose that by "going public"—issuing stock of your company to outside investors who are foaming at the mouth for the chance to buy its shares—you would instantly become one of the richest people in the world. Would you hesitate?

That is exactly what Mark Zuckerberg, the founder of Facebook, did. Many people who start high-tech companies go public as soon as possible to cash in on their riches. But Zuckerberg was reluctant to do so. To understand why, you need to understand the advantages and disadvantages of being a public company.

The main motivation for issuing shares to the public is to raise money so you can grow your business. However, unlike a manufacturer or even an online retailer, Facebook doesn't need major physical resources, it doesn't have inventory, and it doesn't really need much money for marketing. So in the past, the company hasn't had much need for additional cash beyond what it was already generating on its own.

But why not go public anyway, so the company would have some extra cash on hand—and so you personally get rich? As head of a closely held, nonpublic company, Zuckerberg is subject to far fewer regulations than a public company.

> ## OH WELL, I GUESS I'LL GET RICH

Also, the chief executive officer (CEO) of a publicly traded company must respond to shareholder and board of director demands. Prior to going public, Zuckerberg could basically run the company however he wanted to.

For example, consider this recent, huge Facebook transaction. Early in 2012, the company shocked the investment community by purchasing the photo-sharing service Instagram. The purchase was startling both for its speed and price. After considering the purchase over the course of a weekend (while the rest of us were probably wasting time on our Facebook pages), Zuckerberg dropped $1 billion. He basically didn't seek anyone's approval. He thought it was a good idea, so he just did it. The structured decision-making process of a public company would make it very difficult for a public company to move that fast.

Speed is useful, but it is likely that Facebook will make even bigger acquisitions in the future. To survive among the likes of Microsoft, Google, and Apple, it needs lots of cash. To raise that amount of money, the company really needed to go public. So in 2012, Mark Zuckerberg reluctantly made Facebook a public company, thus becoming one of the richest people in the world.

The Navigator

INSIDE CHAPTER 11 . . .

Corporations like Facebook and Google have substantial resources at their disposal. In fact, the corporation is the dominant form of business organization in the United States in terms of sales, earnings, and number of employees. All of the 500 largest U.S. companies are corporations. In this chapter, we look at the essential features of a corporation and explain the accounting for a corporation's capital stock transactions.

The content and organization of the chapter are as follows.

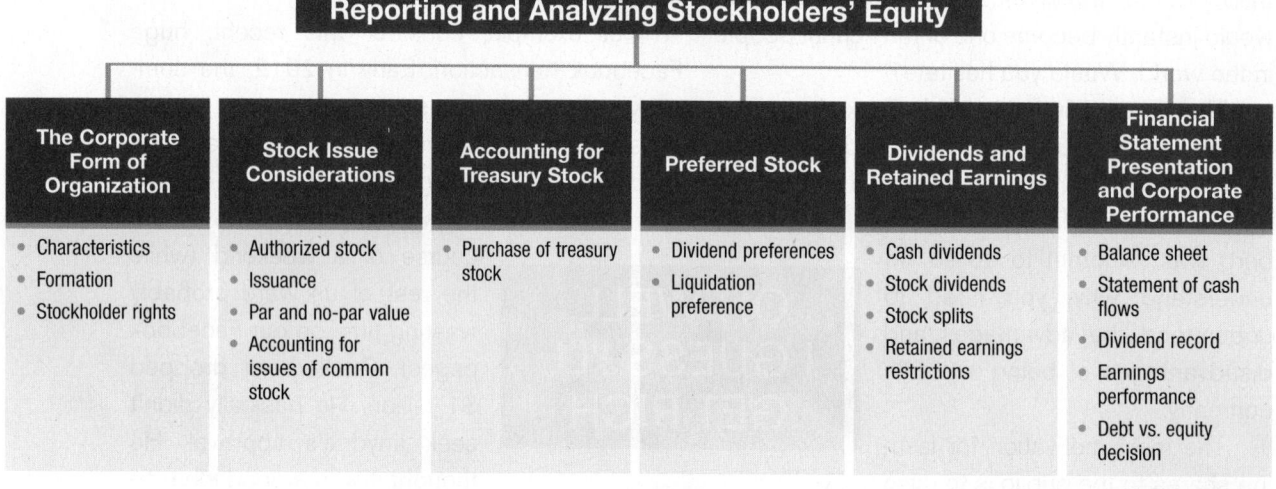

Reporting and Analyzing Stockholders' Equity

The Corporate Form of Organization	Stock Issue Considerations	Accounting for Treasury Stock	Preferred Stock	Dividends and Retained Earnings	Financial Statement Presentation and Corporate Performance
• Characteristics • Formation • Stockholder rights	• Authorized stock • Issuance • Par and no-par value • Accounting for issues of common stock	• Purchase of treasury stock	• Dividend preferences • Liquidation preference	• Cash dividends • Stock dividends • Stock splits • Retained earnings restrictions	• Balance sheet • Statement of cash flows • Dividend record • Earnings performance • Debt vs. equity decision

✔ The Navigator

The Corporate Form of Organization

LEARNING OBJECTIVE 1

Identify and discuss the major characteristics of a corporation.

A corporation is created by law. As a legal entity, a corporation has most of the rights and privileges of a person. The major exceptions relate to privileges that can be exercised only by a living person, such as the right to vote or to hold public office. Similarly, a corporation is subject to the same duties and responsibilities as a person. For example, it must abide by the law and it must pay taxes.

We can classify corporations in a variety of ways. Two common classifications are **by purpose** and **by ownership**. A corporation may be organized for the purpose of making a profit (such as Facebook or General Motors), or it may be a nonprofit charitable, medical, or educational corporation (such as the Salvation Army or the American Cancer Society).

Classification by ownership differentiates publicly held and privately held corporations. A **publicly held corporation** may have thousands of stockholders, and its stock is traded on a national securities market such as the New York Stock Exchange. Examples are IBM, Caterpillar, and General Electric. In contrast, a **privately held corporation**, often referred to as a closely held corporation, usually has only a few stockholders and does not offer its stock for sale to the general public. Privately held companies are generally much smaller than publicly held companies although some notable exceptions exist. Before going public, Facebook was one example. Also, Cargill Inc., a private corporation that trades in grain and other commodities, is one of the largest companies in the United States. This chapter deals primarily with issues related to publicly held companies.

CHARACTERISTICS OF A CORPORATION

Many businesses start as partnerships or sole proprietorships but eventually convert to the corporate form. For example, Nike's founders formed their original organization as a partnership. In 1968, they reorganized the company as a corporation. A number of characteristics distinguish a corporation from sole proprietorships and partnerships. The most important of these characteristics are explained below.

Stockholders
Legal existence separate from owners

Separate Legal Existence

As an entity separate and distinct from its owners, the corporation acts under its own name rather than in the name of its stockholders. Facebook, for example, buys, owns, and sells property, borrows money, and enters into legally binding contracts in its own name. It may also sue or be sued. It pays taxes as a separate entity.

In a partnership, the acts of the owners (partners) bind the partnership. In contrast, the acts of corporate owners (stockholders) do not bind the corporation unless such owners are agents of the corporation. For example, if you own shares of Facebook stock, you do not have the right to purchase inventory for the company unless you are also designated as an agent of the corporation.

Limited Liability of Stockholders

Since a corporation is a separate legal entity, creditors ordinarily have recourse only to corporate assets to satisfy their claims. The liability of stockholders is normally limited to their investment in the corporation. Creditors have no legal claim on the personal assets of the stockholders unless fraud has occurred. Thus, even in the event of bankruptcy of the corporation, stockholders' losses are generally limited to the amount of capital they have invested in the corporation.

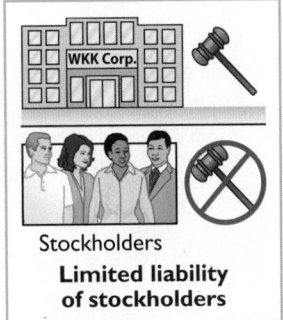

Stockholders
Limited liability of stockholders

Transferable Ownership Rights

Ownership of a corporation is held in shares of capital stock, which are transferable units. Stockholders may dispose of part or all of their interest in a corporation simply by selling their stock. The transfer of an ownership interest in a partnership requires the consent of each partner. In contrast, the transfer of stock is entirely at the discretion of the stockholder. It does not require the approval of either the corporation or other stockholders.

Transferable ownership rights

The transfer of ownership rights among stockholders normally has no effect on the operating activities of the corporation. Nor does it affect the corporation's assets, liabilities, and total stockholders' equity. The transfer of ownership rights is a transaction between individual owners. The company does not participate in the transfer of these ownership rights after the original sale of the capital stock.

Ability to Acquire Capital

It is relatively easy for a corporation to obtain capital through the issuance of stock. Buying stock in a corporation is often attractive to an investor because a stockholder has limited liability and shares of stock are readily transferable. Also, numerous individuals can become stockholders by investing small amounts of money.

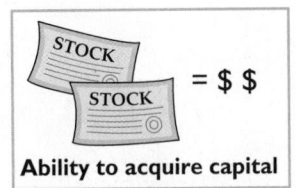

Ability to acquire capital

Continuous Life

The life of a corporation is stated in its charter. The life may be perpetual or it may be limited to a specific number of years. If it is limited, the company extends the period of existence through renewal of the charter. Since a corporation is a separate legal entity, its continuance as a going concern is not affected by the withdrawal, death, or incapacity of a stockholder, employee, or officer. As a result, a successful corporation can have a continuous and perpetual life.

Continuous life

Corporation Management

Although stockholders legally own the corporation, they manage it indirectly through a board of directors they elect. Mark Zuckerberg is the chairman of Facebook's board of directors. The board, in turn, formulates the operating policies for the company. The board also selects officers, such as a president and one or more vice presidents, to execute policy and to perform daily management functions. As a result of the Sarbanes-Oxley Act, the board is required to monitor management's actions closely. Many feel that the failures at Enron, WorldCom, and more recently MF Global could have been avoided by more diligent boards.

Illustration 11-1 depicts a typical organization chart showing the delegation of responsibility.

Illustration 11-1 Corporation organization chart

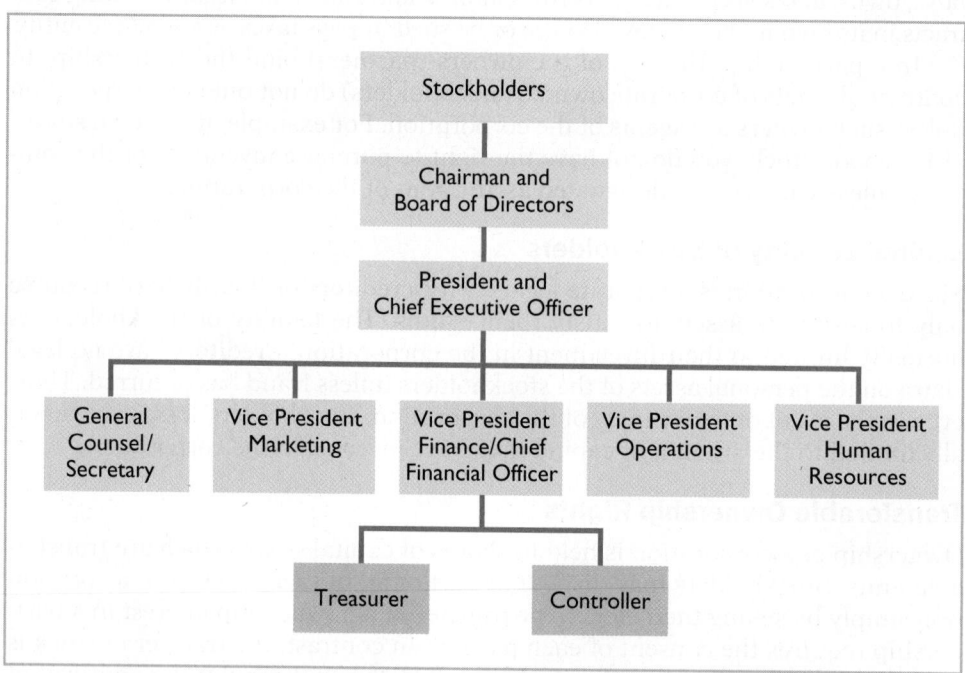

The chief executive officer (CEO) has overall responsibility for managing the business. As the organization chart shows, the CEO delegates responsibility to other officers. The chief accounting officer is the **controller**. The controller (1) maintains the accounting records, (2) maintains an adequate system of internal control, and (3) prepares financial statements, tax returns, and internal reports. The **treasurer** has custody of the corporation's funds and maintains the company's cash position.

Ethics Note Managers who are not owners are often compensated based on the performance of the company. They thus may be tempted to exaggerate company performance by inflating income figures.

The organizational structure of a corporation enables a company to hire professional managers to run the business. On the other hand, the separation of ownership and management often reduces an owner's ability to actively manage the company.

Government Regulations

A corporation is subject to numerous state and federal regulations. For example, state laws usually prescribe the requirements for issuing stock, the distributions of earnings permitted to stockholders, and acceptable methods for buying back and retiring stock. Federal securities laws govern the sale of capital stock to the general public. Also, publicly held corporations must disclose their financial affairs to the Securities and Exchange Commission (SEC) through quarterly and annual reports. The Sarbanes-Oxley Act increased the company's responsibility for the accuracy of these reports. In addition, when a corporate stock is listed and traded on organized securities exchanges, the corporation must comply with the reporting requirements of these exchanges.

People, Planet, and Profit Insight

The Impact of Corporate Social Responsibility

A recent survey conducted by Institutional Shareholder Services, a proxy advisory firm, shows that 83% of investors now believe environmental and social factors can significantly impact shareholder value over the long term. This belief is clearly visible in the rising level of support for shareholder proposals requesting action related to social and environmental issues.

The following table shows that the number of corporate social responsibility (CSR) related shareholder proposals rose from 150 in 2000 to 191 in 2010. Moreover, those proposals received average voting support of 18.4% of votes cast versus just 7.5% a decade earlier.

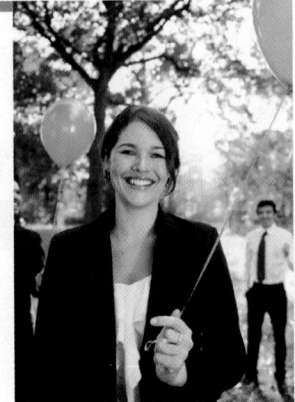

©Robert Churchill/iStockphoto

Trends in Shareholder Proposals on Corporate Responsibility

	2000	2005	2010
Number of proposals voted	150	155	191
Average voting support	7.5%	9.9%	18.4%
Percent proposals receiving >10% support	16.7%	31.2%	52.1%

Source: Investor Responsibility Research Center, Ernst & Young, *Seven Questions CEOs and Boards Should Ask About: "Triple Bottom Line" Reporting.*

? Why are CSR-related shareholder proposals increasing? (See page 620.)

Additional Taxes

Owners of proprietorships and partnerships report their share of earnings on their personal income tax returns. The individual owner then pays taxes on this amount. Corporations, on the other hand, must pay federal and state income taxes as a separate legal entity. These taxes can be substantial. They can amount to as much as 40% of taxable income.

In addition, stockholders are required to pay taxes on cash dividends. Thus, many argue that corporate income is **taxed twice (double taxation)**—once at the corporate level and again at the individual level.

Illustration 11-2 shows the advantages and disadvantages of a corporation compared to a sole proprietorship and partnership.

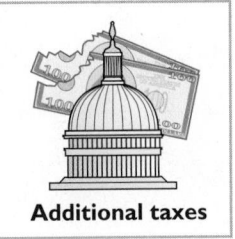

Additional taxes

Advantages	Disadvantages
• Separate legal existence	• Corporation management—separation of ownership and management
• Limited liability of stockholders	• Government regulations
• Transferable ownership rights	• Additional taxes
• Ability to acquire capital	
• Continuous life	
• Corporation management—professional managers	

Illustration 11-2 Advantages and disadvantages of a corporation

Other Forms of Business Organization

A variety of "hybrid" organizational forms—forms that combine different attributes of partnerships and corporations—now exist. For example, one type of corporate form, called an **S corporation**, allows for legal treatment as a corporation but tax treatment as a partnership—that is, no double taxation. Because of changes to the S corporation's rules, more small- and medium-sized businesses now may choose S corporation treatment. One of the primary criteria is that the company cannot have more than 75 shareholders. Other forms of organization include limited partnerships, limited liability partnerships (LLPs), and limited liability companies (LLCs).

DECISION TOOLKIT

DECISION CHECKPOINTS	INFO NEEDED FOR DECISION	TOOL TO USE FOR DECISION	HOW TO EVALUATE RESULTS
Should the company incorporate?	Capital needs, growth expectations, type of business, tax status	Corporations have limited liability, better capital-raising ability, and professional managers. But they suffer from additional taxes, government regulations, and separation of ownership from management.	Must carefully weigh the costs and benefits in light of the particular circumstances.

FORMING A CORPORATION

A corporation is formed by grant of a state charter. The charter is a document that describes the name and purpose of the corporation, the types and number of shares of stock that are authorized to be issued, the names of the individuals that formed the company, and the number of shares that these individuals agreed to purchase. Regardless of the number of states in which a corporation has operating divisions, it is incorporated in only one state. It is to the company's advantage to incorporate in a state whose laws are favorable to the corporate form of business organization. For example, although General Motors has its headquarters in Michigan, it is incorporated in New Jersey. In fact, more and more corporations have been incorporating in states with rules that favor existing management. For example, Gulf Oil changed its state of incorporation to Delaware to thwart possible unfriendly takeovers. There, certain defensive tactics against takeovers can be approved by the board of directors alone, without a vote by shareholders.

Upon receipt of its charter from the state of incorporation, the corporation establishes **by-laws**. The by-laws establish the internal rules and procedures for conducting the affairs of the corporation. Corporations engaged in interstate commerce must also obtain a **license** from each state in which they do business. The license subjects the corporation's operating activities to the general corporation laws of the state.

STOCKHOLDER RIGHTS

When chartered, the corporation begins selling shares of stock. When a corporation has only one class of stock, it is identified as **common stock**. Each share of common stock gives the stockholder the ownership rights pictured in Illustration 11-3. The articles of incorporation or the by-laws state the ownership rights of a share of stock.

Proof of stock ownership is evidenced by a printed or engraved form known as a **stock certificate**. As shown in Illustration 11-4, the face of the certificate shows the name of the corporation, the stockholder's name, the class and special features of the stock, the number of shares owned, and the signatures of authorized corporate officials. Certificates are prenumbered to ensure proper control over their use; they may be issued for any quantity of shares.

Stockholders have the right to:

1. Vote in election of board of directors at annual meeting and vote on actions that require stockholder approval.

2. Share the corporate earnings through receipt of dividends.

3. Keep the same percentage ownership when new shares of stock are issued (**preemptive right**[1]).

4. Share in assets upon liquidation in proportion to their holdings. This is called a **residual claim** because owners are paid with assets that remain after all other claims have been paid.

Illustration 11-3
Ownership rights of stockholders

Illustration 11-4 A stock certificate

Stock Issue Considerations

LEARNING OBJECTIVE 2

Record the issuance of common stock.

Although Facebook incorporated in 2004, it did not sell stock to the public until 2012. At that time, Facebook evidently decided it would benefit from the infusion of cash that a public sale of its shares would bring. When a corporation decides to

---

[1]A number of companies have eliminated the preemptive right because they believe it places an unnecessary and cumbersome demand on management. For example, IBM, by stockholder approval, has dropped its preemptive right for stockholders.

issue stock, it must resolve a number of basic questions: How many shares should it authorize for sale? How should it issue the stock? What value should it assign to the stock? We address these questions in the following sections.

AUTHORIZED STOCK

Authorized stock is the amount of stock that a corporation is authorized to sell as indicated in its charter. If the corporation has sold all of its authorized stock, then it must obtain permission from the state to change its charter before it can issue additional shares.

The authorization of common stock does not result in a formal accounting entry. The reason is that the event has no immediate effect on either corporate assets or stockholders' equity. However, the corporation discloses in the stockholders' equity section of the balance sheet the number of shares authorized.

ISSUANCE OF STOCK

International Note U.S. and U.K. corporations raise most of their capital through millions of outside shareholders and bondholders. In contrast, companies in Germany, France, and Japan acquire financing mostly from large banks or other financial institutions. Consequently, in the latter environment, shareholders are somewhat less important.

A corporation can issue common stock **directly** to investors. Alternatively, it can issue common stock **indirectly** through an investment banking firm that specializes in bringing securities to the attention of prospective investors. Direct issue is typical in closely held companies. Indirect issue is customary for a publicly held corporation.

New issues of stock may be offered for sale to the public through various organized U.S. or foreign securities exchanges. Based on recent figures, the top five exchanges by value of shares traded are the New York Stock Exchange, Nasdaq stock market, London Stock Exchange, Tokyo Stock Exchange, and Euronext.

ANATOMY OF A FRAUD

The president, chief operating officer, and chief financial officer of SafeNet, a software encryption company, were each awarded employee stock options by the company's board of directors as part of their compensation package. Stock options enable an employee to buy a company's stock sometime in the future at the price that existed when the stock option was awarded. For example, suppose that you received stock options today, when the stock price of your company was $30. Three years later, if the stock price rose to $100, you could "exercise" your options and buy the stock for $30 per share, thereby making $70 per share. After being awarded their stock options, the three employees changed the award dates in the company's records to dates in the past, when the company's stock was trading at historical lows. For example, using the previous example, they would choose a past date when the stock was selling for $10 per share, rather than the $30 price on the actual award date. In our example, this would increase the profit from exercising the options to $90 per share.

Total take: $1.7 million

THE MISSING CONTROL

Independent internal verification. The company's board of directors should have ensured that the awards were properly administered. For example, the date on the minutes from the board meeting should be compared to the dates that were recorded for the awards. In addition, the dates should again be confirmed upon exercise.

PAR AND NO-PAR VALUE STOCKS

Par value stock is capital stock that has been assigned a value per share in the corporate charter. Years ago, par value determined the legal capital that must be retained in the business for the protection of corporate creditors. That amount is not available for withdrawal by stockholders. Thus, in the past, most states required the corporation to sell its shares at par or above.

However, the usefulness of par value as a device to protect creditors was limited because par value was often immaterial relative to the value of the company's stock in the securities markets—even at the time of issue. For example, Loews Corporation's par value is $0.01 per share, yet a new issue in a recent year would have sold at a **market price** in the $32 per share range. Thus, par has no relationship with market price. In the vast majority of cases, it is an immaterial amount. As a consequence, today many states do not require a par value. Instead, they use other means to protect creditors.

No-par value stock is capital stock that has not been assigned a value in the corporate charter. No-par value stock is fairly common today. For example, Nike and Procter & Gamble both have no-par stock. In many states, the board of directors assigns a **stated value** to the no-par shares.

Do it!

Indicate whether each of the following statements is true or false.

_____ 1. Similar to partners in a partnership, stockholders of a corporation have unlimited liability.

_____ 2. It is relatively easy for a corporation to obtain capital through the issuance of stock.

_____ 3. The separation of ownership and management is an advantage of the corporate form of business.

_____ 4. The journal entry to record the authorization of capital stock includes a credit to the appropriate capital stock account.

_____ 5. All states require a par value per share for capital stock.

Solution

1. False. The liability of stockholders is normally limited to their investment in the corporation.
2. True.
3. False. The separation of ownership and management is a disadvantage of the corporate form of business.
4. False. The authorization of capital stock does not result in a formal accounting entry.
5. False. Many states do not require a par value.

Related exercise material: **BE11-1** and **Do it! 11-1**.

CORPORATE ORGANIZATION

Action Plan

- Review the characteristics of a corporation and understand which are advantages and which are disadvantages.
- Understand that corporations raise capital through the issuance of stock, which can be par or no-par.

The Navigator

ACCOUNTING FOR ISSUES OF COMMON STOCK

The stockholders' equity section of a corporation's balance sheet includes (1) **paid-in (contributed) capital** and (2) **retained earnings (earned capital)**. The distinction between paid-in capital and retained earnings is important from both a legal and an economic point of view. **Paid-in capital** is the amount stockholders paid to the corporation in exchange for shares of ownership. **Retained earnings** is earned capital held for future use in the business. In this section, we discuss the accounting for paid-in capital. In a later section, we discuss retained earnings.

Helpful Hint Stock is sometimes issued in exchange for services (payment to attorneys or consultants, for example) or for noncash assets (land or buildings). The value recorded for the shares issued is determined by either the market price of the shares or the value of the good or service received, depending upon which amount the company can more readily determine.

Let's now look at how to account for new issues of common stock. The primary objectives in accounting for the issuance of common stock are (1) to identify the specific sources of paid-in capital and (2) to maintain the distinction between paid-in capital and retained earnings. As shown below, **the issuance of common stock affects only paid-in capital accounts**.

As discussed earlier, par value does not indicate a stock's market price. The cash proceeds from issuing par value stock may be equal to, greater than, or less than par value. When a company records the issuance of common stock for cash, it credits the par value of the shares to Common Stock and records in a separate paid-in capital account the portion of the proceeds that is above or below par value.

To illustrate, assume that Hydro-Slide, Inc. issues 1,000 shares of $1 par value common stock at par for cash. The entry to record this transaction is:

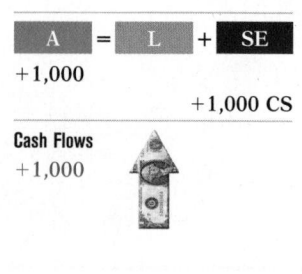

Cash	1,000	
Common Stock		1,000
(To record issuance of 1,000 shares of $1 par common stock at par)		

Now assume Hydro-Slide, Inc. issues an additional 1,000 shares of the $1 par value common stock for cash at $5 per share. The amount received above the par value, in this case $4 ($5 − $1), would be credited to Paid-in Capital in Excess of Par Value. The entry is:

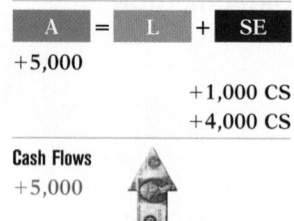

Cash	5,000	
Common Stock (1,000 × $1)		1,000
Paid-in Capital in Excess of Par Value		4,000
(To record issuance of 1,000 shares of common stock in excess of par)		

The total paid-in capital from these two transactions is $6,000. If Hydro-Slide, Inc. has retained earnings of $27,000, the stockholders' equity section of the balance sheet is as shown in Illustration 11-5.

Illustration 11-5
Stockholders' equity—paid-in capital in excess of par value

HYDRO-SLIDE, INC.	
Balance Sheet (partial)	
Stockholders' equity	
Paid-in capital	
Common stock	$ 2,000
Paid-in capital in excess of par value	4,000
Total paid-in capital	6,000
Retained earnings	27,000
Total stockholders' equity	$33,000

Some companies issue no-par stock with a stated value. For accounting purposes, companies treat the stated value in the same way as the par value. For example, if in our Hydro-Slide example the stock was no-par stock with a stated value of $1, the entries would be the same as those presented for the par stock except the term "Par Value" would be replaced with "Stated Value." If a company issues no-par stock that does not have a stated value, then it credits to the Common Stock account the full amount received. In such a case, there is no need for the Paid-in Capital in Excess of Stated Value account.

Investor Insight

How to Read Stock Quotes

Organized exchanges trade the stock of publicly held companies at dollar prices per share established by the interaction between buyers and sellers. For each listed security, the financial press reports the high and low prices of the stock during the year, the total volume of stock traded on a given day, the high and low prices for the day, and the closing market price, with the net change for the day. Facebook is listed on the Nasdaq exchange. Here is a recent listing for Facebook:

	52 Weeks						
Stock	High	Low	Volume	High	Low	Close	Net Change
Facebook	45.00	25.52	30,129,088	32.08	29.41	30.01	−1.93

These numbers indicate the following. The high and low market prices for the last 52 weeks have been $45.00 and $25.52. The trading volume for the day was 30,129,088 shares. The high, low, and closing prices for that date were $32.08, $29.41, and $30.01, respectively. The net change for the day was a decrease of $1.93 per share.

? For stocks traded on organized exchanges, how are the dollar prices per share established? What factors might influence the price of shares in the marketplace? (See page 620.)

Emmanuel Dunand/AFP/Getty Images

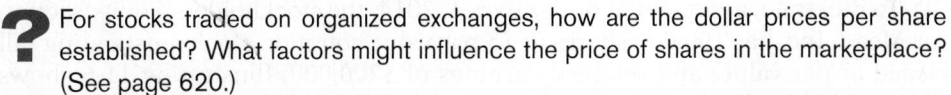 Cayman Corporation issued 100,000 shares of $10 par value common stock for cash at $12 per share on March 1. Journalize the issuance of the shares.

Solution

Mar. 1	Cash		1,200,000	
	Common Stock			1,000,000
	Paid-in Capital in Excess of Par Value			200,000
	(To record issuance of 100,000 shares at $12 per share)			

Related exercise material: **BE11-2, BE11-3, *Do it!* 11-2**, and **E11-1**.

ISSUANCE OF STOCK

Action Plan

- In issuing shares for cash, credit Common Stock for par value per share.
- Credit any additional proceeds in excess of par value to a separate paid-in capital account.

Accounting for Treasury Stock

Treasury stock is a corporation's own stock that has been reacquired by the corporation and is being held for future use. A corporation may acquire treasury stock for various reasons:

1. To reissue the shares to officers and employees under bonus and stock compensation plans.

2. To increase trading of the company's stock in the securities market. Companies expect that buying their own stock will signal that management believes the stock is underpriced, which they hope will enhance its market price.

3. To have additional shares available for use in acquiring other companies.

4. To reduce the number of shares outstanding and thereby increase earnings per share.

LEARNING OBJECTIVE 3

Explain the accounting for the purchase of treasury stock.

A less frequent reason for purchasing treasury shares is to eliminate hostile shareholders by buying them out.

Many corporations have treasury stock. For example, in the United States approximately 65% of companies have treasury stock.[2] In the first quarter of 2007, companies in the Standard & Poor's 500-stock index spent a record of about $118 billion to buy treasury stock. In a recent year, Nike purchased more than 6 million treasury shares. At one point, stock repurchases were so substantial that a study by two Federal Reserve economists suggested that a sharp reduction in corporate purchases of treasury shares might result in a sharp drop in the value of the U.S. stock market.

PURCHASE OF TREASURY STOCK

The purchase of treasury stock is generally accounted for by the **cost method**. This method derives its name from the fact that the Treasury Stock account is maintained at the cost of shares purchased. Under the cost method, **companies increase (debit) Treasury Stock by the price paid to reacquire the shares. Treasury Stock decreases by the same amount when the company later sells the shares**.

To illustrate, assume that on January 1, 2014, the stockholders' equity section for Mead, Inc. has 100,000 shares of $5 par value common stock outstanding (all issued at par value) and retained earnings of $200,000. Illustration 11-6 shows the stockholders' equity section of the balance sheet before purchase of treasury stock.

Illustration 11-6
Stockholders' equity with no treasury stock

MEAD, INC.	
Balance Sheet (partial)	
Stockholders' equity	
Paid-in capital	
Common stock, $5 par value, 400,000 shares authorized,	
100,000 shares issued and outstanding	$500,000
Retained earnings	200,000
Total stockholders' equity	$700,000

On February 1, 2014, Mead acquires 4,000 shares of its stock at $8 per share. The entry is:

Feb.	1	Treasury Stock	32,000	
		Cash		32,000
		(To record purchase of 4,000 shares of treasury stock at $8 per share)		

The Treasury Stock account would increase by the cost of the shares purchased ($32,000). The original paid-in capital account, Common Stock, would not be affected because **the number of issued shares does not change**.

Companies show treasury stock as a deduction from total paid-in capital and retained earnings in the stockholders' equity section of the balance sheet. Illustration 11-7 shows this presentation for Mead, Inc. Thus, the acquisition of treasury stock reduces stockholders' equity.

A = L + SE
−32,000 TS
−32,000

Cash Flows
−32,000

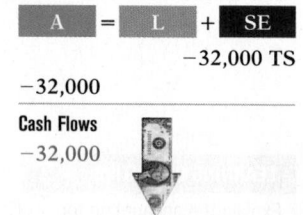

Helpful Hint Treasury Stock is a contra stockholders' equity account.

---

[2]*Accounting Trends & Techniques—2011* (New York: American Institute of Certified Public Accountants).

Illustration 11-7
Stockholders' equity with
treasury stock

MEAD, INC.
Balance Sheet (partial)

Stockholders' equity	
Paid-in capital	
Common stock, $5 par value, 400,000 shares authorized,	
100,000 shares issued and 96,000 shares outstanding	$500,000
Retained earnings	200,000
Total paid-in capital and retained earnings	700,000
Less: Treasury stock (4,000 shares)	32,000
Total stockholders' equity	$668,000

Company balance sheets disclose both the number of shares issued (100,000) and the number in the treasury (4,000). The difference is the number of shares of stock outstanding (96,000). The term **outstanding stock** means the number of shares of issued stock that are being held by stockholders.

In a bold (and some would say risky) move, Reebok at one time bought back nearly a third of its shares. This repurchase of shares dramatically reduced Reebok's available cash. In fact, the company borrowed significant funds to accomplish the repurchase. In a press release, management stated that it was repurchasing the shares because it believed that the stock was severely underpriced. The repurchase of so many shares was meant to signal management's belief in good future earnings.

Skeptics, however, suggested that Reebok's management was repurchasing shares to make it less likely that the company would be acquired by another company (in which case Reebok's top managers would likely lose their jobs). Acquiring companies like to purchase companies with large cash reserves so they can pay off debt used in the acquisition. By depleting its cash, Reebok became a less likely acquisition target.

Ethics Note The purchase of treasury stock reduces the cushion for creditors. To protect creditors, many states require that a portion of retained earnings equal to the cost of the treasury stock purchased be restricted from being paid as dividends.

Do it!

Santa Anita Inc. purchases 3,000 shares of its $50 par value common stock for $180,000 cash on July 1. It expects to hold the shares in the treasury until resold. Journalize the treasury stock transaction.

Solution

July	1	Treasury Stock	180,000	
		Cash		180,000
		(To record the purchase of 3,000 shares		
		at $60 per share)		

Related exercise material: **Do it!** 11-3, E11-2, and E11-5.

TREASURY STOCK

Action Plan

• Record the purchase of treasury stock at cost.

• Report treasury stock as a deduction from stockholders' equity (contra account) at the bottom of the stockholders' equity section.

 The Navigator

Preferred Stock

To appeal to a larger segment of potential investors, a corporation may issue an additional class of stock, called preferred stock. **Preferred stock** has contractual provisions that give it preference or priority over common stock in certain areas. Typically, preferred stockholders have a priority in relation to (1) dividends and (2) assets in the event of liquidation. However, they sometimes do not have voting

LEARNING OBJECTIVE 4
Differentiate preferred stock from common stock.

rights. Facebook had 543 million preferred shares outstanding at the end of 2011, prior to going public. Approximately 6% of U.S. companies have one or more classes of preferred stock.[3]

Like common stock, companies issue preferred stock for cash or for noncash consideration. The entries for these transactions are similar to the entries for common stock. When a corporation has more than one class of stock, each paid-in capital account title should identify the stock to which it relates (e.g., Preferred Stock, Common Stock, Paid-in Capital in Excess of Par Value—Preferred Stock, and Paid-in Capital in Excess of Par Value—Common Stock).

Assume that Stine Corporation issues 10,000 shares of $10 par value preferred stock for $12 cash per share. The entry to record the issuance is:

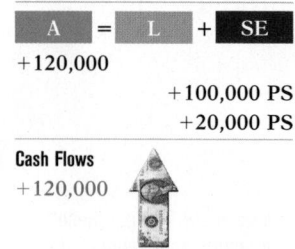

+120,000

+100,000 PS
+20,000 PS

Cash Flows
+120,000

Cash	120,000	
Preferred Stock		100,000
Paid-in Capital in Excess of Par Value—Preferred Stock		20,000
(To record the issuance of 10,000 shares of $10 par value preferred stock)		

Preferred stock has either a par value or no-par value. In the stockholders' equity section of the balance sheet, companies show preferred stock first because of its dividend and liquidation preferences over common stock.

DIVIDEND PREFERENCES

As indicated above, **preferred stockholders have the right to share in the distribution of corporate income before common stockholders**. For example, if the dividend rate on preferred stock is $5 per share, common shareholders cannot receive any dividends in the current year until preferred stockholders have received $5 per share. The first claim to dividends does not, however, **guarantee** dividends. Dividends depend on many factors, such as adequate retained earnings and availability of cash.

For preferred stock, companies state the per share dividend amount as a percentage of the par value of the stock or as a specified amount. For example, EarthLink specifies a 3% dividend.

Cumulative Dividend

Preferred stock contracts often contain a cumulative dividend feature. This feature stipulates that preferred stockholders must be paid both current-year dividends and any unpaid prior-year dividends before common stockholders are paid dividends. When preferred stock is cumulative, preferred dividends not declared in a given period are called dividends in arrears.

To illustrate, assume that Scientific Leasing has 5,000 shares of 7%, $100 par value cumulative preferred stock outstanding. Each $100 share pays a $7 dividend (.07 × $100). The annual dividend is $35,000 (5,000 × $7 per share). If dividends are two years in arrears, preferred stockholders are entitled to receive in the current year the dividends as shown in Illustration 11-8.

Illustration 11-8 Computation of total dividends to preferred stock

Dividends in arrears ($35,000 × 2)	$ 70,000
Current-year dividends	35,000
Total preferred dividends	**$105,000**

[3]*Accounting Trends & Techniques—2011* (New York: American Institute of Certified Public Accountants).

No distribution can be made to common stockholders until Scientific Leasing pays this entire preferred dividend. In other words, companies cannot pay dividends to common stockholders while any preferred stock dividend is in arrears.

Dividends in arrears are not considered a liability. No obligation exists until the board of directors formally "declares" that the corporation will pay a dividend. However, companies should disclose in the notes to the financial statements the amount of dividends in arrears. Doing so enables investors to assess the potential impact of this obligation on the corporation's financial position.

The investment community does not look favorably upon companies that are unable to meet their dividend obligations. As a financial officer noted in discussing one company's failure to pay its cumulative preferred dividend for a period of time, "Not meeting your obligations on something like that is a major black mark on your record."

LIQUIDATION PREFERENCE

Most preferred stocks have a preference on corporate assets if the corporation fails. This feature provides security for the preferred stockholder. The preference to assets may be for the par value of the shares or for a specified liquidating value. For example, Commonwealth Edison issued preferred stock that entitled the holders to receive $31.80 per share, plus accrued and unpaid dividends, in the event of involuntary liquidation. The liquidation preference is used in litigation pertaining to bankruptcy lawsuits involving the respective claims of creditors and preferred stockholders.

Do it!

PREFERRED STOCK DIVIDENDS

MasterMind Corporation has 2,000 shares of 6%, $100 par value preferred stock outstanding at December 31, 2014. At December 31, 2014, the company declared a $60,000 cash dividend. Determine the dividend paid to preferred stockholders and common stockholders under each of the following scenarios.

1. The preferred stock is noncumulative, and the company has not missed any dividends in previous years.

2. The preferred stock is noncumulative, and the company did not pay a dividend in each of the two previous years.

3. The preferred stock is cumulative, and the company did not pay a dividend in each of the two previous years.

Solution

1. The company has not missed past dividends and the preferred stock is noncumulative. Thus, the preferred stockholders are paid only this year's dividends. The dividend paid to preferred stockholders would be $12,000 (2,000 × .06 × $100). The dividend paid to common stockholders would be $48,000 ($60,000 − $12,000).

2. The preferred stock is noncumulative. Thus, past unpaid dividends do not have to be paid. The dividend paid to preferred stockholders would be $12,000 (2,000 × .06 × $100). The dividend paid to common stockholders would be $48,000 ($60,000 − $12,000).

3. The preferred stock is cumulative. Thus, dividends that have been missed (dividends in arrears) must be paid. The dividend paid to preferred stockholders would be $36,000 (3 × 2,000 × .06 × $100). The dividend paid to common stockholders would be $24,000 ($60,000 − $36,000).

Action Plan

• Determine dividends on preferred shares by multiplying the dividend rate times the par value of the stock times the number of preferred shares.

• Understand the cumulative feature: If preferred stock is cumulative, then any missed dividends (dividends in arrears) and the current year's dividend must be paid to preferred stockholders before dividends are paid to common stockholders.

The Navigator

Related exercise material: **Do it!** 11-4.

Dividends

LEARNING OBJECTIVE **5**

Prepare the entries for cash dividends and understand the effect of stock dividends and stock splits.

As noted earlier, a dividend **is a distribution by a corporation to its stock-holders on a pro rata** (proportional to ownership) **basis**. Pro rata means that if you own, say, 10% of the common shares, you will receive 10% of the dividend. Dividends can take four forms: cash, property, scrip (promissory note to pay cash), or stock. Cash dividends, which predominate in practice, and stock dividends, which are declared with some frequency, are the focus of our discussion.

Investors are very interested in a company's dividend practices. In the financial press, **dividends are generally reported quarterly as a dollar amount per share**. (Sometimes they are reported on an annual basis.) For example, the **quarterly** dividend rate in the fourth quarter of 2011 was 36 cents per share for Nike, 15 cents per share for GE, and 24 cents per share for ConAgra Foods. Facebook does not pay dividends.

CASH DIVIDENDS

A cash dividend is a pro rata (proportional to ownership) distribution of cash to stockholders. Cash dividends are not paid on treasury shares. For a corporation to pay a cash dividend, it must have the following.

1. **Retained earnings.** Payment of dividends from retained earnings is legal in all states. In addition, loan agreements frequently constrain companies to pay dividends only from retained earnings. Many states prohibit payment of dividends from legal capital. However, payment of dividends from paid-in capital in excess of par value is legal in some states.

2. **Adequate cash.** Recently, Facebook had a balance in retained earnings of $1,606 million but a cash balance of only $1,512 million. If it had wanted to pay a dividend equal to its retained earnings, Facebook would have had to raise $94 million more in cash. It would have been unlikely to do this because it would not be able to pay this much in dividends in future years. In addition, such a dividend would completely deplete Facebook's balance in retained earnings, so it would not be able to pay a dividend in the next year unless it had positive net income.

3. **Declared dividends.** The board of directors has full authority to determine the amount of income to distribute in the form of dividends. Dividends are not a liability until they are declared.

The amount and timing of a dividend are important issues for management to consider. The payment of a large cash dividend could lead to liquidity problems for the company. Conversely, a small dividend or a missed dividend may cause unhappiness among stockholders who expect to receive a reasonable cash payment from the company on a periodic basis. Many companies declare and pay cash dividends quarterly. On the other hand, a number of high-growth companies pay no dividends, preferring to conserve cash to finance future capital expenditures.

Investors monitor a company's dividend practices. For example, regular dividend boosts in the face of irregular earnings can be a warning signal. Companies with high dividends and rising debt may be borrowing money to pay shareholders. On the other hand, low dividends may not be a negative sign because it may mean the company is reinvesting in itself, which may result in high returns through increases in the stock price. Presumably, investors seeking regular dividends buy stock in companies that pay periodic dividends, and those seeking growth in the stock price (capital gains) buy stock in companies that retain their earnings rather than pay dividends.

Entries for Cash Dividends

Three dates are important in connection with dividends: (1) the declaration date, (2) the record date, and (3) the payment date. Companies make accounting entries on the declaration date and the payment date.

On the declaration date, the board of directors formally authorizes the cash dividend and announces it to stockholders. The declaration of a cash dividend **commits the corporation to a binding legal obligation**. Thus, the company must make an entry to recognize the increase in Cash Dividends and the increase in the liability Dividends Payable.

To illustrate, assume that on December 1, 2014, the directors of Media General declare a $0.50 per share cash dividend on 100,000 shares of $10 par value common stock. The dividend is $50,000 (100,000 × $0.50). The entry to record the declaration is:

Declaration Date

Dec. 1	Cash Dividends	50,000	
	Dividends Payable		50,000
	(To record declaration of cash dividend)		

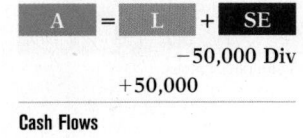

A = L + SE
−50,000 Div
+50,000

Cash Flows
no effect

In Chapter 3, we used an account called Dividends to record a cash dividend. Here, we use the more specific title Cash Dividends to differentiate from other types of dividends, such as stock dividends. Dividends Payable is a current liability. It will normally be paid within the next several months.

At the record date, the company determines ownership of the outstanding shares for dividend purposes. The stockholders' records maintained by the corporation supply this information.

For Media General, the record date is December 22. No entry is required on the record date.

Helpful Hint The record date is important in determining the dividend to be paid to each stockholder.

Record Date

| Dec. 22 | No entry necessary | | |

On the payment date, the company makes cash dividend payments to the stockholders on record as of December 22. It also records the payment of the dividend. If January 20 is the payment date for Media General, the entry on that date is:

Payment Date

Jan. 20	Dividends Payable	50,000	
	Cash		50,000
	(To record payment of cash dividend)		

A = L + SE
−50,000
−50,000

Cash Flows
−50,000

Note that payment of the dividend on the payment date reduces both current assets and current liabilities, but it has no effect on stockholders' equity. The cumulative effect of the **declaration and payment** of a cash dividend on a company's financial statements is to **decrease both stockholders' equity and total assets**.

Palto/iStockphoto

Accounting Across the Organization

Up, Down, and ??

The decision whether to pay a dividend, and how much to pay, is a very important management decision. As the chart below shows, from 2002 to 2007, many companies substantially increased their dividends, and total dividends paid by U.S. companies hit record levels. One reason for the increase is that Congress lowered, from 39% to 15%, the tax rate paid by investors on dividends received, making dividends more attractive to investors.

Then the financial crisis of 2008 occurred. As result, in 2009, 804 companies cut their dividends (see chart), the highest level since Standard & Poor's started collecting data in 1995. In 2010, more companies started to increase their dividends. However, potential higher taxes on dividends coming in the future and the possibility of a low-growth economy may stall any significant increase.

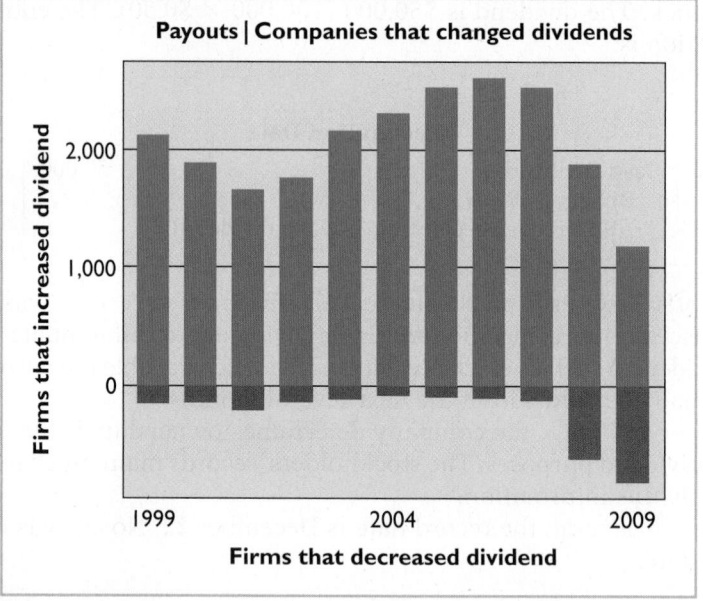

Source: Matt Phillips and Jay Miller, "Last Year's Dividend Slash Was $58 Billion," *Wall Street Journal* (January 8, 2010), p. C5.

 What factors must management consider in deciding how large a dividend to pay? (See page 620.)

STOCK DIVIDENDS

A stock dividend is a pro rata (proportional to ownership) distribution of the corporation's own stock to stockholders. Whereas a cash dividend is paid in cash, a stock dividend is paid in stock. **A stock dividend results in a decrease in retained earnings and an increase in paid-in capital.** Unlike a cash dividend, a stock dividend does not decrease total stockholders' equity or total assets.

Because a stock dividend does not result in a distribution of assets, some view it as nothing more than a publicity gesture. Stock dividends are often issued by companies that do not have adequate cash to issue a cash dividend. These companies may not want to announce that they are not going to be issuing a cash dividend at their normal time to do so. By issuing a stock dividend, they "save face" by giving the appearance of distributing a dividend. Note that since a stock dividend neither increases nor decreases the assets in the company, investors are not receiving anything they didn't already own. In a sense, it is like asking for two pieces of pie and having your host take one piece of pie and cut it into two smaller pieces. You are not better off, but you got your two pieces of pie.

To illustrate a stock dividend, assume that you have a 2% ownership interest in Cetus Inc.; you own 20 of its 1,000 shares of common stock. If Cetus declares a 10% stock dividend, it issues 100 shares (1,000 × 10%) of stock. You receive two shares (2% × 100), but your ownership interest remains at 2% (22 ÷ 1,100). **You now own more shares of stock, but your ownership interest has not changed.** Moreover, the company disburses no cash and assumes no liabilities.

What, then, are the purposes and benefits of a stock dividend? Corporations generally issue stock dividends for one of the following reasons.

1. To satisfy stockholders' dividend expectations without spending cash.
2. To increase the marketability of the stock by increasing the number of shares outstanding and thereby decreasing the market price per share. Decreasing the market price of the stock makes it easier for smaller investors to purchase the shares.
3. To emphasize that the company has permanently reinvested in the business a portion of stockholders' equity, which therefore is unavailable for cash dividends.

When the dividend is declared, the board of directors determines the size of the stock dividend and the value per share to use to record the transaction. In order to meet legal requirements, the per share amount must be at least equal to the par or stated value.

The accounting profession distinguishes between a **small stock dividend** (less than 20%–25% of the corporation's issued stock) and a **large stock dividend** (greater than 20%–25%). It recommends that the company use the **fair value per share** to record small stock dividends. The recommendation is based on the assumption that a small stock dividend will have little effect on the market price of the shares previously outstanding. Thus, many stockholders consider small stock dividends to be distributions of earnings equal to the fair value of the shares distributed. The accounting profession does not specify the value to use to record a large stock dividend. However, companies normally use **par or stated value per share**. Small stock dividends predominate in practice. In Appendix 11A at the end of the chapter, we illustrate the journal entries for small stock dividends.

Effects of Stock Dividends

How do stock dividends affect stockholders' equity? They **change the composition of stockholders' equity** because they result in a transfer of a portion of retained earnings to paid-in capital. However, **total stockholders' equity remains the same**. Stock dividends also have no effect on the par or stated value per share, but the number of shares outstanding increases.

Illustration 11-9 shows the effects that result when Medland Corp. declares a 10% stock dividend on its $10 par common stock when 50,000 shares were outstanding. The market price was $15 per share.

Helpful Hint Because of its effects, a stock dividend is also referred to as *capitalizing retained earnings*.

Illustration 11-9 Stock dividend effects

	Before Dividend	Change	After Dividend
Stockholders' equity			
Paid-in capital			
Common stock, $10 par	$ 500,000	$ 50,000	$ 550,000
Paid-in capital in excess of par value	—	25,000	25,000
Total paid-in capital	500,000	+75,000	575,000
Retained earnings	300,000	−75,000	225,000
Total stockholders' equity	$800,000	$ 0	$800,000
Outstanding shares	50,000	+ 5,000	55,000

In this example, total paid-in capital increased by $75,000 (50,000 shares × 10% × $15), and retained earnings decreased by the same amount. Note also that total stockholders' equity remains unchanged at $800,000. The number of shares increases by 5,000 (50,000 × 10%).

STOCK SPLITS

Helpful Hint A stock split changes the par value per share but does not affect any balances in stockholders' equity.

A **stock split**, like a stock dividend, involves the issuance of additional shares of stock to stockholders according to their percentage ownership. However, **a stock split results in a reduction in the par or stated value per share**. The purpose of a stock split is to increase the marketability of the stock by lowering its market price per share. This, in turn, makes it easier for the corporation to issue additional stock. After hitting a peak of 114 stock splits in 1986, the number of splits in the United States has fallen to about 30 per year. Google announced a 2-for-1 split in 2012 when its stock was selling for $650 per share.

Like a stock dividend, a stock split increases the number of shares owned by a shareholder, but it does not change the percentage of the total company that the shareholder owns. The effects of a 3-for-1 split are shown in Illustration 11-10.

Illustration 11-10 Effect of stock dividend or stock split for stockholders

The effect of a split on market price is generally **inversely proportional** to the size of the split. For example, after a recent 2-for-1 stock split, the market price of Nike's stock fell from $111 to approximately $55.

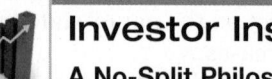 ## Investor Insight

A No-Split Philosophy

Warren Buffett's company, Berkshire Hathaway, has two classes of shares. Until recently, the company had never split either class of stock. As a result, the class A stock had a market price of $97,000 and the class B sold for about $3,200 per share. Because the price per share is so high, the stock does not trade as frequently as the stock of other companies. Buffett has always opposed stock splits because he feels that a lower stock price attracts short-term investors. He appears to be correct. For example, while more than 6 million shares of IBM are exchanged on the average day, only about 1,000 class A shares of Berkshire are traded. Despite Buffett's aversion to splits, in order to accomplish a recent acquisition, Berkshire decided to split its class B shares 50 to 1.

Source: Scott Patterson, "Berkshire Nears Smaller Baby B's," *Wall Street Journal Online* (January 19, 2010).

 Why does Warren Buffett usually oppose stock splits? (See page 620.)

Dietmar Klement/iStockphoto

In a stock split, the company increases the number of shares in the same proportion that it decreases the par or stated value per share. For example, in a

2-for-1 split, the company exchanges one share of $10 par value stock for two shares of $5 par value stock. **A stock split does not have any effect on paid-in capital, retained earnings, and total stockholders' equity.** However, the number of shares outstanding increases. The effects of a 2-for-1 stock split of Medland Corporation's common stock are shown in Illustration 11-11.

Illustration 11-11
Stock split effects

	Before Stock Split	Change	After Stock Split
Stockholders' equity			
Paid-in capital			
Common stock			
(before: 50,000 $10 par shares; after: 100,000 $5 par shares)	$ 500,000		$ 500,000
Paid-in capital in excess of par value	0		0
Total paid-in capital	500,000	$ 0	500,000
Retained earnings	300,000	0	300,000
Total stockholders' equity	$800,000	$ 0	$800,000
Outstanding shares	50,000	+ 50,000	100,000

Because a stock split does not affect the balances in any stockholders' equity accounts, a company **does not need to journalize a stock split**. However, a memorandum entry explaining the effect of the split is typically made.

The differences between the effects of stock dividends and stock splits are shown in Illustration 11-12.

Illustration 11-12 Effects of stock splits and stock dividends differentiated

Item	Stock Dividend	Stock Split
Total paid-in capital	Increase	No change
Total retained earnings	Decrease	No change
Total par value (common stock)	Increase	No change
Par value per share	No change	Decrease
Shares outstanding	Increase	Increase

Do it!

Due to five years of record earnings at Sing CD Corporation, the market price of its 500,000 shares of $2 par value common stock tripled from $15 per share to $45. During this period, paid-in capital remained the same at $2,000,000. Retained earnings increased from $1,500,000 to $10,000,000. President Joan Elbert is considering either a 10% stock dividend or a 2-for-1 stock split. She asks you to show the before-and-after effects of each option on retained earnings.

Solution

The stock dividend amount is $2,250,000 [(500,000 × 10%) × $45]. The new balance in retained earnings is $7,750,000 ($10,000,000 − $2,250,000). The retained earnings balance after the stock split is the same as it was before the split: $10,000,000. The effects on the stockholders' equity accounts are as follows.

	Original Balances	After Dividend	After Split
Paid-in capital	$ 2,000,000	$ 4,250,000	$ 2,000,000
Retained earnings	10,000,000	7,750,000	10,000,000
Total stockholders' equity	$12,000,000	$12,000,000	$12,000,000
Shares outstanding	500,000	550,000	1,000,000

Related exercise material: **BE11-6, BE11-7, Do it! 11-5,** and **E11-7.**

STOCK DIVIDENDS; STOCK SPLITS

Action Plan

- Calculate the stock dividend's effect on retained earnings by multiplying the number of new shares times the market price of the stock (or par value for a large stock dividend).

- Recall that a stock dividend increases the number of shares without affecting total equity.

- Recall that a stock split only increases the number of shares outstanding and decreases the par value per share without affecting total equity.

The Navigator

Retained Earnings

LEARNING OBJECTIVE 6

Identify the items that affect retained earnings.

Retained earnings is net income that a company retains in the business. The balance in retained earnings is part of the stockholders' claim on the total assets of the corporation. It does not, however, represent a claim on any specific asset. Nor can the amount of retained earnings be associated with the balance of any asset account. For example, a $100,000 balance in retained earnings does not mean that there should be $100,000 in cash. The reason is that the company may have used the cash resulting from the excess of revenues over expenses to purchase buildings, equipment, and other assets. Illustration 11-13 shows recent amounts of retained earnings and cash in selected companies.

Illustration 11-13 Retained earnings and cash balances

	(in millions)	
Company	Retained Earnings	Cash
Facebook	$ 1,606	$ 1,512
Google	20,082	10,198
Nike, Inc.	4,885	1,855
Starbucks Coffee Company	2,189	281
Amazon.com	(1,375)	2,539

When expenses exceed revenues, a **net loss** results. In contrast to net income, a net loss decreases retained earnings. In closing entries, a company debits a net loss to the Retained Earnings account. **It does not debit net losses to paid-in capital accounts.** To do so would destroy the distinction between paid-in and earned capital. If cumulative losses and dividends exceed cumulative income over a company's life, a debit balance in Retained Earnings results. A debit balance in Retained Earnings, such as that of Amazon.com in a recent year, is a **deficit**. A company reports a deficit as a deduction in the stockholders' equity section of the balance sheet, as shown in Illustration 11-14.

Illustration 11-14
Stockholders' equity with deficit

Real World	**AMAZON.COM** Balance Sheet (partial) (in millions)	
Stockholders' equity		
Paid-in capital		
Common stock		$ 4
Paid-in capital in excess of par value		3,068
Total paid-in capital		3,072
Accumulated deficit		(1,375)
Total paid-in capital and retained earnings		1,697
Less: Treasury stock		500
Total stockholders' equity		$1,197

RETAINED EARNINGS RESTRICTIONS

The balance in retained earnings is generally available for dividend declarations. Some companies state this fact. In some circumstances, however, there may be **retained earnings restrictions**. These make a portion of the balance currently unavailable for dividends. Restrictions result from one or more of these causes: legal, contractual, or voluntary.

Companies generally disclose retained earnings restrictions in the notes to the financial statements. For example, Tektronix Inc., a manufacturer of electronic measurement devices, recently had total retained earnings of $774 million, but the unrestricted portion was only $223.8 million.

TEKTRONIX INC.
Notes to the Financial Statements

Certain of the Company's debt agreements require compliance with debt covenants. The Company had unrestricted retained earnings of $223.8 million after meeting those requirements.

Illustration 11-15
Disclosure of unrestricted retained earnings

Financial Statement Presentation of Stockholders' Equity

BALANCE SHEET PRESENTATION

LEARNING OBJECTIVE 7
Prepare a comprehensive stockholders' equity section.

In the stockholders' equity section of the balance sheet, companies report paid-in capital and retained earnings and identify the specific sources of paid-in capital. Within paid-in capital, two classifications are recognized:

1. **Capital stock**, which consists of preferred and common stock. Companies show preferred stock before common stock because of its preferential rights. They report information about the par value, shares authorized, shares issued, and shares outstanding for each class of stock.

2. **Additional paid-in capital**, which includes the excess of amounts paid in over par or stated value.

Illustration 11-16 presents the stockholders' equity section of the balance sheet of Graber Inc. The company discloses a retained earnings restriction in the

Illustration 11-16
Comprehensive stockholders' equity section

International Note Like GAAP, under IFRS companies typically disclose separate categories of capital on the balance sheet. However, because of varying accounting treatments of certain transactions (such as treasury stock or asset revaluations), some categories used under IFRS vary from those under GAAP.

GRABER INC.
Balance Sheet (partial)

Stockholders' equity		
Paid-in capital		
Capital stock		
9% preferred stock, $100 par value, cumulative,		
10,000 shares authorized, 6,000 shares issued		
and outstanding		$ 600,000
Common stock, no par, $5 stated value,		
500,000 shares authorized, 400,000 shares		
issued, and 390,000 outstanding		2,000,000
Total capital stock		2,600,000
Additional paid-in capital		
Paid-in capital in excess of par value—preferred stock	$ 30,000	
Paid-in capital in excess of stated value—common stock	1,050,000	
Total additional paid-in capital		1,080,000
Total paid-in capital		3,680,000
Retained earnings (**see Note R**)		1,160,000
Total paid-in capital and retained earnings		4,840,000
Less: Treasury stock (10,000 common shares)		80,000
Total stockholders' equity		$4,760,000

Note R: Retained earnings is restricted for the cost of treasury stock, $80,000.

notes. The stockholders' equity section for Graber Inc. includes most of the accounts discussed in this chapter. The disclosures pertaining to Graber's common stock indicate that 400,000 shares are issued; 100,000 shares are unissued (500,000 authorized less 400,000 issued); and 390,000 shares are outstanding (400,000 issued less 10,000 shares in treasury).

In published annual reports, companies seldom present subclassifications within the stockholders' equity section. Moreover, they often combine and report as a single amount the individual sources of additional paid-in capital. Notes often provide additional detail. Illustration 11-17 is an excerpt from Procter & Gamble Company's balance sheet in a recent year.

Illustration 11-17
Stockholders' equity section

Real World	**PROCTER & GAMBLE COMPANY** Balance Sheet (partial) (in millions)	
	Shareholders' equity	
	Convertible Class A preferred stock, stated value $1 per share (600 shares authorized)	$ 1,406
	Non-voting Class B preferred stock, stated value $1 per share (200 shares authorized)	—
	Common stock, stated value $1 per share (10,000 shares authorized; issued: 3,989.7)	3,990
	Additional paid-in capital	59,030
	Total paid-in capital	64,426
	Reserve for ESOP debt retirement	(1,308)
	Retained earnings	41,797
	Total paid-in capital and retained earnings	104,915
	Accumulated other comprehensive income	617
	Less: Treasury stock, at cost (shares held: 857.8)	38,772
	Total shareholders' equity	$ 66,760

KEEPING AN EYE ON CASH

The balance sheet presents the balances of a company's stockholders' equity accounts at a point in time. Companies report in the "Financing Activities" section of the statement of cash flows information regarding cash inflows and outflows during the year that resulted from equity transactions. The excerpt below presents the cash flows from financing activities from the statement of cash flows of Sara Lee Corporation in a recent year. From this information, we learn that the company's purchases of treasury stock during the period far exceeded its issuances of new common stock, and its financing activities resulted in a net reduction in its cash balance.

Real World	**SARA LEE CORPORATION** Statement of Cash Flows (partial) (in millions)	
	Cash flows from financing activities	
	Issuances of common stock	$ 38
	Purchases of common stock	(686)
	Payments of dividends	(374)
	Borrowings of long-term debt	2,895
	Repayments of long-term debt	(416)
	Short-term (repayments) borrowings, net	(1,720)
	Net cash used in financing activities	$ (263)

Do it!

Jennifer Corporation has issued 300,000 shares of $3 par value common stock. It is authorized to issue 600,000 shares. The paid-in capital in excess of par value on the common stock is $380,000. The corporation has reacquired 15,000 shares at a cost of $50,000 and is currently holding those shares.

The corporation also has 4,000 shares issued and outstanding of 8%, $100 par value preferred stock. It is authorized to issue 10,000 shares. The paid-in capital in excess of par value on the preferred stock is $97,000. Retained earnings is $610,000.

Prepare the stockholders' equity section of the balance sheet.

STOCKHOLDERS' EQUITY SECTION

Solution

JENNIFER CORPORATION
Balance Sheet (partial)

Stockholders' equity		
Paid-in capital		
Capital stock		
8% preferred stock, $100 par value, 10,000 shares authorized, 4,000 shares issued and outstanding	$ 400,000	
Common stock, $3 par value, 600,000 shares authorized, 300,000 shares issued, and 285,000 shares outstanding	900,000	
Total capital stock	1,300,000	
Additional paid-in capital		
Paid-in capital in excess of par value—preferred stock	97,000	
Paid-in capital in excess of par value—common stock	380,000	
Total additional paid-in capital		$ 477,000
Total paid-in capital		1,777,000
Retained earnings		610,000
Total paid-in capital and retained earnings		2,387,000
Less: Treasury stock (15,000 common shares) (at cost)		50,000
Total stockholders' equity		$2,337,000

Action Plan

- Present capital stock first; list preferred stock before common stock.
- Present additional paid-in capital after capital stock.
- Report retained earnings after capital stock and additional paid-in capital.
- Deduct treasury stock from total paid-in capital and retained earnings.

✔ The Navigator

Related exercise material: **BE11-8,** *Do it!* **11-6, E11-8, E11-9,** and **E11-10.**

Measuring Corporate Performance

Investors are interested in both a company's dividend record and its earnings performance. Although those two measures are often parallel, that is not always the case. Thus, investors should investigate each one separately.

LEARNING OBJECTIVE 8

Evaluate a corporation's dividend and earnings performance from a stockholder's perspective.

DIVIDEND RECORD

One way that companies reward stock investors for their investment is to pay them dividends. The **payout ratio** measures the percentage of earnings a company distributes in the form of cash dividends to common stockholders. It is computed by **dividing total cash dividends declared to common shareholders by net income**. Using the information shown below, the payout ratio for Nike in 2011 and 2010 is calculated in Illustration 11-18 (page 594).

	2011	**2010**
Dividends (in millions)	$ 569	$ 515
Net income (in millions)	2,133	1,907

Illustration 11-18 Nike's
payout ratio

Payout Ratio =	$\dfrac{\text{Cash Dividends Declared on Common Stock}}{\text{Net Income}}$	
($ in millions)	**2011**	**2010**
Payout Ratio	$\dfrac{\$569}{\$2,133} = 26.7\%$	$\dfrac{\$515}{\$1,907} = 27.0\%$

Nike's payout ratio was relatively constant at approximately 27%. Companies attempt to set their dividend rate at a level that will be sustainable.

Companies that have high growth rates are characterized by low payout ratios because they reinvest most of their net income in the business. Thus, a low payout ratio is not necessarily bad news. Companies that believe they have many good opportunities for growth, such as Facebook, will reinvest those funds in the company rather than pay dividends. However, low dividend payments, or a cut in dividend payments, might signal that a company has liquidity or solvency problems and is trying to conserve cash by not paying dividends. Thus, investors and analysts should investigate the reason for low dividend payments.

Illustration 11-19 lists recent payout ratios of four well-known companies.

Illustration 11-19
Payout ratios of companies

Company	Payout Ratio
Microsoft	24.5%
Kellogg	43.3%
Facebook	0%
Wal-Mart	49.0%

 DECISION TOOLKIT

DECISION CHECKPOINTS	INFO NEEDED FOR DECISION	TOOL TO USE FOR DECISION	HOW TO EVALUATE RESULTS
What portion of its earnings does the company pay out in dividends?	Net income and total cash dividends on common stock	$\text{Payout ratio} = \dfrac{\text{Cash dividends declared on common stock}}{\text{Net income}}$	A low ratio may suggest that the company is retaining its earnings for investment in future growth.

EARNINGS PERFORMANCE

Another way to measure corporate performance is through profitability. A widely used ratio that measures profitability from the common stockholders' viewpoint is **return on common stockholders' equity (ROE)**. This ratio shows how many dollars of net income a company earned for each dollar of common stockholders' equity. It is computed by dividing net income available to common stockholders (Net income − Preferred dividends) by average common stockholders' equity. Common stockholders' equity is equal to total stockholders' equity minus any equity from preferred stock.

Using the information on the previous page and the additional information presented below, Illustration 11-20 shows Nike's return on common stockholders' equity.

(in millions)	2011	2010
Preferred dividends	$ −0−	$ −0−
Common stockholders' equity	9,843	9,754

Return on Common Stockholders' Equity $=\dfrac{\text{Net Income} - \text{Preferred Dividends}}{\text{Average Common Stockholders' Equity}}$		
($ in millions)	2011	2010
Return on Common Stockholders' Equity	$\dfrac{\$2{,}133 - \$0}{(\$9{,}843 + \$9{,}754)/2} = 21.8\%$	$\dfrac{\$1{,}907 - \$0}{(\$9{,}754 + \$8{,}693.1)/2} = 20.7\%$

Illustration 11-20 Nike's return on common stockholders' equity

From 2010 to 2011, Nike's return on common shareholders' equity increased. As a company grows larger, it becomes increasingly hard to sustain a high return. In Nike's case, since many believe the U.S. market for expensive sports shoes is saturated, it will need to grow either along new product lines, such as hiking shoes and golf equipment, or in new markets, such as Europe and Asia.

DEBT VERSUS EQUITY DECISION

When obtaining long-term capital, corporate managers must decide whether to issue bonds or to sell common stock. Bonds have three primary advantages relative to common stock, as shown in Illustration 11-21.

Bond Financing	Advantages
Ballot	1. **Stockholder control is not affected.** Bondholders do not have voting rights, so current owners (stockholders) retain full control of the company.
Tax Bill	2. **Tax savings result.** Bond interest is deductible for tax purposes; dividends on stock are not.
$ / STOCK	3. **Return on common stockholders' equity may be higher.** Although bond interest expense reduces net income, return on common stockholders' equity often is higher under bond financing because no additional shares of common stock are issued.

Illustration 11-21 Advantages of bond financing over common stock

How does the debt versus equity decision affect the return on common stockholders' equity? Illustration 11-22 shows that the return on common stockholders' equity is affected by the return on assets and the amount of leverage a company uses—that is, by the company's reliance on debt (often measured by the debt to

Illustration 11-22 Components of the return on common stockholders' equity

assets ratio). **If a company wants to increase its return on common stockholders' equity, it can either increase its return on assets or increase its reliance on debt financing.**

To illustrate the potential effect of debt financing on the return on common stockholders' equity, assume that Microsystems Inc. currently has 100,000 shares of common stock outstanding issued at $25 per share and no debt. It is considering two alternatives for raising an additional $5 million. Plan A involves issuing 200,000 shares of common stock at the current market price of $25 per share. Plan B involves issuing $5 million of 12% bonds at face value. Income before interest and taxes will be $1.5 million; income taxes are expected to be 30%. The alternative effects on the return on common stockholders' equity are shown in Illustration 11-23.

Illustration 11-23 Effects on return on common stockholders' equity of issuing debt

	Plan A: Issue stock	**Plan B: Issue bonds**
Income before interest and taxes	$1,500,000	$1,500,000
Interest (12% × $5,000,000)	—	600,000
Income before income taxes	1,500,000	900,000
Income tax expense (30%)	450,000	270,000
Net income	$1,050,000	$ 630,000
Common stockholders' equity	$7,500,000	$2,500,000
Return on common stockholders' equity	14%	25.2%

Note that with long-term debt financing (bonds), net income is $420,000 ($1,050,000 − $630,000) less. However, the return on common stockholders' equity increases from 14% to 25.2% with the use of debt financing because net income is spread over a smaller amount of common stockholders' equity. **In general, as long as the return on assets rate exceeds the rate paid on debt, a company will increase the return on common stockholders' equity by the use of debt.**

After seeing this illustration, you might ask, why don't companies rely almost exclusively on debt financing rather than equity? Debt has one major disadvantage: **Debt reduces solvency. The company locks in fixed payments that it must make in good times and bad. The company must pay interest on a periodic basis and must pay the principal (face value) of the bonds at maturity.** A company with fluctuating earnings and a relatively weak cash position may experience great difficulty in meeting interest requirements in periods of low earnings. In the extreme, this can result in bankruptcy. With common stock financing, on the other hand, the company can decide to pay low (or no) dividends if earnings are low.

DECISION TOOLKIT

DECISION CHECKPOINTS	INFO NEEDED FOR DECISION	TOOL TO USE FOR DECISION	HOW TO EVALUATE RESULTS
What is the company's return on common stockholders' investment?	Earnings available to common stockholders and average common stockholders' equity	$\text{Return on common stockholders' equity} = \dfrac{\text{Net income} - \text{Preferred dividends}}{\text{Average common stockholders' equity}}$	A high measure suggests strong earnings performance from common stockholders' perspective.

USING THE **DECISION TOOLKIT**

adidas is one of Nike's competitors. In such a competitive and rapidly changing environment, one wrong step can spell financial disaster.

Instructions

The following facts are available from adidas's annual report. As a German company, adidas reports under International Financial Reporting Standards (IFRS). Using this information, evaluate its (1) dividend record and (2) earnings performance, and contrast them with those for Nike for 2011 and 2010. Nike's earnings per share were $4.48 in 2011 and $3.93 in 2010.

(in millions)*	2010	2009	2008
Dividends declared	€73	€97	€99
Net income	€567	€245	€642
Preferred dividends	0	0	0
Shares outstanding at end of year	209	209	194
Common stockholders' equity	€4,616	€3,771	€3,386

*Nike has a year-end of May 31, 2011. For comparative purposes, we used adidas's December 31, 2010, data since that represents the closest year-end.

Solution

1. **Dividend record:** A measure to evaluate dividend record is the payout ratio. For adidas, this measure in 2010 and 2009 is calculated as shown below.

	2010	2009
Payout ratio	$\frac{€73}{€567} = 12.9\%$	$\frac{€97}{€245} = 39.6\%$

Nike's payout ratio was 26.7%. adidas's payout ratio dramatically decreased from 2009 to 2010 and was significantly less than Nike's ratio in 2010.

2. **Earnings performance:** There are many measures of earnings performance. Some of those presented thus far in the textbook were earnings per share (page 55) and the return on common stockholders' equity (this chapter). These measures for adidas in 2010 and 2009 are calculated as shown here.

	2010	2009
Earnings per share	$\frac{€567 - 0}{(209 + 209)/2} = €2.71$	$\frac{€245 - 0}{(209 + 194)/2} = €1.22$
Return on common stockholders' equity	$\frac{€567 - 0}{(€4,616 + €3,771)/2} = 13.5\%$	$\frac{€245 - 0}{(€3,771 + €3,386)/2} = 6.8\%$

From 2009 to 2010, adidas's net income improved 130% and its earnings per share increased 122%. Earnings per share should not be compared across companies because the number of shares varies considerably. Thus, we should not compare adidas's earnings per share with Nike's. adidas's return on common stockholders' equity increased from 6.8% to 13.5%.

 The Navigator

Summary of Learning Objectives

1 **Identify and discuss the major characteristics of a corporation.** The major characteristics of a corporation are separate legal existence, limited liability of stockholders, transferable ownership rights, ability to acquire capital, continuous life, corporation management, government regulations, and additional taxes.

2 **Record the issuance of common stock.** When a company records issuance of common stock for cash, it credits the par value of the shares to Common Stock. It records in a separate paid-in capital account the portion of the proceeds that is above par value. When no-par common stock has a stated value, the entries are similar to those for par value stock. When no-par common stock does not have a stated value, the entire proceeds from the issue are credited to Common Stock.

3 **Explain the accounting for the purchase of treasury stock.** Companies generally use the cost method in accounting for treasury stock. Under this approach, a company debits Treasury Stock at the price paid to reacquire the shares.

4 **Differentiate preferred stock from common stock.** Preferred stock has contractual provisions that give it priority over common stock in certain areas. Typically, preferred stockholders have a preference as to (1) dividends and (2) assets in the event of liquidation. However, they sometimes do not have voting rights.

5 **Prepare the entries for cash dividends and understand the effect of stock dividends and stock splits.** Companies make entries for dividends at the declaration date and the payment date. At the declaration date, the entries for a cash dividend are debit Cash Dividends and credit Dividends Payable. The effects of stock dividends and splits are as follows. Small stock dividends transfer an amount equal to the fair value of the shares issued from retained earnings to the paid-in capital accounts. Stock splits reduce the par value per share of the common stock while increasing the number of shares so that the balance in the Common Stock account remains the same.

6 **Identify the items that affect retained earnings.** Additions to retained earnings consist of net income. Deductions consist of net loss and cash and stock dividends. In some instances, portions of retained earnings are restricted, making that portion unavailable for the payment of dividends.

7 **Prepare a comprehensive stockholders' equity section.** In the stockholders' equity section of the balance sheet, companies report paid-in capital and retained earnings and identify specific sources of paid-in capital. Within paid-in capital, companies show two classifications: capital stock and additional paid-in capital. If a corporation has treasury stock, it deducts the cost of treasury stock from total paid-in capital and retained earnings to determine total stockholders' equity.

8 **Evaluate a corporation's dividend and earnings performance from a stockholder's perspective.** A company's dividend record can be evaluated by looking at what percentage of net income it chooses to pay out in dividends, as measured by the dividend payout ratio (dividends divided by net income). Earnings performance is measured with the return on common stockholders' equity (income available to common stockholders divided by average common stockholders' equity).

DECISION TOOLKIT *A SUMMARY*

DECISION CHECKPOINTS	INFO NEEDED FOR DECISION	TOOL TO USE FOR DECISION	HOW TO EVALUATE RESULTS
Should the company incorporate?	Capital needs, growth expectations, type of business, tax status	Corporations have limited liability, better capital-raising ability, and professional managers. But they suffer from additional taxes, government regulations, and separation of ownership from management.	Must carefully weigh the costs and benefits in light of the particular circumstances.
What portion of its earnings does the company pay out in dividends?	Net income and total cash dividends on common stock	$$\text{Payout ratio} = \frac{\text{Cash dividends declared on common stock}}{\text{Net income}}$$	A low ratio may suggest that the company is retaining its earnings for investment in future growth.
What is the company's return on common stockholders' investment?	Earnings available to common stockholders and average common stockholders' equity	$$\text{Return on common stockholders' equity} = \frac{\text{Net income} - \text{Preferred dividends}}{\text{Average common stockholders' equity}}$$	A high measure suggests strong earnings performance from common stockholders' perspective.

Appendix 11A

Entries for Stock Dividends

To illustrate the accounting for stock dividends, assume that Medland Corporation has a balance of $300,000 in retained earnings and declares a 10% stock dividend on its 50,000 shares of $10 par value common stock. The current fair value of its stock is $15 per share. The number of shares to be issued is 5,000 (10% × 50,000), and the total amount to be debited to Retained Earnings is $75,000 (5,000 × $15). The entry to record this transaction at the declaration date is:

LEARNING OBJECTIVE	9
Prepare entries for stock dividends.	

Stock Dividends	75,000	
Common Stock Dividends Distributable		50,000
Paid-in Capital in Excess of Par Value		25,000
(To record declaration of 10% stock dividend)		

A	=	L	+	SE
				−75,000 Div
				+50,000 CS
				+25,000 CS

Cash Flows
no effect

At the declaration date, Medland increases (debits) Stock Dividends for the fair value of the stock issued, increases (credits) Common Stock Dividends Distributable for the par value of the dividend shares (5,000 × $10), and increases (credits) the excess over par (5,000 × $5) to an additional paid-in capital account.

Common Stock Dividends Distributable is a stockholders' equity account. It is not a liability because assets will not be used to pay the dividend. If Medland prepares a balance sheet before it issues the dividend shares, it reports the distributable account in paid-in capital as an addition to common stock issued, as shown in Illustration 11A-1.

Helpful Hint Note that the dividend account title is *distributable*, not *payable*.

Illustration 11A-1 Statement presentation of common stock dividends distributable

MEDLAND CORPORATION	
Balance Sheet (partial)	
Paid-in capital	
Common stock	$500,000
Common stock dividends distributable	**50,000**
Paid-in capital in excess of par—common stock	25,000
Total paid-in capital	$575,000

When Medland issues the dividend shares, it decreases Common Stock Dividends Distributable and increases Common Stock as follows.

Common Stock Dividends Distributable	50,000	
Common Stock		50,000
(To record issuance of 5,000 shares in a stock dividend)		

A	=	L	+	SE
				−50,000 CS
				+50,000 CS

Cash Flows
no effect

Summary of Learning Objective for Appendix 11A

9 **Prepare entries for stock dividends.** To record the declaration of a small stock dividend (less than 20%), debit Stock Dividends for an amount equal to the fair value of the shares issued. Record a credit to a temporary stockholders' equity account—Common Stock Dividends Distributable—for the par value of the shares, and credit the balance to Paid-in Capital in Excess of Par Value. When the shares are issued, debit Common Stock Dividends Distributable and credit Common Stock.

Glossary

Authorized stock *(p. 576)* The amount of stock that a corporation is authorized to sell as indicated in its charter.

Cash dividend *(p. 584)* A pro rata (proportional to ownership) distribution of cash to stockholders.

Charter *(p. 574)* A document that describes a corporation's name and purpose, types of stock and number of shares authorized, names of individuals involved in the formation, and number of shares each individual has agreed to purchase.

Corporation *(p. 570)* A company organized as a separate legal entity, with most of the rights and privileges of a person.

Cumulative dividend *(p. 582)* A feature of preferred stock entitling the stockholder to receive current and unpaid prior-year dividends before common stockholders receive any dividends.

Declaration date *(p. 585)* The date the board of directors formally authorizes the dividend and announces it to stockholders.

Deficit *(p. 590)* A debit balance in Retained Earnings.

Dividend *(p. 584)* A distribution by a corporation to its stockholders on a pro rata (proportional to ownership) basis.

Dividends in arrears *(p. 582)* Preferred dividends that were supposed to be declared but were not declared during a given period.

Legal capital *(p. 577)* The amount of capital that must be retained in the business for the protection of corporate creditors.

No-par value stock *(p. 577)* Capital stock that has not been assigned a value in the corporate charter.

Outstanding stock *(p. 581)* Capital stock that has been issued and is being held by stockholders.

Paid-in capital *(p. 577)* The amount stockholders paid in to the corporation in exchange for shares of ownership.

Par value stock *(p. 577)* Capital stock that has been assigned a value per share in the corporate charter.

Payment date *(p. 585)* The date cash dividend payments are made to stockholders.

Payout ratio *(p. 593)* A measure of the percentage of earnings a company distributes in the form of cash dividends to common stockholders.

Preferred stock *(p. 581)* Capital stock that has contractual preferences over common stock in certain areas.

Privately held corporation *(p. 570)* A corporation that has only a few stockholders and whose stock is not available for sale to the general public.

Publicly held corporation *(p. 570)* A corporation that may have thousands of stockholders and whose stock is traded on a national securities market.

Record date *(p. 585)* The date when the company determines ownership of outstanding shares for dividend purposes.

Retained earnings *(p. 590)* Net income that a company retains in the business.

Retained earnings restrictions *(p. 590)* Circumstances that make a portion of retained earnings currently unavailable for dividends.

Return on common stockholders' equity (ROE) *(p. 594)* A measure of profitability from the stockholders' point of view; computed by dividing net income minus preferred dividends by average common stockholders' equity.

Stated value *(p. 577)* The amount per share assigned by the board of directors to no-par stock.

Stock dividend *(p. 586)* A pro rata (proportional to ownership) distribution of the corporation's own stock to stockholders.

Stock split *(p. 588)* The issuance of additional shares of stock to stockholders accompanied by a reduction in the par or stated value per share.

Treasury stock *(p. 579)* A corporation's own stock that has been reacquired by the corporation and is being held for future use.

Comprehensive Do it!

Rolman Corporation is authorized to issue 1,000,000 shares of $5 par value common stock. In its first year, the company has the following stock transactions.

Jan. 10 Issued 400,000 shares of stock at $8 per share.
Sept. 1 Purchased 10,000 shares of common stock for the treasury at $9 per share.
Dec. 24 Declared a cash dividend of 10 cents per share on common stock outstanding.

Instructions

(a) Journalize the transactions.

(b) Prepare the stockholders' equity section of the balance sheet, assuming the company had retained earnings of $150,600 at December 31.

Solution to Comprehensive Do it!

(a) Jan. 10	Cash	3,200,000	
	Common Stock		2,000,000
	Paid-in Capital in Excess of Par Value		1,200,000
	(To record issuance of 400,000 shares of $5 par value stock)		
Sept. 1	Treasury Stock	90,000	
	Cash		90,000
	(To record purchase of 10,000 shares of treasury stock at cost)		
Dec. 24	Cash Dividends	39,000	
	Dividends Payable		39,000
	(To record declaration of 10 cents per share cash dividend)		

Action Plan

- When common stock has a par value, credit Common Stock for par value and Paid-in Capital in Excess of Par Value for the amount above par value.
- Debit the Treasury Stock account at cost.

(b)
ROLMAN CORPORATION
Balance Sheet (partial)

Stockholders' equity
Paid-in capital
Capital stock
Common stock, $5 par value, 1,000,000 shares
authorized, 400,000 shares issued, 390,000 outstanding $2,000,000
Additional paid-in capital
Paid-in capital in excess of par value—common stock   1,200,000
     Total paid-in capital   3,200,000
Retained earnings   150,600
     Total paid-in capital and retained earnings   3,350,600
     Less: Treasury stock (10,000 shares)   90,000
Total stockholders' equity $3,260,600

 The Navigator

 Self-Test, Brief Exercises, Exercises, Problem Set A, and many more resources are available for practice in WileyPLUS.

Note: All Questions, Exercises, and Problems marked with an asterisk relate to material in the appendix to the chapter.

Self-Test Questions

Answers are on page 620.

(LO 1) 1. Which of these is **not** a major advantage of a corporation?
(a) Separate legal existence.
(b) Continuous life.
(c) Government regulations.
(d) Transferable ownership rights.

(LO 1) 2. A major **disadvantage** of a corporation is:
(a) limited liability of stockholders.
(b) additional taxes.
(c) transferable ownership rights.
(d) None of the above.

(LO 1) 3. Which of these statements is **false**?
(a) Ownership of common stock gives the owner a voting right.

(b) The stockholders' equity section begins with paid-in capital.
(c) The authorization of capital stock does not result in a formal accounting entry.
(d) Legal capital is intended to protect stockholders.

4. ABC Corp. issues 1,000 shares of $10 par value com-(LO 2) mon stock at $12 per share. When the transaction is recorded, credits are made to:
(a) Common Stock $10,000 and Paid-in Capital in Excess of Stated Value $2,000.
(b) Common Stock $12,000.
(c) Common Stock $10,000 and Paid-in Capital in Excess of Par Value $2,000.
(d) Common Stock $10,000 and Retained Earnings $2,000.

(LO 3) **5.** Treasury stock may be repurchased:
   (a) to reissue the shares to officers and employees under bonus and stock compensation plans.
   (b) to signal to the stock market that management believes the stock is underpriced.
   (c) to have additional shares available for use in the acquisition of other companies.
   (d) More than one of the above.

(LO 4) **6.** Preferred stock may have which of the following features?
   (a) Dividend preference.
   (b) Preference to assets in the event of liquidation.
   (c) Cumulative dividends.
   (d) All of the above.

(LO 4) **7.** U-Bet Corporation has 10,000 shares of 8%, $100 par value, cumulative preferred stock outstanding at December 31, 2014. No dividends were declared in 2012 or 2013. If U-Bet wants to pay $375,000 of dividends in 2014, common stockholders will receive:
   (a) $0.   (c) $215,000.
   (b) $295,000.   (d) $135,000.

(LO 5) **8.** Entries for cash dividends are required on the:
   (a) declaration date and the record date.
   (b) record date and the payment date.
   (c) declaration date, record date, and payment date.
   (d) declaration date and the payment date.

(LO 5) **9.** Which of these statements about stock dividends is **true**?
   (a) Stock dividends reduce a company's cash balance.
   (b) A stock dividend has no effect on total stockholders' equity.
   (c) A stock dividend decreases total stockholders' equity.
   (d) A stock dividend ordinarily will increase total stockholders' equity.

(LO 5) **10.** Zealot Inc. has retained earnings of $500,000 and total stockholders' equity of $2,000,000. It has 100,000 shares of $8 par value common stock outstanding, which is currently selling for $30 per share. If Zealot declares a 10% stock dividend on its common stock:
   (a) net income will decrease by $80,000.
   (b) retained earnings will decrease by $80,000 and total stockholders' equity will increase by $80,000.
   (c) retained earnings will decrease by $300,000 and total stockholders' equity will increase by $300,000.
   (d) retained earnings will decrease by $300,000 and total paid-in capital will increase by $300,000.

(LO 7) **11.** In the stockholders' equity section of the balance sheet, common stock:
   (a) is listed before preferred stock.
   (b) is listed after retained earnings.
   (c) is part of paid-in capital.
   (d) is subtracted from treasury stock.

(LO 7) **12.** In the stockholders' equity section, the cost of treasury stock is deducted from:
   (a) total paid-in capital and retained earnings.
   (b) retained earnings.
   (c) total stockholders' equity.
   (d) common stock in paid-in capital.

(LO 8) **13.** The return on common stockholders' equity is usually increased by all of the following, **except**:
   (a) an increase in the return on assets ratio.
   (b) an increase in the use of debt financing.
   (c) an increase in the company's stock price.
   (d) an increase in the company's net income.

(LO 8) **14.** Thomas is nearing retirement and would like to invest in a stock that will provide a good steady income. Thomas should choose a stock with a:
   (a) high current ratio.
   (b) high dividend payout.
   (c) high earnings per share.
   (d) high price-earnings ratio.

(LO 8) **15.** Jackson Inc. reported net income of $186,000 during 2014 and paid dividends of $26,000 on common stock. It also paid dividends on its 10,000 shares of 6%, $100 par value, noncumulative preferred stock. Common stockholders' equity was $1,200,000 on January 1, 2014, and $1,600,000 on December 31, 2014. The company's return on common stockholders' equity for 2014 is:
   (a) 10.0%.   (c) 7.1%.
   (b) 9.0%.   (d) 13.3%.

(LO 8) **16.** If everything else is held constant, earnings per share is increased by:
   (a) the payment of a cash dividend to common shareholders.
   (b) the payment of a cash dividend to preferred shareholders.
   (c) the issuance of new shares of common stock.
   (d) the purchase of treasury stock.

Go to the book's companion website, **www.wiley.com/college/kimmel**, to access additional Self-Test Questions.

 The Navigator

Questions

1. Rob, a student, asks your help in understanding some characteristics of a corporation. Explain each of these to Rob.
   (a) Separate legal existence.
   (b) Limited liability of stockholders.
   (c) Transferable ownership rights.

2. (a) Your friend C. J. Gibson cannot understand how the characteristic of corporate management is both an advantage and a disadvantage. Clarify this problem for C. J.
   (b) Identify and explain two other disadvantages of a corporation.

3. Janie Null believes a corporation must be incorporated in the state in which its headquarters office is located. Is Janie correct? Explain.

4. What are the basic ownership rights of common stockholders in the absence of restrictive provisions?

5. A corporation has been defined as an entity separate and distinct from its owners. In what ways is a corporation a separate legal entity?

6. What are the two principal components of stockholders' equity?

7. The corporate charter of Gagne Corporation allows the issuance of a maximum of 100,000 shares of common stock. During its first 2 years of operation, Gagne sold 70,000 shares to shareholders and reacquired 4,000 of these shares. After these transactions, how many shares are authorized, issued, and outstanding?

8. Which is the better investment—common stock with a par value of $5 per share or common stock with a par value of $20 per share?

9. ⬅ For what reasons might a company like IBM repurchase some of its stock (treasury stock)?

10. Diaz, Inc. purchases 1,000 shares of its own previously issued $5 par common stock for $11,000. Assuming the shares are held in the treasury, what effect does this transaction have on (a) net income, (b) total assets, (c) total paid-in capital, and (d) total stockholders' equity?

11. (a) What are the principal differences between common stock and preferred stock?
    (b) Preferred stock may be cumulative. Discuss this feature.
    (c) How are dividends in arrears presented in the financial statements?

12. Identify the events that result in credits and debits to retained earnings.

13. Indicate how each of these accounts should be classified in the stockholders' equity section of the balance sheet.
    (a) Common Stock.
    (b) Paid-in Capital in Excess of Par Value.
    (c) Retained Earnings.
    (d) Treasury Stock.
    (e) Paid-in Capital in Excess of Stated Value.
    (f) Preferred Stock.

14. What three conditions must be met before a cash dividend is paid?

15. Three dates associated with Goff Company's cash dividend are May 1, May 15, and May 31. Discuss the significance of each date and give the entry at each date.

16. Contrast the effects of a cash dividend and a stock dividend on a corporation's balance sheet.

17. Angie Diltz asks, "Since stock dividends don't change anything, why declare them?" What is your answer to Angie?

18. Deane Corporation has 10,000 shares of $15 par value common stock outstanding when it announces a 3-for-1 split. Before the split, the stock had a market price of $120 per share. After the split, how many shares of stock will be outstanding, and what will be the approximate market price per share?

19. The board of directors is considering a stock split or a stock dividend. They understand that total stockholders' equity will remain the same under either action. However, they are not sure of the different effects of the two actions on other aspects of stockholders' equity. Explain the differences to the directors.

20. ▦ What was the total cost of Tootsie Roll's treasury stock at December 31, 2011? What was the amount of the 2011 cash dividend? What was the total charge to Retained Earnings for the 2011 stock dividend?

21. (a) What is the purpose of a retained earnings restriction?
    (b) Identify the possible causes of retained earnings restrictions.

22. Hatch Inc.'s common stock has a par value of $1 and a current market price of $15. Explain why these amounts are different.

23. ⬅═══╕ What is the formula for the payout ratio? What does it indicate?

24. ⬅ ═══╕ Explain the circumstances under which debt financing will increase the return on common stockholders' equity.

25. Under what circumstances will the return on assets and the return on common stockholders' equity be equal?

26. ⬅ Krause Corp. has a return on assets of 12%. It plans to issue bonds at 8% and use the cash to repurchase stock. What effect will this have on its debt to assets ratio and on its return on common stockholders' equity?

Brief Exercises

BE11-1 Andrea Hanlin is planning to start a business. Identify for Andrea the advantages and disadvantages of the corporate form of business organization.

Cite advantages and disadvantages of a corporation.
(LO 1), **K**

BE11-2 On May 10, Paige Corporation issues 2,500 shares of $5 par value common stock for cash at $13 per share. Journalize the issuance of the stock.

Journalize issuance of par value common stock.
(LO 2), **AP**

BE11-3 On June 1, Tucker Inc. issues 3,000 shares of no-par common stock at a cash price of $7 per share. Journalize the issuance of the shares.

Journalize issuance of no-par common stock.
(LO 2), **AP**

*Journalize issuance of
preferred stock.*
(LO 4), **AP**

BE11-4 Pringle Inc. issues 8,000 shares of $100 par value preferred stock for cash at $106 per share. Journalize the issuance of the preferred stock.

*Prepare entries for a cash
dividend.*
(LO 5), **AP**

BE11-5 Troutman Corporation has 7,000 shares of common stock outstanding. It declares a $1 per share cash dividend on November 1 to stockholders of record on December 1. The dividend is paid on December 31. Prepare the entries on the appropriate dates to record the declaration and payment of the cash dividend.

*Show before-and-after effects
of a stock dividend.*
(LO 5), **AP**

BE11-6 The stockholders' equity section of Maley Corporation's balance sheet consists of common stock ($8 par) $1,000,000 and retained earnings $300,000. A 10% stock dividend (12,500 shares) is declared when the market price per share is $19. Show the before-and-after effects of the dividend on (a) the components of stockholders' equity and (b) the shares outstanding.

*Compare impact of cash
dividend, stock dividend,
and stock split.*
(LO 5), **K**

BE11-7 Indicate whether each of the following transactions would increase (+), decrease (−), or not affect (N/A) total assets, total liabilities, and total stockholders' equity.

Transaction	Assets	Liabilities	Stockholders' Equity
(a) Declared cash dividend.			
(b) Paid cash dividend declared in (a).			
(c) Declared stock dividend.			
(d) Distributed stock dividend declared in (c).			
(e) Split stock 3-for-1.			

*Prepare a stockholders'
equity section.*
(LO 7), **AP**

BE11-8 Leiker Corporation has these accounts at December 31: Common Stock, $10 par, 5,000 shares issued, $50,000; Paid-in Capital in Excess of Par Value $22,000; Retained Earnings $42,000; and Treasury Stock, 500 shares, $11,000. Prepare the stockholders' equity section of the balance sheet.

*Evaluate a company's
dividend record.*
(LO 8), **C**

BE11-9 Mike Haden, president of Haden Corporation, believes that it is a good practice for a company to maintain a constant payout of dividends relative to its earnings. Last year, net income was $600,000, and the corporation paid $120,000 in dividends. This year, due to some unusual circumstances, the corporation had income of $1,600,000. Mike expects next year's net income to be about $700,000. What was Haden Corporation's payout ratio last year? If it is to maintain the same payout ratio, what amount of dividends would it pay this year? Is this necessarily a good idea—that is, what are the pros and cons of maintaining a constant payout ratio in this scenario?

*Calculate the return on
stockholders' equity.*
(LO 8), **AP**

BE11-10 SUPERVALU, one of the largest grocery retailers in the United States, is headquartered in Minneapolis. Suppose the following financial information (in millions) was taken from the company's 2014 annual report: net sales $44,597, net income $393, beginning stockholders' equity $2,581, and ending stockholders' equity $2,887. There were no dividends paid on preferred stock. Compute the return on common stockholders' equity. Provide a brief interpretation of your findings.

*Compare bond financing to
stock financing.*
(LO 8), **AP**

BE11-11 Fugate Inc. is considering these two alternatives to finance its construction of a new $2 million plant:

1. Issuance of 200,000 shares of common stock at the market price of $10 per share.
2. Issuance of $2 million, 6% bonds at face value.

Complete the table and indicate which alternative is preferable.

	Issue Stock	Issue Bond
Income before interest and taxes	$1,500,000	$1,500,000
Interest expense from bonds	_____	_____
Income before income taxes		
Income tax expense (30%)	_____	_____
Net income	$_____	$_____
Outstanding shares	_____	700,000
Earnings per share	$_____	$_____

*Prepare entries for a stock
dividend.*
(LO 9), **AP**

*****BE11-12** Gast Corporation has 200,000 shares of $10 par value common stock outstanding. It declares a 12% stock dividend on December 1 when the market price per share is $17. The dividend shares are issued on December 31. Prepare the entries for the declaration and distribution of the stock dividend.

Do it! Review

Analyze statements about corporate organization.
(LO 1), **C**

Do it! 11-1 Indicate whether each of the following statements is true or false.

_____ 1. The corporation is an entity separate and distinct from its owners.
_____ 2. The liability of stockholders is normally limited to their investment in the corporation.
_____ 3. The relative lack of government regulation is an advantage of the corporate form of business.
_____ 4. There is no journal entry to record the authorization of capital stock.
_____ 5. No-par value stock is quite rare today.

Journalize issuance of stock.
(LO 2), **AP**

Do it! 11-2 Eddy Corporation began operations on April 1 by issuing 55,000 shares of $5 par value common stock for cash at $13 per share. Journalize the issuance.

Journalize treasury stock transaction.
(LO 3), **AP**

Do it! 11-3 Gibbs Corporation purchased 2,000 shares of its $10 par value common stock for $76,000 on August 1. It will hold these in the treasury until resold. Journalize the treasury stock transaction.

Determine dividends paid to preferred and common stockholders.
(LO 4), **AP**

Do it! 11-4 Fusion Corporation has 3,000 shares of 8%, $100 par value preferred stock outstanding at December 31, 2014. At December 31, 2014, the company declared a $105,000 cash dividend. Determine the dividend paid to preferred stockholders and common stockholders under each of the following scenarios.

1. The preferred stock is noncumulative, and the company has not missed any dividends in previous years.
2. The preferred stock is noncumulative, and the company did not pay a dividend in each of the two previous years.
3. The preferred stock is cumulative, and the company did not pay a dividend in each of the two previous years.

Determine effects of stock dividend and stock split.
(LO 5), **AP**

Do it! 11-5 Kosco CD Company has had 4 years of record earnings. Due to this success, the market price of its 400,000 shares of $2 par value common stock has increased from $6 per share to $50. During this period, paid-in capital remained the same at $2,400,000. Retained earnings increased from $1,800,000 to $12,000,000. CEO Al Dryer is considering either (1) a 15% stock dividend or (2) a 2-for-1 stock split. He asks you to show the before-and-after effects of each option on (a) retained earnings and (b) total stockholders' equity.

Prepare stockholders' equity section.
(LO 7), **AP**

Do it! 11-6 Foyle Corporation has issued 100,000 shares of $5 par value common stock. It was authorized 500,000 shares. The paid-in capital in excess of par value on the common stock is $263,000. The corporation has reacquired 7,000 shares at a cost of $46,000 and is currently holding those shares.

The corporation also has 2,000 shares issued and outstanding of 9%, $100 par value preferred stock. It authorized 10,000 shares. The paid-in capital in excess of par value on the preferred stock is $23,000. Retained earnings is $372,000. Prepare the stockholders' equity section of the balance sheet.

Exercises

Journalize issuance of common stock.
(LO 2), **AP**

E11-1 During its first year of operations, Rosa Corporation had these transactions pertaining to its common stock.

> Jan. 10 Issued 30,000 shares for cash at $5 per share.
> July 1 Issued 60,000 shares for cash at $7 per share.

Instructions
(a) Journalize the transactions, assuming that the common stock has a par value of $5 per share.
(b) Journalize the transactions, assuming that the common stock is no-par with a stated value of $1 per share.

Journalize issuance of common stock and preferred stock and purchase of treasury stock.
(LO 2, 3, 4), **AP**

E11-2 Fagan Co. had these transactions during the current period.

> June 12 Issued 80,000 shares of $1 par value common stock for cash of $300,000.
> July 11 Issued 3,000 shares of $100 par value preferred stock for cash at $106 per share.
> Nov. 28 Purchased 2,000 shares of treasury stock for $9,000.

Instructions
Prepare the journal entries for the Fagan Co. transactions shown on page 605.

Journalize preferred stock transactions and indicate statement presentation.
(LO 4, 7), **AP**

E11-3 Meranda Corporation is authorized to issue both preferred and common stock. The par value of the preferred is $50. During the first year of operations, the company had the following events and transactions pertaining to its preferred stock.

Feb. 1 Issued 40,000 shares for cash at $51 per share.
July 1 Issued 60,000 shares for cash at $56 per share.

Instructions
(a) Journalize the transactions.
(b) Post to the stockholders' equity accounts. (Use T-accounts.)
(c) Discuss the statement presentation of the accounts.

Answer questions about stockholders' equity section.
(LO 2, 3, 4, 7), **C**

E11-4 The stockholders' equity section of Leyland Corporation's balance sheet at December 31 is presented here.

LEYLAND CORPORATION
Balance Sheet (partial)

Stockholders' equity	
Paid-in capital	
Preferred stock, cumulative, 10,000 shares authorized,	
6,000 shares issued and outstanding	$ 600,000
Common stock, no par, 750,000 shares authorized,	
580,000 shares issued	2,900,000
Total paid-in capital	3,500,000
Retained earnings	1,158,000
Total paid-in capital and retained earnings	4,658,000
Less: Treasury stock (6,000 common shares)	32,000
Total stockholders' equity	$4,626,000

Instructions
From a review of the stockholders' equity section, answer the following questions.
(a) How many shares of common stock are outstanding?
(b) Assuming there is a stated value, what is the stated value of the common stock?
(c) What is the par value of the preferred stock?
(d) If the annual dividend on preferred stock is $36,000, what is the dividend rate on preferred stock?
(e) If dividends of $72,000 were in arrears on preferred stock, what would be the balance reported for retained earnings?

Prepare correct entries for capital stock transactions.
(LO 2, 3, 4), **AN**

E11-5 Garcia Corporation recently hired a new accountant with extensive experience in accounting for partnerships. Because of the pressure of the new job, the accountant was unable to review what he had learned earlier about corporation accounting. During the first month, he made the following entries for the corporation's capital stock.

May	2	Cash	104,000	
		Capital Stock		104,000
		(Issued 8,000 shares of $10 par value common stock at $13 per share)		
	10	Cash	530,000	
		Capital Stock		530,000
		(Issued 10,000 shares of $20 par value preferred stock at $53 per share)		
	15	Capital Stock	7,200	
		Cash		7,200
		(Purchased 600 shares of common stock for the treasury at $12 per share)		

Instructions
On the basis of the explanation for each entry, prepare the entries that should have been made for the capital stock transactions.

E11-6 On January 1, Vanessa Corporation had 60,000 shares of no-par common stock issued and outstanding. The stock has a stated value of $4 per share. During the year, the following transactions occurred.

Journalize cash dividends and indicate statement presentation.
(LO 5), **AP**

Apr.   1   Issued 9,000 additional shares of common stock for $11 per share.
June 15   Declared a cash dividend of $1.50 per share to stockholders of record on June 30.
July 10   Paid the $1.50 cash dividend.
Dec.   1   Issued 4,000 additional shares of common stock for $12 per share.
        15   Declared a cash dividend on outstanding shares of $1.60 per share to stockholders of record on December 31.

Instructions
(a) Prepare the entries, if any, on each of the three dates that involved dividends.
(b) How are dividends and dividends payable reported in the financial statements prepared at December 31?

E11-7 On October 31, the stockholders' equity section of Pele Company's balance sheet consists of common stock $648,000 and retained earnings $400,000. Pele is considering the following two courses of action: (1) declaring a 5% stock dividend on the 81,000 $8 par value shares outstanding or (2) effecting a 2-for-1 stock split that will reduce par value to $4 per share. The current market price is $17 per share.

Compare effects of a stock dividend and a stock split.
(LO 5), **AP**

Instructions
Prepare a tabular summary of the effects of the alternative actions on the company's stockholders' equity and outstanding shares. Use these column headings: **Before Action**, **After Stock Dividend**, and **After Stock Split**.

E11-8 Wells Fargo & Company, headquartered in San Francisco, is one of the nation's largest financial institutions. Suppose it reported the following selected accounts (in millions) as of December 31, 2014.

Prepare a stockholders' equity section.
(LO 7), **AP**

Retained earnings	$41,563
Preferred stock	8,485
Common stock—$1⅔ par value, authorized 6,000,000,000 shares;	
issued 5,245,971,422 shares	8,743
Treasury stock—67,346,829 common shares	(2,450)
Paid-in capital in excess of par value—common stock	52,878

Instructions
Prepare the stockholders' equity section of the balance sheet for Wells Fargo as of December 31, 2014.

E11-9 The following stockholders' equity accounts, arranged alphabetically, are in the ledger of Roder Corporation at December 31, 2014.

Prepare a stockholders' equity section.
(LO 7), **AP**

Common Stock ($2 stated value)	$1,600,000
Paid-in Capital in Excess of Par Value—Preferred Stock	45,000
Paid-in Capital in Excess of Stated Value—Common Stock	1,050,000
Preferred Stock (8%, $100 par, noncumulative)	600,000
Retained Earnings	1,334,000
Treasury Stock (12,000 common shares)	72,000

Instructions
Prepare the stockholders' equity section of the balance sheet at December 31, 2014.

E11-10 The following accounts appear in the ledger of Polzin Inc. after the books are closed at December 31, 2014.

Prepare a stockholders' equity section.
(LO 7), **AP**

Common Stock (no-par, $1 stated value, 400,000 shares authorized, 250,000 shares issued)	$ 250,000
Paid-in Capital in Excess of Stated Value—Common Stock	1,200,000
Preferred Stock ($50 par value, 8%, 40,000 shares authorized, 14,000 shares issued)	700,000
Retained Earnings	920,000
Treasury Stock (9,000 common shares)	64,000
Paid-in Capital in Excess of Par Value—Preferred Stock	24,000

Instructions

Prepare the stockholders' equity section at December 31, assuming $100,000 of retained earnings is restricted for plant expansion. (Use Note R.)

Calculate ratios to evaluate dividend and earnings performance.

(LO 8), **AP**

E11-11 The following financial information is available for Whitlock Corporation.

(in millions)	2014	2013
Average common stockholders' equity	$2,532	$2,591
Dividends declared for common stockholders	298	611
Dividends declared for preferred stockholders	40	40
Net income	504	555

Instructions

Calculate the payout ratio and return on common stockholders' equity for 2014 and 2013. Comment on your findings.

Calculate ratios to evaluate dividend and earnings performance.

(LO 8), **AP**

E11-12 Suppose the following financial information is available for Walgreen Company.

(in millions)	2014	2013
Average common stockholders' equity	$13,622.5	$11,986.5
Dividends declared for common stockholders	471	394
Dividends declared for preferred stockholders	0	0
Net income	2,006	2,157

Instructions

Calculate the payout ratio and return on common stockholders' equity for 2014 and 2013. Comment on your findings.

Calculate ratios to evaluate profitability and solvency.

(LO 8), **AN**

E11-13 Korsak Corporation decided to issue common stock and used the $300,000 proceeds to redeem all of its outstanding bonds on January 1, 2014. The following information is available for the company for 2013 and 2014.

	2014	2013
Net income	$ 182,000	$ 150,000
Dividends declared for preferred stockholders	8,000	8,000
Average common stockholders' equity	1,000,000	700,000
Total assets	1,200,000	1,200,000
Current liabilities	100,000	100,000
Total liabilities	200,000	500,000

Instructions

(a) Compute the return on common stockholders' equity for both years.

(b) Explain how it is possible that net income increased but the return on common stockholders' equity decreased.

(c) Compute the debt to assets ratio for both years, and comment on the implications of this change in the company's solvency.

Compare issuance of stock financing to issuance of bond financing.

(LO 8), **AN**

E11-14 Atlantic Airlines is considering these two alternatives for financing the purchase of a fleet of airplanes:

1. Issue 50,000 shares of common stock at $40 per share. (Cash dividends have not been paid nor is the payment of any contemplated.)
2. Issue 12%, 10-year bonds at face value for $2,000,000.

It is estimated that the company will earn $800,000 before interest and taxes as a result of this purchase. The company has an estimated tax rate of 30% and has 90,000 shares of common stock outstanding prior to the new financing.

Instructions

Determine the effect on net income and earnings per share for (a) issuing stock and (b) issuing bonds. Assume the new shares or new bonds will be outstanding for the entire year.

Compute ratios and interpret.

(LO 8), **AN**

E11-15 Sandberg Company has $1,000,000 in assets and $1,000,000 in stockholders' equity, with 40,000 shares outstanding the entire year. It has a return on assets of 10%. In the past year, it had net income of $100,000. On January 1, 2014, it issued $400,000 in debt at 4% and immediately repurchased 20,000 shares for $400,000. Management expected that, had it not issued the debt, it would have again had net income of $100,000.

Instructions

(a) Determine the company's net income and earnings per share for 2013 and 2014. (Ignore taxes in your computations.)

(b) Compute the company's return on common stockholders' equity for 2013 and 2014.

(c) Compute the company's debt to assets ratio for 2013 and 2014.

(d) Discuss the impact that the borrowing had on the company's profitability and solvency. Was it a good idea to borrow the money to buy the treasury stock?

E11-16 On January 1, 2014, Wilkens Corporation had $1,200,000 of common stock outstanding that was issued at par and retained earnings of $750,000. The company issued 30,000 shares of common stock at par on July 1 and earned net income of $400,000 for the year.

Journalize stock dividends.
(LO 5, 9), **AP**

Instructions

Journalize the declaration of a 15% stock dividend on December 10, 2014, for the following two independent assumptions.

(a) Par value is $10 and market price is $15.

(b) Par value is $5 and market price is $8.

Exercises: Set B and Challenge Exercises

Visit the book's companion website, at **www.wiley.com/college/kimmel**, and choose the Student Companion site to access Exercise Set B and Challenge Exercises.

Problems: Set A

P11-1A Tidwell Corporation was organized on January 1, 2014. It is authorized to issue 20,000 shares of 6%, $50 par value preferred stock and 500,000 shares of no-par common stock with a stated value of $1 per share. The following stock transactions were completed during the first year.

Journalize stock transactions, post, and prepare paid-in capital section.
(LO 2, 4, 7), **AP**

Jan.	10	Issued 70,000 shares of common stock for cash at $4 per share.
Mar.	1	Issued 12,000 shares of preferred stock for cash at $53 per share.
May	1	Issued 120,000 shares of common stock for cash at $6 per share.
Sept.	1	Issued 5,000 shares of common stock for cash at $5 per share.
Nov.	1	Issued 3,000 shares of preferred stock for cash at $56 per share.

Instructions

(a) Journalize the transactions.

(b) Post to the stockholders' equity accounts. (Use T-accounts.)

(c) Prepare the paid-in capital portion of the stockholders' equity section at December 31, 2014.

(c) Tot. paid-in capital $1,829,000

P11-2A The stockholders' equity accounts of Miley Corporation on January 1, 2014, were as follows.

Journalize transactions, post, and prepare a stockholders' equity section; calculate ratios.
(LO 2, 3, 5, 7, 8), **AP**

Preferred Stock (7%, $100 par noncumulative, 5,000 shares authorized)	$ 300,000
Common Stock ($4 stated value, 300,000 shares authorized)	1,000,000
Paid-in Capital in Excess of Par Value—Preferred Stock	15,000
Paid-in Capital in Excess of Stated Value—Common Stock	480,000
Retained Earnings	688,000
Treasury Stock (5,000 common shares)	40,000

During 2014, the corporation had the following transactions and events pertaining to its stockholders' equity.

Feb.	1	Issued 5,000 shares of common stock for $30,000.
Mar.	20	Purchased 1,000 additional shares of common treasury stock at $7 per share.
Oct.	1	Declared a 7% cash dividend on preferred stock, payable November 1.
Nov.	1	Paid the dividend declared on October 1.

Dec. 1   Declared a $0.50 per share cash dividend to common stockholders of record on December 15, payable December 31, 2014.

      31   Determined that net income for the year was $280,000. Paid the dividend declared on December 1.

Instructions

(a) Journalize the transactions. (Include entries to close net income and dividends to Retained Earnings.)

(b) Enter the beginning balances in the accounts and post the journal entries to the stockholders' equity accounts. (Use T-accounts.)

(c) Tot. paid-in capital $1,825,000

(c) Prepare the stockholders' equity section of the balance sheet at December 31, 2014.

(d) Calculate the payout ratio, earnings per share, and return on common stockholders' equity. (*Note:* Use the common shares outstanding on January 1 and December 31 to determine the average shares outstanding.)

Prepare a stockholders'
equity section.
(LO 7), **AP**

P11-3A On December 31, 2013, Paxson Company had 1,300,000 shares of $5 par common stock issued and outstanding. At December 31, 2013, stockholders' equity had the amounts listed here.

Common Stock	$6,500,000
Additional Paid-in Capital	1,800,000
Retained Earnings	1,200,000

Transactions during 2014 and other information related to stockholders' equity accounts were as follows.

1. On January 10, 2014, issued at $107 per share 120,000 shares of $100 par value, 9% cumulative preferred stock.
2. On February 8, 2014, reacquired 15,000 shares of its common stock for $11 per share.
3. On May 9, 2014, declared the yearly cash dividend on preferred stock, payable June 10, 2014, to stockholders of record on May 31, 2014.
4. On June 8, 2014, declared a cash dividend of $1.20 per share on the common stock outstanding, payable on July 10, 2014, to stockholders of record on July 1, 2014.
5. Net income for the year was $3,600,000.

Instructions

Tot. stockholders' equity $23,153,000

Prepare the stockholders' equity section of Paxson's balance sheet at December 31, 2014.

Reproduce retained earnings
account, and prepare a
stockholders' equity section.
(LO 5, 6, 7), **AP**

P11-4A The ledger of Wade Corporation at December 31, 2014, after the books have been closed, contains the following stockholders' equity accounts.

Preferred Stock (10,000 shares issued)	$1,000,000
Common Stock (300,000 shares issued)	1,500,000
Paid-in Capital in Excess of Par Value—Preferred Stock	200,000
Paid-in Capital in Excess of Stated Value—Common Stock	1,600,000
Retained Earnings	2,860,000

A review of the accounting records reveals this information:

1. Preferred stock is 8%, $100 par value, noncumulative. Since January 1, 2013, 10,000 shares have been outstanding; 20,000 shares are authorized.
2. Common stock is no-par with a stated value of $5 per share; 600,000 shares are authorized.
3. The January 1, 2014, balance in Retained Earnings was $2,380,000.
4. On October 1, 60,000 shares of common stock were sold for cash at $9 per share.
5. A cash dividend of $400,000 was declared and properly allocated to preferred and common stock on November 1. No dividends were paid to preferred stockholders in 2013.
6. Net income for the year was $880,000.
7. On December 31, 2014, the directors authorized disclosure of a $160,000 restriction of retained earnings for plant expansion. (Use Note A.)

Instructions

(a) Reproduce the Retained Earnings account (T-account) for the year.

(b) Tot. paid-in capital $4,300,000

(b) Prepare the stockholders' equity section of the balance sheet at December 31.

Prepare entries for stock
transactions, and prepare a
stockholders' equity section.
(LO 2, 3, 4, 7), **AP**

P11-5A Pringle Corporation has been authorized to issue 20,000 shares of $100 par value, 7%, noncumulative preferred stock and 1,000,000 shares of no-par common stock.

The corporation assigned a $5 stated value to the common stock. At December 31, 2014, the ledger contained the following balances pertaining to stockholders' equity.

Preferred Stock	$ 150,000
Paid-in Capital in Excess of Par Value—Preferred Stock	20,000
Common Stock	2,000,000
Paid-in Capital in Excess of Stated Value—Common Stock	1,520,000
Treasury Stock (4,000 common shares)	36,000
Retained Earnings	82,000

The preferred stock was issued for $170,000 cash. All common stock issued was for cash. In November 4,000 shares of common stock were purchased for the treasury at a per share cost of $9. No dividends were declared in 2014.

Instructions
(a) Prepare the journal entries for the following.
   (1) Issuance of preferred stock for cash.
   (2) Issuance of common stock for cash.
   (3) Purchase of common treasury stock for cash.
(b) Prepare the stockholders' equity section of the balance sheet at December 31, 2014.

(b) Tot. stockholders' equity $3,736,000

P11-6A On January 1, 2014, Kessler Inc. had these stockholders' equity balances.

Prepare a stockholders' equity section.
(LO 7), **AP**

Common Stock, $1 par (2,000,000 shares authorized, 600,000 shares issued and outstanding)	$ 600,000
Paid-in Capital in Excess of Par Value	1,500,000
Retained Earnings	700,000

During 2014, the following transactions and events occurred.

1. Issued 50,000 shares of $1 par value common stock for $3 per share.
2. Issued 60,000 shares of common stock for cash at $4 per share.
3. Purchased 20,000 shares of common stock for the treasury at $3.80 per share.
4. Declared and paid a cash dividend of $207,000.
5. Earned net income of $410,000.

Instructions
Prepare the stockholders' equity section of the balance sheet at December 31, 2014.

Tot. stockholders' equity $3,317,000

P11-7A Cepeda Company manufactures backpacks. During 2014, Cepeda issued bonds at 10% interest and used the cash proceeds to purchase treasury stock. The following financial information is available for Cepeda Company for the years 2014 and 2013.

Evaluate a company's profitability and solvency.
(LO 8), **AP**

	2014	2013
Sales revenue	$ 9,000,000	$ 9,000,000
Net income	2,240,000	2,500,000
Interest expense	500,000	140,000
Tax expense	670,000	750,000
Dividends paid on common stock	890,000	1,026,000
Dividends paid on preferred stock	300,000	300,000
Total assets (year-end)	14,500,000	16,875,000
Average total assets	15,687,500	17,763,000
Total liabilities (year-end)	6,000,000	3,000,000
Avg. total common stockholders' equity	9,400,000	14,100,000

Instructions
(a) Use the information above to calculate the following ratios for both years: (i) return on assets, (ii) return on common stockholders' equity, (iii) payout ratio, (iv) debt to assets ratio, and (v) times interest earned.
(b) Referring to your findings in part (a), discuss the changes in the company's profitability from 2013 to 2014.
(c) Referring to your findings in part (a), discuss the changes in the company's solvency from 2013 to 2014.
(d) Based on your findings in (b), was the decision to issue debt to purchase common stock a wise one?

*Prepare dividend entries,
prepare a stockholders' equity
section, and calculate ratios.
(LO 5, 7, 8, 9), AP*

*P11-8A On January 1, 2014, Everett Corporation had these stockholders' equity accounts.

Common Stock ($10 par value, 70,000 shares issued and outstanding)	$700,000
Paid-in Capital in Excess of Par Value	500,000
Retained Earnings	620,000

During the year, the following transactions occurred.

Jan. 15 Declared a $0.50 cash dividend per share to stockholders of record on January 31, payable February 15.

Feb. 15 Paid the dividend declared in January.

Apr. 15 Declared a 10% stock dividend to stockholders of record on April 30, distributable May 15. On April 15, the market price of the stock was $14 per share.

May 15 Issued the shares for the stock dividend.

Dec. 1 Declared a $0.60 per share cash dividend to stockholders of record on December 15, payable January 10, 2015.

31 Determined that net income for the year was $400,000.

Instructions

(a) Journalize the transactions. (Include entries to close net income and dividends to Retained Earnings.)

(b) Enter the beginning balances and post the entries to the stockholders' equity T-accounts. (*Note:* Open additional stockholders' equity accounts as needed.)

*(c) Tot. stockholders' equity
$2,138,800*

(c) Prepare the stockholders' equity section of the balance sheet at December 31.

(d) Calculate the payout ratio and return on common stockholders' equity.

Problems: Set B

*Journalize stock
transactions, post, and
prepare paid-in capital
section.
(LO 2, 4, 7), AP*

P11-1B Bennis Corporation was organized on January 1, 2014. It is authorized to issue 10,000 shares of 8%, $100 par value preferred stock and 500,000 shares of no-par common stock with a stated value of $1 per share. The following stock transactions were completed during the first year.

Jan. 10 Issued 40,000 shares of common stock for cash at $3.60 per share.

Mar. 1 Issued 5,000 shares of preferred stock for cash at $102 per share.

May 1 Issued 90,000 shares of common stock for cash at $4 per share.

Sept. 1 Issued 10,000 shares of common stock for cash at $4.40 per share.

Nov. 1 Issued 4,000 shares of preferred stock for cash at $103 per share.

Instructions

(a) Journalize the transactions.

(b) Post to the stockholders' equity accounts. (Use T-accounts.)

(c) Tot. paid-in capital $1,470,000

(c) Prepare the paid-in capital section of stockholders' equity at December 31, 2014.

*Journalize transactions, post,
and prepare a stockholders'
equity section; calculate
ratios.
(LO 2, 3, 5, 7, 8), AP*

P11-2B The stockholders' equity accounts of Warden Corporation on January 1, 2014, were as follows.

Preferred Stock (9%, $50 par cumulative, 10,000 shares authorized)	$ 200,000
Common Stock ($1 stated value, 2,000,000 shares authorized)	1,000,000
Paid-in Capital in Excess of Par Value—Preferred Stock	16,000
Paid-in Capital in Excess of Stated Value—Common Stock	1,400,000
Retained Earnings	1,716,000
Treasury Stock (8,000 common shares)	20,000

During 2014 the corporation had these transactions and events pertaining to its stockholders' equity.

Feb. 1 Issued 20,000 shares of common stock for $160,000.

Nov. 10 Purchased 4,000 shares of common stock for the treasury at a cost of $16,000.

Nov. 15 Declared a 9% cash dividend on preferred stock, payable December 15.

Dec. 1 Declared a $0.30 per share cash dividend to common stockholders of record on December 15, payable December 31, 2014.

Dec. 15   Paid the dividend declared on November 15.

     31   Determined that net income for the year was $408,000. The market price of the common stock on this date was $5 per share. Paid the dividend declared on December 1.

Instructions

(a) Journalize the transactions. (Include entries to close net income and dividends to Retained Earnings.)

(b) Enter the beginning balances in the accounts, and post the journal entries to the stockholders' equity accounts. (Use T-accounts.)

(c) Prepare the stockholders' equity section of the balance sheet at December 31, 2014.

(d) Calculate the payout ratio, earnings per share, and return on common stockholders' equity. (*Hint:* Use the common shares outstanding on January 1 and December 31 to determine average shares outstanding.)

(c) Tot. paid-in capital $2,776,000

P11-3B On December 31, 2013, Peabody Company had 820,000 shares of $10 par common stock issued and outstanding. At December 31, 2013, stockholders' equity had the amounts listed here.

Prepare a stockholders' equity section.
(LO 7), **AP**

Common Stock	$8,200,000
Additional Paid-in Capital	2,460,000
Retained Earnings	1,600,000

Transactions during 2014 and other information related to stockholders' equity accounts were as follows.

1. On January 18, 2014, issued at $107 per share 80,000 shares of $100 par value, 7% cumulative preferred stock.
2. On March 23, 2014, reacquired 20,000 shares of its common stock for $15 per share.
3. On May 15, 2014, declared the yearly cash dividend on preferred stock, payable June 12, 2014, to stockholders of record on May 31, 2014.
4. On June 8, 2014, declared a cash dividend of $2.00 per share on the common stock outstanding, payable on July 10, 2014, to stockholders of record on July 1, 2014.
5. Net income for the year was $2,900,000.

Instructions

Prepare the stockholders' equity section of Peabody's balance sheet at December 31, 2014.

Tot. stockholders' equity $21,260,000

P11-4B The post-closing trial balance of Dondec Corporation at December 31, 2014, contains these stockholders' equity accounts.

Reproduce retained earnings account, and prepare a stockholders' equity section.
(LO 5, 6, 7), **AP**

Preferred Stock (6,000 shares issued)	$ 300,000
Common Stock (350,000 shares issued)	3,500,000
Paid-in Capital in Excess of Par Value—Preferred Stock	250,000
Paid-in Capital in Excess of Par Value—Common Stock	520,000
Retained Earnings	720,000

A review of the accounting records reveals this information:

1. Preferred stock is $50 par, 10%, and cumulative; 6,000 shares have been outstanding since January 1, 2013.
2. Authorized stock is 20,000 shares of preferred and 500,000 shares of common with a $10 par value.
3. The January 1, 2014, balance in Retained Earnings was $800,000.
4. On July 1, 20,000 shares of common stock were sold for cash at $16 per share.
5. A cash dividend of $380,000 was declared and properly allocated to preferred and common stock on October 1. No dividends were paid to preferred stockholders in 2013.
6. Net income for the year was $300,000.
7. On December 31, 2014, the directors authorized disclosure of a $150,000 restriction of retained earnings for plant expansion. (Use Note X.)

Instructions

(a) Reproduce the Retained Earnings account (T-account) for the year.

(b) Prepare the stockholders' equity section of the balance sheet at December 31.

(b) Tot. paid-in capital $4,570,000

Prepare entries for stock transactions, and prepare a stockholders' equity section.
(LO 2, 3, 4, 7), **AP**

P11-5B Hartwell Corporation has been authorized to issue 25,000 shares of $100 par value, 8%, noncumulative preferred stock and 1,000,000 shares of no-par common stock. The corporation assigned a $4 stated value to the common stock. At December 31, 2014, the ledger contained the following balances pertaining to stockholders' equity.

Preferred Stock	$ 400,000
Paid-in Capital in Excess of Par Value—Preferred Stock	52,000
Common Stock	2,400,000
Paid-in Capital in Excess of Stated Value—Common Stock	6,600,000
Treasury Stock (40,000 common shares)	680,000
Retained Earnings	3,630,000

The preferred stock was issued for $452,000 cash. All common stock issued was for cash. In November 40,000 shares of common stock were purchased for the treasury at a per share cost of $17. No dividends were declared in 2014.

Instructions
(a) Prepare the journal entries for the following.
   (1) Issuance of preferred stock for cash.
   (2) Issuance of common stock for cash.
   (3) Purchase of common treasury stock for cash.

(b) Tot. stockholders' equity
$12,402,000
(b) Prepare the stockholders' equity section of the balance sheet at December 31, 2014.

Prepare a stockholders' equity section.
(LO 7), **AP**

P11-6B On January 1, 2014, Ferris Inc. had these stockholders' equity balances.

Common Stock, $5 par (2,000,000 shares authorized, 600,000 shares issued and outstanding)	$3,000,000
Paid-in Capital in Excess of Par Value	1,800,000
Retained Earnings	810,000

During 2014, the following transactions and events occurred.
 1. Issued 75,000 shares of $5 par value common stock for $9 per share.
 2. Issued 60,000 shares of common stock for cash at $9.50 per share.
 3. Purchased 25,000 shares of common stock for the treasury at $10 per share.
 4. Declared and paid a cash dividend of $284,000.
 5. Earned net income of $860,000.

Instructions

Tot. stockholders' equity $7,181,000
Prepare the stockholders' equity section of the balance sheet at December 31, 2014.

Evaluate a company's profitability and solvency.
(LO 8), **AP**

P11-7B Hercules Company manufactures raingear. During 2014, Hercules Company decided to issue bonds at 8% interest and then used the cash to purchase a significant amount of treasury stock. The following information is available for Hercules Company.

	2014	2013
Sales revenue	$3,000,000	$3,000,000
Net income	800,000	900,000
Interest expense	120,000	50,000
Tax expense	166,000	190,000
Total assets	5,000,000	5,610,000
Average total assets	5,312,500	6,230,000
Total liabilities	2,000,000	1,200,000
Average total stockholders' equity	3,322,500	5,250,000
Dividends paid on common stock	270,000	300,000
Dividends paid on preferred stock	40,000	40,000

Instructions
(a) Use the information above to calculate the following ratios for both years: (i) return on assets, (ii) return on common stockholders' equity, (iii) payout ratio, (iv) debt to assets ratio, and (v) times interest earned.
(b) Referring to your findings in part (a), discuss the changes in the company's profitability from 2013 to 2014.
(c) Referring to your findings in part (a), discuss the changes in the company's solvency from 2013 to 2014.
(d) Based on your findings in (b), was the decision to issue debt to purchase common stock a wise one?

*P11-8B On January 1, 2014, Lamar Corporation had these stockholders' equity accounts.

Common Stock ($20 par value, 80,000 shares issued and outstanding)	$1,600,000
Paid-in Capital in Excess of Par Value	240,000
Retained Earnings	750,000

Prepare dividend entries, prepare a stockholders' equity section, and calculate ratios.

(LO 5, 7, 8, 9), **AP**

During the year, the following transactions occurred.

Feb. 1 Declared a $1.00 cash dividend per share to stockholders of record on February 15, payable March 1.

Mar. 1 Paid the dividend declared in February.

July 1 Declared a 15% stock dividend to stockholders of record on July 15, distributable July 31. On July 1, the market price of the stock was $25 per share.

31 Issued the shares for the stock dividend.

Dec. 1 Declared a $1 per share dividend to stockholders of record on December 15, payable January 5, 2015.

31 Determined that net income for the year was $500,000. The market price of the common stock on this date was $32.

Instructions

(a) Journalize the transactions. (Include entries to close net income and dividends to Retained Earnings.)

(b) Enter the beginning balances and post the entries to the stockholders' equity T-accounts. (*Note:* Open additional stockholders' equity accounts as needed.)

(c) Prepare the stockholders' equity section of the balance sheet at December 31.

(d) Calculate the payout ratio and return on common stockholders' equity.

(c) Tot. stockholders' equity
$2,918,000

Problems: Set C

Visit the book's companion website, at **www.wiley.com/college/kimmel**, and choose the Student Companion site to access Problem Set C.

Comprehensive Problem

CP11 Klinger Corporation's balance sheet at December 31, 2013, is presented below.

KLINGER CORPORATION
Balance Sheet
December 31, 2013

Cash	$ 24,600	Accounts payable	$ 25,600
Accounts receivable	45,500	Common stock ($10 par)	80,000
Allowance for doubtful		Retained earnings	127,400
accounts	(1,500)		$233,000
Supplies	4,400		
Land	40,000		
Buildings	142,000		
Accumulated depreciation—			
buildings	(22,000)		
	$233,000		

During 2014, the following transactions occurred.

1. On January 1, 2014, Klinger issued 1,200 shares of $40 par, 7% preferred stock for $49,200.

2. On January 1, 2014, Klinger also issued 900 shares of the $10 par value common stock for $21,000.

3. Klinger performed services for $320,000 on account.

4. On April 1, 2014, Klinger collected fees of $36,000 in advance for services to be performed from April 1, 2014, to March 31, 2015.

5. Klinger collected $276,000 from customers on account.
6. Klinger bought $35,100 of supplies on account.
7. Klinger paid $32,200 on accounts payable.
8. Klinger reacquired 400 shares of its common stock on June 1, 2014, for $28 per share.
9. Paid other operating expenses of $188,200.
10. On December 31, 2014, Klinger declared the annual preferred stock dividend and a $1.20 per share dividend on the outstanding common stock, all payable on January 15, 2015.
11. An account receivable of $1,700 which originated in 2013 is written off as uncollectible.

Adjustment data:
1. A count of supplies indicates that $5,900 of supplies remain unused at year-end.
2. Recorded revenue from item 4 above.
3. The allowance for doubtful accounts should have a balance of $3,500 at year end.
4. Depreciation is recorded on the building on a straight-line basis based on a 30-year life and a salvage value of $10,000.
5. The income tax rate is 30%. (*Hint:* Prepare the income statement up to income before taxes and multiply by 30% to compute the amount.)

Instructions
(You may want to set up T-accounts to determine ending balances.)

(b) Totals $740,690

(c) Net income $81,970
   Tot. assets $421,000

(a) Prepare journal entries for the transactions listed above and adjusting entries.
(b) Prepare an adjusted trial balance at December 31, 2014.
(c) Prepare an income statement and a retained earnings statement for the year ending December 31, 2014, and a classified balance sheet as of December 31, 2014.

Continuing Cookie Chronicle

(*Note:* This is a continuation of the Cookie Chronicle from Chapters 1 through 10.)

CCC11 Part 1 Because Natalie has been so successful with Cookie Creations and her friend Curtis Lesperance has been just as successful with his coffee shop, they conclude that they could benefit from each other's business expertise. Curtis and Natalie next evaluate the different types of business organization. Because of the advantage of limited personal liability, they decide to form a corporation.

Natalie and Curtis are very excited about this new business venture. They come to you with information they have gathered about their companies and with a number of questions.

Part 2 After establishing their company's fiscal year to be October 31, Natalie and Curtis began operating Cookie & Coffee Creations Inc. on November 1, 2015. On that date, they issued both preferred and common stock. Natalie and Curtis now want to prepare financial information for the first year of operations.

Go to the book's companion website, at **www.wiley.com/college/kimmel**, to find the completion of this problem.

Broadening Your Perspective

Financial Reporting and Analysis

FINANCIAL REPORTING PROBLEM: *Tootsie Roll Industries, Inc.*

BYP11-1 The stockholders' equity section of Tootsie Roll Industries' balance sheet is shown in the Consolidated Statement of Financial Position in Appendix A. You will also find data relative to this problem on other pages of Appendix A. **(Note that Tootsie Roll has two classes of common stock. To answer the following questions, add the two classes of stock together.)**

Instructions

Answer the following questions.

(a) What is the par or stated value per share of Tootsie Roll's common stock?

(b) What percentage of Tootsie Roll's authorized common stock was issued at December 31, 2011? (Round to the nearest full percent.)

(c) How many shares of common stock were outstanding at December 31, 2010, and at December 31, 2011?

(d) Calculate the payout ratio, earnings per share, and return on common stockholders' equity for 2011.

COMPARATIVE ANALYSIS PROBLEM: *Tootsie Roll vs. Hershey*

BYP11-2 The financial statements of The Hershey Company are presented in Appendix B, following the financial statements for Tootsie Roll in Appendix A.

Instructions

(a) Based on the information in these financial statements, compute the 2011 return on common stockholders' equity, debt to assets ratio, and return on assets for each company.

(b) What conclusions concerning the companies' profitability can be drawn from these ratios? Which company relies more on debt to boost its return to common shareholders?

(c) Compute the payout ratio for each company. Which pays out a higher percentage of its earnings?

RESEARCH CASES

BYP11-3 The March 15, 2010, edition of the *Wall Street Journal* includes an article by Martin Peers entitled "Media's Cash Focus Is Paying Dividends."

Instructions

Read the article and answer the following questions.

(a) What action did Viacom take with its excess cash before it decided to consider paying dividends or stock buybacks?

(b) What percentage of free cash flow does Time Warner pay out in dividends?

(c) Why might Viacom choose to pay a lower dividend and instead use its excess cash for a stock buyback program?

(d) How might the payment of a steady, significant dividend change the nature of shareholders that invest in media companies?

(e) What message might an increased dividend or stock buybacks send to shareholders regarding what the company will do with excess cash now, as opposed to what it used to do with excess cash?

BYP11-4 The November 10, 2011, edition of the *Financial Times* contains an article by Alan Rappeport entitled "McDonald's Looks to Buy More Property."

Instructions

Read the article and answer the following questions.

(a) Why is McDonald's shifting away from leasing its properties toward purchasing them?

(b) What percentage of the land that its stores sit on does McDonald's own? What percentage of its 30,000 restaurant buildings does it own?

(c) William Ackerman was a large McDonald's shareholder. Explain the proposal he had for the company.

(d) What impact would William Ackerman's proposal probably have had on the return on common stockholders' equity?

(e) Why did McDonald's probably choose to decline the Ackerman proposal?

INTERPRETING FINANCIAL STATEMENTS

BYP11-5 Marriott Corporation split into two companies: Host Marriott Corporation and Marriott International. Host Marriott retained ownership of the corporation's vast hotel and other properties, while Marriott International, rather than owning hotels, managed them. The purpose of this split was to free Marriott International from the "baggage" associated with Host Marriott, thus allowing it to be more aggressive in its pursuit of growth. The following information (in millions) is provided for each corporation for their first full year operating as independent companies.

	Host Marriott	Marriott International
Sales revenue	$1,501	$8,415
Net income	(25)	200
Total assets	3,822	3,207
Total liabilities	3,112	2,440
Common stockholders' equity	710	767

Instructions

(a) The two companies were split by the issuance of shares of Marriott International to all share-holders of the previous combined company. Discuss the nature of this transaction.

(b) Calculate the debt to assets ratio for each company.

(c) Calculate the return on assets and return on common stockholders' equity for each company.

(d) The company's debtholders were fiercely opposed to the original plan to split the two compa-nies because the original plan had Host Marriott absorbing the majority of the company's debt. They relented only when Marriott International agreed to absorb a larger share of the debt. Discuss the possible reasons the debtholders were opposed to the plan to split the company.

REAL-WORLD FOCUS

BYP11-6 *Purpose:* Use the stockholders' equity section of an annual report and identify the major components.

Address: **www.annualreports.com**, or go to **www.wiley.com/college/kimmel**

Steps
1. Select a particular company.
2. Search by company name.
3. Follow instructions below.

Instructions

Answer the following questions.

(a) What is the company's name?

(b) What classes of capital stock has the company issued?

(c) For each class of stock:
   (1) How many shares are authorized, issued, and/or outstanding?
   (2) What is the par value?

(d) What are the company's retained earnings?

(e) Has the company acquired treasury stock? How many shares?

Critical Thinking

DECISION-MAKING ACROSS THE ORGANIZATION

BYP11-7 During a recent period, the fast-food chain Wendy's International purchased many treasury shares. This caused the number of shares outstanding to fall from 124 million to 105 mil-lion. The following information was drawn from the company's financial statements (in millions).

	Information for the Year after Purchase of Treasury Stock	Information for the Year before Purchase of Treasury Stock
Net income	$ 193.6	$ 123.4
Total assets	2,076.0	1,837.9
Average total assets	2,016.9	1,889.8
Total common stockholders' equity	1,029.8	1,068.1
Average common stockholders' equity	1,078.0	1,126.2
Total liabilities	1,046.3	769.9
Average total liabilities	939.0	763.7
Interest expense	30.2	19.8
Income taxes	113.7	84.3
Cash provided by operations	305.2	233.8
Cash dividends paid on common stock	26.8	31.0
Preferred stock dividends	0	0
Average number of common shares outstanding	109.7	119.9

Instructions
Use the information provided to answer the following questions.
(a) Compute earnings per share, return on common stockholders' equity, and return on assets for both years. Discuss the change in the company's profitability over this period.
(b) Compute the dividend payout ratio. Also compute the average cash dividend paid per share of common stock (dividends paid divided by the average number of common shares outstanding). Discuss any change in these ratios during this period and the implications for the company's dividend policy.
(c) Compute the debt to assets ratio and times interest earned. Discuss the change in the company's solvency.
(d) Based on your findings in (a) and (c), discuss to what extent any change in the return on common stockholders' equity was the result of increased reliance on debt.
(e) Does it appear that the purchase of treasury stock and the shift toward more reliance on debt were wise strategic moves?

COMMUNICATION ACTIVITY

BYP11-8 Ken Endicott, your uncle, is an inventor who has decided to incorporate. Uncle Ken knows that you are an accounting major at U.N.O. In a recent letter to you, he ends with the question, "I'm filling out a state incorporation application. Can you tell me the difference among the following terms: (1) authorized stock, (2) issued stock, (3) outstanding stock, and (4) preferred stock?"

Instructions
In a brief note, differentiate for Uncle Ken the four different stock terms. Write the letter to be friendly, yet professional.

ETHICS CASES

BYP11-9 The R&D division of Jobe Corp. has just developed a chemical for sterilizing the vicious Brazilian "killer bees" which are invading Mexico and the southern United States. The president of Jobe is anxious to get the chemical on the market because Jobe profits need a boost—and his job is in jeopardy because of decreasing sales and profits. Jobe has an opportunity to sell this chemical in Central American countries, where the laws are much more relaxed than in the United States.

The director of Jobe's R&D division strongly recommends further research in the laboratory to test the side effects of this chemical on other insects, birds, animals, plants, and even humans. He cautions the president, "We could be sued from all sides if the chemical has tragic side effects that we didn't even test for in the lab." The president answers, "We can't wait an additional year for your lab tests. We can avoid losses from such lawsuits by establishing a separate wholly owned corporation to shield Jobe Corp. from such lawsuits. We can't lose any more than our investment in the new corporation, and we'll invest just the patent covering this chemical. We'll reap the benefits if the chemical works and is safe, and avoid the losses from lawsuits if it's a disaster." The following week, Jobe creates a new wholly owned corporation called Windsor Inc., sells the chemical patent to it for $10, and watches the spraying begin.

Instructions
(a) Who are the stakeholders in this situation?
(b) Are the president's motives and actions ethical?
(c) Can Jobe shield itself against losses of Windsor Inc.?

BYP11-10 Osborn Corporation has paid 60 consecutive quarterly cash dividends (15 years). The last 6 months have been a real cash drain on the company, however, as profit margins have been greatly narrowed by increasing competition. With a cash balance sufficient to meet only day-to-day operating needs, the president, Barry Sigle, has decided that a stock dividend instead of a cash dividend should be declared. He tells Osborn's financial vice president, Mandy Drummond, to issue a press release stating that the company is extending its consecutive dividend record with the issuance of a 5% stock dividend. "Write the press release convincing the stockholders that the stock dividend is just as good as a cash dividend," he orders. "Just watch our stock rise when we announce the stock dividend; it must be a good thing if that happens."

Instructions
(a) Who are the stakeholders in this situation?
(b) Is there anything unethical about president Sigle's intentions or actions?
(c) What is the effect of a stock dividend on a corporation's stockholders' equity accounts? Which would you rather receive as a stockholder—a cash dividend or a stock dividend? Why?

ALL ABOUT YOU

BYP11-11 In response to the Sarbanes-Oxley Act, many companies have implemented formal ethics codes. Many other organizations also have ethics codes.

Instructions

Obtain the ethics code from an organization that you belong to (e.g., student organization, business school, employer, or a volunteer organization). Evaluate the ethics code based on how clearly it identifies proper and improper behavior. Discuss its strengths, and how it might be improved.

FASB CODIFICATION ACTIVITY

BYP11-12 If your school has a subscription to the FASB Codification, go to **http://aaahq.org/ ascLogin.cfm** to log in and prepare responses to the following.
(a) What is the stock dividend?
(b) What is a stock split?
(c) At what percentage point does the issuance of additional shares qualify as a stock dividend, as opposed to a stock split?

CONSIDERING PEOPLE, PLANET, AND PROFIT

BYP11-13 The January 19, 2012, edition of the *Wall Street Journal* contains an article by Angus Loten entitled "With New Law, Profits Take a Back Seat."

Instructions

Read the article and answer the following questions.
(a) Summarize the nature of the new law that is discussed in the article.
(b) What do some proponents of the law say is the "biggest value" of the law? How does the article say that this would have impacted Ben & Jerry's?
(c) What are some criticisms of the law?
(d) How does incorporation as a benefit corporation differ from B Corp certification?
(e) What are some of the companies that the article cites as either having adopted benefit corporation standing or are considering it?

Answers to Insight and Accounting Across the Organization Questions

p. 573 The Impact of Corporate Social Responsibility Q: Why are CSR-related shareholder proposals increasing? **A:** The increase in shareholder proposals reflects a growing belief that a company's social and environmental policies correlate strongly with its risk-management strategy and ultimately its financial performance.

p. 579 How to Read Stock Quotes Q: For stocks traded on organized exchanges, how are the dollar prices per share established? What factors might influence the price of shares in the marketplace? **A:** The dollar prices per share are established by the interaction between buyers and sellers of the shares. The prices of shares are influenced by a company's earnings and dividends as well as by factors beyond a company's control, such as changes in interest rates, labor strikes, scarcity of supplies or resources, and politics. The number of willing buyers and sellers (demand and supply) also plays a part in the price of shares.

p. 586 Up, Down, and ?? Q: What factors must management consider in deciding how large a dividend to pay? **A:** Management must consider the size of the company's retained earnings balance, the amount of available cash, the company's expected near-term cash needs, the company's growth opportunities, and what level of dividend the company will be able to sustain based upon its expected future earnings.

p. 588 A No-Split Philosophy Q: Why does Warren Buffett usually oppose stock splits? **A:** Buffett prefers to attract shareholders that make a long-term commitment to his company, as opposed to traders that only hold their investment for a short period of time. He believes that a high stock price discourages short-term investment.

Answers to Self-Test Questions

1. c **2.** b **3.** d **4.** c **5.** d **6.** d **7.** d $375,000 − ($100 × 10,000 × .08 × 3) **8.** d **9.** b **10.** d (100,000 × $30 × .10) **11.** c **12.** a **13.** c **14.** b **15.** b ($186,000 − $60,000) ÷ ((1,200,000 + $1,600,000) ÷ 2) **16.** d

A Look at IFRS

The accounting for transactions related to stockholders' equity, such as issuance of shares, purchase of treasury stock, and declaration and payment of dividends, are similar under both IFRS and GAAP. Major differences relate to terminology used, introduction of items such as revaluation surplus, and presentation of stockholders' equity information.

LEARNING OBJECTIVE 10

Compare the accounting for transactions related to stockholders' equity under GAAP and IFRS.

KEY POINTS

- Under IFRS, the term **reserves** is used to describe all equity accounts other than those arising from contributed capital. This would include, for example, reserves related to retained earnings, asset revaluations, and fair value differences.

- Many countries have a different mix of investor groups than in the United States. For example, in Germany, financial institutions like banks are not only major creditors of corporations but often are the largest corporate stockholders as well. In the United States, Asia, and the United Kingdom, many companies rely on substantial investment from private investors.

- There are often terminology differences for equity accounts. The following summarizes some of the common differences in terminology.

GAAP	IFRS
Common stock	Share capital—ordinary
Stockholders	Shareholders
Par value	Nominal or face value
Authorized stock	Authorized share capital
Preferred stock	Share capital—preference
Paid-in capital	Issued/allocated share capital
Paid-in capital in excess of par value—common stock	Share premium—ordinary
Paid-in capital in excess of par value—preferred stock	Share premium—preference
Retained earnings	Retained earnings or Retained profits
Retained earnings deficit	Accumulated losses
Accumulated other comprehensive income	General reserve and other reserve accounts

As an example of how similar transactions use different terminology under IFRS, consider the accounting for the issuance of 1,000 shares of $1 par value stock for $5 per share. Under IFRS, the entry is as follows.

Cash	5,000	
Share Capital—Ordinary		1,000
Share Premium—Ordinary		4,000

- The accounting for treasury stock differs somewhat between IFRS and GAAP. (However, many of the differences are beyond the scope of this course.) Like GAAP, IFRS does not allow a company to record gains or losses on purchases of its own shares. One difference worth noting is that when a company purchases its own shares, IFRS treats it as a reduction of shareholders' equity but it does not specify which particular equity accounts are to be affected. Therefore, it could be shown as an increase to a contra equity account (Treasury Shares) or a decrease to retained earnings or share capital. IFRS requires that the number of treasury shares held be disclosed.

- A major difference between IFRS and GAAP relates to the account Revaluation Surplus. Revaluation surplus arises under IFRS because companies are permitted to revalue their property, plant, and equipment to fair value under certain circumstances. This account is part of general reserves under IFRS and is not considered contributed capital.

- As indicated earlier, the term **reserves** is used in IFRS to indicate all noncontributed (non–paid-in) capital. Reserves include retained earnings and other comprehensive income items, such as revaluation surplus and unrealized gains or losses on non-trading securities.

- IFRS often uses terms such as **retained profits** or **accumulated profit or loss** to describe retained earnings. The term **retained earnings** is also often used.
- The accounting related to prior period adjustments is essentially the same under IFRS and GAAP. IFRS addresses the accounting for errors in *IAS 8* ("Accounting Policies, Changes in Accounting Estimates, and Errors"). One area where IFRS and GAAP differ in reporting relates to error corrections in previously issued financial statements. While IFRS requires restatement with some exceptions, GAAP does not permit any exceptions.
- Equity is given various descriptions under IFRS, such as shareholders' equity, owners' equity, capital and reserves, and shareholders' funds.

LOOKING TO THE FUTURE

As indicated in earlier discussions, the IASB and the FASB are currently working on a project related to financial statement presentation. An important part of this study is to determine whether certain line items, subtotals, and totals should be clearly defined and required to be displayed in the financial statements. For example, it is likely that the statement of stockholders' equity and its presentation will be examined closely. In addition, the options of how to present other comprehensive income under GAAP will change in any converged standard.

IFRS PRACTICE

IFRS SELF-TEST QUESTIONS

1. Under IFRS, a purchase by a company of its own shares is recorded by:
   (a) an increase in Treasury Shares.
   (b) a decrease in contributed capital.
   (c) a decrease in share capital.
   (d) All of these are acceptable treatments.
2. The term **reserves** is used under IFRS with reference to all of the following **except**:
   (a) gains and losses on revaluation of property, plant, and equipment.
   (b) capital received in excess of the par value of issued shares.
   (c) retained earnings.
   (d) fair value differences.
3. Under IFRS, the amount of capital received in excess of par value on ordinary shares would be credited to:
   (a) Retained Earnings.
   (b) Contributed Capital.
   (c) Share Premium—Ordinary.
   (d) Par value is not used under IFRS.
4. Which of the following is **false**?
   (a) Under GAAP, companies cannot record gains on transactions involving their own shares.
   (b) Under IFRS, companies cannot record gains on transactions involving their own shares.
   (c) Under IFRS, the statement of stockholders' equity is a required statement.
   (d) Under IFRS, a company records a revaluation surplus when it experiences an increase in the price of its common stock.
5. Which of the following does **not** represent a pair of GAAP/IFRS-comparable terms?
   (a) Additional paid-in capital/Share premium.
   (b) Treasury stock/Repurchase reserve.
   (c) Common stock/Share capital—ordinary.
   (d) Preferred stock/Preference shares.

IFRS CONCEPTS AND APPLICATION

IFRS11-1 On May 10, Barone Corporation issues 1,000 shares of $10 par value ordinary shares for cash at $18 per share. Journalize the issuance of the shares.

IFRS11-2 Luther Corporation has the following accounts at December 31, 2014 (in euros): Share Capital—Ordinary, €10 par, 5,000 shares issued, €50,000; Share Premium—Ordinary €10,000; Retained Earnings €45,000; and Treasury Shares—Ordinary, 500 shares, €11,000. Prepare the equity section of the statement of financial position.

IFRS11-3 Vangundy Co. had the following transactions during the current period.

   June 12   Issued 60,000 shares of $1 par value ordinary shares for cash of $375,000.
   July   11   Issued 1,000 shares of $100 par value preference shares for cash at $110 per share.
   Nov. 28   Purchased 2,000 treasury shares for $80,000.

Instructions
Journalize the above transactions.

IFRS11-4 The April 23, 2012, edition of the *Wall Street Journal Online* contains an article by Christopher Bjork entitled "Santander Prepares Record Mexico IPO."

Instructions
Read the article and answer the following questions.
(a) Why is the Spanish lender Santander issuing shares of its Mexican banking subsidiary to the public?
(b) The article suggests that Santander has previously issued shares of subsidiaries in other countries as well. Why does the bank like to do these so-called "local listings"?
(c) In what other countries has Santander done local listings? Why do regulators in those countries like the local listings?
(d) What advantage has Santander had over some of its European rivals in raising funds?

INTERNATIONAL FINANCIAL REPORTING PROBLEM: *Zetar plc*

IFRS11-5 The financial statements of Zetar plc are presented in Appendix C. The company's complete annual report, including the notes to its financial statements, is available in the Investors section at **www.zetarplc.com**.

Instructions
Use the company's annual report to answer the following questions.
(a) Using the information in the statement of changes in equity, prepare the journal entry to record the issuance of ordinary shares during the year ended April 30, 2010.
(b) Compute the company's return on ordinary shareholders' equity for the year ended April 30, 2011.
(c) Examine the equity section of the company's balance sheet. For each item in the equity section, provide the comparable label that would be used under GAAP.

Answers to IFRS Self-Test Questions
1. d **2.** b **3.** c **4.** d **5.** b

Rudi Von Briel/PhotoEdit

CHAPTER 12

STATEMENT OF CASH FLOWS

LEARNING OBJECTIVES

After studying this chapter, you should be able to:

1 Indicate the usefulness of the statement of cash flows.
2 Distinguish among operating, investing, and financing activities.
3 Explain the impact of the product life cycle on a company's cash flows.
4 Prepare a statement of cash flows using the indirect method.
5 Use the statement of cash flows to evaluate a company.

✔ The Navigator

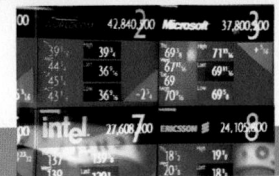
Companies must be ready to respond to changes quickly in order to survive and thrive. This requires careful management of cash. One company that managed cash successfully in its early years was Microsoft. During those years, the company paid much of its payroll with stock options (rights to purchase company stock in the future at a given price) instead of cash. This conserved cash and turned more than a thousand of its employees into millionaires.

In recent years, Microsoft has had a different kind of cash problem. Now that it has reached a more "mature" stage in life, it generates so much cash—roughly $1 billion per month—that it cannot always figure out what to do with it. At one time, Microsoft had accumulated $60 billion.

The company said it was accumulating cash to invest in new opportunities, buy other companies, and pay off pending lawsuits. Microsoft's stockholders complained that holding all this cash was putting a drag on the company's profitability. Why? Because Microsoft had the cash invested in very low-yielding government securities. Stockholders felt that the company either should find new investment projects that would bring higher returns, or return some of the cash to stockholders.

Finally, Microsoft announced a plan to return cash to stockholders by paying a special one-time

GOT CASH?

$32 billion dividend. This special dividend was so large that, according to the U.S. Commerce Department, it caused total personal income in the United States to rise by 3.7% in one month—the largest increase ever recorded by the agency. (It also made the holiday season brighter, especially for retailers in the Seattle area.) Microsoft also doubled its regular annual dividend to $3.50 per share. Further, it announced that it would spend another $30 billion buying treasury stock.

In recent years, Apple also encountered this cash "problem." At the end of 2011, Apple had nearly $100 billion in liquid assets (cash, cash equivalents, and investment securities). At that time, it was generating $37 billion of cash per year from its operating activities but spending only about $7 billion on plant assets and purchases of patents. Shareholders pressured Apple to unload some of this cash. In response, Apple announced that it would begin to pay a quarterly dividend of $2.65 per share and it would buy back up to $10 billion of its stock. Analysts noted that the dividend consumes only $10 billion of cash per year. This leaves Apple wallowing in cash. The rest of us should have such problems.

Source: "Business: An End to Growth? Microsoft's Cash Bonanza," *The Economist* (July 23, 2005), p. 61.

 The Navigator

The balance sheet, income statement, and retained earnings statement do not always show the whole picture of the financial condition of a company or institution. In fact, looking at the financial statements of some well-known companies, a thoughtful investor might ask questions like these: How did Eastman Kodak finance cash dividends of $649 million in a year in which it earned only $17 million? How could United Air Lines purchase new planes that cost $1.9 billion in a year in which it reported a net loss of over $2 billion? How did the companies that spent a combined fantastic $3.4 trillion on mergers and acquisitions in a recent year finance those deals? Answers to these and similar questions can be found in this chapter, which presents the statement of cash flows.

The content and organization of this chapter are as follows.

The Statement of Cash Flows: Usefulness and Format

LEARNING OBJECTIVE **1**

Indicate the usefulness of the statement of cash flows.

The balance sheet, income statement, and retained earnings statement provide only limited information about a company's cash flows (cash receipts and cash payments). For example, comparative balance sheets show the increase in property, plant, and equipment during the year. But, they do not show how the additions were financed or paid for. The income statement shows net income. But, it does not indicate the amount of cash generated by operating activities. The retained earnings statement shows cash dividends declared but not the cash dividends paid during the year. None of these statements presents a detailed summary of where cash came from and how it was used.

USEFULNESS OF THE STATEMENT OF CASH FLOWS

The statement of cash flows reports the cash receipts and cash payments from operating, investing, and financing activities during a period, in a format that reconciles the beginning and ending cash balances. The information in a statement of cash flows helps investors, creditors, and others assess:

1. **The entity's ability to generate future cash flows.** By examining relationships between items in the statement of cash flows, investors make predictions

of the amounts, timing, and uncertainty of future cash flows better than they can from accrual-basis data.

2. **The entity's ability to pay dividends and meet obligations.** If a company does not have adequate cash, it cannot pay employees, settle debts, or pay dividends. Employees, creditors, and stockholders should be particularly interested in this statement because it alone shows the flows of cash in a business.

3. **The reasons for the difference between net income and net cash provided (used) by operating activities.** Net income provides information on the success or failure of a business enterprise. However, some financial statement users are critical of accrual-basis net income because it requires many estimates. As a result, users often challenge the reliability of the number. Such is not the case with cash. Many readers of the statement of cash flows want to know the reasons for the difference between net income and net cash provided by operating activities. Then they can assess for themselves the reliability of the income number.

4. **The cash investing and financing transactions during the period.** By examining a company's investing and financing transactions, a financial statement reader can better understand why assets and liabilities changed during the period.

Ethics Note Though we would discourage reliance on cash flows to the exclusion of accrual accounting, comparing net cash provided by operating activities to net income can reveal important information about the "quality" of reported net income. Such a comparison can reveal the extent to which net income provides a good measure of actual performance.

CLASSIFICATION OF CASH FLOWS

The statement of cash flows classifies cash receipts and cash payments as operating, investing, and financing activities. Transactions and other events characteristic of each kind of activity are as follows.

LEARNING OBJECTIVE 2
Distinguish among operating, investing, and financing activities.

1. **Operating activities** include the cash effects of transactions that create revenues and expenses. They thus enter into the determination of net income.

2. **Investing activities** include (a) cash transactions that involve the purchase or disposal of investments and property, plant, and equipment, and (b) lending money and collecting the loans.

3. **Financing activities** include (a) obtaining cash from issuing debt and repaying the amounts borrowed, and (b) obtaining cash from stockholders, repurchasing shares, and paying dividends.

The operating activities category is the most important. It shows the cash provided by company operations. This source of cash is generally considered to be the best measure of a company's ability to generate sufficient cash to continue as a going concern.

Illustration 12-1 (page 628) lists typical cash receipts and cash payments within each of the three classifications. **Study the list carefully.** It will be very useful in solving homework exercises and problems.

Note the following general guidelines:

1. Operating activities involve income statement items.

2. Investing activities involve cash flows resulting from changes in investments and long-term asset items.

3. Financing activities involve cash flows resulting from changes in long-term liability and stockholders' equity items.

Companies classify as operating activities some cash flows related to investing or financing activities. For example, receipts of investment revenue (interest and dividends) are classified as operating activities. So are payments of interest to lenders. Why are these considered operating activities? **Because companies report these items in the income statement, where results of operations are shown.**

Illustration 12-1 Typical receipt and payment classifications

Operating activities

Investing activities

Financing activities

Types of Cash Inflows and Outflows

Operating activities—Income statement items
Cash inflows:
From sale of goods or services.
From interest received and dividends received.
Cash outflows:
To suppliers for inventory.
To employees for wages.
To government for taxes.
To lenders for interest.
To others for expenses.

Investing activities—Changes in investments and long-term assets
Cash inflows:
From sale of property, plant, and equipment.
From sale of investments in debt or equity securities of other entities.
From collection of principal on loans to other entities.
Cash outflows:
To purchase property, plant, and equipment.
To purchase investments in debt or equity securities of other entities.
To make loans to other entities.

Financing activities—Changes in long-term liabilities and stockholders' equity
Cash inflows:
From sale of common stock.
From issuance of debt (bonds and notes).
Cash outflows:
To stockholders as dividends.
To redeem long-term debt or reacquire capital stock (treasury stock).

International Note The statement of cash flows is very similar under GAAP and IFRS. One difference is that, under IFRS, noncash investing and financing activities are not reported in the statement of cash flows but instead are reported in the notes to the financial statements.

SIGNIFICANT NONCASH ACTIVITIES

Not all of a company's significant activities involve cash. Examples of significant noncash activities are:

1. Direct issuance of common stock to purchase assets.
2. Conversion of bonds into common stock.
3. Direct issuance of debt to purchase assets.
4. Exchanges of plant assets.

Helpful Hint Do not include **noncash** investing and financing activities in the body of the statement of cash flows. Report this information in a separate schedule below the statement of cash flows.

Companies do not report in the body of the statement of cash flows significant financing and investing activities that do not affect cash. Instead, they report these activities in either a **separate schedule** at the bottom of the statement of cash flows or in a **separate note or supplementary schedule** to the financial statements. The reporting of these noncash activities in a separate schedule satisfies the **full disclosure principle**.

In solving homework assignments, you should present significant noncash investing and financing activities in a separate schedule at the bottom of the statement of cash flows. (See the last entry in Illustration 12-2 for an example.)

Accounting Across the Organization

Net *What?*

Net income is not the same as net cash provided by operating activities. The differences are illustrated by the following results from recent annual reports ($ in millions). Note the wide disparity among these companies that all engaged in retail merchandising.

Company	Net Income	Net Cash Provided by Operating Activities
Kohl's Corporation	$ 1,083	$ 1,234
Wal-Mart Stores, Inc.	11,284	20,169
JCPenney Company, Inc.	1,153	1,255
Costco Wholesale Corp.	1,082	2,076
Target Corporation	2,849	4,125

Darren McCollester/Getty Images Inc.

 In general, why do differences exist between net income and net cash provided by operating activities? (See page 684.)

FORMAT OF THE STATEMENT OF CASH FLOWS

The general format of the statement of cash flows presents the results of the three activities discussed previously—operating, investing, and financing—plus the significant noncash investing and financing activities. Illustration 12–2 shows a widely used form of the statement of cash flows.

Illustration 12-2 Format of statement of cash flows

COMPANY NAME
Statement of Cash Flows
Period Covered

Cash flows from operating activities		
(List of individual items)	XX	
Net cash provided (used) by operating activities		XXX
Cash flows from investing activities		
(List of individual inflows and outflows)	XX	
Net cash provided (used) by investing activities		XXX
Cash flows from financing activities		
(List of individual inflows and outflows)	XX	
Net cash provided (used) by financing activities		XXX
Net increase (decrease) in cash		XXX
Cash at beginning of period		XXX
Cash at end of period		XXX
Noncash investing and financing activities		
(List of individual noncash transactions)		XXX

The cash flows from operating activities section always appears first, followed by the investing activities section and then the financing activities section. The sum of the operating, investing, and financing activities sections equals the net increase or decrease in cash for the period. This amount is added to the beginning cash balance to arrive at the ending cash balance—the same amount reported on the balance sheet.

CASH FLOW ACTIVITIES

Action Plan

- Identify the three types of activities used to report all cash inflows and outflows.
- Report as operating activities the cash effects of transactions that create revenues and expenses and enter into the determination of net income.
- Report as investing activities transactions that (a) acquire and dispose of investments and productive long-lived assets and (b) lend money and collect loans.
- Report as financing activities transactions that (a) obtain cash from issuing debt and repay the amounts borrowed and (b) obtain cash from stockholders and pay them dividends.

Do it! During its first week, Duffy & Stevenson Company had these transactions.

1. Issued 100,000 shares of $5 par value common stock for $800,000 cash.
2. Borrowed $200,000 from Castle Bank, signing a 5-year note bearing 8% interest.
3. Purchased two semi-trailer trucks for $170,000 cash.
4. Paid employees $12,000 for salaries and wages.
5. Collected $20,000 cash for services performed.

Classify each of these transactions by type of cash flow activity.

Solution

1. Financing activity
2. Financing activity
3. Investing activity
4. Operating activity
5. Operating activity

Related exercise material: **BE12-1, BE12-2, BE12-3, Do it! 12-1, E12-1,** and **E12-2.**

LEARNING OBJECTIVE 3

Explain the impact of the product life cycle on a company's cash flows.

THE CORPORATE LIFE CYCLE

All products go through a series of phases called the **product life cycle**. The phases (in order of their occurrence) are **introductory phase**, **growth phase**, **maturity phase**, and **decline phase**. The introductory phase occurs at the beginning of a company's life, when it purchases fixed assets and begins to produce and sell products. During the growth phase, the company strives to expand its production and sales. In the maturity phase, sales and production level off. During the decline phase, sales of the product decline due to a weakening in consumer demand.

In the same way that products have life cycles, companies have life cycles as well. Companies generally have more than one product, and not all of a company's products are in the same phase of the product life cycle at the same time. This sometimes makes it difficult to classify a company's phase. Still, we can characterize a company as being in one of the four phases because the majority of its products are in a particular phase.

Illustration 12-3 shows that the phase a company is in affects its cash flows. In the **introductory phase**, we expect that the company will not generate positive cash from operations. That is, cash used in operations will exceed cash generated by operations in the introductory phase. Also, the company spends considerable amounts to purchase productive assets such as buildings and equipment. To support its asset purchases, the company issues stock or debt. Thus, during the introductory phase, we expect negative cash from operations, negative cash from investing, and positive cash from financing.

During the **growth phase**, we expect to see the company start to generate small amounts of cash from operations. During this phase, net cash provided by operating activities on the statement of cash flows is less than net income. One

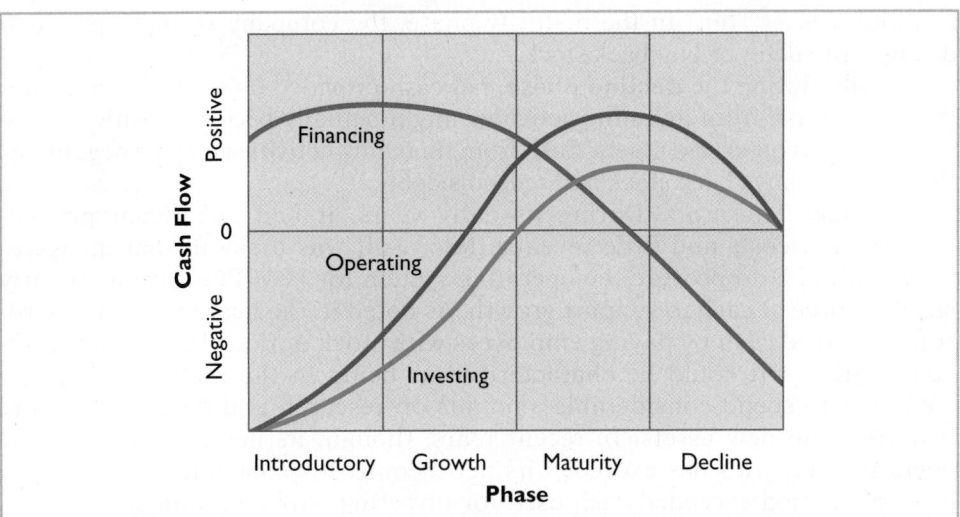

Illustration 12-3 Impact of product life cycle on cash flows

reason net income exceeds cash flow from operations during this period is explained by the difference between the cash paid for inventory and the amount expensed as cost of goods sold. Since the company projects increasing sales, the size of inventory purchases increases. Thus, in the growth phase, the company expenses less inventory on an accrual basis than it purchases on a cash basis. Also, collections on accounts receivable lag behind sales, and accrual sales during a period exceed cash collections during that period. Cash needed for asset acquisitions will continue to exceed net cash provided by operating activities. The company makes up the deficiency by issuing new stock or debt. Thus, in the growth phase, the company continues to show negative cash from investing and positive cash from financing activities.

During the **maturity phase**, net cash provided by operating activities and net income are approximately the same. Cash generated from operations exceeds

Neil Barclay/Retna

Investor Insight

Operating with Negative Cash

Listed here are recent amounts of net income and net cash provided (used) by operating, investing, and financing activities for a variety of companies. The final column suggests the companies' likely phase in the life cycle based on these figures.

Company ($ in millions)	Net Income	Net Cash Provided (Used) by Operating Activities	Net Cash Provided (Used) by Investing Activities	Net Cash Provided (Used) by Financing Activities	Likely Phase in Life Cycle
Amazon.com	$ 476	$1,405	$ (42)	$ (50)	Early maturity
LDK Solar	(144)	(81)	(329)	462	Introductory/ early growth
United States Steel	879	1,745	(4,675)	(1,891)	Maturity
Kellogg	1,103	1,503	(601)	(788)	Early decline
Southwest Airlines	645	2,845	(1,529)	493	Maturity
Starbucks	673	1,331	(1,202)	(172)	Maturity

 Why do companies have negative net cash provided by operating activities during the introductory phase? (See page 684.)

investing needs. Thus, in the maturity phase, the company starts to pay dividends, retire debt, or buy back stock.

Finally, during the **decline phase**, net cash provided by operating activities decreases. Cash from investing activities might actually become positive as the company sells off excess assets. Cash from financing activities may be negative as the company buys back stock and redeems debt.

Consider Microsoft. During its early years, it had significant product development costs and little revenue. Microsoft was lucky in that its agreement with IBM to provide the operating system for IBM PCs gave it an early steady source of cash to support growth. As noted in the Feature Story, Microsoft conserved cash by paying employees with stock options rather than cash. Today, Microsoft could be characterized as being in the maturity phase. It continues to spend considerable amounts on research and development and investment in new assets. In recent years, though, its net cash provided by operating activities has exceeded its net income. Also, cash from operations over this period exceeded cash used for investing, and common stock repurchased exceeded common stock issued. For Microsoft, as for any large company, the challenge is to maintain its growth. In the software industry, where products become obsolete very quickly, the challenge is particularly great.

PREPARING THE STATEMENT OF CASH FLOWS

Companies prepare the statement of cash flows differently from the three other basic financial statements. First, it is not prepared from an adjusted trial balance. It requires detailed information concerning the changes in account balances that occurred between two points in time. An adjusted trial balance will not provide the necessary data. Second, the statement of cash flows deals with cash receipts and payments. As a result, the company **adjusts** the effects of the use of accrual accounting **to determine cash flows**.

The information to prepare this statement usually comes from three sources:

- **Comparative balance sheets.** Information in the comparative balance sheets indicates the amount of the changes in assets, liabilities, and stockholders' equities from the beginning to the end of the period.
- **Current income statement.** Information in this statement helps determine the amount of net cash provided or used by operating activities during the period.
- **Additional information.** Such information includes transaction data that are needed to determine how cash was provided or used during the period.

Preparing the statement of cash flows from these data sources involves three major steps, explained in Illustration 12-4 on the next page.

INDIRECT AND DIRECT METHODS

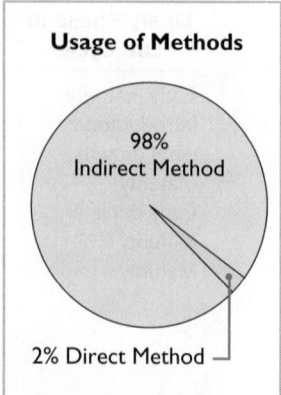

Usage of Methods

98% Indirect Method

2% Direct Method

In order to perform Step 1, a company **must convert net income from an accrual basis to a cash basis**. This conversion may be done by either of two methods: (1) the indirect method or (2) the direct method. **Both methods arrive at the same total amount** for "Net cash provided by operating activities." They differ in **how** they arrive at the amount.

The indirect method adjusts net income for items that do not affect cash to determine net cash provided by operating activities. A great majority of companies (98%) use this method, as shown in the chart on the left.[1] Companies favor

---

[1]*Accounting Trends and Techniques—2011* (New York: American Institute of Certified Public Accountants, 2011).

STEP 1: Determine net cash provided/used by operating activities by converting net income from an accrual basis to a cash basis.

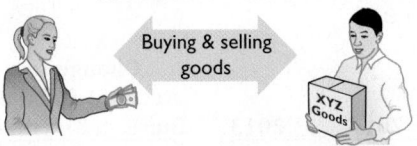

Buying & selling goods

This step involves analyzing not only the current year's income statement but also comparative balance sheets and selected additional data.

STEP 2: Analyze changes in noncurrent asset and liability accounts and record as investing and financing activities, or disclose as noncash transactions.

Investing

Financing

This step involves analyzing comparative balance sheet data and selected additional information for their effects on cash.

STEP 3: Compare the net change in cash on the statement of cash flows with the change in the cash account reported on the balance sheet to make sure the amounts agree.

Year 1 — Year 2 = Difference

The difference between the beginning and ending cash balances can be easily computed from comparative balance sheets.

Illustration 12-4 Three major steps in preparing the statement of cash flows

the indirect method for two reasons. (1) It is easier and less costly to prepare, and (2) it focuses on the differences between net income and net cash flow from operating activities.

The **direct method** shows operating cash receipts and payments. It is prepared by adjusting each item in the income statement from the accrual basis to the cash basis. The FASB has expressed a preference for the direct method but allows the use of either method.

The next section illustrates the more popular indirect method. Appendix 12A illustrates the direct method. Appendix 12B demonstrates an approach that employs T-accounts to prepare the statement of cash flows. Many students find the T-account approach provides a useful structure. We encourage you to give it a try as you walk through the Computer Services example.

Preparation of the Statement of Cash Flows—Indirect Method

LEARNING OBJECTIVE **4**
Prepare a statement of cash flows using the indirect method.

To explain how to prepare a statement of cash flows using the indirect method, we use financial information from Computer Services Company. Illustration 12-5 (page 634) presents Computer Services' current and previous-year balance sheets, its current-year income statement, and related financial information.

Illustration 12-5
Comparative balance sheets, income statement, and additional information for Computer Services Company

COMPUTER SERVICES COMPANY
Comparative Balance Sheets
December 31

Assets	2014	2013	Change in Account Balance Increase/Decrease	
Current assets				
Cash	$ 55,000	$ 33,000	$ 22,000	Increase
Accounts receivable	20,000	30,000	10,000	Decrease
Inventory	15,000	10,000	5,000	Increase
Prepaid expenses	5,000	1,000	4,000	Increase
Property, plant, and equipment				
Land	130,000	20,000	110,000	Increase
Buildings	160,000	40,000	120,000	Increase
Accumulated depreciation—buildings	(11,000)	(5,000)	6,000	Increase
Equipment	27,000	10,000	17,000	Increase
Accumulated depreciation—equipment	(3,000)	(1,000)	2,000	Increase
Total assets	$398,000	$138,000		
Liabilities and Stockholders' Equity				
Current liabilities				
Accounts payable	$ 28,000	$ 12,000	$ 16,000	Increase
Income taxes payable	6,000	8,000	2,000	Decrease
Long-term liabilities				
Bonds payable	130,000	20,000	110,000	Increase
Stockholders' equity				
Common stock	70,000	50,000	20,000	Increase
Retained earnings	164,000	48,000	116,000	Increase
Total liabilities and stockholders' equity	$398,000	$138,000		

COMPUTER SERVICES COMPANY
Income Statement
For the Year Ended December 31, 2014

Sales revenue		$507,000
Cost of goods sold	$150,000	
Operating expenses (excluding depreciation)	111,000	
Depreciation expense	9,000	
Loss on disposal of plant assets	3,000	
Interest expense	42,000	315,000
Income before income tax		192,000
Income tax expense		47,000
Net income		$145,000

Additional information for 2014:
1. Depreciation expense was comprised of $6,000 for building and $3,000 for equipment.
2. The company sold equipment with a book value of $7,000 (cost $8,000, less accumulated depreciation $1,000) for $4,000 cash.
3. Issued $110,000 of long-term bonds in direct exchange for land.
4. A building costing $120,000 was purchased for cash. Equipment costing $25,000 was also purchased for cash.
5. Issued common stock for $20,000 cash.
6. The company declared and paid a $29,000 cash dividend.

We now apply the three steps to the information provided for Computer Services Company.

STEP 1: OPERATING ACTIVITIES

DETERMINE NET CASH PROVIDED/USED BY OPERATING ACTIVITIES BY CONVERTING NET INCOME FROM AN ACCRUAL BASIS TO A CASH BASIS

To determine net cash provided by operating activities under the indirect method, companies **adjust net income in numerous ways**. A useful starting point is to understand **why** net income must be converted to net cash provided by operating activities.

Under generally accepted accounting principles, most companies use the accrual basis of accounting. As you have learned, this basis requires that companies record revenue when the performance obligation is satisfied and record expenses when incurred. Revenues include credit sales for which the company has not yet collected cash. Expenses incurred include some items that it has not yet paid in cash. Thus, under the accrual basis of accounting, net income is not the same as net cash provided by operating activities.

Therefore, under the **indirect method**, companies must adjust net income to convert certain items to the cash basis. The indirect method (or reconciliation method) starts with net income and converts it to net cash provided by operating activities. Illustration 12-6 lists the three types of adjustments.

Net Income +/−	Adjustments	=	Net Cash Provided/ Used by Operating Activities
	• **Add back noncash expenses,** such as depreciation expense, amortization, or depletion.		
	• **Deduct gains and add losses** that resulted from investing and financing activities.		
	• **Analyze changes** to noncash current asset and current liability accounts.		

Illustration 12-6 Three types of adjustments to convert net income to net cash provided by operating activities

We explain the three types of adjustments in the next three sections.

Depreciation Expense

Computer Services' income statement reports depreciation expense of $9,000. Although depreciation expense reduces net income, it does not reduce cash. In other words, depreciation expense is a noncash charge. The company must add it back to net income to arrive at net cash provided by operating activities. Computer Services reports depreciation expense as follows in the statement of cash flows.

Helpful Hint Depreciation is similar to any other expense in that it reduces net income. It differs in that it does not involve a current cash outflow. That is why it must be added back to net income to arrive at net cash provided by operating activities.

Illustration 12-7 Adjustment for depreciation

Cash flows from operating activities	
Net income	$145,000
Adjustments to reconcile net income to net cash provided by operating activities:	
Depreciation expense	**9,000**
Net cash provided by operating activities	$154,000

As the first adjustment to net income in the statement of cash flows, companies frequently list depreciation and similar noncash charges such as amortization of intangible assets, depletion expense, and bad debt expense.

Loss on Disposal of Plant Assets

Illustration 12-1 states that cash received from the sale of plant assets is reported in the investing activities section. Because of this, **companies eliminate from net income all gains and losses resulting from investing activities, to arrive at cash provided by operating activities**.

In our example, Computer Services' income statement reports a $3,000 loss on the disposal of plant assets (book value $7,000, less cash received from sale of equipment $4,000). The company's loss of $3,000 is eliminated in the operating activities section of the statement of cash flows. Illustration 12-8 shows that the $3,000 loss is eliminated by adding $3,000 back to net income to arrive at net cash provided by operating activities.

Illustration 12-8 Adjustment for loss on disposal of plant assets

Cash flows from operating activities		
Net income		$145,000
Adjustments to reconcile net income to net cash provided by operating activities:		
Depreciation expense	$9,000	
Loss on disposal of plant assets	3,000	12,000
Net cash provided by operating activities		$157,000

If a gain on sale occurs, the company deducts the gain from net income in order to determine net cash provided by operating activities. **In the case of either a gain or a loss, companies report the actual amount of cash received from the sale as a source of cash in the investing activities section of the statement of cash flows.**

Changes to Noncash Current Asset and Current Liability Accounts

A final adjustment in reconciling net income to net cash provided by operating activities involves examining all changes in current asset and current liability accounts. The accrual-accounting process records revenues in the period in which the performance obligation is satisfied and expenses in the period incurred. For example, Accounts Receivable reflects amounts owed to the company for sales that have been made but for which cash collections have not yet been received. Prepaid Insurance reflects insurance that has been paid for but which has not yet expired and therefore has not been expensed. Similarly, Salaries and Wages Payable reflects salaries expense that has been incurred but has not been paid.

As a result, we need to adjust net income for these accruals and prepayments to determine net cash provided by operating activities. Thus, we must analyze the change in each current asset and current liability account to determine its impact on net income and cash.

CHANGES IN NONCASH CURRENT ASSETS. The adjustments required for changes in noncash current asset accounts are as follows. **Deduct from net income increases in current asset accounts, and add to net income decreases in**

current asset accounts, to arrive at net cash provided by operating activities. We observe these relationships by analyzing the accounts of Computer Services Company.

DECREASE IN ACCOUNTS RECEIVABLE. Computer Services Company's accounts receivable decreased by $10,000 (from $30,000 to $20,000) during the period. For Computer Services, this means that cash receipts were $10,000 higher than sales revenue. The Accounts Receivable account in Illustration 12-9 shows that Computer Services Company had $507,000 in sales revenue (as reported on the income statement), but it collected $517,000 in cash.

Illustration 12-9 Analysis of Accounts Receivable

	Accounts Receivable			
1/1/12	Balance	30,000	**Receipts from customers**	517,000
	Sales revenue	507,000		
12/31/12	Balance	20,000		

Illustration 12-9 Analysis of Accounts Receivable

As shown in Illustration 12-10, to adjust net income to net cash provided by operating activities, the company adds to net income the decrease of $10,000 in accounts receivable.

Cash flows from operating activities			
Net income			$145,000
Adjustments to reconcile net income to net cash			
provided by operating activities:			
Depreciation expense		$ 9,000	
Loss on disposal of plant assets		3,000	
Decrease in accounts receivable		10,000	
Increase in inventory		(5,000)	
Increase in prepaid expenses		(4,000)	13,000
Net cash provided by operating activities			$158,000

Illustration 12-10
Adjustments for changes in current asset accounts

When the Accounts Receivable balance increases, cash receipts are lower than revenue recorded under the accrual basis. Therefore, the company deducts from net income the amount of the increase in accounts receivable, to arrive at net cash provided by operating activities.

INCREASE IN INVENTORY. Computer Services Company's inventory increased $5,000 (from $10,000 to $15,000) during the period. The change in the Inventory account reflects the difference between the amount of inventory purchased and the amount sold. For Computer Services, this means that the cost of merchandise purchased exceeded the cost of goods sold by $5,000. As a result, cost of goods sold does not reflect $5,000 of cash payments made for merchandise. The company deducts from net income this inventory increase of $5,000 during the period, to arrive at net cash provided by operating activities (see Illustration 12-10). If inventory decreases, the company adds to net income the amount of the change, to arrive at net cash provided by operating activities.

INCREASE IN PREPAID EXPENSES. Computer Services' prepaid expenses increased during the period by $4,000. This means that cash paid for expenses is higher than expenses reported on an accrual basis. In other words, the company has made cash payments in the current period but will not charge expenses to income until future periods (as charges to the income statement). To adjust net income to net cash provided by operating activities, the company deducts from net income the $4,000 increase in prepaid expenses (see Illustration 12-10).

If prepaid expenses decrease, reported expenses are higher than the expenses paid. Therefore, the company adds to net income the decrease in prepaid expense, to arrive at net cash provided by operating activities.

CHANGES IN CURRENT LIABILITIES. The adjustments required for changes in current liability accounts are as follows. **Add to net income increases in current liability accounts, and deduct from net income decreases in current liability accounts, to arrive at net cash provided by operating activities.**

INCREASE IN ACCOUNTS PAYABLE. For Computer Services Company, accounts payable increased by $16,000 (from $12,000 to $28,000) during the period. That means the company received $16,000 more in goods than it actually paid for. As shown in Illustration 12-11 (below), to adjust net income to determine net cash provided by operating activities, the company adds to net income the $16,000 increase in the Accounts Payable account.

DECREASE IN INCOME TAXES PAYABLE. When a company incurs income tax expense but has not yet paid its taxes, it records income taxes payable. A change in the Income Taxes Payable account reflects the difference between income tax expense incurred and income tax actually paid. Computer Services' Income Taxes Payable account decreased by $2,000. That means the $47,000 of income tax expense reported on the income statement was $2,000 less than the amount of taxes paid during the period of $49,000. As shown in Illustration 12-11, to adjust net income to a cash basis, the company must reduce net income by $2,000.

Illustration 12-11
Adjustments for changes in current liability accounts

Cash flows from operating activities		
Net income		$145,000
Adjustments to reconcile net income to net cash provided by operating activities:		
Depreciation expense	$ 9,000	
Loss on disposal of plant assets	3,000	
Decrease in accounts receivable	10,000	
Increase in inventory	(5,000)	
Increase in prepaid expenses	(4,000)	
Increase in accounts payable	16,000	
Decrease in income taxes payable	(2,000)	27,000
Net cash provided by operating activities		$172,000

Illustration 12-11 shows that after starting with net income of $145,000, the sum of all of the adjustments to net income was $27,000. This resulted in net cash provided by operating activities of $172,000.

SUMMARY OF CONVERSION TO NET CASH PROVIDED BY OPERATING ACTIVITIES—INDIRECT METHOD

As shown in the previous illustrations, the statement of cash flows prepared by the indirect method starts with net income. Items are then added or deducted to arrive at net cash provided by operating activities. The required adjustments are of three types:

1. Noncash charges such as depreciation, amortization, and depletion.
2. Gains and losses from investing and financing transactions, such as the sale of plant assets.
3. Changes in noncash current asset and current liability accounts.

Illustration 12-12 provides a summary of these changes.

		Adjustment Required to Convert Net Income to Net Cash Provided by Operating Activities
Noncash charges	Depreciation expense	Add
	Patent amortization expense	Add
Gains and losses	Loss on disposal of plant assets	Add
	Gain on disposal of plant assets	Deduct
Changes in current assets and current liabilities	Increase in current asset account	Deduct
	Decrease in current asset account	Add
	Increase in current liability account	Add
	Decrease in current liability account	Deduct

Illustration 12-12
Adjustments required to convert net income to net cash provided by operating activities

ANATOMY OF A FRAUD

For more than a decade, the top executives at the Italian dairy products company Parmalat engaged in multiple frauds that overstated cash and other assets by more than $1 billion while understating liabilities by between $8 and $12 billion. Much of the fraud involved creating fictitious sources and uses of cash. Some of these activities incorporated sophisticated financial transactions with subsidiaries created with the help of large international financial institutions. However, much of the fraud employed very basic, even sloppy, forgery of documents. For example, when outside auditors requested confirmation of bank accounts (such as a fake $4.8 billion account in the Cayman Islands), documents were created on scanners, with signatures that were cut and pasted from other documents. These were then passed through a fax machine numerous times to make them look real (if difficult to read). Similarly, fictitious bills were created in order to divert funds to other businesses owned by the Tanzi family (who controlled Parmalat).

Total take: Billions of dollars

THE MISSING CONTROL

Independent internal verification. Internal auditors at the company should have independently verified bank accounts and major transfers of cash to outside companies that were controlled by the Tanzi family.

Do it!

Josh's PhotoPlus reported net income of $73,000 for 2014. Included in the income statement were depreciation expense of $7,000 and a gain on disposal of plant assets of $2,500. Josh's comparative balance sheets show the following balances.

NET CASH PROVIDED BY OPERATING ACTIVITIES

	12/31/14	12/31/13
Accounts Receivable	$21,000	$17,000
Accounts Payable	2,200	6,000

Calculate net cash provided by operating activities for Josh's PhotoPlus.

Action Plan

- Add noncash charges such as depreciation back to net income to compute net cash provided by operating activities.
- Deduct gains and add back losses from the disposal of plant assets to compute net cash provided by operating activities.
- Use changes in noncash current asset and current liability accounts to compute net cash provided by operating activities.

The Navigator

Solution

Cash flows from operating activities		
Net income		$73,000
Adjustments to reconcile net income to net cash provided by operating activities:		
Depreciation expense	$ 7,000	
Gain on disposal of plant assets	(2,500)	
Increase in accounts receivable	(4,000)	
Decrease in accounts payable	(3,800)	(3,300)
Net cash provided by operating activities		$69,700

Related exercise material: **BE12-5, BE12-6, BE12-7,** **Do it!** **12-2, E12-4,** and **E12-5.**

Helpful Hint The investing and financing activities are measured and reported the same under both the direct and indirect methods.

Ethics Note Because investors and management bonus contracts often focus on cash flow from operations, some managers have taken unethical actions to artificially increase cash flow from operations. For example, Dynegy restated its statement of cash flows because it had improperly included in operating activities $300 million that should have been reported as financing activities. This increased cash from operating activities by 37%.

Illustration 12-13
Analysis of Equipment

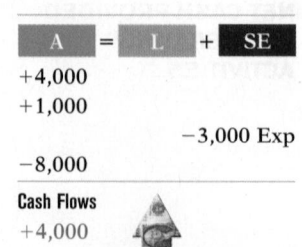

A	=	L	+	SE
+4,000				
+1,000				
				−3,000 Exp
−8,000				

Cash Flows
+4,000

STEP 2: INVESTING AND FINANCING ACTIVITIES

ANALYZE CHANGES IN NONCURRENT ASSET AND LIABILITY ACCOUNTS AND RECORD AS INVESTING AND FINANCING ACTIVITIES, OR DISCLOSE AS NONCASH TRANSACTIONS

INCREASE IN LAND. As indicated from the change in the Land account and the additional information, Computer Services Company purchased land of $110,000 by directly exchanging bonds for land. The exchange of bonds payable for land has no effect on cash. But, it is a significant noncash investing and financing activity that merits disclosure in a separate schedule. (See Illustration 12–14.)

INCREASE IN BUILDINGS. As the additional data indicate, Computer Services Company acquired an office building for $120,000 cash. This is a cash outflow reported in the investing activities section. (See Illustration 12–14.)

INCREASE IN EQUIPMENT. The Equipment account increased $17,000. The additional information explains that this was a net increase that resulted from two transactions: (1) a purchase of equipment of $25,000, and (2) the sale for $4,000 of equipment costing $8,000. These transactions are both investing activities. The company should report each transaction separately. Thus, it reports the purchase of equipment as an outflow of cash for $25,000. It reports the sale as an inflow of cash for $4,000. The T-account below shows the reasons for the change in this account during the year.

Equipment			
1/1/14 Balance	10,000	Cost of equipment sold	8,000
Purchase of equipment	25,000		
12/31/14 Balance	27,000		

The following entry shows the details of the equipment sale transaction.

Cash	4,000	
Accumulated Depreciation	1,000	
Loss on Disposal of Plant Assets	3,000	
Equipment		8,000

INCREASE IN BONDS PAYABLE. The Bonds Payable account increased $110,000. As indicated in the additional information, the company acquired land by directly exchanging bonds for land. It reports this noncash transaction in a separate schedule at the bottom of the statement.

INCREASE IN COMMON STOCK. The balance sheet reports an increase in Common Stock of $20,000. The additional information section notes that this increase resulted from the issuance of new shares of stock. This is a cash inflow reported in the financing activities section.

INCREASE IN RETAINED EARNINGS. Retained earnings increased $116,000 during the year. This increase can be explained by two factors: (1) Net income of $145,000 increased retained earnings and (2) dividends of $29,000 decreased retained earnings. The company adjusts net income to net cash provided by operating activities in the operating activities section. Payment of the dividends (not the declaration) is a **cash outflow that the company reports as a financing activity**.

Helpful Hint When companies issue stocks or bonds for cash, the actual proceeds will appear in the statement of cash flows as a financing inflow (rather than the par value of the stocks or face value of bonds).

Statement of Cash Flows–2014

Using the previous information, we can now prepare a statement of cash flows for 2014 for Computer Services Company, as shown in Illustration 12-14.

STEP 3: NET CHANGE IN CASH

COMPARE THE NET CHANGE IN CASH ON THE STATEMENT OF CASH FLOWS WITH THE CHANGE IN THE CASH ACCOUNT REPORTED ON THE BALANCE SHEET TO MAKE SURE THE AMOUNTS AGREE

Illustration 12-14 indicates that the net change in cash during the period was an increase of $22,000. This agrees with the change in Cash account reported on the balance sheet in Illustration 12-5 (page 634).

Illustration 12-14
Statement of cash flows, 2014—indirect method

COMPUTER SERVICES COMPANY
Statement of Cash Flows–Indirect Method
For the Year Ended December 31, 2014

Cash flows from operating activities			
Net income			$ 145,000
Adjustments to reconcile net income to net cash			
provided by operating activities:			
Depreciation expense		$ 9,000	
Loss on disposal of plant assets		3,000	
Decrease in accounts receivable		10,000	
Increase in inventory		(5,000)	
Increase in prepaid expenses		(4,000)	
Increase in accounts payable		16,000	
Decrease in income taxes payable		(2,000)	27,000
Net cash provided by operating activities			172,000
Cash flows from investing activities			
Sale of equipment		4,000	
Purchase of building		(120,000)	
Purchase of equipment		(25,000)	
Net cash used by investing activities			(141,000)
Cash flows from financing activities			
Issuance of common stock		20,000	
Payment of cash dividends		(29,000)	
Net cash used by financing activities			(9,000)
Net increase in cash			22,000
Cash at beginning of period			33,000
Cash at end of period			$ 55,000
Noncash investing and financing activities			
Issuance of bonds payable to purchase land			$ 110,000

Helpful Hint Note that in the investing and financing activities sections, positive numbers indicate cash inflows (receipts), and negative numbers indicate cash outflows (payments).

© Soubrette/iStockphoto

Accounting Across the Organization

Burning Through Our Cash

Kodak used to dominate the market for photographic film—back when most cameras used film. But when digital cameras arrived, the company's cash flows steadily declined. Investors began to wonder whether Kodak's cash would run out before the company came up with an alternative source of income. Eventually, the company was forced to sell plant assets and intangibles such as patents in order to supplement its cash from operating activities. Finally, Kodak decided to borrow money against its line of credit. Investors in Kodak's stocks and bonds interpreted this as a desperate move (because it further increased the company's debt). The price of its stock and its bonds plummeted. Within months, Kodak had filed for bankruptcy.

Source: Dana Mattioli and Matt Marzemsky, "Clock Ticks as Kodak Burns Cash," *Wall Street Journal* (September 27, 2011).

? What impact did Kodak's sale of plant assets have on its net cash provided by investing activities? (See page 684.)

Using Cash Flows to Evaluate a Company

Traditionally, investors and creditors used ratios based on accrual accounting. These days, cash-based ratios are gaining increased acceptance among analysts. In this section, we review free cash flow and introduce two new measures.

FREE CASH FLOW

In the statement of cash flows, net cash provided by operating activities is intended to indicate the cash-generating capability of the company. Analysts have noted, however, that **cash provided by operating activities fails to take into account that a company must invest in new fixed assets** just to maintain its current level of operations. Companies also must at least **maintain dividends at current levels** to satisfy investors. As we discussed in Chapter 2, the measurement of free cash flow provides additional insight regarding a company's cash-generating ability. Free cash flow describes the net cash provided by operating activities after adjustment for capital expenditures and dividends.

Consider the following example. Suppose that MPC produced and sold 10,000 personal computers this year. It reported $100,000 cash provided by operating activities. In order to maintain production at 10,000 computers, MPC invested $15,000 in equipment. It chose to pay $5,000 in dividends. Its free cash flow was $80,000 ($100,000 − $15,000 − $5,000). The company could use this $80,000 either to purchase new assets, pay off debt, or pay an $80,000 dividend. In practice, free cash flow is often calculated with the formula in Illustration 12-15. Alternative definitions also exist.

Illustration 12-15 Free cash flow

Free Cash Flow	=	Net Cash Provided by Operating Activities	−	Capital Expenditures	−	Cash Dividends

Illustration 12-16 provides basic information excerpted from the 2011 statement of cash flows of Apple (prior to the payment of its first dividends).

Illustration 12-16
Apple's cash flow information
($ in millions)

Real World	**APPLE, INC.** Statement of Cash Flows Information (partial) 2011		
Net cash provided by operating activities			$ 37,529
Cash flows from investing activities			
Additions to property and equipment and intangibles		$ (7,452)	
Purchases of investments		(102,576)	
Sales of investments		49,416	
Acquisitions of companies		(244)	
Maturities of investments		20,437	
Net cash used by investing activities			(40,419)
Cash paid for dividends			-0-

Apple's free cash flow is calculated as shown in Illustration 12-17 (in millions). Apple generated approximately $30 billion of free cash flow. This is a tremendous amount of cash generated in a single year. It is available for the acquisition of new assets, the buyback and retirement of stock or debt, or the payment of dividends.

Illustration 12-17 Calculation of Apple's free cash flow ($ in millions)

Net cash provided by operating activities	$37,529
Less: Expenditures on property, plant, and	
equipment and intangibles	7,452
Dividends paid	-0-
Free cash flow	$30,077

Also note that Apple's cash from operations of $37.5 billion exceeds its 2011 net income of $25.9 billion by $11 billion. This lends additional credibility to Apple's income number as an indicator of potential future performance. If anything, Apple's net income might understate its actual performance. Microsoft's free cash flow for 2011 was $19.5 billion, also an incredible amount of cash.

Do it!

Chicago Corporation issued the following statement of cash flows for 2012. **FREE CASH FLOW**

CHICAGO CORPORATION Statement of Cash Flows–Indirect Method For the Year Ended December 31, 2014		
Cash flows from operating activities		
Net income		$19,000
Adjustments to reconcile net income to net cash		
provided by operating activities:		
Depreciation expense	$ 8,100	
Loss on disposal of plant assets	1,300	
Decrease in accounts receivable	6,900	
Increase in inventory	(4,000)	
Decrease in accounts payable	(2,000)	10,300
Net cash provided by operating activities		29,300
Cash flows from investing activities		
Sale of investments	1,100	
Purchase of equipment	(19,000)	
Net cash used by investing activities		(17,900)

Cash flows from financing activities		
Issuance of stock	10,000	
Payment on long-term note payable	(5,000)	
Payment for dividends	(9,000)	
Net cash used by financing activities		(4,000)
Net increase in cash		7,400
Cash at beginning of year		10,000
Cash at end of year		$17,400

(a) Compute free cash flow for Chicago Corporation. (b) Explain why free cash flow often provides better information than "Net cash provided by operating activities."

Action Plan

• Compute free cash flow as Net cash provided by operating activities — Capital expenditures — Cash dividends.

The Navigator

Solution

(a) Free cash flow = $29,300 − $19,000 − $9,000 = $1,300

(b) Net cash provided by operating activities fails to take into account that a company must invest in new plant assets just to maintain the current level of operation. Companies must also maintain dividends at current levels to satisfy investors. The measurement of free cash flow provides additional insight regarding a company's cash-generating ability.

Related exercise material: **BE12-9, BE12-10, BE12-11, BE12-12, Do it! 12-3, E12-9,** and **E12-10.**

🧰 DECISION TOOLKIT

DECISION CHECKPOINTS	INFO NEEDED FOR DECISION	TOOL TO USE FOR DECISION	HOW TO EVALUATE RESULTS
How much cash did the company generate to either expand operations or pay dividends?	Net cash provided by operating activities, cash spent on fixed assets, and cash dividends	Free cash flow = Net cash provided by operating activities − Capital expenditures − Cash dividends	Significant free cash flow indicates greater potential to finance new investment and pay additional dividends.

KEEPING AN EYE ON CASH

Cash flow is closely monitored by analysts and investors for many reasons and in a variety of ways. One measure that is gaining increased attention is "price to cash flow." This is a variant of the price to earnings (P-E) ratio, which has been a staple of analysts for a long time. The difference is that rather than divide the company's stock price by its earnings per share (an accrual-accounting–based number), the price to cash flow ratio divides the company's stock price by its cash flow per share. A high measure suggests that the stock price is high relative to the company's ability to generate cash. A low measure indicates that the company's stock might be a bargain.

The average price to cash flow ratio for companies in the Standard and Poor's 500-stock index was recently 12.1, when the average price-earnings ratio was 19.9. The following table provides values for some well-known companies in a recent year. While you should not use this measure as the sole factor in choosing a stock, it can serve as a useful screen by which to identify companies that merit further investigation.

Company	Price/Cash Flow	Price/EPS
Microsoft	10.2	11.6
Apple	13.3	14.3
Nike	19.7	23.8
Wal-Mart	8.2	13.0
Ford	1.9	2.2
Jet Blue	3.7	13.6

ASSESSING LIQUIDITY AND SOLVENCY USING CASH FLOWS

Previous chapters have presented ratios used to analyze a company's liquidity and solvency. Many of those ratios used accrual-based numbers from the income statement and balance sheet. In this section, we focus on ratios that are **cash-based** rather than accrual-based. That is, instead of using numbers from the income statement, these ratios use numbers from the statement of cash flows.

As discussed earlier, many analysts are critical of accrual-based numbers because they feel that the adjustment process allows too much management discretion. These analysts like to supplement accrual-based analysis with measures that use the statement of cash flows. One disadvantage of these cash-based measures is that, unlike the more commonly employed accrual-based measures, there are no readily available industry averages for comparison. In the following discussion, we use cash flow-based ratios to analyze Apple. In addition to the cash flow information provided in Illustration 12-16 (page 643), we need the following information related to Apple.

($ in millions)	2011	2010
Current liabilities	$27,970	$20,722
Total liabilities	39,756	27,392

Liquidity

Liquidity is the ability to pay obligations expected to become due within the next year. In Chapter 2, you learned that one measure of liquidity is the **current ratio**: current assets divided by current liabilities. A disadvantage of the current ratio is that it uses year-end balances of current asset and current liability accounts. These year-end balances may not be representative of the company's position during most of the year.

A ratio that partially corrects this problem is the **current cash debt coverage**. It is computed as net cash provided by operating activities divided by average current liabilities. Because net cash provided by operating activities involves the entire year rather than a balance at one point in time, this ratio is often considered a better representation of liquidity on the average day. In general, a value below .40 times is cause for additional investigation of a company's liquidity. Illustration 12-18 shows the current cash debt coverage for Apple, with comparative numbers for Microsoft. For comparative purposes, we have also provided each company's current ratio.

Illustration 12-18 Current cash debt coverage

	$\dfrac{\text{Current Cash}}{\text{Debt Coverage}} = \dfrac{\text{Net Cash Provided by Operating Activities}}{\text{Average Current Liabilities}}$		
($ in millions)	Current cash debt coverage	Current ratio
Apple	$\dfrac{\$37,529}{(\$27,970 + \$20,722)/2} = 1.54$ times	1.60:1
Microsoft	.98 times	2.60:1

Apple's net cash provided by operating activities is 1.54 times its average current liabilities. Microsoft's ratio of .98 times is lower than that of Apple. Both companies far exceed the threshold of .40 times. Keep in mind that both Apple and Microsoft have extraordinary cash positions. For example, many large companies now have current ratios in the range of 1.0. By this standard, Apple's current ratio of 1.60:1 and Microsoft's current ratio of 2.60:1 are both strong.

🧰 DECISION TOOLKIT

DECISION CHECKPOINTS	INFO NEEDED FOR DECISION	TOOL TO USE FOR DECISION	HOW TO EVALUATE RESULTS
Is the company generating sufficient net cash provided by operating activities to meet its current obligations?	Net cash provided by operating activities and average current liabilities	$$\text{Current cash debt coverage} = \frac{\text{Net cash provided by operating activities}}{\text{Average current liabilities}}$$	A high value suggests good liquidity. Since the numerator contains a "flow" measure, it provides a good supplement to the current ratio.

Solvency

Solvency is the ability of a company to survive over the long term. A measure of solvency that uses cash figures is the **cash debt coverage**. It is computed as the ratio of net cash provided by operating activities to total debt as represented by average total liabilities. This ratio indicates a company's ability to repay its liabilities from cash generated from operations—that is, without having to liquidate productive assets such as property, plant, and equipment. A general rule of thumb is that a cash debt coverage below .20 times is cause for additional investigation.

Illustration 12-19 shows the cash debt coverage for Apple and Microsoft for 2011. For comparative purposes, we have also provided the debt to assets ratios for each company.

Illustration 12-19 Cash debt coverage

$$\text{Cash Debt Coverage} = \frac{\text{Net Cash Provided by Operating Activities}}{\text{Average Total Liabilities}}$$

($ in millions)	Cash debt coverage	Debt to assets ratio
Apple	$\dfrac{\$37,529}{(\$39,756 + \$27,392)/2} = 1.12$ times	34%
Microsoft	.59 times	52%

Because Apple has long-term obligations, its cash debt coverage is lower than its current cash debt coverage. Obviously, Apple is very solvent. Microsoft's cash debt coverage of .59 times is not as strong as Apple's but still far exceeds the .20 threshold. Neither the cash nor accrual measures suggest any cause for concern regarding the solvency of either company.

🧰 DECISION TOOLKIT

DECISION CHECKPOINTS	INFO NEEDED FOR DECISION	TOOL TO USE FOR DECISION	HOW TO EVALUATE RESULTS
Is the company generating sufficient net cash provided by operating activities to meet its long-term obligations?	Net cash provided by operating activities and average total liabilities	$$\text{Cash debt coverage} = \frac{\text{Net cash provided by operating activities}}{\text{Average total liabilities}}$$	A high value suggests the company is solvent; that is, it will meet its obligations in the long term.

Investor Insight

We Aren't Going to Fail—Really

When an auditor determines that a company is at risk of failing, the auditor notes this concern about the company's ability to continue as a going concern in its audit opinion. Interestingly, during the first quarter of a recent year, 42% of the companies that filed to go public had such warnings in their audit opinions. At first glance, it would seem strange that a company that is at risk of failing would decide to issue shares to the public. Analysts explained that lenders were reluctant to grant loans due to a very low appetite for risk during and after the financial crisis. As a result, companies that might otherwise have borrowed money to supplement their net cash from operating activities were instead forced to try to raise money by issuing stock.

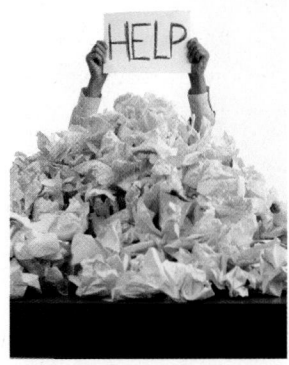

© Kemal Bas/iStockphoto

Source: Maxwell Murphy, "The Big Number: 42," *Wall Street Journal* (April 23, 2012).

 Do you think that issuing stock would be a cost-efficient way for these companies to raise funds? (See page 684.)

 USING THE **DECISION TOOLKIT**

Intel Corporation is the leading producer of computer chips for personal computers. Its primary competitor is AMD. The two are vicious competitors, with frequent lawsuits filed between them. Financial statement data for Intel are provided below.

Instructions

Calculate the following cash-based measures for Intel and compare them with the comparative data for AMD provided on page 648.

1. Free cash flow.
2. Current cash debt coverage.
3. Cash debt coverage.

Real World

INTEL CORPORATION
Balance Sheets
December 31, 2011 and 2010
(in millions)

Assets	2011	2010
Current assets	$25,872	$31,611
Noncurrent assets	45,247	31,575
Total assets	$71,119	$63,186
Liabilities and Stockholders' Equity		
Current liabilities	$12,028	$ 9,327
Long-term liabilities	13,180	4,429
Total liabilities	25,208	13,756
Stockholders' equity	45,911	49,430
Total liabilities and stockholders' equity	$71,119	$63,186

INTEL CORPORATION
Income Statements
For the Years Ended December 31, 2011 and 2010
(in millions)

	2011	2010
Net revenues	$53,999	$43,623
Expenses	41,057	32,159
Net income	$12,942	$11,464

INTEL CORPORATION
Statements of Cash Flows
For the Years Ended December 31, 2011 and 2010
(in millions)

	2011	2010
Net cash provided by operating activities	$ 20,963	$ 16,692
Net cash used for investing activities	(10,301)	(10,539)
Net cash used for financing activities	(11,100)	(4,642)
Net increase (decrease) in cash and cash equivalents	$ (438)	$ 1,511

Note. Cash spent on property, plant, and equipment in 2011 was $10,764. Cash paid for dividends was $4,127.

Comparative data for AMD:

1. Free cash flow $132 million
2. Current cash debt coverage   .22 times
3. Cash debt coverage   .11 times

Solution

1. Intel's free cash flow is $6,072 million ($20,963 − $10,764 − $4,127). AMD's is $132 million. This gives Intel an advantage in the ability to move quickly to invest in new projects.
2. The current cash debt coverage for Intel is calculated as follows.

$$\frac{\$20,963}{(\$12,028 + \$9,327)/2} = 1.96 \text{ times}$$

Compared to AMD's value of .22 times, Intel is significantly more liquid.
3. The cash debt coverage for Intel is calculated as follows.

$$\frac{\$20,963}{(\$25,208 + \$13,756)/2} = 1.08 \text{ times}$$

Compared to AMD's value of .11 times, Intel appears to be significantly more solvent.

✔ The Navigator

Summary of Learning Objectives

1 Indicate the usefulness of the statement of cash flows. The statement of cash flows provides information about the cash receipts, cash payments, and net change in cash resulting from the operating, investing, and financing activities of a company during the period.

2 Distinguish among operating, investing, and financing activities. Operating activities include the cash effects of transactions that enter into the determination of net income. Investing activities involve cash flows resulting from changes in investments and long-term asset items. Financing activities involve cash flows resulting from changes in long-term liability and stockholders' equity items.

3 **Explain the impact of the product life cycle on a company's cash flows.** During the introductory stage, net cash provided by operating activities and net cash from investing activities are negative, and net cash from financing activities is positive. During the growth stage, net cash provided by operating activities becomes positive but is still not sufficient to meet investing needs. During the maturity stage, net cash provided by operating activities exceeds investing needs, so the company begins to retire debt. During the decline stage, net cash provided by operating activities is reduced, net cash from investing activities becomes positive (from selling off assets), and net cash from financing activities becomes more negative.

4 **Prepare a statement of cash flows using the indirect method.** The preparation of a statement of cash flows involves three major steps. (1) Determine net cash provided/used by operating activities by con-

verting net income from an accrual basis to a cash basis. (2) Analyze changes in noncurrent asset and liability accounts and record as investing and financing activities, or disclose as noncash transactions. (3) Compare the net change in cash on the statement of cash flows with the change in the Cash account reported on the balance sheet to make sure the amounts agree.

5 **Use the statement of cash flows to evaluate a company.** A number of measures can be derived by using information from the statement of cash flows as well as the other required financial statements. Free cash flow indicates the amount of cash a company generated during the current year that is available for the payment of dividends or for expansion. Liquidity can be measured with the current cash debt coverage (net cash provided by operating activities divided by average current liabilities). Solvency can be measured by the cash debt coverage (net cash provided by operating activities divided by average total liabilities).

✔ The Navigator

🧰 DECISION TOOLKIT *A SUMMARY*

DECISION CHECKPOINTS	INFO NEEDED FOR DECISION	TOOL TO USE FOR DECISION		HOW TO EVALUATE RESULTS
How much cash did the company generate to either expand operations or pay dividends?	Net cash provided by operating activities, cash spent on fixed assets, and cash dividends	$$\text{Free cash flow} = \text{Net cash provided by operating activities} - \text{Capital expenditures} - \text{Cash dividends}$$		Significant free cash flow indicates greater potential to finance new investment and pay additional dividends.
Is the company generating sufficient net cash provided by operating activities to meet its current obligations?	Net cash provided by operating activities and average current liabilities	$$\text{Current cash debt coverage} = \frac{\text{Net cash provided by operating activities}}{\text{Average current liabilities}}$$		A high value suggests good liquidity. Since the numerator contains a "flow" measure, it provides a good supplement to the current ratio.
Is the company generating sufficient net cash provided by operating activities to meet its long-term obligations?	Net cash provided by operating activities and average total liabilities	$$\text{Cash debt coverage} = \frac{\text{Net cash provided by operating activities}}{\text{Average total liabilities}}$$		A high value suggests the company is solvent; that is, it will meet its obligations in the long term.

Appendix 12A

Statement of Cash Flows—Direct Method

To explain and illustrate the direct method, we will use the transactions of Computer Services Company for 2014, to prepare a statement of cash flows. Illustration 12A-1 (page 650) presents information related to 2014 for Computer Services Company.

LEARNING OBJECTIVE 6
Prepare a statement of cash flows using the direct method.

Illustration 12A-1
Comparative balance sheets, income statement, and additional information for Computer Services Company

COMPUTER SERVICES COMPANY
Comparative Balance Sheets
December 31

Assets	2014	2013	Change in Account Balance Increase/Decrease
Current assets			
Cash	$ 55,000	$ 33,000	$ 22,000 Increase
Accounts receivable	20,000	30,000	10,000 Decrease
Inventory	15,000	10,000	5,000 Increase
Prepaid expenses	5,000	1,000	4,000 Increase
Property, plant, and equipment			
Land	130,000	20,000	110,000 Increase
Buildings	160,000	40,000	120,000 Increase
Accumulated depreciation—buildings	(11,000)	(5,000)	6,000 Increase
Equipment	27,000	10,000	17,000 Increase
Accumulated depreciation—equipment	(3,000)	(1,000)	2,000 Increase
Total assets	$398,000	$138,000	

Liabilities and Stockholders' Equity	2014	2013	
Current liabilities			
Accounts payable	$ 28,000	$ 12,000	$ 16,000 Increase
Income taxes payable	6,000	8,000	2,000 Decrease
Long-term liabilities			
Bonds payable	130,000	20,000	110,000 Increase
Stockholders' equity			
Common stock	70,000	50,000	20,000 Increase
Retained earnings	164,000	48,000	116,000 Increase
Total liabilities and stockholders' equity	$398,000	$138,000	

COMPUTER SERVICES COMPANY
Income Statement
For the Year Ended December 31, 2014

Sales revenue		$507,000
Cost of goods sold	$150,000	
Operating expenses (excluding depreciation)	111,000	
Depreciation expense	9,000	
Loss on disposal of plant assets	3,000	
Interest expense	42,000	315,000
Income before income tax		192,000
Income tax expense		47,000
Net income		$145,000

Additional information for 2014:
1. Depreciation expense was comprised of $6,000 for building and $3,000 for equipment.
2. The company sold equipment with a book value of $7,000 (cost $8,000, less accumulated depreciation $1,000) for $4,000 cash.
3. Issued $110,000 of long-term bonds in direct exchange for land.
4. A building costing $120,000 was purchased for cash. Equipment costing $25,000 was also purchased for cash.
5. Issued common stock for $20,000 cash.
6. The company declared and paid a $29,000 cash dividend.

To prepare a statement of cash flows under the direct approach, we will apply the three steps outlined in Illustration 12-4 (page 633).

STEP 1: OPERATING ACTIVITIES

DETERMINE NET CASH PROVIDED/USED BY OPERATING ACTIVITIES BY CONVERTING NET INCOME FROM AN ACCRUAL BASIS TO A CASH BASIS

Under the **direct method**, companies compute net cash provided by operating activities by **adjusting each item in the income statement** from the accrual basis to the cash basis. To simplify and condense the operating activities section, companies **report only major classes of operating cash receipts and cash payments**. For these major classes, the difference between cash receipts and cash payments is the net cash provided by operating activities. These relationships are as shown in Illustration 12A-2.

Illustration 12A-2 Major classes of cash receipts and payments

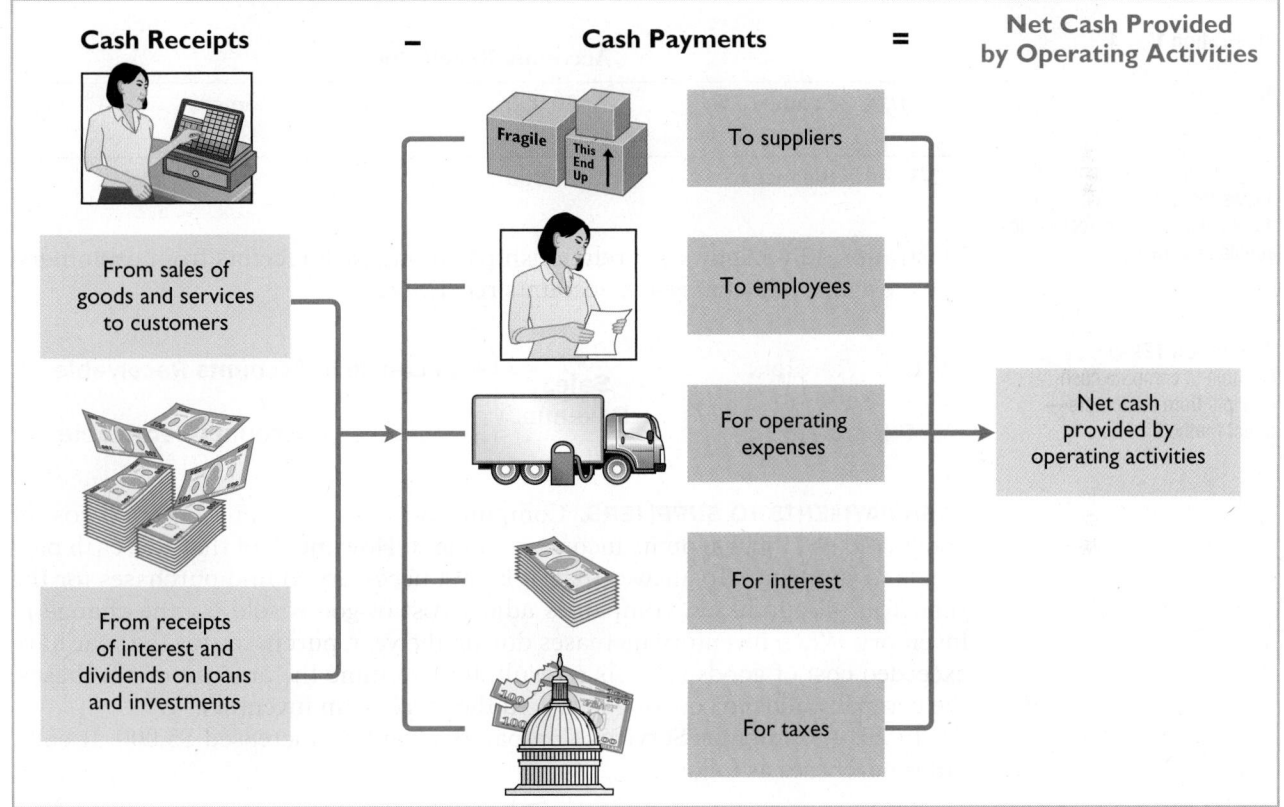

An efficient way to apply the direct method is to analyze the items reported in the income statement in the order in which they are listed. We then determine cash receipts and cash payments related to these revenues and expenses. The following pages present the adjustments required to prepare a statement of cash flows for Computer Services Company using the direct approach.

CASH RECEIPTS FROM CUSTOMERS. The income statement for Computer Services Company reported sales revenue from customers of $507,000. How much of that was cash receipts? To answer that, companies need to consider the change in accounts receivable during the year. When accounts receivable increase during the year, revenues on an accrual basis are higher than cash receipts from customers. Operations led to revenues, but not all of these revenues resulted in cash receipts.

To determine the amount of cash receipts, the company deducts from sales revenue the increase in accounts receivable. On the other hand, there may be a decrease in accounts receivable. That would occur if cash receipts from customers exceeded sales revenue. In that case, the company adds to sales revenue the decrease in accounts receivable. For Computer Services Company, accounts receivable decreased $10,000. Thus, cash receipts from customers were $517,000, computed as shown in Illustration 12A-3.

Illustration 12A-3
Computation of cash receipts from customers

Sales revenue	$ 507,000
Add: Decrease in accounts receivable	10,000
Cash receipts from customers	**$517,000**

Computer Services can also determine cash receipts from customers from an analysis of the Accounts Receivable account, as shown in Illustration 12A-4.

Illustration 12A-4
Analysis of Accounts Receivable

Accounts Receivable				
1/1/14	Balance	30,000	**Receipts from customers**	**517,000**
	Sales revenue	507,000		
12/31/14	Balance	20,000		

Helpful Hint The T-account shows that sales revenue plus decrease in accounts receivables equals cash receipts.

Illustration 12A-5 shows the relationships among cash receipts from customers, sales revenue, and changes in accounts receivable.

Illustration 12A-5
Formula to compute cash receipts from customers—direct method

Cash Receipts from Customers	=	**Sales Revenue**	**+ Decrease in Accounts Receivable** or **− Increase in Accounts Receivable**

CASH PAYMENTS TO SUPPLIERS. Computer Services Company reported cost of goods sold of $150,000 on its income statement. How much of that was cash payments to suppliers? To answer that, it is first necessary to find purchases for the year. To find purchases, companies adjust cost of goods sold for the change in inventory. When inventory increases during the year, purchases for the year have exceeded cost of goods sold. As a result, to determine the amount of purchases, the company adds to cost of goods sold the increase in inventory.

In 2014, Computer Services Company's inventory increased $5,000. It computes purchases as follows.

Illustration 12A-6
Computation of purchases

Cost of goods sold	$ 150,000
Add: Increase in inventory	5,000
Purchases	**$155,000**

After computing purchases, a company can determine cash payments to suppliers. This is done by adjusting purchases for the change in accounts payable. When accounts payable increase during the year, purchases on an accrual basis are higher than they are on a cash basis. As a result, to determine cash payments to suppliers, a company deducts from purchases the increase in accounts payable. On the other hand, if cash payments to suppliers exceed purchases, there may be a decrease in accounts payable. In that case, a company adds to purchases the decrease in accounts payable. For Computer Services Company, cash payments to suppliers were $139,000, computed as follows.

Purchases	$ 155,000
Deduct: Increase in accounts payable	16,000
Cash payments to suppliers	**$139,000**

Illustration 12A-7
Computation of cash payments
to suppliers

Computer Services also can determine cash payments to suppliers from an analysis of the Accounts Payable account, as shown in Illustration 12A-8.

Accounts Payable

Payments to suppliers	139,000	1/1/14	Balance	12,000
			Purchases	155,000
		12/31/14	Balance	28,000

Illustration 12A-8
Analysis of Accounts
Payable

Helpful Hint The T-account
shows that purchases less
increase in accounts payable
equals payments to suppliers.

Illustration 12A-9 shows the relationships among cash payments to suppliers, cost of goods sold, changes in inventory, and changes in accounts payable.

Illustration 12A-9
Formula to compute cash
payments to suppliers—direct
method

CASH PAYMENTS FOR OPERATING EXPENSES. Computer Services reported on its income statement operating expenses of $111,000. How much of that amount was cash paid for operating expenses? To answer that, we need to adjust this amount for any changes in prepaid expenses and accrued expenses payable. For example, if prepaid expenses increased during the year, cash paid for operating expenses is higher than operating expenses reported on the income statement. To convert operating expenses to cash payments for operating expenses, a company adds the increase in prepaid expenses to operating expenses. On the other hand, if prepaid expenses decrease during the year, it deducts the decrease from operating expenses.

Companies must also adjust operating expenses for changes in accrued expenses payable. When accrued expenses payable increase during the year, operating expenses on an accrual basis are higher than they are in a cash basis. As a result, to determine cash payments for operating expenses, a company deducts from operating expenses an increase in accrued expenses payable. On the other hand, a company adds to operating expenses a decrease in accrued expenses payable because cash payments exceed operating expenses.

Computer Services Company's cash payments for operating expenses were $115,000, computed as follows.

Operating expenses	$ 111,000
Add: Increase in prepaid expenses	4,000
Cash payments for operating expenses	**$115,000**

Illustration 12A-10
Computation of cash payments
for operating expenses

Illustration 12A-11 (page 654) shows the relationships among cash payments for operating expenses, changes in prepaid expenses, and changes in accrued expenses payable.

DEPRECIATION EXPENSE AND LOSS ON DISPOSAL OF PLANT ASSETS. Computer Services' depreciation expense in 2014 was $9,000. Depreciation expense is not shown on a statement of cash flows under the direct method because it is a non-

Illustration 12A-11
Formula to compute cash payments for operating expenses—direct method

cash charge. If the amount for operating expenses includes depreciation expense, operating expenses must be reduced by the amount of depreciation to determine cash payments for operating expenses.

The loss on disposal of plant assets of $3,000 is also a noncash charge. The loss on disposal of plant assets reduces net income, but it does not reduce cash. Thus, the loss on disposal of plant assets is not shown on the statement of cash flows under the direct method.

Other charges to expense that do not require the use of cash, such as the amortization of intangible assets, depletion expense, and bad debt expense, are treated in the same manner as depreciation.

CASH PAYMENTS FOR INTEREST. Computer Services reported on the income statement interest expense of $42,000. Since the balance sheet did not include an accrual for interest payable for 2013 or 2014, the amount reported as expense is the same as the amount of interest paid.

CASH PAYMENTS FOR INCOME TAXES. Computer Services reported income tax expense of $47,000 on the income statement. Income taxes payable, however, decreased $2,000. This decrease means that income taxes paid were more than income taxes reported in the income statement. Cash payments for income taxes were, therefore, $49,000 as shown below.

Illustration 12A-12
Computation of cash payments for income taxes

Income tax expense	$ 47,000
Add: Decrease in income taxes payable	2,000
Cash payments for income taxes	**$49,000**

Illustration 12A-13 shows the relationships among cash payments for income taxes, income tax expense, and changes in income taxes payable.

Illustration 12A-13
Formula to compute cash payments for income taxes—direct method

Cash Payments for Income Taxes	=	Income Tax Expense	{	+ Decrease in Income Taxes Payable
				or
				− Increase in Income Taxes Payable

The operating activities section of the statement of cash flows of Computer Services Company is shown in Illustration 12A-14.

Illustration 12A-14
Operating activities section of the statement of cash flows

Cash flows from operating activities		
Cash receipts from customers		$517,000
Less: Cash payments:		
To suppliers	$139,000	
For operating expenses	115,000	
For interest expense	42,000	
For income taxes	49,000	345,000
Net cash provided by operating activities		$172,000

When a company uses the direct method, it must also provide in a **separate schedule** (not shown here) the net cash flows from operating activities as computed under the indirect method.

STEP 2: INVESTING AND FINANCING ACTIVITIES

ANALYZE CHANGES IN NONCURRENT ASSET AND LIABILITY ACCOUNTS AND RECORD AS INVESTING AND FINANCING ACTIVITIES, OR DISCLOSE AS NONCASH TRANSACTIONS

INCREASE IN LAND. As indicated from the change in the Land account and the additional information, Computer Services Company purchased land of $110,000 by directly exchanging bonds for land. The exchange of bonds payable for land has no effect on cash. But, it is a significant noncash investing and financing activity that merits disclosure in a separate schedule. (See Illustration 12A-16.)

Helpful Hint The investing and financing activities are measured and reported the same under both the direct and indirect methods.

INCREASE IN BUILDINGS. As the additional data indicate, Computer Services Company acquired an office building for $120,000 cash. This is a cash outflow reported in the investing activities section. (See Illustration 12A-16.)

INCREASE IN EQUIPMENT. The Equipment account increased $17,000. The additional information explains that this was a net increase that resulted from two transactions: (1) a purchase of equipment of $25,000, and (2) the sale for $4,000 of equipment costing $8,000. These transactions are investing activities. The company should report each transaction separately. The statement in Illustration 12A-16 reports the purchase of equipment as an outflow of cash for $25,000. It reports the sale as an inflow of cash for $4,000. The T-account below shows the reasons for the change in this account during the year.

Equipment			
1/1/14 Balance	10,000	Cost of equipment sold	8,000
Purchase of equipment	25,000		
12/31/14 Balance	27,000		

Illustration 12A-15
Analysis of Equipment

The following entry shows the details of the equipment sale transaction.

Cash	4,000	
Accumulated Depreciation	1,000	
Loss on Disposal of Plant Assets	3,000	
Equipment		8,000

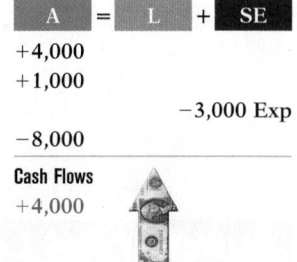

A	=	L	+	SE
+4,000				
+1,000				
				−3,000 Exp
−8,000				

Cash Flows
+4,000

INCREASE IN BONDS PAYABLE. The Bonds Payable account increased $110,000. As indicated in the additional information, the company acquired land by directly exchanging bonds for land. Illustration 12A-16 reports this noncash transaction in a separate schedule at the bottom of the statement.

INCREASE IN COMMON STOCK. The balance sheet reports an increase in Common Stock of $20,000. The additional information section notes that this increase resulted from the issuance of new shares of stock. This is a cash inflow reported in the financing activities section in Illustration 12A-16.

INCREASE IN RETAINED EARNINGS. Retained earnings increased $116,000 during the year. This increase can be explained by two factors: (1) Net income of $145,000 increased retained earnings and (2) dividends of $29,000 decreased retained earnings. The company adjusts net income to net cash provided by operating activities in the operating activities section. **Payment** of the dividends (not the declaration) is a **cash outflow that the company reports as a financing activity in Illustration 12A-16**.

Helpful Hint When companies issue stocks or bonds for cash, the actual proceeds will appear in the statement of cash flows as a financing inflow (rather than the par value of the stocks or face value of bonds).

Statement of Cash Flows—2014

Illustration 12A-16 (page 656) shows the statement of cash flows for Computer Services Company.

Illustration 12A-16
Statement of cash flows,
2014—direct method

COMPUTER SERVICES COMPANY
Statement of Cash Flows—Direct Method
For the Year Ended December 31, 2014

Cash flows from operating activities		
Cash receipts from customers		$ 517,000
Less: Cash payments:		
To suppliers	$ 139,000	
For operating expenses	115,000	
For income taxes	49,000	
For interest expense	42,000	345,000
Net cash provided by operating activities		172,000
Cash flows from investing activities		
Sale of equipment	4,000	
Purchase of building	(120,000)	
Purchase of equipment	(25,000)	
Net cash used by investing activities		(141,000)
Cash flows from financing activities		
Issuance of common stock	20,000	
Payment of cash dividends	(29,000)	
Net cash used by financing activities		(9,000)
Net increase in cash		22,000
Cash at beginning of period		33,000
Cash at end of period		$ 55,000
Noncash investing and financing activities		
Issuance of bonds payable to purchase land		$ 110,000

STEP 3: NET CHANGE IN CASH

COMPARE THE NET CHANGE IN CASH ON THE STATEMENT OF CASH FLOWS WITH THE CHANGE IN THE CASH ACCOUNT REPORTED ON THE BALANCE SHEET TO MAKE SURE THE AMOUNTS AGREE

Illustration 12A-16 indicates that the net change in cash during the period was an increase of $22,000. This agrees with the change in balances in the Cash account reported on the balance sheets in Illustration 12A-1 (page 650).

Summary of Learning Objective for Appendix 12A

6 Prepare a statement of cash flows using the direct method. The preparation of the statement of cash flows involves three major steps: (1) Determine net cash provided/used by operating activities by converting net income from an accrual basis to a cash basis. (2) Analyze changes in noncurrent asset and liability accounts and record as investing and financing activities, or disclose as noncash transactions. (3) Compare the net change in cash on the statement of cash flows with the change in the Cash account reported on the balance sheet to make sure the amounts agree. The direct method reports cash receipts less cash payments to arrive at net cash provided by operating activities.

Appendix 12B

Statement of Cash Flows—T-Account Approach

LEARNING OBJECTIVE 7
Use the T-account approach to prepare a statement of cash flows.

Many people like to use T-accounts to provide structure to the preparation of a statement of cash flows. The use of T-accounts is based on the accounting equation that you learned in Chapter 1. The basic equation is:

$$\text{Assets} = \text{Liabilities} + \text{Equity}$$

Now, let's rewrite the left-hand side as:

$$\text{Cash + Noncash Assets = Liabilities + Equity}$$

Next, rewrite the equation by subtracting Noncash Assets from each side to isolate Cash on the left-hand side:

$$\text{Cash = Liabilities + Equity} - \text{Noncash Assets}$$

Finally, if we insert the Δ symbol (which means "change in"), we have:

$$\Delta \text{ Cash} = \Delta \text{ Liabilities} + \Delta \text{ Equity} - \Delta \text{ Noncash Assets}$$

What this means is that the change in cash is equal to the change in all of the other balance sheet accounts. Another way to think about this is that if we analyze the changes in all of the noncash balance sheet accounts, we will explain the change in the Cash account. This, of course, is exactly what we are trying to do with the statement of cash flows.

To implement this approach, first prepare a large Cash T-account with sections for operating, investing, and financing activities. Then, prepare smaller T-accounts for all of the other noncash balance sheet accounts. Insert the beginning and ending balances for each of these accounts. Once you have done this, then walk through the steps outlined in Illustration 12-4 (page 633). As you walk through the steps, enter debit and credit amounts into the affected accounts. When all of the changes in the T-accounts have been explained, you are done. To demonstrate, we will apply this approach to the example of Computer Services Company that is presented in the chapter. Each of the adjustments in Illustration 12B-1 is numbered so you can follow them through the T-accounts.

1. Post net income as a debit to the operating section of the Cash T-account and a credit to Retained Earnings. Make sure to label all adjustments to the Cash T-account. It also helps to number each adjustment so you can trace all of them if you make an error.

2. Post depreciation expense as a debit to the operating section of Cash and a credit to each of the appropriate accumulated depreciation accounts.

3. Post any gains or losses on the sale of property, plant, and equipment. To do this, it is best to first prepare the journal entry that was recorded at the time of the sale and then post each element of the journal entry. For example, for Computer Services the entry was:

Cash	4,000	
Accumulated Depreciation—Equipment	1,000	
Loss on Disposal of Plant Assets	3,000	
Equipment		8,000

The $4,000 cash entry is a source of cash in the investing section of the Cash account. Accumulated Depreciation—Equipment is debited for $1,000. The Loss on Disposal of Plant Assets is a debit to the operating section of the Cash T-account. Finally, Equipment is credited for $8,000.

4–8. Next, post each of the changes to the noncash current asset and current liability accounts. For example, to explain the $10,000 decline in Computer Services' accounts receivable, credit Accounts Receivable for $10,000 and debit the operating section of the Cash T-account for $10,000.

9. Analyze the changes in the noncurrent accounts. Land was purchased by issuing bonds payable. This requires a debit to Land for $110,000 and a credit to Bonds Payable for $110,000. Note that this is a significant noncash event that requires disclosure at the bottom of the statement of cash flows.

10. Buildings is debited for $120,000, and the investing section of the Cash T-account is credited for $120,000 as a use of cash from investing.

11. Equipment is debited for $25,000 and the investing section of the Cash T-account is credited for $25,000 as a use of cash from investing.

12. Common Stock is credited for $20,000 for the issuance of shares of stock, and the financing section of the Cash T-account is debited for $20,000.

13. Retained Earnings is debited to reflect the payment of the $29,000 dividend, and the financing section of the Cash T-account is credited to reflect the use of Cash.

Illustration 12B-1
T-account approach

Cash

Operating			
(1) Net income	145,000	5,000	Inventory (5)
(2) Depreciation expense	9,000	4,000	Prepaid expenses (6)
(3) Loss on equipment	3,000	2,000	Income taxes payable (8)
(4) Accounts receivable	10,000		
(7) Accounts payable	16,000		
Net cash provided by operating activities	172,000		
Investing			
(3) Sold equipment	4,000	120,000	Purchased building (10)
		25,000	Purchased equipment (11)
		141,000	Net cash used by investing activities
Financing			
(12) Issued common stock	20,000	29,000	Dividend paid (13)
		9,000	Net cash used by financing activities
	22,000		

Accounts Receivable		Inventory		Prepaid Expenses		Land	
30,000		10,000		1,000		20,000	
	10,000 (4)	(5) 5,000		(6) 4,000		(9) 110,000	
20,000		15,000		5,000		130,000	

Buildings		Accumulated Depreciation—Buildings		Equipment		Accumulated Depreciation—Equipment	
40,000			5,000	10,000			1,000
(10) 120,000			6,000 (2)	(11) 25,000	8,000 (3)	(3) 1,000	3,000 (2)
160,000			11,000	27,000			3,000

Accounts Payable		Income Taxes Payable		Bonds Payable		Common Stock		Retained Earnings	
	12,000		8,000		20,000		50,000		48,000
	16,000 (7)	(8) 2,000			110,000 (9)		20,000 (12)		145,000 (1)
	28,000		6,000		130,000		70,000	(13) 29,000	
									164,000

At this point, all of the changes in the noncash accounts have been explained. All that remains is to subtotal each section of the Cash T-account and compare the total change in cash with the change shown on the balance sheet. Once this is done, the information in the Cash T-account can be used to prepare a statement of cash flows.

Summary of Learning Objective for Appendix 12B

7 **Use the T-account approach to prepare a statement of cash flows.** To use T-accounts to prepare the statement of cash flows: (1) prepare a large Cash T-account with sections for operating, investing, and financing activities; (2) prepare smaller T-accounts for all other noncash accounts; (3) insert beginning and ending balances for all accounts; and (4) follows the steps in Illustration 12-4 (page 633), entering debit and credit amounts as needed.

Glossary

Cash debt coverage *(p. 646)* A cash-based ratio used to evaluate solvency, calculated as net cash provided by operating activities divided by average total liabilities.

Current cash debt coverage *(p. 645)* A cash-based ratio used to evaluate liquidity, calculated as net cash provided by operating activities divided by average current liabilities.

Direct method *(p. 633)* A method of determining net cash provided by operating activities by adjusting each item in the income statement from the accrual basis to the cash basis. The direct method shows operating cash receipts and payments.

Financing activities *(p. 627)* Cash flow activities that include (a) obtaining cash from issuing debt and repaying the amounts borrowed and (b) obtaining cash from stockholders, repurchasing shares, and paying dividends.

Free cash flow *(p. 642)* Net cash provided by operating activities after adjusting for capital expenditures and dividends paid.

Indirect method *(p. 632)* A method of preparing a statement of cash flows in which net income is adjusted for

items that do not affect cash, to determine net cash provided by operating activities.

Investing activities *(p. 627)* Cash flow activities that include (a) cash transactions that involve the purchase or disposal of investments and property, plant, and equipment using cash and (b) lending money and collecting the loans.

Operating activities *(p. 627)* Cash flow activities that include the cash effects of transactions that create revenues and expenses and thus enter into the determination of net income.

Product life cycle *(p. 630)* A series of phases in a product's sales and cash flows over time. These phases, in order of occurrence, are introductory, growth, maturity, and decline.

Statement of cash flows *(p. 626)* A basic financial statement that provides information about the cash receipts and cash payments of an entity during a period, classified as operating, investing, and financing activities, in a format that reconciles the beginning and ending cash balances.

Comprehensive Do it!

The income statement for Kosinski Manufacturing Company contains the following condensed information.

KOSINSKI MANUFACTURING COMPANY
Income Statement
For the Year Ended December 31, 2014

Sales revenue		$6,583,000
Operating expenses, excluding depreciation	$4,920,000	
Depreciation expense	880,000	5,800,000
Income before income taxes		783,000
Income tax expense		353,000
Net income		$ 430,000

Included in operating expenses is a $24,000 loss resulting from the sale of machinery for $270,000 cash. Machinery was purchased at a cost of $750,000. The following balances are reported on Kosinski's comparative balance sheet at December 31.

	2014	**2013**
Cash	$672,000	$130,000
Accounts receivable	775,000	610,000
Inventory	834,000	867,000
Accounts payable	521,000	501,000

Income tax expense of $353,000 represents the amount paid in 2014. Dividends declared and paid in 2014 totaled $200,000.

Instructions

(a) Prepare the statement of cash flows using the indirect method.
*(b) Prepare the statement of cash flows using the direct method.

Solution to Comprehensive `Do it!`

Action Plan

- Apply the same data to the preparation of a statement of cash flows under both the indirect and direct methods.
- Note the similarities of the two methods. Both methods report the same information in the investing and financing sections.
- Note the differences between the two methods. The cash flows from operating activities sections report different information, but the amount of net cash provided by operating activities is the same for both methods.

(a)

KOSINSKI MANUFACTURING COMPANY
Statement of Cash Flows—Indirect Method
For the Year Ended December 31, 2014

Cash flows from operating activities		
Net income		$ 430,000
Adjustments to reconcile net income to net cash provided by operating activities:		
Depreciation expense	$ 880,000	
Loss on disposal of plant assets	24,000	
Increase in accounts receivable	(165,000)	
Decrease in inventory	33,000	
Increase in accounts payable	20,000	792,000
Net cash provided by operating activities		1,222,000
Cash flows from investing activities		
Sale of machinery	270,000	
Purchase of machinery	(750,000)	
Net cash used by investing activities		(480,000)
Cash flows from financing activities		
Payment of cash dividends	(200,000)	
Net cash used by financing activities		(200,000)
Net increase in cash		542,000
Cash at beginning of period		130,000
Cash at end of period		$ 672,000

*(b)

KOSINSKI MANUFACTURING COMPANY
Statement of Cash Flows—Direct Method
For the Year Ended December 31, 2014

Cash flows from operating activities		
Cash collections from customers		$6,418,000*
Cash payments:		
For operating expenses	$(4,843,000)**	
For income taxes	(353,000)	(5,196,000)
Net cash provided by operating activities		1,222,000
Cash flows from investing activities		
Sale of machinery	270,000	
Purchase of machinery	(750,000)	
Net cash used by investing activities		(480,000)
Cash flows from financing activities		
Payment of cash dividends	(200,000)	
Net cash used by financing activities		(200,000)
Net increase in cash		542,000
Cash at beginning of period		130,000
Cash at end of period		$ 672,000

Direct-Method Computations:

*Computation of cash collections from customers:	
Sales revenue per the income statement	$6,583,000
Deduct: Increase in accounts receivable	(165,000)
Cash collections from customers	$6,418,000
**Computation of cash payments for operating expenses:	
Operating expenses per the income statement	$4,920,000
Deduct: Loss on disposal of plant assets	(24,000)
Deduct: Decrease in inventories	(33,000)
Deduct: Increase in accounts payable	(20,000)
Cash payments for operating expenses	$4,843,000

The Navigator

Self-Test, Brief Exercises, Exercises, Problem Set A, and many more resources are available for practice in WileyPLUS.

Note: All Questions, Exercises, and Problems marked with an asterisk relate to material in the appendices to the chapter.

Self-Test Questions

Answers are on page 684.

(LO 1) **1.** Which of the following is **incorrect** about the statement of cash flows?
(a) It is a fourth basic financial statement.
(b) It provides information about cash receipts and cash payments of an entity during a period.
(c) It reconciles the ending cash account balance to the balance per the bank statement.
(d) It provides information about the operating, investing, and financing activities of the business.

(LO 1, 2) **2.** Which of the following will **not** be reported in the statement of cash flows?
(a) The net change in plant assets during the year.
(b) Cash payments for plant assets during the year.
(c) Cash receipts from sales of plant assets during the year.
(d) Sources of financing during the period.

(LO 2) **3.** The statement of cash flows classifies cash receipts and cash payments by these activities:
(a) operating and nonoperating.
(b) operating, investing, and financing.
(c) financing, operating, and nonoperating.
(d) investing, financing, and nonoperating.

(LO 2) **4.** Which is an example of a cash flow from an operating activity?
(a) Payment of cash to lenders for interest.
(b) Receipt of cash from the sale of capital stock.
(c) Payment of cash dividends to the company's stockholders.
(d) None of the above.

(LO 2) **5.** Which is an example of a cash flow from an investing activity?
(a) Receipt of cash from the issuance of bonds payable.
(b) Payment of cash to repurchase outstanding capital stock.
(c) Receipt of cash from the sale of equipment.
(d) Payment of cash to suppliers for inventory.

(LO 2) **6.** Cash dividends paid to stockholders are classified on the statement of cash flows as:
(a) operating activities.
(b) investing activities.
(c) a combination of (a) and (b).
(d) financing activities.

(LO 2) **7.** Which is an example of a cash flow from a financing activity?
(a) Receipt of cash from sale of land.
(b) Issuance of debt for cash.
(c) Purchase of equipment for cash.
(d) None of the above

(LO 2) **8.** Which of the following is **incorrect** about the statement of cash flows?
(a) The direct method may be used to report cash provided by operating activities.
(b) The statement shows the net cash provided (used) for three categories of activity.
(c) The operating activities section is the last section of the statement.
(d) The indirect method may be used to report net cash provided by operating activities.

(LO 3) **9.** During the introductory phase of a company's life cycle, one would normally expect to see:
(a) negative cash from operations, negative cash from investing, and positive cash from financing.
(b) negative cash from operations, positive cash from investing, and positive cash from financing.
(c) positive cash from operations, negative cash from investing, and negative cash from financing.
(d) positive cash from operations, negative cash from investing, and positive cash from financing.

Questions 10 through 12 apply only to the indirect method.

(LO 4) **10.** Net income is $132,000, accounts payable increased $10,000 during the year, inventory decreased $6,000 during the year, and accounts receivable increased $12,000 during the year. Under the indirect method, what is net cash provided by operating activities?
(a) $102,000. (c) $124,000.
(b) $112,000. (d) $136,000.

(LO 4) **11.** Items that are added back to net income in determining net cash provided by operating activities under the indirect method do **not** include:
(a) depreciation expense.
(b) an increase in inventory.
(c) amortization expense.
(d) loss on sale of equipment.

(LO 4) **12.** The following data are available for Bill Mack Corporation.

Net income	$200,000
Depreciation expense	40,000
Dividends paid	60,000
Gain on sale of land	10,000
Decrease in accounts receivable	20,000
Decrease in accounts payable	30,000

Net cash provided by operating activities is:
(a) $160,000. (c) $240,000.
(b) $220,000. (d) $280,000.

(LO 4, 6) **13.** The following are data concerning cash received or paid from various transactions for Orange Peels Corporation.

Sale of land	$100,000
Sale of equipment	50,000
Issuance of common stock	70,000
Purchase of equipment	30,000
Payment of cash dividends	60,000

Net cash provided by investing activities is:
(a) $120,000. (c) $150,000.
(b) $130,000. (d) $190,000.

(LO 4, 6) **14.** The following data are available for Retique!

Increase in bonds payable	$100,000
Sale of investment	50,000
Issuance of common stock	60,000
Payment of cash dividends	30,000

Net cash provided by financing activities is:
(a) $90,000. (c) $160,000.
(b) $130,000. (d) $170,000.

(LO 5) **15.** The cash debt coverage is:
(a) a measure of liquidity.
(b) a measure of profitability.
(c) net income divided by average total liabilities.
(d) a measure of solvency.

16. Free cash flow provides an indication of a company's ability to: (LO 5)
(a) generate net income.
(b) generate cash to pay dividends.
(c) generate cash to invest in new capital expenditures.
(d) Both (b) and (c).

Questions 17 and 18 apply only to the direct method.

*17. The beginning balance in accounts receivable is $44,000, the ending balance is $42,000, and sales during the period are $129,000. What are cash receipts from customers? (LO 6)
(a) $127,000. (c) $131,000.
(b) $129,000. (d) $141,000.

*18. Which of the following items is reported on a statement of cash flows prepared by the direct method? (LO 6)
(a) Loss on disposal of plant asset.
(b) Increase in accounts receivable.
(c) Depreciation expense.
(d) Cash payments to suppliers.

Go to the book's companion website, **www.wiley.com/college/kimmel**, to access additional Self-Test Questions. ✔The Navigator

Questions

1. (a) What is a statement of cash flows?
   (b) Mark Paxson maintains that the statement of cash flows is an optional financial statement. Do you agree? Explain.

2. What questions about cash are answered by the statement of cash flows?

3. Distinguish among the three activities reported in the statement of cash flows.

4. (a) What are the sources (inflows) of cash in a statement of cash flows?
   (b) What are the uses (outflows) of cash?

5. Why is it important to disclose certain noncash transactions? How should they be disclosed?

6. Diane Hollowell and Terry Parmenter were discussing the format of the statement of cash flows of Snowbarger Co. At the bottom of Snowbarger's statement of cash flows was a separate section entitled "Noncash investing and financing activities." Give three examples of significant noncash transactions that would be reported in this section.

7. Why is it necessary to use comparative balance sheets, a current income statement, and certain transaction data in preparing a statement of cash flows?

8.
   (a) What are the phases of the corporate life cycle?
   (b) What effect does each phase have on the numbers reported in a statement of cash flows?

9. Based on its statement of cash flows, in what stage of the product life cycle is Tootsie Roll Industries?

10. Contrast the advantages and disadvantages of the direct and indirect methods of preparing the statement of cash flows. Are both methods acceptable? Which method is preferred by the FASB? Which method is more popular?

11. When the total cash inflows exceed the total cash outflows in the statement of cash flows, how and where is this excess identified?

12. Describe the indirect method for determining net cash provided (used) by operating activities.

13. Why is it necessary to convert accrual-basis net income to cash-basis net income when preparing a statement of cash flows?

14. The president of Selby Company is puzzled. During the last year, the company experienced a net loss of $800,000, yet its cash increased $300,000 during the same period of time. Explain to the president how this could occur.

15. Identify five items that are adjustments to convert net income to net cash provided by operating activities under the indirect method.

16. Why and how is depreciation expense reported in a statement of cash flows prepared using the indirect method?

17. Why is the statement of cash flows useful?

18. During 2014, Markowitz Company exchanged $1,700,000 of its common stock for land. Indicate how the transaction would be reported on a statement of cash flows, if at all.

19. Give examples of accrual-based and cash-based ratios to measure each of these characteristics of a company:
(a) Liquidity. (b) Solvency.

*20. Describe the direct method for determining net cash provided by operating activities.

*21. Give the formulas under the direct method for computing (a) cash receipts from customers and (b) cash payments to suppliers.

*22. Detwiler Inc. reported sales of $2 million for 2014. Accounts receivable decreased $150,000 and accounts payable increased $300,000. Compute cash receipts from customers, assuming that the receivable and payable transactions are related to operations.

*23. In the direct method, why is depreciation expense not reported in the cash flows from operating activities section?

Brief Exercises

BE12-1 Each of these items must be considered in preparing a statement of cash flows for Irvin Co. for the year ended December 31, 2014. For each item, state how it should be shown in the statement of cash flows for 2014.
(a) Issued bonds for $200,000 cash.
(b) Purchased equipment for $180,000 cash.
(c) Sold land costing $20,000 for $20,000 cash.
(d) Declared and paid a $50,000 cash dividend.

Indicate statement presentation of selected transactions.
(LO 2), **K**

BE12-2 Classify each item as an operating, investing, or financing activity. Assume all items involve cash unless there is information to the contrary.
(a) Purchase of equipment.
(b) Sale of building.
(c) Redemption of bonds.
(d) Depreciation.
(e) Payment of dividends.
(f) Issuance of capital stock.

Classify items by activities.
(LO 2), **C**

BE12-3 The following T-account is a summary of the cash account of Kemper Company.

Identify financing activity transactions.
(LO 2), **AP**

Cash (Summary Form)

Balance, Jan. 1	8,000		
Receipts from customers	364,000	Payments for goods	200,000
Dividends on stock investments	6,000	Payments for operating expenses	140,000
Proceeds from sale of equipment	36,000	Interest paid	10,000
Proceeds from issuance of		Taxes paid	8,000
bonds payable	300,000	Dividends paid	40,000
Balance, Dec. 31	316,000		

What amount of net cash provided (used) by financing activities should be reported in the statement of cash flows?

BE12-4
(a) Why is net cash provided by operating activities likely to be lower than reported net income during the growth phase?
(b) Why is net cash from investing activities often positive during the late maturity phase and during the decline phase?

Answer questions related to the phases of product life cycle.
(LO 3), **C**

BE12-5 Manuel, Inc. reported net income of $2.5 million in 2014. Depreciation for the year was $160,000, accounts receivable decreased $350,000, and accounts payable decreased $280,000. Compute net cash provided by operating activities using the indirect approach.

Compute net cash provided by operating activities—indirect method.
(LO 4), **AP**

BE12-6 The net income for Freeman Co. for 2014 was $280,000. For 2014, depreciation on plant assets was $70,000, and the company incurred a loss on disposal of plant assets of $28,000. Compute net cash provided by operating activities under the indirect method, assuming there were no other changes in the company's accounts.

Compute net cash provided by operating activities—indirect method.
(LO 4), **AP**

BE12-7 The comparative balance sheets for Lowery Company show these changes in noncash current asset accounts: accounts receivable decrease $80,000, prepaid expenses increase $28,000, and inventories increase $40,000. Compute net cash provided by operating activities using the indirect method, assuming that net income is $186,000.

Compute net cash provided by operating activities—indirect method.
(LO 4), **AP**

Determine cash received from sale of equipment.

(LO 4), **AN**

BE12-8 The T-accounts for Equipment and the related Accumulated Depreciation—Equip. for Coldsmith Company at the end of 2014 are shown here.

Equipment				Accum. Depr.—Equip.			
Beg. bal.	80,000	Disposals	22,000	Disposals	5,100	Beg. bal.	44,500
Acquisitions	41,600					Depr. exp.	12,000
End. bal.	99,600					End. bal.	51,400

In addition, Coldsmith Company's income statement reported a loss on the disposal of plant assets of $3,500. What amount was reported on the statement of cash flows as "cash flow from sale of equipment"?

Calculate cash-based ratios.

(LO 5), **AP**

BE12-9 Suppose during 2014, Cypress Semiconductor Corporation reported net cash provided by operating activities of $89,303,000, cash used in investing of $43,126,000, and cash used in financing of $7,368,000. In addition, cash spent for fixed assets during the period was $25,823,000. Average current liabilities were $251,522,000, and average total liabilities were $286,214,500. No dividends were paid. Calculate these values:
(a) Free cash flow.
(b) Current cash debt coverage.
(c) Cash debt coverage.

Calculate cash-based ratios.

(LO 5), **AP**

BE12-10 Flowers Corporation reported net cash provided by operating activities of $412,000, net cash used by investing activities of $250,000, and net cash provided by financing activities of $70,000. In addition, cash spent for capital assets during the period was $200,000. Average current liabilities were $150,000, and average total liabilities were $225,000. No dividends were paid. Calculate these values:
(a) Free cash flow.
(b) Current cash debt coverage.
(c) Cash debt coverage.

Calculate cash-based ratios.

(LO 5), **AP**

BE12-11 Suppose Canwest Global Communications Corp. reported net cash used by operating activities of $104,539,000 and sales revenue of $2,867,459,000 during 2014. Cash spent on plant asset additions during the year was $79,330,000. Calculate free cash flow.

Calculate and analyze free cash flow.

(LO 5), **AN**

BE12-12 The management of Unruh Inc. is trying to decide whether it can increase its dividend. During the current year, it reported net income of $875,000. It had net cash provided by operating activities of $734,000, paid cash dividends of $92,000, and had capital expenditures of $310,000. Compute the company's free cash flow, and discuss whether an increase in the dividend appears warranted. What other factors should be considered?

Compute receipts from customers—direct method.

(LO 6), **AP**

*BE12-13 Suppose Columbia Sportswear Company had accounts receivable of $299,585,000 at January 1, 2014, and $226,548,000 at December 31, 2014. Assume sales revenue was $1,244,023,000 for the year 2014. What is the amount of cash receipts from customers in 2014?

Compute cash payments for income taxes—direct method.

(LO 6), **AP**

*BE12-14 Kolmer Corporation reported income taxes of $370,000,000 on its 2014 income statement and income taxes payable of $277,000,000 at December 31, 2013, and $528,000,000 at December 31, 2014. What amount of cash payments were made for income taxes during 2014?

Compute cash payments for operating expenses—direct method.

(LO 6), **AP**

*BE12-15 Sellers Corporation reports operating expenses of $90,000, excluding depreciation expense of $15,000 for 2014. During the year, prepaid expenses decreased $7,200 and accrued expenses payable increased $4,400. Compute the cash payments for operating expenses in 2014.

Do it! Review

Classify transactions by type of cash flow activity.

(LO 2), **C**

Do it! 12-1 Morray Corporation had the following transactions.
1. Issued $160,000 of bonds payable.
2. Paid utilities expense.
3. Issued 500 shares of preferred stock for $45,000.
4. Sold land and a building for $250,000.
5. Loaned $30,000 to Dead End Corporation, receiving Dead End's 1-year, 12% note.

Classify each of these transactions by type of cash flow activity (operating, investing, or financing).

Do it! 12-2 RL Photography reported net income of $100,000 for 2014. Included in the income statement were depreciation expense of $6,300, patent amortization expense of $4,000, and a gain on disposal of plant assets of $3,600. RL's comparative balance sheets show the following balances.

Calculate net cash from operating activities.
(LO 4), AP

	12/31/14	12/31/13
Accounts receivable	$21,000	$27,000
Accounts payable	9,200	6,000

Calculate net cash provided by operating activities for RL Photography.

Do it! 12-3 Edelman Corporation issued the following statement of cash flows for 2014.

Compute and discuss free cash flow.
(LO 5), AP

EDELMAN CORPORATION
Statement of Cash Flows—Indirect Method
For the Year Ended December 31, 2014

Cash flows from operating activities		
Net income		$59,000
Adjustments to reconcile net income to net cash provided by operating activities:		
Depreciation expense	$ 9,100	
Decrease in accounts receivable	9,500	
Increase in inventory	(5,000)	
Decrease in accounts payable	(2,200)	
Loss on disposal of plant assets	3,300	14,700
Net cash provided by operating activities		73,700
Cash flows from investing activities		
Sale of investments	3,100	
Purchase of equipment	(24,200)	
Net cash used by investing activities		(21,100)
Cash flows from financing activities		
Issuance of stock	20,000	
Payment on long-term note payable	(10,000)	
Payment for dividends	(13,000)	
Net cash used by financing activities		(3,000)
Net increase in cash		49,600
Cash at beginning of year		13,000
Cash at end of year		$62,600

(a) Compute free cash flow for Edelman Corporation.
(b) Explain why free cash flow often provides better information than "Net cash provided by operating activities."

Exercises

E12-1 Putnam Corporation had these transactions during 2014.
(a) Purchased a machine for $30,000, giving a long-term note in exchange.
(b) Issued $50,000 par value common stock for cash.
(c) Issued $200,000 par value common stock upon conversion of bonds having a face value of $200,000.
(d) Declared and paid a cash dividend of $13,000.
(e) Sold a long-term investment with a cost of $15,000 for $15,000 cash.
(f) Collected $16,000 of accounts receivable.
(g) Paid $18,000 on accounts payable.

Classify transactions by type of activity.
(LO 2), C

Instructions

Analyze the transactions and indicate whether each transaction resulted in a cash flow from operating activities, investing activities, financing activities, or noncash investing and financing activities.

Classify transactions by type of activity.

(LO 2), **C**

E12-2 An analysis of comparative balance sheets, the current year's income statement, and the general ledger accounts of Judd Corp. uncovered the following items. Assume all items involve cash unless there is information to the contrary.

(a) Payment of interest on notes payable.
(b) Exchange of land for patent.
(c) Sale of building at book value.
(d) Payment of dividends.
(e) Depreciation.
(f) Conversion of bonds into common stock.
(g) Receipt of interest on notes receivable.
(h) Issuance of capital stock.
(i) Amortization of patent.
(j) Issuance of bonds for land.
(k) Purchase of land.
(l) Receipt of dividends on investment in stock.
(m) Loss on disposal of plant assets.
(n) Retirement of bonds.

Instructions

Indicate how each item should be classified in the statement of cash flows using these four major classifications: operating activity (indirect method), investing activity, financing activity, and significant noncash investing and financing activity.

Identify phases of product life cycle.

(LO 3), **C**

E12-3 The information in the table is from the statement of cash flows for a company at four different points in time (A, B, C, and D). Negative values are presented in parentheses.

	Point in Time			
	A	**B**	**C**	**D**
Net cash provided by operating activities	$ (60,000)	$ 30,000	$120,000	$ (10,000)
Cash provided by investing activities	(100,000)	25,000	30,000	(40,000)
Cash provided by financing activities	70,000	(90,000)	(50,000)	120,000
Net income	(38,000)	10,000	100,000	(5,000)

Instructions

For each point in time, state whether the company is most likely in the introductory phase, growth phase, maturity phase, or decline phase. In each case, explain your choice.

Prepare the operating activities section—indirect method.

(LO 4), **AP**

E12-4 Cosi Company reported net income of $190,000 for 2014. Cosi also reported depreciation expense of $35,000 and a loss of $5,000 on the disposal of plant assets. The comparative balance sheet shows an increase in accounts receivable of $15,000 for the year, a $17,000 increase in accounts payable, and a $4,000 increase in prepaid expenses.

Instructions

Prepare the operating activities section of the statement of cash flows for 2014. Use the indirect method.

Prepare the operating activities section—indirect method.

(LO 4), **AP**

E12-5 The current sections of Sanford Inc.'s balance sheets at December 31, 2013 and 2014, are presented here. Sanford's net income for 2014 was $153,000. Depreciation expense was $27,000.

	2014	**2013**
Current assets		
Cash	$105,000	$ 99,000
Accounts receivable	80,000	89,000
Inventory	168,000	172,000
Prepaid expenses	27,000	22,000
Total current assets	$380,000	$382,000
Current liabilities		
Accrued expenses payable	$ 15,000	$ 5,000
Accounts payable	85,000	92,000
Total current liabilities	$100,000	$ 97,000

Instructions

Prepare the net cash provided by operating activities section of the company's statement of cash flows for the year ended December 31, 2014, using the indirect method.

E12-6 The following information is available for Ramos Corporation for the year ended December 31, 2014.

Prepare statement of cash flows—indirect method.
(LO 4), AP

Beginning cash balance	$ 45,000
Accounts payable decrease	3,700
Depreciation expense	162,000
Accounts receivable increase	8,200
Inventory increase	11,000
Net income	284,100
Cash received for sale of land at book value	35,000
Cash dividends paid	12,000
Income taxes payable increase	4,700
Cash used to purchase building	289,000
Cash used to purchase treasury stock	26,000
Cash received from issuing bonds	200,000

Instructions

Prepare a statement of cash flows using the indirect method.

E12-7 The three accounts shown below appear in the general ledger of Lauber Corp. during 2014.

Prepare partial statement of cash flows—indirect method.
(LO 4), AN

Equipment

Date		Debit	Credit	Balance
Jan. 1	Balance			160,000
July 31	Purchase of equipment	70,000		230,000
Sept. 2	Cost of equipment constructed	53,000		283,000
Nov. 10	Cost of equipment sold		49,000	234,000

Accumulated Depreciation—Equipment

Date		Debit	Credit	Balance
Jan. 1	Balance			71,000
Nov. 10	Accumulated depreciation on equipment sold	16,000		55,000
Dec. 31	Depreciation for year		28,000	83,000

Retained Earnings

Date		Debit	Credit	Balance
Jan. 1	Balance			105,000
Aug. 23	Dividends (cash)	14,000		91,000
Dec. 31	Net income		72,000	163,000

Instructions

From the postings in the accounts, indicate how the information is reported on a statement of cash flows using the indirect method. The loss on disposal of plant assets was $8,000. (*Hint:* Cost of equipment constructed is reported in the investing activities section as a decrease in cash of $53,000.)

E12-8 Shown below and on the next page are comparative balance sheets for Schmitt Company.

Prepare a statement of cash flows—indirect method, and compute cash-based ratios.
(LO 4, 5), AP

SCHMITT COMPANY
Comparative Balance Sheets
December 31

Assets	2014	2013
Cash	$ 68,000	$ 22,000
Accounts receivable	88,000	76,000
Inventory	167,000	189,000
Land	80,000	100,000
Equipment	260,000	200,000
Accumulated depreciation—equipment	(66,000)	(32,000)
Total	$597,000	$555,000

Liabilities and Stockholders' Equity	2014	2013
Accounts payable	$ 39,000	$ 43,000
Bonds payable	150,000	200,000
Common stock ($1 par)	216,000	174,000
Retained earnings	192,000	138,000
Total	$597,000	$555,000

Additional information:
1. Net income for 2014 was $93,000.
2. Depreciation expense was $34,000.
3. Cash dividends of $39,000 were declared and paid.
4. Bonds payable amounting to $50,000 were redeemed for cash $50,000.
5. Common stock was issued for $42,000 cash.
6. No equipment was sold during 2014.
7. Land was sold for its book value.

Instructions
(a) Prepare a statement of cash flows for 2014 using the indirect method.
(b) Compute these cash-based ratios:
  (1) Current cash debt coverage.
  (2) Cash debt coverage.

Compare two companies by using cash-based ratios.
(LO 5), AN

E12-9 Suppose presented below is 2014 information for PepsiCo, Inc. and The Coca-Cola Company.

($ in millions)	PepsiCo	Coca-Cola
Net cash provided by operating activities	$ 6,796	$ 8,186
Average current liabilities	8,772	13,355
Average total liabilities	22,909	21,491
Net income	5,979	6,906
Sales revenue	43,232	30,990
Capital expenditures	2,128	1,993
Dividends paid	2,732	3,800

Instructions
Using the cash-based measures presented in this chapter, compare the (a) liquidity and (b) solvency of the two companies.

Compare two companies by using cash-based ratios.
(LO 5), AN

E12-10 Information for two companies in the same industry, Patton Corporation and Sager Corporation, is presented here.

	Patton Corporation	Sager Corporation
Net cash provided by operating activities	$ 80,000	$100,000
Average current liabilities	50,000	100,000
Average total liabilities	180,000	250,000
Net income	200,000	200,000
Capital expenditures	40,000	70,000
Dividends paid	5,000	10,000

Instructions
Using the cash-based measures presented in this chapter, compare the (a) liquidity and (b) solvency of the two companies.

Compute cash provided by operating activities—direct method.
(LO 6), AP

*E12-11** Metzger Company completed its first year of operations on December 31, 2014. Its initial income statement showed that Metzger had sales revenue of $198,000 and operating expenses of $83,000. Accounts receivable and accounts payable at year-end were $60,000 and $23,000, respectively. Assume that accounts payable related to operating expenses. Ignore income taxes.

Instructions

Compute net cash provided by operating activities using the direct method.

E12-12 Suppose the 2014 income statement for McDonald's Corporation shows cost of goods sold $5,178.0 million and operating expenses (including depreciation expense of $1,216.2 million) $10,725.7 million. The comparative balance sheet for the year shows that inventory decreased $5.3 million, prepaid expenses increased $42.2 million, accounts payable (merchandise suppliers) increased $15.6 million, and accrued expenses payable increased $199.8 million.

Compute cash payments— direct method.

(LO 6), AP

Instructions

Using the direct method, compute (a) cash payments to suppliers and (b) cash payments for operating expenses.

E12-13 The 2014 accounting records of Rogan Transport reveal these transactions and events.

Compute cash flow from operating activities—direct method.

(LO 6), AP

Payment of interest	$ 10,000	Payment of salaries and wages	$ 53,000
Cash sales	48,000	Depreciation expense	16,000
Receipt of dividend revenue	18,000	Proceeds from sale of vehicles	812,000
Payment of income taxes	12,000	Purchase of equipment for cash	22,000
Net income	38,000	Loss on sale of vehicles	3,000
Payment for merchandise	97,000	Payment of dividends	14,000
Payment for land	74,000	Payment of operating expenses	28,000
Collection of accounts receivable	195,000		

Instructions

Prepare the cash flows from operating activities section using the direct method.

E12-14 The following information is available for Taliaferro Corp. for 2014.

Prepare statement of cash flows—direct method.

(LO 6), AP

Cash used to purchase treasury stock	$ 48,100
Cash dividends paid	21,800
Cash paid for interest	22,400
Net income	464,300
Sales revenue	802,000
Cash paid for taxes	99,000
Cash received from customers	566,100
Cash received from sale of building (at book value)	197,600
Cash paid for operating expenses	77,000
Beginning cash balance	11,000
Cash paid for goods and services	279,100
Cash received from issuing common stock	355,000
Cash paid to redeem bonds at maturity	200,000
Cash paid to purchase equipment	113,200

Instructions

Prepare a statement of cash flows using the direct method.

E12-15 The following information is taken from the 2014 general ledger of Praeger Company.

Calculate cash flows—direct method.

(LO 6), AN

Rent	Rent expense	$ 30,000
	Prepaid rent, January 1	5,900
	Prepaid rent, December 31	7,400
Salaries	Salaries and wages expense	$ 54,000
	Salaries and wages payable, January 1	2,000
	Salaries and wages payable, December 31	8,000
Sales	Sales revenue	$160,000
	Accounts receivable, January 1	16,000
	Accounts receivable, December 31	7,000

Instructions

In each case, compute the amount that should be reported in the operating activities section of the statement of cash flows under the direct method.

Exercises: Set B and Challenge Exercises

Visit the book's companion website, at **www.wiley.com/college/kimmel**, and choose the Student Companion site to access Exercise Set B and Challenge Exercises.

Problems: Set A

Distinguish among operating, investing, and financing activities.

(LO 2), C

P12-1A You are provided with the following transactions that took place during a recent fiscal year.

Transaction	Statement of Cash Flow Activity Affected	Cash Inflow, Outflow, or No Effect?
(a) Recorded depreciation expense on the plant assets.		
(b) Recorded and paid interest expense.		
(c) Recorded cash proceeds from a sale of plant assets.		
(d) Acquired land by issuing common stock.		
(e) Paid a cash dividend to preferred stockholders.		
(f) Paid a cash dividend to common stockholders.		
(g) Recorded cash sales.		
(h) Recorded sales on account.		
(i) Purchased inventory for cash.		
(j) Purchased inventory on account.		

Instructions

Complete the table, indicating whether each item (1) affects operating (O) activities, investing (I) activities, financing (F) activities, or is a noncash (NC) transaction reported in a separate schedule, and (2) represents a cash inflow or cash outflow or has no cash flow effect. Assume use of the indirect approach.

Determine cash flow effects of changes in equity accounts.

(LO 4), AN

P12-2A The following account balances relate to the stockholders' equity accounts of Smoltz Corp. at year-end.

	2014	2013
Common stock, 10,500 and 10,000 shares, respectively, for 2014 and 2013	$160,800	$140,000
Preferred stock, 5,000 shares	125,000	125,000
Retained earnings	300,000	270,000

A small stock dividend was declared and issued in 2014. The market price of the shares was $8,800. Cash dividends were $20,000 in both 2014 and 2013. The common stock has no par or stated value.

Instructions

(a) Net income $58,800

(a) What was the amount of net income reported by Smoltz Corp. in 2014?

(b) Determine the amounts of any cash inflows or outflows related to the common stock and dividend accounts in 2014.

(c) Indicate where each of the cash inflows or outflows identified in (b) would be classified on the statement of cash flows.

P12-3A The income statement of Paxson Company is presented here.

Prepare the operating activities section—indirect method.
(LO 4), **AP**

PAXSON COMPANY
Income Statement
For the Year Ended November 30, 2014

Sales revenue		$7,600,000
Cost of goods sold		
Beginning inventory	$1,900,000	
Purchases	4,400,000	
Goods available for sale	6,300,000	
Ending inventory	1,600,000	
Total cost of goods sold		4,700,000
Gross profit		2,900,000
Operating expenses		
Selling expenses	450,000	
Administrative expenses	700,000	1,150,000
Net income		$1,750,000

Additional information:

1. Accounts receivable decreased $380,000 during the year, and inventory decreased $300,000.
2. Prepaid expenses increased $150,000 during the year.
3. Accounts payable to suppliers of merchandise decreased $350,000 during the year.
4. Accrued expenses payable decreased $100,000 during the year.
5. Administrative expenses include depreciation expense of $110,000.

Instructions
Prepare the operating activities section of the statement of cash flows for the year ended November 30, 2014, for Paxson Company, using the indirect method.

Net cash provided $1,940,000

P12-4A Data for Paxson Company are presented in P12-3A.

Prepare the operating activities section—direct method.
(LO 6), **AP**

Instructions
Prepare the operating activities section of the statement of cash flows using the direct method.

Net cash provided–oper. act. $1,940,000

P12-5A Thornton Company's income statement contained the condensed information below.

Prepare the operating activities section—indirect method.
(LO 4), **AP**

THORNTON COMPANY
Income Statement
For the Year Ended December 31, 2014

Service revenue		$970,000
Operating expenses, excluding depreciation	$614,000	
Depreciation expense	55,000	
Loss on disposal of plant assets	16,000	685,000
Income before income taxes		285,000
Income tax expense		56,000
Net income		$229,000

Thornton's balance sheet contained the comparative data at December 31.

	2014	2013
Accounts receivable	$70,000	$60,000
Accounts payable	41,000	32,000
Income taxes payable	13,000	7,000

Accounts payable pertain to operating expenses.

Instructions
Prepare the operating activities section of the statement of cash flows using the indirect method.

Net cash provided $305,000

*P12-6A   Data for Thornton Company are presented in P12-5A.

Instructions

Prepare the operating activities section of the statement of cash flows using the direct method.

P12-7A   Presented below are the financial statements of Kurtzel Company.

KURTZEL COMPANY
Comparative Balance Sheets
December 31

Assets	2014	2013
Cash	$ 35,000	$ 20,000
Accounts receivable	20,000	14,000
Inventory	28,000	20,000
Property, plant, and equipment	60,000	78,000
Accumulated depreciation	(32,000)	(24,000)
Total	$111,000	$108,000

Liabilities and Stockholders' Equity		
Accounts payable	$ 19,000	$ 15,000
Income taxes payable	7,000	8,000
Bonds payable	17,000	33,000
Common stock	18,000	14,000
Retained earnings	50,000	38,000
Total	$111,000	$108,000

KURTZEL COMPANY
Income Statement
For the Year Ended December 31, 2014

Sales revenue		$242,000
Cost of goods sold		175,000
Gross profit		67,000
Selling expenses	$18,000	
Administrative expenses	6,000	24,000
Income from operations		43,000
Interest expense		3,000
Income before income taxes		40,000
Income tax expense		8,000
Net income		$ 32,000

Additional data:
1. Depreciation expense was $17,500.
2. Dividends declared and paid were $20,000.
3. During the year equipment was sold for $8,500 cash. This equipment cost $18,000 originally and had accumulated depreciation of $9,500 at the time of sale.

Instructions

(a) Prepare a statement of cash flows using the indirect method.
(b) Compute these cash-based measures:
   (1) Current cash debt coverage.
   (2) Cash debt coverage.
   (3) Free cash flow.

*P12-8A   Data for Kurtzel Company are presented in P12-7A. Further analysis reveals the following.
1. Accounts payable pertain to merchandise suppliers.
2. All operating expenses except for depreciation were paid in cash.
3. All depreciation expense is in the selling expense category.
4. All sales and purchases are on account.

Instructions
(a) Prepare a statement of cash flows for Kurtzel Company using the direct method.
(b) Compute these cash-based measures:
    (1) Current cash debt coverage.
    (2) Cash debt coverage.
    (3) Free cash flow.

(a) Net cash provided–oper. act.
$38,500

P12-9A Condensed financial data of Odgers Inc. follow.

Prepare a statement of cash flows—indirect method.
(LO 4), **AP**

ODGERS INC.
Comparative Balance Sheets
December 31

Assets	2014	2013
Cash	$ 80,800	$ 48,400
Accounts receivable	87,800	38,000
Inventory	112,500	102,850
Prepaid expenses	28,400	26,000
Long-term investments	138,000	109,000
Plant assets	285,000	242,500
Accumulated depreciation	(50,000)	(52,000)
Total	$682,500	$514,750

Liabilities and Stockholders' Equity		
Accounts payable	$102,000	$ 67,300
Accrued expenses payable	16,500	21,000
Bonds payable	110,000	146,000
Common stock	220,000	175,000
Retained earnings	234,000	105,450
Total	$682,500	$514,750

ODGERS INC.
Income Statement Data
For the Year Ended December 31, 2014

Sales revenue		$388,460
Less:		
Cost of goods sold	$135,460	
Operating expenses, excluding depreciation	12,410	
Depreciation expense	46,500	
Income tax expense	27,280	
Interest expense	4,730	
Loss on disposal of plant assets	7,500	233,880
Net income		$154,580

Additional information:
1. New plant assets costing $100,000 were purchased for cash during the year.
2. Old plant assets having an original cost of $57,500 and accumulated depreciation of $48,500 were sold for $1,500 cash.
3. Bonds payable matured and were paid off at face value for cash.
4. A cash dividend of $26,030 was declared and paid during the year.

Instructions
Prepare a statement of cash flows using the indirect method.

Net cash provided–oper. act.
$176,930

*P12-10A Data for Odgers Inc. are presented in P12-9A. Further analysis reveals that accounts payable pertain to merchandise creditors.

Prepare a statement of cash flows—direct method.
(LO 6), **AP**

Instructions
Prepare a statement of cash flows for Odgers Inc. using the direct method.

Net cash provided–oper. act.
$176,930

Prepare a statement of cash flows—indirect method.
(LO 4), **AP**

P12-11A The comparative balance sheets for Yanik Company as of December 31 are presented below.

YANIK COMPANY
Comparative Balance Sheets
December 31

Assets	2014	2013
Cash	$ 68,000	$ 45,000
Accounts receivable	50,000	58,000
Inventory	151,450	142,000
Prepaid expenses	15,280	21,000
Land	145,000	130,000
Buildings	200,000	200,000
Accumulated depreciation—buildings	(60,000)	(40,000)
Equipment	225,000	155,000
Accumulated depreciation—equipment	(45,000)	(35,000)
Total	$749,730	$676,000

Liabilities and Stockholders' Equity		
Accounts payable	$ 44,730	$ 36,000
Bonds payable	300,000	300,000
Common stock, $1 par	200,000	160,000
Retained earnings	205,000	180,000
Total	$749,730	$676,000

Additional information:
1. Operating expenses include depreciation expense of $42,000.
2. Land was sold for cash at book value.
3. Cash dividends of $12,000 were paid.
4. Net income for 2014 was $37,000.
5. Equipment was purchased for $92,000 cash. In addition, equipment costing $22,000 with a book value of $10,000 was sold for $8,000 cash.
6. 40,000 shares of $1 par value common stock were issued in exchange for land with a fair value of $40,000.

Instructions

Prepare a statement of cash flows for the year ended December 31, 2014, using the indirect method.

Net cash provided–oper. act.
$94,000

Identify the impact of transactions on ratios.
(LO 5), **C**

P12-12A You are provided with the following transactions that took place during the year.

Transactions	Free Cash Flow ($125,000)	Current Cash Debt Coverage (0.5 times)	Cash Debt Coverage (0.3 times)
(a) Recorded credit sales $2,500.			
(b) Collected $1,900 owed by customers.			
(c) Paid amount owed to suppliers $2,750.			
(d) Recorded sales returns of $500 and credited the customer's account.			
(e) Purchased new equipment $5,000; signed a long-term note payable for the cost of the equipment.			
(f) Purchased a patent and paid $65,000 cash for the asset.			

Instructions

For each transaction listed, indicate whether it will increase (I), decrease (D), or have no effect (NE) on the ratios.

Problems: Set B

P12-1B You are provided with the following transactions that took place during a recent fiscal year.

Distinguish among operating, investing, and financing activities.

(LO 2), C

Transaction	Statement of Cash Flow Activity Affected	Cash Inflow, Outflow, or No Effect?
(a) Purchased shares of common treasury stock.		
(b) Paid a cash dividend to common stockholders.		
(c) Recorded cash sales.		
(d) Recorded sales on account.		
(e) Recorded prepayment of insurance expense.		
(f) Purchased supplies on account.		
(g) Recorded amortization expense on a patent.		
(h) Recorded and received interest revenue.		
(i) Recorded cash proceeds from a sale of plant assets.		
(j) Acquired land by issuing a note payable.		

Instructions

Complete the table indicating whether each item (1) affects operating (O) activities, investing (I) activities, financing (F) activities, or is a noncash (NC) transaction reported in a separate schedule, and (2) represents a cash inflow or cash outflow or has no cash flow effect. Assume use of the indirect approach.

P12-2B The following selected account balances relate to the plant asset accounts of Lazari Inc. at year-end.

Determine cash flow effects of changes in plant asset accounts.

(LO 4), AN

	2014	2013
Accumulated depreciation—buildings	$337,500	$300,000
Accumulated depreciation—equipment	144,000	96,000
Buildings	750,000	750,000
Depreciation expense	99,500	85,500
Equipment	300,000	240,000
Land	120,000	70,000
Loss on disposal of plant assets	6,000	0

Additional information:
1. Lazari purchased $85,000 of equipment and $50,000 of land for cash in 2014.
2. Lazari also sold equipment in 2014.
3. Depreciation expense in 2014 was $37,500 on building and $62,000 on equipment.

Instructions

(a) Determine the amounts of any cash inflows or outflows related to the plant asset accounts in 2014.
(b) Indicate where each of the cash inflows or outflows identified in (a) would be classified on the statement of cash flows.

(a) Cash proceeds $5,000

*Prepare the operating
activities section—indirect
method.*
(LO 4), **AP**

P12-3B The income statement of Hubble Company is presented below.

Additional information:

1. Accounts receivable decreased $290,000 during the year, and inventory increased $140,000.
2. Prepaid expenses increased $175,000 during the year.
3. Accounts payable to merchandise suppliers increased $63,000 during the year.
4. Accrued expenses payable increased $145,000 during the year.

HUBBLE COMPANY
Income Statement
For the Year Ended December 31, 2014

Sales revenue		$5,600,000
Cost of goods sold		
Beginning inventory	$1,780,000	
Purchases	3,430,000	
Goods available for sale	5,210,000	
Ending inventory	1,920,000	
Total cost of goods sold		3,290,000
Gross profit		2,310,000
Operating expenses		
Selling expenses	420,000	
Administrative expense	525,000	
Depreciation expense	105,000	
Amortization expense	15,000	1,065,000
Net income		$1,245,000

Instructions

Net cash provided
$1,548,000

Prepare the operating activities section of the statement of cash flows for the year ended December 31, 2014, for Hubble Company, using the indirect method.

*Prepare the operating activities
section—direct method.*
(LO 6), **AP**

*P12-4B** Data for Hubble Company are presented in P12-3B.

Instructions

Net cash provided
$1,548,000

Prepare the operating activities section of the statement of cash flows using the direct method.

*Prepare the operating
activities section —indirect
method.*
(LO 4), **AP**

P12-5B Mosley Company's income statement contained the condensed information below.

MOSLEY COMPANY
Income Statement
For the Year Ended December 31, 2014

Service revenue		$850,000
Operating expenses, excluding depreciation	$506,000	
Depreciation expense	56,000	
Loss on disposal of plant assets	4,000	566,000
Income before income taxes		284,000
Income tax expense		80,000
Net income		$204,000

Mosley's balance sheet contained the comparative data at December 31, below.

	2014	**2013**
Accounts receivable	$72,000	$65,000
Accounts payable	27,000	35,000
Income taxes payable	23,000	18,000

Accounts payable pertain to operating expenses.

Instructions
Prepare the operating activities section of the statement of cash flows using the indirect method.

Net cash provided
$254,000

P12-6B Data for Mosley Company are presented in P12-5B.

Prepare the operating activities section—direct method.
(LO 6), **AP**

Instructions
Prepare the operating activities section of the statement of cash flows using the direct method.

Net cash provided
$254,000

P12-7B Shown below are the financial statements of Filmore Company.

Prepare a statement of cash flows—indirect method, and compute cash-based ratios.
(LO 4, 5), **AP**

FILMORE COMPANY
Comparative Balance Sheets
December 31

Assets	2014		2013	
Cash		$ 25,000		$ 33,000
Accounts receivable		23,000		14,000
Inventory		41,000		25,000
Property, plant, and equipment	$ 73,000		$ 78,000	
Less: Accumulated depreciation	(27,000)	46,000	(24,000)	54,000
Total		$135,000		$126,000
Liabilities and Stockholders' Equity				
Accounts payable		$ 23,000		$ 46,000
Income taxes payable		26,000		23,000
Bonds payable		20,000		10,000
Common stock		25,000		25,000
Retained earnings		41,000		22,000
Total		$135,000		$126,000

FILMORE COMPANY
Income Statement
For the Year Ended December 31, 2014

Sales revenue		$295,000
Cost of goods sold		194,000
Gross profit		101,000
Selling expenses	$28,000	
Administrative expenses	9,000	37,000
Income from operations		64,000
Interest expense		3,000
Income before income taxes		61,000
Income tax expense		14,000
Net income		$ 47,000

Additional data:
1. Depreciation expense was $6,000.
2. Dividends of $28,000 were declared and paid.
3. During the year, equipment was sold for $10,000 cash. This equipment cost $13,000 originally and had accumulated depreciation of $3,000 at the time of sale.
4. Additional equipment was purchased for $8,000 cash.

Instructions
(a) Prepare a statement of cash flows using the indirect method.
(b) Compute these cash-based measures:

(a) Net cash provided–oper. act.
$8,000

(1) Current cash debt coverage.
(2) Cash debt coverage.
(3) Free cash flow.

Prepare a statement of cash flows—direct method, and compute cash-based ratios.

(LO 5, 6), **AP**

*P12-8B Data for Filmore Company are presented in P12-7B. Further analysis reveals the following.
1. Accounts payable pertains to merchandise creditors.
2. All operating expenses except for depreciation are paid in cash.
3. All depreciation expense is in the selling expense category.
4. All sales and purchases are on account.

Instructions

(a) Net cash provided–oper. act. $8,000

(a) Prepare a statement of cash flows using the direct method.
(b) Compute these cash-based measures:
  (1) Current cash debt coverage.
  (2) Cash debt coverage.
  (3) Free cash flow.

Prepare a statement of cash flows—indirect method.

(LO 4), **AP**

P12-9B Condensed financial data of Turner Inc. follow.

TURNER INC.
Comparative Balance Sheets
December 31

Assets	2014	2013
Cash	$ 37,000	$ 33,000
Accounts receivable	57,000	41,000
Inventories	45,000	48,000
Prepaid expenses	17,000	14,000
Investments	162,000	130,000
Plant assets	580,000	520,000
Accumulated depreciation	(211,000)	(180,000)
Total	$687,000	$606,000

Liabilities and Stockholders' Equity	2014	2013
Accounts payable	$ 44,000	$ 51,000
Accrued expenses payable	21,000	15,000
Bonds payable	180,000	220,000
Common stock	175,000	150,000
Retained earnings	267,000	170,000
Total	$687,000	$606,000

TURNER INC.
Income Statement Data
For the Year Ended December 31, 2014

Sales revenue		$610,000
Less:		
Cost of goods sold	$290,000	
Operating expenses, excluding depreciation	65,000	
Depreciation expense	50,000	
Income tax expense	47,000	
Interest expense	12,000	
Loss on disposal of plant assets	9,000	473,000
Net income		$137,000

Additional information:

1. New plant assets costing $90,000 were purchased for cash during the year.
2. Old plant assets having an original cost of $30,000 were sold for $2,000 cash.
3. Bonds matured and were paid off at face value for cash.
4. A cash dividend of $40,000 was declared and paid during the year.

Instructions
Prepare a statement of cash flows using the indirect method.

Net cash provided–oper. act.
$179,000

*P12-10B Data for Turner Inc. are presented in P12-9B. Further analysis reveals that accounts payable pertain to merchandise creditors.

Prepare a statement of cash flows—direct method.

(LO 6), **AP**

Instructions
Prepare a statement of cash flows for Turner Inc. using the direct method.

Net cash provided–oper. act.
$179,000

P12-11B The comparative balance sheets for Berkler Company as of December 31 are presented below.

Prepare a statement of cash flows—indirect method.

(LO 4), **AP**

BERKLER COMPANY
Comparative Balance Sheets
December 31

Assets	2014	2013
Cash	$ 96,000	$ 78,000
Accounts receivable	76,000	70,000
Inventory	52,000	55,000
Prepaid expenses	22,000	18,000
Land	110,000	144,000
Buildings	300,000	300,000
Accumulated depreciation—buildings	(60,000)	(50,000)
Equipment	264,000	210,000
Accumulated depreciation—equipment	(90,000)	(80,000)
Total	$770,000	$745,000

Liabilities and Stockholders' Equity		
Accounts payable	$ 26,000	$ 35,000
Bonds payable	350,000	400,000
Common stock, $1 par	170,000	120,000
Retained earnings	224,000	190,000
Total	$770,000	$745,000

Additional information:

1. Operating expenses include depreciation expense of $48,000.
2. Land was sold for cash at book value.
3. Cash dividends of $12,000 were paid.
4. Net income for 2014 was $46,000.
5. Equipment was purchased for $88,000 cash. In addition, equipment costing $34,000 with a book value of $6,000 was sold for $9,000 cash.
6. Bonds were converted at face value by issuing 50,000 shares of $1 par value common stock.

Instructions
Prepare a statement of cash flows for the year ended December 31, 2014, using the indirect method.

Net cash provided–oper. act.
$75,000

Identify the impact of transactions on ratios.

(LO 5), C

P12-12B You are provided with the following transactions that took place during the year.

Transactions	Free Cash Flow ($80,000)	Current Cash Debt Coverage (0.7 times)	Cash Debt Coverage (0.4 times)
(a) Recorded cash sales $4,800.			
(b) Sold land for $20,000 cash.			
(c) Declared $6,000 cash dividends.			
(d) Paid $5,800 cash dividends declared last year.			
(e) Paid amount owed to suppliers, $9,400.			
(f) Retired $20,000 convertible bonds payable by issuing common stock.			

Instructions

For each transaction listed above, indicate whether it will increase (I), decrease (D), or have no effect (NE) on the ratios.

Problems: Set C

Visit the book's companion website, at **www.wiley.com/college/kimmel**, and choose the Student Companion site to access Problem Set C.

Continuing Cookie Chronicle

(*Note:* This is a continuation of the Cookie Chronicle from Chapters 1 through 11.)

CCC12 Natalie has prepared the balance sheet and income statement of Cookie & Coffee Creations Inc. and would like you to prepare the statement of cash flows.

> Go to the book's companion website, at **www.wiley.com/college/kimmel**, to find the completion of this problem.

Broadening Your Perspective

Financial Reporting and Analysis

FINANCIAL REPORTING PROBLEM: *Tootsie Roll Industries, Inc.*

BYP12-1 The financial statements of Tootsie Roll Industries are presented in Appendix A.

Instructions

Answer the following questions.

(a) What was the amount of net cash provided by operating activities for 2011? For 2010?

(b) What was the amount of increase or decrease in cash and cash equivalents for the year ended December 31, 2011?
(c) Which method of computing net cash provided by operating activities does Tootsie Roll use?
(d) From your analysis of the 2011 statement of cash flows, was the change in accounts receivable a decrease or an increase? Was the change in inventories a decrease or an increase? Was the change in accounts payable a decrease or an increase?
(e) What was the net cash used by investing activities for 2011?
(f) What was the amount of interest paid in 2011? What was the amount of income taxes paid in 2011?

COMPARATIVE ANALYSIS PROBLEM: *Tootsie Roll vs. Hershey*

BYP12-2 The financial statements of The Hershey Company are presented in Appendix B, following the financial statements for Tootsie Roll Industries in Appendix A.

Instructions
(a) Based on the information in these financial statements, compute these 2011 ratios for each company:
 (1) Current cash debt coverage.
 (2) Cash debt coverage.
(b) What conclusions about the management of cash can you draw from these data?

RESEARCH CASES

BYP12-3 The March 4, 2010, edition of the *Wall Street Journal Online* contains an article by Jeffrey McCracken and Tom McGinty entitled "With Fistfuls of Cash, Firms on Hunt."

Instructions
Read the article and answer the following questions.
(a) How much cash did the nonfinancial (that is, nonbank-like) firms in the Standard and Poor's 500 have at the end of 2009? How big an increase in cash did this represent over the prior year?
(b) What reasons are given in the article for why companies might not want to keep hoarding cash?
(c) What steps did Alcoa take to try to increase the company's cash? Were these efforts successful?
(d) Often, companies issue shares of stock to acquire other companies. This represents a significant noncash transaction. At the time the article was written, why were many companies using cash rather than stock to acquire other companies?
(e) In addition to acquisitions, what other steps can companies take to reduce their cash balances?

BYP12-4 The November 23, 2011, edition of the *Wall Street Journal Online* contains an article by John Jannarone entitled "Backlash from Netflix Buybacks."

Instructions
Read the article and answer the following questions.
(a) What was the stock price for the shares of common stock issued by Netflix in the article? What was the price of the stock a few months previously?
(b) Why did Netflix issue new shares at a time when its stock price was so depressed relative to previous valuations for its stock?
(c) What previous actions had Netflix taken to reduce its cash balance?
(d) What does the article say is the lesson that growth companies should learn from the Netflix example?

INTERPRETING FINANCIAL STATEMENTS

BYP12-5 The incredible growth of Amazon.com has put fear into the hearts of traditional retailers. Its stock price has soared to amazing levels. However, in 2001 many investors were very concerned about whether Amazon would survive since it had never earned a profit and it was burning through cash. Some investors sold, but others decided to hold on to their investment in the company's stock. The following information is taken from the 2001 and 2004 financial statements of Amazon.

($ in millions)	2001	2004
Current assets	$1,207.9	$2,539.4
Total assets	1,637.5	3,248.5
Current liabilities	921.4	1,620.4
Total liabilities	3,077.5	5,096.1
Cash provided by operations	(119.8)	566.6
Capital expenditures	50.3	89.1
Dividends paid	0	0
Net income (loss)	(567.3)	588.5
Average current liabilities	948.2	1,436.6
Average total liabilities	3,090.0	4,773.4

Instructions

(a) Calculate the current ratio and current cash debt coverage for Amazon for 2001 and 2004, and discuss its comparative liquidity.

(b) Calculate the cash debt coverage and the debt to assets ratio for Amazon for 2001 and 2004, and discuss its comparative solvency.

(c) Amazon has avoided purchasing large warehouses. Instead, it has used those of others. In order to increase customer satisfaction, Amazon may have to build its own warehouses. Calculate free cash flow for Amazon for 2001 and 2004, and discuss its ability to purchase warehouses and to finance expansion from internally generated cash.

(d) Based on your findings in parts (a) through (c), can you conclude whether or not Amazon's amazing stock price is justified?

REAL-WORLD FOCUS

BYP12-6 *Purpose:* Use the Internet to view SEC filings.

Address: **biz.yahoo.com/i**, or go to **www.wiley.com/college/kimmel**

Steps
1. Enter a company's name.
2. Choose **Quote**. Answer questions (a) and (b).
3. Choose **Profile**; then choose **SEC**. Answer questions (c) and (d).

Instructions

Answer the following questions.

(a) What company did you select?

(b) What is its stock symbol? What is its selling price?

(c) What recent SEC filings are available for your viewing?

(d) Which filing is the most recent? What is the date?

Critical Thinking

DECISION-MAKING ACROSS THE ORGANIZATION

BYP12-7 Ken Pember and Robyn Mays are examining the following statement of cash flows for Gilbert Company for the year ended January 31, 2014.

GILBERT COMPANY
Statement of Cash Flows
For the Year Ended January 31, 2014

Sources of cash	
From sales of merchandise	$385,000
From sale of capital stock	405,000
From sale of investment (purchased below)	80,000
From depreciation	55,000
From issuance of note for truck	20,000
From interest on investments	6,000
Total sources of cash	951,000

(continues on next page)

Uses of cash	
For purchase of fixtures and equipment	320,000
For merchandise purchased for resale	258,000
For operating expenses (including depreciation)	170,000
For purchase of investment	75,000
For purchase of truck by issuance of note	20,000
For purchase of treasury stock	10,000
For interest on note payable	3,000
Total uses of cash	856,000
Net increase in cash	$ 95,000

Ken claims that Gilbert's statement of cash flows is an excellent portrayal of a superb first year with cash increasing $95,000. Robyn replies that it was not a superb first year. Rather, she says, the year was an operating failure, that the statement is presented incorrectly, and that $95,000 is not the actual increase in cash. The cash balance at the beginning of the year was $140,000.

Instructions
With the class divided into groups, answer the following.
(a) Using the data provided, prepare a statement of cash flows in proper form using the indirect method. The only noncash items in the income statement are depreciation and the gain from the sale of the investment.
(b) With whom do you agree, Ken or Robyn? Explain your position.

COMMUNICATION ACTIVITY

BYP12-8 Jack Werth, the owner-president of Computer Services Company, is unfamiliar with the statement of cash flows that you, as his accountant, prepared. He asks for further explanation.

Instructions
Write him a brief memo explaining the form and content of the statement of cash flows as shown in Illustration 12-14 (page 641).

ETHICS CASE

BYP12-9 Templeton Automotive Corp. is a medium-sized wholesaler of automotive parts. It has 10 stockholders who have been paid a total of $1 million in cash dividends for 8 consecutive years. The board's policy requires that, for this dividend to be declared, net cash provided by operating activities as reported in Templeton Automotive's current year's statement of cash flows must exceed $1 million. President and CEO Rick Hanigan's job is secure so long as he produces annual operating cash flows to support the usual dividend.

At the end of the current year, controller Nick Korte presents president Rick Hanigan with some disappointing news. The net cash provided by operating activities is calculated by the indirect method to be only $970,000. The president says to Nick, "We must get that amount above $1 million. Isn't there some way to increase operating cash flow by another $30,000?" Nick answers, "These figures were prepared by my assistant. I'll go back to my office and see what I can do." The president replies, "I know you won't let me down, Nick."

Upon close scrutiny of the statement of cash flows, Nick concludes that he can get the operating cash flows above $1 million by reclassifying a $60,000, 2-year note payable listed in the financing activities section as "Proceeds from bank loan—$60,000." He will report the note instead as "Increase in payables—$60,000" and treat it as an adjustment of net income in the operating activities section. He returns to the president, saying, "You can tell the board to declare their usual dividend. Our net cash flow provided by operating activities is $1,030,000." "Good man, Nick! I knew I could count on you," exults the president.

Instructions
(a) Who are the stakeholders in this situation?
(b) Was there anything unethical about the president's actions? Was there anything unethical about the controller's actions?
(c) Are the board members or anyone else likely to discover the misclassification?

ALL ABOUT YOU

BYP12-10 In this chapter, you learned that companies prepare a statement of cash flows in order to keep track of their sources and uses of cash and to help them plan for their future cash needs. Planning for your own short- and long-term cash needs is every bit as important as it is for a company.

Instructions

Read the article "Financial 'Uh-oh'? No Problem," at **www.fool.com/savings/shortterm/02.htm**, and answer the following questions.

(a) Describe the three factors that determine how much money you should set aside for short-term needs.

(b) How many months of living expenses does the article suggest to set aside?

(c) Estimate how much you should set aside based upon your current situation. Are you closer to Cliff's scenario or to Prudence's?

FASB CODIFICATION ACTIVITY

BYP12-11 If your school has a subscription to the FASB Codification, go to **http://aaahq.org/ascLogin.cfm** to log in and prepare responses to the following. Use the Master Glossary to determine the proper definitions.

(a) What are cash equivalents?

(b) What are financing activities?

(c) What are investing activities?

(d) What are operating activities?

(e) What is the primary objective for the statement of cash flow? Is working capital the basis for meeting this objective?

(f) Do companies need to disclose information about investing and financing activities that do not affect cash receipts or cash payments? If so, how should such information be disclosed?

Answers to Insight and Accounting Across the Organization Questions

p. 629 Net *What?* Q: In general, why do differences exist between net income and net cash provided by operating activities? **A:** The differences are explained by differences in the timing of the reporting of revenues and expenses under accrual accounting versus cash. Under accrual accounting, companies report revenues when the performance obligation is satisfied, even if cash hasn't been received, and they report expenses when incurred, even if cash hasn't been paid.

p. 631 Operating with Negative Cash Q: Why do companies have negative net cash provided by operating activities during the introductory phase? **A:** During the introductory phase, companies usually spend more on inventory than the amount expensed for cost of goods sold because they are building up inventory and their cash collections frequently lag the amount reported for sales. Therefore, even if companies are reporting positive net income, they frequently report negative net cash provided by operating activities.

p. 642 Burning Through Our Cash Q: What impact did Kodak's sale of plant assets have on its net cash provided by investing activities? **A:** Kodak sold its plant assets to increase its net cash provided by investing activities. This net cash increase allowed Kodak to then invest in new product ideas.

p. 647 We Aren't Going to Fail–Really Q: Do you think that issuing stock would be a cost-efficient way for these companies to raise funds? **A:** When investors are exposed to more risk, they demand a higher return. In the case of stock investments, this means that the investors will pay a lower price in order to get a higher return. Since these companies are at risk of failing, this is a particularly risky investment. As a result, the cash received for new shares would be really low. Therefore, this would not be an efficient source of cash. However, the companies need cash to avoid failing, so they have no choice.

Answers to Self-Test Questions

1. c **2.** a **3.** b **4.** a **5.** c **6.** d **7.** b **8.** c **9.** a **10.** d ($132,000 + $10,000 + $6,000 − $12,000) **11.** b **12.** b ($200,000 + $40,000 − $10,000 + $20,000 − $30,000) **13.** a ($100,000 + $50,000 − $30,000) **14.** b ($100,000 + $60,000 − $30,000) **15.** d **16.** d ***17.** c ($129,000 + ($44,000 − $42,000)) ***18.** d

A Look at IFRS

As in GAAP, the statement of cash flows is a required statement for IFRS. In addition, the content and presentation of an IFRS statement of cash flows is similar to the one used for GAAP. However, the disclosure requirements related to the statement of cash flows are more extensive under GAAP. *IAS 7* ("Cash Flow Statements") provides the overall IFRS requirements for cash flow information.

KEY POINTS

- Companies preparing financial statements under IFRS must prepare a statement of cash flows as an integral part of the financial statements.

- Both IFRS and GAAP require that the statement of cash flows should have three major sections—operating, investing, and financing activities—along with changes in cash and cash equivalents.

- Similar to GAAP, the statement of cash flows can be prepared using either the indirect or direct method under IFRS. In both U.S. and international settings, companies choose for the most part to use the indirect method for reporting net cash flows from operating activities.

- The definition of cash equivalents used in IFRS is similar to that used in GAAP. A major difference is that in certain situations, bank overdrafts are considered part of cash and cash equivalents under IFRS (which is not the case in GAAP). Under GAAP, bank overdrafts are classified as financing activities in the statement of cash flows and are reported as liabilities on the balance sheet.

- IFRS requires that noncash investing and financing activities be excluded from the statement of cash flows. Instead, these noncash activities should be reported elsewhere. This requirement is interpreted to mean that noncash investing and financing activities should be disclosed in the notes to the financial statements instead of in the financial statements. Under GAAP, companies may present this information on the face of the statement of cash flows.

- One area where there can be substantial differences between IFRS and GAAP relates to the classification of interest, dividends, and taxes. The following table indicates the differences between the two approaches.

Item	IFRS	GAAP
Interest paid	Operating or financing	Operating
Interest received	Operating or investing	Operating
Dividends paid	Operating or financing	Financing
Dividends received	Operating or investing	Operating
Taxes paid	Operating—unless specific identification with financing or investing activity	Operating

- Under IFRS, some companies present the operating section in a single line item, with a full reconciliation provided in the notes to the financial statements. This presentation is not seen under GAAP.

- Similar to GAAP, under IFRS companies must disclose the amount of taxes and interest paid. Under GAAP, companies disclose this in the notes to the financial statements. Under IFRS, some companies disclose this information in the notes, but others provide individual line items on the face of the statement. In order to provide this information on the face of the statement, companies first add back the amount of interest expense and tax expense (similar to adding back depreciation expense) and then further down the statement they subtract the cash amount paid for interest and taxes. This treatment can be seen in the statement of cash flows provided for Zetar in Appendix C.

LOOKING TO THE FUTURE

Presently, the FASB and the IASB are involved in a joint project on the presentation and organization of information in the financial statements. One interesting approach, revealed in a published proposal from that project, is that in the future the income statement and balance sheet would adopt headings similar to those of the statement of cash flows. That is, the income statement and balance sheet would be broken into operating, investing, and financing sections.

With respect to the statement of cash flows specifically, the notion of **cash equivalents** will probably not be retained. That is, cash equivalents will not be combined with cash but instead will be reported as a form of highly liquid, low-risk investment. The definition of cash in the existing literature would be retained, and the statement of cash flows would present information on changes in cash only. In addition, the FASB favors presentation of operating cash flows using the direct method only. However, the majority of IASB members express a preference for not requiring use of the direct method of reporting operating cash flows. The two Boards will have to resolve their differences in this area in order to issue a converged standard for the statement of cash flows.

IFRS PRACTICE
IFRS SELF-TEST QUESTIONS

1. Under IFRS, interest paid can be reported as:
   (a) only a financing activity.
   (b) a financing activity or an investing activity.
   (c) a financing activity or an operating activity.
   (d) only an operating activity.
2. IFRS requires that noncash items:
   (a) be reported in the section to which they relate, that is, a noncash investing activity would be reported in the investing section.
   (b) be disclosed in the notes to the financial statements.
   (c) do not need to be reported.
   (d) be treated in a fashion similar to cash equivalents.
3. In the future, it appears likely that:
   (a) the income statement and balance sheet will have headings of operating, investing, and financing, much like the statement of cash flows.
   (b) cash and cash equivalents will be combined in a single line item.
   (c) the IASB will not allow companies to use the direct approach to the statement of cash flows.
   (d) None of the above.
4. Under IFRS:
   (a) taxes are always treated as an operating activity.
   (b) the income statement uses the headings operating, investing, and financing.
   (c) dividends received can be either an operating or investing activity.
   (d) dividends paid can be either an operating or investing activity.
5. Which of the following is **correct**?
   (a) Under IFRS, the statement of cash flows is optional.
   (b) IFRS requires use of the direct approach in preparing the statement of cash flows.
   (c) The majority of companies following GAAP and the majority following IFRS employ the indirect approach to the statement of cash flows.
   (d) Cash and cash equivalents are reported as separate line items under IFRS.

IFRS CONCEPTS AND APPLICATION

IFRS 12-1 Discuss the differences that exist in the treatment of bank overdrafts under GAAP and IFRS.

IFRS12-2 Describe the treatment of each of the following items under IFRS versus GAAP.
   (a) Interest paid.
   (b) Interest received.
   (c) Dividends paid.
   (d) Dividends received.

IFRS 12-3 Explain how the treatment of cash equivalents will probably change in the future.

INTERNATIONAL FINANCIAL REPORTING PROBLEM: *Zetar plc*

IFRS12-4   The financial statements of **Zetar plc** are presented in Appendix C. The company's complete annual report, including the notes to its financial statements, is available in the Investors section at **www.zetarplc.com**.

Instructions
Use the company's annual report to answer the following questions.

(a) In which section (operating, investing, or financing) does Zetar report interest paid?

(b) Explain why the amount that Zetar reports for cash and cash equivalents in its statement of cash flows is negative.

(c) If Zetar reported under GAAP rather than IFRS, how would its treatment of bank overdrafts differ?

(d) Zetar's statement of cash flows reports negative "net movement in working capital" in 2011 of £(6,040) (in thousands). According to the statement of cash flows, what were the components of this "net movement"?

Answers to IFRS Self-Test Questions

1. c **2.** b **3.** a **4.** c **5.** c

The Navigator

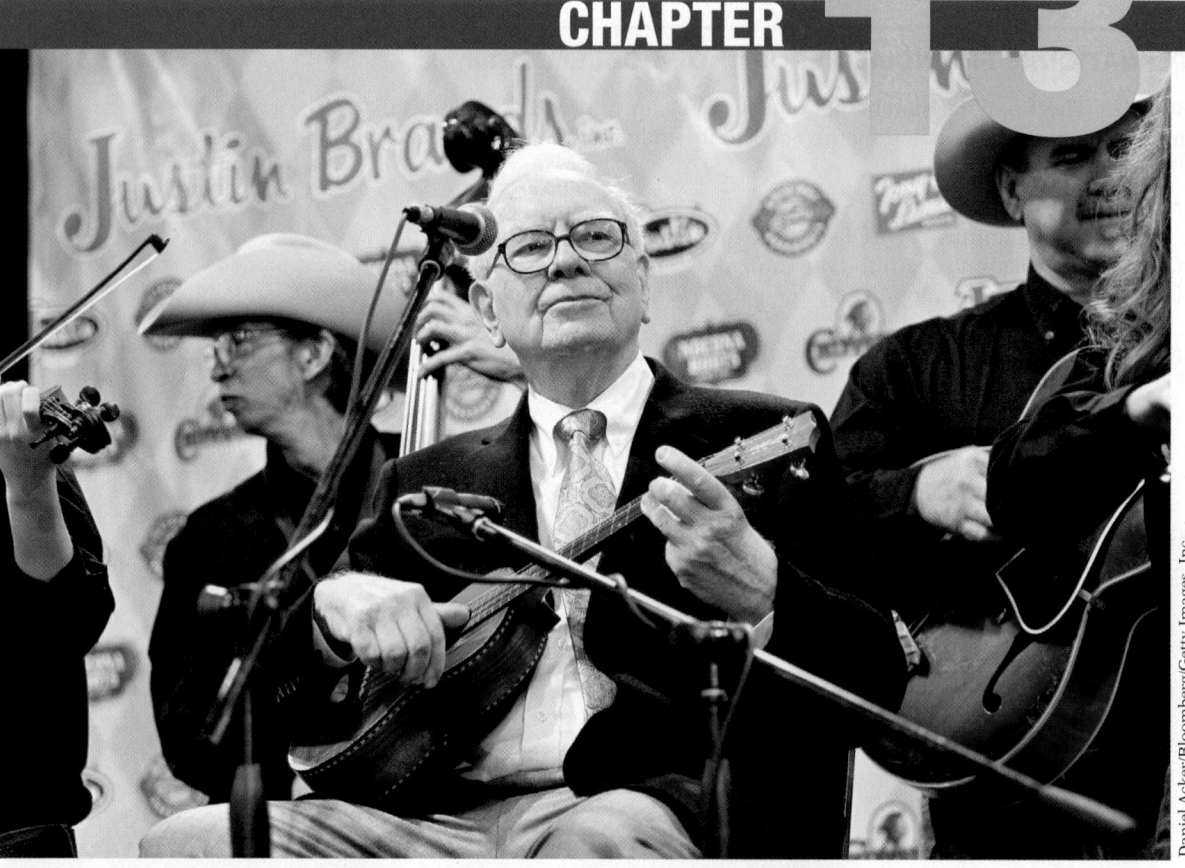

CHAPTER 13

Daniel Acker/Bloomberg/Getty Images, Inc.

✔ The Navigator

- Scan Learning Objectives
- Read Feature Story
- Scan Preview
- Read Text and Answer **Do it!**
  ○ p. 697 ○ p. 700 ○ p. 706 ○ p. 708
- Work Using the Decision Toolkit
- Review Summary of Learning Objectives
- Work Comprehensive **Do it!** p. 725
- Answer Self-Test Questions
- Complete Assignments
- Go to WileyPLUS for practice and tutorials

 Read A Look at IFRS p. 748

FINANCIAL ANALYSIS: THE BIG PICTURE

LEARNING OBJECTIVES

After studying this chapter, you should be able to:

1 Understand the concept of sustainable income.

2 Indicate how irregular items are presented.

3 Explain the concept of comprehensive income.

4 Describe and apply horizontal analysis.

5 Describe and apply vertical analysis.

6 Identify and compute ratios used in analyzing a company's liquidity, solvency, and profitability.

7 Understand the concept of quality of earnings.

✔ The Navigator

A recent issue of *Forbes* magazine listed Warren Buffett as the richest person in the world. His estimated wealth was $62 billion, give or take a few million. How much is $62 billion? If you invested $62 billion in an investment earning just 4%, you could spend $6.8 million per day—every day—forever.

So, how does Buffett spend his money? Basically, he doesn't! He still lives in the same house that he purchased in Omaha, Nebraska, in 1958 for $31,500. He still drives his own car (a Cadillac DTS). And, in case you were thinking that his kids are riding the road to Easy Street, think again. Buffett has committed to donate virtually all of his money to charity before he dies.

IT PAYS TO BE PATIENT

How did Buffett amass this wealth? Through careful investing. Buffett epitomizes a "value investor." He applies the basic techniques he learned in the 1950s from the great value investor Benjamin Graham. He looks for companies that have good long-term potential but are currently underpriced. He invests in companies that have low exposure to debt and that reinvest their earnings for future growth. He does not get caught up in fads or the latest trends.

Buffett sat out on the dot-com mania in the 1990s. When other investors put lots of money into fledgling high-tech firms, Buffett didn't bite because he did not find dot-com companies that met his criteria. He didn't get to enjoy the stock price boom on the way up, but on the other hand, he didn't have to ride the price back down to Earth. When the dot-com bubble burst, everyone else was suffering from investment shock. Buffett swooped in and scooped up deals on companies that he had been following for years.

In 2012, the stock market had again reached near record highs. Buffett's returns had been significantly lagging the market. Only 26% of his investments at that time were in stock, and he was sitting on $38 billion in cash. One commentator noted that "if the past is any guide, just when Buffett seems to look most like a loser, the party is about to end."

If you think you want to follow Buffett's example and transform your humble nest egg into a mountain of cash, be warned. His techniques have been widely circulated and emulated, but never practiced with the same degree of success. You should probably start by honing your financial analysis skills. A good way for you to begin your career as a successful investor is to master the fundamentals of financial analysis discussed in this chapter.

Source: Jason Zweig, "Buffett Is Out of Step," *Wall Street Journal* (May 7, 2012).

INSIDE CHAPTER 13 . . .

We can all learn an important lesson from Warren Buffett: Study companies carefully if you wish to invest. Do not get caught up in fads but instead find companies that are financially healthy. Using some of the basic decision tools presented in this book, you can perform a rudimentary analysis on any company and draw basic conclusions about its financial health. Although it would not be wise for you to bet your life savings on a company's stock relying solely on your current level of knowledge, we strongly encourage you to practice your new skills wherever possible. Only with practice will you improve your ability to interpret financial numbers.

Before we unleash you on the world of high finance, we present a few more important concepts and techniques as well as one more comprehensive review of corporate financial statements. We use all of the decision tools presented in this textbook to analyze a single company, with comparisons to a competitor and industry averages.

The content and organization of Chapter 13 are as follows.

Sustainable Income

Ultimately, the value of a company is a function of its future cash flows. When analysts use this year's net income to estimate future cash flows, they must make sure that this year's net income does not include irregular (i.e., out of the ordinary) revenues, expenses, gains, or losses. Net income adjusted for irregular items is referred to as **sustainable income**. **Sustainable income is the most likely level of income to be obtained in the future.** Sustainable income differs from actual net income by the amount of irregular revenues, expenses, gains, and losses included in this year's net income.

Users are interested in sustainable income because it helps them derive an estimate of future earnings without the "noise" of irregular items. For example, suppose Rye Corporation reports that this year's net income is $500,000 but included in that amount is a once-in-a-lifetime gain of $400,000. In estimating next year's net income for Rye Corporation, we would likely ignore this $400,000 gain and estimate that next year's net income will be in the neighborhood of $100,000. That is, based on this year's results, the company's sustainable income is roughly $100,000. Therefore, identifying irregular items is important if you are going to use reported earnings to estimate a company's value.

In earlier chapters, you learned how to prepare and use a basic multiple-step income statement. In this chapter, we will explain additional components of the income statement as well as a broader measure of performance called

comprehensive income. Illustration 13-1 presents the components of the income statement and comprehensive income; new items are presented in red. When estimating future cash flows, analysts must consider the implications that each of these components has for future cash flows.

Illustration 13-1
Components of the income statement

Income Statement

Sales revenue	$XX
Cost of goods sold	XX
Gross profit	XX
Operating expenses	XX
Income from operations	XX
Other revenues (expenses) and gains (losses)	XX
Income before income taxes	XX
Income tax expense	XX
Income before irregular items	XX
Discontinued operations (net of tax)	XX
Extraordinary items (net of tax)	XX
Net income	XX
Other comprehensive income items (net of tax)	XX
Comprehensive income	$XX

IRREGULAR ITEMS

To help determine sustainable income, we identify irregular items by type on the income statement. There, companies report two types of irregular items:

1. Discontinued operations
2. Extraordinary items

Irregular items are reported net of income taxes. That is, a company first calculates income tax expense for the income before irregular items. Then, it calculates income tax expense for each individual irregular item. The general concept is, "Let the tax follow the income or loss."

Discontinued Operations

To downsize its operations, General Dynamics Corp. sold its missile business to Hughes Aircraft Co. for $450 million. In its income statement, General Dynamics reported the sale in a separate section entitled "Discontinued operations." **Discontinued operations** refers to the disposal of a significant component of a business, such as the elimination of a major class of customers or an entire activity. When the disposal of a significant component occurs, the income statement should report the gain (or loss) from discontinued operations, net of tax.

To illustrate, assume that Rozek Inc. has revenues of $2.5 million and expenses of $1.7 million from continuing operations in 2014. The company has income before income taxes of $800,000. During 2014, the company discontinued and sold its unprofitable chemical division. The loss on disposal of the chemical division (net of $90,000 tax savings) was $210,000. Illustration 13-2 (page 692) shows the income statement presentation, assuming a 30% tax rate on income before income taxes. This presentation clearly indicates the separate effects of continuing operations and discontinued operations on net income.

Illustration 13-2 Statement presentation of discontinued operations

ROZEK INC.
Income Statement (partial)
For the Year Ended December 31, 2014

Income before income taxes	$ 800,000
Income tax expense	240,000
Income before irregular items	560,000
Discontinued operations	
Loss from disposal of chemical division, net of $90,000 income tax savings	(210,000)
Net income	$ 350,000

DECISION TOOLKIT

DECISION CHECKPOINTS	INFO NEEDED FOR DECISION	TOOL TO USE FOR DECISION	HOW TO EVALUATE RESULTS
Has the company sold any major components of its business?	Discontinued operations section of income statement	Anything reported in this section indicates that the company has discontinued a major component of its business.	If a major component has been discontinued, its results during the current period should not be included in estimates of future net income.

Extraordinary Items

Extraordinary items are events and transactions that meet two conditions. They are **unusual in nature** and **infrequent in occurrence**. To be considered **unusual**, the item should be abnormal and only incidentally related to the customary activities of the entity. To be regarded as **infrequent**, the event or transaction should not be reasonably expected to recur in the foreseeable future.

A company must evaluate both criteria in terms of the environment in which it operates. Thus, Weyerhaeuser Co. reported the $36 million in damages to its timberland caused by the eruption of Mount St. Helens as an extraordinary item because the event was both unusual and infrequent. In contrast, Florida Citrus Company does not report frost damage to its citrus crop as an extraordinary item because frost damage is not viewed as infrequent.

Helpful Hint Ordinary gains and losses are reported at pretax amounts in arriving at income before income taxes.

Companies report extraordinary items net of taxes in a separate section of the income statement, immediately below discontinued operations. To illustrate, assume that in 2014 a revolutionary foreign government expropriated property held as an investment by Rozek Inc. If the loss is $70,000 before applicable income tax savings of $21,000, the income statement presentation will show a deduction of $49,000, as in Illustration 13-3.

Illustration 13-3 Statement presentation of extraordinary items

ROZEK INC.
Income Statement (partial)
For the Year Ended December 31, 2014

Income before income taxes	$ 800,000
Income tax expense	240,000
Income before irregular items	560,000
Discontinued operations: Loss from disposal of chemical division, net of $90,000 income tax savings	(210,000)
Extraordinary item: Expropriation of investment, net of $21,000 income tax savings	(49,000)
Net income	$ 301,000

If a transaction or event meets one but not both of the criteria for an extraordinary item, a company should report it as a separate line item in the upper portion of the income statement, rather than in the bottom portion as an extraordinary item. Usually, companies report these items under either "Other revenues and gains" or "Other expenses and losses" at their gross amount (not net of tax). This is true, for example, of gains (losses) resulting from the sale of property, plant, and equipment, as explained in Chapter 9. Illustration 13-4 shows the appropriate classification of extraordinary and ordinary items.

Illustration 13-4
Classification of extraordinary and ordinary items

Extraordinary items

1. Effects of major natural casualties, if rare in the area.

2. Expropriation (takeover) of property by a foreign government.

3. Effects of a newly enacted law or regulation, such as a condemnation action.

Ordinary items

1. Effects of major natural casualties, not uncommon in the area.

2. Write-down of inventories or write-off of receivables.

3. Losses attributable to labor strikes.

4. Gains or losses from sales of property, plant, or equipment.

In summary, in evaluating a company, it generally makes sense to eliminate all irregular items in estimating future sustainable income.

Investor Insight

What Does "Non-Recurring" Really Mean?

Many companies incur restructuring charges as they attempt to reduce costs. They often label these items in the income statement as "non-recurring" charges, to suggest that they are isolated events, unlikely to occur in future periods. The question for analysts is, are these costs really one-time, "non-recurring events" or do they reflect problems that the company will be facing for many periods in the future? If they are one-time events, then they can be largely ignored when trying to predict future earnings.

But, some companies report "one-time" restructuring charges over and over again. For example, Procter & Gamble reported a restructuring charge in 12 consecutive quarters, and Motorola had "special" charges in 14 consecutive quarters. On the other hand, other companies have a restructuring charge only once in a 5- or 10-year period. There appears to be no substitute for careful analysis of the numbers that comprise net income.

© Andrey Armyagov/iStockphoto

 If a company takes a large restructuring charge, what is the effect on the company's current income statement versus future ones? (See page 748.)

DECISION TOOLKIT

DECISION CHECKPOINTS	INFO NEEDED FOR DECISION	TOOL TO USE FOR DECISION	HOW TO EVALUATE RESULTS
Has the company experienced any extraordinary events or transactions?	Extraordinary item section of income statement	Items reported in this section indicate that the company experienced an event that was both unusual and infrequent.	These items should usually be ignored in estimating future net income.

Ethics Note Changes in accounting principle should result in financial statements that are more informative for statement users. They should not be used to artificially improve the reported performance or financial position of the corporation.

CHANGES IN ACCOUNTING PRINCIPLE

For ease of comparison, users of financial statements expect companies to prepare their statements on a basis **consistent** with the preceding period. A change in accounting principle occurs when the principle used in the current year is different from the one used in the preceding year. An example is a change in inventory costing methods (such as FIFO to average-cost). Accounting rules permit a change when management can show that the new principle is preferable to the old principle.

Companies report most changes in accounting principle retroactively.[1] That is, they report both the current period and previous periods using the new principle. As a result, the same principle applies in all periods. This treatment improves the ability to compare results across years.

Larry MacDougal/AP/Wide World Photos

 ### Investor Insight

More Frequent Ups and Downs

In the past, U.S. companies used a method to account for their pension plans that smoothed out the gains and losses on their pension portfolios by spreading gains and losses over multiple years. Many felt that this approach was beneficial because it reduced the volatility of reported net income. However, recently some companies have opted to adopt a method approved by international accounting standard-setters. Under this approach, gains and losses on the pension portfolio affect net income in the period in which they occur. Some of the companies that have adopted this approach are United Parcel Service (UPS), Honeywell International, IBM, AT&T, and Verizon Communications. The CFO at UPS said he favored the new approach because "events that occurred in prior years will no longer distort current-year results. It will result in better transparency by eliminating the noise of past plan performance." When UPS switched, it resulted in a charge of $827 million from the change in accounting principle.

Source: Bob Sechler and Doug Cameron, "UPS Alters Pension-Plan Accounting," *Wall Street Journal* (January 30, 2012).

? When predicting future earnings, how should analysts treat the one-time charge that results from a switch to the different approach for accounting for pension plans? (See page 748.)

 DECISION TOOLKIT

DECISION CHECKPOINTS	INFO NEEDED FOR DECISION	TOOL TO USE FOR DECISION	HOW TO EVALUATE RESULTS
Has the company changed any of its accounting principles?	Effect of change in accounting principle on current and prior periods.	Management indicates that the new principle is preferable to the old principle.	Examine current and prior years' reported income, using new-principle basis to assess trends for estimating future income.

---

[1]An exception to the general rule is a change in depreciation methods. The effects of this change are reported in current and future periods. Discussion of this approach is left for more advanced courses.

COMPREHENSIVE INCOME

Most revenues, expenses, gains, and losses are included in net income. However, certain gains and losses bypass net income. Instead, companies record these items as direct adjustments to stockholders' equity. Many analysts have expressed concern about this practice because they believe it reduces the usefulness of the income statement. To address this concern, the FASB requires companies to report not only net income but also comprehensive income. **Comprehensive income** includes all changes in stockholders' equity during a period except those changes resulting from investments by stockholders and distributions to stockholders.

LEARNING OBJECTIVE   **3**

Explain the concept of comprehensive income.

Illustration of Comprehensive Income

Accounting standards require that companies adjust most investments in stocks and bonds up or down to their market price at the end of each accounting period. For example, assume that during 2014 Stassi Company purchased IBM stock for $10,000 as an investment. At the end of 2014, Stassi was still holding the investment, but the stock's market price was now $8,000. In this case, Stassi is required to reduce the recorded value of its IBM investment by $2,000. The $2,000 difference is an unrealized loss.

Should Stassi include this $2,000 unrealized loss in net income? It depends on whether Stassi classifies the IBM stock as a trading security or an available-for-sale security. A **trading security** is bought and held primarily for sale in the near term to generate income on short-term price differences. Companies report unrealized losses on trading securities in the "Other expenses and losses" section of the income statement. The rationale: It is likely that the company will realize the unrealized loss (or an unrealized gain), so the company should report the loss (gain) as part of net income.

If Stassi did not purchase the investment for trading purposes, it is classified as available-for-sale. **Available-for-sale securities** are held with the intent of selling them sometime in the future. Companies do not include unrealized gains or losses on available-for-sale securities in net income. Instead, they report them as part of "Other comprehensive income." Other comprehensive income is not included in net income. It bypasses net income and is recorded as a direct adjustment to stockholders' equity.

Format

One format for reporting comprehensive income is to report a combined statement of income and comprehensive income.[2] For example, assuming that Stassi Company has a net income of $300,000, the unrealized loss would be reported below net income as follows.

STASSI CORPORATION Combined Statement of Income and Comprehensive Income (partial)	
Net income	$300,000
Unrealized loss on available-for-sale securities	2,000
Comprehensive income	$298,000

Illustration 13-5 Lower portion of combined statement of income and comprehensive income

Companies also report the unrealized loss on available-for-sale securities as a separate component of stockholders' equity. To illustrate, assume Stassi Corporation has common stock of $3,000,000, retained earnings of $1,500,000, and an unrealized loss on available-for-sale securities of $2,000. Illustration 13-6 (page 696) shows the balance sheet presentation of the unrealized loss.

---

[2]Computation of comprehensive income is sometimes shown in a separate statement of comprehensive income or as a section in the stockholders' equity statement.

Illustration 13-6 Unrealized loss in stockholders' equity section

STASSI CORPORATION Balance Sheet (partial)		
Stockholders' equity		
Common stock		$3,000,000
Retained earnings		1,500,000
Total paid-in capital and retained earnings		4,500,000
Less: Unrealized loss on available-for-sale securities		(2,000)
Total stockholders' equity		$4,498,000

Note that the presentation of the loss is similar to the presentation of the cost of treasury stock in the stockholders' equity section. (An unrealized gain would be added in this section of the balance sheet.) Reporting the unrealized gain or loss in the stockholders' equity section serves two important purposes: (1) It reduces the volatility of net income due to fluctuations in fair value, and (2) it informs the financial statement user of the gain or loss that would occur if the company sold the securities at fair value.

Complete Income Statement

The income statement for Pace Corporation in Illustration 13-7 presents the types of items found on this statement, such as net sales, cost of goods sold, operating expenses, and income taxes. In addition, it shows how companies report irregular items and comprehensive income (highlighted in red).

Illustration 13-7 Complete income statement

PACE CORPORATION Income Statement and Statement of Comprehensive Income For the Year Ended December 31, 2014		
Net sales		$440,000
Cost of goods sold		260,000
Gross profit		180,000
Operating expenses		110,000
Income from operations		70,000
Other revenues and gains	$ 5,600	
Other expenses and losses	(9,600)	(4,000)
Income before income taxes		66,000
Income tax expense ($66,000 × 30%)		19,800
Income before irregular items		46,200
Discontinued operations: Gain on disposal of Plastics Division, net of $15,000 income taxes ($50,000 × 30%)		35,000
Extraordinary item: Tornado loss, net of income tax savings $18,000 ($60,000 × 30%)		(42,000)
Net income		39,200
Add: Unrealized gain on available-for-sale securities		10,000
Comprehensive income		$ 49,200

CONCLUDING REMARKS

We have shown that the computation of the correct net income number can be elusive. In assessing the future prospects of a company, some investors focus on income from operations and therefore ignore all irregular and other items. Others use measures such as net income, comprehensive income, or some modified version of one of these amounts.

Do it! In its draft 2014 income statement, AIR Corporation reports income before income taxes $400,000, extraordinary loss due to earthquake $100,000, income taxes $120,000 (not including irregular items), and loss on disposal of discontinued flower division $140,000. The income tax rate is 30%. Prepare a correct income statement, beginning with income before income taxes.

IRREGULAR ITEMS

Solution

AIR CORPORATION
Income Statement (partial)

Income before income taxes	$400,000
Income tax expense	120,000
Income before irregular items	280,000
Discontinued operations	
Loss on disposal of discontinued flower division, net of $42,000 tax savings	(98,000)
Extraordinary earthquake loss net of $30,000 tax savings	(70,000)
Net income	$112,000

Action Plan

- Recall that a loss is extraordinary if it is both unusual and infrequent.
- Disclose the income tax effect of each component of income, beginning with income before any irregular items.
- Show discontinued operations before extraordinary items.

The Navigator

Related exercise material: **BE13-1, BE13-2, BE13-3, Do it! 13-1,** and **E13-1.**

Comparative Analysis

As indicated, in assessing the financial performance of a company, investors are interested in the core or sustainable earnings of a company. In addition, investors are interested in making comparisons from period to period. Throughout this textbook, we have relied on three types of comparisons to improve the decision-usefulness of financial information:

LEARNING OBJECTIVE 4
Describe and apply horizontal analysis.

1. **Intracompany basis.** Comparisons within a company are often useful to detect changes in financial relationships and significant trends. For example, a comparison of Kellogg's current year's cash amount with the prior year's cash amount shows either an increase or a decrease. Likewise, a comparison of Kellogg's year-end cash amount with the amount of its total assets at year-end shows the proportion of total assets in the form of cash.

2. **Intercompany basis.** Comparisons with other companies provide insight into a company's competitive position. For example, investors can compare Kellogg's total sales for the year with the total sales of its competitors in the breakfast cereal area, such as General Mills.

3. **Industry averages.** Comparisons with industry averages provide information about a company's relative position within the industry. For example, financial statement readers can compare Kellogg's financial data with the averages for its industry compiled by financial rating organizations such as Dun & Bradstreet, Moody's, and Standard & Poor's, or with information provided on the Internet by organizations such as Yahoo! on its financial site.

International Note As more countries adopt IFRS, the ability of analysts to compare companies from different countries should improve. However, IFRSs are open to widely varying interpretations. In addition, some countries adopt IFRS "with modifications." As a consequence, most cross-country comparisons are still not as transparent as within-country comparisons.

We use three basic tools in financial statement analysis to highlight the significance of financial statement data:

1. Horizontal analysis
2. Vertical analysis
3. Ratio analysis

In previous chapters, we relied primarily on ratio analysis, supplemented with some basic horizontal and vertical analysis. In the remainder of this section, we introduce more formal forms of horizontal and vertical analysis. In the next section, we review ratio analysis in some detail.

HORIZONTAL ANALYSIS

Horizontal analysis, also known as trend analysis, is a technique for evaluating a series of financial statement data over a period of time. Its purpose is to determine the increase or decrease that has taken place, expressed as either an amount or a percentage. For example, here are recent net sales figures (in thousands) of Chicago Cereal Company:

2011	2010	2009	2008	2007
$11,776	$10,907	$10,177	$9,614	$8,812

If we assume that 2007 is the base year, we can measure all percentage increases or decreases relative to this base-period amount with the formula shown in Illustration 13-8.

Illustration 13-8 Horizontal analysis—computation of changes since base period

$$\frac{\text{Change Since}}{\text{Base Period}} = \frac{\text{Current-Year Amount} - \text{Base-Year Amount}}{\text{Base-Year Amount}}$$

For example, we can determine that net sales for Chicago Cereal increased approximately 9.1% [($9,614 − $8,812) ÷ $8,812] from 2007 to 2008. Similarly, we can also determine that net sales increased by 33.6% [($11,776 − $8,812) ÷ $8,812] from 2007 to 2011.

Alternatively, we can express current-year sales as a percentage of the base period. To do so, we would divide the current-year amount by the base-year amount, as shown in Illustration 13-9.

Illustration 13-9 Horizontal analysis—computation of current year in relation to base year

$$\frac{\text{Current Results in}}{\text{Relation to Base Period}} = \frac{\text{Current-Year Amount}}{\text{Base-Year Amount}}$$

Current-period sales expressed as a percentage of the base period for each of the five years, using 2007 as the base period, are shown in Illustration 13-10.

Illustration 13-10 Horizontal analysis of net sales

CHICAGO CEREAL COMPANY
Net Sales (in thousands)
Base Period 2007

2011	2010	2009	2008	2007
$11,776	$10,907	$10,177	$9,614	$8,812
133.6%	123.8%	115.5%	109.1%	100%

The large increase in net sales during 2008 would raise questions regarding possible reasons for such a significant change. Chicago Cereal's 2008 notes to the financial statements explain that the company completed an acquisition of Elf Foods Company during 2008. This major acquisition would help explain the increase in sales highlighted by horizontal analysis.

To further illustrate horizontal analysis, we use the financial statements of Chicago Cereal Company. Its two-year condensed balance sheets for 2011 and 2010, showing dollar and percentage changes, are presented in Illustration 13-11.

CHICAGO CEREAL COMPANY
Condensed Balance Sheets
December 31 (in thousands)

Illustration 13-11 Horizontal analysis of balance sheets

Assets	2011	2010	Increase (Decrease) during 2011 Amount	Percent
Current assets	$ 2,717	$ 2,427	$ 290	11.9
Property assets (net)	2,990	2,816	174	6.2
Other assets	5,690	5,471	219	4.0
Total assets	$11,397	$10,714	$ 683	6.4
Liabilities and Stockholders' Equity				
Current liabilities	$ 4,044	$ 4,020	$ 24	0.6
Long-term liabilities	4,827	4,625	202	4.4
Total liabilities	8,871	8,645	226	2.6
Stockholders' equity				
Common stock	493	397	96	24.2
Retained earnings	3,390	2,584	806	31.2
Treasury stock (cost)	(1,357)	(912)	(445)	48.8
Total stockholders' equity	2,526	2,069	457	22.1
Total liabilities and stockholders' equity	$11,397	$10,714	$ 683	6.4

Helpful Hint When using horizontal analysis, be sure to examine both dollar amount changes and percentage changes. It is not necessarily bad if a company's earnings are growing at a declining rate. The amount of increase may be the same as or more than the base year, but the percentage change may be less because the base is greater each year.

The comparative balance sheets show that a number of changes occurred in Chicago Cereal's financial position from 2010 to 2011. In the assets section, current assets increased $290,000, or 11.9% ($290 ÷ $2,427), and property assets (net) increased $174,000, or 6.2%. Other assets increased $219,000, or 4.0%. In the liabilities section, current liabilities increased $24,000, or 0.6%, while long-term liabilities increased $202,000, or 4.4%. In the stockholders' equity section, we find that retained earnings increased $806,000, or 31.2%.

Illustration 13-12 presents two-year comparative income statements of Chicago Cereal Company for 2011 and 2010, showing dollar and percentage changes.

CHICAGO CEREAL COMPANY
Condensed Income Statements
For the Years Ended December 31 (in thousands)

Illustration 13-12 Horizontal analysis of income statements

	2011	2010	Increase (Decrease) during 2011 Amount	Percent
Net sales	$11,776	$10,907	$869	8.0
Cost of goods sold	6,597	6,082	515	8.5
Gross profit	5,179	4,825	354	7.3
Selling and administrative expenses	3,311	3,059	252	8.2
Income from operations	1,868	1,766	102	5.8
Interest expense	319	307	12	3.9
Other income (expense), net	(2)	13	(15)	(115.4)
Income before income taxes	1,547	1,472	75	5.1
Income tax expense	444	468	(24)	(5.1)
Net income	$ 1,103	$ 1,004	$ 99	9.9

Helpful Hint Note that, in a horizontal analysis, while the amount column is additive (the total is $99,000), the percentage column is not additive (9.9% is not a total).

Horizontal analysis of the income statements shows the following changes. Net sales increased $869,000, or 8.0% ($869 ÷ $10,907). Cost of goods sold increased $515,000, or 8.5% ($515 ÷ $6,082). Selling and administrative expenses increased $252,000, or 8.2% ($252 ÷ $3,059). Overall, gross profit increased 7.3% and net income increased 9.9%. The increase in net income can be attributed to the increase in net sales and a decrease in income tax expense.

The measurement of changes from period to period in percentages is relatively straightforward and quite useful. However, complications can result in making the computations. If an item has no value in a base year or preceding year and a value in the next year, no percentage change can be computed. Likewise, no percentage change can be computed if a negative amount appears in the base or preceding period and a positive amount exists the following year.

🧰 DECISION TOOLKIT

DECISION CHECKPOINTS	INFO NEEDED FOR DECISION	TOOL TO USE FOR DECISION	HOW TO EVALUATE RESULTS
How do the company's financial position and operating results compare with those of the previous period?	Income statement and balance sheet	Comparative financial statements should be prepared over at least two years, with the first year reported being the base year. Changes in each line item relative to the base year should be presented both by amount and by percentage. This is called **horizontal analysis**.	Significant changes should be investigated to determine the reason for the change.

HORIZONTAL ANALYSIS

 Do it! Summary financial information for Rosepatch Company is as follows.

	December 31, 2014	December 31, 2013
Current assets	$234,000	$180,000
Plant assets (net)	756,000	420,000
Total assets	$990,000	$600,000

Compute the amount and percentage changes in 2014 using horizontal analysis, assuming 2013 is the base year.

Action Plan

• Find the percentage change by dividing the amount of the increase by the 2013 amount (base year).

The Navigator

Solution

	Increase in 2014	
	Amount	**Percent**
Current assets	$ 54,000	30% [($234,000 − $180,000) ÷ $180,000]
Plant assets (net)	336,000	80% [($756,000 − $420,000) ÷ $420,000]
Total assets	$390,000	65% [($990,000 − $600,000) ÷ $600,000]

Related exercise material: **BE13-4, BE13-6, BE13-7, BE13-9, Do it! 13-2,** and **E13-3.**

VERTICAL ANALYSIS

LEARNING OBJECTIVE 5

Describe and apply vertical analysis.

Vertical analysis, also called common-size analysis, is a technique for evaluating financial statement data that expresses each item in a financial statement as a **percentage of a base amount**. For example, on a balance sheet we might express current assets as 22% of total assets (total assets being the base amount).

Or, on an income statement we might express selling expenses as 16% of net sales (net sales being the base amount).

Presented in Illustration 13-13 are the comparative balance sheets of Chicago Cereal for 2011 and 2010, analyzed vertically. The base for the asset items is **total assets**, and the base for the liability and stockholders' equity items is **total liabilities and stockholders' equity**.

Illustration 13-13 Vertical analysis of balance sheets

CHICAGO CEREAL COMPANY
Condensed Balance Sheets
December 31 (in thousands)

	2011		2010	
Assets	**Amount**	**Percent***	**Amount**	**Percent***
Current assets	$ 2,717	23.8	$ 2,427	22.6
Property assets (net)	2,990	26.2	2,816	26.3
Other assets	5,690	50.0	5,471	51.1
Total assets	$11,397	100.0	$10,714	100.0
Liabilities and Stockholders' Equity				
Current liabilities	$ 4,044	35.5	$ 4,020	37.5
Long-term liabilities	4,827	42.4	4,625	43.2
Total liabilities	8,871	77.9	8,645	80.7
Stockholders' equity				
Common stock	493	4.3	397	3.7
Retained earnings	3,390	29.7	2,584	24.1
Treasury stock (cost)	(1,357)	(11.9)	(912)	(8.5)
Total stockholders' equity	2,526	22.1	2,069	19.3
Total liabilities and stockholders' equity	$11,397	100.0	$10,714	100.0

*Numbers have been rounded to total 100%.

In addition to showing the relative size of each category on the balance sheets, vertical analysis can show the percentage change in the individual asset, liability, and stockholders' equity items. In this case, current assets increased $290,000 from 2010 to 2011, and they increased from 22.6% to 23.8% of total assets. Property assets (net) decreased from 26.3% to 26.2% of total assets. Other assets decreased from 51.1% to 50.0% of total assets. Also, retained earnings increased by $806,000 from 2010 to 2011, and total stockholders' equity increased from 19.3% to 22.1% of total liabilities and stockholders' equity. This switch to a higher percentage of equity financing has two causes: First, while total liabilities increased by $226,000, the percentage of liabilities declined from 80.7% to 77.9% of total liabilities and stockholders' equity. Second, retained earnings increased by $806,000, from 24.1% to 29.7% of total liabilities and stockholders' equity. Thus, the company shifted toward equity financing by relying less on debt and by increasing the amount of retained earnings.

Vertical analysis of the comparative income statements of Chicago Cereal, shown in Illustration 13-14 (page 702), reveals that cost of goods sold **as a percentage of net sales** increased from 55.8% to 56.0%, and selling and administrative expenses increased from 28.0% to 28.1%. Net income as a percentage of net sales increased from 9.1% to 9.4%. Chicago Cereal's increase in net income as a percentage of sales is due primarily to the decrease in interest expense and income tax expense as a percentage of sales.

Illustration 13-14 Vertical analysis of income statements

CHICAGO CEREAL COMPANY
Condensed Income Statements
For the Years Ended December 31 (in thousands)

	2011		2010	
	Amount	**Percent***	**Amount**	**Percent***
Net sales	$11,776	100.0	$10,907	100.0
Cost of goods sold	6,597	56.0	6,082	55.8
Gross profit	5,179	44.0	4,825	44.2
Selling and administrative expenses	3,311	28.1	3,059	28.0
Income from operations	1,868	15.9	1,766	16.2
Interest expense	319	2.7	307	2.8
Other income (expense), net	(2)	.0	13	.0
Income before income taxes	1,547	13.2	1,472	13.4
Income tax expense	444	3.8	468	4.3
Net income	$ 1,103	9.4	$ 1,004	9.1

*Numbers have been rounded to total 100%.

Vertical analysis also enables you to compare companies of different sizes. For example, one of Chicago Cereal's competitors is General Mills. General Mills' sales are 1,000 times larger than those of Chicago Cereal. Vertical analysis enables us to meaningfully compare the condensed income statements of Chicago Cereal and General Mills, as shown in Illustration 13-15.

Illustration 13-15 Intercompany comparison by vertical analysis

CONDENSED INCOME STATEMENTS
For the Year Ended December 31, 2011

	Chicago Cereal (in thousands)		General Mills, Inc. (in millions)	
	Amount	**Percent***	**Amount**	**Percent***
Net sales	$11,776	100.0	$14,880	100.0
Cost of goods sold	6,597	56.0	8,927	60.0
Gross profit	5,179	44.0	5,953	40.0
Selling and administrative expenses	3,311	28.1	3,192	21.5
Non-recurring charges and (gains)	0	—	(13)	(0.1)
Income from operations	1,868	15.9	2,774	18.6
Other expenses and revenues (including income taxes)	765	6.5	976	6.5
Net income	$ 1,103	9.4	$ 1,798	12.1

*Numbers have been rounded to total 100%.

Although Chicago Cereal's net sales are much less than those of General Mills, vertical analysis eliminates the impact of this size difference for our analysis. Chicago Cereal has a higher gross profit percentage 44.0%, compared to 40.0% for General Mills. But, Chicago Cereal's selling and administrative expenses are 28.1% of net sales, while those of General Mills are 21.5% of net sales. Looking at net income, we see that General Mills' percentage is higher. Chicago Cereal's net income as a percentage of net sales is 9.4%, compared to 12.1% for General Mills.

ANATOMY OF A FRAUD

This final *Anatomy of a Fraud* box demonstrates that sometimes relationships between numbers can be used by companies to detect fraud. Financial ratios that appear abnormal or statistical abnormalities in the numbers themselves can reveal fraud. For example, the fact that WorldCom's line costs, as a percentage of either total expenses or revenues, differed very significantly from its competitors should have alerted people to the possibility of fraud. Or, consider the case of a bank manager, who cooperated with a group of his friends to defraud the bank's credit card department. The manager's friends would apply for credit cards and then run up balances of slightly less than $5,000. The bank had a policy of allowing bank personnel to write-off balances of less than $5,000 without seeking supervisor approval. The fraud was detected by applying statistical analysis based on Benford's Law. Benford's Law states that in a random collection of numbers, the frequency of lower digits (e.g., 1, 2, or 3) should be much higher than higher digits (e.g., 7, 8, or 9). In this case, bank auditors analyzed the first two digits of amounts written off. There was a spike at 48 and 49, which was not consistent with what would be expected if the numbers were random.

Total take: Thousands of dollars

THE MISSING CONTROL

Independent internal verification. While it might be efficient to allow employees to write off accounts below a certain level, it is important that these write-offs be reviewed and verified periodically. Such a review would likely call attention to an employee with large amounts of write-offs, or in this case, write-offs that were frequently very close to the approval threshold.

Source: Mark J. Nigrini, "I've Got Your Number," *Journal of Accountancy Online* (May 1999).

DECISION TOOLKIT

DECISION CHECKPOINTS	INFO NEEDED FOR DECISION	TOOL TO USE FOR DECISION	HOW TO EVALUATE RESULTS
How do the relationships between items in this year's financial statements compare with those of last year or those of competitors?	Income statement and balance sheet	Each line item on the income statement should be presented as a percentage of net sales, and each line item on the balance sheet should be presented as a percentage of total assets or total liabilities and stockholders' equity. These percentages should be investigated for differences either across years in the same company or in the same year across different companies. This is called **vertical analysis**.	Any significant differences either across years or between companies should be investigated to determine the cause.

Ratio Analysis

In previous chapters, we presented many ratios used for evaluating the financial health and performance of a company. Here, we provide a summary listing of those ratios. (Page references to prior discussions are provided if you feel you need to review any individual ratios.) Appendix 13A provides an example of a comprehensive financial analysis employing these ratios.

LEARNING OBJECTIVE 6
Identify and compute ratios used in analyzing a company's liquidity, solvency, and profitability.

LIQUIDITY RATIOS

Liquidity ratios (Illustration 13-16) measure the short-term ability of the company to pay its maturing obligations and to meet unexpected needs for cash. Short-term creditors such as bankers and suppliers are particularly interested in assessing liquidity.

Illustration 13-16 Summary of liquidity ratios

Liquidity Ratios		
Working capital	Current assets − Current liabilities	p. 58
Current ratio	$\dfrac{\text{Current assets}}{\text{Current liabilities}}$	p. 59
Current cash debt coverage	$\dfrac{\text{Net cash provided by operating activities}}{\text{Average current liabilities}}$	p. 645
Inventory turnover	$\dfrac{\text{Cost of goods sold}}{\text{Average inventory}}$	p. 300
Days in inventory	$\dfrac{\text{365 days}}{\text{Inventory turnover}}$	p. 300
Accounts receivable turnover	$\dfrac{\text{Net credit sales}}{\text{Average net accounts receivable}}$	p. 416
Average collection period	$\dfrac{\text{365 days}}{\text{Accounts receivable turnover}}$	p. 416

SuperStock

 Investor Insight

How to Manage the Current Ratio

The apparent simplicity of the current ratio can have real-world limitations because adding equal amounts to both the numerator and the denominator causes the ratio to decrease.

Assume, for example, that a company has $2,000,000 of current assets and $1,000,000 of current liabilities. Its current ratio is 2:1. If it purchases $1,000,000 of inventory on account, it will have $3,000,000 of current assets and $2,000,000 of current liabilities. Its current ratio decreases to 1.5:1. If, instead, the company pays off $500,000 of its current liabilities, it will have $1,500,000 of current assets and $500,000 of current liabilities. Its current ratio increases to 3:1. Thus, any trend analysis should be done with care because the ratio is susceptible to quick changes and is easily influenced by management.

 How might management influence a company's current ratio? (See page 748.)

SOLVENCY RATIOS

Solvency ratios (Illustration 13-17) measure the ability of the company to survive over a long period of time. Long-term creditors and stockholders are interested in a company's long-run solvency, particularly its ability to pay interest as it comes due and to repay the balance of debt at its maturity.

Illustration 13-17 Summary of solvency ratios

Solvency Ratios		
Debt to assets ratio	$\dfrac{\text{Total liabilities}}{\text{Total assets}}$	p. 60
Cash debt coverage	$\dfrac{\text{Net cash provided by operating activities}}{\text{Average total liabilities}}$	p. 646
Times interest earned	$\dfrac{\text{Net income + Interest expense + Tax expense}}{\text{Interest expense}}$	p. 525
Free cash flow	$\begin{array}{c}\text{Net cash provided}\\\text{by operating activities}\end{array} - \begin{array}{c}\text{Capital}\\\text{expenditures}\end{array} - \begin{array}{c}\text{Cash}\\\text{dividends}\end{array}$	p. 61

PROFITABILITY RATIOS

Profitability ratios (Illustration 13-18) measure the income or operating success of a company for a given period of time. A company's income, or lack of it, affects its ability to obtain debt and equity financing, its liquidity position, and its ability to grow. As a consequence, creditors and investors alike are interested in evaluating profitability. Profitability is frequently used as the ultimate test of management's operating effectiveness.

Illustration 13-18 Summary of profitability ratios

Profitability Ratios

Earnings per share	$\dfrac{\text{Net income} - \text{Preferred dividends}}{\text{Average common shares outstanding}}$	p. 55
Price-earnings ratio	$\dfrac{\text{Stock price per share}}{\text{Earnings per share}}$	p. 707
Gross profit rate	$\dfrac{\text{Gross profit}}{\text{Net sales}}$	p. 248
Profit margin	$\dfrac{\text{Net income}}{\text{Net sales}}$	p. 250
Return on assets	$\dfrac{\text{Net income}}{\text{Average total assets}}$	p. 464
Asset turnover	$\dfrac{\text{Net sales}}{\text{Average total assets}}$	p. 465
Payout ratio	$\dfrac{\text{Cash dividends declared on common stock}}{\text{Net income}}$	p. 594
Return on common stockholders' equity	$\dfrac{\text{Net income} - \text{Preferred dividends}}{\text{Average common stockholders' equity}}$	p. 595

Investor Insight

High Ratings Can Bring Low Returns

Moody's, Standard and Poor's, and Fitch are three big firms that perform financial analysis on publicly traded companies and then publish ratings of the companies' creditworthiness. Investors and lenders rely heavily on these ratings in making investment and lending decisions. Some people feel that the collapse of the financial markets was worsened by inadequate research reports and ratings provided by the financial rating agencies. Critics contend that the rating agencies were reluctant to give large companies low ratings because they feared that by offending them they would lose out on business opportunities. For example, the rating agencies gave many so-called mortgage-backed securities ratings that suggested that they were low risk. Later, many of these very securities became completely worthless. Steps have been taken to reduce the conflicts of interest that lead to these faulty ratings.

Source: Aaron Lucchetti and Judith Burns, "Moody's CEO Warned Profit Push Posed a Risk to Quality of Ratings," *Wall Street Journal Online* (October 23, 2008).

© Ferran Traite Soler/iStockphoto

 Why are credit rating agencies important to the financial markets? (See page 748.)

RATIO ANALYSIS

Action Plan

- Liquidity is the short-term ability of the company to pay its maturing obligations; solvency is the ability to survive over a long period of time; and profitability is the operating success of the company over a period of time.

The Navigator

Do it!

State whether each of the following is an indicator of a company's liquidity, solvency, or profitability.

(a) Cash debt coverage
(b) Average collection period
(c) Working capital
(d) Asset turnover
(e) Payout ratio
(f) Free cash flow

Solution

(a) Solvency   (b) Liquidity   (c) Liquidity   (d) Profitability   (e) Profitability   (f) Solvency

Related exercise material: **BE13-10, BE13-11, BE13-12, BE13-13, BE13-14, BE13-15,** **Do it! 13-3, E13-2, E13-7, E13-8, E13-9, E13-10, E13-11, E13-12,** and **E13-13.**

Quality of Earnings

LEARNING OBJECTIVE 7

Understand the concept of quality of earnings.

The quality of a company's earnings is of extreme importance to analysts. A company that has a high **quality of earnings** provides full and transparent information that will not confuse or mislead users of the financial statements.

Recent accounting scandals suggest that some companies are spending too much time managing their income and not enough time managing their business. Here are some of the factors affecting quality of earnings.

ALTERNATIVE ACCOUNTING METHODS

Variations among companies in the application of generally accepted accounting principles may hamper comparability and reduce quality of earnings. For example, suppose one company uses the FIFO method of inventory costing, while another company in the same industry uses LIFO. If inventory is a significant asset to both companies, it is unlikely that their current ratios are comparable. For example, if General Motors Corporation used FIFO instead of LIFO for inventory valuation, its inventories in a recent year would have been 26% higher, which significantly affects the current ratio (and other ratios as well).

In addition to differences in inventory costing methods, differences also exist in reporting such items as depreciation and amortization. Although these differences in accounting methods might be detectable from reading the notes to the financial statements, adjusting the financial data to compensate for the different methods is often difficult, if not impossible.

PRO FORMA INCOME

Companies whose stock is publicly traded are required to present their income statement following generally accepted accounting principles (GAAP). In recent years, many companies have been also reporting a second measure of income, called pro forma income. **Pro forma income** usually excludes items that the company thinks are unusual or non-recurring. For example, in a recent year, Cisco Systems (a high-tech company) reported a quarterly net loss under GAAP of $2.7 billion. Cisco reported pro forma income for the same quarter as a profit of $230 million. This large difference in profits between GAAP income numbers and pro forma income is not unusual. For example, during one 9-month period, the 100 largest companies on the Nasdaq stock exchange reported a total pro forma income of $19.1 billion but a total loss as measured by GAAP of $82.3 billion—a difference of about $100 billion!

To compute pro forma income, companies generally exclude any items they deem inappropriate for measuring their performance. Many analysts and investors are critical of the practice of using pro forma income because these numbers often make companies look better than they really are. As the financial press noted, pro forma numbers might be called "earnings before bad stuff." Companies, on the other hand, argue that pro forma numbers more clearly indicate sustainable income because they exclude unusual and non-recurring expenses. "Cisco's technique gives readers of financial statements a clear picture of Cisco's normal business activities," the company said in a statement issued in response to questions about its pro forma income accounting.

Recently, the SEC provided some guidance on how companies should present pro forma information. Stay tuned: Everyone seems to agree that pro forma numbers can be useful if they provide insights into determining a company's sustainable income. However, many companies have abused the flexibility that pro forma numbers allow and have used the measure as a way to put their companies in a more favorable light.

IMPROPER RECOGNITION

Because some managers feel pressure from Wall Street to continually increase earnings, they manipulate earnings numbers to meet these expectations. The most common abuse is the improper recognition of revenue. One practice that some companies use is called **channel stuffing**. Offering deep discounts, companies encourage customers to buy early (stuff the channel) rather than later. This boosts earnings in the current period, but it often leads to a disaster in subsequent periods because customers have no need for additional goods. To illustrate, Bristol-Myers Squibb at one time indicated that it used sales incentives to encourage wholesalers to buy more drugs than they needed. As a result, the company had to issue revised financial statements showing corrected revenues and income.

Another practice is the improper capitalization of operating expenses. WorldCom capitalized over $7 billion of operating expenses in order to report positive net income. In other situations, companies fail to report all their liabilities. Enron promised to make payments on certain contracts if financial difficulty developed, but these guarantees were not reported as liabilities. In addition, disclosure was so lacking in transparency that it was impossible to understand what was happening at the company.

PRICE-EARNINGS RATIO

Earnings per share is net income available to common stockholders divided by the average number of common shares outstanding. The market price of a company's stock changes based on investors' expectations about a company's future earnings per share. To compare market prices and earnings across firms, investors calculate the **price-earnings (P-E) ratio**. The P-E ratio divides the market price of a share of common stock by earnings per share.

Illustration 13-19 Formula for price-earnings (P-E) ratio

$$\text{Price-Earnings (P-E) Ratio} = \frac{\text{Stock Price per Share}}{\text{Earnings per Share}}$$

The P-E ratio reflects investors' assessment of a company's future earnings. The ratio of price to earnings will be higher if investors think that earnings will increase substantially in the future and therefore are willing to pay more per share of stock. A low price-earnings ratio often signifies that investors think the company's future earnings will not be strong. In addition, sometimes a low P-E ratio reflects the market's belief that a company has poor-quality earnings.

To illustrate, assume that two identical companies each have earnings per share of $5. Suppose one of the companies manipulated its accounting numbers to achieve the $5 figure. If investors perceive that firm has lower-quality earnings, this perception will be reflected in a lower stock price and, consequently, a lower P-E.

Illustration 13-20 shows earnings per share and P-E ratios for five companies for a recent year. Note the difference in the P-E ratio of General Electric versus Google Inc.

Illustration 13-20 Earnings per share and P-E ratios of various companies

Company	Earnings per Share	Price-Earnings Ratio
Southwest Airlines	$ 0.44	18.6
Google Inc.	13.30	30.8
General Electric	2.17	13.2
Merck	1.49	14.6
Nike	3.70	15.9

QUALITY OF EARNINGS, FINANCIAL STATEMENT ANALYSIS

Do it!

Match each of the following terms with the phrase that it best matches.

Comprehensive income   Vertical analysis
Quality of earnings   Pro forma income
Solvency ratio   Extraordinary items

1. Measures the ability of the company to survive over a long period of time.
2. Usually excludes items that a company thinks are unusual or non-recurring.
3. Includes all changes in stockholders' equity during a period except those resulting from investments by stockholders and distributions to stockholders.
4. Indicates the level of full and transparent information provided to users of the financial statements.
5. Describes events and transactions that are unusual in nature and infrequent in occurrence.
6. Expresses each item within a financial statement as a percentage of a base amount.

Action Plan

• Develop a sound understanding of basic methods used for financial reporting.
• Understand the use of fundamental analysis techniques.

Solution

1. Solvency ratio. Measures the ability of the company to survive over a long period of time.
2. Pro forma income. Usually excludes items that a company thinks are unusual or nonrecurring.
3. Comprehensive income. Includes all changes in stockholders' equity during a period except those resulting from investments by stockholders and distributions to stockholders.
4. Quality of earnings. Indicates the level of full and transparent information provided to users of the financial statements.
5. Extraordinary items. Describes events and transactions that are unusual in nature and infrequent in occurrence.
6. Vertical analysis. Expresses each item within a financial statement as a percentage of a base amount.

✔ The Navigator

Related exercise material: **Do it!** 13-4.

USING THE DECISION TOOLKIT

In analyzing a company, you should always investigate an extended period of time in order to determine whether the condition and performance of the company are changing. The condensed financial statements of Kellogg Company for 2011 and 2010 are presented here.

KELLOGG COMPANY, INC.
Balance Sheets
December 31 (in millions)

Assets	2011	2010
Current assets		
Cash	$ 460	$ 444
Accounts receivable (net)	1,188	1,190
Inventories	1,132	1,056
Other current assets	247	225
Total current assets	3,027	2,915
Property (net)	3,281	3,128
Other assets	5,593	5,804
Total assets	$11,901	$11,847
Liabilities and Stockholders' Equity		
Current liabilities	$ 3,313	$ 3,184
Long-term liabilities	6,826	6,509
Stockholders' equity—common	1,762	2,154
Total liabilities and stockholders' equity	$11,901	$11,847

KELLOGG COMPANY, INC.
Condensed Income Statements
For the Years Ended December 31
(in millions)

	2011	2010
Net sales	$13,198	$12,397
Cost of goods sold	7,750	7,108
Gross profit	5,448	5,289
Selling and administrative expenses	3,472	3,299
Income from operations	1,976	1,990
Interest expense	233	248
Other (income) expense, net	11	–0–
Income before income taxes	1,732	1,742
Income tax expense	503	502
Net income	$ 1,229	$ 1,240

Instructions

Compute the following ratios for Kellogg for 2011 and discuss your findings (2010 values are provided for comparison).
1. Liquidity:
    (a) Current ratio (2010: .92:1).
    (b) Inventory turnover (2010: 7.2 times).
2. Solvency:
    (a) Debt to assets ratio (2010: 82%).
    (b) Times interest earned (2010: 8.0 times).

3. Profitability:
   (a) Return on assets (2010: 10.8%).
   (b) Profit margin (2010: 10.0%).
   (c) Return on common stockholders' equity (2010: 56%).

Solution

1. Liquidity
   (a) Current ratio:

   2011: $\dfrac{\$3,027}{\$3,313} = .91{:}1$ 2010: .92:1

   (b) Inventory turnover:

   2011: $\dfrac{\$7,750}{(\$1,132 + \$1,056)/2} = 7.1$ times   2010: 7.2 times

   We see that between 2010 and 2011, the current ratio declined slightly. The inventory turnover also decreased slightly. Combined these ratios suggest the company's liquidity was basically unchanged.

2. Solvency
   (a) Debt to assets ratio:

   2011: $\dfrac{\$3,313 + \$6,826}{\$11,901} = 85\%$ 2010: 82%

   (b) Times interest earned:

   2011: $\dfrac{\$1,229 + \$503 + \$233}{\$233} = 8.4$ times   2010: 8.0 times

   Kellogg's solvency as measured by the debt to assets ratio increased in 2011, suggesting its solvency declined. However, its times interest earned improved slightly, suggesting its solvency improved.

3. Profitability
   (a) Return on assets:

   2011: $\dfrac{\$1,229}{(\$11,901 + \$11,847)/2} = 10.4\%$ 2010: 10.8%

   (b) Profit margin:

   2011: $\dfrac{\$1,229}{\$13,198} = 9.3\%$ 2010: 10.0%

   (c) Return on common stockholders' equity:

   2011: $\dfrac{\$1,229}{(\$1,762 + \$2,154)/2} = 63\%$ 2010: 56%

   Kellogg's return on assets declined. Its profit margin also declined, but its return on stockholders' equity increased.

✔ The
Navigator

Summary of Learning Objectives

1 **Understand the concept of sustainable income.** Sustainable income refers to a company's ability to sustain its profits from operations.

2 **Indicate how irregular items are presented.** Irregular items—discontinued operations and extraordinary items—are presented on the income statement net of tax below "Income before irregular items" to highlight their unusual nature. Changes in accounting principle are reported retroactively.

3 **Explain the concept of comprehensive income.** Comprehensive income includes all changes in stockholders' equity during a period except those resulting from investments by stockholders and distributions to stockholders. "Other comprehensive income" is added to or subtracted from net income to arrive at comprehensive income.

4 **Describe and apply horizontal analysis.** Horizontal analysis is a technique for evaluating a series of data over a period of time to determine the increase or decrease that has taken place, expressed as either an amount or a percentage.

5 **Describe and apply vertical analysis.** Vertical analysis is a technique that expresses each item in a financial statement as a percentage of a relevant total or a base amount.

6 **Identify and compute ratios used in analyzing a company's liquidity, solvency, and profitability.** Financial ratios are provided in Illustration 13-16 (liquidity), Illustration 13-17 (solvency), and Illustration 13-18 (profitability).

7 **Understand the concept of quality of earnings.** A high quality of earnings provides full and transparent information that will not confuse or mislead users of the financial statements. Issues related to quality of earnings are (1) alternative accounting methods, (2) pro forma income, and (3) improper recognition. The price-earnings (P-E) ratio reflects investors' assessment of a company's future earnings potential.

✔ The Navigator

 DECISION TOOLKIT *A SUMMARY*

DECISION CHECKPOINTS	INFO NEEDED FOR DECISION	TOOL TO USE FOR DECISION	HOW TO EVALUATE RESULTS
Has the company sold any major components of its business?	Discontinued operations section of income statement	Anything reported in this section indicates that the company has discontinued a major component of its business.	If a major component has been discontinued, its results during the current period should not be included in estimates of future net income.
Has the company experienced any extraordinary events or transactions?	Extraordinary item section of income statement	Items reported in this section indicate that the company experienced an event that was both unusual and infrequent.	These items should usually be ignored in estimating future net income.
Has the company changed any of its accounting principles?	Effect of change in accounting principle on current and prior periods.	Management indicates that the new principle is preferable to the old principle.	Examine current and prior years' reported income, using new-principle basis to assess trends for estimating future income.
How do the company's financial position and operating results compare with those of the previous period?	Income statement and balance sheet	Comparative financial statements should be prepared over at least two years, with the first year reported being the base year. Changes in each line item relative to the base year should be presented both by amount and by percentage. This is called **horizontal analysis**.	Significant changes should be investigated to determine the reason for the change.
How do the relationships between items in this year's financial statements compare with those of last year or those of competitors?	Income statement and balance sheet	Each line item on the income statement should be presented as a percentage of net sales, and each line item on the balance sheet should be presented as a percentage of total assets or total liabilities and stockholders' equity. These percentages should be investigated for differences either across years in the same company or in the same year across different companies. This is called **vertical analysis**.	Any significant differences either across years or between companies should be investigated to determine the cause.

Comprehensive Illustration of Ratio Analysis

LEARNING OBJECTIVE 8

Evaluate a company comprehensively using ratio analysis.

In previous chapters, we presented many ratios used for evaluating the financial health and performance of a company. In this appendix, we provide a comprehensive review of those ratios and discuss some important relationships among them. Since earlier chapters demonstrated the calculation of each of these ratios, in this appendix we instead focus on their interpretation. Page references to prior discussions point you to any individual ratios you feel you need to review.

We used the financial information in Illustrations 13A-1 through 13A-4 to calculate Chicago Cereal Company's 2011 ratios. You can use these data to review the computations.

Illustration 13A-1 Chicago Cereal Company's balance sheets

CHICAGO CEREAL COMPANY
Balance Sheets
December 31 (in thousands)

Assets	2011	2010
Current assets		
Cash	$ 524	$ 411
Accounts receivable	1,026	945
Inventory	924	824
Prepaid expenses and other current assets	243	247
Total current assets	2,717	2,427
Property assets (net)	2,990	2,816
Intangibles and other assets	5,690	5,471
Total assets	$11,397	$10,714
Liabilities and Stockholders' Equity		
Current liabilities	$ 4,044	$ 4,020
Long-term liabilities	4,827	4,625
Stockholders' equity—common	2,526	2,069
Total liabilities and stockholders' equity	$11,397	$10,714

Illustration 13A-2 Chicago Cereal Company's income statements

CHICAGO CEREAL COMPANY
Condensed Income Statements
For the Years Ended December 31 (in thousands)

	2011	2010
Net sales	$11,776	$10,907
Cost of goods sold	6,597	6,082
Gross profit	5,179	4,825
Selling and administrative expenses	3,311	3,059
Income from operations	1,868	1,766
Interest expense	319	307
Other income (expense), net	(2)	13
Income before income taxes	1,547	1,472
Income tax expense	444	468
Net income	$ 1,103	$ 1,004

CHICAGO CEREAL COMPANY
Condensed Statements of Cash Flows
For the Years Ended December 31 (in thousands)

	2011	2010
Cash flows from operating activities		
Cash receipts from operating activities	$11,695	$10,841
Cash payments for operating activities	10,192	9,431
Net cash provided by operating activities	1,503	1,410
Cash flows from investing activities		
Purchases of property, plant, and equipment	(472)	(453)
Other investing activities	(129)	8
Net cash used in investing activities	(601)	(445)
Cash flows from financing activities		
Issuance of common stock	163	218
Issuance of debt	2,179	721
Reductions of debt	(2,011)	(650)
Payment of dividends	(475)	(450)
Repurchase of common stock and other items	(645)	(612)
Net cash provided (used) by financing activities	(789)	(773)
Increase (decrease) in cash and cash equivalents	113	192
Cash and cash equivalents at beginning of year	411	219
Cash and cash equivalents at end of year	$ 524	$ 411

Illustration 13A-3 Chicago Cereal Company's statements of cash flows

Additional information:

	2011	2010
Average number of shares (thousands)	418.7	418.5
Stock price at year-end	$52.92	$50.06

Illustration 13A-4 Additional information for Chicago Cereal Company

As indicated in the chapter, we can classify ratios into three types for analysis of the primary financial statements:

1. **Liquidity ratios.** Measures of the short-term ability of the company to pay its maturing obligations and to meet unexpected needs for cash.

2. **Solvency ratios.** Measures of the ability of the company to survive over a long period of time.

3. **Profitability ratios.** Measures of the income or operating success of a company for a given period of time.

As a tool of analysis, ratios can provide clues to underlying conditions that may not be apparent from an inspection of the individual components of a particular ratio. But, a single ratio by itself is not very meaningful. Accordingly, in this discussion we use the following three comparisons.

1. **Intracompany comparisons** covering two years for Chicago Cereal Company (using comparative financial information from Illustrations 13A-1 through 13A-4).

2. **Intercompany comparisons** using General Mills as one of Chicago Cereal's competitors.

3. **Industry average comparisons** based on MSN.com median ratios for manufacturers of flour and other grain mill products and comparisons with other sources. For some of the ratios that we use, industry comparisons are not available. (These are denoted "na.")

LIQUIDITY RATIOS

Liquidity ratios measure the short-term ability of the company to pay its maturing obligations and to meet unexpected needs for cash. Short-term creditors such as bankers and suppliers are particularly interested in assessing liquidity. The measures used to determine the company's short-term debt-paying ability are the current ratio, the current cash debt coverage, the accounts receivable turnover, the average collection period, the inventory turnover, and days in inventory.

1. **Current ratio.** The current ratio expresses the relationship of current assets to current liabilities, computed by dividing current assets by current liabilities. It is widely used for evaluating a company's liquidity and short-term debt-paying ability. The 2011 and 2010 current ratios for Chicago Cereal and comparative data are shown in Illustration 13A-5.

Illustration 13A-5
Current ratio

Ratio	Formula	Indicates	Chicago Cereal 2011	Chicago Cereal 2010	General Mills 2011	Industry 2011	Page in Textbook
Current ratio	Current assets / Current liabilities	Short-term debt-paying ability	.67	.60	1.00	1.20	59

What do the measures tell us? Chicago Cereal's 2011 current ratio of .67 means that for every dollar of current liabilities, it has $0.67 of current assets. We sometimes state such ratios as .67:1 to reinforce this interpretation. Its current ratio—and therefore its liquidity—increased significantly in 2011. It is well below the industry average and that of General Mills.

2. **Current cash debt coverage.** A disadvantage of the current ratio is that it uses year-end balances of current asset and current liability accounts. These year-end balances may not represent the company's current position during most of the year. The current cash debt coverage partially corrects for this problem. It is the ratio of net cash provided by operating activities to average current liabilities. Because it uses net cash provided by operating activities rather than a balance at one point in time, it may provide a better representation of liquidity. Chicago Cereal's current cash debt coverage is shown in Illustration 13A-6.

Illustration 13A-6
Current cash debt coverage

Ratio	Formula	Indicates	Chicago Cereal 2011	Chicago Cereal 2010	General Mills 2011	Industry 2011	Page in Textbook
Current cash debt coverage	Net cash provided by operating activities / Average current liabilities	Short-term debt-paying ability (cash basis)	.37	.39	.54	na	645

This ratio decreased slightly in 2011 for Chicago Cereal. Is the coverage adequate? Probably so. Its operating cash flow coverage of average current liabilities is less than that of General Mills, but it approximates a commonly accepted threshold of .40. No industry comparison is available.

3. **Accounts receivable turnover.** Analysts can measure liquidity by how quickly a company converts certain assets to cash. Low values of the previous ratios can sometimes be compensated for if some of the company's current assets are highly liquid.

   How liquid, for example, are the receivables? The ratio used to assess the liquidity of the receivables is the accounts receivable turnover, which measures the number of times, on average, a company collects receivables during the period. The accounts receivable turnover is computed by dividing net credit sales (net sales less cash sales) by average net accounts receivable during the year. The accounts receivable turnover for Chicago Cereal is shown in Illustration 13A-7.

Illustration 13A-7
Accounts receivable turnover

Ratio	Formula	Indicates	Chicago Cereal 2011	Chicago Cereal 2010	General Mills 2011	Industry 2011	Page in Textbook
Accounts receivable turnover	$\dfrac{\text{Net credit sales}}{\text{Average net accounts receivable}}$	Liquidity of receivables	11.9	12.0	12.4	11.2	416

We have assumed that all Chicago Cereal's sales are credit sales. Its accounts receivable turnover declined slightly in 2011. The turnover of 11.9 times is higher than the industry average of 11.2 times, and slightly lower than General Mills' turnover of 12.4 times.

4. **Average collection period.** A popular variant of the accounts receivable turnover converts it into an average collection period in days. This is done by dividing the accounts receivable turnover into 365 days. The average collection period for Chicago Cereal is shown in Illustration 13A-8.

Illustration 13A-8
Average collection period

Ratio	Formula	Indicates	Chicago Cereal 2011	Chicago Cereal 2010	General Mills 2011	Industry 2011	Page in Textbook
Average collection period	$\dfrac{365 \text{ days}}{\text{Accounts receivable turnover}}$	Liquidity of receivables and collection success	30.7	30.4	29.4	32.6	416

Chicago Cereal's 2011 accounts receivable turnover of 11.9 times is divided into 365 days to obtain approximately 31 days. This means that the average collection period for receivables is about 31 days. Its average collection period is longer than that of General Mills and shorter than that of the industry.

Analysts frequently use the average collection period to assess the effectiveness of a company's credit and collection policies. The general rule is that the collection period should not greatly exceed the credit term period (i.e., the time allowed for payment).

5. **Inventory turnover.** The inventory turnover measures the number of times average inventory was sold during the period. Its purpose is to measure the liquidity of the inventory. A high measure indicates that inventory is being sold and replenished frequently. The inventory turnover is computed by dividing the cost of goods sold by the average inventory during the period. Unless seasonal factors are significant, average inventory can be computed

Illustration 13A-9
Inventory turnover

from the beginning and ending inventory balances. Chicago Cereal's inventory turnover is shown in Illustration 13A-9.

Ratio	Formula	Indicates	Chicago Cereal 2011	Chicago Cereal 2010	General Mills 2011	Industry 2011	Page in Textbook
Inventory turnover	Cost of goods sold / Average inventory	Liquidity of inventory	7.5	7.9	6.5	6.7	300

Chicago Cereal's inventory turnover decreased slightly in 2011. The turnover of 7.5 times is higher than the industry average of 6.7 times and better than General Mills' 6.5 times. Generally, the faster the inventory turnover, the less cash is tied up in inventory and the less the chance of inventory becoming obsolete. Of course, a downside of high inventory turnover is that it sometimes results in lost sales because if a company keeps less inventory on hand, it is more likely to run out of inventory when it is needed.

6. **Days in inventory.** A variant of the inventory turnover is the **days in inventory**, which measures the average number of days inventory is held. The days in inventory for Chicago Cereal is shown in Illustration 13A-10.

Illustration 13A-10
Days in inventory

Ratio	Formula	Indicates	Chicago Cereal 2011	Chicago Cereal 2010	General Mills 2011	Industry 2011	Page in Textbook
Days in inventory	365 days / Inventory turnover	Liquidity of inventory and inventory management	48.7	46.2	56.2	54.5	300

Chicago Cereal's 2011 inventory turnover of 7.5 divided into 365 is approximately 49 days. An average selling time of 49 days is faster than the industry average and faster than that of General Mills. Some of this difference might be explained by differences in product lines across the two companies, although in many ways the types of products of these two companies are quite similar.

Inventory turnovers vary considerably among industries. For example, grocery store chains have a turnover of 10 times and an average selling period of 37 days. In contrast, jewelry stores have an average turnover of 1.3 times and an average selling period of 281 days. Within a company, there may even be significant differences in inventory turnover among different types of products. Thus, in a grocery store the turnover of perishable items such as produce, meats, and dairy products is faster than the turnover of soaps and detergents.

To conclude, nearly all of these liquidity measures suggest that Chicago Cereal's liquidity changed little during 2011. Its liquidity appears acceptable when compared to the industry as a whole and when compared to General Mills.

SOLVENCY RATIOS

Solvency ratios measure the ability of the company to survive over a long period of time. Long-term creditors and stockholders are interested in a company's long-run solvency, particularly its ability to pay interest as it comes due and to repay the face value of debt at maturity. The debt to assets ratio, the times interest earned, and the cash debt coverage provide information about debt-paying ability. In addition, free cash flow provides information about the company's solvency and its ability to pay additional dividends or invest in new projects.

7. **Debt to assets ratio.** The debt to assets ratio measures the percentage of total financing provided by creditors. It is computed by dividing total liabilities (both current and long-term debt) by total assets. This ratio indicates the degree of financial leveraging. It also provides some indication of the company's ability to withstand losses without impairing the interests of its creditors. The higher the percentage of debt to assets, the greater the risk that the company may be unable to meet its maturing obligations. The lower the ratio, the more equity "buffer" is available to creditors if the company becomes insolvent. Thus, from the creditors' point of view, a low ratio of debt to assets is desirable. Chicago Cereal's debt to assets ratio is shown in Illustration 13A-11.

Illustration 13A-11
Debt to assets ratio

Ratio	Formula	Indicates	Chicago Cereal 2011	Chicago Cereal 2010	General Mills 2011	Industry 2011	Page in Textbook
Debt to assets ratio	Total liabilities / Total assets	Percentage of total assets provided by creditors	78%	81%	52%	49%	60

Chicago Cereal's 2011 ratio of 78% means that creditors have provided financing sufficient to cover 78% of the company's total assets. Alternatively, it says that it would have to liquidate 78% of its assets at their book value in order to pay off all of its debts. Its ratio is above the industry average of 49%, as well as that of General Mills. This suggests that it is less solvent than the industry average and General Mills. Chicago Cereal's solvency improved slightly during the year.

The adequacy of this ratio is often judged in light of the company's earnings. Generally, companies with relatively stable earnings, such as public utilities, have higher debt to assets ratios than cyclical companies with widely fluctuating earnings, such as many high-tech companies.

Another ratio with a similar meaning is the **debt to equity ratio**. It shows the relative use of borrowed funds (total liabilities) compared with resources invested by the owners. Because this ratio can be computed in several ways, be careful when making comparisons with it. Debt may be defined to include only the noncurrent portion of liabilities, and intangible assets may be excluded from stockholders' equity (which would equal tangible net worth). If debt and assets are defined as above (all liabilities and all assets), then when the debt to assets ratio equals 50%, the debt to equity ratio is 1:1.

8. **Times interest earned.** The times interest earned (also called interest coverage) indicates the company's ability to meet interest payments as they come due. It is computed by dividing income before interest expense and income taxes by interest expense. Note that this ratio uses income before interest expense and income taxes because this amount represents what is available to cover interest. Chicago Cereal's times interest earned is shown in Illustration 13A-12.

Illustration 13A-12
Times interest earned

Ratio	Formula	Indicates	Chicago Cereal 2011	Chicago Cereal 2010	General Mills 2011	Industry 2011	Page in Textbook
Times interest earned	(Net Income + Interest expense + Tax expense) / Interest expense	Ability to meet interest payments as they come due	5.8	5.8	7.2	19.6	525

For Chicago Cereal, the 2011 interest coverage was 5.8, which indicates that income before interest and taxes was 5.8 times the amount needed for interest expense. This is less than the rate for General Mills, and it is significantly less than the average rate for the industry. The debt to assets ratio decreased for Chicago Cereal during 2011, and its times interest earned held constant.

9. **Cash debt coverage.** The ratio of net cash provided by operating activities to average total liabilities, called the cash debt coverage, is a cash-basis measure of solvency. This ratio indicates a company's ability to repay its liabilities from net cash generated from operating activities without having to liquidate the assets used in its operations. Illustration 13A-13 shows Chicago Cereal's cash debt coverage.

Illustration 13A-13
Cash debt coverage

Ratio	Formula	Indicates	Chicago Cereal 2011	Chicago Cereal 2010	General Mills 2011	Industry 2011	Page in Textbook
Cash debt coverage	Net cash provided by operating activities / Average total liabilities	Long-term debt-paying ability (cash basis)	.17	.17	.13	na	646

An industry average for this measure is not available. Chicago Cereal's .17 is higher than General Mills' .13, and it remained unchanged from 2010. One way of interpreting this ratio is to say that net cash generated from one year of operations would be sufficient to pay off 17% of its total liabilities. If 17% of this year's liabilities were retired each year, it would take approximately 5.9 years to retire all of its debt. It would take General Mills approximately 7.7 years to do so. A general rule of thumb is that a cash debt coverage above .20 is acceptable.

10. **Free cash flow.** One indication of a company's solvency, as well as of its ability to pay dividends or expand operations, is the amount of excess cash it generated after investing in capital expenditures and paying dividends. This amount is referred to as free cash flow. For example, if you generate $100,000 of net cash provided by operating activities but you spend $30,000 on capital expenditures and pay $10,000 in dividends, you have $60,000 ($100,000 − $30,000 − $10,000) to use either to expand operations, pay additional dividends, or pay down debt. Chicago Cereal's free cash flow is shown in Illustration 13A-14.

Illustration 13A-14
Free cash flow

Ratio	Formula	Indicates	Chicago Cereal 2011	Chicago Cereal 2010	General Mills 2011	Industry 2011	Page in Textbook
Free cash flow	Net cash provided by operating activities − Capital expenditures − Cash dividends	Cash available for paying dividends or expanding operations	$556 (in thousands)	$507	$686 (in millions)	na	61

Chicago Cereal's free cash flow increased slightly from 2010 to 2011. During both years, the net cash provided by operating activities was more than enough to allow it to acquire additional productive assets and maintain dividend payments. It could have used the remaining cash to reduce debt if necessary. Given that Chicago Cereal is much smaller than General Mills, we would expect its free cash flow to be substantially smaller, which it is.

PROFITABILITY RATIOS

Profitability ratios measure the income or operating success of a company for a given period of time. A company's income, or the lack of it, affects its ability to obtain debt and equity financing, its liquidity position, and its ability to grow. As a consequence, creditors and investors alike are interested in evaluating profitability. Analysts frequently use profitability as the ultimate test of management's operating effectiveness.

Throughout this textbook, we have introduced numerous measures of profitability. The relationships among measures of profitability are very important. Understanding them can help management determine where to focus its efforts to improve profitability. Illustration 13A-15 diagrams these relationships. Our discussion of Chicago Cereal's profitability is structured around this diagram.

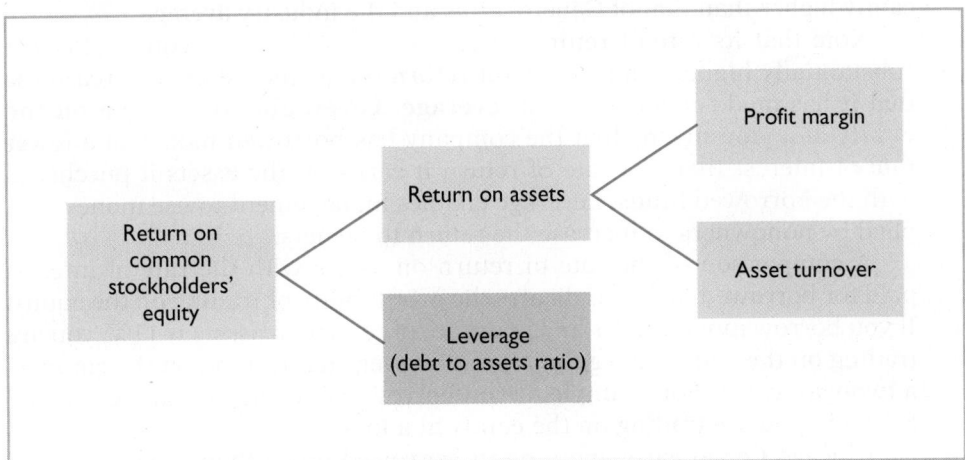

Illustration 13A-15
Relationships among profitability measures

11. **Return on common stockholders' equity (ROE).** A widely used measure of profitability from the common stockholder's viewpoint is the **return on common stockholders' equity (ROE).** This ratio shows how many dollars of net income the company earned for each dollar invested by the owners. It is computed by dividing net income minus any preferred dividends—that is, income available to common stockholders—by average common stockholders' equity. The return on common stockholders' equity for Chicago Cereal is shown in Illustration 13A-16.

Illustration 13A-16 Return on common stockholders' equity

Ratio	Formula	Indicates	Chicago Cereal 2011	Chicago Cereal 2010	General Mills 2011	Industry 2011	Page in Textbook
Return on common stockholders' equity	$\dfrac{\text{Net Income} - \text{Preferred dividends}}{\text{Average common stockholders' equity}}$	Profitability of common stockholders' investment	48%	46%	24%	24%	595

Chicago Cereal's 2011 rate of return on common stockholders' equity is unusually high at 48%. The industry average is 24% and General Mills' return is 24%. In the subsequent sections, we investigate the causes of this high return.

12. **Return on assets.** The return on common stockholders' equity is affected by two factors: the **return on assets** and the degree of leverage. The return on assets measures the overall profitability of assets in terms of the income

earned on each dollar invested in assets. It is computed by dividing net income by average total assets. Chicago Cereal's return on assets is shown in Illustration 13A-17.

Illustration 13A-17
Return on assets

Ratio	Formula	Indicates	Chicago Cereal 2011	Chicago Cereal 2010	General Mills 2011	Industry 2011	Page in Textbook
Return on assets	Net income / Average total assets	Overall profitability of assets	10.0%	9.4%	7.4%	8.7%	464

Chicago Cereal had a 10.0% return on assets in 2011. This rate is significantly higher than that of General Mills and the industry average.

Note that its rate of return on common stockholders' equity (48%) is substantially higher than its rate of return on assets (10%). The reason is that it has made effective use of **leverage**. Leveraging or trading on the equity at a gain means that the company has borrowed money at a lower rate of interest than the rate of return it earns on the assets it purchased with the borrowed funds. Leverage enables management to use money supplied by nonowners to increase the return to owners.

A comparison of the rate of return on assets with the rate of interest paid for borrowed money indicates the profitability of trading on the equity. If you borrow money at 8% and your rate of return on assets is 11%, you are trading on the equity at a gain. Note, however, that trading on the equity is a two-way street: For example, if you borrow money at 11% and earn only 8% on it, you are trading on the equity at a loss.

Chicago Cereal earns more on its borrowed funds than it has to pay in interest. Thus, the return to stockholders exceeds the return on assets because of the positive benefit of leverage. Recall from our earlier discussion that Chicago Cereal's percentage of debt financing, as measured by the ratio of debt to assets (or debt to equity), was higher than General Mills' and the industry average. It appears that Chicago Cereal's high return on common stockholders' equity is due in part to its use of leverage.

13. **Profit margin.** The return on assets is affected by two factors, the first of which is the profit margin. The profit margin, or rate of return on sales, is a measure of the percentage of each dollar of sales that results in net income. It is computed by dividing net income by net sales for the period. Chicago Cereal's profit margin is shown in Illustration 13A-18.

Illustration 13A-18
Profit margin

Ratio	Formula	Indicates	Chicago Cereal 2011	Chicago Cereal 2010	General Mills 2011	Industry 2011	Page in Textbook
Profit margin	Net income / Net sales	Net income generated by each dollar of sales	9.4%	9.2%	9.1%	8.8%	250

Chicago Cereal experienced a slight increase in its profit margin from 2010 to 2011 of 9.2% to 9.4%. Its profit margin was higher than the industry average and that of General Mills.

High-volume (high inventory turnover) businesses such as grocery stores and pharmacy chains generally have low profit margins. Low-volume businesses such as jewelry stores and airplane manufacturers have high profit margins.

14. **Asset turnover.** The other factor that affects the return on assets is the asset turnover. The **asset turnover** measures how efficiently a company uses its assets to generate sales. It is determined by dividing net sales by average total assets for the period. The resulting number shows the dollars of sales produced by each dollar invested in assets. Illustration 13A-19 shows the asset turnover for Chicago Cereal.

Illustration 13A-19
Asset turnover

Ratio	Formula	Indicates	Chicago Cereal 2011	Chicago Cereal 2010	General Mills 2011	Industry 2011	Page in Textbook
Asset turnover	Net sales / Average total assets	How efficiently assets are used to generate sales	1.07	1.02	.80	1.00	465

The asset turnover shows that in 2011, Chicago Cereal generated sales of $1.07 for each dollar it had invested in assets. The ratio rose from 2010 to 2011. Its asset turnover is above the industry average and that of General Mills.

Asset turnover varies considerably among industries. The average asset turnover for utility companies is .45, for example, while the grocery store industry has an average asset turnover of 3.49.

In summary, Chicago Cereal's return on assets increased from 9.4% in 2010 to 10.0% in 2011. Underlying this increase was an increased profitability on each dollar of sales (as measured by the profit margin) and a rise in the sales-generating efficiency of its assets (as measured by the asset turnover). We can analyze the combined effects of profit margin and asset turnover on return on assets for Chicago Cereal as shown in Illustration 13A-20.

Illustration 13A-20
Composition of return on assets

Ratios:	Profit Margin	×	Asset Turnover	=	Return on Assets
	Net Income / Net Sales	×	Net Sales / Average Total Assets	=	Net Income / Average Total Assets
Chicago Cereal					
2011	9.4%	×	1.07 times	=	10.1%*
2010	9.2%	×	1.02 times	=	9.4%

*Difference from value on page 720 due to rounding.

15. **Gross profit rate.** One factor that strongly influences the profit margin is the gross profit rate. The **gross profit rate** is determined by dividing gross profit (net sales less cost of goods sold) by net sales. This rate indicates a company's ability to maintain an adequate selling price above its cost of goods sold.

As an industry becomes more competitive, this ratio declines. For example, in the early years of the personal computer industry, gross profit rates were quite high. Today, because of increased competition and a belief that most brands of personal computers are similar in quality, gross profit rates

Illustration 13A-21
Gross profit rate

have become thin. Analysts should closely monitor gross profit rates over time. Illustration 13A-21 shows Chicago Cereal's gross profit rate.

Ratio	Formula	Indicates	Chicago Cereal 2011	Chicago Cereal 2010	General Mills 2011	Industry 2011	Page in Textbook
Gross profit rate	Gross profit / Net sales	Margin between selling price and cost of goods sold	44%	44%	36%	12%	248

Chicago Cereal's gross profit rate remained constant from 2010 to 2011.

16. **Earnings per share (EPS).** Stockholders usually think in terms of the number of shares they own or plan to buy or sell. Expressing net income earned on a per share basis provides a useful perspective for determining profitability. **Earnings per share** is a measure of the net income earned on each share of common stock. It is computed by dividing net income by the average number of common shares outstanding during the year.

The terms "net income per share" or "earnings per share" refer to the amount of net income applicable to each share of **common stock**. Therefore, when we compute earnings per share, if there are preferred dividends declared for the period, we must deduct them from net income to arrive at income available to the common stockholders. Chicago Cereal's earnings per share is shown in Illustration 13A-22.

Illustration 13A-22
Earnings per share

Ratio	Formula	Indicates	Chicago Cereal 2011	Chicago Cereal 2010	General Mills 2011	Industry 2011	Page in Textbook
Earnings per share (EPS)	(Net income − Preferred dividends) / Average common shares outstanding	Net income earned on each share of common stock	$2.63	$2.40	$2.35	na	55

Note that no industry average is presented in Illustration 13A-22. Industry data for earnings per share are not reported, and in fact the Chicago Cereal and General Mills ratios should not be compared. Such comparisons are not meaningful because of the wide variations in the number of shares of outstanding stock among companies. Chicago Cereal's earnings per share increased 23 cents per share in 2011. This represents a 9.6% increase from the 2010 EPS of $2.40.

17. **Price-earnings ratio.** The **price-earnings ratio** is an oft-quoted statistic that measures the ratio of the market price of each share of common stock to the earnings per share. The price-earnings (P-E) ratio reflects investors' assessments of a company's future earnings. It is computed by dividing the market price per share of the stock by earnings per share. Chicago Cereal's price-earnings ratio is shown in Illustration 13A-23.

Illustration 13A-23
Price-earnings ratio

Ratio	Formula	Indicates	Chicago Cereal 2011	Chicago Cereal 2010	General Mills 2011	Industry 2011	Page in Textbook
Price-earnings ratio	Stock price per share / Earnings per share	Relationship between market price per share and earnings per share	20.1	20.9	16.3	22.8	707

At the end of 2011 and 2010, the market price of Chicago Cereal's stock was $52.92 and $50.06, respectively.

In 2011, each share of Chicago Cereal's stock sold for 20.1 times the amount that was earned on each share. Chicago Cereal's price-earnings ratio is higher than General Mills' ratio of 16.3 and lower than the industry average of 22.8 times. Its higher P-E ratio suggests that the market is more optimistic about Chicago Cereal than about General Mills. However, it might also signal that Chicago Cereal's stock is overpriced. That is a matter for the analyst to determine.

18. **Payout ratio.** The payout ratio measures the percentage of earnings distributed in the form of cash dividends. It is computed by dividing cash dividends declared on common stock by net income. Companies that have high growth rates are characterized by low payout ratios because they reinvest most of their net income in the business. The payout ratio for Chicago Cereal is shown in Illustration 13A-24.

Illustration 13A-24
Payout ratio

Ratio	Formula	Indicates	Chicago Cereal 2011	Chicago Cereal 2010	General Mills 2011	Industry 2011	Page in Textbook
Payout ratio	Cash dividends declared on common stock / Net income	Percentage of earnings distributed in the form of cash dividends	43%	45%	50%	37%	594

The 2011 and 2010 payout ratios for Chicago Cereal are slightly lower than that of General Mills (50%) but higher than the industry average (37%).

Management has some control over the amount of dividends paid each year, and companies are generally reluctant to reduce a dividend below the amount paid in a previous year. Therefore, the payout ratio will actually increase if a company's net income declines but the company keeps its total dividend payment the same. Of course, unless the company returns to its previous level of profitability, maintaining this higher dividend payout ratio is probably not possible over the long run.

Before drawing any conclusions regarding Chicago Cereal's dividend payout ratio, we should calculate this ratio over a longer period of time to evaluate any trends and also try to find out whether management's philosophy regarding dividends has changed recently. The "Selected Financial Data" section of Chicago Cereal's Management Discussion and Analysis shows that over a 5-year period, earnings per share rose 45%, while dividends per share grew only 19%.

In terms of the types of financial information available and the ratios used by various industries, what can be practically covered in this textbook gives you only the "Titanic approach." That is, you are seeing only the tip of the iceberg compared to the vast databases and types of ratio analysis that are available on computers. The availability of information is not a problem. The real trick is to be discriminating enough to perform relevant analysis and select pertinent comparative data.

Summary of Learning Objective for Appendix 13A

8 Evaluate a company comprehensively using ratio analysis. To evaluate a company, ratios (liquidity, solvency, and profitability) provide clues to underlying conditions, but intracompany, intercompany, and industry average comparisons are also needed.

Glossary

Accounts receivable turnover *(p. 715)* A measure of the liquidity of receivables; computed as net credit sales divided by average net accounts receivable.

Asset turnover *(p. 721)* A measure of how efficiently a company uses its assets to generate sales; computed as net sales divided by average total assets.

Available-for-sale securities *(p. 695)* Securities that are held with the intent of selling them sometime in the future.

Average collection period *(p. 715)* The average number of days that receivables are outstanding; calculated as accounts receivable turnover divided into 365 days.

Cash debt coverage *(p. 718)* A cash-basis measure used to evaluate solvency, computed as net cash provided by operating activities divided by average total liabilities.

Change in accounting principle *(p. 694)* Use of an accounting principle in the current year different from the one used in the preceding year.

Comprehensive income *(p. 695)* A measure of income that includes all changes in stockholders' equity during a period except those resulting from investments by stockholders and distributions to stockholders.

Current cash debt coverage *(p. 714)* A cash-basis measure of liquidity; computed as net cash provided by operating activities divided by average current liabilities.

Current ratio *(p. 714)* A measure used to evaluate a company's liquidity and short-term debt-paying ability; calculated as current assets divided by current liabilities.

Days in inventory *(p. 716)* A measure of the average number of days inventory is held; computed as inventory turnover divided into 365 days.

Debt to assets ratio *(p. 717)* A measure of the percentage of total financing provided by creditors; computed as total liabilities divided by total assets.

Discontinued operations *(p. 691)* The disposal of a significant component of a business.

Earnings per share *(p. 722)* The net income earned by each share of common stock; computed as net income less preferred dividends divided by the average common shares outstanding.

Extraordinary items *(p. 692)* Events and transactions that meet two conditions: (1) unusual in nature and (2) infrequent in occurrence.

Free cash flow *(p. 718)* A measure of solvency. Cash remaining from operating activities after adjusting for capital expenditures and dividends paid.

Gross profit rate *(p. 721)* Gross profit expressed as a percentage of sales; computed as gross profit divided by net sales.

Horizontal analysis *(p. 698)* A technique for evaluating a series of financial statement data over a period of time to determine the increase (decrease) that has taken place, expressed as either an amount or a percentage.

Inventory turnover *(p. 715)* A measure of the liquidity of inventory. Measures the number of times average inventory was sold during the period; computed as cost of goods sold divided by average inventory.

Leveraging *(p. 720)* Borrowing money at a lower rate of interest than can be earned by using the borrowed money; also referred to as *trading on the equity*.

Liquidity ratios *(p. 704)* Measures of the short-term ability of the company to pay its maturing obligations and to meet unexpected needs for cash.

Payout ratio *(p. 723)* A measure of the percentage of earnings distributed in the form of cash dividends; calculated as cash dividends declared on common stock divided by net income.

Price-earnings (P-E) ratio *(pp. 707, 722)* A comparison of the market price of each share of common stock to the earnings per share; computed as the market price of the stock divided by earnings per share.

Profitability ratios *(p. 705)* Measures of the income or operating success of a company for a given period of time.

Profit margin *(p. 720)* A measure of the net income generated by each dollar of sales; computed as net income divided by net sales.

Pro forma income *(p. 706)* A measure of income that usually excludes items that a company thinks are unusual or non-recurring.

Quality of earnings *(p. 706)* Indicates the level of full and transparent information that is provided to users of the financial statements.

Return on assets *(p. 719)* A profitability measure that indicates the amount of net income generated by each dollar of assets; calculated as net income divided by average total assets.

Return on common stockholders' equity (ROE) *(p. 719)* A measure of the dollars of net income earned for each dollar invested by the owners; computed as income available to common stockholders divided by average common stockholders' equity.

Solvency ratios *(p. 704)* Measures of the ability of a company to survive over a long period of time, particularly to pay interest as it comes due and to repay the balance of debt at its maturity.

Sustainable income *(p. 690)* The most likely level of income to be obtained in the future; calculated as net income adjusted for irregular items.

Times interest earned *(p. 717)* A measure of a company's solvency and ability to meet interest payments as they come due; calculated as income before interest expense and income taxes divided by interest expense.

Trading on the equity *(p. 720)* See *leveraging*.

Trading securities *(p. 695)* Securities bought and held primarily for sale in the near term to generate income on short-term price differences.

Vertical analysis *(p. 700)* A technique for evaluating financial statement data that expresses each item in a financial statement as a percentage of a base amount.

Comprehensive Do it!

The events and transactions of Dever Corporation for the year ending December 31, 2014, resulted in these data.

Cost of goods sold	$2,600,000
Net sales	4,400,000
Other expenses and losses	9,600
Other revenues and gains	5,600
Selling and administrative expenses	1,100,000
Gain from discontinued division	570,000
Loss from tornado disaster (extraordinary loss)	600,000

Analysis reveals the following.

1. All items are before the applicable income tax rate of 30%.
2. The plastics division was sold on July 1.

Instructions

Prepare an income statement for the year.

Solution to Comprehensive Do it!

DEVER CORPORATION
Income Statement
For the Year Ended December 31, 2014

Net sales		$4,400,000
Cost of goods sold		2,600,000
Gross profit		1,800,000
Selling and administrative expenses		1,100,000
Income from operations		700,000
Other revenues and gains	$ 5,600	
Other expenses and losses	(9,600)	(4,000)
Income before income taxes		696,000
Income tax expense ($696,000 × 30%)		208,800
Income before irregular items		487,200
Discontinued operations: Gain from discontinued division, net of taxes of $171,000 ($570,000 × 30%)		399,000
Extraordinary item: Tornado loss, net of income tax savings $180,000 ($600,000 × 30%)		(420,000)
Net income		$ 466,200

Action Plan

- Remember that material items not typical of operations are reported in separate sections net of taxes.
- Associate income taxes with the item that affects the taxes.
- On a corporation income statement, report income tax expense when there is income before income tax.

 Self-Test, Brief Exercises, Exercises, Problem Set A, and many more resources are available for practice in WileyPLUS.

Self-Test Questions

Answers are on page 748.

All of the Self-Test Questions in this chapter employ decision tools.

(LO 2) **1.** In reporting discontinued operations, the income statement should show in a special section:

(a) gains on the disposal of the discontinued component.
(b) losses on the disposal of the discontinued component.
(c) Neither (a) nor (b).
(d) Both (a) and (b).

(LO 2) **2.** Cool Stools Corporation has income before taxes of $400,000 and an extraordinary loss of $100,000. If the income tax rate is 25% on all items, the income statement should show income before irregular items and an extraordinary loss, respectively, of
(a) $325,000 and $100,000.
(b) $325,000 and $75,000.
(c) $300,000 and $100,000.
(d) $300,000 and $75,000.

(LO 3) **3.** Which of the following would be considered an "Other comprehensive income" item?
(a) Gain on disposal of discontinued operations.
(b) Unrealized loss on available-for-sale securities.
(c) Extraordinary loss related to flood.
(d) Net income.

(LO 4) **4.** In horizontal analysis, each item is expressed as a percentage of the:
(a) net income amount.
(b) stockholders' equity amount.
(c) total assets amount.
(d) base-year amount.

(LO 4) **5.** Adams Corporation reported net sales of $300,000, $330,000, and $360,000 in the years 2012, 2013, and 2014, respectively. If 2012 is the base year, what percentage do 2014 sales represent of the base?
(a) 77%.   (c) 120%.
(b) 108%.   (d) 130%.

(LO 5) **6.** The following schedule is a display of what type of analysis?

	Amount	Percent
Current assets	$200,000	25%
Property, plant, and equipment	600,000	75%
Total assets	$800,000	

(a) Horizontal analysis.   (c) Vertical analysis.
(b) Differential analysis.   (d) Ratio analysis.

(LO 5) **7.** In vertical analysis, the base amount for depreciation expense is generally:
(a) net sales.
(b) depreciation expense in a previous year.
(c) gross profit.
(d) fixed assets.

(LO 6) **8.** Which measure is an evaluation of a company's ability to pay current liabilities?
(a) Current cash debt coverage.
(b) Current ratio.
(c) Both (a) and (b).
(d) None of the above.

(LO 6) **9.** Which measure is useful in evaluating the efficiency in managing inventories?
(a) Inventory turnover.
(b) Days in inventory.
(c) Both (a) and (b).
(d) None of the above.

(LO 6) **10.** Which of these is **not** a liquidity ratio?
(a) Current ratio.
(b) Asset turnover.

(c) Inventory turnover.
(d) Accounts receivable turnover.

(LO 6) **11.** Plano Corporation reported net income $24,000; net sales $400,000; and average assets $600,000 for 2014. What is the 2014 profit margin?
(a) 6%.   (c) 40%.
(b) 12%.   (d) 200%.

Use the following financial statement information as of the end of each year to answer Self-Test Questions 12–16.

	2014	2013
Inventory	$ 54,000	$ 48,000
Current assets	81,000	106,000
Total assets	382,000	326,000
Current liabilities	27,000	36,000
Total liabilities	102,000	88,000
Common stockholders' equity	240,000	198,000
Net sales	784,000	697,000
Cost of goods sold	306,000	277,000
Net income	134,000	90,000
Tax expense	22,000	18,000
Interest expense	12,000	12,000
Dividends paid to preferred stockholders	4,000	4,000
Dividends paid to common stockholders	15,000	10,000

(LO 6) **12.** Compute the days in inventory for 2014.
(a) 64.4 days.   (c) 6 days.
(b) 60.8 days.   (d) 24 days.

(LO 6) **13.** Compute the current ratio for 2014.
(a) 1.26:1.   (c) 0.80:1.
(b) 3.0:1.   (d) 3.75:1.

(LO 6) **14.** Compute the profit margin for 2014.
(a) 17.1%.   (c) 37.9%.
(b) 18.1%.   (d) 5.9%.

(LO 6) **15.** Compute the return on common stockholders' equity for 2014.
(a) 54.2%.   (c) 61.2%.
(b) 52.5%.   (d) 59.4%.

(LO 6) **16.** Compute the times interest earned for 2014.
(a) 11.2 times.   (c) 14.0 times.
(b) 65.3 times.   (d) 13.0 times.

(LO 7) **17.** Which situation below might indicate a company has a low quality of earnings?
(a) The same accounting principles are used each year.
(b) Revenue is recognized when the performance obligation is satisfied.
(c) Maintenance costs are capitalized and then depreciated.
(d) The company's P-E ratio is high relative to competitors.

Go to the book's companion website, **www.wiley.com/college/kimmel**, to access additional Self-Test Questions.

Questions

All of the Questions in this chapter employ decision tools.

1. Explain sustainable income. What relationship does this concept have to the treatment of irregular items on the income statement?

2. Indicate which of the following items would be reported as an extraordinary item on Pitchford Corporation's income statement.
   (a) Loss from damages caused by a volcano eruption in Iona.
   (b) Loss from the sale of short-term investments.
   (c) Loss attributable to a labor strike.
   (d) Loss of inventory from flood damage because a warehouse is located on a flood plain that floods every 5 to 10 years.
   (e) Loss on the write-down of outdated inventory.
   (f) Loss from a foreign government's expropriation of a production facility.
   (g) Loss from damage to a warehouse in southern California from a minor earthquake.

3. Garvey Inc. reported 2013 earnings per share of $3.26 and had no extraordinary items. In 2014, earnings per share on income before extraordinary items was $2.99, and earnings per share on net income was $3.49. Do you consider this trend to be favorable? Why or why not?

4. Hosemer Inc. has been in operation for 3 years and uses the FIFO method of pricing inventory. During the fourth year, Hosemer changes to the average-cost method for all its inventory. How will Hosemer report this change?

5. What amount did Tootsie Roll Industries report as "Other comprehensive earnings" in 2011? By what percentage did Tootsie Roll's "Comprehensive earnings" differ from its "Net earnings"?

6. (a) Jennifer Gorman believes that the analysis of financial statements is directed at two characteristics of a company: liquidity and profitability. Is Jennifer correct? Explain.
   (b) Are short-term creditors, long-term creditors, and stockholders interested in primarily the same characteristics of a company? Explain.

7. (a) Distinguish among the following bases of comparison: intracompany, intercompany and industry averages.
   (b) Give the principal value of using each of the three bases of comparison.

8. Two popular methods of financial statement analysis are horizontal analysis and vertical analysis. Explain the difference between these two methods.

9. (a) If Neer Company had net income of $300,000 in 2013 and it experienced a 24.5% increase in net income for 2014, what is its net income for 2014?
   (b) If 6 cents of every dollar of Neer's revenue is net income in 2013, what is the dollar amount of 2013 revenue?

10. Name the major ratios useful in assessing (a) liquidity and (b) solvency.

11. Tom Vernon is puzzled. His company had a profit margin of 10% in 2014. He feels that this is an indication that the company is doing well. Andrea Travis, his accountant, says that more information is needed to determine the company's financial well-being. Who is correct? Why?

12. What does each type of ratio measure?
    (a) Liquidity ratios.
    (b) Solvency ratios.
    (c) Profitability ratios.

13. What is the difference between the current ratio and working capital?

14. Quick Mart, a retail store, has an accounts receivable turnover of 4.5 times. The industry average is 12.5 times. Does Quick Mart have a collection problem with its receivables?

15. Which ratios should be used to help answer each of these questions?
    (a) How efficient is a company in using its assets to produce sales?
    (b) How near to sale is the inventory on hand?
    (c) How many dollars of net income were earned for each dollar invested by the owners?
    (d) How able is a company to meet interest charges as they fall due?

16. At year-end, the price-earnings ratio of General Motors was 11.3, and the price-earnings ratio of Microsoft was 28.14. Which company did the stock market favor? Explain.

17. What is the formula for computing the payout ratio? Do you expect this ratio to be high or low for a growth company?

18. Holding all other factors constant, indicate whether each of the following changes generally signals good or bad news about a company.
    (a) Increase in profit margin.
    (b) Decrease in inventory turnover.
    (c) Increase in current ratio.
    (d) Decrease in earnings per share.
    (e) Increase in price-earnings ratio.
    (f) Increase in debt to assets ratio.
    (g) Decrease in times interest earned.

19. The return on assets for Espino Corporation is 7.6%. During the same year, Espino's return on common stockholders' equity is 12.8%. What is the explanation for the difference in the two rates?

20. Which two ratios do you think should be of greatest interest in each of the following cases?
    (a) A pension fund considering the purchase of 20-year bonds.
    (b) A bank contemplating a short-term loan.
    (c) A common stockholder.

21. Kono Inc. has net income of $200,000, average shares of common stock outstanding of 40,000,

and preferred dividends for the period of $20,000. What is Kono's earnings per share of common stock? Tim Frye, the president of Kono, believes that the computed EPS of the company is high. Comment.

22. Identify and explain factors that affect quality of earnings.

23. Explain how the choice of one of the following accounting methods over the other raises or lowers a

company's net income during a period of continuing inflation.

(a) Use of FIFO instead of LIFO for inventory costing.

(b) Use of a 6-year life for machinery instead of a 9-year life.

(c) Use of straight-line depreciation instead of declining-balance depreciation.

Brief Exercises

All of the Brief Exercises in this chapter employ decision tools.

Prepare a discontinued operations section of an income statement.
(LO 2), AP

BE13-1 On June 30, Reyes Corporation discontinued its operations in Mexico. On September 1, Reyes disposed of the Mexico facility at a pretax loss of $640,000. The applicable tax rate is 25%. Show the discontinued operations section of Reyes's income statement.

Prepare a corrected income statement with an extraordinary item.
(LO 2), AP

BE13-2 An inexperienced accountant for Fielder Corporation showed the following in Fielder's 2014 income statement: Income before income taxes $300,000; Income tax expense $72,000; Extraordinary loss from flood (before taxes) $80,000; and Net income $168,000. The extraordinary loss and taxable income are both subject to a 30% tax rate. Prepare a corrected income statement beginning with "Income before income taxes."

Indicate how a change in accounting principle is reported.
(LO 2), C

BE13-3 On January 1, 2014, Jenner Inc. changed from the LIFO method of inventory pricing to the FIFO method. Explain how this change in accounting principle should be treated in the company's financial statements.

Prepare horizontal analysis.
(LO 4), AP

BE13-4 Using these data from the comparative balance sheet of Ramirez Company, perform horizontal analysis.

	December 31, 2014	December 31, 2013
Accounts receivable	$ 460,000	$ 400,000
Inventory	780,000	650,000
Total assets	3,164,000	2,800,000

Prepare vertical analysis.
(LO 5), AP

BE13-5 Using the data presented in BE13-4 for Ramirez Company, perform vertical analysis.

Calculate percentage of change.
(LO 4), AP

BE13-6 Net income was $500,000 in 2012, $485,000 in 2013, and $518,400 in 2014. What is the percentage of change from (a) 2012 to 2013, and (b) from 2013 to 2014? Is the change an increase or a decrease?

Calculate net income.
(LO 4), AP

BE13-7 If Francona Company had net income of $382,800 in 2014 and it experienced a 16% increase in net income over 2013, what was its 2013 net income?

Analyze change in net income.
(LO 5), AP

BE13-8 Vertical analysis (common-size) percentages for Capuano Company's sales revenue, cost of goods sold, and expenses are listed here.

Vertical Analysis	**2014**	**2013**	**2012**
Sales revenue	100.0%	100.0%	100.0%
Cost of goods sold	60.5	62.9	64.8
Expenses	26.0	26.6	27.5

Did Capuano's net income as a percent of sales increase, decrease, or remain unchanged over the 3-year period? Provide numerical support for your answer.

Analyze change in net income.
(LO 4), AP

BE13-9 Horizontal analysis (trend analysis) percentages for Roswell Company's sales revenue, cost of goods sold, and expenses are listed here.

Horizontal Analysis	**2014**	**2013**	**2012**
Sales revenue	96.2%	104.8%	100.0%
Cost of goods sold	101.0	98.0	100.0
Expenses	105.6	95.4	100.0

Explain whether Roswell's net income increased, decreased, or remained unchanged over the 3-year period.

BE13-10 Suppose these selected condensed data are taken from recent balance sheets of Bob Evans Farms (in thousands).

Calculate current ratio.
(LO 6), **AP**

	2014	2013
Cash	$ 13,606	$ 7,669
Accounts receivable	23,045	19,951
Inventory	31,087	31,345
Other current assets	12,522	11,909
Total current assets	$ 80,260	$ 70,874
Total current liabilities	$245,805	$326,203

Compute the current ratio for each year and comment on your results.

BE13-11 The following data are taken from the financial statements of Filbert Company.

Evaluate collection of accounts receivable.
(LO 6), **AN**

	2014	2013
Accounts receivable (net), end of year	$ 550,000	$ 540,000
Net sales on account	4,300,000	4,000,000
Terms for all sales are 1/10, n/45		

Compute for each year (a) the accounts receivable turnover and (b) the average collection period. What conclusions about the management of accounts receivable can be drawn from these data? At the end of 2012, accounts receivable was $520,000.

BE13-12 The following data were taken from the income statements of Imhoff Company.

Evaluate management of inventory.
(LO 6), **AN**

	2014	2013
Sales revenue	$6,420,000	$6,240,000
Beginning inventory	960,000	840,000
Purchases	4,840,000	4,661,000
Ending inventory	1,020,000	960,000

Compute for each year (a) the inventory turnover and (b) days in inventory. What conclusions concerning the management of the inventory can be drawn from these data?

BE13-13 Staples, Inc. is one of the largest suppliers of office products in the United States. Suppose it had net income of $738.7 million and sales of $24,275.5 million in 2014. Its total assets were $13,073.1 million at the beginning of the year and $13,717.3 million at the end of the year. What is Staples, Inc.'s (a) asset turnover and (b) profit margin? (Round to two decimals.) Provide a brief interpretation of your results.

Calculate profitability ratios.
(LO 6), **AN**

BE13-14 Voorhees Company has stockholders' equity of $400,000 and net income of $72,000. It has a payout ratio of 18% and a return on assets of 20%. How much did Voorhees pay in cash dividends, and what were its average total assets?

Calculate profitability ratios.
(LO 6), **AN**

BE13-15 Selected data taken from a recent year's financial statements of trading card company Topps Company, Inc. are as follows (in millions).

Calculate cash-basis liquidity and solvency ratios.
(LO 6), **AN**

Net sales	$326.7
Current liabilities, beginning of year	41.1
Current liabilities, end of year	62.4
Net cash provided by operating activities	10.4
Total liabilities, beginning of year	65.2
Total liabilities, end of year	73.2
Capital expenditures	3.7
Cash dividends	6.2

Compute these ratios: (a) current cash debt coverage, (b) cash debt coverage, and (c) free cash flow. Provide a brief interpretation of your results.

Do it! Review

Prepare income statement, including irregular items.
(LO 2), **AP**

Do it! 13-1   In its draft 2014 income statement, Sunflower Corporation reports income before income taxes $500,000, extraordinary loss due to earthquake $180,000, income taxes $200,000 (not including irregular items), and loss on disposal of discontinued music division $24,000. The income tax rate is 40%. Prepare a correct income statement, beginning with income before income taxes.

Prepare horizontal analysis.
(LO 4), **AP**

Do it! 13-2   Summary financial information for Paragon Company is as follows.

	Dec. 31, 2014	Dec. 31, 2013
Current assets	$ 200,000	$ 220,000
Plant assets	1,040,000	780,000
Total assets	$1,240,000	$1,000,000

Compute the amount and percentage changes in 2014 using horizontal analysis, assuming 2013 is the base year.

Identify types of ratio.
(LO 6), **C**

Do it! 13-3   State whether each of the following is an indicator of a company's liquidity, solvency, or profitability.
(a) Price-earnings ratio.
(b) Inventory turnover.
(c) Debt to assets ratio.
(d) Times interest earned.
(e) Return on common stockholders' equity.
(f) Current cash debt coverage.

Match terms relating to quality of earnings and financial statement analysis.
(LO 2, 3, 4, 5, 6, 7), **K**

Do it! 13-4   Match each of the following terms with the phrase that best describes it.

Quality of earnings	Pro forma income
Current ratio	Discontinued operations
Horizontal analysis	Comprehensive income

1. A measure used to evaluate a company's liquidity.
2. Usually excludes items that a company thinks are unusual or non-recurring.
3. Indicates the level of full and transparent information provided to users of the financial statements.
4. The disposal of a significant component of a business.
5. Determines increases or decreases in a series of financial statement data.
6. Includes all changes in stockholders' equity during a period except those resulting from investments by stockholders and distributions to stockholders.

Exercises

⊙━━━━━C All of the Exercises in this chapter employ decision tools.

Prepare irregular items portion of an income statement.
(LO 2), **AP**

E13-1   Utech Company has income before irregular items of $310,000 for the year ended December 31, 2014. It also has the following items (before considering income taxes): (1) an extraordinary fire loss of $60,000 and (2) a gain of $30,000 from the disposal of a division. Assume all items are subject to income taxes at a 30% tax rate.

Instructions
Prepare Utech Company's income statement for 2014, beginning with "Income before irregular items."

Evaluate the effects of unusual or irregular items.
(LO 1, 2, 6), **C**

E13-2   The *Wall Street Journal* routinely publishes summaries of corporate quarterly and annual earnings reports in a feature called the "Earnings Digest." A typical "digest" report takes the following form.

ENERGY ENTERPRISES (A)

	Quarter ending July 31	
	2014	**2013**
Sales revenue	$2,049,000,000	$1,754,000,000
Net income	97,000,000	(a) 68,750,000
EPS: Net income	1.28	0.93

	12 months ending July 31	
	2014	**2013**
Sales revenue	$5,578,500,000	$5,065,300,000
Extraordinary item	(b) 1,900,000	
Net income	102,700,000	(a) 33,250,000
EPS: Net income	1.36	0.48

(a) Includes a net charge of $26,000,000 from loss on the sale of electrical equipment
(b) Extraordinary gain on Middle East property expropriation

The letter in parentheses following the company name indicates the exchange on which Energy Enterprises' stock is traded—in this case, the American Stock Exchange.

Instructions
Answer the following questions.
(a) How was the loss on the electrical equipment reported on the income statement? Was it reported in the fourth quarter of 2013? How can you tell?
(b) Why did the *Wall Street Journal* list the extraordinary item separately?
(c) What is the extraordinary item? Was it included in income for the fourth quarter? How can you tell?
(d) Did Energy Enterprises have an operating loss in any quarter of 2013? Of 2014? How do you know?
(e) Approximately how many shares of stock were outstanding in 2014? Did the number of outstanding shares change from July 31, 2013 to July 31, 2014?
(f) As an investor, what numbers should you use to determine Energy Enterprises' profit margin? Calculate the profit margin for 2013 and 2014 that you consider most useful. Explain your decision.

E13-3 Here is financial information for Spangles Inc.

Prepare horizontal analysis.
(LO 4), **AP**

	December 31, 2014	**December 31, 2013**
Current assets	$106,000	$ 90,000
Plant assets (net)	400,000	350,000
Current liabilities	99,000	65,000
Long-term liabilities	122,000	90,000
Common stock, $1 par	130,000	115,000
Retained earnings	155,000	170,000

Instructions
Prepare a schedule showing a horizontal analysis for 2014, using 2013 as the base year.

E13-4 Operating data for Jacobs Corporation are presented below.

Prepare vertical analysis.
(LO 5), **AP**

	2014	**2013**
Sales revenue	$800,000	$600,000
Cost of goods sold	520,000	408,000
Selling expenses	120,000	72,000
Administrative expenses	60,000	48,000
Income tax expense	30,000	24,000
Net income	70,000	48,000

Instructions
Prepare a schedule showing a vertical analysis for 2014 and 2013.

Prepare horizontal and vertical analyses.
(LO 4, 5), **AP**

E13-5 Suppose the comparative balance sheets of Nike, Inc. are presented here.

NIKE, INC.
Comparative Balance Sheets
May 31
($ in millions)

Assets	2014	2013
Current assets	$ 9,734	$ 8,839
Property, plant, and equipment (net)	1,958	1,891
Other assets	1,558	1,713
Total assets	$13,250	$12,443

Liabilities and Stockholders' Equity		
Current liabilities	$ 3,277	$ 3,322
Long-term liabilities	1,280	1,296
Stockholders' equity	8,693	7,825
Total liabilities and stockholders' equity	$13,250	$12,443

Instructions
(a) Prepare a horizontal analysis of the balance sheet data for Nike, using 2013 as a base. (Show the amount of increase or decrease as well.)
(b) Prepare a vertical analysis of the balance sheet data for Nike for 2014.

Prepare horizontal and vertical analyses.
(LO 4, 5), **AP**

E13-6 Here are the comparative income statements of Eudaley Corporation.

EUDALEY CORPORATION
Comparative Income Statements
For the Years Ended December 31

	2014	2013
Net sales	$598,000	$500,000
Cost of goods sold	477,000	420,000
Gross profit	121,000	80,000
Operating expenses	80,000	44,000
Net income	$ 41,000	$ 36,000

Instructions
(a) Prepare a horizontal analysis of the income statement data for Eudaley Corporation, using 2013 as a base. (Show the amounts of increase or decrease.)
(b) Prepare a vertical analysis of the income statement data for Eudaley Corporation for both years.

Compute liquidity ratios.
(LO 6), **AP**

E13-7 Nordstrom, Inc. operates department stores in numerous states. Suppose selected financial statement data (in millions) for 2014 are presented below.

	End of Year	Beginning of Year
Cash and cash equivalents	$ 795	$ 72
Accounts receivable (net)	2,035	1,942
Inventory	898	900
Other current assets	326	303
Total current assets	$4,054	$3,217
Total current liabilities	$2,014	$1,601

For the year, net credit sales were $8,258 million, cost of goods sold was $5,328 million, and net cash provided by operating activities was $1,251 million.

Instructions
Compute the current ratio, current cash debt coverage, accounts receivable turnover, average collection period, inventory turnover, and days in inventory at the end of the current year.

E13-8 Wyne Incorporated had the following transactions involving current assets and current liabilities during February 2014.

Perform current ratio analysis.

(LO 6), **AP**

Feb.	3	Collected accounts receivable of $15,000.
	7	Purchased equipment for $23,000 cash.
	11	Paid $3,000 for a 1-year insurance policy.
	14	Paid accounts payable of $12,000.
	18	Declared cash dividends, $4,000.

Additional information:
As of February 1, 2014, current assets were $120,000 and current liabilities were $40,000.

Instructions
Compute the current ratio as of the beginning of the month and after each transaction.

E13-9 Kinder Company has these comparative balance sheet data:

Compute selected ratios.

(LO 6), **AP**

KINDER COMPANY
Balance Sheets
December 31

	2014	2013
Cash	$ 15,000	$ 30,000
Accounts receivable (net)	70,000	60,000
Inventory	60,000	50,000
Plant assets (net)	200,000	180,000
	$345,000	$320,000
Accounts payable	$ 50,000	$ 60,000
Mortgage payable (15%)	100,000	100,000
Common stock, $10 par	140,000	120,000
Retained earnings	55,000	40,000
	$345,000	$320,000

Additional information for 2014:
1. Net income was $25,000.
2. Sales on account were $375,000. Sales returns and allowances amounted to $25,000.
3. Cost of goods sold was $198,000.
4. Net cash provided by operating activities was $48,000.
5. Capital expenditures were $25,000, and cash dividends were $10,000.

Instructions
Compute the following ratios at December 31, 2014.
(a) Current ratio.
(b) Accounts receivable turnover.
(c) Average collection period.
(d) Inventory turnover.
(e) Days in inventory.
(f) Cash debt coverage.
(g) Current cash debt coverage.
(h) Free cash flow.

E13-10 Suppose selected comparative statement data for the giant bookseller Barnes & Noble are presented here. All balance sheet data are as of the end of the fiscal year (in millions).

Compute selected ratios.

(LO 6), **AP**

	2014	2013
Net sales	$5,121.8	$5,286.7
Cost of goods sold	3,540.6	3,679.8
Net income	75.9	135.8
Accounts receivable	81.0	107.1
Inventory	1,203.5	1,358.2
Total assets	2,993.9	3,249.8
Total common stockholders' equity	921.6	1,074.7

Instructions
Compute the following ratios for 2014.
(a) Profit margin.
(b) Asset turnover.
(c) Return on assets.
(d) Return on common stockholders' equity.
(e) Gross profit rate.

Compute selected ratios.
(LO 6), **AP**

E13-11   Here is the income statement for Eberle, Inc.

EBERLE, INC.
Income Statement
For the Year Ended December 31, 2014

Sales revenue	$400,000
Cost of goods sold	230,000
Gross profit	170,000
Expenses (including $16,000 interest and $24,000 income taxes)	98,000
Net income	$ 72,000

Additional information:
1. Common stock outstanding January 1, 2014, was 32,000 shares, and 40,000 shares were outstanding at December 31, 2014.
2. The market price of Eberle, Inc., stock was $14 in 2014.
3. Cash dividends of $21,000 were paid, $5,000 of which were to preferred stockholders.

Instructions
Compute the following measures for 2014.
(a) Earnings per share.   (c) Payout ratio.
(b) Price-earnings ratio.   (d) Times interest earned.

Compute amounts from ratios.
(LO 6), **AP**

E13-12   Santo Corporation experienced a fire on December 31, 2014 in which its financial records were partially destroyed. It has been able to salvage some of the records and has ascertained the following balances.

	December 31, 2014	December 31, 2013
Cash	$ 30,000	$ 10,000
Accounts receivable (net)	72,500	126,000
Inventory	200,000	180,000
Accounts payable	50,000	90,000
Notes payable	30,000	60,000
Common stock, $100 par	400,000	400,000
Retained earnings	113,500	101,000

Additional information:
1. The inventory turnover is 3.8 times.
2. The return on common stockholders' equity is 22%. The company had no additional paid-in capital.
3. The accounts receivable turnover is 11.2 times.
4. The return on assets is 18%.
5. Total assets at December 31, 2013, were $605,000.

Instructions
Compute the following for Santo Corporation.
(a) Cost of goods sold for 2014.
(b) Net credit sales for 2014.
(c) Net income for 2014.
(d) Total assets at December 31, 2014.

E13-13 The condensed financial statements of Elliott Company for the years 2013 and 2014 are presented below.

Compute ratios.
(LO 6), **AP**

ELLIOTT COMPANY
Balance Sheets
December 31 (in thousands)

	2014	2013
Current assets		
Cash and cash equivalents	$ 330	$ 360
Accounts receivable (net)	470	400
Inventory	460	390
Prepaid expenses	130	160
Total current assets	1,390	1,310
Property, plant, and equipment (net)	410	380
Investments	10	10
Intangibles and other assets	530	510
Total assets	$2,340	$2,210
Current liabilities	$ 820	$ 790
Long-term liabilities	480	380
Stockholders' equity—common	1,040	1,040
Total liabilities and stockholders' equity	$2,340	$2,210

ELLIOTT COMPANY
Income Statements
For the Year Ended December 31 (in thousands)

	2014	2013
Sales revenue	$3,800	$3,460
Costs and expenses		
Cost of goods sold	970	890
Selling & administrative expenses	2,400	2,330
Interest expense	10	20
Total costs and expenses	3,380	3,240
Income before income taxes	420	220
Income tax expense	168	88
Net income	$ 252	$ 132

Compute the following ratios for 2014 and 2013.
(a) Current ratio.
(b) Inventory turnover. (Inventory on December 31, 2012, was $340.)
(c) Profit margin.
(d) Return on assets. (Assets on December 31, 2012, were $1,900.)
(e) Return on common stockholders' equity. (Equity on December 31, 2012, was $900.)
(f) Debt to assets ratio.
(g) Times interest earned.

Exercises: Set B and Challenge Exercises

Visit the book's companion website, at **www.wiley.com/college/kimmel**, and choose the Student Companion site to access Exercise Set B and Challenge Exercises.

Problems: Set A

⚙══════C All of the Problems in this chapter employ decision tools.

Prepare vertical analysis and comment on profitability.
(LO 5, 6), **AN**

P13-1A   Here are comparative statement data for Prince Company and King Company, two competitors. All balance sheet data are as of December 31, 2014, and December 31, 2013.

	Prince Company		King Company	
	2014	**2013**	**2014**	**2013**
Net sales	$1,849,000		$546,000	
Cost of goods sold	1,063,200		289,000	
Operating expenses	240,000		82,000	
Interest expense	6,800		3,600	
Income tax expense	62,000		28,000	
Current assets	325,975	$312,410	83,336	$ 79,467
Plant assets (net)	526,800	500,000	139,728	125,812
Current liabilities	66,325	75,815	35,348	30,281
Long-term liabilities	113,990	90,000	29,620	25,000
Common stock, $10 par	500,000	500,000	120,000	120,000
Retained earnings	172,460	146,595	38,096	29,998

Instructions

(a)   Prepare a vertical analysis of the 2014 income statement data for Prince Company and King Company.
(b)   ▰▰▰▶ Comment on the relative profitability of the companies by computing the 2014 return on assets and the return on common stockholders' equity for both companies.

Compute ratios from balance sheets and income statements.
(LO 6), **AP**

P13-2A   The comparative statements of Osborne Company are presented here.

OSBORNE COMPANY
Income Statements
For the Years Ended December 31

	2014	**2013**
Net sales	$1,890,540	$1,750,500
Cost of goods sold	1,058,540	1,006,000
Gross profit	832,000	744,500
Selling and administrative expenses	500,000	479,000
Income from operations	332,000	265,500
Other expenses and losses		
Interest expense	22,000	20,000
Income before income taxes	310,000	245,500
Income tax expense	92,000	73,000
Net income	$ 218,000	$ 172,500

OSBORNE COMPANY
Balance Sheets
December 31

Assets	**2014**	**2013**
Current assets		
Cash	$ 60,100	$ 64,200
Debt investments (short-term)	74,000	50,000
Accounts receivable	117,800	102,800
Inventory	126,000	115,500
Total current assets	377,900	332,500
Plant assets (net)	649,000	520,300
Total assets	$1,026,900	$852,800

Liabilities and Stockholders' Equity

Current liabilities		
Accounts payable	$ 160,000	$145,400
Income taxes payable	43,500	42,000
Total current liabilities	203,500	187,400
Bonds payable	220,000	200,000
Total liabilities	423,500	387,400
Stockholders' equity		
Common stock ($5 par)	290,000	300,000
Retained earnings	313,400	165,400
Total stockholders' equity	603,400	465,400
Total liabilities and stockholders' equity	$1,026,900	$852,800

All sales were on account. Net cash provided by operating activities for 2014 was $220,000. Capital expenditures were $136,000, and cash dividends were $70,000.

Instructions
Compute the following ratios for 2014.

(a) Earnings per share.
(b) Return on common stockholders' equity.
(c) Return on assets.
(d) Current ratio.
(e) Accounts receivable turnover.
(f) Average collection period.
(g) Inventory turnover.

(h) Days in inventory.
(i) Times interest earned.
(j) Asset turnover.
(k) Debt to assets.
(l) Current cash debt coverage.
(m) Cash debt coverage.
(n) Free cash flow.

P13-3A Condensed balance sheet and income statement data for Jernigan Corporation are presented here.

Perform ratio analysis, and discuss change in financial position and operating results.

(LO 6), **AN**

JERNIGAN CORPORATION
Balance Sheets
December 31

	2014	2013	2012
Cash	$ 30,000	$ 20,000	$ 18,000
Accounts receivable (net)	50,000	45,000	48,000
Other current assets	90,000	95,000	64,000
Investments	55,000	70,000	45,000
Plant and equipment (net)	500,000	370,000	358,000
	$725,000	$600,000	$533,000
Current liabilities	$ 85,000	$ 80,000	$ 70,000
Long-term debt	145,000	85,000	50,000
Common stock, $10 par	320,000	310,000	300,000
Retained earnings	175,000	125,000	113,000
	$725,000	$600,000	$533,000

JERNIGAN CORPORATION
Income Statements
For the Years Ended December 31

	2014	2013
Sales revenue	$740,000	$600,000
Less: Sales returns and allowances	40,000	30,000
Net sales	700,000	570,000
Cost of goods sold	425,000	350,000
Gross profit	275,000	220,000
Operating expenses (including income taxes)	180,000	150,000
Net income	$ 95,000	$ 70,000

Additional information:

1. The market price of Jernigan's common stock was $7.00, $7.50, and $8.50 for 2012, 2013, and 2014, respectively.
2. You must compute dividends paid. All dividends were paid in cash.

Instructions

(a) Compute the following ratios for 2013 and 2014.
   (1) Profit margin.   (5) Price-earnings ratio.
   (2) Gross profit rate.   (6) Payout ratio.
   (3) Asset turnover.   (7) Debt to assets ratio.
   (4) Earnings per share.

(b) ◼▬▬▶ Based on the ratios calculated, discuss briefly the improvement or lack thereof in the financial position and operating results from 2013 to 2014 of Jernigan Corporation.

Compute ratios; comment on overall liquidity and profitability.
(LO 6), **AN**

P13-4A The following financial information is for Frizell Company.

FRIZELL COMPANY
Balance Sheets
December 31

Assets	2014	2013
Cash	$ 70,000	$ 65,000
Debt investments (short-term)	55,000	40,000
Accounts receivable	104,000	90,000
Inventory	230,000	165,000
Prepaid expenses	25,000	23,000
Land	130,000	130,000
Building and equipment (net)	260,000	185,000
Total assets	$874,000	$698,000

Liabilities and Stockholders' Equity		
Notes payable	$170,000	$120,000
Accounts payable	65,000	52,000
Accrued liabilities	40,000	40,000
Bonds payable, due 2017	250,000	170,000
Common stock, $10 par	200,000	200,000
Retained earnings	149,000	116,000
Total liabilities and stockholders' equity	$874,000	$698,000

FRIZELL COMPANY
Income Statements
For the Years Ended December 31

	2014	2013
Sales revenue	$882,000	$790,000
Cost of goods sold	640,000	575,000
Gross profit	242,000	215,000
Operating expenses	190,000	167,000
Net income	$ 52,000	$ 48,000

Additional information:

1. Inventory at the beginning of 2013 was $115,000.
2. Accounts receivable (net) at the beginning of 2013 were $86,000.
3. Total assets at the beginning of 2013 were $660,000.
4. No common stock transactions occurred during 2013 or 2014.
5. All sales were on account.

Instructions

(a) Indicate, by using ratios, the change in liquidity and profitability of Frizell Company from 2013 to 2014. (*Note:* Not all profitability ratios can be computed nor can cash-basis ratios be computed.)

(b) Given below are three independent situations and a ratio that may be affected. For each situation, compute the affected ratio (1) as of December 31, 2014, and (2) as of December 31, 2015, after giving effect to the situation. Net income for 2015 was $54,000. Total assets on December 31, 2015, were $900,000.

Situation	Ratio
1. 18,000 shares of common stock were sold at par on July 1, 2015.	Return on common stockholders' equity
2. All of the notes payable were paid in 2015.	Debt to assets ratio
3. The market price of common stock was $9 and $12 on December 31, 2014 and 2015, respectively.	Price-earnings ratio

P13-5A Suppose selected financial data of Target and Wal-Mart for 2014 are presented here (in millions).

Compute selected ratios, and compare liquidity, profitability, and solvency for two companies.

(LO 6), AN

	Target Corporation	Wal-Mart Stores, Inc.
Income Statement Data for Year		
Net sales	$65,357	$408,214
Cost of goods sold	45,583	304,657
Selling and administrative expenses	15,101	79,607
Interest expense	707	2,065
Other income (expense)	(94)	(411)
Income tax expense	1,384	7,139
Net income	$ 2,488	$ 14,335
Balance Sheet Data (End of Year)		
Current assets	$18,424	$ 48,331
Noncurrent assets	26,109	122,375
Total assets	$44,533	$170,706
Current liabilities	$11,327	$ 55,561
Long-term debt	17,859	44,089
Total stockholders' equity	15,347	71,056
Total liabilities and stockholders' equity	$44,533	$170,706
Beginning-of-Year Balances		
Total assets	$44,106	$163,429
Total stockholders' equity	13,712	65,682
Current liabilities	10,512	55,390
Total liabilities	30,394	97,747
Other Data		
Average net accounts receivable	$ 7,525	$ 4,025
Average inventory	6,942	33,836
Net cash provided by operating activities	5,881	26,249
Capital expenditures	1,729	12,184
Dividends	496	4,217

Instructions

(a) For each company, compute the following ratios.
 (1) Current ratio.
 (2) Accounts receivable turnover.
 (3) Average collection period.
 (4) Inventory turnover.
 (5) Days in inventory.
 (6) Profit margin.
 (7) Asset turnover.
 (8) Return on assets.
 (9) Return on common stockholders' equity.
 (10) Debt to assets ratio.
 (11) Times interest earned.
 (12) Current cash debt coverage.
 (13) Cash debt coverage.
 (14) Free cash flow.

(b) Compare the liquidity, solvency, and profitability of the two companies.

Problems: Set B

⊙▬▬⊂ All of the Problems in this chapter employ decision tools.

Prepare vertical analysis and comment on profitability.
(LO 5, 6), **AN**

P13-1B Here are comparative statement data for Dean Company and Gerald Company, two competitors. All balance sheet data are as of December 31, 2014, and December 31, 2013.

	Dean Company		Gerald Company	
	2014	**2013**	**2014**	**2013**
Net sales	$350,000		$1,200,000	
Cost of goods sold	175,000		648,000	
Operating expenses	72,000		266,000	
Interest expense	5,000		10,000	
Income tax expense	22,000		54,000	
Current assets	130,000	$100,000	700,000	$650,000
Plant assets (net)	400,000	270,000	1,000,000	750,000
Current liabilities	60,000	58,000	250,000	275,000
Long-term liabilities	50,000	72,000	200,000	150,000
Common stock	340,000	200,000	950,000	700,000
Retained earnings	80,000	40,000	300,000	275,000

Instructions

(a) Prepare a vertical analysis of the 2014 income statement data for Dean Company and Gerald Company.

(b) ▬▬▶Comment on the relative profitability of the companies by computing the return on assets and the return on common stockholders' equity for both companies.

Compute ratios from balance sheets and income statements.
(LO 6), **AP**

P13-2B The comparative statements of Simpson Company are shown below.

SIMPSON COMPANY
Income Statements
For the Years Ended December 31

	2014	**2013**
Net sales	$780,000	$624,000
Cost of goods sold	440,000	405,600
Gross profit	340,000	218,400
Selling and administrative expenses	176,880	149,760
Income from operations	163,120	68,640
Other expenses and losses		
Interest expense	9,920	7,200
Income before income taxes	153,200	61,440
Income tax expense	34,000	14,000
Net income	$119,200	$ 47,440

SIMPSON COMPANY
Balance Sheets
December 31

Assets	**2014**	**2013**
Current assets		
Cash	$ 23,100	$ 21,600
Debt investments (short-term)	44,800	33,000
Accounts receivable	106,200	83,800
Inventory	116,400	74,000
Total current assets	290,500	212,400
Plant assets (net)	485,300	439,600
Total assets	$775,800	$652,000

Liabilities and Stockholders' Equity

Current liabilities		
Accounts payable	$138,200	$132,000
Income taxes payable	25,300	24,000
Total current liabilities	163,500	156,000
Bonds payable	132,000	120,000
Total liabilities	295,500	276,000
Stockholders' equity		
Common stock ($10 par)	150,000	130,000
Retained earnings	330,300	246,000
Total stockholders' equity	480,300	376,000
Total liabilities and stockholders' equity	$775,800	$652,000

All sales were on account. Net cash provided by operating activities was $108,000. Capital expenditures were $47,000, and cash dividends were $30,900.

Instructions

Compute the following ratios for 2014.

(a) Earnings per share.
(b) Return on common stockholders' equity.
(c) Return on assets.
(d) Current ratio.
(e) Accounts receivable turnover.
(f) Average collection period.
(g) Inventory turnover.

(h) Days in inventory.
(i) Times interest earned.
(j) Asset turnover.
(k) Debt to assets ratio.
(l) Current cash debt coverage.
(m) Cash debt coverage.
(n) Free cash flow.

P13-3B The condensed balance sheet and income statement data for Symbiosis Corporation are presented below.

Perform ratio analysis, and discuss change in financial position and operating results.

(LO 6), **AN**

SYMBIOSIS CORPORATION
Balance Sheets
December 31

	2014	2013	2012
Cash	$ 30,000	$ 24,000	$ 20,000
Accounts receivable (net)	110,000	48,000	48,000
Other current assets	80,000	78,000	62,000
Investments	90,000	70,000	50,000
Plant and equipment (net)	503,000	400,000	360,000
	$813,000	$620,000	$540,000
Current liabilities	$ 98,000	$ 75,000	$ 70,000
Long-term debt	130,000	75,000	65,000
Common stock, $10 par	400,000	340,000	300,000
Retained earnings	185,000	130,000	105,000
	$813,000	$620,000	$540,000

SYMBIOSIS CORPORATION
Income Statements
For the Years Ended December 31

	2014	2013
Sales revenue	$800,000	$750,000
Less: Sales returns and allowances	40,000	50,000
Net sales	760,000	700,000
Cost of goods sold	420,000	406,000
Gross profit	340,000	294,000
Operating expenses (including income taxes)	230,000	209,000
Net income	$110,000	$ 85,000

Additional information:
1. The market price of Symbiosis common stock was $5.00, $3.50, and $2.80 for 2012, 2013, and 2014, respectively.
2. You must compute dividends paid. All dividends were paid in cash.

Instructions
(a) Compute the following ratios for 2013 and 2014.

    (1) Profit margin.   (5) Price-earnings ratio.
    (2) Gross profit rate.   (6) Payout ratio.
    (3) Asset turnover.   (7) Debt to assets ratio.
    (4) Earnings per share.

(b) ■━━━▶Based on the ratios calculated, discuss briefly the improvement or lack thereof in the financial position and operating results from 2013 to 2014 of Symbiosis Corporation.

Compute ratios; comment on overall liquidity and profitability.
(LO 6), AN

P13-4B   Financial information for Bradford Company is presented here.

BRADFORD COMPANY
Balance Sheets
December 31

Assets	2014	2013
Cash	$ 50,000	$ 42,000
Debt investments (short-term)	80,000	50,000
Accounts receivable	100,000	77,000
Inventory	410,000	320,000
Prepaid expenses	30,000	31,000
Land	75,000	75,000
Building and equipment (net)	570,000	400,000
Total assets	$1,315,000	$995,000

Liabilities and Stockholders' Equity		
Notes payable	$ 120,000	$ 25,000
Accounts payable	160,000	90,000
Accrued liabilities	50,000	50,000
Bonds payable, due 2014	180,000	100,000
Common stock, $5 par	500,000	500,000
Retained earnings	305,000	230,000
Total liabilities and stockholders' equity	$1,315,000	$995,000

BRADFORD COMPANY
Income Statements
For the Years Ended December 31

	2014	2013
Sales revenue	$1,050,000	$940,000
Cost of goods sold	680,000	635,000
Gross profit	370,000	305,000
Operating expenses	240,000	215,000
Net income	$ 130,000	$ 90,000

Additional information:
1. Inventory at the beginning of 2013 was $330,000.
2. Accounts receivable at the beginning of 2013 were $80,000.
3. Total assets at the beginning of 2013 were $1,175,000.
4. No common stock transactions occurred during 2013 or 2014.
5. All sales were on account.

Instructions
(a) Indicate, by using ratios, the change in liquidity and profitability of the company from 2013 to 2014. (*Note:* Not all profitability ratios can be computed nor can cash-basis ratios be computed.)

(b) Given below are three independent situations and a ratio that may be affected. For each situation, compute the affected ratio (1) as of December 31, 2014, and (2) as of December 31, 2015, after giving effect to the situation. Net income for 2015 was $135,000. Total assets on December 31, 2015, were $1,350,000.

Situation	Ratio
1. 10,000 shares of common stock were sold at par on July 1, 2015.	Return on common stockholders' equity
2. All of the notes payable were paid in 2015.	Debt to assets ratio
3. The market price of common stock on December 31, 2014, was $15. The market price on December 31, 2015, was $18.	Price-earnings ratio

P13-5B Suppose selected financial data of Edgewater Company and The Ritter Company for 2014 are presented here (in millions).

Compute selected ratios, and compare liquidity, profitability, and solvency for two companies.
(LO 6), AN

	Edgewater	Ritter
	Income Statement Data for Year	
Net sales	$1,356.0	$1,436.5
Cost of goods sold	776.3	771.7
Selling and administrative expenses	380.6	605.5
Interest expense	0.1	0.1
Other income (expense)	9.0	.5
Income tax expense	63.6	19.7
Net income	$ 144.4	$ 40.0
	Balance Sheet Data (End of Year)	
Current assets	$ 885.7	$ 617.2
Noncurrent assets	280.8	219.1
Total assets	$1,166.5	$ 836.3
Current liabilities	$ 166.5	$ 218.0
Long-term debt	29.9	41.1
Total stockholders' equity	970.1	577.2
Total liabilities and stockholders' equity	$1,166.5	$ 836.3
	Beginning-of-Year Balances	
Total assets	$1,027.3	$860.4
Total stockholders' equity	830.7	561.7
Current liabilities	187.9	285.6
Total liabilities	196.6	298.7
	Other Data	
Average net accounts receivable	$293.2	$196.1
Average inventory	239.1	194.3
Net cash provided by operating activities	124.5	38.6
Capital expenditures	34.3	30.5
Dividends	20.9	–0–

Instructions
(a) For each company, compute the following ratios.

(1)	Current ratio.	(8)	Return on assets.
(2)	Accounts receivable turnover.	(9)	Return on common stockholders' equity.
(3)	Average collection period.	(10)	Debt to assets ratio.
(4)	Inventory turnover.	(11)	Times interest earned.
(5)	Days in inventory.	(12)	Current cash debt coverage.
(6)	Profit margin.	(13)	Cash debt coverage.
(7)	Asset turnover.	(14)	Free cash flow.

(b) Compare the liquidity, solvency, and profitability of the two companies.

Problems: Set C

Visit the book's companion website, at **www.wiley.com/college/kimmel**, and choose the Student Companion site to access Problem Set C.

Continuing Cookie Chronicle

(*Note:* This is a continuation of the Cookie Chronicle from Chapters 1 through 12.)

CCC13 Natalie and Curtis have comparative balance sheets and income statements for Cookie & Coffee Creations Inc. They have been told that they can use these financial statements to prepare horizontal and vertical analyses, to calculate financial ratios, to analyze how their business is doing, and to make some decisions they have been considering.

Go to the book's companion website, at **www.wiley.com/college/kimmel**, to find the completion of this problem.

Broadening Your Perspective

Financial Reporting and Analysis

FINANCIAL REPORTING PROBLEM: *Tootsie Roll Industries, Inc.*

BYP13-1 Your parents are considering investing in Tootsie Roll Industries common stock. They ask you, as an accounting expert, to make an analysis of the company for them. Fortunately, excerpts from a recent annual report of Tootsie Roll are presented in Appendix A of this textbook.

Instructions
(a) Make a 5-year trend analysis, using 2007 as the base year, of (1) net sales and (2) net earnings. Comment on the significance of the trend results.
(b) Compute for 2011 and 2010 the (1) debt to assets ratio and (2) times interest earned. (See Note 6 for interest expense.) How would you evaluate Tootsie Roll's long-term solvency?
(c) Compute for 2011 and 2010 the (1) profit margin, (2) asset turnover, (3) return on assets, and (4) return on common stockholders' equity. How would you evaluate Tootsie Roll's profitability? Total assets at December 31, 2009, were $836,844,000, and total stockholders' equity at December 31, 2009, was $654,244,000.
(d) What information outside the annual report may also be useful to your parents in making a decision about Tootsie Roll?

COMPARATIVE ANALYSIS PROBLEM: *Tootsie Roll vs. Hershey*

BYP13-2 The financial statements of The Hershey Company are presented in Appendix B, following the financial statements for Tootsie Roll Industries in Appendix A.

Instructions
(a) Based on the information in the financial statements, determine each of the following for each company:
  (1) The percentage increase (i) in net sales and (ii) in net income from 2010 to 2011.
  (2) The percentage increase (i) in total assets and (ii) in total stockholders' equity from 2010 to 2011.
  (3) The earnings per share for 2011.
(b) What conclusions concerning the two companies can be drawn from these data?

RESEARCH CASES

BYP13-3 The April 21, 2008, issue of the *Wall Street Journal Online* included an article by David Reilly entitled "A Way Charges Stay off Bottom Line."

Instructions

Read the article and answer the following questions.

(a) According to the article, how do companies avoid reporting losses on certain types of investment securities in net income?

(b) At what point would these losses be reported in net income?

(c) At the time of the article, what was the total estimated amount of unrealized losses that companies in the Standard and Poor's 500 Stock Index were reporting in equity?

(d) Does the article suggest that these companies are violating accounting standards?

(e) What are the implications of this accounting practice for investors?

BYP13-4 The April 25, 2012, edition of the *Wall Street Journal* contains an article by Spencer Jakab entitled "Amazon's Valuation Is Hard to Justify."

Instructions

Read the article and answer the following questions.

(a) Explain what is meant by the statement that "On a split-adjusted basis, today's share price is the equivalent of $1,166."

(b) The article says that Amazon.com nearly doubled its capital spending on items such as fulfillment centers (sophisticated warehouses where it finds, packages, and ships goods to customers). Discuss the implications that this spending would have on the company's return on assets in the short-term and in the long-term.

(c) How does Amazon's P-E ratio compare to that of Apple, Netflix, and Wal-Mart? What does this suggest about investors' expectations about Amazon's future earnings?

(d) What factor does the article cite as a possible hurdle that might reduce Amazon's ability to raise its operating margin back to previous levels?

INTERPRETING FINANCIAL STATEMENTS

BYP13-5 The Coca-Cola Company and PepsiCo, Inc. provide refreshments to every corner of the world. Suppose selected data from the 2014 consolidated financial statements for The Coca-Cola Company and for PepsiCo, Inc. are presented here (in millions).

	Coca-Cola	PepsiCo
Total current assets	$17,551	$12,571
Total current liabilities	13,721	8,756
Net sales	30,990	43,232
Cost of goods sold	11,088	20,099
Net income	6,824	5,946
Average (net) accounts receivable for the year	3,424	4,654
Average inventories for the year	2,271	2,570
Average total assets	44,595	37,921
Average common stockholders' equity	22,636	14,556
Average current liabilities	13,355	8,772
Average total liabilities	21,960	23,466
Total assets	48,671	39,848
Total liabilities	23,872	23,044
Income taxes	2,040	2,100
Interest expense	355	397
Net cash provided by operating activities	8,186	6,796
Capital expenditures	1,993	2,128
Cash dividends	3,800	2,732

Instructions

(a) Compute the following liquidity ratios for 2014 for Coca-Cola and for PepsiCo and comment on the relative liquidity of the two competitors.

(1) Current ratio.

(2) Accounts receivable turnover.

(3) Average collection period.

(4) Inventory turnover.

(5) Days in inventory.

(6) Current cash debt coverage.

(b) Compute the following solvency ratios for the two companies and comment on the relative solvency of the two competitors.
    (1) Debt to assets ratio.
    (2) Times interest earned.
    (3) Cash debt coverage.
    (4) Free cash flow.

(c) Compute the following profitability ratios for the two companies and comment on the relative profitability of the two competitors.
    (1) Profit margin.
    (2) Asset turnover.
    (3) Return on assets.
    (4) Return on common stockholders' equity.

REAL-WORLD FOCUS

BYP13-6   *Purpose:* To employ comparative data and industry data to evaluate a company's performance and financial position.

Address: **http://www.moneycentral.msn.com/investor/invsub/results/compare.asp**, or go to **www.wiley.com/college/kimmel**

Steps
(1) Identify two competing companies.
(2) Go to the above address.
(3) Type in the first company's stock symbol. (Use "symbol look-up.").
(4) Choose **Ratios**.
(5) Print out the results.
(6) Repeat steps 3–5 for the competitor.

Instructions
(a) Evaluate the company's liquidity relative to the industry averages and to the competitor that you chose.
(b) Evaluate the company's solvency relative to the industry averages and to the competitor that you chose.
(c) Evaluate the company's profitability relative to the industry averages and to the competitor that you chose.

Critical Thinking

DECISION-MAKING ACROSS THE ORGANIZATION

BYP13-7   You are a loan officer for Great Plains Bank of Davenport. Jason Putnam, president of J. Putnam Corporation, has just left your office. He is interested in an 8-year loan to expand the company's operations. The borrowed funds would be used to purchase new equipment. As evidence of the company's debt-worthiness, Putnam provided you with the following facts.

	2014	**2013**
Current ratio	3.1	2.1
Asset turnover	2.8	2.2
Cash debt coverage	.1	.2
Net income	Up 32%	Down 8%
Earnings per share	$3.30	$2.50

Putnam is a very insistent (some would say pushy) man. When you told him that you would need additional information before making your decision, he acted offended and said, "What more could you possibly want to know?" You responded that, at a minimum, you would need complete, audited financial statements.

Instructions

With the class divided into groups, answer the following.

(a) Explain why you would want the financial statements to be audited.

(b) Discuss the implications of the ratios provided for the lending decision you are to make. That is, does the information paint a favorable picture? Are these ratios relevant to the decision?

(c) List three other ratios that you would want to calculate for this company, and explain why you would use each.

COMMUNICATION ACTIVITY

BYP13-8 David Lemay is the chief executive officer of Brenna Electronics. Lemay is an expert engineer but a novice in accounting. Lemay asks you, as an accounting student, to explain (a) the bases for comparison in analyzing Brenna's financial statements and (b) the limitations, if any, in financial statement analysis.

Instructions

Write a memo to David Lemay that explains the basis for comparison and the factors affecting quality of earnings.

ETHICS CASE

BYP13-9 Kelli Rice, president of LR Industries, wishes to issue a press release to bolster her company's image and maybe even its stock price, which has been gradually falling. As controller, you have been asked to provide a list of 20 financial ratios and other operating statistics for LR Industries' first-quarter financials and operations.

Two days after you provide the data requested, Laurie Ellis, the public relations director of LR, asks you to prove the accuracy of the financial and operating data contained in the press release written by the president and edited by Laurie. In the news release, the president highlights the sales increase of 25% over last year's first quarter and the positive change in the current ratio from 1.5:1 last year to 3:1 this year. She also emphasizes that production was up 50% over the prior year's first quarter.

You note that the release contains only positive or improved ratios and none of the negative or deteriorated ratios. For instance, no mention is made that the debt to assets ratio has increased from 35% to 55%, that inventories are up 89%, and that although the current ratio improved, the current cash debt coverage fell from .15 to .05. Nor is there any mention that the reported profit for the quarter would have been a loss had not the estimated lives of LR plant and machinery been increased by 30%. Laurie emphasized, "The Pres wants this release by early this afternoon."

Instructions

(a) Who are the stakeholders in this situation?

(b) Is there anything unethical in the president's actions?

(c) Should you as controller remain silent? Does Laurie have any responsibility?

ALL ABOUT YOU

BYP13-10 In this chapter, you learned how to use many tools for performing a financial analysis of a company. When making personal investments, however, it is most likely that you won't be buying stocks and bonds in individual companies. Instead, when most people want to invest in stock, they buy mutual funds. By investing in a mutual fund, you reduce your risk because the fund diversifies by buying the stock of a variety of different companies, bonds, and other investments, depending on the stated goals of the fund.

Before you invest in a fund, you will need to decide what type of fund you want. For example, do you want a fund that has the potential of high growth (but also high risk), or are you looking for lower risk and a steady stream of income? Do you want a fund that invests only in U.S. companies, or do you want one that invests globally? Many resources are available to help you with these types of decisions.

Instructions

Go to **http://web.archive.org/web/20050210200843/http://www.cnb1.com/invallocmdl.htm** and complete the investment allocation questionnaire. Add up your total points to determine the type of investment fund that would be appropriate for you.

FASB CODIFICATION ACTIVITY

BYP13-11 If your school has a subscription to the FASB Codification, go to **http://aaahq.org/ascLogin.cfm** to log in and prepare responses to the following. Use the Master Glossary for determining the proper definitions.
(a) Discontinued operations.
(b) Extraordinary items.
(c) Comprehensive income.

Answers to Insight and Accounting Across the Organization Questions

p. 693 What Does "Non-Recurring" Really Mean? Q: If a company takes a large restructuring charge, what is the effect on the company's current income statement versus future ones? **A:** The current period's net income can be greatly diminished by a large restructuring charge. The net incomes in future periods can be enhanced because they are relieved of costs (i.e., depreciation and labor expenses) that would have been charged to them.

p. 694 More Frequent Ups and Downs Q: When predicting future earnings, how should analysts treat the one-time charge that results from a switch to the different approach for accounting for pension plans? **A:** Because the change in principle will only happen once, it should be ignored when predicting future earnings. That is, because it will not happen again in future periods, it would not be included in estimates of future results.

p. 704 How to Manage the Current Ratio Q: How might management influence a company's current ratio? **A:** Management can affect the current ratio by speeding up or withholding payments on accounts payable just before the balance sheet date. Management can alter the cash balance by increasing or decreasing long-term assets or long-term debt, or by issuing or purchasing common stock.

p. 705 High Ratings Can Bring Low Returns Q: Why are credit rating agencies important to the financial markets? **A:** Credit rating agencies perform financial analysis on publicly traded companies and then publish research reports and credit ratings. Investors and creditors rely on the information provided by credit rating agencies in making investment and lending decisions.

Answers to Self-Test Questions

1. d **2.** d ($400,000 × .75); ($100,000 × .75) **3.** b **4.** d **5.** c ($360,000 ÷ $300,000) **6.** c **7.** a **8.** c **9.** c **10.** b **11.** a ($24,000 ÷ $400,000) **12.** b ($306,000 ÷ (($54,000 + $48,000)/2)) = 6; 365 ÷ 6 **13.** b ($81,000 ÷ $27,000) **14.** a ($134,000 ÷ $784,000) **15.** d ($134,000 − $4,000) ÷ (($240,000 + $198,000)/2)) **16.** c ($134,000 + $22,000 + $12,000) ÷ $12,000 **17.** c

A Look at IFRS

LEARNING OBJECTIVE 9

Compare the accounting for irregular items and the income statement format under GAAP and IFRS.

The first part of this chapter relates to the income statement and irregular items. As in GAAP, the income statement is a required statement under IFRS. In addition, the content and presentation of an IFRS income statement is similar to the one used for GAAP. *IAS 1* (revised), "Presentation of Financial Statements," provides general guidelines for the reporting of income statement information. In general, the differences in the presentation of financial statement information are relatively minor.

The latter sections of this chapter, dealing with the tools of financial analysis, are the same throughout the world. Techniques such as vertical and horizontal analysis, for example, are tools used by analysts regardless of whether GAAP- or IFRS-related financial statements are being evaluated. In addition, the ratios provided in the textbook are the same ones that are used internationally.

KEY POINTS

- The tools of financial statement analysis covered in this chapter are universal and therefore no significant differences exist in the analysis methods used.

- The basic objectives of the income statement are the same under both GAAP and IFRS. As indicated in the textbook, a very important objective is to ensure that users of the income statement can evaluate the earning power of the company. Earning power is the normal level of income to be obtained in the future. Thus, both the IASB and the FASB are interested in distinguishing normal levels of income from irregular items in order to better predict a company's future profitability.

- The basic accounting for discontinued operations is the same under IFRS and GAAP.

- Under IFRS, there is no classification for extraordinary items. In other words, extraordinary item treatment is prohibited under IFRS. All revenue and expense items are considered ordinary in nature. Disclosure, however, is extensive for items that are considered material to the financial results. Examples are write-downs of inventory or plant assets, or gains and losses on the disposal of plant assets.

- The accounting for changes in accounting principles and changes in accounting estimates are the same for both GAAP and IFRS.

- The income statement under IFRS is referred to as a **statement of comprehensive income**. The statement of comprehensive income can be prepared under the one-statement approach or the two-statement approach.

    Under the one-statement approach, all components of revenue and expense are reported in the income statement. This combined statement of comprehensive income first computes net income or loss, which is then followed by components of other comprehensive income or loss items to arrive at comprehensive income. An example appears below.

WALTER COMPANY
Statement of Comprehensive Income
For the Year Ended December 31, 2014

Sales revenue	$5,100,000
Cost of goods sold	3,800,000
Gross profit	1,300,000
Operating expenses	700,000
Net income	600,000
Other comprehensive income	
Unrealized gain on non-trading securities	75,000
Comprehensive income	$ 675,000

Under the two-statement approach, all the components of revenues and expenses are reported in a traditional income statement **except** for other comprehensive income or loss. In addition, a second statement (the statement of comprehensive income) is then prepared, starting with net income and followed by other comprehensive income or loss items to arrive at comprehensive income. An example of the two-statement approach, using the same data as that used above for Walter Company, appears below.

WALTER COMPANY
Income Statement
For the Year Ended December 31, 2014

Sales revenue	$5,100,000
Cost of goods sold	3,800,000
Gross profit	1,300,000
Operating expenses	700,000
Net income	$ 600,000

WALTER COMPANY	
Statement of Comprehensive Income	
For the Year Ended December 31, 2014	
Net income	$600,000
Other comprehensive income	
Unrealized gain on non-trading securities	75,000
Comprehensive income	$675,000

- GAAP also permits the one-statement or two-statement approach. In addition, GAAP permits a third alternative, which is to show the computation of comprehensive income in the statement of stockholders' equity.

- The issues related to quality of earnings are the same under both GAAP and IFRS. It is hoped that by adopting a more principles-based approach, as found in IFRS, many of the earnings' quality issues will disappear.

LOOKING TO THE FUTURE

The FASB and the IASB are working on a project that would rework the structure of financial statements. Recently, the IASB decided to require a statement of comprehensive income, similar to what was required under GAAP. In addition, another part of this project addresses the issue of how to classify various items in the income statement. A main goal of this new approach is to provide information that better represents how businesses are run. In addition, the approach draws attention away from one number—net income.

IFRS PRACTICE

IFRS SELF-TEST QUESTIONS

1. The basic tools of financial analysis are the same under both GAAP and IFRS **except** that:
   (a) horizontal analysis cannot be done because the format of the statements is sometimes different.
   (b) analysis is different because vertical analysis cannot be done under IFRS.
   (c) the current ratio cannot be computed because current liabilities are often reported before current assets in IFRS statements of financial position.
   (d) None of the above.

2. Under IFRS:
   (a) the reporting of discontinued items is different than GAAP.
   (b) the reporting of extraordinary items is prohibited.
   (c) the reporting of changes in accounting principles is different than under GAAP.
   (d) None of the above.

3. Presentation of comprehensive income must be reported under IFRS in:
   (a) the statement of stockholders' equity.
   (b) the income statement ending with net income.
   (c) the notes to the financial statements.
   (d) a statement of comprehensive income.

4. Parmalane reports the following information:

Sales revenue	$500,000
Cost of goods sold	200,000
Operating expense	40,000
Unrealized loss on non-trading securities	10,000

Parmalane should report the following under the two-statement approach using IFRS:
   (a) net income of $260,000 and comprehensive income of $270,000.
   (b) net income of $270,000 and comprehensive income of $260,000.
   (c) other comprehensive income of $10,000 and comprehensive income of $270,000.
   (d) other comprehensive loss of $10,000 and comprehensive income of 250,000.

5. Assuming the same information as in Question 4, Parmalane should report the following using a one-statement approach under IFRS:
   (a) net income of $260,000 and comprehensive income of $270,000.
   (b) net income of $270,000 and comprehensive income of $260,000.
   (c) other comprehensive income of $10,000 and comprehensive income of $270,000.
   (d) other comprehensive loss of $10,000 and comprehensive income of $250,000.

IFRS CONCEPTS AND APPLICATION

IFRS13-1 Ling Company reports the following information for the year ended December 31, 2014: sales revenue $1,000,000, cost of goods sold $700,000, operating expenses $200,000, and an unrealized gain on non-trading securities of $75,000. Prepare a statement of comprehensive income using the one-statement approach.

IFRS13-2 Assume the same information for Ling Company as in IFRS13-1. Prepare the income statement using the two-statement approach.

INTERNATIONAL FINANCIAL REPORTING PROBLEM: *Zetar plc*

IFRS13-3 The financial statements of Zetar plc are presented in Appendix C. The company's complete annual report, including the notes to its financial statements, is available in the Investors section at **www.zetarplc.com**.

Instructions

Use the company's **2009 annual report** (not the 2011) to answer the following questions.
   (a) The company's income statement reports a loss on discontinued operations. What business did the company discontinue, and why did it choose to discontinue the business?
   (b) For the year ended April 30, 2009, what amount did the company lose on the operation of the discontinued business, and what amount did it lose on disposal?
   (c) What was the total recorded value of the net assets at the date of disposal, and what was the amount of costs incurred to dispose of the business?

Answers to IFRS Self-Test Questions

1. d **2.** b **3.** d **4.** d **5.** d

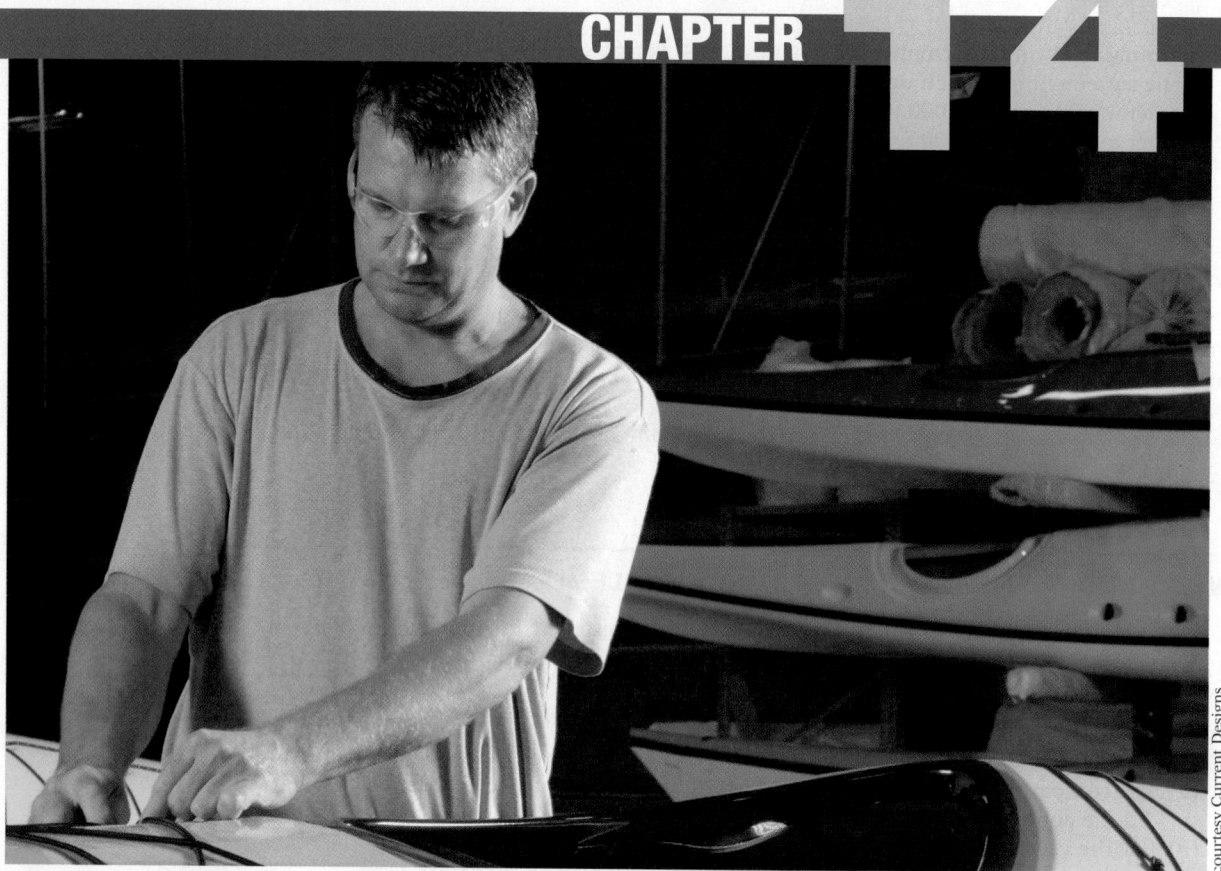

courtesy Current Designs

MANAGERIAL ACCOUNTING

✔ The Navigator

- Scan Learning Objectives
- Read Feature Story
- Scan Preview
- Read Text and Answer **Do it!**
  ○ p. 759 ○ p. 762 ○ p. 765 ○ p. 772
- Work Using the Decision Toolkit
- Review Summary of Learning Objectives
- Work Comprehensive **Do it!** p. 776
- Answer Self-Test Questions
- Complete Assignments
- Go to WileyPLUS for practice and tutorials

LEARNING OBJECTIVES

After studying this chapter, you should be able to:

1 Explain the distinguishing features of managerial accounting.

2 Identify the three broad functions of management.

3 Define the three classes of manufacturing costs.

4 Distinguish between product and period costs.

5 Explain the difference between a merchandising and a manufacturing income statement.

6 Indicate how cost of goods manufactured is determined.

7 Explain the difference between a merchandising and a manufacturing balance sheet.

8 Identify trends in managerial accounting.

✔ The Navigator

Mike Cichanowski grew up on the Mississippi River in Winona, Minnesota. At a young age, he learned to paddle a canoe so he could explore the river. Before long, Mike began crafting his own canoes from bent wood and fiberglass in his dad's garage. Then, when his canoe-making shop outgrew the garage, he moved it into an old warehouse. When that was going to be torn down, Mike came to a critical juncture in his life. He took out a bank loan and built his own small shop, giving birth to the company Wenonah Canoe.

JUST ADD WATER . . . AND PADDLE

Wenonah Canoe soon became known as a pioneer in developing techniques to get the most out of new materials such as plastics, composites, and carbon fibers—maximizing strength while minimizing weight.

In the 1990s, as kayaking became popular, Mike made another critical decision when he acquired Current Designs, a premier Canadian kayak manufacturer. This venture allowed Wenonah to branch out with new product lines while providing Current Designs with much-needed capacity expansion as well as manufacturing expertise. Mike moved Current Designs' headquarters to Minnesota and made a big (and potentially risky) investment in a new production facility. Today, the company's 90 employees produce and sell about 12,000 canoes and kayaks per year, across the country and around the world.

Mike will tell you that business success is "a three-legged stool." The first leg is the knowledge and commitment to make a great product. Wenonah's canoes and Current Designs' kayaks are widely regarded as among the very best. The second leg is the ability to sell your product. Mike's company started off making great canoes, but it took a little longer to figure out how to sell them. The third leg is not something that most of you would immediately associate with entrepreneurial success. It is what goes on behind the scenes—accounting. Good accounting information is absolutely critical to the countless decisions, big and small, that ensure the survival and growth of the company.

Bottom line: No matter how good your product is, and no matter how many units you sell, if you don't have a firm grip on your numbers, you are up a creek without a paddle.

> *Watch the **What Is Managerial Accounting?** video in WileyPLUS for an introduction to managerial accounting and the topics presented in this section of the course.*

Source: www.wenonah.com.

This chapter focuses on issues illustrated in the Feature Story about Current Designs and its parent company Wenonah Canoe. To succeed, the company needs to determine and control the costs of material, labor, and overhead, and understand the relationship between costs and profits. Managers often make decisions that determine their company's fate—and their own. Managers are evaluated on the results of their decisions. Managerial accounting provides tools for assisting management in making decisions and for evaluating the effectiveness of those decisions.

The content and organization of this chapter are as follows.

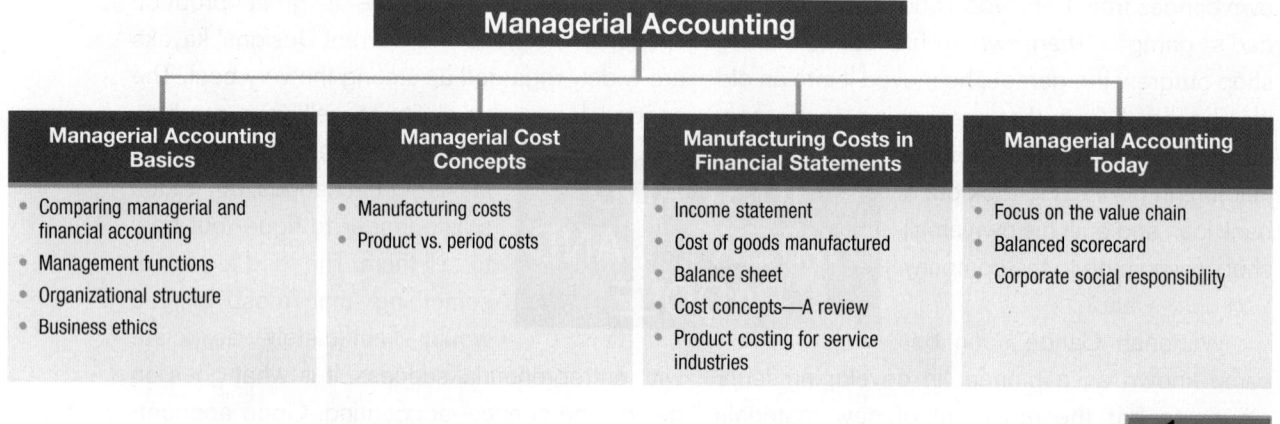

Managerial Accounting			
Managerial Accounting Basics	**Managerial Cost Concepts**	**Manufacturing Costs in Financial Statements**	**Managerial Accounting Today**
• Comparing managerial and financial accounting • Management functions • Organizational structure • Business ethics	• Manufacturing costs • Product vs. period costs	• Income statement • Cost of goods manufactured • Balance sheet • Cost concepts—A review • Product costing for service industries	• Focus on the value chain • Balanced scorecard • Corporate social responsibility

Managerial Accounting Basics

Managerial accounting provides economic and financial information for managers and other internal users. The skills that you will learn in this section of the course will be vital to your future success in business. You don't believe us? Let's look at some examples of some of the crucial activities of employees at Current Designs, and where those activities are addressed in this textbook.

In order to know whether it is making a profit, Current Designs needs accurate information about the cost of each kayak (Chapters 15, 16, and 17). And to stay profitable, Current Designs must adjust the number of kayaks it produces in light of changes in economic conditions and consumer tastes. It then needs to understand how changes in the number of kayaks it produces impact its production costs and profitability (Chapters 18 and 19). Further, Current Designs' managers must often consider alternative courses of action. For example, should the company accept a special order from a customer, produce a particular kayak component internally or outsource it, or continue or discontinue a particular product line (Chapter 20)? Finally, one of the most important, and most difficult, decisions is what price to charge for the kayaks (Appendix J).

In order to plan for the future, Current Designs prepares budgets (Chapter 21), and it then compares its budgeted numbers with its actual results to evaluate performance and identify areas that need to change (Chapters 22 and 23). Finally, it sometimes needs to make substantial investment decisions, such as the building of a new plant or the purchase of new equipment (Chapter 24).

Someday, you are going to face decisions just like these. You may end up in sales, marketing, management, production, or finance. You may work for a company that provides medical care, produces software, or serves up mouth-watering meals. No matter what your position is, and no matter what your product, the skills you acquire in this class will increase your chances of business success. Put another way, in business you can either guess, or you can make an informed decision. As the CEO of Microsoft once noted: "If you're supposed to be making money in business and supposed to be satisfying customers and building market share, there are numbers that characterize those things. And if somebody can't speak to me quantitatively about it, then I'm nervous." This section of the course gives you the skills you need to quantify information so you can make informed business decisions.

COMPARING MANAGERIAL AND FINANCIAL ACCOUNTING

There are both similarities and differences between managerial and financial accounting. First, each field of accounting deals with the economic events of a business. For example, **determining** the unit cost of manufacturing a product is part of managerial accounting. **Reporting** the total cost of goods manufactured and sold is part of financial accounting. In addition, both managerial and financial accounting require that a company's economic events be quantified and communicated to interested parties. Illustration 14-1 summarizes the principal differences between financial accounting and managerial accounting.

> **LEARNING OBJECTIVE 1**
> Explain the distinguishing features of managerial accounting.

Illustration 14-1
Differences between financial and managerial accounting

Feature	Financial Accounting	Managerial Accounting
Primary Users of Reports	External users: stockholders, creditors, and regulators.	Internal users: officers and managers.
Types and Frequency of Reports	Financial statements. Quarterly and annually.	Internal reports. As frequently as needed.
Purpose of Reports	General-purpose.	Special-purpose for specific decisions.
Content of Reports	Pertains to business as a whole. Highly aggregated (condensed). Limited to double-entry accounting and cost data. Generally accepted accounting principles.	Pertains to subunits of the business. Very detailed. Extends beyond double-entry accounting to any relevant data. Standard is relevance to decisions.
Verification Process	Audited by CPA.	No independent audits.

MANAGEMENT FUNCTIONS

Managers' activities and responsibilities can be classified into three broad functions:

1. Planning.
2. Directing.
3. Controlling.

> **LEARNING OBJECTIVE 2**
> Identify the three broad functions of management.

In performing these functions, managers make decisions that have a significant impact on the organization.

Planning requires managers to look ahead and to establish objectives. These objectives are often diverse: maximizing short-term profits and market share, maintaining a commitment to environmental protection, and contributing to social programs. For example, Hewlett-Packard, in an attempt to gain a stronger foothold in the computer industry, has greatly reduced its prices to compete with Dell. A key objective of management is to **add value** to the business under its control. Value is usually measured by the trading price of the company's stock and by the potential selling price of the company.

Directing involves coordinating a company's diverse activities and human resources to produce a smooth-running operation. This function relates to implementing planned objectives and providing necessary incentives to motivate employees. For example, manufacturers such as Campbell Soup Company, General Motors, and Dell must coordinate purchasing, manufacturing, warehousing, and selling. Service corporations such as American Airlines, Federal Express, and AT&T must coordinate scheduling, sales, service, and acquisitions of equipment and supplies. Directing also involves selecting executives, appointing managers and supervisors, and hiring and training employees.

The third management function, **controlling**, is the process of keeping the company's activities on track. In controlling operations, managers determine whether planned goals are being met. When there are deviations from targeted objectives, managers must decide what changes are needed to get back on track. Scandals at companies like Enron, Lucent, and Xerox attest to the fact that companies must have adequate controls to ensure that the company develops and distributes accurate information.

How do managers achieve control? A smart manager in a very small operation can make personal observations, ask good questions, and know how to evaluate the answers. But using this approach in a larger organization would result in chaos. Imagine the president of Current Designs attempting to determine whether the company is meeting its planned objectives, without some record of what has happened and what is expected to occur. Thus, large businesses typically use a formal system of evaluation. These systems include such features as budgets, responsibility centers, and performance evaluation reports—all of which are features of managerial accounting.

Decision-making is not a separate management function. Rather, it is the outcome of the exercise of good judgment in planning, directing, and controlling.

Management Insight
Even the Best Have to Get Better

© Camilla Wisbauer/iStockphoto

Louis Vuitton is a French manufacturer of high-end handbags, wallets, and suitcases. Its reputation for quality and style allows it to charge extremely high prices—for example, $700 for a tote bag. But often in the past, when demand was hot, supply was nonexistent—shelves were empty, and would-be buyers left empty-handed.

Luxury-goods manufacturers used to consider stockouts to be a good thing, but recently Louis Vuitton changed its attitude. The company adopted "lean" processes used by car manufacturers and electronics companies to speed up production of "hot" products. Work is done by flexible teams, with jobs organized based on how long a task takes. By reducing wasted time and eliminating bottlenecks, what used to take 20 to 30 workers eight days to do now takes 6 to 12 workers one day. Also, production employees who used to specialize on a single task on a single product are now multiskilled. This allows them to quickly switch products to meet demand.

To make sure that the factory is making the right products, within a week of a product launch, Louis Vuitton stores around the world feed sales information to the headquarters in France, and production is adjusted accordingly. Finally, the new production processes have also improved quality. Returns of some products are down by two-thirds, which makes quite a difference to the bottom line when the products are pricey.

Source: Christina Passariello, "Louis Vuitton Tries Modern Methods on Factory Lines," *Wall Street Journal* (October 9, 2006).

? What are some of the steps that this company has taken in order to ensure that production meets demand? (See page 797.)

ORGANIZATIONAL STRUCTURE

Most companies prepare **organization charts** to show the interrelationships of activities and the delegation of authority and responsibility within the company. Illustration 14-2 shows a typical organization chart.

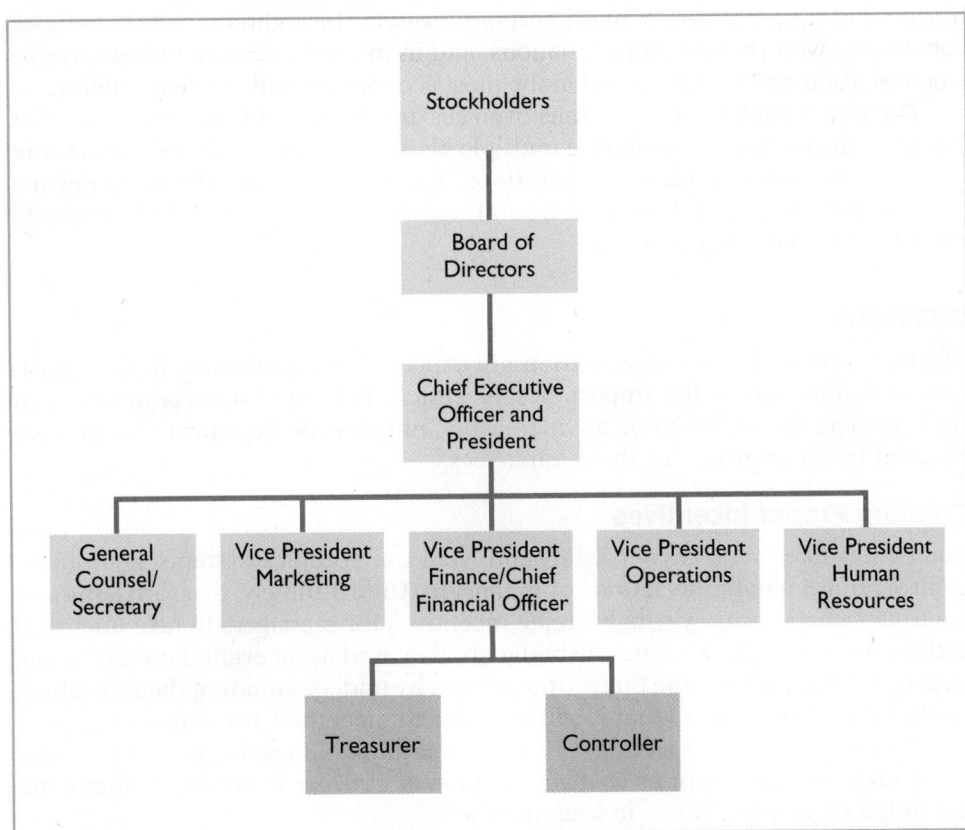

Illustration 14-2 Corporation's organization chart

Stockholders own the corporation, but they manage it indirectly through a board of directors they elect. The board formulates the operating policies for the company or organization. The board also selects officers, such as a president and one or more vice presidents, to execute policy and to perform daily management functions.

The **chief executive officer (CEO)** has overall responsibility for managing the business. As the organization chart above shows, the CEO delegates responsibilities to other officers.

Responsibilities within the company are frequently classified as either line or staff positions. Employees with **line positions** are directly involved in the company's primary revenue-generating operating activities. Examples of line positions include the vice president of operations, vice president of marketing, plant managers, supervisors, and production personnel. Employees with **staff positions** are involved in activities that support the efforts of the line employees. In a company like General Electric or Facebook, employees in finance, legal, and human resources have staff positions. While activities of staff employees are vital to the company, these employees are nonetheless there to serve the line employees who engage in the company's primary operations.

The **chief financial officer (CFO)** is responsible for all of the accounting and finance issues the company faces. The CFO is supported by the **controller** and the **treasurer**. The controller's responsibilities include (1) maintaining the accounting records, (2) maintaining an adequate system of internal control, and (3) preparing financial statements, tax returns, and internal reports. The treasurer has custody of the corporation's funds and is responsible for maintaining the company's cash position.

Also serving the CFO is the internal audit staff. The staff's responsibilities include reviewing the reliability and integrity of financial information provided by the controller and treasurer. Staff members also ensure that internal control systems are functioning properly to safeguard corporate assets. In addition, they investigate compliance with policies and regulations, and in many companies they determine whether resources are being used in the most economical and efficient fashion.

The vice president of operations oversees employees with line positions. For example, the company might have multiple plant managers, each of whom would report to the vice president of operations. Each plant would also have department managers, such as fabricating, painting, and shipping, each of whom would report to the plant manager.

BUSINESS ETHICS

All employees within an organization are expected to act ethically in their business activities. Given the importance of ethical behavior to corporations and their owners (stockholders), an increasing number of organizations provide codes of business ethics for their employees.

Creating Proper Incentives

Companies like Amazon.com, IBM, and Nike use complex systems to monitor, control, and evaluate the actions of managers. Unfortunately, these systems and controls sometimes unwittingly create incentives for managers to take unethical actions. For example, because the budget is also used as an evaluation tool, some managers try to "game" the budgeting process by underestimating their division's predicted performance so that it will be easier to meet their performance targets. On the other hand, if the budget is set at unattainable levels, managers sometimes take unethical actions to meet the targets in order to receive higher compensation or, in some cases, to keep their jobs.

For example, at one time, airline manufacturer Boeing was plagued by a series of scandals including charges of over-billing, corporate espionage, and illegal conflicts of interest. Some long-time employees of Boeing blame the decline in ethics on a change in the corporate culture that took place after Boeing merged with McDonnell Douglas. They suggest that evaluation systems implemented after the merger to evaluate employee performance gave employees the impression that they needed to succeed no matter what actions were required to do so.

As another example, manufacturing companies need to establish production goals for their processes. Again, if controls are not effective and realistic, problems develop. To illustrate, Schering-Plough, a pharmaceutical manufacturer, found that employees were so concerned with meeting production quantity standards that they failed to monitor the quality of the product, and as a result the dosages were often wrong.

Code of Ethical Standards

In response to corporate scandals, the U.S. Congress enacted the Sarbanes-Oxley Act (SOX) to help prevent lapses in internal control. One result of SOX was to clarify top management's responsibility for the company's financial statements. CEOs and CFOs must now certify that financial statements give a fair presentation of the company's operating results and its financial condition. In addition, top managers must certify that the company maintains an adequate system of internal controls to safeguard the company's assets and ensure accurate financial reports.

Another result of SOX is that companies now pay more attention to the composition of the board of directors. In particular, the audit committee of the board of directors must be comprised entirely of independent members (that is, non-employees) and must contain at least one financial expert. Finally, the law substantially increases the penalties for misconduct.

To provide guidance for managerial accountants, the Institute of Management Accountants (IMA) has developed a code of ethical standards, entitled *IMA Statement of Ethical Professional Practice.* Management accountants should not commit acts in violation of these standards. Nor should they condone such acts by others within their organizations. Throughout the remainder of this textbook, we will address various ethical issues managers face.

Do it!

Indicate whether the following statements are true or false.

MANAGERIAL ACCOUNTING CONCEPTS

1. Managerial accountants have a single role within an organization, collecting and reporting costs to management.

2. Financial accounting reports are general-purpose and intended for external users.

3. Managerial accounting reports are special-purpose and issued as frequently as needed.

4. Managers' activities and responsibilities can be classified into three broad functions: cost accounting, budgeting, and internal control.

5. As a result of the Sarbanes-Oxley Act, managerial accounting reports must now comply with generally accepted accounting principles (GAAP).

6. Top managers must certify that a company maintains an adequate system of internal controls.

Solution

1. False. Managerial accountants determine product costs. In addition, managerial accountants are now held responsible for evaluating how well the company is employing its resources. As a result, when the company makes critical strategic decisions, managerial accountants serve as team members alongside personnel from production, marketing, and engineering.

2. True.

3. True.

4. False. Managers' activities are classified into three broad functions: planning, directing, and controlling. Planning requires managers to look ahead to establish objectives. Directing involves coordinating a company's diverse activities and human resources to produce a smooth-running operation. Controlling keeps the company's activities on track.

5. False. SOX clarifies top management's responsibility for the company's financial statements. In addition, top managers must certify that the company maintains an adequate system of internal control to safeguard the company's assets and ensure accurate financial reports.

6. True.

Related exercise material: **BE14-1, BE14-2, BE14-3, E14-1,** and **Do it! 14-1.**

Action Plan

- Understand that managerial accounting is a field of accounting that provides economic and financial information for managers and other internal users.
- Understand that financial accounting provides information for external users.
- Analyze which users require which different types of information.

Managerial Cost Concepts

In order for managers at a company like Current Designs to plan, direct, and control operations effectively, they need good information. One very important type of information is related to costs. Managers should ask questions such as the following.

1. What costs are involved in making a product or providing a service?

2. If we decrease production volume, will costs decrease?

LEARNING OBJECTIVE   3
Define the three classes of manufacturing costs.

3. What impact will automation have on total costs?

4. How can we best control costs?

To answer these questions, managers need reliable and relevant cost information. We now explain and illustrate the various cost categories that companies use.

MANUFACTURING COSTS

Manufacturing consists of activities and processes that convert raw materials into finished goods. Contrast this type of operation with merchandising, which sells merchandise in the form in which it is purchased. Manufacturing costs are classified as direct materials, direct labor, and manufacturing overhead.

Direct Materials

To obtain the materials that will be converted into the finished product, the manufacturer purchases raw materials. **Raw materials** are the basic materials and parts used in the manufacturing process.

Direct Materials

Raw materials that can be physically and directly associated with the finished product during the manufacturing process are direct materials. Examples include flour in the baking of bread, syrup in the bottling of soft drinks, and steel in the making of automobiles. A primary direct material of many Current Designs' kayaks is polyethylene powder. Some of its high-performance kayaks use Kevlar®.

Some raw materials cannot be easily associated with the finished product. These are called indirect materials. Indirect materials have one of two characteristics: (1) They do not physically become part of the finished product (such as lubricants used by Current Designs in its equipment and polishing compounds used for the finishing touches on kayaks). Or, (2) they are impractical to trace to the finished product because their physical association with the finished product is too small in terms of cost (such as cotter pins and lock washers). Companies account for indirect materials as part of **manufacturing overhead**.

Direct Labor

Direct Labor

The work of factory employees that can be physically and directly associated with converting raw materials into finished goods is direct labor. Bottlers at Coca-Cola, bakers at Sara Lee, and equipment operators at Current Designs are employees whose activities are usually classified as direct labor. Indirect labor refers to the work of employees that has no physical association with the finished product, or for which it is impractical to trace costs to the goods produced. Examples include wages of factory maintenance people, factory time-keepers, and factory supervisors. Like indirect materials, companies classify indirect labor as **manufacturing overhead**.

Manufacturing Overhead

Manufacturing overhead consists of costs that are indirectly associated with the manufacture of the finished product. Overhead costs also include manufacturing costs that cannot be classified as direct materials or direct labor. Manufacturing overhead includes indirect materials, indirect labor, depreciation on factory buildings and machines, and insurance, taxes, and maintenance on factory facilities.

One study of manufactured goods found the following magnitudes of the three different product costs as a percentage of the total product cost: direct materials 54%, direct labor 13%, and manufacturing overhead 33%. Note that the direct labor component is the smallest. This component of product cost is dropping substantially because of automation. Companies are working hard to increase productivity by decreasing labor. In some companies, direct labor has become as little as 5% of the total cost.

Alternative Terminology
Some companies use terms such as *factory overhead*, *indirect manufacturing costs*, and *burden* instead of manufacturing overhead.

Allocating direct materials and direct labor costs to specific products is fairly straightforward. Good recordkeeping can tell a company how much plastic it used in making each type of gear, or how many hours of factory labor it took to assemble a part. But allocating overhead costs to specific products presents problems. How much of the purchasing agent's salary is attributable to the hundreds of different products made in the same plant? What about the grease that keeps the machines humming, or the computers that make sure paychecks come out on time? Boiled down to its simplest form, the question becomes: Which products cause the incurrence of which costs? In subsequent chapters, we show various methods of allocating overhead to products.

Management Insight
Why Manufacturing Matters for U.S. Workers

Prior to 2010, U.S. manufacturing employment fell at an average rate of 0.1% per year for 60 years. At the same time, U.S. factory output increased by an average rate of 3.4%. As manufacturers relied more heavily on automation, the number of people they needed declined. However, factory jobs are important because the average wage of a factory worker is $22, twice the average wage of employees in the service sector. Fortunately, manufacturing jobs in the United States increased by 1.2% in 2010, and they are forecast to continue to increase through at least 2015. Why? Because companies like Whirlpool, Caterpillar, and Dow are building huge new plants in the United States to replace old, inefficient U.S. facilities. For many products that are ultimately sold in the United States, it makes more sense to produce them domestically and save on the shipping costs. In addition, these efficient new plants, combined with an experienced workforce, will make it possible to compete with manufacturers in other countries, thereby increasing export potential.

BRIAN SNYDER/Reuters/Landov LLC

Source: Bob Tita, "Whirlpool to Invest in Tennessee Plant," *Wall Street Journal Online* (September 1, 2010); and James R. Hagerty, "U.S. Factories Buck Decline," *Wall Street Journal Online* (January 19, 2011).

 In what ways does the shift to automated factories change the amount and composition of product costs? (See page 797.)

PRODUCT VERSUS PERIOD COSTS

LEARNING OBJECTIVE 4
Distinguish between product and period costs.

Each of the manufacturing cost components—direct materials, direct labor, and manufacturing overhead—are product costs. As the term suggests, **product costs** are costs that are a necessary and integral part of producing the finished product. Companies record product costs, when incurred, as inventory. These costs do not become expenses until the company sells the finished goods inventory. At that point, the company records the expense as cost of goods sold.

Period costs are costs that are matched with the revenue of a specific time period rather than included as part of the cost of a salable product. These are nonmanufacturing costs. Period costs include selling and administrative expenses. In order to determine net income, companies deduct these costs from revenues in the period in which they are incurred.

Alternative Terminology
Product costs are also called *inventoriable costs.*

Illustration 14-3 (page 762) summarizes these relationships and cost terms. Our main concern in this chapter is with product costs.

Illustration 14-3 Product versus period costs

All Costs

Product Costs
Manufacturing Costs

- Direct Materials
- Direct Labor
- Manufacturing Overhead
  - Indirect materials
  - Indirect labor
  - Other indirect costs

Period Costs
Nonmanufacturing Costs

- Selling Expenses
- Administrative Expenses

MANAGERIAL COST CONCEPTS

Action Plan

- Classify as direct materials any raw materials that can be physically and directly associated with the finished product.
- Classify as direct labor the work of factory employees that can be physically and directly associated with the finished product.
- Classify as manufacturing overhead any costs that are indirectly associated with the finished product.

 The Navigator

Do it!

A bicycle company has these costs: tires, salaries of employees who put tires on the wheels, factory building depreciation, lubricants, spokes, salary of factory manager, handlebars, and salaries of factory maintenance employees. Classify each cost as direct materials, direct labor, or overhead.

Solution

Tires, spokes, and handlebars are direct materials. Salaries of employees who put tires on the wheels are direct labor. All of the other costs are manufacturing overhead.

Related exercise material: **BE14-4, BE14-5, BE14-6, BE14-7, E14-2, E14-3, E14-4, E14-5, E14-6, E14-7,** and **Do it!** **14-2.**

Manufacturing Costs in Financial Statements

LEARNING OBJECTIVE **5**

Explain the difference between a merchandising and a manufacturing income statement.

The financial statements of a manufacturer are very similar to those of a merchandiser. For example, you will find many of the same sections and same accounts in the financial statements of Procter & Gamble that you find in the financial statements of Dick's Sporting Goods. The principal differences between their financial statements occur in two places: the cost of goods sold section in the income statement and the current assets section in the balance sheet.

INCOME STATEMENT

Under a periodic inventory system, the income statements of a merchandiser and a manufacturer differ in the cost of goods sold section. Merchandisers compute cost of goods sold by adding the beginning merchandise inventory to the **cost of goods purchased** and subtracting the ending merchandise inventory. Manufacturers compute cost of goods sold by adding the beginning finished goods inventory to the **cost of goods manufactured** and subtracting the ending finished goods inventory. Illustration 14-4 shows these different methods.

Illustration 14-4 Cost of goods sold components

Helpful Hint We assume a periodic inventory system in this illustration.

A number of accounts are involved in determining the cost of goods manufactured. To eliminate excessive detail, income statements typically show only the total cost of goods manufactured. A separate statement, called a Cost of Goods Manufactured Schedule, presents the details. (See the discussion on pages 764–765 and Illustration 14-7.)

Illustration 14-5 shows the different presentations of the cost of goods sold sections for merchandising and manufacturing companies. The other sections of an income statement are similar for merchandisers and manufacturers.

Illustration 14-5 Cost of goods sold sections of merchandising and manufacturing income statements

MERCHANDISING COMPANY Income Statement (partial) For the Year Ended December 31, 2014			MANUFACTURING COMPANY Income Statement (partial) For the Year Ended December 31, 2014		
Cost of goods sold			Cost of goods sold		
Merchandise inventory, Jan. 1	$ 70,000		Finished goods inventory, Jan. 1	$ 90,000	
Cost of goods purchased	650,000		Cost of goods manufactured		
			(see Illustration 14-7)	370,000	
Cost of goods available for sale	720,000		Cost of goods available for sale	460,000	
Less: Merchandise inventory,			Less: Finished goods inventory,		
Dec. 31	400,000		Dec. 31	80,000	
Cost of goods sold	$ 320,000		Cost of goods sold	$ 380,000	

COST OF GOODS MANUFACTURED

An example may help show how companies determine the cost of goods manufactured. Assume that on January 1, Current Designs has a number of kayaks in various stages of production. In total, these partially completed units are called **beginning work in process inventory**. The costs the company assigns to

LEARNING OBJECTIVE 6

Indicate how cost of goods manufactured is determined.

beginning work in process inventory are based on the **manufacturing costs incurred in the prior period**.

Current Designs first incurs manufacturing costs in the current year to complete the work that was in process on January 1. It then incurs manufacturing costs for production of new orders. The sum of the direct materials costs, direct labor costs, and manufacturing overhead incurred in the current year is the total manufacturing costs for the current period.

We now have two cost amounts: (1) the cost of the beginning work in process and (2) the total manufacturing costs for the current period. The sum of these costs is the total cost of work in process for the year.

At the end of the year, Current Designs may have some kayaks that are only partially completed. The costs of these units become the cost of the **ending work in process inventory**. To find the cost of goods manufactured, we subtract this cost from the total cost of work in process. Illustration 14-6 shows the formula for determining the cost of goods manufactured.

Illustration 14-6 Cost of goods manufactured formula

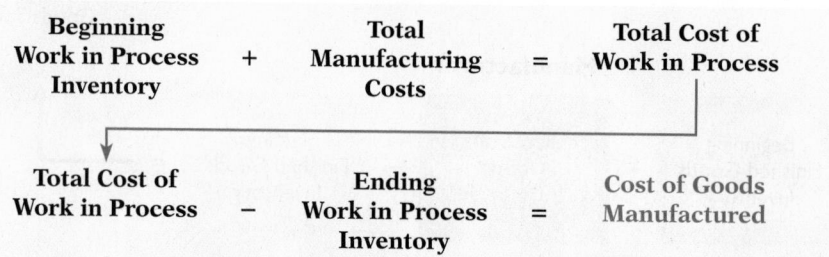

COST OF GOODS MANUFACTURED SCHEDULE

The **cost of goods manufactured schedule** reports cost elements used in calculating cost of goods manufactured. Illustration 14-7 shows the schedule for Current Designs (using assumed data). The schedule presents detailed data for direct materials and for manufacturing overhead.

Illustration 14-7 Cost of goods manufactured schedule

CURRENT DESIGNS
Cost of Goods Manufactured Schedule
For the Year Ended December 31, 2014

Work in process, January 1			$ 18,400
Direct materials			
Raw materials inventory, January 1	$ 16,700		
Raw materials purchases	152,500		
Total raw materials available for use	169,200		
Less: Raw materials inventory, December 31	22,800		
Direct materials used		$146,400	
Direct labor		175,600	
Manufacturing overhead			
Indirect labor	14,300		
Factory repairs	12,600		
Factory utilities	10,100		
Factory depreciation	9,440		
Factory insurance	8,360		
Total manufacturing overhead		54,800	
Total manufacturing costs			376,800
Total cost of work in process			395,200
Less: Work in process, December 31			25,200
Cost of goods manufactured			$370,000

Review Illustration 14-6 and then examine the cost of goods manufactured schedule in Illustration 14-7. You should be able to distinguish between "Total manufacturing costs" and "Cost of goods manufactured." The difference is the effect of the change in work in process during the period.

🧰 DECISION TOOLKIT

DECISION CHECKPOINTS	INFO NEEDED FOR DECISION	TOOL TO USE FOR DECISION	HOW TO EVALUATE RESULTS
Is the company maintaining control over the costs of production?	Cost of material, labor, and overhead	Cost of goods manufactured schedule	Compare the cost of goods manufactured to revenue expected from product sales.

Do it!   The following information is available for Keystone Company.

COST OF GOODS MANUFACTURED

	March 1	March 31
Raw materials inventory	$12,000	$10,000
Work in process inventory	2,500	4,000
Materials purchased in March	$ 90,000	
Direct labor in March	75,000	
Manufacturing overhead in March	220,000	

Prepare the cost of goods manufactured schedule for the month of March.

Solution

KEYSTONE COMPANY
Cost of Goods Manufactured Schedule
For the Month Ended March 31

Work in process, March 1		$ 2,500
Direct materials		
Raw materials, March 1	$ 12,000	
Raw material purchases	90,000	
Total raw materials available for use	102,000	
Less: Raw materials, March 31	10,000	
Direct materials used	$ 92,000	
Direct labor	75,000	
Manufacturing overhead	220,000	
Total manufacturing costs		387,000
Total cost of work in process		389,500
Less: Work in process, March 31		4,000
Cost of goods manufactured		$385,500

Action Plan

- Start with beginning work in process as the first item in the cost of goods manufactured schedule.
- Sum direct materials used, direct labor, and manufacturing overhead to determine total manufacturing costs.
- Sum beginning work in process and total manufacturing costs to determine total cost of work in process.
- Cost of goods manufactured is the total cost of work in process less ending work in process.

The Navigator

Related exercise material: **BE14-8, BE14-10, BE14-11, E14-8, E14-9, E14-10, E14-11, E14-12, E14-13, E14-14, E14-15, E14-16, E14-17,** and **Do it!** **14-3.**

BALANCE SHEET

The balance sheet for a merchandising company shows just one category of inventory. In contrast, the balance sheet for a manufacturer may have three inventory accounts, as shown in Illustration 14-8.

Illustration 14-8 Inventory accounts for a manufacturer

Raw Materials Inventory

Shows the cost of raw materials on hand.

Work in Process Inventory

Shows the cost applicable to units that have been started into production but are only partially completed.

Finished Goods Inventory

Shows the cost of completed goods on hand.

Finished Goods Inventory is to a manufacturer what Merchandise Inventory is to a merchandiser. Each of these classifications represents the goods that the company has available for sale.

The current assets sections presented in Illustration 14-9 contrast the presentations of inventories for merchandising and manufacturing companies. Manufacturing companies generally list their inventories in the order of their liquidity—the order in which they are expected to be realized in cash. Thus, finished goods inventory comes first. The remainder of the balance sheet is similar for the two types of companies.

Illustration 14-9 Current assets sections of merchandising and manufacturing balance sheets

MERCHANDISING COMPANY Balance Sheet December 31, 2014			**MANUFACTURING COMPANY** Balance Sheet December 31, 2014		
Current assets			Current assets		
Cash		$100,000	Cash		$180,000
Receivables (net)		210,000	Receivables (net)		210,000
Merchandise inventory		400,000	Inventories		
Prepaid expenses		22,000	Finished goods	$80,000	
Total current assets		$732,000	Work in process	25,200	
			Raw materials	22,800	128,000
			Prepaid expenses		18,000
			Total current assets		$536,000

Each step in the accounting cycle for a merchandiser applies to a manufacturer. For example, prior to preparing financial statements, manufacturers make adjusting entries. The adjusting entries are essentially the same as those of a merchandiser. The closing entries are also similar for manufacturers and merchandisers.

🧳 DECISION TOOLKIT

DECISION CHECKPOINTS	INFO NEEDED FOR DECISION	TOOL TO USE FOR DECISION	HOW TO EVALUATE RESULTS
What is the composition of a manufacturing company's inventory?	Amount of raw materials, work in process, and finished goods inventories	Balance sheet	Determine whether there are sufficient finished goods, raw materials, and work in process inventories to meet forecasted demand.

COST CONCEPTS—A REVIEW

You have learned a number of cost concepts in this chapter. Because many of these concepts are new, we provide here an extended example for review. Suppose you started your own snowboard factory, Terrain Park Boards. Think that's impossible? Burton Snowboards was started by Jake Burton Carpenter, when he was only 23 years old. Jake initially experimented with 100 different prototype designs before settling on a final design. Then Jake, along with two relatives and a friend, started making 50 boards per day in Londonderry, Vermont. Unfortunately, while they made a lot of boards in their first year, they were only able to sell 300 of them. To get by during those early years, Jake taught tennis and tended bar to pay the bills.

Here are some of the costs that your snowboard factory would incur.

1. The materials cost of each snowboard (wood cores, fiberglass, resins, metal screw holes, metal edges, and ink) is $30.

2. The labor costs (for example, to trim and shape each board using jig saws and band saws) are $40.

3. Depreciation on the factory building and equipment (for example, presses, grinding machines, and lacquer machines) used to make the snowboards is $25,000 per year.

4. Property taxes on the factory building (where the snowboards are made) are $6,000 per year.

5. Advertising costs (mostly online and catalogue) are $60,000 per year.

6. Sales commissions related to snowboard sales are $20 per snowboard.

7. Salaries for factory maintenance employees are $45,000 per year.

8. The salary of the plant manager is $70,000.

9. The cost of shipping is $8 per snowboard.

Illustration 14-10 (page 768) shows how Terrain Park Boards would assign these manufacturing and selling costs to the various categories.

Remember that total manufacturing costs are the sum of the **product costs**— direct materials, direct labor, and manufacturing overhead. If Terrain Park Boards produces 10,000 snowboards the first year, the total manufacturing costs would be $846,000 as shown in Illustration 14-11 (page 768).

Knowing the total manufacturing costs, Terrain Park Boards can compute the manufacturing cost per unit. Assuming 10,000 units, the cost to produce one snowboard is $84.60 ($846,000 ÷ 10,000 units).

In subsequent chapters, we will use extensively the cost concepts discussed in this chapter. So study Illustration 14-10 carefully. If you do not understand any of these classifications, go back and reread the appropriate section in this chapter.

Illustration 14-10
Assignment of costs to cost categories

Terrain Park Boards

	Product Costs			
Cost Item	**Direct Materials**	**Direct Labor**	**Manufacturing Overhead**	**Period Costs**
1. Material cost ($30 per board)	X			
2. Labor costs ($40 per board)		X		
3. Depreciation on factory equipment ($25,000 per year)			X	
4. Property taxes on factory building ($6,000 per year)			X	
5. Advertising costs ($60,000 per year)				X
6. Sales commissions ($20 per board)				X
7. Maintenance salaries (factory facilities) ($45,000 per year)			X	
8. Salary of plant manager ($70,000 per year)			X	
9. Cost of shipping boards ($8 per board)				X

Illustration 14-11
Computation of total manufacturing costs

Cost Number and Item	Manufacturing Cost
1. Material cost ($30 × 10,000)	$ 300,000
2. Labor cost ($40 × 10,000)	400,000
3. Depreciation on factory equipment	25,000
4. Property taxes on factory building	6,000
7. Maintenance salaries (factory facilities)	45,000
8. Salary of plant manager	70,000
Total manufacturing costs	**$846,000**

PRODUCT COSTING FOR SERVICE INDUSTRIES

Much of the U.S. economy has shifted toward an emphasis on services. Today, more than 50% of U.S. workers are employed by service companies. Airlines, marketing agencies, cable companies, and governmental agencies are just a few examples of service companies. How do service companies differ from manufacturing companies? One difference is that services are consumed immediately. For example, when a restaurant produces a meal, that meal is not put in inventory, but it is instead consumed immediately. An airline uses special equipment to provide its product, but again, the output of that equipment is consumed immediately by the customer in the form of a flight. And a marketing agency performs services for its clients that are immediately consumed by the customer in the form of a marketing plan. For a manufacturing company, like Boeing, it often has a long lead time before its airplane is used or consumed by the customer.

This chapter's examples used manufacturing companies because accounting for the manufacturing environment requires the use of the broadest range of accounts. That is, the accounts used by service companies represent a subset of those used by manufacturers because service companies are not producing inventory. Neither the restaurant, the airline, nor the marketing agency discussed above produces an inventoriable product. However, just like a manufacturer, each needs to keep track of the costs of its services in order to know whether it is generating a profit. A successful restaurateur needs to know the cost of each offering on the menu, an airline needs to know the cost of flight service to each destination, and a marketing agency needs to know the cost to develop a marketing plan. Thus, the techniques shown in this chapter, to accumulate manufacturing costs to determine manufacturing inventory, are equally useful for determining the costs of providing services.

For example, let's consider the costs that Hewlett-Packard (HP) might incur on a consulting engagement. A significant portion of its costs would be salaries of consulting personnel. It might also incur travel costs, materials, software costs, and depreciation charges on equipment used by the employees to provide the consulting service. In the same way that it needs to keep track of the cost of manufacturing its computers and printers, HP needs to know what its costs are on each consulting job. It could prepare a cost of services provided schedule similar to the cost of goods manufactured schedule in Illustration 14-7 (page 764). The structure would be essentially the same as the cost of goods manufactured schedule, but section headings would be reflective of the costs of the particular service organization.

Many of the examples we present in subsequent chapters will be based on service companies. To highlight the relevance of the techniques used in this section of the course for service companies, we have placed a service company icon ⚲ next to those items in the text and end-of-chapter materials that relate to nonmanufacturing companies.

Ethics Note Do telecommunications companies have an obligation to provide service to remote or low-user areas for a fee that may be less than the cost of the service?

Service Company Insight

Low Fares but Decent Profits

During 2008, when other airlines were cutting flight service due to the recession, Allegiant Airlines increased capacity by 21%. Sounds crazy, doesn't it? But it must know something, because while the other airlines were losing money, it was generating profits. Consider also that its average one-way fare is only $83. So how does it make money? As a low-budget airline, it focuses on controlling costs. It purchases used planes for $4 million each rather than new planes for $40 million. It flies out of small towns, so wages are low and competition is nonexistent. It only flies a route if its 150-passenger planes are nearly full (it averages about 90% of capacity). If a route isn't filling up, it quits flying it as often or cancels it altogether. It adjusts its prices weekly. The bottom line is that it knows its costs to the penny. Knowing what your costs are might not be glamorous, but it sure beats losing money.

Source: Susan Carey, "For Allegiant, Getaways Mean Profits," *Wall Street Journal Online* (February 18, 2009).

? What are some of the line items that would appear in the cost of services provided schedule of an airline? (See page 797.)

© Stephen Strathdee/iStockphoto

Managerial Accounting Today

The business environment never stands still. Regulations are always changing, global competition continues to intensify, and technology is a source of constant upheaval. In this rapidly changing world, managerial accounting must continue to innovate in order to provide managers with the information they need.

LEARNING OBJECTIVE 8

Identify trends in managerial accounting.

FOCUS ON THE VALUE CHAIN

The **value chain** refers to all business processes associated with providing a product or service. Illustration 14-12 depicts the value chain for a manufacturer. Many of the most significant business innovations in recent years have resulted either directly, or indirectly, from a focus on the value chain. For example, so-called **lean manufacturing**, originally pioneered by Japanese automobile manufacturer Toyota but now widely practiced, reviews all business processes in an effort to increase productivity and eliminate waste, all while continually trying to improve quality.

Illustration 14-12 A
manufacturer's value chain

| Research & development and product design | Acquisition of raw materials | Production | Sales and marketing | Delivery | Customer relations and subsequent services |

Just-in-time (JIT) inventory methods, which have significantly lowered inventory levels and costs for many companies, are one innovation that resulted from the focus on the value chain. Under the JIT inventory method, goods are manufactured or purchased just in time for sale. For example, Dell can deliver a computer within 48 hours of a customer's custom order. However, JIT also necessitates increased emphasis on product quality. Because JIT companies do not have excess inventory on hand, they cannot afford to stop production because of defects or machine breakdowns. If they have to stop production, deliveries will be delayed and customers will be unhappy. For example, a recent design flaw in an Intel computer chip was estimated to cost the company $1 billion in repairs and reduced revenue. As a consequence, many companies now focus on total quality management (TQM) to reduce defects in finished products, with the goal of zero defects. The TQM philosophy has been employed by some of the most successful businesses to improve all aspects of the value chain.

Another innovation, the theory of constraints, involves identification of "bottlenecks"—constraints within the value chain that limit a company's profitability. Once a major constraint has been identified and eliminated, the company moves on to fix the next most significant constraint. General Motors found that by eliminating bottlenecks, it improved its use of overtime labor while meeting customer demand. An application of the theory of constraints is presented in Chapter 19.

Technology has played a big role in the focus on the value chain and the implementation of lean manufacturing. For example, enterprise resource planning (ERP) systems, such as those provided by SAP, provide a comprehensive, centralized, integrated source of information to manage all major business processes—from purchasing, to manufacturing, to sales, to human resources. ERP systems have, in some large companies, replaced as many as 200 individual software packages. In addition, the focus on improving efficiency in the value chain has also resulted in adoption of automated manufacturing processes. Many companies now use computer-integrated manufacturing. These systems often reduce the reliance on manual labor by using robotic equipment. This increases overhead costs as a percentage of total product costs.

As overhead costs increased because of factory automation, the accuracy of overhead cost allocation to specific products became more important. Managerial accounting devised an approach, called activity-based costing (ABC), which allocates overhead based on each product's use of particular activities in making the product. In addition to providing more accurate product costing, ABC also can contribute to increased efficiency in the value chain. For example, suppose one of a company's overhead pools is allocated based on the number of setups that each product requires. If a particular product's cost is high because it is allocated a lot of overhead due to a high number of setups, management will be motivated to try to reduce the number of setups and thus reduce its overhead allocation. ABC is discussed further in Chapter 17.

BALANCED SCORECARD

As companies implement various business practice innovations, managers sometimes focus too enthusiastically on the latest innovation, to the detriment of other areas of the business. For example, by focusing on total quality management, companies sometimes lose sight of cost/benefit considerations. Similarly, in focusing on reducing inventory levels through just-in-time inventory methods, companies sometimes lose sales due to inventory shortages. The balanced scorecard corrects for this limited perspective: This approach uses both financial and nonfinancial measures to evaluate all aspects of a company's operations in an integrated fashion. The performance measures are linked in a cause-and-effect fashion to ensure that they all tie to the company's overall objectives. For example, to increase return on assets, the company could try to increase sales. To increase sales, the company could try to increase customer satisfaction. To increase customer satisfaction, the company could try to reduce product defects. Finally, to reduce product defects, the company could increase employee training. The balanced scorecard, which is discussed further in Chapter 23, is now used by many companies, including Hilton Hotels, Wal-Mart Stores, Inc., and HP.

CORPORATE SOCIAL RESPONSIBILITY

The balanced scorecard attempts to take a broader, more inclusive view of corporate profitability measures. Many companies, however, have begun to evaluate not just corporate profitability but also corporate social responsibility. In addition to profitability, corporate social responsibility considers a company's efforts to employ sustainable business practices with regard to its employees and the environment. This is sometimes referred to as the triple bottom line because it evaluates a company's performance with regard to **people, planet, and profit**. Make no mistake, these companies are still striving to maximize profits—in a competitive world, they won't survive long if they don't. In fact, you might recognize a few of the names on the Forbes.com list of the 100 most sustainable companies in the world. Ever hear of General Electric, adidas, Toyota, Coca-Cola, or Starbucks? These companies have learned that with a long-term, sustainable approach, they can maximize profits while also acting in the best interest of their employees, their communities, and the environment. Throughout this textbook, we discuss situations where real companies use the very skills that you are learning to evaluate decisions from a sustainable perspective.

TRENDS IN MANAGERIAL ACCOUNTING

Match the descriptions that follow with the corresponding terms.

Descriptions:

1. _____ All activities associated with providing a product or service.
2. _____ A method of allocating overhead based on each product's use of activities in making the product.
3. _____ Systems implemented to reduce defects in finished products with the goal of achieving zero defects.
4. _____ A performance-measurement approach that uses both financial and nonfinancial measures, tied to company objectives, to evaluate a company's operations in an integrated fashion.
5. _____ Inventory system in which goods are manufactured or purchased just as they are needed for use.

Terms:

a. Activity-based costing
b. Balanced scorecard
c. Just-in-time (JIT) inventory
d. Total quality management (TQM)
e. Value chain

Action Plan

• Develop a forward-looking view, in order to advise and provide information to various members of the organization.
• Understand current business trends and issues.

Solution

1. e   2. a   3. d   4. b   5. c

Related exercise material: **E14-18** and *Do it!* **14-4.**

USING THE **DECISION TOOLKIT**

Giant Bike Co. Ltd. produces many different models of bicycles. Assume that the market has responded enthusiastically to a new model, the Jaguar. As a result, the company has established a separate manufacturing facility to produce these bicycles. The company produces 1,000 bicycles per month. Giant's monthly manufacturing costs and other data are as follows.

1. Rent on manufacturing equipment (lease cost) $2,000/month
2. Insurance on manufacturing building $750/month
3. Raw materials (frames, tires, etc.) $80/bicycle
4. Utility costs for manufacturing facility $1,000/month
5. Supplies for administrative office $800/month
6. Wages for assembly line workers in manufacturing facility $30/bicycle
7. Depreciation on office equipment $650/month
8. Miscellaneous manufacturing materials (lubricants, solders, etc.) $1.20/bicycle
9. Property taxes on manufacturing building $2,400/year
10. Manufacturing supervisor's salary $3,000/month
11. Advertising for bicycles $30,000/year
12. Sales commissions $10/bicycle
13. Depreciation on manufacturing building $1,500/month

Instructions

(a) Prepare an answer sheet with the following column headings.

	Product Costs			
Cost Item	Direct Materials	Direct Labor	Manufacturing Overhead	Period Costs

Enter each cost item on your answer sheet, placing an "X" mark under the appropriate headings.

(b) Compute total manufacturing costs for the month.

Solution

(a)

	Product Costs			
Cost Item	Direct Materials	Direct Labor	Manufacturing Overhead	Period Costs
1. Rent on manufacturing equipment ($2,000/month)			X	
2. Insurance on manufacturing building ($750/month)			X	
3. Raw materials ($80/bicycle)	X			
4. Manufacturing utilities ($1,000/month)			X	
5. Office supplies ($800/month)				X
6. Wages for assembly workers ($30/bicycle)		X		
7. Depreciation on office equipment ($650/month)				X
8. Miscellaneous manufacturing materials ($1.20/bicycle)			X	
9. Property taxes on manufacturing building ($2,400/year)			X	
10. Manufacturing supervisor's salary ($3,000/month)			X	
11. Advertising cost ($30,000/year)				X
12. Sales commissions ($10/bicycle)				X
13. Depreciation on manufacturing building ($1,500/month)			X	

(b)

Cost Item	Manufacturing Cost
Rent on manufacturing equipment	$ 2,000
Insurance on manufacturing building	750
Raw materials ($80 × 1,000)	80,000
Manufacturing utilities	1,000
Labor ($30 × 1,000)	30,000
Miscellaneous materials ($1.20 × 1,000)	1,200
Property taxes on manufacturing building ($2,400 ÷ 12)	200
Manufacturing supervisor's salary	3,000
Depreciation on manufacturing building	1,500
Total manufacturing costs	$119,650

The Navigator

Summary of Learning Objectives

1 **Explain the distinguishing features of managerial accounting.** The primary users of managerial accounting reports are internal users, who are officers, department heads, managers, and supervisors in the company. Managerial accounting issues internal reports as frequently as the need arises. The purpose of these reports is to provide special-purpose information for a particular user for a specific decision. The content of managerial accounting reports pertains to subunits of the business, may be very detailed, and may extend beyond the double-entry accounting system. The reporting standard is relevance to the decision being made. No independent audits are required in managerial accounting.

2 **Identify the three broad functions of management.** The three functions are planning, directing, and controlling. Planning requires management to look ahead and to establish objectives. Directing involves coordinating the diverse activities and human resources of a company to produce a smooth-running operation. Controlling is the process of keeping the activities on track.

3 **Define the three classes of manufacturing costs.** Manufacturing costs are typically classified as either (1) direct materials, (2) direct labor, or (3) manufacturing overhead. Raw materials that can be physically and directly associated with the finished product during the manufacturing process are called direct materials. The work of factory employees that can be physically and directly associated with converting raw materials into finished goods is considered direct labor. Manufacturing overhead consists of costs that are indirectly associated with the manufacture of the finished product.

4 **Distinguish between product and period costs.** Product costs are costs that are a necessary and integral part of producing the finished product. Product costs are also called inventoriable costs. Under the expense recognition principle, these costs do not become expenses

until the company sells the finished goods inventory. Period costs are costs that are identified with a specific time period rather than with a salable product. These costs relate to nonmanufacturing costs and therefore are not inventoriable costs.

5 **Explain the difference between a merchandising and a manufacturing income statement.** The difference between a merchandising and a manufacturing income statement is in the cost of goods sold section. A manufacturing cost of goods sold section shows beginning and ending finished goods inventories and the cost of goods manufactured.

6 **Indicate how cost of goods manufactured is determined.** Companies add the cost of the beginning work in process to the total manufacturing costs for the current year to arrive at the total cost of work in process for the year. They then subtract the ending work in process from the total cost of work in process to arrive at the cost of goods manufactured.

7 **Explain the difference between a merchandising and a manufacturing balance sheet.** The difference between a merchandising and a manufacturing balance sheet is in the current assets section. The current assets section of a manufacturing company's balance sheet presents three inventory accounts: finished goods inventory, work in process inventory, and raw materials inventory.

8 **Identify trends in managerial accounting.** Managerial accounting has experienced many changes in recent years. Improved practices include a focus on managing the value chain through techniques such as just-in-time inventory, total quality management, activity-based costing, and theory of constraints. The balanced scorecard is now used by many companies in order to attain a more comprehensive view of the company's operations. Finally, companies are now evaluating their performance with regard to their corporate social responsibility.

✔ The Navigator

DECISION TOOLKIT *A SUMMARY*

DECISION CHECKPOINTS	INFO NEEDED FOR DECISION	TOOL TO USE FOR DECISION	HOW TO EVALUATE RESULTS
Is the company maintaining control over the costs of production?	Cost of material, labor, and overhead	Cost of goods manufactured schedule	Compare the cost of goods manufactured to revenue expected from product sales.
What is the composition of a manufacturing company's inventory?	Amount of raw materials, work in process, and finished goods inventories	Balance sheet	Determine whether there are sufficient finished goods, raw materials, and work in process inventories to meet forecasted demand.

Glossary

Activity-based costing (ABC) *(p. 771)* A method of allocating overhead based on each product's use of activities in making the product.

Balanced scorecard *(p. 771)* A performance-measurement approach that uses both financial and nonfinancial measures, tied to company objectives, to evaluate a company's operations in an integrated fashion.

Board of directors *(p. 757)* The group of officials elected by the stockholders of a corporation to formulate operating policies, select officers, and otherwise manage the company.

Chief executive officer (CEO) *(p. 757)* Corporate officer who has overall responsibility for managing the business and delegates responsibilities to other corporate officers.

Chief financial officer (CFO) *(p. 757)* Corporate officer who is responsible for all of the accounting and finance issues of the company.

Controller *(p. 757)* Financial officer responsible for a company's accounting records, system of internal control, and preparation of financial statements, tax returns, and internal reports.

Corporate social responsibility *(p. 771)* The efforts of a company to employ sustainable business practices with regard to its employees and the environment.

Cost of goods manufactured *(p. 764)* Total cost of work in process less the cost of the ending work in process inventory.

Direct labor *(p. 760)* The work of factory employees that can be physically and directly associated with converting raw materials into finished goods.

Direct materials *(p. 760)* Raw materials that can be physically and directly associated with manufacturing the finished product.

Enterprise resource planning (ERP) system *(p. 770)* Software that provides a comprehensive, centralized, integrated source of information used to manage all major business processes.

Indirect labor *(p. 760)* Work of factory employees that has no physical association with the finished product, or for which it is impractical to trace the costs to the goods produced.

Indirect materials *(p. 760)* Raw materials that do not physically become part of the finished product or for which it is impractical to trace to the finished product

because their physical association with the finished product is too small.

Just-in-time (JIT) inventory *(p. 770)* Inventory system in which goods are manufactured or purchased just in time for sale.

Line positions *(p. 757)* Jobs that are directly involved in a company's primary revenue-generating operating activities.

Managerial accounting *(p. 754)* A field of accounting that provides economic and financial information for managers and other internal users.

Manufacturing overhead *(p. 760)* Manufacturing costs that are indirectly associated with the manufacture of the finished product.

Period costs *(p. 761)* Costs that are matched with the revenue of a specific time period and charged to expense as incurred.

Product costs *(p. 761)* Costs that are a necessary and integral part of producing the finished product.

Sarbanes-Oxley Act (SOX) *(p. 758)* Law passed by Congress intended to reduce unethical corporate behavior.

Staff positions *(p. 757)* Jobs that support the efforts of line employees.

Theory of constraints *(p. 770)* A specific approach used to identify and manage constraints in order to achieve the company's goals.

Total cost of work in process *(p. 764)* Cost of the beginning work in process plus total manufacturing costs for the current period. (p. 13).

Total manufacturing costs *(p. 764)* The sum of direct materials, direct labor, and manufacturing overhead incurred in the current period.

Total quality management (TQM) *(p. 770)* Systems implemented to reduce defects in finished products with the goal of achieving zero defects.

Treasurer *(p. 757)* Financial officer responsible for custody of a company's funds and for maintaining its cash position.

Triple bottom line *(p. 771)* The evaluation of a company's social responsibility performance with regard to people, planet, and profit.

Value chain *(p. 770)* All activities that a business processes with providing a product or service.

Comprehensive **Do it!**

Superior Company has the following cost and expense data for the year ending December 31, 2014.

Raw materials, 1/1/14	$ 30,000	Insurance, factory	$ 14,000
Raw materials, 12/31/14	20,000	Property taxes, factory building	6,000
Raw materials purchases	205,000	Sales revenue	1,500,000
Indirect materials	15,000	Delivery expenses	100,000
Work in process, 1/1/14	80,000	Sales commissions	150,000
Work in process, 12/31/14	50,000	Indirect labor	90,000
Finished goods, 1/1/14	110,000	Factory machinery rent	40,000
Finished goods, 12/31/14	120,000	Factory utilities	65,000
Direct labor	350,000	Depreciation, factory building	24,000
Factory manager's salary	35,000	Administrative expenses	300,000

Instructions

(a) Prepare a cost of goods manufactured schedule for Superior Company for 2014.

(b) Prepare an income statement for Superior Company for 2014.

(c) Assume that Superior Company's accounting records show the balances of the following current asset accounts: Cash $17,000, Accounts Receivable (net) $120,000, Prepaid Expenses $13,000, and Short-Term Investments $26,000. Prepare the current assets section of the balance sheet for Superior Company as of December 31, 2014.

Action Plan

- Start with beginning work in process as the first item in the cost of goods manufactured schedule.
- Sum direct materials used, direct labor, and total manufacturing overhead to determine total manufacturing costs.
- Sum beginning work in process and total manufacturing costs to determine total cost of work in process.
- Cost of goods manufactured is the total cost of work in process less ending work in process.
- In the cost of goods sold section of the income statement, show beginning and ending finished goods inventory and cost of goods manufactured.
- In the balance sheet, list manufacturing inventories in the order of their expected realization in cash, with finished goods first.

Solution to Comprehensive **Do it!**

(a)

SUPERIOR COMPANY
Cost of Goods Manufactured Schedule
For the Year Ended December 31, 2014

Work in process, 1/1			$ 80,000
Direct materials			
Raw materials inventory, 1/1	$ 30,000		
Raw materials purchases	205,000		
Total raw materials available for use	235,000		
Less: Raw materials inventory, 12/31	20,000		
Direct materials used		$215,000	
Direct labor		350,000	
Manufacturing overhead			
Indirect labor	90,000		
Factory utilities	65,000		
Factory machinery rent	40,000		
Factory manager's salary	35,000		
Depreciation, factory building	24,000		
Indirect materials	15,000		
Insurance, factory	14,000		
Property taxes, factory building	6,000		
Total manufacturing overhead		289,000	
Total manufacturing costs			854,000
Total cost of work in process			934,000
Less: Work in process, 12/31			50,000
Cost of goods manufactured			$884,000

(b)

SUPERIOR COMPANY
Income Statement
For the Year Ended December 31, 2014

Sales revenue		$1,500,000
Cost of goods sold		
Finished goods inventory, January 1	$110,000	
Cost of goods manufactured	884,000	
Cost of goods available for sale	994,000	
Less: Finished goods inventory, December 31	120,000	
Cost of goods sold		874,000
Gross profit		626,000
Operating expenses		
Administrative expenses	300,000	
Sales commissions	150,000	
Delivery expenses	100,000	
Total operating expenses		550,000
Net income		$ 76,000

(c)

SUPERIOR COMPANY
Balance Sheet (partial)
December 31, 2014

Current assets		
Cash		$ 17,000
Short-term investments		26,000
Accounts receivable (net)		120,000
Inventories		
Finished goods	$120,000	
Work in process	50,000	
Raw materials	20,000	190,000
Prepaid expenses		13,000
Total current assets		$366,000

The Navigator

Self-Test, Brief Exercises, Exercises, Problem Set A, and many more resources are available for practice in WileyPLUS.

Self-Test Questions

Answers are on page 797.

(LO 1) **1.** Managerial accounting:
  (a) is governed by generally accepted accounting principles.
  (b) places emphasis on special-purpose information.
  (c) pertains to the entity as a whole and is highly aggregated.
  (d) is limited to cost data.

2. The management of an organization performs several (LO 2) broad functions. They are:
  (a) planning, directing, and selling.
  (b) planning, directing, and controlling.
  (c) planning, manufacturing, and controlling.
  (d) directing, manufacturing, and controlling.

(LO 2) 3. After passage of the Sarbanes-Oxley Act:
(a) reports prepared by managerial accountants must by audited by CPAs.
(b) CEOs and CFOs must certify that financial statements give a fair presentation of the company's operating results.
(c) the audit committee, rather than top management, is responsible for the company's financial statements.
(d) reports prepared by managerial accountants must comply with generally accepted accounting principles (GAAP).

(LO 3) 4. Direct materials are a:

	Product Cost	Manufacturing Overhead	Period Cost
(a)	Yes	Yes	No
(b)	Yes	No	No
(c)	Yes	Yes	Yes
(d)	No	No	No

(LO 3) 5. Which of the following costs would a computer manufacturer include in manufacturing overhead?
(a) The cost of the disk drives.
(b) The wages earned by computer assemblers.
(c) The cost of the memory chips.
(d) Depreciation on testing equipment.

(LO 3) 6. Which of the following is **not** an element of manufacturing overhead?
(a) Sales manager's salary.
(b) Plant manager's salary.
(c) Factory repairman's wages.
(d) Product inspector's salary.

(LO 4) 7. Indirect labor is a:
(a) nonmanufacturing cost.
(b) raw material cost.
(c) product cost.
(d) period cost.

(LO 4) 8. Which of the following costs are classified as a period cost?
(a) Wages paid to a factory custodian.
(b) Wages paid to a production department supervisor.
(c) Wages paid to a cost accounting department supervisor.
(d) Wages paid to an assembly worker.

(LO 5) 9. For the year, Redder Company has cost of goods manufactured of $600,000, beginning finished goods inventory of $200,000, and ending finished goods inventory of $250,000. The cost of goods sold is:
(a) $450,000.
(b) $500,000.
(c) $550,000.
(d) $600,000.

(LO 5) 10. Cost of goods available for sale is a step in the calculation of cost of goods sold of:
(a) a merchandising company but not a manufacturing company.
(b) a manufacturing company but not a merchandising company.

(c) a merchandising company and a manufacturing company.
(d) neither a manufacturing company nor a merchandising company.

(LO 6) 11. A cost of goods manufactured schedule shows beginning and ending inventories for:
(a) raw materials and work in process only.
(b) work in process only.
(c) raw materials only.
(d) raw materials, work in process, and finished goods.

(LO 6) 12. The formula to determine the cost of goods manufactured is:
(a) Beginning raw materials inventory + Total manufacturing costs − Ending work in process inventory.
(b) Beginning work in process inventory + Total manufacturing costs − Ending finished goods inventory.
(c) Beginning finished good inventory + Total manufacturing costs − Ending finished goods inventory.
(d) Beginning work in process inventory + Total manufacturing costs − Ending work in process inventory.

(LO 7) 13. A manufacturer may report three inventories on its balance sheet: (1) raw materials, (2) work in process, and (3) finished goods. Indicate in what sequence these inventories generally appear on a balance sheet.
(a) (1), (2), (3)
(b) (2), (3), (1)
(c) (3), (1), (2)
(d) (3), (2), (1)

(LO 8) 14. Which of the following managerial accounting techniques attempts to allocate manufacturing overhead in a more meaningful fashion?
(a) Just-in-time inventory.
(b) Total quality management.
(c) Balanced scorecard.
(d) Activity-based costing.

(LO 8) 15. Corporate social responsibility refers to:
(a) the practice by management of reviewing all business processes in an effort to increase productivity and eliminate waste.
(b) an approach used to allocate overhead based on each product's use of activities.
(c) the attempt by management to identify and eliminate constraints within the value chain.
(d) efforts by companies to employ sustainable business practices with regard to employees and the environment.

Go to the book's companion website, **www.wiley.com/college/kimmel**, to access additional Self-Test Questions.

Questions

1. (a) "Managerial accounting is a field of accounting that provides economic information for all interested parties." Do you agree? Explain.
   (b) Joe Delong believes that managerial accounting serves only manufacturing firms. Is Joe correct? Explain.

2. Distinguish between managerial and financial accounting as to (a) primary users of reports, (b) types and frequency of reports, and (c) purpose of reports.

3. How do the content of reports and the verification of reports differ between managerial and financial accounting?

4. In what ways can the budgeting process create incentives for unethical behavior?

5. Linda Olsen is studying for the next accounting midterm examination. Summarize for Linda what she should know about management functions.

6. "Decision-making is management's most important function." Do you agree? Why or why not?

7. Explain the primary difference between line positions and staff positions, and give examples of each.

8. What new rules were enacted under the Sarbanes-Oxley Act to address unethical accounting practices?

9. Tony Andres is studying for his next accounting examination. Explain to Tony what he should know about the differences between the income statements for a manufacturing and for a merchandising company.

10. Jerry Lang is unclear as to the difference between the balance sheets of a merchandising company and a manufacturing company. Explain the difference to Jerry.

11. How are manufacturing costs classified?

12. Mel Finney claims that the distinction between direct and indirect materials is based entirely on physical association with the product. Is Mel correct? Why?

13. Tina Burke is confused about the differences between a product cost and a period cost. Explain the differences to Tina.

14. Identify the differences in the cost of goods sold section of an income statement between a merchandising company and a manufacturing company.

15. The determination of the cost of goods manufactured involves the following factors: (A) beginning work in process inventory, (B) total manufacturing costs, and (C) ending work in process inventory. Identify the meaning of x in the following formulas:
    (a) $A + B = x$
    (b) $A + B - C = x$

16. Sealy Company has beginning raw materials inventory $12,000, ending raw materials inventory $15,000, and raw materials purchases $170,000. What is the cost of direct materials used?

17. Tate Inc. has beginning work in process $26,000, direct materials used $240,000, direct labor $220,000, total manufacturing overhead $180,000, and ending work in process $32,000. What are the total manufacturing costs?

18. Using the data in Question 17, what are (a) the total cost of work in process and (b) the cost of goods manufactured?

19. In what order should manufacturing inventories be listed in a balance sheet?

20. How does the output of manufacturing operations differ from that of service operations?

21. Discuss whether the product costing techniques discussed in this chapter apply equally well to manufacturers and service companies.

22. What is the value chain? Describe, in sequence, the main components of a manufacturer's value chain.

23. What is an enterprise resource planning (ERP) system? What are its primary benefits?

24. Why is product quality important for companies that implement a just-in-time inventory system?

25. Explain what is meant by "balanced" in the balanced scorecard approach.

26. What is activity-based costing, and what are its potential benefits?

Brief Exercises

BE14-1 Complete the following comparison table between managerial and financial accounting.

Distinguish between managerial and financial accounting.
(LO 1), **C**

	Financial Accounting	**Managerial Accounting**
Primary users of reports		
Types of reports		
Frequency of reports		
Purpose of reports		
Content of reports		
Verification process		

Identify important regulatory changes.

(LO 2), C

BE14-2 The Sarbanes-Oxley Act (SOX) has important implications for the financial community. Explain two implications of SOX.

Identify the three management functions.

(LO 2), C

BE14-3 Listed below are the three functions of the management of an organization.

1. Planning   2. Directing   3. Controlling

Identify which of the following statements best describes each of the above functions.

(a) _____ requires management to look ahead and to establish objectives. A key objective of management is to add value to the business.

(b) _____ involves coordinating the diverse activities and human resources of a company to produce a smooth-running operation. This function relates to the implementation of planned objectives.

(c) _____ is the process of keeping the activities on track. Management must determine whether goals are being met and what changes are necessary when there are deviations.

Classify manufacturing costs.

(LO 3), C

BE14-4 Determine whether each of the following costs should be classified as direct materials (DM), direct labor (DL), or manufacturing overhead (MO).

(a) _____ Frames and tires used in manufacturing bicycles.

(b) _____ Wages paid to production workers.

(c) _____ Insurance on factory equipment and machinery.

(d) _____ Depreciation on factory equipment.

Classify manufacturing costs.

(LO 3), C

BE14-5 Indicate whether each of the following costs of an automobile manufacturer would be classified as direct materials, direct labor, or manufacturing overhead.

(a) _____ Windshield.   (e) _____ Factory machinery lubricants.

(b) _____ Engine.   (f) _____ Tires.

(c) _____ Wages of assembly line worker.   (g) _____ Steering wheel.

(d) _____ Depreciation of factory machinery.   (h) _____ Salary of painting supervisor.

Identify product and period costs.

(LO 4), C

BE14-6 Identify whether each of the following costs should be classified as product costs or period costs.

(a) _____ Manufacturing overhead.   (d) _____ Advertising expenses.

(b) _____ Selling expenses.   (e) _____ Direct labor.

(c) _____ Administrative expenses.   (f) _____ Direct material.

Classify manufacturing costs.

(LO 3), C

BE14-7 Presented below are Dieker Company's monthly manufacturing cost data related to its personal computer products.

(a) Utilities for manufacturing equipment $116,000
(b) Raw material (CPU, chips, etc.) $ 85,000
(c) Depreciation on manufacturing building $880,000
(d) Wages for production workers $191,000

Enter each cost item in the following table, placing an "X" under the appropriate headings.

	Product Costs		
	Direct Materials	**Direct Labor**	**Factory Overhead**
(a)			
(b)			
(c)			
(d)			

Compute total manufacturing costs and total cost of work in process.

(LO 6), AP

BE14-8 Francum Company has the following data: direct labor $209,000, direct materials used $180,000, total manufacturing overhead $208,000, and beginning work in process $25,000. Compute (a) total manufacturing costs and (b) total cost of work in process.

Prepare current assets section.

(LO 7), AP

BE14-9 In alphabetical order below are current asset items for Ruiz Company's balance sheet at December 31, 2014. Prepare the current assets section (including a complete heading).

Accounts receivable	$200,000
Cash	62,000
Finished goods	91,000
Prepaid expenses	38,000
Raw materials	73,000
Work in process	87,000

BE14-10 Presented below are incomplete manufacturing cost data. Determine the missing amounts for three different situations.

Determine missing amounts in computing total manufacturing costs.
(LO 6), **AP**

	Direct Materials Used	Direct Labor Used	Factory Overhead	Total Manufacturing Costs
(1)	$40,000	$61,000	$ 50,000	?
(2)	?	$75,000	$140,000	$296,000
(3)	$55,000	?	$111,000	$310,000

BE14-11 Use the same data from BE14–10 above and the data below. Determine the missing amounts.

Determine missing amounts in computing cost of goods manufactured.
(LO 6), **AP**

	Total Manufacturing Cost	Work in Process (1/1)	Work in Process (12/31)	Costs of Goods Manufactured
(1)	?	$120,000	$82,000	?
(2)	$296,000	?	$98,000	$321,000
(3)	$310,000	$463,000	?	$715,000

Do it! Review

Do it! 14-1 Indicate whether the following statements are true or false.

Identify managerial accounting concepts.
(LO 1, 2), **C**

1. Managerial accountants explain and report manufacturing and nonmanufacturing costs, determine cost behaviors, and perform cost-volume-profit analysis, but are not involved in the budget process.
2. Financial accounting reports pertain to subunits of the business and are very detailed.
3. Managerial accounting reports must follow GAAP and are audited by CPAs.
4. Managers' activities and responsibilities can be classified into three broad functions: planning, directing, and controlling.
5. As a result of the Sarbanes-Oxley Act (SOX), top managers must certify that the company maintains an adequate system of internal control.
6. Management accountants follow a code of ethics developed by the Institute of Management Accountants.

Do it! 14-2 A music company has these costs:

Identify managerial cost concepts.
(LO 3, 4), **C**

Advertising	Paper inserts for CD cases
Blank CDs	CD plastic cases
Depreciation of CD image burner	Salaries of sales representatives
	Salaries of factory maintenance employees
Salary of factory manager	Salaries of employees who burn music onto CDs
Factory supplies used	

Classify each cost as a period or a product cost. Within the product cost category, indicate if the cost is part of direct materials (DM), direct labor (DL), or manufacturing overhead (MO).

Do it! 14-3 The following information is available for Fishel Company.

Prepare cost of goods manufactured schedule.
(LO 6), **AP**

	April 1	April 30
Raw materials inventory	$10,000	$14,000
Work in process inventory	5,000	3,500

Materials purchased in April	$ 98,000
Direct labor in April	80,000
Manufacturing overhead in April	180,000

Prepare the cost of goods manufactured schedule for the month of April.

Identify trends in managerial accounting.

(LO 8), **C**

Do it! **14-4** Match the descriptions that follow with the corresponding terms.

Descriptions:

1. _____ Inventory system in which goods are manufactured or purchased just as they are needed for sale.
2. _____ A method of allocating overhead based on each product's use of activities in making the product.
3. _____ Systems that are especially important to firms adopting just-in-time inventory methods.
4. _____ One part of the value chain for a manufacturing company.
5. _____ The U.S. economy is trending toward this.
6. _____ A performance-measurement approach that uses both financial and nonfinancial measures, tied to company objectives, to evaluate a company's operations in an integrated fashion.

Terms:

(a) Activity-based costing
(b) Balanced scorecard
(c) Total quality management (TQM)
(d) Research and development, and product design
(e) Service industries
(f) Just-in-time (JIT) inventory

Exercises

Identify distinguishing features of managerial accounting.

(LO 1), **C**

E14-1 Richard Larkin has prepared the following list of statements about managerial accounting and financial accounting.

1. Financial accounting focuses on providing information to internal users.
2. Analyzing cost-volume-profit relationships is part of managerial accounting.
3. Preparation of budgets is part of financial accounting.
4. Managerial accounting applies only to merchandising and manufacturing companies.
5. Both managerial accounting and financial accounting deal with many of the same economic events.
6. Managerial accounting reports are prepared only quarterly and annually.
7. Financial accounting reports are general-purpose reports.
8. Managerial accounting reports pertain to subunits of the business.
9. Managerial accounting reports must comply with generally accepted accounting principles.
10. Although managerial accountants are expected to behave ethically, there is no code of ethical standards for managerial accountants.

Instructions

Identify each statement as true or false. If false, indicate how to correct the statement.

Classify costs into three classes of manufacturing costs.

(LO 3), **C**

E14-2 Presented below is a list of costs and expenses usually incurred by Barnum Corporation, a manufacturer of furniture, in its factory.

1. Salaries for assembly line inspectors.
2. Insurance on factory machines.
3. Property taxes on the factory building.
4. Factory repairs.
5. Upholstery used in manufacturing furniture.
6. Wages paid to assembly line workers.
7. Factory machinery depreciation.
8. Glue, nails, paint, and other small parts used in production.
9. Factory supervisors' salaries.
10. Wood used in manufacturing furniture.

Instructions

Classify the above items into the following categories: (a) direct materials, (b) direct labor, and (c) manufacturing overhead.

E14-3 Ryan Corporation incurred the following costs while manufacturing its product.

Identify types of cost and explain their accounting.
(LO 3, 4), **C**

Materials used in product	$100,000	Advertising expense	$45,000
Depreciation on plant	60,000	Property taxes on plant	14,000
Property taxes on store	7,500	Delivery expense	21,000
Labor costs of assembly-line workers	110,000	Sales commissions	35,000
Factory supplies used	13,000	Salaries paid to sales clerks	50,000

Instructions

(a) Identify each of the above costs as direct materials, direct labor, manufacturing overhead, or period costs.
(b) Explain the basic difference in accounting for product costs and period costs.

E14-4 Knight Company reports the following costs and expenses in May.

Determine the total amount of various types of costs.
(LO 3, 4), **AP**

Factory utilities	$ 15,500	Direct labor	$69,100
Depreciation on factory		Sales salaries	46,400
equipment	12,650	Property taxes on factory	
Depreciation on delivery trucks	3,800	building	2,500
Indirect factory labor	48,900	Repairs to office equipment	1,300
Indirect materials	80,800	Factory repairs	2,000
Direct materials used	137,600	Advertising	15,000
Factory manager's salary	8,000	Office supplies used	2,640

Instructions

From the information, determine the total amount of:
(a) Manufacturing overhead.
(b) Product costs.
(c) Period costs.

E14-5 Ikerd Company is a manufacturer of personal computers. Various costs and expenses associated with its operations are as follows.

Classify various costs into different cost categories.
(LO 3, 4), **C**

1. Property taxes on the factory building.
2. Production superintendents' salaries.
3. Memory boards and chips used in assembling computers.
4. Depreciation on the factory equipment.
5. Salaries for assembly-line quality control inspectors.
6. Sales commissions paid to sell personal computers.
7. Electrical components used in assembling computers.
8. Wages of workers assembling personal computers.
9. Soldering materials used on factory assembly lines.
10. Salaries for the night security guards for the factory building.

The company intends to classify these costs and expenses into the following categories: (a) direct materials, (b) direct labor, (c) manufacturing overhead, and (d) period costs.

Instructions

List the items (1) through (10). For each item, indicate the cost category to which it belongs.

E14-6 The administrators of Crawford County's Memorial Hospital are interested in identifying the various costs and expenses that are incurred in producing a patient's X-ray. A list of such costs and expenses is presented below.

Classify various costs into different cost categories.
(LO 3), **C**

1. Salaries for the X-ray machine technicians.
2. Wages for the hospital janitorial personnel.
3. Film costs for the X-ray machines.
4. Property taxes on the hospital building.
5. Salary of the X-ray technicians' supervisor.
6. Electricity costs for the X-ray department.
7. Maintenance and repairs on the X-ray machines.

8. X-ray department supplies.
9. Depreciation on the X-ray department equipment.
10. Depreciation on the hospital building.

The administrators want these costs and expenses classified as: (a) direct materials, (b) direct labor, or (c) service overhead.

Instructions

List the items (1) through (10). For each item, indicate the cost category to which the item belongs.

Classify various costs into different cost categories.

(LO 4), **AP**

E14-7 Kwik Delivery Service reports the following costs and expenses in June 2014.

Indirect materials	$ 5,400	Drivers' salaries	$16,000
Depreciation on delivery equipment	11,200	Advertising	3,600
Dispatcher's salary	5,000	Delivery equipment repairs	300
Property taxes on office building	870	Office supplies	650
CEO's salary	12,000	Office utilities	990
Gas and oil for delivery trucks	2,200	Repairs on office equipment	180

Instructions

Determine the total amount of (a) delivery service (product) costs and (b) period costs.

Compute cost of goods manufactured and sold.

(LO 5, 6), **AP**

E14-8 Lopez Corporation incurred the following costs while manufacturing its product.

Materials used in product	$120,000	Advertising expense	$45,000
Depreciation on plant	60,000	Property taxes on plant	14,000
Property taxes on store	7,500	Delivery expense	21,000
Labor costs of assembly-line		Sales commissions	35,000
workers	110,000	Salaries paid to sales	
Factory supplies used	23,000	clerks	50,000

Work in process inventory was $12,000 at January 1 and $15,500 at December 31. Finished goods inventory was $60,000 at January 1 and $45,600 at December 31.

Instructions

(a) Compute cost of goods manufactured.
(b) Compute cost of goods sold.

Determine missing amounts in cost of goods manufactured schedule.

(LO 6), **AP**

E14-9 An incomplete cost of goods manufactured schedule is presented below.

MOLINA COMPANY
Cost of Goods Manufactured Schedule
For the Year Ended December 31, 2014

Work in process (1/1)			$210,000
Direct materials			
Raw materials inventory (1/1)	$?		
Add: Raw materials purchases	158,000		
Total raw materials available for use	?		
Less: Raw materials inventory (12/31)	22,500		
Direct materials used		$190,000	
Direct labor		?	
Manufacturing overhead			
Indirect labor	18,000		
Factory depreciation	36,000		
Factory utilities	68,000		
Total overhead		122,000	
Total manufacturing costs			?
Total cost of work in process			?
Less: Work in process (12/31)			81,000
Cost of goods manufactured			$530,000

Instructions

Complete the cost of goods manufactured schedule for Molina Company.

E14-10 Manufacturing cost data for Copa Company are presented below.

Determine the missing amount of different cost items.
(LO 6), **AN**

	Case A	Case B	Case C
Direct materials used	$ (a)	$68,400	$130,000
Direct labor	57,000	86,000	(g)
Manufacturing overhead	46,500	81,600	102,000
Total manufacturing costs	195,650	(d)	253,700
Work in process 1/1/14	(b)	16,500	(h)
Total cost of work in process	221,500	(e)	337,000
Work in process 12/31/14	(c)	11,000	70,000
Cost of goods manufactured	185,275	(f)	(i)

Instructions

Indicate the missing amount for each letter (a) through (i).

E14-11 Incomplete manufacturing cost data for Colaw Company for 2014 are presented as follows for four different situations.

Determine the missing amount of different cost items, and prepare a condensed cost of goods manufactured schedule.
(LO 6), **AN**

	Direct Materials Used	Direct Labor Used	Manufacturing Overhead	Total Manufacturing Costs	Work in Process 1/1	Work in Process 12/31	Cost of Goods Manufactured
(1)	$127,000	$140,000	$ 87,000	$ (a)	$33,000	$ (b)	$360,000
(2)	(c)	200,000	132,000	450,000	(d)	40,000	470,000
(3)	80,000	100,000	(e)	255,000	60,000	80,000	(f)
(4)	70,000	(g)	75,000	288,000	45,000	(h)	270,000

Instructions

(a) Indicate the missing amount for each letter.

(b) Prepare a condensed cost of goods manufactured schedule for situation (1) for the year ended December 31, 2014.

E14-12 Cepeda Corporation has the following cost records for June 2014.

Prepare a cost of goods manufactured schedule and a partial income statement.
(LO 5, 6), **AP**

Indirect factory labor	$ 4,500	Factory utilities	$ 400
Direct materials used	20,000	Depreciation, factory equipment	1,400
Work in process, 6/1/14	3,000	Direct labor	40,000
Work in process, 6/30/14	3,800	Maintenance, factory equipment	1,800
Finished goods, 6/1/14	5,000	Indirect materials	2,200
Finished goods, 6/30/14	7,500	Factory manager's salary	3,000

Instructions

(a) Prepare a cost of goods manufactured schedule for June 2014.

(b) Prepare an income statement through gross profit for June 2014 assuming sales revenue is $92,100.

E14-13 Joyce Tombert, the bookkeeper for Marks Consulting, a political consulting firm, has recently completed a managerial accounting course at her local college. One of the topics covered in the course was the cost of goods manufactured schedule. Joyce wondered if such a schedule could be prepared for her firm. She realized that, as a service-oriented company, it would have no work in process inventory to consider.

Classify various costs into different categories and prepare cost of services provided schedule.
(LO 4, 5, 6), **AN**

Listed below are the costs her firm incurred for the month ended August 31, 2014.

Supplies used on consulting contracts	$ 1,200
Supplies used in the administrative offices	1,500
Depreciation on equipment used for contract work	900
Depreciation used on administrative office equipment	1,050
Salaries of professionals working on contracts	15,600
Salaries of administrative office personnel	7,700
Janitorial services for professional offices	400
Janitorial services for administrative offices	500
Insurance on contract operations	800
Insurance on administrative operations	900
Utilities for contract operations	1,400
Utilities for administrative offices	1,300

Instructions

(a) Prepare a schedule of cost of contract services provided (similar to a cost of goods manufactured schedule) for the month.

(b) For those costs not included in (a), explain how they would be classified and reported in the financial statements.

Prepare a cost of goods manufactured schedule and a partial income statement.

(LO 5, 6, 7), **AP**

E14-14 The following information is available for Aikman Company.

	January 1, 2014	2014	December 31, 2014
Raw materials inventory	$21,000		$30,000
Work in process inventory	13,500		17,200
Finished goods inventory	27,000		21,000
Materials purchased		$150,000	
Direct labor		220,000	
Manufacturing overhead		180,000	
Sales revenue		910,000	

Instructions

(a) Compute cost of goods manufactured.

(b) Prepare an income statement through gross profit.

(c) Show the presentation of the ending inventories on the December 31, 2014, balance sheet.

(d) How would the income statement and balance sheet of a merchandising company be different from Aikman's financial statements?

Indicate in which schedule or financial statement(s) different cost items will appear.

(LO 5, 6, 7), **C**

E14-15 Chambers Company produces blankets. From its accounting records, it prepares the following schedule and financial statements on a yearly basis.

(a) Cost of goods manufactured schedule.

(b) Income statement.

(c) Balance sheet.

The following items are found in its ledger and accompanying data.

1. Direct labor
2. Raw materials inventory, 1/1
3. Work in process inventory, 12/31
4. Finished goods inventory, 1/1
5. Indirect labor
6. Depreciation on factory machinery
7. Work in process, 1/1
8. Finished goods inventory, 12/31
9. Factory maintenance salaries
10. Cost of goods manufactured
11. Depreciation on delivery equipment
12. Cost of goods available for sale
13. Direct materials used
14. Heat and electricity for factory
15. Repairs to roof of factory building
16. Cost of raw materials purchases

Instructions

List the items (1)–(16). For each item, indicate by using the appropriate letter or letters, the schedule and/or financial statement(s) in which the item will appear.

Prepare a cost of goods manufactured schedule, and present the ending inventories on the balance sheet.

(LO 6, 7), **AP**

E14-16 An analysis of the accounts of Roberts Company reveals the following manufacturing cost data for the month ended June 30, 2014.

Inventories	Beginning	Ending
Raw materials	$9,000	$13,100
Work in process	5,000	7,000
Finished goods	9,000	8,000

Costs incurred: raw materials purchases $54,000, direct labor $47,000, manufacturing overhead $19,900. The specific overhead costs were: indirect labor $5,500, factory insurance $4,000, machinery depreciation $4,000, machinery repairs $1,800, factory utilities $3,100, miscellaneous factory costs $1,500. Assume that all raw materials used were direct materials.

Instructions

(a) Prepare the cost of goods manufactured schedule for the month ended June 30, 2014.

(b) Show the presentation of the ending inventories on the June 30, 2014, balance sheet.

E14-17 Buhler Motor Company manufactures automobiles. During September 2014, the company purchased 5,000 head lamps at a cost of $10 per lamp. Buhler withdrew 4,650 lamps from the warehouse during the month. Fifty of these lamps were used to replace the head lamps in autos used by traveling sales staff. The remaining 4,600 lamps were put in autos manufactured during the month.

Determine the amount of cost to appear in various accounts, and indicate in which financial statements these accounts would appear.

(LO 5, 6, 7), **AP**

Of the autos put into production during September 2014, 90% were completed and transferred to the company's storage lot. Of the cars completed during the month, 70% were sold by September 30.

Instructions

(a) Determine the cost of head lamps that would appear in each of the following accounts at September 30, 2014: Raw Materials, Work in Process, Finished Goods, Cost of Goods Sold, and Selling Expenses.

(b) ✏️⟶ Write a short memo to the chief accountant, indicating whether and where each of the accounts in (a) would appear on the income statement or on the balance sheet at September 30, 2014.

E14-18 The following is a list of terms related to managerial accounting practices.

1. Activity-based costing.
2. Just-in-time inventory.
3. Balanced scorecard.
4. Value chain.

Identify various managerial accounting practices.

(LO 8), **C**

Instructions

Match each of the terms with the statement below that best describes the term.

(a) _____ A performance-measurement technique that attempts to consider and evaluate all aspects of performance using financial and nonfinancial measures in an integrated fashion.

(b) _____ The group of activities associated with providing a product or service.

(c) _____ An approach used to reduce the cost associated with handling and holding inventory by reducing the amount of inventory on hand.

(d) _____ A method used to allocate overhead to products based on each product's use of the activities that cause the incurrence of the overhead cost.

Exercises: Set B and Challenge Exercises

Visit the book's companion website, at **www.wiley.com/college/kimmel**, and choose the Student Companion site to access Exercise Set B and Challenge Exercises.

Problems: Set A

P14-1A Lott Company specializes in manufacturing a unique model of bicycle helmet. The model is well accepted by consumers, and the company has enough orders to keep the factory production at 10,000 helmets per month (80% of its full capacity). Lott's monthly manufacturing cost and other expense data are as follows.

Classify manufacturing costs into different categories and compute the unit cost.

(LO 3, 4), **AP**

Rent on factory equipment	$ 9,000
Insurance on factory building	1,500
Raw materials (plastics, polystyrene, etc.)	75,000
Utility costs for factory	900
Supplies for general office	300
Wages for assembly line workers	53,000
Depreciation on office equipment	800
Miscellaneous materials (glue, thread, etc.)	1,100
Factory manager's salary	5,700
Property taxes on factory building	400
Advertising for helmets	14,000
Sales commissions	10,000
Depreciation on factory building	1,500

Instructions

(a) DM $75,000
DL $53,000
MO $20,100
PC $25,100

(a) Prepare an answer sheet with the following column headings.

| | Product Costs | | | |
Cost Item	Direct Materials	Direct Labor	Manufacturing Overhead	Period Costs

Enter each cost item on your answer sheet, placing the dollar amount under the appropriate headings. Total the dollar amounts in each of the columns.

(b) Compute the cost to produce one helmet.

Classify manufacturing costs into different categories and compute the unit cost.

(LO 3, 4), **AP**

P14-2A Bell Company, a manufacturer of audio systems, started its production in October 2014. For the preceding 3 years, Bell had been a retailer of audio systems. After a thorough survey of audio system markets, Bell decided to turn its retail store into an audio equipment factory.

Raw materials cost for an audio system will total $74 per unit. Workers on the production lines are on average paid $12 per hour. An audio system usually takes 5 hours to complete. In addition, the rent on the equipment used to assemble audio systems amounts to $4,900 per month. Indirect materials cost $5 per system. A supervisor was hired to oversee production; her monthly salary is $3,000.

Factory janitorial costs are $1,300 monthly. Advertising costs for the audio system will be $9,500 per month. The factory building depreciation expense is $7,800 per year. Property taxes on the factory building will be $9,000 per year.

Instructions

(a) DM $111,000
DL $90,000
MO $18,100
PC $9,500

(a) Prepare an answer sheet with the following column headings.

| | Product Costs | | | |
Cost Item	Direct Materials	Direct Labor	Manufacturing Overhead	Period Costs

Assuming that Bell manufactures, on average, 1,500 audio systems per month, enter each cost item on your answer sheet, placing the dollar amount per month under the appropriate headings. Total the dollar amounts in each of the columns.

(b) Compute the cost to produce one audio system.

Indicate the missing amount of different cost items, and prepare a condensed cost of goods manufactured schedule, an income statement, and a partial balance sheet.

(LO 5, 6, 7), **AN**

P14-3A Incomplete manufacturing costs, expenses, and selling data for two different cases are as follows.

| | Case | |
	1	2
Direct materials used	$ 9,600	$ (g)
Direct labor	5,000	8,000
Manufacturing overhead	8,000	4,000
Total manufacturing costs	(a)	16,000
Beginning work in process inventory	1,000	(h)
Ending work in process inventory	(b)	3,000
Sales revenue	24,500	(i)
Sales discounts	2,500	1,400
Cost of goods manufactured	17,000	22,000
Beginning finished goods inventory	(c)	3,300
Goods available for sale	20,000	(j)
Cost of goods sold	(d)	(k)
Ending finished goods inventory	3,400	2,500
Gross profit	(e)	7,000
Operating expenses	2,500	(l)
Net income	(f)	5,000

Instructions

(a) Indicate the missing amount for each letter.

(b) Ending WIP $ 6,600
(c) Current assets $30,000

(b) Prepare a condensed cost of goods manufactured schedule for Case 1.

(c) Prepare an income statement and the current assets section of the balance sheet for Case 1. Assume that in Case 1 the other items in the current assets section are as follows: Cash $4,000, Receivables (net) $15,000, Raw Materials $600, and Prepaid Expenses $400.

P14-4A The following data were taken from the records of Clarkson Company for the fiscal year ended June 30, 2014.

Prepare a cost of goods manufactured schedule, a partial income statement, and a partial balance sheet.
(LO 5, 6, 7), **AP**

Raw Materials		Factory Insurance	$ 4,600
Inventory 7/1/13	$ 48,000	Factory Machinery	
Raw Materials		Depreciation	16,000
Inventory 6/30/14	39,600	Factory Utilities	27,600
Finished Goods		Office Utilities Expense	8,650
Inventory 7/1/13	96,000	Sales Revenue	534,000
Finished Goods		Sales Discounts	4,200
Inventory 6/30/14	75,900	Plant Manager's Salary	58,000
Work in Process		Factory Property Taxes	9,600
Inventory 7/1/13	19,800	Factory Repairs	1,400
Work in Process		Raw Materials Purchases	96,400
Inventory 6/30/14	18,600	Cash	32,000
Direct Labor	139,250		
Indirect Labor	24,460		
Accounts Receivable	27,000		

Instructions

(a) Prepare a cost of goods manufactured schedule. (Assume all raw materials used were direct materials.)

(b) Prepare an income statement through gross profit.

(c) Prepare the current assets section of the balance sheet at June 30, 2014.

(a) CGM $386,910

(b) Gross profit $122,790
(c) Current assets $193,100

P14-5A Phillips Company is a manufacturer of computers. Its controller resigned in October 2014. An inexperienced assistant accountant has prepared the following income statement for the month of October 2014.

Prepare a cost of goods manufactured schedule and a correct income statement.
(LO 5, 6), **AN**

PHILLIPS COMPANY
Income Statement
For the Month Ended October 31, 2014

Sales revenue		$780,000
Less: Operating expenses		
Raw materials purchases	$264,000	
Direct labor cost	190,000	
Advertising expense	90,000	
Selling and administrative salaries	75,000	
Rent on factory facilities	60,000	
Depreciation on sales equipment	45,000	
Depreciation on factory equipment	31,000	
Indirect labor cost	28,000	
Utilities expense	12,000	
Insurance expense	8,000	803,000
Net loss		$ (23,000)

Prior to October 2014, the company had been profitable every month. The company's president is concerned about the accuracy of the income statement. As her friend, you have been asked to review the income statement and make necessary corrections. After examining other manufacturing cost data, you have acquired additional information as follows.

1. Inventory balances at the beginning and end of October were:

	October 1	October 31
Raw materials	$18,000	$29,000
Work in process	16,000	14,000
Finished goods	30,000	45,000

2. Only 75% of the utilities expense and 60% of the insurance expense apply to factory operations. The remaining amounts should be charged to selling and administrative activities.

Instructions

(a) Prepare a schedule of cost of goods manufactured for October 2014.

(b) Prepare a correct income statement for October 2014.

(a) CGM $577,800
(b) NI $ 1,000

Problems: Set B

Classify manufacturing costs into different categories and compute the unit cost.

(LO 3, 4), **AP**

P14-1B Agler Company specializes in manufacturing motorcycle helmets. The company has enough orders to keep the factory production at 1,000 motorcycle helmets per month. Agler's monthly manufacturing cost and other expense data are shown below.

Maintenance costs on factory building	$ 1,500
Factory manager's salary	5,500
Advertising for helmets	8,000
Sales commissions	4,000
Depreciation on factory building	700
Rent on factory equipment	6,000
Insurance on factory building	3,000
Raw materials (plastic, polystyrene, etc.)	25,000
Utility costs for factory	800
Supplies for general office	200
Wages for assembly-line workers	54,000
Depreciation on office equipment	500
Miscellaneous materials (glue, thread, etc.)	2,000

Instructions

(a) DM $25,000
DL $54,000
MO $19,500
PC $12,700

(a) Prepare an answer sheet with the following column headings.

	Product Costs			
Cost Item	Direct Materials	Direct Labor	Manufacturing Overhead	Period Costs

Enter each cost item on your answer sheet, placing the dollar amount under the appropriate headings. Total the dollar amounts in each of the columns.

(b) Compute the cost to produce one motorcycle helmet.

Classify manufacturing costs into different categories and compute the unit cost.

(LO 3, 4), **AP**

P14-2B Elliott Company, a manufacturer of tennis rackets, started production in November 2013. For the preceding 5 years, Elliott had been a retailer of sports equipment. After a thorough survey of tennis racket markets, Elliott decided to turn its retail store into a tennis racket factory.

Raw materials cost for a tennis racket will total $23 per racket. Workers on the production lines are paid on average $15 per hour. A racket usually takes 2 hours to complete. In addition, the rent on the equipment used to produce rackets amounts to $1,300 per month. Indirect materials cost $3 per racket. A supervisor was hired to oversee production; her monthly salary is $3,500.

Janitorial costs are $1,400 monthly. Advertising costs for the rackets will be $8,000 per month. The factory building depreciation expense is $8,400 per year. Property taxes on the factory building will be $9,600 per year.

Instructions

(a) DM $57,500
DL $75,000
MO $15,200
PC $ 8,000

(a) Prepare an answer sheet with the following column headings.

	Product Costs			
Cost Item	Direct Materials	Direct Labor	Manufacturing Overhead	Period Costs

Assuming that Elliott manufactures, on average, 2,500 tennis rackets per month, enter each cost item on your answer sheet, placing the dollar amount per month under the appropriate headings. Total the dollar amounts in each of the columns.

(b) Compute the cost to produce one racket.

Indicate the missing amount of different cost items, and prepare a condensed cost of goods manufactured schedule, an income statement, and a partial balance sheet.

(LO 5, 6, 7), **AN**

P14-3B Incomplete manufacturing costs, expenses, and selling data for two different cases are as follows.

	Case	
	A	B
Direct materials used	$6,300	$ (g)
Direct labor	3,000	4,000
Manufacturing overhead	6,000	5,000

	Case	
	A	**B**
Total manufacturing costs	$ (a)	$16,000
Beginning work in process inventory	1,000	(h)
Ending work in process inventory	(b)	2,000
Sales revenue	22,500	(i)
Sales discounts	1,500	1,200
Cost of goods manufactured	15,800	20,000
Beginning finished goods inventory	(c)	5,000
Goods available for sale	18,300	(j)
Cost of goods sold	(d)	(k)
Ending finished goods inventory	1,200	2,500
Gross profit	(e)	6,000
Operating expenses	2,700	(l)
Net income	(f)	2,200

Instructions

(a) Indicate the missing amount for each letter.

(b) Prepare a condensed cost of goods manufactured schedule for Case A.

(c) Prepare an income statement and the current assets section of the balance sheet for Case A. Assume that in Case A the other items in the current assets section are as follows: Cash $3,000, Receivables (net) $10,000, Raw Materials $700, and Prepaid Expenses $200.

(b) Beg. WIP $ 1,000
(c) Current assets $15,600

P14-4B The following data were taken from the records of Moxie Company for the year ended December 31, 2014.

Prepare a cost of goods manufactured schedule, a partial income statement, and a partial balance sheet.

(LO 5, 6, 7), **AP**

Raw Materials		Factory Insurance	$ 7,400
Inventory 1/1/14	$ 47,000	Factory Machinery	
Raw Materials		Depreciation	7,700
Inventory 12/31/14	44,200	Factory Utilities	12,900
Finished Goods		Office Utilities Expense	8,600
Inventory 1/1/14	85,000	Sales Revenue	465,000
Finished Goods		Sales Discounts	2,500
Inventory 12/31/14	57,800	Plant Manager's Salary	60,000
Work in Process		Factory Property Taxes	6,100
Inventory 1/1/14	9,500	Factory Repairs	800
Work in Process		Raw Materials Purchases	62,500
Inventory 12/31/14	8,000	Cash	18,000
Direct Labor	145,100		
Indirect Labor	18,100		
Accounts Receivable	27,000		

Instructions

(a) Prepare a cost of goods manufactured schedule. (Assume all raw materials used were direct materials.)

(b) Prepare an income statement through gross profit.

(c) Prepare the current assets section of the balance sheet at December 31.

(a) CGM $324,900

(b) Gross profit $ 110,400
(c) Current assets $155,000

P14-5B Ortiz Company is a manufacturer of toys. Its controller resigned in August 2014. An inexperienced assistant accountant has prepared the following income statement for the month of August 2014.

Prepare a cost of goods manufactured schedule and a correct income statement.

(LO 5, 6), **AN**

ORTIZ COMPANY
Income Statement
For the Month Ended August 31, 2014

Sales revenue		$675,000
Less: Operating expenses		
Raw materials purchases	$220,000	
Direct labor cost	160,000	
Advertising expense	75,000	
Selling and administrative salaries	70,000	
Rent on factory facilities	60,000	

Depreciation on sales equipment	50,000	
Depreciation on factory equipment	35,000	
Indirect labor cost	20,000	
Utilities expense	10,000	
Insurance expense	5,000	705,000
Net loss		$ (30,000)

Prior to August 2014, the company had been profitable every month. The company's president is concerned about the accuracy of the income statement. As her friend, you have been asked to review the income statement and make necessary corrections. After examining other manufacturing cost data, you have acquired additional information as follows.

1. Inventory balances at the beginning and end of August were:

	August 1	**August 31**
Raw materials	$19,500	$35,000
Work in process	25,000	21,000
Finished goods	40,000	52,000

2. Only 60% of the utilities expense and 70% of the insurance expense apply to factory operations; the remaining amounts should be charged to selling and administrative activities.

Instructions

(a) CGM $493,000
(b) NL $ (6,500)

(a) Prepare a cost of goods manufactured schedule for August 2014.

(b) Prepare a correct income statement for August 2014.

Problems: Set C

Visit the book's companion website, at **www.wiley.com/college/kimmel**, and choose the Student Companion site to access Problem Set C.

Waterways Continuing Problem

*The **Waterways Problem** starts in this chapter and continues in the remaining chapters. You will find the complete problem for each chapter at the book's companion website.*

(*Note:* The Waterways Problem begins in Chapter 14 and continues in the remaining chapters. You can also find this problem at the book's Student Companion site.)

WCP14   Waterways Corporation is a private corporation formed for the purpose of providing the products and the services needed to irrigate farms, parks, commercial projects, and private lawns. It has a centrally located factory in a U.S. city that manufactures the products it markets to retail outlets across the nation. It also maintains a division that provides installation and warranty servicing in six metropolitan areas.

The mission of Waterways is to manufacture quality parts that can be used for effective irrigation projects that also conserve water. By that effort, the company hopes to satisfy its customers, provide rapid and responsible service, and serve the community and the employees who represent them in each community.

The company has been growing rapidly, so management is considering new ideas to help the company continue its growth and maintain the high quality of its products.

Waterways was founded by Will Winkman, who is the company president and chief executive officer (CEO). Working with him from the company's inception is Will's brother, Ben, whose sprinkler designs and ideas about the installation of proper systems have been a major basis of the company's success. Ben is the vice president who oversees all aspects of design and production in the company.

The factory itself is managed by Todd Senter who hires his line managers to supervise the factory employees. The factory makes all of the parts for the irrigation systems. The purchasing department is managed by Hector Hines.

The installation and training division is overseen by vice president Henry Writer, who supervises the managers of the six local installation operations. Each of these local managers hires his or her own local service people. These service employees are trained by the home office under Henry Writer's direction because of the uniqueness of the company's products.

There is a small human resources department under the direction of Sally Fenton, a vice president who handles the employee paperwork, though hiring is actually performed by the separate departments. Sam Totter is the vice president who heads the sales and marketing area; he oversees 10 well-trained salespeople.

The accounting and finance division of the company is run by Abe Headman, who is the chief financial officer (CFO) and a company vice president. He is a member of the Institute of Management Accountants and holds a certificate in management accounting. He has a small staff of certified public accountants, including a controller and a treasurer, and a staff of accounting input operators who maintain the financial records.

A partial list of Waterways' accounts and their balances for the month of November follows.

Accounts Receivable	$ 275,000
Advertising Expenses	54,000
Cash	260,000
Depreciation—Factory Equipment	16,800
Depreciation—Office Equipment	2,400
Direct Labor	42,000
Factory Supplies Used	16,800
Factory Utilities	10,200
Finished Goods Inventory, November 30	68,800
Finished Goods Inventory, October 31	72,550
Indirect Labor	48,000
Office Supplies Expense	1,600
Other Administrative Expenses	72,000
Prepaid Expenses	41,250
Raw Materials Inventory, November 30	52,700
Raw Materials Inventory, October 31	38,000
Raw Materials Purchases	184,500
Rent—Factory Equipment	47,000
Repairs—Factory Equipment	4,500
Salaries	325,000
Sales Revenue	1,350,000
Sales Commissions	40,500
Work in Process Inventory, October 31	52,700
Work in Process Inventory, November 30	42,000

Instructions

(a) Based on the information given, construct an organizational chart of Waterways Corporation.

(b) A list of accounts and their values are given above. From this information, prepare a cost of goods manufactured schedule, an income statement, and a partial balance sheet for Waterways Corporation for the month of November.

Broadening Your Perspective

Management Decision-Making

Chapters 14–24 contain an exercise based on Current Designs, *the company that was featured at the beginning of this chapter. We are excited to present managerial accounting situations that are based on the operations of a real company. However, to protect the proprietary nature of this information, the amounts in these exercises are realistic but not necessarily the actual data that would be found in Current Designs' accounting records. We sincerely appreciate the cooperation of the people at Current Designs, particularly Mike Cichanowski, Jim Brown, Diane Buswell, and Jake Greseth, who made these exercises possible.*

DECISION-MAKING AT CURRENT DESIGNS

BYP14-1 Mike Cichanowski founded Wenonah Canoe and later purchased Current Designs, a company that designs and manufactures kayaks. The kayak-manufacturing facility is located just a few minutes from the canoe company's headquarters in Winona, Minnesota.

Current Designs makes kayaks using two different processes. (See **www.cdkayak.com/craftsmanship/index.php** for the details of each method.) The rotational molding process uses high temperature to melt polyethylene powder in a closed rotating metal mold to produce a complete kayak hull and deck in a single piece. These kayaks are less labor-intensive and less expensive for the company to produce and sell.

Its other kayaks use the vacuum-bagged composite lamination process (which we will refer to as the composite process). Layers of fiberglass or Kevlar® are carefully placed by hand in a mold and are bonded with resin. Then, a high-pressure vacuum is used to eliminate any excess resin that would otherwise add weight and reduce strength of the finished kayak. These kayaks require a great deal of skilled labor as each boat is individually finished. The exquisite finish of the vacuum-bagged composite kayaks gave rise to Current Designs' tag line, "A work of art, made for life."

Current Designs has the following managers:

Mike Cichanowski, CEO
Diane Buswell, Controller
Deb Welch, Purchasing Manager
Bill Johnson, Sales Manager
Dave Thill, Kayak Plant Manager
Rick Thrune, Production Manager for Composite Kayaks

Instructions
(a) What are the primary information needs of each manager?
(b) Name one special-purpose management accounting report that could be designed for each manager. Include the name of the report, the information it would contain, and how frequently it should be issued.
(c) When Diane Buswell, controller for Current Designs, reviewed the accounting records for a recent period, she noted the following items. Classify each item as a product cost or a period cost. If an item is a product cost, note if it is a direct materials, direct labor, or manufacturing overhead item.

| Payee | Purpose | Product Costs | | | Period Costs |
		Direct Materials	Direct Labor	Manufacturing Overhead	
Winona Agency	Property insurance for the manufacturing plant				
Bill Johnson (sales manager)	Payroll check—payment to sales manager				
Xcel Energy	Electricity for manufacturing plant				
Winona Printing	Price lists for salespeople				
Jim Kaiser (sales representative)	Sales commissions				
Dave Thill (plant manager)	Payroll check—payment to plant manager				
Dana Schultz (kayak assembler)	Payroll check—payment to kayak assembler				
Composite One	Bagging film used when kayaks are assembled; it is discarded after use				
Fastenal	Shop supplies—brooms, paper towels, etc.				
Ravago	Polyethylene powder which is the main ingredient for the rotational molded kayaks				
Winona County	Property taxes on manufacturing plant				
North American Composites	Kevlar® fabric for composite kayaks				
Waste Management	Trash disposal for the company office building				
None	Journal entry to record depreciation of manufacturing equipment				

DECISION-MAKING ACROSS THE ORGANIZATION

BYP14-2 Wendall Company specializes in producing fashion outfits. On July 31, 2014, a tornado touched down at its factory and general office. The inventories in the warehouse and the factory were completely destroyed as was the general office nearby. Next morning, through a careful search of the disaster site, however, Bill Francis, the company's controller, and Elizabeth Walton, the cost accountant, were able to recover a small part of manufacturing cost data for the current month.

"What a horrible experience," sighed Bill. "And the worst part is that we may not have enough records to use in filing an insurance claim."

"It was terrible," replied Elizabeth. "However, I managed to recover some of the manufacturing cost data that I was working on yesterday afternoon. The data indicate that our direct labor cost in July totaled $250,000 and that we had purchased $365,000 of raw materials. Also, I recall that the amount of raw materials used for July was $350,000. But I'm not sure this information will help. The rest of our records are blown away."

"Well, not exactly," said Bill. "I was working on the year-to-date income statement when the tornado warning was announced. My recollection is that our sales in July were $1,240,000 and our gross profit ratio has been 40% of sales. Also, I can remember that our cost of goods available for sale was $770,000 for July."

"Maybe we can work something out from this information!" exclaimed Elizabeth. "My experience tells me that our manufacturing overhead is usually 60% of direct labor."

"Hey, look what I just found," cried Elizabeth. "It's a copy of this June's balance sheet, and it shows that our inventories as of June 30 are Finished goods $38,000, Work in process $25,000, and Raw materials $19,000."

"Super," yelled Bill. "Let's go work something out."

In order to file an insurance claim, Wendall Company must determine the amount of its inventories as of July 31, 2014, the date of the tornado touchdown.

Instructions

With the class divided into groups, determine the amount of cost in the Raw Materials, Work in Process, and Finished Goods inventory accounts as of the date of the tornado touchdown.

MANAGERIAL ANALYSIS

BYP14-3 Tenrack is a fairly large manufacturing company located in the southern United States. The company manufactures tennis rackets, tennis balls, tennis clothing, and tennis shoes, all bearing the company's distinctive logo, a large green question mark on a white flocked tennis ball. The company's sales have been increasing over the past 10 years.

The tennis racket division has recently implemented several advanced manufacturing techniques. Robot arms hold the tennis rackets in place while glue dries, and machine vision systems check for defects. The engineering and design team uses computerized drafting and testing of new products. The following managers work in the tennis racket division:

   Jason Dennis, Sales Manager (supervises all sales representatives)
   Peggy Groneman, Technical Specialist (supervises computer programmers)
   Dave Marley, Cost Accounting Manager (supervises cost accountants)
   Kevin Carson, Production Supervisor (supervises all manufacturing employees)
   Sally Renner, Engineer (supervises all new-product design teams)

Instructions

(a) What are the primary information needs of each manager?
(b) Which, if any, financial accounting report(s) is each likely to use?
(c) Name one special-purpose management accounting report that could be designed for each manager. Include the name of the report, the information it would contain, and how frequently it should be issued.

REAL-WORLD FOCUS

BYP14-4 Anchor Glass Container Corporation, the third largest manufacturer of glass containers in the United States, supplies beverage and food producers and consumer products manufacturers nationwide. Parent company Consumers Packaging Inc. (*Toronto Stock Exchange:* CGC) is a leading international designer and manufacturer of glass containers.

The management discussion on page 796 appeared in a recent annual report of Anchor Glass.

ANCHOR GLASS CONTAINER CORPORATION
Management Discussion

Cost of Products Sold   Cost of products sold as a percentage of net sales was 89.3% in the current year compared to 87.6% in the prior year. The increase in cost of products sold as a percentage of net sales principally reflected the impact of operational problems during the second quarter of the current year at a major furnace at one of the Company's plants, higher downtime, and costs and expenses associated with an increased number of scheduled capital improvement projects, increases in labor, and certain other manufacturing costs (with no corresponding selling price increases in the current year). Reduced fixed costs from the closing of the Streator, Illinois, plant in June of the current year and productivity and efficiency gains partially offset these cost increases.

Instructions
What factors affect the costs of products sold at Anchor Glass Container Corporation?

BYP14-5   The Institute of Management Accountants (IMA) is an organization dedicated to excellence in the practice of management accounting and financial management.

Address: **www.imanet.org**, or go to **www.wiley.com/college/kimmel**

Instructions
At the IMA's home page, locate the answers to the following questions.
(a) How many members does the IMA have, and what are their job titles?
(b) What are some of the benefits of joining the IMA as a student?
(c) Use the chapter locator function to locate the IMA chapter nearest you, and find the name of the chapter president.

Critical Thinking

COMMUNICATION ACTIVITY

BYP14-6   Refer to P14-5A and add the following requirement.

Prepare a letter to the president of the company, Shelly Phillips, describing the changes you made. Explain clearly why net income is different after the changes. Keep the following points in mind as you compose your letter.

1. This is a letter to the president of a company, who is your friend. The style should be generally formal, but you may relax some requirements. For example, you may call the president by her first name.
2. Executives are very busy. Your letter should tell the president your main results first (for example, the amount of net income).
3. You should include brief explanations so that the president can understand the changes you made in the calculations.

ETHICS CASE

BYP14-7   Steve Morgan, controller for Newton Industries, was reviewing production cost reports for the year. One amount in these reports continued to bother him—advertising. During the year, the company had instituted an expensive advertising campaign to sell some of its slower-moving products. It was still too early to tell whether the advertising campaign was successful.

There had been much internal debate as how to report advertising cost. The vice president of finance argued that advertising costs should be reported as a cost of production, just like direct materials and direct labor. He therefore recommended that this cost be identified as manufacturing overhead and reported as part of inventory costs until sold. Others disagreed. Morgan believed that this cost should be reported as an expense of the current period, so as not to overstate net income. Others argued that it should be reported as prepaid advertising and reported as a current asset.

The president finally had to decide the issue. He argued that these costs should be reported as inventory. His arguments were practical ones. He noted that the company was experiencing financial difficulty and expensing this amount in the current period might jeopardize a planned bond offering. Also, by reporting the advertising costs as inventory rather than as prepaid advertising, less attention would be directed to it by the financial community.

Instructions
(a) Who are the stakeholders in this situation?
(b) What are the ethical issues involved in this situation?
(c) What would you do if you were Steve Morgan?

ALL ABOUT YOU

BYP14-8 The primary purpose of managerial accounting is to provide information useful for management decisions. Many of the managerial accounting techniques that you learn in this section of the course will be useful for decisions you make in your everyday life.

Instructions
For each of the following managerial accounting techniques, read the definition provided and then provide an example of a personal situation that would benefit from use of this technique.
(a) Break-even point (page 958).
(b) Budget (page 1082).
(c) Balanced scorecard (page 1211).
(d) Capital budgeting (page 1246).

CONSIDERING YOUR COSTS AND BENEFITS

BYP14-9 As noted in this chapter, because of global competition, companies have become increasingly focused on reducing costs. To reduce costs and remain competitive, many companies are turning to outsourcing. Outsourcing means hiring an outside supplier to provide elements of a product or service rather than producing them internally.

Suppose you are the managing partner in a CPA firm with 30 full-time staff. Larger firms in your community have begun to outsource basic tax-return preparation work to India. Should you outsource your basic tax-return work to India as well? You estimate that you would have to lay off six staff members if you outsource the work. The basic arguments for and against are as follows.

YES: The wages paid to Indian accountants are very low relative to U.S. wages. You will not be able to compete unless you outsource.

NO: Tax-return data is highly sensitive. Many customers will be upset to learn that their data is being emailed around the world.

Instructions
Write a response indicating your position regarding this situation. Provide support for your view.

Answers to Insight and Accounting Across the Organization Questions

p. 756 Even the Best Have to Get Better Q: What are some of the steps that this company has taken in order to ensure that production meets demand? **A:** The company has organized flexible teams, with jobs arranged by the amount of time a task takes. Employees now are multiskilled, so they can switch between tasks and products. Also, the stores now provide sales data more quickly to the manufacturing facility, so that production levels can be changed more quickly in response to demand.

p. 761 Why Manufacturing Matters for U.S. Workers Q: In what ways does the shift to automated factories change the amount and composition of product costs? **A:** As factories become more automated, they become more efficient, increasing output and decreasing cost per unit. The composition of those costs also switches: Factory labor costs decline, and factory overhead costs (e.g., depreciation and maintenance on equipment) increase.

p. 769 Low Fares but Decent Profits Q: What are some of the line items that would appear in the cost of services provided schedule of an airline? **A:** Some of the line items that would appear in the cost of services provided schedule of an airline would be fuel, flight crew salaries, maintenance wages, depreciation on equipment, airport gate fees, and food-service costs.

Answers to Self-Test Questions

1. b **2.** b **3.** b **4.** b **5.** d **6.** a **7.** c **8.** c **9.** c ($200,000 + $600,000 − $250,000) **10.** c **11.** a **12.** d **13.** d **14.** d **15.** d

 Remember to go back to The Navigator box on the chapter opening page and check off your completed work.

Mark Peterson/Redux Pictures

✓ The Navigator

- Scan Learning Objectives
- Read Feature Story
- Scan Preview
- Read Text and answer **Do it!**
  ◯ p. 804 ◯ p. 813 ◯ p. 816 ◯ p. 821
- Work Using the Decision Toolkit
- Review Summary of Learning Objectives
- Work Comprehensive **Do it!** p. 824
- Answer Self-Test Questions
- Complete Assignments
- Go to WileyPLUS for practice and tutorials

JOB ORDER COSTING

LEARNING OBJECTIVES

After studying this chapter, you should be able to:

1 Explain the characteristics and purposes of cost accounting.

2 Describe the flow of costs in a job order cost system.

3 Explain the nature and importance of a job cost sheet.

4 Indicate how the predetermined overhead rate is determined and used.

5 Prepare entries for jobs completed and sold.

6 Distinguish between under- and overapplied manufacturing overhead.

 The Navigator

The financial press is fond of highlighting the fact that, sporting stilettos and leather skirts, Lynn Tilton does not dress like your typical manufacturing executive. Much more important, however, is the fact that her business success is also far from typical. In fact, as the full or partial owner of 74 companies with revenues of more than $8 billion, Tilton is one of the wealthiest female entrepreneurs in the United States. Her company, Patriarch Partners, is sometimes referred to as the largest woman-owned business in America.

Her path to success is an inspiring tale of determination. Tilton started on Wall Street as a single mother, working 15-hour days as she put herself through business school. During years of employment at numerous financial institutions, she developed a knack for analyzing balance sheets and interpreting complex financial information. Eventually, Tilton started her own company, Patriarch Partners, and invested in the debt of a number of distressed companies. She quickly figured out that the only way she was going to make money on those investments was to take control of the companies and try to make them profitable. Thus, seemingly almost by accident, she became the CEO of dozens of failing manufacturing companies. Amazingly, she was able to make these companies profitable when others had given up on them.

As a result of this initial success, Tilton made corporate turn-arounds the focus of her company. Once a business is acquired, she installs a new

SHE SUCCEEDS WHERE OTHERS HAVE FAILED

management team, improves productivity, and identifies new products for the company to produce. For example, she turned a failed paper mill into a producer of alternative fuels, and saved a helicopter company by identifying new customers. When others were fleeing the auto industry, she dove in and bought a number of auto-parts companies.

While she is a tough negotiator, Tilton also has the respect of her workers. Duane Ludgon, a union negotiator says, "Workers really take to Lynn. She's just human and honest with people. I don't say that about many CEOs." In fact, Tilton is a crusader for U.S. manufacturing. She says, "The key to America's future is manufacturing. We simply have to become a country that can make things again."

Not all of her investments are immediate successes. Her investment in a fire-truck manufacturer, American LaFrance, was slow to turn a profit. But everyone involved figured it was only a matter of time before her persistent approach made this fire-truck maker another business that she saved before it went up in smoke.

*Watch the **Making a Hollywood Movie** video in WileyPLUS to learn more about job order costing in the real world.*

Source: Robert Frank, "Tilton Flaunts Her Style at Patriarch," *Wall Street Journal Online* (January 8, 2011).

INSIDE CHAPTER 15 . . .

The Feature Story about Patriarch Partners describes the approach Lynn Tilton uses to turn around a failing company. Accurate costing is critical to this process. For example, in order to submit accurate bids on new jobs and to know whether it profited from past jobs, the company needs a good costing system. This chapter illustrates how these costs are assigned to specific jobs, such as the manufacture of individual fire trucks at one of Tilton's companies, American LaFrance. We begin the discussion in this chapter with an overview of the flow of costs in a job order cost accounting system. We then use a case study to explain and illustrate the documents, entries, and accounts in this type of cost accounting system.

The content and organization of Chapter 15 are as follows.

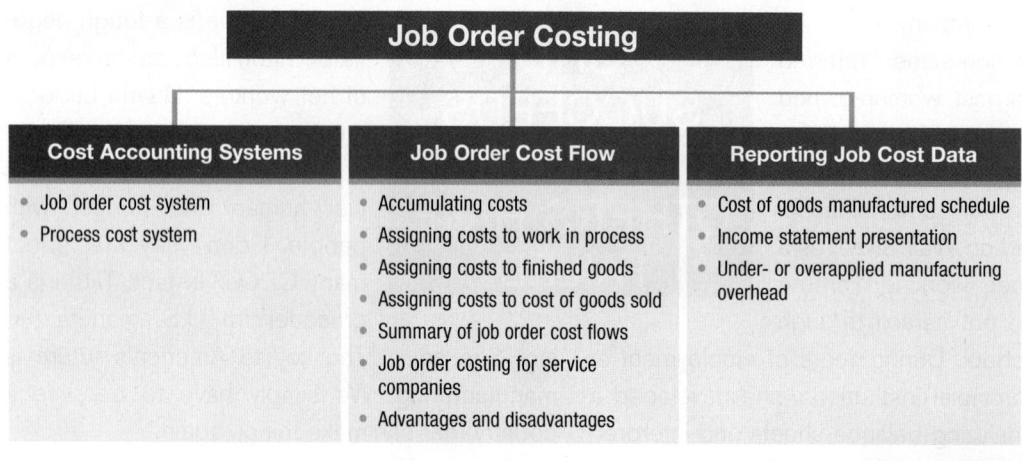

Job Order Costing

Cost Accounting Systems	Job Order Cost Flow	Reporting Job Cost Data
• Job order cost system	• Accumulating costs	• Cost of goods manufactured schedule
• Process cost system	• Assigning costs to work in process	• Income statement presentation
	• Assigning costs to finished goods	• Under- or overapplied manufacturing overhead
	• Assigning costs to cost of goods sold	
	• Summary of job order cost flows	
	• Job order costing for service companies	
	• Advantages and disadvantages	

✔ The Navigator

Cost Accounting Systems

LEARNING OBJECTIVE 1

Explain the characteristics and purposes of cost accounting.

Cost accounting involves measuring, recording, and reporting product costs. Companies determine both the total cost and the unit cost of each product. The accuracy of the product cost information is critical to the success of the company. Companies use this information to determine which products to produce, what price to charge, and the amounts to produce. Accurate product cost information is also vital for effective evaluation of employee performance.

A cost accounting system consists of accounts for the various manufacturing costs. These accounts are fully integrated into the general ledger of a company. An important feature of a cost accounting system is the use of **a perpetual inventory system**. Such a system **provides immediate, up-to-date information on the cost of a product**.

There are two basic types of cost accounting systems: (1) a job order cost system and (2) a process cost system. Although cost accounting systems differ widely from company to company, most involve one of these two traditional product costing systems.

JOB ORDER COST SYSTEM

Under a job order cost system, the company assigns costs to each **job** or to each **batch** of goods. An example of a job is the manufacture of a mainframe computer by IBM, the production of a movie by Disney, or the making of a fire truck by American LaFrance. An example of a batch is the printing of 225 wedding invitations by a local print shop, or the printing of a weekly issue of *Fortune* magazine by a high-tech printer such as Quad Graphics.

An important feature of job order costing is that each job or batch has its own distinguishing characteristics. For example, each house is custom built, each consulting engagement by a CPA firm is unique, and each printing job is different. **The objective is to compute the cost per job.** At each point in manufacturing a product or providing a service, the company can identify the job and its associated costs. A job order cost system measures costs for each completed job, rather than for set time periods. Illustration 15-1 shows the recording of costs in a job order cost system.

Illustration 15-1 Job order cost system

Job Order Cost System
Two Jobs: Wedding Invitations and Menus

Black ink $
Typesetting $
225 Invitations $
225 Envelopes $
Vellum stock, pure white $

Job #9501

Typesetting $
Lamination $
Colored ink $
Yellow stock $
50 Copies $

Job #9502

Each job has distinguishing characteristics and related costs.

PROCESS COST SYSTEM

A company uses a process cost system when it manufactures a large volume of similar products. Production is continuous. Examples of a process cost system are the manufacture of cereal by Kellogg, the refining of petroleum by ExxonMobil, and the production of ice cream by Ben & Jerry's. Process costing accumulates product-related costs **for a period of time** (such as a week or a month) instead of assigning costs to specific products or job orders. In process costing, companies assign the costs to departments or processes for the specified period of time. Illustration 15-2 shows examples of the use of a process cost system. We will discuss the process cost system further in Chapter 16.

Illustration 15-2 Process cost system

Process Cost System
Potato Chips Production

1. Harvest   2. Clean   3. Slice   4. Fry   5. Bag

Similar products are produced over a specified time period.

Can a company use both types of cost systems? Yes. For example, General Motors uses process cost accounting for its standard model cars, such as Malibus and Corvettes, and job order cost accounting for a custom-made limousine for the President of the United States.

The objective of both cost accounting systems is to provide unit cost information for product pricing, cost control, inventory valuation, and financial statement presentation.

Management Insight

Jobs Won, Money Lost

Many companies suffer from poor cost accounting. As a result, they sometimes make products they should not be selling at all, or they buy product components that they could more profitably make themselves. Also, inaccurate cost data leads companies to misallocate capital and frustrates efforts by plant managers to improve efficiency.

For example, consider the case of a diversified company in the business of rebuilding diesel locomotives. The managers thought they were making money, but a consulting firm found that the company had seriously underestimated costs. The company bailed out of the business, and not a moment too soon. Says the consultant who advised the company, "The more contracts it won, the more money it lost." Given that situation, a company cannot stay in business very long!

? What type of costs do you think the company had been underestimating? (See page 843.)

Job Order Cost Flow

LEARNING OBJECTIVE **2**

Describe the flow of costs in a job order cost system.

The flow of costs (direct materials, direct labor, and manufacturing overhead) in job order cost accounting parallels the physical flow of the materials as they are converted into finished goods. As shown in Illustration 15-3, companies first **accumulate** manufacturing costs in the form of raw materials, factory labor, or manufacturing overhead. They then **assign** manufacturing costs to the Work in Process Inventory account. When a job is completed, the company transfers the cost of the job to Finished Goods Inventory. Later when the goods are sold, the company transfers their cost to Cost of Goods Sold.

Illustration 15-3 Flow of costs in job order costing

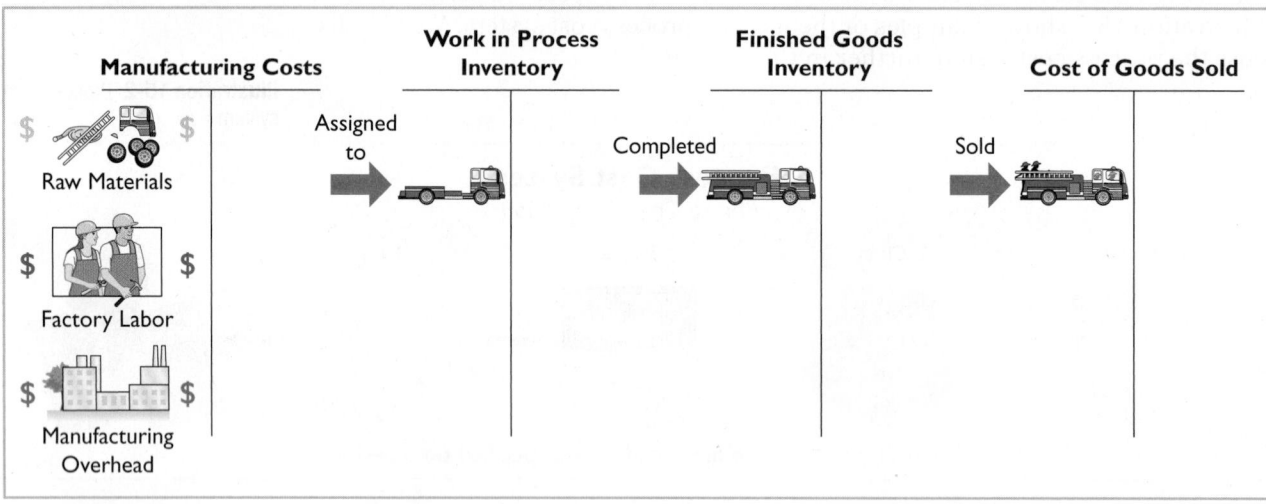

Illustration 15-3 provides a basic overview of the flow of costs in a manufacturing setting. A more detailed presentation of the flow of costs is summarized near the end of this chapter in Illustration 15-15 (page 815). There are two major steps in the flow of costs: (1) **accumulating** the manufacturing costs incurred, and (2) **assigning** the accumulated costs to the work done. The following discussion shows that the company accumulates manufacturing costs incurred by debits to Raw Materials Inventory, Factory Labor, and Manufacturing Overhead.

When the company incurs these costs, it does not attempt to associate the costs with specific jobs. The company makes additional entries to assign manufacturing costs incurred. In the remainder of this chapter, we will use a case study to explain how a job order cost system operates.

ACCUMULATING MANUFACTURING COSTS

To illustrate a job order cost system, we will use the January transactions of Wallace Company, which makes custom electronic sensors for corporate safety applications (such as fire and carbon monoxide) and security applications (such as theft and corporate espionage).

Raw Materials Costs

When Wallace receives the raw materials it has purchased, **it debits the cost of the materials to Raw Materials Inventory**. The company would debit this account for the invoice cost of the raw materials and freight costs chargeable to the purchaser. It would credit the account for purchase discounts taken and purchase returns and allowances. Wallace makes **no effort at this point to associate the cost of materials with specific jobs or orders**.

To illustrate, assume that Wallace purchases 2,000 lithium batteries (Stock No. AA2746) at $5 per unit ($10,000) and 800 electronic modules (Stock No. AA2850) at $40 per unit ($32,000) for a total cost of $42,000 ($10,000 + $32,000). The entry to record this purchase on January 4 is:

	(1)[1]				**Raw Materials Inventory**
Jan. 4	Raw Materials Inventory	42,000			42,000
	Accounts Payable		42,000		
	(Purchase of raw materials on account)				

At this point, Raw Materials Inventory has a balance of $42,000, as shown in the T-account in the margin. As we will explain later in the chapter, the company subsequently assigns direct raw materials inventory to work in process and indirect raw materials inventory to manufacturing overhead.

Factory Labor Costs

Some of a company's employees are involved in the manufacturing process, while others are not. As discussed in Chapter 14, wages and salaries of nonmanufacturing employees are expensed as period costs (e.g., Salaries and Wages Expense). Costs related to manufacturing employees are accumulated in Factory Labor to ensure their treatment as product costs. Factory labor consists of three costs: (1) gross earnings of factory workers, (2) employer payroll taxes on these earnings, and (3) fringe benefits (such as sick pay, pensions, and vacation pay) incurred by the employer. **Companies debit labor costs to Factory Labor as they incur those costs.**

To illustrate, assume that Wallace incurs $32,000 of factory labor costs. Of that amount, $27,000 relates to wages payable and $5,000 relates to payroll taxes payable in February. The entry to record factory labor for the month is:

	(2)				**Factory Labor**
Jan. 31	Factory Labor	32,000			32,000
	Factory Wages Payable		27,000		
	Employer Payroll Taxes Payable		5,000		
	(To record factory labor costs)				

---

[1]The numbers placed above the entries for Wallace Company are used for reference purposes in the summary provided in Illustration 15-15 (page 815).

At this point, Factory Labor has a balance of $32,000, as shown in the T-account in the margin. The company subsequently assigns direct factory labor to work in process and indirect factory labor to manufacturing overhead.

Manufacturing Overhead Costs

A company has many types of overhead costs. If these overhead costs, such as property taxes, depreciation, insurance, and repairs, relate to overhead costs of a nonmanufacturing facility, such as an office building, then these costs are expensed as period costs (e.g., Property Tax Expense, Depreciation Expense, Insurance Expense, and Repairs Expense). If the costs relate to the manufacturing process, then they are accumulated in Manufacturing Overhead, to ensure their treatment as product costs.

Using assumed data, the summary entry for manufacturing overhead in Wallace Company is:

Manufacturing Overhead

13,800	

(3)

Jan. 31	Manufacturing Overhead	13,800	
	Utilities Payable		4,800
	Prepaid Insurance		2,000
	Accounts Payable (for repairs)		2,600
	Accumulated Depreciation		3,000
	Property Taxes Payable		1,400
	(To record overhead costs)		

At this point, Manufacturing Overhead has a balance of $13,800, as shown in the T-account in the margin. The company subsequently assigns manufacturing overhead to work in process.

MANUFACTURING COSTS

Do it!

During the current month, Ringling Company incurs the following manufacturing costs:

(a) Raw material purchases of $4,200 on account.

(b) Incurs factory labor of $18,000. Of that amount, $15,000 relates to wages payable and $3,000 relates to payroll taxes payable.

(c) Factory utilities of $2,200 are payable, prepaid factory insurance of $1,800 has expired, and depreciation on the factory building is $3,500.

Prepare journal entries for each type of manufacturing cost.

Action Plan

• In accumulating manufacturing costs, debit at least one of three accounts: Raw Materials Inventory, Factory Labor, and Manufacturing Overhead.

• Manufacturing overhead costs may be recognized daily. Or manufacturing overhead may be recorded periodically through a summary entry.

✔ The Navigator

Solution

(a)	Raw Materials Inventory	4,200	
	Accounts Payable		4,200
	(Purchases of raw materials on account)		
(b)	Factory Labor	18,000	
	Factory Wages Payable		15,000
	Employer Payroll Taxes Payable		3,000
	(To record factory labor costs)		
(c)	Manufacturing Overhead	7,500	
	Utilities Payable		2,200
	Prepaid Insurance		1,800
	Accumulated Depreciation		3,500
	(To record overhead costs)		

Related exercise material: **BE15-1, BE15-2, E15-1, E15-7, E15-8, E15-11,** and **Do it! 15-1.**

ASSIGNING MANUFACTURING COSTS TO WORK IN PROCESS

Assigning manufacturing costs to work in process results in the following entries.

1. **Debits** made to Work in Process Inventory.
2. **Credits** made to Raw Materials Inventory, Factory Labor, and Manufacturing Overhead.

An essential accounting record in assigning costs to jobs is a **job cost sheet**, as shown in Illustration 15-4. A job cost sheet is a form used to record the costs chargeable to a specific job and to determine the total and unit costs of the completed job.

LEARNING OBJECTIVE **3**

Explain the nature and importance of a job cost sheet.

Illustration 15-4 Job cost sheet

Job Cost Sheet

Job No. _____ Quantity _____
Item _____ Date Requested _____
For _____ Date Completed _____

Date	Direct Materials	Direct Labor	Manufacturing Overhead

Cost of completed job
   Direct materials $ _____
   Direct labor   _____
   Manufacturing overhead   _____
Total cost $ _____
Unit cost (total dollars ÷ quantity) $ _____

Helpful Hint In today's electronic environment, companies typically maintain job cost sheets as computer files.

Companies keep a separate job cost sheet for each job. The job cost sheets constitute the subsidiary ledger for the Work in Process Inventory account. A **subsidiary ledger** consists of individual records for each individual item—in this case, each job. The Work in Process account is referred to as a **control account** because it summarizes the detailed data regarding specific jobs contained in the job cost sheets. **Each entry to Work in Process Inventory must be accompanied by a corresponding posting to one or more job cost sheets.**

Helpful Hint Approvals are an important part of a materials requisition slip because they help to establish individual accountability over inventory.

Raw Materials Costs

Companies assign raw materials costs to jobs when their materials storeroom issues the materials in response to requests. Requests for issuing raw materials are made on a prenumbered materials requisition slip. The materials issued may be used directly on a job, or they may be considered indirect materials. As Illustration 15-5 (page 806) shows, the requisition should indicate the quantity and type of materials withdrawn and the account to be charged. The company will charge direct materials to Work in Process Inventory, and indirect materials to Manufacturing Overhead.

Illustration 15-5 Materials requisition slip

Wallace Company
Materials Requisition Slip

Deliver to: ____Assembly Department____   Req. No.   R247

Charge to: ___Work in Process—Job No. 101___   Date: 1/6/14

Quantity	Description	Stock No.	Cost per Unit	Total
200	Lithium batteries	AA2746	$5.00	$1,000

Requested by *Bruce Howart*   Received by *Herb Crowley*

Approved by *Kap Shin*   Costed by *Heather Remmers*

The company may use any of the inventory costing methods (FIFO, LIFO, or average-cost) in costing the requisitions **to the individual job cost sheets**.

Periodically, the company journalizes the requisitions. For example, if Wallace uses $24,000 of direct materials and $6,000 of indirect materials in January, the entry is:

(4)

Jan. 31	Work in Process Inventory	24,000	
	Manufacturing Overhead	6,000	
	Raw Materials Inventory		30,000
	(To assign materials to jobs and		
	overhead)		

This entry reduces Raw Materials Inventory by $30,000, increases Work in Process Inventory by $24,000, and increases Manufacturing Overhead by $6,000, as shown below.

Illustration 15-6 shows the posting of requisition slip R247 to Job No. 101 and other assumed postings to the job cost sheets for materials. The requisition slips provide the basis for total direct materials costs of $12,000 for Job No. 101, $7,000

for Job No. 102, and $5,000 for Job No. 103. After the company has completed all postings, the sum of the direct materials columns of the job cost sheets (the subsidiary account amounts of $12,000, $7,000, and $5,000) should equal the direct materials debited to Work in Process Inventory (the control account amount of $24,000).

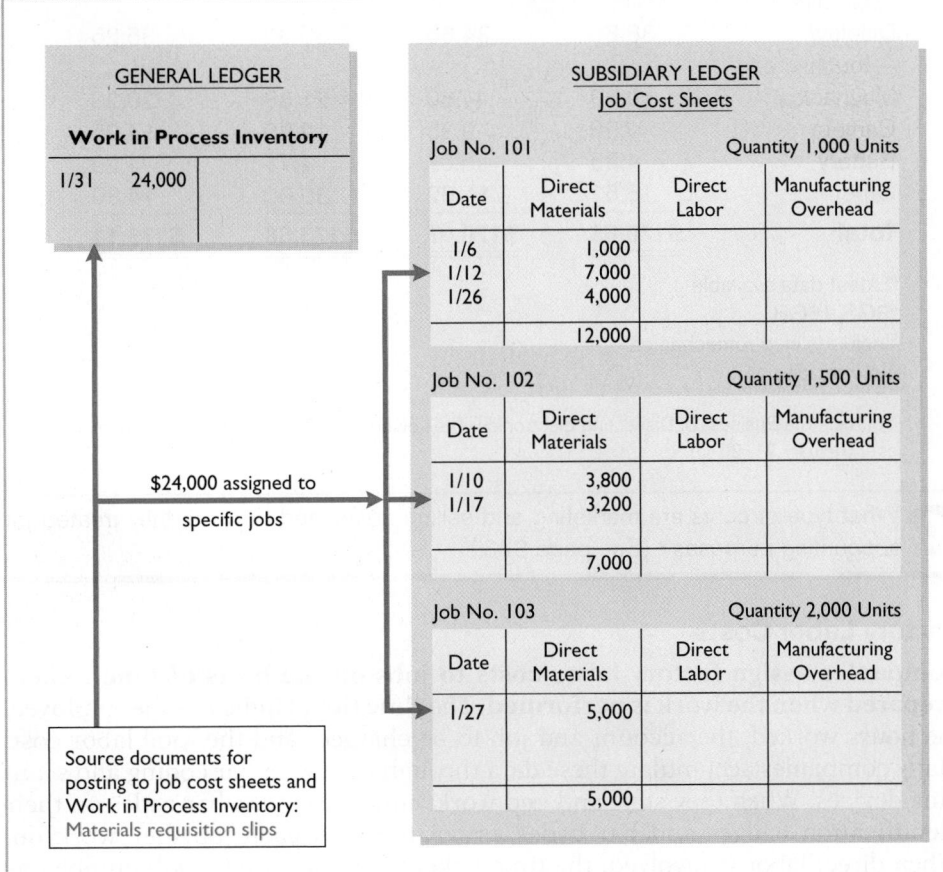

Illustration 15-6 Job cost sheets–direct materials

Helpful Hint Companies post to control accounts monthly, and post to job cost sheets daily.

Helpful Hint Prove the $24,000 direct materials charge to Work in Process Inventory by totaling the charges by jobs:

101	$12,000
102	7,000
103	5,000
	$24,000

Management Insight

The Cost of an iPhone? Just Tear One Apart

All companies need to know what it costs to make their own products—but a lot of companies would also like to know the cost of their competitors' products as well. That's where iSuppli steps in. For a price, iSuppli will tear apart sophisticated electronic devices to tell you what it would cost to replicate. In the case of smart-phones, which often have more than 1,000 tiny components, that is no small feat. As shown in the chart below, components of many smart-phones cost about $170. Assembly is only about another $6.50. The difference between what you pay and the "cost" is not all profit. Consider the additional nonproduction costs of research, design, marketing, patent fees, and selling costs, as shown on page 808.

(Continues)

© TommL/iStockphoto

(Continued)

Sum of the Parts
Cost of components[a], 2009

	Palm Pre	Apple iPhone[b]	Toshiba TG01	Motorola Droid
Integrated circuits	$ 83.96	$ 91.38	$ 68.39	$ 60.83
Display/touchscreen	38.80	34.65	35.30	35.25
Mechanical[c]	19.63	17.80	21.88	20.23
Camera	7.50	9.35	12.80	14.25
Battery	4.25	5.07	4.71	4.25
Other	16.51	11.82	30.60	44.30
Total	**$170.65**	**$170.07**	**$173.68**	**$179.11**

[a]Latest data available
[b]3GS 16GB
[c]Includes electromechanical
Source: iSuppli.

Source: "The Business of Dissecting Electronics: The Lowdown on Teardowns," *The Economist. com* (January 21, 2010).

 What type of costs are marketing and selling costs, and how are they treated for accounting purposes? (See page 843.)

Factory Labor Costs

Companies assign factory labor costs to jobs on the basis of time tickets prepared when the work is performed. The **time ticket** indicates the employee, the hours worked, the account and job to be charged, and the total labor cost. Many companies accumulate these data through the use of bar coding and scanning devices. When they start and end work, employees scan bar codes on their identification badges and bar codes associated with each job they work on. When direct labor is involved, the time ticket must indicate the job number, as shown in Illustration 15-7. The employee's supervisor should approve all time tickets.

Illustration 15-7 Time ticket

Wallace Company
Time Ticket

Date: 1/6/14

Employee: John Nash   Employee No. 124
Charge to: Work in Process   Job No. 101

Time			Hourly Rate	Total Cost
Start	Stop	Total Hours		
0800	1200	4	10.00	40.00

Approved by *Bob Kadler*   Costed by *M Chen*

The time tickets are later sent to the payroll department, which applies the employee's hourly wage rate and computes the total labor cost. Finally, the company journalizes the time tickets. It debits the account Work in Process Inventory for direct labor and debits Manufacturing Overhead for indirect labor. For example, if the $32,000 total factory labor cost consists of $28,000 of direct labor and $4,000 of indirect labor, the entry is:

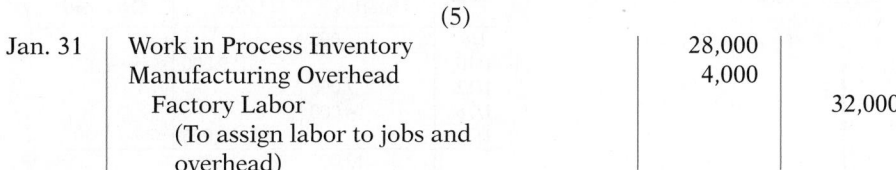

	(5)		
Jan. 31	Work in Process Inventory	28,000	
	Manufacturing Overhead	4,000	
	Factory Labor		32,000
	(To assign labor to jobs and		
	overhead)		

As a result of this entry, Factory Labor is reduced by $32,000 so it has a zero balance, and labor costs are assigned to the appropriate manufacturing accounts. The entry increases Work in Process Inventory by $28,000 and increases Manufacturing Overhead by $4,000, as shown below.

Let's assume that the labor costs chargeable to Wallace's three jobs are $15,000, $9,000, and $4,000. Illustration 15-8 (page 810) shows the Work in Process Inventory and job cost sheets after posting. As in the case of direct materials, the postings to the direct labor columns of the job cost sheets should equal the posting of direct labor to Work in Process Inventory.

MANUFACTURING OVERHEAD COSTS

Companies charge the actual costs of direct materials and direct labor to specific jobs. In contrast, manufacturing **overhead** relates to production operations **as a whole**. As a result, overhead costs cannot be assigned to specific jobs on the basis of actual costs incurred. Instead, companies assign manufacturing overhead to work in process and to specific jobs **on an estimated basis through the use of a predetermined overhead rate**.

The predetermined overhead rate is based on the relationship between estimated annual overhead costs and expected annual operating activity, expressed in terms of a common **activity base**. The company may state the activity in terms of direct labor costs, direct labor hours, machine hours, or any other measure that will provide an equitable basis for applying overhead costs to jobs. Companies establish the predetermined overhead rate at the beginning of the year. Small companies often use a single, company-wide predetermined overhead rate. Large companies often use rates that vary from department to department. The formula for a predetermined overhead rate is shown in Illustration 15-9 (page 810).

LEARNING OBJECTIVE **4**

Indicate how the predetermined overhead rate is determined and used.

Illustration 15-8 Job cost sheets–direct labor

Helpful Hint Prove the $28,000 direct labor charge to Work in Process Inventory by totaling the charges by jobs:

101	$15,000
102	9,000
103	4,000
	$28,000

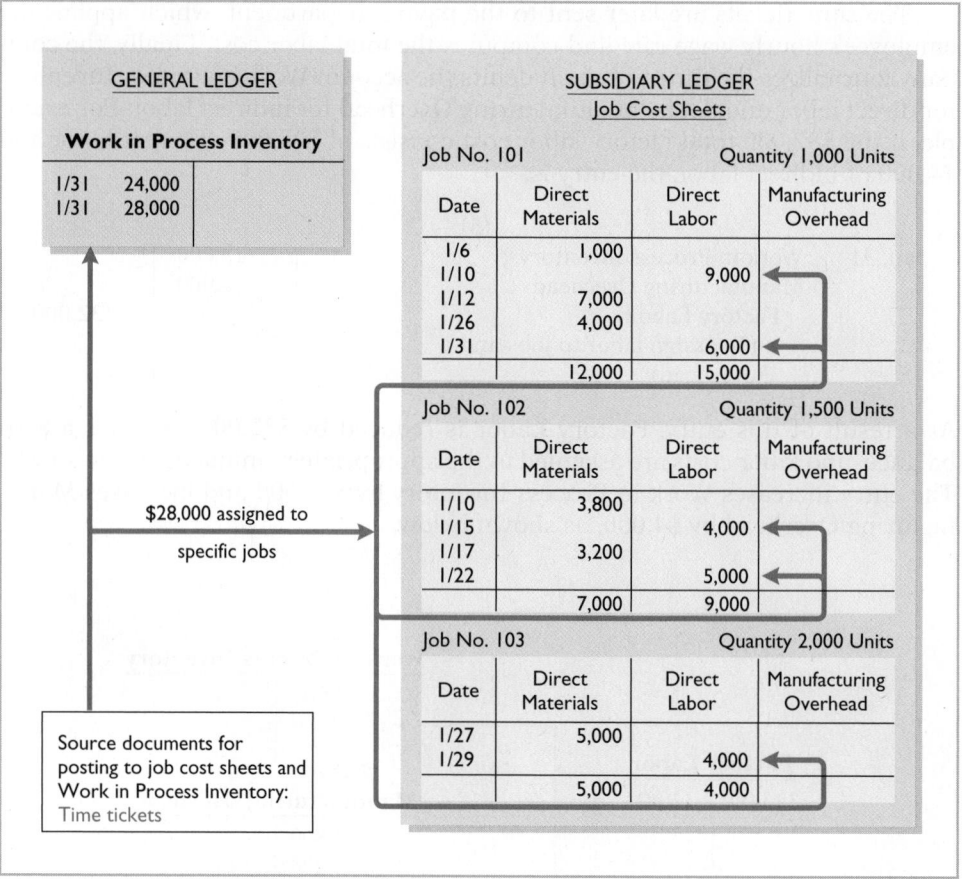

Illustration 15-9 Formula for predetermined overhead rate

$$\text{Estimated Annual Overhead Costs} \div \text{Expected Annual Operating Activity} = \text{Predetermined Overhead Rate}$$

Overhead relates to production operations as a whole. To know what "the whole" is, the logical thing is to wait until the end of the year's operations. At that time, the company knows all of its costs for the period. As a practical matter, though, managers cannot wait until the end of the year. To price products effectively as they are completed, managers need information about product costs of specific jobs completed during the year. Using a predetermined overhead rate enables a cost to be determined for the job immediately. Illustration 15-10 indicates how manufacturing overhead is assigned to work in process.

Illustration 15-10 Using predetermined overhead rates

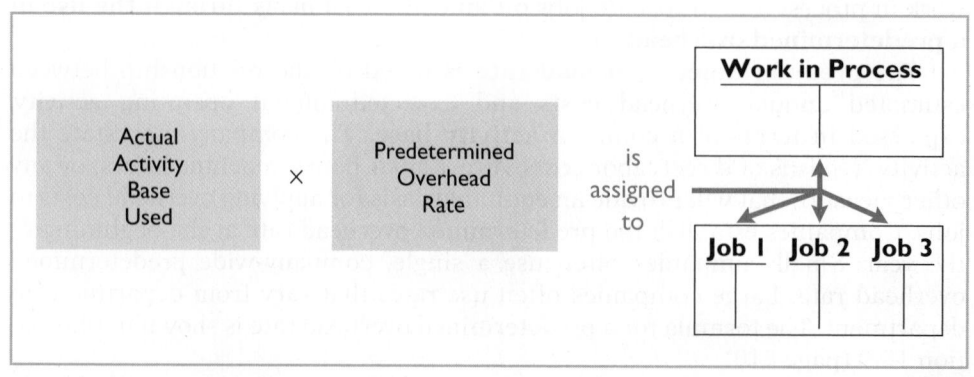

Wallace uses direct labor cost as the activity base. Assuming that the company expects annual overhead costs to be $280,000 and direct labor costs for the year to be $350,000, the overhead rate is 80%, computed as follows.

$$\$280,000 \div \$350,000 = 80\%$$

This means that for every dollar of direct labor, Wallace will assign 80 cents of manufacturing overhead to a job. The use of a predetermined overhead rate enables the company to determine the approximate total cost of each job **when it completes the job**.

Historically, companies used direct labor costs or direct labor hours as the activity base. The reason was the relatively high correlation between direct labor and manufacturing overhead. Today more companies are using **machine hours as the activity base, due to increased reliance on automation in manufacturing operations**. Or, as mentioned in Chapter 14 (and discussed more fully in Chapter 17), many companies now use activity-based costing to more accurately allocate overhead costs based on the activities that give rise to the costs.

A company may use more than one activity base. For example, if a job is manufactured in more than one factory department, each department may have its own overhead rate. In the Feature Story, American LaFrance might use two bases in assigning overhead to fire-truck jobs: direct materials dollars for indirect materials, and direct labor hours for such costs as insurance and supervisors' salaries.

Wallace Company applies manufacturing overhead to work in process when it assigns direct labor costs. It also applies manufacturing overhead to specific jobs at the same time. For January, Wallace applied overhead of $22,400 in response to its assignment of $28,000 of direct labor costs (direct labor cost of $28,000 × 80%). The following entry records this application.

(6)

Jan. 31	Work in Process Inventory	22,400	
	Manufacturing Overhead		22,400
	(To assign overhead to jobs)		

This entry reduces the balance in Manufacturing Overhead and increases Work in Process Inventory by $22,400, as shown below.

Manufacturing Overhead		Work in Process Inventory	
13,800	22,400	24,000	
6,000		28,000	
4,000		22,400	

The overhead that Wallace applies to each job will be 80% of the direct labor cost of the job for the month. Illustration 15-11 (page 812) shows the Work in Process Inventory account and the job cost sheets after posting. Note that the debit of $22,400 to Work in Process Inventory equals the sum of the overhead applied to jobs: Job 101 $12,000 + Job 102 $7,200 + Job 103 $3,200.

At the end of each month, the **balance in Work in Process Inventory should equal the sum of the costs shown on the job cost sheets of unfinished jobs**.

Illustration 15-11 Job cost sheets–manufacturing overhead applied

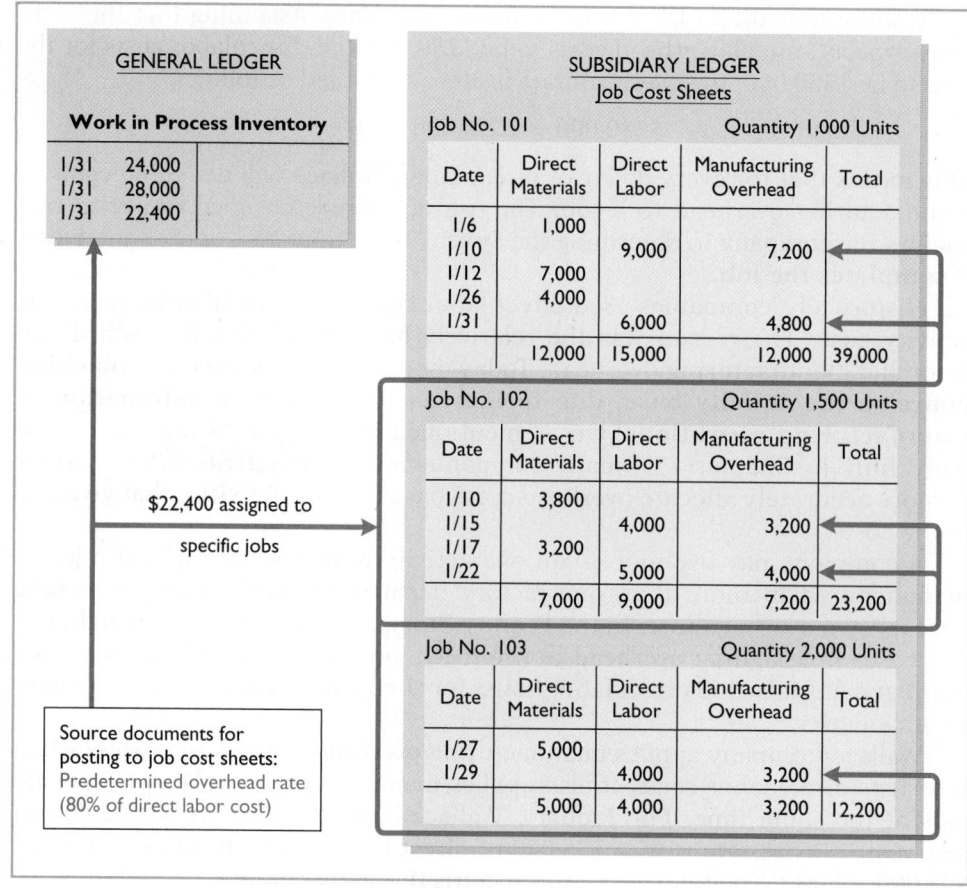

Illustration 15-12 presents proof of the agreement of the control and subsidiary accounts in Wallace. (It assumes that all jobs are still in process.)

Illustration 15-12 Proof of job cost sheets to work in process inventory

Work in Process Inventory			Job Cost Sheets	
Jan. 31	24,000		No. 101	$ 39,000
31	28,000		102	23,200
31	22,400		103	12,200
	74,400	◄		**$74,400**

DECISION TOOLKIT

DECISION CHECKPOINTS	INFO NEEDED FOR DECISION	TOOL TO USE FOR DECISION	HOW TO EVALUATE RESULTS
What is the cost of a job?	Cost of material, labor, and overhead assigned to a specific job	Job cost sheet	Compare costs to those of previous periods and to those of competitors to ensure that costs are in line. Compare costs to expected selling price or service fees charged to determine overall profitability.

Do it!

Danielle Company is working on two job orders. The job cost sheets show the following:

WORK IN PROCESS

Direct materials—Job 120 $6,000; Job 121 $3,600
Direct labor—Job 120 $4,000; Job 121 $2,000
Manufacturing overhead—Job 120 $5,000; Job 121 $2,500

Prepare the three summary entries to record the assignment of costs to Work in Process from the data on the job cost sheets.

Solution

The three summary entries are:		
Work in Process Inventory ($6,000 + $3,600)	9,600	
Raw Materials Inventory		9,600
(To assign materials to jobs)		
Work in Process Inventory ($4,000 + $2,000)	6,000	
Factory Labor		6,000
(To assign labor to jobs)		
Work in Process Inventory ($5,000 + $2,500)	7,500	
Manufacturing Overhead		7,500
(To assign overhead to jobs)		

Action Plan

- Recognize that Work in Process Inventory is the control account for all unfinished job cost sheets.
- Debit Work in Process Inventory for the materials, labor, and overhead charged to the job cost sheets.
- Credit the accounts that were debited when the manufacturing costs were accumulated.

The Navigator

Related exercise material: **BE15-3, BE15-4, BE15-7, E15-2, E15-7, E15-8,** and **Do it! 15-2.**

ASSIGNING COSTS TO FINISHED GOODS

When a job is completed, Wallace summarizes the costs and completes the lower portion of the applicable job cost sheet. For example, if we assume that Wallace completes Job No. 101, a batch of electronic sensors, on January 31, the job cost sheet appears as shown in Illustration 15-13 (page 814).

When a job is finished, Wallace makes an entry to transfer its total cost to finished goods inventory. The entry is as follows.

LEARNING OBJECTIVE 5

Prepare entries for jobs completed and sold.

(7)

Jan. 31	Finished Goods Inventory	39,000	
	Work in Process Inventory		39,000
	(To record completion of		
	Job No. 101)		

This entry increases Finished Goods Inventory and reduces Work in Process Inventory by $39,000, as shown in the T-accounts below.

Work in Process Inventory		**Finished Goods Inventory**	
24,000	39,000 ⟶	39,000	
28,000			
22,400			

Finished Goods Inventory is a control account. It controls individual finished goods records in a finished goods subsidiary ledger. The company posts directly from completed job cost sheets to the receipts columns. Illustration 15-14 (page 814) shows the finished goods inventory record for Job No. 101.

Illustration 15-13 Completed job cost sheet

Job Cost Sheet

Job No. _____ 101 _____   Quantity _____ 1,000 _____
Item _____ Electronic Sensors _____   Date Requested _____ February 5 _____
For _____ Tanner Company _____   Date Completed _____ January 31 _____

Date	Direct Materials	Direct Labor	Manufacturing Overhead
1/6	$ 1,000		
1/10		$ 9,000	$ 7,200
1/12	7,000		
1/26	4,000		
1/31		6,000	4,800
	$12,000	$15,000	$12,000

Cost of completed job		
Direct materials	$	12,000
Direct labor		15,000
Manufacturing overhead		12,000
Total cost	$	39,000
Unit cost ($39,000 ÷ 1,000)	$	39.00

ASSIGNING COSTS TO COST OF GOODS SOLD

Companies recognize cost of goods sold when each sale occurs. To illustrate the entries a company makes when it sells a completed job, assume that on January 31 Wallace sells on account Job 101. The job cost $39,000, and it sold for $50,000. The entries to record the sale and recognize cost of goods sold are:

(8)

Jan. 31	Accounts Receivable	50,000	
	Sales Revenue		50,000
	(To record sale of Job No. 101)		
31	Cost of Goods Sold	39,000	
	Finished Goods Inventory		39,000
	(To record cost of Job No. 101)		

As Illustration 15-14 shows, Wallace records, in the issues section of the finished goods record, the units sold, the cost per unit, and the total cost of goods sold for each job sold.

Illustration 15-14 Finished goods record

Finished Goods.xls

Home Insert Page Layout Formulas Data Review View

P18 — fx

Item: Electronic Sensors   **Job No: 101**

Date	Receipts Units	Cost	Total	Issues Units	Cost	Total	Balance Units	Cost	Total
1/31	1,000	$39	$39,000				1,000	$39	$39,000
1/31				1,000	$39	$39,000			−0−

SUMMARY OF JOB ORDER COST FLOWS

Illustration 15-15 shows a completed flowchart for a job order cost accounting system. All postings are keyed to entries 1–8 in the example presented in the previous pages for Wallace Company.

The cost flows in the diagram can be categorized as one of four types:

- **Accumulation.** The company first accumulates costs by (1) purchasing raw materials, (2) incurring labor costs, and (3) incurring manufacturing overhead costs.
- **Assignment to jobs.** Once the company has incurred manufacturing costs, it must assign them to specific jobs. For example, as it uses raw materials on specific jobs (4), it assigns them to work in process, or treats them as manufacturing overhead if the raw materials cannot be associated with a specific job. Similarly, it either assigns factory labor (5) to work in process, or treats it as manufacturing overhead if the factory labor cannot be associated with a specific job. Finally it assigns manufacturing overhead (6) to work in process using a **predetermined overhead rate**. This deserves emphasis: **Do not assign overhead using actual overhead costs, but instead use a predetermined rate.**
- **Completed jobs.** As jobs are completed (7), the company transfers the cost of the completed job out of work in process inventory into finished goods inventory.
- **When goods are sold.** As specific items are sold (8), the company transfers their cost out of finished goods inventory into cost of goods sold.

Illustration 15-15 Flow of costs in a job order cost system

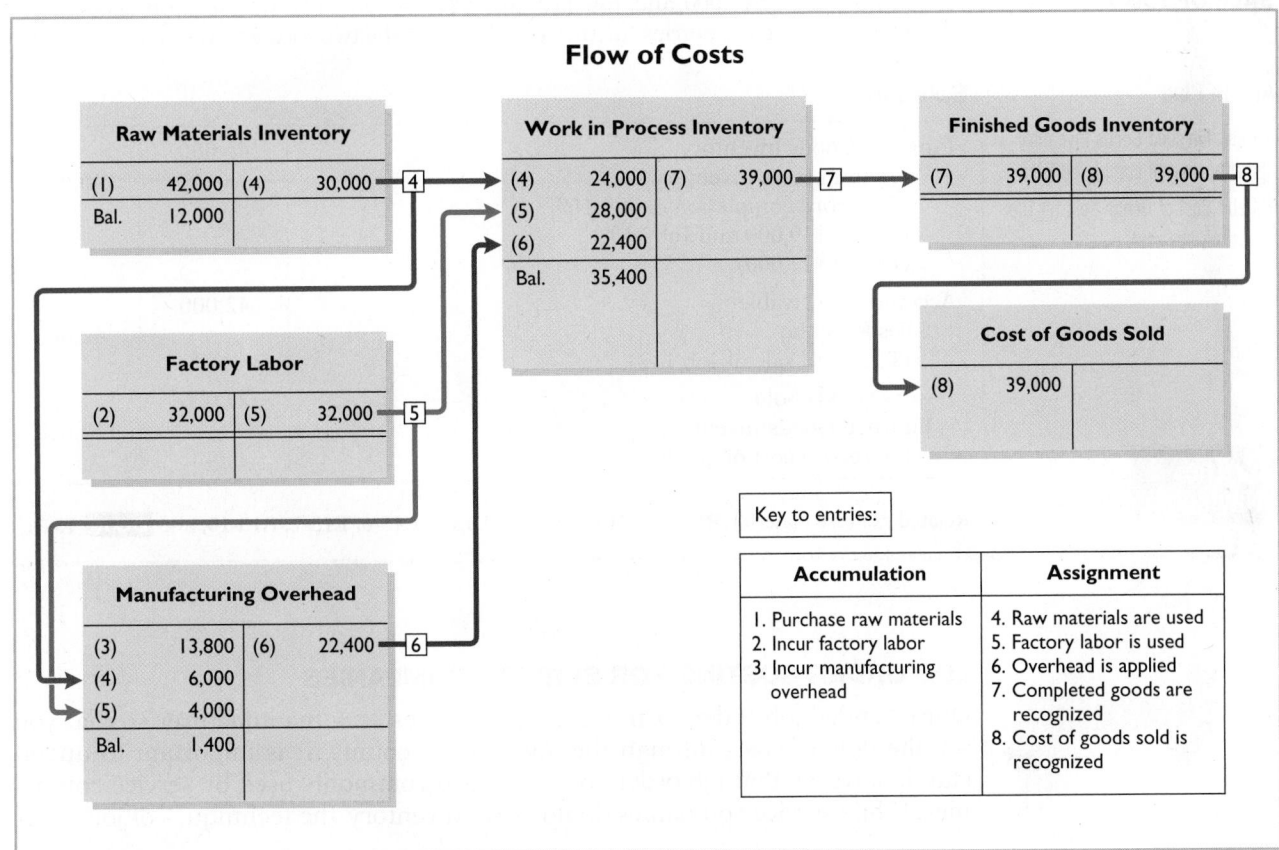

Illustration 15-16 summarizes the flow of documents in a job order cost system.

Illustration 15-16 Flow of documents in a job order cost system

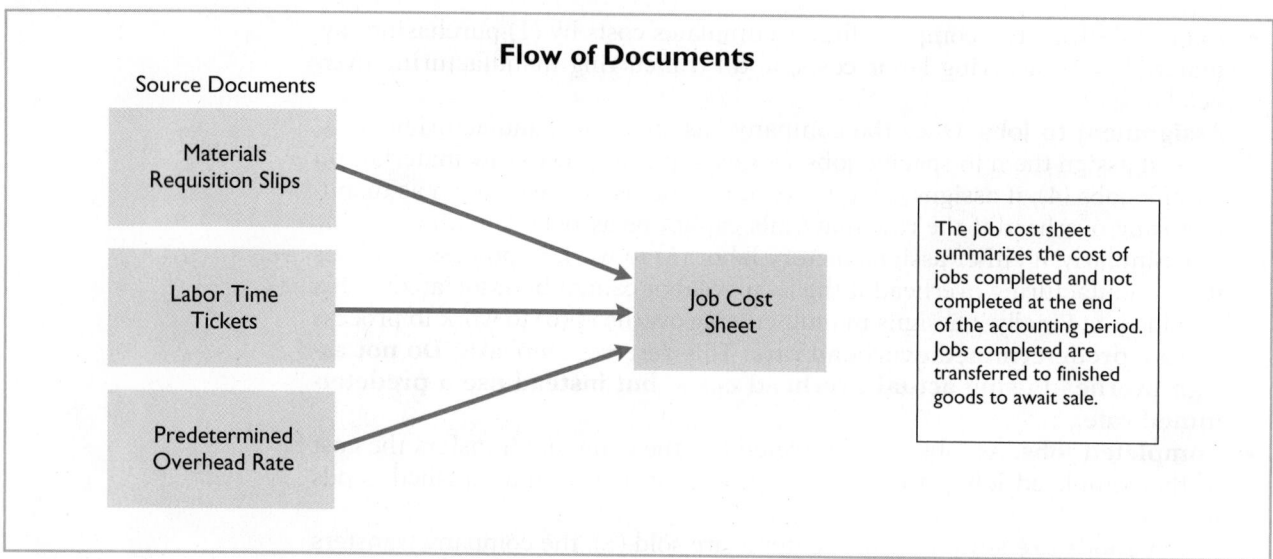

Flow of Documents

Source Documents

Materials Requisition Slips

Labor Time Tickets

Predetermined Overhead Rate

Job Cost Sheet

The job cost sheet summarizes the cost of jobs completed and not completed at the end of the accounting period. Jobs completed are transferred to finished goods to await sale.

COMPLETION AND SALE OF JOBS

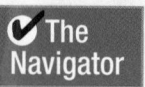

During the current month, Onyx Corporation completed Job 109 and Job 112. Job 109 cost $19,000 and Job 112 cost $27,000. Job 112 was sold on account for $42,000. Journalize the entries for the completion of the two jobs and the sale of Job 112.

Action Plan

• Debit Finished Goods Inventory for the cost of completed jobs.

• Debit Cost of Goods Sold for the cost of jobs sold.

Solution

Finished Goods Inventory	46,000	
Work in Process Inventory		46,000
(To record completion of Job 109, costing $19,000 and Job 112, costing $27,000)		
Accounts Receivable	42,000	
Sales Revenue		42,000
(To record sale of Job 112)		
Cost of Goods Sold	27,000	
Finished Goods Inventory		27,000
(To record cost of goods sold for Job 112)		

The Navigator

Related exercise material: **BE15-8, E15-2, E15-3, E15-4, E15-6, E15-7, E15-10,** and **Do it! 15-3.**

JOB ORDER COSTING FOR SERVICE COMPANIES

Our extended job order costing example focuses on a manufacturer so that you see the flow of costs through the inventory accounts. It is important to understand, however, that job order costing is also commonly used by service companies. While service companies do not have inventory, the techniques of job order costing are still quite useful in many service-industry environments. Consider, for example, the Mayo Clinic (health care), PriceWaterhouseCoopers (accounting), and Goldman Sachs (investment banking). These companies need to keep track of the cost of jobs performed for specific customers to evaluate the profitability of medical treatments, audits, or investment banking engagements.

Many service organizations bill their customers using cost-plus contracts. Cost-plus contracts mean that the customer's bill is the sum of the costs incurred on the job, plus a profit amount that is calculated as a percentage of the costs incurred. In order to minimize conflict with customers and reduce potential contract disputes, service companies that use cost-plus contracts must maintain accurate and up-to-date costing records. Up-to-date cost records enable a service company to immediately notify a customer of cost overruns due to customer requests for changes to the original plan or unexpected complications. Timely recordkeeping allows the contractor and customer to consider alternatives before it is too late.

A service company that uses a job order cost system does not have inventory accounts. It does, however, use an account similar to Work in Process Inventory, referred to here as Service Contracts in Process, to record job costs prior to completion. To illustrate the journal entries for a service company under a job order cost system, consider the following transactions for Frugal Interiors, an interior design company. The entry to record the assignment of $9,000 of supplies to projects ($7,000 direct and $2,000 indirect) is:

Service Contracts in Process	7,000	
Operating Overhead	2,000	
Supplies		9,000
(To assign supplies to projects)		

The entry to record the assignment of service salaries and wages of $100,000 ($84,000 direct and $16,000 indirect) is:

Service Contracts in Process	84,000	
Operating Overhead	16,000	
Service Salaries and Wages		100,000
(To assign personnel costs to projects)		

Frugal Interiors applies operating overhead at a rate of 50% of direct labor costs. The entry to record the application of overhead ($84,000 $\times$ 50%) based on the direct labor costs is:

Service Contracts in Process	42,000	
Operating Overhead		42,000
(To assign operating overhead to projects)		

Finally, upon completion, the job cost sheet of a design project for Sampson Corporation shows a total cost of $34,000. The entry to record completion of this project is:

Cost of Completed Service Contracts	34,000	
Service Contracts in Process		34,000
(To record completion of Sampson project)		

Job cost sheets for a service company keep track of materials, labor, and overhead used on a particular job similar to a manufacturer. A number of exercises at the end of this chapter apply job order costing to service companies.

© Christian Lagereek/iStockphoto

Service Company Insight
Sales Are Nice, but Service Revenue Pays the Bills

Jet engines are one of the many products made by the industrial operations division of General Electric (GE). At prices as high as $30 million per engine, you can bet that GE does its best to keep track of costs. It might surprise you that GE doesn't make much profit on the sale of each engine. So why does it bother making them? Service revenue—during one recent year, about 75% of the division's revenues came from servicing its own products. One estimate is that the $13 billion in aircraft engines sold during a recent three-year period will generate about $90 billion in service revenue over the 30-year life of the engines. Because of the high product costs, both the engines themselves and the subsequent service are most likely accounted for using job order costing. Accurate service cost records are important because GE needs to generate high profit margins on its service jobs to make up for the low margins on the original sale. It also needs good cost records for its service jobs in order to control its costs. Otherwise, a competitor, such as Pratt and Whitney, might submit lower bids for service contracts and take lucrative service jobs away from GE.

Source: Paul Glader, "GE's Focus on Services Faces Test," *Wall Street Journal Online* (March 3, 2009).

? Explain why GE would use job order costing to keep track of the cost of repairing a malfunctioning engine for a major airline. (See page 843.)

ADVANTAGES AND DISADVANTAGES OF JOB ORDER COSTING

An advantage of job order costing is it is more precise in assignment of costs to projects than process costing. For example, assume that a construction company, Juan Company, builds 10 custom homes a year at a total cost of $2,000,000. One way to determine the cost of the homes is to divide the total construction cost incurred during the year by the number of homes produced during the year. For Juan Company, an average cost of $200,000 ($2,000,000 ÷ 10) is computed. If the homes are nearly identical, then this approach is adequate for purposes of determining profit per home. But if the homes vary in terms of size, style, and material types, using the average cost of $200,000 to determine profit per home is inappropriate. Instead, Juan Company should use a job order cost system to determine the specific cost incurred to build each home and the amount of profit made on each. Thus, job order costing provides more useful information for determining the profitability of particular projects and for estimating costs when preparing bids on future jobs.

One disadvantage of job order costing is that it requires a significant amount of data entry. For Juan Company, it is much easier to simply keep track of total costs incurred during the year than it is to keep track of the costs incurred on each job (home built). Recording this information is time-consuming, and if the data is not entered accurately, then the product costs are not accurate. In recent years, technological advances, such as bar-coding devices for both labor costs and materials, have increased the accuracy and reduced the effort needed to record costs on specific jobs. These innovations expand the opportunities to apply job order costing in a wider variety of business settings, thus improving management's ability to control costs and make better informed decisions.

A common problem of all costing systems is how to allocate overhead to the finished product. Overhead often represents more than 50% of a product's cost, and this cost is often difficult to allocate meaningfully to the product. How, for example, is the salary of a project manager allocated to the various homes, which may differ in size, style, and materials used, that she oversees? The accuracy of the job order cost system is largely dependent on the accuracy of the overhead allocation process. Even if the company does a good job of keeping track of the specific amounts of materials and labor used on each job, if the overhead costs are not allocated to individual jobs in a meaningful way, the product costing information is not useful. This issue will be addressed in more detail in Chapter 17.

Reporting Job Cost Data

At the end of a period, companies prepare financial statements that present aggregate data on all jobs manufactured and sold. The cost of goods manufactured schedule in job order costing is the same as in Chapter 14 with one exception: **The schedule shows manufacturing overhead applied, rather than actual overhead costs. The company adds this amount to direct materials and direct labor to determine total manufacturing costs.**

> **LEARNING OBJECTIVE 6**
> Distinguish between under- and overapplied manufacturing overhead.

Companies prepare the cost of goods manufactured schedule directly from the Work in Process Inventory account. Illustration 15-17 shows a condensed schedule for Wallace Company for January.

WALLACE COMPANY
Cost of Goods Manufactured Schedule
For the Month Ending January 31, 2014

Work in process, January 1		$ –0–
Direct materials used	$ 24,000	
Direct labor	28,000	
Manufacturing overhead applied	22,400	
Total manufacturing costs		74,400
Total cost of work in process		74,400
Less: Work in process, January 31		35,400
Cost of goods manufactured		$39,000

Illustration 15-17 Cost of goods manufactured schedule

Note that the cost of goods manufactured ($39,000) agrees with the amount transferred from Work in Process Inventory to Finished Goods Inventory in journal entry No. 7 in Illustration 15-15 (page 815).

The income statement and balance sheet are the same as those illustrated in Chapter 14. For example, Illustration 15-18 shows the partial income statement for Wallace for the month of January.

Helpful Hint Companies usually prepare monthly financial statements for management use only.

Illustration 15-18 Partial income statement

WALLACE COMPANY
Income Statement (partial)
For the Month Ending January 31, 2014

Sales revenue		$50,000
Cost of goods sold		
Finished goods inventory, January 1	$ –0–	
Cost of goods manufactured (see Illustration 15-17)	39,000	
Cost of goods available for sale	39,000	
Less: Finished goods inventory, January 31	–0–	
Cost of goods sold		39,000
Gross profit		$11,000

UNDER- OR OVERAPPLIED MANUFACTURING OVERHEAD

When Manufacturing Overhead has a **debit balance**, overhead is said to be underapplied. Underapplied overhead means that the overhead assigned to work in process is less than the overhead incurred. Conversely, when manufacturing overhead has a **credit balance**, overhead is overapplied. Overapplied overhead means that the overhead assigned to work in process is greater than the overhead incurred. Illustration 15-19 shows these concepts.

Illustration 15-19 Under- and overapplied overhead

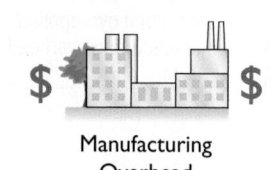

Manufacturing Overhead		If actual is *greater* than applied, manufacturing overhead is underapplied.
Actual (Costs incurred)	Applied (Costs assigned)	If actual is *less* than applied, manufacturing overhead is overapplied.

Manufacturing Overhead

Year-End Balance

At the end of the year, all manufacturing overhead transactions are complete. There is no further opportunity for offsetting events to occur. At this point, Wallace eliminates any balance in Manufacturing Overhead by an adjusting entry. It considers under- or overapplied overhead to be an **adjustment to cost of goods sold**. Thus, Wallace **debits underapplied overhead to Cost of Goods Sold**. It **credits overapplied overhead to Cost of Goods Sold**.

To illustrate, assume that Wallace has a $2,500 credit balance in Manufacturing Overhead at December 31. The adjusting entry for the overapplied overhead is:

Dec. 31	Manufacturing Overhead	2,500	
	Cost of Goods Sold		2,500
	(To transfer overapplied overhead to cost of goods sold)		

After Wallace posts this entry, Manufacturing Overhead has a zero balance. In preparing an income statement for the year, Wallace reports cost of goods sold **after adjusting it** for either under- or overapplied overhead.

Conceptually, some argue, under- or overapplied overhead at the end of the year should be allocated among ending work in process, finished goods, and cost of goods sold. The discussion of this possible allocation approach is left to more advanced courses.

DECISION TOOLKIT

DECISION CHECKPOINTS	INFO NEEDED FOR DECISION	TOOL TO USE FOR DECISION	HOW TO EVALUATE RESULTS
Has the company over- or underapplied overhead for the period?	Actual overhead costs and overhead applied	Manufacturing Overhead account	If the account balance is a credit, overhead applied exceeded actual overhead costs. If the account balance is a debit, overhead applied was less than actual overhead costs.

Do it! For Karr Company, the predetermined overhead rate is 140% of direct labor cost. During the month, Karr incurred $90,000 of factory labor costs, of which $80,000 is direct labor and $10,000 is indirect labor. Actual overhead incurred was $119,000.

Compute the amount of manufacturing overhead applied during the month. Determine the amount of under- or overapplied manufacturing overhead.

APPLIED MANUFACTURING OVERHEAD

Action Plan

- Calculate the amount of overhead applied by multiplying the predetermined overhead rate by actual activity.
- If actual manufacturing overhead is greater than applied, manufacturing overhead is underapplied.
- If actual manufacturing overhead is less than applied, manufacturing overhead is overapplied.

Solution

Manufacturing overhead applied = (140% × $80,000) = $112,000
Underapplied manufacturing overhead = ($119,000 − $112,000) = $7,000

Related exercise material: **BE15-10, E15-5, E15-12, E15-13,** and **Do it!** **15-4.**

USING THE DECISION TOOLKIT

Martinez Building Products Company is one of the largest manufacturers and marketers of unique, custom-made residential garage doors in the United States. It also is a major supplier of industrial and commercial doors, grills, and counter shutters for the new-construction, repair, and remodel markets. Martinez has developed plans for continued expansion of a network of service operations that sell, install, and service manufactured fireplaces, garage doors, and related products.

Martinez uses a job order cost system and applies overhead to production on the basis of direct labor cost. In computing a predetermined overhead rate for the year 2014, the company estimated manufacturing overhead to be $24 million and direct labor costs to be $20 million. In addition, it developed the following information.

Actual Costs Incurred During 2014

Direct materials used	$30,000,000
Direct labor cost incurred	21,000,000
Insurance, factory	500,000
Indirect labor	7,500,000
Factory maintenance	1,000,000
Rent on factory building	11,000,000
Depreciation on factory equipment	2,000,000

Instructions

Answer each of the following.

(a) Why is Martinez Building Products Company using a job order cost system?

(b) On what basis does Martinez allocate its manufacturing overhead? Compute the predetermined overhead rate for 2014.

(c) Compute the amount of the under- or overapplied overhead for 2014.

(d) Martinez had balances in the beginning and ending work in process and finished goods accounts as follows.

	1/1/14	12/31/14
Work in process	$ 5,000,000	$ 4,000,000
Finished goods	13,000,000	11,000,000

Determine the (1) cost of goods manufactured and (2) cost of goods sold for Martinez during 2014. Assume that any under- or overapplied overhead should be included in the cost of goods sold.

(e) During 2014, Job G408 was started and completed. Its cost sheet showed a total cost of $100,000, and the company prices its product at 50% above its cost. What is the price to the customer if the company follows this pricing strategy?

Solution

(a) The company is using a job order cost system because it custom-makes garage doors. Each job has its own distinguishing characteristics. For example, each garage door would be different, and therefore a different cost per garage door can be assigned.

(b) The company allocates its overhead on the basis of direct labor cost. The predetermined overhead rate is 120%, computed as follows.

$$\$24,000,000 \div 20,000,000 = 120\%$$

(c)	Actual manufacturing overhead		$22,000,000
	Applied overhead cost ($21,000,000 × 120%)		25,200,000
	Overapplied overhead		$ 3,200,000

(d) (1)	Work in process, 1/1/14		$ 5,000,000
	Direct materials used	$30,000,000	
	Direct labor	21,000,000	
	Manufacturing overhead applied	25,200,000	
	Total manufacturing costs		76,200,000
	Total cost of work in process		81,200,000
	Less: Work in process, 12/31/14		4,000,000
	Cost of goods manufactured		$77,200,000
(2)	Finished goods inventory, 1/1/14	$13,000,000	
	Cost of goods manufactured (see above)	77,200,000	
	Cost of goods available for sale	90,200,000	
	Finished goods inventory, 12/31/14	11,000,000	
	Cost of goods sold (unadjusted)	79,200,000	
	Less: Overapplied overhead	3,200,000	
	Cost of goods sold	$76,000,000	
(e)	G408 cost	$ 100,000	
	Markup percentage	× 50%	
	Profit	$ 50,000	

The Navigator

Price to customer: $150,000 ($100,000 + $50,000)

Summary of Learning Objectives

1 **Explain the characteristics and purposes of cost accounting.** Cost accounting involves the procedures for measuring, recording, and reporting product costs. From the data accumulated, companies determine the total cost and the unit cost of each product. The two basic types of cost accounting systems are job order cost and process cost.

2 **Describe the flow of costs in a job order cost system.** In job order costing, companies first accumulate manufacturing costs in three accounts: Raw Materials Inventory, Factory Labor, and Manufacturing Overhead. They then assign the accumulated costs to Work in Process Inventory and eventually to Finished Goods Inventory and Cost of Goods Sold.

3 **Explain the nature and importance of a job cost sheet.** A job cost sheet is a form used to record the costs chargeable to a specific job and to determine the total and unit costs of the completed job. Job cost sheets constitute the subsidiary ledger for the Work in Process Inventory control account.

4 **Indicate how the predetermined overhead rate is determined and used.** The predetermined overhead rate is based on the relationship between estimated annual overhead costs and expected annual operating activity. This is expressed in terms of a common activity base, such as direct labor cost. Companies use this rate to assign overhead costs to work in process and to specific jobs.

5 **Prepare entries for jobs completed and sold.** When jobs are completed, companies debit the cost to Finished Goods Inventory and credit it to Work in Process Inventory. When a job is sold, the entries are (a) debit Cash or Accounts Receivable and credit Sales Revenue for the selling price; and (b) debit Cost of Goods Sold and credit Finished Goods Inventory for the cost of the goods.

6 **Distinguish between under- and overapplied manufacturing overhead.** Underapplied manufacturing overhead indicates that the overhead assigned to work in process is less than the overhead incurred. Overapplied overhead indicates that the overhead assigned to work in process is greater than the overhead incurred.

✔ The Navigator

 DECISION TOOLKIT *A SUMMARY*

DECISION CHECKPOINTS	INFO NEEDED FOR DECISION	TOOL TO USE FOR DECISION	HOW TO EVALUATE RESULTS
What is the cost of a job?	Cost of material, labor, and overhead assigned to a specific job	Job cost sheet	Compare costs to those of previous periods and to those of competitors to ensure that costs are in line. Compare costs to expected selling price or service fees charged to determine overall profitability.
Has the company over- or underapplied overhead for the period?	Actual overhead costs and overhead applied	Manufacturing Overhead account	If the account balance is a credit, overhead applied exceeded actual overhead costs. If the account balance is a debit, overhead applied was less than actual overhead costs.

Glossary

Cost accounting *(p. 800)* An area of accounting that involves measuring, recording, and reporting product costs.

Cost accounting system *(p. 800)* Manufacturing-cost accounts that are fully integrated into the general ledger of a company.

Job cost sheet *(p. 805)* A form used to record the costs chargeable to a specific job and to determine the total and unit costs of the completed job.

Job order cost system *(p. 800)* A cost accounting system in which costs are assigned to each job or batch.

Materials requisition slip *(p. 805)* A document authorizing the issuance of raw materials from the storeroom to production.

Overapplied overhead *(p. 820)* A situation in which overhead assigned to work in process is greater than the overhead incurred.

Predetermined overhead rate *(p. 809)* A rate based on the relationship between estimated annual overhead costs and expected annual operating activity, expressed in terms of a common activity base.

Process cost system *(p. 801)* A cost accounting system used when a company manufactures a large volume of similar products.

Time ticket *(p. 808)* A document that indicates the employee, the hours worked, the account and job to be charged, and the total labor cost.

Underapplied overhead *(p. 820)* A situation in which overhead assigned to work in process is less than the overhead incurred.

Comprehensive Do it!

Cardella Company applies overhead on the basis of direct labor costs. The company estimates annual overhead costs will be $760,000, and annual direct labor costs will be $950,000. During February, Cardella works on two jobs: A16 and B17. Summary data concerning these jobs are as follows.

Manufacturing Costs Incurred

Purchased $54,000 of raw materials on account.
Factory labor $76,000, plus $4,000 employer payroll taxes.
Manufacturing overhead exclusive of indirect materials and indirect labor $59,800.

Assignment of Costs

Direct materials: Job A16 $27,000, Job B17 $21,000
Indirect materials: $3,000
Direct labor: Job A16 $52,000, Job B17 $26,000
Indirect labor: $2,000

The company completed Job A16 and sold it on account for $150,000. Job B17 was only partially completed.

Instructions

(a) Compute the predetermined overhead rate.
(b) Journalize the February transactions in the sequence followed in the chapter.
(c) What was the amount of under- or overapplied manufacturing overhead?

Action Plan

- Predetermined overhead rate = Estimated annual overhead cost ÷ Expected annual operating activity.
- In accumulating costs, debit three accounts: Raw Materials Inventory, Factory Labor, and Manufacturing Overhead.
- When Work in Process Inventory is debited, credit one of the three accounts listed above.
- Debit Finished Goods Inventory for the cost of completed jobs. Debit Cost of Goods Sold for the cost of jobs sold.
- Overhead is underapplied when Manufacturing Overhead has a debit balance.

Solution to Comprehensive Do it!

(a)

Estimated annual overhead costs	÷	Expected annual operating activity	=	Predetermined overhead rate
$760,000	÷	$950,000	=	80%

(b)

		(1)		
Feb. 28	Raw Materials Inventory		54,000	
	Accounts Payable			54,000
	(Purchase of raw materials on account)			
		(2)		
28	Factory Labor		80,000	
	Factory Wages Payable			76,000
	Employer Payroll Taxes Payable			4,000
	(To record factory labor costs)			
		(3)		
28	Manufacturing Overhead		59,800	
	Accounts Payable, Accumulated			
	Depreciation, and Prepaid Insurance			59,800
	(To record overhead costs)			
		(4)		
28	Work in Process Inventory		48,000	
	Manufacturing Overhead		3,000	
	Raw Materials Inventory			51,000
	(To assign raw materials to production)			
		(5)		
28	Work in Process Inventory		78,000	
	Manufacturing Overhead		2,000	
	Factory Labor			80,000
	(To assign factory labor to production)			

		(6)		
28	Work in Process Inventory		62,400	
	Manufacturing Overhead			62,400
	(To assign overhead to jobs—			
	80% × $78,000)			

		(7)		
28	Finished Goods Inventory		120,600	
	Work in Process Inventory			120,600
	(To record completion of Job A16: direct			
	materials $27,000, direct labor $52,000,			
	and manufacturing overhead $41,600)			

		(8)		
28	Accounts Receivable		150,000	
	Sales Revenue			150,000
	(To record sale of Job A16)			
28	Cost of Goods Sold		120,600	
	Finished Goods Inventory			120,600
	(To record cost of sale for Job A16)			

(c) Manufacturing Overhead has a debit balance of $2,400 as shown below.

Manufacturing Overhead

(3)	59,800	(6)	62,400
(4)	3,000		
(5)	2,000		
Bal.	2,400		

Thus, manufacturing overhead is underapplied for the month.

 The Navigator

 Self-Test, Brief Exercises, Exercises, Problem Set A, and many more resources are available for practice in WileyPLUS.

Self-Test Questions

Answers are on page 843.

(LO 1) **1.** Cost accounting involves the measuring, recording, and reporting of:
  (a) product costs.
  (b) future costs.
  (c) manufacturing processes.
  (d) managerial accounting decisions.

(LO 1) **2.** A company is more likely to use a job order cost system if:
  (a) it manufactures a large volume of similar products.
  (b) its production is continuous.
  (c) it manufactures products with unique characteristics.
  (d) it uses a periodic inventory system.

(LO 2) **3.** In accumulating raw materials costs, companies debit the cost of raw materials purchased in a perpetual system to:

  (a) Raw Materials Purchases.
  (b) Raw Materials Inventory.
  (c) Purchases.
  (d) Work in Process.

4. When incurred, factory labor costs are debited to: (LO 2)
  (a) Work in Process.
  (b) Factory Wages Expense.
  (c) Factory Labor.
  (d) Factory Wages Payable.

5. The flow of costs in job order costing: (LO 2)
  (a) begins with work in process inventory and ends with finished goods inventory.
  (b) begins as soon as a sale occurs.
  (c) parallels the physical flow of materials as they are converted into finished goods.
  (d) is necessary to prepare the cost of goods manufactured schedule.

(LO 3) 6. Raw materials are assigned to a job when:
- (a) the job is sold.
- (b) the materials are purchased.
- (c) the materials are received from the vendor.
- (d) the materials are issued by the materials storeroom.

(LO 3) 7. The source documents for assigning costs to job cost sheets are:
- (a) invoices, time tickets, and the predetermined overhead rate.
- (b) materials requisition slips, time tickets, and the actual overhead costs.
- (c) materials requisition slips, payroll register, and the predetermined overhead rate.
- (d) materials requisition slips, time tickets, and the predetermined overhead rate.

(LO 3) 8. In recording the issuance of raw materials in a job order cost system, it would be **incorrect** to:
- (a) debit Work in Process Inventory.
- (b) debit Finished Goods Inventory.
- (c) debit Manufacturing Overhead.
- (d) credit Raw Materials Inventory.

(LO 3) 9. The entry when direct factory labor is assigned to jobs is a debit to:
- (a) Work in Process Inventory and a credit to Factory Labor.
- (b) Manufacturing Overhead and a credit to Factory Labor.
- (c) Factory Labor and a credit to Manufacturing Overhead.
- (d) Factory Labor and a credit to Work in Process Inventory.

(LO 4) 10. The formula for computing the predetermined manufacturing overhead rate is estimated annual overhead costs divided by an expected annual operating activity, expressed as:
- (a) direct labor cost.
- (b) direct labor hours.
- (c) machine hours.
- (d) Any of the above.

(LO 4) 11. In Crawford Company, the predetermined overhead rate is 80% of direct labor cost. During the month, Crawford incurs $210,000 of factory labor costs, of which $180,000 is direct labor and $30,000 is indirect labor. Actual overhead incurred was $200,000. The amount of overhead debited to Work in Process Inventory should be:
- (a) $200,000.
- (b) $144,000.
- (c) $168,000.
- (d) $160,000.

(LO 5) 12. Mynex Company completes Job No. 26 at a cost of $4,500 and later sells it for $7,000 cash. A **correct** entry is:

- (a) debit Finished Goods Inventory $7,000 and credit Work in Process Inventory $7,000.
- (b) debit Cost of Goods Sold $7,000 and credit Finished Goods Inventory $7,000.
- (c) debit Finished Goods Inventory $4,500 and credit Work in Process Inventory $4,500.
- (d) debit Accounts Receivable $7,000 and credit Sales Revenue $7,000.

(LO 5) 13. At the end of an accounting period, a company using a job order cost system calculates the cost of goods manufactured:
- (a) from the job cost sheet.
- (b) from the Work in Process Inventory account.
- (c) by adding direct materials used, direct labor incurred, and manufacturing overhead incurred.
- (d) from the Cost of Goods Sold account.

(LO 5) 14. Which of the following statements is **true**?
- (a) Job order costing requires less data entry than process costing.
- (b) Allocation of overhead is easier under job order costing than process costing.
- (c) Job order costing provides more precise costing for custom jobs than process costing.
- (d) The use of job order costing has declined because more companies have adopted automated accounting systems.

(LO 6) 15. At end of the year, a company has a $1,200 debit balance in Manufacturing Overhead. The company:
- (a) makes an adjusting entry by debiting Manufacturing Overhead Applied for $1,200 and crediting Manufacturing Overhead for $1,200.
- (b) makes an adjusting entry by debiting Manufacturing Overhead Expense for $1,200 and crediting Manufacturing Overhead for $1,200.
- (c) makes an adjusting entry by debiting Cost of Goods Sold for $1,200 and crediting Manufacturing Overhead for $1,200.
- (d) makes no adjusting entry because differences between actual overhead and the amount applied are a normal part of job order costing and will average out over the next year.

(LO 6) 16. Manufacturing overhead is underapplied if:
- (a) actual overhead is less than applied.
- (b) actual overhead is greater than applied.
- (c) the predetermined rate equals the actual rate.
- (d) actual overhead equals applied overhead.

Go to the book's companion website, **www.wiley.com/college/kimmel**, to access additional Self-Test Questions. The Navigator

---

Questions

1. (a) Mary Barett is not sure about the difference between cost accounting and a cost accounting system. Explain the difference to Mary.
   (b) What is an important feature of a cost accounting system?

2. (a) Distinguish between the two types of cost accounting systems.
   (b) Can a company use both types of cost accounting systems?

3. What type of industry is likely to use a job order cost system? Give some examples.

4. What type of industry is likely to use a process cost system? Give some examples.

5. Your roommate asks your help in understanding the major steps in the flow of costs in a job order cost system. Identify the steps for your roommate.

6. There are three inventory control accounts in a job order system. Identify the control accounts and their subsidiary ledgers.

7. What source documents are used in accumulating direct labor costs?

8. "Entries to Manufacturing Overhead normally are only made daily." Do you agree? Explain.

9. Stan Kaiser is confused about the source documents used in assigning materials and labor costs. Identify the documents and give the entry for each document.

10. What is the purpose of a job cost sheet?

11. Indicate the source documents that are used in charging costs to specific jobs.

12. Explain the purpose and use of a "materials requisition slip" as used in a job order cost system.

13. Sam Bowden believes actual manufacturing overhead should be charged to jobs. Do you agree? Why or why not?

14. What elements are involved in computing a predetermined overhead rate?

15. How can the agreement of Work in Process Inventory and job cost sheets be verified?

16. Jane Neff believes that the cost of goods manufactured schedule in job order cost accounting is the same as shown in Chapter 1. Is Jane correct? Explain.

17. Matt Litkee is confused about under- and overapplied manufacturing overhead. Define the terms for Matt, and indicate the balance in the manufacturing overhead account applicable to each term.

18. "At the end of the year, under- or overapplied overhead is closed to Income Summary." Is this correct? If not, indicate the customary treatment of this amount.

Brief Exercises

BE15-1 Knox Company begins operations on January 1. Because all work is done to customer specifications, the company decides to use a job order cost system. Prepare a flowchart of a typical job order system with arrows showing the flow of costs. Identify the eight transactions.

Prepare a flowchart of a job order cost accounting system, and identify transactions.
(LO 2), **C**

BE15-2 During January, its first month of operations, Knox Company accumulated the following manufacturing costs: raw materials $4,000 on account, factory labor $6,000 of which $5,200 relates to factory wages payable and $800 relates to payroll taxes payable, and utilities payable $2,000. Prepare separate journal entries for each type of manufacturing cost.

Prepare entries in accumulating manufacturing costs.
(LO 2), **AP**

BE15-3 In January, Knox Company requisitions raw materials for production as follows: Job 1 $900, Job 2 $1,400, Job 3 $700, and general factory use $600. Prepare a summary journal entry to record raw materials used.

Prepare entry for the assignment of raw materials costs.
(LO 3), **AP**

BE15-4 Factory labor data for Knox Company is given in BE15-2. During January, time tickets show that the factory labor of $6,000 was used as follows: Job 1 $2,200, Job 2 $1,600, Job 3 $1,400, and general factory use $800. Prepare a summary journal entry to record factory labor used.

Prepare entry for the assignment of factory labor costs.
(LO 3), **AP**

BE15-5 Data pertaining to job cost sheets for Knox Company are given in BE15-3 and BE15-4. Prepare the job cost sheets for each of the three jobs. (*Note:* You may omit the column for Manufacturing Overhead.)

Prepare job cost sheets.
(LO 3), **AP**

BE15-6 Marquis Company estimates that annual manufacturing overhead costs will be $900,000. Estimated annual operating activity bases are direct labor cost $500,000, direct labor hours 50,000, and machine hours 100,000. Compute the predetermined overhead rate for each activity base.

Compute predetermined overhead rates.
(LO 4), **AP**

BE15-7 During the first quarter, Roland Company incurs the following direct labor costs: January $40,000, February $30,000, and March $50,000. For each month, prepare the entry to assign overhead to production using a predetermined rate of 80% of direct labor cost.

Assign manufacturing overhead to production.
(LO 4), **AP**

BE15-8 In March, Stinson Company completes Jobs 10 and 11. Job 10 cost $20,000 and Job 11 $30,000. On March 31, Job 10 is sold to the customer for $35,000 in cash. Journalize the entries for the completion of the two jobs and the sale of Job 10.

Prepare entries for completion and sale of completed jobs.
(LO 5), **AP**

Prepare entries for service salaries and wages and operating overhead.
(LO 5), **AP**

Prepare adjusting entries for under- and overapplied overhead.
(LO 6), **C**

BE15-9 Preprah Engineering Contractors incurred service salaries and wages of $32,000 ($24,000 direct and $8,000 indirect) on an engineering project. The company applies overhead at a rate of 25% of direct labor. Record the entries to assign service salaries and wages and to apply overhead.

BE15-10 At December 31, balances in Manufacturing Overhead are Shimeca Company—debit $1,200, Garcia Company—credit $900. Prepare the adjusting entry for each company at December 31, assuming the adjustment is made to cost of goods sold.

Do it! Review

Prepare journal entries for manufacturing costs.
(LO 2), **AP**

Do it! 15-1 During the current month, Tomlin Company incurs the following manufacturing costs.

(a) Purchased raw materials of $16,000 on account.

(b) Incurred factory labor of $40,000. Of that amount, $31,000 relates to wages payable and $9,000 relates to payroll taxes payable.

(c) Factory utilities of $3,100 are payable, prepaid factory property taxes of $2,400 have expired, and depreciation on the factory building is $9,500.

Prepare journal entries for each type of manufacturing cost. (Use a summary entry to record manufacturing overhead.)

Assign costs to work in process.
(LO 3, 4), **AP**

Do it! 15-2 Milner Company is working on two job orders. The job cost sheets show the following.

	Job 201	Job 202
Direct materials	$7,200	$9,000
Direct labor	4,000	8,000
Manufacturing overhead	5,200	9,800

Prepare the three summary entries to record the assignment of costs to Work in Process from the data on the job cost sheets.

Prepare entries for completion and sale of jobs.
(LO 5), **AP**

Do it! 15-3 During the current month, Reyes Corporation completed Job 310 and Job 312. Job 310 cost $60,000 and Job 312 cost $50,000. Job 312 was sold on account for $90,000. Journalize the entries for the completion of the two jobs and the sale of Job 312.

Apply manufacturing overhead and determine under- or overapplication.
(LO 6), **AN**

Do it! 15-4 For Eckstein Company, the predetermined overhead rate is 130% of direct labor cost. During the month, Eckstein incurred $100,000 of factory labor costs, of which $85,000 is direct labor and $15,000 is indirect labor. Actual overhead incurred was $115,000. Compute the amount of manufacturing overhead applied during the month. Determine the amount of under- or overapplied manufacturing overhead.

Exercises

Prepare entries for factory labor.
(LO 2, 3), **AP**

E15-1 The gross earnings of the factory workers for Vargas Company during the month of January are $66,000. The employer's payroll taxes for the factory payroll are $8,000. The fringe benefits to be paid by the employer on this payroll are $6,000. Of the total accumulated cost of factory labor, 85% is related to direct labor and 15% is attributable to indirect labor.

Instructions
(a) Prepare the entry to record the factory labor costs for the month of January.
(b) Prepare the entry to assign factory labor to production.

Prepare journal entries for manufacturing costs.
(LO 2, 3, 4, 5), **AP**

E15-2 Stine Company uses a job order cost system. On May 1, the company has a balance in Work in Process Inventory of $3,500 and two jobs in process: Job No. 429 $2,000, and Job No. 430 $1,500. During May, a summary of source documents reveals the following.

Job Number	Materials Requisition Slips		Labor Time Tickets	
429	$2,500		$1,900	
430	3,500		3,000	
431	4,400	$10,400	7,600	$12,500
General use		800		1,200
		$11,200		$13,700

Stine Company applies manufacturing overhead to jobs at an overhead rate of 60% of direct labor cost. Job No. 429 is completed during the month.

Instructions
(a) Prepare summary journal entries to record (i) the requisition slips, (ii) the time tickets, (iii) the assignment of manufacturing overhead to jobs, and (iv) the completion of Job No. 429.
(b) Post the entries to Work in Process Inventory, and prove the agreement of the control account with the job cost sheets. (Use a T-account.)

E15-3 A job order cost sheet for Lowry Company is shown below.

Analyze a job cost sheet and prepare entries for manufacturing costs.
(LO 2, 3, 4, 5), **AP**

Job No. 92			For 2,000 Units
Date	Direct Materials	Direct Labor	Manufacturing Overhead
Beg. bal. Jan. 1	5,000	6,000	5,100
8	6,000		
12		8,000	6,400
25	2,000		
27		4,000	3,200
	13,000	18,000	14,700

Cost of completed job:	
Direct materials	$13,000
Direct labor	18,000
Manufacturing overhead	14,700
Total cost	$45,700
Unit cost ($45,700 ÷ 2,000)	$22.85

Instructions
(a) On the basis of the foregoing data, answer the following questions.
  (1) What was the balance in Work in Process Inventory on January 1 if this was the only unfinished job?
  (2) If manufacturing overhead is applied on the basis of direct labor cost, what overhead rate was used in each year?
(b) Prepare summary entries at January 31 to record the current year's transactions pertaining to Job No. 92.

E15-4 Manufacturing cost data for Orlando Company, which uses a job order cost system, are presented below.

Analyze costs of manufacturing and determine missing amounts.
(LO 2, 6), **AN**

	Case A	Case B	Case C
Direct materials used	$ (a)	$ 83,000	$ 63,150
Direct labor	50,000	140,000	(h)
Manufacturing overhead applied	42,500	(d)	(i)
Total manufacturing costs	145,650	(e)	213,000
Work in process 1/1/14	(b)	15,500	18,000
Total cost of work in process	201,500	(f)	(j)
Work in process 12/31/14	(c)	11,800	(k)
Cost of goods manufactured	192,300	(g)	222,000

Compute the manufacturing overhead rate and under- or overapplied overhead.

(LO 4, 6), **AN**

Analyze job cost sheet and prepare entry for completed job.

(LO 2, 3, 4, 5), **AP**

Instructions

Indicate the missing amount for each letter. Assume that in all cases manufacturing overhead is applied on the basis of direct labor cost and the rate is the same.

E15-5   Duggan Company applies manufacturing overhead to jobs on the basis of machine hours used. Overhead costs are expected to total $325,000 for the year, and machine usage is estimated at 125,000 hours.

For the year, $342,000 of overhead costs are incurred and 130,000 hours are used.

Instructions

(a) Compute the manufacturing overhead rate for the year.
(b) What is the amount of under- or overapplied overhead at December 31?
(c) Prepare the adjusting entry to assign the under- or overapplied overhead for the year to cost of goods sold.

E15-6   A job cost sheet of Sandoval Company is given below.

		Job Cost Sheet		
JOB NO. 469			Quantity 2,500	
ITEM White Lion Cages			Date Requested 7/2	
FOR Todd Company			Date Completed 7/31	
Date	Direct Materials	Direct Labor	Manufacturing Overhead	
7/10	700			
12	900			
15		440	550	
22		380	475	
24	1,600			
27	1,500			
31		540	675	

Cost of completed job:
  Direct materials   _____
  Direct labor   _____

  Manufacturing overhead   _____

Total cost   ══════

Unit cost   ══════

Instructions

(a)   Answer the following questions.
  (1) What are the source documents for direct materials, direct labor, and manufacturing overhead costs assigned to this job?
  (2) What is the predetermined manufacturing overhead rate?
  (3) What are the total cost and the unit cost of the completed job? (Round unit cost to nearest cent.)
(b) Prepare the entry to record the completion of the job.

Prepare entries for manufacturing and nonmanufacturing costs.

(LO 2, 3, 4, 5), **AP**

E15-7   Torre Corporation incurred the following transactions.

1. Purchased raw materials on account $46,300.
2. Raw materials of $36,000 were requisitioned to the factory. An analysis of the materials requisition slips indicated that $6,800 was classified as indirect materials.
3. Factory labor costs incurred were $55,900, of which $51,000 pertained to factory wages payable and $4,900 pertained to employer payroll taxes payable.
4. Time tickets indicated that $50,000 was direct labor and $5,900 was indirect labor.
5. Manufacturing overhead costs incurred on account were $80,500.
6. Depreciation on the company's office building was $8,100.
7. Manufacturing overhead was applied at the rate of 150% of direct labor cost.
8. Goods costing $88,000 were completed and transferred to finished goods.
9. Finished goods costing $75,000 to manufacture were sold on account for $103,000.

Instructions

Journalize the transactions. (Omit explanations.)

E15-8   Enos Printing Corp. uses a job order cost system. The following data summarize the operations related to the first quarter's production.

Prepare entries for manufacturing and nonmanufacturing costs.

(LO 2, 3, 4, 5), **AP**

1. Materials purchased on account $192,000, and factory wages incurred $87,300.
2. Materials requisitioned and factory labor used by job:

Job Number	Materials	Factory Labor
A20	$ 35,240	$18,000
A21	42,920	22,000
A22	36,100	15,000
A23	39,270	25,000
General factory use	4,470	7,300
	$158,000	$87,300

3. Manufacturing overhead costs incurred on account $49,500.
4. Depreciation on factory equipment $14,550.
5. Depreciation on the company's office building was $14,300.
6. Manufacturing overhead rate is 90% of direct labor cost.
7. Jobs completed during the quarter: A20, A21, and A23.

Instructions
Prepare entries to record the operations summarized above. (Prepare a schedule showing the individual cost elements and total cost for each job in item 7.)

E15-9   At May 31, 2014, the accounts of Mantle Company show the following.

Prepare a cost of goods manufactured schedule and partial financial statements.

(LO 2, 5), **AP**

1. May 1 inventories—finished goods $12,600, work in process $14,700, and raw materials $8,200.
2. May 31 inventories—finished goods $9,500, work in process $17,900, and raw materials $7,100.
3. Debit postings to work in process were direct materials $62,400, direct labor $50,000, and manufacturing overhead applied $40,000.
4. Sales revenue totaled $210,000.

Instructions
(a) Prepare a condensed cost of goods manufactured schedule.
(b) Prepare an income statement for May through gross profit.
(c) Indicate the balance sheet presentation of the manufacturing inventories at May 31, 2014.

E15-10   Tierney Company begins operations on April 1. Information from job cost sheets shows the following.

Compute work in process and finished goods from job cost sheets.

(LO 3, 5), **AP**

Job	Manufacturing Costs Assigned			Month
Number	April	May	June	Completed
10	$5,200	$4,400		May
11	4,100	3,900	$2,000	June
12	1,200			April
13		4,700	4,500	June
14		5,900	3,600	Not complete

Job 12 was completed in April. Job 10 was completed in May. Jobs 11 and 13 were completed in June. Each job was sold for 25% above its cost in the month following completion.

Instructions
(a) What is the balance in Work in Process Inventory at the end of each month?
(b) What is the balance in Finished Goods Inventory at the end of each month?
(c) What is the gross profit for May, June, and July?

E15-11   Shown below are the job cost related accounts for the law firm of Jack, Bob, and Will and their manufacturing equivalents:

Prepare entries for costs of services provided.

(LO 2, 4, 5), **AP**

Law Firm Accounts	Manufacturing Firm Accounts
Supplies	Raw Materials
Salaries and Wages Payable	Factory Wages Payable
Operating Overhead	Manufacturing Overhead
Service Contracts in Process	Work in Process
Cost of Completed Service Contracts	Cost of Goods Sold

Cost data for the month of March follow.
1. Purchased supplies on account $1,500.
2. Issued supplies $1,200 (60% direct and 40% indirect).
3. Assigned labor costs based on time cards for the month which indicated labor costs of $60,000 (80% direct and 20% indirect).
4. Operating overhead costs incurred for cash totaled $40,000.
5. Operating overhead is applied at a rate of 90% of direct attorney cost.
6. Work completed totaled $75,000.

Instructions
(a) Journalize the transactions for March. (Omit explanations.)
(b) Determine the balance of the Service Contracts in Process account. (Use a T-account.)

Determine cost of jobs and ending balance in work in process and overhead accounts.

(LO 3, 4, 6), AP

E15-12 Don Lieberman and Associates, a CPA firm, uses job order costing to capture the costs of its audit jobs. There were no audit jobs in process at the beginning of November. Listed below are data concerning the three audit jobs conducted during November.

	Lynn	Brian	Mike
Direct materials	$600	$400	$200
Auditor labor costs	$5,400	$6,600	$3,375
Auditor hours	72	88	45

Overhead costs are applied to jobs on the basis of auditor hours, and the predetermined overhead rate is $50 per auditor hour. The Lynn job is the only incomplete job at the end of November. Actual overhead for the month was $11,000.

Instructions
(a) Determine the cost of each job.
(b) Indicate the balance of the Service Contracts in Process account at the end of November.
(c) Calculate the ending balance of the Operating Overhead account for November.

Determine predetermined overhead rate, apply overhead and determine whether balance under- or overapplied.

(LO 4, 6), AP

E15-13 Pure Decorating uses a job order cost system to collect the costs of its interior decorating business. Each client's consultation is treated as a separate job. Overhead is applied to each job based on the number of decorator hours incurred. Listed below are data for the current year.

Estimated overhead	$920,000
Actual overhead	$942,800
Estimated decorator hours	40,000
Actual decorator hours	40,500

The company uses Operating Overhead in place of Manufacturing Overhead.

Instructions
(a) Compute the predetermined overhead rate.
(b) Prepare the entry to apply the overhead for the year.
(c) Determine whether the overhead was under- or overapplied and by how much.

Exercises: Set B and Challenge Exercises

Visit the book's companion website, at **www.wiley.com/college/kimmel**, and choose the Student Companion site to access Exercise Set B and Challenge Exercises.

Problems: Set A

Prepare entries in a job order cost system and job cost sheets.

(LO 2, 3, 4, 5, 6), AP

P15-1A Degelman Company uses a job order cost system and applies overhead to production on the basis of direct labor costs. On January 1, 2014, Job No. 50 was the only job in process. The costs incurred prior to January 1 on this job were as follows: direct materials

$20,000, direct labor $12,000, and manufacturing overhead $16,000. As of January 1, Job No. 49 had been completed at a cost of $90,000 and was part of finished goods inventory. There was a $15,000 balance in the Raw Materials Inventory account.

During the month of January, Degelman Company began production on Jobs 51 and 52, and completed Jobs 50 and 51. Jobs 49 and 50 were also sold on account during the month for $122,000 and $158,000, respectively. The following additional events occurred during the month.

1. Purchased additional raw materials of $90,000 on account.
2. Incurred factory labor costs of $70,000. Of this amount $16,000 related to employer payroll taxes.
3. Incurred manufacturing overhead costs as follows: indirect materials $17,000; indirect labor $20,000; depreciation expense on equipment $19,000; and various other manufacturing overhead costs on account $16,000.
4. Assigned direct materials and direct labor to jobs as follows.

Job No.	Direct Materials	Direct Labor
50	$10,000	$ 5,000
51	39,000	25,000
52	30,000	20,000

Instructions
(a) Calculate the predetermined overhead rate for 2014, assuming Degelman Company estimates total manufacturing overhead costs of $980,000, direct labor costs of $700,000, and direct labor hours of 20,000 for the year.
(b) Open job cost sheets for Jobs 50, 51, and 52. Enter the January 1 balances on the job cost sheet for Job No. 50.
(c) Prepare the journal entries to record the purchase of raw materials, the factory labor costs incurred, and the manufacturing overhead costs incurred during the month of January.
(d) Prepare the journal entries to record the assignment of direct materials, direct labor, and manufacturing overhead costs to production. In assigning manufacturing overhead costs, use the overhead rate calculated in (a). Post all costs to the job cost sheets as necessary.
(e) Total the job cost sheets for any job(s) completed during the month. Prepare the journal entry (or entries) to record the completion of any job(s) during the month.
(f) Prepare the journal entry (or entries) to record the sale of any job(s) during the month.
(g) What is the balance in the Finished Goods Inventory account at the end of the month? What does this balance consist of?
(h) What is the amount of over- or underapplied overhead?

(e) Job 50, $70,000
Job 51, $99,000

P15-2A For the year ended December 31, 2014, the job cost sheets of Cinta Company contained the following data.

Prepare entries in a job order cost system and partial income statement.
(LO 2, 3, 4, 5, 6), **AN**

Job Number	Explanation	Direct Materials	Direct Labor	Manufacturing Overhead	Total Costs
7640	Balance 1/1	$25,000	$24,000	$28,800	$ 77,800
	Current year's costs	30,000	36,000	43,200	109,200
7641	Balance 1/1	11,000	18,000	21,600	50,600
	Current year's costs	43,000	48,000	57,600	148,600
7642	Current year's costs	58,000	55,000	66,000	179,000

Other data:
1. Raw materials inventory totaled $15,000 on January 1. During the year, $140,000 of raw materials were purchased on account.
2. Finished goods on January 1 consisted of Job No. 7638 for $87,000 and Job No. 7639 for $92,000.
3. Job No. 7640 and Job No. 7641 were completed during the year.
4. Job Nos. 7638, 7639, and 7641 were sold on account for $530,000.
5. Manufacturing overhead incurred on account totaled $120,000.
6. Other manufacturing overhead consisted of indirect materials $14,000, indirect labor $18,000, and depreciation on factory machinery $8,000.

Prepare entries in a job order cost system and cost of goods manufactured schedule.

(LO 2, 3, 4, 5), **AP**

Instructions

(a) Prove the agreement of Work in Process Inventory with job cost sheets pertaining to unfinished work. (*Hint:* Use a single T-account for Work in Process Inventory.) Calculate each of the following, then post each to the T-account: (1) beginning balance, (2) direct materials, (3) direct labor, (4) manufacturing overhead, and (5) completed jobs.

(b) Prepare the adjusting entry for manufacturing overhead, assuming the balance is allocated entirely to Cost of Goods Sold.

(c) Determine the gross profit to be reported for 2014.

P15-3A Stellar Inc. is a construction company specializing in custom patios. The patios are constructed of concrete, brick, fiberglass, and lumber, depending upon customer preference. On June 1, 2014, the general ledger for Stellar Inc. contains the following data.

Raw Materials Inventory	$4,200	Manufacturing Overhead Applied	$32,640
Work in Process Inventory	$5,540	Manufacturing Overhead Incurred	$31,650

Subsidiary data for Work in Process Inventory on June 1 are as follows.

Job Cost Sheets

	Customer Job		
Cost Element	Gannon	Rosenthal	Linton
Direct materials	$ 600	$ 800	$ 900
Direct labor	320	540	580
Manufacturing overhead	400	675	725
	$1,320	$2,015	$2,205

During June, raw materials purchased on account were $4,900, and all wages were paid. Additional overhead costs consisted of depreciation on equipment $700 and miscellaneous costs of $400 incurred on account.

A summary of materials requisition slips and time tickets for June shows the following.

Customer Job	Materials Requisition Slips	Time Tickets
Gannon	$ 800	$ 450
Koss	2,000	800
Rosenthal	500	360
Linton	1,300	1,200
Gannon	300	390
	4,900	3,200
General use	1,500	1,200
	$6,400	$4,400

Overhead was charged to jobs at the same rate of $1.25 per dollar of direct labor cost. The patios for customers Gannon, Rosenthal, and Linton were completed during June and sold for a total of $18,900. Each customer paid in full.

Instructions

(a) Journalize the June transactions: (i) for purchase of raw materials, factory labor costs incurred, and manufacturing overhead costs incurred; (ii) assignment of direct materials, labor, and overhead to production; and (iii) completion of jobs and sale of goods.

(b) Post the entries to Work in Process Inventory.

(d) Cost of goods manufactured $13,840

(c) Reconcile the balance in Work in Process Inventory with the costs of unfinished jobs.

(d) Prepare a cost of goods manufactured schedule for June.

Compute predetermined overhead rates, apply overhead, and calculate under- or overapplied overhead.

(LO 4, 6), **AP**

P15-4A Agassi Company uses a job order cost system in each of its three manufacturing departments. Manufacturing overhead is applied to jobs on the basis of direct labor cost in Department D, direct labor hours in Department E, and machine hours in Department K.

In establishing the predetermined overhead rates for 2014, the following estimates were made for the year.

	Department		
	D	**E**	**K**
Manufacturing overhead	$1,200,000	$1,500,000	$900,000
Direct labor costs	$1,500,000	$1,250,000	$450,000
Direct labor hours	100,000	125,000	40,000
Machine hours	400,000	500,000	120,000

During January, the job cost sheets showed the following costs and production data.

	Department		
	D	**E**	**K**
Direct materials used	$140,000	$126,000	$78,000
Direct labor costs	$120,000	$110,000	$37,500
Manufacturing overhead incurred	$ 99,000	$124,000	$79,000
Direct labor hours	8,000	11,000	3,500
Machine hours	34,000	45,000	10,400

Instructions
(a) Compute the predetermined overhead rate for each department.
(b) Compute the total manufacturing costs assigned to jobs in January in each department.
(c) Compute the under- or overapplied overhead for each department at January 31.

(a) 80%, $12, $7.50
(b) $356,000, $368,000, $193,500
(c) $3,000, $(8,000), $1,000

*Analyze manufacturing
accounts and determine
missing amounts.*
(LO 2, 3, 4, 5, 6), **AN**

P15-5A   Rodman Corporation's fiscal year ends on November 30. The following accounts are found in its job order cost accounting system for the first month of the new fiscal year.

Raw Materials Inventory

Dec. 1	Beginning balance	(a)	Dec. 31	Requisitions	16,850
31	Purchases	19,225			
Dec. 31	Ending balance	7,975			

Work in Process Inventory

Dec. 1	Beginning balance	(b)	Dec. 31	Jobs completed	(f)
31	Direct materials	(c)			
31	Direct labor	8,800			
31	Overhead	(d)			
Dec. 31	Ending balance	(e)			

Finished Goods Inventory

Dec. 1	Beginning balance	(g)	Dec. 31	Cost of goods sold	(i)
31	Completed jobs	(h)			
Dec. 31	Ending balance	(j)			

Factory Labor

Dec. 31	Factory wages	12,025	Dec. 31	Wages assigned	(k)

Manufacturing Overhead

Dec. 31	Indirect materials	1,900	Dec. 31	Overhead applied	(m)
31	Indirect labor	(l)			
31	Other overhead	1,245			

Other data:
1. On December 1, two jobs were in process: Job No. 154 and Job No. 155. These jobs had combined direct materials costs of $9,750 and direct labor costs of $15,000. Overhead was applied at a rate that was 75% of direct labor cost.
2. During December, Job Nos. 156, 157, and 158 were started. On December 31, Job No. 158 was unfinished. This job had charges for direct materials $3,800 and direct labor $4,800, plus manufacturing overhead. All jobs, except for Job No. 158, were completed in December.

3. On December 1, Job No. 153 was in the finished goods warehouse. It had a total cost of $5,000. On December 31, Job No. 157 was the only job finished that was not sold. It had a cost of $4,000.
4. Manufacturing overhead was $230 overapplied in December.

(c) $14,950
(f) $54,150
(i) $55,150

Instructions

List the letters (a) through (m) and indicate the amount pertaining to each letter.

Problems: Set B

Prepare entries in a job order cost system and job cost sheets.

(LO 2, 3, 4, 5, 6), **AP**

P15-1B Pedriani Company uses a job order cost system and applies overhead to production on the basis of direct labor hours. On January 1, 2014, Job No. 25 was the only job in process. The costs incurred prior to January 1 on this job were as follows: direct materials $10,000; direct labor $6,000; and manufacturing overhead $9,000. Job No. 23 had been completed at a cost of $42,000 and was part of finished goods inventory. There was a $5,000 balance in the Raw Materials Inventory account.

During the month of January, the company began production on Jobs 26 and 27, and completed Jobs 25 and 26. Jobs 23 and 25 were sold on account during the month for $63,000 and $74,000, respectively. The following additional events occurred during the month.

1. Purchased additional raw materials of $45,000 on account.
2. Incurred factory labor costs of $33,500. Of this amount, $7,500 related to employer payroll taxes.
3. Incurred manufacturing overhead costs as follows: indirect materials $10,000; indirect labor $9,500; depreciation expense on equipment $12,000; and various other manufacturing overhead costs on account $11,000.
4. Assigned direct materials and direct labor to jobs as follows.

Job No.	Direct Materials	Direct Labor
25	$ 5,000	$ 3,000
26	17,000	12,000
27	13,000	9,000

5. The company uses direct labor hours as the activity base to assign overhead. Direct labor hours incurred on each job were as follows: Job No. 25, 200; Job No. 26, 800; and Job No. 27, 600.

Instructions

(a) Calculate the predetermined overhead rate for the year 2014, assuming Pedriani Company estimates total manufacturing overhead costs of $440,000, direct labor costs of $300,000, and direct labor hours of 20,000 for the year.
(b) Open job cost sheets for Jobs 25, 26, and 27. Enter the January 1 balances on the job cost sheet for Job No. 25.
(c) Prepare the journal entries to record the purchase of raw materials, the factory labor costs incurred, and the manufacturing overhead costs incurred during the month of January.
(d) Prepare the journal entries to record the assignment of direct materials, direct labor, and manufacturing overhead costs to production. In assigning manufacturing overhead costs, use the overhead rate calculated in (a). Post all costs to the job cost sheets as necessary.

(e) Job 25, $37,400
Job 26, $46,600

(e) Total the job cost sheets for any job(s) completed during the month. Prepare the journal entry (or entries) to record the completion of any job(s) during the month.
(f) Prepare the journal entry (or entries) to record the sale of any job(s) during the month.
(g) What is the balance in the Work in Process Inventory account at the end of the month? What does this balance consist of?
(h) What is the amount of over- or underapplied overhead?

P15-2B For the year ended December 31, 2014, the job cost sheets of Dosey Company contained the following data.

Prepare entries in a job order cost system and partial income statement.
(LO 2, 3, 4, 5, 6), **AN**

Job Number	Explanation	Direct Materials	Direct Labor	Manufacturing Overhead	Total Costs
7650	Balance 1/1	$18,000	$20,000	$25,000	$ 63,000
	Current year's costs	32,000	36,000	45,000	113,000
7651	Balance 1/1	12,000	16,000	20,000	48,000
	Current year's costs	30,000	40,000	50,000	120,000
7652	Current year's costs	35,000	68,000	85,000	188,000

Other data:
1. Raw materials inventory totaled $20,000 on January 1. During the year, $100,000 of raw materials were purchased on account.
2. Finished goods on January 1 consisted of Job No. 7648 for $93,000 and Job No. 7649 for $62,000.
3. Job No. 7650 and Job No. 7651 were completed during the year.
4. Job Nos. 7648, 7649, and 7650 were sold on account for $490,000.
5. Manufacturing overhead incurred on account totaled $135,000.
6. Other manufacturing overhead consisted of indirect materials $12,000, indirect labor $16,000, and depreciation on factory machinery $19,500.

Instructions
(a) Prove the agreement of Work in Process Inventory with job cost sheets pertaining to unfinished work. (*Hint:* Use a single T-account for Work in Process Inventory.) Calculate each of the following, then post each to the T-account: (1) beginning balance, (2) direct materials, (3) direct labor, (4) manufacturing overhead, and (5) completed jobs.
(b) Prepare the adjusting entry for manufacturing overhead, assuming the balance is allocated entirely to cost of goods sold.
(c) Determine the gross profit to be reported for 2014.

(a) (1) $111,000
(4) $180,000
Unfinished job 7652,
$188,000

(b) Amount = $2,500

(c) $156,500

P15-3B Robert Perez is a contractor specializing in custom-built jacuzzis. On May 1, 2014, his ledger contains the following data.

Prepare entries in a job order cost system and cost of goods manufactured schedule.
(LO 2, 3, 4, 5), **AP**

Raw Materials Inventory	$30,000
Work in Process Inventory	12,200
Manufacturing Overhead	2,500 (dr.)

The Manufacturing Overhead account has debit totals of $12,500 and credit totals of $10,000. Subsidiary data for Work in Process Inventory on May 1 include:

Job Cost Sheets

Job by Customer	Direct Materials	Direct Labor	Manufacturing Overhead
Stiner	$2,500	$2,000	$1,400
Alton	2,000	1,200	840
Herman	900	800	560
	$5,400	$4,000	$2,800

During May, the following costs were incurred: raw materials purchased on account $4,000, labor paid $7,000, and manufacturing overhead paid $1,400.

A summary of materials requisition slips and time tickets for the month of May reveals the following.

Job by Customer	Materials Requisition Slips	Time Tickets
Stiner	$ 500	$ 400
Alton	600	1,000
Herman	2,300	1,300
Smith	1,900	2,300
	5,300	5,000
General use	1,500	2,000
	$6,800	$7,000

Overhead was charged to jobs on the basis of $0.70 per dollar of direct labor cost. The jacuzzis for customers Stiner, Alton, and Herman were completed during May. The three jacuzzis were sold for a total of $36,000.

Instructions

(a) Prepare journal entries for the May transactions: (i) for purchase of raw materials, factory labor costs incurred, and manufacturing overhead costs incurred; (ii) assignment of raw materials, labor, and overhead to production; and (iii) completion of jobs and sale of goods.

(b) Post the entries to Work in Process Inventory.

(c) Reconcile the balance in Work in Process Inventory with the costs of unfinished jobs.

(d) Prepare a cost of goods manufactured schedule for May.

(d) Cost of goods manufactured $20,190

Compute predetermined overhead rates, apply overhead, and calculate under- or overapplied overhead.

(LO 4, 6), **AP**

P15-4B Net Play Company uses a job order cost system in each of its three manufacturing departments. Manufacturing overhead is applied to jobs on the basis of direct labor cost in Department A, direct labor hours in Department B, and machine hours in Department C.

In establishing the predetermined overhead rates for 2014, the following estimates were made for the year.

| | **Department** | | |
	A	**B**	**C**
Manufacturing overhead	$720,000	$640,000	$900,000
Direct labor cost	$600,000	$100,000	$600,000
Direct labor hours	50,000	40,000	40,000
Machine hours	100,000	120,000	150,000

During January, the job cost sheets showed the following costs and production data.

| | **Department** | | |
	A	**B**	**C**
Direct materials used	$92,000	$86,000	$64,000
Direct labor cost	$48,000	$35,000	$50,400
Manufacturing overhead incurred	$60,000	$60,000	$72,100
Direct labor hours	4,000	3,500	4,200
Machine hours	8,000	10,500	12,600

Instructions

(a) Compute the predetermined overhead rate for each department.

(b) Compute the total manufacturing costs assigned to jobs in January in each department.

(c) Compute the under- or overapplied overhead for each department at January 31.

(a) 120%, $16, $6

(b) $197,600, $177,000, $190,000

(c) $2,400 $4,000, $(3,500)

Analyze manufacturing accounts and determine missing amounts.

(LO 2, 3, 4, 5, 6), **AN**

P15-5B Bell Company's fiscal year ends on June 30. The following accounts are found in its job order cost accounting system for the first month of the new fiscal year.

Raw Materials Inventory

July 1	Beginning balance	19,000	July 31	Requisitions	(a)
31	Purchases	90,400			
July 31	Ending balance	(b)			

Work in Process Inventory

July 1	Beginning balance	(c)	July 31	Jobs completed	(f)
31	Direct materials	80,000			
31	Direct labor	(d)			
31	Overhead	(e)			
July 31	Ending balance	(g)			

Finished Goods Inventory

July 1	Beginning balance	(h)	July 31	Cost of goods sold	(j)
31	Completed jobs	(i)			
July 31	Ending balance	(k)			

Factory Labor

July 31	Factory wages		(l)	July 31	Wages assigned	(m)

Manufacturing Overhead

July 31	Indirect materials	8,900	July 31	Overhead applied		117,000
31	Indirect labor	16,000				
31	Other overhead	(n)				

Other data:
1. On July 1, two jobs were in process: Job No. 4085 and Job No. 4086, with costs of $19,000 and $8,200, respectively.
2. During July, Job Nos. 4087, 4088, and 4089 were started. On July 31, only Job No. 4089 was unfinished. This job had charges for direct materials $2,000 and direct labor $1,500, plus manufacturing overhead. Manufacturing overhead was applied at the rate of 130% of direct labor cost.
3. On July 1, Job No. 4084, costing $145,000, was in the finished goods warehouse. On July 31, Job No. 4088, costing $138,000, was in finished goods.
4. Overhead was $3,000 underapplied in July.

Instructions

List the letters (a) through (n) and indicate the amount pertaining to each letter. Show computations.

(d) $ 90,000
(f) $308,750
(l) $ 106,000

Problems: Set C

Visit the book's companion website, at **www.wiley.com/college/kimmel**, and choose the Student Companion site to access Problem Set C.

Waterways Continuing Problem

(*Note:* This is a continuation of the Waterways Problem from Chapter 14.)

WCP15 Waterways has two major public-park projects to provide with comprehensive irrigation in one of its service locations this month. Job J57 and Job K52 involve 15 acres of landscaped terrain which will require special-order sprinkler heads to meet the specifications of the project. This problem asks you to help Waterways use a job order cost system to account for production of these parts.

Go to the book's companion website, at **www.wiley.com/college/kimmel,** to find the completion of this problem.

Broadening Your Perspective

Management Decision-Making

DECISION-MAKING AT CURRENT DESIGNS

BYP15-1 Huegel Hollow Resort has ordered 20 rotomolded kayaks from Current Designs. Each kayak will be formed in the rotomolded oven, cooled, and then the excess plastic trimmed away. Then, the hatches, seat, ropes, and bungees will be attached to the kayak.

Dave Thill, the kayak plant manager, knows that manufacturing each kayak requires 54 pounds of polyethylene powder and a finishing kit (rope, seat, hardware, etc.). The polyethylene powder used in these kayaks costs $1.50 per pound, and the finishing kits cost $170 each. Each kayak will use two kinds of labor: 2 hours of more-skilled type I labor from people who run the oven and trim the plastic, and 3 hours of less-skilled type II labor from people who attach the hatches and seat and other hardware. The type I employees are paid $15 per hour, and the type II employees are paid $12 per hour. For purposes of this problem, assume that overhead is allocated to all jobs at a rate of 150% of direct labor costs.

Instructions
Determine the total cost of the Huegel Hollow order and the cost of each individual kayak in the order. Identify costs as direct materials, direct labor, or manufacturing overhead.

DECISION-MAKING ACROSS THE ORGANIZATION

BYP15-2   Khan Products Company uses a job order cost system. For a number of months, there has been an ongoing rift between the sales department and the production department concerning a special-order product, TC-1. TC-1 is a seasonal product that is manufactured in batches of 1,000 units. TC-1 is sold at cost plus a markup of 40% of cost.

The sales department is unhappy because fluctuating unit production costs significantly affect selling prices. Sales personnel complain that this has caused excessive customer complaints and the loss of considerable orders for TC-1.

The production department maintains that each job order must be fully costed on the basis of the costs incurred during the period in which the goods are produced. Production personnel maintain that the only real solution to the problem is for the sales department to increase sales in the slack periods.

Andrea Parley, president of the company, asks you as the company accountant to collect quarterly data for the past year on TC-1. From the cost accounting system, you accumulate the following production quantity and cost data.

	Quarter			
Costs	1	2	3	4
Direct materials	$100,000	$220,000	$ 80,000	$200,000
Direct labor	60,000	132,000	48,000	120,000
Manufacturing overhead	105,000	153,000	97,000	125,000
Total	$265,000	$505,000	$225,000	$445,000
Production in batches	5	11	4	10
Unit cost (per batch)	$ 53,000	$ 45,909	$ 56,250	$ 44,500

Instructions
With the class divided into groups, answer the following questions.
(a) What manufacturing cost element is responsible for the fluctuating unit costs? Why?
(b) What is your recommended solution to the problem of fluctuating unit cost?
(c) Restate the quarterly data on the basis of your recommended solution.

MANAGERIAL ANALYSIS

BYP15-3   In the course of routine checking of all journal entries prior to preparing year-end reports, Betty Eller discovered several strange entries. She recalled that the president's son Joe had come in to help out during an especially busy time and that he had recorded some journal entries. She was relieved that there were only a few of his entries, and even more relieved that he had included rather lengthy explanations. The entries Joe made were:

(1)

Work in Process Inventory	25,000	
Cash		25,000

(This is for materials put into process. I don't find the record that we paid for these, so I'm crediting Cash because I know we'll have to pay for them sooner or later.)

(2)

Manufacturing Overhead	12,000	
Cash		12,000

(This is for bonuses paid to salespeople. I know they're part of overhead, and I can't find an account called "Non-Factory Overhead" or "Other Overhead" so I'm putting it in Manufacturing Overhead. I have the check stubs, so I know we paid these.)

(3)

| Wages Expense | 120,000 | |
| Cash | | 120,000 |

(This is for the factory workers' wages. I have a note that payroll taxes are $18,000. I still think that's part of wages expense and that we'll have to pay it all in cash sooner or later, so I credited Cash for the wages and the taxes.)

(4)

| Work in Process Inventory | 3,000 | |
| Raw Materials Inventory | | 3,000 |

(This is for the glue used in the factory. I know we used this to make the products, even though we didn't use very much on any one of the products. I got it out of inventory, so I credited an inventory account.)

Instructions

(a) How should Joe have recorded each of the four events?

(b) If the entry was not corrected, which financial statements (income statement or balance sheet) would be affected? What balances would be overstated or understated?

REAL-WORLD FOCUS

BYP 15-4   Founded in 1970, Parlex Corporation is a world leader in the design and manufacture of flexible interconnect products. Utilizing proprietary and patented technologies, Parlex produces custom flexible interconnects including flexible circuits, polymer thick film, laminated cables, and value-added assemblies for sophisticated electronics used in automotive, telecommunications, computer, diversified electronics, and aerospace applications. In addition to manufacturing sites in Methuen, Massachusetts; Salem, New Hampshire; Cranston, Rhode Island; San Jose, California; Shanghai, China; Isle of Wight, UK; and Empalme, Mexico, Parlex has logistic support centers and strategic alliances throughout North America, Asia, and Europe.

The following information was provided in the company's annual report.

PARLEX COMPANY
Notes to the Financial Statements

The Company's products are manufactured on a job order basis to customers' specifications. Customers submit requests for quotations on each job, and the Company prepares bids based on its own cost estimates. The Company attempts to reflect the impact of changing costs when establishing prices. However, during the past several years, the market conditions for flexible circuits and the resulting price sensitivity haven't always allowed this to transpire. Although still not satisfactory, the Company was able to reduce the cost of products sold as a percentage of sales to 85% this year versus 87% that was experienced in the two immediately preceding years. Management continues to focus on improving operational efficiency and further reducing costs.

Instructions

(a) Parlex management discusses the job order cost system employed by their company. What are several advantages of using the job order approach to costing?

(b) Contrast the products produced in a job order environment, like Parlex, to those produced when process cost systems are used.

BYP15-5   The Institute of Management Accountants sponsors a certification for management accountants, allowing them to obtain the title of Certified Management Accountant.

Address: **www.imanet.org**, or go to **www.wiley.com/college/kimmel**

Steps

1. Go to the site shown above.
2. Choose **CMA Certification**, and then, **Earning & Maintaining Your Credential**.

Instructions

(a) What is the experience qualification requirement?

(b) How many hours of continuing education are required, and what types of courses qualify?

Critical Thinking

COMMUNICATION ACTIVITY

BYP15-6 You are the management accountant for Williams Company. Your company does custom carpentry work and uses a job order cost system. Williams sends detailed job cost sheets to its customers, along with an invoice. The job cost sheets show the date materials were used, the dollar cost of materials, and the hours and cost of labor. A predetermined overhead application rate is used, and the total overhead applied is also listed.

Nancy Kopay is a customer who recently had custom cabinets installed. Along with her check in payment for the work done, she included a letter. She thanked the company for including the detailed cost information but questioned why overhead was estimated. She stated that she would be interested in knowing exactly what costs were included in overhead, and she thought that other customers would, too.

Instructions

Prepare a letter to Ms. Kopay (address: 123 Cedar Lane, Altoona, KS 66651) and tell her why you did not send her information on exact costs of overhead included in her job. Respond to her suggestion that you provide this information.

ETHICS CASE

BYP15-7 LRF Printing provides printing services to many different corporate clients. Although LRF bids most jobs, some jobs, particularly new ones, are negotiated on a "cost-plus" basis. Cost-plus means that the buyer is willing to pay the actual cost plus a return (profit) on these costs to LRF.

Alice Reiley, controller for LRF, has recently returned from a meeting where LRF's president stated that he wanted her to find a way to charge more costs to any project that was on a cost-plus basis. The president noted that the company needed more profits to meet its stated goals this period. By charging more costs to the cost-plus projects and therefore fewer costs to the jobs that were bid, the company should be able to increase its profit for the current year.

Alice knew why the president wanted to take this action. Rumors were that he was looking for a new position and if the company reported strong profits, the president's opportunities would be enhanced. Alice also recognized that she could probably increase the cost of certain jobs by changing the basis used to allocate manufacturing overhead.

Instructions

(a) Who are the stakeholders in this situation?
(b) What are the ethical issues in this situation?
(c) What would you do if you were Alice Reiley?

ALL ABOUT YOU

BYP15-8 Many of you will work for a small business. Some of you will even own your own business. In order to operate a small business, you will need a good understanding of managerial accounting, as well as many other skills. Much information is available to assist people who are interested in starting a new business. A great place to start is the website provided by the Small Business Administration, which is an agency of the federal government whose purpose is to support small business.

Instructions

Go to **www.sba.gov** and in the Small Business Planner, Plan Your Business link, review the material under "Get Ready." Answer the following questions.
(a) What are some of the characteristics required of a small business owner?
(b) What are the top 10 reasons given for business failure?

CONSIDERING YOUR COSTS AND BENEFITS

BYP15-9 After graduating, you might decide to start a small business. As discussed in this chapter, owners of any business need to know how to calculate the cost of their products. In fact, many small businesses fail because they don't accurately calculate their product costs, so they don't know if they are making a profit or losing money—until it's too late.

Suppose that you decide to start a landscape business. You use an old pickup truck that you've fully paid for. You store the truck and other equipment in your parents' barn, and you store trees and shrubs on their land. Your parents will not charge you for the use of these facilities for the first two years, but beginning in the third year they will charge a reasonable rent. Your mother helps you by answering phone calls and providing customers with information. She doesn't charge you for this service, but she plans on doing it for only your first two years in business. In pricing your services, should you include charges for the truck, the barn, the land, and your mother's services when calculating your product cost? The basic arguments for and against are as follows.

> **YES:** If you don't include charges for these costs, your costs are understated and your profit-ability is overstated.
>
> **NO:** At this point, you are not actually incurring costs related to these activities; therefore, you shouldn't record charges.

Instructions

Write a response indicating your position regarding this situation. Provide support for your view.

Answers to Insight and Accounting Across the Organization Questions

p. 802 Jobs Won, Money Lost Q: What type of costs do you think the company had been underes-timating? **A:** It is most likely that the company failed to estimate and track overhead. In a highly diversified company, overhead associated with the diesel locomotive jobs may have been "lost" in the total overhead pool for the entire company.

p. 807 The Cost of an iPhone? Just Tear One Apart Q: What type of costs are marketing and sell-ing costs, and how are they treated for accounting purposes? **A:** Product costs include materials, labor, and overhead. Costs not related to production, such as marketing and selling costs, are period costs which are expensed in the period that they are incurred.

p. 818 Sales Are Nice, but Service Revenue Pays the Bills Q: Explain why GE would use job order costing to keep track of the cost of repairing a malfunctioning engine for a major airline. **A:** GE operates in a competitive environment. Other companies offer competing bids to win service con-tracts on GE's airplane engines. GE needs to know what it costs to repair engines, so that it can present competitive bids while still generating a reasonable profit.

Answers to Self-Test Questions

1. a **2.** c **3.** b **4.** c **5.** c **6.** d **7.** d **8.** b **9.** a **10.** d **11.** b ($180,000 × 80%)
12. c **13.** b **14.** c **15.** c **16.** b

✔ **The Navigator**

✔ Remember to go back to The Navigator box on the chapter opening page and check off your completed work.

CHAPTER 16

Richard B. Levine/Alamy

✔ The Navigator

- Scan Learning Objectives
- Read Feature Story
- Scan Preview
- Read Text and answer **Do it!**
  ○ p. 849 ○ p. 852 ○ p. 856 ○ p. 861
- Work Using the Decision Toolkit
- Review Summary of Learning Objectives
- Work Comprehensive **Do it!** p. 872
- Answer Self-Test Questions
- Complete Assignments
- Go to WileyPLUS for practice and tutorials

PROCESS COSTING

LEARNING OBJECTIVES

After studying this chapter, you should be able to:

1 Understand who uses process cost systems.

2 Explain the similarities and differences between job order cost and process cost systems.

3 Explain the flow of costs in a process cost system.

4 Make the journal entries to assign manufacturing costs in a process cost system.

5 Compute equivalent units.

6 Explain the four steps necessary to prepare a production cost report.

7 Prepare a production cost report.

✔ The Navigator

Ben & Jerry's Homemade, Inc., based in Waterbury, Vermont, started its first ice cream shop in a former gas station in 1978.

Making ice cream is a process—a movement of product from a mixing department to a prepping department to a pint department. The mixing department is where the ice cream is created. In the prep area, the production process adds extras such as cherries and dark chocolate to make plain ice cream into "Cherry Garcia," Ben & Jerry's most popular flavor, or fudge-covered waffle cone pieces and a swirl of caramel for "Stephen Colbert's Americone Dream." The pint department is where the ice cream is actually put into containers. As the product is processed from one department to the next, the appropriate materials, labor, and overhead are added to determine its cost.

"The incoming ingredients from the shipping and receiving departments are stored in certain locations, either in a freezer or dry warehouse," says Beecher Eurich, staff accountant. "As

BEN & JERRY'S TRACKS ITS MIX-UPS

ingredients get added, so do the costs associated with them." How much ice cream is produced? Running plants around the clock, the company produces 18 million gallons a year.

With the company's process cost system, Eurich can tell you how much a certain batch of ice cream costs to make—its materials, labor, and overhead in each of the production departments. She generates reports for the production department heads but makes sure not to overdo it. "You can get bogged down in numbers," says Eurich. "If you're generating a report that no one can use, then that's a waste of time."

It's more likely, though, that Ben & Jerry's production people want to know how efficient they are. Why? Many own stock in the company.

Watch the Jones Soda video in WileyPLUS to learn more about process costing in the real world.

✔ The Navigator

The cost accounting system used by companies such as Ben & Jerry's is **process cost accounting**. In contrast to job order cost accounting, which focuses on the individual job, process cost accounting focuses on the **processes** involved in mass-producing products that are identical or very similar in nature. The primary objective of this chapter is to explain and illustrate process costing.

The content and organization of this chapter are as follows.

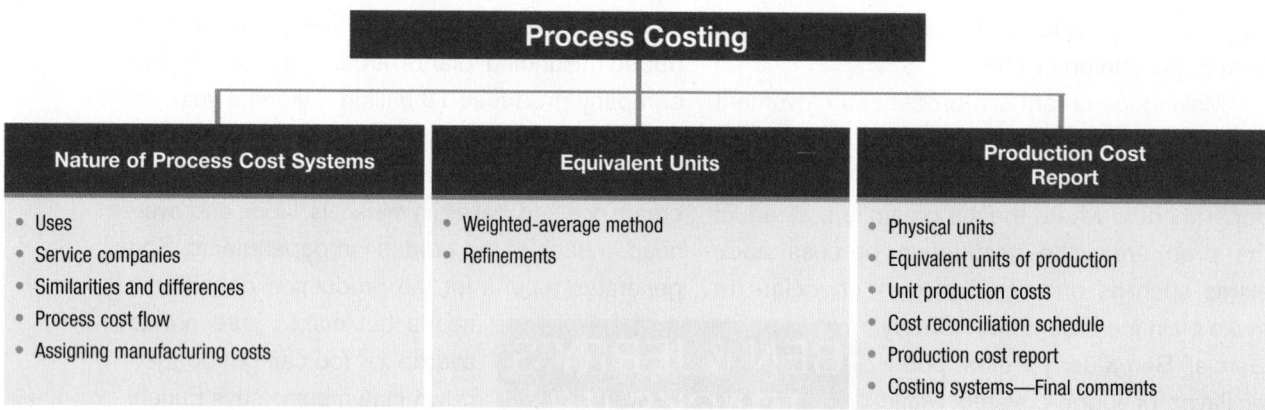

Process Costing		
Nature of Process Cost Systems	**Equivalent Units**	**Production Cost Report**
• Uses	• Weighted-average method	• Physical units
• Service companies	• Refinements	• Equivalent units of production
• Similarities and differences		• Unit production costs
• Process cost flow		• Cost reconciliation schedule
• Assigning manufacturing costs		• Production cost report
		• Costing systems—Final comments

✔ The Navigator

The Nature of Process Cost Systems

USES OF PROCESS COST SYSTEMS

Companies use **process cost systems** to apply costs to similar products that are mass-produced in a continuous fashion. Ben & Jerry's uses a process cost system: Production of the ice cream, once it begins, continues until the ice cream emerges, and the processing is the same for the entire run—with precisely the same amount of materials, labor, and overhead. Each finished pint of ice cream is indistinguishable from another.

A company such as USX uses process costing in the manufacturing of steel. Kellogg and General Mills use process costing for cereal production; ExxonMobil uses process costing for its oil refining. Sherwin Williams uses process costing for its paint products. At a bottling company like Coca-Cola, the manufacturing process begins with the blending of ingredients. Next, automated machinery moves the bottles into position and fills them. The production process then caps, packages, and forwards the bottles to the finished goods warehouse. Illustration 16-1 shows this process.

Illustration 16-1
Manufacturing processes

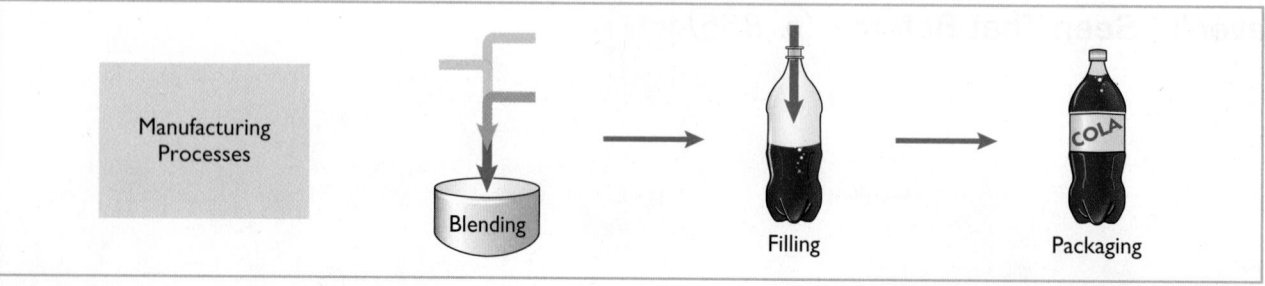

Manufacturing Processes

Blending

Filling

Packaging

For Coca-Cola, as well as the other companies just mentioned, once production begins, it continues until the finished product emerges, and each unit of finished product is like every other unit.

In comparison, a job order cost system assigns costs to a **specific job**. Examples are the construction of a customized home, the making of a motion picture, or the manufacturing of a specialized machine. Illustration 16-2 provides examples of companies that primarily use either a process cost system or a job order cost system.

Illustration 16-2 Process cost and job order cost companies and products

Process Cost System			Job Order Cost System		
Company	**Product**		**Company**	**Product**	
Coca-Cola, PepsiCo	Soft drinks		Young & Rubicam, J. Walter Thompson	Advertising	
ExxonMobil, Royal Dutch Shell	Oil		Walt Disney, Warner Brothers	Motion pictures	
Intel, Advanced Micro Devices	Computer chips		Center Ice Consultants, Ice Pro	Ice rinks	
Dow Chemical, DuPont	Chemicals		Kaiser, Mayo Clinic	Patient health care	

PROCESS COSTING FOR SERVICE COMPANIES

Frequently, when we think of service companies, we think of specific, nonroutine tasks, such as rebuilding an automobile engine, providing consulting services on a business acquisition, or working on a major lawsuit. However, many service companies specialize in performing repetitive, routine aspects of a particular business. For example, auto-care vendors such as Jiffy Lube focus on the routine aspects of car care. H&R Block focuses on the routine aspects of basic tax practice, and many large law firms focus on routine legal services, such as uncomplicated divorces. Service companies that provide specific, nonroutine services will probably benefit from using a job order cost system. Those that perform routine, repetitive services will probably be better off with a process cost system.

SIMILARITIES AND DIFFERENCES BETWEEN JOB ORDER COST AND PROCESS COST SYSTEMS

In a job order cost system, companies assign costs to each job. In a process cost system, companies track costs through a series of connected manufacturing processes or departments, rather than by individual jobs. Thus, companies use process cost systems when they produce a large volume of uniform or relatively homogeneous products. Illustration 16-3 (page 848) shows the basic flow of costs in these two systems.

LEARNING OBJECTIVE 2

Explain the similarities and differences between job order cost and process cost systems.

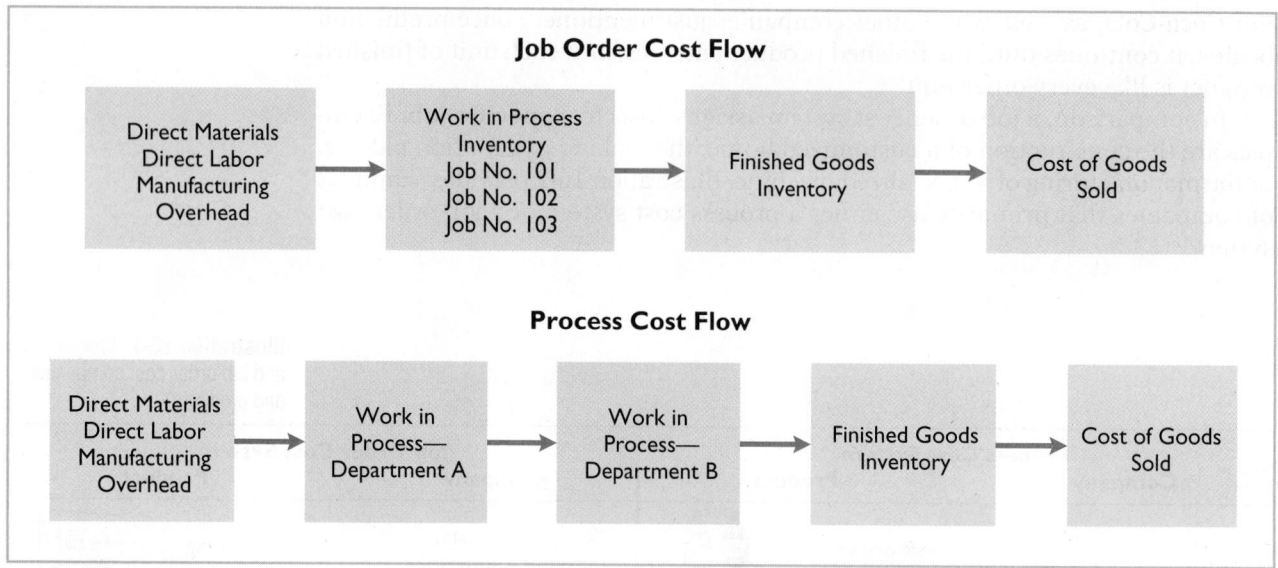

Illustration 16-3 Job order cost and process cost flow

The following analysis highlights the basic similarities and differences between these two systems.

Similarities

Job order cost and process cost systems are similar in three ways:

1. **The manufacturing cost elements.** Both costing systems track three manufacturing cost elements—direct materials, direct labor, and manufacturing overhead.

2. **The accumulation of the costs of materials, labor, and overhead.** Both costing systems debit raw materials to Raw Materials Inventory, factory labor to Factory Labor, and manufacturing overhead costs to Manufacturing Overhead.

3. **The flow of costs.** As noted above, both systems accumulate all manufacturing costs by debits to Raw Materials Inventory, Factory Labor, and Manufacturing Overhead. Both systems then assign these costs to the same accounts—Work in Process, Finished Goods Inventory, and Cost of Goods Sold. **The methods of assigning costs, however, differ significantly.** These differences are explained and illustrated later in the chapter.

Differences

The differences between a job order cost and a process cost system are as follows.

1. **The number of work in process accounts used.** A job order cost system uses only one work in process account. A process cost system uses multiple work in process accounts.

2. **Documents used to track costs.** A job order cost system charges costs to individual jobs and summarizes them in a job cost sheet. A process cost system summarizes costs in a production cost report for each department.

3. **The point at which costs are totaled.** A job order cost system totals costs when the job is completed. A process cost system totals costs at the end of a period of time.

4. **Unit cost computations.** In a job order cost system, the unit cost is the total cost per job divided by the units produced. In a process cost system, the unit cost is total manufacturing costs for the period divided by the units produced during the period.

Illustration 16-4 summarizes the major differences between a job order cost and a process cost system.

Feature	Job Order Cost System	Process Cost System
Work in process accounts	One work in process account	Multiple work in process accounts
Documents used	Job cost sheets	Production cost reports
Determination of total manufacturing costs	Each job	Each period
Unit-cost computations	Cost of each job ÷ Units produced for the job	Total manufacturing costs ÷ Equivalent units produced during the period

Illustration 16-4 Job order versus process cost systems

Do It!

Indicate whether each of the following statements is true or false.

1. A law firm is likely to use process costing for major lawsuits.
2. A manufacturer of paintballs is likely to use process costing.
3. Both job order and process costing determine product costs at the end of a period of time, rather than when a product is completed.
4. Process costing does not keep track of manufacturing overhead.

Solution

1. False.   2. True.   3. False.   4. False.

Related exercise material: **E16-1** and **Do It!** 16-1.

COMPARE JOB ORDER AND PROCESS COST SYSTEMS

Action Plan

- Use job order costing in situations where unit costs are high, unit volume is low, and products are unique.
- Use process costing when there is a large volume of relatively homogeneous products.

✔ The Navigator

PROCESS COST FLOW

Illustration 16-5 shows the flow of costs in the process cost system for Tyler Company. Tyler Company manufactures roller blade and skateboard wheels that it sells to manufacturers and retail outlets. Manufacturing consists of two processes: machining and assembly. The Machining Department shapes, hones, and drills the raw materials. The Assembly Department assembles and packages the parts.

LEARNING OBJECTIVE 3

Explain the flow of costs in a process cost system.

Illustration 16-5 Flow of costs in process cost system

As the flow of costs indicates, the company can add materials, labor, and manufacturing overhead in both the Machining and Assembly departments. When it finishes its work, the Machining Department transfers the partially completed units to the Assembly Department. The Assembly Department finishes the goods and then transfers them to the finished goods inventory. Upon sale, Tyler removes the goods from the finished goods inventory. Within each department, a similar set of activities is performed on each unit processed.

ASSIGNING MANUFACTURING COSTS— JOURNAL ENTRIES

LEARNING OBJECTIVE **4**

Make the journal entries to assign manufacturing costs in a process cost system.

As indicated, the accumulation of the costs of materials, labor, and manufacturing overhead is the same in a process cost system as in a job order cost system. That is, both systems follow these procedures:

- Companies debit all raw materials to Raw Materials Inventory at the time of purchase.
- They debit all factory labor to Factory Labor as the labor costs are incurred.
- They debit overhead costs to Manufacturing Overhead as these costs are incurred.

However, the assignment of the three manufacturing cost elements to Work in Process in a process cost system is different from a job order cost system. Here we'll look at how companies assign these manufacturing cost elements in a process cost system.

Materials Costs

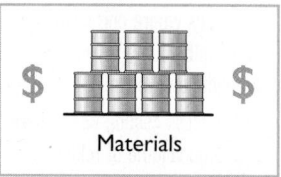

Materials

All raw materials issued for production are a materials cost to the producing department. A process cost system may use materials requisition slips, but **it generally requires fewer requisitions than in a job order cost system, because the materials are used for processes rather than for specific jobs** and therefore typically are for larger quantities.

At the beginning of the first process, a company usually adds most of the materials needed for production. However, other materials may be added at various points. For example, in the manufacture of Hershey candy bars, the chocolate and other ingredients are added at the beginning of the first process, and the wrappers and cartons are added at the end of the packaging process. Tyler Company adds materials at the beginning of each process. Tyler makes the following entry to record the materials used.

Work in Process—Machining	XXXX	
Work in Process—Assembly	XXXX	
Raw Materials Inventory		XXXX
(To record materials used)		

Ice cream maker Ben & Jerry's adds materials in three departments: milk and flavoring in the mixing department, extras such as cherries and dark chocolate in the prepping department, and cardboard containers in the pinting (packaging) department.

Factory Labor Costs

Factory Labor

In a process cost system, as in a job order cost system, companies may use time tickets to determine the cost of labor assignable to production departments. Since they assign labor costs to a process rather than a job, they can obtain, from the payroll register or departmental payroll summaries, the labor cost chargeable to a process.

Labor costs for the Machining Department will include the wages of employees who shape, hone, and drill the raw materials. The entry to assign these costs for Tyler Company is:

Work in Process—Machining	XXXX	
Work in Process—Assembly	XXXX	
Factory Labor		XXXX
(To assign factory labor to production)		

Manufacturing Overhead Costs

The objective in assigning overhead in a process cost system is to allocate the overhead costs to the production departments on an objective and equitable basis. That basis is the activity that "drives" or causes the costs. A primary driver of overhead costs in continuous manufacturing operations is **machine time used**, not direct labor. Thus, companies **widely use machine hours** in allocating manufacturing overhead costs using predetermined overhead rates. Tyler's entry to allocate overhead to the two processes is:

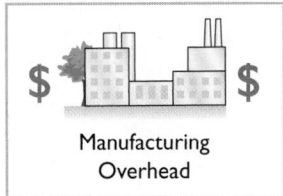

Manufacturing Overhead

Work in Process—Machining	XXXX	
Work in Process—Assembly	XXXX	
Manufacturing Overhead		XXXX
(To assign overhead to production)		

Management Insight

Choosing a Cost Driver

In one of its automated cost centers, Caterpillar feeds work into the cost center, where robotic machines process it and transfer the finished job to the next cost center without human intervention. One person tends all of the machines and spends more time maintaining machines than operating them. In such cases, overhead rates based on direct labor hours may be misleading. Surprisingly, some companies continue to assign manufacturing overhead on the basis of direct labor despite the fact that there is no cause-and-effect relationship between labor and overhead.

iStockphoto

? What is the result if a company uses the wrong "cost driver" to assign manufacturing overhead? (See page 893.)

Transfer to Next Department

At the end of the month, Tyler needs an entry to record the cost of the goods transferred out of the Machining Department. In this case, the transfer is to the Assembly Department, and Tyler makes the following entry.

Work in Process—Assembly	XXXXX	
Work in Process—Machining		XXXXX
(To record transfer of units to the Assembly		
Department)		

Transfer to Finished Goods

When the Assembly Department completes the units, it transfers them to the finished goods warehouse. The entry for this transfer is as follows.

Finished Goods Inventory	XXXXX	
Work in Process—Assembly		XXXXX
(To record transfer of units to finished goods)		

Transfer to Cost of Goods Sold

When Tyler sells the finished goods, it records the cost of goods sold as follows.

Cost of Goods Sold	XXXXX	
Finished Goods Inventory		XXXXX
(To record cost of units sold)		

MANUFACTURING COSTS IN PROCESS COSTING

Do it!

Ruth Company manufactures ZEBO through two processes: blending and bottling. In June, raw materials used were Blending $18,000 and Bottling $4,000. Factory labor costs were Blending $12,000 and Bottling $5,000. Manufacturing overhead costs were Blending $6,000 and Bottling $2,500. The company transfers units completed at a cost of $19,000 in the Blending Department to the Bottling Department. The Bottling Department transfers units completed at a cost of $11,000 to Finished Goods. Journalize the assignment of these costs to the two processes and the transfer of units as appropriate.

Action Plan

- In process cost accounting, keep separate work in process accounts for each process.
- When the costs are assigned to production, debit the separate work in process accounts.
- Transfer cost of completed units to the next process or to Finished Goods.

Solution

The entries are:

Work in Process—Blending	18,000	
Work in Process—Bottling	4,000	
Raw Materials Inventory		22,000
(To record materials used)		
Work in Process—Blending	12,000	
Work in Process—Bottling	5,000	
Factory Labor		17,000
(To assign factory labor to production)		
Work in Process—Blending	6,000	
Work in Process—Bottling	2,500	
Manufacturing Overhead		8,500
(To assign overhead to production)		
Work in Process—Bottling	19,000	
Work in Process—Blending		19,000
(To record transfer of units to the Bottling Department)		
Finished Goods Inventory	11,000	
Work in Process—Bottling		11,000
(To record transfer of units to finished goods)		

Related exercise material: **BE16-1, BE16-2, BE16-3, E16-2, E16-4,** and **Do it!** **16-2.**

The Navigator

Equivalent Units

Suppose you have a work-study job in the office of your college's president, and she asks you to compute the cost of instruction per full-time equivalent student at your college. The college's vice president for finance provides the following information.

LEARNING OBJECTIVE **5**
Compute equivalent units.

Costs:	
Total cost of instruction	$9,000,000
Student population:	
Full-time students	900
Part-time students	1,000

Illustration 16-6 Information for full-time student example

Part-time students take 60% of the classes of a full-time student during the year. To compute the number of full-time equivalent students per year, you would make the following computation.

Full-Time Students	+	**Equivalent Units of Part-Time Students**	=	**Full-Time Equivalent Students**
900	+	(60% × 1,000)	=	1,500

Illustration 16-7 Full-time equivalent unit computation

The cost of instruction per full-time equivalent student is therefore the total cost of instruction ($9,000,000) divided by the number of full-time equivalent students (1,500), which is $6,000 ($9,000,000 ÷ 1,500).

A process cost system uses the same idea, called equivalent units of production. Equivalent units of production measure the work done during the period, expressed in fully completed units. Companies use this measure to determine the cost per unit of completed product.

WEIGHTED-AVERAGE METHOD

The formula to compute equivalent units of production is as follows.

Units Completed and Transferred Out	+	**Equivalent Units of Ending Work in Process**	=	**Equivalent Units of Production**

Illustration 16-8 Equivalent units of production formula

To better understand this concept of equivalent units, consider the following two separate examples.

Example 1. In a specific period, the entire output of Sullivan Company's Blending Department consists of ending work in process of 4,000 units which are 60% complete as to materials, labor, and overhead. The equivalent units of production for the Blending Department are therefore 2,400 units (4,000 × 60%).

Example 2. The output of Kori Company's Packaging Department during the period consists of 10,000 units completed and transferred out, and 5,000 units in ending work in process which are 70% completed. The equivalent units of production are therefore 13,500 [10,000 + (5,000 × 70%)].

This method of computing equivalent units is referred to as the **weighted-average method**. It considers the degree of completion (weighting) of the units completed and transferred out and the ending work in process.

REFINEMENTS ON THE WEIGHTED-AVERAGE METHOD

Kellogg Company has produced Eggo® Waffles since 1970. Three departments produce these waffles: Mixing, Baking, and Freezing/Packaging. The Mixing Department combines dry ingredients, including flour, salt, and baking powder, with liquid ingredients, including eggs and vegetable oil, to make waffle batter. Illustration 16-9 provides information related to the Mixing Department at the end of June.

Illustration 16-9 Information for Mixing Department

MIXING DEPARTMENT

| | | Percentage Complete | |
	Physical Units	Materials	Conversion Costs
Work in process, June 1	100,000	100%	70%
Started into production	800,000		
Total units	900,000		
Units transferred out	700,000		
Work in process, June 30	200,000	100%	60%
Total units	900,000		

Helpful Hint When are separate unit cost computations needed for materials and conversion costs? Answer: Whenever the two types of costs do not occur in the process at the same time.

Ethics Note An unethical manager might use incorrect completion percentages when determining equivalent units. This results in either raising or lowering costs. Since completion percentages are somewhat subjective, this form of income manipulation can be difficult to detect.

Illustration 16-9 indicates that the beginning work in process is 100% complete as to materials cost and 70% complete as to conversion costs. **Conversion costs are the sum of labor costs and overhead costs.** In other words, Kellogg adds both the dry and liquid ingredients (materials) at the beginning of the waffle-making process, and the conversion costs (labor and overhead) related to the mixing of these ingredients are incurred uniformly and are 70% complete. The ending work in process is 100% complete as to materials cost and 60% complete as to conversion costs.

We then use the Mixing Department information to determine equivalent units. **In computing equivalent units, the beginning work in process is not part of the equivalent-units-of-production formula.** The units transferred out to the Baking Department are fully complete as to both materials and conversion costs. The ending work in process is fully complete as to materials, but only 60% complete as to conversion costs. We therefore need to make **two equivalent unit computations**: one for materials, and the other for conversion costs. Illustration 16-10 shows these computations.

Illustration 16-10
Computation of equivalent
units—Mixing Department

MIXING DEPARTMENT

	Equivalent Units	
	Materials	**Conversion Costs**
Units transferred out	700,000	700,000
Work in process, June 30		
200,000 × 100%	200,000	
200,000 × 60%		120,000
Total equivalent units	900,000	820,000

We can refine the earlier formula used to compute equivalent units of production (Illustration 16-8, page 853) to show the computations for materials and for conversion costs, as follows.

Illustration 16-11 Refined
equivalent units of production
formula

Units Completed and Transferred Out– Materials	+	Equivalent Units of Ending Work in Process–Materials	=	Equivalent Units of Production– Materials
Units Completed and Transferred Out– Conversion Costs	**+**	**Equivalent Units of Ending Work in Process–Conversion Costs**	**=**	**Equivalent Units of Production– Conversion Costs**

People, Planet, and Profit Insight
Haven't I Seen That Before?

For a variety of reasons, many companies, including Caterpillar, General Electric, and Eastman Kodak, are making a big push to remanufacture goods that have been thrown away. Items getting a second chance include cell phones, computers, home appliances, car parts, vacuum cleaners, and medical equipment. Businesses have figured out that profit margins on remanufactured goods are significantly higher than on new goods. As commodity prices such as copper and steel increase, reusing parts makes more sense. Also, as more local governments initiate laws requiring that electronics and appliances be recycled rather than thrown away, the cost of remanufacturing declines because the gathering of used goods becomes far more efficient. Besides benefitting the manufacturer, remanufacturing provides goods at a much lower price to consumers, reduces waste going to landfills, saves energy, reuses scarce resources, and reduces emissions. For example, it was estimated that a remanufactured car starter results in about 50% less carbon dioxide emissions than making a new one.

Source: James R. Hagerty and Paul Glader, "From Trash Heap to Store Shelf," *Wall Street Journal Online* (January 24, 2011).

Michael Ventura/Alamy

? In what ways might the relative composition (materials, labor, and overhead) of a remanufactured product's cost differ from that of a newly made product? (See page 893.)

EQUIVALENT UNITS

Do It!

The fabricating department has the following production and cost data for the current month.

Beginning Work in Process	Units Transferred Out	Ending Work in Process
–0–	15,000	10,000

Action Plan

- To measure the work done during the period, expressed in fully completed units, compute equivalent units of production.

- Use the appropriate formula: Units completed and transferred out + Equivalent units of ending work in process = Equivalent units of production.

✔ The Navigator

Materials are entered at the beginning of the process. The ending work in process units are 30% complete as to conversion costs. Compute the equivalent units of production for (a) materials and (b) conversion costs.

Solution

(a) Since materials are entered at the beginning of the process, the equivalent units of ending work in process are 10,000. Thus, 15,000 units + 10,000 units = 25,000 equivalent units of production for materials.

(b) Since ending work in process is only 30% complete as to conversion costs, the equivalent units of ending work in process are 3,000 (30% × 10,000 units). Thus, 15,000 units + 3,000 units = 18,000 equivalent units of production for conversion costs.

Related exercise material: **BE16-5, BE16-10, E16-5, E16-6, E16-8, E16-9, E16-10, E16-11, E16-13, E16-14, E16-15, and Do it! 16-3.**

Production Cost Report

LEARNING OBJECTIVE 6

Explain the four steps necessary to prepare a production cost report.

As mentioned earlier, companies prepare a production cost report for each department. A **production cost report** is the key document that management uses to understand the activities in a department; it shows the production quantity and cost data related to that department. For example, in producing Eggo® Waffles, Kellogg Company uses three production cost reports: Mixing, Baking, and Freezing/Packaging. Illustration 16-12 shows the flow of costs to make an Eggo® Waffle and the related production cost reports for each department.

Illustration 16-12 Flow of costs in making Eggo® Waffles

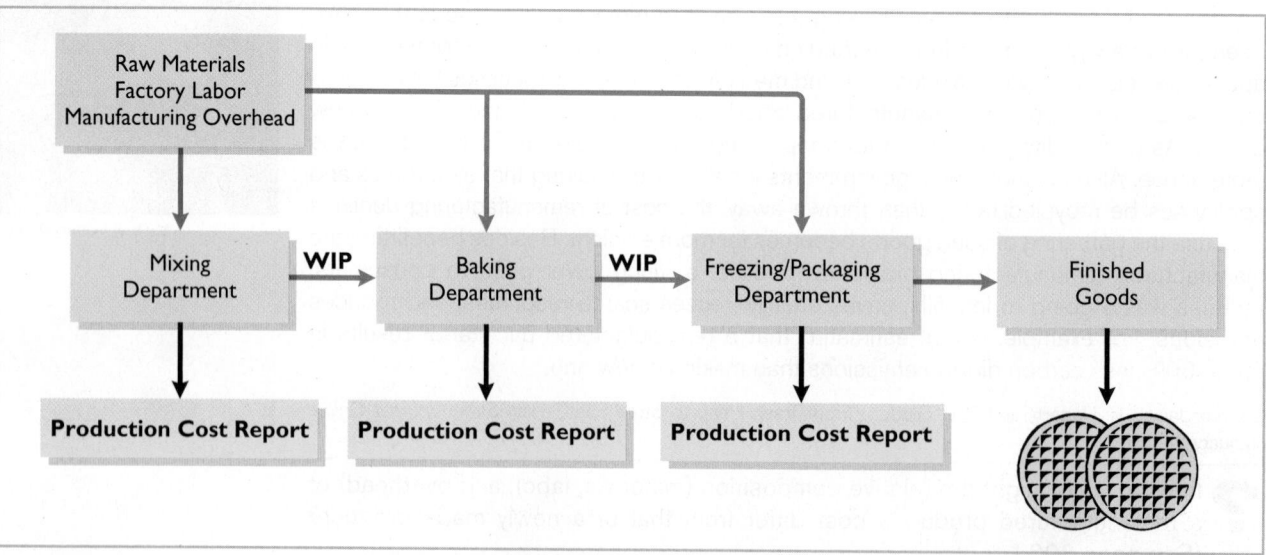

In order to complete a production cost report, the company must perform four steps, which, as a whole, make up the process cost system.

1. Compute the physical unit flow.
2. Compute the equivalent units of production.
3. Compute unit production costs.
4. Prepare a cost reconciliation schedule.

Illustration 16-13 shows assumed data for the Mixing Department at Kellogg Company for the month of June. We will use this information to complete a production cost report for the Mixing Department.

Illustration 16-13 Unit and cost data—Mixing Department

MIXING DEPARTMENT	
Units	
Work in process, June 1	100,000
Direct materials: 100% complete	
Conversion costs: 70% complete	
Units started into production during June	800,000
Units completed and transferred out to Baking Department	700,000
Work in process, June 30	200,000
Direct materials: 100% complete	
Conversion costs: 60% complete	
Costs	
Work in process, June 1	
Direct materials: 100% complete	$ 50,000
Conversion costs: 70% complete	35,000
Cost of work in process, June 1	$ 85,000
Costs incurred during production in June	
Direct materials	$400,000
Conversion costs	170,000
Costs incurred in June	$570,000

COMPUTE THE PHYSICAL UNIT FLOW (STEP 1)

Physical units are the actual units to be accounted for during a period, irrespective of any work performed. To keep track of these units, add the units started (or transferred) into production during the period to the units in process at the beginning of the period. This amount is referred to as the total units to be accounted for.

The total units then are accounted for by the output of the period. The output consists of units transferred out during the period and any units in process at the end of the period. This amount is referred to as the total units accounted for. Illustration 16-14 (page 858) shows the flow of physical units for Kellogg's Mixing Department for the month of June.

Illustration 16-14
Physical unit flow—Mixing
Department

MIXING DEPARTMENT	
	Physical Units
Units to be accounted for	
Work in process, June 1	100,000
Started (transferred) into production	800,000
Total units	**900,000**
Units accounted for	
Completed and transferred out	700,000
Work in process, June 30	200,000
Total units	**900,000**

The records indicate that the Mixing Department must account for 900,000 units. Of this sum, 700,000 units were transferred to the Baking Department and 200,000 units were still in process.

COMPUTE THE EQUIVALENT UNITS OF PRODUCTION (STEP 2)

Helpful Hint Materials are not always added at the beginning of the process. For example, materials are sometimes added uniformly during the process.

Once the physical flow of the units is established, Kellogg must measure the Mixing Department's productivity in terms of equivalent units of production. The Mixing Department adds materials at the beginning of the process, and it incurs conversion costs uniformly during the process. Thus, we need two computations of equivalent units: one for materials and one for conversion costs. The equivalent unit computation is as follows.

Illustration 16-15
Computation of equivalent units—Mixing Department

Helpful Hint Remember that we ignore the beginning work in process in this computation.

	Equivalent Units	
	Materials	**Conversion Costs**
Units transferred out	700,000	700,000
Work in process, June 30		
200,000 × 100%	200,000	
200,000 × 60%		120,000
Total equivalent units	900,000	820,000

COMPUTE UNIT PRODUCTION COSTS (STEP 3)

Armed with the knowledge of the equivalent units of production, we can now compute the unit production costs. **Unit production costs** are costs expressed in terms of equivalent units of production. When equivalent units of production are different for materials and conversion costs, we compute three unit costs: (1) materials, (2) conversion, and (3) total manufacturing.

The computation of total materials cost related to Eggo® Waffles is as follows.

Illustration 16-16 Total
materials cost computation

Work in process, June 1	
Direct materials cost	$ 50,000
Costs added to production during June	
Direct materials cost	400,000
Total materials cost	$450,000

The computation of unit materials cost is as follows.

Total Materials Cost	÷	Equivalent Units of Materials	=	Unit Materials Cost
$450,000	÷	900,000	=	$0.50

Illustration 16-17 Unit materials cost computation

Illustration 16-18 shows the computation of total conversion costs.

Work in process, June 1	
Conversion costs	$ 35,000
Costs added to production during June	
Conversion costs	170,000
Total conversion costs	$205,000

Illustration 16-18 Total conversion costs computation

The computation of unit conversion cost is as follows.

Total Conversion Costs	÷	Equivalent Units of Conversion Costs	=	Unit Conversion Cost
$205,000	÷	820,000	=	$0.25

Illustration 16-19 Unit conversion cost computation

Total manufacturing cost per unit is therefore computed as shown in Illustration 16-20.

Unit Materials Cost	+	Unit Conversion Cost	=	Total Manufacturing Cost per Unit
$0.50	+	$0.25	=	$0.75

Illustration 16-20 Total manufacturing cost per unit

PREPARE A COST RECONCILIATION SCHEDULE (STEP 4)

We are now ready to determine the cost of goods transferred out of the Mixing Department to the Baking Department and the costs in ending work in process. Kellogg charged total costs of $655,000 to the Mixing Department in June, calculated as follows.

Costs to be accounted for	
Work in process, June 1	$ 85,000
Started into production	570,000
Total costs	$655,000

Illustration 16-21 Costs charged to Mixing Department

The company then prepares a cost reconciliation schedule to assign these costs to (a) units transferred out to the Baking Department and (b) ending work in process.

Illustration 16-22 Cost reconciliation schedule—Mixing Department

MIXING DEPARTMENT
Cost Reconciliation Schedule

Costs accounted for		
Transferred out (700,000 × $0.75)		$ 525,000
Work in process, June 30		
Materials (200,000 × $0.50)	$100,000	
Conversion costs (120,000 × $0.25)	30,000	130,000
Total costs		$655,000

Kellogg uses the total manufacturing cost per unit, $0.75, in costing the **units completed** and transferred to the Baking Department. In contrast, the unit cost of materials and the unit cost of conversion are needed in costing **units in process**. The cost reconciliation schedule shows that the total costs accounted for (Illustration 16-22) equal the total costs to be accounted for (Illustration 16-21, page 859).

PREPARING THE PRODUCTION COST REPORT

LEARNING OBJECTIVE 7
Prepare a production cost report.

At this point, Kellogg is ready to prepare the production cost report for the Mixing Department. As indicated earlier, this report is an internal document for management that shows production quantity and cost data for a production department.

There are four steps in preparing a production cost report:

1. Compute the physical unit flow.
2. Compute the equivalent units of production.
3. Compute unit production costs.
4. Prepare a cost reconciliation schedule.

Illustration 16-23 shows the production cost report for the Mixing Department. The report identifies the four steps.

Production cost reports provide a basis for evaluating the productivity of a department. In addition, managers can use the cost data to assess whether unit costs and total costs are reasonable. By comparing the quantity and cost data with predetermined goals, top management can also judge whether current performance is meeting planned objectives.

🧰 DECISION TOOLKIT

DECISION CHECKPOINTS	INFO NEEDED FOR DECISION	TOOL TO USE FOR DECISION	HOW TO EVALUATE RESULTS
What is the cost of a product?	Cost of materials, labor, and overhead assigned to processes used to make the product	Production cost report	Compare costs to previous periods, to competitors, and to expected selling price to evaluate overall profitability.

Illustration 16-23 Production cost report

	Mixing Department.xls				
	Home Insert Page Layout Formulas Data Review View				
	P18 fx				
	A	B	C	D	E
1	**Mixing Department**				
2	**Production Cost Report**				
3	**For the Month Ended June 30, 2014**				
4	**Equivalent Units**				
5		Physical Units	Materials	Conversion Costs	
6	**QUANTITIES**	Step 1	Step 2		
7	Units to be accounted for				
8	Work in process, June 1	100,000			
9	Started into production	800,000			
10	Total units	900,000			
11	Units accounted for				
12	Transferred out	700,000	700,000	700,000	
13	Work in process, June 30	200,000	200,000	120,000	(200,000 × 60%)
14	Total units	900,000	900,000	820,000	
15	**COSTS**				
16	Unit costs Step 3		Materials	Conversion Costs	Total
17	Total cost	(a)	$450,000	$205,000	$655,000
18	Equivalent units	(b)	900,000	820,000	
19	Unit costs [(a) ÷ (b)]		$0.50	$0.25	$0.75
20	Costs to be accounted for				
21	Work in process, June 1				$85,000
22	Started into production				570,000
23	Total costs				$655,000
24	**Cost Reconciliation Schedule** Step 4				
25	Costs accounted for				
26	Transferred out (700,000 × $0.75)				$525,000
27	Work in process, June 30				
28	Materials (200,000 × $0.50)			$100,000	
29	Conversion costs (120,000 × $0.25)			30,000	130,000
30	Total costs				$655,000
31					

Do It!

> In March, Rodayo Manufacturing had the following unit production costs: materials $6 and conversion costs $9. On March 1, it had zero work in process. During March, Rodayo transferred out 12,000 units. As of March 31, 800 units that were 25% complete as to conversion costs and 100% complete as to materials were in ending work in process. Assign the costs to the units transferred out and in process.

COST RECONCILIATION SCHEDULE

Action Plan

- Assign the total manufacturing cost of $15 per unit to the 12,000 units transferred out.
- Assign the materials cost and conversion costs based on equivalent units of production to units in ending work in process.

The Navigator

Solution

The assignment of costs is as follows.

Costs accounted for		
Transferred out (12,000 × $15)		$180,000
Work in process, March 31		
Materials (800 × $6)	$4,800	
Conversion costs (200[a] × $9)	1,800	6,600
Total costs		$186,600

[a]800 × 25%

Related exercise material: **BE16-4, BE16-6, BE16-7, BE16-8, BE16-9, BE16-10, E16-5, E16-6, E16-8, E16-9, E16-10, E16-11, E16-14, E16-15, and Do it! 16-4.**

COSTING SYSTEMS—FINAL COMMENTS

Companies often use a combination of a process cost and a job order cost system. Called operations costing, this hybrid system is similar to process costing in its assumption that standardized methods are used to manufacture the product. At the same time, the product may have some customized, individual features that require the use of a job order cost system.

Consider, for example, the automobile manufacturer Ford Motor Company. Each vehicle at a given plant goes through the same assembly line, but Ford uses different materials (such as seat coverings, paint, and tinted glass) for different vehicles. Similarly, Kellogg's Pop-Tarts® toaster pastries go through numerous standardized processes—mixing, filling, baking, frosting, and packaging. The pastry dough, though, comes in different flavors—plain, chocolate, and graham—and fillings include Smucker's® real fruit, chocolate fudge, vanilla creme, brown sugar cinnamon, and s'mores.

A cost-benefit trade-off occurs as a company decides which costing system to use. A job order cost system, for example, provides detailed information related to the cost of the product. Because each job has its own distinguishing characteristics, the system can provide an accurate cost per job. This information is useful in controlling costs and pricing products. However, the cost of implementing a job order cost system is often expensive because of the accounting costs involved.

On the other hand, for a company like Intel, which makes computer chips, is there a benefit in knowing whether the cost of the one-hundredth chip produced is different from the one-thousandth chip produced? Probably not. An average cost of the product will suffice for control and pricing purposes.

In summary, when deciding to use one of these systems, or a combination system, a company must weigh the costs of implementing the system against the benefits from the additional information provided.

 DECISION TOOLKIT

DECISION CHECKPOINTS	INFO NEEDED FOR DECISION	TOOL TO USE FOR DECISION	HOW TO EVALUATE RESULTS
What costing method should be used?	Type of product or service produced	Cost of accounting system; benefits of additional information	The benefits of providing the additional information should exceed the costs of the accounting system needed to develop the information.

USING THE **DECISION TOOLKIT**

Essence Company manufactures a high-end after-shave lotion, called Eternity, in 10-ounce plastic bottles. Because the market for after-shave lotion is highly competitive, the company is very concerned about keeping its costs under control. Eternity is manufactured through three processes: mixing, filling, and corking. Materials are added at the beginning of the process, and labor and overhead are incurred uniformly throughout each process. The company uses a weighted-average method to cost its product. A partially completed production cost report for the month of May for the Mixing Department is shown below.

ESSENCE COMPANY
Mixing Department
Production Cost Report
For the Month Ended May 31, 2014

| | | Equivalent Units | |
| | Physical | | Conversion |
Quantities	Units	Materials	Costs
Units to be accounted for	Step 1	Step 2	
Work in process, May 1	1,000		
Started into production	2,000		
Total units	3,000		
Units accounted for			
Transferred out	2,200	?	?
Work in process, May 31	800	?	?
Total units	3,000	?	?

| | | | Conversion | |
Costs		Materials	Costs	Total
Unit costs Step 3				
Total cost	(a)	?	?	?
Equivalent units	(b)	?	?	
Unit costs [(a) ÷ (b)]		?	?	?
Costs to be accounted for				
Work in process, May 1				$ 56,300
Started into production				119,320
Total costs				$175,620

Cost Reconciliation Schedule Step 4

Costs accounted for			
Transferred out			?
Work in process, May 31			
Materials		?	
Conversion costs		?	?
Total costs			?

Additional information:
Work in process, May 1, 1000 units

Materials cost, 1,000 units (100% complete)	$49,100	
Conversion costs, 1,000 units (70% complete)	7,200	$ 56,300
Materials cost for May, 2,000 units		$100,000

Work in process, May 31, 800 units, 100% complete as to materials and 50% complete as to conversion costs.

Instructions

(a) Prepare a production cost report for the Mixing Department for the month of May.
(b) Prepare the journal entry to record the transfer of goods from the Mixing Department to the Filling Department.
(c) Explain why Essence Company is using a process cost system to account for its costs.

Solution

(a) A completed production cost report for the Mixing Department is shown below. Computations to support the amounts reported follow the report.

ESSENCE COMPANY
Mixing Department
Production Cost Report
For the Month Ended May 31, 2014

Action Plan

- Compute the physical unit flow–that is, the total units to be accounted for.
- Compute the equivalent units of production.
- Compute the unit production costs, expressed in terms of equivalent units of production.
- Prepare a cost reconciliation schedule, which shows that the total costs accounted for equal the total costs to be accounted for.

Quantities	Physical Units	Equivalent Units Materials	Conversion Costs
Units to be accounted for	Step 1		Step 2
Work in process, May 1	1,000		
Started into production	2,000		
Total units	3,000		
Units accounted for			
Transferred out	2,200	2,200	2,200
Work in process, May 31	800	800	400 (800 × 50%)
Total units	3,000	3,000	2,600

Costs		Materials	Conversion Costs	Total
Unit costs Step 3				
Total cost*	(a)	$149,100	$26,520	$175,620
Equivalent units	(b)	3,000	2,600	
Unit costs [(a) ÷ (b)]		$49.70	$10.20	$59.90
Costs to be accounted for				
Work in process, May 1				$ 56,300
Started into production				119,320
Total costs				$175,620

*Additional computations to support production cost report data:
Materials cost—$49,100 + $100,000
Conversion costs—$7,200 + $19,320 ($119,320 − $100,000)

Cost Reconciliation Schedule Step 4

Costs accounted for			
Transferred out (2,200 × $59.90)			$131,780
Work in process, May 31			
Materials (800 × $49.70)		$39,760	
Conversion costs (400 × $10.20)		4,080	43,840
Total costs			$175,620

(b)

Work in Process—Filling	131,780	
Work in Process—Mixing		131,780

(c) Companies use process cost systems to apply costs to similar products that are mass-produced in a continuous fashion. Essence Company uses a process cost system because production of the after-shave lotion, once it begins, continues until the after-shave lotion emerges. The processing is the same for the entire run—with precisely the same amount of materials, labor, and overhead. Each bottle of Eternity after-shave lotion is indistinguishable from another.

✔ The Navigator

Summary of Learning Objectives

1 **Understand who uses process cost systems.** Companies that mass-produce similar products in a continuous fashion use process cost systems. Once production begins, it continues until the finished product emerges. Each unit of finished product is indistinguishable from every other unit.

2 **Explain the similarities and differences between job order cost and process cost systems.** Job order cost systems are similar to process cost systems in three ways: (1) Both systems track the same cost elements—direct materials, direct labor, and manufacturing overhead. (2) Both accumulate costs in the same accounts—Raw Materials Inventory, Factory Labor, and Manufacturing Overhead. (3) Both assign accumulated costs to the same accounts—Work in Process, Finished Goods Inventory, and Cost of Goods Sold. However, the method of assigning costs differs significantly.

There are four main differences between the two cost systems: (1) A process cost system uses separate accounts for each department or manufacturing process, rather than only one work in process account used in a job order cost system. (2) A process cost system summarizes costs in a production cost report for each department. A job order cost system charges costs to individual jobs and summarizes them in a job cost sheet. (3) Costs are totaled at the end of a time period in a process cost system, but at the completion of a job in a job order cost system. (4) A process cost system calculates unit cost as: Total manufacturing costs for the period ÷ Units produced during the period. A job order cost system calculates unit cost as: Total cost per job ÷ Units produced.

3 **Explain the flow of costs in a process cost system.** A process cost system assigns manufacturing costs for raw materials, labor, and overhead to work in process accounts for various departments or manufacturing processes. It transfers the costs of partially completed units from one department to another as those units move through the manufacturing process. The system

transfers the costs of completed work to Finished Goods Inventory. Finally, when inventory is sold, the system transfers the costs to Cost of Goods Sold.

4 **Make the journal entries to assign manufacturing costs in a process cost system.** Entries to assign the costs of raw materials, labor, and overhead consist of a credit to Raw Materials Inventory, Factory Labor, and Manufacturing Overhead, and a debit to Work in Process for each department. Entries to record the cost of goods transferred to another department are a credit to Work in Process for the department whose work is finished and a debit to the department to which the goods are transferred. The entry to record units completed and transferred to the warehouse is a credit to Work in Process for the department whose work is finished and a debit to Finished Goods Inventory. The entry to record the sale of goods is a credit to Finished Goods Inventory and a debit to Cost of Goods Sold.

5 **Compute equivalent units.** Equivalent units of production measure work done during a period, expressed in fully completed units. Companies use this measure to determine the cost per unit of completed product. Equivalent units are the sum of units completed and transferred out plus equivalent units of ending work in process.

6 **Explain the four steps necessary to prepare a production cost report.** The four steps to complete a production cost report are: (1) Compute the physical unit flow—that is, the total units to be accounted for. (2) Compute the equivalent units of production. (3) Compute the unit production costs, expressed in terms of equivalent units of production. (4) Prepare a cost reconciliation schedule, which shows that the total costs accounted for equal the total costs to be accounted for.

7 **Prepare a production cost report.** The production cost report contains both quantity and cost data for a production department. There are four sections in the report: (1) number of physical units, (2) equivalent units determination, (3) unit costs, and (4) cost reconciliation schedule.

✔ The Navigator

DECISION TOOLKIT *A SUMMARY*

DECISION CHECKPOINTS	INFO NEEDED FOR DECISION	TOOL TO USE FOR DECISION	HOW TO EVALUATE RESULTS
What is the cost of a product?	Costs of materials, labor, and overhead assigned to processes used to make the product	Production cost report	Compare costs to previous periods, to competitors, and to expected selling price to evaluate overall profitability.
Which costing method should be used?	Type of product or service produced	Cost of accounting system; benefits of additional information	The benefits of providing the additional information should exceed the costs of the accounting system needed to develop the information.

FIFO Method

In this chapter, we demonstrated the weighted-average method of computing equivalent units. Some companies use a different method, referred to as the **first-in, first-out (FIFO) method**, to compute equivalent units. The purpose of this appendix is to illustrate how companies use the FIFO method to prepare a production cost report.

EQUIVALENT UNITS UNDER FIFO

Under the FIFO method, companies compute equivalent units on a first-in, first-out basis. Some companies favor the FIFO method because the FIFO cost assumption usually corresponds to the actual physical flow of the goods. Under the FIFO method, companies therefore assume that the beginning work in process is completed before new work is started.

Using the FIFO method, equivalent units are the sum of the work performed to:

1. Finish the units of beginning work in process inventory.
2. Complete the units started into production during the period (referred to as the **units started and completed**).
3. Start, but only partially complete, the units in ending work in process inventory.

Normally, in a process cost system, some units will always be in process at both the beginning and end of the period.

Illustration

Illustration 16A-1 shows the physical flow of units for the Assembly Department of Shutters Inc. In addition, it indicates the degree of completion of the work in process accounts in regard to conversion costs.

Illustration 16A-1
Physical unit flow—Assembly Department

ASSEMBLY DEPARTMENT	
	Physical Units
Units to be accounted for	
Work in process, June 1 (40% complete)	500
Started (transferred) into production	8,000
Total units	8,500
Units accounted for	
Completed and transferred out	8,100
Work in process, June 30 (75% complete)	400
Total units	8,500

In Illustration 16A-1, the units completed and transferred out (8,100) plus the units in ending work in process (400) equal the total units to be accounted for (8,500). Using FIFO, we then compute equivalent units as follows.

1. The 500 units of beginning work in process were 40% complete. Thus, 300 equivalent units (60% × 500 units) were required to complete the beginning inventory.
2. The units started and completed during the current month are the units transferred out minus the units in beginning work in process. For the Assembly Department, units started and completed are 7,600 (8,100 − 500).
3. The 400 units of ending work in process were 75% complete. Thus, equivalent units were 300 (75% × 400).

Equivalent units for the Assembly Department are 8,200, computed as follows.

Illustration 16A-2
Computation of equivalent units—FIFO method

ASSEMBLY DEPARTMENT

Production Data	Physical Units	Work Added This Period	Equivalent Units
Work in process, June 1	500	60%	300
Started and completed	7,600	100%	7,600
Work in process, June 30	400	75%	300
Total	8,500		8,200

COMPREHENSIVE EXAMPLE

To provide a complete illustration of the FIFO method, we will use the data for the Mixing Department at Kellogg Company for the month of June, as shown in Illustration 16A-3.

Illustration 16A-3 Unit and cost data—Mixing Department

MIXING DEPARTMENT

Units	
Work in process, June 1	100,000
Direct materials: 100% complete	
Conversion costs: 70% complete	
Units started into production during June	800,000
Units completed and transferred out to Baking Department	700,000
Work in process, June 30	200,000
Direct materials: 100% complete	
Conversion costs: 60% complete	
Costs	
Work in process, June 1	
Direct materials: 100% complete	$ 50,000
Conversion costs: 70% complete	35,000
Cost of work in process, June 1	$ 85,000
Costs incurred during production in June	
Direct materials	$400,000
Conversion costs	170,000
Costs incurred in June	$570,000

Compute the Physical Unit Flow (Step 1)

Illustration 16A-4 shows the physical flow of units for Kellogg for the month of June for the Mixing Department.

Illustration 16A-4
Physical unit flow—Mixing Department

MIXING DEPARTMENT

	Physical Units
Units to be accounted for	
Work in process, June 1	100,000
Started (transferred) into production	800,000
Total units	900,000
Units accounted for	
Completed and transferred out	700,000
Work in process, June 30	200,000
Total units	900,000

Under the FIFO method, companies often expand the physical units schedule, as shown in Illustration 16A-5 to explain the transferred-out section. As a result, this section reports the beginning work in process and the units started and completed. These two items further explain the completed and transferred-out section.

Illustration 16A-5
Physical unit flow (FIFO)—
Mixing Department

MIXING DEPARTMENT	
	Physical Units
Units to be accounted for	
Work in process, June 1	100,000
Started (transferred) into production	800,000
Total units	900,000
Units accounted for	
Completed and transferred out	
Work in process, June 1	100,000
Started and completed	600,000
	700,000
Work in process, June 30	200,000
Total units	900,000

The records indicate that the Mixing Department must account for 900,000 units. Of this sum, 700,000 units were transferred to the Baking Department and 200,000 units were still in process.

Compute Equivalent Units of Production (Step 2)

As with the method presented in the chapter, once they determine the physical flow of the units, companies need to determine equivalent units of production. The Mixing Department adds materials at the beginning of the process, and it incurs conversion costs uniformly during the process. Thus, Kellogg must make two computations of equivalent units: one for materials and one for conversion costs.

EQUIVALENT UNITS FOR MATERIALS. Since Kellogg adds materials at the beginning of the process, no additional materials costs are required to complete the beginning work in process. In addition, 100% of the materials costs has been incurred on the ending work in process. Thus, the computation of equivalent units for materials is as follows.

Helpful Hint Materials are not always added at the beginning of the process. For example, companies sometimes add materials uniformly during the process.

Illustration 16A-6
Computation of equivalent units—materials

MIXING DEPARTMENT—MATERIALS			
Production Data	**Physical Units**	**Materials Added This Period**	**Equivalent Units**
Work in process, June 1	100,000	–0–	–0–
Started and finished	600,000	100%	600,000
Work in process, June 30	200,000	100%	200,000
Total	900,000		800,000

EQUIVALENT UNITS FOR CONVERSION COSTS The 100,000 units of beginning work in process were 70% complete in terms of conversion costs. Thus, the Mixing Department required 30,000 equivalent units (30% × 100,000 units) of conversion costs to complete the beginning inventory. In addition, the 200,000 units of ending work in process were 60% complete in terms of conversion costs. Thus, the equivalent units for conversion costs is 750,000, computed as follows.

MIXING DEPARTMENT—CONVERSION COSTS			
Production Data	Physical Units	Work Added This Period	Equivalent Units
Work in process, June 1	100,000	30%	30,000
Started and finished	600,000	100%	600,000
Work in process, June 30	200,000	60%	120,000
Total	900,000		750,000

Illustration 16A-7
Computation of equivalent units—conversion costs

Compute Unit Production Costs (Step 3)

Armed with the knowledge of the equivalent units of production, Kellogg can now compute the unit production costs. Unit production costs are costs expressed in terms of equivalent units of production. When equivalent units of production are different for materials and conversion costs, companies compute three unit costs: (1) materials, (2) conversion, and (3) total manufacturing.

Under the FIFO method, the unit costs of production are based entirely on the production costs incurred during the month. Thus, the costs in the beginning work in process are not relevant, because they were incurred on work done in the preceding month. As Illustration 16A-3 (page 867) indicated, the costs incurred during production in June were:

Direct materials	$400,000
Conversion costs	170,000
Total costs	$570,000

Illustration 16A-8
Costs incurred during production in June

Illustration 16A-9 shows the computation of unit materials cost, unit conversion costs, and total unit cost related to Eggo® Waffles.

(1)	Total Materials Cost	÷	Equivalent Units of Materials	=	Unit Materials Cost
	$400,000	÷	800,000	=	$0.50
(2)	Total Conversion Costs	÷	Equivalent Units of Conversion Costs	=	Unit Conversion Cost
	$170,000	÷	750,000	=	$0.227 (rounded)*
(3)	Unit Materials Cost	+	Unit Conversion Cost	=	Total Manufacturing Cost per Unit
	$0.50	+	$0.227	=	$0.727

Illustration 16A-9
Unit cost formulas and computations—Mixing Department

For homework problems, round unit costs to three decimal places.

As shown, the unit costs are $0.50 for materials, $0.227 for conversion costs, and $0.727 for total manufacturing costs.

Prepare a Cost Reconciliation Schedule (Step 4)

Kellogg is now ready to determine the cost of goods transferred out of the Mixing Department to the Baking Department and the costs in ending work in process. The total costs charged to the Mixing Department in June are $655,000, calculated as follows.

Illustration 16A-10 Costs charged to Mixing Department

Costs to be accounted for	
Work in process, June 1	$ 85,000
Started into production	570,000
Total costs	$655,000

Kellogg next prepares a cost reconciliation to assign these costs to (1) units transferred out to the Baking Department and (2) ending work in process. Under the FIFO method, the first goods to be completed during the period are the units in beginning work in process. Thus, the cost of the beginning work in process is always assigned to the goods transferred to the next department (or finished goods, if processing is complete). Under the FIFO method, ending work in process also will be assigned only the production costs incurred in the current period. Illustration 16A-11 shows a cost reconciliation schedule for the Mixing Department.

Illustration 16A-11 Cost reconciliation report

MIXING DEPARTMENT
Cost Reconciliation Schedule

Costs accounted for		
Transferred out		
Work in process, June 1		$ 85,000
Costs to complete beginning work in process		
Conversion costs (30,000 × $0.227)		6,810
Total costs		91,810
Units started and completed (600,000 × $0.727)		435,950*
Total costs transferred out		527,760
Work in process, June 30		
Materials (200,000 × $0.50)	$100,000	
Conversion costs (120,000 × $0.227)	27,240	127,240
Total costs		$655,000

*Any rounding errors should be adjusted in the "Units started and completed" calculation.

As you can see, the total costs accounted for ($655,000 from Illustration 16A-11) equal the total costs to be accounted for ($655,000 from Illustration 16A-10).

Preparing the Production Cost Report

At this point, Kellogg is ready to prepare the production cost report for the Mixing Department. This report is an internal document for management that shows production quantity and cost data for a production department.

As discussed on page 860, there are four steps in preparing a production cost report:

1. Compute the physical unit flow.
2. Compute the equivalent units of production.
3. Compute unit production costs.
4. Prepare a cost reconciliation schedule.

Illustration 16A-12 shows the production cost report for the Mixing Department, with the four steps identified in the report.

As indicated in the chapter, production cost reports provide a basis for evaluating the productivity of a department. In addition, managers can use the cost data to assess whether unit costs and total costs are reasonable. By comparing the quantity and cost data with predetermined goals, top management can also judge whether current performance is meeting planned objectives.

	Mixing Department.xls				
	Home Insert Page Layout Formulas Data Review View				
	P18 ▾ ⨀ *fx*				
	A	B	C	D	E
1	**Mixing Department**				
2	**Production Cost Report**				
3	**For the Month Ended June 30, 2014**				
4		**Equivalent Units**			
5		Physical Units	Materials	Conversion Costs	
6	**QUANTITIES**	Step 1	Step 2		
7	Units to be accounted for				
8	Work in process (WIP), June 1	100,000			
9	Started into production	800,000			
10	Total units	900,000			
11	Units accounted for				
12	Completed and transferred out				
13	Work in process, June 1	100,000	0	30,000	
14	Started and completed	600,000	600,000	600,000	
15	Work in process, June 30	200,000	200,000	120,000	
16	Total units	900,000	800,000	750,000	
17	**COSTS**				
18	Unit costs Step 3		Materials	Conversion Costs	Total
19	Costs in June (excluding beginning WIP) (a)		$400,000	$170,000	$570,000
20	Equivalent units (b)		800,000	750,000	
21	Unit costs [(a) ÷ (b)]		$0.50	$0.227	$0.727
22	Costs to be accounted for				
23	Work in process, June 1				$85,000
24	Started into production				570,000
25	Total costs				$655,000
26	**Cost Reconciliation Schedule** Step 4				
27	Costs accounted for				
28	Transferred out				
29	Work in process, June 1				$85,000
30	Costs to complete beginning work in process				
31	Conversion costs (30,000 × $0.227)				6,810
32	Total costs				91,810
33	Units started and completed (600,000 × $0.727)*				435,950
34	Total costs transferred out				527,760
35	Work in process, June 30				
36	Materials (200,000 × $0.50)			$100,000	
37	Conversions costs (120,000 × $0.227)			27,240	127,240
38	Total costs				$655,000
39	*Any rounding errors should be adjusted in the "Units started and completed."				

Illustration 16A-12 Production cost report—FIFO method

FIFO AND WEIGHTED-AVERAGE

The weighted-average method of computing equivalent units has **one major advantage**: It is simple to understand and apply. In cases where prices do not fluctuate significantly from period to period, the weighted-average method will be very similar to the FIFO method. In addition, companies that have been using just-in-time procedures effectively for inventory control purposes will have minimal inventory balances, and therefore differences between the weighted-average and the FIFO methods will not be material.

Helpful Hint What are the two self-checks in the report? Answer: (1) Total physical units accounted for must equal the total units to be accounted for. (2) Total costs accounted for must equal the total costs to be accounted for.

Conceptually, the FIFO method is superior to the weighted-average method because it measures **current performance** using only costs incurred in the current period. Managers are, therefore, not held responsible for costs from prior periods over which they may not have had control. In addition, the FIFO method **provides current cost information**, which the company can use to establish **more accurate pricing strategies** for goods manufactured and sold in the current period.

Summary of Learning Objective for Appendix 16A

8 **Compute equivalent units using the FIFO method.** Equivalent units under the FIFO method are the sum of the work performed to: (1) Finish the units of beginning work in process inventory, if any; (2) complete the units started into production during the period; and (3) start, but only partially complete, the units in ending work in process inventory.

Glossary

Conversion costs (p. 854) The sum of labor costs and overhead costs.

Cost reconciliation schedule (p. 860) A schedule that shows that the total costs accounted for equal the total costs to be accounted for.

Equivalent units of production (p. 853) A measure of the work done during the period, expressed in fully completed units.

Operations costing (p. 862) A combination of a process cost and a job order cost system, in which products are manufactured primarily by standardized methods, with some customization.

Physical units (p. 857) Actual units to be accounted for during a period, irrespective of any work performed.

Process cost system (p. 846) An accounting system used to apply costs to similar products that are mass-produced in a continuous fashion.

Production cost report (p. 856) An internal report for management that shows both production quantity and cost data for a production department.

Total units (costs) accounted for (p. 857) The sum of the units (costs) transferred out during the period plus the units (costs) in process at the end of the period.

Total units (costs) to be accounted for (p. 857) The sum of the units (costs) started (or transferred) into production during the period plus the units (costs) in process at the beginning of the period.

Unit production costs (p. 858) Costs expressed in terms of equivalent units of production.

Weighted-average method (p. 854) Method of computing equivalent units of production which considers the degree of completion (weighting) of the units completed and transferred out and the ending work in process.

Comprehensive *Do it!*

Karlene Industries produces plastic ice cube trays in two processes: heating and stamping. All materials are added at the beginning of the Heating Department process. Karlene uses the weighted-average method to compute equivalent units.

On November 1, the Heating Department had in process 1,000 trays that were 70% complete. During November, it started into production 12,000 trays. On November 30, 2014, 2,000 trays that were 60% complete were in process.

The following cost information for the Heating Department was also available.

Work in process, November 1:		Costs incurred in November:	
Materials	$ 640	Material	$3,000
Conversion costs	360	Labor	2,300
Cost of work in process, Nov. 1	$1,000	Overhead	4,050

Instructions

(a) Prepare a production cost report for the Heating Department for the month of November 2014, using the weighted-average method.

(b) Journalize the transfer of costs to the Stamping Department.

Solution to Comprehensive Do it!

Action Plan

- Compute the physical unit flow–that is, the total units to be accounted for.
- Compute the equivalent units of production.
- Compute the unit production costs, expressed in terms of equivalent units of production.
- Prepare a cost reconciliation schedule, which shows that the total costs accounted for equal the total costs to be accounted for.

(a)

KARLENE INDUSTRIES
Heating Department
Production Cost Report
For the Month Ended November 30, 2014

| | Physical Units | Equivalent Units | |
		Materials	Conversion Costs
Quantities	Step 1	Step 2	
Units to be accounted for			
Work in process, November 1	1,000		
Started into production	12,000		
Total units	13,000		
Units accounted for			
Transferred out	11,000	11,000	11,000
Work in process, November 30	2,000	2,000	1,200
Total units	13,000	13,000	12,200

Costs		**Materials**	**Conversion Costs**	**Total**
Unit costs Step 3				
Total cost	(a)	$ 3,640*	$ 6,710**	$10,350
Equivalent units	(b)	13,000	12,200	
Unit costs [(a) ÷ (b)]		$0.28	$0.55	$0.83
Costs to be accounted for				
Work in process, November 1				$ 1,000
Started into production				9,350
Total costs				$10,350

*$640 + $3,000
**$360 + $2,300 + $4,050

Cost Reconciliation Schedule   Step 4

Costs accounted for		
Transferred out (11,000 × $0.83)		$ 9,130
Work in process, November 30		
Materials (2,000 × $0.28)	$560	
Conversion costs (1,200 × $0.55)	660	1,220
Total costs		$10,350

(b) Work in Process—Stamping		9,130	
Work in Process—Heating			9,130
(To record transfer of units to the Stamping Department)			

The Navigator

Self-Test, Brief Exercises, Exercises, Problem Set A, and many more resources are available for practice in WileyPLUS.

Note: All Questions, Exercises, and Problems marked with an asterisk relate to material in the appendix to the chapter.

Self-Test Questions

Answers are on page 893.

(LO 1)   **1.** Which of the following items is **not** characteristic of a process cost system?
    (a) Once production begins, it continues until the finished product emerges.
    (b) The products produced are heterogeneous in nature.
    (c) The focus is on continually producing homogeneous products.
    (d) When the finished product emerges, all units have precisely the same amount of materials, labor, and overhead.

(LO 2)   **2.** Indicate which of the following statements is **not** correct.
    (a) Both a job order and a process cost system track the same three manufacturing cost elements—direct materials, direct labor, and manufacturing overhead.
    (b) A job order cost system uses only one work in process account, whereas a process cost system uses multiple work in process accounts.
    (c) Manufacturing costs are accumulated the same way in a job order and in a process cost system.
    (d) Manufacturing costs are assigned the same way in a job order and in a process cost system.

(LO 3)   **3.** In a process cost system, the flow of costs is:
    (a) work in process, cost of goods sold, finished goods.
    (b) finished goods, work in process, cost of goods sold.
    (c) finished goods, cost of goods sold, work in process.
    (d) work in process, finished goods, cost of goods sold.

(LO 4)   **4.** In making journal entries to assign raw materials costs, a company using process costing:
    (a) debits Finished Goods Inventory.
    (b) often debits two or more work in process accounts.
    (c) generally credits two or more work in process accounts.
    (d) credits Finished Goods Inventory.

(LO 4)   **5.** In a process cost system, manufacturing overhead:
    (a) is assigned to finished goods at the end of each accounting period.
    (b) is assigned to a work in process account for each job as the job is completed.
    (c) is assigned to a work in process account for each production department on the basis of a predetermined overhead rate.
    (d) is assigned to a work in process account for each production department as overhead costs are incurred.

(LO 5)   **6.** Conversion costs are the sum of:
    (a) fixed and variable overhead costs.
    (b) labor costs and overhead costs.
    (c) direct material costs and overhead costs.
    (d) direct labor and indirect labor costs.

7. The Mixing Department's output during the period (LO 5) consists of 20,000 units completed and transferred out, and 5,000 units in ending work in process 60% complete as to materials and conversion costs. Beginning inventory is 1,000 units, 40% complete as to materials and conversion costs. The equivalent units of production are:
    (a) 22,600.   (c) 24,000.
    (b) 23,000.   (d) 25,000.

8. In RYZ Company, there are zero units in beginning (LO 6) work in process, 7,000 units started into production, and 500 units in ending work in process 20% completed. The physical units to be accounted for are:
    (a) 7,000.   (c) 7,500.
    (b) 7,360.   (d) 7,340.

9. Mora Company has 2,000 units in beginning work in (LO 6) process, 20% complete as to conversion costs, 23,000 units transferred out to finished goods, and 3,000 units in ending work in process $33\frac{1}{3}\%$ complete as to conversion costs.
    The beginning and ending inventory is fully complete as to materials costs. Equivalent units for materials and conversion costs are, respectively:
    (a) 22,000, 24,000.   (c) 26,000, 24,000.
    (b) 24,000, 26,000.   (d) 26,000, 26,000.

10. Fortner Company has no beginning work in proc- (LO 6) ess; 9,000 units are transferred out and 3,000 units in ending work in process are one-third finished as to conversion costs and fully complete as to materials cost. If total materials cost is $60,000, the unit materials cost is:
    (a) $5.00.
    (b) $5.45 rounded.
    (c) $6.00.
    (d) No correct answer is given.

11. Largo Company has unit costs of $10 for materials (LO 6) and $30 for conversion costs. If there are 2,500 units in ending work in process, 40% complete as to conversion costs, and fully complete as to materials cost, the total cost assignable to the ending work in process inventory is:
    (a) $45,000.   (c) $75,000.
    (b) $55,000.   (d) $100,000.

12. A production cost report: (LO 7)
    (a) is an external report.
    (b) shows both the production quantity and cost data related to a department.

(c) shows equivalent units of production but not physical units.

(d) contains six sections.

(LO 7) **13.** In a production cost report, units to be accounted for are calculated as:

(a) Units started into production + Units in ending work in process.

(b) Units started into production − Units in beginning work in process.

(c) Units transferred out + Units in beginning work in process.

(d) Units started into production + Units in beginning work in process.

(LO 8) ***14.** Hollins Company uses the FIFO method to compute equivalent units. It has 2,000 units in beginning work in process, 20% complete as to conversion costs, 25,000 units started and completed, and 3,000 units in ending work in process, 30% complete as to conversion costs. All units are 100% complete as to materials. Equivalent units for materials and conversion costs are, respectively:

(a) 28,000 and 26,600.

(b) 28,000 and 27,500.

(c) 27,000 and 26,200.

(d) 27,000 and 29,600.

*15. KLM Company uses the FIFO method to compute (LO 8) equivalent units. It has no beginning work in process; 9,000 units are started and completed and 3,000 units in ending work in process are one-third completed. All material is added at the beginning of the process. If total materials cost is $60,000, the unit materials cost is:

(a) $5.00.

(b) $6.00.

(c) $6.67 (rounded).

(d) No correct answer given.

*16. Toney Company uses the FIFO method to compute (LO 3) equivalent units. It has unit costs of $10 for materials and $30 for conversion costs. If there are 2,500 units in ending work in process, 100% complete as to materials and 40% complete as to conversion costs, the total cost assignable to the ending work in process inventory is:

(a) $45,000. (c) $75,000.

(b) $55,000. (d) $100,000.

Go to the book's companion website, **www. wiley.com/college/kimmel**, for additional Self-Test Questions.

Questions

1. Identify which costing system—job order or process cost—the following companies would primarily use: (a) Quaker Oats, (b) Jif Peanut Butter, (c) Gulf Craft (luxury yachts), and (d) Warner Bros. Motion Pictures.

2. Contrast the primary focus of job order cost accounting and of process cost accounting.

3. What are the similarities between a job order and a process cost system?

4. Your roommate is confused about the features of process cost accounting. Identify and explain the distinctive features for your roommate.

5. Sam Bowyer believes there are no significant differences in the flow of costs between job order cost accounting and process cost accounting. Is Bowyer correct? Explain.

6. (a) What source documents are used in assigning (1) materials and (2) labor to production in a process cost system?

(b) What criterion and basis are commonly used in allocating overhead to processes?

7. At Ely Company, overhead is assigned to production departments at the rate of $5 per machine hour. In July, machine hours were 3,000 in the Machining Department and 2,400 in the Assembly Department. Prepare the entry to assign overhead to production.

8. Mark Haley is uncertain about the steps used to prepare a production cost report. State the procedures that are required in the sequence in which they are performed.

9. John Harbeck is confused about computing physical units. Explain to John how physical units to be accounted for and physical units accounted for are determined.

10. What is meant by the term "equivalent units of production"?

11. How are equivalent units of production computed?

12. Coats Company had zero units of beginning work in process. During the period, 9,000 units were completed, and there were 600 units of ending work in process. What were the units started into production?

13. Sanchez Co. has zero units of beginning work in process. During the period, 12,000 units were completed, and there were 500 units of ending work in process one-fifth complete as to conversion cost and 100% complete as to materials cost. What were the equivalent units of production for (a) materials and (b) conversion costs?

14. Hindi Co. started 3,000 units during the period. Its beginning inventory is 500 units one-fourth complete as to conversion costs and 100% complete as to materials costs. Its ending inventory is 300 units one-fifth complete as to conversion costs and 100% complete as to materials costs. How many units were transferred out this period?

15. Clauss Company transfers out 14,000 units and has 2,000 units of ending work in process that are 25% complete. Materials are entered at the beginning of the process and there is no beginning work in process. Assuming unit materials costs of $3 and unit conversion costs of $5, what are the costs to be assigned to units (a) transferred out and (b) in ending work in process?

16. (a) Ann Quinn believes the production cost report is an external report for stockholders. Is Ann correct? Explain.

(b) Identify the sections in a production cost report.

17. What purposes are served by a production cost report?

18. At Trent Company, there are 800 units of ending work in process that are 100% complete as to materials and 40% complete as to conversion costs. If the unit cost of materials is $3 and the total costs assigned to the 800 units is $6,000, what is the per unit conversion cost?

19. What is the difference between operations costing and a process cost system?

20. How does a company decide whether to use a job order or a process cost system?

*21. Soria Co. started and completed 2,000 units for the period. Its beginning inventory is 800 units 25% complete and its ending inventory is 400 units 20% complete. Soria uses the FIFO method to compute equivalent units. How many units were transferred out this period?

*22. Reyes Company transfers out 12,000 units and has 2,000 units of ending work in process that are 25% complete. Materials are entered at the beginning of the process and there is no beginning work in process. Reyes uses the FIFO method to compute equivalent units. Assuming unit materials costs of $3 and unit conversion costs of $7, what are the costs to be assigned to units (a) transferred out and (b) in ending work in process?

Brief Exercises

Journalize entries for accumulating costs.
(LO 4), AP

BE16-1 Weber Company purchases $45,000 of raw materials on account, and it incurs $60,000 of factory labor costs. Journalize the two transactions on March 31 assuming the labor costs are not paid until April.

Journalize the assignment of materials and labor costs.
(LO 4), AP

BE16-2 Data for Weber Company are given in BE16-1. Supporting records show that (a) the Assembly Department used $24,000 of raw materials and $35,000 of the factory labor, and (b) the Finishing Department used the remainder. Journalize the assignment of the costs to the processing departments on March 31.

Journalize the assignment of overhead costs.
(LO 4), AP

BE16-3 Factory labor data for Weber Company are given in BE16-2. Manufacturing overhead is assigned to departments on the basis of 200% of labor costs. Journalize the assignment of overhead to the Assembly and Finishing Departments.

Compute equivalent units of production.
(LO 5), AP

BE16-4 Goode Company has the following production data for selected months.

Month	Beginning Work in Process	Units Transferred Out	Ending Work in Process Units	% Complete as to Conversion Cost
January	–0–	35,000	10,000	40%
March	–0–	40,000	8,000	75
July	–0–	45,000	16,000	25

Compute equivalent units of production for materials and conversion costs, assuming materials are entered at the beginning of the process.

Compute unit costs of production.
(LO 6), AP

BE16-5 In Lopez Company, total material costs are $36,000, and total conversion costs are $54,000. Equivalent units of production are materials 10,000 and conversion costs 12,000. Compute the unit costs for materials, conversion costs, and total manufacturing costs.

Assign costs to units transferred out and in process.
(LO 6), AP

BE16-6 Trek Company has the following production data for April: units transferred out 40,000, and ending work in process 5,000 units that are 100% complete for materials and 40% complete for conversion costs. If unit materials cost is $4 and unit conversion cost is $7, determine the costs to be assigned to the units transferred out and the units in ending work in process.

Compute unit costs.
(LO 6), AP

BE16-7 Production costs chargeable to the Finishing Department in June in Cascio Company are materials $16,000, labor $29,500, overhead $18,000. Equivalent units of production are materials 20,000 and conversion costs 19,000. Compute the unit costs for materials and conversion costs.

Prepare cost reconciliation schedule.
(LO 6), AP

BE16-8 Data for Cascio Company are given in BE16-7. Production records indicate that 18,000 units were transferred out, and 2,000 units in ending work in process were 50% complete as to conversion cost and 100% complete as to materials. Prepare a cost reconciliation schedule.

BE16-9 The Smelting Department of Mathews Company has the following production and cost data for November.

> **Production:** Beginning work in process 2,000 units that are 100% complete as to materials and 20% complete as to conversion costs; units transferred out 8,000 units; and ending work in process 7,000 units that are 100% complete as to materials and 40% complete as to conversion costs.

Compute the equivalent units of production for (a) materials and (b) conversion costs for the month of November.

Compute equivalent units of production.
(LO 5), **AP**

*BE16-10 Sanderson Company has the following production data for March: no beginning work in process, units started and completed 30,000, and ending work in process 5,000 units that are 100% complete for materials and 40% complete for conversion costs. Sanderson uses the FIFO method to compute equivalent units. If unit materials cost is $6 and unit conversion cost is $12, determine the costs to be assigned to the units transferred out and the units in ending work in process. The total costs to be assigned are $594,000.

Assign costs to units transferred out and in process.
(LO 8), **AP**

*BE16-11 Using the data in BE16-10, prepare the cost section of the production cost report for Sanderson Company.

Prepare a partial production cost report.
(LO 7, 8), **AP**

*BE16-12 Production costs chargeable to the Finishing Department in May at Kim Company are materials $8,000, labor $20,000, overhead $18,000, and transferred-in costs $67,000. Equivalent units of production are materials 20,000 and conversion costs 19,000. Kim uses the FIFO method to compute equivalent units. Compute the unit costs for materials and conversion costs. Transferred-in costs are considered materials costs.

Compute unit costs.
(LO 8), **AP**

Do it! Review

Do it! 16-1 Indicate whether each of the following statements is true or false.

1. Many hospitals use job order costing for small, routine medical procedures.
2. A manufacturer of computer flash drives would use a job order cost system.
3. A process cost system uses multiple work in process accounts.
4. A process cost system keeps track of costs on job cost sheets.

Compare job order and process cost systems.
(LO 1, 2), **C**

Do it! 16-2 Kopa Company manufactures CH-21 through two processes: Mixing and Packaging. In July, the following costs were incurred.

	Mixing	**Packaging**
Raw materials used	$10,000	$28,000
Factory labor costs	8,000	36,000
Manufacturing overhead costs	12,000	54,000

Units completed at a cost of $21,000 in the Mixing Department are transferred to the Packaging Department. Units completed at a cost of $106,000 in the Packaging Department are transferred to Finished Goods. Journalize the assignment of these costs to the two processes and the transfer of units as appropriate.

Assign and journalize manufacturing costs.
(LO 4), **AP**

Do it! 16-3 The assembly department has the following production data for the current month.

Beginning Work in Process	**Units Transferred Out**	**Ending Work in Process**
–0–	20,000	12,000

Materials are entered at the beginning of the process. The ending work in process units are 70% complete as to conversion costs. Compute the equivalent units of production for (a) materials and (b) conversion costs.

Compute equivalent units.
(LO 5), **AP**

Do it! 16-4 In March, Kelly Company had the following unit production costs: materials $10 and conversion costs $8. On March 1, it had zero work in process. During March, Kelly transferred out 22,000 units. As of March 31, 4,000 units that were 40% complete as to conversion costs and 100% complete as to materials were in ending work in process.

(a) Compute the total units to be accounted for.
(b) Compute the equivalent units of production.
(c) Prepare a cost reconciliation schedule, including the costs of materials transferred out and the costs of materials in process.

Prepare cost reconciliation schedule.
(LO 6, 7), **AP**

Exercises

E16-1 Robert Mallory has prepared the following list of statements about process cost accounting.

1. Process cost systems are used to apply costs to similar products that are mass-produced in a continuous fashion.
2. A process cost system is used when each finished unit is indistinguishable from another.
3. Companies that produce soft drinks, motion pictures, and computer chips would all use process cost accounting.
4. In a process cost system, costs are tracked by individual jobs.
5. Job order costing and process costing track different manufacturing cost elements.
6. Both job order costing and process costing account for direct materials, direct labor, and manufacturing overhead.
7. Costs flow through the accounts in the same basic way for both job order costing and process costing.
8. In a process cost system, only one work in process account is used.
9. In a process cost system, costs are summarized in a job cost sheet.
10. In a process cost system, the unit cost is total manufacturing costs for the period divided by the equivalent units produced during the period.

Instructions
Identify each statement as true or false. If false, indicate how to correct the statement.

E16-2 Harrelson Company manufactures pizza sauce through two production departments: Cooking and Canning. In each process, materials and conversion costs are incurred evenly throughout the process. For the month of April, the work in process accounts show the following debits.

	Cooking	**Canning**
Beginning work in process	$ –0–	$ 4,000
Materials	21,000	9,000
Labor	8,500	7,000
Overhead	31,500	25,800
Costs transferred in		53,000

Instructions
Journalize the April transactions.

E16-3 The ledger of Custer Company has the following work in process account.

Work in Process—Painting

5/1	Balance	3,590	5/31	Transferred out	?
5/31	Materials	5,160			
5/31	Labor	2,740			
5/31	Overhead	1,380			
5/31	Balance	?			

Production records show that there were 400 units in the beginning inventory, 30% complete, 1,400 units started, and 1,500 units transferred out. The beginning work in process had materials cost of $2,040 and conversion costs of $1,550. The units in ending inventory were 40% complete. Materials are entered at the beginning of the painting process.

Instructions
(a) How many units are in process at May 31?
(b) What is the unit materials cost for May?
(c) What is the unit conversion cost for May?
(d) What is the total cost of units transferred out in May?
(e) What is the cost of the May 31 inventory?

E16-4 Schrager Company has two production departments: Cutting and Assembly. July 1 inventories are Raw Materials $4,200, Work in Process—Cutting $2,900, Work in Process—

Assembly $10,600, and Finished Goods $31,000. During July, the following transactions occurred.

1. Purchased $62,500 of raw materials on account.
2. Incurred $60,000 of factory labor. (Credit Wages Payable.)
3. Incurred $70,000 of manufacturing overhead; $40,000 was paid and the remainder is unpaid.
4. Requisitioned materials for Cutting $15,700 and Assembly $8,900.
5. Used factory labor for Cutting $33,000 and Assembly $27,000.
6. Applied overhead at the rate of $18 per machine hour. Machine hours were Cutting 1,680 and Assembly 1,720.
7. Transferred goods costing $67,600 from the Cutting Department to the Assembly Department.
8. Transferred goods costing $134,900 from Assembly to Finished Goods.
9. Sold goods costing $150,000 for $200,000 on account.

Instructions
Journalize the transactions. (Omit explanations.)

E16-5 In Wayne Company, materials are entered at the beginning of each process. Work in process inventories, with the percentage of work done on conversion costs, and production data for its Sterilizing Department in selected months during 2014 are as follows.

Compute physical units and equivalent units of production.
(LO 5, 6), AP

Month	Beginning Work in Process		Units Transferred Out	Ending Work in Process	
	Units	Conversion Cost%		Units	Conversion Cost%
January	–0–	—	9,000	2,000	60
March	–0–	—	12,000	3,000	30
May	–0–	—	16,000	7,000	80
July	–0–	—	10,000	1,500	40

Instructions
(a) Compute the physical units for January and May.
(b) Compute the equivalent units of production for (1) materials and (2) conversion costs for each month.

E16-6 The Cutting Department of Cassel Company has the following production and cost data for July.

Determine equivalent units, unit costs, and assignment of costs.
(LO 5, 6), AP

Production	Costs	
1. Transferred out 12,000 units.	Beginning work in process	$ –0–
2. Started 3,000 units that are 60% complete as to conversion costs and 100% complete as to materials at July 31.	Materials	45,000
	Labor	16,200
	Manufacturing overhead	18,300

Materials are entered at the beginning of the process. Conversion costs are incurred uniformly during the process.

Instructions
(a) Determine the equivalent units of production for (1) materials and (2) conversion costs.
(b) Compute unit costs and prepare a cost reconciliation schedule.

E16-7 The Sanding Department of Richards Furniture Company has the following production and manufacturing cost data for March 2014, the first month of operation.

Prepare a production cost report.
(LO 5, 6, 7), AP

Production: 9,000 units finished and transferred out; 3,000 units started that are 100% complete as to materials and 20% complete as to conversion costs.

Manufacturing costs: Materials $33,000; labor $24,000; overhead $36,000.

Instructions
Prepare a production cost report.

E16-8 The Blending Department of Luongo Company has the following cost and production data for the month of April.

Determine equivalent units, unit costs, and assignment of costs.
(LO 5, 6), AP

Costs:

Work in process, April 1	
Direct materials: 100% complete	$100,000
Conversion costs: 20% complete	70,000
Cost of work in process, April 1	$170,000
Costs incurred during production in April	
Direct materials	$ 800,000
Conversion costs	365,000
Costs incurred in April	$1,165,000

Units transferred out totaled 17,000. Ending work in process was 1,000 units that are 100% complete as to materials and 40% complete as to conversion costs.

Instructions

(a) Compute the equivalent units of production for (1) materials and (2) conversion costs for the month of April.
(b) Compute the unit costs for the month.
(c) Determine the costs to be assigned to the units transferred out and in ending work in process.

Determine equivalent units, unit costs, and assignment of costs.

(LO 5, 6), **AP**

E16-9 Kostrivas Company has gathered the following information.

Units in beginning work in process	–0–
Units started into production	40,000
Units in ending work in process	6,000
Percent complete in ending work in process:	
Conversion costs	40%
Materials	100%
Costs incurred:	
Direct materials	$72,000
Direct labor	$81,000
Overhead	$101,000

Instructions

(a) Compute equivalent units of production for materials and for conversion costs.
(b) Determine the unit costs of production.
(c) Show the assignment of costs to units transferred out and in process.

Determine equivalent units, unit costs, and assignment of costs.

(LO 5, 6), **AP**

E16-10 Overton Company has gathered the following information.

Units in beginning work in process	20,000
Units started into production	164,000
Units in ending work in process	24,000
Percent complete in ending work in process:	
Conversion costs	60%
Materials	100%
Costs incurred:	
Direct materials	$101,200
Direct labor	$164,800
Overhead	$184,000

Instructions

(a) Compute equivalent units of production for materials and for conversion costs.
(b) Determine the unit costs of production.
(c) Show the assignment of costs to units transferred out and in process.

Compute equivalent units, unit costs, and costs assigned.

(LO 5, 6), **AP**

E16-11 The Polishing Department of Harbin Company has the following production and manufacturing cost data for September. Materials are entered at the beginning of the process.

Production: Beginning inventory 1,600 units that are 100% complete as to materials and 30% complete as to conversion costs; units started during the period are 38,400; ending inventory of 5,000 units 10% complete as to conversion costs.

Manufacturing costs: Beginning inventory costs, comprised of $20,000 of materials and $43,180 of conversion costs; materials costs added in Polishing during the month, $177,200; labor and overhead applied in Polishing during the month, $125,680 and $257,140, respectively.

Instructions

(a) Compute the equivalent units of production for materials and conversion costs for the month of September.

(b) Compute the unit costs for materials and conversion costs for the month.

(c) Determine the costs to be assigned to the units transferred out and in process.

E16-12 David Skaros has recently been promoted to production manager, and so he has just started to receive various managerial reports. One of the reports he has received is the production cost report that you prepared. It showed that his department had 2,000 equivalent units in ending inventory. His department has had a history of not keeping enough inventory on hand to meet demand. He has come to you, very angry, and wants to know why you credited him with only 2,000 units when he knows he had at least twice that many on hand.

Explain the production cost report.

(LO 7), **S**

Instructions

━▰▰▰▶ Explain to him why his production cost report showed only 2,000 equivalent units in ending inventory. Write an informal memo. Be kind and explain very clearly why he is mistaken.

E16-13 The Welding Department of Thorpe Company has the following production and manufacturing cost data for February 2014. All materials are added at the beginning of the process.

Prepare a production cost report.

(LO 5, 6, 7), **AP**

Manufacturing Costs			Production Data		
Beginning work in process			Beginning work in process	15,000 units	
Materials	$18,000			1/10 complete	
Conversion costs	14,175	$ 32,175	Units transferred out	49,000	
Materials		180,000	Units started	45,000	
Labor		52,380	Ending work in process	11,000 units	
Overhead		61,445		1/5 complete	

Instructions

Prepare a production cost report for the Welding Department for the month of February.

E16-14 Remington Shipping, Inc. is contemplating the use of process costing to track the costs of its operations. The operation consists of three segments (departments): receiving, shipping, and delivery. Containers are received at Remington's docks and sorted according to the ship they will be carried on. The containers are loaded onto a ship, which carries them to the appropriate port of destination. The containers are then off-loaded and delivered to the receiving company.

Compute physical units and equivalent units of production.

(LO 5, 6), **AP**

Remington Shipping wants to begin using process costing in the shipping department. Direct materials represent the fuel costs to run the ship, and "Containers in transit" represents work in process. Listed below is information about the shipping department's first month's activity.

Containers in transit, April 1	0
Containers loaded	1,200
Containers in transit, April 30	350, 40% of direct materials and 20% of conversion costs

Instructions

(a) Determine the physical flow of containers for the month.

(b) Calculate the equivalent units for direct materials and conversion costs.

E16-15 Royale Mortgage Company uses a process cost system to accumulate costs in its loan application department. When an application is completed, it is forwarded to the loan department for final processing. The following processing and cost data pertain to September.

Determine equivalent units, unit costs, and assignment of costs.

(LO 5, 6), **AP**

1. Applications in process on September 1, 100
2. Applications started in September, 900
3. Completed applications during September, 800
4. Applications still in process at September 30 were 100% complete as to materials (forms) and 60% complete as to conversion costs.

Beginning WIP:	
Direct materials	$ 1,000
Conversion costs	3,960
September costs:	
Direct materials	$ 4,500
Direct labor	12,000
Overhead	9,340

Materials are the forms used in the application process, and these costs are incurred at the beginning of the process. Conversion costs are incurred uniformly during the process.

Instructions
(a) Determine the equivalent units of service (production) for materials and conversion costs.
(b) Compute the unit costs and prepare a cost reconciliation schedule.

Compute equivalent units, unit costs, and costs assigned.
(LO 6, 8), **AP**

*E16-16 Using the data in E16-15, assume Royale Mortgage Company uses the FIFO method. Also assume that the applications in process on September 1 were 100% complete as to materials (forms) and 40% complete as to conversion costs.

Instructions
(a) Determine the equivalent units of service (production) for materials and conversion costs.
(b) Compute the unit costs and prepare a cost reconciliation schedule.

Determine equivalent units, unit costs, and assignment of costs.
(LO 6, 8), **AP**

*E16-17 The Cutting Department of Keigi Company has the following production and cost data for August.

Production	Costs	
1. Started and completed 8,000 units.	Beginning work in process	$ –0–
2. Started 2,000 units that are 40% completed at August 31.	Materials	45,000
	Labor	14,700
	Manufacturing overhead	16,100

Materials are entered at the beginning of the process. Conversion costs are incurred uniformly during the process. Keigi Company uses the FIFO method to compute equivalent units.

Instructions
(a) Determine the equivalent units of production for (1) materials and (2) conversion costs.
(b) Compute unit costs and show the assignment of manufacturing costs to units transferred out and in work in process.

Compute equivalent units, unit costs, and costs assigned.
(LO 6, 8), **AP**

*E16-18 The Smelting Department of Polzin Company has the following production and cost data for September.

Production: Beginning work in process 2,000 units that are 100% complete as to materials and 20% complete as to conversion costs; units started and finished 9,000 units; and ending work in process 1,000 units that are 100% complete as to materials and 40% complete as to conversion costs.

Manufacturing costs: Work in process, September 1, $15,200; materials added $60,000; labor and overhead $132,000.

Polzin uses the FIFO method to compute equivalent units.

Instructions
(a) Compute the equivalent units of production for (1) materials and (2) conversion costs for the month of September.
(b) Compute the unit costs for the month.
(c) Determine the costs to be assigned to the units transferred out and in process.

*E16-19   The ledger of Hannon Company has the following work in process account.

Answer questions on costs and production.
(LO 6, 8), **AP**

Work in Process—Painting

3/1	Balance	3,680	3/31	Transferred out	?
3/31	Materials	6,600			
3/31	Labor	2,500			
3/31	Overhead	1,150			
3/31	Balance	?			

Production records show that there were 800 units in the beginning inventory, 30% complete, 1,200 units started, and 1,500 units transferred out. The units in ending inventory were 40% complete. Materials are entered at the beginning of the painting process. Hannon uses the FIFO method to compute equivalent units.

Instructions
Answer the following questions.
(a) How many units are in process at March 31?
(b) What is the unit materials cost for March?
(c) What is the unit conversion cost for March?
(d) What is the total cost of units started in February and completed in March?
(e) What is the total cost of units started and finished in March?
(f) What is the cost of the March 31 inventory?

*E16-20   The Welding Department of Majestic Company has the following production and manufacturing cost data for February 2014. All materials are added at the beginning of the process. Majestic uses the FIFO method to compute equivalent units.

Prepare a production cost report for a second process.
(LO 8), **AP**

Manufacturing Costs		Production Data	
Beginning work in process	$ 32,175	Beginning work in process	15,000 units,
Costs transferred in	135,000		10% complete
Materials	57,000	Units transferred out	54,000
Labor	35,100	Units transferred in	64,000
Overhead	68,400	Ending work in process	25,000,
			20% complete

Instructions
Prepare a production cost report for the Welding Department for the month of February. Transferred-in costs are considered materials costs.

Exercises: Set B and Challenge Exercises

Visit the book's companion website, at **www.wiley.com/college/kimmel**, and choose the Student Companion site to access Exercise Set B and Challenge Exercises.

Problems: Set A

P16-1A   Conwell Company manufactures its product, Vitadrink, through two manufacturing processes: Mixing and Packaging. All materials are entered at the beginning of each process. On October 1, 2014, inventories consisted of Raw Materials $26,000, Work in Process—Mixing $0, Work in Process—Packaging $250,000, and Finished Goods $289,000. The beginning inventory for Packaging consisted of 10,000 units that were 50% complete as to conversion costs and fully complete as to materials. During October, 50,000 units were started into production in the Mixing Department and the following transactions were completed.

Journalize transactions.
(LO 3, 4), **AP**

1. Purchased $300,000 of raw materials on account.
2. Issued raw materials for production: Mixing $210,000 and Packaging $45,000.

3. Incurred labor costs of $258,900.
4. Used factory labor: Mixing $182,500 and Packaging $76,400.
5. Incurred $810,000 of manufacturing overhead on account.
6. Applied manufacturing overhead on the basis of $24 per machine hour. Machine hours were 28,000 in Mixing and 6,000 in Packaging.
7. Transferred 45,000 units from Mixing to Packaging at a cost of $979,000.
8. Transferred 53,000 units from Packaging to Finished Goods at a cost of $1,315,000.
9. Sold goods costing $1,604,000 for $2,500,000 on account.

Instructions
Journalize the October transactions.

Complete four steps necessary to prepare a production cost report.
(LO 5, 6, 7), **AP**

P16-2A Rosenthal Company manufactures bowling balls through two processes: Molding and Packaging. In the Molding Department, the urethane, rubber, plastics, and other materials are molded into bowling balls. In the Packaging Department, the balls are placed in cartons and sent to the finished goods warehouse. All materials are entered at the beginning of each process. Labor and manufacturing overhead are incurred uniformly throughout each process. Production and cost data for the Molding Department during June 2014 are presented below.

Production Data	**June**
Beginning work in process units	–0–
Units started into production	22,000
Ending work in process units	2,000
Percent complete—ending inventory	40%

Cost Data	
Materials	$198,000
Labor	53,600
Overhead	112,800
Total	$364,400

Instructions
(a) Prepare a schedule showing physical units of production.
(b) Determine the equivalent units of production for materials and conversion costs.
(c) Compute the unit costs of production.
(d) Determine the costs to be assigned to the units transferred out and in process for June.
(e) Prepare a production cost report for the Molding Department for the month of June.

(c) Materials $9.00
CC $8.00
(d) Transferred
out · $340,000
WIP $ 24,400

Complete four steps necessary to prepare a production cost report.
(LO 5, 6, 7), **AP**

P16-3A Seagren Industries Inc. manufactures in separate processes furniture for homes. In each process, materials are entered at the beginning, and conversion costs are incurred uniformly. Production and cost data for the first process in making two products in two different manufacturing plants are as follows.

	Cutting Department	
	Plant 1	**Plant 2**
Production Data—July	**T12-Tables**	**C10-Chairs**
Work in process units, July 1	–0–	–0–
Units started into production	19,000	16,000
Work in process units, July 31	3,000	500
Work in process percent complete	60	80
Cost Data—July		
Work in process, July 1	$ –0–	$ –0–
Materials	380,000	288,000
Labor	234,200	110,000
Overhead	104,000	96,700
Total	$718,200	$494,700

Instructions

(a) For each plant:
   (1) Compute the physical units of production.
   (2) Compute equivalent units of production for materials and for conversion costs.
   (3) Determine the unit costs of production.
   (4) Show the assignment of costs to units transferred out and in process.
(b) Prepare the production cost report for Plant 1 for July 2014.

(a) (3) T12:
    Materials $20
    CC $19
    (4) T12:
    Transferred
        out $624,000
    WIP $ 94,200

P16-4A Rivera Company has several processing departments. Costs charged to the Assembly Department for November 2014 totaled $2,280,000 as follows.

Assign costs and prepare production cost report.
(LO 5, 6, 7), **AP**

Work in process, November 1		
Materials	$79,000	
Conversion costs	48,150	$ 127,150
Materials added		1,589,000
Labor		225,920
Overhead		337,930

Production records show that 35,000 units were in beginning work in process 30% complete as to conversion costs, 660,000 units were started into production, and 25,000 units were in ending work in process 40% complete as to conversion costs. Materials are entered at the beginning of each process.

Instructions

(a) Determine the equivalent units of production and the unit production costs for the Assembly Department.
(b) Determine the assignment of costs to goods transferred out and in process.
(c) Prepare a production cost report for the Assembly Department.

(b) Transferred
        out $2,211,000
    WIP $ 69,000

P16-5A Morse Company manufactures basketballs. Materials are added at the beginning of the production process and conversion costs are incurred uniformly. Production and cost data for the month of July 2014 are as follows.

Determine equivalent units and unit costs and assign costs.
(LO 5, 6, 7), **AP**

Production Data—Basketballs	Units	Percent Complete
Work in process units, July 1	500	60%
Units started into production	1,250	
Work in process units, July 31	600	40%

Cost Data—Basketballs		
Work in process, July 1		
Materials	$750	
Conversion costs	600	$1,350
Direct materials		2,400
Direct labor		1,580
Manufacturing overhead		1,295

Instructions

(a) Calculate the following.
   (1) The equivalent units of production for materials and conversion costs.
   (2) The unit costs of production for materials and conversion costs.
   (3) The assignment of costs to units transferred out and in process at the end of the accounting period.
(b) Prepare a production cost report for the month of July for the basketballs.

(a) (2) Materials $1.80
    (3) Transferred
        out $4,945
    WIP $1,680

P16-6A Hamilton Processing Company uses a weighted-average process cost system and manufactures a single product—a premium rug shampoo and cleaner. The manufacturing activity for the month of October has just been completed. A partially completed production cost report for the month of October for the Mixing and Cooking Department is shown on the next page.

Compute equivalent units and complete production cost report.
(LO 5, 7), **AP**

Instructions

(a) Prepare a schedule that shows how the equivalent units were computed so that you can complete the "Quantities: Units accounted for" equivalent units section shown in the production cost report, and compute October unit costs.
(b) Complete the "Cost Reconciliation Schedule" part of the production cost report below.

(a) Materials $1.60
    (b) Transferred
        out $282,000
    WIP $ 63,000

HAMILTON PROCESSING COMPANY
Mixing and Cooking Department
Production Cost Report
For the Month Ended October 31

Quantities	Physical Units	Equivalent Units Materials	Equivalent Units Conversion Costs
Units to be accounted for			
Work in process, October 1 (all materials, 70% conversion costs)	20,000		
Started into production	150,000		
Total units	170,000		
Units accounted for			
Transferred out	120,000	?	?
Work in process, October 31 (60% materials, 40% conversion costs)	50,000	?	?
Total units accounted for	170,000	?	?

Costs

Unit costs

	Materials	Conversion Costs	Total
Total cost	$240,000	$105,000	$345,000
Equivalent units	?	?	
Unit costs	$? +	$? =	$?

Costs to be accounted for	
Work in process, October 1	$ 30,000
Started into production	315,000
Total costs	$345,000

Cost Reconciliation Schedule

Costs accounted for		
Transferred out		$?
Work in process, October 31		
Materials	$?	
Conversion costs	?	?
Total costs		$?

Determine equivalent units and unit costs and assign costs for processes; prepare production cost report.

(LO 8), **AP**

*P16-7A Rondeli Company manufactures bicycles and tricycles. For both products, materials are added at the beginning of the production process, and conversion costs are incurred uniformly. Rondeli Company uses the FIFO method to compute equivalent units. Production and cost data for the month of March are as follows.

Production Data—Bicycles	Units	Percent Complete
Work in process units, March 1	200	80%
Units started into production	1,250	
Work in process units, March 31	300	40%

Cost Data—Bicycles	Units	Percent Complete
Work in process, March 1	$19,280	
Direct materials	50,000	
Direct labor	25,500	
Manufacturing overhead	30,000	

Production Data—Tricycles	Units	Percent Complete
Work in process units, March 1	100	75%
Units started into production	800	
Work in process units, March 31	60	25%

Cost Data—Tricycles	
Work in process, March 1	$ 6,125
Direct materials	30,400
Direct labor	15,100
Manufacturing overhead	20,000

Instructions

(a) Calculate the following for both the bicycles and the tricycles.
  (1) The equivalent units of production for materials and conversion costs.
  (2) The unit costs of production for materials and conversion costs.
  (3) The assignment of costs to units transferred out and in process at the end of the accounting period.

(b) Prepare a production cost report for the month of March for the bicycles only.

(a) Bicycles:
  (1) Materials   1,250
  (2) Materials $40
  (3) Transferred
        out $106,780
        WIP $ 18,000

Problems: Set B

P16-1B Wilbury Company manufactures a nutrient, Everlife, through two manufacturing processes: Blending and Packaging. All materials are entered at the beginning of
each process. On August 1, 2014, inventories consisted of Raw Materials $5,000, Work
in Process—Blending $0, Work in Process—Packaging $3,945, and Finished Goods
$7,500. The beginning inventory for Packaging consisted of 500 units, two-fifths com-
plete as to conversion costs and fully complete as to materials. During August, 9,000
units were started into production in Blending, and the following transactions were
completed.

Journalize transactions.
(LO 3, 4), **AP**

1. Purchased $25,000 of raw materials on account.
2. Issued raw materials for production: Blending $18,930 and Packaging $9,140.
3. Incurred labor costs of $25,770.
4. Used factory labor: Blending $15,320 and Packaging $10,450.
5. Incurred $36,500 of manufacturing overhead on account.
6. Applied manufacturing overhead at the rate of $28 per machine hour. Machine hours
   were Blending 900 and Packaging 300.
7. Transferred 8,200 units from Blending to Packaging at a cost of $44,940.
8. Transferred 8,600 units from Packaging to Finished Goods at a cost of $67,490.
9. Sold goods costing $62,000 for $90,000 on account.

Instructions

Journalize the August transactions.

P16-2B Steiner Corporation manufactures water skis through two processes: Molding
and Packaging. In the Molding Department, fiberglass is heated and shaped into the
form of a ski. In the Packaging Department, the skis are placed in cartons and sent to
the finished goods warehouse. Materials are entered at the beginning of both processes.
Labor and manufacturing overhead are incurred uniformly throughout each process.
Production and cost data for the Molding Department for January 2014 are presented
below.

*Complete four steps necessary
to prepare a production cost
report.*
(LO 5, 6, 7), **AP**

Production Data	January
Beginning work in process units	–0–
Units started into production	50,000
Ending work in process units	2,500
Percent complete—ending inventory	40%

Cost Data	January
Materials	$510,000
Labor	92,500
Overhead	150,000
Total	$752,500

Instructions
(a) Compute the physical units of production.
(b) Determine the equivalent units of production for materials and conversion costs.
(c) Compute the unit costs of production.
(d) Determine the costs to be assigned to the units transferred out and in process.
(e) Prepare a production cost report for the Molding Department for the month of January.

(c) Materials $10.20
    CC $5
(d) Transferred out $722,000
    WIP $ 30,500

Complete four steps necessary to prepare a production cost report.
(LO 5, 6, 7), **AP**

P16-3B Borman Corporation manufactures in separate processes refrigerators and freezers for homes. In each process, materials are entered at the beginning and conversion costs are incurred uniformly. Production and cost data for the first process in making two products in two different manufacturing plants are as follows.

	Stamping Department	
	Plant A	Plant B
Production Data—June	R12 Refrigerators	F24 Freezers
Work in process units, June 1	–0–	–0–
Units started into production	20,000	20,000
Work in process units, June 30	4,000	2,500
Work in process percent complete	75	60

Cost Data—June		
Work in process, June 1	$ –0–	$ –0–
Materials	840,000	720,000
Labor	245,000	259,000
Overhead	420,000	292,000
Total	$1,505,000	$1,271,000

(a) (3) R12:
        Materials $42
        CC $35
    (4) R12:
        Transferred
        out $1,232,000
        WIP $ 273,000

Assign costs and prepare production cost report.
(LO 5, 6, 7), **AP**

Instructions
(a) For each plant:
    (1) Compute the physical units of production.
    (2) Compute equivalent units of production for materials and for conversion costs.
    (3) Determine the unit costs of production.
    (4) Show the assignment of costs to units transferred out and in process.
(b) Prepare the production cost report for Plant A for June 2014.

P16-4B Luxman Company has several processing departments. Costs charged to the Assembly Department for October 2014 totaled $1,298,400 as follows.

Work in process, October 1		
Materials	$29,000	
Conversion costs	16,500	$ 45,500
Materials added		1,006,000
Labor		138,900
Overhead		108,000

Production records show that 25,000 units were in beginning work in process 40% complete as to conversion cost, 435,000 units were started into production, and 35,000 units were in ending work in process 40% complete as to conversion costs. Materials are entered at the beginning of each process.

Instructions
(a) Determine the equivalent units of production and the unit production costs for the Assembly Department.

(b) Transferred out $1,211,250
    WIP $ 87,150

(b) Determine the assignment of costs to goods transferred out and in process.
(c) Prepare a production cost report for the Assembly Department.

P16-5B Swinn Company manufactures bicycles. Materials are added at the beginning of the production process, and conversion costs are incurred uniformly. Production and cost data for the month of May are as follows.

Determine equivalent units and unit costs and assign costs.

(LO 5, 6, 7), **AP**

Production Data—Bicycles	Units	Percent Complete
Work in process units, May 1	500	80%
Units started in production	2,000	
Work in process units, May 31	800	40%

Cost Data—Bicycles		
Work in process, May 1 Materials	$15,000	
Conversion costs	18,000	$33,000
Direct materials		50,000
Direct labor		19,020
Manufacturing overhead		33,680

Instructions
(a) Calculate the following.
   (1) The equivalent units of production for materials and conversion.
   (2) The unit costs of production for materials and conversion costs.
   (3) The assignment of costs to units transferred out and in process at the end of the accounting period.
(b) Prepare a production cost report for the month of May for the bicycles.

(2) Materials $26
    CC $35
(3) Transferred
    out $103,700
    WIP $ 32,000

P16-6B Venuchi Cleaner Company uses a weighted-average process cost system and manufactures a single product—an all-purpose liquid cleaner. The manufacturing activity for the month of March has just been completed. A partially completed production cost report for the month of March for the mixing and blending department is shown below.

Compute equivalent units and complete production cost report.

(LO 5, 7), **AP**

VENUCHI CLEANER COMPANY
Mixing and Blending Department
Production Cost Report
For the Month Ended March 31

		Equivalent Units	
Quantities	Physical Units	Materials	Conversion Costs
Units to be accounted for			
Work in process, March 1	10,000		
Started into production	76,000		
Total units	86,000		
Units accounted for			
Transferred out	66,000	?	?
Work in process, March 31 (60% materials, 20% conversion costs)	20,000	?	?
Total units	86,000	?	?

Costs		Conversion	
Unit costs	Materials	Costs	Total
Total cost	$156,000	$98,000	$254,000
Equivalent units	?	?	
Unit costs	$?	+ $?	= $?
Costs to be accounted for			
Work in process, March 1			$ 8,700
Started into production			245,300
Total costs			$254,000

Cost Reconciliation Schedule	Materials	Conversion Costs	Total
Costs accounted for			
Transferred out			$?
Work in process, March 31			
Materials		?	
Conversion costs		$?	?
Total costs			$?

Instructions

(a) Materials $2.00

(a) Prepare a schedule that shows how the equivalent units were computed so that you can complete the "Quantities: Units accounted for" equivalent units section shown in the production cost report above, and compute March unit costs.

(b) Transferred out $224,400
WIP $ 29,600

(b) Complete the "Cost Reconciliation Schedule" part of the production cost report above.

Determine equivalent units and unit costs and assign costs for processes; prepare production cost report.
(LO 8), **AP**

*P16-7B   Holiday Company manufactures basketballs and soccer balls. For both products, materials are added at the beginning of the production process and conversion costs are incurred uniformly. Holiday uses the FIFO method to compute equivalent units. Production and cost data for the month of August are shown below.

Production Data—Basketballs	Units	Percent Complete	Production Data—Soccer Balls	Units	Percent Complete
Work in process units, August 1	500	60%	Work in process units, August 1	200	80%
Units started into production	2,000		Units started into production	2,000	
Work in process units, August 31	600	50%	Work in process units, August 31	150	70%

Cost Data—Basketballs		Cost Data—Soccer Balls	
Work in process, August 1	$1,125	Work in process, August 1	$ 450
Direct materials	1,600	Direct materials	2,800
Direct labor	1,280	Direct labor	1,000
Manufacturing overhead	1,000	Manufacturing overhead	1,394

Instructions

(a) Basketballs:
(1) Materials   2,000
(2) Materials $.80
(3) Transferred out $4,165
     WIP $840

(a) Calculate the following for both the basketballs and the soccer balls.
(1) The equivalent units of production for materials and conversion costs.
(2) The unit costs of production for materials and conversion costs.
(3) The assignment of costs to units transferred out and in process at the end of the accounting period.

(b) Prepare a production cost report for the month of August for the basketballs only.

Problems: Set C

Visit the book's companion website, at **www.wiley.com/college/kimmel**, and choose the Student Companion site to access Problem Set C.

Waterways Continuing Problem

(*Note:* This is a continuation of the Waterways Problem from Chapters 14 through 15.)

WCP16   Because most of the parts for its irrigation systems are standard, Waterways handles the majority of its manufacturing as a process cost system. There are multiple process departments. Three of these departments are the Molding, Cutting, and Welding departments. All items eventually end up in the Packaging department which prepares items for sale in kits or individually. This problem asks you to help Waterways calculate equivalent units and prepare a production cost report.

Go to the book's companion website, at **www.wiley.com/college/kimmel**, to see the completion of this problem.

Broadening Your Perspective

Management Decision-Making

DECISION-MAKING AT CURRENT DESIGNS

BYP16-1 Building a kayak using the composite method is a very labor-intensive process. In the fabrication department, the kayaks go through several steps as employees carefully place layers of Kevlar® in a mold and then use resin to fuse together the layers. The excess resin is removed with a vacuum process, and the upper shell and lower shell are removed from the molds and assembled. The seat, hatch, and other components are added in the finishing department.

At the beginning of April, Current Designs had 30 kayaks in process in the fabrication department. Rick Thrune, the production manager, estimated that about 80% of the material costs had been added to these boats, which were about 50% complete with respect to the conversion costs. The cost of this inventory had been calculated to be $8,400 in materials and $9,000 in conversion costs.

During April, 72 boats were started. At the end of the month, the 35 kayaks in the ending inventory had 20% of the materials and 40% of the conversion costs already added to them.

A review of the accounting records for April showed that materials with a cost of $17,500 had been requisitioned by this department and that the conversion costs for the month were $39,600.

Instructions
Complete a production cost report for April 2014 for the fabrication department using the weighted-average method.

DECISION-MAKING ACROSS THE ORGANIZATION

BYP16-2 Florida Beach Company manufactures suntan lotion, called Surtan, in 11-ounce plastic bottles. Surtan is sold in a competitive market. As a result, management is very cost-conscious. Surtan is manufactured through two processes: mixing and filling. Materials are entered at the beginning of each process, and labor and manufacturing overhead occur uniformly throughout each process. Unit costs are based on the cost per gallon of Surtan using the weighted-average costing approach.

On June 30, 2014, Mary Ritzman, the chief accountant for the past 20 years, opted to take early retirement. Her replacement, Joe Benili, had extensive accounting experience with motels in the area but only limited contact with manufacturing accounting. During July, Joe correctly accumulated the following production quantity and cost data for the Mixing Department.

Production quantities: Work in process, July 1, 8,000 gallons 75% complete; started into production 100,000 gallons; work in process, July 31, 5,000 gallons 20% complete. Materials are added at the beginning of the process.

Production costs: Beginning work in process $88,000, comprised of $21,000 of materials costs and $67,000 of conversion costs; incurred in July: materials $573,000, conversion costs $765,000.

Joe then prepared a production cost report on the basis of physical units started into production. His report showed a production cost of $14.26 per gallon of Surtan. The management of Florida Beach was surprised at the high unit cost. The president comes to you, as Mary's top assistant, to review Joe's report and prepare a correct report if necessary.

Instructions
With the class divided into groups, answer the following questions.
(a) Show how Joe arrived at the unit cost of $14.26 per gallon of Surtan.
(b) What error(s) did Joe make in preparing his production cost report?
(c) Prepare a correct production cost report for July.

MANAGERIAL ANALYSIS

BYP16-3 Harris Furniture Company manufactures living room furniture through two departments: Framing and Upholstering. Materials are entered at the beginning of each process. For May, the following cost data are obtained from the two work in process accounts.

	Framing	Upholstering
Work in process, May 1	$ –0–	$?
Materials	450,000	?
Conversion costs	261,000	330,000
Costs transferred in	–0–	600,000
Costs transferred out	600,000	?
Work in process, May 31	111,000	?

Instructions
Answer the following questions.
(a) If 3,000 sofas were started into production on May 1 and 2,500 sofas were transferred to Uphol-stering, what was the unit cost of materials for May in the Framing Department?
(b) Using the data in (a) above, what was the per unit conversion cost of the sofas transferred to Upholstering?
(c) Continuing the assumptions in (a) above, what is the percentage of completion of the units in process at May 31 in the Framing Department?

REAL-WORLD FOCUS

BYP16-4 Paintball is now played around the world. The process of making paintballs is actually quite similar to the process used to make certain medical pills. In fact, paintballs were previously often made at the same factories that made pharmaceuticals.

Address: **http://video.google.com/videoplay?docid=56864066340713942400,** or go to **www.wiley.com/college/kimmel**

Instructions
View that video at the site listed above and then answer the following questions.
(a) Describe in sequence the primary steps used to manufacture paintballs.
(b) Explain the costs incurred by the company that would fall into each of the following catego-ries: materials, labor, and overhead. Of these categories, which do you think would be the greatest cost in making paintballs?
(c) Discuss whether a paintball manufacturer would use job order costing or process costing.

Critical Thinking

COMMUNICATION ACTIVITY

BYP16-5 Diane Barone was a good friend of yours in high school and is from your home town. While you chose to major in accounting when you both went away to college, she majored in mar-keting and management. You have recently been promoted to accounting manager for the Snack Foods Division of Melton Enterprises, and your friend was promoted to regional sales manager for the same division of Melton. Diane recently telephoned you. She explained that she was familiar with job cost sheets, which had been used by the Special Projects division where she had formerly worked. She was, however, very uncomfortable with the production cost reports prepared by your division. She emailed you a list of her particular questions:

1. Since Melton occasionally prepares snack foods for special orders in the Snack Foods Division, why don't we track costs of the orders separately?
2. What is an equivalent unit?
3. Why am I getting four production cost reports? Isn't there one Work in Process account?

Instructions
Prepare a memo to Diane. Answer her questions, and include any additional information you think would be helpful. You may write informally, but do use proper grammar and punctuation.

ETHICS CASES

BYP16-6 R. B. Dillman Company manufactures a high-tech component that passes through two production processing departments, Molding and Assembly. Department managers are partially compensated on the basis of units of products completed and transferred out relative to units of product put into production. This was intended as encouragement to be efficient and to minimize waste.

Jan Wooten is the department head in the Molding Department, and Tony Ferneti is her quality control inspector. During the month of June, Jan had three new employees who were not yet technically skilled. As a result, many of the units produced in June had minor molding defects. In order to maintain the department's normal high rate of completion, Jan told Tony to pass through inspection and on to the Assembly Department all units that had defects nondetectable to the human eye. "Company and industry tolerances on this product are too high anyway," says Jan. "Less than 2% of the units we produce are subjected in the market to the stress tolerance we've designed into them. The odds of those 2% being any of this month's units are even less. Anyway, we're saving the company money."

Instructions
(a) Who are the potential stakeholders involved in this situation?
(b) What alternatives does Tony have in this situation? What might the company do to prevent this situation from occurring?

CONSIDERING PEOPLE, PLANET, AND PROFIT

BYP16-7 In a recent year, an oil refinery in Texas City, Texas, on the Houston Ship Channel exploded. The explosion killed 14 people and sent a plume of smoke hundreds of feet into the air. The blast started as a fire in the section of the plant that increased the octane of the gasoline that was produced at the refinery. The Houston Ship Channel is the main waterway that allows commerce to flow from the Gulf of Mexico into Houston.

The Texas Commission on Environmental Quality expressed concern about the release of nitrogen oxides, benzene, and other known carcinogens as a result of the blast. Neighbors of the plant complained that the plant had been emitting carcinogens for years and that the regulators had ignored their complaints about emissions and unsafe working conditions.

Instructions
(a) Outline the costs that the company now faces as a result of the accident.
(b) How could the company have reduced the costs associated with the accident?

Answers to Insight and Accounting Across the Organization Questions

p. 851 Choosing a Cost Driver Q: What is the result if a company uses the wrong "cost driver" to assign manufacturing overhead? **A:** Incorrect assignment of manufacturing overhead will result in some products receiving too much overhead and others receiving too little.

p. 855 Haven't I Seen That Before? Q: In what ways might the relative composition (materials, labor, and overhead) of a remanufactured product's cost differ from that of a newly made product? **A:** We would expect that the materials costs would be substantially reduced since the bulk of the physical product is being reused. The labor component might increase, and the level of automation might decrease, since remanufacturing a product requires identification and replacement of malfunctioning components. This process might not be as easily automated as the production of a new product.

Answers to Self-Test Questions

1. b **2.** d **3.** d **4.** b **5.** c **6.** b **7.** b $[20{,}000 + (5{,}000 \times 60\%)]$ **8.** a $(7{,}000 + 0)$ **9.** c $(23{,}000 + 3{,}000)$, $[23{,}000 + (3{,}000 \times 33\frac{1}{3}\%)]$ **10.** a $[\$60{,}000 \div (9{,}000 + 3{,}000)]$ **11.** b $[(\$10 \times 2{,}500) + (\$30 \times 2{,}500 \times 40\%)]$ **12.** b **13.** d ***14.** b $[25{,}000 + (3{,}000 \times 100\%)]$; $[(2{,}000 \times 80\%) + 25{,}000 + (3{,}000 \times 30\%)]$ ***15.** a $[\$60{,}000 \div (9{,}000 + 3{,}000)]$ ***16.** b $[(\$10 \times 2{,}500) + (\$30 \times 2{,}500 \times 40\%)]$

The Navigator

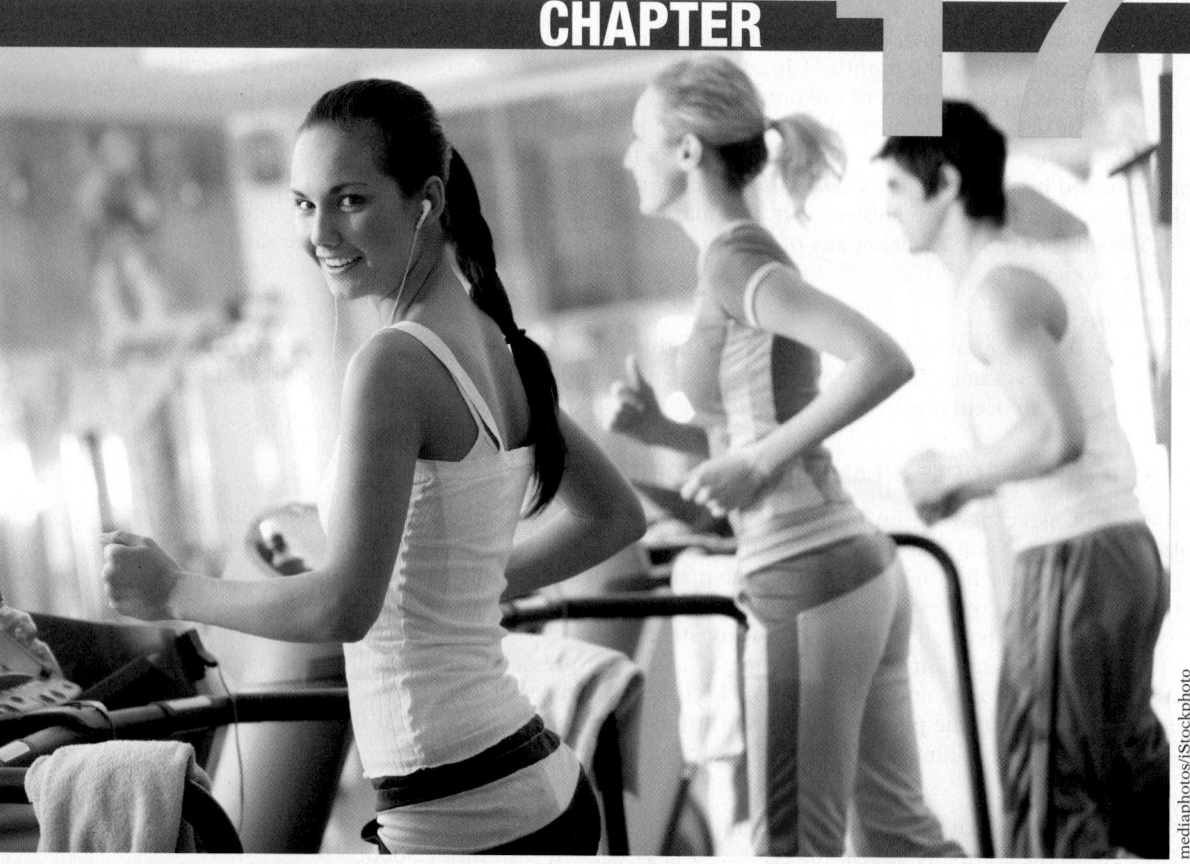

mediaphotos/iStockphoto

ACTIVITY-BASED COSTING

LEARNING OBJECTIVES

After studying this chapter, you should be able to:

1 Recognize the difference between traditional costing and activity-based costing.

2 Identify the steps in the development of an activity-based costing system.

3 Know how companies identify the activity cost pools used in activity-based costing.

4 Know how companies identify and use cost drivers in activity-based costing.

5 Understand the benefits and limitations of activity-based costing.

6 Differentiate between value-added and non–value-added activities.

7 Understand the value of using activity levels in activity-based costing.

8 Apply activity-based costing to service industries.

✔ The Navigator

Do you feel like the whole world is conspiring against your efforts to get in shape? Is it humanly possible to resist the constant barrage of advertisements and fast-food servers who pleasantly encourage us to "supersize" it? Lest we think that we have no allies in our battle against the bulge, consider Precor.

Ever since it made the first ergonomically sound rowing machine in 1980, Precor's sole mission has been to provide exercise equipment. It makes elliptical trainers, exercise bikes, rowing machines, treadmills, multistation strength systems, and many other forms of equipment designed to erase the cumulative effects of a fast-food nation. Its equipment is widely used in Hilton hotels, Gold's Gym franchises, and even in Madonna's Hard Candy fitness center in Moscow.

Building high-quality fitness equipment requires sizable investments by Precor in buildings and machinery. For example, Precor recently moved its facilities from Valencia, California, to Greensboro, North Carolina. In order to reduce costs and minimize environmental impact, the company installed low-flow water fixtures, high-efficiency heating and cooling systems, and state-of-the-art lighting in its $26 million, 230,000-square-foot facility. As a result of these efforts, Precor's new facility received a Leadership in Energy and Efficient Design (LEED) CI Gold Certification.

PRECOR IS ON YOUR SIDE

Because of its huge investments in property, plant, and equipment, overhead costs represent a large percentage of the cost of Precor's exercise equipment. The combination of high overhead costs and a wide variety of products means that it is important that Precor allocates its overhead accurately to its various products. Without accurate cost information, Precor would not know whether its elliptical trainers and recumbent bicycles are making money, whether its AMT 100i adaptive motion trainer is priced high enough to cover its costs, or if its 240i Stretchtrainer is losing money. To increase the accuracy of its costs, Precor uses a method of overhead allocation that focuses on identifying the types of activities that cause the company to incur costs. It then assigns more overhead to those products that rely most heavily on cost-incurring activities. By doing this, the allocation of overhead is less arbitrary than traditional overhead allocation methods. In short, before it can help us burn off the pounds, Precor needs to understand what drives its overhead costs.

Watch the Precor video in WileyPLUS to learn more about activity-based costing in the real world.

Source: www.precor.com.

 The Navigator

As indicated in the Feature Story about Precor, the traditional costing systems described in earlier chapters are not the best answer for every company. Because Precor suspected that the traditional system was masking significant differences in its real cost structure, it sought a new method of assigning costs. Similar searches by other companies for ways to improve operations and gather more accurate data for decision-making have resulted in the development of powerful new management tools, including **activity-based costing (ABC)**. The primary objective of this chapter is to explain and illustrate this concept.

The content and organization of this chapter are as follows.

Activity-Based Costing

Traditional Costing and ABC	Example of ABC versus Traditional Costing	ABC: A Closer Look	ABC in Service Industries
• Traditional costing • Need for a new approach • Activity-based costing	• Identify activities and allocate to cost pools • Identify cost drivers • Compute overhead rates • Assign overhead costs to products • Compare unit costs	• Benefits • Limitations • When to use ABC • Value-added versus non–value-added activities • Classification of activity levels	• Traditional costing example • ABC example

✔ The Navigator

Traditional Costing and Activity-Based Costing

LEARNING OBJECTIVE **1**

Recognize the difference between traditional costing and activity-based costing.

TRADITIONAL COSTING SYSTEMS

It is probably impossible to determine the **exact** cost of a product or service. However, in order to achieve improved management decisions, companies strive to provide decision-makers with the most accurate cost estimates they can. The most accurate estimate of product cost occurs when the costs are traceable directly to the product produced or the service provided. Direct material and direct labor costs are the easiest to trace directly to the product through the use of material requisition forms and payroll time sheets. Overhead costs, on the other hand, are an indirect or common cost that generally cannot be easily or directly traced to individual products or services. Instead, companies use estimates to assign overhead costs to products and services.

Often the most difficult part of computing accurate unit costs is determining the proper amount of **overhead cost** to assign to each product, service, or job. In our coverage of job order costing in Chapter 15 and of process costing in Chapter 16, we used a single or plantwide overhead rate throughout the year for the entire factory operation. That rate was called the **predetermined overhead rate**. For job order costing, we assumed that **direct labor cost** was the relevant activity base for assigning all overhead costs to jobs. For process costing, we assumed that **machine hours** was the relevant activity base for assigning all overhead to the process or department.

The use of direct labor as the activity base made sense when overhead cost allocation systems were first developed. At that time, direct labor made up a large portion of total manufacturing cost. Therefore, it was widely accepted that there was a high correlation between direct labor and the incurrence of overhead cost. As a result, direct labor became the most popular basis for allocating overhead.

Even in today's increasingly automated environment, direct labor is sometimes the appropriate basis for assigning overhead cost to products. It is appropriate to use direct labor when (a) direct labor constitutes a significant part of total product cost, and (b) a high correlation exists between direct labor and changes in the amount of overhead costs. Illustration 17-1 displays a simplified (one-stage) traditional costing system relying on direct labor to assign overhead.

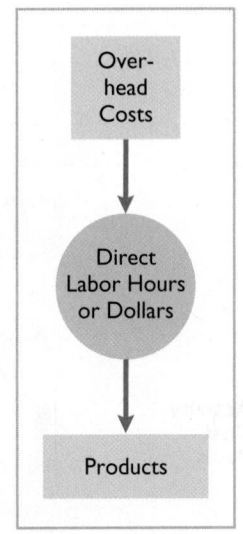

Illustration 17-1 Traditional one-stage costing system

THE NEED FOR A NEW APPROACH

In recent years, manufacturers and service providers have experienced tremendous change. Advances in computerized systems, technological innovation, global competition, and automation have changed the manufacturing environment drastically. As a result, the amount of direct labor used in many industries has greatly decreased, and total overhead costs resulting from depreciation on expensive equipment and machinery, utilities, repairs, and maintenance have significantly increased. When there is not a correlation between direct labor and overhead, it is inappropriate to use plantwide predetermined overhead rates based on direct labor. Companies that use overhead rates based on direct labor when this correlation does not exist experience significant product-cost distortions.

To avoid such distortions, many companies now use machine hours as the basis on which to allocate overhead in an automated manufacturing environment. But even machine hours may not suffice as the only plantwide basis for allocating all overhead. If the manufacturing process is complex, then only multiple allocation bases can result in more accurate product-cost computations. In such situations, managers need to consider an overhead cost allocation method that uses **multiple** bases. That method is **activity-based costing**.

ACTIVITY-BASED COSTING

Broadly, **activity-based costing (ABC)** is an approach for allocating overhead costs. More specifically, ABC allocates overhead to multiple activity cost pools, and it then assigns the activity cost pools to products and services by means of cost drivers. To understand this more clearly, we need to apply some new meanings to the rather common-sounding words that make up the definition: In activity-based costing, an **activity** is any event, action, transaction, or work sequence that incurs costs when producing a product or providing a service. An **activity cost pool** is the overhead cost attributed to a distinct type of activity (e.g., ordering materials or setting up machines). A **cost driver** is any factor or activity that has a direct cause-effect relationship with the resources consumed. The reasoning behind ABC cost allocation is simple: **Products consume activities, and activities consume resources**.

These definitions of terms will become clearer as we look more closely at how ABC works. ABC allocates overhead in a two-stage process. The first stage allocates overhead costs to activity cost pools. (Traditional costing systems, in contrast, allocate these costs to departments or to jobs.) Examples of overhead cost pools are ordering materials, setting up machines, assembling products, and inspecting products.

The second stage assigns the overhead allocated to the activity cost pools to products, using cost drivers. The cost drivers measure the number of individual activities undertaken or performed to produce products or provide services. Examples are number of purchase orders, number of setups, labor hours, and number of inspections. Illustration 17-2 shows examples of activities, and possible cost drivers to measure them, for a company that manufactures two types of abdominal exercise equipment—Ab Benches and Ab Coasters.

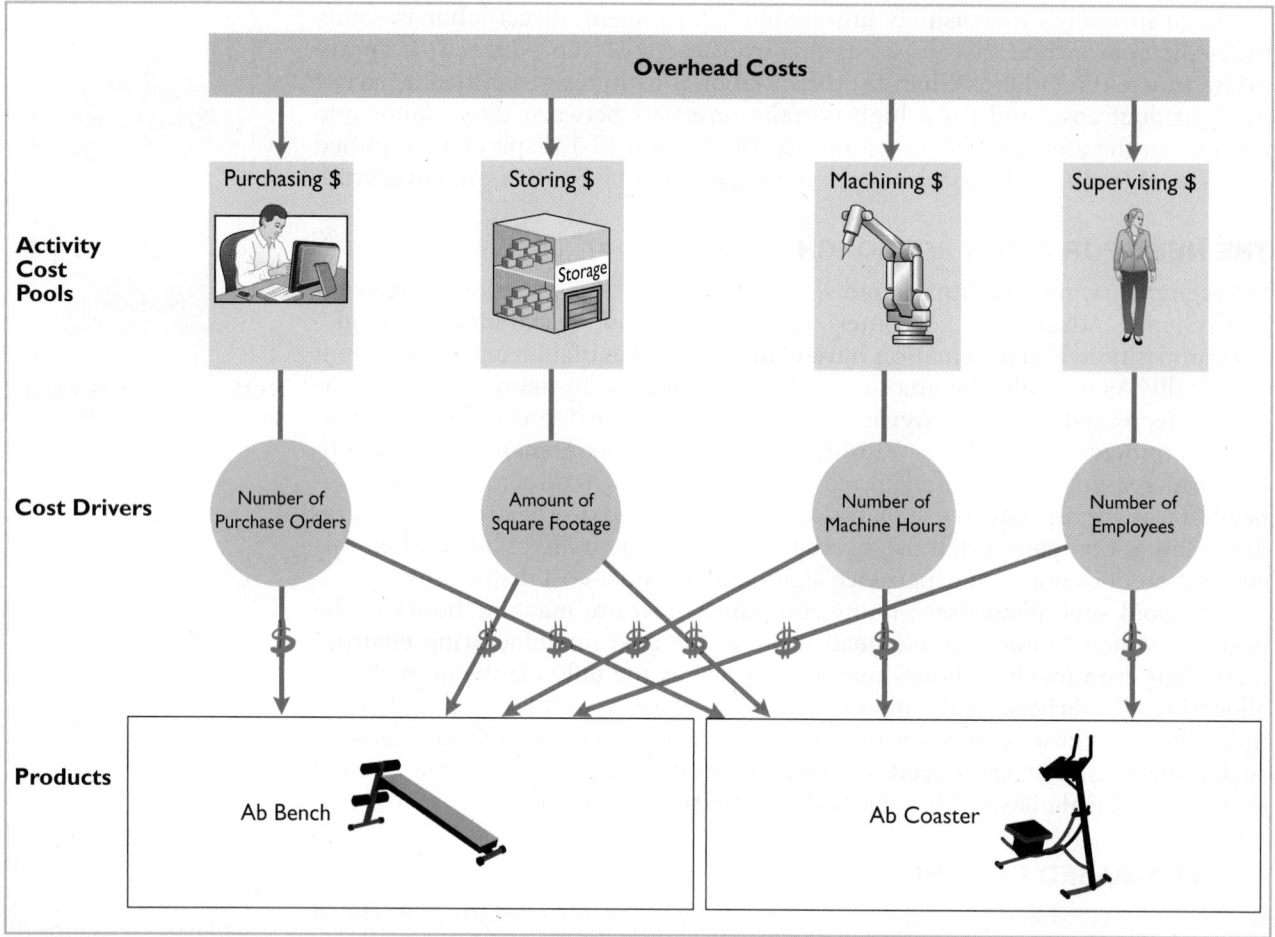

Illustration 17-2 Activities and related cost drivers

In the first step (as shown at the top of Illustration 17-2), the company allocates overhead costs to activity cost pools. In this simplified example, the company has identified four activity cost pools: purchasing, storing, machining, and supervising. After the costs are allocated to the activity cost pools, the company uses cost drivers to determine the costs to assign to the individual products based on each product's use of each activity. For example, if Ab Benches require more activity by the purchasing department, as measured by the number of required purchase orders, then more of the overhead costs from the purchasing pool are allocated to the Ab Benches.

The more complex a product's manufacturing operation, the more activities and cost drivers it is likely to have. If there is little or no correlation between changes in the cost driver and consumption of the overhead cost, inaccurate product costs are inevitable.

Illustration 17-3 shows the design of a more complex activity-based costing system with seven activity cost pools for Lift Jack Company. Lift Jack Company manufactures two automotive jacks—an automobile scissors jack and a truck hydraulic jack.

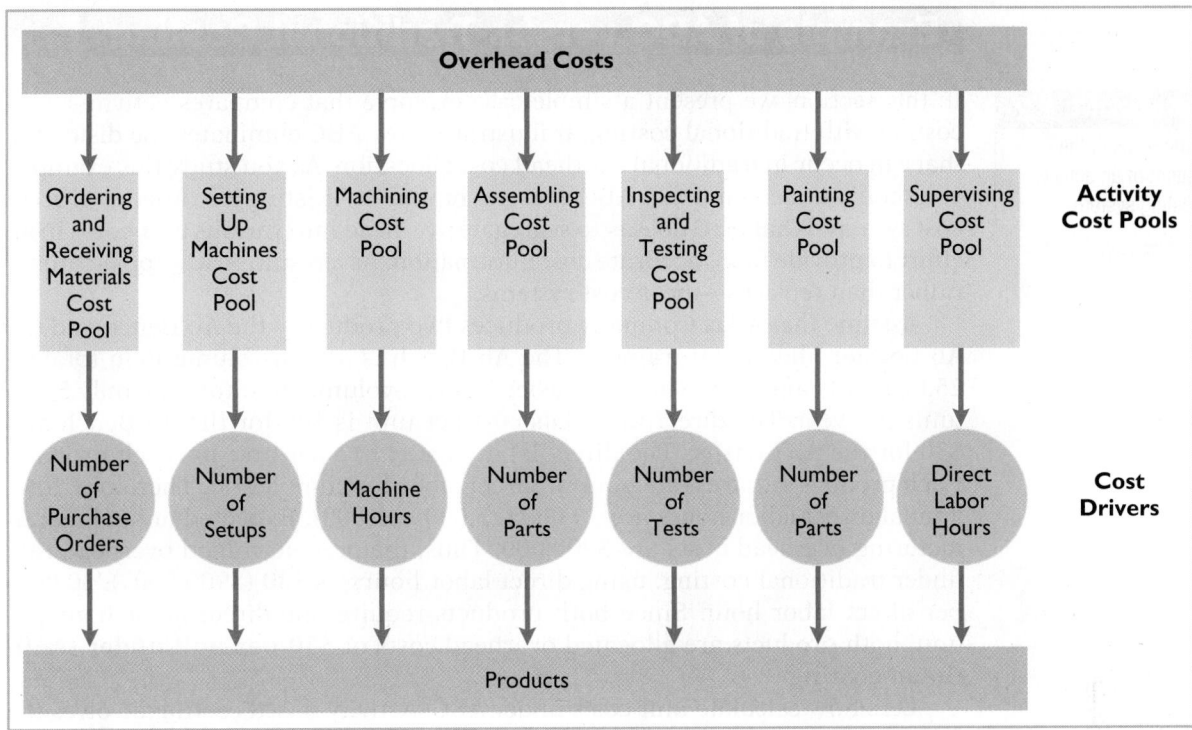

Illustration 17-3 ABC system design—Lift Jack Company

The Lift Jack Company illustration contains seven activity cost pools. In some companies, the number of activities can be substantial. For example, Clark-Hurth (a division of Clark Equipment Company), a manufacturer of axles and transmissions, identified over 170 activities. Compumotor (a division of Parker Hannifin) identified over 80 activities in just the procurement function of its Material Control Department.

Do it!

Indicate whether the following statements are true or false.

COSTING SYSTEMS

1. A traditional costing system allocates overhead by means of multiple overhead rates.
2. Activity-based costing allocates overhead costs in a two-stage process.
3. Direct material and direct labor costs are easier to trace to products than overhead.
4. As manufacturing processes have become more automated, more companies have chosen to allocate overhead on the basis of direct labor costs.
5. In activity-based costing, an activity is any event, action, transaction, or work sequence that incurs cost when producing a product.

Action Plan

- Understand that a traditional costing system allocates overhead on the basis of a single predetermined overhead rate.
- Understand that an ABC system allocates overhead to identified activity cost pools, and then assigns costs to products using related cost drivers that measure the resources consumed.

Solution

1. False.	2. True.	3. True.	4. False.	5. True.

Related exercise material: **BE17-1, BE17-2, E17-1,** and **Do it!** **17-1.**

Example of ABC versus Traditional Costing

In this section, we present a simple case example that compares activity-based costing with traditional costing. It illustrates how ABC eliminates the distortion that can occur in traditional overhead cost allocation. As you study this example, you should understand that ABC does not replace an existing job order or process cost system. What ABC does is to segregate overhead into various cost pools in an effort to provide more accurate cost information. As a result, ABC supplements—rather than replaces—these cost systems.

Assume that Atlas Company produces two products—the Ab Bench and the Ab Coaster abdominal trainers. The Ab Bench is a high-volume item totaling 25,000 units annually. The Ab Coaster is a low-volume item totaling only 5,000 units per year. The direct materials cost per unit is $40 for the Ab Bench and $30 for the Ab Coaster. The direct labor cost is $12 per unit for each product. Each product requires one hour of direct labor for completion. Therefore, total annual direct labor hours are 30,000 (25,000 + 5,000). Expected annual manufacturing overhead costs are $900,000. Thus, the predetermined overhead rate under traditional costing, using direct labor hours, is $30 ($900,000 ÷ 30,000) per direct labor hour. Since both products require one direct labor hour per unit, both products are allocated overhead costs of **$30 per unit under traditional costing**.

Let's now calculate unit costs under ABC. Activity-based costing involves the following four steps.

1. **Identify and classify the activities** involved in the manufacture of specific products, and **allocate overhead to cost pools**.

2. **Identify the cost driver** that has a strong correlation to the costs accumulated in the cost pool.

3. **Compute the activity-based overhead rate** for each cost driver.

4. **Assign overhead costs to products**, using the overhead rates determined for each cost pool (cost per driver).

IDENTIFY AND CLASSIFY ACTIVITIES AND ALLOCATE OVERHEAD TO COST POOLS (STEP 1)

Activity-based costing starts with an analysis of the activities performed to manufacture a product or provide a service. This analysis should identify all resource-consuming activities. It requires documenting every activity undertaken to accomplish a task. Atlas Company identified three activity cost pools: setting up machines, machining, and inspecting.

Next, the system assigns overhead costs directly to the appropriate activity cost pool. For example, all overhead costs directly associated with Atlas Company's machine setups (such as salaries, supplies, and depreciation) would be assigned to the machine setup cost pool. Illustration 17-4 shows the three cost pools, along with the estimated overhead allocated to each cost pool.

Illustration 17-4 Activity cost pools and estimated overhead

Activity Cost Pools	Estimated Overhead
Setting up machines	$300,000
Machining	500,000
Inspecting	100,000
Total	$ 900,000

IDENTIFY COST DRIVERS (STEP 2)

After costs are allocated to the activity cost pools, the company must identify the cost drivers for each cost pool. The cost driver must accurately measure the actual consumption of the activity by the various products. To achieve accurate costing, a **high degree of correlation** must exist between the cost driver and the actual consumption of the overhead costs in the cost pool.

Illustration 17-5 shows the cost drivers identified by Atlas and their total expected use per activity cost pool.

LEARNING OBJECTIVE 4

Know how companies identify and use cost drivers in activity-based costing.

Illustration 17-5 Cost drivers and their expected use

Activity Cost Pools	Cost Drivers	Expected Use of Cost Drivers per Activity
Setting up machines	Number of setups	1,500 setups
Machining	Machine hours	50,000 machine hours
Inspecting	Number of inspections	2,000 inspections

Availability and ease of obtaining data relating to the cost driver is an important factor that must be considered in its selection.

COMPUTE ACTIVITY-BASED OVERHEAD RATES (STEP 3)

Next, the company computes an **activity-based overhead rate** per cost driver by dividing the estimated overhead per activity by the number of cost drivers expected to be used per activity. Illustration 17-6 shows the formula for this computation.

Illustration 17-6 Formula for computing activity-based overhead rate

$$\frac{\text{Estimated Overhead per Activity}}{\text{Expected Use of Cost Drivers per Activity}} = \begin{array}{c}\text{Activity-Based}\\\text{Overhead Rate}\end{array}$$

Atlas Company computes its activity-based overhead rates by using the estimated overhead per activity cost pool, shown in Illustration 17-4, and the expected use of cost drivers per activity, shown in Illustration 17-5. These computations are presented in Illustration 17-7.

Illustration 17-7 Computation of activity-based overhead rates

Activity Cost Pools	Estimated Overhead	÷	Expected Use of Cost Drivers per Activity	=	Activity-Based Overhead Rates
Setting up machines	$300,000		1,500 setups		$200 per setup
Machining	500,000		50,000 machine hours		$10 per machine hour
Inspecting	100,000		2,000 inspections		$50 per inspection
Total	$900,000				

ASSIGN OVERHEAD COSTS TO PRODUCTS (STEP 4)

In assigning overhead costs, it is necessary to know the expected use of cost drivers **for each product**. Because of its low volume, the Ab Coaster requires more setups and inspections than the Ab Bench. Illustration 17-8 (page 902) shows the expected use of cost drivers per product for each of Atlas's products.

Illustration 17-8 Expected use of cost drivers per product

Activity Cost Pools	Cost Drivers	Expected Use of Cost Drivers per Activity	Expected Use of Cost Drivers per Product	
			Ab Bench	**Ab Coaster**
Setting up machines	Number of setups	1,500 setups	500	1,000
Machining	Machine hours	50,000 machine hours	30,000	20,000
Inspecting	Number of inspections	2,000 inspections	500	1,500

To assign overhead costs to each product, Atlas multiplies the activity-based overhead rates per cost driver (Illustration 17-7, page 901) by the number of cost drivers expected to be used per product (Illustration 17-8). Illustration 17-9 shows the overhead cost assigned to each product.

Illustration 17-9 Assignment of activity cost pools to products

Atlas Company.xls

Activity Cost Pools	Ab Bench			Ab Coaster		
	Expected Use of Cost Drivers per Product ×	Activity-Based Overhead Rates =	Cost Assigned	Expected Use of Cost Drivers per Product ×	Activity-Based Overhead Rates =	Cost Assigned
Setting up machines	500	$200	$100,000	1,000	$200	$200,000
Machining	30,000	$10	300,000	20,000	$10	200,000
Inspecting	500	$50	25,000	1,500	$50	75,000
Total costs assigned [(a)]			$425,000			$475,000
Units produced [(b)]			25,000			5,000
Overhead cost per unit [(a)÷(b)]			$17			$95

Under ABC, the overhead cost per unit is $17 for the Ab Bench and $95 for the Ab Coaster. When compared to the $30 per unit overhead charge under traditional costing, ABC shifts costs from the high-volume product (Ab Bench) to the low-volume product (Ab Coaster). This shift occurs because low-volume products often require more special handling, such as machine setups and inspections. This is true for Atlas Company. Thus, the low-volume product frequently is responsible for more overhead costs per unit than is a high-volume product.[1] Assigning overhead using ABC will usually increase the cost per unit for low-volume products as compared to a traditional overhead allocation. Therefore, traditional cost drivers such as direct labor hours are usually not appropriate for assigning overhead costs to low-volume products.

---

[1]Robin Cooper and Robert S. Kaplan, "How Cost Accounting Distorts Product Costs," *Management Accounting* 69, No. 10 (April 1988), pp. 20–27.

COMPARING UNIT COSTS

Illustration 17-10 shows the unit cost for each product under traditional costing.

Illustration 17-10 Computation of unit costs—traditional costing

	Products	
Manufacturing Costs	**Ab Bench**	**Ab Coaster**
Direct materials	$40	$30
Direct labor	12	12
Overhead	30*	30*
Total unit cost	$82	$72

*Predetermined overhead rate × Direct labor hours = $30 × 1 hr. = $30

A comparison of unit manufacturing costs under traditional costing and ABC shows the following significant differences.

Illustration 17-11 Comparison of unit product costs

	Ab Bench		Ab Coaster	
Manufacturing Costs	**Traditional Costing**	**ABC**	**Traditional Costing**	**ABC**
Direct materials	$40	$40	$30	$ 30
Direct labor	12	12	12	12
Overhead	30	17*	30	95*
Total cost per unit	$82	$69	$72	$137
		Overstated $13		Understated $65

*Overhead per Illustration 17-9

The comparison shows that unit costs under traditional costing are significantly distorted. The cost of producing the Ab Bench is overstated by $13 per unit ($82 − $69), and the cost of producing the Ab Coaster is understated by $65 per unit ($137 − $72). These differences are attributable entirely to how Atlas Company assigns manufacturing overhead. A likely consequence of the differences in assigning overhead is that Atlas has been overpricing the Ab Bench and possibly losing market share to competitors. It also has been sacrificing profitability by underpricing the Ab Coaster.

Activity-based costing was pioneered in the United States: John Deere Company coined the term about 25 years ago. Numerous well-known U.S. companies, including IBM, AT&T, Hewlett-Packard, Procter & Gamble, Tektronix, Hughes Aircraft, Caterpillar, and American Express, have adopted ABC. Its use outside the United States, however, is limited. The cost of implementation may discourage some foreign companies.

In Japan, activity-based costing is less widely used. Companies prefer volume measures such as direct labor hours to assign overhead cost to products. Japanese managers are convinced that reducing direct labor is essential to continuous cost reduction. Using direct labor as the basis for overhead allocation forces Japanese companies to watch direct labor more closely.

Oleksiy Maksymenko Photography/
Alamy

Service Company Insight
Traveling Light

Have you flown on an airplane since baggage fees have been implemented? Did the fee make you so mad that you swore that the next time you flew, you would pack fewer clothes so you could use a carry-on bag instead? That is exactly how the airlines hoped that you would react. Baggage handling is extremely labor-intensive. All that tagging, sorting, loading on carts, loading in planes, unloading, and sorting again add up to about $9 per bag. They also have equipment costs: sorters, carts, conveyors, tractors, and storage facilities. That's about another $4 of equipment-related overhead per bag. Finally, there is additional fuel cost of a 40-pound item—about $2 in fuel for a 3-hour flight. These costs add up to $15 ($9 + $4 + $2). Since airlines have implemented their baggage fees, fewer customers are checking bags. Not only does this save the airlines money, it also increases the amount of space available for hauling cargo. An airline can charge at least $80 for hauling a small parcel for same-day delivery service.

Source: Scott McCartney, "What It Costs an Airline to Fly Your Luggage," *Wall Street Journal Online* (November 25, 2008).

? Why do airlines charge even higher rates for heavier bags, bags that are odd shapes (e.g., ski bags), and bags with hazardous materials in them? (see page 943.)

APPLY ABC

 Do it! Casey Company has five activity cost pools and two products. It expects to produce 200,000 units of its automobile scissors jack and 80,000 units of its truck hydraulic jack. Having identified its activity cost pools and the cost drivers for each cost pool, Casey Company accumulated the following data relative to those activity cost pools and cost drivers.

	Annual Overhead Data			Expected Use of Cost Drivers per Product	
Activity Cost Pools	**Cost Drivers**	**Estimated Overhead**	**Expected Use of Cost Drivers per Activity**	**Scissors Jacks**	**Hydraulic Jacks**
Ordering and receiving	Purchase orders	$ 200,000	2,500 orders	1,000	1,500
Machine setup	Setups	600,000	1,200 setups	500	700
Machining	Machine hours	2,000,000	800,000 hours	300,000	500,000
Assembling	Parts	1,800,000	3,000,000 parts	1,800,000	1,200,000
Inspecting and testing	Tests	700,000	35,000 tests	20,000	15,000
		$5,300,000			

Using the above data, do the following.

(a) Prepare a schedule showing the computations of the activity-based overhead rates per cost driver.

(b) Prepare a schedule assigning each activity's overhead cost to the two products.

(c) Compute the overhead cost per unit for each product.

(d) Comment on the comparative overhead cost per unit.

Solution

(a) Computations of activity-based overhead rates per cost driver:

Activity Cost Pools	Estimated Overhead	÷	Expected Use of Cost Drivers per Activity	=	Activity-Based Overhead Rates
Ordering and receiving	$ 200,000		2,500 purchase orders		$80 per order
Machine setup	600,000		1,200 setups		$500 per setup
Machining	2,000,000		800,000 machine hours		$2.50 per machine hour
Assembling	1,800,000		3,000,000 parts		$0.60 per part
Inspecting and testing	700,000		35,000 tests		$20 per test
	$5,300,000				

(b) Assignment of each activity's overhead cost to products using ABC:

Activity Cost Pools	Scissors Jacks Expected Use of Cost Drivers per Product	×	Activity-Based Overhead Rates	=	Cost Assigned	Hydraulic Jacks Expected Use of Cost Drivers per Product	×	Activity-Based Overhead Rates	=	Cost Assigned
Ordering and receiving	1,000		$80		$ 80,000	1,500		$80		$ 120,000
Machine setup	500		$500		250,000	700		$500		350,000
Machining	300,000		$2.50		750,000	500,000		$2.50		1,250,000
Assembling	1,800,000		$0.60		1,080,000	1,200,000		$0.60		720,000
Inspecting and testing	20,000		$20		400,000	15,000		$20		300,000
Total assigned costs					$2,560,000					$2,740,000

(c) Computation of overhead cost per unit:

	Scissors Jack	Hydraulic Jack
Total costs assigned	$2,560,000	$2,740,000
Total units produced	200,000	80,000
Overhead cost per unit	$12.80	$34.25

(d) These data show that the total overhead assigned to 80,000 hydraulic jacks exceeds the overhead assigned to 200,000 scissors jacks. The overhead cost per hydraulic jack is $34.25, but it is only $12.80 per scissors jack.

Related exercise material: **BE17-5, BE17-6, BE17-7, E17-1, E17-2, E17-3, E17-4, E17-5, E17-6, E17-11, and Do it! 17-2.**

✔ The Navigator

Activity-Based Costing: A Closer Look

As the use of activity-based costing has grown, both its practical benefits and its limitations have become apparent.

BENEFITS OF ABC

The primary benefit of ABC is **more accurate product costing**. Here's why:

1. **ABC leads to more cost pools** being used to assign overhead costs to products. Instead of one plantwide pool (or even departmental pools) and a single cost driver, companies use numerous activity cost pools with more relevant cost drivers. Costs are assigned more directly on the basis of the cost drivers used to produce each product.

2. **ABC leads to enhanced control over overhead costs.** Under ABC, companies can trace many overhead costs directly to activities—allowing some indirect

costs to be identified as direct costs. Thus, managers have become more aware of their responsibility to control the activities that generate those costs.

3. **ABC leads to better management decisions.** More accurate product costing should contribute to setting selling prices that can help achieve desired product profitability levels. In addition, more accurate cost data could be helpful in deciding whether to make or buy a product part or component, and sometimes even whether to eliminate a product.

Activity-based costing does not change the amount of overhead costs. What it does do is allocate those overhead costs in a more accurate manner. Furthermore, if the scorekeeping is more realistic and more accurate, managers should be able to better understand cost behavior and overall profitability.

LIMITATIONS OF ABC

Although ABC systems often provide better product cost data than traditional volume-based systems, there are limitations:

1. **ABC can be expensive to use.** The increased cost of identifying multiple activities and applying numerous cost drivers discourages many companies from using ABC. Activity-based costing systems are more complex than traditional costing systems—sometimes significantly more complex. So companies must ask, is the cost of implementation greater than the benefit of greater accuracy? Sometimes it may be. For some companies, there may be no need to consider ABC at all because their existing system is sufficient. If the costs of ABC outweigh the benefits, then the company should not implement ABC.

2. **Some arbitrary allocations continue.** Even though more overhead costs can be assigned directly to products through ABC's multiple activity cost pools, certain overhead costs remain to be allocated by means of some arbitrary volume-based cost driver such as labor or machine hours.

©kryczka/iStockphoto

Service Company Insight
Using ABC to Aid in Employee Evaluation

Although most publicized ABC applications are in manufacturing companies or large service firms, very small service businesses can apply it also. Mahany Welding Supply, a small family-run welding service business in Rochester, New York, used ABC to determine the cost of servicing customers and to identify feasible cost-reduction opportunities.

Application of ABC at Mahany Welding's operations provided information about the five employees who were involved in different activities of revenue generation—i.e., delivery of supplies (rural versus city), welding services, repairs, telephone sales, field or door-to-door sales, repeat business sales, and cold-call sales. Managers applied activity cost pools to the five revenue-producing employees using relevant cost drivers. ABC revealed annual net income (loss) by employee as follows.

Employee #1	$65,431	Employee #4	$(10,957)
Employee #2	$35,154	Employee #5	$(46,180)
Employee #3	$13,731		

This comparative information was an eye-opener to the owner of Mahany Welding—who was Employee #5!

Source: Michael Krupnicki and Thomas Tyson, "Using ABC to Determine the Cost of Servicing Customers," *Management Accounting* (December 31, 1997), pp. 40–46.

? What positive implications does application of ABC have for the employees of this company? (See page 943.)

WHEN TO USE ABC

How does a company know when to use ABC? The presence of one or more of the following factors would point to its possible use:

1. Product lines differ greatly in volume and manufacturing complexity.
2. Product lines are numerous and diverse, and they require differing degrees of support services.
3. Overhead costs constitute a significant portion of total costs.
4. The manufacturing process or the number of products has changed significantly—for example, from labor-intensive to capital-intensive due to automation.
5. Production or marketing managers are ignoring data provided by the existing system and are instead using "bootleg" costing data or other alternative data when pricing or making other product decisions.

The redesign and installation of a product costing system is a significant decision that requires considerable cost and a major effort to accomplish. Therefore, financial managers need to be very cautious and deliberate when initiating changes in costing systems. A key factor in implementing a successful ABC system is the support of top management.

DECISION TOOLKIT

DECISION CHECKPOINTS	INFO NEEDED FOR DECISION	TOOL TO USE FOR DECISION	HOW TO EVALUATE RESULTS
When should we use ABC?	Knowledge of the products or product lines, the manufacturing process, and overhead costs	A detailed and accurate cost accounting system; cooperation between accountants and operating managers	Compare the results under both costing systems. If managers are better able to understand and control their operations using ABC, and the costs are not prohibitive, use of ABC would be beneficial.

VALUE-ADDED VERSUS NON–VALUE-ADDED ACTIVITIES

Some companies that have experienced the benefits of activity-based costing have applied it to a broader range of management activities. **Activity-based management (ABM)** extends the use of ABC from product costing to a comprehensive management tool that focuses on reducing costs and improving processes and decision-making. A refinement of activity-based costing used in ABM is the classification of activities as either value-added or non–value-added.

Value-added activities are those activities of **a company's operations** that increase the perceived worth of a product or service to customers. Examples for the manufacture of Precor exercise equipment include engineering design, machining, assembly, and painting. Examples of value-added activities in a service company include performing surgery at a hospital, providing legal research at a law firm, or delivering packages by a freight company.

Non–value-added activities are those activities that, if eliminated, would not hinder the company's operations or reduce the perceived worth of its product or service. These activities simply **add cost to, or increase the time spent on, a product or service without increasing its perceived value**. One example is inventory storage. If a company eliminated the need to store inventory (for

LEARNING OBJECTIVE 6

Differentiate between value-added and non–value-added activities.

example, through just-in-time inventory processes), it would not hinder its operations or reduce the worth of its product, but it would decrease its product costs. Other examples include moving materials, work in process, or finished goods from one location to another in the plant during the production process; waiting for manufacturing equipment to become available; inspecting goods; and fixing defective goods under warranty.

Companies often use **activity flowcharts** to help identify the ABC activities. Illustration 17-12 shows an activity flowchart. The top part of this flowchart identifies activities as value-added or non–value-added. The value-added activities are highlighted in red. Two rows in the lower part of the flowchart show the number of days spent on each activity. The first row shows the number of days spent on each activity under the current manufacturing process. The second row shows the number of days expected to be spent on each activity under management's proposed reengineered manufacturing process.

HEARTLAND COMPANY
Activity Flowchart

Activities

NVA	NVA	NVA	NVA	VA		NVA	NVA	VA	NVA	NVA	NVA	VA
Receive and Inspect Materials	Move and Store Materials	Move Materials to Production and Wait	Set Up Machines	Machining: Drill	Machining: Lathe	Inspect	Move and Wait	Assembly	Inspect and Test	Move to Storage	Store Finished Goods	Package and Ship

| Current Days | 1 | 12 | 2.5 | 1.5 | 2 | 1 | 0.2 | 6 | 2 | 0.3 | 0.5 | 14 | 1 |

◄──────────── *Total Current Average Time = 44 days* ────────────►

| Proposed Days | 1 | 4 | 1.5 | 1.5 | 2 | 1 | 0.2 | 2 | 2 | 0.3 | 0.5 | 10 | 1 |

◄──────────── *Total Proposed Average Time = 27 days* ────────────►

Proposed reduction in non–value-added time = 17 days

VA = Value-added   NVA = Non–value-added

Illustration 17-12 Flowchart showing value-added and non–value-added activities

The proposed changes would reduce time spent on non–value-added activities by 17 days. This 17-day improvement would be due entirely to moving inventory more quickly through the non–value-added processes—that is, by reducing inventory time in moving, storage, and waiting. The appendix at the end of this chapter discusses a just-in-time inventory system, which some companies use to eliminate non–value-added activities related to inventory.

Not all activities labeled non–value-added are totally wasteful, nor can they be totally eliminated. For example, although inspection time is a non–value-added activity from a customer's perspective, few companies would eliminate their quality control functions. Similarly, moving and waiting time is non–value-added, but it would be impossible to completely eliminate. Nevertheless, when managers recognize the non–value-added characteristic of these activities, they are motivated to minimize them as much as possible. Attention to such matters is part of the growing practice of activity-based management, which helps managers concentrate on **continuous improvement** of operations and activities.

Management Insight

What Does NASCAR Have to Do with Breakfast Cereal?

Often the best way to improve a process is to learn from observing a different process. Production-line technicians from giant food producer General Mills were flown to North Carolina to observe firsthand how race-car pit crews operate. In a NASCAR race, the value-added activity is driving toward the finish line; any time spent in the pit is non–value-added. Every split second saved in the pit increases the chances of winning. From what the General Mills' technicians learned at the car race, as well as other efforts, they were able to reduce setup time from 5 hours to just 20 minutes.

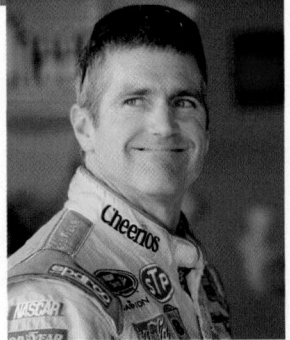

Sam Greenwood/Getty Images, Inc.

? What are the benefits of reducing setup time? (See page 943.)

 Do it!   Classify each of the following activities within a water-ski manufacturer as value-added (VA) or non–value-added (NVA).

1. Inspecting completed skis.
2. Storing raw materials.
3. Machine setups.
4. Installing bindings on skis.
5. Packaging skis for shipment.
6. Reworking defective skis.

Solution

> 1. NVA.   2. NVA.   3. NVA.   4. VA.   5. VA.   6. NVA.

Related exercise material: **BE17-8, BE17-9, E17-13, E17-14, E17-15, E17-16,** and **Do it!** **17-3.**

VALUE-ADDED ACTIVITIES

Action Plan

- Recognize that value-added activities increase the worth of a product or service to customers.
- Understand that non–value-added activities simply add cost to or increase the time spent on a product or service without increasing its market value.

✔ The Navigator

DECISION TOOLKIT

DECISION CHECKPOINTS	INFO NEEDED FOR DECISION	TOOL TO USE FOR DECISION	HOW TO EVALUATE RESULTS
How can activity-based management help managers?	Activities classified as value-added and non–value-added	Activity flowchart	The flowchart should motivate managers to minimize non–value-added activities. Managers should better understand the relationship between activities and the resources they consume.

CLASSIFICATION OF ACTIVITY LEVELS

As mentioned earlier, traditional costing systems are volume-driven—driven by unit-based cost drivers such as direct labor or machine hours. Some activity costs are strictly variable and are caused by the production or acquisition of a single unit of product or the performance of a single unit of service. However, the recognition that other activity costs are not driven by unit-based cost drivers has led to the development of a classification of ABC activities consisting of four levels, as follows.

LEARNING OBJECTIVE   7

Understand the value of using activity levels in activity-based costing.

1. **Unit-level activities** are performed for each unit of production. For example, the assembly of cell phones is a unit-level activity because the amount of assembly the company performs increases with each additional cell phone assembled.

2. **Batch-level activities** are performed every time a company produces another batch of a product. For example, suppose that to start processing a new batch of ice cream, an ice cream producer needs to set up its machines. The amount of time spent setting up machines increases with the number of batches produced, not with the number of units produced.

3. **Product-level activities** are performed every time a company produces a new type of product. For example, before a pharmaceutical company can produce and sell a new type of medicine, it must undergo very substantial product tests to ensure the product is effective and safe. The amount of time spent on testing activities increases with the number of products the company produces.

4. **Facility-level activities** are required to support or sustain an entire production process. Consider, for example, a hospital. The hospital building must be insured and heated, and the property taxes must be paid, no matter how many patients the hospital treats. These costs do not vary as a function of the number of units, batches, or products.

Companies may achieve greater accuracy in overhead cost allocation by recognizing these four different levels of activities and, from them, developing specific activity cost pools and their related cost drivers. Illustration 17-13 graphically displays this four-level activity hierarchy, along with the types of activities and examples of cost drivers for those activities at each level.

Illustration 17-13 Hierarchy of activity levels

Four Levels	Types of Activities	Examples of Cost Drivers
Unit-Level Activities		
	Machine-related Drilling, cutting, milling, trimming, pressing	Machine hours
	Labor-related Assembling, painting, sanding, sewing	Direct labor hours or cost
Batch-Level Activities		
	Equipment setups	Number of setups or setup time
	Purchase ordering	Number of purchase orders
	Inspection	Number of inspections or inspection time
	Material handling	Number of material moves
Product-Level Activities		
	Product design	Number of product designs
	Engineering changes	Number of changes
Facility-Level Activities		
	Plant management salaries	Number of employees managed
	Plant depreciation	Square footage
	Property taxes	Square footage
	Utilities	Square footage

This classification provides managers a structured way of thinking about the relationships between activities and the resources they consume. In contrast, traditional volume-based costing recognizes only unit-level costs. **Failure to recognize this classification of activities is one of the reasons that volume-based cost allocation causes distortions in product costing.**

As indicated earlier, allocating all overhead costs by unit-based cost drivers can send false signals to managers: Dividing batch-, product-, or facility-level costs by the number of units produced gives the mistaken impression that these costs vary with the number of units. **The resources consumed by batch-, product-, and facility-level supporting activities do not vary at the unit level**, nor can managers control them at the unit level. The number of activities performed at the batch level goes up as the **number of batches** rises—not as the number of units within the batches changes. Similarly, the number of product-level activities performed depends on the **number of different products**—not on how many units or batches are produced. Furthermore, facility-sustaining activity costs are not dependent upon the number of products, batches, or units produced. Companies can control batch-, product-, and facility-level costs only by modifying batch-, product-, and facility-level activities.

Do it!

Morgan Toy Company manufactures six primary product lines of toys in its Morganville plant. As a result of an activity analysis, the accounting department has identified eight activity cost pools. Each of the toy products is produced in large batches, with the whole plant devoted to one product at a time. Classify each of the following activities as either unit-level, batch-level, product-level, or facility-level: (a) engineering design, (b) machine setup, (c) toy design, (d) interviews of prospective employees, (e) inspections after each setup, (f) polishing parts, (g) assembling parts, (h) health and safety.

Solution

> (a) product-level. (b) batch-level. (c) product-level. (d) facility-level. (e) batch-level. (f) unit-level. (g) unit-level. (h) facility-level.

Related exercise material: **BE17-10, BE17-11, BE17-12, E17-15, E17-16,** and **Do it! 17-4.**

CLASSIFY ACTIVITY LEVELS

Action Plan

- You should use: **unit-level** activities for each unit of product; **batch-level** activities for each batch of product; **product-level** activities for an entire product line; and **facility-level** activities for across the entire range of products.

✔The Navigator

Activity-Based Costing in Service Industries

Although initially developed and implemented by manufacturers, activity-based costing has been widely adopted in service industries as well. ABC is used by airlines, railroads, hotels, hospitals, banks, insurance companies, telephone companies, and financial services firms. The overall objective of ABC in service firms is no different than it is in a manufacturing company. That objective is to identify the key activities that generate costs and to keep track of how many of those activities are performed for each service provided (by job, service, contract, or customer).

The general approach to identifying activities, activity cost pools, and cost drivers is the same for service companies and for manufacturers. Also, the labeling of activities as value-added and non–value-added, and the attempt to reduce or eliminate non–value-added activities as much as possible, is just as valid in service industries as in manufacturing operations. What sometimes makes implementation of activity-based costing difficult in service industries is that, compared to

LEARNING OBJECTIVE **8**

Apply activity-based costing to service industries.

manufacturers, **a larger proportion of overhead costs are company-wide costs** that cannot be directly traced to specific services provided by the company.

To illustrate the application of activity-based costing to a service company, contrasted to traditional costing, we use a public accounting firm. This illustration is equally applicable to a law firm, consulting firm, architect, or any service firm that performs numerous services for a client as part of a job.

TRADITIONAL COSTING EXAMPLE

Assume that the public accounting firm of Check and Doublecheck prepares the condensed annual budget shown in Illustration 17-14. The firm engages in a number of services, including audit, tax, and computer consulting.

Illustration 17-14 Condensed annual budget of a service firm under traditional costing

CHECK AND DOUBLECHECK, CPAs
Annual Budget

Revenue		$4,000,000
Direct labor	$1,200,000	
Overhead (expected)	600,000	
Total costs		1,800,000
Operating income		$2,200,000

$$\frac{\text{Estimated overhead}}{\text{Direct labor cost}} = \text{Predetermined overhead rate}$$

$$\frac{\$600,000}{\$1,200,000} = 50\%$$

Direct labor is the professional service performed. Under traditional costing, direct labor is the basis for overhead application to each job. As shown in Illustration 17-14, the predetermined overhead rate of 50% is calculated by dividing the total estimated overhead costs by the total direct labor cost. To determine the operating income earned on any job, Check and Doublecheck applies overhead at the rate of 50% of actual direct professional labor costs incurred. For example, assume that Check and Doublecheck records $140,000 of actual direct professional labor cost during its audit of Plano Molding Company, which was billed an audit fee of $260,000. Under traditional costing, using 50% as the rate for applying overhead to the job, Check and Doublecheck would compute applied overhead and operating income related to the Plano Molding Company audit, as shown in Illustration 17-15.

Illustration 17-15 Overhead applied under traditional costing system

CHECK AND DOUBLECHECK, CPAs
Plano Molding Company Audit

Revenue		$260,000
Less: Direct professional labor	$140,000	
Applied overhead (50% × $140,000)	70,000	210,000
Operating income		$ 50,000

This example, under traditional costing, uses only one direct cost item and one overhead application rate.

ACTIVITY-BASED COSTING EXAMPLE

Under **activity-based costing**, Check and Doublecheck distributes its estimated annual overhead costs of $600,000 to three activity cost pools. The firm computes activity-based overhead rates per cost driver by dividing each activity overhead cost pool by the expected number of cost drivers used per activity. Illustration 17-16 shows an annual overhead budget using an ABC system.

CHECK AND DOUBLECHECK, CPAs
Annual Overhead Budget

Activity Cost Pools	Cost Drivers	Estimated Overhead	÷	Expected Use of Cost Drivers per Activity	=	Activity-Based Overhead Rates
Administration	Number of partner-hours	$335,000		3,350		$100 per partner-hour
Customer development	Revenue billed	160,000		$4,000,000		$0.04 per $1 of revenue
Recruiting and training	Direct professional hours	105,000		30,000		$3.50 per hour
		$600,000				

The assignment of the individual overhead activity rates to the actual number of activities used in the performance of the Plano Molding Company audit results in total overhead assigned of $57,200, as shown in Illustration 17-17.

Illustration 17-17 Assigning overhead in a service company

	A	B	C	D	E
1	**CHECK AND DOUBLECHECK, CPAs**				
2	**Plano Molding Company Audit**				
3-5	Activity Cost Pools	Cost Drivers	Actual Use of Drivers	Activity-Based Overhead Rates	Cost Assigned
6	Administration	Number of partner-hours	335	$100.00	$33,500
7	Customer development	Revenue billed	$260,000	$0.04	10,400
8	Recruiting and training	Direct professional hours	3,800	$3.50	13,300
9					$57,200

Under activity-based costing, Check and Doublecheck assigns overhead costs of $57,200 to the Plano Molding Company audit, as compared to $70,000 under traditional costing. Illustration 17-18 compares total costs and operating margins under the two costing systems.

CHECK AND DOUBLECHECK, CPAs
Plano Molding Company Audit

	Traditional Costing		ABC	
Revenue		$260,000		$260,000
Expenses				
Direct professional labor	$140,000		$140,000	
Applied overhead	70,000		57,200	
Total expenses		210,000		197,200
Operating income		$ 50,000		$ 62,800
Profit margin		19.2%		24.2%

The comparison shows that the assignment of overhead costs under traditional costing is distorted. The total cost assigned to performing the audit of Plano Molding Company is greater under traditional costing by $12,800, and the profit margin is significantly lower. Traditional costing understates the profitability of the audit.

Management Insight

ABC Evaluated

Surveys of companies often show ABC usage of approximately 50%. Yet, in recent years, articles about ABC have expressed mixed opinions regarding its usefulness. To evaluate ABC practices and user satisfaction with ABC, a survey was conducted of 348 companies worldwide. Some of the interesting findings included: ABC methods are widely used across the entire value chain, rather than being primarily used to allocate production-specific costs; only 25% of non-ABC companies think they are accurately tracing the costs of activities, while 70% of ABC companies think their company does this well; and respondents felt that ABC provides greater support for financial, operational, and strategic decisions. More than 87% of respondents said that their ideal costing system would include some form of ABC. Since this significantly exceeds the 50% of the respondents actually using it, ABC usage may well increase in the future.

Source: William Stratton, Denis Desroches, Raef Lawson, and Toby Hatch, "Activity-Based Costing: Is It Still Relevant?" *Management Accounting Quarterly* (Spring, 2009), pp. 31–39.

 What might explain why so many companies say that ideally they would use ABC, but they haven't adopted it yet? (See page 943.)

© CGinspiration/iStockphoto

 USING THE **DECISION TOOLKIT**

As mentioned in the Feature Story, Precor manufactures a line of high-end exercise equipment of commercial quality. Assume that the chief accountant has proposed changing from a traditional costing system to an activity-based costing system. The financial vice president is not convinced, so she requests that the next large order for equipment be costed under both systems for purposes of comparison and analysis. An order from Slim-Way Salons, Inc., for 150 low-impact treadmills is received and is identified as the order to be subjected to dual costing. The following cost data relate to the Slim-Way order.

Data relevant to both costing systems

Direct materials	$55,500
Direct labor hours	820
Direct labor rate per hour	$ 18.00

Data relevant to the traditional costing system

Predetermined overhead rate is 300% of direct labor cost.

Data relevant to the activity-based costing system

Activity Cost Pools	Cost Drivers	Activity-Based Overhead Rate	Expected Use of Cost Drivers for Treadmill Order
Engineering design	Engineering hours	$30 per hour	330
Machine setup	Setups	$200 per setup	22
Machining	Machine hours	$25 per hour	732
Assembly	Number of subassemblies	$8 per subassembly	1,500
Packaging and shipping	Packaging/shipping hours	$15 per hour	152
Building occupancy	Machine hours	$6 per hour	732

Instructions

Compute the total cost of the Slim-Way Salons, Inc. order under (a) the traditional costing system and (b) the activity-based costing system. (c) As a result of this comparison, which costing system is Precor likely to adopt? Why?

Solution

(a) Traditional costing system:

Direct materials	$ 55,500
Direct labor (820 × $18)	14,760
Overhead assigned ($14,760 × 300%)	44,280
Total costs assigned to Slim-Way order	$114,540
Number of low-impact treadmills	150
Cost per unit	$ 763.60

(b) Activity-based costing system:

Direct materials		$ 55,500
Direct labor (820 × $18)		14,760
Overhead activities costs:		
Engineering design (330 hours @ $30)	$ 9,900	
Machine setup (22 setups @ $200)	4,400	
Machining (732 machine hours @ $25)	18,300	
Assembly (1,500 subassemblies @ $8)	12,000	
Packaging and shipping (152 hours @ $15)	2,280	
Building occupancy (732 hours @ $6)	4,392	51,272
Total costs assigned to Slim-Way order		$121,532
Number of low-impact treadmills		150
Cost per unit		$ 810.21

(c) Precor will likely adopt ABC because of the difference in the cost per unit (which ABC found to be higher). More importantly, ABC provides greater insight into the sources and causes of the cost per unit. Managers are given greater insight into which activities to control in order to reduce costs. ABC will provide better product costing and greater profitability for the company.

✔ The Navigator

Summary of Learning Objectives

1 Recognize the difference between traditional costing and activity-based costing. A traditional costing system allocates overhead to products on the basis of predetermined plantwide or departmentwide rates such as direct labor or machine hours. An ABC system allocates overhead to identified activity cost pools, and then assigns costs to products using related cost drivers that measure the activities (resources) consumed.

2 Identify the steps in the development of an activity-based costing system. The development of an activity-based costing system involves four steps: (1) Identify and classify the major activities involved in the manufacture of specific products, and allocate manufacturing overhead costs to the appropriate cost pools. (2) Identify the cost driver that has a strong correlation to the costs accumulated in the cost pool. (3) Compute the overhead rate per cost driver. (4) Assign manufac-

turing overhead costs for each cost pool to products or services using the overhead rates.

3 Know how companies identify the activity cost pools used in activity-based costing. To identify activity cost pools, a company must perform an analysis of each operation or process, documenting and timing every task, action, or transaction.

4 Know how companies identify and use cost drivers in activity-based costing. Cost drivers identified for assigning activity cost pools must (a) accurately measure the actual consumption of the activity by the various products and (b) have related data easily available.

5 Understand the benefits and limitations of activity-based costing. Features of ABC that make it a more accurate product costing system include: (1) the increased number of cost pools used to assign overhead, (2) the enhanced control over overhead costs, and (3) the better management decisions it makes possible. The limitations of ABC are (1) the higher analysis and measurement costs that accompany multiple activity centers and cost drivers, and (2) the necessity still to allocate some costs arbitrarily.

6 **Differentiate between value-added and non–value-added activities.** Value-added activities are essential to operations of the business and often increase the worth of a product or service. Non–value-added are non-essential activities that simply add cost to or increase the time spent on a product or service without increasing its market value. Awareness of these classifications encourages managers to reduce or eliminate the time spent on non–value-added activities.

7 **Understand the value of using activity levels in activity-based costing.** Activities may be classified as unit-level, batch-level, product-level, and facility-level. Companies control overhead costs at unit-, batch-, product-, and facility-levels by modifying unit-, batch-, product-, and facility-level activities, respectively. Failure to recognize this classification of levels can result in distorted product costing.

8 **Apply activity-based costing to service industries.** The overall objective of using ABC in service industries is no different than for manufacturing industries—that is, improved costing of services provided (by job, service, contract, or customer). The general approach to costing is the same: analyze operations, identify activities, accumulate overhead costs by activity cost pools, and identify and use cost drivers to assign the cost pools to the services.

✔ The Navigator

🧰 DECISION TOOLKIT *A SUMMARY*

DECISION CHECKPOINTS	INFO NEEDED FOR DECISION	TOOL TO USE FOR DECISION	HOW TO EVALUATE RESULTS
When should we use ABC?	Knowledge of the products or product lines, the manufacturing process, and overhead costs	A detailed and accurate cost accounting system; cooperation between accountants and operating managers	Compare the results under both costing systems. If managers are better able to understand and control their operations using ABC, and the costs are not prohibitive, the use of ABC would be beneficial.
How can activity-based management help managers?	Activities classified as value-added and non–value-added	Activity flowchart	The flowchart should motivate managers to minimize non–value-added activities. Managers should better understand the relationship between activities and the resources they consume.

Appendix 17A

Just-in-Time Processing

LEARNING OBJECTIVE 9
Explain just-in-time (JIT) processing.

Traditionally, continuous process manufacturing has been based on a **just-in-case** philosophy: Inventories of raw materials are maintained just in case some items are of poor quality or a key supplier is shut down by a strike. Similarly, subassembly parts are manufactured and stored just in case they are needed later in the manufacturing process. Finished goods are completed and stored just in case unexpected and rush customer orders are received. This philosophy often results in a "**push approach**," in which raw materials and subassembly parts are pushed through each process. Traditional processing often results in the buildup of extensive manufacturing inventories.

Primarily in response to foreign competition, many U.S. firms have switched to **just-in-time (JIT) processing**. JIT manufacturing is dedicated to having the right amount of materials, parts, or products just as they are needed. JIT first hit the United States in the early 1980s when automobile companies adopted it to compete with foreign automakers. Many companies, including Dell, Caterpillar, and Harley-Davidson, now successfully use JIT. Under JIT processing, companies receive raw materials **just in time** for use in production, they complete sub-assembly parts **just in time** for use in finished goods, and they complete finished goods **just in time** to be sold. Illustration 17A-1 shows the sequence of activities in just-in-time processing.

Illustration 17A-1 Just-in-time processing

OBJECTIVE OF JIT PROCESSING

A primary objective of JIT is to eliminate all manufacturing inventories. Inventories have an adverse effect on net income because they tie up funds and storage space that could be put to more productive uses. JIT strives to eliminate inventories by using a "**pull approach**" in manufacturing. This approach begins with the customer placing an order with the company, which starts the process of pulling the product through the manufacturing process. A computer at the final workstation sends a signal to the preceding workstation. This signal indicates the exact materials (parts and subassemblies) needed to complete the production of a specified product for a specified time period, such as an eight-hour shift. The next-preceding process, in turn, sends its signal to other processes back up the line. The goal is a smooth continuous flow in the manufacturing process, with no buildup of inventories at any point.

ELEMENTS OF JIT PROCESSING

There are three important elements in JIT processing:

Helpful Hint Buyer leverage is important in finding dependable suppliers. Companies like GM and GE have more success than smaller companies.

1. **Dependable suppliers.** Suppliers must be willing to deliver on short notice exact quantities of raw materials according to precise quality specifications (even including multiple deliveries within the same day). Suppliers must also be willing to deliver the raw materials at specified workstations rather than at a central receiving department. This type of purchasing requires constant and direct communication. Such communication is facilitated by an online computer linkage between the company and its suppliers.

2. **A multiskilled work force**. Under JIT, machines are often strategically grouped into work cells or workstations. Much of the work is automated. As a result, one worker may operate and maintain several different types of machines.

Helpful Hint Without its emphasis on quality control, JIT would be impractical or even impossible. In JIT, quality is engineered into the production process.

3. **A total quality control system**. The company must establish total quality control throughout the manufacturing operations. Total quality control means **no defects**. Since the pull approach signals only required quantities, any defects at any workstation will shut down operations at subsequent workstations. Total quality control requires continuous monitoring by both line employees and supervisors at each workstation.

BENEFITS OF JIT PROCESSING

The major benefits of implementing JIT processing are:

1. Significant reduction or elimination of manufacturing inventories.
2. Enhanced product quality.
3. Reduction or elimination of rework costs and inventory storage costs.
4. Production cost savings from the improved flow of goods through the processes.

The effects in many cases have been dramatic. For example, after using JIT for two years, a major division of Hewlett-Packard found that work in process inventories (in dollars) were down 82%, scrap/rework costs were down 30%, space utilization improved by 40%, and labor efficiency improved 50%. As indicated, JIT not only reduces inventory but also enables a manufacturer to produce a better product faster and with less waste.

One of the major accounting benefits of JIT is the elimination of separate raw materials and work in process inventory accounts. These accounts are replaced by **one account**, Raw and In-Process Inventory. All materials and conversion costs are charged to this account. The reduction (or elimination) of in-process inventories results in a simpler computation of equivalent units of production.

Summary of Learning Objective for Appendix 17A

9 **Explain just-in-time (JIT) processing.** JIT is a processing system dedicated to having on hand the right materials and products just at the time they are needed, thereby reducing the amount of inventory and the time inventory is held. One of the principal accounting effects is that one account, Raw and In-Process Inventory, replaces both the raw materials and work-in-process inventory accounts.

✔ The Navigator

Glossary

Activity *(p. 897)* Any event, action, transaction, or work sequence that incurs cost when producing a product or providing a service.

Activity-based costing (ABC) *(p. 897)* An overhead cost-allocation system that allocates overhead to multiple activity cost pools and assigns the activity cost pools to products or services by means of cost drivers that represent the activities used.

Activity-based management (ABM) *(p. 907)* Extends ABC from product costing to a comprehensive management tool that focuses on reducing costs and improving processes and decision-making.

Activity cost pool *(p. 897)* The overhead cost attributed to a distinct type of activity or related activities.

Batch-level activities *(p. 910)* Activities performed for each batch of products rather than for each unit.

Cost driver *(p. 897)* Any factor or activity that has a direct cause–effect relationship with the resources consumed. In ABC, cost drivers are used to assign activity cost pools to products or services.

Facility-level activities *(p. 910)* Activities required to support or sustain an entire production process.

Just-in-time (JIT) processing *(p. 917)* A processing system dedicated to having the right amount of materials, parts, or products arrive as they are needed, thereby reducing the amount of inventory.

Non–value-added activity *(p. 907)* An activity that, if eliminated, would not hinder the company's operations or reduce the perceived worth of its product or service.

Product-level activities *(p. 910)* Activities performed in support of an entire product line, but not always performed every time a new unit or batch of products is produced.

Unit-level activities *(p. 910)* Activities performed for each unit of production.

Value-added activity *(p. 907)* An activity that increases the perceived worth of a product or service to a customer.

Comprehensive Do it!

Spreadwell Paint Company manufactures two high-quality base paints: an oil-based paint and a latex paint. Both are house paints and are manufactured in neutral white color only. Spreadwell sells the white base paints to franchised retail paint and decorating stores where pigments are added to tint (color) the paint as the customer desires. The oil-based paint is made with organic solvents (petroleum products) such as mineral spirits or turpentine. The latex paint is made with water; synthetic resin particles are suspended in the water, and dry and harden when exposed to the air.

Spreadwell uses the same processing equipment to produce both paints in different production runs. Between batches, the vats and other processing equipment must be washed and cleaned.

After analyzing the company's entire operations, Spreadwell's accountants and production managers have identified activity cost pools and accumulated annual budgeted overhead costs by pool as follows.

Activity Cost Pools	Estimated Overhead
Purchasing	$ 240,000
Processing (weighing and mixing, grinding, thinning and drying, straining)	1,400,000
Packaging (quarts, gallons, and 5-gallons)	580,000
Testing	240,000
Storage and inventory control	180,000
Washing and cleaning equipment	560,000
Total annual budgeted overhead	$3,200,000

Following further analysis, activity cost drivers were identified and their expected use by product and activity were scheduled as follows.

Activity Cost Pools	Cost Drivers	Expected Cost Drivers per Activity	Expected Use of Drivers per Product	
			Oil-Based	Latex
Purchasing	Purchase orders	1,500 orders	800	700
Processing	Gallons processed	1,000,000 gallons	400,000	600,000
Packaging	Containers filled	400,000 containers	180,000	220,000
Testing	Number of tests	4,000 tests	2,100	1,900
Storing	Avg. gals. on hand	18,000 gallons	10,400	7,600
Washing	Number of batches	800 batches	350	450

Spreadwell has budgeted 400,000 gallons of oil-based paint and 600,000 gallons of latex paint for processing during the year.

Instructions

(a) Prepare a schedule showing the computations of the activity-based overhead rates.

(b) Prepare a schedule assigning each activity's overhead cost pool to each product.

(c) Compute the overhead cost per unit for each product.

Solution to Comprehensive Do it!

Action Plan

- Identify the major activities that pertain to the manufacture of specific products and allocate manufacturing overhead costs to activity cost pools.
- Identify the cost drivers that accurately measure each activity's contribution to the finished product.
- Compute the activity-based overhead rates.
- Assign manufacturing overhead costs for each activity cost pool to products, using the activity-based overhead rates.

(a) Computations of activity-based overhead rates:

Activity Cost Pools	Estimated Overhead	÷	Expected Use of Cost Drivers	=	Activity-Based Overhead Rates
Purchasing	$ 240,000		1,500 orders		$160 per order
Processing	1,400,000		1,000,000 gallons		$1.40 per gallon
Packaging	580,000		400,000 containers		$1.45 per container
Testing	240,000		4,000 tests		$60 per test
Storing	180,000		18,000 gallons		$10 per gallon
Washing	560,000		800 batches		$700 per batch
	$3,200,000				

(b) Assignment of activity cost pools to products:

Activity Cost Pools	Oil-Based Paint			Latex Paint		
	Expected Use of Drivers	Overhead Rates	Cost Assigned	Expected Use of Drivers	Overhead Rates	Cost Assigned
Purchasing	800	$160	$ 128,000	700	$160	$ 112,000
Processing	400,000	$1.40	560,000	600,000	$1.40	840,000
Packaging	180,000	$1.45	261,000	220,000	$1.45	319,000
Testing	2,100	$60	126,000	1,900	$60	114,000
Storing	10,400	$10	104,000	7,600	$10	76,000
Washing	350	$700	245,000	450	$700	315,000
Total overhead assigned			$1,424,000			$1,776,000

(c) Computation of overhead cost assigned per unit:

	Oil-Based Paint	Latex Paint
Total overhead cost assigned	$1,424,000	$1,776,000
Total gallons produced	400,000	600,000
Overhead cost per gallon	$3.56	$2.96

The Navigator

Self-Test, Brief Exercises, Exercises, Problem Set A, and many more resources are available for practice in WileyPLUS.

Note: All Questions, Exercises, and Problems marked with an asterisk relate to material in the appendix to the chapter.

Self-Test Questions

Answers are on page 943.

(LO 1) **1.** Activity-based costing (ABC):
  (a) can be used only in a process cost system.
  (b) focuses on units of production.
  (c) focuses on activities performed to produce a product.
  (d) uses only a single basis of allocation.

(LO 1) **2.** Activity-based costing:
  (a) is the initial phase of converting to a just-in-time operating environment.
  (b) can be used only in a job order costing system.
  (c) is a two-stage overhead cost allocation system that identifies activity cost pools and cost drivers.
  (d) uses direct labor as its primary cost driver.

(LO 1, 4) **3.** Any activity that causes resources to be consumed is called a:
  (a) just-in-time activity.
  (b) facility-level activity.
  (c) cost driver.
  (d) non–value-added activity.

(LO 2) **4.** The first step in the development of an activity-based costing system is:
  (a) identify and classify activities and allocate overhead to cost pools.
  (b) assign overhead costs to products.
  (c) identify cost drivers.
  (d) compute overhead rates.

(LO 4) **5.** Which of the following would be the **best** cost driver for the assembling cost pool?
  (a) Number of product lines.
  (b) Number of parts.
  (c) Number of orders.
  (d) Amount of square footage.

(LO 4) **6.** The overhead rate for Machine Setups is $100 per setup. Products A and B have 80 and 60 setups, respectively. The overhead assigned to each product is:
  (a) Product A $8,000, Product B $8,000.
  (b) Product A $8,000, Product B $6,000.
  (c) Product A $6,000, Product B $6,000.
  (d) Product A $6,000, Product B $8,000.

(LO 4) **7.** Donna Crawford Co. has identified an activity cost pool to which it has allocated estimated overhead of $1,920,000. It has determined the expected use of cost drivers for that activity to be 160,000 inspections. Widgets require 40,000 inspections, Gadgets 30,000 inspections, and Targets 90,000 inspections. The overhead assigned to each product is:
  (a) Widgets $40,000, Gadgets $30,000, Targets $90,000.
  (b) Widgets $640,000, Gadgets $640,000, Targets $640,000.

  (c) Widgets $360,000, Gadgets $480,000, Targets $1,080,000.
  (d) Widgets $480,000, Gadgets $360,000, Targets $1,080,000.

(LO 5) **8.** A frequently cited limitation of activity-based costing is:
  (a) ABC results in more cost pools being used to assign overhead costs to products.
  (b) certain overhead costs remain to be allocated by means of some arbitrary volume-based cost driver such as labor or machine hours.
  (c) ABC leads to poorer management decisions.
  (d) ABC results in less control over overhead costs.

(LO 5) **9.** A company should consider using ABC if:
  (a) overhead costs constitute a small portion of total product costs.
  (b) it has only a few product lines that require similar degrees of support services.
  (c) direct labor constitutes a significant part of the total product cost and a high correlation exists between direct labor and changes in overhead costs.
  (d) its product lines differ greatly in volume and manufacturing complexity.

(LO 6) **10.** An activity that adds costs to the product but does not increase its perceived market value is a:
  (a) value-added activity.
  (b) cost driver.
  (c) cost/benefit activity.
  (d) non–value-added activity.

(LO 6) **11.** The following activity is value-added:
  (a) Storage of raw materials.
  (b) Moving parts from machine to machine.
  (c) Shaping a piece of metal on a lathe.
  (d) All of the above.

(LO 7) **12.** A relevant facility-level cost driver for heating costs is:
  (a) machine hours. (c) floor space.
  (b) direct material. (d) direct labor cost.

(LO 9) ***13.** Under just-in-time processing:
  (a) raw materials are received just in time for use in production.
  (b) subassembly parts are completed just in time for use in assembling finished goods.
  (c) finished goods are completed just in time to be sold.
  (d) All of the above.

(LO 9) ***14.** The primary objective of just-in-time processing is to:
  (a) accumulate overhead in activity cost pools.
  (b) eliminate or reduce all manufacturing inventories.
  (c) identify relevant activity cost drivers.
  (d) identify value-added activities.

Go to the book's companion website, **www.wiley.com/college/kimmel**, for additional Self-Test Questions.

Questions

1. Under what conditions is direct labor a valid basis for allocating overhead?

2. What has happened in recent industrial history to reduce the usefulness of direct labor as the primary basis for allocating overhead to products?

3. In an automated manufacturing environment, what basis of overhead allocation is frequently more relevant than direct labor hours?

4. What is generally true about overhead allocation to high-volume products versus low-volume products under a traditional costing system?

5. What are the principal differences between activity-based costing (ABC) and traditional product costing?

6. What is the formula for computing activity-based overhead rates?

7. What steps are involved in developing an activity-based costing system?

8. Explain the preparation and use of a value-added/non–value-added activity flowchart in an ABC system.

9. What is an activity cost pool?

10. What is a cost driver?

11. What makes a cost driver accurate and appropriate?

12. What is the formula for assigning activity cost pools to products?

13. What are the benefits of activity-based costing?

14. What are the limitations of activity-based costing?

15. Under what conditions is ABC generally the superior overhead costing system?

16. What refinement has been made to enhance the efficiency and effectiveness of ABC for use in managing costs?

17. Of what benefit is classifying activities as value-added and non–value-added?

18. In what ways is the application of ABC to service industries the same as its application to manufacturing companies?

19. What is the relevance of the classification of levels of activity to ABC?

*20. (a) Describe the philosophy and approach of just-in-time processing.
(b) Identify the major elements of JIT processing.

Brief Exercises

Identify differences between costing systems.
(LO 1), AP

BE17-1 Warner Inc. sells a high-speed retrieval system for mining information. It provides the following information for the year.

	Budgeted	Actual
Overhead cost	$1,000,000	$950,000
Machine hours	50,000	45,000
Direct labor hours	100,000	92,000

Overhead is applied on the basis of direct labor hours. (a) Compute the predetermined overhead rate. (b) Determine the amount of overhead applied for the year. (c) Explain how an activity-based costing system might differ in terms of computing a predetermined overhead rate.

Identify differences between costing systems.
(LO 1), AP

BE17-2 Finney Inc. has conducted an analysis of overhead costs related to one of its product lines using a traditional costing system (volume-based) and an activity-based costing system. Here are its results.

	Traditional Costing	ABC
Sales revenue	$600,000	$600,000
Overhead costs:		
Product RX3	$ 34,000	$ 50,000
Product Y12	36,000	20,000
	$ 70,000	$ 70,000

Explain how a difference in the overhead costs between the two systems may have occurred.

Identify cost drivers.
(LO 4), AP

BE17-3 Storrer Co. identifies the following activities that pertain to manufacturing overhead: materials handling, machine setups, factory machine maintenance, factory supervision, and quality control. For each activity, identify an appropriate cost driver.

BE17-4 Mason Company manufactures four products in a single production facility. The company uses activity-based costing. The following activities have been identified through the company's activity analysis: (a) inventory control, (b) machine setups, (c) employee training, (d) quality inspections, (e) material ordering, (f) drilling operations, and (g) building maintenance.

For each activity, name a cost driver that might be used to assign overhead costs to products.

Identify cost drivers.
(LO 4), **AP**

BE17-5 Mordica Company identifies three activities in its manufacturing process: machine setups, machining, and inspections. Estimated annual overhead cost for each activity is $150,000, $325,000, and $87,500, respectively. The cost driver for each activity and the expected annual usage are number of setups 2,500, machine hours 25,000, and number of inspections 1,750. Compute the overhead rate for each activity.

Compute activity-based overhead rates.
(LO 4), **AP**

BE17-6 Weisman, Inc. uses activity-based costing as the basis for information to set prices for its six lines of seasonal coats. Compute the activity-based overhead rates using the following budgeted data for each of the activity cost pools.

Compute activity-based overhead rates.
(LO 4), **AP**

Activity Cost Pools	Estimated Overhead	Expected Use of Cost Drivers per Activity
Designing	$ 450,000	10,000 designer hours
Sizing and cutting	4,000,000	160,000 machine hours
Stitching and trimming	1,440,000	80,000 labor hours
Wrapping and packing	336,000	32,000 finished units

BE17-7 Hollins, Inc., a manufacturer of computer chips, employs activity-based costing. The budgeted data for each of the activity cost pools is provided below for the year 2014.

Compute activity-based overhead rates.
(LO 4), **AP**

Activity Cost Pools	Estimated Overhead	Expected Use of Cost Drivers per Activity
Ordering and receiving	$ 90,000	12,000 orders
Etching	480,000	60,000 machine hours
Soldering	1,760,000	440,000 labor hours

For 2014, the company had 11,000 orders and used 50,000 machine hours, and labor hours totaled 500,000. What is the total overhead applied?

BE17-8 Rich Novelty Company identified the following activities in its production and support operations. Classify each of these activities as either value-added or non–value-added.

Classify activities as value- or non–value-added.
(LO 6), **AP**

(a) Machine setup. (d) Moving work in process.
(b) Design engineering. (e) Inspecting and testing.
(c) Storing inventory. (f) Painting and packing.

BE17-9 Mendle and Kiner is an architectural firm that is contemplating the installation of activity-based costing. The following activities are performed daily by staff architects. Classify these activities as value-added or non–value-added: (a) designing and drafting, 2.5 hours; (b) staff meetings, 1 hour; (c) on-site supervision, 2 hours; (d) lunch, 1 hour; (e) consultation with client on specifications, 1.5 hours; (f) entertaining a prospective client for dinner, 2 hours.

Classify service company activities as value- or non–value-added.
(LO 6, 8), **AN**

BE17-10 Kwik Pix is a large digital processing center that serves 130 outlets in grocery stores, service stations, camera and photo shops, and drug stores in 16 nearby towns. Kwik Pix operates 24 hours a day, 6 days a week. Classify each of the following activity costs of Kwik Pix as either unit-level, batch-level, product-level, or facility-level.

Classify activities according to level.
(LO 7, 8), **AN**

(a) Color printing materials.
(b) Photocopy paper.
(c) Depreciation of machinery.
(d) Setups for enlargements.
(e) Supervisor's salary.
(f) Ordering materials.
(g) Pickup and delivery.
(h) Commission to dealers.

(i) Insurance on building.
(j) Loading developing machines.

Classify activities according to level.
(LO 7), **AP**

BE17-11 Trammell, Inc. operates 20 injection molding machines in the production of tool boxes of four different sizes, named the Apprentice, the Handyman, the Journeyman, and the Professional. Classify each of the following costs as unit-level, batch-level, product-level, or facility-level.
(a) First-shift supervisor's salary.
(b) Powdered raw plastic.
(c) Dies for casting plastic components.
(d) Depreciation on injection molding machines.
(e) Changing dies on machines.
(f) Moving components to assembly department.
(g) Engineering design.
(h) Employee health and medical insurance coverage.

Compute rates and activity levels.
(LO 4, 7), **AP**

BE17-12 Spin Cycle Company uses three activity pools to apply overhead to its products. Each activity has a cost driver used to allocate the overhead costs to the product. The activities and related overhead costs are as follows: product design $40,000; machining $300,000; and material handling $100,000. The cost drivers and expected use are as follows.

Activities	Cost Drivers	Expected Use of Cost Drivers per Activity
Product design	Number of product changes	10
Machining	Machine hours	150,000
Material handling	Number of setups	100

(a) Compute the predetermined overhead rate for each activity. (b) Classify each of these activities as unit-level, batch-level, product-level, or facility-level.

Do it! Review

Identify characteristics of traditional and ABC costing systems.
(LO 1, 2), **K**

Do it! 17-1 Indicate whether the following statements are true or false.

(a) The reasoning behind ABC cost allocation is that products consume activities and activities consume resources.
(b) Activity-based costing is an approach for allocating direct labor to products.
(c) In today's increasingly automated environment, direct labor is never an appropriate basis for allocating costs to products.
(d) A cost driver is any factor or activity that has a direct cause-effect relationship with resources consumed.
(e) Activity-based costing segregates overhead into various cost pools in an effort to provide more accurate cost information.

Compute activity-based overhead rates and assign overhead using ABC.
(LO 4), **AP**

Do it! 17-2 Flynn Industries has three activity cost pools and two products. It expects to produce 3,000 units of Product BC113 and 1,500 of Product AD908. Having identified its activity cost pools and the cost drivers for each pool, Flynn accumulated the following data relative to those activity cost pools and cost drivers.

	Annual Overhead Data		Expected Use of Cost Drivers per Product		
Activity Cost Pool	Cost Drivers	Estimated Overhead	Expected Use of Cost Drivers per Activity	Product BC113	Product AD908
Machine setup	Setups	$ 16,000	40	25	15
Machining	Machine hours	110,000	5,000	1,000	4,000
Packing	Orders	30,000	500	150	350

Using the above data, do the following:

(a) Prepare a schedule showing the computations of the activity-based overhead rates per cost driver.

(b) Prepare a schedule assigning each activity's overhead cost to the two products.

(c) Compute the overhead cost per unit for each product. (Round to nearest cent.)

(d) Comment on the comparative overhead cost per product.

Do it! 17-3 Classify each of the following activities within a tax-preparation business as value-added (VA) or non–value-added (NVA).

(a) Advertising.

(b) Completing tax returns.

(c) Billing clients.

(d) Answering client questions.

(e) Accompanying clients to audit proceedings.

Classify activities as value- or non–value-added.

(LO 6, 8), **AP**

Do it! 17-4 Adamson Company manufactures four lines of garden tools. As a result of an activity analysis, the accounting department has identified eight activity cost pools. Each of the product lines is produced in large batches, with the whole plant devoted to one product at a time. Classify each of the following activities or costs as either unit-level, batch level, product-level, or facility-level.

Classify activities according to level.

(LO 7), **C**

(a) Machining parts.

(b) Product design.

(c) Plant maintenance.

(d) Machine setup.

(e) Assembling parts.

(f) Purchasing raw materials.

(g) Property taxes.

(h) Painting.

Exercises

E17-1 Wilkins Inc. has two types of handbags: standard and custom. The controller has decided to use a plantwide overhead rate based on direct labor costs. The president has heard of activity-based costing and wants to see how the results would differ if this system were used. Two activity cost pools were developed: machining and machine setup. Presented below is information related to the company's operations.

Assign overhead using traditional costing and ABC.

(LO 1, 4), **AP**

	Standard	**Custom**
Direct labor costs	$50,000	$100,000
Machine hours	1,000	1,000
Setup hours	100	400

Total estimated overhead costs are $270,000. Overhead cost allocated to the machining activity cost pool is $170,000, and $100,000 is allocated to the machine setup activity cost pool.

Instructions

(a) Compute the overhead rate using the traditional (plantwide) approach.

(b) Compute the overhead rates using the activity-based costing approach.

(c) Determine the difference in allocation between the two approaches.

E17-2 Ayala Inc. has conducted the following analysis related to its product lines, using a traditional costing system (volume-based) and an activity-based costing system. Both the traditional and the activity-based costing systems include direct materials and direct labor costs.

Explain difference between traditional and activity-based costing.

(LO 1), **AP**

		Total Costs	
Products	**Sales Revenue**	**Traditional**	**ABC**
Product 540X	$180,000	$55,000	$50,000
Product 137Y	160,000	50,000	35,000
Product 249S	70,000	15,000	35,000

Instructions

(a) For each product line, compute operating income using the traditional costing system.

(b) For each product line, compute operating income using the activity-based costing system.

(c) Using the following formula, compute the percentage difference in operating income for each of the product lines of Ayala: [Operating Income (ABC) − Operating Income (traditional cost)] ÷ Operating Income (traditional cost). (Round the percentage to two decimals.)

(d) Provide a rationale as to why the costs for Product 540X are approximately the same using either the traditional or activity-based costing system.

Assign overhead using traditional costing and ABC.
(LO 1, 4), **AN**

E17-3 American Fabrics has budgeted overhead costs of $990,000. It has allocated overhead on a plantwide basis to its two products (wool and cotton) using direct labor hours which are estimated to be 450,000 for the current year. The company has decided to experiment with activity-based costing and has created two activity cost pools and related activity cost drivers. These two cost pools are: cutting (cost driver is machine hours) and design (cost driver is number of setups). Overhead allocated to the cutting cost pool is $360,000 and $630,000 is allocated to the design cost pool. Additional information related to these pools is as follows.

	Wool	**Cotton**	**Total**
Machine hours	100,000	100,000	200,000
Number of setups	1,000	500	1,500

Instructions

(a) Determine the amount of overhead allocated to the wool product line and the cotton product line using activity-based costing.

(b) What amount of overhead would be allocated to the wool and cotton product lines using the traditional approach, assuming direct labor hours were incurred evenly between the wool and cotton? How does this compare with the amount allocated using ABC in part (a)?

Assign overhead using traditional costing and ABC.
(LO 1, 4), **AN**

E17-4 Altex Inc. manufactures two products: car wheels and truck wheels. To determine the amount of overhead to assign to each product line, the controller, Robert Hermann, has developed the following information.

	Car	**Truck**
Estimated wheels produced	40,000	10,000
Direct labor hours per wheel	1	3

Total estimated overhead costs for the two product lines are $770,000.

Instructions

(a) Compute the overhead cost assigned to the car wheels and truck wheels, assuming that direct labor hours is used to allocate overhead costs.

(b) Hermann is not satisfied with the traditional method of allocating overhead because he believes that most of the overhead costs relate to the truck wheel product line because of its complexity. He therefore develops the following three activity cost pools and related cost drivers to better understand these costs.

Activity Cost Pools	**Expected Use of Cost Drivers**	**Estimated Overhead Costs**
Setting up machines	1,000 setups	$220,000
Assembling	70,000 labor hours	280,000
Inspection	1,200 inspections	270,000

Compute the activity-based overhead rates for these three cost pools.

(c) Compute the cost that is assigned to the car wheels and truck wheels product lines using an activity-based costing system, given the following information.

Expected Use of Cost Drivers per Product		
	Car	**Truck**
Number of setups	200	800
Direct labor hours	40,000	30,000
Number of inspections	100	1,100

(d) What do you believe Hermann should do?

E17-5 Shady Lady sells window coverings (shades, blinds, and awnings) to both commercial and residential customers. The following information relates to its budgeted operations for the current year.

Assign overhead using traditional costing and ABC.
(LO 1, 4), **AP**

	Commercial		Residential	
Revenues		$300,000		$480,000
Direct material costs	$ 30,000		$ 50,000	
Direct labor costs	100,000		300,000	
Overhead costs	85,000	215,000	150,000	500,000
Operating income (loss)		$ 85,000		($ 20,000)

The controller, Peggy Kingman, is concerned about the residential product line. She cannot understand why this line is not more profitable given that the installations of window coverings are less complex for residential customers. In addition, the residential client base resides in close proximity to the company office, so travel costs are not as expensive on a per client visit for residential customers. As a result, she has decided to take a closer look at the overhead costs assigned to the two product lines to determine whether a more accurate product costing model can be developed. Here are the three activity cost pools and related information she developed:

Activity Cost Pools	Estimated Overhead	Cost Drivers
Scheduling and travel	$105,000	Hours of travel
Setup time	70,000	Number of setups
Supervision	60,000	Direct labor cost

Expected Use of Cost Drivers per Product		
	Commercial	Residential
Scheduling and travel	1,000	500
Setup time	450	250

Instructions
(a) Compute the activity-based overhead rates for each of the three cost pools, and determine the overhead cost assigned to each product line.
(b) Compute the operating income for each product line, using the activity-based overhead rates.
(c) What do you believe Peggy Kingman should do?

E17-6 Perdon Corporation manufactures safes—large mobile safes, and large walk-in stationary bank safes. As part of its annual budgeting process, Perdon is analyzing the profitability of its two products. Part of this analysis involves estimating the amount of overhead to be allocated to each product line. The information shown below relates to overhead.

Assign overhead using traditional costing and ABC.
(LO 1, 4), **AN**

	Mobile Safes	Walk-In Safes
Units planned for production	200	50
Material moves per product line	300	200
Purchase orders per product line	450	350
Direct labor hours per product line	800	1,700

Instructions
(a) The total estimated manufacturing overhead was $260,000. Under traditional costing (which assigns overhead on the basis of direct labor hours), what amount of manufacturing overhead costs are assigned to:
  (1) One mobile safe?
  (2) One walk-in safe?
(b) The total estimated manufacturing overhead of $260,000 was comprised of $160,000 for material handling costs and $100,000 for purchasing activity costs. Under activity-based costing (ABC):
  (1) What amount of material handling costs are assigned to:
    (a) One mobile safe?
    (b) One walk-in safe?
  (2) What amount of purchasing activity costs are assigned to:
    (a) One mobile safe?
    (b) One walk-in safe?

(c) Compare the amount of overhead allocated to one mobile safe and to one walk-in safe under the traditional costing approach versus under ABC.

Identify activity cost pools.
(LO 3), **AP**

E17-7 Quik Prints Company is a small printing and copying firm with three high-speed offset printing presses, five copiers (two color and three black-and-white), one collator, one cutting and folding machine, and one fax machine. To improve its pricing practices, owner-manager Terry Morton is installing activity-based accounting. Additionally, Terry employs five employees: two printers/designers, one receptionist/bookkeeper, one salesperson/copy-machine operator, and one janitor/delivery clerk. Terry can operate any of the machines and, in addition to managing the entire operation, he performs the training, designing, selling, and marketing functions.

Instructions

As Quik Prints' independent accountant who prepares tax forms and quarterly financial statements, you have been asked to identify the activities that would be used to accumulate overhead costs for assignment to jobs and customers. Using your knowledge of a small printing and copying firm (and some imagination), identify at least 12 activity cost pools as the start of an activity-based costing system for Quik Prints Company.

Identify activity cost pools and cost drivers.
(LO 3, 4), **AN**

E17-8 Santana Corporation manufactures snowmobiles in its Blue Mountain, Wisconsin, plant. The following costs are budgeted for the first quarter's operations.

Machine setup, indirect materials	$ 4,000
Inspections	16,000
Tests	4,000
Insurance, plant	110,000
Engineering design	140,000
Depreciation, machinery	520,000
Machine setup, indirect labor	20,000
Property taxes	29,000
Oil, heating	19,000
Electricity, plant lighting	21,000
Engineering prototypes	60,000
Depreciation, plant	210,000
Electricity, machinery	36,000
Machine maintenance wages	19,000

Instructions

Classify the above costs of Santana Corporation into activity cost pools using the following: engineering, machinery, machine setup, quality control, factory utilities, maintenance. Next, identify a cost driver that may be used to assign each cost pool to each line of snowmobiles.

Identify activity cost drivers.
(LO 4), **AN**

E17-9 Danny Baden's Verde Vineyards in Oakville, California, produces three varieties of wine: Merlot, Viognier, and Pinot Noir. His winemaster, Russel Hansen, has identified the following activities as cost pools for accumulating overhead and assigning it to products.

1. Culling and replanting. Dead or overcrowded vines are culled, and new vines are planted or relocated. (Separate vineyards by variety.)
2. Tying. The posts and wires are reset, and vines are tied to the wires for the dormant season.
3. Trimming. At the end of the harvest, the vines are cut and trimmed back in preparation for the next season.
4. Spraying. The vines are sprayed with chemicals for protection against insects and fungi.
5. Harvesting. The grapes are hand-picked, placed in carts, and transported to the crushers.
6. Stemming and crushing. Cartfuls of bunches of grapes of each variety are separately loaded into machines which remove stems and gently crush the grapes.
7. Pressing and filtering. The crushed grapes are transferred to presses which mechanically remove the juices and filter out bulk and impurities.
8. Fermentation. The grape juice, by variety, is fermented in either stainless-steel tanks or oak barrels.
9. Aging. The wines are aged in either stainless-steel tanks or oak barrels for one to three years depending on variety.
10. Bottling and corking. Bottles are machine-filled and corked.

11. Labeling and boxing. Each bottle is labeled, as is each nine-bottle case, with the name of the vintner, vintage, and variety.
12. Storing. Packaged and boxed bottles are stored awaiting shipment.
13. Shipping. The wine is shipped to distributors and private retailers.
14. Heating and air-conditioning of plant and offices.
15. Maintenance of buildings and equipment. Printing, repairs, replacements, and general maintenance are performed in the off-season.

Instructions
For each of Verde's 15 activity cost pools, identify a probable cost driver that might be used to assign overhead costs to its three wine varieties.

E17-10 Wilmington, Inc. manufactures five models of kitchen appliances at its Mesa plant. The company is installing activity-based costing and has identified the following activities performed at its Mesa plant.

Identify activity cost drivers.
(LO 4), AN

1. Designing new models.
2. Purchasing raw materials and parts.
3. Storing and managing inventory.
4. Receiving and inspecting raw materials and parts.
5. Interviewing and hiring new personnel.
6. Machine forming sheet steel into appliance parts.
7. Manually assembling parts into appliances.
8. Training all employees of the company.
9. Insuring all tangible fixed assets.
10. Supervising production.
11. Maintaining and repairing machinery and equipment.
12. Painting and packaging finished appliances.

Having analyzed its Mesa plant operations for purposes of installing activity-based costing, Wilmington, Inc. identified its activity cost centers. It now needs to identify relevant activity cost drivers in order to assign overhead costs to its products.

Instructions
Using the activities listed above, identify for each activity one or more cost drivers that might be used to assign overhead to Wilmington's five products.

E17-11 Major Instrument, Inc. manufactures two products: missile range instruments and space pressure gauges. During April, 50 range instruments and 300 pressure gauges were produced, and overhead costs of $94,500 were estimated. An analysis of estimated overhead costs reveals the following activities.

Compute overhead rates and assign overhead using ABC.
(LO 4, 5), AP

Activities	Cost Drivers	Total Cost
1. Materials handling	Number of requisitions	$40,000
2. Machine setups	Number of setups	27,500
3. Quality inspections	Number of inspections	27,000
		$94,500

The cost driver volume for each product was as follows.

Cost Drivers	Instruments	Gauges	Total
Number of requisitions	400	600	1,000
Number of setups	200	300	500
Number of inspections	200	400	600

Instructions
(a) Determine the overhead rate for each activity.
(b) Assign the manufacturing overhead costs for April to the two products using activity-based costing.
(c) ▰▰▰➤ Write a memorandum to the president of Major Instrument explaining the benefits of activity-based costing.

E17-12 Kragan Clothing Company manufactures its own designed and labeled sports attire and sells its products through catalog sales and retail outlets. While Kragan has for years used activity-based costing in its manufacturing activities, it has always used

Assign overhead using traditional costing and ABC.
(LO 1, 4, 6), AP

traditional costing in assigning its selling costs to its product lines. Selling costs have traditionally been assigned to Kragan's product lines at a rate of 70% of direct material costs. Its direct material costs for the month of March for Kragan's "high-intensity" line of attire are $400,000. The company has decided to extend activity-based costing to its selling costs. Data relating to the "high-intensity" line of products for the month of March are as follows.

Activity Cost Pools	Cost Drivers	Overhead Rate	Number of Cost Drivers Used per Activity
Sales commissions	Dollar sales	$0.05 per dollar sales	$900,000
Advertising—TV/Radio	Minutes	$300 per minute	250
Advertising—Newspaper	Column inches	$10 per column inch	2,000
Catalogs	Catalogs mailed	$2.50 per catalog	60,000
Cost of catalog sales	Catalog orders	$1 per catalog order	9,000
Credit and collection	Dollar sales	$0.03 per dollar sales	$900,000

Instructions

(a) Compute the selling costs to be assigned to the "high-intensity" line of attire for the month of March (1) using the traditional product costing system (direct material cost is the cost driver), and (2) using activity-based costing.

(b) By what amount does the traditional product costing system undercost or overcost the "high-intensity" product line?

Assign overhead using traditional costing and ABC; classify activities as value- or non–value-added.

(LO 1, 4, 6), AP

E17-13 Healthy Products, Inc., uses a traditional product costing system to assign overhead costs uniformly to all products. To meet Food and Drug Administration requirements and to assure its customers of safe, sanitary, and nutritious food, Healthy engages in a high level of quality control. Healthy assigns its quality-control overhead costs to all products at a rate of 17% of direct labor costs. Its direct labor cost for the month of June for its low-calorie dessert line is $65,000. In response to repeated requests from its financial vice president, Healthy's management agrees to adopt activity-based costing. Data relating to the low-calorie dessert line for the month of June are as follows.

Activity Cost Pools	Cost Drivers	Overhead Rate	Number of Cost Drivers Used per Activity
Inspections of material received	Number of pounds	$0.80 per pound	6,000 pounds
In-process inspections	Number of servings	$0.33 per serving	10,000 servings
FDA certification	Customer orders	$12.00 per order	420 orders

Instructions

(a) Compute the quality-control overhead cost to be assigned to the low-calorie dessert product line for the month of June (1) using the traditional product costing system (direct labor cost is the cost driver), and (2) using activity-based costing.

(b) By what amount does the traditional product costing system undercost or overcost the low-calorie dessert line?

(c) Classify each of the activities as value-added or non–value-added.

Classify service company activities as value-added or non–value-added.

(LO 6), AN

E17-14 Lasso and Markowitz is a law firm that is initiating an activity-based costing system. Sam Lasso, the senior partner and strong supporter of ABC, has prepared the following list of activities performed by a typical attorney in a day at the firm.

Activities	Hours
Writing contracts and letters	1.5
Attending staff meetings	0.5
Taking depositions	1.0
Doing research	1.0
Traveling to/from court	1.0
Contemplating legal strategy	1.0
Eating lunch	1.0
Litigating a case in court	2.5
Entertaining a prospective client	1.5

Instructions

Classify each of the activities listed by Sam Lasso as value-added or non–value-added, and defend your classification. How much was value-added time and how much was non–value-added?

E17-15 Having itemized its costs for the first quarter of next year's budget, Santana Corporation desires to install an activity-based costing system. First, it identified the activity cost pools in which to accumulate factory overhead. Second, it identified the relevant cost drivers. (This was done in E17-8.)

Classify activities by level. (LO 7), **AN**

Instructions

Using the activity cost pools identified in E17-8, classify each of those cost pools as either unit-level, batch-level, product-level, or facility-level.

E17-16 William Mendel & Sons, Inc. is a small manufacturing company in La Jolla that uses activity-based costing. Mendel & Sons accumulates overhead in the following activity cost pools.

Classify activities by level. (LO 7), **AN**

1. Hiring personnel.
2. Managing parts inventory.
3. Purchasing.
4. Testing prototypes.
5. Designing products.
6. Setting up equipment.
7. Training employees.
8. Inspecting machined parts.
9. Machining.
10. Assembling.

Instructions

For each activity cost pool, indicate whether the activity cost pool would be unit-level, batch-level, product-level, or facility-level.

Exercises: Set B and Challenge Exercises

Visit the book's companion website, at **www.wiley.com/college/kimmel**, and choose the Student Companion site to access Exercise Set B and Challenge Exercises.

Problems: Set A

P17-1A FireOut, Inc. manufactures steel cylinders and nozzles for two models of fire extinguishers: (1) a home fire extinguisher and (2) a commercial fire extinguisher. The home model is a high-volume (54,000 units), half-gallon cylinder that holds 2 1/2 pounds of multi-purpose dry chemical at 480 PSI. The commercial model is a low-volume (10,200 units), two-gallon cylinder that holds 10 pounds of multi-purpose dry chemical at 390 PSI. Both products require 1.5 hours of direct labor for completion. Therefore, total annual direct labor hours are 96,300 or [1.5 hrs. × (54,000 + 10,200)]. Expected annual manufacturing overhead is $1,557,480. Thus, the predetermined overhead rate is $16.17 or ($1,557,480 ÷ 96,300) per direct labor hour. The direct materials cost per unit is $18.50 for the home model and $26.50 for the commercial model. The direct labor cost is $19 per unit for both the home and the commercial models.

The company's managers identified six activity cost pools and related cost drivers and accumulated overhead by cost pool as follows.

Assign overhead using traditional costing and ABC; compute unit costs; classify activities as value- or non–value-added. (LO 1, 4, 6), **AP**

Activity Cost Pools	Cost Drivers	Estimated Overhead	Expected Use of Cost Drivers	Expected Use of Drivers by Product	
				Home	Commercial
Receiving	Pounds	$ 70,350	335,000	215,000	120,000
Forming	Machine hours	150,500	35,000	27,000	8,000
Assembling	Number of parts	412,300	217,000	165,000	52,000
Testing	Number of tests	51,000	25,500	15,500	10,000
Painting	Gallons	52,580	5,258	3,680	1,578
Packing and shipping	Pounds	820,750	335,000	215,000	120,000
		$1,557,480			

Instructions

(a) Unit cost–H.M. $61.76

(a) Under traditional product costing, compute the total unit cost of each product. Prepare a simple comparative schedule of the individual costs by product (similar to Illustration 17-10 on page 903).

(b) Under ABC, prepare a schedule showing the computations of the activity-based overhead rates (per cost driver).

(c) Cost assigned–H.M. $1,069,300

(c) Prepare a schedule assigning each activity's overhead cost pool to each product based on the use of cost drivers. (Include a computation of overhead cost per unit, rounding to the nearest cent.)

(d) Cost/unit–H.M. $57.30

(d) Compute the total cost per unit for each product under ABC.

(e) Classify each of the activities as a value-added activity or a non–value-added activity.

(f) Comment on (1) the comparative overhead cost per unit for the two products under ABC, and (2) the comparative total costs per unit under traditional costing and ABC.

Assign overhead to products using ABC and evaluate decision.

(LO 4), **AP**

P17-2A Schultz Electronics manufactures two large-screen television models: the Royale which sells for $1,600, and a new model, the Majestic, which sells for $1,300. The production cost computed per unit under traditional costing for each model in 2014 was as follows.

Traditional Costing	Royale	Majestic
Direct materials	$ 700	$420
Direct labor ($20 per hour)	120	100
Manufacturing overhead ($38 per DLH)	228	190
Total per unit cost	$1,048	$710

In 2014, Schultz manufactured 25,000 units of the Royale and 10,000 units of the Majestic. The overhead rate of $38 per direct labor hour was determined by dividing total expected manufacturing overhead of $7,600,000 by the total direct labor hours (200,000) for the two models.

Under traditional costing, the gross profit on the models was Royale $552 or ($1,600 − $1,048), and Majestic $590 or ($1,300 − $710). Because of this difference, management is considering phasing out the Royale model and increasing the production of the Majestic model.

Before finalizing its decision, management asks Schultz's controller to prepare an analysis using activity-based costing (ABC). The controller accumulates the following information about overhead for the year ended December 31, 2014.

Activities	Cost Drivers	Estimated Overhead	Expected Use of Cost Drivers	Activity-Based Overhead Rate
Purchasing	Number of orders	$1,200,000	40,000	$30/order
Machine setups	Number of setups	900,000	18,000	$50/setup
Machining	Machine hours	4,800,000	120,000	$40/hour
Quality control	Number of inspections	700,000	28,000	$25/inspection

The cost drivers used for each product were:

Cost Drivers	Royale	Majestic	Total
Purchase orders	17,000	23,000	40,000
Machine setups	5,000	13,000	18,000
Machine hours	75,000	45,000	120,000
Inspections	11,000	17,000	28,000

Instructions

(a) Assign the total 2014 manufacturing overhead costs to the two products using activity-based costing (ABC) and determine the overhead cost per unit.

(b) What was the cost per unit and gross profit of each model using ABC costing?

(c) ✏️➡️ Are management's future plans for the two models sound? Explain.

(a) Royale $4,035,000

(b) Cost/unit–Royale $981.40

P17-3A Thakin Stairs Co. designs and builds factory-made premium wooden stairways for homes. The manufactured stairway components (spindles, risers, hangers, hand rails) permit installation of stairways of varying lengths and widths. All are of white oak wood. Budgeted manufacturing overhead costs for the year 2014 are as follows.

Assign overhead costs using traditional costing and ABC; compare results.
(LO 1, 4), **AN**

Overhead Cost Pools	Amount
Purchasing	$ 69,000
Handling materials	82,000
Production (cutting, milling, finishing)	210,000
Setting up machines	95,000
Inspecting	90,000
Inventory control (raw materials and finished goods)	126,000
Utilities	180,000
Total budgeted overhead costs	$852,000

For the last 4 years, Thakin Stairs Co. has been charging overhead to products on the basis of machine hours. For the year 2014, 100,000 machine hours are budgeted.

Jeremy Nolan, owner-manager of Thakin Stairs Co., recently directed his accountant, Bill Seagren, to implement the activity-based costing system that he has repeatedly proposed. At Jeremy Nolan's request, Bill and the production foreman identify the following cost drivers and their usage for the previously budgeted overhead cost pools.

Activity Cost Pools	Cost Drivers	Expected Use of Cost Drivers
Purchasing	Number of orders	600
Handling materials	Number of moves	8,000
Production (cutting, milling, finishing)	Direct labor hours	100,000
Setting up machines	Number of setups	1,250
Inspecting	Number of inspections	6,000
Inventory control (raw materials and finished goods)	Number of components	168,000
Utilities	Square feet occupied	90,000

Steve Hannon, sales manager, has received an order for 250 stairways from Community Builders, Inc., a large housing development contractor. At Steve's request, Bill prepares cost estimates for producing components for 250 stairways so Steve can submit a contract price per stairway to Community Builders. He accumulates the following data for the production of 250 stairways.

Direct materials	$103,600
Direct labor	$112,000
Machine hours	14,500
Direct labor hours	5,000
Number of purchase orders	60
Number of material moves	800
Number of machine setups	100
Number of inspections	450
Number of components	16,000
Number of square feet occupied	8,000

(b) Cost/stairway $1,356.56

(c) Cost/stairway $1,134.20

Assign overhead costs using traditional costing and ABC; compare results.
(LO 1, 4), **AN**

Instructions

(a) Compute the predetermined overhead rate using traditional costing with machine hours as the basis.

(b) What is the manufacturing cost per stairway under traditional costing? (Round to the nearest cent.)

(c) What is the manufacturing cost per stairway under the proposed activity-based costing? (Round to the nearest cent. Prepare all of the necessary schedules.)

(d) ▰▬▶ Which of the two costing systems is preferable in pricing decisions and why?

P17-4A Benton Corporation produces two grades of wine from grapes that it buys from California growers. It produces and sells roughly 3,000,000 liters per year of a low-cost, high-volume product called CoolDay. It sells this in 600,000 5-liter jugs. Benton also produces and sells roughly 300,000 liters per year of a low-volume, high-cost product called LiteMist. LiteMist is sold in 1-liter bottles. Based on recent data, the CoolDay product has not been as profitable as LiteMist. Management is considering dropping the inexpensive CoolDay line so it can focus more attention on the LiteMist product. The LiteMist product already demands considerably more attention than the CoolDay line.

Jack Eller, president and founder of Benton, is skeptical about this idea. He points out that for many decades the company produced only the CoolDay line and that it was always quite profitable. It wasn't until the company started producing the more complicated LiteMist wine that the profitability of CoolDay declined. Prior to the introduction of LiteMist, the company had simple equipment, simple growing and production procedures, and virtually no need for quality control. Because LiteMist is bottled in 1-liter bottles, it requires considerably more time and effort, both to bottle and to label and box than does CoolDay. The company must bottle and handle 5 times as many bottles of LiteMist to sell the same quantity as CoolDay. CoolDay requires 1 month of aging; LiteMist requires 1 year. CoolDay requires cleaning and inspection of equipment every 10,000 liters; LiteMist requires such maintenance every 600 liters.

Jack has asked the accounting department to prepare an analysis of the cost per liter using the traditional costing approach and using activity-based costing. The following information was collected.

	CoolDay	LiteMist
Direct materials per liter	$0.40	$1.20
Direct labor cost per liter	$0.50	$0.90
Direct labor hours per liter	0.05	0.09
Total direct labor hours	150,000	27,000

Activity Cost Pools	Cost Drivers	Estimated Overhead	Expected Use of Cost Drivers	Expected Use of Cost Drivers Per Product	
				CoolDay	LiteMist
Grape processing	Cart of grapes	$ 145,860	6,600	6,000	600
Aging	Total months	396,000	6,600,000	3,000,000	3,600,000
Bottling and corking	Number of bottles	270,000	900,000	600,000	300,000
Labeling and boxing	Number of bottles	189,000	900,000	600,000	300,000
Maintain and inspect equipment	Number of inspections	240,800	800	350	450
		$1,241,660			

Instructions

Answer each of the following questions. (Round all calculations to three decimal places.)

(a) Cost/liter–C.D. $1.251

(a) Under traditional product costing using direct labor hours, compute the total manufacturing cost per **liter** of both products.

(b) Under ABC, prepare a schedule showing the computation of the activity-based overhead rates (per cost driver).

(c) Cost/liter–C.D. $.241

(c) Prepare a schedule assigning each activity's overhead cost pool to each product, based on the use of cost drivers. Include a computation of overhead cost per liter.

(d) Compute the total manufacturing cost per liter for both products under ABC.

(e) Write a memo to Jack Eller discussing the implications of your analysis for the company's plans. In this memo, provide a brief description of ABC as well as an explanation of how the traditional approach can result in distortions.

P17-5A   Polk and Stoneman is a public accounting firm that offers two primary services, auditing and tax-return preparation. A controversy has developed between the partners of the two service lines as to who is contributing the greater amount to the bottom line. The area of contention is the assignment of overhead. The tax partners argue for assigning overhead on the basis of 40% of direct labor dollars, while the audit partners argue for implementing activity-based costing. The partners agree to use next year's budgeted data for purposes of analysis and comparison. The following overhead data are collected to develop the comparison.

Assign overhead costs to services using traditional costing and ABC; compute overhead rates and unit costs; compare results.

(LO 1, 4, 6, 8), **AN**

Activity Cost Pools	Cost Drivers	Estimated Overhead	Expected Use of Cost Drivers	Expected Use of Cost Drivers Per Service	
				Audit	Tax
Employee training	Direct labor dollars	$216,000	$1,800,000	$1,050,000	$750,000
Typing and secretarial	Number of reports/ forms	76,200	2,500	800	1,700
Computing	Number of minutes	204,000	60,000	25,000	35,000
Facility rental	Number of employees	142,500	40	22	18
Travel	Per expense reports	81,300	Direct	56,000	25,300
		$720,000			

Instructions
(a) Using traditional product costing as proposed by the tax partners, compute the total overhead cost assigned to both services (audit and tax) of Polk and Stoneman.
(b) (1) Using activity-based costing, prepare a schedule showing the computations of the activity-based overhead rates (per cost driver).
   (2) Prepare a schedule assigning each activity's overhead cost pool to each service based on the use of the cost drivers.
(c) Comment on the comparative overhead cost for the two services under both traditional costing and ABC.

(b) (2) Cost assigned–Tax $350,241

(c) Difference–Audit $50,241

Problems: Set B

P17-1B   VideoPlus, Inc. manufactures two types of DVD players, a deluxe model and a standard model. The deluxe model is a multi-format progressive-scan DVD player with networking capability, Dolby digital, and DTS decoder. The standard model's primary feature is progressive-scan. Annual production is 50,000 units for the deluxe and 20,000 units for the standard.

Assign overhead using traditional costing and ABC; compute unit costs; classify activities as value- or non–value-added.

(LO 1, 4, 6), **AP**

Both products require 2 hours of direct labor for completion. Therefore, total annual direct labor hours are 140,000 [2 hrs. × (20,000 + 50,000)]. Expected annual manufacturing overhead is $1,050,000. Thus, the predetermined overhead rate is $7.50 ($1,050,000 ÷ 140,000) per direct labor hour. The direct materials cost per unit is $42 for the deluxe model and $11 for the standard model. The direct labor cost is $18 per unit for both the deluxe and the standard models.

The company's managers identified six activity cost pools and related cost drivers and accumulated overhead by cost pool as follows.

Activity Cost Pool	Cost Driver	Estimated Overhead	Expected Use of Cost Drivers	Expected Use of Drivers by Product	
				Standard	Deluxe
Purchasing	Orders	$ 126,000	400	100	300
Receiving	Pounds	30,000	20,000	4,000	16,000
Assembling	Number of parts	444,000	74,000	20,000	54,000
Testing	Number of tests	115,000	23,000	10,000	13,000
Finishing	Units	140,000	70,000	20,000	50,000
Packing and shipping	Pounds	195,000	80,000	18,000	62,000
		$1,050,000			

(a) Unit cost–Standard $44

(c) Cost assigned–Standard $291,375

(d) Cost/unit–Standard $43.57

Instructions

(a) Under traditional product costing, compute the total unit cost of both products. Prepare a simple comparative schedule of the individual costs by product (similar to Illustration 17-10 on page 903).

(b) Under ABC, prepare a schedule showing the computations of the activity-based overhead rates (per cost driver).

(c) Prepare a schedule assigning each activity's overhead cost pool to each product based on the use of cost drivers. (Include a computation of overhead cost per unit, rounding to the nearest cent.)

(d) Compute the total cost per unit for each product under ABC.

(e) Classify each of the activities as a value-added activity or a non–value-added activity.

(f) Comment on (1) the comparative overhead cost per unit for the two products under ABC, and (2) the comparative total costs per unit under traditional costing and ABC.

Assign overhead to products using ABC and evaluate decision.

(LO 4), **AP**

P17-2B   Kinnard Electronics manufactures two home theater systems: the Elite which sells for $1,400, and a new model, the Preferred, which sells for $1,100. The production cost computed per unit under traditional costing for each model in 2014 was as follows.

Traditional Costing	Elite	Preferred
Direct materials	$600	$320
Direct labor ($20 per hour)	100	80
Manufacturing overhead ($35 per DLH)	175	140
Total per unit cost	$875	$540

In 2014, Kinnard manufactured 20,000 units of the Elite and 10,000 units of the Preferred. The overhead rate of $35 per direct labor hour was determined by dividing total expected manufacturing overhead of $4,900,000 by the total direct labor hours (140,000) for the two models.

Under traditional costing, the gross profit on the models was Elite $525 ($1,400 − $875), and Preferred $560 ($1,100 − $540). Because of this difference, management is considering phasing out the Elite model and increasing the production of the Preferred model.

Before finalizing its decision, management asks Kinnard's controller to prepare an analysis using activity-based costing (ABC). The controller accumulates the following information about overhead for the year ended December 31, 2014.

Activity	Cost Driver	Estimated Overhead	Expected Use of Cost Drivers	Activity-Based Overhead Rate
Purchasing	Number of orders	$ 775,000	25,000	$31
Machine setups	Number of setups	580,000	20,000	29
Machining	Machine hours	3,100,000	100,000	31
Quality control	Number of inspections	445,000	5,000	89

The cost drivers used for each product were:

Cost Driver	Elite	Preferred	Total
Purchase orders	11,250	13,750	25,000
Machine setups	11,000	9,000	20,000
Machine hours	40,000	60,000	100,000
Inspections	2,750	2,250	5,000

(a) Elite $2,152,500

(b) Cost/unit–Elite $807.63

Instructions

(a) Assign the total 2014 manufacturing overhead costs to the two products using activity-based costing (ABC) and determine the overhead cost per unit.

(b) What was the cost per unit and gross profit of each model using ABC costing?

(c) ▬▬▶ Are management's future plans for the two models sound? Explain.

Assign overhead costs using traditional costing and ABC; compare results.

(LO 1, 4), **AN**

P17-3B   Luxury Furniture designs and builds factory-made, premium, wood armoires for homes. All are of white oak. Its budgeted manufacturing overhead costs for the year 2014 are as follows.

Overhead Cost Pools	Amount
Purchasing	$ 45,000
Handling materials	50,000
Production (cutting, milling, finishing)	130,000
Setting up machines	85,000
Inspecting	60,000
Inventory control (raw materials and finished goods)	80,000
Utilities	100,000
Total budgeted overhead costs	$550,000

For the last 4 years, Luxury Furniture has been charging overhead to products on the basis of materials cost. For the year 2014, materials cost of $500,000 were budgeted.

Jim Brigham, owner-manager of Luxury Furniture, recently directed his accountant, Bob Borke, to implement the activity-based costing system that he has repeatedly proposed. At Jim Brigham's request, Bob and the production foreman identify the following cost drivers and their usage for the previously budgeted overhead cost pools.

Overhead Cost Pools	Activity Cost Drivers	Expected Use of Cost Drivers
Purchasing	Number of orders	500
Handling materials	Number of moves	5,000
Production (cutting, milling, finishing)	Direct labor hours	65,000
Setting up machines	Number of setups	1,000
Inspecting	Number of inspections	4,000
Inventory control (raw materials and finished goods)	Number of components	40,000
Utilities	Square feet occupied	50,000

Debbie Steiner, sales manager, has received an order for 12 luxury armoires from Thom's Interior Design. At Debbie's request, Bob prepares cost estimates for producing 12 armoires so Debbie can submit a contract price per armoire to Thom's. He accumulates the following data for the production of 12 armoires.

Direct materials	$5,200
Direct labor	$3,500
Direct labor hours	200
Number of purchase orders	3
Number of material moves	32
Number of machine setups	4
Number of inspections	20
Number of components	640
Number of square feet occupied	320

Instructions
(a) Compute the predetermined overhead rate using traditional costing with materials cost as the basis.
(b) What is the manufacturing cost per armoire under traditional costing?
(c) What is the manufacturing cost per armoire under the proposed activity-based costing? (Prepare all of the necessary schedules.)
(d) ▬▬▶ Which of the two costing systems is preferable in pricing decisions and why?

(b) Cost/armoire $1,201.67
(c) Cost/armoire $1,020.83

P17-4B Merando Corporation produces two grades of wine from grapes that it buys from California growers. It produces and sells roughly 600,000 gallon jugs per year of a low-cost, high-volume product called Valley Fresh. Merando also produces and sells roughly 200,000 gallons per year of a low-volume, high-cost product called Merando Valley. Merando Valley is sold in 1-liter bottles. Based on recent data, the Valley Fresh product has not been as profitable as Merando Valley. Management is considering dropping the inexpensive Valley Fresh line so it can focus more attention on the Merando Valley product. The Merando Valley product already demands considerably more attention than the Valley Fresh line.

Assign overhead costs using traditional costing and ABC; compare results.
(LO 1, 4), **AN**

Frankie Merando, president and founder of Merando, is skeptical about this idea. He points out that for many decades the company produced only the Valley Fresh line, and that it was always quite profitable. It wasn't until the company started producing the more complicated Merando Valley wine that the profitability of Valley Fresh declined. Prior to the introduction of Merando Valley, the company had simple equipment, simple growing and production procedures, and virtually no need for quality control. Because Merando Valley is bottled in 1-liter bottles, it requires considerably more time and effort, both to bottle and to label and box, than does Valley Fresh. The company must bottle and handle 4 times as many bottles of Merando Valley to sell the same quantity as Valley Fresh, since there are approximately 4 liters in a gallon. Valley Fresh requires 1 month of aging; Merando Valley requires 1 year. Valley Fresh requires cleaning and inspection of equipment every 2,500 gallons; Merando Valley requires such maintenance every 250 gallons.

Frankie has asked the accounting department to prepare an analysis of the cost per gallon using the traditional costing approach and using activity-based costing. The following information was collected.

	Valley Fresh	**Merando Valley**
Direct materials per gallon	$1.35	$3.60
Direct labor cost per gallon	$0.75	$1.50
Direct labor hours per gallon	0.05	0.10
Total direct labor hours	30,000	20,000

Activity Cost Pool	**Cost Driver**	**Estimated Overhead**	**Expected Use of Cost Drivers**	**Expected Use of Cost Drivers per Product**	
				Valley Fresh	**Merando Valley**
Grape processing	Cart of grapes	$ 146,000	8,000	6,000	2,000
Aging	Total months	420,000	3,000,000	600,000	2,400,000
Bottling and corking	Number of bottles	210,000	1,400,000	600,000	800,000
Labeling and boxing	Number of bottles	140,000	1,400,000	600,000	800,000
Maintain and inspect equipment	Number of inspections	234,000	1,040	240	800
		$1,150,000			

Instructions

Answer each of the following questions. (Round all calculations to three decimal places.)

(a) Cost/gallon–V.F. $3.25

(a) Under traditional product costing using direct labor hours, compute the total manufacturing cost per **gallon** of both products.

(b) Under ABC, prepare a schedule showing the computation of the activity-based overhead rates (per cost driver).

(c) Cost/gallon–V.F. $0.663

(c) Prepare a schedule assigning each activity's overhead cost pool to each product, based on the use of cost drivers. Include a computation of overhead cost per gallon.

(d) Compute the total manufacturing cost per gallon for both products under ABC.

(e) ━━✏ Write a memo to Frankie Merando discussing the implications of your analysis for the company's plans. In this memo, provide a brief description of ABC as well as an explanation of how the traditional approach can result in distortions.

Assign overhead costs to services using traditional costing and ABC; compute overhead rates and unit costs; compare results.

(LO 1, 4, 6, 8), **AN**

P17-5B Smith and Jones is a law firm that serves both individuals and corporations. A controversy has developed between the partners of the two service lines as to who is contributing the greater amount to the bottom line. The area of contention is the assignment of overhead. The individual partners argue for assigning overhead on the basis of 30% of direct labor dollars, while the corporate partners argue for implementing activity-based costing. The partners agree to use next year's budgeted data for purposes of analysis and comparison. The following overhead data are collected to develop the comparison.

Activity Cost Pool	Cost Driver	Estimated Overhead	Expected Use of Cost Drivers	Expected Use of Cost Drivers per Service	
				Corporate	Individual
Employee training	Direct labor dollars	$120,000	$1,600,000	$900,000	$700,000
Typing and secretarial	Number of reports/ forms	60,000	2,000	500	1,500
Computing	Number of minutes	130,000	40,000	17,000	23,000
Facility rental	Number of employees	100,000	25	14	11
Travel	Per expense reports	70,000	Direct	48,000	22,000
		$480,000			

Instructions

(a) Using traditional product costing, compute the total overhead cost assigned to both services (individual and corporate) of Smith and Jones.

(b) (1) Using activity-based costing, prepare a schedule showing the computations of the activity-based overhead rates (per cost driver).

(2) Prepare a schedule assigning each activity's overhead cost pool to each service based on the use of the cost drivers.

(c) ➡ Comment on the comparative overhead for the two service lines under both traditional costing and ABC.

(b) (2) Cost assigned–
   Individual $238,250

(c) Difference–Corporate
   $28,250

Problems: Set C

Visit the book's companion website, at **www.wiley.com/college/kimmel**, and choose the Student Companion site to access Problem Set C.

Waterways Continuing Problem

(*Note:* This is a continuation of the Waterways Problem from Chapters 14 through 16.)

WCP17 Waterways looked into ABC as a method of costing because of the variety of items it produces and the many different activities in which it is involved. This problem asks you to help Waterways use an activity-based costing system to account for its production activities.

Go to the book's companion website, at **www.wiley.com/college/kimmel**, to find the completion of this problem.

Broadening Your Perspective

Management Decision-Making

DECISION-MAKING AT CURRENT DESIGNS

BYP17-1 As you learned in previous chapters, Current Designs has two main product lines—composite kayaks, which are handmade and very labor-intensive, and rotomolded kayaks, which require less labor but employ more expensive equipment. Current Designs' controller, Diane Buswell, is now evaluating several different methods of assigning overhead to these products. It is important to ensure that costs are appropriately assigned to the company's products. At the same time, the system that is used must not be so complex that its costs are greater than its benefits.

Diane has decided to use the following activities and costs to evaluate the methods of assigning overhead.

Activity	Cost
Designing new models	$121,100
Creating and testing prototypes	152,000
Creating molds for kayaks	188,500
Operating oven for the rotomolded kayaks	40,000
Operating the vacuum line for the composite kayaks	28,000
Supervising production employees	180,000
Curing time (the time that is needed for the chemical processes to finish before the next step in the production process; many of these costs are related to the space required in the building)	190,400
Total	$900,000

As Diane examines the data, she decides that the cost of operating the oven for the rotomolded kayaks and the cost of operating the vacuum line for the composite kayaks can be directly assigned to each of these product lines and do not need to be allocated with the other costs.

Instructions

For purposes of this analysis, assume that Current Designs uses $234,000 in direct labor costs to produce 1,000 composite kayaks and $286,000 in direct labor costs to produce 4,000 rotomolded kayaks each year.

(a) One method of allocating overhead would allocate the common costs to each product line by using an allocation basis such as the number of employees in working on each type of kayak or the amount of factory space used for the production of each type of kayak. Diane knows that about 50% of the area of the plant and 50% of the employees work on the composite kayaks, and the remaining space and other employees work on the rotomolded kayaks. Using this information, and remembering that the cost of operating the oven and vacuum line have been directly assigned, determine the total amount to be assigned to the composite kayak line and the rotomolded kayak line, and the amount to be assigned to each of the units in each line.

(b) Another method of allocating overhead is to use direct labor dollars as an allocation basis. Remembering that the costs of the oven and the vacuum line have been assigned directly to the product lines, allocate the remaining costs using direct labor dollars as the allocation basis. Then, determine the amount of overhead that should be assigned to each unit of each product line using this method.

(c) Activity-based costing requires a cost driver for each cost pool. Use the following information to assign the costs to the product lines using the activity-based costing approach.

Activity	Cost Driver	Driver Amount for Composite Kayaks	Driver Amount for Rotomolded Kayaks
Designing new models	Number of models	3	1
Creating and testing prototypes	Number of prototypes	6	2
Creating molds for kayaks	Number of molds	12	1
Supervising production employees	Number of employees	12	12
Curing time	Number of days of curing time	15,000	2,000

What amount of overhead should be assigned to each composite kayak using this method? What amount of overhead should be assigned to each rotomolded kayak using this method?

(d) Which of the three methods do you think Current Designs should use? Why?

DECISION-MAKING ACROSS THE ORGANIZATION

BYP17-2 East Valley Hospital is a primary medical care facility and trauma center that serves 11 small, rural midwestern communities within a 40-mile radius. The hospital offers all the medical/surgical services of a typical small hospital. It has a staff of 18 full-time doctors and 20 part-time visiting specialists. East Valley has a payroll of 150 employees consisting of technicians, nurses, therapists, managers, directors, administrators, dieticians, secretaries, data processors, and janitors.

Instructions

With the class divided into groups, discuss and answer the following.

(a) Using your (limited, moderate, or in-depth) knowledge of a hospital's operations, identify as many **activities** as you can that would serve as the basis for implementing an activity-based costing system.

(b) For each of the activities listed in (a), identify a **cost driver** that would serve as a valid measure of the resources consumed by the activity.

MANAGERIAL ANALYSIS

BYP17-3 Ideal Manufacturing Company of Sycamore, Illinois, has supported a research and development (R&D) department that has for many years been the sole contributor to the company's new farm machinery products. The R&D activity is an overhead cost center that provides services only to in-house manufacturing departments (four different product lines), all of which produce agricultural/farm/ranch-related machinery products.

The department has never sold its services outside, but because of its long history of success, larger manufacturers of agricultural products have approached Ideal to hire its R&D department for special projects. Because the costs of operating the R&D department have been spiraling uncontrollably, Ideal's management is considering entertaining these outside approaches to absorb the increasing costs. But, (1) management doesn't have any cost basis for charging R&D services to outsiders, and (2) it needs to gain control of its R&D costs. Management decides to implement an activity-based costing system in order to determine the charges for both outsiders and the in-house users of the department's services.

R&D activities fall into four pools with the following annual costs.

Market analysis	$1,050,000
Product design	2,350,000
Product development	3,600,000
Prototype testing	1,400,000

Activity analysis determines that the appropriate cost drivers and their usage for the four activities are:

Activities	Cost Drivers	Total Estimated Drivers
Market analysis	Hours of analysis	15,000 hours
Product design	Number of designs	2,500 designs
Product development	Number of products	90 products
Prototype testing	Number of tests	500 tests

Instructions

(a) Compute the activity-based overhead rate for each activity cost pool.

(b) How much cost would be charged to an in-house manufacturing department that consumed 1,800 hours of market analysis time, was provided 280 designs relating to 10 products, and requested 92 engineering tests?

(c) How much cost would serve as the basis for pricing an R&D bid with an outside company on a contract that would consume 800 hours of analysis time, require 178 designs relating to 3 products, and result in 70 engineering tests?

(d) What is the benefit to Ideal Manufacturing of applying activity-based costing to its R&D activity for both in-house and outside charging purposes?

REAL-WORLD FOCUS

BYP17-4 An article in *Cost Management*, by Kocakulah, Bartlett, and Albin entitled "ABC for Calculating Mortgage Loan Servicing Expenses" (July/August 2009, p. 36), discusses a use of ABC in the financial services industry.

Instructions

Read the article and answer the following questions.

(a) What are some of the benefits of ABC that relate to the financial services industry?

(b) What are three things that the company's original costing method did not take into account?

(c) What were some of the cost drivers used by the company in the ABC approach?

BYP17-5 Activity-based costing methods are constantly being improved upon, and many websites discuss suggestions for improvement. The article in this activity outlines an alternative perspective on activity-based costing.

Address: **http://hbswk.hbs.edu/item/4587.html**, or go to **www.wiley.com/college/kimmel**

Instructions
Read the article provided at the site and answer the following questions.
(a) What concerns do the authors say are raised by "real-world use" of ABC? According to the authors, what benefits have companies enjoyed from the use of ABC?
(b) What method do the authors suggest for estimating practical capacity? How important is it to be precise in this estimate?
(c) Describe the steps that are taken after practical capacity has been estimated.
(d) What is one of the primary benefits obtained by management in the report entitled "ABC, the Time-Driven Way"? What is an example of how this worked for a real company?

Critical Thinking

ETHICS CASE

BYP17-6 Curtis Rich, the cost accountant for Hi-Power Mower Company, recently installed activity-based costing at Hi-Power's St. Louis lawn tractor (riding mower) plant where three models—the 8-horsepower Bladerunner, the 12-horsepower Quickcut, and the 18-horsepower Supercut—are manufactured. Curtis's new product costs for these three models show that the company's traditional costing system had been significantly undercosting the 18-horsepower Supercut. This was due primarily to the lower sales volume of the Supercut compared to the Bladerunner and the Quickcut.

Before completing his analysis and reporting these results to management, Curtis is approached by his friend Ed Gray, who is the production manager for the 18-horsepower Supercut model. Ed has heard from one of Curtis's staff about the new product costs and is upset and worried for his job because the new costs show the Supercut to be losing, rather than making, money.

At first, Ed condemns the new cost system, whereupon Curtis explains the practice of activity-based costing and why it is more accurate than the company's present system. Even more worried now, Ed begs Curtis, "Massage the figures just enough to save the line from being discontinued. You don't want me to lose my job, do you? Anyway, nobody will know."

Curtis holds firm but agrees to recompute all his calculations for accuracy before submitting his costs to management.

Instructions
(a) Who are the stakeholders in this situation?
(b) What, if any, are the ethical considerations in this situation?
(c) What are Curtis's ethical obligations to the company? To his friend?

ALL ABOUT YOU

BYP17-7 There are many resources available on the Web to assist people in time management. Some of these resources are designed specifically for college students.

Instructions
Go to **http://www.dartmouth.edu/~acskills/videos/video_tm.html** (or do an Internet search of Dartmouth's time-management video). Watch the video and then answer the following questions.
(a) What are the main tools of time management for students, and what is each used for?
(b) At what time of day are students most inclined to waste time? What time of day is the best for studying complex topics?
(c) How can employing time-management practices be a "liberating" experience?
(d) Why is goal-setting important? What are the characteristics of good goals, and what steps should you take to help you develop your goals?

CONSIDERING YOUR COSTS AND BENEFITS

BYP17-8 As discussed in the chapter, the principles underlying activity-based costing have evolved into the broader approach known as **activity-based management**. One of the common practices of activity-based management is to identify all business activities, classify each activity as either a value-added or a non–value-added activity, and then try to reduce or eliminate the time spent on non–value-added activities. Consider the implications of applying this same approach to your everyday life, at work and at school. How do you spend your time each day? How much of your day is spent on activities that help you accomplish your objectives, and how much of your day is spent on activities that do not add value?

Many "self-help" books and websites offer suggestions on how to improve your time management. Should you minimize the "non–value-added" hours in your life by adopting the methods suggested by these sources? The basic arguments for and against are as follows.

> **YES:** There are a limited number of hours in a day. You should try to maximize your chances of achieving your goals by eliminating the time that you waste.
>
> **NO:** Life is about more than working yourself to death. Being an efficiency expert doesn't guarantee that you will be happy. Schedules and daily planners are too constraining.

Instructions
Write a response indicating your position regarding this situation. Provide support for your view.

Answers to Insight and Accounting Across the Organization Questions

p. 904 Traveling Light Q: Why do airlines charge even higher rates for heavier bags, bags that are odd shapes (e.g., ski bags), and bags with hazardous materials in them? **A:** Each of these factors increases the costs to the airlines. Heavier baggage is more difficult to handle, thus increasing labor costs. It also uses up more fuel. Bags that are odd shapes complicate handling both for humans and machines. In addition, odd shapes take up more space in the cargo area. Finally, hazardous materials require special handling and storage procedures. All of these factors should be considered by an airline when it decides how much to charge for special baggage.

p. 906 Using ABC to Aid in Employee Evaluation Q: What positive implications does application of ABC have for the employees of this company? **A:** ABC will make these employees more aware of which activities cost the company more money. They will be motivated to reduce their use of these activities in order to improve their individual performance.

p. 909 What Does NASCAR Have to Do with Breakfast Cereal? Q: What are the benefits of reducing setup time? **A:** Setup time is a non–value-added activity. Customers are not willing to pay extra for more setup time. By reducing the time spent on setups, the company can reduce non–value-added costs. Also, by reducing setup time, the company can switch from producing one product to producing a different product more quickly. This enables it to respond to customers' demands more quickly, thus avoiding stockouts.

p. 914 ABC Evaluated Q: What might explain why so many companies say that ideally they would use ABC, but they haven't adopted it yet? **A:** As noted in the chapter, implementation of an ABC system can be very expensive. It may be difficult to justify an expenditure for a system that allocates overhead costs more accurately. The benefits of more accurate costing may not be as obvious as some of the other things a company might spend its money on, such as a machine that produces goods more efficiently.

Answers to Self-Test Questions

1. c **2.** c **3.** c **4.** a **5.** b **6.** b ($100 × 80), ($100 × 60) **7.** d [($1,920,000/160,000) ×40,000], [($1,920,000/160,000) × 30,000)], [($1,920,000/160,000) × 90,000)] **8.** b **9.** d **10.** d **11.** c **12.** c *****13.** d *****14.** b

✔ The Navigator

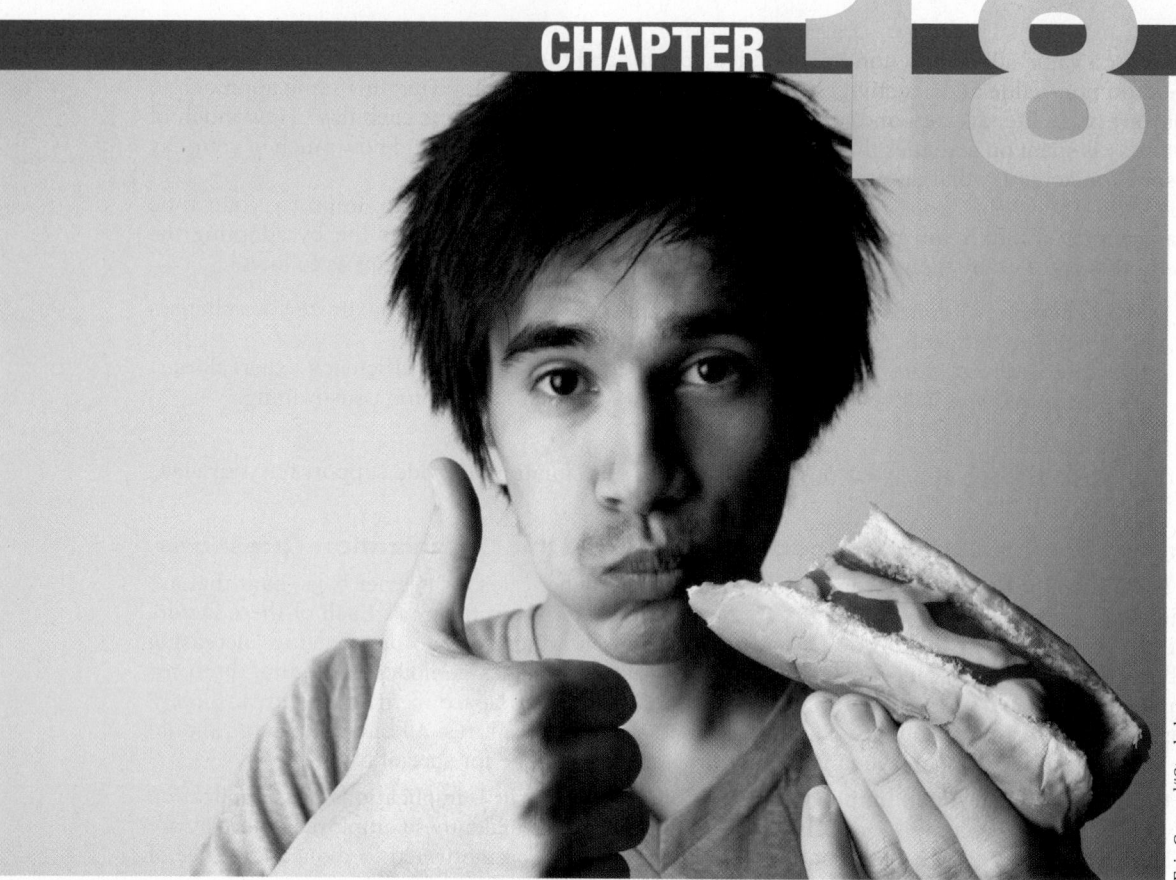

Eric Gerrard/iStockphoto

CHAPTER 18

COST-VOLUME-PROFIT

LEARNING OBJECTIVES

After studying this chapter, you should be able to:

1   Distinguish between variable and fixed costs.

2   Explain the significance of the relevant range.

3   Explain the concept of mixed costs.

4   List the five components of cost-volume-profit analysis.

5   Indicate what contribution margin is and how it can be expressed.

6   Identify the three ways to determine the break-even point.

7   Give the formulas for determining sales required to earn target net income.

8   Define margin of safety, and give the formulas for computing it.

✔ **The Navigator**

- Scan Learning Objectives
- Read Feature Story
- Scan Preview
- Read Text and Answer **Do it!**
  ○ p. 951 ○ p. 954 ○ p. 962 ○ p. 964
- Work Using the Decision Toolkit
- Review Summary of Learning Objectives
- Work Comprehensive **Do it!** p. 967
- Answer Self-Test Questions
- Complete Assignments
- Go to WileyPLUS for practice and tutorials

✔ The Navigator

It wasn't that Jeff Bezos didn't have a good job. He was a vice president at a Wall Street firm. But, he quit his job, moved to Seattle, and started an online retailer, which he named Amazon.com. Like any good entrepreneur, Jeff strove to keep his initial investment small. Operations were run out of his garage. And, to avoid the need for a warehouse, he took orders for books and had them shipped from other distributors' warehouses. One board member recalls how excited the board was whenever an order came in from a customer in a state that Amazon had never serviced before.

DON'T WORRY— JUST GET BIG

By its fourth month, Amazon was selling 100 books a day. In its first full year, it had $15.7 million in sales. The next year, sales increased eightfold. Two years later, sales were $1.6 billion.

Although its sales growth was impressive, Amazon's ability to lose money was equally amazing. One analyst nicknamed it Amazon. bomb, while another, predicting its demise, called it Amazon.toast. Why was it losing money? The company used every available dollar to reinvest in itself. It built massive warehouses and bought increasingly sophisticated (and expensive) computer systems to improve its distribution system. This desire to grow as fast as possible was captured in a T-shirt slogan at its company picnic, which read "Eat another hot dog, get big fast." This buying binge was increasing the company's

fixed costs at a rate that exceeded its sales growth. Skeptics were predicting that Amazon would soon run out of cash. It didn't.

In the fourth quarter of 2010 (only 15 years after its world headquarters were located in a garage), Amazon reported quarterly revenues of $12.95 billion and quarterly income of $416 million. But, even as it announced record profits, its share price fell by 9%. Why? Because although the company was predicting that its sales revenue in the next quarter would increase by at least 28%, it predicted that its operating profit would fall by at least 2% and perhaps by as much as 34%.

The company made no apologies. It explained that it was in the process of expanding from 39 distribution centers to 52. As Amazon's finance chief noted, "You're not as productive on those assets for some time. I'm very pleased with the investments we're making and we've shown over our history that we've been able to make great returns on the capital we invest in." In other words, eat another hot dog.

Watch the Southwest Airlines video in Wiley-PLUS to learn more about cost-volume-profit analysis in the real world.

Source: Christine Frey and John Cook, "How Amazon.com Survived, Thrived and Turned a Profit," *Seattle Post* (January 28, 2008); and Stu Woo, "Sticker Shock Over Amazon Growth," *Wall Street Journal Online* (January 28, 2011).

The Navigator

INSIDE CHAPTER 18 . . .

As the Feature Story indicates, to manage any size business you must understand how costs respond to changes in sales volume and the effect of costs and revenues on profits. A prerequisite to understanding cost-volume-profit (CVP) relationships is knowledge of how costs behave. In this chapter, we first explain the considerations involved in cost behavior analysis. Then, we discuss and illustrate CVP analysis.

The content and organization of Chapter 18 are as follows.

Cost Behavior Analysis

Cost behavior analysis is the study of how specific costs respond to changes in the level of business activity. As you might expect, some costs change, and others remain the same. For example, for an airline company such as Southwest or United, the longer the flight, the higher the fuel costs. On the other hand, Massachusetts General Hospital's costs to staff the emergency room on any given night are relatively constant regardless of the number of patients treated. A knowledge of cost behavior helps management plan operations and decide between alternative courses of action. Cost behavior analysis applies to all types of entities.

The starting point in cost behavior analysis is measuring the key business activities. Activity levels may be expressed in terms of sales dollars (in a retail company), miles driven (in a trucking company), room occupancy (in a hotel), or dance classes taught (by a dance studio). Many companies use more than one measurement base. A manufacturer, for example, may use direct labor hours or units of output for manufacturing costs, and sales revenue or units sold for selling expenses.

For an activity level to be useful in cost behavior analysis, changes in the level or volume of activity should be correlated with changes in costs. The activity level selected is referred to as the activity (or volume) index. The **activity index** identifies the activity that causes changes in the behavior of costs. With an appropriate activity index, companies can classify the behavior of costs in response to changes in activity levels into three categories: variable, fixed, or mixed.

VARIABLE COSTS

Variable costs are costs that vary **in total** directly and proportionately with changes in the activity level. If the level increases 10%, total variable costs will increase 10%. If the level of activity decreases by 25%, variable costs will decrease 25%. Examples of variable costs include direct materials and direct labor for a manufacturer; cost of goods sold, sales commissions, and freight-out for a merchandiser;

and gasoline in airline and trucking companies. A variable cost may also be defined as a cost that **remains the same *per unit* at every level of activity**.

To illustrate the behavior of a variable cost, assume that Damon Company manufactures tablet computers that contain a $10 camera. The activity index is the number of tablet computers produced. As Damon manufactures each tablet, the total cost of cameras used increases by $10. As part (a) of Illustration 18-1 shows, total cost of the cameras will be $20,000 if Damon produces 2,000 tablets, and $100,000 when it produces 10,000 tablets. We also can see that a variable cost remains the same per unit as the level of activity changes. As part (b) of Illustration 18-1 shows, the unit cost of $10 for the cameras is the same whether Damon produces 2,000 or 10,000 tablets.

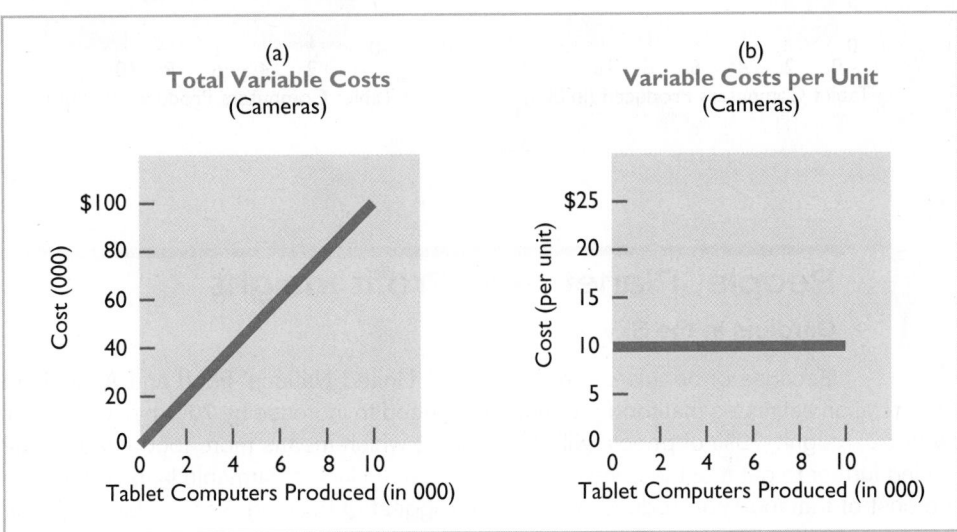

Illustration 18-1 Behavior of total and unit variable costs

Companies that rely heavily on labor to manufacture a product, such as Nike or Reebok, or to provide a service, such as Hilton or Marriott, are likely to have many variable costs. In contrast, companies that use a high proportion of machinery and equipment in producing revenue, such as AT&T or Duke Energy Co., may have few variable costs.

FIXED COSTS

Fixed costs are costs that **remain the same in total** regardless of changes in the activity level. Examples include property taxes, insurance, rent, supervisory salaries, and depreciation on buildings and equipment. Because total fixed costs remain constant as activity changes, it follows that **fixed costs *per unit* vary inversely with activity: As volume increases, unit cost declines, and vice versa**.

To illustrate the behavior of fixed costs, assume that Damon Company leases its productive facilities at a cost of $10,000 per month. Total fixed costs of the facilities will remain constant at every level of activity, as part (a) of Illustration 18-2 (page 948) shows. But, **on a per unit basis, the cost of rent will decline as activity increases**, as part (b) of Illustration 18-2 shows. At 2,000 units, the unit cost per tablet computer is $5 ($10,000 ÷ 2,000). When Damon produces 10,000 tablets, the unit cost of the rent is only $1 per tablet ($10,000 ÷ 10,000).

The trend for many manufacturers is to have more fixed costs and fewer variable costs. This trend is the result of increased use of automation and less use of employee labor. As a result, depreciation and lease charges (fixed costs) increase, whereas direct labor costs (variable costs) decrease.

Illustration 18-2 Behavior of total and unit fixed costs

People, Planet, and Profit Insight

Gardens in the Sky

Because of population increases, the United Nations' Food and Agriculture Organization estimates that food production will need to increase by 70% by 2050. Also, by 2050, roughly 70% of people will live in cities, which means more food needs to be hauled further to get it to the consumer. To address the lack of farmable land and reduce the cost of transporting produce, some have suggested building "vertical farming" sky-scrapers in cities. This sounds great, but do the numbers work? Some variable costs would be reduced. For example, the use of pesticides, herbicides, fuel costs for shipping, and water would all drop. Soil erosion would be a non-issue since plants would be grown hydroponically (in a solution of water and minerals), and land requirements would be reduced because of vertical structures. But, other costs would be higher. First, there is the cost of the building. Also, any multistory building would require artificial lighting for plants on lower floors.

Until these cost challenges can be overcome, it appears that these skyscrapers will not break even. On the other hand, rooftop greenhouses on existing city structures already appear financially viable. For example, a 15,000 square-foot rooftop greenhouse in Brooklyn already produces roughly 30 tons of vegetables per year for local residents.

Source: "Vertical Farming: Does It Really Stack Up?" *The Economist* (December 9, 2010).

 What are some of the variable and fixed costs that are impacted by hydroponic farming? (See page 982.)

© Jani Bryson/iStockphoto

RELEVANT RANGE

LEARNING OBJECTIVE 2

Explain the significance of the relevant range.

In Illustration 18-1 part (a) (page 947), a straight line is drawn throughout the entire range of the activity index for total variable costs. In essence, the assumption is that the costs are **linear**. If a relationship is linear (that is, straight-line), then changes in the activity index will result in a direct, proportional change in the variable cost. For example, if the activity level doubles, the cost doubles.

It is now necessary to ask: Is the straight-line relationship realistic? Does the linear assumption produce useful data for CVP analysis?

In most business situations, a straight-line relationship **does not exist** for variable costs throughout the entire range of possible activity. At abnormally low levels of activity, it may be impossible to be cost-efficient. Small-scale operations may not allow the company to obtain quantity discounts for raw materials or to use specialized labor. In contrast, at abnormally high levels of activity, labor costs may increase sharply because of overtime pay. Also, at high activity levels, materials costs may jump significantly because of excess spoilage caused by worker fatigue.

As a result, in the real world, the relationship between the behavior of a variable cost and changes in the activity level is often **curvilinear**, as shown in part (a) of Illustration 18-3. In the curved sections of the line, a change in the activity index will not result in a direct, proportional change in the variable cost. That is, a doubling of the activity index will not result in an exact doubling of the variable cost. The variable cost may more than double, or it may be less than double.

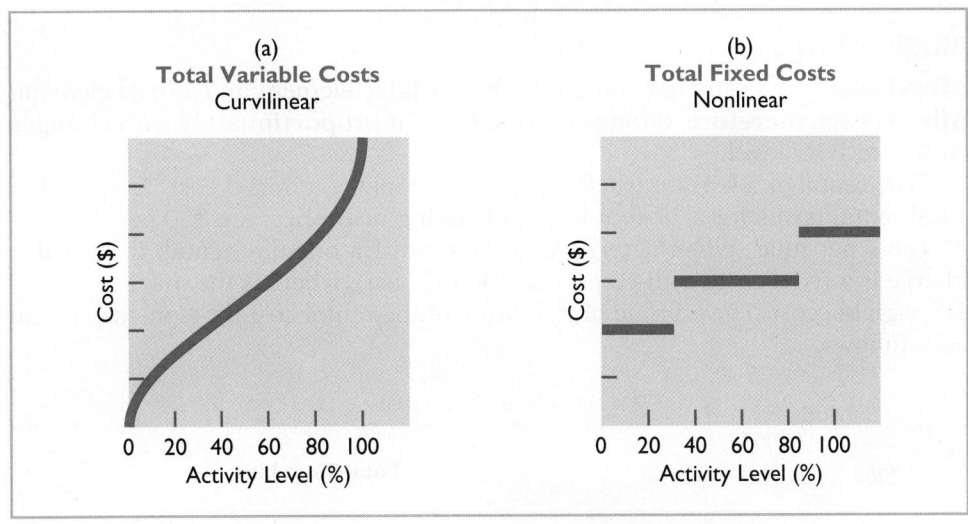

Illustration 18-3 Nonlinear behavior of variable and fixed costs

Total fixed costs also do not have a straight-line relationship over the entire range of activity. Some fixed costs will not change. But it is possible for management to change other fixed costs. For example, in some instances, salaried employees (fixed) are replaced with freelance workers (variable). Illustration 18-3, part (b), shows an example of the behavior of total fixed costs through all potential levels of activity.

For most companies, operating at almost zero or at 100% capacity is the exception rather than the rule. Instead, companies often operate over a somewhat narrower range, such as 40–80% of capacity. The range over which a company expects to operate during a year is called the **relevant range** of the activity index. Within the relevant range, as both diagrams in Illustration 18-4 (page 950) show, a straight-line relationship generally exists for both variable and fixed costs.

Helpful Hint Fixed costs that may be changeable include research, such as new product development, and management training programs.

Alternative Terminology The relevant range is also called the *normal* or *practical range*.

Illustration 18-4 Linear behavior within relevant range

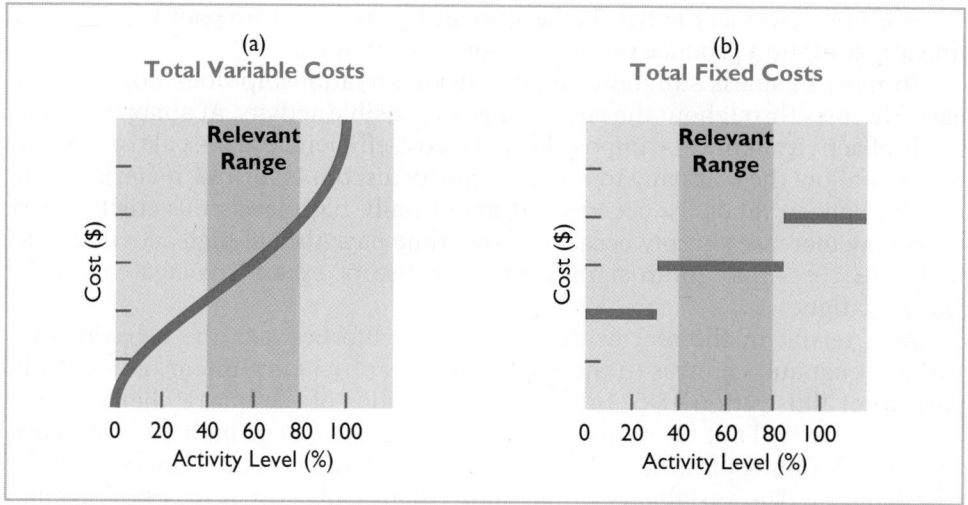

As you can see, although the linear (straight-line) relationship may not be completely realistic, **the linear assumption produces useful data for CVP analysis as long as the level of activity remains within the relevant range**.

MIXED COSTS

Mixed costs are costs that contain both a variable element and a fixed element. **Mixed costs, therefore, change in total but not proportionately with changes in the activity level.**

The rental of a U-Haul truck is a good example of a mixed cost. Assume that local rental terms for a 17-foot truck, including insurance, are $50 per day plus 50 cents per mile. When determining the cost of a one-day rental, the per day charge is a fixed cost (with respect to miles driven), whereas the mileage charge is a variable cost. The graphic presentation of the rental cost for a one-day rental is as follows.

Illustration 18-5 Behavior of a mixed cost

In this case, the fixed-cost element is the cost of having the service available. The variable-cost element is the cost of actually using the service. Another example of a mixed cost is utility costs (electric, telephone, and so on), where there is a flat service fee plus a usage charge.

For purposes of CVP analysis, **mixed costs must be classified into their fixed and variable elements**. How does management make the classification? One possibility is to determine the variable and fixed components each time a mixed cost is incurred. But because of time and cost constraints, this approach is rarely followed. Instead, the usual approach is to collect data on the behavior of the mixed costs at various levels of activity. Analysts then identify the fixed- and variable-cost components. Companies use various types of analysis. One type of analysis, called the **high-low method**, is discussed next. Other methods, such as the scatter diagram method and least squares regression analysis, are more appropriately explained in cost accounting courses.

Do it!

Helena Company reports the following total costs at two levels of production.

	10,000 Units	20,000 Units
Direct materials	$20,000	$40,000
Maintenance	8,000	10,000
Direct labor	17,000	34,000
Indirect materials	1,000	2,000
Depreciation	4,000	4,000
Utilities	3,000	5,000
Rent	6,000	6,000

Classify each cost as variable, fixed, or mixed.

Solution

Direct materials, direct labor, and indirect materials are variable costs.

Depreciation and rent are fixed costs.

Maintenance and utilities are mixed costs.

Related exercise material: **BE18-1, BE18-2, E18-1, E18-2, E18-4,** and **Do it! 18-1.**

TYPES OF COSTS

Action Plan

• Recall that a variable cost varies in total directly and proportionately with each change in activity level.

• Recall that a fixed cost remains the same in total with each change in activity level.

• Recall that a mixed cost changes in total but not proportionately with each change in activity level.

High-Low Method

The high-low method uses the total costs incurred at the high and low levels of activity to classify mixed costs into fixed and variable components. The difference in costs between the high and low levels represents variable costs, since only the variable-cost element can change as activity levels change.

The steps in computing fixed and variable costs under this method are as follows.

1. **Determine variable cost per unit from the following formula.**

$$\text{Change in Total Costs} \div \text{High minus Low Activity Level} = \text{Variable Cost per Unit}$$

Illustration 18-6 Formula for variable cost per unit using high-low method

To illustrate, assume that Metro Transit Company has the following maintenance costs and mileage data for its fleet of buses over a 6-month period.

Illustration 18-7 Assumed maintenance costs and mileage data

Month	Miles Driven	Total Cost	Month	Miles Driven	Total Cost
January	20,000	$30,000	April	50,000	$63,000
February	40,000	48,000	May	30,000	42,000
March	35,000	49,000	June	43,000	61,000

The high and low levels of activity are 50,000 miles in April and 20,000 miles in January. The maintenance costs at these two levels are $63,000 and $30,000, respectively. The difference in maintenance costs is $33,000 ($63,000 − $30,000), and the difference in miles is 30,000 (50,000 − 20,000). Therefore, for Metro Transit, variable cost per unit is $1.10, computed as follows.

$$\$33,000 \div 30,000 = \$1.10$$

2. **Determine the fixed costs by subtracting the total variable costs at either the high or the low activity level from the total cost at that activity level.**

For Metro Transit, the computations are shown in Illustration 18-8.

Illustration 18-8 High-low method computation of fixed costs

				METRO TRANSIT.xls	
Home	Insert	Page Layout	Formulas	Data	Review	View

P18   *fx*

	A	B	C	D
1			**METRO TRANSIT**	
2				**Activity Level**	
3			**High**	**Low**
4	Total cost		$63,000	$30,000
5	Less:	Variable costs		
6		50,000 × $1.10	55,000	
7		20,000 × $1.10		22,000
8	Total fixed costs		$ 8,000	$ 8,000
9				
10				

Maintenance costs are therefore $8,000 per month of fixed costs plus $1.10 per mile of variable costs. This is represented by the following formula:

Maintenance costs = $8,000 + ($1.10 × Miles driven)

For example, at 45,000 miles, estimated maintenance costs would be $8,000 fixed and $49,500 variable ($1.10 × 45,000) for a total of $57,500.

The graph in Illustration 18-9 plots the 6-month data for Metro Transit Company. The red line drawn in the graph connects the high and low data points, and therefore represents the equation that we just solved using the high-low method. The red, "high-low" line intersects the y-axis at $8,000 (the fixed-cost level), and it rises by $1.10 per unit (the variable cost per unit). Note that a completely different line would result if we chose any two of the other data points. That is, by

Illustration 18-9 Scatter plot for Metro Transit Company

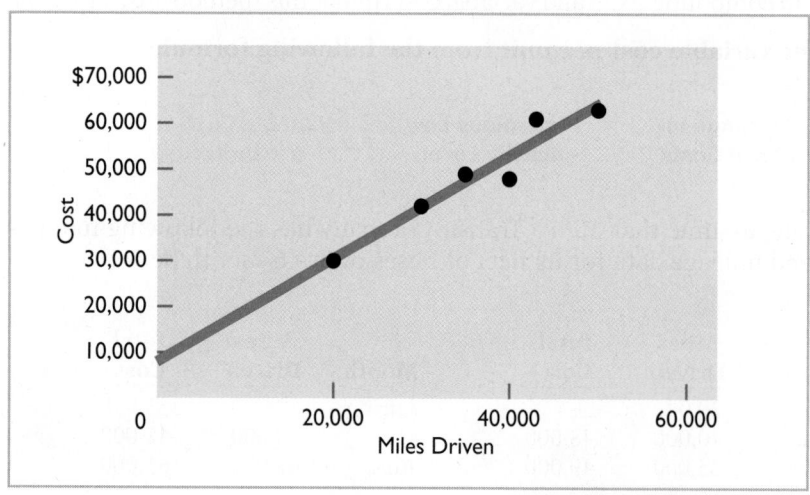

choosing any two other data points, we would end up with a different estimate of fixed costs and a different variable cost per unit. Thus, from this scatter plot, we can see that while the high-low method is simple, the result is rather arbitrary. A better approach, which uses information from all the data points to estimate fixed and variable costs, is called **regression analysis**. A discussion of regression analysis is provided in a supplement on the book's companion website.

Management Insight

Skilled Labor Is Truly Essential

The recession that started in 2008 had devastating implications for employment. But one surprise was that for some manufacturers, the number of jobs lost was actually lower than in previous recessions. One of the main explanations for this was that between 2000 and 2008, many factories adopted lean manufacturing practices. This meant that production relied less on large numbers of low-skilled workers, and more on machines and a few highly skilled workers. As a result of this approach, a single employee was supporting far more dollars in sales. Thus, it would require a larger decline in sales before an employee would need to be laid-off in order to continue to break even. Also, because the employees are highly skilled, employers are reluctant to lose them. Instead of lay-offs, many manufacturers have resorted to cutting employees hours.

Source: Timothy Aeppel and Justin Lahart, "Lean Factories Find It Hard to Cut Jobs Even in a Slump," *Wall Street Journal Online* (March 9, 2009).

 Would you characterize labor costs as being a fixed cost, a variable cost, or something else in this situation? (See page 983.)

pidjoe/iStockphoto

IMPORTANCE OF IDENTIFYING VARIABLE AND FIXED COSTS

Why is it important to segregate costs into variable and fixed elements? The answer may become apparent if we look at the following four business decisions.

1. If American Airlines is to make a profit when it reduces all domestic fares by 30%, what reduction in costs or increase in passengers will be required?
   Answer: To make a profit when it cuts domestic fares by 30%, American Airlines will have to increase the number of passengers or cut its variable costs for those flights. Its fixed costs will not change.

2. If Ford Motor Company meets workers' demands for higher wages, what increase in sales revenue will be needed to maintain current profit levels?
   Answer: Higher wages at Ford Motor Company will increase the variable costs of manufacturing automobiles. To maintain present profit levels, Ford will have to cut other variable costs or increase the price of its automobiles.

3. If United States Steel Corp.'s program to modernize plant facilities through significant equipment purchases reduces the work force by 50%, what will be the effect on the cost of producing one ton of steel?
   Answer: The modernizing of plant facilities at United States Steel Corp. changes the proportion of fixed and variable costs of producing one ton of steel. Fixed costs increase because of higher depreciation charges, whereas variable costs decrease due to the reduction in the number of steelworkers.

4. What happens if Kellogg's increases its advertising expenses but cannot increase prices because of competitive pressure?
   Answer: Sales volume must be increased to cover the increase in fixed advertising costs.

HIGH-LOW METHOD

 Do it! Byrnes Company accumulates the following data concerning a mixed cost, using units produced as the activity level.

Action Plan

- Determine the highest and lowest levels of activity.
- Compute variable cost per unit as: Change in total costs ÷ (High − low activity level) = Variable cost per unit.
- Compute fixed cost as: Total cost − (Variable cost per unit × Units produced) = Fixed cost.

	Units Produced	Total Cost
March	9,800	$14,740
April	8,500	13,250
May	7,000	11,100
June	7,600	12,000
July	8,100	12,460

(a) Compute the variable- and fixed-cost elements using the high-low method.
(b) Estimate the total cost if the company produces 6,000 units.

Solution

(a) Variable cost: ($14,740 − $11,100) ÷ (9,800 − 7,000) = $1.30 per unit
Fixed cost: $14,740 − $12,740 ($1.30 × 9,800 units) = $2,000
or $11,100 − $9,100 ($1.30 × 7,000) = $2,000
(b) Total cost to produce 6,000 units: $2,000 + $7,800 ($1.30 × 6,000) = $9,800

✔ **The Navigator**

Related exercise material: **BE18-3, BE18-4, BE18-5, E18-3, E18-5, E18-6,** and **Do it!** 18-2.

Cost-Volume-Profit Analysis

LEARNING OBJECTIVE 4
List the five components of cost-volume-profit analysis.

Cost-volume-profit (CVP) analysis is the study of the effects of changes in costs and volume on a company's profits. CVP analysis is important in profit planning. It also is a critical factor in such management decisions as setting selling prices, determining product mix, and maximizing use of production facilities.

BASIC COMPONENTS

CVP analysis considers the interrelationships among the components shown in Illustration 18-10.

Illustration 18-10
Components of CVP analysis

| Volume or level of activity | Unit selling prices | Variable costs per unit | Total fixed costs | Sales mix |

The following assumptions underlie each CVP analysis.

1. The behavior of both costs and revenues is linear throughout the relevant range of the activity index.
2. Costs can be classified accurately as either variable or fixed.
3. Changes in activity are the only factors that affect costs.

4. All units produced are sold.

5. When more than one type of product is sold, the sales mix will remain constant. That is, the percentage that each product represents of total sales will stay the same. Sales mix complicates CVP analysis because different products will have different cost relationships. In this chapter, we assume a single product. (In Chapter 19, we relax this assumption.)

When these assumptions are not valid, the CVP analysis may be inaccurate.

CVP INCOME STATEMENT

Because CVP is so important for decision-making, management often wants this information reported in a **cost-volume-profit (CVP) income statement** format for internal use. The CVP income statement classifies costs as variable or fixed and computes a contribution margin. **Contribution margin (CM)** is the amount of revenue remaining after deducting variable costs. It is often stated both as a total amount and on a per unit basis.

> **LEARNING OBJECTIVE 5**
> Indicate what contribution margin is and how it can be expressed.

We will use Vargo Video Company to illustrate a CVP income statement. Vargo Video produces a high-definition digital camcorder with 15× optical zoom and a wide-screen, high-resolution LCD monitor. Relevant data for the camcorders sold by this company in June 2014 are as follows.

Unit selling price of camcorder	$500
Unit variable costs	$300
Total monthly fixed costs	$200,000
Units sold	1,600

Illustration 18-11 Assumed selling and cost data for Vargo Video

The CVP income statement for Vargo Video therefore would be reported as follows.

VARGO VIDEO COMPANY
CVP Income Statement
For the Month Ended June 30, 2014

	Total
Sales (1,600 camcorders)	$ 800,000
Variable costs	480,000
Contribution margin	320,000
Fixed costs	200,000
Net income	$120,000

Illustration 18-12 CVP income statement, with net income

A traditional income statement and a CVP income statement both report the same net income of $120,000. However a traditional income statement does not classify costs as variable or fixed, and therefore it does not report a contribution margin. In addition, sometimes per unit amounts and percentage of sales amounts are shown on a CVP income statement to facilitate CVP analysis. *Homework assignments specify which columns to present.*

In the applications of CVP analysis that follow, we assume that the term "cost" includes all costs and expenses related to production and sale of the product. That is, cost includes manufacturing costs plus selling and administrative expenses.

Contribution Margin per Unit

Illustration 18-14 shows Vargo Video's CVP income statement at the point where net income equals zero. It shows a contribution margin of $200,000, and a contribution margin per unit of $200 ($500 − $300). The formula for **contribution margin per unit** and the computation for Vargo Video are:

Illustration 18-13 Formula for contribution margin per unit

Unit Selling Price	−	Unit Variable Costs	=	Contribution Margin per Unit
$500	−	$300	=	$200

Contribution margin per unit indicates that for every camcorder sold, the selling price exceeds the variable costs by $200. Vargo generates $200 per unit sold to cover fixed costs and contribute to net income. Because Vargo Video has fixed costs of $200,000, it must sell 1,000 camcorders ($200,000 ÷ $200) to cover its fixed costs. At the point where total contribution margin exactly equals fixed costs, Vargo will report net income of zero. At this point, referred to as the **break-even point**, total costs (variable plus fixed) exactly equal total revenue.

Illustration 18-14 CVP income statement, with zero net income

VARGO VIDEO COMPANY
CVP Income Statement
For the Month Ended June 30, 2014

	Total	Per Unit
Sales (1,000 camcorders)	$500,000	$500
Variable costs	300,000	300
Contribution margin	200,000	$200
Fixed costs	200,000	
Net income	$ –0–	

It follows that for every camcorder sold above the break-even point of 1,000 units, **net income increases by the amount of the contribution margin per unit, $200**. For example, assume that Vargo sold one more camcorder, for a total of 1,001 camcorders sold. In this case, Vargo reports net income of $200, as shown in Illustration 18-15.

Illustration 18-15 CVP income statement, with net income and per unit data

VARGO VIDEO COMPANY
CVP Income Statement
For the Month Ended June 30, 2014

	Total	Per Unit
Sales (1,001 camcorders)	$500,500	$500
Variable costs	300,300	300
Contribution margin	200,200	$200
Fixed costs	200,000	
Net income	$ 200	

Contribution Margin Ratio

Some managers prefer to use a contribution margin ratio in CVP analysis. The contribution margin ratio is the contribution margin expressed as a percentage of sales, as shown in Illustration 18-16.

VARGO VIDEO COMPANY
CVP Income Statement
For the Month Ended June 30, 2014

	Total	Percent of Sales
Sales (1,001 camcorders)	$500,500	100%
Variable costs	300,300	60
Contribution margin	200,200	40%
Fixed costs	200,000	
Net income	$ 200	

Illustration 18-16 CVP income statement, with net income and percent of sales data

Alternatively, the contribution margin ratio is the contribution margin per unit divided by the unit selling price. For Vargo Video, the ratio is as follows.

Contribution Margin per Unit	÷	Unit Selling Price	=	Contribution Margin Ratio
$200	÷	$500	=	40%

Illustration 18-17 Formula for contribution margin ratio

The contribution margin ratio of 40% means that Vargo generates 40 cents of contribution margin with each dollar of sales. That is, $0.40 of each sales dollar (40% × $1) is available to apply to fixed costs and to contribute to net income.

This expression of contribution margin is very helpful in determining the effect of changes in sales on net income. For example, if Vargo's sales increase $100,000, net income will increase $40,000 (40% × $100,000). Thus, by using the contribution margin ratio, managers can quickly determine increases in net income from any change in sales.

We can also see this effect through a CVP income statement. Assume that Vargo Video's current sales are $500,000 and it wants to know the effect of a $100,000 (200-unit) increase in sales. Vargo prepares a comparative CVP income statement analysis as follows.

Illustration 18-18
Comparative CVP income statements

VARGO VIDEO COMPANY
CVP Income Statements
For the Month Ended June 30, 2014

	No Change			With Change		
	Total	Per Unit	Percent of Sales	Total	Per Unit	Percent of Sales
Sales	$ 500,000	$ 500	100%	$ 600,000	$ 500	100%
Variable costs	300,000	300	60	360,000	300	60
Contribution margin	200,000	$200	40%	240,000	$200	40%
Fixed costs	200,000			200,000		
Net income	$ –0–			$ 40,000		

The $40,000 increase in net income can be calculated on either a contribution margin per unit basis (200 units × $200 per unit) or using the contribution margin ratio times the increase in sales dollars (40% × $100,000). Note that the contribution margin per unit and contribution margin as a percentage of sales remain unchanged by the increase in sales.

Study these CVP income statements carefully. The concepts presented in these statements are used extensively in this and later chapters.

🧰 DECISION TOOLKIT

DECISION CHECKPOINTS	INFO NEEDED FOR DECISION	TOOL TO USE FOR DECISION	HOW TO EVALUATE RESULTS
What was the contribution toward fixed costs and income from each unit sold?	Selling price per unit and variable cost per unit	Contribution margin per unit = Unit selling price − Unit variable cost	Every unit sold will increase income by the contribution margin.
What was the increase in income as a result of an increase in sales?	Contribution margin per unit and unit selling price	Contribution margin ratio = Contribution margin per unit ÷ Unit selling price	Every dollar of sales will increase income by the contribution margin ratio.

BREAK-EVEN ANALYSIS

A key relationship in CVP analysis is the level of activity at which total revenues equal total costs (both fixed and variable)—the **break-even point**. At this volume of sales, the company will realize no income but will suffer no loss. The process of finding the break-even point is called **break-even analysis**. Knowledge of the break-even point is useful to management when it decides whether to introduce new product lines, change sales prices on established products, or enter new market areas.

The break-even point can be:

1. Computed from a mathematical equation.
2. Computed by using contribution margin.
3. Derived from a cost-volume-profit (CVP) graph.

The break-even point can be expressed either in **sales units** or **sales dollars**.

Mathematical Equation

The first line of Illustration 18-19 shows a common equation used for CVP analysis. When net income is set to zero, this equation can be used to calculate the break-even point.

Illustration 18-19 Basic CVP equation

Required Sales	−	Variable Costs	−	Fixed Costs	=	Net Income
$500Q	−	$300Q	−	$200,000	=	$0

As shown in Illustration 18-14 (page 956), net income equals zero when the contribution margin (sales minus variable costs) is equal to fixed costs.

To reflect this, Illustration 18-20 rewrites the equation with contribution margin (sales minus variable costs) on the left side, and fixed costs and net income on the right. We can compute the break-even point **in units** by **using unit selling prices** and **unit variable costs**. The computation for Vargo Video is:

Illustration 18-20
Computation of break-even point in units

Required Sales	−	Variable Costs	−	Fixed Costs	=	Net Income
$500Q	−	$300Q	−	$200,000	=	$0
$500Q	−	$300Q	=	$200,000	+	$0
$200Q	=	$200,000				

$$Q = \frac{\$200,000}{\$200} = \frac{\text{Fixed Costs}}{\text{Contribution Margin per Unit}}$$

$$Q = 1{,}000 \text{ units}$$

where

Q	=	sales volume in units
$500	=	selling price
$300	=	variable costs per unit
$200,000	=	total fixed costs

Thus, Vargo Video must sell 1,000 units to break even.

To find the amount of **sales dollars** required to break even, we multiply the units sold at the break-even point times the selling price per unit, as shown below.

$$1{,}000 \times \$500 = \$500{,}000 \text{ (break-even sales dollars)}$$

Contribution Margin Technique

Many managers employ the contribution margin to compute the break-even point.

CONTRIBUTION MARGIN IN UNITS. The final step in Illustration 18-20 divides fixed costs by the contribution margin per unit (highlighted in red). Thus, rather than walk through all of the steps of the equation approach, we can simply employ this formula shown in Illustration 18-21.

Fixed Costs	÷	Contribution Margin per Unit	=	Break-Even Point in Units
$200,000	÷	$200	=	1,000 units

Why does this formula work? The contribution margin per unit is the net amount by which each sale exceeds the variable costs per unit. Every sale generates this much money to pay off fixed costs. Consequently, if we divide fixed costs by the contribution margin per unit, we know how many units we need to sell to break even.

CONTRIBUTION MARGIN RATIO. As we will see in the next chapter, when a company has numerous products, it is not practical to determine the contribution margin per unit for each product. In this case, using the contribution margin ratio is very useful for determining the break-even point in total dollars (rather than units). Recall that the contribution margin ratio is the amount of contribution margin that is generated from each dollar of sales. Therefore, to determine the sales dollars needed to cover fixed costs, we divide fixed costs by the contribution margin ratio, as shown in Illustration 18-22.

Fixed Costs	÷	Contribution Margin Ratio	=	Break-Even Point in Dollars
$200,000	÷	40%	=	$500,000

To apply this formula to Vargo, consider that its 40% contribution margin ratio means that for every dollar sold, it generates 40 cents of contribution margin. The question is, how many dollars of sales does Vargo need in order to generate total contribution margin of $200,000 to pay off fixed costs? We divide the fixed costs of $200,000 by the 40 cents of contribution margin generated by each dollar of sales to arrive at $500,000 ($200,000 ÷ 40%). To prove this result, if we generate 40 cents of contribution margin for each dollar of sales, then the total contribution margin generated by $500,000 in sales is $200,000 ($500,000 × 40%).

Service Company Insight

Charter Flights Offer a Good Deal

The Internet is wringing inefficiencies out of nearly every industry. While commercial aircraft spend roughly 4,000 hours a year in the air, chartered aircraft are flown only 500 hours annually. That means that they are sitting on the ground—not making any money—about 90% of the time. One company, FlightServe, saw a business opportunity in that fact. For about the same cost as a first-class ticket, FlightServe decided to match up executives with charter flights in small "private jets." The executive would get a more comfortable ride and could avoid the hassle of big airports. Flight-Serve noted that the average charter jet has eight seats. When all eight seats were full, the company would have an 80% profit margin. It would break even at an average of 3.3 full seats per flight.

Source: "Jet Set Go," *The Economist* (March 18, 2000), p. 68.

? How did FlightServe determine that it would break even with 3.3 seats full per flight? (See page 983.)

Digital Vision/Getty Images

Graphic Presentation

An effective way to find the break-even point is to prepare a break-even graph. Because this graph also shows costs, volume, and profits, it is referred to as a **cost-volume-profit (CVP) graph.**

As the CVP graph in Illustration 18-23 shows, sales volume is recorded along the horizontal axis. This axis should extend to the maximum level of expected sales. Both total revenues (sales) and total costs (fixed plus variable) are recorded on the vertical axis.

The construction of the graph, using the data for Vargo Video, is as follows.

1. Plot the sales line, starting at the zero activity level. For every camcorder sold, total revenue increases by $500. For example, at 200 units, sales are $100,000. At the upper level of activity (1,800 units), sales are $900,000. The revenue line is assumed to be linear through the full range of activity.

2. Plot the total fixed costs using a horizontal line. For the camcorders, this line is plotted at $200,000. The fixed costs are the same at every level of activity.

3. Plot the total-cost line. This starts at the fixed-cost line at zero activity. It increases by the variable costs at each level of activity. For each camcorder, variable costs are $300. Thus, at 200 units, total variable costs are $60,000, and the total cost is $260,000. At 1,800 units, total variable costs are $540,000, and total cost is $740,000. On the graph, the amount of the variable costs can be derived from the difference between the total-cost and fixed-cost lines at each level of activity.

Illustration 18-23 CVP graph

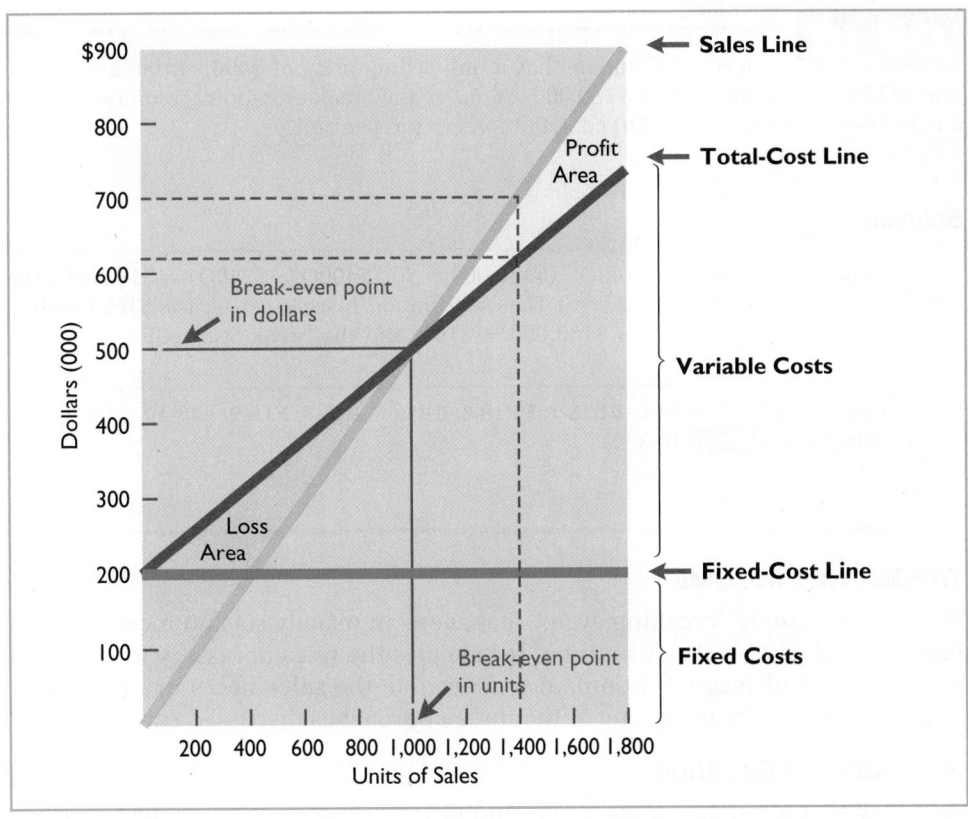

4. Determine the break-even point from the intersection of the total-cost line and the sales line. The break-even point in dollars is found by drawing a horizontal line from the break-even point to the vertical axis. The break-even point in units is found by drawing a vertical line from the break-even point to the horizontal axis. For the camcorders, the break-even point is $500,000 of sales, or 1,000 units. At this sales level, Vargo Video will cover costs but make no profit.

The CVP graph also shows both the net income and net loss areas. Thus, the amount of income or loss at each level of sales can be derived from the sales and total-cost lines.

A CVP graph is useful because the effects of a change in any element in the CVP analysis can be quickly seen. For example, a 10% increase in selling price will change the location of the sales line. Likewise, the effects on total costs of wage increases can be quickly observed.

DECISION TOOLKIT

DECISION CHECKPOINTS	INFO NEEDED FOR DECISION	TOOL TO USE FOR DECISION	HOW TO EVALUATE RESULTS
At what amount of sales does a company cover its costs?	Unit selling price, unit variable cost, and total fixed costs	Break-even point analysis *In units:* $$\text{Break-even point} = \frac{\text{Fixed costs}}{\text{Unit contribution margin}}$$ *In dollars:* $$\text{Break-even point} = \frac{\text{Fixed costs}}{\text{Contribution margin ratio}}$$	Below the break-even point, the company is unprofitable.

BREAK-EVEN ANALYSIS

Do it!

Lombardi Company has a unit selling price of $400, variable costs per unit of $240, and fixed costs of $180,000. Compute the break-even point in units using (a) a mathematical equation and (b) contribution margin per unit.

Action Plan

• Apply the formula:
Sales = Variable costs + Fixed costs + Net income.

• Apply the formula:
Fixed costs ÷ Contribution margin per unit = Break-even point in units.

The Navigator

Solution

(a) The equation is $400Q − $240Q − $180,000 = $0; ($400Q − $240Q) = $180,000. The break-even point in units is 1,125. (b) The contribution margin per unit is $160 ($400 − $240). The formula therefore is $180,000 ÷ $160, and the break-even point in units is 1,125.

Related exercise material: **BE18-6, BE18-7, BE18-8, BE18-9, E18-8, E18-9, E18-10, E18-11, E18-12, E18-13,** and **Do it! 18-3.**

TARGET NET INCOME

Rather than simply "breaking even," management usually sets an income objective often called **target net income**. It indicates the sales necessary to achieve a specified level of income. Companies determine the sales necessary to achieve target net income by using one of the three approaches discussed earlier.

Mathematical Equation

We know that at the break-even point no profit or loss results for the company. By adding an amount for target net income to the same basic equation, we obtain the following formula for determining required sales.

Illustration 18-24 Formula for required sales to meet target net income

Required Sales	−	Variable Costs	−	Fixed Costs	=	Target Net Income

Recall that once the break-even point has been reached so that fixed costs are covered, each additional unit sold increases net income by the amount of the contribution margin per unit. We can rewrite the equation with contribution margin (sales minus variable costs) on the left-hand side, and fixed costs and net income on the right. Assuming that target net income is $120,000 for Vargo Video, the computation of required sales in units is as follows.

Illustration 18-25 Computation of required sales

Required Sales	−	Variable Costs	−	Fixed Costs	=	Target Net Income
$500Q	−	$300Q	−	$200,000	=	$120,000
$500Q	−	$300Q	=	$200,000	+	$120,000

$$\$200Q = \$200,000 + \$120,000$$

$$Q = \frac{\$200,000 + \$120,000}{\$200} = \frac{\text{Fixed Costs} + \text{Net Target Income}}{\text{Contribution Margin per Unit}}$$

$$Q = 1,600$$

where

Q	=	sales volume
$500	=	selling price
$300	=	variable costs per unit
$200,000	=	total fixed costs
$120,000	=	target net income

Vargo must sell 1,600 units to achieve target net income of $120,000. The sales dollars required to achieve the target net income is found by multiplying the units sold by the unit selling price [(1,600 × $500) = $800,000].

Contribution Margin Technique

As in the case of break-even sales, we can compute in either units or dollars the sales required to meet target net income. The formula to compute required sales in units for Vargo Video using the contribution margin per unit can be seen in the final step of the equation approach in Illustration 18-25 (shown in red). We simply divide the sum of fixed costs and target net income by the contribution margin per unit. Illustration 18-26 shows this for Vargo.

$\left(\begin{array}{c}\textbf{Fixed Costs +}\\\textbf{Target Net Income}\end{array}\right)$	÷	Contribution Margin per Unit	=	Required Sales in Units
($200,000 + $120,000)	÷	$200	=	1,600 units

Illustration 18-26 Formula for required sales in units using contribution margin per unit

To achieve its desired target net income of $120,000, Vargo must sell 1,600 camcorders.

The formula to compute the required sales in dollars for Vargo Video using the contribution margin ratio is shown below.

$\left(\begin{array}{c}\textbf{Fixed Costs +}\\\textbf{Target Net Income}\end{array}\right)$	÷	Contribution Margin Ratio	=	Required Sales in Dollars
($200,000 + $120,000)	÷	40%	=	$800,000

Illustration 18-27 Formula for required sales in dollars using contribution margin ratio

To achieve its desired target net income of $120,000, Vargo must generate sales of $800,000.

Graphic Presentation

We also can use the CVP graph in Illustration 18-23 (on page 961) to find the sales required to meet target net income. In the profit area of the graph, the distance between the sales line and the total-cost line at any point equals net income. We can find required sales by analyzing the differences between the two lines until the desired net income is found.

For example, suppose Vargo Video sells 1,400 camcorders. Illustration 18-23 shows that a vertical line drawn at 1,400 units intersects the sales line at $700,000 and the total cost line at $620,000. The difference between the two amounts represents the net income (profit) of $80,000.

MARGIN OF SAFETY

Margin of safety is the difference between actual or expected sales and sales at the break-even point. It measures the "cushion" that a particular level of sales provides. It tells us how far sales could fall before the company begins operating at a loss. The margin of safety is expressed in dollars or as a ratio.

The formula for stating the **margin of safety in dollars** is actual (or expected) sales minus break-even sales. Assuming that actual (expected) sales for Vargo Video are $750,000, the computation is:

LEARNING OBJECTIVE 8
Define margin of safety, and give the formulas for computing it.

Actual (Expected) Sales	−	Break-Even Sales	=	Margin of Safety in Dollars
$750,000	−	$500,000	=	$250,000

Illustration 18-28 Formula for margin of safety in dollars

Vargo's margin of safety is $250,000. Its sales could fall $250,000 before it operates at a loss.

The **margin of safety ratio** is the margin of safety in dollars divided by actual (or expected) sales. The formula and computation for determining the margin of safety ratio are:

Illustration 18-29 Formula for margin of safety ratio

Margin of Safety in Dollars	÷	Actual (Expected) Sales	=	Margin of Safety Ratio
$250,000	÷	$750,000	=	33%

This means that the company's sales could fall by 33% before it would be operating at a loss.

The higher the dollars or the percentage, the greater the margin of safety. Management continuously evaluates the adequacy of the margin of safety in terms of such factors as the vulnerability of the product to competitive pressures and to downturns in the economy.

Yael/Retna

Service Company Insight

How a Rolling Stones' Tour Makes Money

Computation of break-even and margin of safety is important for service companies. Consider how the promoter for the Rolling Stones' tour used the break-even point and margin of safety. For example, one outdoor show should bring 70,000 individuals for a gross of $2.45 million. The promoter guarantees $1.2 million to the Rolling Stones. In addition, 20% of gross goes to the stadium in which the performance is staged. Add another $400,000 for other expenses such as ticket takers, parking attendants, advertising, and so on. The promoter also shares in sales of T-shirts and memorabilia for which the promoter will net over $7 million during the tour. From a successful Rolling Stones' tour, the promoter could make $35 million!

 What amount of sales dollars are required for the promoter to break even? (See page 983.)

BREAK-EVEN, MARGIN OF SAFETY, TARGET NET INCOME

Action Plan

- Apply the formula for the break-even point in dollars.
- Apply the formulas for the margin of safety in dollars and the margin of safety ratio.
- Apply the formula for the required sales in dollars.

 The Navigator

Do it!

Zootsuit Inc. makes travel bags that sell for $56 each. For the coming year, management expects fixed costs to total $320,000 and variable costs to be $42 per unit. Compute the following: (a) break-even point in dollars using the contribution margin (CM) ratio; (b) the margin of safety and margin of safety ratio assuming actual sales are $1,382,400; and (c) the sales dollars required to earn net income of $410,000.

Solution

(a) Contribution margin ratio = [($56 − $42) ÷ $56] = 25%
Break-even sales in dollars = $320,000 ÷ 25% = $1,280,000

(b) Margin of safety = $1,382,400 − $1,280,000 = $102,400
Margin of safety ratio = $102,400 ÷ $1,382,400 = 7.4%

(c) Required sales in dollars = ($320,000 + $410,000) ÷ 25% = $2,920,000

Related exercise material: **BE18-10, BE18-11, BE18-12, E18-14, E18-15, E18-16,** and **Do it! 18-4.**

USING THE DECISION TOOLKIT

B.T. Hernandez Company, maker of high-quality flashlights, has experienced steady growth over the last 6 years. However, increased competition has led Mr. Hernandez, the president, to believe that an aggressive campaign is needed next year to maintain the company's present growth. The company's accountant has presented Mr. Hernandez with the following data for the current year, 2013, for use in preparing next year's advertising campaign.

Cost Schedules

Variable costs	
Direct labor per flashlight	$ 8.00
Direct materials	4.00
Variable overhead	3.00
Variable cost per flashlight	$15.00
Fixed costs	
Manufacturing	$ 25,000
Selling	40,000
Administrative	70,000
Total fixed costs	$135,000
Selling price per flashlight	$25.00
Sales, 2013 (20,000 flashlights)	$500,000

Mr. Hernandez has set the sales target for the year 2014 at a level of $550,000 (22,000 flashlights).

Instructions

(Ignore any income tax considerations.)
(a) What is the operating income for 2013?
(b) What is the contribution margin per unit for 2013?
(c) What is the break-even point in units for 2013?
(d) Mr. Hernandez believes that to attain the sales target in the year 2014, the company must incur an additional selling expense of $10,000 for advertising in 2014, with all other costs remaining constant. What will be the break-even point in sales dollars for 2014 if the company spends the additional $10,000?
(e) If the company spends the additional $10,000 for advertising in 2014, what is the sales level in dollars required to equal 2013 operating income?

Solution

(a)
Sales		$500,000
Less:		
Variable costs (20,000 flashlights × $15)	300,000	
Fixed costs	135,000	
Operating income		$ 65,000

(b)
Selling price per flashlight	$25
Variable cost per flashlight	15
Contribution margin per unit	$10

(c) Fixed costs ÷ Contribution margin per unit = Break-even point in units $135,000 ÷ $10 = 13,500 units

(d) Fixed costs ÷ Contribution margin ratio = Break-even point in dollars $145,000* ÷ 40%** = $362,500

*Fixed costs (from 2013)	$135,000
Additional advertising expense	10,000
Fixed costs (2014)	$145,000

**Contribution margin ratio = Contribution margin per unit ÷ Unit selling price 40% = $10 ÷ $25

(e) Required sales = (Fixed costs + Target net income) ÷ Contribution margin ratio
$525,000 = ($145,000 + $65,000) ÷ 40%

Summary of Learning Objectives

1 **Distinguish between variable and fixed costs.** Variable costs are costs that vary in total directly and proportionately with changes in the activity index. Fixed costs are costs that remain the same in total regardless of changes in the activity index.

2 **Explain the significance of the relevant range.** The relevant range is the range of activity in which a company expects to operate during a year. It is important in CVP analysis because the behavior of costs is assumed to be linear throughout the relevant range.

3 **Explain the concept of mixed costs.** Mixed costs increase in total but not proportionately with changes in the activity level. For purposes of CVP analysis, mixed costs must be classified into their fixed and variable elements. One method that management may use to classify these costs is the high-low method.

4 **List the five components of cost-volume-profit analysis.** The five components of CVP analysis are (a) volume or level of activity, (b) unit selling prices, (c) variable costs per unit, (d) total fixed costs, and (e) sales mix.

5 **Indicate what contribution margin is and how it can be expressed.** Contribution margin is the amount of revenue remaining after deducting variable costs. It is identified in a CVP income statement, which classifies costs as variable or fixed. It can be expressed as a total amount, as a per unit amount, or as a ratio.

6 **Identify the three ways to determine the break-even point.** The break-even point can be (a) computed from a mathematical equation, (b) computed by using a contribution margin technique, and (c) derived from a CVP graph.

7 **Give the formulas for determining sales required to earn target net income.** The general formula for required sales is: Required sales − Variable costs − Fixed costs = Target net income. Two other formulas are Required sales in units = (Fixed costs + Target net income) ÷ Contribution margin per unit, and Required sales in dollars = (Fixed costs + Target net income) ÷ Contribution margin ratio.

8 **Define margin of safety, and give the formulas for computing it.** Margin of safety is the difference between actual or expected sales and sales at the break-even point. The formulas for margin of safety are Actual (expected) sales − Break-even sales = Margin of safety in dollars; Margin of safety in dollars ÷ Actual (expected) sales = Margin of safety ratio.

✔ The Navigator

🧰 DECISION TOOLKIT *A SUMMARY*

DECISION CHECKPOINTS	INFO NEEDED FOR DECISION	TOOL TO USE FOR DECISION	HOW TO EVALUATE RESULTS
What was the contribution toward fixed costs and income from each unit sold?	Selling price per unit and variable cost per unit	$\text{Contribution margin per unit} = \text{Unit selling price} - \text{Unit variable cost}$	Every unit sold will increase income by the contribution margin.
What was the increase in income as a result of an increase in sales?	Contribution margin per unit and unit selling price	$\text{Contribution margin ratio} = \text{Contribution margin per unit} \div \text{Unit selling price}$	Every dollar of sales will increase income by the contribution margin ratio.
At what amount of sales does a company cover its costs?	Unit selling price, unit variable cost, and total fixed costs	Break-even point analysis *In units:* $\text{Break-even point} = \dfrac{\text{Fixed costs}}{\text{Unit contribution margin}}$ *In dollars:* $\text{Break-even point} = \dfrac{\text{Fixed costs}}{\text{Contribution margin ratio}}$	Below the break-even point, the company is unprofitable.

Glossary

Activity index *(p. 946)* The activity that causes changes in the behavior of costs.

Break-even point *(p. 956)* The level of activity at which total revenues equal total costs.

Contribution margin (CM) *(p. 955)* The amount of revenue remaining after deducting variable costs.

Contribution margin per unit *(p. 956)* The amount of revenue remaining per unit after deducting variable costs; calculated as unit selling price minus unit variable cost.

Contribution margin ratio *(p. 957)* The percentage of each dollar of sales that is available to apply to fixed costs and contribute to net income; calculated as contribution margin per unit divided by unit selling price.

Cost behavior analysis *(p. 946)* The study of how specific costs respond to changes in the level of business activity.

Cost-volume-profit (CVP) analysis *(p. 954)* The study of the effects of changes in costs and volume on a company's profits.

Cost-volume-profit (CVP) graph *(p. 960)* A graph showing the relationship between costs, volume, and profits.

Cost-volume-profit (CVP) income statement *(p. 955)* A statement for internal use that classifies costs as fixed or variable and reports contribution margin in the body of the statement.

Fixed costs *(p. 947)* Costs that remain the same in total regardless of changes in the activity level.

High-low method *(p. 951)* A mathematical method that uses the total costs incurred at the high and low levels of activity to classify mixed costs into fixed and variable components.

Margin of safety *(p. 963)* The difference between actual or expected sales and sales at the break-even point.

Mixed costs *(p. 950)* Costs that contain both a variable- and a fixed-cost element and change in total but not proportionately with changes in the activity level.

Relevant range *(p. 949)* The range of the activity index over which the company expects to operate during the year.

Target net income *(p. 962)* The income objective set by management.

Variable costs *(p. 946)* Costs that vary in total directly and proportionately with changes in the activity level.

Comprehensive Do it!

Mabo Company makes calculators that sell for $20 each. For the coming year, management expects fixed costs to total $220,000 and variable costs to be $9 per unit.

Instructions

(a) Compute break-even point in units using the mathematical equation.
(b) Compute break-even point in dollars using the contribution margin (CM) ratio.
(c) Compute the margin of safety percentage assuming actual sales are $500,000.
(d) Compute the sales required in dollars to earn net income of $165,000.

Solution to Comprehensive Do it!

(a) Sales − Variable costs − Fixed costs = Net income
$$\$20Q - \$9Q - \$220,000 = \$0$$
$$\$11Q = \$220,000$$
$$Q = 20,000 \text{ units}$$

(b) Contribution margin per unit = Unit selling price − Unit variable costs
$$\$11 = \$20 - \$9$$
Contribution margin ratio = Contribution margin per unit ÷ Unit selling price
$$55\% = \$11 \div \$20$$
Break-even point in dollars = Fixed costs ÷ Contribution margin ratio
$$= \$220,000 \div 55\%$$
$$= \$400,000$$

(c) Margin of safety = $\dfrac{\text{Actual sales} - \text{Break-even sales}}{\text{Actual sales}}$

$$= \frac{\$500,000 - \$400,000}{\$500,000}$$

$$= 20\%$$

(d) Required sales − Variable costs − Fixed costs = Net income
$$\$20Q - \$9Q - \$220,000 = \$165,000$$
$$\$11Q = \$385,000$$
$$Q = 35,000 \text{ units}$$
35,000 units × $20 = $700,000 required sales

Action Plan

• Know the formulas.
• Recognize that variable costs change with sales volume; fixed costs do not.
• Avoid computational errors.

The Navigator

Self-Test, Brief Exercises, Exercises, Problem Set A, and many more resources are available for practice in WileyPLUS.

Self-Test Questions

Answers are on page 983.

(LO 1) **1.** Variable costs are costs that:
 (a) vary in total directly and proportionately with changes in the activity level.
 (b) remain the same per unit at every activity level.
 (c) Neither of the above.
 (d) Both (a) and (b) above.

(LO 2) **2.** The relevant range is:
 (a) the range of activity in which variable costs will be curvilinear.
 (b) the range of activity in which fixed costs will be curvilinear.
 (c) the range over which the company expects to operate during a year.
 (d) usually from zero to 100% of operating capacity.

(LO 3) **3.** Mixed costs consist of a:
 (a) variable-cost element and a fixed-cost element.
 (b) fixed-cost element and a controllable-cost element.
 (c) relevant-cost element and a controllable-cost element.
 (d) variable-cost element and a relevant-cost element.

(LO 3) **4.** Your phone service provider offers a plan that is classified as a mixed cost. The cost per month for 1,000 minutes is $50. If you use 2,000 minutes this month, your cost will be:
 (a) $50.   (c) more than $100.
 (b) $100.   (d) between $50 and $100.

(LO 3) **5.** Kendra Corporation's total utility costs during the past year were $1,200 during its highest month and $600 during its lowest month. These costs corresponded with 10,000 units of production during the high month and 2,000 units during the low month. What are the fixed and variable components of its utility costs using the high-low method?
 (a) $0.075 variable and $450 fixed.
 (b) $0.120 variable and $0 fixed.
 (c) $0.300 variable and $0 fixed.
 (d) $0.060 variable and $600 fixed.

(LO 4) **6.** Which of the following is **not** involved in CVP analysis?
 (a) Sales mix.
 (b) Unit selling prices.
 (c) Fixed costs per unit.
 (d) Volume or level of activity.

(LO 5) **7.** When comparing a traditional income statement to a CVP income statement:
 (a) net income will always be greater on the traditional statement.
 (b) net income will always be less on the traditional statement.
 (c) net income will always be identical on both.
 (d) net income will be greater or less depending on the sales volume.

(LO 5) **8.** Contribution margin:
 (a) is revenue remaining after deducting variable costs.
 (b) may be expressed as contribution margin per unit.
 (c) is selling price less cost of goods sold.
 (d) Both (a) and (b) above.

(LO 5) **9.** Cournot Company sells 100,000 wrenches for $12 a unit. Fixed costs are $300,000, and net income is $200,000. What should be reported as variable expenses in the CVP income statement?
 (a) $700,000.   (c) $500,000.
 (b) $900,000.   (d) $1,000,000.

(LO 6) **10.** Gossen Company is planning to sell 200,000 pliers for $4 per unit. The contribution margin ratio is 25%. If Gossen will break even at this level of sales, what are the fixed costs?
 (a) $100,000.   (c) $200,000.
 (b) $160,000.   (d) $300,000.

(LO 6) **11.** Brownstone Company's contribution margin ratio is 30%. If Brownstone's sales revenue is $100 greater than its break-even sales in dollars, its net income:
 (a) will be $100.
 (b) will be $70.
 (c) will be $30.
 (d) cannot be determined without knowing fixed costs.

(LO 7) **12.** The mathematical equation for computing required sales to obtain target net income is: Required sales =
 (a) Variable costs + Target net income.
 (b) Variable costs + Fixed costs + Target net income.
 (c) Fixed costs + Target net income.
 (d) No correct answer is given.

(LO 8) **13.** Margin of safety is computed as:
 (a) Actual sales − Break-even sales.
 (b) Contribution margin − Fixed costs.
 (c) Break-even sales − Variable costs.
 (d) Actual sales − Contribution margin.

(LO 8) **14.** Marshall Company had actual sales of $600,000 when break-even sales were $420,000. What is the margin of safety ratio?
 (a) 25%.   (c) 33⅓%.
 (b) 30%.   (d) 45%.

Go to the book's companion website, **www.wiley.com/college/kimmel**, for additional Self-Test Questions.

 ✔ The Navigator

Questions

1. (a) What is cost behavior analysis?
   (b) Why is cost behavior analysis important to management?

2. (a) Scott Winter asks your help in understanding the term "activity index." Explain the meaning and importance of this term for Scott.
   (b) State the two ways that variable costs may be defined.

3. Contrast the effects of changes in the activity level on total fixed costs and on unit fixed costs.

4. J. P. Alexander claims that the relevant range concept is important only for variable costs.
   (a) Explain the relevant range concept.
   (b) Do you agree with J. P.'s claim? Explain.

5. "The relevant range is indispensable in cost behavior analysis." Is this true? Why or why not?

6. Adam Antal is confused. He does not understand why rent on his apartment is a fixed cost and rent on a Hertz rental truck is a mixed cost. Explain the difference to Adam.

7. How should mixed costs be classified in CVP analysis? What approach is used to effect the appropriate classification?

8. At the high and low levels of activity during the month, direct labor hours are 90,000 and 40,000, respectively. The related costs are $165,000 and $100,000. What are the fixed and variable costs at any level of activity?

9. "Cost-volume-profit (CVP) analysis is based entirely on unit costs." Do you agree? Explain.

10. Faye Dunn defines contribution margin as the amount of profit available to cover operating expenses. Is there any truth in this definition? Discuss.

11. Marshall Company's GWhiz calculator sells for $40. Variable costs per unit are estimated to be $26. What are the contribution margin per unit and the contribution margin ratio?

12. "Break-even analysis is of limited use to management because a company cannot survive by just breaking even." Do you agree? Explain.

13. Total fixed costs are $26,000 for Daz Inc. It has a contribution margin per unit of $15, and a contribution margin ratio of 25%. Compute the break-even sales in dollars.

14. Peggy Turnbull asks your help in constructing a CVP graph. Explain to Peggy (a) how the break-even point is plotted, and (b) how the level of activity and dollar sales at the break-even point are determined.

15. Define the term "margin of safety." If Revere Company expects to sell 1,250 units of its product at $12 per unit, and break-even sales for the product are $13,200, what is the margin of safety ratio?

16. Huang Company's break-even sales are $500,000. Assuming fixed costs are $180,000, what sales volume is needed to achieve a target net income of $90,000?

17. The traditional income statement for Pace Company shows sales $900,000, cost of goods sold $600,000, and operating expenses $200,000. Assuming all costs and expenses are 70% variable and 30% fixed, prepare a CVP income statement through contribution margin.

Brief Exercises

BE18-1 Monthly production costs in Pesavento Company for two levels of production are as follows.

Classify costs as variable, fixed, or mixed.
(LO 1, 3), **C**

Cost	2,000 Units	4,000 Units
Indirect labor	$10,000	$20,000
Supervisory salaries	5,000	5,000
Maintenance	4,000	7,000

Indicate which costs are variable, fixed, and mixed, and give the reason for each answer.

BE18-2 For Lodes Company, the relevant range of production is 40–80% of capacity. At 40% of capacity, a variable cost is $4,000 and a fixed cost is $6,000. Diagram the behavior of each cost within the relevant range assuming the behavior is linear.

Diagram the behavior of costs within the relevant range.
(LO 2), **AN**

BE18-3 For Hunt Company, a mixed cost is $15,000 plus $18 per direct labor hour. Diagram the behavior of the cost using increments of 500 hours up to 2,500 hours on the horizontal axis and increments of $15,000 up to $60,000 on the vertical axis.

Diagram the behavior of a mixed cost.
(LO 3), **AN**

BE18-4 Bruno Company accumulates the following data concerning a mixed cost, using miles as the activity level.

Determine variable- and fixed-cost elements using the high-low method.
(LO 3), **AP**

	Miles Driven	Total Cost		Miles Driven	Total Cost
January	8,000	$14,150	March	8,500	$15,000
February	7,500	13,500	April	8,200	14,490

Compute the variable- and fixed-cost elements using the high-low method.

Determine variable- and fixed-cost elements using the high-low method.
(LO 3), AP

BE18-5 Stiever Corp. has collected the following data concerning its maintenance costs for the past 6 months.

	Units Produced	Total Cost
July	18,000	$32,000
August	32,000	48,000
September	36,000	55,000
October	22,000	38,000
November	40,000	66,100
December	38,000	62,000

Compute the variable- and fixed-cost elements using the high-low method.

Determine missing amounts for contribution margin.
(LO 5), AN

BE18-6 Determine the missing amounts.

	Unit Selling Price	Unit Variable Costs	Contribution Margin per Unit	Contribution Margin Ratio
1.	$640	$352	(a)	(b)
2.	$300	(c)	$93	(d)
3.	(e)	(f)	$325	25%

Prepare CVP income statement.
(LO 5), AP

BE18-7 Radial Inc. had sales of $2,400,000 for the first quarter of 2014. In making the sales, the company incurred the costs and expenses shown below.

	Variable	Fixed
Cost of goods sold	$920,000	$440,000
Selling expenses	70,000	45,000
Administrative expenses	86,000	98,000

Prepare a CVP income statement for the quarter ended March 31, 2014.

Compute the break-even point.
(LO 6), AP

BE18-8 Rice Company has a unit selling price of $520, variable costs per unit of $286, and fixed costs of $163,800. Compute the break-even point in units using (a) the mathematical equation and (b) contribution margin per unit.

Compute the break-even point.
(LO 6), AP

BE18-9 Acorn Corp. had total variable costs of $180,000, total fixed costs of $170,000, and total revenues of $300,000. Compute the required sales in dollars to break even.

Compute sales for target net income.
(LO 7), AP

BE18-10 For Flynn Company, variable costs are 70% of sales, and fixed costs are $195,000. Management's net income goal is $75,000. Compute the required sales in dollars needed to achieve management's target net income of $75,000. (Use the contribution margin approach.)

Compute the margin of safety and the margin of safety ratio.
(LO 8), AP

BE18-11 For Stevens Company, actual sales are $1,000,000 and break-even sales are $840,000. Compute (a) the margin of safety in dollars and (b) the margin of safety ratio.

Compute the required sales in units for target net income.
(LO 7), AP

BE18-12 Deines Corporation has fixed costs of $480,000. It has a unit selling price of $6, unit variable costs of $4.40, and a target net income of $1,500,000. Compute the required sales in units to achieve its target net income.

Do it! Review

Classify types of costs.
(LO 1, 3), C

Do it! 18-1 Helena Company reports the following total costs at two levels of production.

	5,000 Units	10,000 Units
Indirect labor	$ 3,000	$ 6,000
Property taxes	7,000	7,000
Direct labor	28,000	56,000
Direct materials	22,000	44,000
Depreciation	4,000	4,000
Utilities	5,000	7,000
Maintenance	9,000	11,000

Classify each cost as variable, fixed, or mixed.

Do it! 18-2 Westerville Company accumulates the following data concerning a mixed cost, using units produced as the activity level.

	Units Produced	Total Cost
March	10,000	$18,000
April	9,000	16,650
May	10,500	18,580
June	8,800	16,200
July	9,500	17,100

Compute costs using high-low method and estimate total cost.

(LO 3), AP

(a) Compute the variable- and fixed-cost elements using the high-low method.
(b) Estimate the total cost if the company produces 9,200 units.

Do it! 18-3 Larissa Company has a unit selling price of $250, variable costs per unit of $170, and fixed costs of $140,000. Compute the break-even point in units using (a) the mathematical equation and (b) contribution margin per unit.

Compute break-even point in units.

(LO 6), AP

Do it! 18-4 Presto Company makes radios that sell for $30 each. For the coming year, management expects fixed costs to total $220,000 and variable costs to be $18 per unit.
(a) Compute the break-even point in dollars using the contribution margin (CM) ratio.
(b) Compute the margin of safety ratio assuming actual sales are $800,000.
(c) Compute the sales dollars required to earn net income of $140,000.

Compute break-even point, margin of safety ratio, and sales for target net income.

(LO 6, 7, 8), AP

Exercises

E18-1 Turgro Company manufactures a single product. Annual production costs incurred in the manufacturing process are shown below for two levels of production.

Define and classify variable, fixed, and mixed costs.

(LO 1, 3), C

	Costs Incurred			
Production in Units	**5,000**		**10,000**	
Production Costs	**Total Cost**	**Cost/ Unit**	**Total Cost**	**Cost/ Unit**
Direct materials	$8,000	$1.60	$16,000	$1.60
Direct labor	9,500	1.90	19,000	1.90
Utilities	2,000	0.40	3,500	0.35
Rent	4,000	0.80	4,000	0.40
Maintenance	800	0.16	1,100	0.11
Supervisory salaries	1,000	0.20	1,000	0.10

Instructions
(a) Define the terms variable costs, fixed costs, and mixed costs.
(b) Classify each cost above as either variable, fixed, or mixed.

E18-2 Shingle Enterprises is considering manufacturing a new product. It projects the cost of direct materials and rent for a range of output as shown below.

Diagram cost behavior, determine relevant range, and classify costs.

(LO 1, 2), C

Output in Units	Rent Expense	Direct Materials
1,000	$ 5,000	$ 4,000
2,000	5,000	7,200
3,000	8,000	9,000
4,000	8,000	12,000
5,000	8,000	15,000
6,000	8,000	18,000
7,000	8,000	21,000
8,000	8,000	24,000
9,000	10,000	29,300
10,000	10,000	35,000
11,000	10,000	44,000

Instructions

(a) Diagram the behavior of each cost for output ranging from 1,000 to 11,000 units.
(b) Determine the relevant range of activity for this product.
(c) Calculate the variable costs per unit within the relevant range.
(d) Indicate the fixed cost within the relevant range.

Determine fixed and variable costs using the high-low method and prepare graph.
(LO 1, 3), **AN**

E18-3 The controller of Furgee Industries has collected the following monthly expense data for use in analyzing the cost behavior of maintenance costs.

Month	Total Maintenance Costs	Total Machine Hours
January	$2,500	300
February	3,000	350
March	3,600	500
April	4,500	690
May	3,200	400
June	4,900	700

Instructions

(a) Determine the fixed- and variable-cost components using the high-low method.
(b) Prepare a graph showing the behavior of maintenance costs, and identify the fixed- and variable-cost elements. Use 100-hour increments and $1,000 cost increments.

Classify variable, fixed, and mixed costs.
(LO 1, 3), **C**

E18-4 Family Furniture Corporation incurred the following costs.

1. Wood used in the production of furniture.
2. Fuel used in delivery trucks.
3. Straight-line depreciation on factory building.
4. Screws used in the production of furniture.
5. Sales staff salaries.
6. Sales commissions.
7. Property taxes.
8. Insurance on buildings.
9. Hourly wages of furniture craftsmen.
10. Salaries of factory supervisors.
11. Utilities expense.
12. Telephone bill.

Instructions

Identify the costs above as variable, fixed, or mixed.

Determine fixed and variable costs using the high-low method and prepare graph.
(LO 1, 3), **AP**

E18-5 The controller of Dousmann Industries has collected the following monthly expense data for use in analyzing the cost behavior of maintenance costs.

Month	Total Maintenance Costs	Total Machine Hours
January	$2,750	3,500
February	3,000	4,000
March	3,600	6,000
April	4,500	7,900
May	3,200	5,000
June	5,000	8,000

Instructions

(a) Determine the fixed- and variable-cost components using the high-low method.
(b) Prepare a graph showing the behavior of maintenance costs, and identify the fixed- and variable-cost elements. Use 2,000-hour increments and $1,000 cost increments.

Determine fixed, variable, and mixed costs.
(LO 1, 3), **AP**

E18-6 PCB Corporation manufactures a single product. Monthly production costs incurred in the manufacturing process are shown below for the production of 3,000 units. The utilities and maintenance costs are mixed costs. The fixed portions of these costs are $300 and $200, respectively.

Production in Units	3,000
Production Costs	
Direct materials	$ 7,500
Direct labor	18,000
Utilities	2,100
Property taxes	1,000
Indirect labor	4,500
Supervisory salaries	1,900
Maintenance	1,100
Depreciation	2,400

Instructions

(a) Identify the above costs as variable, fixed, or mixed.

(b) Calculate the expected costs when production is 5,000 units.

E18-7 Jim Taylor wants Taylor Company to use CVP analysis to study the effects of changes in costs and volume on the company. Taylor has heard that certain assumptions must be valid in order for CVP analysis to be useful.

Explain assumptions underlying CVP analysis.

(LO 4), K

Instructions

 Prepare a memo to Jim Taylor concerning the assumptions that underlie CVP analysis.

E18-8 All That Blooms provides environmentally friendly lawn services for homeowners. Its operating costs are as follows.

Compute break-even point in units and dollars.

(LO 5, 6), AP

Depreciation	$1,400 per month
Advertising	$200 per month
Insurance	$2,000 per month
Weed and feed materials	$12 per lawn
Direct labor	$10 per lawn
Fuel	$2 per lawn

All That Blooms charges $60 per treatment for the average single-family lawn.

Instructions

Determine the company's break-even point in (a) number of lawns serviced per month and (b) dollars.

E18-9 The Green Acres Inn is trying to determine its break-even point. The inn has 50 rooms that it rents at $60 a night. Operating costs are as follows.

Compute break-even point.

(LO 5, 6), AP

Salaries	$6,200 per month
Utilities	$1,100 per month
Depreciation	$1,000 per month
Maintenance	$100 per month
Maid service	$11 per room
Other costs	$28 per room

Instructions

Determine the inn's break-even point in (a) number of rented rooms per month and (b) dollars.

E18-10 In the month of March, Style Salon services 560 clients at an average price of $120. During the month, fixed costs were $21,024 and variable costs were 60% of sales.

Compute contribution margin and break-even point.

(LO 5, 6), AP

Instructions

(a) Determine the contribution margin in dollars, per unit, and as a ratio.

(b) Using the contribution margin technique, compute the break-even point in dollars and in units.

Compute break-even point.

(LO 5, 6), AP

E18-11 Kare Kars provides shuttle service between four hotels near a medical center and an international airport. Kare Kars uses two 10-passenger vans to offer 12 round trips per day. A recent month's activity in the form of a cost-volume-profit income statement is shown on page 974.

Fare revenues (1,440 fares)		$36,000
Variable costs		
Fuel	$ 5,040	
Tolls and parking	3,100	
Maintenance	860	9,000
Contribution margin		27,000
Fixed costs		
Salaries	12,700	
Depreciation	1,300	
Insurance	1,000	15,000
Net income		$12,000

Instructions
(a) Calculate the break-even point in (1) dollars and (2) number of fares.
(b) Without calculations, determine the contribution margin at the break-even point.

Compute variable costs per unit, contribution margin ratio, and increase in fixed costs.
(LO 5, 6), **AP**

E18-12 In 2013, Manhoff Company had a break-even point of $350,000 based on a selling price of $5 per unit and fixed costs of $112,000. In 2014, the selling price and the variable costs per unit did not change, but the break-even point increased to $420,000.

Instructions
(a) Compute the variable costs per unit and the contribution margin ratio for 2013.
(b) Compute the increase in fixed costs for 2014.

Prepare CVP income statements.
(LO 5, 6), **AP**

E18-13 Cannes Company has the following information available for September 2014.

Unit selling price of video game consoles	$ 400
Unit variable costs	$ 275
Total fixed costs	$52,000
Units sold	600

Instructions
(a) Compute the contribution margin per unit.
(b) Prepare a CVP income statement that shows both total and per unit amounts.
(c) Compute Cannes' break-even point in units.
(d) Prepare a CVP income statement for the break-even point that shows both total and per unit amounts.

Compute various components to derive target net income under different assumptions.
(LO 6, 7), **AP**

E18-14 Naylor Company had $210,000 of net income in 2013 when the selling price per unit was $150, the variable costs per unit were $90, and the fixed costs were $570,000. Management expects per unit data and total fixed costs to remain the same in 2014. The president of Naylor Company is under pressure from stockholders to increase net income by $52,000 in 2014.

Instructions
(a) Compute the number of units sold in 2013.
(b) Compute the number of units that would have to be sold in 2014 to reach the stockholders' desired profit level.
(c) Assume that Naylor Company sells the same number of units in 2014 as it did in 2013. What would the selling price have to be in order to reach the stockholders' desired profit level?

Compute net income under different alternatives.
(LO 7), **AP**

E18-15 Cottonwood Company reports the following operating results for the month of August: sales $400,000 (units 5,000); variable costs $210,000; and fixed costs $90,000. Management is considering the following independent courses of action to increase net income.

1. Increase selling price by 10% with no change in total variable costs or units sold.
2. Reduce variable costs to 45% of sales.

Instructions

Prepare a CVP graph and compute break-even point and margin of safety.
(LO 6, 8), **AP**

Compute the net income to be earned under each alternative. Which course of action will produce the highest net income?

E18-16 Glacial Company estimates that variable costs will be 62.5% of sales, and fixed costs will total $600,000. The selling price of the product is $4.

Instructions

(a) Prepare a CVP graph, assuming maximum sales of $3,200,000. (*Note:* Use $400,000 increments for sales and costs and 100,000 increments for units.)

(b) Compute the break-even point in (1) units and (2) dollars.

(c) Compute the margin of safety in (1) dollars and (2) as a ratio, assuming actual sales are $2 million.

E18-17   Oak Bucket Co., a manufacturer of wood buckets, had the following data for 2013:

Determine contribution margin ratio, break-even point in dollars, and margin of safety.

(LO 5, 6, 7, 8), **AP**

Sales	2,600 units
Sales price	$40 per unit
Variable costs	$16 per unit
Fixed costs	$19,500

Instructions

(a) What is the contribution margin ratio?

(b) What is the break-even point in dollars?

(c) What is the margin of safety in dollars and as a ratio?

(d) If the company wishes to increase its total dollar contribution margin by 30% in 2014, by how much will it need to increase its sales if all other factors remain constant?

(CGA adapted)

Exercises: Set B and Challenge Exercises

Visit the book's companion website, at **www.wiley.com/college/kimmel**, and choose the Student Companion site to access Exercise Set B and Challenge Exercises.

Problems: Set A

P18-1A   Telly Savalas owns the Bonita Barber Shop. He employs four barbers and pays each a base rate of $1,000 per month. One of the barbers serves as the manager and receives an extra $500 per month. In addition to the base rate, each barber also receives a commission of $4.50 per haircut.

Determine variable and fixed costs, compute break-even point, prepare a CVP graph, and determine net income.

(LO 1, 3, 5, 6), **AN**

Other costs are as follows.

Advertising	$200 per month
Rent	$1,100 per month
Barber supplies	$0.30 per haircut
Utilities	$175 per month plus $0.20 per haircut
Magazines	$25 per month

Telly currently charges $10 per haircut.

Instructions

(a) Determine the variable costs per haircut and the total monthly fixed costs.

(b) Compute the break-even point in units and dollars.

(c) Prepare a CVP graph, assuming a maximum of 1,800 haircuts in a month. Use increments of 300 haircuts on the horizontal axis and $3,000 on the vertical axis.

(d) Determine net income, assuming 1,700 haircuts are given in a month.

(a) VC $5

P18-2A   Jorge Company bottles and distributes B-Lite, a diet soft drink. The beverage is sold for 50 cents per 16-ounce bottle to retailers, who charge customers 75 cents per bottle. For the year 2014, management estimates the following revenues and costs.

Prepare a CVP income statement, compute break-even point, contribution margin ratio, margin of safety ratio, and sales for target net income.

(LO 5, 6, 7, 8), **AN**

Sales	$1,800,000	Selling expenses—variable	$70,000
Direct materials	430,000	Selling expenses—fixed	65,000
Direct labor	360,000	Administrative expenses—	
Manufacturing overhead—		variable	20,000
variable	380,000	Administrative expenses—	
Manufacturing overhead—		fixed	60,000
fixed	280,000		

Instructions

(a) Prepare a CVP income statement for 2014 based on management's estimates. (Show column for total amounts only.)

(b) Compute the break-even point in (1) units and (2) dollars.

(c) Compute the contribution margin ratio and the margin of safety ratio. (Round to nearest full percent.)

(d) Determine the sales dollars required to earn net income of $180,000.

P18-3A Dousmann Corp.'s sales slumped badly in 2014. For the first time in its history, it operated at a loss. The company's income statement showed the following results from selling 500,000 units of product: sales $2,500,000; total costs and expenses $2,600,000; and net loss $100,000. Costs and expenses consisted of the amounts shown below.

	Total	Variable	Fixed
Cost of goods sold	$2,140,000	$1,540,000	$600,000
Selling expenses	250,000	92,000	158,000
Administrative expenses	210,000	68,000	142,000
	$2,600,000	$1,700,000	$900,000

Management is considering the following independent alternatives for 2015.

1. Increase unit selling price 20% with no change in costs, expenses, and sales volume.
2. Change the compensation of salespersons from fixed annual salaries totaling $150,000 to total salaries of $60,000 plus a 5% commission on sales.

Instructions

(a) Compute the break-even point in dollars for 2014.

(b) Compute the break-even point in dollars under each of the alternative courses of action. (Round all ratios to nearest full percent.) Which course of action do you recommend?

P18-4A Mary Willis is the advertising manager for Bargain Shoe Store. She is currently working on a major promotional campaign. Her ideas include the installation of a new lighting system and increased display space that will add $24,000 in fixed costs to the $270,000 currently spent. In addition, Mary is proposing that a 5% price decrease ($40 to $38) will produce a 20% increase in sales volume (20,000 to 24,000). Variable costs will remain at $24 per pair of shoes. Management is impressed with Mary's ideas but concerned about the effects that these changes will have on the break-even point and the margin of safety.

Instructions

(a) Compute the current break-even point in units, and compare it to the break-even point in units if Mary's ideas are used.

(b) Compute the margin of safety ratio for current operations and after Mary's changes are introduced. (Round to nearest full percent.)

(c) Prepare a CVP income statement for current operations and after Mary's changes are introduced. (Show column for total amounts only.) Would you make the changes suggested?

P18-5A Mozena Corporation has collected the following information after its first year of sales. Sales were $1,500,000 on 100,000 units; selling expenses $250,000 (40% variable and 60% fixed); direct materials $511,000; direct labor $290,000; administrative expenses $270,000 (20% variable and 80% fixed); manufacturing overhead $350,000 (70% variable and 30% fixed). Top management has asked you to do a CVP analysis so that it can make plans for the coming year. It has projected that unit sales will increase by 10% next year.

Instructions

(a) Compute (1) the contribution margin for the current year and the projected year, and (2) the fixed costs for the current year. (Assume that fixed costs will remain the same in the projected year.)

(b) Compute the break-even point in units and sales dollars for the current year.

(c) The company has a target net income of $200,000. What is the required sales in dollars for the company to meet its target?

(d) If the company meets its target net income number, by what percentage could its sales fall before it is operating at a loss? That is, what is its margin of safety ratio?

P18-6A Kaiser Industries carries no inventories. Its product is manufactured only when a customer's order is received. It is then shipped immediately after it is made. For its fiscal year ended October 31, 2014, Kaiser's break-even point was $1.3 million. On sales of $1.2 million, its income statement showed a gross profit of $180,000, direct materials cost of $400,000, and direct labor costs of $500,000. The contribution margin was $180,000, and variable manufacturing overhead was $50,000.

Determine contribution margin ratio, break-even point, and margin of safety.
(LO 1, 5, 7, 8), **E**

Instructions
(a) Calculate the following:
   (1) Variable selling and administrative expenses.
   (2) Fixed manufacturing overhead.
   (3) Fixed selling and administrative expenses.
(b) Ignoring your answer to part (a), assume that fixed manufacturing overhead was $100,000 and the fixed selling and administrative expenses were $80,000. The marketing vice president feels that if the company increased its advertising, sales could be increased by 25%. What is the maximum increased advertising cost the company can incur and still report the same income as before the advertising expenditure?

(a) (2) $70,000

(CGA adapted)

Problems: Set B

P18-1B The Sasoon Barber Shop employs four barbers. One barber, who also serves as the manager, is paid a salary of $3,000 per month. The other barbers are paid $1,500 per month. In addition, each barber is paid a commission of $3 per haircut. Other monthly costs are store rent $700 plus 60 cents per haircut, depreciation on equipment $400, barber supplies 40 cents per haircut, utilities $300, and advertising $100. The price of a haircut is $10.

Determine variable and fixed costs, compute break-even point, prepare a CVP graph, and determine net income.
(LO 1, 3, 5, 6), **AN**

Instructions
(a) Determine the variable costs per haircut and the total monthly fixed costs.
(b) Compute the break-even point in units and dollars.
(c) Prepare a CVP graph, assuming a maximum of 1,800 haircuts in a month. Use increments of 300 haircuts on the horizontal axis and $3,000 increments on the vertical axis.
(d) Determine the net income, assuming 1,800 haircuts are given in a month.

(a) VC $4

P18-2B All Frute Company bottles and distributes Frute Ade, a fruit drink. The beverage is sold for 50 cents per 16-ounce bottle to retailers, who charge customers 70 cents per bottle. For the year 2014, management estimates the following revenues and costs.

Prepare a CVP income statement, compute break-even point, contribution margin ratio, margin of safety ratio, and sales for target net income.
(LO 5, 6, 7, 8), **AN**

Sales	$2,500,000	Selling expenses—variable	$ 80,000
Direct materials	360,000	Selling expenses—fixed	250,000
Direct labor	450,000	Administrative expenses—	
Manufacturing overhead—		variable	40,000
variable	270,000	Administrative expenses—	
Manufacturing overhead—		fixed	150,000
fixed	380,000		

Instructions
(a) Prepare a CVP income statement for 2014 based on management's estimates. (Show column for total amounts only.)
(b) Compute the break-even point in (1) units and (2) dollars.
(c) Compute the contribution margin ratio and the margin of safety ratio.
(d) Determine the sales dollars required to earn net income of $624,000.

(b) (1) 3,000,000 units
(c) CM ratio 52%

P18-3B Olgivie Company had a bad year in 2013. For the first time in its history, it operated at a loss. The company's income statement showed the following results from selling 60,000 units of product: sales $1,800,000; total costs and expenses $2,010,000; and net loss $210,000. Costs and expenses consisted of the amounts shown on page 978.

Compute break-even point under alternative courses of action.
(LO 5, 6), **E**

	Total	Variable	Fixed
Cost of goods sold	$1,350,000	$ 930,000	$420,000
Selling expenses	480,000	125,000	355,000
Administrative expenses	180,000	115,000	65,000
	$2,010,000	$1,170,000	$840,000

Management is considering the following independent alternatives for 2014.

1. Increase unit selling price 25% with no change in costs, expenses, and sales volume.
2. Change the compensation of salespersons from fixed annual salaries totaling $200,000 to total salaries of $20,000 plus a 5% commission on net sales.
3. Purchase new high-tech factory machinery that will change the proportion between variable and fixed cost of goods sold to 50:50.

Instructions

(a) Compute the break-even point in dollars for 2013.
(b) Compute the break-even point in dollars under each of the alternative courses of action. (Round all ratios to nearest full percent.) Which course of action do you recommend?

(b) Alternative 1, $1,750,000

Compute break-even point and margin of safety ratio, and prepare a CVP income statement before and after changes in business environment.

(LO 5, 6, 8), **E**

P18-4B Alma Ortiz is the advertising manager for CostLess Shoe Store. She is currently working on a major promotional campaign. Her ideas include the installation of a new lighting system and increased display space that will add $18,000 in fixed costs to the $216,000 currently spent. In addition, Alma is proposing that a 10% price decrease (from $30 to $27) will produce an increase in sales volume from 20,000 to 24,000 units. Variable costs will remain at $12 per pair of shoes. Management is impressed with Alma's ideas but concerned about the effects that these changes will have on the break-even point and the margin of safety.

Instructions

(a) Compute the current break-even point in units, and compare it to the break-even point in units if Alma's ideas are used.

(b) Current margin of safety ratio 40%

(b) Compute the margin of safety ratio for current operations and after Alma's changes are introduced. (Round to nearest full percent.)
(c) Prepare a CVP income statement for current operations and after Alma's changes are introduced. (Show column for total amounts only.) Would you make the changes suggested?

Compute break-even point and margin of safety ratio, and prepare a CVP income statement before and after changes in business environment.

(LO 5, 6, 7, 8), **AN**

P18-5B Isaac Corporation has collected the following information after its first year of sales. Sales were $1,800,000 on 100,000 units; selling expenses $400,000 (30% variable and 70% fixed); direct materials $456,000; direct labor $250,000; administrative expenses $484,000 (50% variable and 50% fixed); manufacturing overhead $480,000 (40% variable and 60% fixed). Top management has asked you to do a CVP analysis so that it can make plans for the coming year. It has projected that unit sales will increase by 20% next year.

Instructions

(a) Compute (1) the contribution margin for the current year and the projected year, and (2) the fixed costs for the current year. (Assume that fixed costs will remain the same in the projected year.)

(b) 150,000 units

(b) Compute the break-even point in units and sales dollars.
(c) The company has a target net income of $213,000. What is the required sales in dollars for the company to meet its target?
(d) If the company meets its target net income number, by what percentage could its sales fall before it is operating at a loss? That is, what is its margin of safety ratio?
(e) The company is considering a purchase of equipment that would reduce its direct labor costs by $100,000 and would change its manufacturing overhead costs to 10% variable and 90% fixed (assume total manufacturing overhead cost is $480,000, as above). It is also considering switching to a pure commission basis for its sales staff. This would change selling expenses to 80% variable and 20% fixed (assume total selling expense is $400,000, as above). Compute (1) the contribution margin and (2) the contribution margin ratio, and recompute (3) the break-even point in sales dollars. Comment on the effect each of management's proposed changes has on the break-even point.

P18-6B Mega Electronix carries no inventories. Its product is manufactured only when a customer's order is received. It is then shipped immediately after it is made. For its fiscal year ended October 31, 2014, Mega's break-even point was $2.4 million. On sales of $2 million, its income statement showed a gross profit of $400,000, direct materials cost of $600,000, and direct labor costs of $700,000. The contribution margin was $150,000, and variable manufacturing overhead was $200,000.

Determine contribution margin ratio, break-even point, and margin of safety.

(LO 1, 5, 7, 8), E

Instructions
(a) Calculate the following:
   1. Variable selling and administrative expenses.
   2. Fixed manufacturing overhead.
   3. Fixed selling and administrative expenses.
(b) Ignoring your answer to part (a), assume that fixed manufacturing overhead was $100,000 and the fixed selling and administrative expenses were $80,000. The marketing vice president feels that if the company increased its advertising, sales could be increased by 15%. What is the maximum increased advertising cost the company can incur and still report the same income as before the advertising expenditure?

(a) 2. $100,000

(CGA adapted)

Problems: Set C

Visit the book's companion website, at **www.wiley.com/college/kimmel**, and choose the Student Companion site to access Problem Set C.

Waterways Continuing Problem

(*Note:* This is a continuation of the Waterways Problem from Chapters 14 through 17.)

WCP18 The Vice President for Sales and Marketing at Waterways Corporation is planning for production needs to meet sales demand in the coming year. He is also trying to determine how the company's profits might be increased in the coming year. This problem asks you to use cost-volume-profit concepts to help Waterways understand contribution margins of some of its products and to decide whether to mass-produce certain products.

Go to the book's companion website, **www.wiley.com/college/kimmel**, to find the remainder of this problem.

Broadening Your Perspective

Management Decision-Making

DECISION-MAKING AT CURRENT DESIGNS

BYP18-1 Bill Johnson, sales manager, and Diane Buswell, controller, at Current Designs are beginning to analyze the cost considerations for one of the composite models of the kayak division. They have provided the following production and operational costs necessary to produce one composite kayak.

Kevlar®	$250 per kayak
Resin and supplies	$100 per kayak
Finishing kit (seat, rudder, ropes, etc.)	$170 per kayak
Labor	$420 per kayak
Selling and administrative expenses—variable	$400 per kayak
Selling and administrative expenses—fixed	$119,700 per year
Manufacturing overhead—fixed	$240,000 per year

Bill and Diane have asked you to provide a cost-volume-profit analysis, to help them finalize the budget projections for the upcoming year. Bill has informed you that the selling price of the composite kayak will be $2,000.

Instructions
(a) Calculate variable costs per unit.
(b) Determine the contribution margin per unit.
(c) Using the contribution margin per unit, determine the break-even point in units for this product line.
(d) Assume that Current Designs plans to earn $270,600 on this product line. Using the contribution margin per unit, calculate the number of units that need to be sold to achieve this goal.
(e) Based on the most recent sales forecast, Current Designs plans to sell 1,000 units of this model. Using your results from part (c), calculate the margin of safety and the margin of safety ratio.

DECISION-MAKING ACROSS THE ORGANIZATION

BYP18-2 Creative Ideas Company has decided to introduce a new product. The new product can be manufactured by either a capital-intensive method or a labor-intensive method. The manufacturing method will not affect the quality of the product. The estimated manufacturing costs by the two methods are as follows.

	Capital-Intensive	Labor-Intensive
Direct materials	$5 per unit	$5.50 per unit
Direct labor	$6 per unit	$8.00 per unit
Variable overhead	$3 per unit	$4.50 per unit
Fixed manufacturing costs	$2,524,000	$1,550,000

Creative Ideas' market research department has recommended an introductory unit sales price of $32. The incremental selling expenses are estimated to be $502,000 annually plus $2 for each unit sold, regardless of manufacturing method.

Instructions
With the class divided into groups, answer the following.
(a) Calculate the estimated break-even point in annual unit sales of the new product if Creative Ideas Company uses the:
  (1) Capital-intensive manufacturing method.
  (2) Labor-intensive manufacturing method.
(b) Determine the annual unit sales volume at which Creative Ideas Company would be indifferent between the two manufacturing methods.
(c) Explain the circumstance under which Creative Ideas should employ each of the two manufacturing methods.

(CMA adapted)

MANAGERIAL ANALYSIS

BYP18-3 The condensed income statement for the Peri and Paul partnership for 2014 is as follows.

PERI AND PAUL COMPANY
Income Statement
For the Year Ended December 31, 2014

Sales (240,000 units)		$1,200,000
Cost of goods sold		800,000
Gross profit		400,000
Operating expenses		
Selling	$280,000	
Administrative	150,000	430,000
Net loss		($30,000)

A cost behavior analysis indicates that 75% of the cost of goods sold are variable, 42% of the selling expenses are variable, and 40% of the administrative expenses are variable.

Instructions
(Round to nearest unit, dollar, and percentage, where necessary. Use the CVP income statement format in computing profits.)

(a) Compute the break-even point in total sales dollars and in units for 2014.

(b) Peri has proposed a plan to get the partnership "out of the red" and improve its profitability. She feels that the quality of the product could be substantially improved by spending $0.25 more per unit on better raw materials. The selling price per unit could be increased to only $5.25 because of competitive pressures. Peri estimates that sales volume will increase by 25%. What effect would Peri's plan have on the profits and the break-even point in dollars of the partnership? (Round the contribution margin ratio to two decimal places.)

(c) Paul was a marketing major in college. He believes that sales volume can be increased only by intensive advertising and promotional campaigns. He therefore proposed the following plan as an alternative to Peri's: (1) Increase variable selling expenses to $0.59 per unit, (2) lower the selling price per unit by $0.25, and (3) increase fixed selling expenses by $40,000. Paul quoted an old marketing research report that said that sales volume would increase by 60% if these changes were made. What effect would Paul's plan have on the profits and the break-even point in dollars of the partnership?

(d) Which plan should be accepted? Explain your answer.

REAL-WORLD FOCUS

BYP18-4 The Coca-Cola Company hardly needs an introduction. A line taken from the cover of a recent annual report says it all: If you measured time in servings of Coca-Cola, "a billion Coca-Cola's ago was yesterday morning." On average, every U.S. citizen drinks 363 8-ounce servings of Coca-Cola products each year. Coca-Cola's primary line of business is the making and selling of syrup to bottlers. These bottlers then sell the finished bottles and cans of Coca-Cola to the consumer.

In the annual report of Coca-Cola, the information shown below was provided.

THE COCA-COLA COMPANY
Management Discussion

Our gross margin declined to 61 percent this year from 62 percent in the prior year, primarily due to costs for materials such as sweeteners and packaging.

The increases [in selling expenses] in the last two years were primarily due to higher marketing expenditures in support of our Company's volume growth.

We measure our sales volume in two ways: (1) gallon shipments of concentrates and syrups and (2) unit cases of finished product (bottles and cans of Coke sold by bottlers).

Instructions

Answer the following questions.

(a) Are sweeteners and packaging a variable cost or a fixed cost? What is the impact on the contribution margin of an increase in the per unit cost of sweeteners or packaging? What are the implications for profitability?

(b) In your opinion, are marketing expenditures a fixed cost, variable cost, or mixed cost to The Coca-Cola Company? Give justification for your answer.

(c) Which of the two measures cited for measuring volume represents the activity index as defined in this chapter? Why might Coca-Cola use two different measures?

BYP18-5 The May 21, 2010, edition of the *Wall Street Journal* includes an article by Jeffrey Trachtenberg entitled "E-Books Rewrite Bookselling."

Instructions

Read the article and answer the following questions.

(a) What aspect of Barnes and Noble's current structure puts it at risk if electronic books become a significant portion of book sales?

(b) What was Barnes and Noble's primary competitive advantage in a "paper book" world? How has this advantage been eliminated by e-books?

(c) What event do the authors say might eventually be viewed as the big turning point for e-books?

(d) What amount does Barnes and Noble earn on a $25 hardcover book? How much would it likely earn on an e-book version of the same title? What implications does this have for Barnes and Noble versus its competitors?

(e) What two mistakes does the author suggest that Barnes and Noble made that left it ill-prepared for an e-book environment?

Critical Thinking

COMMUNICATION ACTIVITY

BYP18-6 Your roommate asks for your help on the following questions about CVP analysis formulas.
(a) How can the mathematical equation for break-even sales show both sales units and sales dollars?
(b) How do the formulas differ for contribution margin per unit and contribution margin ratio?
(c) How can contribution margin be used to determine break-even sales in units and in dollars?

Instructions
Write a memo to your roommate stating the relevant formulas and answering each question.

ETHICS CASE

BYP18-7 Scott Bestor is an accountant for Westfield Company. Early this year, Scott made a highly favorable projection of sales and profits over the next 3 years for Westfield's hot-selling computer PLEX. As a result of the projections Scott presented to senior management, the company decided to expand production in this area. This decision led to dislocations of some plant personnel who were reassigned to one of the company's newer plants in another state. However, no one was fired, and in fact the company expanded its work force slightly.

Unfortunately, Scott rechecked his computations on the projections a few months later and found that he had made an error that would have reduced his projections substantially. Luckily, sales of PLEX have exceeded projections so far, and management is satisfied with its decision. Scott, however, is not sure what to do. Should he confess his honest mistake and jeopardize his possible promotion? He suspects that no one will catch the error because sales of PLEX have exceeded his projections, and it appears that profits will materialize close to his projections.

Instructions
(a) Who are the stakeholders in this situation?
(b) Identify the ethical issues involved in this situation.
(c) What are the possible alternative actions for Scott? What would you do in Scott's position?

ALL ABOUT YOU

BYP18-8 Cost-volume-profit analysis can also be used in making personal financial decisions. For example, the purchase of a new car is one of your biggest personal expenditures. It is important that you carefully analyze your options.

Suppose that you are considering the purchase of a hybrid vehicle. Let's assume the following facts: The hybrid will initially cost an additional $4,500 above the cost of a traditional vehicle. The hybrid will get 40 miles per gallon of gas, and the traditional car will get 30 miles per gallon. Also, assume that the cost of gas is $3.60 per gallon.

Instructions
Using the facts above, answer the following questions.
(a) What is the variable gasoline cost of going one mile in the hybrid car? What is the variable cost of going one mile in the traditional car?
(b) Using the information in part (a), if "miles" is your unit of measure, what is the "contribution margin" of the hybrid vehicle relative to the traditional vehicle? That is, express the variable cost savings on a per-mile basis.
(c) How many miles would you have to drive in order to break even on your investment in the hybrid car?
(d) What other factors might you want to consider?

Answers to Insight and Accounting Across the Organization Questions

p. 948 Gardens in the Sky Q: What are some of the variable and fixed costs that are impacted by hydroponic farming? **A:** Compared to traditional methods, hydroponic farming would reduce the use of pesticides, herbicides, fuel, and water. Soil erosion would be eliminated, and land requirements would drop. But, fixed costs related to constructing greenhouses, suitable vertical planters, as well as investments in artificial lighting could be high.

p. 953 Skilled Labor Is Truly Essential Q: Would you characterize labor costs as being a fixed cost, a variable cost, or something else in this situation? **A:** Because these labor costs are essentially unchanged for most levels of production, they are primarily fixed. However, it could be described as being a "step function." If production gets too far outside the normal range, workers' hours will change. If production goes too low, hours are cut, and if it goes too high, overtime hours are needed.

p. 960 Charter Flights Offer a Good Deal Q: How did FlightServe determine that it would break even with 3.3 seats full per flight? **A:** FlightServe determined its break-even point with the following formula: Fixed costs ÷ Contribution margin per seat occupied = Break-even point in seats.

p. 964 How a Rolling Stones' Tour Makes Money Q: What amount of sales dollars are required for the promoter to break even?

A: Fixed costs = $1,200,000 + $400,000 = $1,600,000
Contribution margin ratio = 80%
Break-even sales = $1,600,000 ÷ .80 = $2,000,000

Answers to Self-Test Questions

1. d   **2.** c   **3.** a   **4.** d   **5.** a [($1,200 − $600) ÷ (10,000 − 2,000)]   **6.** c   **7.** c   **8.** d
9. a [(100,000 × $12) − $300,000 − $200,000]   **10.** c (200,000 × $4 × 25%)   **11.** c ($100 × 30%)
12. b   **13.** a   **14.** b [($600,000 − $420,000) ÷ $600,000]

The Navigator

✔ **Remember to go back to The Navigator box on the chapter opening page and check off your completed work.**

CHAPTER 19

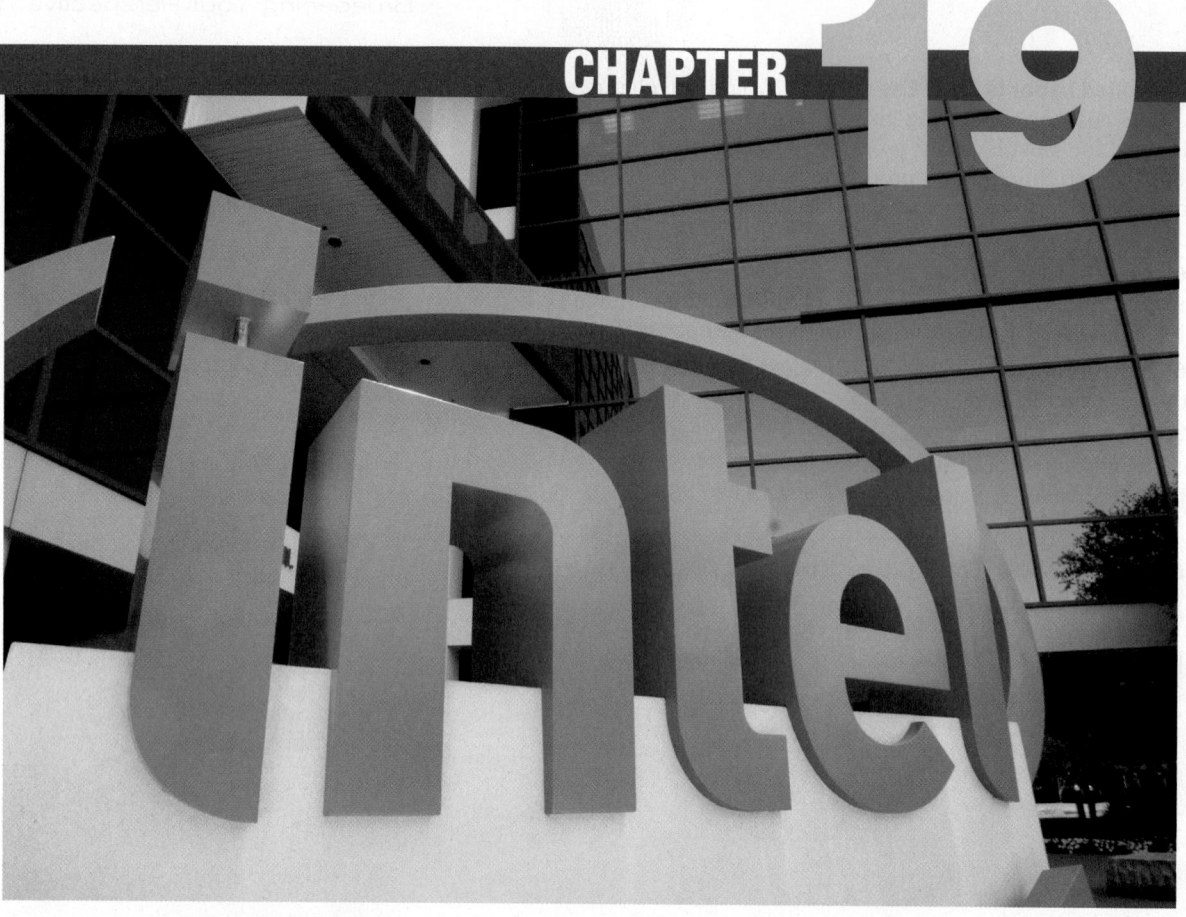

Paul Sakuma/©AP/Wide World Photos

COST-VOLUME-PROFIT ANALYSIS: ADDITIONAL ISSUES

LEARNING OBJECTIVES

After studying this chapter, you should be able to:

1 Describe the essential features of a cost-volume-profit income statement.

2 Apply basic CVP concepts.

3 Explain the term sales mix and its effects on break-even sales.

4 Determine sales mix when a company has limited resources.

5 Understand how operating leverage affects profitability.

✔ The Navigator

Intel doesn't do things half-way. If you own a PC, then there is a roughly 85% chance that the microprocessor chip that runs your machine was made by Intel. In fact, for as long as most people can remember, Intel has had at least an 85% share of the market for PC computer chips. That doesn't mean, however, that life is easy for Intel. Its earnings swings, like everything else about the company, are major league. Consider these two *Wall Street Journal* headlines: "Intel's Net Plunges as Demand Dries Up" and then, only slightly more than a year later, "Intel Earnings Set High Bar."

If Intel is so dominant in the computer chip market, why does it experience such huge swings in its earnings? First, to produce computer chips, Intel must continually make huge investments in sophisticated equipment. Now, consider what you learned in the previous chapter. The higher a company's fixed costs, the more units it must sell to break even. In this chapter, you will learn that if a company has high fixed costs as a percentage of total costs, then its earnings will be very susceptible to economic swings.

Another way of saying this is that when the economy gets the sniffles, Intel gets the flu. A drop in Intel's sales results in a disproportionately large drop in its profits. For example, during a recent quarter when Intel's sales fell 23%, its profits fell 90%. On the other hand, the minute the economy turns upward, Intel's profits do a sharp about-face. After the recent downturn, Intel's sales jumped 44%. While this was a nice bump in sales, consider what happened to its net income. Its net income increased by almost 10 times as much—nearly 400%.

Is there anything that Intel can do to tame this roller coaster ride? It can try to change its cost structure by reducing its reliance on fixed costs. But to do this, it would have to rely more heavily on outside suppliers rather than producing its own chips. Intel is probably reluctant to make this change because it would lose some of its control over product quality.

RAPID REPLAY

Watch the Whole Foods video in WileyPLUS to learn more about the use of cost-volume-profit analysis in a changing business environment.

Source: Don Clark and Ben Worthen, "Intel's Net Plunges as Demand Dries Up," *Wall Street Journal Online* (January 16, 2009); and Don Clark, "Intel Earnings Set High Bar," *Wall Street Journal Online* (April 13, 2010).

✔ The Navigator

INSIDE CHAPTER 19 . . .

As the Feature Story about Intel suggests, the relationship between a company's fixed and variable costs can have a huge impact on its profitability. In particular, the trend toward cost structures dominated by fixed costs has significantly increased the volatility of many companies' net income. The purpose of this chapter is to demonstrate additional uses of cost-volume-profit analysis in making sound business decisions.

The content and organization of this chapter are as follows.

Cost-Volume-Profit Analysis: Additional Issues

Cost-Volume-Profit (CVP) Review	Sales Mix	Cost Structure and Operating Leverage
• Basic concepts • Basic computations • CVP and changes in the business environment	• Break-even sales in units • Break-even sales in dollars • Sales mix with limited resources	• Effect on contribution margin ratio • Effect on break-even point • Effect on margin of safety ratio • Operating leverage

✔ The Navigator

Cost-Volume-Profit (CVP) Review

LEARNING OBJECTIVE 1

Describe the essential features of a cost-volume-profit income statement.

As indicated in Chapter 18, cost-volume-profit (CVP) analysis is the study of the effects of changes in costs and volume on a company's profit. CVP analysis is important to profit planning. It is also a critical factor in determining product mix, maximizing use of production facilities, and setting selling prices.

BASIC CONCEPTS

Because CVP is so important for decision-making, management often wants this information reported in a CVP income statement format for internal use. The CVP income statement classifies costs as **variable** or **fixed** and computes a contribution margin. **Contribution margin** is the amount of revenue remaining after deducting variable costs. It is often stated both as a total amount and on a per unit basis.

Illustration 19-1 presents the CVP income statement for Vargo Video (which was shown in Illustration 18-12, on page 955). Note that Vargo's sales included 1,600 camcorders at $500 per unit.

Illustration 19-1 Basic CVP income statement

VARGO VIDEO COMPANY
CVP Income Statement
For the Month Ended June 30, 2014

	Total	Per Unit
Sales (1,600 camcorders)	$ 800,000	$ 500
Variable costs	480,000	300
Contribution margin	320,000	$200
Fixed costs	200,000	
Net income	$120,000	

Companies often prepare detailed CVP income statements. The CVP income statement in Illustration 19-2 uses the same base information as that presented in Illustration 19-1 but provides more detailed information (using assumed data) about the composition of expenses.

VARGO VIDEO COMPANY
CVP Income Statement
For the Month Ended June 30, 2014

	Total	Per Unit
Sales		$ 800,000	$ 500
Variable expenses			
Cost of goods sold	$400,000		
Selling expenses	60,000		
Administrative expenses	20,000		
Total variable expenses		480,000	300
Contribution margin		320,000	$200
Fixed expenses			
Cost of goods sold	120,000		
Selling expenses	40,000		
Administrative expenses	40,000		
Total fixed expenses		200,000	
Net income		$120,000	

Illustration 19-2 Detailed CVP income statement

Helpful Hint The appendix to this chapter provides additional discussion of income statements used for decision-making.

In the applications of CVP analysis that follow, we assume that the term "cost" includes all costs and expenses related to production and sale of the product. That is, **cost includes manufacturing costs plus selling and administrative expenses**.

Do it!

Garner Inc. sold 20,000 units and recorded sales of $800,000 for the first quarter of 2014. In making the sales, the company incurred the following costs and expenses.

CVP INCOME STATEMENT

	Variable	Fixed
Cost of goods sold	$250,000	$110,000
Selling expenses	100,000	25,000
Administrative expenses	82,000	73,000

(a) Prepare a CVP income statement for the quarter ended March 31, 2014.

(b) Compute the contribution margin per unit.

(c) Compute the contribution margin ratio.

Solution

(a)

GARNER INC.
Income Statement
For the Quarter Ended March 31, 2014

Sales (20,000 units)		$800,000
Variable expenses		
Cost of goods sold	$250,000	
Selling expenses	100,000	
Administrative expenses	82,000	
Total variable expenses		432,000
Contribution margin		368,000

Action Plan

- Use the CVP income statement format.
- Use the formula for contribution margin per unit.
- Use the formula for the contribution margin ratio.

Fixed expenses		
Cost of goods sold	110,000	
Selling expenses	25,000	
Administrative expenses	73,000	
Total fixed expenses		208,000
Net income		$160,000

(b) Contribution margin per unit:
$368,000 ÷ 20,000 units = $18.40 per unit.

(c) Contribution margin ratio:
$368,000 ÷ $800,000 = 46% (or $18.40 ÷ $40 = 46%).

The Navigator

Related exercise material: **BE19-1, BE19-2,** and **Do it!** **19-1.**

BASIC COMPUTATIONS

Before we introduce additional issues of CVP analysis, let's review some of the basic concepts that you learned in Chapter 18, specifically break-even analysis, target net income, and margin of safety.

Break-Even Analysis

Vargo Video's CVP income statement (Illustration 19-2) shows that total contribution margin (sales minus variable expenses) is $320,000, and the company's contribution margin per unit is $200. Recall that contribution margin can also be expressed in the form of the **contribution margin ratio** (contribution margin divided by sales), which in the case of Vargo is 40% ($200 ÷ $500).

Illustration 19-3 demonstrates how to compute Vargo's break-even point in units (using contribution margin per unit).

Illustration 19-3 Break-even point in units

Fixed Costs	÷	Contribution Margin per Unit	=	Break-Even Point in Units
$200,000	÷	$200	=	1,000 units

Illustration 19-4 shows the computation for the break-even point in dollars (using contribution margin ratio).

Illustration 19-4 Break-even point in dollars

Fixed Costs	÷	Contribution Margin Ratio	=	Break-Even Point in Dollars
$200,000	÷	.40	=	$500,000

When a company is in its early stages of operation, its primary goal is to break even. Failure to break even will lead eventually to financial failure.

Target Net Income

Once a company achieves break-even, it then sets a sales goal that will generate a target net income. For example, assume that Vargo's management has a target net income of $250,000. Illustration 19-5 shows the required sales in units to achieve its target net income.

Illustration 19-5 Target net income in units

(Fixed Costs + Target Net Income)	÷	Contribution Margin per Unit	=	Required Sales in Units
($200,000 + $250,000)	÷	$200	=	2,250 units

Illustration 19-6 uses the contribution margin ratio to compute the required sales in dollars.

Illustration 19-6 Target net income in dollars

(Fixed Costs + Target Net Income)	÷	**Contribution Margin Ratio**	=	**Required Sales in Dollars**
($200,000 + $250,000)	÷	.40	=	$1,125,000

In order to achieve net income of $250,000, Vargo has to sell 2,250 camcorders, for a total price of $1,125,000.

Margin of Safety

Another measure managers use to assess profitability is the margin of safety. The **margin of safety** tells us **how far sales can drop** before the company will be operating at a loss. Managers like to have a sense of how much cushion they have between their current situation and operating at a loss. This can be expressed in dollars or as a ratio. In Illustration 19-2, for example, Vargo reported sales of $800,000. At that sales level, its margin of safety in dollars and as a ratio are as follows.

Illustration 19-7 Margin of safety in dollars

Actual (Expected) Sales	−	**Break-Even Sales**	=	**Margin of Safety in Dollars**
$800,000	−	$500,000	=	$300,000

As shown in Illustration 19-8, Vargo's sales could drop by $300,000, or 37.5%, before the company would operate at a loss.

Illustration 19-8 Margin of safety ratio

Margin of Safety in Dollars	÷	**Actual (Expected) Sales**	=	**Margin of Safety Ratio**
$300,000	÷	$800,000	=	37.5%

CVP AND CHANGES IN THE BUSINESS ENVIRONMENT

To better understand how CVP analysis works, let's look at three independent situations that might occur at Vargo Video. Each case uses the original camcorder sales and cost data, which were:

Illustration 19-9 Original camcorder sales and cost data

Unit selling price	$500
Unit variable cost	$300
Total fixed costs	$200,000
Break-even sales	$500,000 or 1,000 units

Case I

A competitor is offering a 10% discount on the selling price of its camcorders. Management must decide whether to offer a similar discount.

Question: What effect will a 10% discount on selling price have on the break-even point for camcorders?

Answer: A 10% discount on selling price reduces the selling price per unit to $450 [$500 − ($500 × 10%)]. Variable costs per unit remain unchanged at $300. Thus, the contribution margin per unit is $150. Assuming no change in fixed costs, break-even sales are 1,333 units, computed as follows.

Illustration 19-10 Computation of break-even sales in units

Fixed Costs	÷	Contribution Margin per Unit	=	Break-Even Sales
$200,000	÷	$150	=	1,333 units (rounded)

For Vargo Video, this change requires monthly sales to increase by 333 units, or 33⅓%, in order to break even. In reaching a conclusion about offering a 10% discount to customers, management must determine how likely it is to achieve the increased sales. Also, management should estimate the possible loss of sales if the competitor's discount price is not matched.

Case II

To meet the threat of foreign competition, management invests in new robotic equipment that will lower the amount of direct labor required to make camcorders. The company estimates that total fixed costs will increase 30% and that variable cost per unit will decrease 30%.

Question: What effect will the new equipment have on the sales volume required to break even?

Answer: Total fixed costs become $260,000 [$200,000 + (30% × $200,000)]. The variable cost per unit becomes $210 [$300 − (30% × $300)]. The new break-even point is approximately 897 units, computed as shown below.

Illustration 19-11 Computation of break-even sales in units

Fixed Costs	÷	Contribution Margin per Unit	=	Break-Even Sales
$260,000	÷	($500 − $210)	=	897 units (rounded)

These changes appear to be advantageous for Vargo Video. The break-even point is reduced by approximately 10%, or 100 units.

Case III

Vargo's principal supplier of raw materials has just announced a price increase. The higher cost is expected to increase the variable cost of camcorders by $25 per unit. Management decides to hold the line on the selling price of the camcorders. It plans a cost-cutting program that will save $17,500 in fixed costs per month. Vargo is currently realizing monthly net income of $80,000 on sales of 1,400 camcorders.

Question: What increase in units sold will be needed to maintain the same level of net income?

Answer: The variable cost per unit increases to $325 ($300 + $25). Fixed costs are reduced to $182,500 ($200,000 − $17,500). Because of the change in variable cost, the contribution margin per unit becomes $175 ($500 − $325). The required number of units sold to achieve the target net income is computed as follows.

Illustration 19-12 Computation of required sales

(Fixed Costs + Target Net Income)	÷	Contribution Margin per Unit	=	Required Sales in Units
($182,500 + $80,000)	÷	$175	=	1,500

To achieve the required sales, Vargo Video will have to sell 1,500 camcorders, an increase of 100 units. If this does not seem to be a reasonable expectation, management will either have to make further cost reductions or accept less net income if the selling price remains unchanged.

We hope that the concepts reviewed in this section are now familiar to you. We are now ready to examine additional ways that companies use CVP analysis to assess profitability and to help in making effective business decisions.

Management Insight

Don't Just Look—Buy Something

When analyzing an Internet business, analysts closely watch the so-called "conversion rate." This rate is calculated by dividing the number of people who actually take action at an Internet site (buy something) by the total number of people who visit the site. Average conversion rates are from 3% to 5%. A rate below 2% is poor, while a rate above 10% is great.

Conversion rates have an obvious effect on the break-even point. Suppose you spend $10,000 on your site, and you attract 5,000 visitors. If you get a 2% conversion rate (100 purchases), your site costs $100 per purchase ($10,000 ÷ 100). A 4% conversion rate gets you down to a cost of $50 per transaction, and an 8% conversion rate gets you down to $25. Studies show that conversion rates increase if the site has an easy-to-use interface, fast-performing screens, a convenient ordering process, and advertising that is both clever and clear.

Warchi/iStockphoto

Source: J. William Gurley, "The One Internet Metric That Really Counts" *Fortune* (March 6, 2000), p. 392.

 Besides increasing their conversion rates, what steps can online merchants use to lower their break-even points? (See page 1038.)

🧰 DECISION TOOLKIT

DECISION CHECKPOINTS	INFO NEEDED FOR DECISION	TOOL TO USE FOR DECISION	HOW TO EVALUATE RESULTS
How can a company use CVP analysis to improve profitability?	Data on what effect a price change, a fixed-cost change, or a trade-off between fixed and variable costs would have on volume and costs	Measurement of income at new volume levels	If profitability increases under proposed change, adopt change.

Do it!   Krisanne Company reports the following operating results for the month of June.   **CVP ANALYSIS**

KRISANNE COMPANY
CVP Income Statement
For the Month Ended June 30, 2014

	Total	Per Unit
Sales (5,000 units)	$300,000	$60
Variable costs	180,000	36
Contribution margin	120,000	$24
Fixed expenses	100,000	
Net income	$ 20,000	

To increase net income, management is considering reducing the selling price by 10%, with no changes to unit variable costs or fixed costs. Management is confident that this change will increase unit sales by 25%.

Using the contribution margin technique, compute the break-even point in units and dollars and margin of safety in dollars (a) assuming no changes to sales price or costs, and (b) assuming changes to sales price and volume as described above. (c) Comment on your findings.

Action Plan

- Apply the formula for the break-even point in units.
- Apply the formula for the break-even point in dollars.
- Apply the formula for the margin of safety in dollars.

Solution

(a) Assuming no changes to sales price or costs:
   Break-even point in units = 4,167 units (rounded) ($100,000 ÷ $24).
   Break-even point in sales dollars = $250,000 ($100,000 ÷ .40^a).
   Margin of safety in dollars = $50,000 ($300,000 − $250,000).

   ^{a}$24 ÷ $60.

(b) Assuming changes to sales price and volume:
   Break-even point in units = 5,556 units (rounded) ($100,000 ÷ $18^b).
   Break-even point in sales dollars = $300,000 ($100,000 ÷ ($18 ÷ $54)).
   Margin of safety in dollars = $37,500 ($337,500^c − $300,000).

   ^{b}$60 − (.10 × $60) − 36 = $18.
   ^{c}5,000 + (.25 × 5,000) = 6,250 units, 6,250 units × $54 = $337,500.

(c) The increase in the break-even point and the decrease in the margin of safety indicate that management should not implement the proposed change. The increase in sales volume will result in contribution margin of $112,500 (6,250 × $18), which is $7,500 less than the current amount.

✔ The Navigator

Related exercise material: **BE19-3, BE19-4, BE19-5, BE19-6, E19-1, E19-2, E19-3, E19-4, E19-5,** and **Do it!** 19-2.

Sales Mix

To this point, our discussion of CVP analysis has assumed that a company sells only one product. However, most companies sell multiple products. When a company sells many products, it is important that management understand its sales mix.

Sales mix is the relative percentage in which a company sells its multiple products. For example, if 80% of Hewlett Packard's unit sales are printers and the other 20% are PCs, its sales mix is 80% printers to 20% PCs.

Sales mix is important to managers because different products often have substantially different contribution margins. For example, Ford's SUVs and F150 pickup trucks have higher contribution margins compared to its economy cars. Similarly, first-class tickets sold by United Airlines provide substantially higher contribution margins than coach-class tickets. Intel's sales of computer chips for netbook computers have increased, but the contribution margin on these chips is lower than for notebook and desktop PCs.

BREAK-EVEN SALES IN UNITS

Companies can compute break-even sales for a mix of two or more products by determining the **weighted-average unit contribution margin of all the products**. To illustrate, assume that Vargo Video sells not only camcorders but high-definition TVs as well. Vargo sells its two products in the following amounts: 1,500 camcorders and 500 TVs. The sales mix, expressed as a percentage of the 2,000 total units sold, is as follows.

Illustration 19-13 Sales mix as a function of units sold

Camcorders	**TVs**
1,500 units ÷ 2,000 units = 75%	500 units ÷ 2,000 units = 25%

That is, 75% of the 2,000 units sold are camcorders, and 25% of the 2,000 units sold are TVs.

Illustration 19-14 shows additional information related to Vargo Video. The unit contribution margin for camcorders is $200, and for TVs it is $500. Vargo's fixed costs total $275,000.

Illustration 19-14 Per unit data—sales mix

Unit Data	Camcorders	TVs
Selling price	$500	$1,000
Variable costs	300	500
Contribution margin	$200	$500
Sales mix—units	75%	25%
Fixed costs = $275,000		

To compute break-even for Vargo, we must determine the weighted-average unit contribution margin for the two products. We use the **weighted-average** contribution margin because Vargo sells three times as many camcorders as TVs. As a result, in determining an average unit contribution margin, three times as much weight should be placed on the contribution margin of the camcorders as on the TVs. Therefore, the camcorders must be counted three times for every TV sold. The weighted-average contribution margin for a sales mix of 75% camcorders and 25% TVs is $275, which is computed as follows.

Illustration 19-15 Weighted-average unit contribution margin

Camcorders			**TVs**			
$\left(\begin{array}{c}\text{Unit} \\ \text{Contribution} \\ \text{Margin}\end{array}\right.$	×	$\left.\begin{array}{c}\text{Sales Mix} \\ \text{Percentage}\end{array}\right)$	+ $\left(\begin{array}{c}\text{Unit} \\ \text{Contribution} \\ \text{Margin}\end{array}\right.$	×	$\left.\begin{array}{c}\text{Sales Mix} \\ \text{Percentage}\end{array}\right)$ =	$\begin{array}{c}\text{Weighted-Average} \\ \text{Unit Contribution} \\ \text{Margin}\end{array}$
($200	×	.75)	+ ($500	×	.25) =	$275

Similar to our calculation in the single-product setting, we can compute the break-even point in units by dividing the fixed costs by the weighted-average unit contribution margin. Then, we use the weighted-average unit contribution margin of $275 to compute the break-even point in unit sales. The computation of break-even sales in units for Vargo Video, assuming $275,000 of fixed costs, is as follows.

Illustration 19-16 Break-even point in units

Fixed Costs	÷	Weighted-Average Unit Contribution Margin	=	Break-Even Point in Units
$275,000	÷	$275	=	1,000 units

Illustration 19-16 shows the break-even point for Vargo Video is 1,000 units—camcorders and TVs combined. Management needs to know how many of these 1,000 units are camcorders and how many are TVs. Applying the sales mix percentages that we computed previously of 75% for camcorders and 25% for TVs, these 1,000 units would be comprised of 750 camcorders (.75 × 1,000 units) and 250 TVs (.25 × 1,000). This can be verified by the computations in Illustration 19-17, which shows that the total contribution margin is $275,000 when 1,000 units are sold, which equals the fixed costs of $275,000.

Illustration 19-17 Break-even proof—sales units

Product	Unit Sales	×	Unit Contribution Margin	=	Total Contribution Margin
Camcorders	750	×	$200	=	$ 150,000
TVs	250	×	500	=	125,000
	1,000				**$275,000**

Management should continually review the company's sales mix. At any level of units sold, **net income will be greater if higher contribution margin units are sold, rather than lower contribution margin units**. For Vargo Video, the TVs produce the higher contribution margin. Consequently, if Vargo sells 300 TVs and 700 camcorders, net income would be higher than in the current sales mix even though total units sold are the same.

An analysis of these relationships shows that a shift from low-margin sales to high-margin sales may increase net income even though there is a decline in total units sold. Likewise, a shift from high- to low-margin sales may result in a decrease in net income even though there is an increase in total units sold.

DECISION TOOLKIT

DECISION CHECKPOINTS	INFO NEEDED FOR DECISION	TOOL TO USE FOR DECISION	HOW TO EVALUATE RESULTS
How many units of product A and product B do we need to sell to break even?	Fixed costs, weighted-average unit contribution margin, sales mix	$$\text{Break-even point in units} = \frac{\text{Fixed costs}}{\text{Weighted-average unit contribution margin}}$$	To determine number of units of product A and B, allocate total units based on sales mix.

BREAK-EVEN SALES IN DOLLARS

The calculation of the break-even point presented for Vargo Video in the previous section works well if a company has only a **small number** of products. In contrast, consider 3M, the maker of Post-it Notes, which has more than 30,000 products. In order to calculate the break-even point for 3M using a weighted-average unit contribution margin, we would need to calculate 30,000 different unit contribution margins. That is not realistic.

Therefore, for a company with many products, we calculate the break-even point in terms of sales dollars (rather than units sold), using sales information for divisions or product lines (rather than individual products). This requires that we compute sales mix as a percentage of total dollars sales (rather than units sold) and we compute the contribution margin ratio (rather than contribution margin per unit).

To illustrate, suppose that Kale Garden Supply Company has two divisions—Indoor Plants and Outdoor Plants. Each division has hundreds of different types of plants and plant-care products. Illustration 19-18 provides information necessary for determining the sales mix percentages for the two divisions of Kale Garden Supply.

Illustration 19-18
Cost-volume-profit data for Kale Garden Supply

	Indoor Plant Division	Outdoor Plant Division	Total
Sales	$ 200,000	$ 800,000	$1,000,000
Variable costs	120,000	560,000	680,000
Contribution margin	$ 80,000	$ 240,000	$ 320,000
Sales mix percentage (Division sales ÷ Total sales)	$\frac{\$\ 200,000}{\$1,000,000} = .20$	$\frac{\$\ 800,000}{\$1,000,000} = .80$	

As shown in Illustration 19-19, the contribution margin ratio for the combined company is 32%, which is computed by dividing the total contribution margin by total sales.

Illustration 19-19 Contribution margin ratio for each division

	Indoor Plant Division	Outdoor Plant Division	Total
Contribution margin ratio (Contribution margin ÷ Sales)	$\frac{\$\ 80,000}{\$200,000} = .40$	$\frac{\$240,000}{\$800,000} = .30$	$\frac{\$\ 320,000}{\$1,000,000} = .32$

It is useful to note that the contribution margin ratio of 32% is a weighted average of the individual contribution margin ratios of the two divisions (40% and 30%). To illustrate, in Illustration 19-20 we multiply each division's contribution margin ratio by its sales mix percentage, based on dollar sales, and then sum these amounts. As shown later, the calculation in Illustration 19-20 is useful because it enables us to determine how the break-even point changes when the sales mix changes.

Illustration 19-20 Calculation of weighted-average contribution margin

Indoor Plant Division			Outdoor Plant Division			
(Contribution Margin Ratio	×	Sales Mix Percentage)	+ (Contribution Margin Ratio	×	Sales Mix Percentage)	= Weighted-Average Contribution Margin Ratio
(.40	×	.20)	+ (.30	×	.80)	= .32

Kale Garden Supply's break-even point in dollars is then computed by dividing its fixed costs of $300,000 by the weighted-average contribution margin ratio of 32%, as shown in Illustration 19-21 (page 996).

Illustration 19-21 Calculation of break-even point in dollars

Fixed Costs	÷	Weighted-Average Contribution Margin Ratio	=	Break-Even Point in Dollars
$300,000	÷	.32	=	$937,500

The break-even point is based on the sales mix of 20% to 80%. We can determine the amount of sales contributed by each division by multiplying the sales mix percentage of each division by the total sales figure. Of the company's total break-even sales of $937,500, a total of $187,500 (.20 × $937,500) will come from the Indoor Plant Division, and $750,000 (.80 × $937,500) will come from the Outdoor Plant Division.

What would be the impact on the break-even point if a higher percentage of Kale Garden Supply's sales were to come from the Indoor Plant Division? Because the Indoor Plant Division enjoys a higher contribution margin ratio, this change in the sales mix would result in a higher weighted-average contribution margin ratio, and consequently a lower break-even point in dollars. For example, if the sales mix changes to 50% for the Indoor Plant Division and 50% for the Outdoor Plant Division, the weighted-average contribution margin ratio would be 35% [(.40 × .50) + (.30 × .50)]. The new, lower, break-even point is $857,143 ($300,000 ÷ .35). The opposite would occur if a higher percentage of sales were expected from the Outdoor Plant Division. As you can see, the information provided using CVP analysis can help managers better understand the impact of sales mix on profitability.

dem10/iStockphoto

Service Company Insight

Healthy for You, and Great for the Bottom Line

Zoom Kitchen, a chain of four restaurants in the Chicago area, is known for serving sizable portions of meat and potatoes. But the company's management is quite pleased with the fact that during the past four years, salad sales have increased from 18% of its sales mix to 40%. Why are they pleased? Because the contribution margin on salads is much higher than on meat. The restaurant made a conscious effort to encourage people to buy more salads by offering an interesting assortment of salad ingredients including jicama, beets, marinated mushrooms, grilled tuna, and carved turkey. Management has to be very sensitive to contribution margin—it costs about $600,000 to open up a new Zoom Kitchen restaurant.

Source: Amy Zuber, "Salad Sales 'Zoom' at Meat-and-Potatoes Specialist," *Nation's Restaurant News* (November 12, 2001), p. 26.

 Why do you suppose restaurants are so eager to sell beverages and desserts? (See page 1039.)

DECISION TOOLKIT

DECISION CHECKPOINTS	INFO NEEDED FOR DECISION	TOOL TO USE FOR DECISION	HOW TO EVALUATE RESULTS
How many dollars of sales are required from each division in order to break even?	Fixed costs, weighted-average contribution margin ratio, sales mix	$$\text{Break-even point in dollars} = \frac{\text{Fixed costs}}{\text{Weighted-average contribution margin ratio}}$$	To determine the sales dollars required from each division, allocate the total break-even sales using the sales mix.

Do it! Manzeck Bicycles International produces and sells three different types of mountain bikes. Information regarding the three models is shown below.

	Pro	Intermediate	Standard	Total
Units sold	5,000	10,000	25,000	40,000
Selling price	$800	$500	$350	
Variable costs	$500	$300	$250	

The company's total fixed costs to produce the bicycles are $7,500,000.

(a) Determine the sales mix as a function of units sold for the three products.

(b) Determine the weighted-average unit contribution margin.

(c) Determine the total number of units that the company must produce to break even.

(d) Determine the number of units of each model that the company must produce to break even.

Action Plan

- The sales mix is the relative percentage of each product sold in units.
- The weighted-average unit contribution margin is the sum of the per unit contribution margins multiplied by the respective sales mix percentage.
- Determine the break-even point in units by dividing the fixed costs by the weighted-average unit contribution margin.
- Determine the number of units of each model to produce by multiplying the total break-even units by the respective sales mix percentage for each product.

Solution

(a) The sales mix percentages as a function of units sold are:

Pro	Intermediate	Standard
5,000/40,000 = 12.5%	10,000/40,000 = 25%	25,000/40,000 = 62.5%

(b) The weighted-average unit contribution margin is:

$[.125 \times (\$800 - \$500)] + [.25 \times (\$500 - \$300)] + [.625 \times (\$350 - \$250)] = \$150$

(c) The break-even point in units is:

$\$7,500,000 \div \$150 = 50,000 \text{ units}$

(d) The break-even units to produce for each product are:

Pro:	50,000 units × 12.5%	=	6,250 units
Intermediate:	50,000 units × 25%	=	12,500 units
Standard:	50,000 units × 62.5%	=	31,250 units
			50,000 units

Related exercise material: **BE19-7, BE19-8, BE19-9, BE19-10, E19-6, E19-7, E19-8, E19-9, E19-10, and Do it! 19-3.**

DETERMINING SALES MIX WITH LIMITED RESOURCES

In the previous discussion, we assumed a certain sales mix and then determined the break-even point given that sales mix. We now discuss how limited resources influence the sales-mix decision.

Everyone's resources are limited. The limited resource may be floor space in a retail department store, or raw materials, direct labor hours, or machine capacity in a manufacturing company. When a company has limited resources, management must decide which products to make and sell in order to maximize net income.

To illustrate, recall that Vargo manufactures camcorders and TVs. The limiting resource is machine capacity, which is 3,600 hours per month. Relevant data consist of the following.

	Camcorders	TVs
Contribution margin per unit	$200	$500
Machine hours required per unit	.2	.625

LEARNING OBJECTIVE   4

Determine sales mix when a company has limited resources.

Illustration 19-22 Contribution margin and machine hours

Helpful Hint CM alone is not enough to make this decision. The key factor is CM per unit of limited resource.

The TVs may appear to be more profitable since they have a higher contribution margin per unit ($500) than the camcorders ($200). However, the camcorders take fewer machine hours to produce than the TVs. Therefore, it is necessary to find the **contribution margin per unit of limited resource**—in this case, contribution margin per machine hour. This is obtained by dividing the contribution margin per unit of each product by the number of units of the limited resource required for each product, as shown in Illustration 19-23.

Illustration 19-23 Contribution margin per unit of limited resource

	Camcorders	TVs
Contribution margin per unit (a)	$200	$500
Machine hours required (b)	0.2	0.625
Contribution margin per unit of limited resource [(a) ÷ (b)]	$1,000	$800

The computation shows that the camcorders have a higher contribution margin per unit of limited resource. This would suggest that, given sufficient demand for camcorders, Vargo should shift the sales mix to produce more camcorders or increase machine capacity.

As indicated in Illustration 19-23, the constraint for the production of the TVs is the larger number of machine hours needed to produce them. In addressing this problem, we have taken the limited number of machine hours as a given and have attempted to maximize the contribution margin given the constraint. One question that Vargo should ask, however, is whether this constraint can be reduced or eliminated. If Vargo is able to increase machine capacity from 3,600 hours to 4,200 hours, the additional 600 hours could be used to produce either the camcorders or TVs. The total contribution margin under each alternative is found by multiplying the machine hours by the contribution margin per unit of limited resource, as shown below.

Illustration 19-24 Incremental analysis—computation of total contribution margin

	Camcorders	TVs
Machine hours (a)	600	600
Contribution margin per unit of limited resource (b)	$ 1,000	$ 800
Contribution margin [(a) × (b)]	$600,000	$480,000

From this analysis, we can see that to maximize net income, all of the increased capacity should be used to make and sell the camcorders.

Vargo's manufacturing constraint might be due to a bottleneck in production or to poorly trained machine operators. In addition to finding ways to solve those problems, the company should consider other possible solutions, such as outsourcing part of the production, acquiring additional new equipment (discussed in Chapter 24), or striving to eliminate any non–value-added activities (see Chapter 17). As discussed in Chapter 14, this approach to evaluating constraints is referred to as the theory of constraints. The **theory of constraints** is a specific approach used to identify and manage constraints in order to achieve the company's goals. According to this theory, a company must continually identify its constraints and find ways to reduce or eliminate them, where appropriate.

Management Insight

Something Smells

When fragrance sales went flat, retailers turned up the heat on fragrance manufacturers. They reduced the amount of floor space devoted to fragrances, leaving fragrance manufacturers fighting each other for the smaller space. The retailer doesn't just choose the fragrance with the highest contribution margin. Instead, it chooses the fragrance with the highest contribution margin per square foot for a given period of time. In this game, a product with a lower contribution margin, but a higher turnover, could well be the winner.

? What is the limited resource for a retailer, and what implications does this have for sales mix? (See page 1039.)

Liv Friis-Larsen/iStockphoto

 ## DECISION TOOLKIT

DECISION CHECKPOINTS	INFO NEEDED FOR DECISION	TOOL TO USE FOR DECISION	HOW TO EVALUATE RESULTS
How many units of product A and B should we produce in light of a limited resource?	Contribution margin per unit, limited resource required per unit	$\dfrac{\text{Contribution margin per unit of limited resource}}{} = \dfrac{\text{Contribution margin per unit}}{\text{Limited resource per unit}}$	Any additional capacity of limited resource should be applied toward the product with higher contribution margin per unit of limited resource.

Do it!

SALES MIX WITH LIMITED RESOURCES

Carolina Corporation manufactures and sells three different types of high-quality sealed ball bearings. The bearings vary in terms of their quality specifications—primarily with respect to their smoothness and roundness. They are referred to as Fine, Extra-Fine, and Super-Fine bearings. Machine time is limited. More machine time is required to manufacture the Extra-Fine and Super-Fine bearings. Additional information is provided below.

	Product		
	Fine	**Extra-Fine**	**Super-Fine**
Selling price	$6.00	$10.00	$16.00
Variable costs and expenses	4.00	6.50	11.00
Contribution margin	$2.00	$ 3.50	$ 5.00
Machine hours required	0.02	0.04	0.08

(a) Ignoring the machine time constraint, what strategy would appear optimal?

(b) What is the contribution margin per unit of limited resource for each type of bearing?

(c) If additional machine time could be obtained, how should the additional capacity be used?

Solution

(a) The Super-Fine bearings have the highest contribution margin per unit. Thus, ignoring any manufacturing constraints, it would appear that the company should shift toward production of more Super-Fine units.

Action Plan

• Calculate the contribution margin per unit of limited resource for each product.

Action Plan (cont'd.)

- Apply the formula for the contribution margin per unit of limited resource.
- To maximize net income, shift sales mix to the product with the highest contribution margin per unit of limited resource.

The Navigator

(b) The contribution margin per unit of limited resource (machine hours) is calculated as:

	Fine	Extra-Fine	Super-Fine
$\dfrac{\text{Contribution margin per unit}}{\text{Limited resource consumed per unit}}$	$\dfrac{\$2}{.02} = \$100$	$\dfrac{\$3.5}{.04} = \$87.50$	$\dfrac{\$5}{.08} = \$62.50$

(c) The Fine bearings have the highest contribution margin per unit of limited resource even though they have the lowest contribution margin per unit. Given the resource constraint, any additional capacity should be used to make Fine bearings.

Related exercise material: **BE19-11, E19-11, E19-12, E19-13,** and **Do it!** 19-4.

Cost Structure and Operating Leverage

LEARNING OBJECTIVE **5**
Understand how operating leverage affects profitability.

Cost structure refers to the relative proportion of fixed versus variable costs that a company incurs. Cost structure can have a significant effect on profitability. For example, computer equipment manufacturer Cisco Systems has substantially reduced its fixed costs by choosing to outsource much of its production. By minimizing its fixed costs, Cisco is now less susceptible to economic swings. However, as the following discussion shows, its reduced reliance on fixed costs has also reduced its ability to experience the incredible profitability that it used to have during economic booms.

The choice of cost structure should be carefully considered. There are many ways that companies can influence their cost structure. For example, by acquiring sophisticated robotic equipment, many companies have reduced their use of manual labor. Similarly, some brokerage firms, such as E*Trade, have reduced their reliance on human brokers and have instead invested heavily in computers and online technology. In so doing, they have increased their reliance on fixed costs (through depreciation on the robotic equipment or computer equipment) and reduced their reliance on variable costs (the variable employee labor cost). Alternatively, some companies have reduced their fixed costs and increased their variable costs by outsourcing their production. Nike, for example, does very little manufacturing but instead outsources the manufacture of nearly all of its shoes. It has consequently converted many of its fixed costs into variable costs and therefore changed its cost structure.

Consider the following example of Vargo Video and one of its competitors, New Wave Company. Both make camcorders. Vargo Video uses a traditional, labor-intensive manufacturing process. New Wave Company has invested in a completely automated system. The factory employees are involved only in setting up, adjusting, and maintaining the machinery. Illustration 19-25 shows CVP income statements for each company.

Illustration 19-25 CVP income statements for two companies

	Vargo Video	New Wave Company
Sales	$800,000	$800,000
Variable costs	480,000	160,000
Contribution margin	320,000	640,000
Fixed costs	200,000	520,000
Net income	$120,000	$120,000

Both companies have the same sales and the same net income. However, because of the differences in their cost structures, they differ greatly in the risks and rewards related to increasing or decreasing sales. Let's evaluate the impact of cost structure on the profitability of the two companies.

EFFECT ON CONTRIBUTION MARGIN RATIO

First let's look at the contribution margin ratio. Illustration 19-26 shows the computation of the contribution margin ratio for each company.

Illustration 19-26 Contribution margin ratio for two companies

	Contribution Margin	÷	Sales	=	Contribution Margin Ratio
Vargo Video	$320,000	÷	$800,000	=	.40
New Wave	$640,000	÷	$800,000	=	.80

Because of its lower variable costs, New Wave has a contribution margin ratio of 80% versus only 40% for Vargo. That means that with every dollar of sales, New Wave generates 80 cents of contribution margin (and thus an 80-cent increase in net income), versus only 40 cents for Vargo. However, it also means that for every dollar that sales decline, New Wave loses 80 cents in net income, whereas Vargo will lose only 40 cents. New Wave's cost structure, which relies more heavily on fixed costs, makes it more sensitive to changes in sales revenue.

EFFECT ON BREAK-EVEN POINT

The difference in cost structure also affects the break-even point. The break-even point for each company is calculated in Illustration 19-27.

Illustration 19-27 Computation of break-even point for two companies

	Fixed Costs	÷	Contribution Margin Ratio	=	Break-Even Point in Dollars
Vargo Video	$200,000	÷	.40	=	$500,000
New Wave	$520,000	÷	.80	=	$650,000

New Wave needs to generate $150,000 ($650,000 − $500,000) more in sales than Vargo before it breaks even. This makes New Wave riskier than Vargo because a company cannot survive for very long unless it at least breaks even.

EFFECT ON MARGIN OF SAFETY RATIO

We can also evaluate the relative impact that changes in sales would have on the two companies by computing the margin of safety ratio. Illustration 19-28 shows the computation of the **margin of safety ratio** for the two companies.

Illustration 19-28 Computation of margin of safety ratio for two companies

	(Actual Sales	−	Break-Even Sales)	÷	Actual Sales	=	Margin of Safety Ratio
Vargo Video	($800,000	−	$500,000)	÷	$800,000	=	.38
New Wave	($800,000	−	$650,000)	÷	$800,000	=	.19

The difference in the margin of safety ratio also reflects the difference in risk between the two companies. Vargo could sustain a 38% decline in sales before it would be operating at a loss. New Wave could sustain only a 19% decline in sales before it would be "in the red."

OPERATING LEVERAGE

Operating leverage refers to the extent to which a company's net income reacts to a given change in sales. Companies that have higher fixed costs relative to variable costs have higher operating leverage. When a company's sales revenue is increasing, high operating leverage is a good thing because it means that profits will increase rapidly. But when sales are declining, too much operating leverage can have devastating consequences.

Degree of Operating Leverage

How can we compare operating leverage between two companies? The **degree of operating leverage** provides a measure of a company's earnings volatility and can be used to compare companies. Degree of operating leverage is computed by dividing contribution margin by net income. This formula is presented in Illustration 19-29 and applied to our two manufacturers of camcorders.

Illustration 19-29 Computation of degree of operating leverage

	Contribution Margin	÷	Net Income	=	Degree of Operating Leverage
Vargo Video	$320,000	÷	$120,000	=	2.67
New Wave	$640,000	÷	$120,000	=	5.33

New Wave's earnings would go up (or down) by about two times (5.33 ÷ 2.67 = 1.99) as much as Vargo's with an equal increase (or decrease) in sales. For example, suppose both companies experience a 10% decrease in sales. Vargo's net income will decrease by 26.7% (2.67 × 10%), while New Wave's will decrease by 53.3% (5.33 × 10%). Thus, New Wave's higher operating leverage exposes it to greater earnings volatility risk.

You should be careful not to conclude from this analysis that a cost structure that relies on higher fixed costs, and consequently has higher operating leverage, is necessarily bad. Some have suggested that Internet radio company Pandora has limited potential for growth in its profitability because it has very little operating leverage. When its revenues grow, its variable costs (fees it pays for the right to use music) grow proportionally. When used carefully, operating leverage can add considerably to a company's profitability. For example, computer equipment manufacturer Komag enjoyed a 66% increase in net income when its sales increased by only 8%. As one commentator noted, "Komag's fourth quarter illustrates the company's significant operating leverage; a small increase in sales leads to a big profit rise." However, as our illustration demonstrates, increased reliance on fixed costs increases a company's risk.

Michele Wassell/Age Fotostock America, Inc.

Service Company Insight

There Is Something About a Train

Warren Buffett, arguably the most successful investor in history, recently bought a new train set—for $44 billion. The sage from Omaha bought Burlington Northern Railroad for an amount that exceeded its market price by 31%. At a time when the rest of the investing public was obsessed with technology companies like Facebook and Twitter, what could Buffett possibly see in a railroad? What he sees is a business whose costs are between 50–60% fixed. With such high fixed costs, railways have huge operating leverage. And because he bought the railroad at the bottom of a recession, when the economy turns around, Burlington could take off as well. Add to that the fact that railroad transport is very energy-efficient, and it has high barriers to entry. So, as energy prices increase, more people will turn to the rails, but there are a limited number of railways. Makes sense to me.

Source: Liam Denning, "Buffett's Unusual Train of Thought," *Wall Street Journal* (November 4, 2009).

 Why did Warren Buffett think that this was a good time to invest in railroad stocks? (See page 1039.)

DECISION TOOLKIT

DECISION CHECKPOINTS	INFO NEEDED FOR DECISION	TOOL TO USE FOR DECISION	HOW TO EVALUATE RESULTS
How sensitive is the company's net income to changes in sales?	Contribution margin and net income	Degree of operating leverage $= \dfrac{\text{Contribution margin}}{\text{Net income}}$	Reports the change in net income that will occur with a given change in sales. A high degree of operating leverage means that the company's net income is very sensitive to changes in sales.

 # USING THE DECISION TOOLKIT

Rexfield Corp. is contemplating a huge investment in automated mass-spectrometers for its medical laboratory testing services. Its current process relies heavily on the expertise of a high number of lab technicians. The new equipment would employ a computer expert system that integrates much of the decision process and knowledge base that is used by a skilled lab technician.

Rex Field, the company's CEO, has requested that an analysis of projected results using the old technology versus the new technology be done for the coming year. The accounting department has prepared the following CVP income statements for use in your analysis.

	Old	New
Sales	$2,000,000	$2,000,000
Variable costs	1,400,000	600,000
Contribution margin	600,000	1,400,000
Fixed costs	400,000	1,200,000
Net income	$ 200,000	$ 200,000

Instructions

Use the information provided above to do the following.

(a) Compute the degree of operating leverage for the company under each scenario, and discuss your results.

(b) Compute the break-even point in dollars and margin of safety ratio for the company under each scenario, and discuss your results.

Solution

(a)

	Contribution Margin	÷	Net Income	=	Degree of Operating Leverage
Old	$600,000	÷	$200,000	=	3
New	$1,400,000	÷	$200,000	=	7

The degree of operating leverage measures the company's sensitivity to changes in sales. By switching to a cost structure dominated by fixed costs, the company would significantly increase its operating leverage. As a result, with a percentage change in sales, its percentage change in net income would be 2.33 times as much (7 ÷ 3) under the new structure as it would under the old.

(b) To compute the break-even point in sales dollars, we need first to compute the contribution margin ratio under each scenario. Under the old structure, the contribution margin ratio would be .30 ($600,000 ÷ $2,000,000), and under the new it would be .70 ($1,400,000 ÷ $2,000,000).

	Fixed Costs	÷	Contribution Margin Ratio	=	Break-Even Point in Dollars
Old	$400,000	÷	.30	=	$1,333,333
New	$1,200,000	÷	.70	=	$1,714,286

Because the company's fixed costs would be substantially higher under the new cost structure, its break-even point would increase significantly, from $1,333,333 to $1,714,286. A higher break-even point is riskier because it means that the company must generate higher sales to be profitable.

The margin of safety ratio tells how far sales can fall before the company is operating at a loss.

	$\left(\begin{array}{c}\text{Actual}\\\text{Sales}\end{array}\right.$	$-$	$\left.\begin{array}{c}\text{Break-Even}\\\text{Sales}\end{array}\right)$	$\div$	Actual Sales	$=$	Margin of Safety Ratio
Old	($2,000,000	$-$	$1,333,333)	$\div$	$2,000,000	$=$	.33
New	($2,000,000	$-$	$1,714,286)	$\div$	$2,000,000	$=$	.14

The Navigator

Under the old structure, sales could fall by 33% before the company would be operating at a loss. Under the new structure, sales could fall by only 14%.

Summary of Learning Objectives

1 **Describe the essential features of a cost-volume-profit income statement.** The CVP income statement classifies costs and expenses as variable or fixed and reports contribution margin in the body of the statement.

2 **Apply basic CVP concepts.** Contribution margin is the amount of revenue remaining after deducting variable costs. It can be expressed as a per unit amount or as a ratio. The break-even point in units is fixed costs divided by contribution margin per unit. The break-even point in dollars is fixed costs divided by the contribution margin ratio. These formulas can also be used to determine units or sales dollars needed to achieve target net income, simply by adding target net income to fixed costs before dividing by the contribution margin. Margin of safety indicates how much sales can decline before the company is operating at a loss. It can be expressed in dollar terms or as a percentage.

3 **Explain the term sales mix and its effects on break-even sales.** Sales mix is the relative proportion in which each product is sold when a company sells more than one product. For a company with a small number of products, break-even sales in units is determined by using the weighted-average unit contribution margin of all the products. If the company sells many different products, then calculating the break-even point using unit information is not practical. Instead, in a company with many products, break-even sales in dollars is calculated using the weighted-average contribution margin ratio.

4 **Determine sales mix when a company has limited resources.** When a company has limited resources, it is necessary to find the contribution margin per unit of limited resource. This amount is then multiplied by the units of limited resource to determine which product maximizes net income.

5 **Understand how operating leverage affects profitability.** Operating leverage refers to the degree to which a company's net income reacts to a change in sales. Operating leverage is determined by a company's relative use of fixed versus variable costs. Companies with high fixed costs relative to variable costs have high operating leverage. A company with high operating leverage will experience a sharp increase (decrease) in net income with a given increase (decrease) in sales. The degree of operating leverage can be measured by dividing contribution margin by net income.

The Navigator

DECISION TOOLKIT *A SUMMARY*

DECISION CHECKPOINTS	INFO NEEDED FOR DECISION	TOOL TO USE FOR DECISION	HOW TO EVALUATE RESULTS
How can a company use CVP analysis to improve profitability?	Data on what effect a price change, a fixed-cost change, or a trade-off between fixed and variable costs would have on volume and costs	Measurement of income at new volume levels	If profitability increases under proposed change, adopt change.
How many units of product A and product B do we need to sell to break even?	Fixed costs, weighted-average unit contribution margin, sales mix	$\begin{array}{c}\text{Break-}\\\text{even}\\\text{point in}\\\text{units}\end{array} = \dfrac{\text{Fixed costs}}{\begin{array}{c}\text{Weighted-average}\\\text{unit contribution}\\\text{margin}\end{array}}$	To determine number of units of product A and B, allocate total units based on sales mix.

DECISION CHECKPOINTS	INFO NEEDED FOR DECISION	TOOL TO USE FOR DECISION	HOW TO EVALUATE RESULTS
How many dollars of sales are required from each division in order to break even?	Fixed costs, weighted-average contribution margin ratio, sales mix	$$\text{Break-even point in dollars} = \frac{\text{Fixed costs}}{\text{Weighted-average contribution margin ratio}}$$	To determine the sales dollars required from each division, allocate the total break-even sales using the sales mix.
How many units of product A and B should we produce in light of a limited resource?	Contribution margin per unit, limited resource required per unit	$$\text{Contribution margin per unit of limited resource} = \frac{\text{Contribution margin per unit}}{\text{Limited resource per unit}}$$	Any additional capacity of limited resource should be applied toward the product with higher contribution margin per unit of limited resource.
How sensitive is the company's net income to changes in sales?	Contribution margin and net income	$$\text{Degree of operating leverage} = \frac{\text{Contribution margin}}{\text{Net income}}$$	Reports the change in net income that will occur with a given change in sales. A high degree of operating leverage means that the company's net income is very sensitive to changes in sales.

Appendix 19A

Absorption Costing versus Variable Costing

In the earlier chapters, we classified both variable and fixed manufacturing costs as product costs. In job order costing, for example, a job is assigned the costs of direct materials, direct labor, and **both** variable and fixed manufacturing overhead. This costing approach is referred to as **full** or **absorption costing**. It is so named because all manufacturing costs are charged to, or absorbed by, the product. Absorption costing is the approach used for external reporting under generally accepted accounting principles.

An alternative approach is to use **variable costing**. Under variable costing, only direct materials, direct labor, and variable manufacturing overhead costs are considered product costs. Companies recognize fixed manufacturing overhead costs as period costs (expenses) when incurred. The difference between absorption costing and variable costing is shown graphically as follows.

> **LEARNING OBJECTIVE 6**
> Explain the difference between absorption costing and variable costing.

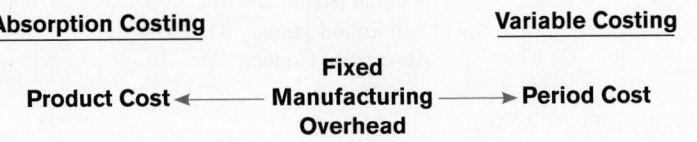

Illustration 19A-1 Difference between absorption costing and variable costing

Under both absorption and variable costing, selling and administrative expenses are period costs.

Companies may not use variable costing for external financial reports because generally accepted accounting principles require that fixed manufacturing overhead be accounted for as a product cost.

EXAMPLE COMPARING ABSORPTION COSTING WITH VARIABLE COSTING

To illustrate absorption and variable costing, assume that Premium Products Corporation manufactures a polyurethane sealant, called Fix-It, for car windshields.

Relevant data for Fix-It in January 2014, the first month of production, are as shown below.

Illustration 19A-2 Sealant sales and cost data for Premium Products Corporation

Selling price	$20 per unit.
Units	Produced 30,000; sold 20,000; beginning inventory zero.
Variable unit costs	Manufacturing $9 (direct materials $5, direct labor $3, and variable overhead $1). Selling and administrative expenses $2.
Fixed costs	Manufacturing overhead $120,000. Selling and administrative expenses $15,000.

The per unit manufacturing cost under each costing approach is computed in Illustration 19A-3.

Illustration 19A-3 Computation of per unit manufacturing cost

Type of Cost	Absorption Costing	Variable Costing
Direct materials	$ 5	$5
Direct labor	3	3
Variable manufacturing overhead	1	1
Fixed manufacturing overhead ($120,000 ÷ 30,000 units produced)	4	0
Manufacturing cost per unit	$13	$9

The manufacturing cost per unit is $4 higher ($13 − $9) for absorption costing. This occurs because fixed manufacturing overhead costs are a product cost under absorption costing. Under variable costing, they are, instead, a period cost, and so they are expensed. Based on these data, each unit sold and each unit remaining in inventory is costed under absorption costing at $13 and under variable costing at $9.

Absorption Costing Example

Illustration 19A-4 shows the income statement for Premium Products using absorption costing. It shows that cost of goods manufactured is $390,000, computed by multiplying the 30,000 units produced times the manufacturing cost per

Illustration 19A-4 Absorption costing income statement

Helpful Hint The income statement format in Illustration 19A-4 is the same as that used under generally accepted accounting principles.

PREMIUM PRODUCTS CORPORATION
Income Statement
For the Month Ended January 31, 2014
Absorption Costing

Sales (20,000 units × $20)		$400,000
Cost of goods sold		
Inventory, January 1	$ –0–	
Cost of goods manufactured (30,000 units × $13)	390,000	
Cost of goods available for sale	390,000	
Inventory, January 31 (10,000 units × $13)	130,000	
Cost of goods sold (20,000 units × $13)		260,000
Gross profit		140,000
Variable selling and administrative expenses (20,000 × $2)	40,000	
Fixed selling and administrative expenses	15,000	55,000
Net income		$ 85,000

unit of $13 (see Illustration 19A-3). Cost of goods sold is $260,000, after subtracting ending inventory of $130,000. Under absorption costing, $40,000 of the fixed overhead (10,000 units × $4) is deferred to a future period as part of the cost of ending inventory.

Variable Costing Example

As Illustration 19A-5 shows, companies use the cost-volume-profit format in preparing a variable costing income statement. The variable manufacturing cost of $270,000 is computed by multiplying the 30,000 units produced times variable manufacturing cost of $9 per unit (see Illustration 19A-3). As in absorption costing, both variable and fixed selling and administrative expenses are treated as period costs.

Illustration 19A-5 Variable costing income statement

PREMIUM PRODUCTS CORPORATION
Income Statement
For the Month Ended January 31, 2014
Variable Costing

Sales (20,000 units × $20)		$400,000
Variable cost of goods sold		
Inventory, January 1	$ –0–	
Variable cost of goods manufactured		
(30,000 units × $9)	270,000	
Variable cost of goods available for sale	270,000	
Inventory, January 31 (10,000 units × $9)	90,000	
Variable cost of goods sold	180,000	
Variable selling and administrative expenses		
(20,000 units × $2)	40,000	220,000
Contribution margin		180,000
Fixed manufacturing overhead	120,000	
Fixed selling and administrative expenses	15,000	135,000
Net income		$ 45,000

Helpful Hint Note the difference in the computation of the ending inventory: $9 per unit here, $13 per unit in Illustration 19A-4.

There is one primary difference between variable and absorption costing: **Under variable costing, companies charge the fixed manufacturing overhead as an expense in the current period.** Fixed manufacturing overhead costs of the current period, therefore, are not deferred to future periods through the ending inventory. As a result, absorption costing will show a **higher net income number** than variable costing **whenever units produced exceed units sold.** This difference can be seen in the income statements in Illustrations 19A-4 and 19A-5. There is a $40,000 difference in the ending inventories ($130,000 under absorption costing versus $90,000 under variable costing). Under absorption costing, $40,000 of the fixed overhead costs (10,000 units × $4) has been deferred to a future period as part of inventory. In contrast, under variable costing, all fixed manufacturing costs are expensed in the current period.

As shown, when units produced exceed units sold, income under absorption costing is **higher.** When units produced are less than units sold, income under absorption costing is **lower.** When units produced and sold are the same, net income will be **equal** under the two costing approaches. In this case, there is no increase in ending inventory. So fixed overhead costs of the current period are not deferred to future periods through the ending inventory.

AN EXTENDED EXAMPLE

To further illustrate the concepts underlying absorption and variable costing, we will look at an extended example using Overbay Inc., a manufacturer of small airplane drones. We assume that production volume stays the same each year over the 3-year period, but the number of units sold varies each year.

2013 Results

As indicated in Illustration 19A-6 below, the variable manufacturing cost per drone is $240,000, and the fixed manufacturing overhead cost per drone is $60,000 (assuming 10 drones). Total manufacturing cost per drone under absorption costing is therefore $300,000 ($240,000 + $60,000). Overbay also has variable selling and administrative expenses of $5,000 per drone. The fixed selling and administrative expenses are $80,000.

Illustration 19A-6 Information for Overbay Inc.

	2013	2014	2015
Volume information			
Drones in beginning inventory	0	0	2
Drones produced	10	10	10
Drones sold	10	10	10
Drones in ending inventory	0	2	0
Financial information			
Selling price per drone	$400,000		
Variable manufacturing cost per drone	$240,000		
Fixed manufacturing overhead for the year	$600,000		
Fixed manufacturing overhead per drone	$ 60,000 ($600,000 ÷ 10)		
Variable selling and administrative expenses per drone	$ 5,000		
Fixed selling and administrative expenses	$ 80,000		

An absorption costing income statement for 2013 for Overbay Inc. is shown in Illustration 19A-7.

Illustration 19A-7 Absorption costing income statement—2013

OVERBAY INC.
Income Statement
For the Year Ended December 31, 2013
Absorption Costing

Sales (10 drones × $400,000)		$4,000,000
Cost of goods sold (10 drones × $300,000)		3,000,000
Gross profit		1,000,000
Variable selling and administrative expenses (10 drones × $5,000)	$50,000	
Fixed selling and administrative expenses	80,000	130,000
Net income		$ 870,000

Overbay reports net income of $870,000 under absorption costing.

Under a variable costing system, the income statement follows a cost-volume-profit (CVP) format. In this case, the manufacturing cost is comprised solely of the variable manufacturing costs of $240,000 per drone. The fixed manufacturing overhead costs of $600,000 for the year are expensed in 2013. As in absorption costing, the fixed and variable selling and administrative expenses are period costs expensed in 2013. A variable costing income statement for Overbay Inc. for 2013 is shown in Illustration 19A-8.

OVERBAY INC. Income Statement For the Year Ended December 31, 2013 Variable Costing		
Sales (10 drones × $400,000)		$4,000,000
Variable cost of goods sold		
(10 drones × $240,000)	$2,400,000	
Variable selling and administrative expenses		
(10 drones × $5,000)	50,000	2,450,000
Contribution margin		1,550,000
Fixed manufacturing overhead	600,000	
Fixed selling and administrative expenses	80,000	680,000
Net income		$ 870,000

As shown in Illustration 19A-8, the variable costing net income of $870,000 is the same as the absorption costing net income computed in Illustration 19A-7. **When the numbers of units produced and sold are the same, net income is equal under the two costing approaches.** Because no increase in ending inventory occurs, no fixed manufacturing overhead costs incurred in 2013 are deferred to future periods using absorption costing.

2014 Results

In 2014, Overbay produced 10 drones but sold only eight drones. As a result, there are two drones in ending inventory. The absorption costing income statement for 2014 is shown in Illustration 19A-9.

OVERBAY INC. Income Statement For the Year Ended December 31, 2014 Absorption Costing		
Sales (8 drones × $400,000)		$3,200,000
Cost of goods sold (8 drones × $300,000)		2,400,000
Gross profit		800,000
Variable selling and administrative expenses		
(8 drones × $5,000)	$40,000	
Fixed selling and administrative expenses	80,000	120,000
Net income		$ 680,000

Under absorption costing, the ending inventory of two drones is $600,000 ($300,000 × 2). Each unit of ending inventory includes $60,000 of fixed manufacturing overhead. Therefore, fixed manufacturing overhead costs of $120,000 ($60,000 × 2 drones) are deferred until a future period.

The variable costing income statement for 2014 is shown in Illustration 19A-10 (page 1010).

OVERBAY INC. Income Statement For the Year Ended December 31, 2014 Variable Costing		
Sales (8 drones × $400,000)		$3,200,000
Variable cost of goods sold		
(8 drones × $240,000)	$1,920,000	
Variable selling and administrative expenses		
(8 drones × $5,000)	40,000	1,960,000
Contribution margin		1,240,000
Fixed manufacturing overhead	600,000	
Fixed selling and administrative expenses	80,000	680,000
Net income		$ 560,000

As shown, when units produced (10) exceeds units sold (8), net income under absorption costing ($680,000) is higher than net income under variable costing ($560,000). The reason: The cost of the ending inventory is higher under absorption costing than under variable costing. In 2014, under absorption costing, fixed manufacturing overhead of $120,000 is deferred and carried to future periods as part of inventory. Under variable costing, the $120,000 is expensed in the current period and, therefore the difference in the two net income numbers is $120,000 ($680,000 − $560,000).

2015 Results

In 2015, Overbay produced 10 drones and sold 12 (10 drones from the current year's production and 2 drones from the beginning inventory). As a result, there are no drones in ending inventory. The absorption costing income statement for 2015 is shown in Illustration 19A-11.

OVERBAY INC. Income Statement For the Year Ended December 31, 2015 Absorption Costing		
Sales (12 drones × $400,000)		$4,800,000
Cost of goods sold (12 drones × $300,000)		3,600,000
Gross profit		1,200,000
Variable selling and administrative expenses		
(12 drones × $5,000)	$60,000	
Fixed selling and administrative expenses	80,000	140,000
Net income		$1,060,000

Fixed manufacturing costs of $720,000 ($60,000 × 12 drones) are expensed as part of cost of goods sold in 2015. This $720,000 includes $120,000 of fixed manufacturing costs incurred during 2014 and included in beginning inventory, plus $600,000 of fixed manufacturing costs incurred during 2015. Given this result for the absorption costing statement, what would you now expect the result to be under variable costing? Let's take a look.

The variable costing income statement for 2015 is shown in Illustration 19A-12.

OVERBAY INC.
Income Statement
For the Year Ended December 31, 2015
Variable Costing

Sales (12 drones × $400,000)		$4,800,000
Variable cost of goods sold		
(12 drones × $240,000)	$2,880,000	
Variable selling and administrative expenses		
(12 drones × $5,000)	60,000	2,940,000
Contribution margin		1,860,000
Fixed manufacturing overhead	600,000	
Fixed selling and administrative expenses	80,000	680,000
Net income		$1,180,000

When Drones produced (10) are less than Drones sold (12), net income under absorption costing ($1,060,000) is less than net income under variable costing ($1,180,000). This difference of $120,000 ($1,180,000 − $1,060,000) results because $120,000 of fixed manufacturing overhead costs in beginning inventory are charged to 2015 under absorption costing. Under variable costing, there is no fixed manufacturing overhead cost in beginning inventory.

Illustration 19A-13 summarizes the results of the three years.

Net Income under Two Costing Approaches

	2013 Production = Sales	2014 Production > Sales	2015 Production < Sales
Absorption costing	$870,000	$ 680,000	$1,060,000
Variable costing	870,000	560,000	1,180,000
Difference	$ –0–	$120,000	$(120,000)

This relationship between production and sales and its effect on net income under the two costing approaches is shown graphically in Illustration 19A-14.

DECISION-MAKING CONCERNS

LEARNING OBJECTIVE **8**
Discuss the merits of absorption versus variable costing for management decision-making.

Generally accepted accounting principles require that absorption costing be used for the costing of inventory for external reporting purposes. Net income measured under GAAP (absorption costing) is often used internally to evaluate performance, justify cost reductions, or evaluate new projects. Some companies, however, have recognized that net income calculated using GAAP does not highlight differences between variable and fixed costs and may lead to poor business decisions. Consequently, these companies use variable costing for internal reporting purposes. The following discussion and example highlight a significant problem related to the use of absorption costing for decision-making purposes.

When production exceeds sales, absorption costing reports a higher net income than variable costing. The reason is that some fixed manufacturing costs are not expensed in the current period but are deferred to future periods as part of inventory. As a result, management may be tempted to overproduce in a given period in order to increase net income. Although net income will increase, this decision to overproduce may not be in the company's best interest.

Suppose, for example, a division manager's compensation is based upon the division's net income. In such a case, the manager may decide to meet the net income targets by increasing production. While this overproduction may increase the manager's compensation, the buildup of inventories in the long run will lead to additional costs to the company. Variable costing avoids this situation because net income under variable costing is unaffected by changes in production levels, as the following illustration shows.

Warren Lund, a division manager of Walker Enterprises, is under pressure to boost the performance of the Lighting Division in 2014. Unfortunately, recent profits have not met expectations. The expected sales for this year are 20,000 units. As he plans for the year, Warren has to decide whether to produce 20,000 or 30,000 units. The following facts are available for the division.

Illustration 19A-15 Facts for Lighting Division—2014

Beginning inventory	0
Expected sales in units	20,000
Selling price per unit	$15
Variable manufacturing cost per unit	$6
Fixed manufacturing overhead cost (total)	$60,000
Fixed manufacturing overhead costs per unit	
Based on 20,000 units	$3 per unit ($60,000 ÷ 20,000 units)
Based on 30,000 units	$2 per unit ($60,000 ÷ 30,000 units)
Total manufacturing cost per unit	
Based on 20,000 units	$9 per unit ($6 variable + $3 fixed)
Based on 30,000 units	$8 per unit ($6 variable + $2 fixed)
Variable selling and administrative expenses per unit	$1
Fixed selling and administrative expenses	$15,000

Illustration 19A-16 presents the division's results based upon the two possible levels of output under absorption costing.

If the Lighting Division produces 20,000 units, its net income under absorption costing is $85,000. If it produces 30,000 units, its net income is $105,000. By producing 30,000 units, the division has inventory of 10,000 units. This excess inventory causes net income to increase $20,000 because $20,000 of fixed costs

LIGHTING DIVISION
Income Statement
For the Year Ended December 31, 2014
Absorption Costing

	20,000 Produced	30,000 Produced
Sales (20,000 units × $15)	$300,000	$ 300,000
Cost of goods sold	180,000*	160,000**
Gross profit	120,000	140,000
Variable selling and administrative expenses (20,000 units × $1)	20,000	20,000
Fixed selling and administrative expenses	15,000	15,000
Net income	$ 85,000	$105,000

*20,000 units × $9
**20,000 units × $8

(10,000 units × $2) are not charged to the current year, but are deferred to future periods.

What do you think Warren Lund might do in this situation? Given his concern about the profit numbers of the Lighting Division, he may be tempted to increase production. Although this increased production will increase 2014 net income, it may be costly to the company in the long run.

Now let's evaluate the same situation under variable costing. A variable costing income statement is shown for production at both 20,000 and 30,000 units, using the information from Illustration 19A-15.

LIGHTING DIVISION
Income Statement
For the Year Ended December 31, 2014
Variable Costing

	20,000 Produced	30,000 Produced
Sales (20,000 units × $15)	$300,000	$300,000
Variable cost of goods sold (20,000 units × $6)	120,000	120,000
Variable selling and administrative expenses (20,000 units × $1)	20,000	20,000
Contribution margin	160,000	160,000
Fixed manufacturing overhead	60,000	60,000
Fixed selling and administrative expenses	15,000	15,000
Net income	$ 85,000	$ 85,000

From this example, we see that under variable costing, net income is not affected by the number of units produced. Net income is $85,000 whether the division produces 20,000 or 30,000 units. Why? Because fixed manufacturing overhead is treated as a period expense. Unlike absorption costing, no fixed manufacturing overhead is deferred through inventory buildup. Therefore, under variable costing, production does not increase income; sales do. As a result, if the company uses variable costing, managers like Warren Lund cannot affect profitability by increasing production.

POTENTIAL ADVANTAGES OF VARIABLE COSTING

Variable costing has a number of potential advantages relative to absorption costing:

1. Net income computed under variable costing is unaffected by changes in production levels. As a result, it is much easier to understand the impact of fixed and variable costs on the computation of net income when variable costing is used.

2. The use of variable costing is consistent with the cost-volume-profit material presented in Chapters 18 and 19.

3. Net income computed under variable costing is closely tied to changes in sales levels (not production levels), and therefore provides a more realistic assessment of the company's success or failure during a period.

4. The presentation of fixed and variable cost components on the face of the variable costing income statement makes it easier to identify these costs and understand their effect on the business. Under absorption costing, the allocation of fixed costs to inventory makes it difficult to evaluate the impact of fixed costs on the company's results.

Companies that use just-in-time processing techniques to minimize their inventories will not have significant differences between absorption and variable costing net income.

VARIABLE COSTING

Do it!

Franklin Company produces and sells tennis balls. The following costs are available for the year ended December 31, 2014. The company has no beginning inventory. In 2014, 8,000,000 units were produced, but only 7,500,000 units were sold. The unit selling price was $0.50 per ball. Costs and expenses were:

Variable costs per unit	
Direct materials	$0.10
Direct labor	0.05
Variable manufacturing overhead	0.08
Variable selling and administrative expenses	0.02
Annual fixed costs and expenses	
Manufacturing overhead	$500,000
Selling and administrative expenses	100,000

(a) Compute the manufacturing cost of one unit of product using variable costing.

(b) Prepare a 2014 income statement for Franklin Company using variable costing.

Action Plan

• Recall that under variable costing, only variable manufacturing costs are treated as manufacturing (product) costs.

Solution

(a) The cost of one unit of product under variable costing would be:

Direct materials	$0.10
Direct labor	0.05
Variable manufacturing overhead	0.08
	$0.23

(b) The variable costing income statement would be as follows.

Action Plan (cont'd.)

- Subtract all fixed costs, both manufacturing overhead and selling and administrative expenses, as period costs.

FRANKLIN COMPANY
Income Statement
For the Year Ended December 31, 2014
Variable Costing

Sales (7,500,000 × $0.50)		$3,750,000
Variable cost of goods sold (7,500,000 × $0.23)	$1,725,000	
Variable selling and administrative expenses (7,500,000 × .02)	150,000	1,875,000
Contribution margin		1,875,000
Fixed manufacturing overhead	500,000	
Fixed selling and administrative expenses	100,000	600,000
Net income		$1,275,000

Related exercise material: **BE19-16, BE19-17, BE19-18, BE19-19, E19-17, E19-18,** and **E19-19.**

 The Navigator

Summary of Learning Objectives for Appendix 19A

6 Explain the difference between absorption costing and variable costing. Under absorption costing, fixed manufacturing costs are product costs. Under variable costing, fixed manufacturing costs are period costs.

7 Discuss net income effects under absorption costing versus variable costing. If production volume exceeds sales volume, net income under absorption costing will exceed net income under variable costing by the amount of fixed manufacturing costs included in ending inventory that results from units produced but not sold during the period. If production volume is less than sales volume, net income under absorption costing will be less than under variable costing by the

amount of fixed manufacturing costs included in the units sold during the period that were not produced during the period.

8 Discuss the merits of absorption versus variable costing for management decision-making. The use of variable costing is consistent with cost–volume–profit analysis. Net income under variable costing is unaffected by changes in production levels. Instead, it is closely tied to changes in sales. The presentation of fixed costs in the variable costing approach makes it easier to identify fixed costs and to evaluate their impact on the company's profitability.

 The Navigator

Glossary

Absorption costing (p. 1005) A costing approach in which all manufacturing costs are charged to the product.

Cost structure (p. 1000) The relative proportion of fixed versus variable costs that a company incurs.

Degree of operating leverage (p. 1002) A measure of the extent to which a company's net income reacts to a change in sales. It is calculated by dividing contribution margin by net income.

Operating leverage (p. 1001) The extent to which a company's net income reacts to a change in sales. Operating

leverage is determined by a company's relative use of fixed versus variable costs.

Sales mix (p. 992) The relative percentage in which a company sells its multiple products.

Theory of constraints (p. 998) A specific approach used to identify and manage constraints in order to achieve the company's goals.

Variable costing (p. 1005) A costing approach in which only variable manufacturing costs are product costs, and fixed manufacturing costs are period costs (expenses).

Comprehensive Do it!

Francis Corporation manufactures and sells three different types of water-sport wake-boards. The boards vary in terms of their quality specifications—primarily with respect to their smoothness and finish. They are referred to as Smooth, Extra-Smooth, and Super-Smooth boards. Machine time is limited. More machine time is required to manufacture the Extra-Smooth and Super-Smooth boards. Additional information is provided below.

	Product		
	Smooth	**Extra-Smooth**	**Super-Smooth**
Selling price	$60	$100	$160
Variable costs and expenses	50	75	130
Contribution margin	$10	$ 25	$ 30
Machine hours required	0.25	0.40	0.60
Total fixed costs: $234,000			

Instructions

Answer each of the following questions.

(a) Ignoring the machine time constraint, what strategy would appear optimal?

(b) What is the contribution margin per unit of limited resource for each type of board?

(c) If additional machine time could be obtained, how should the additional capacity be used?

Action Plan

• To determine how best to use a limited resource, calculate the contribution margin per unit of limited resource for each product type.

The Navigator

Solution to Comprehensive Do it!

(a) The Super-Smooth boards have the highest contribution margin per unit. Thus, ignoring any manufacturing constraints, it would appear that the company should shift toward production of more Super-Smooth units.

(b) The contribution margin per unit of limited resource is calculated as:

	Smooth	Extra-Smooth	Super-Smooth
$\dfrac{\text{Contribution margin per unit}}{\text{Limited resource consumed per unit}}$	$\dfrac{\$10}{.25} = \$40$	$\dfrac{\$25}{.40} = \$62.50$	$\dfrac{\$30}{.60} = \$50$

(c) The Extra-Smooth boards have the highest contribution margin per unit of limited resource. Given the resource constraint, any additional capacity should be used to make Extra-Smooth boards.

WILEY PLUS

Self-Test, Brief Exercises, Exercises, Problem Set A, and many more resources are available for practice in WileyPLUS.

Note: All Questions, Exercises, and Problems marked with an asterisk relate to material contained in the appendix to the chapter.

Self-Test Questions

Answers are on page 1039.

(LO 1) 1. Which one of the following is the format of a CVP income statement?
(a) Sales − Variable costs = Fixed costs + Net income.
(b) Sales − Fixed costs − Variable costs − Operating expenses = Net income.
(c) Sales − Cost of goods sold − Operating expenses = Net income.

(d) Sales − Variable costs − Fixed costs = Net income.

2. Croc Catchers calculates its contribution margin to (LO 1, 2) be less than zero. Which statement is **true**?
(a) Its fixed costs are less than the variable costs per unit.
(b) Its profits are greater than its total costs.
(c) The company should sell more units.
(d) Its selling price is less than its variable costs.

(LO 2) 3. Which one of the following describes the break-even point?
   (a) It is the point where total sales equals total variable plus total fixed costs.
   (b) It is the point where the contribution margin equals zero.
   (c) It is the point where total variable costs equal total fixed costs.
   (d) It is the point where total sales equals total fixed costs.

(LO 1) 4. The following information is available for Chap Company.

Sales	$350,000
Cost of goods sold	$120,000
Total fixed expenses	$60,000
Total variable expenses	$100,000

   Which amount would you find on Chap's CVP income statement?
   (a) Contribution margin of $250,000.
   (b) Contribution margin of $190,000.
   (c) Gross profit of $230,000.
   (d) Gross profit of $190,000.

(LO 2) 5. Gabriel Corporation has fixed costs of $180,000 and variable costs of $8.50 per unit. It has a target income of $268,000. How many units must it sell at $12 per unit to achieve its target net income?
   (a) 51,429 units.   (c) 76,571 units.
   (b) 128,000 units.   (d) 21,176 units.

(LO 2) 6. Mackey Corporation has fixed costs of $150,000 and variable costs of $9 per unit. If sales price per unit is $12, what is break-even sales in dollars?
   (a) $200,000.   (c) $480,000.
   (b) $450,000.   (d) $600,000.

(LO 3) 7. Sales mix is:
   (a) important to sales managers but not to accountants.
   (b) easier to analyze on absorption costing income statements.
   (c) a measure of the relative percentage of a company's variable costs to its fixed costs.
   (d) a measure of the relative percentage in which a company's products are sold.

(LO 3) 8. Net income will be:
   (a) greater if more higher-contribution margin units are sold than lower-contribution margin units.
   (b) greater if more lower-contribution margin units are sold than higher-contribution margin units.
   (c) equal as long as total sales remain equal, regardless of which products are sold.
   (d) unaffected by changes in the mix of products sold.

(LO 4) 9. If the contribution margin per unit is $15 and it takes 3.0 machine hours to produce the unit, the contribution margin per unit of limited resource is:
   (a) $25.   (c) $4.
   (b) $5.   (d) None of the above.

(LO 4) 10. MEM manufactures two products. Product X has a contribution margin of $26 and requires 4 hours of machine time. Product Y has a contribution margin of $14 and requires 2 hours of machine time. Assuming that machine time is limited to 3,000 hours, how should it allocate the machine time to maximize its income?
   (a) Use 1,500 hours to produce X and 1,500 hours to produce Y.
   (b) Use 2,250 hours to produce X and 750 hours to produce Y.
   (c) Use 3,000 hours to produce only X.
   (d) Use 3,000 hours to produce only Y.

(LO 4) 11. When a company has a limited resource, it should apply additional capacity of that resource to providing more units of the product or service that has:
   (a) the highest contribution margin.
   (b) the highest selling price.
   (c) the highest gross profit.
   (d) the highest contribution margin per unit of that limited resource.

(LO 5) 12. The degree of operating leverage:
   (a) can be computed by dividing total contribution margin by net income.
   (b) provides a measure of the company's earnings volatility.
   (c) affects a company's break-even point.
   (d) All of the above.

(LO 5) 13. A high degree of operating leverage:
   (a) indicates that a company has a larger percentage of variable costs relative to its fixed costs.
   (b) is computed by dividing fixed costs by contribution margin.
   (c) exposes a company to greater earnings volatility risk.
   (d) exposes a company to less earnings volatility risk.

(LO 5) 14. Stevens Company has a degree of operating leverage of 3.5 at a sales level of $1,200,000 and net income of $200,000. If Stevens' sales fall by 10%, Stevens can be expected to experience a:
   (a) decrease in net income of $70,000.
   (b) decrease in contribution margin of $7,000.
   (c) decrease in operating leverage of 35%.
   (d) decrease in net income of $175,000.

*15. Fixed manufacturing overhead costs are recognized as: (LO 6)
   (a) period costs under absorption costing.
   (b) product costs under absorption costs.
   (c) product costs under variable costing.
   (d) part of ending inventory costs under both absorption and variable costing.

*16. Net income computed under absorption costing will be: (LO 6)
   (a) higher than net income under variable costing in all cases.
   (b) equal to net income under variable costing in all cases.
   (c) higher than net income under variable costing when units produced are greater than units sold.
   (d) higher than net income under variable costing when units produced are less than units sold.

Go to the book's companion website, **www.wiley.com/college/kimmel**, for additional Self-Test Questions.

Questions

1. What is meant by CVP analysis?

2. Provide three examples of management decisions that benefit from CVP analysis.

3. Distinguish between a traditional income statement and a CVP income statement.

4. Describe the features of a CVP income statement that make it more useful for management decision-making than the traditional income statement that is prepared for external users.

5. The traditional income statement for Wheat Company shows sales $900,000, cost of goods sold $500,000, and operating expenses $200,000. Assuming all costs and expenses are 75% variable and 25% fixed, prepare a CVP income statement through contribution margin.

6. If management chooses to reduce its selling price to match that of a competitor, how will the break-even point be affected?

7. What is meant by the term *sales mix*? How does sales mix affect the calculation of the break-even point?

8. Performance Company sells two types of performance tires. The lower-priced model is guaranteed for only 50,000 miles; the higher-priced model is guaranteed for 150,000 miles. The unit contribution margin on the higher-priced tire is twice as high as that of the lower-priced tire. If the sales mix shifts so that the company begins to sell more units of the lower-priced tire, explain how the company's break-even point in units will change.

9. What approach should be used to calculate the break-even point of a company that has many products?

10. How is the contribution margin per unit of limited resource computed?

11. What is the theory of constraints? Provide some examples of possible constraints for a manufacturer.

12. What is meant by "cost structure?" Explain how a company's cost structure affects its break-even point.

13. What is operating leverage? How does a company increase its operating leverage?

14. How does the replacement of manual labor with automated equipment affect a company's cost structure? What implications does this have for its operating leverage and break-even point?

15. What is a measure of operating leverage, and how is it calculated?

16. Pine Company has a degree of operating leverage of 8. Fir Company has a degree of operating leverage of 4. Interpret these measures.

*17. Distinguish between absorption costing and variable costing.

*18. (a) What is the major rationale for the use of variable costing?
    (b) Discuss why variable costing may not be used for financial reporting purposes.

*19. Doc Rowan Corporation sells one product, its waterproof hiking boot. It began operations in the current year and had an ending inventory of 8,500 units. The company sold 20,000 units throughout the year. Fixed manufacturing overhead is $5 per unit, and total manufacturing cost per unit is $20 (including fixed manufacturing overhead costs). What is the difference in net income between absorption and variable costing?

*20. If production equals sales, what, if any, is the difference between net income under absorption costing versus under variable costing?

*21. If production is greater than sales, how does absorption costing net income differ from variable costing net income?

*22. In the long run, will net income be higher or lower under variable costing compared to absorption costing?

Brief Exercises

Determine missing amounts for contribution margin.

(LO 1, 2), **AN**

BE19-1 Determine the missing amounts.

	Unit Selling Price	Unit Variable Costs	Contribution Margin per Unit	Contribution Margin Ratio
1.	$250	$180	(a)	(b)
2.	$500	(c)	$300	(d)
3.	(e)	(f)	$330	30%

Prepare CVP income statement.

(LO 1, 2), **AP**

BE19-2 Hamby Inc. has sales of $2,000,000 for the first quarter of 2014. In making the sales, the company incurred the following costs and expenses.

	Variable	Fixed
Cost of goods sold	$760,000	$600,000
Selling expenses	95,000	60,000
Administrative expenses	79,000	66,000

Prepare a CVP income statement for the quarter ended March 31, 2014.

BE19-3 Wesland Corp. had total variable costs of $175,000, total fixed costs of $120,000, and total revenues of $250,000. Compute the required sales in dollars to break even.

Compute the break-even point.
(LO 1, 2), **AP**

BE19-4 Dilts Company has a unit selling price of $400, variable costs per unit of $250, and fixed costs of $210,000. Compute the break-even point in units using (a) the mathematical equation and (b) contribution margin per unit.

Compute the break-even point.
(LO 1, 2), **AP**

BE19-5 For Ortega Company, variable costs are 60% of sales, and fixed costs are $210,000. Management's net income goal is $60,000. Compute the required sales needed to achieve management's target net income of $60,000. (Use the mathematical equation approach.)

Compute sales for target net income.
(LO 1, 2), **AP**

BE19-6 For Kosko Company actual sales are $1,200,000 and break-even sales are $960,000. Compute (a) the margin of safety in dollars and (b) the margin of safety ratio.

Compute the margin of safety and the margin of safety ratio.
(LO 1, 2), **AP**

BE19-7 Markowis Corporation sells three different models of mosquito "zapper." Model A12 sells for $50 and has variable costs of $40. Model B22 sells for $100 and has variable costs of $70. Model C124 sells for $400 and has variable costs of $300. The sales mix of the three models is: A12, 60%; B22, 15%; and C124, 25%. What is the weighted-average unit contribution margin?

Compute weighted-average unit contribution margin based on sales mix.
(LO 3), **AP**

BE19-8 Information for Markowis Corporation is given in BE19-7. If the company has fixed costs of $213,000, how many units of each model must the company sell in order to break even?

Compute break-even point in units for company with multiple products.
(LO 3), **AP**

BE19-9 Peine Candle Supply makes candles. The sales mix (as a percentage of total dollar sales) of its three product lines is birthday candles 30%, standard tapered candles 50%, and large scented candles 20%. The contribution margin ratio of each candle type is shown below.

Compute break-even point in dollars for company with multiple product lines.
(LO 3), **AP**

Candle Type	Contribution Margin Ratio
Birthday	20%
Standard tapered	20%
Large scented	45%

(a) What is the weighted-average contribution margin ratio?
(b) If the company's fixed costs are $440,000 per year, what is the dollar amount of each type of candle that must be sold to break even?

BE19-10 Faune Furniture Co. consists of two divisions, Bedroom Division and Dining Room Division. The results of operations for the most recent quarter are:

Determine weighted-average contribution margin.
(LO 3), **AP**

	Bedroom Division	Dining Room Division	Total
Sales	$500,000	$750,000	$1,250,000
Variable costs	225,000	450,000	675,000
Contribution margin	$275,000	$300,000	$ 575,000

(a) Determine the company's sales mix.
(b) Determine the company's weighted-average contribution margin ratio.

BE19-11 In Briggs Company, data concerning two products are contribution margin per unit—Product A $12, Product B $15; machine hours required for one unit—Product A 2, Product B 3. Compute the contribution margin per unit of limited resource for each product.

Show allocation of limited resources.
(LO 4), **AP**

BE19-12 Sam's Shingle Corporation is considering the purchase of a new automated shingle-cutting machine. The new machine will reduce variable labor costs but will increase depreciation expense. Contribution margin is expected to increase from $200,000 to $240,000. Net income is expected to be the same at $40,000. Compute the degree of operating leverage before and after the purchase of the new equipment. Interpret your results.

Compute degree of operating leverage.
(LO 5), **AP**

BE19-13 Presented on the next page are variable costing income statements for Logan Company and Morgan Company. They are in the same industry, with the same net incomes, but different cost structures.

Compute break-even point with change in operating leverage.
(LO 5), **AP**

	Logan Co.	Morgan Co.
Sales	$200,000	$200,000
Variable costs	80,000	50,000
Contribution margin	120,000	150,000
Fixed costs	60,000	90,000
Net income	$ 60,000	$ 60,000

Compute the break-even point in dollars for each company and comment on your findings.

Determine contribution margin from degree of operating leverage.
(LO 5), **AP**

BE19-14 The degree of operating leverage for Montana Corp. and APK Co. are 1.6 and 5.4, respectively. Both have net incomes of $50,000. Determine their respective contribution margins.

Show allocation of limited resources.
(LO 4), **AP**

BE19-15 Ger Corporation manufactures two products with the following characteristics.

	Contribution Margin per Unit	Machine Hours Required for Production
Product 1	$42	.15 hours
Product 2	$35	.10 hours

If Ger's machine hours are limited to 2,000 per month, determine which product it should produce.

Compute product costs under variable costing.
(LO 6), **AP**

*****BE19-16** The Rock Company produces basketballs. It incurred the following costs during the year.

Direct materials	$14,400
Direct labor	$25,600
Fixed manufacturing overhead	$12,000
Variable manufacturing overhead	$32,400
Selling costs	$21,000

What are the total product costs for the company under variable costing?

Compute product costs under absorption costing.
(LO 6), **AP**

*****BE19-17** Information concerning The Rock Company is provided in BE19-16. What are the total product costs for the company under absorption costing?

Determine manufacturing cost per unit under absorption and variable costing.
(LO 6), **AP**

*****BE19-18** Burns Company incurred the following costs during the year: direct materials $20 per unit; direct labor $14 per unit; variable manufacturing overhead $15 per unit; variable selling and administrative costs $8 per unit; fixed manufacturing overhead $128,000; and fixed selling and administrative costs $10,000. Burns produced 8,000 units and sold 6,000 units. Determine the manufacturing cost per unit under (a) absorption costing and (b) variable costing.

Compute net income under absorption and variable costing.
(LO 7), **AP**

*****BE19-19** ✏️ Howser Company's fixed overhead costs are $4 per unit, and its variable overhead costs are $8 per unit. In the first month of operations, 50,000 units are produced, and 48,000 units are sold. Write a short memo to the chief financial officer explaining which costing approach will produce the higher income and what the difference will be.

Do it! Review

Prepare CVP income statement and compute contribution margin.
(LO 1), **AP**

Do it! 19-1 Amanda Inc. sold 10,000 units and recorded sales of $400,000 for the first month of 2014. In making the sales, the company incurred the following costs and expenses.

	Variable	Fixed
Cost of goods sold	$184,000	$70,000
Selling expenses	40,000	30,000
Administrative expenses	16,000	50,000

(a) Prepare a CVP income statement for the month ended January 31, 2014.
(b) Compute the contribution margin per unit.
(c) Compute the contribution margin ratio.

Do it! 19-2   Queensland Company reports the following operating results for the month of April.

QUEENSLAND COMPANY
CVP Income Statement
For the Month Ended April 30, 2014

	Total	Per Unit
Sales (9,000 units)	$450,000	$50
Variable costs	270,000	30
Contribution margin	180,000	$20
Fixed expenses	150,000	
Net income	$ 30,000	

Management is considering the following course of action to increase net income: Reduce the selling price by 4%, with no changes to unit variable costs or fixed costs. Management is confident that this change will increase unit sales by 20%.

Using the contribution margin technique, compute the break-even point in units and dollars and margin of safety in dollars:

(a) Assuming no changes to selling price or costs, and
(b) Assuming changes to sales price and volume as described above.

Comment on your findings.

Do it! 19-3   Snow Cap Springs produces and sells water filtration systems for homeowners. Information regarding its three models is shown below.

	Basic	Basic Plus	Premium	Total
Units sold	750	450	300	1,500
Selling price	$250	$400	$800	
Variable costs	$195	$288	$416	

The company's total fixed costs to produce the filtration systems are $165,480.

(a) Determine the sales mix as a function of units sold for the three products.
(b) Determine the weighted-average unit contribution margin.
(c) Determine the total number of units that the company must produce to break even.
(d) Determine the number of units of each model that the company must produce to break even.

Do it! 19-4   Eye Spy Corporation manufactures and sells three different types of binoculars. They are referred to as Good, Better, and Best binoculars. Grinding and polishing time is limited. More time is required to grind and polish the lenses used in the Better and Best binoculars. Additional information is provided below.

	Product		
	Good	Better	Best
Selling price	$90.00	$330.00	$900.00
Variable costs and expenses	50.00	180.00	480.00
Contribution margin	$40.00	$150.00	$420.00
Grinding and polishing time required	0.5 hrs	1.5 hrs	6 hrs

(a) Ignoring the time constraint, what strategy would appear to be optimal?
(b) What is the contribution margin per unit of limited resource for each type of binocular?
(c) If additional grinding and polishing time could be obtained, how should the additional capacity be used?

Exercises

Compute break-even point and margin of safety.

(LO 2), **AP**

E19-1 The Bonita Inn is trying to determine its break-even point. The inn has 75 rooms that are rented at $60 a night. Operating costs are as follows.

Salaries	$8,800 per month
Utilities	2,400 per month
Depreciation	1,500 per month
Maintenance	800 per month
Maid service	8 per room
Other costs	37 per room

Instructions
(a) Determine the inn's break-even point in (1) number of rented rooms per month and (2) dollars.
(b) If the inn plans on renting an average of 50 rooms per day (assuming a 30-day month), what is (1) the monthly margin of safety in dollars and (2) the margin of safety ratio?

Compute contribution margin, break-even point, and margin of safety.

(LO 2), **AP**

E19-2 In the month of June, Jose Hebert's Beauty Salon gave 4,000 haircuts, shampoos, and permanents at an average price of $30. During the month, fixed costs were $16,800 and variable costs were 75% of sales.

Instructions
(a) Determine the contribution margin in dollars, per unit and as a ratio.
(b) Using the contribution margin technique, compute the break-even point in dollars and in units.
(c) Compute the margin of safety in dollars and as a ratio.

Compute net income under different alternatives.

(LO 2), **AP**

E19-3 Norton Company reports the following operating results for the month of August: sales $310,000 (units 5,000); variable costs $210,000; and fixed costs $75,000. Management is considering the following independent courses of action to increase net income.

1. Increase selling price by 10% with no change in total variable costs or sales volume.
2. Reduce variable costs to 58% of sales.
3. Reduce fixed costs by $20,000.

Instructions
Compute the net income to be earned under each alternative. Which course of action will produce the highest net income?

Compute break-even point and prepare CVP income statement.

(LO 2), **AP**

E19-4 Comfi Airways, Inc., a small two-plane passenger airline, has asked for your assistance in some basic analysis of its operations. Both planes seat 10 passengers each, and they fly commuters from Comfi's base airport to the major city in the state, Metropolis. Each month, 40 round-trip flights are made. Shown below is a recent month's activity in the form of a cost-volume-profit income statement.

Fare revenues (400 fares)		$48,000
Variable costs		
Fuel	$14,000	
Snacks and drinks	800	
Landing fees	2,000	
Supplies and forms	1,200	18,000
Contribution margin		30,000
Fixed costs		
Depreciation	3,000	
Salaries	15,000	
Advertising	500	
Airport hangar fees	1,750	20,250
Net income		$ 9,750

Instructions
(a) Calculate the break-even point in (1) dollars and (2) number of fares.
(b) Without calculations, determine the contribution margin at the break-even point.
(c) If fares were decreased by 10%, an additional 100 fares could be generated. However, total variable costs would increase by 20%. Should the fare decrease be adopted?

E19-5 Hall Company had sales in 2014 of $1,560,000 on 60,000 units. Variable costs totaled $720,000, and fixed costs totaled $500,000.

  A new raw material is available that will decrease the variable costs per unit by 25% (or $3.00). However, to process the new raw material, fixed operating costs will increase by $150,000. Management feels that one-half of the decline in the variable costs per unit should be passed on to customers in the form of a sales price reduction. The marketing department expects that this sales price reduction will result in a 5% increase in the number of units sold.

Prepare a CVP income statement before and after changes in business environment.
(LO 2), **AP**

Instructions
Prepare a projected CVP income statement for 2014 (a) assuming the changes have not been made, and (b) assuming that changes are made as described.

E19-6 Yard Tools manufactures lawnmowers, weed-trimmers, and chainsaws. Its sales mix and contribution margin per unit are as follows.

Compute break-even point in units for a company with more than one product.
(LO 3), **AP**

	Sales Mix	Contribution Margin per Unit
Lawnmowers	20%	$30
Weed-trimmers	50%	$20
Chainsaws	30%	$40

Yard Tools has fixed costs of $4,200,000.

Instructions
Compute the number of units of each product that Yard Tools must sell in order to break even under this product mix.

E19-7 Qwik Repairs has over 200 auto-maintenance service outlets nationwide. It provides primarily two lines of service: oil changes and brake repair. Oil change–related services represent 70% of its sales and provide a contribution margin ratio of 20%. Brake repair represents 30% of its sales and provides a 60% contribution margin ratio. The company's fixed costs are $16,000,000 (that is, $80,000 per service outlet).

Compute service line break-even point and target net income in dollars for a company with more than one service.
(LO 3), **AN**

Instructions
(a) Calculate the dollar amount of each type of service that the company must provide in order to break even.
(b) The company has a desired net income of $60,000 per service outlet. What is the dollar amount of each type of service that must be provided by each service outlet to meet its target net income per outlet?

E19-8 Express Delivery is a rapidly growing delivery service. Last year, 80% of its revenue came from the delivery of mailing "pouches" and small, standardized delivery boxes (which provides a 20% contribution margin). The other 20% of its revenue came from delivering non-standardized boxes (which provides a 70% contribution margin). With the rapid growth of Internet retail sales, Express believes that there are great opportunities for growth in the delivery of non-standardized boxes. The company has fixed costs of $12,000,000.

Compute break-even point in dollars for a company with more than one service.
(LO 3), **AN**

Instructions
(a) What is the company's break-even point in total sales dollars? At the break-even point, how much of the company's sales are provided by each type of service?
(b) The company's management would like to hold its fixed costs constant but shift its sales mix so that 60% of its revenue comes from the delivery of non-standardized boxes and the remainder from pouches and small boxes. If this were to occur, what would be the company's break-even sales, and what amount of sales would be provided by each service type?

E19-9 Palmer Golf Accessories sells golf shoes, gloves, and a laser-guided range-finder that measures distance. Shown below are unit cost and sales data.

Compute break-even point in units for a company with multiple products.
(LO 3), **AP**

	Pairs of Shoes	Pairs of Gloves	Range-Finder
Unit sales price	$100	$30	$260
Unit variable costs	60	10	200
Unit contribution margin	$ 40	$20	$ 60
Sales mix	30%	60%	10%

Fixed costs are $630,000.

Instructions

(a) Compute the break-even point in units for the company.
(b) Determine the number of units to be sold at the break-even point for each product line.
(c) Verify that the mix of sales units determined in (b) will generate a zero net income.

Determine break-even point in dollars for two divisions.
(LO 3), **AP**

E19-10 Personal Electronix sells iPads and iPods. The business is divided into two divisions along product lines. CVP income statements for a recent quarter's activity are presented below.

	iPad Division	iPod Division	Total
Sales	$600,000	$400,000	$1,000,000
Variable costs	420,000	260,000	680,000
Contribution margin	$180,000	$140,000	320,000
Fixed costs			120,000
Net income			$ 200,000

Instructions

(a) Determine sales mix percentage and contribution margin ratio for each division.
(b) Calculate the company's weighted-average contribution margin ratio.
(c) Calculate the company's break-even point in dollars.
(d) Determine the sales level in dollars for each division at the break-even point.

Compute contribution margin and determine the product to be manufactured.
(LO 4), **AN**

E19-11 Spencer Company manufactures and sells three products. Relevant per unit data concerning each product are given below.

	Product		
	A	**B**	**C**
Selling price	$8	$12	$15
Variable costs and expenses	$3	$10	$12
Machine hours to produce	2	1	2

Instructions

(a) Compute the contribution margin per unit of the limited resource (machine hours) for each product.
(b) Assuming 1,500 additional machine hours are available, which product should be manufactured?
(c) Prepare an analysis showing the total contribution margin if the additional hours are (1) divided equally among the products, and (2) allocated entirely to the product identified in (b) above.

Compute contribution margin and determine the products to be manufactured.
(LO 4), **AN**

E19-12 Dalton Inc. produces and sells three products. Unit data concerning each product is shown below.

	Product		
	D	**E**	**F**
Selling price	$200	$300	$250
Direct labor costs	30	80	35
Other variable costs	95	80	145

The company has 2,000 hours of labor available to build inventory in anticipation of the company's peak season. Management is trying to decide which product should be produced. The direct labor hourly rate is $10.

Instructions

(a) Determine the number of direct labor hours per unit.
(b) Determine the contribution margin per direct labor hour.
(c) Determine which product should be produced and the total contribution margin for that product.

Compute contribution margin and determine the products to be manufactured.
(LO 4), **AN**

E19-13 Billings Company manufactures and sells two products. Relevant per unit data concerning each product follow.

	Product	
	Basic	**Deluxe**
Selling price	$40	$52
Variable costs	$20	$22
Machine hours	.5	.8

Instructions

(a) Compute the contribution margin per machine hour for each product.

(b) If 1,000 additional machine hours are available, which product should Billings manufacture?

(c) Prepare an analysis showing the total contribution margin if the additional hours are:
  (1) Divided equally between the products.
  (2) Allocated entirely to the product identified in part (b).

E19-14 The CVP income statements shown below are available for Armstrong Company and Contador Company.

Compute degree of operating leverage and evaluate impact of alternative cost structures on net income.

(LO 5), AN

	Armstrong Co.	**Contador Co.**
Sales	$500,000	$500,000
Variable costs	240,000	50,000
Contribution margin	260,000	450,000
Fixed costs	160,000	350,000
Net income	$100,000	$100,000

Instructions

(a) Compute the degree of operating leverage for each company and interpret your results.

(b) Assuming that sales revenue increases by 10%, prepare a variable costing income statement for each company.

(c) Discuss how the cost structure of these two companies affects their operating leverage and profitability.

E19-15 Arquitectos Interiores of Juarez, Mexico, is contemplating a major change in its cost structure. Currently, all of its drafting work is performed by skilled draftsmen. Alfonso Jiminez, Arquitectos' owner, is considering replacing the draftsmen with a computerized drafting system. However, before making the change, Alfonso would like to know the consequences of the change, since the volume of business varies significantly from year to year. Shown below are CVP income statements for each alternative.

Compute degree of operating leverage and evaluate impact of alternative cost structures on net income and margin of safety.

(LO 5), AN

	Manual System	**Computerized System**
Sales	$1,500,000	$1,500,000
Variable costs	1,200,000	600,000
Contribution margin	300,000	900,000
Fixed costs	50,000	650,000
Net income	$ 250,000	$ 250,000

Instructions

(a) Determine the degree of operating leverage for each alternative.

(b) Which alternative would produce the higher net income if sales increased by $150,000?

(c) Using the margin of safety ratio, determine which alternative could sustain the greater decline in sales before operating at a loss.

E19-16 An investment banker is analyzing two companies that specialize in the production and sale of candied yams. Traditional Yams uses a labor-intensive approach, and Auto-Yams uses a mechanized system. CVP income statements for the two companies are shown below.

Compute degree of operating leverage and impact on net income of alternative cost structures.

(LO 5), AN

	Traditional Yams	**Auto-Yams**
Sales	$400,000	$400,000
Variable costs	320,000	160,000
Contribution margin	80,000	240,000
Fixed costs	30,000	190,000
Net income	$ 50,000	$ 50,000

The investment banker is interested in acquiring one of these companies. However, she is concerned about the impact that each company's cost structure might have on its profitability.

Instructions

(a) Calculate each company's degree of operating leverage. Determine which company's cost structure makes it more sensitive to changes in sales volume.

(b) Determine the effect on each company's net income if sales decrease by 15% and if sales increase by 10%. Do not prepare income statements.

(c) Which company should the investment banker acquire? Discuss.

Compute product cost and prepare an income statement under variable and absorption costing.

(LO 6), **AP**

*E19-17 Felde Company builds custom fishing lures for sporting goods stores. In its first year of operations, 2014, the company incurred the following costs.

Variable Costs per Unit	
Direct materials	$7.50
Direct labor	$2.45
Variable manufacturing overhead	$5.80
Variable selling and administrative expenses	$3.90

Fixed Costs per Year	
Fixed manufacturing overhead	$225,000
Fixed selling and administrative expenses	$240,100

Felde Company sells the fishing lures for $25. During 2014, the company sold 80,000 lures and produced 90,000 lures.

Instructions

(a) Assuming the company uses variable costing, calculate Felde's manufacturing cost per unit for 2014.

(b) Prepare a variable costing income statement for 2014.

(c) Assuming the company uses absorption costing, calculate Felde's manufacturing cost per unit for 2014.

(d) Prepare an absorption costing income statement for 2014.

Determine ending inventory under variable costing and determine whether absorption or variable costing would result in higher net income.

(LO 6, 7), **AN**

*E19-18 Langdon Company produced 9,000 units during the past year, but only 8,200 of the units were sold. The following additional information is also available.

Direct materials used	$79,000
Direct labor incurred	$30,000
Variable manufacturing overhead	$21,500
Fixed manufacturing overhead	$45,000
Fixed selling and administrative expenses	$70,000
Variable selling and administrative expenses	$10,000

There was no work in process inventory at the beginning of the year, nor did Langdon have any beginning finished goods inventory.

Instructions

(a) What would be Langdon Company's finished goods inventory cost on December 31 under variable costing?

(b) Which costing method, absorption or variable costing, would show a higher net income for the year? By what amount?

Compute manufacturing cost under absorption and variable costing and explain difference.

(LO 6), **AN**

*E19-19 Creative Crates Co. produces wooden crates used for shipping products by ocean liner. In 2014, Creative incurred the following costs.

Wood used in crate production	$54,000
Nails (considered insignificant and a variable expense)	$ 350
Direct labor	$38,000
Utilities for the plant:	
$1,500 each month,	
plus $0.40 for each kilowatt-hour used each month	
Rent expense for the plant for the year	$21,400

Assume Creative used an average 500 kilowatt-hours each month over the past year.

Instructions

(a) What is Creative's total manufacturing cost if it uses a variable costing approach?
(b) What is Creative's total manufacturing cost if it uses an absorption costing approach?
(c) What accounts for the difference in manufacturing costs between these two costing approaches?

Exercises: Set B and Challenge Exercises

Visit the book's companion website, at **www.wiley.com/college/kimmel**, and choose the Student Companion site to access Exercise Set B and Challenge Exercises.

Problems: Set A

P19-1A Fredonia Inc. had a bad year in 2013. For the first time in its history, it operated at a loss. The company's income statement showed the following results from selling 80,000 units of product: net sales $2,000,000; total costs and expenses $1,740,000; and net loss $135,000. Costs and expenses consisted of the following.

Compute break-even point under alternative courses of action.
(LO 1, 2), **AN**

	Total	Variable	Fixed
Cost of goods sold	$1,468,000	$ 950,000	$ 518,000
Selling expenses	517,000	92,000	425,000
Administrative expenses	150,000	58,000	92,000
	$2,135,000	$1,100,000	$1,035,000

Management is considering the following independent alternatives for 2014.

1. Increase unit selling price 25% with no change in costs and expenses.
2. Change the compensation of salespersons from fixed annual salaries totaling $200,000 to total salaries of $40,000 plus a 5% commission on net sales.
3. Purchase new high-tech factory machinery that will change the proportion between variable and fixed cost of goods sold to 50:50.

Instructions

(a) Compute the break-even point in dollars for 2014.
(b) Compute the break-even point in dollars under each of the alternative courses of action. (Round to the nearest dollar.) Which course of action do you recommend?

(b) (2) $2,187,500

P19-2A Lorge Corporation has collected the following information after its first year of sales. Sales were $1,500,000 on 100,000 units; selling expenses $250,000 (40% variable and 60% fixed); direct materials $511,000; direct labor $290,000; administrative expenses $270,000 (20% variable and 80% fixed); manufacturing overhead $350,000 (70% variable and 30% fixed). Top management has asked you to do a CVP analysis so that it can make plans for the coming year. It has projected that unit sales will increase by 10% next year.

Compute break-even point and margin of safety ratio, and prepare a CVP income statement before and after changes in business environment.
(LO 1, 2), **AN**

Instructions

(a) Compute (1) the contribution margin for the current year and the projected year, and (2) the fixed costs for the current year. (Assume that fixed costs will remain the same in the projected year.)
(b) Compute the break-even point in units and sales dollars for the first year.

(b) 157,000 units

(c) The company has a target net income of $200,000. What is the required sales in dollars for the company to meet its target?
(d) If the company meets its target net income number, by what percentage could its sales fall before it is operating at a loss? That is, what is its margin of safety ratio?
(e) The company is considering a purchase of equipment that would reduce its direct labor costs by $104,000 and would change its manufacturing overhead costs to 30%

(e) (3) $1,735,714

variable and 70% fixed (assume total manufacturing overhead cost is $350,000, as above). It is also considering switching to a pure commission basis for its sales staff. This would change selling expenses to 90% variable and 10% fixed (assume total selling expense is $250,000, as above). Compute (1) the contribution margin and (2) the contribution margin ratio, and recompute (3) the break-even point in sales dollars. Comment on the effect each of management's proposed changes has on the break-even point.

Determine sales mix with limited resources.

(LO 4), **AN**

P19-3A Tanek Industries manufactures and sells three different models of wet-dry shop vacuum cleaners. Although the shop vacs vary in terms of quality and features, all are good sellers. Tanek is currently operating at full capacity with limited machine time.

Sales and production information relevant to each model follows.

| | Product | | |
	Economy	Standard	Deluxe
Selling price	$30	$50	$100
Variable costs and expenses	$14	$15	$46
Machine hours required	.5	.8	1.6

Instructions

(a) Ignoring the machine time constraint, which single product should Tanek Industries produce?

(b) Economy $32

(b) What is the contribution margin per unit of limited resource for each product?

(c) If additional machine time could be obtained, how should the additional time be used?

Determine break-even sales under alternative sales strategies and evaluate results.

(LO 3), **AN**

P19-4A The Hillside Inn is a restaurant in Flagstaff, Arizona. It specializes in southwestern style meals in a moderate price range. Phil Weld, the manager of Hillside, has determined that during the last 2 years the sales mix and contribution margin ratio of its offerings are as follows.

	Percent of Total Sales	Contribution Margin Ratio
Appetizers	15%	50%
Main entrees	50%	25%
Desserts	10%	50%
Beverages	25%	80%

Phil is considering a variety of options to try to improve the profitability of the restaurant. His goal is to generate a target net income of $117,000. The company has fixed costs of $1,053,000 per year.

Instructions

(a) Total sales $2,600,000

(a) Calculate the total restaurant sales and the sales of each product line that would be necessary to achieve the desired target net income.

(b) Total sales $3,375,000

(b) Phil believes the restaurant could greatly improve its profitability by reducing the complexity and selling price of its entrees to increase the number of clients that it serves. It would then more heavily market its appetizers and beverages. He is proposing to reduce the contribution margin ratio on the main entrees to 10% by dropping the average selling price. He envisions an expansion of the restaurant that would increase fixed costs by $585,000. At the same time, he is proposing to change the sales mix to the following.

	Percent of Total Sales	Contribution Margin Ratio
Appetizers	25%	50%
Main entrees	25%	10%
Desserts	10%	50%
Beverages	40%	80%

Compute the total restaurant sales, and the sales of each product line that would be necessary to achieve the desired target net income.

(c) Suppose that Phil reduces the selling price on entrees and increases fixed costs as proposed in part (b), but customers are not swayed by the marketing efforts and the sales mix remains what it was in part (a). Compute the total restaurant sales and the sales of each product line that would be necessary to achieve the desired target net income. Comment on the potential risks and benefits of this strategy.

P19-5A The following CVP income statements are available for Viejo Company and Nuevo Company.

Compute degree of operating leverage and evaluate impact of operating leverage on financial results.

(LO 5), **AN**

	Viejo Company	Nuevo Company
Sales	$500,000	$500,000
Variable costs	280,000	180,000
Contribution margin	220,000	320,000
Fixed costs	180,000	280,000
Net income	$ 40,000	$ 40,000

Instructions

(a) Compute the break-even point in dollars and the margin of safety ratio for each company.

(b) Compute the degree of operating leverage for each company and interpret your results.

(c) Assuming that sales revenue increases by 20%, prepare a CVP income statement for each company.

(d) Assuming that sales revenue decreases by 20%, prepare a CVP income statement for each company.

(e) ✏️➡ Discuss how the cost structure of these two companies affects their operating leverage and profitability.

(a) BE, Viejo $409,091
    BE, Nuevo $437,500

(b) DOL, Viejo 5.5
    DOL, Nuevo 8.0

P19-6A Bonita Beauty Corporation manufactures cosmetic products that are sold through a network of sales agents. The agents are paid a commission of 18% of sales. The income statement for the year ending December 31, 2014, is as follows.

Determine contribution margin, break-even point, target sales, and degree of operating leverage.

(LO 2, 5), **AN**

BONITA BEAUTY CORPORATION
Income Statement
For the Year Ended December 31, 2014

Sales		$75,000,000
Cost of goods sold		
Variable	$31,500,000	
Fixed	8,610,000	40,110,000
Gross margin		34,890,000
Selling and marketing expenses		
Commissions	13,500,000	
Fixed costs	10,260,000	23,760,000
Operating income		$11,130,000

The company is considering hiring its own sales staff to replace the network of agents. It will pay its salespeople a commission of 8% and incur additional fixed costs of $7.5 million.

Instructions

(a) Under the current policy of using a network of sales agents, calculate the Bonita Beauty Corporation's break-even point in sales dollars for the year 2014.

(b) Calculate the company's break-even point in sales dollars for the year 2014 if it hires its own sales force to replace the network of agents.

(c) Calculate the degree of operating leverage at sales of $75 million if (1) Bonita Beauty uses sales agents, and (2) Bonita Beauty employs its own sales staff. Describe the advantages and disadvantages of each alternative.

(d) Calculate the estimated sales volume in sales dollars that would generate an identical net income for the year ending December 31, 2014, regardless of whether Bonita Beauty Corporation employs its own sales staff and pays them an 8% commission or continues to use the independent network of agents.

(a) $47,175

(c) (2) 3.37

(CMA-Canada adapted)

Prepare income statements under absorption costing and variable costing for a company with beginning inventory, and reconcile differences.

(LO 6, 7), **AN**

(a) 2014 $3,500,000

(b) 2014 $2,750,000

P19-7A Gardner Company produces plastic that is used for injection-molding applications such as gears for small motors. In 2013, the first year of operations, Gardner produced 4,000 tons of plastic and sold 2,500 tons. In 2014, the production and sales results were exactly reversed. In each year, the selling price per ton was $2,000, variable manufacturing costs were 15% of the sales price of units produced, variable selling expenses were 10% of the selling price of units sold, fixed manufacturing costs were $2,000,000, and fixed administrative expenses were $500,000.

Instructions

(a) Prepare income statements for each year using variable costing. (Use the format from Illustration 19A-5.)

(b) Prepare income statements for each year using absorption costing. (Use the format from Illustration 19A-4.)

(c) Reconcile the differences each year in net income under the two costing approaches.

(d) ▬▬▶ Comment on the effects of production and sales on net income under the two costing approaches.

Prepare absorption and variable costing income statements and reconcile differences between absorption and variable costing income statements when sales level and production level change. Discuss relative usefulness of absorption costing versus variable costing.

(LO 6, 7, 8), **AN**

P19-8A Dilithium Batteries is a division of Enterprise Corporation. The division manufactures and sells a long-life battery used in a wide variety of applications. During the coming year, it expects to sell 60,000 units for $30 per unit. Nyota Uthura is the division manager. She is considering producing either 60,000 or 90,000 units during the period. Other information is presented in the schedule.

Division Information for 2014

Beginning inventory	0
Expected sales in units	60,000
Selling price per unit	$30
Variable manufacturing costs per unit	$12
Fixed manufacturing overhead costs (total)	$540,000
Fixed manufacturing overhead costs per unit:	
Based on 60,000 units	$9 per unit ($540,000 ÷ 60,000)
Based on 90,000 units	$6 per unit ($540,000 ÷ 90,000)
Manufacturing costs per unit:	
Based on 60,000 units	$21 per unit ($12 variable + $9 fixed)
Based on 90,000 units	$18 per unit ($12 variable + $6 fixed)
Variable selling and administrative expenses	$2
Fixed selling and administrative expenses (total)	$50,000

(a) 90,000 units: NI $550,000

(b) 90,000 units: NI $370,00

Instructions

(a) Prepare an absorption costing income statement, with one column showing the results if 60,000 units are produced and one column showing the results if 90,000 units are produced.

(b) Prepare a variable costing income statement, with one column showing the results if 60,000 units are produced and one column showing the results if 90,000 units are produced.

(c) Reconcile the difference in net incomes under the two approaches and explain what accounts for this difference.

(d) ▬▬▶ Discuss the relative usefulness of the variable costing income statements versus the absorption costing income statements for decision-making and for evaluating the manager's performance.

Problems: Set B

Compute break-even point under alternative courses of action.

(LO 1, 2), **AN**

P19-1B McCure Corporation had a bad year in 2013, operating at a loss for the first time in its history. The company's income statement showed the following results from selling 200,000 units of product: net sales $2,400,000; total costs and expenses $2,472,000; and net loss $72,000. Costs and expenses consisted of the following.

	Total	Variable	Fixed
Cost of goods sold	$1,486,000	$1,070,000	$416,000
Selling expenses	681,000	356,000	325,000
Administrative expenses	305,000	110,000	195,000
	$2,472,000	$1,536,000	$936,000

Management is considering the following independent alternatives for 2014.
1. Increase unit selling price 25% with no change in costs and expenses.
2. Change the compensation of salespersons from fixed annual salaries totaling $170,000 to total salaries of $50,000 plus a 6% commission on net sales.
3. Purchase new high-tech factory machinery that will change the proportion between variable and fixed cost of goods sold to 40:60.

Instructions
(a) Compute the break-even point in dollars for 2014.
(b) Compute the break-even point in dollars under each of the alternative courses of action. Which course of action do you recommend? Round to the nearest dollar.

(b) (2) $2,720,000

P19-2B Huber Corporation has collected the following information after its first year of sales. Sales were $1,000,000 on 40,000 units; selling expenses $200,000 (30% variable and 70% fixed); direct materials $327,000; direct labor $190,000; administrative expenses $250,000 (30% variable and 70% fixed); manufacturing overhead $240,000 (20% variable and 80% fixed). Top management has asked you to do a CVP analysis so that it can make plans for the coming year. It has projected that unit sales will increase by 20% next year.

Compute break-even point and margin of safety ratio, and prepare a CVP income statement before and after changes in business environment.
(LO 1, 2), AN

Instructions
(a) Compute (1) the contribution margin for the current year and the projected year, and (2) the fixed costs for the current year. (Assume that fixed costs will remain the same in the projected year.)
(b) Compute the break-even point in units and sales dollars for the current year.
(c) The company has a target net income of $120,000. What is the required sales in dollars for the company to meet its target?
(d) If the company meets its target net income number, by what percentage could its sales fall before it is operating at a loss? That is, what is its margin of safety ratio?
(e) The company is considering a purchase of equipment that would reduce its direct labor costs by $90,000 and would change its manufacturing overhead costs to 10% variable and 90% fixed (assume total manufacturing overhead cost is $240,000, as above). It is also considering switching to a pure commission basis for its sales staff. This would change selling expenses to 80% variable and 20% fixed (assume total selling expense is $200,000, as above). Compute (1) the contribution margin and (2) the contribution margin ratio, and (3) recompute the break-even point in sales dollars. Comment on the effect each of management's proposed changes has on the break-even point.

(b) 67,600 units

(e) (3) $1,372,611

P19-3B Keppel Corporation manufactures and sells three different models of exterior doors. Although the doors vary in terms of quality and features, all are good sellers. Keppel is currently operating at full capacity with limited machine time.

Determine sales mix with limited resources.
(LO 4), AN

Sales and production information relevant to each model is shown below.

	Product		
	Economy	Standard	Deluxe
Selling price	$270	$450	$650
Variable costs and expenses	$144	$260	$430
Machine hours required	.6	.8	1.1

Instructions
(a) Ignoring the machine time constraint, which single product should Keppel produce?
(b) What is the contribution margin per unit of limited resource for each product?
(c) If additional machine time could be obtained, how should the additional time be used?

(b) Economy $210

Determine break-even sales under alternative sales strategies and evaluate results.

(LO 3), **AN**

P19-4B The Eatery is a restaurant in DeKalb, Illinois. It specializes in deluxe sandwiches in a moderate price range. Michael Raye, the manager of The Eatery, has determined that during the last 2 years the sales mix and contribution margin ratio of its offerings are as follows.

	Percent of Total Sales	Contribution Margin Ratio
Appetizers	15%	60%
Main entrees	60%	25%
Desserts	10%	40%
Beverages	15%	80%

Michael is considering a variety of options to try to improve the profitability of the restaurant. His goal is to generate a target net income of $176,000. The company has fixed costs of $352,000 per year.

Instructions

(a) Total sales, $1,320,000

(a) Calculate the total restaurant sales and the sales of each product line that would be necessary to achieve the desired target net income.

(b) Total sales, $1,600,000

(b) Michael believes the restaurant could greatly improve its profitability by reducing the complexity and selling price of its entrees to increase the number of clients that it serves. It would then more heavily market its appetizers and beverages. He is proposing to reduce the contribution margin ratio on the main entrees to 10% by dropping the average selling price and increasing the contribution margin ratio on desserts to 50% by reducing costs. He envisions an expansion of the restaurant that would increase fixed costs by 50%. At the same time, he is proposing to change the sales mix to the following.

	Percent of Total Sales	Contribution Margin Ratio
Appetizers	25%	60%
Main entrees	40%	10%
Desserts	10%	50%
Beverages	25%	80%

Compute the total restaurant sales, and the sales of each product line that would be necessary to achieve the desired target net income.

(c) Total sales, $2,200,000

(c) Suppose that Michael reduces the selling price on entrees and increases fixed costs as proposed in part (b), but customers are not swayed by the marketing efforts and the sales mix remains what it was in part (a). Compute the total restaurant sales and the sales of each product line that would be necessary to achieve the desired target net income. Comment on the potential risks and benefits of this strategy.

Compute degree of operating leverage and evaluate impact of operating leverage on financial results.

(LO 5), **AN**

P19-5B The following variable costing income statements are available for Lyte Company and Darke Company.

	Lyte Company	Darke Company
Sales	$1,000,000	$1,000,000
Variable costs	600,000	200,000
Contribution margin	400,000	800,000
Fixed costs	200,000	600,000
Net income	$ 200,000	$ 200,000

Instructions

(a) BE Lyte $500,000
BE Darke $750,000

(a) Compute the break-even point in dollars and the margin of safety ratio for each company.

(b) DOL, Lyte 2.0
DOL, Darke 4.0

(b) Compute the degree of operating leverage for each company and interpret your results.

(c) Assuming that sales revenue increases by 30%, prepare a variable costing income statement for each company.

(d) Assuming that sales revenue decreases by 30%, prepare a variable costing income statement for each company.

(e) ▭▬▬▶ Discuss how the cost structure of these two companies affects their operating leverage and profitability.

P19-6B   Peaches and Cream Corporation manufactures cosmetic products that are sold through a network of sales agents. The agents are paid a commission of 16.25% of sales. The income statement for the year ending December 31, 2014, is shown below.

Determine contribution margin, break-even point, target sales, and degree of operating leverage.
(LO 2, 5), **AN**

PEACHES AND CREAM CORPORATION
Income Statement
For the Year Ended December 31, 2014

Sales		$120,000,000
Cost of goods sold		
Variable	$58,500,000	
Fixed	11,000,000	69,500,000
Gross margin		50,500,000
Selling and marketing expenses		
Commissions	19,500,000	
Fixed costs	10,000,000	29,500,000
Operating income		$ 21,000,000

The company is considering hiring its own sales staff to replace the network of agents. It will pay its salespeople a commission of 10% and incur additional fixed costs of $12.0 million.

Instructions

(a) Under the current policy of using a network of sales agents, calculate the Peaches and Cream Corporation's break-even point in sales dollars for the year 2014.

(a) $60,000

(b) Calculate the company's break-even point in sales dollars for the year 2014 if it hires its own sales force to replace the network of agents.

(c) Calculate the degree of operating leverage at sales of $120 million if (1) Peaches and Cream uses sales agents, and (2) Peaches and Cream employs its own sales staff. Describe the advantages and disadvantages of each alternative.

(c) (2) 3.0

(d) Calculate the estimated sales volume in sales dollars that would generate an identical net income for the year ending December 31, 2014, regardless of whether Peaches and Cream Corporation employs its own sales staff and pays them a 10% commission as well as incurring additional fixed costs of $12.0 million, or continues to use the independent network of agents.

(CMA Canada-adapted)

*P19-7B   FAB produces fabrics that are used for clothing and other applications. In 2013, the first year of operations, FAB produced 500,000 yards of fabric and sold 400,000 yards. In 2014, the production and sales results were exactly reversed. In each year, selling price per yard was $2.50, variable manufacturing costs were 30% of the sales price of units produced, variable selling expenses were 10% of the selling price of units sold, fixed manufacturing costs were $400,000, and fixed administrative expenses were $100,000.

Prepare income statements under absorption costing and variable costing for a company with beginning inventory, and reconcile differences.
(LO 6, 7), **AN**

Instructions

(a) Prepare income statements for each year using variable costing. (Use the format from Illustration 19A-10.)

(a) 2013 Net income $100,000

(b) Prepare income statements for each year using absorption costing. (Use the format from Illustration 19A-11.)

(b) 2013 Net income $180,000

(c) Reconcile the differences each year in income from operations under the two costing approaches.

(d) ▭▬▬▶ Comment on the effects of production and sales on net income under the two costing approaches.

Prepare absorption and variable costing income statements and reconcile differences between absorption and variable costing income statements when sales level and production level change. Discuss relative usefulness of absorption costing versus variable costing.
(LO 6, 7, 8), **AN**

P19-8B   Electricoil is a division of Meier Products Corporation. The division manufactures and sells an electric coil used in a wide variety of applications. During the coming year, it expects to sell 200,000 units for $9 per unit. Mark Barnes is the division manager. He is considering producing either 200,000 or 250,000 units during the period. Other information is presented in the schedule on the next page.

Division Information for 2014

Beginning inventory	0
Expected sales in units	200,000
Selling price per unit	$9
Variable manufacturing costs per unit	$3
Fixed manufacturing overhead costs (total)	$500,000

Fixed manufacturing overhead costs per unit:

Based on 200,000 units	$2.50 per unit ($50,000 ÷ 200,000)
Based on 250,000 units	$2.00 per unit ($500,000 ÷ 250,000)

Manufacturing costs per unit:

Based on 200,000 units	$5.50 per unit ($3 variable + $2.50 fixed)
Based on 250,000 units	$5.00 per unit ($3 variable + $2.00 fixed)
Variable selling and administrative expense	$0.40
Fixed selling and administrative expense (total)	$15,000

Instructions

(a) 250,000 produced
NI, $705,000

(a) Prepare an absorption costing income statement, with one column showing the results if 200,000 units are produced and one column showing the results if 250,000 units are produced.

(b) 250,000 produced
NI, $605,000

(b) Prepare a variable costing income statement, with one column showing the results if 200,000 units are produced and one column showing the results if 250,000 units are produced.

(c) Reconcile the difference in net incomes under the two approaches and explain what accounts for this difference.

(d)   Discuss the relative usefulness of the variable costing income statements versus the absorption costing income statements for decision-making and for evaluating the manager's performance.

Problems: Set C

Visit the book's companion website, at **www.wiley.com/college/kimmel**, and choose the Student Companion site to access Problem Set C.

Waterways Continuing Problem

(*Note:* This is a continuation of the Waterways Problem from Chapters 14 through 18.)

WCP19   This problem asks you to perform break-even analysis based on Waterways' sales mix and to make sales mix decisions related to Waterways' use of its productive facilities. An optional extension of the problem (related to the chapter appendix) also asks you to prepare a variable costing income statement and an absorption costing income statement.

Go to the book's companion website, **www.wiley.com/college/kimmel**, to find the remainder of this problem.

Broadening Your Perspective

Management Decision-Making

DECISION-MAKING AT CURRENT DESIGNS

BYP19-1   Current Designs manufactures two different types of kayaks, rotomolded kayaks and composite kayaks. The following information is available for each product line.

	Rotomolded	Composite
Sales price/unit	$950	$2,000
Variable costs/unit	$570	$1,340

The company's fixed costs are $820,000. An analysis of the sales mix identifies that rotomolded kayaks make up 80% of the total units sold.

Instructions
(a) Determine the weighted-average unit contribution margin for Current Designs.
(b) Determine the break-even point in units for Current Designs and identify how many units of each type of kayak will be sold at the break-even point. (Round to the nearest whole number.)
(c) Assume that the sales mix changes, and rotomolded kayaks now make up 70% of total units sold. Calculate the total number of units that would need to be sold to earn a net income of $2,000,000 and identify how many units of each type of kayak will be sold at this level of income. (Round to the nearest whole number.)
(d) Assume that Current Designs will have sales of $3,000,000 with two-thirds of the sales dollars in rotomolded kayaks and one-third of the sales dollars in composite kayaks. Assuming $660,000 of fixed costs are allocated to the rotomolded kayaks and $160,000 to the composite kayaks, prepare a CVP income statement for each product line.
(e) Using the information in part (d), calculate the degree of operating leverage for each product line and interpret your findings. (Round to two decimal places.)

DECISION-MAKING ACROSS THE ORGANIZATION

BYP19-2 E-Z Seats manufactures swivel seats for customized vans. It currently manufactures 10,000 seats per year, which it sells for $500 per seat. It incurs variable costs of $200 per seat and fixed costs of $2,000,000. It is considering automating the upholstery process, which is now largely manual. It estimates that if it does so, its fixed costs will be $3,000,000, and its variable costs will decline to $100 per seat.

Instructions
With the class divided into groups, answer the following questions.
(a) Prepare a CVP income statement based on current activity.
(b) Compute contribution margin ratio, break-even point in dollars, margin of safety ratio, and degree of operating leverage based on current activity.
(c) Prepare a CVP income statement assuming that the company invests in the automated upholstery system.
(d) Compute contribution margin ratio, break-even point in dollars, margin of safety ratio, and degree of operating leverage assuming the new upholstery system is implemented.
(e) Discuss the implications of adopting the new system.

MANAGERIAL ANALYSIS

BYP19-3 For nearly 20 years, Specialized Coatings has provided painting and galvanizing services for manufacturers in its region. Manufacturers of various metal products have relied on the quality and quick turnaround time provided by Specialized Coatings and its 20 skilled employees. During the last year, as a result of a sharp upturn in the economy, the company's sales have increased by 30% relative to the previous year. The company has not been able to increase its capacity fast enough, so Specialized Coatings has had to turn work away because it cannot keep up with customer requests.

Top management is considering the purchase of a sophisticated robotic painting booth. The booth would represent a considerable move in the direction of automation versus manual labor. If Specialized Coatings purchases the booth, it would most likely lay off 15 of its skilled painters. To analyze the decision, the company compiled production information from the most recent year and then prepared a parallel compilation assuming that the company would purchase the new equipment and lay off the workers. Those data are shown below. As you can see, the company projects that during the last year it would have been far more profitable if it had used the automated approach.

	Current Approach	**Automated Approach**
Sales	$2,000,000	$2,000,000
Variable costs	1,500,000	1,000,000
Contribution margin	500,000	1,000,000
Fixed costs	380,000	800,000
Net income	$ 120,000	$ 200,000

Instructions

(a) Compute and interpret the contribution margin ratio under each approach.
(b) Compute the break-even point in sales dollars under each approach. Discuss the implications of your findings.
(c) Using the current level of sales, compute the margin of safety ratio under each approach and interpret your findings.
(d) Determine the degree of operating leverage for each approach at current sales levels. How much would the company's net income decline under each approach with a 10% decline in sales?
(e) At what level of sales would the company's net income be the same under either approach?
(f) Discuss the issues that the company must consider in making this decision.

REAL-WORLD FOCUS

BYP19-4   In a recent report, the Del Monte Foods Company reported three separate operating segments: consumer products (which includes a variety of canned foods including tuna, fruit, and vegetables); pet products (which includes pet food and snacks and veterinary products); and soup and infant-feeding products (which includes soup, broth, and infant feeding and pureed products).

In its annual report, Del Monte uses absorption costing. As a result, information regarding the relative composition of its fixed and variable costs is not available. We have assumed that $860.3 million of its total operating expenses of $1,920.3 million are fixed and have allocated the remaining variable costs across the three divisions. Sales data, along with assumed expense data, are provided below.

	(in millions)	
	Sales	**Variable Costs**
Consumer products	$1,031.8	$ 610
Pet products	837.3	350
Soup and infant-feeding products	302.0	100
	$2,171.1	$1,060

Instructions

(a) Compute each segment's contribution margin ratio and the sales mix.
(b) Using the information computed in part (a), compute the company's break-even point in dollars, and then determine the amount of sales that would be generated by each division at the break-even point.

BYP19-5   The external financial statements published by publicly traded companies are based on absorption cost accounting. As a consequence, it is very difficult to gain an understanding of the relative composition of the companies' fixed and variable costs. It is possible, however, to learn about a company's sales mix and the relative profitability of its various divisions. This exercise looks at the financial statements of FedEx Corporation.

Address: **www.fedex.com/us/investorrelations**, or go to **www.wiley.com/college/kimmel**

Steps

1. Go to the site above.
2. Under "Financial Documents," choose "Annual Reports."
3. Choose "2008 Annual Report."

Instructions

(a) Read page 25 of the report under the heading "Description of Business." What are the three primary product lines of the company? What does the company identify as the key factors affecting operating results?
(b) Page 36 of the report lists the operating expenses of FedEx Ground. Assuming that rentals, depreciation, and "other" are all fixed costs, prepare a variable costing income statement for 2008, and compute the division's contribution margin ratio and the break-even point in dollars.
(c) Page 73, Note 13 ("Business segment information") provides additional information regarding the relative profitability of the three business segments.
   (i) Calculate the sales mix for 2006 and 2008. (*Note:* Exclude "other" when you calculate total revenue.)

(ii) The company does not provide the contribution margin for each division, but it does provide "operating margin" (operating income divided by revenues) on pages 34, 36, and 37. List these for each division for 2006 and 2008.

(iii) Assuming that the "operating margin" (operating income divided by revenues) moves in parallel with each division's contribution margin, how has the shift in sales mix affected the company's profitability from 2006 to 2008?

BYP19-6 The June 8, 2009, edition of the *Wall Street Journal* has an article by JoAnn Lublin entitled "Smart Balance Keeps Tight Focus on Creativity."

Instructions
Read the article and answer the following questions.
(a) Describe Smart Balance's approach to employment and cost structure.
(b) What function does it keep "in-house"?
(c) Based on the discussion in this chapter, what are the advantages to Smart Balance's approach?
(d) Based on the discussion in this chapter, what are the disadvantages to Smart Balance's approach?

Critical Thinking

COMMUNICATION ACTIVITY

BYP19-7 Easton Corporation makes two different boat anchors—a traditional fishing anchor and a high-end yacht anchor—using the same production machinery. The contribution margin of the yacht anchor is three times as high as that of the other product. The company is currently operating at full capacity and has been doing so for nearly two years. Bjorn Borg, the company's CEO, wants to cut back on production of the fishing anchor so that the company can make more yacht anchors. He says that this is a "no-brainer" because the contribution margin of the yacht anchor is so much higher.

Instructions
Write a short memo to Bjorn Borg describing the analysis that the company should do before it makes this decision and any other considerations that would affect the decision.

ETHICS CASE

BYP19-8 Brett Stern was hired during January 2014 to manage the home products division of Hi-Tech Products. As part of his employment contract, he was told that he would get $5,000 of additional bonus for every 1% increase that the division's profits exceeded those of the previous year.

Soon after coming on board, Brett met with his plant managers and explained that he wanted the plants to be run at full capacity. Previously, the plant had employed just-in-time inventory practices and had consequently produced units only as they were needed. Brett stated that under previous management the company had missed out on too many sales opportunities because it didn't have enough inventory on hand. Because previous management had employed just-in-time inventory practices, when Brett came on board there was virtually no beginning inventory. The selling price and variable costs per unit remained the same from 2013 to 2014. Additional information is provided below.

	2013	2014
Net income	$ 300,000	$ 525,000
Units produced	25,000	30,000
Units sold	25,000	25,000
Fixed manufacturing overhead costs	$1,350,000	$1,350,000
Fixed manufacturing overhead costs per unit	$ 54	$ 45

Instructions
(a) Calculate Brett's bonus based upon the net income shown above.
(b) Recompute the 2013 and 2014 results using variable costing.
(c) Recompute Brett's 2014 bonus under variable costing.
(d) Were Brett's actions unethical? Do you think any actions need to be taken by the company?

ALL ABOUT YOU

BYP19-9 Many of you will some day own your own business. One rapidly growing opportunity is no-frills workout centers. Such centers attract customers who want to take advantage of state-of-the-art fitness equipment but do not need the other amenities of full-service health clubs. One way to own your own fitness business is to buy a franchise. Snap Fitness is a Minnesota-based business that offers franchise opportunities. For a very low monthly fee ($26, without an annual contract), customers can access a Snap Fitness center 24 hours a day.

The Snap Fitness website (**www.snapfitness.com**) indicates that start-up costs range from $60,000 to $184,000. This initial investment covers the following pre-opening costs: franchise fee, grand opening marketing, leasehold improvements, utility/rent deposits, and training.

Instructions
(a) Suppose that Snap Fitness estimates that each location incurs $4,000 per month in fixed operating expenses plus $1,460 to lease equipment. A recent newspaper article describing no-frills fitness centers indicated that a Snap Fitness site might require only 300 members to break even. Using the information provided above and your knowledge of CVP analysis, estimate the amount of variable costs. (When performing your analysis, assume that the only fixed costs are the estimated monthly operating expenses and the equipment lease.)
(b) Using the information from part (a), what would monthly sales in members and dollars have to be to achieve a target net income of $3,640 for the month?
(c) Provide five examples of variable costs for a fitness center.
(d) Go to a fitness-business website, such as Curves, Snap Fitness, or Anytime Fitness, and find information about purchasing a franchise. Summarize the franchise information needed to decide whether entering into a franchise agreement would be a good idea.

CONSIDERING PEOPLE, PLANET, AND PROFIT

BYP19-10 Many politicians, scientists, economists, and businesspeople have become concerned about the potential implications of global warming. The largest source of the emissions thought to contribute to global warming is from coal-fired power plants. The cost of alternative energy has declined, but it is still higher than coal. In 1980, wind-power electricity cost 80 cents per kilowatt hour. Using today's highly efficient turbines with rotor diameters of up to 125 meters, the cost can be as low as 4 cents (about the same as coal), or as much as 20 cents in places with less wind.

Some people have recently suggested that conventional cost comparisons are not adequate because they do not take environmental costs into account. For example, while coal is a very cheap energy source, it is also a significant contributor of greenhouse gases. Should environmental costs be incorporated into decision formulas when planners evaluate new power plants? The basic arguments for and against are as follows.

> **YES:** As long as environmental costs are ignored, renewable energy will appear to be too expensive relative to coal.
>
> **NO:** If one country decides to incorporate environmental costs into its decision-making process but other countries do not, the country that does so will be at a competitive disadvantage because its products will cost more to produce.

Instructions
Write a response indicating your position regarding this situation. Provide support for your view.

Answers to Insight and Accounting Across the Organization Questions

p. 991 Don't Just Look–Buy Something Q: Besides increasing their conversion rates, what steps can online merchants use to lower their break-even points? **A:** In theory, one of the principal advantages of online retailers is that they can minimize their investment in "bricks and mortar" and thus minimize their fixed costs. Some online merchants never even handle the merchandise they sell. Instead, they simply provide a centralized location for customers to view merchandise and to place orders. The online retailer then forwards the order to the supplier, and the supplier ships it directly to the customer.

However, some online merchants who originally planned on employing this model have since found it necessary to build their own warehouses and distribution centers to ensure timely and dependable product delivery. This increases their fixed costs and consequently increases their break-even point.

p. 996 Healthy for You, and Great for the Bottom Line Q: Why do you suppose restaurants are so eager to sell beverages and desserts? **A:** There is a reason why servers at restaurants keep your beverage glass full, and why they wave the dessert tray in your face at the end of the meal. Both of these items traditionally have very high contribution margins and require very minimal investments in fixed costs. As a consequence, they are a great mechanism by which a company can hit its break-even point.

p. 999 Something Smells Q: What is the limited resource for a retailer, and what implications does this have for sales mix? **A:** For retailers, the limited resource is not just shelf space, but shelf space per day. At first, you might think that a product that is small and has a high contribution margin would be the product of choice. But, you also have to factor in the amount of time that a product sits on the shelf.

For example, suppose Products A and B are the same size. Product A has twice the contribution margin as product B, but A sits on the shelf five times as long as product B. In this case, once time spent on the shelf is taken into account, B's superior turnover more than makes up for its lower contribution margin.

p. 1002 There Is Something About a Train Q: Why did Warren Buffett think that this was a good time to invest in railroad stocks? **A:** Railroads have extremely high fixed costs. Mr. Buffett bought Burlington Northern Railroad at the bottom of a recession. He is counting on the railroad's high operating leverage to provide large profits once the economy rebounds.

Answers to Self-Test Questions

1. d **2.** d **3.** a **4.** a ($350,000 − $100,000) **5.** b [($180,000 + $268,000) ÷ ($12 − $8.50)]
6. d [$150,000 ÷ ($3 ÷ $12)] **7.** d **8.** a **9.** b ($15 ÷ 3.0) **10.** d [($26 ÷ 4) < ($14 ÷ 2)]
11. d **12.** d **13.** c **14.** a ($200,000 × 3.5 × 10%) ***15.** b ***16.** c

The Navigator

CHAPTER 20

© Izabela Habur/iStockphoto

✔ The Navigator

- Scan Learning Objectives
- Read Feature Story
- Scan Preview
- Read Text and Answer **Do it!**
  ◯ p. 1046 ◯ p. 1048 ◯ p. 1052
  ◯ p. 1056
- Work Using the Decision Toolkit
- Review Summary of Learning Objectives
- Work Comprehensive **Do it!** p. 1059
- Answer Self-Test Questions
- Complete Assignments
- Go to WileyPLUS for practice and tutorials

INCREMENTAL ANALYSIS

LEARNING OBJECTIVES

After studying this chapter, you should be able to:

1. Identify the steps in management's decision-making process.
2. Describe the concept of incremental analysis.
3. Identify the relevant costs in accepting an order at a special price.
4. Identify the relevant costs in a make-or-buy decision.
5. Identify the relevant costs in determining whether to sell or process materials further.
6. Identify the relevant costs to be considered in repairing, retaining, or replacing equipment.
7. Identify the relevant costs in deciding whether to eliminate an unprofitable segment or product.

✔ The Navigator

When is a manufacturer not a manufacturer? When it outsources. An extension of the classic "make or buy" decision, outsourcing involves hiring other companies to make all or part of a product or to perform services. Who is outsourcing? Nike, General Motors, Sara Lee, and Hewlett-Packard, to name a few. Even a recent trade journal article for small cabinet-makers outlined the pros and cons of building cabinet doors and drawers internally, or outsourcing them to other shops.

Gibson Greetings, Inc., one of the country's largest sellers of greeting cards, has experienced both the pros and cons of outsourcing. In April one year, it announced it would outsource the manufacturing of all of its cards and gift wrap. Gibson's stock price shot up quickly because investors believed the strategy could save the company $10 million a year, primarily by reducing manufacturing costs. But later in the same year, Gibson got a taste of the negative side of outsourcing: When one of its suppliers was unable to meet its production schedule, about $20 million of Christmas cards went to stores a month later than scheduled.

Outsourcing is often a point of dispute in labor negotiations. Although many of the jobs lost to outsourcing go overseas, that is not always the case. In fact, a recent trend is to hire out work to vendors located close to the company. This reduces shipping costs and can improve coordination of efforts.

One company that has benefited from local outsourcing is Solectron Corporation in Silicon Valley. It makes things like cell phones, printers, and computers for high-tech companies in the region. To the surprise of many, it has kept thousands of people employed in California rather than watching those jobs go overseas. What is its secret? It produces high-quality products efficiently. Solectron has to be efficient because it operates on a very thin profit margin—that is, it makes a tiny amount of money on each part—but it makes millions and millions of parts. It has proved the logic of outsourcing as a management decision, both for the companies for which it makes parts and for its owners and employees.

MAKE IT OR BUY IT?

Watch the Method video in WileyPLUS to learn more about incremental analysis in the real world.

✔ The Navigator

INSIDE CHAPTER 20 . . .

An important purpose of management accounting is to provide managers with relevant information for decision-making. Companies of all sorts must make product decisions. Philip Morris decided to cut prices to raise market share. Oral-B Laboratories opted to produce a new, higher-priced ($5) toothbrush. General Motors discontinued making the Buick Riviera and announced the closure of its Oldsmobile Division. Quaker Oats decided to sell off a line of beverages, at a price more than $1 billion less than it paid for that product line only a few years before. Ski manufacturers like Dynastar had to decide whether to use their limited resources to make snowboards instead of downhill skis.

This chapter explains management's decision-making process and a decision-making approach called incremental analysis. The use of incremental analysis is demonstrated in a variety of situations.

The content and organization of this chapter are as follows.

Management's Decision-Making Process

LEARNING OBJECTIVE 1

Identify the steps in management's decision-making process.

Making decisions is an important management function. Management's decision-making process does not always follow a set pattern because decisions vary significantly in their scope, urgency, and importance. It is possible, though, to identify some steps that are frequently involved in the process. These steps are shown in Illustration 20-1 below.

Accounting's contribution to the decision-making process occurs primarily in Steps 2 and 4—evaluating possible courses of action, and reviewing results. In

Illustration 20-1
Management's decision-making process

Step 2, for each possible course of action, relevant revenue and cost data are provided. These show the expected overall effect on net income. In Step 4, internal reports are prepared that review the actual impact of the decision.

In making business decisions, management ordinarily considers both financial and nonfinancial information. **Financial** information is related to revenues and costs and their effect on the company's overall profitability. **Nonfinancial** information relates to such factors as the effect of the decision on employee turnover, the environment, or the overall image of the company in the community. (These are considerations that we touched on in our Chapter 1 discussion of corporate social responsibility.) Although nonfinancial information can be as important as financial information, we will focus primarily on financial information that is relevant to the decision.

INCREMENTAL ANALYSIS APPROACH

Decisions involve a choice among alternative courses of action. Suppose you face the personal financial decision of whether to purchase or lease a car. The financial data relate to the cost of leasing versus the cost of purchasing. For example, leasing would involve periodic lease payments; purchasing would require "up-front" payment of the purchase price. In other words, the financial data relevant to the decision are the data that would vary in the future among the possible alternatives. The process used to identify the financial data that change under alternative courses of action is called incremental analysis. In some cases, you will find that when you use incremental analysis, both costs **and** revenues will vary. In other cases, only costs **or** revenues will vary.

Just as your decision to buy or lease a car will affect your future financial situation, similar decisions, on a larger scale, will affect a company's future. Incremental analysis identifies the probable effects of those decisions on future earnings. Such analysis inevitably involves estimates and uncertainty. Gathering data for incremental analyses may involve market analysts, engineers, and accountants. In quantifying the data, the accountant is expected to produce the most reliable information available at the time the decision must be made.

> **LEARNING OBJECTIVE 2**
> Describe the concept of incremental analysis.

> **Alternative Terminology**
> Incremental analysis is also called *differential analysis* because the analysis focuses on differences.

HOW INCREMENTAL ANALYSIS WORKS

The basic approach in incremental analysis is illustrated in the following example.

Illustration 20-2 Basic approach in incremental analysis

	A	B	C	D
		Alternative A	**Alternative B**	**Net Income Increase (Decrease)**
2	Revenues	$125,000	$110,000	$ (15,000)
3	Costs	100,000	80,000	20,000
4	Net income	$ 25,000	$ 30,000	$ 5,000
5				

This example compares alternative B with alternative A. The net income column shows the differences between the alternatives. In this case, incremental revenue will be $15,000 less under alternative B than under alternative A. But a

$20,000 incremental cost saving will be realized.[1] Thus, alternative B will produce $5,000 more net income than alternative A.

In the following pages, you will encounter three important cost concepts used in incremental analysis, as defined and discussed in Illustration 20-3.

Illustration 20-3 Key cost concepts in incremental analysis

- **Relevant cost**   In incremental analysis, the only factors to be considered are those costs and revenues that differ across alternatives. Those factors are called **relevant costs**. Costs and revenues that do not differ across alternatives can be ignored when trying to choose between alternatives.

- **Opportunity cost**   Often in choosing one course of action, the company must give up the opportunity to benefit from some other course of action. For example, if a machine is used to make one type of product, the benefit of making another type of product with that machine is lost. This lost benefit is referred to as **opportunity cost**.

- **Sunk cost**   Costs that have already been incurred and will not be changed or avoided by any present or future decisions are referred to as **sunk costs**. For example, the amount you spent in the past to purchase or repair a machine should have no bearing on your decision whether to buy a new machine. **Sunk costs are not relevant costs.**

Incremental analysis sometimes involves changes that at first glance might seem contrary to your intuition. For example, sometimes variable costs **do not change** under the alternative courses of action. Also, sometimes fixed costs **do change**. For example, direct labor, normally a variable cost, is not an incremental cost in deciding between two new factory machines if each asset requires the same amount of direct labor. In contrast, rent expense, normally a fixed cost, is an incremental cost in a decision whether to continue occupancy of a building or to purchase or lease a new building.

It is also important to understand that **the approaches to incremental analysis discussed in this chapter do not take into consideration the time value of money**. That is, amounts to be paid or received in future years are not discounted for the cost of interest. Time value of money is addressed in Chapter 24 and Appendix D.

---

[1]Although income taxes are sometimes important in incremental analysis, they are ignored in the chapter for simplicity's sake.

Service Company Insight

That Letter from AmEx Might Not Be a Bill

No doubt every one of you has received an invitation from a credit card company to open a new account—some of you have probably received three in one day. But how many of you have received an offer of $300 to close out your credit card account? American Express decided to offer some of its customers $300 if they would give back their credit card. You could receive the $300 even if you hadn't paid off your balance yet, as long as you agreed to give up your credit card.

Source: Aparajita Saha-Bubna and Lauren Pollock, "AmEx Offers Some Holders $300 to Pay and Leave," *Wall Street Journal Online* (February 23, 2009).

 What are the relevant costs that American Express would need to know in order to determine to whom to make this offer? (See page 1079.)

Tina Spruce/iStockphoto

Types of Incremental Analysis

A number of different types of decisions involve incremental analysis. The more common types of decisions are whether to:

LEARNING OBJECTIVE 3
Identify the relevant costs in accepting an order at a special price.

1. Accept an order at a special price.
2. Make or buy component parts or finished products.
3. Sell products or process them further.
4. Repair, retain, or replace equipment.
5. Eliminate an unprofitable business segment or product.

We will consider each of these types of decisions in the following pages.

ACCEPT AN ORDER AT A SPECIAL PRICE

Sometimes a company may have an opportunity to obtain additional business if it is willing to make a major price concession to a specific customer. To illustrate, assume that Sunbelt Company produces 100,000 Smoothie blenders per month, which is 80% of plant capacity. Variable manufacturing costs are $8 per unit. Fixed manufacturing costs are $400,000, or $4 per unit. The Smoothie blenders are normally sold directly to retailers at $20 each. Sunbelt has an offer from Kensington Co. (a foreign wholesaler) to purchase an additional 2,000 blenders at $11 per unit. Acceptance of the offer would not affect normal sales of the product, and the additional units can be manufactured without increasing plant capacity. What should management do?

If management makes its decision on the basis of the total cost per unit of $12 ($8 variable + $4 fixed), the order would be rejected because costs per unit ($12) would exceed revenues per unit ($11) by $1 per unit. However, since the units can be produced within existing plant capacity, the special order **will not increase fixed costs**. Let's identify the relevant data for the decision. First, the variable manufacturing costs will increase $16,000 ($8 × 2,000). Second, the expected revenue will increase $22,000 ($11 × 2,000). Thus, as shown in Illustration 20-4 (page 1046), Sunbelt will increase its net income by $6,000 by accepting this special order.

Helpful Hint This is a good example of different costs for different purposes. In the long run all costs are relevant, but for this decision only costs that change are relevant.

Incremental Analysis - Accepting an order at a special price.xls

Home Insert Page Layout Formulas Data Review View

P18   *fx*

	A	B	C	D
1		**Reject Order**	**Accept Order**	**Net Income Increase (Decrease)**
2	Revenues	$0	$22,000	$ 22,000
3	Costs	0	16,000	(16,000)
4	Net income	$0	$ 6,000	$ 6,000
5				

Illustration 20-4 Incremental analysis—accepting an order at a special price

Two points should be emphasized: First, we assume that sales of the product in other markets **would not be affected by this special order**. If other sales were affected, then Sunbelt would have to consider the lost sales in making the decision. Second, if Sunbelt is operating **at full capacity**, it is likely that the special order would be rejected. Under such circumstances, the company would have to expand plant capacity. In that case, the special order would have to absorb these additional fixed manufacturing costs, as well as the variable manufacturing costs.

SPECIAL ORDERS

Do It! Cobb Company incurs costs of $28 per unit ($18 variable and $10 fixed) to make a product that normally sells for $42. A foreign wholesaler offers to buy 5,000 units at $25 each. Cobb will incur additional shipping costs of $1 per unit. Compute the increase or decrease in net income Cobb will realize by accepting the special order, assuming Cobb has excess operating capacity. Should Cobb Company accept the special order?

Action Plan

- Identify all revenues that will change as a result of accepting the order.
- Identify all costs that will change as a result of accepting the order, and net this amount against the change in revenues.

Solution

	Reject	Accept	Net Income Increase (Decrease)
Revenue	$-0-	$125,000*	$125,000
Costs	-0-	95,000**	(95,000)
Net income	$-0-	$ 30,000	$ 30,000

*5,000 × $25
**(5,000 × $18) + (5,000 × $1)

The analysis indicates net income will increase by $30,000; therefore, Cobb Company should accept the special order.

The Navigator

Related exercise material: **BE20-3, E20-2, E20-3, E20-4,** and **Do It!** **20-1.**

MAKE OR BUY

LEARNING OBJECTIVE **4**

Identify the relevant costs in a make-or-buy decision.

When a manufacturer assembles component parts in producing a finished product, management must decide whether to make or buy the components. The decision to buy parts or services is often referred to as outsourcing. For example, as discussed in the Feature Story, a company such as General Motors Corporation may either make or buy the batteries, tires, and radios used in its cars. Similarly, Hewlett-Packard Corporation may make or buy the electronic circuitry, cases, and printer heads for its printers. Boeing recently sold some of its commercial aircraft factories in an effort to cut production costs and focus instead on engineering and final assembly rather than manufacturing. The decision to make or buy components should be made on the basis of incremental analysis.

Baron Company makes motorcycles and scooters. It incurs the following annual costs in producing 25,000 ignition switches for scooters.

Direct materials	$ 50,000
Direct labor	75,000
Variable manufacturing overhead	40,000
Fixed manufacturing overhead	60,000
Total manufacturing costs	$225,000
Total cost per unit ($225,000 ÷ 25,000)	$9.00

Illustration 20-5 Annual product cost data

Instead of making its own switches, Baron Company might purchase the ignition switches from Ignition, Inc. at a price of $8 per unit. What should management do?

At first glance, it appears that management should purchase the ignition switches for $8 rather than make them at a cost of $9. However, a review of operations indicates that if the ignition switches are purchased from Ignition, Inc., **all** of Baron's variable costs but only $10,000 of its fixed manufacturing costs will be eliminated (avoided). Thus, $50,000 of the fixed manufacturing costs will remain if the ignition switches are purchased. The relevant costs for incremental analysis, therefore, are as shown below.

Illustration 20-6 Incremental analysis—make or buy

	A	B	C	D
		Make	**Buy**	**Net Income Increase (Decrease)**
2	Direct materials	$ 50,000	$ 0	$ 50,000
3	Direct labor	75,000	0	75,000
4	Variable manufacturing costs	40,000	0	40,000
5	Fixed manufacturing costs	60,000	50,000	10,000
6	Purchase price (25,000 × $8)	0	200,000	(200,000)
7	Total annual cost	$225,000	$250,000	$ (25,000)

Incremental Analysis - Make or buy.xls
Home | Insert | Page Layout | Formulas | Data | Review | View
P18   fx

This analysis indicates that Baron Company would incur $25,000 of additional costs by buying the ignition switches rather than making them. Therefore, Baron should continue to make the ignition switches even though the total manufacturing cost is $1 higher per unit than the purchase price. The primary cause of this result is that, even if the company purchases the ignition switches, it will still have fixed costs of $50,000 to absorb.

Opportunity Cost

The foregoing make-or-buy analysis is complete only if it is assumed that the productive capacity used to make the ignition switches cannot be converted to another purpose. If there is an opportunity to use this productive capacity in some other manner, then this opportunity cost must be considered. As indicated earlier, **opportunity cost** is the potential benefit that may be obtained by following an alternative course of action.

To illustrate, assume that through buying the switches, Baron Company can use the released productive capacity to generate additional income of $38,000

Ethics Note In the make-or-buy decision, it is important for management to take into account the social impact of its choice. For instance, buying may be the most economically feasible solution, but such action could result in the closure of a manufacturing plant that employs many good workers.

from producing a different product. This lost income is an additional cost of continuing to make the switches in the make-or-buy decision. This opportunity cost is therefore added to the "Make" column for comparison. As shown in Illustration 20-7, it is now advantageous to buy the ignition switches. The company's income would increase by $13,000.

Illustration 20-7 Incremental analysis—make or buy, with opportunity cost

Incremental Analysis - Make or buy with opportunity cost.xls			
	A	B	C	D
		Make	**Buy**	**Net Income Increase (Decrease)**
2	Total annual cost	$225,000	$250,000	$(25,000)
3	Opportunity cost	38,000	0	38,000
4	Total cost	$263,000	$250,000	$ 13,000
5				

The qualitative factors in this decision include the possible loss of jobs for employees who produce the ignition switches. In addition, management must assess how well the supplier will be able to satisfy the company's quality control standards at the quoted price per unit.

Service Company Insight

Giving Away the Store?

In an earlier chapter, we discussed Amazon.com's incredible growth. However, some analysts have questioned whether some of the methods that Amazon uses to increase its sales make good business sense. For example, a few years ago, Amazon initiated a "Prime" free-shipping subscription program. For a $79 fee per year, Amazon's customers get free shipping on as many goods as they want to buy. At the time, CEO Jeff Bezos promised that the program would be costly in the short-term but benefit the company in the long-term. Six years later, it was true that Amazon's sales had grown considerably. It was also estimated that its Prime customers buy two to three times as much as non-Prime customers. But, its shipping costs rose from 2.8% of sales to 4% of sales, which is remarkably similar to the drop in its gross margin from 24% to 22.3%. Perhaps even less easy to justify is a proposal by Mr. Bezos to start providing a free Internet movie-streaming service to Amazon's Prime customers. Perhaps some incremental analysis is in order?

Source: Martin Peers, "Amazon's Prime Numbers," *Wall Street Journal Online* (February 3, 2011).

? What are the relevant revenues and costs that Amazon should consider relative to the decision whether to offer the Prime free-shipping subscription? (See page 1079.)

© klenger/iStockphoto

MAKE OR BUY

Do It!

Juanita Company must decide whether to make or buy some of its components for the appliances it produces. The costs of producing 166,000 electrical cords for its appliances are as follows.

Direct materials	$90,000	Variable overhead	$32,000
Direct labor	$20,000	Fixed overhead	$24,000

Instead of making the electrical cords at an average cost per unit of $1.00 ($166,000 ÷ 166,000), the company has an opportunity to buy the cords at $0.90 per unit. If the company purchases the cords, all variable costs and one-fourth of the fixed costs will be eliminated.

(a) Prepare an incremental analysis showing whether the company should make or buy the electrical cords. (b) Will your answer be different if the released productive capacity will generate additional income of $5,000?

Solution

(a)

	Make	**Buy**	**Net Income Increase (Decrease)**
Direct materials	$ 90,000	$ –0–	$ 90,000
Direct labor	20,000	–0–	20,000
Variable manufacturing costs	32,000	–0–	32,000
Fixed manufacturing costs	24,000	18,000*	6,000
Purchase price	–0–	149,400**	(149,400)
Total cost	$166,000	$167,400	$ (1,400)

*.75 × $24,000
**$166,000 × .90

This analysis indicates that Juanita Company will incur $1,400 of additional costs if it buys the electrical cords rather than making them.

(b)

	Make	**Buy**	**Net Income Increase (Decrease)**
Total cost	$166,000	$167,400	$(1,400)
Opportunity cost	5,000	–0–	5,000
Total cost	$171,000	$167,400	$ 3,600

Yes, the answer is different: The analysis shows that net income will be increased by $3,600 if Juanita Company purchases the electrical cords rather than making them.

Related exercise material: **BE20-4, E20-5, E20-6, E20-7, E20-8**, and **Do it!** **20-2**.

Action Plan

• Look for the costs that change.
• Ignore the costs that do not change.
• Use the format in the chapter for your answer.
• Recognize that opportunity cost can make a difference.

The Navigator

SELL OR PROCESS FURTHER

Many manufacturers have the option of selling products at a given point in the production cycle or continuing to process with the expectation of selling them at a later point at a higher price. For example, a bicycle manufacturer such as Trek could sell its bicycles to retailers either unassembled or assembled. A furniture manufacturer such as Ethan Allen could sell its dining room sets to furniture stores either unfinished or finished. The sell-or-process-further decision should be made on the basis of incremental analysis. The basic decision rule is: **Process further as long as the incremental revenue from such processing exceeds the incremental processing costs**.

LEARNING OBJECTIVE 5

Identify the relevant costs in determining whether to sell or process materials further.

Single-Product Case

Assume, for example, that Woodmasters Inc. makes tables. It sells unfinished tables for $50. The cost to manufacture an unfinished table is $35, computed as follows.

Direct materials	$15
Direct labor	10
Variable manufacturing overhead	6
Fixed manufacturing overhead	4
Manufacturing cost per unit	$35

Illustration 20-8 Per unit cost of unfinished table

Helpful Hint Current net income is known. Net income from processing further is an estimate. In making its decision, management could add a "risk" factor for the estimate.

Woodmasters currently has unused productive capacity that is expected to continue indefinitely. Some of this capacity could be used to finish the tables and sell them at $60 per unit. For a finished table, direct materials will increase $2 and direct labor costs will increase $4. Variable manufacturing overhead costs will increase by $2.40 (60% of direct labor). No increase is anticipated in fixed manufacturing overhead.

Should the company sell the unfinished tables, or should it process them further? The incremental analysis on a per unit basis is as follows.

	Incremental Analysis - Sell or process further.xls		
	Home Insert Page Layout Formulas Data Review View		
P18	fx		
	A	B	C	D

	A	B Sell Unfinished	C Process Further	D Net Income Increase (Decrease)
1				
2	Sales price per unit	$50.00	$60.00	$10.00
3	Cost per unit			
4	Direct materials	15.00	17.00	(2.00)
5	Direct labor	10.00	14.00	(4.00)
6	Variable manufacturing overhead	6.00	8.40	(2.40)
7	Fixed manufacturing overhead	4.00	4.00	0.00
8	Total	35.00	43.40	(8.40)
9	Net income per unit	$15.00	$16.60	$ 1.60
10				

Illustration 20-9 Incremental analysis—sell or process further

It would be advantageous for Woodmasters to process the tables further. The incremental revenue of $10.00 from the additional processing is $1.60 higher than the incremental processing costs of $8.40.

Multiple-Product Case

Sell-or-process-further decisions are particularly applicable to production processes that produce multiple products simultaneously. In many industries, a number of end-products are produced from a single raw material and a common production process. These multiple end-products are commonly referred to as **joint products**. For example, in the meat-packing industry, Armour processes a cow or pig to produce meat, internal organs, hides, bones, and fat. In the petroleum industry, ExxonMobil refines crude oil to produce gasoline, lubricating oil, kerosene, paraffin, and ethylene.

Illustration 20-10 presents a joint product situation for Marais Creamery involving a decision **to sell or process further** cream and skim milk. Cream and skim milk are joint products that result from the processing of raw milk.

Illustration 20-10 Joint production process—Creamery

Marais incurs many costs prior to the manufacture of the cream and skim milk. All costs incurred prior to the point at which the two products are separately identifiable (the **split-off point**) are called joint costs. For purposes of determining the cost of each product, joint product costs must be allocated to the individual products. This is frequently done based on the relative sales value of the joint products. While this allocation is important for determination of product cost, **it is irrelevant for any sell-or-process-further decisions**. The reason is that these **joint product costs are sunk costs.** That is, they have already been incurred, and they cannot be changed or avoided by any subsequent decision.

Illustration 20-11 provides the daily cost and revenue data for Marais Creamery related to cream and cottage cheese.

Illustration 20-11 Cost and revenue data per day for cream

Costs (per day)	
Joint cost allocated to cream	$ 9,000
Cost to process cream into cottage cheese	10,000
Revenues from Products (per day)	
Cream	$19,000
Cottage cheese	27,000

From this information, we can determine whether the company should simply sell the cream or process it further into cottage cheese. Illustration 20-12 shows the necessary analysis. Note that the joint cost that is allocated to the cream is not included in this decision. It is not relevant to the decision because it is a sunk cost. It has been incurred in the past and will remain the same no matter whether the cream is subsequently processed into cottage cheese or not.

Illustration 20-12 Analysis of whether to sell cream or process into cottage cheese

			Incremental Analysis - Sell or process further - Cottage cheese.xls
	Home Insert Page Layout Formulas Data Review View		
	P18	fx	
	A	B	C	D
1		Sell	Process Further	Net Income Increase (Decrease)
2	Sales per day	$19,000	$27,000	$ 8,000
3	Cost per day to process cream into cottage cheese	0	10,000	(10,000)
4		$19,000	$ 17,000	$ (2,000)
5				

From this analysis, we can see that Marais should not process the cream further because it will sustain an incremental loss of $2,000.

Illustration 20-13 provides the daily cost and revenue data for the company related to skim milk and condensed milk.

Illustration 20-13 Cost and revenue data per day for skim milk

Costs (per day)	
Joint cost allocated to skim milk	$ 5,000
Cost to process skim milk into condensed milk	8,000
Revenues from Products (per day)	
Skim milk	$11,000
Condensed milk	26,000

Illustration 20-14 shows that Marais Company should process the skim milk into condensed milk, as it will increase net income by $7,000.

		Incremental Analysis - Sell or process further - Skim milk or process condensed milk.xls		
	A	Sell (B)	Process Further (C)	Net Income Increase (Decrease) (D)
1		**Sell**	**Process Further**	**Net Income Increase (Decrease)**
2	Sales per day	$11,000	$26,000	$15,000
3	Cost per day to process skim milk into condensed milk	0	8,000	(8,000)
4		$11,000	$18,000	$ 7,000
5				

Illustration 20-14 Analysis of whether to sell skim milk or process into condensed milk

Again, note that the $5,000 of joint cost allocated to the skim milk is irrelevant in deciding whether to sell or process further. Why? The joint cost remains the same, whether or not further processing is performed.

It is important to understand that these decisions need to be reevaluated as market conditions change. For example, if the price of skim milk increases relative to the price of condensed milk, it may become more profitable to sell the skim milk rather than process it into condensed milk. Consider also oil refineries. As market conditions change, they must constantly re-assess which products to produce from the oil they receive at their plants.

SELL OR PROCESS FURTHER

Do it!

Easy Does It manufactures unpainted furniture for the do-it-yourself (DIY) market. It currently sells a child's rocking chair for $25. Production costs are $12 variable and $8 fixed. Easy Does It is considering painting the rocking chair and selling it for $35. Variable costs to paint each chair are expected to be $9, and fixed costs are expected to be $2.

Prepare an analysis showing whether Easy Does It should sell unpainted or painted chairs.

Action Plan

- Identify the revenues that will change as a result of painting the rocking chair.
- Identify all costs that will change as a result of painting the rocking chair, and net the amount against the revenues.

The Navigator

Solution

	Sell	Process Further	Net Income Increase (Decrease)
Revenues	$25	$35	$10
Variable costs	12	21	(9)
Fixed costs	8	10	(2)
Net income	$ 5	$ 4	$ (1)

The analysis indicates that the rocking chair should be sold unpainted because net income per chair will be $1 greater.

Related exercise material: **BE20-5, BE20-6, E20-9, E20-10, E20-11, E20-12,** and **Do it! 20-3.**

REPAIR, RETAIN, OR REPLACE EQUIPMENT

LEARNING OBJECTIVE 6
Identify the relevant costs to be considered in repairing, retaining, or replacing equipment.

Management often has to decide whether to continue using an asset, repair, or replace it. For example, Delta Airlines must decide whether to replace old jets with new, more fuel-efficient ones. To illustrate, assume that Jeffcoat Company has a factory machine that originally cost $110,000. It has a balance in Accumulated Depreciation of $70,000, so its book value is $40,000. It has a remaining useful life of four years. The company is considering replacing this machine with a new machine. A new machine is available that costs $120,000. It is expected to have zero salvage value at the end of its four-year useful life. If the new machine is acquired, variable manufacturing costs are expected to decrease from $160,000 to $125,000 annually, and the old unit could be sold for $5,000. The incremental analysis for the **four-year period** is as follows.

Illustration 20-15
Incremental analysis—retain or replace equipment

	Incremental Analysis - Retain or replace equipment.xls						
	Home Insert Page Layout Formulas Data Review View						
	P18	*fx*					
	A	B	C	D	E	F	
1		Retain Equipment		Replace Equipment		Net Income Increase (Decrease)	
2	Variable manufacturing costs	$640,000 ᵃ		$500,000 ᵇ		$140,000	
3	New machine cost			120,000		(120,000)	
4	Sale of old machine			(5,000)		5,000	
5	Total	$640,000		$615,000		$ 25,000	
6							
7	ᵃ(4 years × $160,000)						
8	ᵇ(4 years × $125,000)						
9							

In this case, it would be to the company's advantage to replace the equipment. The lower variable manufacturing costs due to replacement more than offset the cost of the new equipment. Note that the $5,000 received from the sale of the old machine is relevant to the decision because it will only be received if the company chooses to replace its equipment. In general, any trade-in allowance or cash disposal value of existing assets is relevant to the decision to retain or replace equipment.

One other point should be mentioned regarding Jeffcoat's decision: **The book value of the old machine does not affect the decision**. Book value is a **sunk cost**, which is a cost that cannot be changed by any present or future decision. **Sunk costs are not relevant in incremental analysis.** In this example, if the asset is retained, book value will be depreciated over its remaining useful life. Or, if the new unit is acquired, book value will be recognized as a loss of the current period. Thus, the effect of book value on current and future earnings is the same regardless of the replacement decision.

Sometimes, decisions regarding whether to replace equipment are clouded by behavioral decision-making errors. For example, suppose a manager spent $90,000 repairing a machine two months ago. Now, suppose that the machine breaks down again today. The manager might be inclined to think that, because the company recently spent a large amount of money to repair the machine, the machine should now be repaired rather than replaced. However, the amount spent in the past to repair the machine is irrelevant to the current decision. It is a sunk cost.

Similarly, suppose a manager spent $5,000,000 to purchase a new machine. Six months later, a new machine comes on the market that is significantly more efficient than the one recently purchased. The manager might be inclined to think that he or she should not buy the new machine because of the recent purchase. In fact, the manager might fear that buying a different machine so quickly might call into question the merit of the previous decision. Again, the fact that the company recently bought a new machine is not relevant. Instead, the manager should use incremental analysis to determine whether the savings generated by the efficiencies of the new machine would justify its purchase.

ELIMINATE AN UNPROFITABLE SEGMENT OR PRODUCT

Management sometimes must decide whether to eliminate an unprofitable business segment or product. For example, in recent years, many airlines quit servicing certain cities or cut back on the number of flights. Goodyear quit producing several brands in the low-end tire market. Again, the key is to **focus on the relevant costs—the data that change under the alternative courses of action**. To illustrate, assume that Venus Company manufactures tennis racquets in three models: Pro, Master, and Champ. Pro and Master are profitable lines. Champ (highlighted in red in the table below) operates at a loss. Condensed income statement data are as follows.

Illustration 20-16 Segment income data

	Pro	Master	Champ	Total
Sales	$800,000	$300,000	$100,000	$1,200,000
Variable costs	520,000	210,000	90,000	820,000
Contribution margin	280,000	90,000	10,000	380,000
Fixed costs	80,000	50,000	30,000	160,000
Net income	$200,000	$ 40,000	$ (20,000)	$ 220,000

Helpful Hint A decision to discontinue a segment based solely on the bottom line—net loss—is inappropriate.

You might think that total net income will increase by $20,000 to $240,000 if the unprofitable Champ line of racquets is eliminated. However, **net income may actually decrease if the Champ line is discontinued**. The reason is that the fixed costs allocated to the Champ racquets will have to be absorbed by the other products. To illustrate, assume that the $30,000 of fixed costs applicable to the unprofitable segment are allocated ⅔ to the Pro model and ⅓ to the Master model if the Champ model is eliminated. Fixed costs will increase to $100,000 ($80,000 + $20,000) in the Pro line and to $60,000 ($50,000 + $10,000) in the Master line. The revised income statement is:

Illustration 20-17 Income data after eliminating unprofitable product line

	Pro	Master	Total
Sales	$800,000	$300,000	$1,100,000
Variable costs	520,000	210,000	730,000
Contribution margin	280,000	90,000	370,000
Fixed costs	100,000	60,000	160,000
Net income	$180,000	$ 30,000	$ 210,000

Illustration 20-18 Incremental analysis— eliminating unprofitable segment with no reduction in fixed costs

Total net income has decreased $10,000 ($220,000 − $210,000). This result is also obtained in the following incremental analysis of the Champ racquets.

Incremental Analysis - Eliminating an unprofitable segment.xls

Home   Insert   Page Layout   Formulas   Data   Review   View

P18   fx

	A	B	C	D
1		Continue	Eliminate	Net Income Increase (Decrease)
2	Sales	$100,000	$ 0	$(100,000)
3	Variable costs	90,000	0	90,000
4	Contribution margin	10,000	0	(10,000)
5	Fixed costs	30,000	30,000	0
6	Net income	$(20,000)	$(30,000)	$ (10,000)
7				

The loss in net income is attributable to the Champ line's contribution margin ($10,000) that will not be realized if the segment is discontinued.

Assume the same facts as above, except now assume that $22,000 of the fixed costs attributed to the Champ line can be eliminated if the line is discontinued. Illustration 20-19 presents the incremental analysis based on this revised assumption.

Illustration 20-19
Incremental analysis—eliminating unprofitable segment with reduction in fixed costs

Incremental Analysis - Eliminating an unprofitable segment.xls

	A	B	C	D
		Continue	Eliminate	Net Income Increase (Decrease)
2	Sales	$100,000	$ 0	$(100,000)
3	Variable costs	90,000	0	90,000
4	Contribution margin	10,000	0	(10,000)
5	Fixed costs	30,000	8,000	22,000
6	Net income	$(20,000)	$(8,000)	$ 12,000

In this case, because the company is able to eliminate some of its fixed costs by eliminating the division, it can increase its net income by $12,000. **This occurs because the $22,000 savings that results from the eliminated fixed costs exceeds the $10,000 in lost contribution margin by $12,000 ($22,000 − $10,000).**

In deciding on the future status of an unprofitable segment, management should consider the effect of elimination on related product lines. It may be possible for continuing product lines to obtain some or all of the sales lost by the discontinued product line. In some businesses, services or products may be linked—for example, free checking accounts at a bank, or coffee at a donut shop. In addition, management should consider the effect of eliminating the product line on employees who may have to be discharged or retrained.

Management Insight

Time to Move to a New Neighborhood?

If you have ever moved, then you know how complicated and costly it can be. Now consider what it would be like for a manufacturing company with 260 employees and a 170,000-square-foot facility to move from southern California to Idaho. That is what Buck Knives did in order to save its company from financial ruin. Electricity rates in Idaho were half those in California, workers' compensation was one-third the cost, and factory wages were 20% lower. Combined, this would reduce manufacturing costs by $600,000 per year. Moving the factory would cost about $8.5 million, plus $4 million to move key employees. Offsetting these costs was the estimated $11 million selling price of the California property. Based on these estimates, the move would pay for itself in three years.

Ultimately, the company received only $7.5 million for its California property, only 58 of 75 key employees were willing to move, construction was delayed by a year which caused the new plant to increase in price by $1.5 million, and wages surged in Idaho due to low unemployment. Despite all of these complications, though, the company considers the move a great success.

Source: Chris Lydgate, "The Buck Stopped," *Inc. Magazine* (May 2006), pp. 87–95.

? What were some of the factors that complicated the company's decision to move? How should the company have incorporated such factors into its incremental analysis? (See page 1079.)

Max Blain/iStockphoto

**UNPROFITABLE
SEGMENTS**

Do it!

Lambert, Inc. manufactures several types of accessories. For the year, the knit hats and scarves line had sales of $400,000, variable expenses of $310,000, and fixed expenses of $120,000. Therefore, the knit hats and scarves line had a net loss of $30,000. If Lambert eliminates the knit hats and scarves line, $20,000 of fixed costs will remain. Prepare an analysis showing whether the company should eliminate the knit hats and scarves line.

Action Plan

- Identify the revenues that will change as a result of eliminating a product line.
- Identify all costs that will change as a result of eliminating a product line, and net the amount against the revenues.

 The Navigator

Solution

	Continue	Eliminate	Net Income Increase (Decrease)
Sales	$400,000	$ 0	$(400,000)
Variable costs	310,000	0	310,000
Contribution margin	90,000	0	(90,000)
Fixed costs	120,000	20,000	100,000
Net income	$ (30,000)	$(20,000)	$ 10,000

The analysis indicates that Lambert should eliminate the knit hats and scarves line because net income will increase $10,000.

Related exercise material: **BE20-8, E20-15, E20-16, E20-17,** and **Do it! 20-4.**

🧰 DECISION TOOLKIT

DECISION CHECKPOINTS	INFO NEEDED FOR DECISION	TOOL TO USE FOR DECISION	HOW TO EVALUATE RESULTS
Which alternative should the company choose?	All relevant costs including opportunity cost	Compare relevant cost of each alternative	Choose the alternative that maximizes net income

OTHER CONSIDERATIONS IN DECISION-MAKING

Qualitative Factors

In this chapter, we have focused primarily on the quantitative factors that affect a decision—those attributes that can be easily expressed in terms of numbers or dollars. However, many of the decisions involving incremental analysis have important qualitative features. Though not easily measured, they should not be ignored.

Consider, for example, the potential effects of the make-or-buy decision or of the decision to eliminate a line of business on existing employees and the community in which the plant is located. The cost savings that may be obtained from outsourcing or from eliminating a plant should be weighed against these qualitative attributes. One example would be the cost of lost morale that might result. Al "Chainsaw" Dunlap was a so-called "turnaround" artist who went into many companies, identified inefficiencies (using incremental analysis techniques), and tried to correct these problems to improve corporate profitability. Along the way, he laid off thousands of employees at numerous companies. As head of Sunbeam, it was Al Dunlap who lost his job because his Draconian approach failed to improve Sunbeam's profitability. It was widely reported that Sunbeam's employees openly rejoiced for days after his departure. Clearly, qualitative factors can matter.

Relationship of Incremental Analysis and Activity-Based Costing

In Chapter 17, we noted that many companies have shifted to activity-based costing to allocate overhead costs to products. The primary reason for using activity-based costing is that it results in a more accurate allocation of overhead. The concepts presented in this chapter are completely consistent with the use of activity-based costing. In fact, activity-based costing will result in better identification of relevant costs and, therefore, better incremental analysis.

Management Insight

What Is the Real Cost of Packaging Options?

The existence of excess plant capacity is frequently the incentive for management to add new products. Adding one new product may not add much incremental cost. But continuing to add products will at some point create new constraints, perhaps requiring additional investments in people, equipment, and facilities.

The effects of product and product line proliferation are generally understood. But the effect on incremental overhead costs of changes in servicing customers is less understood. For example, if a company newly offers its customers the option of product delivery by case or by pallet, the new service may appear to be simple and low in cost. But, if the manufacturing process must be realigned to package in two different forms; if two sets of inventory records must be maintained; and if warehousing, handling, and shipping require two different arrangements or sets of equipment, the additional costs of this new option could be as high as a whole new product. If the customer service option were adopted for all products, the product line could effectively be doubled—but so might many overhead costs.

Source: Elizabeth Haas Edersheim and Joan Wilson, "Complexity at Consumer Goods Companies: Naming and Taming the Beast," *Journal of Cost Management* (Fall 1992), pp. 26–36.

© Baloncici/iStockphoto

? If your marketing director suggests that, in addition to selling your cereal in a standard size box, you should sell a jumbo size and an individual size, what issues must you consider? (See page 1079.)

 ## USING THE DECISION TOOLKIT

Suppose Hewlett-Packard Company (HP) must decide whether to make or buy some of its components from Solectron Corp. The cost of producing 50,000 electrical connectors for its printers is $110,000, broken down as follows.

Direct materials	$60,000	Variable manufacturing overhead	$12,000
Direct labor	$30,000	Fixed manufacturing overhead	$ 8,000

Instead of making the electrical connectors at an average cost per unit of $2.20 ($110,000 ÷ 50,000), HP has an opportunity to buy the connectors at $2.15 per unit. If the connectors are purchased, all variable costs and one-half of the fixed costs will be eliminated.

Instructions

(a) Prepare an incremental analysis showing whether HP should make or buy the electrical connectors.

(b) Will your answer be different if the released productive capacity resulting from the purchase of the connectors will generate additional income of $25,000?

Solution

(a)

	Make	Buy	Net Income Increase (Decrease)
Direct materials	$ 60,000	$ –0–	$ 60,000
Direct labor	30,000	–0–	30,000
Variable manufacturing costs	12,000	–0–	12,000
Fixed manufacturing costs	8,000	4,000*	4,000
Purchase price	–0–	107,500**	(107,500)
Total cost	$110,000	$111,500	$ (1,500)

*$8,000 × .50; **$2.15 × 50,000

This analysis indicates that HP will incur $1,500 of additional costs if it buys the electrical connectors. HP therefore would choose to make the connectors.

(b)

	Make	Buy	Net Income Increase (Decrease)
Total cost	$110,000	$111,500	$ (1,500)
Opportunity cost	25,000	–0–	25,000
Total cost	$135,000	$111,500	$23,500

Yes, the answer is different. The analysis shows that if additional capacity is released, net income will be increased by $23,500 if the electrical connectors are purchased. In this case, HP would choose to purchase the connectors.

✔ The Navigator

Summary of Learning Objectives

1 Identify the steps in management's decision-making process. Management's decision-making process consists of (a) identifying the problem and assigning responsibility for the decision, (b) determining and evaluating possible courses of action, (c) making the decision, and (d) reviewing the results of the decision.

2 Describe the concept of incremental analysis. Incremental analysis identifies financial data that change under alternative courses of action. These data are relevant to the decision because they will vary in the future among the possible alternatives.

3 Identify the relevant costs in accepting an order at a special price. The relevant costs are those that change if the order is accepted. The relevant information in accepting an order at a special price is the difference between the variable manufacturing costs to produce the special order and expected revenues. Any changes in fixed costs, opportunity cost, or other incremental costs or savings (such as additional shipping) should be considered.

4 Identify the relevant costs in a make-or-buy decision. In a make-or-buy decision, the relevant costs are (a) the variable manufacturing costs that will be saved as well as changes to fixed manufacturing costs, (b) the purchase price, and (c) opportunity cost.

5 Identify the relevant costs in determining whether to sell or process materials further. The decision rule for whether to sell or process materials further is: Process further as long as the incremental revenue from processing exceeds the incremental processing costs.

6 Identify the relevant costs to be considered in repairing, retaining, or replacing equipment. The relevant costs to be considered in determining whether equipment should be repaired, retained, or replaced are the effects on variable costs and the cost of the new equipment. Also, any disposal value of the existing asset must be considered.

7 Identify the relevant costs in deciding whether to eliminate an unprofitable segment or product. In deciding whether to eliminate an unprofitable segment or product, the relevant costs are the variable costs that drive the contribution margin, if any, produced by the segment or product. Disposition of the segment's or the product's fixed expenses and opportunity cost must also be considered.

✔ The Navigator

DECISION TOOLKIT A SUMMARY

DECISION CHECKPOINTS	INFO NEEDED FOR DECISION	TOOL TO USE FOR DECISION	HOW TO EVALUATE RESULTS
Which alternative should the company choose?	All relevant costs including opportunity cost	Compare the relevant cost of each alternative	Choose the alternative that maximizes net income.

Glossary

Incremental analysis *(p. 1043)* The process of identifying the financial data that change under alternative courses of action.

Joint costs *(p. 1051)* For joint products, all costs incurred prior to the point at which the two products are separately identifiable (known as the **split-off point**).

Joint products *(p. 1050)* Multiple end-products produced from a single raw material and a common production process.

Opportunity cost *(p. 1044)* The potential benefit that is lost when one course of action is chosen rather than an alternative course of action.

Relevant costs *(p. 1044)* Those costs and revenues that differ across alternatives.

Sunk cost *(p. 1044)* A cost that cannot be changed or avoided by any present or future decision.

Comprehensive *Do it!*

Walston Company produces kitchen cabinets for homebuilders across the western United States. The cost of producing 5,000 cabinets is as follows.

Materials	$ 500,000
Labor	250,000
Variable overhead	100,000
Fixed overhead	400,000
Total	$1,250,000

Walston also incurs selling expenses of $20 per cabinet. Wellington Corp. has offered Walston $165 per cabinet for a special order of 1,000 cabinets. The cabinets would be sold to homebuilders in the eastern United States and thus would not conflict with Walston's current sales. Selling expenses per cabinet would be only $5 per cabinet. Walston has available capacity to do the work.

Instructions

(a) Prepare an incremental analysis for the special order.

(b) Should Walston accept the special order? Why or why not?

Solution to Comprehensive *Do it!*

(a) Relevant costs per unit would be:

Materials	$500,000/5,000 = $100
Labor	250,000/5,000 = 50
Variable overhead	100,000/5,000 = 20
Selling expenses	5
Total relevant cost per unit	$175

	Reject Order	Accept Order	Net Income Increase (Decrease)
Revenues	$0	$165,000	$165,000
Costs	0	175,000	(175,000)
Net income	$0	$ (10,000)	$ (10,000)

(b) Walston should reject the offer. The incremental benefit of $165 per cabinet is less than the incremental cost of $175. By accepting the order, Walston's net income would actually decline by $10,000.

Action Plan

- Determine the relevant cost per unit of the special order.
- Identify the relevant costs and revenues for the units to be produced.
- Compare the results related to accepting the special order versus rejecting the special order.

The Navigator

Self-Test Questions

Answers are on page 1079.

(LO 1)
1. Three of the steps in management's decision-making process are (1) review results of decision, (2) determine and evaluate possible courses of action, and (3) make the decision. The steps are prepared in the following order:
   (a) (1), (2), (3).   (c) (2), (1), (3).
   (b) (3), (2), (1).   (d) (2), (3), (1).

(LO 2)
2. Incremental analysis is the process of identifying the financial data that:
   (a) do not change under alternative courses of action.
   (b) change under alternative courses of action.
   (c) are mixed under alternative courses of action.
   (d) No correct answer is given.

(LO 1, 2)
3. In making business decisions, management ordinarily considers:
   (a) quantitative factors but not qualitative factors.
   (b) financial information only.
   (c) both financial and nonfinancial information.
   (d) relevant costs, opportunity cost, and sunk costs.

(LO 2)
4. A company is considering the following alternatives:

	Alternative A	Alternative B
Revenues	$50,000	$50,000
Variable costs	24,000	24,000
Fixed costs	12,000	15,000

Which of the following are relevant in choosing between these alternatives?
   (a) Revenues, variable costs, and fixed costs.
   (b) Variable costs and fixed costs.
   (c) Variable costs only.
   (d) Fixed costs only.

(LO 3)
5. It costs a company $14 of variable costs and $6 of fixed costs to produce product Z200 that sells for $30. A foreign buyer offers to purchase 3,000 units at $18 each. If the special offer is accepted and produced with unused capacity, net income will:
   (a) decrease $6,000.   (c) increase $12,000.
   (b) increase $6,000.   (d) increase $9,000.

(LO 3)
6. It costs a company $14 of variable costs and $6 of fixed costs to produce product Z200. Product Z200 sells for $30. A buyer offers to purchase 3,000 units at $18 each. The seller will incur special shipping costs of $5 per unit. If the special offer is accepted and produced with unused capacity, net income will:
   (a) increase $3,000.   (c) decrease $12,000.
   (b) increase $12,000.   (d) decrease $3,000.

(LO 3)
7. Jobart Company is currently operating at full capacity. It is considering buying a part from an outside supplier rather than making it in-house. If Jobart purchases the part, it can use the released productive capacity to generate additional income of $30,000

from producing a different product. When conducting incremental analysis in this make-or-buy decision, the company should:
   (a) ignore the $30,000.
   (b) add $30,000 to other costs in the "Make" column.
   (c) add $30,000 to other costs in the "Buy" column.
   (d) subtract $30,000 from the other costs in the "Make" column.

(LO 4)
8. In a make-or-buy decision, relevant costs are:
   (a) manufacturing costs that will be saved.
   (b) the purchase price of the units.
   (c) the opportunity cost.
   (d) All of the above.

(LO 4)
9. Derek is performing incremental analysis in a make-or-buy decision for Item X. If Derek buys Item X, he can use its released productive capacity to produce Item Z. Derek will sell Item Z for $12,000 and incur production costs of $8,000. Derek's incremental analysis should include an opportunity cost of:
   (a) $12,000.   (c) $4,000.
   (b) $8,000.   (d) $0.

(LO 5)
10. The decision rule in a sell-or-process-further decision is process further as long as the incremental revenue from processing exceeds:
   (a) incremental processing costs.
   (b) variable processing costs.
   (c) fixed processing costs.
   (d) No correct answer is given.

(LO 5)
11. Walton, Inc. makes an unassembled product that it currently sells for $55. Production costs are $20. Walton is considering assembling the product and selling it for $68. The cost to assemble the product is estimated at $12. What decision should Walton make?
   (a) Sell before assembly; net income per unit will be $12 greater.
   (b) Sell before assembly; net income per unit will be $1 greater.
   (c) Process further; net income per unit will be $13 greater.
   (d) Process further; net income per unit will be $1 greater.

(LO 6)
12. In a decision to retain or replace equipment, the book value of the old equipment is a (an):
   (a) opportunity cost.   (c) incremental cost.
   (b) sunk cost.   (d) marginal cost.

(LO 7)
13. If an unprofitable segment is eliminated:
   (a) net income will always increase.
   (b) variable expenses of the eliminated segment will have to be absorbed by other segments.
   (c) fixed expenses allocated to the eliminated segment will have to be absorbed by other segments.
   (d) net income will always decrease.

(LO 7) **14.** A segment of Hazard Inc. has the following data.

Sales	$200,000
Variable expenses	140,000
Fixed expenses	100,000

If this segment is eliminated, what will be the effect on the remaining company? Assume that 50% of the fixed expenses will be eliminated and the rest will be allocated to the segments of the remaining company.
(a) $120,000 increase.   (c) $50,000 increase.
(b) $10,000 decrease.   (d) $10,000 increase.

Go to the book's companion website, **www.wiley.com/college/kimmel**, for additional Self-Test Questions.

Questions

1. What steps are frequently involved in management's decision-making process?

2. Your roommate, Anna Polis, contends that accounting contributes to most of the steps in management's decision-making process. Is your roommate correct? Explain.

3. "Incremental analysis involves the accumulation of information concerning a single course of action." Do you agree? Why?

4. Sydney Greene asks for your help concerning the relevance of variable and fixed costs in incremental analysis. Help Sydney with her problem.

5. What data are relevant in deciding whether to accept an order at a special price?

6. Emil Corporation has an opportunity to buy parts at $9 each that currently cost $12 to make. What manufacturing costs are relevant to this make-or-buy decision?

7. Define the term "opportunity cost." How may this cost be relevant in a make-or-buy decision?

8. What is the decision rule in deciding whether to sell a product or process it further?

9. What are joint products? What accounting issue results from the production process that creates joint products?

10. How are allocated joint costs treated when making a sell-or-process-further decision?

11. Your roommate, Gale Dunham, is confused about sunk costs. Explain to your roommate the meaning of sunk costs and their relevance to a decision to retain or replace equipment.

12. Huang Inc. has one product line that is unprofitable. What circumstances may cause overall company net income to be lower if the unprofitable product line is eliminated?

Brief Exercises

BE20-1   The steps in management's decision-making process are listed in random order below. Indicate the order in which the steps should be executed.

_____	Make a decision.	_____	Review results of the decision.
_____	Identify the problem and assign responsibility.	_____	Determine and evaluate possible courses of action.

Identify the steps in management's decision-making process.
(LO 1), AP

BE20-2   Bogart Company is considering two alternatives. Alternative A will have revenues of $160,000 and costs of $100,000. Alternative B will have revenues of $180,000 and costs of $125,000. Compare Alternative A to Alternative B showing incremental revenues, costs, and net income.

Determine incremental changes.
(LO 2), AP

BE20-3   At Jaymes Company, it costs $30 per unit ($20 variable and $10 fixed) to make a product at full capacity that normally sells for $45. A foreign wholesaler offers to buy 3,000 units at $25 each. Jaymes will incur special shipping costs of $2 per unit. Assuming that Jaymes has excess operating capacity, indicate the net income (loss) Jaymes would realize by accepting the special order.

Determine whether to accept a special order.
(LO 3), AP

BE20-4   Manson Industries incurs unit costs of $8 ($5 variable and $3 fixed) in making a subassembly part for its finished product. A supplier offers to make 10,000 of the assembly part at $6 per unit. If the offer is accepted, Manson will save all variable costs but no fixed costs. Prepare an analysis showing the total cost saving, if any, Manson will realize by buying the part.

Determine whether to make or buy a part.
(LO 4), AP

BE20-5   Chudrick Inc. makes unfinished bookcases that it sells for $62. Production costs are $36 variable and $10 fixed. Because it has unused capacity, Chudrick is considering finishing the bookcases and selling them for $70. Variable finishing costs are expected to be $7 per unit with no increase in fixed costs. Prepare an analysis on a per unit basis showing whether Chudrick should sell unfinished or finished bookcases.

Determine whether to sell or process further.
(LO 5), AP

Determine whether to sell or process further, joint products.
(LO 5), **AP**

BE20-6   Each day, Adama Corporation processes 1 ton of a secret raw material into two resulting products, AB1 and XY1. When it processes 1 ton of the raw material, the company incurs joint processing costs of $60,000. It allocates $25,000 of these costs to AB1 and $35,000 of these costs to XY1. The resulting AB1 can be sold for $100,000. Alternatively, it can be processed further to make AB2 at an additional processing cost of $45,000, and sold for $150,000. Each day's batch of XY1 can be sold for $95,000. Alternatively, it can be processed further to create XY2, at an additional processing cost of $50,000, and sold for $130,000. Discuss what products Adama Corporation should make.

Determine whether to retain or replace equipment.
(LO 6), **AP**

BE20-7   Kobe Company has a factory machine with a book value of $90,000 and a remaining useful life of 5 years. It can be sold for $30,000. A new machine is available at a cost of $300,000. This machine will have a 5-year useful life with no salvage value. The new machine will lower annual variable manufacturing costs from $600,000 to $500,000. Prepare an analysis showing whether the old machine should be retained or replaced.

Determine whether to eliminate an unprofitable segment.
(LO 7), **AP**

BE20-8   Lisah, Inc., manufactures golf clubs in three models. For the year, the Big Bart line has a net loss of $10,000 from sales $200,000, variable costs $180,000, and fixed costs $30,000. If the Big Bart line is eliminated, $20,000 of fixed costs will remain. Prepare an analysis showing whether the Big Bart line should be eliminated.

Do it! Review

Evaluate special order.
(LO 3), **AN**

Do it! 20-1   Maize Company incurs a cost of $35 per unit, of which $20 is variable, to make a product that normally sells for $58. A foreign wholesaler offers to buy 6,000 units at $30 each. Maize will incur additional costs of $3 per unit to imprint a logo and to pay for shipping. Compute the increase or decrease in net income Maize will realize by accepting the special order, assuming Maize has sufficient excess operating capacity. Should Maize Company accept the special order?

Evaluate make-or-buy opportunity.
(LO 4), **AN**

Do it! 20-2   Rubble Company must decide whether to make or buy some of its components. The costs of producing 60,000 switches for its generators are as follows.

Direct materials	$30,000	Variable overhead	$45,000
Direct labor	$42,000	Fixed overhead	$60,000

Instead of making the switches at an average cost of $2.95 ($177,000 ÷ 60,000), the company has an opportunity to buy the switches at $2.70 per unit. If the company purchases the switches, all the variable costs and one-fourth of the fixed costs will be eliminated.

(a) Prepare an incremental analysis showing whether the company should make or buy the switches. (b) Would your answer be different if the released productive capacity will generate additional income of $34,000?

Sell or process further.
(LO 5), **AP**

Do it! 20-3   Mesa Verde manufactures unpainted furniture for the do-it-yourself (DIY) market. It currently sells a table for $75. Production costs are $40 variable and $10 fixed. Mesa Verde is considering staining and sealing the table to sell it for $100. Variable costs to finish each table are expected to be $17, and fixed costs are expected to be $3.

Prepare an analysis showing whether Mesa Verde should sell unpainted or finished tables.

Analyze whether to eliminate unprofitable segment.
(LO 7), **AP**

Do it! 20-4   Gator Corporation manufactures several types of accessories. For the year, the gloves and mittens line had sales of $500,000, variable expenses of $370,000, and fixed expenses of $150,000. Therefore, the gloves and mittens line had a net loss of $20,000. If Gator eliminates the line, $38,000 of fixed costs will remain.

Prepare an analysis showing whether the company should eliminate the gloves and mittens line.

Exercises

E20-1 Ortega has prepared the following list of statements about decision-making and incremental analysis.

Analyze statements about decision-making and incremental analysis.
(LO 1, 2), **C**

1. The first step in management's decision-making process is, "Determine and evaluate possible courses of action."
2. The final step in management's decision-making process is to actually make the decision.
3. Accounting's contribution to management's decision-making process occurs primarily in evaluating possible courses of action and in reviewing the results.
4. In making business decisions, management ordinarily considers only financial information because it is objectively determined.
5. Decisions involve a choice among alternative courses of action.
6. The process used to identify the financial data that change under alternative courses of action is called incremental analysis.
7. Costs that are the same under all alternative courses of action sometimes affect the decision.
8. When using incremental analysis, some costs will always change under alternative courses of action, but revenues will not.
9. Variable costs will change under alternative courses of action, but fixed costs will not.

Instructions

Identify each statement as true or false. If false, indicate how to correct the statement.

E20-2 Gruden Company produces golf discs which it normally sells to retailers for $7 each. The cost of manufacturing 20,000 golf discs is:

Use incremental analysis for special-order decision.
(LO 3), **AN**

Materials	$ 10,000
Labor	30,000
Variable overhead	20,000
Fixed overhead	40,000
Total	$100,000

Gruden also incurs 5% sales commission ($0.35) on each disc sold.

McGee Corporation offers Gruden $4.80 per disc for 5,000 discs. McGee would sell the discs under its own brand name in foreign markets not yet served by Gruden. If Gruden accepts the offer, its fixed overhead will increase from $40,000 to $46,000 due to the purchase of a new imprinting machine. No sales commission will result from the special order.

Instructions

(a) Prepare an incremental analysis for the special order.
(b) Should Gruden accept the special order? Why or why not?
(c) What assumptions underlie the decision made in part (b)?

E20-3 Leno Company manufactures toasters. For the first 8 months of 2014, the company reported the following operating results while operating at 75% of plant capacity:

Use incremental analysis for special order.
(LO 3), **AN**

Sales (350,000 units)	$4,375,000
Cost of goods sold	2,600,000
Gross profit	1,775,000
Operating expenses	840,000
Net income	$ 935,000

Cost of goods sold was 70% variable and 30% fixed; operating expenses were 75% variable and 25% fixed.

In September, Leno Company receives a special order for 15,000 toasters at $7.60 each from Centro Company of Ciudad Juarez. Acceptance of the order would result in an additional $3,000 of shipping costs but no increase in fixed operating expenses.

Instructions

(a) Prepare an incremental analysis for the special order.
(b) ━━▶ Should Leno Company accept the special order? Why or why not?

Use incremental analysis for special order.

(LO 3), **AN**

E20-4 Klean Fiber Company is the creator of Y-Go, a technology that weaves silver into its fabrics to kill bacteria and odor on clothing while managing heat. Y-Go has become very popular as an undergarment for sports activities. Operating at capacity, the company can produce 1,000,000 undergarments of Y-Go a year. The per unit and the total costs for an individual garment when the company operates at full capacity are as follows.

	Per Undergarment	Total
Direct materials	$2.00	$2,000,000
Direct labor	0.75	750,000
Variable manufacturing overhead	1.00	1,000,000
Fixed manufacturing overhead	1.50	1,500,000
Variable selling expenses	0.25	250,000
Totals	$5.50	$5,500,000

The U.S. Army has approached Klean Fiber and expressed an interest in purchasing 250,000 Y-Go undergarments for soldiers in extremely warm climates. The Army would pay the unit cost for direct materials, direct labor, and variable manufacturing overhead costs. In addition, the Army has agreed to pay an additional $1 per undergarment to cover all other costs and provide a profit. Presently, Klean Fiber is operating at 70% capacity and does not have any other potential buyers for Y-Go. If Klean Fiber accepts the Army's offer, it will not incur any variable selling expenses related to this order.

Instructions

Using incremental analysis, determine whether Klean Fiber should accept the Army's offer.

Use incremental analysis for make-or-buy decision.

(LO 4), **AN**

E20-5 Schopp Inc. has been manufacturing its own shades for its table lamps. The company is currently operating at 100% of capacity, and variable manufacturing overhead is charged to production at the rate of 70% of direct labor cost. The direct materials and direct labor cost per unit to make the lamp shades are $4 and $5, respectively. Normal production is 30,000 table lamps per year.

A supplier offers to make the lamp shades at a price of $12.75 per unit. If Schopp Inc. accepts the supplier's offer, all variable manufacturing costs will be eliminated, but the $45,000 of fixed manufacturing overhead currently being charged to the lamp shades will have to be absorbed by other products.

Instructions

(a) Prepare the incremental analysis for the decision to make or buy the lamp shades.
(b) Should Schopp Inc. buy the lamp shades?
(c) Would your answer be different in (b) if the productive capacity released by not making the lamp shades could be used to produce income of $25,000?

Use incremental analysis for make-or-buy decision.

(LO 4), **E**

E20-6 Jobs, Inc. has recently started the manufacture of Tri-Robo, a three-wheeled robot that can scan a home for fires and gas leaks and then transmit this information to a mobile phone. The cost structure to manufacture 20,000 Tri-Robos is as follows.

	Cost
Direct materials ($50 per robot)	$1,000,000
Direct labor ($40 per robot)	800,000
Variable overhead ($6 per robot)	120,000
Allocated fixed overhead ($30 per robot)	600,000
Total	$2,520,000

Jobs is approached by Tienh Inc., which offers to make Tri-Robo for $115 per unit or $2,300,000.

Instructions

(a) Using incremental analysis, determine whether Jobs should accept this offer under each of the following independent assumptions.
   (1) Assume that $405,000 of the fixed overhead cost can be reduced (avoided).
   (2) Assume that none of the fixed overhead can be reduced (avoided). However, if the robots are purchased from Tienh Inc., Jobs can use the released productive resources to generate additional income of $405,000.

(b) Describe the qualitative factors that might affect the decision to purchase the robots from an outside supplier.

E20-7   Gibbs Company purchases sails and produces sailboats. It currently produces 1,200 sailboats per year, operating at normal capacity, which is about 80% of full capacity. Gibbs purchases sails at $250 each, but the company is considering using the excess capacity to manufacture the sails instead. The manufacturing cost per sail would be $100 for direct materials, $80 for direct labor, and $100 for overhead. The $100 overhead is based on $78,000 of annual fixed overhead that is allocated using normal capacity.

Prepare incremental analysis for make-or-buy decision.
(LO 4), E

The president of Gibbs has come to you for advice. "It would cost me $280 to make the sails," she says, "but only $250 to buy them. Should I continue buying them, or have I missed something?"

Instructions
(a) Prepare a per unit analysis of the differential costs. Briefly explain whether Gibbs should make or buy the sails.
(b) If Gibbs suddenly finds an opportunity to rent out the unused capacity of its factory for $77,000 per year, would your answer to part (a) change? Briefly explain.
(c) Identify three qualitative factors that should be considered by Gibbs in this make-or-buy decision.

(CGA adapted)

E20-8   Innova uses 1,000 units of the component IMC2 every month to manufacture one of its products. The unit costs incurred to manufacture the component are as follows.

Prepare incremental analysis concerning make-or-buy decision.
(LO 4), E

Direct materials	$ 65.00
Direct labor	45.00
Overhead	126.50
Total	$236.50

Overhead costs include variable material handling costs of $6.50, which are applied to products on the basis of direct material costs. The remainder of the overhead costs are applied on the basis of direct labor dollars and consist of 60% variable costs and 40% fixed costs.

A vendor has offered to supply the IMC2 component at a price of $200 per unit.

Instructions
(a) Should Innova purchase the component from the outside vendor if Innova's capacity remains idle?
(b) Should Innova purchase the component from the outside vendor if it can use its facilities to manufacture another product? What information will Innova need to make an accurate decision? Show your calculations.
(c) What are the qualitative factors that Innova will have to consider when making this decision?

(CGA adapted)

E20-9   Rachel Rey recently opened her own basketweaving studio. She sells finished baskets in addition to the raw materials needed by customers to weave baskets of their own. Rachel has put together a variety of raw material kits, each including materials at various stages of completion. Unfortunately, owing to space limitations, Rachel is unable to carry all varieties of kits originally assembled and must choose between two basic packages.

Use incremental analysis for further processing of materials decision.
(LO 5), AN

The basic introductory kit includes undyed, uncut reeds (with dye included) for weaving one basket. This basic package costs Rachel $14 and sells for $30. The second kit, called Stage 2, includes cut reeds that have already been dyed. With this kit the customer need only soak the reeds and weave the basket. Rachel is able to produce the second kit by using the basic materials included in the first kit and adding one hour of her own time, which she values at $18 per hour. Because she is more efficient at cutting and dying reeds than her average customer, Rachel is able to make two kits of the dyed reeds, in one hour, from one kit of undyed reeds. The Stage 2 kit sells for $35.

Instructions
Determine whether Rachel's basketweaving shop should carry the basic introductory kit with undyed and uncut reeds or the Stage 2 kit with reeds already dyed and cut. Prepare an incremental analysis to support your answer.

Determine whether to sell or process further, joint products.
(LO 5), **AN**

E20-10 Stahl Inc. produces three separate products from a common process costing $100,000. Each of the products can be sold at the split-off point or can be processed further and then sold for a higher price. Shown below are cost and selling price data for a recent period.

	Sales Value at Split-Off Point	Cost to Process Further	Sales Value after Further Processing
Product 10	$60,000	$100,000	$190,000
Product 12	15,000	30,000	35,000
Product 14	55,000	150,000	215,000

Instructions
(a) Determine total net income if all products are sold at the split-off point.
(b) Determine total net income if all products are sold after further processing.
(c) Using incremental analysis, determine which products should be sold at the split-off point and which should be processed further.
(d) Determine total net income using the results from (c) and explain why the net income is different from that determined in (b).

Determine whether to sell or process further, joint products.
(LO 5), **AN**

E20-11 Chen Minerals processes materials extracted from mines. The most common raw material that it processes results in three joint products: Larco, Marco, and Narco. Each of these products can be sold as is, or each can be processed further and sold for a higher price. The company incurs joint costs of $180,000 to process one batch of the raw material that produces the three joint products. The following cost and sales information is available for one batch of each product.

	Sales Value at Split-Off Point	Allocated Joint Costs	Cost to Process Further	Sales Value of Processed Product
Larco	$200,000	$40,000	$110,000	$300,000
Marco	300,000	60,000	85,000	400,000
Narco	405,000	80,000	250,000	800,000

Instructions
Determine whether each of the three joint products should be sold as is, or processed further.

Prepare incremental analysis for whether to sell or process materials further.
(LO 5), **E**

E20-12 A company manufactures three products using the same production process. The costs incurred up to the split-off point are $200,000. These costs are allocated to the products on the basis of their sales value at the split-off point. The number of units produced, the selling prices per unit of the three products at the split-off point and after further processing, and the additional processing costs are as follows.

Product	Number of Units Produced	Selling Price at Split-Off	Selling Price after Processing	Additional Processing Costs
D	4,000	$10.00	$15.00	$14,000
E	6,000	11.60	16.20	20,000
F	2,000	19.40	22.60	9,000

Instructions
(a) Which information is relevant to the decision on whether or not to process the products further? Explain why this information is relevant.
(b) Which product(s) should be processed further and which should be sold at the split-off point?
(c) Would your decision be different if the company was using the quantity of output to allocate joint costs? Explain.

(CGA adapted)

Use incremental analysis for retaining or replacing equipment decision.
(LO 6), **E**

E20-13 On January 2, 2013, Benson Hospital purchased a $100,000 special radiology scanner from Picard Inc. The scanner had a useful life of 4 years and was estimated to have no disposal value at the end of its useful life. The straight-line method of depreciation is used on this scanner. Annual operating costs with this scanner are $105,000.

Approximately one year later, the hospital is approached by Dyno Technology salesperson, Meg Ryan, who indicated that purchasing the scanner in 2013 from Picard Inc.

was a mistake. She points out that Dyno has a scanner that will save Benson Hospital $30,000 a year in operating expenses over its 3-year useful life. She notes that the new scanner will cost $110,000 and has the same capabilities as the scanner purchased last year. The hospital agrees that both scanners are of equal quality. The new scanner will have no disposal value. Ryan agrees to buy the old scanner from Benson Hospital for $40,000.

Instructions

(a) If Benson Hospital sells its old scanner on January 2, 2014, compute the gain or loss on the sale.
(b) Using incremental analysis, determine if Benson Hospital should purchase the new scanner on January 2, 2014.
(c) Explain why Benson Hospital might be reluctant to purchase the new scanner, regardless of the results indicated by the incremental analysis in (b).

E20-14 Johnson Enterprises uses a computer to handle its sales invoices. Lately, business has been so good that it takes an extra 3 hours per night, plus every third Saturday, to keep up with the volume of sales invoices. Management is considering updating its computer with a faster model that would eliminate all of the overtime processing.

Use incremental analysis for retaining or replacing equipment decision.
(LO 6), **AN**

	Current Machine	New Machine
Original purchase cost	$15,000	$25,000
Accumulated depreciation	$ 6,000	—
Estimated annual operating costs	$25,000	$20,000
Useful life	5 years	5 years

If sold now, the current machine would have a salvage value of $6,000. If operated for the remainder of its useful life, the current machine would have zero salvage value. The new machine is expected to have zero salvage value after 5 years.

Instructions

Should the current machine be replaced?

E20-15 Judy Jean, a recent graduate of Rolling's accounting program, evaluated the operating performance of Artie Company's six divisions. Judy made the following presentation to Artie's board of directors and suggested the Huron Division be eliminated. "If the Huron Division is eliminated," she said, "our total profits would increase by $26,000."

Use incremental analysis concerning elimination of division.
(LO 7), **AN**

	The Other Five Divisions	Huron Division	Total
Sales	$1,664,200	$100,000	$1,764,200
Cost of goods sold	978,520	76,000	1,054,520
Gross profit	685,680	24,000	709,680
Operating expenses	527,940	50,000	577,940
Net income	$ 157,740	$ (26,000)	$ 131,740

In the Huron Division, cost of goods sold is $61,000 variable and $15,000 fixed, and operating expenses are $26,000 variable and $24,000 fixed. None of the Huron Division's fixed costs will be eliminated if the division is discontinued.

Instructions

Is Judy right about eliminating the Huron Division? Prepare a schedule to support your answer.

E20-16 Cawley Company makes three models of tasers. Information on the three products is given below.

Use incremental analysis for elimination of a product line.
(LO 7), **AN**

	Tingler	Shocker	Stunner
Sales	$300,000	$500,000	$200,000
Variable expenses	150,000	200,000	145,000
Contribution margin	150,000	300,000	55,000
Fixed expenses	120,000	230,000	95,000
Net income	$ 30,000	$ 70,000	$ (40,000)

Fixed expenses consist of $300,000 of common costs allocated to the three products based on relative sales, and additional fixed expenses of $30,000 (Tingler), $80,000 (Shocker), and $35,000 (Stunner). The common costs will be incurred regardless of how many models are produced. The other fixed expenses would be eliminated if a model is phased out.

James Watt, an executive with the company, feels the Stunner line should be discontinued to increase the company's net income.

Instructions
(a) Compute current net income for Cawley Company.
(b) Compute net income by product line and in total for Cawley Company if the company discontinues the Stunner product line. (*Hint:* Allocate the $300,000 common costs to the two remaining product lines based on their relative sales.)
(c) Should Cawley eliminate the Stunner product line? Why or why not?

Prepare incremental analysis concerning keeping or dropping a product to maximize operating income.
(LO 2, 7), **AN**

E20-17 Twyla Company operates a small factory in which it manufactures two products: C and D. Production and sales results for last year were as follows.

	C	D
Units sold	9,000	20,000
Selling price per unit	$95	$75
Variable cost per unit	50	40
Fixed cost per unit	22	22

For purposes of simplicity, the firm averages total fixed costs over the total number of units of C and D produced and sold.

The research department has developed a new product (E) as a replacement for product D. Market studies show that Twyla Company could sell 10,000 units of E next year at a price of $115; the variable cost per unit of E is $40. The introduction of product E will lead to a 10% increase in demand for product C and discontinuation of product D. If the company does not introduce the new product, it expects next year's results to be the same as last year's.

Instructions
Should Twyla Company introduce product E next year? Explain why or why not. Show calculations to support your decision.

(CMA-Canada adapted)

Identify relevant costs for different decisions.
(LO 3, 4, 5, 6, 7), **C**

E20-18 The costs listed below relate to a variety of different decision situations.

Cost	Decision
1. Unavoidable fixed overhead	Eliminate an unprofitable segment
2. Direct labor	Make or buy
3. Original cost of old equipment	Equipment replacement
4. Joint production costs	Sell or process further
5. Opportunity cost	Accepting a special order
6. Segment manager's salary	Eliminate an unprofitable segment (manager will be terminated)
7. Cost of new equipment	Equipment replacement
8. Incremental production costs	Sell or process further
9. Direct materials	Equipment replacement (the amount of materials required does not change)
10. Rent expense	Purchase or lease a building

Instructions
For each cost listed above, indicate if it is relevant or not to the related decision. For those costs determined to be irrelevant, briefly explain why.

Exercises: Set B and Challenge Exercises

Visit the book's companion website, at **www.wiley.com/college/kimmel**, and choose the Student Companion site to access Exercise Set B and Challenge Exercises.

Problems: Set A

P20-1A ShurShot Sports Inc. manufactures basketballs for the National Basketball Association (NBA). For the first 6 months of 2014, the company reported the following operating results while operating at 80% of plant capacity and producing 120,000 units.

	Amount
Sales	$4,800,000
Cost of goods sold	3,600,000
Selling and administrative expenses	405,000
Net income	$ 795,000

Use incremental analysis for special order and identify nonfinancial factors in the decision.

(LO 3), E

Fixed costs for the period were cost of goods sold $960,000, and selling and administrative expenses $225,000.

In July, normally a slack manufacturing month, ShurShot Sports receives a special order for 10,000 basketballs at $27 each from the Greek Basketball Association (GBA). Acceptance of the order would increase variable selling and administrative expenses $0.50 per unit because of shipping costs but would not increase fixed costs and expenses.

Instructions
(a) Prepare an incremental analysis for the special order.
(b) Should ShurShot Sports Inc. accept the special order? Explain your answer.
(c) What is the minimum selling price on the special order to produce net income of $4.00 per ball?
(d) ➤ What nonfinancial factors should management consider in making its decision?

(a) NI increase $30,000

P20-2A The management of Shatner Manufacturing Company is trying to decide whether to continue manufacturing a part or to buy it from an outside supplier. The part, called CISCO, is a component of the company's finished product.

The following information was collected from the accounting records and production data for the year ending December 31, 2014.
1. 8,000 units of CISCO were produced in the Machining Department.
2. Variable manufacturing costs applicable to the production of each CISCO unit were: direct materials $4.80, direct labor $4.30, indirect labor $0.43, utilities $0.40.
3. Fixed manufacturing costs applicable to the production of CISCO were:

Use incremental analysis related to make or buy, consider opportunity cost, and identify nonfinancial factors.

(LO 4), E

Cost Item	Direct	Allocated
Depreciation	$2,100	$ 900
Property taxes	500	200
Insurance	900	600
	$3,500	$1,700

All variable manufacturing and direct fixed costs will be eliminated if CISCO is purchased. Allocated costs will have to be absorbed by other production departments.
4. The lowest quotation for 8,000 CISCO units from a supplier is $80,000.
5. If CISCO units are purchased, freight and inspection costs would be $0.35 per unit, and receiving costs totaling $1,300 per year would be incurred by the Machining Department.

Instructions
(a) Prepare an incremental analysis for CISCO. Your analysis should have columns for (1) Make CISCO, (2) Buy CISCO, and (3) Net Income Increase/(Decrease).
(b) Based on your analysis, what decision should management make?
(c) Would the decision be different if Shatner Company has the opportunity to produce $3,000 of net income with the facilities currently being used to manufacture CISCO? Show computations.
(d) ➤ What nonfinancial factors should management consider in making its decision?

(a) NI (decrease) $(1,160)

(c) NI increase $1,840

P20-3A Sutton Industrial Products Inc. (SIPI) is a diversified industrial-cleaner processing company. The company's Verde plant produces two products: a table cleaner and a floor cleaner from a common set of chemical inputs (CDG). Each week 900,000 ounces of chemical input are processed at a cost of $210,000 into 600,000 ounces of floor cleaner

Determine if product should be sold or processed further.

(LO 5), AN

and 300,000 ounces of table cleaner. The floor cleaner has no market value until it is converted into a polish with the trade name FloorShine. The additional processing costs for this conversion amount to $240,000.

FloorShine sells at $20 per 30-ounce bottle. The table cleaner can be sold for $18 per 25-ounce bottle. However, the table cleaner can be converted into two other products by adding 300,000 ounces of another compound (TCP) to the 300,000 ounces of table cleaner. This joint process will yield 300,000 ounces each of table stain remover (TSR) and table polish (TP). The additional processing costs for this process amount to $100,000. Both table products can be sold for $14 per 25-ounce bottle.

The company decided not to process the table cleaner into TSR and TP based on the following analysis.

| | Table Cleaner | Process Further | | |
		Table Stain Remover (TSR)	Table Polish (TP)	Total
Production in ounces	300,000	300,000	300,000	
Revenue	$216,000	$168,000	$168,000	$336,000
Costs:				
CDG costs	70,000*	52,500	52,500	105,000**
TCP costs	0	50,000	50,000	100,000
Total costs	70,000	102,500	102,500	205,000
Weekly gross profit	$146,000	$ 65,500	$ 65,500	$131,000

*If table cleaner is not processed further, it is allocated 1/3 of the $210,000 of CDG cost, which is equal to 1/3 of the total physical output.
**If table cleaner is processed further, total physical output is 1,200,000 ounces. TSR and TP combined account for 50% of the total physical output and are each allocated 25% of the CDG cost.

Instructions
(a) Determine if management made the correct decision to not process the table cleaner further by doing the following.
  (1) Calculate the company's total weekly gross profit assuming the table cleaner is not processed further.
  (2) Calculate the company's total weekly gross profit assuming the table cleaner is processed further.
  (3) Compare the resulting net incomes and comment on management's decision.
(b) Using incremental analysis, determine if the table cleaner should be processed further.

(CMA adapted)

(2) Gross profit $186,000

Compute gain or loss, and determine if equipment should be replaced.

(LO 6), S

P20-4A Last year (2013), Richter Condos installed a mechanized elevator for its tenants. The owner of the company, Ron Richter, recently returned from an industry equipment exhibition where he watched a computerized elevator demonstrated. He was impressed with the elevator's speed, comfort of ride, and cost efficiency. Upon returning from the exhibition, he asked his purchasing agent to collect price and operating cost data on the new elevator. In addition, he asked the company's accountant to provide him with cost data on the company's elevator. This information is presented below.

	Old Elevator	New Elevator
Purchase price	$120,000	$160,000
Estimated salvage value	0	0
Estimated useful life	5 years	4 years
Depreciation method	Straight-line	Straight-line
Annual operating costs other than depreciation:		
Variable	$ 35,000	$ 10,000
Fixed	23,000	8,500

Annual revenues are $240,000, and selling and administrative expenses are $29,000, regardless of which elevator is used. If the old elevator is replaced now, at the beginning of 2014, Richter Condos will be able to sell it for $25,000.

Instructions
(a) Determine any gain or loss if the old elevator is replaced.
(b) Prepare a 4-year summarized income statement for each of the following assumptions:
    (1) The old elevator is retained.
    (2) The old elevator is replaced.
(c) Using incremental analysis, determine if the old elevator should be replaced.
(d) ▬▬▶ Write a memo to Ron Richter explaining why any gain or loss should be ignored in the decision to replace the old elevator.

(b) (2) NI $539,000
(c) NI increase $23,000

P20-5A Gutierrez Company has four operating divisions. During the first quarter of 2014, the company reported aggregate income from operations of $213,000 and the following divisional results.

Prepare incremental analysis concerning elimination of divisions.
(LO 7), **AN**

	Division			
	I	**II**	**III**	**IV**
Sales	$250,000	$200,000	$500,000	$450,000
Cost of goods sold	200,000	192,000	300,000	250,000
Selling and administrative expenses	75,000	60,000	60,000	50,000
Income (loss) from operations	$ (25,000)	$ (52,000)	$140,000	$150,000

Analysis reveals the following percentages of variable costs in each division.

	I	**II**	**III**	**IV**
Cost of goods sold	75%	90%	80%	75%
Selling and administrative expenses	40	70	50	60

Discontinuance of any division would save 50% of the fixed costs and expenses for that division.

Top management is very concerned about the unprofitable divisions (I and II). Consensus is that one or both of the divisions should be discontinued.

Instructions
(a) Compute the contribution margin for Divisions I and II.
(b) Prepare an incremental analysis concerning the possible discontinuance of (1) Division I and (2) Division II. What course of action do you recommend for each division?
(c) Prepare a columnar condensed income statement for Gutierrez Company, assuming Division II is eliminated. (Use the CVP format.) Division II's unavoidable fixed costs are allocated equally to the continuing divisions.
(d) Reconcile the total income from operations ($213,000) with the total income from operations without Division II.

(a) I $70,000

(c) Income III $133,800

Problems: Set B

P20-1B Morello Inc. manufactures basketballs for the National Basketball Association (NBA). For the first 6 months of 2014, the company reported the following operating results while operating at 90% of plant capacity and producing 90,000 units.

Use incremental analysis for special order and identify nonfinancial factors in decision.
(LO 3), **E**

	Amount	**Per Unit**
Sales	$4,500,000	$50
Cost of goods sold	3,060,000	34
Selling and administrative expenses	360,000	4
Net income	$1,080,000	$12

Fixed costs for the period were cost of goods sold $900,000, and selling and administrative expenses $180,000.

In July, normally a slack manufacturing month, Morello receives a special order for 10,000 basketballs at $30 each from the Chinese Basketball Association (CBA). Acceptance of the order would increase variable selling and administrative expenses $0.50 per unit because of shipping costs but would not increase fixed costs and expenses.

Instructions

(a) NI increase $35,000

(a) Prepare an incremental analysis for the special order.
(b) Should Morello Inc. accept the special order?
(c) What is the minimum selling price on the special order to produce net income of $5.50 per ball?
(d) ▪◼═══▶ What nonfinancial factors should management consider in making its decision?

Use incremental analysis related to make or buy; consider opportunity cost and identify nonfinancial factors.
(LO 4), **E**

P20-2B The management of Gill Corporation is trying to decide whether to continue manufacturing a part or to buy it from an outside supplier. The part, called FIZBE, is a component of the company's finished product.

The following information was collected from the accounting records and production data for the year ending December 31, 2014.

1. 5,000 units of FIZBE were produced in the Machining Department.
2. Variable manufacturing costs applicable to the production of each FIZBE unit were: direct materials $4.75, direct labor $4.60, indirect labor $0.45, utilities $0.35.
3. Fixed manufacturing costs applicable to the production of FIZBE were:

Cost Item	Direct	Allocated
Depreciation	$1,100	$ 900
Property taxes	500	200
Insurance	900	600
	$2,500	$1,700

All variable manufacturing and direct fixed costs will be eliminated if FIZBE is purchased. Allocated costs will have to be absorbed by other production departments.

4. The lowest quotation for 5,000 FIZBE units from a supplier is $56,000.
5. If FIZBE units are purchased, freight and inspection costs would be $0.30 per unit, and receiving costs totaling $500 per year would be incurred by the Machining Department.

Instructions

(a) NI (decrease) ($4,750)

(a) Prepare an incremental analysis for FIZBE. Your analysis should have columns for (1) Make FIZBE, (2) Buy FIZBE, and (3) Net Income Increase/Decrease.
(b) Based on your analysis, what decision should management make?

(c) NI increase $1,250

(c) Would the decision be different if Gill Corporation has the opportunity to produce $6,000 of net income with the facilities currently being used to manufacture FIZBE? Show computations.
(d) ▪◼═══▶ What nonfinancial factors should management consider in making its decision?

Determine if product should be sold or processed further.
(LO 5), **AN**

P20-3B Ohio Household Products Co. (OHPC) is a diversified household-cleaner processing company. The company's Mishawaka plant produces two products: an appliance cleaner and a general-purpose cleaner from a common set of chemical inputs (NPR). Each week 1,000,000 ounces of chemical input are processed at a cost of $200,000 into 750,000 ounces of appliance cleaner and 250,000 ounces of general-purpose cleaner. The appliance cleaner has no market value until it is converted into a polish with the trade name Shine Brite. The additional processing costs for this conversion amount to $300,000. Shine Brite sells at $15 per 25-ounce bottle. The general-purpose cleaner can be sold for $20 per 20-ounce bottle. However, the general-purpose cleaner can be converted into two other products by adding 250,000 ounces of another compound (PST) to the 250,000 ounces of general-purpose cleaner. This joint process will yield 250,000 ounces each of premium cleaner (PC) and premium stain remover (PSR). The additional processing costs for this process amount to $140,000. Both premium products can be sold for $16 per 20-ounce bottle.

The company decided not to process the general-purpose cleaner into PC and PSR based on the following analysis.

| | General-Purpose Cleaner | Process Further | | |
		Premium Cleaner (PC)	Premium Stain Remover (PSR)	Total
Production in ounces	250,000	250,000	250,000	
Revenue	$250,000	$200,000	$200,000	$400,000
Costs:				
NPR costs	50,000*	40,000	40,000	80,000**
PST costs	0	70,000	70,000	140,000
Total costs	50,000	110,000	110,000	220,000
Weekly gross profit	$200,000	$ 90,000	$ 90,000	$180,000

*If general-purpose cleaner is not processed further, it is allocated 1/4 of the $200,000 of NPR cost, which is equal to 1/4 of the total physical output.
**If general-purpose cleaner is processed further, total physical output is 1,250,000 ounces. PC and PSR combined account for 40% of the total output and are each allocated 20% of the NPR cost.

Instructions

(a) Determine if management made the correct decision to not process the general-purpose cleaner further by doing the following.
  (1) Calculate the company's total weekly gross profit assuming the general-purpose cleaner is not processed further.
  (2) Calculate the company's total weekly gross profit assuming the general-purpose cleaner is processed further.
  (3) Compare the resulting net incomes and comment on management's decision.
(b) Using incremental analysis, determine if the general-purpose cleaner should be processed further.

(a) (2) Gross profit $210,000

(CMA adapted)

P20-4B   Last year (2013), Simmons Company installed new factory equipment. The owner of the company, Gene Simmons, recently returned from an industry equipment exhibition where he watched computerized equipment demonstrated. He was impressed with the equipment's speed and cost efficiency. Upon returning from the exhibition, he asked his purchasing agent to collect price and operating cost data on the new equipment. In addition, he asked the company's accountant to provide him with cost data on the company's equipment. This information is presented below.

Compute gain or loss, and determine if equipment should be replaced.
(LO 6), S

	Old Equipment	New Equipment
Purchase price	$210,000	$250,000
Estimated salvage value	0	0
Estimated useful life	5 years	4 years
Depreciation method	Straight-line	Straight-line
Annual operating costs other than depreciation:		
Variable	$50,000	$12,000
Fixed	30,000	5,000

Annual revenues are $360,000, and selling and administrative expenses are $45,000, regardless of which equipment is used. If the old equipment is replaced now, at the beginning of 2014, Simmons Company will be able to sell it for $58,000.

Instructions

(a) Determine any gain or loss if the old equipment is replaced.
(b) Prepare a 4-year summarized income statement for each of the following assumptions:
  (1) The old equipment is retained.
  (2) The old equipment is replaced.
(c) Using incremental analysis, determine if the old equipment should be replaced.
(d) ━━▶ Write a memo to Gene Simmons explaining why any gain or loss should be ignored in the decision to replace the old equipment.

(b) (2) NI $832,000
(c) NI increase $60,000

Prepare incremental analysis concerning elimination of divisions.
(LO 7), **AN**

P20-5B Panda Corporation has four operating divisions. During the first quarter of 2014, the company reported aggregate income from operations of $129,000 and the divisional results shown below.

| | **Division** | | | |
	I	**II**	**III**	**IV**
Sales	$510,000	$400,000	$310,000	$170,000
Cost of goods sold	300,000	250,000	270,000	156,000
Selling and administrative expenses	60,000	80,000	75,000	70,000
Income (loss) from operations	$150,000	$ 70,000	$ (35,000)	$ (56,000)

Analysis reveals the following percentages of variable costs in each division.

	I	**II**	**III**	**IV**
Cost of goods sold	70%	80%	70%	90%
Selling and administrative expenses	40	50	60	70

Discontinuance of any division would save 50% of the fixed costs and expenses for that division.

Top management is very concerned about the unprofitable divisions (III and IV). Consensus is that one or both of the divisions should be discontinued.

Instructions

(a) III $76,000

(a) Compute the contribution margin for Divisions III and IV.

(b) Prepare an incremental analysis concerning the possible discontinuance of (1) Division III and (2) Division IV. What course of action do you recommend for each division?

(c) II $63,900

(c) Prepare a columnar condensed income statement for Panda Corporation, assuming Division IV is eliminated. (Use the CVP format.) Division IV's unavoidable fixed costs are allocated equally to the continuing divisions.

(d) Reconcile the total income from operations ($129,000) with the total income from operations without Division IV.

Problems: Set C

Visit the book's companion website, at **www.wiley.com/college/kimmel**, and choose the Student Companion site to access Problem Set C.

Waterways Continuing Problem

(This is a continuation of the Waterways Problem from Chapters 14 through 19.)

WCP20 Waterways Corporation is considering various business opportunities. It wants to make the best use of its production facilities to maximize income. This problem asks you to help Waterways do incremental analysis on these various opportunities.

> Go to the book's companion website, **www.wiley.com/college/kimmel**, to find the remainder of this problem.

Broadening Your Perspective

Management Decision-Making

DECISION-MAKING AT CURRENT DESIGNS

BYP20-1 Current Designs faces a number of important decisions that require incremental analysis. Consider each of the following situations independently.

Situation 1

Recently, Mike Cichanowski, owner and CEO of Current Designs, received a phone call from the president of a brewing company. He was calling to inquire about the possibility of Current Designs producing "floating coolers" for a promotion his company was planning. These coolers resemble a kayak but are about one-third the size. They are used to float food and beverages while paddling down the river on a weekend leisure trip. The company would be interested in purchasing 100 coolers for the upcoming summer. It is willing to pay $250 per cooler. The brewing company would pick up the coolers upon completion of the order.

Mike met with Diane Buswell, controller, to identify how much it would cost Current Designs to produce the coolers. After careful analysis, the following costs were identified.

Direct materials	$80/unit	Variable overhead	$20/unit
Direct labor	$60/unit	Fixed overhead	$1,000

Current Designs would be able to modify an existing mold to produce the coolers. The cost of these modifications would be approximately $2,000.

Instructions

(a) Prepare an incremental analysis to determine whether Current Designs should accept this special order to produce the coolers.
(b) Discuss additional factors that Mike and Diane should consider if Current Designs is currently operating at full capacity.

Situation 2

Current Designs is always working to identify ways to increase efficiency while becoming more environmentally conscious. During a recent brainstorming session, one employee suggested to Diane Buswell, controller, that the company should consider replacing the current rotomold oven as a way to realize savings from reduced energy consumption. The oven operates on natural gas, using 17,000 therms of natural gas for an entire year. A new, energy-efficient rotomold oven would operate on 15,000 therms of natural gas for an entire year. After seeking out price quotes from a few suppliers, Diane determined that it would cost approximately $250,000 to purchase a new, energy-efficient rotomold oven. She determines that the expected useful life of the new oven would be 10 years, and it would have no salvage value at the end of its useful life. Current Designs would be able to sell the current oven for $10,000.

Instructions

(a) Prepare an incremental analysis to determine if Current Designs should purchase the new rotomold oven, assuming that the average price for natural gas over the next 10 years will be $0.65 per therm.
(b) Diane is concerned that natural gas prices might increase at a faster rate over the next 10 years. If the company projects that the average natural gas price of the next 10 years could be as high as $0.85 per therm, discuss how that might change your conclusion in (a).

Situation 3

One of Current Designs' competitive advantages is found in the ingenuity of its owner and CEO, Mike Cichanowski. His involvement in the design of kayak molds and production techniques has led to Current Designs being recognized as an industry leader in the design and production of kayaks. This ingenuity was evident in an improved design of one of the most important components of a kayak, the seat. The "Revolution Seating System" is a one-of-a-kind, rotating axis seat that gives unmatched, full-contact, under-leg support. It is quickly adjustable with a lever-lock system that allows for a customizable seat position that maximizes comfort for the rider.

Having just designed the "Revolution Seating System," Current Designs must now decide whether to produce the seats internally or buy them from an outside supplier. The costs for Current Designs to produce the seats are as follows.

Direct materials	$20/unit	Direct labor	$15/unit
Variable overhead	$12/unit	Fixed overhead	$20,000

Current Designs will need to produce 3,000 seats this year; 25% of the fixed overhead will be avoided if the seats are purchased from an outside vendor. After soliciting prices from outside suppliers, the company determined that it will cost $50 to purchase a seat from an outside vendor.

Instructions

(a) Prepare an incremental analysis showing whether Current Designs should make or buy the "Revolution Seating System."

(b) Would your answer in (a) change if the productive capacity released by not making the seats could be used to produce income of $20,000?

DECISION-MAKING ACROSS THE ORGANIZATION

BYP20-2   Aurora Company is considering the purchase of a new machine. The invoice price of the machine is $140,000, freight charges are estimated to be $4,000, and installation costs are expected to be $6,000. Salvage value of the new equipment is expected to be zero after a useful life of 5 years. Existing equipment could be retained and used for an additional 5 years if the new machine is not purchased. At that time, the salvage value of the equipment would be zero. If the new machine is purchased now, the existing machine would have to be scrapped. Aurora's accountant, Lisah Huang, has accumulated the following data regarding annual sales and expenses with and without the new machine.

1. Without the new machine, Aurora can sell 12,000 units of product annually at a per unit selling price of $100. If the new machine is purchased, the number of units produced and sold would increase by 10%, and the selling price would remain the same.
2. The new machine is faster than the old machine, and it is more efficient in its usage of materials. With the old machine the gross profit rate will be 25% of sales, whereas the rate will be 30% of sales with the new machine.
3. Annual selling expenses are $180,000 with the current equipment. Because the new equipment would produce a greater number of units to be sold, annual selling expenses are expected to increase by 10% if it is purchased.
4. Annual administrative expenses are expected to be $100,000 with the old machine, and $113,000 with the new machine.
5. The current book value of the existing machine is $36,000. Aurora uses straight-line depreciation.

Instructions

With the class divided into groups, prepare an incremental analysis for the 5 years showing whether Aurora should keep the existing machine or buy the new machine. (Ignore income tax effects.)

MANAGERIAL ANALYSIS

BYP20-3   MiniTek manufactures private-label small electronic products, such as alarm clocks, calculators, kitchen timers, stopwatches, and automatic pencil sharpeners. Some of the products are sold as sets, and others are sold individually. Products are studied as to their sales potential, and then cost estimates are made. The Engineering Department develops production plans, and then production begins. The company has generally had very successful product introductions. Only two products introduced by the company have been discontinued.

One of the products currently sold is a multi-alarm clock. The clock has four alarms that can be programmed to sound at various times and for varying lengths of time. The company has experienced a great deal of difficulty in making the circuit boards for the clocks. The production process has never operated smoothly. The product is unprofitable at the present time, primarily because of warranty repairs and product recalls. Two models of the clocks were recalled, for example, because they sometimes caused an electric shock when the alarms were being shut off. The Engineering Department is attempting to revise the manufacturing process, but the revision will take another 6 months at least.

The clocks were very popular when they were introduced, and since they are private-label, the company has not suffered much from the recalls. Presently, the company has a very large order for several items from Kmart Stores. The order includes 5,000 of the multi-alarm clocks. When the company suggested that Kmart purchase the clocks from another manufacturer, Kmart threatened to rescind the entire order unless the clocks were included.

The company has therefore investigated the possibility of having another company make the clocks for them. The clocks were bid for the Kmart order based on an estimated $6.90 cost to manufacture:

Circuit board, 1 each @ $2.00	$2.00
Plastic case, 1 each @ $0.80	0.80
Alarms, 4 @ $0.15 each	0.60
Labor, 15 minutes @ $12/hour	3.00
Overhead, $2.00 per labor hour	0.50

MiniTek could purchase clocks to fill the Kmart order for $10 from Trans-Tech Asia, a Korean manufacturer with a very good quality record. Trans-Tech has offered to reduce the price to $7.50 after MiniTek has been a customer for 6 months, placing an order of at least 1,000 units per month. If MiniTek becomes a "preferred customer" by purchasing 15,000 units per year, the price would be reduced still further to $4.50.

Omega Products, a local manufacturer, has also offered to make clocks for MiniTek. They have offered to sell 5,000 clocks for $5 each. However, Omega Products has been in business for only 6 months. They have experienced significant turnover in their labor force, and the local press has reported that the owners may face tax evasion charges soon. The owner of Omega Products is an electronic engineer, however, and the quality of the clocks is likely to be good.

If MiniTek decides to purchase the clocks from either Trans-Tech or Omega, all the costs to manufacture could be avoided, except a total of $5,000 in overhead costs for machine depreciation. The machinery is fairly new, and has no alternate use.

Instructions

(a) What is the difference in profit under each of the alternatives if the clocks are to be sold for $14.50 each to Kmart?

(b) What are the most important nonfinancial factors that MiniTek should consider when making this decision?

(c) What do you think MiniTek should do in regard to the Kmart order? What should it do in regard to continuing to manufacture the multi-alarm clocks? Be prepared to defend your answer.

REAL-WORLD FOCUS

BYP20-4 Founded in 1983, Beverly Hills Fan Company is located in Woodland Hills, California. With 23 employees and sales of less than $10 million, the company is relatively small. Management feels that there is potential for growth in the upscale market for ceiling fans and lighting. They are particularly optimistic about growth in Mexican and Canadian markets.

Presented below is information from the president's letter in the company's annual report.

BEVERLY HILLS FAN COMPANY
President's Letter

An aggressive product development program was initiated during the past year resulting in new ceiling fan models planned for introduction this year. Award winning industrial designer Ron Rezek created several new fan models for the Beverly Hills Fan and L.A. Fan lines, including a new Showroom Collection, designed specifically for the architectural and designer markets. Each of these models has received critical acclaim, and order commitments for this year have been outstanding. Additionally, our Custom Color and special order fans continued to enjoy increasing popularity and sales gains as more and more customers desire fans that match their specific interior decors. Currently, Beverly Hills Fan Company offers a product line of over 100 models of contemporary, traditional, and transitional ceiling fans.

Instructions

(a) What points did the company management need to consider before deciding to offer the special-order fans to customers?

(b) How would incremental analysis be employed to assist in this decision?

BYP20-5 Outsourcing by both manufacturers and service companies is becoming increasingly common. There are now many firms that specialize in outsourcing consulting.

Address: www.alsbridge.com, or go to **www.wiley.com/college/kimmel**

Instructions

Go to the Web page of Alsbridge, Inc. at the address shown above, and answer the following questions.

(a) What are some of the types of outsourcing for which the company provides assistance?

(b) What is insourcing?

(c) What are some of the potential benefits of insourcing?

Critical Thinking

COMMUNICATION ACTIVITY

BYP20-6 Hank Jewell is a production manager at a metal fabricating plant. Last night, he read an article about a new piece of equipment that would dramatically reduce his division's costs. Hank was very excited about the prospect, and the first thing he did this morning was to bring the article to his supervisor, Preston Thiese, the plant manager. The following conversation occurred:

Hank: Preston, I thought you would like to see this article on the new PDD1130; they've made some fantastic changes that could save us millions of dollars.

Preston: I appreciate your interest, Hank, but I actually have been aware of the new machine for two months. The problem is that we just bought a new machine last year. We spent $2 million on that machine, and it was supposed to last us 12 years. If we replace it now, we would have to write its book value off of the books for a huge loss. If I go to top management now and say that I want a new machine, they will fire me. I think we should use our existing machine for a couple of years, and then when it becomes obvious that we have to have a new machine, I will make the proposal.

Instructions

Hank just completed a course in managerial accounting, and he believes that Preston is making a big mistake. Write a memo from Hank to Preston explaining Preston's decision-making error.

ETHICS CASE

BYP20-7 Blake Romney became Chief Executive Officer of Peters Inc. two years ago. At the time, the company was reporting lagging profits, and Blake was brought in to "stir things up." The company has three divisions, electronics, fiber optics, and plumbing supplies. Blake has no interest in plumbing supplies, and one of the first things he did was to put pressure on his accountants to reallocate some of the company's fixed costs away from the other two divisions to the plumbing division. This had the effect of causing the plumbing division to report losses during the last two years; in the past it had always reported low, but acceptable, net income. Blake felt that this reallocation would shine a favorable light on him in front of the board of directors because it meant that the electronics and fiber optics divisions would look like they were improving. Given that these are "businesses of the future," he believed that the stock market would react favorably to these increases, while not penalizing the poor results of the plumbing division. Without this shift in the allocation of fixed costs, the profits of the electronics and fiber optics divisions would not have improved. But now the board of directors has suggested that the plumbing division be closed because it is reporting losses. This would mean that nearly 500 employees, many of whom have worked for Peters their whole lives, would lose their jobs.

Instructions

(a) If a division is reporting losses, does that necessarily mean that it should be closed?
(b) Was the reallocation of fixed costs across divisions unethical?
(c) What should Blake do?

ALL ABOUT YOU

BYP20-8 Managerial accounting techniques can be used in a wide variety of settings. As we have frequently pointed out, you can use them in many personal situations. They also can be useful in trying to find solutions for societal issues that appear to be hard to solve.

Instructions

Read the *Fortune* article, "The Toughest Customers: How Hardheaded Business Metrics Can Help the Hard-core Homeless," by Cait Murphy, available at **http://money.cnn.com/magazines/fortune/fortune_archive/2006/04/03/8373067/index.htm**. Answer the following questions.

(a) How does the article define "chronic" homelessness?
(b) In what ways does homelessness cost a city money? What are the estimated costs of a chronic homeless person to various cities?
(c) What are the steps suggested to address the problem?
(d) What is the estimated cost of implementing this program in New York? What results have been seen?
(e) In terms of incremental analysis, frame the relevant costs in this situation.

CONSIDERING YOUR COSTS AND BENEFITS

BYP20-9 School costs money. Is this an expenditure that you should have avoided? A year of tuition at a public four-year college costs about $8,655, and a year of tuition at a public two-year college costs about $1,359. If you did not go to college, you might avoid mountains of school-related debt. In fact, each year, about 600,000 students decide to drop out of school. Many of them never return. Suppose that you are working two jobs and going to college, and that you are not making ends meet. Your grades are suffering due to your lack of available study time. You feel depressed. Should you drop out of school?

YES: You can always go back to school. If your grades are bad and you are depressed, what good is school doing you anyway?

NO: Once you drop out, it is very hard to get enough momentum to go back. Dropping out will dramatically reduce your long-term opportunities. It is better to stay in school, even if you take only one class per semester. While you cannot go back and redo your initial decision, you can look at some facts to evaluate the wisdom of your decision.

Instructions

Write a response indicating your position regarding this situation. Provide support for your view.

Answers to Insight and Accounting Across the Organization Questions

p. 1045 That Letter from AmEx Might Not Be a Bill Q: What are the relevant costs that American Express would need to know in order to determine to whom to make this offer? **A:** Clearly, American Express would make this offer to those customers that are most likely to default on their bills. The most important relevant cost would be the "expected loss" that an at-risk customer posed. If a customer has a high probability of defaulting and if the expected loss exceeds the $300 cost, then American Express can probably save money by paying that customer to quit using its card so that the customer doesn't incur an even bigger bill.

p. 1048 Giving Away the Store? Q: What are the relevant revenues and costs that Amazon should consider relative to the decision whether to offer the Prime free-shipping subscription? **A:** The relevant revenues to consider would be the estimated change in revenue that would result from offering free shipping and the $79 annual fee for a Prime subscription. The relevant costs would be the estimated additional shipping costs that the company would incur.

p. 1055 Time to Move to a New Neighborhood? Q: What were some of the factors that complicated the company's decision to move? How should the company have incorporated such factors into its incremental analysis? **A:** The company received only $7.5 million for its California property, only 58 of 75 key employees were willing to move, construction was delayed by a year which caused the new plant to increase in price by $1.5 million, and wages surged in Idaho due to low unemployment. In performing incremental analysis of the decision to move, a company should perform sensitivity analysis. This would include evaluating the impact on the decision if all costs were, for example, 10% higher than expected or if cost savings were 10% lower than expected.

p. 1057 What Is the Real Cost of Packaging Options? Q: If your marketing director suggests that, in addition to selling your cereal in a standard-size box, you should sell a jumbo size and an individual size, what issues must you consider? **A:** In evaluating this decision, you should identify the incremental revenues as well as incremental costs. The marketing manager is most likely focusing on the fact that by offering alternative packaging options, the company can market the product to a broader range of customers. However, alternative packaging options will also result in additional costs. It will increase the number of setups, require different types of storage and handling, and increase the need for additional storage space for the packages and the packaged products.

Answers to Self-Test Questions

1. d **2.** b **3.** c **4.** d **5.** c (3,000 × $4) **6.** d [$18 − ($14 + $5)] × 3,000 **7.** b **8.** d **9.** c ($12,000 − $8,000) **10.** a **11.** d [($68 − $55) − $12] **12.** b **13.** c **14.** b (.5 × $100,000) − ($200,000 − $140,000)

The Navigator

Remember to go back to The Navigator box on the chapter opening page and check off your completed work.

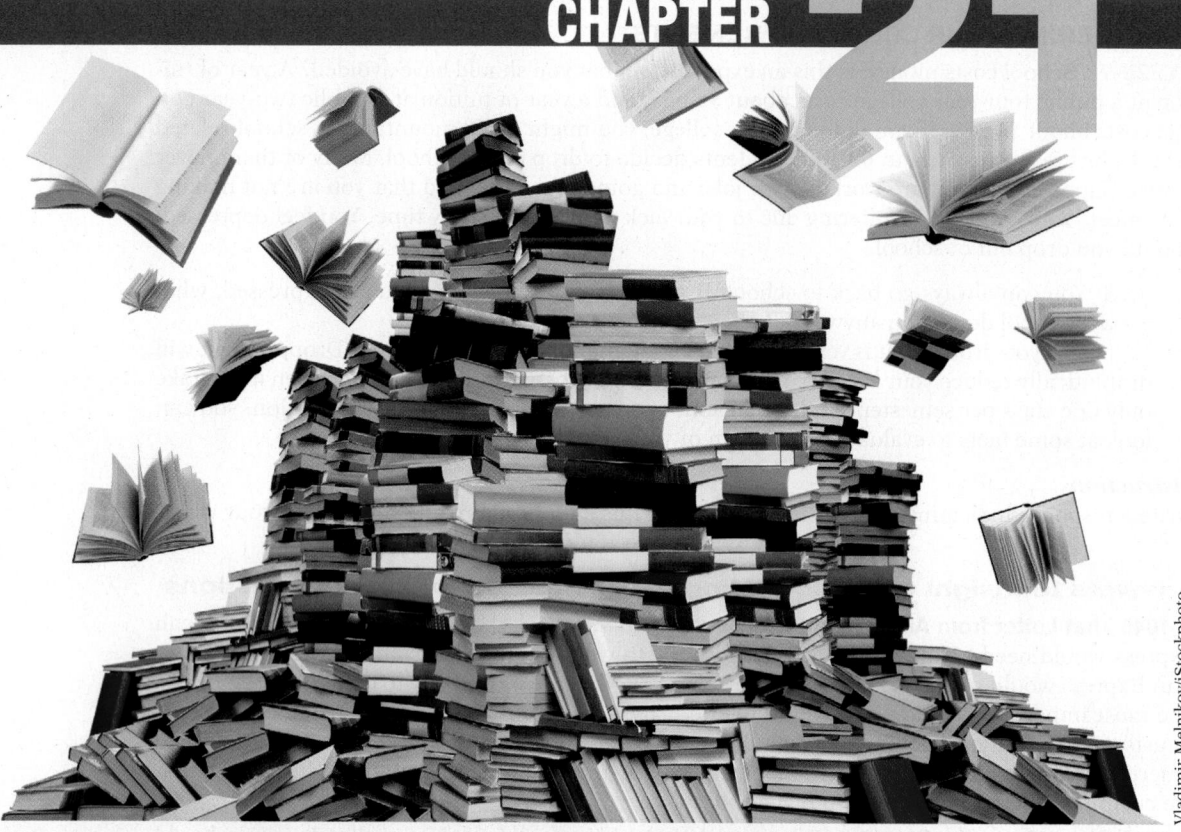

CHAPTER 21

Vladimir Melnikov/iStockphoto

BUDGETARY PLANNING

✔ The Navigator

- Scan Learning Objectives
- Read Feature Story
- Scan Preview
- Read Text and Answer **Do it!**
  ◯ p. 1087 ◯ p. 1090 ◯ p. 1092
  ◯ p. 1097 ◯ p. 1102
- Work Using the Decision Toolkit
- Review Summary of Learning Objectives
- Work Comprehensive **Do it!** 1 p. 1108
  2 p. 1110
- Answer Self-Test Questions
- Complete Assignments
- Go to WileyPLUS for practice and tutorials

LEARNING OBJECTIVES

After studying this chapter, you should be able to:

1. Indicate the benefits of budgeting.
2. State the essentials of effective budgeting.
3. Identify the budgets that comprise the master budget.
4. Describe the sources for preparing the budgeted income statement.
5. Explain the principal sections of a cash budget.
6. Indicate the applicability of budgeting in nonmanufacturing companies.

So you came up with a great idea for a product. You started a company, and you are selling stuff so fast that you can barely keep up. No problem, right? However, without proper planning and budgeting, your success could be short-lived. In some cases, failure is actually brought on by rapid, uncontrolled growth.

One such example was online discount bookseller, www.Positively-You.com. One of the website's co-founders, Lyle Bowline, had never run a business. However, his experience as an assistant director of an entrepreneurial center had provided him with knowledge about the do's and don'ts of small business. To minimize costs, he started the company small and simple. He invested $5,000 in computer equipment and ran the business out of his basement. In the early months, even though sales were only about $2,000 a month, the company actually made a profit because it kept its costs low (a feat few other dot-coms could boast of).

Things changed dramatically when the company received national publicity in the financial press. Suddenly, the company's sales increased to $50,000 a month—fully 25 times the previous level. The "simple" little business suddenly needed a business plan, a strategic plan, and a budget. It needed to rent office space and to hire employees.

Initially, members of a local book club donated time to help meet the sudden demand. Some put in so much time that eventually the company hired them. Quickly, the number of paid employees ballooned. The sudden growth necessitated detailed planning and budgeting.

THE NEXT AMAZON.COM? NOT QUITE

The need for a proper budget was accentuated by the fact that the company's gross profit was only 16 cents on each dollar of goods sold. This meant that after paying for its inventory, the company had only 16 cents of every dollar to cover its remaining operating costs.

Unfortunately, the company never got things under control. Within a few months, sales had plummeted to $12,000 per month. At this level of sales, the company could not meet the mountain of monthly expenses that it had accumulated in trying to grow. Ironically, the company's sudden success, and the turmoil it created, appears to have been what eventually caused the company to fail.

Watch the Babycakes video in WileyPLUS to learn more about budgetary planning in the real world. ✔The Navigator

As the Feature Story about Positively-You.com indicates, budgeting is critical to financial well-being. As a student, you budget your study time and your money. Families budget income and expenses. Governmental agencies budget revenues and expenditures. Businesses use budgets in planning and controlling their operations.

Our primary focus in this chapter is budgeting—specifically, how budgeting is used as a **planning tool** by management. Through budgeting, it should be possible for management to maintain enough cash to pay creditors, to have sufficient raw materials to meet production requirements, and to have adequate finished goods to meet expected sales.

The content and organization of Chapter 21 are as follows.

Budgeting Basics

LEARNING OBJECTIVE 1

Indicate the benefits of budgeting.

One of management's major responsibilities is planning. As explained in Chapter 14, **planning** is the process of establishing company-wide objectives. A successful organization makes both long-term and short-term plans. These plans establish the objectives of the company and the proposed way of accomplishing them.

A budget is a formal written statement of management's plans for a specified future time period, expressed in financial terms. It represents the primary method of communicating agreed-upon objectives throughout the organization. Once adopted, a budget becomes an important basis for evaluating performance. It promotes efficiency and serves as a deterrent to waste and inefficiency. We consider the role of budgeting as a **control device** in Chapter 22.

BUDGETING AND ACCOUNTING

Accounting information makes major contributions to the budgeting process. From the accounting records, companies can obtain historical data on revenues, costs, and expenses. These data are helpful in formulating future budget goals.

Normally, accountants have the responsibility for presenting management's budgeting goals in financial terms. In this role, they translate management's plans and communicate the budget to employees throughout the company. They prepare periodic budget reports that provide the basis for measuring performance and comparing actual results with planned objectives. The budget itself, and the administration of the budget, however, are entirely management responsibilities.

THE BENEFITS OF BUDGETING

The primary benefits of budgeting are:

1. It requires all levels of management to **plan ahead** and to formalize goals on a recurring basis.

2. It provides **definite objectives** for evaluating performance at each level of responsibility.

3. It creates an **early warning system** for potential problems so that management can make changes before things get out of hand.

4. It facilitates the **coordination of activities** within the business. It does this by correlating the goals of each segment with overall company objectives. Thus, the company can integrate production and sales promotion with expected sales.

5. It results in greater **management awareness** of the entity's overall operations and the impact on operations of external factors, such as economic trends.

6. It **motivates personnel** throughout the organization to meet planned objectives.

A budget is an aid to management; it is not a substitute for management. A budget cannot operate or enforce itself. Companies can realize the benefits of budgeting only when managers carefully administer budgets.

ESSENTIALS OF EFFECTIVE BUDGETING

Effective budgeting depends on a **sound organizational structure**. In such a structure, authority and responsibility for all phases of operations are clearly defined. Budgets based on **research and analysis** are more likely to result in realistic goals that will contribute to the growth and profitability of a company. And, the effectiveness of a budget program is directly related to its **acceptance by all levels of management**.

> **LEARNING OBJECTIVE 2**
> State the essentials of effective budgeting.

Once adopted, the budget is an important tool for evaluating performance. Managers should systematically and periodically review variations between actual and expected results to determine their cause(s). However, individuals should not be held responsible for variations that are beyond their control.

LENGTH OF THE BUDGET PERIOD

The budget period is not necessarily one year in length. **A budget may be prepared for any period of time.** Various factors influence the length of the budget period. These factors include the type of budget, the nature of the organization, the need for periodic appraisal, and prevailing business conditions.

The budget period should be long enough to provide an attainable goal under normal business conditions. Ideally, the time period should minimize the impact of seasonal or cyclical fluctuations. On the other hand, the budget period should not be so long that reliable estimates are impossible.

The **most common budget period is one year**. The annual budget, in turn, is often supplemented by monthly and quarterly budgets. Many companies use **continuous 12-month budgets**. These budgets drop the month just ended and add a future month. One advantage of continuous budgeting is that it keeps management planning a full year ahead.

Thinkstock/Comstock/Getty Images, Inc.

Accounting Across the Organization
Businesses Often Feel Too Busy to Plan for the Future

A study by Willard & Shullman Group Ltd. found that fewer than 14% of businesses with less than 500 employees do an annual budget or have a written business plan. For many small businesses, the basic assumption is that, "As long as I sell as much as I can, and keep my employees paid, I'm doing OK." A few small business owners even say that they see no need for budgeting and planning. Most small business owners, though, say that they understand that budgeting and planning are critical for survival and growth. But given the long hours that they already work addressing day-to-day challenges, they also say that they are "just too busy to plan for the future."

? Describe a situation in which a business "sells as much as it can" but cannot "keep its employees paid." (See page 1130.)

THE BUDGETING PROCESS

The development of the budget for the coming year generally starts several months before the end of the current year. The budgeting process usually begins with the collection of data from each organizational unit of the company. Past performance is often the starting point from which future budget goals are formulated.

The budget is developed within the framework of a **sales forecast**. This forecast shows potential sales for the industry and the company's expected share of such sales. Sales forecasting involves a consideration of various factors: (1) general economic conditions, (2) industry trends, (3) market research studies, (4) anticipated advertising and promotion, (5) previous market share, (6) changes in prices, and (7) technological developments. The input of sales personnel and top management is essential to the sales forecast.

In small companies like Positively-You.com, the budgeting process is often informal. In larger companies, a **budget committee** has responsibility for coordinating the preparation of the budget. The committee ordinarily includes the president, treasurer, chief accountant (controller), and management personnel from each of the major areas of the company, such as sales, production, and research. The budget committee serves as a review board where managers can defend their budget goals and requests. Differences are reviewed, modified if necessary, and reconciled. The budget is then put in its final form by the budget committee, approved, and distributed.

BUDGETING AND HUMAN BEHAVIOR

A budget can have a significant impact on human behavior. If done well, it can inspire managers to higher levels of performance. However, if done poorly, budgets can discourage additional effort and pull down the morale of managers. Why do these diverse effects occur? The answer is found in how the budget is developed and administered.

In developing the budget, each level of management should be invited to participate. This "bottom-to-top" approach is referred to as **participative budgeting**. One advantage of participative budgeting is that lower-level managers have more detailed knowledge of their specific area and thus are able to provide more accurate budgetary estimates. Also, when lower-level managers participate in the budgeting process, they are more likely to perceive the resulting budget as fair. The overall goal is to reach agreement on a budget that the managers consider fair and achievable, but that also meets the corporate goals set by top management. When this goal is met, the budget will provide positive motivation for the managers. In contrast, if managers view the budget as unfair and unrealistic, they may feel discouraged and uncommitted to budget goals. The risk of having unrealistic budgets is generally greater when the budget is developed from top management down to lower management than vice versa. Illustration 21-1 graphically displays the flow of budget data from bottom to top under participative budgeting.

Illustration 21-1 Flow of budget data under participative budgeting

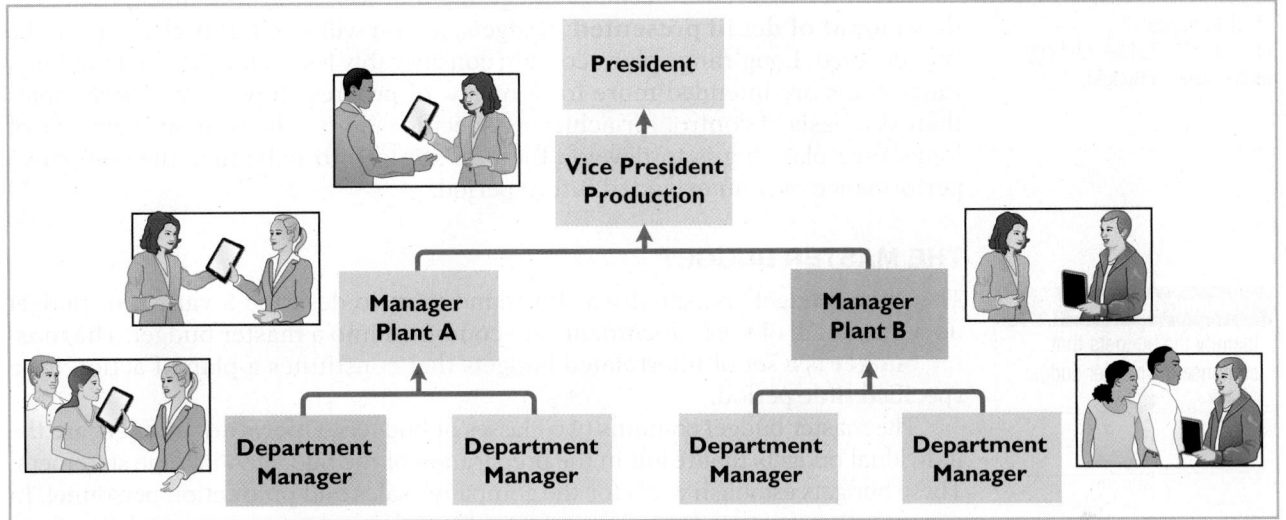

For example, at one time, in an effort to revive its plummeting stock, Time Warner's top management determined and publicly announced bold new financial goals for the coming year. Unfortunately, these goals were not reached. The next year, the company got a new CEO who said the company would now actually set reasonable goals that it could meet. The new budgets were developed with each operating unit setting what it felt were optimistic but attainable goals. In the words of one manager, using this approach created a sense of teamwork.

Participative budgeting does, however, have potential disadvantages. First, the "give and take" of participative budgeting is time-consuming (and thus more costly). Under a "top-down" approach, the budget is simply developed by top management and then dictated to lower-level managers. A second disadvantage is that participative budgeting can foster budgetary "gaming" through budgetary slack. Budgetary slack occurs when managers intentionally underestimate budgeted revenues or overestimate budgeted expenses in order to make it easier to achieve budgetary goals. To minimize budgetary slack, higher-level managers must carefully review and thoroughly question the budget projections provided to them by employees whom they supervise.

For the budget to be effective, top management must completely support the budget. The budget is an important basis for evaluating performance. It also can be used as a positive aid in achieving projected goals. The effect of an evaluation is positive when top management tempers criticism with advice and assistance. In contrast, a manager is likely to respond negatively if top management uses the budget exclusively to assess blame. A budget should not be used as a pressure device to force improved performance. In sum, a budget can be a manager's friend or a foe.

Ethics Note Unrealistic budgets can lead to unethical employee behavior such as cutting corners on the job or distorting internal financial reports.

BUDGETING AND LONG-RANGE PLANNING

Budgeting and long-range planning are not the same. One important difference is the **time period involved**. The maximum length of a budget is usually one year, and budgets are often prepared for shorter periods of time, such as a month or a quarter. In contrast, long-range planning usually encompasses a period of at least five years.

A second significant difference is in **emphasis**. Budgeting focuses on achieving specific short-term goals, such as meeting annual profit objectives. Long-range

Helpful Hint In comparing a budget with a long-range plan: (1) Which has more detail? (2) Which is done for a longer period of time? (3) Which is more concerned with short-term goals?
Answers: (1) Budget. (2) Long-range plan. (3) Budget.

planning, on the other hand, identifies long-term goals, selects strategies to achieve those goals, and develops policies and plans to implement the strategies. In long-range planning, management also considers anticipated trends in the economic and political environment and how the company should cope with them.

The final difference between budgeting and long-range planning relates to the **amount of detail presented**. Budgets, as you will see in this chapter, can be very detailed. Long-range plans contain considerably less detail. The data in long-range plans are intended more for a review of progress toward long-term goals than as a basis of control for achieving specific results. The primary objective of long-range planning is to develop the best strategy to maximize the company's performance over an extended future period.

THE MASTER BUDGET

LEARNING OBJECTIVE 3
Identify the budgets that comprise the master budget.

The term "budget" is actually a shorthand term to describe a variety of budget documents. All of these documents are combined into a master budget. The **master budget** is a set of interrelated budgets that constitutes a plan of action for a specified time period.

The master budget contains two classes of budgets. **Operating budgets** are the individual budgets that result in the preparation of the budgeted income statement. These budgets establish goals for the company's sales and production personnel. In contrast, **financial budgets** focus primarily on the cash resources needed to fund expected operations and planned capital expenditures. Financial budgets include the capital expenditure budget, the cash budget, and the budgeted balance sheet.

Illustration 21-2 pictures the individual budgets included in a master budget, and the sequence in which they are prepared. The company first develops the

Illustration 21-2 Components of the master budget

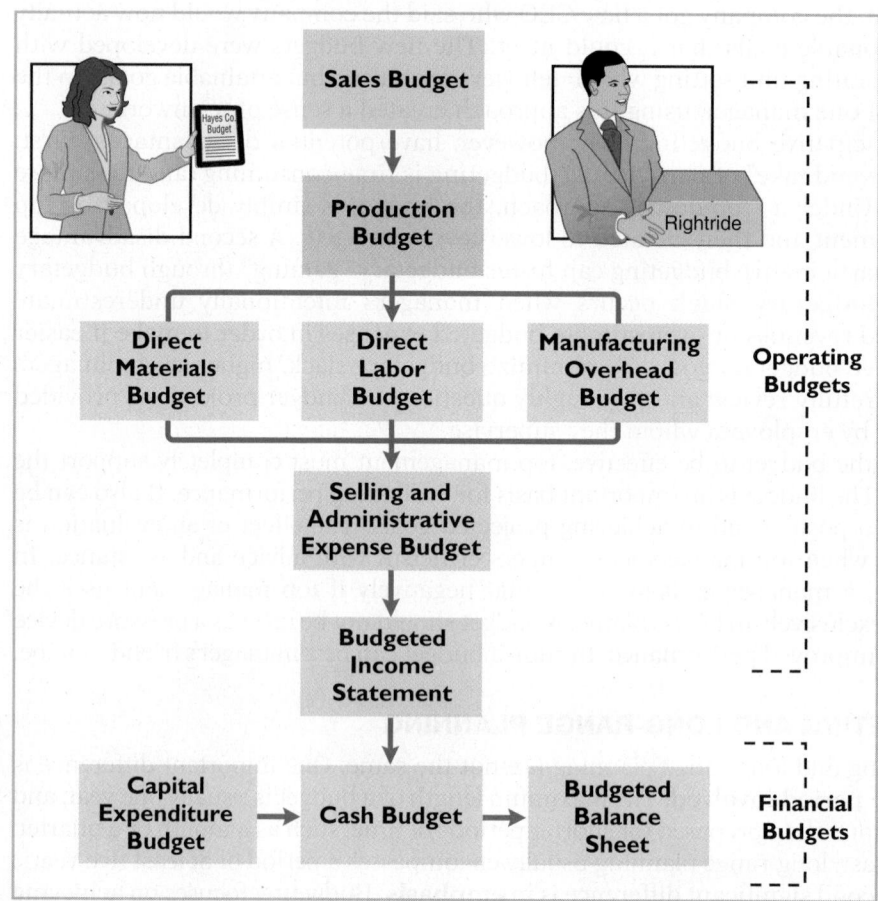

operating budgets, beginning with the sales budget. Then, it prepares the financial budgets. We will explain and illustrate each budget shown in Illustration 21-2 except the capital expenditure budget. That budget is discussed under the topic of capital budgeting in Chapter 24.

Do it!

BUDGET TERMINOLOGY

Use this list of terms to complete the sentences that follow.

Long-range planning	Participative budgeting
Sales forecast	Operating budgets
Master budget	Financial budgets

1. A _____ shows potential sales for the industry and a company's expected share of such sales.

2. _____ are used as the basis for the preparation of the budgeted income statement.

3. The _____ is a set of interrelated budgets that constitutes a plan of action for a specified time period.

4. _____ identifies long-term goals, selects strategies to achieve these goals, and develops policies and plans to implement the strategies.

5. Lower-level managers are more likely to perceive results as fair and achievable under a _____ approach.

6. _____ focus primarily on the cash resources needed to fund expected operations and planned capital expenditures.

Action Plan

- Understand the budgeting process, including the importance of the sales forecast.
- Understand the difference between an operating budget and a financial budget.
- Differentiate budgeting from long-range planning.
- Realize that the master budget is a set of interrelated budgets.

Solution

1. Sales forecast.	4. Long-range planning.
2. Operating budgets.	5. Participative budgeting.
3. Master budget.	6. Financial budgets.

Related exercise material: **BE21-1, E21-1,** and **Do it! 21-1.**

Preparing the Operating Budgets

We use a case study of Hayes Company in preparing the operating budgets. Hayes manufactures and sells a single product, an ergonomically designed bike seat with multiple customizable adjustments, called the Rightride. The budgets are prepared by quarters for the year ending December 31, 2014. Hayes Company begins its annual budgeting process on September 1, 2013, and it completes the budget for 2014 by December 1, 2013.

SALES BUDGET

As shown in the master budget in Illustration 21-2, **the sales budget is prepared first**. Each of the other budgets depends on the sales budget. The sales budget is derived from the sales forecast. It represents management's best estimate of sales revenue for the budget period. An inaccurate sales budget may adversely affect net income. For example, an overly optimistic sales budget may result in excessive inventories that may have to be sold at reduced prices. In contrast, an unduly pessimistic sales budget may result in loss of sales revenue due to inventory shortages.

For example, at one time Amazon.com significantly underestimated demand for its e-book reader, the Kindle. As a consequence, it did not produce enough

Helpful Hint For a retail or manufacturing company, what is the starting point in preparing the master budget, and why? Answer: The sales budget is the starting point for the master budget. It sets the level of activity for other functions such as production and purchasing.

Kindles and was completely sold out well before the holiday shopping season. Not only did this represent a huge lost opportunity for Amazon.com, but it exposed it to potential competitors, who were eager to provide customers with alternatives to the Kindle.

Forecasting sales is challenging. For example, consider the forecasting challenges faced by major sports arenas, whose revenues depend on the success of the home team. Madison Square Garden's revenues from April to June were $193 million during a year when the Knicks made the NBA playoffs. But revenues were only $133.2 million a couple of years later when the team did not make the playoffs. Or, consider the challenges faced by Hollywood movie producers in predicting the complicated revenue stream produced by a new movie. Movie theater ticket sales represent only 20% of total revenue. The bulk of revenue comes from global sales, DVDs, video-on-demand, merchandising products, and videogames, all of which are difficult to forecast.

The sales budget is prepared by multiplying the expected unit sales volume for each product by its anticipated unit selling price. Hayes Company expects sales volume to be 3,000 units in the first quarter, with 500-unit increases in each succeeding quarter. Illustration 21-3 shows the sales budget for the year, by quarter, based on a sales price of $60 per unit.

Illustration 21-3 Sales budget

	Home	Insert	Page Layout	Formulas	Data	Review	View	

	A	B	C	D	E	F
1		HAYES COMPANY				
2		Sales Budget				
3		For the Year Ending December 31, 2014				
4				Quarter		
5		1	2	3	4	Year
6	Expected unit sales	3,000	3,500	4,000	4,500	15,000
7	Unit selling price	× $60	× $60	× $60	× $60	× $60
8	Total sales	$180,000	$210,000	$240,000	$270,000	$900,000

Some companies classify the anticipated sales revenue as cash or credit sales and by geographical regions, territories, or salespersons.

PRODUCTION BUDGET

The **production budget** shows the number of units of a product to produce to meet anticipated sales demand. Production requirements are determined from the following formula.[1]

Illustration 21-4 Production requirements formula

$$\begin{array}{c}\text{Budgeted}\\\text{Sales Units}\end{array} + \begin{array}{c}\text{Desired Ending}\\\text{Finished}\\\text{Goods Units}\end{array} - \begin{array}{c}\text{Beginning}\\\text{Finished}\\\text{Goods Units}\end{array} = \begin{array}{c}\text{Required}\\\text{Production}\\\text{Units}\end{array}$$

Units of Finished Goods Inventory

Beg. Inv.	
Required Prod. Units	Sales
End. Inv.	

A realistic estimate of ending inventory is essential in scheduling production requirements. Excessive inventories in one quarter may lead to cutbacks in production and employee layoffs in a subsequent quarter. On the other

---

[1]This formula ignores any work in process inventories, which are assumed to be nonexistent in Hayes Company.

hand, inadequate inventories may result either in added costs for overtime work or in lost sales. Hayes Company believes it can meet future sales requirements by maintaining an ending inventory equal to 20% of the next quarter's budgeted sales volume. For example, the ending finished goods inventory for the first quarter is 700 units (20% × anticipated second-quarter sales of 3,500 units). Illustration 21-5 shows the production budget.

Illustration 21-5 Production budget

	Units of Finished Goods Inventory (1st Qtr.)	
	600	
	3,100	3,000
	700	

A	B	C	D	E	F	G	H	I	J
	HAYES COMPANY								
	Production Budget								
	For the Year Ending December 31, 2014								
				Quarter					
	1		2		3		4		Year
Expected unit sales (Illustration 21-3)	3,000		3,500		4,000		4,500		
Add: Desired ending finished goods units[a]	700		800		900		1,000 [b]		
Total required units	3,700		4,300		4,900		5,500		
Less: Beginning finished goods units	600 [c]		700		800		900		
Required production units	3,100		3,600		4,100		4,600		15,400
[a]20% of next quarter's sales									
[b]Expected 2015 first-quarter sales, 5,000 units × 20%									
[c]20% of estimated first-quarter 2014 sales units									

The production budget, in turn, provides the basis for the budgeted costs for each manufacturing cost element, as explained in the following pages.

Service Company Insight

The Implications of Budgetary Optimism

Companies aren't the only ones that have to estimate revenues. Governments at all levels (e.g., local, state or federal) prepare annual budgets. Most are required to submit balanced budgets, that is, estimated revenues are supposed to cover anticipated expenditures. Unfortunately, estimating government revenues can be as difficult as, or even more difficult than, estimating company revenues. The accuracy of government estimates is most critical during economic downturns. If governments fail to anticipate lower revenues during the planning stage, they then often have to make much larger, more disruptive cuts than would have been originally necessary.

For example, during 2009, the median state government overestimated revenues by 10.2%, with four state governments missing by more than 25%. What makes estimation so difficult for these governments? Most states rely on income taxes, which fluctuate widely with economic gyrations. Some states rely on sales taxes, which are problematic because the laws regarding sales taxes haven't adjusted for the shift from manufacturing to service companies and from brick-and-mortar stores to online sales.

Source: Conor Dougherty, "States Fumble Revenue Forecasts," *Wall Street Journal Online* (March 2, 2011).

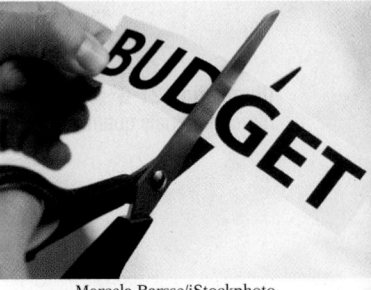

Marcela Barsse/iStockphoto

? Why is it important that government budgets accurately estimate future revenues during economic downturns? (See page 1130.)

PRODUCTION BUDGET

Do it!

Becker Company estimates that 2014 unit sales will be 12,000 in quarter 1, 16,000 in quarter 2, and 20,000 in quarter 3, at a unit selling price of $30. Management desires to have ending finished goods inventory equal to 15% of the next quarter's expected unit sales. Prepare a production budget by quarter for the first six months of 2014.

Action Plan

- Begin with budgeted sales in units.
- Add desired ending finished goods inventory.
- Subtract beginning finished goods inventory.

The Navigator

Solution

Becker Company Production Budget.xls

Home   Insert   Page Layout   Formulas   Data   Review   View

P18   fx

	A	B	C	D	E	F
1		**BECKER COMPANY**				
2		**Production Budget**				
3		**For the Six Months Ending June 30, 2014**				
4			Quarter			
5			1		2	Six Months
6	Expected unit sales	12,000		16,000		
7	Add: Desired ending finished goods	2,400		3,000		
8	Total required units	14,400		19,000		
9	Less: Beginning finished goods inventory	1,800		2,400		
10	Required production units	12,600		16,600		29,200

Related exercise material: **BE21-3, E21-4, E21-6,** and **Do it! 21-2.**

DIRECT MATERIALS BUDGET

The **direct materials budget** shows both the quantity and cost of direct materials to be purchased. The quantities of direct materials are derived from the following formula.

Illustration 21-6 Formula for direct materials quantities

Direct Materials Units Required for Production	+	Desired Ending Direct Materials Units	−	Beginning Direct Materials Units	=	Required Direct Materials Units to Be Purchased

Units of Direct Materials

Beg. Inv.	
Direct Materials to Prod.	Direct Materials Required for Prod.
End. Inv.	

After the company determines the number of units to purchase, it can compute the budgeted cost of direct materials to be purchased. It does so by multiplying the required units of direct materials by the anticipated cost per unit.

The desired ending inventory is again a key component in the budgeting process. For example, inadequate inventories could result in temporary shutdowns of production. Because of its close proximity to suppliers, Hayes Company maintains an ending inventory of raw materials equal to 10% of the next quarter's production requirements. The manufacture of each Rightride requires 2 pounds of raw materials, and the expected cost per pound is $4. Illustration 21-7 shows the direct materials budget. Assume that the desired ending direct materials amount is 1,020 pounds for the fourth quarter of 2014.

	Hayes Company Direct Materials Budget.xls							
Home	Insert	Page Layout	Formulas	Data	Review	View		

P18   *fx*

	A	B C D E F G H I J K				
1		**HAYES COMPANY**				
2		Direct Materials Budget				
3		For the Year Ending December 31, 2014				
4		Quarter				
5		1	2	3	4	Year
6	Units to be produced (Illustration 21-5)	3,100	3,600	4,100	4,600	
7	Direct materials per unit	× 2	× 2	× 2	× 2	
8	Total pounds needed for production	6,200	7,200	8,200	9,200	
9	Add: Desired ending direct materials (pounds)[a]	720	820	920	1,020	
10	Total materials required	6,920	8,020	9,120	10,220	
11	Less: Beginning direct materials (pounds)	620 [b]	720	820	920	
12	Direct materials purchases	6,300	7,300	8,300	9,300	
13	Cost per pound	× $4	× $4	× $4	× $4	
14	Total cost of direct materials purchases	$25,200	$29,200	$33,200	$37,200	$124,800
15						
16	[a]10% of next quarter's production requirements					
17	[b]10% of estimated first-quarter pounds needed for production					
18						

Units of Direct Materials (1st Qtr.)

620	
6,300	6,200
720	

Illustration 21-7 Direct materials budget

Management Insight

Betting That Prices Won't Fall

Sometimes things happen that cause managers to reevaluate their normal purchasing patterns. Consider, for example, the predicament that businesses faced when the price of many raw materials recently skyrocketed. Rubber, cotton, oil, corn, wheat, steel, copper, and spices—prices for seemingly everything were going straight up. Anticipating that prices might continue to go up, many managers decided to stockpile much larger quantities of raw materials to avoid paying even higher prices in the future. For example, after cotton prices rose 92%, one manager of a printed T-shirt manufacturer decided to stockpile a huge supply of plain T-shirts in anticipation of additional price increases. While he normally has about 30 boxes of T-shirts in inventory, he purchased 2,500 boxes.

Source: Liam Pleven and Matt Wirz, "Companies Stock Up as Commodities Prices Rise," *Wall Street Journal Online* (February 3, 2011).

© William Wang/iStockphoto

? What are the potential downsides of stockpiling a huge amount of raw materials? (See page 1131.)

MASTER BUDGET

Action Plan

- Know the form and content of the sales budget.
- Prepare the sales budget first, as the basis for the other budgets.
- Determine the units that must be produced to meet anticipated sales.
- Know how to compute the beginning and ending finished goods units.
- Determine the materials required to meet production needs.
- Know how to compute the beginning and ending direct materials units.

Do it! Soriano Company is preparing its master budget for 2014. Relevant data pertaining to its sales, production, and direct materials budgets are as follows.

Sales. Sales for the year are expected to total 1,200,000 units. Quarterly sales, as a percentage of total sales, are 20%, 25%, 30%, and 25%, respectively. The sales price is expected to be $50 per unit for the first three quarters and $55 per unit beginning in the fourth quarter. Sales in the first quarter of 2015 are expected to be 10% higher than the budgeted sales for the first quarter of 2014.

Production. Management desires to maintain the ending finished goods inventories at 25% of the next quarter's budgeted sales volume.

Direct materials. Each unit requires 3 pounds of raw materials at a cost of $5 per pound. Management desires to maintain raw materials inventories at 5% of the next quarter's production requirements. Assume the production requirements for the first quarter of 2015 are 810,000 pounds.

Prepare the sales, production, and direct materials budgets by quarters for 2014.

Solution

Soriano Company Sales Budget.xls

SORIANO COMPANY
Sales Budget
For the Year Ending December 31, 2014

	Quarter				Year
	1	2	3	4	
Expected unit sales	240,000	300,000	360,000	300,000	1,200,000
Unit selling price	× $50	× $50	× $50	× $55	—
Total sales	$12,000,000	$15,000,000	$18,000,000	$16,500,000	$61,500,000

Soriano Company Production Budget.xls

SORIANO COMPANY
Production Budget
For the Year Ending December 31, 2014

	Quarter				Year
	1	2	3	4	
Expected unit sales	240,000	300,000	360,000	300,000	
Add: Desired ending finished goods units[a]	75,000	90,000	75,000	66,000 [b]	
Total required units	315,000	390,000	435,000	366,000	
Less: Beginning finished goods units	60,000 [c]	75,000	90,000	75,000	
Required production units	255,000	315,000	345,000	291,000	1,206,000

[a]25% of next quarter's unit sales
[b]Estimated first-quarter 2015 sales units: 240,000 + (240,000 × 10%) = 264,000: 264,000 × 25%
[c]25% of estimated first-quarter 2014 sales units (240,000 × 25%)

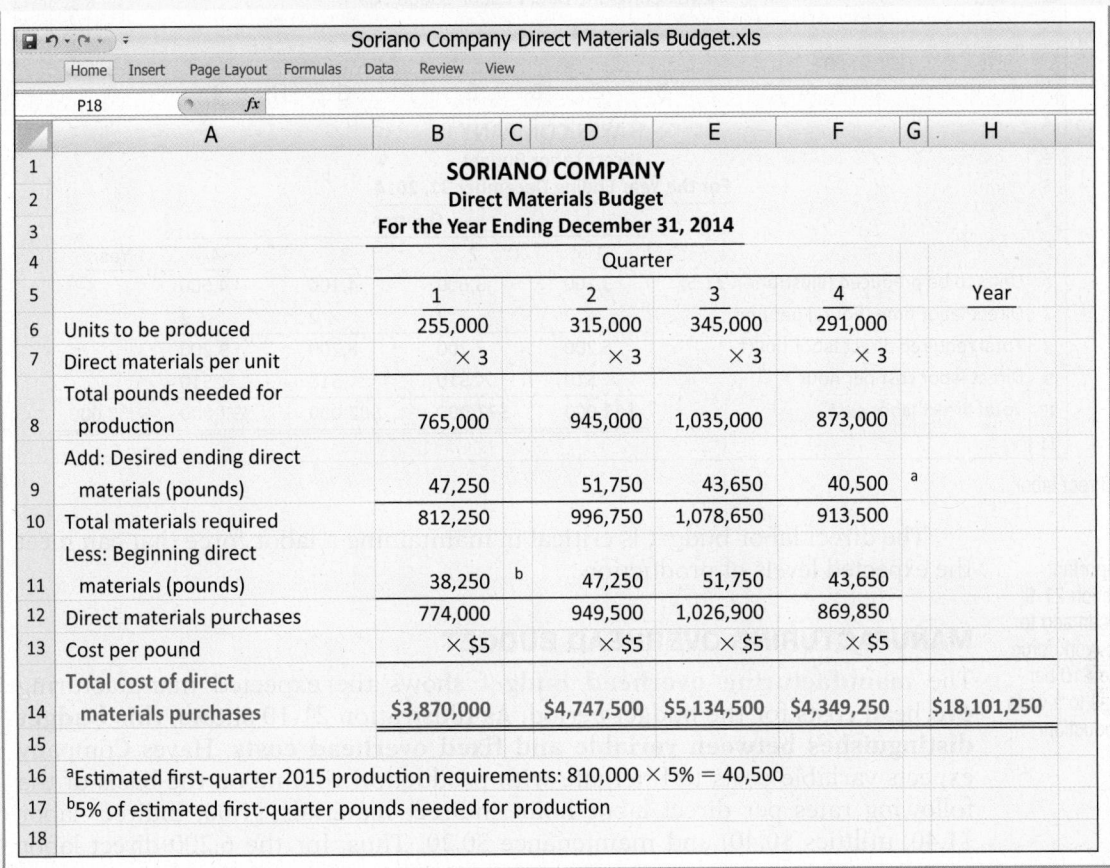

		B	C	D	E	F	G	H
	A							

SORIANO COMPANY
Direct Materials Budget
For the Year Ending December 31, 2014

		Quarter						Year
		1		**2**	**3**	**4**		
6	Units to be produced	255,000		315,000	345,000	291,000		
7	Direct materials per unit	× 3		× 3	× 3	× 3		
8	Total pounds needed for production	765,000		945,000	1,035,000	873,000		
9	Add: Desired ending direct materials (pounds)	47,250		51,750	43,650	40,500	a	
10	Total materials required	812,250		996,750	1,078,650	913,500		
11	Less: Beginning direct materials (pounds)	38,250	b	47,250	51,750	43,650		
12	Direct materials purchases	774,000		949,500	1,026,900	869,850		
13	Cost per pound	× $5		× $5	× $5	× $5		
14	Total cost of direct materials purchases	$3,870,000		$4,747,500	$5,134,500	$4,349,250		$18,101,250
15								
16	aEstimated first-quarter 2015 production requirements: 810,000 × 5% = 40,500							
17	b5% of estimated first-quarter pounds needed for production							
18								

Related exercise material: **BE21-2, BE21-3, BE21-4, E21-2, E21-3, E21-4, E21-5, E21-6,** and
Do it! 21-3.

DIRECT LABOR BUDGET

Like the direct materials budget, the **direct labor budget** contains the quantity (hours) and cost of direct labor necessary to meet production requirements. The total direct labor cost is derived from the following formula.

Units to Be Produced	×	Direct Labor Time per Unit	×	Direct Labor Cost per Hour	=	Total Direct Labor Cost

Illustration 21-8 Formula for direct labor cost

Direct labor hours are determined from the production budget. At Hayes Company, two hours of direct labor are required to produce each unit of finished goods. The anticipated hourly wage rate is $10. Illustration 21-9 (page 1094) shows these data.

Illustration 21-9 Direct labor budget

Helpful Hint An important assumption in Illustration 21-9 is that the company can add to and subtract from its work force as needed so that the $10 per hour labor cost applies to a wide range of possible production activity.

The direct labor budget is critical in maintaining a labor force that can meet the expected levels of production.

MANUFACTURING OVERHEAD BUDGET

The **manufacturing overhead budget** shows the expected manufacturing overhead costs for the budget period. As Illustration 21-10 shows, **this budget distinguishes between variable and fixed overhead costs**. Hayes Company expects variable costs to fluctuate with production volume on the basis of the following rates per direct labor hour: indirect materials $1.00, indirect labor $1.40, utilities $0.40, and maintenance $0.20. Thus, for the 6,200 direct labor

Illustration 21-10
Manufacturing overhead budget

hours to produce 3,100 units, budgeted indirect materials are $6,200 (6,200 × $1), and budgeted indirect labor is $8,680 (6,200 × $1.40). Hayes also recognizes that some maintenance is fixed. The amounts reported for fixed costs are assumed for our example. The accuracy of budgeted overhead cost estimates can be greatly improved by employing activity-based costing.

At Hayes Company, overhead is applied to production on the basis of direct labor hours. Thus, as Illustration 21-10 shows, the budgeted annual rate is $8 per hour ($246,400 ÷ 30,800).

SELLING AND ADMINISTRATIVE EXPENSE BUDGET

Hayes Company combines its operating expenses into one budget, the **selling and administrative expense budget**. This budget projects anticipated selling and administrative expenses for the budget period. This budget (Illustration 21-11) also classifies expenses as either variable or fixed. In this case, the variable expense rates per unit of sales are sales commissions $3 and freight-out $1. Variable expenses per quarter are based on the unit sales from the sales budget (Illustration 21-3, page 1088). For example, Hayes expects sales in the first quarter to be 3,000 units. Thus, Sales Commissions Expense is $9,000 (3,000 × $3), and Freight-Out is $3,000 (3,000 × $1). Fixed expenses are based on assumed data.

Illustration 21-11 Selling and administrative expense budget

Hayes Company Manufacturing Selling and Administrative Expense Budget.xls

	B	C	D	E	F
HAYES COMPANY					
Selling and Administrative Expense Budget					
For the Year Ending December 31, 2014					
	Quarter				
	1	2	3	4	Year
Budgeted sales in units (Illustration 21-3)	3,000	3,500	4,000	4,500	15,000
Variable expenses					
Sales commissions ($3 per unit)	$ 9,000	$10,500	$12,000	$13,500	$ 45,000
Freight-out ($1 per unit)	3,000	3,500	4,000	4,500	15,000
Total variable expenses	12,000	14,000	16,000	18,000	60,000
Fixed expenses					
Advertising	5,000	5,000	5,000	5,000	20,000
Sales salaries	15,000	15,000	15,000	15,000	60,000
Office salaries	7,500	7,500	7,500	7,500	30,000
Depreciation	1,000	1,000	1,000	1,000	4,000
Property taxes and insurance	1,500	1,500	1,500	1,500	6,000
Total fixed expenses	30,000	30,000	30,000	30,000	120,000
Total selling and administrative expenses	$42,000	$44,000	$46,000	$48,000	$180,000

BUDGETED INCOME STATEMENT

The **budgeted income statement** is the important end-product of the operating budgets. This budget indicates the expected profitability of operations for the budget period. The budgeted income statement provides the basis for evaluating company performance. Budgeted income statements often act as a call to action. For example, a board member at XM Satellite Radio Holdings felt that budgeted costs were too high relative to budgeted revenues. When management refused to

LEARNING OBJECTIVE 4
Describe the sources for preparing the budgeted income statement.

cut its marketing and programming costs, the board member resigned. He felt that without the cuts, the company risked financial crisis.

As you would expect, the budgeted income statement is prepared from the various operating budgets. For example, to find the cost of goods sold, Hayes Company must first determine the total unit cost of producing one Rightride, as follows.

Illustration 21-12
Computation of total unit cost

Cost of One Rightride

Cost Element	Illustration	Quantity	Unit Cost	Total
Direct materials	21-7	2 pounds	$ 4.00	$ 8.00
Direct labor	21-9	2 hours	$10.00	20.00
Manufacturing overhead	21-10	2 hours	$ 8.00	16.00
Total unit cost				$44.00

Hayes Company then determines cost of goods sold by multiplying the units sold by the unit cost. Its budgeted cost of goods sold is $660,000 (15,000 × $44). All data for the income statement come from the individual operating budgets except the following: (1) interest expense is expected to be $100, and (2) income taxes are estimated to be $12,000. Illustration 21-13 shows the budgeted income statement.

Illustration 21-13 Budgeted income statement

HAYES COMPANY
Budgeted Income Statement
For the Year Ending December 31, 2014

Sales (Illustration 21-3)	$900,000
Cost of goods sold (15,000 × $44)	660,000
Gross profit	240,000
Selling and administrative expenses (Illustration 21-11)	180,000
Income from operations	60,000
Interest expense	100
Income before income taxes	59,900
Income tax expense	12,000
Net income	$ 47,900

DECISION TOOLKIT

DECISION CHECKPOINTS	INFO NEEDED FOR DECISION	TOOL TO USE FOR DECISION	HOW TO EVALUATE RESULTS
Has the company met its targets for sales, production expenses, selling and administrative expenses, and net income?	Sales forecasts, inventory levels, projected materials, labor, overhead, and selling and administrative requirements	Master budget—a set of interrelated budgets including sales, production, materials, labor, overhead, and selling and administrative budgets	Results are favorable if revenues exceed budgeted amounts, or if expenses are less than budgeted amounts.

Do it!

Soriano Company is preparing its budgeted income statement for 2014. Relevant data pertaining to its sales, production, and direct materials budgets can be found in the **Do it!** exercise on pages 1092–1093.

In addition, Soriano budgets 0.5 hours of direct labor per unit, labor costs at $15 per hour, and manufacturing overhead at $25 per direct labor hour. Its budgeted selling and administrative expenses for 2014 are $12,000,000.

(a) Calculate the budgeted total unit cost. (b) Prepare the budgeted income statement for 2014.

Solution

(a)

Cost Element	Quantity	Unit Cost	Total
Direct materials	3.0 pounds	$ 5	$ 15.00
Direct labor	0.5 hours	$15	7.50
Manufacturing overhead	0.5 hours	$25	12.50
Total unit cost			$35.00

(b)

SORIANO COMPANY
Budgeted Income Statement
For the Year Ending December 31, 2014

Sales (1,200,000 units from sales budget, page 1092)	$61,500,000
Cost of goods sold (1,200,000 × $35.00/unit)	42,000,000
Gross profit	19,500,000
Selling and administrative expenses	12,000,000
Net income	$ 7,500,000

Action Plan

- Recall that total unit cost consists of direct materials, direct labor, and manufacturing overhead.
- Recall that direct materials costs are included in the direct materials budget.
- Know the form and content of the income statement.
- Use the total unit sales information from the sales budget to compute annual sales and cost of goods sold.

The Navigator

Related exercise material: **BE21-8, E21-11, E21-13,** and **Do it! 21-4.**

Preparing the Financial Budgets

As shown in Illustration 21-2 (page 1086), the financial budgets consist of the capital expenditure budget, the cash budget, and the budgeted balance sheet. We will discuss the capital expenditure budget in Chapter 24. The other budgets are explained in the following sections.

LEARNING OBJECTIVE 5
Explain the principal sections of a cash budget.

CASH BUDGET

The cash budget shows anticipated cash flows. Because cash is so vital, this budget is often considered to be the most important financial budget.

The cash budget contains three sections (cash receipts, cash disbursements, and financing) and the beginning and ending cash balances, as shown in Illustration 21-14 (page 1098).

The **cash receipts section** includes expected receipts from the company's principal source(s) of revenue. These are usually cash sales and collections from customers on credit sales. This section also shows anticipated receipts of interest and dividends, and proceeds from planned sales of investments, plant assets, and the company's capital stock.

Illustration 21-14 Basic form of a cash budget

Helpful Hint Why is the cash budget prepared after the other budgets are prepared? Answer: Because the information generated by the other budgets dictates the expected inflows and outflows of cash.

Illustration 21-14 Basic form of a cash budget

ANY COMPANY Cash Budget	
Beginning cash balance	$X,XXX
Add: Cash receipts (itemized)	X,XXX
Total available cash	X,XXX
Less: Cash disbursements (itemized)	X,XXX
Excess (deficiency) of available cash over cash disbursements	X,XXX
Financing	X,XXX
Ending cash balance	$X,XXX

The **cash disbursements section** shows expected cash payments. Such payments include direct materials, direct labor, manufacturing overhead, and selling and administrative expenses. This section also includes projected payments for income taxes, dividends, investments, and plant assets.

The **financing section** shows expected borrowings and the repayment of the borrowed funds plus interest. Companies need this section when there is a cash deficiency or when the cash balance is below management's minimum required balance.

Data in the cash budget are prepared in sequence. The ending cash balance of one period becomes the beginning cash balance for the next period. Companies obtain data for preparing the cash budget from other budgets and from information provided by management. In practice, cash budgets are often prepared for the year on a monthly basis.

To minimize detail, we will assume that Hayes Company prepares an annual cash budget by quarters. Its cash budget is based on the following assumptions.

1. The January 1, 2014, cash balance is expected to be $38,000. Hayes wishes to maintain a balance of at least $15,000.

2. Sales (Illustration 21-3, page 1088): 60% are collected in the quarter sold and 40% are collected in the following quarter. Accounts receivable of $60,000 at December 31, 2013, are expected to be collected in full in the first quarter of 2014.

3. Short-term investments are expected to be sold for $2,000 cash in the first quarter.

4. Direct materials (Illustration 21-7, page 1091): 50% are paid in the quarter purchased and 50% are paid in the following quarter. Accounts payable of $10,600 at December 31, 2013, are expected to be paid in full in the first quarter of 2014.

5. Direct labor (Illustration 21-9, page 1094): 100% is paid in the quarter incurred.

6. Manufacturing overhead (Illustration 21-10, page 1094) and selling and administrative expenses (Illustration 21-11, page 1095): All items except depreciation are paid in the quarter incurred.

7. Management plans to purchase a truck in the second quarter for $10,000 cash.

8. Hayes makes equal quarterly payments of its estimated annual income taxes.

9. Loans are repaid in the earliest quarter in which there is sufficient cash (that is, when the cash on hand exceeds the $15,000 minimum required balance).

In preparing the cash budget, it is useful to prepare schedules for collections from customers (assumption No. 2) and cash payments for direct materials (assumption No. 4). These schedules are shown in Illustrations 21-15 and 21-16.

HAYES COMPANY
Schedule of Expected Collections from Customers

	Sales[a]	Collections by Quarter			
		1	**2**	**3**	**4**
Accounts receivable, 12/31/13		$ 60,000			
First quarter	$180,000	108,000[b]	$ 72,000[c]		
Second quarter	210,000		126,000	$ 84,000	
Third quarter	240,000			144,000	$ 96,000
Fourth quarter	270,000				162,000
Total collections		$168,000	$198,000	$228,000	$258,000

[a]Per Illustration 21-3; [b]$180,000 × .60; [c]$180,000 × .40

Illustration 21-15 Collections from customers

HAYES COMPANY
Schedule of Expected Payments for Direct Materials

	Purchases[a]	Payments by Quarter			
		1	**2**	**3**	**4**
Accounts payable, 12/31/13		$10,600			
First quarter	$25,200	12,600[b]	$12,600[c]		
Second quarter	29,200		14,600	$14,600	
Third quarter	33,200			16,600	$16,600
Fourth quarter	37,200				18,600
Total payments		$23,200	$27,200	$31,200	$35,200

[a]Per Illustration 21-7; [b]$25,200 × .50; [c]$25,200 × .50

Illustration 21-16 Payments for direct materials

Illustration 21-17 (page 1100) shows the cash budget for Hayes Company. The budget indicates that Hayes will need $3,000 of financing in the second quarter to maintain a minimum cash balance of $15,000. Since there is an excess of available cash over disbursements of $22,500 at the end of the third quarter, the borrowing, plus $100 interest, is repaid in this quarter.

Service Company Insight
Without a Budget, Can the Games Begin?

Behind the grandeur of the Olympic Games lies a huge financial challenge—how to keep budgeted costs in line with revenues. For example, the 2006 Winter Olympics in Turin, Italy, narrowly avoided going into bankruptcy before the Games even started. In order for the event to remain solvent, organizers canceled glitzy celebrations and shifted promotional responsibilities to an Italian state-run agency. Despite these efforts, after the Games were over, the Italian government created a lottery game to cover its financial losses.

As another example, organizers of the 2002 Winter Olympics in Salt Lake City cut budgeted costs by $200 million shortly before the events began. According to the chief operating and financial officer, the organizers went through every line item in the budget, sorting each one into "must have" versus "nice to have." As a result, the Salt Lake City Games produced a surplus of $100 million.

Source: Gabriel Kahn and Roger Thurow, "In Turin, Paying for Games Went Down to the Wire," *Wall Street Journal* (February 10, 2006).

 Why does it matter whether the Olympic Games exceed their budget? (See page 1131.)

Marianna Day Massey/
Zuma Press/NewsCom

Hayes Company Cash Budget.xls

	A	B	C	D	E	F	G	H	I	J

HAYES COMPANY
Cash Budget
For the Year Ending December 31, 2014

	Assumption	Quarter			
		1	2	3	4
6 Beginning cash balance	1	$ 38,000	$ 25,500	$ 15,000	$ 19,400
7 Add: Receipts					
8 Collections from customers	2	168,000	198,000	228,000	258,000
9 Sale of securities	3	2,000	0	0	0
10 Total receipts		170,000	198,000	228,000	258,000
11 Total available cash		208,000	223,500	243,000	277,400
12 Less: Disbursements					
13 Direct materials	4	23,200	27,200	31,200	35,200
14 Direct labor	5	62,000	72,000	82,000	92,000
15 Manufacturing overhead	6	53,300 [a]	56,300	59,300	62,300
16 Selling and administrative expenses	6	41,000 [b]	43,000	45,000	47,000
17 Purchase of truck	7	0	10,000	0	0
18 Income tax expense	8	3,000	3,000	3,000	3,000
19 Total disbursements		182,500	211,500	220,500	239,500
20 Excess (deficiency) of available cash over cash disbursements		25,500	12,000	22,500	37,900
21 Financing					
22 Add: Borrowings		0	3,000	0	0
23 Less: Repayments including interest	9	0	0	3,100	0
24 Ending cash balance		$ 25,500	$ 15,000	$ 19,400	$ 37,900
25					
26 [a]$57,100 − $3,800 depreciation					
27 [b]$42,000 − $1,000 depreciation					

Illustration 21-17 Cash budget

A cash budget contributes to more effective cash management. It shows managers when additional financing is necessary well before the actual need arises. And, it indicates when excess cash is available for investments or other purposes.

🧰 DECISION TOOLKIT

DECISION CHECKPOINTS	INFO NEEDED FOR DECISION	TOOL TO USE FOR DECISION	HOW TO EVALUATE RESULTS
Is the company going to need to borrow funds in the coming quarter?	Beginning cash balance, cash receipts, cash disbursements, and desired cash balance	Cash budget	The company will need to borrow money if the cash budget indicates a projected cash deficiency of available cash over cash disbursements for the quarter.

BUDGETED BALANCE SHEET

The **budgeted balance sheet** is a projection of financial position at the end of the budget period. This budget is developed from the budgeted balance sheet for the preceding year and the budgets for the current year. Pertinent data from the budgeted balance sheet at December 31, 2013, are as follows.

Buildings and equipment	$182,000	Common stock	$225,000
Accumulated depreciation	$ 28,800	Retained earnings	$ 46,480

Illustration 21-18 shows Hayes Company's budgeted balance sheet at December 31, 2014.

Illustration 21-18 Budgeted balance sheet

HAYES COMPANY
Budgeted Balance Sheet
December 31, 2014

Assets

Cash		$ 37,900
Accounts receivable		108,000
Finished goods inventory		44,000
Raw materials inventory		4,080
Buildings and equipment	$192,000	
Less: Accumulated depreciation	48,000	144,000
Total assets		$337,980

Liabilities and Stockholders' Equity

Accounts payable	$ 18,600
Common stock	225,000
Retained earnings	94,380
Total liabilities and stockholders' equity	$337,980

The computations and sources of the amounts are explained below.

Cash: Ending cash balance $37,900, shown in the cash budget (Illustration 21-17, page 1100).

Accounts receivable: 40% of fourth-quarter sales $270,000, shown in the schedule of expected collections from customers (Illustration 21-15, page 1099).

Finished goods inventory: Desired ending inventory 1,000 units, shown in the production budget (Illustration 21-5, page 1089) times the total unit cost $44 (shown in Illustration 21-12, page 1096).

Raw materials inventory: Desired ending inventory 1,020 pounds, times the cost per pound $4, shown in the direct materials budget (Illustration 21-7, page 1091).

Buildings and equipment: December 31, 2013, balance $182,000, plus purchase of truck for $10,000 (Illustration 21-17, page 1100).

Accumulated depreciation: December 31, 2013, balance $28,800, plus $15,200 depreciation shown in manufacturing overhead budget (Illustration 21-10, page 1094) and $4,000 depreciation shown in selling and administrative expense budget (Illustration 21-11, page 1095).

Accounts payable: 50% of fourth-quarter purchases $37,200, shown in schedule of expected payments for direct materials (Illustration 21-16, page 1099).

Common stock: Unchanged from the beginning of the year.

Retained earnings: December 31, 2013, balance $46,480, plus net income $47,900, shown in budgeted income statement (Illustration 21-13, page 1096).

After budget data are entered into the computer, Hayes prepares the various budgets (sales, cash, etc.), as well as the budgeted financial statements. Using spreadsheets, management can also perform "what if" (sensitivity) analyses based on different hypothetical assumptions. For example, suppose that sales managers project that sales will be 10% higher in the coming quarter. What impact does this change have on the rest of the budgeting process and the financing needs of the business? The impact of the various assumptions on the budget is quickly determined by the spreadsheet. Armed with these analyses, managers make more informed decisions about the impact of various projects. They also anticipate future problems and business opportunities. As seen in this chapter, budgeting is an excellent use of electronic spreadsheets.

CASH BUDGET

Do it!

Martian Company management wants to maintain a minimum monthly cash balance of $15,000. At the beginning of March, the cash balance is $16,500, expected cash receipts for March are $210,000, and cash disbursements are expected to be $220,000. How much cash, if any, must be borrowed to maintain the desired minimum monthly balance?

Action Plan

- Write down the basic form of the cash budget, starting with the beginning cash balance, adding cash receipts for the period, deducting cash disbursements, and identifying the needed financing to achieve the desired minimum ending cash balance.

- Insert the data given into the outlined form of the cash budget.

The Navigator

Solution

MARTIAN COMPANY
Cash Budget
For the Month Ending March 31, 2014

Beginning cash balance	$ 16,500
Add: Cash receipts for March	210,000
Total available cash	226,500
Less: Cash disbursements for March	220,000
Excess of available cash over cash disbursements	6,500
Financing	8,500
Ending cash balance	$ 15,000

To maintain the desired minimum cash balance of $15,000, Martian Company must borrow $8,500 of cash.

Related exercise material: **BE21-9, E21-13, E21-14, E21-15, E21-16,** and **Do it! 21-5.**

Budgeting in Nonmanufacturing Companies

LEARNING OBJECTIVE 6

Indicate the applicability of budgeting in nonmanufacturing companies.

Budgeting is not limited to manufacturers. Budgets are also used by merchandisers, service companies, and not-for-profit organizations.

MERCHANDISERS

As in manufacturing operations, the sales budget for a merchandiser is both the starting point and the key factor in the development of the master budget. The major differences between the master budgets of a merchandiser and a manufacturer are these:

1. A merchandiser **uses a merchandise purchases budget instead of a production budget**.
2. A merchandiser **does not use the manufacturing budgets (direct materials, direct labor, and manufacturing overhead)**.

The merchandise purchases budget shows the estimated cost of goods to be purchased to meet expected sales. The formula for determining budgeted merchandise purchases is:

Illustration 21-19
Merchandise purchases formula

Budgeted Cost of Goods Sold	+	Desired Ending Merchandise Inventory	−	Beginning Merchandise Inventory	=	Required Merchandise Purchases

To illustrate, assume that the budget committee of Lima Company is preparing the merchandise purchases budget for July 2014. It estimates that budgeted sales will be $300,000 in July and $320,000 in August. Cost of goods sold is expected to be 70% of sales—that is, $210,000 in July (.70 × $300,000) and $224,000 in August (.70 × $320,000). The company's desired ending inventory is 30% of the following month's cost of goods sold. Required merchandise purchases for July are $214,200, computed as follows.

Illustration 21-20
Merchandise purchases budget

LIMA COMPANY
Merchandise Purchases Budget
For the Month Ending July 31, 2014

Budgeted cost of goods sold ($300,000 × 70%)	$ 210,000
Add: Desired ending merchandise inventory ($224,000 × 30%)	67,200
Total	277,200
Less: Beginning merchandise inventory ($210,000 × 30%)	63,000
Required merchandise purchases for July	**$214,200**

When a merchandiser is departmentalized, it prepares separate budgets for each department. For example, a grocery store prepares sales budgets and purchases budgets for each of its major departments, such as meats, dairy, and produce. The store then combines these budgets into a master budget for the store. When a retailer has branch stores, it prepares separate master budgets for each store. Then, it incorporates these budgets into master budgets for the company as a whole.

SERVICE COMPANIES

In a service company, such as a public accounting firm, a law office, or a medical practice, the critical factor in budgeting is **coordinating professional staff needs with anticipated services**. If a firm is overstaffed, several problems may result: Labor costs are disproportionately high. Profits are lower because of the additional salaries. Staff turnover sometimes increases because of lack of challenging work. In contrast, if a service company is understaffed, it may lose revenue because existing and prospective client needs for service cannot be met. Also, professional staff may seek other jobs because of excessive work loads.

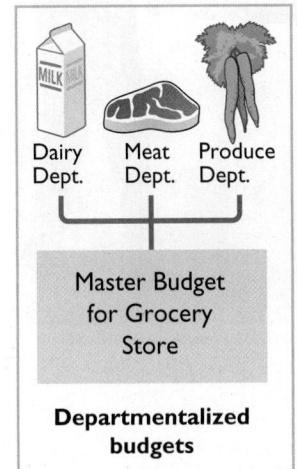

Dairy Dept. Meat Dept. Produce Dept.

Master Budget for Grocery Store

Departmentalized budgets

Service companies can obtain budget data for service revenue from **expected output** or **expected input**. When output is used, it is necessary to determine the expected billings of clients for services provided. In a public accounting firm, for example, output is the sum of its billings in auditing, tax, and consulting services. When input data are used, each professional staff member projects his or her billable time. The firm then applies billing rates to billable time to produce expected service revenue.

NOT-FOR-PROFIT ORGANIZATIONS

Budgeting is just as important for not-for-profit organizations as for profit-oriented businesses. The budget process, however, is different. In most cases, not-for-profit entities budget **on the basis of cash flows (expenditures and receipts), rather than on a revenue and expense basis**. Further, the starting point in the process is usually expenditures, not receipts. For the not-for-profit entity, management's task generally is to find the receipts needed to support the planned expenditures. The activity index is also likely to be significantly different. For example, in a not-for-profit entity, such as a university, budgeted faculty positions may be based on full-time equivalent students or credit hours expected to be taught in a department.

For some governmental units, voters approve the budget. In other cases, such as state governments and the federal government, legislative approval is required. After the budget is adopted, it must be followed. Overspending is often illegal. In governmental budgets, authorizations tend to be on a line-by-line basis. That is, the budget for a municipality may have a specified authorization for police and fire protection, garbage collection, street paving, and so on. The line-item authorization of governmental budgets significantly limits the amount of discretion management can exercise. The city manager often cannot use savings from one line item, such as street paving, to cover increased spending in another line item, such as snow removal.

©ZUMA Press/Newscom/NewsCom

Service Company Insight
Budget Shortfalls as Far as the Eye Can See

All organizations need to stick to budgets. The Museum of Contemporary Art in Los Angeles learned this the hard way. Over a 10-year period, its endowment shrunk from $50 million to $6 million as its newly hired director strove to build the museum's reputation through spending. The director consistently ran budget deficits, which eventually threatened the museum's survival.

The most recent recession has created budgeting challenges for nearly all governmental agencies. Tax revenues dropped rapidly as earnings declined and unemployment skyrocketed. At the same time, sources of debt financing dried up. To meet a projected shortfall of nearly $50 billion, California proposed to cut the school year by five days, give state workers two unpaid days off per month, and raise the state's sales tax percentage. Even Princeton University, with the largest endowment per student of any U.S. university ($2 million per student), experienced a 25% drop in the value of its endowment when the financial markets plunged. Because the endowment supports 45% of the university's $1.25 billion budget, when the endowment fell the university had to make cuts. Many raises were capped at $2,000, administrative budgets were cut by 5%, and major construction projects were put on hold.

Source: Edward Wyatt and Jori Finkel, "Soaring in Art, Museum Trips over Finances," *Wall Street Journal Online* (December 4, 2008); and Stu Woo, "California's Plans to Close Gap Become More Drastic," *Wall Street Journal Online* (January 8, 2009); and John Hechinger, "Princeton Cuts Budget as Endowment Slides," *Wall Street Journal Online* (January 9, 2009).

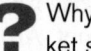 Why would a university's budgeted scholarships probably fall when the stock market suffers a serious drop? (See page 1131.)

USING THE DECISION TOOLKIT

The University of Wisconsin and its subunits must prepare budgets. One unique subunit of the University of Wisconsin is Babcock Ice Cream, a functioning producer of dairy products (and famous, at least on campus, for its delicious ice cream).

Assume that Babcock Ice Cream prepares monthly cash budgets. Relevant data from assumed operating budgets for 2014 are:

	January	February
Sales	$460,000	$412,000
Direct materials purchases	185,000	210,000
Direct labor	70,000	85,000
Manufacturing overhead	50,000	65,000
Selling and administrative expenses	85,000	95,000

Babcock sells its ice cream in shops on campus, as well as to local stores. Collections are expected to be 75% in the month of sale, and 25% in the month following sale. Babcock pays 60% of direct materials purchases in cash in the month of purchase, and the balance due in the month following the purchase. All other items above are paid in the month incurred. (Depreciation has been excluded from manufacturing overhead and selling and administrative expenses.)

Other data:

(1) Sales: December 2013, $320,000
(2) Purchases of direct materials: December 2013, $175,000
(3) Other receipts: January—Donation received, $2,000
    February—Sale of used equipment, $4,000
(4) Other disbursements: February—Purchased equipment, $10,000
(5) Repaid debt: January, $30,000

The company's cash balance on January 1, 2014, is expected to be $50,000. The company wants to maintain a minimum cash balance of $45,000.

Instructions

(a) Prepare schedules for (1) expected collections from customers and (2) expected payments for direct materials purchases for January and February.
(b) Prepare a cash budget for January and February in columnar form.

Solution

(a) (1)

Expected Collections from Customers

	Sales	January	February
December	$320,000	$ 80,000	$ 0
January	460,000	345,000	115,000
February	412,000	0	309,000
Totals		$425,000	$424,000

(2)

Expected Payments for Direct Materials

	Purchases	January	February
December	$175,000	$ 70,000	$ 0
January	185,000	111,000	74,000
February	210,000	0	126,000
Totals		$181,000	$200,000

(b)

BABCOCK ICE CREAM
Cash Budget
For the Two Months Ending February 28, 2014

	January	February
Beginning cash balance	$ 50,000	$ 61,000
Add: Receipts		
Collections from customers	425,000	424,000
Donations received	2,000	0
Sale of used equipment	0	4,000
Total receipts	427,000	428,000
Total available cash	477,000	489,000
Less: Disbursements		
Direct materials	181,000	200,000
Direct labor	70,000	85,000
Manufacturing overhead	50,000	65,000
Selling and administrative expenses	85,000	95,000
Purchase of equipment	0	10,000
Total disbursements	386,000	455,000
Excess (deficiency) of available cash over cash disbursements	91,000	34,000
Financing		
Add: Borrowings	0	11,000
Less: Repayments	30,000	0
Ending cash balance	$ 61,000	$ 45,000

Summary of Learning Objectives

1 **Indicate the benefits of budgeting.** The primary advantages of budgeting are that it (a) requires management to plan ahead, (b) provides definite objectives for evaluating performance, (c) creates an early warning system for potential problems, (d) facilitates coordination of activities, (e) results in greater management awareness, and (f) motivates personnel to meet planned objectives.

2 **State the essentials of effective budgeting.** The essentials of effective budgeting are (a) sound organizational structure, (b) research and analysis, and (c) acceptance by all levels of management.

3 **Identify the budgets that comprise the master budget.** The master budget consists of the following budgets: (a) sales, (b) production, (c) direct materials, (d) direct labor, (e) manufacturing overhead, (f) selling and administrative expense, (g) budgeted income statement, (h) capital expenditure budget, (i) cash budget, and (j) budgeted balance sheet.

4 **Describe the sources for preparing the budgeted income statement.** The budgeted income statement is prepared from (a) the sales budget; (b) the budgets for direct materials, direct labor, and manufacturing overhead; and (c) the selling and administrative expense budget.

5 **Explain the principal sections of a cash budget.** The cash budget has three sections (receipts, disbursements, and financing) and the beginning and ending cash balances.

6 **Indicate the applicability of budgeting in nonmanufacturing companies.** Budgeting may be used by merchandisers for development of a merchandise purchases budget. In service companies, budgeting is a critical factor in coordinating staff needs with anticipated services. In not-for-profit organizations, the starting point in budgeting is usually expenditures, not receipts.

DECISION TOOLKIT A SUMMARY

DECISION CHECKPOINTS	INFO NEEDED FOR DECISION	TOOL TO USE FOR DECISION	HOW TO EVALUATE RESULTS
Has the company met its targets for sales, production expenses, selling and administrative expenses, and net income?	Sales forecasts, inventory levels, projected materials, labor, overhead, and selling and administrative requirements	Master budget—a set of interrelated budgets including sales, production, materials, labor, overhead, and selling and administrative budgets	Results are favorable if revenues exceed budgeted amounts, or if expenses are less than budgeted amounts.
Is the company going to need to borrow funds in the coming quarter?	Beginning cash balance, cash receipts, cash disbursements, and desired cash balance	Cash budget	The company will need to borrow money if the cash budget indicates a projected cash deficiency of available cash over cash disbursements for the quarter.

Glossary

Budget (p. 1082) A formal written statement of management's plans for a specified future time period, expressed in financial terms.

Budget committee (p. 1084) A group responsible for coordinating the preparation of the budget.

Budgetary slack (p. 1085) The amount by which a manager intentionally underestimates budgeted revenues or overestimates budgeted expenses in order to make it easier to achieve budgetary goals.

Budgeted balance sheet (p. 1101) A projection of financial position at the end of the budget period.

Budgeted income statement (p. 1095) An estimate of the expected profitability of operations for the budget period.

Cash budget (p. 1097) A projection of anticipated cash flows.

Direct labor budget (p. 1093) A projection of the quantity and cost of direct labor necessary to meet production requirements.

Direct materials budget (p. 1090) An estimate of the quantity and cost of direct materials to be purchased.

Financial budgets (p. 1086) Individual budgets that focus primarily on the cash resources needed to fund expected operations and planned capital expenditures.

Long-range planning (p. 1085) A formalized process of identifying long-term goals, selecting strategies to achieve those goals, and developing policies and plans to implement the strategies.

Manufacturing overhead budget (p. 1094) An estimate of expected manufacturing overhead costs for the budget period.

Master budget (p. 1086) A set of interrelated budgets that constitutes a plan of action for a specific time period.

Merchandise purchases budget (p. 1103) The estimated cost of goods to be purchased by a merchandiser to meet expected sales.

Operating budgets (p. 1086) Individual budgets that result in a budgeted income statement.

Participative budgeting (p. 1084) A budgetary approach that starts with input from lower-level managers and works upward so that managers at all levels participate.

Production budget (p. 1088) A projection of the units that must be produced to meet anticipated sales.

Sales budget (p. 1087) An estimate of expected sales revenue for the budget period.

Sales forecast (p. 1084) The projection of potential sales for the industry and the company's expected share of such sales.

Selling and administrative expense budget (p. 1095) A projection of anticipated selling and administrative expenses for the budget period.

Comprehensive Do it! 1

Barrett Company has completed all operating budgets other than the income statement for 2014. Selected data from these budgets follow.

Sales: $300,000
Purchases of raw materials: $145,000
Ending inventory of raw materials: $15,000
Direct labor: $40,000
Manufacturing overhead: $73,000, including $3,000 of depreciation expense
Selling and administrative expenses: $36,000 including depreciation expense of $1,000
Interest expense: $1,000
Principal payment on note: $2,000
Dividends declared: $2,000
Income tax rate: 30%

Other information:

Assume that the number of units produced equals the number sold.
Year-end accounts receivable: 4% of 2014 sales.
Year-end accounts payable: 50% of ending inventory of raw materials.
Interest, direct labor, manufacturing overhead, and selling and administrative expenses other than depreciation are paid as incurred.
Dividends declared and income taxes for 2014 will not be paid until 2015.

BARRETT COMPANY
Balance Sheet
December 31, 2013

Assets

Cash		$20,000
Raw materials inventory		10,000
Equipment	$40,000	
Less: Accumulated depreciation	4,000	36,000
Total assets		$66,000

Liabilities and Stockholders' Equity

Accounts payable	$ 5,000	
Notes payable	22,000	
Total liabilities		$27,000
Common stock	25,000	
Retained earnings	14,000	39,000
Total liabilities and stockholders' equity		$66,000

Instructions

(a) Calculate budgeted cost of goods sold.
(b) Prepare a budgeted income statement for the year ending December 31, 2014.
(c) Prepare a budgeted balance sheet as of December 31, 2014.

Action Plan

- Recall that beginning raw materials inventory plus purchases less ending raw materials inventory equals direct materials used.

Solution to Comprehensive Do it! 1

(a) Beginning raw materials + Purchases − Ending raw materials = Cost of direct materials used ($10,000 + $145,000 − $15,000 = $140,000)
   Direct materials used + Direct labor + Manufacturing overhead = Cost of goods sold ($140,000 + $40,000 + $73,000 = $253,000)

(b)

BARRETT COMPANY
Budgeted Income Statement
For the Year Ending December 31, 2014

Sales		$300,000
Cost of goods sold		253,000
Gross profit		47,000
Selling and administrative expenses	$36,000	
Interest expense	1,000	37,000
Income before income tax expense		10,000
Income tax expense (30%)		3,000
Net income		$ 7,000

(c)

BARRETT COMPANY
Budgeted Balance Sheet
December 31, 2014

Assets

Cash[(1)]		$17,500
Accounts receivable (4% × $300,000)		12,000
Raw materials inventory		15,000
Equipment	$40,000	
Less: Accumulated depreciation	8,000	32,000
Total assets		$76,500

[(1)]Beginning cash balance		$ 20,000
Add: Collections from customers		
(96% × $300,000 sales)		288,000
Total available cash		308,000
Less: Disbursements		
Direct materials ($5,000 + $145,000 − $7,500)	$142,500	
Direct labor	40,000	
Manufacturing overhead	70,000	
Selling and administrative expenses	35,000	
Total disbursements		287,500
Excess of available cash over cash disbursements		20,500
Financing		
Less: Repayment of principal and interest		3,000
Ending cash balance		$ 17,500

Liabilities and Stockholders' Equity

Accounts payable (50% × $15,000)	$ 7,500	
Income taxes payable	3,000	
Dividends payable	2,000	
Note payable	20,000	
Total liabilities		$32,500
Common stock	25,000	
Retained earnings[(2)]	19,000	44,000
Total liabilities and stockholders' equity		$76,500

[(2)]Beginning retained earnings + Net income − Dividends declared = Ending retained
earnings ($14,000 + $7,000 − $2,000 = $19,000)

- Prepare the budgeted income statement before the budgeted balance sheet.
- Use the standard form of a cash budget to determine cash on the budgeted balance sheet.
- Add budgeted depreciation expense to accumulated depreciation at the beginning of the year to determine accumulated depreciation on the budgeted balance sheet.
- Add budgeted net income to retained earnings from the beginning of the year and subtract dividends declared to determine retained earnings on the budgeted balance sheet.
- Verify that total assets equal total liabilities and stockholders' equity on the budgeted balance sheet.

Comprehensive Do it! 2

Action Plan

- Know the form and content of the sales budget.
- Prepare the sales budget first as the basis for the other budgets.
- Determine the units that must be produced to meet anticipated sales.
- Know how to compute the beginning and ending finished goods units.

Asheville Company is preparing its master budget for 2014. Relevant data pertaining to its sales and production budgets are as follows.

Sales. Sales for the year are expected to total 2,100,000 units. Quarterly sales, as a percentage of total sales, are 15%, 25%, 35%, and 25%, respectively. The sales price is expected to be $70 per unit for the first three quarters and $75 per unit beginning in the fourth quarter. Sales in the first quarter of 2015 are expected to be 10% higher than the budgeted sales volume for the first quarter of 2014.

Production. Management desires to maintain ending finished goods inventories at 20% of the next quarter's budgeted sales volume.

Instructions

Prepare the sales budget and production budget by quarters for 2014.

Solution to Comprehensive Do it! 2

ASHEVILLE COMPANY
Sales Budget
For the Year Ending December 31, 2014

	Quarter				
	1	**2**	**3**	**4**	**Year**
Expected unit sales	315,000	525,000	735,000	525,000	2,100,000
Unit selling price	× $70	× $70	× $70	× $75	—
Total sales	$22,050,000	$36,750,000	$51,450,000	$39,375,000	$149,625,000

ASHEVILLE COMPANY
Production Budget
For the Year Ending December 31, 2014

	Quarter				
	1	**2**	**3**	**4**	**Year**
Expected unit sales	315,000	525,000	735,000	525,000	
Add: Desired ending finished goods units	105,000	147,000	105,000	69,300[a]	
Total required units	420,000	672,000	840,000	594,300	
Less: Beginning finished goods units	63,000[b]	105,000	147,000	105,000	
Required production units	357,000	567,000	693,000	489,300	2,106,300

[a]Estimated first-quarter 2015 sales volume 315,000 + (315,000 × 10%) = 346,500; 346,500 × 20%
[b]20% of estimated first-quarter 2014 sales units (315,000 × 20%)

✔ The Navigator

Self-Test Questions

Answers are on page 1131.

(LO 1) **1.** Which of the following is **not** a benefit of budgeting?
  (a) Management can plan ahead.
  (b) An early warning system is provided for potential problems.
  (c) It enables disciplinary action to be taken at every level of responsibility.
  (d) The coordination of activities is facilitated.

(LO 1) **2.** A budget:
  (a) is the responsibility of management accountants.
  (b) is the primary method of communicating agreed-upon objectives throughout an organization.
  (c) ignores past performance because it represents management's plans for a future time period.
  (d) may promote efficiency but has no role in evaluating performance.

(LO 2) **3.** The essentials of effective budgeting do **not** include:
  (a) top-down budgeting.
  (b) management acceptance.
  (c) research and analysis.
  (d) sound organizational structure.

(LO 2) **4.** Compared to budgeting, long-range planning generally has the:
  (a) same amount of detail.
  (b) longer time period.
  (c) same emphasis.
  (d) same time period.

(LO 3) **5.** A sales budget is:
  (a) derived from the production budget.
  (b) management's best estimate of sales revenue for the year.
  (c) not the starting point for the master budget.
  (d) prepared only for credit sales.

(LO 3) **6.** The formula for the production budget is budgeted sales in units plus:
  (a) desired ending merchandise inventory less beginning merchandise inventory.
  (b) beginning finished goods units less desired ending finished goods units.
  (c) desired ending direct materials units less beginning direct materials units.
  (d) desired ending finished goods units less beginning finished goods units.

(LO 3) **7.** Direct materials inventories are kept in pounds in Byrd Company, and the total pounds of direct materials needed for production is 9,500. If the beginning inventory is 1,000 pounds and the desired ending inventory is 2,200 pounds, the total pounds to be purchased is:
  (a) 9,400.   (c) 9,700.
  (b) 9,500.   (d) 10,700.

(LO 3) **8.** The formula for computing the direct labor budget is to multiply the direct labor cost per hour by the:
  (a) total required direct labor hours.
  (b) physical units to be produced.
  (c) equivalent units to be produced.
  (d) No correct answer is given.

(LO 4) **9.** Each of the following budgets is used in preparing the budgeted income statement **except** the:
  (a) sales budget.
  (b) selling and administrative budget.
  (c) capital expenditure budget.
  (d) direct labor budget.

(LO 4) **10.** The budgeted income statement is:
  (a) the end-product of the operating budgets.
  (b) the end-product of the financial budgets.
  (c) the starting point of the master budget.
  (d) dependent on cash receipts and cash disbursements.

(LO 5) **11.** The budgeted balance sheet is:
  (a) developed from the budgeted balance sheet for the preceding year and the budgets for the current year.
  (b) the last operating budget prepared.
  (c) used to prepare the cash budget.
  (d) All of the above.

(LO 5) **12.** The format of a cash budget is:
  (a) Beginning cash balance + Cash receipts + Cash from financing − Cash disbursements = Ending cash balance.
  (b) Beginning cash balance + Cash receipts − Cash disbursements +/− Financing = Ending cash balance.
  (c) Beginning cash balance + Net income − Cash dividends = Ending cash balance.
  (d) Beginning cash balance + Cash revenues − Cash expenses = Ending cash balance.

(LO 5) **13.** Expected direct materials purchases in Read Company are $70,000 in the first quarter and $90,000 in the second quarter. Forty percent of the purchases are paid in cash as incurred, and the balance is paid in the following quarter. The budgeted cash payments for purchases in the second quarter are:
  (a) $96,000.   (c) $78,000.
  (b) $90,000.   (d) $72,000.

(LO 6) **14.** The budget for a merchandiser differs from a budget for a manufacturer because:
  (a) a merchandise purchases budget replaces the production budget.
  (b) the manufacturing budgets are not applicable.
  (c) None of the above.
  (d) Both (a) and (b) above.

(LO 6) 15. In most cases, not-for-profit entities:
  (a) prepare budgets using the same steps as those used by profit-oriented businesses.
  (b) know budgeted cash receipts at the beginning of a time period, so they budget only for expenditures.
  (c) begin the budgeting process by budgeting expenditures rather than receipts.

  (d) can ignore budgets because they are not expected to generate net income.

Go to the book's companion website, **www.wiley.com/college/kimmel**, for additional Self-Test Questions.

Questions

1. (a) What is a budget?
   (b) How does a budget contribute to good management?

2. Kate Cey and Joe Coulter are discussing the benefits of budgeting. They ask you to identify the primary advantages of budgeting. Comply with their request.

3. Jane Gilligan asks your help in understanding the essentials of effective budgeting. Identify the essentials for Jane.

4. (a) "Accounting plays a relatively unimportant role in budgeting." Do you agree? Explain.
   (b) What responsibilities does management have in budgeting?

5. What criteria are helpful in determining the length of the budget period? What is the most common budget period?

6. Lori Wilkins maintains that the only difference between budgeting and long-range planning is time. Do you agree? Why or why not?

7. What is participative budgeting? What are its potential benefits? What are its potential disadvantages?

8. What is budgetary slack? What incentive do managers have to create budgetary slack?

9. Distinguish between a master budget and a sales forecast.

10. What budget is the starting point in preparing the master budget? What may result if this budget is inaccurate?

11. "The production budget shows both unit production data and unit cost data." Is this true? Explain.

12. Alou Company has 20,000 beginning finished goods units. Budgeted sales units are 160,000. If management desires 15,000 ending finished goods units, what are the required units of production?

13. In preparing the direct materials budget for Quan Company, management concludes that required purchases are 64,000 units. If 52,000 direct materials units are required in production and there are 9,000 units of beginning direct materials, what is the desired units of ending direct materials?

14. The production budget of Justus Company calls for 80,000 units to be produced. If it takes 45 minutes to make one unit and the direct labor rate is $16 per hour, what is the total budgeted direct labor cost?

15. Ortiz Company's manufacturing overhead budget shows total variable costs of $198,000 and total fixed costs of $162,000. Total production in units is expected to be 150,000. It takes 20 minutes to make one unit, and the direct labor rate is $15 per hour. Express the manufacturing overhead rate as (a) a percentage of direct labor cost, and (b) an amount per direct labor hour.

16. Everly Company's variable selling and administrative expenses are 12% of net sales. Fixed expenses are $50,000 per quarter. The sales budget shows expected sales of $200,000 and $240,000 in the first and second quarters, respectively. What are the total budgeted selling and administrative expenses for each quarter?

17. For Goody Company, the budgeted cost for one unit of product is direct materials $10, direct labor $20, and manufacturing overhead 80% of direct labor cost. If 25,000 units are expected to be sold at $65 each, what is the budgeted gross profit?

18. Indicate the supporting schedules used in preparing a budgeted income statement through gross profit for a manufacturer.

19. Identify the three sections of a cash budget. What balances are also shown in this budget?

20. Noterman Company has credit sales of $600,000 in January. Past experience suggests that 40% is collected in the month of sale, 50% in the month following the sale, and 10% in the second month following the sale. Compute the cash collections from January sales in January, February, and March.

21. What is the formula for determining required merchandise purchases for a merchandiser?

22. How may expected revenues in a service company be computed?

Brief Exercises

Prepare a diagram of a master budget.
(LO 3), **AN**

BE21-1 Chicksaw Company uses the following budgets: Balance Sheet, Capital Expenditure, Cash, Direct Labor, Direct Materials, Income Statement, Manufacturing Overhead, Production, Sales, and Selling and Administrative. Prepare a diagram of the interrelationships of the budgets in the master budget. Indicate whether each budget is an operating or a financial budget.

BE21-2 Palermo Company estimates that unit sales will be 10,000 in quarter 1; 12,000 in quarter 2; 15,000 in quarter 3; and 18,000 in quarter 4. Using a sales price of $70 per unit, prepare the sales budget by quarters for the year ending December 31, 2014.

Prepare a sales budget.
(LO 3), AP

BE21-3 Sales budget data for Palermo Company are given in BE21-2. Management desires to have an ending finished goods inventory equal to 25% of the next quarter's expected unit sales. Prepare a production budget by quarters for the first 6 months of 2014.

Prepare a production budget for 2 quarters.
(LO 3), AP

BE21-4 Perine Company has 2,000 pounds of raw materials in its December 31, 2013, ending inventory. Required production for January and February of 2014 are 4,000 and 5,000 units, respectively. Two pounds of raw materials are needed for each unit, and the estimated cost per pound is $6. Management desires an ending inventory equal to 25% of next month's materials requirements. Prepare the direct materials budget for January.

Prepare a direct materials budget for 1 month.
(LO 3), AP

BE21-5 For Mize Company, units to be produced are 5,000 in quarter 1 and 6,000 in quarter 2. It takes 1.6 hours to make a finished unit, and the expected hourly wage rate is $15 per hour. Prepare a direct labor budget by quarters for the 6 months ending June 30, 2014.

Prepare a direct labor budget for 2 quarters.
(LO 3), AP

BE21-6 For Roche Inc., variable manufacturing overhead costs are expected to be $20,000 in the first quarter of 2014, with $5,000 increments in each of the remaining three quarters. Fixed overhead costs are estimated to be $40,000 in each quarter. Prepare the manufacturing overhead budget by quarters and in total for the year.

Prepare a manufacturing overhead budget.
(LO 3), AP

BE21-7 Noble Company classifies its selling and administrative expense budget into variable and fixed components. Variable expenses are expected to be $22,000 in the first quarter, and $4,000 increments are expected in the remaining quarters of 2014. Fixed expenses are expected to be $40,000 in each quarter. Prepare the selling and administrative expense budget by quarters and in total for 2014.

Prepare a selling and administrative expense budget.
(LO 3), AP

BE21-8 North Company has completed all of its operating budgets. The sales budget for the year shows 50,000 units and total sales of $2,250,000. The total unit cost of making one unit of sales is $25. Selling and administrative expenses are expected to be $300,000. Income taxes are estimated to be $210,000. Prepare a budgeted income statement for the year ending December 31, 2014.

Prepare a budgeted income statement for the year.
(LO 4), AP

BE21-9 Bruno Industries expects credit sales for January, February, and March to be $200,000, $260,000, and $300,000, respectively. It is expected that 75% of the sales will be collected in the month of sale, and 25% will be collected in the following month. Compute cash collections from customers for each month.

Prepare data for a cash budget.
(LO 5), AP

BE21-10 Moore Wholesalers is preparing its merchandise purchases budget. Budgeted sales are $400,000 for April and $480,000 for May. Cost of goods sold is expected to be 65% of sales. The company's desired ending inventory is 20% of the following month's cost of goods sold. Compute the required purchases for April.

Determine required merchandise purchases for 1 month.
(LO 6), AP

Do it! Review

Do it! 21-1 Use this list of terms to complete the sentences that follow.

Identify budget terminology.
(LO 2, 3), K

Long-range plans	Participative budgeting
Sales forecast	Operating budgets
Master budget	Financial budgets

1. _____ establish goals for the company's sales and production personnel.
2. The _____ is a set of interrelated budgets that constitutes a plan of action for a specified time period.
3. _____ reduces the risk of having unrealistic budgets.
4. _____ include the cash budget and the budgeted balance sheet.
5. The budget is formed within the framework of a _____ .
6. _____ contain considerably less detail than budgets.

Production budget.
(LO 3), **AP**

Do it! 21-2 Zeller Company estimates that 2014 unit sales will be 20,000 in quarter 1, 24,000 in quarter 2, and 29,000 in quarter 3, at a unit selling price of $20. Management desires to have ending finished goods inventory equal to 10% of the next quarter's expected unit sales. Prepare a production budget by quarter for the first 6 months of 2014.

Prepare sales, production, and direct materials budgets.
(LO 3), **AP**

Do it! 21-3 Ash Creek Company is preparing its master budget for 2014. Relevant data pertaining to its sales, production, and direct materials budgets are as follows.

Sales. Sales for the year are expected to total 1,000,000 units. Quarterly sales are 20%, 20%, 30%, and 30%, respectively. The sales price is expected to be $40 per unit for the first three quarters and $45 per unit beginning in the fourth quarter. Sales in the first quarter of 2015 are expected to be 20% higher than the budgeted sales for the first quarter of 2014.

Production. Management desires to maintain the ending finished goods inventories at 25% of the next quarter's budgeted sales volume.

Direct materials. Each unit requires 2 pounds of raw materials at a cost of $12 per pound. Management desires to maintain raw materials inventories at 10% of the next quarter's production requirements. Assume the production requirements for the first quarter of 2015 are 450,000 pounds.

Prepare the sales, production, and direct materials budgets by quarters for 2014.

Calculate budgeted total unit cost and prepare budgeted income statement.
(LO 4), **AP**

Do it! 21-4 Ash Creek Company is preparing its budgeted income statement for 2014. Relevant data pertaining to its sales, production, and direct materials budgets can be found in **Do it!** 21-3.

In addition, Ash Creek budgets 0.3 hours of direct labor per unit, labor costs at $15 per hour, and manufacturing overhead at $20 per direct labor hour. Its budgeted selling and administrative expenses for 2014 are $6,000,000.

(a) Calculate the budgeted total unit cost.
(b) Prepare the budgeted income statement for 2014.

Determine amount of financing needed.
(LO 5), **AP**

Do it! 21-5 Batista Company management wants to maintain a minimum monthly cash balance of $20,000. At the beginning of April, the cash balance is $25,000, expected cash receipts for April are $245,000, and cash disbursements are expected to be $255,000. How much cash, if any, must be borrowed to maintain the desired minimum monthly balance?

Exercises

Explain the concept of budgeting.
(LO 1, 2, 3), **C**

E21-1 Adler Company has always done some planning for the future, but the company has never prepared a formal budget. Now that the company is growing larger, it is considering preparing a budget.

Instructions ━━▶

Write a memo to Jim Dixon, the president of Adler Company, in which you define budgeting, identify the budgets that comprise the master budget, identify the primary benefits of budgeting, and discuss the essentials of effective budgeting.

Prepare a sales budget for 2 quarters.
(LO 3), **AP**

E21-2 Edington Electronics Inc. produces and sells two models of pocket calculators, XQ-103 and XQ-104. The calculators sell for $15 and $25, respectively. Because of the intense competition Edington faces, management budgets sales semiannually. Its projections for the first 2 quarters of 2014 are as follows.

| | Unit Sales | |
Product	Quarter 1	Quarter 2
XQ-103	20,000	22,000
XQ-104	12,000	15,000

No changes in selling prices are anticipated.

Instructions

Prepare a sales budget for the 2 quarters ending June 30, 2014. List the products and show for each quarter and for the 6 months, units, selling price, and total sales by product and in total.

E21-3 Garza and Neely, CPAs, are preparing their service revenue (sales) budget for the coming year (2014). The practice is divided into three departments: auditing, tax, and consulting. Billable hours for each department, by quarter, are provided below.

Prepare a sales budget for 4 quarters.
(LO 3, 6), **AP**

Department	Quarter 1	Quarter 2	Quarter 3	Quarter 4
Auditing	2,300	1,600	2,000	2,400
Tax	3,000	2,200	2,000	2,500
Consulting	1,500	1,500	1,500	1,500

Average hourly billing rates are auditing $80, tax $90, and consulting $100.

Instructions

Prepare the service revenue (sales) budget for 2014 by listing the departments and showing for each quarter and the year in total, billable hours, billable rate, and total revenue.

E21-4 Turney Company produces and sells automobile batteries, the heavy-duty HD-240. The 2014 sales forecast is as follows.

Prepare quarterly production budgets.
(LO 3), **AP**

Quarter	HD-240
1	5,000
2	7,000
3	8,000
4	10,000

The January 1, 2014, inventory of HD-240 is 2,000 units. Management desires an ending inventory each quarter equal to 40% of the next quarter's sales. Sales in the first quarter of 2015 are expected to be 25% higher than sales in the same quarter in 2014.

Instructions

Prepare quarterly production budgets for each quarter and in total for 2014.

E21-5 Dallas Industries has adopted the following production budget for the first 4 months of 2014.

Prepare a direct materials purchases budget.
(LO 3), **AP**

Month	Units	Month	Units
January	10,000	March	5,000
February	8,000	April	4,000

Each unit requires 2 pounds of raw materials costing $2 per pound. On December 31, 2013, the ending raw materials inventory was 4,000 pounds. Management wants to have a raw materials inventory at the end of the month equal to 20% of next month's production requirements.

Instructions

Prepare a direct materials purchases budget by month for the first quarter.

E21-6 On January 1, 2014, the Hardin Company budget committee has reached agreement on the following data for the 6 months ending June 30, 2014.

Prepare production and direct materials budgets by quarters for 6 months.
(LO 3), **AP**

Sales units: First quarter 5,000; second quarter 6,000; third quarter 7,000.

Ending raw materials inventory: 40% of the next quarter's production requirements.

Ending finished goods inventory: 25% of the next quarter's expected sales units.

Third-quarter production: 7,200 units.

The ending raw materials and finished goods inventories at December 31, 2013, follow the same percentage relationships to production and sales that occur in 2014. Three pounds of raw materials are required to make each unit of finished goods. Raw materials purchased are expected to cost $4 per pound.

Instructions

(a) Prepare a production budget by quarters for the 6-month period ended June 30, 2014.
(b) Prepare a direct materials budget by quarters for the 6-month period ended June 30, 2014.

Prepare raw materials purchase budget in dollars.
(LO 3), **AP**

E21-7 Chandler Ltd. estimates sales for the second quarter of 2014 will be as follows.

Month	Units
April	2,550
May	2,475
June	2,390

The target ending inventory of finished products is as follows.

March 31	2,000
April 30	2,230
May 31	2,200
June 30	2,310

Two units of material are required for each unit of finished product. Production for July is estimated at 2,700 units to start building inventory for the fall sales period. Chandler's policy is to have an inventory of raw materials at the end of each month equal to 50% of the following month's production requirements.

Raw materials are expected to cost $4 per unit throughout the period.

Instructions

Calculate the May raw materials purchases in dollars.

(CGA adapted)

Prepare a direct labor budget.
(LO 3), **AP**

E21-8 Rodriguez, Inc., is preparing its direct labor budget for 2014 from the following production budget based on a calendar year.

Quarter	Units	Quarter	Units
1	20,000	3	35,000
2	25,000	4	30,000

Each unit requires 1.5 hours of direct labor.

Instructions

Prepare a direct labor budget for 2014. Wage rates are expected to be $16 for the first 2 quarters and $18 for quarters 3 and 4.

Prepare production and direct labor budgets.
(LO 3), **AP**

E21-9 Donnegal Company makes and sells artistic frames for pictures. The controller is responsible for preparing the master budget and has accumulated the following information for 2014.

	January	February	March	April	May
Estimated unit sales	12,000	14,000	10,000	11,000	11,000
Sales price per unit	$50.00	$47.50	$47.50	$47.50	$47.50
Direct labor hours per unit	2.0	2.0	1.5	1.5	1.5
Wage per direct labor hour	$8.00	$8.00	$8.00	$9.00	$9.00

Donnegal has a labor contract that calls for a wage increase to $9.00 per hour on April 1. New labor-saving machinery has been installed and will be fully operational by March 1.

Donnegal expects to begin the year with 17,600 frames on hand and has a policy of carrying an end-of-month inventory of 100% of the following month's sales, plus 40% of the second following month's sales.

Instructions

Prepare a production budget and a direct labor budget for Donnegal Company by month and for the first quarter of the year. The direct labor budget should include direct labor hours.

(CMA-Canada adapted)

Prepare a manufacturing overhead budget for the year.
(LO 3), **AP**

E21-10 Atlanta Company is preparing its manufacturing overhead budget for 2014. Relevant data consist of the following.

Units to be produced (by quarters): 10,000, 12,000, 14,000, 16,000.

Direct labor: time is 1.5 hours per unit.

Variable overhead costs per direct labor hour: indirect materials $0.80; indirect labor $1.20; and maintenance $0.50.

Fixed overhead costs per quarter: supervisory salaries $35,000; depreciation $15,000; and maintenance $12,000.

Instructions

Prepare the manufacturing overhead budget for the year, showing quarterly data.

E21-11 Duncan Company combines its operating expenses for budget purposes in a selling and administrative expense budget. For the first 6 months of 2014, the following data are available.

1. Sales: 20,000 units quarter 1; 22,000 units quarter 2.
2. Variable costs per dollar of sales: sales commissions 5%, delivery expense 2%, and advertising 4%.
3. Fixed costs per quarter: sales salaries $10,000, office salaries $8,000, depreciation $4,200, insurance $1,500, utilities $800, and repairs expense $500.
4. Unit selling price: $20.

Prepare a selling and administrative expense budget for 2 quarters.
(LO 3), **AP**

Instructions

Prepare a selling and administrative expense budget by quarters for the first 6 months of 2014.

E21-12 Fuqua Company's sales budget projects unit sales of part 198Z of 10,000 units in January, 12,000 units in February, and 13,000 units in March. Each unit of part 198Z requires 4 pounds of materials, which cost $2 per pound. Fuqua Company desires its ending raw materials inventory to equal 40% of the next month's production requirements, and its ending finished goods inventory to equal 20% of the next month's expected unit sales. These goals were met at December 31, 2013.

Prepare a production and a direct materials budget.
(LO 3), **AP**

Instructions

(a) Prepare a production budget for January and February 2014.
(b) Prepare a direct materials budget for January 2014.

E21-13 Dalby Company has accumulated the following budget data for the year 2014.

1. Sales: 30,000 units, unit selling price $85.
2. Cost of one unit of finished goods: direct materials 2 pounds at $5 per pound, direct labor 3 hours at $15 per hour, and manufacturing overhead $5 per direct labor hour.
3. Inventories (raw materials only): beginning, 10,000 pounds; ending, 15,000 pounds.
4. Selling and administrative expenses: $200,000.
5. Income taxes: 30% of income before income taxes.

Prepare a budgeted income statement for the year.
(LO 4), **AP**

Instructions

(a) Prepare a schedule showing the computation of cost of goods sold for 2014.
(b) Prepare a budgeted income statement for 2014.

E21-14 Danner Company expects to have a cash balance of $45,000 on January 1, 2014. Relevant monthly budget data for the first 2 months of 2014 are as follows.

Prepare a cash budget for 2 months.
(LO 5), **AP**

Collections from customers: January $85,000, February $150,000.

Payments for direct materials: January $50,000, February $75,000.

Direct labor: January $30,000, February $45,000. Wages are paid in the month they are incurred.

Manufacturing overhead: January $21,000, February $25,000. These costs include depreciation of $1,500 per month. All other overhead costs are paid as incurred.

Selling and administrative expenses: January $15,000, February $20,000. These costs are exclusive of depreciation. They are paid as incurred.

Sales of marketable securities in January are expected to realize $12,000 in cash. Danner Company has a line of credit at a local bank that enables it to borrow up to $25,000. The company wants to maintain a minimum monthly cash balance of $20,000.

Instructions

Prepare a cash budget for January and February.

E21-15 Aaron Corporation is projecting a cash balance of $30,000 in its December 31, 2013, balance sheet. Aaron's schedule of expected collections from customers for the first quarter of 2014 shows total collections of $180,000. The schedule of expected payments for direct materials for the first quarter of 2014 shows total payments of $41,000. Other information gathered for the first quarter of 2014 is sale of equipment $3,000; direct labor $70,000, manufacturing overhead $35,000, selling and administrative expenses $45,000;

Prepare a cash budget.
(LO 5), **AP**

and purchase of securities $14,000. Aaron wants to maintain a balance of at least $25,000 cash at the end of each quarter.

Instructions

Prepare a cash budget for the first quarter.

Prepare cash budget for a month.
(LO 5), AN

E21-16 The controller of Trenshaw Company wants to improve the company's control system by preparing a month-by-month cash budget. The following information is for the month ending July 31, 2014.

June 30, 2014, cash balance	$45,000
Dividends to be declared on July 15*	12,000
Cash expenditures to be paid in July for operating expenses	40,800
Amortization expense in July	4,500
Cash collections to be received in July	90,000
Merchandise purchases to be paid in cash in July	56,200
Equipment to be purchased for cash in July	20,000

*Dividends are payable 30 days after declaration to shareholders of record on the declaration date.

Trenshaw Company wants to keep a minimum cash balance of $25,000.

Instructions

(a) Prepare a cash budget for the month ended July 31, 2014, and indicate how much money, if any, Trenshaw Company will need to borrow to meet its minimum cash requirement.

(b) Explain how cash budgeting can reduce the cost of short-term borrowing.

(CGA adapted)

Prepare schedules of expected collections and payments.
(LO 5), AP

E21-17 LRF Company's budgeted sales and direct materials purchases are as follows.

	Budgeted Sales	**Budgeted D.M. Purchases**
January	$200,000	$30,000
February	220,000	36,000
March	270,000	40,000

LRF's sales are 30% cash and 70% credit. Credit sales are collected 10% in the month of sale, 50% in the month following sale, and 36% in the second month following sale; 4% are uncollectible. LRF's purchases are 50% cash and 50% on account. Purchases on account are paid 40% in the month of purchase, and 60% in the month following purchase.

Instructions

(a) Prepare a schedule of expected collections from customers for March.

(b) Prepare a schedule of expected payments for direct materials for March.

Prepare schedules for cash receipts and cash payments, and determine ending balances for balance sheet.
(LO 5, 6), AP

E21-18 Green Landscaping Inc. is preparing its budget for the first quarter of 2014. The next step in the budgeting process is to prepare a cash receipts schedule and a cash payments schedule. To that end the following information has been collected.

Clients usually pay 60% of their fee in the month that service is provided, 30% the month after, and 10% the second month after receiving service.

Actual service revenue for 2013 and expected service revenues for 2014 are November 2013, $80,000; December 2013, $90,000; January 2014, $100,000; February 2014, $120,000; March 2014, $140,000.

Purchases of landscaping supplies (direct materials) are paid 60% in the month of purchase and 40% the following month. Actual purchases for 2013 and expected purchases for 2014 are December 2013, $14,000; January 2014, $12,000; February 2014, $15,000; March 2014, $18,000.

Instructions

(a) Prepare the following schedules for each month in the first quarter of 2014 and for the quarter in total:

(1) Expected collections from clients.

(2) Expected payments for landscaping supplies.

(b) Determine the following balances at March 31, 2014:
   (1) Accounts receivable.
   (2) Accounts payable.

E21-19 Lager Dental Clinic is a medium-sized dental service specializing in family dental care. The clinic is currently preparing the master budget for the first 2 quarters of 2014. All that remains in this process is the cash budget. The following information has been collected from other portions of the master budget and elsewhere.

Prepare a cash budget for 2 quarters.

(LO 5, 6), **AP**

Beginning cash balance	$ 30,000
Required minimum cash balance	25,000
Payment of income taxes (2nd quarter)	4,000
Professional salaries:	
1st quarter	140,000
2nd quarter	140,000
Interest from investments (2nd quarter)	7,000
Overhead costs:	
1st quarter	75,000
2nd quarter	100,000
Selling and administrative costs, including	
$2,000 depreciation:	
1st quarter	50,000
2nd quarter	70,000
Purchase of equipment (2nd quarter)	50,000
Sale of equipment (1st quarter)	12,000
Collections from clients:	
1st quarter	230,000
2nd quarter	380,000
Interest payments (2nd quarter)	400

Instructions

Prepare a cash budget for each of the first two quarters of 2014.

E21-20 In May 2014, the budget committee of Grand Stores assembles the following data in preparation of budgeted merchandise purchases for the month of June.

1. Expected sales: June $500,000, July $600,000.
2. Cost of goods sold is expected to be 75% of sales.
3. Desired ending merchandise inventory is 30% of the following (next) month's cost of goods sold.
4. The beginning inventory at June 1 will be the desired amount.

Prepare a purchases budget and budgeted income statement for a merchandiser.

(LO 6), **AP**

Instructions

(a) Compute the budgeted merchandise purchases for June.
(b) Prepare the budgeted income statement for June through gross profit.

Exercises: Set B and Challenge Exercises

Visit the book's companion website, at **www.wiley.com/college/kimmel**, and choose the Student Companion site to access Exercise Set B and Challenge Exercises.

Problems: Set A

P21-1A Glendo Farm Supply Company manufactures and sells a pesticide called Snare. The following data are available for preparing budgets for Snare for the first 2 quarters of 2014.

1. Sales: quarter 1, 30,000 bags; quarter 2, 42,000 bags. Selling price is $60 per bag.
2. Direct materials: each bag of Snare requires 4 pounds of Gumm at a cost of $3.80 per pound and 6 pounds of Tarr at $1.50 per pound.
3. Desired inventory levels:

Prepare budgeted income statement and supporting budgets.

(LO 3, 4), **AP**

Type of Inventory	January 1	April 1	July 1
Snare (bags)	8,000	15,000	18,000
Gumm (pounds)	9,000	10,000	13,000
Tarr (pounds)	14,000	20,000	25,000

4. Direct labor: direct labor time is 15 minutes per bag at an hourly rate of $16 per hour.
5. Selling and administrative expenses are expected to be 15% of sales plus $175,000 per quarter.
6. Income taxes are expected to be 30% of income from operations.

Your assistant has prepared two budgets: (1) The manufacturing overhead budget shows expected costs to be 150% of direct labor cost. (2) The direct materials budget for Tarr shows the cost of Tarr purchases to be $297,000 in quarter 1 and $439,500 in quarter 2.

Instructions

Net income $601,720
Cost per bag $ 34.20

Prepare the budgeted income statement for the first 6 months and all required operating budgets by quarters. (*Note:* Use variable and fixed in the selling and administrative expense budget.) Do not prepare the manufacturing overhead budget or the direct materials budget for Tarr.

Prepare sales, production, direct materials, direct labor, and income statement budgets.

(LO 3, 4), AP

P21-2A Deleon Inc. is preparing its annual budgets for the year ending December 31, 2014. Accounting assistants furnish the data shown below.

	Product JB 50	Product JB 60
Sales budget:		
Anticipated volume in units	400,000	200,000
Unit selling price	$20	$25
Production budget:		
Desired ending finished goods units	30,000	15,000
Beginning finished goods units	25,000	10,000
Direct materials budget:		
Direct materials per unit (pounds)	2	3
Desired ending direct materials pounds	30,000	10,000
Beginning direct materials pounds	40,000	15,000
Cost per pound	$3	$4
Direct labor budget:		
Direct labor time per unit	0.4	0.6
Direct labor rate per hour	$12	$12
Budgeted income statement:		
Total unit cost	$13	$20

An accounting assistant has prepared the detailed manufacturing overhead budget and the selling and administrative expense budget. The latter shows selling expenses of $560,000 for product JB 50 and $360,000 for product JB 60, and administrative expenses of $540,000 for product JB 50 and $340,000 for product JB 60. Income taxes are expected to be 30%.

Instructions

(a) Total sales $13,000,000
(b) Required production units:
    JB 50, 405,000
    JB 60, 205,000
(c) Total cost of direct materials purchases $4,840,000
(d) Total direct labor cost $3,420,000
(e) Net income $1,400,000

Prepare the following budgets for the year. Show data for each product. Quarterly budgets should not be prepared.

(a) Sales
(b) Production
(c) Direct materials
(d) Direct labor
(e) Income statement (*Note:* Income taxes are not allocated to the products.)

Prepare sales and production budgets and compute cost per unit under two plans.

(LO 3, 4), E

P21-3A Marsh Industries had sales in 2013 of $6,400,000 and gross profit of $1,100,000. Management is considering two alternative budget plans to increase its gross profit in 2014.

Plan A would increase the selling price per unit from $8.00 to $8.40. Sales volume would decrease by 10% from its 2013 level. Plan B would decrease the selling price per unit by $0.50. The marketing department expects that the sales volume would increase by 100,000 units.

At the end of 2013, Marsh has 38,000 units of inventory on hand. If Plan A is accepted, the 2014 ending inventory should be equal to 5% of the 2014 sales. If Plan B is accepted, the ending inventory should be equal to 60,000 units. Each unit produced will cost $1.80 in direct labor, $1.30 in direct materials, and $1.20 in variable overhead. The fixed overhead for 2014 should be $1,895,000.

Instructions
(a) Prepare a sales budget for 2014 under each plan.
(b) Prepare a production budget for 2014 under each plan.
(c) Compute the production cost per unit under each plan. Why is the cost per unit different for each of the two plans? (Round to two decimals.)
(d) Which plan should be accepted? (*Hint:* Compute the gross profit under each plan.)

(c) Unit cost:
    Plan A $6.94
    Plan B $6.36
(d) Gross profit:
    Plan A $1,051,200
    Plan B $1,026,000

P21-4A   Colter Company prepares monthly cash budgets. Relevant data from operating budgets for 2014 are:

Prepare cash budget for 2 months.
(LO 5), AP

	January	February
Sales	$360,000	$400,000
Direct materials purchases	120,000	125,000
Direct labor	90,000	100,000
Manufacturing overhead	70,000	75,000
Selling and administrative expenses	79,000	85,000

All sales are on account. Collections are expected to be 50% in the month of sale, 30% in the first month following the sale, and 20% in the second month following the sale. Sixty percent (60%) of direct materials purchases are paid in cash in the month of purchase, and the balance due is paid in the month following the purchase. All other items above are paid in the month incurred except for selling and administrative expenses that include $1,000 of depreciation per month.

Other data:

1. Credit sales: November 2013, $250,000; December 2013, $320,000.
2. Purchases of direct materials: December 2013, $100,000.
3. Other receipts: January—collection of December 31, 2013, notes receivable $15,000;
        February—proceeds from sale of securities $6,000.
4. Other disbursements: February—payment of $6,000 cash dividend.

The company's cash balance on January 1, 2014, is expected to be $60,000. The company wants to maintain a minimum cash balance of $50,000.

Instructions
(a) Prepare schedules for (1) expected collections from customers and (2) expected payments for direct materials purchases for January and February.
(b) Prepare a cash budget for January and February in columnar form.

(a) January:
    collections $326,000
    payments $112,000
(b) Ending cash balance:
    January $51,000
    February $50,000

P21-5A   The budget committee of Litwin Company collects the following data for its San Miguel Store in preparing budgeted income statements for May and June 2014.

Prepare purchases and income statement budgets for a merchandiser.
(LO 6), AP

1. Sales for May are expected to be $800,000. Sales in June and July are expected to be 5% higher than the preceding month.
2. Cost of goods sold is expected to be 75% of sales.
3. Company policy is to maintain ending merchandise inventory at 15% of the following month's cost of goods sold.
4. Operating expenses are estimated to be:

Sales salaries	$30,000 per month
Advertising	6% of monthly sales
Delivery expense	3% of monthly sales
Sales commissions	5% of monthly sales
Rent expense	$5,000 per month
Depreciation	$800 per month
Utilities	$600 per month
Insurance	$500 per month

5. Income taxes are estimated to be 30% of income from operations.

(a) Purchases:
   May $604,500
   June $634,725
(b) Net income:
   May $35,770
   June $38,850

Prepare budgeted income statement and balance sheet.

(LO 4, 5), **AP**

Instructions

(a) Prepare the merchandise purchases budget for each month in columnar form.

(b) Prepare budgeted income statements for each month in columnar form. Show in the statements the details of cost of goods sold.

P21-6A   Krause Industries' balance sheet at December 31, 2013, is presented below.

KRAUSE INDUSTRIES
Balance Sheet
December 31, 2013
Assets

Current assets		
Cash		$ 7,500
Accounts receivable		82,500
Finished goods inventory (1,000 units)		15,000
Total current assets		105,000
Property, plant, and equipment		
Equipment	$40,000	
Less: Accumulated depreciation	10,000	30,000
Total assets		$135,000

Liabilities and Stockholders' Equity

Liabilities		
Notes payable		$ 25,000
Accounts payable		45,000
Total liabilities		70,000
Stockholders' equity		
Common stock	$40,000	
Retained earnings	25,000	
Total stockholders' equity		65,000
Total liabilities and stockholders' equity		$135,000

Additional information accumulated for the budgeting process is as follows. Budgeted data for the year 2014 include the following.

	4th Qtr. of 2014	Year 2014 Total
Sales budget (8,000 units at $32)	$76,800	$256,000
Direct materials used	17,000	62,500
Direct labor	12,500	50,900
Manufacturing overhead applied	10,000	48,600
Selling and administrative expenses	18,000	75,000

To meet sales requirements and to have 3,000 units of finished goods on hand at December 31, 2014, the production budget shows 9,000 required units of output. The total unit cost of production is expected to be $18. Krause Industries uses the first-in, first-out (FIFO) inventory costing method. Selling and administrative expenses include $4,000 for depreciation on equipment. Interest expense is expected to be $3,500 for the year. Income taxes are expected to be 40% of income before income taxes.

All sales and purchases are on account. It is expected that 60% of quarterly sales are collected in cash within the quarter and the remainder is collected in the following quarter. Direct materials purchased from suppliers are paid 50% in the quarter incurred and the remainder in the following quarter. Purchases in the fourth quarter were the same as the materials used. In 2014, the company expects to purchase additional equipment costing $9,000. It expects to pay $8,000 on notes payable plus all interest due and payable to December 31 (included in interest expense $3,500, above). Accounts payable at December 31, 2014, include amounts due suppliers (see above) plus other accounts payable of $6,500. In 2014, the company expects to declare and pay an $8,000 cash dividend.

Unpaid income taxes at December 31 will be $5,000. The company's cash budget shows an expected cash balance of $6,980 at December 31, 2014.

Instructions

Prepare a budgeted income statement for 2014 and a budgeted balance sheet at December 31, 2014. In preparing the income statement, you will need to compute cost of goods manufactured (direct materials + direct labor + manufacturing overhead) and finished goods inventory (December 31, 2014).

Net income	$ 32,700
Total assets	$126,700

Problems: Set B

P21-1B   Mercer Farm Supply Company manufactures and sells a fertilizer called Basic II. The following data are available for preparing budgets for Basic II for the first 2 quarters of 2014.

Prepare budgeted income statement and supporting budgets.

(LO 3, 4), **AP**

1. Sales: quarter 1, 40,000 bags; quarter 2, 50,000 bags. Selling price is $63 per bag.
2. Direct materials: each bag of Basic II requires 5 pounds of Crup at a cost of $3.80 per pound and 10 pounds of Dert at $1.50 per pound.
3. Desired inventory levels:

Type of Inventory	January 1	April 1	July 1
Basic II (bags)	10,000	15,000	20,000
Crup (pounds)	9,000	12,000	15,000
Dert (pounds)	15,000	20,000	25,000

4. Direct labor: direct labor time is 15 minutes per bag at an hourly rate of $12 per hour.
5. Selling and administrative expenses are expected to be 10% of sales plus $150,000 per quarter.
6. Income taxes are expected to be 30% of income from operations.

Your assistant has prepared two budgets: (1) The manufacturing overhead budget shows expected costs to be 100% of direct labor cost. (2) The direct materials budget for Dert which shows the cost of Dert to be $682,500 in quarter 1 and $832,500 in quarter 2.

Instructions

Prepare the budgeted income statement for the first 6 months of 2014 and all required supporting budgets by quarters. (*Note:* Use variable and fixed in the selling and administrative expense budget.) Do not prepare the manufacturing overhead budget or the direct materials budget for Dert.

Net income	$842,100
Cost per bag	$ 40.00

P21-2B   Urbina Inc. is preparing its annual budgets for the year ending December 31, 2014. Accounting assistants furnish the following data.

Prepare sales, production, direct materials, direct labor, and income statement budgets.

(LO 3, 4), **AP**

	Product LN 35	Product LN 40
Sales budget:		
Anticipated volume in units	400,000	240,000
Unit selling price	$25	$35
Production budget:		
Desired ending finished goods units	20,000	25,000
Beginning finished goods units	30,000	15,000
Direct materials budget:		
Direct materials per unit (pounds)	2	3
Desired ending direct materials pounds	50,000	10,000
Beginning direct materials pounds	40,000	20,000
Cost per pound	$2	$3
Direct labor budget:		
Direct labor time per unit	0.5	0.75
Direct labor rate per hour	$12	$12
Budgeted income statement:		
Total unit cost	$12	$22

An accounting assistant has prepared the detailed manufacturing overhead budget and the selling and administrative expense budget. The latter shows selling expenses of $750,000 for product LN 35 and $580,000 for product LN 40, and administrative expenses of $420,000 for product LN 35 and $380,000 for product LN 40. Income taxes are expected to be 30%.

Instructions

Prepare the following budgets for the year. Show data for each product. You do not need to prepare quarterly budgets.

(a) Sales (d) Direct labor
(b) Production (e) Income statement (*Note:* Income taxes are
(c) Direct materials not allocated to the products.)

P21-3B Ogleby Industries has sales in 2013 of $5,600,000 (800,000 units) and gross profit of $1,344,000. Management is considering two alternative budget plans to increase its gross profit in 2014.

Plan A would increase the selling price per unit from $7.00 to $7.60. Sales volume would decrease by 5% from its 2013 level. Plan B would decrease the selling price per unit by 5%. The marketing department expects that the sales volume would increase by 150,000 units.

At the end of 2013, Ogleby has 70,000 units on hand. If Plan A is accepted, the 2014 ending inventory should be equal to 90,000 units. If Plan B is accepted, the ending inventory should be equal to 100,000 units. Each unit produced will cost $2.00 in direct materials, $1.50 in direct labor, and $0.50 in variable overhead. The fixed overhead for 2014 should be $980,000.

Instructions

(a) Prepare a sales budget for 2014 under (1) Plan A and (2) Plan B.
(b) Prepare a production budget for 2014 under (1) Plan A and (2) Plan B.
(c) Compute the cost per unit under (1) Plan A and (2) Plan B. Explain why the cost per unit is different for each of the two plans. (Round to two decimals.)
(d) Which plan should be accepted? (*Hint:* Compute the gross profit under each plan.)

P21-4B Derby Company prepares monthly cash budgets. Relevant data from operating budgets for 2014 are:

	January	February
Sales	$350,000	$400,000
Direct materials purchases	110,000	120,000
Direct labor	85,000	115,000
Manufacturing overhead	60,000	75,000
Selling and administrative expenses	75,000	80,000

All sales are on account. Collections are expected to be 60% in the month of sale, 25% in the first month following the sale, and 15% in the second month following the sale. Thirty percent (30%) of direct materials purchases are paid in cash in the month of purchase, and the balance due is paid in the month following the purchase. All other items above are paid in the month incurred. Depreciation has been excluded from manufacturing overhead and selling and administrative expenses.

Other data:

1. Credit sales: November 2013, $200,000; December 2013, $290,000.
2. Purchases of direct materials: December 2013, $90,000.
3. Other receipts: January—collection of December 31, 2013, interest receivable $3,000; February—proceeds from sale of securities $5,000.
4. Other disbursements: February—payment of $20,000 for land.

The company's cash balance on January 1, 2014, is expected to be $50,000. The company wants to maintain a minimum cash balance of $40,000.

Instructions

(a) Prepare schedules for (1) expected collections from customers and (2) expected payments for direct materials purchases.
(b) Prepare a cash budget for January and February in columnar form.

Margin notes (left column):

(a) Total sales $18,400,000
(b) Required production units:
 LN 35, 390,000
(c) Total cost of direct materials purchases $3,800,000
(d) Total direct labor cost $4,590,000
(e) Net income $4,333,000

Prepare sales and production budgets and compute cost per unit under two plans.
(LO 3, 4), **E**

(c) Unit cost:
 Plan A $5.26
 Plan B $5.00
(d) Gross profit:
 Plan A $1,778,400
 Plan B $1,567,500

Prepare cash budget for 2 months.
(LO 5), **AP**

(a) January:
 collections $312,500
 payments $96,000
(b) Ending cash balance:
 January $49,500
 February $40,000

P21-5B The budget committee of Widner Company collects the following data for its Westwood Store in preparing budgeted income statements for July and August 2014.

Prepare purchases and income statement budgets for a merchandiser.
(LO 6), **AP**

1. Expected sales: July $400,000, August $450,000, September $500,000.
2. Cost of goods sold is expected to be 65% of sales.
3. Company policy is to maintain ending merchandise inventory at 15% of the following month's cost of goods sold.
4. Operating expenses are estimated to be:

Sales salaries	$50,000 per month
Advertising	5% of monthly sales
Delivery expense	2% of monthly sales
Sales commissions	4% of monthly sales
Rent expense	$3,000 per month
Depreciation	$700 per month
Utilities	$500 per month
Insurance	$300 per month

5. Income taxes are estimated to be 30% of income from operations.

Instructions
(a) Prepare the merchandise purchases budget for each month in columnar form.
(b) Prepare budgeted income statements for each month in columnar form. Show the details of cost of goods sold in the statements.

(a) Purchases:
   July $264,875
   August $297,375
(b) Net income:
   July $29,050
   August $37,450

Problems: Set C

Visit the book's companion website, at **www.wiley.com/college/kimmel**, and choose the Student Companion site to access Problem Set C.

Waterways Continuing Problem

(This is a continuation of the Waterways Problem from Chapters 14 through 20.)

WCP21 Waterways Corporation is preparing its budget for the coming year, 2014. The first step is to plan for the first quarter of that coming year. The company has gathered information from its managers in preparation of the budgeting process. This problem asks you to prepare the various budgets that comprise the master budget for 2014.

> Go to the book's companion website, at **www.wiley.com/college/kimmel**, to find the completion of this problem.

Broadening Your Perspective

Management Decision-Making

DECISION-MAKING AT CURRENT DESIGNS

BYP21-1 Diane Buswell is preparing the 2013 budget for one of Current Designs' rotomolded kayaks. Extensive meetings with members of the sales department and executive team have resulted in the following unit sales projections for 2013.

Quarter 1	1,000 kayaks
Quarter 2	1,500 kayaks
Quarter 3	750 kayaks
Quarter 4	750 kayaks

Current Designs' policy is to have finished goods ending inventory in a quarter equal to 20% of the next quarter's anticipated sales. Preliminary sales projections for 2014 are 1,100 units for the first quarter and 1,500 units for the second quarter. Ending inventory of finished goods at December 31, 2012, will be 200 rotomolded kayaks.

Production of each kayak requires 54 pounds of polyethylene powder and a finishing kit (rope, seat, hardware, etc.). Company policy is that the ending inventory of polyethylene powder should be 25% of the amount needed for production in the next quarter. Assume that the ending inventory of polyethylene powder on December 31, 2012, is 19,400 pounds. The finishing kits can be assembled as they are needed. As a result, Current Designs does not maintain a significant inventory of the finishing kits.

The polyethylene powder used in these kayaks costs $1.50 per pound, and the finishing kits cost $170 each. Production of a single kayak requires 2 hours of time by more experienced, type I employees and 3 hours of finishing time by type II employees. The type I employees are paid $15 per hour, and the type II employees are paid $12 per hour.

Selling and administrative expenses for this line are expected to be $45 per unit sold plus $7,500 per quarter. Manufacturing overhead is assigned at 150% of labor costs.

Instructions

Prepare the production budget, direct materials budget, direct labor budget, manufacturing overhead budget, and selling and administrative budget for this product line by quarter and in total for 2013.

DECISION-MAKING ACROSS THE ORGANIZATION

BYP21-2 Palmer Corporation operates on a calendar-year basis. It begins the annual budgeting process in late August when the president establishes targets for the total dollar sales and net income before taxes for the next year.

The sales target is given first to the marketing department. The marketing manager formulates a sales budget by product line in both units and dollars. From this budget, sales quotas by product line in units and dollars are established for each of the corporation's sales districts. The marketing manager also estimates the cost of the marketing activities required to support the target sales volume and prepares a tentative marketing expense budget.

The executive vice president uses the sales and profit targets, the sales budget by product line, and the tentative marketing expense budget to determine the dollar amounts that can be devoted to manufacturing and corporate office expense. The executive vice president prepares the budget for corporate expenses. She then forwards to the production department the product-line sales budget in units and the total dollar amount that can be devoted to manufacturing.

The production manager meets with the factory managers to develop a manufacturing plan that will produce the required units when needed within the cost constraints set by the executive vice president. The budgeting process usually comes to a halt at this point because the production department does not consider the financial resources allocated to be adequate.

When this standstill occurs, the vice president of finance, the executive vice president, the marketing manager, and the production manager meet together to determine the final budgets for each of the areas. This normally results in a modest increase in the total amount available for manufacturing costs and cuts in the marketing expense and corporate office expense budgets. The total sales and net income figures proposed by the president are seldom changed. Although the participants are seldom pleased with the compromise, these budgets are final. Each executive then develops a new detailed budget for the operations in his or her area.

None of the areas has achieved its budget in recent years. Sales often run below the target. When budgeted sales are not achieved, each area is expected to cut costs so that the president's profit target can be met. However, the profit target is seldom met because costs are not cut enough. In fact, costs often run above the original budget in all functional areas (marketing, production, and corporate office).

The president is disturbed that Palmer has not been able to meet the sales and profit targets. He hired a consultant with considerable experience with companies in Palmer's industry. The consultant reviewed the budgets for the past 4 years. He concluded that the product line sales budgets were reasonable and that the cost and expense budgets were adequate for the budgeted sales and production levels.

Instructions

With the class divided into groups, answer the following.
(a) Discuss how the budgeting process employed by Palmer Corporation contributes to the failure to achieve the president's sales and profit targets.
(b) Suggest how Palmer Corporation's budgeting process could be revised to correct the problems.
(c) Should the functional areas be expected to cut their costs when sales volume falls below budget? Explain your answer.

(CMA adapted)

MANAGERIAL ANALYSIS

BYP21-3 Elliot & Hesse Inc. manufactures ergonomic devices for computer users. Some of its more popular products include glare screens (for computer monitors), keyboard stands with wrist rests, and carousels that allow easy access to discs. Over the past 5 years, it experienced rapid growth, with sales of all products increasing 20% to 50% each year.

Last year, some of the primary manufacturers of computers began introducing new products with some of the ergonomic designs, such as glare screens and wrist rests, already built in. As a result, sales of Elliot & Hesse's accessory devices have declined somewhat. The company believes that the disc carousels will probably continue to show growth, but that the other products will probably continue to decline. When the next year's budget was prepared, increases were built into research and development so that replacement products could be developed or the company could expand into some other product line. Some product lines being considered are general-purpose ergonomic devices including back supports, foot rests, and sloped writing pads.

The most recent results have shown that sales decreased more than was expected for the glare screens. As a result, the company may have a shortage of funds. Top management has therefore asked that all expenses be reduced 10% to compensate for these reduced sales. Summary budget information is as follows.

Direct materials	$240,000
Direct labor	110,000
Insurance	50,000
Depreciation	90,000
Machine repairs	30,000
Sales salaries	50,000
Office salaries	80,000
Factory salaries (indirect labor)	50,000
Total	$700,000

Instructions

Using the information above, answer the following questions.
(a) What are the implications of reducing each of the costs? For example, if the company reduces direct materials costs, it may have to do so by purchasing lower-quality materials. This may affect sales in the long run.
(b) Based on your analysis in (a), what do you think is the best way to obtain the $70,000 in cost savings requested? Be specific. Are there any costs that cannot or should not be reduced? Why?

REAL-WORLD FOCUS

BYP21-4 Network Computing Devices, Inc. was founded in 1988 in Mountain View, California. The company develops software products such as X-terminals, Z-mail, PC X-ware, and related hardware products. The following is a discussion by management in its annual report.

NETWORK COMPUTING DEVICES, INC.
Management Discussion

The Company's operating results have varied significantly, particularly on a quarterly basis, as a result of a number of factors, including general economic conditions affecting industry demand for computer products, the timing and market acceptance of new product introductions by the Company and its competitors, the timing of significant orders from large customers, periodic changes in product pricing and discounting due to competitive factors, and the availability of key components, such as video monitors and electronic subassemblies, some of which require substantial order lead times. The Company's operating results may fluctuate in the future as a result of these and other factors, including the Company's success in developing and introducing new products, its product and customer mix, and the level of competition which it experiences. The Company operates with a small backlog. Sales and operating results, therefore, generally depend on the volume and timing of orders received, which are difficult to forecast. The Company has experienced slowness in orders from some customers during the first quarter of each calendar year due to budgeting cycles common in the computer industry. In addition, sales in Europe typically are adversely affected in the third calendar quarter as many European customers reduce their business activities during the month of August.

Due to the Company's rapid growth rate and the effect of new product introductions on quarterly revenues, these seasonal trends have not materially impacted the Company's results of operations to date. However, as the Company's product lines mature and its rate of revenue growth declines, these seasonal factors may become more evident. Additionally, the Company's international sales are denominated in U.S. dollars, and an increase or decrease in the value of the U.S. dollar relative to foreign currencies could make the Company's products less or more competitive in those markets.

Instructions
(a) Identify the factors that affect the budgeting process at Network Computing Devices, Inc.
(b) Explain the additional budgeting concerns created by the international operations of the company.

BYP21-5 Information regarding many approaches to budgeting can be found on the Web. The following activity investigates the merits of "zero-based" budgeting, as discussed by Michael LaFaive, Director of Financial Policy of the Mackinac Center for Public Policy.

Address: www.mackinac.org/article.aspx?ID=5928, or go to **www.wiley.com/college/kimmel**

Instructions
Read the article at the website and answer the following questions.
(a) How does zero-based budgeting differ from standard budgeting procedures?
(b) What are some potential advantages of zero-based budgeting?
(c) What are some potential disadvantages of zero-based budgeting?
(d) How often do departments in Oklahoma undergo zero-based budgeting?

Critical Thinking

COMMUNICATION ACTIVITY

BYP21-6 In order to better serve their rural patients, Drs. Joe and Rick Parcells (brothers) began giving safety seminars. Especially popular were their "emergency-preparedness" talks given to farmers. Many people asked whether the "kit" of materials the doctors recommended for common farm emergencies was commercially available.

After checking with several suppliers, the doctors realized that no other company offered the supplies they recommended in their seminars, packaged in the way they described. Their wives, Megan and Sue, agreed to make a test package by ordering supplies from various medical supply companies and assembling them into a "kit" that could be sold at the seminars. When these kits proved a runaway success, the sisters-in-law decided to market them. At the advice of their accountant, they organized this venture as a separate company, called Life Protection Products (LPP), with Megan Parcells as CEO and Sue Parcells as Secretary-Treasurer.

LPP soon started receiving requests for the kits from all over the country, as word spread about their availability. Even without advertising, LPP was able to sell its full inventory every month. However, the company was becoming financially strained. Megan and Sue had about $100,000 in savings, and they invested about half that amount initially. They believed that this venture would allow them to make money. However, at the present time, only about $30,000 of the cash remains, and the company is constantly short of cash.

Megan has come to you for advice. She does not understand why the company is having cash flow problems. She and Sue have not even been withdrawing salaries. However, they have rented a local building and have hired two more full-time workers to help them cope with the increasing demand. They do not think they could handle the demand without this additional help.

Megan is also worried that the cash problems mean that the company may not be able to support itself. She has prepared the cash budget shown below. All seminar customers pay for their products in full at the time of purchase. In addition, several large companies have ordered the kits for use by employees who work in remote sites. They have requested credit terms and have been allowed to pay in the month following the sale. These large purchasers amount to about 25% of the sales at the present time. LPP purchases the materials for the kits about 2 months ahead of time. Megan and Sue are considering slowing the growth of the company by simply purchasing less materials, which will mean selling fewer kits.

The workers are paid weekly. Megan and Sue need about $15,000 cash on hand at the beginning of the month to pay for purchases of raw materials. Right now they have been using cash from their savings, but as noted, only $30,000 is left.

Instructions

Write a response to Megan Parcells. Explain why LPP is short of cash. Will this company be able to support itself? Explain your answer. Make any recommendations you deem appropriate.

LIFE PROTECTION PRODUCTS
Cash Budget
For the Quarter Ending June 30, 2014

	April	May	June
Cash balance, beginning	$15,000	$15,000	$15,000
Cash received			
From prior month sales	5,000	7,500	12,500
From current sales	15,000	22,500	37,500
Total cash on hand	35,000	45,000	65,000
Cash payments			
To employees	3,000	3,000	3,000
For products	25,000	35,000	45,000
Miscellaneous expenses	5,000	6,000	7,000
Postage	1,000	1,000	1,000
Total cash payments	34,000	45,000	56,000
Cash balance	$ 1,000	$ 0	$ 9,000
Borrow from savings	$14,000	$15,000	$ 1,000
Borrow from bank?	$ 0	$ 0	$ 5,000

ETHICS CASE

BYP21-7 You are an accountant in the budgetary, projections, and special projects department of Fernetti Conductor, Inc., a large manufacturing company. The president, Richard Brown, asks you on very short notice to prepare some sales and income projections covering the next 2 years of the company's much heralded new product lines. He wants these projections for a series of speeches he is making while on a 2-week trip to eight East Coast brokerage firms. The president hopes to bolster Fernetti's stock sales and price.

You work 23 hours in 2 days to compile the projections, hand-deliver them to the president, and are swiftly but graciously thanked as he departs. A week later, you find time to go over some of your computations and discover a miscalculation that makes the projections grossly overstated. You quickly inquire about the president's itinerary and learn that he has made half of his speeches and has half yet to make. You are in a quandary as to what to do.

Instructions
(a) What are the consequences of telling the president of your gross miscalculations?
(b) What are the consequences of not telling the president of your gross miscalculations?
(c) What are the ethical considerations to you and the president in this situation?

ALL ABOUT YOU

BYP21-8 In order to get your personal finances under control, you need to prepare a personal budget. Assume that you have compiled the following information regarding your expected cash flows for a typical month.

Rent payment	$ 500	Miscellaneous costs	$210
Interest income	50	Savings	50
Income tax withheld	300	Eating out	150
Electricity bill	85	Telephone and Internet costs	125
Groceries	100	Student loan payments	375
Wages earned	2,500	Entertainment costs	250
Insurance	100	Transportation costs	150

Instructions
Using the information above, prepare a personal budget. In preparing this budget, use the format found at **http://financialplan.about.com/cs/budgeting/l/blbudget.htm**. Just skip any unused line items.

CONSIDERING YOUR COSTS AND BENEFITS

BYP21-9 You might hear people say that they "need to learn to live within a budget." The funny thing is that most people who say this haven't actually prepared a personal budget, nor do they intend to. Instead, what they are referring to is a vaguely defined, poorly specified collection of rough ideas of how much they should spend on various aspects of their lives. However, you can't live within or even outside of something that doesn't exist. With that in mind, let's take a look at one aspect of personal-budget templates.

Many personal-budget worksheet templates that are provided for college students treat student loans as an income source. See, for example, the template provided at **http://financialplan. about.com/cs/budgeting/l/blmocolbud.htm**. Based on your knowledge of accounting, is this correct?

YES: Student loans provide a source of cash, which can be used to pay costs. As the saying goes, "It all spends the same." Therefore, student loans are income.

NO: Student loans must eventually be repaid; therefore, they are not income. As the name suggests, they are loans.

Instructions
Write a response indicating your position regarding this situation. Provide support for your view.

Answers to Insight and Accounting Across the Organization Questions

p. 1084 Businesses Often Feel Too Busy to Plan for the Future Q: Describe a situation in which a business "sells as much as it can" but cannot "keep its employees paid." **A:** If sales are made to customers on credit and collection is slow, the company may find that it does not have enough cash to pay employees or suppliers. Without these resources, the company will fail to survive.

p. 1089 The Implications of Budgetary Optimism Q: Why is it important that government budgets accurately estimate future revenues during economic downturns? **A:** Accuracy of government revenue estimates is especially important during economic downturns because most governments must balance their budgets. If anticipated revenues in one period do not match expectations, then the shortfall must be made up in the next period. This can result in much steeper, more disruptive cuts than might have been necessary had the government anticipated the revenue decline more accurately and consequently started cutting expenditures sooner.

p. 1091 Betting That Prices Won't Fall Q: What are the potential downsides of stockpiling a huge amount of raw materials? **A:** If prices continue to go up, these managers will avoid paying higher prices until their inventory runs out. However, it is a risky strategy. First of all, prices fluctuate. If a price goes up by 90% in a year, it can also go down by 90%. If this happens, the managers will be stuck with overpriced raw materials. Second, if the economy slows down, it might take a lot longer to sell their inventory than they had planned. There are many costs associated with holding large quantities of inventory. The additional storage, insurance, and handling costs can be very expensive, and obsolescence can occur.

p. 1099 Without a Budget, Can the Games Begin? Q: Why does it matter whether the Olympic Games exceed their budget? **A:** If the Olympic Games exceed their budget, taxpayers of the sponsoring community and country will end up footing the bill. Depending on the size of the losses, and the resources of the community, this could produce a substantial burden. As a result, other communities might be reluctant to host the Olympics in the future.

p. 1104 Budget Shortfalls as Far as the Eye Can See Q: Why would a university's budgeted scholarships probably fall when the stock market suffers a serious drop? **A:** Scholarships typically cannot be paid out of the "principal" portion of donations made to scholarship endowment funds. Instead, scholarships are usually funded through earnings generated by endowment investments. Any excess earnings above current-year scholarship needs can be used for scholarships in subsequent years. But a serious drop in the value of endowment investments can wipe out previous earnings, in some cases completely eliminating funds available for scholarships.

Answers to Self-Test Questions

1. c 2. b 3. a 4. b 5. b 6. d 7. d (9,500 + 2,200 − 1,000) 8. a 9. c
10. a 11. a 12. b 13. c [($70,000 × 60%) + ($90,000 × 40%)] 14. d 15. c

CHAPTER 22

Marcus Clackson/iStockphoto

✔ The Navigator

- Scan Learning Objectives
- Read Feature Story
- Scan Preview
- Read Text and Answer **Do it!**
  ○ p. 1142 ○ p. 1144 ○ p. 1155
  ○ p. 1159
- Work Using the Decision Toolkit
- Review Summary of Learning Objectives
- Work Comprehensive **Do it!** p. 1165
- Answer Self-Test Questions
- Complete Assignments
- Go to WileyPLUS for practice and tutorials

BUDGETARY CONTROL AND RESPONSIBILITY ACCOUNTING

LEARNING OBJECTIVES

After studying this chapter, you should be able to:

1 Describe the concept of budgetary control.

2 Evaluate the usefulness of static budget reports.

3 Explain the development of flexible budgets and the usefulness of flexible budget reports.

4 Describe the concept of responsibility accounting.

5 Indicate the features of responsibility reports for cost centers.

6 Identify the content of responsibility reports for profit centers.

7 Explain the basis and formula used in evaluating performance in investment centers.

✔ The Navigator

Vancouver teenager Brian Scudamore needed to raise money to pay his way through college. With $700 and a strong desire to do it on his own, he established a junk removal company. Fifteen years later, 1-800-GOT-JUNK? had 113 franchise partners across Canada and the United States, and projected revenues of more than $60 million.

"It was a high-school business project that was out of control," says Cameron Herold, vice president of operations.

While the exponential growth of 1-800-GOT-JUNK? may seem unwieldy (at one point it had five consecutive years of 100-percent compounded growth), it has in fact involved sound financial planning, budgeting, and cash management. The company only spends money it has; it has no outside investors or debt.

Managing this growth involves forecasting everything by creating a "painted picture" of what the company will look like in three years. The company knows its staffing plans, training requirements, and overhead and office space needs well in advance. "That filters back to our budgeting process," Mr. Herold says. "We'll sit down and say, 'If this is where we're going, what

TURNING TRASH INTO TREASURE

are all the components of that?' . . . Then we bring it back to zero and say, 'What's it going to cost us? Where does it fit into the budget?'"

Key to the company's growth management was the introduction of franchising. "We chose franchising because our franchise partners would actually finance our growth," Mr. Herold says. In addition to the initial franchise fee, franchisees pay the head office 8 percent of their sales, plus another 7 percent to run the centralized call center.

While the company has used franchising to manage growth, a frugal approach to day-to-day costs has also been integral to its budgeting success. "We're always looking for ways to cut costs," Mr. Herold says. This includes establishing strategic relationships with the local coffee shop, doing regular cost analyses of office equipment and changing suppliers when needed, and buying office furniture in bulk from liquidators at 10 cents on the dollar. "All those little things start to really add up," he says.

Watch the Tribeca Grand video in WileyPLUS to learn more about budgeting in the real world.

✔ The Navigator

In contrast to Chapter 21, we now consider how budgets are used by management to control operations. In the Feature Story on 1-800-GOT-JUNK?, we saw that management uses the budget to adapt to the business environment. This chapter focuses on two aspects of management control: (1) budgetary control and (2) responsibility accounting.

The content and organization of Chapter 22 are as follows.

Budgetary Control and Responsibility Accounting

Budgetary Control	Static Budget Reports	Flexible Budgets	Responsibility Accounting	Types of Responsibility Centers
• Budget reports	• Examples	• Why flexible budgets?	• Controllable vs. noncontrollable	• Cost centers
• Control activities	• Uses and limitations	• Development	• Performance evaluation	• Profit centers
• Reporting systems		• Case study	• Reporting system	• Investment centers
		• Reports		

✔ The Navigator

Budgetary Control

LEARNING OBJECTIVE 1
Describe the concept of budgetary control.

One of management's functions is to control company operations. Control consists of the steps taken by management to see that planned objectives are met. We now ask: How do budgets contribute to control of operations?

The use of budgets in controlling operations is known as **budgetary control**. Such control takes place by means of **budget reports** that compare actual results with planned objectives. The use of budget reports is based on the belief that planned objectives lose much of their potential value without some monitoring of progress along the way. Just as your professors give midterm exams to evaluate your progress, top management requires periodic reports on the progress of department managers toward their planned objectives.

Budget reports provide management with feedback on operations. The feedback for a crucial objective, such as having enough cash on hand to pay bills, may be made daily. For other objectives, such as meeting budgeted annual sales and operating expenses, monthly budget reports may suffice. Budget reports are prepared as frequently as needed. From these reports, management analyzes any differences between actual and planned results and determines their causes. Management then takes corrective action, or it decides to modify future plans. Budgetary control involves the activities shown in Illustration 22-1.

Budgetary control works best when a company has a formalized reporting system. The system does the following:

1. Identifies the name of the budget report, such as the sales budget or the manufacturing overhead budget.
2. States the frequency of the report, such as weekly or monthly.
3. Specifies the purpose of the report.
4. Indicates the primary recipient(s) of the report.

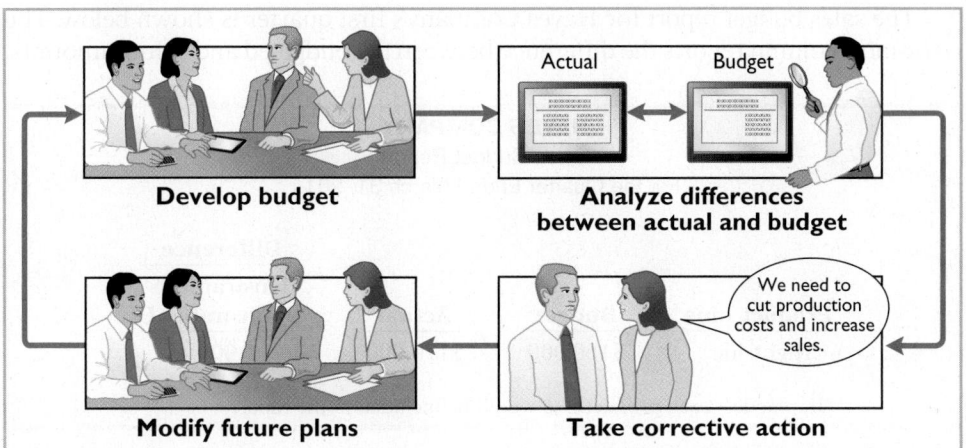

Illustration 22-1 Budgetary control activities

Illustration 22-2 provides a partial budgetary control system for a manufacturing company. Note the frequency of the reports and their emphasis on control. For example, there is a daily report on scrap and a weekly report on labor.

Illustration 22-2 Budgetary control reporting system

Name of Report	Frequency	Purpose	Primary Recipient(s)
Sales	Weekly	Determine whether sales goals are met	Top management and sales manager
Labor	Weekly	Control direct and indirect labor costs	Vice president of production and production department managers
Scrap	Daily	Determine efficient use of materials	Production manager
Departmental overhead costs	Monthly	Control overhead costs	Department manager
Selling expenses	Monthly	Control selling expenses	Sales manager
Income statement	Monthly and quarterly	Determine whether income goals are met	Top management

Static Budget Reports

You learned in Chapter 21 that the master budget formalizes management's planned objectives for the coming year. When used in budgetary control, each budget included in the master budget is considered to be static. A **static budget** is a projection of budget data **at one level of activity**. These budgets do not consider data for different levels of activity. As a result, companies always compare actual results with budget data at the activity level that was used in developing the master budget.

LEARNING OBJECTIVE 2

Evaluate the usefulness of static budget reports.

EXAMPLES

To illustrate the role of a static budget in budgetary control, we will use selected data prepared for Hayes Company in Chapter 21. Budget and actual sales data for the Rightride product in the first and second quarters of 2014 are as follows.

Illustration 22-3 Budget and actual sales data

Sales	First Quarter	Second Quarter	Total
Budgeted	$180,000	$210,000	$390,000
Actual	179,000	199,500	378,500
Difference	$ 1,000	$ 10,500	$ 11,500

The sales budget report for Hayes Company's first quarter is shown below. The right-most column reports the difference between the budgeted and actual amounts.

Illustration 22-4 Sales budget report—first quarter

HAYES COMPANY
Sales Budget Report
For the Quarter Ended March 31, 2014

			Difference
			Favorable F
Product Line	Budget	Actual	Unfavorable U
Rightride[a]	$180,000	$179,000	$1,000 U

[a]In practice, each product line would be included in the report.

Alternative Terminology The difference between budget and actual is sometimes called a *budget variance.*

The report shows that sales are $1,000 under budget—an unfavorable result. This difference is less than 1% of budgeted sales ($1,000 ÷ $180,000 = .0056). Top management's reaction to unfavorable differences is often influenced by the materiality (significance) of the difference. Since the difference of $1,000 is immaterial in this case, we assume that Hayes Company management takes no specific corrective action.

Illustration 22-5 shows the budget report for the second quarter. It contains one new feature: cumulative year-to-date information. This report indicates that sales for the second quarter are $10,500 below budget. This is 5% of budgeted sales ($10,500 ÷ $210,000). Top management may now conclude that the difference between budgeted and actual sales requires investigation.

HAYES COMPANY
Sales Budget Report
For the Quarter Ended June 30, 2014

	Second Quarter			Year-to-Date		
			Difference			Difference
			Favorable F			Favorable F
Product Line	Budget	Actual	Unfavorable U	Budget	Actual	Unfavorable U
Rightride	$210,000	$199,500	$10,500 U	$390,000	$378,500	$11,500 U

Illustration 22-5 Sales budget report—second quarter

Management's analysis should start by asking the sales manager the cause(s) of the shortfall. Managers should consider the need for corrective action. For example, management may decide to spur sales by offering sales incentives to customers or by increasing the advertising of Rightrides. Or, if management concludes that a downturn in the economy is responsible for the lower sales, it may modify planned sales and profit goals for the remainder of the year.

USES AND LIMITATIONS

From these examples, you can see that a master sales budget is useful in evaluating the performance of a sales manager. It is now necessary to ask: Is the master budget appropriate for evaluating a manager's performance in controlling costs? Recall that in a static budget, data are not modified or adjusted, regardless of changes in activity. It follows, then, that a static budget is appropriate in evaluating a manager's effectiveness in controlling costs when:

1. The actual level of activity closely approximates the master budget activity level, and/or
2. The behavior of the costs in response to changes in activity is fixed.

Static budgets report a single level of activity

A static budget report is, therefore, appropriate for **fixed manufacturing costs** and for **fixed selling and administrative expenses**. But, as you will see shortly, static budget reports may not be a proper basis for evaluating a manager's performance in controlling variable costs.

Flexible Budgets

In contrast to a static budget, which is based on one level of activity, a flexible budget projects budget data for various levels of activity. In essence, **the flexible budget is a series of static budgets at different levels of activity**. The flexible budget recognizes that the budgetary process is more useful if it is adaptable to changed operating conditions.

Flexible budgets can be prepared for each of the types of budgets included in the master budget. For example, Marriott Hotels can budget revenues and net income on the basis of 60%, 80%, and 100% of room occupancy. Similarly, American Van Lines can budget its operating expenses on the basis of various levels of truck-miles driven. Duke Energy can budget revenue and net income on the basis of estimated billions of kwh (kilowatt hours) of residential, commercial, and industrial electricity generated. In the following pages, we will illustrate a flexible budget for manufacturing overhead.

Flexible budgets are static budgets at different activity levels

WHY FLEXIBLE BUDGETS?

Assume that you are the manager in charge of manufacturing overhead in the Assembly Department of Barton Robotics. In preparing the manufacturing overhead budget for 2014, you prepare the following static budget based on a production volume of 10,000 units of robotic controls.

Illustration 22-6 Static overhead budget

BARTON ROBOTICS	
Manufacturing Overhead Budget (Static)	
Assembly Department	
For the Year Ended December 31, 2014	
Budgeted production in units (robotic controls)	10,000
Budgeted costs	
Indirect materials	$ 250,000
Indirect labor	260,000
Utilities	190,000
Depreciation	280,000
Property taxes	70,000
Supervision	50,000
	$1,100,000

Helpful Hint The master budget described in Chapter 21 is based on a static budget.

Fortunately for the company, the demand for robotic controls has increased, and Barton produces and sells 12,000 units during the year, rather than 10,000. You are elated: Increased sales means increased profitability, which should mean a bonus or a raise for you and the employees in your department. Unfortunately, a comparison of Assembly Department actual and budgeted costs has put you on the spot. The budget report is shown on page 1138.

This comparison uses budget data based on the original activity level (10,000 robotic controls). It indicates that the Assembly Department is significantly **over budget** for three of the six overhead costs. There is a total unfavorable difference of $132,000, which is 12% over budget ($132,000 ÷ $1,100,000). Your supervisor

Helpful Hint A static budget is not useful for performance evaluation if a company has substantial variable costs.

Illustration 22-7 Overhead static budget report

		Barton Robotics.xls			
Home	Insert	Page Layout	Formulas	Data	Review	View
	P18	fx			

	A	B	C	D	E
1		**BARTON ROBOTICS**			
2		**Manufacturing Overhead Static Budget Report**			
3		**For the Year Ended December 31, 2014**			
4				Difference	
5		Budget	Actual	Favorable - F Unfavorable - U	
6	Production in units	10,000	12,000		
7					
8	Costs				
9	Indirect materials	$ 250,000	$ 295,000	$ 45,000	U
10	Indirect labor	260,000	312,000	52,000	U
11	Utilities	190,000	225,000	35,000	U
12	Depreciation	280,000	280,000	0	
13	Property taxes	70,000	70,000	0	
14	Supervision	50,000	50,000	0	
15		$1,100,000	$1,232,000	$132,000	U
16					

is very unhappy! Instead of sharing in the company's success, you may find yourself looking for another job. What went wrong?

When you calm down and carefully examine the manufacturing overhead budget, you identify the problem: The budget data are not relevant! At the time the budget was developed, the company anticipated that only 10,000 units would be produced, **not** 12,000. Comparing actual with budgeted variable costs is meaningless. As production increases, the budget allowances for variable costs should increase proportionately. The variable costs in this example are indirect materials, indirect labor, and utilities.

Analyzing the budget data for these costs at 10,000 units, you arrive at the following per unit results.

Illustration 22-8 Variable costs per unit

Item	Total Cost	Per Unit
Indirect materials	$250,000	$25
Indirect labor	260,000	26
Utilities	190,000	19
	$700,000	$70

Illustration 22-9 calculates the budgeted variable costs at 12,000 units.

Illustration 22-9 Budgeted variable costs, 12,000 units

Item	Computation	Total
Indirect materials	$25 × 12,000	$300,000
Indirect labor	26 × 12,000	312,000
Utilities	19 × 12,000	228,000
		$840,000

Because fixed costs do not change in total as activity changes, the budgeted amounts for these costs remain the same. Illustration 22-10 shows the budget report based on the flexible budget for **12,000 units** of production. (Compare this with Illustration 22-7.)

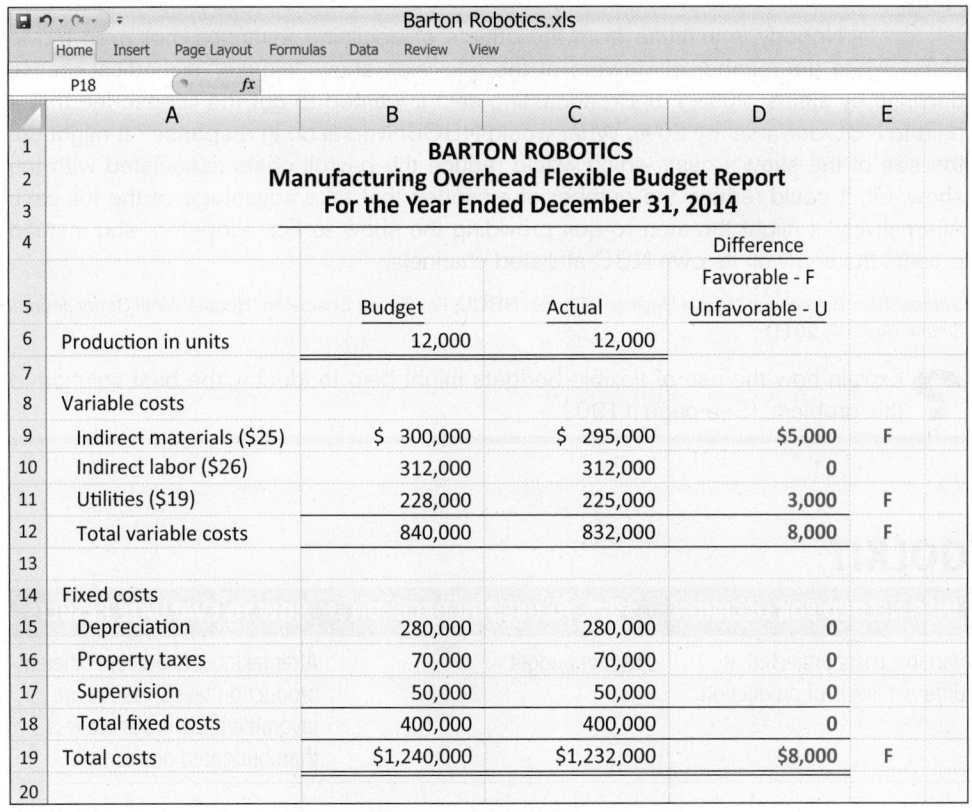

Illustration 22-10 Overhead flexible budget report

BARTON ROBOTICS
Manufacturing Overhead Flexible Budget Report
For the Year Ended December 31, 2014

	Budget	Actual	Difference Favorable - F Unfavorable - U	
Production in units	12,000	12,000		
Variable costs				
Indirect materials ($25)	$ 300,000	$ 295,000	$5,000	F
Indirect labor ($26)	312,000	312,000	0	
Utilities ($19)	228,000	225,000	3,000	F
Total variable costs	840,000	832,000	8,000	F
Fixed costs				
Depreciation	280,000	280,000	0	
Property taxes	70,000	70,000	0	
Supervision	50,000	50,000	0	
Total fixed costs	400,000	400,000	0	
Total costs	$1,240,000	$1,232,000	$8,000	F

This report indicates that the Assembly Department's costs are **under budget**—a favorable difference. Instead of worrying about being fired, you may be in line for a bonus or a raise after all! As this analysis shows, the only appropriate comparison is between actual costs at 12,000 units of production and budgeted costs at 12,000 units. Flexible budget reports provide this comparison.

DEVELOPING THE FLEXIBLE BUDGET

The flexible budget uses the master budget as its basis. To develop the flexible budget, management uses the following steps.

1. Identify the activity index and the relevant range of activity.
2. Identify the variable costs, and determine the budgeted variable cost per unit of activity for each cost.
3. Identify the fixed costs, and determine the budgeted amount for each cost.
4. Prepare the budget for selected increments of activity within the relevant range.

The activity index chosen should significantly influence the costs being budgeted. For manufacturing overhead costs, for example, the activity index is usually the same as the index used in developing the predetermined overhead rate—that is, direct labor hours or machine hours. For selling and administrative expenses, the activity index usually is sales or net sales.

The choice of the increment of activity is largely a matter of judgment. For example, if the relevant range is 8,000 to 12,000 direct labor hours, increments of 1,000 hours may be selected. The flexible budget is then prepared for each increment within the relevant range.

Service Company Insight

Just What the Doctor Ordered?

Nobody is immune from the effects of declining revenues—not even movie stars. When the number of viewers of the television show "House," a medical drama, declined by almost 20%, Fox Broadcasting said it wanted to cut the license fee that it paid to NBCUniversal by 20%. What would NBCUniversal do in response? It might cut the size of the show's cast, which would reduce the payroll costs associated with the show. Or, it could reduce the number of episodes that take advantage of the full cast. Alternatively, it might threaten to quit providing the show to Fox altogether and instead present the show on its own NBC-affiliated channels.

Source: Sam Schechner, "Media Business Shorts: NBCU, Fox Taking Scalpel to 'House,'" *Wall Street Journal Online* (April 17, 2011).

? Explain how the use of flexible budgets might help to identify the best solution to this problem. (See page 1190.)

🧰 DECISION TOOLKIT

DECISION CHECKPOINTS	INFO NEEDED FOR DECISION	TOOL TO USE FOR DECISION	HOW TO EVALUATE RESULTS
Are the increased costs resulting from increased production reasonable?	Variable costs projected at different levels of production	Flexible budget	After taking into account different production levels, results are favorable if expenses are less than budgeted amounts.

FLEXIBLE BUDGET—A CASE STUDY

To illustrate the flexible budget, we use Fox Company. Fox's management uses a **flexible budget for monthly comparisons** of actual and budgeted manufacturing overhead costs of the Finishing Department. The master budget for the year ending December 31, 2014, shows expected **annual** operating capacity of 120,000 direct labor hours and the following overhead costs.

Illustration 22-11 Master budget data

Variable Costs		Fixed Costs	
Indirect materials	$180,000	Depreciation	$180,000
Indirect labor	240,000	Supervision	120,000
Utilities	60,000	Property taxes	60,000
Total	$480,000	Total	$360,000

The four steps for developing the flexible budget are applied as follows.

STEP 1. Identify the activity index and the relevant range of activity. The activity index is direct labor hours. The relevant range is 8,000–12,000 direct labor hours per **month**.

STEP 2. Identify the variable costs, and determine the budgeted variable cost per unit of activity for each cost. There are three variable costs. The variable cost per unit is found by dividing each total budgeted cost by the direct labor hours used in preparing the annual master budget (120,000 hours). For Fox Company, the computations are:

Illustration 22-12
Computation of variable cost
per direct labor hour

Variable Costs	Computation	Variable Cost per Direct Labor Hour
Indirect materials	$180,000 ÷ 120,000	$1.50
Indirect labor	$240,000 ÷ 120,000	2.00
Utilities	$ 60,000 ÷ 120,000	0.50
Total		$4.00

STEP 3. Identify the fixed costs, and determine the budgeted amount for each cost. There are three fixed costs. Since Fox desires **monthly budget data**, it divides each annual budgeted cost by 12 to find the monthly amounts. For Fox Company, the monthly budgeted fixed costs are depreciation $15,000, supervision $10,000, and property taxes $5,000.

STEP 4. Prepare the budget for selected increments of activity within the relevant range. Management prepares the budget in increments of 1,000 direct labor hours.

Illustration 22-13 shows Fox's flexible budget.

Illustration 22-13 Monthly overhead flexible budget

	A	B	C	D	E	F
1	FOX COMPANY					
2	Monthly Manufacturing Overhead Flexible Budget					
3	Finishing Department					
4	For Months During the Year 2014					
5	Activity level					
6	Direct labor hours	8,000	9,000	10,000	11,000	12,000
7	Variable costs					
8	Indirect materials ($1.50)ᵃ	$12,000ᵇ	$13,500	$15,000	$16,500	$18,000
9	Indirect labor ($2.00)ᵃ	16,000ᶜ	18,000	20,000	22,000	24,000
10	Utilities ($0.50)ᵃ	4,000ᵈ	4,500	5,000	5,500	6,000
11	Total variable costs	32,000	36,000	40,000	44,000	48,000
12	Fixed costs					
13	Depreciation	15,000	15,000	15,000	15,000	15,000
14	Supervision	10,000	10,000	10,000	10,000	10,000
15	Property taxes	5,000	5,000	5,000	5,000	5,000
16	Total fixed costs	30,000	30,000	30,000	30,000	30,000
17	Total costs	$62,000	$66,000	$70,000	$74,000	$78,000
18						
19	ᵃCost per direct labor hour; ᵇ8,000 x $1.50; ᶜ8,000 x $2.00; ᵈ8,000 x $0.50					

Fox uses the formula below to determine total budgeted costs at any level of activity.

Illustration 22-14 Formula for total budgeted costs

$$\text{Fixed Costs} + \text{Variable Costs*} = \text{Total Budgeted Costs}$$

*Total variable cost per unit of activity × Activity level.

For Fox, fixed costs are $30,000, and total variable cost per direct labor hour is $4 ($1.50 + $2.00 + $0.50). At 9,000 direct labor hours, total budgeted costs are

Helpful Hint Using the data given for Fox, what amount of total costs would be budgeted for 10,600 direct labor hours? Answer: $30,000 fixed + $42,400 variable (i.e., 10,600 × $4) = $72,400 total.

$66,000 [$30,000 + ($4 × 9,000)]. At 8,622 direct labor hours, total budgeted costs are $64,488 [$30,000 + ($4 × 8,622)].

Total budgeted costs can also be shown graphically, as in Illustration 22-15. In the graph, the horizontal axis represents the activity index, and costs are indicated on the vertical axis. The graph highlights two activity levels (10,000 and 12,000). As shown, total budgeted costs at these activity levels are $70,000 [$30,000 + ($4 × 10,000)] and $78,000 [$30,000 + ($4 × 12,000)], respectively.

Illustration 22-15 Graphic flexible budget data highlighting 10,000 and 12,000 activity levels

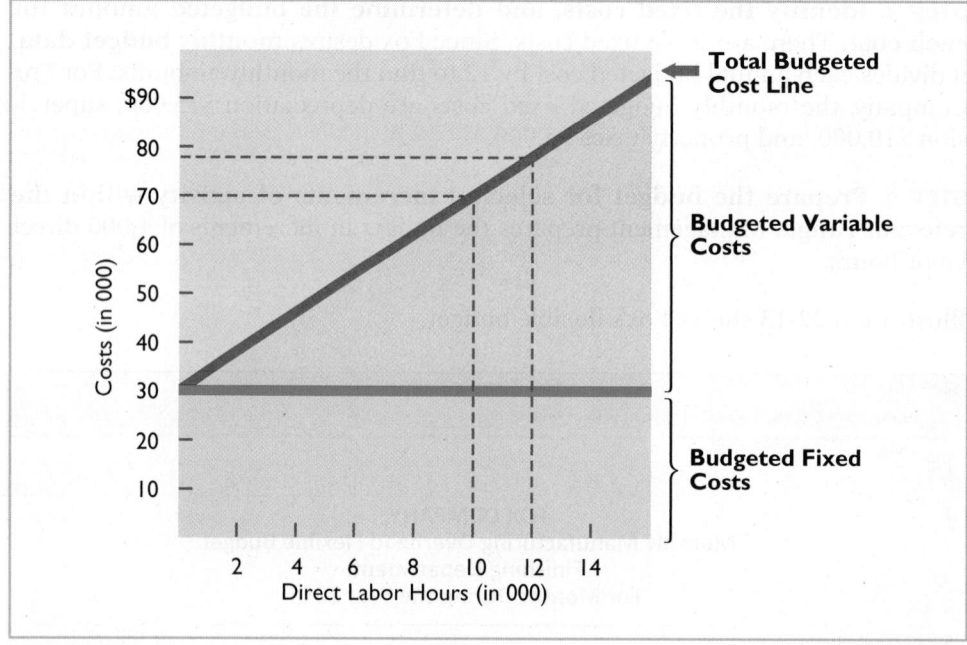

FLEXIBLE BUDGETS **Do It!** In Strassel Company's flexible budget graph, the fixed cost line and the total budgeted cost line intersect the vertical axis at $36,000. The total budgeted cost line is $186,000 at an activity level of 50,000 direct labor hours. Compute total budgeted costs at 30,000 direct labor hours.

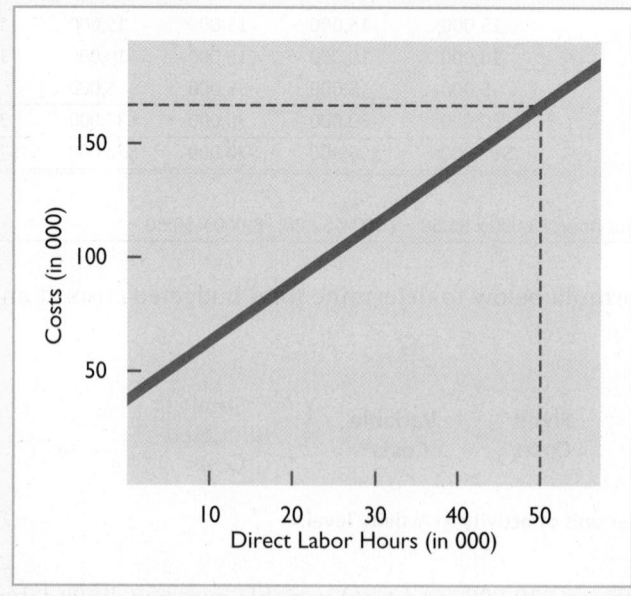

Solution

Using the graph, fixed costs are $36,000, and variable costs are $3 per direct labor hour [($186,000 − $36,000) ÷ 50,000]. Thus, at 30,000 direct labor hours, total budgeted costs are $126,000 [$36,000 + ($3 × 30,000)].

Related exercise material: **BE22-4, E22-3, E22-5,** and **Do it!** 22-1.

FLEXIBLE BUDGET REPORTS

Flexible budget reports are another type of internal report. The flexible budget report consists of two sections: (1) production data for a selected activity index, such as direct labor hours, and (2) cost data for variable and fixed costs. The report provides a basis for evaluating a manager's performance in two areas: production control and cost control. Flexible budget reports are widely used in production and service departments.

Illustration 22-16 shows a budget report for the Finishing Department of Fox Company for the month of January. In this month, 9,000 hours are worked. The budget data are therefore based on the flexible budget for 9,000 hours in Illustration 22-13 (page 1141). The actual cost data are assumed.

Illustration 22-16 Overhead flexible budget report

FOX COMPANY
Manufacturing Overhead Flexible Budget Report
Finishing Department
For the Month Ended January 31, 2014

	Budget at 9,000 DLH	Actual costs at 9,000 DLH	Difference Favorable - F Unfavorable - U	
Direct labor hours (DLH)				
Variable costs				
Indirect materials ($1.50)[a]	$13,500	$14,000	$ 500	U
Indirect labor ($2.00)[a]	18,000	17,000	1,000	F
Utilities ($0.50)[a]	4,500	4,600	100	U
Total variable costs	36,000	35,600	400	F
Fixed costs				
Depreciation	15,000	15,000	0	
Supervision	10,000	10,000	0	
Property taxes	5,000	5,000	0	
Total fixed costs	30,000	30,000	0	
Total costs	$66,000	$65,600	$ 400	F

[a]Cost per direct labor hour

How appropriate is this report in evaluating the Finishing Department manager's performance in controlling overhead costs? The report clearly provides a reliable basis. Both actual and budget costs are based on the activity level worked during January. Since variable costs generally are incurred directly by the department, the difference between the budget allowance for those hours and the actual costs is the responsibility of the department manager.

In subsequent months, Fox Company will prepare other flexible budget reports. For each month, the budget data are based on the actual activity level attained. In February that level may be 11,000 direct labor hours, in July 10,000, and so on.

Note that this flexible budget is based on a single cost driver. A more accurate budget often can be developed using the activity-based costing concepts explained in Chapter 17.

©Eric Isselee/iStockphoto

Service Company Insight
Budgets and the Exotic Newcastle Disease

Exotic Newcastle Disease, one of the most infectious bird diseases in the world, kills so swiftly that many victims die before any symptoms appear. When it broke out in Southern California, it could have spelled disaster for the San Diego Zoo. "We have one of the most valuable collections of birds in the world, if not *the* most valuable," says Paula Brock, CFO of the Zoological Society of San Diego, which operates the zoo.

Bird exhibits were closed to the public for several months (the disease, which is harmless to humans, can be carried on clothes and shoes). The tires of arriving delivery trucks were sanitized, as were the shoes of anyone visiting the zoo's nonpublic areas. Zookeeper uniforms had to be changed and cleaned daily. And ultimately, the zoo, with $150 million in revenues, spent almost half a million dollars on quarantine measures.

It worked: No birds got sick. Better yet, the damage to the rest of the zoo's budget was minimized by another protective measure: the monthly budget reforecast. "When we get a hit like this, we still have to find a way to make our bottom line," says Brock. Thanks to a new planning process Brock had introduced a year earlier, the zoo's scientists were able to raise the financial alarm as they redirected resources to ward off the disease. "Because we had timely awareness," she says, "we were able to make adjustments to weather the storm."

Budget reforecasting is nothing new. (The San Diego Zoo's annual static budget was behind the times before Brock took over as CFO.) But the reaction of the zoo's staff shows the benefits of Brock's immediate efforts to link strategy to the process. It's a move long touted by consultants as a key way to improve people's involvement in budgeting.

"To keep your company on a path, it has to have some kind of map," says Brock. "The budgeting-and-planning process is that map. I cannot imagine an organization feeling in control if it didn't have that sort of discipline."

Source: Tim Reason, "Budgeting in the Real World," *CFO Magazine* (July 12, 2005), *www.cfodirect.com/ cfopublic.nsf/vContentPrint/649A82C8FF8AB06B85257037004* (accessed July 2005).

? What is the major benefit of tying a budget to the overall goals of the company? (See page 1190.)

FLEXIBLE BUDGET REPORTS

Do it!

Lawler Company expects to produce 40,000 units of product CV93 during the current year. Budgeted variable manufacturing costs per unit are direct materials $6, direct labor $15, and overhead $24. Annual budgeted fixed manufacturing overhead costs are $120,000 for depreciation and $60,000 for supervision.

In the current month, Lawler produced 5,000 units and incurred the following costs: direct materials $33,900, direct labor $74,200, variable overhead $120,500, depreciation $10,000, and supervision $5,000.

Prepare a flexible budget report. (*Note:* You do not have to prepare the heading.) Were costs controlled?

Solution

	Lawler Company.xls			
	Home Insert Page Layout Formulas Data Review View			
	P18 fx			
	A	B	C	D	
1				Difference	
2		Budget at	Actual costs at	Favorable - F	
3	Units produced	5,000 units	5,000 units	Unfavorable - U	
4					
5	Variable costs				
6	Direct materials ($6)	$ 30,000	$ 33,900	$3,900	U
7	Direct labor ($15)	75,000	74,200	800	F
8	Overhead ($24)	120,000	120,500	500	U
9	Total variable costs	225,000	228,600	3,600	U
10					
11	Fixed costs				
12	Depreciation	10,000	10,000	0	
13	Supervision	5,000	5,000	0	
14	Total fixed costs	15,000	15,000	0	
15	Total costs	$240,000	$243,600	$3,600	U
16					
17					

The responsibility report indicates that actual direct labor was only about 1% different from the budget, and overhead was less than half a percent different. Both appear to have been well-controlled.

This was not the case for direct materials. Its 13% unfavorable difference should probably be investigated.

Actual fixed costs had no difference from budget and were well-controlled.

Related exercise material: **BE22-5, E22-4, E22-6, E22-7, E22-8, E22-10, and Do it! 22-2.**

Action Plan

- Use budget for actual units produced.
- Classify each cost as variable or fixed.
- Determine monthly fixed costs by dividing annual amounts by 12.
- Determine the difference as favorable or unfavorable.
- Determine the difference in total variable costs, total fixed costs, and total costs.

✔ The Navigator

Responsibility Accounting

Like budgeting, responsibility accounting is an important part of management accounting. **Responsibility accounting** involves accumulating and reporting costs (and revenues, where relevant) on the basis of the manager who has the authority to make the day-to-day decisions about the items. Under responsibility accounting, a manager's performance is evaluated on matters directly under that manager's control. Responsibility accounting can be used at every level of management in which the following conditions exist.

LEARNING OBJECTIVE 4
Describe the concept of responsibility accounting.

1. Costs and revenues can be directly associated with the specific level of management responsibility.

2. The costs and revenues can be controlled by employees at the level of responsibility with which they are associated.

3. Budget data can be developed for evaluating the manager's effectiveness in controlling the costs and revenues.

Illustration 22-17 depicts levels of responsibility for controlling costs.

Illustration 22-17
Responsibility for controllable costs at varying levels of management

Helpful Hint All companies use responsibility accounting. Without some form of responsibility accounting, there would be chaos in discharging management's control function.

Under responsibility accounting, any individual who controls a specified set of activities can be a responsibility center. Thus, responsibility accounting may extend from the lowest level of control to the top strata of management. Once responsibility is established, the company first measures and reports the effectiveness of the individual's performance for the specified activity. It then reports that measure upward throughout the organization.

Responsibility accounting is especially valuable in a decentralized company. **Decentralization** means that the control of operations is delegated to many managers throughout the organization. The term **segment** is sometimes used to identify an area of responsibility in decentralized operations. Under responsibility accounting, companies prepare segment reports periodically, such as monthly, quarterly, and annually, to evaluate managers' performance.

Responsibility accounting is an essential part of any effective system of budgetary control. The reporting of costs and revenues under responsibility accounting differs from budgeting in two respects:

1. A distinction is made between controllable and noncontrollable items.

2. Performance reports either emphasize or include only items controllable by the individual manager.

Responsibility accounting applies to both profit and not-for-profit entities. For-profit entities seek to maximize net income. Not-for-profit entities wish to provide services as efficiently as possible.

Management Insight

Competition versus Collaboration

Many compensation and promotion programs encourage competition among employees for pay raises. To get ahead you have to perform better than your fellow employees. While this may encourage hard work, it does not foster collaboration, and it can lead to distrust and disloyalty. Such results have led some companies to believe that cooperation and collaboration are essential in order to succeed in today's environment. For example, division managers might increase collaboration (and reduce costs) by sharing design and marketing resources or by jointly negotiating with suppliers. In addition, companies can reduce the need to hire and lay off employees by sharing employees across divisions as human resource needs increase and decrease.

As a consequence, many companies now explicitly include measures of collaboration in their performance measures. For example, Procter & Gamble measures collaboration in employees' annual performance reviews. At Cisco Systems the assessment of an employee's teamwork can affect the annual bonus by as much as 20%.

Source: Carol Hymowitz, "Rewarding Competitors Over Collaboration No Longer Makes Sense," *Wall Street Journal* (February 13, 2006).

© Marek Uliasz/iStockphoto

 How might managers of separate divisions be able to reduce division costs through collaboration? (See page 1190.)

CONTROLLABLE VERSUS NONCONTROLLABLE REVENUES AND COSTS

All costs and revenues are controllable at some level of responsibility within a company. This truth underscores the adage by the CEO of any organization that "the buck stops here." Under responsibility accounting, the critical issue is **whether the cost or revenue is controllable at the level of responsibility with which it is associated**. A cost over which a manager has control is called a controllable cost. From this definition, it follows that:

1. All costs are controllable by top management because of the broad range of its authority.
2. Fewer costs are controllable as one moves down to each lower level of managerial responsibility because of the manager's decreasing authority.

In general, **costs incurred directly by a level of responsibility are controllable at that level**. In contrast, costs incurred indirectly and allocated to a responsibility level are noncontrollable costs at that level.

Helpful Hint Are there more or fewer controllable costs as you move to higher levels of management?
Answer: More.

PRINCIPLES OF PERFORMANCE EVALUATION

Performance evaluation is at the center of responsibility accounting. It is a management function that compares actual results with budget goals. It involves both behavioral and reporting principles.

Helpful Hint The longer the time span, the more likely that the cost becomes controllable.

Management By Exception

Management by exception means that top management's review of a budget report is focused either entirely or primarily on differences between actual results and planned objectives. This approach enables top management to focus on problem areas. For example, many companies now use online reporting systems for employees to file their travel and entertainment expense reports. In addition to cutting reporting time in half, the online system enables managers to quickly analyze variances from travel budgets. This cuts down on expense account "padding" such as spending too much on meals or falsifying documents for costs that were never actually incurred.

Management by exception does not mean that top management will investigate every difference. For this approach to be effective, there must be guidelines for identifying an exception. The usual criteria are materiality and controllability.

MATERIALITY. Without quantitative guidelines, management would have to investigate every budget difference regardless of the amount. Materiality is usually expressed as a percentage difference from budget. For example, management may set the percentage difference at 5% for important items and 10% for other items. Managers will investigate all differences either over or under budget by the specified percentage. Costs over budget warrant investigation to determine why they were not controlled. Likewise, costs under budget merit investigation to determine whether costs critical to profitability are being curtailed. For example, if maintenance costs are budgeted at $80,000 but only $40,000 is spent, major unexpected breakdowns in productive facilities may occur in the future.

Alternatively, a company may specify a single percentage difference from budget for all items and supplement this guideline with a minimum dollar limit. For example, the exception criteria may be stated at 5% of budget or more than $10,000.

CONTROLLABILITY OF THE ITEM. Exception guidelines are more restrictive for controllable items than for items the manager cannot control. In fact, there may be no guidelines for noncontrollable items. For example, a large unfavorable difference between actual and budgeted property tax expense may not be flagged for investigation because the only possible causes are an unexpected increase in the tax rate or in the assessed value of the property. An investigation into the difference would be useless: The manager cannot control either cause.

Behavioral Principles

The human factor is critical in evaluating performance. Behavioral principles include the following.

1. **Managers of responsibility centers should have direct input into the process of establishing budget goals of their area of responsibility.** Without such input, managers may view the goals as unrealistic or arbitrarily set by top management. Such views adversely affect the managers' motivation to meet the targeted objectives.

2. **The evaluation of performance should be based entirely on matters that are controllable by the manager being evaluated.** Criticism of a manager on matters outside his or her control reduces the effectiveness of the evaluation process. It leads to negative reactions by a manager and to doubts about the fairness of the company's evaluation policies.

3. **Top management should support the evaluation process.** As explained earlier, the evaluation process begins at the lowest level of responsibility and extends upward to the highest level of management. Managers quickly lose faith in the process when top management ignores, overrules, or bypasses established procedures for evaluating a manager's performance.

4. **The evaluation process must allow managers to respond to their evaluations.** Evaluation is not a one-way street. Managers should have the opportunity to defend their performance. Evaluation without feedback is both impersonal and ineffective.

5. The evaluation should identify both good and poor performance. Praise for good performance is a powerful motivating factor for a manager. This is especially true when a manager's compensation includes rewards for meeting budget goals.

Reporting Principles

Performance evaluation under responsibility accounting should be based on certain reporting principles. These principles pertain primarily to the internal reports that provide the basis for evaluating performance. Performance reports should:

1. Contain only data that are controllable by the manager of the responsibility center.

2. Provide accurate and reliable budget data to measure performance.

3. Highlight significant differences between actual results and budget goals.

4. Be tailor-made for the intended evaluation.

5. Be prepared at reasonable time intervals.

In recent years, companies have come under increasing pressure from influential shareholder groups to do a better job of linking executive pay to corporate performance. For example, software maker Siebel Systems unveiled a new incentive plan after lengthy discussions with the California Public Employees' Retirement System. One unique feature of the plan is that managers' targets will be publicly disclosed at the beginning of each year for investors to evaluate.

Management Insight
Flexible Manufacturing Requires Flexible Accounting

Flexible budgeting is useful because it enables managers to evaluate performance in light of changing conditions. But the ability to react quickly to changing conditions is even more important. Among automobile manufacturing facilities in the U.S., nobody's plants are more flexible than Honda. The manufacturing facilities of some auto companies can make slight alterations to the features of a vehicle in response to changes in demand for particular features. But for most plants, to switch from production of one type of vehicle to a completely different type of vehicle, when demand for types of vehicles shifts, typically takes months and costs hundreds of millions of dollars. But at the Honda plant, the switch takes minutes. For example, it takes about five minutes to install different hand-like parts on the robots so they can switch from making Civic compacts to the longer, taller CR-V crossover. This ability to adjust quickly to changing demand gave Honda a huge advantage when gas prices surged and demand for more fuel-efficient cars increased quickly.

Source: Kate Linebaugh, "Honda's Flexible Plants Provide Edge," *Wall Street Journal Online* (September 23, 2008).

© Chris Ratcliffe/Bloomberg/
Getty Images

 What implications do these improvements in production capabilities have for management accounting information and performance evaluation within the organization? (See page 1190.)

RESPONSIBILITY REPORTING SYSTEM

A responsibility reporting system involves the preparation of a report for each level of responsibility in the company's organization chart. To illustrate such a system, we use the partial organization chart and production departments of Francis Chair Company in Illustration 22-18 (page 1150).

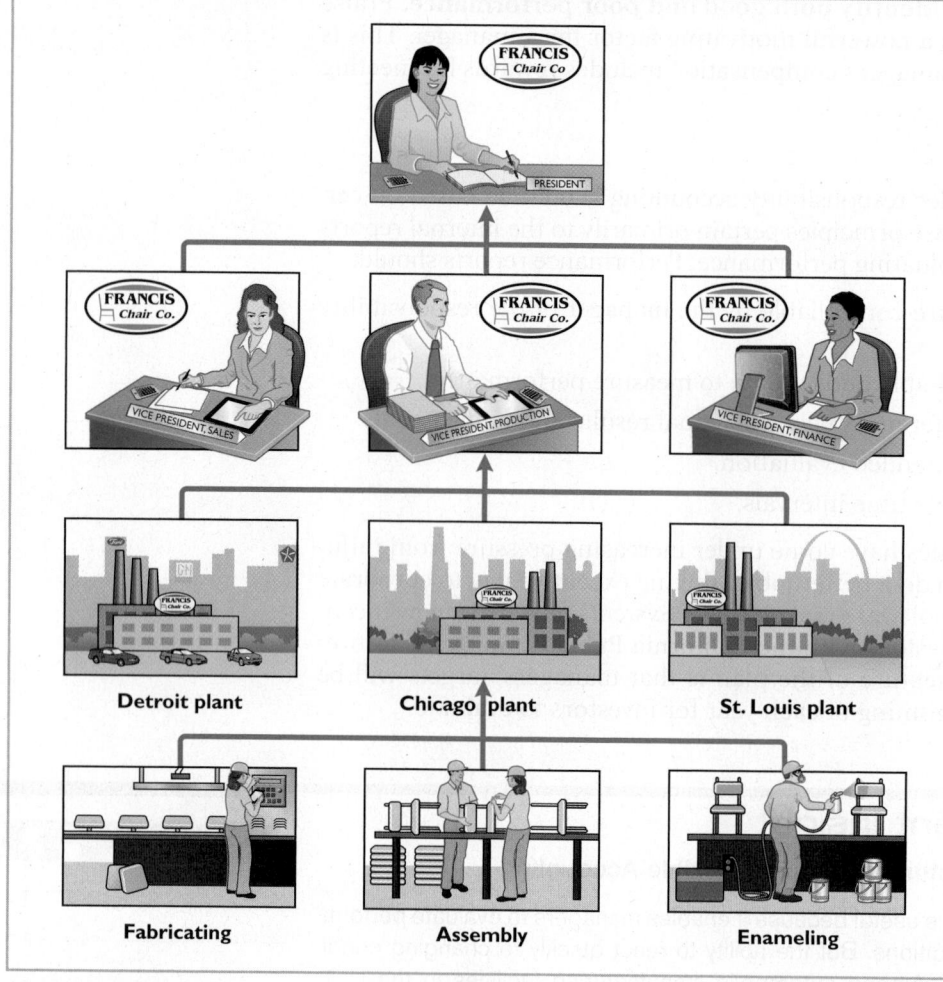

Report A
President sees summary data of vice presidents.

Report B
Vice president sees summary of controllable costs in his/her functional area.

Report C
Plant manager sees summary of controllable costs for each department in the plant.

Report D
Department manager sees controllable costs of his/her department.

Illustration 22-18 Partial organization chart

The responsibility reporting system begins with the lowest level of responsibility for controlling costs and moves upward to each higher level. Illustration 22-19 details the connections between levels.

A brief description of the four reports for Francis Chair Company is as follows.

1. **Report D** is typical of reports that go to department managers. Similar reports are prepared for the managers of the Fabricating, Assembly, and Enameling Departments.

2. **Report C** is an example of reports that are sent to plant managers. It shows the costs of the Chicago plant that are controllable at the second level of responsibility. In addition, Report C shows summary data for each department that is controlled by the plant manager. Similar reports are prepared for the Detroit and St. Louis plant managers.

3. **Report B** illustrates the reports at the third level of responsibility. It shows the controllable costs of the vice president of production and summary data on the three assembly plants for which this officer is responsible. Similar reports are prepared for the vice presidents of sales and finance.

4. **Report A** is typical of reports that go to the top level of responsibility—the president. It shows the controllable costs and expenses of this office and summary data on the vice presidents that are accountable to the president.

Illustration 22-19
Responsibility reporting system

Report A
President sees summary data of vice presidents.

Report A.xls

Home | Insert | Page Layout | Formulas | Data | Review | View

P18   fx

	A	B	C	D	E
1		**Report A**			
2					
3	To President			Month: January	
4	Controllable Costs:	Budget	Actual	Fav/Unfav	
5	President	$ 150,000	$ 151,500	$ 1,500	U
6	Vice Presidents:				
7	Sales	185,000	187,000	2,000	U
8	Production	1,179,000	1,186,300	7,300	U
9	Finance	100,000	101,000	1,000	U
10	Total	$1,614,000	$1,625,800	$11,800	U
11					

Report B
Vice president sees summary of controllable costs in his/her functional area.

Report B.xls

Home | Insert | Page Layout | Formulas | Data | Review | View

P18   fx

	A	B	C	D	E
1		**Report B**			
2					
3	To Vice President Production			Month: January	
4	Controllable Costs:	Budget	Actual	Fav/Unfav	
5	VP Production	$ 125,000	$ 126,000	$ 1,000	U
6	Assembly Plants:				
7	Detroit	420,000	418,000	2,000	F
8	Chicago	304,000	309,300	5,300	U
9	St. Louis	330,000	333,000	3,000	U
10	Total	$1,179,000	$1,186,300	$ 7,300	U
11					

Report C
Plant manager sees summary of controllable costs for each department in the plant.

Report C.xls

Home | Insert | Page Layout | Formulas | Data | Review | View

P18   fx

	A	B	C	D	E
1		**Report C**			
2					
3	To Plant Manager-Chicago			Month: January	
4	Controllable Costs:	Budget	Actual	Fav/Unfav	
5	Chicago Plant	$110,000	$113,000	$3,000	U
6	Departments:				
7	Fabricating	84,000	85,300	1,300	U
8	Enameling	62,000	64,000	2,000	U
9	Assembly	48,000	47,000	1,000	F
10	Total	$304,000	$309,300	$5,300	U
11					

Report D
Department manager sees controllable costs of his/her department.

Report D.xls

Home | Insert | Page Layout | Formulas | Data | Review | View

P18   fx

	A	B	C	D	E
1		**Report D**			
2					
3	To Fabricating Dept. Manager			Month: January	
4	Controllable Costs:	Budget	Actual	Fav/Unfav	
5	Direct Materials	$20,000	$20,500	$ 500	U
6	Direct Labor	40,000	41,000	1,000	U
7	Overhead	24,000	23,800	200	F
8	Total	$84,000	$85,300	$1,300	U
9					

A responsibility reporting system permits management by exception at each level of responsibility. And, each higher level of responsibility can obtain the detailed report for each lower level of responsibility. For example, the vice president of production in the Francis Chair Company may request the Chicago plant manager's report because this plant is $5,300 over budget.

This type of reporting system also permits comparative evaluations. In Illustration 22-19, the Chicago plant manager can easily rank the department managers' effectiveness in controlling manufacturing costs. Comparative rankings provide further incentive for a manager to control costs.

Types of Responsibility Centers

There are three basic types of responsibility centers: cost centers, profit centers, and investment centers. These classifications indicate the degree of responsibility the manager has for the performance of the center.

Helpful Hint (1) Is the jewelry department of Macy's department store a profit center or a cost center? (2) Is the props department of a movie studio a profit center or a cost center?
Answers: (1) Profit center. (2) Cost center.

A cost center incurs costs (and expenses) but does not directly generate revenues. Managers of cost centers have the authority to incur costs. They are evaluated on their ability to control costs. **Cost centers are usually either production departments or service departments.** Production departments participate directly in making the product. Service departments provide only support services. In a Ford Motor Company automobile plant, the welding, painting, and assembling departments are production departments. Ford's maintenance, cafeteria, and human resources departments are service departments. All of them are cost centers.

A profit center incurs costs (and expenses) and also generates revenues. Managers of profit centers are judged on the profitability of their centers. Examples of profit centers include the individual departments of a retail store, such as clothing, furniture, and automotive products, and branch offices of banks.

Like a profit center, an investment center incurs costs (and expenses) and generates revenues. In addition, an investment center has control over decisions regarding the assets available for use. Investment center managers are evaluated on both the profitability of the center and the rate of return earned on the funds invested. Investment centers are often associated with subsidiary companies. Utility Duke Energy has operating divisions such as electric utility, energy trading, and natural gas. Investment center managers control or significantly influence investment decisions related to such matters as plant expansion and entry into new market areas. Illustration 22-20 depicts the three types of responsibility centers.

Illustration 22-20 Types of responsibility centers

Types of Responsibility Centers

Expenses

Cost Center

Expenses & Revenues

Profit Center

Expenses & Revenues & Return on Investment

Investment Center

RESPONSIBILITY ACCOUNTING FOR COST CENTERS

The evaluation of a manager's performance for cost centers is based on his or her ability to meet budgeted goals for controllable costs. **Responsibility reports for cost centers compare actual controllable costs with flexible budget data.**

Illustration 22-21 shows a responsibility report. The report is adapted from the flexible budget report for Fox Company in Illustration 22-16 (page 1143). It assumes that the Finishing Department manager is able to control all manufacturing overhead costs except depreciation, property taxes, and his own monthly salary of $6,000. The remaining $4,000 ($10,000 − $6,000) of supervision costs are assumed to apply to other supervisory personnel within the Finishing Department, whose salaries are controllable by the manager.

LEARNING OBJECTIVE 5
Indicate the features of responsibility reports for cost centers.

Illustration 22-21
Responsibility report for a cost center

Controllable Costs	Budget	Actual	Difference Favorable - F Unfavorable - U	
Indirect materials	$13,500	$14,000	$ 500	U
Indirect labor	18,000	17,000	$1,000	F
Utilities	4,500	4,600	100	U
Supervision	4,000	4,000	0	
	$40,000	$39,600	$ 400	F

FOX COMPANY
Finishing Department
Responsibility Report
For the Month Ended January 31, 2014

The report in Illustration 22-21 includes **only controllable costs**, and no distinction is made between variable and fixed costs. The responsibility report continues the concept of management by exception. In this case, top management may request an explanation of the $1,000 favorable difference in indirect labor and/or the $500 unfavorable difference in indirect materials.

RESPONSIBILITY ACCOUNTING FOR PROFIT CENTERS

To evaluate the performance of a profit center manager, upper management needs detailed information about both controllable revenues and controllable costs. The operating revenues earned by a profit center, such as sales, are controllable by the manager. All variable costs (and expenses) incurred by the center are also controllable by the manager because they vary with sales. However, to determine the controllability of fixed costs, it is necessary to distinguish between direct and indirect fixed costs.

LEARNING OBJECTIVE 6
Identify the content of responsibility reports for profit centers.

Direct and Indirect Fixed Costs

A profit center may have both direct and indirect fixed costs. Direct fixed costs relate specifically to one center and are incurred for the sole benefit of that center. Examples of such costs include the salaries established by the profit center manager for supervisory personnel and the cost of a timekeeping department for the center's employees. Since these fixed costs can be traced directly to a center, they are also called **traceable costs**. **Most direct fixed costs are controllable by the profit center manager.**

In contrast, indirect fixed costs pertain to a company's overall operating activities and are incurred for the benefit of more than one profit center. Management allocates indirect fixed costs to profit centers on some type of equitable basis. For example, property taxes on a building occupied by more than one center may be allocated on the basis of square feet of floor space used by each center. Or, the costs of a company's human resources department may be allocated to profit centers on the basis of the number of employees in each center. Because these fixed costs apply to more than one center, they are also called **common costs**. **Most indirect fixed costs are not controllable by the profit center manager.**

Helpful Hint Recognize that we are emphasizing *financial* measures of performance. These days companies are also making an effort to stress *nonfinancial* performance measures such as product quality, labor productivity, market growth, materials' yield, manufacturing flexibility, and technological capability.

Responsibility Report

The responsibility report for a profit center shows budgeted and actual **controllable revenues and costs**. The report is prepared using the cost-volume-profit income statement explained in Chapter 18. In the report:

1. Controllable fixed costs are deducted from contribution margin.
2. The excess of contribution margin over controllable fixed costs is identified as controllable margin.
3. Noncontrollable fixed costs are not reported.

Illustration 22-22 shows the responsibility report for the manager of the Marine Division, a profit center of Mantle Company. For the year, the Marine Division also had $60,000 of indirect fixed costs that were not controllable by the profit center manager.

Illustration 22-22
Responsibility report for profit center

MANTLE COMPANY
Marine Division
Responsibility Report
For the Year Ended December 31, 2014

	Budget	Actual	Difference Favorable - F Unfavorable - U	
Sales	$1,200,000	$1,150,000	$50,000	U
Variable costs				
Cost of goods sold	500,000	490,000	10,000	F
Selling and administrative	160,000	156,000	4,000	F
Total	660,000	646,000	14,000	F
Contribution margin	540,000	504,000	36,000	U
Controllable fixed costs				
Cost of goods sold	100,000	100,000	0	
Selling and administrative	80,000	80,000	0	
Total	180,000	180,000	0	
Controllable margin	$ 360,000	$ 324,000	$36,000	U

Controllable margin is considered to be the best measure of the manager's performance **in controlling revenues and costs**. The report in Illustration 22-22 shows that the manager's performance was below budgeted expectations by 10% ($36,000 ÷ $360,000). Top management would likely investigate the causes of this unfavorable result. Note that the report does not show the Marine Division's noncontrollable fixed costs of $60,000. These costs would be included in a report on the profitability of the profit center.

Management also may choose to see **monthly** responsibility reports for profit centers. In addition, responsibility reports may include cumulative year-to-date results.

DECISION TOOLKIT

DECISION CHECKPOINTS	INFO NEEDED FOR DECISION	TOOL TO USE FOR DECISION	HOW TO EVALUATE RESULTS
Have the individual managers been held accountable for the costs and revenues under their control?	Review costs and revenues, where the individual manager has authority to make day-to-day decisions about the items	Responsibility reports focused on cost centers, profit centers, and investment centers as appropriate	Compare budget to actual costs and revenues for controllable items.

Do it!

PROFIT CENTER RESPONSIBILITY REPORT

Midwest Division operates as a profit center. It reports the following for the year:

	Budget	Actual
Sales	$1,500,000	$1,700,000
Variable costs	700,000	800,000
Controllable fixed costs	400,000	400,000
Noncontrollable fixed costs	200,000	200,000

Prepare a responsibility report for the Midwest Division for December 31, 2014.

Solution

Action Plan

- Deduct variable costs from sales to show contribution margin.
- Deduct controllable fixed costs from the contribution margin to show controllable margin.
- Do not report noncontrollable fixed costs.

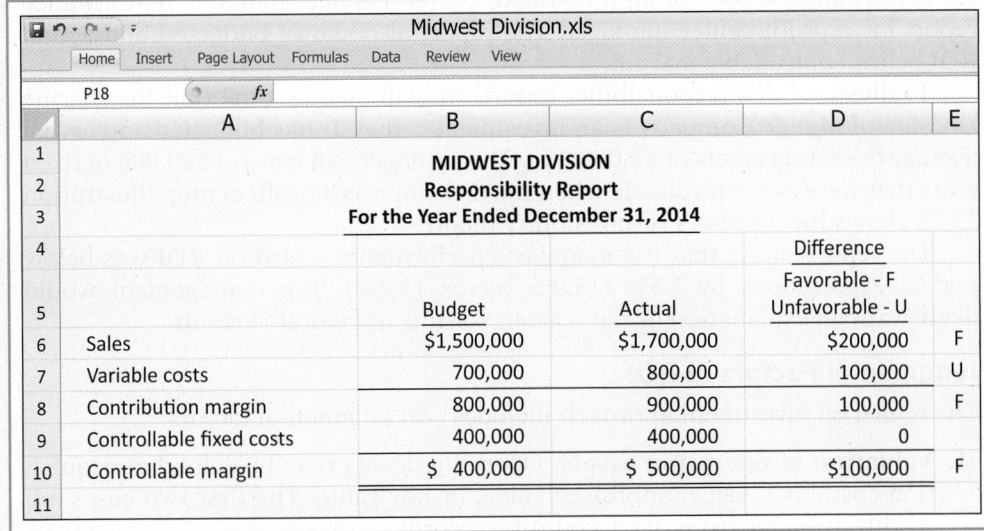

MIDWEST DIVISION
Responsibility Report
For the Year Ended December 31, 2014

	Budget	Actual	Difference Favorable - F Unfavorable - U	
Sales	$1,500,000	$1,700,000	$200,000	F
Variable costs	700,000	800,000	100,000	U
Contribution margin	800,000	900,000	100,000	F
Controllable fixed costs	400,000	400,000	0	
Controllable margin	$ 400,000	$ 500,000	$100,000	F

 The Navigator

Related exercise material: **BE 22-7, E22-15, and Do it! 22-3.**

RESPONSIBILITY ACCOUNTING FOR INVESTMENT CENTERS

LEARNING OBJECTIVE 7

Explain the basis and formula used in evaluating performance in investment centers.

As explained earlier, an investment center manager can control or significantly influence the investment funds available for use. Thus, the primary basis for evaluating the performance of a manager of an investment center is **return on investment (ROI)**. The return on investment is considered to be a useful performance measurement because it shows the **effectiveness of the manager in utilizing the assets at his or her disposal**.

Return on Investment (ROI)

The formula for computing ROI for an investment center, together with assumed illustrative data, is shown in Illustration 22-23.

Illustration 22-23 ROI formula

Controllable Margin	÷	Average Operating Assets	=	Return on Investment (ROI)
$1,000,000	÷	$5,000,000	=	20%

Both factors in the formula are controllable by the investment center manager. Operating assets consist of current assets and plant assets used in operations by the center and controlled by the manager. Nonoperating assets such as idle plant assets and land held for future use are excluded. Average operating assets are usually based on the cost or book value of the assets at the beginning and end of the year.

Responsibility Report

The scope of the investment center manager's responsibility significantly affects the content of the performance report. Since an investment center is an independent entity for operating purposes, **all fixed costs are controllable by its manager**. For example, the manager is responsible for depreciation on investment center assets. Therefore, more fixed costs are identified as controllable in the performance report for an investment center manager than in a performance report for a profit center manager. The report also shows budgeted and actual ROI below controllable margin.

To illustrate this responsibility report, we will now assume that the Marine Division of Mantle Company is an investment center. It has budgeted and actual average operating assets of $2,000,000. The manager can control $60,000 of fixed costs that were not controllable when the division was a profit center. Illustration 22-24 shows the division's responsibility report.

The report shows that the manager's performance based on ROI was below budget expectations by 1.8% (15.0% versus 13.2%). Top management would likely want an explanation of the reasons for this unfavorable result.

Judgmental Factors in ROI

The return on investment approach includes two judgmental factors:

1. **Valuation of operating assets.** Operating assets may be valued at acquisition cost, book value, appraised value, or fair value. The first two bases are readily available from the accounting records.

2. **Margin (income) measure.** This measure may be controllable margin, income from operations, or net income.

Illustration 22-24
Responsibility report for investment center

		Mantle Company.xls			
Home	Insert	Page Layout	Formulas	Data	Review	View

	A	B	C	D	E
1		**MANTLE COMPANY**			
2		**Marine Division**			
3		**Responsibility Report**			
4		**For the Year Ended December 31, 2014**			
5				Difference	
6		Budget	Actual	Favorable - F Unfavorable - U	
7	Sales	$ 1,200,000	$ 1,150,000	$ 50,000	U
8	Variable costs				
9	Cost of goods sold	500,000	490,000	10,000	F
10	Selling and administrative	160,000	156,000	4,000	F
11	Total	660,000	646,000	14,000	F
12	Contribution margin	540,000	504,000	36,000	U
13	Controllable fixed costs				
14	Cost of goods sold	100,000	100,000	0	
15	Selling and administrative	80,000	80,000	0	
16	Other fixed costs	60,000	60,000	0	
17	Total	$ 240,000	$ 240,000	0	
18	Controllable margin	$ 300,000	$ 264,000	$ 36,000	U
19	Return on investment	15.0%	13.2%	1.8%	U
20		(a)	(b)	(c)	
21					
22		(a) $ 300,000 / $2,000,000	(b) $ 264,000 / $2,000,000	(c) $ 36,000 / $2,000,000	
23					

Each of the alternative values for operating assets can provide a reliable basis for evaluating a manager's performance as long as it is consistently applied between reporting periods. However, the use of income measures other than controllable margin will not result in a valid basis for evaluating the performance of an investment center manager.

Improving ROI

The manager of an investment center can improve ROI by increasing controllable margin, and/or reducing average operating assets. To illustrate, we will use the following assumed data for the Laser Division of Berra Company.

Illustration 22-25 Assumed data for Laser Division

Sales	$2,000,000
Variable costs	1,100,000
Contribution margin (45%)	900,000
Controllable fixed costs	300,000
Controllable margin (a)	$ 600,000
Average operating assets (b)	$5,000,000
Return on investment (a) ÷ (b)	12%

INCREASING CONTROLLABLE MARGIN. Controllable margin can be increased by increasing sales or by reducing variable and controllable fixed costs as follows.

1. **Increase sales 10%.** Sales will increase $200,000 ($2,000,000 × .10). Assuming no change in the contribution margin percentage of 45%, contribution margin will increase $90,000 ($200,000 × .45). Controllable margin will increase by the same amount because controllable fixed costs will not change. Thus, controllable margin becomes $690,000 ($600,000 + $90,000). The new ROI is 13.8%, computed as follows.

Illustration 22-26 ROI computation—increase in sales

$$ROI = \frac{\text{Controllable margin}}{\text{Average operating assets}} = \frac{\$690,000}{\$5,000,000} = 13.8\%$$

An increase in sales benefits both the investment center and the company if it results in new business. It would not benefit the company if the increase was achieved at the expense of other investment centers.

2. **Decrease variable and fixed costs 10%.** Total costs decrease $140,000 [($1,100,000 + $300,000) × .10]. This reduction results in a corresponding increase in controllable margin. Thus, controllable margin becomes $740,000 ($600,000 + $140,000). The new ROI is 14.8%, computed as follows.

Illustration 22-27 ROI computation—decrease in costs

$$ROI = \frac{\text{Controllable margin}}{\text{Average operating assets}} = \frac{\$740,000}{\$5,000,000} = 14.8\%$$

This course of action is clearly beneficial when the reduction in costs is the result of eliminating waste and inefficiency. But, a reduction in costs that results from cutting expenditures on vital activities, such as required maintenance and inspections, is not likely to be acceptable to top management.

REDUCING AVERAGE OPERATING ASSETS. Assume that average operating assets are reduced 10% or $500,000 ($5,000,000 × .10). Average operating assets become $4,500,000 ($5,000,000 − $500,000). Since controllable margin remains unchanged at $600,000, the new ROI is 13.3%, computed as follows.

Illustration 22-28 ROI computation—decrease in operating assets

$$ROI = \frac{\text{Controllable margin}}{\text{Average operating assets}} = \frac{\$600,000}{\$4,500,000} = 13.3\%$$

Reductions in operating assets may or may not be prudent. It is beneficial to eliminate overinvestment in inventories and to dispose of excessive plant assets. However, it is unwise to reduce inventories below expected needs or to dispose of essential plant assets.

Accounting Across the Organization

Does Hollywood Look at ROI?

If Hollywood were run like a real business, where things like return on investment mattered, there would be one unchallenged, sacred principle that studio chieftains would never violate: Make lots of G-rated movies.

No matter how you slice the movie business—by star vehicles, by budget levels, or by sequels or franchises—by far the best return on investment comes from the not-so-glamorous world of G-rated films. The problem is, these movies represent only 3% of the total films made in a typical year.

Take 2003: According to Motion Picture Association of America statistics, of the 940 movies released that year, only 29 were G-rated. Yet the highest-grossing movie of the year, *Finding Nemo*, was G-rated. . . . On the flip side are the R-rated films, which dominate the total releases and yet yield the worst return on investment. A whopping 646 R-rated films were released in 2003—69% of the total output—but only four of the top-20 grossing movies of the year were R-rated films.

This trend—G-rated movies are good for business but underproduced; R-rated movies are bad for business, and yet overdone—is something that has been driving economists batty for the past several years.

Source: David Grainger, "The Dysfunctional Family-Film Business," *Fortune* (January 10, 2005), pp. 20–21.

© YinYang/iStockphoto

 What might be the reason that movie studios do not produce G-rated movies as much as R-rated ones? (See page 1191.)

DECISION TOOLKIT

DECISION CHECKPOINTS	INFO NEEDED FOR DECISION	TOOL TO USE FOR DECISION	HOW TO EVALUATE RESULTS
Has the investment center performed up to expectations?	Controllable margin (contribution margin minus controllable fixed costs), and average investment center operating assets	Return on investment	Compare actual ROI to expected ROI.

 The service division of Metro Industries reported the following results for 2014.

PERFORMANCE EVALUATION

Sales	$400,000
Variable costs	320,000
Controllable fixed costs	40,800
Average operating assets	280,000

Management is considering the following independent courses of action in 2015 in order to maximize the return on investment for this division.

1. Reduce average operating assets by $80,000, with no change in controllable margin.

2. Increase sales $80,000, with no change in the contribution margin percentage.

(a) Compute the controllable margin and the return on investment for 2014.

(b) Compute the controllable margin and the expected return on investment for each proposed alternative.

Action Plan

- Recall key formulas: Sales − Variable costs = Contribution margin.
- Contribution margin ÷ Sales = Contribution margin percentage.
- Contribution margin − Controllable fixed costs = Controllable margin.
- Return on investment = Controllable margin ÷ Average operating assets.

Solution

(a) Return on investment for 2014

Sales	$400,000
Variable costs	320,000
Contribution margin	80,000
Controllable fixed costs	40,800
Controllable margin	$ 39,200

$$\text{Return on investment} \quad \frac{\$39,200}{\$280,000} = 14\%$$

(b) Expected return on investment for alternative 1:

$$\frac{\$39,200}{\$280,000 - \$80,000} = 19.6\%$$

Expected return on investment for alternative 2:

Sales ($400,000 + $80,000)	$480,000
Variable costs ($320,000/$400,000 × $480,000)	384,000
Contribution margin	96,000
Controllable fixed costs	40,800
Controllable margin	$ 55,200

$$\text{Return on investment} \quad \frac{\$55,200}{\$280,000} = 19.7\%$$

Related exercise material: **BE22-8, BE22-9, BE22-10, E22-16, E22-17,** and **Do it!** 22-4.

USING THE DECISION TOOLKIT

The manufacturing overhead budget for Reebles Company contains the following items.

Variable costs	
Indirect materials	$25,000
Indirect labor	12,000
Maintenance expenses	10,000
Manufacturing supplies	6,000
Total variable	$53,000
Fixed costs	
Supervision	$17,000
Inspection costs	1,000
Insurance expenses	2,000
Depreciation	15,000
Total fixed	$35,000

The budget was based on an estimated 2,000 units being produced. During November, 1,500 units were produced, and the following costs incurred.

	Variable costs	
	Indirect materials	$25,200
	Indirect labor	13,500
	Maintenance expenses	8,200
	Manufacturing supplies	5,100
	Total variable	$52,000
	Fixed costs	
	Supervision	$19,300
	Inspection costs	1,200
	Insurance expenses	2,200
	Depreciation	14,700
	Total fixed	$37,400

Instructions

(a) Determine which items would be controllable by Ed Lopat, the production manager. (Assume "supervision" excludes Lopat's own salary.)
(b) How much should have been spent during the month for the manufacture of the 1,500 units?
(c) Prepare a flexible manufacturing overhead budget report for Mr. Lopat.
(d) Prepare a responsibility report. Include only the costs that would have been controllable by Mr. Lopat. In an attached memo, describe clearly for Mr. Lopat the areas in which his performance needs to be improved.

Solution

(a) Ed Lopat should be able to control all the variable costs and the fixed costs of supervision and inspection. Insurance and depreciation ordinarily are not the responsibility of the department manager.
(b) The total variable cost per unit is $26.50 ($53,000 ÷ 2,000). The total budgeted cost during the month to manufacture 1,500 units is variable costs $39,750 (1,500 × $26.50) plus fixed costs ($35,000), for a total of $74,750 ($39,750 + $35,000).
(c)

REEBLES COMPANY
Production Department
Manufacturing Overhead Budget Report (Flexible)
For the Month Ended November 30, 2014

	Budget at 1,500 Units	Actual at 1,500 Units	Difference Favorable F Unfavorable U
Variable costs			
Indirect materials ($12.50)	$18,750	$25,200	$ 6,450 U
Indirect labor ($6)	9,000	13,500	4,500 U
Maintenance ($5)	7,500	8,200	700 U
Manufacturing supplies ($3)	4,500	5,100	600 U
Total variable	39,750	52,000	12,250 U
Fixed costs			
Supervision	17,000	19,300	2,300 U
Inspection	1,000	1,200	200 U
Insurance	2,000	2,200	200 U
Depreciation	15,000	14,700	300 F
Total fixed	35,000	37,400	2,400 U
Total costs	$74,750	$89,400	$14,650 U

(d) Because a production department is a cost center, the responsibility report should include only the costs that are controllable by the production manager. In this type of report, no distinction is made between variable and fixed costs. Budget data in the report should be based on the units actually produced.

REEBLES COMPANY
Production Department
Manufacturing Overhead Responsibility Report
For the Month Ended November 30, 2014

Controllable Costs	Budget	Actual	Difference Favorable F Unfavorable U
Indirect materials	$18,750	$25,200	$ 6,450 U
Indirect labor	9,000	13,500	4,500 U
Maintenance	7,500	8,200	700 U
Manufacturing supplies	4,500	5,100	600 U
Supervision	17,000	19,300	2,300 U
Inspection	1,000	1,200	200 U
Total	$57,750	$72,500	$14,750 U

To: Mr. Ed Lopat, Production Manager

From: _____, Vice President of Production

Subject: Performance Evaluation for the Month of November

Your performance in controlling costs that are your responsibility was very disappointing in the month of November. As indicated in the accompanying responsibility report, total costs were $14,750 over budget. On a percentage basis, costs were 26% over budget. As you can see, actual costs were over budget for every cost item. In three instances, costs were significantly over budget (indirect materials 34%, indirect labor 50%, and supervision 14%).

   Ed, it is imperative that you get costs under control in your department as soon as possible.

   I think we need to talk about ways to implement more effective cost control measures. I would like to meet with you in my office at 9 a.m. on Wednesday to discuss possible alternatives.

✔ The Navigator

Summary of Learning Objectives

1 **Describe the concept of budgetary control.** Budgetary control consists of (a) preparing periodic budget reports that compare actual results with planned objectives, (b) analyzing the differences to determine their causes, (c) taking appropriate corrective action, and (d) modifying future plans, if necessary.

2 **Evaluate the usefulness of static budget reports.** Static budget reports are useful in evaluating the progress toward planned sales and profit goals. They are also appropriate in assessing a manager's effectiveness in controlling costs when (a) actual activity closely approximates the master budget activity level, and/or (b) the behavior of the costs in response to changes in activity is fixed.

3 **Explain the development of flexible budgets and the usefulness of flexible budget reports.** To develop the flexible budget it is necessary to: (a) Identify the activity index and the relevant range of activity. (b) Identify the variable costs, and determine the budgeted variable cost per unit of activity for each cost. (c) Identify the fixed costs, and determine the budgeted amount for each cost. (d) Prepare the budget for selected increments of activity within the relevant range. Flexible budget reports permit an evaluation of a manager's performance in controlling production and costs.

4 **Describe the concept of responsibility accounting.** Responsibility accounting involves accumulating and reporting revenues and costs on the basis of the individual manager who has the authority to make the day-to-day decisions about the items. The evaluation of a manager's performance is based on the matters directly under the manager's control. In responsibility accounting, it is necessary to distinguish between controllable and non-controllable fixed costs and to identify three types of responsibility centers: cost, profit, and investment.

5 **Indicate the features of responsibility reports for cost centers.** Responsibility reports for cost centers compare actual costs with flexible budget data. The reports show only controllable costs, and no distinction is made between variable and fixed costs.

6 **Identify the content of responsibility reports for profit centers.** Responsibility reports show contribution margin, controllable fixed costs, and controllable margin for each profit center.

7 **Explain the basis and formula used in evaluating performance in investment centers.** The primary basis for evaluating performance in investment centers is return on investment (ROI). The formula for computing ROI for investment centers is: Controllable margin ÷ Average operating assets.

✔ The Navigator

DECISION TOOLKIT *A SUMMARY*

DECISION CHECKPOINTS	INFO NEEDED FOR DECISION	TOOL TO USE FOR DECISION	HOW TO EVALUATE RESULTS
Are the increased costs resulting from increased production reasonable?	Variable costs projected at different levels of production	Flexible budget	After taking into account different production levels, results are favorable if expenses are less than budgeted amounts.
Have the individual managers been held accountable for the costs and revenues under their control?	Relevant costs and revenues, where the individual manager has authority to make day-to-day decisions about the items	Responsibility reports focused on cost centers, profit centers, and investment centers as appropriate	Compare budget to actual costs and revenues for controllable items.
Has the investment center performed up to expectations?	Controllable margin (contribution margin minus controllable fixed costs), and average investment center operating assets	Return on investment	Compare actual ROI to expected ROI.

Appendix 22A

Residual Income—Another Performance Measurement

Although most companies use ROI in evaluating their investment performance, ROI has a significant disadvantage. To illustrate, let's look at the Electronics Division of Pujols Company. It has an ROI of 20% computed as follows.

LEARNING OBJECTIVE 8

Explain the difference between ROI and residual income.

Controllable Margin	÷	Average Operating Assets	=	Return on Investment (ROI)
$1,000,000	÷	$5,000,000	=	20%

Illustration 22A-1 ROI formula

The Electronics Division is considering producing a new product, a GPS device (hereafter referred to as Tracker), for its boats. To produce Tracker, operating assets will have to increase $2,000,000. Tracker is expected to generate an additional $260,000 of controllable margin. Illustration 22A-2 shows how Tracker will effect ROI.

Illustration 22A-2 ROI comparison

	Without Tracker	Tracker	With Tracker
Controllable margin (a)	$1,000,000	$ 260,000	$1,260,000
Average operating assets (b)	$5,000,000	$2,000,000	$7,000,000
Return on investment [(a) ÷ (b)]	20%	13%	18%

The investment in Tracker reduces ROI from 20% to 18%.

Let's suppose that you are the manager of the Electronics Division and must make the decision to produce or not produce Tracker. If you were evaluated using ROI, you probably would not produce Tracker because your ROI would drop from 20% to 18%. The problem with this ROI analysis is that it ignores an important variable, the minimum rate of return on a company's operating assets.

The **minimum rate of return** is the rate at which the Electronics Division can cover its costs and earn a profit. Assuming that the Electronics Division has a minimum rate of return of 10%, it should invest in Tracker because its ROI of 13% is greater than 10%.

RESIDUAL INCOME COMPARED TO ROI

To evaluate performance using the minimum rate of return, companies use the residual income approach. **Residual income** is the income that remains after subtracting from the controllable margin the minimum rate of return on a company's average operating assets. The residual income for Tracker would be computed as follows.

Illustration 22A-3 Residual income formula

Controllable Margin	−	Minimum Rate of Return × Average Operating Assets	=	Residual Income
$260,000	−	10% × $2,000,000	=	$60,000

As shown, the residual income related to the Tracker investment is $60,000. Illustration 22A-4 indicates how residual income changes as the additional investment is made.

Illustration 22A-4 Residual income comparison

	Without Tracker	Tracker	With Tracker
Controllable margin (a)	$1,000,000	$260,000	$1,260,000
Average operating assets × 10% (b)	500,000	200,000	700,000
Residual income [(a) − (b)]	$ 500,000	$ 60,000	$ 560,000

This example illustrates how performance evaluation based on ROI can be misleading and can even cause managers to reject projects that would actually increase income for the company. As a result, many companies such as Coca-Cola, Briggs and Stratton, Eli Lilly, and Siemens AG use residual income (or a variant often referred to as economic value added) to evaluate investment alternatives and measure company performance.

RESIDUAL INCOME WEAKNESS

It might appear from the above discussion that the goal of any company should be to maximize the total amount of residual income in each division. This goal, however, ignores the fact that one division might use substantially fewer assets to attain the same level of residual income as another division. For example, we know that to produce Tracker, the Electronics Division of Pujols Company used $2,000,000 of average operating assets to generate $260,000 of controllable margin. Now let's say a different division produced a product called SeaDog, which used $4,000,000 to generate $460,000 of controllable margin, as shown in Illustration 22A-5.

Illustration 22A-5 Comparison of two products

	Tracker	SeaDog
Controllable margin (a)	$260,000	$460,000
Average operating assets × 10% (b)	200,000	400,000
Residual income [(a) − (b)]	$ 60,000	$ 60,000

If the performance of these two investments were evaluated using residual income, they would be considered equal: Both products have the same total residual income. This ignores, however, the fact that SeaDog required **twice** as many operating assets to achieve the same level of residual income.

Summary of Learning Objective for Appendix 22A

8 **Explain the difference between ROI and residual income.** ROI is controllable margin divided by average operating assets. Residual income is the income that remains after subtracting the minimum rate of return on a company's average operating assets. ROI sometimes provides misleading results because profitable investments are often rejected when the investment reduces ROI but increases overall profitability.

✔ The Navigator

Glossary

Budgetary control *(p. 1134)* The use of budgets to control operations.

Controllable cost *(p. 1147)* A cost over which a manager has control.

Controllable margin *(p. 1154)* Contribution margin less controllable fixed costs.

Cost center *(p. 1152)* A responsibility center that incurs costs but does not directly generate revenues.

Decentralization *(p. 1146)* Control of operations is delegated to many managers throughout the organization.

Direct fixed costs *(p. 1153)* Costs that relate specifically to a responsibility center and are incurred for the sole benefit of the center.

Flexible budget *(p. 1137)* A projection of budget data for various levels of activity.

Indirect fixed costs *(p. 1154)* Costs that are incurred for the benefit of more than one profit center.

Investment center *(p. 1152)* A responsibility center that incurs costs, generates revenues, and has control over decisions regarding the assets available for use.

Management by exception *(p. 1147)* The review of budget reports by top management focused entirely or primarily on differences between actual results and planned objectives.

Noncontrollable costs *(p. 1147)* Costs incurred indirectly and allocated to a responsibility center that are not controllable at that level.

Profit center *(p. 1152)* A responsibility center that incurs costs and also generates revenues.

Residual income *(p. 1164)* The income that remains after subtracting from the controllable margin the minimum rate of return on a company's average operating assets.

Responsibility accounting *(p. 1145)* A part of management accounting that involves accumulating and reporting revenues and costs on the basis of the manager who has the authority to make the day-to-day decisions about the items.

Responsibility reporting system *(p. 1149)* The preparation of reports for each level of responsibility in the company's organization chart.

Return on investment (ROI) *(p. 1156)* A measure of management's effectiveness in utilizing assets at its disposal in an investment center.

Segment *(p. 1146)* An area of responsibility in decentralized operations.

Static budget *(p. 1135)* A projection of budget data at one level of activity.

Comprehensive Do it!

Glenda Company uses a flexible budget for manufacturing overhead based on direct labor hours. For 2014, the master overhead budget for the Packaging Department based on 300,000 direct labor hours was as follows.

Variable Costs		Fixed Costs	
Indirect labor	$360,000	Supervision	$ 60,000
Supplies and lubricants	150,000	Depreciation	24,000
Maintenance	210,000	Property taxes	18,000
Utilities	120,000	Insurance	12,000
	$840,000		$114,000

During July, 24,000 direct labor hours were worked. The company incurred the following variable costs in July: indirect labor $30,200, supplies and lubricants $11,600, maintenance $17,500, and utilities $9,200. Actual fixed overhead costs were the same as monthly budgeted fixed costs.

Instructions

Prepare a flexible budget report for the Packaging Department for July.

Action Plan

- Classify each cost as variable or fixed.
- Compute the budgeted cost per direct labor hour for all variable costs.
- Use budget data for actual direct labor hours worked.
- Determine the difference between budgeted and actual costs.
- Identify the difference as favorable or unfavorable.
- Determine the difference in total variable costs, total fixed costs, and total costs.

Solution to Comprehensive Do it!

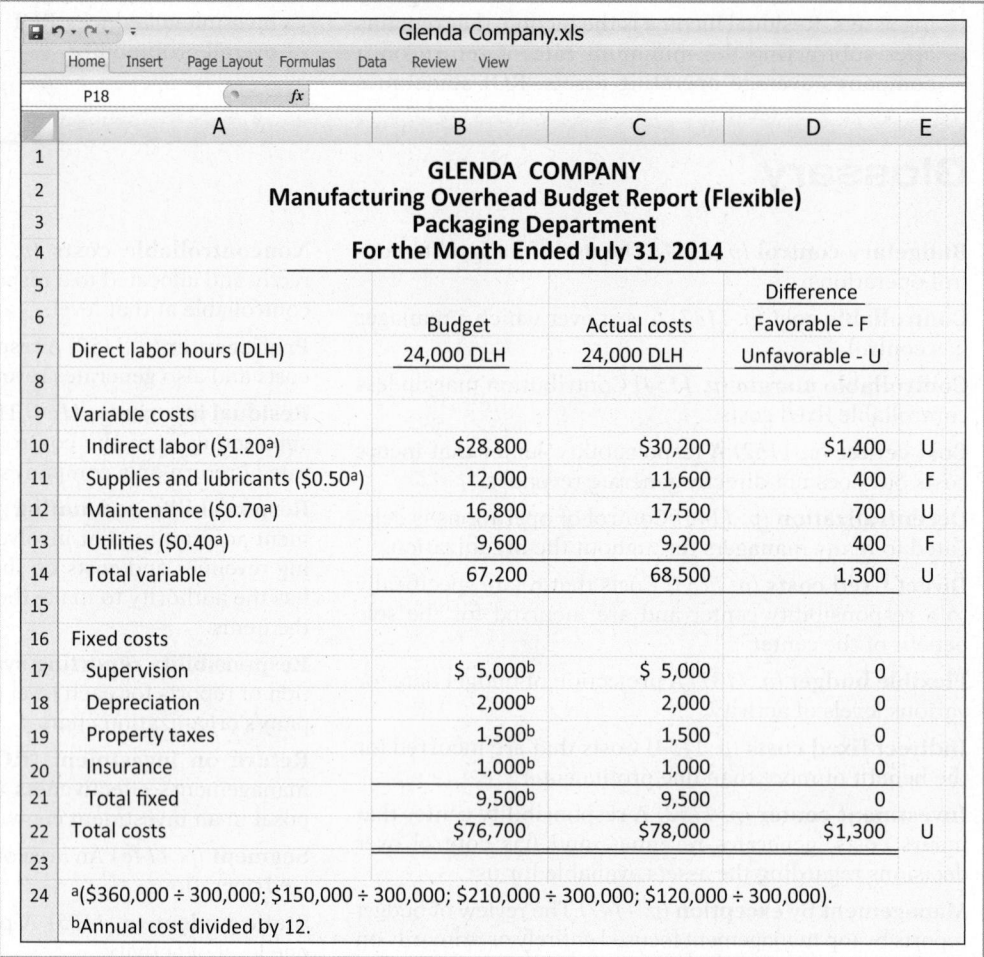

GLENDA COMPANY
Manufacturing Overhead Budget Report (Flexible)
Packaging Department
For the Month Ended July 31, 2014

	Budget	Actual costs	Difference Favorable - F Unfavorable - U	
Direct labor hours (DLH)	24,000 DLH	24,000 DLH		
Variable costs				
Indirect labor ($1.20a)	$28,800	$30,200	$1,400	U
Supplies and lubricants ($0.50a)	12,000	11,600	400	F
Maintenance ($0.70a)	16,800	17,500	700	U
Utilities ($0.40a)	9,600	9,200	400	F
Total variable	67,200	68,500	1,300	U
Fixed costs				
Supervision	$ 5,000b	$ 5,000	0	
Depreciation	2,000b	2,000	0	
Property taxes	1,500b	1,500	0	
Insurance	1,000b	1,000	0	
Total fixed	9,500b	9,500	0	
Total costs	$76,700	$78,000	$1,300	U

a($360,000 ÷ 300,000; $150,000 ÷ 300,000; $210,000 ÷ 300,000; $120,000 ÷ 300,000).
bAnnual cost divided by 12.

The Navigator

WILEY PLUS **Self-Test, Brief Exercises, Exercises, Problem Set A, and many more resources are available for practice in WileyPLUS.**

Note: All Questions, Exercises, and Problems marked with an asterisk relate to material in the appendix to the chapter.

Self-Test Questions

Answers are on page 1191.

(LO 1) 1. Budgetary control involves all but one of the following:
(a) modifying future plans.
(b) analyzing differences.
(c) using static budgets.
(d) determining differences between actual and planned results.

2. Budget reports are prepared: (LO 1)
(a) daily.
(b) weekly.
(c) monthly.
(d) All of the above.

3. A production manager in a manufacturing company (LO 1) would most likely receive a:
(a) sales report.
(b) income statement.

(c) scrap report.

(d) shipping department overhead report.

(LO 2) **4.** A static budget is:

(a) a projection of budget data at several levels of activity within the relevant range of activity.

(b) a projection of budget data at a single level of activity.

(c) compared to a flexible budget in a budget report.

(d) never appropriate in evaluating a manager's effectiveness in controlling costs.

(LO 2) **5.** A static budget is useful in controlling costs when cost behavior is:

(a) mixed.   (c) variable.

(b) fixed.   (d) linear.

(LO 3) **6.** At zero direct labor hours in a flexible budget graph, the total budgeted cost line intersects the vertical axis at $30,000. At 10,000 direct labor hours, a horizontal line drawn from the total budgeted cost line intersects the vertical axis at $90,000. Fixed and variable costs may be expressed as:

(a) $30,000 fixed plus $6 per direct labor hour variable.

(b) $30,000 fixed plus $9 per direct labor hour variable.

(c) $60,000 fixed plus $3 per direct labor hour variable.

(d) $60,000 fixed plus $6 per direct labor hour variable.

(LO 3) **7.** At 9,000 direct labor hours, the flexible budget for indirect materials is $27,000. If $28,000 of indirect materials costs are incurred at 9,200 direct labor hours, the flexible budget report should show the following difference for indirect materials:

(a) $1,000 unfavorable.   (c) $400 favorable.

(b) $1,000 favorable.   (d) $400 unfavorable.

(LO 4) **8.** Under responsibility accounting, the evaluation of a manager's performance is based on matters that the manager:

(a) directly controls.

(b) directly and indirectly controls.

(c) indirectly controls.

(d) has shared responsibility for with another manager.

(LO 4) **9.** Responsibility centers include:

(a) cost centers.   (c) investment centers.

(b) profit centers.   (d) All of the above.

(LO 5) **10.** Responsibility reports for cost centers:

(a) distinguish between fixed and variable costs.

(b) use static budget data.

(c) include both controllable and noncontrollable costs.

(d) include only controllable costs.

11. The accounting department of a manufacturing com- (LO 5) pany is an example of:

(a) a cost center.   (c) an investment center.

(b) a profit center.   (d) a contribution center.

12. To evaluate the performance of a profit center man- (LO 6) ager, upper management needs detailed information about:

(a) controllable costs.

(b) controllable revenues.

(c) controllable costs and revenues.

(d) controllable costs and revenues and average operating assets.

13. In a responsibility report for a profit center, control- (LO 6) lable fixed costs are deducted from contribution margin to show:

(a) profit center margin.

(b) controllable margin.

(c) net income.

(d) income from operations.

14. In the formula for return on investment (ROI), the (LO 7) factors for controllable margin and operating assets are, respectively:

(a) controllable margin percentage and total operating assets.

(b) controllable margin dollars and average operating assets.

(c) controllable margin dollars and total assets.

(d) controllable margin percentage and average operating assets.

15. A manager of an investment center can improve (LO 7) ROI by:

(a) increasing average operating assets.

(b) reducing sales.

(c) increasing variable costs.

(d) reducing variable and/or controllable fixed costs.

Go to the book's companion website, **www. wiley.com/college/kimmel**, for additional Self-Test Questions.

 The Navigator

Questions

1. (a) What is budgetary control?

(b) Fred Barone is describing budgetary control. What steps should be included in Fred's description?

2. The following purposes are part of a budgetary reporting system: (a) Determine efficient use of materials. (b) Control overhead costs. (c) Determine whether income objectives are being met. For each purpose, indicate the name of the report, the frequency of the report, and the primary recipient(s) of the report.

3. How may a budget report for the second quarter differ from a budget report for the first quarter?

4. Ken Bay questions the usefulness of a master sales budget in evaluating sales performance. Is there justification for Ken's concern? Explain.

5. Under what circumstances may a static budget be an appropriate basis for evaluating a manager's effectiveness in controlling costs?

6. "A flexible budget is really a series of static budgets." Is this true? Why?

7. The static manufacturing overhead budget based on 40,000 direct labor hours shows budgeted indirect labor costs of $54,000. During March, the department incurs $64,000 of indirect labor while working 45,000 direct labor hours. Is this a favorable or unfavorable performance? Why?

8. A static overhead budget based on 40,000 direct labor hours shows Factory Insurance $6,500 as a fixed cost. At the 50,000 direct labor hours worked in March, factory insurance costs were $6,300. Is this a favorable or unfavorable performance? Why?

9. Megan Pedigo is confused about how a flexible budget is prepared. Identify the steps for Megan.

10. Cali Company has prepared a graph of flexible budget data. At zero direct labor hours, the total budgeted cost line intersects the vertical axis at $20,000. At 10,000 direct labor hours, the line drawn from the total budgeted cost line intersects the vertical axis at $85,000. How may the fixed and variable costs be expressed?

11. The flexible budget formula is fixed costs $50,000 plus variable costs of $4 per direct labor hour. What is the total budgeted cost at (a) 9,000 hours and (b) 12,345 hours?

12. What is management by exception? What criteria may be used in identifying exceptions?

13. What is responsibility accounting? Explain the purpose of responsibility accounting.

14. Eve Rooney is studying for an accounting examination. Describe for Eve what conditions are necessary for responsibility accounting to be used effectively.

15. Distinguish between controllable and noncontrollable costs.

16. How do responsibility reports differ from budget reports?

17. What is the relationship, if any, between a responsibility reporting system and a company's organization chart?

18. Distinguish among the three types of responsibility centers.

19. (a) What costs are included in a performance report for a cost center? (b) In the report, are variable and fixed costs identified?

20. How do direct fixed costs differ from indirect fixed costs? Are both types of fixed costs controllable?

21. Jane Nott is confused about controllable margin reported in an income statement for a profit center. How is this margin computed, and what is its primary purpose?

22. What is the primary basis for evaluating the performance of the manager of an investment center? Indicate the formula for this basis.

23. Explain the ways that ROI can be improved.

24. Indicate two behavioral principles that pertain to (a) the manager being evaluated and (b) top management.

*25. What is a major disadvantage of using ROI to evaluate investment and company performance?

*26. What is residual income, and what is one of its major weaknesses?

Brief Exercises

Prepare static budget report.
(LO 2), **AP**

BE22-1 For the quarter ended March 31, 2014, Maris Company accumulates the following sales data for its product, Garden-Tools: $310,000 budget; $305,000 actual. Prepare a static budget report for the quarter.

Prepare static budget report for 2 quarters.
(LO 2), **AP**

BE22-2 Data for Maris Company are given in BE22-1. In the second quarter, budgeted sales were $380,000, and actual sales were $384,000. Prepare a static budget report for the second quarter and for the year to date.

Show usefulness of flexible budgets in evaluating performance.
(LO 3), **E**

BE22-3 In Paige Company, direct labor is $20 per hour. The company expects to operate at 10,000 direct labor hours each month. In January 2014, direct labor totaling $204,000 is incurred in working 10,400 hours. Prepare (a) a static budget report and (b) a flexible budget report. Evaluate the usefulness of each report.

Prepare a flexible budget for variable costs.
(LO 3), **AP**

BE22-4 Gundy Company expects to produce 1,200,000 units of Product XX in 2014. Monthly production is expected to range from 80,000 to 120,000 units. Budgeted variable manufacturing costs per unit are direct materials $5, direct labor $6, and overhead $8. Budgeted fixed manufacturing costs per unit for depreciation are $2 and for supervision are $1. Prepare a flexible manufacturing budget for the relevant range value using 20,000 unit increments.

Prepare flexible budget report.
(LO 3), **AN**

BE22-5 Data for Gundy Company are given in BE22-4. In March 2014, the company incurs the following costs in producing 100,000 units: direct materials $525,000, direct labor $596,000, and variable overhead $805,000. Actual fixed costs were equal to budgeted fixed costs. Prepare a flexible budget report for March. Were costs controlled?

Prepare a responsibility report for a cost center.
(LO 5), **AP**

BE22-6 In the Assembly Department of Hannon Company, budgeted and actual manufacturing overhead costs for the month of April 2014 were as follows.

	Budget	**Actual**
Indirect materials	$16,000	$14,300
Indirect labor	20,000	20,600
Utilities	10,000	10,850
Supervision	5,000	5,000

All costs are controllable by the department manager. Prepare a responsibility report for April for the cost center.

BE22-7 Elbert Company accumulates the following summary data for the year ending December 31, 2014, for its Water Division, which it operates as a profit center: sales— $2,000,000 budget, $2,080,000 actual; variable costs—$1,000,000 budget, $1,060,000 actual; and controllable fixed costs—$300,000 budget, $305,000 actual. Prepare a responsibility report for the Water Division.

Prepare a responsibility report for a profit center.

(LO 6), AP

BE22-8 For the year ending December 31, 2014, Cobb Company accumulates the following data for the Plastics Division which it operates as an investment center: contribution margin—$700,000 budget, $710,000 actual; controllable fixed costs—$300,000 budget, $302,000 actual. Average operating assets for the year were $2,000,000. Prepare a responsibility report for the Plastics Division beginning with contribution margin.

Prepare a responsibility report for an investment center.

(LO 7), AP

BE22-9 For its three investment centers, Kaspar Company accumulates the following data:

Compute return on investment using the ROI formula.

(LO 7), AP

	I	**II**	**III**
Sales	$2,000,000	$4,000,000	$ 4,000,000
Controllable margin	1,300,000	2,000,000	3,600,000
Average operating assets	5,000,000	8,000,000	12,000,000

Compute the return on investment (ROI) for each center.

BE22-10 Data for the investment centers for Kaspar Company are given in BE22-9. The centers expect the following changes in the next year: (I) increase sales 15%; (II) decrease costs $400,000; (III) decrease average operating assets $500,000. Compute the expected return on investment (ROI) for each center. Assume center I has a contribution margin percentage of 70%.

Compute return on investment under changed conditions.

(LO 7), AP

*BE22-11 Voorhees, Inc. reports the following financial information.

Compute ROI and residual income.

(LO 8), AP

Average operating assets	$3,000,000
Controllable margin	$ 660,000
Minimum rate of return	10%

Compute the return on investment and the residual income.

*BE22-12 Presented below is information related to the Southern Division of Lumber, Inc.

Compute ROI and residual income.

(LO 8), AP

Contribution margin	$1,200,000
Controllable margin	$ 800,000
Average operating assets	$4,000,000
Minimum rate of return	15%

Compute the Southern Division's return on investment and residual income.

Do it! Review

Do it! 22-1 In Pargo Company's flexible budget graph, the fixed cost line and the total budgeted cost line intersect the vertical axis at $90,000. The total budgeted cost line is $330,000 at an activity level of 50,000 direct labor hours. Compute total budgeted costs at 65,000 direct labor hours.

Compute total budgeted costs in flexible budget.

(LO 3), AP

Prepare and evaluate a flexible budget report.
(LO 3), **AP**

Do it! 22-2 Mussatto Company expects to produce 50,000 units of product IOA during the current year. Budgeted variable manufacturing costs per unit are direct materials $7, direct labor $13, and overhead $18. Annual budgeted fixed manufacturing overhead costs are $96,000 for depreciation and $45,600 for supervision.

In the current month, Mussatto produced 6,000 units and incurred the following costs: direct materials $38,850, direct labor $76,440, variable overhead $116,640, depreciation $8,000, and supervision $4,000.

Prepare a flexible budget report. (*Note:* You do not need to prepare the heading.) Were costs controlled?

Prepare a responsibility report.
(LO 6), **AP**

Do it! 22-3 The Wellstone Division operates as a profit center. It reports the following for the year.

	Budget	Actual
Sales	$2,000,000	$1,860,000
Variable costs	800,000	760,000
Controllable fixed costs	550,000	550,000
Noncontrollable fixed costs	250,000	250,000

Prepare a responsibility report for the Wellstone Division at December 31, 2014.

Compute ROI and expected return on investments.
(LO 7), **AP**

Do it! 22-4 The service division of Raney Industries reported the following results for 2013.

Sales	$500,000
Variable costs	300,000
Controllable fixed costs	75,000
Average operating assets	625,000

Management is considering the following independent courses of action in 2014 in order to maximize the return on investment for this division.

1. Reduce average operating assets by $125,000, with no change in controllable margin.
2. Increase sales $100,000, with no change in the contribution margin percentage.

(a) Compute the controllable margin and the return on investment for 2013. (b) Compute the controllable margin and the expected return on investment for each proposed alternative.

Exercises

Understand the concept of budgetary control.
(LO 1, 2, 3), **K**

E22-1 Mike Trusler has prepared the following list of statements about budgetary control.
1. Budget reports compare actual results with planned objectives.
2. All budget reports are prepared on a weekly basis.
3. Management uses budget reports to analyze differences between actual and planned results and determine their causes.
4. As a result of analyzing budget reports, management may either take corrective action or modify future plans.
5. Budgetary control works best when a company has an informal reporting system.
6. The primary recipients of the sales report are the sales manager and the vice president of production.
7. The primary recipient of the scrap report is the production manager.
8. A static budget is a projection of budget data at one level of activity.
9. Top management's reaction to unfavorable differences is not influenced by the materiality of the difference.
10. A static budget is not appropriate in evaluating a manager's effectiveness in controlling costs unless the actual activity level approximates the static budget activity level or the behavior of the costs is fixed.

Instructions

Identify each statement as true or false. If false, indicate how to correct the statement.

E22-2 Crede Company budgeted selling expenses of $30,000 in January, $35,000 in February, and $40,000 in March. Actual selling expenses were $31,200 in January, $34,525 in February, and $46,000 in March.

Prepare and evaluate static budget report.

(LO 2), **AN**

Instructions

(a) Prepare a selling expense report that compares budgeted and actual amounts by month and for the year to date.

(b) What is the purpose of the report prepared in (a), and who would be the primary recipient?

(c) What would be the likely result of management's analysis of the report?

E22-3 Thome Company uses a flexible budget for manufacturing overhead based on direct labor hours. Variable manufacturing overhead costs per direct labor hour are as follows.

Prepare flexible manufacturing overhead budget.

(LO 3), **AP**

Indirect labor	$1.00
Indirect materials	0.60
Utilities	0.40

Fixed overhead costs per month are supervision $4,000, depreciation $1,200, and property taxes $800. The company believes it will normally operate in a range of 7,000–10,000 direct labor hours per month.

Instructions

Prepare a monthly manufacturing overhead flexible budget for 2014 for the expected range of activity, using increments of 1,000 direct labor hours.

E22-4 Using the information in E22-3, assume that in July 2014, Thome Company incurs the following manufacturing overhead costs.

Prepare flexible budget reports for manufacturing overhead costs, and comment on findings.

(LO 3), **AN**

Variable Costs		**Fixed Costs**	
Indirect labor	$8,800	Supervision	$4,000
Indirect materials	5,300	Depreciation	1,200
Utilities	3,200	Property taxes	800

Instructions

(a) Prepare a flexible budget performance report, assuming that the company worked 9,000 direct labor hours during the month.

(b) Prepare a flexible budget performance report, assuming that the company worked 8,500 direct labor hours during the month.

(c) ▭▬▶ Comment on your findings.

E22-5 DeWitt Company uses flexible budgets to control its selling expenses. Monthly sales are expected to range from $170,000 to $200,000. Variable costs and their percentage relationship to sales are sales commissions 6%, advertising 4%, traveling 3%, and delivery 2%. Fixed selling expenses will consist of sales salaries $35,000, depreciation on delivery equipment $7,000, and insurance on delivery equipment $1,000.

Prepare flexible selling expense budget.

(LO 3), **AP**

Instructions

Prepare a monthly flexible budget for each $10,000 increment of sales within the relevant range for the year ending December 31, 2014.

E22-6 The actual selling expenses incurred in March 2014 by DeWitt Company are as follows.

Prepare flexible budget reports for selling expenses.

(LO 3), **AN**

Variable Expenses		**Fixed Expenses**	
Sales commissions	$11,000	Sales salaries	$35,000
Advertising	6,900	Depreciation	7,000
Travel	5,100	Insurance	1,000
Delivery	3,450		

Instructions

(a) Prepare a flexible budget performance report for March using the budget data in E22-5, assuming that March sales were $170,000.

(b) Prepare a flexible budget performance report, assuming that March sales were $180,000.

(c) ▭▬▶ Comment on the importance of using flexible budgets in evaluating the performance of the sales manager.

Prepare flexible budget report for cost center.

(LO 3), AP

E22-7 Kitchen Help Inc. (KHI) is a manufacturer of toaster ovens. To improve control over operations, the president of KHI wants to begin using a flexible budgeting system, rather than use only the current master budget. The following data are available for KHI's expected costs at production levels of 90,000, 100,000, and 110,000 units.

Variable costs	
Manufacturing	$6 per unit
Administrative	$4 per unit
Selling	$2 per unit
Fixed costs	
Manufacturing	$160,000
Administrative	$ 80,000

Instructions

(a) Prepare a flexible budget for each of the possible production levels: 90,000, 100,000, and 110,000 units.

(b) If KHI sells the toaster ovens for $16 each, how many units will it have to sell to make a profit of $200,000 before taxes?

(CGA adapted)

Prepare flexible budget report; compare flexible and static budgets.

(LO 2, 3), E

E22-8 Rensing Groomers is in the dog-grooming business. Its operating costs are described by the following formulas:

Grooming supplies (variable)	$y = \$0 + \$5x$
Direct labor (variable)	$y = \$0 + \$14x$
Overhead (mixed)	$y = \$10,000 + \$1x$

Milo, the owner, has determined that direct labor is the cost driver for all three categories of costs.

Instructions

(a) Prepare a flexible budget for activity levels of 550, 600, and 700 direct labor hours.

(b) ✏️➡ Explain why the flexible budget is more informative than the static budget.

(c) Calculate the total cost per direct labor hour at each of the activity levels specified in part (a).

(d) The groomers at Rensing normally work a total of 650 direct labor hours during each month. Each grooming job normally takes a groomer 1.3 hours. Milo wants to earn a profit equal to 40% of the costs incurred. Determine what he should charge each pet owner for grooming.

(CGA adapted)

Prepare flexible budget and responsibility report for manufacturing overhead.

(LO 3, 5), AP

E22-9 Lowell Company's manufacturing overhead budget for the first quarter of 2014 contained the following data.

Variable Costs		**Fixed Costs**	
Indirect materials	$12,000	Supervisory salaries	$36,000
Indirect labor	10,000	Depreciation	7,000
Utilities	8,000	Property taxes and insurance	8,000
Maintenance	6,000	Maintenance	5,000

Actual variable costs were indirect materials $13,900, indirect labor $9,500, utilities $8,700, and maintenance $5,000. Actual fixed costs equaled budgeted costs except for property taxes and insurance, which were $8,400. The actual activity level equaled the budgeted level.

All costs are considered controllable by the production department manager except for depreciation, and property taxes and insurance.

Instructions

(a) Prepare a manufacturing overhead flexible budget report for the first quarter.

(b) Prepare a responsibility report for the first quarter.

Prepare flexible budget report, and answer question.

(LO 2, 3), E

E22-10 As sales manager, Joe Batista was given the following static budget report for selling expenses in the Clothing Department of Soria Company for the month of October.

SORIA COMPANY
Clothing Department
Budget Report
For the Month Ended October 31, 2014

	Budget	Actual	Difference Favorable F Unfavorable U
Sales in units	8,000	10,000	2,000 F
Variable expenses			
Sales commissions	$ 2,400	$ 2,600	$ 200 U
Advertising expense	720	850	130 U
Travel expense	3,600	4,100	500 U
Free samples given out	1,600	1,400	200 F
Total variable	8,320	8,950	630 U
Fixed expenses			
Rent	1,500	1,500	–0–
Sales salaries	1,200	1,200	–0–
Office salaries	800	800	–0–
Depreciation—autos (sales staff)	500	500	–0–
Total fixed	4,000	4,000	–0–
Total expenses	$12,320	$12,950	$ 630 U

As a result of this budget report, Joe was called into the president's office and congratulated on his fine sales performance. He was reprimanded, however, for allowing his costs to get out of control. Joe knew something was wrong with the performance report that he had been given. However, he was not sure what to do, and comes to you for advice.

Instructions
(a) Prepare a budget report based on flexible budget data to help Joe.
(b) Should Joe have been reprimanded? Explain.

E22-11 Kirkland Plumbing Company is a newly formed company specializing in plumbing services for home and business. The owner, Lenny Kirkland, had divided the company into two segments: Home Plumbing Services and Business Plumbing Services. Each segment is run by its own supervisor, while basic selling and administrative services are shared by both segments.

Prepare and discuss a responsibility report.
(LO 3, 5), **AP**

Lenny has asked you to help him create a performance reporting system that will allow him to measure each segment's performance in terms of its profitability. To that end, the following information has been collected on the Home Plumbing Services segment for the first quarter of 2014.

	Budget	Actual
Service revenue	$25,000	$26,000
Allocated portion of:		
Building depreciation	11,000	11,000
Advertising	5,000	4,200
Billing	3,500	3,000
Property taxes	1,200	1,000
Material and supplies	1,600	1,200
Supervisory salaries	9,000	9,500
Insurance	4,000	3,600
Wages	3,000	3,250
Gas and oil	2,800	3,400
Equipment depreciation	1,500	1,300

Instructions
(a) Prepare a responsibility report for the first quarter of 2014 for the Home Plumbing Services segment.
(b) ▬▬▶ Write a memo to Lenny Kirkland discussing the principles that should be used when preparing performance reports.

State total budgeted cost formulas, and prepare flexible budget graph.
(LO 3), **AP**

E22-12 Venetian Company has two production departments, Fabricating and Assembling. At a department managers' meeting, the controller uses flexible budget graphs to explain total budgeted costs. Separate graphs based on direct labor hours are used for each department. The graphs show the following.

1. At zero direct labor hours, the total budgeted cost line and the fixed cost line intersect the vertical axis at $50,000 in the Fabricating Department and $40,000 in the Assembling Department.
2. At normal capacity of 50,000 direct labor hours, the line drawn from the total budgeted cost line intersects the vertical axis at $150,000 in the Fabricating Department, and $120,000 in the Assembling Department.

Instructions
(a) State the total budgeted cost formula for each department.
(b) Compute the total budgeted cost for each department, assuming actual direct labor hours worked were 53,000 and 47,000, in the Fabricating and Assembling Departments, respectively.
(c) Prepare the flexible budget graph for the Fabricating Department, assuming the maximum direct labor hours in the relevant range is 100,000. Use increments of 10,000 direct labor hours on the horizontal axis and increments of $50,000 on the vertical axis.

Prepare reports in a responsibility reporting system.
(LO 4, 5), **AP**

E22-13 Fultz Company's organization chart includes the president; the vice president of production; three assembly plants—Dallas, Atlanta, and Tucson; and two departments within each plant—Machining and Finishing. Budget and actual manufacturing cost data for July 2014 are as follows.

Finishing Department—Dallas: direct materials $41,500 actual, $44,000 budget; direct labor $83,400 actual, $82,000 budget; manufacturing overhead $51,000 actual, $49,200 budget.

Machining Department—Dallas: total manufacturing costs $220,000 actual, $219,000 budget.

Atlanta Plant: total manufacturing costs $424,000 actual, $421,000 budget.

Tucson Plant: total manufacturing costs $494,200 actual, $496,500 budget.

The Dallas plant manager's office costs were $95,000 actual and $92,000 budget. The vice president of production's office costs were $132,000 actual and $130,000 budget. Office costs are not allocated to departments and plants.

Instructions
Using the format on page 1151, prepare the reports in a responsibility system for:
(a) The Finishing Department—Dallas.
(b) The plant manager—Dallas.
(c) The vice president of production.

Prepare a responsibility report for a cost center.
(LO 5), **AN**

E22-14 The Mixing Department manager of Malone Company is able to control all overhead costs except rent, property taxes, and salaries. Budgeted monthly overhead costs for the Mixing Department, in alphabetical order, are:

Indirect labor	$12,000	Property taxes	$ 1,000
Indirect materials	7,700	Rent	1,800
Lubricants	1,675	Salaries	10,000
Maintenance	3,500	Utilities	5,000

Actual costs incurred for January 2014 are indirect labor $12,250; indirect materials $10,200; lubricants $1,650; maintenance $3,500; property taxes $1,100; rent $1,800; salaries $10,000; and utilities $6,400.

Instructions
(a) Prepare a responsibility report for January 2014.
(b) What would be the likely result of management's analysis of the report?

Compute missing amounts in responsibility reports for three profit centers, and prepare a report.
(LO 6), **AN**

E22-15 Deitz Inc. has three divisions which are operated as profit centers. Actual operating data for the divisions listed alphabetically are as follows.

Operating Data	Women's Shoes	Men's Shoes	Children's Shoes
Contribution margin	$250,000	(3)	$180,000
Controllable fixed costs	100,000	(4)	(5)
Controllable margin	(1)	$ 90,000	95,000
Sales	600,000	450,000	(6)
Variable costs	(2)	320,000	250,000

Instructions
(a) Compute the missing amounts. Show computations.
(b) Prepare a responsibility report for the Women's Shoes Division assuming (1) the data are for the month ended June 30, 2014, and (2) all data equal budget except variable costs which are $10,000 over budget.

E22-16 The Sports Equipment Division of Harrington Company is operated as a profit center. Sales for the division were budgeted for 2014 at $900,000. The only variable costs budgeted for the division were cost of goods sold ($440,000) and selling and administrative ($60,000). Fixed costs were budgeted at $100,000 for cost of goods sold, $90,000 for selling and administrative, and $70,000 for noncontrollable fixed costs. Actual results for these items were:

Prepare a responsibility report for a profit center, and compute ROI.
(LO 6, 7), AP

Sales	$880,000
Cost of goods sold	
Variable	408,000
Fixed	105,000
Selling and administrative	
Variable	61,000
Fixed	66,000
Noncontrollable fixed	90,000

Instructions
(a) Prepare a responsibility report for the Sports Equipment Division for 2014.
(b) Assume the division is an investment center, and average operating assets were $1,000,000. The noncontrollable fixed costs are controllable at the investment center level. Compute ROI.

E22-17 The West Division of Nieto Company reported the following data for the current year.

Compute ROI for current year and for possible future changes.
(LO 7), AP

Sales	$3,000,000
Variable costs	1,980,000
Controllable fixed costs	600,000
Average operating assets	5,000,000

Top management is unhappy with the investment center's return on investment (ROI). It asks the manager of the West Division to submit plans to improve ROI in the next year. The manager believes it is feasible to consider the following independent courses of action.

1. Increase sales by $320,000 with no change in the contribution margin percentage.
2. Reduce variable costs by $150,000.
3. Reduce average operating assets by 4%.

Instructions
(a) Compute the return on investment (ROI) for the current year.
(b) Using the ROI formula, compute the ROI under each of the proposed courses of action. (Round to one decimal.)

E22-18 The Dinkle and Frizell Dental Clinic provides both preventive and orthodontic dental services. The two owners, Reese Dinkle and Anita Frizell, operate the clinic as two separate investment centers: Preventive Services and Orthodontic Services. Each of them is in charge of one of the centers: Reese for Preventive Services and Anita for Orthodontic Services. Each month, they prepare an income statement for the two centers to evaluate performance and make decisions about how to improve the operational efficiency and profitability of the clinic.

Prepare a responsibility report for an investment center.
(LO 7), AP

Recently, they have been concerned about the profitability of the Preventive Services operations. For several months, it has been reporting a loss. The responsibility report for the month of May 2014 is shown on page 1176.

	Actual	Difference from Budget
Service revenue	$ 40,000	$1,000 F
Variable costs		
Filling materials	5,000	100 U
Novocain	3,900	100 U
Supplies	1,900	350 F
Dental assistant wages	2,500	–0–
Utilities	500	110 U
Total variable costs	13,800	40 F
Fixed costs		
Allocated portion of receptionist's salary	3,000	200 U
Dentist salary	9,800	400 U
Equipment depreciation	6,000	–0–
Allocated portion of building depreciation	15,000	1,000 U
Total fixed costs	33,800	1,600 U
Operating income (loss)	$ (7,600)	$ 560 U

In addition, the owners know that the investment in operating assets at the beginning of the month was $82,400, and it was $77,600 at the end of the month. They have asked for your assistance in evaluating their current performance reporting system.

Instructions

(a) Prepare a responsibility report for an investment center as illustrated in the chapter.

(b) Write a memo to the owners discussing the deficiencies of their current reporting system.

Prepare missing amounts in responsibility reports for three investment centers.

(LO 7), AN

E22-19 The Pletcher Transportation Company uses a responsibility reporting system to measure the performance of its three investment centers: Planes, Taxis, and Limos. Segment performance is measured using a system of responsibility reports and return on investment calculations. The allocation of resources within the company and the segment managers' bonuses are based in part on the results shown in these reports.

Recently, the company was the victim of a computer virus that deleted portions of the company's accounting records. This was discovered when the current period's responsibility reports were being prepared. The printout of the actual operating results appeared as follows.

	Planes	Taxis	Limos
Service revenue	$?	$500,000	$?
Variable costs	5,500,000	?	300,000
Contribution margin	?	250,000	480,000
Controllable fixed costs	1,500,000	?	?
Controllable margin	?	80,000	240,000
Average operating assets	25,000,000	?	1,500,000
Return on investment	13%	10%	?

Instructions

Determine the missing pieces of information above.

Compare ROI and residual income.

(LO 8), AN

*E22-20 Presented below is selected information for three regional divisions of Medina Company.

	Divisions		
	North	West	South
Contribution margin	$ 300,000	$ 500,000	$ 400,000
Controllable margin	$ 140,000	$ 360,000	$ 210,000
Average operating assets	$1,000,000	$2,000,000	$1,500,000
Minimum rate of return	13%	16%	10%

Instructions

(a) Compute the return on investment for each division.
(b) Compute the residual income for each division.
(c) Assume that each division has an investment opportunity that would provide a rate of return of 16%.
  (1) If ROI is used to measure performance, which division or divisions will probably make the additional investment?
  (2) If residual income is used to measure performance, which division or divisions will probably make the additional investment?

*E22-21   Presented below is selected financial information for two divisions of Yono Brewing.

Fill in information related to ROI and residual income.
(LO 8), **AN**

	Lager	Lite Lager
Contribution margin	$500,000	$ 300,000
Controllable margin	200,000	(c)
Average operating assets	(a)	$1,200,000
Minimum rate of return	(b)	13%
Return on investment	20%	(d)
Residual income	$100,000	$ 204,000

Instructions

Supply the missing information for the lettered items.

Exercises: Set B and Challenge Exercises

Visit the book's companion website, at **www.wiley.com/college/kimmel**, and choose the Student Companion site to access Exercise Set B and Challenge Exercises.

Problems: Set A

P22-1A   Cook Company estimates that 300,000 direct labor hours will be worked during the coming year, 2014, in the Packaging Department. On this basis, the budgeted manufacturing overhead cost data, shown below, are computed for the year.

Prepare flexible budget and budget report for manufacturing overhead.
(LO 3), **AN**

Fixed Overhead Costs		Variable Overhead Costs	
Supervision	$ 96,000	Indirect labor	$126,000
Depreciation	72,000	Indirect materials	90,000
Insurance	30,000	Repairs	54,000
Rent	24,000	Utilities	72,000
Property taxes	18,000	Lubricants	18,000
	$240,000		$360,000

It is estimated that direct labor hours worked each month will range from 27,000 to 36,000 hours.

During October, 27,000 direct labor hours were worked and the following overhead costs were incurred.

Fixed overhead costs: supervision $8,000, depreciation $6,000, insurance $2,460, rent $2,000, and property taxes $1,500.

Variable overhead costs: indirect labor $12,432, indirect materials $7,680, repairs $4,800, utilities $6,840, and lubricants $1,920.

Instructions

(a) Prepare a monthly manufacturing overhead flexible budget for each increment of 3,000 direct labor hours over the relevant range for the year ending December 31, 2014.
(b) Prepare a flexible budget report for October.
(c) ▬▬▶ Comment on management's efficiency in controlling manufacturing overhead costs in October.

(a) Total costs: DLH 27,000, $52,400; DLH 36,000, $63,200
(b) Total $1,232 U

Prepare flexible budget, budget report, and graph for manufacturing overhead.

(LO 3), **E**

P22-2A Zelmer Company manufactures tablecloths. Sales have grown rapidly over the past 2 years. As a result, the president has installed a budgetary control system for 2014. The following data were used in developing the master manufacturing overhead budget for the Ironing Department, which is based on an activity index of direct labor hours.

Variable Costs	Rate per Direct Labor Hour	Annual Fixed Costs	
Indirect labor	$0.40	Supervision	$48,000
Indirect materials	0.50	Depreciation	18,000
Factory utilities	0.30	Insurance	12,000
Factory repairs	0.20	Rent	30,000

The master overhead budget was prepared on the expectation that 480,000 direct labor hours will be worked during the year. In June, 41,000 direct labor hours were worked. At that level of activity, actual costs were as shown below.

> Variable—per direct labor hour: indirect labor $0.44, indirect materials $0.48, factory utilities $0.32, and factory repairs $0.25.

> Fixed: same as budgeted.

Instructions

(a) Total costs: 35,000 DLH, $58,000; 50,000 DLH, $79,000

(b) Budget $66,400 Actual $70,090

(a) Prepare a monthly manufacturing overhead flexible budget for the year ending December 31, 2014, assuming production levels range from 35,000 to 50,000 direct labor hours. Use increments of 5,000 direct labor hours.
(b) Prepare a budget report for June comparing actual results with budget data based on the flexible budget.
(c) Were costs effectively controlled? Explain.
(d) State the formula for computing the total budgeted costs for the Ironing Department.
(e) Prepare the flexible budget graph, showing total budgeted costs at 35,000 and 45,000 direct labor hours. Use increments of 5,000 direct labor hours on the horizontal axis and increments of $10,000 on the vertical axis.

State total budgeted cost formula, and prepare flexible budget reports for 2 time periods.

(LO 2, 3), **AN**

P22-3A Hill Company uses budgets in controlling costs. The August 2014 budget report for the company's Assembling Department is as follows.

HILL COMPANY
Budget Report
Assembling Department
For the Month Ended August 31, 2014

Manufacturing Costs	Budget	Actual	Difference Favorable F Unfavorable U
Variable costs			
Direct materials	$ 48,000	$ 47,000	$1,000 F
Direct labor	54,000	51,200	2,800 F
Indirect materials	24,000	24,200	200 U
Indirect labor	18,000	17,500	500 F
Utilities	15,000	14,900	100 F
Maintenance	6,000	6,200	200 U
Total variable	165,000	161,000	4,000 F
Fixed costs			
Rent	12,000	12,000	–0–
Supervision	17,000	17,000	–0–
Depreciation	6,000	6,000	–0–
Total fixed	35,000	35,000	–0–
Total costs	$200,000	$196,000	$4,000 F

The monthly budget amounts in the report were based on an expected production of 60,000 units per month or 720,000 units per year. The Assembling Department manager is pleased with the report and expects a raise, or at least praise for a job well done. The company president, however, is unhappy with the results for August because only 58,000 units were produced.

Instructions

(a) State the total monthly budgeted cost formula.

(b) Prepare a budget report for August using flexible budget data. Why does this report provide a better basis for evaluating performance than the report based on static budget data?

(b) Budget $194,500

(c) In September, 64,000 units were produced. Prepare the budget report using flexible budget data, assuming (1) each variable cost was 10% higher than its actual cost in August, and (2) fixed costs were the same in September as in August.

(c) Budget $211,000
     Actual $212,100

P22-4A   Clarke Inc. operates the Patio Furniture Division as a profit center. Operating data for this division for the year ended December 31, 2014, are as shown below.

Prepare responsibility report for a profit center.
(LO 6), AN

	Budget	**Difference from Budget**
Sales	$2,500,000	$50,000 F
Cost of goods sold		
Variable	1,300,000	41,000 F
Controllable fixed	200,000	3,000 U
Selling and administrative		
Variable	220,000	6,000 U
Controllable fixed	50,000	2,000 U
Noncontrollable fixed costs	70,000	4,000 U

In addition, Clarke incurs $180,000 of indirect fixed costs that were budgeted at $175,000. Twenty percent (20%) of these costs are allocated to the Patio Furniture Division.

Instructions

(a) Prepare a responsibility report for the Patio Furniture Division for the year.

(b) ⟶ Comment on the manager's performance in controlling revenues and costs.

(c) Identify any costs excluded from the responsibility report and explain why they were excluded.

(a) Contribution margin
     $85,000 F
     Controllable margin
     $80,000 F

P22-5A   Suppan Company manufactures a variety of tools and industrial equipment. The company operates through three divisions. Each division is an investment center. Operating data for the Home Division for the year ended December 31, 2014, and relevant budget data are as follows.

Prepare responsibility report for an investment center, and compute ROI.
(LO 7), E

	Actual	**Comparison with Budget**
Sales	$1,400,000	$100,000 favorable
Variable cost of goods sold	675,000	55,000 unfavorable
Variable selling and administrative expenses	125,000	25,000 unfavorable
Controllable fixed cost of goods sold	170,000	On target
Controllable fixed selling and administrative expenses	80,000	On target

Average operating assets for the year for the Home Division were $2,000,000 which was also the budgeted amount.

Instructions

(a) Prepare a responsibility report (in thousands of dollars) for the Home Division.

(b) Evaluate the manager's performance. Which items will likely be investigated by top management?

(a) Controllable margin:
     Budget $330;
     Actual $350

(c) Compute the expected ROI in 2014 for the Home Division, assuming the following independent changes to actual data.

(1) Variable cost of goods sold is decreased by 5%.

(2) Average operating assets are decreased by 10%.

(3) Sales are increased by $200,000, and this increase is expected to increase contribution margin by $85,000.

P22-6A   Durham Company uses a responsibility reporting system. It has divisions in Denver, Seattle, and San Diego. Each division has three production departments: Cutting, Shaping, and Finishing. The responsibility for each department rests with a manager who reports to the division production manager. Each division manager reports to the vice

Prepare reports for cost centers under responsibility accounting, and comment on performance of managers.
(LO 4), AN

president of production. There are also vice presidents for marketing and finance. All vice presidents report to the president.

In January 2014, controllable actual and budget manufacturing overhead cost data for the departments and divisions were as shown below.

Manufacturing Overhead	Actual	Budget
Individual costs—Cutting Department—Seattle		
Indirect labor	$ 73,000	$ 70,000
Indirect materials	47,900	46,000
Maintenance	20,500	18,000
Utilities	20,100	17,000
Supervision	22,000	20,000
	$183,500	$171,000
Total costs		
Shaping Department—Seattle	$158,000	$148,000
Finishing Department—Seattle	210,000	205,000
Denver division	678,000	673,000
San Diego division	722,000	715,000

Additional overhead costs were incurred as follows: Seattle division production manager—actual costs $52,500, budget $51,000; vice president of production—actual costs $65,000, budget $64,000; president—actual costs $76,400, budget $74,200. These expenses are not allocated.

The vice presidents who report to the president, other than the vice president of production, had the following expenses.

Vice President	Actual	Budget
Marketing	$133,600	$130,000
Finance	109,000	104,000

Instructions

(a) (1) $12,500 U
(2) $29,000 U
(3) $42,000 U
(4) $52,800 U

(a) Using the format on page 1151, prepare the following responsibility reports.
    (1) Manufacturing overhead—Cutting Department manager—Seattle division.
    (2) Manufacturing overhead—Seattle division manager.
    (3) Manufacturing overhead—vice president of production.
    (4) Manufacturing overhead and expenses—president.
(b) Comment on the comparative performances of:
    (1) Department managers in the Seattle division.
    (2) Division managers.
    (3) Vice presidents.

Compare ROI and residual income.

(LO 8), **AN**

*P22-7A Delby Industries has manufactured prefabricated houses for over 20 years. The houses are constructed in sections to be assembled on customers' lots. Delby expanded into the precut housing market when it acquired Jensen Company, one of its suppliers. In this market, various types of lumber are precut into the appropriate lengths, banded into packages, and shipped to customers' lots for assembly. Delby designated the Jensen Division as an investment center.

Delby uses return on investment (ROI) as a performance measure with investment defined as average operating assets. Management bonuses are based in part on ROI. All investments are expected to earn a minimum rate of return of 18%. Jensen's ROI has ranged from 20.1% to 23.5% since it was acquired. Jensen had an investment opportunity in 2014 that had an estimated ROI of 19%. Jensen management decided against the investment because it believed the investment would decrease the division's overall ROI.

Selected financial information for Jensen are presented below. The division's average operating assets were $12,300,000 for the year 2014.

JENSEN DIVISION
Selected Financial Information
For the Year Ended December 31, 2014

Sales	$26,000,000
Contribution margin	9,100,000
Controllable margin	2,583,000

Instructions

(a) Calculate the following performance measures for 2014 for the Jensen Division.
    (1) Return on investment (ROI).
    (2) Residual income.
(b) ━━▶ Would the management of Jensen Division have been more likely to accept the investment opportunity it had in 2014 if residual income were used as a performance measure instead of ROI? Explain your answer.

(CMA adapted)

Problems: Set B

P22-1B Speier Company estimates that 240,000 direct labor hours will be worked during 2014 in the Assembly Department. On this basis, the following budgeted manufacturing overhead data are computed.

Prepare flexible budge and budget report for manufacturing overhead.
(LO 3), **AN**

Variable Overhead Costs		Fixed Overhead Costs	
Indirect labor	$ 72,000	Supervision	$ 75,600
Indirect materials	48,000	Depreciation	30,000
Repairs	36,000	Insurance	12,000
Utilities	24,000	Rent	9,600
Lubricants	12,000	Property taxes	6,000
	$192,000		$133,200

It is estimated that direct labor hours worked each month will range from 18,000 to 24,000 hours.

During January, 20,000 direct labor hours were worked and the following overhead costs were incurred.

Variable Overhead Costs		Fixed Overhead Costs	
Indirect labor	$ 6,200	Supervision	$ 6,300
Indirect materials	3,600	Depreciation	2,500
Repairs	2,300	Insurance	1,000
Utilities	1,700	Rent	850
Lubricants	1,050	Property taxes	500
	$14,850		$11,150

Instructions

(a) Prepare a monthly flexible manufacturing overhead budget for each increment of 2,000 direct labor hours over the relevant range for the year ending December 31, 2014.
(b) Prepare a manufacturing overhead budget report for January.
(c) ━━▶ Comment on management's efficiency in controlling manufacturing overhead costs in January.

(a) Total costs: 18,000 DLH, $25,500; 24,000 DLH, $30,300
(b) Budget $27,100 Actual $26,000

P22-2B Gonzalez Company produces one product, Olpe. Because of wide fluctuations in demand for Olpe, the Assembly Department experiences significant variations in monthly production levels.

Prepare flexible budget, budget report, and graph for manufacturing overhead.
(LO 3), **E**

The annual master manufacturing overhead budget is based on 300,000 direct labor hours. In July, 27,500 labor hours were worked. The master manufacturing overhead budget for the year and the actual overhead costs incurred in July are as follows.

Overhead Costs	Master Budget (annual)	Actual in July
Variable		
Indirect labor	$300,000	$26,000
Indirect materials	150,000	11,350
Utilities	90,000	8,050
Maintenance	60,000	5,400
Fixed		
Supervision	144,000	12,000
Depreciation	96,000	8,000
Insurance and taxes	60,000	5,000
Total	$900,000	$75,800

(a) Total costs: 22,500 DLH, $70,000; 30,000 DLH, $85,000

(b) Budget $80,000
Actual $75,800

Instructions

(a) Prepare a monthly flexible overhead budget for the year ending December 31, 2014, assuming monthly production levels range from 22,500 to 30,000 direct labor hours. Use increments of 2,500 direct labor hours.

(b) Prepare a budget report for the month of July 2014, comparing actual results with budget data based on the flexible budget.

(c) ✏️➡ Were costs effectively controlled? Explain.

(d) State the formula for computing the total monthly budgeted costs in the Gonzalez Company.

(e) Prepare the flexible budget graph showing total budgeted costs at 25,000 and 27,500 direct labor hours. Use increments of 5,000 on the horizontal axis and increments of $10,000 on the vertical axis.

State total budgeted cost formula, and prepare flexible budget reports for 2 time periods.

(LO 2, 3), **AN**

P22-3B Hardesty Company uses budgets in controlling costs. The May 2014 budget report for the company's Packaging Department is as follows.

HARDESTY COMPANY
Budget Report
Packaging Department
For the Month Ended May 31, 2014

Manufacturing Costs	Budget	Actual	Difference Favorable F Unfavorable U
Variable costs			
Direct materials	$ 40,000	$ 41,000	$1,000 U
Direct labor	45,000	47,300	2,300 U
Indirect materials	15,000	15,200	200 U
Indirect labor	12,500	13,000	500 U
Utilities	10,000	9,600	400 F
Maintenance	7,500	8,000	500 U
Total variable	130,000	134,100	4,100 U
Fixed costs			
Rent	10,000	10,000	–0–
Supervision	7,000	7,000	–0–
Depreciation	4,000	4,000	–0–
Total fixed	21,000	21,000	–0–
Total costs	$151,000	$155,100	$4,100 U

The monthly budget amounts in the report were based on an expected production of 50,000 units per month or 600,000 units per year.

The company president was displeased with the department manager's performance. The department manager, who thought he had done a good job, could not understand the unfavorable results. In May, 55,000 units were produced.

Instructions

(a) State the total budgeted cost formula.

(b) Prepare a budget report for May using flexible budget data. Why does this report provide a better basis for evaluating performance than the report based on static budget data?

(c) In June, 40,000 units were produced. Prepare the budget report using flexible budget data, assuming (1) each variable cost was 20% less in June than its actual cost in May, and (2) fixed costs were the same in the month of June as in May.

(b) Budget $164,000

(c) Budget $125,000
Actual $128,280

Prepare responsibility report for a profit center.

(LO 6), **AN**

P22-4B Guzman Inc. operates the Home Appliance Division as a profit center. Operating data for this division for the year ended December 31, 2014, are shown on the next page.

	Budget	Difference from Budget
Sales	$2,400,000	$90,000 U
Cost of goods sold		
Variable	1,200,000	58,000 U
Controllable fixed	200,000	8,000 F
Selling and administrative		
Variable	240,000	8,000 F
Controllable fixed	60,000	3,000 U
Noncontrollable fixed costs	50,000	2,000 U

In addition, Guzman incurs $150,000 of indirect fixed costs that were budgeted at $155,000. Twenty percent (20%) of these costs are allocated to the Home Appliance Division. None of these costs are controllable by the division manager.

Instructions

(a) Prepare a responsibility report for the Home Appliance Division (a profit center) for the year.

(b) ➤ Comment on the manager's performance in controlling revenues and costs.

(c) Identify any costs excluded from the responsibility report and explain why they were excluded.

(a) Contribution margin
$140,000 U
Controllable margin
$135,000 U

P22-5B Strauss Company manufactures a variety of garden and lawn equipment. The company operates through three divisions. Each division is an investment center. Operating data for the Lawnmower Division for the year ended December 31, 2014, and relevant budget data are as follows.

Prepare responsibility report for an investment center, and compute ROI.

(LO 7), E

	Actual	Comparison with Budget
Sales	$2,900,000	$150,000 unfavorable
Variable cost of goods sold	1,400,000	100,000 unfavorable
Variable selling and administrative expenses	300,000	40,000 favorable
Controllable fixed cost of goods sold	270,000	On target
Controllable fixed selling and administrative expenses	140,000	On target

Average operating assets for the year for the Lawnmower Division were $5,000,000, which was also the budgeted amount.

Instructions

(a) Prepare a responsibility report (in thousands of dollars) for the Lawnmower Division.

(b) Evaluate the manager's performance. Which items will likely be investigated by top management?

(c) Compute the expected ROI in 2014 for the Lawnmower Division, assuming the following independent changes.

(1) Variable cost of goods sold is decreased by 20%.

(2) Average operating assets are decreased by 24%.

(3) Sales are increased by $700,000, and this increase is expected to increase contribution margin by $260,000.

(a) Controllable margin:
Budget $1,000
Actual $790

P22-6B Gore Company uses a responsibility reporting system. It has divisions in San Francisco, Phoenix, and Tulsa. Each division has three production departments: Cutting, Shaping, and Finishing. The responsibility for each department rests with a manager who reports to the division production manager. Each division manager reports to the vice president of production. There are also vice presidents for marketing and finance. All vice presidents report to the president.

In January 2014, controllable actual and budget manufacturing overhead cost data for the departments and divisions were as shown on the next page.

Prepare reports for cost centers under responsibility accounting, and comment on performance of managers.

(LO 4), AN

Manufacturing Overhead	Actual	Budget
Individual costs—Cutting Department—Phoenix		
Indirect labor	$ 95,000	$ 90,000
Indirect materials	62,700	61,000
Maintenance	27,400	25,000
Utilities	25,200	20,000
Supervision	31,000	28,000
	$241,300	$224,000
Total costs		
Shaping Department—Phoenix	$190,000	$177,000
Finishing Department—Phoenix	250,000	245,000
San Francisco division	724,000	715,000
Tulsa division	760,000	750,000

Additional overhead costs were incurred as follows: Phoenix division production manager—actual costs $73,100, budget $70,000; vice president of production—actual costs $72,000, budget $70,000; president—actual costs $94,200, budget $91,300. These expenses are not allocated.

The vice presidents, who report to the president (other than the vice president of production), had the following expenses.

Vice President	Actual	Budget
Marketing	$167,200	$160,000
Finance	125,000	120,000

Instructions

(a) (1) $17,300 U
    (2) $38,400 U
    (3) $59,400 U
    (4) $74,500 U

(a) Using the format on page 1151, prepare the following responsibility reports.
(1) Manufacturing overhead—Cutting Department manager—Phoenix division.
(2) Manufacturing overhead—Phoenix division manager.
(3) Manufacturing overhead—vice president of production.
(4) Manufacturing overhead and expenses—president.
(b) Comment on the comparative performances of:
(1) Department managers in the Phoenix division.
(2) Division managers.
(3) Vice presidents.

Compare ROI and residual income.

(LO 8), **AN**

*P22-7B Walton Industries has manufactured prefabricated garages for over 20 years. The garages are constructed in sections to be assembled on customers' lots. Walton expanded into the precut housing market when it acquired Washington Enterprises, one of its suppliers. In this market, various types of lumber are precut into the appropriate lengths, banded into packages, and shipped to customers' lots for assembly. Walton designated the Washington Division as an investment center.

Walton uses return on investment (ROI) as a performance measure, with investment defined as average operating assets. Management bonuses are based in part on ROI. All investments are expected to earn a minimum rate of return of 15%. Washington's ROI has ranged from 19.9% to 23.3% since it was acquired. Washington had an investment opportunity in 2014 that had an estimated ROI of 18%. Washington's management decided against the investment because it believed the investment would decrease the division's overall ROI.

Selected financial information for Washington is presented below. The division's average operating assets were $7,500,000 for the year 2014.

WASHINGTON DIVISION
Selected Financial Information
For the Year Ended December 31, 2014

Sales	$16,000,000
Contribution margin	5,600,000
Controllable margin	1,500,000

Instructions

(a) Calculate the following performance measures for 2014 for the Washington Division.
   (1) Return on investment (ROI).
   (2) Residual income.
(b) ✏️ Would the management of Washington have been more likely to accept the investment opportunity it had in 2014 if residual income were used as a performance measure instead of ROI? Explain your answer.

Problems: Set C

Visit the book's companion website, at **www.wiley.com/college/kimmel**, and choose the Student Companion site to access Problem Set C.

Waterways Continuing Problem

(*Note:* This is a continuation of the Waterways Problem from Chapters 14 through 21.)

WCP22 Waterways Corporation is continuing its budget preparations. This problem gives you static budget information as well as actual overhead costs, and asks you to calculate amounts related to budgetary control and responsibility accounting.

> Go to the book's companion website, at **www.wiley.com/college/kimmel**, to find the completion of this problem.

Broadening Your Perspective

Management Decision-Making

DECISION-MAKING AT CURRENT DESIGNS

BYP22-1 The Current Designs staff has prepared the annual manufacturing budget for the roto-molded line based on an estimated annual production of 4,000 kayaks during 2013. Each kayak will require 54 pounds of polyethylene powder and a finishing kit (rope, seat, hardware, etc.). The polyethylene powder used in these kayaks costs $1.50 per pound, and the finishing kits cost $170 each. Each kayak will use two kinds of labor—2 hours of type I labor from people who run the oven and trim the plastic, and 3 hours of work from type II workers who attach the hatches and seat and other hardware. The type I employees are paid $15 per hour, and the type II are paid $12 per hour.

Manufacturing overhead is budgeted at $396,000 for 2013, broken down as follows.

Variable costs	
Indirect materials	$ 40,000
Manufacturing supplies	53,800
Maintenance and utilities	88,000
	181,800
Fixed costs	
Supervision	90,000
Insurance	14,400
Depreciation	109,800
	214,200
Total	$396,000

During the first quarter, ended March 31, 2013, 1,050 units were actually produced with the following costs.

Polyethylene powder	$ 87,000
Finishing kits	178,840
Type I labor	31,500
Type II labor	39,060
Indirect materials	10,500
Manufacturing supplies	14,150
Maintenance and utilities	26,000
Supervision	20,000
Insurance	3,600
Depreciation	27,450
Total	$438,100

Instructions

(a) Prepare the annual manufacturing budget for 2013, assuming that 4,000 kayaks will be produced.

(b) Prepare the flexible budget for manufacturing for the quarter ended March 31, 2013. Assume activity levels of 900, 1,000, and 1,050 units.

(c) Assuming the rotomolded line is treated as a profit center, prepare a flexible budget report for manufacturing for the quarter ended March 31, 2013, when 1,050 units were produced.

DECISION-MAKING ACROSS THE ORGANIZATION

BYP22-2 Green Pastures is a 400-acre farm on the outskirts of the Kentucky Bluegrass, specializing in the boarding of broodmares and their foals. A recent economic downturn in the thoroughbred industry has led to a decline in breeding activities, and it has made the boarding business extremely competitive. To meet the competition, Green Pastures planned in 2014 to entertain clients, advertise more extensively, and absorb expenses formerly paid by clients such as veterinary and blacksmith fees.

The budget report for 2014 is presented below. As shown, the static income statement budget for the year is based on an expected 21,900 boarding days at $25 per mare. The variable expenses per mare per day were budgeted: feed $5, veterinary fees $3, blacksmith fees $0.25, and supplies $0.55. All other budgeted expenses were either semifixed or fixed.

During the year, management decided not to replace a worker who quit in March, but it did issue a new advertising brochure and did more entertaining of clients.[1]

GREEN PASTURES
Static Budget Income Statement
For the Year Ended December 31, 2014

	Actual	Master Budget	Difference
Number of mares	52	60	8 U
Number of boarding days	19,000	21,900	2,900 U
Sales	$380,000	$547,500	$167,500 U
Less: Variable expenses			
Feed	104,390	109,500	5,110 F
Veterinary fees	58,838	65,700	6,862 F
Blacksmith fees	4,984	5,475	491 F
Supplies	10,178	12,045	1,867 F
Total variable expenses	178,390	192,720	14,330 F
Contribution margin	201,610	354,780	153,170 U

---

[1]Data for this case are based on Hans Sprohge and John Talbott, "New Applications for Variance Analysis," *Journal of Accountancy* (AICPA, New York), April 1989, pp. 137–141.

	Actual	Master Budget	Difference
Less: Fixed expenses			
Depreciation	40,000	40,000	–0–
Insurance	11,000	11,000	–0–
Utilities	12,000	14,000	2,000 F
Repairs and maintenance	10,000	11,000	1,000 F
Labor	88,000	95,000	7,000 F
Advertisement	12,000	8,000	4,000 U
Entertainment	7,000	5,000	2,000 U
Total fixed expenses	180,000	184,000	4,000 F
Net income	$ 21,610	$170,780	$149,170 U

Instructions

With the class divided into groups, answer the following.
(a) Based on the static budget report:
  (1) What was the primary cause(s) of the loss in net income?
  (2) Did management do a good, average, or poor job of controlling expenses?
  (3) Were management's decisions to stay competitive sound?
(b) Prepare a flexible budget report for the year.
(c) Based on the flexible budget report, answer the three questions in part (a) above.
(d) What course of action do you recommend for the management of Green Pastures?

MANAGERIAL ANALYSIS

BYP22-3 Lanier Company manufactures expensive watch cases sold as souvenirs. Three of its sales departments are Retail Sales, Wholesale Sales, and Outlet Sales. The Retail Sales Department is a profit center. The Wholesale Sales Department is a cost center. Its managers merely take orders from customers who purchase through the company's wholesale catalog. The Outlet Sales Department is an investment center because each manager is given full responsibility for an outlet store location. The manager can hire and discharge employees, purchase, maintain, and sell equipment, and in general is fairly independent of company control.

Mary Gammel is a manager in the Retail Sales Department. Stephen Flott manages the Wholesale Sales Department. Jose Gomez manages the Golden Gate Club outlet store in San Francisco. The following are the budget responsibility reports for each of the three departments.

	Budget		
	Retail Sales	Wholesale Sales	Outlet Sales
Sales	$ 750,000	$ 400,000	$200,000
Variable costs			
Cost of goods sold	150,000	100,000	25,000
Advertising	100,000	30,000	5,000
Sales salaries	75,000	15,000	3,000
Printing	10,000	20,000	5,000
Travel	20,000	30,000	2,000
Fixed costs			
Rent	50,000	30,000	10,000
Insurance	5,000	2,000	1,000
Depreciation	75,000	100,000	40,000
Investment in assets	1,000,000	1,200,000	800,000

	Actual Results		
	Retail Sales	**Wholesale Sales**	**Outlet Sales**
Sales	$ 750,000	$ 400,000	$200,000
Variable costs			
Cost of goods sold	192,000	122,000	26,500
Advertising	100,000	30,000	5,000
Sales salaries	75,000	15,000	3,000
Printing	10,000	20,000	5,000
Travel	14,000	21,000	1,500
Fixed costs			
Rent	40,000	50,000	12,300
Insurance	5,000	2,000	1,000
Depreciation	80,000	90,000	56,000
Investment in assets	1,000,000	1,200,000	800,000

Instructions

(a) Determine which of the items should be included in the responsibility report for each of the three managers.

(b) Compare the budgeted measures with the actual results. Decide which results should be called to the attention of each manager.

REAL-WORLD FOCUS

BYP22-4 Computer Associates International, Inc., the world's leading business software company, delivers the end-to-end infrastructure to enable e-business through innovative technology, services, and education. Computer Associates has 19,000 employees worldwide and recently had revenue of over $6 billion.

Presented below is information from the company's annual report.

COMPUTER ASSOCIATES INTERNATIONAL, INC.
Management Discussion

The Company has experienced a pattern of business whereby revenue for its third and fourth fiscal quarters reflects an increase over first- and second-quarter revenue. The Company attributes this increase to clients' increased spending at the end of their calendar year budgetary periods and the culmination of its annual sales plan. Since the Company's costs do not increase proportionately with the third- and fourth-quarters' increase in revenue, the higher revenue in these quarters results in greater profit margins and income. Fourth-quarter profitability is traditionally affected by significant new hirings, training, and education expenditures for the succeeding year.

Instructions

(a) Why don't the company's costs increase proportionately as the revenues increase in the third and fourth quarters?

(b) What type of budgeting seems appropriate for the Computer Associates situation?

BYP22-5 There are many useful resources regarding budgeting available on websites. The following activity investigates the results of a comprehensive budgeting study.

Address: **http://www.accountingweb.com/whitepapers/centage_ioma.pdf**, or go to **www.wiley.com/college/kimmel**

Instructions

Go to the address above and then answer the following questions.

(a) What are cited as the two most common "pain points" of budgeting?

(b) What percentage of companies that participated in the survey said that they prepare annual budgets? Of those that prepare budgets, what percentage say that they start the budgeting process by first generating sales projections?

(c) What is the most common amount of time for the annual budgeting process?

(d) When evaluating variances from budgeted amounts, what was the most commonly defined range of acceptable tolerance levels?

(e) The study defines three types of consequences for varying from budgeted amounts. How does it describe "severe" consequences?

Critical Thinking

COMMUNICATION ACTIVITY

BYP22-6 The manufacturing overhead budget for Fleming Company contains the following items.

Variable costs		Fixed costs	
Indirect materials	$22,000	Supervision	$17,000
Indirect labor	12,000	Inspection costs	1,000
Maintenance expense	10,000	Insurance expense	2,000
Manufacturing supplies	6,000	Depreciation	15,000
Total variable	$50,000	Total fixed	$35,000

The budget was based on an estimated 2,000 units being produced. During the past month, 1,500 units were produced, and the following costs incurred.

Variable costs		Fixed costs	
Indirect materials	$22,500	Supervision	$18,400
Indirect labor	13,500	Inspection costs	1,200
Maintenance expense	8,200	Insurance expense	2,200
Manufacturing supplies	5,000	Depreciation	14,700
Total variable	$49,200	Total fixed	$36,500

Instructions

(a) Determine which items would be controllable by Fred Bedner, the production manager.

(b) How much should have been spent during the month for the manufacture of the 1,500 units?

(c) Prepare a flexible manufacturing overhead budget report for Mr. Bedner.

(d) Prepare a responsibility report. Include only the costs that would have been controllable by Mr. Bedner. Assume that the supervision cost above includes Mr. Bedner's salary of $10,000, both at budget and actual. In an attached memo, describe clearly for Mr. Bedner the areas in which his performance needs to be improved.

ETHICS CASE

BYP22-7 American Products Corporation participates in a highly competitive industry. In order to meet this competition and achieve profit goals, the company has chosen the decentralized form of organization. Each manager of a decentralized investment center is measured on the basis of profit contribution, market penetration, and return on investment. Failure to meet the objectives established by corporate management for these measures has not been acceptable and usually has resulted in demotion or dismissal of an investment center manager.

An anonymous survey of managers in the company revealed that the managers feel the pressure to compromise their personal ethical standards to achieve the corporate objectives. For example, at certain plant locations there was pressure to reduce quality control to a level which could not assure that all unsafe products would be rejected. Also, sales personnel were encouraged to use questionable sales tactics to obtain orders, including gifts and other incentives to purchasing agents.

The chief executive officer is disturbed by the survey findings. In his opinion, such behavior cannot be condoned by the company. He concludes that the company should do something about this problem.

Instructions

(a) Who are the stakeholders (the affected parties) in this situation?

(b) Identify the ethical implications, conflicts, or dilemmas in the above described situation.

(c) What might the company do to reduce the pressures on managers and decrease the ethical conflicts?

(CMA adapted)

ALL ABOUT YOU

BYP22-8   It is one thing to prepare a personal budget; it is another thing to stick to it. Financial planners have suggested various mechanisms to provide support for enforcing personal budgets. One approach is called "envelope budgeting."

Instructions
Read the article provided at **http://en.wikipedia.org/wiki/Envelope_budgeting**, and answer the following questions.
(a) Summarize the process of envelope budgeting.
(b) Evaluate whether you think you would benefit from envelope budgeting. What do you think are its strengths and weaknesses relative to your situation?

CONSIDERING YOUR COSTS AND BENEFITS

BYP22-9   Preparing a personal budget is a great first step toward control over your personal finances. It is especially useful to prepare a budget when you face a big decision. For most people, the biggest decision they will ever make is whether to purchase a house. The percentage of people in the United States who own a home is high compared to many other countries. This is partially the result of U.S. government programs and incentives that encourage home ownership. For example, the interest on a home mortgage is tax-deductible.

Before purchasing a house, you should first consider whether buying it is the best choice for you. Suppose you just graduated from college and are moving to a new community. Should you immediately buy a new home?

YES: If I purchase a home, I am making my housing cost more like a "fixed cost," thus minimizing increases in my future housing costs. Also, I benefit from the appreciation in my home's value. Although recent turbulence in the economy has caused home prices in many communities to decline, I know that over the long term, home prices have increased across the country.

NO: I just moved to a new town, so I don't know the housing market. I am new to my job, so I don't know whether I will like it or my new community. Also, if my job does go well, it is likely that my income will increase in the next few years, so I will able to afford a better house if I wait. Therefore, the flexibility provided by renting is very valuable to me at this point in my life.

Instructions
Write a response indicating your position regarding this situation. Provide support for your view.

Answers to Insight and Accounting Across the Organization Questions

p. 1140 Just What the Doctor Ordered? Q: Explain how the use of flexible budgets might help to identify the best solution to this problem. **A:** A fixed budget assumes a particular level of activity. In the case of television shows, the number of viewers can impact revenues and costs. NBCUniversal could prepare alternative budgets at varying levels of activities and assume various cost structures depending on the number of cast members and other factors. Experimenting with different scenarios could help the network identify an approach that maintains an acceptable level of income as revenues decline.

p. 1144 Budgets and the Exotic Newcastle Disease Q: What is the major benefit of tying a budget to the overall goals of the company? **A:** People working on a budgeting process that is clearly guided and focused by strategic goals spend less time arguing about irrelevant details and more time focusing on the items that matter.

p. 1147 Competition versus Collaboration Q: How might managers of separate divisions be able to reduce division costs through collaboration? **A:** Division managers might reduce costs by sharing design and marketing resources or by jointly negotiating with suppliers. In addition, they can reduce the need to hire and lay off employees by sharing staff across divisions as human resource needs change.

p. 1149 Flexible Manufacturing Requires Flexible Accounting Q: What implications do these improvements in production capabilities have for management accounting information and performance evaluation within the organization? **A:** In order to maximize the potential of flexible manufacturing facilities, managers need to be supplied with information on a more frequent basis. In turn, the tools used to evaluate performance need to take into account what information management had at its disposal, and what decisions were made in response to this information.

p. 1159 Does Hollywood Look at ROI? Q: What might be the reason that movie studios do not produce G-rated movies as much as R-rated ones? **A:** Perhaps Hollywood believes that big-name stars or large budgets, both of which are typical of R-rated movies, sell movies. However, one study recently concluded, "We can't find evidence that stars help movies, and we can't find evidence that bigger budgets increase return on investment." Some film companies are going out of their way to achieve at least a PG rating.

Answers to Self-Test Questions

1. c **2.** d **3.** c **4.** b **5.** b **6.** a ($90,000 − $30,000) ÷ 10,000 **7.** d $28,000 − [9,200 × ($2,700 ÷ 9,000)] **8.** a **9.** d **10.** d **11.** a **12.** c **13.** b **14.** b **15.** d

Bloomberg/Getty Images

STANDARD COSTS AND BALANCED SCORECARD

LEARNING OBJECTIVES

After studying this chapter, you should be able to:

1 Distinguish between a standard and a budget.

2 Identify the advantages of standard costs.

3 Describe how companies set standards.

4 State the formulas for determining direct materials and direct labor variances.

5 State the formula for determining the total manufacturing overhead variance.

6 Discuss the reporting of variances.

7 Prepare an income statement for management under a standard costing system.

8 Describe the balanced scorecard approach to performance evaluation.

✔ **The Navigator**

- Scan Learning Objectives
- Read Feature Story
- Scan Preview
- Read Text and Answer **Do it!**
  ◯ p. 1200 ◯ p. 1204 ◯ p. 1209
  ◯ p. 1213
- Work Using the Decision Toolkit
- Review Summary of Learning Objectives
- Work Comprehensive **Do it!** p. 1222
- Answer Self-Test Questions
- Complete Assignments
- Go to WileyPLUS for practice and tutorials

✔ The Navigator

When Howard Schultz purchased a small Seattle coffee-roasting business in 1987, he set out to create a new kind of company. He thought the company should sell coffee by the cup in its store, in addition to the bags of roasted beans it already sold. He also felt that the store shouldn't just sell coffee but also a pleasant atmosphere and experience. Schultz saw the store as a place where you could order a beverage, custom-made to your unique tastes, in an environment that would give you the sense that you had escaped, if only momentarily, from the chaos we call life. Finally, Schultz believed that the company would prosper if employees shared in its success.

In a little more than 20 years, Howard Schultz's company, Starbucks, grew from that one store to over 17,000 locations in 54 countries. That is an incredible rate of growth, and it didn't happen by accident. While Starbucks does everything it can to maximize the customer's experience, behind the scenes it needs to control costs. Consider the almost infinite options of beverage combinations and variations at Starbucks. The company must determine the most efficient way to make each beverage, it

80,000 DIFFERENT CAFFEINATED COMBINATIONS

must communicate these methods in the form of standards to its employees, and it must then evaluate whether those standards are being met.

Schultz's book, *Onward: How Starbucks Fought for Its Life Without Losing Its Soul*, describes a painful period in which Starbucks had to close 600 stores and lay off thousands of employees. However, when a prominent shareholder suggested that the company eliminate its employee health-care plan, as so many other companies had done, Schultz refused. The health-care plan represented one of the company's most tangible commitments to employee well-being as well as to corporate social responsibility. Schultz feels strongly that providing health care to the company's employees is an essential part of the standard cost of a cup of Starbucks' coffee.

Watch the Starbucks video in WileyPLUS to learn more about how the company sets standards. Watch the Southwest Airlines video in WileyPLUS to learn more about the use of the balanced scorecard in the real world.

✔ The Navigator

Standards are a fact of life. You met the admission standards for the school you are attending. The vehicle that you drive had to meet certain governmental emissions standards. The hamburgers and salads that you eat in a restaurant have to meet certain health and nutritional standards before they can be sold. As described in our Feature Story, Starbucks has standards for the costs of its materials, labor, and overhead. The reason for standards in these cases is very simple. They help to ensure that overall product quality is high while keeping costs under control.

In this chapter, we continue the study of controlling costs. You will learn how to evaluate performance using standard costs and a balanced scorecard.

The content and organization of Chapter 23 are as follows.

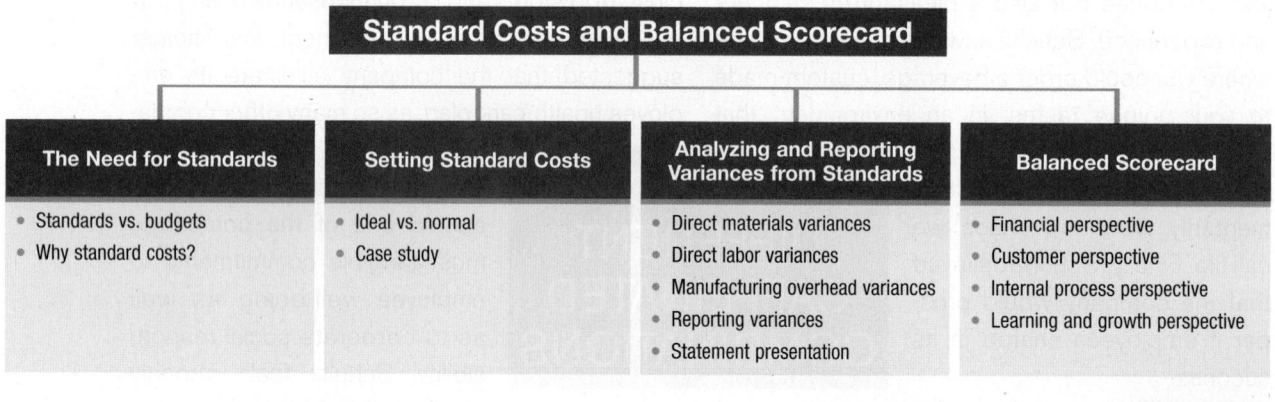

Standard Costs and Balanced Scorecard			
The Need for Standards	**Setting Standard Costs**	**Analyzing and Reporting Variances from Standards**	**Balanced Scorecard**
• Standards vs. budgets • Why standard costs?	• Ideal vs. normal • Case study	• Direct materials variances • Direct labor variances • Manufacturing overhead variances • Reporting variances • Statement presentation	• Financial perspective • Customer perspective • Internal process perspective • Learning and growth perspective

✔ The Navigator

The Need for Standards

LEARNING OBJECTIVE 1

Distinguish between a standard and a budget.

Standards are common in business. Those imposed by government agencies are often called **regulations**. They include the Fair Labor Standards Act, the Equal Employment Opportunity Act, and a multitude of environmental standards. Standards established internally by a company may extend to personnel matters, such as employee absenteeism and ethical codes of conduct, quality control standards for products, and standard costs for goods and services. In managerial accounting, standard costs are predetermined unit costs, which companies use as measures of performance.

We will focus on manufacturing operations in this chapter. But you should also recognize that standard costs also apply to many types of service businesses as well. For example, a fast-food restaurant such as McDonald's knows the price it should pay for pickles, beef, buns, and other ingredients. It also knows how much time it should take an employee to flip hamburgers. If the company pays too much for pickles or if employees take too much time to prepare Big Macs, McDonald's notices the deviations and takes corrective action. Not-for-profit entities, such as universities, charitable organizations, and governmental agencies, also may use standard costs as measures of performance.

DISTINGUISHING BETWEEN STANDARDS AND BUDGETS

Both **standards** and **budgets** are predetermined costs, and both contribute to management planning and control. There is a difference, however, in the way the terms are expressed. A standard is a **unit** amount. A budget is a **total** amount. Thus, it is customary to state that the **standard cost** of direct labor for a unit of product is, say, $10. If the company produces 5,000 units of the product, the $50,000 of direct labor is the **budgeted** labor cost. A standard is the budgeted **cost per unit** of product. A standard is therefore concerned with each individual cost component that makes up the entire budget.

There are important accounting differences between budgets and standards. Except in the application of manufacturing overhead to jobs and processes, budget data are not journalized in cost accounting systems. In contrast, as we illustrate in the appendix to this chapter, standard costs may be incorporated into cost accounting systems. Also, a company may report its inventories at standard cost in its financial statements, but it would not report inventories at budgeted costs.

WHY STANDARD COSTS?

Standard costs offer a number of advantages to an organization, as shown in Illustration 23-1.

Advantages of Standard Costs

Facilitate management planning

Promote greater economy by making employees more "cost-conscious"

Useful in setting selling prices

Contribute to management control by providing basis for evaluation of cost control

Useful in highlighting variances in management by exception

Simplify costing of inventories and reduce clerical costs

Illustration 23-1
Advantages of standard costs

The organization will realize these advantages only when standard costs are carefully established and prudently used. Using standards solely as a way to place blame can have a negative effect on managers and employees. To minimize this effect, many companies offer wage incentives to those who meet the standards.

Setting Standard Costs

The setting of standard costs to produce a unit of product is a difficult task. It requires input from all persons who have responsibility for costs and quantities. To determine the standard cost of direct materials, management consults purchasing agents, product managers, quality control engineers, and production supervisors. In setting the standard cost for direct labor, managers obtain pay rate data from the payroll department. Industrial engineers generally determine the labor time requirements. The managerial accountant provides important input for the standard-setting process by accumulating historical cost data and by knowing how costs respond to changes in activity levels.

To be effective in controlling costs, standard costs need to be current at all times. Thus, standards are under continuous review. They should change whenever managers determine that the existing standard is not a good measure of performance. Circumstances that warrant revision of a standard include changed wage rates resulting from a new union contract, a change in product specifications, or the implementation of a new manufacturing method.

IDEAL VERSUS NORMAL STANDARDS

Companies set standards at one of two levels: ideal or normal. Ideal standards represent optimum levels of performance under perfect operating conditions. Normal standards represent efficient levels of performance that are attainable under expected operating conditions.

Some managers believe ideal standards will stimulate workers to ever-increasing improvement. However, most managers believe that ideal standards lower the morale of the entire workforce because they are difficult, if not impossible, to meet. Very few companies use ideal standards.

Ethics Note When standards are set too high, employees sometimes feel pressure to consider unethical practices to meet these standards.

Most companies that use standards set them at a normal level. Properly set, normal standards should be **rigorous but attainable**. Normal standards allow for rest periods, machine breakdowns, and other "normal" contingencies in the production process. In the remainder of this chapter, we will assume that standard costs are set at a normal level.

© Rebecca Ellis/iStockphoto

Accounting Across the Organization

How Do Standards Help a Business?

A number of organizations, including corporations, consultants, and governmental agencies, share information regarding performance standards in an effort to create a standard set of measures for thousands of business processes. The group, referred to as the Open Standards Benchmarking Collaborative, includes IBM, Procter and Gamble, the U.S. Navy, and the World Bank. Companies that are interested in participating can go to the group's website and enter their information.

Source: William M. Bulkeley, "Business, Agencies to Standardize Their Benchmarks," *Wall Street Journal* (May 19, 2004).

? How will the creation of such standards help a business or organization? (See page 1242.)

A CASE STUDY

To establish the standard cost of producing a product, it is necessary to establish standards for each manufacturing cost element—direct materials, direct labor, and manufacturing overhead. The standard for each element is derived from the standard price to be paid and the standard quantity to be used.

To illustrate, we use an extended example. Xonic Beverage Company uses standard costs to measure performance at the production facility of its caffeinated energy drink, Xonic Tonic. Xonic produces one-gallon containers of concentrated syrup that it sells to coffee and smoothie shops, and other retail outlets. The syrup is mixed with ice water or ice "slush" before serving. The potency of the beverage varies depending on the amount of concentrated syrup used.

Direct Materials

The direct materials price standard is the cost per unit of direct materials that should be incurred. This standard is based on the purchasing department's best estimate of the **cost of raw materials**. This cost is frequently based on current purchase prices. The price standard also includes an amount for related costs such as receiving, storing, and handling. The materials price standard per pound of material for Xonic Tonic is:

Item	Price
Purchase price, net of discounts	$ 2.70
Freight	0.20
Receiving and handling	0.10
Standard direct materials price per pound	**$3.00**

Illustration 23-2 Setting direct materials price standard

The direct materials quantity standard is the quantity of direct materials that should be used per unit of finished goods. This standard is expressed as a physical measure, such as pounds, barrels, or board feet. In setting the standard, management considers both the quality and quantity of materials required to manufacture the product. The standard includes allowances for unavoidable waste and normal spoilage. The standard quantity per unit for Xonic Tonic is as follows.

Item	Quantity (Pounds)
Required materials	3.5
Allowance for waste	0.4
Allowance for spoilage	0.1
Standard direct materials quantity per unit	**4.0**

Illustration 23-3 Setting direct materials quantity standard

The standard direct materials cost per unit is the standard direct materials price times the standard direct materials quantity. For Xonic, the standard direct materials cost per gallon of Xonic Tonic is $12.00 ($3 $\times$ 4 pounds).

Direct Labor

The direct labor price standard is the rate per hour that should be incurred for direct labor. This standard is based on current wage rates, adjusted for anticipated changes such as cost of living adjustments (COLAs). The price standard also generally includes employer payroll taxes and fringe benefits, such as paid holidays and vacations. For Xonic, the direct labor price standard is as follows.

Alternative Terminology The direct labor price standard is also called the *direct labor rate standard*.

Illustration 23-4 Setting direct labor price standard

Item	Price
Hourly wage rate	$ 12.50
COLA	0.25
Payroll taxes	0.75
Fringe benefits	1.50
Standard direct labor rate per hour	**$15.00**

Alternative Terminology The direct labor quantity standard is also called the *direct labor efficiency standard*.

The **direct labor quantity standard** is the time that should be required to make one unit of the product. This standard is especially critical in labor-intensive companies. Allowances should be made in this standard for rest periods, cleanup, machine setup, and machine downtime. For Xonic, the direct labor quantity standard is as follows.

Illustration 23-5 Setting direct labor quantity standard

Item	Quantity (Hours)
Actual production time	1.5
Rest periods and cleanup	0.2
Setup and downtime	0.3
Standard direct labor hours per unit	**2.0**

The standard direct labor cost per unit is the standard direct labor rate times the standard direct labor hours. For Xonic, the standard direct labor cost per gallon is $30 ($15 × 2 hours).

Manufacturing Overhead

For manufacturing overhead, companies use a **standard predetermined overhead rate** in setting the standard. This overhead rate is determined by dividing budgeted overhead costs by an expected standard activity index. For example, the index may be standard direct labor hours or standard machine hours.

As discussed in Chapter 17, many companies employ activity-based costing (ABC) to allocate overhead costs. Because ABC uses multiple activity indices to allocate overhead costs, it results in a better correlation between activities and costs incurred than do other methods. As a result, the use of ABC can significantly improve the usefulness of standard costing for management decision-making.

Xonic uses standard direct labor hours as the activity index. The company expects to produce 13,200 gallons of Xonic Tonic during the year at normal capacity. **Normal capacity** is the average activity output that a company should experience over the long run. Since it takes two direct labor hours for each gallon, total standard direct labor hours are 26,400 (13,200 gallons × 2 hours).

At normal capacity of 26,400 direct labor hours, overhead costs are expected to be $132,000. Of that amount, $79,200 are variable and $52,800 are fixed. Illustration 23-6 shows computation of the standard predetermined overhead rates for Xonic.

Calculating the overhead rate

Overhead ÷ Standard activity index

Illustration 23-6 Computing predetermined overhead rates

Budgeted Overhead Costs	Amount	÷	Standard Direct Labor Hours	=	Overhead Rate per Direct Labor Hour
Variable	$ 79,200		26,400		$3.00
Fixed	52,800		26,400		2.00
Total	$132,000		26,400		$5.00

The standard manufacturing overhead rate per unit is the predetermined overhead rate times the activity index quantity standard. For Xonic, which uses direct labor hours as its activity index, the standard manufacturing overhead rate per gallon of Xonic Tonic is $10 ($5 × 2 hours).

Total Standard Cost per Unit

After a company has established the standard quantity and price per unit of product, it can determine the total standard cost. The total standard cost per unit is the sum of the standard costs of direct materials, direct labor, and manufacturing overhead. The total standard cost per gallon of Xonic Tonic is $52, as shown on the following standard cost card.

Illustration 23-7 Standard cost per gallon of Xonic Tonic

Product: Xonic Tonic	Unit Measure: Gallon		
Manufacturing Cost Elements	Standard Quantity ×	Standard Price =	Standard Cost
Direct materials	4 pounds	$ 3.00	$12.00
Direct labor	2 hours	$15.00	30.00
Manufacturing overhead	2 hours	$ 5.00	10.00
			$52.00

The company prepares a standard cost card for each product. This card provides the basis for determining variances from standards.

Management Insight

How Can We Make Susan's Chili Profitable?

Susan's Chili Factory manufactures and sells chili. The cost of manufacturing Susan's chili consists of the costs of raw materials, labor to convert the basic ingredients to chili, and overhead. Managers need to develop three standards for materials: (1) What should be the formula (mix) of ingredients for one gallon of chili? (2) What should be the normal wastage (or shrinkage) for the individual ingredients? (3) What should be the standard cost for the individual ingredients that go into the chili?

Susan's Chili Factory also illustrates how managers can use standard costs in controlling costs. Suppose that summer droughts have reduced crop yields. As a result, prices have doubled for beans, onions, and peppers. In this case, actual costs will be significantly higher than standard costs, which will cause management to evaluate the situation. Similarly, assume that poor maintenance caused the onion-dicing blades to become dull. As a result, usage of onions to make a gallon of chili tripled. Because this deviation is quickly highlighted through standard costs, managers can take corrective action promptly.

Manuel Gutjahri/iStockphoto

Source: Adapted from David R. Beran, "Cost Reduction Through Control Reporting," *Management Accounting* (April 1982), pp. 29–33.

 How might management use this raw materials cost information? (See page 1242.)

STANDARD COSTS

Action Plan

• Know that standard costs are predetermined unit costs.

• To establish the standard cost of producing a product, establish the standard for each manufacturing cost element—direct materials, direct labor, and manufacturing overhead.

• Compute the standard cost for each element from the standard price to be paid and the standard quantity to be used.

The Navigator

Do it!

Ridette Inc. accumulated the following standard cost data concerning product Cty31.

Direct materials per unit: 1.5 pounds at $4 per pound
Direct labor per unit: 0.25 hours at $13 per hour.
Manufacturing overhead: predetermined rate is 120% of direct labor cost.

Compute the standard cost of one unit of product Cty31.

Solution

Manufacturing Cost Element	Standard Quantity	×	Standard Price	=	Standard Cost
Direct materials	1.5 pounds		$4.00		$ 6.00
Direct labor	0.25 hours		$13.00		3.25
Manufacturing overhead	120% of direct labor cost		$3.25		3.90
Total					$13.15

Related exercise material: **BE23-2, BE23-3, E23-1, E23-2, E23-3,** and **Do it! 23-1.**

Analyzing and Reporting Variances from Standards

LEARNING OBJECTIVE 4

State the formulas for determining direct materials and direct labor variances.

One of the major management uses of standard costs is to identify variances from standards. **Variances** are the differences between total actual costs and total standard costs.

To illustrate, assume that in producing 1,000 gallons of Xonic Tonic in the month of June, Xonic incurred the following costs.

Illustration 23-8 Actual production costs

Direct materials	$13,020
Direct labor	31,080
Variable overhead	6,500
Fixed overhead	4,400
Total actual costs	$55,000

Companies determine total standard costs by multiplying the units produced by the standard cost per unit. The total standard cost of Xonic Tonic is $52,000 (1,000 gallons × $52). Thus, the total variance is $3,000, as shown below.

Illustration 23-9 Computation of total variance

Actual costs	$55,000
Less: Standard costs	52,000
Total variance	$ 3,000

Note that the variance is expressed in total dollars, and not on a per unit basis.

When actual costs exceed standard costs, the variance is **unfavorable**. The $3,000 variance in June for Xonic Tonic is unfavorable. An unfavorable variance has a negative connotation. It suggests that the company paid too much for one or more of the manufacturing cost elements or that it used the elements inefficiently.

If actual costs are less than standard costs, the variance is **favorable**. A favorable variance has a positive connotation. It suggests efficiencies in incurring manufacturing costs and in using direct materials, direct labor, and manufacturing overhead.

However, be careful. A favorable variance could be obtained by using inferior materials. In printing wedding invitations, for example, a favorable variance could result from using an inferior grade of paper. Or, a favorable variance might be achieved in installing tires on an automobile assembly line by tightening only half of the lug bolts. A variance is not favorable if the company has sacrificed quality control standards.

To interpret a variance, you must analyze its components. A variance can result from differences related to the cost of materials, labor, or overhead. Illustration 23-10 shows that the total variance is the sum of the materials, labor, and overhead variances.

Alternative Terminology In business, the term *variance* is also used to indicate differences between total budgeted and total actual costs.

Materials Variance + Labor Variance + Overhead Variance = Total Variance

Illustration 23-10 Components of total variance

In the following discussion, you will see that the materials variance and the labor variance are the sum of variances resulting from price differences and quantity differences. Illustration 23-11 shows a format for computing the price and quantity variances.

Illustration 23-11 Breakdown of materials or labor variance into price and quantity variances

Note that the left side of the matrix is actual cost (actual quantity times actual price). The right hand is standard cost (standard quantity times standard price). The only additional element you need in order to compute the price and quantity variances is the middle element, the actual quantity at the standard price.

DIRECT MATERIALS VARIANCES

Part of Xonic's total variance of $3,000 is due to a materials variance. In completing the order for 1,000 gallons of Xonic Tonic, the company used 4,200 pounds of direct materials. The direct materials were purchased at a price of $3.10 per unit. From Illustration 23-3, we know that Xonic's standards require it to use 4 pounds of materials per gallon produced, so it should have only used 4,000 (4 × 1,000) pounds of direct materials to produce 1,000 gallons. Illustration 23-2 shows that the standard cost of each pound of direct materials is $3 instead of the $3.10 actually paid. Illustration 23-12 shows that the total materials variance is computed as the difference between the amount paid (actual quantity times actual price) and the amount that should have been paid based on standards (standard quantity times standard price of materials).

Illustration 23-12 Formula for total materials variance

Actual Quantity × Actual Price (AQ) × (AP)	−	Standard Quantity × Standard Price (SQ) × (SP)	=	Total Materials Variance (TMV)
(4,200 × $3.10)	−	(4,000 × $3.00)	=	$1,020 U

Thus, for Xonic, the total materials variance is $1,020 ($13,020 − $12,000) unfavorable.

The total materials variance could be caused by differences in the price paid for the materials or by differences in the amount of materials used. Illustration 23-13 shows that the total materials variance is the sum of the materials price variance and the materials quantity variance.

Illustration 23-13 Components of total materials variance

Materials Price Variance + **Materials Quantity Variance** = **Total Materials Variance**

The materials price variance results from a difference between the actual price and the standard price. Illustration 23-14 shows that the materials price variance is computed as the difference between the actual amount paid (actual quantity of materials times actual price) and the standard amount that should have been paid for the materials used (actual quantity of materials times standard price).[1]

Illustration 23-14 Formula for materials price variance

Actual Quantity × Actual Price (AQ) × (AP)	−	Actual Quantity × Standard Price (AQ) × (SP)	=	Materials Price Variance (MPV)
(4,200 × $3.10)	−	(4,200 × $3.00)	=	$420 U

Helpful Hint
The alternative formula is:

$$\boxed{AQ} \times \boxed{AP - SP} = \boxed{MPV}$$

For Xonic, the materials price variance is $420 ($13,020 − $12,600) unfavorable.

The price variance can also be computed by multiplying the actual quantity purchased by the difference between the actual and standard price per unit. The computation in this case is 4,200 × ($3.10 − $3.00) = $420 U.

As seen in Illustration 23-13, the other component of the materials variance is the quantity variance. The quantity variance results from differences between the amount of material actually used and the amount that should have been used. As shown in Illustration 23-15, the materials quantity variance is computed as the difference between the standard cost of the actual quantity (actual quantity times standard price) and the standard cost of the amount that should have been used (standard quantity times standard price for materials).

Illustration 23-15 Formula for materials quantity variance

Actual Quantity × Standard Price (AQ) × (SP)	−	Standard Quantity × Standard Price (SQ) × (SP)	=	Materials Quantity Variance (MQV)
(4,200 × $3.00)	−	(4,000 × $3.00)	=	$600 U

---

[1]Assume that all materials purchased during the period are used in production and that no units remain in inventory at the end of the period.

Thus, for Xonic, the materials quantity variance is $600 ($12,600 − $12,000) unfavorable.

The quantity variance can also be computed by applying the standard price to the difference between actual and standard quantities used. The computation in this example is $3.00 × (4,200 − 4,000) = $600 U.

The total materials variance of $1,020 U, therefore, consists of the following.

Materials price variance	$ 420 U
Materials quantity variance	600 U
Total materials variance	**$1,020 U**

Illustration 23-16 Summary of materials variances

Companies sometimes use a matrix to analyze a variance. **When the matrix is used, a company computes the amounts using the formulas for each cost element first and then computes the variances.** Illustration 23-17 shows the completed matrix for the direct materials variance for Xonic. The matrix provides a convenient structure for determining each variance.

Illustration 23-17 Matrix for direct materials variances

Causes of Materials Variances

What are the causes of a variance? The causes may relate to both internal and external factors. The investigation of a **materials price variance usually begins in the purchasing department**. Many factors affect the price paid for raw materials. These include availability of quantity and cash discounts, the quality of the materials requested, and the delivery method used. To the extent that these factors are considered in setting the price standard, the purchasing department is responsible for any variances.

However, a variance may be beyond the control of the purchasing department. Sometimes, for example, prices may rise faster than expected. Moreover,

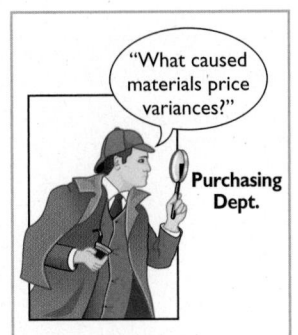

"What caused materials price variances?"

Purchasing Dept.

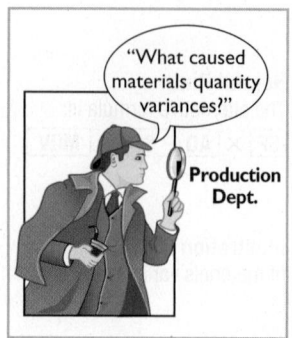

"What caused materials quantity variances?"

Production Dept.

actions by groups over which the company has no control, such as the OPEC nations' oil price increases, may cause an unfavorable variance. For example, during a recent year, Kraft Foods and Kellogg Company both experienced unfavorable materials price variances when the cost of dairy and wheat products jumped unexpectedly. There are also times when a production department may be responsible for the price variance. This may occur when a rush order forces the company to pay a higher price for the materials.

The starting point for determining the cause(s) of a significant **materials quantity variance is in the production department**. If the variances are due to inexperienced workers, faulty machinery, or carelessness, the production department is responsible. However, if the materials obtained by the purchasing department were of inferior quality, then the purchasing department is responsible.

🧰 DECISION TOOLKIT

DECISION CHECKPOINTS	INFO NEEDED FOR DECISION	TOOL TO USE FOR DECISION	HOW TO EVALUATE RESULTS
Has management accomplished its price and quantity objectives regarding materials?	Actual cost and standard cost of materials	Materials price and materials quantity variances	Positive (favorable) variances suggest that price and quantity objectives have been met.

DIRECT MATERIALS VARIANCES

Action Plan

Use the formulas for computing each of the materials variances:

- Total materials variance
  = (AQ × AP) − (SQ × SP)
- Materials price variance
  = (AQ × AP) − (AQ × SP)
- Materials quantity variance
  = (AQ × SP) − (SQ × SP)

✔ The Navigator

Do it! The standard cost of Wonder Walkers includes two units of direct materials at $8.00 per unit. During July, the company buys 22,000 units of direct materials at $7.50 and uses those materials to produce 10,000 Wonder Walkers. Compute the total, price, and quantity variances for materials.

Solution

Standard quantity = 10,000 × 2.
Substituting amounts into the formulas, the variances are:

Total materials variance = (22,000 × $7.50) − (20,000 × $8.00) = $5,000 unfavorable
Materials price variance = (22,000 × $7.50) − (22,000 × $8.00) = $11,000 favorable
Materials quantity variance = (22,000 × $8.00) − (20,000 × $8.00) = $16,000 unfavorable

Related exercise material: **BE23-4, E23-5, and Do it! 23-2.**

DIRECT LABOR VARIANCES

The process of determining direct labor variances is the same as for determining the direct materials variances. In completing the Xonic Tonic order, the company incurred 2,100 direct labor hours at an average hourly rate of $14.80. The standard hours allowed for the units produced were 2,000 hours (1,000 gallons × 2 hours). The standard labor rate was $15 per hour.

The total labor variance is the difference between the amount actually paid for labor versus the amount that should have been paid. Illustration 23-18 shows that the total labor variance is computed as the difference between the amount actually paid for labor (actual hours times actual rate) and the amount that should have been paid (standard hours times standard rate for labor).

Actual Hours		**Standard Hours**		**Total Labor**
× Actual Rate	**−**	**× Standard Rate**	**=**	**Variance**
(AH) × (AR)		**(SH) × (SR)**		**(TLV)**
(2,100 × $14.80)	−	(2,000 × $15.00)	=	$1,080 U

Illustration 23-18 Formula for total labor variance

The total labor variance is $1,080 ($31,080 − $30,000) unfavorable.

The total labor variance is caused by differences in the labor rate or difference in labor hours. Illustration 23-19 shows that the total labor variance is the sum of the labor price variance and the labor quantity variance.

Labor Price Variance	**+**	**Labor Quantity Variance**	**=**	**Total Labor Variance**

Illustration 23-19 Components of total labor variance

The labor price variance results from the difference between the rate paid to workers versus the rate that was supposed to be paid. Illustration 23-20 shows that the labor price variance is computed as the difference between the actual amount paid (actual hours times actual rate) and the amount that should have been paid for the number of hours worked (actual hours times standard rate for labor).

Actual Hours		**Actual Hours**		**Labor Price**
× Actual Rate	**−**	**× Standard Rate**	**=**	**Variance**
(AH) × (AR)		**(AH) × (SR)**		**(LPV)**
(2,100 × $14.80)	−	(2,100 × $15.00)	=	$420 F

Illustration 23-20 Formula for labor price variance

For Xonic, the labor price variance is $420 ($31,080 − $31,500) favorable.

The labor price variance can also be computed by multiplying actual hours worked by the difference between the actual pay rate and the standard pay rate. The computation in this example is 2,100 × ($15.00 − $14.80) = $420 F.

The other component of the total labor variance is the labor quantity variance. The labor quantity variance results from the difference between the actual number of labor hours and the number of hours that should have been worked for the quantity produced. Illustration 23-21 shows that the labor quantity variance is computed as the difference between the amount that should have been paid for the hours worked (actual hours times standard rate) and the amount that should have been paid for the amount of hours that should have been worked (standard hours times standard rate for labor).

Helpful Hint
The alternative formula is:
$$\boxed{AH} \times \boxed{AR - SR} = \boxed{LPV}$$

Actual Hours		**Standard Hours**		**Labor Quantity**
× Standard Rate	**−**	**× Standard Rate**	**=**	**Variance**
(AH) × (SR)		**(SH) × (SR)**		**(LQV)**
(2,100 × $15.00)	−	(2,000 × $15.00)	=	$1,500 U

Illustration 23-21 Formula for labor quantity variance

Thus, for Xonic, the labor quantity variance is $1,500 ($31,500 − $30,000) unfavorable.

The same result can be obtained by multiplying the standard rate by the difference between actual hours worked and standard hours allowed. In this case, the computation is $15.00 × (2,100 − 2,000) = $1,500 U.

Helpful Hint
The alternative formula is:
$$\boxed{SR} \times \boxed{AH - SH} = \boxed{LQV}$$

The total direct labor variance of $1,080 U, therefore, consists of:

Illustration 23-22 Summary of labor variances

Labor price variance	$ 420 F
Labor quantity variance	1,500 U
Total direct labor variance	**$1,080 U**

Illustration 23-23 Matrix for direct labor variances

These results can also be obtained from the matrix in Illustration 23-23.

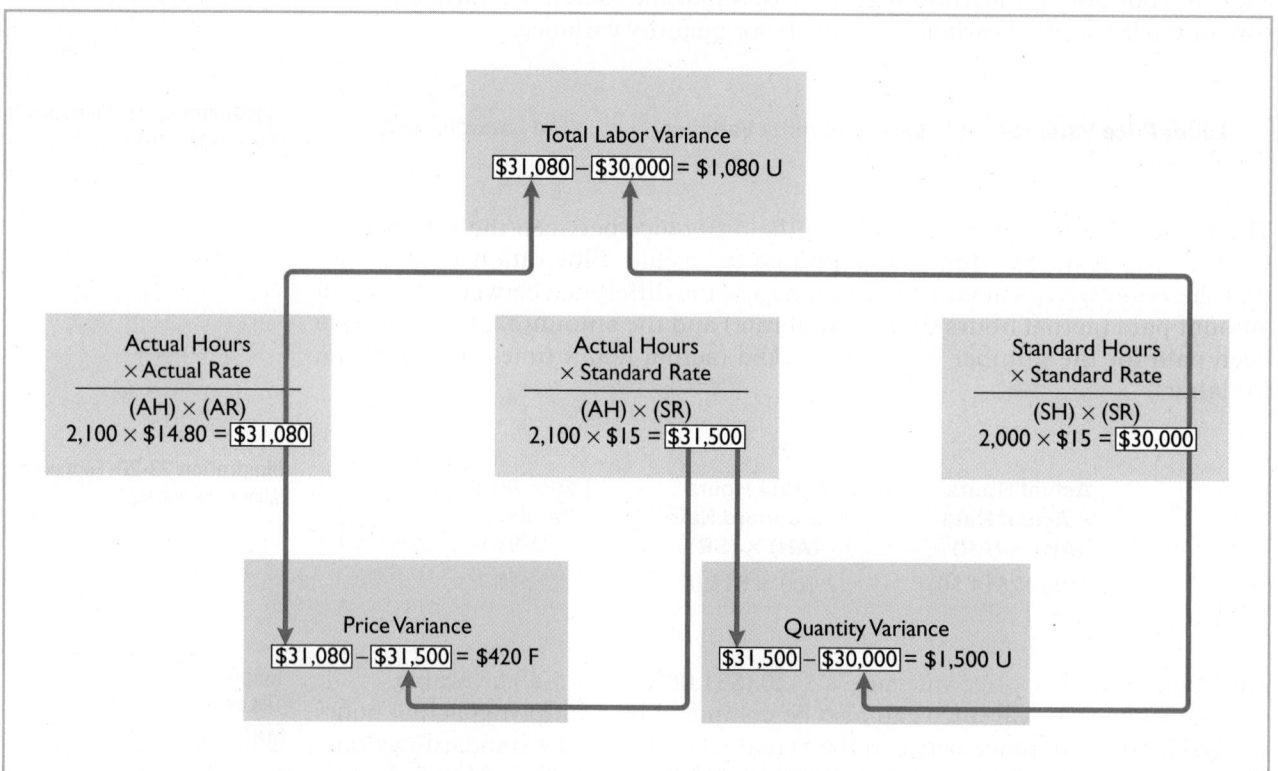

Causes of Labor Variances

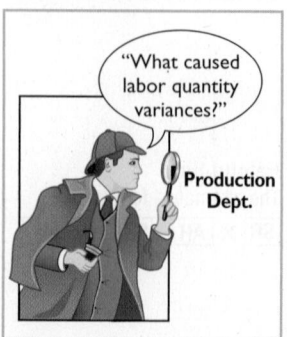

Labor price variances usually result from two factors: (1) paying workers **different wages than expected**, and (2) **misallocation of workers**. In companies where pay rates are determined by union contracts, labor price variances should be infrequent. When workers are not unionized, there is a much higher likelihood of such variances. The responsibility for these variances rests with the manager who authorized the wage change.

Misallocation of the workforce refers to using skilled workers in place of unskilled workers and vice versa. The use of an inexperienced worker instead of an experienced one will result in a favorable price variance because of the lower pay rate of the unskilled worker. An unfavorable price variance would result if a skilled worker were substituted for an inexperienced one. The production department generally is responsible for labor price variances resulting from misallocation of the workforce.

Labor quantity variances relate to the **efficiency of workers**. The cause of a quantity variance generally can be traced to the production department. The causes of an unfavorable variance may be poor training, worker fatigue, faulty machinery, or carelessness. These causes are the responsibility of the **production department**. However, if the excess time is due to inferior materials, the responsibility falls outside the production department.

DECISION TOOLKIT

DECISION CHECKPOINTS	INFO NEEDED FOR DECISION	TOOL TO USE FOR DECISION	HOW TO EVALUATE RESULTS
Has management accomplished its price and quantity objectives regarding labor?	Actual cost and standard cost of labor	Labor price and labor quantity variances	Positive (favorable) variances suggest that price and quantity objectives have been met.

MANUFACTURING OVERHEAD VARIANCES

The **total overhead variance** is the difference between the actual overhead costs and overhead costs applied based on standard hours allowed for the amount of goods produced. As indicated in Illustration 23-8 (page 1200), Xonic incurred overhead costs of $10,900 to produce 1,000 gallons of Xonic Tonic in June. The computation of the actual overhead is comprised of a variable and a fixed component. Illustration 23-24 shows this computation.

> **LEARNING OBJECTIVE** 5
>
> State the formula for determining the total manufacturing overhead variance.

Variable overhead	$ 6,500
Fixed overhead	4,400
Total actual overhead	**$10,900**

Illustration 23-24 Actual overhead costs

To find the total overhead variance in a standard costing system, we determine the overhead costs applied based on standard hours allowed. **Standard hours allowed** are the hours that **should** have been worked for the units produced. Overhead costs for Xonic Tonic are applied based on direct labor hours. Because it takes two hours of direct labor to produce one gallon of Xonic Tonic, for the 1,000-gallon Xonic Tonic order, the standard hours allowed are 2,000 hours (1,000 gallons × 2 hours). We then apply the predetermined overhead rate to the 2,000 standard hours allowed.

Recall from Illustration 23-6 (page 1198) that the amount of budgeted overhead costs at normal capacity of $132,000 was divided by normal capacity of 26,400 direct labor hours, to arrive at a predetermined overhead rate of $5 ($132,000 ÷ 26,400). The predetermined rate of $5 is then multiplied by the 2,000 standard hours allowed, to determine the overhead costs applied.

Illustration 23-25 shows the formula for the total overhead variance and the calculation for Xonic for the month of June.

Actual Overhead	−	Overhead Applied*	=	Total Overhead Variance
$10,900	−	$10,000	=	$900 U
($6,500 + $4,400)		($5 × 2,000 hours)		

*Based on standard hours allowed.

Illustration 23-25 Formula for total overhead variance

Thus, for Xonic, the total overhead variance is $900 unfavorable.

The overhead variance is generally analyzed through a price and a quantity variance. (These computations are discussed in more detail in advanced courses.) The name usually given to the price variance is the **overhead controllable variance**; the quantity variance is referred to as the **overhead volume variance**. Appendix 23B discusses how the total overhead variance can be broken down into these two variances.

Causes of Manufacturing Overhead Variances

One reason for an overhead variance relates to over- or underspending on overhead items. For example, overhead may include indirect labor for which a company paid wages higher than the standard labor price allowed. Or, the price of electricity to run the company's machines increased, and the company did not anticipate this additional cost. Companies should investigate any spending variances, to determine whether they will continue in the future. Generally, the responsibility for these variances rests with the production department.

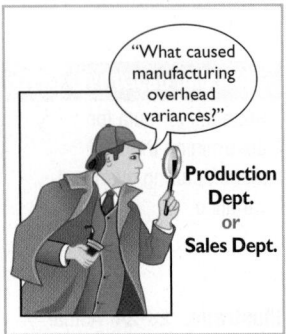

"What caused manufacturing overhead variances?"

Production Dept. or **Sales Dept.**

The overhead variance can also result from the inefficient use of overhead. For example, because of poor maintenance, a number of the manufacturing machines are experiencing breakdowns on a consistent basis, leading to reduced production. Or, the flow of materials through the production process is impeded because of a lack of skilled labor to perform the necessary production tasks, due to a lack of planning. In both of these cases, the production department is responsible for the cause of these variances. On the other hand, overhead can also be underutilized because of a lack of sales orders. When the cause is a lack of sales orders, the responsibility rests outside the production department. For example, at one point Chrysler experienced a very significant unfavorable overhead variance because plant capacity was maintained at excessively high levels, due to overly optimistic sales forecasts.

DECISION TOOLKIT

DECISION CHECKPOINTS	INFO NEEDED FOR DECISION	TOOL TO USE FOR DECISION	HOW TO EVALUATE RESULTS
Has management accomplished its objectives regarding manufacturing overhead?	Actual cost and standard cost of manufacturing overhead	Total manufacturing overhead variance	Positive (favorable) variances suggest that manufacturing overhead objectives have been met.

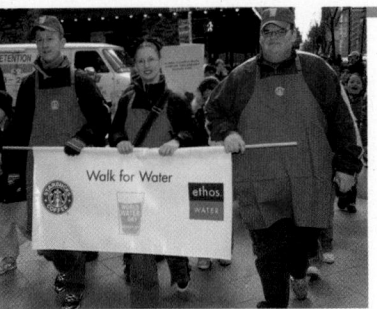

Archer Colin/SiPA/NewsCom

People, Planet, and Profit Insight

What's Brewing at Starbucks?

It is one thing for a company to say it is committed to corporate social responsibility. It is another thing for the company to actually spell out measurable goals. Recently, Starbucks published its 10th annual *Global Responsibility Report* in which it describes its goals, achievements, and even its shortcomings related to corporate social responsibility. For example, the company achieved its goal of getting more than 50% of its electricity from renewable sources. It then set its sights higher by setting a goal of 100% within five years. The company also has numerous goals related to purchasing coffee from sources that are certified as responsibly grown and ethically traded; providing funds for loans to coffee farmers; and partnerships with Conservation International to provide training to farmers on ecologically friendly growing. Further, the company reduced water consumption by more than 20% in a two-year period. Finally, it made a significant investment in programs to increase recycling of paper and plastic at its stores.

The report also candidly explains that the company did not meet its goal to cut energy consumption by 25%. It also fell far short of its goal of getting customers to reuse their cups. In those instances where it didn't achieve its goals, Starbucks set new goals and described steps it would take to achieve them. You can view the company's *Global Responsibility Report* at **www.starbucks.com/2010report.**

Source: "Starbucks Launches 10th Global Responsibility Report," *Business Wire* (April 18, 2011).

 What implications does Starbucks' commitment to corporate social responsibility have for the standard cost of a cup of coffee? (See page 1242.)

Do it! The standard cost of Product YY includes 3 hours of direct labor at $12.00 per hour. The predetermined overhead rate is $20.00 per direct labor hour. During July, the company incurred 3,500 hours of direct labor at an average rate of $12.40 per hour and $71,300 of manufacturing overhead costs. It produced 1,200 units.

(a) Compute the total, price, and quantity variances for labor. (b) Compute the total overhead variance.

LABOR AND MANUFACTURING OVERHEAD VARIANCES

Action Plan

- Use the formulas for computing each of the variances:
  Total labor variance =
  (AH × AR) − (SH × SR)
  Labor price variance =
  (AH × AR) − (AH × SR)
  Labor quantity variance =
  (AH × SR) − (SH × SR)
  Total overhead variance =
  Actual overhead −
  Overhead applied*

*Based on standard hours allowed.

Solution

Substituting amounts into the formulas, the variances are:

(a) Total labor variance = (3,500 × $12.40) − (3,600 × $12.00) = $200 unfavorable
   Labor price variance = (3,500 × $12.40) − (3,500 × $12.00) = $1,400 unfavorable
   Labor quantity variance = (3,500 × $12.00) − (3,600 × $12.00) = $1,200 favorable

(b) Total overhead variance = $71,300 − $72,000* = $700 favorable

   *3,600 hours × $20.00

Related exercise material: **BE23-5, BE23-6, E23-4, E23-6, E23-7, E23-8, E23-11,** and **Do it! 23-3.**

 The Navigator

REPORTING VARIANCES

All variances should be reported to appropriate levels of management as soon as possible. The sooner managers are informed, the sooner they can evaluate problems and take corrective action.

The form, content, and frequency of variance reports vary considerably among companies. One approach is to prepare a weekly report for each department that has primary responsibility for cost control. Under this approach, materials price variances are reported to the purchasing department, and all other variances are reported to the production department that did the work. The following report for Xonic, with the materials for the Xonic Tonic order listed first, illustrates this approach.

LEARNING OBJECTIVE 6

Discuss the reporting of variances.

XONIC
Variance Report—Purchasing Department
For Week Ended June 8, 2014

Type of Materials	Quantity Purchased	Actual Price	Standard Price	Price Variance	Explanation
X100	4,200 lbs.	$3.10	$3.00	$ 420 U	Rush order
X142	1,200 units	2.75	2.80	60 F	Quantity discount
A85	600 doz.	5.20	5.10	60 U	Regular supplier on strike
Total price variance				**$420 U**	

Illustration 23-26 Materials price variance report

The explanation column is completed after consultation with the purchasing department manager.

Variance reports facilitate the principle of "management by exception" explained in Chapter 22. For example, the vice president of purchasing can use the report shown above to evaluate the effectiveness of the purchasing department manager. Or, the vice president of production can use production department variance reports to determine how well each production manager is controlling costs. In using variance reports, top management normally looks for **significant variances**. These may be judged on the basis of some quantitative measure, such as more than 10% of the standard or more than $1,000.

STATEMENT PRESENTATION OF VARIANCES

LEARNING OBJECTIVE 7

Prepare an income statement for management under a standard costing system.

In income statements **prepared for management** under a standard cost accounting system, **cost of goods sold is stated at standard cost and the variances are disclosed separately**. Unfavorable variances increase cost of goods sold, while favorable variances decrease cost of goods sold. Illustration 23-27 shows the presentation of variances in an income statement. This income statement is based on the production and sale of 1,000 units of Xonic Tonic at $70 per unit. It also assumes selling and administrative costs of $3,000. Observe that each variance is shown, as well as the total net variance. In this example, variations from standard costs reduced net income by $3,000.

Illustration 23-27
Variances in income statement for management

XONIC		
Income Statement		
For the Month Ended June 30, 2014		
Sales revenue		$70,000
Cost of goods sold (at standard)		52,000
Gross profit (at standard)		18,000
Variances		
Materials price	$ 420 U	
Materials quantity	600 U	
Labor price	420 F	
Labor quantity	1,500 U	
Overhead	900 U	
Total variance unfavorable		3,000
Gross profit (actual)		15,000
Selling and administrative expenses		3,000
Net income		$12,000

Standard costs may be used in financial statements prepared for stockholders and other external users. The costing of inventories at standard costs is in accordance with generally accepted accounting principles when there are no significant differences between actual costs and standard costs. Hewlett-Packard and Jostens, Inc., for example, report their inventories at standard costs. However, if there are significant differences between actual and standard costs, the financial statements must report inventories and cost of goods sold at actual costs.

It is also possible to show the variances in an income statement prepared in the variable costing (CVP) format. To do so, it is necessary to analyze the overhead variances into variable and fixed components. This type of analysis is explained in cost accounting textbooks.

Balanced Scorecard

LEARNING OBJECTIVE 8

Describe the balanced scorecard approach to performance evaluation.

Financial measures (measurement of dollars), such as variance analysis and return on investment (ROI), are useful tools for evaluating performance. However, many companies now supplement these financial measures with nonfinancial measures to better assess performance and anticipate future results. For example, airlines like Delta, American, and United use capacity utilization as an important measure to understand and predict future performance. Newspaper publishers such as the *New York Times* and the *Chicago Tribune* use circulation figures as another measure by which to assess performance. Penske Automotive Group, the owner of 300 dealerships, rewards executives for meeting employee retention targets. Illustration 23-28 lists some key nonfinancial measures used in various industries.

Industry	Measure
Automobiles	Capacity utilization of plants.
	Average age of key assets.
	Impact of strikes.
	Brand-loyalty statistics.
Computer Systems	Market profile of customer end-products.
	Number of new products.
	Employee stock ownership percentages.
	Number of scientists and technicians used in R&D.
Chemicals	Customer satisfaction data.
	Factors affecting customer product selection.
	Number of patents and trademarks held.
	Customer brand awareness.
Regional Banks	Number of ATMs by state.
	Number of products used by average customer.
	Percentage of customer service calls handled by interactive voice response units.
	Personnel cost per employee.
	Credit card retention rates.

Source: Financial Accounting Standards Board, *Business Reporting: Insights into Enhancing Voluntary Disclosures* (Norwalk, Conn.: FASB, 2001).

Illustration 23-28
Nonfinancial measures used in various industries

Most companies recognize that both financial and nonfinancial measures can provide useful insights into what is happening in the company. As a result, many companies now use a broad-based measurement approach, called the **balanced scorecard**, to evaluate performance. The balanced scorecard incorporates financial and nonfinancial measures in an integrated system that links performance measurement with a company's strategic goals. Nearly 50% of the largest companies in the United States, including Unilever, Chase, and Wal-Mart Stores Inc., are using the balanced scorecard approach.

The balanced scorecard evaluates company performance from a series of "perspectives." The four most commonly employed perspectives are as follows.

1. The financial perspective is the most traditional view of the company. It employs financial measures of performance used by most firms.

2. The customer perspective evaluates the company from the viewpoint of those people who buy its products or services. This view compares the company to competitors in terms of price, quality, product innovation, customer service, and other dimensions.

3. The internal process perspective evaluates the internal operating processes critical to success. All critical aspects of the value chain—including product development, production, delivery, and after-sale service—are evaluated to ensure that the company is operating effectively and efficiently.

4. The **learning and growth perspective** evaluates how well the company develops and retains its employees. This would include evaluation of such things as employee skills, employee satisfaction, training programs, and information dissemination.

Within each perspective, the balanced scorecard identifies objectives that contribute to attainment of strategic goals. Illustration 23-29 shows examples of objectives within each perspective.

Illustration 23-29
Examples of objectives within the four perspectives of balanced scorecard

Perspective		Objective
Financial		Return on assets
		Net income
		Credit rating
		Share price
		Profit per employee
Customer		Percentage of customers who would recommend product
		Customer retention
		Response time per customer request
		Brand recognition
		Customer service expense per customer
Internal Process		Percentage of defect-free products
		Stockouts
		Labor utilization rates
		Waste reduction
		Planning accuracy
Learning and Growth		Percentage of employees leaving in less than one year
		Number of cross-trained employees
		Ethics violations
		Training hours
		Reportable accidents

The objectives are linked across perspectives in order to tie performance measurement to company goals. The financial-perspective objectives are normally set first, and then objectives are set in the other perspectives in order to accomplish the financial goals.

For example, within the financial perspective, a common goal is to increase profit per dollars invested as measured by ROI. In order to increase ROI, a customer-perspective objective might be to increase customer satisfaction as measured by the percentage of customers who would recommend the product to a friend. In order to increase customer satisfaction, an internal-process-perspective objective might be to increase product quality as measured by the percentage of defect-free units. Finally, in order to increase the percentage of defect-free units, the learning-and-growth-perspective objective might be to reduce factory employee turnover as measured by the percentage of employees leaving in under one year.

Illustration 23-30 illustrates this linkage across perspectives.

Illustration 23-30 Linked process across balanced scorecard perspectives

Through this linked process, the company can better understand how to achieve its goals and what measures to use to evaluate performance.

In summary, the balanced scorecard does the following:

1. Employs both **financial and nonfinancial measures**. (For example, ROI is a financial measure; employee turnover is a nonfinancial measure.)

2. **Creates linkages** so that high-level corporate goals can be communicated all the way down to the shop floor.

3. **Provides measurable objectives for nonfinancial measures** such as product quality, rather than vague statements such as "We would like to improve quality."

4. Integrates all of the company's goals into a single performance measurement system, so that **an inappropriate amount of weight will not be placed on any single goal**.

Service Company Insight
It May Be Time to Fly United Again

Many of the benefits of a balanced scorecard approach are evident in the improved operations at United Airlines. At the time it filed for bankruptcy, United had a reputation for some of the worst service in the airline business. But when Glenn Tilton took over as United's chief executive officer, he recognized that things had to change.

He implemented an incentive program that allows all of United's 63,000 employees to earn a bonus of 2.5% or more of their wages if the company "exceeds its goals for on-time flight departures and for customer intent to fly United again." After instituting this program, the company's on-time departures were among the best, its customer complaints were reduced considerably, and the number of customers who said that they would fly United again was at its highest level ever.

Source: Susan Carey, "Friendlier Skies: In Bankruptcy, United Airlines Forges a Path to Better Service," *Wall Street Journal* (June 15, 2004).

 Which of the perspectives of a balanced scorecard were the focus of United's CEO? (See page 1243.)

Gene Chutka/IStockphoto

Do it!

Indicate which of the four perspectives in the balanced scorecard is most likely associated with the objectives that follow.

1. Percentage of repeat customers.
2. Number of suggestions for improvement from employees.
3. Contribution margin.
4. Brand recognition.
5. Number of cross-trained employees.
6. Amount of setup time.

Solution

1. Customer perspective.
2. Learning and growth perspective.
3. Financial perspective.
4. Customer perspective.
5. Learning and growth perspective.
6. Internal process perspective.

Related exercise material: **BE23-7, E23-17,** and **Do it! 23-4.**

BALANCED SCORECARD

Action Plan

- The financial perspective employs traditional financial measures of performance.

- The customer perspective evaluates company performance as seen by the people who buy its products or services.

- The internal process perspective evaluates the internal operating processes critical to success.

- The learning and growth perspective evaluates how well the company develops and retains its employees.

✔ The Navigator

USING THE **DECISION TOOLKIT**

Assume that during the past month, Sanford produced 10,000 cartons of Liquid ACCENT® highlighters. Liquid ACCENT® offers a translucent barrel and cap with a visible ink supply for see-through color. The special fluorescent ink is fade- and water-resistant. Each carton contains 100 boxes of markers, and each box contains five markers. The markers come in boxes of one of five fluorescent colors—orange, blue, yellow, green, and pink—and in a five-color set.

Assume the following additional facts: The standard cost for one carton of 500 markers is as follows.

Manufacturing Cost Elements	Standard Quantity	×	Price	=	Cost
Direct materials					
Tips (boxes of 500)	500	×	$ 0.03	=	$ 15.00
Translucent barrels and caps (boxes of 500)	500	×	$ 0.09	=	45.00
Fluorescent ink (100 oz. containers)	100 oz.	×	$ 0.32	=	32.00
Total direct materials					92.00
Direct labor	0.25 hours	×	$ 9.00	=	2.25
Overhead	0.25 hours	×	$48.00	=	12.00
					$106.25

During the month, the following transactions occurred in manufacturing the 10,000 cartons of highlighters.

1. Purchased 10,000 boxes of tips for $148,000 ($14.80 per 500 tips); purchased 10,200 boxes of translucent barrels and caps for $453,900 ($44.50 per 500 barrels and caps); and purchased 9,900 containers of fluorescent ink for $328,185 ($33.15 per 100 ounces).
2. All materials purchased during the period were used to make markers during the period.
3. 2,300 direct labor hours were worked at a total labor cost of $20,240 (an average hourly rate of $8.80).
4. Variable manufacturing overhead incurred was $34,600, and fixed overhead incurred was $84,000.

The manufacturing overhead rate of $48.00 is based on a normal capacity of 2,600 direct labor hours. The total budget at this capacity is $83,980 fixed and $40,820 variable.

Instructions

Determine whether Sanford met its price and quantity objectives relative to materials, labor, and overhead.

Solution

To determine whether Sanford met its price and quantity objectives, compute the total variance and the variances for direct materials and direct labor, and calculate the total variance for manufacturing overhead.

Total Variance

Actual cost incurred:		
Direct materials		
Tips	$148,000	
Translucent barrels and caps	453,900	
Fluorescent ink	328,185	
Total direct materials		$ 930,085
Direct labor		20,240
Overhead		118,600
Total actual costs		1,068,925
Less: Standard cost (10,000 × $106.25)		1,062,500
Total variance		$ 6,425 U

Direct Materials Variances

Total	= $930,085	−	$920,000 (10,000 × $92)	=	$10,085 U
Price (Tips)	= $148,000 (10,000 × $14.80)	−	$150,000 (10,000 × $15.00)	=	$ 2,000 F
Price (Barrels and caps)	= $453,900 (10,200 × $44.50)	−	$459,000 (10,200 × $45.00)	=	$ 5,100 F
Price (Ink)	= $328,185 (9,900 × $33.15)	−	$316,800 (9,900 × $32.00)	=	$11,385 U
Quantity (Tips)	= $150,000 (10,000 × $15.00)	−	$150,000 (10,000 × $15.00)	=	$ 0
Quantity (Barrels and caps)	= $459,000 (10,200 × $45.00)	−	$450,000 (10,000 × $45.00)	=	$ 9,000 U
Quantity (Ink)	= $316,800 (9,900 × $32.00)	−	$320,000 (10,000 × $32.00)	=	$ 3,200 F

Direct Labor Variances

Total	=	$20,240 (2,300 × $8.80)	−	$22,500 (2,500* × $9.00)	= $ 2,260 F
Price	=	$20,240 (2,300 × $8.80)	−	$20,700 (2,300 × $9.00)	= $ 460 F
Quantity	=	$20,700 (2,300 × $9.00)	−	$22,500 (2,500* × $9.00)	= $ 1,800 F

*10,000 × .25

Overhead Variance

Total	=	$118,600 ($84,000 + $34,600)	−	$120,000 (2,500 × $48)	= $ 1,400 F

Sanford's total variance was an unfavorable $6,425. The unfavorable materials variance outweighed the favorable labor and overhead variances. The primary determinants were an unfavorable price variance for ink and an unfavorable quantity variance for barrels and caps.

Summary of Learning Objectives

1 Distinguish between a standard and a budget. Both standards and budgets are predetermined costs. The primary difference is that a standard is a unit amount, whereas a budget is a total amount. A standard may be regarded as the budgeted cost per unit of product.

2 Identify the advantages of standard costs. Standard costs offer a number of advantages. They (a) facilitate management planning, (b) promote greater economy, (c) are useful in setting selling prices, (d) contribute to management control, (e) permit "management by exception," and (f) simplify the costing of inventories and reduce clerical costs.

3 Describe how companies set standards. The direct materials price standard should be based on the delivered cost of raw materials plus an allowance for receiving and handling. The direct materials quantity standard should establish the required quantity plus an allowance for waste and spoilage.

The direct labor price standard should be based on current wage rates and anticipated adjustments such as COLAs. It also generally includes payroll taxes and fringe benefits. Direct labor quantity standards should be based on required production time plus an allowance for rest periods, cleanup, machine setup, and machine downtime.

For manufacturing overhead, a standard predetermined overhead rate is used. It is based on an expected standard activity index such as standard direct labor hours or standard machine hours.

4 State the formulas for determining direct materials and direct labor variances. The formulas for the direct materials variances are:

$$\left(\begin{array}{c}\text{Actual quantity}\\ \times \text{ Actual price}\end{array}\right) - \left(\begin{array}{c}\text{Standard quantity}\\ \times \text{ Standard price}\end{array}\right) = \begin{array}{c}\text{Total}\\ \text{materials}\\ \text{variance}\end{array}$$

$$\left(\begin{array}{c}\text{Actual quantity}\\ \times \text{ Actual price}\end{array}\right) - \left(\begin{array}{c}\text{Actual quantity}\\ \times \text{ Standard price}\end{array}\right) = \begin{array}{c}\text{Materials}\\ \text{price}\\ \text{variance}\end{array}$$

$$\left(\begin{array}{c}\text{Actual quantity}\\ \times \text{ Standard price}\end{array}\right) - \left(\begin{array}{c}\text{Standard quantity}\\ \times \text{ Standard price}\end{array}\right) = \begin{array}{c}\text{Materials}\\ \text{quantity}\\ \text{variance}\end{array}$$

The formulas for the direct labor variances are:

$$\left(\begin{array}{c}\text{Actual hours}\\ \times \text{ Actual rate}\end{array}\right) - \left(\begin{array}{c}\text{Standard hours}\\ \times \text{ Standard rate}\end{array}\right) = \begin{array}{c}\text{Total}\\ \text{labor}\\ \text{variance}\end{array}$$

$$\left(\begin{array}{c}\text{Actual hours}\\ \times \text{ Actual rate}\end{array}\right) - \left(\begin{array}{c}\text{Actual hours}\\ \times \text{ Standard rate}\end{array}\right) = \begin{array}{c}\text{Labor}\\ \text{price}\\ \text{variance}\end{array}$$

$$\left(\begin{array}{c}\text{Actual hours}\\ \times \text{ Standard rate}\end{array}\right) - \left(\begin{array}{c}\text{Standard hours}\\ \times \text{ Standard rate}\end{array}\right) = \begin{array}{c}\text{Labor}\\ \text{quantity}\\ \text{variance}\end{array}$$

5 State the formula for determining the total manufacturing overhead variance. The formula for the total manufacturing overhead variance is:

$$\left(\begin{array}{c}\text{Actual}\\ \text{overhead}\end{array}\right) - \left(\begin{array}{c}\text{Overhead}\\ \text{applied at}\\ \text{standard hours}\\ \text{allowed}\end{array}\right) = \begin{array}{c}\text{Total overhead}\\ \text{variance}\end{array}$$

6 Discuss the reporting of variances. Variances are reported to management in variance reports. The reports facilitate management by exception by highlighting significant differences.

7 Prepare an income statement for management under a standard costing system. Under a standard costing system, an income statement prepared for management will report cost of goods sold at standard cost and then disclose each variance separately.

8 **Describe the balanced scorecard approach to performance evaluation.** The balanced scorecard incorporates financial and nonfinancial measures in an integrated system that links performance measurement and a company's strategic goals. It employs four perspectives: financial, customer, internal process, and learning and growth. Objectives are set within each of these perspectives that link to objectives within the other perspectives.

✔ The Navigator

🧰 DECISION TOOLKIT *A SUMMARY*

DECISION CHECKPOINTS	INFO NEEDED FOR DECISION	TOOL TO USE FOR DECISION	HOW TO EVALUATE RESULTS
Has management accomplished its price and quantity objectives regarding materials?	Actual cost and standard cost of materials	Materials price and materials quantity variances	Positive (favorable) variances suggest that price and quantity objectives have been met.
Has management accomplished its price and quantity objectives regarding labor?	Actual cost and standard cost of labor	Labor price and labor quantity variances	Positive (favorable) variances suggest that price and quantity objectives have been met.
Has management accomplished its objectives regarding manufacturing overhead?	Actual cost and standard cost of manufacturing overhead	Total manufacturing overhead variance	Positive (favorable) variances suggest that manufacturing overhead objectives have been met.

Appendix 23A

Standard Cost Accounting System

LEARNING OBJECTIVE | **9**

Identify the features of a standard cost accounting system.

A **standard cost accounting system** is a double-entry system of accounting. In this system, companies use standard costs in making entries, and they formally recognize variances in the accounts. Companies may use a standard cost system with either job order or process costing.

In this appendix, we will explain and illustrate a **standard cost, job order cost accounting system**. The system is based on two important assumptions:

1. Variances from standards are recognized at the earliest opportunity.
2. The Work in Process account is maintained exclusively on the basis of standard costs.

In practice, there are many variations among standard cost systems. The system described here should prepare you for systems you see in the "real world."

JOURNAL ENTRIES

We will use the transactions of Xonic to illustrate the journal entries. Note as you study the entries that the major difference between the entries here and those for the job order cost accounting system in Chapter 15 is the **variance accounts**.

1. Purchase raw materials on account for $13,020 when the standard cost is $12,600.

Raw Materials Inventory	12,600	
Materials Price Variance	420	
Accounts Payable		13,020
(To record purchase of materials)		

Xonic debits the inventory account for actual quantities at standard cost. This enables the perpetual materials records to show actual quantities. Xonic debits the price variance, which is unfavorable, to Materials Price Variance.

2. Incur direct labor costs of $31,080 when the standard labor cost is $31,500.

Factory Labor	31,500	
Labor Price Variance		420
Factory Wages Payable		31,080
(To record direct labor costs)		

Like the raw materials inventory account, Xonic debits Factory Labor for actual hours worked at the standard hourly rate of pay. In this case, the labor variance is favorable. Thus, Xonic credits Labor Price Variance.

3. Incur actual manufacturing overhead costs of $10,900.

Manufacturing Overhead	10,900	
Accounts Payable/Cash/Acc. Depreciation		10,900
(To record overhead incurred)		

The controllable overhead variance (see Appendix 23B) is not recorded at this time. It depends on standard hours applied to work in process. This amount is not known at the time overhead is incurred.

4. Issue raw materials for production at a cost of $12,600 when the standard cost is $12,000.

Work in Process Inventory	12,000	
Materials Quantity Variance	600	
Raw Materials Inventory		12,600
(To record issuance of raw materials)		

Xonic debits Work in Process Inventory for standard materials quantities used at standard prices. It debits the variance account because the variance is unfavorable. The company credits Raw Materials Inventory for actual quantities at standard prices.

5. Assign factory labor to production at a cost of $31,500 when standard cost is $30,000.

Work in Process Inventory	30,000	
Labor Quantity Variance	1,500	
Factory Labor		31,500
(To assign factory labor to jobs)		

Xonic debits Work in Process Inventory for standard labor hours at standard rates. It debits the unfavorable variance to Labor Quantity Variance. The credit to Factory Labor produces a zero balance in this account.

6. Apply manufacturing overhead to production $10,000.

Work in Process Inventory	10,000	
Manufacturing Overhead		10,000
(To assign overhead to jobs)		

Xonic debits Work in Process Inventory for standard hours allowed multiplied by the standard overhead rate.

7. Transfer completed work to finished goods $52,000.

Finished Goods Inventory	52,000	
Work in Process Inventory		52,000
(To record transfer of completed work to		
finished goods)		

In this example, both inventory accounts are at standard cost.

8. Sell the 1,000 gallons of Xonic Tonic for $70,000.

Accounts Receivable	70,000	
Cost of Goods Sold	52,000	
Sales		70,000
Finished Goods Inventory		52,000
(To record sale of finished goods and the cost of goods sold)		

The company debits Cost of Goods Sold at standard cost. Gross profit, in turn, is the difference between sales and the standard cost of goods sold.

9. Recognize unfavorable total overhead variance:

Overhead Variance	900	
Manufacturing Overhead		900
(To recognize overhead variances)		

Prior to this entry, a debit balance of $900 existed in Manufacturing Overhead. This entry therefore produces a zero balance in the Manufacturing Overhead account. The information needed for this entry is often not available until the end of the accounting period.

LEDGER ACCOUNTS

Illustration 23A-1 shows the cost accounts for Xonic after posting the entries. Note that five variance accounts are included in the ledger. The remaining accounts are the same as those illustrated for a job order cost system in Chapter 15, in which only actual costs were used.

Illustration 23A-1 Cost accounts with variances

Helpful Hint All debit balances in variance accounts indicate unfavorable variances; all credit balances indicate favorable variances.

Summary of Learning Objective for Appendix 23A

9 **Identify the features of a standard cost accounting system.** In a standard cost accounting system, companies journalize and post standard costs, and they maintain separate variance accounts in the ledger.

✔ The Navigator

Appendix 23B

A Closer Look at Overhead Variances

As indicated in the chapter, the total overhead variance is generally analyzed through a price variance and a quantity variance. The name usually given to the price variance is the **overhead controllable variance**; the quantity variance is referred to as the **overhead volume variance**.

LEARNING OBJECTIVE **10**
Compute overhead controllable and volume variance.

OVERHEAD CONTROLLABLE VARIANCE

The overhead controllable variance shows whether overhead costs are effectively controlled. To compute this variance, the company compares actual overhead costs incurred with budgeted costs for the **standard hours allowed**. The budgeted costs are determined from a flexible manufacturing overhead budget. The concepts related to a flexible budget were discussed in Chapter 22.

For Xonic, the budget formula for manufacturing overhead is variable manufacturing overhead cost of $3 per hour of labor plus fixed manufacturing overhead costs of $4,400 ($52,800 ÷ 12, per Illustration 23-6 on page 1198). Illustration 23B-1 shows the monthly flexible budget for Xonic.

Illustration 23B-1 Flexible budget using standard direct labor hours

A	B	C	D	E
XONIC				
Flexible Manufacturing Overhead Monthly Budget				
Activity Index				
Standard direct labor hours	1,800	2,000	2,200	2,400
Costs				
Variable costs				
Indirect materials	$1,800	$ 2,000	$ 2,200	$ 2,400
Indirect labor	2,700	3,000	3,300	3,600
Utilities	900	1,000	1,100	1,200
Total variable costs	5,400	6,000	6,600	7,200
Fixed costs				
Supervision	3,000	3,000	3,000	3,000
Depreciation	1,400	1,400	1,400	1,400
Total fixed costs	4,400	4,400	4,400	4,400
Total costs	$9,800	$10,400	$11,000	$11,600

As shown, the budgeted costs for 2,000 standard hours are $10,400 ($6,000 variable and $4,400 fixed).

Illustration 23B-2 (page 1220) shows the formula for the overhead controllable variance and the calculation for Xonic at 1,000 units of output (2,000 standard labor hours).

Illustration 23B-2 Formula for overhead controllable variance

Actual Overhead	−	Overhead Budgeted*	=	Overhead Controllable Variance
$10,900 ($6,500 + $4,400)	−	$10,400 ($6,000 + $4,400)	=	$500 U

*Based on standard hours allowed.

The overhead controllable variance for Xonic is $500 unfavorable.

Most controllable variances are associated with variable costs, which are controllable costs. Fixed costs are often known at the time the budget is prepared and are therefore not as likely to deviate from the budgeted amount. In Xonic's case, all of the overhead controllable variance is due to the difference between the actual variable overhead costs ($6,500) and the budgeted variable costs ($6,000).

Management can compare actual and budgeted overhead for each manufacturing overhead cost that contributes to the controllable variance. In addition, management can develop cost and quantity variances for each overhead cost, such as indirect materials and indirect labor.

OVERHEAD VOLUME VARIANCE

The overhead volume variance is the difference between normal capacity hours and standard hours allowed times the fixed overhead rate. The overhead volume variance relates to whether fixed costs were under- or overapplied during the year. For example, the overhead volume variance answers the question of whether Xonic effectively used its fixed costs. If Xonic produces less Xonic Tonic than normal capacity would allow, an unfavorable variance results. Conversely, if Xonic produces more Xonic Tonic than what is considered normal capacity, a favorable variance results.

The formula for computing the overhead volume variance is as follows.

Illustration 23B-3 Formula for overhead volume variance

Fixed Overhead Rate	×	(Normal Capacity Hours	−	Standard Hours Allowed)	=	Overhead Volume Variance

To illustrate the fixed overhead rate computation, recall that Xonic budgeted fixed overhead cost for the year of $52,800 (Illustration 23-6 on page 1198). At normal capacity, 26,400 standard direct labor hours are required. The fixed overhead rate is therefore $2 per hour ($52,800 ÷ 26,400 hours).

Xonic produced 1,000 units of Xonic Tonic in June. The standard hours allowed for the 1,000 gallons produced in June is 2,000 (1,000 gallons × 2 hours). For Xonic, normal capacity for June is 1,100, so standard direct labor hours for June at normal capacity is 2,200 (26,400 annual hours ÷ 12 months). The computation of the overhead volume variance in this case is as follows.

Illustration 23B-4 Computation of overhead volume variance for Xonic

Fixed Overhead Rate	×	(Normal Capacity Hours	−	Standard Hours Allowed)	=	Overhead Volume Variance
$2	×	(2,200	−	2,000)	=	$400 U

In Xonic's case, a $400 unfavorable volume variance results. The volume variance is unfavorable because Xonic produced only 1,000 gallons rather than the normal capacity of 1,100 gallons in the month of June. As a result, it underapplied fixed overhead for that period.

In computing the overhead variances, it is important to remember the following.

1. Standard hours allowed are used in each of the variances.
2. Budgeted costs for the controllable variance are derived from the flexible budget.
3. The controllable variance generally pertains to variable costs.
4. The volume variance pertains solely to fixed costs.

Summary of Learning Objective for Appendix 23B

10 **Compute overhead controllable and volume variance.** The total overhead variance is generally analyzed through a price variance and a quantity variance. The name usually given to the price variance is the overhead controllable variance. The quantity variance is referred to as the overhead volume variance.

Glossary

Balanced scorecard *(p. 1211)* An approach that incorporates financial and nonfinancial measures in an integrated system that links performance measurement and a company's strategic goals.

Customer perspective *(p. 1211)* A viewpoint employed in the balanced scorecard to evaluate the company from the perspective of those people who buy and use its products or services.

Direct labor price standard *(p. 1197)* The rate per hour that should be incurred for direct labor.

Direct labor quantity standard *(p. 1198)* The time that should be required to make one unit of product.

Direct materials price standard *(p. 1197)* The cost per unit of direct materials that should be incurred.

Direct materials quantity standard *(p. 1197)* The quantity of direct materials that should be used per unit of finished goods.

Financial perspective *(p. 1211)* A viewpoint employed in the balanced scorecard to evaluate a company's performance using financial measures.

Ideal standards *(p. 1196)* Standards based on the optimum level of performance under perfect operating conditions.

Internal process perspective *(p. 1211)* A viewpoint employed in the balanced scorecard to evaluate the effectiveness and efficiency of a company's value chain, including product development, production, delivery, and after-sale service.

Labor price variance *(p. 1205)* The difference between the actual hours times the actual rate and the actual hours times the standard rate for labor.

Labor quantity variance *(p. 1205)* The difference between actual hours times the standard rate and standard hours times the standard rate for labor.

Learning and growth perspective *(p. 1212)* A viewpoint employed in the balanced scorecard to evaluate how well a company develops and retains its employees.

Materials price variance *(p. 1202)* The difference between the actual quantity times the actual price and the actual quantity times the standard price for materials.

Materials quantity variance *(p. 1202)* The difference between the actual quantity times the standard price and the standard quantity times the standard price for materials.

Normal capacity *(p. 1198)* The average activity output that a company should experience over the long run.

Normal standards *(p. 1196)* Standards based on an efficient level of performance that are attainable under expected operating conditions.

Overhead controllable variance *(p. 1219)* The difference between actual overhead incurred and overhead budgeted for the standard hours allowed.

Overhead volume variance *(p. 1220)* The difference between normal capacity hours and standard hours allowed times the fixed overhead rate.

Standard cost accounting system *(p. 1216)* A double-entry system of accounting in which standard costs are used in making entries, and variances are recognized in the accounts.

Standard costs *(p. 1194)* Predetermined unit costs which companies use as measures of performance.

Standard hours allowed *(p. 1207)* The hours that should have been worked for the units produced.

Standard predetermined overhead rate *(p. 1198)* An overhead rate determined by dividing budgeted overhead costs by an expected standard activity index.

Total labor variance *(p. 1204)* The difference between actual hours times the actual rate and standard hours times the standard rate for labor.

Total materials variance *(p. 1202)* The difference between the actual quantity times the actual price and the standard quantity times the standard price of materials.

Total overhead variance *(p. 1207)* The difference between actual overhead costs and overhead costs applied to work done, based on standard hours allowed.

Variances *(p. 1200)* The differences between total actual costs and total standard costs.

Comprehensive Do it!

Manlow Company makes a cologne called Allure. The standard cost for one bottle of Allure is as follows.

| | | Standard | | |
Manufacturing Cost Elements	Quantity	×	Price	=	Cost
Direct materials	6 oz.	×	$ 0.90	=	$ 5.40
Direct labor	0.5 hrs.	×	$12.00	=	6.00
Manufacturing overhead	0.5 hrs.	×	$ 4.80	=	2.40
					$13.80

During the month, the following transactions occurred in manufacturing 10,000 bottles of Allure.

1. 58,000 ounces of materials were purchased at $1.00 per ounce.
2. All the materials purchased were used to produce the 10,000 bottles of Allure.
3. 4,900 direct labor hours were worked at a total labor cost of $56,350.
4. Variable manufacturing overhead incurred was $15,000 and fixed overhead incurred was $10,400.

The manufacturing overhead rate of $4.80 is based on a normal capacity of 5,200 direct labor hours. The total budget at this capacity is $10,400 fixed and $14,560 variable.

Instructions

(a) Compute the total variance and the variances for direct materials and direct labor elements.

(b) Compute the total variance for manufacturing overhead.

Action Plan

- Check to make sure the total variance and the sum of the individual variances are equal.
- Find the price variance first, then the quantity variance.
- Base budgeted overhead costs on flexible budget data.
- Base overhead applied on standard hours allowed.
- Ignore actual hours worked in computing overhead variances.

The Navigator

Solution to Comprehensive Do it!

(a)   **Total Variance**

Actual costs incurred	
Direct materials	$ 58,000
Direct labor	56,350
Manufacturing overhead	25,400
	139,750
Standard cost (10,000 × $13.80)	138,000
Total variance	$ 1,750 U

Direct Materials Variances

Total   = $58,000 (58,000 × $1.00) − $54,000 (60,000 × $0.90) = $4,000 U
Price   = $58,000 (58,000 × $1.00) − $52,200 (58,000 × $0.90) = $5,800 U
Quantity = $52,200 (58,000 × $0.90) − $54,000 (60,000 × $0.90) = $1,800 F

Direct Labor Variances

Total   = $56,350 (4,900 × $11.50) − $60,000 (5,000 × $12.00) = $3,650 F
Price   = $56,350 (4,900 × $11.50) − $58,800 (4,900 × $12.00) = $2,450 F
Quantity = $58,800 (4,900 × $12.00) − $60,000 (5,000 × $12.00) = $1,200 F

(b)   **Overhead Variance**

Total   = $25,400 ($15,000 + $10,400) − $24,000 (5,000 × $4.80) = $1,400 U

Self-Test, Brief Exercises, Exercises, Problem Set A, and many more resources are available for practice in WileyPLUS.

Note: All Questions, Exercises, and Problems marked with an asterisk relate to material in the appendices to the chapter.

Self-Test Questions

Answers are on page 1243.

(LO 1) **1.** Standards differ from budgets in that:
(a) budgets but not standards may be used in valuing inventories.
(b) budgets but not standards may be journalized and posted.
(c) budgets are a total amount and standards are a unit amount.
(d) only budgets contribute to management planning and control.

(LO 1) **2.** Standard costs:
(a) are imposed by governmental agencies.
(b) are predetermined unit costs which companies use as measures of performance.
(c) can be used by manufacturing companies but not by service or not-for-profit companies.
(d) All of the above.

(LO 2) **3.** The advantages of standard costs include all of the following **except**:
(a) management by exception may be used.
(b) management planning is facilitated.
(c) they may simplify the costing of inventories.
(d) management must use a static budget.

(LO 3) **4.** Normal standards:
(a) allow for rest periods, machine breakdowns, and setup time.
(b) represent levels of performance under perfect operating conditions.
(c) are rarely used because managers believe they lower workforce morale.
(d) are more likely than ideal standards to result in unethical practices.

(LO 3) **5.** The setting of standards is:
(a) a managerial accounting decision.
(b) a management decision.
(c) a worker decision.
(d) preferably set at the ideal level of performance.

(LO 4) **6.** Each of the following formulas is correct **except**:
(a) Labor price variance = (Actual hours × Actual rate) − (Actual hours × Standard rate).
(b) Total overhead variance = Actual overhead − Overhead applied.
(c) Materials price variance = (Actual quantity × Actual price) − (Standard quantity × Standard price).
(d) Labor quantity variance = (Actual hours × Standard rate) − (Standard hours × Standard rate).

(LO 4) **7.** In producing product AA, 6,300 pounds of direct materials were used at a cost of $1.10 per pound. The standard was 6,000 pounds at $1.00 per pound. The direct materials quantity variance is:
(a) $330 unfavorable. (c) $600 unfavorable.
(b) $300 unfavorable. (d) $630 unfavorable.

(LO 4) **8.** In producing product ZZ, 14,800 direct labor hours were used at a rate of $8.20 per hour. The standard was 15,000 hours at $8.00 per hour. Based on these data, the direct labor:
(a) quantity variance is $1,600 favorable.
(b) quantity variance is $1,600 unfavorable.
(c) price variance is $2,960 favorable.
(d) price variance is $2,960 unfavorable.

(LO 5) **9.** Which of the following is **correct** about the total overhead variance?
(a) Budgeted overhead and budgeted overhead applied are the same.
(b) Total actual overhead is composed of variable overhead, fixed overhead, and period costs.
(c) Standard hours actually worked are used in computing the variance.
(d) Standard hours allowed for the work done is the measure used in computing the variance.

(LO 5) **10.** The formula for computing the total overhead variance is:
(a) actual overhead less overhead applied.
(b) overhead budgeted less overhead applied.
(c) actual overhead less overhead budgeted.
(d) No correct answer is given.

(LO 6) **11.** Which of the following is **incorrect** about variance reports?
(a) They facilitate "management by exception."
(b) They should only be sent to the top level of management.
(c) They should be prepared as soon as possible.
(d) They may vary in form, content, and frequency among companies.

(LO 6) **12.** In using variance reports to evaluate cost control, management normally looks into:
(a) all variances.
(b) favorable variances only.
(c) unfavorable variances only.
(d) both favorable and unfavorable variances that exceed a predetermined quantitative measure such as a percentage or dollar amount.

(LO 7) 13. Generally accepted accounting principles allow a company to:
- (a) report inventory at standard cost but cost of goods sold must be reported at actual cost.
- (b) report cost of goods sold at standard cost but inventory must be reported at actual cost.
- (c) report inventory and cost of goods sold at standard cost as long as there are no significant differences between actual and standard cost.
- (d) report inventory and cost of goods sold only at actual costs; standard costing is never permitted.

(LO 8) 14. Which of the following would **not** be an objective used in the customer perspective of the balanced scorecard approach?
- (a) Percentage of customers who would recommend product to a friend.
- (b) Customer retention.
- (c) Brand recognition.
- (d) Earnings per share.

*15. Which of the following is **incorrect** about a standard cost accounting system? (LO 9)
- (a) It is applicable to job order costing.
- (b) It is applicable to process costing.
- (c) It reports only favorable variances.
- (d) It keeps separate accounts for each variance.

*16. The formula to compute the overhead volume variance is: (LO 10)
- (a) Fixed overhead rate × (Standard hours − Actual hours).
- (b) Fixed overhead rate × (Normal capacity hours − Actual hours).
- (c) Fixed overhead rate × (Normal capacity hours − Standard hours allowed).
- (d) (Variable overhead rate + Fixed overhead rate) × (Normal capacity hours − Standard hours allowed).

Go to the book's companion website, **www.wiley.com/college/kimmel**, for additional Self-Test Questions.

 The Navigator

Questions

1. (a) "Standard costs are the expected total cost of completing a job." Is this correct? Explain.
   (b) "A standard imposed by a governmental agency is known as a regulation." Do you agree? Explain.

2. (a) Explain the similarities and differences between standards and budgets.
   (b) Contrast the accounting for standards and budgets.

3. Standard costs facilitate management planning. What are the other advantages of standard costs?

4. Contrast the roles of the management accountant and management in setting standard costs.

5. Distinguish between an ideal standard and a normal standard.

6. What factors should be considered in setting (a) the direct materials price standard and (b) the direct materials quantity standard?

7. "The objective in setting the direct labor quantity standard is to determine the aggregate time required to make one unit of product." Do you agree? What allowances should be made in setting this standard?

8. How is the predetermined overhead rate determined when standard costs are used?

9. What is the difference between a favorable cost variance and an unfavorable cost variance?

10. In each of the following formulas, supply the words that should be inserted for each number in parentheses.
   (a) (Actual quantity × (1)) − (Standard quantity × (2)) = Total materials variance
   (b) ((3) × Actual price) − (Actual quantity × (4)) = Materials price variance
   (c) (Actual quantity × (5)) − ((6) × Standard price) = Materials quantity variance

11. In the direct labor variance matrix, there are three factors: (1) Actual hours × Actual rate, (2) Actual hours × Standard rate, and (3) Standard hours × Standard rate. Using the numbers, indicate the formulas for each of the direct labor variances.

12. Mikan Company's standard predetermined overhead rate is $9 per direct labor hour. For the month of June, 26,000 actual hours were worked, and 27,000 standard hours were allowed. How much overhead was applied?

13. How often should variances be reported to management? What principle may be used with variance reports?

14. What circumstances may cause the purchasing department to be responsible for both an unfavorable materials price variance and an unfavorable materials quantity variance?

15. What are the four perspectives used in the balanced scorecard? Discuss the nature of each, and how the perspectives are linked.

16. Kerry James says that the balanced scorecard was created to replace financial measures as the primary mechanism for performance evaluation. He says that it uses only nonfinancial measures. Is this true?

17. What are some examples of nonfinancial measures used by companies to evaluate performance?

18. (a) How are variances reported in income statements prepared for management? (b) May standard costs be used in preparing financial statements for stockholders? Explain.

*19. (a) Explain the basic features of a standard cost accounting system. (b) What type of balance will exist in the variance account when (1) the materials price variance is unfavorable and (2) the labor quantity variance is favorable?

*20. If the $9 per hour overhead rate in Question 12 includes $5 variable, and actual overhead costs were $248,000, what is the overhead controllable variance for June? The normal capacity hours were 28,000. Is the variance favorable or unfavorable?

*21. What is the purpose of computing the overhead volume variance? What is the basic formula for this variance?

*22. Alma Ortiz does not understand why the overhead volume variance indicates that fixed overhead costs are under- or overapplied. Clarify this matter for Alma.

*23. John Hsu is attempting to outline the important points about overhead variances on a class examination. List four points that John should include in his outline.

Brief Exercises

BE23-1 Perez Company uses both standards and budgets. For the year, estimated production of Product X is 500,000 units. Total estimated cost for materials and labor are $1,300,000 and $1,700,000. Compute the estimates for (a) a standard cost and (b) a budgeted cost.

Distinguish between a standard and a budget.
(LO 1), AP

BE23-2 Tang Company accumulates the following data concerning raw materials in making one gallon of finished product: (1) Price—net purchase price $2.30, freight-in $0.20, and receiving and handling $0.10. (2) Quantity—required materials 3.6 pounds, allowance for waste and spoilage 0.4 pounds. Compute the following.
(a) Standard direct materials price per gallon.
(b) Standard direct materials quantity per gallon.
(c) Total standard materials cost per gallon.

Set direct materials standard.
(LO 3), AP

BE23-3 Labor data for making one gallon of finished product in Tang Company are as follows: (1) Price—hourly wage rate $13.00, payroll taxes $0.80, and fringe benefits $1.20. (2) Quantity—actual production time 1.1 hours, rest periods and cleanup 0.25 hours, and setup and downtime 0.15 hours. Compute the following.
(a) Standard direct labor rate per hour.
(b) Standard direct labor hours per gallon.
(c) Standard labor cost per gallon.

Set direct labor standard.
(LO 3), AP

BE23-4 Simba Company's standard materials cost per unit of output is $10 (2 pounds × $5). During July, the company purchases and uses 3,200 pounds of materials costing $16,192 in making 1,500 units of finished product. Compute the total, price, and quantity materials variances.

Compute direct materials variances.
(LO 4), AP

BE23-5 Hartley Company's standard labor cost per unit of output is $22 (2 hours × $11 per hour). During August, the company incurs 2,100 hours of direct labor at an hourly cost of $10.80 per hour in making 1,000 units of finished product. Compute the total, price, and quantity labor variances.

Compute direct labor variances.
(LO 4), AP

BE23-6 In October, Roby Company reports 21,000 actual direct labor hours, and it incurs $118,000 of manufacturing overhead costs. Standard hours allowed for the work done is 20,400 hours. The predetermined overhead rate is $6 per direct labor hour. Compute the total overhead variance.

Compute total overhead variance.
(LO 5), AP

BE23-7 The four perspectives in the balanced scorecard are (1) financial, (2) customer, (3) internal process, and (4) learning and growth. Match each of the following objectives with the perspective it is most likely associated with: (a) Plant capacity utilization. (b) Employee work days missed due to injury. (c) Return on assets. (d) Brand recognition.

Match balanced scorecard perspectives.
(LO 8), AP

*****BE23-8** Journalize the following transactions for Combs Company.
(a) Purchased 6,000 units of raw materials on account for $11,500. The standard cost was $12,000.
(b) Issued 5,600 units of raw materials for production. The standard units were 5,800.

Journalize materials variances.
(LO 9), AP

*****BE23-9** Journalize the following transactions for Dewey, Inc.
(a) Incurred direct labor costs of $24,000 for 3,000 hours. The standard labor cost was $25,500.
(b) Assigned 3,000 direct labor hours costing $24,000 to production. Standard hours were 3,150.

Journalize labor variances.
(LO 9), AP

Compute the overhead controllable variance.
(LO 10), AP

*BE23-10   Some overhead data for Roby Company are given in BE23-6. In addition, the flexible manufacturing overhead budget shows that budgeted costs are $4 variable per direct labor hour and $50,000 fixed. Compute the overhead controllable variance.

Compute overhead volume variance.
(LO 10), AP

*BE23-11   Using the data in BE23-6 and BE23-10, compute the overhead volume variance. Normal capacity was 25,000 direct labor hours.

Do it! Review

Compute standard cost.
(LO 3), AP

Do it! 23-1   Jacque Company accumulated the following standard cost data concerning product I-Tal.

Direct materials per unit: 2 pounds at $5 per pound
Direct labor per unit: 0.2 hours at $15 per hour
Manufacturing overhead: Predetermined rate is 125% of direct labor cost

Compute the standard cost of one unit of product I-Tal.

Compute materials variance.
(LO 4), AP

Do it! 23-2   The standard cost of product 777 includes 2 units of direct materials at $6.00 per unit. During August, the company bought 29,000 units of materials at $6.30 and used those materials to produce 16,000 units. Compute the total, price, and quantity variances for materials.

Compute labor and manufacturing overhead variances.
(LO 4, 5), AP

Do it! 23-3   The standard cost of product 5252 includes 1.9 hours of direct labor at $14.00 per hour. The predetermined overhead rate is $22.00 per direct labor hour. During July, the company incurred 4,100 hours of direct labor at an average rate of $14.30 per hour and $81,300 of manufacturing overhead costs. It produced 2,000 units.

(a) Compute the total, price, and quantity variances for labor. (b) Compute the total overhead variance.

Match balance scorecard perspectives and their objectives.
(LO 8), C

Do it! 23-4   Indicate which of the four perspectives in the balanced scorecard is most likely associated with the objectives that follow.
   1. Ethics violations.
   2. Credit rating.
   3. Customer retention.
   4. Stockouts.
   5. Reportable accidents.
   6. Brand recognition.

Exercises

Compute budget and standard.
(LO 1, 2, 3), AP

E23-1   Shannon Company is planning to produce 2,000 units of product in 2014. Each unit requires 3 pounds of materials at $5 per pound and a half-hour of labor at $15 per hour. The overhead rate is 70% of direct labor.

Instructions
(a) Compute the budgeted amounts for 2014 for direct materials to be used, direct labor, and applied overhead.
(b) Compute the standard cost of one unit of product.
(c) What are the potential advantages to a corporation of using standard costs?

Compute standard materials costs.
(LO 3), AP

E23-2   Hank Itzek manufactures and sells homemade wine, and he wants to develop a standard cost per gallon. The following are required for production of a 50-gallon batch.

3,000 ounces of grape concentrate at $0.06 per ounce
54 pounds of granulated sugar at $0.30 per pound
60 lemons at $0.60 each
50 yeast tablets at $0.25 each
50 nutrient tablets at $0.20 each
2,600 ounces of water at $0.005 per ounce

Hank estimates that 4% of the grape concentrate is wasted, 10% of the sugar is lost, and 25% of the lemons cannot be used.

Instructions

Compute the standard cost of the ingredients for one gallon of wine. (Carry computations to two decimal places.)

E23-3 Kimm Company has gathered the following information about its product.

Compute standard cost per unit.
(LO 3), **AP**

Direct materials. Each unit of product contains 4.5 pounds of materials. The average waste and spoilage per unit produced under normal conditions is 0.5 pounds. Materials cost $5 per pound, but Kimm always takes the 2% cash discount all of its suppliers offer. Freight costs average $0.25 per pound.

Direct labor. Each unit requires 2 hours of labor. Setup, cleanup, and downtime average 0.3 hours per unit. The average hourly pay rate of Kimm's employees is $12. Payroll taxes and fringe benefits are an additional $3 per hour.

Manufacturing overhead. Overhead is applied at a rate of $7 per direct labor hour.

Instructions

Compute Kimm's total standard cost per unit.

E23-4 Monte Services, Inc. is trying to establish the standard labor cost of a typical oil change. The following data have been collected from time and motion studies conducted over the past month.

Compute labor cost and labor quantity variance.
(LO 3, 4), **AP**

Actual time spent on the oil change	1.0 hour
Hourly wage rate	$12
Payroll taxes	10% of wage rate
Setup and downtime	20% of actual labor time
Cleanup and rest periods	30% of actual labor time
Fringe benefits	25% of wage rate

Instructions

(a) Determine the standard direct labor hours per oil change.
(b) Determine the standard direct labor hourly rate.
(c) Determine the standard direct labor cost per oil change.
(d) If an oil change took 1.6 hours at the standard hourly rate, what was the direct labor quantity variance?

E23-5 The standard cost of Product B manufactured by MIT Company includes three units of direct materials at $5.00 per unit. During June, 29,000 units of direct materials are purchased at a cost of $4.70 per unit, and 29,000 units of direct materials are used to produce 9,500 units of Product B.

Compute materials price and quantity variances.
(LO 4), **AP**

Instructions

(a) Compute the total materials variance and the price and quantity variances.
(b) Repeat (a), assuming the purchase price is $5.15 and the quantity purchased and used is 28,000 units.

E23-6 Lewis Company's standard labor cost of producing one unit of Product DD is 4 hours at the rate of $12.00 per hour. During August, 40,600 hours of labor are incurred at a cost of $12.15 per hour to produce 10,000 units of Product DD.

Compute labor price and quantity variances.
(LO 4), **AP**

Instructions

(a) Compute the total labor variance.
(b) Compute the labor price and quantity variances.
(c) Repeat (b), assuming the standard is 4.1 hours of direct labor at $12.25 per hour.

E23-7 Nona Inc., which produces a single product, has prepared the following standard cost sheet for one unit of the product.

Compute materials and labor variances.
(LO 4), **AP**

Direct materials (8 pounds at $2.50 per pound)	$20
Direct labor (3 hours at $12.00 per hour)	$36

During the month of April, the company manufactures 235 units and incurs the following actual costs.

Direct materials purchased and used (1,900 pounds)	$5,035
Direct labor (700 hours)	$8,260

Instructions

Compute the total, price, and quantity variances for materials and labor.

Compute the materials and labor variances and list reasons for unfavorable variances.

(LO 4), **AN**

E23-8 The following direct materials and direct labor data pertain to the operations of Laurel Company for the month of August.

Costs		Quantities	
Actual labor rate	$13 per hour	Actual hours incurred and used	4,150 hours
Actual materials price	$128 per ton	Actual quantity of materials purchased and used	1,220 tons
Standard labor rate	$12.50 per hour	Standard hours used	4,300 hours
Standard materials price	$130 per ton	Standard quantity of materials used	1,200 tons

Instructions

(a) Compute the total, price, and quantity variances for materials and labor.
(b) ▬▬► Provide two possible explanations for each of the unfavorable variances calculated above, and suggest where responsibility for the unfavorable result might be placed.

Determine amounts from variance report.

(LO 4), **AN**

E23-9 You have been given the following information about the production of Horatio Co., and are asked to provide the plant manager with information for a meeting with the vice president of operations.

	Standard Cost Card
Direct materials (5 pounds at $4 per pound)	$20.00
Direct labor (0.8 hours at $10)	8.00
Variable overhead (0.8 hours at $3 per hour)	2.40
Fixed overhead (0.8 hours at $7 per hour)	5.60
	$36.00

The following is a variance report for the most recent period of operations.

		Variances	
Costs	Total Standard Cost	Price	Quantity
Direct materials	$405,000	$5,175 F	$9,000 U
Direct labor	180,000	3,840 U	6,000 U

Instructions

(a) How many units were produced during the period?
(b) How many pounds of raw materials were purchased and used during the period?
(c) What was the actual cost per pound of raw materials?
(d) How many actual direct labor hours were worked during the period?
(e) What was the actual rate paid per direct labor hour?

(CGA adapted)

Prepare a variance report for direct labor.

(LO 4, 6), **AP**

E23-10 During March 2014, Toby Tool & Die Company worked on four jobs. A review of direct labor costs reveals the following summary data.

Job Number	Actual		Standard		Total Variance
	Hours	Costs	Hours	Costs	
A257	221	$4,420	225	$4,500	$ 80 F
A258	450	9,450	430	8,600	850 U
A259	300	6,180	300	6,000	180 U
A260	116	2,088	110	2,200	112 F
Total variance					$838 U

Analysis reveals that Job A257 was a repeat job. Job A258 was a rush order that required overtime work at premium rates of pay. Job A259 required a more experienced replacement worker on one shift. Work on Job A260 was done for one day by a new trainee when a regular worker was absent.

Instructions

Prepare a report for the plant supervisor on direct labor cost variances for March. The report should have columns for (1) Job No., (2) Actual Hours, (3) Standard Hours, (4) Quantity Variance, (5) Actual Rate, (6) Standard Rate, (7) Price Variance, and (8) Explanation.

E23-11 Manufacturing overhead data for the production of Product H by Smart Company are as follows.

Compute overhead variance.

(LO 5), AN

Overhead incurred for 52,000 actual direct labor hours worked	$263,000
Overhead rate (variable $3; fixed $2) at normal capacity of 54,000 direct labor hours	$5
Standard hours allowed for work done	51,000

Instructions

Compute the total overhead variance.

E23-12 Byrd Company produces one product, a putter called GO-Putter. Byrd uses a standard cost system and determines that it should take one hour of direct labor to produce one GO-Putter. The normal production capacity for this putter is 100,000 units per year. The total budgeted overhead at normal capacity is $850,000 comprised of $250,000 of variable costs and $600,000 of fixed costs. Byrd applies overhead on the basis of direct labor hours.

Compute overhead variances.

(LO 5), AP

During the current year, Byrd produced 95,000 putters, worked 94,000 direct labor hours, and incurred variable overhead costs of $256,000 and fixed overhead costs of $600,000.

Instructions

(a) Compute the predetermined variable overhead rate and the predetermined fixed overhead rate.
(b) Compute the applied overhead for Byrd for the year.
(c) Compute the total overhead variance.

E23-13 Wales Company purchased (at a cost of $10,800) and used 2,400 pounds of materials during May. Wales's standard cost of materials per unit produced is based on 2 pounds per unit at a cost $5 per pound. Production in May was 1,070 units.

Compute variances for materials.

(LO 4), AP

Instructions

(a) Compute the total, price, and quantity variances for materials.
(b) Assume Wales also had an unfavorable labor quantity variance. What is a possible scenario that would provide one cause for the variances computed in (a) and the unfavorable labor quantity variance?

E23-14 Picard Landscaping plants grass seed as the basic landscaping for business campuses. During a recent month, the company worked on three projects (Remington, Chang, and Wyco). The company is interested in controlling the materials costs, namely the grass seed, for these plantings projects.

Prepare a variance report.

(LO 4, 6), AP

In order to provide management with useful cost control information, the company uses standard costs and prepares monthly variance reports. Analysis reveals that the purchasing agent mistakenly purchased poor-quality seed for the Remington project. The Chang project, however, received higher-than-standard-quality seed that was on sale. The Wyco project received standard-quality seed. However, the price had increased and a new employee was used to spread the seed.

Shown below are quantity and cost data for each project.

	Actual		Standard		Total
Project	**Quantity**	**Costs**	**Quantity**	**Costs**	**Variance**
Remington	500 lbs.	$1,200	460 lbs.	$1,150	$ 50 U
Chang	400	920	410	1,025	105 F
Wyco	550	1,430	480	1,200	230 U
Total variance					$175 U

Instructions

(a) Prepare a variance report for the purchasing department with the following columns: (1) Project, (2) Actual Pounds Purchased, (3) Actual Price, (4) Standard Price, (5) Price Variance, and (6) Explanation.

(b) Prepare a variance report for the production department with the following columns: (1) Project, (2) Actual Pounds, (3) Standard Pounds, (4) Standard Price, (5) Quantity Variance, and (6) Explanation.

Complete variance report.
(LO 6), **AP**

E23-15 Burte Corporation prepared the following variance report.

BURTE CORPORATION
Variance Report—Purchasing Department
For the Week Ended January 9, 2014

Type of Materials	Quantity Purchased	Actual Price	Standard Price	Price Variance	Explanation
Rogue11	? lbs.	$5.20	$5.00	$5,000 ?	Price increase
Storm17	7,000 oz.	?	3.30	1,050 U	Rush order
Beast29	22,000 units	0.40	?	440 F	Bought larger quantity

Instructions

Fill in the appropriate amounts or letters for the question marks in the report.

Prepare income statement for management.
(LO 7), **AP**

E23-16 Fisk Company uses a standard cost accounting system. During January, the company reported the following manufacturing variances.

Materials price variance	$1,200 U	Labor quantity variance	$750 U
Materials quantity variance	800 F	Overhead variance	800 U
Labor price variance	550 U		

In addition, 8,000 units of product were sold at $8 per unit. Each unit sold had a standard cost of $5. Selling and administrative expenses were $8,000 for the month.

Instructions

Prepare an income statement for management for the month ended January 31, 2014.

Identify performance evaluation terminology.
(LO 3, 8), **C**

E23-17 The following is a list of terms related to performance evaluation.

1. Balanced scorecard
2. Variance
3. Learning and growth perspective
4. Nonfinancial measures
5. Customer perspective
6. Internal process perspective
7. Ideal standards
8. Normal standards

Instructions

Match each of the following descriptions with one of the terms above.

(a) The difference between total actual costs and total standard costs.

(b) An efficient level of performance that is attainable under expected operating conditions.

(c) An approach that incorporates financial and nonfinancial measures in an integrated system that links performance measurement and a company's strategic goals.

(d) A viewpoint employed in the balanced scorecard to evaluate how well a company develops and retains its employees.

(e) An evaluation tool that is not based on dollars.

(f) A viewpoint employed in the balanced scorecard to evaluate the company from the perspective of those people who buy its products or services.

(g) An optimum level of performance under perfect operating conditions.

(h) A viewpoint employed in the balanced scorecard to evaluate the efficiency and effectiveness of the company's value chain.

Journalize entries in a standard cost accounting system.
(LO 9), **AP**

*E23-18 Vista Company installed a standard cost system on January 1. Selected transactions for the month of January are as follows.

1. Purchased 18,000 units of raw materials on account at a cost of $4.50 per unit. Standard cost was $4.40 per unit.

2. Issued 18,000 units of raw materials for jobs that required 17,500 standard units of raw materials.

3. Incurred 15,300 actual hours of direct labor at an actual rate of $5.00 per hour. The standard rate is $5.50 per hour. (Credit Factory Wages Payable.)

4. Performed 15,300 hours of direct labor on jobs when standard hours were 15,400.
5. Applied overhead to jobs at the rate of 100% of direct labor cost for standard hours allowed.

Instructions

Journalize the January transactions.

*E23-19 Stiller Company uses a standard cost accounting system. Some of the ledger accounts have been destroyed in a fire. The controller asks your help in reconstructing some missing entries and balances.

Answer questions concerning missing entries and balances.
(LO 4, 5, 9), **AN**

Instructions

Answer the following questions.

(a) Materials Price Variance shows a $2,000 unfavorable balance. Accounts Payable shows $128,000 of raw materials purchases. What was the amount debited to Raw Materials Inventory for raw materials purchased?

(b) Materials Quantity Variance shows a $3,000 favorable balance. Raw Materials Inventory shows a zero balance. What was the amount debited to Work in Process Inventory for direct materials used?

(c) Labor Price Variance shows a $1,500 favorable balance. Factory Labor shows a debit of $140,000 for wages incurred. What was the amount credited to Factory Wages Payable?

(d) Factory Labor shows a credit of $140,000 for direct labor used. Labor Quantity Variance shows a $900 favorable balance. What was the amount debited to Work in Process for direct labor used?

(e) Overhead applied to Work in Process totaled $165,000. If the total overhead variance was $1,200 favorable, what was the amount of overhead costs debited to Manufacturing Overhead?

*E23-20 Data for Nona Inc. are given in E23-7.

Journalize entries for materials and labor variances.
(LO 9), **AP**

Instructions

Journalize the entries to record the materials and labor variances.

*E23-21 The information shown below was taken from the annual manufacturing overhead cost budget of Samantha Company.

Compute manufacturing overhead variances and interpret findings.
(LO 10), **AN**

Variable manufacturing overhead costs	$34,650
Fixed manufacturing overhead costs	$19,800
Normal production level in labor hours	16,500
Normal production level in units	4,125
Standard labor hours per unit	4

During the year, 4,000 units were produced, 16,100 hours were worked, and the actual manufacturing overhead was $55,000. Actual fixed manufacturing overhead costs equaled budgeted fixed manufacturing overhead costs. Overhead is applied on the basis of direct labor hours.

Instructions

(a) Compute the total, fixed, and variable predetermined manufacturing overhead rates.
(b) Compute the total, controllable, and volume overhead variances.
(c) ✏️➤ Briefly interpret the overhead controllable and volume variances computed in (b).

*E23-22 The loan department of Calgary Bank uses standard costs to determine the overhead cost of processing loan applications. During the current month, a fire occurred, and the accounting records for the department were mostly destroyed. The data shown below were salvaged from the ashes.

Compute overhead variances.
(LO 10), **AN**

Standard variable overhead rate per hour	$9
Standard hours per application	2
Standard hours allowed	2,000
Standard fixed overhead rate per hour	$6
Actual fixed overhead cost	$12,600
Variable overhead budget based on standard hours allowed	$18,000
Fixed overhead budget	$12,600
Overhead controllable variance	$ 1,200 U

Instructions
(a) Determine the following.
   (1) Total actual overhead cost.
   (2) Actual variable overhead cost.
   (3) Variable overhead costs applied.
   (4) Fixed overhead costs applied.
   (5) Overhead volume variance.
(b) Determine how many loans were processed.

Compute variances.
(LO 10), **AP**

*E23-23 Alona Company's overhead rate was based on estimates of $200,000 for over-head costs and 20,000 direct labor hours. Alona's standards allow 2 hours of direct labor per unit produced. Production in May was 900 units, and actual overhead incurred in May was $19,000. The overhead budgeted for 1,800 standard direct labor hours is $17,600 ($5,000 fixed and $12,600 variable).

Instructions
(a) Compute the total, controllable, and volume variances for overhead.
(b) What are possible causes of the variances computed in part (a)?

Exercises: Set B and Challenge Exercises

Visit the book's companion website, at **www.wiley.com/college/kimmel**, and choose the Student Companion site to access Exercise Set B and Challenge Exercises.

Problems: Set A

Compute variances.
(LO 4, 5), **AP**

P23-1A Costello Corporation manufactures a single product. The standard cost per unit of product is shown below.

Direct materials—1 pound plastic at $7.00 per pound	$ 7.00
Direct labor—1.6 hours at $12.00 per hour	19.20
Variable manufacturing overhead	12.00
Fixed manufacturing overhead	4.00
Total standard cost per unit	$42.20

The predetermined manufacturing overhead rate is $10 per direct labor hour ($16.00 ÷ 1.6). It was computed from a master manufacturing overhead budget based on normal production of 8,000 direct labor hours (5,000 units) for the month. The master budget showed total variable costs of $60,000 ($7.50 per hour) and total fixed overhead costs of $20,000 ($2.50 per hour). Actual costs for October in producing 4,900 units were as follows.

Direct materials (5,100 pounds)	$ 36,720
Direct labor (7,500 hours)	93,750
Variable overhead	59,700
Fixed overhead	21,000
Total manufacturing costs	$211,170

The purchasing department buys the quantities of raw materials that are expected to be used in production each month. Raw materials inventories, therefore, can be ignored.

Instructions
(a) MPV $1,020 U
(a) Compute all of the materials and labor variances.
(b) Compute the total overhead variance.

P23-2A Ayala Corporation accumulates the following data relative to jobs started and finished during the month of June 2014.

Compute variances, and prepare income statement.
(LO 4, 5, 7), **AP**
XLS

Costs and Production Data	Actual	Standard
Raw materials unit cost	$2.25	$2.10
Raw materials units used	10,600	10,000
Direct labor payroll	$120,960	$120,000
Direct labor hours worked	14,400	15,000
Manufacturing overhead incurred	$189,500	
Manufacturing overhead applied		$189,000
Machine hours expected to be used at normal capacity		42,500
Budgeted fixed overhead for June		$55,250
Variable overhead rate per machine hour		$3.00
Fixed overhead rate per machine hour		$1.30

Overhead is applied on the basis of standard machine hours. Three hours of machine time are required for each direct labor hour. The jobs were sold for $400,000. Selling and administrative expenses were $40,000. Assume that the amount of raw materials purchased equaled the amount used.

Instructions

(a) Compute all of the variances for (1) direct materials and (2) direct labor.
(b) Compute the total overhead variance.
(c) Prepare an income statement for management. (Ignore income taxes.)

(a) LQV $4,800 F

P23-3A Hopkins Clothiers is a small company that manufactures tall-men's suits. The company has used a standard cost accounting system. In May 2014, 11,200 suits were produced. The following standard and actual cost data applied to the month of May when normal capacity was 14,000 direct labor hours. All materials purchased were used.

Compute and identify significant variances.
(LO 4, 5, 6), **AN**

Cost Element	Standard (per unit)	Actual
Direct materials	8 yards at $4.40 per yard	$375,575 for 90,500 yards ($4.15 per yard)
Direct labor	1.2 hours at $13.40 per hour	$200,220 for 14,200 hours ($14.10 per hour)
Overhead	1.2 hours at $6.10 per hour (fixed $3.50; variable $2.60)	$49,000 fixed overhead $37,000 variable overhead

Overhead is applied on the basis of direct labor hours. At normal capacity, budgeted fixed overhead costs were $49,000, and budgeted variable overhead was $36,400.

Instructions

(a) Compute the total, price, and quantity variances for (1) materials and (2) labor.
(b) Compute the total overhead variance.
(c) ✏➤ Which of the materials and labor variances should be investigated if management considers a variance of more than 4% from standard to be significant?

(a) MPV $22,625 F

P23-4A Kansas Company uses a standard cost accounting system. In 2014, the company produced 28,000 units. Each unit took several pounds of direct materials and 1.6 standard hours of direct labor at a standard hourly rate of $12.00. Normal capacity was 50,000 direct labor hours. During the year, 117,000 pounds of raw materials were purchased at $0.92 per pound. All materials purchased were used during the year.

Answer questions about variances.
(LO 4, 5), **AN**

Instructions

(a) If the materials price variance was $3,510 favorable, what was the standard materials price per pound?
(b) If the materials quantity variance was $4,750 unfavorable, what was the standard materials quantity per unit?
(c) What were the standard hours allowed for the units produced?
(d) If the labor quantity variance was $7,200 unfavorable, what were the actual direct labor hours worked?
(e) If the labor price variance was $9,080 favorable, what was the actual rate per hour?
(f) If total budgeted manufacturing overhead was $360,000 at normal capacity, what was the predetermined overhead rate?

(b) 4.0 pounds

(f) $7.20 per DLH

(g) What was the standard cost per unit of product?

(h) How much overhead was applied to production during the year?

(i) Using one or more answers above, what were the total costs assigned to work in process?

Compute variances, prepare an income statement, and explain unfavorable variances.
(LO 4, 5, 7), **AP**

P23-5A Pace Labs, Inc. provides mad cow disease testing for both state and federal governmental agricultural agencies. Because the company's customers are governmental agencies, prices are strictly regulated. Therefore, Pace Labs must constantly monitor and control its testing costs. Shown below are the standard costs for a typical test.

Direct materials (2 test tubes @ $1.46 per tube)	$ 2.92
Direct labor (1 hour @ $24 per hour)	24.00
Variable overhead (1 hour @ $6 per hour)	6.00
Fixed overhead (1 hour @ $10 per hour)	10.00
Total standard cost per test	$42.92

The lab does not maintain an inventory of test tubes. Therefore, the tubes purchased each month are used that month. Actual activity for the month of November 2014, when 1,500 tests were conducted, resulted in the following.

Direct materials (3,050 test tubes)	$ 4,209
Direct labor (1,600 hours)	36,800
Variable overhead	7,400
Fixed overhead	15,000

Monthly budgeted fixed overhead is $14,000. Revenues for the month were $75,000, and selling and administrative expenses were $5,000.

Instructions

(a) Compute the price and quantity variances for direct materials and direct labor.

(b) Compute the total overhead variance.

(c) Prepare an income statement for management.

(d) Provide possible explanations for each unfavorable variance.

(a) LQV $2,400 U

Journalize and post standard cost entries, and prepare income statement.
(LO 4, 5, 7, 9), **AP**

***P23-6A** Jorgensen Corporation uses standard costs with its job order cost accounting system. In January, an order (Job No. 12) for 1,900 units of Product B was received. The standard cost of one unit of Product B is as follows.

Direct materials	3 pounds at $1.00 per pound	$ 3.00
Direct labor	1 hour at $8.00 per hour	8.00
Overhead	2 hours (variable $4.00 per machine hour;	
	fixed $2.25 per machine hour)	12.50
Standard cost per unit		$23.50

Normal capacity for the month was 4,200 machine hours. During January, the following transactions applicable to Job No. 12 occurred.

1. Purchased 6,200 pounds of raw materials on account at $1.05 per pound.
2. Requisitioned 6,200 pounds of raw materials for Job No. 12.
3. Incurred 2,000 hours of direct labor at a rate of $7.80 per hour.
4. Worked 2,000 hours of direct labor on Job No. 12.
5. Incurred manufacturing overhead on account $25,000.
6. Applied overhead to Job No. 12 on basis of standard machine hours allowed.
7. Completed Job No. 12.
8. Billed customer for Job No. 12 at a selling price of $65,000.

Instructions

(a) Journalize the transactions.

(b) Post to the job order cost accounts.

(c) Prepare the entry to recognize the total overhead variance.

(d) Prepare the January 2014 income statement for management. Assume selling and administrative expenses were $2,000.

(d) NI $15,890

*P23-7A   Using the information in P23-1A, compute the overhead controllable variance and the overhead volume variance.

Compute overhead controllable and volume variances.
(LO 10), **AP**

*P23-8A   Using the information in P23-2A, compute the overhead controllable variance and the overhead volume variance.

Compute overhead controllable and volume variances.
(LO 10), **AP**

*P23-9A   Using the information in P23-3A, compute the overhead controllable variance and the overhead volume variance.

Compute overhead controllable and volume variances.
(LO 10), **AP**

*P23-10A   Using the information in P23-5A, compute the overhead controllable variance and the overhead volume variance.

Compute overhead controllable and volume variances.
(LO 10), **AP**

Problems: Set B

P23-1B   Buil Corporation manufactures a single product. The standard cost per unit of product is as follows.

Compute variances.
(LO 4, 5), **AP**

Direct materials—2 pounds of plastic at $6 per pound	$12
Direct labor—2 hours at $13 per hour	26
Variable manufacturing overhead	7
Fixed manufacturing overhead	5
Total standard cost per unit	$50

The master manufacturing overhead budget for the month based on normal productive capacity of 20,000 direct labor hours (10,000 units) shows total variable costs of $70,000 ($3.50 per labor hour) and total fixed costs of $50,000 ($2.50 per labor hour). Normal productive capacity is 20,000 direct labor hours. Overhead is applied on the basis of direct labor hours. Actual costs for November in producing 9,700 units were as follows.

Direct materials (20,000 pounds)	$119,000
Direct labor (19,600 hours)	256,760
Variable overhead	68,800
Fixed overhead	50,000
Total manufacturing costs	$494,560

The purchasing department normally buys the quantities of raw materials that are expected to be used in production each month. Raw materials inventories, therefore, can be ignored.

Instructions
(a) Compute all of the materials and labor variances.
(b) Compute the total overhead variance.

(a) MPV $1,000 F

P23-2B   Huang Company uses a standard cost accounting system to account for the manufacture of exhaust fans. In July 2014, it accumulates the following data relative to 1,800 units started and finished.

Compute variances, and prepare income statement.
(LO 4, 5, 7), **AP**

Cost and Production Data	Actual	Standard
Raw materials		
Units purchased	21,000	
Units used	21,000	22,000
Unit cost	$3.70	$3.50
Direct labor		
Hours worked	3,450	3,600
Hourly rate	$11.50	$12.00
Manufacturing overhead		
Incurred	$94,800	
Applied		$100,800

Manufacturing overhead was applied on the basis of direct labor hours. Normal capacity for the month was 3,400 direct labor hours. At normal capacity, budgeted overhead costs were $16 per labor hour variable and $12 per labor hour fixed. Total budgeted fixed overhead costs were $40,800.

Jobs finished during the month were sold for $270,000. Selling and administrative expenses were $20,000.

Instructions

(a) LQV $1,800 F

(a) Compute all of the variances for (1) direct materials and (2) direct labor.

(b) Compute the total overhead variance.

(c) Prepare an income statement for management. (Ignore income taxes.)

Compute and identify significant variances.

(LO 4, 5, 6), **AN**

P23-3B Zimmerman Clothiers manufactures women's business suits. The company uses a standard cost accounting system. In March 2014, 15,700 suits were made. The following standard and actual cost data applied to the month of March when normal capacity was 20,000 direct labor hours. All materials purchased were used in production.

Cost Element	Standard (per unit)	Actual
Direct materials	5 yards at $6.75 per yard	$547,200 for 76,000 yards ($7.20 per yard)
Direct labor	1.0 hours at $11.45 per hour	$165,760 for 14,800 hours ($11.20 per hour)
Overhead	1.0 hours at $9.40 per hour (fixed $6.25; variable $3.15)	$120,000 fixed overhead $49,000 variable overhead

Overhead is applied on the basis of direct labor hours. At normal capacity, budgeted fixed overhead costs were $125,000, and budgeted variable overhead costs were $63,000.

Instructions

(a) MPV $34,200 U

(a) Compute the total, price, and quantity variances for (1) materials and (2) labor.

(b) Compute the total overhead variance.

(c) ▬▬▶ Which of the materials and labor variances should be investigated if management considers a variance of more than 5% from standard to be significant?

Answer questions about variances.

(LO 4, 5), **AN**

P23-4B Beta Company uses a standard cost accounting system. In 2014, 45,000 units were produced. Each unit took several pounds of direct materials and 2 standard hours of direct labor at a standard hourly rate of $12.00. Normal capacity was 86,000 direct labor hours. During the year, 200,000 pounds of raw materials were purchased at $1.00 per pound. All materials purchased were used during the year.

Instructions

(a) If the materials price variance was $10,000 unfavorable, what was the standard materials price per pound?

(b) 5.0 pounds

(b) If the materials quantity variance was $23,750 favorable, what was the standard materials quantity per unit?

(c) What were the standard hours allowed for the units produced?

(d) If the labor quantity variance was $10,080 unfavorable, what were the actual direct labor hours worked?

(e) If the labor price variance was $18,168 favorable, what was the actual rate per hour?

(f) $8.30 per DLH

(f) If total budgeted manufacturing overhead was $713,800 at normal capacity, what was the predetermined overhead rate per direct labor hour?

(g) What was the standard cost per unit of product?

(h) How much overhead was applied to production during the year?

(i) Using selected answers above, what were the total costs assigned to work in process?

Compute variances, prepare an income statement, and explain unfavorable variances.

(LO 4, 5, 7), **AP**

P23-5B Bonita Labs performs steroid testing services to high schools, colleges, and universities. Because the company deals solely with educational institutions, the price of each test is strictly regulated. Therefore, the costs incurred must be carefully monitored and controlled. Shown below are the standard costs for a typical test.

Direct materials (1 petri dish @ $1.80 per dish)	$ 1.80
Direct labor (0.5 hours @ $20.50 per hour)	10.25
Variable overhead (0.5 hours @ $8 per hour)	4.00
Fixed overhead (0.5 hours @ $5 per hour)	2.50
Total standard cost per test	$18.55

The lab does not maintain an inventory of petri dishes. Therefore, the dishes purchased each month are used that month. Actual activity for the month of May 2014, when 2,500 tests were conducted, resulted in the following.

Direct materials (2,530 dishes)	$ 5,060
Direct labor (1,240 hours)	26,040
Variable overhead	10,100
Fixed overhead	5,700

Monthly budgeted fixed overhead is $6,000. Revenues for the month were $55,000, and selling and administrative expenses were $2,000.

Instructions
(a) Compute the price and quantity variances for direct materials and direct labor.
(b) Compute the total overhead variance.
(c) Prepare an income statement for management.
(d) Provide possible explanations for each unfavorable variance.

(a) LQV $205 F

***P23-6B**   Frio Company uses standard costs with its job order cost accounting system. In January, an order (Job No. 84) was received for 5,500 units of Product D. The standard cost of 1 unit of Product D is as follows.

Journalize and post standard cost entries, and prepare income statement.
(LO 4, 5, 7, 9), **AP**

Direct materials—1.5 pounds at $4.00 per pound	$ 6.00
Direct labor—1 hour at $9.00 per hour	9.00
Overhead—1 hour (variable $7.40; fixed $8.00)	15.40
Standard cost per unit	$30.40

Overhead is applied on the basis of direct labor hours. Normal capacity for the month of January was 6,000 direct labor hours. During January, the following transactions applicable to Job No. 84 occurred.

1. Purchased 8,100 pounds of raw materials on account at $3.70 per pound.
2. Requisitioned 8,100 pounds of raw materials for production.
3. Incurred 5,200 hours of direct labor at $9.20 per hour.
4. Worked 5,200 hours of direct labor on Job No. 84.
5. Incurred $87,500 of manufacturing overhead on account.
6. Applied overhead to Job No. 84 on the basis of direct labor hours.
7. Transferred Job No. 84 to finished goods.
8. Billed customer for Job No. 84 at a selling price of $270,000.

Instructions
(a) Journalize the transactions.
(b) Post to the job order cost accounts.
(c) Prepare the entry to recognize the total overhead variance.
(d) Prepare the January 2014 income statement for management. Assume selling and administrative expenses were $60,000.

(d) NI $44,690

***P23-7B**   Using the information in P23-1B, compute the overhead controllable variance and the overhead volume variance.

Compute overhead controllable and volume variances.
(LO 10), **AP**

***P23-8B**   Using the information in P23-2B, compute the overhead controllable variance and the overhead volume variance.

Compute overhead controllable and volume variances.
(LO 10), **AP**

***P23-9B**   Using the information in P23-3B, compute the overhead controllable variance and the overhead volume variance.

Compute overhead controllable and volume variances.
(LO 10), **AP**

***P23-10B**   Using the information in P23-5B, compute the overhead controllable variance and the overhead volume variance.

Compute overhead controllable and volume variances.
(LO 10), **AP**

Problems: Set C

Visit the book's companion website, at **www.wiley.com/college/kimmel**, and choose the Student Companion site to access Problem Set C.

Waterways Continuing Problem

(This is a continuation of the Waterways Problem from Chapters 14 through 22.)

WCP23   Waterways Corporation uses very stringent standard costs in evaluating its manufacturing efficiency. These standards are not "ideal" at this point, but management is working toward that as a goal. This problem asks you to calculate and evaluate the company's variances.

> Go to the book's companion website, at **www.wiley.com/college/kimmel**, to find the completion of this problem.

Broadening Your Perspective

Management Decision-Making

DECISION-MAKING AT CURRENT DESIGNS

BYP23-1   The executive team at Current Designs has gathered to evaluate the company's operations for the last month. One of the topics on the agenda is the special order from Huegel Hollow, which was presented in BYP2-1. Recall that Current Designs had a special order to produce a batch of 20 kayaks for a client, and you were asked to determine the cost of the order and the cost per kayak.

Mike Cichanowski asked the others if the special order caused any particular problems in the production process. Dave Thill, the production manager, made the following comments: "Since we wanted to complete this order quickly and make a good first impression on this new customer, we had some of our most experienced type I workers run the rotomold oven and do the trimming. They were very efficient and were able to complete that part of the manufacturing process even more quickly than the regular crew. However, the finishing on these kayaks required a different technique than what we usually use, so our type II workers took a little longer than usual for that part of the process."

Deb Welch, who is in charge of the purchasing function, said, "We had to pay a little more for the polyethylene powder for this order because the customer wanted a color that we don't usually stock. We also ordered a little extra since we wanted to make sure that we had enough to allow us to calibrate the equipment. The calibration was a little tricky, and we used all of the powder that we had purchased. Since the number of kayaks in the order was fairly small, we were able to use some rope and other parts that were left over from last year's production in the finishing kits. We've seen a price increase for these components in the last year, so using the parts that we already had in inventory cut our costs for the finishing kits."

Instructions

(a) Based on the comments above, predict whether each of the following variances will be favorable or unfavorable. If you don't have enough information to make a prediction, use "NEI" to indicate "Not Enough Information."

(1) Quantity variance for polyethylene powder.
(2) Price variance for polyethylene powder.
(3) Quantity variance for finishing kits.
(4) Price variance for finishing kits.
(5) Quantity variance for type I workers.
(6) Price variance for type I workers.
(7) Quantity variance for type II workers.
(8) Price variance for type II workers.

(b) Diane Buswell examined some of the accounting records and reported that Current Designs purchased 1,200 pounds of pellets for this order at a total cost of $2,040. Twenty (20) finishing kits were assembled at a total cost of $3,240. The payroll records showed that the type I employees worked 38 hours on this project at a total cost of $570. The type II finishing employees worked 65 hours at a total cost of $796.25. A total of 20 kayaks were produced for this order.

    The standards that had been developed for this model of kayak were used in BYP15-1 and are reproduced here. For each kayak:

54 pounds of polyethylene powder at $1.50 per pound

1 finishing kit (rope, seat, hardware, etc.) at $170

2 hours of type I labor from people who run the oven and trim the plastic at a standard wage rate of $15 per hour

3 hours of type II labor from people who attach the hatches and seat and other hardware at a standard wage rate of $12 per hour.

Calculate the eight variances that are listed in part (a) of this problem.

DECISION-MAKING ACROSS THE ORGANIZATION

BYP23-2 Milton Professionals, a management consulting firm, specializes in strategic planning for financial institutions. James Hahn and Sara Norton, partners in the firm, are assembling a new strategic planning model for use by clients. The model is designed for use on most personal computers and replaces a rather lengthy manual model currently marketed by the firm. To market the new model, James and Sara will need to provide clients with an estimate of the number of labor hours and computer time needed to operate the model. The model is currently being test-marketed at five small financial institutions. These financial institutions are listed below, along with the number of combined computer/labor hours used by each institution to run the model one time.

Financial Institutions	Computer/Labor Hours Required
Midland National	25
First State	45
Financial Federal	40
Pacific America	30
Lakeview National	30
Total	170
Average	34

    Any company that purchases the new model will need to purchase user manuals for the system. User manuals will be sold to clients in cases of 20, at a cost of $320 per case. One manual must be used each time the model is run because each manual includes a nonreusable computer-accessed password for operating the system. Also required are specialized computer forms that are sold only by Milton. The specialized forms are sold in packages of 250, at a cost of $60 per package. One application of the model requires the use of 50 forms. This amount includes two forms that are generally wasted in each application due to printer alignment errors. The overall cost of the strategic planning model to clients is $12,000. Most clients will use the model four times annually.

    Milton must provide its clients with estimates of ongoing costs incurred in operating the new planning model, and would like to do so in the form of standard costs.

Instructions

With the class divided into groups, answer the following.
(a) What factors should be considered in setting a standard for computer/labor hours?
(b) What alternatives for setting a standard for computer/labor hours might be used?
(c) What standard for computer/labor hours would you select? Justify your answer.
(d) Determine the standard materials cost associated with the user manuals and computer forms for each application of the strategic planning model.

MANAGERIAL ANALYSIS

*BYP23-3   Ana Carillo and Associates is a medium-sized company located near a large metropolitan area in the Midwest. The company manufactures cabinets of mahogany, oak, and other fine woods for use in expensive homes, restaurants, and hotels. Although some of the work is custom, many of the cabinets are a standard size.

One such non-custom model is called Luxury Base Frame. Normal production is 1,000 units. Each unit has a direct labor hour standard of 5 hours. Overhead is applied to production based on standard direct labor hours. During the most recent month, only 900 units were produced; 4,500 direct labor hours were allowed for standard production, but only 4,000 hours were used. Standard and actual overhead costs were as follows.

	Standard (1,000 units)	Actual (900 units)
Indirect materials	$ 12,000	$ 12,300
Indirect labor	43,000	51,000
(Fixed) Manufacturing supervisors salaries	22,500	22,000
(Fixed) Manufacturing office employees salaries	13,000	12,500
(Fixed) Engineering costs	27,000	25,000
Computer costs	10,000	10,000
Electricity	2,500	2,500
(Fixed) Manufacturing building depreciation	8,000	8,000
(Fixed) Machinery depreciation	3,000	3,000
(Fixed) Trucks and forklift depreciation	1,500	1,500
Small tools	700	1,400
(Fixed) Insurance	500	500
(Fixed) Property taxes	300	300
Total	$144,000	$150,000

Instructions

(a) Determine the overhead application rate.
(b) Determine how much overhead was applied to production.
(c) Calculate the total overhead variance, controllable variance, and volume variance.
(d) Decide which overhead variances should be investigated.
(e) Discuss causes of the overhead variances. What can management do to improve its performance next month?

REAL-WORLD FOCUS

BYP23-4   Glassmaster Company is organized as two divisions and one subsidiary. One division focuses on the manufacture of filaments such as fishing line and sewing thread; the other division manufactures antennas and specialty fiberglass products. Its subsidiary manufactures flexible steel wire controls and molded control panels.

The annual report of Glassmaster provides the following information.

GLASSMASTER COMPANY
Management Discussion

Gross profit margins for the year improved to 20.9% of sales compared to last year's 18.5%. All operations reported improved margins due in large part to improved operating efficiencies as a result of cost reduction measures implemented during the second and third quarters of the fiscal year and increased manufacturing throughout due to higher unit volume sales. Contributing to the improved margins was a favorable materials price variance due to competitive pricing by suppliers as a result of soft demand for petrochemical-based products. This favorable variance is temporary and will begin to reverse itself as stronger worldwide demand for commodity products improves in tandem with the economy. Partially offsetting these positive effects on profit margins were competitive pressures on sales prices of certain product lines. The company responded with pricing strategies designed to maintain and/or increase market share.

Instructions
(a) Is it apparent from the information whether Glassmaster utilizes standard costs?
(b) Do you think the price variance experienced should lead to changes in standard costs for the next fiscal year?

BYP23-5 The Balanced Scorecard Institute **(www.balancedscorecard.org)** is a great resource for information about implementing the balanced scorecard. One item of interest provided at its website is an example of a balanced scorecard for a regional airline.

Address: **http://www.balancedscorecard.org/portals/0/pdf/regional_airline.pdf**, or go to **www.wiley.com/college/kimmel**

Instructions

Go to the address above and answer the following questions.
(a) What are the objectives identified for the airline for each perspective?
(b) What measures are used for the objectives in the customer perspective?
(c) What initiatives are planned to achieve the objective in the learning perspective?

BYP23-6 The December 22, 2009, edition of the *Wall Street Journal* has an article by Kevin Kelliker entitled "In Risky Move, GM to Run Plants Around Clock."

Instructions

Read the article and answer the following questions.
(a) According to the article, what is the normal industry standard for plants to be considered operating at full capacity?
(b) What ideal standard is the company hoping to achieve?
(c) What reasons are given in the article for why most companies do not operate a third shift? How does GM propose to overcome these issues?
(d) What are some potential drawbacks of the midnight shift? What implications does this have for variances from standards?
(e) What potential sales/marketing disadvantage does the third shift create?

Critical Thinking

COMMUNICATION ACTIVITY

BYP23-7 The setting of standards is critical to the effective use of standards in evaluating performance.

Instructions

Explain the following in a memo to your instructor.
(a) The comparative advantages and disadvantages of ideal versus normal standards.
(b) The factors that should be included in setting the price and quantity standards for direct materials, direct labor, and manufacturing overhead.

ETHICS CASE

BYP23-8 At Symond Company, production workers in the Painting Department are paid on the basis of productivity. The labor time standard for a unit of production is established through periodic time studies conducted by Douglas Management Consultants. In a time study, the actual time required to complete a specific task by a worker is observed. Allowances are then made for preparation time, rest periods, and cleanup time. Bill Carson is one of several veterans in the Painting Department.

Bill is informed by Douglas that he will be used in the time study for the painting of a new product. The findings will be the basis for establishing the labor time standard for the next 6 months. During the test, Bill deliberately slows his normal work pace in an effort to obtain a labor time standard that will be easy to meet. Because it is a new product, the Douglas representative who conducted the test is unaware that Bill did not give the test his best effort.

Instructions
(a) Who was benefited and who was harmed by Bill's actions?
(b) Was Bill ethical in the way he performed the time study test?
(c) What measure(s) might the company take to obtain valid data for setting the labor time standard?

ALL ABOUT YOU

BYP23-9   From the time you first entered school many years ago, instructors have been measuring and evaluating you by imposing standards. In addition, many of you will pursue professions that administer professional examinations to attain recognized certification. Recently, a federal commission presented proposals suggesting all public colleges and universities should require standardized tests to measure their students' learning.

Instructions

Read the article at **www.signonsandiego.com/uniontrib/20060811/news_1n11colleges.html**, and answer the following questions.
(a) What areas of concern did the panel's recommendations address?
(b) What are possible advantages of standard testing?
(c) What are possible disadvantages of standard testing?
(d) Would you be in favor of standardized tests?

CONSIDERING YOUR COSTS AND BENEFITS

BYP23-10   Do you think that standard costs are used only in making products like wheel bearings and hamburgers? Think again. Standards influence virtually every aspect of our lives. For example, the next time you call to schedule an appointment with your doctor, ask the receptionist how many minutes the appointment is scheduled for. Doctors are under increasing pressure to see more patients each day, which means the time spent with each patient is shorter. As insurance companies and employers push for reduced medical costs, every facet of medicine has been standardized and analyzed. Doctors, nurses, and other medical staff are evaluated in every part of their operations to ensure maximum efficiency. While keeping medical treatment affordable seems like a worthy goal, what are the potential implications for the quality of health care? Does a focus on the bottom line result in a reduction in the quality of health care?

A simmering debate has centered on a very basic question: To what extent should accountants, through financial measures, influence the type of medical care that you receive? Suppose that your local medical facility is in danger of closing because it has been losing money. Should the facility put in place incentives that provide bonuses to doctors if they meet certain standard-cost targets for the cost of treating specific ailments?

> **YES:** If the facility is in danger of closing, then someone should take steps to change the medical practices to reduce costs. A closed medical facility is of no use to me, my family, or the community.
>
> **NO:** I don't want an accountant deciding the right medical treatment for me. My family and I deserve the best medical care.

Instructions

Write a response indicating your position regarding this situation. Provide support for your view.

Answers to Insight and Accounting Across the Organization Questions

p. 1196 How Do Standards Help a Business? Q: How will the creation of such standards help a business or organization? **A:** A business or organization may use the data to compare its performance relative to others with regard to common practices such as processing a purchase order or filling a sales order. Armed with this information, an organization can determine which areas to focus on with improvement campaigns.

p. 1199 How Can We Make Susan's Chili Profitable? Q: How might management use this raw materials cost information? **A:** Management might decide to increase the price of its chili. Or, it might revise its recipes to use cheaper ingredients. Or, it might eliminate some products until ingredients are available at costs closer to standard. Regarding the waste due to dull blades, management should reconsider its maintenance policy, to balance the cost of maintenance versus the cost of wasted product.

p. 1208 What's Brewing at Starbucks? Q: What implications does Starbucks' commitment to corporate social responsibility have for the standard cost of a cup of coffee? **A:** Starbucks' *Global Responsibility Report* explicitly describes its goals related to corporate social responsibility. By including measurable objectives, it signals that it is committed to meeting these goals. As a consequence of setting measurable objectives, when the company determines the standard costs of its products, it needs to factor in the costs of these programs. For example, if renewable energy costs more per kilowatt, then the company must include this added cost in its determination of its products' costs.

p. 1213 It May Be Time to Fly United Again Q: Which of the perspectives of a balanced scorecard were the focus of United's CEO? **A:** Improving on-time flight departures is an objective within the internal process perspective. Customer intent to fly United again is an objective within the customer perspective.

Answers to Self-Test Questions

1. c **2.** b **3.** d **4.** a **5.** b **6.** c **7.** b $[(6,300 \times \$1.00) - (6,000 \times \$1.00)]$
8. a $[(14,800 \times \$8.00) - (15,000 \times \$8.00)]$ **9.** d **10.** a **11.** b **12.** d **13.** c
14. d ***15.** c ***16.** c

Engel & Gielen/Look/Getty Images, Inc.

CHAPTER 24

PLANNING FOR CAPITAL INVESTMENTS

LEARNING OBJECTIVES

After studying this chapter, you should be able to:

1 Discuss capital budgeting evaluation, and explain inputs used in capital budgeting.

2 Describe the cash payback technique.

3 Explain the net present value method.

4 Identify the challenges presented by intangible benefits in capital budgeting.

5 Describe the profitability index.

6 Indicate the benefits of performing a post-audit.

7 Explain the internal rate of return method.

8 Describe the annual rate of return method.

✔ The Navigator

Do you own a boat? Maybe it's a nice boat, but how many swimming pools, movie theaters, shopping malls, or restaurants does it have on board? If you are in the cruise-line business, like Holland America Line, you need all of these amenities and more just to stay afloat. Holland America Line is considered by many to be the leader of the premium luxury-liner segment.

Carnival Corporation, which owns Holland America Line and other cruise lines, is one of the largest vacation companies in the world. During one recent three-year period, Carnival spent more than $3 billion per year on capital expenditures. Those are big numbers, but keep in mind that Carnival estimates that at any given time there are 270,000 people (200,000 customers and 70,000 crew) on one of its 100 ships somewhere in the world.

The cruise industry is a tricky business. When times are good, customers are looking for ways to splurge. But when times get tough, people are more inclined to take a trip in a minivan than a

FLOATING HOTELS

luxury yacht. So timing your investment properly is important. For example, during one stretch of solid global economic growth, many cruise lines decided to add capacity. The industry built 14 new ships at a total price of $4.7 billion. (That's an average price of about $330 million.) But, it takes up to three years to build one of these giant vessels. Unfortunately, by the time these ships were completed, the economy was in a nose-dive.

To maintain passenger numbers, cruise prices had to be cut by up to 40%. While the lower prices attracted lots of customers, that wasn't enough to offset an overall decline in revenue of 10% in the middle of the recession. The industry had added capacity at just the wrong time.

Watch the Holland America Line video in WileyPLUS to learn more about capital budgeting in the real world.

Companies like Holland America Line must constantly determine how to invest their resources. Other examples: Dell announced plans to spend $1 billion on data centers for cloud computing. Exxon announced that two wells off the Brazilian coast, which it had spent hundreds of millions to drill, would produce no oil. Renault and Nissan spent over $5 billion during a nearly 20-year period to develop electric cars, such as the Leaf.

The process of making such capital expenditure decisions is referred to as **capital budgeting**. Capital budgeting involves choosing among various capital projects to find the one(s) that will maximize a company's return on its financial investment. The purpose of this chapter is to discuss the various techniques used to make effective capital budgeting decisions.

The content and organization of this chapter are as follows.

The Capital Budgeting Evaluation Process

Many companies follow a carefully prescribed process in capital budgeting. At least once a year, top management requests proposals for projects from each department. A capital budgeting committee screens the proposals and submits its findings to the officers of the company. The officers, in turn, select the projects they believe to be most worthy of funding. They submit this list of projects to the board of directors. Ultimately, the directors approve the capital expenditure budget for the year. Illustration 24-1 shows this process.

The involvement of top management and the board of directors in the process demonstrates the importance of capital budgeting decisions. These decisions often have a significant impact on a company's future profitability. In fact, poor capital budgeting decisions can cost a lot of money. Such decisions have even led to the bankruptcy of some companies.

CASH FLOW INFORMATION

In this chapter, we will look at several methods that help companies make effective capital budgeting decisions. Most of these methods employ **cash flow numbers**, rather than accrual accounting revenues and expenses. Remember from your financial accounting course that accrual accounting records **revenues** and **expenses**, rather than cash inflows and cash outflows. In fact, revenues and

1. Project proposals are requested from departments, plants, and authorized personnel.

2. Proposals are screened by a capital budget committee.

3. Officers determine which projects are worthy of funding.

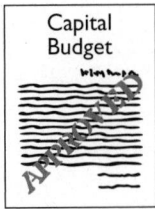

4. Board of directors approves capital budget.

Illustration 24-1 Corporate capital budget authorization process

expenses measured during a period often differ significantly from their cash flow counterparts. Accrual accounting has advantages over cash accounting in many contexts. **For purposes of capital budgeting, though, estimated cash inflows and outflows are the preferred inputs.** Why? Because ultimately the value of all financial investments is determined by the value of cash flows received and paid.

Sometimes cash flow information is not available. In this case, companies can make adjustments to accrual accounting numbers to estimate cash flow. Often, they estimate net annual cash flow by adding back depreciation expense to net income. Depreciation expense is added back because it is an expense that does not require an outflow of cash. By adding back to net income the depreciation expense that was deducted in determining net income, companies approximate net annual cash flow. Suppose, for example, that Reno Company's net income of $13,000 includes a charge for depreciation expense of $26,000. Its estimated net annual cash flow would be $39,000 ($13,000 + $26,000).

Illustration 24-2 lists some typical cash outflows and inflows related to equipment purchase and replacement.

Illustration 24-2 Typical cash flows relating to capital budgeting decisions

Cash Outflows

Initial investment
Repairs and maintenance
Increased operating costs
Overhaul of equipment

Cash Inflows

Sale of old equipment
Increased cash received from customers
Reduced cash outflows related to operating costs
Salvage value of equipment

These cash flows are the inputs that are considered relevant in capital budgeting decisions.

The capital budgeting decision, under any technique, depends in part on a variety of considerations:

- **The availability of funds:** Does the company have unlimited funds, or will it have to ration capital investments?
- **Relationships among proposed projects:** Are proposed projects independent of each other, or does the acceptance or rejection of one depend on the acceptance or rejection of another?

- **The company's basic decision-making approach:** Does the company want to produce an accept-reject decision or a ranking of desirability among possible projects?
- **The risk associated with a particular project:** How certain are the projected returns? The certainty of estimates varies with such issues as market considerations or the length of time before returns are expected.

ILLUSTRATIVE DATA

For our initial discussion of quantitative capital budgeting techniques, we will use a continuing example, which will enable us to compare the results of the various techniques. Assume that Stewart Shipping Company is considering an investment of $130,000 in new equipment. The new equipment is expected to last 10 years. It will have a zero salvage value at the end of its useful life. The annual cash inflows are $200,000, and the annual cash outflows are $176,000. Illustration 24-3 summarizes these data.

Illustration 24-3 Investment information for Stewart Shipping example

Initial investment	$130,000
Estimated useful life	10 years
Estimated salvage value	–0–
Estimated annual cash flows	
Cash inflows from customers	$200,000
Cash outflows for operating costs	176,000
Net annual cash flow	$ 24,000

In the following two sections, we will examine two popular techniques for evaluating capital investments: cash payback and the net present value method.

Cash Payback

The **cash payback technique** identifies the time period required to recover the cost of the capital investment from the net annual cash flow produced by the investment. Illustration 24-4 presents the formula for computing the cash payback period assuming equal annual cash flows.

Illustration 24-4 Cash payback formula

Cost of Capital Investment	÷	Net Annual Cash Flow	=	Cash Payback Period

Helpful Hint Net annual cash flow can also be approximated by "Net cash provided by operating activities" from the statement of cash flows.

The cash payback period in the Stewart Shipping example is 5.42 years, computed as follows.

$$\$130,000 \div \$24,000 = 5.42 \text{ years}$$

The evaluation of the payback period is often related to the expected useful life of the asset. For example, assume that at Stewart Shipping a project is unacceptable if the payback period is longer than 60% of the asset's expected useful life. The 5.42-year payback period in this case is a bit over 50% of the project's expected useful life. Thus, the project is acceptable.

It follows that when the payback technique is used to decide among acceptable alternative projects, **the shorter the payback period, the more attractive the investment**. This is true for two reasons: First, the earlier the investment is recovered, the sooner the company can use the cash funds for other purposes.

Second, the risk of loss from obsolescence and changed economic conditions is less in a shorter payback period.

The preceding computation of the cash payback period assumes **equal** net annual cash flows in each year of the investment's life. In many cases, this assumption is not valid. In the case of **uneven** net annual cash flows, the company determines the cash payback period when the cumulative net cash flows from the investment equal the cost of the investment.

To illustrate, assume that Chen Company proposes an investment in a new website that is estimated to cost $300,000. Illustration 24-5 shows the proposed investment cost, net annual cash flows, cumulative net cash flows, and the cash payback period.

Year	Investment	Net Annual Cash Flow	Cumulative Net Cash Flow
0	$300,000		
1		$ 60,000	$ 60,000
2		90,000	150,000
3		90,000	240,000
4		120,000	360,000
5		100,000	460,000

Cash payback period = 3.5 years

Illustration 24-5
Computation of cash payback period—unequal cash flows

As Illustration 24-5 shows, at the end of year 3, cumulative net cash flow of $240,000 is less than the investment cost of $300,000, but at the end of year 4 the cumulative cash inflow of $360,000 exceeds the investment cost. The cash flow needed in year 4 to equal the investment cost is $60,000 ($300,000 − $240,000). Assuming the cash inflow occurred evenly during year 4, we then divide this amount by the net annual cash flow in year 4 ($120,000) to determine the point during the year when the cash payback occurs. Thus, we get 0.50 ($60,000/$120,000), or half of the year, and the cash payback period is 3.5 years.

The cash payback technique may be useful as an initial screening tool. It may be the most critical factor in the capital budgeting decision for a company that desires a fast turnaround of its investment because of a weak cash position. It also is relatively easy to compute and understand.

However, cash payback should not ordinarily be the only basis for the capital budgeting decision because it **ignores the expected profitability of the project**. To illustrate, assume that Projects A and B have the same payback period, but Project A's useful life is double the useful life of Project B. Project A's earning power, therefore, is twice as long as Project B's. A further—and major—disadvantage of this technique is that it **ignores the time value of money**.

Do it! Watertown Paper Corporation is considering adding another machine for the manufacture of corrugated cardboard. The machine would cost $900,000. It would have an estimated life of 6 years and no salvage value. The company estimates that annual cash inflows would increase by $400,000 and that annual cash outflows would increase by $190,000. Compute the cash payback period.

CASH PAYBACK PERIOD

Action Plan

- Annual cash inflows − Annual cash outflows = Net annual cash flow.
- Cash payback period = Cost of capital investment/Net annual cash flow.

Solution

Estimated annual cash inflows	$400,000
Estimated annual cash outflows	190,000
Net annual cash flow	$210,000

Cash payback period = $900,000/$210,000 = 4.3 years.

Related exercise material: **BE 24-1** and **Do it!** 24-1.

 The Navigator

Net Present Value Method

LEARNING OBJECTIVE 3

Explain the net present value method.

Recognition of the time value of money can make a significant difference in the long-term impact of the capital budgeting decision. For example, cash flows that occur early in the life of an investment will be worth more than those that occur later—because of the time value of money. Therefore, it is useful to recognize the timing of cash flows when evaluating projects.

Capital budgeting techniques that take into account both the time value of money and the estimated net cash flow from an investment are called **discounted cash flow techniques**. They are generally recognized as the most informative and best conceptual approaches to making capital budgeting decisions. The expected net cash flow used in discounting cash flows consists of the annual net cash flows plus the estimated liquidation proceeds (salvage value) when the asset is sold for salvage at the end of its useful life.

The primary discounted cash flow technique is the **net present value method**. A second method, discussed later in the chapter, is the **internal rate of return**. At this point, before you read on, **we recommend that you examine Appendix D** at the end of the textbook to review time value of money concepts, upon which these methods are based.

The **net present value (NPV) method** involves discounting net cash flows to their present value and then comparing that present value with the capital outlay required by the investment. The difference between these two amounts is referred to as **net present value (NPV)**. Company management determines what interest rate to use in discounting the future net cash flows. This rate, often referred to as the **discount rate** or **required rate of return**, is discussed in a later section.

The NPV decision rule is this: **A proposal is acceptable when net present value is zero or positive**. At either of those values, the rate of return on the investment equals or exceeds the required rate of return. When net present value is negative, the project is unacceptable. Illustration 24-6 shows the net present value decision criteria.

Illustration 24-6 Net present value decision criteria

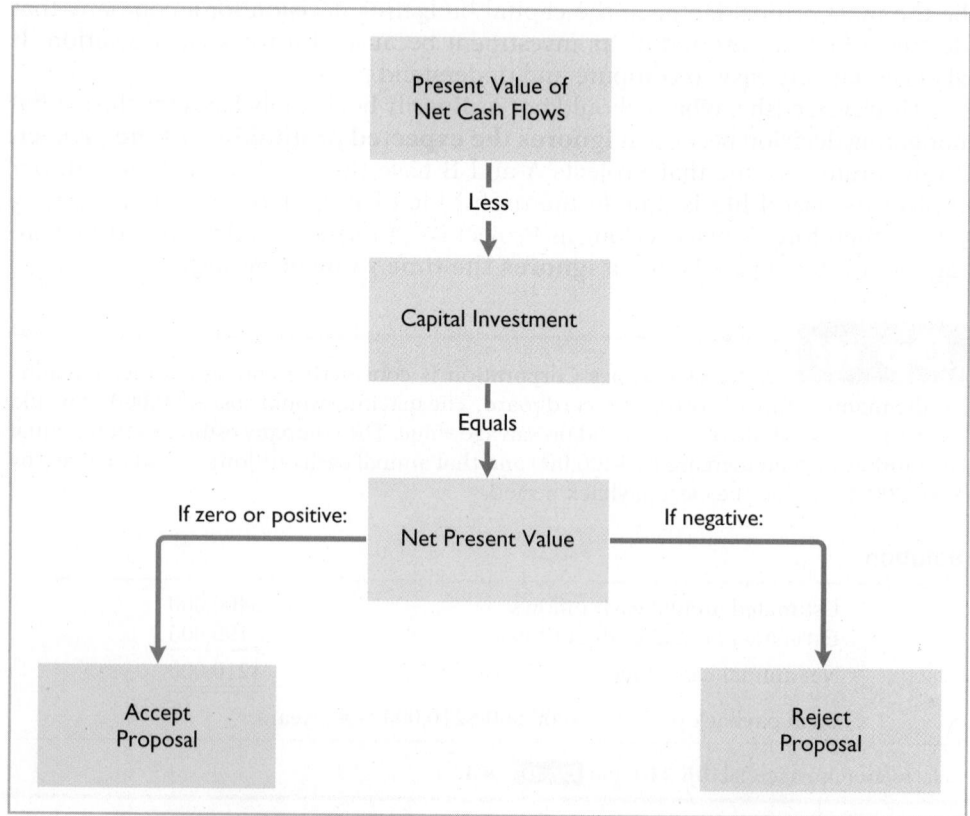

When making a selection among acceptable proposals, **the higher the positive net present value, the more attractive the investment**. The application of this method to two cases is described in the next two sections. In each case, we will assume that the investment has no salvage value at the end of its useful life.

EQUAL ANNUAL CASH FLOWS

In our Stewart Shipping Company example, the company's net annual cash flows are $24,000. If we assume this amount **is uniform over the asset's useful life**, we can compute the present value of the net annual cash flows by using the present value of an annuity of 1 for 10 payments (from Table 4, Appendix D). Assuming a discount rate of 12%, the present value of net cash flows are as shown in Illustration 24-7 (rounded to the nearest dollar).

Helpful Hint The ABC Co. expects equal cash flows over an asset's 5-year useful life. What discount factor should it use in determining present values if management wants (1) a 12% return or (2) a 15% return? Answer: Using Table 4, the factors are (1) 3.60478 and (2) 3.35216.

	Present Value at 12%
Discount factor for 10 periods	5.65022
Present value of net cash flows: $24,000 × 5.65022	**$135,605**

Illustration 24-7 Computation of present value of equal net annual cash flows

The analysis of the proposal by the net present value method is as follows.

	12%
Present value of net cash flows	$135,605
Capital investment	130,000
Net present value	**$ 5,605**

Illustration 24-8 Computation of net present value—equal net annual cash flows

The proposed capital expenditure is acceptable at a required rate of return of 12% because the net present value is positive.

UNEQUAL ANNUAL CASH FLOWS

When net annual cash flows are unequal, we cannot use annuity tables to calculate their present value. Instead, we use tables showing the **present value of a single future amount for each annual cash flow**.

To illustrate, assume that Stewart Shipping Company expects the same total net cash flows of $240,000 over the life of the investment. But because of a declining market demand for the new product over the life of the equipment, the net annual cash flows are higher in the early years and lower in the later years. The present value of the net annual cash flows is calculated as follows, using Table 3 in Appendix D.

Helpful Hint Appendix D demonstrates the use of a financial calculator to solve time value of money problems.

Year	Assumed Net Annual Cash Flows	Discount Factor 12%	Present Value 12%
	(1)	(2)	(1) × (2)
1	$ 34,000	.89286	$ 30,357
2	30,000	.79719	23,916
3	27,000	.71178	19,218
4	25,000	.63552	15,888
5	24,000	.56743	13,618
6	22,000	.50663	11,146
7	21,000	.45235	9,499
8	20,000	.40388	8,078
9	19,000	.36061	6,852
10	18,000	.32197	5,795
	$240,000		$144,367

Illustration 24-9 Computation of present value of unequal annual cash flows

Therefore, the analysis of the proposal by the net present value method is as follows.

Illustration 24-10 Computation of net present value—unequal annual cash flows

	12%
Present value of net cash flows	$144,367
Capital investment	130,000
Net present value	**$ 14,367**

In this example, the present value of the net cash flows is greater than the $130,000 capital investment. Thus, the project is acceptable at a 12% required rate of return. The difference between the present values using the 12% rate under equal cash flows ($135,605) and unequal cash flows ($144,367) is due to the pattern of the flows. Since more money is received sooner under this particular uneven cash flow scenario, its present value is greater.

© Pictafolio/iStockphoto

 Management Insight

Can You Hear Me—Better?

What's better than 3G wireless service? 4G. But the question for wireless service providers is whether customers will be willing to pay extra for that improvement. Verizon has already spent billions on the upgrade, but customer usage might be slow in coming. First, there aren't that many 4G-compatible devices, and coverage will be spotty. Also, most applications don't really need higher speeds. Verizon is hoping that its investment in 4G works out better than its $23 billion investment in its FIOS fiber-wired network for TV and ultrahigh-speed Internet. One analyst estimates that the present value of each FIOS customer is $800 less than the cost of the connection.

Source: Martin Peers, "Investors: Beware Verizon's Generation GAP," *Wall Street Journal Online* (January 26, 2010).

? Based on the potentially slow initial adoption of 4G by customers, how might the conclusions of a cash payback analysis of Verizon's 4G investment differ from a present value analysis? (See page 1282.)

CHOOSING A DISCOUNT RATE

Now that you understand how companies apply the net present value method, it is logical to ask a related question: How is a discount rate (required rate of return) determined in real capital budgeting decisions? In most instances, a company uses a required rate of return equal to its **cost of capital**—that is, the rate that it must pay to obtain funds from creditors and stockholders.

Helpful Hint Cost of capital is the rate that management expects to pay on all borrowed and equity funds. It does not relate to the cost of funding a *specific* project.

The cost of capital is a weighted average of the rates paid on borrowed funds as well as on funds provided by investors in the company's common stock and preferred stock. If management believes a project is riskier than the company's usual line of business, the discount rate should be increased. That is, the discount rate has two elements, a cost of capital element and a risk element. Often, companies assume the risk element is equal to zero.

Using an incorrect discount rate can lead to incorrect capital budgeting decisions. Consider again the Stewart Shipping example in Illustration 24-8, where we used a discount rate of 12%. Suppose that this rate does not take into account the fact that this project is riskier than most of the company's investments. A more appropriate discount rate, given the risk, might be 15%. Illustration 24-11 compares the net present values at the two rates. At the higher, more appropriate discount rate of 15%, the net present value is negative, and the company should reject the project (discount factors from Appendix D, Table 4).

	Present Values at Different Discount Rates	
	12%	**15%**
Discount factor for 10 payments	5.65022	5.01877
Present value of net cash flows:		
$24,000 × 5.65022	$135,605	
$24,000 × 5.01877		$120,450
Capital investment	130,000	130,000
Positive (negative) net present value	$ 5,605	$ (9,550)

The discount rate is often referred to by alternative names, including the **required rate of return**, the **hurdle rate**, and the **cutoff rate**. Determination of the cost of capital varies somewhat depending on whether the entity is a for-profit or not-for-profit business. Calculation of the cost of capital is discussed more fully in advanced accounting and finance courses.

SIMPLIFYING ASSUMPTIONS

In our examples of the net present value method, we have made a number of simplifying assumptions:

- **All cash flows come at the end of each year.** In reality, cash flows will come at uneven intervals throughout the year. However, it is far simpler to assume that all cash flows come at the end (or in some cases the beginning) of the year. In fact, this assumption is frequently made in practice.
- **All cash flows are immediately reinvested in another project that has a similar return.** In most capital budgeting situations, companies receive cash flows during each year of a project's life. In order to determine the return on the investment, some assumption must be made about how the cash flows are reinvested in the year that they are received. It is customary to assume that cash flows received are reinvested in some other project of similar return until the end of the project's life.
- **All cash flows can be predicted with certainty.** The outcomes of business investments are full of uncertainty, as the Holland America Line Feature Story shows. There is no way of knowing how popular a new product will be, how long a new machine will last, or what competitors' reactions might be to changes in a product. But, in order to make investment decisions, analysts must estimate future outcomes. In this chapter, we have assumed that future amounts are known with certainty.[1] In reality, little is known with certainty. More advanced capital budgeting techniques deal with uncertainty by considering the probability that various outcomes will occur.

> **Do it!**
>
> Watertown Paper Corporation is considering adding another machine for the manufacture of corrugated cardboard. The machine would cost $900,000. It would have an estimated life of 6 years and no salvage value. The company estimates that annual cash inflows would increase by $400,000 and that annual cash outflows would increase by $190,000. Management has a required rate of return of 9%. Calculate the net present value on this project and discuss whether it should be accepted.

NET PRESENT VALUE

---

[1] One exception is a brief discussion of sensitivity analysis later in the chapter.

Action Plan

- Estimated annual cash inflows — Estimated annual cash outflows = Net annual cash flow.

- Use the NPV technique to calculate the difference between net cash flows and the initial investment.

- Accept the project if the net present value is positive.

Solution

Estimated annual cash inflows	$400,000		
Estimated annual cash outflows	190,000		
Net annual cash flow	$210,000		

	Cash Flow	9% Discount Factor	Present Value
Present value of net annual cash flows	$210,000	4.48592[a]	$942,043
Capital investment			900,000
Net present value			$ 42,043

[a]Table 4, Appendix D, 9%, 6 years

Since the net present value is greater than zero, Watertown should accept the project.

Related exercise material: **BE24-2, BE24-3, E24-1, E24-2, E24-3,** and **Do it!** **24-2.**

COMPREHENSIVE EXAMPLE

Best Taste Foods is considering investing in new equipment to produce fat-free snack foods. Management believes that although demand for fat-free foods has leveled off, fat-free foods are here to stay. The following estimated costs, cost of capital, and cash flows were determined in consultation with the marketing, production, and finance departments.

Illustration 24-12 Investment information for Best Taste Foods example

Initial investment	$1,000,000
Cost of equipment overhaul in 5 years	$200,000
Salvage value of equipment in 10 years	$20,000
Cost of capital (discount rate)	15%
Estimated annual cash flows	
Cash inflows received from sales	$500,000
Cash outflows for cost of goods sold	$200,000
Maintenance costs	$30,000
Other direct operating costs	$40,000

Remember that we are using cash flows in our analysis, not accrual revenues and expenses. Thus, for example, the direct operating costs would not include depreciation expense, since depreciation expense does not use cash. Illustration 24-13 presents the computation of the net annual cash flows of this project.

Illustration 24-13 Computation of net annual cash flow

Cash inflows received from sales	$ 500,000
Cash outflows for cost of goods sold	(200,000)
Maintenance costs	(30,000)
Other direct operating costs	(40,000)
Net annual cash flow	**$230,000**

Illustration 24-14 shows computation of the net present value for this proposed investment (discount factors from Appendix D, Table 4).

Event	Time Period	Cash Flow	×	15% Discount Factor	=	Present Value
Equipment purchase	0	$1,000,000		1.00000		$(1,000,000)
Equipment overhaul	5	200,000		.49718		(99,436)
Net annual cash flow	1–10	230,000		5.01877		1,154,317
Salvage value	10	20,000		.24719		4,944
Net present value						$ **59,825**

Illustration 24-14 Computation of net present value for Best Taste Foods investment

Because the net present value of the project is positive, Best Taste should accept the project.

 DECISION TOOLKIT

DECISION CHECKPOINTS	INFO NEEDED FOR DECISION	TOOL TO USE FOR DECISION	HOW TO EVALUATE RESULTS
Should the company invest in a proposed project?	Cash flow estimates, discount rate	Net present value = Present value of net cash flows less capital investment	The investment is financially acceptable if net present value is positive.

Additional Considerations

Now that you understand how the net present value method works, we can add some "additional wrinkles." Specifically, these are the impact of intangible benefits, a way to compare mutually exclusive projects, refinements that take risk into account, and the need to conduct post-audits of investment projects.

LEARNING OBJECTIVE **4**
Identify the challenges presented by intangible benefits in capital budgeting.

INTANGIBLE BENEFITS

The NPV evaluation techniques employed thus far rely on tangible costs and benefits that can be relatively easily quantified. Some investment projects, especially high-tech projects, fail to make it through initial capital budget screens because only the project's tangible benefits are considered. **Intangible benefits** might include increased quality, improved safety, or enhanced employee loyalty. By ignoring intangible benefits, capital budgeting techniques might incorrectly eliminate projects that could be financially beneficial to the company.

To avoid rejecting projects that actually should be accepted, analysts suggest two possible approaches:

1. Calculate net present value ignoring intangible benefits. Then, if the NPV is negative, ask whether the project offers any intangible benefits that are worth at least the amount of the negative NPV.

2. Project rough, conservative estimates of the value of the intangible benefits, and incorporate these values into the NPV calculation.

Example

Assume that Berg Company is considering the purchase of a new mechanical robot to be used for soldering electrical connections. Illustration 24-15 (page 1256) shows the estimates related to this proposed purchase (discount factors from Appendix D, Table 4).

Illustration 24-15 Investment information for Berg Company example

Initial investment	$200,000
Annual cash inflows	$ 50,000
Annual cash outflows	20,000
Net annual cash flow	**$ 30,000**
Estimated life of equipment	10 years
Discount rate	12%

	Cash Flows	×	12% Discount Factor	=	Present Value
Present value of net annual cash flows	$30,000	×	5.65022	=	$169,507
Initial investment					200,000
Net present value					**$(30,493)**

Based on the negative net present value of $30,493, the proposed project is not acceptable. This calculation, however, ignores important information. First, the company's engineers believe that purchasing this machine will dramatically improve the quality of electrical connections in the company's products. As a result, future warranty costs will be reduced. Also, the company believes that this higher quality will translate into higher future sales. Finally, the new machine will be much safer than the previous one.

Berg can incorporate this new information into the capital budgeting decision in the two ways discussed earlier. First, management might simply ask whether the reduced warranty costs, increased sales, and improved safety benefits have an estimated total present value to the company of at least $30,493. If yes, then the project is acceptable.

Alternatively, analysts can estimate the annual cash flows of these benefits. In our initial calculation, we assumed each of these benefits to have a value of zero. It seems likely that their actual values are much higher than zero. Given the difficulty of estimating these benefits, however, conservative values should be assigned to them. If, after using conservative estimates, the net present value is positive, Berg should accept the project.

To illustrate, assume that Berg estimates that improved sales will increase cash inflows by $10,000 annually as a result of an increase in perceived quality. Berg also estimates that annual cost outflows would be reduced by $5,000 as a result of lower warranty claims, reduced injury claims, and missed work. Consideration of the intangible benefits results in the following revised NPV calculation (discount factors from Appendix D, Table 4).

Illustration 24-16 Revised investment information for Berg Company example, including intangible benefits

Initial investment	$200,000
Annual cash inflows (revised)	$ 60,000 ($50,000 + $10,000)
Annual cash outflows (revised)	15,000 ($20,000 − $5,000)
Net annual cash flow	**$ 45,000**
Estimated life of equipment	10 years
Discount rate	12%

	Cash Flows	×	12% Discount Factor	=	Present Value
Present value of net annual cash flows	$45,000	×	5.65022	=	$254,260
Initial investment					200,000
Net present value					**$ 54,260**

Using these conservative estimates of the value of the additional benefits, Berg should accept the project.

Ethics Insight

It Need Not Cost an Arm and a Leg

Most manufacturers say that employee safety matters above everything else. But how many back up this statement with investments that improve employee safety? Recently, a woodworking hobbyist, who also happens to be a patent attorney with a Ph.D. in physics, invented a mechanism that automatically shuts down a power saw when the saw blade comes in contact with human flesh. The blade stops so quickly that only minor injuries result.

Power saws injure 40,000 Americans each year, and 4,000 of those injuries are bad enough to require amputation. Therefore, one might think that power-saw companies would be lined up to incorporate this mechanism into their saws. But, in the words of one power-tool company, "Safety doesn't sell." Since existing saw manufacturers were unwilling to incorporate the device into their saws, eventually the inventor started his own company to build the devices and sell them directly to businesses that use power saws.

Source: Melba Newsome, "An Edgy New Idea," *Time: Inside Business* (May 2006), p. A16.

? In addition to the obvious humanitarian benefit of reducing serious injuries, how else might the manufacturer of this product convince potential customers of its worth? (See page 1282.)

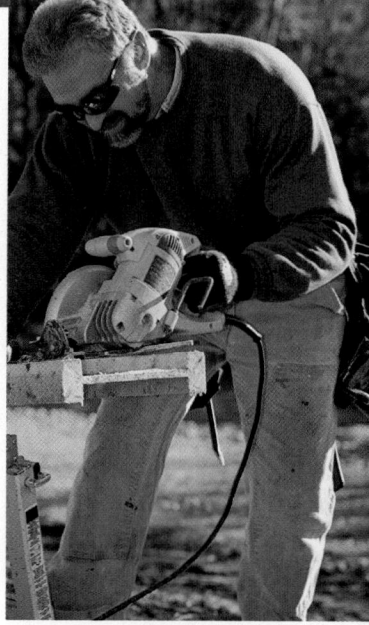

Carol Gering/iStockphoto

PROFITABILITY INDEX FOR MUTUALLY EXCLUSIVE PROJECTS

In theory, companies should accept all projects with positive NPVs. However, companies rarely are able to adopt all positive-NPV proposals. First, proposals often are **mutually exclusive**. This means that if the company adopts one proposal, it would be impossible also to adopt the other proposal. For example, a company may be considering the purchase of a new packaging machine and is looking at various brands and models. It needs only one packaging machine. Once the company has determined which brand and model to purchase, the others will not be purchased—even though they also may have positive net present values.

> **LEARNING OBJECTIVE 5**
> Describe the profitability index.

Even in instances where projects are not mutually exclusive, managers often must choose between various positive-NPV projects because of **limited resources**. For example, the company might have ideas for two new lines of business, each of which has a projected positive NPV. However, both of these proposals require skilled personnel, and the company determines that it will not be able to find enough skilled personnel to staff both projects. Management will have to choose the project it thinks is a better option.

When choosing between alternative proposals, it is tempting simply to choose the project with the higher NPV. Consider the following example of two mutually exclusive projects. Each is assumed to have a 10-year life and a 12% discount rate (discount factors from Appendix D, Tables 3 and 4). Illustration 24-17 shows the estimates for each project and the computation of the present value of the net annual cash flows.

	Project A	Project B
Initial investment	$40,000	$ 90,000
Net annual cash inflow	10,000	19,000
Salvage value	5,000	10,000
Present value of net annual cash flows		
($10,000 × 5.65022) + ($5,000 × .32197)	58,112	
($19,000 × 5.65022) + ($10,000 × .32197)		110,574

Illustration 24-17 Investment information for mutually exclusive projects

Illustration 24-18 computes the net present values of Project A and Project B by subtracting the initial investment from the present value of the net annual cash flows.

Illustration 24-18 Net present value computation

	Project A	Project B
Present value of net annual cash flows	$ 58,112	$110,574
Initial investment	40,000	90,000
Net present value	$18,112	$ 20,574

Project B has the higher NPV, and so it would seem that the company should adopt B. Note, however, that Project B also requires more than twice the original investment of Project A. In choosing between the two projects, the company should also include in its calculations the amount of the original investment.

One relatively simple method of comparing alternative projects is the **profitability index**. This method takes into account both the size of the original investment and the discounted cash flows. The profitability index is calculated by dividing the present value of net cash flows that occur after the initial investment by the amount of the initial investment.

Illustration 24-19 Formula for profitability index

$$\frac{\text{Present Value of}}{\text{Net Cash Flows}} \div \frac{\text{Initial}}{\text{Investment}} = \frac{\text{Profitability}}{\text{Index}}$$

The profitability index allows comparison of the relative desirability of projects that require differing initial investments. Note that any project with a positive NPV will have a profitability index above 1. The profitability index for each of the mutually exclusive projects is calculated below.

Illustration 24-20 Calculation of profitability index

$$\text{Profitability Index} = \frac{\text{Present Value of Net Cash Flows}}{\text{Initial Investment}}$$

Project A	Project B
$\dfrac{\$58,112}{\$40,000} = 1.45$	$\dfrac{\$110,574}{\$90,000} = 1.23$

In this case, the profitability index of Project A exceeds that of Project B. Thus, Project A is more desirable. Again, if these were not mutually exclusive projects and if resources were not limited, then the company should invest in both projects since both have positive NPVs. Additional considerations related to preference decisions are discussed in more advanced courses.

DECISION TOOLKIT

DECISION CHECKPOINTS	INFO NEEDED FOR DECISION	TOOL TO USE FOR DECISION	HOW TO EVALUATE RESULTS
Which investment proposal should a company accept?	Estimated cash flows and discount rate for each proposal	$\text{Profitability index} = \dfrac{\text{Present value of net cash flows}}{\text{Initial investment}}$	The investment proposal with the highest profitability index should be accepted.

RISK ANALYSIS

A simplifying assumption made by many financial analysts is that projected results are known with certainty. In reality, projected results are only estimates based upon the forecaster's belief as to the most probable outcome. One approach for dealing with such uncertainty is **sensitivity analysis**. Sensitivity analysis uses a number of outcome estimates to get a sense of the variability among potential returns. An example of sensitivity analysis was presented in Illustration 24-11 (page 1253), where we illustrated the impact on NPV of different discount rate assumptions. A higher-risk project would be evaluated using a higher discount rate.

Similarly, to take into account that more distant cash flows are often more uncertain, a higher discount rate can be used to discount more distant cash flows. Other techniques to address uncertainty are discussed in advanced courses.

Management Insight
Wide-Screen Capacity

Matjaz Boncina/iStockphoto

Building a new factory to produce 50- and even 60-inch TV screens can cost $4 billion. But for more than 10 years, manufacturers of these screens have continued to build new plants. By building so many plants, they have expanded productive capacity at a rate that has exceeded the demand for big-screen TVs. In fact, during one recent year, the supply of big-screen TVs was estimated to exceed demand by 12%, rising to 16% in the future. One state-of-the-art plant built by Sharp was estimated to be operating at only 50% of capacity. Experts say that the price of big-screen TVs will have to fall much further than they already have before demand may eventually catch up with productive capacity.

Source: James Simms, "Sharp's Payoff Delayed," *Wall Street Journal Online* (September 14, 2010).

 What implications does the excess capacity have for the cash payback and net present value calculations of these investments? (See page 1282.)

POST-AUDIT OF INVESTMENT PROJECTS

Any well-run organization should perform an evaluation, called a post-audit, of its investment projects after their completion. A post-audit is a thorough evaluation of how well a project's actual performance matches the original projections. An example of a post-audit is seen in a situation that occurred at Campbell Soup. The company made the original decision to invest in the Intelligent Quisine line based on management's best estimates of future cash flows. During the development phase of the project, Campbell hired an outside consulting firm to evaluate the project's potential for success. Because actual results during the initial years were far below the estimated results and because the future also did not look promising, the project was terminated.

LEARNING OBJECTIVE 6
Indicate the benefits of performing a post-audit.

Performing a post-audit is important for a variety of reasons. First, if managers know that the company will compare their estimates to actual results, they will be more likely to submit reasonable and accurate data when they make investment proposals. This clearly is better for the company than for managers to submit overly optimistic estimates in an effort to get pet projects approved. Second, as seen with Campbell Soup, a post-audit provides a formal mechanism by which the company can determine whether existing projects should be supported or terminated. Third, post-audits improve future investment proposals because, by evaluating past successes and failures, managers improve their estimation techniques.

A post-audit involves the same evaluation techniques used in making the original capital budgeting decision—for example, use of the NPV method. The difference is that, in the post-audit, analysts insert actual figures, where known, and they revise estimates of future amounts based on new information. The managers responsible for the estimates used in the original proposal must explain the reasons for any significant differences between their estimates and actual results.

Post-audits are not foolproof. In the case of Campbell Soup, some observers suggested that the company was too quick to abandon the project. Industry analysts suggested that with more time and more advertising expenditures, the company might have enjoyed success.

© Don Bayley/iStockphoto

Management Insight
Seeing the Big Picture

Inaccurate trend forecasting and market positioning are more detrimental to capital investment decisions than using the wrong discount rate. Ampex patented the VCR but failed to see its market potential. Westinghouse made the same mistake with the flat-screen video display. More often, companies adopt projects or businesses only to discontinue them in response to market changes. Texas Instruments announced it would stop manufacturing computer chips, after it had made substantial capital investments that enabled it to become one of the world's leading suppliers. The company dropped out of some 12 business lines in only a few years.

Source: World Research Advisory Inc. (London, August 1998), p. 4.

? How important is the choice of discount rate in making capital budgeting decisions? (See page 1282.)

Other Capital Budgeting Techniques

Some companies use capital budgeting techniques other than, or in addition to, the cash payback and net present value methods. In this section, we will briefly discuss these other approaches.

INTERNAL RATE OF RETURN METHOD

LEARNING OBJECTIVE 7
Explain the internal rate of return method.

The **internal rate of return (IRR) method** differs from the net present value method in that it finds the **interest yield of the potential investment**. The **internal rate of return (IRR)** is the interest rate that will cause the present value of the proposed capital expenditure to equal the present value of the expected net annual cash flows (that is, NPV equal to zero). Because it recognizes the time value of money, the internal rate of return method is (like the NPV method) a discounted cash flow technique.

How do we determine the internal rate of return? One way is to use a financial calculator (see Appendix D, page D-14) or computerized spreadsheet to solve for this rate. Or, we can use a trial-and-error procedure.

To illustrate, assume that Stewart Shipping Company is considering the purchase of a new front-end loader at a cost of $244,371. Net annual cash flows from this loader are estimated to be $100,000 a year for three years. To determine the internal rate of return on this front-end loader, the company finds the discount rate that results in a net present value of zero. As Illustration 24-21 shows, at a rate of return of 10%, Stewart Shipping has a positive net present value of $4,315. At a rate of return of 12%, it has a negative net present value of $4,188. At an 11% rate, the net present value is zero. Therefore, 11% is the internal rate of return for this investment (discount factors from Appendix D, Table 3).

Illustration 24-21 Estimation of internal rate of return

Year	Net Annual Cash Flows	Discount Factor 10%	Present Value 10%	Discount Factor 11%	Present Value 11%	Discount Factor 12%	Present Value 12%
1	$100,000	.90909	$ 90,909	.90090	$ 90,090	.89286	$ 89,286
2	$100,000	.82645	82,645	.81162	81,162	.79719	79,719
3	$100,000	.75132	75,132	.73119	73,119	.71178	71,178
			248,686		244,371		240,183
Less: Initial investment			244,371		244,371		244,371
Net present value			$ 4,315		$ –0–		$ (4,188)

An easier approach to solving for the internal rate of return can be used if the net annual cash flows are **equal**, as in the Stewart Shipping example. In this special case, we can find the internal rate of return using the following formula.

| **Capital Investment** | ÷ | **Net Annual Cash Flows** | = | **Internal Rate of Return Factor** |

Illustration 24-22 Formula for internal rate of return—even cash flows

Applying this formula to the Stewart Shipping example, we find:

$$\$244{,}371 \div \$100{,}000 = 2.44371$$

We then look up the factor 2.44371 in Table 4 of Appendix D in the three-payment row and find it under 11%. Row 3 is reproduced below for your convenience.

Table 4 Present Value of an Annuity of 1

(n) Payments	4%	5%	6%	7%	8%	9%	10%	11%	12%	15%
3	2.77509	2.72325	2.67301	2.62432	2.57710	2.53130	2.48685	**2.44371**	2.40183	2.28323

Recognize that if the cash flows are **uneven**, then a trial-and-error approach or a financial calculator or computerized spreadsheet must be used.

Once managers know the internal rate of return, they compare it to the company's required rate of return (the discount rate). The IRR decision rule is as follows: **Accept the project when the internal rate of return is equal to or greater than the required rate of return. Reject the project when the internal rate of return is less than the required rate of return.** Illustration 24-23 shows these relationships. The internal rate of return method is widely used in practice, largely because most managers find the internal rate of return easy to interpret.

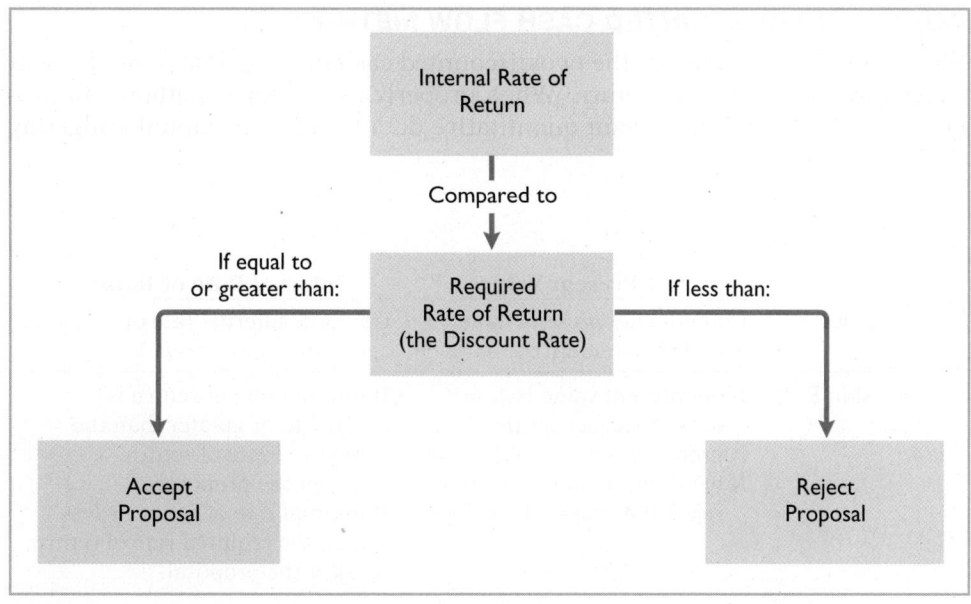

Illustration 24-23 Internal rate of return decision criteria

DECISION TOOLKIT

DECISION CHECKPOINTS	INFO NEEDED FOR DECISION	TOOL TO USE FOR DECISION	HOW TO EVALUATE RESULTS
Should the company invest in a proposed project?	Estimated cash flows and the required rate of return (hurdle rate)	Internal rate of return = Interest rate that results in a net present value of zero	If the internal rate of return exceeds the required rate of return for the project, then the project is financially acceptable.

INTERNAL RATE OF RETURN

Action Plan

- Estimated annual cash inflows − Estimated annual cash outflows = Net annual cash flow.

- Capital investment/Net annual cash flows = Internal rate of return factor.

- Look up the factor in the present value of an annuity table to find the internal rate of return.

- Accept the project if the internal rate of return is equal to or greater than the required rate of return.

Do it! Watertown Paper Corporation is considering adding another machine for the manufacture of corrugated cardboard. The machine would cost $900,000. It would have an estimated life of 6 years and no salvage value. The company estimates that annual cash inflows would increase by $400,000 and that annual cash outflows would increase by $190,000. Management has a required rate of return of 9%. Calculate the internal rate of return on this project and discuss whether it should be accepted.

Solution

Estimated annual cash inflows	$400,000
Estimated annual cash outflows	190,000
Net annual cash flow	$210,000

$900,000/210,000 = 4.285714. Using Table 4 of Appendix D and the factors that correspond with the six-payment row, 4.285714 is between the factors for 10% and 11%. Since the project has an internal rate that is greater than 10% and the required rate of return is only 9%, the project should be accepted.

Related exercise material: **BE24-7, BE24-8, E24-5, E24-6, E24-7,** and **Do it! 24-3.**

COMPARING DISCOUNTED CASH FLOW METHODS

Illustration 24-24 compares the two discounted cash flow methods—net present value and internal rate of return. When properly used, either method will provide management with relevant quantitative data for making capital budgeting decisions.

Illustration 24-24 Comparison of discounted cash flow methods

	Net Present Value	**Internal Rate of Return**
1. Objective	Compute net present value (a dollar amount).	Compute internal rate of return (a percentage).
2. Decision Rule	If net present value is zero or positive, accept the proposal. If net present value is negative, reject the proposal.	If internal rate of return is equal to or greater than the required rate of return, accept the proposal. If internal rate of return is less than the required rate of return, reject the proposal.

ANNUAL RATE OF RETURN METHOD

The final capital budgeting technique we will look at is the annual rate of return method. It is based directly on accrual accounting data rather than on cash flows. It indicates **the profitability of a capital expenditure** by dividing expected annual net income by the average investment. Illustration 24-25 shows the formula for computing annual rate of return.

LEARNING OBJECTIVE 8
Describe the annual rate of return method.

$$\frac{\text{Expected Annual}}{\text{Net Income}} \div \frac{\text{Average}}{\text{Investment}} = \frac{\text{Annual Rate}}{\text{of Return}}$$

Illustration 24-25 Annual rate of return formula

Assume that Reno Company is considering an investment of $130,000 in new equipment. The new equipment is expected to last five years and have zero salvage value at the end of its useful life. Reno uses the straight-line method of depreciation for accounting purposes. The expected annual revenues and costs of the new product that will be produced from the investment are:

Sales		$200,000
Less: Costs and expenses		
Manufacturing costs (exclusive of depreciation)	$132,000	
Depreciation expense ($130,000 ÷ 5)	26,000	
Selling and administrative expenses	22,000	180,000
Income before income taxes		20,000
Income tax expense		7,000
Net income		$ 13,000

Illustration 24-26 Estimated annual net income from Reno Company's capital expenditure

Reno's expected annual net income is $13,000. Average investment is derived from the formula shown below.

$$\frac{\text{Original Investment} + \text{Value at End of Useful Life}}{2} = \text{Average Investment}$$

Illustration 24-27 Formula for computing average investment

The value at the end of useful life is equal to the asset's salvage value, if any. For Reno, average investment is $65,000 [($130,000 + $0) ÷ 2]. The expected annual rate of return for Reno's investment in new equipment is therefore 20%, computed as follows.

$$\$13,000 \div \$65,000 = 20\%$$

Management then compares the annual rate of return with its required rate of return for investments of similar risk. The required rate of return is generally based on the company's cost of capital. The decision rule is: **A project is acceptable if its rate of return is greater than management's required rate of return. It is unacceptable when the reverse is true.** When companies use the rate of return technique in deciding among several acceptable projects, **the higher the rate of return for a given risk, the more attractive the investment**.

The principal advantages of this method are the simplicity of its calculation and management's familiarity with the accounting terms used in the computation. A major limitation of the annual rate of return method is that it does not consider the time value of money. For example, no consideration is given as to whether cash inflows will occur early or late in the life of the investment. As explained in Appendix D recognition of the time value of money can make a significant difference between the future value and the discounted present value of

Helpful Hint A capital budgeting decision based on only one technique may be misleading. It is often wise to analyze an investment from a number of different perspectives.

an investment. A second disadvantage is that this method relies on accrual accounting numbers rather than expected cash flows.

ANNUAL RATE OF RETURN

Do it!

Watertown Paper Corporation is considering adding another machine for the manufacture of corrugated cardboard. The machine would cost $900,000. It would have an estimated life of 6 years and no salvage value. The company estimates that annual revenues would increase by $400,000 and that annual expenses excluding depreciation would increase by $190,000. It uses the straight-line method to compute depreciation expense. Management has a required rate of return of 9%. Compute the annual rate of return.

Action Plan

- Expected annual net income = Annual revenues − Annual expenses (including depreciation expense).
- Annual rate of return = Expected annual net income/Average investment.
- Average investment = (Original investment + Value at end of useful life)/2.

The Navigator

Solution

Revenues		$400,000
Less:		
Expenses (excluding depreciation)	$190,000	
Depreciation ($900,000/6 years)	150,000	340,000
Annual net income		$ 60,000

Average investment = ($900,000 + 0)/2 = $450,000.
Annual rate of return = $60,000/$450,000 = 13.3%.

Since the annual rate of return (13.33%) is greater than Watertown's required rate of return (9%), the proposed project is acceptable.

Related exercise material: **BE24-9, E24-8, E24-9, E24-10, E24-11,** and **Do it! 24-4.**

USING THE **DECISION TOOLKIT**

Campbell Soup is considering expanding its international presence. It sells 38% of the soup consumed in the United States but only 2% of soup worldwide. Thus, the company believes that it has great potential for international sales. Recently, 20% of Campbell's sales were in foreign markets (and nearly all of that was in Europe). Its goal is to have 30% of its sales be in foreign markets. In order to accomplish this goal, the company will have to invest heavily.

In recent years, Campbell has spent between $300 and $400 million on capital expenditures. Suppose that Campbell is interested in expanding its South American presence by building a new production facility. After considering tax, marketing, labor, transportation, and political issues, Campbell has determined that the most desirable location is either in Buenos Aires or Rio de Janeiro. The following estimates have been provided. (All amounts are stated in U.S. dollars.)

	Buenos Aires	Rio de Janeiro
Initial investment	$2,500,000	$1,400,000
Estimated useful life	20 years	20 years
Annual revenues (accrual)	$500,000	$380,000
Annual expenses (accrual)	$200,000	$180,000
Annual cash inflows	$550,000	$430,000
Annual cash outflows	$222,250	$206,350
Estimated salvage value	$500,000	$0
Discount rate	9%	9%

Instructions

Evaluate each of these mutually exclusive proposals employing (a) cash payback, (b) net present value, (c) the profitability index, (d) the internal rate of return, and (e) annual rate of return. Discuss the implications of your findings.

Solution

	Buenos Aires	**Rio de Janeiro**
(a) Cash payback	$\dfrac{\$2,500,000}{\$327,750^*} = 7.63$ years	$\dfrac{\$1,400,000}{\$223,650^{**}} = 6.26$ years

*$550,000 − $222,250; **$430,000 − $206,350

(b) Net present value
Present value of net cash flows

	Buenos Aires	Rio de Janeiro
$327,750 × 9.12855 =	$2,991,882	$223,650 × 9.12855 = $2,041,600
$500,000 × 0.17843 =	89,215	
	3,081,097	
Less: Initial investment	2,500,000	1,400,000
Net present value	$ 581,097	$ 641,600

(c) Profitability index

$$\dfrac{\$3,081,097}{\$2,500,000} = 1.23 \qquad \dfrac{\$2,041,600}{\$1,400,000} = 1.46$$

(d) Internal rate of return: The internal rate of return can be approximated by experimenting with different discount rates to see which one comes the closest to resulting in a net present value of zero. Doing this, we find that Buenos Aires has an internal rate of return of approximately 12%, while the internal rate of return of the Rio de Janeiro location is approximately 15% as shown below. Rio, therefore, is preferable.

	Buenos Aires				**Rio de Janeiro**		
Internal rate of return							
Cash Flows	×	**12% Discount Factor**	=	**Present Value**	**Cash Flows**	×	**15% Discount Factor**	=	**Present Value**

Cash Flows	×	**12% Discount Factor**	=	**Present Value**	**Cash Flows**	×	**15% Discount Factor**	=	**Present Value**
$327,750	×	7.46944	=	$2,448,109	$223,650	×	6.25933	=	$1,399,899
$500,000	×	0.10367	=	51,835					
				$2,499,944					
Less: Capital investment				2,500,000					1,400,000
Net present value				$ (56)					$ (101)

(e) Annual rate of return

Average investment

$$\dfrac{(\$2,500,000 + \$500,000)}{2} = \$1,500,000 \qquad \dfrac{(\$1,400,000 + \$0)}{2} = \$700,000$$

Annual rate of return

$$\dfrac{\$300,000^*}{\$1,500,000} = .20 = 20\% \qquad \dfrac{\$200,000^{**}}{\$700,000} = .286 = 28.6\%$$

*$500,000 − $200,000; **$380,000 − $180,000

Implications: Although the annual rate of return is higher for Rio de Janeiro, this method has the disadvantage of ignoring time value of money, as well as using accrual numbers rather than cash flows. The cash payback of Rio de Janeiro is also shorter, but this method also ignores the time value of money. Thus, while these two methods can be used for a quick assessment, neither should be relied upon as the sole evaluation tool.

From the net present value calculation, it would appear that the two projects are nearly identical in their acceptability. However, the profitability index indicates that the Rio de Janeiro investment is far more desirable because it generates its cash flows with a much smaller initial investment. A similar result is found by using the internal rate of return. Overall, assuming that the company will invest in only one project, it would appear that the Rio de Janeiro project should be chosen.

✔ The
Navigator

Summary of Learning Objectives

1 **Discuss capital budgeting evaluation, and explain inputs used in capital budgeting.** Management gathers project proposals from each department; a capital budget committee screens the proposals and recommends worthy projects. Company officers decide which projects to fund, and the board of directors approves the capital budget. In capital budgeting, estimated cash inflows and outflows, rather than accrual-accounting numbers, are the preferred inputs.

2 **Describe the cash payback technique.** The cash payback technique identifies the time period required to recover the cost of the investment. The formula when net annual cash flows are equal is: Cost of capital investment ÷ Estimated net annual cash flow = Cash payback period. The shorter the payback period, the more attractive the investment.

3 **Explain the net present value method.** The net present value method compares the present value of future cash inflows with the capital investment to determine net present value. The NPV decision rule is: Accept the project if net present value is zero or positive. Reject the project if net present value is negative.

4 **Identify the challenges presented by intangible benefits in capital budgeting.** Intangible benefits are difficult to quantify and thus are often ignored in capital budgeting decisions. This can result in incorrectly rejecting some projects. One method for considering intangible benefits is to calculate the NPV, ignoring intangible benefits. If the resulting NPV is below zero, evaluate whether the benefits are worth at least the amount of the negative net present value. Alternatively,

intangible benefits can be incorporated into the NPV calculation, using conservative estimates of their value.

5 **Describe the profitability index.** The profitability index is a tool for comparing the relative merits of alternative capital investment opportunities. It is computed as: Present value of net cash flows ÷ Initial investment. The higher the index, the more desirable the project.

6 **Indicate the benefits of performing a post-audit.** A post-audit is an evaluation of a capital investment's actual performance. Post-audits create an incentive for managers to make accurate estimates. Post-audits also are useful for determining whether a company should continue, expand, or terminate a project. Finally, post-audits provide feedback that is useful for improving estimation techniques.

7 **Explain the internal rate of return method.** The objective of the internal rate of return method is to find the interest yield of the potential investment, which is expressed as a percentage rate. The IRR decision rule is: Accept the project when the internal rate of return is equal to or greater than the required rate of return. Reject the project when the internal rate of return is less than the required rate of return.

8 **Describe the annual rate of return method.** The annual rate of return uses accrual accounting data to indicate the profitability of a capital investment. It is calculated as: Expected annual net income ÷ Amount of the average investment. The higher the rate of return, the more attractive the investment.

DECISION TOOLKIT *A SUMMARY*

DECISION CHECKPOINTS	INFO NEEDED FOR DECISION	TOOL TO USE FOR DECISION	HOW TO EVALUATE RESULTS
Should the company invest in a proposed project?	Cash flow estimates, discount rate	Net present value = Present value of net cash flows less capital investment	The investment is financially acceptable if net present value is positive.
Which investment proposal should a company accept?	Estimated cash flows and discount rate for each proposal	Profitability index = $\dfrac{\text{Present value of net cash flows}}{\text{Initial investment}}$	The investment proposal with the highest profitability index should be accepted.
Should the company invest in a proposed project?	Estimated cash flows and the required rate of return (hurdle rate)	Internal rate of return = Interest rate that results in a net present value of zero	If the internal rate of return exceeds the required rate of return for the project, then the project is financially acceptable.

Glossary

Annual rate of return method (*p. 1263*) The determination of the profitability of a capital expenditure, computed by dividing expected annual net income by the average investment.

Capital budgeting (*p. 1246*) The process of making capital expenditure decisions in business.

Cash payback technique (*p. 1248*) A capital budgeting technique that identifies the time period required to recover the cost of a capital investment from the net annual cash flow produced by the investment.

Cost of capital (*p. 1252*) The average rate of return that the firm must pay to obtain funds from creditors and stockholders.

Discounted cash flow technique (*p. 1250*) A capital budgeting technique that considers both the estimated net cash flows from the investment and the time value of money.

Discount rate (*p. 1250*) The interest rate used in discounting the future net cash flows to determine present value.

Internal rate of return (IRR) (*p. 1260*) The interest rate that will cause the present value of the proposed capital expenditure to equal the present value of the expected net annual cash flows.

Internal rate of return (IRR) method (*p. 1260*) A method used in capital budgeting that results in finding the interest yield of the potential investment.

Net present value (NPV) (*p. 1250*) The difference that results when the original capital outlay is subtracted from the discounted net cash flows.

Net present value (NPV) method (*p. 1250*) A method used in capital budgeting in which net cash flows are discounted to their present value and then compared to the capital outlay required by the investment.

Post-audit (*p. 1259*) A thorough evaluation of how well a project's actual performance matches the original projections.

Profitability index (*p. 1258*) A method of comparing alternative projects that takes into account both the size of the investment and its discounted future net cash flows. It is computed by dividing the present value of net future cash flows by the initial investment.

Required rate of return (*p. 1263*) The rate of return management expects on investments; also called the *discount rate* or *cost of capital*.

Comprehensive Do it!

Cornfield Company is considering a long-term capital investment project in laser equipment. This will require an investment of $280,000, and it will have a useful life of 5 years. Annual net income is expected to be $16,000 a year. Depreciation is computed by the straight-line method with no salvage value. The company's cost of capital is 10%. (*Hint:* Assume cash flows can be computed by adding back depreciation expense.)

Instructions

(Round all computations to two decimal places.)

(a) Compute the cash payback period for the project. (Round to two decimals.)

(b) Compute the net present value for the project. (Round to nearest dollar.)

(c) Compute the annual rate of return for the project.

(d) Should the project be accepted? Why?

Solution to Comprehensive Do it!

(a) $280,000 ÷ $72,000 ($16,000 + $56,000) = 3.89 years

(b)

	Present Value at 10%
Discount factor for 5 payments	3.79079
Present value of net cash flows: $72,000 × 3.79079	$272,937
Capital investment	280,000
Negative net present value	$ (7,063)

(c) $16,000 ÷ $140,000 ($280,000 ÷ 2) = 11.4%

(d) The annual rate of return of 11.4% is good. However, the cash payback period is 78% of the project's useful life, and net present value is negative. The recommendation is to reject the project.

Action Plan

• Calculate the time it will take to pay back the investment: cost of the investment divided by net annual cash flows.

• When calculating NPV, remember that net annual cash flow equals annual net income plus annual depreciation expense.

• Be careful to use the correct discount factor in using the net present value method.

• Calculate the annual rate of return: expected annual net income divided by average investment.

 The Navigator

Self-Test, Brief Exercises, Exercises, Problem Set A, and many more resources are available for practice in WileyPLUS.

Self-Test Questions

Answers are on page 1283.

(LO 1) **1.** Which of the following is **not** an example of a capital budgeting decision?
  (a) Decision to build a new plant.
  (b) Decision to renovate an existing facility.
  (c) Decision to buy a piece of machinery.
  (d) All of these are capital budgeting decisions.

(LO 1) **2.** What is the order of involvement of the following parties in the capital budgeting authorization process?
  (a) Plant managers, officers, capital budget committee, board of directors.
  (b) Board of directors, plant managers, officers, capital budget committee.
  (c) Plant managers, capital budget committee, officers, board of directors.
  (d) Officers, plant managers, capital budget committee, board of directors.

(LO 2) **3.** What is a weakness of the cash payback approach?
  (a) It uses accrual-based accounting numbers.
  (b) It ignores the time value of money.
  (c) It ignores the useful life of alternative projects.
  (d) Both (b) and (c) are true.

(LO 2) **4.** Siegel Industries is considering two capital budgeting projects. Project A requires an initial investment of $48,000. It is expected to produce net annual cash flows of $7,000. Project B requires an initial investment of $75,000 and is expected to produce net annual cash flows of $12,000. Using the cash payback technique to evaluate the two projects, Siegel should accept:
  (a) Project A because it has a shorter cash payback period.
  (b) Project B because it has a shorter cash payback period.
  (c) Project A because it requires a smaller initial investment.
  (d) Project B because it produces a larger net annual cash flow.

(LO 3) **5.** Which is a true statement regarding using a higher discount rate to calculate the net present value of a project?
  (a) It will make it less likely that the project will be accepted.
  (b) It will make it more likely that the project will be accepted.
  (c) It is appropriate to use a higher rate if the project is perceived as being less risky than other projects being considered.
  (d) It is appropriate to use a higher rate if the project will have a short useful life relative to other projects being considered.

6. A positive net present value means that the: (LO 3)
  (a) project's rate of return is less than the cutoff rate.
  (b) project's rate of return exceeds the required rate of return.
  (c) project's rate of return equals the required rate of return.
  (d) project is unacceptable.

7. Which of the following is **not** an alternative name for (LO 3) the discount rate?
  (a) Hurdle rate.
  (b) Required rate of return.
  (c) Cutoff rate.
  (d) All of these are alternative names for the discount rate.

8. If a project has intangible benefits whose value is (LO 4) hard to estimate, the best thing to do is:
  (a) ignore these benefits, since any estimate of their value will most likely be wrong.
  (b) include a conservative estimate of their value.
  (c) ignore their value in your initial net present value calculation, but then estimate whether their potential value is worth at least the amount of the net present value deficiency.
  (d) Either (b) or (c) is correct.

9. An example of an intangible benefit provided by a (LO 4) capital budgeting project is:
  (a) the salvage value of the capital investment.
  (b) a positive net present value.
  (c) a decrease in customer complaints due to poor quality.
  (d) an internal rate of return greater than zero.

10. The following information is available for a potential (LO 5) capital investment.

Initial investment	$80,000
Salvage value	10,000
Net annual cash flow	14,820
Net present value	18,112
Useful life	10 years

The potential investment's profitability index (rounded to two decimals) is:
  (a) 5.40.   (c) 1.23.
  (b) 1.19.   (d) 1.40.

11. A post-audit of an investment project should be (LO 6) performed:
  (a) on all significant capital expenditure projects.
  (b) on all projects that management feels might be financial failures.
  (c) on randomly selected projects.
  (d) only on projects that enjoy tremendous success.

(LO 7) **12.** A project should be accepted if its internal rate of return exceeds:
(a) zero.
(b) the rate of return on a government bond.
(c) the company's required rate of return.
(d) the rate the company pays on borrowed funds.

(LO 7) **13.** The following information is available for a potential capital investment.

Initial investment	$60,000
Net annual cash flow	15,400
Net present value	3,143
Useful life	5 years

The potential investment's internal rate of return is approximately:
(a) 5%.
(b) 10%.
(c) 4%.
(d) 9%.

(LO 8) **14.** Which of the following is **incorrect** about the annual rate of return technique?
(a) The calculation is simple.
(b) The accounting terms used are familiar to management.
(c) The timing of the cash inflows is not considered.
(d) The time value of money is considered.

15. The following information is available for a potential (LO 8) capital investment.

Initial investment	$120,000
Annual net income	15,000
Net annual cash flow	27,500
Salvage value	20,000
Useful life	8 years

The potential investment's annual rate of return is approximately:
(a) 21%.
(b) 15%.
(c) 30%.
(d) 39%.

Go to the book's companion website, **www. wiley.com/college/kimmel**, for additional Self-Test Questions.

 ✔The Navigator

Questions

1. Describe the process a company may use in screening and approving the capital expenditure budget.

2. What are the advantages and disadvantages of the cash payback technique?

3. Tom Wells claims the formula for the cash payback technique is the same as the formula for the annual rate of return technique. Is Tom correct? What is the formula for the cash payback technique?

4. Two types of present value tables may be used with the discounted cash flow techniques. Identify the tables and the circumstance(s) when each table should be used.

5. What is the decision rule under the net present value method?

6. Discuss the factors that determine the appropriate discount rate to use when calculating the net present value.

7. What simplifying assumptions were made in the chapter regarding calculation of net present value?

8. What are some examples of potential intangible benefits of investment proposals? Why do these intangible benefits complicate the capital budgeting evaluation process? What might happen if intangible benefits are ignored in a capital budgeting decision?

9. What steps can be taken to incorporate intangible benefits into the capital budget evaluation process?

10. What advantages does the profitability index provide over direct comparison of net present value when comparing two projects?

11. What is a post-audit? What are the potential benefits of a post-audit?

12. Identify the steps required in using the internal rate of return method when the net annual cash flows are equal.

13. El Cajon Company uses the internal rate of return method. What is the decision rule for this method?

14. What are the strengths of the annual rate of return approach? What are its weaknesses?

15. Your classmate, Mike Dawson, is confused about the factors that are included in the annual rate of return technique. What is the formula for this technique?

16. Sveta Pace is trying to understand the term "cost of capital." Define the term and indicate its relevance to the decision rule under the internal rate of return technique.

Brief Exercises

BE24-1 Bella Company is considering purchasing new equipment for $450,000. It is expected that the equipment will produce net annual cash flows of $50,000 over its 10-year useful life. Annual depreciation will be $45,000. Compute the cash payback period.

Compute the cash payback period for a capital investment.
(LO 2), **AP**

BE24-2 Hsung Company accumulates the following data concerning a proposed capital investment: cash cost $215,000, net annual cash flows $40,000, present value factor of cash inflows for 10 years 5.65 (rounded). Determine the net present value, and indicate whether the investment should be made.

Compute net present value of an investment.
(LO 3), **AN**

Compute net present value of an investment.
(LO 3), AP

BE24-3 Magic Corporation, an amusement park, is considering a capital investment in a new exhibit. The exhibit would cost $136,000 and have an estimated useful life of 5 years. It will be sold for $65,000 at that time. (Amusement parks need to rotate exhibits to keep people interested.) It is expected to increase net annual cash flows by $25,000. The company's borrowing rate is 8%. Its cost of capital is 10%. Calculate the net present value of this project to the company.

Compute net present value of an investment and consider intangible benefits.
(LO 3, 4), AN

BE24-4 Caine Bottling Corporation is considering the purchase of a new bottling machine. The machine would cost $200,000 and has an estimated useful life of 8 years with zero salvage value. Management estimates that the new bottling machine will provide net annual cash flows of $34,000. Management also believes that the new bottling machine will save the company money because it is expected to be more reliable than other machines, and thus will reduce downtime. How much would the reduction in downtime have to be worth in order for the project to be acceptable? Assume a discount rate of 9%. (*Hint:* Calculate the net present value.)

Compute net present value and profitability index.
(LO 3, 5), AN

BE24-5 Beacon Company is considering two different, mutually exclusive capital expenditure proposals. Project A will cost $400,000, has an expected useful life of 10 years, a salvage value of zero, and is expected to increase net annual cash flows by $70,000. Project B will cost $280,000, has an expected useful life of 10 years, a salvage value of zero, and is expected to increase net annual cash flows by $50,000. A discount rate of 9% is appropriate for both projects. Compute the net present value and profitability index of each project. Which project should be accepted?

Perform a post-audit.
(LO 6), AN

BE24-6 Quillen Company is performing a post-audit of a project completed one year ago. The initial estimates were that the project would cost $250,000, would have a useful life of 9 years, zero salvage value, and would result in net annual cash flows of $46,000 per year. Now that the investment has been in operation for 1 year, revised figures indicate that it actually cost $260,000, will have a useful life of 11 years, and will produce net annual cash flows of $39,000 per year. Evaluate the success of the project. Assume a discount rate of 10%.

Calculate internal rate of return.
(LO 7), AP

BE24-7 Horowitz Company is evaluating the purchase of a rebuilt spot-welding machine to be used in the manufacture of a new product. The machine will cost $176,000, has an estimated useful life of 7 years, a salvage value of zero, and will increase net annual cash flows by $33,740. What is its approximate internal rate of return?

Calculate internal rate of return.
(LO 7), AN

BE24-8 Viera Corporation is considering investing in a new facility. The estimated cost of the facility is $2,045,000. It will be used for 12 years, then sold for $716,000. The facility will generate annual cash inflows of $400,000 and will need new annual cash outflows of $150,000. The company has a required rate of return of 7%. Calculate the internal rate of return on this project, and discuss whether the project should be accepted.

Compute annual rate of return.
(LO 8), AP

BE24-9 Mecha Oil Company is considering investing in a new oil well. It is expected that the oil well will increase annual revenues by $130,000 and will increase annual expenses by $70,000 including depreciation. The oil well will cost $470,000 and will have a $10,000 salvage value at the end of its 10-year useful life. Calculate the annual rate of return.

Do it! Review

Compute the cash payback period for an investment.
(LO 2), AP

Do it! 24-1 Wallowa Company is considering a long-term investment project called ZIP. ZIP will require an investment of $120,000. It will have a useful life of 4 years and no salvage value. Annual cash inflows would increase by $80,000, and annual cash outflows would increase by $40,000. Compute the cash payback period.

Calculate net present value of an investment.
(LO 3), AN

Do it! 24-2 Wallowa Company is considering a long-term investment project called ZIP. ZIP will require an investment of $120,000. It will have a useful life of 4 years and no salvage value. Annual cash inflows would increase by $80,000, and annual cash outflows would increase by $40,000. The company's required rate of return is 12%. Calculate the net present value on this project and discuss whether it should be accepted.

Do it! 24-3   Wallowa Company is considering a long-term investment project called ZIP. ZIP will require an investment of $120,000. It will have a useful life of 4 years and no salvage value. Annual cash inflows would increase by $80,000, and annual cash outflows would increase by $40,000. The company's required rate of return is 12%. Calculate the internal rate of return on this project and discuss whether it should be accepted.

Calculate internal rate of return.
(LO 7), **AN**

Do it! 24-4   Wallowa Company is considering a long-term investment project called ZIP. ZIP will require an investment of $120,000. It will have a useful life of 4 years and no salvage value. Annual revenues would increase by $80,000, and annual expenses (excluding depreciation) would increase by $40,000. Wallowa uses the straight-line method to compute depreciation expense. The company's required rate of return is 12%. Compute the annual rate of return.

Calculate annual rate of return.
(LO 8), **AP**

Exercises

E24-1   Palo Alto Corporation is considering purchasing a new delivery truck. The truck has many advantages over the company's current truck (not the least of which is that it runs). The new truck would cost $56,000. Because of the increased capacity, reduced maintenance costs, and increased fuel economy, the new truck is expected to generate cost savings of $7,500. At the end of 8 years the company will sell the truck for an estimated $27,000. Traditionally the company has used a rule of thumb that a proposal should not be accepted unless it has a payback period that is less than 50% of the asset's estimated useful life. Larry Newton, a new manager, has suggested that the company should not rely solely on the payback approach, but should also employ the net present value method when evaluating new projects. The company's cost of capital is 8%.

Compute cash payback and net present value.
(LO 2, 3), **AN**

Instructions
(a) Compute the cash payback period and net present value of the proposed investment.
(b) Does the project meet the company's cash payback criteria? Does it meet the net present value criteria for acceptance? Discuss your results.

E24-2   Doug's Custom Construction Company is considering three new projects, each requiring an equipment investment of $22,000. Each project will last for 3 years and produce the following net annual cash flows.

Compute cash payback period and net present value.
(LO 2, 3), **AN**

Year	AA	BB	CC
1	$ 7,000	$10,000	$13,000
2	9,000	10,000	12,000
3	12,000	10,000	11,000
Total	$28,000	$30,000	$36,000

The equipment's salvage value is zero, and Doug uses straight-line depreciation. Doug will not accept any project with a cash payback period over 2 years. Doug's required rate of return is 12%.

Instructions
(a) Compute each project's payback period, indicating the most desirable project and the least desirable project using this method. (Round to two decimals and assume in your computations that cash flows occur evenly throughout the year.)
(b) Compute the net present value of each project. Does your evaluation change? (Round to nearest dollar.)

E24-3   Hiland Inc. manufactures snowsuits. Hiland is considering purchasing a new sewing machine at a cost of $2.45 million. Its existing machine was purchased five years ago at a price of $1.8 million; six months ago, Hiland spent $55,000 to keep it operational. The existing sewing machine can be sold today for $260,000. The new sewing machine

Calculate net present value and apply decision rule.
(LO 3), **AN**

would require a one-time, $85,000 training cost. Operating costs would decrease by the following amounts for years 1 to 7:

Year	
1	$390,000
2	400,000
3	411,000
4	426,000
5	434,000
6	435,000
7	436,000

The new sewing machine would be depreciated according to the declining-balance method at a rate of 20%. The salvage value is expected to be $350,000. This new equipment would require maintenance costs of $100,000 at the end of the fifth year. The cost of capital is 9%.

Instructions

Use the net present value method to determine whether Hiland should purchase the new machine to replace the existing machine, and state the reason for your conclusion.

(CGA adapted)

Compute net present value and profitability index.
(LO 3, 5), **AN**

E24-4 BAK Corp. is considering purchasing one of two new diagnostic machines. Either machine would make it possible for the company to bid on jobs that it currently isn't equipped to do. Estimates regarding each machine are provided below.

	Machine A	Machine B
Original cost	$75,500	$180,000
Estimated life	8 years	8 years
Salvage value	–0–	–0–
Estimated annual cash inflows	$20,000	$40,000
Estimated annual cash outflows	$5,000	$10,000

Instructions

Calculate the net present value and profitability index of each machine. Assume a 9% discount rate. Which machine should be purchased?

Determine internal rate of return.
(LO 7), **AN**

E24-5 Eisler Corporation is involved in the business of injection molding of plastics. It is considering the purchase of a new computer-aided design and manufacturing machine for $430,000. The company believes that with this new machine it will improve productivity and increase quality, resulting in an increase in net annual cash flows of $101,000 for the next 6 years. Management requires a 10% rate of return on all new investments.

Instructions

Calculate the internal rate of return on this new machine. Should the investment be accepted?

Calculate cash payback period, internal rate of return, and apply decision rules.
(LO 2, 7), **AN**

E24-6 BSU Inc. wants to purchase a new machine for $29,300, excluding $1,500 of installation costs. The old machine was bought five years ago and had an expected economic life of 10 years without salvage value. This old machine now has a book value of $2,000, and BSU Inc. expects to sell it for that amount. The new machine would decrease operating costs by $7,000 each year of its economic life. The straight-line depreciation method would be used for the new machine, for a six-year period with no salvage value.

Instructions

(a) Determine the cash payback period.
(b) Determine the approximate internal rate of return.
(c) Assuming the company has a required rate of return of 10%, state your conclusion on whether the new machine should be purchased.

(CGA adapted)

Determine internal rate of return.
(LO 7), **AN**

E24-7 Ueker Company is considering three capital expenditure projects. Relevant data for the projects are as follows.

Project	Investment	Annual Income	Life of Project
22A	$240,000	$16,700	6 years
23A	270,000	20,600	9 years
24A	280,000	17,500	7 years

Annual income is constant over the life of the project. Each project is expected to have zero salvage value at the end of the project. Ueker Company uses the straight-line method of depreciation.

Instructions
(a) Determine the internal rate of return for each project. Round the internal rate of return factor to three decimals.
(b) If Ueker Company's required rate of return is 11%, which projects are acceptable?

E24-8 Pierre's Hair Salon is considering opening a new location in French Lick, California. The cost of building a new salon is $300,000. A new salon will normally generate annual revenues of $70,000, with annual expenses (including depreciation) of $41,500. At the end of 15 years the salon will have a salvage value of $80,000.

Calculate annual rate of return.
(LO 8), AP

Instructions
Calculate the annual rate of return on the project.

E24-9 Brady Service Center just purchased an automobile hoist for $35,000. The hoist has an 8-year life and an estimated salvage value of $3,000. Installation costs and freight charges were $3,300 and $700, respectively. Brady uses straight-line depreciation.

The new hoist will be used to replace mufflers and tires on automobiles. Brady estimates that the new hoist will enable his mechanics to replace five extra mufflers per week. Each muffler sells for $72 installed. The cost of a muffler is $36, and the labor cost to install a muffler is $12.

Compute cash payback period and annual rate of return.
(LO 2, 8), AP

Instructions
(a) Compute the cash payback period for the new hoist.
(b) Compute the annual rate of return for the new hoist. (Round to one decimal.)

E24-10 Vilas Company is considering a capital investment of $190,000 in additional productive facilities. The new machinery is expected to have a useful life of 5 years with no salvage value. Depreciation is by the straight-line method. During the life of the investment, annual net income and net annual cash flows are expected to be $12,000 and $50,000, respectively. Vilas has a 12% cost of capital rate, which is the required rate of return on the investment.

Compute annual rate of return, cash payback period, and net present value.
(LO 2, 3, 8), AP

Instructions
(Round to two decimals.)
(a) Compute (1) the cash payback period and (2) the annual rate of return on the proposed capital expenditure.
(b) Using the discounted cash flow technique, compute the net present value.

E24-11 BAP Corporation is reviewing an investment proposal. The initial cost and estimates of the book value of the investment at the end of each year, the net cash flows for each year, and the net income for each year are presented in the schedule below. All cash flows are assumed to take place at the end of the year. The salvage value of the investment at the end of each year is equal to its book value. There would be no salvage value at the end of the investment's life.

Calculate payback, annual rate of return, and net present value.
(LO 2, 3, 8), AP

Investment Proposal

Year	Initial Cost and Book Value	Annual Cash Flows	Annual Net Income
0	$105,000		
1	70,000	$45,000	$10,000
2	42,000	40,000	12,000
3	21,000	35,000	14,000
4	7,000	30,000	16,000
5	0	25,000	18,000

BAP Corporation uses a 12% target rate of return for new investment proposals.

Instructions
(a) What is the cash payback period for this proposal?
(b) What is the annual rate of return for the investment?
(c) What is the net present value of the investment?

(CMA-Canada adapted)

Exercises: Set B and Challenge Exercises

Visit the book's companion website, at **www.wiley.com/college/kimmel**, and choose the Student Companion site to access Exercise Set B and Challenge Exercises.

Problems: Set A

Compute annual rate of return, cash payback, and net present value.
(LO 2, 3, 8), **AN**

P24-1A   Henkel Company is considering three long-term capital investment proposals. Each investment has a useful life of 5 years. Relevant data on each project are as follows.

	Project Kilo	**Project Lima**	**Project Oscar**
Capital investment	$150,000	$165,000	$200,000
Annual net income:			
Year 1	14,000	18,000	27,000
2	14,000	17,000	23,000
3	14,000	16,000	21,000
4	14,000	12,000	13,000
5	14,000	9,000	12,000
Total	$ 70,000	$ 72,000	$ 96,000

Depreciation is computed by the straight-line method with no salvage value. The company's cost of capital is 15%. (Assume that cash flows occur evenly throughout the year.)

Instructions
(a) Compute the cash payback period for each project. (Round to two decimals.)
(b) Compute the net present value for each project. (Round to nearest dollar.)
(c) Compute the annual rate of return for each project. (Round to two decimals.) (*Hint:* Use average annual net income in your computation.)
(d) Rank the projects on each of the foregoing bases. Which project do you recommend?

(b) L $(4,016); O $2,163

Compute annual rate of return, cash payback, and net present value.
(LO 2, 3, 8), **AN**

P24-2A   Lon Timur is an accounting major at a midwestern state university located approximately 60 miles from a major city. Many of the students attending the university are from the metropolitan area and visit their homes regularly on the weekends. Lon, an entrepreneur at heart, realizes that few good commuting alternatives are available for students doing weekend travel. He believes that a weekend commuting service could be organized and run profitably from several suburban and downtown shopping mall locations. Lon has gathered the following investment information.

1. Five used vans would cost a total of $75,000 to purchase and would have a 3-year useful life with negligible salvage value. Lon plans to use straight-line depreciation.
2. Ten drivers would have to be employed at a total payroll expense of $48,000.
3. Other annual out-of-pocket expenses associated with running the commuter service would include Gasoline $16,000, Maintenance $3,300, Repairs $4,000, Insurance $4,200, Advertising $2,500.
4. Lon has visited several financial institutions to discuss funding. The best interest rate he has been able to negotiate is 15%. Use this rate for cost of capital.
5. Lon expects each van to make ten round trips weekly and carry an average of six students each trip. The service is expected to operate 30 weeks each year, and each student will be charged $12.00 for a round-trip ticket.

Instructions
(a) (1) $5,000

(b) (1) 2.5 years

(a) Determine the annual (1) net income and (2) net annual cash flows for the commuter service.
(b) Compute (1) the cash payback period and (2) the annual rate of return. (Round to two decimals.)
(c) Compute the net present value of the commuter service. (Round to the nearest dollar.)
(d) ▄▄▄➤ What should Lon conclude from these computations?

P24-3A Goltra Clinic is considering investing in new heart-monitoring equipment. It has two options: Option A would have an initial lower cost but would require a significant expenditure for rebuilding after 4 years. Option B would require no rebuilding expenditure, but its maintenance costs would be higher. Since the Option B machine is of initial higher quality, it is expected to have a salvage value at the end of its useful life. The following estimates were made of the cash flows. The company's cost of capital is 8%.

Compute net present value, profitability index, and internal rate of return.

(LO 3, 5, 7), **AN**

	Option A	Option B
Initial cost	$160,000	$227,000
Annual cash inflows	$70,000	$80,000
Annual cash outflows	$30,000	$26,000
Cost to rebuild (end of year 4)	$50,000	$0
Salvage value	$0	$8,000
Estimated useful life	7 years	7 years

Instructions
(a) Compute the (1) net present value, (2) profitability index, and (3) internal rate of return for each option. (*Hint:* To solve for internal rate of return, experiment with alternative discount rates to arrive at a net present value of zero.)
(b) Which option should be accepted?

(a) (1) NPV A $11,503
(3) IRR B 15%

P24-4A Jane's Auto Care is considering the purchase of a new tow truck. The garage doesn't currently have a tow truck, and the $60,000 price tag for a new truck would represent a major expenditure. Jane Austen, owner of the garage, has compiled the estimates shown below in trying to determine whether the tow truck should be purchased.

Compute net present value considering intangible benefits.

(LO 3, 4), **E**

Initial cost	$60,000
Estimated useful life	8 years
Net annual cash flows from towing	$8,000
Overhaul costs (end of year 4)	$6,000
Salvage value	$12,000

Jane's good friend, Rick Ryan, stopped by. He is trying to convince Jane that the tow truck will have other benefits that Jane hasn't even considered. First, he says, cars that need towing need to be fixed. Thus, when Jane tows them to her facility, her repair revenues will increase. Second, he notes that the tow truck could have a plow mounted on it, thus saving Jane the cost of plowing her parking lot. (Rick will give her a used plow blade for free if Jane will plow Rick's driveway.) Third, he notes that the truck will generate goodwill; people who are rescued by Jane's tow truck will feel grateful and might be more inclined to use her service station in the future or buy gas there. Fourth, the tow truck will have "Jane's Auto Care" on its doors, hood, and back tailgate—a form of free advertising wherever the tow truck goes. Rick estimates that, at a minimum, these benefits would be worth the following.

Additional annual net cash flows from repair work	$3,000
Annual savings from plowing	750
Additional annual net cash flows from customer "goodwill"	1,000
Additional annual net cash flows resulting from free advertising	750

The company's cost of capital is 9%.

Instructions
(a) Calculate the net present value, ignoring the additional benefits described by Rick. Should the tow truck be purchased?
(b) Calculate the net present value, incorporating the additional benefits suggested by Rick. Should the tow truck be purchased?
(c) Suppose Rick has been overly optimistic in his assessment of the value of the additional benefits. At a minimum, how much would the additional benefits have to be worth in order for the project to be accepted?

(a) NPV $(13,950)

(b) NPV $16,491

P24-5A Goldbloom Corp. is thinking about opening a soccer camp in southern California. To start the camp, Goldbloom would need to purchase land and build four soccer fields and a sleeping and dining facility to house 150 soccer players. Each year, the camp would be run for 8 sessions of 1 week each. The company would hire college soccer players as coaches. The camp attendees would be male and female soccer players ages 12–18. Property values in southern California have enjoyed a steady increase in value. It

Compute net present value and internal rate of return with sensitivity analysis.

(LO 3, 7), **E**

is expected that after using the facility for 20 years, Goldbloom can sell the property for more than it was originally purchased for. The following amounts have been estimated.

Cost of land	$300,000
Cost to build soccer fields, dorm and dining facility	$600,000
Annual cash inflows assuming 150 players and 8 weeks	$940,000
Annual cash outflows	$840,000
Estimated useful life	20 years
Salvage value	$1,500,000
Discount rate	8%

Instructions

(a) NPV $403,640

(a) Calculate the net present value of the project.

(b) To gauge the sensitivity of the project to these estimates, assume that if only 125 players attend each week, annual cash inflows will be $800,000 and annual cash outflows will be $750,000. What is the net present value using these alternative estimates? Discuss your findings.

(c) Assuming the original facts, what is the net present value if the project is actually riskier than first assumed and an 11% discount rate is more appropriate?

(d) IRR 12%

(d) Assume that during the first 5 years, the annual net cash flows each year were only $40,000. At the end of the fifth year, the company is running low on cash, so management decides to sell the property for $1,332,000. What was the actual internal rate of return on the project? Explain how this return was possible given that the camp did not appear to be successful.

Problems: Set B

Compute annual rate of return, cash payback, and net present value.

(LO 2, 3, 8), **AN**

P24-1B The Borders and Noble partnership is considering three long-term capital investment proposals. Each investment has a useful life of 5 years. Relevant data on each project are as follows.

	Project Mary	Project Winnie	Project Sarah
Capital investment	$140,000	$175,000	$190,000
Annual net income:			
Year 1	$10,000	$12,500	$19,000
2	10,000	12,000	16,000
3	10,000	11,000	14,000
4	10,000	8,000	9,000
5	10,000	6,000	8,000
Total	$50,000	$49,500	$66,000

Depreciation is computed by the straight-line method with no salvage value. The company's cost of capital is 12%. (Assume cash flows occur evenly throughout the year.)

Instructions

(a) Compute the cash payback period for each project. (Round to two decimals.)

(b) M $(3,018); S $(3,075)

(b) Compute the net present value for each project. (Round to nearest dollar.)

(c) Compute the annual rate of return for each project. (Round to two decimals.) (*Hint:* Use average annual net income in your computation.)

(d) Rank the projects on each of the foregoing bases. Which project do you recommend?

Compute annual rate of return, cash payback, and net present value.

(LO 2, 3, 8), **AN**

P24-2B Ben Paul is an accounting major at a western university located approximately 60 miles from a major city. Many of the students attending the university are from the metropolitan area and visit their homes regularly on the weekends. Ben, an entrepreneur at heart, realizes that few good commuting alternatives are available for students doing weekend travel. He believes that a weekend commuting service could be organized and run profitably from several suburban and downtown shopping mall locations. Ben has gathered the following investment information.

1. Five used vans would cost a total of $90,000 to purchase and would have a 3-year useful life with negligible salvage value. Ben plans to use straight-line depreciation.

2. Ten drivers would have to be employed at a total payroll expense of $43,000.

3. Other annual out-of-pocket expenses associated with running the commuter service would include Gasoline $26,000, Maintenance $4,000, Repairs $5,300, Insurance $4,500, Advertising $2,200.
4. Ben desires to earn a return of 15% on his investment.
5. Ben expects each van to make ten round trips weekly and carry an average of six students each trip. The service is expected to operate 32 weeks each year, and each student will be charged $15 for a round-trip ticket.

Instructions
(a) Determine the annual (1) net income and (2) net annual cash flows for the commuter service.

(a) (1) $29,000

(b) Compute (1) the cash payback period and (2) the annual rate of return. (Round to two decimals.)

(b) (1) 1.53 years

(c) Compute the net present value of the commuter service. (Round to the nearest dollar.)
(d) ━━▶ What should Ben conclude from these computations?

P24-3B Platteville Eye Clinic is considering investing in new optical-scanning equipment. It has two options: Option A would have an initial lower cost but would require a significant expenditure for rebuilding after 3 years. Option B would require no rebuilding expenditure, but its maintenance costs would be higher. Since the Option B machine is of initial higher quality, it is expected to have a salvage value at the end of its useful life. The following estimates were made of the cash flows. The company's cost of capital is 11%.

Compute net present value, profitability index, and internal rate of return.
(LO 3, 5, 7), **AN**

	Option A	Option B
Initial cost	$100,000	$160,000
Annual cash inflows	$56,000	$60,000
Annual cash outflows	$24,000	$24,000
Cost to rebuild (end of year 3)	$53,000	$0
Salvage value	$0	$24,000
Estimated useful life	6 years	6 years

Instructions
(a) Compute the (1) net present value, (2) profitability index, and (3) internal rate of return for each option. (*Hint:* To solve for internal rate of return, experiment with alternative discount rates to arrive at a net present value of zero.)
(b) Which option should be accepted?

(a) (1) NPV A $(3,376)
(3) IRR B 12%

P24-4B Isaac's Auto Repair is considering the purchase of a new tow truck. The garage doesn't currently have a tow truck, and the $65,000 price tag for a new truck would represent a major expenditure for the garage. Isaac Mayer, owner of the garage, has compiled the following estimates in trying to determine whether to purchase the truck.

Compute net present value considering intangible benefits.
(LO 3, 4), **E**

Initial cost	$65,000
Estimated useful life	8 years
Net annual cash inflows from towing	$9,600
Overhaul costs (end of year 4)	$7,000
Salvage value	$16,000

Isaac's good friend, Brad Jolie, stopped by. He is trying to convince Isaac that the tow truck will have other benefits that Isaac hasn't even considered. First, he says, cars that need towing need to be fixed. Thus, when Isaac tows them to his facility his repair revenues will increase. Second, he notes that the tow truck could have a plow mounted on it, thus saving Isaac the cost of plowing his parking lot. (Brad will give him a used plow blade for free if Isaac will plow Brad's driveway.) Third, he notes that the truck will generate goodwill; that is, people who are rescued by Isaac and his tow truck will feel grateful and might be more inclined to use his service station in the future or buy gas there. Fourth, the tow truck will have "Isaac's Auto Repair" on its doors, hood, and back tailgate—a form of free advertising wherever the tow truck goes.

Brad estimates that, at a minimum, these benefits would be worth the following.

Additional annual net cash flows from repair work	$2,600
Annual savings from plowing	600
Additional annual net cash flows from customer "goodwill"	1,200
Additional annual net cash flows resulting from free advertising	500

The company's cost of capital is 10%.

Instructions

(a) NPV $(11,102)

(a) Calculate the net present value, ignoring the additional benefits described by Brad. Should the tow truck be purchased?

(b) NPV $15,039

(b) Calculate the net present value, incorporating the additional benefits suggested by Brad. Should the tow truck be purchased?

(c) Suppose Brad has been overly optimistic in his assessment of the value of the additional benefits. At a minimum, how much would the additional benefits have to be worth in order for the project to be accepted?

Compute net present value and internal rate of return with sensitivity analysis.

(LO 3, 7), **E**

P24-5B Lewis Corp. is thinking about opening a basketball camp in Texas. In order to start the camp, the company would need to purchase land and build eight basketball courts and a dormitory-type sleeping and dining facility to house 110 basketball players. Each year, the camp would be run for 8 sessions of 1 week each. The company would hire college basketball players as coaches. The camp attendees would be male and female basketball players ages 12 to 18. Property values in Texas have enjoyed a steady increase in value. It is expected that after using the facility for 20 years, Lewis can sell the property for more than it was originally purchased for. The amounts shown below have been estimated.

Cost of land	$200,000
Cost to build dorm and dining facility	$350,000
Annual cash inflows assuming 110 players and 8 weeks	$700,000
Annual cash outflows	$570,000
Estimated useful life	20 years
Salvage value	$700,000
Discount rate	12%

Instructions

(a) NPV $493,596

(a) Calculate the net present value of the project.

(b) To gauge the sensitivity of the project to these estimates, assume that if only 90 campers attend each week, annual cash inflows will be $570,000 and annual cash outflows will be $508,000. What is the net present value using these alternative estimates? Discuss your findings.

(c) Assuming the original facts, what is the net present value if the project is actually riskier than first assumed, and a 15% discount rate is more appropriate?

(d) IRR 15%

(d) Assume that during the first 5 years the annual net cash inflows each year were only $65,000. At the end of the fifth year, the company is running low on cash, so management decides to sell the property for $668,000. What was the actual internal rate of return on the project? Explain how this return was possible given that the camp did not appear to be successful.

Problems: Set C

Visit the book's companion website, at **www.wiley.com/college/kimmel**, and choose the Student Companion site to access Problem Set C.

Waterways Continuing Problem

(This is a continuation of the Waterways Problem from Chapters 14 through 23.)

WCP24 Waterways Corporation puts much emphasis on cash flow when it plans for capital investments. The company chose its discount rate of 8% based on the rate of return it must pay its owners and creditors. Using that rate, Waterways then uses different methods to determine the best decisions for making capital outlays. Waterways is considering buying five new backhoes to replace the backhoes it now has. This problem asks you to evaluate that decision, using various capital budgeting techniques.

Go to the book's companion website, at **www.wiley.com/college/kimmel**, to find the remainder of this problem.

Broadening Your Perspective

Management Decision-Making

DECISION-MAKING AT CURRENT DESIGNS

BYP24-1 A company that manufactures recreational pedal boats has approached Mike Cichanowski to ask if he would be interested in using Current Designs' rotomold expertise and equipment to produce some of the pedal boat components. Mike is intrigued by the idea and thinks it would be an interesting way of complementing the present product line.

One of Mike's hesitations about the proposal is that the pedal boats are a different shape than the kayaks that Current Designs produces. As a result, the company would need to buy an additional rotomold oven in order to produce the pedal boat components. This project clearly involves risks, and Mike wants to make sure that the returns justify the risks. In this case, since this is a new venture, Mike thinks that a 15% discount rate is appropriate to use to evaluate the project.

As an intern at Current Designs, Mike has asked you to prepare an initial evaluation of this proposal. To aid in your analysis, he has provided the following information and assumptions.

1. The new rotomold oven will have a cost of $256,000, a salvage value of $0, and an 8-year useful life. Straight-line depreciation will be used.
2. The projected revenues, costs, and results for each of the 8 years of this project are as follows.

Sales		$220,000
Less:		
Manufacturing costs	$140,000	
Depreciation	32,000	
Shipping and administrative costs	22,000	194,000
Income before income taxes		26,000
Income tax expense		10,800
Net income		$ 15,200

Instructions
(a) Compute the annual rate of return. (Round to two decimal places.)
(b) Compute the payback period. (Round to two decimal places.)
(c) Compute the NPV using a discount rate of 9%. (Round to nearest dollar.) Should the proposal be accepted using this discount rate?
(d) Compute the NPV using a discount rate of 15%. (Round to nearest dollar.) Should the proposal be accepted using this discount rate?

DECISION-MAKING ACROSS THE ORGANIZATION

BYP24-2 Luang Company is considering the purchase of a new machine. Its invoice price is $122,000, freight charges are estimated to be $3,000, and installation costs are expected to be $5,000. Salvage value of the new machine is expected to be zero after a useful life of 4 years. Existing equipment could be retained and used for an additional 4 years if the new machine is not purchased. At that time, the salvage value of the equipment would be zero. If the new machine is purchased now, the existing machine would be scrapped. Luang's accountant, Lisa Hsung, has accumulated the following data regarding annual sales and expenses with and without the new machine.

1. Without the new machine, Luang can sell 10,000 units of product annually at a per unit selling price of $100. If the new unit is purchased, the number of units produced and sold would increase by 25%, and the selling price would remain the same.
2. The new machine is faster than the old machine, and it is more efficient in its usage of materials. With the old machine the gross profit rate will be 28.5% of sales, whereas the rate will be 30% of sales with the new machine.
3. Annual selling expenses are $160,000 with the current equipment. Because the new equipment would produce a greater number of units to be sold, annual selling expenses are expected to increase by 10% if it is purchased.

4. Annual administrative expenses are expected to be $100,000 with the old machine, and $112,000 with the new machine.

5. The current book value of the existing machine is $40,000. Luang uses straight-line depreciation.

6. Luang's management has a required rate of return of 15% on its investment and a cash payback period of no more than 3 years.

Instructions

With the class divided into groups, answer the following. (Ignore income tax effects.)

(a) Calculate the annual rate of return for the new machine. (Round to two decimals.)

(b) Compute the cash payback period for the new machine. (Round to two decimals.)

(c) Compute the net present value of the new machine. (Round to the nearest dollar.)

(d) On the basis of the foregoing data, would you recommend that Luang buy the machine? Why?

MANAGERIAL ANALYSIS

BYP24-3 Hawke Skateboards is considering building a new plant. Bob Skerritt, the company's marketing manager, is an enthusiastic supporter of the new plant. Lucy Liu, the company's chief financial officer, is not so sure that the plant is a good idea. Currently, the company purchases its skateboards from foreign manufacturers. The following figures were estimated regarding the construction of a new plant.

Cost of plant	$4,000,000	Estimated useful life	15 years
Annual cash inflows	4,000,000	Salvage value	$2,000,000
Annual cash outflows	3,540,000	Discount rate	11%

Bob Skerritt believes that these figures understate the true potential value of the plant. He suggests that by manufacturing its own skateboards the company will benefit from a "buy American" patriotism that he believes is common among skateboarders. He also notes that the firm has had numerous quality problems with the skateboards manufactured by its suppliers. He suggests that the inconsistent quality has resulted in lost sales, increased warranty claims, and some costly lawsuits. Overall, he believes sales will be $200,000 higher than projected above, and that the savings from lower warranty costs and legal costs will be $60,000 per year. He also believes that the project is not as risky as assumed above, and that a 9% discount rate is more reasonable.

Instructions

Answer each of the following.

(a) Compute the net present value of the project based on the original projections.

(b) Compute the net present value incorporating Bob's estimates of the value of the intangible benefits, but still using the 11% discount rate.

(c) Compute the net present value using the original estimates, but employing the 9% discount rate that Bob suggests is more appropriate.

(d) Comment on your findings.

REAL-WORLD FOCUS

BYP24-4 Tecumseh Products Company has its headquarters in Tecumseh, Michigan. It describes itself as "a global multinational corporation producing mechanical and electrical components essential to industries creating end-products for health, comfort, and convenience." The following was excerpted from the management discussion and analysis section of a recent annual report.

TECUMSEH PRODUCTS COMPANY
Management Discussion and Analysis

The company has invested approximately $50 million in a scroll compressor manufacturing facility in Tecumseh, Michigan. After experiencing setbacks in developing a commercially acceptable scroll compressor, the Company is currently testing a new generation of scroll product. The Company is unable to predict when, or if, it will offer a scroll compressor for commercial sale, but it does anticipate that reaching volume production will require a significant additional investment. Given such additional investment and current market conditions, management is currently reviewing its options with respect to scroll product improvement, cost reductions, joint ventures and alternative new products.

Instructions

Discuss issues the company should consider and techniques the company should employ to determine whether to continue pursuing this project.

BYP24-5   Campbell Soup Company is an international provider of soup products. Management is very interested in continuing to grow the company in its core business, while "spinning off" those businesses that are not part of its core operation.

Address: **www.campbellsoups.com**, or go to **www.wiley.com/college/kimmel**

Steps
1. Go to the home page of Campbell Soup Company at the address shown above.
2. Choose the current annual report.

Instructions

Review the financial statements and management's discussion and analysis, and answer the following questions.

(a) What was the total amount of capital expenditures in the current year, and how does this amount compare with the previous year?
(b) What interest rate did the company pay on new borrowings in the current year?
(c) Assume that this year's capital expenditures are expected to increase cash flows by $42 million. What is the expected internal rate of return (IRR) for these capital expenditures? (Assume a 10-year period for the cash flows.)

Critical Thinking

COMMUNICATION ACTIVITY

BYP24-6   Refer back to E24-9 to address the following.

Instructions

Prepare a memo to Maria Fierro, your supervisor. Show your calculations from E24-9, (a) and (b). In one or two paragraphs, discuss important nonfinancial considerations. Make any assumptions you believe to be necessary. Make a recommendation based on your analysis.

ETHICS CASE

BYP24-7   NuComp Company operates in a state where corporate taxes and workers' compensation insurance rates have recently doubled. NuComp's president has just assigned you the task of preparing an economic analysis and making a recommendation relative to moving the entire operation to Missouri. The president is slightly in favor of such a move because Missouri is his boyhood home and he also owns a fishing lodge there.

You have just completed building your dream house, moved in, and sodded the lawn. Your children are all doing well in school and sports and, along with your spouse, want no part of a move to Missouri. If the company does move, so will you because the town is a one-industry community and you and your spouse will have to move to have employment. Moving when everyone else does will cause you to take a big loss on the sale of your house. The same hardships will be suffered by your coworkers, and the town will be devastated.

In compiling the costs of moving versus not moving, you have latitude in the assumptions you make, the estimates you compute, and the discount rates and time periods you project. You are in a position to influence the decision singlehandedly.

Instructions

(a) Who are the stakeholders in this situation?
(b) What are the ethical issues in this situation?
(c) What would you do in this situation?

ALL ABOUT YOU

BYP24-8   Numerous articles have been written that identify early warning signs that you might be getting into trouble with your personal debt load. You can find many good articles on this topic on the Web.

Instructions
Find an article that identifies early warning signs of personal debt trouble. Write up a summary of the article and bring your summary and the article to class to share.

CONSIDERING YOUR COSTS AND BENEFITS

BYP24-9 The March 31, 2011, edition of the *Wall Street Journal* includes an article by Russell Gold entitled "Solar Gains Traction—Thanks to Subsidies."

Instructions
Read the article and answer the following questions.

(a) What was the total cost of the solar panels installed? What was the "out-of-pocket" cost to the couple?

(b) Using the total annual electricity bill of $5,000 mentioned in the story, what is the cash payback of the project using the total cost? What is the cash payback based on the "out-of-pocket" cost?

(c) Solar panel manufactures estimate that solar panels can last up to 40 years with only minor maintenance costs. Assuming no maintenance costs, a 6% rate of interest, a more conservative 20-year life, and zero salvage value, what is the net present value of the project based on the total cost? What is the net present value of the project based on the "out-of-pocket" cost?

(d) What was the wholesale price of panels per watt at the time the article was written? At what price per watt does the article say that subsidies will no longer be needed? Does this price appear to be achievable?

Answers to Insight and Accounting Across the Organization Questions

p. 1252 Can You Hear Me–Better? Q: Based on the potentially slow initial adoption of 4G by customers, how might the conclusions of a cash payback analysis of Verizon's 4G investment differ from a present value analysis? **A:** If the initial adoption of 4G by customers is slow, then the amount of cash received in the early years will be low. This would lengthen the cash payback period, making it unlikely that the investment would get high marks with this test. However, the long-run potential of 4G is probably quite high as more people switch to smart phones and consequently increase their use of services that benefit from a high-speed connection. These later cash flows may well be large enough that they provide a positive net present value amount.

p. 1257 It Need Not Cost an Arm and a Leg Q: In addition to the obvious humanitarian benefit of reducing serious injuries, how else might the manufacturer of this product convince potential customers of its worth? **A:** Serious injuries cost employers huge sums, which can sometimes force small companies out of business. In addition to the obvious humanitarian benefit, the manufacturer can demonstrate that this device is a sound financial investment in terms of reduced health-care and workers' compensation costs and fewer hours missed due to injury. Also, as the device gains wider acceptance, employers that do not have the device may ultimately be found negligent with regard to worker safety.

p. 1259 Wide-Screen Capacity Q: What implications does the excess capacity have for the cash payback and net present value calculations of these investments? **A:** Because the companies have excess capacity, they are not selling as many units as expected. Also, to increase sales, they are being forced to cut selling prices in order to sell units. Therefore, the revenues that they generate are lower than the amounts that would have been estimated when the plants were planned and built. This means that cash payback periods are longer and net present values are lower than desired levels.

p. 1260 Seeing the Big Picture Q: How important is the choice of discount rate in making capital budgeting decisions? **A:** The point of this discussion is that errors in implementation, as well as the accuracy of the estimated future benefits and costs as measured by cash inflows and outflows, are what matter the most when making capital expenditure decisions. While the choice of discount rates will result in incremental differences in present value calculations, "missing the big picture" has the potential to cause much bigger decision errors. Underestimating potential future cash inflows can result in missed opportunities. Underestimating future costs can result in failed investments.

Answers to Self-Test Questions

1. d **2.** c **3.** d **4.** b ($48,000 ÷ $7,000) > ($75,000 ÷ $12,000) **5.** a **6.** b **7.** d
8. d **9.** c **10.** c ($18,112 + $80,000) ÷ $80,000 **11.** a **12.** c **13.** d ($60,000 ÷ $15,400) = IRR factor **14.** d **15.** a $15,000 ÷ [($120,000 + $20,000) ÷ 2]

✔ **Remember to go back to The Navigator box on the chapter opening page and check off your completed work.**

SPECIMEN FINANCIAL STATEMENTS: TOOTSIE ROLL INDUSTRIES, INC.

The Annual Report

Once each year, a corporation communicates to its stockholders and other interested parties by issuing a complete set of audited financial statements. The **annual report**, as this communication is called, summarizes the financial results of the company's operations for the year and its plans for the future. Many annual reports are attractive, multicolored, glossy public relations pieces, containing pictures of corporate officers and directors as well as photos and descriptions of new products and new buildings. Yet the basic function of every annual report is to report financial information, almost all of which is produced by the corporation's accounting system.

The content and organization of corporate annual reports have become fairly standardized. Excluding the public relations part of the report (pictures, products, and propaganda), the following items are the traditional financial portions of the annual report:

> Financial Highlights
> Letter to the Stockholders
> Management's Discussion and Analysis
> Financial Statements
> Notes to the Financial Statements
> Management's Report on Internal Control
> Management Certification of Financial Statements
> Auditor's Report
> Supplementary Financial Information

In this appendix, we illustrate current financial reporting with a comprehensive set of corporate financial statements that are prepared in accordance with generally accepted accounting principles and audited by an international independent certified public accounting firm. We are grateful for permission to use the actual financial statements and other accompanying financial information from the annual report of a large, publicly held company, Tootsie Roll Industries, Inc.

The financial information herein is reprinted with permission from the Tootsie Roll Industries, Inc. 2011 Annual Report. The complete financial statements for Tootsie Roll Industries are also available on the book's companion website at **www.wiley.com/college/kimmel**.

Corporate Profile

Tootsie Roll Industries, Inc. has been engaged in the manufacture and sale of confectionery products for 115 years. Our products are primarily sold under the familiar brand names: Tootsie Roll, Tootsie Roll Pops, Caramel Apple Pops, Child's Play, Charms, Blow Pop, Blue Razz, Cella's chocolate covered cherries, Tootsie Dots, Tootsie Crows, Junior Mints, Junior Caramels, Charleston Chew, Sugar Daddy, Sugar Babies, Andes, Fluffy Stuff cotton candy, Dubble Bubble, Razzles, Cry Baby, Nik-L-Nip and EI Bubble.

Melvin J. Gordon, Chairman and Chief Executive Officer and Ellen R. Gordon, President and Chief Operating Officer.

Corporate Principles

We believe that the differences among companies are attributable to the caliber of their people, and therefore we strive to attract and retain superior people for each job.

We believe that an open family atmosphere at work combined with professional management fosters cooperation and enables each individual to maximize his or her contribution to the Company and realize the corresponding rewards.

We do not jeopardize long-term growth for immediate, short-term results.

We maintain a conservative financial posture in the deployment and management of our assets.

We run a trim operation and continually strive to eliminate waste, minimize cost and implement performance improvements.

We invest in the latest and most productive equipment to deliver the best quality product to our customers at the lowest cost.

We seek to outsource functions where appropriate and to vertically integrate operations where it is financially advantageous to do so.

We view our well known brands as prized assets to be aggressively advertised and promoted to each new generation of consumers.

We conduct business with the highest ethical standards and integrity which are codified in the Company's "Code of Business Conduct and Ethics."

Letter to the Stockholders

Nearly every annual report contains a letter to the stockholders from the chairman of the board or the president, or both. This letter typically discusses the company's accomplishments during the past year and highlights significant events such as mergers and acquisitions, new products, operating achievements, business philosophy, changes in officers or directors, financing commitments, expansion plans, and future prospects. The letter to the stockholders signed by Melvin J. Gordon, Chairman of the Board and Chief Executive Officer, and Ellen R. Gordon, President and Chief Operating Officer, of Tootsie Roll Industries is shown on the next pages.

To Our Shareholders

Net product sales in 2011 were a record $528 million, surpassing the previous record of $517 million set in 2010. The Company had another strong Halloween selling season and sales gains were achieved across many of our core brands. Sales benefited from successful promotional programs, new distribution and selected price increases.

Net earnings in 2011 were $44 million compared to $53 million in 2010. The decline in net earnings is primarily due to significantly higher raw material and packaging costs in 2011. While we endeavor to maintain the Company's profitability by adjusting prices in response to rising costs, we are mindful of the competitive value positioning of our products in the market place. We also remain true to the principles enumerated on the facing page, which have guided the Company for many years.

We focus in particular on the principles of taking a long-term perspective, reinvesting in our operations and our brands and maintaining a conservative financial posture. We believe that these principles have served the Company and its shareholders well over the years and we remain committed to them.

Financial Highlights

	December 31,	
	2011	**2010**
	(in thousands except per share data)	
Net Product Sales	$528,369	$517,149
Net Earnings	43,938	53,063
Working Capital	153,846	176,662
Net Property, Plant and Equipment	212,162	215,492
Shareholders' Equity	665,935	667,408
Average Shares Outstanding*	57,892	58,685
Per Share Items*		
Net Earnings	$ 0.76	$ 0.90
Cash Dividends Paid	.32	.32

*Adjusted for stock dividends.

Highlights in 2011 include:

- $16 million was invested in capital expenditures for property, plant and equipment.
- Cash dividends were paid for the sixty-ninth consecutive year.
- Our forty-seventh consecutive annual 3% stock dividend was distributed.
- 708,235 shares of our common stock were repurchased in the open market for an aggregate price of $18 million.
- The above actions were taken entirely with internally generated funds, and the Company remains essentially debt free.

As of December 31, 2011, the Company had $186 million in cash and investments. These financial resources enable us to continue distributing cash dividends to our shareholders, repurchasing our stock on the open market and reinvesting in operating assets and in our brands, including new products. We are also prepared to consider and respond to appropriate business acquisition opportunities as they may arise.

Sales and Marketing

Consumers have many tempting choices in the candy aisle and retailers are highly selective as to the products they stock. We have found that consumers respond well to the many high quality/high value brands in our portfolio. Additionally, the high percentage of sell-throughs and attractive margins of our items are appealing to the trade. This was evident once again in 2011. We used carefully targeted promotional initiatives to help move our products into distribution and to subsequently move them off the retail shelf. Our diverse portfolio of highly recognizable brands remains popular across all channels of trade.

Our broad range of offerings includes something for virtually every major consumer demographic, which we continue to refine and evolve to meet changing consumer preferences and the demands of the trade in today's fluctuating market place. We remain vigilant in keeping our products contemporary even as they retain their iconic character.

Halloween is a major selling season in our primary market, the United States, for a number of product categories including candy. It is a magical time of fun, family togetherness, gatherings and parties, evoking feelings of excitement and nostalgia. Our sales in the third quarter are centered on this popular holiday and are nearly double those of any other quarter during the year.

In 2011, we posted strong Halloween sales in the grocery, mass merchandiser, warehouse club, dollar store and drug store classes of trade. Our line of packaged goods, including straight goods as well as large bags of Child's Play and other mixed assortments, are offered in a number of merchandising presentations and are especially popular during this season. Other traditional merchandising presentations such as shippers, pallet packs and display ready cases contributed to Halloween sales.

Outside of Halloween, we continued our position of leadership in the theater box category. This category is no longer limited to the "big screen" venue and has developed into a major format for everyday candy purchases. Two new offerings in this important category were added to our line in 2011.

Blow Pop Minis' New Theater Box

Blow Pop Minis, bite-sized candy tablets, each with a real Blow Pop bubble gum center, were extended into the theater box format. Popular and portable, this "Blow Pop with no stick!" includes four of the most popular Blow Pop flavors in each box, enveloped in a protective sealed pouch for added freshness. Blow Pop Minis continue to be a sales growth driver.

Raspberry Cremes

Another winning addition to our theater box line was Tootsie Roll Raspberry Cremes. These delicious morsels feature a luscious, creamy raspberry center encased in a thin shell of pure dark chocolate. A perfect snacking indulgence for people on the go!

Tear Jerker Mini Pops

We also extended our market leadership position in the lollipop category with the introduction of Tear Jerkers Mini Pops. This exciting new addition to our bagged line packs a super sour punch into each pop! The assortment includes six tangy flavors in a laydown bag with eye catching graphics and great consumer appeal. Pucker up!

Giant Sugar Daddy

As big as we are in the lollipop category, in 2011 we introduced our biggest entry ever in the category—the Giant Sugar Daddy! This novelty item consists of a full pound of luscious caramel on a real wooden stick packaged in the familiar yellow and red Sugar Daddy wrapper and shape. The Giant Sugar Daddy makes a fun gift or an all-day good treat.

Andes Mint Truffles

The Andes line was expanded with a delicious new seasonal offering. Andes Mint Truffles are beautifully packaged in a festive Christmas-themed red box highlighted with gold ornaments and featuring a decorative green foil tree topper. The individually wrapped treats feature a delicious truffle mint center that melts in your mouth. Perfect for holiday gift giving!

The Dubble Bubble Nostalgic Big Bar was a new addition to the Dubble Bubble line in 2011. The wrapper features nostalgic graphics and is made of foil for lasting freshness. The Big Bar is a foot-long rope of bubble blowing fun.

Dubble Bubble Big Bar

Our popular line of novelty fun banks grew with the addition of two new items in 2011. The Dubble Bubble bank was launched in a patriotic red, white and blue motif and the Tootsie Roll bank took on a nostalgic tone with old-fashioned graphics at a price point that makes it an old-fashioned value. All of our banks feature a slotted lid so when the candy is gone you can begin to save for the next one. Fun you can bank on!

Advertising and Public Relations

Having been described as "elegant in its simplicity" for more than 40 years the Tootsie Pop "How Many Licks?" television ad has presented viewers with both an intriguing challenge and a clear concept of the product and its value proposition to several generations of consumers. In 2011, this ad was showcased in an exhibit at the Chicago Museum of Broadcast Communications.

The iconic ad, featuring the wise old Mr. Owl advising a young boy that indeed three licks was all it took before the inevitable crunch! when he bit his way to the middle of the Tootsie Pop, was culled from over 100,000 spots in the museum's archives and was selected as one of the 100 best commercials over the last six decades.

Dubble Bubble Patriotic and Tootsie Roll Nostalgic Banks

The ad has led to an inestimable number of experiments and trials, ranging from innovative licking machines built by physics students that counted strokes with scientific precision, to informal personal licking trials communicated to us in many thousands of consumer letters. Despite this massive amount of research, the provocative question posed by the announcer: "How many licks does it take to get to the Tootsie Roll center of a Tootsie Pop?" remains unanswered. So, as the commercial states, "the world may never know."

This message has been extended to social media, and in 2011 the Company continued to bring new users into the Tootsie Roll and Tootsie Pops franchises with a digital media campaign targeting moms with kids. Featuring our own "Mr. Owl" character, banner ads, online video ads, and search ads directed consumers to the brands' Facebook pages. There, consumers could send Halloween e-cards featuring our brands, play customized games and share photos and stories with their Facebook friends.

Additionally, several of our products were featured in special interest programs on the History Channel, the Travel Channel and the Food Channel. These programs are quite popular with viewing audiences and are often repeated, generating extensive recurring exposure and interest in the featured brands.

Purchasing

The markets for the majority of the Company's key ingredients, including corn syrup, edible oils, gum base, cocoa powder and sugar, rose sharply to record or near record levels in 2011. Likewise, the cost of many of our principle packaging materials, including corrugated, film and wax paper, increased over 2010. These input cost increases were well in excess of the price increases we implemented in 2011.

Competitive bidding, selective hedging and forward purchasing as well as leveraging our high volume of purchases are some of the means we use to manage costs to the greatest extent possible in an upward commodity and packaging materials price environment.

Operations and Supply Chain

We continue to invest capital and resources in projects that support evolving customer/consumer preferences and distribution patterns, promote growing product lines, improve quality and maximize efficiency across our operations. It is our goal to be the low cost producer in the categories in which we compete. As technology advances, we are constantly on the lookout for new cost saving process enhancements as they become feasible and financially justified.

We have also made a major commitment to information technology, and in 2011 the final phase of a comprehensive enterprise resource planning system was implemented. Investment in leading edge equipment and technology is one of our key corporate principles and we believe it has resulted in the Company's success and profitability over many years.

International

Sales in Mexico declined somewhat and operating income also declined, as price increases taken during the year were not sufficient to recover cost increases. Our export sales to the Canadian market decreased due to inventory reductions by a distributor.

Export sales to other countries were lower in 2011, though we continue to believe that the broad assortment of well-known brands that we offer will, over the long run, appeal to consumers in a variety of foreign markets and venues. Accordingly, we continue to actively cultivate these opportunities in over 40 foreign countries.

In Appreciation

We wish to express our appreciation to our many loyal employees, customers, suppliers, sales brokers and distributors throughout the world for their support during the past year. We also thank our fellow shareholders for their support in today's challenging business environment. We remain committed to the pursuit of excellence in every aspect of our business in order to ensure the Company's success both in the near term and far into the future.

Melvin J Gordon

Melvin J. Gordon
Chairman of the Board and
Chief Executive Officer

Ellen R Gordon

Ellen R. Gordon
President and
Chief Operating Officer

Management Discussion and Analysis

The management discussion and analysis (MD&A) section covers three financial aspects of a company: its results of operations, its ability to pay near-term obligations, and its ability to fund operations and expansion. Management must highlight favorable or unfavorable trends and identify significant events and uncertainties that affect these three factors. This discussion obviously involves a number of subjective estimates and opinions. The MD&A section of Tootsie Roll's annual report is presented below.

Management's Discussion and Analysis of Financial Condition and Results of Operations

(in thousands except per share, percentage and ratio figures)

FINANCIAL REVIEW

This financial review discusses the Company's financial condition, results of operations, liquidity and capital resources, significant accounting policies and estimates, new accounting pronouncements, market risks and other matters. It should be read in conjunction with the Consolidated Financial Statements and related footnotes that follow this discussion.

FINANCIAL CONDITION

The Company's overall financial position remains very strong as a result of its 2011 net product sales, net earnings and related cash flows provided by operating activities.

During 2011, the Company's net product sales increased from $517,149 in 2010 to $528,369 in 2011, an increase of $11,220 or 2.2%. Cash flows from operating activities totaled $50,390 in 2011 compared to $82,805 in 2010. The Company used its 2011 cash flows to pay cash dividends of $18,407, purchase and retire $18,190 of its outstanding shares, and make capital expenditures of $16,351.

The Company's net working capital was $153,846 at December 31, 2011 compared to $176,662 at December 31, 2010 reflecting a $37,364 decrease in cash and cash equivalents. As of December 31, 2011, the Company's aggregate cash, cash equivalents and investments, including all long-term investments in marketable securities, was $185,668 compared to $188,433 at December 31, 2010, a decrease of $2,765. The aforementioned includes $41,768 and $38,504 in trading securities as of December 31, 2011 and 2010, respectively. The Company invests in trading securities to provide an economic hedge for its deferred compensation liabilities, as further discussed herein and in Note 7 to the Consolidated Financial Statements.

Shareholders' equity decreased from $667,408 at December 31, 2010 to $665,935 as of December 31, 2011, principally reflecting 2011 net earnings of $43,938, less cash dividends and share repurchases of $18,407 and $18,190, respectively, and $8,740 of other comprehensive loss which is summarized in Note 12 to the Consolidated Financial Statements.

The Company has a relatively straight-forward financial structure and has historically maintained a conservative financial position. Except for an immaterial amount of operating leases, the Company has no special financing arrangements or "off-balance sheet" special purpose entities. Cash flows from operations plus maturities of short-term investments are expected to be adequate to meet the Company's overall financing needs, including capital expenditures, in 2012. Periodically, the Company considers possible acquisitions, and if the Company were to pursue and complete such an acquisition, that could result in bank borrowings or other financing.

Results of Operations

2011 vs. 2010

Net product sales were $528,369 in 2011 compared to $517,149 in 2010, an increase of $11,220 or 2.2%. This increase principally reflects sales price increases during 2011 which were required to recover some of our rising input costs as discussed below. Although price increases were made throughout 2011, most became effective during mid-fourth quarter 2011 after the Company's large pre-Halloween selling season, and therefore, a substantial portion of the benefits of such price increases will be realized in 2012.

Product cost of goods sold were $365,225 in 2011 compared to $349,334 in 2010, an increase of $15,891 or 4.5%. Product cost of goods sold includes $44 and $770 in certain deferred compensation expenses in 2011 and 2010, respectively. These deferred compensation expenses principally result from changes in the market value of investments and investment income from trading securities relating to compensation deferred in previous years and are not reflective of current operating results. Adjusting for the aforementioned, product cost of goods sold increased from $348,564 in 2010 to $365,181 in 2011, an increase of $16,617 or 4.8%. As a percent of net product sales, these adjusted costs increased from 67.4% in 2010 to 69.1% in 2011, an increase of 1.7% as a percent of net product sales. The Company was adversely affected by significantly higher input costs, including approximately $17,300 and $2,800 of unit cost increases in ingredients and packaging materials, respectively, in 2011 compared to 2010. The Company generally experienced significant cost increases in sugar, corn syrup, cocoa, edible oils, dairy and gum base inputs resulting in higher cost of goods sold as a percentage of sales.

Selling, marketing and administrative expenses were $108,276 in 2011 compared to $106,316 in 2010, an increase of $1,960 or 1.8%. Selling, marketing and administrative expenses reflect a $15 decrease and $2,594 increase in certain deferred compensation expenses in 2011 and 2010, respectively. These deferred compensation expenses principally result from changes in the market value of investments and investment income from trading securities relating to compensation deferred in previous years and are not reflective of current operating results. Adjusting for the aforementioned, selling, marketing and administrative expenses increased from $103,722 in 2010 to $108,291 in 2011, an increase of $4,569 or 4.4%. As a percent of net product sales, these adjusted expenses increased slightly from 20.1% of net product sales in 2010 to 20.5% of net product sales in 2011.

Selling, marketing and administrative expenses include $45,849 and $43,034 of freight, delivery and warehousing expenses in 2011 and 2010, respectively. These expenses increased from 8.3% of net product sales in 2010 to 8.7% of net product sales in 2011, principally reflecting an 8.7% increase in freight and delivery costs for trucking carriers including higher fuel surcharges for diesel fuel.

The Company believes that the carrying values of its trademarks and goodwill have indefinite lives as they are expected to generate cash flows indefinitely. In accordance with current accounting guidance, goodwill and indefinite-lived intangible assets are assessed at least annually for impairment as of December 31 or whenever events or circumstances indicate that the carrying values may not be recoverable from future cash flows. No impairments were recorded in 2011 or 2010.

The fair values of indefinite lived intangible assets are primarily assessed using the present value of estimated future cash flows. Management believes that all assumptions used for the impairment tests are consistent with those utilized by market participants performing similar valuations. The Company's fair value estimates based on these assumptions were used to prepare projected financial information which it believes to be reasonable. Actual future results may differ from those projections and the differences could be material. Holding all other assumptions constant at the test date, a 100 basis point increase in the discount rate or a 100 basis point decrease in the royalty rate would reduce the fair value of certain trademarks by approximately 16% and 11%, respectively. Individually, a 100 basis point increase in the discount rate would indicate a potential impairment of approximately $2,000 as of December 31, 2011; however, if the royalty rate were decreased by 100 basis points no potential impairment would be indicated as of December 31, 2011.

Earnings from operations were $57,966 in 2011 compared to $64,710 in 2010, a decrease of $6,744. Earnings from operations includes $29 and $3,364 in certain deferred compensation expenses in 2011 and 2010, respectively. As discussed above, these deferred compensation expenses relate to changes in deferred compensation liabilities resulting from corresponding changes in the market value of trading securities and related investment income that hedge these liabilities. Adjusting for these deferred compensation expenses, operating earnings were $57,995 and $68,074 in 2011 and 2010, respectively, a decrease of $10,079 or 14.8%. This decrease in earnings from operations principally reflects significantly higher ingredient costs and resulting lower gross profit margins, as well as higher freight and delivery expenses as discussed above.

Management believes the comparisons presented in the preceding paragraphs after adjusting for changes in deferred compensation are more reflective of the underlying operations of the Company.

Other income (expense), net was $2,946 in 2011 compared to $8,358 in 2010, a decrease of $5,412. This decrease principally reflects a $3,335 decrease in net gains and related investment income on trading securities of $29 and $3,364 in 2011 and 2010 which is discussed above. These trading securities were substantially offset by a like amount of expense in aggregate product cost of goods sold and selling, marketing, and administrative expenses in the respective years as discussed above. Foreign exchange gains in 2011 decreased $1,992 which includes a decrease in net realized gains on foreign currency hedging. Other income (expense), net also includes the operating losses of $194 and $342 for 2011 and 2010, respectively, relating to the Company's equity method investment in two 50% owned foreign companies.

As of December 31, 2011 and 2010, the Company's long-term investments include $7,453 and $6,775 ($13,550 original cost), respectively, of Jefferson County Alabama Sewer Revenue Refunding Warrants, originally purchased with an insurance-backed AAA rating. This is an auction rate security (ARS) that is classified as an available for sale security. Representatives of Jefferson County and the bond holders were unable to reach a settlement agreement, and therefore the County filed for bankruptcy in 2011. Due to adverse events related to Jefferson County and its bond insurance carrier, Financial Guaranty Insurance Company (FGIC), as well as events in the credit markets, the auctions for this ARS failed in 2008 through 2011 (and subsequent to December 31, 2011). As such, the Company estimated the fair value of this ARS as of December 31, 2011 and 2010 utilizing a valuation model with Level 3 inputs, as defined by guidance and discussed in Note 10 to the Consolidated Financial Statements. This valuation model considered, among others items, recent third-party trading and sales prices, the credit risk of the municipality and collateral underlying the ARS, the credit risk of the bond insurer, interest rates, and the amount and timing of expected future cash flows including assumptions about the market expectation of the next successful auction or a restructured security that is likely to be issued as a result of the municipality's bankruptcy.

During the fourth quarter of 2008, the Company determined that the market decline in fair value of its Jefferson County ARS became other-than-temporarily impaired, as defined, and recorded a pre-tax impairment of $5,140. During 2011 and 2010, the Company further evaluated this investment and concluded that additional increases and (declines) in the market value were temporary because it was not related to further credit impairment and recorded $678 and $(935), respectively, as adjustments to accumulated other comprehensive gain (loss). The Company has classified this ARS as non-current and has included it in long-term investments on the Consolidated Statements of Financial Position at December 31, 2011 and 2010 because the Company believes that the current financial conditions, including bankruptcy filing, of Jefferson County and the stressed financial condition of FGIC, as well as the conditions in the auction rate securities market, may take more than twelve months to resolve. Future evaluations of the fair value of this ARS could also result in additional other-than-temporary classification of declines in market value, and therefore result in additional charges to earnings. The Company continues to receive all contractual interest payments on this ARS on a timely basis, it is insured by FGIC and the Company has the intent and ability to hold this ARS until recovery of its amortized cost basis. The Company is not currently able to predict the outcome of this bankruptcy, or the amount and timing of net proceeds it may ultimately recover.

The consolidated effective tax rate was 27.9% and 27.4% in 2011 and 2010, respectively. At December 31, 2011, the Company has approximately $66,740 of foreign subsidiary tax loss carry-forwards expiring in future years 2014 through 2031. The Company has concluded that it is more-likely-than-not that it would realize the deferred tax assets relating to such tax operating loss carry-forwards because it is expected that sufficient levels of taxable income will be generated during the carry-forward periods.

Net earnings were $43,938 in 2011 compared to $53,063 in 2010, and earnings per share were $.76 and $.90 in 2011 and 2010, respectively, a decrease of $.14 or 15.6%. Earnings per share benefited from the reduction in average shares outstanding resulting from purchases of the Company's common stock (the "Common Stock") in the open market by the Company. Average shares outstanding decreased from 58,685 in 2010 to 57,892 in 2011.

2010 vs. 2009

Net product sales were $517,149 in 2010 compared to $495,592 in 2009, an increase of $21,557 or 4.3%. This increase principally reflects organic growth in volume, including product line extensions.

Product cost of goods sold were $349,334 in 2010 compared to $319,775 in 2009, an increase of $29,559 or 9.2%. Product cost of goods sold reflects a $228 decrease in certain deferred compensation expenses in 2010 compared to 2009. This decrease principally results from changes in the market value of investments in trading securities relating to compensation deferred in previous years and is not reflective of current operating results. Adjusting for the aforementioned, product cost of goods sold as a percentage of net product sales increased from 64.3% in 2009 to 67.4% in 2010, an increase of 3.1% as a percent of net product sales. The Company was adversely affected by significantly higher input costs, including approximately $16,600 of ingredient unit cost increases in 2010 compared to 2009. However, packaging material unit costs favorably decreased by approximately $800 in 2010. The Company generally experienced significant cost increases in sugar, cocoa, edible oils and dairy inputs, however, the Company experienced favorable declines in corn syrup.

Selling, marketing and administrative expenses were $106,316 in 2010 compared to $103,755 in 2009, an increase of $2,561 or 2.5%. Selling, marketing and administrative expenses reflect a $932 decrease in certain deferred compensation expense in 2010 compared to 2009. This decrease reflects changes in the market value of investments in trading securities and related investment income relating to compensation deferred in previous years and is not reflective of current operating results. Adjusting for the aforementioned, selling, marketing and administrative expenses increased from $100,230 in 2009 to $103,722 in 2010, an increase of $3,492 or 3.5%. As a percent of net product sales, these expenses decreased slightly from 20.2% of net product sales in 2009 to 20.1% of net product sales in 2010.

Selling, marketing and administrative expenses include $43,034 and $38,628 of freight, delivery and warehousing expenses in 2010 and 2009, respectively. These expenses increased from 7.8% of net product sales in 2009 to 8.3% of net product sales in 2010, primarily due to increases in warehousing expenses and an 11.3% increase in freight and delivery costs for trucking carriers including higher surcharges for diesel fuel.

Earnings from operations were $64,710 in 2010 compared to $60,949 in 2009, a decrease of $3,761. Earnings from operations reflect a $3,364 increase in certain deferred compensation expenses in 2010 compared to a $4,524 increase in 2009. As discussed above, these deferred compensation expenses relate to changes in deferred compensation liabilities resulting from corresponding changes in the market value of trading securities and related investment income that hedge these liabilities. Adjusting for these changes in deferred compensation, and excluding the non-recurring $14,000 non-cash impairment charge in 2009 relating to trademarks, operating earnings were $68,074 and $79,473 in 2010 and 2009, respectively, a decrease of $11,399 or 14.3%. This decrease in earnings from operations principally reflects significantly higher ingredient costs and resulting lower gross profit margins, as well as higher freight and delivery expenses as discussed above.

Management believes the comparisons presented in the preceding paragraphs after adjusting for changes in deferred compensation are more reflective of the underlying operations of the Company.

Other income (expense), net was $8,358 in 2010 compared to $2,100 in 2009, an increase of $6,258. This increase principally reflects a pre-tax impairment charge of $4,400 in 2009 to write down to market value the Company's equity method investment combined with a $3,139 increase in foreign exchange gains in 2010. The increase in foreign exchange gains consists primarily of net realized gains on foreign currency hedging. Other income (expense), net also includes gains on trading securities and related investment income of $3,364 and $4,524 in 2010 and 2009, respectively. These trading securities gains principally reflect market appreciation in the equity markets and related investment income in the respective years and were substantially offset by a like amount of expense in aggregate product cost of goods sold and selling, marketing, and administrative expenses in the respective years as discussed above. Other income (expense), net also includes the operating losses of $342 and $233 for 2010 and 2009, respectively, relating to the Company's equity method investment in two 50% owned foreign companies.

As of December 31, 2010 and 2009, the Company's long-term investments include $6,775 and $7,710 ($13,550 original cost), respectively, of Jefferson County Alabama Sewer Revenue Refunding Warrants. The Company estimated the fair value of this ARS as of December 31, 2010 and 2009 utilizing a valuation model with Level 3 inputs, as defined by guidance. During 2010 and 2009, the Company recorded $935 and $700, respectively, as a charge to accumulated other comprehensive loss.

The consolidated effective tax rate was 27.4% and 15.7% in 2010 and 2009, respectively. The increase in the effective income tax rate from the prior year reflects the release of Canadian income tax valuation allowances during 2009. Prior to fourth quarter 2009, Canadian income tax valuation allowances were recorded against Canadian deferred tax assets as a result of losses generated in 2009 and prior years. Because management determined that the Canadian net operating loss (NOL) carry-forward benefits were more-likely-than-not realizable as of December 31, 2009, the Company reversed approximately $10,700 of valuation allowances as a credit to income tax expense as of December 31, 2009.

Net earnings were $53,063 in 2010 compared to $53,157 in 2009, and earnings per share were $.90 and $.89 in 2010 and 2009, respectively, an increase of $.01 or 1%. Earnings per share benefited from the reduction in average shares outstanding resulting from Common Stock purchases in the open market by the Company. Average shares outstanding decreased from 59,425 in 2009 to 58,685 in 2010.

LIQUIDITY AND CAPITAL RESOURCES

Cash flows from operating activities were $50,390, $82,805 and $76,994 in 2011, 2010 and 2009, respectively. The $32,415 decrease in cash flows from operating activities from 2010 to 2011 primarily reflects the 2011 decrease in net earnings, increased accounts receivables and inventories, and decreases in income taxes payable and deferred.

During 2008 the Company contributed $16,050 to a VEBA trust to fund the estimated future costs of certain employee health, welfare and other benefits. The Company used the funds, as well as investment income in this VEBA trust, to pay the actual cost of such benefits during 2010, 2011 and will continue to do so through 2012. At December 31, 2011, the VEBA trust held $6,424 of aggregate cash, cash equivalents and investments; this asset value is included in prepaid expenses in the Company's current and other long-term assets.

Cash flows from investing activities reflect capital expenditures of $16,351, $12,813, and $20,831 in 2011, 2010 and 2009, respectively, including $3,025 related to the 2011 purchase of warehouse space and land planned for future use. The 2011, 2010 and 2009 capital additions include $727, $1,682 and $2,326, respectively, relating to computer systems and related implementation.

The Company had no bank borrowing or repayments in 2009, 2010, or 2011, and had no outstanding bank borrowings as of December 31, 2010 or 2011.

Financing activities include Common Stock purchases and retirements of $18,190, $22,881, and $20,723 in 2011, 2010 and 2009, respectively. Cash dividends of $18,407, $18,130, and $17,825 were paid in 2011, 2010 and 2009, respectively. The increase in cash dividends each year reflects the annual 3% stock dividend issued in each of these years less the effects of Common Stock purchases and retirements.

SIGNIFICANT ACCOUNTING POLICIES AND ESTIMATES

Preparation of the Company's financial statements involves judgments and estimates due to uncertainties affecting the application of accounting policies, and the likelihood that different amounts would be reported under different conditions or using different assumptions. The Company bases its estimates on historical experience and other assumptions, as discussed herein, that it believes are reasonable. If actual amounts are ultimately different from previous estimates, the revisions are included in the Company's results of operations for the period in which the actual amounts become known. The Company's significant accounting policies are discussed in Note 1 to the Consolidated Financial Statements.

Following is a summary and discussion of the more significant accounting policies which management believes to have a significant impact on the Company's operating results, financial position, cash flows and footnote disclosure.

Revenue recognition

Revenue, net of applicable provisions for discounts, returns, allowances and certain advertising and promotional costs, is recognized when products are delivered to customers based on a customer purchase order, and collectability is reasonably assured. The accounting for promotional costs is discussed under "Customer incentive programs, advertising and marketing" below.

Provisions for bad debts are recorded as selling, marketing and administrative expenses. Write-offs of bad debts did not exceed 0.1% of net product sales in each of 2011, 2010 and 2009, and accordingly, have not been significant to the Company's financial position or results of operations.

Intangible assets

The Company's intangible assets consist primarily of acquired trademarks and goodwill. In accordance with accounting guidance, goodwill and other indefinite-lived assets are not amortized, but are instead subjected to annual testing for impairment unless certain triggering events or circumstances are noted. The Company performs its annual impairment testing as of December 31. The Company may utilize third-party professional valuation firms to assist in the determination of valuation of certain intangibles.

The impairment test is performed by comparing the carrying value of the asset with its estimated fair value, which is calculated using estimates, including discounted projected future cash flows. If the carrying value exceeds the fair value, the second step of the process is necessary. The second step measures the difference between the carrying value and implied fair value of goodwill. These projected future cash flows are dependent on a number of factors including the execution of business plans, achievement of projected sales, including but not limited to future price increases, projected operating margins, and projected capital expenditures. Such operating results are also dependent upon future ingredient and packaging material costs, exchange rates for products manufactured or sold in foreign countries, operational efficiencies, cost savings initiatives, and competitive factors. Although the majority of the Company's trademarks relate to well established brands with a long history of consumer acceptance, projected cash flows are inherently uncertain. A change in the assumptions underlying the impairment analysis, including but not limited to a reduction in projected cash flows, the use of a different discount rate to discount future cash flows or a different royalty rate applied to the Company's trademarks, could cause impairment in the future.

Customer incentive programs, advertising and marketing

Advertising and marketing costs are recorded in the period to which such costs relate. The Company does not defer the recognition of any amounts on its consolidated balance sheet with respect to such costs. Customer incentives and other promotional costs are recorded at the time of sale based upon incentive program terms and historical utilization statistics, which are generally consistent from year to year.

The liabilities associated with these programs are reviewed quarterly and adjusted if utilization rates differ from management's original estimates. Such adjustments have not historically been material to the Company's operating results.

Split dollar officer life insurance

The Company provides split dollar life insurance benefits to certain executive officers and records an asset principally equal to the cumulative premiums paid. The Company will fully recover these premiums in future years under the terms of the plan. The Company retains a collateral assignment of the cash surrender values and policy death benefits payable to insure recovery of these premiums.

Valuation of long-lived assets

Long-lived assets, primarily property, plant and equipment are reviewed for impairment as events or changes in business circumstances occur indicating that the carrying value of the asset may not be recoverable. The estimated cash flows produced by assets or asset groups, are compared to the asset carrying value to determine whether impairment exists. Such estimates involve considerable management judgment and are based upon assumptions about expected future operating performance. As a result, actual cash flows could differ from management's estimates due to changes in business conditions, operating performance, and economic and competitive conditions.

Income taxes

Deferred income taxes are recognized for future tax effects of temporary differences between financial and income tax reporting using tax rates in effect for the years in which the differences are expected to reverse. The Company records valuation allowances in situations where the realization of deferred tax assets, including those relating to net operating tax losses, is not more-likely-than-not; and the Company adjusts and releases such valuation allowances when realization becomes more-likely-than-not as defined by accounting guidance. The Company periodically reviews assumptions and estimates of the Company's probable tax obligations and effects on its liability for uncertain tax positions, using informed judgment which may include the use of third-party consultants, advisors and legal counsel, and historical experience.

Valuation of investments

Investments, primarily municipal bonds, mutual funds and equity method investments are reviewed for impairment at each reporting period by comparing the carrying value or amortized cost to the fair market value. The Company may utilize third-party professional valuation firms as necessary to assist in the determination of the value of investments using a valuation model with Level 3 inputs as defined. In the event that an investment security's fair value is below carrying value or amortized cost, the Company will record an other-than-temporary impairment or a temporary impairment based on accounting guidance.

Other matters

In the opinion of management, other than contracts for foreign currency forwards and raw materials, including currency and commodity hedges and outstanding purchase orders for packaging, ingredients, supplies, and operational services, all entered into in the ordinary course of business, the Company does not have any significant contractual obligations or future commitments. The Company's outstanding contractual commitments as of December 31, 2011, all of which are generally normal and recurring in nature, are summarized in the chart on page 13.

RECENT ACCOUNTING PRONOUNCEMENTS

In May 2011, the Financial Accounting Standards Board (FASB) issued Accounting Standards Update (ASU) 2011-04, "Fair Value Measurement (Topic 820): Amendments to Achieve Common Fair Value Measurement and Disclosure Requirements in U.S. GAAP and International Financial Reporting Standards (IFRS)." ASU 2011-04 represents converged guidance between U.S. GAAP and IFRS resulting in common requirements for measuring fair value and for disclosing information about fair value measurements. This new guidance will be effective for fiscal years beginning after December 15, 2011 and subsequent interim periods. The Company is currently assessing the impact, if any, on the consolidated financial statements.

In June 2011, the FASB issued ASU 2011-05, "Presentation of Comprehensive Income." ASU 2011-05 requires us to present components of other comprehensive income and of net income in one continuous statement of comprehensive income or in two separate, but consecutive, statements. The option to report other comprehensive income within the statement of equity has been removed. This new presentation of comprehensive income will be effective for fiscal years beginning after December 15, 2011 and subsequent interim periods.

In September 2011, the FASB issued ASU 2011-08, "Testing Goodwill for Impairment". The revised standard is intended to simplify how entities test goodwill for impairment. Under certain circumstances, a two-step impairment test may be unnecessary. The revised standard is effective for annual and interim goodwill impairment tests performed for fiscal years beginning after December 15, 2011. The Company currently believes there will be no impact on its consolidated financial statements.

In September 2011, FASB issued ASU 2011-09, "Compensation-Retirement Benefits-Multiemployer Plans" which amends the guidance in ASC 715-80. The amendments in ASU 2011-09 provide additional disclosure requirements for entities which participate in multi-employer pension plans. The purpose of the new disclosures is to provide financial statement users with information about an employer's level of participation in and the financial health of significant plans. The new disclosures are effective for annual periods ending after December 15, 2011. There will be no impact on the Company's consolidated financial statements as the changes relate only to additional disclosures.

MARKET RISKS

The Company is exposed to market risks related to commodity prices, interest rates, investments in marketable securities, equity price and foreign exchange.

The Company's ability to forecast the direction and scope of changes to its major input costs is impacted by significant volatility in crude oil, sugar, corn, soybean and edible oils, cocoa and dairy products markets. The prices of these commodities are influenced by changes in global demand, changes in weather and crop yields, changes in governments' farm policies, including mandates for ethanol and bio-fuels, and environmental matters, including global warming, and fluctuations in the U.S. dollar relative to dollar-denominated commodities in world markets. The Company believes that its competitors face the same or similar challenges.

In order to address the impact of rising input and other costs, the Company periodically reviews each item in its product portfolio to ascertain if price increases, weight declines (indirect price increases) or other actions should be taken. These reviews include an evaluation of the risk factors relating to market place acceptance of such changes and their potential effect on future sales volumes. In addition, the estimated cost of packaging modifications associated with weight changes is evaluated. The Company also maintains ongoing cost reduction and productivity improvement programs under which cost savings initiatives are encouraged and progress monitored. The Company is not able to accurately predict the outcome of these cost savings initiatives and their effects on its future results.

Commodity future and foreign currency forward contracts

Commodity price risks relate to ingredients, primarily sugar, cocoa, chocolate, corn syrup, dextrose, soybean and edible oils, milk, whey and gum base ingredients. The Company believes its competitors face similar risks, and the industry has historically adjusted prices to compensate for adverse fluctuations in commodity costs. The Company, as well as competitors in the confectionery industry, have taken actions, including price increases and selective product weight declines (indirect price increases) to mitigate rising input costs for ingredients, energy, freight and delivery. Although management seeks to substantially recover cost increases over the long-term, there is risk that price increases and weight declines cannot be fully passed on to customers and, to the extent they are passed on, they could adversely affect customer and consumer acceptance and resulting sales volume.

The Company utilizes commodity futures contracts and commodity options contracts as well as annual supply agreements to hedge and plan for anticipated purchases of certain ingredients, including sugar, in order to mitigate commodity cost fluctuation. The Company also may purchase forward foreign exchange contracts to hedge its costs of manufacturing certain products in Canada for sale and distribution in the United States, and periodically does so for purchases of equipment or raw materials from foreign suppliers. Such commodity futures, commodity options and currency forward contracts are cash flow hedges and are effective as hedges as defined by accounting guidance. The unrealized gains and losses on such contracts are deferred as a component of accumulated other comprehensive loss and are recognized as a component of product cost of goods sold when the related inventory is sold.

The potential change in fair value of commodity and foreign currency derivative instruments held by the Company at December 31, 2011, assuming a 10% change in the underlying contract price, was $1,761. The analysis only includes commodity and foreign currency derivative instruments and, therefore, does not consider the offsetting effect of changes in the price of the underlying commodity or foreign currency. This amount is not significant compared with the net earnings and shareholders' equity of the Company.

Interest rates

Interest rate risks primarily relate to the Company's investments in tax exempt marketable securities, including ARS, with maturities or auction dates of generally up to three years.

The majority of the Company's investments, which are classified as available for sale, have historically been held until they mature, which limits the Company's exposure to interest rate fluctuations. The accompanying chart summarizes the maturities of the Company's investments in debt securities at December 31, 2011.

Less than 1 year	$10,854
1–2 years	17,753
2–3 years	29,133
Over 3 years	7,504
Total	$65,244

The Company's outstanding debt at December 31, 2011 and 2010 was $7,500 in an industrial revenue bond in which interest rates reset each week based on the current market rate. Therefore, the Company does not believe that it has significant interest rate risk with respect to its interest bearing debt.

Investment in marketable securities

As stated above, the Company invests primarily in tax exempt marketable securities, including ARS, with maturities or auction dates generally up to three years. The Company utilizes professional money managers and maintains investment policy guidelines which emphasize quality and liquidity in order to minimize the potential loss exposures that could result in the event of a default or other adverse event, including failed auctions.

However, given events in the municipal bond and ARS markets, including failed auctions, the Company continues to monitor these investments and markets, as well as its investment policies. Nonetheless, the financial markets have been experiencing unprecedented events in recent years, and future outcomes are less predictable than in the past.

Equity price

Equity price risk relates to the Company's investments in mutual funds which are principally used to fund and hedge the Company's deferred compensation liabilities. At December 31, 2011, the Company has investments in mutual funds, classified as trading securities, of $41,768. Any change in the fair value of these trading securities is completely offset by a corresponding change in the respective hedged deferred compensation liability.

Foreign currency

Foreign currency risk principally relates to the Company's foreign operations in Canada and Mexico, as well as periodic purchase commitments of machinery and equipment from foreign sources.

Certain of the Company's Canadian manufacturing costs, including local payroll and plant operations, and a portion of its packaging and ingredients are sourced in Canadian dollars. The Company may purchase Canadian forward contracts to receive Canadian dollars at a specified date in the future and uses its Canadian dollar collections on Canadian sales as a partial hedge of its overall Canadian manufacturing obligations sourced in Canadian dollars. The Company also periodically purchases and holds Canadian dollars to facilitate the risk management of these currency changes.

From time to time, the Company may use foreign exchange forward contracts and derivative instruments to mitigate its exposure to foreign exchange risks, as well as those related to firm commitments to purchase equipment from foreign vendors. As of December 31, 2011, the Company held foreign exchange forward contracts with a fair value of $205.

RISK FACTORS

The Company's operations and financial results are subject to a number of risks and uncertainties that could adversely affect the Company's operating results and financial condition. Significant risk factors, without limitations that could impact the Company, are the following: (i) significant competitive activity, including advertising, promotional and price competition, and changes in consumer demand for the Company's products; (ii) fluctuations in the cost and availability of commodities and ingredients, and packaging materials, and the ability to recover cost increases through product sales price increases; (iii) inherent risks in the marketplace, including uncertainties about trade and consumer acceptance of price increases and seasonal events such as Halloween; (iv) the effect of acquisitions on the Company's results of operations and financial condition; (v) the effect of changes in foreign currencies on the Company's foreign subsidiaries operating results, and the effect of the fluctuation of the Canadian dollar on products manufactured in Canada and marketed and sold in the United States in U.S. dollars; (vi) the Company's reliance on third party vendors for various goods and services, including commodities used for ingredients that are primarily grown or sourced from foreign locations; (vii) the Company's ability to successfully implement new production processes and lines, and new computer software systems; (viii) the effect of changes in assumptions, including discount rates, sales growth and profit margins and the capability to pass along higher ingredient and other input costs through price increases, relating to the Company's impairment testing and analysis of its goodwill and trademarks; (ix) changes in the confectionery marketplace including actions taken by major retailers and customers; (x) customer, consumer and competitor response to marketing programs and price and product weight adjustments, and new products; (xi) dependence on significant customers, including the volume and timing of their purchases, and availability of shelf space; (xii) increases in energy costs, including freight and delivery, that cannot be passed along to customers through increased prices due to competitive reasons; (xiii) any significant labor stoppages, strikes or production interruptions; (xiv) changes in governmental laws and regulations including taxes and tariffs; (xv) the adverse effects should the Company either voluntarily or involuntarily recall its product(s) from the marketplace; (xvi) the risk that the market value of Company's investments could decline including being classified as "other-than-temporary" as defined; (xvii) the Company's dependence on its enterprise resource planning computer system to manage its supply chain and customer deliveries, and the risk that the Company's information technology systems fail to perform adequately or the Company is unable to protect such information technology systems against data corruption, cyber-based attacks or network security breaches; and (xviii) the potential effects of current and future macroeconomic conditions and geopolitical events.

Forward-looking statements

This discussion and certain other sections contain forward-looking statements that are based largely on the Company's current expectations and are made pursuant to the safe harbor provision of the Private Securities Litigation Reform Act of 1995. Forward-looking statements can be identified by the use of words such as "anticipated," "believe," "expect," "intend," "estimate," "project," and other words of similar meaning in connection with a discussion of future operating or financial performance and are subject to certain factors, risks, trends and uncertainties that could cause actual results and achievements to differ materially from those expressed in the forward-looking statements. Such factors, risks, trends and uncertainties which in some instances are beyond the Company's control, include the overall competitive environment in the Company's industry, changes in assumptions and judgments discussed above under the heading "Significant Accounting Policies and Estimates", and factors identified and referred to above under the heading "Risk Factors."

The risk factors identified and referred to above are believed to be significant factors, but not necessarily all of the significant factors that could cause actual results to differ from those expressed in any forward-looking statement. Readers are cautioned not to place undue reliance on such forward-looking statements, which are made only as of the date of this report. The Company undertakes no obligation to update such forward-looking statements.

Open Contractual Commitments as of December 31, 2011

Payable in	Total	Less than 1 Year	1 to 3 Years	3 to 5 Years	More than 5 Years
Commodity hedges	$ 4,557	$ 4,538	$ 19	$ —	$ —
Foreign currency hedges	13,044	13,044	—	—	—
Purchase obligations	10,373	10,373	—	—	—
Interest bearing debt	7,500	—	—	—	7,500
Operating leases	3,926	1,047	1,836	1,043	—
Total	$39,400	$29,002	$1,855	$1,043	$7,500

Note: Commodity hedges and foreign currency hedges reflect the amounts at which the Company will settle the related contracts. The above amounts exclude deferred income tax liabilities of $43,521, liabilities for uncertain tax positions of $8,345, postretirement health care and life insurance benefits of $26,108 and deferred compensation and other liabilities of $48,092 because the timing of payments relating to these items cannot be reasonably determined.

Financial Statements and Accompanying Notes

The standard set of financial statements consists of (1) a comparative income statement for three years, (2) a comparative balance sheet for two years, (3) a comparative statement of cash flows for three years, (4) a statement of retained earnings (or stockholders' equity) for three years, and (5) a set of accompanying notes that are considered an integral part of the financial statements. The auditor's report, unless stated otherwise, covers the financial statements and the accompanying notes. The financial statements and accompanying notes plus some supplementary data and analyses for Tootsie Roll Industries follow.

CONSOLIDATED STATEMENTS OF

Earnings, Comprehensive Earnings and Retained Earnings

TOOTSIE ROLL INDUSTRIES, INC. AND SUBSIDIARIES (in thousands except per share data)

	For the year ended December 31,		
	2011	2010	2009
Net product sales	$528,369	$517,149	$495,592
Rental and royalty revenue	4,136	4,299	3,739
Total revenue	532,505	521,448	499,331
Product cost of goods sold	365,225	349,334	319,775
Rental and royalty cost	1,038	1,088	852
Total costs	366,263	350,422	320,627
Product gross margin	163,144	167,815	175,817
Rental and royalty gross margin	3,098	3,211	2,887
Total gross margin	166,242	171,026	178,704
Selling, marketing and administrative expenses	108,276	106,316	103,755
Impairment charges	—	—	14,000
Earnings from operations	57,966	64,710	60,949
Other income (expense), net	2,946	8,358	2,100
Earnings before income taxes	60,912	73,068	63,049
Provision for income taxes	16,974	20,005	9,892
Net earnings	$ 43,938	$ 53,063	$ 53,157
Net earnings	$ 43,938	$ 53,063	$ 53,157
Other comprehensive earnings (loss)	(8,740)	1,183	2,845
Comprehensive earnings	$ 35,198	$ 54,246	$ 56,002
Retained earnings at beginning of year	$135,866	$147,687	$144,949
Net earnings	43,938	53,063	53,157
Cash dividends	(18,360)	(18,078)	(17,790)
Stock dividends	(47,175)	(46,806)	(32,629)
Retained earnings at end of year	$114,269	$135,866	$147,687
Earnings per share	$ 0.76	$ 0.90	$ 0.89
Average Common and Class B Common shares outstanding	57,892	58,685	59,425

(The accompanying notes are an integral part of these statements.)

CONSOLIDATED STATEMENTS OF

Financial Position

TOOTSIE ROLL INDUSTRIES, INC. AND SUBSIDIARIES (in thousands except per share data)

Assets

	December 31,	
	2011	**2010**
CURRENT ASSETS:		
Cash and cash equivalents	$ 78,612	$115,976
Investments	10,895	7,996
Accounts receivable trade, less allowances of $1,731 and $1,531	41,895	37,394
Other receivables	3,391	9,961
Inventories:		
Finished goods and work-in-process	42,676	35,416
Raw materials and supplies	29,084	21,236
Prepaid expenses	5,070	6,499
Deferred income taxes	578	689
Total current assets	212,201	235,167
PROPERTY, PLANT AND EQUIPMENT, at cost:		
Land	21,939	21,619
Buildings	107,567	102,934
Machinery and equipment	322,993	307,178
Construction in progress	2,598	9,243
	455,097	440,974
Less—Accumulated depreciation	242,935	225,482
Net property, plant and equipment	212,162	215,492
OTHER ASSETS:		
Goodwill	73,237	73,237
Trademarks	175,024	175,024
Investments	96,161	64,461
Split dollar officer life insurance	74,209	74,441
Prepaid expenses	3,212	6,680
Equity method investment	3,935	4,254
Deferred income taxes	7,715	9,203
Total other assets	433,493	407,300
Total assets	$857,856	$857,959

Liabilities and Shareholders' Equity

	December 31,	
	2011	**2010**
CURRENT LIABILITIES:		
Accounts payable	$ 10,683	$ 9,791
Dividends payable	4,603	4,529
Accrued liabilities	43,069	44,185
Total current liabilities	58,355	58,505
NONCURRENT LIABILITES:		
Deferred income taxes	43,521	47,865
Postretirement health care and life insurance benefits	26,108	20,689
Industrial development bonds	7,500	7,500
Liability for uncertain tax positions	8,345	9,835
Deferred compensation and other liabilities	48,092	46,157
Total noncurrent liabilities	133,566	132,046
SHAREHOLDERS' EQUITY		
Common stock, $.69-4/9 par value— 120,000 shares authorized— 36,479 and 36,057, respectively, issued	25,333	25,040
Class B common stock, $.69-4/9 par value—40,000 shares authorized— 21,025 and 20,466, respectively, issued	14,601	14,212
Capital in excess of par value	533,677	505,495
Retained earnings, per accompanying statement	114,269	135,866
Accumulated other comprehensive loss	(19,953)	(11,213)
Treasury stock (at cost)—71 shares and 69 shares, respectively	(1,992)	(1,992)
Total shareholders' equity	665,935	667,408
Total liabilities and shareholders' equity	$857,856	$857,959

(The accompanying notes are an integral part of these statements.)

CONSOLIDATED STATEMENTS OF

Cash Flows

TOOTSIE ROLL INDUSTRIES, INC. AND SUBSIDIARIES (in thousands)

	For the year ended December 31,		
	2011	**2010**	**2009**
CASH FLOWS FROM OPERATING ACTIVITIES:			
Net earnings	$ 43,938	$ 53,063	$53,157
Adjustments to reconcile net earnings to net cash provided by operating activities:			
Depreciation	19,229	18,279	17,862
Impairment charges	—	—	14,000
Impairment of equity method investment	—	—	4,400
Loss from equity method investment	194	342	233
Amortization of marketable security premiums	1,267	522	320
Changes in operating assets and liabilities:			
Accounts receivable	(5,448)	717	(5,899)
Other receivables	3,963	(2,373)	(2,088)
Inventories	(15,631)	(1,447)	455
Prepaid expenses and other assets	5,106	4,936	5,203
Accounts payable and accrued liabilities	84	2,180	(2,755)
Income taxes payable and deferred	(5,772)	2,322	(12,543)
Postretirement health care and life insurance benefits	2,022	1,429	1,384
Deferred compensation and other liabilities	3,146	2,525	2,960
Other	(708)	310	305
Net cash provided by operating activities	50,390	82,805	76,994
CASH FLOWS FROM INVESTING ACTIVITIES:			
Capital expenditures	(16,351)	(12,813)	(20,831)
Net purchases of trading securities	(3,234)	(2,902)	(1,713)
Purchase of available for sale securities	(39,252)	(9,301)	(11,331)
Sale and maturity of available for sale securities	7,680	8,208	17,511
Net cash used in investing activities	(51,157)	(16,808)	(16,364)
CASH FLOWS FROM FINANCING ACTIVITIES:			
Shares purchased and retired	(18,190)	(22,881)	(20,723)
Dividends paid in cash	(18,407)	(18,130)	(17,825)
Net cash used in financing activities	(36,597)	(41,011)	(38,548)
Increase (decrease) in cash and cash equivalents	(37,364)	24,986	22,082
Cash and cash equivalents at beginning of year	115,976	90,990	68,908
Cash and cash equivalents at end of year	$ 78,612	$115,976	$90,990
Supplemental cash flow information:			
Income taxes paid	$ 16,906	$ 20,586	$22,364
Interest paid	$ 38	$ 49	$ 182
Stock dividend issued	$ 47,053	$ 46,683	$32,538

(The accompanying notes are an integral part of these statements.)

Notes to Consolidated Financial Statements ($ in thousands except per share data)

TOOTSIE ROLL INDUSTRIES, INC. AND SUBSIDIARIES

NOTE 1—SIGNIFICANT ACCOUNTING POLICIES:

Basis of consolidation:

The consolidated financial statements include the accounts of Tootsie Roll Industries, Inc. and its wholly-owned subsidiaries (the Company), which are primarily engaged in the manufacture and sales of candy products. All significant intercompany transactions have been eliminated.

The preparation of financial statements in conformity with generally accepted accounting principles in the United States of America requires management to make estimates and assumptions that affect the reported amounts of assets and liabilities and disclosure of contingent assets and liabilities at the date of the financial statements and the reported amounts of revenues and expenses during the reporting period. Actual results could differ from those estimates.

Revenue recognition:

Products are sold to customers based on accepted purchase orders which include quantity, sales price and other relevant terms of sale. Revenue, net of applicable provisions for discounts, returns, allowances and certain advertising and promotional costs, is recognized when products are delivered to customers and collectability is reasonably assured. Shipping and handling costs of $45,850, $43,034, and $38,628 in 2011, 2010 and 2009, respectively, are included in selling, marketing and administrative expenses. Accounts receivable are unsecured. Revenues from a major customer aggregated approximately 23.3%, 21.4% and 22.9% of net product sales during the years ended December 31, 2011, 2010 and 2009, respectively.

Cash and cash equivalents:

The Company considers temporary cash investments with an original maturity of three months or less to be cash equivalents.

Investments:

Investments consist of various marketable securities with maturities of generally up to three years. The Company classifies debt and equity securities as either available for sale or trading. Available for sale securities are not actively traded by the Company and are carried at fair value. The Company follows current fair value measurement guidance and unrealized gains and losses on these securities are excluded from earnings and are reported as a separate component of shareholders' equity, net of applicable taxes, until realized or other than temporarily impaired. Trading securities relate to deferred compensation arrangements and are carried at fair value with gains or losses included in other income (expense), net. The Company invests in trading securities to economically hedge changes in its deferred compensation liabilities.

The Company regularly reviews its investments to determine whether a decline in fair value below the cost basis is other than temporary. If the decline in fair value is judged to be other than temporary, the cost basis of the security is written down to fair value and the amount of the write-down is included in other income (expense), net. Further information regarding the fair value of the Company's investments is included in Note 10 to the Consolidated Financial Statements.

Derivative instruments and hedging activities:

Authoritative guidance requires qualitative disclosures about objectives and strategies for using derivatives, quantitative disclosures about fair value amounts of derivative instruments and related gains and losses, and disclosures about credit-risk-related contingent features in derivative agreements.

From time to time, the Company enters into commodity futures, commodity options contracts and foreign currency forward contracts. Commodity futures and options are intended and are effective as hedges of market price risks associated with the anticipated purchase of certain raw materials (primarily sugar). Foreign currency forward contracts are intended and are effective as hedges of the Company's exposure to the variability of cash flows, primarily related to the foreign exchange rate changes of products manufactured in Canada and sold in the United States, and periodic equipment purchases from foreign suppliers denominated in a foreign currency. The Company does not engage in trading or other speculative use of derivative instruments. Further information regarding derivative instruments and hedging activities is included in Note 11 to the Consolidated Financial Statements.

Inventories:

Inventories are stated at cost, not to exceed market. The cost of substantially all of the Company's inventories ($67,339 and $52,863 at December 31, 2011 and 2010, respectively) has been determined by the last-in, first-out (LIFO) method. The excess of current cost over LIFO cost of inventories approximates $24,043 and $19,379 at December 31, 2011 and 2010, respectively. The cost of certain foreign inventories ($4,421 and $3,789 at December 31, 2011 and 2010, respectively) has been determined by the first-in, first-out (FIFO) method. Rebates, discounts and other cash consideration received from vendors related to inventory purchases is reflected as a reduction in the cost of the related inventory item, and is therefore reflected in cost of sales when the related inventory item is sold.

Property, plant and equipment:

Depreciation is computed for financial reporting purposes by use of the straight-line method based on useful lives of 20 to 35 years for buildings and 5 to 20 years for machinery and equipment. Depreciation expense was $19,229, $18,279 and $17,862 in 2011, 2010 and 2009, respectively.

Carrying value of long-lived assets:

The Company reviews long-lived assets to determine if there are events or circumstances indicating that the amount of the asset reflected in the Company's balance sheet may not be recoverable. When such indicators are present, the Company compares the carrying value of the long-lived asset, or asset group, to the future undiscounted cash flows of the underlying assets to determine if an impairment exists. If applicable, an impairment charge would be recorded to write down the carrying value to its fair value. The determination of fair value involves the use of estimates of future cash flows that involve considerable management judgment and are based upon assumptions about expected future operating performance. The actual cash flows could differ from management's estimates due to changes in business conditions, operating performance, and economic conditions. No impairment charges of long-lived assets were recorded by the Company during 2011, 2010 and 2009.

Postretirement health care and life insurance benefits:

The Company provides certain postretirement health care and life insurance benefits. The cost of these postretirement benefits is accrued during employees' working careers. The Company also provides split dollar life benefits to certain executive officers. The Company records an asset equal to the cumulative insurance premiums paid that will be recovered upon the death of covered employees or earlier under the terms of the plan. No premiums were paid in 2011, 2010 and 2009.

Goodwill and intangible assets:

In accordance with authoritative guidance, goodwill and intangible assets with indefinite lives are not amortized, but rather tested for impairment at least annually unless certain interim triggering events or circumstances require more frequent testing. All trademarks have been assessed by management to have indefinite lives because they are expected to generate cash flows indefinitely. The Company has completed its annual impairment testing of its goodwill and trademarks at December 31 of each of the years presented. As of December 31, 2009, management ascertained that certain trademarks were impaired, and recorded a pre-tax charge of $14,000. No impairments of intangibles were recorded in 2011 and 2010.

This determination is made by comparing the carrying value of the asset with its estimated fair value, which is calculated using estimates including discounted projected future cash flows. If the carrying value of goodwill exceeds the fair value, a second step would measure the carrying value and implied fair value of goodwill. Management believes that all assumptions used for the impairment tests are consistent with those utilized by market participants performing similar valuations.

Income taxes:

Deferred income taxes are recorded and recognized for future tax effects of temporary differences between financial and income tax reporting. The Company records valuation allowances in situations where the realization of deferred tax assets is not more-likely-than-not. Federal income taxes are provided on the portion of income of foreign subsidiaries that is expected to be remitted to the U.S. and become taxable, but not on the portion that is considered to be permanently invested in the foreign subsidiary.

Foreign currency translation:

The U.S. dollar is used as the functional currency where a substantial portion of the subsidiary's business is indexed to the U.S. dollar or where its manufactured products are principally sold in the U.S. All other foreign subsidiaries use the local currency as their functional currency. Where the U.S. dollar is used as the functional currency, foreign currency remeasurements are recorded as a charge or credit to other income (expense), net in the statement of earnings. Where the foreign local currency is used as the functional currency, translation adjustments are recorded as a separate component of accumulated other comprehensive (loss).

Equity method investment:

The Company's 50% interest in two foreign companies is accounted for using the equity method. The Company records an increase in its investment to the extent of its share of earnings, and reduces its investment to the extent of losses and dividends received. No dividends were paid in 2011, 2010 and 2009.

As of December 31, 2009, management determined that the fair value of the asset was less than the carrying value. As a result, the Company recorded a pre-tax impairment charge of $4,400 in the fourth quarter 2009, resulting in an adjusted carrying value of $4,961 as of December 31, 2009. The fair value was primarily assessed using the present value of estimated future cash flows. No impairments were recorded in 2011 and 2010.

Comprehensive earnings:

Comprehensive earnings includes net earnings, foreign currency translation adjustments and unrealized gains/losses on commodity and/or foreign currency hedging contracts, available for sale securities and certain postretirement benefit obligations.

Earnings per share:

A dual presentation of basic and diluted earnings per share is not required due to the lack of potentially dilutive securities under the Company's simple capital structure. Therefore, all earnings per share amounts represent basic earnings per share.

The Class B Common Stock has essentially the same rights as Common Stock, except that each share of Class B Common Stock has ten votes per share (compared to one vote per share of Common Stock), is not traded on any exchange, is restricted as to transfer and is convertible on a share-for-share basis, at any time and at no cost to the holders, into shares of Common Stock which are traded on the New York Stock Exchange.

Use of estimates:

The preparation of consolidated financial statements in conformity with accounting principles generally accepted in the U.S. requires management to make estimates and assumptions that affect the amounts reported. Estimates are used when accounting for sales discounts, allowances and incentives, product liabilities, assets recorded at fair value, income taxes, depreciation, amortization, employee benefits, contingencies and intangible asset and liability valuations. For instance, in determining the annual post-employment benefit costs, the Company estimates the cost of future health care benefits. Actual results may or may not differ from those estimates.

Retrospective application of change in accounting principle:

During the fourth quarter of fiscal 2011, the Company changed the method used to compute the LIFO value of its domestic inventories. The change was largely driven by the fact that the Company has made changes in the business model over the last several years to achieve efficiencies in manufacturing, distribution and marketing processes and therefore combined multiple LIFO pools into a single LIFO pool to better reflect these changes. The Company has applied this change retrospectively, adjusting all prior periods presented. The cumulative effect of the change on retained earnings as of January 1, 2009, was a reduction of $174, with offsets to inventories and deferred taxes. For 2010, inventories and deferred income taxes reflect decreases of $2,424 and $878, respectively. For 2010 and 2009, product cost of goods sold increased $1,021 and $1,130, respectively; provision for income taxes decreased $370 and $409, respectively.

Recent accounting pronouncements:

In May 2011, the Financial Accounting Standards Board (FASB) issued Accounting Standards Update (ASU) 2011-04, "Fair Value Measurement (Topic 820): Amendments to Achieve Common Fair Value Measurement and Disclosure Requirements in U.S. GAAP and International Financial Reporting Standards (IFRS)." ASU 2011-04 represents converged guidance between U.S. GAAP and IFRS resulting in common requirements for measuring fair value and for disclosing information about fair value measurements. This new guidance will be effective for fiscal years beginning after December 15, 2011 and subsequent interim periods. The Company is currently assessing the impact, if any, on the consolidated financial statements.

In June 2011, the FASB issued ASU 2011-05, "Presentation of Comprehensive Income." ASU 2011-05 requires the Company to present components of other comprehensive income and of net income in one continuous statement of comprehensive income, or in two separate, but consecutive statements. The option to report other comprehensive income within the statement of equity has been removed. This new presentation of comprehensive income will be effective for fiscal years beginning after December 15, 2011 and subsequent interim periods.

In September 2011, the FASB issued ASU 2011-08, "Testing Goodwill for Impairment". The revised standard is intended to simplify how entities test goodwill for impairment. Under certain circumstances, a two-step impairment test may be unnecessary. The revised standard is effective for annual and interim goodwill impairment tests performed for fiscal years beginning after December 15, 2011. The Company currently believes there will be no impact on its consolidated financial statements.

In September 2011, FASB issued ASU 2011-09, "Compensation-Retirement Benefits-Multiemployer Plans" which amends the guidance in ASC 715-80. The amendments in ASU 2011-09 provide additional disclosure requirements for entities which participate in multi-employer pension plans. The purpose of the new disclosures is to provide financial statement users with information about an employer's level of participation in and the financial health of significant plans. The new disclosures are effective for annual periods ending after December 15, 2011. There will be no impact on the Company's consolidated financial statements as the changes relate only to additional disclosures.

NOTE 2—ACCRUED LIABILITIES:

Accrued liabilities are comprised of the following:

	December 31,	
	2011	2010
Compensation	$ 8,817	$ 9,750
Other employee benefits	2,004	2,030
Taxes, other than income	1,954	1,966
Advertising and promotions	20,568	20,775
Other	9,726	9,664
	$43,069	$44,185

NOTE 3—INDUSTRIAL DEVELOPMENT BONDS:

Industrial development bonds are due in 2027. The average floating interest rate was 0.3% and 0.4% in 2011 and 2010, respectively. See Note 10 to the Consolidated Financial Statements for fair value disclosures.

NOTE 4—INCOME TAXES:
The domestic and foreign components of pretax income are as follows:

	2011	2010	2009
Domestic	$56,651	$59,308	$68,649
Foreign	4,261	13,760	(5,600)
	$60,912	$73,068	$63,049

The provision for income taxes is comprised of the following:

	2011	2010	2009
Current:			
Federal	$15,568	$10,251	$21,836
Foreign	559	806	500
State	863	1,455	1,665
	16,990	12,512	24,001
Deferred:			
Federal	(1,230)	5,622	(432)
Foreign	1,221	2,518	(12,987)
State	(7)	(647)	(690)
	(16)	7,493	(14,109)
	$16,974	$20,005	$ 9,892

Significant components of the Company's net deferred tax liability at year end were as follows:

	December 31,	
	2011	2010
Deferred tax assets:		
Accrued customer promotions	$ 1,920	$ 1,634
Deferred compensation	15,593	11,602
Postretirement benefits	9,139	6,596
Other accrued expenses	6,347	5,475
Foreign subsidiary tax loss carry forward	16,406	16,582
Tax credit carry forward	841	978
Realized capital losses	1,349	—
Unrealized capital loss	6,401	6,566
	57,996	49,433
Valuation reserve	(2,190)	(686)
Total deferred tax assets	$55,806	$48,747
Deferred tax liabilities:		
Depreciation	$35,103	$32,376
Deductible goodwill and trademarks	38,635	35,790
Accrued export company commissions	4,649	4,532
Employee benefit plans	2,248	3,506
Inventory reserves	1,733	1,871
Prepaid insurance	289	377
Accounts receivable	733	624
Deferred gain on sale of real estate	7,644	7,644
Total deferred tax liabilities	$91,034	$86,720
Net deferred tax liability	$35,228	$37,973

At December 31, 2011, the Company recognized $3,854 of benefits related to capital loss carry forwards. The carry forward losses will begin to expire in 2013. A valuation allowance has been established for the carry forward losses to reduce the future income tax benefits to amounts expected to be realized.

At December 31, 2011 the Company recognized $841 of benefits related to foreign subsidiary tax credit carry forwards. The carry forward credits expire in 2017. A valuation allowance has been established for the carry forward losses to reduce the future income tax benefits to amounts expected to be realized.

At December 31, 2011, the tax benefits of foreign subsidiary tax loss carry forwards expiring by year are as follows: $697 in 2014, $2,672 in 2015, $366 in 2026, $640 in 2027, $6,578 in 2028, $4,681 in 2029 and $772 in 2031.

Certain out of period items have been included in the 2011 provision that are immaterial individually and in the aggregate. The effective income tax rate differs from the statutory rate as follows:

	2011	2010	2009
U.S. statutory rate	35.0%	35.0%	35.0%
State income taxes, net	1.2	1.1	1.7
Exempt municipal bond interest	(0.5)	(0.4)	(0.7)
Foreign tax rates	(0.4)	(2.0)	(4.9)
Release of prior period valuation allowances	—	—	(13.3)
Qualified domestic production activities deduction	(2.5)	(2.6)	(2.0)
Tax credits receivable	(0.4)	(0.2)	(0.4)
Adjustment of deferred tax balances	(1.7)	—	—
Reserve for uncertain tax benefits	(0.6)	(2.3)	1.3
Other, net	(2.2)	(1.2)	(1.0)
Effective income tax rate	27.9%	27.4%	15.7%

In connection with the acquisition in 2004 of Concord Confections, a Canadian subsidiary, the Company established an inter-company financing structure which included a loan from the U.S. parent to the Canadian subsidiary. By December of 2006, significant operating losses had accumulated in Canada and management determined that the realization of the net operating loss carry forward benefits was not more-likely-than-not, and provided a full tax valuation allowance. Consistent with relevant accounting guidance, these benefits continued to be reserved through 2008 and through the third quarter of 2009.

In December of 2008, a new U.S./Canada income tax treaty (Treaty) was ratified which effectively denies certain inter-company interest benefits to the U.S. shareholder of a Canadian company. Accordingly, in December of 2009, the Company decided to recapitalize its Canadian operations effective January 1, 2010. During the fourth quarter of 2009, the Company considered all of the evidence and relevant accounting guidance related to this recapitalization and based on reasonable assumptions, the Company concluded that it was more-likely-than-not that it would realize substantially all of the deferred tax assets related to the Canadian net operating loss carry forward benefits because it is expected that sufficient levels of income will be generated in the foreseeable future. As a result, the Company released $8.4 million of prior period valuation allowances and $2.3 million of allowances that were provided through the first nine months of 2009.

The Treaty also introduced a phase out of the withholding tax on payments from Canada to the U.S. allowing the Company to qualify for a zero percent withholding rate in 2010 if certain requirements of the Treaty were met. On January 4, 2010, the Canadian subsidiary repaid accrued interest to its U.S. parent in a manner consistent with these requirements. As a result, $1.5 million of withholding taxes accrued for 2007 and 2008 and through the third quarter of 2009 were released in the fourth quarter of 2009.

The Company has not provided for U.S. federal or foreign withholding taxes on $6,410 and $4,787 of foreign subsidiaries' undistributed earnings as of December 31, 2011 and December 31, 2010, respectively, because such earnings are considered to be permanently reinvested. It is not practicable to determine the amount of income taxes that would be payable upon remittance of the undistributed earnings.

The Company recognizes interest and penalties related to unrecognized tax benefits in the provision for income taxes on the Consolidated Statements of Earnings.

At December 31, 2011 and 2010, the Company had unrecognized tax benefits of $6,804 and $8,138, respectively. Included in this balance is $4,199 and $4,949, respectively, of unrecognized tax benefits that, if recognized, would favorably affect the annual effective income tax rate. As of December 31, 2011 and 2010, $1,541 and $1,697, respectively, of interest and penalties were included in the liability for uncertain tax positions.

A reconciliation of the beginning and ending balances of the total amounts of unrecognized tax benefits is as follows:

	2011	2010	2009
Unrecognized tax benefits at January 1	$8,138	$14,370	$13,069
Increases in tax positions for the current year	320	632	2,661
Reductions in tax positions for lapse of statute of limitations	(668)	(1,122)	(514)
Reductions in tax positions for withdrawal of positions previously taken	—	(5,256)	—
Reductions in tax positions for effective settlements	(986)	(486)	(846)
Unrecognized tax benefits at December 31	$6,804	$ 8,138	$14,370

The Company is subject to taxation in the U.S. and various state and foreign jurisdictions. The Company remains subject to examination by U.S. federal and state and foreign tax authorities for the years 2008 through 2010. With few exceptions, the Company is no longer subject to examinations by tax authorities for the year 2007 and prior.

The Company is currently subject to a U.S. federal examination for tax year 2009. The field work has not yet concluded and the Company is unable to determine the outcome at this time. The Company's Canadian subsidiary is currently subject to examination by the Canada Revenue Agency for tax years 2005 and 2006. The Company is unable to determine the outcome of the examination at this time. In addition, the Company is currently subject to various state tax examinations. One of the state examinations has been effectively settled and the corresponding liability for unrecognized tax benefits has been reduced. Although the Company is unable to determine the ultimate outcome of the ongoing examinations, the Company believes that its liability for uncertain tax positions relating to these jurisdictions for such years is adequate.

Beginning in 2008, statutory income tax rates in Canada will be reduced five percentage points with the final rate reduction coming in 2014. Accordingly in 2009, the Company's Canadian subsidiary has revalued its deferred tax assets and liabilities based on the rate in effect for the year the differences are expected to reverse.

NOTE 5—SHARE CAPITAL AND CAPITAL IN EXCESS OF PAR VALUE:

	Common Stock		Class B Common Stock		Treasury Stock		Capital in Excess of Par Value
	Shares (000's)	Amount	Shares (000's)	Amount	Shares (000's)	Amount	
Balance at January 1, 2009	35,658	$24,762	19,357	$13,442	(65)	$(1,992)	$470,927
Issuance of 3% stock dividend	1,064	739	580	403	(2)	—	31,396
Conversion of Class B common shares to common shares	18	12	(18)	(12)	—	—	—
Purchase and retirement of common shares	(938)	(651)	—	—	—	—	(20,073)
Balance at December 31, 2009	35,802	24,862	19,919	13,833	(67)	(1,992)	482,250
Issuance of 3% stock dividend	1,070	743	597	414	(2)	—	45,526
Conversion of Class B common shares to common shares	50	35	(50)	(35)	—	—	—
Purchase and retirement of common shares	(865)	(600)	—	—	—	—	(22,281)
Balance at December 31, 2010	36,057	25,040	20,466	14,212	(69)	(1,992)	505,495
Issuance of 3% stock dividend	1,077	748	612	426	(2)	—	45,880
Conversion of Class B common shares to common shares	53	37	(53)	(37)	—	—	—
Purchase and retirement of common shares	(708)	(492)	—	—	—	—	(17,698)
Balance at December 31, 2011	36,479	$25,333	21,025	$14,601	(71)	$(1,992)	$533,677

Average shares outstanding and all per share amounts included in the financial statements and notes thereto have been adjusted retroactively to reflect annual three percent stock dividends.

While the Company does not have a formal or publicly announced Company Common Stock purchase program, the Company's board of directors periodically authorizes a dollar amount for such share purchases.

Based upon this policy, shares were purchased and retired as follows:

Year	Total Number of Shares Purchased (000's)	Average Price Paid Per Share
2011	708	$25.64
2010	865	$26.41
2009	938	$22.05

NOTE 6—OTHER INCOME (EXPENSE), NET:

Other income (expense), net is comprised of the following:

	2011	2010	2009
Interest and dividend income	$1,087	$ 879	$1,439
Gains (losses) on trading securities relating to deferred compensation plans	29	3,364	4,524
Interest expense	(121)	(142)	(243)
Impairment of equity method investment	—	—	(4,400)
Equity method investment loss	(194)	(342)	(233)
Foreign exchange gains (losses)	2,098	4,090	951
Capital gains (losses)	(277)	(28)	(38)
Miscellaneous, net	274	537	100
	$2,946	$8,358	$2,100

As of December 31, 2009, management determined that the carrying value of an equity method investment was impaired as a result of accumulated losses from operations and review of future expectations. The Company recorded a pre-tax impairment charge of $4,400 resulting in an adjusted carrying value of $4,961 as of December 31, 2009. The fair value was primarily assessed using the present value of estimated future cash flows.

NOTE 7—EMPLOYEE BENEFIT PLANS:

Pension plans:

The Company sponsors defined contribution pension plans covering certain non-union employees with over one year of credited service. The Company's policy is to fund pension costs accrued based on compensation levels. Total pension expense for 2011, 2010 and 2009 approximated $4,011, $4,196 and $4,178, respectively. The Company also maintains certain profit sharing and retirement savings-investment plans. Company contributions in 2011, 2010 and 2009 to these plans were $1,024, $1,043 and $1,011, respectively.

The Company also contributes to multi-employer defined benefit pension plan for certain of its union employees under a collective bargaining agreement which expires on September 30, 2012, as follows:

Plan name: Bakery and Confectionery Union and Industry International Pension Fund

Employer Identification Number and plan number: 52-6118572, plan number 001

Funded Status as of the most recent year available: 86.51% funded as of January 1, 2010

The Company's contributions to such plan: $2,046, $1,923 and $1,633 in 2011, 2010 and 2009, respectively

Plan status: Not in reorganization and not insolvent as of December 31, 2010

Although the Company has been advised that the plan is currently in an underfunded status, the relative position of each employer associated with the multi-employer plan with respect to the actuarial present value of benefits and net plan assets is not determinable by the Company. The Company's annual contributions do not exceed 5% of total contributions to the Plan.

Deferred compensation:

The Company sponsors three deferred compensation plans for selected executives and other employees: (i) the Excess Benefit Plan, which restores retirement benefits lost due to IRS limitations on contributions to tax-qualified plans, (ii) the Supplemental Plan, which allows eligible employees to defer the receipt of eligible compensation until designated future dates and (iii) the Career Achievement Plan, which provides a deferred annual incentive award to selected executives. Participants in these plans earn a return on amounts due them based on several investment options, which mirror returns on underlying investments (primarily mutual funds). The Company economically hedges its obligations under the plans by investing in the actual underlying investments. These investments are classified as trading securities and are carried at fair value. At December 31, 2011 and 2010, these investments totaled $41,768 and $38,504, respectively. All gains and losses and related investment income in these investments, which are recorded in other income (expense), net, are equally offset by corresponding increases and decreases in the Company's deferred compensation liabilities.

Postretirement health care and life insurance benefit plans:

The Company provides certain postretirement health care and life insurance benefits for corporate office and management employees based upon their age, years of service, date of hire and if they agree to contribute a portion of the cost as determined by the Company. The Company has the right to modify or terminate these benefits and does not fund postretirement health care and life insurance benefits in advance of payments for benefit claims. The Company is currently contemplating changes to its postretirement health care and life insurance benefits with the intention of reducing the Company's cost of providing such benefits. These changes are likely to include increasing retiree premium contributions, reducing and eliminating certain benefits, and taking steps to ensure that the Company does not become subject to the excise tax on high value coverage instituted by the Patient Protection and Affordability Act. The Company is not presently able to determine the effects of such changes on its financial statements.

Amounts recognized in accumulated other comprehensive loss (pre-tax) at December 31, 2011 are as follows:

Prior service credit	$ (626)
Net actuarial loss	8,255
Net amount recognized in accumulated other comprehensive loss	$7,629

The estimated actuarial loss and prior service credit to be amortized from accumulated other comprehensive income into net periodic benefit cost during 2012 are $1,146 and $(125), respectively.

The changes in the accumulated postretirement benefit obligation at December 31, 2011 and 2010 consist of the following:

	December 31,	
	2011	2010
Benefit obligation, beginning of year	$20,689	$16,674
Service cost	831	696
Interest cost	1,117	958
Actuarial loss	3,898	2,714
Benefits paid	(427)	(353)
Benefit obligation, end of year	$26,108	$20,689

Net periodic postretirement benefit cost included the following components:

	2011	2010	2009
Service cost—benefits attributed to service during the period	$ 831	$ 696	$ 704
Interest cost on the accumulated postretirement benefit obligation	1,117	958	853
Net amortization	501	128	140
Net periodic postretirement benefit cost	$2,449	$1,782	$1,697

For measurement purposes, the 2012 annual rate of increase in the per capita cost of covered health care benefits was assumed to be 8.2% for pre-age 65 retirees, post 65 retirees and for prescription drugs; these rates were assumed to decrease gradually to 5.0% for 2019 and remain at that level thereafter. The health care cost trend rate assumption has a significant effect on the amounts reported. The weighted-average discount rate used in determining the accumulated postretirement benefit obligation was 4.31% and 5.47% at December 31, 2011 and 2010, respectively.

Increasing or decreasing the health care trend rates by one percentage point in each year would have the following effect:

	1% Increase	1% Decrease
Postretirement benefit obligation	$6,247	$(4,277)
Total of service and interest cost components	$ 484	$ (320)

The Company estimates future benefit payments will be $574, $710, $882, $993 and $1,095 in 2012 through 2016, respectively, and a total of $7,002 in 2017 through 2020. The future benefit payments are net of the annual Medicare Part D subsidy of approximately $1,094 beginning in 2012.

NOTE 8—COMMITMENTS:

Rental expense aggregated $1,042, $1,152 and $1,180 in 2011, 2010 and 2009, respectively.

Future operating lease commitments are not significant.

NOTE 9—SEGMENT AND GEOGRAPHIC INFORMATION:

The Company operates as a single reportable segment encompassing the manufacture and sale of confectionery products. Its principal manufacturing operations are located in the United States and Canada, and its principal market is the United States. The Company also manufactures and sells confectionery products in Mexico, and exports products to Canada and other countries worldwide.

The following geographic data includes net product sales summarized on the basis of the customer location and long-lived assets based on their physical location:

	2011	2010	2009
Net product sales:			
United States	$487,185	$471,714	$455,517
Foreign	41,184	45,435	40,075
	$528,369	$517,149	$495,592
Long-lived assets:			
United States	$170,173	$172,087	$176,044
Foreign	41,989	43,405	44,677
	$212,162	$215,492	$220,721

NOTE 10—FAIR VALUE MEASUREMENTS:

Current accounting guidance defines fair value as the price that would be received in the sale of an asset or paid to transfer a liability in an orderly transaction between market participants at the measurement date. Guidance requires disclosure of the extent to which fair value is used to measure financial assets and liabilities, the inputs utilized in calculating valuation measurements, and the effect of the measurement of significant unobservable inputs on earnings, or changes in net assets, as of the measurement date. Guidance establishes a three-level valuation hierarchy based upon the transparency of inputs utilized in the measurement and valuation of financial assets or liabilities as of the measurement date. Level 1 inputs include quoted prices for identical instruments and are the most observable. Level 2 inputs include quoted prices for similar assets and observable inputs such as interest rates, foreign currency exchange rates, commodity rates and yield curves. Level 3 inputs are not observable in the market and include management's own judgments about the assumptions market participants would use in pricing the asset or liability. The use of observable and unobservable inputs is reflected in the hierarchy assessment disclosed in the table below.

As of December 31, 2011 and 2010, the Company held certain financial assets that are required to be measured at fair value on a recurring basis. These included derivative hedging instruments related to the foreign currency forward contracts and purchase of certain raw materials, investments in trading securities and available for sale securities, including an auction rate security (ARS). The Company's available for sale and trading securities principally consist of municipal bonds and mutual funds that are publicly traded.

The following tables present information about the Company's financial assets measured at fair value as of December 31, 2011 and 2010, and indicate the fair value hierarchy and the valuation techniques utilized by the Company to determine such fair value:

	Estimated Fair Value December 31, 2011			
	Total	Input Levels Used		
	Fair Value	Level 1	Level 2	Level 3
Cash and equivalents	$ 78,612	$ 78,612	$ —	$ —
Auction rate security	7,453	—	—	7,453
Available-for-sale securities, excluding the auction rate security	57,835	—	57,835	—
Foreign currency forward contracts	205	—	205	—
Commodity futures contracts	203	203	—	—
Commodity options contracts	—	—	—	—
Trading securities	41,768	41,768	—	—
Total assets measured at fair value	$186,076	$120,583	$58,040	$7,453

	Estimated Fair Value December 31, 2010			
	Total	Input Levels Used		
	Fair Value	Level 1	Level 2	Level 3
Cash and equivalents	$115,976	$115,976	$ —	$ —
Auction rate security	6,775	—	—	6,775
Available-for-sale securities, excluding the auction rate security	27,178	—	27,178	—
Foreign currency forward contracts	942	—	942	—
Commodity futures contracts	2,310	2,310	—	—
Commodity options contracts	5,369	5,369	—	—
Trading securities	38,504	38,504	—	—
Total assets measured at fair value	$197,054	$162,159	$28,120	$6,775

Available for sale securities which utilize level 2 inputs consist primarily of municipal bonds, which are valued based on quoted market prices or alternative pricing sources with reasonable level of price transparency.

A summary of the aggregate fair value, gross unrealized gains, gross unrealized losses, realized losses and amortized cost basis of the Company's investment portfolio by major security type is as follows:

	December 31, 2011				
	Amortized	Fair	Unrealized		Realized
Available for Sale:	Cost	Value	Gains	Losses	Losses
Auction rate security	$ 8,410	$ 7,453	$ —	$ (957)	$ —
Municipal bonds	57,389	57,791	402	—	—
Mutual funds	45	44	—	(1)	—
	$65,844	$65,288	$402	$ (958)	$ —

	December 31, 2010				
	Amortized	Fair	Unrealized		Realized
Available for Sale:	Cost	Value	Gains	Losses	Losses
Auction rate security	$ 8,410	$ 6,775	$ —	$(1,635)	$ —
Municipal bonds	27,073	27,122	49	—	—
Mutual funds	56	56	—	—	—
	$35,539	$33,953	$ 49	$(1,635)	$ —

As of December 31, 2011, the Company's long-term investments included an auction rate security, Jefferson County Alabama Sewer Revenue Refunding Warrants, reported at a fair value of $7,453, after reflecting a $5,140 other-than-temporary impairment and a $957 temporary, as defined, decline in market value against its $13,550 par value. This other-than-temporary impairment was recorded in other income (expense), net in 2008. In 2008, this auction rate security was determined to be other-than-temporarily impaired due to the duration and severity of the decline in fair value. The Company estimated the fair value of this auction rate security utilizing a valuation model with Level 3 inputs.

This valuation model considered, among other items, the credit risk of the collateral underlying the auction rate security, the credit risk of the bond insurer, interest rates, and the amount and timing of expected future cash flows including the Company's assumption about the market expectation of the next successful auction. See also the Management's Discussion and Analysis of Financial Condition and Results of Operations regarding Jefferson County auction rate security.

The Company classified this auction rate security as non-current and has included it in long-term investments on the Consolidated Statements of Financial Position at December 31, 2011 and 2010 because the Company believes that the current condition of the auction rate security market may take more than twelve months to improve.

The following table presents additional information about the Company's financial instruments (all ARS) measured at fair value on a recurring basis using Level 3 inputs at December 31, 2011 and 2010:

	2011	2010
Balance at January 1	$6,775	$7,710
Unrealized loss recognized in other comprehensive loss	678	(935)
Balance at December 31	$7,453	$6,775

The $7,500 carrying amount of the Company's industrial revenue development bonds at December 31, 2011 and 2010 approximates its estimated fair value as the bonds have a floating interest rate.

In addition to assets and liabilities that are recorded at fair value on a recurring basis, guidance requires the Company to record assets and liabilities at fair value on a nonrecurring basis generally as a result of impairment charges. Assets measured at fair value on a nonrecurring basis during 2009 are summarized below:

	Pre-Impairment Cost Basis	2009 Impairment Charge	New Cost Basis	Level 1	Level 2	Level 3
Equity method investment	$ 9,361	$ 4,400	$ 4,961	$ —	$ —	$ 4,961
Trademarks	189,024	14,000	175,024	—	—	175,024
Total	$198,385	$18,400	$179,985	$ —	$ —	$179,985

Twelve Months Ended December 31, 2009 — Level Used to Determine New Cost Basis

As discussed in Note 6, during the fourth quarter of 2009 the Company recognized an impairment of $4,400 in an equity method investment based on Level 3 inputs.

As discussed in Note 13, during the fourth quarter of 2009 the Company recognized a trademark impairment of $14,000 based on Level 3 inputs.

NOTE 11—DERIVATIVE INSTRUMENTS AND HEDGING ACTIVITIES:

From time to time, the Company uses derivative instruments, including foreign currency forward contracts, commodity futures contracts and commodity option contracts, to manage its exposures to foreign exchange and commodity prices. Commodity futures contracts and most commodity option contracts are intended and effective as hedges of market price risks associated with the anticipated purchase of certain raw materials (primarily sugar). Foreign currency forward contracts are intended and effective as hedges of the Company's exposure to the variability of cash flows, primarily related to the foreign exchange rate changes of products manufactured in Canada and sold in the United States, and periodic equipment purchases from foreign suppliers denominated in a foreign currency. The Company does not engage in trading or other speculative use of derivative instruments.

The Company recognizes all derivative instruments as either assets or liabilities at fair value in the Consolidated Statements of Financial Position. Derivative assets are recorded in other receivables and derivative liabilities are recorded in accrued liabilities. The Company uses either hedge accounting or mark-to-market accounting for its derivative instruments. Derivatives that qualify for hedge accounting are designated as cash flow hedges by formally documenting the hedge relationships, including identification of the hedging instruments, the hedged items and other critical terms, as well as the Company's risk management objectives and strategies for undertaking the hedge transaction.

Changes in the fair value of the Company's cash flow hedges are recorded in accumulated other comprehensive loss, net of tax, and are reclassified to earnings in the periods in which earnings are affected by the hedged item. Substantially all amounts reported in accumulated other comprehensive loss for commodity derivatives are expected to be reclassified to cost of goods sold. Substantially all amounts reported in accumulated other comprehensive loss for foreign currency derivatives are expected to be reclassified to other income (expense), net.

The following table summarizes the Company's outstanding derivative contracts and their effects on its Consolidated Statements of Financial Position at December 31, 2011 and 2010:

December 31, 2011

	Notional Amounts	Assets	Liabilities
Derivatives designated as hedging instruments:			
Foreign currency forward contracts	$13,044	$205	$ —
Commodity futures contracts	4,557	341	(138)
Commodity option contracts	—	—	—
Total derivatives		$546	$(138)

December 31, 2010

	Notional Amounts	Assets	Liabilities
Derivatives designated as hedging instruments:			
Foreign currency forward contracts	$ 3,572	$ 942	$ —
Commodity futures contracts	4,407	2,310	—
Commodity option contracts	10,344	5,481	(112)
Total derivatives		$8,733	$(112)

The effects of derivative instruments on the Company's Consolidated Statement of Earnings, Comprehensive Earnings and Retained Earnings for years ended December 31, 2011 and 2010 are as follows:

	For Year Ended December 31, 2011		
	Gain (Loss) Recognized in OCI	Gain (Loss) Reclassified from Accumulated OCI into Earnings	Gain (Loss) on Amount Excluded from Effectiveness Testing Recognized in Earnings
Foreign currency forward contracts	$ 317	$1,054	$—
Commodity futures contracts	4,674	6,782	—
Commodity option contracts	(5,388)	(305)	—
Total	$ (397)	$7,531	$—

	For Year Ended December 31, 2010		
	Gain (Loss) Recognized in OCI	Gain (Loss) Reclassified from Accumulated OCI into Earnings	Gain (Loss) on Amount Excluded from Effectiveness Testing Recognized in Earnings
Foreign currency forward contracts	$ 467	$3,199	$—
Commodity futures contracts	2,120	(191)	—
Commodity option contracts	4,726	(357)	—
Total	$7,313	$2,651	$—

For the years ended December 31, 2011 and 2010, the Company recognized a loss of $0 and $1,613 in earnings, respectively, related to mark-to-market accounting for certain commodity option contacts.

NOTE 12—COMPREHENSIVE EARNINGS (LOSS):

The following table sets forth information with respect to accumulated other comprehensive earnings (loss):

	Foreign Currency Translation Adjustment	Unrealized Gain (Loss) on		Postretirement and Pension Benefits	Accumulated Other Comprehensive Earning (Loss)
		Investments	Derivatives		
Balance at January 1, 2009	$(14,292)	$ 191	$ 220	$(1,360)	$(15,241)
Unrealized gains (losses)	1,183	(709)	4,341	109	4,924
(Gains) losses reclassified to net earnings	—	—	(1,015)	—	(1,015)
Tax effect	(118)	263	(1,232)	23	(1,064)
Net of tax amount	1,065	(446)	2,094	132	2,845
Balance at December 31, 2009	(13,227)	(255)	2,314	(1,228)	(12,396)
Unrealized gains (losses)	856	(1,179)	7,313	(3,007)	3,983
(Gains) losses reclassified to net earnings	—	—	(2,651)	—	(2,651)
Tax effect	135	435	(1,724)	1,005	(149)
Net of tax amount	991	(744)	2,938	(2,002)	1,183
Balance at December 31, 2010	(12,236)	(999)	5,252	(3,230)	(11,213)
Unrealized gains (losses)	(2,496)	1,030	(397)	(3,092)	(4,955)
(Gains) losses reclassified to net earnings	—	—	(7,531)	—	(7,531)
Tax effect	46	(382)	2,933	1,149	3,746
Net of tax amount	(2,450)	648	(4,995)	(1,943)	(8,740)
Balance at December 31, 2011	$(14,686)	$ (351)	$ 257	$(5,173)	$(19,953)

NOTE 13—GOODWILL AND INTANGIBLE ASSETS:

All of the Company's intangible indefinite-lived assets are trademarks.

The changes in the carrying amount of trademarks for 2011 and 2010 were as follows:

	2011	2010
Original cost	$193,767	$193,767
Accumulated impairment losses as of January 1	(18,743)	(18,743)
Balance at January 1	$175,024	$175,024
Current year impairment losses	—	—
Balance at December 31	$175,024	$175,024
Accumulated impairment losses as of December 31	$ (18,743)	$ (18,743)

As of December 31, 2009, management ascertained certain trademarks were impaired, and recorded a pre-tax charge of $14,000. The principal driver of this impairment charge was an increase in the discount rate required by market participants. The fair value of indefinite-lived intangible assets was primarily assessed using the present value of estimated future cash flows.

The Company has no accumulated impairment losses of goodwill.

Auditor's Report

All publicly held corporations, as well as many other businesses and organizations (both profit and not-for-profit, large and small), engage the services of independent certified public accountants (CPAs) for the purpose of obtaining an objective, expert report on their financial statements. Based on a comprehensive examination of the company's accounting system, accounting records, and the financial statements, the outside CPA issues the auditor's report.

The standard auditor's report should identify who and what was audited and indicate the responsibilities of management and the auditor relative to the financial statements. The report should clearly state that the audit was conducted in accordance with generally accepted auditing standards and discusses the nature and limitations of the audit. Finally, the report should express an informed opinion as to (1) the fairness of the financial statements and (2) their conformity with generally accepted accounting principles. The report of PricewaterhouseCoopers LLP appearing in Tootsie Roll's annual report is shown below.

Report of Independent Registered Public Accounting Firm

To the Board of Directors and Shareholders of Tootsie Roll Industries, Inc.:

In our opinion, the accompanying consolidated statements of financial position and the related consolidated statements of earnings, comprehensive earnings and retained earnings, and of cash flows present fairly, in all material respects, the financial position of Tootsie Roll Industries, Inc. and its subsidiaries at December 31, 2011 and December 31, 2010, and the results of their operations and their cash flows for each of the three years in the period ended December 31, 2011 in conformity with accounting principles generally accepted in the United States of America. Also in our opinion, the Company maintained, in all material respects, effective internal control over financial reporting as of December 31, 2011, based on criteria established in *Internal Control—Integrated Framework* issued by the Committee of Sponsoring Organizations of the Treadway Commission (COSO). The Company's management is responsible for these financial statements, for maintaining effective internal control over financial reporting and for its assessment of the effectiveness of internal control over financial reporting, included in Management's Report on Internal Control over Financial Reporting on page 27 of the 2011 Annual Report to Shareholders. Our responsibility is to express opinions on these financial statements and on the Company's internal control over financial reporting based on our integrated audits. We conducted our audits in accordance with the standards of the Public Company Accounting Oversight Board (United States). Those standards require that we plan and perform the audits to obtain reasonable assurance about whether the financial statements are free of material misstatement and whether effective internal control over financial reporting was maintained in all material respects. Our audits of the financial statements included examining, on a test basis, evidence supporting the amounts and disclosures in the financial statements, assessing the accounting principles used and significant estimates made by management, and evaluating the overall financial statement presentation. Our audit of internal control over financial reporting included obtaining an understanding of internal control over financial reporting, assessing the risk that a material weakness exists, and testing and evaluating the design and operating effectiveness of internal control based on the assessed risk. Our audits also included performing such other procedures as we considered necessary in the circumstances. We believe that our audits provide a reasonable basis for our opinions.

As discussed in Note 1 to the consolidated financial statements, the Company changed the manner in which it accounts for LIFO inventories in 2011.

A company's internal control over financial reporting is a process designed to provide reasonable assurance regarding the reliability of financial reporting and the preparation of financial statements for external purposes in accordance with generally accepted accounting principles. A company's internal control over financial reporting includes those policies and procedures that (i) pertain to the maintenance of records that, in reasonable detail, accurately and fairly reflect the transactions and dispositions of the assets of the company; (ii) provide reasonable assurance that transactions are recorded as necessary to permit preparation of financial statements in accordance with generally accepted accounting principles, and that receipts and expenditures of the company are being made only in accordance with authorizations of management and directors of the company; and (iii) provide reasonable assurance regarding prevention or timely detection of unauthorized acquisition, use, or disposition of the company's assets that could have a material effect on the financial statements.

Because of its inherent limitations, internal control over financial reporting may not prevent or detect misstatements. Also, projections of any evaluation of effectiveness to future periods are subject to the risk that controls may become inadequate because of changes in conditions, or that the degree of compliance with the policies or procedures may deteriorate.

PricewaterhouseCoopers LLP

Chicago, IL
February 29, 2012

Performance Graph

The following performance graph compares the cumulative total shareholder return on the Company's Common Stock for a five-year period (December 31, 2006 to December 31, 2011) with the cumulative total return of Standard & Poor's 500 Stock Index ("S&P 500") and the Dow Jones Industry Food Index ("Peer Group," which includes the Company), assuming (i) $100 invested on December 31 of the first year of the chart in each of the Company's Common Stock, S&P 500 and the Dow Jones Industry Food Index and (ii) the reinvestment of dividends.

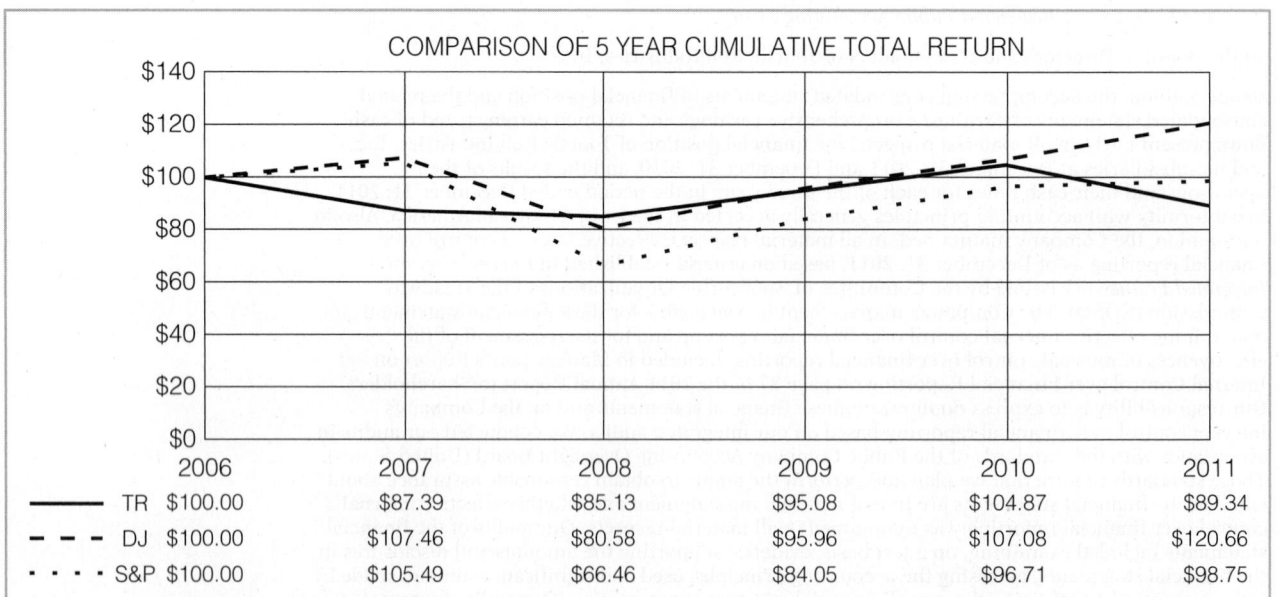

	2006	2007	2008	2009	2010	2011
TR	$100.00	$87.39	$85.13	$95.08	$104.87	$89.34
DJ	$100.00	$107.46	$80.58	$95.96	$107.08	$120.66
S&P	$100.00	$105.49	$66.46	$84.05	$96.71	$98.75

COMPARISON OF 5 YEAR CUMULATIVE TOTAL RETURN

Management's Report on Internal Control and Management Certifications of Financial Statements

The Sarbanes-Oxley Act requires managers of publicly traded companies to establish and maintain systems of internal control on the company's financial reporting processes. In addition, the act requires the company's top management to provide certifications regarding the accuracy of the financial statements. The reports of Tootsie Roll are shown below.

Management's Report on Internal Control Over Financial Reporting

The management of Tootsie Roll Industries, Inc. is responsible for establishing and maintaining adequate internal control over financial reporting, as such term is defined in the Securities Exchange Act of 1934 (SEC) Rule 13a-15(f). Our management conducted an evaluation of the effectiveness of the Company's internal control over financial reporting as of December 31, 2011 as required by SEC Rule 13a-15(c). In making this assessment, we used the criteria established in *Internal Control—Integrated Framework* issued by the Committee of Sponsoring Organizations of the Treadway Commission (the COSO criteria). Based on our evaluation under the COSO criteria, our management concluded that our internal control over financial reporting was effective as of December 31, 2011.

The effectiveness of the Company's internal control over financial reporting as of December 31, 2011 has been audited by PricewaterhouseCoopers LLP, an independent registered public accounting firm, as stated in their report which appears on page 26.

Tootsie Roll Industries, Inc.

Chicago, Illinois
February 29, 2012

Quarterly Financial Data (Unaudited)

TOOTSIE ROLL INDUSTRIES, INC. AND SUBSIDIARIES

	First	Second	Third	Fourth	Year
	(Thousands of dollars except per share data)				
2011					
Net product sales	$108,323	$104,884	$186,784	$128,378	$528,369
Product gross margin	34,799	33,898	54,554	39,893	163,144
Net earnings	8,330	6,486	18,855	10,267	43,938
Net earnings per share	0.14	0.11	0.33	0.18	0.76
2010					
Net product sales	$103,244	$105,026	$191,045	$117,834	$517,149
Product gross margin	34,909	35,450	61,649	35,807	167,815
Net earnings	9,068	8,309	26,245	9,441	53,063
Net earnings per share	0.15	0.14	0.45	0.16	0.90

The results for the quarters presented reflect the retrospective application of a change in accounting principle for inventory valuation and the related effects on product gross margin, net earnings and net earnings per share as discussed in Note 1 to the Consolidated Financial Statements. Product gross margin reflects increases (decreases) of $517, $504, and $811 for the three quarters of 2011 and $(212), $(216), $(375) and $(218) for the four quarters of 2010. Net earnings reflect increases (decreases) $330, $321, and $517 for the three quarters of 2011 and $(136), $(138), $(239) and $(138) for four quarters of 2010. Net earnings per share increased .01 per share for the third quarter of 2011 and decreased .01 per share for the first quarter of 2010. All other quarters remain unchanged as reported.

Net earnings per share is based upon average outstanding shares as adjusted for 3% stock dividends issued during the second quarter of each year and revision of net earnings as discussed above. The sum of the per share amounts may not equal annual amounts due to rounding.

2011-2010 QUARTERLY SUMMARY OF TOOTSIE ROLL INDUSTRIES, INC. STOCK PRICES AND DIVIDENDS PER SHARE

STOCK PRICES*

	2011		2010	
	High	**Low**	**High**	**Low**
1st Qtr	$29.45	$27.06	$28.24	$25.88
2nd Qtr	$29.68	$27.78	$28.04	$23.65
3rd Qtr	$29.80	$23.52	$25.95	$23.34
4th Qtr	$25.95	$22.85	$29.84	$24.64

*NYSE—Closing Price

Estimated Number of shareholders at February 2012:

Common Stock	18,000
Class B Common Stock	5,000

DIVIDENDS

	2011	**2010**
1st Qtr	$.08	$.08
2nd Qtr	$.08	$.08
3rd Qtr	$.08	$.08
4th Qtr	$.08	$.08

NOTE: In addition to the above cash dividends, a 3% stock dividend was issued on April 7, 2011 and April 8, 2010. Cash dividends are restated to reflect 3% stock dividends.

Financial Highlights

Companies often present the financial highlights section inside the front cover of the annual report or on its first two pages. This section generally reports the total or per share amounts for five to ten financial items for the current year and one or more previous years.

Five Year Summary of Earnings and Financial Highlights

TOOTSIE ROLL INDUSTRIES, INC. AND SUBSIDIARIES

(Thousands of dollars except per share, percentage and ratio figures)

(See management's comments starting on page 5)

	2011	2010	2009	2008	2007
Sales and Earnings Data (2)(3)(4)(5)					
Net product sales	$528,369	$517,149	$495,592	$492,051	$492,742
Product gross margin	163,144	167,815	175,817	158,055	165,456
Interest expense	121	142	243	378	53
Provision for income taxes	16,974	20,005	9,892	16,347	25,401
Net earnings	43,938	53,063	53,157	38,880	52,175
% of net product sales	8.3%	10.3%	10.7%	7.9%	10.6%
% of shareholders' equity	6.6%	8.0%	8.1%	6.1%	8.1%
Per Common Share Data (1)(3)(4)(5)					
Net earnings	$ 0.76	$ 0.90	$ 0.89	$ 0.65	$ 0.85
Cash dividends declared	0.32	0.32	0.32	0.32	0.32
Stock dividends	3%	3%	3%	3%	3%
Additional Financial data (1)(2)(3)(4)(5)					
Working capital	$153,846	$176,662	$154,409	$129,694	$142,163
Net cash provided by operating activities	50,390	82,805	76,994	57,533	90,148
Net cash provided by (used in) investing activities	(51,157)	(16,808)	(16,364)	(7,565)	(43,429)
Net cash used in financing activities	(36,597)	(41,011)	(38,548)	(38,666)	(44,842)
Property, plant & equipment additions	16,351	12,813	20,831	34,355	14,767
Net property, plant & equipment	212,162	215,492	220,721	217,628	201,401
Total assets	857,856	857,959	836,844	813,252	813,134
Long-term debt	7,500	7,500	7,500	7,500	7,500
Shareholders' equity	665,935	667,408	654,244	636,847	640,204
Average shares outstanding	57,892	58,685	59,425	60,152	61,580

(1) Per Common share data and average shares outstanding adjusted for annual 3% stock dividends.

(2) Certain reclassifications have been made to prior year numbers to conform to current year presentation.

(3) The 2009 data included the release of tax valuation allowances, charges related to the impairment of an equity method investment and impairment charges related to certain trademarks as discussed in Notes 4, 6 and 13 to the Consolidated Financial Statements, respectively.

(4) The 2008 data included a charge for the other-than-temporary impairment of an ARS. Further information is included in Note 10 to the Consolidated Financial Statements.

(5) Reflects the increase (decrease) retrospective application of a change in accounting principle for inventory valuation for the following:

	2010	2009	2008	2007
Product gross margin	$(1,021)	$(1,130)	$(682)	$409
Provision for income taxes	(370)	(409)	(247)	148
Net earnings	(651)	(721)	(435)	261
Net earnings per share	(0.02)	(0.02)	—	0.01
Working capital	(2,424)	(1,403)	(273)	409
Total assets	(2,424)	(1,403)	(273)	409
Shareholders' equity	(1,546)	(895)	(174)	261

SPECIMEN FINANCIAL STATEMENTS: THE HERSHEY COMPANY

THE HERSHEY COMPANY

CONSOLIDATED STATEMENTS OF INCOME

For the years ended December 31, In thousands of dollars except per share amounts	2011	2010	2009
Net Sales	**$6,080,788**	$5,671,009	$5,298,668
Costs and Expenses:			
Cost of sales	**3,548,896**	3,255,801	3,245,531
Selling, marketing and administrative	**1,477,750**	1,426,477	1,208,672
Business realignment and impairment (credits) charges, net	**(886)**	83,433	82,875
Total costs and expenses	**5,025,760**	4,765,711	4,537,078
Income before Interest and Income Taxes	**1,055,028**	905,298	761,590
Interest expense, net	**92,183**	96,434	90,459
Income before Income Taxes	**962,845**	808,864	671,131
Provision for income taxes	**333,883**	299,065	235,137
Net Income	**$ 628,962**	$ 509,799	$ 435,994
Net Income Per Share—Basic—Class B Common Stock	**$ 2.58**	$ 2.08	$ 1.77
Net Income Per Share—Diluted—Class B Common Stock	**$ 2.56**	$ 2.07	$ 1.77
Net Income Per Share—Basic—Common Stock	**$ 2.85**	$ 2.29	$ 1.97
Net Income Per Share—Diluted—Common Stock	**$ 2.74**	$ 2.21	$ 1.90
Cash Dividends Paid Per Share:			
Common Stock	**$ 1.3800**	$1.2800	$ 1.1900
Class B Common Stock	**1.2500**	1.1600	1.0712

The notes to consolidated financial statements are an integral part of these statements and are included in Hershey's 2011 Annual Report, available at **www.thehersheycompany.com**.

THE HERSHEY COMPANY

CONSOLIDATED BALANCE SHEETS

December 31,	2011	2010
In thousands of dollars		
ASSETS		
Current Assets:		
Cash and cash equivalents.	$ 693,686	$ 884,642
Accounts receivable—trade.	399,499	390,061
Inventories	648,953	533,622
Deferred income taxes.	136,861	55,760
Prepaid expenses and other.	167,559	141,132
Total current assets.	2,046,558	2,005,217
Property, Plant and Equipment, Net	1,559,717	1,437,702
Goodwill	516,745	524,134
Other Intangibles	111,913	123,080
Deferred Income Taxes	38,544	21,387
Other Assets	138,722	161,212
Total assets	$4,412,199	$4,272,732
LIABILITIES AND STOCKHOLDERS' EQUITY		
Current Liabilities:		
Accounts payable	$ 420,017	$ 410,655
Accrued liabilities	612,186	593,308
Accrued income taxes	1,899	9,402
Short-term debt	42,080	24,088
Current portion of long-term debt	97,593	261,392
Total current liabilities.	1,173,775	1,298,845
Long-term Debt	1,748,500	1,541,825
Other Long-term Liabilities.	617,276	494,461
Total liabilities	3,539,551	3,335,131
Commitments and Contingencies	—	—
Stockholders' Equity:		
The Hershey Company Stockholders' Equity		
Preferred Stock, shares issued: none in 2011 and 2010.	—	—
Common Stock, shares issued: 299,269,702 in 2011 and 299,195,325 in 2010	299,269	299,195
Class B Common Stock, shares issued: 60,632,042 in 2011 and 60,706,419 in 2010	60,632	60,706
Additional paid-in capital.	490,817	434,865
Retained earnings.	4,699,597	4,374,718
Treasury—Common Stock shares, at cost: 134,695,826 in 2011 and 132,871,512 in 2010	(4,258,962)	(4,052,101)
Accumulated other comprehensive loss	(442,331)	(215,067)
The Hershey Company stockholders' equity	849,022	902,316
Noncontrolling interests in subsidiaries	23,626	35,285
Total stockholders' equity	872,648	937,601
Total liabilities and stockholders' equity	$4,412,199	$4,272,732

THE HERSHEY COMPANY

CONSOLIDATED STATEMENTS OF CASH FLOWS

For the years ended December 31, In thousands of dollars	2011	2010	2009
Cash Flows Provided from (Used by) Operating Activities			
Net income	$628,962	$509,799	$ 435,994
Adjustments to reconcile net income to net cash provided from operations:			
Depreciation and amortization	215,763	197,116	182,411
Stock-based compensation expense, net of tax of $15,127, $17,413 and $19,223, respectively	28,341	32,055	34,927
Excess tax benefits from stock-based compensation	(13,997)	(1,385)	(4,455)
Deferred income taxes	33,611	(18,654)	(40,578)
Gain on sale of trademark licensing rights, net of tax of $5,962	(11,072)	—	—
Business realignment and impairment charges, net of tax of $18,333, $20,635 and $38,308, respectively	30,838	77,935	60,823
Contributions to pension plans	(8,861)	(6,073)	(54,457)
Changes in assets and liabilities, net of effects from business acquisitions and divestitures:			
Accounts receivable—trade	(9,438)	20,329	46,584
Inventories	(115,331)	(13,910)	74,000
Accounts payable	7,860	90,434	37,228
Other assets and liabilities	(205,809)	13,777	293,272
Net Cash Provided from Operating Activities	580,867	901,423	1,065,749
Cash Flows Provided from (Used by) Investing Activities			
Capital additions	(323,961)	(179,538)	(126,324)
Capitalized software additions	(23,606)	(21,949)	(19,146)
Proceeds from sales of property, plant and equipment	312	2,201	10,364
Proceeds from sale of trademark licensing rights	20,000	—	—
Business acquisitions	(5,750)	—	(15,220)
Net Cash (Used by) Investing Activities	(333,005)	(199,286)	(150,326)
Cash Flows Provided from (Used by) Financing Activities			
Net change in short-term borrowings	10,834	1,156	(458,047)
Long-term borrowings	249,126	348,208	—
Repayment of long-term debt	(256,189)	(71,548)	(8,252)
Proceeds from lease financing agreement	47,601	—	—
Cash dividends paid	(304,083)	(283,434)	(263,403)
Exercise of stock options	184,411	92,033	28,318
Excess tax benefits from stock-based compensation	13,997	1,385	4,455
Contributions from noncontrolling interests in subsidiaries	—	10,199	7,322
Repurchase of Common Stock	(384,515)	(169,099)	(9,314)
Net Cash (Used by) Financing Activities	(438,818)	(71,100)	(698,921)
(Decrease) Increase in Cash and Cash Equivalents	(190,956)	631,037	216,502
Cash and Cash Equivalents as of January 1	884,642	253,605	37,103
Cash and Cash Equivalents as of December 31	$693,686	$884,642	$ 253,605
Interest Paid	$ 97,892	$ 97,932	$ 91,623
Income Taxes Paid	292,315	350,948	252,230

THE HERSHEY COMPANY
CONSOLIDATED STATEMENTS OF STOCKHOLDERS' EQUITY

In thousands of dollars	Preferred Stock	Common Stock	Class B Common Stock	Additional Paid-in Capital	Retained Earnings	Treasury Common Stock	Accumulated Other Comprehensive Income (Loss)	Noncontrolling Interests in Subsidiaries	Total Stockholders' Equity
Balance as of January 1, 2009	$—	$299,190	$60,711	$352,375	$3,975,762	$(4,009,931)	$(359,908)	$31,745	$349,944
Net income					435,994				435,994
Other comprehensive income							157,064		157,064
Comprehensive income									593,058
Dividends:									
Common Stock, $1.19 per share					(198,371)				(198,371)
Class B Common Stock, $1.0712 per share					(65,032)				(65,032)
Conversion of Class B Common Stock into Common Stock		2	(2)						—
Incentive plan transactions				(355)		4,762			4,407
Stock-based compensation				44,704					44,704
Exercise of stock options				(2,046)		34,854			32,808
Repurchase of Common Stock						(9,314)			(9,314)
Noncontrolling interests in subsidiaries								8,135	8,135
Balance as of December 31, 2009		299,192	60,709	394,678	4,148,353	(3,979,629)	(202,844)	39,880	760,339
Net income					509,799				509,799
Other comprehensive loss							(12,223)		(12,223)
Comprehensive income									497,576
Dividends:									
Common Stock, $1.28 per share					(213,013)				(213,013)
Class B Common Stock, $1.16 per share					(70,421)				(70,421)
Conversion of Class B Common Stock into Common Stock		3	(3)						—
Incentive plan transactions				(7,453)		10,239			2,786
Stock-based compensation				40,630					40,630
Exercise of stock options				7,010		86,388			93,398
Repurchase of Common Stock						(169,099)			(169,099)
Noncontrolling interests in subsidiaries								(4,595)	(4,595)
Balance as of December 31, 2010		299,195	60,706	434,865	4,374,718	(4,052,101)	(215,067)	35,285	937,601
Net income					628,962				628,962
Other comprehensive loss							(227,264)		(227,264)
Comprehensive income									401,698
Dividends:									
Common Stock, $1.38 per share					(228,269)				(228,269)
Class B Common Stock, $1.25 per share					(75,814)				(75,814)
Conversion of Class B Common Stock into Common Stock		74	(74)						—
Incentive plan transactions				(15,844)		14,306			(1,538)
Stock-based compensation				40,439					40,439
Exercise of stock options				31,357		163,348			194,705
Repurchase of Common Stock						(384,515)			(384,515)
Noncontrolling interests in subsidiaries								(11,659)	(11,659)
Balance as of December 31, 2011	$—	$299,269	$60,632	$490,817	$4,699,597	$(4,258,962)	$(442,331)	$23,626	$872,648

SPECIMEN FINANCIAL STATEMENTS: ZETAR plc

Consolidated income statement

FOR THE YEAR ENDED 30 APRIL 2011

	Note	2011 Adjusted[1] results £'000	2011 Adjusting items £'000	2011 Total £'000	2010 Adjusted[1] results £'000	2010 Adjusting items £'000	2010 Total £'000
Revenue	5	**134,998**	–	**134,998**	131,922	–	131,922
Cost of sales		**(107,677)**	–	**(107,677)**	(105,112)	–	(105,112)
Gross profit		**27,321**	–	**27,321**	26,810	–	26,810
Distribution costs		**(5,550)**	–	**(5,550)**	(5,495)	–	(5,495)
Administrative expenses:							
– other administrative expenses		**(14,271)**	**(267)**	**(14,538)**	(14,003)	–	(14,003)
– amortisation of intangible assets	15	–	**(170)**	**(170)**	–	(299)	(299)
– share-based payments	10	–	**(330)**	**(330)**	–	(287)	(287)
Operating profit		**7,500**	**(767)**	**6,733**	7,312	(586)	6,726
Finance income	9	**3**	–	**3**	11	–	11
Finance costs	9	**(793)**	**(308)**	**(1,101)**	(968)	201	(767)
Profit from continuing operations before taxation		**6,710**	**(1,075)**	**5,635**	6,355	(385)	5,970
Tax on profit from continuing activities	11	**(1,764)**	**108**	**(1,656)**	(1,722)	20	(1,702)
Net result from continuing operations		**4,946**	**(967)**	**3,979**	4,633	(365)	4,268
Net result from discontinued operations	34	–	**503**	**503**	–	–	–
Profit for the year		**4,946**	**(464)**	**4,482**	4,633	(365)	4,268
Basic earnings per share (p)	13			**35.1**			32.6
Diluted earnings/per share (p)	13			**34.9**			32.6
Adjusted basic earnings per share (p)[1]	13	**38.7**			35.4		
Adjusted diluted earnings per share (p)[1]	13	**38.5**			35.4		

[1] Adjusted operating profit and adjusted earnings per share are stated before one-off items, amortisation of intangible assets, share-based payments and the fair value movement on financial instruments.

Consolidated statement of comprehensive income

FOR THE YEAR ENDED 30 APRIL 2011

	2011 Total £'000	2010 Total £'000
Profit for the year	**4,482**	4,268
Other comprehensive income:		
– currency translation differences	**245**	(917)
Other comprehensive income	**245**	(917)
Total comprehensive income for the year	**4,727**	3,351
Attributable to:		
– owners of the parent	**4,727**	3,351

The accompanying notes and accounting policies, which form an integral part of the financial statements, are included in Zetar's 2011 Annual Report, available at the company's website, **www.zetarplc.com**.

Consolidated balance sheet
AT 30 APRIL 2011

	Note	2011 £'000	2010 £'000
Non-current assets			
Goodwill	14	30,520	30,342
Other intangible assets	15	140	309
Property, plant and equipment	16	16,583	14,886
Deferred tax asset	22	149	213
		47,392	45,750
Current assets			
Inventories	17	16,453	16,039
Trade and other receivables	18	24,935	19,062
Cash at bank	27	4,282	4,257
		45,670	39,358
Total assets		93,062	85,108
Current liabilities			
Trade and other payables	19	(25,075)	(25,176)
Deferred consideration	12	(38)	–
Current tax liabilities		(620)	(524)
Obligations under finance leases	20	(75)	(90)
Derivative financial instruments	30	(157)	(406)
Borrowings and overdrafts	21	(14,509)	(12,885)
		(40,474)	(39,081)
Net current assets		5,196	277
Non-current liabilities			
Deferred consideration		–	(300)
Deferred tax liabilities	22	(1,750)	(1,605)
Obligations under finance leases	20	(15)	(77)
Borrowings and overdrafts	21	(4,536)	(2,290)
		(6,301)	(4,272)
Total liabilities		(46,775)	(43,353)
Net assets		46,287	41,755
Equity			
Share capital	23	1,324	1,324
Share premium account	24	28,266	28,266
Merger reserve		3,411	3,411
Equity reserve	25	2,664	2,089
Retained earnings	25	10,622	6,665
Total equity attributable to equity holders of the parent		46,287	41,755

The financial statements were approved by the Board for issue on 20 July 2011

IAN BLACKBURN
CHIEF EXECUTIVE

MARK STOTT
GROUP FINANCE DIRECTOR

Consolidated cash flow statement
FOR THE YEAR ENDED 30 APRIL 2011

	Note	2011 £'000	2010 £'000
Cash flow from operating activities			
Profit from continuing operations before taxation		5,635	5,970
Finance costs		1,101	767
Interest income		(3)	(11)
Share-based payments		330	287
Depreciation	6	2,267	2,337
Loss/(profit) on sale of plant and equipment	6	9	(113)
Amortisation of intangible assets	6	170	299
Net movement in working capital		(6,040)	(179)
Decrease/(increase) in inventories		72	(1,720)
(Increase)/decrease in receivables		(5,295)	128
(Decrease)/increase in payables		(817)	1,413
Total cash flow from operations		3,469	9,357
Net interest paid	9	(1,347)	(957)
Tax paid		(1,369)	(1,415)
Total cash flow from operating activities		753	6,985
Cash flow from investing activities			
Purchase of property, plant and equipment		(3,789)	(2,098)
Proceeds from sale of plant and equipment		45	259
Disposal of subsidiary		500	–
Total cash impact of acquisitions		(848)	(220)
Acquisition of business		(483)	(220)
Net borrowings assumed on acquisition		(365)	
Net cash flow from investing activities		(4,092)	(2,059)
Cash flow from financing activities			
Net proceeds from issue of ordinary share capital		–	14
Purchase of own shares		(525)	(250)
Proceeds from new borrowings		7,000	–
Repayment of borrowings		(5,174)	(2,545)
Finance lease repayments		(91)	(214)
Net cash flow from financing activities		1,210	(2,995)
Net (decrease)/increase in cash and cash equivalents		(2,129)	1,931
Cash and cash equivalents at beginning of the year		(6,608)	(8,127)
Effect of foreign exchange rate movements		96	(412)
Cash and cash equivalents at the end of the year		(8,641)	(6,608)
Cash and cash equivalents comprise:			
– cash at bank	27	4,282	4,257
– bank overdraft	27	(12,923)	(10,865)
		(8,641)	(6,608)

Consolidated statement of changes in equity
FOR THE YEAR ENDED 30 APRIL 2011

	Attributable to equity holders of the parent					
	Share capital £'000	Share premium account £'000	Merger reserve £'000	Equity reserve £'000	Retained earnings £'000	Total £'000
Balance at 1 May 2009	1,324	28,252	3,411	2,719	2,647	38,353
Comprehensive income						
Profit for the year	–	–	–	–	4,268	4,268
Other comprehensive income						
Exchange (loss) on translation of foreign operations	–	–	–	(917)	–	(917)
Total other comprehensive income	–	–	–	(917)	–	(917)
Total comprehensive income	–	–	–	(917)	4,268	3,351
Transactions with owners:						
– issue of new ordinary shares	–	14	–	–	–	14
– purchase of own shares	–	–	–	–	(250)	(250)
– share-based payment charge	–	–	–	287	–	287
Total transactions with owners	–	14	–	287	(250)	51
Balance at 30 April 2010	1,324	28,266	3,411	2,089	6,665	41,755
Comprehensive income						
Profit for the year	–	–	–	–	4,482	4,482
Other comprehensive income						
Exchange gain on translation of foreign operations	–	–	–	245	–	245
Total other comprehensive income	–	–	–	245	–	245
Total comprehensive income	–	–	–	245	4,482	4,727
Transactions with owners:						
– purchase of own shares	–	–	–	–	(525)	(525)
– share-based payment charge	–	–	–	330	–	330
Total transactions with owners	–	–	–	330	(525)	(195)
Balance at 30 April 2011	1,324	28,266	3,411	2,664	10,622	46,287

TIME VALUE OF MONEY

LEARNING OBJECTIVES

After studying this appendix, you should be able to:

1 Distinguish between simple and compound interest.

2 Solve for future value of a single amount.

3 Solve for future value of an annuity.

4 Identify the variables fundamental to solving present value problems.

5 Solve for present value of a single amount.

6 Solve for present value of an annuity.

7 Compute the present value of notes and bonds.

8 Use a financial calculator to solve time value of money problems.

Nature of Interest

LEARNING OBJECTIVE 1

Distinguish between simple and compound interest.

Would you rather receive $1,000 today or a year from now? You should prefer to receive the $1,000 today because you can invest the $1,000 and earn interest on it. As a result, you will have more than $1,000 a year from now. What this example illustrates is the concept of the **time value of money**. Everyone prefers to receive money today rather than the same amount in the future because of the interest factor.

Interest is payment for the use of another person's money. It is the difference between the amount borrowed or invested (called the **principal**) and the amount repaid or collected. The amount of interest to be paid or collected is usually stated as a rate over a specific period of time. The rate of interest is generally stated as an annual rate.

The amount of interest involved in any financing transaction is based on three elements:

1. **Principal (p):** The original amount borrowed or invested.
2. **Interest Rate (i):** An annual percentage of the principal.
3. **Time (n):** The number of years that the principal is borrowed or invested.

SIMPLE INTEREST

Simple interest is computed on the principal amount only. It is the return on the principal for one period. Simple interest is usually expressed as shown in Illustration D-1.

Illustration D-1 Interest computation

Interest	=	Principal p	$\times$	Rate i	$\times$	Time n

For example, if you borrowed $5,000 for 2 years at a simple interest rate of 12% annually, you would pay $1,200 in total interest, computed as follows.

$$\text{Interest} = p \times i \times n$$
$$= \$5,000 \times .12 \times 2$$
$$= \$1,200$$

COMPOUND INTEREST

Compound interest is computed on principal **and** on any interest earned that has not been paid or withdrawn. It is the return on (or growth of) the principal for two or more time periods. Compounding computes interest not only on the principal but also on the interest earned to date on that principal, assuming the interest is left on deposit.

To illustrate the difference between simple and compound interest, assume that you deposit $1,000 in Bank Two, where it will earn simple interest of 9% per year, and you deposit another $1,000 in Citizens Bank, where it will earn compound interest of 9% per year compounded annually. Also assume that in both cases you will not withdraw any cash until three years from the date of deposit. Illustration D-2 shows the computation of interest to be received and the accumulated year-end balances.

Illustration D-2 Simple versus compound interest

Bank Two				Citizens Bank		
Simple Interest Calculation	Simple Interest	Accumulated Year-End Balance		Compound Interest Calculation	Compound Interest	Accumulated Year-End Balance
Year 1 $1,000.00 × 9%	$ 90.00	$1,090.00		Year 1 $1,000.00 × 9%	$ 90.00	$1,090.00
Year 2 $1,000.00 × 9%	90.00	$1,180.00		Year 2 $1,090.00 × 9%	98.10	$1,188.10
Year 3 $1,000.00 × 9%	90.00	$1,270.00		Year 3 $1,188.10 × 9%	106.93	$1,295.03
	$ 270.00		→ $25.03 ← Difference		$ 295.03	

Note in Illustration D-2 that simple interest uses the initial principal of $1,000 to compute the interest in all three years. Compound interest uses the accumulated balance (principal plus interest to date) at each year-end to compute interest in the succeeding year—which explains why your compound interest account is larger.

Obviously, if you had a choice between investing your money at simple interest or at compound interest, you would choose compound interest, all other things—especially risk—being equal. In the example, compounding provides $25.03 of additional interest income. For practical purposes, compounding assumes that unpaid interest earned becomes a part of the principal, and the accumulated balance at the end of each year becomes the new principal on which interest is earned during the next year.

Illustration D-2 indicates that you should invest your money at a bank that compounds interest. Most business situations use compound interest. Simple interest is generally applicable only to short-term situations of one year or less.

Future Value Concepts

FUTURE VALUE OF A SINGLE AMOUNT

The **future value of a single amount** is the value at a future date of a given amount invested, assuming compound interest. For example, in Illustration D-2, $1,295.03 is the future value of the $1,000 investment earning 9% for

LEARNING OBJECTIVE 2

Solve for future value of a single amount.

three years. The $1,295.03 could be determined more easily by using the following formula.

Illustration D-3 Formula for future value

$$FV = p \times (1 + i)^n$$

where:

FV = future value of a single amount
p = principal (or present value; the value today)
i = interest rate for one period
n = number of periods

The $1,295.03 is computed as follows.

$$
\begin{aligned}
FV &= \quad p \quad \times (1 + i)^n \\
&= \$1{,}000 \times (1 + .09)^3 \\
&= \$1{,}000 \times 1.29503 \\
&= \$1{,}295.03
\end{aligned}
$$

The 1.29503 is computed by multiplying (1.09 × 1.09 × 1.09). The amounts in this example can be depicted in the time diagram shown in Illustration D-4.

Illustration D-4 Time diagram

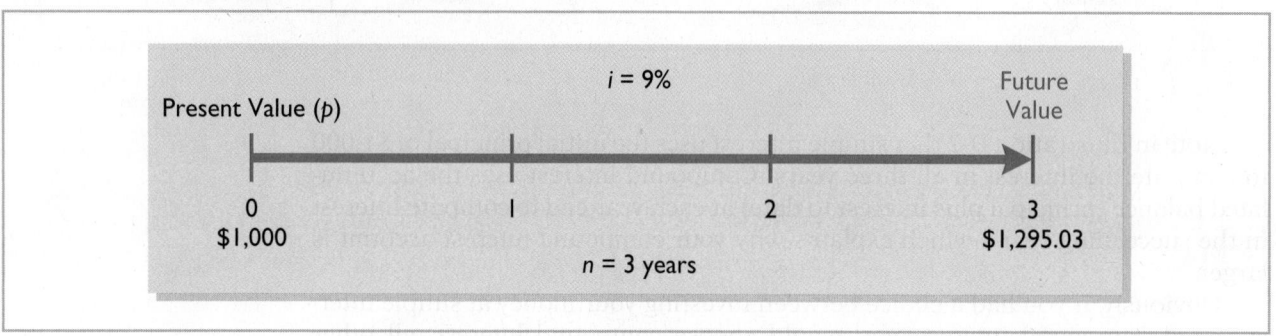

Another method used to compute the future value of a single amount involves a compound interest table. This table shows the future value of 1 for n periods. Table 1 on the next page is such a table.

In Table 1, n is the number of compounding periods, the percentages are the periodic interest rates, and the 5-digit decimal numbers in the respective columns are the future value of 1 factors. In using Table 1, you would multiply the principal amount by the future value factor for the specified number of periods and interest rate. For example, the future value factor for two periods at 9% is 1.18810. Multiplying this factor by $1,000 equals $1,188.10—which is the accumulated balance at the end of year 2 in the Citizens Bank example in Illustration D-2. The $1,295.03 accumulated balance at the end of the third year can be calculated from Table 1 by multiplying the future value factor for three periods (1.29503) by the $1,000.

The demonstration problem in Illustration D-5 (page D-4) shows how to use Table 1.

TABLE 1   **Future Value of 1**

(n) Periods	4%	5%	6%	7%	8%	9%	10%	11%	12%	15%
0	1.00000	1.00000	1.00000	1.00000	1.00000	1.00000	1.00000	1.00000	1.00000	1.00000
1	1.04000	1.05000	1.06000	1.07000	1.08000	1.09000	1.10000	1.11000	1.12000	1.15000
2	1.08160	1.10250	1.12360	1.14490	1.16640	1.18810	1.21000	1.23210	1.25440	1.32250
3	1.12486	1.15763	1.19102	1.22504	1.25971	1.29503	1.33100	1.36763	1.40493	1.52088
4	1.16986	1.21551	1.26248	1.31080	1.36049	1.41158	1.46410	1.51807	1.57352	1.74901
5	1.21665	1.27628	1.33823	1.40255	1.46933	1.53862	1.61051	1.68506	1.76234	2.01136
6	1.26532	1.34010	1.41852	1.50073	1.58687	1.67710	1.77156	1.87041	1.97382	2.31306
7	1.31593	1.40710	1.50363	1.60578	1.71382	1.82804	1.94872	2.07616	2.21068	2.66002
8	1.36857	1.47746	1.59385	1.71819	1.85093	1.99256	2.14359	2.30454	2.47596	3.05902
9	1.42331	1.55133	1.68948	1.83846	1.99900	2.17189	2.35795	2.55803	2.77308	3.51788
10	1.48024	1.62889	1.79085	1.96715	2.15892	2.36736	2.59374	2.83942	3.10585	4.04556
11	1.53945	1.71034	1.89830	2.10485	2.33164	2.58043	2.85312	3.15176	3.47855	4.65239
12	1.60103	1.79586	2.01220	2.25219	2.51817	2.81267	3.13843	3.49845	3.89598	5.35025
13	1.66507	1.88565	2.13293	2.40985	2.71962	3.06581	3.45227	3.88328	4.36349	6.15279
14	1.73168	1.97993	2.26090	2.57853	2.93719	3.34173	3.79750	4.31044	4.88711	7.07571
15	1.80094	2.07893	2.39656	2.75903	3.17217	3.64248	4.17725	4.78459	5.47357	8.13706
16	1.87298	2.18287	2.54035	2.95216	3.42594	3.97031	4.59497	5.31089	6.13039	9.35762
17	1.94790	2.29202	2.69277	3.15882	3.70002	4.32763	5.05447	5.89509	6.86604	10.76126
18	2.02582	2.40662	2.85434	3.37993	3.99602	4.71712	5.55992	6.54355	7.68997	12.37545
19	2.10685	2.52695	3.02560	3.61653	4.31570	5.14166	6.11591	7.26334	8.61276	14.23177
20	2.19112	2.65330	3.20714	3.86968	4.66096	5.60441	6.72750	8.06231	9.64629	16.36654

John and Mary Rich invested $20,000 in a savings account paying 6% interest at the time their son, Mike, was born. The money is to be used by Mike for his college education. On his 18th birthday, Mike withdraws the money from his savings account. How much did Mike withdraw from his account?

Present Value (p)   i = 6%   Future Value = ?

0   1   2   3   4   5   6   7   8   9   10   11   12   13   14   15   16   17   18

$20,000

n = 18 years

Answer: The future value factor from Table 1 is 2.85434 (18 periods at 6%). The future value of $20,000 earning 6% per year for 18 years is **$57,086.80** ($20,000 × 2.85434).

Illustration D-5
Demonstration problem—Using Table 1 for *FV* of 1

FUTURE VALUE OF AN ANNUITY

The preceding discussion involved the accumulation of only a single principal sum. Individuals and businesses frequently encounter situations in which a **series** of equal dollar amounts are to be paid or received at evenly spaced time intervals (periodically), such as loans or lease (rental) contracts. Such payments or receipts of equal dollar amounts are referred to as **annuities**.

LEARNING OBJECTIVE **3**

Solve for future value of an annuity.

The **future value of an annuity** is the sum of all the payments (receipts) plus the accumulated compound interest on them. In computing the future value of an annuity, it is necessary to know (1) the interest rate, (2) the number of compounding periods, and (3) the amount of the periodic payments or receipts.

To illustrate the computation of the future value of an annuity, assume that you invest $2,000 at the end of each year for three years at 5% interest compounded annually. This situation is depicted in the time diagram in Illustration D-6.

Illustration D-6 Time diagram for a three-year annuity

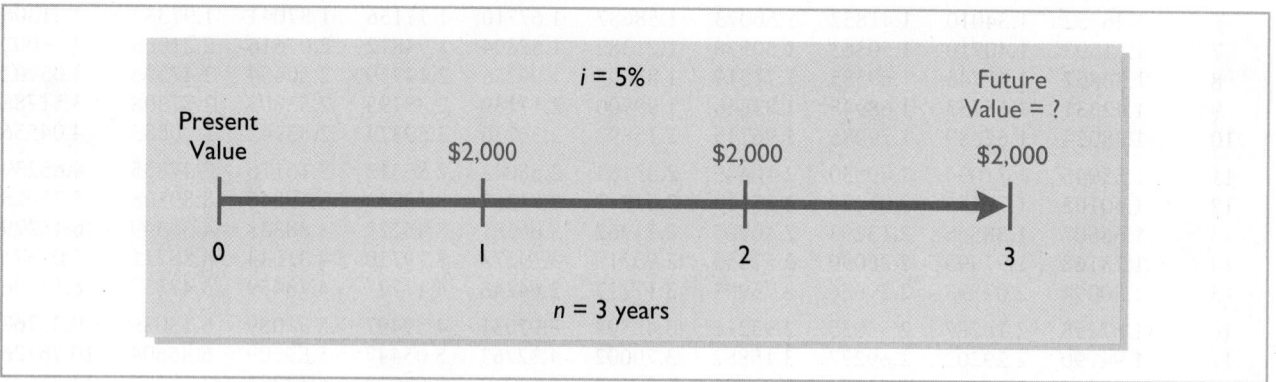

The $2,000 invested at the end of year 1 will earn interest for two years (years 2 and 3), and the $2,000 invested at the end of year 2 will earn interest for one year (year 3). However, the last $2,000 investment (made at the end of year 3) will not earn any interest. The future value of these periodic payments could be computed using the future value factors from Table 1, as shown in Illustration D-7.

Illustration D-7 Future value of periodic payment computation

Invested at End of Year	Number of Compounding Periods	Amount Invested	×	Future Value of 1 Factor at 5%	=	Future Value
1	2	$2,000	×	1.10250		$2,205
2	1	$2,000	×	1.05000		2,100
3	0	$2,000	×	1.00000		2,000
				3.15250		$6,305

The first $2,000 investment is multiplied by the future value factor for two periods (1.1025) because two years' interest will accumulate on it (in years 2 and 3). The second $2,000 investment will earn only one year's interest (in year 3) and therefore is multiplied by the future value factor for one year (1.0500). The final $2,000 investment is made at the end of the third year and will not earn any interest. Thus $n = 0$ and the future value factor is 1.00000. Consequently, the future value of the last $2,000 invested is only $2,000 since it does not accumulate any interest.

Calculating the future value of each individual cash flow is required when the periodic payments or receipts are not equal in each period. However, when the periodic payments (receipts) are **the same in each period**, the future value can be computed by using a future value of an annuity of 1 table. Table 2 (page D-6) is such a table.

TABLE 2   Future Value of an Annuity of 1

(n) Periods	4%	5%	6%	7%	8%	9%	10%	11%	12%	15%
1	1.00000	1.00000	1.00000	1.0000	1.00000	1.00000	1.00000	1.00000	1.00000	1.00000
2	2.04000	2.05000	2.06000	2.0700	2.08000	2.09000	2.10000	2.11000	2.12000	2.15000
3	3.12160	3.15250	3.18360	3.2149	3.24640	3.27810	3.31000	3.34210	3.37440	3.47250
4	4.24646	4.31013	4.37462	4.4399	4.50611	4.57313	4.64100	4.70973	4.77933	4.99338
5	5.41632	5.52563	5.63709	5.7507	5.86660	5.98471	6.10510	6.22780	6.35285	6.74238
6	6.63298	6.80191	6.97532	7.1533	7.33592	7.52334	7.71561	7.91286	8.11519	8.75374
7	7.89829	8.14201	8.39384	8.6540	8.92280	9.20044	9.48717	9.78327	10.08901	11.06680
8	9.21423	9.54911	9.89747	10.2598	10.63663	11.02847	11.43589	11.85943	12.29969	13.72682
9	10.58280	11.02656	11.49132	11.9780	12.48756	13.02104	13.57948	14.16397	14.77566	16.78584
10	12.00611	12.57789	13.18079	13.8164	14.48656	15.19293	15.93743	16.72201	17.54874	20.30372
11	13.48635	14.20679	14.97164	15.7836	16.64549	17.56029	18.53117	19.56143	20.65458	24.34928
12	15.02581	15.91713	16.86994	17.8885	18.97713	20.14072	21.38428	22.71319	24.13313	29.00167
13	16.62684	17.71298	18.88214	20.1406	21.49530	22.95339	24.52271	26.21164	28.02911	34.35192
14	18.29191	19.59863	21.01507	22.5505	24.21492	26.01919	27.97498	30.09492	32.39260	40.50471
15	20.02359	21.57856	23.27597	25.1290	27.15211	29.36092	31.77248	34.40536	37.27972	47.58041
16	21.82453	23.65749	25.67253	27.8881	30.32428	33.00340	35.94973	39.18995	42.75328	55.71747
17	23.69751	25.84037	28.21288	30.8402	33.75023	36.97351	40.54470	44.50084	48.88367	65.07509
18	25.64541	28.13238	30.90565	33.9990	37.45024	41.30134	45.59917	50.39593	55.74972	75.83636
19	27.67123	30.53900	33.75999	37.3790	41.44626	46.01846	51.15909	56.93949	63.43968	88.21181
20	29.77808	33.06595	36.78559	40.9955	45.76196	51.16012	57.27500	64.20283	72.05244	102.44358

Table 2 shows the future value of 1 to be received periodically for a given number of periods. It assumes that each payment is made at the **end** of each period. We can see from Table 2 that the future value of an annuity of 1 factor for three periods at 5% is 3.15250. The future value factor is the total of the three individual future value factors was shown in Illustration D-7. Multiplying this amount by the annual investment of $2,000 produces a future value of $6,305.

The demonstration problem in Illustration D-8 shows how to use Table 2.

Illustration D-8
Demonstration problem—Using Table 2 for *FV* of an annuity of 1

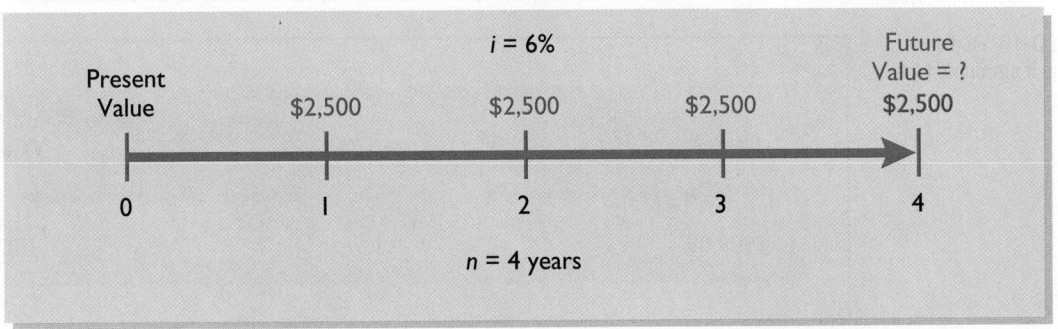

John and Char Lewis' daughter, Debra, has just started high school. They decide to start a college fund for her and will invest **$2,500** in a savings account at the end of each year she is in high school (4 payments total). The account will earn 6% interest compounded annually. How much will be in the college fund at the time Debra graduates from high school?

$i = 6\%$

Present Value ... $2,500 ... $2,500 ... $2,500 ... $2,500 ... Future Value = ?

0   1   2   3   4

$n = 4$ years

Answer: The future value factor from Table 2 is 4.37462 (4 periods at 6%). The future value of $2,500 invested each year for 4 years at 6% interest is **$10,936.55** ($2,500 × 4.37462).

Present Value Concepts

PRESENT VALUE VARIABLES

LEARNING OBJECTIVE 4

Identify the variables fundamental to solving present value problems.

The present value is the value now of a given amount to be paid or received in the future, assuming compound interest. The present value, like the future value, is based on three variables: (1) the dollar amount to be received (future amount), (2) the length of time until the amount is received (number of periods), and (3) the interest rate (the discount rate). The process of determining the present value is referred to as discounting the future amount.

In this textbook, we use present value computations in measuring several items. For example, Chapter 10 computed the present value of the principal and interest payments to determine the market price of a bond. In addition, determining the amount to be reported for notes payable and lease liabilities involves present value computations.

PRESENT VALUE OF A SINGLE AMOUNT

LEARNING OBJECTIVE 5

Solve for present value of a single amount.

To illustrate present value, assume that you want to invest a sum of money today that will provide $1,000 at the end of one year. What amount would you need to invest today to have $1,000 one year from now? If you want a 10% rate of return, the investment or present value is $909.09 ($1,000 ÷ 1.10). The formula for calculating present value is shown in Illustration D-9.

Illustration D-9 Formula for present value

$$\text{Present Value} = \text{Future Value} \div (1 + i)^n$$

The computation of $1,000 discounted at 10% for one year is as follows.

$$
\begin{aligned}
PV &= FV \div (1 + i)^n \\
&= \$1{,}000 \div (1 + .10)^1 \\
&= \$1{,}000 \div 1.10 \\
&= \$909.09
\end{aligned}
$$

The future amount ($1,000), the discount rate (10%), and the number of periods (1) are known. The variables in this situation can be depicted in the time diagram in Illustration D-10.

Illustration D-10 Finding present value if discounted for one period

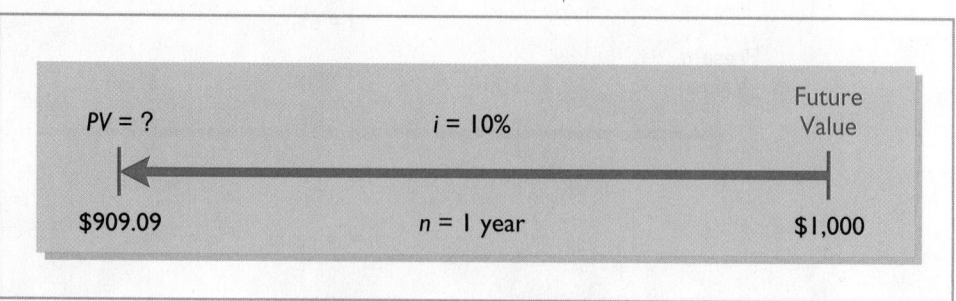

If the single amount of $1,000 is to be received **in two years** and discounted at 10% [$PV = \$1{,}000 \div (1 + .10)^2$], its present value is $826.45 [($1,000 ÷ 1.21), depicted as shown in Illustration D-11 on the next page.

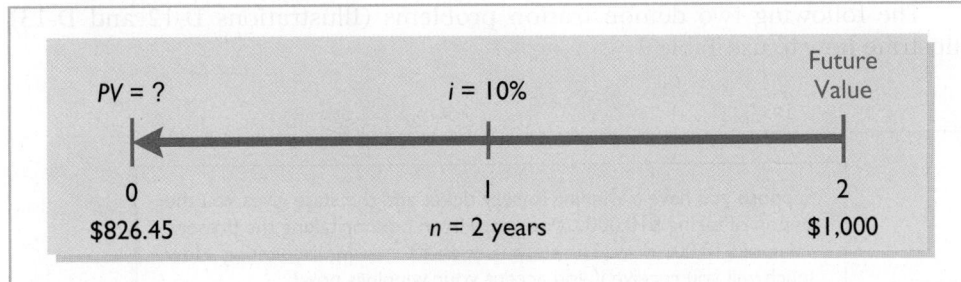

Illustration D-11 Finding present value if discounted for two periods

The present value of 1 may also be determined through tables that show the present value of 1 for n periods. In Table 3 below, n is the number of discounting periods involved. The percentages are the periodic interest rates or discount rates, and the 5-digit decimal numbers in the respective columns are the present value of 1 factors.

When using Table 3, the future value is multiplied by the present value factor specified at the intersection of the number of periods and the discount rate.

TABLE 3   Present Value of 1

(n) Periods	4%	5%	6%	7%	8%	9%	10%	11%	12%	15%
1	.96154	.95238	.94340	0.93458	.92593	.91743	.90909	.90090	.89286	.86957
2	.92456	.90703	.89000	0.87344	.85734	.84168	.82645	.81162	.79719	.75614
3	.88900	.86384	.83962	0.81630	.79383	.77218	.75132	.73119	.71178	.65752
4	.85480	.82270	.79209	0.76290	.73503	.70843	.68301	.65873	.63552	.57175
5	.82193	.78353	.74726	0.71299	.68058	.64993	.62092	.59345	.56743	.49718
6	.79031	.74622	.70496	0.66634	.63017	.59627	.56447	.53464	.50663	.43233
7	.75992	.71068	.66506	0.62275	.58349	.54703	.51316	.48166	.45235	.37594
8	.73069	.67684	.62741	0.58201	.54027	.50187	.46651	.43393	.40388	.32690
9	.70259	.64461	.59190	0.54393	.50025	.46043	.42410	.39092	.36061	.28426
10	.67556	.61391	.55839	0.50835	.46319	.42241	.38554	.35218	.32197	.24719
11	.64958	.58468	.52679	0.47509	.42888	.38753	.35049	.31728	.28748	.21494
12	.62460	.55684	.49697	0.44401	.39711	.35554	.31863	.28584	.25668	.18691
13	.60057	.53032	.46884	0.41496	.36770	.32618	.28966	.25751	.22917	.16253
14	.57748	.50507	.44230	0.38782	.34046	.29925	.26333	.23199	.20462	.14133
15	.55526	.48102	.41727	0.36245	.31524	.27454	.23939	.20900	.18270	.12289
16	.53391	.45811	.39365	0.33873	.29189	.25187	.21763	.18829	.16312	.10687
17	.51337	.43630	.37136	0.31657	.27027	.23107	.19785	.16963	.14564	.09293
18	.49363	.41552	.35034	0.29586	.25025	.21199	.17986	.15282	.13004	.08081
19	.47464	.39573	.33051	0.27615	.23171	.19449	.16351	.13768	.11611	.07027
20	.45639	.37689	.31180	0.25842	.21455	.17843	.14864	.12403	.10367	.06110

For example, the present value factor for one period at a discount rate of 10% is .90909, which equals the $909.09 ($1,000 × .90909) computed in Illustration D-10. For two periods at a discount rate of 10%, the present value factor is .82645, which equals the $826.45 ($1,000 × .82645) computed previously.

Note that a higher discount rate produces a smaller present value. For example, using a 15% discount rate, the present value of $1,000 due one year from now is $869.57 versus $909.09 at 10%. Also note that the further removed from the present the future value is, the smaller the present value. For example, using the same discount rate of 10%, the present value of $1,000 due in **five years** is $620.92. The present value of $1,000 due in **one year** is $909.09, a difference of $288.17.

The following two demonstration problems (Illustrations D-12 and D-13) illustrate how to use Table 3.

Illustration D-12
Demonstration problem–Using Table 3 for *PV* of 1

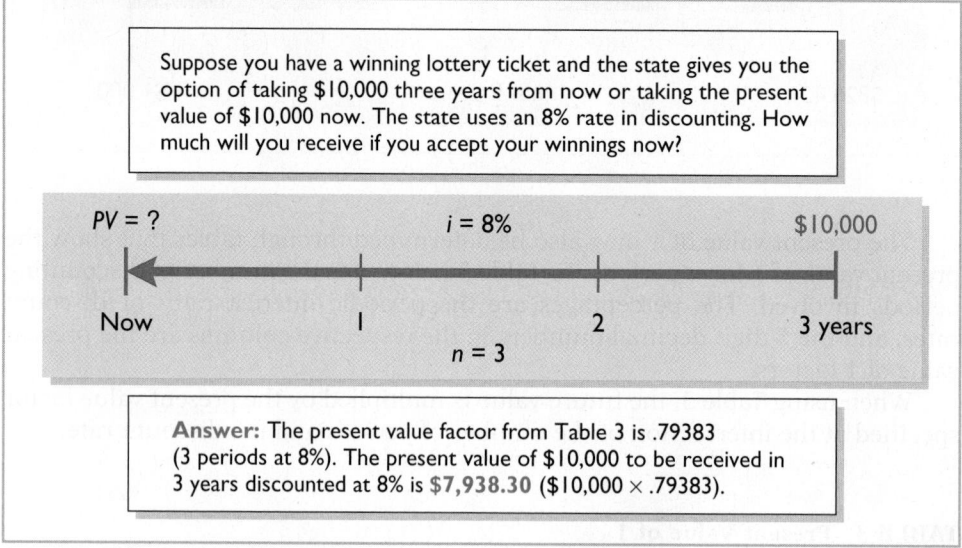

Suppose you have a winning lottery ticket and the state gives you the option of taking $10,000 three years from now or taking the present value of $10,000 now. The state uses an 8% rate in discounting. How much will you receive if you accept your winnings now?

PV = ?   i = 8% $10,000

Now   1   2   3 years
                        n = 3

Answer: The present value factor from Table 3 is .79383 (3 periods at 8%). The present value of $10,000 to be received in 3 years discounted at 8% is **$7,938.30** ($10,000 × .79383).

Illustration D-13
Demonstration problem–Using Table 3 for *PV* of 1

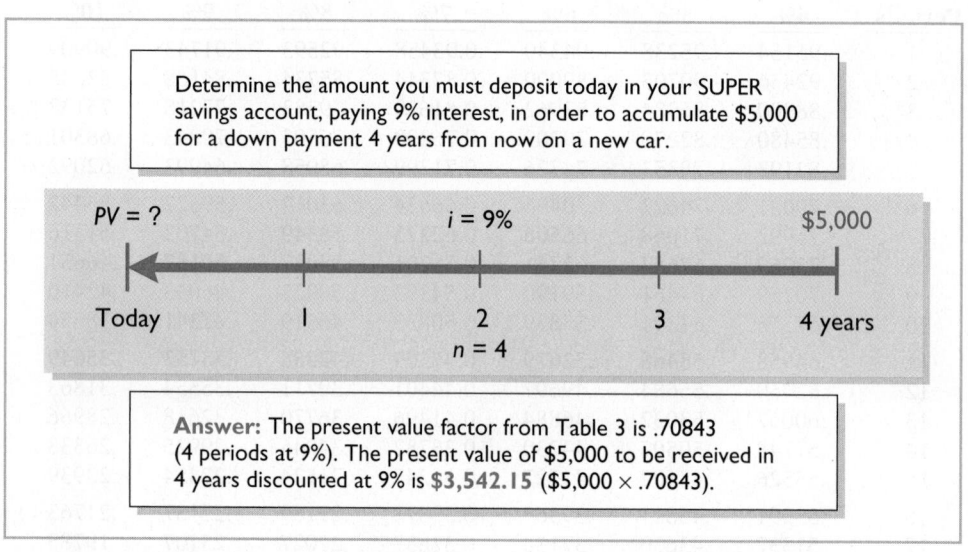

Determine the amount you must deposit today in your SUPER savings account, paying 9% interest, in order to accumulate $5,000 for a down payment 4 years from now on a new car.

PV = ?   i = 9% $5,000

Today   1   2   3   4 years
                            n = 4

Answer: The present value factor from Table 3 is .70843 (4 periods at 9%). The present value of $5,000 to be received in 4 years discounted at 9% is **$3,542.15** ($5,000 × .70843).

PRESENT VALUE OF AN ANNUITY

The preceding discussion involved the discounting of only a single future amount. Businesses and individuals frequently engage in transactions in which a series of equal dollar amounts are to be received or paid at evenly spaced time intervals (periodically). Examples of a series of periodic receipts or payments are loan agreements, installment sales, mortgage notes, lease (rental) contracts, and pension obligations. As discussed earlier, these periodic receipts or payments are **annuities**.

The **present value of an annuity** is the value now of a series of future receipts or payments, discounted assuming compound interest. In computing the present value of an annuity, it is necessary to know (1) the discount rate, (2) the number of discount periods, and (3) the amount of the periodic receipts or payments. To illustrate the computation of the present value of an annuity, assume that you will receive $1,000 cash annually for three years at a time when the discount rate is 10%. This situation is depicted in the time diagram in Illustration D-14. Illustration D-15 shows computation of the present value in this situation.

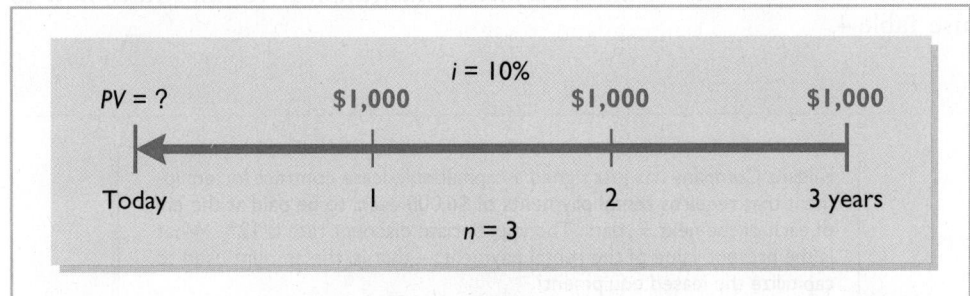

Illustration D-14 Time diagram for a three-year annuity

Future Amount	×	Present Value of 1 Factor at 10%	=	Present Value
$1,000 (one year away)		.90909		$ 909.09
1,000 (two years away)		.82645		826.45
1,000 (three years away)		.75132		751.32
		2.48686		$2,486.86

Illustration D-15 Present value of a series of future amounts computation

This method of calculation is required when the periodic cash flows are not uniform in each period. However, when the future receipts are the same in each period, an annuity table can be used. As illustrated in Table 4 below, an annuity table shows the present value of 1 to be received periodically for a given number of periods.

TABLE 4   Present Value of an Annuity of 1

(n) Periods	4%	5%	6%	7%	8%	9%	10%	11%	12%	15%
1	.96154	.95238	.94340	0.93458	.92593	.91743	.90909	.90090	.89286	.86957
2	1.88609	1.85941	1.83339	1.80802	1.78326	1.75911	1.73554	1.71252	1.69005	1.62571
3	2.77509	2.72325	2.67301	2.62432	2.57710	2.53130	2.48685	2.44371	2.40183	2.28323
4	3.62990	3.54595	3.46511	3.38721	3.31213	3.23972	3.16986	3.10245	3.03735	2.85498
5	4.45182	4.32948	4.21236	4.10020	3.99271	3.88965	3.79079	3.69590	3.60478	3.35216
6	5.24214	5.07569	4.91732	4.76654	4.62288	4.48592	4.35526	4.23054	4.11141	3.78448
7	6.00205	5.78637	5.58238	5.38989	5.20637	5.03295	4.86842	4.71220	4.56376	4.16042
8	6.73274	6.46321	6.20979	5.97130	5.74664	5.53482	5.33493	5.14612	4.96764	4.48732
9	7.43533	7.10782	6.80169	6.51523	6.24689	5.99525	5.75902	5.53705	5.32825	4.77158
10	8.11090	7.72173	7.36009	7.02358	6.71008	6.41766	6.14457	5.88923	5.65022	5.01877
11	8.76048	8.30641	7.88687	7.49867	7.13896	6.80519	6.49506	6.20652	5.93770	5.23371
12	9.38507	8.86325	8.38384	7.94269	7.53608	7.16073	6.81369	6.49236	6.19437	5.42062
13	9.98565	9.39357	8.85268	8.35765	7.90378	7.48690	7.10336	6.74987	6.42355	5.58315
14	10.56312	9.89864	9.29498	8.74547	8.24424	7.78615	7.36669	6.98187	6.62817	5.72448
15	11.11839	10.37966	9.71225	9.10791	8.55948	8.06069	7.60608	7.19087	6.81086	5.84737
16	11.65230	10.83777	10.10590	9.44665	8.85137	8.31256	7.82371	7.37916	6.97399	5.95424
17	12.16567	11.27407	10.47726	9.76322	9.12164	8.54363	8.02155	7.54879	7.11963	6.04716
18	12.65930	11.68959	10.82760	10.05909	9.37189	8.75563	8.20141	7.70162	7.24967	6.12797
19	13.13394	12.08532	11.15812	10.33560	9.60360	8.95012	8.36492	7.83929	7.36578	6.19823
20	13.59033	12.46221	11.46992	10.59401	9.81815	9.12855	8.51356	7.96333	7.46944	6.25933

Table 4 shows that the present value of an annuity of 1 factor for three periods at 10% is 2.48685.[1] This present value factor is the total of the three individual present value factors, as shown in Illustration D-15. Applying this amount to the annual cash flow of $1,000 produces a present value of $2,486.85.

The following demonstration problem (Illustration D-16) illustrates how to use Table 4.

Illustration D-16
Demonstration problem–Using Table 4 for *PV* of an annuity of 1

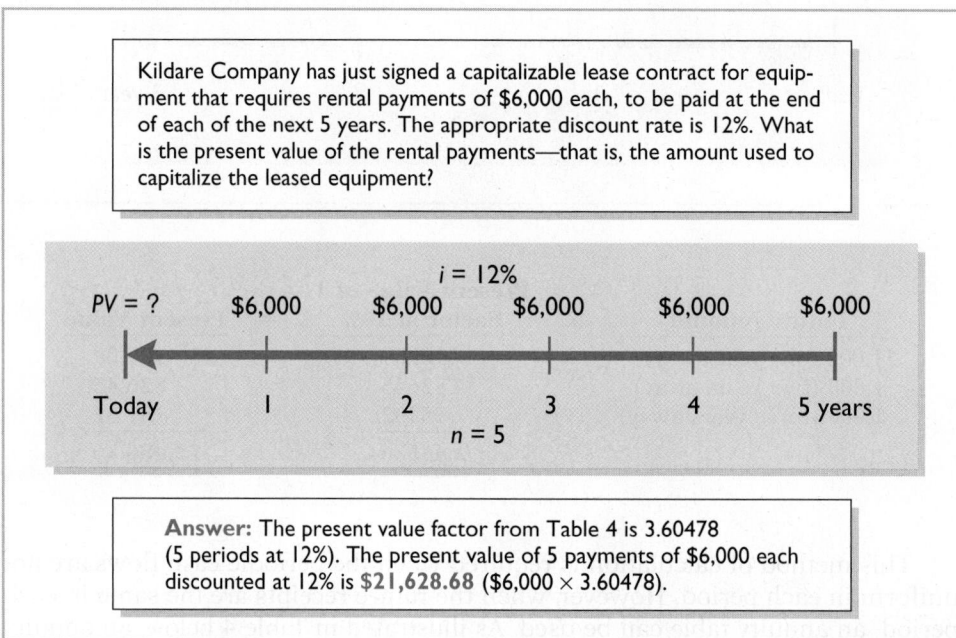

Kildare Company has just signed a capitalizable lease contract for equipment that requires rental payments of $6,000 each, to be paid at the end of each of the next 5 years. The appropriate discount rate is 12%. What is the present value of the rental payments—that is, the amount used to capitalize the leased equipment?

Answer: The present value factor from Table 4 is 3.60478 (5 periods at 12%). The present value of 5 payments of $6,000 each discounted at 12% is **$21,628.68** ($6,000 × 3.60478).

TIME PERIODS AND DISCOUNTING

In the preceding calculations, the discounting was done on an annual basis using an annual interest rate. Discounting may also be done over shorter periods of time such as monthly, quarterly, or semiannually.

When the time frame is less than one year, it is necessary to convert the annual interest rate to the applicable time frame. Assume, for example, that the investor in Illustration D-14 received $500 **semiannually** for three years instead of $1,000 annually. In this case, the number of periods becomes six (3 × 2), the discount rate is 5% (10% ÷ 2), the present value factor from Table 4 is 5.07569 (6 periods at 5%), and the present value of the future cash flows is $2,537.85 (5.07569 × $500). This amount is slightly higher than the $2,486.86 computed in Illustration D-15 because interest is computed twice during the same year. That is, during the second half of the year, interest is earned on the first half-year's interest.

COMPUTING THE PRESENT VALUE OF A LONG-TERM NOTE OR BOND

LEARNING OBJECTIVE **7**

Compute the present value of notes and bonds.

The present value (or market price) of a long-term note or bond is a function of three variables: (1) the payment amounts, (2) the length of time until the amounts are paid, and (3) the discount rate. Our illustration (on the next page) uses a five-year bond issue.

---

[1]The difference of .00001 between 2.48686 and 2.48685 is due to rounding.

The first variable (dollars to be paid) is made up of two elements: (1) a series of interest payments (an annuity) and (2) the principal amount (a single sum). To compute the present value of the bond, both the interest payments and the principal amount must be discounted—two different computations. The time diagrams for a bond due in five years are shown in Illustration D-17.

Illustration D-17 Present value of a bond time diagram

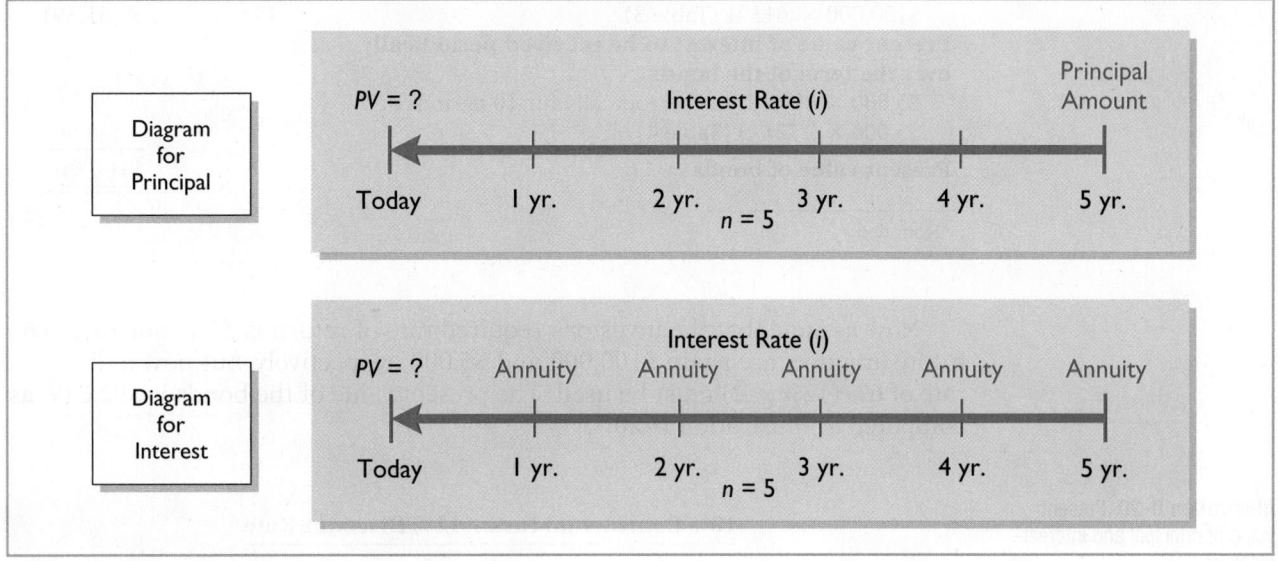

When the investor's market interest rate is equal to the bond's contractual interest rate, the present value of the bonds will equal the face value of the bonds. To illustrate, assume a bond issue of 10%, five-year bonds with a face value of $100,000 with interest payable **semiannually** on January 1 and July 1. If the discount rate is the same as the contractual rate, the bonds will sell at face value. In this case, the investor will receive (1) $100,000 at maturity and (2) a series of ten $5,000 interest payments [($100,000 × 10%) ÷ 2] over the term of the bonds. The length of time is expressed in terms of interest periods—in this case—10, and the discount rate per interest period, 5%. The following time diagram (Illustration D-18) depicts the variables involved in this discounting situation.

Illustration D-18 Time diagram for present value of a 10%, five-year bond paying interest semiannually

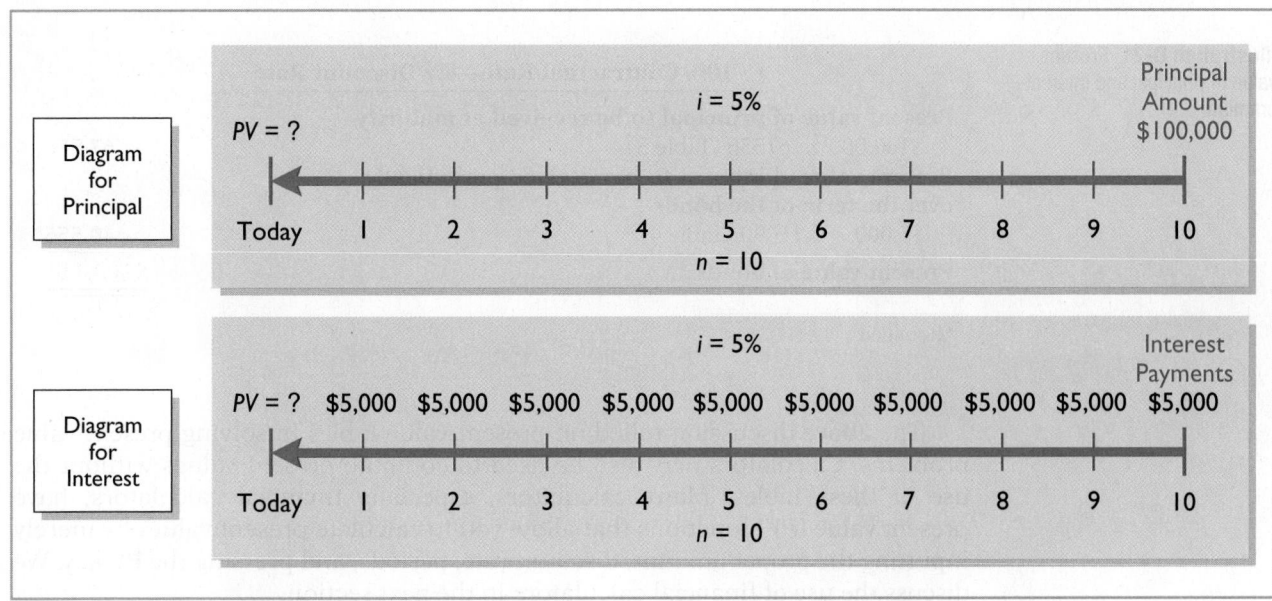

Illustration D-19 shows the computation of the present value of these bonds.

Illustration D-19 Present value of principal and interest–face value

10% Contractual Rate—10% Discount Rate	
Present value of principal to be received at maturity	
$100,000 × PV of 1 due in 10 periods at 5%	
$100,000 × .61391 (Table 3)	$ 61,391
Present value of interest to be received periodically	
over the term of the bonds	
$5,000 × PV of 1 due periodically for 10 periods at 5%	
$5,000 × 7.72173 (Table 4)	38,609*
Present value of bonds	$100,000

*Rounded

Now assume that the investor's required rate of return is 12%, not 10%. The future amounts are again $100,000 and $5,000, respectively, but now a discount rate of 6% (12% ÷ 2) must be used. The present value of the bonds is $92,639, as computed in Illustration D-20.

Illustration D-20 Present value of principal and interest–discount

10% Contractual Rate—12% Discount Rate	
Present value of principal to be received at maturity	
$100,000 × .55839 (Table 3)	$ 55,839
Present value of interest to be received periodically	
over the term of the bonds	
$5,000 × 7.36009 (Table 4)	36,800*
Present value of bonds	$92,639

*Rounded

Conversely, if the discount rate is 8% and the contractual rate is 10%, the present value of the bonds is $108,111, computed as shown in Illustration D-21.

Illustration D-21 Present value of principal and interest–premium

10% Contractual Rate—8% Discount Rate	
Present value of principal to be received at maturity	
$100,000 × .67556 (Table 3)	$ 67,556
Present value of interest to be received periodically	
over the term of the bonds	
$5,000 × 8.11090 (Table 4)	40,555*
Present value of bonds	$108,111

*Rounded

The above discussion relied on present value tables in solving present value problems. Calculators may also be used to compute present values without the use of these tables. Many calculators, especially financial calculators, have present value (*PV*) functions that allow you to calculate present values by merely inputting the proper amount, discount rate, periods, and pressing the PV key. We discuss the use of financial calculators in the next section.

Using Financial Calculators

Business professionals, once they have mastered the underlying concepts in sections 1 and 2, often use a financial calculator to solve time value of money problems. In many cases, they must use calculators if interest rates or time periods do not correspond with the information provided in the compound interest tables.

To use financial calculators, you enter the time value of money variables into the calculator. Illustration D-22 shows the five most common keys used to solve time value of money problems.[2]

Illustration D-22 Financial calculator keys

where:

N = number of periods
I = interest rate per period (some calculators use I/YR or i)
PV = present value (occurs at the beginning of the first period)
PMT = payment (all payments are equal, and none are skipped)
FV = future value (occurs at the end of the last period)

In solving time value of money problems in this appendix, you will generally be given three of four variables and will have to solve for the remaining variable. The fifth key (the key not used) is given a value of zero to ensure that this variable is not used in the computation.

PRESENT VALUE OF A SINGLE SUM

To illustrate how to solve a present value problem using a financial calculator, assume that you want to know the present value of $84,253 to be received in five years, discounted at 11% compounded annually. Illustration D-23 depicts this problem.

Illustration D-23 Calculator solution for present value of a single sum

Illustration D-23 shows you the information (inputs) to enter into the calculator: N = 5, I = 11, PMT = 0, and FV = 84,253. You then press PV for the answer: −$50,000. As indicated, the PMT key was given a value of zero because a series of payments did not occur in this problem.

---

[2]On many calculators, these keys are actual buttons on the face of the calculator. On others, they appear on the display after the user accesses a present value menu.

Plus and Minus

The use of plus and minus signs in time value of money problems with a financial calculator can be confusing. Most financial calculators are programmed so that the positive and negative cash flows in any problem offset each other. In the present value problem above, we identified the $84,253 future value initial investment as a positive (inflow); the answer −$50,000 was shown as a negative amount, reflecting a cash outflow. If the 84,253 were entered as a negative, then the final answer would have been reported as a positive 50,000.

Hopefully, the sign convention will not cause confusion. If you understand what is required in a problem, you should be able to interpret a positive or negative amount in determining the solution to a problem.

Compounding Periods

In the problem above, we assumed that compounding occurs once a year. Some financial calculators have a default setting, which assumes that compounding occurs 12 times a year. You must determine what default period has been programmed into your calculator and change it as necessary to arrive at the proper compounding period.

Rounding

Most financial calculators store and calculate using 12 decimal places. As a result, because compound interest tables generally have factors only up to five decimal places, a slight difference in the final answer can result. In most time value of money problems, the final answer will not include more than two decimal places.

PRESENT VALUE OF AN ANNUITY

To illustrate how to solve a present value of an annuity problem using a financial calculator, assume that you are asked to determine the present value of rental receipts of $6,000 each to be received at the end of each of the next five years, when discounted at 12%, as pictured in Illustration D-24.

Illustration D-24 Calculator solution for present value of an annuity

Inputs:	5	12	?	6,000	0
	N	I	PV	PMT	FV
Answer:			−21,628.66		

In this case, you enter N = 5, I = 12, PMT = 6,000, FV = 0, and then press PV to arrive at the answer of −$21,628.66.

USEFUL APPLICATIONS OF THE FINANCIAL CALCULATOR

With a financial calculator, you can solve for any interest rate or for any number of periods in a time value of money problem. Here are some examples of these applications.

Auto Loan

Assume you are financing the purchase of a used car with a three-year loan. The loan has a 9.5% stated annual interest rate, compounded monthly. The price of the car is $6,000, and you want to determine the monthly payments, assuming that the payments start one month after the purchase. This problem is pictured in Illustration D-25.

Illustration D-25 Calculator solution for auto loan payments

To solve this problem, you enter N = 36 (12 × 3), I = 9.5, PV = 6,000, FV = 0, and then press PMT. You will find that the monthly payments will be $192.20. Note that the payment key is usually programmed for 12 payments per year. Thus, you must change the default (compounding period) if the payments are other than monthly.

Mortgage Loan Amount

Let's say you are evaluating financing options for a loan on a house. You decide that the maximum mortgage payment you can afford is $700 per month. The annual interest rate is 8.4%. If you get a mortgage that requires you to make monthly payments over a 15-year period, what is the maximum home loan you can afford? Illustration D-26 depicts this problem.

Illustration D-26 Calculator solution for mortgage amount

You enter N = 180 (12 × 15 years), I = 8.4, PMT = −700, FV = 0, and press PV. With the payments-per-year key set at 12, you find a present value of $71,509.81— the maximum home loan you can afford, given that you want to keep your mortgage payments at $700. Note that by changing any of the variables, you can quickly conduct "what-if" analyses for different situations.

Summary of Learning Objectives

1 **Distinguish between simple and compound interest.** Simple interest is computed on the principal only, while compound interest is computed on the principal and any interest earned that has not been withdrawn.

2 **Solve for future value of a single amount.** Prepare a time diagram of the problem. Identify the principal amount, the number of compounding periods, and the interest rate. Using the future value of 1 table, multiply the principal amount by the future value factor specified at the intersection of the number of periods and the interest rate.

3 **Solve for future value of an annuity.** Prepare a time diagram of the problem. Identify the amount of the periodic payments, the number of compounding periods, and the interest rate. Using the future value of an annuity of 1 table, multiply the amount of the payments by the future value factor specified at the intersection of the number of periods and the interest rate.

4 **Identify the variables fundamental to solving present value problems.** The following three variables are fundamental to solving present value problems: (1) the future amount, (2) the number of periods, and (3) the interest rate (the discount rate).

5 Solve for present value of a single amount. Prepare a time diagram of the problem. Identify the future amount, the number of discounting periods, and the discount (interest) rate. Using the present value of a single amount table, multiply the future amount by the present value factor specified at the intersection of the number of periods and the discount rate.

6 Solve for present value of an annuity. Prepare a time diagram of the problem. Identify the amount of future periodic receipts or payment (annuities), the number of discounting periods, and the discount (interest) rate. Using the present value of an annuity of 1 table, multiply the amount of the annuity by the present value factor specified at the intersection of the number of periods and the interest rate.

7 Compute the present value of notes and bonds. Determine the present value of the principal amount: Multiply the principal amount (a single future amount) by the present value factor (from the present value of 1 table) intersecting at the number of periods

(number of interest payments) and the discount rate. Determine the present value of the series of interest payments: Multiply the amount of the interest payment by the present value factor (from the present value of an annuity of 1 table) intersecting at the number of periods (number of interest payments) and the discount rate. Add the present value of the principal amount to the present value of the interest payments to arrive at the present value of the note or bond.

8 Use a financial calculator to solve time value of money problems. Financial calculators can be used to solve the same and additional problems as those solved with time value of money tables. Enter into the financial calculator the amounts for all of the known elements of a time value of money problem (periods, interest rate, payments, future or present value), and it solves for the unknown element. Particularly useful situations involve interest rates and compounding periods not presented in the tables.

Glossary

Annuity *(p. D-4)* A series of equal dollar amounts to be paid or received at evenly spaced time intervals (periodically).

Compound interest *(p. D-2)* The interest computed on the principal and any interest earned that has not been paid or withdrawn.

Discounting the future amount(s) *(p. D-7)* The process of determining present value.

Future value of a single amount *(p. D-2)* The value at a future date of a given amount invested, assuming compound interest.

Future value of an annuity *(p. D-5)* The sum of all the payments or receipts plus the accumulated compound interest on them.

Interest *(p. D-1)* Payment for the use of another person's money.

Present value *(p. D-7)* The value now of a given amount to be paid or received in the future assuming compound interest.

Present value of an annuity *(p. D-9)* The value now of a series of future receipts or payments, discounted assuming compound interest.

Principal *(p. D-1)* The amount borrowed or invested.

Simple interest *(p. D-1)* The interest computed on the principal only.

 PLUS Self-Test, Brief Exercises, Exercises, Problem Set A, and many more resources are available for practice in WileyPLUS.

Brief Exercises

(Use tables to solve exercises BED-1 to BED-23.)

Compute the future value of a single amount.

(LO 2), **AP**

BED-1 Jerry Rees invested $8,000 at 5% annual interest, and left the money invested without withdrawing any of the interest for 12 years. At the end of the 12 years, Jerry withdrew the accumulated amount of money. (a) What amount did Jerry withdraw, assuming the investment earns simple interest? (b) What amount did Jerry withdraw, assuming the investment earns interest compounded annually?

BED-2 For each of the following cases, indicate (a) to what interest rate columns and (b) to what number of periods you would refer in looking up the future value factor.

Use future value tables.
(LO 2, 3), **C**

(1) In Table 1 (future value of 1):

	Annual Rate	Number of Years Invested	Compounded
Case A	6%	3	Annually
Case B	8%	4	Semiannually

(2) In Table 2 (future value of an annuity of 1):

	Annual Rate	Number of Years Invested	Compounded
Case A	5%	8	Annually
Case B	6%	6	Semiannually

BED-3 Mayer Company signed a lease for an office building for a period of 12 years. Under the lease agreement, a security deposit of $9,200 is made. The deposit will be returned at the expiration of the lease with interest compounded at 4% per year. What amount will Mayer receive at the time the lease expires?

Compute the future value of a single amount.
(LO 2), **AP**

BED-4 Ekman Company issued $1,000,000, 10-year bonds and agreed to make annual sinking fund deposits of $78,000. The deposits are made at the end of each year into an account paying 5% annual interest. What amount will be in the sinking fund at the end of 10 years?

Compute the future value of an annuity.
(LO 3), **AP**

BED-5 Terry and Jessica Benedict invested $6,000 in a savings account paying 4% annual interest when their daughter, Kristi, was born. They also deposited $1,000 on each of her birthdays until she was 18 (including her 18th birthday). How much was in the savings account on her 18th birthday (after the last deposit)?

Compute the future value of a single amount and of an annuity.
(LO 2, 3), **AP**

BED-6 Jeff Farris borrowed $34,000 on July 1, 2014. This amount plus accrued interest at 9% compounded annually is to be repaid on July 1, 2019. How much will Jeff have to repay on July 1, 2019?

Compute the future value of a single amount.
(LO 2), **AP**

BED-7 For each of the following cases, indicate (a) to what interest rate columns and (b) to what number of periods you would refer in looking up the discount rate.

Use present value tables.
(LO 5, 6), **C**

(1) In Table 3 (present value of 1):

	Annual Rate	Number of Years Involved	Discounts per Year
Case A	12%	6	Annually
Case B	10%	11	Annually
Case C	6%	9	Semiannually

(2) In Table 4 (present value of an annuity of 1):

	Annual Rate	Number of Years Involved	Number of Payments Involved	Frequency of Payments
Case A	12%	20	20	Annually
Case B	10%	5	5	Annually
Case C	8%	4	8	Semiannually

BED-8 (a) What is the present value of $28,000 due 9 periods from now, discounted at 10%?

(b) What is the present value of $28,000 to be received at the end of each of 6 periods, discounted at 9%?

Determine present values.
(LO 5, 6), **AP**

BED-9 Elmdale Company is considering an investment that will return a lump sum of $750,000 five years from now. What amount should Elmdale Company pay for this investment to earn a 9% return?

Compute the present value of a single amount investment.
(LO 5), **AP**

Compute the present value of a single amount investment.
(LO 5), **AP**

BED-10 Orear Company earns 10% on an investment that will return $480,000 eight years from now. What is the amount Orear should invest now to earn this rate of return?

Compute the present value of an annuity investment.
(LO 6), **AP**

BED-11 Dayton Company is considering investing in an annuity contract that will return $45,000 annually at the end of each year for 15 years. What amount should Dayton Company pay for this investment if it earns a 5% return?

Compute the present value of an annuity investment.
(LO 6), **AP**

BED-12 Nolasko Enterprises earns 8% on an investment that pays back $90,000 at the end of each of the next 6 years. What is the amount Nolasko Enterprises invested to earn the 8% rate of return?

Compute the present value of bonds.
(LO 5, 6, 7), **AP**

BED-13 Kirby Railroad Co. is about to issue $300,000 of 10-year bonds paying a 9% interest rate, with interest payable semiannually. The discount rate for such securities is 8%. How much can Kirby expect to receive for the sale of these bonds?

Compute the present value of bonds.
(LO 5, 6, 7), **AP**

BED-14 Assume the same information as BED-13 except that the discount rate was 10% instead of 8%. In this case, how much can Kirby expect to receive from the sale of these bonds?

Compute the present value of a note.
(LO 5, 6, 7), **AP**

BED-15 Robertson Company receives a $64,000, 6-year note bearing interest of 6% (paid annually) from a customer at a time when the discount rate is 8%. What is the present value of the note received by Robertson?

Compute the present value of bonds.
(LO 5, 6, 7), **AP**

BED-16 Jimenez Enterprises issued 9%, 8-year, $2,600,000 par value bonds that pay interest semiannually on October 1 and April 1. The bonds are dated April 1, 2014, and are issued on that date. The discount rate of interest for such bonds on April 1, 2014, is 10%. What cash proceeds did Jimenez receive from issuance of the bonds?

Compute the present value of a machine for purposes of making a purchase decision.
(LO 6, 7), **AP**

BED-17 Phil Emley owns a garage and is contemplating purchasing a tire retreading machine for $18,000. After estimating costs and revenues, Phil projects a net cash flow from the retreading machine of $3,300 annually for 8 years. Phil hopes to earn a return of 10% on such investments. What is the present value of the retreading operation? Should Phil purchase the retreading machine?

Compute the present value of a note.
(LO 6), **AP**

BED-18 Jamison Company issues an 8%, 5-year mortgage note on January 1, 2014, to obtain financing for new equipment. Land is used as collateral for the note. The terms provide for semiannual installment payments of $46,850. What were the cash proceeds received from the issuance of the note?

Compute the maximum price to pay for a machine.
(LO 6, 7), **AP**

BED-19 Pendley Company is considering purchasing equipment. The equipment will produce the following cash flows: Year 1, $38,000; Year 2, $40,000; and Year 3, $50,000. Pendley requires a minimum rate of return of 10%. What is the maximum price Pendley should pay for this equipment?

Compute the interest rate on a single amount.
(LO 5), **AN**

BED-20 If Barbara Oxford invests $4,172.65 now and she will receive $10,000 at the end of 15 years, what annual rate of interest will Barbara earn on her investment? (*Hint:* Use Table 3.)

Compute the number of periods of a single amount.
(LO 5), **AN**

BED-21 Blake Mohr has been offered the opportunity of investing $25,490 now. The investment will earn 10% per year and at the end of that time will return Blake $80,000. How many years must Blake wait to receive $80,000? (*Hint:* Use Table 3.)

Compute the interest rate on an annuity.
(LO 6), **AN**

BED-22 Amanda Tevis made an investment of $9,128.55. From this investment, she will receive $1,000 annually for the next 20 years starting one year from now. What rate of interest will Amanda's investment be earning for her? (*Hint:* Use Table 4.)

Compute the number of periods of an annuity.
(LO 6), **AN**

BED-23 Kelly Reading invests $5,146.12 now for a series of $1,000 annual returns beginning one year from now. Kelly will earn a return of 11% on the initial investment. How many annual payments of $1,000 will Kelly receive? (*Hint:* Use Table 4.)

Determine interest rate.
(LO 8), **AP**

BED-24 Julie Vopat wishes to invest $18,000 on July 1, 2014, and have it accumulate to $50,000 by July 1, 2024. Use a financial calculator to determine at what exact annual rate of interest Julie must invest the $18,000.

Determine interest rate.
(LO 8), **AP**

BED-25 On July 17, 2014, Billy Prater borrowed $60,000 from his grandfather to open a clothing store. Starting July 17, 2020, Billy has to make 10 equal annual payments of $8,860 each to repay the loan. Use a financial calculator to determine what interest rate Billy is paying.

BED-26   As the purchaser of a new house, Manuel Rodriguez has signed a mortgage note to pay the Nashville National Bank and Trust Co. $8,400 every 6 months for 20 years, at the end of which time he will own the house. At the date the mortgage is signed, the purchase price was $198,000 and Rodriguez made a down payment of $20,000. The first payment will be made 6 months after the date the mortgage is signed. Using a financial calculator, compute the exact rate of interest earned on the mortgage by the bank.

Determine interest rate.
(LO 8), **AP**

BED-27   Using a financial calculator, solve for the unknowns in each of the following situations.
(a) On June 1, 2014, Linda Cuningham purchases lakefront property from her neighbor, Donald Fancher, and agrees to pay the purchase price in seven payments of $16,000 each, the first payment to be payable June 1, 2015. (Assume that interest compounded at an annual rate of 6.9% is implicit in the payments.) What is the purchase price of the property?
(b) On January 1, 2014, Noonan Corporation purchased 200 of the $1,000 face value, 7% coupon, 10-year bonds of Lumley Inc. The bonds mature on January 1, 2022, and pay interest annually beginning January 1, 2015. Noonan purchased the bonds to yield 8.65%. How much did Noonan pay for the bonds?

Various time value of money situations.
(LO 8), **AP**

BED-28   Using a financial calculator, provide a solution to each of the following situations.
(a) Tina Deboer owes a debt of $42,000 from the purchase of her new sport utility vehicle. The debt bears annual interest of 7.8% compounded monthly. Tina wishes to pay the debt and interest in equal monthly payments over 8 years, beginning one month hence. What equal monthly payments will pay off the debt and interest?
(b) On January 1, 2014, Danny Herron offers to buy Mark Jacobs' used snowmobile for $8,000, payable in five equal annual installments, which are to include 7.25% interest on the unpaid balance and a portion of the principal. If the first payment is to be made on December 31, 2014, how much will each payment be?

Various time value of money situations.
(LO 8), **AP**

REPORTING AND ANALYZING INVESTMENTS

LEARNING OBJECTIVES

After studying this appendix, you should be able to:

1 Identify the reasons corporations invest in stocks and debt securities.

2 Explain the accounting for debt investments.

3 Explain the accounting for stock investments.

4 Describe the purpose and usefulness of consolidated financial statements.

5 Indicate how debt and stock investments are valued and reported in the financial statements.

6 Distinguish between short-term and long-term investments.

Why Corporations Invest

Corporations purchase investments in debt or equity securities generally for one of three reasons. First, a corporation may **have excess cash** that it does not need for the immediate purchase of operating assets. For example, many companies experience seasonal fluctuations in sales. A Cape Cod marina has more sales in the spring and summer than in the fall and winter. The reverse is true for an Aspen ski shop. Thus, at the end of an operating cycle, many companies may have cash on hand that is temporarily idle until the start of another operating cycle. These companies may invest the excess funds to earn—through interest and dividends—a greater return than they would get by just holding the funds in the bank. Illustration E-1 shows the role that such temporary investments play in the operating cycle.

Illustration E-1 Temporary investments and the operating cycle

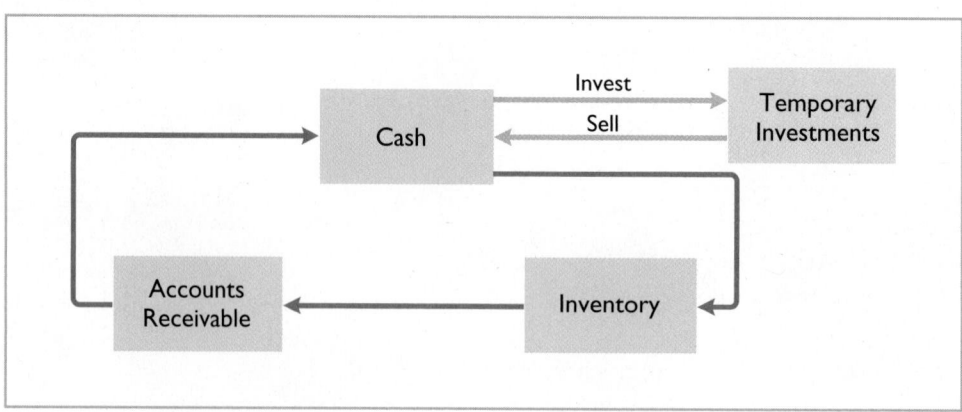

A second reason some companies such as banks purchase investments is to generate **earnings from investment income**. Although banks make most of their earnings by lending money, they also generate earnings by investing in debt and equity securities. Banks purchase investment securities because loan demand varies both seasonally and with changes in the economic climate. Thus, when loan demand is low, a bank must find other uses for its cash.

Some companies attempt to generate investment income through speculative investments. That is, they are speculating that the investment will increase in value and thus result in positive returns. Therefore, they invest primarily in the common stock of other corporations.

Third, companies also invest for **strategic reasons**. A company may purchase a noncontrolling interest in another company in a related industry in which it wishes to establish a presence. Alternatively, a company can exercise some influence over one of its customers or suppliers by purchasing a significant, but not controlling, interest in that company. Or, a corporation may choose to purchase a controlling interest in another company in order to enter a new industry without incurring the costs and risks associated with starting from scratch.

In summary, businesses invest in other companies for the reasons shown in Illustration E-2.

Reason	Typical Investment
To house excess cash until needed	Low-risk, highly liquid, short-term securities such as government-issued securities
To generate earnings *I need 1,000 Treasury bills by tonight.* BANK	Banks and financial institutions often purchase debt securities, while mutual funds and index funds purchase both debt and stock securities
To meet strategic goals	Stocks of companies in a related industry or in an unrelated industry that the company wishes to enter

Illustration E-2 Why corporations invest

Accounting for Debt Investments

Debt investments are investments in government and corporation bonds. In accounting for debt investments, companies must make entries to record (1) the acquisition, (2) the interest revenue, and (3) the sale.

LEARNING OBJECTIVE **2**
Explain the accounting for debt investments.

RECORDING ACQUISITION OF BONDS

At acquisition, debt investments are recorded at cost. Cost includes all expenditures necessary to acquire these investments, such as the price paid plus brokerage fees (commissions), if any.

For example, assume that Kuhl Corporation acquires 50 Doan Inc. 8%, 10-year, $1,000 bonds on January 1, 2014, at a cost of $50,000. Kuhl records the investment as:

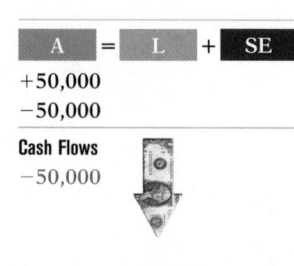

Jan.	1	Debt Investments	50,000	
		Cash		50,000
		(To record purchase of 50 Doan Inc. bonds)		

RECORDING BOND INTEREST

The Doan Inc. bonds pay interest of $2,000 semiannually on July 1 and January 1 ($50,000 \times 8\% \times \frac{1}{2}$). The entry for the receipt of interest on July 1 is:

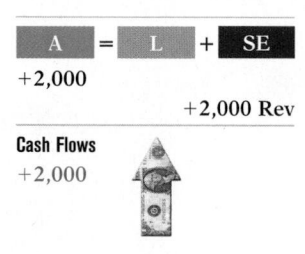

July	1	Cash	2,000	
		Interest Revenue		2,000
		(To record receipt of interest on Doan Inc. bonds)		

If Kuhl Corporation's fiscal year ends on December 31, it accrues the interest of $2,000 earned since July 1. The adjusting entry is:

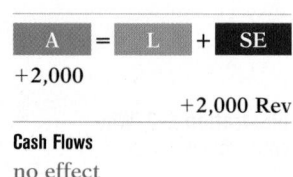

Dec.	31	Interest Receivable	2,000	
		Interest Revenue		2,000
		(To accrue interest on Doan Inc. bonds)		

Kuhl reports Interest Receivable as a current asset in the balance sheet. It reports Interest Revenue under "Other revenues and gains" in the income statement.
    Kuhl records receipt of the interest on January 1 as follows.

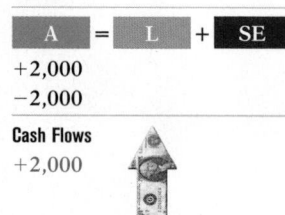

Jan.	1	Cash	2,000	
		Interest Receivable		2,000
		(To record receipt of accrued interest)		

A credit to Interest Revenue at this time would be incorrect. Why? Because the company earned and accrued the interest revenue in the preceding accounting period.

RECORDING SALE OF BONDS

Helpful Hint The accounting for short-term debt investments and long-term debt investments is similar. Any exceptions are discussed in more advanced courses.

When Kuhl sells the bond investments, it credits the investment account for the cost of the bonds. The company records as a gain or loss any difference between the net proceeds from the sale (sales price less brokerage fees) and the cost of the bonds.
    Assume, for example, that Kuhl Corporation receives net proceeds of $54,000 on the sale of the Doan Inc. bonds on January 1, 2015, after receiving the interest due. Since the securities cost $50,000, Kuhl has realized a gain of $4,000. It records the sale as follows.

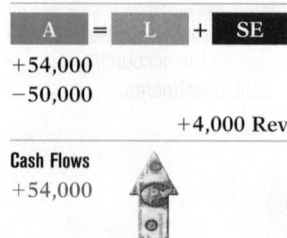

Jan.	1	Cash	54,000	
		Debt Investments		50,000
		Gain on Sale of Debt Investments		4,000
		(To record sale of Doan Inc. bonds)		

Kuhl reports the gain on the sale of debt investments under "Other revenues and gains" in the income statement and reports losses under "Other expenses and losses."

Accounting for Stock Investments

Stock investments are investments in the capital stock of corporations. When a company holds stock (and/or debt) of several different corporations, the group of securities is an **investment portfolio**.

The accounting for investments in common stock depends on the extent of the investor's influence over the operating and financial affairs of the issuing corporation (the **investee**). Illustration E-3 shows the general guidelines.

Investor's Ownership Interest in Investee's Common Stock	Presumed Influence on Investee	Accounting Guidelines
Less than 20%	Insignificant	Cost method
Between 20% and 50%	Significant	Equity method
More than 50%	Controlling	Consolidated financial statements

Illustration E-3 Accounting guidelines for stock investments

Companies are required to use judgment instead of blindly following the guidelines.[1] We explain and illustrate the application of each guideline next.

HOLDINGS OF LESS THAN 20%

In the accounting for stock investments of less than 20%, companies use the cost method. Under the cost method, companies record the investment at cost and recognize revenue only when cash dividends are received.

Recording Acquisition of Stock

At acquisition, stock investments are recorded at cost. Cost includes all expenditures necessary to acquire these investments, such as the price paid plus brokerage fees (commissions), if any.

Assume, for example, that on July 1, 2014, Sanchez Corporation acquires 1,000 shares (10% ownership) of Beal Corporation common stock at $40 per share. The entry for the purchase is:

July	1	Stock Investments	40,000	
		Cash		40,000
		(To record purchase of 1,000 shares of		
		Beal common stock)		

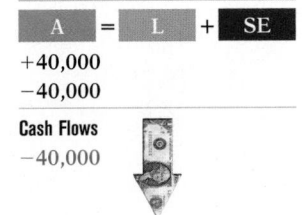

A = L + SE
+40,000
−40,000

Cash Flows
−40,000

---

[1]Among the factors that companies should consider in determining an investor's influence are whether (1) the investor has representation on the investee's board of directors, (2) the investor participates in the investee's policy-making process, (3) there are material transactions between the investor and the investee, and (4) the common stock held by other stockholders is concentrated or dispersed.

Recording Dividends

During the time the company holds the stock, it makes entries for any cash dividends received. Thus, if Sanchez Corporation receives a $2 per share dividend on December 31, the entry is:

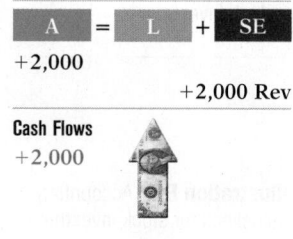

A = L + SE
+2,000
          +2,000 Rev

Cash Flows
+2,000

Dec. 31	Cash (1,000 × $2)	2,000	
	Dividend Revenue		2,000
	(To record receipt of a cash dividend)		

Sanchez reports Dividend Revenue under "Other revenues and gains" in the income statement.

Recording Sale of Stock

When a company sells a stock investment, it recognizes the difference between the net proceeds from the sale (sales price less brokerage fees) and the cost of the stock as a gain or a loss.

Assume, for instance, that Sanchez Corporation receives net proceeds of $39,500 on the sale of its Beal Corporation stock on February 10, 2015. Because the stock cost $40,000, Sanchez has incurred a loss of $500. It records the sale as:

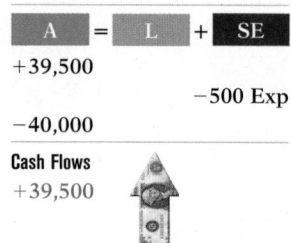

A = L + SE
+39,500
          −500 Exp
−40,000

Cash Flows
+39,500

Feb. 10	Cash	39,500	
	Loss on Sale of Stock Investments	500	
	Stock Investments		40,000
	(To record sale of Beal common stock)		

Sanchez reports the loss account under "Other expenses and losses" in the income statement and shows a gain on sale under "Other revenues and gains."

HOLDINGS BETWEEN 20% AND 50%

When an investor company owns only a small portion of the shares of stock of another company, the investor cannot exercise control over the investee. But when an investor owns between 20% and 50% of the common stock of a corporation, it is presumed that the investor has significant influence over the financial and operating activities of the investee. The investor probably has a representative on the investee's board of directors. Through that representative, the investor begins to exercise some control over the investee—and the investee company in some sense becomes part of the investor company.

For example, even prior to purchasing all of Turner Broadcasting, Time Warner owned 20% of Turner. Because it exercised significant control over major decisions made by Turner, Time Warner used an approach called the equity method. Under the **equity method, the investor records its share of the net income of the investee in the year when it is earned**. An alternative might be to delay recognizing the investor's share of net income until a cash dividend is declared. But that approach would ignore the fact that the investor and investee are, in some sense, one company, making the investor better off by the investee's earned income.

Under the equity method, the company initially records the investment in common stock at cost. After that, it adjusts the investment account **annually** to show the investor's equity in the investee. Each year, the investor does the following. (1) It increases (debits) the investment account and increases (credits) revenue for its share of the investee's net income.[2] (2) The investor also decreases (credits) the investment account for the amount of dividends received. The investment account is reduced for dividends received because payment of a dividend decreases the net assets of the investee.

Recording Acquisition of Stock

Assume that Milar Corporation acquires 30% of the common stock of Beck Company for $120,000 on January 1, 2014. The entry to record this transaction is:

Jan. 1	Stock Investments		120,000	
	Cash			120,000
	(To record purchase of Beck common stock)			

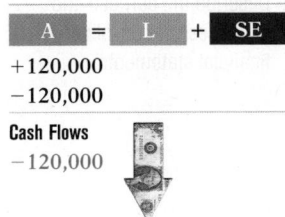

A = L + SE
+120,000
−120,000

Cash Flows
−120,000

Recording Revenue and Dividends

For 2014, Beck reports net income of $100,000. It declares and pays a $40,000 cash dividend. Milar must record (1) its share of Beck's income, $30,000 (30% × $100,000), and (2) the reduction in the investment account for the dividends received, $12,000 (30% × $40,000). The entries are:

(1)

Dec. 31	Stock Investments		30,000	
	Revenue from Stock Investments			30,000
	(To record 30% equity in Beck's 2014 net income)			

A = L + SE
+30,000
+30,000 Rev

Cash Flows
no effect

(2)

Dec. 31	Cash		12,000	
	Stock Investments			12,000
	(To record dividends received)			

A = L + SE
+12,000
−12,000

Cash Flows
+12,000

After Milar posts the transactions for the year, the investment and revenue accounts are as shown in Illustration E-4.

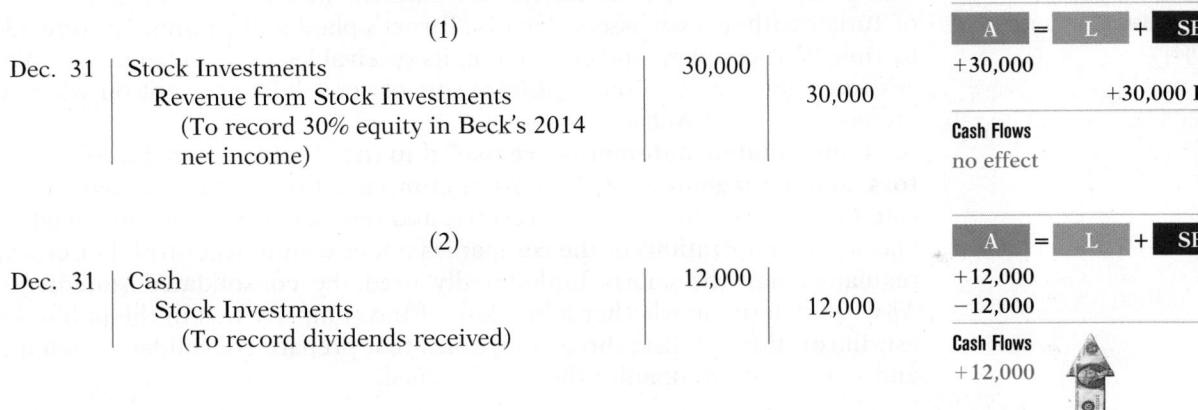

Stock Investments				Revenue from Stock Investments	
Jan. 1	120,000	Dec. 31	12,000	Dec. 31	30,000
Dec. 31	30,000				
Dec. 31 Bal.	138,000				

Illustration E-4 Investment and revenue accounts after posting

During the year, the investment account increased by $18,000. This $18,000 is Milar's 30% equity in the $60,000 increase in Beck's retained earnings ($100,000 − $40,000). In addition, Milar reports $30,000 of revenue from its investment, which is 30% of Beck's net income of $100,000.

---

[2]Conversely, the investor increases (debits) a loss account and decreases (credits) the investment account for its share of the investee's net loss.

Note that the difference between reported revenue under the cost method and reported revenue under the equity method can be significant. For example, Milar would report only $12,000 of dividend revenue (30% × $40,000) if it used the cost method.

HOLDINGS OF MORE THAN 50%

A company that owns more than 50% of the common stock of another entity is known as the **parent company**. The entity whose stock is owned by the parent company is called the **subsidiary (affiliated) company**. Because of its stock ownership, the parent company has a **controlling interest** in the subsidiary company.

When a company owns more than 50% of the common stock of another company, it usually prepares **consolidated financial statements**. Consolidated financial statements present the assets and liabilities controlled by the parent company. They also present the total revenues and expenses of the subsidiary companies. Companies prepare consolidated statements **in addition to** the financial statements for the individual parent and subsidiary companies.

Helpful Hint If the parent (A) has three wholly owned subsidiaries (B, C, and D), there are four separate legal entities but only one economic entity from the viewpoint of the shareholders of the parent company.

As noted earlier, prior to acquiring all of Turner Broadcasting, Time Warner accounted for its investment in Turner using the equity method. Time Warner's net investment in Turner was reported in a single line item—Other investments. After the merger, Time Warner instead consolidated Turner's results with its own. Under this approach, Time Warner included the individual assets and liabilities of Turner with its own assets. That is, Turner's plant and equipment were added to Time Warner's plant and equipment, its receivables were added to Time Warner's receivables, and so on. A similar sort of consolidation went on when AOL merged with Time Warner.

Consolidated statements are useful to the stockholders, board of directors, and management of the parent company. Consolidated statements indicate to creditors, prospective investors, and regulatory agencies the magnitude and scope of operations of the companies under common control. For example, regulators and the courts undoubtedly used the consolidated statements of AT&T to determine whether a breakup of the company was in the public interest. Illustration E-5 lists three companies that prepare consolidated statements and some of the companies they have owned.

Illustration E-5 Examples of consolidated companies and their subsidiaries

PepsiCo	Cendant	The Walt Disney Company
Frito-Lay	Howard Johnson	Capital Cities/ABC, Inc.
Tropicana	Ramada Inn	Disneyland, Disney World
Quaker Oats	Century 21	Mighty Ducks
Pepsi-Cola	Coldwell Banker	Anaheim Angels
Gatorade	Avis	ESPN

Valuing and Reporting Investments

The value of debt and stock investments may fluctuate greatly during the time they are held. For example, in a 12-month period, the stock of Time Warner hit a high of $58\frac{1}{2}$ and a low of 9. In light of such price fluctuations, how should companies value investments at the balance sheet date? Valuation could be at cost, at fair value, or at the lower-of-cost-or-market value.

Many people argue that fair value offers the best approach because it represents the expected cash realizable value of securities. Fair value is the amount for which a security could be sold in a normal market. Others counter that unless a security is going to be sold soon, the fair value is not relevant because the price of the security will likely change again.

CATEGORIES OF SECURITIES

For purposes of valuation and reporting at a financial statement date, debt and stock investments are classified into three categories of securities:

1. **Trading securities** are bought and held primarily for sale in the near term to generate income on short-term price differences.

2. **Available-for-sale securities** are held with the intent of selling them sometime in the future.

3. **Held-to-maturity securities** are debt securities that the investor has the intent and ability to hold to maturity.[3]

Illustration E-6 shows the valuation guidelines for these securities. **These guidelines apply to all debt securities and to those stock investments in which the holdings are less than 20%.**

International Note A recent U.S. accounting standard gives companies the "option" of applying fair value accounting, rather than historical cost, to certain types of assets and liabilities. This makes U.S. accounting closer to international standards.

Illustration E-6 Valuation guidelines

Trading	Available-for-sale	Held-to-maturity

Trading	Available-for-sale	Held-to-maturity
At fair value with changes reported in net income	At fair value with changes reported in the stockholders' equity section	At amortized cost

Trading Securities

Trading securities are held with the intention of selling them in a short period of time (generally less than a month). **Trading** means frequent buying and selling. As indicated in Illustration E-6, companies adjust trading securities to fair value at the end of each period (an approach referred to as mark-to-market accounting). They report changes from cost **as part of net income**. The changes are reported as **unrealized gains or losses** because the securities have not been sold. The unrealized gain or loss is the difference between the **total cost** of trading securities and their **total fair value**. Companies classify trading securities as a current asset.

---

[3]This category is provided for completeness. The accounting and valuation issues related to held-to-maturity securities are discussed in more advanced accounting courses.

As an example, Illustration E-7 shows the costs and fair values for investments classified as trading securities for Pace Corporation on December 31, 2014. Pace Corporation has an unrealized gain of $7,000 because total fair value ($147,000) is $7,000 greater than total cost ($140,000).

Illustration E-7 Valuation of trading securities

Trading Securities, December 31, 2014

Investments	Cost	Fair Value	Unrealized Gain (Loss)
Yorkville Company bonds	$ 50,000	$ 48,000	$(2,000)
Kodak Company stock	90,000	99,000	9,000
Total	$140,000	$147,000	$ 7,000

Helpful Hint Companies report an unrealized gain or loss in the income statement because of the likelihood that the securities will be sold at fair value since they are a short-term investment.

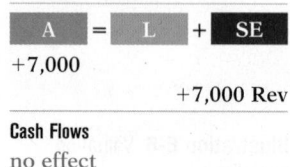

+7,000

　　　　　　+7,000 Rev

Cash Flows
no effect

The fact that trading securities are a short-term investment increases the likelihood that Pace will sell them at fair value for a gain. Pace records fair value and the unrealized gain through an adjusting entry at the time it prepares financial statements. In this entry, the company uses a valuation allowance account, Fair Value Adjustment—Trading, to record the difference between the total cost and the total fair value of the securities. The adjusting entry for Pace Corporation is:

Dec. 31	Fair Value Adjustment—Trading	7,000	
	Unrealized Gain—Income		7,000
	(To record unrealized gain on trading securities)		

The use of the Fair Value Adjustment—Trading account enables the company to maintain a record of the investment cost. Actual cost is needed to determine the gain or loss realized when the securities are sold. The company adds the debit balance (or subtracts a credit balance) of the Fair Value Adjustment—Trading account to the cost of the investments to arrive at a fair value for the trading securities.

The fair value of the securities is the amount companies report on the balance sheet. They report the unrealized gain on the income statement under "Other revenues and gains." The term **income** in the account title indicates that the gain affects net income. If the total cost of the trading securities is greater than total fair value, an unrealized loss has occurred. In such a case, the adjusting entry is a debit to Unrealized Loss—Income and a credit to Fair Value Adjustment—Trading. Companies report the unrealized loss under "Other expenses and losses" in the income statement.

The fair value adjustment account is carried forward into future accounting periods. No entries are made to this account during the period. At the end of each reporting period, a company adjusts the balance in the account to the difference between cost and fair value at that time. It closes the Unrealized Gain—Income account or Unrealized Loss—Income account at the end of the reporting period.

Available-for-Sale Securities

As indicated earlier, available-for-sale securities are held with the intent of selling them sometime in the future. If the intent is to sell the securities within the next year or operating cycle, a company classifies the securities as current assets in the balance sheet. Otherwise, it classifies them as long-term assets in the investments section of the balance sheet.

Companies also report available-for-sale securities at fair value. The procedure for determining fair value and unrealized gain or loss for these securities is the same as that for trading securities. To illustrate, assume that Elbert Corporation has two securities that are classified as available-for-sale. Illustration E-8 provides information on the cost, fair value, and amount of the unrealized gain or loss on December 31, 2014. There is an unrealized loss of $9,537 because total cost ($293,537) is $9,537 more than total fair value ($284,000).

Available-for-Sale Securities, December 31, 2014			
Investments	**Cost**	**Fair Value**	**Unrealized Gain (Loss)**
Campbell Soup Corporation 8% bonds	$ 93,537	$103,600	$10,063
Hershey Foods stock	200,000	180,400	(19,600)
Total	$293,537	$284,000	$(9,537)

Illustration E-8 Valuation of available-for-sale securities

BALANCE SHEET PRESENTATION

For balance sheet presentation, companies must classify investments as either short-term or long-term.

Short-Term Investments

Short-term investments (also called **marketable securities**) are securities held by a company that are (1) **readily marketable** and (2) **intended to be converted into cash** within the next year or operating cycle, whichever is longer. Investments that do not meet **both criteria** are classified as long-term investments.

Both the adjusting entry and the reporting of the unrealized loss from Elbert's available-for-sale securities differ from those illustrated for trading securities. The differences result because these securities are not going to be sold in the near term. Thus, prior to actual sale it is much more likely that changes in fair value may reverse the unrealized loss. Therefore, Elbert does not report an unrealized loss in the income statement. Instead, the company reports it as a **separate component of stockholders' equity**. In the adjusting entry, Elbert identifies the fair value adjustment account with available-for-sale securities, and identifies the unrealized gain or loss account with stockholders' equity. The adjusting entry for Elbert Corporation to record the unrealized loss of $9,537 is:

LEARNING OBJECTIVE 6

Distinguish between short-term and long-term investments.

Dec. 31	Unrealized Gain or Loss—Equity	9,537	
	Fair Value Adjustment—Available-for-Sale		9,537
	(To record unrealized loss on available-for-sale securities)		

If total fair value exceeds total cost, Elbert would record the adjusting entry as an increase (debit) to Fair Value Adjustment—Available-for-Sale and a credit to Unrealized Gain or Loss—Equity.

For available-for-sale securities, the company carries forward the Unrealized Gain or Loss—Equity account to future periods. At each future balance sheet date, the account is adjusted with the fair value adjustment account to show the difference between cost and fair value at that time.

Helpful Hint The entry is the same regardless of whether the securities are considered short-term or long-term.

$$A = L + SE$$
$$-9,537 \text{ Eq}$$
$$-9,537$$

Cash Flows
no effect

Ethics Note Recently, the SEC accused investment bank Morgan Stanley of overstating the value of certain bond investments by $75 million. The SEC stated that, in applying fair value accounting, Morgan Stanley used its own more optimistic assumptions rather than relying on external pricing sources.

Helpful Hint Trading securities are always classified as short-term. Available-for-sale securities can be either short-term or long-term.

READILY MARKETABLE. An investment is readily marketable when it can be sold easily whenever the need for cash arises. Short-term paper[4] meets this criterion because a company can readily sell it to other investors. Stocks and bonds traded on organized securities markets, such as the New York Stock Exchange, are readily marketable because they can be bought and sold daily. In contrast, there may be only a limited market for the securities issued by small corporations and no market for the securities of a privately held company.

INTENT TO CONVERT. Intent to convert means that management intends to sell the investment within the next year or operating cycle, whichever is longer. Generally, this criterion is satisfied when the investment is considered a resource that the company will use whenever the need for cash arises. For example, a ski resort may invest idle cash during the summer months with the intent to sell the securities to buy supplies and equipment shortly before the next winter season. This investment is considered short-term even if lack of snow cancels the next ski season and eliminates the need to convert the securities into cash as intended.

Because of their high liquidity, companies list short-term investments immediately below Cash in the current assets section of the balance sheet. Short-term investments are reported at fair value. For example, Weber Corporation would report its trading securities as shown in Illustration E-9.

Illustration E-9 Balance sheet presentation of short-term investments

WEBER CORPORATION	
Balance Sheet (partial)	
Current assets	
Cash	$21,000
Short-term investments, at fair value	**60,000**

Long-Term Investments

Companies generally report long-term investments in a separate section of the balance sheet immediately below "Current assets," as shown in Illustration E-10. Long-term investments in available-for-sale securities are reported at fair value. Investments in common stock accounted for under the equity method are reported at equity.

Illustration E-10 Balance sheet presentation of long-term investments

WEBER CORPORATION	
Balance Sheet (partial)	
Investments	
Bond sinking fund	$100,000
Investments in stock of less than 20% owned	
companies, at fair value	50,000
Investment in stock of 20%–50% owned	
company, at equity	150,000
Total investments	$300,000

---

[4]Short-term paper includes (1) certificates of deposits (CDs) issued by banks, (2) money market certificates issued by banks and savings and loan associations, (3) Treasury bills issued by the U.S. government, and (4) commercial paper issued by corporations with good credit ratings.

PRESENTATION OF REALIZED
AND UNREALIZED GAIN OR LOSS

Companies must present in the financial statements gains and losses on investments, whether realized or unrealized. In the income statement, companies report gains and losses, as well as interest and dividend revenue, in the nonoperating activities section under the categories listed in Illustration E-11.

Other Revenue and Gains	Other Expenses and Losses
Interest Revenue	Loss on Sale of Investments
Dividend Revenue	Unrealized Loss—Income
Gain on Sale of Investments	
Unrealized Gain—Income	

Illustration E-11
Nonoperating items related to investments

As indicated earlier, companies report an unrealized gain or loss on available-for-sale securities as a separate component of stockholders' equity. To illustrate, assume that Muzzillo Inc. has common stock of $3,000,000, retained earnings of $1,500,000, and an unrealized loss on available-for-sale securities of $100,000. Illustration E-12 shows the financial statement presentation of the unrealized loss.

Illustration E-12 Unrealized loss in stockholders' equity section

MUZZILLO INC.
Balance Sheet (partial)

Stockholders' equity	
Common stock	$3,000,000
Retained earnings	1,500,000
Total paid-in capital and retained earnings	4,500,000
Less: **Unrealized loss on available-for-sale securities**	100,000
Total stockholders' equity	$4,400,000

Note that the presentation of the loss is similar to the presentation of the cost of treasury stock in the stockholders' equity section. (It decreases stockholders' equity.) An unrealized gain would be added in this section. Reporting the unrealized gain or loss in the stockholders' equity section serves two important purposes. (1) It reduces the volatility of net income due to fluctuations in fair value. (2) It informs the financial statement user of the gain or loss that would occur if the company sold the securities at fair value.

Companies must report, as part of a more inclusive measure called **comprehensive income**, items such as unrealized gains and losses on available-for-sale securities, which affect stockholders' equity but are not included in the calculation of net income. For example, Tootsie Roll reported other comprehensive loss in 2011 of $8,740,000. Note 12 to Tootsie Roll's financial statements shows that one component of this amount was unrealized gains and losses on investment securities. Comprehensive income is discussed more fully in Chapter 13.

STATEMENT OF CASH FLOWS PRESENTATION

As shown previously in Illustrations E-9, E-10, and E-12, the balance sheet presents a company's investment accounts at a point in time. The "Investing activities" section of the statement of cash flows reports information on the cash inflows and outflows during the period that resulted from investment transactions.

Illustration E-13 presents the cash flows from investing activities from a recent statement of cash flows of The Walt Disney Company. From this information, we learn that Disney received $1,530 million from the sale or redemption of investments during the year.

Illustration E-13 Statement of cash flows presentation of investment activities

Real World	THE WALT DISNEY COMPANY Statement of Cash Flows (partial) (in millions)	
	Investing Activities	
	Investments in parks, resorts and other property	$(1,566)
	Acquisitions	(588)
	Dispositions	—
	Proceeds from sale of investments	**1,530**
	Other	6
	Cash used by investing activities	$ (618)

Summary of Learning Objectives

1 Identify the reasons corporations invest in stocks and debt securities. Corporations invest for three common reasons. (a) They have excess cash. (b) They view investment income as a significant revenue source. (c) They have strategic goals such as gaining control of a competitor or supplier or moving into a new line of business.

2 Explain the accounting for debt investments. Entries for investments in debt securities are required when companies purchase bonds, receive or accrue interest, and sell bonds.

3 Explain the accounting for stock investments. Entries for investments in common stock are required when companies purchase stock, receive dividends, and sell stock. When ownership is less than 20%, the cost method is used—the investment is recorded at cost. When ownership is between 20% and 50%, the equity method should be used—the investor records its share of the net income of the investee in the year it is earned. When ownership is more than 50%, consolidated financial statements should be prepared.

4 Describe the purpose and usefulness of consolidated financial statements. When a company owns more than 50% of the common stock of another company, consolidated financial statements are usually prepared. These statements are especially useful to the stockholders, board of directors, and management of the parent company.

5 Indicate how debt and stock investments are valued and reported in the financial statements. Investments in debt and stock securities are classified as trading, available-for-sale, or held-to-maturity for valuation and reporting purposes. Trading securities are reported as current assets at fair value, with changes from cost reported in net income. Available-for-sale securities are also reported at fair value, with the changes from cost reported in stockholders' equity. Available-for-sale securities are classified as short-term or long-term depending on their expected realization.

6 Distinguish between short-term and long-term investments. Short-term investments are securities held by a company that are readily marketable and intended to be converted to cash within the next year or operating cycle, whichever is longer. Investments that do not meet both criteria are classified as long-term investments.

Glossary

Available-for-sale securities (p. E-8) Securities that are held with the intent of selling them sometime in the future.

Consolidated financial statements (p. E-7) Financial statements that present the assets and liabilities controlled by the parent company and the total revenues and expenses of the subsidiary companies.

Controlling interest (p. E-7) Ownership of more than 50% of the common stock of another entity.

Cost method (p. E-4) An accounting method in which the investment in common stock is recorded at cost and revenue is recognized only when cash dividends are received.

Debt investments (p. E-2) Investments in government and corporation bonds.

Equity method (p. E-5) An accounting method in which the investment in common stock is initially recorded at cost, and the investment account is then adjusted annually to show the investor's equity in the investee.

Fair value *(p. E-8)* Amount for which a security could be sold in a normal market.

Held-to-maturity securities *(p. E-8)* Debt securities that the investor has the intent and ability to hold to maturity.

Long-term investments *(p. E-10)* Investments that are not readily marketable or that management does not intend to convert into cash within the next year or operating cycle, whichever is longer.

Mark-to-market *(p. E-8)* A method of accounting for certain investments that requires that they be adjusted to their fair value at the end of each period.

Parent company *(p. E-7)* A company that owns more than 50% of the common stock of another entity.

Short-term investments (marketable securities) *(p. E-10)* Investments that are readily marketable and intended to be converted into cash within the next year or operating cycle, whichever is longer.

Stock investments *(p. E-4)* Investments in the capital stock of corporations.

Subsidiary (affiliated) company *(p. E-7)* A company in which more than 50% of its stock is owned by another company.

Trading securities *(p. E-8)* Securities bought and held primarily for sale in the near term to generate income on short-term price differences.

 Self-Test, Brief Exercises, Exercises, Problem Set A, and many more resources are available for practice in WileyPLUS.

Self-Test Questions

Answers are at the end of the appendix.

(LO 1) **1.** Which of the following is **not** a primary reason why corporations invest in debt and equity securities?
   (a) They wish to gain control of a competitor.
   (b) They have excess cash.
   (c) They wish to move into a new line of business.
   (d) They are required to by law.

(LO 2) **2.** Debt investments are initially recorded at:
   (a) cost.
   (b) cost plus accrued interest.
   (c) book value.
   (d) None of the above

(LO 2) **3.** Stan Free Company sells debt investments costing $26,000 for $28,000 plus accrued interest that has been recorded. In journalizing the sale, credits are:
   (a) Debt Investments and Loss on Sale of Debt Investments.
   (b) Debt Investments, Gain on Sale of Debt Investments, and Bond Interest Receivable.
   (c) Stock Investments and Bond Interest Receivable.
   (d) The correct answer is not given.

(LO 3) **4.** Karen Duffy Company receives net proceeds of $42,000 on the sale of stock investments that cost $39,500. This transaction will result in reporting in the income statement a:
   (a) loss of $2,500 under "Other expenses and losses."
   (b) loss of $2,500 under "Operating expenses."
   (c) gain of $2,500 under "Other revenues and gains."
   (d) gain of $2,500 under "Operating revenues."

(LO 3) **5.** The equity method of accounting for long-term investments in stock should be used when the investor has significant influence over an investee and owns:

   (a) between 20% and 50% of the investee's common stock.
   (b) 20% or more of the investee's bonds.
   (c) more than 50% of the investee's common stock.
   (d) less than 20% of the investee's common stock.

(LO 3) **6.** Assume that Horicon Corp. acquired 25% of the common stock of Sheboygan Corp. on January 1, 2014, for $300,000. During 2014, Sheboygan Corp. reported net income of $160,000 and paid total dividends of $60,000. If Horicon uses the equity method to account for its investment, the balance in the investment account on December 31, 2014, will be:
   (a) $300,000.   (c) $400,000.
   (b) $325,000.   (d) $340,000.

(LO 3) **7.** Using the information in Question 6, what entry would Horicon make to record the receipt of the dividend from Sheboygan?
   (a) Debit Cash and credit Revenue from Stock Investments.
   (b) Debit Dividends and credit Revenue from Stock Investments.
   (c) Debit Cash and credit Stock Investments.
   (d) Debit Cash and credit Dividend Revenue.

(LO 3) **8.** You have a controlling interest if:
   (a) you own more than 20% of a company's stock.
   (b) you are the president of the company.
   (c) you use the equity method.
   (d) you own more than 50% of a company's stock.

(LO 4) **9.** Which of these statements is **false**?
   Consolidated financial statements are useful to:
   (a) determine the profitability of specific subsidiaries.
   (b) determine the aggregate profitability of companies under common control.

(c) determine the breadth of a parent company's operations.

(d) determine the full extent of aggregate obligations of companies under common control.

(LO 5) **10.** At the end of the first year of operations, the total cost of the trading securities portfolio is $120,000 and the total fair value is $115,000. What should the financial statements show?

(a) A reduction of an asset of $5,000 and a realized loss of $5,000.

(b) A reduction of an asset of $5,000 and an unrealized loss of $5,000 in the stockholders' equity section.

(c) A reduction of an asset of $5,000 in the current assets section and an unrealized loss of $5,000 under "Other expenses and losses."

(d) A reduction of an asset of $5,000 in the current assets section and a realized loss of $5,000 under "Other expenses and losses."

(LO 5) **11.** In the balance sheet, Unrealized Gain or Loss—Equity is reported as a:

(a) contra asset account.

(b) contra stockholders' equity account.

(c) loss in the income statement.

(d) loss in the retained earnings statement.

(LO 5) **12.** If a company wants to increase its reported income by manipulating its investment accounts, which should it do?

(a) Sell its "winner" trading securities and hold its "loser" trading securities.

(b) Hold its "winner" trading securities and sell its "loser" trading securities.

(c) Sell its "winner" available-for-sale securities and hold its "loser" available-for-sale securities.

(d) Hold its "winner" available-for-sale securities and sell its "loser" available-for-sale securities.

(LO 5) **13.** At December 31, 2014, the fair value of available-for-sale securities is $41,300 and the cost is $39,800. At January 1, 2014, there was a credit balance of $900 in the Fair Value Adjustment—Available-for-Sale account. The required adjusting entry would be:

(a) Debit Fair Value Adjustment—Available-for-Sale for $1,500, and credit Unrealized Gain or Loss—Equity for $1,500.

(b) Debit Fair Value Adjustment—Available-for-Sale for $600, and credit Unrealized Gain or Loss—Equity for $600.

(c) Debit Fair Value Adjustment—Available-for-Sale for $2,400, and credit Unrealized Gain or Loss—Equity for $2,400.

(d) Debit Unrealized Gain or Loss—Equity for $2,400, and credit Fair Value Adjustment—Available-for-Sale for $2,400.

(LO 6) **14.** To be classified as short-term investments, debt investments must be readily marketable and be expected to be sold within:

(a) 3 months from the date of purchase.

(b) the next year or operating cycle, whichever is shorter.

(c) the next year or operating cycle, whichever is longer.

(d) the operating cycle.

Questions

1. What are the reasons that companies invest in securities?

2. (a) What is the cost of an investment in bonds?
   (b) When is interest on bonds recorded?

3. Jill Glendo is confused about losses and gains on the sale of debt investments. Explain these issues to Jill:
   (a) How the gain or loss is computed.
   (b) The statement presentation of gains and losses.

4. Townsend Company sells bonds that cost $40,000 for $45,000, including $1,000 of accrued interest. In recording the sale, Townsend books a $5,000 gain. Is this correct? Explain.

5. What is the cost of an investment in stock?

6. To acquire Engels Corporation stock, Kaiser Co. pays $61,500 in cash. What entry should be made for this investment, assuming the stock is readily marketable?

7. (a) When should a long-term investment in common stock be accounted for by the equity method?
   (b) When is revenue recognized under the equity method?

8. Upson Corporation uses the equity method to account for its ownership of 30% of the common stock of Holland Packing. During 2014, Holland reported a net income of $80,000 and declares and pays cash dividends of $10,000. What recognition should Upson Corporation give to these events?

9. What constitutes "significant influence" when an investor's financial interest is less than 50%?

10. Distinguish between the cost and equity methods of accounting for investments in stocks.

11. What are consolidated financial statements?

12. What are the valuation guidelines for trading and available-for-sale investments at a balance sheet date?

13. Erica Pike is the controller of D-Products, Inc. At December 31, the company's investments in trading securities cost $74,000 and have a fair value of $70,000. Indicate how Erica would report these data in the financial statements prepared on December 31.

14. Using the data in Question 13, how would Erica report the data if the investments were long-term and the securities were classified as available-for-sale?

15. Napa Company's investments in available-for-sale securities at December 31 show total cost of $202,000 and total fair value of $210,000. Prepare the adjusting entry.

16. Using the data in Question 15, prepare the adjusting entry, assuming the securities are classified as trading securities.

17. ◐══════◖ Where is Unrealized Gain or Loss—Equity reported on the balance sheet?

18. What purposes are served by reporting Unrealized Gains (Losses)—Equity in the stockholders' equity section?

19. Ginavan Wholesale Supply owns stock in Kriley Corporation, which it intends to hold indefinitely because of some negative tax consequences if sold. Should the investment in Kriley be classified as a short-term investment? Why?

Brief Exercises

BEE-1 Sprague Corporation purchased debt investments for $40,800 on January 1, 2014. On July 1, 2014, Sprague received cash interest of $1,660. Journalize the purchase and the receipt of interest. Assume no interest has been accrued.

Journalize entries for debt investments.
(LO 2), **AP**

BEE-2 On August 1, Frost Company buys 1,000 shares of ABC common stock for $35,600 cash. On December 1, the stock investments are sold for $38,000 in cash. Journalize the purchase and sale of the common stock.

Journalize entries for stock investments.
(LO 3), **AP**

BEE-3 Bass Company owns 25% of Petit Company. For the current year, Petit reports net income of $150,000 and declares and pays a $60,000 cash dividend. Record Bass's equity in Petit's net income and the receipt of dividends from Petit.

Journalize transactions under the equity method.
(LO 3), **AP**

BEE-4 Cost and fair value data for the trading securities of Dobler Company at December 31, 2014, are $62,000 and $59,600, respectively. Prepare the adjusting entry to record the securities at fair value.

Prepare adjusting entry using fair value.
(LO 5), **AP**

BEE-5 For the data presented in BEE-4, show the financial statement presentation of the trading securities and related accounts.

Indicate statement presentation using fair value.
(LO 6), **AN**

BEE-6 In its first year of operations, Mallein Corporation purchased available-for-sale stock securities costing $72,000 as a long-term investment. At December 31, 2014, the fair value of the securities is $69,000. Prepare the adjusting entry to record the securities at fair value.

Prepare adjusting entry using fair value.
(LO 5), **AP**

BEE-7 For the data presented in BEE-6, show the financial statement presentation of the securities and related accounts. Assume the securities are noncurrent.

Indicate statement presentation using fair value.
(LO 6), **AN**

BEE-8 Rhoads Corporation has these long-term investments: common stock of Wenn Co. (10% ownership) held as available-for-sale securities, cost $108,000, fair value $112,000; common stock of Thomas Inc. (30% ownership), cost $210,000, equity $230,000; and a bond sinking fund of $150,000. Prepare the investments section of the balance sheet.

Prepare investments section of balance sheet.
(LO 6), **AP**

Exercises

EE-1 Maurer Corporation had these transactions pertaining to debt investments:

Jan. 1 Purchased 90 10%, $1,000 Landis Co. bonds for $90,000 cash. Interest is payable semiannually on July 1 and January 1.
July 1 Received semiannual interest on Landis Co. bonds.
July 1 Sold 30 Landis Co. bonds for $32,000.

Journalize debt investment transactions, and accrue interest.
(LO 2), **AP**

Instructions
(a) Journalize the transactions.
(b) Prepare the adjusting entry for the accrual of interest at December 31.

EE-2 Soils Company had these transactions pertaining to stock investments:

Feb. 1 Purchased 1,200 shares of JB common stock (2% of outstanding shares) for $8,400.
July 1 Received cash dividends of $2 per share on JB common stock.
Sept. 1 Sold 500 shares of JB common stock for $5,400.
Dec. 1 Received cash dividends of $1 per share on JB common stock.

Journalize stock investment transactions, and explain income statement presentation.
(LO 3), **AN**

Instructions

(a) Journalize the transactions.

(b) Explain how dividend revenue and the gain (loss) on sale should be reported in the income statement.

Journalize transactions for investments in stock.

(LO 3), AP

EE-3 Kurzon Inc. had these transactions pertaining to investments in common stock:

Jan.	1	Purchased 1,200 shares of Fulten Corporation common stock (5% of outstanding shares) for $59,200 cash.
July	1	Received a cash dividend of $7 per share.
Dec.	1	Sold 900 shares of Fulten Corporation common stock for $47,200 cash.
	31	Received a cash dividend of $7 per share.

Instructions

Journalize the transactions.

Journalize and post trans-actions under the equity method.

(LO 3), AP

EE-4 On January 1, Lambert Corporation purchased a 25% equity investment in Dougherty Corporation for $150,000. At December 31, Dougherty declared and paid a $80,000 cash dividend and reported net income of $380,000.

Instructions

(a) Journalize the transactions.

(b) Determine the amount to be reported as an investment in Dougherty stock at December 31.

Journalize entries under cost and equity methods.

(LO 3), AP

EE-5 These are two independent situations:

1. Eusey Cosmetics acquired 12% of the 300,000 shares of common stock of High Fashion at a total cost of $14 per share on March 18, 2014. On June 30, High declared and paid a $75,000 dividend. On December 31, High reported net income of $244,000 for the year. At December 31, the market price of High Fashion was $16 per share. The stock is classified as available-for-sale.

2. Dickson Inc. obtained significant influence over Kiner Corporation by buying 25% of Kiner's 30,000 outstanding shares of common stock at a total cost of $11 per share on January 1, 2014. On June 15, Kiner declared and paid a cash dividend of $35,000. On December 31, Kiner reported a net income of $120,000 for the year.

Instructions

Prepare all the necessary journal entries for 2014 for (a) Eusey Cosmetics and (b) Dickson Inc.

Prepare adjusting entry to record fair value, and indicate statement presentation.

(LO 5, 6), AP

EE-6 At December 31, 2014, the trading securities for Puckett, Inc. are as follows.

Security	Cost	Fair Value
A	$18,100	$16,000
B	12,500	14,800
C	23,000	18,000
Total	$53,600	$48,800

Instructions

(a) Prepare the adjusting entry at December 31, 2014, to report the securities at fair value.

(b) Show the balance sheet and income statement presentation at December 31, 2014, after adjustment to fair value.

Prepare adjusting entry to record fair value, and indicate statement presentation.

(LO 5, 6), AN

EE-7 Data for investments in stock classified as trading securities are presented in EE-6. Assume instead that the investments are classified as available-for-sale securities with the same cost and fair value data. The securities are considered to be a long-term investment.

Instructions

(a) Prepare the adjusting entry at December 31, 2014, to report the securities at fair value.

(b) Show the statement presentation at December 31, 2014, after adjustment to fair value.

(c) ━━━▶ Jayne Parks, a member of the board of directors, does not understand the reporting of the unrealized gains or losses on trading securities and available-for-sale securities. Write a letter to Ms. Parks explaining the reporting and the purposes it serves.

EE-8 Swisher Company has these data at December 31, 2014:

Securities	Cost	Fair Value
Trading	$110,000	$122,000
Available-for-sale	100,000	96,000

Prepare adjusting entries for fair value, and indicate statement presentation for two classes of securities.

(LO 5, 6), **AN**

The available-for-sale securities are held as a long-term investment.

Instructions
(a) Prepare the adjusting entries to report each class of securities at fair value.
(b) Indicate the statement presentation of each class of securities and the related unrealized gain (loss) accounts.

Problems

PE-1 Moore Farms is a grower of hybrid seed corn for DeKalb Genetics Corporation. It has had two exceptionally good years and has elected to invest its excess funds in bonds. The following selected transactions relate to bonds acquired as an investment by Moore Farms, whose fiscal year ends on December 31.

Journalize debt investment transactions.

(LO 2, 5, 6), **AN**

2014

Jan.	1	Purchased at par $600,000 of Vandiver Corporation 10-year, 7% bonds dated January 1, 2014, directly from the issuing corporation.
July	1	Received the semiannual interest on the Vandiver bonds.
Dec. 31		Accrual of interest at year-end on the Vandiver bonds.

Assume that all intervening transactions and adjustments have been properly recorded and the number of bonds owned has not changed from December 31, 2014, to December 31, 2016.

2017

Jan.	1	Received the semiannual interest on the Vandiver bonds.
Jan.	1	Sold $300,000 of Vandiver bonds at 110.
July	1	Received the semiannual interest on the Vandiver bonds.
Dec. 31		Accrual of interest at year-end on the Vandiver bonds.

Instructions
Journalize the listed transactions for the years 2014 and 2017.

PE-2 In January 2014, the management of Weast Company concludes that it has sufficient cash to purchase some short-term investments in debt and stock securities. During the year, the following transactions occurred.

Journalize investment transactions, prepare adjusting entry, and show financial statement presentation.

(LO 2, 3, 5, 6), **AN**

Feb.	1	Purchased 1,200 shares of ALF common stock for $51,600.
Mar.	1	Purchased 500 shares of LNC common stock for $18,500.
Apr.	1	Purchased 70 $1,000, 8% CRT bonds for $70,000. Interest is payable semiannually on April 1 and October 1.
July	1	Received a cash dividend of $0.80 per share on the ALF common stock.
Aug.	1	Sold 200 shares of ALF common stock at $42 per share.
Sept.	1	Received $2 per share cash dividend on the LNC common stock.
Oct.	1	Received the semiannual interest on the CRT bonds.
Oct.	1	Sold the CRT bonds for $75,700.

At December 31, the fair values of the ALF and LNC common stocks were $39 and $30 per share, respectively.

Instructions
(a) Journalize the transactions and post to the accounts Debt Investments and Stock Investments. (Use the T-account form.)
(b) Prepare the adjusting entry at December 31, 2014, to report the investments at fair value. All securities are considered to be trading securities.
(c) Show the balance sheet presentation of investment securities at December 31, 2014.
(d) Identify the income statement accounts and give the statement classification of each account.

Journalize transactions, prepare adjusting entry for stock investments, and show balance sheet presentation.

(LO 3, 5, 6), **AN**

PE-3 On December 31, 2013, Ogleby Associates owned the following securities that are held as long-term investments.

Common Stock	Shares	Cost
A Co.	1,000	$48,000
B Co.	5,000	36,000
C Co.	1,200	24,000

On this date, the total fair value of the securities was equal to its cost. The securities are not held for influence or control over the investees. In 2014, the following transactions occurred.

July	1	Received $2.00 per share semiannual cash dividend on B Co. common stock.
Aug.	1	Received $0.50 per share cash dividend on A Co. common stock.
Sept.	1	Sold 1,000 shares of B Co. common stock for cash at $9 per share.
Oct.	1	Sold 300 shares of A Co. common stock for cash at $53 per share.
Nov.	1	Received $1 per share cash dividend on C Co. common stock.
Dec.	15	Received $0.50 per share cash dividend on A Co. common stock.
	31	Received $2.20 per share semiannual cash dividend on B Co. common stock.

At December 31, the fair values per share of the common stocks were A Co. $47, B Co. $7, and C Co. $24.

Instructions

(a) Journalize the 2014 transactions and post to the account Stock Investments. (Use the T-account form.)

(b) Prepare the adjusting entry at December 31, 2014, to show the securities at fair value. The stock should be classified as available-for-sale securities.

(c) Show the balance sheet presentation of the investments and the unrealized gain (loss) at December 31, 2014. At this date, Ogleby Associates has common stock $2,000,000 and retained earnings $1,200,000.

Prepare entries under cost and equity methods, and prepare memorandum.

(LO 3), **AN**

PE-4 Farwell Company acquired 30% of the outstanding common stock of Ingold Inc. on January 1, 2014, by paying $1,800,000 for 60,000 shares. Ingold declared and paid a $0.50 per share cash dividend on June 30 and again on December 31, 2014. Ingold reported net income of $800,000 for the year.

Instructions

(a) Prepare the journal entries for Farwell Company for 2014, assuming Farwell cannot exercise significant influence over Ingold. (Use the cost method.)

(b) Prepare the journal entries for Farwell Company for 2014, assuming Farwell can exercise significant influence over Ingold. (Use the equity method.)

(c) ▬▬▶ The board of directors of Farwell Company is confused about the differences between the cost and equity methods. Prepare a memorandum for the board that explains each method and shows in tabular form the account balances under each method at December 31, 2014.

Journalize stock transactions, and show balance sheet presentation.

(LO 3, 5, 6), **AN**

PE-5 Here is Kline Company's portfolio of long-term available-for-sale securities at December 31, 2013:

	Cost
1,400 shares of Tabares Inc. common stock	$73,500
1,200 shares of Munoz Corporation common stock	84,000
800 shares of H. Hogan Corporation preferred stock	33,600

On December 31, the total cost of the portfolio equaled the total fair value. Kline had the following transactions related to the securities during 2014.

Jan.	20	Sold 1,400 shares of Tabares Inc. common stock at $55 per share.
	28	Purchased 400 shares of $10 par value common stock of M. Powell Corporation at $78 per share.
	30	Received a cash dividend of $1.25 per share on Munoz Corporation common stock.
Feb.	8	Received cash dividends of $0.40 per share on H. Hogan Corporation preferred stock.
	18	Sold all 800 shares of H. Hogan preferred stock at $35 per share.

July 30 Received a cash dividend of $1.10 per share on Munoz Corporation common stock.

Sept. 6 Purchased an additional 600 shares of the $10 par value common stock of M. Powell Corporation at $82 per share.

Dec. 1 Received a cash dividend of $1.50 per share on M. Powell Corporation common stock.

At December 31, 2014, the fair values of the securities were:

Munoz Corporation common stock	$65 per share
M. Powell Corporation common stock	$77 per share

Kline uses separate account titles for each investment, such as Investment in Munoz Corporation Common Stock.

Instructions
(a) Prepare journal entries to record the transactions.
(b) Post to the investment accounts. (Use separate T-accounts for each investment.)
(c) Prepare the adjusting entry at December 31, 2014, to report the portfolio at fair value.
(d) Show the balance sheet presentation at December 31, 2014.

PE-6 The following data, presented in alphabetical order, are taken from the records of Wellman Corporation.

Prepare a balance sheet.
(LO 6), **AP**

Accounts payable	$ 150,000
Accounts receivable	90,000
Accumulated depreciation—buildings	180,000
Accumulated depreciation—equipment	52,000
Allowance for doubtful accounts	6,000
Bonds payable (10%, due 2025)	350,000
Buildings	900,000
Cash	63,000
Common stock ($5 par value; 500,000 shares authorized, 240,000 shares issued)	$1,200,000
Debt investments	400,000
Discount on bonds payable	20,000
Dividends payable	50,000
Equipment	275,000
Goodwill	190,000
Income taxes payable	70,000
Inventory	170,000
Land	410,000
Notes payable (due 2015)	70,000
Paid-in capital in excess of par value	464,000
Prepaid insurance	16,000
Retained earnings	310,000
Stock investments (Lawton Inc. stock, 30% ownership, at equity)	240,000
Stock investments (short-term, at fair value)	128,000

Instructions
Prepare a balance sheet at December 31, 2014.

Answers to Self-Test Questions

1. d **2.** a **3.** b **4.** c **5.** a **6.** b $300,000 + (($160,000 − $60,000) × .25) **7.** c **8.** d
9. a **10.** c **11.** b **12.** c **13.** c ($41,300 − $39,800) + $900 **14.** c

COMPANY INDEX

Please note any entries for pages within Appendices F-J may be found at the book's companion website,
www.wiley.com/college/kimmel.

SUBJECT INDEX

Please note any entries for pages within Appendices F–J may be found at the book's companion website, www.wiley.com/college/kimmel.

RAPID REVIEW
Chapter Content

ACCOUNTING CONCEPTS (Chapters 2–4)

Fundamental Qualities	Enhancing Qualities	Assumptions	Principles	Constraint
Relevance	Comparability	Monetary unit	Historical cost	Materiality
Faithful representation	Consistency	Economic entity	Fair value	
	Verifiability	Periodicity	Full disclosure	
	Timeliness	Going concern	Revenue recognition	
	Understandability	Accrual basis	Expense recognition	

BASIC ACCOUNTING EQUATION (Chapter 3)

INVENTORY (Chapters 5 and 6)

Ownership

Freight Terms	Ownership of goods on public carrier resides with:
FOB Shipping point	Buyer
FOB Destination	Seller

ADJUSTING ENTRIES (Chapter 4)

	Type	Adjusting Entry	
Deferrals	1. Prepaid expenses	Dr. Expenses	Cr. Assets
	2. Unearned revenues	Dr. Liabilities	Cr. Revenues
Accruals	1. Accrued revenues	Dr. Assets	Cr. Revenues
	2. Accrued expenses	Dr. Expenses	Cr. Liabilities

Note: Each adjusting entry will affect one or more income statement accounts and one or more balance sheet accounts.

Interest Computation

Interest = Face value of note × Annual interest rate × Time in terms of one year

CLOSING ENTRIES (Chapter 4)

Purpose

1. Update the Retained Earnings account in the ledger by transferring net income (loss) and dividends to retained earnings.
2. Prepare the temporary accounts (revenue, expense, dividends) for the next period's postings by reducing their balances to zero.

Perpetual vs. Periodic Journal Entries

Event	Perpetual	Periodic
Purchase of goods	Inventory Cash (A/P)	Purchases Cash (A/P)
Freight (shipping point)	Inventory Cash	Freight-In Cash
Return of goods	Cash (or A/P) Inventory	Cash (or A/P) Purchase Returns and Allowances
Sale of goods	Cash (or A/R) Sales Cost of Goods Sold Inventory	Cash (or A/R) Sales No entry
End of period	No entry	Closing or adjusting entry required

ACCOUNTING CYCLE (Chapter 4)

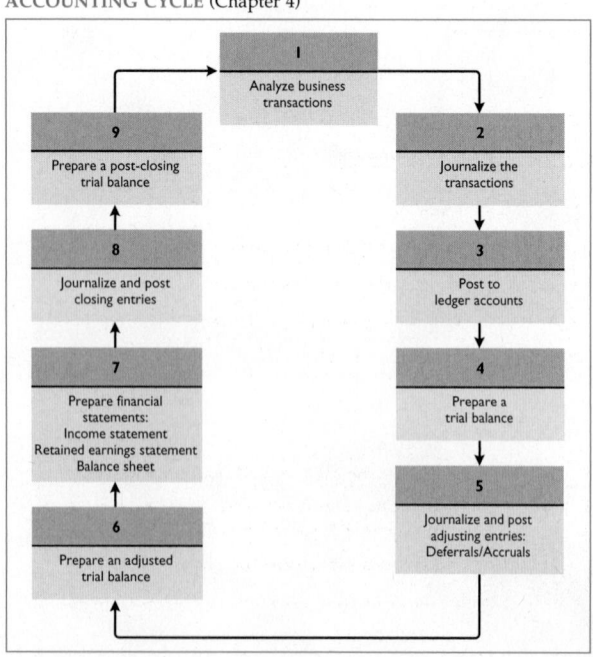

FRAUD, INTERNAL CONTROL, AND CASH (Chapter 7)

Principles of Internal Control

Establishment of responsibility
Segregation of duties
Documentation procedures
Physical controls
Independent internal verification
Human resource controls

The Fraud Triangle

Opportunity

Financial pressure

Rationalization

Bank Reconciliation

Bank	Books
Balance per bank statement Add: Deposits in transit	Balance per books Add: Unrecorded credit memoranda from bank statement
Deduct: Outstanding checks	Deduct: Unrecorded debit memoranda from bank statement
Adjusted cash balance	Adjusted cash balance

Note: 1. Errors should be offset (added or deducted) on the side that made the error.
2. Adjusting journal entries should only be made for items affecting books.

STOP AND CHECK: Does the adjusted cash balance in the Cash account equal the reconciled balance?

RECEIVABLES (Chapter 8)

Two Methods to Account for Uncollectible Accounts

Direct write-off method	Record bad debt expense when the company determines a particular account to be uncollectible.
Allowance method	At the end of each period, estimate the amount of uncollectible receivables. Debit Bad Debt Expense and credit Allowance for Doubtful Accounts in an amount that results in a balance in the allowance account equal to the estimate of uncollectibles. As specific accounts become uncollectible, debit Allowance for Doubtful Accounts and credit Accounts Receivable.

Steps to Manage Accounts Receivable

1. Determine to whom to extend credit.
2. Establish a payment period.
3. Monitor collections.
4. Evaluate the receivables balance.
5. Accelerate cash receipts from receivables when necessary.

PLANT ASSETS (Chapter 9)

Computation of Annual Depreciation Expense

Straight-line	$\dfrac{\text{Cost} - \text{Salvage value}}{\text{Useful life (in years)}}$
*Declining-balance	Book value at beginning of year × Declining balance rate* *Declining-balance rate = 1 ÷ Useful life (in years)
*Units-of-activity	$\dfrac{\text{Depreciable cost}}{\text{Useful life (in units)}} \times$ Units of activity during year

*Appendix coverage.

Note: If depreciation is calculated for partial periods, the straight-line and declining-balance methods must be adjusted for the relevant proportion of the year. Multiply the annual depreciation expense by the number of months expired in the year divided by 12 months.

BONDS (Chapter 10)

Premium	Market interest rate < Contractual interest rate
Face Value	Market interest rate = Contractual interest rate
Discount	Market interest rate > Contractual interest rate

Computation of Annual Bond Interest Expense

Interest expense = Interest paid (payable) + Amortization of discount
(OR − Amortization of premium)

*Straight-line amortization	$\dfrac{\text{Bond discount (premium)}}{\text{Number of interest periods}}$	
*Effective-interest amortization (preferred method)	Bond interest expense	Bond interest paid
	Carrying value of bonds at beginning of period × Effective-interest rate	Face amount of bonds × Contractual interest rate

*Appendix coverage.

STOCKHOLDERS' EQUITY (Chapter 11)

No-Par Value vs. Par Value Stock Journal Entries

No-Par Value	Par Value

Cash
    Common Stock
	Cash
	    Common Stock (par value)
	    Paid-in Capital in Excess of Par Value

Comparison of Dividend Effects

	Cash	Common Stock	Retained Earnings
Cash dividend	↓	No effect	↓
Stock dividend	No effect	↑	↓
Stock split	No effect	No effect	No effect

*Appendix coverage.

STATEMENT OF CASH FLOWS (Chapter 12)

Cash flows from operating activities (**indirect method**)

Net income		
Add:	Amortization and depreciation	$ X
	Losses on disposals of assets	X
	Decreases in current assets	X
	Increases in current liabilities	X
Deduct:	Increases in current assets	(X)
	Decreases in current liabilities	(X)
	Gains on disposals of assets	(X)
Net cash provided (used) by operating activities		$ X

Cash flows from operating activities (**direct method**)

Cash receipts
  (Examples: from sales of goods and services to customers, from receipts of interest and dividends) $ X
Cash payments
  (Examples: to suppliers, for operating expenses, for interest, for taxes)   (X)
Net cash provided (used) by operating activities $ X

FINANCIAL STATEMENT ANALYSIS (Chapter 13)

Discontinued operations	Income statement (presented separately after "Income from continuing operations")
Extraordinary items	Income statement (presented separately after "Discontinued operations")
Changes in accounting principle	In most instances, use the new method in current period and restate previous years' results using new method. For changes in depreciation and amortization methods, use the new method in the current period but do not restate previous periods.

Income Statement and Comprehensive Income

Sales revenue	$ XX
Cost of goods sold	XX
Gross profit	XX
Operating expenses	XX
Income from operations	XX
Other revenues (expenses) and gains (losses)	XX
Income before income taxes	XX
Income tax expense	XX
Income before irregular items	XX
Irregular items (net of tax)	**XX**
Net income	**XX**
Other comprehensive income items (net of tax)	**XX**
Comprehensive income	**$ XX**

MANAGERIAL ACCOUNTING (Chapter 14)

Characteristics of Managerial Accounting

Primary users	Internal users
Reports	Internal reports issued as needed
Purpose	Special purpose for a particular user
Content	Pertains to subunits, may be detailed, use of relevant data
Verification	No independent audits

Types of Manufacturing Costs

Direct materials	Raw materials directly associated with finished product
Direct labor	Work of employees directly associated with turning raw materials into finished product
Manufacturing overhead	Costs indirectly associated with manufacture of finished product

JOB ORDER AND PROCESS COSTING (Chapters 15 and 16)

Types of Accounting Systems

Job order	Costs are assigned to each unit or each batch of goods
Process cost	Costs are applied to similar products that are mass-produced in a continuous fashion

Job Order and Process Cost Flow

ACTIVITY-BASED COSTING (Chapter 17)

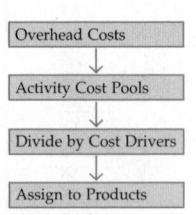

Activity-based costing involves the following four steps:
1. Identify and classify the major activities involved in the manufacture of specific products, and allocate the manufacturing overhead costs to the appropriate cost pools.
2. Identify the cost driver that has a strong correlation to the costs accumulated in the cost pool.
3. Compute the overhead rate for each cost driver.
4. Assign manufacturing overhead costs for each cost pool to products, using the overhead rates (cost per driver).

COST-VOLUME-PROFIT (Chapters 18 and 19)

Types of Costs

Variable costs	Vary in total directly and proportionately with changes in activity level
Fixed costs	Remain the same in total regardless of change in activity level
Mixed costs	Contain both a fixed and a variable element

CVP Income Statement Format

	Total	Per Unit
Sales	$xx	$xx
Variable costs	xx	xx
Contribution margin	xx	$xx
Fixed costs	xx	
Net income	$xx	

$$\text{Contribution margin per unit} = \text{Unit selling price} - \text{Unit variable costs}$$

$$\text{Break-even point in units} = \text{Fixed costs} \div \text{Unit contribution margin*}$$

$$\text{Break-even point in dollars} = \text{Fixed costs} \div \text{Contribution margin ratio*}$$

$$\text{Required sales in units for target net income} = (\text{Fixed costs} + \text{Target net income}) \div \text{Contribution margin per unit}$$

$$\text{Degree of operating leverage} = \text{Contribution margin} \div \text{Net income}$$

*For multiple products, use weighted-average.

INCREMENTAL ANALYSIS (Chapter 20)

1. Identify the relevant costs associated with each alternative. **Relevant costs** are those costs and revenues that differ across alternatives. Choose the alternative that maximizes net income.
2. **Opportunity costs** are those benefits that are given up when one alternative is chosen instead of another one. Opportunity costs are relevant costs.
3. **Sunk costs** have already been incurred and will not be changed or avoided by any future decision. Sunk costs are not relevant costs.

BUDGETS (Chapter 21)

Components of the Master Budget

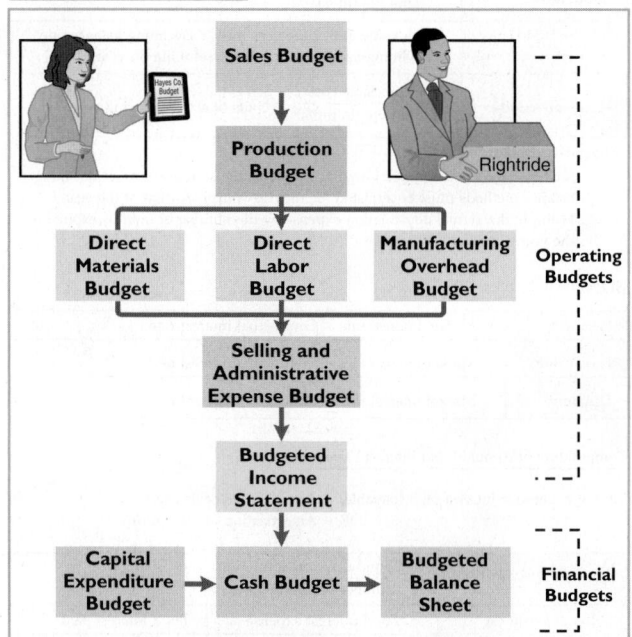

RESPONSIBILITY ACCOUNTING (Chapter 22)

Types of Responsibility Centers

Cost	Profit	Investment
Expenses only	Expenses and Revenues	Expenses and Revenues and ROI

Return on Investment

$$\text{Return on investment (ROI)} = \text{Investment center controllable margin} \div \text{Average investment center operating assets}$$

RAPID REVIEW
Chapter Content

STANDARD COSTS (Chapter 23)

Standard Cost Variances

$$\begin{array}{|c|}\text{Total}\\\text{materials}\\\text{variance}\end{array} = \begin{array}{c}\text{Materials}\\\text{price}\\\text{variance}\end{array} + \begin{array}{c}\text{Materials}\\\text{quantity}\\\text{variance}\end{array}$$

$$\begin{array}{|c|}\text{Total}\\\text{labor}\\\text{variance}\end{array} = \begin{array}{c}\text{Labor}\\\text{price}\\\text{variance}\end{array} + \begin{array}{c}\text{Labor}\\\text{quantity}\\\text{variance}\end{array}$$

$$\begin{array}{|c|}\text{Total}\\\text{overhead}\\\text{variance}\end{array} = \begin{array}{c}\text{Overhead}\\\text{controllable}\\\text{variance}\end{array} + \begin{array}{c}\text{Overhead}\\\text{volume}\\\text{variance}\end{array}$$

Materials price variance $= \boxed{AQ \times AP} - \boxed{AQ \times SP}$

Materials quantity variance $= \boxed{AQ \times SP} - \boxed{SQ \times SP}$

Labor price variance $= \boxed{AH \times AR} - \boxed{AH \times SR}$

Labor quantity variance $= \boxed{AH \times SR} - \boxed{SH \times SR}$

* Overhead controllable variance $= \boxed{\text{Actual overhead}} - \boxed{\text{Overhead budgeted}}$

* Overhead volume variance $= \boxed{\text{Fixed overhead rate}} \times \boxed{\begin{array}{c}\text{Normal capacity} -\\\text{Standard hours allowed}\end{array}}$

*Appendix coverage.

Balanced Scorecard

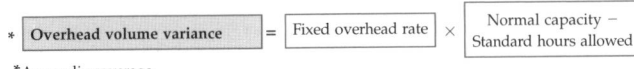

Linked process across perspectives:

Financial → Customer → Internal Process → Learning and Growth

CAPITAL BUDGETING (Chapter 24)

Annual Rate of Return

$$\begin{array}{|c|}\text{Annual rate}\\\text{of return}\end{array} = \begin{array}{c}\text{Expected annual}\\\text{net income}\end{array} \div \begin{array}{c}\text{Average}\\\text{investment}\end{array}$$

Cash Payback

$$\begin{array}{|c|}\text{Cash payback}\\\text{period}\end{array} = \begin{array}{c}\text{Cost of capital}\\\text{investment}\end{array} \div \begin{array}{c}\text{Annual}\\\text{cash inflow}\end{array}$$

Discounted Cash Flow Approaches

Net Present Value	Internal Rate of Return
Compute net present value (a dollar amount). If net present value is zero or positive, accept the proposal. If net present value is negative, reject the proposal.	Compute internal rate of return (a percentage). If internal rate of return is equal to or greater than the minimum required rate of return, accept the proposal. If internal rate of return is less than the minimum rate, reject the proposal.

INVESTMENTS (Appendix E)

Comparison of Long-Term Bond Investment and Liability Journal Entries

Event	Investor	Investee
Purchase / issue of bonds	Debt Investments 　Cash	Cash 　Bonds Payable
Interest receipt / payment	Cash 　Interest Revenue	Interest Expense 　Cash

Comparison of Cost and Equity Methods of Accounting for Long-Term Stock Investments

Event	Cost	Equity
Acquisition	Stock Investments 　Cash	Stock Investments 　Cash
Investee reports earnings	No entry	Stock Investments 　Investment Revenue
Investee pays dividends	Cash 　Dividend Revenue	Cash 　Stock Investments

PRICING (Appendix J)

External Pricing

$$\begin{array}{|c|}\text{Markup}\\\text{percentage}\end{array} = \begin{array}{c}\text{Desired ROI}\\\text{per unit}\end{array} \div \begin{array}{c}\text{Total}\\\text{unit cost}\end{array}$$

$$\begin{array}{|c|}\text{Target selling}\\\text{price per unit}\end{array} = \text{Total unit cost} + \left(\begin{array}{c}\text{Total}\\\text{unit cost}\end{array} \times \begin{array}{c}\text{Markup}\\\text{percentage}\end{array}\right)$$

Transfer Pricing

$$\begin{array}{|c|}\text{Minimum}\\\text{transfer price}\end{array} = \text{Variable cost} + \text{Opportunity cost}$$

RAPID REVIEW
Financial Statements

Order of Preparation	Date
1. Income statement	For the period ended
2. Retained earnings statement	For the period ended
3. Balance sheet	As of the end of the period
4. Statement of cash flows	For the period ended

Income Statement (perpetual inventory system)

Name of Company Income Statement For the Period Ended		
Sales		
Sales revenue	$ X	
Less: Sales returns and allowances	X	
Sales discounts	X	
Net sales		$ X
Cost of goods sold		X
Gross profit		X
Operating expenses		
(Examples: store salaries, advertising, delivery, rent, depreciation, utilities, insurance)		X
Income from operations		X
Other revenues and gains		
(Examples: interest, gains)	X	
Other expenses and losses		
(Examples: interest, losses)	X	X
Income before income taxes		X
Income tax expense		X
Net income		$ X

Income Statement (periodic inventory system)

Name of Company Income Statement For the Period Ended			
Sales			
Sales revenue		$ X	
Less: Sales returns and allowances		X	
Sales discounts		X	
Net sales			$ X
Cost of goods sold			
Beginning inventory		X	
Purchases	$ X		
Less: Purchase returns and allowances	X		
Net purchases	X		
Add: Freight-in	X		
Cost of goods purchased		X	
Cost of goods available for sale		X	
Less: Ending inventory		X	
Cost of goods sold			X
Gross profit			X
Operating expenses			
(Examples: store salaries, advertising, delivery, rent, depreciation, utilities, insurance)			X
Income from operations			X
Other revenues and gains			
(Examples: interest, gains)		X	
Other expenses and losses			
(Examples: interest, losses)		X	X
Income before income taxes			X
Income tax expense			X
Net income			$ X

Retained Earnings Statement

Name of Company Retained Earnings Statement For the Period Ended	
Retained earnings, beginning of period	$ X
Add: Net income (or deduct net loss)	X
	X
Deduct: Dividends	X
Retained earnings, end of period	$ X

STOP AND CHECK: Net income (loss) presented on the retained earnings statement must equal the net income (loss) presented on the income statement.

Balance Sheet

Name of Company Balance Sheet As of the End of the Period			
Assets			
Current assets			
(Examples: cash, short-term investments, accounts receivable, inventory, prepaids)			$ X
Long-term investments			
(Examples: investments in bonds, investments in stocks)			X
Property, plant, and equipment			
Land		$ X	
Buildings and equipment	$ X		
Less: Accumulated depreciation	X	X	X
Intangible assets			X
Total assets			$ X
Liabilities and Stockholders' Equity			
Liabilities			
Current liabilities			
(Examples: notes payable, accounts payable, accruals, unearned revenues, current portion of notes payable)			$ X
Long-term liabilities			
(Examples: notes payable, bonds payable)			X
Total liabilities			X
Stockholders' equity			
Common stock			X
Retained earnings			X
Total liabilities and stockholders' equity			$ X

STOP AND CHECK: Total assets on the balance sheet must equal total liabilities plus stockholders' equity; and, ending retained earnings on the balance sheet must equal ending retained earnings on the retained earnings statement.

Statement of Cash Flows

Name of Company Statement of Cash Flows For the Period Ended	
Cash flows from operating activities	
(*Note:* May be prepared using the direct or indirect method)	
Net cash provided (used) by operating activities	$ X
Cash flows from investing activities	
(Examples: purchase / sale of long-term assets)	
Net cash provided (used) by investing activities	X
Cash flows from financing activities	
(Examples: issue / repayment of long-term liabilities, issue of stock, payment of dividends)	
Net cash provided (used) by financing activities	X
Net increase (decrease) in cash	X
Cash at beginning of the period	X
Cash at end of the period	$ X

STOP AND CHECK: Cash at end of the period on the statement of cash flows must equal cash presented on the balance sheet.